D1806323

B 4 399334 6

Council
of Europe

Conseil
de L'Europe

EUDISED
European Educational
Research Yearbook
1993

K·G·Saur
München · New Providence · London · Paris
1995

Linguistic and technical editing:
Kees Broekhof (SVO)
Sheilah Tanner (Council of Europe)

Die Deutsche Bibliothek – CIP-Einheitsaufnahme

EUDISED European educational research yearbook / Council
of Europe. – München ; New York ; London ; Paris : Saur.
1993 (1995) – Erscheint jährl. – Aufnahme nach 1993 (1995)

1995 by K.G. Saur Verlag München
A Reed Reference Publishing Company

Printed and bound in the Federal Republic of Germany.

Online access to the EUDISED database is provided by the
Information Retrieval Service of the European Space Agency (ESA/IRS).

Typesetting by Peter Peregrinus Ltd., Stevenage, United Kingdom
Printed by WS Druckerei, Bodenheim
Bound by Buchbinderei Schaumann, Darmstadt

ISBN 3-598-23460-0
ISSN 0947-5826

Contents

NATIONAL AGENCIES / AGENCES NATIONALES

AUSTRIA / AUTRICHE
Ms Elfriede TAJALLI
Bundesministerium für Unterricht und
Kunst, Abt. I/6b, Minoritenplatz 5,
Postfach 65, 1014 WIEN
tel: +43 1 53120 3520
fax: +43 1 53120 3535

BELGIUM / BELGIQUE
M. Luc STOOPS
Ministerie van de Vlaamse Gemeenschap
Departement Onderwijs
Centrum voor Informatie en
Documentatie
Koningsstraat 71
B-1000 BRUSSEL
tel: +32 2 219 82 19
fax: +32 2 219 77 73

BULGARIA / BULGARIE
Ms Reneta CHRISTOVA PERGUELOVA
Centre d'Information et de Calcul
Ministère de l'éducation et de la science
rue Bigla 52, 1ère étage
SOFIA

CROATIA / CROATIE
Ms Maja BRATANI–
Zavod za Lingvistiku
Filizofskoga fakulteta Sveu-ili-ta u
Zagrebu
Salajeva 3
HR-4100 ZAGREB
tel: +385 41 620 011, 620 142
fax: +385 41 513 834

CYPRUS / CHYPRE
M. Andreas SKOTINOS
Pedagogical Institute
PO Box 512, NICOSIA
tel: +357 2 303 466
fax: +357 2 445 021

**CZECH REPUBLIC / REPUBLIQUE
TCHEQUE**
Ms Stanislava BRO-OVÁ
Státní Pedagogická knihovna
Komenského
-stav pro informace ve vzd-lávání
Mikulandská 5
CZ-116 74 PRAHA 1
tel: +422 294 062
fax: +422 267 137

DENMARK / DANEMARK
Mr. Michael SØGAARD LARSEN
Danmarks Pædagogiske Bibliotek
Lersø Parkallé 101, 2100 KØBENHAVN Ø
tel: +45 39 29 82 11
fax: +45 39 29 42 06

ESTONIA / ESTONIE
Ms Reet NEUDORF
Ministry of Culture and Education
11 Tönismägi Street
EE-0100 TALINN
tel: +372 2 44 08 28
fax: +373 6 31 12 13

FINLAND / FINLANDE
Ms Liisa HUGHES
Institute for Educational Research,
University of Jyväskylä, PO Box 35,
40351 JYVÄSKYLÄ 10
tel: +358 41 601 211
fax: +358 41 603 201

FRANCE
M. Philippe CHAMPY
Mme. M-E. BOURGEOIS
Département ressources et communications
Service banque de données
Institut National de Recherche pédagogique
29 rue d'Ulm, 75230 PARIS CEDEX 05
tel: +33 46 34 91 57
fax: +33 43 54 32 01

GERMANY / ALLEMAGNE
Ms D. LEWERENZ
Sekretariat der Ständigen Konferenz der
Kultusminister der Länder, Nassestrasse
8, 53113 BONN 1
tel: +49 228 501-0

GREECE / GRECE
Professor Christopher CHARALAMBAKIS
University of Athens
44 Hippokratous Street, 10680 ATHENS
tel: +30 36 40 719
fax: +30 36 40 719

HUNGARY / HONGROIE
Ms Katalin VARGA
Dr. Zsuzsanna CELLER
Országos Pedagógiai Könyvtár és
Muzeum
Honvéd u. 19, BP PF 49 1363
H-BUDAPEST
tel: +36 1 126 862
fax: +36 1 112 6862

ICELAND / ISLANDE
Professor Thorolfur THORLINDSSON
Institute for Educational Research
Sudurlandsbraut 6, 108 REYKJAVIK
tel: +354 91 678 166
fax: +354 91 678 185

IRELAND / IRLANDE
Dr. Thomas KELLAGHAN
Educational Research Centre
St. Patrick's College
Drumcondra, DUBLIN 9

ITALY / ITALIE
Ms Antonella TURCHI
Biblioteca di Documentazione pedagogica
Via M Buonarroti 10, 501 22 FIRENZE
tel: +39 55 234 6106
fax: +39 55 242 884

LATVIA / LETTONIE
Ms Tatyana KOKE
University of Latvia
Department of Education and Psychology
Kronvalda boulv., RIGA, LV-1010
tel: +371 2 322 918
fax: +371 2 883 0039

LITHUANIE / LITUANIE
Mr.Algirdas BUDREVICIUS
Centre of Informatics and Forecasting
1 Suvalk-, 2600 VILNIUS
tel: +370 88 1927
fax: +370 88 1884

LUXEMBOURG
Ministère de l'Education Nationale,
Service d'Innovation et de Recherche
pédagogiques, Section de la
Documentation
29 rue Aldringen, L-2926 LUXEMBOURG
tel: +352 478 5128
fax: +352 478 5130

MALTA / MALTE
Dr. George BONNICI
Resource Centre, Centre for
Communication Technology
University of Malta, M-MSIDA
tel: +356 333 903-6
fax: +356 336 450

NETHERLANDS / PAYS-BAS
Mr. Kees BROEKHOF
Institute for Educational Research
in the Netherlands (SVO)
Sweelinckplein 14, NL-2517 GK
THE HAGUE
tel: +31 070 346 9679
fax: +31 070 360 9951

NORWAY / NORVEGE
Mr. Arne GUNDERSEN
Ministry of Education, Research & Church
affairs, Akersgaten 42, Postboks 8119
Dep
0032 OSLO
tel: +47 2 234 7439
fax: +47 2 234 9540

POLAND / POLOGNE
Ms Anna SMOCZYNSKA
Institute for Educational Research
Gorczewska 8, PL-01-180 WARSAW
fax: +48 22 32 1895

PORTUGAL
Professor Bártolo PAIVA CAMPOS
Institute of Educational Innovation
Trav. Terras Sant'Ana 15, P-1200 LISBOA
tel: +351 1 692970
fax: +351 1 690731

ROMANIA / ROUMANIE
Ms Iuliana MIHALCEA
Biblioteca Centrala Pedagogica
Str. Zalomit nr. 1, Sector 1
R-BUCHAREST
tel: +40 1 312 14 47
fax: +40 1 311 13 28

RUSSIAN FEDERATION / FEDERATION DE RUSSIE
Ms Larissa SAMOVOLNOVA
Department of Informatization of
Education
Ministry of Education of the Russian
Federation
Chistoprudny bvd. 6, 101856 MOSCOW
tel: +3592 95 923 57 68
fax: +3592 95 924 69 89

SLOVAK REPUBLIC / REPUBLIQUE SLOVAQUE
Ms Marta IVANOVÁ
Ms Vera CHUDIKOVA
Institute of Information and Prognoses
of Education, Youth and Sport
Staré Grunty 52
842 44 BRATISLAVA
tel: +427 726 521
fax: +427 726 180

SLOVENIA / SLOVENIE
Professor Vili ROGAN
Zavod RS za -olstvo in -port
Poljanska 28, 61000 LJUBLJANA
tel: +386 61 133 266
fax: +386 61 310 267

SPAIN / ESPAGNE
Servicio de Documentación
CIDE,Ministerio de Educación y Ciencia
Ciudad Universitaire, E-28040 MADRID

SWEDEN / SUEDE
Ms EVA TROTZIG
National Library of Psychology and
Education
Frescati Hagväg 10, Box 50063
104 50 STOCKHOLM
tel: +46 08 15 18 20
fax: +46 08 15 55 81

SWITZERLAND / SUISSE
Dr. Armin GRETLER
Swiss Coordination Centre for Research
in Education
Entfelderstrasse 61, CH-5000 AARAU
tel: +41 064 21 21 80
fax: +41 064 22 94 72

TURKEY / TURQUIE
Ms Aytaç YILDIZELI
The Scientific and Technical Research
Council of Turkey
TÜBITAK / TÜRDOK
Atatürk Bulvari 221, Kavaklidere
TR-06100 ANKARA
tel: +90 4 426 04 89
fax: +90 4 427 23 92

UNITED KINGDOM / ROYAUME-UNI
England,Scotland and Wales
Dr. Seamus HEGARTY
The National Foundation for Educational
Research in England and Wales
The Mere, Upton Park
Slough, GB-Berks SL1 2DQ
tel: +44 0753 574 123
fax: +44 0753 691 632

Northern Ireland
Ms Anne SUTHERLAND
NICER Applied Education Research Unit
School of Education
The Queen's University of Belfast
BELFAST BT7 1NN
tel: +44 0232 245 133 ext. 3311
fax: +44 0232 239 263

* * * *

ALBANIA / ALBANIE
Agency in creation

The following ISO codes are used in the country index:

AUT Austria; BEL Belgium; BG Bulgaria; CYP Cyprus; HR Croatia; CS Czech Republic; DNK Denmark; EE Estonia; FIN Finland; FRA France; DEU Germany; GRC Greece; HU Hungary; ISL Iceland; IRL Ireland; ITA Italy; LV Latvia; LIE Liechtenstein; LT Lithuania; LUX Luxembourg, MTL Malta; NLD Netherlands; NOR Norway; POL Poland; PRT Portugal; RO Romania; RU Russian Federation; SK Slovakia; SI Slovenia; ESP Spain; SWE Sweden; CHE Switzerland; TUR Turkey; GBR United Kingdom; XCE Council of Europe.

Ces codes ISO sont utilisés dans l'Indexe par pays:

DEU Allemagne; AUT Autriche; BEL Belgique; BG Bulgarie; HR Croatie; CYP Chypre; DNK Danemark; ESP Espagne; EE Estonie; FIN Finlande; FR France; GRC Grèce; HU Hongroie; IRL Ireland; ISL Islande; ITA Italy; LV Lettonie; LIE Liechtenstein; LT Lituanie; LUX Luxembourg; MLT Malte; NOR Norvège; NLD Pays-Bas; POL Pologne; PRT Portugal; CS République Tchèque; RO Roumanie, GBR Royaume-Uni; RU Russie; SK Slovaquie; SI Slovenie; CHE Suisse; SWE Suède; TUR Turquie; XCE Conseil de l'Europe.

INTRODUCTION

by Philippe CHAMPY
Chairman of the EUDISED Data Network Group

Reference works, such as yearbooks or catalogues, deserve more than other publications to be presented to readers. For three reasons. Firstly, these works should not be judged out of context. They have a background, and have been produced out of well defined institutional frameworks. The context should be made explicit because it throws light on the objectives of this kind of work. It is important to explain briefly what exactly is the **EUDISED Data Network Group** of the Council of Europe and the origin of the **European Educational Research Yearbook.** Secondly, readers should be able to evaluate the value of the information which is offered to them. To this end, they should not only be able to identify disparities in the collection and selection of data, but also know something of the intellectual and technical background which determines the processing of information. The second part of this introduction recalls the method used in the EUDISED Data Network to list educational research in the thirty odd countries concerned. Readers will then more easily understand the form and content of this **Yearbook.** Lastly, it seems essential that besides having access to the regular information provided with each piece of research, a general synthesis should be available for comparative purposes. This is the intention behind the third part, which gives an overview of the total number of research items indicated in this first issue of the **European Educational Research Yearbook.**

1. THE EUDISED DATA NETWORK OF THE COUNCIL OF EUROPE

In creating the EUDISED network twenty years ago, the Council of Europe's pioneering spirit demonstrated political support to educational research. This support has not been without influence on the growth movement in this vast field of research, and continues in a similar way today. This innovative action has made it possible to define the shape of an area difficult to delimit because of its pluridisciplinarity and its multiple bases in human and social sciences, the diversity of its subjects and methodologies, and the huge variation in development and organization in different countries. Moreover, the high level of social implications in a large part of its work incites or sustains professional and social debate.

The Council of Europe has thus accompanied a great movement of thought, harbinger of the future for the European education area, still in its gestation period. Moreover, there are considerable stakes at issue behind the simple collection and distribution of information on European educational research (this idea was the „raison d'être" of the creation of EUDISED network at the beginning of the 1970s, and remains its primary objective); the development of illuminative educational thought, the true base of the European education area.

Since its creation, in the framework of the work programme of the Council for Cultural Cooperation, the EUDISED network has supported the efforts of numerous countries to bring together national resources in the field of educational research and capitalise the results. Thanks to this impetus, the institutionalisation of specialised information has been enlarged, and frontiers difficult to cross in the field of education and training have been penetrated. This international work has been achieved by respect of common norms, and in using the same multilingual Thesaurus, the **EUDISED Thesaurus,** which became, in 1980, the **European Education Thesaurus** following a coproduction agreement between the Council of Europe and the European Union (European Economic Commission). This Thesaurus is henceforth a European reference. Its updating, within the EUDISED network, is assured by the Thesaurus Management Group which works in tandem with the Data Network Group.

In this way the EUDISED network, which has national agencies in more than 30 countries, centralises descriptions of educational research in the EUDISED database. It makes it possible to have a retrospective view over a period of twenty years. The network circulates information on an international level through two major routes; on the one hand, online access to the database at the European Space Agency (ESA/IRS) host, operating since 1983, and on the other hand the publication of the EUDISED R&D Bulletin of which 48 numbers have appeared between 1974 and 1994. The present **European Educational Research Yearbook** succeeds this earlier quarterly publication. Its new annual rhythm of publication is better adjusted to research programmes. This first edition of the **Yearbook** corresponds to numbers 49 to 52 of the **Bulletin.** It contains information collected in 1993, that is to say 2,084 research descriptions.

2. THE COLLECTION AND THE PROCESSING OF INFORMATION IN THE EUDISED NETWORK.

National agencies have responsibility for collecting and processing the research descriptions in each country. Sometimes they draw from existing national databases. In the majority of cases, they carry out research work themselves, by means of questionnaires sent direct to research teams, or by any other suitable means. These agencies are to be found in various institutional contexts (central Ministry administration, national information and documentation institutions, national research institutions, etc.).

Contrary to preconceived ideas, the collection and bringing up to date of information on ongoing research is not easy. The difficulty is for both scientific and institutional reasons. In this context, the situation from one country to another can be quite different. From a scientific point of view, it is the pluriannual character of research which represents the principal difficulty. At the time of its annual „photograph" of educational research, the EUDISED network is liable to encounter research at one of the three stages of its existence; its initiation, its execution, and the final phase of results. The aim of the network is to capture each piece of research if possible at the initial stage, and for a second time at the final stage. The first „portrait" can be taken from real life, as it is; but of necessity, it remains brief. The second „portrait" can be more detailed; it can on the other hand be judged too late in relation to current events. The results of the annual collection of the network resembles a photograph album bringing together a successive number of „portraits" recently begun, on the way, or finished. To this can be added older „portraits" of research which have up until then escaped the camera. In relation to current events, the time lag is inevitable. On the other hand, the album is irreplaceable in order to have a retrospective overview and to define the emergence of a theme.

Possible institutional obstacles to the collection of data are well known; diversity and compartmentalization of research structures at national level which hold up the rapid circulation of information, the preoccupation with confidentiality in the initial phase of the research, the rejection by researchers of enquiry procedures judged too tedious, the fragility of certain EUDISED national agencies, etc.

Once identified, each piece of research is described by means of information fields entered on to a standard worksheet. From an intellectual point of view, the research is indexed by using descriptors taken from the **European Education Thesaurus**. Each piece of research is also the object of a summary, which aims to bring out its hypothesis, its methodology and its results. Any relevant publications are also listed. These diverse pieces of information together form the entry which appears in the **Yearbook.** The entries are edited in English, French or German, and are subject to a centralised editorial supervision.

For convenience, the research is presented in the **Yearbook** according to main themes (also called terminographs), following the structure of the Thesaurus. A list of correlated research can be found at the of each group of terminographs. Three indexes complete the work; an index of names, a subject index (in the nine languages of the Thesaurus) and a country index.

3. GENERAL SURVEY OF THE RESEARCH PRESENTED IN THE YEARBOOK.

Within the limits of this introduction, three indicators seem pertinent for a global approach towards the research for which the descriptions were collected in 1993; the distribution of research by country, the distribution according to the themes in the Thesaurus, and the distribution according to the length of the research.

Table 1 reports on the **distribution of research by country**. It allows a geographic approach. This table invites three comments:

a. Several national agencies did not provide information in 1993 because of disruptions in their functioning (Denmark, Finland, Hungary, Iceland, Luxembourg, Malta, Portugal, Spain, Sweden): one new agency has not yet provided information (Lithuania).

b. Amongst the 23 national agencies having provided information, the United Kingdom alone represented more than half the research (58.6%). 13 countries represented less than 1% (Albania, Belgium, Bulgaria, Cyprus, Estonia, Greece, Ireland, Latvia, Norway, Roumania, Russia, Slovakia, Slovenia). Three countries represented between 1 and 1.9% (Italy, Poland, Turkey), three countries between 2 and 4.9% (Austria, the Czech Republic, Switzerland), and three countries between 5 and 10,9% (France, Germany and Holland).

c. These figures beg the question of the representativity or the exhaustivity of the information. Do the disproportions between the countries reflect important differences between the potentials in educational research at national level, or do they come from an increasing effect due to the unequal efficiency of the collection of data in different countries? Most of the Central and Eastern European countries have joined the EUDISED network. National agencies are being constituted. As far as Western and Northern European countries are concerned, it seems that data collection is not always carried out at the same level, which can distort comparisons. It also seems that recognition of educational research is unequal from one country to another: very strong and very traditional in the United Kingdom, it is nevertheless limited elsewhere to the most established professional research. The figures should therefore be regarded with caution.

Table 1: Distribution of research by country (N = 2084)

Country	number	%	Country	number	%	Country	number	%
Albania	1	0,05	Hungary	–	–	Roumania	5	0,30
Austria	75	3,60	Iceland	–	–	Russia	12	0,60
Belgium	15	0,70	Ireland	5	0,25	Slovakia	11	0,50
Bulgaria	6	0,30	Italy	40	1,90	Slovenia	4	0,20
Cyprus	13	0,60	Latvia	2	0,10	Spain	–	–
Czech Republic	48	2,30	Lithuania	–	–	Sweden	–	–
Denmark	–	–	Luxembourg	–	–	Switzerland	44	2,10
Estonia	13	0,60	Malta	–	–	Turkey	28	1,30
Finland	–	–	Netherlands	127	6,10	United Kingdom	1222	58,60
France	145	7,00	Norway	20	100	Council of Europe	4	0,20
Germany	213	10,20	Poland	25	1,20			
Greece	6	0,30	Portugal	–	–			

Table 2 gives the **distribution of research by the main themes** of the thesaurus (terminographs). It is difficult to draw any conclusions concerning the disciplinary and methodological approach in educational research because the themes are above all attached to the subject of the research.

As one would expect, school systems (from a pedagogical, curriculum, didactic, political, etc.
point of view) is the dominant subject (67.8% of research cumulating themes nos. 01, 02, 03, 04, 05, 06, 07, 08, 09, 10, 11, 12, 13, 14, 15, 34, 35, 36. Subjects of a psychological nature concern about a tenth of the research (19, 20, 21, 22, 23, 24). Subjects of sociological nature concern about a twentieth of the research (27, 28, 29, 30, 31). But these two proportions do not reflect the importance of these approaches in the study of school systems. Vocational training, education of adults, as well as the link between the education system and the economy account for approximately 10% of the research (32,33, 34).

Table 2: Distribution of research according to the thesaurus structure (N = 2084)

Thesaurus themes (microthesauri)	Number	%	Thesaurus themes (microthesauri)	Number	%
01 Teaching and training	167	8,00	22 Affectivity and feeling	5	0,20
02 Learning	51	2,40	23 Behaviour incentive	31	1,50
03 Principles of education	127	6,10	24 Behaviour	40	2,00
04 System of education	240	11,50	25 Safety and health	11	0,50
05 Administration of education	90	4,30	26 Handicap and handicapped	87	4,20
06 Evaluation	109	5,20	27 Interrelations	38	1,80
07 Building	7	0,30	28 Groups and organizations	10	0,50
08 Equipment	9	0,40	29 Socio-cultural environment	46	2,20
09 Curriculum	38	1,80	30 Demographic environment	5	0,20
10 Content of education	116	5,60	31 Family environment	8	0,40
11 Sciences and technology	104	5,00	32 Economic environment	30	1,40
12 Social sciences	54	2,60	33 Labour environment	131	6,30
13 Language sciences	161	7,80	34 Profession and personnel	61	3,00
14 Philosophy and religion	16	0,80	35 Administration	18	0,90
15 Art	22	1,00	36 Public authority	22	1,00
16 Research	24	1,10	37 International organizations	1	0,05
17 Information and communication technologies	22	1,00	38 Africa	2	0,10
18 Information source	18	0,90	39 America	–	–
19 Personality development	48	2,30	40 Asia/Middle East/Oceania	12	0,60
20 Cognitive process	60	2,90	41 Europe	2	0,10
21 Personality	40	2,00	42 Regions	1	0,05

Table 3 gives the **distribution of research according to its duration and by theme.**
This table provides invaluable chronological information, and allows a glimpse of the large diversity existing between the research reported in this volume. It appears that half the research (49.2%) lasts from one to three years, and three quarters (74.7%) lasts from one to five years. Research without a final date (13.2%) corresponds either to recent research, older research which has overrun five years, or research of which the final date is not known. The first two cases seem to be the most frequent.

Table 3 : Distribution of research according to duration and by theme (N = 2084)

	1 to 2 years	2 to 3 years	3 to 4 years	4 to 5 years	More than 5 years	Without final date		Total		1 to 2 years	2 to 3 years	3 to 4 years	4 to 5 years	More than 5 years	Without final date	Total
01	47	39	33	21	12	15		167	22	2	–	–	1	1	1	5
02	11	11	8	6	5	10		51	23	4	11	7	3	3	3	31
03	33	34	18	18	13	11		127	24	14	10	6	2	3	5	40
04	86	50	34	21	28	21		240	25	5	–	–	2	2	2	11
05	27	24	14	5	9	11		90	26	22	23	9	8	11	14	87
06	35	19	23	7	14	11		109	27	7	7	7	6	4	7	38
07	3	–	2	–	1	1		7	28	2	2	3	1	2	–	10
08	2	3	1	1	2	–		9	29	16	11	8	1	3	7	46
09	9	4	4	10	7	4		38	30	1	–	1	–	2	1	5
10	34	22	12	13	17	18		116	31	4	2	–	1	–	1	8
11	28	21	13	8	16	18		104	32	10	9	2	1	1	7	30
12	9	8	11	8	13	5		54	33	49	26	16	9	9	22	131
13	31	35	28	14	33	20		161	34	26	10	10	5	9	1	61
14	4	4	3	3	–	2		16	35	5	6	4	–	1	2	18
15	4	2	2	6	5	3		22	36	8	2	8	2	2	–	22
16	11	5	2	2	3	1		24	37	1	1	–	–	–	–	2
17	9	5	3	1	–	4		22	38	–	1	1	–	–	–	2
18	5	3	1	4	2	3		18	39	–	–	–	–	–	–	–
19	7	7	9	8	2	15		48	40	–	1	4	3	4	–	12
20	11	6	8	6	8	21		60	41	–	–	1	–	1	–	2
21	17	4	5	3	4	7		40	42	–	–	–	–	1	–	1
									Total	599	427	329	210	253	274	2084
									%	28,7	20,5	15,4	10,1	12,1	13,2	100

4. CONCLUSION.

With the first issue of this **Yearbook,** the scientific community and the educational community possess an instrument of information on European educational research. This instrument can reveal new approaches and innovations at the same time as proven knowledge. It can also serve as an observatory of scientific activity. It can finally permit researchers to get to know each other better, researchers and decision-makers to make acquaintance, and to bring about fruitful working relationships.

This first volume is an experiment which owes a great deal to the past. Improvements as regards form as well as content will be introduced in the next edition, and production techniques will be entirely renewed. That is why remarks and suggestions will be very welcome.

INTRODUCTION

par Philippe CHAMPY
président du groupe Réseau de données Eudised

Les ouvrages de référence, comme les annuaires ou les répertoires, méritent plus que d'autres d'être présentés aux lecteurs. Pour trois séries de raisons. En premier lieu, ces ouvrages ne doivent pas être considérés dans l'absolu. Ils ont une histoire et sont produits dans des cadres institutionnels déterminés. Ce contexte doit être explicité car il éclaire les objectifs de ce type d'ouvrages. Dans une première partie, il a donc paru indispensable d'exposer brièvement ce qu'est le **réseau Eudised** du Conseil de l'Europe à l'origine du présent **Annuaire européen de la recherche en éducation**. En second lieu, les lecteurs doivent pouvoir évaluer la valeur de l'information qui leur est délivrée. À cette fin, ils doivent non seulement pouvoir identifier les biais introduits dans la collecte et la sélection des données, mais aussi connaître l'arrière-plan intellectuel et technique qui conditionne le traitement de l'information. La deuxième partie de cette introduction rappelle la méthode en usage dans le réseau Eudised pour répertorier les recherches en éducation dans la trentaine de pays européens concernés. Les lecteurs comprendront mieux le contenu et la forme même de cet **Annuaire**. Enfin, il a paru essentiel que par-delà les informations ponctuelles qui sont présentées sur chaque recherche en particulier, l'on puisse disposer de quelques données générales de synthèse à des fins de comparaison. C'est le sens de la troisième partie qui donne un aperçu global du corpus des recherches signalées dans cette première livraison de l'**Annuaire européen de la recherche en éducation**.

1. LE RÉSEAU EUDISED DU CONSEIL DE L'EUROPE

En créant le réseau Eudised il y a une vingtaine d'années, le Conseil de l'Europe a manifesté un soutien politique pionnier à la recherche en éducation, soutien qui n'a pas été sans influence sur le mouvement de croissance de ce vaste champ de recherche jusqu'à aujourd'hui. Cette action novatrice a permis de mieux dessiner les contours d'un secteur difficile à cerner à cause de sa pluridisciplinarité et de ses ancrages multiples dans les sciences humaines et sociales, de la diversité de ses objets et de ses méthodologies, de la grande variété de ses développements et de son organisation selon les pays. En outre, la forte implication sociale d'une bonne partie de ses travaux suscitent ou alimentent des débats d'opinion.

Le Conseil a ainsi accompagné un grand mouvement de pensée, porteur d'avenir pour l'espace européen de l'éducation aujourd'hui en gestation. En effet, derrière le projet de collecter et de faire circuler l'information sur les recherches en éducation en Europe (idée qui fut à l'origine de la création du réseau Eudised au début des années 70 et qui demeure son objectif premier), se profile un enjeu considérable : le développement d'une **pensée éducative éclairée**, véritable socle d'un espace européen de l'éducation.

Depuis sa création dans le cadre du programme de travail du Conseil de la Coopération Culturelle, le réseau Eudised a favorisé et appuyé les efforts de maints pays pour rassembler les ressources nationales dans le domaine de la recherche en éducation et en capitaliser les résultats. Grâce à cette impulsion, il a permis à l'information spécialisée d'être davantage institutionnalisée et de franchir plus facilement les frontières encore souvent très étanches dans les domaines de l'éducation et de la formation. Ce travail international a été réalisé en respectant des normes communes et en utilisant un même thésaurus multilingue, le **Thésaurus Eudised** devenu, en 1980, à la suite d'un accord de coproduction entre le Conseil de l'Europe et la Commission des Communautés européennes, le **Thésaurus européen de l'éducation**. Ce thésaurus fait désormais autorité en Europe. Au sein du réseau Eudised, sa mise à jour est assurée par le groupe Gestion du thésaurus qui agit parallèlement au groupe Réseau de données.

Ainsi le réseau Eudised qui dispose d'agences nationales dans plus de trente pays centralise les signalements des recherches en éducation dans la banque de données Eudised. Il rend dès lors possible un regard rétrospectif sur une période de vingt ans. Le réseau fait circuler les informations au niveau international en recourant à deux voies principales : d'une part, l'accès en ligne à la banque de données sur le serveur de l'Agence spatiale européenne (ESA/IRS) depuis 1983, et, d'autre part, la publication du **Bulletin Eudised R & D** dont 48 numéros ont paru de 1974 à 1994. Le présent **Annuaire européen de la recherche en éducation** prend la suite de cette publication trimestrielle. Son rythme de parution annuel est mieux ajusté à celui des programmes de recherche. Cette première livraison de l'**Annuaire** correspond aux numéros 49 à 52 du **Bulletin**. Elle contient les informations collectées en 1993, soit 2084 signalements de recherche.

2. LA COLLECTE ET LE TRAITEMENT DE L'INFORMATION DANS LE RÉSEAU EUDISED

Ce sont les agences nationales qui sont chargées de collecter et de traiter le signalement des recherches dans chaque pays. Parfois elles puisent dans des banques de données nationales préexistantes. Dans la majorité des cas, elles procèdent elles-mêmes à un travail original de collecte des données par voie d'enquête directe auprès des équipes de recherche ou par tout autre moyen jugé opportun. Ces agences sont inscrites dans des contextes institutionnels très divers (administration centrale de ministères, institutions nationales d'information et de documentation, institutions nationales de recherche, etc.).

Contrairement à une idée reçue, la collecte et la mise à jour de l'information concernant les recherches vivantes ne sont pas aisées. La difficulté tient à des raisons scientifiques et à des raisons institutionnelles. À cet égard, la situation d'un pays à l'autre est relativement contrastée. Du point de vue scientifique, c'est le caractère pluriannuel de la recherche qui représente la principale difficulté. Lors de sa photographie annuelle de la recherche en éducation, le réseau Eudised peut rencontrer les recherches à l'une des trois phases de leur existence : la phase de lancement, la phase d'exécution ou la phase finale des résultats. L'ambition du réseau est de capter chaque recherche si possible une première fois dans la phase initiale et une seconde fois dans la phase terminale. Le premier " portrait " pourra être pris sur le vif ; mais il restera nécessairement sommaire. Le second " portrait " sera plus détaillé ; il pourra en revanche être jugé trop tardif par rapport à l'actualité du jour. La collecte annuelle du réseau s'apparente donc à un album de photographies réunissant des " portraits " successifs de recherches à leur début, en cours ou achevées, auxquels s'ajoutent des " portraits " plus anciens de recherches qui avaient jusqu'alors échappé à l'objectif. Par rapport à l'actualité immédiate, le décalage est inévitable. Par contre, pour jeter un regard rétrospectif et circonscrire l'émergence d'un thème, l'album est irremplaçable.

Les éventuels obstacles institutionnels à la collecte des données sont plus connus : diversité et cloisonnement des structures de recherche au niveau national qui empêchent la circulation rapide des informations, souci d'une certaine confidentialité dans la phase initiale de la recherche, rejet par les chercheurs de procédures d'enquête jugées fastidieuses, fragilité de certaines agences nationales Eudised, etc.

Une fois identifiée, chaque recherche est décrite à travers un ensemble de champs d'information rassemblés dans un bordereau normalisé. Du point de vue intellectuel, elle est indexée à l'aide de descripteurs extraits du **Thésaurus européen de l'éducation.** Chaque recherche fait également l'objet d'un résumé qui s'attache à dégager ses hypothèses, sa méthodologie et ses résultats. Sont signalées aussi les publications qui en sont issues. Ce sont ces diverses informations qui forment le corps des notices publiées dans cet **Annuaire.** Elles sont rédigées en anglais, français ou allemand et donnent lieu à un contrôle éditorial centralisé.

Pour plus de commodité, les recherches sont présentées dans cet **Annuaire** par grandes thématiques (appelées aussi terminogrammes) d'après la structure du thésaurus. À la fin de chacune d'elles, une liste de corrélats signale les recherches voisines. Trois index complètent l'ouvrage : un index des noms cités, un index des matières (dans les neuf langues du thésaurus) et un index par pays.

3. APERÇU GLOBAL SUR LES RECHERCHES PRÉSENTÉES DANS L'ANNUAIRE

Dans les limites de cette introduction, trois indicateurs paraissent pertinents pour une approche globale des recherches dont les signalements ont été collectés en 1993 : la répartition des recherches par pays, leur répartition selon les thématiques du thésaurus, leur répartition selon la durée.

Le **tableau 1** rend compte de la **répartition des recherches par pays.** Il permet une approche géographique. Ce tableau suscite trois commentaires :

1°) Plusieurs agences nationales anciennes n'ont pas fourni d'information en 1993 à cause de perturbations dans leur fonctionnement (Danemark, Espagne, Finlande, Hongrie, Islande, Luxembourg, Malte, Portugal, Suède) ; une agence récente n'a pas encore fourni d'information (Lituanie).

2°) Parmi les 23 agences nationales ayant fourni de l'information, le Royaume-Uni représente à lui seul plus de la moitié des recherches (58,6 %). 13 pays représentent chacun moins de 1 % (Albanie, Belgique, Bulgarie, Chypre, Estonie, Grèce, Irlande, Lettonie, Norvège, Roumanie, Russie, Slovaquie, Slovénie), 3 pays représentent entre 1 et 1,9 % (Italie, Pologne, Turquie), 3 pays entre 2 et 4,9 % (Autriche, Suisse, République tchèque), 3 pays entre 5 et 10,9 % (Allemagne, France, Pays-Bas).

3°) Ces chiffres incitent à se poser la question de la représentativité ou de l'exhaustivité des informations. Les disproportions constatées entre les pays reflètent-elles des différences importantes entre les potentiels de recherche en éducation au niveau national ou proviennent-elles d'un effet grossissant dû à l'inégale efficacité de la collecte des données selon les pays ? La plupart des pays d'Europe centrale et orientale viennent de rejoindre le réseau Eudised. Les agences nationales y sont en cours de constitution. Pour les pays d'Europe occidentale et nordique, il semble que la collecte ne soit pas toujours assurée au même niveau, ce qui peut fausser les comparaisons. Il semble aussi que la reconnaissance de la recherche en éducation soit inégale d'un pays à l'autre : très forte et ancienne au Royaume-Uni, elle se limite ailleurs à la recherche professionnelle la plus établie. Les chiffres doivent donc être utilisés avec beaucoup de précaution.

Tableau 1 : Répartition des recherches par pays (N = 2084)

Pays	Nombre	%	Pays	Nombre	%	Pays	Nombre	%
Albanie	1	0,05	Hongrie	-	-	Roumanie	5	0,30
Allemagne	213	10,20	Irlande	5	0,25	Royaume-Uni	1222	58,60
Autriche	75	3,60	Islande	-	-	Russie	12	0,60
Belgique	15	0,70	Italie	40	1,90	Slovaquie	11	0,50
Bulgarie	6	0,30	Lettonie	2	0,10	Slovénie	4	0,20
Chypre	13	0,60	Lituanie	-	-	Suède	-	-
Danemark	-	-	Luxembourg	-	-	Suisse	44	2,10
Espagne	-	-	Malte	-	-	Tchèque (Rép.)	48	2,30
Estonie	13	0,60	Norvège	20	1,00	Turquie	28	1,30
Finlande	-	-	Pays-Bas	127	6,10	Conseil de l'Europe	4	0,20
France	145	7,00	Pologne	25	1,20			
Grèce	6	0,30	Portugal	-	-			

Le **tableau 2** donne la **répartition des recherches par grandes thématiques** du thésaurus (les terminogrammes). Il est difficile d'en tirer des conclusions concernant les approches disciplinaires et méthodologiques des recherches en éducation puisque les thématiques s'attachent davantage aux objets de recherche.

Comme il est logique, le système scolaire (sous les aspects pédagogique, curriculaire, didactique, politique, etc.) est l'objet dominant (67,8 % des recherches en cumulant les thématiques 01, 02, 03, 04, 05, 06, 07, 08, 09, 10, 11, 12, 13, 14, 15, 34, 35, 36). Les objets d'ordre psychologique concernent environ un dixième des recherches (19, 20, 21, 22, 23, 24), les objets d'ordre sociologique concernent environ un vingtième des recherches (27, 28, 29, 30, 31). Mais ces deux proportions ne reflètent pas l'importance de ces approches dans l'étude du système scolaire. Le domaine de la formation professionnelle et de la formation d'adultes ainsi que le lien du système éducatif avec l'économie concernent environ 10 % des recherches (32, 33, 34).

Tableau 2 : Répartition des recherches selon la structure du thésaurus (N = 2084)

Thématique du thésaurus	Nombre	%	Thématique du thésaurus	Nombre	%
01 Enseignement et formation	167	8,00	22 Affectivité et sentiment	5	0,20
02 Acquisition de connaissances	51	2,40	23 Motivation du comportement	31	1,50
03 Principes d'éducation	127	6,10	24 Comportement	40	2,00
04 Système d'enseignement	240	11,50	25 Santé	11	0,50
05 Administration de l'enseignement	90	4,30	26 Handicap	87	4,20
06 Evaluation	109	5,20	27 Interrelations	38	1,80
07 Bâtiment	7	0,30	28 Groupes et organisations	10	0,50
08 Équipement	9	0,40	29 Environnement socio-culturel	46	2,20
09 Programme d'études	38	1,80	30 Environnement démographique	5	0,20
10 Contenu de l'éducation	116	5,60	31 Milieu familial	8	0,40
11 Sciences et technologie	104	5,00	32 Environnement économique	30	1,40
12 Sciences sociales	54	2,60	33 Environnement du travail	131	6,30
13 Sciences du langage	161	7,80	34 Profession et personnel	61	3,00
14 Philosophie et religion	16	0,80	35 Administration	18	0,90
15 Art	22	1,00	36 Administration publique	22	1,00
16 Recherche	24	1,10	37 Organisations internationales	1	0,05
17 Systèmes d'information	22	1,00	38 Afrique	2	0,10
18 Source d'information	18	0,90	39 Amérique	-	-
19 Développement de la personnalité	48	2,30	40 Asie/Moyen-Orient/Océanie	12	0,60
20 Processus cognitif	60	2,90	41 Europe	2	0,10
21 Personnalité	40	2,00	42 Régions	1	0,05

Le **tableau 3** donne la **répartition des recherches selon la durée et par thématiques**. Ce tableau fournit des indications chronologiques très précieuses et laisse entrevoir la grande diversité existant entre les recherches signalées dans ce volume. Il apparaît que la moitié des recherches (49,2 %) durent de 1 à 3 ans, les trois quarts (74,7 %) durent de 1 à 5 ans. Les recherches sans date de fin (13,2 %) correspondent soit à des recherches récentes, soit à des recherches anciennes dont la durée dépasse 5 ans, soit à des recherches dont la date de fin est ignorée. Les deux premiers cas sont apparemment les plus fréquents.

Tableau 3 : Répartition des recherches selon la durée et par thématiques (N = 2084)

	1 à 2 ans	2 à 3 ans	3 à 4 ans	4 à 5 ans	Plus de 5 ans	Sans date de fin	Total		1 à 2 ans	2 à 3 ans	3 à 4 ans	4 à 5 ans	Plus de 5 ans	Sans date de fin	Total
01	47	39	33	21	12	15	167	22	2	-	-	1	1	1	5
02	11	11	8	6	5	10	51	23	4	11	7	3	3	3	31
03	33	34	18	18	13	11	127	24	14	10	6	2	3	5	40
04	86	50	34	21	28	21	240	25	5	-	-	2	2	2	11
05	27	24	14	5	9	11	90	26	22	23	9	8	11	14	87
06	35	19	23	7	14	11	109	27	7	7	7	6	4	7	38
07	3	-	2	-	1	1	7	28	2	2	3	1	2	-	10
08	2	3	1	1	2	-	9	29	16	11	8	1	3	7	46
09	9	4	4	10	7	4	38	30	1	-	1	-	2	1	5
10	34	22	12	13	17	18	116	31	4	2	-	1	-	1	8
11	28	21	13	8	16	18	104	32	10	9	2	1	1	7	30
12	9	8	11	8	13	5	54	33	49	26	16	9	9	22	131
13	31	35	28	14	33	20	161	34	26	10	10	5	9	1	61
14	4	4	3	3	-	2	16	35	5	6	4	-	1	2	18
15	4	2	2	6	5	3	22	36	8	2	8	2	2	-	22
16	11	5	2	2	3	1	24	37	1	1	-	-	-	-	2
17	9	5	3	1	-	4	22	38	-	1	1	-	-	-	2
18	5	3	1	4	2	3	18	39	-	-	-	-	-	-	-
19	7	7	9	8	2	15	48	40	-	1	4	3	4	-	12
20	11	6	8	6	8	21	60	41	-	-	1	-	1	-	2
21	17	4	5	3	4	7	40	42	-	-	-	-	1	-	1
								Total	599	427	329	210	253	274	2084
								%	28,7	20,5	15,4	10,1	12,1	13,2	100

4. CONCLUSION

Avec la première livraison de cet **Annuaire**, la communauté scientifique et la communauté éducative disposent d'un outil d'information sur la recherche européenne en éducation. Cet outil peut faire connaître les approches nouvelles, les innovations, en même temps que les connaissances certifiées. Il peut aussi servir d'observatoire de l'activité scientifique. Il peut enfin permettre aux chercheurs entre eux, aux chercheurs et aux décideurs entre eux, de mieux se connaître et d'engager des relations de travail fructueuses.

Ce volume est un premier essai qui doit encore beaucoup au passé. Des améliorations dans la forme comme dans le contenu seront apportées lors de la prochaine édition dont les conditions de production seront largement rénovées. C'est pourquoi les remarques et les propositions seront les bienvenues.

Serial number ⟶

Country in which the
research is/was carried out

Title of the research project

C = completed

Researcher ⟶

Institution where the
research is/was carried out

Abstract ⟶

Publication(s)

985 A pre-school intervention programme for disadvantaged children.
IEC 1969—1976 ⟵ ——————————————— Dates of the research
Kellaghan, Thomas.   project
Inst: Educational Research Centre.
St. Patrick's College, IE-Dublin 9.
Fin: Department of Education of Irish government; Van Leer Foun-   Source of finance
dation, The Hague.
cognitive development; compensatory education; deprived; early read-
ing; family environment; pre-school education; primary education;
socially handicapped développement cognitif; éducation compen- ⟵ EUDISED descriptors
satoire; défavorisé; lecture précoce; milleu familial; éducation pré-
scolaire; enseignement primaire; handicapé social
    In 1969, an experimental pre-school for three- and four-year old
children was set up in a disadvantaged area in central Dublin which
had a history of high educational failure. The major aim of the pre-
school was to assist in the development of the cognitive skills of the
children and by so doing prepare them for the work of the primary
school. A curriculum designed to foster cognitive development...

Kellaghan, T. Intelligence and achievement in a disadvantaged population: A cross-lagged pannel analysis. *Irish Journal of Education,* 1973,
7, 23—28.

Kellaghan, T. *The evaluation of an intervention programme for disad-*
vantaged children. Windsor: NFER, 1977. (ISBN 0 85633 124 4).

Research title in the original language

O = Ongoing

Research supervisor ⟶

990 Barns initiativ pa lagstadiat (Children's initiative in primary
schools)
SE O 1975—1980
Krook, Ylva, Malmros, Asa   Institution where the
Sup: Andersson, Bengt-Erik.   research is/was carried
Inst. Pedagogiska Institutionen, Department of Educational and Psy-   out
chological Research, Fack, S-100 26, Stockholm 34.
Stockholm School of Education, Fack, S-100 26, Stockholm 34. ⟵ Parent institution
Fin: The National Board of Education.
primary education; activity method; child development; learning proc-
ess; work attitude; work environment; developmental psychology;
motivation; interest; satisfaction; theory of education
enseignement primaire; méthode active; développement de l'enfant;
apprentissage; attitude envers le travail; milieu de travail; psychologie
du développement; motivation; intérêt; satisfaction; théorie de
l'éducation
    The project is based on Piaget's theories of development. The child
has a drive to learn and a spontaneous wish to...

Intitulé de la recherche

Numéro d'ordre

Pays où la recherche est/était conduite

C = recherche achevée

Etablissement où la recherche est/etait conduite

Source de financement

1067 Contribution à une étude psychologique générale et différentielle de conduites cognitives en situation habituelle.

FR C 1970—1976. ⟵——————————————— *Dates de la recherche*

Gillet, Bernard. ⟵——————————————— *Chercheur*

Sup: Reuchlin, Maurice. ⟵ *Directeur de recherche*

Inst: Institut National d'Orientation Professionnelle, Service de Recherche, 41 rue Gay Lussac, 75005 Paris

Conservatoire National des Arts et Métiers (CNAM), 292, rue Saint-Martin, 75141 Paris Cedex 03. ⟵——————————— *Etablissement du tuteur*

Fin: C.N.A.M.-Ecole Pratique des Hautes Etudes 3a Section—C.N.R.S. (ERA 79). Université Paris V.

vocational training; cognitive process; logical thinking; upper secondary; electrical engineering; problem solving

formation professionnelle; processus cognitif; pensée logique; secondaire deuxième cycle; électrotechnique; résolution de problème

    Les conduites cognitives habituelles, etudiées ici, sont le raisonnement de techniciens en électronique en cours de formation. Ce sont des élèves d'établissements techniques qui préparent le baccalauréat ⟵—— *Analyse* de technicians en électronique F2. Ils sont confrontés ici à des exercices, de type scolaire...

Publication(s)

Publ: Gillet, Bernard. Premières difficultés dans l'apprentissage de l'électronique. In: *L'Orientation scolaire et professionnelle*, 1975, 4, no 2, pp. 109-135.

Gillet, Bernard. Psychopédagogie de l'enseignement des objets techniques. In: *Bulletin de l'Enseignement technique et de la formation professionnelle* no. 17, février 1975, 17 p., et In: *Bulletin de Psychologie*, 1974—75, XXVIII, no. 319 pp. 948—955.

1038 Elaboration d'un programme grammatical en vue de l'enseignement de l'anglais dans les quatre premières années de l'enseignement secondaire français.

FRO 1976—1979

O = recherche en cours

Samuel, Jane; Bailly, Danièle; Barrie, Bill; Cureau, Jean; Luc, Christiane; Marandet, Jesu; Prevoteau, Solange.

Sup: Legrand, Louis.

Inst: Département des études et recherches appliquées aux enseignements généraux et à la vie scolaire. Section Langues vivantes, 29 rue d'Ulm, 75230 Paris Cedex 05.

Institut National de Recherche Pédagogique.

Fin: Ministère de l'Education.

Descripteurs EUDISED

English; secondary school; teaching programme; lexicon; grammar

anglais; école secondaire; programme d'enseignement; lexique; grammaire

    La recherche a pour buts: l'harmonisation du programme lexical et du programme grammatical, la recherche de progressions pédagogiques dans l'enseignement d'un...

EUROPEAN EDUCATION YEARBOOK 1993

01 TEACHING AND TRAINING – ENSEIGNEMENT ET FORMATION – UNTERRICHT UND AUSBILDUNG

11683   16-19 mathematics support materials project.
GBR   1993
Research Date(s): 1991-1992
Everton, C.
Inst: Leicester University, School of Education, University Road, Leicester LE1 7RH, United Kingdom.
Fin: Trustees of the School Mathematics Project.
teaching aid; mathematics; post-compulsory education
moyen d'enseignement; mathématiques; enseignement postobligatoire
PROJECT DESCRIPTION
 The aim is to research and produce support materials for teachers using 16-19 mathematics. The end product is to be a set of three booklets. Trialling of the booklets will be carried out by asking pertinent questions and building up a set of answer data.

11684   Adapting tutoring systems to students' learning styles.
GBR   1993
Research Date(s): 1989-1993
Del Soldato, T.
Sup: Du Boulay, J.
Inst: Sussex University, School of Cognitive and Computing Sciences, Sussex House, Falmer, Brighton BN1 9RH, United Kingdom.
Fin: Brazilian Council for Scientific and Technological Development (CNPq).
didactic use of computer; artificial intelligence; educational software; cognitive style
usage didactique de l'ordinateur; intelligence artificielle; didacticiel; style cognitif
PROJECT DESCRIPTION
 The purpose of this project is to investigate the possibilities of adapting computer-assisted instruction to students' learning styles. Usually tutoring systems adjust their instructional planning according to what knowledge the learner has acquired, neglecting how the student acquired such knowledge. Several aspects of learning systems (e.g. level of confidence, anxiety, independence vs. need of constant help, toleration to challenge) will be considered by the instructional planner, aiming to motivate the student and enrich the teaching interaction. As a result of this project, the core of a learning style adaptable tutoring system should be implemented.

11685   Adult learning at work.
GBR   1993
Research Date(s): 1991-1992
Frank, F.
Sup: Hamilton, M.
Inst: Lancaster University, Department of Educational Research, Centre for the Study of Education and Training, Cartmel College, Bailrigg, Lancaster LA1 4YW, United Kingdom.
Fin: Leverhulme Trust.
basic training; adult education; literacy; employee; in-service training
formation de base; éducation des adultes; alphabétisation; salarié; formation en cours d'emploi
PROJECT DESCRIPTION
 The aim of this project is to chart the contemporary process of workplace literacy schemes, making the process more viable and aiding its growth. Three main case studies with other minor ones are being used plus a sample of 100 telephone interviews with employers in the North West, in small and large sized companies. The case studies will include interviews with students, union representatives, management and college staff involved at each site. Questionnaires are also being circulated to groups of students and group discussions with students and union representatives have been organised. Loosely structured interviews will lead to qualitative data. Telephone interviews will be carried out with the organisation personnel responsible for training, to ascertain the companies' attitudes to workplace basic education training. Results and conclusions of the research will be presented in a way which is accessible to employers and trade unions and which will set out practical ways in which these groups can proceed to set up workplace basic education schemes. A longer report will be produced for the Leverhulme Trust.

11686   Aide à domicile: emplois et formation en Bourgogne.
FRA   1993
Research Date(s): 1987-1989
Danrey, Jean.
Inst: Université de Dijon, UER Faculté des sciences économiques et de gestion, CNRS UPR/29 et GDR/996, Institut de recherche sur l'économie de l'éducation, BP 138, 21004 Dijon Cedex, France.
Fin: Délégation régionale à la formation professionnelle de Bourgogne; Conseil régional de Bourgogne.
in-service training; unskilled worker; occupational qualification
formation en cours d'emploi; travailleur non-qualifié; qualification professionnelle
PROJECT DESCRIPTION
 Objectifs: Dans le secteur d'activité "aide ménagère à domicile" les travailleurs sont généralement dotés d'un faible niveau de formation, d'où la création récente d'un diplôme national: le CAFAD (novembre 1988) qui valide le savoir-faire et les connaissances acquises par le personnel en cours d'emploi. L'étude tente de cerner l'ampleur et les caractéristiques de ce nouveau marché de la formation continue.
 Méthodologie: Evaluation des besoins des employés et des actions de formation prises en charge par les Pouvoirs publics et/ou les employeurs.
 Résultats: le CAFAD ne saurait régler tous les problèmes de formation. En amont il convient d'abord de lutter contre l'illettrisme des salariés afin de leur permettre d'accéder à une formation qui valide un premier palier de qualification. En aval il est nécessaire de mettre en place une politique de formation pour faire face aux situations de dépendance ou de perte d'autonomie.

Publ: Danrey, Jean. *Aide à domicile: emplois et formation en Bourgogne.* IREDU: Rapport à la Délégation régionale à la formation professionnelle de Bourgogne, 1989, 100p.

11687   Analyse de l'apprentissage et évaluation des activités de remédiation.
FRA   1993
Research Date(s): 1987-1991
Rapiau, Marie-Thérèse.
Inst: Université de Dijon, UER Faculté des sciences économiques et de gestion, CNRS UPR/29 et GDR/996, Institut de recherche sur l'économie de l'éducation, BP 138, 21004 Dijon Cedex, France.
apprenticeship; alternating training; technical education; remedial teaching; knowledge level
apprentissage professionnel; formation alternée; enseignement technique; soutien pédagogique; niveau de connaissances
PROJECT DESCRIPTION
 Objectifs: La loi du 23 juillet 1987 a lancé un mouvement de rénovation et de promotion de l'apprentissage en créant une filière complète de formation par alternance (niveaux V, IV, III). La recherche engagée sur l'apprentissage d'une part examine comment se situe l'évolution antérieure de l'apprentissage par rapport aux modes alternatifs de formation dans les établissements techniques ainsi que la place que pourront prendre les formations alternées dans les nouveaux schémas de développement des enseignements professionnels ("bacs pro"). Il s'agit de savoir sur quelles lignes de partage peuvent s'établir les rapports entre les différents types de formation. Cette nouvelle concurrence entre l'apprentissage et l'enseignement technique se fera à un niveau d'acquisitions des élèves plus élevé.
 Méthodologie: Les travaux permettent d'évaluer l'efficacité interne des formations en apprentissage notamment au niveau des formes d'aide aux élèves et de leurs coûts associés dans la perspective de porter le niveau final de ces formations au niveau III. Ces travaux sont complétés par des études d'insertion sur le marché du travail, en effectuant des analyses secondaires d'enquêtes existantes.

Publ: Rapiau, Marie-Thérèse. *Efficacité interne, efficacité externe des for-mations techniques courtes (CAP, BEP, Apprentissage): le cas des métiers de la coiffure et de l'hôtellerie.* IREDU, 1989, 14p.

Rapiau, Marie-Thérèse. *La formation par alternance de niveau V: forma-tion, insertion professionnelle, quelle relation.* IREDU-CEREQ, 1990, 13p.

Rapiau, Marie-Thérèse. *L'apprentissage de niveau V: formation, insertion professionnelle.* In: *Savoir,* n° 2, 1990, pp. 281-289.

Rapiau, Marie-Thérèse. *Le commerce: activité économique, formations, emplois.* Rapport à la délégation régionale de l'ANPE 1990, 68p.

Rapiau, Marie-Thérèse. Formation et insertion des apprentis de niveau V, quelle relation établir? In: *La revue de l'économie sociale,* 1990, pp. 269-280.

Rapiau, Marie-Thérèse. *Les mesures de la production scolaire en appren-tissage: méthode générale, première version.* IREDU, document interne, 1991, 11p.

11688 Analyse en effecten van uitleg door medeleerlingen en leer-krachten bij een complexe taak. (Analysis and effects of fellow pupils' and teachers' explanations in the performance of complex tasks.)
NLD 1994
Research Date(s): 1993
Ros, A.A.
Inst: RION Instituut voor Onderwijsonderzoek (RION Institute for Educa-tional Research), P.O. Box 1286, 9701 BG Groningen, Netherlands.
Rijksuniversiteit Groningen (State University of Groningen), P.O. Box 72, 9700 AB Groningen, Netherlands
Fin: SVO het Instituut voor Onderzoek van het Onderwijs.
teaching method; transfer of learning; teacher role; pupil; cooperation
méthode pédagogique; transfert pédagogique; rôle de l'enseignant; élève; coopération
PROJECT DESCRIPTION
   Background: A doctoral study has shown that in the upper years of primary school cooperative learning hardly occurs in situations where pupils jointly perform a task. Teachers do not object, however, against pupils asking each other for explanations. Little is known about the effec-tiveness of this approach. Pupils may receive more feedback from their fellow pupils - and more frequently -, but much depends on the quality of this feedback in comparison with the explanations that can be provided by the teacher.
   Aims: (1) To determine to what extent pupils, in comparison with teach-ers, use in their explanations particular elements that have been defined by Mehan and Riel (1982); (2) to explore the relationships among the ele-ments in the explanation and the explanatory strategies used by pupils.
   Methods: Experiment.
   Design: In a quasi-experimental design teachers and pupils will be asked to explain a specific task. The study will be conducted in ten primary schools, involving ten teachers, 60 pupils who give an explanation and 90 pupils who receive an explanation. Of each teacher, three explanations will be observed. Conditions and task instructions will be standardized. Pretests and posttests will be conducted to measure any improvement in the performance levels of pupils who give and pupils who receive explana-tions. Three aspects of explanation will be distinguished: (1) the presence or absence of a particular element in the explanation; (2) the frequency with which an element occurs in the explanation; and (3) the sequence in which explanatory elements occur.

11689 Arbeidsmarktrelevantie en rendement PBVE. (Labour mar-ket relevance and output of adult education courses.)
NLD 1994
Research Date(s): 1989-1992
Onstenk, J.H.A.M.; Wilbrink, B.; Babeliowsky, M.L.B.; Felix, C.
Inst: Stichting Centrum voor Onderwijsonderzoek (SCO) (Centre for Educa-tional Research), Grote Bickersstraat 72, 1013 KS Amsterdam, Netherlands.
Universiteit van Amsterdam (University of Amsterdam), P.O. Box 19268, 1000 GG Amsterdam, Netherlands
Fin: SVO het Instituut voor Onderzoek van het Onderwijs.
vocational training; adult education; training-employment relationship; employment opportunities
formation professionnelle; éducation des adultes; relation formation-emploi; chances d'obtenir un emploi
PROJECT DESCRIPTION
   Background: In 1987 the "Vocationally-Oriented Adult Education" (PBVE) projects were launched. With these projects it is hoped to establish greater coherence in course offerings and to improve the links between adult education courses and the labour market. The aim is to offer the less privileged a type of training that gives them a better chance on the labour market. Course planning and delivery take place at the regional level. The PBVE philosophy includes two elements that may to some extent be contradictory: the need to take account of the needs of the labour market and the need to take account of the needs of specific target groups. It is the task of PBVE course providers to unite these two goals. The regula-tions governing PBVE courses give the course providers ample scope for their own interpretation of the concept of "labour market relevance".
   Aim: The study aimed to clarify the concept of "labour market relevance" as it is used in the context of PBVE courses. More specifically, the following research questions were addressed: (1) How do course prov-iders attempt to ensure that the courses they offer have relevance for the labour market opportunities of their target groups? (2) How valid and how reliable are the assessments of the course providers regarding the labour market relevance of the PBVE courses?
   Methods: Content analysis; instrument development; questionnaire survey.
   Results: Due to rapid developments in the field of PBVE policy, the Regional Manpower Services Board (RBA) is now responsible for assessing the labour market relevance of PBVE courses. The courses as such have largely been incorporated in the work of the Regional Education Office (RBO). Thus, a more rigid distinction has been established between training supply and demand. The various forms of cooperation that have been developed with regard to PBVE allow for a reasonably reliable and valid assessment of the labour market relevance of the courses. The position of the PBVE coordinators, between training supply and demand, plays a major part in this. A reasonable degree of consensus has been reached about a course supply that has relevance both for the labour market and for the target group. Furthermore, it is possible to form a fairly valid judgement of former participants' success on the labour market. On the other hand, there is dissatisfaction about the available information on which this judgement has to be based, especially where specific aspects of labour market relevance are concerned, such as the opportunities for dis-crete target groups, assessment of the level of training, and comparison with qualifications offered outside the PBVE system.

Publ: Onstenk, J.H.A.M.; et al. *Arbeidsmarktrelevantie van het PBVE-aanbod.* Amsterdam: SCO, 1991, 201p.

11690 Befaehigung zum Verstehen von Tabellen und Schemata bei Schuelern der Primarstufe. (Primary school pupils' ability to under-stand tables and schematic drawings.)
DEU 1993
Research Date(s): 1990-1993
Schmidt, S.
Sup: Nestler, K.
Inst: Paedagogische Hochschule Halle-Koethen, Abt. Koethen FB Primar-schullehrerausbildung, Fachgebiet Psychologie, Lohmannstrasse 23, O-4370 Koethen.
primary education; pupil; comprehension; cognitive ability; didactics; dia-gram; graph
enseignement primaire; élève; compréhension; aptitude cognitive; didac-tique; diagramme; graphique
PROJECT DESCRIPTION
   Inhalt: Konstatierende Untersuchungen zum Verstehen von unterschied-lich gestalteten Tabellen (Variable: Groesse, Informationsdichte, Struk-turiertheit, Bekanntheit) in Abhaengigkeit von Personenvariablen. Hypothetisch wird z.B. ein Zusammenhang zwischen einem optimalen Konzentriertheitsgrad der Grafik und ihrer Strukturiertheit einerseits und unterschiedlichen Verstehenstiefen (Faktenerfassung und Inferenzbildung) andererseits angenommen. Kognitive Lernervoraussetzungen und Bekanntheit des Inhalts werden als Einflussgroessen untersucht. Aus-bildungsexperimente mit Schuelern der Klasse 4 zur zielgerichteten Qualifizierung des Tabellenverstaendnisses sollen Hinweise auf didaktisch-methodische Konsequenzen ergeben.
   Geographischer Raum: Sachsen-Anhalt.
   Vorgehensweise: Verstehenstheoretische Ansaetze (Engelkamp, Mandl, Schnotz, Ballstaedt, Baumann), theoretische Modelle zur Lehrstrategie des Aufsteigens vom Abstrakten zum Konkreten (Dawydow, Lompscher) und Interiorisationstheorie (Galperin). Untersuchungsdesign: (Quasi-)Experiment.
   Datengewinnung: Gruppenbefragung (Stichprobe: 360; Schueler der Klasse 4; Auswahlverfahren: willkuerlich). Experiment (dito. Stichprobe: 20; Schueler der Klasse 4; Auswahlverfahren: bewusst). Primaererhebung: Feldarbeit von Mitarbeitern des Projektes durchgefuehrt.
   Auswertung: Varianzanalyse; Clusteranalyse. Datenaufbereitung: Pruef-statistische Verfahren.

11691 Begleituntersuchung 'Fachakademien'. (A study on 'Fachakademien' (vocational academies).)
AUT 1993
Research Date(s): 1991-1995
Jonke, Edith; Freundlinger, Alfred; Hoellinger, Herwig; Thum-Kraft, Monika; Eckstein, Wolf-Erich.
Inst: Institut fuer Bildungsforschung der Wirtschaft, Rainergasse 38, A-1050 Wien.
Fin: Wirtschaftsfoerderungsinstitut der Handelskammer.
further training; vocational school; occupational qualification; vocational education
formation complémentaire; école professionnelle; qualification profession-nelle; enseignement professionnel

PROJECT DESCRIPTION

Die vom Wirtschaftsfoerderungsinstitut ins Leben gerufenen und im Herbst 1991 erstmals beginnenden Fachakademien, die zur Hoeherqualifizierung begabter LehrabsolventInnen entwickelt wurden, sollen ueber drei Jahre hinweg (= Dauer der Fachakademie) begleitend untersucht werden.

Die Untersuchung ist in vier Teile gegliedert: 1. Dokumentation 2. Befragung aller Studierenden (dreimal), der Kursleiter (dreimal), der Abbrecher und der Betriebe mittels Fragebogen (schriftlich). Dieser Teil wird mit Hilfe statistischer Verfahren und der EDV ausgewertet. 3. Leitsaetze fuer das paedagogische Konzept und 4. Recherche der rechtlichen Stellung im oesterreichischen Ausbildungsrecht und im weiteren in der Europaeischen Gemeinschaft.

11692 Betriebliche Berufsausbildung: Lern- und Verhaltensschwierigkeiten. (In-house vocational training: learning and behavioural difficulties.)
DEU 1993
Research Date(s): 1991-1992
Schwark, W.; Elsaesser, T.; Uhl, H.; Zenke, K.
Inst: Paedagogische Hochschule Ludwigsburg, Postfach 220, D-7140 Ludwigsburg.
Fin: Land Baden-Wuerttemberg Ministerium fuer Wissenschaft und Kunst.
vocational training; enterprise; learning difficulty; behaviour; in-service training
formation professionnelle; entreprise; difficulté de l'apprentissage; comportement; formation en cours d'emploi
PROJECT DESCRIPTION

Inhalt: Teil I: Kategorisierung und Operationalisierung von Lern- und Verhaltensschwierigkeiten. Teil II: Entwicklung praeventiver und interventionistischer Massnahmen (ab 1/93).

Datengewinnung: Gruppendiskussion (Auszubildende im 1. Jahr). Muendliche Befragung (dito). Expertengespraech (Ausbilder und Ausbildungsleiter). Aktenanalyse (betriebliche Beurteilungen).

11693 Betriebliche Weiterbildung fuer Ausbildungspersonal (BeWAP). (In-company further training for training personnel (BeWAP).)
DEU 1993
Research Date(s): 1988-1992
Fischer, A.; Herget, C.; Jehlicka, W.; Schubert, H.; Wussow, W.
Sup: Dikau, J.
Inst: Freie Universitaet Berlin, FB Erziehungs- und Unterrichtswissenschaften, Institut fuer Arbeits- und Berufspaedagogik WE 04, Arnimallee 9, D-1000 Berlin 33.
Fin: Land Berlin Senatsverwaltung fuer Schule, Berufsbildung und Sport.
training of trainers; further training; enterprise; training need; curriculum development; in-plant training
formation des formateurs; formation complémentaire; entreprise; besoin de formation; élaboration de programmes d'études; stage en entreprise
PROJECT DESCRIPTION

Inhalt: Ermittlung des Weiterbildungsbedarfs fuer Ausbilder, vor allem in Klein- und Mittelbetrieben; Entwicklung von Lehr- und Lernmaterial: Ausbilderzeitschrift (2x monatlich), Kompakthefte zu Themenbausteinen, Erprobungsseminare mit Kursleiterbroschueren; Durchfuehrung von Erprobungsseminaren mit Auswertung; Nachbefragung bei Lesern und Experten; Literaturanalyse.

Geographischer Raum: Berlin.

Vorgehensweise: Ausbilderqualifizierung zur Beseitigung erwachsenenpaedagogischer (berufspaedagogischer) Defizite bedarf neuer didaktischer/kommunikativer Ansaetze.

11694 Bilgisayar eğitimi ve bilgisayar destekli öğretime ilişkin öğretmen görüşlerinin değerlendirilmesi. (Teachers' perceptions of computer education and computer-assisted instruction (CAI).)
TUR 1994
Research Date(s): 1988-1989
Hızal, Alişan.
Inst: Anadolu Üniversitesi Eğitim Fakültesi (University of Anatolia, Faculty of Education), Eskişehir, Turkey.
didactic use of computer; education system; teacher behaviour; further education of teachers
usage didactique de l'ordinateur; système d'enseignement; comportement de l'enseignant; perfectionnement des enseignants
PROJECT DESCRIPTION

The support of teachers is important for the success of new teaching and learning systems based on new technologies. However, teachers tend to be less supportive of projects about which their opinion was not asked. Before introducing an innovation in education, a study should be made of teachers' views about the innovation concerned and their perceptions of the preconditions for its implementation.

The research was conducted to determine teachers' readiness, attitudes, expectations and suggestions with regard to computers, computer education and computer-assisted instruction (CAI). Data were collected with the help of a specially developed questionnaire which was given to 709 teachers from primary and secondary schools in the province of Eskişehir.

Results: Ten percent of teachers have a computer, 80 per cent would like to have one and 75 per cent think that computers are a necessity. Teachers support the introduction of CAI in Turkish schools. They feel that the use of computers in teaching has been accepted relatively late in Turkey because of shortages resulting from economic difficulties and because Turkish society has been insufficiently prepared. According to the teachers in the survey, computer education and CAI should be started in primary school or from the beginning of secondary school. Teachers should be trained in the fields of computer education and CAI. For this reason, computer training and CAI courses should be included in pre-service and in-service teacher training programmes. The respondents also indicated that it would be convenient if CAI was first started in the fields of science and mathematics. They expect that an inadequate infrastructure (electricity, buildings, etc.) will have a detrimental effect on CAI. They also note a lack of literature on CAI in Turkey. Furthermore, they say it would be useful to implement computer education and CAI in Turkish. It is proposed to train a team of experts who would prepare computer programs.

11695 CHECK (Continuing Higher Education Consulting Kit).
DEU 1993
Research Date(s): 1988-1992
Brinker, J.; Mitzlaff, H.; Foellmer, H.; Kraft-Dittmar, A.; Dittmar, S.
Sup: Fritsch, H.
Inst: Fernuniversitaet-Gesamthochschule Hagen, Zentrales Institut fuer Fernstudienforschung -ZIFF-, Humpertstr. 11a, D-5800 Hagen.
Fin: Institution; Bundesanstalt fuer Arbeit.
distance study; further training; educational guidance; educational need; information system
enseignement à distance; formation complémentaire; orientation pédagogique; besoin d'éducation; système d'information
PROJECT DESCRIPTION

Inhalt: Die vom Zentralen Institut fuer Fernstudienforschung entwickelte und in einigen Studienzentren/ Bildungsberatungstellen eingesetzte Datenbank fuer Angebote wissenschaftlicher Weiterbildung soll ergaenzt werden um einen vorgeschalteten Baustein zur Weiterbildungsberatung. Hierbei soll sichergestellt werden, dass dem Nachfrager nur die fuer seine persoenliche Situation in Frage kommenden Angebote praesentiert werden.

Geographischer Raum: BRD.

Vorgehensweise: Grosse Datenmengen lassen sich durch vorgeschaltete Filter auf sinnvolle Mengen reduzieren. Der theoretische Ansatz ist, dass solche Filter personenbezogen in einer Art Bildungs-Anamnese-Dialog aufgebaut werden, um dem so entstandenen Weiterbildungsprofil entsprechende Angebote zuzuordnen und durch anschliessende Befragung auszuwerten. Untersuchungsdesign: (Quasi-)Experiment.

Datengewinnung: Integrierte Datenbank-Nutzer-Befragung (Weiterbildungsinteressenten in Studienzentren; Auswahlverfahren: total). Datenerstellung auf der Basis von bereits vorliegenden Materialien wie Texten, Akten, Statistiken.

Auswertung: Datenaufbereitung: Verknuepfung verschiedener Datensaetze (record linkage).

Publ: Huelsmann, Thomas. *Wissenschaftliche Weiterbildung. Wissenschaftliche Weiterbildungsmoeglichkeiten aus der Weiterbildungsdatenbank CHECK (Continuing Higher Education Consulting Kit).* Hagen 1991.
Standort: UuStB Koeln(38)-920109058.

11696 Classroom-based multimedia authoring tools.
GBR 1993
Research Date(s): 1992-1993
Whalley, P.; Moar, M.
Inst: Open University, Institute of Educational Technology, Walton Hall, Milton Keynes MK7 6AA, United Kingdom.
Fin: National Council for Educational Technology; Stirling Microsystems.
didactic use of computer; authoring system; multimedia system
usage didactique de l'ordinateur; système-auteur; système multimédia
PROJECT DESCRIPTION

The proposed project is concerned with children's use of the dynamic representations made possible by the newly available multimedia tools. With the micros affordable by schools, it is now possible to capture high-quality colour images, sound, and short video clips. The purpose of this project is to develop an authoring tool for integrating these components which will be accessible to young children with a wide range of abilities, and to indicate ways in which it could enhance their work.

Considerable success has already been achieved in the classroom with a prototype of the proposed system. The researchers intend to further refine the software to better incorporate video, and to provide detailed documentation as to how the various components of a dynamic document can be created, manipulated and finally assembled together.

Technology, even if it is freely available, is of no use if it can not be integrated into classroom practice. The selection, organisation and presentation of learned materials is seen as a valuable part of current educational practice in British classrooms. Documenting how the software environment, together with paper-based planning tools, can enable and extend these activities is seen as an important part of the project. Examples of completed projects on topics such as the 'rain cycle' and 'digestion' will be included, both in their final state and in the form of separate image and sound components.

Publ: Moar, M. The construction of dynamic documents by children. In: *Proceedings of the 'East-West conference on emerging computer technologies in education*, Moscow, April 1992.

11697   Communication Aids for Language and Learning (CALL).
GBR   1993
Research Date(s): 1986-
Aitken, S.; Millar, S.; Nisbet, P.; Sutherland, E.
Sup: Entwistle, N.
Inst: Edinburgh University, Department of Education, CALL Centre, 4 Buccleuch Place, Edinburgh EH8 9JT, United Kingdom.
Fin: Scottish Office Education Department.
teaching aid; communication; handicapped; new technologies
moyen d'enseignement; communication; handicapé; nouvelles technologies
PROJECT DESCRIPTION

This is a research and development project, including service delivery, offering help in assessing what communication aids or teaching programmes are needed for learners with disabilities. Development work includes investigation of how these aids might be incorporated within, and contribute towards, curriculum development. Research is carried out into a wide range of aspects of communication difficulty and technology, with development of new microelectronic and computing systems to exploit new technologies. Support is given to clients and carers in tailoring and using the chosen system. Activities cover a Scotland-wide assessment service; information, demonstrations and advice and loan services. Training is offered through the media of seminars, awareness training, short and long term secondments for training of professionals including teachers, psychologists, social workers, programmers and technicians. 1991/1992 projects include assessment-related work; training-related work; smart wheelchair-related work; and functional communication-related work.

Publ: Aitken, S. Me and my therapists. In: *The Scottish Child*, Winter 1987, pp. 16-17.
Aitken, S. Computer aided instruction with the multiply impaired. In: *Journal of Mental Deficiency Research*, No 32/1988, pp. 257-263.
Buultjens, M. & Aitken, S. Assessment of vision in multiply impaired children. In: *British Journal of Special Education*, No 14/1987, pp. 112-114.
A comprehensive report pack and a set of research papers are available from the researcher.

11698   Comparative analysis of national and foreign programmes in the field of computer education: the development of new information technologies in teaching.
RUS   1994
Research Date(s): 1991-1992
Lobanov, Y.I.
Inst: Research Institute for Higher Education, 103062, Moscow, K-62, Podsosensky per. 20, Russia.
State Committee for Higher Education Institutions, 113833, Moscow, M-230, Lysinovskja str. 51, Russia
teaching method; concept formation; higher education; computer science; assessment
méthode pédagogique; formation de concept; enseignement supérieur; informatique; appréciation
PROJECT DESCRIPTION

The study proposes the use of adaptive management in computer education, involving assessment of students' achievement through deductive conceptual models. In assessing the quality of students' work the emphasis is not on the reproduction of theoretical knowledge, but on the ability to use the knowledge acquired in solving practical tasks.

It is proposed to use expert consulting systems to foster in students/specialists the integration of conceptual knowledge gained from different disciplines and to encourage them to develop a global system of concepts. Moreover, expert consulting systems make it possible to organize and develop existing teaching programmes. Ways of presenting conceptual knowledge were tested in different areas.

Publ: Lobanov, Y.I. Resources for ensuring the effectiveness of self-education of specialists. In: *Postdiploma education: demands, problems and tendencies*. M., NIIVO, 1992.
Kovalenko, V.Y.; Koltsova, N.Y.; Lobanov, Y.I.; et al. *The data bases of education purposes*. Information review. M., NIIVO, 1992.
Barabanshikov, Y.I.; Kasimas, R.Y. & Lobanov, Y.I. *Didactic basis of computer education of articles. Scientific achievements and progressive experience in the sphere of higher education*. M., NIIVO, 1992.
Kogdov, N.M. & Lobanov, Y.I. *Encyclopaedic dictionary for Automatic Educational Systems (AOC)*. Ukrainian encyclopaedia. Kiev, 1992.

11699   Comparison of examination results of Business Studies students who have/have not intercalated a year to see if the extramural experience affects results.
GBR   1993
Research Date(s): 1989-1993
Marsland, J.
Inst: Bradford University, Management Centre, Emm Lane, Bradford BD9 UJL, United Kingdom.
alternating training; undergraduate study; commercial training; practice period; achievement
formation alternée; supérieur premier cycle; formation commerciale; stage pratique; rendement
PROJECT DESCRIPTION

This research is a comparison of the results of courses run by the Management Centre at Bradford University. For several years the department has run both traditional and 'sandwich' undergraduate courses in parallel. Direct comparison of results from the two is difficult since the syllabuses are not identical. However, in recent years an appreciable number (10-15%) of the three-year course students have voluntarily intercalated a year of industrial experience. Examination marks and degree classifications will be examined to see whether performance in the final year of the course is affected by the break for practical experience.

11700   "CompReha" - Computerunterstuetzter Unterricht fuer die Rehabilitation. ("CompReha": computer-aided teaching for rehabilitation.)
DEU   1993
Research Date(s): 1988-1993
Albrecht, W.; Fraunholz, W.; Lakaszus, W.; Zimmermann, H.
Sup: Schroeder, M.
Inst: Universitaet Koblenz-Landau, Abt. Koblenz, FB 03 Naturwissenschaften, Mathematisches Institut, Rheinau 3-4, D-5400 Koblenz; Universitaet Koblenz-Landau, Abt. Koblenz, Institut fuer Mediendidaktik, Rheinau 3-4, D-5400 Koblenz; Gesellschaft fuer die Verknuepfung Informatischer und Sozialpaedagogischer Arbeitsfelder VISA e.V., Postfach, D-5400 Koblenz; Neurologisches Rehabilitationszentrum fuer Jugendliche, Postfach, D-5414 Vallendar.
didactic use of computer; brain injury; rehabilitation
usage didactique de l'ordinateur; lésion cérébrale; réadaptation
PROJECT DESCRIPTION

Inhalt: Entwicklung eines interaktiven Lernsystems zum Thema "Zahlbegriff" fuer den Unterricht von Gehirnverletzten waehrend der Rehabilitation.

Vorgehensweise: Geplant ist die Erstellung eines Sets von Lern- und Uebungsbausteinen (Programme) zur Vermittlung des Zahlbegriffs, mit deren Hilfe gezielt individuelle Defizite von Gehirnverletzten, die sich in der zweiten Phase der Rehabilitation befinden, aufgearbeitet werden koennen; die didaktische Konzeption der Bausteine zielt zunaechst auf die Integration in die therapeutische Arbeit des Walter-Poppelreuter-Hauses in Vallendar; dort soll spaeter - begleitend zur Entwicklung - der Pretest des Sets erfolgen.

11701   Computer-assisted learning in the teaching of reading.
GBR   1993
Research Date(s): 1988-1992
Davidson, J.
Sup: Lewis, E.; Noyes, P.
Inst: Cheltenham & Gloucester College of Higher Education, Faculty of Education and Health, The Park, Cheltenham GL50 2QF, United Kingdom.
didactic use of computer; reading; teaching method; primary education
usage didactique de l'ordinateur; lecture; méthode pédagogique; enseignement primaire
PROJECT DESCRIPTION

This research will develop and evaluate a computer-aided learning system for the teaching of reading incorporating recent advances in digitised speech output. This simulates the usual reading instruction process where the teacher provides individual assistance to the learner by spoken prompts. Scanning techniques now enable pages of reading books already in use in primary classrooms to be displayed on a microcomputer and a child's voice is recorded, digitised and used to provide the speech. These prompts are issued when the child highlights words or whole pages with which he or she may be having difficulty. This system has the advantage of providing additional reading practice with an infinitely patient non-judgemental listener and avoids the humiliation that some children experience when seen to fail in front of a skilled reader.

The initial reaction from pupils and teachers has been favourable, largely due to the clarity of the voice and the fact that teachers can use books which are already used in their schools and do not therefore need to change dramatically their approach to reading. The results of initial trials undertaken in Gloucestershire primary schools comparing groups of children using the system with control groups have shown the system to be of benefit in the teaching of reading. These comparisons are made by recording improved performance in standardised reading tests and measurements of sight vocabulary. The improvement goes beyond the immediate situation and evidence suggests it influences general reading attainment. Work has now started in the area of helping children who have had difficulty in learning to read.

11702 Computer-based modelling across the curriculum.
GBR 1993
Research Date(s): 1989-1992
Hoyles, C.; Tagg, W.; Stevenson, I.; Hassell, D.
Inst: London University, Institute of Education, Department of Mathematics, Statistics and Computing, 20 Bedford Way, London WC1H OAL, United Kingdom.
Fin: Training, Enterprise & Education Directorate.
didactic use of computer; software; model
usage didactique de l'ordinateur; logiciel; modèle
PROJECT DESCRIPTION
The aim of the project is to develop materials to support the use of the computer as a tool for modelling in the following subjects: mathematics, business studies, science and geography. A major objective will be to use modelling with teachers in order to develop curriculum materials for classroom use. The intention is to use generic software (rather than content-specific software) which can be adapted for use across the curriculum, in order to enhance pupil and teacher understanding of the modelling process as it is relevant to different knowledge domains, and in order that pupils themselves can create and interpret their own models.

11703 Computer in der Schule: die Schweiz im Vergleich mit 18 anderen Bildungssystemen. (L'ordinateur dans l'enseignement: la Suisse en comparaison avec 18 autres systèmes éducatifs.)
CHE 1994
Research Date(s): 1985-1991
Pelgrum, Willem J.; Plomp, Tjeerd; Niederer, Ruedi; Gretler, Armin; et al.
Inst: Schweizerische Koordinationsstelle für Bildungsforschung (IEA member for Switzerland), Entfelderstrasse 61, 5000 Aarau, Schweiz.
didactic use of computer; computer; educational administration; comparative research; primary education; secondary education
usage didactique de l'ordinateur; ordinateur; administration de l'enseignement; recherche comparative; enseignement primaire; enseignement secondaire
PROJECT DESCRIPTION
Die "International Association for the Evaluation of Educational Achievement (IEA)", deren Hauptquartier sich im niederländischen Haag befindet, wurde 1959 gegründet; sie hat seither eine ganze Reihe international vergleichender Forschungsprojekte im Bildungsbereich durchgeführt und sich grosses Ansehen und ausserordentliche Kompetenzen auf diesem Gebiet erworben. Die COMPED-Studie (Computers in Education) wurde 1985 beschlossen und ist zweiphasig angelegt. In der ersten Phase (Datenerhebung 1989) ging es um eine deskriptive Analyse des Standes der Computer-einführung in den 19 beteiligten Bildungssystemen. Die zweite Phase (Erhebung 1992) soll im Sinne einer Longitudinalstudie die Dynamik der Veränderungen erfassen, gleichzeitig aber auch Schülerleistungen in Abhängigkeit der gewählten Einführungsstrategien und Verwendungsweisen erheben.
Die Ergebnisse der ersten Phase, an welcher sich auch die Schweiz beteiligt hat (das Projektmanagement für die Schweiz lag bei der ETH Zürich), sind mittlerweile (auf englisch) publiziert worden. (Es liegt zudem eine deutsch- und französischsprachige Publikation der ETHZ vor, die aber nur die schweizerische Situation beschreibt).
Die internationale Vergleichsstudie zeigt, dass - von gewissen nationalen Verschiedenheiten einmal abgesehen - die Hauptprobleme in den 19 untersuchten Bildungssytemen dieselben sind. Das innovative Potential des Computers im Unterricht kann erst zur Geltung kommen, wenn zum einer qualitativ hochstehende und für Unterrichtszwecke geeignete Software zur Verfügung steht und zum andern den Lehrern beigebracht worden ist, wie sie diese Software verwenden und in ihr unterrichtliches Handeln vollauf integrieren können. In allzu vielen Schulen, in der Schweiz wie anderswo, wird sehr viel Wissen über den Computer vermittelt, während die Schülerinnen und Schüler kaum darauf trainiert werden, den Rechner für die Lösung praktischer Probleme zu verwenden.

Publ: Niederer, Ruedi & Frey, Karl (Hrsg.). *Informatik und Computernutzung im schweizerischen Bildungswesen: Bestandesaufnahme 1989 = Informatique et utilisation de l'ordinateur dans les écoles suisses: état de situation 1989.* Zürich: ETHZ Zürich, Informatikdienste, 1990, 120 Seiten.
Pelgrum, Willem J. & Plomp, Tjeerd. *The use of computers in education worldwide: results from the IEA "Computers in education" survey in 19 educational systems.* Oxford; New York; Seoul; Tokio: Pergamon, 1991, 179p.

11704 Computerdidaktik in der Sonderpädagogik. (Didactique de l'informatique en pédagogie curative.)
CHE 1994
Research Date(s): 1990-1992
Bonfranchi, Riccardo (Im Davidsboden 10, 4056 Basel, Schweiz).
didactic use of computer; special education; learning difficulty

usage didactique de l'ordinateur; enseignement spécial; difficulté de l'apprentissage
PROJECT DESCRIPTION
Der Computer hat in den letzten Jahren auch in den Sonderschulen zunehmend an Bedeutung gewonnen. Dies ist eine Auswirkung des gesellschaftlichen Prozesses, der die Informatik zu einer Schlüsseltechnologie hat werden lassen. Da die Informatik alle Lebensbereiche mehr oder weniger stark durchdringt, entsteht die Notwendigkeit und die Legitimation, Informatik auch im Bereich der Sonderschulen in den Unterricht einzuführen. Damit wiederum ergibt sich die Notwendigkeit, das Fach oder besser die Aktivität Informatik, mit und am Computer durchgeführt, hinsichtlich der Besonderheiten des Sonderschulwesens didaktisch zu durchleuchten. Den Problemen, die dabei entstehen, und der Frage, wie sie von Praktikern oder innerhalb von Forschungsprojekten gelöst worden sind bzw. welche Perspektiven sich in diesem Bereich abzeichnen, ist der Autor - Dozent an einer Ausbildungsstätte für Lehrkräfte für geistig Behinderte - in einem auf eigener Initiative basierenden Projekt nachgegangen.
Im ersten Teil seines Berichts - "Informatikunterricht in der Sonderpädagogik" - geht es um didaktische Fragen. Behandelt werden vorerst die Rahmenbedingungen und die Ziele des Informatikunterrichts in der Sonderpädagogik, sodann die Inhalte, die Unterrichtsmethoden und schliesslich die Medien (Hardware und Software).
Der zweite Teil ist betitelt mit "Computereinsatz bei verschiedenen Behinderungsarten". Mit dieser Einteilung nach Behindertengruppen will der Autor nicht einer separierenden Heil- und Sonderpädagogik das Wort reden; er ist aber bei der Sichtung des umfangreichen vorliegenden Materials zum Schluss gekommen, dass die Einsatzmöglichkeiten des Computers je nach Behinderung extrem unterschiedlich sein können.
Ein Kapitel über mögliche Anwendungsformen des Computers in der Sozialpädagogik und ein Exkurs über die Auswirkungen industrieller Revolutionen auf lernschwächere Menschen runden die Arbeit ab. Eine umfangreiche Bibliographie vermittelt eine Ahnung von der Fülle des Materials, das zum Thema heute bereits vorhanden ist.

Publ: Bonfranchi, Riccardo. *Computer-Didaktik in der Sonderpädagogik.* Luzern: Schweizerische Zentralstelle für Heilpädagogik (SZH), 1992, 190 Seiten.

11705 Computernutzung im Fachunterricht. (L'utilisation de l'ordinateur dans l'enseignement des disciplines.)
CHE 1994
Research Date(s): 1990-1992
Niederer, Ruedi.
Inst: ETH Zürich, Abteilung für Informatik, 8092 Zürich, Schweiz.
didactic use of computer; computer; didactics; teacher
usage didactique de l'ordinateur; ordinateur; didactique; enseignant
PROJECT DESCRIPTION
Diese Untersuchung zur Verwendung des Computers im Fachunterricht der schweizerischen Sekundarstufen I (die zur Pflichtschulzeit gehört) und II (allgemeinbildende oder berufsbildende nachobligatorische Schulen) basiert auf einer vertieften Auswertung der Daten, die im Rahmen des schweizerischen Beitrags an das internationale Projekt "Computers in Education" der IEA erhoben worden sind.
Laut den Ergebnissen der Studie ist die Verwendung des Computers im Fachunterricht marginal. Zwar erhalten drei Viertel der Schülerinnen und Schüler auf der Sekundarstufe I und nahezu alle auf der Sekundarstufe II eine Einführung in die Arbeit mit dem Computer. Im Fachunterricht sieht es anders aus: nur eine Lehrperson auf sieben setzt im Verlauf des Schuljahres den Computer in den Fächern Mathematik, Naturwissenschaften oder Muttersprache ein. Kommt noch dazu, dass es vorwiegend die Lehrperson selber ist, die sich an den Computer setzt, um etwas zu demonstrieren.
Erwähnen wir ein paar Faktoren, die sich auf die Häufigkeit der Computernutzung auswirken. Zuerst einmal ist der Typ zu nennen: Macintosh-Computer werden signifikant häufiger genutzt als MS-DOS-Computer. Dies hat wohl auch damit zu tun, dass die Lehrer mit MS-DOS-Maschinen schon selber deutlich häufiger Probleme mit ihrer Software haben als Kollegen, die mit Macs ausgerüstet sind. Auch nach Schultyp gibt es Unterschiede: an Gymnasien setzen 25 Prozent der Mathematik-, Naturkunde- oder Muttersprachlehrer den Computer im Unterricht ein, in gewerblich industriellen Berufsschulen 17 Prozent, an der Sekundarstufe I 15 Prozent. Überraschenderweise erst am Schluss kommen die kaufmännischen Berufsschulen. Bei den Fächern schwingt Mathematik obenaus. Textverarbeitung in den sprachlichen Fächern scheint kaum ein Thema zu sein; hier beträgt der Wert 11 Prozent. Die Naturwissenschaften liegen mit 16 Prozent dazwischen. An welchem Ort die Computer stehen, ist wichtig: sind sie schon im Klassenzimmer, werden sie doppelt so häufig gebraucht wie Computer in einem separaten Informatikzimmer.
Die Computernutzung scheint bei den Lehrpersonen Männersache zu sein. Lehrerinnen besuchten im Durchschnitt acht Kursstunden Informatik; bei den Männern ist dieser Wert fünfmal höher. Ein ähnliches Bild zeigt sich bei den Lehrpersonen, die noch nie einen Informatikkurs besucht haben: bei den Lehrern beträgt deren Prozentsatz 20 Prozent, bei den Lehrerinnen 41 Prozent.

Publ: Niederer, Ruedi. *Computernutzung im Fachunterricht*. Zürich: ETH Zürich, Departement Informatik, 1992, 118 Seiten (Informatik und Computernutzung im schweizerischen Bildungswesen; 2).

11706 Computers in nursery schools.
GBR 1993
Research Date(s): 1989-1992
Grant, C.
Inst: Heriot-Watt University, Moray House Institute of Education, Holyrood Road, Edinburgh EH8 8AQ, United Kingdom.
didactic use of computer; nursery school
usage didactique de l'ordinateur; école maternelle
PROJECT DESCRIPTION
    The aim of the research is to examine the use of computers in the context of the nursery classroom whether in a nursery school or a nursery class attached to a primary school. This will involve: (1) establishing the policy of Her Majesty's Inspectorate (HMI) as regards the use of computers in the nursery classroom context; (2) establishing regional policy/guidelines on the use of computers in nursery classrooms; (3) establishing the number of nursery classrooms where computers are used, identifying the type of computer used and times available; (4) identifying the degree of computer training given to teachers of nursery classes by the colleges where they were originally trained; (5) examining the amount and nature of inservice training offered by Scottish regions; and (6) examining the amount and nature of in-service training offered by colleges.

11707 Computers in teaching history.
GBR 1993
Research Date(s): 1991-1992
Hillis, P.; Munro, R.
Inst: Jordanhill College of Education, Division of Social Studies, Southbrae Drive, Jordanhill, Glasgow G13 1PP, United Kingdom.
Fin: Scottish Office Education Department.
didactic use of computer; data base; history
usage didactique de l'ordinateur; banque de données; histoire
PROJECT DESCRIPTION
    The aims of the project are: (1) to provide a range of curricular material to help primary and secondary schools use census databases; (2) and to compile a rateable value database for parts of Glasgow in 1881 for use with Scottish Vocational Education Council (SCOTVEC) modules.

11708 Computing in physical education.
GBR 1993
Research Date(s): 1991-1992
Sharp, R.
Inst: Jordanhill College of Education, Division of PE, Sport and Outdoor Education, Southbrae Drive, Glasgow, G13 1PP, United Kingdom.
didactic use of computer; physical education
usage didactique de l'ordinateur; éducation physique
PROJECT DESCRIPTION
    This project aims to identify the computing requirements of physical education (PE) teachers in Scotland with regard to the AppleMac computer.

11709 The construction of dynamic documents by children.
GBR 1993
Research Date(s): 1989-1993
Moar, M.
Sup: Whalley, P.
Inst: Open University, Institute of Educational Technology, Walton Hall, Milton Keynes MK7 6AA, United Kingdom.
Fin: Economic and Social Research Council.
didactic use of computer; project method
usage didactique de l'ordinateur; pédagogie du projet
PROJECT DESCRIPTION
    Project work seeks to encourage the pupils' freedom to investigate a subject. It requires the selection, organisation and presentation of learned materials and as such is seen as a valuable part of current educational practice in British classrooms. Typically, the end product of a project is a document consisting of text together with appropriate graphics. It is now possible however to produce dynamic computer-based documents in the classroom, which incorporate moving images, text and sound.
    The thesis explores this possibility by looking briefly at the cognitive effects of producing media in an educational context and considering the representational qualities of such dynamic documents. The development of a methodology for dynamic document use based on conventional classroom practice is described, and suggestions for future research are made.
Publ: Moar, M. The construction of dynamic documents by children. In: *Proceedings of the 'East-West Conference on Emerging Computer Technologies for Education*, Moscow, April 1992.

11710 The debriefing process in active learning.
GBR 1993
Research Date(s): 1990-1993
Harwood, D.

Inst: Warwick University, Faculty of Educational Studies, Department of Science Education, Coventry CV4 7AL, United Kingdom.
Fin: Warwickshire Local Education Authority.
activity method; teaching method; conversation; teacher-pupil relation; teacher role; interaction
méthode active; méthode pédagogique; conversation; relation maître-élève; rôle de l'enseignant; interaction
PROJECT DESCRIPTION
    Previous research has shown that the teacher becomes the focus of interaction in active learning whenever he or she is present with the teaching group. This research aims to study the nature of the teacher's statements and questions during the debriefing process and identify the effects they have upon pupil participation. Teachers who are experienced in active learning, have volunteered to participate. The 'debriefing' phase of the lesson will be videotaped and transcribed. As a result of collaboration between teacher and researcher, a commentary will be written to accompany the transcript. Guidelines for debriefing 'active learning' will be identified.
Publ: Harwood, D.L. *Guidelines for debriefing active learning: an interim report*. Coventry: University of Warwick/Warwickshire Local Education Authority, 1991. (Available from the author).

11711 Design of Electronic Performance Support Systems.
GBR 1993
Research Date(s): 1991-1994
Banerji, A.
Sup: Barker, P.; Manji, K.
Inst: Teesside University, School of Computing and Mathematics, Interactive Systems Research Group, Borough Road, Middlesbrough, Cleveland TS1 3BA, United Kingdom.
didactic use of computer; training type; optical storage; expert system; educational technology; work environment
usage didactique de l'ordinateur; type de formation; mémoire optique; système-expert; technologie de l'éducation; milieu de travail
PROJECT DESCRIPTION
    An Electronic Performance Support System (EPSS) is an approach to integrating hardware, software and end-user interfaces in order to produce more useful computer-based information delivery systems that embed various types of job performance aid. Essentially, an EPSS is intended to be a computer-based job performance aid that is able to provide 'just-in-time' (JIT) training and an enhanced interactive performance support environment. This environment provides various types of information, data, images, advice, assistance and guidance in order to permit an employee to perform his/her job with minimum support and intervention from others. The concept of JIT training is derived from the JIT inventory control methods adopted by the Japanese and accepted as a new productivity standard. It can be viewed as an evolution of computer-based training (CBT) delivery stages - from 'off-the-job' training through 'prior-to-job-performance' training to the approach of learning while doing a job using an EPSS.
    Research into basic EPSS techniques has been taking place within the School of Computing and Mathematics at Teesside University. Interest in this area has arisen as a result of the School's organising research into the application of computer-based training and the development of interactive job performance aids.
    The objective of this current project is to investigate the potential utility of EPSS techniques and to formulate a set of design and fabrication guidelines to facilitate their creation within industrial and commercial environments. The four avenues of investigation currently explored involve the use of on-line help systems; full-text retrieval packages; expert systems; and intelligent simulation environments, in order to augment the use of CBT within the interactive work environment of an employee. This project will also explore the use of compact disc read-only memory (CD-ROM) as a means of embedding and delivering EPSS facilities to end-users.
Publ: Barker, P.G. Computer-based training in India. In: *International Journal of Computers in Adult Education and Training*, Vol 2, No 3/1991, pp. 213-224.
Barker, P.G. Designing interactive learning systems. In: *Educational & Training Technology International*, Vol 27, No 2, pp. 125-145, May.
Barker, P.G. Developing competence through CBT. Paper presented at AETT '91 International Conference, Polytechnic of Wales, Pontypridd, 2-5 April, 1991.

11712 Designing instructional text.
GBR 1993
Research Date(s): 1970-
Hartley, J.
Inst: Keele University, Department of Psychology, Keele, Staffordshire ST5 5BG, United Kingdom.
teaching aid; textbook
moyen d'enseignement; manuel d'enseignement
PROJECT DESCRIPTION
    This research focuses on the design of instructional text - mainly in the form of printed materials - which enables the reader to do or to understand

something. The research covers three areas: (1) the layout of such materials; (2) the language of such materials; and (3) the use of structural devices which enable people to find their way about a piece of text. Work with layout stresses the importance of using the 'white space' systematically in order to convey the underlying structure of text. Work with language suggests the importance of simpler wording. Work with 'access structures' indicates how devices such as headings and summaries can aid recall. Recently the research has shifted its focus of interest from work with printed text to work with braille, audio-taped instruction, and electronic text.

Publ: Hartley, J. Text design and the setting up of Braille. In: *Information Design Journal*, Vol 5/1989, pp. 183-190.
Hartley, J. Textbook design: current status and future directions. In: *International Journal of Educational Research*, Vol 14/1990, pp. 533-541.
Hartley, J. Author, printer, reader, listener: four sources of confusion when listening to tabular/diagrammatic information. In: *British Journal of Visual Impairment*, Vol VIII, 1990, pp. 51-53.
Hartley, J. Psychology, writing and computers. In: *Visible Language*, Vol 25, 1991, pp. 339-375.
Hartley, S. The layout of computer-based test? In: Sassoon, R. (ed.). *Computers and Typology*. Oxford: Intellect Books, 1992.

11713 Developing teaching materials on the international politics of the environment.
GBR 1993
Research Date(s): 1990-1991
Hocking, B.
Inst: Coventry University, Priory Street, Coventry CV1 5FB, United Kingdom.
teaching aid; environmental study; international studies
moyen d'enseignement; étude du milieu; études internationales
PROJECT DESCRIPTION
  The aim of the project is to develop teaching materials on the subject of the environment as an issue on the international agenda. These will comprise a bibliography and a course guide which can be used in the context of traditional courses or self-learning environments.

11714 Development of curriculum-based resources.
GBR 1993
Research Date(s): 1982-
Crowther, N.
Inst: Heriot-Watt University, Moray House Institute of Education, Holyrood Road, Edinburgh EH8 8AQ, United Kingdom.
Fin: Resources for Environmental and Social Studies Teaching (RESST); Moray House Institute of Education.
teaching aid; filmstrip; environmental study
moyen d'enseignement; film fixe; étude du milieu
PROJECT DESCRIPTION
  Since 1982 a series of filmstrips for schools have been published under the collective title 'Habitats in Scotland'. Each is accompanied by a teacher's booklet. Initially the publications were made to meet the curriculum resource needs of specialist teachers of outdoor and environmental education. Increasingly in recent years the resource needs of primary teachers, identified by the Primary Education Development Project (PEDP), have been a major outlet for sales. Work continues on reprinting and updating previous titles in addition to the completion of the remaining titles in the series. The focus of continuing research is the production of teaching resources for the 5-14 Environmental Studies Syllabus.

Publ: Crowther, N. *Seashore and coastal habitats*. Edinburgh: Moray House, 1984.
Crowther, N. *Mountains and moorlands*. Edinburgh: Moray House, 1985.
Crowther, N. *Freshwater habitats*. Edinburgh: Moray House, 1987.
Crowther, N. *Woodlands in Scotland*. 2nd edition. Edinburgh: Moray House, 1988.

11715 Diagnostische Erfassung und Foerderung technisch-kreativer Problemloeseleistungen bei Jugendlichen. (Training and promotion of technical creativity among gifted young people at the intermediate secondary school level.)
DEU 1993
Research Date(s): 1989-1991
Enzinger, A.; Hany, G.
Sup: Hany, E.; Heller, K.
Inst: Universitaet Muenchen, Fak. fuer Psychologie und Paedagogik, Institut fuer Empirische Paedagogik und Paedagogische Psychologie - Paedagogische Psychologie, und Psychologische Diagnostik-, Leopoldstrasse 13, D-8000 Muenchen 40.
Fin: Bildung und Begabung e.V.; Cornelsen Stiftung Lehren und Lernen.
teaching method; adolescent; creativity; technical education; talent; cognitive ability; problem solving
méthode pédagogique; adolescent; créativité; enseignement technique; talent; aptitude cognitive; résolution de problème
PROJECT DESCRIPTION

Inhalt: Folgende Ziele werden angestrebt: (1) Schulpraktisch: Die Foerderung begabter Schueler auf dem Gebiet physikalisch-technischen Problemloesens. (2) Anwendungsbezogen: Die Klaerung der Frage, ob die Vermittlung kreativer Kompetenzen oder bereichsspezifischen Wissens wichtiger ist fuer den Problemloeseerfolg (Diskussion formale vs. materiale Bildung). (3) Theoriebezogen: Untersuchung des Aufbaus bereichsspezifischen Wissens durch solche Instruktionstechniken, dass es fuer Problemloesungen optimal zur Verfuegung steht. Inhaltlich geht es um Probleme betriebswirtschaftlicher Optimierung eines Warenlagers, das mit Fischertechnik-Baumaterialien simuliert und mit einem Computerprogramm gesteuert wird.
  Geographischer Raum: Deutschland (Bayern).
  Vorgehensweise: Empirisch-statistischer Ansatz, von der Expertenbefragung (knowledge engineering zur physikalischen Wissensdomaene) ueber kontrollierte Experimentaluntersuchungen zu einem Trainingsprogramm mit verschiedenen Experimental- und Kontrollgruppen; kognitive Instruktionspsychologie; Problemloeseforschung. Untersuchungsdesign: Querschnittserhebung; (Quasi-)Experiment.
  Datengewinnung: Experiment (Stichprobe: 60; SchuelerInnen der 7.-9. Klasse Gymnasium; Auswahlverfahren: willkuerlich). Psychologischer Test (Stichprobe: 60; SchuelerInnen der 7.-9. Klasse Gymnasium; Auswahlverfahren: willkuerlich). Primaererhebung: Feldarbeit von Mitarbeitern des Projektes durchgefuehrt.
  Auswertung: Varianzanalyse; Regressionsanalyse. Datenaufbereitung: Aggregierung oder Disaggregierung.

11716 Didaktik der Stochastik fuer Realschulen. (A stochastics teaching method for intermediate schools.)
DEU 1993
Research Date(s): 1991-1993
Koelbl, I.
Inst: Universitaet Rostock, Mathematisch-Naturwissenschaftliche Fakultaet, Lehrstuhl fuer Didaktik des Mathematikunterrichts, Universitaetsplatz 1, O-2500 Rostock.
teaching; mathematics; didactics; thinking; teaching method; secondary school
enseignement; mathématiques; didactique; pensée; méthode pédagogique; école secondaire
PROJECT DESCRIPTION
  Inhalt: Ziel und Inhalt eines Lehrgangs Stochastik fuer den Mathematikunterricht in Realschulen; didaktisch-methodische Vorgehensweisen im Unterricht; fachuebergreifende Probleme der Stochastik im Unterricht; Entwicklung einer stochastischen Denkweise bei Schuelern.
  Geographischer Raum: Mecklenburg.
  Vorgehensweise: Theoretische Erarbeitung grundlegender Ideen und deren (teilweisen) Ueberpruefung in der Schulpraxis.

11717 Didaktische Materialien fuer vorschulische Verkehrserziehung. (Didactic materials for pre-school road safety education.)
DEU 1993
Research Date(s): 1991-1992
Feldmann, K.
Inst: Fachhochschule Fulda, FB Sozialpaedagogik, Marquardtstrasse 35, D-6400 Fulda.
Fin: Daimler-Benz AG.
teaching aid; pre-school education; didactics; road safety education; curriculum; educational innovation
moyen d'enseignement; éducation préscolaire; didactique; éducation à la sécurité routière; programme d'études; innovation pédagogique
PROJECT DESCRIPTION
  Inhalt: Innovation und Evaluation vorschulischer Verkehrserziehung; dynamisches Curriculum fuer "Eltern-Erzieher-Kind"-Seminare; "Sicherheitserziehung": Verkehrserziehung als Teil einer allgemeinen Sicherheitserziehung.
  Geographischer Raum: Deutschland.
  Vorgehensweise: Empirische Untersuchung zur Situation der o.a. Thematik; Handlungsorientierter Ansatz; action research; Theorie-Praxis-Projekt.

11718 Didaktische Weiterentwicklung der ausbildungsbegleitenden Hilfen (abH) - Anpassung und Fortschreibung von abH-Konzepten. (Didactic development of training support resources; modification and updating of such resources.)
DEU 1993
Research Date(s): 1992
Selzer, H.
Inst: Didaktisches Labor H.M. Selzer, Rosengasse 3, D-8834 Pappenheim 2.
in-service training; adolescent; apprenticeship; didactics; underachievement; teaching aid
formation en cours d'emploi; adolescent; apprentissage professionnel; didactique; rendement déficient; moyen d'enseignement
PROJECT DESCRIPTION
  Inhalt: Ausbildungsbegleitende Hilfen nehmen fuer einen groesser werdenden Personenkreis an Bedeutung zu. Im Rahmen der Ausschoepfung

aller Ausbildungsressourcen sind zwei Veraenderungstendenzen einflussgebend auf die Arbeit der abH: Tendenz 1: Zahlreiche eher leistungsschwache Jugendliche entscheiden sich derzeit fuer eine Berufsausbildung. Tendenz 2: Mehr Jugendliche waehlen Ausbildungsberufe oberhalb ihres Leistungsniveaus. AbH brauchen ein fortgeschriebenes Didaktikkonzept, um die erweiterten Aufgaben in Zukunft erfuellen zu koennen. Dazu zaehlen: Modifizierung der didaktischen Instrumente, insbesondere die Modifizierung der Lernorganisation und der Lernmedien; Einbeziehung fachpraktischer Lernoperationen in die abH. Untersuchungsziel: Erstellung von Defizitanalysen; Weiterentwicklung und Intensivierung der abH-Methoden; Anpassung an die veraenderten Beduerfnisse der In-Anspruch-Nehmer.

Vorgehensweise: Zur Unterstuetzung der didaktischen Bedarfserhebung aus der Anamnese der den Modellversuchsgruppen zugeordneten Jugendlichen wird eine regional begrenzte Traegerbefragung geplant. Untersuchungsdesign: qualitative Forschung.

Datengewinnung: Expertengespraech, Befragung (abH-Traeger in Bayern; Auswahlverfahren: bewusst). Primaererhebung: Feldarbeit von Mitarbeitern des Projektes durchgefuehrt.

11719 Die Anfaenge einer Neuorientierung der politischen Bildung in der DDR 1989/1990. (The beginnings of reorientation in political education in the GDR 1989/1990.)
DEU 1993
Research Date(s): 1990-1993
Gellert, W.
Sup: Gericke, H.
Inst: Paedagogische Hochschule Magdeburg, Institut fuer Sozialwissenschaften i.G., Virchowstr. 24, O-3040 Magdeburg.
political education; German DR; history; educational reform; civics
éducation politique; Allemagne RDA; histoire; réforme de l'enseignement; instruction civique
PROJECT DESCRIPTION
Inhalt: Ende der Staatsbuergerkunde, Vorschlaege und Projekte zur Neugestaltung, Anfaenge des Gesellschaftskundeunterrichts 1990.
Untersuchter Zeitraum: 1989-1990.

11720 Die Nachhaltigkeit von Vorhaben der beruflichen Bildung. (The permanence of vocational training projects.)
DEU 1993
Research Date(s): 1990-1992
Resch, A.
Sup: Stockmann, R.
Inst: Universitaet Mannheim, Fak. fuer Sozialwissenschaften, Lehrstuhl fuer Methoden der empirischen Sozialforschung und angewandte Soziologie, Seminargebaeude A5, D-6800 Mannheim.
Fin: Deutsche Gesellschaft fuer Technische Zusammenarbeit -GTZ- GmbH.
vocational education; developing country; development aid; South America; Central America
enseignement professionnel; pays en développement; aide au développement; Amérique du Sud; Amérique centrale
PROJECT DESCRIPTION
Inhalt: Das Vorhaben soll dazu beitragen, den Kenntnisstand ueber die Nachhaltigkeit von Entwicklungsprojekten der Technischen Zusammenarbeit anhand einer Ex-post-Untersuchung von 15 Berufsbildungsprojekten zu erhoehen. Dabei werden folgende Ziele angestrebt: Eine Bestandsaufnahme und Bewertung der Nachhaltigkeit der Projekte (Erstellung einer Nachhaltigkeitsbilanz); eine Untersuchung der Einflussfaktoren, die auf die Nachhaltigkeit eines Projekts (in positiver wie negativer Hinsicht) massgeblich einwirken (tendenziell Ursache-Wirkungsanalyse); aus den ermittelten Befunden werden Schlussfolgerungen gezogen, die fuer die Auswahl-, Planungs-, Durchfuehrungs- und Evaluierungspraxis bei TZ-Projekten relevant sind ("lessons learned").
Geographischer Raum: Sued- und Mittelamerika.
Untersuchter Zeitraum: 1960-1990.
Vorgehensweise: Fuer die Untersuchung wurde ein Analyseraster entwickelt, das auf drei theoretischen Ueberlegungen aufbaut: einem Lebenszyklusmodell fuer Entwicklungshilfeprojekte; einem mehrdimensionalen Nachhaltigkeitsbegriff; einem systemtheoretischen Wirkungsmodell. Untersuchungsdesign: Methodenforschung; Evaluationsstudie.
Datengewinnung: Standardisiertes Interview (Stichprobe: 2500; Schueler, Lehrer, Absolventen, Betriebsleiter; Auswahlverfahren: total. Stichprobe: 2500; Schueler, Lehrer, Absolventen, Betriebsleiter; Auswahlverfahren: willkuerlich). Nicht-standardisiertes Interview (Stichprobe: 200; ehemalige Projektmitarbeiter, Counterparts etc.; Auswahlverfahren: bewusst). Beobachtung (Stichprobe: 15; Projektbesuche -Werkstatt, Unterricht-; Auswahlverfahren: total). Aktenanalyse (Stichprobe: 15; Akten und Berichte ueber die ausgewaehlten Projekte; Auswahlverfahren: total). Primaererhebung: Feldarbeit von Mitarbeitern des Projektes durchgefuehrt.

Publ: Stockmann, R. & Resch, Annnegret. *Die Nachhaltigkeit von Vorhaben der beruflichen Bildung in Lateinamerika.* GTZ-Zwischenbericht, Mannheim 1991.

11721 Die Weiterbildungsoffensive (WBO) im Berufsbildungsbereich. (Mesures spéciales en faveur du perfectionnement professionnel.)
CHE 1994
Research Date(s): 1990-1996
Schmitter, Christoph; et al.
Inst: Bundesamt für Industrie, Gewerbe und Arbeit (BIGA), Bundesgasse 8, 3003 Bern, Schweiz.
Fin: Schweizerische Eidgenossenschaft.
further training; vocational education; vocational training; educational policy; educational provision; financing
formation complémentaire; enseignement professionnel; formation professionnelle; politique de l'éducation; scolarisation; financement
PROJECT DESCRIPTION
Im Frühjahr 1990 hat das schweizerische Parlament die sogennante Weiterbildungsoffensive (offizielle Bezeichnung: "Sondermassnahmen zugunsten der beruflichen und universitären Weiterbildung und Förderung neuer Technologien im Fertigungsbereich (CIM)") lanciert. Dieses landesweite Impulsprogramm besteht darin, dass während sechs Jahren Sondermassnahmen zugunsten der beruflichen Weiterbildung unterstützt werden. Die Beiträge ergänzen die allgemeine Förderung aufgrund des Berufsbildungsgesetzes. Es handelt sich um Beiträge an die Kantone, an Verbände der Arbeitgeber und der Arbeitnehmer sowie an öffentliche und private Institutionen, die ohne Erwerbszweck Ziele der beruflichen Weiterbildung verfolgen. In erster Linie sollen Projekte unterstützt werden, die in Konzeption und Ausführung neuartig sind, analoge Aktivitäten bei Dritten anregen und Chance auf eine Weiterführung nach Auslaufen des Impulsprogramms haben.

Die Weiterbildungsoffensive ist gut gestartet. Im Herbst 1990 wurde das BIGA, dem die Koordination oblag, mit Gesuchen überschwemmt. Am Ende der ersten Eingabefrist, dem 31. Oktober 1990 (es gibt jährlich zwei Eingabetermine, den 31. März und den 31. Oktober) lagen 373 Gesuche vor. 1991 kamen weitere 120 Gesuche dazu. 208 dieser 493 Gesuche waren Ende 1991 bewilligt; vom Gesamtkredit von 162 Millionen Franken waren damit 35,6 Millionen zugesprochen.

Eine Analyse der eingereichten und bewilligten Gesuche zeigt, dass die Gesuchsteller fast ausnahmslos mit ihren Vorhaben primär partikulare Interessen vertreten haben. Projekte "von allgemeinem oder übergeordnetem Interesse" sind selten. Immerhin sind gegen Ende der betrachteten Periode einige Anträge zu Vorhaben eingegangen, die eine ganze Branche oder eine Region betreffen, organisatorisch breit abgestützt sind und von verschiedenen Gruppen gemeinsam getragen werden. Die Gesuche stammen aus 23 Kantonen (allen mit Ausnahme der beiden Appenzell und des Kantons Glarus). Dennoch gibt es grosse Unausgewogenheiten. Besonders bedauerlich ist, dass 90 Prozent der Gesuche, die bewilligt werden konnten, aus der Deutschschweiz stammen. Auch stammt der weitaus grösste Teil der eingereichten und bewilligten Gesuche aus bildungspolitischen Zentren. Wenn auch klar ist, dass der Sitz des Trägers grundsätzlich wenig darüber aussagt, wo das Projekt schliesslich seine Wirkung entfaltet, kann aufgrund der Projektkonzepte dennoch geschlossen werden, dass die überwiegende Zahl der Bildungsveranstaltungen in den Städten und nicht in ländlichen Gebieten angeboten werden.

Publ: Schmitter, Christoph. Die Weiterbildungsoffensive im Berufsbildungsbereich: eine Zwischenbilanz. In: *Volkswirtschaft*, 2/92, S. 40-43.
Schmitter, Christoph. Mesures spéciales en faveur du perfectionnement professionel: bilan intermédiaire. In: *Vie économique*, 2/92, p. 40-43.

11722 Die Wettbewerbsfaehigkeit der amerikanischen Wirtschaft und das System der beruflichen Bildung in den USA. (The competitive capacity of American industry and the vocational training system in the USA.)
DEU 1993
Research Date(s): 1991-1993
Jaschner, P.
Sup: Holtfrerich, C.
Inst: Freie Universitaet Berlin, ZI John-F.-Kennedy-Institut fuer Nordamerikastudien, Abt. Wirtschaft Nordamerikas, Lansstrasse 5-9, D-1000 Berlin 33.
Fin: Deutsche Forschungsgemeinschaft.
vocational education; education system; USA; economic conditions; competition
enseignement professionnel; système d'enseignement; Etats-Unis; conditions économiques; concurrence
PROJECT DESCRIPTION
Geographischer Raum: USA.
Vorgehensweise: Untersuchungsdesign: qualitative Forschung.

11723 DISCOURSE: Design & Interactive Specification of Courseware.
GBR 1993
Research Date(s): 1992-1994
Johnson, R.; Goodyear, P.
Inst: Lancaster University, Department of Educational Research, Cartmel College, Bailrigg, Lancaster LA1 4YW, United Kingdom.

Fin: European Community DELTA Programme.
didactic use of computer; teaching aid; computer; educational software
usage didactique de l'ordinateur; moyen d'enseignement; ordinateur; didacticiel
PROJECT DESCRIPTION

The goal of DISCOURSE is to build a set of computer-based tools to help the producers of computer-based learning materials work through the early stages of courseware design. Tools will be built to help with representing subject matter, teaching strategies and characteristics of target learners. Courseware designers will be able to work with a variety of presentational possibilities, including multimedia simulations. The project builds on earlier work in the EC DELTA projects TOSKA and Simulate. The lead partner for DISCOURSE is Dornier (part of Deutsche Aerospace).

11724 Doorstroom van O- & S-cursussen naar primair leerlingwezen. (Transfer from bridging courses to elementary apprenticeship training.)
NLD 1994
Research Date(s): 1992-1993
Babeliowsky, M.
Inst: Stichting Centrum voor Onderwijsonderzoek (SCO) (Centre for Educational Research), Grote Bickersstraat 72, 1013 KS Amsterdam, Netherlands.
Universiteit van Amsterdam (University of Amsterdam), P.O. Box 19268, 1000 GG Amsterdam, Netherlands
Fin: SVO het Instituut voor Onderzoek van het Onderwijs.
apprenticeship; training course; performance; vocational preparation; wastage
apprentissage professionnel; cours de formation; performance; initiation à la profession; déperdition d'effectifs
PROJECT DESCRIPTION

Background: An increasing number of orientation and bridging courses are being organized to enable specific target populations to enrol in elementary training courses and thus to obtain a basic qualification. In 1991 Research for Policy made a study of participation in such courses in the area of apprenticeship training. That study did not pay attention to the number of course participants who transfer to apprenticeship training.

Aim: To examine how far orientation and bridging courses succeed in preparing young people for entry into apprenticeship training.

Design: To establish the courses' success rates, three existing sets of data will be used. These will be supplemented by data from 10 apprenticeship training schools on the school careers of former bridging course participants. On the basis of the school files, four cohorts of apprentices will be formed. Interviews will be held with 32 apprentices, selected on the basis of specific school career characteristics. On account of their role in the guidance provided to apprentices, a number of "regional consultants" will be asked for their views. In the study of factors that facilitate or impede the transfer to apprenticeship training, a distinction will be made between individual, educational and labour market factors.

11725 Effectieve instructiemethoden voor schrijf- en leesvaardigheid in het Voortgezet onderwijs. (Effective instructional methods for reading and writing in secondary schools.)
NLD 1994
Research Date(s): 1992
Overmaat, A.M.; Glopper, K. de; Rijlaardsam, G.C.W.
Sup: Hout-Wolters, B.H.A.M.
Inst: Stichting Centrum voor Onderwijsonderzoek (SCO) (Centre for Educational Research), Grote Bickersstraat 72, 1013 KS Amsterdam, Netherlands.
Universiteit van Amsterdam (University of Amsterdam), P.O. Box 19268, 1000 GG Amsterdam, Netherlands
Fin: SVO het Instituut voor Onderzoek van het Onderwijs.
teaching method; reading; writing
méthode pédagogique; lecture; écriture
PROJECT DESCRIPTION

Background: This doctoral dissertation is based on two earlier studies of reading and writing skills. One investigated the effects of two experimental programmes for teaching text structure, the other examined the use of giving a detailed instruction in text schemata for specific types of text. In spite of a number of shared characteristics - population, design, pedagogical approach - the two studies lack a common theoretical framework.

Aim: To place the two studies in a common theoretical framework, with a view to (1) describing similarities in the instructional content and the pedagogical approach used and (2) explaining the strong effects of the experimental methods.

11726 The effectiveness of new curriculum models for initial vocational training.
GBR 1993
Research Date(s): 1991-1992
Raffe, D.; Howieson, C.

Inst: Edinburgh University, Centre for Educational Sociology, 7 Buccleuch Place, Edinburgh EH8 9JT, United Kingdom.
Fin: European Community PETRA Programme.
vocational training; curriculum; modular training; cross-national research
formation professionnelle; programme d'études; formation modulaire; recherche transnationale
PROJECT DESCRIPTION

The purpose of this research is to investigate the main objectives for modularisation and related reforms such as certification in different countries, and to assess the variation of the success of such policies across different institutional contexts and different national circumstances.

11727 The effects of information technology on the sequencing and development of concept acquisition, particularly in open-ended, creative situations.
GBR 1993
Research Date(s): 1990-1994
Wells, C.
Sup: Kemp, A.; Hopper, G.
Inst: Reading University, Department of Arts and Humanities in Education, Bulmershe Court, Woodlands Avenue, Earley, Reading RG6 1HY, United Kingdom.
didactic use of computer; creative activities; concept formation; cognitive process; writing; art
usage didactique de l'ordinateur; activités créatrices; formation de concept; processus cognitif; écriture; art
PROJECT DESCRIPTION

A preliminary study has been completed over a period of one year in a primary school with very good access to computer facilities. Work in creative areas, particularly in creative writing and in art, was monitored throughout the year - both with and without the use of the computer. Children from ages 5 to 11 were involved, though more detailed observations were made of a group of 30 9-10 year olds. This data, once analysed, will enable the focusing of particular sequencing and developmental trends in the main research.

11728 The effects of the National Curriculum on infant teachers and their practice.
GBR 1993
Research Date(s): 1989-1992
Hull, B.
Sup: Gipps, C.
Inst: Hertfordshire University, School of Humanities and Education, Wall Hall Campus, Aldenham, Watford WD2 8AT, United Kingdom.
Fin: Hatfield Polytechnic.
teaching; nursery school; teacher; occupational status
enseignement; école maternelle; enseignant; statut professionnel
PROJECT DESCRIPTION

The research aims to investigate the extent to which infant teachers respond to change, in particular the requirements of the National Curriculum. Case studies involving six teachers in two schools were carried out, employing techniques of participant observation and interviewing over a two year period. The results are currently being evaluated and set in a context which looks at the image of teachers of young children through history and literature. This theme is developed into an examination of the growth of professionalism with regard to infant teachers, and with particular reference to gender inequalities in education, posing the hypothesis that infant teaching has suffered from low status because of its relationship to the education of girls and the social position of women in society.

Publ: Hull, B. The National Curriculum: its effects on infant teachers and their practice. In: *Early Years*, Vol 2, No 1/1990, pp. 39-44, Autumn.

11729 Einsatz von CBT (Computer-Based Training) als Bestandteil multimedialen Lernens in der Erwachsenenbildung. (Use of CBT (Computer-Based Training) as a multimedia learning component in adult education.)
DEU 1993
Research Date(s): 1991-1994
Boy, D.
Sup: Huber, G.
Inst: Universitaet Koblenz-Landau, Abt. Koblenz, Institut fuer Mediendidaktik, Rheinau 3-4, D-5400 Koblenz.
adult education; learning process; computer application; didactic use of computer
éducation des adultes; apprentissage; application informatique; usage didactique de l'ordinateur
PROJECT DESCRIPTION

Inhalt: Entwicklung eines interaktiven Lernsystems zum Thema "Personalbeschaffung" fuer den Einsatz in der Erwachsenenbildung.

11730 Einsatz von Fallstudien und Unternehmensplanspielen an Fachhochschulen im Fachbereich Wirtschaft. (Use of case studies and management games in the economic departments of technical colleges.)
DEU 1993
Research Date(s): 1991-1992
Hennig.
Sup: Noetzel, R.
Inst: Institut fuer betriebliche Forschung und Praxis e.V., Felix-Nussbaum-Strasse 7, D-4500 Osnabrueck; Universitaet Osnabrueck, FB Wirtschaftswissenschaften, Fachgebiet BWL, insb. Absatz, Marketing, Rolandstr. 8, D-4500 Osnabrueck.
educational game; economics; operational research; university; learning; simulation; teaching method; case study
jeu éducatif; science économique; recherche opérationnelle; université; acquisition de connaissances; simulation; méthode pédagogique; étude de cas
PROJECT DESCRIPTION
Inhalt: Einsatz von Fallstudien; Einsatz von Unternehmensplanspielen; spezielle Vorteile der Methoden.
Geographischer Raum: Bundesrepublik Deutschland.
Untersuchter Zeitraum: 1992.
Vorgehensweise: Untersuchungsdesign: Evaluationsstudie.
Datengewinnung: Postalische Befragung (Stichprobe: 29; 43 Fachbereiche Wirtschaft; Auswahlverfahren: total). Befragung (dito). Primaererhebung: Feldarbeit von Mitarbeitern des Projektes durchgefuehrt.
Auswertung: Datenaufbereitung: Aggregierung oder Disaggregierung.

11731 Enterprise Education: Scottish Enterprise funded package writing.
GBR 1993
Research Date(s): 1991-1992
Twiddle, B.; MacDonald, D.; Semple, S.; Cantlay, D.
Inst: Jordanhill College of Education, Division of Primary Education, Southbrae Drive, Jordanhill, Glasgow G13 1PP, United Kingdom.
Fin: Scottish Enterprise.
teaching aid; self-instruction; primary education; enterprise
moyen d'enseignement; auto-enseignement; enseignement primaire; entreprise
PROJECT DESCRIPTION
This project aims to prepare two packages: (1) to examine the previous 'industrial' experience of students and to prepare a self-study package to enable them to make best use of their experiences; (2) to examine the scope for Enterprise Education in 5-14.

11732 Entwicklung eines Anwenderkurses im Bereich der integrierten Software fuer die Produktionsplanung und -steuerung. (Development of a course for users of integrated software for production planning and control.)
DEU 1993
Research Date(s): 1990-1993
Eichacker, S.
Sup: Scheer, A.
Inst: Universitaet Saarbruecken, FB 02 Wirtschaftswissenschaft, Fachrichtung BWL, insb. Wirtschaftsinformatik, Postfach, D-6600 Saarbruecken.
Fin: Kommission der Europaeischen Gemeinschaften.
further training; software; curriculum development; industry; computer application; control technology; small and medium entreprise
formation complémentaire; logiciel; élaboration de programmes d'études; industrie; application informatique; technologie de contrôle; petite ou moyenne entreprise
PROJECT DESCRIPTION
Inhalt: Das Projekt wird seit September 1990 vom Institut fuer Wirtschaftsinformatik (IWi) und den Handwerkskammern Luxemburg, des Saarlandes und Trier bearbeitet. Ziel des Projektes ist die Entwicklung und Umsetzung eines Schulungskonzeptes zur systemneutralen Qualifizierung der Anwender von PPS-Systemen. Mit der Schulung sollen solide theoretische Kenntnisse ueber die einem PPS-System zugrundeliegenden Planungs-und Steuerungsphilosophie vermittelt werden. Durch die Bearbeitung von Fallstudien mit Hilfe eines PPS-Systems wird das vermittelte Basiswissen vertieft. Zielgruppe der Schulungsmassnahmen sind die Mitarbeiter von Klein- und Mittelunternehmen (KMU). Wichtige Projektschritte sind: (a) Analyse der Ist-Situation in Klein- und Mittelunternehmen und die sich daraus ergebenden Anforderungen an den Einsatz von PPS-Systemen. (b) Erarbeitung eines Schulungskonzeptes unter Beruecksichtigung der bisher angebotenen Schulungsmassnahmen der Handwerkskammern. (c) Auswahl einer geeigneten Schulungssoftware. (d) Erstellung von Schulungsunterlagen und -hilfsmitteln.
Publ: Nuettgens, M.; Eichacker, S. & Scheer, A.-W. *Qualifizierungskonzept fuer Klein- und Mittelunternehmen (KMU).* (Veroeffentlichungen des Instituts fuer Wirtschaftsinformatik, H. 75) Saarbruecken 1991.

11733 Entwicklung eines erweiterten Lernaufgabenkonzeptes fuer erfahrungsgeleitete Taetigkeitsanteile in der computergestuetzten Arbeit. (Development of an extended concept of learning tasks for experience-based activities in computer-aided work.)
DEU 1993
Research Date(s): 1990-1992
Krogoll, T.; Wilke-Schnaufer, J.
Inst: Fraunhofer-Institut fuer Arbeitswirtschaft und Organisation -IAO-, Nobelstrasse 12 C, D-7000 Stuttgart 80.
Fin: Deutsche Forschungsanstalt fuer Luft- und Raumfahrt -DLR- Projekttraeger des Programms "Arbeit und Technik".
didactic use of computer; enterprise; in-service training; further training; computer application; teaching method
usage didactique de l'ordinateur; entreprise; formation en cours d'emploi; formation complémentaire; application informatique; méthode pédagogique
PROJECT DESCRIPTION
Inhalt: Ein Modellbetrieb der Metallbranche (Blechbearbeitung) wird bei der Umstellung von herkoemmlicher Fertigung zu moderner, qualifizierter Gruppenarbeit begleitet. Es werden neuartige Lernaufgabensysteme in Anlehnung an die Methode CLAUS entwickelt. Die notwendigen Qualifizierungsmassnahmen werden gemeinsam mit den Betroffenen in mehrern Schritten fuer drei Einzelarbeitsaufgaben und eine die Gruppenarbeit speziell charakterisierenden Kernaufgabe (Kooperations-und Planungserfordernisse) ausgearbeitet und durchgefuehrt. Die Betreuung im Betrieb reicht ueber eine arbeitsbegleitende Schulung bis zur systematischen Uebergabe der Handbuecher fuer Schulungen durch Dritte. Im Vordergrund steht der besondere Aspekt der Beteiligung sowie der Nutzung von Erfahrungswissen im Prozess der produktionsnahen, dezentralen Qualifizierung. In einem weiteren Modellbetrieb wird ein CNC-Pilotkurs entwickelt, der unter dem besonderen Aspekt des Erhalts des Erfahrungswissens der Facharbeiter steht, die von konventioneller auf CNC-Arbeit umlernen.
Publ: Krogoll, T. & Wilke-Schnaufer, J. Die Arbeitsaufgabe als Referenzpunkt fuer Konzepte der betrieblichen Qualifizierung und Beteiligung. In: *Tagungsband "Europaeisches Symposium Qualifikation: Schluessel fuer eine soziale Innovation" 16.-19.9.1991.* Bremen: ITB 1991.

11734 Entwicklung faehigkeitsgerechter Differenzierungsmassnahmen im Mathematikunterricht des 7. Schuljahres. (Differentiation according to ability in seventh form mathematics classes.)
DEU 1993
Research Date(s): 1991-1992
Grosmann, U.; Buck, E.
Sup: Viet, U.
Inst: Universitaet Osnabrueck, FB Mathematik, Informatik, Fachgebiet Mathematik, LS Didaktik der Mathematik, Albrechtstrasse 28, D-4500 Osnabrueck.
Fin: Institution; Arbeitsamt Osnabrueck.
differentiated teaching; performance; guidance period; lower secondary; mathematics
pédagogie differenciée; performance; cycle d'orientation; secondaire premier cycle; mathématiques
PROJECT DESCRIPTION
Inhalt: Durch breite Erhebungen in Orientierungsstufen vermuten wir, dass Empfehlungen und Kurszuweisungen starke sozial- und entwicklungspsychologische Ursachen haben. Es soll untersucht werden, ob Differenzierungsmassnahmen auf Faehigkeitsbasis, weitgehend abstrahierend von Schulleistung und Arbeitsverhalten, in der Lage sind, die Schulleistung, Motivation und das Interesse am Fach zu verbessern.
Geographischer Raum: Bundesrepublik Deutschland.
Vorgehensweise: Empirisch; kognitionswissenschaftlich. Untersuchungsdesign: Methodenforschung; Fallstudie; Evaluationsstudie; qualitative Forschung; Unterrichtsforschung.
Datengewinnung: Nicht-standardisiertes Interview (Stichprobe: 22; 7. Klassen; Auswahlverfahren: Zufall). Gruppendiskussion (dito). Gruppenbefragung (dito). Teilnehmende Beobachtung (dito). Beobachtung (dito). Inhaltsanalyse (dito). Psychologischer Test (dito). Primaererhebung: Feldarbeit von Mitarbeitern des Projektes durchgefuehrt.
Auswertung: Clusteranalyse; formale Begriffsanalyse. Datenaufbereitung: Datenedition (z.B. Aufbau von Datenbanken).

11735 Entwicklung und Erprobung einer Seminarkonzeption fuer Ausbilder am Arbeitsplatz (Ausbildungsbeauftragte). (Development and testing of a seminar concept for on-the-job instructors.)
DEU 1993
Research Date(s): 1991-1993
Unseld, G.; Abele, T.; Behrens, B.
Sup: Henecka, H.
Inst: Paedagogische Hochschule Heidelberg, FB 04 Fach Soziologie, Keplerstrasse 87, D-6900 Heidelberg.
Fin: Paedagogische Hochschule Freiburg, Arbeitskreis Paedagogische Hochschulen - Wirtschaft in Baden-Wuerttemberg.
vocational training; training of trainers; didactics; occupational qualification; enterprise; in-service training

formation professionnelle; formation des formateurs; didactique; qualification professionnelle; entreprise; formation en cours d'emploi
PROJECT DESCRIPTION

Inhalt: Ausbildungsbeauftragte betreuen Jugendliche und junge Erwachsene in den Phasen der Berufsausbildung, die an einem Arbeitsplatz im Betrieb selbst stattfinden. Sie nehmen damit regelmaessig eine Anleitungstaetigkeit neben ihrer eigentlichen Aufgabe im Betrieb wahr. Ihre Qualifikation ist heterogen; in der Regel verfuegen sie ueber keine berufspaedagogische Qualifikation, die den Anforderungen der Ausbildereignungsverordnung entspricht. Ziel des Projekts ist der Aufbau und die Systematisierung einer berufspaedagogischen Grundqualifikation fuer die Ausbildungsbeauftragten. Vorhandene Wissensbestaende und Faehigkeiten sollen ergaenzt und weiterentwickelt werden. Die Faehigkeit zur selbstaendigen praktischen Umsetzung berufspaedagogischer Konzepte soll entwickelt werden; damit soll die verbreitete Unsicherheit bezueglich der Lerninhalte und Handlungskonzepte abgebaut werden. Die angestrebte Grundqualifikation fuer Ausbildungsbeauftragte richtet sich vor allem auf drei Bereiche: - methodisch-didaktischer Bereich; - kommunikativ-sozialer Bereich; - personaler Bereich.

Vorgehensweise: Situationsanalyse: Sekundaeranalyse vorliegender Untersuchungen; Analyse von Ausbildungsverordnungen; Interviews und Workshop mit Ausbildungsbeauftragten; Entwicklung eines Seminarkonzeptes und dessen Erprobung. Untersuchungsdesign: Fallstudie; Evaluationsstudie; qualitative Forschung.

11736 Entwicklung und Erprobung eines Curriculums zur Integration der Oekologie in die wirtschaftswissenschaftliche Ausbildung. (Development and testing of a curriculum for the integration of ecology in economics training.)
DEU 1993
Research Date(s): 1990-1992
Tiebler, P.; Antes, R.
Sup: Feess-Doerr, E.
Inst: European Business, School Institut fuer Oekologie und Unternehmensfuehrung, Schloss Reichartshausen, D-6227 Oestrich-Winkel.
Fin: Bundesministerium fuer Bildung und Wissenschaft.
curriculum development; ecology; environment; economics; university studies
élaboration de programmes d'études; écologie; environnement; science économique; études universitaires
PROJECT DESCRIPTION

Inhalt: Entwicklung und Erprobung eines Curriculums zur Integration der Oekologie in die wirtschaftswissenschaftliche Ausbildung mit dem Ziel, die umweltbezogene Handlungskompetenz der Studienabgaenger zu erhoehen. Die Notwendigkeit des Forschungsprojekts ergibt sich aus der Hypothese, dass die aktuelle wirtschaftswissenschaftliche Ausbildung nicht hinreichend ist, um das differenzierte oekonomische Instrumentarium zur Bewaeltigung des Umweltproblems zufriedenstellend auszuschoepfen. Der Begriff der "Integration" bringt zum Ausdruck, dass es nicht nur um den Aufbau eines Wahlpflichtfachs, sondern auch und gerade um die verstaerkte Vermittlung von Umweltaspekten innerhalb der allgemeinen wirtschaftswissenschaftlichen Ausbildung geht. Dies folgt aus der durch empirische Erhebungen gestuetzten Einschaetzung, dass die Umweltthematik in den meisten Arbeitsfeldern von Oekonomen in Wirtschaft, Politik und Verwaltung einen steigenden Stellenwert einnehmen wird und ein Verstaendnis der elementaren Zusammenhaenge daher nicht den Absolventen umweltoekonomischer Spezialveranstaltungen vorbehalten sein sollte. Gleichzeitig bietet erst die Vermittlung von Grundkenntnissen im Rahmen des allgemeinen Studiums die Moeglichkeit zur Implementierung eines gehaltvollen Wahlpflichtfachs. Geprueft werden soll, inwieweit die vorhandenen Methoden und Instrumente der oekonomischen Theorie auf Umweltfragen angewendet werden koennen und wo moeglicherweise neue Ansaetze gefunden werden muessen. Das Forschungsprojekt bezieht sich ausschliesslich auf die wirtschaftswissenschaftliche Hochschulausbildung, so dass die Entwicklung eines interdisziplinaeren umweltbezogenen Studienganges nicht intendiert ist. Dies beschreibt lediglich die Aufgaben des Forschungsprojekts und impliziert weder eine Wertung noch den vollstaendigen Ausschluss naturwissenschaftlich-technischer Zusammenhaenge, sofern diese auch fuer Wirtschaftswissenschaftler fuer unverzichtbar gehalten werden und als Voraussetzung in interdisziplinaeren Teams mit umweltbezogenen Aufgabenstellungen in Industrie, Dienstleistungsbetrieben und Behoerden angesehen werden. Vor diesem Hintergrund besteht die Zielsetzung des Forschungsprojekts darin, curriculare Bausteine fuer drei Typen von Lehrveranstaltungen zu erarbeiten und zu erproben: (1) Pflichtfaecher des wirtschaftswissenschaftlichen Studiums, fuer die Moeglichkeiten einer Bezugnahme auf umweltbezogene Fragestellungen untersucht werden. Dies bezieht sich gleichermassen auf die Betriebs- wie Volkswirtschaftslehre. (2) Aufbau eines Wahlpflichtfachs mit dem Arbeitstitel "Betriebliche Umweltoekonomie", in dem auch auf die Vermittlung praxisbezogener Faehigkeiten Wert gelegt wird. Die Betonung der betriebswirtschaftlichen gegenueber der volkswirtschaftlichen Perspektive im Wahlpflichtfach ist zum einen darauf zurueckzufuehren, dass die volkswirtschaftliche Umweltoekonomie auf eine laengere Tradition zurueck-

blicken kann und entsprechend weiter vorgeschritten ist und erklaert sich zum anderen daraus, dass es sich beim Projektnehmer um eine wissenschaftliche Hochschule mit primaer betriebswirtschaftlicher Ausrichtung handelt. (3) Der dritte Veranstaltungstyp schliesslich zielt aus den genannten Gruenden auf die Darstellung elementarer naturwissenschaftlich-technischer Grundkenntnisse.

11737 Entwicklung und Erprobung eines Fortbildungsprogramms fuer das Personal der beruflichen Weiterbildung in den neuen Laendern. (Development and testing of a further training programme for vocational trainers in the new German states.)
DEU 1993
Research Date(s): 1991-1994
Reutter, G.; Bruening, G.
Sup: Nader, D.
Inst: Deutscher Volkshochschulverband e.V., Paedagogische Arbeitsstelle, Holzhausenstrasse 21, D-6000 Frankfurt am Main 1.
Fin: Bundesministerium fuer Bildung und Wissenschaft.
further training; German DR; vocational training; training of trainers; training personnel; curriculum development
formation complémentaire; Allemagne RDA; formation professionnelle; formation des formateurs; personnel de formation; élaboration de programmes d'études
PROJECT DESCRIPTION

Inhalt: Aufgabe des Projektes ist die Qualifizierung von Mitarbeiterinnen und Mitarbeitern in der beruflichen Weiterbildung in den Bereichen: (a) Planung und Konzeptentwicklung von Foerder-, Fortbildungs- und Umschulungsmassnahmen. (b) Unterrichten und Unterweisen in beruflichen Weiterbildungsangeboten. (c) Organisation und regionale Kooperation. (d) Aufbau von Qualifizierungs- und Beschaeftigungsgesellschaften. Das Projekt entwickelt, erprobt und evaluiert Fortbildungs- und Beratungskonzeptionen und fuehrt Fortbildungsveranstaltungen durch. Es werden sowohl teambezogene als auch themenorientierte Seminare durchgefuehrt. Die Fortbildungs- und Beratungsaktivitaeten werden durch die Herausgabe schriftlicher Praxismaterialien unterstuetzt.

Vorgehensweise: Beratung der Traeger und der Arbeitsverwaltung; Aufbau regionaler Kooperationsnetze; Themenorientierte Seminare; Themenbezogene Beratung und Fortbildung.

11738 Entwicklung und Erprobung ganzheitlicher Lernansaetze in der Umweltbildung in Kooperation zwischen Betrieb und Berufsschule. (Development and testing of holistic learning concepts for environmental education programmes for vocational school-industry partnerships.)
DEU 1993
Research Date(s): 1992-1994
Drees, G.
Sup: Paetzold, G.
Inst: Universitaet Dortmund, FB Erziehungswissenschaften und Biologie, Institut fuer Allg., Vgl. und Berufspaedagogik, Emil-Figge-Str. 50, D-4600 Dortmund 50.
Fin: Institution; Land Nordrhein-Westfalen Kultusministerium.
vocational school; curriculum development; learning; further training; enterprise; environment; cooperation
école professionnelle; élaboration de programmes d'études; acquisition de connaissances; formation complémentaire; entreprise; environnement; coopération
PROJECT DESCRIPTION

Inhalt: Hauptfrage: Kann Auszubildenden durch "ganzheitliche" Ausbildungskonzepte, die eine enge Lernortkooperation zwischen Betrieb und Berufsschule vorsehen, im Rahmen von handlungsorientierten, erfahrungsbezogenen Projekten eine breite Umweltkompetenz vermittelt werden? Einzelfragen: (1) Welche berufspaedagogischen Intentionen muss eine berufliche Umweltbildung aufnehmen? Wie muessen die methodischen Ansaetze aussehen? Welche Rolle spielt dabei die Lernortkooperation? (2) Welche inhaltlichen und organisatorischen Voraussetzungen sind in Betrieben und Berufsschulen zu schaffen, um lernortuebergreifende umweltbezogene Ausbildungsinhalte kooperativ zu vermitteln? (3) Welche Kooperationsstrukturen zwischen Betrieb und Berufsschule koennen die Basis fuer ein handlungsorientiertes Lernen bilden? (4) Wie kann von den berufsbildenden Schulen auf kommunaler bzw. regionaler Ebene eine Koordinationsfunktion bei der Lernortkooperation in der beruflichen Umweltbildung uebernommen werden? (5) Kann von der Akademie fuer Jugend und Beruf eine ueberregionale Agenturfunktion wahrgenommen werden, die den Aufbau regionaler und lokaler Verbundstrukturen zwischen Betrieben und Berufsschulen zur Umsetzung einer ganzheitlichen Umweltbildung durch Beratung, Koordination sowie Fortbildungen und Materialentwicklung foerdert? (6) Welche Projekte koennen einen Beitrag dazu leisten, ein umfassendes Verstaendnis fuer oekologische Zusammenhaenge herzustellen und umweltbewusstes Handeln zu foerdern? (7) Welchen Zeitrahmen und welche Zeitorganisation sind fuer oekologischen Projektausschulunterricht bzw. in der betrieblichen Ausbildung anzusetzen?

Geographischer Raum: Nordrhein-Westfalen, Brandenburg, Sachsen.

Vorgehensweise: Teilnehmende Beobachtung; Gespraechskreise; Beratung; kommunikative Validierung. Untersuchungsdesign: Fallstudie; Evaluationsstudie; Querschnittserhebung; qualitative Forschung.

Datengewinnung: Primaererhebung: Feldarbeit von Mitarbeitern des Projektes durchgefuehrt.

11739 Entwicklung und Erprobung von Curriculumelementen fuer ein Modell Fort- und Weiterbildung fuer ehrenamtliche Taetigkeit im Bereich der Altenhilfe. (Development and testing of curricular elements for a model of further and advanced training for voluntary geriatric work.)
DEU 1993
Research Date(s): 1991-1992
Dallinger, U.; Wassmuth, R.
Sup: Veelken, L.
Inst: Forschungsgesellschaft fuer Gerontologie e.V., Schwanenwall 31-35, D-4600 Dortmund 1.
Fin: Land Nordrhein-Westfalen Ministerium fuer Arbeit, Gesundheit und Soziales.
further training; curriculum development; elderly person; social work; personnel; voluntary work
formation complémentaire; élaboration de programmes d'études; personne âgée; travail social; personnel; travail volontaire
PROJECT DESCRIPTION
Inhalt: Ziel des Projektes ist es durch Fort- und Weiterbildung ehrenamtlich Taetiger in der Altenarbeit die Qualitaet und Attraktivitaet ehrenamtlicher Mitarbeit, verstanden als soziale Partizipation, zu steigern. Besondere Augenmerke liegen auf der Qualifizierung der Person des (potentiellen) ehrenamtlichen Mitarbeiters, auf der Eroeffnung neuer Arbeitsfelder ehrenamtlicher Taetigkeit im Bereich der Altenarbeit, sowie auf Aspekten der Verbesserung der Kooperation zwischen ehrenamtlichen und hauptamtlichen Mitarbeitern. Durch eine wissenschaftliche Begleitung soll die Effizienz des Projektes sowohl in Hinblick auf Verbesserungen und Innovationen in der Praxis der Altenarbeit als auch auf relevante persoenliche Veraenderungen der Teilnehmer ueberprueft werden.
Geographischer Raum: Dortmund.
Vorgehensweise: Untersuchungsdesign: Querschnittserhebung; qualitative Forschung; Literaturanalyse.
Datengewinnung: Postalische Befragung (Stichprobe: 260; Ehrenamtliche der Stadt Dortmund; Auswahlverfahren: total). Gruppendiskussion (Stichprobe: 15; Teilnehmer einer Fortbildungsveranstaltung; Auswahlverfahren: Zufall). Nicht-standardisiertes Interview (Stichprobe: 5; Ehrenamtliche der Stadt Dortmund; Auswahlverfahren: bewusst). Expertengespraech (Stichprobe: 7; Mitarbeiter aus der Altenhilfe, Altenarbeit; Auswahlverfahren: bewusst). Standardisiertes Interview Stichprobe: 70; Ehrenamtliche der Stadt Dortmund; Auswahlverfahren: Quota). Primaererhebung: Feldarbeit von Mitarbeitern des Projektes durchgefuehrt.
Auswertung: Faktorenanalyse, Varianzanalyse.

11740 Erfolgsfaktor Hochschulstudium. (University studies as a factor for success.)
DEU 1993
Research Date(s): 1991-1992
Friese, M.; Lotz, U.
Sup: Hoerschgen, H.
Inst: Universitaet Hohenheim, Fak. 05 Wirtschafts- und Sozialwissenschaften, Institut fuer BWL, LS Absatzwirtschaft, Postfach 700562, D-7000 Stuttgart 70.
university studies; economics; transition from school to work; career; success; occupational success
études universitaires; science économique; passage à la vie active; carrière; réussite; réussite professionnelle
PROJECT DESCRIPTION
Inhalt: Untersuchung der Zusammenhaenge zwischen dem Studium der Wirtschaftswissenschaften an der Universitaet Hohenheim, dem Berufseinstieg und dem beruflichen Werdegang.
Vorgehensweise: Repraesentative empirische Erhebung in Form einer schriftlichen Befragung von Absolventen der Wirtschaftswissenschaften der Universitaet Hohenheim. Untersuchungsdesign: Methodenforschung.
Datengewinnung: Postalische Befragung (Stichprobe: ca. 1100; Absolventen der Wirtschaftswissenschaften der Universitaet Hohenheim; Auswahlverfahren: bewusst). Primaererhebung: Feldarbeit von Mitarbeitern des Projektes durchgefuehrt.
Auswertung: alle gaengigen Verfahren uni-, bi- und multivariater Datenanalyse.

11741 Erzieherinnen - Ausbildung in Niedersachsen. (Educators - training in Lower Saxony.)
DEU 1993
Research Date(s): 1991-1992
Geisler, D.
Sup: Dippelhofer-Stiem, B.
Inst: Institut Frau und Gesellschaft, Walter-Gieseking-Str. 14, D-3000 Hannover 1.
Fin: Bundesanstalt fuer Arbeit; Land Niedersachsen.

vocational education; sciences of education; Lower Saxony; European community; woman; university studies
enseignement professionnel; sciences de l'éducation; Basse-Saxe; Communauté européenne; femme; études universitaires
PROJECT DESCRIPTION
Inhalt: Die Studie moechte Einblick in die Bildungsziele und Berufsvorbereitung sowie die fachlichen und persoenlichen Anforderungen des Ausbildungsganges in Niedersachsen vermitteln. Dabei sollen die impliziten und expliziten curricularen Inhalte analysiert und die Probleme und Desiderate in diesem, vorwiegend von jungen Frauen frequentierten Lernfeld naeher benannt werden. Vor dem Hintergrund von Professionalisierungstendenzen ist beabsichtigt, wissenschaftlich untermauerte Argumentationshilfen fuer die ideelle und materielle Aufwertung dieses Berufes bereitzustellen. Mit Blick auf die Oeffnung des EG-Binnenmarktes 1993 ist dies zugleich ein Schritt in die wissenschaftliche Analyse des Ausbildungsganges und ein Anstoss zur Diskussion ueber die moegliche Anbindung des Elementarbereiches an das allgemeine Bildungswesen.
Geographischer Raum: Niedersachsen.
Vorgehensweise: Inhaltsanalyse von Rahmenrichtlinien, Studien- und Pruefungsordnungen sowie Lehrplaenen; Expertengespraeche auf der Grundlage der inhaltsanalytischen Ergebnisse.
Datengewinnung: Expertengespraech (Lehrkraefte von Ausbildungseinrichtungen). Inhaltsanalyse (Ausbildungsvoraussetzungen und -inhalte, Berufsbild).

11742 Evaluatie van "onderwijs op maat" in het basisonderwijs. (Evaluation of "tailored instruction" in primary schools.)
NLD 1994
Research Date(s): 1992-1993
Houtveen, A.A.M.
Inst: Interdisciplinair Sociaal-wetenschappelijk Onderzoeksinstituut, Afdeling Onderwijs (ISOR) (Interdisciplinary Research Institute for the Social Sciences, Department of Educational Research), P.O. Box 80140, 3508 TC Utrecht, Netherlands.
Rijksuniversiteit Utrecht (State University of Utrecht), P.O. Box 80125, 3508 TC Utrecht, Netherlands
Fin: SVO het Instituut voor Onderzoek van het Onderwijs.
teaching method; differentiated teaching; evaluation; primary education
méthode pédagogique; pédagogie differenciée; évaluation; enseignement primaire
PROJECT DESCRIPTION
Background: "Tailored instruction" occurs when a school's educational efforts are a response to the specific needs of individual pupils. One of the tasks of the Primary Education Evaluation Committee is to describe and evaluate current practice in tailored teaching in schools. Existing information on differentiated teaching dates back to the period before the reform of primary education (the integration of nursery and primary schools in 1985).
Aim: (1) To describe current forms of tailored instruction in primary schools; (2) to identify factors that advance or hinder the realization of tailored instruction.
Design: Questionnaires will be given to teachers in primary years 3, 5 and 7 and the headteachers of 381 schools selected by the Primary Education Evaluation Committee. The evaluation will focus on: outcomes, educational content, process (instruction and organization) and context. Teachers will be given questions about tailored instruction in reading, mathematics and world studies. Headteachers will be asked about the organization of teaching, the context in which the school operates and school characteristics. Additional evaluative data will be collected from school inspectors with the help of a checklist.

11743 Evaluation des Projekts "Student und Arbeitswelt". (Evaluation of the project "Students and the world of work".)
DEU 1993
Research Date(s): 1991-1993
Bewyl, W.
Inst: Universitaet Koeln, Erziehungswissenschaftliche Fakultaet, Seminar fuer Sozialwissenschaften, Abt. Wirtschaftswissenschaft und ihre Didaktik, Gronewaldstrasse 2, D-5000 Koeln 41.
in-plant training; student; sciences of education; qualification; further training
stage en entreprise; étudiant; sciences de l'éducation; qualification; formation complémentaire
PROJECT DESCRIPTION
Inhalt: Beschreibung, Bewertung und Verbesserung des Projekts, in dessen Rahmen Diplompaedagogik-StudentInnen ihre Eignung und Neigung fuer eine Taetigkeit in Wirtschaftsunternehmen ueberpruefen (8-woechiges Betriebspraktikum) sowie Zusatzqualifikationen erwerben. Zielsetzung ist die Verbesserung der Praktikumsorganisation durch die Hochschule und durch die Praktikumsgeber sowie des zusaetzlichen Lehrangebotes. Sekundaer geht es um die Erforschung des Berufsfeldes unternehmensinterner sowie unternehmensnaher Aus- und Weiterbildung.
Geographischer Raum: Grossraum Koeln.
Untersuchter Zeitraum: 1989-1993.

Vorgehensweise: Praxiszentrierte, responsive Evaluation. Untersuchungsdesign: Fallstudie; Evaluationsstudie.

Datengewinnung: Standardisiertes Interview (Stichprobe: 50; alle PraktikantInnen 1989-1992; Auswahlverfahren: total. Stichprobe: 20; alle Praktikumsbetriebe; Auswahlverfahren: total). Gruppendiskussion (dito). Primaererhebung: Feldarbeit von Mitarbeitern des Projektes durchgefuehrt; Datenerstellung auf der Basis von bereits vorliegenden Materialien wie Texten, Akten, Statistiken.

11744 Evaluation einer berufsbegleitenden Fortbildungsmassnahme "Leitungstaetigkeit in Kindertagesstaetten". (Evaluation of an in-service training programme "Management activities in day nurseries".)
DEU 1993
Research Date(s): 1991-1994
Seeger, D.
Sup: Holodynski, M.
Inst: Universitaet Bielefeld, Fak. fuer Psychologie und Sportwissenschaft, Abt. Psychologie, Postfach 100131, D-4800 Bielefeld.
Fin: Institution; Arbeitsamt Bielefeld.
in-service training; further training; nursery school; managerial staff; job requirements; qualification
formation en cours d'emploi; formation complémentaire; école maternelle; personnel d'encadrement; qualification requise pour l'emploi; qualification
PROJECT DESCRIPTION
Inhalt: Die evaluierte Fortbildung hat Modellcharakter, da darin fuer Leitungskraefte in Vorschuleinrichtungen eine systematische Ausbildung in spezifischen Fuehrungsqualifikationen durchgefuehrt wird, die auf das Anforderungsprofil des Taetigkeitsfeldes "Kindertagesstaette" zugeschnitten sind und die das Problem der effektiven Umsetzung des Fuehrungswissens vor Ort direkt zum Fortbildungsinhalt hat. Entsprechend werden deutliche Verbesserungen bzgl. der Fuehrungsqualifikationen der Leiterinnen erwartet, insbesondere in Organisationsplanung und Mitarbeiterfuehrung angesichts steigender Anforderungen an die elementaren Bildungseinrichtungen. Die Ueberpruefung der Fortbildungseffektivitaet ist Gegenstand der begleitenden Evaluation. Dabei werden sowohl subjektive Masse (Frageboegen) wie Verhaltensmasse (Video- und Zeitbudgetanalyse) eingesetzt.

Vorgehensweise: Taetigkeits- und Handlungstheorie; Feldforschung; Handlungsforschung. Untersuchungsdesign: Evaluationsstudie; (Quasi-)Experiment.

Datengewinnung: Aktenanalyse (Stichprobe: 2 X 15; Leiterinnen von Kindertagesstaetten in Bielefeld; Auswahlverfahren: bewusst). Inhaltsanalyse (dito). Videoaufnahmen (dito). Zeitbudgetanalyse (dito). Befragung (Stichprobe: 2 X 15; Leiterinnen von Kindertagesstaetten in Bielefeld; Auswahlverfahren: bewusst. Stichprobe: 320; Mitarbeiterinnen von Kindertagesstaetten in Bielefeld; Auswahlverfahren: total). Primaererhebung: Feldarbeit von Mitarbeitern des Projektes durchgefuehrt.

Auswertung: Faktorenanalyse; Varianzanalyse. Datenaufbereitung: Aggregierung oder Disaggregierung; Zeitreihe(n).

11745 An evaluation of area learning support teams and observation of cooperative teaching.
GBR 1993
Research Date(s): 1990-1991
Munn, P.; Allan, J.
Inst: Scottish Council for Research in Education, 15 St John Street, Edinburgh EH8 8JR, United Kingdom.
Fin: Scottish Office Education Department; Dumfries and Galloway Region.
team teaching; special education; learning difficulty; teaching method
enseignement en équipe; enseignement spécial; difficulté de l'apprentissage; méthode pédagogique
PROJECT DESCRIPTION
The project, based in Dumfries and Galloway, has two distinctive strands. The first of these evaluated the effectiveness of a new initiative for learning support provision. The second phase focuses on cooperative teaching strategies for meeting the needs of pupils with learning difficulties.
Publ: Allan, J. *Providing learning support through area teams.* SCRE Spotlights Series, No 34, Edinburgh: Scottish Council for Research in Education, 1992.
Allan, J. & Munn, P. *Teaming up: area teams for learning support.* SCRE Research Report Series, No 38, Edinburgh: Scottish Council for Research in Education, 1992.

11746 An evaluation of home computers in adult distance education.
GBR 1993
Research Date(s): 1988-1993
Kirkup, G.; Kirkwood, A.; Jones, A.
Inst: Open University, Institute of Educational Technology, Walton Hall, Milton Keynes MK7 6AA, United Kingdom.
didactic use of computer; distance study; open university; microcomputer
usage didactique de l'ordinateur; enseignement à distance; télé-université; micro-ordinateur

PROJECT DESCRIPTION
This is an investigation of the effects of compulsory use of a personal computer by students studying particular courses in the undergraduate programme of the Open University. Students were sampled during their studies in 1988, 1989, 1990 and 1991. Issues of interest include: access and availability of equipment; costs; the effect of introducing home-based computing on study habits; content difficulty; and the impact on family of computer in home. Teaching staff are also researched to discover the effects on contact with students and teaching load.
Research methods include: survey questionnaires; interviews; and self-completion journals.
Publ: Kirkwood, A. & Kirkup, G. Access to computing for home-based students. In: *Studies in Higher Education,* Vol 16, No 3/1991.
Kirkup, G. Computer conferencing and gender. In: *Computers in Adult Education and Training,* Vol 2, No 2/1991.
Jones, A.; Kirkup, G.; Kirkwood, A. & Mason, R. Providing computing for distance learners: a strategy for home use. In: *Computers and Education,* No 18/1992, pp. 1-3.
Kirkup, G.; Jones, A. & Kirkwood, A. *Personal computers for distance learning.* London: Paul Chapman, 1992.

11747 Evaluation of the National Oracy Project.
GBR 1993
Research Date(s): 1990-1993
Keiner, J.; Grugeon, A.
Inst: Reading University, Department of Education Studies and Management, Bulmershe Court, Woodlands Avenue, Earley, Reading RG6 1HY, United Kingdom; Bedford College of Higher Education, Cauldwell Street, Bedford MK24 9AH, United Kingdom.
Fin: National Curriculum Council.
oral work; oral expression; assessment
exercice oral; expression orale; appréciation
PROJECT DESCRIPTION
The National Oracy Project was established to promote good practice in oral work across the curriculum and to develop appropriate modes of assessment for pupils aged 3 to 18 years. This evaluation of the National Oracy Project aims to explore the extent to which the Project's work fulfils its stated aims. A case study approach has been adopted, drawing on a selection of seven local authority consortia of teacher-based groups involved in the Project, in conjunction with studies of the National Project Team to examine the Project's relationship with the National Curriculum Council and other national educational policy bodies; and publications and other data emerging from the Project. Methods used include analysis of published material and other documents; field visits and interviews; and participant observation. Results and conclusions will be published in a final report.

11748 Evaluation of the second year of the Training Credits pilot: three case studies.
GBR 1993
Research Date(s): 1992-1993
Sims, D.; Harland, J.; Tomlins, B.; Twitchin, R.
Sup: Stoney, S.
Inst: National Foundation for Educational Research, The Mere, Upton Park, Slough SL1 2DQ, United Kingdom.
Fin: Department of Employment.
vocational training; credits; vocational guidance; transition from school to work
formation professionnelle; unités capitalisables; orientation professionnelle; passage à la vie active
PROJECT DESCRIPTION
This evaluation sought to explore any changes in attitudes, culture and practice amongst young people, school staff, careers staff, employers and training providers which may have occurred as a result of the introduction of the Training Credits (TC) pilot and since the first round of evaluations. The project has focused on the extent to which the original aims of the Training Credits pilots have been achieved, how much progress has been made in overcoming difficulties identified from the first-year evaluations and making practical recommendations to assist in the further development of the pilots.
The three case studies employed the following research methods: postal questionnaires, telephone and face-to-face interviews, and group discussions. Key groups of people targeted in each area and the number in each questionnaire sample were as follows: Year 11 students (200), Year 12 students (50), young people (200 TC-users; up to 50 non-TC users) and training providers (25). Interviews were conducted with up to 20 operational personnel such as Training and Enterprise Councils (TECs), local education authority (LEA) and Careers Service staff and 100 employers (50 TC-users; 50 non-TC users).
Broadly, findings indicate that TECs are making strenuous efforts to promote the Training Credits pilot but are finding that outcomes and impact are being seriously constrained by the current recession. The main outcomes from the project will be three case-study reports and one overall national report.

11749 Evaluering av begynneropplæring. (Evaluation of basic instruction in reading and writing.)
NOR 1994
Research Date(s): 1992-1994
Madssen, Kjell-Arild.
Inst: Volda Lærerhögskole (Volda College of Education), 6100 Volda, Norway.
Fin: NAVF/RSF.
beginning learning; basic education; reading; writing; mathematics; curriculum
enseignement initial; éducation de base; lecture; écriture; mathématiques; programme d'études
PROJECT DESCRIPTION
  The study examines the intentions of the curriculum for basic instruction in years 0 to 3 and the way these intentions are perceived and realized by teachers. The focus will be on reading, writing and mathematics. Research methods will include content analysis of curriculum plans, questionnaires, interviews and classroom observations.

Publ: A full list of publications can be obtained on request from the research institute.

11750 Evangelische Erwachsenenbildung in Stadt- und Landgemeinden. (Protestant adult education in urban and rural communities.)
DEU 1993
Research Date(s): 1991-1992
Dieckhoff, K.
Sup: Faber, W.
Inst: Universitaet Bamberg, Fak. Paedagogik, Philosophie, Psychologie, Fach Erwachsenenbildung, Markusplatz 3 Marcus-Haus, D-8600 Bamberg.
adult education; didactics; church; motivation; content of education
éducation des adultes; didactique; église; motivation; contenu de l'éducation
PROJECT DESCRIPTION
  Inhalt: Inhaltliche Interessen, Bildungsmotive und didaktische Praeferenzen der Teilnehmer evangelischer Erwachsenenbildung im Zusammenhang mit ihren demographischen Merkmalen, ihrer kirchlichen Bindung und anderen Aktivitaeten.
  Geographischer Raum: Bundesrepublik Deutschland (alte Bundeslaender).
  Vorgehensweise: Postalische Befragung mit standardisierten Fragebogen. Untersuchungsdesign: Querschnittserhebung.
  Datengewinnung: Postalische Befragung (Stichprobe: ca. 2.500; Teilnehmer an Bildungsveranstaltungen; Auswahlverfahren: willkuerlich). Primaererhebung: Feldarbeit von Mitarbeitern des Projektes durchgefuehrt.
  Auswertung: Kreuztabellen.

11751 An examination of Language Experience Approach (LEA) to teaching reading development and its use in second language learning.
GBR 1993
Research Date(s): 1986-1991
Lo, A.
Sup: Byram, M.
Inst: Durham University, School of Education, Leazes Road, Durham DH1 1TA, United Kingdom.
teaching method; language teaching; foreign languages; reading; secondary education
méthode pédagogique; enseignement des langues; langues étrangères; lecture; enseignement secondaire
PROJECT DESCRIPTION
  This is a critical survey of the literature on language experience approaches to reading development and writing with particular reference to their use in second language learning. The research includes a case study of the introduction and development of language experience approaches with students in a secondary school in Hong Kong. The evaluation of the study utilises a range of qualitative approaches, observations, self-reporting, written materials and some formal and informal assessments of attainment.

11752 Feedback: its effects on procedural and conceptual knowledge for problem solving strategies.
GBR 1993
Research Date(s): 1991-1994
Cope, P.; Simmons, M.
Inst: Stirling University, Department of Education, Stirling FK9 4LA, United Kingdom.
Fin: Economic and Social Research Council.
didactic use of computer; feedback; logo; problem solving; teaching method; educational innovation
usage didactique de l'ordinateur; rétroaction; logo; résolution de problème; méthode pédagogique; innovation pédagogique
PROJECT DESCRIPTION

The aims of the research are: (1) to investigate the effects of changing the instructional environment on the problem-solving strategies of children using Logo microworlds; (2) to measure the effect of such changes of strategy on the development of conceptual knowledge; (3) to determine which aspects of conceptual knowledge relating to rotation and angle will enhance pupils' ability to solve simple geometry problems using a screen turtle; (4) to invesitigate effective ways of teaching these aspects of rotation and angle.
  The background to this research is a general concern about the way in which young children interact with a Logo-based system. Effective use of Logo requires the development of mathematical knowledge about basic aspects of turtle geometry such as angle, rotation and distance. Such knowledge is a combination of both procedural and conceptual knowledge and although it is assumed that such knowledge can be developed through the use of Logo itself, this is by no means certain. Ideally, the development of knowledge about turtle geometry is one in which procedural knowledge and conceptual knowledge develop together. But in Logo the constant availability of feedback may have a profound effect on the development of knowledge.
  There are three phases to the study. Study 1 takes a sample of 60 children aged between 10 and 12. Groups are matched on the basis of a pre-test and thereafter are exposed to different kinds of feedback. Data collection is by taped transcripts and spooled output files. Study 2 takes the most appropriate principles of feedback found in Study 1 to develop structured Logo sessions. Study 3 compares computer-based and non-computer-based teaching strategies of angle and rotation concepts.

Publ: Cope, P.; Smith, H. & Simmons, M. Misconceptions concerning rotation and angle in LOGO. In: *Journal of Computer Assisted Learning*, Vol 8, No 1/1992, pp. 16-24.
Cope, P. & Simmons, M. Children's exploration of rotation and angle in limited LOGO microworlds. In: *Computers in Education*, Vol 16, No 2/1992, pp. 133-141.

11753 Foerderung deduktiven und induktiven Urteilens. (Promotion of deductive and inductive judgment.)
DEU 1993
Research Date(s): 1991-1993
Hinnersmann, H.
Sup: Bredenkamp, J.
Inst: Universitaet Bonn, Philosophische Fakultaet, Psychologisches Institut, LS Allg. Psychologie, Roemerstrasse 164, D-5300 Bonn 1.
Fin: Deutsche Forschungsgemeinschaft.
didactic use of computer; lower secondary; pupil; thinking; problem solving; mathematics; logical thinking
usage didactique de l'ordinateur; secondaire premier cycle; élève; pensée; résolution de problème; mathématiques; pensée logique
PROJECT DESCRIPTION
  Inhalt: Evaluation eines z. T. computergestuetzten Trainingsprogramms fuer Schueler der 7./ 8. Klassenstufe. Trainingsziele sind: Foerderung des Verstaendnisses fuer das Rationale von deduktiven Schluessen und Wahrscheinlichkeitsurteilen; Vermittlung der Strategie der externen analogen Problemrepraesentation; Foerderung eines flexibel-reflexiven Denkstils; Minimierung von Urteilsverzerrungen (z.B. belief bias, confirmation bias, overconfidence, hindsight bias, konjunktiver Fehler, Basisraten-Fehler).
  Vorgehensweise: Schlussfolgerungen auf der Basis mentaler Modelle (Johnson-Laird); kognitiver Bias und Urteilsheuristiken (Kahnemann und Tversky); active open-mindedness (J. Baron). Untersuchungsdesign: Evaluationsstudie; (Quasi-)Experiment.
  Datengewinnung: Experiment (Stichprobe: 64; Schueler der 7./ 8. Klasse; Auswahlverfahren: willkuerlich). Primaererhebung: Feldarbeit von Mitarbeitern des Projektes durchgefuehrt.
  Auswertung: Varianzanalyse; verteilungsfreie Verfahren.

11754 Further development on interactive video.
GBR 1993
Research Date(s): 1990-
Kennett, D.; Al-seaidy, H.
Sup: Burghes, D.
Inst: Exeter University, School of Education, St Luke's, Heavitree Road, Exeter EX1 2LU, United Kingdom.
teaching aid; mathematics; motivation; interactive video
moyen d'enseignement; mathématiques; motivation; vidéo interactive
PROJECT DESCRIPTION
  The main aim of the research is to evaluate a mathematics teaching interactive video package called School Disco. The evaluation concentrates on the motivational and attainment based aspects. For the purpose of conducting the evaluation process, several tests have been applied. Technical and educational points which might have a direct or indirect effect on pupil motivation have been detected. Other aims of the research are to explore the extent to which interactive video material could be employed within an educational system.

11755 Gender differences in educational computing in the humanities.

GBR 1993

Research Date(s): 1991-1993

Colley, A.

Sup: Hargreaves, D.

Inst: Leicester University, Department of Psychology, University Road, Leicester LE1 7RH, United Kingdom.

Fin: Leverhulme Trust.

didactic use of computer; sex difference; humanities; information technology

usage didactique de l'ordinateur; différence de sexe; études littéraires; technologie de l'information

PROJECT DESCRIPTION

Although Information Technology (IT) has become an important part of education at all levels, there is clear evidence that girls receive less benefit from IT. Research shows that boys are more interested in computers, and that they use them more at home and at school. Computers are widely used in the male-dominated areas of science and technology but they are now making a significant impact in the arts, in subject areas which traditionally have attracted girls.

This project uses a large scale survey method (N=1,500) to investigate secondary school boys' and girls' interest in, attitudes towards and use of IT in English and music in which new technologies are increasingly being used. Previous research has found that girls are likely to perform better in science and technology subjects in single-sex schools, where they do not feel in competition with their male peers. A comparison will therefore be made between pupils in co-educational and single-sex schools. Gender stereotyping has prevented many girls from developing an interest in science and technology. The project will provide valuable information which can be used to ensure that girls do not miss out on technological advancements in the humanities.

11756 Handreichungen zum Lehrgang CNC-Drehen als Ergebnisse eines Modellversuchs sowie CNC-Lernmaterialien fuer die Aus- und Weiterbildung. (Suggestions for a CNC turning course as the outcome of a pilot project and CNC learning material for basic and further training.)

DEU 1993

Research Date(s): 1990-1992

Selzer, H.

Inst: Didaktisches Labor H.M. Selzer, Rosengasse 3, D-8834 Pappenheim 2.

Fin: Kolping-Bildungswerk Landesverband Bayern, Wissenschaftliche Begleitung Modellversuch Neue Technologien in der beruflichen Bildung fuer benachteiligte Jugendliche.

vocational training; adolescent; deprived; learning difficulty; cognitive ability; remedial teaching

formation professionnelle; adolescent; défavorisé; difficulté de l'apprentissage; aptitude cognitive; soutien pédagogique

PROJECT DESCRIPTION

Inhalt: Der Modellversuch zur Foerderung der beruflichen Bildung benachteiligter Jugendlicher hat didaktische und konzeptionelle Erkenntnisse ausgewertet; diese werden umgesetzt in Arbeitsmaterialien fuer Auszubildende sowie fuer junge Erwachsene im Weiterbildungsbereich. Thematisch eingegrenzt sind die Untersuchungen auf CNC-(Computer Numerical Control)Drehen. Die besonderen Foerdermassnahmen zur erfolgreichen Unterweisung von teilweise lernbeeintraechtigten und schwach ausbildungsmotivierten Jugendlichen fuehrten zu einer intensivierten didaktischen Konzeption mit zwei Auspraegungen: Auspraegung A: Im Rahmen des ersten Ausbildungsjahres werden CNC-Basiskompetenzen vermittelt, auf die im zweiten und dritten Ausbildungsjahr die ausbildenden Industrieunternehmen aufbauen. Auspraegung S: Im Rahmen einer Vollausbildung (in Metallberufen) erhalten die Jugendlichen eine CNC-Grundausbildung. Entscheidend fuer die Didaktik dieses Ansatzes sind Projektorientierung, Foerderung der Handlungskompetenzen, haeufiger Wechsel von kognitiven Lernsituationen und Handlungsphasen an der CNC-Maschine. Die Zielorientierung liegt auf der zu vermittelnden Handlungskompetenz.

Geographischer Raum: Augsburg und Schweinfurt.

Untersuchter Zeitraum: 1989 bis 1991.

Vorgehensweise: Insgesamt standen vier Ausbildungsjahrgaenge mit je ca. 12 Teilnehmern zur wissenschaftlichen Beobachtung; im Zuge didaktischer Konkretisierung wurden die didaktischen Annahmen schrittweise modifiziert und auf die Lernbeduerfnisse der beteiligten Jugendlichen angepasst: im Sinne einer bedarfsgeleiteten didaktischen Optimierung. Untersuchungsdesign: qualitative Forschung.

Datengewinnung: Begleituntersuchung und Leistungsmessung (insgesamt 4 Ausbildungsgruppen).

11757 Het gebruik van vingers en de vijfstructuur bij het automatiseren tot twintig. (The usage of fingers and five-structures in automatizing up to 20.)

NLD 1994

Research Date(s): 1991-1992

Eerde, H.A.A. van; Berg, W. van den; Woerd, E.D.H.M. te.

Inst: Rotterdams Instituut voor Sociologisch en Bestuurskundig Onderzoek (RISBO) (Rotterdam Institute for Sociological, Environmental and Public Administration Research), P.O. Box 1738, 3000 DR Rotterdam, Netherlands.

Erasmus Universiteit Rotterdam (Erasmus University Rotterdam), P.O. Box 1738, 3000 DR Rotterdam, Netherlands

Fin: SVO het Instituut voor Onderzoek van het Onderwijs.

teaching method; teaching programme; calculation; achievement; primary education

méthode pédagogique; programme d'enseignement; calcul; rendement; enseignement primaire

PROJECT DESCRIPTION

Background: Research findings show that children in the 7-9 age range do not attain the objectives for basic calculations up to 20 within the set time. In the draft national programme for arithmetic instruction an important place is assigned to the usage of five-structures in the teaching and learning of basic facts. The present study is concerned with an evaluation of the implementation and the effectiveness of a curriculum based on five-structures.

Aim: To examine the use of five-structures in the teaching of basic facts up to 20; to evaluate an arithmetic programme based on the usage of five-structures and the fingers for automatizing basic facts.

Design: A group of 8-year-old pupils who had difficulty in mastering basic facts up to 20 were divided into three groups: one was given additional instruction using five-structures (F); one was given additional instruction based on rote learning (R); and one was given no additional instruction (C). Group tests were administered on four occasions to measure the effect of the instructional programme.

Results: No significant differences in learning gains were found between the F group and the R group, although certain tendencies were observed. Even though in the F programme there was little time to let the newly acquired skills sink in, the learning gains in the F group appeared to equal those of the R group. This means that the F group performed relatively better. Furthermore, the assumption seems justified that the F group has learned more from the programme than can be measured by the tests that were used.

(This is an updating of EUDISED no. 44/10582).

Publ: Berg, W. van den & Eerde, D. van. *Geef me de vijf: een onderzoek naar de waarde van de vijfstructuur voor het leren automatiseren van de optel- en aftrektafels tot twintig.* Rotterdam: RISBO, 1992, 104p., appendix 169p.

11758 Huiswerk maken bij de televisie of geluidsmedia: een descriptieve voorstudie. (Doing homework in front of the television or sound media: a descriptive preliminary study.)

NLD 1994

Research Date(s): 1993

Beentjes, J.W.J.

Sup: Voort, T.H.A. van der.

Inst: Sectie Kind en Media (Child and Media Section), P.O. Box 9555, 2300 RB Leiden, Netherlands.

Rijksuniversiteit Leiden (State University of Leiden), P.O. Box 9555, 2300 RB Leiden, Netherlands

Fin: SVO het Instituut voor Onderzoek van het Onderwijs.

homework; mass media; pupil attitude; opinion; achievement

devoirs; médias; attitude de l'élève; opinion; rendement

PROJECT DESCRIPTION

Background: Many pupils do their homework with a television or radio playing in the background. Teachers as well as parents are wondering whether this has a detrimental effect on the pupils' homework. There have been laboratory experiments which examined the effect of background media on the performance of cognitive tasks, but the results have limited relevance for the homework situation of Dutch secondary school pupils.

Aims: To gather information about (a) the types of homework pupils do, (b) the media playing in the background while pupils are doing their homework and (c) the degree to which homework assignments and background media take up pupils' attention.

Methods: Questionnaire survey, semi-structured interviews.

Design: Semi-structured interviews will be conducted with 20 pupils in the second or fourth year of various types of secondary school (ranging from pre-vocational to pre-university). On the basis of the interviews a pilot questionnaire will be constructed about doing homework in the presence of background media and pupils' perceptions thereof. Twenty-four pupils in the target group will be asked to complete the pilot questionnaire while thinking aloud. The definitive questionnaire will be administered in classrooms to a total of 2,000 pupils.

11759 Human-computer interfaces to reactive graphical images.
GBR 1993
Research Date(s): 1990-1993
Lamont, C.
Sup: Barker, P.; Manji, K.
Inst: Teesside University, School of Computing and Mathematics, Interactive Systems Research Group, Borough Road, Middlesbrough, Cleveland TS1 3BA, United Kingdom.
Fin: Science and Engineering Research Council; A.P. Chesters and Associates.
didactic use of computer; man-machine interface; interactive video; educational software
usage didactique de l'ordinateur; interface homme-machine; vidéo interactive; didacticiel
PROJECT DESCRIPTION
   A reactive graphical image is one that changes its form when pointed at by a computer user using a mouse or a touch screen. Such reactive graphical images can be combined with multimedia presentations (the blending of moving video, sound, and graphics in one display environment) to form the basis of effective interactive multimedia courseware for use in the computer-based training (CBT) industries. Work has initially been undertaken to provide custom editors within the PC/PILOT and PROPI authoring environments. A custom editor is designed to enhance the authoring capability of a CBT production environment by allowing parameters to be embedded within a lesson to access external material and devices. Such methods can enhance the usability and training value of a CBT lesson. Initially, custom editors have been built to incorporate videodisc still images or moving video sequences into a lesson, and for displaying graphics images on a remote terminal. However, because videodisc technology is based on analog data, it cannot effectively provide variable speed motion with continued sound synchronisation and effective graphics overlays. Thus the thrust of multimedia technology development is to provide all these features in one digital environment. Future custom editors will be built to take full advantage of this digital video interactive (DVI) technology. Once the full range of graphical custom editors has been designed and built, evaluations will be conducted to assess the quality of design and the usability of the products that are generated. Extensive end-user evaluations will also be conducted in order that a set of models and guidelines which reflect good design practice can be derived from the research.

11760 Identifikation und Foerderung begabter Ingenieurstudenten. (Identification and support of gifted engineering students.)
DEU 1993
Research Date(s): 1988-1993
Finze, F.; Pietrzyk, U.
Sup: Arnold, W.
Inst: Technische Universitaet Dresden, Fak. Geistes- und Sozialwissenschaften, Institut fuer Psychologie, Mommsenstr. 13, O-8027 Dresden; Technische Universitaet Dresden, Fak. Erziehungswissenschaften, Institut fuer Berufspaedagogik, Mommsenstr. 13, O-8027 Dresden.
engineering; student; technical ability; talent; aptitude
ingénierie; étudiant; capacité technique; talent; aptitude
PROJECT DESCRIPTION
   Inhalt: Gibt es eine Spezifik technischer Begabung? Welche Identifikationshilfen koennen angeboten werden? Welche Foerdermodelle sind im universitaeren Bereich am geeignetsten? Wann sollte universitaere Foerderung einsetzen (z.B. schon in der Schule)?
   Vorgehensweise: Ausgangspunkt ist das Begabungsmodell von Renzulli und Monks; darauf aufbauend erfolgten empirische Felduntersuchungen und retrospektiven Befragungen; das Problem wird interdisziplinaer unter psychologischem und paedagogischem Aspekt erarbeitet. Untersuchungsdesign: Methodenforschung; Fallstudie; Querschnittserhebung; retrospektive Daten.
   Datengewinnung: Standardisiertes Interview (Stichprobe: 80; Studenten TU Dresden -Meisterschueler-; Auswahlverfahren: total). Nicht-standardisiertes Interview (dito). Befragung (dito). Aktenanalyse (dito). Psychologischer Test (dito). Postalische Befragung (Stichprobe: 80; Studenten TU Dresden -Meisterschueler-; Auswahlverfahren: total. Stichprobe: 200; Hochschullehrer -gesamte BRD-; Auswahlverfahren: bewusst). Primaererhebung: Feldarbeit von Mitarbeitern des Projektes durchgefuehrt; Datenerstellung auf der Basis von bereits vorliegenden Materialien wie Texten, Akten, Statistiken.
   Auswertung: Deskriptive und Teststatistik. Datenaufbereitung: Verlaufsdaten (event history data).

11761 Implications of moving towards a more resource-based approach to teaching.
GBR 1993
Research Date(s): 1990-1992
Jackson, S.
Inst: Heriot-Watt University, Moray House Institute of Education, Holyrood Road, Edinburgh EH8 8AQ, United Kingdom.
teaching method; teaching aid; teacher role
méthode pédagogique; moyen d'enseignement; rôle de l'enseignant
PROJECT DESCRIPTION
   The aim of the research is to examine the implications of a move towards a more resource-based teaching approach. This will include looking at the implications for: (i) the role of the teacher; (ii) departmental and school administration; (iii) development of materials; and (iv) assessment. The research will look at the extent to which similar or different implications can be identified in different subject areas.
   The project also involves the preparation of teaching materials and this includes a video package for preservice and inservice courses. The package is based upon a case study (The James Young High School, Livingston) outlining how the Design Technology Department have implemented a resource-based approach. During the production of these materials there has been collaboration with British Petroleum who have used some of the material to produce a video package highlighting the high-quality design and craft work taking place at the school.
Publ: Jackson, S. & Barrett, P. Resource based learning - what does it mean in terms of Standard Grade teaching across the curriculum. Scottish Educational Research Association (SERA) Conference, 1991, St Andrews University.

11762 Industrial placements in Belgium.
GBR 1993
Research Date(s): 1989-1991
French, D.
Inst: Coventry University, Centre for Communication Studies, Gosford Street, Coventry CV1 5RZ, United Kingdom.
Fin: Belgian Government; European Community COMMETT Programme; University of Liege; Coventry University.
work experience; in-plant training; university industry relationship; Belgium
expérience du travail; stage en entreprise; relation université-entreprise; Belgique
PROJECT DESCRIPTION
   The project investigates student experience of industrial placements and the perception of the value, operational problems, etc. of such placements on the part of students, academic staff and placement hosts. It concentrates on communication/media studies but its conclusions have more general application.

11763 Informatique et formation: les nouvelles technologies de l'information (NTI).
FRA 1993
Research Date(s): 1987-
Léonhardt, Jean-Louis; Bessière, Christian; Vacherand-Revel, Jacqueline; Baker, Michaël; Balacheff, Nicolas.
Inst: Ministère de la recherche, CNRS UPR/5411 et GDR/28, Institut de recherche en pédagogie de l'économie et en audio-visuel pour la communication dans les sciences sociales, 93 Chemin des Mouilles, BP 167, 69130 Ecully Cedex, France.
new technologies; information technology; technological change; information dissemination; computer science; training type; learning; didactic use of computer; multimedia method
nouvelles technologies; technologie de l'information; changement technologique; diffusion de l'information; informatique; type de formation; acquisition de connaissances; usage didactique de l'ordinateur; moyen multimédia
PROJECT DESCRIPTION
   Objectifs: Il s'agit d'étudier les problèmes de fond que posent l'application et le fonctionnement des nouvelles technologies de l'information (NTI) dans le domaine des pratiques de formation. Il s'agit de déterminer comment les possibilités et contraintes du système machine NTI et les interactions personne-machine qu'il ménage, commandent la spécification par l'auteur-spécialiste de la connaissance, du contenu à intégrer, dans un contexte multimédia. Quelles sont les caractéristiques requises du système pour intégrer la connaissance à transmettre? Comment la connaissance y est-elle introduite? Comment s'en sert-on? Deux champs de pratiques sont privilégiés où se développe la problématique de l'outil de création et de son usage: (1) les NTI multimédia intégrant l'informatique et l'audiovisuel; (2) les activités de génie didacticiel.
   Méthodologie: La méthode mise en oeuvre assure la continuité entre recherche et applications: elle permet de créer un terrain où l'analyse et l'évaluation des usages sont évaluées, analysées et alimentent en retour les recherches en amont.
   Résultats: Les résultats de recherche sont de nature différente: des outils logiciels destinés à la production de didacticiels multimédias, la définition de structures informatiques spécifiques de la transmission des connaissances.
Publ: Léonhardt, Jean-Louis. *MINIGR: un éditeur graphique pour l'interactivité.* Rapport interne. CNRS IRPEACS, 1987.
Bessière, Christian. *EDP: un éditeur pédagogique pour l'interactivité.* Rapport interne. CNRS IRPEACS, 1988.
Bessière, Christian & Vacherand-Revel, Jacqueline. *Jouer du graphique pour faire... autre chose.* In: Tucker, R.N. *Interactive media. The human issues,* vol. 2. Amsterdam: Kogan, 1989.

Bessière, Christian & Vacherand-Revel, Jacqueline. L'interaction graphique et la prise en compte des différences entre usagers dans la formation d'adultes assistée par ordinateur. In: *Informatique et différences individuelles*, PUL, 1990, pp. 21-52.

11764 Innere Differenzierung in Fachklassen der Berufsschule. (Internal differentiation into specialized classes in part-time vocational schools.)
DEU 1993
Research Date(s): 1989-1992
Arnold, R.
Inst: Universitaet Kaiserslautern, FB Sozial- und Wirtschaftswissenschaften, Fachgebiet Paedagogik, insb. Berufs- und Arbeitspaedagogik, Pfaffenbergstrasse 95, D-6750 Kaiserslautern.
Fin: Land Rheinland-Pfalz Kultusministerium; Bund-Laender-Kommission fuer Bildungsplanung und Forschungsfoerderung.
vocational education; didactics; industrial training; differentiation; model
enseignement professionnel; didactique; formation industrielle; différenciation; modèle
PROJECT DESCRIPTION
Inhalt: Erprobung eines Modells. Exemplarische Entwicklung differenzierungsdidaktischer Materialien fuer gewerblich-technische Fachrichtungen.
Geographischer Raum: Rheinland-Pfalz.
Vorgehensweise: Empirisch-analytische Begleitforschung (Schuelerbefragung, Lehrerbefragung) ergaenzt um qualitative Methoden (Interviews). Untersuchungsdesign: Evaluationsstudie; qualitative Forschung.
Datengewinnung: Primaererhebung: Feldarbeit von Mitarbeitern des Projektes durchgefuehrt.
Auswertung: Korrelations-, Faktorenanalyse.

Publ: Arnold, R. Innere Differenzierung in Fachklassen der Berufsschule - 10 Hinweise fuer die Entwicklung eines pragmatischen Konzeptes. In: *Zeitschrift fuer Berufs- und Wirtschaftspaedagogik*, Bd. 87, 1991, H. 1, S. 32-44.

11765 Intégration de l'outil informatique dans l'enseignement des disciplines.
FRA 1993
Research Date(s): 1986-
Jean, Françoise.
Sup: Grandbastien, Monique.
Inst: Ministère de l'éducation nationale, Mission académique à la formation des personnels de l'éducation nationale (Nancy), Rectorat, 2 rue Philippe de Gueldres, CO 013, 54035 Nancy Cedex, France.
didactic use of computer; teaching method; teacher education
usage didactique de l'ordinateur; méthode pédagogique; formation des enseignants
PROJECT DESCRIPTION
Objectifs: Il s'agit de cerner le rôle des outils informatiques dans l'enseignement des disciplines. Plusieurs hypothèses sous-tendent cette recherche action: (1) l'utilisation de l'outil informatique permet de rendre l'enseignement plus efficace; (2) l'informatique est un outil pédagogique comme un autre: il doit être intégré dans les séquences pédagogiques; (3) la formation des enseignants est importante mais après une phase d'appropriation technique du matériel, il s'avère nécessaire de construire des stratégies pour l'intégration dans la pratique quotidienne: la diffusion d'expériences auprès des collègues semble être un moyen privilégié. Au préalable une définition de la "séquence pédagogique" est donnée.
Méthodologie: Production en équipes disciplinaires de séquences pédagogiques intégrant l'informatique; mise en oeuvre de ces séquences dans les classes des enseignants "expérimentateurs" associés, avec observations sur le terrain; mise en commun des observations, analyse, réajustements, réexpérimentations; réflexion intergroupe sur la méthodologie, les problèmes rencontrés, l'apport de l'informatique pour développer les capacités transdisciplinaires.
Résultats: La mise en cohérence des spécificités de l'ordinateur, du but visé dans l'activité et de la situation pédagogique mise en place a permis de dresser une typologie des utilisations pédagogiques de l'informatique.

Publ: Collection *Fenêtre active*. CRDP de Nancy.
Jean, Françoise. Mettre l'outil informatique au service des disciplines. In: *EPI*, n° 51, 1988, pp. 117-122.

11766 Interdisziplinaere Kommunikation in der wissenschaftlichen Weiterbildung. (Interdisciplinary communication in further scientific training.)
DEU 1993
Research Date(s): 1992
Ballstaedt, S.; Reinhard, P.; Wagner, G.
Sup: Rentschler, M.; Rottlaender, E.
Inst: Deutsches Institut fuer Fernstudien -DIFF- an der Universitaet, Konrad-Adenauer-Str. 40-44, D-7400 Tuebingen.
further training; distance study; content of education; science education; social sciences; interdisciplinary approach; communication
formation complémentaire; enseignement à distance; contenu de l'éducation; éducation scientifique; sciences sociales; interdisciplinarité; communication
PROJECT DESCRIPTION
Inhalt: Im Rahmen der Weiterbildungsforschung sollen Bedingungen und Probleme der interdisziplinaeren Kommunikation exemplarisch analysiert werden. Die Untersuchungsergebnisse sollen Kriterien liefern fuer die adressatengerechte Erarbeitung eines Weiterbildungsprojekts fuer das Fernstudium zum Thema Boden. Mit diesen Entwicklungsarbeiten sollen die interdisziplinaere Vernetzung von naturwissenschaftlichen und geistes- bzw. sozialwissenschaftlichen Wissensbestaenden konkret vorgestellt sowie interdisziplinaere Arbeits-und Denkweise im Sinne wissenschaftspropaedeutischen Vorgehens dargestellt werden.
Vorgehensweise: Die Forschungsarbeiten befassen sich mit Unterschieden in der mentalen Verarbeitung wissenschaftlicher Texte bei Vertretern der beteiligten Disziplinen (exemplarisch: Biologie und Geschichte) und der Auswirkung dieser Unterschiede auf interdisziplinaere Kommunikation. Die der Untersuchung zugrundeliegenden Texte sind Teile der zu entwickelnden schriftlichen Fernstudieneinheiten. Untersuchungsdesign: Fallstudie; (Quasi-)Experiment.
Datengewinnung: Standardisiertes Interview (Stichprobe: 10; Studenten der Biologie bzw. Geschichte; Auswahlverfahren: bewusst). Experiment (Stichprobe: 10; Studenten der Biologie bzw. Geschichte; Auswahlverfahren: bewusst). Primaererhebung: Feldarbeit von Mitarbeitern des Projektes durchgefuehrt.

11767 "Internationales Lernen" - Veraenderung von Lebenssituation und Orientierung Jugendlicher im Kontext der europaeischen Entwicklung - Jugendforschung als Basis fuer die Verbesserung von Bildungsarbeit. ("International learning" - Changes in the life situation and orientation of young people in the context of European development: youth research as a basis for improving educational work.)
DEU 1993
Research Date(s): 1991-1994
Horn, H.; Leiprecht, R.; Marvakis, A.; Spona, A.; Tsiakalos, G.; Navridis, K.; Papathanasiou, A.; Svob, M.
Sup: Held, J.
Inst: Universitaet Tuebingen, Fak. fuer Sozial- und Verhaltenswissenschaften, Institut fuer Erziehungswissenschaft 01, Arbeitsbereich Paedagogische Psychologie, Muenzgasse 22-30, D-7400 Tuebingen.
adolescent; political education; learning; international education; Europe; nationalism
adolescent; éducation politique; acquisition de connaissances; éducation internationale; Europe; nationalisme
PROJECT DESCRIPTION
Inhalt: Ziel des Projekts ist es, auf der Basis von Jugendforschung (quantitativ und qualitativ) konzeptuelle und praktikable Bildungs- und Lernansaetze zu entwickeln und modellhaft zu erproben. Exemplarische Praxis, Praxisforschung und vergleichende Jugendforschung werden so miteinander kombiniert, dass die Forschungsergebnisse direkt fuer die Bildungsarbeit nutzbar gemacht werden koennen. "Internationales Lernen" richtet sich vor allem gegen nationalistische Orientierungen. Dass diese bei Jugendlichen in zukunftstraechtiger Ausbildung nicht geringer sind, als bei benachteiligten Jugendlichen wurde von uns nachgewiesen.
Geographischer Raum: Mittlerer Neckarraum, Raum Leipzig, Riga, Saloniki, Ioanina, Athen, Amsterdam.
Untersuchter Zeitraum: 1991 bis 1995.
Vorgehensweise: Grundlegend ist die Kritische Psychologie; angestrebt wird eine Verbindung von psychologischer und soziologischer Theorie; wir streben eine Methodenkombination an. Untersuchungsdesign: Querschnittserhebung; qualitative Forschung.
Datengewinnung: Standardisiertes Interview (Stichprobe: 600; jugendliche Arbeitnehmer Deutschland-West; Auswahlverfahren: Quota. Stichprobe: 300; Jugendliche Arbeitnehmer Deutschland-Ost; Auswahlverfahren: Quota. Stichprobe: 200; jugendliche Arbeitnehmer Lettland; Auswahlverfahren: Quota. Stichprobe: 400; jugendliche Arbeitnehmer Griechenland; Auswahlverfahren: Quota. Stichprobe: 400; jugendliche Arbeitnehmer Niederlande; Auswahlverfahren: Quota). Primaererhebung: Feldarbeit von Mitarbeitern des Projektes durchgefuehrt.
Auswertung: Faktorenanalyse und nicht-parametrische Verfahren.
Datenaufbereitung: Verknuepfung verschiedener Datensaetze (record linkage).

Publ: Held; Horn; Leiprecht & Marvakis. "*Du musst so handeln, dass Du Gewinn machst...*" - Empirische Untersuchungen und theoretische Ueberlegungen zu politisch rechten Orientierungen jugendlicher Arbeitnehmer. DISS-Texte Nr. 18, Dortmund 1991.

11768 The interrelationship of verbal and visual narrative: its importance as a teaching tool.
GBR 1993
Research Date(s): 1984-1992
Cox, C.
Sup: Burgess, A.

Inst: London University, Institute of Education, Department of English and Media Studies, 20 Bedford Way, London WC1H OAL, United Kingdom.
teaching method; visual learning; verbal learning; image; narration; writing
méthode pédagogique; apprentissage visuel; apprentissage verbal; image; narration; écriture
PROJECT DESCRIPTION

This project aims to make better use of visual materials to improve writing techniques across the ability range. Following a review of the existing literature, an analysis of a cartoon story drawn by three eighth-year pupils on an expressive arts course was carried out. The use of illustration with narrative and its role in early reading was also analysed. Work has also been carried out with mixed ability multi-ethnic groups.

11769   Investigating in the social subjects.
GBR   1993
Research Date(s): 1991
Munn, P.; Holroyd, C.
Inst: Scottish Council for Research in Education, 15 St John Street, Edinburgh EH8 8JR, United Kingdom.
Fin: Scottish Office Education Department.
teaching method; project; examination; social studies
méthode pédagogique; projet; examen; études sociales
PROJECT DESCRIPTION

An exploration of the demands which 'investigations' at Standard Grade make on staff and pupils. The research aims at the identification of good practice in terms of school administration, teaching and learning.
Publ: Holroyd, C. *Investigating in the social subjects*. SCRE Research Report Series, No 34. Edinburgh: Scottish Council for Research in Education, 1992.
Holroyd, C. *Investigating in the social subjects*. SCRE Spotlights Series, No 35. Edinburgh: Scottish Council for Research in Education, 1992.

11770   An investigation into the social and educational impact of project work in GCSE.
GBR   1993
Research Date(s): 1990-1991
Reid, I.; Wiegand, P.
Inst: Loughborough University of Technology, Department of Education, Loughborough LE11 3TU, Leeds University, School of Education, Leeds LS2 9JT, United Kingdom.
project method; teaching method; individual work
pédagogie du projet; méthode pédagogique; travail individuel
PROJECT DESCRIPTION

This is an investigation into project work in General Certificate of Secondary Education (GCSE) subjects. The first stage involves the analysis of questionnaires completed by some 400 pupils who completed GCSEs in the summer of 1990. The second stage involves parents and teachers. The thrust of the investigation is to review the impact of project work on pupils and the extent to which factors of social background and gender affect attitudes and performance. It will also look at the overall demands and level of co-ordination of such coursework by level of ability and subject choice.

11771   Jugend und Berufsausbildung in Deutschland. (Young people and vocational training in Germany.)
DEU   1993
Research Date(s): 1991-1997
Beer, D.; Schweikert, K.; Granato, M.; Mabedank, G.; Meissner, V.
Inst: Bundesinstitut fuer Berufsbildung, Fehrbelliner Platz 3, D-1000 Berlin 31.
vocational training; youth; German DR; occupational choice; youth attitude; apprentice; aspiration
formation professionnelle; jeunesse; Allemagne RDA; choix d'une profession; attitude de la jeunesse; apprenti; aspiration
PROJECT DESCRIPTION

Inhalt: Ueber die Situation von Auszubildenden in der frueheren Bundesrepublik sind in den letzten Jahren, durch das Bundesinstitut u.a. mit der Studie "Jugend, Ausbildung und Beruf", eine Reihe von Untersuchungen durchgefuehrt worden. Diese Forschungstradition des BIBB hat dazu gefuehrt, dass umfangreiche Erkenntnisse zu den Einstellungen der Jugendlichen, zum Stellenwert von Berufsausbildung und Arbeit, zu ihrer Zukunftssicht gewonnen wurden. In bezug auf die neuen Bundeslaender liegen zu dieser Thematik keinerlei Erkenntnisse vor. Durch die jahrzehntelange Vorgabe von Zielen sozialistischer Erziehung mit einem wenig differenzierten gesellschaftlichen Normengefuege stellt sich die Frage, welche Einstellungen die Jugendlichen in der ehemaligen DDR insbesondere zu Berufsausbildung, Arbeit und Zukunft im Laufe ihrer Sozialisation entwickelt haben und welche Auswirkungen die derzeitige gesellschaftliche und wirtschaftliche Umwaelzung auf ihre beruflichen und allgemeinen Lebensziele hat. Auf dieser Basis laesst sich dann eine Vergleichbarkeit mit Jugendlichen aus den alten Bundeslaendern herstellen.

Das Projekt zielt auf die Analyse des Zusammenhangs zwischen Berufswahl, Zugang zur Berufsausbildung, die Berufsausbildung und ihre strukturellen Gegebenheiten und der Faehigkeit der Jugendlichen zur Entwicklung von Zukunftsperspektiven auf der Grundlage eines zunehmend differenzierten Normengefueges in einer sich drastisch veraendernden Lebenswelt. Die Jugendlichen in den neuen Bundeslaendern stehen nunmehr einem System neuer Berufe und Ausbildungsgaenge gegenueber, in die sie nicht unmittelbar und staatlich einmuenden koennen. Sie haben ihre Berufswahl nun selbstaendig und eigenverantwortlich zu treffen und individuelle Strategien zu entwickeln, um einen Ausbildungsplatz zu finden. Dies wird erschwert dadurch, dass das Angebot an betrieblichen Ausbildungsplaetzen noch nicht ausreicht, die Nachfrage zu decken. Die in diesem geplanten Projekt erzielten Ergebnisse zur Situation der Jugendlichen in den neuen Bundeslaendern sind zu vergleichen mit einer aktualisierten Situationsanalyse von Auszubildenden der alten Bundeslaender. Damit ist zugleich die Moeglichkeit gegeben, im 10-Jahresvergleich Veraenderungen auch in den alten Bundeslaendern nachzuvollziehen.

Ziel des Forschungsprojekts sind Sammlung und Interpretation fundierter und repraesentativer Befunde in ganz Deutschland zu: (a) Stellenwert von Beruf, Berufsausbildung und Arbeit fuer die Lebensplanung der Jugendlichen; (b) Berufswahl und Berufszugang; (c) Erfahrungen mit Wirkungen der Berufsausbildung auf die Jugendlichen; (d) Lebenslage und Perspektiven; (e) Wechselwirkungen von beruflicher Qualifizierung bzw. Nichtqualifizierung mit der Perspektiventwicklung von Jugendlichen. Zentrale Forschungshypothese ist, dass wirtschaftlicher und gesellschaftlicher Wandel die Integration in das Ausbildungssystem bestimmen. Es wird dabei davon ausgegangen, dass berufliche Qualifizierung die Lebenschancen der Jugendlichen entscheidend verbessert. Durch den Vergleich der Situation von Auszubildenden und Unversorgten in den neuen Bundeslaendern soll der Stellenwert beruflicher Qualifizierung fuer die Lebenslage (Lebensplanung) von Jugendlichen analysiert werden.

11772   Kenmerken van krachtige leeromgevingen. (Features of powerful learning environments.)
NLD   1994
Research Date(s): 1993-1994
Kanselaar, G.
Inst: Interdisciplinair Sociaal-wetenschappelijk Onderzoeksinstituut, Afdeling Onderwijs (ISOR) (Interdisciplinary Research Institute for the Social Sciences, Department of Educational Research), P.O. Box 80140, 3508 TC Utrecht, Netherlands.
Rijksuniversiteit Utrecht (State University of Utrecht), P.O. Box 80125, 3508 TC Utrecht, Netherlands
Fin: SVO het Instituut voor Onderzoek van het Onderwijs.
didactic use of computer; educational technology; science education; secondary education; teacher role; teaching method
usage didactique de l'ordinateur; technologie de l'éducation; éducation scientifique; enseignement secondaire; rôle de l'enseignant; méthode pédagogique
PROJECT DESCRIPTION

Background: Recent developments in the field of technology as well as in instructional and learning psychology have made it possible to design challenging and powerful learning environments in which the teacher and the pupils go through an exploratory learning process together. This requires a great deal on the part of the teacher. The more open environments that are currently available give teachers varying degrees of freedom, as a result of which individual teachers' scope for decision making is increasing.

Aim: To obtain an insight into the possibilities and the limitations of teachers to function as designers of challenging and powerful learning environments.

Methods: Bibliographic research, case study, participant observation, audiovisual observation, structured interview, logs, tests.

Design: A literature survey will be conducted on the features of powerful learning environments and an analysis will be made of relevant computer environments. Four case studies will be conducted, with three parallel replications per study. Per "case", three science teachers will be involved for each type of secondary education. The teachers will twice be asked to design a powerful, computer-assisted learning environment for a selected topic. The first time they will not be given specific training; the second time they will receive instruction and training in the theoretical principles underlying powerful learning environments.

11773   Konstatierende Untersuchung und Ausbildungsexperiment zur Verarbeitung von Stoerstellen in komplizierten Texten in Klasse 3 und 5. (Confirmatory study and teaching experiment for overcoming difficulties in complex texts in primary years 3 and 5.)
DEU   1993
Research Date(s): 1989-1992
Knoll, S.
Sup: Nestler, K.
Inst: Paedagogische Hochschule Halle-Koethen, Abt. Koethen, FB Primarschullehrerausbildung, Fachgebiet Psychologie, Lohmannstrasse 23, O-4370 Koethen.
teaching method; pupil; reading; comprehension; cognitive ability; primary education; performance; reading difficulty
méthode pédagogique; élève; lecture; compréhension; aptitude cognitive; enseignement primaire; performance; difficulté de lecture

PROJECT DESCRIPTION

Inhalt: Konstatierende Untersuchungen zum Verstehen von stoerstellenbehafteten Texten (Variable: Kompliziertheitsgrad von Texten, struktureller Aufbau, Makro-, Mikrostruktur, Stoerstellen auf Wort- und Satzebene) in Abhaengigkeit von Personenvariablen. Vergleich zweier Altersstufen bezueglich der Reproduktionsleistungen und der Verstehenstiefe. Hypothese: Befaehigung der Schueler zu verbessertem Textverstehen durch Training metakognitiver Komponenten ist mit Erlangung der Lesefaehigkeit moeglich und notwendig. Ausbildungsexperiment mit Schuelern der Klasse 3 unter dem Aspekt verschiedener meth. Vorgehensweisen bei der Erkennung und Aufloesung von Stoerstellen im Text. Beruecksichtigung der Lernvoraussetzungen, Vorwissen und Lesefaehigkeit als Einflussgroessen beim Textverstehen.

Geographischer Raum: Sachsen-Anhalt.

Vorgehensweise: Verstehenstheoretische bzw. kognitionspsychologische Ansaetze (Engelkamp, Schnotz, Mandl, Anderson, Groeben, Baumann, Nestler), Modell der Lehrstrategie des Aufsteigens vom Abstrakten zum Konkreten (Dawydow, Lompscher) und Interiorisationstheorie (Galperin). Untersuchungsdesign: (Quasi-)Experiment.

Datengewinnung: Gruppenbefragung (Stichprobe: 100; Schueler Klasse 3; Auswahlverfahren: willkuerlich. Stichprobe: 100, Schueler der Klasse 5; Auswahlverfahren: willkuerlich). Experiment (dito. Stichprobe: 60; Schueler Klasse 3; Auswahlverfahren: bewusst). Primaererhebung: Feldarbeit von Mitarbeitern des Projektes durchgefuehrt.

Auswertung: Varianzanalyse; Korrelations- und Regressionsstatistik. Datenaufbereitung: Pruefstatistik.

11774 Lehrlingsausbildung in Nigeria. (Apprenticeship training in Nigeria.)
DEU 1993
Research Date(s): 1992-1993
Adam, S.
Sup: Boehm, U.
Inst: Universitaet Bremen, FB 09 Human- und Sozialwissenschaften, InterdisziplinaeresAufbaustudium Dritte Welt, Postfach 330440, D-2800 Bremen 33.
Fin: Deutsche Forschungsgemeinschaft.
vocational training; small and medium entreprise; occupational qualification; developing country; apprenticeship; Nigeria
formation professionnelle; petite ou moyenne entreprise; qualification professionnelle; pays en développement; apprentissage professionnel; Nigeria
PROJECT DESCRIPTION

Inhalt: Welche Kompetenzen werden in Kleinbetrieben benoetigt? Wie werden diese Kompetenzen erworben? Welchen quantitativen und qualitativen Einfluss hat die staatliche Foerderung? Ist das staatliche Foerderprogramm ein tragfaehiger Ansatz zur Entwicklung eines Dualen Systems?

Geographischer Raum: Ibadan/Nigeria.

Vorgehensweise: Interkulturelle Berufsbildungsforschung.

Datengewinnung: Standardisiertes Interview (Stichprobe: 240; Kleinbetriebe). Primaererhebung: Feldarbeit von Mitarbeitern des Projektes durchgefuehrt.

Auswertung: Multiple Regression.

11775 Lernambulanz Steyr. (The Steyr remedial teaching centre.)
AUT 1993
Research Date(s): 1992-
Leeb, Hans; Kiesenhofer, Emma; Fischer, Karl; Seyfried, Peter; Rothschedl, Erich.
Inst: Abteilung fuer Schulpsychologie und Bildungsberatung, Stifterstrasse 29, A-4020 Linz.
Landesschulrat fuer Oberoesterreich, Stifterstrasse 29, A-4020 Linz
remedial teaching; psychological service; learning difficulty
soutien pédagogique; service psychologique; difficulté de l'apprentissage
PROJECT DESCRIPTION

Aufbau einer Foerderambulanz; Koordination saemtlicher Foerdereinrichtungen: Sprachbetreuung, Therapeutische Intervention, Logopaedie, Legasthenie, Beratung usw. Es wird auch eine Entwicklung neuer Foerdermethoden durchgefuehrt.

Es werden Interviews, Tests, schriftliche Befragungen und teilnehmende Beobachtung verwendet.

Eine Beschreibung des Gesamtprojekts liegt vor.

11776 Lernprogramm zur Umweltbildung an kaufmaennischen Schulen (LUKAS). (Learning programme for environmental education at commercial colleges (LUKAS).)
DEU 1993
Research Date(s): 1991-1994
Flottmann, H.; Brettschneider, V.
Sup: Siggemeier, M.; Kaiser, F.
Inst: Universitaet-Gesamthochschule Paderborn, FB 05 Wirtschaftswissenschaften, Fach Wirtschaftswissenschaften und Didaktik der Wirtschaftslehre, Warburger Str. 100, D-4790 Paderborn.
vocational school; commercial training; environment; didactics; learning; environmental study
école professionnelle; formation commerciale; environnement; didactique; acquisition de connaissances; étude du milieu
PROJECT DESCRIPTION

Inhalt: Wie ist die Ausgangssituation hinsichtlich der Vermittlung von Fragen des Umweltschutzes der beruflichen Bildung? Welche fachwissenschaftlichen und paedagogisch-didaktischen Ansaetze zum Umweltschutz gibt es? Welche paedagogisch-didaktischen Massnahmen sind geeignet, die Jugendlichen zu umweltbewusstem Verhalten und Handeln anzuleiten? Welche schulorganisatorischen Rahmenbedingungen sind zu beachten? Welche Unterrichtsfaecher sind vorrangig geeignet, die Aufgabe der Umwelterziehung zu uebernehmen? Welche Lernhilfen und Unterrichtsmaterialien gibt es und welche sind neu zu entwickeln und zu erproben? Wie und in welchem Umfang sind die Ergebnisse uebertragbar? In welchem Umfang ergeben sich fuer die Lehrplaene inhaltliche Veraenderungen?

Geographischer Raum: RP Detmold.

Untersuchter Zeitraum: 1991-1994.

Vorgehensweise: Handlungsforschung: Qualitative Unterrichtsforschung, die neben der Beobachtung, Erhebung, Entwicklung und Bewertung von Konzepten zur Umweltbildung an kaufmaennischen Schulen die Zusammenarbeit mit den Lehrern der Schulen anstrebt, an denen die entwickelten Konzeptionen erprobt und umgesetzt werden. Untersuchungsdesign: Methodenforschung; Evaluationsstudie; qualitative Forschung; (Quasi-)Experiment.

Datengewinnung: Gruppendiskussion, teilnehmende Beobachtung, Aktenanalyse (Schueler der hoeheren Berufsfachschule, Ausbildung zum Einzelhandelskaufmann/zur Einzelhandelskauffrau). Primaererhebung: Feldarbeit von Mitarbeitern des Projektes durchgefuehrt.

Auswertung: Qualitative Analyse. Datenaufbereitung: Verknuepfung verschiedener Datensaetze (record linkage).

Publ: Brettschneider, V. & Kaiser, F.J. Projekt: Verbraucher und Umweltfragen als zukunftsorientierter Unternehmenspolitik. In: *Arbeiten und Lernen, Wirtschaft*, H. 2, 1991.
Kaiser, F.J. & Brettschneider, V. Die Bewaeltigung komplexer Gestaltungsaufgaben in schulischen Modellunternehmen - dargestellt am Beispiel des Projektes: Die Einrichtung einer "Abteilung fuer Verbraucher- und Umweltfragen". In: Achtenhagen, F. (Hrsg.): *Kongressband zum Internationalen Symposium: Mehrdimensionale Lehr-Lern-Arrangements - Lernen, Denken, Handeln in komplexen beruflichen Situationen.* Goettingen 1991.
Kaiser, F.J.; Brettschneider, V. & Preuss, V. Die Einrichtung einer Abteilung fuer Verbraucher- und Umweltfragen in schulischen Modellunternehmen (Lernbuero) - Ein Beitrag zur Verbraucher- und Umwelterziehung im Fach Buerowirtschaft. In: *Forum Buerowirtschaft*, H. 4, 1991.
Kaiser, F.J.; Brettschneider, V. & Preuss, V. Die Bewaeltigung mehrdimensionaler Aufgaben im komplexen System schulischer Modellunternehmen - Ein Beitrag zur Verbraucher- und Umwelterziehung in berufsbildenden Schulen. In: *Wirtschaft und Gesellschaft im Beruf*, H. 6, 1991.

11777 Making efficient use of microcomputers in teaching mathematics to gifted children in the Jordanian primary schools.
GBR 1993
Research Date(s): 1989-1993
Mahmoud, T.
Sup: Galloway, D.
Inst: Durham University, School of Education, Leazes Road, Durham DH1 1TA, United Kingdom.
didactic use of computer; Jordan; mathematics; gifted; individualized teaching
usage didactique de l'ordinateur; Jordanie; mathématiques; doué; enseignement individualisé
PROJECT DESCRIPTION

The study offers a critical examination of concepts of giftedness, in the context of mathematics. It presents a framework for the development of computer-based programmes of individualized education for the mathematically gifted. It tests the framework by pilot studies in a sample of schools in Jordan.

11778 Management in the primary school class.
GBR 1993
Research Date(s): 1990-1992
Wragg, C.
Sup: Wragg, E.; Ackland, J.
Inst: Exeter University, School of Education, St Luke's, Heavitree Road, Exeter EX1 2LU, United Kingdom.
class management; primary education; teaching
conduite de la classe; enseignement primaire; enseignement
PROJECT DESCRIPTION

This research into classroom management is based upon a study of over 200 lessons given by teachers in the South West of England, Manchester and London. It includes over 400 interviews with pupils and an analysis of over 1,000 teacher questions and responses.

11779 Marketing PICKUP in Europe.
GBR 1993
Research Date(s): 1990-1991
Stainsby, R.; Snook, C.
Sup: Neville, C.
Inst: Lowestoft College, St Peter's Street, Lowestoft, Suffolk NR32 2NB, United Kingdom.
Fin: Further Education Unit.
vocational training; marketing; training course; technical education; industrial training
formation professionnelle; mercatique; cours de formation; enseignement technique; formation industrielle
PROJECT DESCRIPTION

Lowestoft College has developed considerable expertise in fibre optics over a period of four years. With Professional, Industrial and Commercial Updating (PICKUP) backing, a conference has been held and a certificated short course programme has been developed which has been supported by local and national firms dealing in fibre optics. The College perceives that there is a market available on the European mainland for its courses.

The aims of the project are to identify fibre optic training and certification currently available in West Germany and the Netherlands; to examine the level of expertise in English language of the target population; to carry out a survey of the pricing of similar short course provision in these countries; to look at course delivery in site, in conjunction with equipment suppliers and training establishments; and to prepare a model for further education colleges for marketing PICKUP courses in Europe.

Methods used to establish contacts and links in West Germany and the Netherlands will include correspondence, telephone and visits. The outcomes of the project will be to establish a network of firms in West Germany and the Netherlands for the marketing of the short course programme; to provide a coordinated set of information on equivalence of providers and certification, awareness and response to 1993, a year plan of trade fairs and exhibitions and a dossier of support available to UK colleges and firms wishing to benefit from the College's experience. A report will provide the model for marketing PICKUP courses in Europe.

11780 Material for a literature and politics course.
GBR 1993
Research Date(s): 1990-1991
Taylor, K.
Inst: Coventry University, Department of Languages, Politics and History, Priory Street, Coventry CV1 5FB, United Kingdom.
teaching aid; literature; political education; undergraduate study
moyen d'enseignement; littérature; éducation politique; supérieur premier cycle
PROJECT DESCRIPTION

This research will involve collecting course materials for a new third year undergraduate course on literature and politics, with particular reference to Britain and Europe in the contemporary period, and also to changing ideas and values in view of the rapid changes in East/West Europe.

11781 The MEDA project (Methodologie d'Evaluation des Didacticiels pour les Adultes).
GBR 1993
Research Date(s): 1987-1991
Saunders, M.; Machell, J.; Lewis, R.
Inst: Lancaster University, Department of Educational Research, Centre for the Study of Education and Training, Cartmel College, Bailrigg, Lancaster LA1 4YW, United Kingdom.
Fin: European Community EUROTECNET Programme.
teaching aid; didactic use of computer; educational software; evaluation
moyen d'enseignement; usage didactique de l'ordinateur; didacticiel; évaluation
PROJECT DESCRIPTION

MEDA is a collaborative European Community funded project, involving participants from France, Belgium, Germany, Italy and the United Kingdom which began in 1987. Stage 1 of the project involved surveys of users of training courseware evaluation throughout Europe. Stage 2 of MEDA had as its objective the development of a generic evaluation tool for computer-based training courseware. The team have now developed both a text-based and software version of the MEDA tool. Stage 3 involved disseminating the MEDA tool throughout Europe.

11782 Medienerziehung im Kindergarten: Paedagogische Grundlagen und praktische Handreichungen. (Media education in nurseries: pedagogic principles and practical activities.)
DEU 1993
Research Date(s): 1990-1993
Feil, C.; Lehnig, U.
Inst: Deutsches Jugendinstitut e.V., Freibadstrasse 30, D-8000 Muenchen 90.
Fin: Institution; Bundesministerium fuer Bildung und Wissenschaft.
nursery school; media education; pre-school child; teacher education; further training; didactics
école maternelle; éducation aux médias; enfant d'âge préscolaire; formation des enseignants; formation complémentaire; didactique
PROJECT DESCRIPTION

Inhalt: Im Projekt "Medienerziehung im Kindergarten: Paedagogische Grundlagen und praktische Handreichungen" soll eine informative, systematische und orientierende Zusammenschau von Forschungsergebnissen, Konzepten und praktischen Vorschlaegen zur Medienerziehung von drei- bis sechsjaehrigen Kindern erarbeitet werden. Dabei soll ein Handbuch fuer die Medienerziehung im Kindergarten erstellt werden, das sowohl fuer die praktische Arbeit mit Kindern als auch fuer die Aus- und Fortbildung von Erzieherinnen einsetzbar ist. Zielvorstellung des Projektes ist es, Grundlagen zu schaffen fuer: ganzheitliche Interpretationshilfen und Handlungsperspektiven bei medienbezogenen Schwierigkeiten im Kindergarten; die Versachlichung des Verhaeltnisses zwischen Erzieherinnen und Eltern, vor allem im Hinblick auf den haeuslichen Medienkonsum; das Verstehen des medienbezogenen Verhaltens von Kindern; medienpaedagogische Aktivitaeten, d.h. fuer die Erziehung zu einer aktiven, durch produktiven Umgang gekennzeichneten Nutzung von Medien durch Kinder; die Durchfuehrung medienbezogener Projekte oder fuer den themenbezogenen Medieneinsatz.

Vorgehensweise: Aufbauend auf die Ergebnisse des Projektes "Medienerfahrungen von Kindern" und in Zusammenarbeit mit Medienexperten aus verschiedenen Wissenschaftsdisziplinen und der paedagogischen Fachbasis sollen Leitlinien fuer eine situationsorientierte medienpaedagogische Praxis konkretisiert und Praxismaterialien evaluiert werden.

Publ: Barthelmes, Juergen; Feil, Christine & Furtner-Kallmuenzer, Maria. *Medienerfahrungen von Kindern im Kindergarten. Spiele - Gespraeche - Soziale Beziehungen.* Muenchen, 1991.

11783 Méthodologie des histoires de vie et formation de formateurs.
FRA 1993
Research Date(s): 1988-1990
Pineau, Gaston.
Inst: Université de Tours, UFR Arts et sciences humaines, Laboratoire des sciences de l'éducation et de la formation, 3 rue des Tanneurs, bureau 405, 37041 Tours Cedex, France.
biography; training of trainers; teaching method; methodology
biographie; formation des formateurs; méthode pédagogique; méthodologie
PROJECT DESCRIPTION

Objectifs: Il s'agit d'identifier les méthodologies pratiques émergentes et de développer les capacités de théorisation des formateurs-acteurs.

Méthodologie: Recherche-action-formation à partir de sept pratiques d'utilisation des histoires de vie en formation de formateurs dans le grand Ouest français.

Résultats: Elaboration d'une carte méthodologique présentant les opérations majeures.

Publ: Pineau, Gaston. Germination des histoires de vie en formation de formateurs. In: *Education-formation.* (Union de Liège), n° 217-218, 1990, pp. 69-78.
Pineau, Gaston & Jobert, Guy (Eds). *Les histoires de vie,* Actes du Colloque les histoires de vie en formation (5-7 juin 1986). Paris: L'Harmattan, tome 1 *Utilisation pour la formation,* 1989, 239p.; tome 2 *Approches multidisciplinaires,* 1989, 285p.

11784 Metodologie per la gestione e la produzione di sistemi didattici adattivi. (Methods for the management and development of adaptive education systems.)
ITA 1994
Research Date(s): 1992-
Midoro, Vittorio; Besio, Serenella; Doretti, Lorenzo; Frau, Elena.
Sup: Trentin, Guglielmo.
Inst: Istituto per le Tecnologie Didattiche - ITD (Institute for Educational Technology), Via all'Opera Pia 11, 16145 Genova, Italy.
Consiglio Nazionale delle Ricerche - CNR (National Research Council), Piazzale Aldo Moro 7, 00185 Roma, Italy
teaching method; didactic use of computer; teaching aid; educational software; interface; test construction; evaluation; computer-assisted examination
méthode pédagogique; usage didactique de l'ordinateur; moyen d'enseignement; didacticiel; interface; construction de tests; évaluation; examen assisté par ordinateur
PROJECT DESCRIPTION

The project builds on the studies conducted by the Institute for Educational Technology on the use of computers in the management of learning evaluation tests. These studies were conducted in order to define a particular test development method on which was then based the DELFI system, a software system able to assist authors of assessment tests in the development phases.

The study aims to generalize the methods used by DELFI, extending them to the problem of the management and development of adaptive education systems, not only oriented towards the assessment of knowledge but also towards learning, exercises, and simulation.

The study will be based on the use of hypertext techniques, both in use and the development of multimedia educational material. To this end, on the one hand, theoretical models will be constructed, defining how to guide and assist the student in the use of educational material. On the other hand, guidelines for the production of adaptive education systems will be sketched, based on the models and methods studied.

The study will develop along the following lines: (1) study of a model of an adaptive education system that is able to carry out diverse educational strategies in an individualized manner; (2) study of the management of individual strategies; (3) definition of the developmental phases of adaptive education systems, based on the models and methods studied; (4) use of the DBLM (Database of Learning Materials) in the production and management of multimedia learning materials used by the adaptive learning system.

11785 Microcomputer use in the primary school.
GBR 1993
Research Date(s): 1988-1993
Jackson, A.
Inst: Hertfordshire University, School of Humanities and Education, Wall Hall Campus, Aldenham, Watford WD2 8AT, United Kingdom.
didactic use of computer; microcomputer
usage didactique de l'ordinateur; micro-ordinateur
PROJECT DESCRIPTION
This is an extension of research commenced at postgraduate level. It investigates some of the psychological variables which influence children's performance during microcomputer-based problem solution when working alone or in groups. It also considers the current uses of microcomputers in primary education, and factors which affect use. Previous surveys have revealed that microcomputers are primarily used for group rather than individualised instruction in the primary school. This research addresses the question of why, and whether groups of children show superior performance compared to children working alone on a series of mathematical problems.

All experiments have been, and will be conducted in primary schools working with 10- to 11-year old children. Performance is examined in terms of (1) time to problem solution; (2) number of moves to solution; (3) types of moves made. Over 300 children have been tested in 5 experiments so far.

Initial results indicate that groups of 3 children do show superior on-task decision making to individuals. There was an indication that group interaction could be more beneficial for performance over and above the provision of a software-based 'help-facility'.

Further investigations will include (1) differences in decision-making strategy between groups and individuals, and (2) the conditions under which intragroup discussion is beneficial to performance.

Publ: Jackson, A.; Fletcher, B.(C) & Messer, D.J. Effects of experience on microcomputer use in primary schools: results of a second survey. In: *Journal of Computer Assisted Learning*, Vol 4, No 4, pp. 214-226, December 1988.
Jackson, A. Are three heads better than one? An investigation of children solving microcomputer based problems. Paper presented to the XXIV International Congress of Psychology, Sydney, Australia, August 1988.
Jackson, A.; Fletcher, B.(C) & Messer, D.J. When talking doesn't help: an investigation of microcomputer based group problem solving. Invited paper for Special Issue of *International Journal of Educational Research*. A full list of publications is available from the researcher.

11786 Modulair beroepsonderwijs: verschijningsvormen en effecten. (Modular vocational courses: types and effects.)
NLD 1994
Research Date(s): 1992
Meesterberends-Harms, G.J.
Sup: Creemers, B.P.M.; Koster, K.B.
Inst: RION Instituut voor Onderwijsonderzoek (RION Institute for Educational Research), P.O. Box 1286, 9701 BG Groningen, Netherlands.
Rijksuniversiteit Groningen (State University of Groningen), P.O. Box 72, 9700 AB Groningen, Netherlands
Fin: SVO het Instituut voor Onderzoek van het Onderwijs.
modular training; vocational education; alternating training; apprenticeship; motivation for studies; achievement
formation modulaire; enseignement professionnel; formation alternée; apprentissage professionnel; motivation pour les études; rendement
PROJECT DESCRIPTION
Background and aim: The research builds on two previous studies of modular-type instruction: one on different types of modular courses in vocational secondary education and apprenticeship training and one on the relationships between a modular course organization and pupil motivation, progress and dropout rates. The aim is to integrate the results of both studies in the form of a doctoral dissertation.

Design: A description will be made of the various definitions of modularity in the literature. Short-term and long-term expectations with regard to modular training and its effects on pupils will be discussed. On the basis of the findings of the two previous studies, the various types of modular courses and outcomes at pupil level (motivation, progress) will be presented. To gauge pupils' perceptions of modular-type instruction, secondary analyses will be performed on data obtained in one of the two earlier projects.

11787 Moeglichkeiten und Grenzen der Akademisierung der Lehrerbildung im Pflegebereich in Abhaengigkeit von der Entwicklung einer Pflegewissenschaft. (Possibilities and limitations of academicizing teacher training in the nursing sector in relation to the development of nursing as a science.)
DEU 1993
Research Date(s): 1990-1992
Witte, A.
Inst: Akademie fuer Altenpflegelehrer und Krankenpflegelehrer, Schussengasse 14, D-7000 Stuttgart 50.
teacher education; university studies; academic degree; medical service; branch of study; care; medical treatment
formation des enseignants; études universitaires; grade universitaire; service médical; filière d'études; soin; traitement médical
PROJECT DESCRIPTION
Inhalt: Es wird untersucht, inwieweit Pflegewissenschaft in der BRD bereits an wissenschaftlichen Hochschulen betrieben wird, welche laufenden oder geplanten Projekte zur Einrichtung von Studiengaengen auf welchem Wissenschaftsstand im internationalen Vergleich aufbauen und wie sie fachkompetent personell ausgestattet sind. Des weiteren wird untersucht, welche Fachkompetenzen die Absolventen der Studiengaenge erreichen und wie diese mit den wachsenden Anforderungen des Berufsfeldes korrespondieren.

Vorgehensweise: Vergleichende Analyse.

Publ: Witte, A. "Dem Wuenschbaren steht das Machbare entgegen...". Probleme der Akademisierung der Pflege (6 Thesen). In: Rabe-Kleberg, U.; Krueger, H.; Karsten, M.E. & Bals, T. (Hrsg.). *Dienstleistungsberufe in Krankenpflege, Altenpflege und Kindererziehung. Pro Person. Ausbildung - Taetigkeitsfelder - Professionalisierung. Ergebnisse und Materialien.* Bielefeld: KT-Verl. 1991.
Witte, A. Fachhochschule fuer Pflegeberufe? Ein Versuch zur Nieveaubestimmung. In: *Die Schwester/ Der Pfleger*, Jg. 29, 1990, H. 3.
Witte, A. Der Bedarf an Altenpflegelehrern wird um 50 Prozent steigen. Perspektiven zur Weiterbildung in der Altenpflege. In: *Altenpflege*, Jg. 15, 1990, H. 2, S. 106-111.
Witte, A. Wissenschaftler fuer die Wissenschaft, aber fuer den Nachwuchs "Lehrer erster Klasse". In: Bischoff-Wanner, C. (Hrsg.). *Die Zukunft hat begonnen. Neue Wege in der Lehrerausbildung fuer Pflegeberufe.* Melsungen: Bibliomed Verl. 1992.

11788 Motivation and collaboration in computer-assisted learning of chemistry.
GBR 1993
Research Date(s): 1991-1994
Issroff, K.
Sup: Scanlon, E.; Jones, A.
Inst: Open University, Institute of Educational Technology, Walton Hall, Milton Keynes MK7 6AA, United Kingdom.
Fin: Economic and Social Research Council.
didactic use of computer; learning process; group learning; motivation; chemistry
usage didactique de l'ordinateur; apprentissage; pédagogie de groupe; motivation; chimie
PROJECT DESCRIPTION
This research aims to investigate the motivation of secondary school students learning from computers in different learning situations. Motivation appears to change when students use computers for learning, especially when working collaboratively. In order to investigate the nature of this different motivation, quantitative and qualitative motivational indices can be measured. Quantitative indices refer to the students' behaviours during learning, while qualitative indices refer to their feelings and attitudes towards the learning. Studies of cooperative learning at the computer have focused predominantly on the cognitive aspects of the interaction and results have not been conclusive. By investigating the psychological environment which surrounds the computer, it may be possible to explain some aspects of the cooperative learning process.

The main study involves 15 individuals and 30 pairs learning chemistry from a computer. There is pre- and post-testing of both cognitive and motivational factors and the sessions are video-taped for quantitative motivational indices. It is hoped that the results of this research will provide guidelines for designers of educational software, and educators in setting up effective computer-assisted learning situations and help us to understand the processes which occur when students work at the computer in different learning situations.

Publ: Issroff, K. *Cooperative computer-assisted learning.* CITE Report No 173. Milton Keynes: Open University, Institute of Educational Technology, 1992.

Issroff, K. *Motivation and computer-assisted learning.* CITE Report No 174. Milton Keynes: Open University, Institute of Educational Technology, 1992.

11789 Multi-media course in Italian language.
GBR 1993
Research Date(s): 1986-
Jones, D.; Orsini-Jones, M.
Inst: Coventry University, School of International Studies and Law, Priory Street, Coventry CV1 5FB, United Kingdom.
multimedia method; training course; Italian language; teaching aid
moyen multimédia; cours de formation; langue italienne; moyen d'enseignement
PROJECT DESCRIPTION
  The aim is to prepare a course for the teaching of Italian language which would be suitable for use in this institution. It will need to make use of audio and video recording facilities and computer programs as well as written material, and to be usable with limited input from teaching staff. Work is currently progressing on a beginners course, but it is hoped ultimately to produce an integrated course for three years.

11790 Organisation beruflicher Weiterbildung fuer CIM und flexible Arbeitssysteme. (Organization of further vocational training for CIM and flexible work systems.)
DEU 1993
Research Date(s): 1992-1994
Eichener, V.; Huppertz, M.; Bauerdick, J.
Sup: Heinze, R.
Inst: Universitaet Bochum, Fak. fuer Sozialwissenschaft, Sektion Soziologie, LS Soziologie 02, Postfach 102148, D-4630 Bochum 1.
Fin: Institution; Deutsche Forschungsgemeinschaft.
vocational training; further training; control technology; new technologies; study method; enterprise
formation professionnelle; formation complémentaire; technologie de contrôle; nouvelles technologies; méthode de travail; entreprise
PROJECT DESCRIPTION
  Inhalt: Das Projekt untersucht, welche Bedarfe die Flexibilisierung der Produktion, der Einsatz moderner Technologien sowie die Einfuehrung flexibler teilautonomer Arbeitssysteme im Fertigungsbereich von kleinen und mittelgrossen Betrieben des Maschinen- und Anlagenbaus an berufliche Weiterbildung stellen. Aufgrund dieser Bedarfsanalyse wird die Interaktion von Betrieben, Weiterbildungsanbietern und intermediaeren Akteuren analysiert. Auf der betrieblichen Ebene stehen die Defizite bzw. Probleme, die dieser Interaktion erwachsen, im Vordergrund. Auf der Ebene der Weiterbildungsanbieter wird untersucht, wie diese veraenderte Weiterbildungsbedarfe ermitteln, von welchen Determinanten die Weiterbildungsangebote bestimmt werden, welche Entwicklungstendenzen die Weiterbildungsangebote aufweisen und wie diese Angebote von den Betrieben genutzt und bewertet werden. Nach einer Defizitanalyse sollen Steuerungsinstrumente zur Gewaehrleistung eines Weiterbildungsangebots erarbeitet werden, das bedarfsgerecht und antizipativ ist, weil hoehere Qualifikationspotentiale bessere Voraussetzungen fuer technische und arbeitsorganisatorische Innovationen schaffen.
  Vorgehensweise: Das Projekt basiert auf Ansaetzen der Industrie-, Arbeits-, Organisations- und Verbaendesoziologie. Handlungstheoretische Ansaetze werden durch institutionstheoretische Ansaetze und den Ansatz figurationaler Verflechtung ergaenzt, wobei Interdependenzbeziehungen innerhalb der Organisationen und zwischen Akteuren verschiedener Organisationen analysiert werden. Die zu untersuchenden Organisationen und ihre Akteure kommen im Bereich der beruflichen Weiterbildung aufgrund ihrer jeweiligen Eigeninteressen und Restriktionen nicht zu einer optimalen Abstimmung, so dass externe Steuerungsleistungen durch intermediaere Akteure als Ausweg gesehen werden. Untersuchungsdesign: Fallstudie; Evaluationsstudie.
  Datengewinnung: Nicht-standardisiertes Interview (betriebliche Funktionstraeger -einschliesslich Arbeitnehmer-, Mitarbeiter in teilautonomen flexiblen Fertigungssystemen; Auswahlverfahren: bewusst). Expertengespraech (betriebliche Funktionstraeger -einschliesslich Arbeitnehmer-, Mitarbeiter in teilautonomen flexiblen Fertigungssystemen; Auswahlverfahren: bewusst. Funktionstraeger von Weiterbildungsanbietern; Auswahlverfahren: bewusst. Funktionstraeger intermediaerer Akteure; Auswahlverfahren: bewusst). Aktenanalyse (Dokumente von Weiterbildungsanbietern; Auswahlverfahren: bewusst). Auswerten der Daten der Panel-Studie des SFB 187 (Gesamtheit der Fertigungsbetriebe im Maschinen- und Anlagenbau mit mehr als 20 Mitarbeitern). Primaererhebung: Feldarbeit von Mitarbeitern des Projektes durchgefuehrt; Datenerstellung auf der Basis von bereits vorliegenden Materialien wie Texten, Akten, Statistiken.

11791 PALM (Pupil Autonomy in Learning with Micros) Extension.
GBR 1993
Research Date(s): 1990-1991
Davies, R.
Inst: University of East Anglia, School of Education, Norwich NR4 7TJ, United Kingdom.

Fin: National Council for Educational Technology.
didactic use of computer; self-instruction; discovery learning; teaching method; information technology
usage didactique de l'ordinateur; auto-enseignement; apprentissage par la découverte; méthode pédagogique; technologie de l'information
PROJECT DESCRIPTION
  Between 1988 and 1990, the PALM (Pupil Autonomy in Learning with Micros) project was undertaken to support information technology development in schools using action research methods. The aim was to explore the possibility of improving teaching and learning in the classroom supported by microcomputers. It also aimed to use classroom-based action research to investigate and develop pedagogies that were most appropriate for working with the new technologies. The term 'autonomy' was used because its problematic nature served to stimulate enquiry.
  The extension project is a feasibility study to investigate the extent to which it is possible to disseminate PALM project methods to other local education authorities.

11792 Perparesite e programit te ri te matematikes per zgjidhjen e problemeve ne shkollen fillore. (Priorities of the new mathematics curriculum for problem solving in primary school.)
ALB 1994
Research Date(s): 1992-1993
Koci, Erlira.
Sup: Minga, Aleko.
Inst: Instuti i Studimeve Pedagogjike (Institute of Pedagogical Studies), Rruga "Naim Frasheri" no 37, Tirana, Albania.
teaching method; problem solving; achievement; primary education; mathematics; curriculum
méthode pédagogique; résolution de problème; rendement; enseignement primaire; mathématiques; programme d'études
PROJECT DESCRIPTION
  Background: A critical point in mathematics curricula has always been the element of problem solving. Five years ago it was decided to introduce a new mathematics curriculum in primary schools. One of the main goals of this curriculum is to foster attitudes towards mathematics that enable pupils to acquire problem solving strategies. Furthermore, the problems presented in the new curriculum are more closely linked to pupils' everyday experiences and the real world around them.
  Aim: To assess the possibilities that the new mathematics curriculum offers to pupils with regard to problem solving.
  Research questions: (1) What factors hindered the understanding of problem solving in the previous curriculum? (2) To what extent does the new curriculum promote pupils' problem solving skills?
  Design: The new curriculum was piloted in 73 classrooms. For each experimental class there was a control class. Various observations and tests were conducted in each class. A number of teachers were interviewed about their opinion of the results.
  Results: The new mathematics curriculum is characterized by a predominantly heuristic approach to problem solving. The presentation of the problem solving process actively involves all pupils in reaching creative solutions; it helps them to reason, to analyse, to reflect and to explain their thinking. The pupils succeed in understanding the text of the problems. They are able to check themselves step-by-step while solving a problem. They have no difficulty with problems with extraneus information, problems with incomplete information, problems to which there is no solution, and tasks of the type "find as many ... as possible", "create a problem by yourself", etc. The way in which the problems are dealt with enhances the pupils' motivation and their confidence in their problem solving skills.
  Publ: Koci, E. Kushte te reja per zhvillimin e te menduarit logjik te nxenesve ne matematike. In: *Revista pedagogjike* 4/1992, pp. 27-31.

11793 Planning for differentiation in the primary classroom.
GBR 1993
Research Date(s): 1990-1991
Evans, G.; Eynon, A.
Inst: Trinity College, Carmarthen, Dyfed SA31 3EP, United Kingdom.
Fin: Curriculum Council for Wales.
differentiation; teaching method; primary education
différenciation; méthode pédagogique; enseignement primaire
PROJECT DESCRIPTION
  This research will explore strategies for plannning for differentiated work. It is intended for children in primary schools to match their abilities and needs.

11794 Probleme und Entwicklungsperspektiven der Kooperation zwischen den Berufsbildungsstaetten. (Problems and development perspectives in the cooperation between vocational training institutions.)
DEU 1993
Research Date(s): 1991-1993
Walden, G.; Brandes, H.; Koedderitzsch, G.
Inst: Bundesinstitut fuer Berufsbildung, Fehrbelliner Platz 3, D-1000 Berlin 31.

vocational training; apprentice; educational institution; in-service training; cooperation

formation professionnelle; apprenti; établissement d'enseignement; formation en cours d'emploi; coopération

PROJECT DESCRIPTION

Inhalt: Das geplante Projekt soll einen Beitrag zur Verbesserung der Kooperation zwischen den Berufsbildungsstaetten leisten. Hierzu sollen zunaechst in einer Bestandsaufnahme bewaehrte Kooperationsformen zwischen den Berufsbildungsstaetten erfasst werden. Aufbauend auf dieser Bestandsaufnahme sollen Vorschlaege und Hilfen zur Kooperation zwischen den Berufsbildungsstaetten entwickelt werden. Dabei sind Moeglichkeiten aufzuzeigen, wie in der Praxis bewaehrte Kooperationsformen allgemein zugaenglich gemacht werden koennen. Zusaetzlich sollen Arbeitshilfen fuer die Praxis (z.B. Darstellung typischer Probleme mit Loesungsansaetzen, Sammlung von Fallbeispielen mit Vorbildcharakter) entwickelt werden. Durch eine effektivere Kooperation koennen die Bedingungen fuer Ausbilder und Auszubildende verbessert und neuen Qualifikationsanforderungen sowie Erwartungen der Betriebe gegenueber den Berufsschulen besser Rechnung getragen werden. Ausserdem koennen Ausbildungsplatzkapazitaeten in den Regionen besser genutzt werden. Zentrale Forschungshypothese des Projektes ist: Es gibt in der Praxis bewaehrte Kooperationsformen, die erfasst, systematisiert und allgemein zugaenglich gemacht werden koennen, um so zu einer Verbesserung der Kooperationspraxis insgesamt beizutragen.

11795 Proefstation Informatietechnologie Basisonderwijs. (Research Station - Primary Education Information Technology.)
NLD 1994
Research Date(s): 1992-1993
Zoelen, E.M. van.
Inst: Interdisciplinair Sociaal-wetenschappelijk Onderzoeksinstituut, Afdeling Onderwijs (ISOR) (Interdisciplinary Research Institute for the Social Sciences, Department of Educational Research), P.O. Box 80140, 3508 TC Utrecht, Netherlands.
Rijksuniversiteit Utrecht (State University of Utrecht), P.O. Box 80125, 3508 TC Utrecht, Netherlands
Fin: SVO het Instituut voor Onderzoek van het Onderwijs.
didactic use of computer; primary education; quality of education; evaluation
usage didactique de l'ordinateur; enseignement primaire; qualité de l'éducation; évaluation
PROJECT DESCRIPTION

Background: In May 1990 the project "Research Station - Primary Education Information Technology" was launched at the Dr. D. Bosschool in Utrecht. Since August 1992 the funds that the Ministry of Education makes available for this project are being administered by SVO, the Institute for Educational Research in the Netherlands. SVO has asked the ISOR, the Institute of Social Research at the Department of Education of the State University of Utrecht, to draw up a research plan to support the execution and the evaluation of the project for the period August 1992 - August 1993.

Aim: The approach and the practical value of Computer-Managed Instruction (CMI) will be critically tested at an "ordinary" primary school; in the short term, the focus will be on the adoption and implementation of computers for personal and educational use.

Design: Activities and developments (meetings, trainings and practical sessions) will be monitored and registered on a weekly basis. Informal talks will be had with teachers, the head teacher, the advisor and the project leader. In addition, informal classroom observations will be carried out. Every six months the state of affairs will be charted in a standardized way, involving interviews with teachers, the head teacher, and the advisor as well as questionnaires to teachers. Teachers and the head teacher will be asked to keep logs on the use of CMI at the classroom and school level.

11796 Pupil opinion: a contribution to child-centred theory and to curriculum and staff development.
GBR 1993
Research Date(s): 1984-1991
Logan, A.
Sup: Daws, P.; Livingston, R.
Inst: Ulster University, Faculty of Education, Cromore Road, Coleraine, County Londonderry BT52 1SA, United Kingdom.
teaching method; pupil attitude; teacher-pupil relation
méthode pédagogique; attitude de l'élève; relation maître-élève
PROJECT DESCRIPTION

The concept of child-centredness in education can be viewed as an aspect of the wider movement to extend human rights to some of those who had hitherto been denied respect as persons; in this instance pupils. The advent of a centralised, statutory curriculum in Britain in the late 1980s has presented child-centredness with a series of challenges. However, pupils in schools, the only bona fide customers in the education system, claim when consulted, that teachers must protect the child-cen-

tred dimension in their teaching practice if pupils are to succeed and if learning is to be accessible to them.

This thesis argues that one of the most practical and manageable ways of achieving this is to consult with pupils in a meaningful way. The thesis creates a context for the consideration of child-centredness, examines previous research that has been built on pupil views, suggests a model for consultation with pupils and presents their confidential responses.

Analysis of the resultant data, especially qualitative data, suggests not only that pupils can respond with intelligence and concern but also that their opinions can inform and enhance the practice of every teacher, regardless of style or philosophy. Finally, this thesis shows that the use of pupil views within a process of curriculum review and staff development can contribute to the theory of child-centredness, adds significantly to teachers' underlying understandings of their job, and helps to ensure effective teaching, happy learning and an improvement in standards.

11797 Pupils' workloads in years 1-12.
BUL 1994
Research Date(s): 1991-1994
Ivanova, A.; Kukusheva, V.; Milovanova, V.
Sup: Naidenov, G.
Inst: National Centre for Educational and Science Studies, Tzarigradsko Chossé 125, 1113 Sofia, Bulgaria.
Fin: Ministry of Education and Science.
school activities; pupil; social change; content of education
activités scolaires; élève; changement social; contenu de l'éducation
PROJECT DESCRIPTION

Variety in the educational activities of pupils is of great importance for the efficiency of their work, as it benefits both their capacity for work as well as the development of their personalities. Given the present conditions of social change, the study seeks to examine the workload of pupils in various domains and to propose new forms of education that are appropriate for the new situation.

Aims: To establish a clear picture of pupils' workloads; to analyse and compare relevant data from earlier studies; to establish regularities in the development of pupils' workloads, problems and prospects in education.

Research questions: (1) What kind of changes have taken place during the last 20 years in the pupils' workloads? (2) How do recent socio-economic changes affect pupils, their adjustment, their expectations and desires? (3) To what extent does the education system meet pupils' interests and desires?

Sample: 3,300 pupils.

Methods: Chronocards with a questionnaire for pupils in years 1-12; checklist for teachers.

11798 Qualitaet beruflicher Weiterbildung. (The quality of further vocational training.)
DEU 1993
Research Date(s): 1991-1992
Schade, A.; Weymann, V.; Peters, A.
Sup: Weymann, A.
Inst: Universitaet Bremen, EMPAS Institut fuer Empirische und Angewandte Soziologie, Postfach 330440, D-2800 Bremen 33.
Fin: Bundesministerium fuer Bildung und Wissenschaft.
in-service training; further training; electronic data processing; training course; quality of education
formation en cours d'emploi; formation complémentaire; traitement électronique des données; cours de formation; qualité de l'éducation
PROJECT DESCRIPTION

Inhalt: Pruefung der Qualitaet von berufsbegleitenden EDV-Kursen. Erarbeitung von Empfehlungen zur Auswahl von EDV-Kursen. Als Grundlagen dienen: (1) Marktuebersicht fuer berufsbegleitende EDV-Kurse fuer die ausgewaehlten Maerkte Bremen, Frankfurt/M., Berlin, Schwerin. (2) Vergleich der von den Veranstaltern angebotenen EDV-Kurse in bezug auf Kosten und verschiedene Leistungsmerkmale. (3) Untersuchung des Informationsgehaltes von schriftlichen Unterlagen (z.B. Kursprogramme). (4) Teilnehmende Beobachtung in EDV-Kursen. (5) Befragung von Kursteilnehmern. (6) Verdeckte Inspektion bei Anbietern von EDV-Kursen (teilnehmende Beobachtung). (7) Expertengespraeche.

Geographischer Raum: Bremen, Berlin, Frankfurt/ M., Schwerin.

Vorgehensweise: Untersuchungsdesign: Evaluationsstudie.

Datengewinnung: Aktenanalyse (Stichprobe: 120; schriftliche Kursunterlagen von EDV-Kursen; Auswahlverfahren: total. Stichprobe: 120; schriftliche Kursunterlagen von EDV-Kursen; Auswahlverfahren: Quota). Teilnehmende Beobachtung (Stichprobe: 60; Anbieter von EDV-Kursen; Auswahlverfahren: bewusst. Stichprobe: 25; EDV-Kurse; Auswahlverfahren: bewusst). Befragung (Stichprobe: 1.000; Teilnehmer an EDV-Kursen; Auswahlverfahren: willkuerlich). Expertengespraech (Stichprobe: ca. 5; Experten; Auswahlverfahren: bewusst). Primaererhebung: Feldarbeit von Mitarbeitern des Projektes durchgefuehrt; Datenerstellung auf der Basis von bereits vorliegenden Materialien wie Texten, Akten, Statistiken.

11799 Qualitaet der Lehre an der Universitaet Kaiserslautern. (The quality of teaching at Kaiserslautern university.)
DEU 1993
Research Date(s): 1991-1992
Barz, A.; Miethig, T.
Inst: Universitaet Kaiserslautern, FB Sozial- und Wirtschaftswissenschaften, Fachgebiet Politikwissenschaft, Pfaffenbergstrasse 95, D-6750 Kaiserslautern.
university; teaching profession; teacher; evaluation; vocational training; teaching quality
université; profession d'enseignant; enseignant; évaluation; formation professionnelle; qualité de l'enseignement
PROJECT DESCRIPTION
   Inhalt: Stellenwert und Qualitaet der Lehre an der Universitaet Kaiserslautern in der Sicht von Professoren, Mitarbeitern und Studenten.
   Geographischer Raum: Kaiserslautern.
   Vorgehensweise: Methoden: Evaluation ueber Interviews mit den genannten Zielgruppen, repraesentative Umfrage. Untersuchungsdesign: Fallstudie; Evaluationsstudie; Querschnittserhebung.
   Datengewinnung: Expertengespraech (Stichprobe: 140; Professoren, Fachstudienberater; Auswahlverfahren: total). Nicht-Standardisiertes Interview (Stichprobe: 13; Fachschaften, politisch-organisierte Gruppen; Auswahlverfahren: total). Postalische Befragung (Stichprobe: 1000; Studenten; Auswahlverfahren: Quota). Aktenanalyse (Stichprobe: 1000; Studenten; Auswahlverfahren: bewusst). Primaererhebung: Feldarbeit von Mitarbeitern des Projektes durchgefuehrt; Datenerstellung auf der Basis von bereits vorliegenden Materialien wie Texten, Akten, Statistiken.
   Auswertung: Haeufigkeitstabellen; Kontingenzanalyse. Datenaufbereitung: Zeitreihe(n); Verknuepfung verschiedener Datensaetze (record linkage).

11800 Qualitative thinking in tertiary education.
GBR 1993
Research Date(s): 1991-1994
Fitzgerald, D.
Sup: Morgan, A.
Inst: Open University, Institute of Educational Technology, Walton Hall, Milton Keynes MK7 6AA, United Kingdom.
teaching method; learning strategy; learning process; post-secondary education
méthode pédagogique; stratégie d'apprentissage; apprentissage; enseignement postsecondaire
PROJECT DESCRIPTION
   This research looks at approaches to teaching and consequent learning outcomes in tertiary education students, to investigate what techniques might be implemented in order to develop students' independence in thinking. The background work centres on research which suggests three fundamental approaches to learning (surface, strategic, deep) used by students. It will examine how it may be possible to aspire towards deep learning, i.e. how might critical thinking be instantiated into the learning process. How to think rather than what to know is the underlying rationale.

11801 Quel dispositif de formation pour les maîtres d'apprentissage.
FRA 1993
Research Date(s): 1990-1994
Savy, Françoise; Maubant, Philippe.
Inst: Institut national de recherches et d'applications pédagogiques, 2 rue des Champs Prévois, 21100 Dijon, France.
Fin: Délégation à la formation professionnelle.
apprenticeship; tutor; training of trainers; teacher-pupil relation; agricultural training
apprentissage professionnel; tuteur de formation; formation des formateurs; relation maître-élève; formation agricole
PROJECT DESCRIPTION
   Objectifs: En général, la formation des maîtres d'apprentissage ne prend pas suffisamment en compte ce qui se passe au sein même de la relation maître d'apprentissage-apprenti. Partant d'une étude sur l'approche globale de cette relation, nous proposons de vérifier certaines hypothèses: nécessité (1) de partir des représentations des maîtres d'apprentissage sur la formation, l'apprenti, le métier, (2) de faire un apport d'informations, (3) de suivre (d'accompagner) la relation maître d'apprentissage-apprenti dans le temps.
   Méthodologie: Recherche action conduite avec une dizaine de centres de formation qui forment de futurs ouvriers et employés d'entreprises horticoles.
   Publ: Savy, Françoise. *Un dispositif de formation à la communication pour les maîtres d'apprentissage.* Dijon: INRAP, décembre 1990.

11802 Rahmenbedingungen beruflicher Umschulungen. (Conditions for vocational retraining.)
DEU 1993
Research Date(s): 1991-1994
Kuenzel, B.
Sup: Nenniger, P.
Inst: Universitaet Kiel, Philosophische Fakultaet, Institut fuer Paedagogik, Hermann-Rodewald-Str. 9, D-2300 Kiel.
vocational education; retraining; commercial training; curriculum development; teaching method
enseignement professionnel; recyclage; formation commerciale; élaboration de programmes d'études; méthode pédagogique
PROJECT DESCRIPTION
   Inhalt: Die Rahmenbedingungen beruflicher Umschulung, insbesondere im kaufmaennischen Bereich, sollen auf ihre Effizienz ueberprueft werden. Ausgangspunkt hierfuer ist die Frage, ob Umschulungskonzepte, wie sie heute angeboten werden, optimale Lernergebnisse erbringen koennen. Ziel dieser Arbeit soll es sein, alternative Umschulungskonzepte zu erstellen. Insbesondere bezueglich neuer Curriculare (z.B. Einbeziehung von Schluesselqualifikationen) neuer Lern-und Lehrmethoden als auch neuer Lernorte. In diesem Zusammenhang spielt der Kostengesichtspunkt eine nicht unwesentliche Rolle.
   Geographischer Raum: Bundesrepublik Deutschland.

11803 Retraining under conditions of industrial restructuring.
CHE 1993
Research Date(s): 1992-
Alfthan, T.
Sup: Lee, E.
Inst: Training Policy and Programme Development Branch, Training Department, International Labour Office, 1211 Geneva, Switzerland.
retraining; technological change; industrialization; manpower need; training need; training programme
recyclage; changement technologique; industrialisation; besoin de main-d'oeuvre; besoin de formation; programme de formation
PROJECT DESCRIPTION
   Background: The nature of adjustment and the need for retraining programmes differ between countries, depending on their initial conditions and the economic and social policies they have pursued. Adjustment has been effective in some industrial and rapidly industrializing countries, where governments have introduced training and retraining programmes to match the emerging pattern of enterprises' needs for new skills and qualifications. Other countries, which have pursued protective industrial policies, face important adjustment challenges and major policy and institutional reform. Economic liberalization has forced yet other countries to shift resources from capital-intensive production to more labour-intensive, informal employment for which retraining is needed.
   Aims: To examine retraining programmes in countries undergoing structural adjustment so as to identify the best available training approaches under varying conditions.
   Design: A first phase will involve case studies illustrative of the models mentioned above. In a second phase, the findings of the case studies will be synthesized and conclusions drawn on: how training needs have been identified; the main modes of programme implementation; outcomes of the programmes (employment after retraining, cost-effectiveness and equity); effectiveness of different types of retraining programmes.

11804 Ricerca di pedagogia comparata sull'insegnamento dell'informatica nella scuola dell'obbligo di alcuni Paesi esteri (Francia e Inghilterra). (Comparative study on the teaching of information technology in compulsory schools in Italy, France and England.)
ITA 1993
Research Date(s): 1989
Rosati, L.; Maggiore, E.; Sebastiani, D.; Menna, V.; Sacchi, S.; Boriosi, M.P.; Gardner, S.
Sup: Leoni, R.
Inst: Centro Studi "Progresso Pedagogico" (Centre of "Progressive Pedagogy" Studies), Via Borghetto di Prejo 70, 06100 Perugia, Italy; Via Beuco 71, 00100 Roma, Italy.
Fin: Ministero della Pubblica Istruzione, Ufficio Studi e Programmazione.
didactic use of computer; compulsory education; cross-national research; computer
usage didactique de l'ordinateur; enseignement obligatoire; recherche transnationale; ordinateur
PROJECT DESCRIPTION
   Aims: The main goal of this research was to provide information on the use of computers in school, through a comparative examination of the situations in England and France. Other objectives were to show the extensive possibilities of the computer as a "teaching machine" and as a "machine that teaches" that can be used to: get to know pupils and the socio-cultural environment in which they live; furnish basic knowledge; assess results; plan teaching activities and educational projects; manage groups and control individual learning paths; acquire technologies directed toward the rehabilitation and re-education of the handicapped.
   Methods: Translation and analysis of syllabi and texts in France and England; construction of diagrams and tables related to technological aspects and the types of software used in French and English schools.
   Results: Compared to England and France, where computers have been introduced throughout the system, the Italian system is blocked at the theoretical level. There is an urgent need to introduce computers in Italian

schools. The technological training of teachers should be improved in order to enable them to use the computer critically and creatively. The various types of computer and the various languages were compared. It is recommended to use one type of hardware.

11805 The role of information technology in the education of socially handicapped children.
GBR 1993
Research Date(s): 1989-1993
Wood, A.
Sup: Jotham, R.
Inst: Nottingham University, Department of Adult Education, 14-22 Shakespeare Street, Nottingham NG1 4FJ, United Kingdom.
didactic use of computer; information technology; special education; special school; socially handicapped
usage didactique de l'ordinateur; technologie de l'information; enseignement spécial; centre d'éducation spéciale; handicapé social
PROJECT DESCRIPTION
   Particular topics in numeracy and literacy areas are taught to groups of children in a special school for maladjusted children in formats which (a) do not use information technology (IT); and (b) use IT extensively. Observers who are normally present in classes record characteristics such as attention span systematically for individual children in order to establish primary data for comparison.

11806 The role of the workplace in the work experience triangle with particular reference to transferable skills.
GBR 1993
Research Date(s): 1991-1993
Sommerlad, E.
Inst: Tavistock Institute of Human Relations, Evaluation Development and Review Unit, The Tavistock Centre, 120 Belsize Lane, London NW3 5BA, United Kingdom.
Fin: European Community PETRA Programme.
work experience; in-service training; skill; transfer of learning; cross-national research
expérience du travail; formation en cours d'emploi; compétence; transfert pédagogique; recherche transnationale
PROJECT DESCRIPTION
   Alternance arrangements generally recognise three elements: off-the-job education and training, on-the-job training and the link between them. The focus of the research is to explore the workplace as an environment for learning and to draw out the implications of workplace diversity for off-the-job education and the links between on-the-job and off-the-job. The specific questions being addressed are: (1) What feasibilities do different workplace settings offer for acquiring skills that are transferable? (2) In what ways can the acquisition of transferable skills be maximised in different work settings? (3) How is this mediated or influenced by different labour markets or industrial relations?
   The research includes: (i) secondary analysis of existing data and literature review; (ii) development of conceptual models and typologies; and (iii) a cross-national comparative element (Netherlands and Italy).

11807 School links and exchanges in Europe.
XCE 1993
Research Date(s): 1992
Rowles, D.
school exchange; school travel; school visit; Europe; European dimension; seminar; Council of Europe
échange scolaire; voyage scolaire; visite scolaire; Europe; dimension européenne; séminaire; Conseil de l'Europe
COLLECTED WORKS - Conference proceedings
   Seminar on School links and exchanges in Europe, Brighton (United Kingdom), 14-16 November 1991. This seminar was organised in the context of the Council of Europe Network on School Links and Exchanges, enlarged by the additional membership of a number of Central and Eastern European countries. These countries now face the problem of revising and reviewing the school curriculum in order to ensure it is suited to the needs of young poeple in the 21st century.
   More and more pupils currently in secondary schools will spend an increasing part of their working lives and leisure time in an extended community of European nations brought even closer together by progress in communication and transport. Therefore, schools, colleges and other educational institutions, as well as the governmental and non-governmental organisations which advise and support them, need to build upon current developments in the field of international links, visits and exchanges, thus ensuring that regular and meaningful contacts among young people from all of the participating countries should become the norm rather than the exception.
   The major preoccupations arising out of the seminar were centred around the following issues: (1) establishing a network for school exchanges; (2) devising a framework for in-service teacher training; (3) increasing the involvement of Eastern and Central European countries; and (4) devising new approaches to links and exchanges. The present report contains: the background to the recently published Council of Europe

Handbook on school links and exchanges; summaries of contributions on current practice in various countries and the European dimension in the curriculum; discussion of common problems; examples of good practice and a number of recommendations for consideration by the Council of Europe.

11808 Seniorenbildung im kirchlichen Arbeitsfeld (Schleswig-Holstein). (Education for senior citizens in a church setting (Schleswig-Holstein).)
DEU 1993
Research Date(s): 1990-1992
Gaertig, A.
Sup: Dieckmann, J.
Inst: Paedagogische Hochschule Kiel, Seminar fuer Soziologie, Olshausenstrasse 75, D-2300 Kiel.
church; elderly person; adult education; Schleswig-Holstein; evaluation
église; personne âgée; éducation des adultes; Schleswig-Holstein; évaluation
PROJECT DESCRIPTION
   Inhalt: Die im kirchlichen Arbeitsfeld bereits erbrachte Seniorenbildung verlangt die Erstellung wissenschaftlicher Bewertungskriterien, die auch fuer die anderen Bildungstraeger verwendbar werden.
   Geographischer Raum: Schleswig-Holstein.
   Vorgehensweise: Ermittlung von Beduerfnisstrukturen in der Altenbildung, narratives Interview. Untersuchungsdesign: qualitative Forschung.
   Datengewinnung: Nicht-standardisiertes Interview (Stichprobe: ca. 100; Senioren, Seniorinnen, ca. 8 kirchliche Fuehrungskraefte; Auswahlverfahren: bewusst). Primaererhebung: Feldarbeit von Mitarbeitern des Projektes durchgefuehrt.

11809 The share-a-book project.
GBR 1993
Research Date(s): 1988-
Miller, L.
Sup: Campbell, R.; Trendall, C.
Inst: Hertfordshire University, School of Humanities and Education, Wall Hall Campus, Aldenham, Watford WD2 8AT, United Kingdom.
pre-reading; reading; pre-school education; parent participation
préparation à la lecture; lecture; éducation préscolaire; participation des parents
PROJECT DESCRIPTION
   The project has arisen from the growing awareness of insights on learning to read to be gained by observing young children's earliest interactions with print and the increasing recognition of the role of the home environment and parental involvement in promoting early literacy development. A successful initiative in this area has been the introduction of shared reading schemes in primary schools, which recognise the importance of parents reading to and sharing books with their children. The share-a-book scheme has been extended into pre-school. The principles embodied in the concept of shared reading schemes could be viewed as a pre-cursor to such a scheme.
   The research focused upon the implementation and evaluation of a share-a-book scheme in a community playgroup and involved a group of 40 pre-school children and their parents. Evaluation relates to the children's emerging literacy skills and linked features of the home background. The viability of the scheme was evaluated for Cambridgeshire library service. Quantitative and qualitative methods of data collection were used. These included: (i) recording the number of books loaned and parental comments on these; (ii) a pre/post questionnaire relating to the children's emerging literacy skills and related features of the home background; (iii) pre and post testing of the children's concepts about print.
   The first phase of the project has been completed. A further phase is concerned with the continuity of literacy experiences between the pre-school and the beginning of primary school.
Publ: Miller, L. Sharing books in the pre-school: what is it all about? In: *Early Years*, Vol 11, No 1/1990, pp. 13-17.
Miller, L. Literacy development in young children: continuities between home and school. In: *Early Education*, No 4, Autumn 1991.

11810 SIMULATE: Simulation Authoring Tools Environment.
GBR 1993
Research Date(s): 1989-1991
Goodyear, P.; Self, J.
Inst: Lancaster University, Department of Educational Research, Cartmel College, Bailrigg, Lancaster LA1 4YW, United Kingdom.
didactic use of computer; simulation; authoring system
usage didactique de l'ordinateur; simulation; système-auteur
PROJECT DESCRIPTION
   The general topic of SIMULATE is learning and instruction with computer simulations and even more specifically, authoring for learning and instruction with computer simulations. Computer simulations are seen as a vehicle for acquiring knowledge and skills in an active way, by providing the learner an exploratory environment. In this respect computer simulations used in an educational environment are different from general courseware,

because they are not aimed at substituting the individual, experienced, teacher, but offer new teaching opportunities.

The starting point of the project is the observation that in order to be effective, simulations require the presence of an instructor to monitor the performance of the student and to provide support, both directive and non-directive. For open-learning situations this would mean embedding the simulation into an adaptive learning environment, capable of functioning in the above respects as a human tutor. The SIMULATE sub-project will deliver requirements and (global) specifications for an authoring environment (also) called SIMULATE (SIMULation Authoring Tools Environment), that can be used to create simulations embedded in an intelligent learning environment. In this document a simulation with such an environment will be called an ISLE (Intelligent Simulation Learning Environment).

Publ: Goodyear, P. & Tait, K. Learning with computer based simulations: tutoring and student modelling requirements for an intelligent learning advisor. In: Carretero, M. et al. (eds.). *Learning and Instruction.* Oxford: Pergamon Press, 1990.
Goodyear, P. The provision of tutorial support for learning with computer-based simulations. In: De Corte, E. (ed.). *Computer-based Learning Environments and Problem Solving.* Belgium: Springer Verlag, 1990.
Goodyear, P.; Ronteltap, T. & Van Kouwen, A. Intelligent support for simulation-based learning: tutoring at the discussion level. Paper presented at the 3rd European Seminar on Intelligent Tutoring Systems, December 1990, Denmark, Aarhus.
Goodyear, P. Development of learning technology at the European level. In: *Educational and Training Technology International,* Vol 26, No 4/1989, pp. 335-341.

11811 Spezielle Medienfragen im Fernstudienbereich: eine vergleichende Untersuchung. (The use of special media in graduate correspondence courses: a comparative study.)
DEU 1993
Research Date(s): 1992-1994
Doerfert, F.
Inst: Fernuniversitaet-Gesamthochschule Hagen, Zentrales Institut fuer Fernstudienforschung -ZIFF-, Humpertstr. 11a, D-5800 Hagen.
distance study; didactics; teaching aid; evaluation
enseignement à distance; didactique; moyen d'enseignement; évaluation
PROJECT DESCRIPTION
Inhalt: Erforschung und Evaluation der Medienpraxis ausgewaehlter Fernlehrinstitute. Die Auswahl der Institute erfolgt aufgrund vorhergehender Untersuchungen.
Geographischer Raum: international.
Vorgehensweise: Empirisch/sekundaeranalytisch.

11812 Språklige minoriteter og skolefaglig læring som et betingelsesavhengig fenomen. (Teaching methods and materials for linguistic minority children.)
NOR 1994
Research Date(s): 1992-1995
Yzerk, Kiamil Zihni.
Inst: Universitetet i Oslo, Pedagogisk Forskningsinstitutt (University of Oslo, Institute for Educational Research), PB 1092 Blindern, 0317 Oslo, Norway.
Fin: NAVF/RSF.
teaching method; teaching aid; national minority; bilingualism; learning
méthode pédagogique; moyen d'enseignement; minorité nationale; bilinguisme; acquisition de connaissances
PROJECT DESCRIPTION
The study focuses on the working methods, teaching methods and teaching aids that are used in language teaching and theoretical instruction of linguistic minority pupils. Through an empirical examination (using both qualitative and quantitative methods) it is hoped to gain insight into the effects of specific methods and instructional materials on linguistic minority pupils in primary school. An important part of the project consists of identifying and describing suitable and unsuitable working methods, teaching methods and teaching aids.

11813 Staff development in higher education.
GBR 1993
Research Date(s): 1990-1994
Riddell, B.
Sup: Daines, J.; Graham, B.
Inst: Nottingham University, Department of Adult Education, 14-22 Shakespeare Street, Nottingham NG4 4FJ, United Kingdom; University of British Columbia, 5597 Iona Drive, Vancouver, Canada.
teaching technique; teaching method; university; further education of teachers
technique pédagogique; méthode pédagogique; université; perfectionnement des enseignants
PROJECT DESCRIPTION
This research is aimed at addressing the issue of teacher-centred versus learner-centred approaches to teaching/instruction. The research uses participants in 'instructor training' workshops as subjects. Using a case study

method, it will seek to establish the antecedents and ongoing effects of training, experience and self-reflection upon teaching approaches. In particular, it will seek to identify changes in values, attitudes and beliefs of participants towards more learner-centred approaches to university teaching.

11814 Struktur und Entwicklung des Ausbildungsstellenangebots in ausgewaehlten Regionen der neuen Bundeslaender. (Structure and development of the supply of trainee places in selected regions in the new German states.)
DEU 1993
Research Date(s): 1992-1994
Wolfinger, C.; Schober, K.
Inst: Institut fuer Arbeitsmarkt- und Berufsforschung der Bundesanstalt fuer Arbeit -IAB-, Regensburgerstrasse 104, D-8500 Nuernberg.
Fin: Bundesanstalt fuer Arbeit.
vocational training; training supply; education system; place of work; German DR
formation professionnelle; offre de formation; système d'enseignement; lieu de travail; Allemagne RDA
PROJECT DESCRIPTION
Inhalt: Struktur der Ausbildungstraeger/-einrichtungen in der Region; Ausbildungsleistungen in der und fuer die Region, u.a. auch im Hinblick auf den erforderlichen beruflichen Strukturwandel; Entwicklungsperspektiven der Traeger/Einrichtungen im Hinblick auf ihren kuenftigen Beitrag zur Berufsausbildung in der Region; Identifizierung moeglicher Defizite in der regionalen Ausbildungsversorgung oder im Hinblick auf bestimmte Zielgruppen der Berufsbildungspolitik; Auswirkunen der staatlichen Programme zur Ausbildungsplatzsicherung auf die Herausbildung regionaler Traegerstrukturen in der Berufsausbildung sowie auf die Etablierung und Funktionsweise des dualen Ausbildungssystems in Ostdeutschland.
Geographischer Raum: Ostdeutschland.

11815 Student and peer tutoring in Wales.
GBR 1993
Research Date(s): 1991-1994
Saunders, D.
Inst: Glamorgan University, Enterprise Unit, Pontypridd, Mid Glamorgan CF37 1DL, United Kingdom.
Fin: BP (Chemicals) Baglan Bay.
peer group teaching; student; Wales
enseignement mutuel; étudiant; Pays de Galles
PROJECT DESCRIPTION
The student and peer tutoring in Wales initiative involves four higher education centres which are sending their students into schools to help teachers in the delivery of the curriculum as well as to provide positive role models for pupils. The project examines assessment issues and strategies emerging from student and peer tutoring, as well as numerous other developments emerging out of links between universities or institutes and local schools.

Publ: Saunders, D. Peer tutoring in higher education. In: *Studies in Higher Education,* Vol 17, No 2/1992, pp. 211-217.

11816 Studieneingangsbedingungen. (Entry requirements in higher education.)
DEU 1993
Research Date(s): 1991-1993
Schaale, D.
Inst: Humboldt Universitaet Berlin, FB 04 Erziehungswissenschaften, Institut fuer Hochschulforschung und Hochschuldidaktik, Unter den Linden 9, O-1086 Berlin.
German DR; Berlin; university studies; admission requirements; access to education
Allemagne RDA; Berlin; études universitaires; conditions d'admission; accès à l'éducation
PROJECT DESCRIPTION
Inhalt: Ermittlung von Studienvoraussetzungen von Studienanfaengern an der Humboldt-Universitaet zu Berlin 1991; Pilotuntersuchung zur Pruefung des Fragebogens und der Organisation der Untersuchung (1991) fuer das international vergleichende Projekt "Access to Higher Education" (Oesterreich, Italien, CSFR, Polen, Jugoslawien). Entwicklung des Zugangs im Vergleich zu Hochschulen der alten Bundeslaender: Differenzen in Herkunftsbedingungen, Erwartungshaltung, Studienmotiven.
Geographischer Raum: Berlin (Humboldt-Univ.).
Untersuchter Zeitraum: 1990-1993.
Vorgehensweise: Untersuchungsdesign: Fallstudie; Querschnitterhebung; Panel.
Datengewinnung: Befragung (Stichprobe: 400; Studienanfaenger der Humboldt-Universitaet; Auswahlverfahren: Zufall). Postalische Befragung (Stichprobe: 4.000; Studienanfaenger der Humboldt-Universitaet; Auswahlverfahren: total). Primaererhebung: Feldarbeit von Mitarbeitern des Projektes durchgefuehrt.
Auswertung: Faktorenanalyse. Datenaufbereitung: Zeitreihe(n); Verknuepfung verschiedener Datensaetze (record linkage).

11817   A study of technological capability as manifest in secondary school pupils' project work.
GBR   1993
Research Date(s): 1989-1991
Lewis, I.
Sup: Jenkins, E.; Donnelly, J.
Inst: Leeds University, School of Education, Leeds LS2 9JT, United Kingdom.
Fin: Leeds University: School of Education; Sheffield Local Education Authority.
project method; technology; secondary education; ability
pédagogie du projet; technologie; enseignement secondaire; capacité
PROJECT DESCRIPTION
   The study is an exploration of 'the technology project' with particular attention being given to its origination, development and closure. An attempt is made to establish the criteria used by pupils in, for example, choosing one solution/design criterion in preference to another, evaluating/apraising their project as it develops. The work is based on an ethnographic study of pupils in classes in five Sheffield schools. A sample size of about 10 pupils is likely to be involved.

11818   Supervision als paedagogische Handlungsform in Prozessen berufsbezogener Weiterbildung. (Supervision as a pedagogic activity in in-service further training processes.)
DEU   1993
Research Date(s): 1991-1995
Fernkorn, E.
Sup: Doerry, G.
Inst: Freie Universitaet Berlin, FB Erziehungs- und Unterrichtswissenschaften, Institut fuer Kleinkind-, Erwachsenen- und Sozialpaedagogik WE 05, Arnimallee 12, D-1000 Berlin.
vocational training; further training; didactics; sciences of education; methodology; model; supervision
formation professionnelle; formation complémentaire; didactique; sciences de l'éducation; méthodologie; modèle; surveillance
PROJECT DESCRIPTION
   Inhalt: Begruendung von Supervision im Kontext berufsbezogener Weiterbildung auf der Grundlage eines Bildungsbegriffes und didaktischer Prinzipien. Ueberpruefung theoretischer Ansaetze und methodischer Konzeptionen von Supervision im Hinblick auf ihre Verwendbarkeit fuer die Weiterbildung. Entwurf eines Entwicklungsmodells Supervision in der berufsbezogenen Weiterbildung. Konsequenzen fuer die Professionalisierung im Weiterbildungsbereich.
   Vorgehensweise: Theoretisch-hermeneutisch; Fallanalysen. Untersuchungsdesign: Fallstudie; Evaluationsstudie; qualitative Forschung.
   Datengewinnung: Nicht-standardisiertes Interview (Stichprobe: 5; Weiterbildungsseminare; Auswahlverfahren: bewusst). Expertengespraech (dito). Teilnehmende Beobachtung (dito). Primaererhebung: Feldarbeit von Mitarbeitern des Projektes durchgefuehrt.

11819   Technische Bildung und oekologisches Lernen im Jugendalter. (Technical training and ecological learning in youth.)
DEU   1993
Research Date(s): 1992-1993
Wahler, P.
Sup: Lappe, L.
Inst: Deutsches Jugendinstitut e.V., Freibadstrasse 30, D-8000 Muenchen 90.
Fin: Institution; Bundesministerium fuer Bildung und Wissenschaft.
technical education; youth; study method; learning process; ecology; vocational training
enseignement technique; jeunesse; méthode de travail; apprentissage; écologie; formation professionnelle
PROJECT DESCRIPTION
   Inhalt: Das Projekt untersucht den Zusammenhang zwischen dem Einsatz neuer Produktions-und Arbeitstechniken und umweltbezogenen Lernprozessen bei Jugendlichen. Es will einen Beitrag leisten zur Begruendung eines technikorientierten und oekologisch fundierten Lernkonzeptprozesses fuer berufliche Bildungsprozesse.
   Geographischer Raum: Bundesrepublik Deutschland.
   Vorgehensweise: Literaturaufarbeitung.

11820   Theoretische Grundlegung fuer eine Didaktik, den Erstleseunterricht mit musikalischen Mitteln zu erweitern, um das Auftreten von Leserechtschreibschwaechen zu verringern. (Theoretical principles for an initial reading instruction method using music media with a view to reducing the incidence of dyslexia.)
DEU   1993
Research Date(s): 1990-1993
Rosbach, A.
Sup: Bruhn, H.
Inst: Paedagogische Hochschule Kiel, Institut fuer Musik und ihre Didaktik, Olshausenstrasse 75, D-2300 Kiel.
reading; primary education; didactics; dyslexia; music
lecture; enseignement primaire; didactique; dyslexie; musique

PROJECT DESCRIPTION
   Inhalt: Besser Lesen- und Schreibenlernen mit Musik? Die Zusammenhaenge zwischen Sprache und Musik konnten schon in vielen empirischen Untersuchungen und vereinzelt auch in projekten mit vermehrtem Musikunterricht dargestellt und behandelt werden. Als theoretische Grundlage dieser Arbeit dient ein Modell, das den Zusammenhang zwischen Sprache und Musik aus kognitionspsychologischer Sicht erklaert. Vor diesem Hintergrund entstehen neue Ziele fuer den Schulmusikunterricht, die als Ergaenzung zu einem methodenintegrierenden Erstlesewerk das Erlernen vom Lesen und Schreiben erleichtern und angenehmer gestalten.
   Vorgehensweise: Untersuchungsdesign: Evaluationsstudie; Didaktik.
   Datengewinnung: Standardisiertes Interview, Gruppenbefragung, psychologischer Test (Stichprobe: 27; SchuelerInnen 2. Klasse; Auswahlverfahren: total. Stichprobe: 184; SchuelerInnen 2. Klasse; Auswahlverfahren: total). Primaererhebung: Feldarbeit von Mitarbeitern des Projektes durchgefuehrt.
   Auswertung: Faktorenanalyse; Varianzanalyse.
Publ: Bruhn, Herbert. *Die Beziehung zwischen musikalischen und schriftsprachlichen Faehigkeiten. Bericht ueber eine empirische Studie an 184 Kindern aus der 2. Klasse von fuenf schleswig-holsteinischen Grundschulen.* Kiel 1991. Standort: UuStB Koeln(38)-920109029.
Bruhn, Herbert. *Singen in der ersten Grundschulklasse. Ueber eine Beziehung zwischen musikalischen Faehigkeiten und dem Erstunterricht in Lesen und Schreiben.* Kiel 1990. Standort: UuStB Koeln(38)-920109030.

11821   The trainer's workbench.
GBR   1993
Research Date(s): 1990-
Lefrere, P.
Inst: Open University, Institute of Educational Technology, Walton Hall, Milton Keynes MK7 6AA, United Kingdom.
didactic use of computer; educational technology; distance study
usage didactique de l'ordinateur; technologie de l'éducation; enseignement à distance
PROJECT DESCRIPTION
   The project aims at a partial codification, for proof of concept purposes, of open learning expertise, with a view to developing rule-based systems. A prototype system will provide on-the-job help with the design and evaluation of learning materials, including computer-assisted learning.

11822   Tutoring from colleges to schools.
GBR   1993
Research Date(s): 1990-1993
Hughes, J.
Sup: Goodlad, S.
Inst: London University, Imperial College of Science, Technology and Medicine, Humanities Programme, Mechanical Engineering Building, Exhibition Road, London SW7 3BX, United Kingdom.
Fin: British Petroleum (BP) Aiming for a College Education Initiative.
peer group teaching; teaching method; science education; mathematics; technology; tutor
enseignement mutuel; méthode pédagogique; éducation scientifique; mathématiques; technologie; tuteur de formation
PROJECT DESCRIPTION
   The aim of the project is to promote peer tutoring schemes, similar to Imperial College's 'Pimlico Connection', around the United Kingdom. This is when volunteer students from further or higher education act as tutors in local primary and secondary schools often in science, mathematics and technology lessons. The professional teacher uses them as an extra, and valuable, teaching resource. The student tutors provide positive role models to the school pupils and in doing so it is hoped to increase the aspiration for them to stay on in education and training beyond age 16. Students acquire communication, organisational and problem-solving skills as well as self-confidence. Student tutoring involves volunteer students going into local primary and secondary schools on a sustained and systematic basis. From the original Pimlico Connection Scheme the number has risen to 96 similar programmes.
Publ: Goodlad, S. & Hirst, B. *Explorations in peer tutoring.* Oxford: Blackwell, 1990.
Hughes, J.C. *Tutoring: students as tutors in school.* London: BP Educational Service, 1992.
Hughes, J.C. (ed.). *Tutoring Resource Pack.* London: BP Educational Service, 1991.

11823   Tvorba interaktivních výukových programů pro multimediální systémy. (The creation of interactive instructional programs for multimedia systems.)
CSK   1994
Research Date(s): 1991-1993
Zochová, Zdenka; Dohnal, Gejza; Kolek, Lubomír; Vávra, Stanislav; Sýkora, Richard; Zlatník, Čeněk.
Sup: Bartošek, Miroslav; Rýdl, Josef.
Inst: České vysoké technické, Audiovizuální a technické centrum (Czech Technical University, Audiovisual and Technological Centre), Trojanova 13, 120 00 Praha 2, Czech Republic.

Ministerstvo školství, mládeže a tělovýchovy České republiky (Ministry of Education, Youth and Physical Education of the Czech Republic), Karmelitská ul. 5, 110 00 Praha 1, Czech Republic
didactic use of computer; multimedia system; problem solving; mathematics
usage didactique de l'ordinateur; système multimédia; résolution de problème; mathématiques
PROJECT DESCRIPTION
Aims: The project was concerned with the creation of instructional programs aimed at regulating learning during the solving of complex tasks. The programs use diagnostic functions for the regulation of students' activities and foster an independent and creative attitude towards complex problem solving. Part of the project was concerned with the integrated use of computer and video recorder and the development of peripheral devices and software.

Results: The project resulted in the construction of: (1) a program model for a computer-video recorder system based on a psychological theory of learning; (2) an interface connecting the computer and the video recorder; (3) computer programs for controlling the system as a whole; (4) two instructional programs: "linear differential equation of the first order - rectilinear motion" and "linear analytic geometry in space - application".

Publ: Zochová, Zdenka a kol. *Tvorba inteligentních výukových programů pro multimediální systémy, zpráva výzkumného úkolu 13/16.* Praha: ČVUT, 1991, 33p.
Zochová, Zdenka a kol. *Tvorba interaktivních výukových programů pro multimediální systémy a zpráva výzkumného úkolu č. 2-III-12-92.* Praha: ČVUT, 1992, 29p.
Kolek, Lubomír; Sýkora, Richard; Vávra, Stanislav & Zochová, Zdenka. Interactive Educational Programs. In: *Proceedings of the International Workshop on CAL and Simulation Technologies.* Praha: ČVUT, 1991, pp. 33-35.
Dohnal, Gejza. Some generalizations of Rasch's Logist Response Model. In: *Proceedings of the International Workshop on CAL and Simulation Technologies.* Praha: ČVUT, 1991, pp. 29-32.
Kolek, Lubomír; Sýkora, Richard; Vávra, Stanislav & Zochová, Zdenka. Interactive programs for multimedia systems. In: *Proceedings of the International Conference on Trans-European Cooperation in Engineering Education.* Praha: ČVUT, 1992, pp. 234-236.

11824 Ueberbetriebliches Ausbildungszentrum "Oberes Erzgebirge". (Interplant training centre "Oberes Erzgebirge".)
DEU 1993
Research Date(s): 1992-1995
Ullmann, J.; Petermann, S.; Kruse, W.
Sup: Thomas, W.
Inst: Technische Universitaet Chemnitz, FB Erziehungswissenschaften, Postfach 964, O-9010 Chemnitz; Landesinstitut Sozialforschungsstelle Dortmund, Rheinlanddamm 199, D-4600 Dortmund 1.
Fin: Bundesministerium fuer Bildung und Wissenschaft.
vocational training; training centre; occupational qualification; interplant training; economic conditions
formation professionnelle; centre de formation; qualification professionnelle; formation interfirmes; conditions économiques
PROJECT DESCRIPTION
Inhalt: Berufsausbildung entsprechend des Strukturwandels in der Wirtschaft. Berufliche Qualifizierung als Motor der Produktionsmodernisierung. Neue berufspaedagogische Konzepte in der Ausbildung. Realisierung eines Ausbildungszentrums.
Geographischer Raum: Oberes Erzgebirge (Annaberg, Aue, Marienberg).
Vorgehensweise: Innovationstransfer Berufsbildung in der Wirtschaft unter den spezifischen Bedingungen der Region.

11825 Ujumise tehnika ja vôistlustegevuse taktika optimaalsed mudelid. (Improving methods of teaching and learning swimming.)
EST 1994
Research Date(s): 1975-
Haljand, R.
Inst: Tallinna Pedagoogikaülikool (Tallinn Pedagogical University), 0102 Tallinn, Narva mnt. 25, Estonia.
Fin: Ülikooli riigieelarve; Lepingud erinevate partneritega.
teaching method; videorecording; competitive sport; swimming; didactic use of computer
méthode pédagogique; enregistrement sur magnétoscope; sport de compétition; natation; usage didactique de l'ordinateur
PROJECT DESCRIPTION
The aim of this investigation was to improve swimming skills through improved swimming instruction and learning methods for all age levels and swimming performance levels. It was hypothesized that a new learning system and new control methods would lead to better results than traditional methods. Instructional methods included video registration and analysis by computer, using digital parameters and graphical images. The results are positive for all age groups and levels of performance of swimmers in Estonia, Finland and Russia.

Publ: *How to develop Olympic level swimmers.* Helsinki, 1982.

11826 Undervisningsstrategier i heterogene klasser - idealer og realiteter. (Teaching strategies in heterogeneous classes - ideals and realities.)
NOR 1994
Research Date(s): 1992-1994
Skaalvik, Einar M.
Inst: Pedagogisk Institutt (Department of Education), 7055 Dragvoll, Norway.
Fin: NAVF/RSF.
teaching method; teaching practice; teaching style; teacher behaviour; heterogeneous class; class size
méthode pédagogique; pratique pédagogique; style pédagogique; comportement de l'enseignant; classe hétérogène; dimension de la classe
PROJECT DESCRIPTION
Aim: The aim of the project is to gain knowledge about how teachers in primary school try to solve the problem of large and heterogeneous classes. What kinds of strategies do they use and what is the pedagogical philosophy behind these strategies? How do the different strategies influence the pupils?
Methods: Classroom observation, interviews with teachers and pupils and analysis of pupils' responses.
The descriptions of the various strategies may later be used as an idea bank in educational development work. Results from the project will be published through articles, a project report and seminars.

11827 The use of computers to teach mathematics.
GBR 1993
Research Date(s): 1988-
Moscardini, A.; Curran, D.; Middleton, W.; Bloor, C.; Prior, D.
Inst: Sunderland University, School of Computing and Information Studies, Priestman Building, Green Terrace, Sunderland SR1 3SD, United Kingdom.
Fin: Training, Enterprise & Education Directorate.
didactic use of computer; information technology; mathematics; university studies; undergraduate study; engineering; sciences; handicapped
usage didactique de l'ordinateur; technologie de l'information; mathématiques; études universitaires; supérieur premier cycle; ingénierie; sciences; handicapé
PROJECT DESCRIPTION
A laboratory has been set up for teaching mathematics to 300-400 first year undergraduate engineering and science students. The laboratory has replaced a large amount of material previously taught by lectures. The work has also been extended to include teaching the mathematically unadapted and, more recently, teaching the disabled.

Publ: Middleton, W. Innovative applications of CAL to the teaching of the mathematically unadapted. In: *Conference Proceedings, CAL 90,* Barcelona, 1990.

11828 Use of games in the teaching of mathematics.
GBR 1993
Research Date(s): 1985-1991
Cornelius, M.
Inst: Durham University, School of Education, Leazes Road, Durham DH1 1TA, United Kingdom.
educational game; mathematics; teaching aid
jeu éducatif; mathématiques; moyen d'enseignement
PROJECT DESCRIPTION
This research is concerned with the history of games and their use in investigational work in the teaching of mathematics. The aim of the research is to stimulate pupil investigations in mathematics through the use of board games. Details of board games from a wide range of civilisations and periods have been identified and described. Mathematical activities based on these games have been devised and piloted with pupils. Methods used included classroom trials with investigations based on games.

Publ: Bell, R. & Cornelius, M.L. *Board games around the world: a resource book for mathematical investigations.* Cambridge: Cambridge University Press, 1988.
Cornelius, M.L. & Parr, A. *What's your game?: a resource book for mathematical activities.* Cambridge: Cambridge University Press, 1991.

11829 The use of microcomputers in British schools, the implications for their use in Turkish schools and the improvement of computer-assisted learning in Turkish schools.
GBR 1993
Research Date(s): 1985-1991
Akkoyunlu, B.
Sup: Ball, D.
Inst: Leicester University, School of Education, University Road, Leicester LE1 7RH, United Kingdom.
Fin: Hacettepe University.
didactic use of computer; comparative education; cross-national research; Turkey
usage didactique de l'ordinateur; éducation comparée; recherche transnationale; Turquie
PROJECT DESCRIPTION

Computer-assisted instruction is a new area for study and practice in Turkey. Research studies are very limited and qualified personnel are scarce. Utilisation of computers has a relatively long history in some countries such as England, the USA, Japan and the Netherlands, and there is a considerable amount of experience and accumulated knowledge in the use of computers for education.

By reviewing research studies and investigating practices and the present status of computer-assisted instruction in the other countries the study aims to achieve the following objectives: (1) to draw relevant lessons of experience for Turkish computer-assisted instruction practices in order to establish a sound ground for implementation and development; (2) to suggest procedures and methods which will fit the Turkish educational system for the development of the use of microcomputers for instruction; (3) to provide criteria and a frame of reference for evaluating the practices of computer-assisted instruction in Turkey.

The data will be gathered in two ways: (1) by reviewing and analysing the literature on computer-assisted instruction and by drawing implications for the Turkish case; (2) by conducting some case studies in which different approaches are utilised for the implementation of computer-assisted or computer-based instruction. For data collection, an observation list, questionnaires and interview techniques will be employed. The full design of the study will be completed by collaborative and co-operative work with related members of the School of Education at Leicester University.

11830   The use of microcomputers in Saudi secondary schools.
GBR   1993
Research Date(s): 1989-1991
Almajid, A.
Sup: Reid, D.
Inst: Manchester University, School of Education, Oxford Road, Manchester M13 9PL, United Kingdom.
didactic use of computer; microcomputer; Saudi Arabia; software
usage didactique de l'ordinateur; micro-ordinateur; Arabie Saoudite; logiciel
PROJECT DESCRIPTION

The use of microcomputers in Saudi secondary schools is ineffectual. Problems centre around the software, which is not Arabized and therefore causes difficulty, around the Saudi information technology (IT) curriculum. This is program-focused. The thesis argues the case for an applications-based strategy.

11831   L'utilisation des logiciels de traitement de texte pour le développement de la maîtrise de la production écrite.
FRA   1993
Research Date(s): 1989-
Raisky, Claude.
Inst: Institut national de recherches et d'applications pédagogiques, 2 rue des Champs Prévois, 21100 Dijon, France.
Fin: Ministère de l'agriculture, Direction générale de l'enseignement et de la recherche.
teaching method; written expression; word processing; microcomputer; lower secondary; agricultural training
méthode pédagogique; expression écrite; traitement de texte; micro-ordinateur; secondaire premier cycle; formation agricole
PROJECT DESCRIPTION

Objectifs: En 1989, une recherche a été conduite à l'INRAP, sous la direction du Laboratoire d'étude des acquisitions et du développement pour évaluer les effets de l'utilisation d'un traitement de texte par des élèves durant leur formation. Les résultats obtenus nous invitent à construire des expérimentations à la fois plus fines et plus vastes. L'objectif final est, dans la mesure où nous pouvons montrer que l'usage du traitement de texte en formation modifie chez les sujets les procédures d'écriture, de formuler des conseils d'utilisation auprès des enseignants, d'élaborer des séquences pédagogiques. Le public visé est constitué des élèves du cycle court de l'enseignement technique agricole. Les résultats pourront ête ensuite étendus à d'autres publics.

11832   Uued suunad inglise keele õpetamisel Tallinna Pedagoogikaülikoolis. (New perspectives of English language teaching at the Tallinn Pedagogical University.)
EST   1994
Research Date(s): 1991-1992
Alas, E.; Liiv, S.; Rebane, E.; Taiger, A.
Inst: Tallinna Pedagoogikaülikool (Tallinn Pedagogical University), 0102 Tallinn, Narva mnt. 25, Estonia.
language teaching; foreign languages; further education of teachers; English language; training need
enseignement des langues; langues étrangères; perfectionnement des enseignants; langue anglaise; besoin de formation
PROJECT DESCRIPTION

The aim of the research was to study: English language teaching in the Tallinn Pedagogical University's Department of English; the teaching of English as a foreign language in other departments and schools; and the needs for in-service training among school teachers. The study was prompted by the increasing number of international contacts of the Estonian Republic and the growing motivation among Estonians to learn English. As there is a shortage of English language teachers in schools, existing needs for in-service training were investigated with the help of a questionnaire.

The results of the study were presented by four members of the research group at the 10th Anniversary Oral Skills Workshop "Symposium on Language Centre Teaching and Research" in Helsinki, October 9-11, 1992.

11833   Verteilte Systeme fuer Tele- und Gruppenarbeit. (Distributed systems for telework and group work.)
DEU   1993
Research Date(s): 1991-1994
Seitz, R.
Sup: Bodendorf, F.
Inst: Universitaet Erlangen-Nuernberg, Wirtschafts- und Sozialwissenschaftliche Fakultaet, Betriebswirtschaftliches Institut, LS BWL, insb. Wirtschaftsinformatik 02, Lange Gasse 20, D-8500 Nuernberg.
Fin: Freistaat Bayern Bayerisches Staatsministerium fuer Unterricht, Kultus, Wissenschaft und Kunst.
data processing; learning; university studies; decentralization; electronic data processing; educational software; hardware
traitement des données; acquisition de connaissances; études universitaires; décentralisation; traitement électronique des données; didacticiel; matériel informatique
PROJECT DESCRIPTION

Inhalt: Dezentralisierung von DV-Ausbildungssystemen. Elektronische Kommunikation zwischen Lernenden und Lehrenden. Aufbau einer hard- und softwaretechnischen Kommunikationsinfrastruktur zur Erforschung von Tele- und Gruppenarbeit in der Hochschulausbildung.

Vorgehensweise: Literaturstudien; Telearbeitsmodelle; Gruppenarbeitsmodelle; prototypische Realisierung von Loesungen. Untersuchungsdesign: Modellversuch.

11834   Verteiltes wissensbasiertes CBT. (Distributed knowledge-based CBT.)
DEU   1993
Research Date(s): 1991-1994
Langer, K.
Sup: Bodendorf, F.
Inst: Universitaet Erlangen-Nuernberg, Wirtschafts- und Sozialwissenschaftliche Fakultaet, Betriebswirtschaftliches Institut, LS BWL, insb. Wirtschaftsinformatik 02, Lange Gasse 20, D-8500 Nuernberg.
Fin: Diehl GmbH Abt. Systemtechnik; Bundesministerium fuer Forschung und Technologie.
didactic use of computer; teaching programme; model; multimedia system
usage didactique de l'ordinateur; programme d'enseignement; modèle; système multimédia
PROJECT DESCRIPTION

Inhalt: Schwerpunkte des Projektes liegen auf der wissensbasierten Repraesentation von Lehrstoff, Tutorial und Benutzermodell fuer computerunterstuetzten Unterricht (CBT) in verteilten Systemen. Unter verteiltem CBT wird die (kooperative) Unterrichtung mehrerer Personen in einer vernetzten Systemumgebung verstanden.

Vorgehensweise: Einer Fixierung des theoretischen Ansatzes zur CBT-Wissensrepraesentation folgt eine prototypische Validierung der zu erarbeitenden Konzepte nach einem Client-Server-Modell.

11835   Weiterbildung betrieblicher Weiterbildner der neuen Bundeslaender. (Further training for in-house instructors in companies in the new German states.)
DEU   1993
Research Date(s): 1992-1994
Petermann, S.; Polster, A.; Fuchs, D.; Huebner, R.
Sup: Thomas, W.
Inst: Technische Universitaet Chemnitz, FB Erziehungswissenschaften, Postfach 964, O-9010 Chemnitz.
Fin: Bundesministerium fuer Bildung und Wissenschaft.
further training; training of trainers; enterprise; German DR; educational need; educational provision
formation complémentaire; formation des formateurs; entreprise; Allemagne RDA; besoin d'éducation; scolarisation
PROJECT DESCRIPTION

Inhalt: Erhebung des spezifischen Weiterbildungsbedarfs von betrieblichen Weiterbildnern der fuenf neuen Laender. Exakte Abbildung der Berufsrollen im Bereich der betrieblichen Weiterbildung der fuenf neuen Laender. Berufsrollenspezifische Erarbeitung von modularen Qualifizierungsangeboten (Trainings) zur Effektivierung betrieblichen Weiterbildungsgeschehens in den neuen Bundeslaendern. Umsetzung dieses Modells.

Geographischer Raum: Fuenf neue Bundeslaender.

Vorgehensweise: Handlungs- und erfahrungsorientiertes Lernen.

11836 Weiterbildung von Aussiedlern unter besonderer Beruecksichtigung fachuebergreifender Kompetenzen. (Further education for immigrants, with particular reference to cross-disciplinary competencies.)
DEU 1993
Research Date(s): 1991-1993
Kuehn, G.
Inst: Bundesinstitut fuer Berufsbildung, Fehrbelliner Platz 3, D-1000 Berlin 31.
further training; foreign worker; occupational integration; social integration; language; socio-cultural activities
formation complémentaire; travailleur étranger; intégration professionnelle; intégration sociale; langage; activités socioculturelles
PROJECT DESCRIPTION

Inhalt: Als allgemeines Forschungsziel ist die Verbesserung von Weiterbildungsmassnahmen fuer Aussiedler vor allen Dingen durch eine besondere Beruecksichtigung fachuebergreifender Kompetenzen in der Weiterbildung und durch eine Abstimmung unterschiedlicher Massnahmen und Inhalte im Bereich der soziokulturellen, sprachlichen und beruflichen Bildung anzufuehren. Folgende Forschungshypothesen werden zugrundegelegt: (a) Die verschiedenen Aussiedlergruppen weisen aufgrund andersartiger Sozialisationsverlaeufe in den einzelnen Herkunftslaendern Differenzierungen in ihrer Qualifikationsstrukturen und in ihren Verhaltensmuster auf, was noch nicht hinreichend in den Massnahmen Beruecksichtigung gefunden hat. (b) Soziokulturelle, sprachliche und berufliche Eingliederungsveranstaltungen werden in der Praxis oft noch ohne Bezug zueinander durchgefuehrt. (c) Fachuebergreifende Kompetenzen sind u.a. neben der Sprachkompetenz wesentliche Voraussetzungen fuer eine rasche berufliche Eingliederung von Aussiedlern in die hiesige Lebens- und Arbeitswelt, die erfahrungsgemaess viele Aussiedler nicht vorweisen. Als Arbeitsergebnis sollen Empfehlungen und Handreichungen unter den genannten Gesichtspunkten zur praktischen Ausgestaltung von Weiterbildung fuer die Bildungseinrichtungen und mit Aussiedlern befassten Institutionen vorgelegt werden.

11837 Weiterbildung von un- und angelernten Arbeitnehmern in kleinen und mittleren Betrieben der Staedte Wuppertal, Remscheid und Solingen. (Further training for unskilled and semi-skilled workers in small and medium-sized companies in Wuppertal, Remscheid and Solingen.)
DEU 1993
Research Date(s): 1991-1994
Witzgall, E.
Inst: AIQ Dortmund e.V., Arbeit Innovation Qualifikation, Bornstr. 50, D-4600 Dortmund 1.
Fin: Bundesinstitut fuer Berufsbildung; Stadt Wuppertal Amt fuer Wirtschafts- und Verkehrsfoerderung; Stadt Remscheid; Stadt Solingen Amt fuer Stadtentwicklung und Wirtschaftsfoerderung.
further training; North Rhine-Westphalia; vocational education; in-service training; unskilled worker; small and medium entreprise
formation complémentaire; Rhénanie du Nord-Westphalie; enseignement professionnel; formation en cours d'emploi; travailleur non-qualifié; petite ou moyenne entreprise
PROJECT DESCRIPTION

Inhalt: Wissenschaftliche Begleitung des Modellversuchs im ausserschulischen Bereich der Berufsbildung. Evaluation, Unterstuetzung und Erprobung beim Aufbau eines regionalen Weiterbildungssystems. Konzipierung und Erprobung von Qualifizierungsmassnahmen am Arbeitsplatz.

Geographischer Raum: Wuppertal, Remscheid, Solingen.

Vorgehensweise: Literaturauswertung; Leitfadeninterviews in interessierten Betrieben und Institutionen; Analyse qualifizierungsrelevanter Taetigkeiten; Teilnehmende Beobachtung von Qualifizierungsmassnahmen. Untersuchungsdesign: Fallstudie.

Datengewinnung: Primaererhebung: Feldarbeit von Mitarbeitern des Projektes durchgefuehrt.

11838 Wissenschaftliche Begleitung des Modellversuchs "Faecheruebergreifender Unterricht in der Berufsschule". (Evaluation research for the pilot project "Cross-curricular teaching at vocational schools".)
DEU 1993
Research Date(s): 1991-1995
Schelten, A.
Inst: Technische Universitaet Muenchen, Fak. fuer Wirtschafts- und Sozialwissenschaften, Institut fuer Psychologie und Erziehungswissenschaften, LS Paedagogik, Lothstrasse 17, D-8000 Muenchen 2.
Fin: Bund-Laender-Kommission fuer Bildungsplanung und Forschungsfoerderung.
vocational education; teaching method; qualification; electrical engineering; integrated curriculum
enseignement professionnel; méthode pédagogique; qualification; électrotechnique; programme d'études intégré
PROJECT DESCRIPTION

Inhalt: Welche Methoden/Verfahren sind besonders geeignet, Schluesselqualifikationen zu vermitteln? Die Untersuchungen konzentrieren sich auf die Berufsfelder Metall- und Elektrotechnik.

Geographischer Raum: Bayern.

Vorgehensweise: Auf der Grundlage der Handlungsregulation werden Verlaufsuntersuchungen zur Evaluation faecheruebergreifenden Unterrichts durchgefuehrt. Untersuchungsdesign: Evaluationsstudie.

Datengewinnung: Teilnehmende Beobachtung (2 Unterrichtsversuche mit ca. 50 Unterrichtsstunden an 2 beruflichen Schulen je Versuchsjahr; Auswahlverfahren: Quota). Aktenanalyse (dito). Inhaltsanalyse (dito). Primaererhebung: Feldarbeit von Mitarbeitern des Projektes durchgefuehrt.

Publ: Schelten, Andreas. *Einfuehrung in die Berufspaedagogik.* Stuttgart: Steiner 1991.
Schelten, Andreas. Faecheruebergreifender Unterricht in der Berufsschule. In: *Verband der Lehrer an beruflichen Schulen - VBB aktuell*, 1, 1991.

11839 Wissenschaftliche Begleitung zum Modellversuch "Bausteine zur ueberfachlichen Qualifizierung von Ausbildern und Auszubildenden in der chemischen Industrie mit den Schwerpunkten Oekologie und soziales Lernen". (Evaluation research for the pilot project "Materials for the cross-disciplinary training of educators and learners in the chemical industry, with a special focus on ecology and social learning".)
DEU 1993
Research Date(s): 1989-1992
Marggraf, C.; Felfe, J.; Neumann, U.
Sup: Lipemann, D.
Inst: Freie Universitaet Berlin, FB Erziehungs- und Unterrichtswissenschaften, Institut fuer Psychologie WE 07, Habelschwerdter Allee 45, D-1000 Berlin 33.
Fin: Bundesministerium fuer Bildung und Wissenschaft.
vocational training; further training; training of trainers; chemistry; industry; social learning; ecology
formation professionnelle; formation complémentaire; formation des formateurs; chimie; industrie; apprentissage social; écologie
PROJECT DESCRIPTION

Inhalt: Die Ziele der Evaluation ergeben sich aus den fuer den Modellversuch konzipierten Zielen: (1) Erwerb ueberfachlicher und berufsuebergreifender Qualifikationen bei Auszubildenden und Ausbildern. (2) Weiterbildung der haupt- und nebenamtlichen Ausbilder ("Training of Trainers") bezueglich methodischer, didaktischer und sozialer Kompetenzen. (3) Verstaerkte Integration zwischen zentraler und dezentraler Ausbildung unter Beruecksichtigung fachlicher als auch ueberfachlicher Qualifikationen. (4) Einsatz neuer Lehr- und Lernformen unter Beruecksichtigung organisationaler und individueller Rahmenbedingungen.

Datengewinnung: Standardisiertes Interview (Stichprobe: 60; Ausbilder). Expertengespraech (Stichprobe: ca. 10; Ausbildungsleiter). Befragung (Stichprobe: ca. 2000; Auszubildende, alle aus der chemischen Industrie).

11840 Wissenschaftliche Begleituntersuchung des Modellversuches "Entwicklung und Erprobung ganzheitlicher Lernansaetze in der kaufmaennischen Berufsausbildung am Beispiel des Ausbildungsberufs 'Versicherungskaufmann/ -frau'". (Evaluation research for the pilot project "Development and testing of holistic learning concepts in further commercial training, with particular reference to the occupation of insurance clerk".)
DEU 1993
Research Date(s): 1991-1995
Theis, C.
Inst: Universitaet Saarbruecken, FB 06 Sozial- und Umweltwissenschaften, Fachrichtung Erziehungswissenschaft, Stadtwald Bau 8, D-6600 Saarbruecken.
Fin: Bund-Laender-Kommission fuer Bildungsplanung und Forschungsfoerderung.
commercial training; vocational training; insurance; teaching method; curriculum
formation commerciale; formation professionnelle; assurances; méthode pédagogique; programme d'études
PROJECT DESCRIPTION

Inhalt: (1) Modellversuch: a) Ermittlung von lernpsychologischen Kriterien fuer einen Berufsschulunterricht; b) Erarbeitung von Merkmalen zur Gestaltung von Lehrplaenen; c) Bestimmung von unterrichtsmethodischen Ansaetzen; d) organisatorische Umgestaltungen; e) Entwicklung neuer Formen der Zusammenarbeit von Schule und Praxis; f) Ueberpruefung von Leistungsmessung und Leistungsbewertung; g) Auswirkungen auf die Lehrerfortbildung. (2) Wissenschaftliche Begleituntersuchung: Das Konzept der Themenzentrierten Interaktion und des lebendigen Lernens nach R. Cohn ist als theoretische Orientierung geeignet fuer a) die Gestaltung des Unterrichts zur fachlichen, sozialen und persoenlichkeitsbezogenen Kompetenzerweiterung der SchuelerInnen; b) die Kooperation der beteiligten Lehrer; c) die Fortbildung, begleitende Beratung und Supervision des Lehrerteams; d) die Dokumentation und kritische Analyse des Modellversuchs.

Geographischer Raum: Saarbruecken.

Untersuchter Zeitraum: 1991-1994.

Vorgehensweise: Themenzentrierte Interaktion (TZI); qualitative Sozialforschung; Evaluation; entwicklungsorientiert; Handlungsforschungselemente durch teilehmende Beobachtung; Beratung. Untersuchungsdesign: Methodenforschung; Fallstudie; Evaluationsstudie; qualitative Forschung.

Datengewinnung: Nicht-standardisiertes Interview, Gruppendiskussion, Befragung, teilnehmende Beobachtung, Beobachtung, Aktenanalyse (Stichprobe: 20; SchuelerInnen der Berufsschulklasse; Auswahlverfahren: total. Stichprobe: 4; LehrerInnen, die in dieser Klasse unterrichten; Auswahlverfahren: total). Expertengespraech, Befragung, Aktenanalyse (Stichprobe: 5; Versicherungsbetriebe im Saarland, in denen die Modellversuchsschueler arbeiten; Auswahlverfahren: total). Primaererhebung: Feldarbeit von Mitarbeitern des Projektes durchgefuehrt.

Auswertung: u.a. systematische Inhaltsanalyse.

Publ: Hoffmann, Elke; Theis, Christiane & Becker, Stefanie. Arbeitslose und ihre Kinder: Ein Thema fuer universitaere Forschung (und) mit gesellschaftlichem Handlungsbedarf. In: *Beitraege der Arbeitskammer des Saarlandes. Aufwachsen mit Arbeitslosigkeit - keine Chance fuer die Kinder?* Jg. 4, 1991, Nr. 3, S. 1-10.

11841 Work-based learning for academic credit.
GBR 1993
Research Date(s): 1990-1994
Alston, P.; Carhart, J.; Robertson, D.; Pegg, R.; Major, D.; Jackson, S.; Lunt, P.
Inst: Chester College of Higher Education, Cheyney Road, Chester CH1 4BJ, United Kingdom.
Fin: Learning from Experience Trust.
work experience; university industry relationship; credits; experiential learning; higher education
expérience du travail; relation université-entreprise; unités capitalisables; apprentissage par la pratique; enseignement supérieur
PROJECT DESCRIPTION

The aim of the project is to work in collaboration with three higher education institutions (Chester College of Higher Education, Liverpool Polytechnic and Liverpool University), to develop the use of work placements as academic components of first degree programmes as an option for students not on designated sandwich courses. The project will: (1) provide them with experience of the world of work, opportunities for taking initiatives and developing their independence; (2) provide them with the opportunity of gaining academic credit towards their degree from learning derived from experience in an employer site; (3) provide additional examples of ways to extend the range of mainstream curricula with higher education to meet the requirements of employment; and (4) to enhance partnerships between higher education and employers.

11842 A working arrangement: student work experience placements.
GBR 1993
Research Date(s): 1990-1991
Cowley, V.
Sup: Lewis, P.
Inst: Cheltenham & Gloucester College of Higher Education, Faculty of Business and Finance Management, Oxstalls Campus, Oxstalls Lane, Gloucester GL2 9HW, United Kingdom.
work experience; student; practice period; employer; attitude
expérience du travail; étudiant; stage pratique; employeur; attitude
PROJECT DESCRIPTION

This is an investigation into student work experience placements. Employers are being asked what they get out of work experience arrangements; who, in their view, benefits most from them; and how far their expectations of students are realised. They are also being invited to describe how they plan in advance for work placements, and how they believe colleges can best assist them in this task and in making the arrangements work well for all parties.

11843 The workings of multidisciplinary teams in special education.
GBR 1993
Research Date(s): 1991-1995
Lacey, P.
Sup: Upton, G.
Inst: Birmingham University, School of Education, Edgbaston, Birmingham B15 2TT, United Kingdom.
teaching method; integrated curriculum; special education; team teaching
méthode pédagogique; programme d'études intégré; enseignement spécial; enseignement en équipe
PROJECT DESCRIPTION

This is an investigation into the workings of multidisciplinary teams in special education. The emphasis will be on how they function, the amount of collaboration possible, the way in which the curriculum is influenced by such a team and the training necessary for effective cross-discipline work. The main aims for the research are: (1) to investigate the workings of multidisciplinary teams in the field of special education, and (2) to draw together examples of good practice for dissemination through courses and written work.

Methods of research will include observation and interview of team members and pupils in schools and local education authorities. Questionnaires will also be used but the main emphasis will be on case studies and accounts. As the 1988 Education Reform Act is likely to have a considerable effect upon the financing of specialist professionals in special education, there will be due emphasis on the changes monitored over the four years given to this research.

11844 Yabancı dil öğretiminde programlı öğretim uygulaması. (The effectiveness of programmed instruction in foreign language teaching.)
TUR 1994
Research Date(s): 1987-1988
Yaşar, Şefik.
Sup: Çilenti, Kamuran.
Inst: Anadolu Üniversitesi, Sosyal Bilimler Enstitüsü (University of Anatolia, Institute of Social Sciences), Eğitim Fakültesi, Eskişehir, Turkey.
programmed learning; language teaching; English language
enseignement programmé; enseignement des langues; langue anglaise
PROJECT DESCRIPTION

Aim: This research was carried out to test the effectiveness of the programmed instruction method in comparison with conventional instruction in English as a foreign language in Anadolu secondary schools.

Design: A pretest-posttest design was used. The sample consisted of 56 subjects matched for all the variables except the independent one (instruction method), who were equally divided into an experimental group and a control group. The experimental group studied English by the programmed instruction method, whereas the control group studied the same texts with the help of the teacher. Both groups were given a pretest before the intervention and a posttest afterwards. The study was conducted in the 1987-1988 school year.

Results: Pupils in the programmed instruction course were significantly more successful in vocabulary acquisition than those in the conventionally taught course. There was no significant difference between the two groups in the acquisition of grammar or in general language success in English as a foreign language.

11845 Young people's experience of National Certificate Modules.
GBR 1993
Research Date(s): 1988-1991
Croxford, L.; Howieson, C.
Sup: McPherson, A.
Inst: Edinburgh University, Centre for Educational Sociology, 7 Buccleuch Place, Edinburgh EH8 9JT, United Kingdom.
Fin: Scottish Education Department.
post-compulsory education; curriculum research; modular training; youth attitude; educational provision
enseignement postobligatoire; recherche sur les programmes d'études; formation modulaire; attitude de la jeunesse; scolarisation
PROJECT DESCRIPTION

The project will analyse data from the Scottish Young People's Surveys (1985-1989) to ascertain the impact and development of the 16+ programme among young people. The analyses will cover five broad areas: National Certificate Modules in context, whether educational, social, occupational or geographical; trends between the first and third Action Plan year groups; progression into, within and out of the modular system; attitudes to the National Certificate; and modules within schools.

Publ: A full list of publications is available from the research institute.

11846 Žiakova interpretácia sveta ako východisko pre výchovu a vzdelávanie. (Pupils' interpretations of the world as a starting point for education and training.)
CSK 1993
Research Date(s): 1991-1993
Gavora, Peter; Blašková, Silvia; Jelínková, Dagmar; Semjanová, Ivana; Sawicki, Silvester.
Sup: Holkovič, Lubomír.
Inst: Ústav experimentálnej pedagogiky SAV (Institute of Experimental Pedagogy, Slovak Academy of Sciences), 851 01 Bratislava, Mánesovo nám. 1, Czech and Slovak Federal Republic.
Slovenská akadémia vied (Slovak Academy of Sciences), 811 04 Bratislava, Štefánikova ul. 49, Czech and Slovak Federal Republic
Fin: Government of the Slovak Republic.
teaching method; primary education; pupil; perception; personality development
méthode pédagogique; enseignement primaire; élève; perception; développement de la personnalité
PROJECT DESCRIPTION

Background: Research has shown that children's views, or interpretations, of the world can serve as a basis for humanizing the teaching process and for the development of pupils as individuals. On the other hand, it has been found that teaching at primary schools in the Czech and

Slovak Republic has a manipulative character and lacks humanistic elements.

Methods: The basic possibilities of using pupils' interpretations of the world in teaching and training have been set down. An analysis was made of qualitative research methods and their use for the study. Elements of qualitative research were used for the first time in educational research in Slovakia.

Preliminary results: With the help of qualitative research methods, data have been obtained on how primary school pupils interpret certain phenomena in the world around them. Possibilities for the development and cultivation of children's interpretation of these phenomena in an educational setting have been explored. A "dramatic game" has been developed and used as the effective device for the cultivation of children's interpretations.

Publ: Gavora, P. Naivné teórie diet'at'a a ich pedagogické využitie. In: Pedagogika, XLI 1992, č.1, pp. 95-102.

11847 Zum Problem der Aneignung didaktischen Theoriewissens in der Lehrerausbildung - aufgezeigt an biologiedidaktischen Begriffen. (On the problem of acquiring theoretical didactic knowledge in teacher training, with particular reference to didactic biological concepts.)
DEU 1993
Research Date(s): 1991-1995
Mende, P.
Sup: Dauzenroth, E.; Berck, K.
Inst: Universitaet Giessen, FB 15 Biologie, Institut fuer Biologiedidaktik, Karl-Gloeckner-Strasse 21 C, D-6300 Giessen; Universitaet Giessen, FB 04 Erziehungswissenschaften, Institut fuer Bildungsforschung und Paedagogik des Auslands, Karl-Gloeckner-Strasse 21 B, D-6300 Giessen.
teacher education; didactics; biology; theory; terminology
formation des enseignants; didactique; biologie; théorie; terminologie
PROJECT DESCRIPTION
Inhalt: Ansatzpunkt fuer die Ueberlegungen ist der Anspruch der Wissenschaftlichkeit der Biologiedidaktik. Wenn auch noch kein geschlossenes Theoriekonzept - etwa gar empirisch abgesichert - in der noch jungen Wissenschaft entwickelt ist, so hat sie doch fuer ihre Theorieaussagen eine spezifische Begrifflichkeit hervorgebracht. Dieses Begriffsrepertoire ist offenbar Anlass fuer Probleme beim Aneignen eines auch fuer die spaetere Berufspraxis notwendigen Theoriewissens. Dementsprechend sind als erster Untersuchungsschritt Begriffsmengenanalysen bei Lehrbuechern fuer Biologiedidaktik vorgesehen. Durch vergleichende Betrachtungen soll versucht werden, die vermutete Begriffsvielfalt zu entwirren und ggfs. im Sinne eines Grundbegriffsrepertoires zu reduzieren. Soll hier durch vergleichende Analyse abgeleitet werden, ueber welches Begriffswissen Lehramtsstudenten am Ende ihrer Ausbildung verfuegen sollen, so ist in einem zweiten - diesmal empirischen - Untersuchungsschritt daran gedacht, Studenten hoeherer Semester auf ihr Begriffswissen hin zu befragen. Untersuchungen auf diesem Sektor didaktischer Forschung liegen unseres Wissens bisher nicht vor. In einem ggfs. dritten Teilabschnitt der vorgesehenen Arbeit waere schliesslich empirisch zu ueberpruefen und abzusichern, wieweit an ausgewaehlten Begriffsdefinitionen deutlich wird, welche Rolle der Verstaendlichkeit didaktischer Texte bei der Aneignung von Theorie zukommt.
Geographischer Raum: Bundesrepublik Deutschland.
Untersuchter Zeitraum: 1970-1992.
Vorgehensweise: Didaktisches Theoriewissen manifestiert sich u.a. im Gebrauch und im Verstaendnis eines adaequaten didaktischen Begriffsrepertoires. Ueber empirische Erhebungen soll herausgefunden werden, wieweit ein solches am Ende des Lehramtsstudiums ausgepraegt ist und inwieweit die didaktische Kompendienliteratur einen Betrag dazu zu leisten vermag. Untersuchungsdesign: Evaluationsstudie.
Datengewinnung: Befragung (Lehramtsstudenten in Examenssemestern; Auswahlverfahren: Quota). Aktenanalyse (Kompendienliteratur zur Biologiedidaktik, weitere Datensaetze; Auswahlverfahren: total). Primaererhebung: Feldarbeit von Mitarbeitern des Projektes durchgefuehrt; Datenerstellung auf der Basis von bereits vorliegenden Materialien wie Texten, Akten, Statistiken.
Auswertung: Quantitative Analyse, ggfs. Varianzanalyse.

11848 Zur Psychologie des Literaturunterrichts (von der Psychologie zur Dramaturgie des Literaturunterrichts). (On the psychology of teaching literature (from the psychology of teaching literature to its dramaturgy).)
DEU 1993
Research Date(s): 1989-1993
Barz, A.
Sup: Brekle, W.
Inst: Paedagogische Hochschule Leipzig, FB Deutsche Sprache und Literatur, WB Fachdidaktik, Methodiken des Deutschunterrichts, Karl-Heine-Str. 22b, O-7031 Leipzig.
teaching; literature; media education; German language
enseignement; littérature; éducation aux médias; langue allemande

PROJECT DESCRIPTION
No abstract supplied.

Publ: Barz, Andre. Die Bedeutung kunst- und rezeptionspsychologischer Erkenntnisse fuer die literaturaesthetische Bildung und Erziehung unter besonderer Beruecksichtigung der kuenstlerisch-produktiven (Schueler-) Taetigkeit: ein theoretischer Ansatz. In: *5. Seminar der Nachwuchswissenschaftler des Interdisziplinaeren Zentrums Unterrichtsforschung der Paed. Hochschule Leipzig*. Leipzig 1990, S. 24-26.
Barz, Andre & Kohn, Werner. Kommunikationskultur und Medienerziehung - Anmerkungen zu einem Konzept literatur- und medienaesthetischer Bildung (Teil 1). In: *Wissenschaftliche Zeitschrift der Paedagogischen Hochschule Leipzig*, 1991, I, S. 130-147.
Barz, Andre & Kohn, Werner. Kuenstlerisch-produktive Taetigkeiten und Medienpaedagogik - ein Antagonismus?. In: *Jugendliche Medienerziehung in Leipzig*. Leipzig 1991, S. 92-102.
Barz, Andre & Kohn, Werner. Video - gehasst und geliebt. In: *Hortheute*. Berlin, 2, 1991, 4, S. 23-24.
Barz, Andre. Medien und Spiel. In: *Hortheute*. Berlin, 2, 1991, 4, S. 9-10.

11849 Zur Situation der Fort- und Weiterbildung in der Altenarbeit: Bestandsaufnahme, Evaluierung und Entwicklung von Qualitaetsstandards. (On the situation of further and advanced training in geriatric care: current situation, evaluation and development of quality standards.)
DEU 1993
Research Date(s): 1991-1993
Koch, A.
Sup: Kuehnert, S.
Inst: Forschungsgesellschaft fuer Gerontologie e.V., Schwanenwall 31-35, D-4600 Dortmund 1.
Fin: Kuratorium Deutsche Altershilfe e.V.
vocational training; elderly person; social work; personnel; educational need; care; further training
formation professionnelle; personne âgée; travail social; personnel; besoin d'éducation; soin; formation complémentaire
PROJECT DESCRIPTION
Inhalt: Informationsbasis ueber den Bestand an Fort- und Weiterbildungsangebot fuer Mitarbeiter in der Altenarbeit; Analyse der derzeitigen Fort- und Weiterbildungspraxis und ihrer konzeptionellen Grundlagen; Entwicklung von Beurteilungskriterien zum Fortbildungsbedarf und der Fortbildungsqualitaet.
Geographischer Raum: Bundesrepublik Deutschland.
Untersuchter Zeitraum: 1990-1991.

Fortbildung fuer Polizeidienststellen im Bereich Gewalt gegen Frauen (Further education for police personnel on the subject of violence against women) .... see no. 13732

The implementation of local education authority curriculum policies in two metropolitan authorities .... see no. 13735

02 LEARNING – ACQUISITION DE CONNAISSANCES – LERNEN

11850 Access to the National Curriculum for pupils with severe and complex learning difficulties.
GBR 1993
Research Date(s): 1989
Mittler, P.
Inst: Manchester University, School of Education, Centre for Educational Guidance and Special Needs, Oxford Road, Manchester M13 9PL, United Kingdom.
Fin: Manchester Education Committee.
learning difficulty; special education; common core curriculum
difficulté de l'apprentissage; enseignement spécial; tronc commun
PROJECT DESCRIPTION
Starting with the 'broad, balanced and relevant' curriculum of the Education Reform Act 1988, in-depth studies have been carried out with the aim of demonstrating ways in which programmes of study and cross-curricular elements can be integrated with core and foundation subjects to meet the individual needs of children with severe and complex learning difficulties. Statements of attainment for the core subjects have been broken down for Key Stage 1 of the National Curriculum.
Publ: Fagg, S.; Aherne, P.; Skelton, S. & Thorburn, A. *Entitlement for all in practice: towards a broad, balanced and relevant curriculum for pupils with severe and complex learning difficulties in the 1990s.* London: Fulton, 1990.
Fagg, S. & Skelton, S. *Science for all.* London: Fulton, 1990.
Aherne, P. & Thorburn, A. *Mathematics for all: an interactive approach within level 1.* London: Fulton, 1990.
Aherne, P. & Thorburn, A. *Communication for all: a cross-curricular skill involving interactions between speaker and listener.* London: Fulton, 1990.
Mount, H. & Ackerman, D. *Technology for all.* London: Fulton, 1991.

11851 Anschaulich-praktisches Lernen in der Lernortverbindung Museum - Betrieb - Schule. (Visual and practical learning in the combined educational setting of museums - companies - schools.)
DEU 1993
Research Date(s): 1991-1994
Ziefuss, H.; Oberhusen, R.; Hollstein, B.; Ziefuss, H.
Inst: Universitaet Hamburg FB 06 Erziehungswissenschaft, Von-Melle-Park 8, D-2000 Hamburg 13.
learning; enterprise; school; museum; discovery learning; model
acquisition de connaissances; entreprise; école; musée; apprentissage par la découverte; modèle
PROJECT DESCRIPTION
Inhalt: Die zentrale Fragestellung des Projektes lautet, ob und inwieweit sich die Schule ausserschulischen Lernorten oeffnen soll und unter welchen Bedingungen diese Oeffnung zu einer neuen Qualitaet des Lernens fuehren kann, die wir mit den Begriffen "anschaulich-praktisch" und "historisch-genetisch" beschreiben wollen. Dabei gehen wir davon aus, dass jeder Lernort ueber eine fuer ihn typische Lernumgebung verfuegt, die das Lernen von Zusammenhaengen und Sinngehalten lernortspezifisch erleichtert bzw. erschwert, und dass deshalb "Grenzoeffnungen" zwischen den Lernorten erforderlich sind. Das Forschungsvorhaben moechte dazu beitragen, Modelle sinnvoller Grenzoeffnungen zu erkunden und die lernorttypischen Lernverhaltensweisen fuer allgemeines Lernen zusammenzufuehren.
Vorgehensweise: Entwickelnd; empirisch; handlungsorientierte Lernforschung.
Datengewinnung: Standardisiertes Interview (Stichprobe: 20; LehrerInnen und Museumsfachleute). Befragung (ca. 100; Museen; Auswahlverfahren: bewusst. Stichprobe: ca. 200; LehrerInnen; Auswahlverfahren: Zufall). Beobachtung (Stichprobe: ca. 100; Museen; Auswahlverfahren: bewusst. Stichprobe: ca. 200; LehrerInnen; Auswahlverfahren: Zufall).

11852 Antimetopisi pedion me mathisiakes diskolies apo tous daskalous tis dimotikis ekpethefsis sta scholia tis polis tis Lefkosias. (Teachers' approaches to pupils' learning difficulties in primary schools in Nicosia.)
CYP 1993
Research Date(s): 1991
Archontaki, Manolis; Kyriakou, Tsambikas.
Inst: Pedagogiko Instituto (Pedagogical Institute), P.O. Box 512, Nicosia, Cyprus.
learning difficulty; reading difficulty; teaching method; special school teacher; teacher behaviour
difficulté de l'apprentissage; difficulté de lecture; méthode pédagogique; éducateur spécialisé; comportement de l'enseignant
PROJECT DESCRIPTION
Background and aims: The problem of children with learning difficulties concerns teachers in their everyday teaching practice. The aim of this research study was to investigate and analyse how primary school teachers deal with children with learning difficulties in the classroom. More specifically, the research had the following aims: (1) to determine the number of primary school children in Nicosia who, according to their teachers, have learning difficulties in reading, understanding, writing, spelling and arithmetic; (2) to list and examine the methods teachers use to evaluate learning difficulties; (3) to list and examine the specific actions teachers undertake in dealing with children with learning difficulties; (4) to investigate how teachers evaluate their own teaching methods and (5) to list teachers' suggestions on how to cope with children with learning difficulties in Cyprus.
Methods: A questionnaire was distributed among the randomly selected sample. In all, 238 questionnaires were distributed to teachers in 38 primary schools in Nicosia; 171 questionnaires were returned (response rate: 71.8%).
Results: Statistical analysis showed that only 15 out of the 171 respondents (8.9%) had attended seminars relevant to special needs and only four had attended seminars on learning difficulties. According to the teachers' responses, 11.24% of primary school pupils have learning difficulties: 4.7% have difficulties in reading, 7.7% in understanding, 5.2% in writing, 9.6% in spelling and 8.9% in arithmetic. Some pupils have difficulties in more than one subject. Sixteen teachers said that a special programme for helping children with difficulties was being applied in their classroom; 32 teachers (19%) stated that they themselves were using a special programme. Of the latter group, only four (12.9%) had attended special seminars on learning difficulties.
The teachers who had the opportunity to observe a special programme being applied in their classroom made significantly different statements than the other teachers. Their suggestions included: placing children with learning difficulties in mixed-ability groups, preparing specific work for these children, using special instructional materials, changing the pupils' class if necessary.
It was also found that most teachers who are having to deal with children with learning difficulties ask help from their headmasters, not from specialists in this field. The main factors influencing the ways in which teachers deal with these children are the teacher's gender and the number of children with learning difficulties in the classroom. Teachers expressed a need for more in-service training on the subject of learning difficulties, more help from specialists and more information about learning difficulties for parents. To an open-ended question inviting suggestions from teachers, most respondents replied that these children should be encouraged and helped in the classroom. The presence of a specialist teacher for children with learning difficulties was considered essential.

11853 An approach to music teaching with people with learning difficulties which emphasises collaborative teaching.
GBR 1993
Research Date(s): 1988-1992
Megee, M.
Sup: Evans, D.; Smith, M.
Inst: South Devon College of Arts and Technology, Newton Road, Torquay TQ2 5BY, United Kingdom; Exeter University, School of Education, St Luke's, Heavitree Road, Exeter EX1 2LU, United Kingdom.
learning difficulty; music education; special education; teaching method; self-esteem
difficulté de l'apprentissage; éducation musicale; enseignement spécial; méthode pédagogique; estime de soi
PROJECT DESCRIPTION
The study demonstrates positive changes in the self-esteem of students with severe and moderate learning difficulties, attending a weekly group for composing and performing music. The experimental groups consisted of a total of 12 students, aged 16-19 against a control group of six students. Tests used were Piers-Harris; Gurney's Revised Self-Esteem Inventory and Intellectual Achievement Rating Scale. All the students attend full-time at a local authority further education college.

11854 Cognitive impairments in children with arithmetical learning disabilities.
GBR 1993
Research Date(s): 1990-1993
Walker, P.; Hitch, G.; Lewis, C.
Inst: University of Central Lancashire, Corporation Street, Preston PR1 2TQ, United Kingdom; Manchester University, Department of Psychology, Oxford Road, Manchester M13 9PL, United Kingdom.
Fin: Medical Research Council.
learning difficulty; arithmetic; cognitive development
difficulté de l'apprentissage; arithmétique; développement cognitif
PROJECT DESCRIPTION

38

This project aims to discover why some children of normal intelligence have great difficulty with elementary arithmetic. In some cases arithmetical difficulties are associated with reading problems, in others they occur in isolation. The project will identify children with arithmetical learning disability and will investigate cognitive impairments in different subgroups using tasks designed to explore working memory, the part of the cognitive system responsible for storing and manipulating temporary information.

The hypothesis is that children with specific arithmetical difficulties have impaired working memory for visuo-spatial information, whereas children with learning problems in both arithmetic and reading have impaired working memory for phonological information. These deficits will be analysed in relation to the way working memory normally develops in order to distinguish developmental lag from other kinds of abnormality. The researchers will test the prediction that different kinds of impairment to working memory are related to the kinds of difficulty children experience in simple arithmetic tasks.

The results will contribute to diagnosis and assessment of arithmetical learning disabilities, and to the planning of more effective remediation.

11855   Collaborative learning and equal opportunities.
GBR   1993
Research Date(s): 1991-
Matthews, B.; Thumpston, G.
Inst: London University, Goldsmiths' College, Faculty of Education, Lewisham Way, New Cross, London SE14 6NW, United Kingdom.
group work; group learning; interaction; intergroup relations; discussion; equal opportunity
travail par équipe; pédagogie de groupe; interaction; relations intergroupes; discussion; égalité de chances
PROJECT DESCRIPTION

There has been an increasing emphasis on collaborative learning in all aspects of education. Within the National Curriculum, evaluation of pupils discussing and taking part in group work is now statutory. In particular, recent research projects have shown how important the discussion of ideas is to children learning about science and other subjects. The action research is to find ways of: studying interactions; finding strategies that will enable pupils to be aware of their interactions; finding strategies that will enable pupils to change the ways they discuss; encouraging greater learning of all pupils; encouraging girls and boys to see each other as full people, rather than to relate to each other through stereotypes; encouraging pupils from all ethnic backgrounds to see each other as full people, rather than to relate to each other through stereotypes. The project is focused on all curriculum areas in primary and secondary schools, but will also apply to adults. As it is an action research project set in the classroom, it is possible that local education authorities will be interested.

11856   Denk- en leeraktiviteiten demonstreren in (K)MBO. (Demonstrating thinking and learning activities in vocational secondary schools.)
NLD   1994
Research Date(s): 1992-1998
Sanden, J.M.M. van der; Brussel, F. van; Vermunt, J.; Teurlings, Ch.
Inst: Vakgroep Psychologie, Sectie Onderwijs- en Opleidingspsychologie (Department of Psychology), P.O. Box 92153, 5000 LE Tilburg, Netherlands.
Katholieke Universiteit Brabant (Catholic University of Brabant), P.O. Box 92153, 5000 LE Tilburg, Netherlands
Fin: SVO het Instituut voor Onderzoek van het Onderwijs.
learning strategy; teaching method; vocational training; thinking; learning
stratégie d'apprentissage; méthode pédagogique; formation professionnelle; pensée; acquisition de connaissances
PROJECT DESCRIPTION

Background: It is characteristic of many educational situations that the thinking and learning activities of teachers and pupils remain largely implicit. It is not unlikely that this seriously impedes the development of adequate mental representations of the subject matter, of relevant thinking and learning activities, and of the role these activities can play in the subject matter area concerned. There is a lack of empirical evidence on the potential effect of demonstrating thinking and learning activities at the secondary vocational level (MBO).

Aim: (1) To determine the effect of demonstrating and making explicit relevant thinking and learning activities in vocational training on the students' knowledge of these activities, on the usage of this knowledge and on achievement levels; (2) to examine the effect of demonstrating thinking and learning activities in instructional programmes designed according to the Leittext method and elaboration theory.

Design: Five empirical studies will be conducted in secondary vocational schools, focusing on commercial and technical courses. An adjusted version of the Learning Styles Inventory will be examined for validity and reliability. It will be attempted to establish which subject-specific activities (including acquisition, monitoring, evaluation) are essential in thinking, learning and working in the courses under study, i.e. word processing (a part of commercial training) and programming computer-controlled metal work machines (as part of technical training). Subsequently, the thinking

and learning activities that are not or little practised by students will be made explicit and demonstrated.

11857   Developmental analysis of dyslexia in childhood.
GBR   1993
Research Date(s): 1989-1994
Snowling, M.; Goulandris, N.
Inst: London University, University College London, Department of Psychology, Gower Street, London WC1E 6BT, United Kingdom; National Hospitals' College of Speech Sciences, Chandler House, 2 Wakefield Street, London WC1N 1PG, United Kingdom.
Fin: Medical Research Council.
dyslexia; reading difficulty; learning difficulty
dyslexie; difficulté de lecture; difficulté de l'apprentissage
PROJECT DESCRIPTION

The development of 24 dyslexic children (reading at the 6, 7 and 8 year levels) is being closely monitored, and compared with a control gorup of average readers. Experimental investigations have included qualitative comparisons of their literacy skills and phonological processing abilities. The consistency of their reading has been investigated to explore the status of the lexical reading system of the dyslexic and normal readers.

Preliminary evidence suggests that the dyslexics are less consistent in their reading behaviour even when processing familiar words.

Publ: Snowling, M.; Hulme, C. & Goulandris, N. Phonological coding in deficits in dyslexia. In: Hales, G. (ed.). *Meeting points in dyslexia. Proceedings of the First International Conference of the British Dyslexia Association*. Reading: British Dyslexia Association, 1990, pp. 93-97.

11858   Dialogvideo in der Softwareschulung - Ein Lernen im Medienverbund. (Dialogue video for software training: multimedia learning.)
DEU   1993
Research Date(s): 1989-1992
Jung, M.
Sup: Fricke, R.
Inst: Technische Universitaet Braunschweig, FB 08 Philosophie und Sozialwissenschaften, Seminar fuer Paedagogik, Wendenring 1, D-3300 Braunschweig.
Fin: Institution; Deutsche Bundespost Posttechnisches Zentralamt Zentralstelle fuer Arbeitssicherheit u. Ergonomie.
multimedia system; interactive video; learning; success; adult education
système multimédia; vidéo interactive; acquisition de connaissances; réussite; éducation des adultes
PROJECT DESCRIPTION

Inhalt: (1) Hat Video einen Einfluss auf den Lernerfolg? (2) Wie laesst sich die Aktivitaet der Lerner foerdern? Die Fragestellungen beziehen sich auf das Lernen Erwachsener in Hinblick auf den Lernerfolg. Sie sind von grosser praktischer Bedeutung, da Videoproduktionen sehr kostenintensiv sind.

Vorgehensweise: Selbstgesteuertes Lernen; Lerner sind abhaengig von Lernumwelt; Gestaltung von Medien (z. B. Lernprogramme). Untersuchungsdesign: Evaluationsstudie.

Datengewinnung: Experiment (Stichprobe: 80; Erwachsene im Angestelltenverhaeltnis; Auswahlverfahren: bewusst). Sekundaeranalyse bereits vorhandener maschinenlesbarer Datensaetze; Datenerstellung auf der Basis von bereits vorliegenden Materialien wie Texten, Akten, Statistiken.
Auswertung: Varianzanalyse (3-faktoriell).

Publ: Jung, M.H. Dialogvideo in der Softwareschulung. In: "Abstracts" der 3. Tagung "Paedagogische Psychologie", vom 25.9.-27.9.91 in Koeln.

11859   Dyslexia and mathematics.
GBR   1993
Research Date(s): 1988-
Miles, T.
Inst: University College of North Wales, Department of Psychology, College Road, Bangor, Gwynedd LL57 2DG, United Kingdom.
dyslexia; learning difficulty; mathematics
dyslexie; difficulté de l'apprentissage; mathématiques
PROJECT DESCRIPTION

It is hypothesised that the mathematical difficulties of dyslexics are a consequence of the same anomaly of development which affects their literary skills. It has been shown (Pritchard et al., 1989) that 15 dyslexic boys aged 12 to 14 had fewer 'number facts' available than a suitably matched control.

Work is now in progress on the time needed by dyslexics and matched control to carry out different types of mathematical operations. Data on the mathematical performance of over 12,000 10 year-olds (Child Health and Education Study), including some dyslexics, are in the process of being analysed.

Publ: Miles, T.R. Dyslexia and mathematics. In: *Ace Reports*, No 16/1989, pp. 16-20.
Pritchard, R.A.; Miles, T.R.; Chinn, S.J. & Taggart, A.T. Dyslexia and knowledge of number facts. In: *Links*, Vol 14, No 3/1989, pp. 17-20.

Miles, T.R. & Miles, E. (eds.). *Dyslexia and Mathematics*. London: Routledge, 1991.

11860 Dyslexia research project.

GBR 1993

Research Date(s): 1990-1993

Tod, J.

Sup: Jones, L.; Abbott, P.

Inst: Harris City Technology College, The Dyslexia Centre, 9 Maberley Road, Upper Norwood, London SE19 2JH, United Kingdom; Canterbury Christ Church College, North Holmes Road, Canterbury CT1 1QU, United Kingdom.

Fin: Department for Education.

dyslexia; special education; learning difficulty

dyslexie; enseignement spécial; difficulté de l'apprentissage

PROJECT DESCRIPTION

A three year research project has been set up at the Dyslexia Centre of Harris City Technology College in Upper Norwood, South London. The research body is Harris City Technology College in conjunction with Christchurch College, Canterbury. The aim of the new centre is the development of best practice in the teaching of dyslexic students; the provision of special teacher training in this area of learning difficulty; and the undertaking of research and development in the use of technology and materials appropriate to the teaching of dyslexic students.

The aims of the project are: (1) to measure the progress over three academic years of a group of pupils entering the Harris CTC in September 1990, diagnosed as having the specific learning difficulty known as dyslexia, using a range of approaches designed to enable these pupils to participate fully and effectively in the City Technology College curriculum which includes access to the National Curriculum; (2) to devise new approaches and resource materials in order to test their value for pupils in the Harris CTC and to enable the Centre to develop resource materials for a wide use with the CTC age group (11-18); (3) to develop the use of information technology and work with dyslexic pupils in the Harris CTC and to disseminate good practice in this respect. The project runs from 1 November 1990 to 31 October 1993.

11861 Enquête sur les apprentis des cinq départements de la Région Pays de Loire.

FRA 1993

Research Date(s): 1986-

Baudelot, Christian; Creusen, Joseph; Rame, Sébastien; Tarin, Laurence.

Inst: Laboratoire d'études et de recherches sociologiques sur la classe ouvrière, Université de Nantes, UFR Institut d'histoire et de sociologie, Chemin de la Sensive-du-Tertre, BP 1025, 44036 Nantes Cedex, France.

apprenticeship; apprentice; school career; social origin

apprentissage professionnel; apprenti; cursus scolaire; origine sociale

PROJECT DESCRIPTION

Objectifs: Cette enquête menée en collaboration avec la Direction régionale de l'INSEE concerne l'ensemble des jeunes entrés en apprentissage dans l'un des centres de formation d'adultes (CFA) des cinq départements des Pays de Loire en octobre 1984 (soit environ 8000 individus).

Méthodologie: Quatre opérations sont actuellement en cours: (1) dépouillement et exploitation des données figurant sur les 8000 contrats d'apprentissage; (2) dépouillement des réponses à une enquête postale en 1988 afin de connaître la situation occupée par ces jeunes quatre ans après leur entrée en apprentissage ainsi que leurs itinéraires; (3) enquête intensive par questionnaires auprès d'un échantillon de 1000 apprentis en deuxième année de centre de formation d'adultes en 1988-1989 des cinq départements aux fins de connaître les caractéristiques sociales, professionnelles et scolaires des apprentis et de leur famille; (4) monographie des comportements des élèves et des façons dont ils vivent leur apprentissage par voie d'observations et d'entretiens dans un centre de formation d'adultes.

Publ: Baudelot, Christian; Creusen, Joseph; Bouqsim, O.; Fourage, C.; Rame, S. & Tarin, L. Apprentissage: un peu d'histoire, de géographie et de sociologie. In: *Statistique et développement*, Revue régionale de l'INSEE, février 1989, n° 81.

Apprentis dans la région des Pays de la Loire. Nantes: INSEE, avril 1990, Rapport d'enquête.

Baudelot, Christian; Creusen, Joseph; Rame, Sébastien & Tarin, Laurence. Etre apprenti en 1990. In: *Education et formations*, n° 24, novembre 1990.

11862 Erschliessung komplexer Inhalte. (Development of complex educational contents.)

DEU 1993

Research Date(s): 1990-1992

Wedekind, J.; Mangold, K.; Walser, W.

Inst: Deutsches Institut fuer Fernstudien -DIFF- an der Universitaet, Konrad-Adenauer-Str. 40-44, D-7400 Tuebingen.

learning; simulation; didactic use of computer; automatic teaching; self-instruction; model

acquisition de connaissances; simulation; usage didactique de l'ordinateur; enseignement automatisé; auto-enseignement; modèle

PROJECT DESCRIPTION

Inhalt: Durch Computersimulationen und Modellbildungssystemen sollen komplexe Inhalte (Struktur und Verhalten dynamischer Systeme, statistische Methoden) fuer das angeleitete Selbststudium erschlossen werden. Insbesondere sollen Moeglichkeiten der grafischen Repraesentation und Interaktion zur Unterstuetzung der Lernenden untersucht werden.

Vorgehensweise: Fallstudien und Evaluation des unterrichtspraktischen Einsatzes.

Publ: Klueser, J.; Walser, W. & Wedekind, J. Hierarchistisches Modellieren komplexer Systeme. In: Gorny, P. (Hrsg.). *Informatik: Wege zur Vielfalt beim Lehren und Lernen*. Berlin: Springer 1991, S. 244-250.

11863 Feedback, peer interaction and adult intervention in initial logo learning.

GBR 1993

Research Date(s): 1990-1994

Hughes, M.

Inst: Exeter University, School of Education, St Luke's, Heavitree Road, Exeter EX1 2LU, United Kingdom.

Fin: Economic and Social Research Council.

learning process; feedback; interaction; didactic use of computer; child; adult; logo

apprentissage; rétroaction; interaction; usage didactique de l'ordinateur; enfant; adulte; logo

PROJECT DESCRIPTION

The overall aim of the research is to increase our understanding of children's learning, and of the effects on learning of outside agencies such as feedback, peers and adults. The research will study children learning to control the Logo Turtle in view of the theoretical and curricular relevance of this activity. The specific research objectives are: (1) to compare children learning in four conditions (a) alone (b) with a peer (c) with an adult and (d) with an adult and a peer, looking at the effects of these conditions on task performance and on aspects of learning; (2) to examine the nature of the feedback provided by the system and to look at its effect on children's learning in the individual condition; (3) to analyse the interaction taking place within the peer and adult conditions, looking in particular at interaction concerned with planning and feedback, and to assess its effects on learning; (4) to examine the effects of age and gender on the above issues, by using children aged 4, 7 and 11, and by including same-sex and mixed-sex pairs in the peer conditions.

11864 Group work with computers.

GBR 1993

Research Date(s): 1988-1992

Hoyles, C.; Healy, S.; Pozzi, S.; Eraut, M.; Petch, R.

Inst: London University, Institute of Education, Department of Mathematics, Statistics and Computing, 20 Bedford Way, London WC1H 0AL, United Kingdom; Sussex University, Institute of Continuing & Professional Education, Sussex House, Falmer, Brighton BN1 9RH, United Kingdom.

Fin: Economic and Social Research Council.

group work; group learning; teaching method; didactic use of computer

travail par équipe; pédagogie de groupe; méthode pédagogique; usage didactique de l'ordinateur

PROJECT DESCRIPTION

Because of the scarcity of computers, pupils using them frequently work in groups. However, the potential of groupwork is rarely exploited, and collaborative learning in such groups happens more by chance than design. There are some compelling theoretical reasons for believing that groupwork has considerable potential for the enhancement of learning. Psychologists believe that for some learning goals and tasks, groupwork is likely to be more effective than individual learning.

This project seeks to provide guidance to teachers seeking to gain the maximum benefit from the use of computers. It focuses on seven questions: (1) For what types of learning goal is groupwork with computers most appropriate? (2) What is its potential contribution to the curriculum? (3) How can computer and non-computer based tasks be designed which facilitate groupwork? (4) Is it possible to identify criteria for task design, group management and their interrelationships, for effective groupwork to be established? (5) What kinds of group are best for achieving particular goals? (6) How can such groupwork best be prepared for, implemented and evaluated? (7) Is training in collaborative groupwork a significant advantage?.

Publ: Eraut, M. & Hoyles, C. Groupwork with computers, *ESRC Occasional Paper: INTER/3/88*. University of Lancaster, Department of Psychology, 1988.

Eraut, M. & Hoyles, C. Groupwork with computers. In: *Journal of Computer Assisted Learning*, Vol 5, No 1/1989, pp. 12-24.

Hoyles, C.; Healy, L. & Pozzi, S. *Groupwork with computers: final report to the ESRC*, July 1992.

Hoyles, C.; Healy, L. & Pozzi, S. Computer-based group as vehicles for learning mathematics. In: *Proceedings of the Fifteenth International Conference for the Psychology of Mathematics Education*, Vol 11/1991, pp. 9165-9172, Italy.

11865 Het verbeteren van zelfregulatievaardigheden via geïsoleerde en geïntegreerde training. (Improving self-regulation skills through isolated and integrated training.)
NLD 1994
Research Date(s): 1992-1994
Simons, P.R.J.; Kluvers, C.; Aarnoutse, C.; Vermunt, J.D.H.M.; Voeten, M.
Sup: Boekaerts, M.
Inst: Vakgroep Onderwijskunde (Department of Education), P.O. Box 9103, 6500 HD Nijmegen, Netherlands.
Katholieke Universiteit Nijmegen (Catholic University of Nijmegen), P.O. Box 9102, 6500 HC Nijmegen, Netherlands
Fin: SVO het Instituut voor Onderzoek van het Onderwijs.
independent work; transfer of learning; achievement; study method
travail indépendant; transfert pédagogique; rendement; méthode de travail
PROJECT DESCRIPTION

Background: The study is an extension of the project "Self-Regulation and Computer-Assisted Instruction". That project has so far yielded the following products: (1) a computer-controlled test procedure that tests nine self-regulatory skills related to study-reading; (2) a questionnaire on self-regulation strategies related to study-reading (IRS); (3) a questionnaire on learning and regulation styles (ILS). In consultation with other members of the committee coordinating the research it has been decided to conduct an additional longitudinal study, exploring any changes in the relationships between self-regulation, motivation and perception of the environment. The study is particularly concerned with (a) the direct effect of training on the ability to use trained skills and (b) transfer effects.

Aim: To explore the effects of training modules in which self-regulation skills can be integrated into study skills instruction and subject instruction, with a view to offering an insight into the desirability or otherwise of integrated study skills instruction.

Design: In the first year four studies will be executed in which four training modules will be evaluated. These modules will deal with: pupils' ability to choose learning goals; their ability to select learning activities related to these goals; their ability to ask for support in time; and one other subject. The research will continually focus on the effect of training in self-regulation on these component skills and on motivation. Pre- and post-measurements will be conducted with the help of the CAI test procedure, the IRS, the ILS, and motivation measurements with pupils and teachers in the first two secondary school years. Each of the four studies will use an experimental group of 100 pupils and a control group of 50 pupils. In the second year two training groups will be used: one will receive training without links to other school subjects, the other will be given a combination of study skills instruction and integrated study skills instruction. Study skills will be taught with the help of the training modules examined in the preceding year. One control group will be used that will not be trained in study skills. If possible, classes will be randomly assigned to the experimental and control groups. Pre- and post-measurements will be carried out as in the first year of the project, supplemented by achievement tests and transfer measurements.

11866 The historical development of selected principles in mechanics and the relationship with growth of understanding in students.
GBR 1993
Research Date(s): 1989-1993
Roper, T.
Sup: Orton, A.
Inst: Leeds University, School of Education, Leeds LS2 9JT, United Kingdom.
learning process; physics; comprehension
apprentissage; physique; compréhension
PROJECT DESCRIPTION

The development of the principles of mechanics throughout history has been slow and faltering. The same can be said about the growth of understanding of these principles in students. The study aims to investigate the relationship between the historical development and the growth of understanding.

11867 How do computers best help children and adults to overcome learning difficulties?
GBR 1993
Research Date(s): 1990-1991
Hawkridge, D.; Vincent, T.
Inst: Open University, Institute of Educational Technology, Walton Hall, Milton Keynes MK7 6AA, United Kingdom.
Fin: Nuffield Foundation.
learning difficulty; special education; handicapped; didactic use of computer
difficulté de l'apprentissage; enseignement spécial; handicapé; usage didactique de l'ordinateur
PROJECT DESCRIPTION

This project reports and evaluates recent United Kingdom experience of using computers in schools and colleges to aid children and adults with learning difficulties caused by a wide range of physical, sensory and psy-chological disabilities, in their study of the curriculum. Fieldwork was carried out by selected teachers, advisory teachers, further education coordinators and adult educators, working under the principal researchers' direction. Each person selected was asked to compile a critical account of recent experience, particularly the best current practice, in his or her institution or district.

Chapters were written by the principal researchers incorporating material from the fieldwork accounts, and sent to the fieldworkers for comment. Additional chapters were written by the principal researchers to provide context and a broad view of the state of the art, together with commentary.

The study's main audience is likely to be those engaged in helping children and adults with learning difficulties: parents, policy-makers, administrators, principals, advisory teachers, advisors and teachers; staff and students in teacher training institutions. It will also be of interest to some adult students with learning difficulties.

Publ: Hawkridge, D. & Vincent, T. *Learning difficulties and computers: access to the curriculum*. London: Jessica Kingsley Publishers, 1992.

11868 The humanization of higher education.
RUS 1994
Research Date(s): 1991-1992
Kohanovich, L.I.
Inst: Research Institute for Higher Education, 103062, Moscow, K-62, Podsosensky per. 20, Russia.
State Committee for Higher Education Institutions, 113833, Moscow, M-230, Lysinovskja str. 51, Russia
higher education; teaching method
enseignement supérieur; méthode pédagogique
PROJECT DESCRIPTION

The study explored the principles of a humanitarian type of education in higher education. Problems examined included psychological, pedagogical and methodological aspects of humanitarian education.

Publ: Kohanovich, L.I.; Shahova, R.F.; Ivanovskaya, I.P.; et al. *Humanization of education: trends and problems*. M., NIIVO, 1992.
Ivanovskaya, I.P. & Fathullin, M.F. *Humanizing higher education and the students' public opinion*. M., NIIVO, 1992.
Kohanovich, L.I.; Shahova, R.F.; Migalin, L.N.; et al. *Scholarly achievement and experience in higher education*. M., NIIVO, 1993.
Intelligentsia and morals. M., NIIVO, 1993.

11869 Improving student achievement through promoting effective learning.
GBR 1993
Research Date(s): 1990-1991
Tait, H.; Thompson, S.
Sup: Entwistle, N.
Inst: Edinburgh University, Department of Education, Centre for Research on Learning and Instruction, 10-12 Buccleuch Place, Edinburgh EH8 9JT, United Kingdom.
Fin: Scottish Office Education Department.
learning strategy; higher education; teaching method; educational innovation; predictive evaluation; achievement
stratégie d'apprentissage; enseignement supérieur; méthode pédagogique; innovation pédagogique; évaluation prédictive; rendement
PROJECT DESCRIPTION

By promoting effective learning, student achievement should be improved. A significant part of this project involved producing a set of guidelines for teaching staff in higher education to allow them to explore alternative ideas and approaches to entry qualifications, previous knowledge, study skills, syllabus content, teaching methods, assessment and institutional policies for supporting teaching and learning. The guidelines are not intended to be in any way prescriptive, but rather to provide an opportunity for staff to reflect on their current policies and practices in the light of the latest research findings. A separate part of the project aimed to develop an Approach to Studying Inventory which could be used mid-way through the first term of a first year course to identify students who may be at risk of failing due to inappropriate study habits and inadequate skills. A computer program was developed to display scores on three dimensions graphically, and to identify students at risk of failure by means of a 'prediction function'. Further development work of the inventory is underway, and is planned for the computer program 'StudentView', if funding becomes available.

Publ: Entwistle, N.J.; Tait, H. & Thompson, S. *Improving student achievement through promoting effective learning*. Final Report to the Scottish Office Education Department, 1992. Available from Edinburgh University, Centre for Research on Learning and Instruction.
Entwistle, N.J.; Thompson, S. & Tait, H. *Guidelines for promoting effective learning in higher education*. Final Report to the Scottish Office Education Department, 1992. Available from Edinburgh University, Centre for Research on Learning and Instruction.
Odor, P. *StudentView - an interactive graphical system for analysing and exploring student questionnaire data*. User handbook, demonstrator ver-

sion. Available from Edinburgh University, Centre for Research on Learning and Instruction.

11870 Inquiry into key psychological concepts used to characterise features of learning and teaching, especially in mathematics.
GBR 1993
Research Date(s): 1987-
Davis, A.
Inst: Durham University, School of Education, Leazes Road, Durham DH1 1TA, United Kingdom.
learning process; cognitive process; philosophy of education; concept; mathematics
apprentissage; processus cognitif; philosophie de l'éducation; concept; mathématiques
PROJECT DESCRIPTION

This research argues that learning may be seen as the acquisition of knowledge and understanding, and/or the acquisition of abilities, capacities and skills. Research into the degree to which the curriculum offered to pupils 'matches' their current level of knowledge etc. relies on certain conceptions of knowledge, belief, understanding, ability, skill, and so on. Ideas behind the National Curriculum, especially with regard to assessment, also rely upon certain characteristics of the changes in pupils that occur when learning takes place.

The research consists of a wide ranging conceptual/philosophical investigation into the adequacy of these conceptions and characterisations. Empirical research of others is sometimes reviewed and referred to, but the argument being pursued is that at least some of this research is an expensive irrelevance, based tacitly on conceptually inadequate foundations.

Publ: Davis, A.J. Ability and learning. In: *Journal of Philosophy of Education*, Vol 22/1988.
Davis, A.J. Logical defects of the TGAT Report. In: *British Journal of Educational Studies*, Vol XXXVIII, No 3/1990, pp. 237-250.

11871 Integratie-activiteiten bij het leren. (Integration activities in learning.)
NLD 1994
Research Date(s): 1992-1996
Simons, P.R.J.
Inst: Vakgroep Onderwijskunde (Department of Education), P.O. Box 9103, 6500 HD Nijmegen, Netherlands.
Katholieke Universiteit Nijmegen (Catholic University of Nijmegen), P.O. Box 9102, 6500 HC Nijmegen, Netherlands
Fin: SVO het Instituut voor Onderzoek van het Onderwijs.
cognitive process; learning process; integration; memory; learning strategy
processus cognitif; apprentissage; intégration; mémoire; stratégie d'apprentissage
PROJECT DESCRIPTION

Background: Integration in learning refers to the establishment and the strengthening of links between different types of information (conceptual, episodic and procedural) in the long-term memory. Although various educational-psychological theories stress the importance of integration-oriented learning activities, there exists little empirical evidence to support this view.

Aim: (1) To determine the necessity of integrating acquired knowledge and skills for their retention and application; (2) to explore possibilities for teaching integration activities and thus to improve, through training, academic achievement levels.

Design: The first experiment will involve one experimental group and two control groups (each group N=50). Five computer-controlled lessons will be presented to the experimental group, requiring subjects to undertake various types of integration activities. The first control group will be offered the same learning material without activation of integration. Learning time will not be restricted, neither in the experimental group, nor in the first control group. As it is expected that activation of integration will lead to an extension of the amount of learning time, a fixed amount of learning time will be set for the second control group. This will enable a cost-benefit analysis to be made of the amount of learning time and gains in learning. In the second experiment two types of integration activity will be compared. Use will be made of two experimental groups (each group N=50). The third experiment will investigate the effectiveness of a training programme whereby pupils are taught integration activities. One experimental group (N=40) and one control group (N=40) will be used.

11872 Jugend - Freizeit - Technik: Kompetenzerwerb im alltaeglichen Technikumgang unter besonderer Beruecksichtigung von Freizeit als Lernort. (Youth - leisure - technology: acquisition of competence in everyday use of technology, with particular reference to leisure as an educational setting.)
DEU 1993
Research Date(s): 1990-1992
Bruns, T.; Sessar, H.
Sup: Schatz, H.; Schatz-Bergfeld, M.
Inst: Rhein-Ruhr-Institut fuer Sozialforschung und Politikberatung e.V. - RISP- an der Uni, Heinrich-Lersch-Str. 15, D-4100 Duisburg 1.

Fin: Bundesministerium fuer Forschung und Technologie.
concomitant learning; youth; leisure; technical ability; new technologies; computer literacy
apprentissage fortuit; jeunesse; loisir; capacité technique; nouvelles technologies; initiation à l'informatique
PROJECT DESCRIPTION

Inhalt: Vor dem Hintergrund der fortschreitenden Technisierung des Alltags gewinnt Freizeit als "Lernort" fuer Technikaneignung und -nutzung eine zunehmende Bedeutung. Gerade Jugendliche nehmen im freizeitlichen Kontext ohne Scheu neue Techniken wie beispielsweise den Computer oder neue Geraete der Unterhaltungselektronik in Gebrauch, reagieren aber andererseits sehr sensibel auf das Gefaehrdungspotential neuer Grosstechnologien, deren technische und soziale Beherrschbarkeit ihnen zweifelhaft erscheint. Diese differenzierten Einstellungen von Jugendlichen zur Technik lassen vermuten, dass Jugendliche eigene bzw. "eigensinnige" Technikumgangsformen ausbilden und diese auch lebens- und berufsperspektivisch nutzen. Im Mittelpunkt der Untersuchung steht dementsprechend die Herausbildung und der Erwerb von Technikkompetenz von Jugendlichen im freizeitlichen Kontext. Dieser Prozess ist eingebettet in den Sozialisationsprozess der Adoleszenzphase und die je spezifische individuelle Auspraegung von Identitaet und gesellschaftlicher Integration. Technikkompetenz ist Handlungsressource und Handlungspotential fuer die Orientierung und Realitaetsverarbeitung in einer technisierten Umwelt.

Geographischer Raum: Duisburger Raum.

Vorgehensweise: Handlungs- und sozialisationstheoretischer Ansatz; explorative Untersuchung. Untersuchungsdesign: Fallstudie; qualitative Forschung.

Datengewinnung: Nicht-standardisiertes Interview (Stichprobe: ca. 40; Jugendliche im Alter zwischen 16 und 19 Jahren; Auswahlverfahren: Quota. Stichprobe: ca. 40; Jugendliche im Alter zwischen 16 und 19 Jahren; Auswahlverfahren: bewusst). Gruppendiskussion (dito). Expertengespraech (dito). Primaererhebung: Feldarbeit von Mitarbeitern des Projektes durchgefuehrt.

Auswertung: Inhaltsanalyse, Clusteranalyse.

Publ: Schatz, H. & Schatz-Bergfeld, M. Jugend-Freizeit-Technik: Kompetenzerwerb im alltaeglichen Technikumgang unter besonderer Beruecksichtigung von Freizeit als Lernort. In: VDI-Technologiezentrum Physikalische Technologien. Projekttraeger Technikfolgenabschaetzung (Hrsg.). *Technikfolgenabschaetzung. Projektpraesentationen zum Foerderschwerpunkt "Wechselwirkungen zwischen Arbeit, Technik und Freizeit".* Duesseldorf, 1991, S. 15-21.

11873 Komplexní a multidisciplinární péče o děti s vývojovými poruchami učení a chování. (Care for children with learning and behavioural difficulties.)
CSK 1994
Research Date(s): 1992-1994
Martincová, Nora; Susová, Ilona; Preiss, Marek; Juřička, Jan; Novák, Jaromír; Teslíková, Jitka.
Sup: Voděrková, Irena.
Inst: Ministerstvo školství, mládeže a tělovýchovy ČR (Ministry of Education, Youth and Physical Education), Karmelitská 7, 118 13 Praha 1, Czech Republic.
learning difficulty; child development; guidance; diagnosis; therapy; mentally handicapped; deviant behaviour
difficulté de l'apprentissage; développement de l'enfant; orientation; diagnostic; thérapie; handicapé mental; comportement déviant
PROJECT DESCRIPTION

The research is divided into three stages. (1) The theoretical part deals with the development of learning functions and developmental difficulties related to learning. Special terminology and etiology will be examined, as well as developmental difficulties of behaviour. Czech and foreign approaches to dealing with the learning problems of children with developmental difficulties will be studied. (2) In the second part, diagnostic criteria and methods will be defined and American diagnostic tests verified. (3) The third part will focus on re-education, compensatory and therapeutic methods that can be used with children with learning and behavioural difficulties.

The results will be used to integrate diagnostic processes and to improve the quality of care and educational and psychological guidance for these handicapped children.

11874 Korrektive Lesetechnologie, Korrektive Schreibtechnologie. (Corrective reading technology, corrective writing technology.)
AUT 1993
Research Date(s): 1988-
Karl, Helmut W.
Inst: Institute Helmut W. Karl, Tuerkenstrasse 29, A-1090 Wien; Freies Paedagogisches Zentrum, Tuerkenstrasse 29, A-1090 Wien.
learning difficulty; remedial teaching; dyslexia; dysorthography; private tutor; teaching aid
difficulté de l'apprentissage; soutien pédagogique; dyslexie; dysorthographie; précepteur; moyen d'enseignement
PROJECT DESCRIPTION

Eine durch angeborene Legasthenie nicht plausibel erklaerbar grosse Zahl von SchuelerInnen zwischen acht und dreizehn Jahren leidet unter Lese- und Schreibschwaeche. Inhaltliche Ziele des Projektes sind: (a) Leicht erlernbare Verfahren zur Diagnose und Linderung einer erworbenen Lese- und Schreibschwaeche zu entwickeln, die rasche Linderung bis voellige Behebung der Schwaechen gewaehrleisten, getrennt in die Bereiche Lesen und Schreiben; (b) Lehr- und Unterrichtsmittel zu entwickeln, die solche Verfahren unterstuetzen; (c) Richtlinien zu erarbeiten, die erworbene Lese- und Schreibschwaeche verhindern helfen.

Es erfolgte die systematische Beobachtung, das Erfassen und Auswerten von fuer die Zielsetzung relevanten Daten zur Entwicklung, Modifikation und Korrektur der angestrebten Verfahren, sowie das systematische 'Testen' der so entwickelten Verfahren. Es werden jaehrlich ca. 50 Pflicht-schuelerInnen zwischen acht und zwoelf Jahren ohne eigene Selektion (nur solche, deren Eltern oder LehrerIn um Besserung besorgt sind) einbezogen.

Es handelt sich um systematisch-analytische Methoden- Entwicklung (Verfahrens-Entwicklung).

Verfahren und Material fuer 'Lesetraining' brachten seit 1980 in mehr als 80% der Faelle eine statistische Verbesserung um eine Schulstufe durch je zehn bis zwoelf Stunden Training. Aehnliche Resultate im 'Schreibtraining', allerdings erst seit 1988.

Publ: Karl, Helmut W. *Korrektive Lesetechnologie.* Academe, Eigenverlag, Wien, 1988.

11875   Krise oder Risiko: zwei Perspektiven der Selbstbeschreibung moderner Gesellschaften.   (Crisis or risk: two alternative self-descriptions of modern societies.)
DEU   1993
Research Date(s): 1991-1992
Halfmann, J.; Japp, K.
Inst: Universitaet Osnabrueck, FB Sozialwissenschaften, Fachgebiet Soziologie, Seminarstr. 33, D-4500 Osnabrueck.
society; learning; communication theory; sociology
société; acquisition de connaissances; théorie de la communication; sociologie
PROJECT DESCRIPTION
Inhalt: Diskussion der kommunikationstheoretischen und der systemtheoretischen Gesellschaftstheorien unter dem Gesichtspunkt der Voraussetzungen und Folgen kollektiven Lernens.
Vorgehensweise: Soziologische Systemtheorie.

11876   Læringsstrategier i lærerutdanningen.   (Learning strategies in teacher education.)
NOR   1994
Research Date(s): 1992-1994
Hauge, Trond Eiliv.
Inst: Universitet i Oslo, Senter for Lærerutdanning og Skoletjeneste (University of Oslo, Centre for Teacher Education and In-Service Training), Postboks 1099 Blindern, 0316 Oslo, Norway.
Fin: NAVF/RSF.
learning strategy; learning; student teacher; teacher education; teaching practice
stratégie d'apprentissage; acquisition de connaissances; élève-maître; formation des enseignants; pratique pédagogique
PROJECT DESCRIPTION
The project aims to discover and analyse the strategies used by student teachers in learning and acquiring knowledge during their teacher training at SLS (Senter for lærerutdanning og skoletjeneste), both at the intended and at the implemented level. The purpose is to gain an insight into the factors that influence and form new teachers' conceptions of learning and teaching, and to provide a basis for reflection and for the revision of goals and contents in the teaching and counselling of student teachers in a changing society that continuously sets new demands for teachers.

The project is based on constructivist learning theories, hermeneutics, subject didactics, teacher thinking research and theories of philosophy of knowledge. The project is inspired by local didactic R & D programmes at SLS, and a national research programme on mentoring and knowledge acquisition in in-service teacher education.

The focus is on: (1) the student teacher's own learning history and theory of teaching practice; (2) the strategies employed by the student in learning pedagogical theory and subject didactics at SLS, and the implementation of the knowledge thus acquired during school practice; (3) the student's own teaching strategies in the classroom.

Three selected cohorts with a background in science, social science and foreign language (English) have been followed throughout their teacher training and have been subjected to intensive qualitative research. In addition, a survey has been made of all the SLS students (questionnaires at the beginning and at the end of their training), both to extract generalizations based on a broader set of data, as well as to form a backcloth for the case studies of the three cohorts.

Publ: A full list of publications can be obtained on request from the research institute.

11877   Learning and the pace of lessons.
GBR   1993
Research Date(s): 1989-
Preece, P.
Inst: Exeter University, School of Education, St Luke's, Heavitree Road, Exeter EX1 2LU, United Kingdom.
learning pace; time-factor; ability; achievement; model construction
rythme d'apprentissage; facteur temps; capacité; rendement; construction de modèle
PROJECT DESCRIPTION
An algebraic model relating the rate of learning to the pace of teaching and to pupil ability has been developed. The model accounts well for prior data on learning at different speeds and accurately predicts the learning deficit for able pupils taught in heterogeneous classes. The model can predict the changes of pace and learning from lesson to lesson. A direct investigation of the interrelationship of learning, ability and pace has been carried out with 40 undergraduate education students, using foreign language vocabulary items. Some qualitative features of the theoretical model were supported.

Publ: Preece, P.F.W. Learning and the pace of lessons: a theoretical model. In: *British Journal of Mathematical and Statistical Psychology,* Vol 43/1990, pp. 1-6.
Preece, P.F.W. Imitatio Physicae. In: *British Educational Research Journal,* Vol 16/1990, pp. 297-304.
Preece, P.F.W. Foreign language vocabulary learning and the pace of instruction. In: *The Teacher Trainer,* Vol 5, No 2/1991, pp. 21-22.

11878   Learning styles and education management.
GBR   1993
Research Date(s): 1988-1992
Seymour, R.
Inst: Crewe and Alsager College of Higher Education, Department of Education Management, Hassall Road, Alsager, Stoke on Trent ST7 2HL, United Kingdom.
learning strategy; cognitive style; management education; educational administration; managerial staff
stratégie d'apprentissage; style cognitif; formation à la gestion; administration de l'enseignement; personnel d'encadrement
PROJECT DESCRIPTION
This research uses the work of Honey and Mumford on learning styles and applies it to the education sector. Education management norms have been derived to compare with other management groups. Follow-up work has been carried out on a sample from the original research group to analyse individual changes and review these against the background of learning development and organisational environment. A learning diagnostic questionnaire was used and important indicators were found for the training and development of middle managers in schools. Further work is in progress on the use of learning styles in relation to students' study choices within a flexible, negotiated programme for the M.Sc. degree in Education Management.

Publ: Seymour, R. & West-Burnham, J. Learning styles and education management: part one. In: *International Journal of Educational Management,* Vol 3, No 4/1989, pp. 19-25, December.
Seymour, R. & West-Burnham, J. Learning styles and education management: part two. In: *International Journal of Educational Management,* Vol 4, No 4/1990, pp. 22-26, December.

11879   Lern- und Arbeitstechniken von Studienanfaengern an Fachhochschulen - Methoden zu ihrer Erfassung, Evaluation und Optimierung.   (Methods for the acquisition, evaluation and optimization of learning and working techniques for first-year students at technical colleges.)
DEU   1993
Research Date(s): 1992-1994
Herkert, P.
Inst: Fachhochschule Furtwangen, FB Wirtschafts- und Sozialwissenschaften, Gerwigstrasse 11, D-7743 Furtwangen.
learning process; study method; student; university studies; learning strategy
apprentissage; méthode de travail; étudiant; études universitaires; stratégie d'apprentissage
PROJECT DESCRIPTION
Inhalt: Ziel: Lern- und Arbeitsweise von Studienanfaengern erfassen, analysieren und evaluieren, um Methoden zur Optimierung des studentischen Lernens und/oder professoralen Lehrens zu entwickeln. Fragestellung: (1) Wie gehen Studienanfaenger mit komplexen Lernaufgaben um? (Lernmethoden/Arbeitsorganisation/Zeitplanung/Gruppenarbeit) (2) Wo gibt es Defizite? Korrelation mit Noten? (3) Welche Optimierungsstrategien lassen sich entwickeln?
Untersuchter Zeitraum: 1992-1994.
Vorgehensweise: Wissenspsychologie (kognitive Stile); Lernpsychologie (Info-Aufnahme); Verhaltenspsychologie (Verstaerker); Erfassungsmethoden: Fragebogen, Interviews, Verhaltensbeobachtung. Unter-

suchungsdesign: Evaluationsstudie; Querschnittserhebung; qualitative Forschung.

Datengewinnung: Standardisiertes Interview (Stichprobe: ca. 150; Studenten im 1. Semester techn. Faecher; Auswahlverfahren: total. Stichprobe: ca. 150; Studenten im 7. Semester techn. Faecher; Auswahlverfahren: total). Gruppenbefragung (dito). Psychologischer Test (dito). Teilnehmende Beobachtung (Stichprobe: ca. 150; Studenten im 1. Semester techn. Faecher; Auswahlverfahren: total). Primaererhebung: Feldarbeit von Mitarbeitern des Projektes durchgefuehrt; Sekundaeranalyse bereits vorhandener maschinenlesbarer Datensaetze.

Auswertung: Korrelation; Varianzanalyse; Repression; Faktorenanalyse. Datenaufbereitung: Datenedition (z.B. Aufbau von Datenbanken); Aggregierung oder Disaggregierung; Verknuepfung verschiedener Datensaetze (record linkage).

11880   Lernen und Fertigen. (Learning and manufacturing.)
DEU   1993
Research Date(s): 1991-1993
Frevel, A.
Sup: Volkholz, V.
Inst: Gesellschaft fuer Arbeitsschutz- und Humanisierungsforschung, Hollaendische Reihe 4, D-2000 Hamburg 50.
Fin: Deutsche Forschungsanstalt fuer Luft- und Raumfahrt -DLR- Projekttraeger des Programms "Arbeit und Technik".
learning; enterprise; work experience; employee; new technologies; curriculum; small and medium entreprise
acquisition de connaissances; entreprise; expérience du travail; salarié; nouvelles technologies; programme d'études; petite ou moyenne entreprise
PROJECT DESCRIPTION
Inhalt: Unter Nutzung betrieblicher Ressourcen sollen technische, organisatorische und paedagogische Konzepte entwickelt werden, die es ermoeglichen, die durch den Einsatz neuer Techniken erforderlichen Qualifizierungsmassnahmen so zu gestalten, dass vorhandenes Erfahrungswissen insbesondere aelterer Arbeitnehmer in den Unternehmen erhalten und entwickelt werden kann. Wesentlich ist dabei die Zielstellung, dass diese Konzepte nach Ende der oeffentlichen Anschubfinanzierung auf privatwirtschaftlicher Grundlage unter den oekonomischen Bedingungen kleiner und mittlerer Betriebe als "Selbstlaeufer" fortgefuehrt werden koennen. Wissenschaftliche Begleitung und Unterstuetzung des Projekts "Stabilisierung aelterer Arbeiter in Klein-und Mittelbetrieben durch werkstattgerechte CNC-Technik" der Fa. Keller, Wuppertal. Evaluation der Schulungs- und Beratungsmassnahmen durch Einbeziehung uebergreifender Aspekte, Konzipierung und Unterstuetzung integrativer Produktionskonzepte (Technik, Organisation, Paedagogik). Analyse der Transfer-Oekonomie bei der Personalentwicklung aelterer Arbeitnehmer in Klein- und Mittelbetrieben in der Gesamtkonzeption der Integration von Lernen und Fertigen. Unterstuetzung der Qualifizierung von Metallfacharbeitern in der DDR. Kooperation zusaetzlich mit ATB Institut Arbeit, Technik, Bildung (Chemnitz) und Institut fuer Arbeitspsychologie der TU Dresden.

Vorgehensweise: Evaluation von Schulungsmassnahmen durch Kursbegleitung; Einzelinterviews; standardisierte Befragung von Teilnehmern und Trainern; BMS-Erhebung; betriebliche Fallstudien einschliesslich Expertengespraechen und Interview; Literatur-und Dokumentenanalyse.

11881   The nature of teacher-student interaction in active and student-centred approaches: an inservice course in a college of further education.
GBR   1993
Research Date(s): 1989-1991
Harwood, D.
Inst: Warwick University, Faculty of Educational Studies, Department of Science Education, Coventry CV4 7AL, United Kingdom.
learning process; discovery learning; teaching method; activity method; interaction
apprentissage; apprentissage par la découverte; méthode pédagogique; méthode active; interaction
PROJECT DESCRIPTION
Student-centred learning has emerged as a parallel, though related, development to 'active learning'. In this research, tapes and transcripts of an inservice course for lecturers in a college of further education are being studied, in order to identify patterns of interaction in student-centred approaches.

11882   Onderzoek naar cognitieve structuren en taalvaardigheden in gesproken en geschreven (vak)talen ten behoeve van het tweede-vak-taalonderwijs. (Cognitive structures and language skills in vocational training.)
NLD   1994
Research Date(s): 1993-1994
Overmaat, A.M.
Inst: Stichting Centrum voor Onderwijsonderzoek (SCO) (Centre for Educational Research), Grote Bickersstraat 72, 1013 KS Amsterdam, Netherlands.
Universiteit van Amsterdam (University of Amsterdam), P.O. Box 19268, 1000 GG Amsterdam, Netherlands

Fin: SVO het Instituut voor Onderzoek van het Onderwijs.
learning; vocational education; cognition; cognitive development; language development; language for special purposes
acquisition de connaissances; enseignement professionnel; cognition; développement cognitif; développement du langage; langage de spécialité
PROJECT DESCRIPTION
Background: Many students entering apprenticeship courses or senior secondary vocational training (MBO) lack the cognitive structures that are required for these courses. The Feuerstein's Instrumental Enrichment (FIE) programme aims to develop cognitive structures and to link them to language structures, starting from a situation that demands little in terms of students' language skills. It is not sufficiently clear how such linkage can best take place. That is why, prior to the main study, a preliminary study is conducted which aims at the integration of the FIE programme into specific curricular areas.

Aim: To examine how vocational training and cognitive training can best be linked; to establish the feasibility of some experimental links; to make recommendations, on the basis of the outcomes, for the main study.

Design: Previous experiences with the integration of the FIE programme in vocational training will be listed. Both the enrichment programmes and the curricula for some subject areas will be analysed; possibilities for linking them will be explored. Model lessons will be described and tested. On the basis of the findings, guidelines will be formulated for the design of lesson plans for the main study. Research objectives will be further defined, agreements will be made with schools to ensure cooperation, and the design of the main study will be elaborated.

11883   Onderzoek van structuren en concepten in de schoolvakken met het oog op het aanleren van specifieke taal- en denkstructuren in het vakkengeïntegreerde taalonderwijs. (Investigation into structures and concepts in school subjects with a view to teaching specific linguistic and cognitive structures in integrated language instruction.)
BEL   1994
Research Date(s): 1990-
Vanmaele, L.; Wielemans, K.
Sup: Lowyck, J.
Inst: Centrum voor instructiepsychologie en technologie (Centre for Instruction Psychology and Technology), Tiensestraat 102, 3000 Leuven, Belgium.
Katholieke Universiteit Leuven (Catholic University of Leuven), Naamsestraat 22, 3000 Leuven, Belgium
Fin: Departement Onderwijs, Fonds voor Kollektief en Fundamenteel Onderzoek op Ministerieel Initiatief.
learning process; cognitive process; curriculum subject; textbook; content analysis; teaching language
apprentissage; processus cognitif; matière d'enseignement; manuel d'enseignement; analyse de contenu; langue d'enseignement
PROJECT DESCRIPTION
Aim: The ultimate aim of this study of the content and linguistic characteristics of school subjects is to optimize teaching and learning processes. One of the premises is that both the language used by the teacher in verbal instruction and the language in textbooks play a crucial role in these processes.

Methods: A theoretical framework is constructed to enable the analysis of the content and the linguistic characteristics of textbooks. This is done in through: (1) an examination of the literature for classification systems and classification criteria for scientific disciplines; (2) the construction of a provisional analysis grid, followed by an analysis of characteristics of groups of disciplines; (3) an analysis of distinct scientific disciplines in the research literature and corresponding subjects in textbooks.

Publ: Lowyck, J.; Vanmaele, L. & Wielemans, K. *Taal- en denkstructuren in schoolvakken: op zoek naar een theoretisch kader: rapport 1.* Leuven: KUL, Onderzoekscentrum voor instructiepsychologie en technologie, 1991, 64p.

11884   Oppimisega toimetuleku tingimused Eestimaa kasvatustegelikkuses: sotsiaalse keskkonna seisund kasvatuse sotsiaalse taustana. (Conditions for learning and Estonian educational reality: the social environment as the background to social education.)
EST   1994
Research Date(s): 1989-1994
Kruusvall, J.; Kera, S.; Kuurme, T.; Vôhandu, E.; Liimets, A.; Vernik, E.-M.; Orn, J.; et al.
Inst: Tallinna Pedagoogikaülikool (Tallinn Pedagogical University), 0102 Tallinn, Narva mnt. 25, Estonia.
Fin: EV Haridusministeerium.
learning conditions; social environment; school-community relation; teacher-pupil relation; pupil attitude; teacher behaviour
conditions d'apprentissage; milieu social; relation école-collectivité; relation maître-élève; attitude de l'élève; comportement de l'enseignant
PROJECT DESCRIPTION
The study examines educational relations as a condition for learning and a regulator of learning. The focus is on the possibilities of the school system to create the conditions for multifunctional learning. It is hypothe-

sized that in the post-socialist society the nature of educational relations lies at the core of educational reality and that pupils will be better learners if the learning process is built upon social relations.

The aims of the study are: (1) to examine the parameters determining educational relations; (2) to analyse the conditions for multifunctional learning; (3) to determine the degree of dependence between the social actors in schools; (4) to examine the attitude and communicative readiness of pupils and teachers; (5) to examine the social competence of pupils and teachers.

Methods: Interview, observation, questionnaire, secondary analysis.

Publ: *Haridusuuendus - mis, miks ja kuidas?* Tallinn, 1992.

11885 Outcomes of experiential learning.
GBR 1993
Research Date(s): 1974–
Hall, E.; Hall, C.
Inst: Nottingham University, School of Education, Centre for the Study of Human Relations, University Park, Nottingham NG7 2RD, United Kingdom.
Fin: Nottingham University: School of Education; Universities Funding Council; Enterprise in Higher Education.
experiential learning; interpersonal relations
apprentissage par la pratique; relations interpersonnelles
PROJECT DESCRIPTION

This is an ongoing project which examines the outcomes of experiential interpersonal skills training programmes which have been developed over the years at the Centre for the Study of Human Relations at the University of Nottingham. A series of studies have been conducted, partly associated with four Ph.D. students. All of the evaluations have involved experienced teachers who attended six-day residential courses or extended award bearing courses to gain an M.Ed. or an Advanced Diploma.

Data has been collected before, during and up to three years after the courses. Data was collected using standardised questionnaires, interviews, diaries of critical incidents, outcomes of goal setting, learning journals and data collected during experiential exercises during the courses.

A consistent pattern has emerged over several studies. The participants reported significant changes in both their personal and professional lives. These changes involved reports of reductions in stress, a greater sense of control over one's life and a shift to a more humanistic approach to discipline issues. These changes involved relationships with both students and colleagues. There was also a strong 'Sleeper effect' in several of the studies in which a significant improvement was obtained at the end of the course, followed by a much more substantial increase one year later.

Publ: Hall, E.; Woodhouse, D.A. & Wooster, A.D. An evaluation of inservice courses in human relations. In: *British Journal of Inservice Education*, Vol 11, No 1/1984, pp. 55-60.
Woodhouse, D.A.; Hall, E. & Wooster, D.A. Taking control of stress in teaching. In: *British Journal of Educational Psychology*, Vol 55, Part 2, 1985, pp. 119-123.
Hall, E. & Hall, C.A. *Human relations in education.* London: Routledge, 1988.
Hall, E.; Hall, C.A. & Leech, A. *A scripted fantasy in the classroom.* London: Routledge, 1990.

11886 Picture-text interaction in children's learning of science.
GBR 1993
Research Date(s): 1985–
Reid, D.
Inst: Manchester University, School of Education, Oxford Road, Manchester M13 9PL, United Kingdom.
visual learning; science education; learning process
apprentissage visuel; éducation scientifique; apprentissage
PROJECT DESCRIPTION

The Picture Superiority Effect (PSE) is ambiguous. What are the variables which contribute to it? The investigations are data-driven and school-based to optimise ecological validity. Typically between 100 and 200 13-14 year old children are given memory recall tasks of science comprehension.

Use of microcomputers has shown that PSE is enhanced when the material to be learned is present redundantly in both picture and text, the learning task is memory-based, the structure of the picture is optimised in terms of those perceptual elements known to direct or attract attention and the learner is trained how to use pictures in relation to the text.

Publ: A full list of publications is available from the researcher.

11887 PINGIST PINKI: Handlungsorientierungen fuer Lehrerbildner und Lehrer. (PINGIST PINKI: normative orientations for teacher trainers and teachers.)
DEU 1993
Research Date(s): 1991-1994
Kala, U.; Orn, J.; Queis, D.
Sup: Altermann, K.
Inst: Paedagogische Hochschule Magdeburg, Institut fuer Paedagogik i.G., Lennestrasse 64, O-3010 Magdeburg.
learning; teaching; teacher; pupil; cross-national research; comparative research

acquisition de connaissances; enseignement; enseignant; élève; recherche transnationale; recherche comparative
PROJECT DESCRIPTION

Inhalt: Das Projekt untersucht die Lernmethoden, die Lebensweise, die Lebensperspektive und die Entwicklungsfaktoren und -bedingungen der Schulkinder und -jugend der genannten Laender. Mit einer hohen Untersuchungspopulation wird eine Zustandsanalyse erstellt, aus der Handlungsorientierungen fuer Lehrerbildner und Lehrer abgeleitet werden.

Geographischer Raum: Deutschland, Estland, Finnland, Schweden, Holland, Kasachstan.

Untersuchter Zeitraum: 1991-1994 (vorerst).

Vorgehensweise: Untersuchungsdesign: Methodenforschung; Querschnittserhebung; retrospektive Daten; qualitative Forschung.

Datengewinnung: Expertengespraech. Befragung. Teilnehmende Beobachtung. Aktenanalyse. Inhaltsanalyse. Primaererhebung: Feldarbeit von Mitarbeitern des Projektes durchgefuehrt; Sekundaeranalyse bereits vorhandener maschinenlesbarer Datensaetze. Datenerstellung auf der Basis von bereits vorliegenden Materialien wie Texten, Akten, Statistiken.

Auswertung: Faktorenanalyse.

11888 Praktisches Lernen in der Schule. (Practical learning at school.)
DEU 1993
Research Date(s): 1982-1992
Beutel, W.; Konrad, F.; Mack, W.; Schiller, A.; Schoenig, W.; Schubert, G.; Schweitzer, F.; et al.
Sup: Flitner, A.; Fauser, P.
Inst: Universitaet Tuebingen, Fak. fuer Sozial- und Verhaltenswissenschaften, Institut fuer Erziehungswissenschaft 01, Arbeitsbereich Schulpaedagogik, Muenzgasse 22-30, D-7400 Tuebingen.
Fin: Robert Bosch Stiftung GmbH.
discovery learning; school; sciences of education; child; experiential learning
apprentissage par la découverte; école; sciences de l'éducation; enfant; apprentissage par la pratique
PROJECT DESCRIPTION

Inhalt: Foerderung des praktischen Lernens in den Schulen und theoretische Aufarbeitung der in den Schulprojekten gewonnenen Erkenntnisse sowie Diskussion in der Erziehungswissenschaft. Praktisches Lernen meint einen staerkeren Praxisbezug des Lernens sowohl im Blick auf das lernende Kind (Eigentaetigkeit) als auch auf die gesellschaftliche Praxis, fuer die schulisches Lernen offen sein sollte. Praktisches Lernen zielt auf die Entwicklung einer pluralen und dezentral organisierten Schullandschaft.

Datengewinnung: Aktenanalyse (Stichprobe: ca. 100; kooperierende Schulen 1983-1988; Auswahlverfahren: willkuerlich. Stichprobe: ca. 200; kooperierende Schulen 1988-1992; Auswahlverfahren: willkuerlich). Datenerstellung auf der Basis von bereits vorliegenden Materialien wie Texten, Akten, Statistiken.

Publ: Beutel, W. & Fauser, P. (Hrsg.). *Demokratisch Handeln. Dokumentation des Kolloquiums "Schule der Demokratie" vom 24.-26.09.1989.* Tuebingen 1990.
Frommer, H. & Koersgen, S. *Ueber das Fach hinaus. Fachuebergreifender Unterricht, praktisches Lernen, paedagogische Tradition.* Duesseldorf 1989.
Fauser, P.; Konrad, F.-M. & Woeppel, J. (Hrsg.). *Lern-Arbeit. Arbeitslehre als praktisches Lernen.* Weinheim 1989.
Fauser, P.; Fintelmann, K.J. & Flitner, A. (Hrsg.). *Lernen mit Kopf und Hand. Berichte und Anstoesse zum praktischen Lernen in der Schule.* Weinheim 1983/1990.
Umfangreiche Literaturliste liegt beim Institut vor.

11889 The principle of economy in learning and teaching mathematics.
GBR 1993
Research Date(s): 1987-1992
Hewitt, D.
Sup: Mason, J.
Inst: Birmingham University, School of Education, Edgbaston, Birmingham B15 2TT, United Kingdom; Open University, Faculty of Mathematics, Walton Hall, Milton Keynes MK7 6AA, United Kingdom.
learning strategy; learning process; mathematics; teaching method; child
stratégie d'apprentissage; apprentissage; mathématiques; méthode pédagogique; enfant
PROJECT DESCRIPTION

This research concerns the recognition of economy as a factor in the learning and teaching of mathematics. Economy in this context refers to the personal use of one's time and energy in order to achieve a particular aim, ability or understanding. Very young children learn skills and develop abilities before entering the formal environment of a classroom; they learn at a rate that adults consider impressive and much of their learning remains learnt for the rest of their life. The researcher has identified aspects of the way in which young children use themselves in gaining these abilities, and compared these with ways pupils are often asked to work in mathematics classrooms.

The research is mainly based on observations of children both in and out of classroom situations. Conclusions are likely to identify ways children use themselves in learning efficiently and the consequences these may have on styles of teaching mathematics.

Publ: Hewitt, D. Memory. In: *Mathematics Teaching*, No 118, pp. 18-20, March 1987.
Hewitt, D. Gaining time. In: *Mathematics Teaching*, No 119, pp. 9-11, June 1987.
Hewitt, D. Fickle. In: *Mathematics Teaching*, No 125, pp. 14-15, December 1988.
Hewitt, D. Forcing awareness. In: *Micromath*, Vol 5, No 1, pp. 27-29, Spring 1989.

11890 Segmentation ability and patterns of reading failure: the nature of the relationship.
GBR 1993
Research Date(s): 1992-1993
Johnston, R.
Sup: Holligan, C.
Inst: St Andrews University, Department of Psychology, St Andrews, Fife KY16 9AJ, United Kingdom; Craigie College of Education, Beech Grove, Ayr KA8 OSR, United Kingdom.
Fin: Wellcome Trust.
reading difficulty; dyslexia; reading; word recognition
difficulté de lecture; dyslexie; lecture; reconnaissance des mots
PROJECT DESCRIPTION
The aim of this research is to examine: (a) how poor readers recognise words; (b) in what way this is qualitatively distinct from that of normal readers; and (c) why this leads to impaired nonword reading. A study is also being made of poor readers' memory difficulties, and the importance of visual skills to the early stages of reading development.

11891 Skolens kunnskapsinnhold og elevenes subjektive læringsprosesser. (School content knowledge and pupils' subjective learning processes.)
NOR 1994
Research Date(s): 1992-1993
Imsen, Gunn.
Inst: Universitetet i Trondheim, Norsk Senter for Barneforskning (University of Trondheim, Norwegian Centre for Child Research), 7055 Dragvoll, Norway.
Fin: NAVF/RSF.
learning process; learning; knowledge
apprentissage; acquisition de connaissances; connaissance
PROJECT DESCRIPTION
Much has been written about a "gap" or culture conflict between pupils' lives and the theoretical and structured world of the school. What can be revealed about this gap? How do pupils perceive the content knowledge that is taught in school?
The theoretical frame of reference is constructivistic, emphasizing knowledge as socially constructed, with some ideas from linguistic and post-structuralistic theory. The empirical part consists of qualitative in-depth studies, with classroom observation, interviews with students (13-16 years old) and workbook analysis. Various school subjects are studied during a six-month field work.
The project focuses on the social construction of knowledge in a range of classroom settings and the qualitative dimensions that seem important in pupils' social and personal construction of meaning. The project will be of interest for research and theory building about school learning, as well as school administration, teaching and teacher education.

11892 Sosialisering til læring: om begynnerstudenters mestring av læringskulturen ved universitetet. (Socialization to learning: how students learn and learn to learn at the university.)
NOR 1994
Research Date(s): 1992-1994
Havnes, Anton.
Inst: Universitetet i Oslo, Pedagogisk Forskningsinstitutt (University of Oslo, Institute for Educational Research), PB 1092 Blindern, 0317 Oslo, Norway.
Fin: NAVF/RSF.
learning; learning conditions; quality of education; student behaviour; university studies; learning theory
acquisition de connaissances; conditions d'apprentissage; qualité de l'éducation; comportement de l'étudiant; études universitaires; théorie de l'apprentissage
PROJECT DESCRIPTION
Questions concerning the quality of higher education call for different kinds of measures, for example changes in the financing of university studies and changes in curricula, teaching methods and students' working conditions. Another aspect of the problem is the way students cope with the learning culture at the university. This study focuses on how students contribute to the quality of their studies by their participation in the learning environment. The respondents in the project are first-year students. It

is also intended to discuss how the conclusions of the study can be fed back to students.
The objectives of the project are: (1) to gain "inside" information on students' experiences with learning at the university; (2) to describe students' perceptions of education and learning; (3) to describe students' opportunities to influence their own learning; (4) to contribute to the development of theories of learning that have practical relevance for learners.

11893 Specific learning difficulties (dyslexia): challenges and responses.
GBR 1993
Research Date(s): 1988-1991
Pumfrey, P.; Reason, R.
Inst: Manchester University, School of Education, Centre for Educational Guidance and Special Needs, Oxford Road, Manchester M13 9PL, United Kingdom.
Fin: Division of Educational and Child Psychology of the British Psychological Society.
learning difficulty; dyslexia; special education
difficulté de l'apprentissage; dyslexie; enseignement spécial
PROJECT DESCRIPTION
This is a national enquiry mounted in 1988 by the Division of Educational and Child Psychology of the British Psychological Society. A team of nine qualified and experienced educational psychologists from eight local education authorities were involved under the co-ordination of Professor Pumfrey and Mrs Reason, the authors of the final report.
The inquiry had two main aims: (1) to provide a wide-ranging account of current theory and research with regard to specific learning difficulties; and, (2) to investigate relevant educational and policies and practices.
The historical context was reviewed and key theoretical and practical issues considered. A comprehensive review of psychological, psychoeducational and psychomedical theory and research was undertaken. Relevant educational policies and practices were surveyed covering: (a) policies of local education authorities; (b) practices of educational psychologists; and (c) policies of examination boards on dispensations for pupils deemed to have specific learning difficulties. The views of a wide range of voluntary bodies and professional organisations were sought in relation to the concept of specific learning difficulties, identification and assessment, prevention, teaching methods and the provision of resources.
Publ: Pumfrey, P.D. & Reason, R. *Specific learning difficulties (dyslexia): challenges and responses.* Windsor: NFER-Nelson, 1991.
Pumfrey, P.D. Introduction: purposes, context and scope of a National Enquiry. In: *Abstracts of the Annual Conference of the British Psychological Society*, pp. 12, April 1991.
Pumfrey, P.D. Identifying and alleviating specific learning difficulties (dyslexia): Issues and implications for LEA's, professionals and parents. In: *Educational Psychology in Practice*, Vol 6, No 4/1991, pp. 222-228.
Pumfrey, P.D. & Reason, R. A national enquiry 1989. Specific learning difficulties (dyslexia): challenges, responses and recommendations, further details. In: *Division of Educational and Child Psychology Newsletter*, No 33/1989, pp. 14-16.

11894 Specific learning difficulties (Dyslexia) project.
GBR 1993
Research Date(s): 1990-1993
Diniz, F.; Reid, G.
Inst: Heriot-Watt University, Moray House Institute of Education, Holyrood Road, Edinburgh EH8 8AQ, United Kingdom.
Fin: Scottish Dyslexia Trust.
dyslexia; learning difficulty; reading difficulty; teacher education; special education
dyslexie; difficulté de l'apprentissage; difficulté de lecture; formation des enseignants; enseignement spécial
PROJECT DESCRIPTION
The aims of the research are to investigate the potential for developments in teacher education to meet the needs of those concerned about the education of children with specific learning difficulties associated with dyslexia.

11895 Support arrangements for primary school children who experience difficulty learning to read - help or hinderance?
GBR 1993
Research Date(s): 1992-
Feiler, A.
Sup: Webster, A.
Inst: Bath College of Higher Education, Newton Park, Newton St Loe, Bath BA2 9BN, United Kingdom; Bristol University, School of Education, 35 Berkeley Square, Bristol BS8 1JA, United Kingdom.
reading difficulty; special education; remedial teaching
difficulté de lecture; enseignement spécial; soutien pédagogique
PROJECT DESCRIPTION
One aim of this research will be to establish how much help is provided for children with reading difficulties in primary schools and the nature of this help. A related aim will then be to establish the effect that internal and

external arrangements for helping such children have on the amount and quality of support provided. In other words, does the presence of 'special arrangements' (either internal or external to the school) result in class teachers providing levels of support similar to those before these arrangements were made, more help, or less? A related aim will be to explore the quality of support once help is provided. Does this tend to result in children being given tasks that are less stimulating, where the emphasis is on decoding and on processing texts for information rather than on reading texts that are imaginative and expressive?

It is intended that teachers and children from six primary schools will participate in this investigation - which will be carried out by interviewing, observation and analysing school records.

11896   A survey of learner training for language learning.
GBR   1993
Research Date(s): 1991-1992
Dickinson, L.
Inst: Heriot-Watt University, Moray House Institute of Education, Scottish Centre for Education Overseas, Holyrood Road, Edinburgh EH8 8AQ, United Kingdom.
learning process; learning strategy; language teaching; cognitive style
apprentissage; stratégie d'apprentissage; enseignement des langues; style cognitif
PROJECT DESCRIPTION

Learner training is concerned with helping learners consider the factors that affect their learning and with helping them to discover the learning strategies which suit them best. It focuses learners' attention on the process of learning so that the emphasis is on how to learn rather than what to learn. Though this is a relatively new development in language teaching and learning, there are indications that there is a growing interest in many parts of the world. This research aims to survey a broad sample of language teaching institutions to gauge the interest in learner training, to discover the varying meanings given to the term and to establish a network of individuals and institutions with an interest in learner training.

11897   Teaching and learning strategies in multi-ethnic further education classrooms.
GBR   1993
Research Date(s): 1989-1991
Roberts, C.; Kapoor, S.; Garnett, C.
Inst: Thames Valley University, Faculty of Humanities and Languages, 1 The Grove, London W5 5DX, United Kingdom.
Fin: Training, Enterprise and Education Directorate.
learning strategy; teaching method; ethnic minority; vocational education
stratégie d'apprentissage; méthode pédagogique; minorité ethnique; enseignement professionnel
PROJECT DESCRIPTION

The aim of the project is to establish what teaching and learning strategies contribute to the progress and achievement of ethnic minority students in work-related further education classes and to develop some staff training materials. Four London colleges will be visited on a regular basis and the researchers will work closely with four Business and Technical Education Councils (BTEC) lecturers who have agreed to participate in the project as teacher/researchers. Audio and video recordings will be made in the classroom and interviews carried out with lecturers and students. The second part of the project is the development of staff training materials. These will include case studies and a video.

11898   Tools for exploratory learning programme.
GBR   1993
Research Date(s): 1988-1991
Bliss, J.; Ogborn, J.
Inst: London University, King's College, 552 King's Road, London SW10 0UA, United Kingdom; London University, Institute of Education, 20 Bedford Way, London WC1H 0AL, United Kingdom.
Fin: Economic and Social Research Council.
discovery learning; didactic use of computer; educational software
apprentissage par la découverte; usage didactique de l'ordinateur; didacticiel
PROJECT DESCRIPTION

The aim of this research is to examine whether or not computer tools facilitate different types of reasoning in two different modes of learning. Exploratory learning is defined as the learning that occurs when children use software tools containing representations or models of a specific domain. Expressive learning occurs when children are given the facility to represent their own ideas about the domain. Preliminaries will be a teaching session for familiarisation with the computer, followed by a session to teach the children how to use the relevant software.

The main study will be composed of a preliminary interview to record pupils' spontaneous reasoning in the domain area. Children will be then set an extended task in which they will use the software followed by a final interview to examine their reasoning. The tasks will be designed to call on reasoning in one of the three areas: quantitative; semi-quantitative; and qualitative. The rationale of tasks will be to create 'what if' situations, that is to ask children to explore or express alternatives to reach a specific goal.

Approximately 2,000 children will be sampled in the course of the study. These children will be in the age range 11 to 14 years from middle or secondary schools. During the study the children will work in same sex friendship pairs on one specific task, using one particular software tool. The interviews will be transcribed, as will any conversation between the children. These transcriptions together with observational data will form the basis of the data to be analysed. The data will be qualitatively analysed using systemic networks.

Publ: Bliss, J. & Ogborn, J. Tools for exploratory learning. In: *Journal of Computer Assisted Learning*, Vol 5, No 1/1989, pp. 37-50.
Ogborn, J. Computational modelling: a link between mathematics and other subjects. In: Blum, W. et al. *Modelling, applications and applied problems solving*. Hemel Hempstead: Horwood (Ellis), 1989.
Miller, R.; Ogborn, J.; Turner, J.; Briggs, J.H. & Brough, D.R. Towards a tool to support semi-quantitative modelling. In: *Proceedings of International Conference on Advanced Research on Computers in Education, July 1990*. Tokyo: Gakashuin University, 1990.

11899   Transfervermogen en instructie.   (Transfer ability and instruction.)
NLD   1994
Research Date(s): 1992-1993
Hoeven-van Doornum, A.A. van der.
Sup: Simons, P.R.J.; Buis, Th.J.M.N.
Inst: Instituut voor Toegepaste Sociale wetenschappen (ITS) (Institute for Applied Social Sciences), P.O. Box 9048, 6500 KJ Nijmegen, Netherlands. Katholieke Universiteit Nijmegen (Catholic University of Nijmegen), P.O. Box 9102, 6500 HC Nijmegen, Netherlands
Fin: SVO het Instituut voor Onderzoek van het Onderwijs.
learning strategy; flexibility; transfer of learning; teaching method; teacher behaviour
stratégie d'apprentissage; flexibilité; transfert pédagogique; méthode pédagogique; comportement de l'enseignant
PROJECT DESCRIPTION

Background: Rapid developments in society are placing increasing demands on people's cognitive flexibility and transfer ability, i.e. the skills that are needed to apply previously acquired knowledge to new situations. Pupils need to be prepared for these changing demands. That is why it is expected that in education the traditional emphasis on "teaching" will gradually be replaced by an emphasis on "learning" and "learning to learn". This study has links with research on transfer ability, independent learning, learning to learn and studies of educational quality.

Aim: (1) To examine conditions and factors that foster cognitive flexibility and transfer ability in pupils; (2) to find out how these conditions and factors may be translated into effective teaching behaviours; (3) to identify teacher characteristics that contribute to effective instructional behaviour.

Design: Literature surveys will be carried out on three topics. (1) Pupil characteristics. The concepts of "cognitive flexibility" and "transfer ability" will be described systematically on the basis of national and international literature. (2) Teacher behaviour. Pedagogical and domain-specific principles for effective instructional behaviours will be identified and brought together in a descriptive model. (3) Characteristics of teachers and instructional contexts. Variables that play a role in the implementation of the behaviours found under (2) will be identified and brought together in a model. Study visits will be made to Germany and United Kingdom. On the basis of the results of the literature surveys several alternative scenarios will be proposed for the implementation of instructional behaviours. These scenarios will be assessed by a panel of about 25 representatives and experts from the fields of education and industrial training by telephone questionnaire.

11900   Verhoging onderwijskwaliteit door beheersingsleren. (Improving the quality of education through mastery learning.)
BEL   1994
Research Date(s): 1989-1991
de Ruyck, B.
Sup: Dyck, W.
Inst: Departement Didactiek en Kritiek (Department of Didactics and Critique), Universiteitsplein 1, 2610 Wilrijk, Belgium. Universitaire Instelling Antwerpen, UIA (University Institution Antwerp, UIA) Universiteitsplein 1, 2610 Wilrijk, Belgium
Fin: Departement Onderwijs, Fonds voor Kollektief en Fundamenteel Onderzoek op Ministerieel Initiatief.
mastery learning; quality of education; achievement gain
pédagogie de la maîtrise; qualité de l'éducation; progrès scolaire
PROJECT DESCRIPTION

Aims: (1) To develop a method for improving pupil performance; (2) to describe and investigate the factors that influence achievement in primary and secondary schools.

Methods: In seven experimental schools (primary and secondary) instruction was given, followed by intermittent formative self-evaluation. The schools were compared with control schools by means of pretests and posttests.

Hypothesis: Pupils in the experimental schools will: (1) obtain higher average scores; (2) show less wide differences in performance levels; (3) develop more positive attitudes towards school and learning.

Results: The performance levels of the experimental and control groups were compared. The expectation that pupils would perform better through self-evaluation was not confirmed.

Publ: Dyck, W. & de Ruyck, B. *Verhoging onderwijskwaliteit door beheersingleren. Een onderzoek in het basis- en secundair onderwijs.* Antwerpen: UIA, 1990, 304p.

03 PRINCIPLES OF EDUCATION – PRINCIPES D'EDUCATION – BILDUNGSPRINZIP

11901 Accelerated access to higher education from science and technology based industries.
GBR 1993
Research Date(s): 1990-1992
Dodd, J.
Sup: Taylor, R.; Williamson, W.
Inst: Leeds University, Adult Education Centre, 37 Harrow Road, Middlesbrough, Cleveland TS5 5NT, United Kingdom; Durham University, Department of Adult and Continuing Education, 32 Old Elvet, Durham DH1 3HN, United Kingdom.
Fin: Training, Enterprise and Education Directorate.
access to education; higher education; technician; admission requirements
accès à l'éducation; enseignement supérieur; technicien; conditions d'admission
PROJECT DESCRIPTION

The project arose from discussions of adult education provision in the Teesside area involving the departments concerned at Durham and Leeds universities. The aim was to facilitate entry into undergraduate courses by staff from the science and technology based industries, in conjunction with ICI, British Steel and Tioxide (UK).

Admissions tutors in the relevant departments of both universities were consulted individually on their attitudes towards, and experience of, mature students having non-standard entry qualifications. Whilst they were favourably disposed towards such students, concern was expressed that although most satisfied the general Matriculation requirement they did not necessarily meet specific entry requirements for individual courses, and that there was a general weakness in mathematics.

A survey of technicians on Teesside and in Leeds produced 360 returns of a questionnaire which showed that more than half were interested in proceeding into higher education and most of these had at least the minimum educational qualifications to do so, but the vast majority wished to do so on a part-time basis.

A detailed investigation of the nature of mathematical provision at sub-degree level, including the running of two short courses on Teesside, produced two levels of mathematics acceptable to tutors. These were incorporated into a modular access programme including biology, chemistry and physics, a suitable selection from which was agreed by tutors as qualifying for admission. Forty students are now following the programme in Leeds or Middlesbrough. An Apel procedure is being developed to identify suitable candidates for entry with advanced standing.

11902 Accès des bacheliers à l'enseignement supérieur.
FRA 1993
Research Date(s): 1989-
Guénard, Christine; Ricci, H.; Chenin, J.F.
Inst: Université de Dijon, UER Faculté des sciences économiques et de gestion, CNRS UPR/29 et GDR/996, Institut de recherche sur l'économie de l'éducation, BP 138, 21004 Dijon Cedex, France.
access to education; higher education; educational guidance; choice of studies; student sociology
accès à l'éducation; enseignement supérieur; orientation pédagogique; choix des études; sociologie de l'étudiant
PROJECT DESCRIPTION
Objectifs: L'enquête ACCES est un dispositif permettant d'appréhender le passage du secondaire au supérieur et de rendre transparents les processus d'orientation à la fin de l'enseignement secondaire.

Méthodologie: Les intentions d'inscription dans l'enseignement supérieur de 13300 élèves de terminales des lycées publics, privés et agricoles de l'académie de Dijon ont été recensées en mai 1990. En novembre 1990, une seconde interrogation permet de connaître l'orientation définitive de 7900 bacheliers.

Résultats: Parmi ces jeunes, 90% suivent une formation dans l'enseignement supérieur, dont 38% en première année de Diplôme d'études universitaires générales et 29% en Brevet de Technicien supérieur. Plus de la moitié des diplômés sont inscrits à l'Université, l'Université de Bourgogne accueillant 42% des bacheliers, 3321 bacheliers se retrouvent dans la formation souhaitée. Les premiers résultats montrent une différenciation des poursuites d'études selon le type de diplôme obtenu, selon le sexe, selon le département d'origine.

D'autres analyses sont réalisées pour connaître l'impact de différents facteurs comme la série du baccalauréat, l'âge, le sexe, l'origine sociale et géographique. La cohorte de jeunes entrés non seulement à l'université mais dans les autres formations supérieures est suivie sur une période de trois années afin d'effectuer un bilan du déroulement de leurs études, de leurs réussites ou réorientations.

Publ: Guégnard, C.; Ricci, H. & Chenin, J.F. *Accès à l'enseignement supérieur en Bourgogne: premiers résultats.* Document CIA-CER-EQ/ONISEP/SSR, octobre 1990, 4p.
Guégnard, C. & Ricci, H. *Accès à l'enseignement supérieur en Bourgogne; les bacheliers: situation en novembre 1990.* Document CIA-CER-EQ/ONISEP/SSR, avril 1991, 4p.

11903 Access coordinators in institutions of higher education in the United Kingdom.
GBR 1993
Research Date(s): 1990-1991
Parry, G.; Thompson, A.
Inst: City University, Centre for Continuing Education, Northampton Square, London EC1V OHB, United Kingdom.
Fin: Universities Funding Council.
access to education; adult education; higher education
accès à l'éducation; éducation des adultes; enseignement supérieur
PROJECT DESCRIPTION
This is a one-year research project investigating the role of access coordinators in higher education who have responsibility for extending and supporting the participation of mature and non-traditional students. The first phase used a questionnaire to heads of continuing education in all universities, polytechnics and colleges to collect baseline data on patterns of provision and activity. The second phase involved the identification of a small number of institutions for more qualitative and detailed investigation using case study methods.
Publ: Thompson, A. & Parry, G. *Access coordinators in higher education.* London: City University, 1992.

11904 Access to higher education in Xinjiang Uyghur Autonomous Region, China, 1949-1987.
GBR 1993
Research Date(s): 1987-1991
Aishiding, H.
Sup: Little, A.
Inst: London University, Institute of Education, Department of International & Comparative Education, 20 Bedford Way, London WC1H OAL, United Kingdom.
access to education; higher education; equal opportunity; ethnic group; China

accès à l'éducation; enseignement supérieur; égalité de chances; groupe ethnique; Chine
PROJECT DESCRIPTION
Despite tremendous achievements in the quantitative expansion of education, there have been problems of equality in higher education for the various ethnic groups in the Uyghur Autonomous Region of Xinjiang (UARX). This study is aimed at examining some of these problems which are concomitant with the expansion since the revolution. According to various definitions in the international literature, equality in higher education refers to a wide range of issues such as equal access to the system, which includes equal provision of facilities; equal participation in the system or the probability of survival and equal attainment throughout the system. In other words, equality of output or in the performance of the applicants and equal opportunity which applies to the value of education in its achieving equal access to jobs, income, political power and social networks. All of these can vary in their effects for citizens in the different regions, e.g. urban and rural; for men and women; for the different ethnic groups; for the different socio-economic groups and for the physically healthy and the disabled. This study confines itself to the equality of access to higher education for Han-Chinese and non-Han people (refers to Uyghurs, Kazaks, Kirghiz, Hui, Mongols, Sibo, etc.) in UARX between 1949 and 1987.

11905 Access to Information on Multi-cultural Education Resources (AIMER).
GBR 1993
Research Date(s): 1987-
Abbas, S.
Inst: Reading University, Reading and Language Information Centre, Bulmershe Court, Woodlands Avenue, Earley, Reading RG6 1HY, United Kingdom.
intercultural education; teaching aid; data base
éducation interculturelle; moyen d'enseignement; banque de données
PROJECT DESCRIPTION
AIMER is a database project which offers students, teachers, advisers and others information on multicultural antiracist teaching materials. In recent years there has been a proliferation of booklets, packs and other resources produced within local education authorities (LEAs) and other organisations. AIMER acts as a clearing house for materials of this kind. In addition to a postal inquiry service, it publishes resource lists on a wide range of topics which are updated on an annual basis. It is possible to buy either individual resource lists or the whole set at a substantial discount in the form of a single volume, 'Photocopiable resources to support the multicultural dimension of the National Curriculum'.
Publ: A publications list is available on request.

11906 Alternatives in education - an analysis of past and present educational policies and ideologies and suggested alternatives for the future.
GBR 1993
Research Date(s): 1990-1992
Tomlinson, S.
Inst: Lancaster University, Department of Educational Research, Cartmel College, Bailrigg, Lancaster LA1 4YW, United Kingdom.
Fin: Leverhulme Trust.
educational policy; comparative education; history of education; ideology
politique de l'éducation; éducation comparée; histoire de l'éducation; idéologie
PROJECT DESCRIPTION
The research will develop a critical analysis of educational policies from 1944 to 1988, with a focus on the failures of the 'left' and the influence of the 'right' in terms of ideology. The working out of the Education Reform Act 1988 in terms of policy and practice will be examined and suggestions for alternative educational policies based on particular values will be put forward. A study will be made of European education systems, particularly Germany, and the possibility of a future European education system explored.

11907 Ambulante begeleiding: werkvormen en opbrengsten. (Peripatetic supervision: methods and results.)
NLD 1994
Research Date(s): 1992-1995
Kool, E.; Venne, L. van de.
Sup: Rijswijk, C.M. van; Wolf, J.C. van der.
Inst: Stichting Centrum voor Onderwijsonderzoek (SCO) (Centre for Educational Research), Grote Bickersstraat 72, 1013 KS Amsterdam, Netherlands.
Universiteit van Amsterdam (University of Amsterdam), P.O. Box 19268, 1000 GG Amsterdam, Netherlands
Fin: SVO het Instituut voor Onderzoek van het Onderwijs.
educational guidance; special education; secondary education; peripatetic teacher; supervision
orientation pédagogique; enseignement spécial; enseignement secondaire; enseignant itinérant; surveillance
PROJECT DESCRIPTION

Background: Peripatetic supervision consists of additional support for special needs pupils in mainstream schools who without this support would have to be referred to a special school. The support is provided by teachers who are employed by the school board of a special school; the financial resources involved are allocated to that school. This regulation dates back to 1985 and is regarded as a means whereby the links between special and mainstream schools may be strengthened and the growth of the special education sector may be curbed.

Aim: To examine the effectiveness of models of peripatetic supervision (differentiated by type of special school and by type of supervision ("traditional" vs. "preventive")) at pupil, teacher and school level; to investigate the conditions under which different models are applied.

Design: In the first phase a questionnaire survey will be conducted among all special schools in the Netherlands (N=900) in order to collect quantitative data on types of supervision and amounts of time devoted to supervision. The second phase will focus on a selection of 50 special schools, exploring in particular the working methods, the effect of supervision at pupil, teacher and school level, and any problems that are encountered in practice. Data will be collected from supervisors (N=50), teachers (N=50), school heads (N=25) and pupils (N=100) with the help of questionnaires and interviews. In the third phase all special schools will be asked to comment on the feasibility of implementing the more effective methods on a larger scale.

11908 Analfabetismul functional si educatia de bază a adultilor în România. (Functional illiteracy and adult basic education in Romania.)
ROM 1994
Research Date(s): 1991-1995
Lită, Ana; Anghel, Florentina.
Sup: Bîrzea, Cezar.
Inst: Institutul de Stiinte ale Educatiei (Institute for Educational Sciences), str. Stirbei Vodă 37, 70732 Bucharest, Romania.
Ministerul Învătământului (Ministry of Education), str. General Berthelot 28-30, Bucharest, Romania
illiteracy; reading; writing; adult education; basic education
analphabétisme; lecture; écriture; éducation des adultes; éducation de base
PROJECT DESCRIPTION

Background: UNESCO is interested in an international perspective on functional illiteracy. As one of its members, Romania is trying to implement the Canadian methodology of realizing a study on this topic during the transition period.

Aims: To identify the incidence of functional illiteracy in Romania and to elaborate remedial programmes.

Design: The study consists of three complementary stages: (1) a survey of adult education (20-35 years old), which aims to gather statistical information on the incidence of functional illiteracy in Romania; (2) elaboration of remedial literacy programmes and assessment of their effect; (3) elaboration of recommendations for the reform of compulsory education on the basis of the results of the two previous stages.

Sample: The survey will use four target populations: (1) young people who, having completed compulsory education, are called for military service; (2) young people from urban areas (16-35 years old), searching employment; (3) graduates of "vocational high schools"; (4) young people from rural areas.

11909 Analisi della domanda e della funzionalità del servizio scolastico. (Analysis of the demand for education and the functioning of the education system.)
ITA 1994
Research Date(s): 1989-1991
Medina, A.; Guazzini, G.; Saddemi, L.; Gigante, M.
Sup: Rossi, Giampaolo.
Inst: Centro di Ricerche Sociali ed Istituzionali - CeRSI (Centre for Social and Institutional Research), Via S. Agata 14, 06100 Perugia, Italy.
Consiglio Nazionale delle Ricerche - CNR (National Research Council), Piazzale Aldo Moro 7, 00185 Roma, Italy
quality of education; education system; demand for education; opinion; parental attitude; satisfaction
qualité de l'éducation; système d'enseignement; demande d'éducation; opinion; attitude des parents; satisfaction
PROJECT DESCRIPTION

The study offers a complex view of the functioning of the education system at the provincial level, from nursery school to upper secondary school. The analysis has revealed the low level of uniformity in the education system in Italy and the shortcomings in some Provinces. Indicators such as timetables, class sizes, pupil-teacher ratios, split schedules, unfit buildings, and repeating were examined. Through a questionnaire survey of a sample of 1,500 families, levels of satisfaction with the use and the role of the school in the education process of young people were revealed.

11910 Anregung und Unterstuetzung von Lernprozessen erwachsener Analphabeten mit dem Computer. (Stimulation and support of learning processes in illiterate adults working with computers.)
DEU 1993
Research Date(s): 1989-1992
Angyal, E.; Tymister, U.
Sup: Eigler, G.
Inst: Universitaet Freiburg, Philosophische Fakultaet, 01 Seminar fuer Erziehungswissenschaft, Werthmannplatz, D-7800 Freiburg im Breisgau.
Fin: Deutsche Forschungsgemeinschaft.
illiteracy; adult; cognitive ability; didactic use of computer; reading; spelling; learning process
analphabétisme; adulte; aptitude cognitive; usage didactique de l'ordinateur; lecture; orthographe; apprentissage
PROJECT DESCRIPTION

Inhalt: Ermittlung kognitiver Strategien im Bereich des Lese-, Rechtschreiberwerbs bei Erwachsenen. Vermittlung von Lernstrategien, die das Loesen von Lese-, Rechtschreibproblemen steuern. Entwicklung eines computerunterstuetzten Lernprogramms zum Erwerb der Problemloesesestrategien beim Rechtschreiben. Gestaltung und Einsatzmoeglichkeiten des Programms: Lerner koennen die Problemloesesestrategien erwerben durch ein erwachsenengerechtes und lebensnahgestaltetes Lernprogramm. Texte aus alltaeglichen Schreibsituationen werden bearbeitet. Anregen eines aktiven Lernprozesses: selbstgesteuertes Lernen wird unterstuetzt durch mehrstufiges Rueckmeldesystem. Ergebnisse: Die angewandten Rechtschreibstrategien werden mit Hilfe eines Protokollsystems, das mit dem Lernprogramm gekoppelt ist, ausgewertet.

Vorgehensweise: Untersuchungsdesign: Fallstudie; qualitative Forschung.

Datengewinnung: Teilnehmende Beobachtung (Stichprobe: 3x3; VHS-Kurs Freiburg; Auswahlverfahren: bewusst). Primaererhebung: Feldarbeit von Mitarbeitern des Projektes durchgefuehrt; Sekundaeranalyse bereits vorhandener maschinenlesbarer Datensaetze.

Publ: Eigler, G. Funktionaler Analphabetismus - auch ein psychologisch-erziehungs-wissenschaftliches Problem. In: *Unterrichtswissenschaft*, 2, 1990, S. 146-160.
Tymister, U. Arbeiten mit Analphabeten in Volkshochschulen. In: *Unterrichtswissenschaft*, 2, 1990.

11911 The application of quality management principles to learning.
GBR 1993
Research Date(s): 1991-1993
Hughes, T.; Williams, T.
Sup: Hibberd, P.; Gronow, S.
Inst: Glamorgan University, Department of Property and Development Studies, Pontypridd, Mid Glamorgan CF37 1DL, United Kingdom.
Fin: Department of Employment.
quality of education; training-employment relationship; vocational education; job requirements
qualité de l'éducation; relation formation-emploi; enseignement professionnel; qualification requise pour l'emploi
PROJECT DESCRIPTION

In vocational courses there are two principle customers whose needs are to be satisfied; the students and the employers. Research has shown that these needs are difficult to define and equally difficult to satisfy. The aims of the research are therefore to: (1) identify the key personal and technical skills necessary in professional quantity surveying practice; (2) develop a simulation-based teaching vehicle on the basis of (1) above; and (3) use quality management principles to monitor and improve the learning experience.

Publ: Hughes, T. & Williams, T. *Quality Assurance, a Framework to Build on*. Oxford: Blackwell Scientific Publications, 1991.
Hughes, T. & Williams, T. Learning by experience: integrated learning materials based on a construction project. In: *Building Technology and Management*, Vol 18, 1991, pp. 56-64, Kuala Lumpur, Building Technology Society.

11912 Arbeidsmarktindicatoren ten behoeve van het emancipatiebeleid. (Labour market indicators for equal opportunity policies.)
NLD 1993
Research Date(s): 1990-1991
Lodder, B.J.H.; Loo, P.J.E. van de; Ramaekers, G.W.M.; Velden, R.K.W. van der.
Inst: ROA Researchcentrum voor Onderwijs en Arbeidsmarkt, Universiteit Limburg (Research Centre for Education and the Labour Market, University of Limburg), P.O. Box 616, 6200 MD Maastricht, Netherlands.
equal opportunity; labour market; graduate; employment opportunities
égalité de chances; marché du travail; étudiant diplômé; chances d'obtenir un emploi
PROJECT DESCRIPTION

Under a contract from the Board of Governors of the University of Limburg, ROA conducted research into the present situation and trends in sex inequality on the labour market. The information presented covers both national data relating to disciplines relevant for the University of Limburg, and data on the position which the University's graduates attain on the labour market.

Publ: *Arbeidsmarktindicatoren ten behoeve van het emancipatiebeleid aan de Rijksuniversiteit Limburg* (Labour market indicators for the equal opportunities policy at the University of Limburg), ROA-R-1991/7.

11913 Bazı derslerin liselerdeki öğrenci, öğretmen, danışman ve yöneticilerin psikolojik danışma ve rehberlik hizmetlerinden beklentilerine etkisi. (The expectations of pupils, teachers, counsellors and administrators of the service for psychological counselling and guidance.)
TUR 1994
Research Date(s): 1991
Özdemir, Ibrahim Etem.
Sup: Özgüven, I. Ethem.
Inst: Hacettepe Üniversitesi, Eğitim Fakültesi, Psikolojik Hizmetler Bölümü (Hacettepe University, Faculty of Education, Department of Psychological Services), 06532 Beytepe, Ankara, Turkey.
guidance; guidance service; psychological service; expectancy; pupil; teacher; managerial staff; guidance officer
orientation; service d'orientation; service psychologique; attente; élève; enseignant; personnel d'encadrement; orienteur
PROJECT DESCRIPTION
The study examined the expectations of counselling held by pupils, teachers, counsellors and administrators in state secondary schools which offer psychological counselling and guidance services. It was also attempted to identify essential differences between the expectations of different groups.

The sample consisted of 325 pupils, 97 teachers, 76 counsellors, and 33 heads of schools in the area of Ankara in the 1987-1988 school year. Expectations were measured with the help of the specially developed "Inventory of Expectations from Psychological Counselling and Guidance Services". A "Personal Information Questionnaire" was designed to gather information on some characteristics of the groups of respondents. In the analysis of the data, the t-test technique was used.

Results showed that girls, younger pupils, higher class pupils, and pupils living in urban areas held higher expectations of psychological counselling and guidance services than boys, older pupils, lower class pupils and pupils from rural backgrounds.

As regards the expectations of teaching staff, it was found that teachers with a specific educational background, teachers of vocational courses and philosophy-related courses, and teachers who have taken counselling courses in pre-service or in-service training hold higher expectations than teachers with opposite characteristics. The expectations of women teachers, older teachers, and teachers with a high level of professional experience did not differ significantly from those of teachers with opposite characteristics.

The expectations of counsellors who had not taken guidance courses during their studies were significantly higher than those of counsellors who had taken such courses. The expectations of female counsellors, counsellors in the domains of psychological counselling, guidance-related and philosophy-related counselling, professionally experienced counsellors, counsellors who took in-service guidance courses, older counsellors and faculty graduate counsellors did not differ significantly from the expectations of counsellors with opposite characteristics.

Younger administrators and administrators who had taken guidance courses as part of in-service training held higher expectations than administrators with opposite characteristics. The expectations of faculty graduate administrators, highly experienced administrators and administrators who had taken guidance courses during their studies did not differ significantly from those of administrators with opposite characteristics.

11914 Bewaeltigung von Uebergangssituationen im Jugendalter. (Dealing with transitional situations in adolescence.)
DEU 1993
Research Date(s): 1989-1992
Bauch, D.
Sup: Kirsch, B.
Inst: Universitaet Potsdam, FB Psychologie, Am Neuen Palais, O-1571 Potsdam.
guidance; adolescent; school leaving; secondary education; university studies
orientation; adolescent; fin de scolarité; enseignement secondaire; études universitaires
PROJECT DESCRIPTION
Inhalt: Gibt es Moeglichkeiten (in Form eines Arbeitsblattes oder Trainings), die den Uebergang in eine zum Abitur fuehrende Bildungseinrichtung fuer den Schueler erleichtern? Im Ergebnis liegt ein praxisrelevanter Beitrag fuer den paedagogischen Alltag vor: ein Arbeitsmaterial fuer Schueler und ein sozialpsychologisch orientiertes Trainingsprogramm.
Geographischer Raum: Land Thueringen (ehem. Bezirk Gera).
Untersuchter Zeitraum: 1990.

Vorgehensweise: Der theoretische Ansatz basiert auf Auffassungen von Haan, Lazarus und Launier zum Sachverhalt 'Coping' auf Aussagen von S.H. Filipp zur Bewaeltigung von Krisen und Aussagen von Seiffge-Krenke, die generell die Fragestellung Jugendalter und Bewaeltigung ansprechen. Untersuchungsdesign: Fallstudie; (Quasi-)Experiment.
Datengewinnung: Gruppenbefragung (Stichprobe: 125; Schueler der 11. Klasse, die neu an eine zum Abitur fuehrende Bildungseinrichtung immatriiulert wurden; Auswahlverfahren: willkuerlich. Stichprobe: 214; Schueler der 9. und 11. Klasse, die neu an eine zum Abitur fuehrende Bildungseinrichtung immatriiulert wurden; Auswahlverfahren: willkuerlich). Experiment (Stichprobe: 214; Schueler der 9. und 11. Klasse, die neu an eine zum Abitur fuerende Bildungseinrichtung immatriiulert wurden; Auswahlverfahren: willkuerlich. Nicht-standardisiertes Interview dito). Gruppendiskussion (dito). Primaererhebung: Feldarbeit von Mitarbeitern des Projektes durchgefuehrt.
Auswertung: Rangkorrelation nach Spearman; Chi-Quadrat-Berechnung; Medianberechnung.

11915 Bilingual-bikulturelle und multikulturelle Kindergärten: wissenschaftliche Begleitung eines Pilotprojekts in Basel. (Jardins d'enfants bilingues-biculturels et multiculturels: accompagnement scientifique d'une expérience-pilote à Bâle.)
CHE 1994
Research Date(s): 1991-1992
Allemann-Ghionda, Cristina (Wollbacherstrasse 1, 4058 Basel, Schweiz).
Erziehungsdepartement Basel-Stadt, Münsterplatz 1, 4051 Basel, Schweiz
intercultural education; pre-school education; child of foreign national; bilingual education
éducation interculturelle; éducation préscolaire; enfant d'étranger; enseignement bilingue
PROJECT DESCRIPTION
Die Idee, einen Kindergarten zweisprachig zu führen, enstand, als man nach innovativen und praktikablen Lösungen für zwei stadtbaslerische Kindergärten suchte, die von relativ grossen Populationen anderssprachiger Kinder aus in der Nähe gelegenen Kinderkrippen (in einem Fall eine spanische, im andern eine italienische) besucht werden.

Im "italienisch-deutschen" Kindergarten arbeiteten zwei Kindergärtnerinnen vollzeitig; eine davon war italienische Muttersprache (eine Tessinerin). Die Anzahl der Kinder stieg in der Beobachtungszeit von 13 auf 18. Der "spanisch-deutsche" Kindergarten wurde von 23 Kindern besucht, 12 im ersten und 11 im zweiten Jahr. Diese Kinder wurden von drei zu je 80 Prozent angestellten Kindergärtnerinnen betreut; zwar waren alle deutscher Muttersprache, aber eine hatte längere Zeit in Lateinamerika gearbeitet und sprach fliessend Spanisch.

Aus einer Reihe von Gründen wurden in den wissenschaftlich zu begleitenden Versuch auch zwei multinational und multikulturell zusammengestzte Kindergärten einbezogen. Gemeinsam waren den vier Institutionen zwei Merkmale: Blockzeiten und eine Führung im Team (drei Zweier- und aus Gründen der Kinderzahlen ein Dreierteam). Die wissenschaftliche Begleitung setzte im Oktober 1991 ein und endete im Juni 1992 mit der Abgabe eines Forschungsberichts. In der Zwischenzeit konzentrierte sich dei Begleitarbeit auf Anstrengungen in den Bereichen Aus- und Weiterbildung, Organisation des Erfahrungsaustauschs, gemeinsame Konzeptentwicklung, Erarbeitung von Unterrichtseinheiten usw. Phasenweise arbeiteten drei Studentinnen des Romanischen Seminars der Universität Basel im Rahmen ihrer Seminar-arbeiten im Projekt mit.

Die aus den Schlussfolgerungen sich ergebenden Vorschläge betreffen einen Ausbau der pädagogischen Unterstützung der fremdsprachigen Kinder durch Personen mit gleicher Muttersprache wie sie, die Vermehrung der durch Teams geleiteten Kindergärten, eine zeitliche Verlängerung der wissenschaftlichen Begleitung sowie Massnahmen im Bereich der Aus- und Weiterbildung. Solche Dinge kosten natürlich etwas; es darf jedoch davon ausgegangen werden, dass es sich dabei um Investitionen handelt, die sich im Lauf der späteren Beschulung der Kinder wieder auszahlen werden.

Publ: Allemann-Ghionda, Cristina. *Pilotprojekt Bilingual-bikulturelle und multikulturelle Kindergärten*. Basel: Erziehungsdepartement, Juni 1992, 28 Seiten + Anhänge.

11916 Bringing teachers to the centre of the stage: a study of secondary school teachers' responses to curriculum change in mathematics.
GBR 1993
Research Date(s): 1985-1991
Nolder, R.
Sup: Johnson, D.
Inst: Loughborough University of Technology, Department of Education, Loughborough LE11 3TU, United Kingdom; London University, King's College, Centre for Educational Studies, Cornwall House Annexe, Waterloo Road, London SE1 3TY, United Kingdom.
educational reform; curriculum development; teacher behaviour
réforme de l'enseignement; élaboration de programmes d'études; comportement de l'enseignant
PROJECT DESCRIPTION

The research aims to examine the ways in which teachers respond to changes in classroom practice demanded of them in the course of radical curriculum change in mathematics. The fieldwork was carried out from 1985 to 1988 when various changes were being introduced into the secondary methematics curriculum largely in connection with the new examination at 16 plus, the General Certificate of Secondary Education.

The research falls into the category of interpretivist research. It focuses on teachers in two mathematics departments (N=8, of 12 in the two schools). Qualitative research methods are used; the main research strategy is participant observation. Data have been collected in the form of field notes, documentation and audiotapes of interviews. A network which represents a set of 11 interrelated concepts associated with professional change (including competence, confidence, control and constraints on professional practice) has been developed from the data. This network has served as an analytic tool, firstly to monitor professional change for two case study subjects and secondly to identify commonalities and differences in responses to change among teachers in the study.

From the analyses an empirically based model of the process of accelerated professional development associated with radical change has been developed. The model comprises five stages: anticipation, immersion, coping, consolidation, and extension.

Publ: Nolder, R.B. Responding to change. In: Pimm, D. (ed.). *Mathematics, Teachers and Children*. London: Hodder and Stoughton, 1988.
Nolder, R.B. & Tytherleigh, B. R2MC: a springboard to curriculum change. In: *British Journal of Inservice Education*, Vol 16, No 1/1990, pp. 14-22.
Nolder, R.B. Accommodating curriculum change in mathematics: teachers' dilemmas. In: *Proceedings of the 14th Annual Conference of the International Group for the Psychology of Mathematical Education*, Oaxtepec, Mexico, Vol 1, 1990, pp. 167-174.

11917 Budoucnost vzdělávání a školství v obnovené demokratické společnosti a ve sjednocující se Evropě. (The future of education in a renewed democratic society and a united Europe.)
CSK 1994
Research Date(s): 1990-1992
Kotásek, J.; Helus, Z.; Pitha, P.; Cerná, M.; Vyskočilová, M.; Kalous, J.; Solfronk, J.; Průcha, J.
Inst: Pedagogická fakulta Univerzity Karlovy (Charles University, Faculty of Education), M.D. Rettigové 4, 116 39 Praha 1, Czech Republic.
Ministerstvo školství, mládeže a tělovýchovy (Ministry of Education, Youth and Physical Education), Karmelitská 7, 118 00 Praha 1, Czech Republic
educational reform; educational policy; development of education; Europe
réforme de l'enseignement; politique de l'éducation; développement de l'éducation; Europe
PROJECT DESCRIPTION
Aim: The research consisted of a programme of expert studies presenting alternative proposals for educational reform and innovation in the next decade.
Results: The results of the project, including 16 expert reports, have been submitted to the Czech Ministry of Education, Youth and Physical Education.
Publ: Rozvaha o školství a vzdělanosti a jejich dalším vývoji v českých zemích. In: *Učitelské noviny*. 1991/33, příloha Obzor.
Pedagogika, 42, 1992/1.
Expertní studie k Rozvaze o školství a vzdělanosti a jejich dalším vývoji v českých zemích. In: *Učitelské noviny*, 1991/45, příloha Obzor.

11918 The caring school.
GBR 1993
Research Date(s): 1988-1993
Fletcher-Campbell, F.
Sup: Straughan, R.
Inst: Reading University, Faculty of Education and Community Studies, Bulmershe Court, Woodlands Avenue, Earley, Reading RG6 1HY, United Kingdom.
guidance; teacher-pupil relation; school; social role
orientation; relation maître-élève; école; rôle social
PROJECT DESCRIPTION
Most schools claim to be caring institutions but it is not clear as to how this claim should be interpreted. The research analyses accounts in the literature and as given by a small sample of secondary headteachers. A philosophical analysis of the concept of the caring school is then undertaken before practical recommendations for schools' policy and practice are made.

11919 Changes in the classroom experience of Inner London pupils.
GBR 1993
Research Date(s): 1992-1994
Plewis, I.
Inst: London University, Institute of Education, Thomas Coram Research Unit, 41 Brunswick Square, London WC1N 1AZ, United Kingdom.
Fin: Economic and Social Research Council.
educational reform; nursery school; classroom arrangement; primary school; curriculum research; learning conditions; urban school

réforme de l'enseignement; école maternelle; arrangement de la salle de classe; école primaire; recherche sur les programmes d'études; conditions d'apprentissage; école urbaine
PROJECT DESCRIPTION
The focus of this project is on infant schools, and on measuring changes in pupils' experiences in them following the changes introduced by the Education Reform Act. Comparisons will be made with data obtained at the Thomas Coram Research Unit (TCRU) in 1984/1985. The project will concentrate on how much time pupils spend on different parts of the curriculum, and how much of the mathematics curriculum they experience. It will also look at classroom organisation in terms of how pupils are grouped for mathematics and how this varies over time. As well as looking at changes in pupils' experiences at a time of considerable change in the educational system, the project will contribute to the development of theory about factors influencing children's learning, and to the development of statistical methods for the analysis of longitudinal data sets in educational research.

11920 The changing impact of a policy initiative: a multilevel analysis of TVEI.
GBR 1993
Research Date(s): 1990-1991
Raffe, D.; McPherson, A.; Paterson, L.
Inst: Edinburgh University, Centre for Educational Sociology, 7 Buccleuch Place, Edinburgh EH8 9JT, United Kingdom.
Fin: Economic and Social Research Council.
educational policy; vocational education; technical education; evaluation
politique de l'éducation; enseignement professionnel; enseignement technique; évaluation
PROJECT DESCRIPTION
The project aims to examine the effects of the pilot TVEI (Technical and Vocational Education Initiative) on attainment, truancy, staying-on, employment, training and attitudinal outcomes. The study will use data from the Scottish Young People's Survey.
Publ: A bibliography of published work and further details of the project are available.

11921 The changing impact of a policy initiative: a multilevel analysis of TVEI.
GBR 1993
Research Date(s): 1990-1991
Paterson, L.; Raffe, D.
Inst: Edinburgh University, Centre for Educational Sociology, 7 Buccleuch Place, Edinburgh EH8 9JT, United Kingdom.
Fin: Economic and Social Research Council.
educational policy; technical education; vocational education; transition from school to work
politique de l'éducation; enseignement technique; enseignement professionnel; passage à la vie active
PROJECT DESCRIPTION
The purpose of this research is to examine the effects of the pilot Technical and Vocational Education Initiative (TVEI) on attainment, truancy, staying-on, employment, training and attitudinal outcomes. The study will use data from the Scottish Young People's Survey.

11922 Comparaisons des inégalités sociales de scolarisation dans quatre pays européens et en France au cours des trente dernières années.
FRA 1993
Research Date(s): 1987-1991
Mingat, Alain; Duru-Bellat, Marie.
Inst: Université de Dijon, UER Faculté des sciences économiques et de gestion, CNRS UPR/29 et GDR/996, Institut de recherche sur l'économie de l'éducation, BP 138, 21004 Dijon Cedex, France.
equal opportunity; comparative education; education system; schooling rate; cross-national research
égalité de chances; éducation comparée; système d'enseignement; taux de scolarisation; recherche transnationale
PROJECT DESCRIPTION
Objectifs: L'analyse en termes de différenciations sociales de cursus scolaires peut être organisée autour de la séparation entre ce qui tient d'une part à l'ouverture d'ensemble du système (aspect structurel) et ce qui tient d'autre part aux différenciations sociales à niveau d'ouverture donnée du système (aspect sélectivité). Cette distinction est au coeur de la politique publique pour plus d'équité à l'école, car les voies de la démocratisation sociale passent essentiellement par une meilleure équité au sein du système si bien que l'analyse des différenciations sociales à niveau de développement éducatif donné devient la question d'intérêt central.
Méthodologie: On estime intéressant d'identifier comment les différences de fonctionnement engendrent des inégalités sociales plus ou moins marquées. Pour cela on adopte une approche macro-économique mobilisant des comparaisons internationales: Italie, Royaume-Uni, Suisse et France. Cette approche se prête à des comparaisons dans le temps et ceci a été fait pour les trente dernières années sur des données françaises.

Publ: Duru-Bellat, Marie & Mingat, Alain. *Mobiliser des comparaisons pour analyser les effets sociaux du fonctionnement du système et des mécanismes d'orientation: dans l'espace, sur plusieurs pays européens: dans le temps, en France au cours des 20 dernières années.* IREDU, fév. 1991, 28p.

Duru-Bellat, Marie & Mingat, Alain. *Comparaison des procédures et processus d'orientation et analyse de leurs effets dans plusieurs pays européens et en France au cours des 20 dernières années.* IREDU, Rapport pour la Fédération de l'éducation nationale, juin 1991, 57p.

11923   Counselling in different settings.
GBR   1993
Research Date(s): 1992-1993
Rees, W.
Inst: University College of North Wales, School of Education, Deiniol Road, Bangor, Gwynedd LL57 2UW, United Kingdom.
guidance; guidance officer; skill
orientation; orienteur; compétence
PROJECT DESCRIPTION
   The aim of this research is to discover whether there is a common core of counselling skills and approaches in different settings. Interviews have been taped and transcribed with hospital chaplains, hospital social workers, probation officers, drugs workers, and student counsellors.

11924   Das Museum aus sozialhistorischer und psychoanalytischer Sicht. (A socio-historical and psychoanalytical view of museums.)
DEU   1993
Research Date(s): 1989-1993
Pazzini, K.; Fliedl, G.
Inst: Universitaet Lueneburg, FB 01 Erziehungswissenschaften, Lehrgebiet Werken, Aesthetische Erziehung, Postfach 2440, D-2120 Lueneburg.
didactics; museum; sciences of education; aesthetic education; art
didactique; musée; sciences de l'éducation; éducation esthétique; art
PROJECT DESCRIPTION
   Inhalt: Funktionen des Museums, die in der gegenwaertigen Tendenz der Musealisierung in den Hintergrund getreten sind, "vergessen" wurden, aber dennoch institutionell wirksam sind. Konsequenzen fuer Ausstellungsdidaktik, Museumspaedagogik.
   Vorgehensweise: Hermeneutik; Psychoanalyse.
Publ: Pazzini, Karl-Josef. Tod im Museum. Ueber eine gewisse Naehe von Paedagogik, Museum und Tod. In: Groppe, Hans-Hermann; Juergensen, Frank (Hrsg.). *Gegenstaende der Fremdheit. Museale Grenzgaenge.* Marburg: Jonas Verl. 1989, S. 124 ff.
Pazzini, Karl-Josef. ders. Beitrag. In: Zacharias, W. (Hg.). *Zeitphaenomen Musealisierung. Das Verschwinden der Gegenwart und die Konstruktion der Erinnerung.* Essen: Klartext 1990, S. 83-98.
Pazzini, Karl-Josef. Reanimation oder die Furcht vor Rache und Wiederkehr. In: *Saarbruecker Hefte. Industriekultur und Industriearchaeologie.* 64, 11, 1990, S. 61-69.

11925   De derde fase van de OVB-BO-cohortonderzoeken. (Third phase of the primary education cohort studies conducted as part of the evaluation of the Educational Priority Policy (OVB).)
NLD   1994
Research Date(s): 1992-1994
Mulder, L.; Werf, M.P.C. van der.
Inst: Instituut voor Toegepaste Sociale wetenschappen (ITS) (Institute for Applied Social Sciences), P.O. Box 9048, 6500 KJ Nijmegen, Netherlands.
Katholieke Universiteit Nijmegen (Catholic University of Nijmegen), P.O. Box 9102, 6500 HC Nijmegen, Netherlands
Fin: SVO het Instituut voor Onderzoek van het Onderwijs.
educational policy; primary education; evaluation; ethnic minority; achievement
politique de l'éducation; enseignement primaire; évaluation; minorité ethnique; rendement
PROJECT DESCRIPTION
   Background: The aim of the Educational Priority Policy (OVB) is to improve the achievements and the school careers of pupils from disadvantaged backgrounds. In order to ascertain to what extent this goal is being reached and to identify the determining factors in this context, an extensive "OVB evaluation programme" was started in 1987. The core of this programme consists of a series of longitudinal investigations of successive cohorts of pupils in primary years 4, 6 and 8 and of the schools they attend. Every two years, data are collected from the schools, the pupils and the parents. The present investigation concerns the third phase of the longitudinal evaluation studies.
   Aim: To examine: how the OVB is being implemented; what results are being achieved; what changes, if any, have taken place in the course of time.
   Design: The study will focus in principle on the same schools that participated in the previous two phases of the cohort studies. At pupil level data will be gathered from all pupils in years 4, 6 and 8. Only the fourth-year pupils, to whom the tests will be administered, constitute a new cohort. Some of the data on the pupils in years 6 and 8 are already available from the previous phases. Information will be collected on how

OVB facilities are being deployed. Data will be gathered on characteristics of school effectiveness, taking Scheerens' theory (1989) as a basis. Twenty Islamic primary schools will participate in the study.

11926   De kwaliteit van het kleuteronderwijs: een onderzoek naar de samenhang tussen de pedagogisch-didactische aanpak, de processen en de ontwikkelingseffecten. (The quality of pre-school education: an exploration of the relationships between teaching methods, process variables and outcomes.)
BEL   1994
Research Date(s): 1989-1991
Nijsmans, I.; et al.
Sup: Laevers, F.
Inst: Departement Pedagogische Wetenschappen (Department of Educational Sciences), Vesaliusstraat 2, 3000 Leuven, Belgium.
Katholiek Universiteit Leuven (Catholic University of Leuven), Naamsestraat 22, 3000 Leuven, Belgium
Fin: Departement Onderwijs, Fonds voor Kollektief en Fundamenteel Onderzoek op Ministerieel Initiatief.
didactics; learning process; teaching quality; achievement measurement; pre-school education
didactique; apprentissage; qualité de l'enseignement; mesure du rendement; éducation préscolaire
PROJECT DESCRIPTION
   Aim: The aim of this research is to develop a strategy (instruments and methodology) to assess the quality of educational provisions for young children. The variables explored are located in three domains. The teaching method aspect concerns: teacher style (with three dimensions: responsiveness to feeling, providing autonomy, giving stimulating impulses), use of time (total class time vs. time available for activities) and degree of child initiative at the level of the class day organisation. The process variables are: performed activities, cognitive processes, degree of involvement (i.e. intensity of the activity) and degree of emotional well-being. The outcomes - which will be measured in a pretest posttest design - concern: prearithmetic skills, language development, physical knowledge and social cognition.
   Sample: The study was conducted in 12 pre-school classes (5-year-olds). These represented a wide range of pre-school practice, varying from traditional to innovative. In every class, 12 children were selected, taking into account their gender and social background with a view to achieving a balanced distribution.
   Results: The major contribution of the project bears on the development of a methodology to chart relevant aspects of pre-school teaching methods and process factors. The instruments enable a detailed description to be made of crucial dimensions of the quality of pre-school education and bring to light wide differences between the classes in the sample. One of the most striking results is the significant correlation between the degree of child initiative and involvement. The highest degrees of involvement were found in classes where the "Experiential Education" model (developed in Leuven) was implemented.
   As regards the analysis of the relationships between method/process and outcomes, the data are rather confusing. The need for a critical, qualitative, in-depth analysis of the tests and the test situation is emphasized. The motivational conditions surrounding the measurement of outcomes require particular attention. These problems seem to be connected with the young age of the children involved.
Publ: Vandevenne, F. *De ontwikkeling van basisinzichten m.b.t. de psycho-sociale wereld bij kleuters: literatuuronderzoek en ontwerp van een instrument.* Leuven: KUL, Afdeling Didactiek, 1990, 156p. + appendices.
Van Laethem, I. *Fysische kennis bij kleuters: literatuuronderzoek en ontwikkeling van een instrument.* Leuven: KUL, Afdeling Didactiek, 1990, 162p. + appendices.

11927   De onderwijspositie van leerlingen uit OVB-cohort 88-8 in het derde jaar van het voortgezet onderwijs. (The position in education of the 88-8 Educational Priority Policy cohort in the third secondary school year.)
NLD   1994
Research Date(s): 1992-1993
Mulder, L.; Suhre, C.J.M.
Sup: Tesser, P.; Werf, M. van der.
Inst: Instituut voor Toegepaste Sociale wetenschappen (ITS) (Institute for Applied Social Sciences), P.O. Box 9048, 6500 KJ Nijmegen, Netherlands.
Katholieke Universiteit Nijmegen (Catholic University of Nijmegen), P.O. Box 9102, 6500 HC Nijmegen, Netherlands
Fin: SVO het Instituut voor Onderzoek van het Onderwijs.
equal opportunity; educational policy; achievement; social environment; school career
égalité de chances; politique de l'éducation; rendement; milieu social; cursus scolaire
PROJECT DESCRIPTION
   Background: In the 1988-1989 school year the first round of measurements took place as part of the longitudinal evaluation of the Educational

Priority Policy which aims to improve the educational opportunities of disadvantaged pupils. In the evaluation, the achievements and the school careers of consecutive cohorts of primary school pupils are being monitored. About half of all pupils who were in the final year of primary school in 1988 (the 88-8 cohort) have been followed through to secondary school.

Aim: To examine the effect of the Educational Priority Policy on the school careers of the target population in the third year of secondary schooling.

Design: Data will be collected on over 5,000 pupils in the third secondary school year. Questionnaires will be sent to the head teachers or the administrative departments of the schools concerned. Information will be collected on: type of school, classroom, target pupils' report card marks for Dutch and mathematics, average marks for Dutch and mathematics in these pupils' classes, pupils' choices of specializations and course options, and absence rates. In the case of pupils who have left their school, the name and address of the school to which they transferred will be asked.

11928 Developing emancipatory curricula in primary schools.
GBR 1993
Research Date(s): 1990-1993
Morrison, K.
Sup: Gilliland, J.
Inst: Durham University, School of Education, Leazes Road, Durham DH1 1TA, United Kingdom.
educational theory; primary education; curriculum development; emancipation
théorie de l'éducation; enseignement primaire; élaboration de programmes d'études; émancipation
PROJECT DESCRIPTION

The study critiques the work of Jurgen Habermas and indicates how it may be used to inform a debate on developing emancipation through primary school curricula. Issues in the sociology of knowledge are addressed which bridge the gap between Habermasian theory and school curricula. A case study of the National Curriculum of England and Wales is undertaken, focussing particularly on cross-curricular issues. A short empirical research is undertaken to attempt to complete an analysis of the contribution of Habermas to curriculum theory and practice.

11929 Developing models of educational accountability.
GBR 1993
Research Date(s): 1987-
Jesson, D.; Mayston, D.
Inst: Sheffield University, Division of Education, 388 Glossop Road, Sheffield S10 2TN, United Kingdom; York University, Department of Economics and Related Studies, York YO1 5DD, United Kingdom.
quality of education; education system; secondary education; performance; measurement technique; model
qualité de l'éducation; système d'enseignement; enseignement secondaire; performance; technique de mesure; modèle
PROJECT DESCRIPTION

The research attempts to model the ouptuts of the secondary educational system using techniques drawn from the theory of production functions in economics. A major concern is to accommodate a wide variety of 'outputs', which, whilst including examination results, are capable of embracing other 'performance indicators'. The initial thrust has been to contrast the interpretations of previous studies using regression analysis with those obtained using data envelope analysis applied to inter-LEA (local education authority) studies. The phase now opening explores the potential at the intra-LEA level.

Publ: Jesson, D.; Mayston, D. & Smith, P. Performance assessment in the education sector: educational and economic perspectives. In: *Oxford Review of Education*, Vol 13, No 3/1987, pp. 249-266.
Jesson, D. & Mayston, D. Developing models of educational accountability. In: *Oxford Review of Education*, Vol 14, No 3/1988, pp. 321-339.

11930 Developing tools to measure the outcomes of guidance.
GBR 1993
Research Date(s): 1992-1993
Christophers, U.
Sup: Stoney, S.; Whetton, C.
Inst: National Foundation for Educational Research, The Mere, Upton Park, Slough SL1 2DQ, United Kingdom.
Fin: Department of Employment.
guidance; vocational guidance; measurement technique
orientation; orientation professionnelle; technique de mesure
PROJECT DESCRIPTION

The aim of the project is to produce valid and reliable instruments for measuring the outcomes of vocational or careers guidance. Vocational guidance is increasingly seen as a requirement in a range of effective employment strategies. Guidance is one of a number of services offered through Training and Enterprise Councils and subject to systematic evaluation. Currently, methods of evaluating guidance rely on measures of customer satisfaction and/or numbers of clients seen.

The new instruments are intended to provide alternative and more objective measures. The present-day theoretical formulation of careers guidance provided the starting point for this new approach. The process of guidance involves assisting clients themselves to achieve as good a match as may be possible between their interests and skills and their job aspirations, bearing in mind the opportunities open to them. An additional aim is to foster the transition skills which will stand clients in good stead in their job search now and at other times in their lives. Four areas, therefore, are frequently addressed in guidance: Opportunity Awareness; Self-Awareness; Decision Making Skills; and Transition Skills. The new instrument probes the extent to which learning in these areas has occurred and how well this persists.

A national trial involving 1,500 clients has been undertaken and clients will be followed up after two weeks and after three months to discover how the guidance affected their job search and employment status.

An additional aim of the project is to produce a diagnostic tool, which, when used during guidance, will assist workers in pinpointing a client's particular areas of difficulty. It is likely that the instrument devised will be published. The title of the new instrument is the Measure of Guidance Outcomes (MGO).

11931 Didaktische Planung und Gestaltung von Lehrveranstaltungen. (The didactic planning and organization of lectures.)
AUT 1993
Research Date(s): 1989-1992
Schilling, Michael; Csanyi, Gottfried S.; Sturm, Michael.
Inst: Bundeskonferenz des wissenschaftlichen und kuenstlerischen Personals der Oesterreichischen Universitaeten, Liechtensteinstrasse 22A, A-1090 Wien; Oesterreichische Gesellschaft fuer Hochschuldidaktik, Strozzigasse 2, A-1080 Wien.
Fin: Bundesministerium fuer Wissenschaft und Forschung.
didactics; university studies; teaching method; teaching aid; content of education; lecture
didactique; études universitaires; méthode pédagogique; moyen d'enseignement; contenu de l'éducation; exposé
PROJECT DESCRIPTION

1988 hat die Didaktikkommission der Bundeskonferenz des wissenschaftlichen und kuenstlerischen Personals der oesterreichischen Universitaeten eine Projektreihe mit dem Ziel gestartet, fuer Hochschullehrende 'Materialien zur Verbesserung von Lehrveranstaltungen' zu konzipieren und herauszugeben. Nach der Veroeffentlichung der Materialienmappe I zum Thema 'Rueckmeldungen' (1988; 2. ueberarbeitete Auflage 1990) wird in der Materialienmappe II 'Planung und Gestaltung von Lehrveranstaltungen' hochschuldidaktisches Grundwissen in praxisorientierter Form vermittelt. Im 1. Abschnitt werden Fragen behandelt, die fuer didaktische Entscheidungen offenstehen (Festlegung von Lehrzielen, Auswahl von Inhalten und Methoden, Medieneinsatz sowie Leistungsbeurteilung). Einzelne didaktische Elemente werden im 2. Abschnitt vorgestellt und in ihren Moeglichkeiten und Grenzen, Vor- und Nachteilen diskutiert. Eine Auswahl einfach handhabbarer Medien rundet die Mappe ab. Insgesamt sollen damit den Lehrenden Orientierungshilfen fuer den Einsatz und die Kombination didaktischer Elemente geboten werden.

Es wurden qualitative Interviews durchgefuehrt und eine Materialiensammlung angelegt.

Publ: Csanyi, Gottfried S. & Sturm, Michael. *Materialien zur Verbesserung von Lehrveranstaltungen. Teil 2: Planung und Gestaltung.* Herausgegeben von der Didaktikkommission der Bundeskonferenz des wissenschaftlichen und kuenstlerischen Personals der oesterreichischen Universitaeten. Wien 1992.

11932 Ecoles d'hier et d'aujourd'hui.
FRA 1993
Research Date(s): 1980-1987
Peneff, Jean.
Inst: Université de Nantes, UFR Institut d'histoire et de sociologie, CNRS URA/889 et GDR/55, Laboratoire d'études et de recherches sociologiques sur la classe ouvrière, Chemin de la Sensive-du-Tertre, BP 1025, 44036 Nantes Cedex, France.
public education; private education; educational provision; working class; history of education
enseignement public; enseignement privé; scolarisation; classe ouvrière; histoire de l'éducation
PROJECT DESCRIPTION

Objectifs: Ensemble de travaux constituant une contribution importante à l'histoire de la scolarisation populaire: La division école laïque-école confessionnelle dans l'ouest. Deux contributions apportent un éclairage local et historique de ces divisions, tout en les resituant dans une perspective à long terme de l'évolution de la scolarisation réelle. (1) Autobiographies d'enseignants d'écoles publiques et privées. Les individus y apparaissent très proches par l'origine sociale et le style de vie, mais séparés par les conditions de leur formation, de leur carrière et de leur travail. Dans une région où la concurrence entre les écoles est vive, chacun milite pour son école. (2) Trois monographies de trois écoles primaires respectivement situées dans le Morbihan, en Loire-Atlantique et en Vendée. De l'observation minutieuse de la vie quotidienne dans ces écoles, du dépouillement de leurs archives et de la comptabilité des entrées et des sorties, s'impose une image de la scolarité réelle très différente de celle que nous a léguée la tradition républicaine. Ce n'est qu'immédiatement avant la guerre de 1939 que la scolarisation primaire a vraiment concerné la quasi-totalité d'une génération. Nombreuses et efficaces ont en effet été de 1880 à 1940 les forces, à la fois populaires et patronales, qui ont résisté à la généralisation de cette scolarisation.

Publ: Peneff, Jean. *Ecoles publiques, écoles privées dans l'ouest, 1880-1950*. Paris: L'Harmattan, 1987.

Peneff, Jean. Autobiographies d'enseignants d'écoles publiques et privées. In: *Cahiers du LERSCO*, janvier 1987, n° 8.

11933 Educatie '92: naar een behoeftendekkend aanbod en beter gecoördineerd beleid inzake Permanente Vorming in Vlaaderen. (Education '92: towards a need-oriented supply and a better coordinated policy for continuing education in Flanders (Belgium).)
BEL 1994
Research Date(s): 1990-1992
Van Damme, D.; et al.
Sup: Leirman, W.; Faché, W.
Inst: Afdeling Sociale Pedagogiek en Gezinspedagogiek (Unit of Social Pedagogy and Family Pedagogy), Vesaliusstraat 2, 3000 Leuven, Belgium; Seminarie en Laboratorium voor Jeugdwelzijn en Volwassenenvorming (Seminar and Laboratorium for Youth Welfare and Adult Education), H. Dunantlaan 2, 9000 Gent, Belgium.
Katholieke Universiteit Leuven (Catholic University of Leuven), Naamsestraat 22, 3000 Leuven, Belgium; Rijksuniversiteit Gent (State University of Gent), Sint-Pietersnieuwstraat 25, 9000 Gent, Belgium
Fin: Departement Onderwijs, Fonds voor Kollektief en Fundamenteel Onderzoek op Ministerieel Initiatief.
continuing education; educational policy; educational need; adult education
éducation permanente; politique de l'éducation; besoin d'éducation; éducation des adultes
PROJECT DESCRIPTION
This project was set up as a policy-oriented Delphi survey about continuing education in Flanders (the Dutch-speaking part of Belgium). 300 experts from policy, practice and research as well as external commentators were asked to complete three questionnaires in three rounds. "Problem representativeness" was the most important criterion for the selection of respondents; 130 persons participated at least once.
Two important questions had to be answered: (1) What does a need-oriented offer of continuing education look like? (2) How can policy makers improve coordination in order to build up an integrated system of continuing education in Flanders? For the first question, the main problems adults are having to deal with today were identified. The results served as a basis for an attempt to formulate an adequate educational response to these problems. The policy question is two-sided. On the one hand there is the question of how existing educational domains can improve cooperation in order to achieve an integrated educational system. On the other hand there is the question of which policy makers have the responsibility to organize a better coordinated policy for continuing education in Flanders.
At the end of the project, the most important results were presented to and discussed by 100 experts from the respondents' group during a discussion day. The final report contains suggestions for policy and practice.
Publ: Gehre, G. et al. *Educatie '92: naar een behoeftendekkend aanbod en beter gecoördineerd beleid inzake permanente vorming in Vlaanderen.* Leuven, Gent: KUL, Afdeling Sociale Pedagogiek & RUG, Seminarie voor Jeugdwelzijn en Volwassenvorming, 1992, 146p. + summary (12p.).

11934 Education and social change with special reference to Nigerian women (particularly the Igbo).
GBR 1993
Research Date(s): 1989-
Uzoigwe, F.
Sup: Brock, C.
Inst: Hull University, School of Education, Cottingham Road, Hull HU6 7RX, United Kingdom.
equal opportunity; women's education; Nigeria
égalité de chances; éducation des femmes; Nigeria
PROJECT DESCRIPTION
Nigeria embraced western-style education in the early 1940s. Unlike many developing countries, Nigeria is a very big country with a population of well over a million people. There are over 300 languages in Nigeria and the main ethnic groups are: the Hausa/Fulani in the north, the Yoruba in the west and the Igbo in the east. Since the advent of western education no serious study has been undertaken with a view to determining whether or not Nigerian women and girls have had the same educational opportunities as men and boys, and also whether western-style education has enhanced or jeopardised the status of women in Nigeria.
In this study a vigorous attempt is being made to assess the educational status of women - firstly in global terms, in order to understand and appreciate more realistically the Nigerian situation; bearing in mind the findings of the United Nations, which show that women constitute the

greater percentage of the world's illiterates and that the rate is much higher among the women in the developing countries. In the case of Nigeria for instance, in 1984 the Federal Ministry of Education indicated that the adult illiteracy rate stood at 65%. It should, however, be borne in mind that in Nigeria a number of factors, including heavy domestic chores and child marriages, have over the years militated against the formal education of women and girls. Generally, the women in the northern part of Nigeria have lagged behind their counterparts in other parts of the country educationally, because the north is predominantly Moslem and certain demands are made on the women. For example, some women have to go into purdals and some girls are withdrawn from educational institutions at puberty. However, it is noteworthy that any measures designed to reduce female illiteracy rates in Nigeria (there are more illiterate women than men) must take into account informal methods of education, such as adult education, especially with regard to rural women.

11935 The education system in England and Wales.
GBR 1993
Research Date(s): 1991-1992
Hough, R.
Inst: Loughborough University of Technology, Department of Education, Loughborough LE11 3TU, United Kingdom.
educational policy; educational reform; education system; educational planning; regional planning
politique de l'éducation; réforme de l'enseignement; système d'enseignement; planification de l'éducation; planification régionale
PROJECT DESCRIPTION
This research is surveying developments in the education system in England and Wales with emphasis on changes since the Education Reform Act 1988. The research includes: The Department of Education and Science; local education authorities; the Education Reform Act 1988; the comprehensive school; the private sector of education; the education of the 16-19 age group and the further education sector; and higher education. In each case the project studies recent changes, especially those stemming directly from the Education Reform Act, and considers the effects and consequences.
Publ: Hough, J.R. *The education system in England and Wales: a synopsis.* Papers in Education Series. Loughborough University of Technology, Department of Education, 1991.

11936 Edukacja a humanistyka: kompetencja edukacyjna nauczyciela i ucznia. (Education and humanities: teachers' and pupils' educational competence.)
POL 1994
Research Date(s): 1988-1992
Biłos, Edward; Pluta, Andrzej; Bauć, Piotr.
Inst: Instytut Pedagogiki i Psychologii, Zakład Pedagogiki Ogólnej, Wyższa Szkoła Pedagogiczna (Institute of Education and Psychology, General Education Division, Pedagogical University), Jasnogórska 64, 42-200 Czestochowa, Poland.
Ministerstwo Edukacji Narodowej (Ministry of National Education), Al. I Armii Wojska Polskiego 25, 00-918 Warszawa, Poland; Komitet Badań Naukowych (Committee for Scientific Research), Wspólna 1/3, Warszawa, Poland
didactics; educational theory; humanities; teaching aptitude; learning aptitude
didactique; théorie de l'éducation; études littéraires; aptitude à l'enseignement; aptitude aux études
PROJECT DESCRIPTION
The aim is to recognize the nature and the structure of a didactic function. Having defined the didactic function as a complex subjective-rational activity, which is controlled by the autonomous social consciousness (didactic culture), the researchers aim at the development of a didactic theory (didactic norms and directives), which would be opposed to modern didactic ideas, and which could grasp the essential aspect of the cultural didactic function through the reconstruction of educational competence of the teacher and the pupil.
Methods: The researchers have applied a humanistic interpretation with a view to reconstructing existing education ideas and the principle of correspondence substantially correcting the epistemological fragment.
Preliminary results: The structure of the subjective-rational didactic function, called by the researchers a "didactic sequence", has been recognized and described. Above 400 educational activities have been developed and reconstructed at all education levels and in all types of education. On the basis of the research findings, curricula for the integrated subject General Pedagogy (General Pedagogy + Theory of Education + General Didactics), as well as the Polish language teaching methodology, have been developed. Since the academic year 1990/1991 these curricula have been implemented at the following faculties: Childcare Pedagogy, Mathematics, Physics, Chemistry, Pedagogy of Work, and the Polish language teaching methodology at the faculty of the Polish Philology. At present, research into pupils' educational competence is being carried out, as well as research into the structural-didactic system of the relationships between

didactic functions of the teacher and the pupil (teaching-learning processes).

Publ: Biłos, Edward. *Wypowiedzenia pytajne w nauczaniu jezyka polskiego.* Czestochowa: 1992, 196p.

Pluta, Andrzej. On the Application of the Notion of Pedagogical Culture. In: Kmita, Jerzy; Zamiara, Krystyna (eds.). *Visions of culture and the Models of Cultural Sciences.* Amsterdam: Atlanta, 1989, pp. 243-259.

Pluta, Andrzej. Uwagi o funkcjonalnych powiazaniach badań pedagogicznych i dydaktycznych z praktyka edukacyjna. In: *Dydaktyka literatury.* Vol. X. Zielona Góra: 1989, pp. 111-113.

Pluta, Andrzej. Edukacja - Światopoglad - Dydaktyka. In: *Ruch Pedagogiczny,* 4/1989, pp. 18-51.

Pluta, Andrzej. *Edukacja a kultura.* Czestochowa: 1992, 173p. (A full list of publications is available from the researchers.).

11937 The effectiveness of Access courses.
GBR 1993
Research Date(s): 1991-1993
Munn, P.; Robinson, R.; Johnstone, M.
Inst: Scottish Council for Research in Education, 15 St John Street, Edinburgh EH8 8JR, United Kingdom.
Fin: Leverhulme Trust.
access to education; quality of education; higher education; adult education
accès à l'éducation; qualité de l'éducation; enseignement supérieur; éducation des adultes
PROJECT DESCRIPTION
The aim of this project is to assess the effectiveness of science and social science Access courses in preparing adults for degree-level study. The research will provide a greater understanding of the strengths and weaknesses of Access courses, as well as recommendations for good practice both in Access courses themselves and in higher education responsiveness to Access students.

11938 The effectiveness of bilingual education in Wales.
GBR 1993
Research Date(s): 1992-1995
Baker, C.
Inst: University College of North Wales, School of Education, Deiniol Road, Bangor, Gwynedd LL57 2UW, United Kingdom.
bilingual education; Welsh language; language teaching; teaching language; educational policy; aims of education
enseignement bilingue; langue galloise; enseignement des langues; langue d'enseignement; politique de l'éducation; finalité de l'éducation
PROJECT DESCRIPTION
The project will look at the results of computer analysis of the 1991 Census on the Welsh language, studying spatial, age, oracy/literacy trends alongside immigration/emigration and the effects on Welsh language educational provision. The major focus of the project will be the relationship of these trends to Welsh medium education and the implications for present and future educational policy. The project will also include a historical perspective of the growth of bilingual education in Wales from 1939 to the present; the National Curriculum and Assessment and the implications for bilingual education in Wales; county policies for Welsh language in education and the provision of Welsh medium teaching; recent conflicts and controversies over the Welsh language; perspectives of Inspectorate reports on Welsh medium teaching; Welsh medium curriculum development projects; the provision of Welsh medium education in higher education and further education; Welsh language media and voluntary bodies such as Urdd and Ysgolion Meithrin.

11939 Ekspansjonen i privat höyskolesektor - en utvikling uten styring? (Expansion in private higher education - a development out of control?)
NOR 1994
Research Date(s): 1992-1994
Amdam, Rolv Petter.
Inst: BI Handelshöyskolen i Oslo (Norwegian School of Management), PB 580, 1301 Sandvika, Norway.
Fin: NORAS.
private education; educational policy; decision making; higher education
enseignement privé; politique de l'éducation; prise de décision; enseignement supérieur
PROJECT DESCRIPTION
Background: There has been a remarkable expansion in private higher education compared to the little attention that private education has received in higher education policy.
Aim: The project aims to study where the decisions have been made that have led to this strong dominance of private colleges for education within the fields of economics and information technology. The project will study whether this expansion is the result of developments outside the control of political decision-makers or whether it results from an underlying strategy which aims at the development of a compound system for education and of which delegating the decision-making process forms a part.

11940 Elaborarea unui sistem interactiv de orientarea carierei. (Development of an interactive system for career guidance.)
ROM 1994
Research Date(s): 1992-1995
Tăsică, Luminita-Gabriela; Marinescu, Gabriela; Niculescu, Cătălina; Ardelean, Eugenia.
Sup: Klein, Maria-Magdalena.
Inst: Institutul de Stiinte ale Educatiei (Institute for Educational Sciences), str. Stirbei Vodă 37, 70732 Bucharest, Romania.
Ministerul Învătământului (Ministry of Education), str. General Berthelot 28-30, Bucharest, Romania
guidance; guidance service; occupational choice; occupational qualification; labour market; personality development
orientation; service d'orientation; choix d'une profession; qualification professionnelle; marché du travail; développement de la personnalité
PROJECT DESCRIPTION
Background: In Romania there is at present no comprehensive national source for career guidance. Information about labour market requirements and information derived from educational and occupational prognoses is not available to young people. Career decisions are based upon traditional family influence and exam results rather than on informed choice. As a result, most youth are forced to use incomplete and often inaccurate information about their career options in a rapidly changing economic and social environment.
Aims: To build a system that will provide young people with accurate and complete information about their abilities and the qualifications required on the labour market.
Design: Initially, the project will focus on psychological tests (abilities, interests, personality) and the development of materials to inform pupils and teachers about this new form of support for those taking a career decision. The next step will be to collect and disseminate in a uniform and structured manner information (including occupational profiles and related educational requirements) that will help individuals to explore their career options. It is also hoped to set up a national database with this information, which would also include tests of abilities and interests, labour market demands, and available forms of training. This database will be experimented and validated for use in careers counselling in guidance centres.

11941 Elaboration of didactic aspects of the reform of higher education.
RUS 1994
Research Date(s): 1991-1992
Yaroshenko, N.G.
Sup: Fokin, Y.T.
Inst: Research Institute for Higher Education, 103062, Moscow, K-62, Podsosensky per. 20, Russia.
State Committee for Higher Education Institutions, 113833, Moscow, M-230, Lysinovskja str. 51, Russia
educational reform; higher education; education system; teaching model
réforme de l'enseignement; enseignement supérieur; système d'enseignement; modèle didactique
PROJECT DESCRIPTION
The study aimed to contribute to the reform of higher education within the wider framework of the Russian education system. A new classification of educational characteristics was elaborated. Furthermore, specific features of organizational/didactic models were defined and achievement standards for specialized secondary education were outlined.
The results of the study can be used in higher education, especially in activity-oriented teaching.

Publ: Semushina, L.G.; Yaroshenko, N.G.; Zaitseva, Z.A.; et al. *Study of the development of specialized secondary education under new socio-economic conditions.* Information review. M., NIIVO, 1992, 52p.

Semushina, L.G. *Theoretical foundations of professional education and training in specialized secondary education establishments.* Doctoral thesis.

Fokin, Y.G. *The purpose of higher education in the system of people's education in Russia.* A collection of research works on "Youth, education, market", M., NIIVO, 1992.

11942 Elaborazione di un gioco di simulazione per l'orientamento scolastico e professionale nelle scuole medie. (Elaboration of a simulation game for educational and vocational guidance in lower secondary schools.)
ITA 1993
Research Date(s): 1988-1989
Panizzi, G.
Inst: Centro Nazionale Italiano Tecnologie Educative - CNITE (Italian Centre of Educational Technology), Via Marche 84, 00187 Roma, Italy.
Fin: Ministero della Pubblica Istruzione, Ufficio Studi e Programmazione.
guidance; lower secondary; simulation game; educational game
orientation; secondaire premier cycle; jeu de simulation; jeu éducatif
PROJECT DESCRIPTION

Aims: The research comprises three complementary projects which aim to enable lower secondary school teachers to stay up-to-date on modern techniques in the field of education and training.

The projects are: (1) the elaboration of a simulation model for teachers in lower secondary schools; (2) research and experimentation focusing on the techniques and instruments available for the evaluation of training and simulation activities; (3) a project to update lower secondary school teachers on distance training activities.

At this stage, only the first project has been accomplished. A simulation game has been devised for both educational and vocational counselling in lower secondary schools. The game is called SEXTANT and is seen as an instrument for giving guidance in a particular direction, not for setting a specific goal.

Methods: The study has a theoretical premise and makes reference to similar experiences. It examines the principal variants in the planning of simulation games. It describes in detail the internal structure of the game and its different stages, giving further explanation of the teaching evaluation materials and commenting on the guidance participants. Three reports have been published: (1) preliminary results; (2) the organizer's (or teachers's) text; (3) the player's (or pupil's) text.

Results: The introductory section summarizes the theoretical premises regarding educational and vocational counselling and implements some practical techniques such as guidance, counselling, problem solving, and role playing. Next, the study explains the procedures of the game. (a) The player (pupil) chooses a role on the basis of acquired knowledge about professional profiles and economic sectors. The various players have to interact and establish relations between themselves and the guidance counsellors. They are required to discuss the reasons why they choose one sector instead of another. (b) The organizer (teacher) inserts a guidance counsellor or teacher in the game in order to put him or her on more equal footing, as a player, with the pupil.

The manual allows for the enrichment of the game with other information.

11943 Equal opportunities and social justice.
GBR 1993
Research Date(s): 1990-1991
Griffiths, M.; McBride, R.; Weiner, G.
Inst: Nottingham University, Department of Adult Education, 14-22 Shakespeare Street, Nottingham NG1 4FJ, United Kingdom; University of East Anglia, School of Education, Norwich NR4 7TJ, United Kingdom; South Bank University, 103 Borough Road, London SE1 OAA, United Kingdom.
equal opportunity; justice; social change; social class
égalité de chances; justice; changement social; classe sociale
PROJECT DESCRIPTION

This is a theoretical and philosophical examination of the central concepts and their relationship to teacher development in the 1990s. The work as a whole will include an investigation of the concept of justice and social justice, to inequality with reference to race, class, sexuality, etc. Key themes will include: the importance of focusing on both individuals and groups as a unit of analysis; the significance of metaphors of balance and harmony and their possible inappropriateness in a dynamic society; and changing meanings of the notion of justice across time and place. These themes will be used to illuminate evidence about inequalities in modern British society. The implications for policy will be drawn out and formulated in terms of an education agenda for the 1990s.

11944 Equal opportunities policies in schools and colleges post local management developments from the 1988 Education Act.
GBR 1993
Research Date(s): 1991-1994
Mardle, G.; Colclough, P.; Shain, F.; Modiba, M.
Inst: Keele University, Department of Education, Keele, Staffordshire ST5 5BG, United Kingdom.
equal opportunity; educational policy; educational reform; educational legislation
égalité de chances; politique de l'éducation; réforme de l'enseignement; législation scolaire
PROJECT DESCRIPTION

In the past, policy initiation in the education system has in general been the responsibility of either the government or the local education authority. Under the 1988 Education Act this has changed. Secondary schools and further education colleges now have control over their budgets and also a far higher degree of control over certain policy initiatives. Within the context of many other pressures this has led to a degree of inertia in certain areas. In particular, the development of equal opportunity policies has been affected.

The aim of this investigation is to examine, via questionnaire and case study material, the effects of current legislation in the area of equal opportunity policy in schools and colleges. The focus of attention starts with the political aspects of the problem. It then goes on to examine the way in which such policies in the areas of gender, race and disability are seen by the participants, developed in the institutions and the methods deployed in

putting them into practice. It is hoped that the results and conclusions of the study will enable more institutions to develop and implement such policies.

11945 Equity aspects of training policy.
CHE 1993
Research Date(s): 1992-
Lee, E.; Goodale, G.; Plett, P.
Inst: Training Policy and Programme Development Branch, Training Department, International Labour Office, 1211 Geneva, Switzerland.
equal opportunity; developing country; government policy; educational policy
égalité de chances; pays en développement; politique gouvernementale; politique de l'éducation
PROJECT DESCRIPTION

Background: Little research has been undertaken on equity aspects of training policy in developing countries. In order to remedy this situation, it is proposed to set up an analytical framework with a view to defining equity issues in training and provide methodological guidelines to measure their effects. In addition, another analytical framework will be set up specifically for analysis of gender-related equity issues.

Aim: The aim of the frameworks will be to guide the formulation of equitable training policies. In this context, questions such as the amount of resources allocated to training and criteria for access to training opportunities will be considered.

The methodological guidelines will cover issues such as what equity considerations need to be taken into account, the types of data which need to be consulted, possible future data generation needs and how data should be interpreted.

Gender equity aspects of training policy and systems will be approached through case studies from which a conceptual framework for policy makers will be drawn. Here, the training system will be examined, as well as legislation, present policies, expenditures, participation of females, provision of training and post-training outcomes.

The results of the research will be published as one or more working papers.

11946 Establishing access to the tertiary curriculum for adults with special educational needs.
GBR 1993
Research Date(s): 1987-1992
Cooper, A.
Sup: Jotham, R.
Inst: Nottingham University, Department of Adult Education, 14-22 Shakespeare Street, Nottingham NG1 4FJ, United Kingdom; Derby Tertiary College, Wilmorton Campus, Wilmorton, Derby DE2 8UG, United Kingdom.
access to education; post-compulsory education; special education; mentally handicapped
accès à l'éducation; enseignement postobligatoire; enseignement spécial; handicapé mental
PROJECT DESCRIPTION

The purpose of the project is to evaluate the effectiveness of an educational support centre for special needs students located within a college of further education. Methodology involves regular consultation with the Centre staff, students and management staff.

11947 Ethnizität und Multilingualismus: Grundlagenforschung zur Interkulturellen Pädagogik. (Ethnicité et multilinguisme: recherche fondamentale dans le domaine de la pédagogie interculturelle.)
CHE 1994
Research Date(s): 1988-1991
Steiner, Gitta (Grellingerstrasse 12, 4052 Basel, Schweiz).
Fin: Schweizerischer Nationalfonds zur Förderung der wissenschaftlichen Forschung.
intercultural education; national minority; cross-national research; philosophy of education
éducation interculturelle; minorité nationale; recherche transnationale; philosophie de l'éducation
PROJECT DESCRIPTION

Die Forscherin hat sich während ihres dreijährigen Forschungsaufenthalts an den Universitäten London, Toronto und Berkeley (Kalifornien) mit der Entwicklung der interkulturellen Pädagogik in Grossbritannien, Kanada und den USA befasst. In jedem der drei Länder hat sie sich vornehmlich einem Thema gewidmet.

In England - am Beispiel der Städte Leeds, Bradford und London - ging es um den Paradigmenwechsel von einer interkulturellen zu einer antirassistischen Erziehung, der schwerpunktmässig in den Jahren von 1983 bis 1989 vollzogen wurde.

In Kanada ging es um die Umsetzung des staatlich geförderten Multikulturalismus. Die Autorin untersuchte die Organisation der `heritage classes` (mit Unterricht in der Herkunftssprache) an den Schulen Torontos und diskutiert sie im Rahmen der kanadischen Multikulturalismus-Debatte. Sie zeichnet ferner die diskursiven Brüche in der kanadischen Multikulturalismus-Debatte von 1976 (Entstehung der Multikulturalismus-Richtlinie) bis ans Ende der achtziger Jahre nach.

In den USA interessierte der Einzug multikultureller Bildungskonzepte an den Universitäten (Fallstudien: die kalifornischen Universitäten Berkeley und Stanford), zugleich aber auch die negativen Reaktionen (Verunglimpfung unter dem Stichwort der "political correctness"), die sie hervorriefen.

Der Autorin scheint die US-amerikanische Multikulturalisierungsbewegung besonders interessant für die Grundlagenforschung auf dem Gebiet der interkulturellen Pädagogik. Diese Bewegung stellt eine explizite Verbindung zum Dekonstruktivismus her. Die Autorin begründet, weshalb sie es als sinnvoll erachtet, das Konzept des "miniority discourse" - welches in dekonstruktivistischen Ansätzen formuliert und in der feministischen Theorie weiterentwickelt wurde - in die interkulturelle Diskussion des deutschen Sprachraums aufzunehmen. In ihrer Optik ist es eine Alternative zum kulturvergleichenden Ansatz der hiesigen Pädagogik, deren Ethnizitätsparadigma laut ihr dazu beiträgt, dass die Eingewanderten als die kulturell Anderen konstruiert und damit exotisiert, entmündigt und ghettosisiert werden.

Publ: Steiner-Khamsi, Gita. *Multikulturelle Bildungspolitik in der Postmoderne*. Opladen: Leske & Budrich, 1992, 239 S.

11948 Evaluation du premier cycle "délocalisé" de Nevers.

FRA 1993
Research Date(s): 1989-
Duru-Bellat, Marie; Jarousse, Jean-Pierre; Rapiau, Marie-Thérèse.
Inst: Université de Dijon, UER Faculté des sciences économiques et de gestion, CNRS UPR/29 et GDR/996, Institut de recherche sur l'économie de l'éducation, BP 138, 21004 Dijon Cedex, France.
Fin: Conseil régional de Bourgogne.
educational policy; undergraduate study; success; cost-benefit analysis; content of education; regional planning
politique de l'éducation; supérieur premier cycle; réussite; analyse coût-bénéfice; contenu de l'éducation; planification régionale
PROJECT DESCRIPTION
Objectifs: L'évaluation du degré d'atteinte des objectifs poursuivis par le Ministère ou à l'échelon local pour les premiers cycles universitaires "délocalisés", est structurée autour d'un certain nombre de questions: (1) incidence sur les comportements d'orientation des usagers; (2) incidence sur le contenu des formations et les modalités de la réussite; (3) incidence en termes financiers. Au terme de la recherche, un bilan coût-avantage d'une scolarité en antenne pour l'étudiant et aussi pour les collectivités et une évaluation de cette politique publique de délocalisation sont menés.

11949 Evaluation of the introduction of a national framework for the recognition of Access Courses to higher education in England and Wales and Northern Ireland.

GBR 1993
Research Date(s): 1990-1991
Parry, G.; Davies, P.
Inst: City University, Centre for Continuing Education, Northampton Square, London EC1V OHB, United Kingdom.
Fin: TEED; FEU; DES; UDACE.
access to education; adult education; higher education; recurrent education; recognition of qualifications
accès à l'éducation; éducation des adultes; enseignement supérieur; éducation récurrente; reconnaissance des qualifications
PROJECT DESCRIPTION
This research was a twenty month study of the introduction of the CNAA/CVCP (Council for National Academic Awards/Committee of Vice Chancellors and Principals) national framework for the recognition of Access Courses to higher education. The research project aimed to trace the origin, development and impact of the framework as a means of extending opportunities for adults without conventional qualifications to participate in higher education.

The first phase focused on the first round of approvals of authorised validating agencies and involved content analysis of published documents and interview and observational studies of the central body. The extended phase focused on subsequent rounds of approvals and case studies of selected authorised validating agencies to monitor the impact of the framework at local level and in relation to Access Course providers and students.

The study involved both formative and summative evaluation and results and conclusions were disseminated through an interim and final report.

Publ: Parry, G. & Davies, P. *Framing Access*. Leicester: UDACE, 1991.
Parry, G. & Davies, P. The National Evaluation Study: some issues from the first report. In: *Journal of Access Studies*, Vol 6, No 1/1991, pp. 65-71.
Davies, P. & Parry, G. Central intentions and local interpretations: implementing national arrangements for the recognition of Access Courses. In: *Journal of Access Studies*, Vol 7, No 1/1992, pp. 42-60.
Parry, G. & Davies, P. *Kitemarking Access*. London DEU, 1992.

11950 Expanding horizons: multicultural and international education in the South West of England.

GBR 1993
Research Date(s): 1992-1995
Leedham, W.
Sup: Hannan, A.; Halstead, M.
Inst: Plymouth University, Rolle Faculty of Education, Douglas Avenue, Exmouth EX8 2AT, United Kingdom.
Fin: Polytechnics and Colleges Funding Council.
intercultural education; common core curriculum; cultural pluralism
éducation interculturelle; tronc commun; pluralisme culturel
PROJECT DESCRIPTION
The research examines one aspect of the relationship between a system of state education and the society which supports and funds it. The United Kingdom is a multicultural and multiracial society, one of many such societies in a diverse and changing world, but the National Curriculum introduced recently makes few specific references to this broader picture. Much will be left to the initiative of individual schools and teachers.

The research looks at the effects of greater centralisation on the one hand, and the need for state schools to provide an education appropriate for all pupils on the other. It focuses on examples of good practice in multicultural and international education in what is mainly a 'white' area (the South West of England) and asks: is a more centralised curriculum necessarily a more relevant one, as the legislators claim?.

11951 Experimentálny prístup k tvorbe výchovno - vzdelávacieho prostredia. (An experimental educational environment.)

CSK 1993
Research Date(s): 1991-1993
Cvik, Peter; Dančová, Dagmar; Gogal', Alexander; Holčík, Milan; Šimončičová, Marta; Večeríková, Mária; Ruisel, Imrich; et al.
Inst: Ústav experimentálnej pedagogiky SAV (Institute of Experimental Pedagogy, Slovak Academy of Sciences), 851 01 Bratislava, Mánesovo nám. 1, Czech and Slovak Federal Republic.
Slovenská akadémia vied (Slovak Academy of Sciences), 811 04 Bratislava, Štefánikova ul. 49, Czech and Slovak Federal Republic
experimental education; teaching method; experimentation; learning conditions
pédagogie expérimentale; méthode pédagogique; expérimentation; conditions d'apprentissage
PROJECT DESCRIPTION
Background: In an experimental teaching environment the researchers are working on the innovation of teaching methods (more games, competition, team work, abolition of assessment during the school year, closer contacts with parents, etc.), while observing regulations governing content (changes are possible only in line with the instructions of the Slovak Ministry of Education and Science) and form (restricted to the integration of lessons concerning work in a computer laboratory). The researchers propose a more extensive utilization of teaching aids.

The impact of the experimental environment is measured in terms of its effect on such aspects as pupil independence, team work, problem solving skills (with practical intelligence as a normative category), and the motivation of pupils. Special attention will be given to changes in teachers' individual conceptions of the educational process.

Aim: The research aims to identify changes brought about by the experimental environment and to compare the experimental and the traditional educational environment, paying special attention to the child as the subject of education and training.

11952 Forecasting the demand for higher education specialists.

RUS 1994
Research Date(s): 1991-1992
Yatsenko, V.Y.
Sup: Zuyev, V.M.
Inst: Research Institute for Higher Education, 103062, Moscow, K-62, Podsosensky per. 20, Russia.
State Committee for Higher Education Institutions, 113833, Moscow, M-230, Lysinovskja str. 51, Russia
educational reform; higher education; forecasting; manpower need
réforme de l'enseignement; enseignement supérieur; prévision; besoin de main-d'oeuvre
PROJECT DESCRIPTION
The study sought to develop new approaches to forecasting in the field of higher education. These approaches take into account the new relations in the developing market economy and they enable forecasts to be made of the demand for higher education specialists during the transition period.

Forecasts have been made of developments in higher education across the Russian Federation.

On the basis of foreign experiences, recommendations have been made regarding the integration of higher education into regional structures of education, economics and science. A study was made of the methodological and practical aspects of forecasting regional demand for qualified specialists in this field.

Problems related to the regionalization of higher education in the Russian Federation as a result of higher education legislation issued by the President of the Russian Federation and the Supreme Soviet have been identified.

Publ: Pugach, V.F. *Pedagogical higher education in Russia: the staff problem.* M., NIIVO, 1992.

Gorodetskaya, O.L.; Yatsenko, U.Y. & Korolyeva, L.V. *Prognosis of staff assessment in cultural institutions in Russia.* M., NIIVO, 1992.

Bokov, V.V.; Dzhalalov, S.; Ananyev, M.A.; et al. Papers of the international conference "Economics and higher education management" (Krasnogorsk, May 1992).

Dzhalalov, S. & Yatsenko, V.Y. *Economics of higher education under the conditions of developing market relations.* M., NIIVO, 1993.

(A complete list is available from the researcher.).

11953 The Freinet Movement in its international context.

GBR 1993

Research Date(s): 1987-1993

Beattie, N.

Inst: Liverpool University, Department of Education, PO Box 147, Liverpool L69 3BX, United Kingdom.

educational theory; history of education; comparative education; cross-national research

théorie de l'éducation; histoire de l'éducation; éducation comparée; recherche transnationale

PROJECT DESCRIPTION

The aim is to explore the Freinet Movement, which has been central to most 'progressive' developments in French education, over the period 1920 to the present day and to describe and discuss its cross-national impact. This has been considerable in some areas (e.g. Italy post-1945, Portugal post-1974) and nil in others (e.g. United Kingdom). By placing a very broad movement of opinion and practice in its cultural and historical context, this long-term enquiry should produce some clarification of elusive culture-bound ideas such as 'progressive' and 'international' dissemination.

11954 Good schools, effective schools: judgements and their history.

GBR 1993

Research Date(s): 1989-1993

Silver, H.

Inst: Plymouth University, Rolle Faculty of Education, Douglas Avenue, Exmouth EX8 2AT, United Kingdom.

quality of education; comparative education; history of education; educational research

qualité de l'éducation; éducation comparée; histoire de l'éducation; recherche en éducation

PROJECT DESCRIPTION

This is a study of the development of research interests in effective schools and school differences in the 1970s-1980s, in the United States and Britain, in a historical context. The investigation covers perceptions of what has constituted a good school, who has had the power to define what is good, and the criteria that have been used for different kinds of schooling. It considers the difference between 19th and earlier 20th century judgements about the quality of schooling and the research-based interest in effective schools after the decline in confidence in the outcomes of schooling in the late 1960s and early 1970s. It looks at the implementation of effective schools criteria in individual American states and in Congressional legislation in 1988. The study will also examine alternatives to school reform based on the effective schools research - in the US essential and accelerated schools and forms of restructuring, and in the UK government-sponsored approaches to curricula and assessment.

The study is mainly document-based, except for visits to Connecticut, Rhode Island and Washington DC to visit administrators and schools.

Publ: Silver, H. Poverty and effective schools. In: *Journal of Education Policy*, Vol 6, No 3/1991, pp. 271-285.

Silver, H. *Educational research and the policy environment: the case of 'effective schools'.* Liber amoricum for H. Remak, Indiana University, 1991.

11955 The Gramscian theory of education: a critical study of the development of educational theory.

GBR 1993

Research Date(s): 1988-1995

Kaskaris, I.

Sup: Hartley, J.

Inst: Dundee University, Centre for Continuing Education, Dundee DD1 4HN, United Kingdom.

educational theory

théorie de l'éducation

PROJECT DESCRIPTION

This research aims to generate a theory of education which, firstly, provides a critical analysis of the positivism underlying much educational theory; secondly, to analyse the post-modern semiotic reaction to this,

with a view to pointing up its largely de-politicised, ahistorical essence; and to suggest a convergence of Gramscian theory and critical theory.

11956 Het gebruik van "performance indicatoren" in het onderzoek van de overgangsproblematiek S.O.-H.O. en bij de evaluatie van het zelfstudiecentrum als begeleidingsinitiatief. (The use of performance indicators in the study of problems in the transition from secondary to higher education and in the evaluation of the Centre for Self-Instruction as a guidance service.)

BEL 1994

Research Date(s): 1989-1990

Schatteman, A.; Crabbé, C.

Sup: Loccufier, S.; Eisendrath, H.

Inst: Centrum voor Zelfstudie en Begeleiding (Centre for Self-Instruction and Educational Guidance), Pleinlaan 2, 1050 Brussel, Belgium.

Vrije Universiteit Brussel (Free University of Brussels), Pleinlaan 2, 1050 Brussel, Belgium

Fin: Departement Onderwijs, Fonds voor Kollektief en Fundamenteel Onderzoek op Ministerieel Initiatief.

guidance; measurement; study method; self-instruction; student; evaluation

orientation; mesure; méthode de travail; auto-enseignement; étudiant; évaluation

PROJECT DESCRIPTION

The overall aim was to improve, with the help of qualitative and quantitative performance indicators, the effectiveness of the remedial study service offered by the Centre for Self-Instruction to first-year students at the Free University of Brussels. The study, initially scheduled to last four years, sought to set up a coherent and effective action scheme, but was cut down by the government to two years.

Methods: The effectiveness of student guidance can only be measured if the final results (at the end of the first year and after graduation) can be compared to the conditions of the student at the start of the first year (secondary school achievement, previous knowledge and skills). To this end, a data base was set up in which all this information was stored. Besides quantitative data, the following qualitative information was collected: motivation, perceptions of study, study methods (in mathematics, physics and biology), cognitive styles. To measure these aspects, pre-tests were used as well as the instrument of J. Vermunt and F. Van Rijswijk (1988).

Results: Different methods for study guidance were described (formative evaluation, interactive study groups, etc.). Due to the reduction in the project's duration, the collected data could not be analysed.

Publ: Schatteman, A. & Crabbé, C. *Het gebruik van "performance indicatoren" in het onderzoek van de overgangsproblematiek S.O.-H.O. en bij de evaluatie van het zelfstudiecentrum als begeleidingsinitiatief: eindverslag.* VUB, Centrum voor Zelfstudie en Begeleiding, 1992, 90p.

11957 I prosphora tis kinonikis agogis sti Demotiki ke Mesi Ekpedefsi. (The contribution of social education to primary and secondary education.)

CYP 1993

Research Date(s): 1992-

Persianis, P.; Yiangou, N.

Inst: Pedagogiko Instituto (Pedagogical Institute), P.O. Box 512, Nicosia, Cyprus.

aims of education; community education; socialization; perception; teacher; primary education; secondary education

finalité de l'éducation; éducation sociale; socialisation; perception; enseignant; enseignement primaire; enseignement secondaire

PROJECT DESCRIPTION

Background and aims: One of the most important aims of the school is to provide social education to pupils, to facilitate their socialization. Still, to date no research has been conducted to investigate to what extent schools accomplish this aim. The present study investigates: (a) how primary and secondary teachers view social education; (b) current practice in social education; (c) the help teachers receive and/or expect from others.

More specifically, the study examines: (1) teachers' interpretations of the concept of "social education"; (2) the importance teachers attach to pupils' social education; (3) the factors teachers consider important for the success of the social education; (4) the approaches and procedures they use; (5) the means and aids they have at their disposal; (6) the activities that, according to teachers, promote social education; (7) the evaluation of the results of their efforts and their own perceptions of them; (8) the help they receive and their expectations regarding external factors.

Methodology: Data collection was based on a combination of interviews and questionnaires. The questionnaire was given to a random sample of 687 primary school teachers, head teachers and secondary school teachers. It consisted of two parts: part A concerned demographic characteristics; part B concerned subjects' perceptions of social education, the methods and aids they use, and the help they expect from external factors.

11958 I symberifora ton mathiton Mesis Ekpedefsis opos parousiazete sta vivlia paraptomaton ton scholion ke se singrisi me tis antilipsis ton diefthindon, ton ekpedeftikon ke ton mathiton. (Pupils' misbehaviour reported as discipline problems conceptually interpreted by headmasters, teachers and pupils in secondary schools.)
CYP 1993
Research Date(s): 1988-1991
Yiangou, Niki.
Inst: Pedagogiko Instituto (Pedagogical Institute), P.O. Box 512, Nicosia, Cyprus.
discipline; misconduct; punishment; perception; opinion; secondary school; pupil; teacher
discipline; déviance scolaire; punition; perception; opinion; école secondaire; élève; enseignant
PROJECT DESCRIPTION
This is an updating of EUDISED entry 40/9476.

Results: The research shows that headmasters, teachers and pupils have a clear concept of the situation in our schools - Gymnasia as well as Lycea. Regarding the most frequent discipline problems, the picture presented by the school record books for disciplinary offences is in agreement with the views expressed by teachers and pupils. Most cases of disciplinary offences are associated with male pupils. The offences mainly concern female teachers. The most frequent type of offence in Gymnasia is misbehaviour. In Lycea indecent appearance and misbehaviour outside the school premises are the most frequent.

A number of teaching staff believe that the main factors causing pupil misbehaviour are lack of motivation, the teacher's personality, and pupils' home environments. According to headmasters, the main factors are lack of motivation, teachers' attitudes, the teacher's personality, and the pupils' home environment. Assistant headmasters believe that the main factors are the family, the personality of the teacher, lack of motivation and the context of the subject. Teachers consider as main factors the family, lack of motivation, and the teacher's personality.

Although there is agreement on the fact that lack of motivation and the teacher's personality are main factors influencing pupil behaviour, there are statistically significant differences between the views of headmasters and teachers regarding the factor "teacher's attitude". As regards the effectiveness of positive and negative measures which would render the problem less acute, headmasters, teachers and pupils attach more importance to positive rather than negative measures.

The measures considered to be most effective by both teachers and pupils are corrective disciplinary measures administered in private, while a reprimand in class is seen as the least effective measure. This reflects the importance attributed to the respect for the pupil's personality. Headmasters consider a reprimand, dismissal from classes, and referral of the case to their authority to be effective measures. They consider a reprimand in the presence of the parent or guardian to be less effective.

There is a consensus of opinion among assistant headmasters and teachers. Both groups view a reprimand in the presence of a parent or guardian as an effective measure. They regard a reprimand in class, dismissal from classes and referring the case to the headmaster as less effective measures. Their views are in direct contrast to those held by headmasters.

11959 Identification and evaluation of innovatory curriculum development approaches in higher education.
BUL 1994
Research Date(s): 1991-1993
Stoycheva, K.; Peychev, A.
Sup: Georgieva, P.
Inst: National Centre for Educational and Science Studies, Tzarigradsko Chossé 125, 1113 Sofia, Bulgaria.
Fin: National Science and Research Fund.
development of education; curriculum development; evaluation; university studies; quality of education
développement de l'éducation; élaboration de programmes d'études; évaluation; études universitaires; qualité de l'éducation
PROJECT DESCRIPTION
Background: As the needs of society are changing drastically, the objectives of higher education, the concepts of teaching, the methods of instruction and the criteria for evaluation must also change. The present project is concerned with the process of improving the quality of education in Bulgarian universities.

Aims: (1) To identify the differing approaches towards curriculum development among university teaching staff; (2) to evaluate the relationship between curriculum innovation and curriculum development approaches among university teaching staff.

Design: A questionnaire is developed aimed at examining theoretically derived models for curriculum development. The research instrument will be piloted during the 1991-1992 academic year. A general study of the curriculum development approaches among university staff is planned for the 1992-1993 academic year. Data will be collected through questionnaire, observation and interviews. Data analysis methods will include descriptive analyses, supplemented by univariate and multi-variate analyses of group differences and factor and cluster analyses.

Sample: Academic staff at all levels: presidents, vice-presidents, deans, faculty members.

11960 Identifying and developing a quality ethos for teaching in higher education.
GBR 1993
Research Date(s): 1991-1993
Williams, G.
Inst: London University, Institute of Education, Department of Policy Studies, 20 Bedford Way, London WC1H 0AL, United Kingdom.
Fin: Leverhulme Trust.
teaching quality; quality of education; higher education
qualité de l'enseignement; qualité de l'éducation; enseignement supérieur
PROJECT DESCRIPTION
The primary aim of the project is to increase understanding of quality in higher education teaching by a systematic series of surveys of students, academics, administrators and employers of graduates.

11961 The impact of local management of schools.
GBR 1993
Research Date(s): 1991-1993
Thomas, H.; Arnott, M.; Bullock, A.
Inst: Birmingham University, School of Education, Edgbaston, Birmingham B15 2TT, United Kingdom.
Fin: National Association of Head Teachers.
educational reform; educational administration
réforme de l'enseignement; administration de l'enseignement
PROJECT DESCRIPTION
The project aims to describe and analyse the impact of Local Management of Schools. This includes the immediate impact in relation to local education authority approaches to delegation, and the impact on roles of headteachers and deputy headteachers.

The methods to be used are quantitative analysis of a questionnaire sent to 2000 headteachers in England and Wales and qualitative analysis of interviews with school personnel.

11962 The impact of the Education Reform Act - 1988 on the further education curriculum.
GBR 1993
Research Date(s): 1990-1992
Herrman, S.; Johnson, M.
Sup: Williets, D.
Inst: Further Education Unit, Citadel Place, Pinworth Street, London SE11 5EH, United Kingdom.
educational reform; vocational education; curriculum development; post-compulsory education
réforme de l'enseignement; enseignement professionnel; élaboration de programmes d'études; enseignement postobligatoire
PROJECT DESCRIPTION
The purpose of this project is: (i) to analyse and appraise the changes in the further education curriculum over an initial 3-year period; and (ii) throughout the period of the project, to keep local education authorities and colleges informed of significant developments and outcomes, either generally or on specific curricular issues.

The Education Reform Act - 1988 is one of a number of significant influences on the further education curriculum. It requires every local education authority to prepare and submit for the Secretary of State's approval a scheme providing for: (i) the principles and procedures which the authority will use to plan the educational provision to be made in the further and higher education colleges which it maintains or substantially assists; (ii) the determination of an annual budget for each of those colleges; and (iii) the delegation by the authority of the management of the budget to the governing body of the college, where such delegation is required or permitted under the scheme. The general criteria which the Secretary of State expects to apply in considering the schemes submitted will include the following: (i) that each scheme should give colleges as much freedom as possible to manage their affairs and allocate their resources as they think best within the strategic framework set by the local education authority; (ii) that each scheme should promote responsiveness by colleges to the changing needs of students, employers and the local community; (iii) that each scheme should give colleges appropriate incentives to earn additional income by providing course and other services and facilities for the local community, including in particular the business community.

The Further Education Unit's remit is to review and evaluate the further education curriculum and to determine priorities and recommend improvements. In this context and in line with the Further Education Unit's current strategies on curriculum planning, management and evaluation, and on market penetration, the Unit proposes to undertake an analysis of the curriculum impact of the Education Reform Act. The project aims to assess the changes in the range, balance, processes and perceived quality of the post-16 curriculum which occur during the first 3-year period of operation of measures derived from the Education Reform Act. Whilst it is recognised that the legislation is one significant influence on the further education curriculum, there are other influences. Interim bulletins or guidance notes on formative issues, will be disseminated by the Further Education Unit at appropriate times throughout the project and a final report will assess the development of the further education curriculum during the early years of the implementation of the Education Reform Act in further education.

11963 Implementing educational changes in primary schools with particular reference to small schools.
GBR 1993
Research Date(s): 1990-1993
Waugh, D.
Sup: Gorwood, B.
Inst: Hull University, School of Education, Cottingham Road, Hull HU6 7RX, United Kingdom.
educational reform; educational legislation; primary school; school size; small school
réforme de l'enseignement; législation scolaire; école primaire; dimension de l'école; école de taille réduite
PROJECT DESCRIPTION
The research takes the form of questionnaire and survey work on the methods used, and problems encountered, when primary schools attempt to meet the requirements of the 1988 Education Reform Act. A survey of around 200 schools has been undertaken and a number of case studies made. The aim of the research is to determine whether school size affects the ability to implement change. It is hoped that recommendations can be made, which will draw upon examples of 'good practice', to enable schools to fulfil legal requirements in an educationally acceptable way.

11964 Improving access to education for young black adults.
GBR 1993
Research Date(s): 1987-1992
Eggleston, S.; Lashley, H.
Inst: Warwick University, Faculty of Educational Studies, Coventry CV4 7AL, United Kingdom; Reading University, Faculty of Education and Community Studies, Bulmershe Court, Woodlands Avenue, Earley, Reading RG6 1HY, United Kingdom.
Fin: Further Education Unit.
access to education; ethnic group; vocational education; quality of education
accès à l'éducation; groupe ethnique; enseignement professionnel; qualité de l'éducation
PROJECT DESCRIPTION
The general aim of this research project is to prepare a directory of projects with details of their curriculum arrangements; short-term evaluation focusing on quality of training; placement of trainees; content and organization of curriculum; access criteria and opportunity for further advanced training; and jobs obtained.
The research work will be organized in Northern and Southern Regions divided by the Midlands; Coventry being the northern limit of the Southern Region and Birmingham/Leicester the southern end of the Northern Region. A base for each regional research associate is provided in London (Southern Region) and Manchester (Northern Region) at the relevant Replan offices. The Directorate and Administration of the project is based at Warwick University.

11965 Improving the quality of education for all.
GBR 1993
Research Date(s): 1990-1994
Ainscow, M.; Hopkins, D.; Southworth, G.; West, M.
Inst: Cambridge University, Institute of Education, Shaftesbury Road, Cambridge CB2 2BX, United Kingdom.
Fin: Local Education Authority contributions; Participating schools; Cambridge University.
quality of education; development of education
qualité de l'éducation; développement de l'éducation
PROJECT DESCRIPTION
The aim of this study is to prodce and evaluate a model of school development, and a programme of support, that strengthens a school's ability to provide quality education for all its pupils. Currently the project involves 25 schools in the South East of England and in Yorkshire. The team from Cambridge provide training and support for school coordinators who, in turn, support project activities in other schools.
Current research questions are: (1) What strategies facilitate policy development in schools? (2) what are the social experiences that characterise the cultures of 'moving schools'? (3) What is the impact of our intervention? Work is also going on to explore new methodologies to map the process of change in schools.

Publ: Ainscow, M. & Hopkins, D. Aboard the 'moving school'. In: *Educational Leadership*, Vol 50, No 3/1992, pp. 79-83.

11966 Interkulturelle Begegnungen auf Jugendsprachreisen in England. (Inter-cultural meetings on language trips to England for young people.)
DEU 1993
Research Date(s): 1991-1992
Dietl, B.; Fleckenstein, E.; Goettsch, M.; Kaercher, E.
Sup: Lutz, R.; Roemhild, R.
Inst: Universitaet Frankfurt, FB 09 Klassische Philologie und Kunstwissenschaften, Institut fuer Kulturanthropologie und Europaeische Ethnologie, Bettinaplatz 5, D-6000 Frankfurt am Main.
Fin: Studienkreis fuer Tourismus, Modellseminare.
intercultural education; adolescent; England; language teaching; vacation course; cultural exchange
éducation interculturelle; adolescent; Angleterre; enseignement des langues; cours de vacances; échange culturel
PROJECT DESCRIPTION
Inhalt: Sind Sprachreisen, insbesondere im Jugendbereich, eine Moeglichkeit kultureller Begegnung, die zu einer Auseinandersetzung mit dem Fremden fuehren und somit zu einem Verstehen beitragen? Die Ergebnisse der Studie, die praxisbegleitend erhoben wurden, im Verlauf von Jugendsprachreisen naemlich, sollen in die methodische und inhaltliche Arbeit eines Traegers von Jugendsprachreisen einfliessen, um die beabsichtigte Auseinandersetzung mit der fremden Kultur zu effektivieren.
Geographischer Raum: Sued-West-England.
Vorgehensweise: Arbeit auf der Grundlage ethnologischer Feldforschung (methodisch). Untersuchungsdesign: Fallstudie.
Datengewinnung: Standardisiertes Interview (Stichprobe: 100; Sprachschueler; Auswahlverfahren: total). Nicht-standardisiertes Interview (dito). Teilnehmende Beobachtung (dito). Primaererhebung: Feldarbeit von Mitarbeitern des Projektes durchgefuehrt.

11967 Internationale vergelijking onderwijsemancipatiebeleid met bijzondere aandacht voor het beleid van scholen. (International comparison of equal opportunities policies in education with particular reference to school policies.)
NLD 1994
Research Date(s): 1992
Dekkers, H.
Sup: Jungbluth, P.
Inst: Instituut voor Toegepaste Sociale wetenschappen (ITS) (Institute for Applied Social Sciences), P.O. Box 9048, 6500 KJ Nijmegen, Netherlands. Katholieke Universiteit Nijmegen (Catholic University of Nijmegen), P.O. Box 9102, 6500 HC Nijmegen, Netherlands
Fin: SVO het Instituut voor Onderzoek van het Onderwijs.
equal opportunity; educational policy; cross-national research; Western Europe; girl
égalité de chances; politique de l'éducation; recherche transnationale; Europe occidentale; jeune fille
PROJECT DESCRIPTION
Background: A major aim of equal opportunity policies in education in the Netherlands is to help girls attain economic independence by preparing them for a place on the labour market. Girls are encouraged to take science subjects and to enroll in technical courses. The educational problems of girls in the Netherlands are comparable to those of girls in other Western European countries: they attain about the same level of education as boys, but the subjects and courses they choose do not give them the most favourable opportunities for a high position on the labour market. Dissatisfaction with the allegedly one-sided approach of equal opportunity policies in education and their demonstrably limited results has prompted this study of equal opportunity policies in the countries surrounding the Netherlands.
Aim: To study equal opportunity policies in education in a number of Western European countries; to investigate aspects of the labour market in these countries; and to determine what initiatives have been successful.
Design: A list will be made of policy initiatives that have been taken in the past five years in Great Britain, Germany, Denmark, Norway, and Sweden. The responsible ministries, committees or local authorities will be approached for written information on their policies. They will also be asked for the names and addresses of other institutions or individuals that might be able to provide relevant information on policies and the scientific evaluation of these policies. Searches will be conducted in international documentary systems for additional information. Projects that are relevant for the Dutch situation will be studied more closely to determine their transferability.

11968 Investigation into what factors pre-dispose students to seek counselling with special reference to: subject bias, special categories of college entry and history of mental instability.
GBR 1993
Research Date(s): 1991-1992
Adams, T.; Grandison, S.
Inst: London University, Goldsmiths' College, Department of Continuing and Community Education, New Cross, London SE14 6NW, United Kingdom.

guidance; student behaviour; higher education
orientation; comportement de l'étudiant; enseignement supérieur
PROJECT DESCRIPTION

Data collected by Goldsmiths' Counselling Service over the last three years profiles a number of factors which the case-load presents. With regard to strategies of resourcing and academic pastoral support the data moves beyond an equation of student numbers and counselling hours. Relevant factors so far identified are that subject bias can appear to influence student stability; that special categories of students (e.g. mature) can cause considerable stress on the counselling provision; and that aspects of the psychological backgrounds of vulnerable students can lead to the service responding to problems that are reactivated through study.

In order to address the essential responsibilities of the Counselling Service provision the present study aims to evaluate students' specific needs by investigating what factors pre-dispose students to seek counselling. By appropriating the preliminary data, special reference is given in the study to subject bias, categories of college entry and history of mental instability. Research on student counselling services has been largely conducted by practising counsellors upon their own services. Such relatively small-scale research has resulted in a dearth of comparative studies across services. The present study is a comparative study made of the case-loads of counselling services in three institutions in the first instance. On identifying the small sample of services, students' specific needs are accessed by means of a semi-structured interview schedule, through which a base of information evolves and from which the final field work questions can be structured. The design of the pilot questionnaires will incorporate attitudes to and expectations of the counselling service, i.e. how the perception of student counselling consumerism affect the service provision. As a pilot study this research initiative will be broadened in scope at a national level.

11969   An investigation the support/counselling provision needed for the mature student compared to younger students.
GBR   1993
Research Date(s):   1991-1995
Walters, M.
Sup: Nichol, B.
Inst: North Cheshire College, Padgate Campus, Fearnhead Lane, Warrington WA2 0DB, United Kingdom; Manchester University, School of Education, Oxford Road, Manchester M13 9PL, United Kingdom.
guidance; adult education; higher education
orientation; éducation des adultes; enseignement supérieur
PROJECT DESCRIPTION

Mature students, by re-entering education, have already made major choices. These choices may have been influenced or precipitated by major life incidents, some traumatic, e.g. redundancy, divorce, bereavement, failure or loss. Students have tremendous commitment to making a success of their venture; they may or may not, however, have come to terms with their changing circumstances, self-image, aspirations and present role. Their positive drive and energy, therefore, may be dissipated by their underlying problems, which sometimes have to be addressed and resolved to enable their energy to be recharged and channelled into academic work.

The objective of the research is to investigate whether there is a difference in the support/counselling provision needed for the mature student compared to younger students. The methods used will, on the whole, be qualitative rather than quantitative. It will involve in-depth interviews of students and of student counsellors and careers advisors; and case studies which may be journalistic, quantitative or evaluative. Surveys will be carried out on: students' problems; students' evaluation of student services; and student services, including counsellors and careers advisors.

11970   Labour's education policy.
GBR   1993
Research Date(s):   1991-1993
Demaine, J.
Inst: Loughborough University of Technology, Department of Education, Loughborough LE11 3TU, United Kingdom.
educational policy; political party
politique de l'éducation; parti politique
PROJECT DESCRIPTION

This is a study of the Labour Party's education policy in the recent past and for the future.

11971   Lage en hoge transfer bij wiskundig probleemoplossen. (Transfer in mathematical problem solving.)
NLD   1994
Research Date(s):   1993-1994
Riemersma, F.S.J.; Meijer, J.
Inst: Stichting Centrum voor Onderwijsonderzoek (SCO) (Centre for Educational Research), Grote Bickersstraat 72, 1013 KS Amsterdam, Netherlands.
Universiteit van Amsterdam (University of Amsterdam), P.O. Box 19268, 1000 GG Amsterdam, Netherlands
Fin: SVO het Instituut voor Onderzoek van het Onderwijs.

transfer of learning; problem solving; mathematics
transfert pédagogique; résolution de problème; mathématiques
PROJECT DESCRIPTION

Background: In ordinary mathematics teaching there is usually a low level of transfer, i.e. the learning situation and the situation in which the acquired knowledge is applied are much alike. The problem with a low level of transfer is that it has limited scope. It is generally considered desirable that pupils learn to apply their knowledge to a wide range of situations (i.e., a high level of transfer). This study is mainly concerned with the latter type of transfer.

Aims: (1) To gather empirical knowledge on transfer in mathematical problem solving; (2) to examine to what extent and under what conditions supplementary instruction (in the form of phased help in solving problems) leads to improved pupil performance.

Design: A programme of problem-based mathematics instruction will be integrated with standardized help for solving mathematics problems. A range of problems accompanied by "phased help" will be developed, based on the view that the more help a pupil needs, the more specific it should be. This approach will be elaborated as a six-weeks' experimental programme which will be part of the ordinary curriculum. A pretest post-test design will be used in which pupils will be randomly assigned to the experimental or the control group (N=46 per group).

11972   Law improvement project.
GBR   1993
Research Date(s):   1990-1992
Cameron, K.
Inst: Jordanhill College of Education, Division of Social Work, Southbrae Drive, Jordanhill, Glasgow G13 1PP, United Kingdom.
Fin: Central Council for Education and Training in Social Work.
quality of education; social worker; law
qualité de l'éducation; travailleur social; droit
PROJECT DESCRIPTION

The aim of this project is to improve the standards of law teaching on social work courses throughout Britain.

11973   Leerling- en keuzebegeleiding bij de basisvorming. (Pupil counselling and careers guidance and the national core curriculum for the lower secondary level.)
NLD   1994
Research Date(s):   1991-1992
Bos, K.T.; Velden, L.F.J. van der; Amelsvoort, H.W.C.H. van; Vermeulen, C.J.A.J.
Inst: Onderzoek Centrum Toegepaste Onderwijskunde (OCTO) (Research Centre of the Department of Educational Technology), P.O. Box 217, 7500 AE Enschede, Netherlands.
Universiteit Twente (Twente University), P.O. Box 217, 7500 AE Enschede, Netherlands
Fin: SVO het Instituut voor Onderzoek van het Onderwijs.
educational guidance; vocational guidance; common core curriculum
orientation pédagogique; orientation professionnelle; tronc commun
PROJECT DESCRIPTION

Background: With the introduction of basic education (a common core curriculum for the lower secondary level), the government pursues the following objectives: improving the quality of education, reducing inequality of opportunities, and making schools more responsive to developments in society. To be able to attain these goals, schools will need an adequate system of pupil counselling and careers guidance. This system will have to be incorporated in the entire school organization and will have to be implemented consistently. At present these matters are given little systematic attention in secondary schools, especially careers guidance.

Aim: To investigate the requirements of pupil counselling and careers guidance in the context of the core curriculum for lower secondary education; to examine to what extent schools are equipped to make the needed adjustments when the core curriculum is introduced; to indicate what action secondary schools must take to establish an adequate system of pupil guidance.

Methods: Literature survey, structured interviews, case study, content analysis, questionnaire survey.

Results: A gap was found to exist between current provision for pupil guidance and counselling and the provision needed when the core curriculum is introduced. A large number of schools are adequately equipped to adjust their provision according to the guidelines of the core curriculum; however, external support and extension of facilities are considered necessary.

(This is an updating of EUDISED no. 44/10675).

Publ: Bos, K.T. et al. *Leerling- en keuzebegeleiding bij de basisvorming.* Enschede: OCTO, 1993, 151p.

Bos, K.T. et al. Intensievere keuzebegeleiding in de basisvorming heeft veel consequenties: vooral behoefte aan bijscholing en een zwaardere begeleidingsstructuur. In: *Didaktief*, 1993/3, pp. 17-18.

11974 Lernzielformulierungen bei zentralen Prüfungen. (Définition des objectifs pédagogiques dans le cadre d'examens centralisés.)
CHE 1994
Research Date(s): 1987-1992
Saxer-Büchi, Urs.
Sup: Dubs, Rolf; Metzger, Christoph.
Inst: Hochschule St. Gallen für Wirtschafts-, Rechts- und Sozialwissenschaften (HSG), Institut für Wirtschaftspädagogik, Guisanstrasse 9, 9010 St. Gallen, Schweiz.
teaching objective; commercial training; docimology; examination
objectif pédagogique; formation commerciale; docimologie; examen
PROJECT DESCRIPTION
Die Einführung neuer Lehrpläne wurd häufig durch die Trägheit von Bildungssystemen behindert. Ein Mittel, die Umsetzung von Innovationen in diesem Bereich zu fördern, besteht in der zentralen Prüfung des neu verlangten Unterrichsstoffs. Dieser Schritt wurde an den kaufmännischen Berufsschulen der Schweiz getan, wo 1987 ein neuer Lehrplan in Kraft trat und 1989 zentrale Prüfungen eingeführt wurden (erstmalige Durchführung 1990). Im Bereich des Betriebs- und Rechtskundeunterrichts, auf den sich die hier vorgestellte Arbeit beschränkt, wechselten die Ausbildungsziele mit dem neuen Lehrplan von rein kaufmännischen Fertigkeiten weg in Richtung auf ein allgemeineres Verständnis wirtschaftlicher und gesellschaftlicher Fragestellungen. Diese Öffnung wie auch die Einführung zentraler Prüfungen schufen Unsicherheit sowohl auf seiten der Lehrerinnen und Lehrer bezüglich des zu vermittelnden Stoffs wie auch bei den Schülerinnen und Schülern in bezug auf das, was sie für die Lehrabschlussprüfung zu lernen hatten. Diese Unsicherheit hat einiges zu tun mit der Interpretationsbedürftigkeit der Lehrplanvorgaben.

In dieser Situation nahm sich der Autor vor, Möglichkeiten zur Verbesserung der Lage zu erkunden und gegeneinander abzuwägen. Ein Schwergewicht legte er auf die Frage nach dem Grad der Ausformulierung bzw. der Offenheit der Lehrzielvorgaben, welche die Unterrichtenden zu akzeptieren gewillt sind oder wünschen. Im Rahmen der Doktorarbeit wurden unter anderem zehn Möglichkeiten von Massnahmen in einer schriftlichen Befragung (N = 600) dem Lehrpersonal im Bereich Betriebs- und Rechtskunde unterbreitet. In seinen Schlussfolgerungen empfiehlt der Autor, für zwei Drittel der Unterrichtszeit solle der zu behandelnde Stoff verbindlich vorgeschrieben werden, während das restliche Drittel den Lehrpersonen zur freien Verfügung stehen solle. Weitere Empfehlungen betreffen eine Individualisierung des Unterrichts und eine Professionalisierung bei der Erstellung der zentralisierten Abschlussprüfungen.

Publ: Saxer-Büchi, Urs. *Lernzielformulierungen bei zentralen Prüfungen: eine empirische Untersuchung an kaufmännischen Berufsschulen.* Bamberg: Difo, 1992, 283 Seiten (Dissertation St. Gallen Nr. 1341).

11975 Likhet og/eller kvalitet: grunnskolens dilemma i dagens Europa. (Equality versus quality: the dilemma of primary schools in today's Europe.)
NOR 1994
Research Date(s): 1992-1994
Harbo, Torstein.
Inst: Universitetet i Oslo, Pedagogisk Forskningsinstitutt (University of Oslo, Institute for Educational Research), PB 1092 Blindern, 0317 Oslo, Norway.
Fin: NAVF/RSF; Faglitterær forfatterforening.
quality of education; equal opportunity; primary education; cross-national research
qualité de l'éducation; égalité de chances; enseignement primaire; recherche transnationale
PROJECT DESCRIPTION
Several European countries are facing the dilemma of, on the one hand, striving for more equality in schools - in a political-ideological or pedagogical-organizational sense - and, on the other, aiming at improving educational quality. The study aims to establish under what conditions there is question of both, and under what conditions there is question of one or the other. The study will be comparative and contemporary. The countries considered are: England, France, Germany, Lithuania and Norway.

Publ: A full list of publications can be obtained on request from the research institute.

11976 Literacy in the community.
GBR 1993
Research Date(s): 1989-1991
Barton, D.; Hamilton, M.
Inst: Lancaster University, Department of Linguistics and Modern English Language, Cartmel College, Bailrigg, Lancaster LA1 4YW, United Kingdom.
Fin: Economic and Social Research Council.
literacy; adult; society
alphabétisation; adulte; société
PROJECT DESCRIPTION
This project will investigate the role of literacy in adult life in contemporary Britain, by means of ethnographic interviews and observation. It will document the everyday practical uses of literacy in the household and in the community and examine how they interface with school and work. The

aim is to extend the view of literacy which currently informs educational practice at all levels and to contribute to the debate on levels of literacy in our society. The focus will be on literacy 'practices' or 'events' and on exploring the social meanings of literacy to the people involved.

Publ: A series of working papers are available on request from the researcher.

11977 Literacy screening analyses.
GBR 1993
Research Date(s): 1986-
Reece, D.
Inst: Berkshire County Council, Education Department, Information Technology Management, Shire Hall, Shinfield Park, Reading RG2 9XD, United Kingdom.
literacy; achievement; educational planning; resource allocation; educational need
alphabétisation; rendement; planification de l'éducation; affectation des ressources; besoin d'éducation
PROJECT DESCRIPTION
Each year a survey of the literacy capabilities of children in the 7+ and 9+ year groups is undertaken: (1) to identify those children in need of particular help; and (2) to use the results at school level as an index of educational needs in the school. This index is combined with indices of social needs, based on census variables and free school meals, to give a score for the school. This is used to help allocate discretionary teaching resources.

11978 Local education authority support for continuity and progression in the 5-16 curriculum.
GBR 1993
Research Date(s): 1992-1994
Dickson, P.; Lee, B.
Inst: National Foundation for Educational Research, The Mere, Upton Park, Slough SL1 2DQ, United Kingdom.
didactic continuity; primary education; secondary education; curriculum development; common core curriculum
continuité didactique; enseignement primaire; enseignement secondaire; élaboration de programmes d'études; tronc commun
PROJECT DESCRIPTION
The introduction of the National Curriculum and associated assessment has provided a new context for the activities which have been traditionally undertaken to ensure curriculum continuity, within school and on transfer between school phases. The research aims to investigate continuity from two different perspectives: the support provided by local education authorities (LEAs) and the measures taken at school level.

Through the use of six case studies, based on 'families' of schools, and a questionnaire survey of LEAs, information will be sought on: (1) strategies for promoting continuity in different LEA contexts; (2) collaboration and arrangements for transfer between school phases; and (3) methods used for promoting continuity within schools and subject areas.

The findings of the research will be disseminated through workshops for participants and a project report.

11979 Local management of schools and racial equality.
GBR 1993
Research Date(s): 1992-1993
Troyna, B.
Inst: Warwick University, Faculty of Educational Studies, Coventry CV4 7AL, United Kingdom.
Fin: Commission for Racial Equality.
equal opportunity; racial integration; racial discrimination; educational administration
égalité de chances; intégration raciale; discrimination raciale; administration de l'enseignement
PROJECT DESCRIPTION
The research explores how the recent educational reforms have affected the status of (and commitment to) racial equality issues in a local education authority and a sample of its secondary schools.

11980 Making your way through secondary school: pupils' experiences of teaching and learning.
GBR 1993
Research Date(s): 1991-1995
Rudduck, J.; Harris, S.
Inst: Sheffield University, Division of Education, 388 Glossop Road, Sheffield S10 2TN, United Kingdom.
Fin: Economic and Social Research Council.
quality of education; secondary education; pupil attitude; school career
qualité de l'éducation; enseignement secondaire; attitude de l'élève; cursus scolaire
PROJECT DESCRIPTION
The project is one of a number of parallel research studies funded as part of the initiative 'Innovation and change in education: the quality of teaching and learning'. The broad aims of the research are to: (1) collect contextualised information about pupils' experiences of teaching and learning as they

move through their final years of secondary schooling; (2) contribute to knowledge and understanding of the ways in which pupils perceive, make sense of and respond to the teaching and learning opportunities that their school provides. The specific aim is to examine pupils' experiences of and reactions to teaching and learning in relation to the concept of 'school career'.

The research is being conducted in a single comprehensive school in three separate local education authorities (LEAs). It is developmental, using a longitudinal, interview-based design and concentrates on one cohort of pupils in each school, who were 12 years old at the start of the research and will be 16 years at the end. The data is contextualised through information gathered in interviews with teachers, observation and the analysis of school records and documents.

Fieldwork already undertaken over four terms has included: interviews with headteachers and members of senior management teams; interviews with the form tutor, subject teachers and pupils within the target classes, and interviews with the nominated school contact person. The researchers have also attended key events (e.g. parents' evenings) which affect their target group.

11981 Migration und Erziehung in multikulturellen Gesellschaften: europäische Modelle im Wandel. (Migration et éducation dans les sociétés multiculturelles: les modèles européens en changement.)
CHE 1994
Research Date(s): 1992-1995
Allemann-Ghionda, Cristina (Wollbacherstrasse 1, 4058 Basel, Schweiz).
Sup: Oelkers, Jürgen.
intercultural education; child of foreign national; migrant
éducation interculturelle; enfant d'étranger; migrant
PROJECT DESCRIPTION

Diese Habilitationsarbeit, die unter dem Patronat der Nationalen schweizerischen UNESCO-Kommission steht, befasst sich mit der Erziehung in den multikulturellen Gesellschaften der westeuropäischen Einwanderungsländer vor dem Hintergrund der qualitativen und quantitativen Veränderungen, denen sich das Phänomen Migration ebenso ausgesetzt sieht wie die Bildungssysteme, die gefordert sind, mit der kulturellen und sprachlichen Vielfalt ihrer Benutzer zu Rande zu kommen. Dieser Wandel ist zurückzuführen auf die tiefgreifenden geopolitischen Veränderungen in Mittel- und Osteuropa, auf die vermehrte Immigration aus Asien und Afrika, aber auch auf die Neuregelung der Beziehungen zwischen den europäischen Ländern (Vertiefung und Erweiterung der Europäischen Gemeinschaft). Alle diese Veränderungen machen eine Neubewertung der sprachlichen und kulturellen Vielfalt in Schule und Gesellschaft dringlich, und sie haben Folgen sowohl auf die Organisation wie auch auf die Inhalte des Unterrichts.

Vor diesem Hintergrund werden Modelle und Konzepte der Beschulung von Migrantenkindern in vier europäischen Ländern analysiert; es sind dies Deutschland, Frankreich, Italien und die Schweiz. Alle diese Länder sind hoch industrialisiert und kennen starke (und wachsende) Populationen von Arbeitsmigranten. Zudem entsprechen die drei nichtschweizerischen Länder den wichtigen drei schweizerischen Sprachregionen. Die Aufmerksamkeit richtet sich vor allem auf die Entwicklungen ab Mitte der achtziger Jahre; es wird angenommen, dass sie mehr oder weniger direkte Konsequenzen der obernerwähnten geopolitischen Veränderungen sind.

Die vergleichende Analyse will Fragen wie folgende beantworten: Welche Konzepte und pädagogischen Optionen tragen am ehesten dazu bei, den Schulerfolg von zugewanderten Kindern zu verbessern? In welcher Weise gelingt die gemeinsame Schulung von international gemischten Schulpopulationen am ehesten? Welche Konzepte setzen sich in Theorie und Praxis am adäquatesten mit den im ersten Absatz erwähnten Entwicklungen auseinander, und auf welchen Paradigmata basieren sie?

Vorgegangen wird mit der Analyse von Modellversuchen auf der Ebene der Primarschulen in den erwähnten Ländern; weiter werden bildungspolitische Dokumente, Schulstatistiken usw. herangezogen.

11982 Modellentwicklung fuer eine oeffentliche bilinguale Schule der Zehn- bis Vierzehnjaehrigen. (Developing a model of state bilingual schools for the 10-14 age bracket.)
AUT 1993
Research Date(s): 1992-1996
Bierbaumer, Peter; Conrad, Barbara; Kovatschitsch, Christa; Fleischmann, Elisabeth; Poelzleitner, Elisabeth; Heindler, Dagmar; Grogger, Guenter.
Inst: Institut fuer Anglistik, Heinrichstrasse 36, A-8010 Graz.
Universitaet Graz, Heinrichstrasse 36, A-8010 Graz; International Bilingual School, Klusemannstrasse 25, A-8053 Graz
Fin: Fonds zur Foerderung der wissenschaftlichen Forschung.
bilingual education; international school; internationalism
enseignement bilingue; école internationale; internationalisme
PROJECT DESCRIPTION

Durch politische, oekonomische und soziale Veraenderungen in Europa gewinnen fremdsprachliche und interkulturelle Kompetenz immer mehr an Bedeutung. International reagiert man vermehrt durch Schulen mit bilingualem Profil, das heisst mit zweisprachigem Fachunterricht, auf diese neuen Anforderungen an das Bildungswesen. In Oesterreich wird dieser

Weg noch zaghaft beschritten: es gibt erst ein oeffentliches bilinguales internationales Gymnasium in Graz, doch besteht bundesweit bereits enormes Interesse daran. Die Entwicklung methodisch-didaktischer Grundlagen fuer den bilingualen Unterricht steckt im gesamten deutschen Sprachraum noch in den Anfaengen. Sie soll mit diesem Projekt durch die wissenschaftliche Begleitung, Evaluierung und Dokumentierung der gesamten Unterstufe der Graz International Bilingual School in den Jahren 1992 bis 1996 entscheidend vorangetrieben werden.

11983 Modernité et illettrisme: enquêtes en Suisse et à Genève.
CHE 1994
Research Date(s): 1989-1991
Girod, Roger (5 Chemin de la Boule, 1232 Confignon, Suisse); Sjollema, Frederik.
Inst: Université de Genève, Département de sociologie, 5 rue St-Ours, 1211 Genève 4, Suisse.
Fin: Fonds national suisse de la recherche scientifique.
illiteracy; knowledge level; adult
analphabétisme; niveau de connaissances; adulte
PROJECT DESCRIPTION

Dans le cadre d'un programme de recherche, soutenu par le Fonds national et consacré à l'illettrisme en Suisse, trois enquêtes quantitatives ont été menées, deux à Genève et une dans l'ensemble de la Suisse. La première enquête quantitative a concerné 1401 personnes domiciliées dans le canton de Genève depuis deux ans au moins, âgées de 20 ans ou plus et tirées au sort. Pour arriver à ce nombre de contacts, fixé d'avance, il a fallu utiliser 4361 adresses. Parmi les personnes sollicitées, 1012 ont refusé un rendez-vous. Les autres étaient malades, trop âgées, jamais là ou n'ont pu être atteintes pour d'autres raisons. L'enquête 2 a complété la première; elle a été mené d'une part auprès des personnes qui, dans la première enquête, se situaient au bas de l'échelle de performances et d'autre part auprès d'un groupe témoin choisis parmi les autres répondants de l'enquête 1. Ces enquêtes portaient sur les connaissances intellectuelles de base de la population, ainsi que sur des questions relatives à la politique, l'informatique et les langues. L'enquête 3 a concerné un échantillon représentatif de la population suisse de 15 ans et plus (N = 1040 répondants); elle n'a porté que sur les connaissances en lecture, écriture et calcul.

Voici trois exemples de résultats: 90,9% des répondants ont su additionner 4 fr. 30 plus 2 fr. 85; 79,5% ont su trouver dans l'annuaire le numéro de téléphone d'une agence locale d'une banque et la noter (enquête suisse). Près de la moitié de la population genevoise titulaire d'un passeport suisse n'a pas réussi à comprendre un graphique simple illustrant les explications adressées par le Conseil fédéral aux électeurs et électrices (enquête genevoise).

Selon les résultats de ces enquêtes, les semi-illettrés - autour de 5% ou de 10% des adultes, ou plus encore suivant les critères utilisés - se recrutent en majorité hors des catégories sociales les plus nettement défavorisées. La plupart sont des Suisses. Généralement, leur scolarité a été, d'après ce qu'ils disent, normale. A Genève, la moitié des répondants des degrés de performance inférieurs ne se souviennent pas d'avoir doublé à l'école obligatoire. La plupart de ces personnes estiment en outre n'avoir pas été des élèves particulièrement faibles.

Il n'y a toutefois pas que les illettrés et semi-illettrés qui ne lisent pas. Cela permet de supposer que, dans de nombreux milieux, il n'est pas trop difficile de se tirer d'affaire sans avoir à lire, écrire ou calculer, et ceci même lorsqu'il s'agit de faire face à des tâches dont l'accomplissement nécessiterait normalement la maîtrise de ces compétences.

Publ: Girod, Roger & Sjollema, Frederik. *Modernité et illettrisme: enquêtes (Suisse, Genève)*. Lausanne: Réalités sociales, septembre 1992 (Cahiers du Centre d'étude de la politiques sociale).

11984 Modernité et illettrisme: études de cas.
CHE 1994
Research Date(s): 1989-1991
Girod, Roger (5 Chemin de la Boule, 1232 Confignon, Suisse); Lenoir Françoise; Orihuela-Burnat, Ana-Maria.
Inst: Université de Genève, Département de sociologie, 5 rue St-Ours, 1211 Genève 4, Suisse.
Fin: Fonds national suisse de la recherche scientifique.
illiteracy; adult; social integration
analphabétisme; adulte; intégration sociale
PROJECT DESCRIPTION

Ces études qualitatives font partie d'un programme de recherche sur l'illettrisme. Ce programme, qui a bénéficié d'une aide du Fonds national suisse de la recherche scientifique, a comporté notamment des sondages, l'un à l'échelle de la population adulte de toute la Suisse et deux autres sur la population adulte du canton de Genève. La présente information se défère à la partie qualitative de cette recherche. Le but principal des enquêtes qualitatives était de décrire le vécu des "analphabètes fonctionnels" en ce qui concerne leur rapport à l'écrit. Plus exactement, comment l'analphabète fonctionnel perçoit-il l'importance et l'utilité de la lecture, de l'écriture et du calcul dans la vie de tous les jours, comment se débrouille-til face à l'écrit et quelles stratégies ou tactiques met-il en œuvre pour contourner l'écrit?

Dans leurs rapports de recherche, les auteures parviennent à la conclusion que, bien que les illettrés qu'elles ont observés fonctionnent et soient intégrés socialement sur le plan des pratiques quotidiennes, ils sont cependant atteints dans leur identité et se sentent dévalorisés à cause de leur handicap. Ils ont intériorisé les valeurs d'une société fondée sur le clivage entre l'intellectuel et le manuel. Il est également intéressant de remarquer que l'aspiration à sortir de la dépendance d'autrui, engendrée nécessairement par l'illettrisme, est rare: on n'a guère trouvé d'illettrés qui entreprennent ou désirent entreprendre des démarches pour apprendre à lire et écrire mieux dans ce but. Les motivations sont plutôt liées à des aspirations professionnelles, à l'acquisition de qualifications donnant accès à des métiers jugés supérieurs.

Pour les personnes interviewées, c'est donc l'accès au travail ou au métier qui représente le facteur primordial d'insertion sociale. La disparition progressive, de nos jours, des emplois sans qualification pourrait dès lors constituer le facteur d'exclusion le plus menaçant pour l'analphabète fonctionnel.

Publ: Lenoir, Françoise. *Analyse qualitative de l'illettrisme fonctionnel: étude de cas sur la base d'entretiens approfondis.* Genève: Université de Genève, Département de sociologie, juin 1991, 83p.

Orihuela-Burnat, Ana-Maria. *L'analphabétisme fonctionnel: études de cas.* Genève: Université de Genève, Département de sociologie, décembre 1991, 37p.

Orihuela-Burnat, Ana-Maria. *L'analphabétisme fonctionnel: études de cas: les apprentis.* Genève: Université de Genève, Département de sociologie, janvier 1992, 32p.

11985   Moray House Institute of Education policy on equal opportunities (disability and race): curricular implementation.
GBR   1993
Research Date(s): 1990-1992
Diniz, F.
Inst: Heriot-Watt University, Moray House Institute of Education, Holyrood Road, Edinburgh EH8 8AQ, United Kingdom.
equal opportunity; access to education; handicapped; race; curriculum development
égalité de chances; accès à l'éducation; handicapé; race; élaboration de programmes d'études
PROJECT DESCRIPTION
The main aim of this research is to monitor the curricular implementation of the Institute's policy on Equal Opportunity (Disability and Race). The curricular dimension is regarded as a major strategy for students and staff to develop critical perspectives on discrimination, in relation to disability and race.

11986   Multicultural education after ERA: concerns and challenges for the 1990s.
GBR   1993
Research Date(s): 1991-1993
Taylor, M.; Bagley, C.
Sup: Stoney, S.
Inst: National Foundation for Educational Research, The Mere, Upton Park, Slough SL1 2DQ, United Kingdom.
intercultural education; educational policy; ethnic relations
éducation interculturelle; politique de l'éducation; relations ethniques
PROJECT DESCRIPTION
The values underpinning the Education Reform Act 1988 (ERA) and the structures and targets set by the implementation of the National Curriculum and Local Management of Schools (LMS) have raised new issues and challenges in the realisation of equal opportunities in the translation of multicultural antiracist policies into practice. This project has sought to be diagnostic and responsive by establishing current concerns among local education authorities (LEAs) and identifying promising developmental strategies in relation to institutional, training and curricular issues.

The research has had three phases: a national questionnaire, interviews, and thematic case studies. Initially the project identified LEA concerns, constraints and challenges for multicultural antiracist education in post-ERA developments. As a result, five themes formed the focus of subsequent research: (1) the implementation of Section 11 changes; (2) Training and Enterprise Councils (TECs) and the Ethnic Minority Grant; (3) equal opportunities in governor training; (4) the issues of cultural diversity in Religious Education and the Standing Advisory Councils on Religious Education (SACREs); and (5) managing quality and equality - the permeation of multicultural antiracist education in school inspections.

Research dissemination has occurred during the project and included ongoing publications, seminars, conference presentations and talks to various audiences.

Publ: Taylor, M.J. *Multicultural Antiracist Education After ERA: Concerns, Constraints and Challenges.* NFER, 1992.

Taylor, M.J. *Equality after ERA?* NFER, 1992.

Bagley, C.A. *Back to the Future: Section 11 of the Local Government Act 1966: Local Education Authorities and Multicultural/Antiracist Education.* NFER, 1992.

Bagley, C.A. *An Enterprising Initiative? Training and Enterprising Councils and the Ethnic Minority Grant.* NFER, 1993.

11987   Multicultural education: images at primary level.
GBR   1993
Research Date(s): 1988-1993
Brown, M.
Sup: Wright, C.; Fogelman, K.
Inst: Leicester University, School of Education, University Road, Leicester LE1 7RH, United Kingdom.
Fin: Overstone Park Kindergarten & Preparatory School.
cultural integration; ethnic minority; intercultural education
intégration culturelle; minorité ethnique; éducation interculturelle
PROJECT DESCRIPTION
Is concern about minority pupils a worthy matter or are there more pressing problems in education? What does multicultural education mean in terms of actual school practice? Who is referred to when we use the term 'ethnic minority'? In this study an observational research will be conducted, with the aim of analysing attitudes and views of teachers and pupils of given primary schools. Three types of school will be researched and formal and informal interviews with individuals and groups of teachers and pupils will be conducted. Records and reports will also be assessed in order to discover views on multicultural education and to ascertain if school experiences of ethnic minority pupils in the various schools are similar. It will also be decided whether the internal system of the schools and their teaching methods have differential effects on the pupils of ethnic minority.

The three different types of school examined are: (a) large primary schools in inner city areas (Birmingham and London) where there exists a high percentage of pupils from ethnic minority backgrounds. In these schools multicultural educational techniques are used to an extreme to cater for 'supposed needs' especially in the area of language development; (b) primary schools in developing towns (Northampton and Cambridge) where pupils of multiethnic backgrounds attend on a smaller scale, and multicultural teaching methods and practices are incorporated in the curriculum successfully; (c) rural primary schools where heads and teachers alike believe that multicultural education is not needed in their school as no pupils of multiethnic backgrounds attend and they find multicultural education baffling, misleading and foreign.

The study prompts questions in relation to the degree of multicultural awareness and practices observed in schools.

11988   Návrh koncepce vzdělání na obecné a základní škole. (The design of education in primary and lower secondary schools.)
CSK   1994
Research Date(s): 1992-1993
Janoušková, Eva; Smejkalová, Adriena; Müllerová, Jana; Brant, Jiří.
Sup: Roušal, Antonín; Vrbová, Marie.
Inst: Výzkumný ústav pedagogický (Research Institute of Education), Strojírenská 386, 155 21 Praha 5 - Zličín, Czech Republic.
Ministerstvo školství, mládeže a tělovýchovy ČR (Ministry of Education, Youth and Physical Education), Karmelitská 7, 118 13 Praha 1, Czech Republic
general education; compulsory education; primary education; lower secondary; curriculum; pupil; personality development
enseignement général; enseignement obligatoire; enseignement primaire; secondaire premier cycle; programme d'études; élève; développement de la personnalité
PROJECT DESCRIPTION
This is an expert study aimed at the solution of some key issues of the educational programme for youth of compulsory school age, focusing especially on the functions of primary schools. The project involves the design of frameworks for dynamic teaching plans and curricula for compulsory and optional subjects, with a special emphasis on the development of pupils' personalities and taking account of their individual abilities, aspirations and orientations.

Methods: The study will be conducted in close cooperation with educational practitioners on the basis of experimentation and evaluation in several primary schools.

Publ: Janoušková, Eva a kol. *Návrh koncepce vzdělávání na obecné a základní škole. Výchozí podkladová studie k řešení grantového úkolu MŠMT ČR.* Praha; Výzkumný ústav pedagogický 1992, 73p.

11989   New Directions in Education Policy Sociology.
GBR   1993
Research Date(s): 1993
Shilling, C.; Ball, S.
Inst: Southampton University, Department of Sociology and Social Policy, Highfield, Southampton SO9 5NH, United Kingdom; London University, King's College, Centre for Educational Studies, Cornwall House Annexe, Waterloo Road, London SE1 3TY, United Kingdom.
Fin: Nuffield Foundation.

educational policy; educational sociology
politique de l'éducation; sociologie de l'éducation
PROJECT DESCRIPTION

'New Directions in Education Policy Sociology' is a Nuffield Foundation funded conference taking place in March 1993. It is also intended that the Conference proceedings will (in part) contribute to a book, with the same title, addressing theoretical and methodological issues in the field of education policy sociology.

11990   The new government and management of education.
GBR   1993
Research Date(s): 1990-1994
Ranson, S.; Thomas, H.; Ribbins, P.
Inst: Birmingham University, School of Education, Edgbaston, Birmingham B15 2TT, United Kingdom.
Fin: Economic and Social Research Council.
educational reform; educational administration; economics of education
réforme de l'enseignement; administration de l'enseignement; économie de l'éducation
PROJECT DESCRIPTION

The implementation of the 1988 Education Reform Act over four to five years provides a unique opportunity to study the emergence of a new system of government for education. This research proposes to develop knowledge and understanding of that system. It will focus upon understanding the tension within the new system between its principal characteristics of administrative regulation and public choice and accountability.

The research will analyse the emerging patterns of administration (financial staffing and curriculum procedures) and public choice (open enrolment, opting out and accountability systems) in the new system of government as it is implemented. A theoretical model will be developed which seeks to explain the development and change of the new system of government by identifying key factors; their purposes and strategies; their resource ownership and interests; their roles and relationships in the system; patterns of conflict and cooperation; and the emerging structure of power, influence and control. The unique opportunity to study a system as it develops over time requires a longitudinal research design which enables the team to understand 'diachronic' as well as 'synchronic' characteristics of the emerging system.

This research intends to clarify types of emergent system of educational government and will enable a study of how the nature of institutional management may be shaped by the context in which they are located. This subsequent study will wish to investigate the effects of the changes on the roles of governors, headteachers and staff, the distribution of educational opportunities and standards of pupil achievement.

11991   OECD (Organisation for Economic Co-operation and Development) education indicators on attitudes and expectations.
GBR   1993
Research Date(s): 1990-1992
MacBeath, J.; Weir, A.
Inst: Jordanhill College of Education, Division of Education and Psychology, Southbrae Drive, Glasgow G13 1PP, United Kingdom.
Fin: Scottish Office Education Department.
aims of education; attitude; survey; educational research
finalité de l'éducation; attitude; enquête; recherche en éducation
PROJECT DESCRIPTION

The aims of this project are to: (1) examine surveys and polls of attitudes to and expectations of schooling in Britain with a view to identifying key performance indicators of international relevance; and (2) produce a digest and bibliography of the research based on parents', pupils' and teachers' expectations of schools.

11992   Open learning methods in chemistry.
GBR   1993
Research Date(s): 1988-
Brattan, D.
Inst: University of Central Lancashire, Corporation Street, Preston PR1 2TQ, United Kingdom.
Fin: University of Central Lancashire; Pickup; Enterprise.
open education; chemistry; teaching aid; educational software
éducation ouverte; chimie; moyen d'enseignement; didacticiel
PROJECT DESCRIPTION

This study is concerned with the preparation, use of, and evaluation of open learning texts, video and computer based materials, in physical and analytical chemistry. The main aims are to evaluate a change to learning rather than teaching methods and to examine ways of increasing access to higher education. Evaluation will be by interview and questionnaire.

11993   Opting for grant-maintained status: a study of policy-making in education.
GBR   1993
Research Date(s): 1989-1992
Halpin, D.; Fitz, J.

Inst: Warwick University, Faculty of Educational Studies, Coventry CV4 7AL, United Kingdom; University of Wales College of Cardiff, School of Education, 42 Park Place, Cardiff CF1 3BB, United Kingdom.
Fin: Economic and Social Research Council.
school autonomy; educational policy; educational reform; educational administration; grant
autonomie scolaire; politique de l'éducation; réforme de l'enseignement; administration de l'enseignement; allocation financière
PROJECT DESCRIPTION

This research aims to explore the origins and implementation of the government's grant-maintained schools policy. The policy will be investigated in the context of other government initiatives, in education and elsewhere, which are intended to enhance competition between providing institutions and to extend 'consumer' choice in the area of public and welfare services. Data collected in the course of the research will aid the conceptualisation of the education policy-making process. The project also aims to contribute to current theoretical debates in the area of policy research.

The research features the extensive use of interviews with individuals involved in making and implementing policy, both centrally and at local education authority level. In addition, the impact of grant-maintained schools will be investigated by intensive research in selected areas involving research within grant-maintained schools and other adjacent schools as well as interviews with pupils and their parents about their perceptions of schools and education in light of the policy and other related provisions of the Education Reform Act 1988.

Publ: Halpin, D. & Fitz, J. Researching grant-maintained schools. In: *Journal of Education Policy*, Vol 5, No 2/1990, pp. 167-180.
Fitz, J.; Halpin, D. & Power, S. Grant-maintained schools: a third force in education? In: *Forum*, Vol 33, No 2/1991, pp. 36-38.
Fitz, J. & Halpin, D. From a policy idea to a workable scheme: grant-maintained schools and the DES. In: *International Studies in Sociology of Education*, Vol 1, 1991.
Halpin, D.; Fitz, J. & Power, S. Local education authorities and the grant-maintained schools policy. In: *Educational Management and Administration*, Vol 19, No 4/1991, pp. 233-242.

11994   Policy and practice in multicultural education in Canada and Great Britain.
GBR   1993
Research Date(s): 1990-1991
Redfern, A.; Edwards, V.
Inst: Reading University, Faculty of Education and Community Studies, Bulmershe Court, Woodlands Avenue, Earley, Reading RG6 1HY, United Kingdom.
Fin: Canadian Government: Department of External Affairs.
intercultural education; educational policy; multilingualism; language teaching; cross-national research
éducation interculturelle; politique de l'éducation; multilinguisme; enseignement des langues; recherche transnationale
PROJECT DESCRIPTION

This is a comparative analysis of British and Canadian multicultural education policies and practices. In particular the study will look at: (1) policy development which is responsive to the needs of a multilingual, multicultural school population; (2) strategies for providing language support for children in the process of acquiring English; and (3) the planning and management of multicultural, multilingual classroom resources.

The research will be a mixture of observation of classroom practices; interviews with teachers, principals and policy-makers and administrators; and analysis of published policy papers. The sample consists of the principals and staff of two elementary and two high schools, and the trustees, superintendants and other administrators of a board of education. Staff at York University and the Ontario Institute for Studies in Education are also involved.

11995   Policy development and the provision of Access courses.
GBR   1993
Research Date(s): 1988-1992
Field, J.
Inst: Warwick University, Faculty of Educational Studies, Department of Continuing Education, Continuing Education Research Centre, Coventry CV4 7AL, United Kingdom.
Fin: Universities Funding Council.
access to education; adult education; higher education
accès à l'éducation; éducation des adultes; enseignement supérieur
PROJECT DESCRIPTION

During the 1980s, Access courses emerged as a major new contribution to expanding and broadening participation in higher education. The project is exploring the process of innovation by which Access courses were and are still being established; and will investigate the impact upon decision-making and implementation of recent changes in the governance and planning of further and higher education and training (e.g. Training and Enterprise Councils, Access recognition procedures, the new Funding

Councils in further and higher education, and the single European market for highly skilled labour).
Publ: Field, J.; Harragan, S. & Smith, G. *Struggling to learn: the financial situation of Access students.* Derby: Forum for Access Studies, 1990.

11996 Policy, practice and provision for children with specific learning difficulties.
GBR 1993
Research Date(s): 1990-1992
Duffield, J.
Sup: Riddell, S.; Brown, S.
Inst: Stirling University, Department of Education, Stirling FK9 4LA, United Kingdom.
Fin: Scottish Office Education Department.
educational policy; educational provision; special education; learning difficulty
politique de l'éducation; scolarisation; enseignement spécial; difficulté de l'apprentissage
PROJECT DESCRIPTION
The project is intended to provide an overview of policy and provision for children with specific learning difficulties in the Scottish regions. The central concern is to understand how the problem is conceptualised by professionals, voluntary organisations and parents and to analyse the way in which different forms of provision arise from these conceptualisations. Interviews with principal psychologists, education officers, advisers, voluntary organisations and teacher educators are being undertaken, followed by surveys of the views of pre-service teachers, inservice teachers and parents. Case studies of particular ways of meeting the needs of children with specific learning difficulties are being undertaken during the final phase of the project.

11997 Preparation for life: TVEI and equal opportunities (gender).
GBR 1993
Research Date(s): 1990-1993
New, S.
Sup: Summerfield, P.; Mason, J.
Inst: Lancaster University, Department of Educational Research, Cartmel College, Bailrigg, Lancaster LA1 4YW, United Kingdom.
equal opportunity; vocational education; technical education; transition from school to work
égalité de chances; enseignement professionnel; enseignement technique; passage à la vie active
PROJECT DESCRIPTION
From its inception, the Technical and Vocational Education Initiative (TVEI) included, as a central objective, a commitment to the promotion of equal opportunities for boys and girls within pilot schemes. Using a triangulated case study approach, this research seeks to explore, within a theoretical framework informed by feminist research and theory on gender and education, the development, implementation and impact of TVEI equal opportunities policy and practice in one local education authority (LEA), from the dual perspectives of (a) policymakers (both at local authority and school level) and (b) the young people involved in the second year of the pilot scheme. With regard to the former perspective, methods have included the analysis of archive documentation and interviews with key local authority personnel; and with regard to the latter, the analysis of careers service destinations data, questionnaire data and data from in-depth interviews, conducted at various stages up to two-and-a-half years after leaving school.
In particular, the research seeks to understand the nature of the underlying philosophy/philosophies reflected in the equal opportunities developments of the LEA in question, and the impact this has had on the young people involved, and the implications of this for the promotion of equal opportunities work within a feminist framework.
Publ: New, S.J. *The destinations of 1989 leavers from the five TVEI pilot schools.* (Working Paper). City of Salford Education Department (14-19 Development Unit), 1990.
New, S.J. *The Salford school leavers survey: a report based on the experiences of 1989 leavers from the five TVEI pilot schools.* (Working Paper). City of Salford Education Department (14-19 Development Unit), 1990.

11998 Problems and possibilities of managing small secondary schools (circa 400) as a result of the Education Reform Act 1988.
GBR 1993
Research Date(s): 1990-1993
Richmond, J.
Sup: Thomas, H.
Inst: Birmingham University, School of Education, Edgbaston, Birmingham B15 2TT, United Kingdom.
educational reform; educational administration; school size; small school
réforme de l'enseignement; administration de l'enseignement; dimension de l'école; école de taille réduite
PROJECT DESCRIPTION
The Education Reform Act 1988 has implications for the management and size of schools within a local authority. Her Majesty's Inspectorate has suggested that four-form entry schools may be the minimum under Local Management of Schools, yet many secondary schools fall below this minimum. In order to examine the problems and possibilities for the management of such schools, the proposed research will be both qualititative and quantitative in approach. Key issues of the 1988 Act will be reviewed and consideration given to the requirements of the Government through the Department of Education and Science, those of the local education authority as well as the needs of small schools themselves.

11999 Problems with right wing education policy.
GBR 1993
Research Date(s): 1987-1992
Demaine, J.
Inst: Loughborough University of Technology, Department of Education, Loughborough LE11 3TU, United Kingdom.
educational policy; educational reform; political philosophy
politique de l'éducation; réforme de l'enseignement; philosophie politique
PROJECT DESCRIPTION
The research examines right wing arguments on educational provision, including the notion of a voucher scheme and the introduction of elements of a 'free market' into public sector education. It examines right wing arguments on 'gradualism' as a means of securing educational reform. The research examines arguments put forward by the Right on the idea of a General Teaching Council, on the teacher labour market, and on the status of teachers.
Publ: Demaine, J. Teachers' work, curriculum and the New Right. In: *British Journal of Sociology of Education*, Vol 9, No 3/1988, pp. 247-264.
Demaine, J. Privatisation by stealth: New Right Education Policy. In: *ACE (Advisory Centre for Education) Bulletin*, No 28/1989, Advisory Centre for Education, pp. 5-7.
Demaine, J. A General Teaching Council and the status of teachers. In: *ACE (Advisory Centre for Education) Bulletin*, No 32/1989, Advisory Centre for Education, pp. 3-5.
Demaine, J. The reform of secondary education. In: Hindness, B. (ed.). *Reactions to the Right.* London: Routledge, 1990.

12000 Projekt Alternatívneho vysokého školstva na Slovensku v spolupráci so zahraničím. (Non-university higher education in Slovakia: an international cooperative project.)
SVK 1994
Research Date(s): 1991-1995
Hrabinská, M.; Štefančík, J.
Sup: Harach, L'.
Inst: Ústav informácií a prognóz školstva, mládeže a telovýchovy (Institute of Information and Prognoses of Education, Youth and Sport), Staré grunty 52, 842 44 Bratislava, Slovak Republic.
Ministerstvo školstva a vedy SR (Ministry of Education and Science of the Slovak Republic), Hlboká 2, 813 30 Bratislava, Slovak Republic
educational reform; vocational education; higher education; experimental school; curriculum development
réforme de l'enseignement; enseignement professionnel; enseignement supérieur; école expérimentale; élaboration de programmes d'études
PROJECT DESCRIPTION
Background and aims: The project aims to contribute to the diversification of higher education in Slovakia by creating a new type of higher education: professional higher education. The new type of higher education involves the transformation of six selected specialized secondary schools (in cooperation with the Netherlands) and will also be offered within the framework of existing universities (in cooperation with Germany). The project is also concerned with the evaluation of the experimental phase.
Professional higher education institutions will offer a course programme of three-and-a-half to four years' duration. As courses will be of a vocational nature and highly specialized, graduates from these courses will be highly skilled specialists who will be able to adapt themselves to concrete workplace conditions according to the needs of society.
Design: The experimental courses were started in the academic year 1992/1993 at several university faculties (the Faculty of Materials and Technology in Trnava at the Slovac Technical University in Bratislava; the Faculty of Economics at Matej Bel University in Banská Bystrica and the Faculty of Professional Studies at Technical University in Košice), based on specialized secondary schools (Commercial Academy in Bratislava, Hotel Management Academy in Piešt'any, Commercial Academy in Dolný Kubín). Teaching will also start at the Secondary Nursing School in Martin and the Secondary School of Engineering in Košice. The focus of the project is on the development of legislation and training and the in-service training of managerial and teaching staff in the new establishments.

12001 Psychology and pedagogy: investigations into the relationships between principles of psychology of human learning and practical teaching and the supervision of practical teaching in teacher training.
GBR 1993
Research Date(s): 1983-
Stones, E.

Inst: Birmingham University, School of Psychology, Edgbaston, Birmingham B15 2TT, United Kingdom.
pedagogical theory; learning psychology; learning theory; teacher education; teaching practice; supervision; educational psychology
courant pédagogique; psychologie de l'apprentissage; théorie de l'apprentissage; formation des enseignants; pratique pédagogique; surveillance; psychologie de l'éducation
PROJECT DESCRIPTION
The work comprises a variety of investigations by experienced teachers into different aspects of pedagogy and employing different approaches. Qualitative as well quantitative data are sought for. Surveys of current practice are complemented by empirical work exploring the effects of theory-based practical pedagogical intervention into the teaching of a wide variety of subjects. Experiments are predominantly naturalistic, clinical, learning-based and outcome-oriented case studies involving small groups of teachers or student teachers and their pupils.

Publ: Stones, E. *Supervision in teacher education: a counselling and pedagogical approach.* London: Methuen, 1984.
Stones, E. Teaching practice supervision: bridge between theory and practice. In: *European Journal of Teacher Education*, Vol 10, No 1/1987, pp. 67-69.
Stones, E. Pedagogical studies in the theory and practice of teacher education. In: *Oxford Review of Education*, Vol 15, No 1/1989 pp. 3-15.
A full list of publications is available from the researcher.

12002 La qualité du dispositif rénové de formation professionnelle continue en agriculture.
FRA 1993
Research Date(s): 1989-1990
Clément, Jacqueline; Danrey, Jean; Henriot, Marie-Odile; Gateau, Francis.
Sup: Orivel, François; Savy, Hervé.
Inst: Institut national de promotion supérieure agricole, Département éducation permanente, 1 rue des Champs Prévois, 21000 Dijon, France; Université de Dijon, UER Faculté des sciences économiques et de gestion, CNRS UPR/29 et GDR/996, Institut de recherche sur l'économie de l'éducation, BP 138, 21004 Dijon Cedex, France.
Fin: Délégation à la formation professionnelle.
continuing education; vocational training; certificate; educational reform; teaching quality; credits; agricultural training
éducation permanente; formation professionnelle; diplôme; réforme de l'enseignement; qualité de l'enseignement; unités capitalisables; formation agricole
PROJECT DESCRIPTION
Objectifs: Le dispositif de formation professionnelle continue agricole est engagé dans une profonde évolution, au travers de la transformation du Brevet professionnel agricole (BPA) en un diplôme en unités capitalisables (UC), qui concerne maintenant les deux tiers de l'appareil. Cette transformation a-t-elle entraîné une augmentation de la qualité de l'offre de formation? Les démarches qualité du monde de l'entreprise sont-elles applicables à la formation?
Méthodologie: Trois séries d'investigations ont été conduites entre dispositifs traditionnel et rénové: une analyse comparative du devenir professionnel des anciens stagiaires et de leur opinion sur le déroulement de la formation; une analyse comparative des principes d'organisation curriculaire; une analyse comparative des coûts et de leur couverture.
Résultats: Le dispositif UC s'appuie directement sur les principes d'une démarche qualité. Il a permis une amélioration significative de l'adéquation entre la demande et l'offre de formation, avec des différences selon les sites. Une augmentation de la valorisation des potentialités du système est possible.

Publ: Savy, Hervé; Clément, Jacqueline; Danrey, Jean; Gateau, Francis; Henriot, Marie-Odile & Orivel, François. *La qualité du système rénové de formation professionnelle continue agricole.* Dijon: INPSA/IREDU, Avr. 1991, 140p.

12003 Racism and multicultural education.
GBR 1993
Research Date(s): 1988-1995
Demaine, J.
Inst: Loughborough University of Technology, Department of Education, Loughborough LE11 3TU, United Kingdom.
intercultural education; racial integration; racism; ethnic group
éducation interculturelle; intégration raciale; racisme; groupe ethnique
PROJECT DESCRIPTION
The research examines the arguments surrounding the notions of multicultural and antiracist education with particular reference to the pedagogic practice. The research is also concerned with the ways in which terms and categories are deployed in analyses, and discussion of differences in educational achievement between social groups whose identity is usually specified in terms of 'race' or 'ethnicity'.

Publ: Demaine, J. & Kadowala, D. Multicultural and antiracist education: the unnecessary divide. In: *Curriculum*, Vol 9, No 2/1988, pp. 99-102.

Demaine, J. Race, categorisation and educational achievement. In: *British Journal of Sociology of Education*, Vol 10, No 2/1989, pp. 195-214.

12004 The reconstruction and transfer of learning: teaching for effective learning in higher education.
GBR 1993
Research Date(s): 1989-1993
Machell, J.
Sup: Saunders, M.
Inst: Lancaster University, Department of Educational Research, Centre for the Study of Education and Training, Cartmel College, Bailrigg, Lancaster LA1 4YW, United Kingdom.
transfer of learning; higher education; learning; learning strategy; teaching method
transfert pédagogique; enseignement supérieur; acquisition de connaissances; stratégie d'apprentissage; méthode pédagogique
PROJECT DESCRIPTION
'Transfer of learning' is a much used but misused phrase. 'Transfer' represents a facile, inflexible and surface approach to learning which has limited use value. In contrast 'reconstructing learning' - applying previous learning creatively in new contexts - offers far more potential benefits and it is this ability, rather than simple transfer, which instructional strategies should aim to develop.
The research will: (1) identify the key differences between transfer and reconstruction; (2) establish connections between current educational concerns and reconstruction; (3) examine key theories of learning which contribute to an understanding of reconstruction; (4) explore the ways in which teaching in higher education facilitate reconstruction; (5) discuss the implications of reconstructions for teaching methods in higher education.

12005 Research and evaluation of Cheshire LEA's Technical and Vocational Education Initiative (TVEI), Inservice Education and Training (INSET) & Education Support Grant (ESG) programmes.
GBR 1993
Research Date(s): 1989-1991
Burgess, R.
Sup: Gleeson, D.
Inst: Keele University, Department of Education, Keele, Staffordshire ST5 5BG, United Kingdom.
Fin: Cheshire Local Education Authority.
educational policy; educational innovation; technical education; vocational education; further education of teachers; grant
politique de l'éducation; innovation pédagogique; enseignement technique; enseignement professionnel; perfectionnement des enseignants; allocation financière
PROJECT DESCRIPTION
The aim is to provide an up-to-date case study analysis of a small group of schools (secondary, primary and special) and a further education institution, in order to evaluate the impact of Technical and Vocational Education Initiative (TVEI), Inservice Education and Training (INSET) and Education Support Grant (ESG) initiatives on staff development and teaching and learning processes.

12006 Rozvoj školstva v Českej a Slovenskej federatívnej republike v rokoch 1991-1992. (Development of education in the Czech and Slovak Federal Republic in the period 1991-1992.)
SVK 1994
Research Date(s): 1992
Belišová, E.; Dzurko, J.; Ferenčíková, A.; Horváth, S.; Ivanová, M.; Kobyda, F.; Kulich, D.; et al.
Sup: Hrabinská, M.
Inst: Ústav informácií a prognóz školstva, mládeže a telovýchovy (Institute of Information and Prognoses of Education, Youth and Sport), Staré grunty 52, 842 44 Bratislava, Slovak Republic.
Ministerstvo školstva a vedy SR (Ministry of Education and Science of the Slovak Republic), Hlboká 2, 813 30 Bratislava, Slovak Republic
development of education; education system; educational policy; educational reform; educational innovation; report
développement de l'éducation; système d'enseignement; politique de l'éducation; réforme de l'enseignement; innovation pédagogique; rapport
PROJECT DESCRIPTION
Background and aim: The research aimed to elaborate a national report on the development of education in the CSFR in the period 1990-1992 for the 43rd session of the International Conference on Education in Geneva. More specifically, the aim was to describe the reforms that have taken place in education in the light of the following acts: the Amendment of Primary and Secondary Education Act; the Higher Education Act; the State Government and Local Education Authorities Act.
The changes that have taken place in the concept, content, scope and conditions of different parts of the educational system are scrutinized in the following chapters: Pre-school education; Primary education; Secondary schools; Special education; School inspection; Higher education; Administration and management; Financing; Environmental education; Adult education; Education for cultural development; Initial and in-service teacher education; Educational research; International regional and bilateral

cooperation in the sphere of education; Implementation of the plan of action to eradicate illiteracy by the year 2000; Declaration and framework for action adopted by the World Conference on Education for All and Recommendation No. 77 of the International Conference on Education; Basic statistical data.

Design: Data were collected during the 1991-1992 school year. The appendix to the national report presents the basic statistical data on individual elements of the education system.

Publ: Hrabinská, M. (ed.). *Development of Education 1990-1992. The Czech and Slovak Federal Republic.* ÚIP ŠMT, Bratislava, 1992, 110p.

12007 Schulkultur - ein Schulversuch. (School culture - a pilot project.)
AUT 1993
Research Date(s): 1990-1994
Porcham, Werner; Prackwieser, Kurt; Schlichtherle, Andreas; Kuenz, Irmgard; Egger, Gerlinde; Weingruber, Viktor.
Inst: Uebungshauptschule der Paedagogischen Akademie des Bundes, Pastorstrasse 5-7, A-6020 Innsbruck.
Paedagogische Akademie des Bundes in Tirol, Pastorstrasse 5-7, A-6020 Innsbruck
Fin: Bundesministerium fuer Unterricht und Kunst.
intercultural education; socio-cultural activities; experimentation; language development
éducation interculturelle; activités socioculturelles; expérimentation; développement du langage
PROJECT DESCRIPTION
Der dritte Abschnitt des Schulversuchs steht unter dem Motto 'anderen Kulturen begegnen und andere Kulturen verstehen'. Schwerpunkte im Programm sind: 1. Aus dem 'Schonraum' Familie - Schule hinaustreten und mit dem Ungewohnten, Fremden umgehen lernen. 2. Kontakte mit Personen und Institutionen aus anderen Kulturkreisen aufnehmen. 3. Kreative Sprachentwicklung als Hilfestellung zur Bewaeltigung von Unsicherheit und Angst in interkulturellen Begegnungssituationen anregen. 4. Den geplanten Schueleraustausch mit Grossbritannien (4. Schuljahr) kooperativ vorbereiten.

Die Begleitung des Schulversuchs ist auf der Basis der Handlungsforschung zu sehen, wobei die Erkundungen (schriftliche und muendliche Befragung, Beobachtung und Tests) ausgewertet werden und sofort nachher Einfluss auf die weitere Gestaltung des Versuchs haben. Da die Versuchsgruppe klein ist und die Uebungshauptschule eine ganz besondere Schule ist, ist es uns viel wichtiger, den Fortgang in diesem Versuch zu erkunden, als schon jetzt moegliche Verallgemeinerungen zu finden.

Es handelt sich um Schulversuchsbegleitung im Stil einer Handlungsforschung, um den Fortgang des Versuchs zu unterstuetzen.

In der 1. Klasse lag der Schwerpunkt in der Erweiterung der Gemeinschaftsfaehigkeit, in der die Klasse als Ort der Begegnung und Zeit von Erlebnissen kognitiv, affektiv und psychomotorisch erlebt werden soll. Gemeinsames Erleben, Arbeiten, Reden und Feiern soll gezielt in den Unterricht eingebaut werden. In der 2. Klasse ist das Schwerpunktthema 'Lernen ist ungleich Angst'. Die SchuelerInnen sollen Moeglichkeiten und Grenzen der eigenen Leistungsfaehigkeit richtig einschaetzen, ihre Lernbereitschaft foerdern und Leistungsanforderungen ohne Angst bewaeltigen.

Publ: Porcham, Werner & Schlichtherle, Andreas. Schulkultur - ein Schulversuch. In: *Tiroler Schule*, 1991, Heft 1, S. 30-31.
Porcham, Werner & Schlichtherle, Andreas. Schuleintritt. In: *Tiroler Schule*, Heft 2, S. 29-33.
Porcham, Werner. Schulkultur - ein Schulversuch an der Uebungshauptschule der Paedagogischen Akademie des Bundes in Tirol. In: *Schule und Leben*. 1992, Heft 2, S. 84-91.

12008 Schulpsychologie - Bildungsberatung. (School psychology - educational counselling.)
AUT 1993
Research Date(s): 1990-1992
Sedlak, Franz; Steurer-Kerbl, Lydia; Aigner, Harald; Eibner, Anton; Leeb, Hans Paul; Tursky, Ingrid; Helbock, Maria.
Inst: Abteilung fuer Schulpsychologie und Bildungsberatung, Minoritenplatz 5, A-1014 Wien.
Bundesministerium fuer Unterricht und Kunst, Minoritenplatz 5, A-1014 Wien
educational guidance; school psychologist; mental health
orientation pédagogique; psychologue scolaire; santé mentale
PROJECT DESCRIPTION
Zu den vielseitigen Anliegen der Schulpsychologie- Bildungsberatung gehoeren die folgenden: Die aktive Mitgestaltung des kommunikativen Klimas in der Schule ('Soziales Lernen', 'Schule ohne Angst und Aggression', Gespraechsplattformen im Rahmen der Schulpartnerschaft, Managertraining fuer Fuehrungskraefte im Schulbereich etc.); praeventive und innovative Aktivitaeten fuer das System Schule (Untersuchungen, Grundlagenforschung, Rueckmeldungen an das System, Foerderung bzw. Unterstuetzung systematischer Weiterentwicklungen wie z.B. Schulautonomie, aber auch kritisches Engagement bei problematischen Tendenzen in Schule und Gesellschaft); Einsatz des fachlichen Erfahrungsschatzes fuer das Individuum (Schueler und Schuelerinnen, Eltern, Lehrer und Lehrerinnen, Schulleiter und Schulleiterinnen etc.), das im System eine Stuetze, Orientierungshilfe, Begleitung, Betreuung oder Behandlung braucht, oder aber auch als etikettierter Patient eines stoeranfaelligen Systems Schutz gegenueber Forderungen der Umwelt (Schule, Familie, Leistungsgesellschaft) benoetigt. In allen Bereichen kommen theoretisches Grundlagenwissen, Erkenntnisse der Allgemeinen und der Differentiellen Psychologie, insbesondere aber die in der Angewandten Psychologie gesammelten und weiterentwickelten Wissensbestaende und Fertigkeiten zum Tragen (z.B. Betriebspsychologie, Organisationspsychologie, Gesundheitspsychologie, Klinische Psychologie usw.). Auch das psychotherapeutische Know-How wird bedeutender.

Publ: Sedlak, Franz (Hrsg.). *Schulpsychologie - Bildungsberatung.* Paedagogischer Verlag Eugen Ketterl. Wien 1992.

12009 The Scottish educational reforms and teachers' theories of teaching and learning.
GBR 1993
Research Date(s): 1992-1994
Brown, S.; Drever, E.; Swann, J.
Inst: Stirling University, Department of Education, Stirling FK9 4LA, United Kingdom.
Fin: Economic and Social Research Council.
educational reform; common core curriculum; curriculum development; teacher; teaching practice
réforme de l'enseignement; tronc commun; élaboration de programmes d'études; enseignant; pratique pédagogique
PROJECT DESCRIPTION
The Scottish reforms for curriculum, assessment and national testing for 5 to 14 year olds are likely to influence teachers' ideas about teaching and learning. In this context, the project aims to explore teachers' assumptions about children's learning, how teachers interpret the differences among pupils (in the new atmosphere which emphasises 'attainment targets') and the ways in which they cater for these differences. The work focuses on two curriculum areas within the new reforms: mathematics (which has national testing) and environmental studies (which does not).

Twenty teachers in eight schools are involved, with classes of 6, 8, 12 and 14 year olds. The research methods include classroom observation (responsive and systematic), interviews with teachers (open-ended and semi-structured), an analysis of curriculum documents and of other support. Particular attention is being paid to the impact of the reforms on teachers' goals. For instance, do they now emphasise 'progress' more than 'activity' goals? There is also concern with teachers' conceptions of how pupils influence these goals and the actions taken to achieve them. The project will explore in depth: teachers' explicit use of 'attainment targets', their strategies of assessment and remediation, and evidence about how they think about children's learning.

12010 Scottish Wider Access Programme study.
GBR 1993
Research Date(s): 1991-1992
Munn, P.; Johnstone, M.; Lowden, K.
Inst: Scottish Council for Research in Education, 15 St John Street, Edinburgh EH8 8JR, United Kingdom.
Fin: Scottish Office Education Department.
access to education; adult education; higher education
accès à l'éducation; éducation des adultes; enseignement supérieur
PROJECT DESCRIPTION
This project complements the Leverhulme Access study by focusing on a survey of 100 Access students. It will identify any problems which Access students experience in their courses and in transition to higher education and will explore the effective ways of dealing with them and identify measures to increase the success rates of Access students.

12011 Self-governance, grant-maintained schools and educational identities.
GBR 1993
Research Date(s): 1992-1994
Halpin, D.; Fitz, J.
Inst: Warwick University, Faculty of Educational Studies, Coventry CV4 7AL, United Kingdom; University of Wales, College of Cardiff, School of Education, 42 Park Place, Cardiff CF1 3BB, United Kingdom.
Fin: Economic and Social Research Council.
school autonomy; educational administration; grant; financing
autonomie scolaire; administration de l'enseignement; allocation financière; financement
PROJECT DESCRIPTION
The main aim of this research is to explore the extent to which self-governance arising from grant-maintained (GM) status has contributed to innovation and change within education. The specific objectives are: (1) to investigate the impact of self-governance on the distribution of power and control in GM school management structures and practices including its effects on specialisation within the division of labour amongst teaching and non-teaching staff in GM schools and teachers' perceptions of their work and professional status, and its consequences for relations between GM

schools and their former local education authorities (LEAs); (2) to compare the management structures and practices found in GM schools with those of other schools in order to: (a) explore the extent to which different forms of self-governance have consequences for the organisation to teaching and learning; and (b) clarify whether the educational experiences offered by GM schools arise from self-governance as much as from perceived financial advantages that GM status may afford; (3) to explore the extent to which organisational differences between GM and other schools foster diversity of pupil experience of schooling and contribute to differentiated and stratified educational identities.

12012 Škola jako významný prostředek v procesu formování mladé generace. (School as an instrument in the education of the young generation.)
CSK 1994
Research Date(s): 1991-1994
Pelikán, J.; Vališová, A.; Novotná, M.; Kasíková, H.; Valenta, J.; Kota, J.; Rýdl, K.; Poláčková, V.
Sup: Homolka, J.
Inst: Filosofická fakulta Univerzity Karlovy (Charles University, Faculty of Arts, Department of Education), nám. J. Palacha 2, 110 00 Praha 1, Czech Republic.
development of education; education system; educational reform; educational theory; teacher education
développement de l'éducation; système d'enseignement; réforme de l'enseignement; théorie de l'éducation; formation des enseignants
PROJECT DESCRIPTION
The aim of the study is to examine: the influence of the social environment on pupils' personalities; the possibilities for alternative schools in the Czech education system; the possibility of recruiting educational science graduates into the teaching profession; the current state of educational theory regarding secondary schools, higher education, and teacher education. The wider aim is to develop educational theory, secondary school teacher education and educational research and evaluation in the Czech Republic.
Design: The study is conducted in collaboration with educational institutions in Germany, former Yugoslavia, Austria, France, England and the USA. A range of theoretical and empirical methods is used.
Publ: Vališová, A. *Asertivita v rodině a ve škole.* Praha: H&H, 1992, 156p.
Pelikán, J. *Metodologie výzkumu osobnosti středoškoského profesora a jeho pedagogického působení.* Praha: SPN, 1991, 150p.
Vališová, A. *Výchova k práci s knihou a s ostatními informačními prameny.* In: *Pedagogická Revue,* 2/1991.
Kasíková, H. *Humanizace v učitelské přípravě.* In: *Pedagogická Revue,* 1/1991.
Pelikán, J. *Některé problémy pedagogické interakce z hlediska výchovně vzdělávacího procesu.* In: *Pedagogika,* 1/1991.

12013 Socialisation of elites.
GBR 1993
Research Date(s): 1990-1992
Banks, M.; Roker, D.
Inst: Sheffield University, Department of Psychology, Sheffield S10 2TN, United Kingdom.
Fin: Economic and Social Research Council.
private education; occupational aspiration; work attitude; socialization; elite
enseignement privé; aspirations professionnelles; attitude envers le travail; socialisation; élite
PROJECT DESCRIPTION
The aim of this project is to assess the effects of private education on occupational aspirations and attitudes. The researchers carried out a secondary analysis of the Youthscan data base which consists of the 1970 birth cohort of 15,000 births.

12014 Student publishing in adult literacy.
GBR 1993
Research Date(s): 1991-1992
O'Rourke, R.
Sup: Mace, J.
Inst: London University, Goldsmiths' College, Department of Continuing and Community Education, Lewisham Way, New Cross, London SE14 6NW, United Kingdom.
Fin: Leverhulme Trust.
literacy; adult education; written expression; composition; author; publication
alphabétisation; éducation des adultes; expression écrite; composition littéraire; auteur; publication
PROJECT DESCRIPTION
Adult literacy in the UK adopted a practice (from the mid 1970s) of publishing reading material written by literacy students themselves. There has been some evidence to show that this practice gave new confidence both to the student authors and to their readers and that it is a practice which since the late 1980s appears to be in decline.

The study aims to establish the rationale, extent, and educational effects of the practice of publishing writing by adult literacy students in the UK and to examine the staff development implications of these. It is a national study which will consist of: (a) a literature search (both of theoretical work on writing development, and of the publications which have resulted from student writing); (b) visits and interviews with tutors and students at a sample of 20 centres across the UK; (c) a postal questionnaire of 200+ tutors and organisers in literacy programmes; (d) interviews/group events with up to 6 groups of 12 students each; (e) a national consultative conference on the draft report.

12015 A study of the management and implementation of educational change in primary schools.
GBR 1993
Research Date(s): 1990-1994
Waugh, D.
Sup: Gorwood, B.
Inst: Hull University, School of Education, Cottingham Road, Hull HU6 7RX, United Kingdom.
educational reform; primary school; school size; small school; educational administration
réforme de l'enseignement; école primaire; dimension de l'école; école de taille réduite; administration de l'enseignement
PROJECT DESCRIPTION
The research involves a study of primary schools of different sizes, but is concerned principally with those with 100 pupils or fewer. Case studies will be made and a questionnaire has been used to enable comparisons to be drawn between schools of varying sizes and the effects of educational reform upon them. The following will be considered: management of curriculum change; collaboration with other schools; resources and facilities; scope for delegation of responsibility by headteachers; the role of the headteacher; professional development of teaching staff; secretarial and other ancillary assistance; and classroom and school organisation.

12016 A study of the relationship between intentions and outcomes of policy initiatives related to women's education and training.
GBR 1993
Research Date(s): 1991-1995
Malcolm, J.
Inst: Leeds University, Department of Adult Continuing Education, Study of Continuing Education Unit, Leeds LS2 9JT, United Kingdom.
educational policy; women's education; continuing education; access to education; aims of education
politique de l'éducation; éducation des femmes; éducation permanente; accès à l'éducation; finalité de l'éducation
PROJECT DESCRIPTION
This study will investigate the relationship between government policy initiatives and the provision and outcomes of continuing education aimed mainly at women. It will attempt to establish whether the outcomes of, e.g. access courses, employment training and 'positive action' courses run over the last 15 years are in accordance with their publicly espoused purposes. The strategies adopted in such initiatives will be critically examined in terms of their roots in the policy process, their rationale and the consequences for women students and for educational institutions. The study will analyse the link, if it exists, between educational programmes directed at women and longer-term changes in their social and economic position as a group.

12017 Les "Théories implicites de l'orientation" chez le lycéen et le professeur de lycée.
FRA 1992
Research Date(s): 1990-1991
Dumora, Bernadette; Vern, Claudine.
Sup: Bruchon-Schweitzer, Marilou.
Inst: Université de Bordeaux II, UFR Sciences sociales et psychologiques, Laboratoire de psychologie, Domaine universitaire, Esplanade des Antilles Bât.E, 33405 Talence, France.
educational guidance; teacher behaviour; general education; vocational education
orientation pédagogique; comportement de l'enseignant; enseignement général; enseignement professionnel
PROJECT DESCRIPTION
Objectifs: Analyse des "théories implicites de l'orientation", du lycéen et du professeur de lycée: différences en fonction de la filière d'enseignement (visée générale ou visée professionnelle) ou similarité, symétrie, correspondance entre "théories" du lycéen et "théories" du professeur. Le champ théorique de référence: les théories implicites de l'orientation et la théorie de la rationalisation en psychologie sociale.
Méthodologie: Entretiens et interviews de groupes auprès de professeurs et d'élèves de lycées d'enseignement général et technique: Analyses de contenu (analyse propositionnelle du discours: Ghiglione, Matalon, Bacri); Elaboration de protocoles et de graphes.

12018   The transition to democracy and educational change in contemporary Chile and post-Franco Spain.
GBR   1993
Research Date(s): 1990-1992
Richmond, M.
Sup: Brock, C.
Inst: Hull University, School of Education, Cottingham Road, Hull HU6 7RX, United Kingdom.
educational policy; Chile; Spain; politics; government policy; democracy; educational reform
politique de l'éducation; Chili; Espagne; politique; politique gouvernementale; démocratie; réforme de l'enseignement
PROJECT DESCRIPTION
Located within two main sub-fields of educational inquiry (comparative education and the politics of education), the study aims to ascertain and understand the effects of transitions to democracy upon education and also the role of education within such transitions. Given its vital involvement in social and cultural reproduction, education may reveal itself to be a particularly sensitive field for registering the changes associated with a shift away from authoritarianism towards more democratic forms of policy. This sensitivity (its extent and character) will constitute the primary focus of the study. An examination of Chile and Spain affords an opportunity to explore whether or not there are structural similarities or parallels within the process of democratic transition and associated educational change in different countries. Study of the two national experiences is further justified by the possibility that Spain's transition may have furnished lessons for later transitions in Latin America in particular, such as that in Chile. Fieldwork in both countries will focus upon the main primary and secondary written sources of information and upon interviews with government officials and significant personnel within non-governmental organisations.

12019   Umweltbewusstsein und Umweltverhalten - Zum sozialen Vakuum in der Umwelterziehung und Umweltbildung. (Ecological awareness and behaviour: on the social vacuum in environmental education and training.)
DEU   1993
Research Date(s): 1991-1992
Krol, G.
Inst: Universitaet Muenster, FB 06 Sozialwissenschaften, Institut fuer Wirtschaftswissenschaft und ihre Didaktik, Fliednerstrasse 21, D-4400 Muenster.
aims of education; environment; social behaviour
finalité de l'éducation; environnement; comportement social
PROJECT DESCRIPTION
Inhalt: Umwelterziehung und Umweltbildung basieren auf dem zentralen Paradigma, dass eine Foerderung des Umweltbewusstseins sich in umweltvertraeglicheren Verhaltensweisen niederschlagen wird. Dieses Paradigma laesst die Faktoren aus dem Blickfeld geraten, die der Umsetzung eines gesteigerten Umweltbewusstseins in konkretes Verhalten auf allen Ebenen unserer Gesellschaft entgegenstehen. Sie sind Gegenstand der oekonomischen Analyse der Umweltprobleme. Ziel der Arbeit ist es, die Relevanz der umweltoekonomischen Erklaerungs- und Loesungsansaetze fuer Umwelterziehung und Umweltbildung herauszuarbeiten und zu ueberpruefen, inwieweit diese konstruktiven Problemsichten bei den Multiplikatoren (Lehrern, Studierenden) praesent sind.
Vorgehensweise: Untersuchungsdesign: Panel; qualitative Forschung.
Datengewinnung: Befragung (Lehrer an allgemeinbildenden Schulen des Landes Nordrhein-Westfalen; Auswahlverfahren: Zufall). Primaererhebung: Feldarbeit von Mitarbeitern des Projektes durchgefuehrt.

Publ: Krol, G.-J. Begruendung eines eigenstaendigen sozialoekonomischen Beitrags zur Umweltbildung und Umwelterziehung - Lehrerbefragung zur Umwelterziehung. In: Eulefeld, G.; Bolscho, D.; Seybold, H. (Hrsg.). *Umweltbewusstsein und Umwelterziehung.* Kiel: IPN 1991, S. 135-171.
Krol, G.-J. Umweltprobleme aus oekonomischer Sicht - Zur Relevanz der Umweltoekonomie fuer die Umwelterziehung. In: May, H. (Hrsg.). *Handbuch der oekonomischen Bildung.* Muenchen 1991.

12020   Une approche multimédia pour l'orientation scolaire et professionnelle.
FRA   1993
Research Date(s): 1988-1992
Lemercier, Denis.
Inst: Ministère de l'éducation, Conservatoire national des arts et métiers, Ecole pratique des Hautes Etudes et Université de Paris V, Institut national d'études du travail et d'orientation professionnelle - Service de recherche, 41 rue Gay-Lussac, 75005 Paris, France.
educational guidance; vocational guidance; audiovisual method; data base; information system; multimedia method; maturity; choice of studies; occupational choice
orientation pédagogique; orientation professionnelle; méthode audiovisuelle; banque de données; système d'information; moyen multimédia; maturité; choix des études; choix d'une profession

PROJECT DESCRIPTION
Objectifs: La recherche porte sur l'étude des conditions d'accès, d'exploitation et d'intégration par les élèves d'un ensemble diversifié d'informations dans le contexte multimedia (ordinateur, vidéo-disque, bandes-vidéo, minitel, fiches auto-documentaires). Elle vise plus particulièrement à mesurer l'apport spécifique de l'image et des banques de données dans une stratégie de recherche d'informations sur les métiers et les filières scolaires. Elle s'efforce de faire une étude critique des produits existants et de formuler des propositions visant à faciliter l'introduction de tels systèmes dans un environnement scolaire ou extra-scolaire. Les hypothèses d'ordre psychologique mettent en liaison le degré d'activité de l'élève sur le dispositif et le développement de la maturité du projet scolaire et professionnel.
Méthodologie: Un groupe contrôle et un groupe expérimental ont été constitués. Le groupe expérimental comprend des élèves de 3ème de quatre collèges (2 en région parisienne, 1 dans le Nord, 1 en Bretagne) qui possèdent le matériel nécessaire et une équipe enseignante qui a les conditions pour participer à l'expérimentation. Le questionnaire utilisé pour mesurer l'évolution de la maturité du projet a été utilisé dans une étude antérieure. En outre des grilles d'observation des élèves ont été élaborées et ont été utilisées, par les enseignants des établissements concernés. Enfin des questionnaires de connaissances portant sur le système de formation ont été mis au point.

12021   Vývoj vzdelanostnej úrovne obyvateľstva v Slovenskej republike. (Development of the educational level of the population in the Slovak Republic by the year 2000.)
SVK   1994
Research Date(s): 1990-1992
Beňo, M.; Csicsayová, M.; Khun, P.; Kociánová, M.; Letková, K.
Sup: Harach, Ľ.
Inst: Ústav informácií a prognóz školstva, mládeže a telovýchovy (Institute of Information and Prognoses of Education, Youth and Sport), Staré grunty 52, 842 44 Bratislava, Slovak Republic.
Ministerstvo školstva a vedy SR (Ministry of Education and Science of the Slovak Republic), Hlboká 2, 813 30 Bratislava, Slovak Republic
development of education; society; primary education; secondary education; aims of education; social change; forecasting
développement de l'éducation; société; enseignement primaire; enseignement secondaire; finalité de l'éducation; changement social; prévision
PROJECT DESCRIPTION
Background: The research started from the hypothesis that the development of the Slovak Republic is dependent on the educational level of the population.
Aims: (1) To identify and examine new criteria for the aims and content of education and training in view of the social changes caused by the transition to a pluralist and democratic system and a market economy; (2) to examine the conditions that will influence the level of education and training in the long term and to propose criteria that should be considered in prognoses of education, training and the school system.
Research question: What are the educational aspects of the development of the cultural level of the population in the Slovak Republic?
Design: The problem was examined from three perspectives: philosophical, educational and demographic. The final report of the research describes the basic philosophical principles of education in the democratic society and the possibility of their application in the Slovak education system. Relevant issues are discussed under the following headings: (a) conditions for achieving the optimum level of education; (b) education and training in the pluralist and democratic society; (c) defining the aims and tasks of education and training in primary and secondary schools; (d) the educational level of the population in the Slovak Republic - prognosis up to the year 2010.

Publ: Beňo, M. *Pedagogické aspekty vývoja vzdelanostnej úrovne obyvateľstva Slovenskej republiky.* (Educational aspects of the development of educational standards of the population of the Slovak Republic.) Bratislava, ÚIP ŠMT, 1991, 113p.
Beňo, M. Škola a politika. (School and policy.) In: *Nové slovo*, 1991, No. 93, p. 3.
Khun, P. *Základní východiska filosofie výchovy demokratické společnosti a možnost jejich aplikace ve výchovném systému Slovenské republiky.* (Philosophical principles of education in the democratic society and possibilities of their application in the education system of the Slovak Republic.) Bratislava, ÚIP ŠMT, 1991, 25p.
Khun, P. Základní východiska filosofie výchovy v demokratické společnosti. (Philosophical principles of education in the democratic society.) In: *Pedagogická revue*, XLIV, 1992, pp. 218-231.
Kocianová, M.; Letková, K. & Csicsayová, M. *Vzdelanostná úroveň obyvateľstva Slovenskej republiky. Prognóza do roku 2010.* (Educational level of the population of the Slovak republic. Prognosis until 2010.) Bratislava, ÚIP ŠMT, 1991, 84p.

12022 Welche Bildung brauchen HTL-Ingenieure? (Quelle formation pour les ingénieurs ETS?)
CHE 1994
Research Date(s): 1991-
Feierabend, Urs J.
Sup: Oser, Fritz.
Inst: Universität Freiburg, Pädagogisches Institut, Route des Fougères, 1700 Freiburg, Schweiz.
Liberal education; technological sciences; curriculum
culture générale; sciences technologiques; programme d'études
PROJECT DESCRIPTION
Diese Dissertation wird sich in erster Linie mit der der Frage auseinandersetzen, wieviel und welche Allgemeinbildung an den Höheren Technischen Lehranstalten der Schweiz vermittelt werden soll. Diese Fragestellung wird von verschiedenen Seiten angegangen werden. So sollen die klassischen, aber auch modernere Bildungstheorien herangezogen werden, wobei der Autor den Arbeiten von Klafki einen speziellen Platz einzuräumen gedenkt. Vermutlich das Herstück der Arbeit wird aber in einer schriftlichen Befragung von Dozenten und ehemaligen wie gegenwärtigen Studierenden an den Höheren Technischen Lehranstalten von Biel (wo der Autor selbst unterrichtete), Burgdorf und Winterthur bestehen sowie in einer Reihe von Einzelinterviews mit Managern aus der Privatwirtschaft.
Noch unklar ist im gegenwärtigen Zeitpunkt, wie sehr die aktuellen Reformbestrebungen im Bereich der Berufsbildung (Berufsmatur, Fachhochschulen) berücksichtigt werden können. Eine Frage, die sicher behandelt werden wird, ist jene der besseren didaktischen Qualifizierung der HTL-Dozenten.

12023 Well-being and education.
GBR 1993
Research Date(s): 1991-1994
Kim, J.
Sup: Wringe, C.
Inst: Keele University, Department of Education, Keele, Staffordshire ST5 5BG, United Kingdom.
aims of education; philosophy of education; health; mental health
finalité de l'éducation; philosophie de l'éducation; santé; santé mentale
PROJECT DESCRIPTION
This is a philosophical study examining the concept of well-being as an educational aim. Various conceptions of well-being will be examined, a distinction established between material welfare and a broader conception of well-being, and the links between this conception of well-being and education explored.

12024 Widening access to human resources disciplines: developing opportunities for ethnic minority students at the University of Leeds.
GBR 1993
Research Date(s): 1991-1992
Gardiner, J.
Sup: Taylor, R.
Inst: Leeds University, Department of Adult Continuing Education, Leeds LS2 9JT, United Kingdom.
Fin: Department of Employment via Focus Educational Consultancy.
access to education; equal opportunity; higher education; ethnic minority
accès à l'éducation; égalité de chances; enseignement supérieur; minorité ethnique
PROJECT DESCRIPTION
The project is part of a national collaborative action research project on widening access to higher education. The aims are to: (1) evaluate strategies for pre-degree and degree course curriculum change in the social sciences and humanities which enhance access to degree programmes for black/ethnic minority mature students; (2) gather evidence on and evaluate the experiences of non-traditional students from different ethnic backgrounds on access and degree coures; (3) analyse the results of ethnic monitoring of applications, offers and acceptances for undergraduate places at the University of Leeds; and (4) disseminate the project results.
Methods used include: (1) participant observation of curriculum development processes; (2) content analysis of structured interviews; and (3) statistical analysis of ethnic monitoring and course outcomes data.

12025 Wissen von "Erziehung" und "Paedagogik" im erziehungswissenschaftlichen und paedagogischen Diskurs in Deutschland 1945-1989. (Knowledge of "education" and "pedagogics" in the pedagogic debate in Germany 1945-1989.)
DEU 1993
Research Date(s): 1992-1994
Fritzke, C.; Appoltshauser, M.; Gatzemann, T.
Sup: Menck, P.
Inst: Universitaet-Gesamthochschule Siegen, FB 02 Erziehungswissenschaft, Psychologie, Sportwissenschaft, Fach Erziehungswissenschaft, LS Erziehungswissenschaft, Adolf-Reichwein-Strasse 2, D-5900 Siegen 21; Universitaet Halle-Wittenberg, Postfach, O-4050 Halle.
Fin: Deutsche Forschungsgemeinschaft.
sciences of education; German DR; Germany - Federal Republic; knowledge; education system; history of education
sciences de l'éducation; Allemagne RDA; Allemagne RFA; connaissance; système d'enseignement; histoire de l'éducation
PROJECT DESCRIPTION
Inhalt: Rekonstruktion und Interpretation des erziehungswissenschaftlichen Diskurses: Themen, ueber die kommuniziert wird und Kategorien, mit denen soziale Tatsachen als "Erziehung" bestimmt werden. Dabei soll geprueft werden, ob es Unterschiede im Blick auf die sozialen Kontexte (BRD - DDR) sowie zeitliche Entwicklung gibt. Unterschiede werden vor dem Hintergrund der Entwicklung und Struktur des Erziehungssystems und des Systems der Erziehungswissenschaft bzw. Paedagogik interpretiert.
Materialbasis: Aufsaetze von Professoren fuer Erziehungswissenschaft/Paedagogik in je zwei Zeitschriften aus der BRD sowie der DDR (eine eher wissenschaftlich, eine eher schulpraktisch orientierte). Datenbasis: (1) Aufsatztitel; (2) Saetze ueber "Erziehung" sowie "Paedagogik"/"Erziehungswissenschaft" in den Aufsaetzen.
Geographischer Raum: Deutschland.
Untersuchter Zeitraum: 1945-1989.
Vorgehensweise: Untersuchungsdesign: retrospektive Daten.
Datengewinnung: Inhaltsanalyse (Professoren fuer Erziehungswissenschaft/Paedagogik als Autoren in 4 fuehrenden Fachzeitschriften; Auswahlverfahren: total). Datenerstellung auf der Basis von bereits vorliegenden Materialien wie Texten, Akten, Statistiken.
Auswertung: Kontingenz- und Korrelationsstatistik.

12026 Working with parents to promote early literacy development.
GBR 1993
Research Date(s): 1988-1991
Hannon, P.
Inst: Sheffield University, Division of Education, 388 Glossop Road, Sheffield S10 2TN, United Kingdom.
Fin: European Commission; Department of Education and Science.
literacy; reading; early childhood education; pre-school child; parent participation
alphabétisation; lecture; éducation de la prime enfance; enfant d'âge préscolaire; participation des parents
PROJECT DESCRIPTION
The project is the United Kingdom's contribution to the European Communities' Action Research Programme on the Prevention and Combatting of Illiteracy and is linked to 16 others in the member states. It aims to develop methods of working with parents of preschool children to promote literacy development in the early stages. The focus is on children's learning at home, but both home-based and school-based methods are being explored through a set of 14 case studies of families. The project team has adopted an emergent literacy perspective and has attempted to share it with parents, some in distinctly disadvantaged circumstances. The outcomes will be descriptions of methods to be shared with other workers, and a qualitative evaluation of their feasibility and impact which may lead to future experimental studies.

Publ: Hannon, P. Parental involvement in preschool literacy development. In: Wray, D. (ed.). *Emerging partnerships: current research in language and literacy.* BERA (British Educational Research Association) Dialogues in Education, 4. Clevedon, Avon: Multilingual Matters, 1990.
Weinberger, J.; Hannon, P. & Nutbrown, C. *Ways of working with parents to promote early literacy development.* USDE (University of Sheffield, Division of Education) Papers in Education, 14. Sheffield: University of Sheffield, Division of Education, 1990.
Hannon, P.; Weinberger, J. & Nutbrown, C. A study of work with parents to promote early literacy development. In: *Research Papers in Education*, Vol 6, No 2/1991, pp. 77-97.
Nutbrown, C.; Hannon, P. & Weinberger, J. Training teachers to work with parents to promote early literacy development. In: *International Journal of Early Childhood*, Vo, 23, No 2/1991, pp. 1-10.

12027 Zarys dydaktyki geografii. (An outline of the didactics of geography.)
POL 1994
Research Date(s): 1986-1992
Desperak, Jerzy; Kadziołka, Jan; Skwarcan, Mariola; Zajac, Stanisław; Zołnierz, Alfred.
Sup: Piskorz, Sławomir.
Inst: Wyższa Szkoła Pedagogiczna, Instytut Geografii, Zakład Dydaktyki Geografii (Higher School of Education, Geography Department, Unit of Geography Didactics), 30 084 Kraków, Podchorażych 2, Poland.
Wyższa Szkoła Pedagogiczna (Higher School of Education), 85 064 Bydgoszcz, Chodkiewicza 30, Poland
Fin: Ministerstwo Edukacji Narodowej.
didactics; geography; aims of education; teaching method
didactique; géographie; finalité de l'éducation; méthode pédagogique
PROJECT DESCRIPTION
Aim: To prepare a modern academic handbook on the didactics of geography against a background of general theories of instruction and geography as earth science.

Planned content of the handbook: introduction (subject, aims, sources, research methods, history of didactics of geography), aims of geography teaching, curricula, choice and patterns of subject matter content, teaching methods, didactic devices, lessons, school trips and homework, achievement testing, evaluation, optional activities, the geography teacher.

It is expected that a modern academic handbook on the didactics of geography will increase the efficiency of teacher training; furthermore, it may contribute to the development of instructional models for particular subjects.

Methods: Study of literature, document analysis, indirect and direct observation, natural and laboratory experiments, interview and inquiry.

Results: The first edition of "An outline of Didactics of Geography" and a monograph entitled "The Aims of Geography Teaching" have been published as a result of the project.

Publ: Zając, Stanisław. *Cele nauczania geografii.* Kraków Wydawnictwo Naukowe WSP, 1991, 148p.

Piskorz, Sławomir (ed.). *Zarys dydaktyki geografii.* Kraków: Wydawnictwo Naukowe WSP, 1992, 295p.

04 SYSTEM OF EDUCATION – SYSTEME D'ENSEIGNEMENT – BILDUNGSWESEN

12028 41st European Teachers' Seminar on education against violence: the potential of fair play in sport.
XCE 1993
Research Date(s): 1988
McIntosh, Peter C.
teacher education; training workshop; competitive sport; content of education; physical education; Council of Europe
formation des enseignants; atelier de formation; sport de compétition; contenu de l'éducation; éducation physique; Conseil de l'Europe
COLLECTED WORKS - Conference proceedings

41st European Teachers' Seminar on education against violence: the potential of fair play in sport, Donaueschingen (Germany), 10–15 October 1988. The Sports Section of the Directorate of Education, Culture and Sport of the Council of Europe has carried out a number of projects in the area of violence and fair play in sport. Another Section, concerned with education furthered these efforts in this seminar for teachers. This report includes background information, summaries of the lectures, results of the group work by participants, and conclusions by the director of the Seminar. Six lectures were given. The first set the scene by giving a definition of "what makes people violent". The second discussed the effects that our emphasis on victory and success has on students. The third demonstrated the many variables which act on students and which teachers have to deal with in sport. The fourth gave the results of three research studies carried out on a group of competitive squash players over a period of three years. The fifth investigated sportsmanship in the Netherlands and how to encourage it. The final lecture covered a study carried out in Liverpool, analysing children's essays on football. Four groups of participants discussed: child development of fair play; concretisation; cooperation and fair play. One group's report is reproduced in full, two others were combined together to produce a list of recommendations.

12029 Abstimmung und Steuerung von Bildung und Beschaeftigung in Japan (im Rahmen des Projektverbundes: Wechselbeziehungen zwischen Bildungs- und Beschaeftigungssystem in Japan in vergleichender Perspektive). (Coordination and control of education and employment in Japan (as part of the series of projects: "Interrelationships between education and employment systems in Japan, a comparative view").)
DEU 1993
Research Date(s): 1991-1995
Fuerstenberg, F.

Inst: Universitaet Bonn, Philosophische Fakultaet, Seminar fuer Soziologie, Adenauerallee 98a, D-5300 Bonn 1.
Fin: Volkswagen Stiftung.
education system; employment; labour market; Japan; educational policy; employment policy
système d'enseignement; emploi; marché du travail; Japon; politique de l'éducation; politique de l'emploi
PROJECT DESCRIPTION

Inhalt: Geklaert werden soll, in welchem Ausmass und in welchen Bereichen ordnungspolitische Rahmenbedingungen und -setzungen, groessere bildungs- und beschaeftigungspolitische Entscheidungen, Verhandlungen zwischen verschiedenen Instrumenten von Bildung und Beschaeftigung und verschiedene Einzelregelungen oder unabhaengige Einzelentscheidungen der verschiedenen Akteure fuer die "Abstimmung" von Bildungs- und Beschaeftigungssystem ausschlaggebend sind.

Geographischer Raum: Japan.

Vorgehensweise: Handlungsfeldanalyse mit besonderer Beruecksichtigung von Kontrollmechanismen und Integrationsprozessen. Untersuchungsdesign: qualitative Forschung.

Datengewinnung: Expertengespraech, Aktenanalyse, Befragung (Bildungsinstitutionen, Verbaende, Ministerien). Primaererhebung: Feldarbeit von Mitarbeitern des Projektes durchgefuehrt; Datenerstellung auf der Basis von bereits vorliegenden Materialien wie Texten, Akten, Statistiken.

12030 Access and delivery in continuing educational training: a survey of contemporary literature.
GBR 1993
Research Date(s): 1992
Bridge, H.; Salt, H.
Sup: Morgan, W.; Davies, J.
Inst: Nottingham University, Department of Adult Education, Centre for Research into the Education of Adults, 14-22 Shakespeare Street, Nottingham NG1 4FJ, United Kingdom.
Fin: Department of Employment.
post-compulsory education; adult education; continuing education; access to education; vocational training
enseignement postobligatoire; éducation des adultes; éducation permanente; accès à l'éducation; formation professionnelle
PROJECT DESCRIPTION

The aim of this research has been to produce a report and a select annotated bibliography to support the work of those with an interest in access and delivery in continuing education and training. A broad definition is taken to mean learning and training opportunites taken up after compulsory education has been completed. The research identifies literature, assesses its relevance and accessibility and reviews its content. It focuses on material relating to the United Kingdom, published since 1985, dealing with the 18-55 age group.

12031 Access to learning and accreditation in Work-Related Further Education.
GBR 1993
Research Date(s): 1990-1991
Carroll, S.
Sup: Dixon, K.; Haldane, A.
Inst: Further Education Unit, Citadel Place, Pinworth Street, London SE11 5EH, United Kingdom.
Fin: Training, Enterprise and Education Directorate.
vocational education; course programme; teaching method; post-compulsory education; access to education
enseignement professionnel; programme de cours; méthode pédagogique; enseignement postobligatoire; accès à l'éducation
PROJECT DESCRIPTION

A substantial number of projects related to flexible learning have been supported by the Work-Related Further Education Development Fund and its predecessors. Most have encouraged innovative developments locally but some could provide extra benefits through wider dissemination of outcomes. Recent studies have shown colleges making progress and generally positive staff attitudes, but further help would accelerate the process of embedding flexible learning. The need for colleges to be responsive to the requirements of individual learners, emphasised by the introduction of National Vocational Qualifications and the possibility of a 'common core' curriculum, has led many colleges to commence the transition from conventional modes of delivery to the implementation of flexible learning across the curriculum and across institutions.

The aims of this project are: (a) to provide the information base on which a national overview of the Work-Related Further Education flexible learning developments programme might be taken; (b) to give detailed consideration to the strategy required to achieve the implementation of this overview approach. It will provide information and an analysis in order to assess how the Work-Related Further Education Development Fund might operate more effectively to promote speedier advances in flexible learning across the country; and ensure coherence within the Fund and with likely future local education authority and Training and Education Council strategies.

12032 An action project designed to promote the development of mentors in the context of initial teacher training (ITT) teaching practice.
GBR 1993
Research Date(s): 1987-1992
Jones, B.
Sup: Pope, M.
Inst: Kingston University, Faculty of Education, Kingston Hill Centre, Kingston Hill, Kingston upon Thames, Surrey KT2 7LB, United Kingdom.
teacher education; teaching practice; training of trainers; supervision
formation des enseignants; pratique pédagogique; formation des formateurs; surveillance
PROJECT DESCRIPTION
This is a quantitative research project designed to illuminate and promote staff development in the context of largely school-based initial teacher training. The sample is relatively small, but the quantitative methods of research have generated a great deal of relevant information. The research is based on enabling practitioners to reflect on this practice, with use made of interviews, video-taping, practical counselling sessions, case studies of particular school instances and leading to collaborative staff development. This research will also look at links with inservice education of teachers (INSET) provision, again of a collaborative nature.

12033 Action research in initial teacher training.
GBR 1993
Research Date(s): 1989-1991
Macintyre, C.
Inst: Heriot-Watt University, Moray House Institute of Education, Holyrood Road, Edinburgh EH8 8AQ, United Kingdom.
teacher education; student teacher; researcher
formation des enseignants; élève-maître; chercheur
PROJECT DESCRIPTION
The aims of this research at Moray House Institute of Education are to: (a) develop written and visual materials; (b) help student teachers become effective action researchers in the classroom; (c) help the teachers who have responsibility for overseeing the students to guide and support them appropriately; and (d) help college tutors to supervise the students' action research. This is being done by studying the experiences and evaluations of four cohorts of final-year students, their teachers and their supervisors and constantly producing and amending materials to facilitate and enrich their task.

12034 An action research study into the role of a mathematics coordinator in a primary school.
GBR 1993
Research Date(s): 1985-1993
Atkinson, S.
Sup: McIntyre, D.; Lewis, I.
Inst: Westminster College, North Hinksey, Oxford OX2 9AT, United Kingdom; Oxford University, Department of Educational Studies, 15 Norham Gardens, Oxford OX2 6PY, United Kingdom.
further education of teachers; primary education; mathematics
perfectionnement des enseignants; enseignement primaire; mathématiques
PROJECT DESCRIPTION
The role of the mathematics coordinator is explored in the context of school-based Inservice Education and Training of Teachers (INSET). The research looks at changes that took place in a primary school over three years; the ways that teachers coped with change; what the facilitating role of the coordinator involved; and when the facilitating was most successful. The nature of action research is discussed in relation to the feasibility of the concept of teacher-researcher and to the nature of the teacher's 'self' in a demanding situation.

12035 Adult education in the United Kingdom and China.
GBR 1993
Research Date(s): 1992-1993
Jones, D.
Sup: Stephens, M.
Inst: Nottingham University, Department of Adult Education, 14-22 Shakespeare Street, Nottingham NG1 4FJ, United Kingdom.
adult education; comparative education; China; United Kingdom
éducation des adultes; éducation comparée; Chine; Royaume-Uni
PROJECT DESCRIPTION
Working with colleagues at Shandung Teachers University, it is intended to carry out a comparative study of adult education in the United Kingdom and China which will examine: (a) theories and philosophies of adult education; (b) organisation and structure of adult education; (c) aims and purposes of adult education; (d) target groups; (e) institutions for adult education; (f) teaching methods; (g) developments and trends in adult education.

12036 Adult education: provision, guidance and progression.
GBR 1993
Research Date(s): 1991-1993
Munn, P.; Blair, A.; Lowden, K.; Powney, J.; McPake, J.; Arney, N.
Inst: Scottish Council for Research in Education, 15 St John Street, Edinburgh EH8 8JR, United Kingdom.
Fin: Scottish Office Education Department.
adult education; educational guidance; access to education; educational provision
éducation des adultes; orientation pédagogique; accès à l'éducation; scolarisation
PROJECT DESCRIPTION
The research will be carried out in four studies. It will provide a broad-based national picture of opportunities for progression and of guidance while enabling more detailed information on adults' experiences and on the operation of particular systems to be collected. The four studies are: (1) case studies of adults' experiences of guidance, provision and progression, Scottish Council for Research in Education (SCRE) and Scottish Community Education Council (SCEC); (2) a survey of opportunities for progression, focusing particularly on inter-sector links and on links between formal and informal services, together with in-depth analysis of opportunities for progression within one region; (3) a survey of guidance provision together with in-depth analysis of a small number of new initiatives and an assessment of user experience (SCRE); and (4) a special study of adults in schools, investigating the opinions of adults and of the schools about the advantages of this form of provision (SCRE).

12037 Adult employment training in four regions (East Midlands, South Wales, Bremen, and Baden Wurttemberg).
GBR 1993
Research Date(s): 1990-1993
Morgan, W.
Inst: Nottingham University, Department of Adult Education, Centre for Research into the Education of Adults, 14-22 Shakespeare Street, Nottingham NG1 4FJ, United Kingdom.
Fin: Universities Funding Council.
continuing education; vocational education; adult education; educational need; comparative education; United Kingdom; Germany
éducation permanente; enseignement professionnel; éducation des adultes; besoin d'éducation; éducation comparée; Royaume-Uni; Allemagne
PROJECT DESCRIPTION
The research concentrates upon: (i) the changing continuing education needs of the regions; (ii) the impact of the 1993 single market; and (iii) the possibility of a European model emerging from British-German experience.

12038 Allgemeinbildung an schweizerischen gewerblichen Berufsschulen. (L'enseignement des branches de culture générale dans les écoles professionnelles des arts et métiers en Suisse.)
CHE 1994
Research Date(s): 1988-1991
Pflüger, Michael.
Sup: Dubs, Rolf.
Inst: Hochschule St. Gallen für Wirtschafts-, Rechts- und Sozialwissenschaften, Institut für Wirtschaftspädagogik, Guisanstrasse 9, 9010 St. Gallen, Schweiz.
vocational education; general education; curriculum; educational reform
enseignement professionnel; enseignement général; programme d'études; réforme de l'enseignement
PROJECT DESCRIPTION
Diese Dissertation zu Handen der Hochschule St. Gallen beschreibt die Ursprünge, die gegenwärtige Situation und die Zukunftsperspektiven des allgemeinbildenden Unterrichts an gewerblichen Berufsschulen der Schweiz. Angesichts der Tatsache, dass dieser Bereich des Unterrichts gegenwärtig den Gegenstand von Schulversuchen und Reformbemühungen bildet, ist ein wichtiger Teil der Dissertation verschiedenen Szenarien und Varianten einer solchen Reform gewidmet. Die in Diskussion befindlichen Varianten unterscheiden sich vor allem hinsichtlich des Grades von Offenheit der neu zu entwickelnden Lehrpläne (soll der allgemeinbildende Unterricht sich an einer Fächerstruktur orientieren oder eher an thematischen Achsen und Schwerpunkten, die exemplarisch und multidisziplinär zu behandeln wären?). Der Autor spricht sich nicht eindeutig für eine bestimmte Variante aus, sondern zeigt die jeweiligen Vor- und Nachteile der vorgeschlagenen Lösungen auf. Die Arbeit basiert vor allem auf einer Analyse einschlägiger Dokumente und Literatur. Zwar wurden in einem empirischen Teil Lehrmeister, Berufsleute, Technikumsabsolventen, ein Direktor einer Berufsschule sowie Eltern von Lehrlingen befragt; die Stichprobe (N total = 29) ist aber wohl zu gering, als dass sich daraus "harte" Schlussfolgerungen ableiten liessen.

Publ: Pflüger, Michael. *Allgemeinbildung an schweizerischen gewerblichen Berufsschulen: Geschichte - Zustand - Perspektiven.* Bamberg: Difo, 1991, 237 Seiten (Dissertation St. Gallen 1281).

12039 Analyse comparative des systèmes scolaires des pays d'Asie.
FRA 1993
Research Date(s): 1988-1989
Mingat, Alain; Tan, J.P.
Inst: Université de Dijon, UER Faculté des sciences économiques et de gestion, CNRS UPR/29 et GDR/996, Institut de recherche sur l'économie de l'éducation, BP 138, 21004 Dijon Cedex, France.
Fin: Banque mondiale.
education system; education budget; Asia; comparative education
système d'enseignement; budget de l'éducation; Asie; éducation comparée
PROJECT DESCRIPTION
Objectifs: Il s'agit de mener une analyse comparative des systèmes scolaires des 16 principaux pays d'Asie. Les pays de ce continent présentent en effet un intérêt particulier en raison de la très grande variété qu'on y trouve dans les modes d'organisation et de financement et en raison des situations particulières qu'on y trouve. Cela dit, bien que l'objectif concerne principalement les pays d'Asie, pour lesquels de nombreuses données ont été extraites dans un nombre important de rapports (généralement non publiés), l'échantillon de pays a été étendu pour ce qui concerne les données générales disponibles dans les banques de données de la Banque mondiale et de l'UNESCO.
Méthodologie: Le travail entrepris concerne bien sûr les pays d'Asie en cherchant à déterminer les forces et les faiblesses du système scolaire de chacun des pays étudiés. Il s'agit plus encore de mobiliser les données collectées pour profiter de l'analyse comparative et mettre en évidence des relations fondamentales qu'il n'est pas possible d'analyser dans le cadre d'un pays unique. De nombreux résultats ont été obtenus par cette analyse comparative.
Résultats: Deux résultats illustratifs: Il a été observé qu'il existait globalement une relation très faible entre l'effort financier effectué par un pays et le niveau de développement de son système d'enseignement. Dans la perspective comparative, les estimations économétriques montrent qu'il existe en réalité beaucoup d'espaces de liberté dans l'organisation et la structure du financement de l'école et que les résultats obtenus par le système scolaire dépendent certes des contraintes budgétaires mais aussi pour une large part des choix politiques pris dans le pays. De même, un résultat, qui pourrait être considéré par certains comme paradoxal, est que le niveau global d'équité dans le système scolaire (qu'on l'apprécie par l'accès à des scolarisations plus longues ou par la distribution des crédits publics pour l'éducation) est meilleur dans les pays qui font davantage appel au financement privé dans l'enseignement supérieur et ont une structure d'organisation moins centralisée.

Publ: Mingat, Alain & Tan, J.P. *Educational development in Asia: a comparative study with special emphasis on cost and financing issues.* Rapport à la Banque mondiale, mai 1989, 184p.

12040 Analyse der Berufsschule. (An analysis of vocational schools.)
AUT 1993
Research Date(s): 1992-1993
Schneeberger, Arthur; Eckstein, Wolf-Erich; Haintz-Klemm, Gertrude.
Inst: Institut fuer Bildungsforschung der Wirtschaft, Rainergasse 38, A-1050 Wien.
Fin: Bundeswirtschaftskammer.
vocational school; apprenticeship; training-employment relationship; vocational education; quality of education
école professionnelle; apprentissage professionnel; relation formation-emploi; enseignement professionnel; qualité de l'éducation
PROJECT DESCRIPTION
Ziel des Projekts ist es, die Qualitaet des Berufsschulunterrichts und insbesondere den Bezug zwischen Berufsschule und beruflicher Praxis zu analysieren. Hierzu werden Lehrabsolventen (Jahrgang 1991), Lehrberechtigte, Berufsschullehrer und Berufsschuldirektoren befragt.
Es werden schriftliche Befragungen durchgefuehrt.

12041 Analysis of foreign experiences in dealing with problem situations in higher education.
RUS 1994
Research Date(s): 1991-1992
Galagan, A.I.
Sup: Zuyev, V.M.
Inst: Research Institute for Higher Education, 103062, Moscow, K-62, Podsosensky per. 20, Russia.
State Committee for Higher Education Institutions, 113833, Moscow, M-230, Lysinovskja str. 51, Russia
higher education; educational policy; cross-national research
enseignement supérieur; politique de l'éducation; recherche transnationale
PROJECT DESCRIPTION
The aim of the study was to examine how foreign countries solve problem situations in their higher education systems.
An examination was made of relevant experiences in the USA, Japan, Germany, Great Britain, France, Canada and Poland. The findings were subjected to analysis and generalization.

The results of the study have been used in the work on higher education legislation and in the training of educationalists in Russia. The results are also used to facilitate the regionalization of higher education in Russia.

Publ: Galagan, A.I.; Zeikovich, K.N.; Tarasyuk, L.N.; et al. *The peculiarities of training teaching staff in foreign countries.* Information review. M., NIIVO, 1992.
Tarasyuk, L.N. *The development of the education system in Canada.* Information review. M., NIIVO, 1992.
Pokladok, Y.B. & Spasskaya, V.V. *The evolution of university autonomy in European countries.* Information review. M., NIIVO, 1992.
Spasskaya, V.V. *The experience of higher education in Poland under market conditions.* Information review. M., NIIVO, 1992.
(A complete list can be obtained from the researcher.).

12042 An analysis of government policy for teachers' professional development in Scotland: 1979-1990.
GBR 1993
Research Date(s): 1986-
Hartley, J.
Inst: Dundee University, Centre for Continuing Education, Dundee DD1 4HN, United Kingdom.
further education of teachers; Scotland; teaching profession; government policy
perfectionnement des enseignants; Ecosse; profession d'enseignant; politique gouvernementale
PROJECT DESCRIPTION
An analysis of government documentation and research on teachers' continuing professional development, informed by critical theory.

Publ: Hartley, J.D. Structural isomorphism and the management of consent in education. In: *Journal of Education Policy*, Vol 1, No 3/1986, pp. 229-237.
Hartley, J.D. Tests, tasks and Taylorism: a model T approach to the management of education. In: *Journal of Education Policy*, Vol 5, No 1/1990, pp. 67-76.
Hartley, J.D. Beyond collaboration: the management of professional development in Scotland. In: *British Journal of Education for Teaching*, Vol 10, No 2/1989, pp. 253-261.
Hartley, J.D. Beyond competency: a socio-technical model of continuing professional education. In: *British Journal of Inservice Education*, Vol 16, No 1/1990, pp. 66-70.

12043 Analysis of the adult education problem in Taiwan, Republic of China: a comparative study of adult education between Taiwan and England and its implications in Taiwan.
GBR 1993
Research Date(s): 1991-1994
Yang, K-T.
Sup: Jones, D.; Stephens, M.
Inst: Nottingham University, Department of Adult Education, 14-22 Shakespeare Street, Nottingham NG1 4FJ, United Kingdom.
Fin: Government of Taiwan.
adult education; Taiwan; comparative education; university; United Kingdom
éducation des adultes; Taiwan; éducation comparée; université; Royaume-Uni
PROJECT DESCRIPTION
This is a comparative study of university adult education in the United Kingdom and China. Questionnaires and semi-structured interviews will be used to collect data on attitudes towards univeristy adult education. All departments of adult education in the United Kingdom will be contacted and a selection in China.

12044 Analysis of the Semi-Higher Education Colleges.
BGR 1994
Research Date(s): 1992-1993
Angelov, G.; Popov, L.; Popova, D.
Sup: Evtimov, I.
Inst: National Centre for Educational and Science Studies, Tzarigradsko Chossé 125, 1113 Sofia, Bulgaria.
Fin: Ministry of Education and Science.
vocational education; higher education; number of pupils; economic conditions
enseignement professionnel; enseignement supérieur; effectifs scolaires; conditions économiques
PROJECT DESCRIPTION
Background: The Semi-Higher Educational Institutes in Bulgaria can be compared to the Colleges for Further Education in England. They offer courses in: mechanical engineering, chemistry, atomic energy, transport, microelectronics, mining and metallurgy, communication and tourism, teacher training and nursing. During the last few years the number of students in these institutions has fallen drastically due to the economic crisis as well as structural economic changes which are related to the transition towards a market economy. The technical institutes are the most seriously affected, which shows that industry has been hit hardest by the

economic crisis. Most of these institutes are in danger of being closed, and the Ministry of Education and Science is looking for ways to help them.

Aims: The aim of the research was to find out how teachers and students perceive the education offered by the institutions; how they view the quality of the vocational preparation provided and the prospects for the professions concerned. Another aim was to elicit teachers' and students' views regarding the future destiny of the institutes and their chances of surviving in the conditions of crisis.

Research questions: How do students and teachers assess the curricula of the institutes? Can the institutes be integrated with universities? Can they be transformed into specialized schools or is it better to close them down? Do students believe they will find work in their field after graduation? Do students have the money to pay for their education and are they willing to pay for it?

Design: Analysis of statistical information on the numbers of candidates, the students who entered, those who left and graduated, as well as data on unemployment among graduates, survey of teachers and students.

Hypothesis: The drastic fall in the number of students entering Semi-Higher Educational Institutes is not caused by a decline in educational quality, but by structural economic changes and unemployment among specialists in industrial and other areas. At the same time, the economic crisis has revealed the shortcomings of this type of education, which is not flexible enough to adjust its curricula or to offer an alternative to students.

Sample: 1,040 students and 445 teachers.

Results: It appears that the economic crisis is the general reason why fewer students enrol at Semi-Higher Educational Institutions. Besides this general reason, wide differences exist among institutes. Most institutes meet their students' needs for a professional type of education. Students look upon this sort of education as a compensation, because of their failure to get into university. Teachers and students think current difficulties could be overcome by integrating the institutes with universities. This would help the institutes to respond more flexibly to the changing requirements of vocational education and would create better opportunities for the students who wish to continue their education. Teacher training institutes and institutes training industrial specialists are particularly interested in integrating with the universities. Institutes for nurse training and tourism insist on remaining independent.

12045 Analýza a prognoza rozvoja základného a stredného školstva v SR. (The development of primary and secondary education: analysis and prognosis.)
CSK 1993
Research Date(s): 1991-1992
Ondrejkovič, Peter; Gavora, Peter; Kratochvílová, Milka; Rosa, Vladimír; Hrabinská, Mária; Khuna, Pavel; Letková, Katarína; Branecký, Oldrich.
Sup: Majtán, Michal.
Inst: Ústav informácií a prognóz školstva, mládeže a telovýchovy (Institute of Information and Prognoses of Education, Youth and Sports), Staré Grunty 52, 842 44 Bratislava, Czech and Slovak Federal Republic.
Ministerstvo školstva, mládeže a športu Slovenskej republiky (Ministry of Education, Youth and Sports of Slovak Republic), Hlboká 2, 813 30 Bratislava, Czech and Slovak Federal Republic
Fin: Ústav experimentálnej pedagogiky -SAV; Filozofická fakulta UK-Katedra pedagogiky; Ústredné inšpekčné centrum.
education system; educational policy; primary education; secondary education; development of education
système d'enseignement; politique de l'éducation; enseignement primaire; enseignement secondaire; développement de l'éducation
PROJECT DESCRIPTION

The aims of the research are: (a) to identify key problems in the system of education and training, to classify these problems and to offer proposals for their solution; (b) to inform debates by the government and Parliament of the Slovak Republic on the new education law; (c) to study the current state of the art of a number of scientific disciplines and to stimulate their development, especially philosophy, sociology of education (aims of education, status of teachers in society), economics of education (financing and qualitative criteria for financing), educational forecasting (forecasting model, forecasting of teachers' needs), empirical educational research (research methods) and information science; (d) to synthesize the results of individual research studies and to coordinate work on qualitative and quantitative aspects of education.

Methods: The study will be carried out through team work and participation in work conducted at higher education institutions. Foreign experts will be asked for advice. Seminars and discussions will be organized.

The results will be used in educational legislation.

12046 Annual survey of new Open University courses.
GBR 1993
Research Date(s): 1991-1992
Womphrey, R.; Calder, J.
Inst: Open University, Institute of Educational Technology, Walton Hall, Milton Keynes MK7 6AA, United Kingdom.
open university; distance study; quality of education; survey
télé-université; enseignement à distance; qualité de l'éducation; enquête

PROJECT DESCRIPTION

Each year the Open University surveys its students in order to acquaint the University with the reactions of students to course materials and services. As the University is a distance-teaching institution, the self-completion questionnaires are mailed to the students. A survey of all undergraduate courses in first presentation is carried out at the end of the courses. The samples vary from 200 to 800 undergraduates who all receive a mailed self-completion survey report form, followed by two reminders. The survey results assist the allocation of resources to courses, and the improvement of the design of courses.

12047 Assessing the ability of school leavers in Swaziland to use process skills.
GBR 1993
Research Date(s): 1988-1991
Putsoa, B.
Sup: Campbell, R.
Inst: York University, Department of Educational Studies, Heslington, York YO1 5DD, United Kingdom.
Fin: British Council Technical Assistance to Swaziland.
school leaver; transition from school to work; Swaziland; science education
élève sortant; passage à la vie active; Swaziland; éducation scientifique
PROJECT DESCRIPTION

The study was motivated by the fact that only a minority of school leavers in Swaziland proceed into institutions of higher education at the end of high school. The more fortunate among the remaining majority are either absorbed into professional training institutions or move straight into the adult world of work. The less fortunate join the mainstream of the unemployed.

The study aimed to find out the extent to which school science may be of use to school leavers in coping cognitively with the experiences they will encounter in the future. Would they rely on the concepts and objective processes that characterize the sciences to interpret the events and situations that arise? This assessment attempted to account for the time and effort spent in teaching and learning science by showing the extent to which it is likely to be used by those who have experienced it.

Paper and pencil tests were used in the assessment. A total of 45 questions were designed with the specific purpose of re-enacting the experiences of junior secondary school science and converting them to portray everyday events and experiences in the Swazi environment. Each of the 45 questions was distributed among school leavers in sample schools in such a way that each participating school leaver received 10 questions containing the 10 processes being assessed. The sample comprised all fifth-formers in the 20 schools which were selected, so that all regions and types of schools in the country were represented. The sample represented 40% of the target group at the time when the study began, i.e. 1,088 school leavers. The pupils' responses were then analysed.

12048 Ausserfamiliäre Betreuung in der Stadt St. Gallen. (Prise en charge extra-familiale dans la ville de St-Gall.)
CHE 1994
Research Date(s): 1988-1991
Zeugin, Peter; Landert, Charles.
Inst: IPSO Sozialforschung, Heuelstrasse 21, Postfach 153, 8030 Zürich, Schweiz.
Schulamt St. Gallen, Scheffelstrasse 2, 9000 St. Gallen, Schweiz
day care; social policy; educational policy; out-of-school education
mode de garde; politique sociale; politique de l'éducation; éducation extra-scolaire
PROJECT DESCRIPTION

1987 wurden in St. Gallen - nach Ablehnung einer Initiative auf Einführung von Tagesschulen - verschiedene politische Vorstösse lanciert, die einen Ausbau der ausserfamiliären Betreuung zum Ziel hatten. Im Hinblick auf die Erarbeitung eines Grundkonzepts für diesen Bereich der Sozialpolitik erteilte die Stadt St. Gallen der IPSO, einer privaten Firma für Sozialforschung, den Auftrag, eine Analyse der Bedürfnisse vorzunehmen und weitere Entscheidungsgrundlagen bereitzustellen.

Für ihre Studie der Problematik griff die IPSO zum Mittel von Befragungen und analysierte Dokumente und statistisches Material, das bei der Stadtverwaltung vorlag, und stellte Beobachtungen in den bestehenden Kinderhorten an. Bei der Beschreibung des erweiterten Kontexts der Probleme konnte sie auch auf Material zurückgreifen, welches sie in andern Aufträgen erarbeitet hatte. Der den St. Galler Behörden eingereichte Bericht beschreibt zum einen die Art und Weise, wie St. Galler Jugendliche ihre Freizeit verbringen; der grösste Teil des Berichts ist aber einer Analyse der Stadt nach Quartieren gewidmet: durchschnittliche Einkommen, durchschnittliche Haushaltsgrössen, Anzahl Kinder im Vorschul-, Kindergarten- und Schulalter, Heirats- und Scheidungsquoten, Anteile an Einelternfamilien, Anzahl Jugendlicher, deren Sozialisation mit Risiken behaftet erscheint, Anteile an deutsch- und nicht deutschsprachigen Ausländern usw. Aus diesen Daten werden Nachfragewerte für Krippen und Horte errechnet.

Die Studie der IPSO hat einer vom St. Galler Stadtrat eingesetzten Projektgruppe bei ihrem Auftrag geholfen, ein Grundkonzept für die ausserfamiliäre Betreuung im Schulaltersbereich (in Zusammenarbeit mit IPSO-Vertretern) zu erarbeiten. Dieses wurde von der Legislative im Frühjahr 1992 zustimmend zur Kenntnis genommen. Die erwähnte Stadtanalyse soll in Zukunft regelmässig aktualisiert werden; die künftigen Analysen werden Daten liefern, die einerseits zur Evaluation der getroffenen Massnahmen dienen können, andererseits Entscheidungsgrundlagen bereitstellen für das, was noch zu tun bleibt.

Publ: Stadt St. Gallen (Hrsg.). *Ausserfamiliäre Betreuung in der Stadt St. Gallen*. St. Gallen: Juni 1991, 124 Seiten.

Stadt St. Gallen (Hrsg.). *Grundkonzept ausserfamiliäre Betreuung im Schulaltersbereich in der Stadt St. Gallen*. St. Gallen: Februar 1992, 15 Seiten.

12049   B.Ed. Primary and Scottish Wider Access Programme - monitoring student progress.
GBR   1993
Research Date(s): 1991-1992
Turner, D.; Kidd, J.; Adams, F.
Inst: Heriot-Watt University, Moray House Institute of Education, Holyrood Road, Edinburgh EH8 8AQ, United Kingdom.
teacher education; student teacher; adult education; access to education; student behaviour
formation des enseignants; élève-maître; éducation des adultes; accès à l'éducation; comportement de l'étudiant
PROJECT DESCRIPTION
The study is intended to establish a formative baseline for a subsequent study of a cohort of Scottish Wider Access Programme students over the duration of a college B.Ed. Primary course. It will attempt to examine the course experience of Access students in terms of: (a) teaching, learning and assessment/placement demands; (b) social integration and participation in collegiate life; and (c) academic and other forms of counselling. It will also attempt to draw comparisons with the experiences of Access students across colleges and across professions, e.g. nursing.
The project will use a combination of: (a) empirical study of product data relating to entry and transit (eventually exit) characteristics; and (b) illuminative approaches. These will include questionnaires and interviews for students and providers within and without college.

12050   Becoming a postgraduate science student.
GBR   1993
Research Date(s): 1992-1994
Burgess, R.; Pole, C.; Sprokkereef, A.
Inst: Warwick University, Faculty of Educational Studies, Centre for Educational Development, Appraisal and Research, Coventry CV4 7AL, United Kingdom.
Fin: Economic and Social Research Council.
post-graduate study; science education; student; socialization
supérieur troisième cycle; éducation scientifique; étudiant; socialisation
PROJECT DESCRIPTION
This project examines postgraduate training in three disciplinary fields in the sciences: physics, mathematics, and engineering. The key issue to be addressed is: what is the process of becoming a postgraduate science student? Case study data will be collected regarding the first year of postgraduate training in nine departments in the United Kingdom, three in each discipline examined.
The aims and objectives of the project are: (1) to provide data on the process of socialization in the first year of postgraduate study, covering such themes as: student choice and selection; admission procedures; the selection and focusing of a research topic; taught course work; supervision; monitoring; and assessment; (2) to provide evidence on the range of postgraduate training in the light of the data obtained above; (3) to compare the different types of research training within and between disciplines; (4) to explore the implications of the research evidence for policy and practice regarding research training in the natural sciences in the United Kingdom.
The main method of social investigation will be through unstructured interviews and observation. The research will result in nine departmental case studies; three disciplinary case studies; and a thematic report. In the latter comparisons will be made with the work conducted by the Centre for Educational Development, Appraisal and Research (CEDAR) on first-year social science postgraduate students.

12051   Begleitforschung zum Modellversuch 'Studienzirkel in Oberoesterreich'. (Research on the pilot project 'A study circle in Upper Austria'.)
AUT   1993
Research Date(s): 1992-1994
Maass, Juergen; Karlsson, Lars.
Inst: Institut fuer Mathematik, Altenbergerstrasse 69, A-4040 Linz.
Universitaet Linz, Altenbergerstrasse 69, A-4040 Linz
Fin: Jubilaeumsfonds der Oesterreichischen Nationalbank.
adult education; pilot project; development of education
éducation des adultes; projet-pilote; développement de l'éducation
PROJECT DESCRIPTION
Studienzirkel heisst das in Schweden vorherrschende und sehr erfolgreiche Modell fuer Erwachsenenbildung. In Oberoesterreich wird ab Herbst

1992 versucht, dieses Modell fuer Oesterreich zu adaptieren. Die Begleitforschung soll die in Oberoesterreich gesammelten Erfahrungen fuer spaetere Adaptionsversuche in ganz Oesterreich zugaenglich machen. Darueber hinaus sollen bisherige Versuche mit Studienzirkeln in Oesterreich erfasst werden. Auf der wissenschaftlichen Ebene sollen an diesem Beispiel auch prinzipielle Fragen der Uebertragbarkeit eines Bildungsmodells von einem Land in ein anderes reflektiert werden.
Es werden Frageboegen ausgegeben und strukturierte Interviews mit den OrganisatorInnen durchgefuehrt. 300 Stunden Tonbandaufzeichnungen von Studienzirkeltreffen dienen als Unterlage.
Das Datenmaterial wird empirischen und qualitativen Analysen unterzogen.

Publ: Karlsson, Lars & Maass, Juergen. Studienzirkel in Oberoesterreich - ein Modellversuch mit Begleitforschung. In: *Die Oesterreichische Volkshochschule*, Dezember 1992.

12052   Below average attainment project.
GBR   1993
Research Date(s): 1991-1993
Hewitt, C.; Hamill, P.; Robertson, P.
Inst: Jordanhill College of Education, Division of Special Educational Needs, Southbrae Drive, Jordanhill, Glasgow G13 1PP, United Kingdom.
Fin: Scottish Office Education Department.
special education; socially handicapped; learning difficulty
enseignement spécial; handicapé social; difficulté de l'apprentissage
PROJECT DESCRIPTION
This project aims to describe and evaluate the variety of services designed to support the progress of pupils with learning difficulties and social disadvantage.

12053   The benefit from the Focus Learning Centre.
GBR   1993
Research Date(s): 1990-1992
McMellin, I.
Inst: Jordanhill College of Education, Division of Community Education, Southbrae Drive, Glasgow G13 1PP, United Kingdom.
Fin: Jordanhill College; Ayr Division, Strathclyde Local Education Authority.
adult education; attitude
éducation des adultes; attitude
PROJECT DESCRIPTION
The study aims to identify the benefits adult participants perceive they have gained by undertaking educational opportunities at the Focus Community Learning Centre, by reflecting back at least one year since initial participation. Interviews will be carried out and analysis of these undertaken.

12054   Berufliche Weiterbildung und Europaeische Integration. (Further vocational training and European integration.)
AUT   1993
Research Date(s): 1991-1993
Schedler, Klaus; Blumberger, Walter; Jenny, Ulrike; Poller, Bettina.
Inst: Institut fuer Bildungsforschung der Wirtschaft, Rainergasse 38, A-1050 Wien; Institut fuer Berufs- und Erwachsenenbildungsforschung, Stifterstrasse 28, A-4020 Linz.
Fin: Bundesministerium fuer Arbeit und Soziales.
education system; further training; community policy; educational planning
système d'enseignement; formation complémentaire; politique communautaire; planification de l'éducation
PROJECT DESCRIPTION
Stand und Strukturen der beruflichen Weiterbildungssysteme in Europa bzw. die Handlungsbefugnisse der Europaeischen Gemeinschaften sollen anhand verschiedener Komplexe analysiert werden. Komplexe sind: Auswirkungen der Europaeischen Integration und des Binnenmarktes auf die berufliche Weiterbildung; die Bildungspolitik der Europaeischen Gemeinschaften; zur Abgrenzung massgeblicher Begriffsmerkmale beruflicher Weiterbildung; europaeische Integration und berufliche Weiterbildung anhand der Vergleichslaender Deutschland, Daenemark, Niederlande, Grossbritannien; zwischenstaatlicher Vergleich; Schlussfolgerungen fuer Oesterreich. Zielsetzung ist es, aufgrund der Ergebnisse der Laenderstudien und unter Beruecksichtigung der Kompetenzen der Europaeischen Gemeinschaften im Bereich der beruflichen Weiterbildung Implikationen und Empfehlungen fuer die oesterreichische Weiterbildungslandschaft zu treffen.
Es werden Literaturrecherchen durchgefuehrt.

12055   Beyond training - adult education in the workplace.
GBR   1993
Research Date(s): 1990-1992
Cox, D.; Hannah, J.
Inst: Nottingham University, Department of Adult Education, 14-22 Shakespeare Street, Nottingham NG1 4FJ, United Kingdom.
Fin: National Westminster Bank Research Fund.
workers' education; adult education; demand for education
éducation ouvrière; éducation des adultes; demande d'éducation

PROJECT DESCRIPTION

The project will undertake an investigation of the demand for adult education opportunities within a sample of the working population of the East Midlands. A questionnaire will be distributed to establish the dimensions of need amongst a sample of employees in the region.

12056 Cardiff Collegiate Faculty of Education: provision of routes to graduate status for certificated teachers.
GBR 1993
Research Date(s): 1985-1993
Loudon, M.
Sup: Allsobrook, D.
Inst: University of Wales College of Cardiff, School of Education, 21 Senghennydd Road, Cardiff CF2 4YG, United Kingdom.
teacher education; graduate; student teacher
formation des enseignants; étudiant diplômé; élève-maître
PROJECT DESCRIPTION

The research examines the significance of attainment of graduate status for participants - both providers and students.

12057 Case study of staff development in a large comprehensive school.
GBR 1993
Research Date(s): 1987-1991
Metcalfe, C.
Sup: Lazonby, J.
Inst: York University, Department of Educational Studies, Heslington, York YO1 5DD, United Kingdom.
further education of teachers; peer group teaching; teacher; comprehensive secondary school
perfectionnement des enseignants; enseignement mutuel; enseignant; école secondaire polyvalente
PROJECT DESCRIPTION

The objective of the research is to make a major case study of staff development in a large, purpose-built comprehensive school with a particular focus on the emergence of a scheme of peer counselling as a means of individual and institutional development. The study involves the use of qualitative interview; questionnaires and other forms of research may be used.

12058 Chancen und Probleme der Zusammenarbeit von Lehrpersonen in integrativen Kindergärten und Schulklassen. (La collaboration des enseignant-e-s dans les classes enfantines et primaires intégratives: chances et problèmes.)
CHE 1994
Research Date(s): 1990-1992
Haeberlin, Urs; Jenni-Fuchs, Elisabeth; Moser Opitz, Elisabeth.
Inst: Universität Freiburg, Heilpädagogisches Institut, Petrus-Canisius-Gasse 21, 1700 Freiburg, Schweiz.
Fin: Schweizerischer Nationalfonds zur Förderung der wissenschaftlichen Forschung.
special education; individualization; remedial teaching; integration; cooperation
enseignement spécial; individualisation; soutien pédagogique; intégration; coopération
PROJECT DESCRIPTION

Diese Untersuchung fügt sich ein in den Rahmen einer Reihe von Forschungsarbeiten über die Wirkungen separierender und integrierender Lehrformen auf lernbehinderte Schüler (Forschungsprogramm INTSEP). Das Programm INTSEP bzw. die vergleichende Evaluation der beiden zentralen Ansätze einer Pädagogik für Lernende mit besonderen Bedürfnissen (integrierend vs. separierend) hat sich in den letzten sechs Jahren kontinuierlich zum eigentlichen Arbeitsschwerpunkt des Heilpädagogischen Instituts der Universität Freiburg entwickelt. In der Praxis hat sich die Gestaltung der Zusammenarbeit zwischen den Lehrpersonen als wichtiger Schlüssel zum Gelingen integrativer Schulung erwiesen. Denn die integrative Unterrichtsform, wo das Kind mit besonderen Bedürfnissen in der "Normalklasse" bleibt und punktuelle Unterstützung kriegt, bedingt natürlich ein gut koordiniertes Zusammenwirken zwischen Klassenlehrerin oder -lehrer und den Spezialisten (im Bereich Psychologie, Legasthenie, Logopädie, Psychomotorik usw).

Das INTSEP-Programm ist allgemein eher als empirisch-analytische Forschung konzipiert. Die hier vorgestellte Arbeit hingegen basiert auf der qualitativen Auswertung von ausführlichen Gesprächen mit Lehrpersonen auf Kindergarten- und Primarschulstufe, die nach dem integrativen Modell arbeiten, und mit den mit ihnen zusammenarbeitenden Sonderpädagoginnen und -pädagogen. Die Auswertung der Gespräche gibt Hinweise auf einige Bedingungen für einen Erfolg integrativen Unterrichtens. So sollten etwa die reguläre Lehrperson und die für die Sondermassnahmen zuständige Person über eine gemeinsame Vision eines integrierenden Schul- und Gesellschaftsmodells verfügen; sie müssen einander als gleichberechtigte Partner gegenüberstehen (was sich auch auf der Ebene der Besoldung ausdrücken müsste...); das neue, auf der erwähnten Vision basierende Rollen- und Aufgabenverständnis muss sich in Ausbildung, Pflichtenheft und Anforderungsprofil aller beteiligten Partner niederschlagen. Eine

Hauptschwierigkeit liegt jedoch in der Tatsache, dass die Prinzipien von Humanisierung und Individualisierung den gezwungenermassen bürokratischen Prinzipien eines öffentlichen Bildungswesens zuwiderlaufen, gemäss welchen ein jeder nach denselben, von der Allgemeinheit abgesegneten und kontrollierbaren Verfahrensnormen behandelt werden soll.

Publ: Haeberlin, Urs; Jenni-Fuchs, Elisabeth & Moser Opitz, Elisabeth. *Zusammenarbeit: Wie Lehrpersonen Kooperation zwischen Regel- und Sonderpädagogik in integrativen Kindergärten und Schulklassen erfahren.* Bern: Haupt, 1992, 173 Seiten (Beiträge zur Heil- und Sonderpädagogik; 13).

12059 Change in teacher education: an Anglo-Soviet study.
GBR 1993
Research Date(s): 1991-1992
Pullin, R.; Poppleton, P.
Inst: Sheffield University, Division of Education, 388 Glossop Road, Sheffield S10 2TN, United Kingdom.
Fin: Sheffield University; The British Council.
teacher education; comparative education; educational reform; USSR
formation des enseignants; éducation comparée; réforme de l'enseignement; URSS
PROJECT DESCRIPTION

The content, process and organisation of initial teacher education is now a key item on the government's agenda for change following the debate on teaching quality and the legislative changes in the Education Reform Act 1988. These will seek to bring about greater centralised control of the teaching profession, and ultimately, greater uniformity in preparation for it.

The aim of the first stage of this exploratory study is to seek the views of those most concerned: teachers, employers and administrators on the impact on initial teacher education of the Education Reform Act and other changes that have affected schools. The ultimate aim is a more comprehensive study that will assess the nature and direction of desired change and lead to a programme for its implementation.

This study runs parallel to a similar one being conducted by colleagues in the USSR as part of a collaborative research agreement between the University of Sheffield and the Academy of Pedagogical Sciences, Moscow, USSR. Soviet teacher education has also been under pressure to change, though in opposite directions, from total centralisation to relative autonomy. Both studies will enable the researchers to draw up a number of priority statements which represent a wide range of views and which can then be put to larger representative groups of 'consumers' in each country.

12060 Changing modes of professionalism? A case study of teacher education in transition.
GBR 1993
Research Date(s): 1993-1995
Whitty, G.; Furlong, J.; Barton, L.; Miles, S.
Inst: London University, Institute of Education, Department of Policy Studies, Health and Education Research Unit, 20 Bedford Way, London WC1H 0AL, United Kingdom.
Fin: Economic and Social Research Council.
teacher education; teaching profession; educational reform
formation des enseignants; profession d'enseignant; réforme de l'enseignement
PROJECT DESCRIPTION

This project will build upon the earlier Modes of Teacher Education Project. Using baseline data from that project, it will explore the nature and impact of current changes in initial teacher education in England and Wales. The study will focus on the experience, outcomes and costs of teacher training in the new modes required by government policy. It will also consider how far the new approaches foster new conceptions of professionalism and professionality.

12061 The City Technology College initiative with particular reference to the establishment of a City Technology College on Teesside.
GBR 1993
Research Date(s): 1989-1993
Abbott, I.
Inst: Warwick University, Faculty of Educational Studies, Coventry CV4 7AL, United Kingdom.
technical education; urban school; school-community relation
enseignement technique; école urbaine; relation école-collectivité
PROJECT DESCRIPTION

The study aims to assess the effectiveness and impact of a city technology college on the educational system of a deprived urban area, particularly the effect the college will have on the local education authority schools within the locality. The means of collecting data will include in-depth interviews, observation and the use of questionnaires and surveys. Specifically extensive contacts have been made with the institutions and individuals involved in this process. It is expected that a wide range of issues will be identified including the role of the industrial sponsors, the position of the local authority, the effect on schools and colleges, the response of teachers and the impact on parents, pupils and staff involved in the college. The study will be looking at a rapidly developing area and it is expected that it will provide data which will be of use in determining future policy decisions.

Publ: Abbott, I.D. British and American approaches to science and technology. In: *Education and Training*, Vol 33, No 1/1991, pp. 5-7.
Abbott, I.D. School industry links: an American perspective. In: *Head Teachers Review*, pp. 10-12, Winter 1991.

12062 La comparaison des systèmes d'enseignement supérieur français et espagnol.
FRA 1993
Research Date(s): 1987-1989
Lassibille, Gérard.
Inst: Université de Dijon, UER Faculté des sciences économiques et de gestion, CNRS UPR/29 et GDR/996, Institut de recherche sur l'économie de l'éducation, BP 138, 21004 Dijon Cedex, France.
education system; comparative education; France; Spain; education budget; higher education; comparative achievement
système d'enseignement; éducation comparée; France; Espagne; budget de l'éducation; enseignement supérieur; rendement comparé
PROJECT DESCRIPTION
Objectifs: Il s'agit de mettre en rapport les modes d'organisation des systèmes d'enseignement supérieur français et espagnol et de retracer les changements quantitatifs qui ont affecté les secteurs universitaires dans chaque pays.
Méthodologie: La comparaison porte (1) sur l'évolution de la demande d'éducation supérieure et sur celle des flux de diplômés produits, (2) sur les moyens humains et financiers qui sont mis à la disposition de chacun des secteurs pour les années 1969-1979 (les ressources publiques affectées à l'enseignement supérieur ne sont pas recensées en Espagne depuis 10 ans).
Résultats: Les universités espagnoles disposent, aujourd'hui, d'une autonomie que n'ont pas les universités françaises, l'offre de formation aux étudiants est plus diversifiée en France qu'en Espagne; les effectifs de l'enseignement supérieur ont cru dans des proportions tout à fait considérables en Espagne, mais les filières à finalité professionnelle n'ont pas attiré les jeunes de façon aussi massive qu'en France. Le recrutement des personnels enseignants a augmenté davantage en Espagne qu'en France. En 1979 l'effort public en faveur de l'enseignement supérieur est nettement plus faible en Espagne même si sur la période 1969-1979 les ressources affectées à ce secteur ont augmenté plus en Espagne qu'en France.
Publ: Lassibille, Gérard & Navarro-Gomez, Lucia. *L'enseignement supérieur en Espagne et en France: une comparaison chiffrée.* IREDU: Rapport d'action intégrée franco-espagnole, 1989, 24p.

12063 A comparative study of outcomes and process in English higher education.
GBR 1993
Research Date(s): 1991-1993
Knight, P.
Inst: Lancaster University, Department of Educational Research, Cartmel College, Bailrigg, Lancaster LA1 4YW, United Kingdom.
higher education; quality of education; comparative analysis; performance
enseignement supérieur; qualité de l'éducation; analyse comparative; performance
PROJECT DESCRIPTION
This is a comparative study of the outcomes of higher education institutions and universities. Although there has been plentiful research into student learning in higher education, and consequent recommendations for effective teaching, it does not readily allow explanation of the performance of public sector institutions in the 1980s. In a decade where student expenditure has remained below that of the university sector (allowing for research funding), when public sector student numbers have burgeoned, and when staff-student ratios have become less favourable, the number and proportion of 2:1 and 1st class degrees have also grown on a sector-wide basis as compared to universities. The study attempts to find out why this should be the case. The focus is upon academic departments teaching the same subject. The usual forms of input and process data are to be collected, but close attention is being given also to the structure of courses; to observation of teaching; and to the assessment of student performance leading to degree classification. The working hypothesis is that there are general, distinct differences in the teaching/learning processes in the two sectors (university:public).

12064 A comparative study of school-based, school-focused and college-based approaches to teacher education.
GBR 1993
Research Date(s): 1990-1994
Hill, D.
Sup: Whitty, G.
Inst: West Sussex Institute of Higher Education, The Dome, Upper Bognor Road, Bognor Regis PO21 1HR, United Kingdom; London University, Goldsmiths' College, Faculty of Education, Lewisham Way, New Cross, London SE14 6NW, United Kingdom.
teacher education; educational policy; philosophy
formation des enseignants; politique de l'éducation; philosophie

PROJECT DESCRIPTION
This research aims to examine and evaluate contemporary developments in teacher education, and to explore the possibilities of developing a left radical analysis of teacher education policy, using a model of the critical reflective practitioner and teacher educator as 'transformative intellectual'.
The main objectives of this study are to: (1) ascertain and evaluate the nature of a variety of routes to teacher education; (2) critique radical left, radical right and liberal perspectives on teacher education and schooling; (3) elicit novice teachers' reactions to key elements and issues in their training programmes; (4) identify elements and approaches that facilitate the development of critical reflective approaches to teacher education and schooling; (5) assist in the development of radical left policies for teacher education.
Publ: Hill, D. Thatcherism, teacher eduation and the suppression of critical thought. In: *Liberal Education and General Educator*, Issue 64, pp. 36-39, Winter 1989/90.
Clay, J.; Cole, M. & Hill, D. Black achievement in initial teacher education: how do we proceed into the 1990s. In: *Multicultural Teaching*, Vol 8, No 3/1990, pp. 31-35, Summer.
Hill, D. Local management of schools. In: *New Socialist*, October/November 1990.
Hill, D. The Hillcole Group. In: *Forum*, Vol 33, No 2/1990, pp. 58-59, Spring.
Hillcole Group What's Left in teacher education?. In: Chitty, C. (ed.). *Changing the future: redprint for education.* London: Tufnell Press, 1991.

12065 Competence-based teacher training for the primary years: a comparative approach.
GBR 1993
Research Date(s): 1992-1996
Payne, G.
Sup: Hannan, A.; Silver, H.
Inst: Plymouth University, Rolle Faculty of Education, Douglas Avenue, Exmouth EX8 2AT, United Kingdom; University of the West of England at Bristol, Coldharbour Lane, Frenchay, Bristol BS16 1QY, United Kingdom.
teacher education; educational reform; management
formation des enseignants; réforme de l'enseignement; gestion
PROJECT DESCRIPTION
The aim of the investigation is, generally, to contribute to our understanding of the management of change in initial teacher education. The specific aims are to: (1) analyse proposals over the past 10 years to change primary teacher training with particular reference to moves to introduce a competence-based approach; (2) undertake a national survey of how such change has been managed; (3) investigate in depth the experiences of a number of institutions selected to illustrate the range of responses; and (4) undertake a comparative study of two institutions in the process of adaptation.
This research will focus on the management of change in initial teacher training (ITT) for the primary years, in particular on proposals for introducing competence-based training. Development of the research will be through a number of stages: (1) an analysis of the wide range of proposals over the past 10 years to change primary teacher training; (2) a national questionnaire survey of ITT providers (postal questionnaire to the 94 institutions offering ITT courses); (3) follow-up interviews with a selection of institutions; and (4) a comparative case study of the experience of change in two institutions.

12066 Concepts in fundamental science: development, interpretation and communication.
GBR 1993
Research Date(s): 1977-
Counihan, M.
Inst: Southampton University, Faculty of Educational Studies, Department of Adult Education, Highfield, Southampton SO9 5NH, United Kingdom.
adult education; science education; concept; comprehension
éducation des adultes; éducation scientifique; concept; compréhension
PROJECT DESCRIPTION
This is a continuing programme of research on fundamental science in the context of adult education. It is concerned with the development and interpretation of concepts, their relevance, and their communication. The central focus is on cosmological and subnuclear phenomena, and on how these matters can or should be interpreted to improve public understanding of science. The output from this research has taken the form of public course programmes, and is intended to be published in book form.

12067 Continuation of Scottish Young People's Survey.
GBR 1993
Research Date(s): 1990-1992
McPherson, A.; Raffe, D.; Lamb, J.; Jones, G.; Middleton, L.
Inst: Edinburgh University, Centre for Educational Sociology, 7 Buccleuch Place, Edinburgh EH8 9JT, United Kingdom.
Fin: Scottish Education Department.
school leaver; Scotland; post-compulsory education; transition from school to work; youth employment

élève sortant; Ecosse; enseignement postobligatoire; passage à la vie active; emploi des jeunes
PROJECT DESCRIPTION

The biennial series of surveys of Scottish school leavers is to be continued.

Publ: A bibliography of published work is available.

12068   Continuation of Scottish Young People's Survey.
GBR   1993
Research Date(s): 1990-
McPherson, A.; Raffe, D.; Lamb, J.; Middleton, L.
Inst: Edinburgh University, Centre for Educational Sociology, 7 Buccleuch Place, Edinburgh EH8 9JT, United Kingdom.
Fin: Scottish Education Department.
school leaver; secondary education; survey; transition from school to work; youth employment
élève sortant; enseignement secondaire; enquête; passage à la vie active; emploi des jeunes
PROJECT DESCRIPTION

The biennial series of surveys of Scottish school leavers is to be continued.

Publ: A bibliography of published work is available.

12069   Continuing education and organisation change in universities.
GBR   1993
Research Date(s): 1990-1993
Duke, C.
Inst: Warwick University, Faculty of Educational Studies, Department of Continuing Education, Continuing Education Research Centre, Coventry CV4 7AL, United Kingdom.
Fin: Universities Funding Council; Training, Enterprise & Education Directorate.
continuing education; university; adult education
éducation permanente; université; éducation des adultes
PROJECT DESCRIPTION

This is a study of change in university continuing education in Britain as a window into change in higher education generally. The traditional, often marginalised, extramural departments are giving way to new structures and arrangements. Continuing education is gaining a much wider meaning and being 'mainstreamed' in policy and organisation. The research studies these trends and processes, and considers implications for higher education generally.

Publ: Duke, C. Restructuring for better service in continuing university education. In: New Education, Vol 13, No 1/1991, pp. 57-68.
Duke, C. University continuing education: identities, prospects and perspectives. In: Fieldhouse, R. (ed.). The organisation of continuing education in universities. UDACE, 1991.
Duke, C. Lifelong education and the universities of the United Kingdom. In: Higher Education in Europe, Vol XVI, No 1/1991, pp. 46-55.

12070   Continuing education practice in Canada and the United Kingdom: a case study of Calgary and Leeds Universities.
GBR   1993
Research Date(s): 1988-1992
Taylor, R.
Inst: Leeds University, Department of Adult Continuing Education, Leeds LS2 9JT, United Kingdom.
Fin: Alberta/Leeds Exchange Scheme.
continuing education; adult education; comparative education; Canada
éducation permanente; éducation des adultes; éducation comparée; Canada
PROJECT DESCRIPTION

Continuing education provision in Canada and the United Kingdom operates on different models. This research analyses assumptions, priorities, models, financing, curriculum approaches and outcomes in the two countries, using case study material for Calgary and Leeds.

12071   Das berufliche Bildungswesen in der Republik Oesterreich. (Vocational education in the Republic of Austria.)
AUT   1993
Research Date(s): 1990-1991
Schedler, Klaus; Blumberger, Walter.
Inst: Institut fuer Bildungsforschung der Wirtschaft, Rainergasse 38, A-1050 Wien; Institut fuer Berufs- und Erwachsenenbildungsforschung, Stifterstrasse 28, A-4020 Linz.
Fin: Bundeskanzleramt; Bundesministerium fuer Arbeit und Soziales; Bundesministerium fuer Unterricht und Kunst; Bundesministerium fuer Wissenschaft und Forschung, Bundeswirtschaftskammer, Arbeiterkammer Oberoesterreich; Vereinigung Oesterreichischer Industrieller.
vocational education; education system; Austria
enseignement professionnel; système d'enseignement; Autriche
PROJECT DESCRIPTION

Der Bericht beinhaltet ausgehend von einer allgemeinen Darstellung der Republik Oesterreich in bezug auf staatlichen Aufbau, Sozialpartnerschaft,

Bevoelkerungsstand und -entwicklung, Wirtschaftsstruktur und Arbeitsmarkt, einen Ueberblick ueber das oesterreichische Bildungssystem. Der Schwerpunkt liegt auf dem beruflichen Bildungswesen: Lehre und Berufsausbildung in Schulen. Weiters wird auch auf das allgemeinbildende Schulwesen, Hochschulen und Erwachsenenbildung und die Vielfalt der Kompetenzen (Administration) und Finanzierungsformen eingegangen. Den Abschluss bildet ein bildungspolitischer Ausblick.

Die empirische Praxis bildeten Experteninterviews.

Publ: Vorlagebericht an das Europaeische Zentrum fuer die Foerderung der Berufsbildung (Cedefop). Wien, Dezember 1991.

12072   Day care and later development.
GBR   1993
Research Date(s): 1988-1991
Hennessy, E.; Martin, S.
Sup: Melhuish, E.; Moss, P.
Inst: London University, Institute of Education, Thomas Coram Research Unit, 41 Brunswick Square, London WC1N 1AZ, United Kingdom.
Fin: Department of Health.
day care; child development; cognitive development
mode de garde; développement de l'enfant; développement cognitif
PROJECT DESCRIPTION

The day care project, which finished in 1988, was concerned with single and dual-career families over the first three years of the child's life. The current project is a follow-up of these families, which aims to answer substantial questions about the usage and effects of day care, and also parental employment over the subsequent three years. The children in the study are now attending primary school, and the implications of this for dual-career families are being examined. The project also considers the implications of different types of early day care experience for the child's socio-emotional and cognitive development at the age of six. The project staff are visiting 243 families remaining in the day care project when the children are six years old. The mothers are to be interviewed, particularly about child care and employment histories over the last three years. The children's cognitive development is assessed using standardised psychometric measure, their socio-emotional development by questionnaires which are completed by the mother and class teacher.

Publ: Brannen, J. & Moss, P. New mothers at work: employment and childcare. London: Unwin, 1988.

12073   De werking van de volwasseneneducatiemarkt. (The continuing education market: patterns and functions.)
NLD   1994
Research Date(s): 1990-1992
Brandsma, T.F.; Peters, F.J.M.
Inst: Onderzoek Centrum Toegepaste Onderwijskunde (OCTO) (Research Centre of the Department of Educational Technology), P.O. Box 217, 7500 AE Enschede, Netherlands.
Universiteit Twente (Twente University), P.O. Box 217, 7500 AE Enschede, Netherlands
Fin: SVO het Instituut voor Onderzoek van het Onderwijs.
adult education; demand for education; educational provision; educational research
éducation des adultes; demande d'éducation; scolarisation; recherche en éducation
PROJECT DESCRIPTION

Background: Since the 1980s participation in adult education courses has gone up by 20%. In policy circles, too, the interest in adult education is growing. The initial socio-cultural orientation of the courses (with an emphasis on self-development) has gradually made way for a more socio-economic orientation (improving one's position on the labour market). In industry, too, continuing education is coming to be recognized more and more as a management tool. Adult education is thus increasingly seen as a market and as a field for investment. At the same time, there are signs of certain shortcomings in this market.

Aim: The study consisted of a review of national and international literature with the aim to provide an overview of the current body of knowledge concerning a range of aspects of the adult education market, as well as the interrelations between those aspects and their influence on the workings of the adult education market.

Results: There are still gaps in our knowledge of how the adult education market works. Little is known about why some aspects of the adult education market do not function properly; the competing explanations that are given lack a sound empirical foundation. Dutch research on adult education is fragmentary and lacks a sound theoretical basis. This is one of the reasons why insufficient reserach evidence is available on the interrelationships between distinct components of the adult education market.

(This is an updating of EUDISED no. 43/10235).

Publ: Brandsma, T.F. et al. De werking van de volwasseneneducatiemarkt. Enschede, OCTO, 1992, 167p.

12074 Defining high-quality preschool provision in Belgium and Britain.
GBR 1993
Research Date(s): 1991-1992
David, T.
Inst: Warwick University, Faculty of Educational Studies, Coventry CV4 7AL, United Kingdom.
Fin: The Nuffield Foundation.
early childhood education; pre-school education; educational provision; quality of education; comparative education; Belgium; United Kingdom
éducation de la prime enfance; éducation préscolaire; scolarisation; qualité de l'éducation; éducation comparée; Belgique; Royaume-Uni
PROJECT DESCRIPTION
Using a variety of research methods (document searches, interviews, observations), the research will explore the views of parents, staff, children and politicians, concerning preschool provision in Belgium and Britain. In particular the research will address issues involved in the rationale underpinning different forms of provision, definitions of quality, and what each situation indicates about the position of young children in that society. The research will also contribute to debates on research methods.

The sample will comprise: 20 parents in each country; 20 children in each country; 20 providers in each country; and politicians representing different political parties in each country.

12075 Degree specialism and pedagogic understanding in primary PGCE courses.
GBR 1993
Research Date(s): 1991-1992
Knight, P.
Inst: Lancaster University, Department of Educational Research, Cartmel College, Bailrigg, Lancaster LA1 4YW, United Kingdom.
teacher education; post-graduate study; main subject; teaching method; pedagogical theory
formation des enseignants; supérieur troisième cycle; matière principale; méthode pédagogique; courant pédagogique
PROJECT DESCRIPTION
The question is whether students who enter primary Postgraduate Certificate in Education (PGCE) courses with history or geography degrees show any greater grasp of the pedagogy of those subjects either at the start of the course, or at the end of it. The hypothesis is that the subject teaching methods element of the PGCEs will not make a difference, and that differences apparent on entry will be reproduced on exit.

Students in three institutions were given questionnaires about geography and history - the subjects and their pedagogy - on entry to the course, and will do the same questionnaires on completion. In addition, during the course they undertake a planning exercise and an evaluation exercise, in both of which they are required to apply their grasp of primary geography and primary history to lifelike teaching problems.

Reports will be published separately for geography and history and will be written by the colleagues in the institutions concerned. Lancaster University is co-ordinating the project.

12076 Democratic approaches to initial teacher education.
GBR 1993
Research Date(s): 1988-1991
Mercer, D.
Inst: Sunderland University, School of Education, Hammerton Hall, Gray Road, Sunderland SR2 7EE, United Kingdom.
teacher education; learning strategy; group learning; teaching method
formation des enseignants; stratégie d'apprentissage; pédagogie de groupe; méthode pédagogique
PROJECT DESCRIPTION
This is a study of a variety of student-centred approaches in initial teacher education. These include a democratic learning approach, partnership supervision in the teaching practice and student profiling.

Publ: Mercer, D. & Abbott, I. Democratic learning in initial teacher education: a comparative study. In: *Educational Review*, Vol 41, No 1/1989, pp. 3-8.
Mercer, D. & Abbott, I. Democratic learning in initial teacher education: partnership supervision in the teaching practice. In: *Journal of Education for Teaching*, Vol 15, No 2/1989, pp. 141-148.

12077 Der Umbau des Bildungswesens in den neuen Bundeslaendern. (Reorganization of the education system in the new German states.)
DEU 1993
Research Date(s): 1991-1995
Fuchs, H.
Sup: Reuter, L.
Inst: Universitaet der Bundeswehr Hamburg, FB Paedagogik, Professur fuer Erziehungswissenschaft, insb. Bildungspolitik, Hostenhofweg 85, D-2000 Hamburg 70.
education system; German DR; educational reform
système d'enseignement; Allemagne RDA; réforme de l'enseignement

PROJECT DESCRIPTION
Inhalt: Darstellung und Analyse der Umbauprozesse im Bildungswesen der neuen Bundeslaender, Voraussetzungen, Verlauf und Folgen des Wandels; Darstellung und Analyse der Reformdiskussion gesellschaftlich relevanter Gruppen der DDR/ der neuen Bundeslaender und ihrer Auswirkungen auf die Neugestaltung des Bildungswesens. Frage: gibt es trotz offensichtlichem Wandel (versteckte) Kontinuitaeten? Wenn ja, wo und wie wirken sich diese aus?

Geographischer Raum: Neue Bundeslaender und Berlin.

Untersuchter Zeitraum: 1989 ff.

Vorgehensweise: Untersuchungsdesign: Fallstudie; Evaluationsstudie; Trend; qualitative Forschung.

Datengewinnung: Aktenanalyse (Stichprobe: ueber 500; Artikel und Aufsaetze regionaler und ueberregionaler Tages- und Wochenzeitungen; Auswahlverfahren: Zufall. Gesetze, Verordnungen, Erlasse der neuen Bundeslaender). Nicht-standardisiertes Interview, Expertengespraech, postalische Befragung, Befragung (Stichprobe: jedesmal ueber 50; Gespraeche und Interviews mit Bildungsexperten, Angehoerigen der Bildungsverwaltung etc.; Auswahlverfahren: bewusst). Primaererhebung: Feldarbeit von Mitarbeitern des Projektes durchgefuehrt.

Auswertung: Datenaufbereitung: Verlaufsdaten (event history data).

12078 Description and evaluation of an educational intervention to assist learning-disabled adults into employment and independent living.
GBR 1993
Research Date(s): 1990-1992
Orbell, S.
Inst: Dundee University, Centre for Continuing Education, Dundee DD1 4HN, United Kingdom.
Fin: Scottish Office, Home and Health Department.
special education; training centre; learning difficulty; access to education; basic education; minimum competencies; adult education
enseignement spécial; centre de formation; difficulté de l'apprentissage; accès à l'éducation; éducation de base; fundamentum; éducation des adultes
PROJECT DESCRIPTION
The aim of this project is to describe the experiences of the first group of trainees entering a newly opened training centre. It will describe: (1) the needs of trainees; and (2) the activities undertaken by trainees, identifying the methods and difficulties associated with operationalising supported employment training. The project will also longitudinally assess the outcomes of training including (a) employment; (b) independent living; (c) perceived competence and (d) self-esteem.

The sample consists of 39 adults, aged 16 - 25, with mild or moderate mental handicap. Data collected include project records and staff assessments. Personal interviews with trainees are of two kinds: (a) semi-structured interviews to identify living skills, social activities, aspirations, work motivation; and (b) quantitative instruments designed to measure perceived competence, self-esteem, social comparisons.

12079 Developing a joint BA Honours course in International Studies and Business Studies.
GBR 1993
Research Date(s): 1990-1992
Hocking, B.
Inst: Coventry University, Priory Street, Coventry CV1 5FB, United Kingdom.
undergraduate study; commercial training; international studies
supérieur premier cycle; formation commerciale; études internationales
PROJECT DESCRIPTION
The purpose of the project is to develop a course which focuses on the international context in which modern business operates and, thereby, provides a broader educational experience than is the case with most undergraduate courses in business studies.

12080 Developing information technology in a primary Post-Graduate Certificate of Education course.
GBR 1993
Research Date(s): 1992-1994
Pickford, A.
Inst: Chester College of Higher Education, Cheyney Road, Chester CH1 4BJ, United Kingdom.
teacher education; student teacher; information technology
formation des enseignants; élève-maître; technologie de l'information
PROJECT DESCRIPTION
The aim of the project is to identify the factors affecting student competence in information technology in relation to the teaching practice experience of Post-Graduate Certificate of Education (PGCE) students. The research will also consider the kinds of positive interventions which can be made by a teacher training institution and those personal characteristics of students which might lead to the development of information technology capability. The sample size is approximately 50 PGCE students (primary). The study uses questionnaires and direct observation by tutors.

12081 Developing policy in the field of special educational needs for the 1990s.
GBR 1993
Research Date(s): 1992-1995
Wedell, K.; Norwich, B.
Inst: London University, Institute of Education, Department of Educational Psychology and Special Educational Needs, 20 Bedford Way, London WC1H OAL, United Kingdom.
Fin: B & G Cadbury Trust; Economic and Social Research Council.
special education; educational policy
enseignement spécial; politique de l'éducation
PROJECT DESCRIPTION
The project is concerned with the preparation and publication of policy papers on special educational needs provision.

12082 Developing school-based services for children with severe learning difficulties and challenging behaviour.
GBR 1993
Research Date(s): 1992-1993
Cook, M.
Sup: Upton, G.; Harris, J.
Inst: Birmingham University, School of Education, Edgbaston, Birmingham B15 2TT, United Kingdom; British Institute of Learning Disabilities, Wolverhampton Road, Kidderminster, Worcestershire DY10 3PP, United Kingdom.
Fin: Mental Health Foundation.
special education; in-service training; learning difficulty; behaviour disorder; problem child; intervention
enseignement spécial; formation en cours d'emploi; difficulté de l'apprentissage; trouble du comportement; enfant perturbé; intervention
PROJECT DESCRIPTION
The general aim of the project is to improve the quality of school-based services for children with severe learning difficulties who present various forms of challenging behaviour. More specifically it involves: (a) collaboration with teachers and care staff in special schools for children with severe learning difficulties in the design and implementation of a range of strategies for the management and amelioration of challenging behaviour in schools; (b) monitoring and evaluating different intervention strategies to identify those which can be most effectively employed in schools; and (c) developing an in-service training programme which will assist teachers and other staff in working more effectively with children with challenging behaviour.
The study is being carried out in two phases. In the first phase five schools are involved in the development of the intervention strategies which will be evaluated in phase two in a further five schools.

12083 The development, implementation and evaluation of a model of practice in art and design teacher education.
GBR 1993
Research Date(s): 1991-1996
Hall, J.
Sup: Adelman, C.
Inst: Reading University, Department of Arts and Humanities in Education, Bulmershe Court, Woodlands Avenue, Earley, Reading RG6 1HY, United Kingdom.
teacher education; student teacher; art education
formation des enseignants; élève-maître; éducation artistique
PROJECT DESCRIPTION
This is a longitudinal study of a sample of beginning teachers of art and design, following them through a one year post-graduate course of initial teacher education and into their first teaching appointments. The research will investigate the effectiveness of the Post-Graduate Certificate of Education (PGCE) Art and Design Course at Reading University, and the processes through which beginning teachers learn to teach and go on to develop and improve their practice.
Publ: Hall, J. The roles of practising teachers and university lecturers in the initial training of teachers of art and design. In: *Journal of Art and Design Education*, Vol 10, No 3/1991, pp. 317-327.

12084 Development of a distance learning course for teachers of children with speech and language disorders.
GBR 1993
Research Date(s): 1981-1991
Miller, C.
Sup: Upton, G.
Inst: Birmingham University, School of Education, Edgbaston, Birmingham B15 2TT, United Kingdom.
Fin: Department of Education and Science.
distance study; course programme; further education of teachers; speech defect; communication
enseignement à distance; programme de cours; perfectionnement des enseignants; trouble de la parole; communication
PROJECT DESCRIPTION
The aims of the research are to investigate teachers' needs regarding speech and language disorders and to develop a distance learning course based on the identified needs. The questionnaire used to identify needs and discussions with trainers lead to modifications in the balance of the syllabus for the course.
Publ: Mason, H. & Miller, C. Training teachers of children with special needs at a distance. In: Upton, G. (ed.). *Staff training and special educational needs: innovatory strategies and models of delivery*. London: David Fulton, 1991.

12085 Differential provision for children with special educational needs in ordinary schools.
GBR 1993
Research Date(s): 1986-
Bennett, S.; Trotter, A.
Inst: Exeter University, School of Education, St Luke's, Heavitree Road, Exeter EX1 2LU, United Kingdom.
Fin: Economic and Social Research Council.
special education; pupil integration; slow learning; educational need; guidance
enseignement spécial; intégration scolaire; apprentissage lent; besoin d'éducation; orientation
PROJECT DESCRIPTION
The aim of the study is to investigate the effects of various kinds of provision made for children with special educational needs at secondary level. Three main systems were investigated - the support base, withdrawal, and in-class support. Children were selected at primary level who were deemed to be in need of special educational needs provision at secondary school. Their entry into secondary school and subsequent performance was closely monitored. Along with details of their academic performance, the research includes the views of their parents and the children themselves.

12086 Distance education and the humanities.
GBR 1993
Research Date(s): 1975-
Chambers, E.; Durbridge, N.
Inst: Open University, Institute of Educational Technology, Walton Hall, Milton Keynes MK7 6AA, United Kingdom.
Fin: Open University.
distance study; open university; adult education; humanities
enseignement à distance; télé-université; éducation des adultes; études littéraires
PROJECT DESCRIPTION
This is an investigation of all aspects of adult students' encounters with distance courses in the Humanities. To date most research has been done into beginning students (i.e. those taking an interdisciplinary Foundation course) and those studying philosophy and music. The research covers: students' expectations of and attitudes to studying; students' acquisition of study skills; the particular problems facing students new to the study of philosophy (and, in 1992, literature, art history, music and history).
The methods used are: survey questionnaires, large and small samples; interviews; small samples; institutional data (e.g. drop out, examination pass rates etc.).
Publ: Chambers, E.A. A project component in architectural history. In: Henderson, E. & Nathenson, M. (eds.). *Independent learning in higher education*. Englewood Cliffs, New Jersey: Prentice-Hall Inc., 1984.
Chambers, E.A. & Durbridge, N. Preparing for the examination. In: *A102 An Arts Foundation Course, Units 31-32*. Milton Keynes: Open University Press, 1987.
Chambers, E.A. Improving Foundation Level study at the Open University through Evaluation of student experience. In: *Proceedings of the CNAA Conference 'Academic Quality Assurance'*. London: CNAA, 1991.

12087 Distance learning in Central Nervous Systems (CNS) psychiatry.
GBR 1993
Research Date(s): 1991-1992
Blicharski, J.
Sup: Harden, R.
Inst: Dundee University, Centre for Medical Education, Ninewells Hospital and Medical School, Dundee DD1 9SY, United Kingdom.
Fin: Glaxo Group Research Ltd.
distance study; pharmaceutics; management education
enseignement à distance; pharmacie; formation à la gestion
PROJECT DESCRIPTION
As part of Glaxo's continued research in the field of central nervous system pharmacology, Glaxo have commissioned the Centre for Medical Education, Dundee to develop a distance learning programme aimed at senior managers within Glaxo. This programme will inform managers of the pharmacological significance of a new drug, ondansetron, and how it can be used in a variety of disorders. Development of an educational strategy to explain often complex theories and terminology will be accompanied by assessments for each topic module. Information will be presented at four levels of complexity, allowing readers to obtain information at a level appropriate to their needs.

12088   Drama and special needs.
GBR   1993
Research Date(s): 1990-1991
Kempe, A.
Sup: Weller, M.
Inst: Reading University, Department of Arts and Humanities in Education, Bulmershe Court, Woodlands Avenue, Earley, Reading RG6 1HY, United Kingdom.
Fin: Technical and Vocational Education Initiative (TVEI) syndicate.
special education; learning difficulty; teaching method; educational need; drama
enseignement spécial; difficulté de l'apprentissage; méthode pédagogique; besoin d'éducation; art dramatique
PROJECT DESCRIPTION
The research syndicate will be made up of three teachers in a special school, (the Avenue School, Reading), two university lecturers and a small number of Postgraduate Certificate of Education (PGCE) drama students. The project will aim to find ways of enabling young people with a variety of special educational needs to engage with drama as an expressive and performing art. The practical work will be trialled with one group of 11 to 12 year olds with moderate learning difficulties and one group of 15 to 17 year olds with various physical and learning difficulties. A report documenting all of the practical project and referring it to the available theory in the field will be produced.
Publ: Kempe, A. Learning both ways. In: *British Journal of Special Education*, Vol 18, No 4/1991, pp. 137-139.

12089   Du projet-élèves à la pédagogie du projet.
FRA   1993
Research Date(s): 1991-1992
Huber, Michel; Duny, André; Chaix, Michèle.
Sup: Huberman, Michael.
Inst: Institut national de recherches et d'applications pédagogiques, 2 rue des Champs Prévois, 21100 Dijon, France.
teacher education; achievement motivation; in-service training; teaching practice; project method
formation des enseignants; motivation d'accomplissement; formation en cours d'emploi; pratique pédagogique; pédagogie du projet
PROJECT DESCRIPTION
Objectifs: On organise auprès des enseignants un stage mettant en oeuvre des pratiques constructivistes suscitant un certain déséquilibre cognitif et favorisant l'intégration d'outils pédagogiques. On fait l'hypothèse que ce stage est susceptible d'avoir un impact positif sur les pratiques et de permettre une meilleure maîtrise de la conduite de projets-élèves et que cela renforce la motivation des élèves en donnant un véritable sens à leur apprentissage et crée de meilleures conditions de structuration en suscitant une plus grande confiance en eux.
Méthodologie: (1) Entretien préalable avec une vingtaine d'enseignants de la région Provence Alpes Côte d'Azur avec observation de séquences de classe, puis stage de cinq jours et second entretien permettant d'évaluer la portée du stage, possibilité d'un suivi lors d'un second-stage de deux jours; (2) entretien préalable avec les élèves de deux classes de quatrième, deux autres classes de quatrième servent de classes-témoins, conduite de projets-élèves par les maîtres formés par le stage; (3) second entretien avec les élèves des deux quatrièmes afin d'évaluer l'impact de la conduite de ces projets par les élèves et le niveau de leurs acquisitions; (4) comparaison avec les élèves des deux classes témoins.

12090   Educating teachers to be intellectuals: a study of an attempt to enable preservice primary teachers to develop as critically reflective practitioners.
GBR   1993
Research Date(s): 1990-1995
Mackenzie, R.
Sup: Hannan, A.; Taylor, G.
Inst: Plymouth University, Rolle Faculty of Education, Douglas Avenue, Exmouth EX8 2AT, United Kingdom.
teacher education; teaching profession; probationary teacher; intellectual; teacher status
formation des enseignants; profession d'enseignant; enseignant stagiaire; intellectuel; statut de l'enseignant
PROJECT DESCRIPTION
The concept of the reflective practitioner has been explored and extended in a critical direction, and the investigation has been both conceptual and empirical. The case for teachers to act as transformative intellectuals rather than State technicians has been argued within the context of a period of cultural and legislative change in society and in relation to primary school practices developed beyond the ideological polarisations of the past period.
The empirical part of the investigation is based on an attempt to incorporate the concept of teachers as intellectuals in a B.Ed. Educational Studies course component entitled 'Teachers and Children of the Future'. The course aims to support emerging teachers in developing a personal philosophy of education within collegial frameworks so that contemporary challenges should not swamp them personally or professionally. Action research has been used to investigate the aims, content, pedagogy and outcomes of the course which 80 B.Ed. students have now completed.
A smaller group of ex-students, now newly qualified teachers (NQTs), are assisting a follow through into the first year of teaching: the aspiration is to compare and contrast the conceptual and empirical positions of the course with the experienced realities of being an NQT in the 1990s.

12091   Education with unwaged adults as community adult education.
GBR   1993
Research Date(s): 1985-1991
Johnston, R.
Inst: Southampton University, Faculty of Educational Studies, Department of Adult Education, Highfield, Southampton SO9 5NH, United Kingdom.
adult education; community education; unemployed
éducation des adultes; éducation sociale; chômeur
PROJECT DESCRIPTION
This thesis focuses primarily on two action-research projects with unwaged adults carried out between 1985 and 1988. The heart of the thesis consists of the published reports of the projects 'Exploring the Educational Needs of Unwaged Adults' and 'Negotiating the Curriculum with Unwaged Adults'. Additional material sets out to put this research into its historical context, to reflect critically on its developing methodology and to learn from it in the context of the 1990s. An attempt is made to ground the research in the historical context of the previous debates concerning ideology and curriculum in community-based adult education and their influence on the growth of educational intiatives with unwaged adults, particularly those projects sponsored through Replan in the mid-1980s. The thesis also includes a reflexive methodological critique of the two projects. It concludes by relating the work and findings of the projects to the emerging educational context of the 1990s and identifying the lessons that can be learned for the future development of Community Adult Education.
Publ: Johnston, R.A. *Exploring the educational needs of unwaged adults.* Leicester: NIACE, 1987.
Johnston, R.A.; Jacobs, M. & McWilliam, I. *Negotiating the curriculum with unwaged adults.* London: Further Education Unit, 1989.
Johnston, R.A. Education and unwaged adults: relevance, social control and empowerment. In: Allen, G. & Martin, I. (eds.). *Education and community: the politics of practice.* Poole: Cassell, 1992.
Johnston, R.A. Outreach work with unemployed and unwaged adults. In: *Adult Education*, Vol 60, No 1/1987. pp. 58-65.

12092   Effecten stopzetting planprocedure (voortgezet) speciaal onderwijs. (Effects of the discontinuation of the special education planning procedure.)
NLD   1994
Research Date(s): 1992
Esch, W.J.M. van; Laemers, M.; Oudenhoven, D.; Vrieze, G.
Inst: Instituut voor Toegepaste Sociale wetenschappen (ITS) (Institute for Applied Social Sciences), P.O. Box 9048, 6500 KJ Nijmegen, Netherlands. Katholieke Universiteit Nijmegen (Catholic University of Nijmegen), P.O. Box 9102, 6500 HC Nijmegen, Netherlands
Fin: SVO het Instituut voor Onderzoek van het Onderwijs.
special education; educational policy; school distribution
enseignement spécial; politique de l'éducation; carte scolaire
PROJECT DESCRIPTION
Background: In February 1991 the planning procedure for special school was suspended by law. This means that for an indefinite period no new special schools will be funded by the government. An important argument underlying this decision was that the level of provision was adequate and that there was no need for further extension. By suspending the planning procedure it is hoped to prevent an imbalance between the growth of the ordinary and special primary education.
Aim: To examine whether the suspension of the planning procedure has had a negative effect on the possibility to found schools and, if so, whether these negative effects are sufficiently compensated for by the exceptions provided in the Special Education Interim Act.
Methods: Structured questionnaires (provincial authority officials, local authority officials, representatives of school board unions), interviews (local authority officials, representatives of school board unions, government officials).
Results: There is still a need for new provisions for special schools. The number of problems encountered by the respondents is limited. Schools look for alternative solutions to educational problems within the scope afforded by current laws and regulations. The problems that do occur are serious. Nearly three quarters of the local authorities that experience negative consequences as a result of the discontinuation of the planning procedure think that regulations concerning exceptional situations offer insufficient compensation. An important consequence of the suspension of the planning procedure is that new emerging parties do not have access to the special school market.

Publ: Esch, W. van & Vrieze, G. *De gevolgen van de stopzetting van de planprocedure ISOVSO*. Nijmegen: ITS, 1992, 70p.
Vrieze, G. & Esch, W. van. Procedures en gemeenten onderschatten gevolgen stopzetting planprocedure speciaal onderwijs: scholen vaak gedwongen om naar weinig ideale alternatieven te zoeken. In: *Didaktief* 1993/4, pp. 16-17.

12093 Effectiveness of nurse teacher training related to experience since qualifying.
GBR 1993
Research Date(s): 1992-1993
Nolan, R.
Inst: University of Wales College of Cardiff, School of Education, Senghennydd Road, Cardiff CF2 4AG, United Kingdom.
training of trainers; teacher education; nurse; health service personnel; quality of education
formation des formateurs; formation des enseignants; infirmier; personnel médical; qualité de l'éducation
PROJECT DESCRIPTION
This project aims to determine how effective nurse teacher training at University of Wales College of Cardiff and elsewhere was in relation to experience. The sample comprises a random selection of nurse/midwifery teachers who qualified over the past four years taken from college records and via contacts from other centres.

12094 The efficient use of talent in the expansion of Scottish higher education.
GBR 1993
Research Date(s): 1992-1993
Paterson, L.
Sup: McPherson, A.
Inst: Edinburgh University, Centre for Educational Sociology, 7 Buccleuch Place, Edinburgh EH8 9JT, United Kingdom.
Fin: The Leverhulme Trust.
higher education; post-compulsory education; educational opportunities
enseignement supérieur; enseignement postobligatoire; chances d'éducation
PROJECT DESCRIPTION
The object of the research is to investigate the scope for exploiting untapped talent among young people (aged under 20) as a result of the fundamental changes affecting Scottish higher education.
Publ: A full list of publications is available.

12095 Einheitlichkeit und Differenzierung im Schulwesen. (Uniformity and differentiation in the school system.)
DEU 1993
Research Date(s): 1992-1993
Wigger, L.; Mietz, C.; Fuhrmann, E.; Walter, K.
Sup: Paschen, H.
Inst: Universitaet Bielefeld, Fak. fuer Paedagogik, Fach Allg. Erziehungswissenschaft, Universitaetsstrasse 25, D-4800 Bielefeld 1.
Fin: Deutsche Forschungsgemeinschaft.
school system; differentiation; educational policy; German DR; Germany - Federal Republic; history of education
système scolaire; différenciation; politique de l'éducation; Allemagne RDA; Allemagne RFA; histoire de l'éducation
PROJECT DESCRIPTION
Inhalt: Erhebung, Dokumentation und Analyse der Begruendungen und Begruendungspotentiale bildungspolitischer Entscheidungen zum Problem "Einheitlichkeit und Differenzierung im Schulwesen" in der Bundesrepublik Deutschland und der DDR. Entwicklung einer problemspezifischen Topik von Argumenten. Entwicklung eines Gewichtungsmodells fuer Entscheidungsbegruendungen.
Geographischer Raum: Bundesrepublik Deutschland und DDR.
Untersuchter Zeitraum: 1945-1991.
Vorgehensweise: Argumentationsanalyse. Untersuchungsdesign: qualitative Forschung.
Datengewinnung: Aktenanalyse. Inhaltsanalyse. Datenerstellung auf der Basis von bereits vorliegenden Materialien wie Texten, Akten, Statistiken.

12096 Enterprise in vocational education and training.
GBR 1993
Research Date(s): 1988-1991
McLean, M.
Inst: Durham University, University Business School, Old Shire Hall, Durham DH1 3HP, United Kingdom.
Fin: Training, Enterprise & Education Directorate; British Steel.
vocational education; vocational training; teaching aid; experiential learning; post-compulsory education
enseignement professionnel; formation professionnelle; moyen d'enseignement; apprentissage par la pratique; enseignement postobligatoire
PROJECT DESCRIPTION
The aim of this project was to research, develop, pilot and disseminate active-learning materials to embed enterprising approaches to the delivery of vocational courses in further education. Fourteen colleges of further education were involved in the piloting of the materials. Information was gathered by observation of lecturers and students in the classroom situation and feedback was also given during workshop sessions. Initially a review of literature was undertaken, followed by in-depth interviews with 'enterprise' practitioners.

12097 Entwicklung der Studiensituation und studentische Orientierungen. (Development of students' situations and orientations.)
DEU 1993
Research Date(s): 1982-
Sandberger, J.; Ramm, M.; Simeaner, H.
Sup: Bargel, T.
Inst: Universitaet Konstanz, Sozialwissenschaftliche Fakultaet, Arbeitsgemeinschaft Hochschulforschung, Universitaetsstr. 10, D-7750 Konstanz.
Fin: Bundesministerium fuer Bildung und Wissenschaft; Bundesanstalt fuer Arbeit.
university; educational planning; university studies; educational policy; trend; student life; student behaviour
université; planification de l'éducation; études universitaires; politique de l'éducation; tendance; vie étudiante; comportement de l'étudiant
PROJECT DESCRIPTION
Inhalt: Dauerbeobachtung der Studiensituation und studentischer Orientierungen in den 80er und 90er Jahren; Analyse von Trends und Stabilitaeten; Frueherkennung von Problemzonen, Informationen fuer Hochschulen, Hochschulplanung und Hochschulpolitik.
Geographischer Raum: Bundesrepublik Deutschland, ab 1992 einschl. neue Laender.
Untersuchter Zeitraum: ab 1982.
Vorgehensweise: Surveyforschung. Untersuchungsdesign: Trend.
Datengewinnung: Standardisiertes Interview (Stichprobe: 7817; Studierende im WS 82/83 an 10 Hochschulen; Auswahlverfahren: Zufall. Stichprobe: 10037; Studierende im WS 84/85 an 14 Hochschulen; Auswahlverfahren: Zufall. Stichprobe: 9852; Studierende im WS 86/87 an 14 Hochschulen; Auswahlverfahren: Zufall. Stichprobe: 8812; Studierende im WS 89/90 an 14 Hochschulen; Auswahlverfahren: Zufall). Primaererhebung: Feldarbeit von Mitarbeitern des Projektes durchgefuehrt.
Auswertung: Ueblische statistische Auswertungsverfahren einschliesslich Strukturgleichungsmodelle. Datenaufbereitung: Verknuepfung verschiedener Datensaetze (record linkage).
Publ: Bargel, T.; Framhein-Peisert, G. & Sandberger, J.-U. Studienerfahrungen und studentische Orientierungen in den 80er Jahren. In: *Studien zu Bildung und Wissenschaft 86*. Bonn: 1989.

12098 European adult education directory project (Northern Ireland).
GBR 1993
Research Date(s): 1991-1992
O'Reilly, B.
Inst: Ulster University at Jordanstown, Regional Curriculum Base, Shore Road, Newtownabbey, County Antrim BT37 0QB, United Kingdom.
Fin: European Bureau of Adult Education.
adult education; directory; comparative education
éducation des adultes; répertoire; éducation comparée
PROJECT DESCRIPTION
The aim of the project is to map out a description of the whole system of adult education in each of the European Community countries, to identify and provide an overview of organisations in the field of general non-vocational adult education and to provide a directory of the findings.
Publ: O'Reilly, B. & Young, E. *Adult education directory preliminary report: Northern Ireland*. Jordanstown: Regional Curriculum Base, 1991.

12099 Evaluatie van de driejarige opleiding in het Pedagogisch Hoger Onderwijs. (Evaluation of the three-year training course in primary teacher training colleges.)
BEL 1994
Research Date(s): 1990-
Pittoors, T.; Robben, D.
Sup: Janssens, S.
Inst: Afdeling Didactiek, Onderzoekscentrum voor Lerarenopleiding (Department of Didactics, Research Centre for Teacher Training), Vesaliusstraat 2, 3000 Leuven, Belgium.
Katholieke Universiteit Leuven (Catholic University of Leuven), Naamsestraat 22, 3000 Leuven, Belgium
Fin: Departement Onderwijs, Fonds voor Kollektief en Fundamenteel Onderzoek op Ministerieel Initiatief.
teacher education; primary education; educational reform; content of education; student; personal interest; educational need
formation des enseignants; enseignement primaire; réforme de l'enseignement; contenu de l'éducation; étudiant; intérêt personnel; besoin d'éducation
PROJECT DESCRIPTION

Aim: This evaluative study investigates to what extent the reformed primary teaching training course corresponds to the model of personalized teacher education.

Research questions: (1) What is the content of current primary teacher training? (2) What are the concerns of student teachers during their training, and how do these concerns develop? (3) How far does the training course respond to the students' concerns?

Methods: The present situation in primary teacher training, reformed since 1984, is described on the basis of questionnaires completed by about 90 educationalists in 30 colleges, followed by interviews. The criterion whereby the teacher training course is evaluated is the "personalized teacher education" model of Francis Fuller (1974). This model provides a framework for a training programme based on the knowledge that student teachers go through different stages of concern: student, self, task and pupil concerns. The concerns of 69 student teachers from two colleges (but divided over the three grades), were gathered through weekly log-keeping and an interview every six weeks.

Preliminary results: The data so far collected need to be further processed and classified. Comparison of the description of current training practice and the students' concerns will show to what degree the present training course responds to these concerns. The final report will include policy-oriented recommendations.

Publ: Pittoors, T. & Robben, D. *Evaluatie van de driejarige opleiding in het Pedagogisch Hoger Onderwijs: rapport van het eerste werkingsjaar*. Leuven: KUL, Onderzoekscentrum voor Lerarenopleiding, 1991, 68p. + appendix (6p.).

12100   Evaluating rural adult learning.
GBR   1993
Research Date(s): 1990-1991
Chase, M.; Donajgrodzki, A.; Harrison, B.; Murphy, B.
Inst: Leeds University, Department of Adult Continuing Education, Leeds LS2 9JT, United Kingdom.
Fin: Universities Funding Council.
adult education; continuing education; non-formal education; rural area
éducation des adultes; éducation permanente; éducation non-formelle; zone rurale
PROJECT DESCRIPTION

This project aims to evaluate the educational content and delivery of 'non-educational' agencies in rural areas. It provides an assessment of mature learning activity in rural areas: how adults learn, where, for what purposes and to what effect. It highlights current good practice at the interface of non-formal and statutory continuing education provision.

12101   Evaluation of a teacher training package designed to enhance pupils' self-image.
GBR   1993
Research Date(s): 1990-1993
Charlton, A.; Leo, E.; Indoe, D.; James, J.
Inst: Cheltenham & Gloucester College of Higher Education, Faculty of Education and Health, The Park, Cheltenham GL50 2QF, United Kingdom.
further education of teachers; pupil attitude; self-concept; training programme
perfectionnement des enseignants; attitude de l'élève; conception de soi; programme de formation
PROJECT DESCRIPTION

The research involves an evaluation of an inservice teacher training package constructed by the researchers. The package - EASI Teaching Package (Enhancement Approaches with the Self-Image) - is designed to assist teachers to improve the self-image of their pupils. Evaluation will incorporate a pre-/post intervention design. Seventy-two teachers (drawn from nine primary schools) are to constitute the intervention group. They will receive the EASI Teaching Programme (4 one and a half hour meetings) over a 4 week period. A comparison group (similar size/type to the intervention group) will receive no special treatment. Pre-/post evaluations will utilise indices of teachers' classroom behaviour, and pupils' self-image reports and behavioural functioning.

12102   An evaluation of current British policy concerning postgraduate overseas students.
GBR   1993
Research Date(s): 1990-1993
Bo, J.
Sup: Morgan, W.; Muckle, J.
Inst: Nottingham University, Department of Adult Education, Centre for Research into the Education of Adults, 14-22 Shakespeare Street, Nottingham NG1 4FJ, United Kingdom.
Fin: Overseas Research Studentship; British Council.
foreign student; post-graduate; higher education; educational policy
étudiant étranger; étudiant niveau postuniversitaire; enseignement supérieur; politique de l'éducation
PROJECT DESCRIPTION

The research is a study of overseas student issues from a host country perspective. It focuses on the 'managing' of the growth of incoming postgraduate students and on the extent to which the needs and obligations perceived and accepted by the policy-making machinery shape the experience of students. The costs and benefits to the host country are considered in both immediate and longer terms.

12103   Evaluation of Derbyshire College B.Ed (Hon) Initial Degree.
GBR   1993
Research Date(s): 1987-1991
Roberts, R.; McKean, R.
Sup: Littler, G.; Dale, A.
Inst: Derbyshire College of Higher Education, Western Road, Mickleover, Derby DE3 5GX, United Kingdom.
teacher education; bachelors degree; evaluation; higher education
formation des enseignants; diplôme universitaire (1er cycle); évaluation; enseignement supérieur
PROJECT DESCRIPTION

The aims of this research project are to evaluate the B.Ed Hons degree at Derbyshire College for a number of different research perceptions, and in doing so to provide the faculty and the validating body with data upon which sound judgements can be made about the standing and the future of the degree; and to provide course management with data upon which valid course development can be based. The evaluation is based on the experience of the cohort of 1987 entry students and associated staff within the college and off-site, in particular teaching practice schools.

The mode of enquiry is through 'whole college evaluation' and 'research-based teaching' together with 'process evaluation' facilitated by the employment of a research assistant. The case study will cover approximately 120 students and 30+ staff.

12104   An evaluation of distance learning Inservice Education and Training of Teachers (INSET) in Wales.
GBR   1993
Research Date(s): 1989-
Banks, F.
Inst: University College of Swansea, Department of Education, Hendrefoilan, Swansea SA2 7NB, United Kingdom.
Fin: University of Wales.
further education of teachers; distance study; teacher behaviour; quality of education
perfectionnement des enseignants; enseignement à distance; comportement de l'enseignant; qualité de l'éducation
PROJECT DESCRIPTION

The problems of geographical isolation and the small number of teachers requiring Inservice Education and Training of Teachers (INSET) in some curriculum areas make distance learning an attractive option for many Welsh local education authorities. The study seeks to illuminate both effective course design and good practice in local education authority (LEA) management of teacher support.

Teachers in Wales, from all LEAs, involved in (initially) one distance learning INSET programme have been interviewed about their perceived progress and satisfaction with the course, its delivery, and the extent to which they think the course will alter their practice. An attempt will be made to design an evaluation method which will include a longitudinal study of how teachers change over time following an INSET experience. They were asked to give factual details of patterns of study and use of the materials. The INSET coordinators from the corresponding LEAs have been asked to supply details of the support they are prepared to give to the teachers in terms of fees, expenses, free time, etc., and have been interviewed to gather their opinion of the effectiveness of the programmes.

12105   Evaluation of information technology teacher training development programme.
GBR   1993
Research Date(s): 1989-1992
Blackman, S.; Brown, A.
Inst: Surrey University, Department of Educational Studies, Guildford GU2 5XH, United Kingdom.
Fin: Training Agency: TVEI Unit.
technical education; vocational education; teacher education; information technology
enseignement technique; enseignement professionnel; formation des enseignants; technologie de l'information
PROJECT DESCRIPTION

The Technical and Vocational Education Initiative (TVEI) Unit funded a major programme (of eight projects) to help teachers make more effective use of Information Technology (IT) in teaching and learning. This project aims to provide formative evaluation and support to all components of the programme. Methods used include the use of a rolling feedback strategy to support individual projects and to facilitate progress of the programme as a whole. The results of the research will be made available to those outside the programme at the end of the project.

Publ: Brown, A.J. Support for and management of information technology in schools. In: *Proceedings of the Seventh International Conference on Technology and Education*, Vol 2, 1992.

12106 Evaluation of Technical & Vocational Education Initiative developments.
GBR 1993
Research Date(s): 1989-1994
Gleeson, D.; Russell, V.
Inst: Keele University, Department of Education, Keele, Staffordshire ST5 5BG, United Kingdom.
Fin: Hereford & Worcester Local Education Authority.
technical education; vocational education
enseignement technique; enseignement professionnel
PROJECT DESCRIPTION
This is an evaluation of the Technical & Vocational Education Initiative (TVEI) in a local education authority, with the specific purpose of initiating and supporting practitioner research.

12107 Evaluation of the Lancashire Licensed Teachers Scheme.
GBR 1993
Research Date(s): 1992-1993
McHugh, G.
Sup: Saunders, M.
Inst: Lancaster University, Department of Educational Research, Centre for the Study of Education and Training, Cartmel College, Bailrigg, Lancaster LA1 4YW, United Kingdom.
Fin: Lancashire Local Education Authority.
teacher education; teaching profession
formation des enseignants; profession d'enseignant
PROJECT DESCRIPTION
This is a brief evaluation of the Lancashire Licensed Teachers Scheme which has been jointly delivered by Lancashire Local Education Authority and the two collaborating colleges of education, which has been running since September 1991.

12108 Evaluation of the licensed teacher route to Qualified Teacher Status.
GBR 1993
Research Date(s): 1990-1992
Macneil, M.
Sup: Stoney, S.
Inst: National Foundation for Educational Research, The Mere, Upton Park, Slough SL1 2DQ, United Kingdom.
Fin: Department for Education.
teacher education; student teacher; teaching profession
formation des enseignants; élève-maître; profession d'enseignant
PROJECT DESCRIPTION
The evaluation of the new licensed teacher route to Qualified Teacher Status (QTS) has aimed to provide a detailed overview of the structure and operation of this route and to monitor its effects and implications at local education authority (LEA), training institution and school level.
The evaluation has been conducted mainly through case-study and survey methods, with some background documentary analysis. Three surveys have been conducted during 1991, designed to investigate the experience of schools in implementing this route, with questionnaires for licensed teachers, their headteachers, and mentors. A further two surveys conducted in 1992, were designed to explore the roles of local education authorities and institutions of higher education (IHEs). The case-study work has focused on interviews with the key personnel involved in the training of licensed teachers, within a wide representation of different ways of implementing the licensed teachers route.
A final report was presented to the Department for Education in Autumn 1992 and dissemination opportunities are being considered.

12109 Evaluation of the Lothian Region Technical and Vocational Education Initiative (TVEI) Extension.
GBR 1993
Research Date(s): 1989-1994
Black, H.; Malcolm, H.
Inst: Scottish Council for Research in Education, 15 St John Street, Edinburgh EH8 8JR, United Kingdom.
Fin: Lothian Region.
technical education; vocational education
enseignement technique; enseignement professionnel
PROJECT DESCRIPTION
The team provides an ongoing evaluation service to Lothian's Technical and Vocational Education Initiative (TVEI) Extension project - contact with the project being sustained through membership of the TVEI Evaluation Group. Evaluative studies and other services are negotiated throughout the lifetime of the evaluation. Three specific topics identified to date are: the project's school/college week; mechanisms for neighbourhood management group activity and ideas sharing; and curriculum auditing.

12110 Evaluierung des Studiums der internationalen Berufspaedagogik am Beispiel einer jemenitischen Stipendiatengruppe. (Evaluation of international occupational pedagogics courses, with particular reference to a group of stipendiaries from Yemen.)
DEU 1993
Research Date(s): 1991-1993
Przyklenk, K.
Sup: Noelker, H.
Inst: Gesamthochschule-Universitaet Kassel, FB 02 Berufspaedagogik, Polytechnik, Arbeitswissenschaft, Fach Berufs- und Wirtschaftsspaedagogik, Heinrich-Plett-Strasse 40, D-3500 Kassel.
Fin: Deutsche Stiftung fuer internationale Entwicklung.
university studies; vocational education; sciences of education; foreign student; scholarship; didactics
études universitaires; enseignement professionnel; sciences de l'éducation; étudiant étranger; bourse d'études; didactique
PROJECT DESCRIPTION
Inhalt: Erfolgs- und Qualitaetserhebung - Curriculum kritisch (hochschuldidaktisch).
Geographischer Raum: Kassel.
Untersuchter Zeitraum: 1988-1991.
Vorgehensweise: Qualitative Evaluationsforschung. Untersuchungsdesign: Methodenforschung; Fallstudie.
Datengewinnung: Gruppendiskussion (Stichprobe: 7; Stipendiatengruppe; Auswahlverfahren: total. Stichprobe: 3; wissenschaftliche Mitarbeiter; Auswahlverfahren: total. Stichprobe: 6; Tutoren; Auswahlverfahren: total). Expertengespraech (Stichprobe: 2; Lehrkoerper; Auswahlverfahren: total). Inhaltsanalyse (Stichprobe: 7; Berichte/Examen; Auswahlverfahren: total). Primaererhebung: Feldarbeit von Mitarbeitern des Projektes durchgefuehrt; Datenerstellung auf der Basis von bereits vorliegenden Materialien wie Texten, Akten, Statistiken.
Auswertung: Interpretation.

12111 Experiential learning in initial teacher education.
GBR 1993
Research Date(s): 1990-1995
Tyler, K.
Inst: Loughborough University of Technology, Department of Education, Loughborough LE11 3TU, United Kingdom.
teacher education; experiential learning; learning process
formation des enseignants; apprentissage par la pratique; apprentissage
PROJECT DESCRIPTION
This is an investigation into experiential learning in teacher education. The work will focus on the development of interpersonal skills within an experiential workshop setting with primary Post-Graduate Certificate of Education (PGCE) students, and the relevance of such an approach to the students' overall preparation for teaching in a primary school.

12112 Exploring the gender gap in primary schools.
IRL 1994
Research Date(s): 1990-1993
Lewis, Mary.
Inst: Educational Research Centre, St Patrick's College, Dublin 9, Ireland.
coeducational school; boys' school; girls' school; sex difference; sex role; stereotype; teacher behaviour
école mixte; école de garçons; école de filles; différence de sexe; rôle sexuel; stéréotype; comportement de l'enseignant
PROJECT DESCRIPTION
A national survey involving 600 primary schools was carried out to examine provision and practices relating to gender in single-sex and mixed schools. Information was obtained in postal questionnaires from principals and teachers at junior, middle, and senior levels in the primary cycle.
Gender differences were found in the staffing structures of schools, in some aspects of provision, and in how girls and boys are perceived and treated by their teachers. The differences were found to vary by sex category of school. Provision in boys' schools is poorer in the creative and expressive arts, nature study and sex education. In girls' schools, which tend to be staffed entirely by female teachers, team sports are less well developed. Sex-stereotyping in the practices and perceptions of teachers is more marked in senior than in junior classes. Teachers in mixed schools, more frequently than teachers in single-sex schools, perceive differences between the genders in a variety of behavioural characteristics.

12113 Fitting into institutions.
GBR 1992
Research Date(s): 1990-1991
Crawford, E.
Inst: Moray House College, Centre for Leisure Research, Holyrood Road, Edinburgh EH8 8AQ, United Kingdom.
school; teacher-pupil relation
école; relation maître-élève
PROJECT DESCRIPTION
The aims of the research are to examine the experience of students in placement schools; examine the experience of schools accepting students; identify institutional factors (as opposed to personal factors) which affect

the experience of both parties; evaluate these factors with regard to beneficial and detrimental aspects of the experiences and develop induction and preparation procedures and compare with present preparation techniques.

12114 Fitting into institutions.
GBR 1993
Research Date(s): 1990-1992
Crawford, E.
Inst: Heriot-Watt University, Moray House Institute of Education, Holyrood Road, Edinburgh EH8 8AQ, United Kingdom.
teacher education; student teacher; teaching experience; teaching practice
formation des enseignants; élève-maître; expérience de l'enseignement; pratique pédagogique
PROJECT DESCRIPTION
The aims of the research are to: (1) examine the experience of teacher education students in placement schools; (2) examine the experience of schools accepting students; (3) identify institutional factors (as opposed to personal factors) which affect the experience of both parties; (4) evaluate these factors with regard to beneficial and detrimental aspects of the experiences; and (5) develop induction and preparation procedures and compare with present preparation techniques.

12115 Focused mentoring for the National Curriculum.
GBR 1993
Research Date(s): 1992
McNamara, D.
Inst: Hull University, School of Education, Cottingham Road, Hull HU6 7RX, United Kingdom.
Fin: Paul Hamlyn Foundation.
teacher education; teaching practice; student teacher; supervision; training personnel
formation des enseignants; pratique pédagogique; élève-maître; surveillance; personnel de formation
PROJECT DESCRIPTION
The study aims to explore the contributions which teacher trainers (tutors) and teachers responsible for the student teachers during periods of school practice (mentors) make to students' practical preparations for teaching. The study will focus upon the teaching of mathematics at all four key stages of the National Curriculum. A case study design is being adopted, supplemented by classroom observation and focused interviews.

12116 Follow-up study on the initial training of newly qualified teachers - a feasibility study.
GBR 1993
Research Date(s): 1991-1992
Powney, J.; Harlen, W.; Martin, S.; Holroyd, C.
Inst: Scottish Council for Research in Education, 15 St John Street, Edinburgh EH8 8JR, United Kingdom.
Fin: Department of Education and Science.
teacher education; college of education; probationary teacher; student teacher; teaching post; initial employment
formation des enseignants; centre de formation des enseignants; enseignant stagiaire; élève-maître; poste d'enseignement; premier emploi
PROJECT DESCRIPTION
This study, initiated by the Council for the Accreditation of Teacher Education, and financed by the Department of Education and Science (DES) will focus on the match between initial teacher training and the requirements of the first posts held by newly qualified teachers.
Evidence will be sought about current practices in Northern Ireland, Wales and England of tracking students from their initial teacher training through their early professional experience and how such information could or does provide feedback to their initial training institutions. Informants will include newly qualified teachers and staff from initial teacher training institutions, local education authorities/Library Boards and schools.
From the evidence collected by questionnaire and interview in the initial stage of the project, the research team will draft a framework for a possible national scheme to follow up initial teacher training. This framework will be the basis for a series of discussions with small groups exploring the feasibility, desirability, nature, content and cost of a possible national scheme. In this consultative exercise, the discussion groups will involve representatives from Northern Ireland, Wales and England drawn from the same categories of informants as the first stage of the project.
The outcome of the study will be recommendations to the DES on the feasibility of a national scheme for intitial training institutions to appraise their effectiveness by tracking their newly qualified teachers as they begin their careers.

12117 Fonctionnement des établissements scolaires et efficacité d'ensemble du système.
FRA 1993
Research Date(s): 1990-1991
Ballion, Robert.

Inst: Ecole des hautes études en sciences sociales, CNRS URA/985, Centre d'analyse et d'intervention sociologiques, 54 Bd Raspail, 75270 Paris Cedex 06, France.
Fin: Ministère de l'éducation, Direction de l'évaluation et de la prospective.
education system; educational institution; questionnaire; OECD; achievement measurement
système d'enseignement; établissement d'enseignement; questionnaire; OCDE; mesure du rendement
PROJECT DESCRIPTION
Objectifs: Il s'agit de construire un cadre d'analyse des établissements scolaires permettant de mesurer les facteurs d'efficacité.
Méthodologie: Recherche internationale faite dans le cadre de l'OCDE; un travail en commission aboutit à la réalisation d'un questionnaire.

Publ: *Fonctionnement des établissements et efficacité d'ensemble du système. Projet indicateur de l'enseignement.* Paris: OCDE-CERI, 1991.

12118 Formation continue des enseignant-e-s de langue des écoles de commerce et des écoles professionnelles commerciales en Suisse.
CHE 1993
Research Date(s): 1991-1993
Schurmans, Marie-Noëlle; Bezzola, Graziella; Stahl, Anne; Sedioli, Peter; Tettamanti, Enrico.
Inst: Université de Genève, Faculté de psychologie et des sciences de l'éducation (FPSE), 11 route de Drize, 1227 Carouge, Suisse.
Office fédéral de l'industrie, des arts et métiers et du travail (OFIAMT), Bundesgasse 8, 3003 Berne, Suisse
further education of teachers; commercial training; language teaching; educational need; teacher
perfectionnement des enseignants; formation commerciale; enseignement des langues; besoin d'éducation; enseignant
PROJECT DESCRIPTION
L'Office fédéral de l'industrie, des arts et métiers et du travail (OFIAMT) a mandaté une équipe de recherche de réaliser une enquête portant sur les besoins de formation continue des enseignant-e-s de langue des écoles de commerce et des écoles professionnelles commerciales en Suisse. La démarche d'enquête se déroule en quatre temps.
Après la première phase, durant laquelle le contexte a été étudié (formation initiale des enseignant-e-s, programmes de formation continue, développement historique de ces programmes, types d'enseignement, etc.), les personnes menant cette recherche ont contacté un premier échantillon (réduit) se composant de personnel enseignant, de responsables de formation et d'experts, ceci afin d'explorer le terrain au travers d'interviews qualitatives.
Dans une troisième phase, un questionnaire a été adressé à tous les enseignant-e-s de langue dans les écoles de commerce ou écoles professionnelles commerciales en Suisse (N = env. 3000). La première partie de ce questionnaire concerne la formation initiale, les conditions d'exercice de la profession, la situation familiale, la période de la carrière - des éléments donc qui sont censés déterminer l'attitude face aux offres de formation. La seconde partie vise l'étude des représentations sociales de la formation continue par associations de mots.
Une quatrième phase, encore à venir, se fera encore une fois au moyen d'entretiens qualitatifs auprès d'un certain nombre de personnes contactées dans la deuxième phase. Il s'agira d'approfondir l'un ou l'autre point résultant de l'analyse des réponses aux questionnaires.

12119 Graduate education in the United Kingdom.
GBR 1993
Research Date(s): 1991-1992
Kogan, M.; Becher, R.; Henkel, M.
Inst: Brunel University, Department of Government, Uxbridge UB8 3PH, United Kingdom; Sussex University, Institute of Continuing and Professional Education, Sussex House, Falmer, Brighton BN1 9RH, United Kingdom.
Fin: The Nuffield Foundation.
graduate study; educational policy; higher education
supérieur deuxième cycle; politique de l'éducation; enseignement supérieur
PROJECT DESCRIPTION
The research concerns developments in British higher education at two levels. The recent history of the policy of graduate education is reviewed with a view to creating a policy analysis in which the conflicting objectives of graduate education are analysed; the governmental machinery for generating policy in graduate education described; and the relationship between graduate education and staffing of higher education put under scrutiny. This part of the study leads to the critique of existing policies and proposals for their improvement.
The second level of the study is that of micro-analyses of graduate education in different disciplinary areas. The analysis includes a summation of the essential characteristics of the discipline concerned, the way in which it recruits its students, the extent to which there is pre-requisite structured training before research is undertaken; the expectations within the discipline, and the relationship between graduate training and recruitment for higher education staffing and cognate professions.

The methods involved are a study of secondary sources and interviews at both levels.

12120   Graduates becoming primary teachers: a study of the development of reflective professionalism by graduates following a school-based one-year primary course in initial teacher education.
GBR   1993
Research Date(s): 1987-1991
Heaney, S.
Sup: Golby, M.
Inst: Chester College of Higher Education, Cheyney Road, Chester CH1 4BJ, United Kingdom; Exeter University, Department of Education, St Luke's, Exeter EX1 2LU, United Kingdom.
teacher education; student teacher; teaching profession; probationary teacher
formation des enseignants; élève-maître; profession d'enseignant; enseignant stagiaire
PROJECT DESCRIPTION
    Case study material will be assembled in order to examine the development of reflective professionalism in graduates following a one-year school-based course of initial teacher training. Work will be done with sequential intakes, over three or more years, of 25 in number.

12121   Heilpädagogischer Stützunterricht: Ergebnisse einer Meinungsumfrage in Deutschfreiburg.   (L'appui pédagogique: résultats d'une enquête dans la partie alémanique du canton de Fribourg.)
CHE   1994
Research Date(s): 1991-1992
Niedermann, Albin; Bless, Gérard; Sassenroth, Martin; Delacrétaz, Caroline; Emmenegger, Brigitte; Schmid, Chantal.
Inst: Universität Freiburg, Heilpädagogisches Institut, Abteilung Schulische Heilpädagogik, Petrus-Canisius-Gasse 21, 1700 Freiburg, Schweiz.
special education; remedial teaching; educational provision; integration
enseignement spécial; soutien pédagogique; scolarisation; intégration
PROJECT DESCRIPTION
    Der Heilpädagogische Stützunterricht (sonderpädagogische Betreuung schulschwacher Kinder im Rahmen ihrer Normalklasse) wurde im deutschsprachigen Teil des Kantons Freiburg 1989 eingeführt. Gemäss dem Freiburger Modell richtet sich die Massnahme nur an Kinder in ländlichen Gebieten, wo die Schülerzahlen zu gering sind, als dass Sonderklassen geführt werden könnten, bzw. wo die Führung von Sonderklassen für die meisten Kinder extrem lange Schulwege mit sich brächte. Gemäss den herrschenden freiburgischen Vorstellungen ist Unterricht in Sonderklassen aber nach wie vor die optimale Form der Unterstützung, und der Heilpädagogische Stützunterricht beschränkt sich deshalb auf die ersten drei Schuljahre; bis dann soll ein Kind entweder seinen Rückstand aufgeholt haben oder dann einer Kleinklasse zugewiesen werden. Im Schuljahr 1990/1991, als die hier beschriebene Untersuchung stattfand, betraf der Heilpädagogische Stützunterricht insgesamt 24 Kinder in acht deutschfreiburgischen Gemeinden.
    Die hier beschriebene Meinungsumfrage bei den Betroffenen wurde von drei Studentinnen durchgeführt, die sich selber zu schulischen Heilpädagoginnen ausbilden lassen. Es wurden etwa 60 jeweils rund 40 Minuten dauernde Interviews mit Eltern, Lehrpersonen, Expertinnen und Experten sowie Behördemitgliedern geführt. Die Auswertung zeigt etwa, dass der Heilpädagogische Stützunterricht als taugliches Instrument anerkannt wird. Eine Ausdehnung wird gewünscht, und zwar sowohl was die Quantität der Interventionen je Kind betrifft wie auch auf die Schuljahre 4 bis 6; Kinder, die dank Unterstützung dem Normalunterricht folgen können, sollten weiterhin von der Massnahme profitieren können, und die Sonderklasse sollte jenen vorbehalten bleiben, die auch mit Stützunterricht dem "Normalunterricht" nicht zu folgen vermögen. Von Expertenseite vor allem wird einer weiter gehenden Ausdehnung das Wort geredet: Heilpädagogischer Stützunterricht sollte in allen Gemeinden möglich sein, ungeachtet ihrer Einwohner- und Schülerzahlen, da das Axiom von der Überlegenheit der gesonderten Schulung keine Gültigkeit mehr beanspruchen kann. Eine solche Ausdehnung des Modells würde aber eine vertiefte Auseinandersetzung mit dem Integrationsgedanken an der Basis bedingen: eine Anerkennung des Rechts der Kinder auf Verschiedenheit und eine Durchsetzung des Gedankens, dass nicht notwendigerweise alle Kinder zur gleichen Zeit und im gleichen Rhythmus das gleiche zu lernen brauchen.
Publ: Niedermann, Albin; Bless, Gérard & Sassenroth, Martin. *Heilpädagogischer Stützunterricht: Ergebnisse einer Meinungsumfrage in Deutschfreiburg.* Luzern: SZH/SPC, 1992, 48 Seiten (Edition SZH; Aspekte; Nr. 44).

12122   Higher education in the Czech and Slovak Federal Republic: a guide for foreign students.
CSK   1993
Research Date(s): 1992
Hrabinská, Mária; Tollingerová, Dana; Halberštát, Ladislav.
Inst: Ústav informácií a prognóz školstva, mládeže a telovýchovy (Institute of Information and Prognoses of Education, Youth and Sports), Staré Grunty 52, 842 44 Bratislava, Czech and Slovak Federal Republic; Centre for Higher Education Studies, U Lužickeho semináře 13, 118 00 Prague 1-Malá Strana, Czech and Slovak Federal Republic. Ministerstvo školstva, mládeže a športu Slovenskej republiky (Ministry of Education, Youth and Sports of the Slovak Republic), Hlboka 2, 813 30 Bratislava, Czech and Slovak Federal Republic; Ministerstvo školstva, mládeže a telovýchovy Českej republiky (Ministry of Education, Youth and Sports of the Czech Republic), Hlboká 2, 813 30 Bratislava, Czech and Slovak Federal Republic; Karmelitská 8, 118 00 Prague 1, Czech and Slovak Federal Republic.
Fin: Tempus Office, Bratislava.
higher education; university; university faculty; reference book; university studies
enseignement supérieur; université; faculté universitaire; ouvrage de référence; études universitaires
PROJECT DESCRIPTION
    The aim of this work was to prepare a publication which would provide detailed information on the higher education system in the Czech and Slovak Federal Republic (CSFR). The publication would be aimed at foreign readers, especially those interested in course programmes in higher education institutions in the CSFR.
    The work resulted in a guide which is divided into three parts. The first part includes information about: courses at individual universities, requirements for entrance examinations, state final examinations, recognition of foreign certificates and degrees, accommodation and student services. This part also contains diagrams of course programmes.
    The second part is devoted to information about: the history of individual universities, their organizational and administrative structure, and basic statistical data.
    The third part of the guide contains: various directories of higher education institutes in the CSFR, a description of regional structures of higher education in the CSFR, a list of Czechoslovak embassies, a list of other important addresses, and basic statistical data.

12123   Hudba 20. století v přípravě učitelů hudební výchovy. (Twentieth-century music in music teacher education courses.)
CSK   1994
Research Date(s): 1991-1993
Drábek, V.; Petrová, E.; Duzbaba, O.; Rob, J.; Palkovská, J.; Hurník, L.
Sup: Helus, Z.
Inst: Pedagogická fakulta Univerzity Karlovy (Charles University, Faculty of Education), M.D. Rettigové 4, 116 39 Praha 1, Czech Republic. Ministerstvo školství, mládeže a tělovýchovy (Ministry of Education, Youth and Physical Education), Karmelitská 7, 118 00 Praha 1, Czech Republic
teacher education; music education; curriculum development
formation des enseignants; éducation musicale; élaboration de programmes d'études
PROJECT DESCRIPTION
    Background: The current historical approach to teaching music fails to realize the full potential of music education. Because music teachers have insufficient knowledge of contemporary music, they refuse to deal with music that can make a significant contribution to the development of children's ideas and emotions. Teachers need to be prepared to deal effectively with contemporary music in the classroom.
    Aims: The project aims to update the content, forms and methods of music teacher education in faculties of education, with a view to strengthening the position of contemporary music in the music education curriculum. More specifically, the research seeks to: (1) fill the gap in music teachers' knowledge through a description of trends in the development of artificial and non-artificial 20th-century music; and (2) to define appropriate methods for teaching this topic.
    Hypothesis: Appreciation of the stylistic pluralism of 20th-century music requires an understanding of different musical systems, i.e. the ability to "retune" oneself to different codes of music language. These codes, as models of musical communication, can best be learnt through creative musical activities.
Publ: Sborník, *Tvořivost jako základní dimenze moderní hudební pedagogiky.* Praha: SVI Pedagogické fakulty UK, 1992, 182p.

12124   Hudson Shaw and the university extension movement.
GBR   1993
Research Date(s): 1988-1994
Marriott, J.
Inst: Leeds University, School of Education, Leeds LS2 9JT, United Kingdom.
adult education; history of education; workers' education; biography; educationalist
éducation des adultes; histoire de l'éducation; éducation ouvrière; biographie; pédagogue
PROJECT DESCRIPTION
    This research is a biography of G.W. Hudson Shaw. Although Shaw was always acknowledged as one of the greatest figures of the Oxford Extension Movement, he has not received serious biographical attention. The study will set the record right about his origins, his early life and per-

sonal/family circumstances. It will treat him as the epitome of the Oxford Extension Movement, and examine the origins and character of his educational beliefs and commitments. Leading sub-themes will be: use of the ideas of John Ruskin; the attitude to working-class education and the effects of a changing political climate; relations to the early Workers' Educational Association (WEA); his position as an ordained clergyman of the Church of England; his relationship to Maude Royden, feminist and advocate of female ordination. The method of research is conventionally historical and biographical.

12125 Humboldt Universitaet - Freie Universitaet: ein Vergleich der Entwicklung der unterschiedlichen Funktionen und der Beschraenkungen der Autonomien und der Dysfunktionen der beiden Berliner Universitaeten. (Humboldt Universitaet - Freie Universitaet: a comparison of the development of the different functions and the restrictions of the autonomy and the shortcomings of the two Berlin universities.)

DEU 1993

Research Date(s): 1991-1993

Rabehl, B.; et al.

Sup: Loennendonker, S.

Inst: Freie Universitaet Berlin, ZI fuer Sozialwissenschaftliche Forschung, Malteserstr. 74-100, D-1000 Berlin 46.

university; Berlin; Germany - Federal Republic; German DR; autonomy; educational administration

université; Berlin; Allemagne RFA; Allemagne RDA; autonomie; administration de l'enseignement

PROJECT DESCRIPTION

Geographischer Raum: Berlin.

12126 The idea of 'university extension' across the English-speaking world, 1867-1914.

GBR 1993

Research Date(s): 1991-1993

Coles, J.

Sup: Marriott, J.

Inst: Leeds University, School of Education, Leeds LS2 9JT, United Kingdom.

Fin: Leverhulme Trust.

adult education; continuing education; history of education; comparative education

éducation des adultes; éducation permanente; histoire de l'éducation; éducation comparée

PROJECT DESCRIPTION

The project continues an earlier Leverhulme-funded enquiry into the intercultural links between adult education in England and Germany since the late 19th century. Earlier research revealed the brief but significant influence of the English idea of 'university extension' (a form of adult education) in Germany and Austria. It also became clear that a more substantial 'export' of this idea was to other parts of the English-speaking world.

The new project is investigating the export of university extension philosophy and method to the United States, as evidenced in the work of the American Society for the Extension of University Teaching (Philadelphia) and the new University of Chicago. The influence of the American Chautauqua system (a form of summer school) on English adult education will also be studied. The export of university extension to British Empire countries (primarily Australasia, but also Canada and Cape Colony) will also be investigated.

12127 The identification of the feasibility of the preparation of Master of Arts (MA) Dissertations in distance mode in developing countries.

GBR 1993

Research Date(s): 1990-1992

Dickinson, N.

Inst: Heriot-Watt University, Moray House Institute of Education, Holyrood Road, Edinburgh EH8 8AQ, United Kingdom.

distance study; academic degree; developing country

enseignement à distance; grade universitaire; pays en développement

PROJECT DESCRIPTION

The aims of the research are: (a) to identify the feasibility of preparing and writing Master of Arts (MA) dissertations in distance mode; and (b) to identify the areas of difficulty in writing dissertations in distance mode in respect of resources, local supervision, external (Moray House) supervision, and time factors. The project aims to identify difficulties inherent in distance learning and in country dissertation mixing and to seek solutions.

12128 Il problema dell'efficacia/efficienza del sistema di istruzione: individuazione di soluzioni organizzative adeguate per la scuola secondaria superiore. (The problem of the efficiency/effectiveness of the education system: organizational solutions for upper secondary schools.)

ITA 1993

Research Date(s): 1990-1991

Muscella, F.; Proserpio, S.; Tacchi, E.M.; Guzzi, V.; Garavelli, M.A.; Ravotto, P.F.; Vimercati, M.

Sup: Cesareo, V.

Inst: Dipartimento di Sociologia, Università Cattolica di Milano (Department of Sociology, Catholic University of Milan), Largo A. Gemelli 1, 20123 Milano, Italy.

Fin: Ministero della Pubblica Istruzione, Ufficio Studi e Programmazione.

education system; upper secondary; quality of education; aims of education; assessment; school; performance

système d'enseignement; secondaire deuxième cycle; qualité de l'éducation; finalité de l'éducation; appréciation; école; performance

PROJECT DESCRIPTION

Aims: The study examines the problem of the efficiency/effectiveness of the education system, first along general lines and then with particular reference to the Italian situation. The aims are: to identify a basic structural model; to describe an experimental educational project in an Italian upper secondary school; and to propose some alternatives for the interpretation of the upper secondary school model and for organizational innovation.

Methods: Identification of the problem, formulation of the hypothesis, investigation, analysis and critical discussion of the data, presentation of results, conclusions, and proposals.

Results: The study starts by identifying the theoretical framework and the norms in practice. Within this framework, it examines how upper secondary schools function. Conclusions are drawn. Following an examination of the most relevant literature, the study elaborates a scheme to which the Italian upper school can be related. Subsequently, the study explores the organizational dimension of the school, possible models, educational autonomy, and innovation. It goes on to examine the organizational model of the traditional Italian school, pointing out the principal problems: rigidity, limited possibility for the use of human resources, and a lack of checks and evaluative assessments of the efficacy of educational procedures. The study concludes with the analysis of new organizational models such as: open systems, relations between the school and the environment, problems connected to the realization of innovation.

12129 L'impact de la formation sur les trajectoires des adultes peu qualifiés: une approche contextuelle.

FRA 1993

Research Date(s): 1990-

Foudi, Rachid; Stankiewicz, François; Trelcat, Marie-Hélène.

Inst: Université de Lille I, Centre lillois d'études et de recherches sociologiques et économiques, CNRS URA/345, Laboratoire de sociologie du travail, de l'éducation et de l'emploi, Institut de Sociologie, 59655 Villeneuve d'Ascq Cedex, France.

Fin: Ministère de la recherche et de la technologie, Programme technologie, emploi, travail; Agence nationale pour l'emploi; CNRS-IFRESI.

adult education; unskilled worker; unemployed; vocational training; employee; comparative achievement

éducation des adultes; travailleur non-qualifié; chômeur; formation professionnelle; salarié; rendement comparé

PROJECT DESCRIPTION

Objectifs: Le contexte dans lequel la formation est délivrée détermine de façon essentielle son efficacité ou plus généralement la nature de son impact. De ce point de vue, on doit s'attendre à ce que le contenu de la formation mais aussi les transformations qu'elle est susceptible d'opérer diffèrent de façon sensible selon que la formation s'appliquera à des individus en situation d'emploi, de licenciement économique ou de chômage.

Méthodologie: Différentes investigations sont menées relatives à différents contextes: (1) exploitation de matériaux d'enquêtes collectés auprès de chômeurs de longue durée du Bassin minier de la Région Nord-Pas de Calais pour reconstituer les trajectoires professionnelles suivies; (2) enquête auprès d'une vingtaine d'entreprises sensibilisées au problème de la formation des salariés ayant un bas niveau de qualification de la région Nord-Pas de Calais; (3) enquête auprès des demandeurs d'emploi de la région Nord-Pas de Calais entrés en formation ou ayant retrouvé un emploi.

Publ: Foudi, Rachid; Stankiewicz, François & Trelcat, Marie-Hélène. *L'impact de la formation sur les trajectoires des adultes peu qualifiés: une approche contextuelle.* Rapport au Ministère de la recherche et de la technologie, janvier-novembre 1990.

12130 The implications for nursing education in Cyprus commensurate with joining the European Community: a problem study.

GBR 1993

Research Date(s): 1991-1994

Antoniou, M.

Sup: Nolan, R.

Inst: University of Wales, College of Cardiff School of Education, Sengennhydd Road, Cardiff CF2 4AG, United Kingdom; Nicosia General Hospital, School of Nursing, Nicosia, Cyprus.

vocational education; nurse; comparative research; Cyprus; United Kingdom

enseignement professionnel; infirmier; recherche comparative; Chypre; Royaume-Uni

PROJECT DESCRIPTION

The research aims to explore the changes required for nursing education in Cyprus commensurate with the EC directive re. nursing to be implemented in 1993. The study will compare nurse education in Cyprus with the changes in the United Kingdom in the implementation of Project 2000 and the need to conform to the EC directives as Cyprus has applied to join the European Community.

12131 Improving the problem solving skills of learners in vocational programmes.
GBR   1993
Research Date(s): 1991-1992
Soden, R.; Holmes, S.; Dumbleton, P.
Inst: Jordanhill College of Education, Scottish School of Further Education, Southbrae Drive, Jordanhill, Glasgow G13 1PP, United Kingdom.
Fin: Scottish Office Education Department; Training, Enterprise & Education Directorate.
vocational education; problem solving; thinking; further education of teachers; post-compulsory education
enseignement professionnel; résolution de problème; pensée; perfectionnement des enseignants; enseignement postobligatoire
PROJECT DESCRIPTION

This project aims to illuminate the staff development required to enable further education lecturers to provide a 'thinking curriculum' in catering, hairdressing, text processing and electrical circuit work.

12132 Indagine sulla sperimentazione dei Programmi P.N.I. di matematica e fisica in Abruzzo. (A study of the experiment in Abruzzo with mathematics and physics programmes developed as part of the National Computer Science Project (PNI).)
ITA   1994
Research Date(s): 1991
Verini, Antonio; et al.
Inst: Istituto Regionale Ricerca Sperimentazione e Aggiornamento Educativi d'Abruzzo - IRRSAE (Regional Institute for Educational Research, Innovation and Teacher Training - Abruzzo), Via Aldo Moro 30, 67100 L'Aquila, Italy.
Ministero della Pubblica Istruzione (Ministry of Education), Viale Trastevere 76, 00100 Roma, Italy
further education of teachers; upper secondary; physics; mathematics; teaching programme; experimental education
perfectionnement des enseignants; secondaire deuxième cycle; physique; mathématiques; programme d'enseignement; pédagogie expérimentale
PROJECT DESCRIPTION

The study investigated all upper secondary schools in the region through the use of three questionnaires: (1) for teachers experimenting with the programme; (2) for teachers not engaged in the experiment; (3) for the experimentation of the PNI mathematics and physics programmes currently underway in schools of the region.

The contribution IRRSAE could make in the wider framework of the PNI would be to offer support courses to teachers participating in the experiment. The overall aim was to organize the participation of IRRSAE Abruzzo in the PNI with regard to the needs of Abruzzo schools and the current situation in these schools. More specific objectives were: (1) to provide a clear picture of the PNI experiment in Abruzzo; (2) to ascertain the willingness of mathematics and physics teachers to participate in support courses.

Results: The results have been compiled in a report which has been used to devise a way for IRRSAE Abruzzo to provide support to teachers participating in the experiment.

12133 Indagine sulle scuole italiane all'estero. (Investigation of Italian schools abroad.)
ITA   1993
Research Date(s): 1988-1989
Bolognini, S.; Iori, A.; Marrazzo, A.; Venditti, C.
Sup: De Napoli, D.
Inst: Istituto di Studi Politici "S. Pio V" (Institute of Political Studies "S. Pio V"), Piazza Navoria 93, 00186 Roma, Italy.
Fin: Ministero della Pubblica Istruzione, Ufficio Studi e Programmazione.
foreign school; international relations; international understanding; educational policy; abroad; study abroad
école à l'étranger; relations internationales; compréhension internationale; politique de l'éducation; à l'étranger; études à l'étranger
PROJECT DESCRIPTION

Aims: The study examined the general principles that inspire the activities of Italian schools, both state and private, outside Italy. More specifi-

cally, the study aimed to describe the historical, cultural, and social context in which Italian policies regarding schools abroad have developed.

Methods: The investigation involved a contrastive analysis of the real situation and several ideological viewpoints. Questionnaires were used, consisting of ten open-ended questions. The theoretical-ideological aspects were taken from documents. The focus was on criteria of exemplariness, interdependence and selectivity.

Results: Italian schools abroad aim at promoting and diffusing the Italian language and culture in the Italian community living abroad as well as in the host country. They encourage the integration of Italian pupils and Italian educational institutions in the local cultural and socio-economic community, while maintaining contact with the native culture, language and society in general. They aim to foster a critical spirit in pupils, taking as a model the Italian pedagogical system based on the harmonious integration of humanist and technical-scientific culture. They value the factors of cohesion between the two societies, minimizing those of diversity. They reflect the principal shortcomings of Italian schools, such as a low degree of professionalism among locally recruited teaching staff. The tendencies observed can be ascribed to: a predisposition to bilateral cultural agreements, cooperation with local schools and the local community in integration processes, and the establishment of an ever-increasing number of bilingual schools.

12134 Individual action plan project.
GBR   1993
Research Date(s): 1991-1995
Tomley, D.
Inst: Leicester University, School of Education, University Road, Leicester LE1 7RH, United Kingdom.
Fin: Training, Enterprise & Education Directorate.
teacher education; post-graduate study
formation des enseignants; supérieur troisième cycle
PROJECT DESCRIPTION

The project aims to introduce the process of Action Planning within the PGCE (Postgraduate Certificate of Education) courses at Leicester University. The project will follow the PGCE students who secure posts locally for two years, to see how individual action planning is built upon during their induction period.

12135 L'informatica al servizio dei giovani della formazione empirica. (L'informatique au service des jeunes en formation professionnelle élémentaire.)
CHE   1994
Research Date(s): 1990-1993
Schürch, Dieter; Reggiori, Renato; Thierstein, Christof; Lupi, Monica; Antognini, Cesare.
Inst: Istituto svizzero di pedagogia per la formazione professionale (ISPFP), Sezione dip lingua italiana, Via Besso 84, 6900 Lugano-Massagno, Suisse.
Fin: Ufficio federale delle arti e mestieri, dell'industria e del lavoro.
vocational education; computer; vocational training; didactic use of computer; teaching aid
enseignement professionnel; ordinateur; formation professionnelle; usage didactique de l'ordinateur; moyen d'enseignement
PROJECT DESCRIPTION

Les nouvelles technologies informatiques ont profondément bouleversé le monde du travail et elles apparaissent évidemment aussi dans les écoles. Partout on peut constater des efforts visant à initier formateurs et élèves aux nouvelles méthodes de travail. A première vue, les innovations semblent favoriser surtout les jeunes qui disposent non seulement de la motivation de base, mais aussi des moyens intellectuels qui facilitent l'assimilation de connaissances nouvelles. L'introduction de l'informatique semble donc élargir le fossé entre les "bons" et les "mauvais" élèves. La recherche présentée ici veut attirer l'attention sur les jeunes de la seconde catégorie. Il s'agit de trouver la stratégie optimale pour intégrer l'ordinateur dans l'enseignement professionnel donné aux apprentis en formation élémentaire et de voir, par exemple, si un enseignement assisté par ordinateur pourrait aider l'élève à s'approprier des connaissances que l'école obligatoire n'a pas réussi à lui communiquer. Le projet consiste en un cours-pilote systématiquement observé et évalué, dont chaque phase est planifiée sur la base des résultats de la phase antérieure. Il est réalisé grâce au soutien financier de la Confédération dans le cadre des mesures spéciales en faveur du perfectionnement professionnel.

Publ: ISPFP. *L'informatica al servizio dei giovani della formazione empirica: rapporto intermedio.* Massagno, luglio 1991, 25p. + allegati.
ISPFP. *L'informatica al servizio dei giovani della formazione empirica: secondo rapporto intermedio.* Massagno, luglio 1992, 41p. + allegati.

12136 Initial teacher training and professional development within dimensions of classroom activity ambiguity.
GBR   1993
Research Date(s): 1990-1997
Simco, N.
Sup: Smith, L.
Inst: Lancaster University, Department of Educational Research, Cartmel College, Bailrigg, Lancaster LA1 4YW, United Kingdom.

teacher education; student teacher; teaching practice; teaching style; directed activities
formation des enseignants; élève-maître; pratique pédagogique; style pédagogique; activités dirigées

PROJECT DESCRIPTION

The research seeks to illuminate aspects of the professional development of students undergoing initial teacher training. In particular it aims to richly describe classrooms where students are operating and to draw from this description common strands of professional progress made by beginning teachers. The study has as a central focus the development made along two dimensions of activity, namely the degree of activity openness enabled and the degree of teacher clarity in delivering activity. In this respect activity will be described in four 'cells': activity which is open and clear; activity which is closed and clear; activity which is open and vague; activity which is closed and vague.

The empirical work has an ecological approach, allowing issues to emerge for semi-structured observation and pre and post activity interviews with student teachers and children. In essence it is a longitudinal study which focuses on the professional progress of four students during teaching practices at various times in their training. These case studies represent the first stage of the research. This stage attempts to be purely descriptive. From this description a second prescriptive stage is likely to emerge.

12137 INSET for school reorganisation in Hull: analysis and evaluation.
GBR 1993
Research Date(s): 1989-1993
Tydeman, M.
Sup: Spence, B.
Inst: Hull University, School of Education, Cottingham Road, Hull HU6 7RX, United Kingdom.
further education of teachers; educational planning; training programme
perfectionnement des enseignants; planification de l'éducation; programme de formation

PROJECT DESCRIPTION

In September 1988 the organisation of the school system in the city of Hull was changed from transferring children between phases of education at the ages of 9 and 13 to transfer at 11 and 16. This reorganisation involved the simultaneous reallocation into different types of school of more than 2,100 teachers employed in the city in August 1988. The LEA (local education authority) recognised that the effective implementation of this reorganisation could only be achieved with the aid of a co-ordinated and sustained INSET (in-service education and training) programme for all affected staff. The programme lasted from 1985 to 1988 and it was instituted as a compulsory INSET programme for all teachers. Large scale INSET programmes have not been adequately researched before. This analysis and evaluation of Hull reorganisation INSET aims to provide information on four topics of value to decision makers who are involved in the planning, negotiation and delivery of large scale INSET programmes: the extent to which the programme achieved its stated objectives; its replicability; its effectiveness; its value for the teachers involved.

12138 Institutional ethos.
GBR 1993
Research Date(s): 1991-
Tymms, P.; Cosford, B.; Dunnett, A.; Draper, J.; Knowles, I.
Inst: Heriot-Watt University, Moray House Institute of Education, Holyrood Road, Edinburgh EH8 8AQ, United Kingdom.
educational institution; higher education; cultural identity
établissement d'enseignement; enseignement supérieur; identité culturelle

PROJECT DESCRIPTION

The aim of the project is to investigate the 'ethos' of the Institute with a view to (a) establishing how people who work in it experience the Institute, with a particular emphasis on how shared or distinct perceptions of ethos are; and (b) identifying a set of performance indicators upon which a long-term strategy to monitor Institutional ethos can be designed.

Data was initially collected through interview from a range of people including students and academic and support staff. This interview data has been analysed to highlight key issues and as the basis for the development of questionnaires on ethos issues which will be circulated to: (a) Institute staff (academic and support); (b) Institute students; (c) staff and students at two other institutions (one a university, one a two campus college) for comparative purposes. Associations will be sought between views on the Institute regarding relationships, academic atmosphere and social opportunities role within the organisation and other, individual characteristics.

12139 International education in international schools: developing a consensus of opinion.
GBR 1993
Research Date(s): 1987-1992
Jonietz, P.
Sup: Harris, N.
Inst: Brunel University, Department of Education and Design, Runnymede Campus, Englefield Green, Egham TW20 0JZ, United Kingdom.

international school; education system; international education; comparative analysis; cross-national research
école internationale; système d'enseignement; éducation internationale; analyse comparative; recherche transnationale

PROJECT DESCRIPTION

This research explores how international schools appear diverse in location, size, population, funding and governing body, but are similar in goals, objectives, and curricula. It will then enquire whether teachers, administrators, and parents can reach consensus on the thesis that international schools establish an educational system because they are similar to each other and different from national systems.

Schools in Frankfurt, London, and Washington, D.C. each serve as research sites. This is because they each have a well-established community base, an experienced multinational faculty, a multinational, multicultural student body, English as the language of instruction, and European Council of International Schools accreditation. They have also adopted the International Baccalaureate diploma to cut across cultures and boundaries.

The research employs triangulation through archive review, interviews, and questionnaires to demonstrate consensus on how these international schools are related to traditional definitions of international education, as well as to a larger organizational system of international education.

12140 The international reception of British university extension 1885-1925.
GBR 1993
Research Date(s): 1990-1992
Steele, G.
Sup: Marriott, J.
Inst: Leeds University, Department of Adult Continuing Education, Leeds LS2 9JT, United Kingdom.
Fin: Universities Funding Council.
continuing education; adult education; comparative education; history of education
éducation permanente; éducation des adultes; éducation comparée; histoire de l'éducation

PROJECT DESCRIPTION

The aim is to discover the extent of the influence of British 'university extension'. The research will examine and analyse the wide variety of adult educational practices in Europe which appeared during the 1890s which were called 'university extension' and attempts to assess their relationship to the British model. Sources of the research are primarily archival, including reports of international conferences published in Britain and France, reports in British and American university extension journals, collections of papers and memoirs. A chronology of the development of university extension in Europe (excluding Germany) will be attempted, this will try to create a typology of occurrences. The research will also isolate and describe significant features of the development including the objectives of university extension, the role of radical and liberal university lecturers, the international networking and solidarising of schoolteachers as a profession, the relation of adult education to national and workers' movements, scientific and objective education and the nature of cultural borrowing.

Publ: Steele, T. Metropolitan extensions: a comparison of two moments in the export of British University Adult Education, Europe 1890-1910 and Africa 1945-1955. In: Marriott, J.S.M. & Hake, B. (eds). Leeds Studies in the Education of Adults, Proceedings of the Leiden Conference of Intercultural Adult Education, 1992.

12141 Inventarisatie van het volwassenenonderwijs. (Inventory of adult education.)
NLD 1994
Research Date(s): 1990-1991
Velden, R.K.W. van der; Willems, E.J.T.A.
Inst: ROA Researchcentrum voor Onderwijs en Arbeidsmarkt, Universiteit Limburg (Research Centre for Education and the Labour Market, University of Limburg), P.O. Box 616, 6200 MD Maastricht, Netherlands.
Fin: Ministry of Education and Science.
adult education; data base
éducation des adultes; banque de données

PROJECT DESCRIPTION

Commissioned by the Ministry of Education and Science, the study lists and analyses data bases in the Netherlands that can be used in analysing the working of the market for adult education.

Publ: Velden, R.K.W. van der & Willems, E.J.T.A. Volwasseneneducatie. Een inventarisatie van bestaande databestanden (Adult Education. An inventory of existing data bases), ROA-W-1991/4 (ISBN 90-5321-073-3).

12142 Investigating a framework for mathematics teacher education: an action research study.
GBR 1993
Research Date(s): 1985-1992
Haggarty, L.
Sup: McIntyre, D.
Inst: Oxford University, Department of Educational Studies, 15 Norham Gardens, Oxford OX2 6PY, United Kingdom.
teacher education; mathematics; student teacher; supervision

formation des enseignants; mathématiques; élève-maître; surveillance
PROJECT DESCRIPTION

The aim of the research was to set up and investigate a model of school-based initial teacher education, working as university tutor in partnership with mathematics mentors in schools. The setting up and testing of the model was done within a framework of action research and the first cycle of the research was concerned with establishing a partnership with school supervisors acting as mentors; and also designing and testing a mathematics curriculum programme which satisfied the principles of the Internship Scheme, being implemented at Oxford University. Results from this work suggested that the hypothetical solution had gone according to plan.

However, it was discovered that mentors had not been able to implement two fairly fundamental aspects of the model, so in the second cycle of the research, attention was focused on the mentors, in an attempt to discover how each approached their agreed role. Content analysis was used as a major research method in order to determine the nature of conversations between mentors and interns (students) in schools. Results suggested that whilst mentors were taking many of the agreed actions, they were also interpreting their roles in quite different ways.

The third cycle of the research focused on the mathematics interns and, taking an ethnographic approach, asked what and how interns learn within the model of teacher education. Whilst many of the findings are consistent with those in the research literature, this research identifies important issues about both school-based models of teacher education and beginning teachers' learning.

Publ: Davies, C. & Haggarty, L. Learning to teach. In: Benton, P. (ed.). *Internship: integration and partnership in initial teacher training*. London: Gulbenkian Foundation, 1989.
Haggarty, L. Investigating a new framework for mathematics teacher education: an action research study. In: *Proceedings of the British Society for the Research into Learning Mathematics*, 1988.
Bachhouse, J.K. & Haggarty, L. An 'Internship' approach to the initial training of mathematics teachers. Paper presented at ICME in Budapest, 1988.
Haggarty, L. PGCE: a new approach. In: *Mathematics Teaching*, No 124/1988, pp. 42-43, September.

12143 Investigating the effectiveness of continuing education.
GBR 1993
Research Date(s): 1991-1994
Day, C.; Ellis, C.; Sutton, I.
Inst: Nottingham University, School of Education, University Park, Nottingham NG7 2RD, United Kingdom.
Fin: Universities Funding Council.
continuing education; adult education; further education of teachers; vocational training
éducation permanente; éducation des adultes; perfectionnement des enseignants; formation professionnelle
PROJECT DESCRIPTION

Much research has focused upon developing continuing education provision in adult education, inservice training for teachers and industrial and professional training. The aim of this research is to examine critically these theories in practice, and to evaluate both independently and through comparison their effectiveness in terms of client/consumer expectations, relevance of course provision to client need and its effects on professional and institutional growth.

12144 Investigation of the effects of different Inservice Education and Training of Teachers (INSET) experiences on teachers' understanding and perception of their role in teaching science at the elementary level (in US schools).
GBR 1993
Research Date(s): 1988-1992
Hall, J.
Sup: Hamilton, D.
Inst: Liverpool University, Department of Education, PO Box 147, Liverpool L69 3BX, United Kingdom.
further education of teachers; science education; learning process; teacher role; primary education
perfectionnement des enseignants; éducation scientifique; apprentissage; rôle de l'enseignant; enseignement primaire
PROJECT DESCRIPTION

Twenty-four elementary school teachers in Vermont, USA, were involved in an extensive summer workshop run by primary science specialists from England in 1987. Eighteen have continued follow-up work consisting of a 13-week series of meetings. Inservice work has been directed at enabling teachers to encourage children's use of process skills in science activities. Teachers' understanding of these skills and their role in learning has been monitored during the course. Some instruments have also been used with teachers involved in a conventional inservice course in elementary science in the USA and with a group of teachers in England, for comparison.

12145 JITOL: Just In Time Open Learning.
GBR 1993
Research Date(s): 1992-1994
Goodyear, P.
Inst: Lancaster University, Department of Educational Research, Cartmel College, Bailrigg, Lancaster LA1 4YW, United Kingdom.
Fin: European Community DELTA Programme.
distance study; open education; telecommunication; computer network; Europe; in-service training
enseignement à distance; éducation ouverte; télécommunication; réseau informatique; Europe; formation en cours d'emploi
PROJECT DESCRIPTION

JITOL aims to explore the use of electronic communications networks and multimedia computer conferencing in order to support continuing professional development and updating by skilled workers distributed throughout Europe. The lead partner in the project is NeuropeLab (in Archamps, France). Other partners include Logica, DEC, Credit Agricole and the universities of Lisbon and Namur.

Publ: Lewis, R.; Goodyear, P. & Boder, A. *Just In Time Open Learning: a DELTA project outline*. Archamps, France: NeuropeLab, 1992. (Occasional Paper 92/1).

12146 Kinder in altersgemischten Gruppen (0-6 Jahre) im Kinderhaus Sebastianstrasse Ingolstadt. (Children in mixed-age groups (0 to 6 years) in the Sebastianstrasse day care centre in Ingolstadt.)
DEU 1993
Research Date(s): 1991-1994
Erath, P.
Inst: Katholische Universitaet Eichstaett, Fak. fuer Sozialwesen, Studiengang Sozialwesen, Ostenstrasse 28, D-8078 Eichstaett.
Fin: Buergerhilfe Ingolstadt e. V.; Stadt Ingolstadt.
nursery school; pre-school education; educational planning; sciences of education; grouping
école maternelle; éducation préscolaire; planification de l'éducation; sciences de l'éducation; groupement
PROJECT DESCRIPTION

Inhalt: Erprobung paedagogischer Methoden bei der Tagesbetreuung von Kindern im Vorschulalter in altersgemischten Gruppen (0-6) unter besonderer Beruecksichtigung der Forderungen der Rahmenplaene (Art. 4.7 BayKiG bzw. 4. DVBayKiG).

Vorgehensweise: Begleitforschung; quantitative und qualitative Methoden.

12147 Koncepce a problémy zvláštní školy. (Special education: concepts and issues.)
CSK 1994
Research Date(s): 1991-1992
Kubová, Libuše; Švarcová, Iva.
Sup: Teplá, Marta; Petrů, Eva.
Inst: Výzkumný ústav pedagogický (Research Institute of Education), Strojírenská 386, 155 21 Praha 5 - Zličín, Czech Republic.
Ministerstvo školství, mládeže a tělovýchovy ČR (Ministry of Education, Youth and Physical Education), Karmelitská 7, 118 13 Praha 1, Czech Republic
special education; mentally handicapped; curriculum subject; interdisciplinary approach; content of education; educational need
enseignement spécial; handicapé mental; matière d'enseignement; interdisciplinarité; contenu de l'éducation; besoin d'éducation
PROJECT DESCRIPTION

Aim: To contribute to the improvement of the education of mentally handicapped pupils and their psychophysical development. It is felt the present education system does not adequately respond to the special education needs of handicapped pupils.

Methods: (1) Teacher questionnaires; (2) consultation with specialists.

The first stage of the project is to result in a report outlining a new conception of special education (January 1992). The second phase is to result in a teaching programme for special education (June 1992). The evaluation of both parts of the project will be the subject of a separate study.

Publ: Kubová, Libuše a kol. *Učební osnovy zvláštní školy*. 1. verze. MŠMT ČR čj. 18 314/92 - 21. Praha: Výzkumný ústav pedagogický v Praze, 1992.

12148 Kształcenie nauczycieli dla szkół podstawowych w Uniwersytecie w Linköping. (Teacher preparation for compulsory schools in Linköping University.)
POL 1994
Research Date(s): 1992
Szczepska-Pustkowska, Maria; Lewartowska-Zychowicz, Małgorzata; Szkudlarek, Tomasz.
Sup: Rutkowiak, Joanna.
Inst: Uniwersytet Gdański, Instytut Pedagogiki (University of Gdańsk, Institute for Education), 80-952 Gdańsk, Krzywoustego 19, Poland.

Uniwersytet w Linköping, Szwecja (Linköping University, Sweden), 581 83 Linköping, Sweden
teacher education; university; student teacher; teaching method
formation des enseignants; université; élève-maître; méthode pédagogique
PROJECT DESCRIPTION

The research was part of a project undertaken by Linköping University to evaluate their newly introduced teacher training scheme. It was based on the "peer review" approach.

The research started from a theoretical analysis of teacher training approaches, in which three models were formulated: a scientific model, a practical model, and a holistic "practice-of-thinking" model. On the basis of curriculum content analysis it was assumed that the practical model would prevail in the Linköping University teacher training programme. However, detailed qualitative research (observation, interviews and questionnaires involving a total of 59 student teachers and academic staff) showed the holistic "practice-of-thinking" model to be dominant. This finding led to conclusions concerning cultural factors that underlie teacher training curricula. Even though holistic thinking was not visibly dominant in the teacher training curriculum, it prevailed in the attitudes of teachers and students.

Publ: Rutkowiak, Joanna; Szczepska-Pustkowska, Maria; Szkudlarek, Tomasz & Lewartowska-Zychowicz, Małgorzata. *Teacher preparation for compulsory schools in Linköping University.* Linköping: Linköping University Press, 1993.

12149 Å lære å bli naturfaglærer. (Learning to be a natural science teacher.)
NOR 1994
Research Date(s): 1992-1994
Jordell, Karl Yvvind.
Inst: Universitetet i Oslo, Pedagogisk Forskningsinstitutt (University of Oslo, Institute for Educational Research), PB 1092 Blindern, 0317 Oslo, Norway.
Fin: NAVF/RSF.
student teacher; teacher education; learning process; teacher behaviour; occupational integration
élève-maître; formation des enseignants; apprentissage; comportement de l'enseignant; intégration professionnelle
PROJECT DESCRIPTION

Aim: To investigate how distinct components in teacher education influence the student teacher and to establish the importance of persons (colleagues and pupils) and the school structure for the development "reflected experience" and the mastery of basic professional functions by newly qualified teachers entering the teaching profession.

Design: The focus will be on the development of "reflected experience" in biology teachers as regards the teaching of biology and natural science as well as the development of attitudes towards these subjects, especially regarding the way teachers and pupils actively construct an understanding of scientific phenomena.

Method: In cooperation with researchers from the USA (University of Wisconsin, Madison) and Norwegian teacher training institutes, about 20 teacher students with a background in biology/natural sciences will be interviewed and observed in the final part of their training. Half of this group will also be interviewed and observed in their first year of teaching at school.

12150 Lancaster Technical and Vocational Education Initiative evaluation programme.
GBR 1993
Research Date(s): 1984-
Helsby, G.; Saunders, M.
Inst: Lancaster University, Department of Educational Research, Centre for the Study of Education and Training, Cartmel College, Bailrigg, Lancaster LA1 4YW, United Kingdom.
Fin: LEAs Consortium; Employment Department/(MSC/Training Agency).
vocational education; technical education; educational policy
enseignement professionnel; enseignement technique; politique de l'éducation
PROJECT DESCRIPTION

The focus of the work has varied over the lifetime of the project, being based upon a consortium of 15 local education authorities (LEAs) under Technical and Vocational Education Initiative (TVEI) pilot, and a consortium of seven LEAs under TVEI extension. During TVEI pilot the researchers investigated the effect of TVEI upon students, teachers and institutions. This work included widescale student surveys amongst some 7,000 TVEI and non-TVEI students, as well as qualitative inquiry. Areas of particular interest included profiling, work experience, technology, cross-curriculum developments and teaching and learning strategies. During TVEI extension the focus was particularly upon the use of teacher-generated performance indicators as a route into self-evaluation. More recently the researchers have undertaken an investigation of the TVEI effect, including its impact upon whole institutional working and its influence upon change.

Publ: A complete list of publications is available from the researchers.

12151 Langfristige Effekte schulischer Separation. (Effets à long terme de la ségrégation scolaire.)
CHE 1994
Research Date(s): 1988-1991
Blöchlinger, Hermann (Vogelsbergstrasse 28, 9240 Uzwil, Schweiz).
Sup: Stoll, François.
special education; remedial teaching; slow learner; integration
enseignement spécial; soutien pédagogique; esprit lent; intégration
PROJECT DESCRIPTION

Diese Dissertation geht mit einem Längsschnittdesign der Frage nach, ob es mittel- bis langfristig sinnvoller ist, ein Kind mit Schulschwierigkeiten in der Normalklasse zu belassen oder in eine Sonderklasse einzuweisen. Der Autor hat standardisiert Interviews mit zwei Gruppen von Männern - Frauen waren in der Stichprobe keine vertreten - im Alter zwischen 23 und 35 Jahren geführt. Die erste Gruppe bestand aus 23 ehemaligen Hilfsschülern, die einer Lernbehinderung wegen sonderbeschult wurden; die zweite Gruppe bestand aus Männern, bei denen während der Schulzeit eine solche Massnahme ebenfalls angezeigt erschien, aber aus dem einen oder anderen Grund nicht in die Praxis umgesetzt wurde. Die Interviews mit einer Dauer von durchschnittlich zwei bis drei Stunden betrafen die folgenden Bereiche: familiäre Situation, Schullaufbahn, aktuelle schulische Fähigkeiten (Test über Lesen, Schreiben und Rechnen), berufliche Laufbahn, Sozialstatus, Arbeitszufriedenheit, militärische Karriere, physische und psychische Befindlichkeit, Selbstbild und Selbstwertgefühl, gesellschaftliche Partizipation, Lebenszufriedenheit und Straffälligkeit.

Der Autor betont, dass die von ihm untersuchten Personen nicht die leistungsschwächsten unter den damaligen Hilfsschülern gewesen seien, eher im Gegenteil. Für Fälle wie sie, die sich laut traditioneller schulpsychologischer Praxis an der Grenze zwischen Normalschulfähigkeit und Hilfsschulbedürftigkeit bewegen, kommt er jedoch aufgrund der gefundenen langfristigen Effekte zu einem eindeutigen Schluss: für diese Schüler ist es längerfristig von Vorteil, wenn sie in der angestammten Klasse verbleiben können. Dies entbindet die Schule natürlich nicht davon, ihnen mit Stützmassnahmen unter die Arme zu greifen. Für schwerere Fälle der Lernbehinderung hält er eine Beschulung in einem geschützten Raum, also in Sonderklassen, durchaus für nützlich.

Publ: Blöchlinger, Hermann. *Langfristige Effekte schulischer Separation.* Luzern: Schweizerische Zentralstelle für Heilpädagogik (SZH), 1991, 163 Seiten.

12152 The Leeds adult learners at work project.
GBR 1993
Research Date(s): 1991-1993
Payne, J.
Sup: Ward, K.; Forrester, K.
Inst: Leeds University, Department of Adult Continuing Education, Leeds LS2 9JT, United Kingdom.
Fin: Universities Funding Council.
workers' education; adult education; employee; continuing education
éducation ouvrière; éducation des adultes; salarié; éducation permanente
PROJECT DESCRIPTION

The aims of the project are to study work-based learning to: (1) identify existing schemes and facilities by which employers cater for the continuing general education and training of their employees; (2) determine the factors that affect the success of such schemes; (3) explore the theoretical issues emerging which relate to adult learning at the workplace; (4) examine the policy issues relating to the development of lifelong learning; and (5) make international comparisons. In practical terms this will involve: gathering information about existing schemes; visiting existing schemes, together with interested individuals and organisations; and selecting a number of schemes in different kinds of enterprise for more detailed evaluation. Newsletters, journal articles and a final report will be produced.

12153 Lehrerarbeit auf dem Weg zur paedagogischen Professionalitaet. (The teacher's work on the road to pedagogic professionalism.)
DEU 1993
Research Date(s): 1991-1993
Burkard, C.
Sup: Bauer, K.
Inst: Universitaet Dortmund, FB Erziehungswissenschaften und Biologie, Institut fuer Schulentwicklungsforschung -IFS-, Rheinlanddamm 199, D-4600 Dortmund.
Fin: Deutsche Forschungsgemeinschaft.
teacher education; sciences of education; further training; theory
formation des enseignants; sciences de l'éducation; formation complémentaire; théorie
PROJECT DESCRIPTION

Inhalt: In Fallstudien an ausgewaehlten Lehrergruppen wird mittels teilnehmender Beobachtung und narrativer Interviews versucht, Logiken professionellen Handelns zu rekonstruieren und -unter Beruecksichtigung sozialwissenschaftlicher Gegenwartsdiagnosen - die tatsaechlichen Arbeitsaufgaben unterschiedlicher Lehrergruppen zu ermitteln. Von besonderem Interesse ist dabei fuer den Antragsteller der Bezug der Lehrerinnen und

Lehrer zur erziehungswissenschaftlichen Theorie und Empirie. Es soll eine empirische Basis und praxisnahe Theorie zur gezielten Foerderung paedagogischer Professionalitaet in Aus- und Weiterbildung von Lehrerinnen und Lehrern sowie von Lehrerberatern geschaffen werden.

Vorgehensweise: Ethnographische Feldstudie. Untersuchungsdesign: Fallstudie.

Datengewinnung: Primaererhebung: Feldarbeit von Mitarbeitern des Projektes durchgefuehrt.

12154 Leicestershire Technical and Vocational Education Initiative Extension evaluation project.
GBR 1993
Research Date(s): 1991-1992
Reid, I.; Wild, P.; Blease, D.; Busher, H.; Zanker, N.
Inst: Loughborough University of Technology Department of Education, Loughborough LE11 3TU, United Kingdom.
Fin: Leicestershire County Council.
vocational education; technical education
enseignement professionnel; enseignement technique
PROJECT DESCRIPTION

This project sets out to draw conclusions on the effectiveness of the Technical and Vocational Education Initiative Extension scheme (TVEI (E)) in promoting a change of pedagogy and content in the 14-18 curriculum. This evaluation is expected to provide valuable information collected from schools, teachers, pupils and parents through illustrative case accounts and analysis of numerical returns of students: (1) uptake on pre-vocational/vocational courses; and (2) involvement in areas such as flexible learning, information technology, residential/work experience and records of achievement. A sample size of 69 schools and colleges covers the whole local education authority, surveyed initially by questionnaire and followed up through semi-structured interviews.

12155 Leicestershire Technical and Vocational Education Initiative Extension evaluation consultancy.
GBR 1993
Research Date(s): 1991-1992
Reid, I.; Blease, D.; Wild, P.; Busher, H.
Inst: Loughborough University of Technology, Department of Education, Loughborough LE11 3TU, United Kingdom.
Fin: Leicestershire County Council.
vocational education; technical education; quality of education; achievement control
enseignement professionnel; enseignement technique; qualité de l'éducation; contrôle du rendement
PROJECT DESCRIPTION

This project provides consultancy for institutions in the final year of the Technical and Vocational Education Initiative Extension (TVEI (E)) in order to sustain and develop their monitoring and evaluation programmes. The consultancy programme is based on a supporting cascade model involving skills acquisition and dissemination. Fourteen institutions are actively involved.

12156 Leren van lager opgeleide werknemers, ouder dan 35 jaar. (Learning by workers (aged above 35) with a low level of education.)
NLD 1994
Research Date(s): 1990-1991
Onstenk, J.H.A.M.; Felix, C.; Gijtenbeek, J.
Inst: Stichting Centrum voor Onderwijsonderzoek (SCO) (Centre for Educational Research), Grote Bickersstraat 72, 1013 KS Amsterdam, Netherlands.·
Universiteit van Amsterdam (University of Amsterdam), P.O. Box 19268, 1000 GG Amsterdam, Netherlands
Fin: SVO het Instituut voor Onderzoek van het Onderwijs.
industrial training; vocational training; in-service training; adult education; participation; motivation for studies; level of education; employee
formation industrielle; formation professionnelle; formation en cours d'emploi; éducation des adultes; participation; motivation pour les études; niveau d'enseignement; salarié
PROJECT DESCRIPTION

Background: According to employers' organizations and government officials, technological innovations and increasing competition on the world market necessitate action to improve general levels of education and to boost participation in education. The Ministry of Education considers the participation rates of adults, especially those with a low level of education, much too low. At present an overall proportion of about 15-18% of employees participate in in-service training; 4% are on industrial training courses. Participation rates of older employees (over 35) and employees with a low level of education are much lower.

Aim: To examine current and forecasted rates of participation in training by employees with a low level of education, aged above 35, with a view to informing policy.

Results: Rates of participation in any type of education or training are generally very low among the group studied, especially among those who have not been educated above primary or junior secondary vocational level. This is not so much caused by a lack of ability or interest, as by a lack of a

suitable training supply. Workers generally hold positive attitudes towards training, as long as it is clearly linked to their work and a number of specific conditions are met.

(This is an updating of EUDISED no. 43/10246).

Publ: Onstenk, J.H.A.M. et al. *Deelname aan scholing door lager opgeleide werknemers.* Amsterdam: SCO, 1991, 173p.

12157 The Leverhulme Primary Project.
GBR 1993
Research Date(s): 1989-1992
Carre, C.
Sup: Wragg, E.; Bennett, S.
Inst: Exeter University, School of Education, St Luke's, Heavitree Road, Exeter EX1 2LU, United Kingdom.
Fin: The Leverhulme Trust.
teacher education; class management; teaching quality
formation des enseignants; conduite de la classe; qualité de l'enseignement
PROJECT DESCRIPTION

The nature and quality of teacher education is the subject of much current debate and research has highlighted the importance of the quality of classroom activity and of teacher competences. An initial national survey reflected current concerns amongst teachers' views of their competences to teach the National Curriculum. The project's research programme into various aspects of primary education is divided into two strands: (1) The classroom management strand has as its major aim to conduct research into teachers' professional skills, by studying teachers both in class and under experimental conditions. Several hundred lessons have been observed and a cluster of studies conducted. These have considered such matters as: teachers' first encounters with new classes, either at the beginning of the year or at the start of teaching practice; the handling of disruption; the management of professional skills like questioning and explaining; strategies used by supply teachers; pupils' views of discipline; teachers' management of their subject knowledge. Techniques used include live observation of lessons, interviews, questionnaires and the use of photographs to analyse decision-making strategies. (2) The development of the teacher competence strand questions the role of teacher knowledge in teaching quality, defined in terms of competences. Research was conducted on student teachers (N=59) taking the Post Graduate Certificate in Education and were from four specialisms: maths, science, music and early years. A sample (N=24) was randomly selected for in-depth observation and interview. A number of data-gathering formats were used to collect information on changes in student teachers' understanding of three knowledge bases (i.e. subject knowledge, pedagogical subject matter, beliefs and ideologies). The impact of teaching experiences and the course has been monitored.

A follow-up study is being conducted on a small sample, through the first year of teaching.

Publ: Trotter, A. & Wragg, E.C. A Study of Supply Teachers. In: *Research Papers in Education*, Vol 5, No 3/1990, pp. 251-276.
Dunne, E. & Bennett, N. *Talking and Learning in Groups.* London: Macmillan, 1990.
Bennett, S.N.; Wragg, E.C. & Carre, C.G. Primary Teachers and the National Curriculum. In: *Junior Education*, Vol 15, No 11, November 1991.
Carter, D.S.G. & Carre, C.G. Gender differences in primary teachers' self estimates of their competence to teach National Curriculum Science. In: *Australian Educational Researcher*, Vol 18, No 2/1991.
Bennett, S.N.; Wragg, E.C.; Carre, C.G. & Carter, D. A longitudinal study of primary teachers' perceived competence in, and concerns about, National Curriculum implementation. In: *Research Papers in Education*, Vol 7, No 1/1992.

12158 Life history and initial teacher education.
GBR 1993
Research Date(s): 1988-1992
Sikes, P.; Troyna, B.
Inst: Warwick University, Faculty of Educational Studies, Coventry CV4 7AL, United Kingdom.
teacher education; teaching profession; student teacher; teacher behaviour
formation des enseignants; profession d'enseignant; élève-maître; comportement de l'enseignant
PROJECT DESCRIPTION

Research evidence suggests that many teachers continue, consciously or otherwise, to make important decisions about the organization, orientation and delivery of the formal and informal curricula on grounds which are racist, sexist and discriminatory in a range of other ways. Should we therefore succumb to a system of teacher education/training in which these practices could well be reproduced systematically? Or should we, instead, develop preservice courses geared towards the development of a teaching force which reflects in a critical manner on taken-for-granted assumptions, which can articulate reasons for co-testing some of the conventional wisdoms about pupils, their interests and abilities, and which, ultimately, might influence future cohorts?

In contrast to recent calls for the dismemberment of Initial Teacher Education (ITE) courses, as they are presently constituted, the researchers argue for the introduction of life history methods as a strategy for facilitating the transition from pupil to teacher status. The study draws on the researchers' experiences of using this strategy with a group of first-year students following an ITE course. Follow-up studies of these students were made throughout their course.

Publ: Troyna, B. & Sikes, P. Putting the 'why' back into teacher education. In: *Forum*, Vol 32, No 1/1989.

Sikes, P. & Troyna, B. True stories: a case study in the use of life history in Initial Teacher Education. In: *Educational Review*, Vol 43, No 1/1991, pp. 3-16.

12159 Life in post-compulsory classrooms.
GBR 1993
Research Date(s): 1991-1992
Bloomer, M.
Inst: Exeter University, School of Education, St Luke's, Heavitree Road, Exeter EX1 2LU, United Kingdom.
post-compulsory education; classroom; learning conditions; teacher; student; perception
enseignement postobligatoire; salle de classe; conditions d'apprentissage; enseignant; étudiant; perception
PROJECT DESCRIPTION
Despite massive changes to the 14-19 curriculum, classroom life in the post-compulsory (16-19) sector of education is vastly under-represented in research literature and a great deal of what does exist is informed as much by inferences from grand curriculum designs ('it is planned to happen, therefore it happens') as by any systematic study. This study is the first stage of a research programme which aims to gain insights into students' and teachers' experiences of teaching and learning, and to provide evidence of the effects of 'educational planning/provision' upon student learning. The aims are: (1) to enable the researchers to deepen their insights into teachers' and students' experiences of classroom life in order that a more substantial project can be planned; (2) to develop such materials and skills as will be necessary to discharge the full project; and (3) to establish a network of teacher fieldworkers.

The pilot study will be based at a tertiary college. Initially, it will focus on A-level students but will broaden out to include other types of course. Semi-structured observations of class meetings and follow-up interviews with students and teachers will yield the data for this exploratory, pilot study. In addition, certain information will be obtained from college records. These data will inform and guide the choice of concepts, categories and hypotheses that will shape the full project. A number of teachers at the college will participate in the project as field workers and, ultimately, as full partners in the research.

12160 Local education authority policy and practices in supporting special education provision in schools.
GBR 1993
Research Date(s): 1990-1992
Fletcher-Campbell, F.
Sup: Bradley, J.
Inst: National Foundation for Educational Research, The Mere, Upton Park, Slough SL1 2DQ, United Kingdom.
special education; educational policy; local government; educational planning; educational need; educational provision
enseignement spécial; politique de l'éducation; administration locale; planification de l'éducation; besoin d'éducation; scolarisation
PROJECT DESCRIPTION
The research aims to: (1) document and analyse local education authorities' (LEAs') current policies for special educational needs (SEN); (2) examine the nature of special support as policy is realised in practice; (3) identify Inservice Education and Training of Teachers (INSET) needs and provision; (4) investigate the effect of the Education Reform Act 1988 on SEN provision; and (5) consider the ways in which LEAs monitor and evaluate their SEN provision.

In the initial phase, all LEAs in England and Wales were invited to submit any documentation relating to SEN. In the second phase, a small number of LEAs are being studied in depth. Issues being focused on are: structure and management of support services; assessment; monitoring and evaluation; INSET and resourcing.

12161 Local evaluation of Technical and Vocational Education Initiative (TVEI), TVEI-Related Inservice Training (TRIST) and Grant-Related INSET (GRIST).
GBR 1993
Research Date(s): 1985-1993
McLean, M.
Sup: Gleeson, D.
Inst: Keele University, Department of Education, Keele, Staffordshire ST5 5BG, United Kingdom.
Fin: Staffordshire LEA; Training, Enterprise & Education Directorate.
vocational education; technical education; further education of teachers

enseignement professionnel; enseignement technique; perfectionnement des enseignants
PROJECT DESCRIPTION
The study looks at the background and development of the Technical and Vocational Education Initiative (TVEI) and TVEI-Related Inservice Training (TRIST) in local institutions. The research adopts an action-oriented approach to evaluation, involving formative methods of reporting. Reports will be sent to the schools and colleges involved.

Publ: Gleeson, D. *TVEI and secondary education*. Buckingham: Open University Press, 1988.

Gleeson, D. *The paradox of training: making progress out of crisis*. Buckingham: Open University Press, 1989.

12162 The management of politically, or financially expedient change in a college of further education.
GBR 1993
Research Date(s): 1988-1992
Proctor, J.
Sup: Gray, H.
Inst: Lancaster University, Department of Educational Research, Cartmel College, Bailrigg, Lancaster LA1 4YW, United Kingdom.
post-compulsory education; educational administration; educational reform
enseignement postobligatoire; administration de l'enseignement; réforme de l'enseignement
PROJECT DESCRIPTION
The research concerns the management of change within a college of further education. It focuses particularly on the processes of change which result from policies adopted primarily as a political or financial expedient. The research draws on varied case study materials spanning the period from 1975 to 1990. It is possible to make a comparison between two distinct leadership styles and two distinct management structures. These materials are related to minutes of Local Authority committees to deepen the perspective of explanations of events. The case study is also contrasted with the management of non-consensus policies in the National Health Service and with other case studies of change in further education.

The study argues that in a period of accelerated change the 'integrative' model of policy information is insufficient to explain the complexity of the change process. The study emphasises the subjective responses of college members to policies which are imposed because of decisions taken outwith the college, but posits that although these responses are related to personal experience they are to an extent consensual and predictable since they also relate to the 'climate' of the college, to the expected behaviour of the executive and to common human responses when dealing with stress. The study is illustrated by references to attempts to implement particular policies, including equal opportunity policies as they relate to racial minorities and to women, and the development of open learning.

Publ: Proctor, J. Literature review. In: *The assessment of management competences*. CNAA, BTEC, Department of Employment (Training), 1990.

Powney, J.; Proctor, J. & Crowcroft, C. Opening up the debate. In: *Assessing Management Competence, final report*. CNAA, BTEC, Department of Employment (Training), 1991.

Proctor, J. & Powney, J. The standard of qualification in management education: unresolved questions. In: *Higher Education Review*, Vol 23, No 3/1991.

Proctor, J. *Managers working for patients: using competences in management development*, NHSTD, 1991.

Proctor, J. & Jackson, C. *Women managers in the NHS: a celebration of success*. Department of Health, NHSME, Women's Unit, 1992.

12163 The management of the Technical and Vocational Education Initiative within post-16 institutions in Hampshire.
GBR 1993
Research Date(s): 1988-1991
Hobrough, J.; McCann, J.
Sup: Evans, K.
Inst: Surrey University, Department of Educational Studies, Guildford GU2 5XH, United Kingdom.
Fin: Hampshire Local Education Authority.
technical education; vocational education; post-secondary education; educational administration
enseignement technique; enseignement professionnel; enseignement post-secondaire; administration de l'enseignement
PROJECT DESCRIPTION
The research programme is designed to analyse the perceptions of the Technical and Vocational Education Intitiative (TVEI) coordinators in relation to management structures adopted within post-16 institutions. A general/institutional summary is obtained using interviews, documented by a verified-reporting technique. Perceptions of senior managers and TVEI coordinators are obtained using repertory grids, concept maps, and information models.

Comparisons between 11-18 schools, sixth-form colleges, technical colleges and tertiary colleges will be made. Some comparison between Hampshire and 'distant' case studies will also be completed.

12164 Managing Chart Continuing Vocational Training.
NLD 1994
Research Date(s): 1991-1992
Brandsma, T.F.; Dam, J.W. van; Grip, A. de.
Inst: ROA Researchcentrum voor Onderwijs en Arbeidsmarkt, Universiteit Limburg (Research Centre for Education and the Labour Market, University of Limburg), P.O. Box 616, 6200 MD Maastricht, Netherlands.
Fin: Ministry of Education and Science.
vocational training; continuing education
formation professionnelle; éducation permanente
PROJECT DESCRIPTION
Under a contract from the Ministry of Education and Science and in cooperation with the Research Centre of the Department of Educational Technology of the University of Twente (OCTO), ROA is responsible for a "Managing Chart" with regard to the availability in the Netherlands of a number of indicators in the field of vocational training.
This exploratory study takes place as part of the FORCE programme of the Task Force on Human Resources, Education, Training, and Youth, of the European Community.
The research is particularly examining the definitions and classifications to be used as the basis of the indicators that will be generated for the Netherlands.
Publ: *Continuing Vocational Training in the Netherlands: Managing Chart,* ROA & OCTO (Research Centre of the Department of Educational Technology, University of Twente), Enschede & Maastricht, January 1992.

12165 Managing chart permanent beroepsonderwijs. (Managing chart continuing vocational training.)
NLD 1993
Research Date(s): 1991-1992
Brandsma, T.F.; Dam, J.W. van; Grip, A. de.
Inst: ROA Researchcentrum voor Onderwijs en Arbeidsmarkt, Universiteit Limburg (Research Centre for Education and the Labour Market, University of Limburg), P.O. Box 616, 6200 MD Maastricht, Netherlands.
Fin: Ministry of Education and Science.
continuing education; vocational training; educational provision
éducation permanente; formation professionnelle; scolarisation
PROJECT DESCRIPTION
Under a contract from the Ministry of Education and Science and in cooperation with the Research Centre of the Department of Educational Technology (OCTO) of the University of Twente, ROA is responsible for a "Managing Chart" with regard to the availability in the Netherlands of a number of indicators in the field of vocational training. This exploratory study takes place as part of the FORCE programme of the Task Force on Human Resources, Education, Training, and Youth, of the European Community. The research is particularly examining the definitions and classifications to be used as the basis for the indicators that will be generated for the Netherlands.
Publ: *Continuing Vocational Training in the Netherlands; Managing Chart,* ROA & OCTO, Enschede & Maastricht, January, 1992.

12166 Managing staff development in schools.
GBR 1993
Research Date(s): 1989-1991
Busher, H.
Inst: Loughborough University of Technology, Department of Education, Loughborough LE11 3TU, United Kingdom.
further education of teachers; working conditions; teaching profession; teaching personnel
perfectionnement des enseignants; conditions de travail; profession d'enseignant; corps enseignant
PROJECT DESCRIPTION
The research has sought to explore: (1) how teachers have responded to the 1987 conditions of service, through the use of semi-structured interviews; and (2) how the professional development necessary to help teachers meet these new conditions is being organised. Questionnaires and document searches are also being used.
Publ: Busher, H.C. Managing compulsory INSET under teachers' new conditions of service. In: *Educational Management & Administration,* Vol 18, No 3/1990, pp. 39-45.
Busher, H.C. Towards a systematic management of professional staff development in schools. In: Wallace, G. (ed.). *Local Management of schools: research and experience.* BERA dialogs No 6. Multilingual Matters, 1992.
Busher, H.C. & Saran, R. *Teachers and their conditions of employment: a study in the politics of schools.* London: Kogan Page, 1992.

12167 Mature women entrants to teaching: an analysis of the process of adjustment to the student role in the four-year B.Ed. course.
GBR 1993
Research Date(s): 1989-1994
Duncan, D.
Sup: Burgess, R.

Inst: Nene College, Faculty of Education, Health and Science, Moulton Park, Northampton NN2 7AL, United Kingdom; Warwick University, Faculty of Educational Studies, Coventry CV4 7AL, United Kingdom.
teacher education; adult education; women's education; student teacher; student behaviour; student life
formation des enseignants; éducation des adultes; éducation des femmes; élève-maître; comportement de l'étudiant; vie étudiante
PROJECT DESCRIPTION
The research study has two distinct aims: (1) To investigate mature candidates' previous career and work experiences and the factors leading to a decision to pursue a career in the teaching profession; (2) to identify the problems, resource needs and learning needs of mature students in the first year of the B.Ed. course. A case study approach will be used to chart the socialisation process of 26 mature women into the student role in the first year of the B.Ed. course (1991-1992).
The research will be conducted using mainly qualitative research methods. Much of the data will be gathered via tape-recorded interviews using a 'structured conversation' approach. Interviews will be conducted at key points of their first year (before entry; once in each of the three terms; and at the end of the post-examination period of the first year) in order to identify the changes which have occurred in their behaviour, and in their perceptions of the student role in the first year of a teacher training course.

12168 Mentors in education and training.
GBR 1993
Research Date(s): 1991-1993
Davies, J.
Inst: Plymouth University, Enterprise Unit, 92 Cobourg Street, Plymouth PL4 8AA, United Kingdom.
training of trainers; further education of teachers; supervision; training need; trainer
formation des formateurs; perfectionnement des enseignants; surveillance; besoin de formation; formateur
PROJECT DESCRIPTION
Mentors were introduced into Plymouth University's inservice Certificate in Education course in 1985 as a means of providing a link betweenthe students' course of study and their place of work. As mentors have come to take an increasingly important role in education and training, so a need for mentor training has been identified. In order to design coherent training programmes, it is essential to have a clear view of the roles of both mentors and protégés. Through the literature, this research aims to clarify and identify established roles, to create a typology, and to suggest training programmes appropriate to the different roles.

12169 Modele zarzadzania edukacja przedszkolna a efekty wychowania w Wielkiej Brytanii, Szwecji i USA. (Models of organization and management of pre-school provision and their effects on the child's development in Great Britain, Sweden and the USA.)
POL 1994
Research Date(s): 1991-1993
Karwowska-Struczyk, Małgorzata.
Inst: Instytut Badań Edukacyjnych (Institute for Educational Research), Górczewska 8, 01-180 Warszawa, Poland.
pre-school education; educational administration; decision making; school-community relation; parent-school relation
éducation préscolaire; administration de l'enseignement; prise de décision; relation école-collectivité; relation parents-école
PROJECT DESCRIPTION
Aims: (1) to describe the various organizational forms of pre-school provision in Great Britain, Sweden and the USA, to present their dependence on local and governmental authorities in such fields as: management, financial support, control and guidelines (curriculum); (2) to present the way in which pre-school education developed in these countries, its history, as well as the political and economic features which influence pre-school provision; (3) to present the effects of pre-school experiences on the development of young children.
Main questions: (1) Who has the primary responsibility for making decisions concerning policy and organization of pre-school provision? (2) What are the types of pre-school provision? (3) How do ideology and research influence the state of early provision? (4) What are the main goals and activities of early education programmes? (5) What are the connections between pre-school provision and the local community? (6) Are parents involved in pre-school institutions? (7) What are the effects of various types of pre-school institutions? (8) What factors do they depend on? (the children's home background, parental involvement, frequency, duration and attendance, staff, etc.).
Theoretical background: Bronfenbrenner's concentric circle model of the ecology of human development is used as a theoretical framework for analysing the influences of various factors on the life of the young child.
Methods: (1) Questionnaire for contextual information; (2) literature study.
Publ: Karwowska-Struczyk, Małgorzata. Co rodzice myśla o przedszkolu? In: *Wychowanie w Przedszkolu,* 10/1991, pp. 451-457.

Karwowska-Struczyk, Małgorzata. Wychowanie przedszkolne w Szwecji i W. Brytanii. In: *Wychowanie w Przedszkolu*, 8/1991, pp. 330-339.

12170 Models of the primary teacher in use in primary B.Ed. courses.
GBR 1993
Research Date(s): 1990-1991
Clemson, D.
Inst: Liverpool John Moores University, School of Education and Community Studies, I.M. Marsh Campus, Barkhill Road, Liverpool L17 6BD, United Kingdom.
Fin: Liverpool Polytechnic.
teacher education; course programme; curriculum development
formation des enseignants; programme de cours; élaboration de programmes d'études
PROJECT DESCRIPTION
The education and training of teachers is currently of central concern to both trainers and national governments. The inception of accreditation demands through the Council for the Accreditation of Teacher Education (CATE) has caused widespread re-organisation of teacher education courses. The focus of this research activity is the Primary B.Ed. (Council for National Academic Awards (CNAA) validated courses only) and the ways in which course writers depict the model of the primary teacher which underpins their course. Possible tensions between desired models and externally provided, or approved, models will be explored. Data will be assembled from course documents, CATE criteria, and other formal/official groups and publications.

12171 Modes of teacher education: towards a basis for comparison.
GBR 1993
Research Date(s): 1991-1992
Whitty, G.; Furlong, J.; Barton, L.; Miles, S.
Inst: London University, Institute of Education, Department of Policy Studies, Health and Education Research Unit, 20 Bedford Way, London WC1H 0AL, United Kingdom; Sheffield University, Division of Education, 388 Glossop Road, Sheffield S10 2TN, United Kingdom; Cambridge University, Department of Education, The Old Schools, United Kingdom.
Fin: Economic and Social Research Council.
teacher education; college of education; cost of education
formation des enseignants; centre de formation des enseignants; coût de l'éducation
PROJECT DESCRIPTION
This project is designed to provide a sharper focus to current policy debates about the future of teacher education, using a national survey of all courses of initial training in England and Wales, and a detailed study of a sample of 50 courses across a variety of routes to Qualified Teacher Status (QTS). The project will provide an up-to-date database on the nature and costs of different approaches to teacher education and the models of professionalism that they seek to engender.
Publ: Whitty, G. et al. Initial teacher education in England and Wales. In: *Cambridge Journal of Education*, Vol 22, No 3/1992, pp. 293-306.
Barrett, E. et al. New routes to Qualified Teacher Status. In: *Cambridge Journal of Education*, Vol 22, No 3/1992, pp. 323-335.

12172 Multi-professional support for young adults with special needs.
GBR 1993
Research Date(s): 1988-1991
Maychell, K.
Sup: Bradley, J.
Inst: National Foundation for Educational Research, The Mere, Upton Park, Slough SL1 2DQ, United Kingdom.
special education; training need; youth; local government; cooperation
enseignement spécial; besoin de formation; jeunesse; administration locale; coopération
PROJECT DESCRIPTION
The need for cooperation among various services involved in supporting young people with special needs has long been recognised. Yet relatively few examples may be cited of cooperative action to meet the needs of these young people in their transition from school or college to adult life.
The study aimed to: (1) identify relevant models of inter-professional working; (2) ascertain how they relate to desired objectives in terms of supporting young people as they progress from school or college to continuing education and training; and (3) highlight the lessons for practice elsewhere. It also aimed to make an assessment of the type of training that would facilitate the introduction and development of cooperative working relationships.
The first phase involved identifying those local authorities where cooperative working was being planned or already in existence in order to gain information on their development and operation. On the basis of the information gathered, a number of initiatives were selected for detailed investigation in phase two, involving extended field visits to each location.

The final report documents the range of initiatives studied, analyses these for their relevance to the practice of cooperative working in other locations, and provides information to guide future policy and practice.
Publ: Maychell, K. & Bradley, J. *Preparing for partnership: multi-agency support for special needs.* Slough: NFER, 1991.

12173 National Council for Vocational Qualifications (NCVQ) Fellowship.
GBR 1993
Research Date(s): 1990-1994
Lawton, D.
Inst: London University, Institute of Education, Department of Curriculum Studies, 20 Bedford Way, London WC1H 0AL, United Kingdom.
Fin: National Council for Vocational Qualifications.
vocational education; qualification
enseignement professionnel; qualification
PROJECT DESCRIPTION
This four year project is to examine impact and take-up of the new framework for National Vocational Qualifications (NVQs); it examines and supports the technical processes required to develop and implement NVQs as well as providing a critique of policy and strategy formation in vocational qualifications in the United Kingdom.

12174 The nature and use of the enquiry project in short award-bearing courses for primary school teachers.
GBR 1993
Research Date(s): 1992-1993
Dadds, M.
Inst: Cambridge University, Institute of Education, Shaftesbury Road, Cambridge CB2 2BX, United Kingdom.
further education of teachers
perfectionnement des enseignants
PROJECT DESCRIPTION
The research is exploring the variety of classroom and school development issues upon which primary school teachers focus when conducting their self-chosen project on short courses at the Cambridge Institute of Education. The research is also studying the practical links that teachers make between their self-chosen projects and the work of colleagues in their schools where links are being made. The research looks at the demands which this places on the in-service teachers as disseminators and change agents. It is seeking to understand what knowledge,. personal skills, personal qualities and competencies are needed for teachers to make successful links. The research also seeks to identify factors within the in-service course and the school that support, or hinder, teachers in these demands.

Questionnaires have raised data from students on four short award-bearing courses. Follow-up interviews with a small sample of teachers are being conducted over a period of a year. Interviews will be sought with a small sample of colleagues in the in-service teachers' schools.

12175 Navrhovaný systém dalšího vzdělávání učitelů a servisní střediska v regionu. (The in-service teacher education system and the regional services centres.)
CSK 1994
Research Date(s): 1991-1992
Kohnová, J.; Dostálová, R.
Inst: Pedagogická fakulta Univerzity Karlovy (Charles University, Faculty of Education), M.D. Rettigové 4, 116 39 Praha 1, Czech Republic.
Ministerstvo školství, mládeže a tělovýchovy (Ministry of Education, Youth and Physical Education), Karmelitská 7, 118 00 Praha 1, Czech Republic
further education of teachers; in-service training; teaching profession; continuing education; educational legislation
perfectionnement des enseignants; formation en cours d'emploi; profession d'enseignant; éducation permanente; législation scolaire
PROJECT DESCRIPTION
Aim: To conduct for the Czech Ministry of Education, Youth and Physical Education: (1) a survey of the main components of in-service teacher education that need to be developed and (2) a survey of recent organizational and legislative developments in the field of in-service teacher training.
Hypothesis: The forms of in-service training and the conditions under which it takes place have an influence on its quality and outcomes.
Methods: Study and analysis of foreign literature; analysis of relevant Czech legislation in the field of in-service teacher training.
Results: Concrete recommendations to the ministry regarding: the definition of a concept of life-long education; the implementation of a legal framework for the in-service training of teachers and other education professionals; an analysis of the Czech education system, focusing on the structure of the teaching profession and the quality of teachers; and the specification of different types of in-service training.

12176 The needs of mature entrants in higher and further education.
GBR 1993
Research Date(s): 1990-1991
Munn, P.; MacDonald, C.; Lowden, K.
Inst: Scottish Council for Research in Education, 15 St John Street, Edinburgh EH8 8JR, United Kingdom.
Fin: Scottish Office Education Department.
adult education; student; higher education; selection
éducation des adultes; étudiant; enseignement supérieur; sélection
PROJECT DESCRIPTION
The research focuses on the identification and effectiveness of innovative approaches in supporting the needs of mature entrants in higher and further education and on ways of attracting potential adult returners back into education and training. It builds on previous work in these areas, concentrating on case-study approaches in higher and further education institutions to complement our larger-scale survey work. The case studies have concentrated on areas where there has traditionally been difficulty in attracting mature students, i.e. engineering, electronics, mathematics and sciences. A telephone survey of potential returners has supplemented the case-study work.
Publ: Munn, P.; MacDonald, C. & Lowden, K. *Helping adult students cope: mature students on science, mathematics and engineering courses.* SCRE Research Report Series, No 39. Edinburgh: Scottish Council for Research in Education, 1992.

12177 OECD integration project: pupils with special educational needs.
GBR 1993
Research Date(s): 1991
Munn, P.; Allan, J.
Inst: Scottish Council for Research in Education, 15 St John Street, Edinburgh EH8 8JR, United Kingdom.
Fin: National Foundation for Educational Research; Organisation for Economic Cooperation and Development (OECD).
special education; special school; pupil integration; OECD
enseignement spécial; centre d'éducation spéciale; intégration scolaire; OCDE
PROJECT DESCRIPTION
A number of case studies of the integration policies and practice of schools in the UK will be undertaken as the UK contribution to Phase II of the OECD/CERI project 'Integration in the school'. The project's concern is with resourcing, access to the National Curriculum and the role of the special school. SCRE has been subcontracted to undertake the Scottish case study.

12178 An open university for women in Saudi Arabia: problems and prospects.
GBR 1993
Research Date(s): 1986-1990
Al Rawat, H.
Sup: Simmons, C.
Inst: Loughborough University of Technology, Department of Education, Loughborough LE11 3TU, United Kingdom; King Saud University, The College of Education, Riyadh, Saudi Arabia.
open university; distance study; women's education; Saudi Arabia
télé-université; enseignement à distance; éducation des femmes; Arabie Saoudite
PROJECT DESCRIPTION
This study investigates the prospects of setting up an open university for women in Saudi Arabia against the background of the problems which Saudi women face in pursuing higher education. A review is given of the development of modern public education for women since its beginning in 1960, with emphasis on the more recent development of higher education for women. The position of women in Islam and in contemporary Saudi society is examined as this has influenced their access to higher education. Three open universities in the United Kingdom, Thailand and Pakistan are described (the latter in an Islamic country). A questionnaire was devised in order to gather data on attitudes to the setting up of an open university for women in Saudi Arabia, on perceptions of its feasibility, and on possible obstacles to its foundation. The questionnaire also included a section on the most suitable model for an open university for women in Saudi Arabia. The questionnaire was distributed in government bodies and higher educational establishments in Saudi Arabia to policy makers, academics and female students.
An analysis of the data reveals a very positive response to the setting up of an open university for women in Saudi Arabia. Respondents, however, demonstrated a realistic awareness of the problems of gaining public acceptance for a new type of higher education in a time of restrictions on government spending. Finally, on the basis of the findings a proposal is being made for the setting up of an open university for women in Saudi Arabia.
Publ: Al Rawat, H.S. & Simmons, C.V. The education of women in Saudi Arabia. In: *Comparative Education*, Vol 27, No 3/1991, pp. 287-295.

12179 Organization and economic foundations for the development of scientific technical education.
RUS 1994
Research Date(s): 1991-1992
Kagermanyan, V.S.
Sup: Tsesnek, L.S.
Inst: Research Institute for Higher Education, 103062, Moscow, K-62, Podsosensky per. 20, Russia.
State Committee for Higher Education Institutions, 113833, Moscow, M-230, Lysinovskja str. 51, Russia
technical education; higher education; development of education; economics of education
enseignement technique; enseignement supérieur; développement de l'éducation; économie de l'éducation
PROJECT DESCRIPTION
The study aimed to contribute to the development of technical and engineering education in Russia. An analysis was made of organizational and economic aspects of the development of scientific technical education. On the basis of scientific evidence, recommendations have been made as to the organizational and economic basis that is needed for an effective training system for future specialists in the fields of research and engineering. The main structural components of this type of education were defined as well as the ways and means for their development.
Publ: Kagermanyan, V.S.; Tsesnec, L.S.; Gorunov, M.G.; et al. *Scientific-technological education: ideas, state of the art and perspectives of development.* Information review, M., NIIVO, 1992.
Savelyev, A.Y.; Kagermanyan, V.S. & Gorunov, M.G. *Training of engineers under new social and economic conditions.* Sevastopol, 1992.

12180 Orta öğretim ders programlarında temel kültür derslerinin yeri ve rolü. (The place and role of core cultural subjects in the secondary school curriculum.)
TUR 1994
Research Date(s): 1990
Dirik, Zahit.
Sup: Variş, Fatma.
Inst: Uludağ Üniversitesi, Sosyal Bilimler Enstitüsü (Uludağ University, Institute of Social Sciences), Görükle Kampusu, Bursa, Turkey.
secondary education; common core curriculum; main subject; curriculum development
enseignement secondaire; tronc commun; matière principale; élaboration de programmes d'études
PROJECT DESCRIPTION
This research investigated core cultural subjects in the secondary school curriculum in terms of their conceptual and practical features.
The study was descriptive and fell into three parts. In the first part the evolution of the secondary school curriculum was surveyed from a conceptual perspective (in the West) and a historical perspective (in Turkey). Similarities and differences were emphasized. In the second part, 17 schools in the Bursa region were selected for a questionnaire survey. Questionnaires were administered to teachers, administrators and pupils to elicit views on the core cultural curriculum. Respondents approved of the following common compulsory subjects: Turkish language and literature, mathematics, history, foreign languages, physics and chemistry. Common core subjects are: music, painting, physical education and sports, and foreign languages, followed by mathematics, physics and chemistry.
Today, the secondary school curriculum is strongly dependent on the university entrance examinations. The study emphasizes this dependence and invites those involved to offer solutions.

12181 Participation in education and training: age group 16-19.
GBR 1993
Research Date(s): 1992-1993
Richardson, W.
Inst: Warwick University, Faculty of Educational Studies, Coventry CV4 7AL, United Kingdom.
Fin: Economic and Social Research Council.
post-compulsory education; vocational education; access to education; motivation for studies
enseignement postobligatoire; enseignement professionnel; accès à l'éducation; motivation pour les études
PROJECT DESCRIPTION
A research seminar will convene on six occasions over two years. Six designated themes are identified: (1) determinants of individuals' decisions; (2) qualifications as a predictor of post-education destination; (3) funding structures; (4) the status of qualifications; (5) access; (6) quality in teaching and learning.

12182 Patterns of local education authority inservice education and training of teachers (INSET) organisation.
GBR 1993
Research Date(s): 1991-1993
Harland, J.; Kinder, K.
Sup: Bradley, J.

Inst: National Foundation for Educational Research, The Mere, Upton Park, Slough SL1 2DQ, United Kingdom.

further education of teachers; in-service training; training supply; educational policy; local government

perfectionnement des enseignants; formation en cours d'emploi; offre de formation; politique de l'éducation; administration locale

PROJECT DESCRIPTION

Recent changes in in-service education and training of teachers (INSET) funding arrangements have resulted in local education authorities (LEAs) adopting a wide range of strategies for the planning and delivery of professional development activities. The research mapped the major types and patterns of LEA INSET organisation with the intent of developing guidelines on good practice. A national survey of INSET coordinators was followed by case study work in five LEAs exhibiting different types of INSET policy and practice. The views of LEA and school staff was sought on the benefits, problems and effectiveness of the varying approaches to INSET. A report on the project will be produced.

12183   Pedagogicheskoe znanie v obrazovanii uchitelja. (The pedagogical knowledge base in teacher education.)
LAT   1994
Research Date(s): 1990-1993
Kurilova, T.
Sup: Nikandrov, N.
Inst: Latvijas Universitate (University of Latvia), Kronvalda boulv. 4, Riga, 1010 Latvia.
Krievijas Pedagogijas Akademija (Russian Academy of Pedagogical Sciences), 119905, Pogodinskaja 8, Moscow, Russia
teacher education; educational theory; comparative analysis; cross-national research
formation des enseignants; théorie de l'éducation; analyse comparative; recherche transnationale
PROJECT DESCRIPTION

The project consists of a comparative analysis of the evolution of pedagogical theory in pre-service teacher training in countries representing different political, social and cultural systems and different epistemological styles, viz. Marxist-Leninist, liberal-pragmatic, and classical European.

The study addresses the following questions: To what extent should teacher training be based on the apprenticeship concept? How many and what subjects should be included in the pedagogical component of teacher training? What sources should be used as a knowledge base for teaching? What is the relationship between theory and practice in teacher education? What is the relationship between teachers' personal pedagogical knowledge and their classroom experience?.

Publ: Kurilova, T. Pedagogical training of teachers in Russia: historiographical analyses. In: *Soviet pedagogy*, 1/1991, pp. 81-87.

12184   Pegagogiska tehnologija universitates studentu sagatavosanai skolotaja profesijai. (Development of an educational technology for the preparation of university students for the teaching profession.)
LAT   1994
Research Date(s): 1991-1992
Koke, T.; Shpona, A.; et al.
Sup: Kula, M.
Inst: Latvijas Universitate (University of Latvia), Kronvalda boulv. 4, Riga, 1010 Latvia.
Zinatnu Akademija (Academy of Science), Turgeneva str. 19, Riga, 1018 Latvia
teacher education; educational reform; educational technology; teacher education
formation des enseignants; réforme de l'enseignement; technologie de l'éducation; formation des enseignants
PROJECT DESCRIPTION

Teacher education in Latvia is currently being reformed to respond to the needs of a democratic society. Changes in the training of teachers are urgently needed to stabilize the education system. This means that the pedagogical content of teacher training needs to be revised in order to make optimum use of students' abilities, to foster students' responsibility for their own learning and to prepare students for independent and efficient lifelong learning.

This study sought to contribute to the revision of teacher education programmes on the basis of an analysis of literature on educational technology and past and contemporary experiences of teachers in Latvia. Data were collected through questionnaires, interviews and experiments.

It was found that the most vital element in developing an effective educational technology is the definition of the problem. The main conclusion was that during the theoretical phase of their training, student teachers should develop the ability to formulate problems, to decide what objectives they wish to achieve, to look at phenomena from a particular perspective and to use "tacit knowledge".

12185   Permanentní inovace ekologické výchovy ve vysokoškolské přípravě učitelů chemie. (Continuous innovation of environmental education in chemistry teacher education.)
CSK   1994
Research Date(s): 1992-1996
Neiser, Jan; Zvolský, J.; Dluhoš, L.
Sup: Herčík, M.; Kvasničková, D.
Inst: Ostravská univerzita, Přírodovědecká fakulta, katedra chemie (Ostrava University, Faculty of Natural Sciences, Department of Chemistry), Bráfova 7, 701 00 Ostrava, Czech Republic.
Ministerstvo školství, mládeže a tělovýchovy (Ministry of Education, Youth and Physical Education), Karmelitská 7, 118 00 Praha 1, Czech Republic
teacher education; further education of teachers; quality of education; environmental study; chemistry
formation des enseignants; perfectionnement des enseignants; qualité de l'éducation; étude du milieu; chimie
PROJECT DESCRIPTION

The research project seeks to update the environmental education courses for chemistry student teachers in university faculties of education and natural sciences and in colleges of education.

The project comprises: (1) a comparative study of current practice in environmental education in the Czech Republic and in some selected European countries; (2) the preparation of a design for the innovation and updating of environmental education courses; (3) a study of the use of mobile equipment for the analysis of emissions in environmental education in chemistry teacher training and in chemistry teaching in primary and secondary schools; (4) a study of the use of computer technology for environmental education in chemistry teacher training (computerized model, database and expert system); (5) testing of the proposed improvements in practice in selected subjects in the Chemistry Department of the Faculty of Natural Sciences at Ostrava University; (6) further testing and extension of the project through in-service training for chemistry teachers (seminars for teachers in the Moravosilesian region).

Publ: Neiser, J. & Zvolský, J. *Ekologická výchova ve vysokoškolské přípravě učitelů chemie.* Sborník mezinárodní konference. Fulnek: 17-18.9.1992.

12186   Playgroups' study.
GBR   1993
Research Date(s): 1987-1991
Lloyd, E.; Statham, J.
Sup: Moss, P.; Melhuish, E.
Inst: London University, Institute of Education, Thomas Coram Research Unit, 41 Brunswick Square, London WC1N 1AZ, United Kingdom.
Fin: Department of Health.
pre-school education; pre-school child; educational provision
éducation préscolaire; enfant d'âge préscolaire; scolarisation
PROJECT DESCRIPTION

The first stage of this project examines the pattern of pre-school provision nationally, looking especially at the role of playgroups within it, and at the relationship between playgroups and other under-fives services. Some of the data for this stage comes from an analysis of national statistics, but the main component is a study of 25 local authorities in England, or roughly a quarter of the total. Each area has been visited, and key workers in the Education Department, Social Services Department, and the Preschool Playgroups Association (PPA) interviewed. The second stage is a detailed study of playgroups in contrasting areas, both rural and urban. Approximately 20 playgroups will be selected in each area, taken from the local authority register so as not to confine the sample to PPA members. This stage is based on interviews with around 200 mothers; and on interviews with playgroup leaders, covering such issues as resources, training, parental involvement, methods of management, and liaison with the local authority. It is also intended during this stage to do some exploratory work on children's experiences in different playgroups, using observational methods.

Publ: Lloyd, E. et al. A review of research on playgroups. In: *Early Child Development and Care*, Vol 43, pp. 77-99, March 1989.

12187   Põhikooli õpetajate ettevalmistamise õppekava projekteerimine. (Curriculum development for secondary school teacher training.)
EST   1994
Research Date(s): 1992-1997
Salundi, M.; Kreitzberg, P.; Muoni, H.; et al.
Inst: Tartu ülikool (Tartu University), 2400 Tartu, üliooli 18, Estonia.
Fin: Tartu ülikool; Haridusinnovatsiooni fond.
teacher education; further education of teachers; in-service training; curriculum development; lower secondary
formation des enseignants; perfectionnement des enseignants; formation en cours d'emploi; élaboration de programmes d'études; secondaire premier cycle
PROJECT DESCRIPTION

Middle school teachers in Estonia teach three subjects. Their pre-service training consists of 160 weeks of training, focused on the acquisition of subject matter knowledge. Middle schools are now developing towards a greater degree of independence. Changes in the content and the management of secondary education require changes in the following fields: (1) curriculum and instructional materials; (2) pre-service teacher training; (3) in-service teacher training.

12188 Positive approaches to discipline in inner-city schools.
GBR 1993
Research Date(s): 1990-1991
Gillborn, D.; Rudduck, J.; Nixon, J.
Inst: Sheffield University, Division of Education, 388 Glossop Road, Sheffield S10 2TN, United Kingdom.
Fin: Department of Education and Science.
urban school; quality of education; behaviour; discipline
école urbaine; qualité de l'éducation; comportement; discipline
PROJECT DESCRIPTION
    Inner-city schools are likely, for a number of familiar reasons, to present the greatest challenge to the building and sustaining of a supportive and orderly environment for working. Carefully contextualised accounts of good practice in schools which have different pasts, localities, characters and problems, can powerfully demonstrate the possibilities that are open to all schools staffs. It is now more than a decade since Her Majesty's Inspectorate (HMI) published 'Ten good schools'. Department of Education and Science, HMI. *Ten good schools: a secondary school inquiry: a discussion paper by some members of HM Inspectorate of Schools*, 1977). In the United States of America, Lightfoot's 'The good high school', (Lightfoot, S.L. *The good high school: portraits of character and culture.* New York: Basic, 1983) has made a considerable impact on people's perceptions of schools and their achievements. This study will build on these models by using detailed studies of six inner city schools to identify and explore what HMI have called 'the complex and difficult task of achieving and maintaining high standards of behaviour and discipline'.

12189 Pozvoj profesního růstu pedagogických pracovníků a jeho hodnocení.   (Professional development of teaching staff and its evaluation.)
CSK 1994
Research Date(s): 1991
Singule, František; Mukařovdká, Hana; Procházka, Vladimír; Kloub, Josef; Muchová, Marie; Novotný, Vladimír; Žiška, Vítězslav; et al.
Sup: Sýkora, Václav.
Inst: Ústřední ústav pro vzdělávání pedagogických pracovníků (Central Institute for Teacher Education), Myslíkova 7, 110 00 Praha 1, Czechoslovakia.
Ministerstvo školství, mládeže a tělovýchovy (Ministry of Education, Youth and Physical Eduation), Karmelitská 8, 110 00 Praha 1, Czechoslovakia
further education of teachers; teacher appraisal; salary; teacher status
perfectionnement des enseignants; évaluation sur l'enseignant; traitement; statut de l'enseignant
PROJECT DESCRIPTION
    Aims: To study the professional development of educators in developed countries and to work out a project for the Czech Republic.
    The research was prompted by the debate on the accreditation system in the Czech Republic. During the research the theme was enlarged, as the problem had to be examined in relation with the status of teachers. The synthesis of the different studies led to the design of a project on the accreditation system for teachers in the Czech Republic. The system is connected with salaries and should motivate the teachers to enrol in inservice training.

Publ: Sýkora, V. & Marinková, H. Učitel a reforma školství. In: *Učitel matematiky, fyziky, informatiky. Zpravodaj. MPS JČMF*, 4/1992.

12190 Practical psychiatry in primary care.
GBR 1993
Research Date(s): 1991-1992
Rudland, J.
Sup: Harden, R.
Inst: Dundee University, Centre for Medical Education, Ninewells Hospital and Medical School, Dundee DD1 9SY, United Kingdom.
Fin: SmithKline Beecham Pharmaceuticals Ltd.
distance study; psychiatry; health service personnel
enseignement à distance; psychiatrie; personnel médical
PROJECT DESCRIPTION
    This programme is being developed with the aim of improving the practical psychiatry skills of medical practitioners (GPs). It comprises resource booklets containing sections on depression and anxiety, alcohol abuse, marital and sexual problems, the difficult patient and special problems. The booklets will utilise latent image printing to offer immediate feedback to the participants. Participants will also receive a series of management problems in which decisions have to be taken concerning diagnosis and treatment. Participants' responses to these problems will be returned on a pre-printed card to the Centre for Medical Education. On receipt of the card a personalised commentary on the given responses will be sent to the participants.

12191 Preparing teachers for organisational change: an evaluation of a programme of compulsory inservice training in readiness for the re-organisation of a school system.
GBR 1993
Research Date(s): 1989-1993
Tydeman, M.
Sup: Spence, B.
Inst: Hull University, School of Education, Cottingham Road, Hull HU6 7RX, United Kingdom.
further education of teachers; in-service training; educational reform; training programme; educational administration
perfectionnement des enseignants; formation en cours d'emploi; réforme de l'enseignement; programme de formation; administration de l'enseignement
PROJECT DESCRIPTION
    In September 1988 the organisation of the school system in the city of Hull was changed from transferring children between phases of education at the ages of 9 to 13 to transfer at 11 and 16. This re-organisation involved the simultaneous reallocation into different types of school of 2,000 teachers employed in the city in August 1988. The local education authority recognised that the effective implementation of this re-organisation could only be achieved with the aid of a coordinated and sustained inservice education of teachers (INSET) programme for all affected staff. The programme lasted from 1985 to 1988 and it was remarkable in the history of INSET in five main respects: (1) it involved the sustained daily release of 3% of the teaching force in the city; (2) it was a compulsory programme for all the teachers; (3) it was a systematic programme which was based upon, and supportive of, a city-wide philosophy and policy; (4) it was a centralised programme; and (5) it was planned as an integral part of the re-organisation preparation.
    Large-scale INSET programmes have not been adequately researched before. This evaluation of Hull re-organiation INSET aims to provide information of value to decision makers who are involved in the planning, negotiation and delivery of large-scale INSET programmes based upon a description of the programme, judgements of the extent to which it achieved its stated objectives and the teachers' views of its value to them.

12192 Preparing teachers for student placement.
GBR 1993
Research Date(s): 1990-1991
Cosford, B.
Inst: Heriot-Watt University, Moray House Institute of Education, Holyrood Road, Edinburgh EH8 8AQ, United Kingdom.
teacher education; student teacher; teaching practice; teaching experience; supervision
formation des enseignants; élève-maître; pratique pédagogique; expérience de l'enseignement; surveillance
PROJECT DESCRIPTION
    An investigation of the feasibility and effectiveness of a programme designed to prepare teachers for having a student on placement. In particular to test the Planning, Implementation, Evaluation (PIEC) model, within a context as a framework for developing the teacher's role on placement.

12193 Prevenzione difficolt di apprendimento - Scuola Materna. (Prevention of learning problems in nursery school children.)
ITA 1994
Research Date(s): 1989-
Di Orio, F.; Gargiulo, V.; De Lellis, M.
Sup: Verini, Antonio.
Inst: Istituto Regionale di Ricerca Sperimentazione e Aggiornamento Educativi d'Abruzzo - IRRSAE (Regional Institute for Educational Research, Innovation and Teacher Training, Abruzzo), Via Aldo Moro 30, 67100 L'Aquila, Italy.
Ministero della Pubblica Istruzione (Ministry of Public Education), Viale Trastevere 76, 00100 Roma, Italy
teacher education; further education of teachers; pre-school education; compensatory education; learning difficulty; social handicap
formation des enseignants; perfectionnement des enseignants; éducation préscolaire; éducation compensatoire; difficulté de l'apprentissage; handicap social
PROJECT DESCRIPTION
    Aim: To contribute to the professional development of teachers with respect to alleviating disadvantages (for instance, prevention of learning disabilities) in nursery school children.
    Design: (1) Study of the topic and collecting documentation; (2) updating of nursery school teachers and an evaluation of their attitudes; (3) experimental phase: choice of a regional sample, analysis of the initial situation, methodological-didactic planning, realization; (4) evaluation of the results of the experiment; (5) definition of innovatory modules.
    Hypothesis: By compensating for social disadvantage it is possible to prevent learning difficulties.
    Sample: Nursery schools in the region.
    Methods: Action research.

12194 Probleme der Reorganisation der beruflichen/betrieblichen Weiterbildung fuer die unteren und mittleren Qualifikationsebenen in den fuenf neuen Bundeslaendern. (Problems in reorganizing further vocational/in-house training for people with lower and middle level qualifications in the five new German states.)
DEU 1993
Research Date(s): 1991-1994
Broeker, A.; Kramer, G.
Sup: Lipsmeier, A.; Dobischat, R.
Inst: Universitaet Karlsruhe, Fak. fuer Geistes- und Sozialwissenschaften, Institut fuer Berufspaedagogik, Kaiserstrasse 12, D-7500 Karlsruhe.
Fin: Bundesministerium fuer Bildung und Wissenschaft.
vocational education; further training; in-service training; enterprise; didactics; German DR
enseignement professionnel; formation complémentaire; formation en cours d'emploi; entreprise; didactique; Allemagne RDA
PROJECT DESCRIPTION
Inhalt: Zentrale Aufgabe des Forschungsprojektes ist es, die prozessualen Wandlungen in der Destruktion bzw. Destabilisierung und der zugleich synchron verlaufenden Reorganisation und Stabilisierung der beruflichen und betrieblichen Weiterbildung unter veraenderten Rahmenbedingungen in der ehemaligen DDR im Hinblick auf die institutionell-organisatorischen und konzeptionellen (curricular und didaktisch-methodisch) Wirkungsebenen zu untersuchen. Das Projekt bezieht betriebliche Strategien, Veraenderungen im Bereich der Weiterbildung sowie subjektive Aspekte der potentiellen Weiterbildungsteilnehmer ein.
Geographischer Raum: Ostdeutschland.
Vorgehensweise: In einer Themenfindungsphase werden die Auswertung sekundaer-statistischer Materialien und Einzelfallstudien in ausgewaehlten Regionen und Branchen Zielstellungen und Methoden praezisiert und ausgestaltet; der Schwerpunkt der Empirie in der Hauptphase bildet eine Panel-Befragung (in Verbindung mit dem SOFI), flankiert von Fallstudien und Materialauswertungen.
Datengewinnung: Standardisiertes Interview; Expertengespraech; Befragung; Aktenanalyse. Untersuchungsdesign: Fallstudie.

12195 Processes and outcomes of the introduction of comprehensive schools in England and Wales.
GBR 1993
Research Date(s): 1991-1992
Fogelman, K.; Reeder, D.; Crook, D.
Inst: Leicester University, School of Education, University Road, Leicester LE1 7RH, United Kingdom.
Fin: Spenser Foundation.
comprehensive secondary school; secondary education; history of education; educational reform; England; Wales
école secondaire polyvalente; enseignement secondaire; histoire de l'éducation; réforme de l'enseignement; Angleterre; Pays de Galles
PROJECT DESCRIPTION
This research looks at the processes and outcomes of the introduction of comprehensive schools in England and Wales. Ten representative authorities are being studied and Duke University, North Carolina (collaborating in the project) are working on data gathered by the National Child Development Study.

12196 Professional bodies: education and training and the labour market.
GBR 1993
Research Date(s): 1989-
Trotman-Dickenson, D.
Inst: Glamorgan University, Business School, Pontypridd, Mid Glamorgan CF37 1DL, United Kingdom.
vocational education; professional association; comparative education; cross-national research; Europe
enseignement professionnel; association professionnelle; éducation comparée; recherche transnationale; Europe
PROJECT DESCRIPTION
This research is concerned with professional education and training in the United Kingdom and other countries in Europe. Comparisons with France and Germany have been made and implications of a free market in professional services in the European Community are being examined. The research has been extended to study the market for professional services in Central and Eastern Europe.

Publ: Trotman-Dickenson, D.I. The response of professional bodies to changing needs. In: *Higher Education Review*, Vol 22, No 1/1989, pp. 47-62.
Trotman-Dickenson, D.I. Developing and measuring competence. In: *Proceedings of the Association of Education and Training Technology*, 1991.
Trotman-Dickenson, D.I. Professional bodies and poicies in the anticipation and the aftermath of 1992. In: *The Royal Bank of Scotland Quarterly Review* 29, September 1990.

12197 Professional development of adult educators in south east London.
GBR 1993
Research Date(s): 1991-1993
Clyne, P.
Sup: Coben, D.
Inst: London University, Goldsmiths' College, Department of Continuing and Community Education, Lewisham Way, New Cross, London SE14 6NW, United Kingdom.
Fin: Universities Funding Council.
further education of teachers; adult education; teacher; educational need; continuing education
perfectionnement des enseignants; éducation des adultes; enseignant; besoin d'éducation; éducation permanente
PROJECT DESCRIPTION
This project seeks to research the need for professional development of adult educators in south east London. This will be done through consultation with other providers of adult and continuing education in a range of settings including the new local education authorities, health authorities, social services and others. The aim will be to develop the curriculum and appropriate accreditation and transferability and to begin to provide short courses.

12198 Przygotowanie studentów kierunków nauczycielskich do twórczej pracy zawodowejstan aktualny i próby innowacji. (Preparation of students in pedagogical faculties for creative work and attempts at innovation.)
POL 1994
Research Date(s): 1993-1994
Giza, Teresa.
Inst: Instytut Pedagogiki, Wyższa Szkoła Pedagogiczna w Kielcach (Institute of Pedagogy, Higher School of Education in Kielce), 25-029 Kielce, Krakowska 11, Poland.
teacher education; college of education; educational innovation; creativity; student teacher
formation des enseignants; centre de formation des enseignants; innovation pédagogique; créativité; élève-maître
PROJECT DESCRIPTION
Aim: (1) To make a diagnosis of the efficiency of the training of student teachers in pedagogical universities; (2) to construct an innovatory design of teacher education; (3) to experiment this design.
Design: Diagnostic studies were carried out in three pedagogical universities: in Kielce, Słupsk and Kraków. The innovatory design that was developed involves the introduction of an optional subject called "pedagogics of creativity" which will be piloted from October 1993 to February 1994 with fourth-year students. The following items are included in the programme: exercises in fluency and flexibility, interpersonal training, simulation games, elements of psychodrama, training for the perception of pedagogical problems and sensitivity to problems, training in nonverbal communication.
Methods: In the diagnostic part: questionnaire and interview. In the experimental part: S. Popek Kahn Test, J.P. Guilford Creative Thinking Test, Situation Test, Sensitivity to Pedagogical Problems Test.
Results: Preliminary results show that the information levels and creative thinking abilities of students in pedagogical faculties are very low. Teachers are not prepared for creative work at school. This applies to all of the universities examined. It is expected that the introduction of experimental classes will raise the level of creative thinking and activity amongst prospective teachers.

Publ: Giza, Teresa. Innowacje pedagogiczne jako zjawisko wieloaspektowe. In: *Kieleckie Studia Pedagogiczne i Psychologiczne*, 6/1992, pp. 23-29.
Giza, Teresa. Przygotowanie studentów kierunków nauczycielskich do twórczej pracy zawodowej. In: *Materiały z konferencji nt. "Kierunki rozwoju pedagogiki wczesnoszkolnej"*. Kielce: Wyd.WSP, 1993, pp. 88-102.

12199 Quality assurance in continuing professional education.
GBR 1993
Research Date(s): 1990-1992
Todd, F.; Tovey, P.
Inst: Leeds University, Department of Continuing Professional Education, Leeds LS2 9NG, United Kingdom.
Fin: Universities Funding Council.
continuing education; vocational education; quality of education; evaluation
éducation permanente; enseignement professionnel; qualité de l'éducation; évaluation
PROJECT DESCRIPTION
United Kingdom universities offer programmes of continuing professional education for a wide range of professional groups. The clientele for continuing professional education (CPE) includes professional institutions, employers and individual professionals. A substantial proportion of such programmes comprises short, intensive courses which are not credit-rated and which are planned and held outside existing university course monitor-

ing mechanisms. In the context of an increasing interest in quality assurance procedures (including the setting up of the Committee of Vice-Chancellors and Principals' academic audit unit) this project will explore the quality assurance mechanisms that are or could be used in (primarily university-based) CPE provision.

The research will explore current practice in this field by universities. It will examine quality assurance procedures used in other sectors (e.g. the construction industry, social services and health care) and will assess the applicability of such methods and concepts (e.g. the use of British Standard 5750) to university-based CPE.

Data will be collected through questionnaires to all university CPE providers, to a sample of academic departments which provide CPE independently and to certain professional institutions, employers, and clients. Interviews will be used to follow up key issues in greater depth. Consultancy advice will be taken on quality assurance procedures outside higher education. The aims will be to produce recommendations on good practice and the results of the research will be discussed through workshops and/or conferences as well as through papers and publications.

12200 Quality in initial teacher training - an examination of course structure within selected institutions.
GBR 1993
Research Date(s): 1991-1992
Ducker, P.
Sup: Wilson, J.
Inst: Bishop Grosseteste College, Newport, Lincoln LN1 3DY, United Kingdom.
teacher education; evaluation; quality of education; teaching method
formation des enseignants; évaluation; qualité de l'éducation; méthode pédagogique
PROJECT DESCRIPTION

This research involves an examination of the present initial teacher training course structure that exists within Bishop Grosseteste College and similar institutions. It will examine methods of delivery within the course, and the use of teaching staff to facilitate a more cost-effective course structure that allows a flexible arrangement (with regard to the group tutor system and the need to provide specialist inputs) within a four year BEd (Bachelor of Education) and one year PGCE (Post Graduate Certificate of Education) programme.

The research process involves action research methods through the examination of a sample of teaching groups within Bishop Grosseteste College and other institutions, the collection of data through observation and field notes, interviews, questionnaires and the use of statistical evidence from similar research, if available. The researcher aims to identify, monitor and evaluate elements which affect the quality of student-teacher education.

12201 Racial equality and initial teacher education.
GBR 1993
Research Date(s): 1993-1994
Troyna, B.; Siraj-Blatchford, I.
Inst: Warwick University, Faculty of Educational Studies, Coventry CV4 7AL, United Kingdom.
Fin: Leverhulme Trust.
teacher education; college of education; racial integration; racial discrimination; equal opportunity
formation des enseignants; centre de formation des enseignants; intégration raciale; discrimination raciale; égalité de chances
PROJECT DESCRIPTION

Three case studies of initial teacher education institutions will be undertaken. Using multiple data collection procedures, the research will try to establish the salience of racial equality in these institutions.

12202 Recherche et professionnalisation dans l'enseignement supérieur.
FRA 1993
Research Date(s): 1991-
Demailly, Lise.
Sup: Caspar, Pierre; Barbier, Jean-Marie.
Inst: Université de Lille I, Centre lillois d'études et de recherches sociologiques et économiques, CNRS URA/345, Laboratoire de sociologie du travail, de l'éducation et de l'emploi, Institut de Sociologie, 59655 Villeneuve d'Ascq Cedex, France.
Fin: Ministère de l'éducation, Direction de la recherche et des études doctorales (DRED).
vocational education; higher education; branch of study; research; engineer; teacher; trainer
enseignement professionnel; enseignement supérieur; filière d'études; recherche; ingénieur; enseignant; formateur
PROJECT DESCRIPTION

Objectifs: Dans le cadre du réseau DRED, il s'agit: (1) d'identifier les différents types de filières dans lesquelles se produit un des processus institutionnels suivants: universitarisation de filières professionnalisées, création de filières professionnalisées en marge des filières académiques,

introduction de la "recherche" comme outil de formation professionnelle; et (2) de dégager les conditions d'émergence de ces filières.

Méthodologie: Les terrains d'observation sont des formations d'ingérieurs, d'enseignants, de travailleurs sociaux, de responsables de communication ou de gestion des ressources humaines, de formateurs d'adultes. Le LASTREE prend en charge deux terrains spécifiques: formations universitaires à la communication d'entreprise et formations des enseignants en Instituts universitaires de formation des maîtres (IUFM).

12203 Réforme de l'enseignement des branches de culture générale dans les écoles professionnelles.
CHE 1994
Research Date(s): 1988-1994
Berset, Jean-Etienne; Ammann, Beat; Wiebel, Bernhard; Wenger, Bernhard; et al.
Sup: Natsch, Rudolf.
Inst: Office fédéral de l'industrie, des arts et métiers et du travail (OFIAMT), Bundesgasse 8, 3003 Berne, Suisse.
vocational education; general education; curriculum; educational reform
enseignement professionnel; enseignement général; programme d'études; réforme de l'enseignement
PROJECT DESCRIPTION

En automne 1988, après avoir consulté et réuni des représentants de tous les milieux concernés, l'OFIAMT a créé une commission chargée de s'attaquer à la réforme de l'enseignement des branches de culture générale dans les écoles professionnelles. Un groupe de travail de cette commission a ensuite élaboré un rapport, présenté en juillet 1990, qui contenait des indications quant aux objectifs à poursuivre dans le processus de réforme, ceci tant du point de vue des contenus que de celui de l'organisation. Conformément aux recommandations de ce groupe, l'OFIAMT a mis sur pied une structure tripartite chargée de poursuivre le travail de réforme. Il y a d'abord la Direction du projet, ensuite le Groupe de planification et enfin le Groupe de validation, dans lequel toutes les écoles professionnelles de Suisse sont représentées; ce dernier groupe doit assurer entre autres les contacts avec la pratique. Les résultats de chaque phase de travail sont discutés par le Groupe de validation. Si ce groupe réagit positivement, la phase est validée. Il appartient ensuite à la direction du projet de donner son feu vert pour la phase suivante. Certaines recommandations touchant aux contenus des programmes ont également été approuvées; l'enseignement général rénové ne sera plus, en partie du moins, subdivisé en branches; il sera orienté vers l'action, axé sur des thèmes, et pluridisciplinaire.

Pour la phase de travail actuellement en cours, le Groupe de planification s'est divisé en quatre sous-groupes qui élaborent chacun un projet de plan d'études. Un sous-groupe est basé en Suisse romande (Neuchâtel), un autre au Tessin et deux en Suisse alémanique (l'un à Zurich, l'autre à Berne). Ces groupes s'organisent de manière autonome et peuvent faire appel, en fonction des besoins, à des conseillers scientifiques en matière de pédagogie. En août, les projets seront présentés en trois langues au groupe de validation. Le processus de validation durera jusqu'en octobre. Les résultats des travaux ainsi validés seront soumis à la Direction du projet par le Groupe de planification. En cas d'accord de la Direction du projet, une esquisse d'un nouveau plan d'études sera vraisemblablement élaborée sur la base des quatre plans-pilote jusqu'en mai 1993, et le reste de l'année sera consacré à la consultation des milieux intéressés. Si tout va bien, les nouveaux programmes pourront entrer en vigueur au début de l'anné scolaire 1994/1995.

Publ: BIGA-Arbeitsgruppe "Reform Allgemeinbildender Unterricht; Arbeitsgruppe Unterrichtsinhalte. *Inhaltliche und organisatorische Zielvorstellungen für die Reform des allgemeinbildenden Unterrichts: Bericht und Anträge.* Bern, Juli 1990, 18 Seiten.

12204 Reorganising further education: the tertiary option.
GBR 1993
Research Date(s): 1990-1991
Tomlins, B.
Sup: Stoney, S.
Inst: National Foundation for Educational Research, The Mere, Upton Park, Slough SL1 2DQ, United Kingdom.
post-secondary education; educational institution; educational administration; educational reform
enseignement postsecondaire; établissement d'enseignement; administration de l'enseignement; réforme de l'enseignement
PROJECT DESCRIPTION

Since the first tertiary college was established at Exeter in 1970, demographic changes and constraints on local authority spending have encouraged other authorities to consider reorganising educational provision for 16-19 year olds along tertiary lines, and there are now more than 70 tertiary colleges. Much of the literature on tertiary systems is based on personal accounts of tertiary reorganisation and provision. The project seeks to provide a broad-based and objective assessment of the tertiary option. It aims to explore the variety of approaches to tertiary reorganisation to be found in different local authorities and to provide a fund of data and set of guidelines on the management of tertiary systems.

Interviews have been conducted with senior local education authority officers and college principals in fifteen tertiary authorities, and more detailed case study work carried out in seven authorities. Approaches and experiences in all other tertiary and non-tertiary authorities are being explored by means of questionnaires.

A literature review and final report of the project have been published.

Publ: Tomlins, B. & Miles, J. *Reorganising post-16 education: the tertiary option.* Slough: NFER, 1991.

12205 Ressursbruk og produksjon i institusjoner for höyere utdanning. (Productivity in higher education.)
NOR 1994
Research Date(s): 1992-1993
Hernæs, Erik.
Inst: Stiftelsen for Samfunns- og Næringslivsforskning (Centre for Research in Economics and Business Administration), Gaustadalléen 21, 0371 Oslo, Norway.
Fin: NORAS.
higher education; performance; productivity
enseignement supérieur; performance; productivité
PROJECT DESCRIPTION

The project will undertake a productivity analysis of higher education with the help of a database for higher education which is currently being constructed. A related purpose of the project is to test this database and to give recommendations for its structure. Data envelopment analysis (DEA) as well as other methods will be used in the analysis. The unit of analysis will be departments, and variation in productivity will be related to organizational and other characteristics, in order to understand and provide a basis for decision-making in the field of higher education, or even to make policy recommendations. Part of this process will be to provide an empirical basis for a budget model which is being set up for the Ministry of Education, Research and Church Affairs.

Publ: Dalen, D.M.; Hernæs, E.; Norli, Y.; et al. *Om analyse av effektivitet i höyere utdanning.* Oslo: SNF, 1993, 39p. (Arbeidsnotater 46/1993).

12206 Reviewing post-16 provision in four occupational sectors.
GBR 1993
Research Date(s): 1990-1991
Gray, L.; Warrender, A.-M.; Latcham, J.
Inst: Staff College, Coombe Lodge, Blagdon, Bristol BS18 6RG, United Kingdom.
Fin: Gloucestershire Local Education Authority.
post-compulsory education; training-employment relationship; transition from school to work; demand for education; educational provision
enseignement postobligatoire; relation formation-emploi; passage à la vie active; demande d'éducation; scolarisation
PROJECT DESCRIPTION

This research will involve a review of current and future demand for post-16 provision of education and training in the sectors of agriculture and horticulture, art and design, caring and the motor vehicle industry.

12207 The role of a change agent in the introduction of a new curriculum in technical teacher training.
GBR 1993
Research Date(s): 1990-1994
Thompson, W.
Sup: Sands, M.
Inst: Nottingham University, School of Education, University Park, Nottingham NG7 2RD, United Kingdom.
teacher education; curriculum development; innovation
formation des enseignants; élaboration de programmes d'études; innovation
PROJECT DESCRIPTION

The research stems from the researcher's involvement as a consultant in a large project in an overseas country. This was to introduce a new teacher training curriculum into four faculties of technical/vocational teacher training, based upon common, core subjects/modules, that would apply in all faculties. It involved major structural and equipment refurbishment and the provision of new equipment.

The basic method is the use of case studies based upon observation as a full participator. Curriculum documents, discussion papers, questionnaires, minutes of meetings, project documents, will be used as the database. Major themes to be considered will be the management of the project, role of consultancy and individual consultants, working methods of consultants, development of curriculum, development of faculty management resources and facilities.

Comparison will be made with published accounts of other similar projects undertaken in overseas countries. From this an hypotheses about the role of change agents in similar situations will be generated.

12208 The role of the local education authority in the professional development of new teachers.
GBR 1993
Research Date(s): 1992-1993
Earley, P.; Harland, J.; Kinder, K.

Inst: National Foundation for Educational Research, The Mere, Upton Park, Slough SL1 2DQ, United Kingdom.
teacher education; further education of teachers; probationary teacher; local government
formation des enseignants; perfectionnement des enseignants; enseignant stagiaire; administration locale
PROJECT DESCRIPTION

Awareness of the potentially powerful role of local education authorities (LEAs) and schools in programmes of professional development for new teachers has been heightened following the introduction of the new training routes to Qualified Teacher Status (QTS), the proposed changes in the nature and content of initial teacher training courses and the abolition of probation. A growing number of LEAs and schools are offering induction and training programmes designed to ensure the continuing development of the professional skills and competencies currently required of new teachers, not least in the delivery of the National Curriculum.

This 18-month study is employing both survey and case study research methods to investigate the role of the LEAs in the extension of initial training. It intends to analyse the professional development programmes offered to new teachers and seek perceptions of the range of professionals involved on their effects and outcomes. The main aim of the research is to contribute to the improvement of the quality of support offered to new teachers. More specifically, the research has three aims: (i) to gather a broad base of information from all LEAs on their structures and procedures for training and supporting new teachers; (ii) to collect more detailed information from selected authorities and schools on professional development programmes in practice; and (iii) to ascertain the perceptions of a wide range of providers and practitioners on the benefits, problems and overall effectiveness of the various approaches to the induction and development of new teachers.

The research will begin with a series of exploratory interviews in several LEAs to gather initial perspectives from key training personnel on the main issues relating to the induction and professional development of new teachers. The material collected from these interviews, complemented by the findings from recent research studies, will be used to develop a questionnaire which will be sent to each authority. An interim report based on the questionnaire findings will be available by autumn 1992.

In the next phase of the research, interviews will be held with LEA personnel to clarify and expand upon the questionnaire data. About six LEAs will then be chosen for case study investigation. In each case study location, interviews will be held with relevant LEA personnel and all documentation relating to the professional development of new teachers will be collected. A sample of schools will be selected to represent the primary and secondary sectors as well as grant-maintained schools within each LEA. The work in the schools will involve interviews with headteachers, INSET coordinators, staff with responsibility for the guidance and support of new teachers, and the new teachers themselves. It will, of course, be important to ensure that teachers following different routes to QTS are included in the sample. The particular emphasis during the case study phase will be on collecting more detailed information on the content and delivery of training and support programmes in the selected LEAs and schools, whilst also focusing on emerging issues. A final report, drawing on both the survey and case study evidence will be produced at the end of the project.

Publ: Earley, P. *Beyond initial teacher training: induction and the role of the LEA.* Slough: NFER, 1992.

12209 The role of the mentor in initial teacher education.
GBR 1993
Research Date(s): 1992-1993
Furlong, J.
Inst: University College of Swansea, Department of Education, Hendrefoilan, Swansea SA2 7NB, United Kingdom.
Fin: Paul Hamlyn Foundation.
teacher education; supervision
formation des enseignants; surveillance
PROJECT DESCRIPTION

This is an in-depth study of the work of eight 'mentors' in different programmes of initial teacher education.

12210 Rozšiřující studium učitelství všeobecně vzdělávacího předmětu pro absolventy neučitelských studijních oborů (zahr. DPS). (Rationalization of the preparation of university graduates for the teaching profession.)
CSK 1994
Research Date(s): 1992-1993
Mošna, F.; Jesenská, Z.; Mojžišová, J.; Sýkora, V.; Holada, K.; Boučková, V.; Dostál, P.
Sup: Nagy, J.
Inst: Pedagogická fakulta Univerzity Karlovy (Charles University, Faculty of Education), M.D. Rettigové 4, 116 39 Praha 1, Czech Republic.
Ministerstvo školství, mládeže a tělovýchovy (Ministry of Education, Youth and Physical Education), Karmelitská 7, 118 00 Praha 1, Czech Republic
teacher education; graduate; qualification; curriculum development

formation des enseignants; étudiant diplômé; qualification; élaboration de programmes d'études
PROJECT DESCRIPTION

Aim: The aim of the study is to rationalize the preparation of university graduates for the teaching profession. As a result of this rationalization, graduates interested in entering the teaching profession will no longer be required to complete two subjects as part of their teacher training programme.

Results: The project has resulted in the design of two-semester and four-semester Bachelor of Education courses, comprising instruction in philosophical and psychological subjects as well as educational theory and practice.

12211 Rural Schools Curriculum Enhancement National Evaluation (SCENE) project.
GBR 1993
Research Date(s): 1988-1991
Galton, M.; Fogelman, K.; Hargreaves, L.; Cavendish, S.
Inst: Leicester University, School of Education, University Road, Leicester LE1 7RH, United Kingdom.
Fin: Department of Education and Science.
rural school; regional cooperation; curriculum development
école rurale; coopération régionale; élaboration de programmes d'études
PROJECT DESCRIPTION

The rural SCENE (Schools Curriculum Enhancement National Evaluation) project is evaluating 14 pilot projects using education support grants (ESGs) to extend the range or improve the quality of the curriculum in rural primary schools. The various local authority pilot projects have used a range of strategies to achieve this, e.g. the use of clustering of schools to share resources and inservice provision, the employment of coordinators and advisory teachers with varying duties and the provision of transport to bring children from small schools together into larger peer groupings. The grants were provided for three to five years.

Six case studies of schools in local education authorities which used similar strategies are being conducted. The data collection includes interviews; questionnaires to ESG and non-ESG schools; classroom observation of children's activities and projective activities for children. Major themes which are emerging include the history of school cooperation within areas and the effectiveness of 'working alongside' as an inservice method.

12212 Sample enhancement for the 1991 Scottish Young People's Survey.
GBR 1993
Research Date(s): 1990-1991
Raffe, D.; McPherson, A.
Inst: Edinburgh University, Centre for Educational Sociology, 7 Buccleuch Place, Edinburgh EH8 9JT, United Kingdom.
Fin: Economic and Social Research Council.
school leaver; transition from school to work; Scotland; youth employment; post-compulsory education
élève sortant; passage à la vie active; Ecosse; emploi des jeunes; enseignement postobligatoire
PROJECT DESCRIPTION

The project aims to support enhancement of the sampling fraction of the 1991 Scottish Young People's Survey.

Publ: A bibliography of published work and further details of the project are available.

12213 School-based teacher training: a comparative case study of an Articled Teacher course and a one-year Post-Graduate Certificate in Education (PGCE) course.
GBR 1993
Research Date(s): 1991-1994
Cashmore, C.
Sup: Hannan, A.; Halstead, J.
Inst: Plymouth University, Rolle Faculty of Education, Douglas Avenue, Exmouth EX8 2AT, United Kingdom; University College of Swansea, Department of Education, Hendrefoilan, Swansea SA2 7NB, United Kingdom.
teacher education; post-graduate; student teacher; teaching profession
formation des enseignants; étudiant niveau postuniversitaire; élève-maître; profession d'enseignant
PROJECT DESCRIPTION

The aim of the study is to consider recent moves to develop school based teacher training and in particular to carry out a comparative case study of the Articled Teacher course and a more traditional one-year Post-Graduate Certificate of Education (PGCE) course based at Rolle Faculty of Education, University of Plymouth, concentrating on the 1991 intake.

The study will be an evaluation based on the 'illuminative' approach using participant observation, questionnaires and interviews. There are 12 Articled Teachers and 75 students on the one-year course, of which 12 will be studied in detail.

12214 School/Industry Compacts: the translation of an American model to England.
GBR 1993
Research Date(s): 1988-
Ferguson, S.
Inst: Liverpool University, Department of Education, PO Box 147, Liverpool L69 3BX, United Kingdom.
vocational education; industry; school; cooperation; comparative education; USA
enseignement professionnel; industrie; école; coopération; éducation comparée; Etats-Unis
PROJECT DESCRIPTION

The Boston Compact has been used as a model for school/industry compacts in the United Kingdom which have been promoted by government, industry and local authorities since late 1987. This research builds upon first-hand knowledge of the original Boston Compact to make comments upon the applicability of this American model to the English education setting.

12215 SchuelerInnen an Alternativschulen und Regelschulen: ein Vergleich. (A comparison of pupils in alternative schools and regular schools.)
AUT 1993
Research Date(s): 1991-1993
Fischer-Kowalski, Marina; Pelikan, Johanna; Drasch, Wolfgang; Schandl, Heinz; Wieger, Maria.
Inst: Abteilung fuer Schule und gesellschaftliches Lernen, Seidengasse 13, A-1070 Wien.
Institut fuer interdisziplinaere Forschung und Fortbildung, Seidengasse 13, A-1070 Wien
Fin: Bundesministerium fuer Unterricht und Kunst.
alternative school; experimental education; parent participation; comparative analysis
école alternative; pédagogie expérimentale; participation des parents; analyse comparative
PROJECT DESCRIPTION

Alternativschulen stellen in Oesterreich eine autonome Schulform dar. Sie folgen nur zum Teil dem oesterreichischen Lehrplan und organisieren sich nach basisdemokratischen Modellen der Lehrer-Schueler-Eltern Kooperation. Sie werden jedoch nur von einem sehr kleinen Teil der Bevoelkerung in Anspruch genommen, der Grossteil weiss nichts von ihrer Existenz. Trotzdem erwecken sie Kontroversen. Man koennte ihnen die Rolle eines Modells, eines Experiments, eines Schulversuchs - allerdings ungefoerdert - zuschreiben. Was bisher fehlte, waren objektivierbare Anhaltspunkte, was die besonderen Leistungen, die Staerken und Defizite von Alternativschulen ausmacht, ebenso wie ein Erfahrungsaustausch zwischen 'Alternativschulen' und 'Regelschulen'. Diese Studie stellt sich die Frage, wie sich die Schulerfahrungen von Eltern und Kindern an beiden Schulformen unterscheiden und welche Auswirkungen das hat. Diese Fragen sollen im Rahmen von exemplarischen Teilstudien, ueberwiegend an Volksschulen, untersucht werden. Aus den folgenden Teilstudien sollen mit Hilfe des Beirats und der Lehrer und Eltern der Schulen fuenf bis sechs Themen ausgewaehlt werden: Schulangst, Interesse und Neugierverhalten, Soziale Kompetenzen/Selbststaendigkeit, Soziale Kompetenzen/Konfliktaustragung und Problemloesungsstrategien, Sexualitaet und geschlechtsspezifisches Verhalten, Schulleistungen, Moralentwicklung und Gerechtigkeitssinn, Schule als seelische Belastung fuer Kinder, Erkrankungshaeufigkeit/Gesundheitszustand, Elternwuensche/Elternaengste im Vergleich, Zukunft von Alternativschulen.

In die Fragebogenerhebung werden die Eltern von 53 AlternativschuelerInnen und die Eltern von 36 RegelschuelerInnen (Volksschule) einbezogen. Die experimentelle Situation in neun Klassen von Alternativschulen mit durchschnittlich sieben Kindern, in vier Regelschulklassen mit durchschnittlich 23 Kindern und in zwei Vergleichsgruppen von RegelschuelerInnen mit neun Kindern (Volksschule) wird in einem Beobachtungsprotokoll festgehalten. Interviews mit LehrerInnen und Lehrherrn von ehemaligen AlternativschuelerInnen sind geplant. Ausserdem sollen standardisierte Tests (Rechtschreibung und Rechnen) an der Gesamtpopulation der Wiener alternativen VolksschuelerInnen - 95 Kinder - sowie eine soziolinguistische Analyse von 15 Tonbandaufnahmen durchgefuehrt werden.

Es werden Methoden der empirischen Sozialforschung verwendet.

Folgende Zwischenergebnisse liegen vor: 1. Sozialstatistische Erfassung der Alternativschuleltern: Die Population der Eltern von AlternativschuelerInnen lebt in unkonventionelleren Familienverhaeltnissen als die Restbevoelkerung (hoeherer Anteil alleinerziehender Muetter, nichteheliche Lebensgemeinschaften) und verfuegt ueber ein ueberdurchschnittliches Bildungsniveau und eine hohe berufliche Qualifikation bei unter dem Durchschnitt liegendem Einkommen. In einem Vergleich der Einstellungen von Eltern von AlternativschuelerInnen bzw. Eltern von SchuelerInnen der Regelschule (mit aehnlichem sozialem Hintergrund) zu beiden Schultypen nehmen beide Elterngruppen die Alternativschule positiver wahr. 2. Eine experimentelle Studie zur sozialen Kompetenz (insbesondere Konfliktaustragung und Problemloesungsstrategie) von RegelschuelerInnen und AlternativschuelerInnen ergibt bei den AlternativschuelerInnen ein einheitliches Bild: sie sind faehig, Diskussionen und Entscheidungsprozesse als Gruppe, ohne Hilfe von Erwachsenen, zu initiieren und zu strukturieren. In Regelschulklassen gibt es eine viel groessere Spannbreite an Verhaltensmustern. Der/die einzelne LehrerIn ist anscheinend ausschlaggebend.

Publ: 1. und 2. Zwischenbericht zum Projekt 'SchuelerInnen an Alternativschulen und Regelschulen - Ein Vergleich'.

12216 Schulung von Multiplikatorinnen in den neuen Bundeslaendern. (Training female "multiplicators" in the new German states.)
DEU 1993
Research Date(s): 1991-1993
Ellebrecht, I.; Sessar-Karpp, E.; Kirchner, M.; Schiersmann, C.
Inst: Deutscher Frauenring e.V., FrauenTechnikZentrum, Normannenweg 2, D-2000 Hamburg 26.
Fin: Bundesministerium fuer Bildung und Wissenschaft.
German DR; in-service training; further training; vocational guidance
Allemagne RDA; formation en cours d'emploi; formation complémentaire; orientation professionnelle
PROJECT DESCRIPTION
Inhalt: Berufsbegleitende Fortbildung von Multiplikatorinnen im Weiterbildungsbereich in den neuen Bundeslaendern und Fortbildung von Weiterbildungsberaterinnen.
Geographischer Raum: Ostdeutschland.
Vorgehensweise: Uebliche Methoden der empirischen Sozialforschung.
Datengewinnung: Standardisiertes Interview (Stichprobe: ca. 10; Weiterbildungseinrichtungen in den neuen Bundeslaendern). Gruppendiskussion (Stichprobe: ca. 10; Weiterbildungseinrichtungen in den neuen Bundeslaendern). Expertengespraech (Stichprobe: ca. 10; Weiterbildungseinrichtungen in den neuen Bundeslaendern). Befragung (Stichprobe: ca. 10; Weiterbildungseinrichtungen in den neuen Bundeslaendern). Beobachtung (Stichprobe: ca. 10; Weiterbildungseinrichtungen in den neuen Bundeslaendern).

12217 Schulvergleich BRD - UdSSR. (Comparison of schools in the Federal Republic of Germany and the Soviet Union.)
DEU 1993
Research Date(s): 1990-1992
Novikov, L.; Ruecker, H.; Scheerer, H.; Schneider, H.
Sup: Glowka, D.
Inst: Universitaet Muenster, FB 09 Erziehungswissenschaft, Institut fuer Erziehungswissenschaft, 01 Abt. Vgl. Erziehungswissenschaft, Georgskommende 26, D-4400 Muenster.
Fin: Deutsche Forschungsgemeinschaft.
education system; school; teaching method; USSR; Germany; general education; comparative education
système d'enseignement; école; méthode pédagogique; URSS; Allemagne; enseignement général; éducation comparée
PROJECT DESCRIPTION
Inhalt: Vergleich von je drei allgemeinbildenden Schulen in Deutschland und in Russland. Erprobung eines Modells qualitativer differentieller Schulforschung im interkulturellen Vergleich. Erwartung von deutlichen Unterschieden in der Unterrichtsmethodik (Laenderdifferenzen groesser als die Schuldifferenzen).
Geographischer Raum: Schulen in Muenster, Wulfen, Moskau, Rjasan.
Untersuchter Zeitraum: 1991.
Vorgehensweise: Versuch einer ganzheitlichen Erfassung der Qualitaet von Schulen (Schule als "Kultur"); Kombination von strukturierten Beobachtungen (insbesondere Unterrichtsbeobachtung); Datenerhebung ueber Fragebogen und Interviews. Untersuchungsdesign: Fallstudie; qualitative Forschung; interkulturell vergleichend.
Datengewinnung: Gruppenbefragung (Stichprobe: 400; Schueler von 18 Klassen; Auswahlverfahren: total. Stichprobe: 400; Eltern von 18 Klassen; Auswahlverfahren: total. Stichprobe: 200; Lehrer von 6 Schulen; Auswahlverfahren: total). Nicht-standardisiertes Interview (Stichprobe: 20; Schueler und Lehrer aus 6 Schulen; Auswahlverfahren: willkuerlich). Beobachtung (Stichprobe: 120; Unterrichtsstunden aus 6 Schulen; Auswahlverfahren: bewusst). Primaererhebung: Feldarbeit von Mitarbeitern des Projektes durchgefuehrt.
Auswertung: Multivariate Verfahren. Datenaufbereitung: Aufschliessung von Video-Aufzeichnungen von Unterricht.

12218 Schulzentrierte Lehrerfortbildung. (School-centred in-service training of teachers.)
AUT 1993
Research Date(s): 1992-
Juna, Johanna; Scheutl, Karl.
Inst: Paedagogisches Institut der Stadt Wien, Burggasse 14-16, A-1070 Wien.
further education of teachers; dyslexia; individualized teaching; remedial teaching
perfectionnement des enseignants; dyslexie; enseignement individualisé; soutien pédagogique
PROJECT DESCRIPTION
In den letzten zwei Jahren wurde an einer Ganztagsschule die Grundausbildung zum Legasthenikerbetreuer durchgefuehrt. Die Schule als Standort

der Lehrerfortbildung bot die Moeglichkeit, das Umsetzen des in der Vorlesung Gebotenen in die Praxis zu beobachten. Auf Wunsch der KolleginInnen wurden fuer das Schuljahr 1992/1993 Arbeitsgruppen installiert, die sich vor allem mit der Individualisierung im Unterricht beschaeftigen.

In die Untersuchung werden zwei erste Klassen, eine zweite Klasse und zwei Legasthenikerkurse einbezogen. Die Arbeit mit dem Schulleiter begleitet das Projekt.

Die Evaluation erfolgt durch die Methode der Aktionsforschung (action research).

12219 Special needs in primary schools.
GBR 1993
Research Date(s): 1989-
Rouse, M.
Sup: Balshaw, M.
Inst: Cambridge University, Institute of Education, Shaftesbury Road, Cambridge CB2 2BX, United Kingdom.
Fin: Six Local Education Authorities.
special education; primary education; cooperation; integration; further education of teachers; local government
enseignement spécial; enseignement primaire; coopération; intégration; perfectionnement des enseignants; administration locale
PROJECT DESCRIPTION
This project investigates the effects of the government-funded National Priority Area (NPA) courses designed to help schools in meeting special educational needs. A collaborative initiative was established six years ago between higher education (Cambridge Institute of Education) and a number of local education authorities (LEAs). The initiative linked individual development for teachers with institutional development for their schools with the active participation of the LEAs.

Follow-up evaluation by survey, case study and other ethnographic methods across five LEAs has. indicated successful implementation of school change and growth for individual participants.

Publ: Rouse, M. & Balshaw, M. Collaborative INSET and special educational needs. In: Upton, G. (ed.). *Staff development for special educational needs.* London: David Fulton, 1991.
Rouse, M. Effective INSET: the role of the outsider. In: McLaughlin, C. & Rouse, M. (eds.). *Supporting schools.* London: David Fulton, 1991.

12220 Special needs in the classroom.
GBR 1993
Research Date(s): 1988-1995
Ainscow, M.
Inst: Cambridge University, Institute of Education, Shaftesbury Road, Cambridge CB2 2BX, United Kingdom.
Fin: UNESCO.
special education; teacher education; teaching aid; integration; cross-national research
enseignement spécial; formation des enseignants; moyen d'enseignement; intégration; recherche transnationale
PROJECT DESCRIPTION
The aim of this project is to develop and disseminate teacher education materials that can be used to help student teachers and experienced teachers cater for pupil diversity in mainstream schools. The research involves an international resource team. Intensive action research was carried out in 1990-1991 in eight countries. This has led to the development of a resource pack, video programmes and a coordinator's guide. On the basis of this formative research the materials are now being used in over 30 countries.

Major national action research projects involving the project materials and ideas are currently underway in China, India, Spain and Thailand. Developments are also being introduced in the Middle East, South America and Africa. All of these developments involve further action research to refine the theoretical basis of the materials.

Publ: Ainscow, M. Special needs in the classroom: the development of teacher education resource pack. In: *International Journal of Special Education*, Vol 5, No 1/1990, pp. 13-20.
Ainscow, M. Teacher education as a strategy for developing inclusive schools. In: Slee, R. (ed.). *The politics of integration.* London: Falmer Press, 1993.
Ainscow, M. Teacher development and special needs: some lessons from the UNESCO project 'Special needs in the classroom'. In: Mittler, P. et al. (eds.). *World yearbook of education.* London: Kogan Page, 1993.
Ainscow, M. *Special needs in the classroom: a teacher education guide.* Paris: UNESCO, 1993.

12221 Spring 1991 and Autumn 1991 Scottish Young People's Surveys.
GBR 1993
Research Date(s): 1990-1992
Middleton, L.; McPherson, A.; Lamb, J.; Jones, G.; Hughes, J.; Brannen, K.; Fairgrieve, J.
Sup: Raffe, D.

Inst: Edinburgh University, Centre for Educational Sociology, 7 Buccleuch Place, Edinburgh EH8 9JT, United Kingdom.

Fin: Scottish Education Department; Department of Employment; Industry Department for Scotland; Training Agency.

school leaver; transition from school to work; Scotland; youth employment; post-compulsory education

élève sortant; passage à la vie active; Ecosse; emploi des jeunes; enseignement postobligatoire

PROJECT DESCRIPTION

Three further postal surveys in the SYPS (Scottish Young People's Survey) series will be conducted. A 10% national sample of young people who started S4 in 1989, and an overlapping 10% sample of leavers from the 1989/1990 session, will be surveyed in Spring 1991. The latter will extend the biennial sequence of leavers' surveys since 1977. A 10% sample of young people who started S4 in 1987, which was surveyed in the Spring 1989 SYPS, will be surveyed again in Autumn 1991.

Publ: A bibliography of published work and further details of the project are available.

12222 Spring 1991 and autumn 1991 Scottish Young People's Surveys.

GBR 1993

Research Date(s): 1990-1992

Raffe, D.; Lamb, J.; Jones, G.; Hughes, J.; Brannen, K.; Fairgrieve, J.; Middleton, L.

Sup: McPherson, A.

Inst: Edinburgh University, Centre for Educational Sociology, 7 Buccleuch Place, Edinburgh EH8 9JT, United Kingdom.

Fin: Scottish Office, Education Department; Department of Employment; Industry Department for Scotland; Training, Enterprise & Education Directorate.

labour market; youth employment; career; school career; survey; school leaver; vocational education; post-compulsory education; Scotland

marché du travail; emploi des jeunes; carrière; cursus scolaire; enquête; élève sortant; enseignement professionnel; enseignement postobligatoire; Ecosse

PROJECT DESCRIPTION

Three further postal surveys in the Scottish Young People's Survey (SYPS) series will be conducted. A 10% national sample of young people who started S4 in 1989, and an overlapping 10% sample of leavers from the 1989/1990 session, will be surveyed in spring 1991. The latter will extend the biennial sequence of leavers surveys since 1977. A 10% sample of young people who started S4 in 1987, which was surveyed in the spring 1989 SYPS, will be surveyed again in autumn 1991.

Publ: A full list of publications is available.

12223 Student evaluation of teaching in higher education in the UK.

GBR 1993

Research Date(s): 1991-1993

Demaine, J.

Inst: Loughborough University of Technology, Department of Education, Loughborough LE11 3TU, United Kingdom.

higher education; teaching quality

enseignement supérieur; qualité de l'enseignement

PROJECT DESCRIPTION

This is an investigation into student evaluation of teaching in higher education in the United Kingdom.

12224 Student teachers' perceptions of stressful situations in schools.

GBR 1993

Research Date(s): 1991-1994

Macintyre, C.

Inst: Heriot-Watt University, Moray House Institute of Education, Holyrood Road, Edinburgh EH8 8AQ, United Kingdom.

student teacher; teacher education; teaching practice; mental stress; student behaviour

élève-maître; formation des enseignants; pratique pédagogique; tension mentale; comportement de l'étudiant

PROJECT DESCRIPTION

Most student teachers expect to have anxious, even stressful times during their weeks on school placement as they build relationships with teachers, children and tutors, learn to teach and have continuous assessment. Some cope very well; they may even find short periods of anxiety or stress stimulating if there is a fairly immediate and successful outcome. But others find that stress builds to an unacceptable level, that of distress and they fail to cope. This can have devastating and possibly long lasting results. What then are the factors which cause student teachers stress/distress? Are there ways (coping strategies) in which they can be helped to cope?

This research intends to address these questions by asking student teachers to reflect on their practice and report their level of anxiety stress/distress, to articulate if they can name the factors that caused them stress and to evaluate the coping strategies they used. Having identified the students' perceptions and their successful coping strategies the

research will then find if these can usefully be shared with other students to alleviate their problems. Finally the student teachers in the next cohort at Moray House will be asked whether knowledge of coping strategies helped them to select appropriately and so helped to reduce the level of stress to at least an acceptable degree.

12225 Students, supervisors and the social science research training process.

GBR 1993

Research Date(s): 1990-1991

Acker, S.; Hill, T.; Black, E.

Inst: Bristol University, School of Education, 35 Berkeley Square, Bristol BS8 1JA, United Kingdom.

Fin: Economic and Social Research Council.

graduate study; research; social sciences; student; supervision

supérieur deuxième cycle; recherche; sciences sociales; étudiant; surveillance

PROJECT DESCRIPTION

This project is one of four qualitative studies funded by the Economic and Social Research Council to investigate the experiences of research students in social science departments. The project's theoretical contributions will be to greater understanding of the social science research student supervision process, through collecting data on policies, practices, experiences and expectations from both students and supervisors. The supervisor-student relationship is conceptualised as a teaching-learning interaction embedded in a framework of contextual factors, including structures and cultures of departments and disciplines.

An additional anticipated outcome is a practical contribution to academic staff development. In the British model of social science graduate education the supervisor plays a key role, yet training for supervisors is minimal. This project will help discover from experienced supervisors what, in their opinion, is 'good practice' and from less experienced ones, what they would like to learn. The main part of the study will consist of in-depth interviews with a sample of supervisors and research students in eight or nine departments. A particular focus will be upon the disciplines of psychology and education, although several other subjects will be represented. The approach is qualitative; the data will be combed for themes with the aid of a suitable microcomputer and software package.

12226 Study of mature entrants to teaching.

GBR 1993

Research Date(s): 1991-1992

Munn, P.; Johnstone, M.

Inst: Scottish Council for Research in Education, 15 St John Street, Edinburgh EH8 8JR, United Kingdom.

Fin: Scottish Office Education Department.

teacher education; supply of teachers; student teacher; teaching profession; secondary education; adult; recruitment

formation des enseignants; offre d'enseignants; élève-maître; profession d'enseignant; enseignement secondaire; adulte; recrutement

PROJECT DESCRIPTION

The overall aim of the research is to address the question: why are there not more mature student entrants to secondary teaching and what could be done to attract more mature entrants to teaching? This question will be addressed by collecting evidence through three separate surveys of: (1) mature secondary teaching students at colleges of education, at Stirling University, and on Scottish Wider Access Programme (SWAP) secondary teaching courses; (2) a sample of final-year mature students in higher education; and (3) mature people who enquired about secondary teaching but did not apply.

12227 A study of pre-school education in the Republic of Ireland with particular reference to those pre-schools which are listed by the Irish Pre-School Playgroups Association in Cork City and County.

GBR 1993

Research Date(s): 1989-1992

Douglas, F.

Sup: McClelland, V.

Inst: Hull University, School of Education, Cottingham Road, Hull HU6 7RX, United Kingdom.

pre-school education; Ireland; educational provision

éducation préscolaire; Irlande; scolarisation

PROJECT DESCRIPTION

Over the years there has been protracted discussion on the provision of pre-school education for children in the Republic of Ireland. Generally this has proceeded without prior knowledge of what actually goes on within the various pre-school establishments yet with the number of working mothers ever on the increase it is of the utmost importance that information be available to parents and educators alike.

This study is an attempt to redress this lack of understanding with respect to pre-school children in Cork City and County. It is intended to: (1) obtain information; (2) answer practical questions on pre-school provision; and (3) study the effects of present pre-school facilities on children. It is intended also to offer recommendations for future development. The methodology of the study is ethnographic and is based on observation in 24 pre-schools in Cork City and County. A nationwide questionnaire is used to lace these observations in context.

12228 A study of teaching methods in a college of higher education.
GBR 1993
Research Date(s): 1990-1991
Noyes, P.
Inst: Cheltenham & Gloucester College of Higher Education, Faculty of Education and Health, The Park, Cheltenham GL50 2QF, United Kingdom.
further education of teachers; higher education; teaching method
perfectionnement des enseignants; enseignement supérieur; méthode pédagogique
PROJECT DESCRIPTION
This research will identify the teaching needs of new members of academic staff in the Faculty of Education and Health at Cheltenham & Gloucester College of Higher Education, by means of paired observation and discussion groups. Action research techniques are then being used to develop and monitor teaching methods. Nine academic staff are involved and the direction of the project will depend upon identified needs and decisions reached during discussion.

12229 The supplementary school and its role in inner-city London.
GBR 1993
Research Date(s): 1988-1991
McCalman, L.
Sup: Andrews, R.
Inst: Hull University, School of Education, Cottingham Road, Hull HU6 7RX, United Kingdom.
special education; ethnic group; urban environment; urban school
enseignement spécial; groupe ethnique; milieu urbain; école urbaine
PROJECT DESCRIPTION
The study hopes to achieve two goals. Its primary objective is to explain the role of Afro-Caribbean Supplementary Schools in inner-city London. Their funding, curriculum, opportunities for assessment and profiling, and education direction in terms of policy will be looked at. Emphasis will be placed on the curriculum of these schools, the recruitment of pupils, the quality of staff and measures for assessing the programme. The second objective of the study is to show that with the implementation of the National Curriculum, the Supplementary Schools will have to expand their roles to encompass changes in education.

12230 Support of mentors in the classroom.
GBR 1993
Research Date(s): 1991-1992
Naish, M.; Watkins, C.
Inst: London University, Institute of Education, Department of Educational Psychology and Special Educational Needs, 20 Bedford Way, London WC1H OAL, United Kingdom.
Fin: Paul Hamlyn Foundation.
teacher education; student teacher; supervision
formation des enseignants; élève-maître; surveillance
PROJECT DESCRIPTION
The Institute of Education Post-Graduate Certificate of Education (PGCE) is developing an area-based approach to teacher education, involving school teachers in initial teacher education. Linked teachers in the schools require training and support. This project will isolate their needs, develop training and support and evaluate processes and outcomes.

12231 Supporting teachers, supporting children with special educational needs: an exploration of the partnership between class teachers and support teachers.
GBR 1993
Research Date(s): 1986-
Harland, L.
Sup: Gipps, C.
Inst: London University, Institute of Education, Department of Curriculum Studies, 20 Bedford Way, London WC1H OAL, United Kingdom; Greenwich University, Avery Hill Campus, Bexley Road, Eltham, London SE9 2PQ, United Kingdom.
special education; teacher; assistant; cooperation
enseignement spécial; enseignant; assistant; coopération
PROJECT DESCRIPTION
The role of the support teacher is changing extensively. It is assumed that the move from withdrawing children with special educational needs from the classroom, towards working within the classroom, with the accompanying need to advise/consult the class teacher, has resulted in a qualitative improvement of educational provisions for these children. Questions are proposed which will explore the nature of the partnership between support teacher and class teachers. It is intended to uncover some of the tensions which accompany the work of the support teacher. So far there has been little evaluation of any possible improvement in educational provision for children with special educational needs which may have been accounted for by support teacher/class teacher collaboration.

12232 Survey of 50% of Grampian Leavers.
GBR 1993
Research Date(s): 1990-1991
Raffe, D.; Lamb, J.; Middleton, L.
Sup: McPherson, A.
Inst: Edinburgh University, Centre for Educational Sociology, 7 Buccleuch Place, Edinburgh EH8 9JT, United Kingdom.
Fin: Grampian Regional Council.
school leaver; transition from school to work; vocational education; labour market; secondary education; youth employment
élève sortant; passage à la vie active; enseignement professionnel; marché du travail; enseignement secondaire; emploi des jeunes
PROJECT DESCRIPTION
The research team will conduct a survey of 50% of pupils in the Grampian Region in the fourth year of secondary school in session 1989-1990 to provide reliable information on education and training.
Publ: A full list of publications is available.

12233 Systém dalšího vzdělávání učitelů a servisních středisek pro učitele v regionu. (The in-service teacher education system and the regional service centres for teachers.)
CSK 1994
Research Date(s): 1992
Kohnová, Jana; Dostálová, Radmila; et al.
Sup: Helus, Zdeněk.
Inst: Ústav rozvoje školství a postgraduálních studií UK (Institute of educational development and postgraduate studies), Msylíkova 7, 110 00 Praha 1, Czech Republic.
Ministerstvo školství, mládeže a tělovýchovy (Ministry of Education, Youth and Physical Education), Karmelitská 7, 118 12 Praha 1, Czech Republic
further education of teachers; educational reform; training cost; educational legislation
perfectionnement des enseignants; réforme de l'enseignement; coût de la formation; législation scolaire
PROJECT DESCRIPTION
Aim: To conduct a survey of the main components of the in-service teacher training system in order to describe the organization of past and present in-service training provision and relevant legislation; to make recommendations to the Ministry of Education, especially with regard to the lifelong education of teachers; to examine the legislative and financial conditions related to in-service teacher training.
Publ: Kohnová, Jana & Dostálová, Radmila. *Systém dalšího vzdělávání učitelů a servisní střediska pro učitele v regionu.* Praha: 1992, 196p.

12234 Systemstruktur der Weiterbildung in den neuen Bundeslaendern. (Structure of the further training system in the new German states.)
DEU 1993
Research Date(s): 1992
Faulstich, P.
Inst: Gesamthochschule-Universitaet Kassel, Kontaktstelle fuer wissenschaftliche Weiterbildung, Moenchebergstrasse 19, D-3500 Kassel.
Fin: Max-Traeger-Stiftung.
further training; German DR; educational policy; educational need
formation complémentaire; Allemagne RDA; politique de l'éducation; besoin d'éducation
PROJECT DESCRIPTION
Inhalt: Ueberblick ueber die wichtigsten Traeger und Einrichtungen; Identifikation moeglicher Perspektiven; Problemkatalog fuer Anknuepfungspunkte politischen und administrativen Handelns.
Vorgehensweise: Sekundaeranalyse statistischen Materials; Interviews. Untersuchungsdesign: Querschnittserhebung; qualitative Forschung.
Datengewinnung: Nicht-standardisiertes Interview (Stichprobe: 20; Experteninterviews mit Entscheidungstraegern). Primaererhebung: Feldarbeit von Mitarbeitern des Projektes durchgefuehrt.

12235 Szkolnictwo prywatne w Polsce (1918-1993). (Private schools in Poland (1918-1993).)
POL 1994
Research Date(s): 1989-1994
Ratuś, Bronisław.
Inst: Zakład Teorii Wychowania i Pedagogiki Porównawczej, Wyższa Szkoła Pedagogiczna (Department of Educational Theory and Comparative Education, Higher School of Education), 65 625 Zielona Góra, Wojska Polskiego 69, Poland.
private school; history of education; social change; government policy; educational policy
école privée; histoire de l'éducation; changement social; politique gouvernementale; politique de l'éducation
PROJECT DESCRIPTION
Aims: (a) To define the place of private schools in the Polish educational tradition and the scope they were given in Poland in various historical periods; (b) to present the revival of private schools in Poland in the period of political transformation; (c) to examine the pedagogical problems of private schools in Poland in times of socio-political change; (d) to analyse

the attitudes of the authorities towards private schools in totalitarian and liberal-democratic systems; (e) to attempt to define the prospects of private schooling in Poland.

Methods: Document analysis (both from a historical and pedagogical viewpoint) of archives, newspapers, statistical yearbooks and other statistical documents published between 1918 and 1993, legal acts, etc.; questionnaire, interview, observation.

12236 Szkoły społeczne jako placówki alternatywne. (Civic schools as alternative educational institutions.)

POL 1994

Research Date(s): 1991-1992

Rusakowska, Daniela; Jung-Miklaszewska, Joanna.

Inst: Instytut Badań Edukacyjnych (Institute for Educational Research), 01-180 Warszawa, Górczewska 8, Poland.

Ministerstwo Edukacji Narodowej (Ministry of National Education), 00-918 Warszawa, Aleja Szucha 25, Poland

Fin: Komitet Badań Edukacyjnych.

private school; non-state school; alternative school; school autonomy; learning conditions; parent role

école privée; école non-étatique; école alternative; autonomie scolaire; conditions d'apprentissage; rôle des parents

PROJECT DESCRIPTION

Background and aims: "Civic" schools, a type of private schools that were established in post-war Poland at the end of the 1980s, enjoy considerable social interest, accompanied by hopes that these schools will prove better than the state-maintained schools. This project examined the performance of civic schools on the basis of the following questions: (1) What are learning conditions like in civic schools? (2) To what extent do parents influence school performance? Are these schools subjected to social control? (3) To what extent are teachers and pupils allowed to influence curricula and the school organization? (4) How independent are these schools and how is this independence used?

Hypotheses: (1) Civic schools provide conditions that benefit the physical and mental development of their pupils; (2) parents have little influence on school performance; their role is limited to creating the necessary financial conditions; (3) the decision as to what to teach and how to teach is taken by the teachers; (4) civic schools enjoy increasing autonomy, but they make insufficient use of it.

Design: Postal questionnaires were sent to all civic schools that were operational in December 1991.

12237 Teacher competencies and professional development.

GBR 1993

Research Date(s): 1991-1993

Rowe, M.; Tanner, H.; Davies, L.; Morgan-Jones, P.; Prichard, J.

Inst: University College of Swansea, Department of Education, Hendrefoilan, Swansea SA2 7NB, United Kingdom.

Fin: University of Wales.

teacher education; student teacher; student record; achievement; minimum competencies

formation des enseignants; élève-maître; dossier académique; rendement; fundamentum

PROJECT DESCRIPTION

Action research is being conducted in Swansea, Aberystwyth and Bangor to develop a framework of competencies for use in initial teacher education. Techniques and documentation are being developed to establish records of achievement for student teachers. The success of the competencies and records of achievement will then be evaluated.

12238 Teaching and learning strategies in the extension of TVEI in Scotland.

GBR 1993

Research Date(s): 1989-1991

Black, H.; Malcolm, H.; Blair, A.; Latta, J.; Zaklukiewicz, S.

Inst: Scottish Council for Research in Education, 15 St John Street, Edinburgh EH8 8JR, United Kingdom.

Fin: Training, Enterprise and Education Directorate.

vocational education; technical education; learning strategy; teaching method

enseignement professionnel; enseignement technique; stratégie d'apprentissage; méthode pédagogique

PROJECT DESCRIPTION

This research seeks to evaluate the changes in and impact of teaching and learning strategies in the Technical and Vocational Education Initiative (TVEI) extension in Scotland. Five questions will be addressed: (1) What strategies for teaching, learning and assessment are used in schools and colleges to deliver TVEI in selected areas of the curriculum, and how effectively is assessment integrated with teaching and learning? (2) What claims are made for these teaching, learning and assessment strategies, particularly in relation to their preparing young people for adult and working life? (3) To what extent are these strategies supportive of the aspiration of TVEI? (4) What impact do they have on student achievements which will be of value to them in adult and working life, both in terms of formal qualifications and other characteristics? (5) How does 'what is taught' and

'how it is taught' articulate with other aspects of the management of the curriculum in Scottish education?

The research will identify examples of interesting and effective practice in five Round Two and Round Three TVEI projects through a series of related stages leading through progressive focusing to a small set of case studies. There are five stages. Stages 1 and 2 will provide an overview of practice, Stage 1 through a documentary analysis and Stage 2 through interviews with key individuals. Stage 3 will involve a questionnaire analysis of the nature and extent of practice identified in the first two stages. Stage 4 will comprise visits to and interviews with the key staff of a short list of possible units for case study. Stage 5 will provide the most substantial set of data through intensive case studies of practice using interviews, observation of classroom and other relevant work, and questionnaires.

Publ: Black, H.D.; et al. *Staff development in teaching and learning.* SCRE Project Report 27, 1991.

Black, H.D.; et al. *Teaching and learning in an 'Education for Life' Programme.* SCRE Project Report 29, 1991.

Black, H.D.; et al. *Teaching and learning staff development.* SCRE Project Report 30, 1991.

Black, H.D.; et al. *The spread of resource-based learning methods.* SCRE Project Report 32, 1991.

Black, H.D.; et al. *Changing teaching, changing learning.* SCRE/Employment Department, 1991.

A full list of publications is available from the researchers.

12239 Technical and Vocational Education in Initial Teacher Training.

GBR 1993

Research Date(s): 1991-

Glover, D.; Gleeson, D.; Gough, G.

Sup: Brighouse, T.

Inst: Keele University, Department of Education, Keele, Staffordshire ST5 5BG, United Kingdom.

Fin: Training, Enterprise & Education Directorate.

technical education; vocational education; teacher education

enseignement technique; enseignement professionnel; formation des enseignants

PROJECT DESCRIPTION

This action-oriented study of the Technical and Vocational Education Initiative (TVEI) in Initial Teacher (IT) education adopts a qualitative approach looking at management of change and developmental perspectives.

Publ: Gleeson, D. *Training and its Alternatives.* Buckingham: Open University Press, 1991.

Gleeson, D. & Brighouse, T.R.P. How to manage change in colleges. In: *Polytechnics & Colleges: an illustrative study.* London: Training, Enterprise Education Directorate.

12240 The Technical and Vocational Education Initiative in initial teacher training.

GBR 1993

Research Date(s): 1989-1992

Naish, M.; Young, M.

Inst: London University, Institute of Education, Department of Economics, Geography and Business Education, 20 Bedford Way, London WC1H OAL, United Kingdom.

Fin: Training, Enterprise & Education Directorate.

teacher education; vocational education; technical education

formation des enseignants; enseignement professionnel; enseignement technique

PROJECT DESCRIPTION

The Technical & Vocational Education Initiative (TVEI) in the Initial Teacher Training (ITT) project is funded by the Training Enterprise & Education Directorate as a pilot project to consider the implications of TVEI for ITT. The focus is on staff development and, through that, course development. The project is sponsoring a number of mini research projects which are being undertaken by PGCE (Postgraduate Certificate in Education) staff and will feed into proposals for course development. These proposals will be trialled and evaluated in order to ascertain their viability for implementation in the course.

12241 The Technical and Vocational Education Initiative (TVEI) in initial teacher training.

GBR 1993

Research Date(s): 1989-1991

Shipstone, D.

Inst: Nottingham University, School of Education, University Park, Nottingham NG7 2RD, United Kingdom.

Fin: Training Agency.

teacher education; further education of teachers; technical education; vocational education

formation des enseignants; perfectionnement des enseignants; enseignement technique; enseignement professionnel

PROJECT DESCRIPTION

This research and development project has a substantial staff development component and focuses upon the changes that have taken place within education in the 14-18 age range through the impetus provided by the Technical and Vocational Education Initiative (TVEI). Many School of Education lecturers engage in research studies within five broad themes: new technology learning; personal and social education, guidance and profiling; industry links and work experience; and equal opportunities.

Publications will take the form of workshop materials and case studies to be used on initial and inservice training courses; research papers and monographs dealing with aspects of education which have been particularly influenced by TVEI.

12242 Technical and Vocational Education Initiative.
GBR 1993
Research Date(s): 1989-1991
Thomson, S.
Inst: Liverpool John Moores University, School of Education and Community Studies, I.M. Marsh Campus, Barkhill Road, Liverpool L17 6BD, United Kingdom.
Fin: Training Agency.
vocational education; technical education
enseignement professionnel; enseignement technique
PROJECT DESCRIPTION
The main themes of this project examining the Technical and Vocational Education Initiative include: (1) active learning strategies; (2) profiling and Records of Achievement; (3) information technology and the curriculum; and (4) links between education and the world of work.

12243 Technical and Vocational Education Initiative (TVEI) evaluation project.
GBR 1993
Research Date(s): 1988-1993
McLean, M.; Siggers, T.
Sup: Gleeson, D.
Inst: Keele University, Department of Education, Keele, Staffordshire ST5 5BG, United Kingdom.
Fin: Training, Enterprise and Education Directorate; Staffordshire LEA.
technical education; vocational education
enseignement technique; enseignement professionnel
PROJECT DESCRIPTION
The aim of the study is to evaluate the county-wide extension of the Technical and Vocational Education Initiative (TVEI) in Staffordshire and to provide independent and impartial assessment of a cluster-based strategy, how it affects school and college curriculum, organization, community, links with employers and other support services across the county. The research adopts an action-oriented approach to evaluation, involving formative methods of reporting.

12244 Technical and Vocational Education Initiative (TVEI) local evaluation.
GBR 1993
Research Date(s): 1984-1991
Germon, S.
Sup: Evans, K.
Inst: Surrey University, Department of Educational Studies, Guildford GU2 5XH, United Kingdom.
Fin: Surrey, Kingston, Sutton, Berkshire, West Sussex Local Education Authorities.
technical education; vocational education; transition from school to work; training-employment relationship
enseignement technique; enseignement professionnel; passage à la vie active; relation formation-emploi
PROJECT DESCRIPTION
In setting up the Technical and Vocational Education Initiative (TVEI), the Manpower Services Commission (MSC) stipulated that each local education authority operating in a pilot scheme should make arrangements for it to be evaluated by an independent local evaluator. The purpose of the local evaluation has been to undertake research into a key aspect of the pilot schemes in operation and feed back the results to those involved at managerial level, in order to aid future planning. Local evaluation also gives an independent unbiased viewpoint at 'grassroots' level.

Methods have been mainly questionnaire survey and in-depth interview. Topics for research have varied, responding to local needs, and include: (1) pupils' perceptions at varying stages during their progress through TVEI schemes; (2) the employment dimension, in which the value and use of TVEI to former pupils now in employment, and employers' knowledge and perspectives on TVEI, were investigated; (3) the impact on TVEI schools and colleges, which explored the outcomes of TVEI in comparison with anticipation, achievements, barriers to change and areas for future development, as perceived by key participants. These studies, in particular, informed not only the pilot schemes but also those consortia engaged in developing TVEI extension plans, by highlighting the lessons learned.

12245 Technical education, 1880-1914, with particular reference to the printing trade.
GBR 1993
Research Date(s): 1986-1992
Henry, M.
Sup: Jenkins, E.; Sharp, P.
Inst: Leeds University, School of Education, Leeds LS2 9JT, United Kingdom.
technical education; history of education; printing; vocational education
enseignement technique; histoire de l'éducation; imprimerie; enseignement professionnel
PROJECT DESCRIPTION
The study uses a range of primary sources to examine the origins, nature and development of technical education for the printing industry from 1880 to 1914. The study is placed in the broader context of the technical education movement and addresses the questions concerned with the politics of curriculum design and innovation in the area of vocational education. It also examines the relationship between employers and employees and evaluates the effect of technical education classes upon the education and training of printers.
Publ: Henry, M. The nineteenth-century printing apprenticeship: elements of change. In: Myers, R. & Harris, M. (eds.). *Aspects of printing from 1600.* Headington: Oxford Polytechnic Press, 1987.

12246 Teorie a koncepce počátečního vyučování. (Theory and concept of primary education.)
CSK 1994
Research Date(s): 1991-1992
Vyskočilová, H.; Vánová, R.; Spilková, V.; Uhlířová, J.; Křivánek, Z.; Wildová, R.; Táborský, P.
Sup: Helus, Z.
Inst: Pedagogická fakulta Univerzity Karlovy (Charles University, Faculty of Education), M.D. Rettigové 4, 116 39 Praha 1, Czech Republic.
Ministerstvo školství, mládeže a tělovýchovy (Ministry of Education, Youth and Physical Education), Karmelitská 7, 118 00 Praha 1, Czech Republic
primary education; educational reform; educational theory; Czechoslovakia; history of education
enseignement primaire; réforme de l'enseignement; théorie de l'éducation; Tchécoslovaquie; histoire de l'éducation
PROJECT DESCRIPTION
The study was concerned with theoretical issues related to the reform of primary education and addressed a number of relevant issues in this context, such as: a prognosis of primary education, the concept of primary education, theories of moral education at the primary level, sex education in primary school, elementary curriculum subjects, teaching in primary school, and the history of primary education between the two world wars in Czechoslovakia. The study was conducted from a comparative, historical point of view.
Publ: Vyskočilová, H. *Návrh koncepce základní školy. Expertizní studie.* Praha, 1992, 15p.

12247 Territorial justice and nursery education provision in England and Wales.
GBR 1993
Research Date(s): 1990-
Farrell, C.
Sup: Boyne, G.; Baker, C.
Inst: Glamorgan University, Business School, Pontypridd, Mid Glamorgan CF37 1DL, United Kingdom.
early childhood education; nursery school; regional planning; educational provision; demand for education
éducation de la prime enfance; école maternelle; planification régionale; scolarisation; demande d'éducation
PROJECT DESCRIPTION
The aim of this project is to measure the need for, and the provision of, nursery education facilities in local authority areas in England and Wales. This involves the construction of a model of service need and service provision, and the evaluation of the extent of territorial justice. This assessment is based on a statistical analysis of the relationship between service need and service provision. The project examines the reasons for spatial variations in provision and assesses the impact of local financial resources, party politics, private sector provision and day care services upon the level of local authority provision of nursery education.

12248 Tertiary education in West Glamorgan Local Education Authority.
GBR 1993
Research Date(s): 1989-1991
Cunnington, J.; Tomlinson, J.; Elford, G.
Inst: Warwick University, Faculty of Educational Studies, Coventry CV4 7AL, United Kingdom; West Glamorgan Local Education Authority, Education Department, County Hall, Swansea SA1 3SN, United Kingdom.
Fin: West Glamorgan Local Education Authority.
post-compulsory education; quality of education; regional planning; local government

enseignement postobligatoire; qualité de l'éducation; planification régionale; administration locale

PROJECT DESCRIPTION

West Glamorgan Local Education Authority (LEA) sponsored this project to investigate and report upon the effectiveness of their Tertiary Education Policy. The four colleges serve a population of about 360,000 and have 75 per cent of all 16-19 year-old students and 100 per cent 19+ students in further education.

The research has included an account of the history of the development of policy 1974-1986; the founding of the colleges 1986-1989; and a review of the quality of outcomes according to a number of parameters. The report was submitted to West Glamorgan LEA in December 1991.

Publ: Tomlinson, J.; Cunnington, J. & Elford, G. *Tertiary education in West Glamorgan Local Education Authority*. Coventry: Warwick University/West Glamorgan LEA, 1991.

12249 To initiate a distance learning undergraduate degree course in information and library studies.
GBR 1993
Research Date(s): 1992-1993
Preston, G.; Barber, J.
Sup: Baggs, C.
Inst: University College of Wales, Aberystwyth Department of Information and Library Studies, Llanbadarn Fawr, Aberystwyth, Dyfed SY23 3AS, United Kingdom.
Fin: Universities Funding Council.
distance study; adult education; library science; information science
enseignement à distance; éducation des adultes; bibliothéconomie; science de l'information
PROJECT DESCRIPTION

In the light of current moves towards providing greater opportunities for mature adults with non-traditional educational qualifications to gain access to higher education, and the Universities Funding Council's (UFC) programme to encourage flexibility in course provision, it was proposed to set up a research and development programme to initiate a distance learning undergraduate degree course in information and library studies.

The aim of the project is to investigate the scope and management of current distance learning provision; to evaluate the relative merits of different methods of course provision, including developments in educational technology; to look at methods of assessment for student-centred learning; and to develop quality control mechanisms appropriate for academic and professional validation.

High attrition rates experienced in some models of distance learning provision make it important to assess how inherent problems such as student support and adequate resourcing may be overcome. This will lead to the design of a course aimed at mature non-traditional entrants currently or recently employed in a library or information environment, who wish to gain a professional qualification. The production of student-centred learning packages will involve research into developing Computer-Assisted Learning (CAL) and video-conferencing to supplement traditional print-based materials.

12250 Towards the effective inclusive school.
GBR 1993
Research Date(s): 1992-1993
Rouse, M.; Florian, L.; Hardman, M.
Inst: Cambridge University, Institute of Education, Shaftesbury Road, Cambridge CB2 2BX, United Kingdom; University of Utah, Department of Special Education, Milton Bennion Hall, Salt Lake City, Utah 84112, USA; University of Maryland, College Park, Department of Special EducatioN, USA.
Fin: State of Utah.
special education; handicapped; integration; USA
enseignement spécial; handicapé; intégration; Etats-Unis
PROJECT DESCRIPTION

The State of Utah (USA) has been committed for a number of years to the development of inclusive schools in which all pupils, regardless of disability, will be educated. This evaluation and research project by the State investigated the outcomes of the initiative and the progress made to full inclusion.

Initial findings indicate progress in a range of significant areas in certain parts of the State. Barriers to change, as well as an account of innovative practice, are included in the final report.

Publ: Florian, L. & Rouse, M. *Utah's inclusive schools*. Report to the Utah State Department of Education, Salt Lake City, Utah, 1993.

12251 Training for special educational needs in Sandwell and Coventry.
GBR 1993
Research Date(s): 1990-1991
Heathcote, G.
Inst: Crewe & Alsager College of Higher Education, Health Research and Development Unit, Hassell Road, Alsager, Stoke on Trent ST7 2HL, United Kingdom.

Fin: Replan; National Institute for Adult Education; Training, Enterprise & Education Directorate.
special education; vocational training; training supply; training need
enseignement spécial; formation professionnelle; offre de formation; besoin de formation
PROJECT DESCRIPTION

Action research conducted in two Metropolitan districts to improve the 'match' between training opportunities and special educational needs.

12252 The training the trainers approach to staff development project.
GBR 1993
Research Date(s): 1988-1991
Robertson, P.; McGinley, L.; MacDonald, D.
Sup: Smith, I.; Rand, J.
Inst: Jordanhill College of Education, Division of Inservice Training, Southbrae Drive, Jordanhill, Glasgow G13 1PP, United Kingdom.
Fin: Scottish Office Education Department.
training of trainers; further education of teachers; training type
formation des formateurs; perfectionnement des enseignants; type de formation
PROJECT DESCRIPTION

The 'training of trainers' approach has been widely used in educational innovation in Scotland, however, there has been no formal evaluation of this approach. In response to this the Scottish Office Education Department has funded an evaluative study to ascertain the effectiveness of the model within education.

The aim of the project is to identify, and further test by action research, a set of factors which contribute to the effective management and operation of 'training of trainers' staff development strategies. The project is designed in three stages. The initial stage is a detailed literature survey, a survey of recent and current course provision, research into the pilot School Board Initiative, intensive study of several cases, the forming of hypotheses to be used in consultancy and action research with School Board Initiatives. The second stage consists of consultancy involvement with three major courses and post-course evaluations. Finally there will be post-course follow-ups with participants and others in client relationships with course providers.

Outcomes of the project will include papers designed for education personnel who plan or present staff development programmes, a project bulletin - a Checklist for Training of Trainers Programmes, and a final report for the Scottish Office Education Department.

12253 Transition to college.
GBR 1993
Research Date(s): 1990-1992
Page, C.
Inst: Heriot-Watt University, Moray House Institute of Education, Holyrood Road, Edinburgh EH8 8AQ, United Kingdom.
student; higher education; student behaviour; student life
étudiant; enseignement supérieur; comportement de l'étudiant; vie étudiante
PROJECT DESCRIPTION

This research will provide evidence about the nature of the transition to Moray House, as experienced by new students, which could help this Institute (and other colleges) make wise decisions on future planning in the areas of teaching and learning, advising and counselling, residence, college ethos and health education. The researcher will also address such questions as: to what extent does the new student experience homesickness; how is this related to links with home (e.g. letters, home events missed, vacations etc.); what preparation for the transition was experienced; and in what ways does homesickness affect course work.

12254 Tripartism and education in 20th century Britain.
GBR 1993
Research Date(s): 1987-1995
McCulloch, G.
Inst: Lancaster University, Department of Educational Research, Cartmel College, Bailrigg, Lancaster LA1 4YW, United Kingdom.
secondary education; history of education; school system; educational policy
enseignement secondaire; histoire de l'éducation; système scolaire; politique de l'éducation
PROJECT DESCRIPTION

This research project is designed to explore the tripartite distinctions in educational provision in 20th century Britain, and how they have been reconstructed and developed in the final decades of the century. The theme of 'education for leadership' originally associated with the 19th century public school has been one focus of the research. The attempts to promote a 'respectable' form of technical education, for example through the post-war secondary technical schools, has provided another. Lastly, the tradition of working class schooling seen in the central schools and secondary modern schools is an important theme for further research. Continuities and shifts in emphasis underlying policy documents such as Hadow in the 1920s, Spens in the 1930s, Norwood in the 1940s, and

Crowther in the 1950s are explored. The relationships between these and the educational policies of the 1980s-1990s are another aspect of the research project.

Publ: McCulloch, G. *The secondary technical school: a usable past?* London: Falmer Press, 1989.

McCulloch, G. *Philosophers and kings: education for leadership in modern England*. Cambridge: Cambridge University Press, 1991.

12255 Türkiye'de öğretmen yetiştirme ve isdihdam şartları. (Teacher training and employment conditions in Turkey.)
TUR 1994
Research Date(s): 1992
Dilaver, H. Hüseyin.
Sup: Koçer, Hasan Ali.
Inst: Ankara Üniversitesi, Sosyal Bilimler Enstitüsü (University of Ankara, Institute of Social Sciences), 06590 Ankara, Turkey.
teacher education; employment; teaching profession; working conditions
formation des enseignants; emploi; profession d'enseignant; conditions de travail
PROJECT DESCRIPTION
This research examined the views of school heads, teachers and ministerial officials on teacher training and employment conditions in Turkey.

The population of the research included the heads and teaching staff of schools that fall under the responsibility of the Ministry of Education. Through stratified sampling, a selection was made of 12 cities where such schools are situated. From each city, 15 heads and 40 teachers were selected. In addition, top administrators of the central organization of the Ministry of Education were included in the sample.

Questionnaires pertaining to teacher training and employment conditions were developed by the researcher and administered to the groups mentioned above. Responses were analysed in terms of frequencies, percentages, means, and standard deviations.

Results: Shortcomings were mentioned in the following areas: teacher training and employment conditions, student selection, pre-service education, in-service education, teacher recruitment, teacher distribution and rotation, and the socio-economic situation of teachers.

12256 TVEI local evaluation.
GBR 1993
Research Date(s): 1986-1992
Rand, J.
Inst: Jordanhill College of Education, Division of Inservice Training, Southbrae Drive, Glasgow G13 1PP, United Kingdom.
Fin: local authorities.
technical education; vocational education; evaluation
enseignement technique; enseignement professionnel; évaluation
PROJECT DESCRIPTION
The college has been responsible for the local evaluation of former Technical and Vocational Education Initiative (TVEI) pilot projects. The format and nature of the research tasks have varied from project to project, the primary focus has been to help projects identify development needs.

12257 The Two Degrees - a comparative study of former students and first post headteacher satisfaction with initial teacher education at Charlotte Mason College.
GBR 1993
Research Date(s): 1989-1993
Hegarty, P.
Inst: Charlotte Mason College, Department of Professional Studies, Ambleside, Cumbria LA22 9BB, United Kingdom.
teacher education; student teacher; satisfaction; bachelors degree
formation des enseignants; élève-maître; satisfaction; diplôme universitaire (1er cycle)
PROJECT DESCRIPTION
The Council for the Accreditation of Teacher Education (CATE) criteria for primary initial teacher education have occasioned very significant changes in B.Ed applied teacher education courses. This study aims to illuminate the levels of student and first post headteacher satisfaction with students' initial training.

The methods include surveys of the whole output from Charlotte Mason College of the last two cohorts of Applied B.Ed and the first two cohorts of Subject Studies B.Ed, and observations and interviews with a small sample each year.

12258 Uitstroom PBVE. (Characteristics of leavers from Adult Elementary Vocational Education projects.)
NLD 1994
Research Date(s): 1990-1991
Boer, P.R. den.
Inst: RION Instituut voor Onderwijsonderzoek (RION Institute for Educational Research), P.O. Box 1286, 9701 BG Groningen, Netherlands.
Rijksuniversiteit Groningen (State University of Groningen), P.O. Box 72, 9700 AB Groningen, Netherlands
Fin: SVO het Instituut voor Onderzoek van het Onderwijs.
vocational education; adult education; employment; career; labour market

enseignement professionnel; éducation des adultes; emploi; carrière; marché du travail
PROJECT DESCRIPTION
Background: Improving educational provision is a central element in government policies aimed at reducing unemployment. In 1987 the Adult Elementary Vocational Education (PBVE) projects were started. Coordination of educational activities takes place per region, of which there are 48. An earlier study examined the results of the projects in 18 regions. As that study focused on the most experienced regions, in terms of contacts with the regular education field, it is feared that the outcomes may be biased. In order to obtain a more complete picture of the results of the PBVE projects, the present study focuses on the other 30 regions.

Aim: To examine what benefit participants derive from Adult Elementary Vocational Education (PBVE) courses.

Methods: Telephone survey of 320 former participants who had left PBVE six months earlier and 307 former participants who had left 12-18 months earlier.

Results: 57% of course participants find a job within 12-18 months after finishing the course. This finding corroborates earlier research evidence. This decline in unemployment rates among PBVE participants and the promising educational careers of those who move on to higher-level courses warrant the conclusion that the PBVE projects constitute a major instrument for improving the labour market position of participants. Problems that occur concern: dropout rates (40%); declining levels of motivation as a result of negative experiences on the labour market; and relatively poor outcomes among immigrants, women and long-term unemployed people. These problems might be solved if a more concrete prospect of employment was offered and more attention given to the content of the practical training that is provided as part of the course.

(This is an updating of EUDISED no. 44/10525).

Publ: Boer, P.R. den. *De uitstroom uit de PBVE in kaart gebracht*. Groningen: RION, 1991, 140p.

12259 University extension and national education.
GBR 1993
Research Date(s): 1988-1994
Marriott, J.
Inst: Leeds University, School of Education, Leeds LS2 9JT, United Kingdom.
workers' education; adult education; history of education
éducation ouvrière; éducation des adultes; histoire de l'éducation
PROJECT DESCRIPTION
This research is a policy and organisational study of the university extension system (1873-1914) which argues that the movement cannot be adequately understood in terms of the later concept of 'adult education'. The aspirations and efforts of extension are presented in the context of changing attitudes towards secondary, technical and higher education, and in the light of its aims of becoming a recognised element within 'national education'. Also emphasised is the implicit shaping of policy by the internal organisational problems of the movement. Sub-themes include: the search for financial aid from the State; the relation to technical instruction; the relation to secondary education and the training of teachers; involvement in local institutes for higher education; historical application of organisation theory. The method used is historical; the analysis draws additionally on the sociology of organisations.

12260 Unqualified school leaver.
GBR 1993
Research Date(s): 1991
Young, M.
Inst: London University, Institute of Education, Department of Policy Studies, Centre for Post Sixteen Education, 20 Bedford Way, London WC1H 0AL, United Kingdom.
Fin: British Gas.
school leaver; transition from school to work; unqualified young people; post-compulsory education
élève sortant; passage à la vie active; jeune sans qualification; enseignement postobligatoire
PROJECT DESCRIPTION
The project involved an extensive literature review of research and evaluation of policy initiatives in Britain in the last decade as well as a section on comparative studies of participation in post-compulsory education in France and Germany. Its outcome was a report that included a number of proposals for how future research might be linked more closely both to policy evaluation as well as to the aspirations and needs of young people.

Publ: Mortimore, J. The unqualified school leaver. In: Young, M. (ed.). *Post-16 Education Centre Report*, No 8/1992.

12261 The use of performance indicators in the evaluation of educational institutions.
GBR 1993
Research Date(s): 1989-1992
Wakelin, M.
Sup: Brighouse, T.; Wringe, C.

Inst: Keele University, Department of Education, Keele, Staffordshire ST5 5BG, United Kingdom.
educational institution; evaluation; performance; quality of education
établissement d'enseignement; évaluation; performance; qualité de l'éducation
PROJECT DESCRIPTION

Current use of performance indicators is to be surveyed and evaluated in relation to currently proposed educational aims. Their validity as a measure of educational effectiveness and their effect on the performance of teachers and institutions will be assessed.

12262 Vervolg evaluatie APS-project voor ontwikkeling van PABO's. (Evaluation of a development project on primary teacher education.)
NLD 1994
Research Date(s): 1993
Houtveen, A.A.M.; Booij, N.
Inst: Interdisciplinair Sociaal-wetenschappelijk Onderzoeksinstituut, Afdeling Onderwijs (ISOR) (Interdisciplinary Research Institute for the Social Sciences, Department of Educational Research), P.O. Box 80140, 3508 TC Utrecht, Netherlands.
Rijksuniversiteit Utrecht (State University of Utrecht), P.O. Box 80125, 3508 TC Utrecht, Netherlands
Fin: SVO het Instituut voor Onderzoek van het Onderwijs.
teacher education; educational innovation; primary education
formation des enseignants; innovation pédagogique; enseignement primaire
PROJECT DESCRIPTION

Background: In the academic year 1989/1990 the Non-denominational Educational Advisory Centre (APS) started the Primary Teacher Education project, which is scheduled to last until 1994/1995. The project aims to help Primary Teacher Education Institutes (PABOs) solve educational and organizational problems. The present study concerns the evaluation of the innovations introduced in the year 1992/1993.

Aim: To examine: how far the PABOs that participate in the project have developed; how far the innovations that have been implemented can be regarded as solutions to problems; how far the networks that have emerged are able to manage themselves; and how far innovations are visible at the student level.

Design: On the basis of document analyses and talks, case descriptions will be made of six PABOs. Two rounds of interviews will be held with coordinators, teachers and students. Within the project, three networks have emerged. Interviews will be held at the network level. A questionnaire survey will be conducted among all students starting the second course year in 1992, eliciting attitudes towards the training they receive and the use of aids and resources. Learner reports will be compiled of the first and second year students in the three PABOs that have progressed the furthest in the implementation of the project. Teachers and coordinators will also be given questionnaires. Two conferences will be organized.

12263 Vocational education.
GBR 1993
Research Date(s): 1984-1991
Shilling, C.
Inst: Southampton University, Department of Sociology and Social Policy, Highfield, Southampton SO9 5NH, United Kingdom.
vocational education; technical education; work experience
enseignement professionnel; enseignement technique; expérience du travail
PROJECT DESCRIPTION

The project is concerned with an investigation into the structure, organisation and content of vocational education and education-industry relations in England and Wales. The first part of the proejct involved analysing the historical development of vocational schooling. The second part concentrated on the actual operation of vocational schemes with a particular focus on the National Technical and Vocational Education Initiative (TVEI), the Mini-Enterprises in Schools Project and a local education authority scheme called the Schools Vocational Programme. This second part of the research is based on observation and interviews with project directors, teachers, students and employers.

Publ: Shilling, C. *Schooling for work in capitalist Britain.* Lewes: Falmer Press, 1989.
Shilling, C. The mini-enterprise in schools project: a new stage in education-industry relations. In: *Journal of Education Policy*, Vol 4, No 2/1989, pp. 115-124.
Shilling, C. & Dale, R. (eds.). *The TVEI story: policy, practice and preparation for the workplace.* Milton Keynes: Open University Press, 1990.
Shilling, C. Labouring at school: work experience in the TVEI. In: *Work, Employment and Society*, Vol 5, No 1/1991, pp. 59-80.

12264 VOTEC - The Development of Vocational and Technical Education and Training.
AUT 1993
Research Date(s): 1990-1993
Schedler, Klaus.

Inst: Institut fuer Bildungsforschung der Wirtschaft, Rainergasse 38, A-1050 Wien.
Fin: Bundesministerium fuer wirtschaftliche Angelegenheiten.
vocational education; economic development; technical education
enseignement professionnel; développement économique; enseignement technique
PROJECT DESCRIPTION

Das Projekt VOTEC (The Development of Vocational and Technical Education and Training) wurde von der OECD angeregt. Ziel des laufenden Forschungsvorhabens ist es aufzuzeigen, welche aktuellen Herausforderungen in den einzelnen Laendern zu welchen Aenderungen in den jeweiligen beruflichen Bildungssystemen fuehren. Der Schwerpunkt liegt dabei auf Bildungsgaengen des Sekundarbereichs II. Die auf mehrere Jahre ausgelegte Arbeit gliedert sich im wesentlichen in drei Phasen. Phase I behandelt die Beschreibung der Entwicklungen der letzten 20 Jahre bis zur politischen Umsetzung von konkreten Massnahmen. Dieser Teil, der in Kooperation mit dem Bundesministerium fuer wirtschaftliche Angelegenheiten erarbeitet wurde, konnte mittlerweile fuer Oesterreich abgeschlossen werden. In Phase II geht es um die Zusammenstellung von Fallbeispielen fuer eine Auswahl von Branchen in Oesterreich. Auch dieser Teil wird gemeinsam mit dem Bundesministerium fuer wirtschaftliche Angelegenheiten erarbeitet werden. In der anschliessenden Phase III sollen die Ergebnisse der vorangegangenen Arbeiten auf nationaler Ebene zusammengefasst und evaluiert werden.

12265 What do Muslim children need from the education system?
GBR 1993
Research Date(s): 1991-1993
Parker-Jenkins, M.
Inst: Nottingham University, School of Education, University Park, Nottingham NG7 2RD, United Kingdom.
denominational school; Islam; religion; religious education; women's education; girls' school
école confessionnelle; islamisme; religion; éducation religieuse; éducation des femmes; école de filles
PROJECT DESCRIPTION

This case study of the Muslim Girls' High School, by Leicester, will provide an insight into an unexplored area which has recently provoked educational debate in Britain and abroad: the lack of understanding between the State educational system and the Muslim community. Adopting an ethnographic approach, the study aims to examine educational provision in non-maintained Muslim schools and to consider the extent to which the maintained school sector is able to accommodate Muslim needs.

The two-year project will comprise four stages of work. Firstly, initial research of the Muslim Girls' High School, Leicester, visits to other Muslim schools in Britain to provide comparative analysis, and in-depth interviewing of interested parties; educationalists; clergy; academics; and community leaders. Finally, the production of a report, study guide and articles for publication, offering practical solutions to the problems of educating Muslim children within State schools and in accordance with parents' religious convictions.

The education system is presently being criticised by 'Muslims' who see an incompatibility between values taught at home and those at school. Although voluntary-aided status may be granted to Muslim schools in the future, there will still be a large element of Muslim children who remain in regular maintained schools. Accommodating their educational needs will continue to be a pressing concern for educationalists and this research will provide a direct contribution to knowledge in the field of cultural diversity.

Publ: Parker-Jenkins, M. Muslim matters: exploring the educational needs of the Muslim child. In: *New Community*, Vol 17, No 4/1991.

12266 What is the experience of Muslim girls in a Muslim school in Britain? An ethnographic study with proposals for change.
GBR 1993
Research Date(s): 1993-1995
Parker-Jenkins, M.
Inst: Nottingham University, School of Education, University Park, Nottingham NG7 2RD, United Kingdom.
Fin: Economic and Social Research Council.
denominational school; Islam; religion; religious education; women's education; girl
école confessionnelle; islamisme; religion; éducation religieuse; éducation des femmes; jeune fille
PROJECT DESCRIPTION

Muslims comprise the third largest religious group in Britain today, after Roman Catholics and Anglicans. Whilst multi-racial, multi-cultural and multi-lingual in nature, they are united by the faith dimension of their lives. The powerful revival of Islamic Fundamentalism of late has deeply affected the thinking of Muslim minority groups in the West. The education system has been criticised by Muslims, who see an incompatibility between values taught at home and those at school.

The objective of this research is to make a study of Muslim education as offered by a selected Muslim girls' independent school and to accumulate new and timely information. Other research aims are to examine the cognitive basis of Islamic education and the selection of knowledge.

The research methodology is predominantly ethnographic with an in-depth study of a girls' Muslim school and shorter studies of five other Muslim schools for comparative analysis. Following the traditions of ethnography, the research aims to examine the experience of Muslim girls in a Muslim school. Furthermore, proposals for change will be explored, outlining areas concerning the educational needs of Muslim children within the maintained school system. The study involves six Muslim and six non-Muslim schools and is conducted by a small team of researchers comprising both Muslims and non-Muslims.

A report will be published profiling educational provision within a Muslim school with recommendations for the maintained school system.

12267 Young people's experience of National Certificate Modules.
GBR 1993
Research Date(s): 1988-1991
Raffe, D.; Croxford, L.; Howieson, C.
Sup: McPherson, A.
Inst: Edinburgh University, Centre for Educational Sociology, 7 Buccleuch Place, Edinburgh EH8 9JT, United Kingdom.
Fin: Scottish Education Department.
post-compulsory education; secondary education; modular training; youth attitude
enseignement postobligatoire; enseignement secondaire; formation modulaire; attitude de la jeunesse
PROJECT DESCRIPTION

The project will analyse data from the Scottish Young People's Surveys (1985-1989) to ascertain the impact and development of the 16+ programme among young people. The analyses will cover five broad areas: National Certificate modules in context, whether educational, social, occupational or geographical; trends between the first and third Action Plan year groups; progression into, within, and out of the modular system; attitudes to the National Certificate; and modules within schools.
Publ: A full list of publications is available.

05   ADMINISTRATION OF EDUCATION – ADMINISTRATION DE L'ENSEIGNEMENT – BILDUNGSVERWALTUNG

12268   L'allocation du temps en cours d'études: le cas des étudiants espagnols.
FRA   1993
Research Date(s): 1986-1991
Lassibille, Gérard; Navarro-Gomez, Lucia.
Inst: Université de Dijon, UER Faculté des sciences économiques et de gestion, CNRS UPR/29 et GDR/996, Institut de recherche sur l'économie de l'éducation, BP 138, 21004 Dijon Cedex, France.
Fin: Institut du développement régional de l'Université de Séville.
time-budget; student sociology; Spain; higher education
budget-temps; sociologie de l'étudiant; Espagne; enseignement supérieur
PROJECT DESCRIPTION
Objectifs: Cette recherche considère le facteur temps des étudiants comme étant au centre du processus de production d'éducation.
Méthodologie: Les éléments empiriques de la recherche s'appuient sur les données d'une enquête de budget-temps réalisée auprès de 1800 étudiants de l'Université de Malaga (premier et second cycles des Facultés de Science économique et de gestion, de droit, de philosophie et lettres, de science et de médecine et première année des Ecoles universitaires de gestion et d'ingéniérie).
Résultats: L'enquête détaille les caractéristiques individuelles des élèves, leur milieu familial, leur situation académique et leur réussite à certains examens. Elle détaille aussi avec précision la distribution du temps des étudiants en dix-huit postes observés au cours d'une semaine. A partir de cette source d'information on donne la mesure du temps consacré par les étudiants aux activités académiques et non académiques, lors de leur passage à l'Université.
Publ: Lassibille, Gérard & Navarro-Gomez, Lucia. La utilizacion del tiempo de los estudiantes. IREDU: Rapport à l'Instituto de Desarollo Regional de l'Université de Séville, juin 1988, 43p.
Lassibille, Gérard & Navarro-Gomez, Lucia. El valor del tiempo en la Universidad. Universidad de Malaga, Colleccion Textos Minimos, Malaga, janvier 1991, 79p.

12269   Analyse des disparités géographiques de scolarisation en France.
FRA   1993
Research Date(s): 1988-1990
Mingat, Alain; Richard, Marc.
Inst: Université de Dijon, UER Faculté des sciences économiques et de gestion, CNRS UPR/29 et GDR/996, Institut de recherche sur l'économie de l'éducation, BP 138, 21004 Dijon Cedex, France.
Fin: Conseil général du département des Ardennes.
geographic distribution; regional inequality; schooling rate; demand for education; training supply; France
répartition géographique; disparité régionale; taux de scolarisation; demande d'éducation; offre de formation; France
PROJECT DESCRIPTION
Objectifs: On vérifie que les différents départements ne connaissent pas le même niveau de développement de leur système scolaire par la comparaison directe des taux d'accès au baccalauréat ou des taux de scolarisation à un âge donné post-scolarité obligatoire. Ces différences ont une variété de raisons qui peuvent se grouper de façon globale entre des facteurs de demande d'une part et des facteurs d'offre de l'autre.
Méthodologie: Les facteurs de demande peuvent être connus au niveau départemental, alors que les facteurs d'offre peuvent difficilement être appréhendés directement sur un plan empirique. Le travail a consisté à estimer, par des procédures économétriques, des taux simulés de scolarisation (aux niveaux de la classe de 4ème et de 2nde, en 1982 et 1988) qui permettent de raisonner, à population départementale donnée, et à les confronter avec les taux effectifs. Les écarts mesurent alors les différences dans les carrières scolaires d'élèves socialement comparables et s'interprètent en terme de sur ou sous scolarisation nette associée à des effets d'offre.
Résultats: Les écarts restent tout à fait substantiels, des départements sont spécialement favorisés, d'autres au contraire en situation de sous-scolrisation manifeste. Le rapport analyse également les dotations en personnel en quantité et en qualité. Outre les analyses globales inter-départementales, le rapport propose des profils monographiques de chaque département.
Publ: Mingat, Alain & Richard, Marc. *Disparités géographiques de scolarisation en classe de 4e et de 2nde; volume 1: Analyses interdépartementales.* IREDU, document interne, 1990, 91p.

12270   The applicability of total quality management to the management of schools.
GBR   1993
Research Date(s): 1990-1994
West-Burnham, J.
Sup: Seymour, R.; James, L.
Inst: Crewe & Alsager College of Higher Education, Department of Education Management, Hassall Road, Alsager, Stoke on Trent ST7 2HL, United Kingdom.
educational administration; management; quality of education
administration de l'enseignement; gestion; qualité de l'éducation
PROJECT DESCRIPTION
Total Quality Management (TQM) has emerged in the 1980s as the most powerful tool for organisational review and development. This research seeks to explore the extent to which the principles of TQM are applicable to school management. The research model is based on the researcher's book *Managing quality in schools: a TQM approach* as a basis for examining perceptions of quality, identifying and analysing existing relevant practice and developing a model that is applicable in schools. The book includes an invitation to respond to the writer - this will generate an opportunity sample. The writer has been engaged by a number of local education authorities to run courses on quality management - participants in these courses will be used as a sample for follow-up work in order to review the principles and practices identified in the book.
Publ: West-Burnham, J. *Managing quality in schools: a TQM approach.* Harlow: Longman Press, 1992.

12271   Attitudes towards 'economic course' provision in the public further education sector.
GBR   1993
Research Date(s): 1989-1993
Robinson, P.
Sup: Marriott, J.
Inst: Leeds University, School of Education, Leeds LS2 9JT, Bradford & Ilkley Community College, Great Horton Road, Bradford BD1 1AY, United Kingdom.
economics of education; educational administration; cost of education; educational institution
économie de l'éducation; administration de l'enseignement; coût de l'éducation; établissement d'enseignement
PROJECT DESCRIPTION
During the 1980s the further education (FE) sector has come under increasing pressure to operate within the context of a 'New Right Market Economy'. The purpose of this research is to enquire into and collect information about people's perceptions of how economic course provision within FE can be developed more effectively. Given a context of increasing competitiveness from other public and private agencies, the research aims to examine the attitudes of staff in terms of their willingness to embrace this current entrepreneurial philosophy, as well as to further consider present management and administrative structures in order to assess the degree to which these existing structures may hinder or facilitate flexible responses to commercial demands.
The research has an ethnographic base and will aim to interview respondents from four sample areas: college managers and administrators; college staff academic and technical, other local training providers; and industrial managers. An initial pilot project took place within Bradford & Ilkley Community College during the academic year 1989/1990 and five subsequent research projects were developed during the following 18 months.

12272   Autonome Weiterbildung.   (Independence in further education.)
AUT   1993
Research Date(s): 1992-1993
Fritzer, Eva; Reumueller, Alfred; Larcher, Dietmar; Mathes, Reinhard; Klien, Gabi; Odrei, Ilse.
Inst: Institut fuer Weiterbildung, Sterneckstrasse 15, A-9010 Klagenfurt; Zentrum fuer Schulversuche und Schulentwicklung, Universitaetsstrasse 70, A-9020 Klagenfurt.
Universitaet fuer Bildungswissenschaften, Universitaetsstrasse 65-67, A-9020 Klagenfurt; Bundesministerium fuer Unterricht und Kunst, Minoritenplatz 5, A-1014 Wien
school autonomy; parent participation; teacher participation
autonomie scolaire; participation des parents; participation de l'enseignant
PROJECT DESCRIPTION
Partnerschaftliche Entwicklung einer kleinstaedtischen Volksschule unter Einbeziehung des gesamten Lehrkoerpers, der Eltern und des Umfelds - im Sinne der Schulautonomiebestimmungen.
Es wird die gesamte Population einbezogen.
Das Vorgehen entspricht den Methoden der Handlungsforschung.

12273   Berkshire school pupil forecasting system.
GBR   1993
Research Date(s): 1976-
Reece, D.

Inst: Berkshire County Council, Education Department, Information Technology Management, Shire Hall, Shinfield Park, Reading RG2 9XD, United Kingdom.
number of pupils; forecasting; regional planning
effectifs scolaires; prévision; planification régionale
PROJECT DESCRIPTION

The objective of the Berkshire school pupil forecasting system is to predict numbers of pupils of each age group in every Berkshire school, for up to 10 years ahead. The basic approach in forecasting is the 'cohort trend' method, where changes observed to cohorts of pupils over previous years are applied in the future. Recent enhancements to the system include: (1) the prediction of primary school entry (i.e. 5 year old) age pupils by relating intakes to the past and predicted resident population of the school catchment area, using data from the Research and Intelligence Unit's Population Estimation and Projection Models; and (2) prediction of intakes to secondary schools by using data from the Education Department's computerised Secondary School Allocation System. Forecasts are produced annually using pupil numbers in January.

12274 La collaborazione scuola-famiglia per l'orientamento degli alunni. (School-home collaboration in pupil guidance.)
ITA 1993
Research Date(s): 1990-1991
Travaglia, G.; Alcini, P.; Richiedei, G.; Borrelli, M.; Mellano, M.
Sup: Sgobino, L.
Inst: Istituto di Ricerche e Studi sull'Educazione e la Famiglia - IRSEF (Institute of Research and Study on Education and the Family), Via Soana 22, 00183 Roma, Italy.
Fin: Ministero della Pubblica Istruzione, Ufficio Studi e Programmazione.
choice of school; upper secondary; parent-pupil relation; parent-school relation; educational guidance; choice of studies
choix d'une école; secondaire deuxième cycle; relation parents-élève; relation parents-école; orientation pédagogique; choix des études
PROJECT DESCRIPTION

Aims: The study examined how pupils arrive at a choice for an upper secondary school. It looked at the types of collaboration that exist between the school and the family in the guidance of pupils and focused in particular on the level of involvement of parents, pupils, and peers and the relative influence of these three components on the eventual choice.

Methods: The study used three open-answer questionnaires: one to pupils, one to parents, and one to teachers. The administration of 1,000 questionnaires took place by geographical area and by category. The research was divided into two parts and resulted in a report comprising nine brief chapters and a conclusion.

Results: Tabulation and elaboration of the data show that youth look for support either from the family or from the school. However, the response from these two educational entities appears ambiguous. There is, in fact, a mutual delegation of responsibilities that is caused by a mistaken conception of the guidance process. Delegation of responsibilities to psychology and sociology experts is a noteworthy phenomenon, even if one takes into consideration geographical differences (it occurs more frequently in the north than in the central part of Italy). Parents tend to delegate their responsibilities to the school, partly out of the fear of interfering with the authority of teachers. In consequence, they remain entirely uninformed about issues related to upper secondary school choice. Teachers tend to look at the informative rather than the vocational aspects of guidance. There is a striking gap between school and the world of work in all three geographical areas and all three categories concerned.

12275 A conceptual model for the functioning of higher education during the transition to a market economy.
RUS 1994
Research Date(s): 1991-1992
Voronin, A.A.
Sup: Zuyev, V.M.
Inst: Research Institute for Higher Education, 103062, Moscow, K-62, Podsosensky per. 20, Russia.
State Committee for Higher Education Institutions, 113833, Moscow, M-230, Lysinovskja str. 51, Russia
economics of education; educational reform; higher education; economic conditions
économie de l'éducation; réforme de l'enseignement; enseignement supérieur; conditions économiques
PROJECT DESCRIPTION

The study sought to improve the functioning of higher education in Russia during the transition to a market economy. An analysis was made of political and socio-economic aspects of the functioning of higher education. An economic model for the functioning of higher education during the transition period was elaborated. Recommendations were made regarding the need for extra resources to finance higher education. Economic models for specialized secondary schools and professional technological schools were elaborated.

Publ: Zuyev, V.M.; Zuyeva, T.V.; Nikulin, I.I. & Voronin, A.A. *The formation of a system of retraining specialists in other spheres of work under*

the circumstances of the transitional period. Information review, M., NIIVO, 1992.
Popov, Y.N. Educational services and the market economy. In: *Russian Economics Journal*, N6, 1992.
Voronin, A.A.; Nikulin, I.I.; Popov, Y.N.; et al. *Youth, education, market economy.* M., NIIVO, 1992.
Popov, Y.N.; Klimova, N.V.; Ostapchenko, V.D.; et al. *Economics of higher education during the transition to a market economy.* M., NIIVO, 1993.
(A complete list can be obtained from the researcher.).

12276 Coût et financement de l'enseignement supérieur en France.
FRA 1993
Research Date(s): 1987-1989
Eicher, Jean-Claude.
Inst: Université de Dijon, UER Faculté des sciences économiques et de gestion, CNRS UPR/29 et GDR/996, Institut de recherche sur l'économie de l'éducation, BP 138, 21004 Dijon Cedex, France.
education budget; France; higher education; cost of education; cost-benefit analysis; forecasting; cross-national research
budget de l'éducation; France; enseignement supérieur; coût de l'éducation; analyse coût-bénéfice; prévision; recherche transnationale
PROJECT DESCRIPTION

Objectifs: Faisant suite à des travaux menés à l'IREDU à la fin des années 70 et au début des années 80, ces recherches explorent l'évolution du financement de l'enseignement supérieur français.

Méthodologie: Comparaisons internationales et analyses des transformations des structures de l'enseignement supérieur français.

Résultats: (1) La baisse des crédits publics par élève observée entre la fin des années 60 et la fin des années 70 plaçait la France très au dessous de la moyenne des pays développés quelque soit l'indice d'effort utilisé. (2) On observe le développement rapide des filières courtes à finalité professionnelle tant à l'intérieur que (surtout) à l'extérieur des universités, l'apparition de filières longues professionnalisées et plus généralement la diversification des filières universitaires, le développement explosif et anarchique d'un secteur privé d'enseignement supérieur de qualité souvent faible. (3) La baisse de la qualité des études universitaires traditionnelles entraîne la nécessité tant d'une augmentation de l'effort financier public que d'une diversification des financements qui permettrait d'accroître l'autonomie des établissements.

Publ: Eicher, Jean-Claude. La France dépense-t-elle trop peu pour son enseignement supérieur? In: *Revue française des finances publiques*, n° 27, sept. 1989.

12277 Les coûts de l'enseignement pré-scolaire au Brésil.
FRA 1993
Research Date(s): 1987-1989
Paul, Jean-Jacques.
Inst: Université de Dijon, UER Faculté des sciences économiques et de gestion, CNRS UPR/29 et GDR/996, Institut de recherche sur l'économie de l'éducation, BP 138, 21004 Dijon Cedex, France.
education budget; cost of education; Brazil; pre-school education; association; local government; equal opportunity; access to education
budget de l'éducation; coût de l'éducation; Brésil; éducation préscolaire; association; administration locale; égalité de chances; accès à l'éducation
PROJECT DESCRIPTION

Objectifs: Les pays en développement font généralement face à une double série de problèmes: la scolarisation universelle n'est pas atteinte au niveau de l'enseignement primaire; les ressources consacrées à la fonction éducative ne peuvent pas augmenter. La situation du Brésil est différente du cadre général, on observe un taux de scolarisation pour les premières années du primaire (proche de 100%) mais également un taux de déperdition particulièrement élevé. Une des hypothèses retenues est qu'il faut réduire les inégalités d'accès à l'enseignement pré-scolaire pour une meilleure réussite au niveau du primaire. La solution envisagée par l'Etat de Sao-Paulo est d'augmenter les capacités d'accueil, en confiant l'administration des nouveaux établissements aux municipalités et organisations non gouvernementales (ONG). L'hypothèse était que le coût de ces organisations est moindre, il s'agissait donc de tester la véracité des hypothèses relatives aux résultats des organisations non gouvernementales.

Méthodologie: Evaluation des coûts respectifs des écoles maternelles des municipalités et des organisations non gouvernementales et identification du type de public accueilli auprès d'un échantillon de 31 institutions (vingt et une d'ONG et dix municipales).

Résultats: Le coût unitaire annuel des maternelles d'organisations non gouvernementales apparaît supérieur à celui des maternelles municipales mais le temps d'accueil quotidien des premières est plus élevé; les maternelles d'ONG accueillent un public plus pauvre que les municipales. C'est par leurs capacités à mobiliser des fonds privés et par le type du public accueilli que les ONG représentent des partenaires potentiels pour le programme d'extension de l'enseignement pré-scolaire.

Publ: Paul, Jean-Jacques. *Os custos do pre-escola em São Paulo.* Rapport pour le Secrétariat de l'éducation de l'Etat de Sao Paulo, janvier 1989, 15p.

12278 Coûts et efficacité dans l'enseignement supérieur malien.
FRA 1993
Research Date(s): 1987-1990
Cuenin, Serge; Orivel, François.
Inst: Université de Dijon, UER Faculté des sciences économiques et de gestion, CNRS UPR/29 et GDR/996, Institut de recherche sur l'économie de l'éducation, BP 138, 21004 Dijon Cedex, France.
education budget; Mali; cost-benefit analysis; level of education
budget de l'éducation; Mali; analyse coût-bénéfice; niveau d'enseignement
PROJECT DESCRIPTION
Objectifs: Le système éducatif malien est entré, depuis une dizaine d'années, dans une phase de récession longue qui conduit, inéluctablement, par sa dynamique interne, à une baisse des taux de scolarisation à tous les niveaux. Ce phénomène grave n'a été perçu que pour l'enseignement primaire essentiellement parce que la supression des débouchés traditionnels des diplômés (emplois dans la fonction publique) l'a occulté.
Méthodologie: Le travail entrepris a consisté à analyser en premier lieu la démographie scolaire malienne à tous les niveaux d'études afin de disposer des éléments de base pour porter un diagnostic sur ce système éducatif. Ce travail a été complété par une analyse des coûts et du financement aux principaux niveaux d'études.
Résultats: Cette analyse a mis en évidence les caractéristiques principales de l'enseignement: (1) trop faible part des ressources de l'Etat accordée à l'enseignement primaire alors qu'une part excessive est accordée aux aides sociales en faveur des étudiants; (2) faibles salaires des enseignants, ce qui entraîne la recherche d'activités secondaires et une moindre motivation; (3) surcapacité des infrastructures d'accueil dans les deuxième et troisième degrés, ce qui entraîne des coûts de fonctionnement récurrents; (4) inadéquation formation-emploi qui touche plus sévèrement les diplômés pré-supérieurs car les employeurs ont une préférence relative pour les diplômes les plus élevés.
A partir de ce constat, un certain nombre de mesures ont été proposées afin de rééquilibrer l'effort de l'Etat en faveur de l'enseignement primaire, le freinage de la progression des effectifs dans les deuxième et troisième degrés devant être mis à profit pour réallouer les ressources correspondantes vers l'enseignement du premier degré.
Publ: Orivel, François & Perrot, Jean. *Coûts, financement et efficacité des enseignements supérieur et secondaire au Mali.* IREDU: Rapport pour la Banque mondiale, déc. 1988, 35p. et annexes.
Cuénin, Serge. *Les besoins en maîtres: un essai de prévision dans le cas d'un pays en développement: le Mali.* IREDU: Rapport pour le Ministère de l'éducation nationale du Mali, nov. 1990, 40p.

12279 A cross-case study of actors' perceptions of key aspects of policy realization in sixth-form colleges.
GBR 1993
Research Date(s): 1989-1992
Stopper, M.
Sup: Spence, B.
Inst: Hull University, School of Education, Cottingham Road, Hull HU6 7RX, United Kingdom.
post-compulsory education; general education; guidance; aims of education
enseignement postobligatoire; enseignement général; orientation; finalité de l'éducation
PROJECT DESCRIPTION
The growth of the sixth-form college as a focus for post-16 provision, has created opportunities for examining what given institutions appear to have achieved from the perspective of both students and staff. Studies of the sixth-form have been related hitherto to areas such as: students' views of what the aims and objectives of sixth-form education ought to be; what they regard as the aims and objectives actually pursued by teachers; and the views of teachers as to the importance of particular aims and objectives. Little work has, however, been done on comparing the views of staff and students towards what has actually been achieved in these terms.
The present research concentrates upon two key areas: (1) general education; (2) pastoral provision, which represent dimensions of the common concern for educating the 'whole person'. It draws upon multiple data sources and methods, including documentary analysis, unstructured interview, participant observation and questionnaire and seeks to represent actors' construction of reality in selected institutions.

12280 Cross phase continuity and progression project: transition from primary to secondary school.
GBR 1993
Research Date(s): 1990-1992
Munro, R.
Inst: Jordanhill College of Education, Division of Business & Computer Education, Southbrae Drive, Jordanhill, Glasgow G13 1PP, United Kingdom.
Fin: Apple Computer UK; Strathclyde Regional Council.
transitional class; primary education; secondary education; teaching aid
classe de transition; enseignement primaire; enseignement secondaire; moyen d'enseignement

PROJECT DESCRIPTION
The aims of this project are to: (1) improve the social and educational links between secondary schools and their associated primary schools and with senior classes of these primary schools; (2) promote social and educational links between secondary school departments; (3) create an educational structure that will motivate pupils and enhance learning; (4) evaluate the effects of computer technology as an aid to learning; (5) ease the transition between primary and secondary schools. Various software packages and teaching materials have been produced by the pilot project which will now be tested (and refined) in a number of invited schools in Glasgow.

12281 Curriculum development in technical and vocational education in Saudi Arabia related to students' needs, perceptions and expectations.
GBR 1993
Research Date(s): 1991-1993
Obeid, S.
Sup: Nolan, R.
Inst: University of Wales, College of Cardiff School of Education, Senghennydd Road, Cardiff CF2 4AG, United Kingdom.
Fin: Saudia Arabia Ministry of Education.
wastage; dropout; technical education; vocational education; curriculum development; educational need; Saudi Arabia
déperdition d'effectifs; abandon d'études; enseignement technique; enseignement professionnel; élaboration de programmes d'études; besoin d'éducation; Arabie Saoudite
PROJECT DESCRIPTION
This is a study that aims to determine the cause of student wastage in technical and vocational education institutes in Saudi Arabia as a basis of the need for curriculum development.

12282 De organisatie van een centrale directie in het Voortgezet onderwijs. (The introduction of central management teams in secondary schools.)
NLD 1994
Research Date(s): 1992
Kuijk, J. van; Pelkmans, A.
Sup: Pouwels, J.
Inst: Instituut voor Toegepaste Sociale wetenschappen (ITS) (Institute for Applied Social Sciences), P.O. Box 9048, 6500 KJ Nijmegen, Netherlands. Katholieke Universiteit Nijmegen (Catholic University of Nijmegen), P.O. Box 9102, HC Nijmegen, Netherlands
Fin: SVO het Instituut voor Onderzoek van het Onderwijs.
educational administration; head teacher; managerial staff; secondary school
administration de l'enseignement; chef d'établissement; personnel d'encadrement; école secondaire
PROJECT DESCRIPTION
Background: With the introduction of the staff budget system, "complex" combined secondary schools will be given the opportunity to form a central management team, a type of shared leadership by maximally three persons. These schools will have to comply with the following formula: (c x 100) + y $\geq$ 1000, in which c = "complexity" (i.e. the number of types of school represented in the combined school concerned) and y = number of pupils. The central management team has already been introduced as a management structure in senior secondary vocational education (MBO) and in higher vocational education (HBO). With its pending introduction in general secondary education, there is a growing need for information among head teachers and school boards about the possibilities it offers.
Aim: To examine, on the basis of experiences in MBO, what problems need to be solved before the central management team can be introduced as a management structure in general secondary schools.
Design: The research population comprises the heads, deputy heads and the members of the governing bodies and participation councils of MBO schools and general secondary schools. The sample will consist of five MBO schools that have been working with a central management team for some time and 10 general secondary schools that are being managed similarly or that have or have had the intention to install a central management team. Data will be collected through interviews, topic lists, and document analysis. Experiences in MBO schools will be compared with the situation in general secondary schools.

12283 De toekomst van het leerlingwezen. (The future of apprenticeship training.)
NLD 1993
Research Date(s): 1992-1993
Grip, A. de; Berendsen, H.; Dekker, R.J.P.
Inst: ROA Researchcentrum voor Onderwijs en Arbeidsmarkt, Universiteit Limburg (Research Centre for Education and the Labour Market, University of Limburg), P.O. Box 616, 6200 MD Maastricht, Netherlands.
Fin: Ministry of Education and Science.
number of pupils; apprentice; apprenticeship; training need; training supply
effectifs scolaires; apprenti; apprentissage professionnel; besoin de formation; offre de formation
PROJECT DESCRIPTION

This research focuses on the extent to which the supply of apprentices in apprenticeship training in the near future may fall short of the target for each sector. Forecasts will be made of the expected numbers of apprentices entering and leaving apprenticeship training. An estimate will also be made of dropout rates.

The analyses will be carried out at the level of the various apprenticeship supervisory boards. Furthermore, if possible, a number of central indicators will be presented, related to the take-up of apprenticeships in the various trades (distribution of entrants by type of previous training and the proportion of women and adults among new apprentices).

The study will result in a basic forecast of the expected numbers of entrants for the years 1993-2001, supplemented by a number of alternative scenarios for changes in dropout rates and an increase in the participation of women and adults. Separate figures will be provided for elementary and advanced apprenticeship training.

12284 Decision-making and school policy: a case study of a primary school at a time of rapid change.
GBR 1993
Research Date(s): 1991-1994
Hayes, D.
Sup: Hannan, A.; Holt, D.
Inst: Plymouth University, Rolle Faculty of Education, Douglas Avenue, Exmouth EX8 2AT, United Kingdom.
educational administration; primary school; educational reform; decision making
administration de l'enseignement; école primaire; réforme de l'enseignement; prise de décision
PROJECT DESCRIPTION
The case study focuses upon the decision-making process within a combined first and middle school in the South West of England. It aims to provide a perspective on the involvement of staff and governors in the process in the light of the rapidly changing circumstances created through government education legislation.

Data have been gained during 1991 and 1992 through non-participant observation at staff meetings and governors' meetings, through formal and informal discussions with staff, and through familiarity with school management structures and procedures.

Data analysis indicates that the rapidity of change has placed a considerable strain upon the headteacher and staff, jeopardising the carefully designed management system established within the school, and creating insufficient opportunity for reflection upon, implementation, and subsequent amendment of decisions taken. The extent of teacher participation has varied according to the priority given to an issue by the staff and their beliefs about the genuineness of the consultation process. The need to act swiftly has sometimes obliged the headteacher to pre-empt full staff consultation by presenting, in consultation with governors and senior staff, a limited range of options or a single alternative, thereby undermining her preference for joint decision-making and collegial relations among staff.

12285 Les dépenses publiques pour l'enseignement universitaire et le taux de rendement fiscal.
FRA 1993
Research Date(s): 1987-1989
Perrot, Jean.
Inst: Université de Dijon, UER Faculté des sciences économiques et de gestion, CNRS UPR/29 et GDR/996, Institut de recherche sur l'économie de l'éducation, BP 138, 21004 Dijon Cedex, France.
education budget; higher education; fees; taxation; cost-benefit analysis
budget de l'éducation; enseignement supérieur; droits de scolarité; fiscalité; analyse coût-bénéfice
PROJECT DESCRIPTION
Objectifs: Ce travail est réalisé en collaboration avec C. Lemelin de l'Université du Québec à Montréal. L'Etat en tant qu'agent économique conçoit que les dépenses publiques d'éducation peuvent donner naissance à un flux de rentrées fiscales supplémentaires ce qui rend possible le calcul d'un taux de rendement fiscal. Ce compte budgétaire de long terme rapprochant coûts et bénéfices pour l'Etat peut servir deux préoccupations bien distinctes: L'Etat réalise-t-il une opération rentable en finançant, en partie, le coût de l'enseignement supérieur? Quelles conséquences aurait une modification du financement de l'Etat, notamment quelles seraient les répercussions sur le rendement fiscal d'une augmentation des droits de scolarité?

Résultats: Des estimations qui sont proposées, il ressort que l'augmentation des droits de scolarité, présentée souvent comme une des solutions au problème du développement des universités, s'avère être une mesure à manier avec précaution. A court terme cela permet de dégager des recettes supplémentaires, à long terme on assiste à une réduction du nombre d'étudiants et l'Etat perd les bénéfices fiscaux de ceux qui auraient sans cette décision poursuivi leurs études.

Publ: Perrot, Jean. Les dépenses publiques pour l'enseignement universitaire et le taux de rendement fiscal: le cas de la France. In: *Revue économique*, vol. 42, n° 1, janv. 1991, pp. 111-132.

12286 Derugulering: noden en mogelijkheden voor het beheer van onderwijsinstellingen. (Deregulation: needs and possibilities for school management.)
BEL 1994
Research Date(s): 1990-1991
Buelens, M.; Devos, G.
Inst: De Vlerick School voor Management (Vlerick School for Management), Sint-Pietersnieuwstraat 184, 9000 Gent, Belgium.
Universiteit Gent (University of Gent), Sint-Pietersnieuwstraat 25, 9000 Gent, Belgium
Fin: Departement Onderwijs, Fonds voor Kollektief en Fundamenteel Onderzoek op Ministerieel Initiatief.
educational administration; school autonomy; school; management; central government
administration de l'enseignement; autonomie scolaire; école; gestion; administration centrale
PROJECT DESCRIPTION
In this project deregulation is defined as reducing the number of legal rules and regulations, with a view to decreasing state intervention and increasing school autonomy.

The aim of the project is to answer the following questions: (1) Under what organizational conditions can deregulation be effective, enabling schools to use the available scope for policy-making? (2) In which sectors of school policy do school heads consider deregulation desirable? The research was limited to secondary schools and concentrated on the following dimensions of school policy: personnel management, financial management, management of the infrastructure, the curriculum and the pedagogical mission of the school.

Methods: 27 school heads were interviewed by means of an open questionnaire. These data were supplemented by secondary information material, such as school periodicals and notes. To investigate the relationship between organization characteristics and the utilization of the scope for policy-making, use was made of the "quantum view model" of Miller and Friesen.

Results: A description was made of the scope for policy-making for schools under present central regulations. The relationship between organizational characteristics and schools' use of their scope for policy-making was also described. These data have been used to classify schools into three organizational types: the pupil-oriented, the subject-oriented and the rule-oriented school.

Publ: Buelens, M. & Devos, G. *Derugulering: noden en mogelijkheden voor het beheer van onderwijsinstellingen: eindrapport*. Gent: Vlerick school voor management, 1992, 133p.

12287 The development of a newly formed comprehensive school.
GBR 1993
Research Date(s): 1988-1991
Bell, L.
Inst: Warwick University, Faculty of Educational Studies, Coventry CV4 7AL, United Kingdom.
Fin: The Nuffield Foundation.
amalgamation of schools; comprehensive secondary school; educational planning
regroupement d'écoles; école secondaire polyvalente; planification de l'éducation
PROJECT DESCRIPTION
This study provides a description of the closure of three comprehensive schools, their amalgamation into one new school, and the strategies used by those within the school to cope with this process. It goes on to examine the initial impact of the Education Reform Act 1988 on the school. The research uses interviews, observation and documentary sources.

12288 The development of managerialism in Scottish education since 1945.
GBR 1993
Research Date(s): 1988-1993
Murray, R.
Sup: Hartley, J.
Inst: Dundee University, Centre for Continuing Education, Dundee DD1 4HN, United Kingdom.
educational administration; management; Scotland
administration de l'enseignement; gestion; Ecosse
PROJECT DESCRIPTION
The study examines the increasing tendency in Scottish education to use industrial and corporate modes of management in education since 1945.

12289 Devolved management of schools.
GBR 1993
Research Date(s): 1992-1994
Adler, M.; Raab, C.; Munn, P.
Inst: Edinburgh University, Old College, South Bridge, Edinburgh EH8 9YL, United Kingdom; Scottish Council for Research in Education, 15 St John Street, Edinburgh EH8 8JR, United Kingdom.
Fin: Economic and Social Research Council.
educational administration; parent participation; parent-school relation

administration de l'enseignement; participation des parents; relation parents-école

PROJECT DESCRIPTION

This project aims to compare the impact of parental participation and Local Management of Schools on parents, teachers, education authorities and government in England and Scotland. It will also analyse the changes in relationships between those involved, and assess their significance for educational provision.

12290 Die Schullaufbahnentscheidung in der 4. Schulstufe (Nachfolgeuntersuchung bei Grazer Eltern). (School career decisions in the fourth year (a follow-up survey among parents in Graz).)

AUT 1993

Research Date(s): 1991-1992

Seel, Helmut; Bachmann, Gerhild.

Inst: Institut fuer Erziehungswissenschaften, Hans-Sachs-Gasse 3, A-8010 Graz.

Universitaet Graz, Hans-Sachs-Gasse 3, A-8010 Graz

choice of school; post-compulsory education; parental attitude

choix d'une école; enseignement postobligatoire; attitude des parents

PROJECT DESCRIPTION

Um regelmaessig und fortlaufend ueber aktuelle Entwicklungen im Schulbereich zu informieren, fuehrte das Institut fuer Erziehungswissenschaften der Karl-Franzens-Universtaet Graz, Abteilung Schulpaedagogik, im Schuljahr 1990/1991 eine Nachfolgeuntersuchung zu der im Schuljahr 1989/1990 durchgefuehrten Erhebung "Die Schullaufbahnentscheidung in der 4. Schulstufe (Untersuchung bei Grazer Eltern)" durch. In einem eigens entwickelten Fragebogen gaben 321 Eltern mit einem Kind in der 4. Schulstufe Auskunft ueber ihre Ueberlegungen, die bei der Schullaufbahnentscheidung fuer ihr Kind eine Rolle gespielt haben, nannten die wichtigsten Faehigkeiten, die die Schule ihrem Kind vermitteln sollte, aeusserten sich zu grundsaetzlichen Bildungsfragen und Fragen der Schulsituation und -entwicklung und beurteilten die Schulformen Hauptschule und allgemeinbildende hoehere Schule-Unterstufe in einem Polaritaetsprofil, einer Methode, die den subjektiven Bedeutungsgehalt eines Begriffs fassbar zu machen trachtet, indem er verschiedenen Eigenschaftspaaren zugeordnet wird. Vorrangiger Gegenstand der Untersuchung war es, aktuelle Daten im Vergleich zu den Ergebnissen des Vorjahres zu praesentieren und zu diskutieren. Explorativ wurden auch Einstellungen der Eltern zu Fragen des Computereinsatzes in der Grundschule erhoben.

Es wurde eine schriftliche Befragung durchgefuehrt. Fuer die Stichprobenauswahl wurde ein mehrstufiger Auswahlplan realisiert. Nach dem Zufallsprinzip wurden von den 55 oeffentlichen Grazer Volksschulen je nach Groesse der siebzehn Grazer Schulbezirke eine bzw. zwei Schulen ausgewaehlt und innerhalb dieser Schulen eine der 4. Schulklassen. Insgesamt wurden 23 Schulen mit 371 SchuelerInnen in die Untersuchung einbezogen. 321 Elternfrageboegen gelangten in die Endauswertung (Ruecklaufquote 86,5 %).

Die statistischen Analysen der Fragebogen konnten unter Zuhilfenahme des Statistikprogrammpakets SPSS-PC 3.0 auf der Computeranlage des Instituts fuer Erziehungswissenschaften durchgefuehrt werden. Chi-Quadrat-Analyse, t-Tests, Frequenztabellen und graphische Darstellungen kamen zur Anwendung. Die offene Frage 11 des Fragebogens wurde inhaltsanalystisch ausgewertet.

In der Rangfolge der wichtigsten Hauptmotive der Schullaufbahnentscheidung ergab sich keine Aenderung zur Vorjahrsuntersuchung. Von den Eltern wurden der Wunsch der Kinder, der Ruf einer Schule als gute Ausbildungsinstitution, die mit einem bestimmten Schultyp verbundenen Aufstiegsmoeglichkeiten bzw. das mit einem bestimmten Schultyp verbundene soziale Ansehen und die raeumliche Naehe der Schule als wichtigste Krierien fuer ihre Entscheidung genannt. Zukuenftigen Eltern von HauptschuelerInnen ist auch die Moeglichkeit einer raschen Eingliederung in den Arbeitsprozess sehr wichtig. Im Polaritaetsprofil zeigte sich eine positivere Bewertung der allgemeinbildenden hoeheren Schule-Unterstufe.

Publ: Bachmann, Gerhild. *Die Schullaufbahnentscheidung in der 4. Schulstufe (Nachfolgeuntersuchung bei Grazer Eltern)*. Forschungsbericht des Instituts fuer Erziehungswissenschaften, Abteilung Schulpaedagogik. Graz 1992.

12291 Economic decision-making models on non-advanced further education.

GBR 1993

Research Date(s): 1989-1993

Shepherson, D.

Sup: Thomas, H.

Inst: Birmingham University, School of Education, Edgbaston, Birmingham B15 2TT, United Kingdom.

economics of education; educational planning; resource allocation; decision making; curriculum; post-compulsory education

économie de l'éducation; planification de l'éducation; affectation des ressources; prise de décision; programme d'études; enseignement postobligatoire

PROJECT DESCRIPTION

The relationship between resource decisions and curriculum decision processes will be examined in the context created by the local authority role in creating a framework for strategic planning, as influenced by the Local Authority Act and the Education Reform Act. At the centre of the analysis will be an opportunity cost model of decision making. It is expected that quantitative data will be collected reflecting commonly used performance indicators. This will be analysed in the context of qualitative data, based upon interviews, relating to the perceptions of individuals on their valuations of resource and curriculum alternatives.

12292 Economy, education and ecumenism 1931-1984.

GBR 1993

Research Date(s): 1988-1991

Owen, D.

Sup: McClelland, V.

Inst: Hull University, School of Education, Cottingham Road, Hull HU6 7RX, United Kingdom.

educational administration; denominational school; economics of education; Christian education; church; governing body; history of education

administration de l'enseignement; école confessionnelle; économie de l'éducation; éducation chrétienne; église; direction administrative; histoire de l'éducation

PROJECT DESCRIPTION

The contribution of the churches to education has been conspicuous by a pattern of discord, even hostility, from the earliest years of the last century, when the setting for their work was permeated by division. Social division, political division and religious division formed a perpetuating circle. The question was posed by Russell that perhaps it was necessary to have several different and separate churches and chapels to reach out to several different social classes. Could a united church have served a divided society? By the middle of the twentieth century a number of the denominational schools were giving concern to the local authorities; many of the buildings were old and considered inadequate to modern educational requirements. The chief concern was that most of the religious bodies lacked the financial means to maintain their schools. The research considers the approaches of the education authorities and the religious bodies towards the provision of education in parts of Lincolnshire by the establishment of joint Anglican and Methodist controlled schools.

12293 Education in the United Arab Emirates: an examination of selected themes and issues with reference to the 'small country' context.

GBR 1993

Research Date(s): 1989-1992

Biggs, M.

Sup: Brock, C.

Inst: Hull University, School of Education, Cottingham Road, Hull HU6 7RX, United Kingdom.

educational provision; United Arab Emirates; educational policy; development of education

scolarisation; Emirats arabes unis; politique de l'éducation; développement de l'éducation

PROJECT DESCRIPTION

The United Arab Emirates (UAE) is a group of seven small sheikdoms, previously known as the Trucial States whilst under British tutelage. Since their independence in 1971, and aided by the oil wealth of certain emirates, the UAE has undergone a period of unprecedented growth and modernisation. It has progressed from relative obscurity and poverty into a modern well serviced country of international recognition with one of the highest per capita incomes in the world. Education has always been assigned an important role in this process of modernisation. This research outlines educational provision in the UAE in both an historical and contemporary context. It further discusses important factors that influence the style of educational provision at all levels in both the state and private sectors such as Islam, demography, gender, manpower, pluralism, and 'small country' issues.

12294 Educational management in developing countries.

GBR 1993

Research Date(s): 1990-

Harber, C.; Davies, L.

Inst: Birmingham University, School of Education, Edgbaston, Birmingham B15 2TT, United Kingdom.

educational administration; educational policy; developing country

administration de l'enseignement; politique de l'éducation; pays en développement

PROJECT DESCRIPTION

This is a qualitative research project that uses observation, semi-structured interviews and documentation to explore the realities of school management in developing societies. It pays particular attention to the social, economic, political and cultural context in which schools operate and the ways in which this affects the attitudes and behaviour of key participants including headteachers, teachers, parents and pupils.

Publ: Davies, L. *Equity and efficiency: school management in an international context*. London: Falmer Press, 1990.

Dadey, A. & Harber, C. *Training and professional support for Headship in Africa*. London: Commonwealth Secretariat, 1991.

12295 Educational management, teacher evaluation and teacher autonomy.
GBR 1993
Research Date(s): 1986-1993
Toy, K.
Sup: Wringe, C.
Inst: Keele University, Department of Education, Keele, Staffordshire ST5 5BG, United Kingdom.
educational administration; teacher autonomy; teacher appraisal
administration de l'enseignement; liberté de l'enseignant; évaluation sur l'enseignant
PROJECT DESCRIPTION
This is principally a conceptual and library study. Theories of educational management and teacher evaluation are to be explored in relation to a concept of teacher autonomy. Historical and current expectations and practice will be examined in the light of available documentary evidence, and a small number of exemplary case studies may be undertaken.

12296 Effecten stopzetting planprocedure (voortgezet) speciaal onderwijs. (Effects of the discontinuation of the special education planning procedure.)
NLD 1994
Research Date(s): 1992
Laemers, M.; Oudenhoven, D.
Sup: Esch, W. van.
Inst: Instituut voor Toegepaste Sociale wetenschappen (ITS) (Institute for Applied Social Sciences), P.O. Box 9048, 6500 KJ Nijmegen, Netherlands. Katholieke Universiteit Nijmegen (Catholic University of Nijmegen), P.O. Box 9102, 6500 HC Nijmegen, Netherlands
Fin: SVO het Instituut voor Onderzoek van het Onderwijs.
school distribution; special school; educational policy; legislation
carte scolaire; centre d'éducation spéciale; politique de l'éducation; législation
PROJECT DESCRIPTION
Background: One of the measures that were taken in 1988 as part of the government's policy to curb the growth of the special education sector was to stop the planning procedure for the distribution and reshuffling of special schools. This means that, for the time being, the government will not fund any new special schools. Hereby it is hoped to prevent an imbalance between the growth of the ordinary and special sectors of education.

Aim: To examine whether the discontinuation of the planning procedure has had a negative effect on the possibility to found schools and, if so, whether these negative effects are sufficiently compensated for by the exceptions provided in the Special Education Interim Act.

Design: Provincial authority officials who are responsible for special education will be interviewed with the help of a semi-structured questionnaire. Additional data will be collected, through interviews and questionnaires, from representatives from municipalities that provide special education, representatives from municipalities that do not offer special education and that experience problems as a result of the discontinuation of the planning procedure, and representatives from three special school board unions. One or several government official(s) will be interviewed by telephone.

12297 Effectiveness of different kinds of literacy provision.
GBR 1993
Research Date(s): 1989-1991
Francis, H.; Abell, S.
Inst: London University, Institute of Education, Department of Educational Psychology and Special Educational Needs, 20 Bedford Way, London WC1H 0AL, United Kingdom.
Fin: Adult Literacy & Basic Skills Unit.
educational provision; adult education; basic education; literacy; evaluation
scolarisation; éducation des adultes; éducation de base; alphabétisation; évaluation
PROJECT DESCRIPTION
Three main types of provision were identified in eight participating local education authorities (LEAs). Each was examined for evidence of student satisfaction and benefit and for student, staffing, organisation and teaching factors which influenced student experience and outcomes. Little evidence emerged which differentiated clearly between styles, but overall a number of issues were identified which must be taken into account in evaluating provision in order to improve it.

Publ: Abell, S. *Effective approaches in adult literacy: research into evaluating the effectiveness of different styles of provision in adult literacy*. London: ALBSU, 1992.

12298 The effects of the Education Reform Act 1988: formula funding of schools.
GBR 1993
Research Date(s): 1990-1991
Levacic, R.; Marren, E.
Inst: Open University, Walton Hall, Milton Keynes MK7 6AA, United Kingdom.
Fin: Economic and Social Research Council.
educational administration; economics of education; budgetary control; budget; school; resource allocation; reform
administration de l'enseignement; économie de l'éducation; contrôle budgétaire; budget; école; affectation des ressources; réforme
PROJECT DESCRIPTION
The study addresses two key questions, the first at local education authority (LEA) level and the second at school level: (1) how does formula funding affect the budgets which different types of schools receive compared to the previous 'historic' or 'traditional' method of funding? and (2) how do schools respond to changes in the level and character of their funding? The project is assessing the extent to which official intentions of the Local Management of Schools (LMS) legislation that schools should be better able to allocate resources efficiently and according to educational priorities are being fulfilled.

A case study approach is used. One county LEA is studied and within that eleven schools have been selected to represent pairs of schools 'winning' and 'losing' in relation to changes in their budgets due to formula funding and to cover the different phases. The methods used are (1) collection and analysis of documents from LEA and schools on budget data and decisions relating to the allocation of finance; (2) statistical analysis of numerical data on financial and related resource variables; (3) interviews with teachers, school and LEA finance officers and governors. Observation of meetings - the latter almost entirely in schools.

Publ: Levacic, R. Management of schools: aims, scope and impact. In: *Educational Management and Administration*, Vol 20, No 1/1992, pp. 16-29.

12299 Einschaetzung der Schulaufsicht durch Lehrer. (Assessment of the school inspectorate by teachers.)
DEU 1993
Research Date(s): 1991-1992
Gebel; Mauser; Rosenbusch, H.
Inst: Universitaet Bamberg, Fak. Paedagogik, Philosophie, Psychologie, Fach Schulpaedagogik, Steinertstrasse 1, D-8600 Bamberg.
inspection; teacher; educational reform; inspector
inspection; enseignant; réforme de l'enseignement; inspecteur
PROJECT DESCRIPTION
Inhalt: Durch eine empirische Untersuchung soll herausgefunden werden, wie Lehrer in Bayern die aktuelle Schulaufsicht, insbesondere in Form von Schulratsbesuchen einschaetzen und wie sie bestimmten Reformversuchen gegenueberstehen. Die Ergebnisse werden mit einer vergleichbaren eigenen Untersuchung von 1975 konfrontiert (Laengsschnittstudie).

Geographischer Raum: Bayern.

Vorgehensweise: Deskriptives empirisches Verfahren.

12300 Les enseignements moyens général et technique au Bénin.
FRA 1993
Research Date(s): 1987-1989
Rasera, Jean-Bernard.
Inst: Université de Dijon, UER Faculté des sciences économiques et de gestion, CNRS UPR/29 et GDR/996, Institut de recherche sur l'économie de l'éducation, BP 138, 21004 Dijon Cedex, France.
Fin: Banque mondiale.
cost of education; Benin; technical education; occupational integration; certificate; comparative achievement; general education; cost-benefit analysis
coût de l'éducation; Bénin; enseignement technique; intégration professionnelle; diplôme; rendement comparé; enseignement général; analyse coût-bénéfice
PROJECT DESCRIPTION
Objectifs: Cette recherche a bénéficié d'une collaboration étroite avec la Direction des études et de la planification du Ministère des enseignements moyens et supérieurs du Bénin. Son objectif est de comparer l'insertion professionnelle des titulaires de diplômes d'enseignement technique (CAP industriels et CAP commerciaux) avec l'insertion professionnelle des titulaires du diplôme d'enseignement général (BEPC) pour effectuer ensuite une analyse coûts-bénéfices des deux types d'enseignement.

Méthodologie: Trois enquêtes sont réalisées: (1) sur l'insertion de 2500 diplômés CAP ou BEPC des années 1980 à 1986; (2) sur les flux d'embauches et de débauchages de 24 entreprises pendant la période de 1980-1986; (3) sur les coûts d'enseignement dans les établissements.

Résultats: La conclusion principale dément la supériorité du titulaire d'un CAP (notamment industriel) sur le titulaire du BEPC dans la quête d'un emploi que ce soit dans le secteur moderne de l'économie ou dans le secteur informel. L'analyse des coûts de l'enseignement technique fait apparaître que la prise en compte de l'amortissement du matériel majore de plus de 28% des coûts unitaires déjà nettement plus élevés que ceux de l'enseignement général. Le taux de rendement interne social de l'enseignement technique est plus élevé que celui de l'enseignement général (17% contre 3%).

Publ: Rasera, Jean-Bernard. *Les enseignements moyens général et technique au Bénin: devenir des diplômés, coûts et rendements internes des études.* IREDU - Banque mondiale, février 1989, 56p. et ann.

12301 Entscheidungshilfen zum Vergleich von Angeboten in der beruflichen Weiterbildung. (Comparison of further vocational training courses to facilitate choice of training.)
DEU 1993
Research Date(s): 1991-1993
Balli, C.; Bardeleben, R.; Berger, K.; Holzschuh, J.; Scholz, D.
Sup: Stockmann, R.
Inst: Bundesinstitut fuer Berufsbildung, Fehrbelliner Platz 3, D-1000 Berlin 31.
educational provision; further training; vocational education; educational need; cost of education; choice of training; information; guidance
scolarisation; formation complémentaire; enseignement professionnel; besoin d'éducation; coût de l'éducation; choix de la formation; information; orientation
PROJECT DESCRIPTION
Inhalt: Das Projekt verfolgt das Ziel, ein Instrumentarium fuer den deskriptiven Vergleich und die Entscheidung ueber berufliche Weiterbildungsmassnahmen zu entwickeln. Mit den im Projekt entwickelten und erprobten Instrumentarien soll Dritten die Moeglichkeit gegeben werden, Weiterbildungsangebote selbst zu pruefen. Damit kann den Beteiligten am Weiterbildungsmarkt ein Mittel an die Hand gegeben werden, sich mehr Transparenz zu verschaffen. Schliesslich soll potentiellen Nachfragern entscheidungsrelevante Unterschiede (z.B. Abschlussart, Ausstattung, Preis und Dauer) bei vergleichbaren Weiterbildungsveranstaltungen bewusst gemacht werden. Dazu sollen Checklisten als Entscheidungshilfen fuer Weiterbildungsberater und -nachfrager entwickelt werden; dabei sollen insbesondere auch adressatenspezifische Formen des Bedarfs an Information und Beratung untersucht werden. So kann die Rationalitaet der Teilnahmeentscheidungen erhoeht und die Anbieterkonkurrenz gefoerdert werden.
Die zentrale Forschungshypothese lautet: Zwischen vergleichbaren Angeboten gibt es erhebliche qualitative und quantitative Unterschiede, die unter dem Aspekt rationaler Weiterbildungsentscheidung fuer die Nachfragenden nicht transparent sind, aber transparent gemacht werden koennen.

12302 Entwicklung von Begleitmaterialien zu den Rahmenrichtlinien Mathematik auf dem Gebiet der Stochastik fuer Lehrer und Schueler. (Development of materials for basic directives for mathematics in the field of stochastic theory for teachers and pupils.)
DEU 1993
Research Date(s): 1991-1992
Sill, H.
Inst: Universitaet Rostock, Abt. Guestrow Mathematisch-Naturwissenschaftliche Fakultaet, Lehrstuhl Didaktik der Mathematik, Goldberger Str. 12, O-2600 Guestrow.
Fin: Institution; Land Mecklenburg-Vorpommern Landesinst. für Schule und Ausbildung.
curriculum development; mathematics; teacher education; further training; statistics; statistical method
élaboration de programmes d'études; mathématiques; formation des enseignants; formation complémentaire; statistique; méthode statistique
PROJECT DESCRIPTION
Inhalt: Konzipierung eines Stochastik-Curriculums; Entwicklung und Erprobung von Materialien fuer die Lehrerfort- und -weiterbildung; Schwerpunkte: Verbindung von Statistik und Wahrscheinlichkeitsrechnung, Moeglichkeiten der explorativen Datenanalyse, Entwicklung eines Modells zur Beschreibung zufaelliger Erscheinungen.
Geographischer Raum: Mecklenburg-Vorpommern.
Vorgehensweise: Zugang zu stochastischem Denken ueber die Analyse von Daten; Entwicklung "statistischen Denkens".

12303 Evaluation and monitoring at local education authority level.
GBR 1993
Research Date(s): 1991-1993
Maychell, K.
Sup: Bradley, J.
Inst: National Foundation for Educational Research, The Mere, Upton Park, Slough SL1 2DQ, United Kingdom.
inspection; evaluation; school
inspection; évaluation; école
PROJECT DESCRIPTION
Local education authorities (LEAs) have a statutory duty to inspect schools. The Department of Education and Science require LEAs to define their policy for inspection, including details of procedures, reporting and roles of LEA personnel. School development plans, classroom observation,

performance indicators, and the use of information technology to assist analysis and reporting all have a place within the national picture, along with school self-evaluation by heads and teachers.
The research has three main aims: (1) to gather detailed information on the operation of a range of LEA monitoring and evaluation strategies; (2) to carry out a national survey of LEAs and schools that would provide useful information when developing evaluation and monitoring strategies; (3) to provide practical information and guidance to assist LEAs in the future development of good practice in this area of their work.
The first phase of the research involves case study investigation in six LEAs. These reflect the range of strategies currently being used or planned by LEAs. Each case study involves interviews with headteachers and LEA officers as well as examination of LEA and school documentation. The second phase comprises two questionnaire surveys - one to all LEAs and the other to a representative sample of 500 schools. The purpose of these is to provide a national picture on all aspects of policy and practice with regard to inspection, evaluation and monitoring and to describe the successes, problems and issues emerging for LEAs and schools.

12304 Evaluation de la double vacation au primaire: l'exemple du Niger.
FRA 1993
Research Date(s): 1987-1989
Duru-Bellat, Marie; Jarousse, Jean-Pierre.
Inst: Université de Dijon, UER Faculté des sciences économiques et de gestion, CNRS UPR/29 et GDR/996, Institut de recherche sur l'économie de l'éducation, BP 138, 21004 Dijon cedex, France.
arrangement of school time; cost of education; comparative achievement; Niger; primary education
aménagement du temps scolaire; coût de l'éducation; rendement comparé; Niger; enseignement primaire
PROJECT DESCRIPTION
Objectifs: L'organisation en double vacation confie à un même maître la responsabilité de deux cohortes d'élèves sur la base d'un emploi du temps allégé. L'intérêt de la formule dépend de l'impact pédagogique et financier respectifs des différents éléments de l'arbitrage. Cette recherche vise à documenter ces différents points sur la base d'une évaluation d'une expérience de double vacation au Niger.
Méthodologie: L'évaluation a porté sur 52 cohortes à la rentrée 1988-1989 dans les classes de Cours d'initiation (première classe du primaire).
Résultats: La comparaison entre la formule de double vacation et les classes témoins montre que le niveau des acquisitions est proche autorisant pour la formule double vacation par un plus faible coût unitaire un gain en terme quantitatif à un niveau de qualité raisonnable. Cependant la connaissance de l'effet de la taille des classes sur les acquisitions des élèves fait du maintien du système d'enseignement en vacation unique un moyen de gérer l'arbitrage qualité-quantité dans l'expansion du système scolaire. De nouveaux tests trois ans après éprouvent le caractère durable de ces premiers résultats.

Publ: Duru-Bellat, Marie & Jarousse, Jean-Pierre. *Evaluation de la double vacation dans l'enseignement primaire au Niger.* IREDU: Rapport pour le Ministère de l'éducation nationale de la République du Niger, septembre 1989, 56p.

12305 Evaluation of a local education inspectorate.
GBR 1993
Research Date(s): 1989-1994
Gleeson, D.; Russell, V.
Inst: Keele University, Department of Education, Keele, Staffordshire ST5 5BG, United Kingdom.
Fin: Hereford & Worcester Local Education Authority.
inspection; local government
inspection; administration locale
PROJECT DESCRIPTION
This project involves an investigation of the changing role of the inspectorate in one local education authority using interview and observation approaches.

12306 Evaluation of information technology systems used to support administration in schools.
GBR 1993
Research Date(s): 1989-
Wild, P.
Sup: Richardson, S.
Inst: Loughborough University of Technology, Department of Education, Loughborough LE11 3TU, United Kingdom.
educational administration; information technology; computer
administration de l'enseignement; technologie de l'information; ordinateur
PROJECT DESCRIPTION
A consequence of the Education Reform Act 1988 (ERA) is the need for information technology (IT) systems to support the Local Management of Schools (LMS). It is well known from research in the commercial and industrial sectors that the success rate for the implementation of such systems is as low as 20%. If the IT systems being installed in schools are to achieve their potential in helping to administer, or, more importantly,

manage the working of the school then it is essential that some evaluation of the systems is carried out.

A methodology developed at the Human Sciences and Advanced Technology (HUSAT) Research Institute at Loughborough University, called the User Acceptance Audit, is being modified for the school environment. A detailed task analysis is required of the management and administration within the schools so that the evaluation tool developed by HUSAT can be made context sensitive. The final outcome should be an 'evaluation package' which could be used by local education authorities and/or individual schools to assess the potential barriers to successful implementation.

Publ: Wild, P.; Scivier, J.E. & Richardson, S.J. Evaluating information technology-supported Local Management of Schools: the User Acceptability Audit. In: *Education Management and Administration*, Vol 20, No 1/1992, pp. 40-48.

12307 An evaluation of the Dorset Local Education Authority Inspectorate.

GBR 1993
Research Date(s): 1991-1992
Clift, P.; Morris, B.
Inst: Southampton University, Faculty of Educational Studies, Assessment and Evaluation Unit, Highfield, Southampton SO9 5NH, United Kingdom.
Fin: Dorset Local Education Authority.
inspection; local government
inspection; administration locale
PROJECT DESCRIPTION

The Dorset Local Education Authority (LEA) Advisory Service was converted to an Inspectorate with effect from 1st January 1990, following a period of 'cascaded' training organised by the Centre for Advisor and Inspector Development (CAID). In the summer of 1991, the Unit was invited to design and carry out an evaluation of the work of the Inspectorate to date, reporting to the Chief Inspector, the Chief Education Officer and Elected Members.

The issues to be addressed, as agreed with the Chief Inspector are: (i) How effective is the Inspectorate in collecting evidence concerning the quality of education in Dorset schools? (ii) What performance indicators are used by the Inspectorate and how valid are they for judging the educational effectiveness of schools? (iii) How acceptable to schools are the judgements made? (iv) How useful to the LEA administrators and elected members is the evidence of educational effectiveness provided in inspectors' reports? (v) How efficient is the internal communication within the Inspectorate? (vi) How effective are role and task differentiation within the Inspectorate? (vii) To what extent and in what ways do the activities of the Inspectorate foster the development of Dorset schools? (viii) How effective is the advisory teacher support offered to schools as a direct consequence of inspectors' visits? (ix) Other issues arising during the investigation.

A sample of ten Dorset schools is included (primary, secondary, special) which have been involved in all aspects of the Inspectorate's activity. The main methods of investigation are: documentary analysis, interviews with headteachers, governors, members of the LEA evaluation panel (elected members) and inspectors, and questionnaires to all the teachers in the ten schools.

12308 Evolution of the role, structure and operations of senior management groups in universities.

GBR 1993
Research Date(s): 1988-1991
Davies, J.
Inst: Anglia Polytechnic University, Anglia Business School, Centre for Higher Education Management, Danbury Park Conference Centre, Danbury Park, Chelmsford CM3 4AT, United Kingdom.
Fin: Anglia Business School and five institutions concerned.
educational administration; university; management; managerial staff
administration de l'enseignement; université; gestion; personnel d'encadrement
PROJECT DESCRIPTION

The research aims to: (1) monitor the evolution of senior management teams in five universities over a three year period; (2) produce a classification of types of senior management teams; (3) identify the situational factors underpinning the development of the various types; and (4) indicate the operational characteristics associated with each type, and the consequences for institutional processes.

The research is based on five universities engaged in the transformation of its senior management structures and processes, using a combination of case study and action research methods, with the principal investigator acting as participant observer in the change process.

The principal types of structure that have been identified are: (1) traditional model; (2) general management academic sector model; (3) loose brief troubleshooter model; (4) functional policy coordinator model; (5) functional executive/presidential model. Differences are apparent in terms of the role and style of vice-chancellor; the power and authority of pro-vice-chancellors; the style of operation of team; institutional processes for planning, resource allocation; and interaction with academic units and administration.

12309 Evoluzione demografica e perdita di "risorse" del sistema scolastico. (Demographic change and the loss of resources in the education system.)

ITA 1993
Research Date(s): 1989
Ceccanti, S.
Sup: Allulli, G.
Inst: Centro Studi Investimenti Sociali - CENSIS (Centre for Social Studies and Investments), Piazza di Novella 2, 00199 Roma, Italy.
Fin: Ministero della Pubblica Istruzione, Ufficio Studi e Programmazione.
economics of education; educational administration; schooling; educational provision; attendance; development of education; educational innovation; quality of education
économie de l'éducation; administration de l'enseignement; scolarité; scolarisation; fréquentation; développement de l'éducation; innovation pédagogique; qualité de l'éducation
PROJECT DESCRIPTION

Aim: To identify and analyse the key phenomena that have characterized schools in Italy in the last ten years, with particular attention to the evolution of school attendance, demographic decline, decentralization, dispersion of schooling, experimentation and innovation, and the availability and utilization of resources.

Methods: Analysis of official data; generation of tables, graphs, flow charts, tabulations and comments; preparation of a report, divided into three chapters articulated in four, five or six parts, and supplemented by an introduction and a conclusion.

Results: In the 1980s the use of the school has both diminished and changed qualitatively. Upper secondary schools, especially the technical and vocational schools, registered remarkable growth. On the other hand, there was a persistent drive towards decentralization. The contrast between northern and southern Italy remained virtually unchanged. Reforms at the political-institutional level remained blocked, while there was a remarkable innovative push at the local level: experimentation, spontaneous innovation, relations between schools and the labour market, research into professionalism.

From the few international comparisons that exist, Italian schools appear deficient in the scientific area and seem to be moving at two different speeds: high in the productive sector and low in the public and service sectors.

Prospects for the future are related to the positive aspects (school autonomy, overcoming the spontaneous phase of initiative, reward of those who are truly useful) and the negative aspects (the lack of a "guiding principle" for experimentation and for the evaluation of the effectiveness of schools).

12310 Le financement de l'enseignement post-obligatoire.

FRA 1993
Research Date(s): 1980-
Eicher, Jean-Claude; Cuenin, Serge; Lassibille, Gérard; Orivel, François.
Inst: Université de Dijon, UER Faculté des sciences économiques et de gestion, CNRS UPR/29 et GDR/996, Institut de recherche sur l'économie de l'éducation, BP 138, 21004 Dijon Cedex, France.
education budget; post-compulsory education; comparative education; higher education; financing; cost of education
budget de l'éducation; enseignement postobligatoire; éducation comparée; enseignement supérieur; financement; coût de l'éducation
PROJECT DESCRIPTION

Objectifs: L'IREDU mène depuis une vingtaine d'années des recherches sur le coût de l'éducation. Ces travaux ont d'abord porté sur la France et ont été empiriques. Mais ils ont très rapidement donné naissance à des réflexions d'ordre méthodologique et conceptuel sur la nature du coût en éducation, les catégories pertinentes, les modes de mesure. Parmi les catégorisations, celle qui part des différents payeurs s'est révélée particulièrement utile, en raison d'une part de l'absence d'informations fiables sur la contribution de certains d'entre eux - familles, collectivités locales -, d'autre part de la crise qui incite à une réflexion nouvelle sur les modes de financement.

Méthodologie: Cette réflexion s'oriente surtout dans deux directions: (1) Recensement des principales innovations en matière de financement de l'enseignement post-obligatoire, évaluation de celles-ci en termes d'efficacité, d'équité et aussi de transférabilité dans des pays différents par l'organisation du système d'enseignement, les habitudes sociales et le niveau de développement et propositions en faveur d'un financement mixte public-privé, du développement des systèmes de prêts aux étudiants et de modes de financement permettant aux établissements d'avoir un assez large degré d'autonomie. (2) Etude pour le Comité national pour le développement des grandes écoles sur les coûts unitaires des diplômés dans les formations supérieures scientifiques françaises (Grandes écoles d'ingénieurs et Unités de formation et de recherche scientifiques des universités). Cette étude comporte un échantillon de 15 grandes écoles et de quatre départements scientifiques de l'Université de Bourgogne. Elle étudie les principaux déterminants de la variation des coûts unitaires et montre l'importance de la taille des groupes d'étudiants et du taux d'échec aux examens sur les coûts de production des diplômés.

Publ: Eicher, Jean-Claude. The financial crisis and its consequences in European higher education. In: *Higher Education Policy*, 1990, vol. 3, n° 4, pp. 26-29.

12311 Le financement de l'enseignement supérieur espagnol.
FRA 1993
Research Date(s): 1986-
Lassibille, Gérard; Navarro-Gomez, Lucia.
Inst: Université de Dijon, UER Faculté des sciences économiques et de gestion, CNRS UPR/29 et GDR/996, Institut de recherche sur l'économie de l'éducation, BP 138, 21004 Dijon Cedex, France.
education budget; Spain; higher education; national budget; regional administration; cost of education; financing
budget de l'éducation; Espagne; enseignement supérieur; budget de l'Etat; administration régionale; coût de l'éducation; financement
PROJECT DESCRIPTION

Objectifs: Cette recherche s'inscrit dans le cadre du programme de coopération franco-espagnol Mercure. Elle a pour but d'analyser dans le détail les formes de financement de l'enseignement supérieur espagnol et d'évaluer les processus d'allocation des ressources à ce niveau d'études. Plus précisément la recherche vise à identifier la participation précise de l'Etat, des Communautés autonomes, des entreprises et des familles au financement des dépenses des établissements sur la base de budgets qui permettent dans le même temps d'évaluer avec rigueur le coût des différentes activités d'enseignement.

Méthodologie: Les données proviennent de l'examen des budgets de l'Etat et des budgets des Communautés autonomes qui ont une responsabilité dans la conduite de la politique d'enseignement supérieur (Andalousie, Iles canaries, Catalogne, Navarre, Pays basques, Valence). Ces informations sont complétées par les données d'une enquête adressée aux recteurs de 40 universités espagnoles sur les ressources et dépenses des établissements universitaires (depuis la loi de réforme universitaire) et les sommes et aides affectées aux étudiants.

12312 Financial management in education.
GBR 1993
Research Date(s): 1990-1992
Hough, J.
Inst: Loughborough University of Technology, Department of Education, Loughborough LE11 3TU, United Kingdom.
Fin: UNESCO.
economics of education; education budget; educational administration; budgetary control; financial resources; developing country; comparative research
économie de l'éducation; budget de l'éducation; administration de l'enseignement; contrôle budgétaire; ressources financières; pays en développement; recherche comparative
PROJECT DESCRIPTION

The project surveys financial management in education with particlar reference to Third World countries. Topics included are: characteristics of financial management; how developed are current financial management systems; cash management; budgeting and budget practices; school site budgeting; project budgeting; zero-based budgeting; control of costs; accounting and double entry book-keeping; and planning, programming, budgeting, evaluation assessments (PPBES).

12313 Forecasting student enrolments for further education colleges.
GBR 1993
Research Date(s): 1990-1991
Pardey, D.
Inst: Staff College, Coombe Lodge, Blagdon, Bristol BS18 6RG, United Kingdom.
registration; post-compulsory education; forecasting; number of pupils
inscription; enseignement postobligatoire; prévision; effectifs scolaires
PROJECT DESCRIPTION

This research is an analysis of forecasting methodologies used in deriving enrolment projections for further education plans at college and local education authority level.

12314 The framework for Local Management of Schools: a study of local education authorities' approved Local Management of Schools schemes.
GBR 1993
Research Date(s): 1990-1991
Thomas, G.
Sup: Levacic, R.
Inst: Open University, School of Education, Walton Hall, Milton Keynes MK7 6AA, United Kingdom.
educational administration; educational planning; school autonomy
administration de l'enseignement; planification de l'éducation; autonomie scolaire
PROJECT DESCRIPTION

This is a survey of Local Management of Schools schemes approved by the Department of Education and Science (DES) for implementation in 1990/1991, and is supplemented by data from Section 42 financial statements. The study analyses 82 schemes for England and Wales from a total of 103. The aspects of schemes surveyed are: (1) the extent of delegation of management responsibilities to schools; (2) age-weighted element of the formula; (3) other elements; (4) financial regulations; (5) monitoring and evaluation. It includes detailed statistical tables reproducing the data base of financial and formula variables for all the authorities surveyed. An additional aspect of the study investigated the changes to local education authorities' original Local Management of Schools submissions required by the DES before the schemes were finally approved.

Publ: Thomas, G. *The framework for local management of schools: a study of local education authorities' approved local management of schools schemes.* Milton Keynes: Open University, 1991.
Thomas, G. & Levacic, R. Centralising in order to decentralise? DES scrutiny and approval of LMS schemes. In: *Journal of Educational Policy*, Vol 6, No 4/1991, pp. 401-416.

12315 The funding of schools after the 1988 Education Reform Act.
GBR 1993
Research Date(s): 1990-1993
Thomas, H.; Bullock, A.
Inst: Birmingham University, School of Education, Edgbaston, Birmingham B15 2TT, United Kingdom.
Fin: Leverhulme Trust.
economics of education; education budget; educational administration; financing; resource allocation; local government
économie de l'éducation; budget de l'éducation; administration de l'enseignement; financement; affectation des ressources; administration locale
PROJECT DESCRIPTION

The principal aims of this study are to describe and analyse the pattern of resource distribution in local education authorities; to examine the change in priorities as the system moves from one method of funding to another; to investigate the relationship between the resource priorities of the local education authority and those of the school and inquire into the rationale of resource decisions. The methods used are: quantitative analysis of local education authority budgetary data and school level budgetary data; and interviews and self-completed question schedules with personnel in schools.

Publ: Thomas, H. & Bullock, A.D. *The flawed formulae.* Vol 1, No 3/1991, pp. 5-6.

12316 Fusie- en vernieuwingsprocessen in het MBO. (Innovation and mergers in senior secondary vocational education.)
NLD 1994
Research Date(s): 1990-1991
Pelkmans, A.; Vries, B. de; Vrieze, G.
Sup: Krogt, F. van der; Pouwels, J.P.A.
Inst: Instituut voor Toegepaste Social wetenschappen (ITS) (Institute for Applied Social Sciences), P.O. Box 9048, 6500 KJ Nijmegen, Netherlands. Katholieke Universiteit Nijmegen (Catholic University of Nijmegen), P.O. Box 9102, 6500 HC Nijmegen, Netherlands
Fin: SVO het Instituut voor Onderzoek van het Onderwijs.
amalgamation of schools; vocational education; educational innovation
regroupement d'écoles; enseignement professionnel; innovation pédagogique
PROJECT DESCRIPTION

Background: The preparations for mergers of schools as part of the operation "Sector Formation and Innovation in Senior Secondary Education" (the "SVM operation") were concluded in March 1990. In August 1990 122 senior secondary vocational education (MBO) institutions embarked on the second phase of the operation, the phase following the mergers. The remaining small number of institutions entered this phase in August 1991. At present there are 143 "new" MBO institutions as a result of the SVM operation.

Aim: To examine current practice in teaching and management in the new MBO institutions in the second phase of the SVM operation.

Methods: Case study; questionnaire survey; telephone survey.

Results: Since the completion of the large-scale merger operation nearly all MBO institutions are engaged in innovatory educational activities. Only 5% of the 122 institutions that were formed in the years 1990-1991 are not engaged in innovation. Innovatory activities generally concern the intake and guidance of new students, the organization of teaching (modularity, flexibility), the integration of short and long courses and the improvement of overall performance levels. Furthermore, the schools are making attempts to be more responsive to the needs of the labour market, for instance by strengthening the practical component of the courses. As a rule, innovations are not carried out across the institution as a whole, but within a specific branch or department. External support is called in for about 25% of innovatory activities.

(This is an updating of EUDISED no. 41/9764).

Publ: Pelkmans, A. et al. *De V van SVM.* Nijmegen: ITS, 1991, 124p.
De V van SVM. In: *BVE-Informatie*, 3/1992, pp. 19-21.

12317   Going grant-maintained: a case study of change from a management perspective.
GBR   1993
Research Date(s): 1992-1996
Cavendish, M.
Sup: Hellawell, D.
Inst: University of Central England in Birmingham, Faculty of Education, Centre for Advanced Studies in Education, Westbourne Road, Edgbaston, Birmingham B15 3TN, United Kingdom.
educational administration; school autonomy
administration de l'enseignement; autonomie scolaire
PROJECT DESCRIPTION
   The investigation will cover a three-year period (1990-1993) during which the researcher's school will become grant-maintained. The intention is to develop an interpretive account of the management of change over the period, examining roles, structures and processes of management.

12318   Grunnskolen mellom statlig og kommunal styring og forhandlingssystem/avtaleverk.   (Governance and corporatism in the Norwegian school system.)
NOR   1994
Research Date(s): 1992-1995
Lauvdal, Torunn.
Inst: Oppland Distriktshögskole, Institutt for Pedagogikk og Sosialfag (Oppland College, Institute for Education and Social Work), PB 1004 Skurva, 2601 Lillehammer, Norway.
Fin: NORAS.
educational administration; decision making; public administration; teachers' organization; local government
administration de l'enseignement; prise de décision; administration publique; organisation d'enseignants; administration locale
PROJECT DESCRIPTION
   The main purpose of this research project is to provide more knowledge about the "steering" interplay between the hierarchical state and municipality system of primary and secondary school administration and the corporatist system of negotiations/agreements between state/municipalities and teachers' unions (about working hours, working conditions, wages, administration, etc.).
   The first part of the project studies reforms in two municipalities that are aimed at increasing and tightening local (municipality-level) political and administrative control over schools. It is intended to reveal how state governance (legislation and regulations) and agreements negotiated by the state and teachers' unions are experienced as limiting local autonomy. The second part of the study will consist of a closer study of some cases observed in the first part. Special attention will be paid to their background, the way they developed in the light of the role of the corporative system and the relation and interplay between legal-hierarchical and corporative decision-making in the education system.

Publ: Lauvdal, Torunn. Avtaleverk og forhandlingssystem mellom sentralt og lokalt nivå. In: *Konferansrapport*. Oslo: PUF, 1992, pp. 83-101.

12319   Il tempo prolungato nell'esperienza delle scuole medie della Campania.   (Experiences with extended school time in the lower secondary schools in Campania.)
ITA   1994
Research Date(s): 1990
Domenghini, Alessio; Moncini, Valerio.
Sup: Lanzetti, Clemente.
Inst: Istituto Regionale di Ricerca, Sperimentazione e Aggiornamento Educativi per la Campania - IRRSAE (Regional Institute for Educational Research, Innovation and Teacher Training - Campania), Via G. Melisurgo 4, 80133 Napoli, Italy.
Ministero della Pubblica Istruzione (Ministry of Education), Viale Trastevere 76, 00100 Roma, Italy
time-table; school day; teaching time; teaching quality
emploi du temps; journée scolaire; temps d'enseignement; qualité de l'enseignement
PROJECT DESCRIPTION
   Objectives: To investigate experiences with extended school time in lower secondary schools in Campania.
   Methods: The research was carried out through the administration of a closed-response questionnaire to teachers of extended time classes and school heads. The study concentrated above all on teachers.
   Results: The results have been presented in a final report. On the basis of the findings, it is possible to reflect on the experiments carried out, to evaluate them critically, and to set forth research proposals regarding functional organizational and educational models and effective teacher behaviour in lower secondary schools.

Publ: Monelli Perucci, F. Considerazioni conclusive e prospettiche. In: AA.VV., Tempo Prolungato: Situazione e Prospettive, *Quaderni IRRSAE Lombardia*, n. 17, p. 197.

12320   L'impact de la crise économique sur les systèmes éducatifs.
FRA   1993
Research Date(s): 1988-1990
Orivel, François; Rasera, Jean-Bernard; Eicher, Jean-Claude; Lassibille, Gérard; Navarro-Gomez, Maria-Lucia.
Inst: Université de Dijon, UER Faculté des sciences économiques et de gestion, CNRS UPR/29 et GDR/996, Institut de recherche sur l'économie de l'éducation, BP 138, 21004 Dijon Cedex, France.
education budget; crisis of education; forecasting; educational policy; economic conditions
budget de l'éducation; crise de l'enseignement; prévision; politique de l'éducation; conditions économiques
PROJECT DESCRIPTION
   Objectifs: Le but de ces travaux est d'examiner la nature réelle de la "crise de l'éducation" et la relation entre celle-ci et la crise économique pour prévoir les évolutions souhaitables des politiques éducatives. Il est courant d'établir une relation de cause à effet entre la crise économique et la "crise de l'éducation", relation qui serait d'ordre financier. Or, l'analyse des évolutions des grands agrégats (PIB/tête, dépenses d'éducation, quantité de services éducatifs) rend sujet à caution une telle relation, à moins de dire que la poursuite d'une croissance économique forte eût permis de satisfaire les besoins croissants des systèmes éducatifs.
   Méthodologie et résultats: L'analyse des flux de demande et des déterminants, des coûts unitaires en éducation montre plutôt que, pour l'essentiel, la "crise de l'éducation" se serait produite de toutes façons, même sans crise économique. La tendance séculaire à l'augmentation du coût par élève dans l'enseignement traditionnel, l'incapacité croissante de ce dernier à satisfaire les besoins de publics nouveaux en forte croissance dans les pays développés, la pression de la demande elle-même poussée en partie par l'explosion démographique dans beaucoup de pays du tiers monde, entraînent nécessairement des tensions et des déséquilibres. La "crise de l'éducation" se manifeste aussi par une baisse de la qualité qui tend à prendre un caractère catastrophique, dans certains pays en développement, surtout en Afrique au sud du Sahara. Compte-tenu de ces constatations et des perspectives de croissance relativement pessimistes, notamment dans les pays en développement, il est possible de suggérer et/ou de prévoir les politiques de nature à contrer ces phénomènes, en ce qui concerne tant le financement de l'éducation que le choix des technologies.

Publ: Orivel, François & Rasera, Jean-Bernard. La scuola in economie che non crescono. In: *Mondoperaiò*, n° 6, juin 1988, pp. 47-50.
Eicher, Jean-Claude. La crise financière dans les systèmes d'enseignement. In: *Actes du colloque Vingt-cinquième anniversaire de l'IIPE des 28 novembre - 2 décembre 1988*. Paris: IIPE, 1989.
Lassibille, Gérard & Navarro-Gomez, Maria-Lucia. Horizon 2000: Prévisions des dépenses d'éducation primaire dans les pays en développement. In: *Perspectives*, 1990, n° 4, pp. 565-577.

12321   Individuelle Kosten der beruflichen Weiterbildung unter Beruecksichtigung von Nutzenaspekten.   (Individual costs and benefits of further vocational training.)
DEU   1993
Research Date(s): 1991-1993
Dahm, T.; Bardeleben, R.; Holzschuh, J.; Ruebsaat, R.; Stockmann, R.
Inst: Bundesinstitut fuer Berufsbildung, Fehrbelliner Platz 3, D-1000 Berlin 31.
cost of education; cost-benefit analysis; further training; vocational education; educational policy
coût de l'éducation; analyse coût-bénéfice; formation complémentaire; enseignement professionnel; politique de l'éducation
PROJECT DESCRIPTION
   Inhalt: Das Projekt verfolgt folgende Ziele: (1) Ermittlung der durchschnittlichen individuellen beruflichen Weiterbildungskosten pro Jahr, differenziert z.B. nach Massnahmetypen, Unterrichtsformen, beruflicher Stellung, Geschlecht. (2) Hochrechnung der individuellen Kosten fuer alle Teilnehmer an beruflichen Weiterbildungsmassnahmen zur Verbesserung der Basis fuer bildungspolitische Entscheidungen. (3) Differenzierte Dokumentation der individuellen Weiterbildungskosten nach Art, Hoehe und Struktur sowie der individuellen Weiterbildungsfinanzierung. (4) Analyse und Darstellung der Kosten-Nutzen-Erwartungen und Kosten-Nutzen-Realisierungen als Grundlage rationaler Kosten-Nutzen-Abwaegungen fuer potentielle Weiterbildungsteilnehmer.
   Die forschungsleitenden Hypothesen sind: (a) Die individuellen Kosten der Teilnahme an beruflichen Weiterbildungsmassnahmen uebersteigen die bisherigen Schaetzungen erheblich. (b) Hoehe, Art und Struktur der individuellen beruflichen Weiterbildungskosten werden vom Massnahmetyp, von der Unterrichtsform, der beruflichen Stellung sowie auch von der Entfernung zwischen Wohn- und Mahssnahmeort des Teilnehmers beeinflusst. (c) Die Weiterbildungsbereitschaft haengt von Kosten-Nutzen-Ueberlegungen bzw. von Kosten-Nutzen-Relationen ab. (d) Den potentiellen Teilnehmern ist das tatsaechliche Ausmass der Weiterbildungskosten und des Nutzens nicht hinlaenglich bekannt, um eine rationale Kosten-Nutzen-Abwaegung vornehmen zu koennen.

12322 Les instruments de gestion de l'enseignement des disciplines scientifiques : objectifs, curriculums, évaluation. Problèmes théoriques et méthodologiques.
FRA 1993
Research Date(s): 1988-
Brousseau, Guy; Martinand, Jean-Louis; Bodin, Antoine; Chevallard, Yvon; Colomb, Jacques; Cornu, Bernard; Douady, Régine; et al.
Inst: Ministère de la recherche, Centre national de la recherche scientifique, CNRS GDR/71, Didactique et acquisition des connaissances scientifiques, Laboratoire PSYDEE, Université de Paris V, 46 rue Saint-Jacques, 75005 Paris, France.
curriculum; scientific studies; textbook; teaching objective
programme d'études; études scientifiques; manuel d'enseignement; objectif pédagogique
PROJECT DESCRIPTION
Objectifs: Ce thème, selon le principe des groupes de recherche du Centre national de la recherche scientifique, est supporté par les travaux de plusieurs équipes. Il s'agit de recherches tendant à mettre à jour les mécanismes locaux et globaux de la transposition didactique en conjuguant différentes approches: théorique, méthodologique et expérimentale. Plusieurs synthèses ont été faites de travaux portant sur l'objet didactique de la gestion du système d'enseignement, à savoir le curriculum des élèves: (1) les nouveaux programmes et manuels, les référentiels et les différentes évaluations; (2) les instruments d'études centrés sur les conceptions des élèves ou celles des enseignants et ceux centrés sur les objectifs et les manuels d'enseignement, les réformes; (3) la théorisation du fonctionnement des curriculums, les indices du fonctionnement et des dysfonctionnements, l'étude des modélisations utilisés dans les pays anglo-saxons.

Publ: Bodin, Antoine. Dossiers d'évaluation (EVAPM), 1989, 1990, 1991.
Bodin, Antoine. Techniques susceptibles de faciliter les diagnostics individuels et collectifs. In: *Petit x*, 1991, n° 125, pp. 5-24.
Martinand, Jean-Louis. Le domaine didactique: construction des contenus et appropriation des connaissances. In: *Le transfert des connaissances en sciences et techniques.* Université de Montpellier II, 1990, pp. 29-36.
Martinand, Jean-Louis. Travailler les contenus en physique, chimie, technologie. In: *Approche de la didactique*, 1991, Paris: ADAPT, 1991, pp. 33-39.
(Une liste complète est disponible auprès des chercheurs.).

12323 International recruiting of student-athletes by American universities.
GBR 1993
Research Date(s): 1985-1991
Bale, J.
Inst: Keele University, Department of Education, Keele, Staffordshire ST5 5BG, United Kingdom.
selection; athletics; admission; university; USA
sélection; athlétisme; admission; université; Etats-Unis
PROJECT DESCRIPTION
The project seeks to identify the extent of recruitment of foreign student-athletes by US universities and the experience of such recruits while resident in the United States of America.

Publ: Bale, J.R. The international recruiting game: foreign student athletes in American universities. In: Bondi, E. & Matthews, H. (eds.). *Educational society: social, political and geographical perspectives.* London: Routledge, 1988.
Bale, J.R. Alien student-athletes in American higher education; locational decision-making and sojourn abroad. In: *Physical Education Review*, Vol 10, No 2/1987, pp. 81-93.
Bale, J.R. Foreign students in NCAA Division 1 universities; an empirical study of six men's sports. In: *Journal of Comparative Physical Education and Sport*, Vol 10, No 1/1988, pp. 21-31.
Bale, J.R. *The Brawn Drain: foreign student-athletes in American universities.* Urbana: University of Illinois Press, 1991.

12324 Komparative studier av utdanningsledelse i Russland og Baltikum. (Comparative studies of educational management in Russia and the Baltic republics.)
NOR 1994
Research Date(s): 1992-1994
Tjeldvoll, Arild.
Inst: Universitetet i Oslo, Pedagogisk Forskningsinstitutt (University of Oslo, Institute for Educational Research), PB 1092 Blindern, 0317 Oslo, Norway.
Fin: NAVF/RSF.
educational administration; comparative research; cross-national research; educational reform; politics
administration de l'enseignement; recherche comparative; recherche transnationale; réforme de l'enseignement; politique
PROJECT DESCRIPTION

Aim: The aim is to study the consequences of historical political developments and recent ideological changes for the administrative structure of the education systems of Russia, Estonia, Latvia and Lithuania.
Design: Central, regional and local levels will all be studied with a view to understanding the content of relevant plans and actions. Data will be collected through interviews, document analysis and observation of management practice. To avoid language problems, it will be attempted to cooperate with researchers in the countries under study.

12325 Law, education and social control: the case of non-school attendance.
GBR 1993
Research Date(s): 1988-
Gleeson, D.; Carlen, P.; Wardough, J.
Inst: Keele University, Department of Education, Keele, Staffordshire ST5 5BG, United Kingdom.
Fin: Economic and Social Research Council.
legislation; absenteeism; social control
législation; absentéisme; régulation sociale
PROJECT DESCRIPTION
This study looks at the processing of non-school attendance in relation to inter-agency links: education, law, social and welfare services.

12326 Local management in schools: the three year review.
GBR 1993
Research Date(s): 1991-1992
Thompson, Q.; Keys, W.
Sup: Evans, M.
Inst: Chartered Institute of Public Finance and Accountancy (CIPFA), The LMS Initiative, 3 Robert Street, London WC2N 6BH, United Kingdom; Coopers & Lybrand Deloitte, Plumtree Court, London EC4A AHT, United Kingdom; National Foundation for Educational Research, The Mere, Upton Park, Slough SL1 2DQ, United Kingdom.
Fin: Department of Education and Science; Consortium of Local Education Authorities.
educational administration; educational policy; economics of education; local government; financing
administration de l'enseignement; politique de l'éducation; économie de l'éducation; administration locale; financement
PROJECT DESCRIPTION
A study into the formula funding of schools and the related management issues that currently face local education authorities (LEAs), to provide them with timely and practical information on the issues they will wish - and be required - to review as part of the three year review of Local Management of Schools (LMS) schemes, due to be completed in autumn 1992. The study will look forward to examine the delegation of responsibilities and the management issues from both the LEAs' viewpoint and from the perspective of schools. This will include the scope and means of delegation, the facility for sending policy signals to schools, and the mechanisms for monitoring performance and for operating quality control. It will also cover formula funding in depth as a distribution mechanism, in terms of its impact on education policy in schools and by reference to its technical construction.

Publ: The LMS Initiative. Local management of schools: a study into formula funding and management issues. Prepared by Coopers & Lybrand Deloitte and NFER. London: CIPFA, 1992.

12327 Local Management of Schools.
GBR 1993
Research Date(s): 1991-1993
Demaine, J.
Inst: Loughborough University of Technology, Department of Education, Loughborough LE11 3TU, United Kingdom.
educational administration; educational reform
administration de l'enseignement; réforme de l'enseignement
PROJECT DESCRIPTION
A study of the effects of Local Management of Schools (LMS) on a select group of schools in England.

12328 Local management of secondary schools in Berkshire - an evaluation.
GBR 1993
Research Date(s): 1989-1993
Dawkins, J.
Sup: Fidler, B.
Inst: Reading University, Faculty of Education and Community Studies, Bulmershe Court, Woodlands Avenue, Earley, Reading RG6 1HY, United Kingdom.
Fin: Berkshire Local Education Authority.
educational administration; secondary school; educational reform
administration de l'enseignement; école secondaire; réforme de l'enseignement
PROJECT DESCRIPTION
The aim of this research is to monitor and evaluate the implementation of Local Management of Schools (LMS) in secondary schools in Berkshire

to assess over the initial period if the quality of education in those schools has been enhanced by the provision of LMS. The researcher will aim to: (i) keep abreast of, and include current research in terms of a developing national perspective of the implementation of LMS; (ii) to detail within Berkshire the changes planned within the Local Education Authority (LEA) as direct result of delegated budgets in secondary schools; (iii) evaluate (by means of a detailed case study of three secondary schools) the LMS pilot scheme; (iv) evaluate three further (non-pilot) schools as case studies; and (v) conclude whether the quality of education has been enhanced by the provision of LMS. Research will be carried out through questionnaires and follow-up interviews of LEA officers and governors, teachers and administrators from at least six secondary schools.

12329   Management cultures within primary schools.
GBR   1993
Research Date(s): 1989-1993
Braund, C.
Sup: Hoy, C.
Inst: Manchester University, School of Education, Oxford Road, Manchester M13 9PL, United Kingdom.
Fin: Crewe & Alsager College of Higher Education.
educational administration; school environment; primary school
administration de l'enseignement; milieu scolaire; école primaire
PROJECT DESCRIPTION
   The aim of this study is to illuminate concepts of culture within primary schools, in relation to their management. It will involve a wide ranging review of literature and industrial comparatives, extended by empirical techniques used to verify and/or clarify school cultures.

12330   Management information services.
GBR   1993
Research Date(s): 1991
Southworth, G.
Inst: Cambridge University, Institute of Education, Shaftesbury Road, Cambridge CB2 2BX, United Kingdom.
Fin: Department of Education and Science.
educational administration; information technology; secretary; head teacher; attitude; office automation
administration de l'enseignement; technologie de l'information; secrétaire; chef d'établissement; attitude; bureautique
PROJECT DESCRIPTION
   The objectives of the study were: to discover how staff in schools were encountering and responding to information technology and its impact on school management; to analyse and report the main findings emerging from this data; and to outline some conclusion and directions for further investigation.
   The study investigated headteachers' and secretaries' views concerning Management Information Services (MIS) in a sample of 20 small primary schools across East Anglia. Research was undertaken by four fieldworkers using structured interviews. The study focused on equipment, training and support, problems and challenges, in-school effects, financial and school management.
   Emerging themes were: lack of storage space; the isolation of school secretaries; problems of finding sufficient time to familiarise oneself with the equipment; the way implementation relies upon the goodwill of the secretary, the changing role and responsibility of the secretary and, to a lesser degree, the headteacher.

Publ: Southworth, G. Management Information Services for small primary schools: a report for School Management Task Force. Chelmsford: East Anglia Regional Curriculum, 1991.

12331   Management training needs of technical institutions in Africa.
GBR   1993
Research Date(s): 1990-1991
Foster, B.
Inst: Staff College, Coombe Lodge, Blagdon, Bristol BS18 6RG, United Kingdom.
training need; management education; Africa
besoin de formation; formation à la gestion; Afrique
PROJECT DESCRIPTION
   The aim of this project is to identify management and management training needs in relation to organisational development for technical institutions in Africa, and to devise appropriate training interventions and resources.

12332   Managing the implementation of the National Curriculum.
GBR   1993
Research Date(s): 1990-1993
James, M.
Sup: Seymour, R.
Inst: Crewe & Alsager College of Higher Education, Hassall Road, Alsager, Stoke on Trent ST7 2HL, United Kingdom.

educational administration; common core curriculum; integrated curriculum; curriculum development; reform; development of education
administration de l'enseignement; tronc commun; programme d'études intégré; élaboration de programmes d'études; réforme; développement de l'éducation
PROJECT DESCRIPTION
   This research examines the introduction of the National Curriculum as an exercise in the management of change. Literature reviews have been carried out on curriculum theory, a centrally controlled curriculum and various perspectives on the National Curriculum as well as educational change. The question of cross curricularity and subject overlap has emerged as extremely important. Five secondary schools will be studied. Interviews with the headteacher and deputy and the heads of science, geography and technology will take place. Data will then be collated and analysed to compare 'real world' perceptions and problems with the theoretical perspectives of the literature review.
   It is hoped that 'good practice' guidelines and additional knowledge on the management of change will emerge.

12333   Mature students' perceptions and performance of polytechnic degree courses.
GBR   1993
Research Date(s): 1991-1994
Fulton, O.
Inst: Lancaster University, Department of Educational Research, Cartmel College, Bailrigg, Lancaster LA1 4YW, United Kingdom.
Fin: Economic and Social Research Council.
educational need; student; higher education; adult; student behaviour
besoin d'éducation; étudiant; enseignement supérieur; adulte; comportement de l'étudiant
PROJECT DESCRIPTION
   Because of the increasing number of places available, coupled with the drop in birth rate more mature students enter higher education. However, they often face difficulties such as poor educational background and a more complex personal background. Such difficulties have been studied but not acted upon because mature students have been seen as a homogeneous group and their problems considered accordingly.
   Although research has shown that mature students' examination results compare favourably with traditional entry students, the researcher believes that they could perform better and, equally importantly, could enjoy their courses more if their particular needs were considered. Using a broadly phenomenological perspective, the researcher contends that within polytechnics many mature students do not get the type of education that best fits their needs, needs which have been created by their past experiences. By studying different types of courses, with their contrasting styles and philosophies of teaching, in relation to categories of mature students we may better understand their needs.
   The research will involve statistical analysis of questionnaires from around 600 mature degree students. Students' perceptions of higher education courses and the teaching styles used will be examined, and these perceptions related to their social and academic backgrounds and degree classification in order to establish any relationship between them. The findings will be used to assess through modelling the strength of the relationships between the various elements of the research, and thus gain an overview of the effects of specific types of courses on categories of mature students.

12334   Models of effective management in schools.
GBR   1993
Research Date(s): 1991-1992
Bolam, R.; McMahon, A.; Pocklington, K.; Weindling, R.
Inst: Bristol University, School of Education, National Development Centre for Educational Management & Policy, 35 Berkeley Square, Bristol BS8 1JA, United Kingdom.
Fin: Department of Education and Science - School Management Task Force.
educational administration; management; cross-national research; primary school; secondary school
administration de l'enseignement; gestion; recherche transnationale; école primaire; école secondaire
PROJECT DESCRIPTION
   The research will aim to: (i) identify examples of management structures and processes which staff of these schools have recognised as effective practice; and (ii) identify international comparisons of management structures and processes which add to our understanding of effective practice.
   The research falls into two distinct phases. Phase 1 is a questionnaire survey of staff in a sample of 40 primary and 20 secondary schools. In Phase 2, 12 of these schools will be selected for detailed case study. Information about international school management structures and processes will be gathered mainly through a review of the relevant literature.

12335 The modern inspectorate: HM Inspectorate of schools 1944-91.
GBR 1993
Research Date(s): 1987-1992
Dunford, J.
Sup: Goodings, R.
Inst: Durham University, School of Education, Leazes Road, Durham DH1 1TA, United Kingdom.
inspection; history of education; central government; local government; school
inspection; histoire de l'éducation; administration centrale; administration locale; école
PROJECT DESCRIPTION
The twin aims of Her Majesty's Inspecorate (HMI) - advice and inspection - have dominated the work of HMI since 1944, but the balance between the two aims has frequently shifted. This study chronicles the history of HMI since 1944, placing it in the context of its earlier history and studying its effect on other parts of the education system - schools, colleges, local education authorities, higher and further education institutions and the Department of Education and Science (DES). The relationship between HMI and the DES is studied with particular reference to the independence of HMI. The research includes interviews with senior inspectors and local authority officials.
Publ: Goodings, R.F. & Dunford, J.E. Her Majesty's Inspectorate of Schools, 1839-1989: the question of independence. In: *Journal of Educational Administration and History*, Vol XXII, No 1, pp. 1-8, January 1990.

12336 Monitoring and evaluation of new funding mechanisms in higher education.
GBR 1993
Research Date(s): 1988-1991
Woodhall, M.; Mace, J.; Loder, C.
Sup: Williams, G.
Inst: London University, Institute of Education, Department of Policy Studies, Centre for Higher Education Studies, 20 Bedford Way, London WC1H 0AL, United Kingdom.
Fin: Department of Education and Science.
economics of education; financial resources; financing; higher education
économie de l'éducation; ressources financières; financement; enseignement supérieur
PROJECT DESCRIPTION
The Education Reform Act (1988) brought about radical changes in the method of funding on the basis of contracts, rather than grants. The principal aims of the research are to: (1) examine the rationale for alternative models of funding higher education within the general framework of contractual responsibility by institutions to their funding bodies; (2) evaluate the operation and effects of funding arrangements prior to 1988 which contain contractual obligations between higher education institutions and funding bodies; (3) propose ways of monitoring the effects of new funding mechanisms, including identifying the data requirements for measurement of output or institutional performance; (4) monitor the introduction of the new funding arrangements, in order to provide a basis for the full-scale evaluation of the system, once it is fully operational. Broadly, this stage of the project will involve three activities: (a) discussions with Finance Officers and other senior administrators in universities, colleges and polytechnics to identify categories of activities subject to contractual arrangements; (b) a postal questionnaire to all higher education institutions seeking information on the extent of the activities identified and the institutional responses to them; (c) the selection of a limited number of examples, probably about 25, which would be the subject of detailed case studies to examine the educational and other implications of different funding mechanisms.

12337 Nové trendy riadenia výchovy a vzdelávania v demokratickej spoločnosti a rozhodujúce postavenie učiteľov pri ich realizácii. (New trends in educational administration and teacher training in a democratic society and their implications for the role of the teacher.)
CSK 1993
Research Date(s): 1992-1994
Kolláriková, Zuzana; Špánik, Miroslav; Matúšová, Silvia.
Sup: Obdržálek, Zdenek.
Inst: Pedagogická fakulta UK, Katedra pedagogiky (Comenius University, Faculty of Education, Department of Pedagogy), 813 34 Bratislava, Moskovská 3, Czech and Slovak Federal Republic.
Ústredné metodické centrum MŠaV SR (Central Methodology Centre, Ministry of Education and Science of the Slovak Republic), 800 00 Bratislava, Záhradnícka 93, Czech and Slovak Federal Republic
educational administration; teacher education; teacher role; educational reform; social change; education system
administration de l'enseignement; formation des enseignants; rôle de l'enseignant; réforme de l'enseignement; changement social; système d'enseignement
PROJECT DESCRIPTION
Background: Given the new social conditions which have developed in Slovakia and Czecho-Slovakia since 1989, there is a need for the definition of concepts and contents for the creation of a new education system, including teacher training, and a new administrative structure. Such a definition would take place on the basis of empirical research, comparison of relevant experiences inside and outside Europe, as well as theoretical considerations.
Aim: The investigation has the following aims: (1) To describe and compare the organization and management of education in selected European and non-European countries, with a view to (a) identifying examples of good practice that have relevance for the current situation in the Czech and Slovak Republic and (b) constructing a basis for the study of problems related to the organization and management of teacher training; (2) to contribute to the elaboration of a theoretical basis for the management of education which will serve (a) as a basis for the improvement of educational administrative practice, (b) as training material for student teachers and school administrators; (3) to conduct empirical and theoretical research into the phenomena that have generated the current social and working climate in schools and to study the relationships between these phenomena, as a starting point for the definition of optimum approaches to school management; (4) to examine the basic problems of today's teachers from a managerial viewpoint and to work out, on this basis, teacher training strategies or models which will provide a basis for efficient teaching practice.

12338 Observatoire de la vie étudiante.
FRA 1993
Research Date(s): 1991-
Molinari, Jean-Paul; Lecomte, Monique.
Sup: Baudelot, Christian.
Inst: Université de Nantes, UFR Institut d'histoire et de sociologie, CNRS URA/889 et GDR/55, Laboratoire d'études et de recherches sociologiques sur la classe ouvrière, Chemin de la Sensive-du-Tertre, BP 1025, 44036 Nantes Cedex, France.
student sociology; higher education; student life
sociologie de l'étudiant; enseignement supérieur; vie étudiante
PROJECT DESCRIPTION
Objectifs: Plusieurs enquêtes sur la condition étudiante et les modes de vie des étudiants sont développées et la création d'un observatoire nantais de la vie étudiante est réalisée depuis février 1990. La première enquête de l'observatoire porte sur l'abandon de leurs études par les étudiants de premier cycle.
Publ: Molinari, Jean-Paul. Les étudiants. Nantes: LERSCO, mai 1991.

12339 Parental choice of school.
GBR 1993
Research Date(s): 1991-1994
Wikeley, F.
Sup: Hughes, M.; Golby, M.
Inst: Exeter University, School of Education, St Luke's, Heavitree Road, Exeter EX1 2LU, United Kingdom.
choice of school; parents; parent-school relation; marketing
choix d'une école; parents; relation parents-école; mercatique
PROJECT DESCRIPTION
This research involves the use of case study to identify criteria used by parents in choosing schools and to explore how these can help schools in marketing themselves.

12340 Parents and National Curriculum: criteria of parental choice of primary school.
GBR 1993
Research Date(s): 1989-
Hughes, M.
Sup: Golby, M.
Inst: Exeter University, School of Education, St Luke's, Heavitree Road, Exeter EX1 2LU, United Kingdom.
Fin: Leverhulme Trust.
choice of school; primary school; parents; parent-school relation
choix d'une école; école primaire; parents; relation parents-école
PROJECT DESCRIPTION
In the present political climate it is becoming increasingly important for schools to make themselves attractive to parents. In order to do this it would be advantageous for them to know how parents choose a school and on what criteria that choice is based.
The research will concentrate on parental choice of primary school. It will select from the sample being used by the wider research project 'Parents and the National Curriculum', some parents for a case study approach. The whole sample consists of a wide range of parents in differing socio-economic circumstances. They all have a child who started school in the year 1988/1989 and have been interviewed four times in two years. The complete interview, which was semi-structured, covered several aspects of the changes taking place in their children's schooling at the present time. This research will look in depth at the criteria they used, and how those criteria were chosen in their decision as to which primary schools their children would attend.
It is hoped that by looking closely at the cases of a few parents it will be possible to identify differences in the choice process. In this way it is hoped

to develop a paradigm which illuminates the process and would enable schools to better target potential parents.

Publ: Hughes, M.; Wikeley, F. & Nash, P. *Parents and the National Curriculum: an interim report*. Exeter University, 1990.

Hughes, M.; Wikeley, F. & Nash, P. *Parents and SATs: a second interim report from the project Parents and the National Curriculum*. Exeter University, School of Education, 1991.

Hughes, M.; Wikeley, F. & Nash, P. Parents in the new era: myth and reality. In: Merthens, F. & Vass, J. (eds.). *Impact Issues: Discursive Interruptions in Curriculum Practice*. London: Falmer, 1991.

Hughes, M.; Wikeley, F. & Nash, P. Business partners. In: *Times Educational Supplement*, 5 January 1990.

12341   The politics of working in secondary schools.
GBR   1993
Research Date(s): 1987-1992
Busher, H.
Inst: Loughborough University of Technology, Department of Education, Loughborough LE11 3TU, United Kingdom.
educational administration; teacher behaviour; interaction
administration de l'enseignement; comportement de l'enseignant; interaction
PROJECT DESCRIPTION

This research aims to look at the interaction between individuals and institutions (between individuals and groups of individuals in institutions) when implementing and negotiating changes in secondary schools. The research is small scale and has been carried out ethnographically. It has explored the different interpretations that participants give to the same events. It has focused on time periods when people were most likely to notice dysfunctions between personal views of education and institutionally sustained views of education. The study has focused on six main participants, on how they perceived their work in their schools and how their colleagues perceived them working. The research has made use of tape-recorded semi-structured interviews, of classroom observation, and of enriched interviews (using video-recordings of teacher activity to trigger discussion). Some 30 interviews in all were conducted during the course of one academic year.

Tentative conclusions are that school organisations can be adequately described using a political systems model and that the management of schools is an intensely political process rather than a mechanistically rational one.

12342   Promotion, abandon et redoublement dans les systèmes éducatifs africains.
FRA   1993
Research Date(s): 1987-1989
Orivel, François; Perrot, Jean.
Inst: Université de Dijon, UER Faculté des sciences économiques et de gestion, CNRS UPR/29 et GDR/996, Institut de recherche sur l'économie de l'éducation, BP 138, 21004 Dijon Cedex, France.
wastage; Africa; repeating; dropout; primary education; achievement
déperdition d'effectifs; Afrique; redoublement; abandon d'études; enseignement primaire; rendement
PROJECT DESCRIPTION

Objectifs: L'analyse des flux d'élèves dans les pays africains laisse apparaître des différences encore plus importantes que dans les pays développés: (1) la propension à redoubler est significativement plus élevée en Afrique francophone qu'elle ne l'est en Afrique anglophone; (2) les abandons en cours d'études sont nombreux et beaucoup d'élèves n'atteignent pas la dernière année du primaire. L'analyse de cette diversité est abordée ici sous l'angle économique et au niveau collectif.

Méthodologie: Partant des hypothèses sur la liaison entre les taux de redoublement et d'abandon on réalise des simulations montrant comment une cohorte de 1000 élèves traverse le système éducatif. Un coefficient de gaspillage est défini: c'est le rapport entre le temps gaspillé et le nombre total d'années-élèves utilisées dans le système éducatif.

Résultats: On trouve un coefficient de 4,7% pour un taux de redoublement de 5% et de 50% pour un taux de redoublement de 40%, ce qui signifie que, pour les nombreux pays d'Afrique francophone où les taux de redoublement sont de l'ordre de 30% on peut considérer que l'organisation retenue conduit à un gaspillage compris entre 1/3 et la moitié des années-élèves utilisées. En diminuant ces taux de redoublement, un pays peut réaliser des économies substantielles.

Publ: Perrot, Jean & Orivel, François. *Promotion, abandon et redoublement dans les systèmes éducatifs africains*. IREDU, 17p.

12343   Reducing the cost of technical and vocational education.
GBR   1993
Research Date(s): 1991-1992
Gray, L.; Warrender, A.-M.
Inst: Staff College, Coombe Lodge, Blagdon, Bristol BS18 6RG, United Kingdom.
Fin: Overseas Development Administration.
cost of education; technical education; vocational education; developing country; cross-national research
coût de l'éducation; enseignement technique; enseignement professionnel; pays en développement; recherche transnationale
PROJECT DESCRIPTION

The research project examined policies of national governments and international donor agencies in seeking to reduce the costs and improve the effectiveness of technical education provision at national and local levels. It examined policies concerning equipment provision, the use of centralised workshops, repair and maintenance procedures, and the effective deployment of technical support. It reviewed experiments in encouraging the adoption of competence-based learning strategies, the use of institutionally managed labour market signalling, and the collection, analysis and comparison of cost data within and between training institutions in ways which are compatible with existing administrative systems, and do not demand more sophisticated computerised management information systems. It also looked at project management issues, initial appraisal techniques and the planning framework within which technical and vocational institutions operate. The researchers reviewed the literature on aid projects for technical and vocational education/training, and examined at first hand the work of international donor agencies, and the impact of that work in one African and one Asian country.

12344   Resourcing Sheffield schools.
GBR   1993
Research Date(s): 1991-1992
Levacic, R.; Jesson, D.
Inst: Open University, School of Education, Walton Hall, Milton Keynes MK7 6AA, United Kingdom; Sheffield University, Division of Education, 388 Glossop Road, Sheffield S10 2TN, United Kingdom.
Fin: Sheffield Education Authority.
education budget; economics of education; educational planning
budget de l'éducation; économie de l'éducation; planification de l'éducation
PROJECT DESCRIPTION

The project is constructing a school funding formula which meets the requirements of the Education Reform Act 1988 and which is based on a needs assessment for educating pupils aged 3-18 at schools with different characteristics. A major source of evidence for constructing the model is a survey of current patterns of resource use in Sheffield Education Authority's 32 secondary schools, 191 primary schools and 6 colleges. This will be supplemented by professional assessment of resource requirements to construct an activity-led resourcing model to provide age-weightings for the funding formula.

12345   The role of the senior management team in secondary schools.
GBR   1993
Research Date(s): 1991-1993
Wallace, M.
Sup: Bolam, R.
Inst: Bristol University, School of Education, National Development Centre for Educational Management & Policy, 35 Berkeley Square, Bristol BS8 1JA, United Kingdom.
Fin: Economic and Social Research Council.
educational administration; secondary school; managerial staff
administration de l'enseignement; école secondaire; personnel d'encadrement
PROJECT DESCRIPTION

The aim of this research is to examine how senior management teams manage secondary schools within a context of educational reform and to identify approaches to teamwork which appear to be effective. Senior managers in secondary schools may face a greater need than hitherto to co-ordinate their work so as to effectively orchestrate the implementation of multiple innovations.

The research will be conducted in two local education authorities (LEAs). In each LEA, case studies will be carried out during the summer of 1991 in three schools where all members of the senior management team express a strong commitment to teamwork. A longitudinal case study will be undertaken in one of these schools.

12346   School management in conditions of stringency.
GBR   1993
Research Date(s): 1990-
Davies, L.; Harber, C.
Inst: Birmingham University, School of Education, Edgbaston, Birmingham B15 2TT, United Kingdom.
educational administration; education budget; resource allocation; developing country; developed country
administration de l'enseignement; budget de l'éducation; affectation des ressources; pays en développement; pays développé
PROJECT DESCRIPTION

Managers of schools in countries with limited or declining budgets for education face conditions and problems in their institutions which are rarely addressed by conventional educational administration literature. Shortages of resources of all kinds (teachers, training, textbooks, equipment, furniture), levels of pay which can compromise full commitment to the work of teaching, and communication and transport problems may characterise a number of Third World countries as well as some declining First World ones. Together with widely divergent expectations of authority and the role of the headteacher, this may mean that images of school management are called for which are radically different from the models in much administrative theory. There is little systematically collected evidence either about problems faced by schools operating in economically constrained circumstances or about the management strategies which are actually used for coping with them. However, it is probable that the internal reality of very tightly budgeted schools will depart significantly from the prescriptions for 'effective' management found in Western-based management textbooks.

The research aims to gather case study evidence on the reality of school organisation in selected Third World countries. Clearly, there can be no single objective and valid view of how a school operates. Rather, the same features of school organisation will be viewed and assessed by different participants in the process. The research therefore uses qualitative methods to examine the perceptions of key participants within school management - headteachers, deputies and senior teachers. A cumulative bank of such case studies of schools can develop a grounded theory around themes relevant for future management training. The aim is therefore to encourage portrayal of the real contexts of school life in order to (a) critically challenge the imposition of Western-based educational administration principles; and (b) derive relevant management images and strategies which do not necessarily rely on full levels of school financing.

Publ: Davies, L. Equity or efficiency? School management in an international context. London: Falmer Press, 1990.

12347 Schoolkeuzemotieven van kinderen in het basisonderwijs. (Motives determining choice of school in the transfer from primary to secondary education.)

NLD 1994
Research Date(s): 1993-1994
Derriks, M.F.G.
Sup: Roede, E.; Eck, E. van.
Inst: Stichting Centrum voor Onderwijsonderzoek (SCO) (Centre for Educational Research), Grote Bickersstraat 72, 1013 KS Amsterdam, Netherlands.
Universiteit van Amsterdam (University of Amsterdam), P.O. Box 19268, 1000 GG Amsterdam, Netherlands
Fin: SVO het Instituut voor Onderzoek van het Onderwijs.
choice of school; pupil; parent role; teacher role; secondary school
choix d'une école; élève; rôle des parents; rôle de l'enseignant; école secondaire
PROJECT DESCRIPTION

Background: The question of what factors have an influence on the transition from primary to secondary school has been studied from various angles. The emphasis is usually on the motives underlying the choice for a particular type of education. Little is known about the motives for choosing a particular school and about the children's say in this matter.

Aim: To examine what factors are important for children, parents and teachers in choosing a secondary school.

Design: Questionnaires will be sent to all secondary schools in four geographical areas, asking for information on the transfer of pupils from primary to secondary school in the last three years. The parents (n=400), teachers (n=16) and final-year pupils (n=400) from at least 24 primary schools will be given questionnaires on two occasions to collect information on the factors that play a part in selecting a secondary school. Indepth interviews will be conducted with 16 children and their parents and teachers on three occasions.

12348 Self-managing schools - a practical way forward for secondary schools.

GBR 1993
Research Date(s): 1990-1993
Hemmings, N.
Sup: Seymour, R.
Inst: Crewe & Alsager College of Higher Education, Department of Education Management, Hassall Road, Alsager, Stoke on Trent ST7 2HL, United Kingdom.
Fin: Stoke on Trent Local Education Authority.
educational administration; educational reform; school autonomy; secondary school
administration de l'enseignement; réforme de l'enseignement; autonomie scolaire; école secondaire
PROJECT DESCRIPTION

The research aims to consider some of the practical effects of school management in the light of the Education Reform Act 1988 (ERA), in particular focusing upon the ways secondary schools have adapted to the new challenges that ERA has presented. A case study of representative schools has begun.

12349 Strategic management and development in educational organisation.

GBR 1993
Research Date(s): 1990-
Burt, G.
Inst: Open University, Institute of Educational Technology, Walton Hall, Milton Keynes MK7 6AA, United Kingdom.
educational administration; management; university
administration de l'enseignement; gestion; université
PROJECT DESCRIPTION

There is a growing attention to 'management' in educational organisations. However it is important that fashionable management ideas should not be accepted uncritically. The project studies the strategic process at the Open University noting the presence of structural and political dimensions. Special attention is given to studying the values and ethics dimensions.

12350 Structure d'accueil pour la petite enfance dans la région morgienne.

CHE 1994
Research Date(s): 1989-1991
Richard-de Paolis, Paola; Pecorini, Muriel; Meyer, Gil; Spack, Annelyse; Berz, Candid; Troutot, Pierre-Yves.
Inst: Ecole d'études sociales et pédagogiques (EESP), Isabelle-de-Montolieu 19, C.P. 70, 1000 Lausanne 24, Suisse.
Commune de Morges, 1110 Morges, Suisse
educational administration; pre-school child; day nursery; nursery school; educational provision
administration de l'enseignement; enfant d'âge préscolaire; crèche; école maternelle; scolarisation
PROJECT DESCRIPTION

Dans cette étude mandatée par la Commune de Morges, il s'est agi de recenser, dans la région morgienne, les besoins exprimés en matière d'accueil pour la petite enfance et les structures mises en place pour les satisfaire, d'analyser les représentations relatives aux fonctions des différents lieux d'accueil et de fournir des indications quant aux priorités dans les modalités d'intervention appropriées aux attentes des utilisateurs et des professionnels concernés. Ont été retenues les diverses formes d'accueil destinées à la population enfantine, soit les institutions (nursery, garderie, halte-garderie, jardin d'enfants, unité d'accueil pour écoliers) et le placement familial à la journée, assuré par les mamans de jour agréées par le Service de protection de la jeunesse. Le recensement des lieux d'accueil comporte une description de leurs fonctions ainsi que de leur capacité d'accueil et de leur fréquentation. Cette dernière est complétée par une analyse des caractéristiques socio-démographiques des usagers. Ont également été recensés les services directement ou indirectement concernés par le placement des enfants: services sociaux publics ou privés considérés comme des lieux ressources pour des demandes d'informations, d'orientations, voire de dépannages. La représentation de la fonction des lieux d'accueil et de l'adéquation de ces lieuz aux attentes et expériences est abordée dans deux enquêtes réalisées auprès des professionnels des institutions et auprès de 420 parents utilisateurs. Il s'est agi d'évaluer le type de demandes formulées par les parents, mais aussi d'estimer l'importance de la demande non satisfaite.

Le rapport sur le projet est conçu de manière à être directement utile aux personnes qui, à Morges comme dans beaucoup d'autres régions de Suisse, sont confrontées à des choix en matière de politique social pour l'enfance.

Publ: Richard-de Paolis, Paola; Pecorini, Muriel; Meyer, Gil; Spack, Annelyse; Berz, Candid. *Accueil de la petite enfance: une enquête régionale.* Lausanne: Ecole d'études sociales et pédagogiques (EESP), 1992, 185 pages (Cahiers de l'EESP; 12).

12351 Study of independent further and higher education.

GBR 1993
Research Date(s): 1991-1993
Williams, G.; Loder, C.
Inst: London University, Institute of Education, Department of Policy Studies, 20 Bedford Way, London WC1H 0AL, United Kingdom.
Fin: Department of Education and Science.
educational provision; private education; post-secondary education; higher education
scolarisation; enseignement privé; enseignement postsecondaire; enseignement supérieur
PROJECT DESCRIPTION

The Centre for Higher Education Studies is undertaking a survey of independent further and higher education in Great Britain in order to provide information on: (1) number and type of institutions; (2) number and characteristics of students (including age, sex, mode of study and domicile); (3) range of courses offered; (4) number and range of qualifications obtained by students; and (5) sources of financial support for students (e.g. grants under PICKUP, sponsorship by employers, mandatory and discretionary awards from local education authorities and training vouchers.

12352 Term of birth and special educational placement: the impact of assessment procedures in a local education authority.
GBR 1993
Research Date(s): 1989-1991
Pumfrey, P.; Ward, J.
Inst: Manchester University, School of Education, Centre for Educational Guidance and Special Needs, Oxford Road, Manchester M13 9PL, United Kingdom; University of Victoria, Faculty of Education, Victoria V8W 3N4, British Columbia, Canada.
admission; special school; special education; school entry age; birth
admission; centre d'éducation spéciale; enseignement spécial; âge d'entrée à l'école; naissance
PROJECT DESCRIPTION
One source of unplanned systematic bias in the selection of pupils for special educational placement has been the tendency for children born in the final term of the school year to be over-represented among those designated mildly retarded or as having moderate learning difficulties, and educated in special schools. The issue of selection bias relates to a more general problem area in education, the so-called 'relative-age' effect.

The present study was undertaken to ascertain whether a relative-age bias is currently evident in children in segregated special education placement and, if it exists, whether it is confined to particular groups. Of particular interest in this study are comparisons with the earlier data obtained in the same local education authority before the implementation of the Education Act 1981 in April, 1983. Data were obtained concerning 1,192 pupils attending 14 special schools in a local education authority. Analyses by 'term of birth' and 'age group' were carried out.

At each age level no significant association between term of birth and the expected frequencies was identified. A comparison between term of birth and frequency of special educational placement in 1974 and the present study at three age levels was also carried out. In 1974 the association differed markedly from the expected theoretical frequencies. In the current data, no significant association was identified. The importance of the use of monthly age allowances in the selection procedures is identified as an important factor in this change in pattern over time.

Publ: Pumfrey, P.D. & Ward, J. Term of birth and special educational placement: the impact of assessment procedures in an LEA. In: *Research in Education*, No 46/1991, pp. 61-71, November.

12353 Three longitudinal studies of medical student selection.
GBR 1993
Research Date(s): 1990-1994
McManus, I.; Richards, P.; Vincent, C.
Inst: London University, Imperial College of Science, Technology and Medicine, St Mary's Hospital Medical School, Norfolk Place, Paddington, London W2 1PG, United Kingdom.
Fin: Leverhulme Trust.
selection; medicine; admission requirements; student; higher education
sélection; médecine; conditions d'admission; étudiant; enseignement supérieur
PROJECT DESCRIPTION
This project is an assessment of the process of medical student selection at five medical schools, for admission in October 1981 with follow-up of the entrants between October 1981 and October 1986.

12354 The use of teachers' time.
GBR 1993
Research Date(s): 1990-1991
Campbell, R.; Neill, S.
Inst: Warwick University, Faculty of Educational Studies, Policy Analysis Unit, Coventry CV4 7AL, United Kingdom.
Fin: Assistant Masters and Mistresses Association.
arrangement of school time; teaching time; teacher; primary school; secondary school; hours of work
aménagement du temps scolaire; temps d'enseignement; enseignant; école primaire; école secondaire; heures de travail
PROJECT DESCRIPTION
The aim of the project is to analyse the time that teachers spend on work, using five broad categories: teaching; preparation; inservice training; administration; and other activities. The analysis is related to education policy, including the delivery of the National Curriculum. Ninety-five key stage 1 teachers, and 300 secondary school teachers are participating by completing a daily time diary and questionnaire. Analysis is by a specially written program. A sub-sample of 24 key stage 1 teachers is being followed up by interviews.

Publ: Campbell, R.J. & Neill, S.St.J. *Thirteen hundred and thirty days: final report of a pilot study of teacher time in key stage 1.* Warwick: University of Warwick, Department of Education, Policy Analysis Unit, 1990.
Campbell, R.J. et al. *Workloads, achievement and stress. Two follow-up studies of teacher time in key stage 1.* Warwick: University of Warwick, Department of Education, Policy Analysis Unit, 1991.

Campbell, R.J. & Neill, S.St.J. *The workloads of secondary school teachers.* Final report. Warwick: University of Warwick, Department of Education, Policy Analysis Unit, 1991.

12355 Verwijzing van leerlingen naar speciaal onderwijs en terugplaatsing in de stad Utrecht. (Referral of pupils to special education and returning of special education pupils to mainstream education in the city of Utrecht.)
NLD 1994
Research Date(s): 1992-1993
Oudenhoven, D.; Petersen, B.
Inst: Instituut voor Toegepaste Sociale wetenschappen (ITS) (Institute for Applied Social Sciences), P.O. Box 9048, 6500 KJ Nijmegen, Netherlands. Katholieke Universiteit Nijmegen (Catholic University of Nijmegen), P.O. Box 9102, 6500 HC Nijmegen, Netherlands
Fin: SVO het Instituut voor Onderzoek van het Onderwijs.
admission; special education; innovation; number of pupils
admission; enseignement spécial; innovation; effectifs scolaires
PROJECT DESCRIPTION
Background: For some time in Utrecht various kinds of activities have taken place in the context of innovation in mainstream education. Some of these activities have been initiated by local authorities, others by central authorities. The activities are aimed at: reducing referrals from ordinary to special education; promoting the return of special school pupils to mainstream schools; and improving the quality of mainstream education (special needs provision in ordinary schools). It is the task of the Utrecht School Advisory Centre Foundation (SAC) to help schools carry out their innovatory activities. It is unclear whether the activities undertaken so far have produced the desired results, because no systematic data are available.

Aim: To examine the movement of pupils between the sectors of special and mainstream education during the past ten years in and around Utrecht; to identify specific changes, if any, as a result of innovatory activities.

Design: The research population consists of those pupils who have been referred to special schools in Utrecht since 1982 (and whose records are available) and all 20 Utrecht special schools as well as the schools - inside and outside Utrecht - which these pupils attended before they were referred to special education. The pupils' files will supply most of the data on: size and type of special school, denomination of mainstream school attended prior to referral, socio-economic status, ethnic background, year of referral, agency that referred the pupil. These data will be entered in a data file and will be supplemented by data on the entire Utrecht primary school population over the period 1982-1992. One or several staff of the SAC will be interviewed about primary education and special needs provision in ordinary primary schools in Utrecht.

12356 The work of primary school teachers.
GBR 1993
Research Date(s): 1991-1992
Campbell, R.; Neill, S.
Inst: Warwick University, Faculty of Educational Studies, Policy Analysis Unit, Coventry CV4 7AL, United Kingdom.
Fin: Association of Education Committees Trust.
arrangement of school time; teaching time; teacher; primary school; hours of work
aménagement du temps scolaire; temps d'enseignement; enseignant; école primaire; heures de travail
PROJECT DESCRIPTION
The aim of the project is to analyse the time spent on work by primary school teachers, using a 29-item coding system and a daily log of time spent working. The sample comprises one teacher from each key stage in every primary school in three Midlands local authorities. The aim is to relate the findings to education policy, especially the implementation of the National Curriculum.

12357 Zagotavljenje kontinuitete vzgojno-izobraževalnega dela na prehodu iz vrtca v šolo. (Transition from pre-school to primary school.)
SVN 1994
Research Date(s): 1992-1994
Vonta, Tatjana; Cerar, Marjeta; Furjan, Tatjana; Mohorčič, Lidija; Hrovat, Ana; Prešeren, Tatjan; Vodnik, Ivanka; et al.
Inst: Pedagoški inštitut pri Univerzi v Ljubljani (Educational Research Institute, University of Ljubljana), Gerbičeva 62, 61111 Ljubljana, Slovenia. Univerza v Ljubljani (University of Ljubljana), Kongresni trg 15, 61000 Ljubljana, Slovenia
Fin: Ministrstvo za znanost in tehnologijo; Ministrstvo za šolstvo in šport; Ministrstvo za delo, družino in socialne zadeve; Mestni sekretariat za družbene dejavnosti mesta Ljubljane.
entry to school; quality of education; primary education; teaching model; school environment
entrée à l'école; qualité de l'éducation; enseignement primaire; modèle didactique; milieu scolaire
PROJECT DESCRIPTION
Background and aims: Continuity in the educational process is one of the main factors determining the quality of learning and the quality of chil-

dren's lives today and tomorrow. The problem addressed by this research is the transition from pre-school to primary school - a problem that has become more urgent since the lowering of the school entry age. The aim of the project is also to contribute to a friendlier and more effective organization of children's lives in the transition from pre-school to primary school and to examine the relations between pre-school and primary school in respect of teaching programmes, content of education, teaching methods, teaching personnel and institutional organization, since previously relations were formal only. The aim is to improve provision in this sector of education and thus to create a positive emotional and motivational climate for effective learning.

Design: Three models of entry into primary school have been designed with it is hoped to help children during the transition period. The main characteristic of the models is the involvement of pre-school teachers in school work. Thus, the children are offered a new role in the school environment: there is room for making mistakes, sharing personal experiences, and acquiring, using and assessing knowledge at a reasonable pace. In pre-school institutions new forms of cooperation with primary schools are being developed and parents are prepared for their children's entry to school. The pre-school education curriculum is being reformed with a view to improving equal opportunities and enhancing the interaction and participation of children and parents in the education process.

Sample and methods: The models are introduced and evaluated in one pre-school institution and one primary school. Some 20 practitioners collaborate in the construction, introduction and assessment of the innovations. An action research approach is used, with an emphasis on triangulation and using also experimental and descriptive methods.

Results: In the school year 1992/1993 the first model was introduced in primary school. The children entered school as a group, together with their pre-school teacher. The primary school teacher had to adapt to this group. Consequently, the climate in the school was emotionally favourable; developmentally oriented teaching methods from pre-school were transferred to primary school. A qualitative analysis has shown that parents and children feel that the model offers a safe school environment. Children display a high degree of expressiveness, creativity and persistence in task fulfillment.

Publ: Vonta, T. Spreminjanje vzgojnega procesa v vrtcu. In: *Educa*. 1-2/1992, pp. 9-15.
Vonta, T. Spreminjanje vzgojnega procesa v vrtcu. In: *Educa*. 6/1993, pp. 419-429.

06 EVALUATION – EVALUATION – EVALUATION

12358 Achievements and competence of Standard Grades 3-6.
GBR 1993
Research Date(s): 1991-1992
Black, H.; Devine, M.; Hall, J.; Martin, S.
Inst: Scottish Council for Research in Education, 15 St John Street, Edinburgh EH8 8JR, United Kingdom.
Fin: Scottish Office Education Department.
examination; achievement; English language; mathematics
examen; rendement; langue anglaise; mathématiques
PROJECT DESCRIPTION
    The research aims to describe: the actual language and mathematics competence of pupils gaining grades 3, 4, 5 and 6 in Standard Grade

English and Mathematics; and the competence shown in school work by pupils failing to achieve at least grade 6 in Standard Grade English and Mathematics. It will also identify changes in grade-related criteria which might lead to improvements in the teaching of basic competence in language and mathematics.

12359   Advanced Courses Development Programme.
GBR   1993
Research Date(s): 1990-1991
Black, H.; Hall, J.; Martin, S.
Inst: Scottish Council for Research in Education, 15 St John Street, Edinburgh EH8 8JR, United Kingdom.
Fin: Scottish Office Education Department.
examination; curriculum development
examen; élaboration de programmes d'études
PROJECT DESCRIPTION
   The main aim of the project is to evaluate the Advanced Courses Development Programme with regard to its overall effectiveness. It will examine the actual process of developing the Higher National units used in advanced courses and will also concern the product of this process, and the actual units and courses themselves. Each of these two concerns will focus on aspects such as criteria for good practice, strengths and weaknesses, and articulation with other qualifications.

12360   Allgemeine und differentielle Praediktoren aussergewoehnlicher Leistungen (im Rahmen des Projekts: Retrospektive Befragung erwachsener Begabter nach ihrer Jugend- und Schulzeit). (General and differential predictors of exceptional achievement (as part of the project: Retrospective survey on the youth and school life of gifted adults).)
DEU   1993
Research Date(s): 1989-1993
Sieglen, J.
Sup: Trost, G.; Todt, E.
Inst: Universitaet Giessen, FB 06 Psychologie Professur fuer Paedagogische Psychologie, Otto-Behaghel-Strasse 10, D-6300 Giessen; Institut fuer Test- und Begabungsforschung der Studienstiftung des deutschen Volkes, Koblenzer Strasse 77, D-5300 Bonn 2.
achievement; adolescent; success; career; sciences; technology; gifted
rendement; adolescent; réussite; carrière; sciences; technologie; doué
PROJECT DESCRIPTION
   Inhalt: Welche Verhaltensweisen und Eigenschaften Heranwachsender stehen im Zusammenhang mit deren spaeteren beruflichen Leistungen? Wie lassen sich aussergewoehnliche Leistungen in den Berufsfeldern Wissenschaft, Technik und Wirtschaft schon waehrend der Schulzeit voraussagen? Welche Rolle spielen Umwelt- und Familieneinfluesse im Vergleich zu Persoenlichkeits- oder kognitiven Merkmalen?
   Geographischer Raum: alte Bundeslaender.
   Untersuchter Zeitraum: 1.12.1989 - Mitte 1993.
   Vorgehensweise: Identifikation einer Gruppe von Personen mit aussergewoehnlichen beruflichen Leistungen innerhalb der Gesamtstichprobe; Vergleich der Spitzengruppe mit der Gesamtstichprobe bezueglich einer Vielzahl von Aspekten der Jugend-, Schul- und Ausbildungszeit. Untersuchungsdesign: Methodenforschung; Querschnittserhebung; Panel; retrospektive Daten.
   Datengewinnung: Postalische Befragung (Stichprobe: 9.000; Abiturjahrgang 1974; Auswahlverfahren: Quota. Stichprobe: 800; Stipendiaten des Abiturjahrgangs 1974; Auswahlverfahren: total. Stichprobe: 400; Stipendiaten des Abiturjahrgangs 1964; Auswahlverfahren: total. Stichprobe: 400; Stipendiaten des Abiturjahrgangs 1954; Auswahlverfahren: total). Primaererhebung: Feldarbeit von Mitarbeitern des Projektes durchgefuehrt; Sekundaeranalyse bereits vorhandener maschinenlesbarer Datensaetze.
   Auswertung: Deskriptive Statistiken; parametrische und nicht-parametrische Gruppenvergleiche; Faktorenanalyse; Diskriminanzanalyse; loglineare Modelle. Datenaufbereitung: Aggregierung oder Disaggregierung.

12361   Analysis of examination results.
GBR   1993
Research Date(s): 1981-
Reece, D.
Inst: Berkshire County Council, Education Department, Information Technology Management, Shire Hall, Shinfield Park, Reading RG2 9XD, United Kingdom.
examination; achievement measurement; performance; comparative analysis
examen; mesure du rendement; performance; analyse comparative
PROJECT DESCRIPTION
   Information is received from NCER (National Consortium for Examination Results) and examination results are analysed by subject, sex and school and a combination of the three. These are in the form of detailed tabulations, summary measures of performance and 'profiles' for schools. Results for examinations taken at different times are matched together to produce overall summaries of attainment. Information on the ethnic origin of candidates is added to the results, which are also analysed by ethnicity.

12362   Appraising appraisal: quality control and quality assurance.
GBR   1993
Research Date(s): 1991-1992
Hutchinson, B.
Inst: Ulster University at Jordanstown, Department of Inservice Education, Shore Road, Newtownabbey, County Antrim, BT37 0QB, United Kingdom.
teacher appraisal; higher education; teaching personnel
évaluation sur l'enseignant; enseignement supérieur; corps enseignant
PROJECT DESCRIPTION
   The project is investigating the processes of staff appraisal, quality control and assurance in the University of Ulster. The two principal methods of data collection are (a) documentary evidence; (b) semi-structured interview. Transcripts of the interviews and the draft report are cleared with the contributors before the interim and final reports are published. The evidence collected is analysed using the methods of triangulation and critical analysis.

12363   The assessment of art at first degree level: a comparative study of the principles and methods underlying assessment of fine art students in Athens and Leicester.
GBR   1993
Research Date(s): 1988-
Kypreou, I.
Sup: Allison, B.; Mason, R.
Inst: De Montford University, Department of Education, Centre for Postgraduate Teacher Education, Scraptoft Campus, Scraptoft, Leicester LE7 9SU, United Kingdom.
assessment; art education; fine arts; academic degree
appréciation; éducation artistique; Beaux-Arts; grade universitaire
PROJECT DESCRIPTION
   The study sets out to determine: (a) the role theories of art criticism play in the assessment of fine art students at first degree level; (b) whether assessment procedures in two fine art institutions (Leicester - documented procedures, Athens - non-documented procedures) can be described relative to major theories of art criticism; and (c) the extent to which the differing procedures of assessment utilised in the two institutions are subject to or are affected by the theoretical positions adopted by individual examiners. Fieldwork (observation, interview and questionnaire) will be carried out in the two institutions.

12364   Assessment of competence in general practice.
GBR   1993
Research Date(s): 1988-1993
Mulholland, H.
Inst: Dundee University, Centre for Medical Education, Ninewells Hospital and Medical School, Dundee DD1 9SY, United Kingdom.
Fin: Royal College of General Practitioners; Department of Health; European Community.
assessment; medicine; doctor; examination
appréciation; médecine; médecin; examen
PROJECT DESCRIPTION
   The research was designed to improve the reliability and validity of the Membership Examination of the Royal College of General Practitioners (RCGP). Results of the last five years were analysed (for approximately 2,000 candidates each year) and recommendations made as to changes in numbers and types of questions in the existing papers. Two new types of test were developed: (1) the Critical Reading Paper in which candidates have to read, critically evaluate and discuss applications of scientific journal articles and of printed material of a variety of forms; (2) the simulated surgery, in which candidates are placed in conditions which simulate as far as possible real surgery conditions and are assessed on their competence in consultation. This part of the research is now being continued with funding from the European Community. The second stage of the project is to develop a method of assessing consultation skills in general practice. This part of the project is being carried on in conjunction with the Department of General Practice at the University of Leicester and the Free University of Amsterdam.
Publ: Lockie, C. (ed.). *The MRCGP Examination*, Occasional Paper, No 46. London Royal College of General Practitioners, 1990.

12365   Assessment of Performance Unit in design and technology: aimed at monitoring the performance of 15 year old pupils in design and technology.
GBR   1993
Research Date(s): 1985-1991
Kimbell, R.; Stables, K.; Patterson, J.; Wheeler, A.
Sup: Kelly, A.
Inst: London University, Goldsmiths' College, Faculty of Education, Lewisham Way, New Cross, London SE14 6NW, United Kingdom.
Fin: School Examinations and Assessment Council.
achievement; assessment; craft; technology
rendement; appréciation; artisanat; technologie
PROJECT DESCRIPTION
   The Assessment of Performance Unit was established in 1975 with the prime task of surveying and monitoring levels of achievement in schools.

Progressively the concern became to understand why pupils performed in the ways they did; teasing out learning blocks and helping teachers to enhance the learning of their pupils.

The Design and Technology Project set out to: (a) identify those aspects of an understanding of both design and technology most likely to be reflected in primary and secondary schools; (b) to consider when and where abilities in design and technology appear in the school curriculum; (c) to suggest how those aspects of pupils' development might be assessed; (d) develop a test of capability; (e) administer this test to 2% of a 15 year old cohort in England, Wales and Northern Ireland (1988-1989); and (f) analyse data and report on strengths/weaknesses in relation to a variety of background variables.

The sample used was 10,000 - 2% of all 15 year old pupils from schools throughout the United Kingdom. A pilot survey (1987-1988) was made using short term (90 minute) pencil/paper activities to establish the viability of the test design and the form of the main survey activities. Information was gathered from schools on curriculum matters. The main survey (1988-1989) consisted of: case records of extended activity (on GCSE project); short term (90 minute) pencil/paper activities; extended half day modelling activities involving real materials and allowing collaboration between pupils; and collection of data on schools and pupils.

Publ: *Learning through design and technology: the APU model*, Leaflet No 1, School Examination and Assessment Council, 1990.
The assessment of performance in design and technology: final report, School Examination and Assessment Council, 1991.

12366   Baseline assessment at age 4+.

GBR   1993
Research Date(s): 1991-1994
Strand, S.
Inst: London Borough of Wandsworth, Education Department, Professional Centre, Franciscan Road, Tooting, London SW17 8HE, United Kingdom.
Fin: Wandsworth Local Education Authority.
initial assessment; entry to school; school entry age; child development; problem child
évaluation initiale; entrée à l'école; âge d'entrée à l'école; développement de l'enfant; enfant perturbé
PROJECT DESCRIPTION

Wandsworth LEA (local education authority) is instigating a baseline assessment for every pupil starting full-time education in a reception class in a Wandsworth school. The aims of the assessment are: (i) to provide structured materials to support teachers in identifying children with problems in their first term of school; (ii) to identify children for further diagnostic assessment or referral to LEA support agencies (e.g. Integrated Support Service, Educational Psychology Service); (iii) to act as a baseline against which to evaluate the child's progress at the end of National Curriculum Key Stage 1.

Baseline will consist of two elements: (i) a teacher-completed checklist giving detailed background information on the child, and an assessment of the child's social and emotional development, motor skills, attainment in oral language, early reading and writing, mathematics and science; (ii) a shortened form of the Linguistic Awareness for Reading Readiness (LARR) Test. Both assessments will be completed by the classroom teacher during the course of the child's first term in school.

A borough-wide pilot involving over 2,000 pupils in 63 schools started in Autumn term 1992. The LEA will evaluate the reliability and concurrent validity of baseline in an interim report in 1993. This will include investigating the relationship between pupil attainment and gender, home language/s, ethnic group, family size, birth order and age (summer born). The final report, evaluating the predictive validity of baseline, will be compiled when the cohort have completed their Key Stage 1 assessment in 1994.

Publ: Copies of Baseline materials are available from the researcher.

12367   Begeleiding van doctoraatsstudenten positieve wetenschappen in België en andere Europese landen. (Supervision of science research students in Belgium and other European countries.)

BEL   1994
Research Date(s): 1988-1989
Brown, G.; et al.
Sup: De Jaegere, S.
Inst: Laboratorium Scheikunde (Laboratory of Chemistry), Celestijnenlaan 200F, 3030 Leuven (Heverlee), Belgium.
Katholieke Universiteit Leuven (Catholic University of Leuven), Naamsestraat 22, 3000 Leuven, Belgium
Fin: Departement Onderwijs, Fonds voor Kollektief en Fundamenteel Onderzoek op Ministerieel Initiatief.
doctorate; biology; physics; chemistry; guidance; comparative research; motivation; duration of studies
doctorat; biologie; physique; chimie; orientation; recherche comparative; motivation; durée des études
PROJECT DESCRIPTION

Aims: This international study concerns a particular, important part of higher education: PhD training in science. An examination is conducted of

the circumstances under which research training takes place in Europe, more specifically in Belgium, the United Kingdom, Germany and the Netherlands. Each of these four countries is represented by two universities.

Methods: In order to obtain information on PhD research, two questionnaires, one for supervisors and one for PhD students, were designed in five languages. The study focused on chemistry, biology and physics. 1135 persons (790 students and 345 supervisors) completed the questionnaire.

Results: Supervisors' and PhD students' opinions on the main characteristics of PhD training, PhD supervision and PhD programmes form the bulk of the results of the study. The data were analysed by computer with the help of the Statistical Analysis System (SAS). The analysis shows similarities and differences regarding PhD training and supervision between countries, universities, subjects, supervisors, students, and sexes. The final report tries to answer the following questions: (1) Who enters a PhD programme and why? (2) How is supervision generally carried out, and what factors are important in the supervision process? (3) Are there any difficulties or weaknesses that are experienced by most postgraduate students? (4) How long does it take to complete a PhD?.

Publ: Brown, G.; De Jaegere, S.; Lapiere, D. et al. *Supervision of science research students: views of science supervisors and science research students on methods and attitudes in Belgium, The United Kingdom, Germany and The Netherlands.* Leuven: KU Leuven, 1991, 114p.

12368   Beschrijvende analyses VOCL leerjaar 3. (Descriptive analyses of the "VOCL" cohort: year three.)

NLD   1994
Research Date(s): 1992-1993
Werf, M.P.C. van der; Driessen, G.W.J.M.
Inst: Instituut voor Toegepaste Sociale wetenschappen (ITS) (Institute for Applied Social Sciences), P.O. Box 9048, 6500 KJ Nijmegen, Netherlands; RION Instituut voor Onderwijsonderzoek (RION Institute for Educational Research), P.O. Box 1286, 9701 BG Groningen, Netherlands.
Katholieke Universiteit Nijmegen (Catholic University of Nijmegen), P.O. Box 9102, 6500 HC Nijmegen, Netherlands; Rijksuniversiteit Groningen (State University of Groningen), P.O. Box 72, 9700 AB Groningen, Netherlands
Fin: SVO het Instituut voor Onderzoek van het Onderwijs.
achievement; school career; educational policy; evaluation; quality of education; lower secondary
rendement; cursus scolaire; politique de l'éducation; évaluation; qualité de l'éducation; secondaire premier cycle
PROJECT DESCRIPTION

Background: As part of the evaluation of the Educational Priority Policy (OVB) and the planned evaluation of the future national core curriculum for lower secondary schools (which will be introduced in August 1993) a cohort study was started in the school year 1989/1990, involving the participation of 381 secondary schools, including 73 educational priority area schools. The currently available data set of this cohort study covers the first three years of secondary school. As a sequel to the analyses that have been performed on the data concerning the first secondary school year, additional analyses will be carried out.

Aim: To assess the quality of education and the pupils' achievement levels from the perspective of the objectives of the national core curriculum for lower secondary schools and the Educational Priority Policy (OVB).

Design: The available data will be analysed for differences between schools. The analyses will be performed at school, classroom and pupil level. Relationships between school, classroom and pupil characteristics will be examined. Prior to the analysis of pupils' achievement levels and careers, a dropout analysis will be carried out on the data concerning the school years 1990/1991 and 1991/1992.

12369   Bildungsverlaeufe im Jugendalter. (Educational careers in youth.)

DEU   1993
Research Date(s): 1991-1992
Schnabel, K.
Sup: Roeder, P.
Inst: Max-Planck-Institut fuer Bildungsforschung, Lentzeallee 94, D-1000 Berlin 33.
school career; comparative achievement; youth; Germany - Federal Republic; German DR; vocational training; performance; achievement motivation
cursus scolaire; rendement comparé; jeunesse; Allemagne RFA; Allemagne RDA; formation professionnelle; performance; motivation d'accomplissement
PROJECT DESCRIPTION

Inhalt: Schulische Bildungsverlaeufe und ihre Determinanten im Vergleich alte/ neue Bundeslaender; internationale Leistungsvergleiche im Sekundarschulbereich; Schulmotivationsentwicklung im Jugendalter.

Vorgehensweise: Untersuchungsdesign: Querschnittserhebung; Panel.

Datengewinnung: Standardisiertes Interview (Stichprobe: 8000; SchuelerInnen 7. Schuljahr; Auswahlverfahren: Zufall. Stichprobe: 8000; SchuelerInnen 7. Schuljahr; Auswahlverfahren: Quota). Primaererhebung:

Feldarbeit von Mitarbeitern des Projektes durchgefuehrt; Sekundaeranalyse bereits vorhandener maschinenlesbarer Datensaetze.

Auswertung: Mehrebenenanalyse. Datenaufbereitung: Aggregierung oder Disaggregierung.

12370 Central Support Unit: the Assessment of Achievement Programme.
GBR 1993
Research Date(s): 1987-1994
Thorpe, G.; Pollard, J.; Whitcombe, D.; Bichard, A.
Inst: Scottish Council for Research in Education, 15 St John Street, Edinburgh EH8 8JR, United Kingdom.
Fin: Scottish Office Education Department.
assessment; achievement; achievement measurement; educational research
appréciation; rendement; mesure du rendement; recherche en éducation
PROJECT DESCRIPTION
The Central Support Unit (CSU) has been funded by the Scottish Office Education Department to provide the technical support and infra-structure for its Assessment of Achievement Programme (AAP). The AAP is a systematic programme, designed to monitor pupil attainment. Individual teams with knowledge and expertise in the particular subject under study are established to have responsibility for the content-specific part of the projects.

The CSU provides technical support to all projects across the subject spectrum. This support includes: advice on experimental design; sampling; liaison with schools; collation, distribution and collection of test materials; computing the desired analyses and advising on the statistics of these. Part of the general support of the AAP will incorporate the development and continuous updating of a set of guidelines for AAP projects. These guidelines will assist the project teams in the efficient design of their assessment programmes, will offer a repertoire of analytic approaches designed to enable the teams to extract different kinds of information from their data, and will make practical suggestions which will help to overcome anticipated difficulties.

Publ: *Noticeboard* - a newsletter for schools and Feedback booklets covering the 1989 science and 1990 mathematics surveys are available from the Scottish Council for Research in Education.

12371 Cognitive assessment of maladjusted children.
GBR 1993
Research Date(s): 1985-1991
Pont, H.
Sup: Shepherd, J.
Inst: Aberdeen University, Department of Psychology, Taylor Building, King's College, Aberdeen AB9 2UB, United Kingdom.
cognitive test; cognitive development; maladjustment; assessment; problem child; social learning
test cognitif; développement cognitif; inadaptation; appréciation; enfant perturbé; apprentissage social
PROJECT DESCRIPTION
A cognitive social learning approach to assessment is based on the belief that social behaviour is determined by the individual's expectations and beliefs about a situation, and is under the control of mediating processes such as self-control or reflective ability. The need therefore is to focus on what a person constructs in specific situations rather than to infer general explanatory traits as merely to describe behaviour. Within the terms of the above approach several areas of cognitive social functioning were identified as being of particular significance in the study of behaviourally and/or emotionally disturbed children, e.g. self-perception, perception of problem behaviour, perception of others and inter-personal problem-solving skills.

The present study includes an in-depth assessment of 40 children in a residential special school for emotionally/behaviourally disturbed children in the above areas together with a full professional and current behaviour assessment. Performance of the target group is compared with normal controls and a group of problem behaviour controls from a List D setting to identify differences in functioning.

12372 Consortium for assessment and testing in schools - English key stage 3.
GBR 1993
Research Date(s): 1989-1992
Furlong, J.
Inst: London University, Institute of Education, Consortium for Assessment and Testing in Schools, 20 Bedford Way, London WC1H OAL, United Kingdom.
Fin: School Examinations and Assessment Council.
assessment; achievement test; English language; lower secondary; test construction
appréciation; test de rendement; langue anglaise; secondaire premier cycle; construction de tests
PROJECT DESCRIPTION
The Consortium for Assessment and Testing in Schools (CATS) was formed in January 1989 to develop standard assessment tasks for the National Curriculum at key stage 1. The Consortium comprises the Insti-

tute, the University of London Examinations and Assessment Council and Hodder & Stoughton Publishers. To develop standard assessment tasks for pupils at the end of key stage 3 (age 14), the Consortium was joined by two other schools of the University: Goldsmiths' College and King's College. The assessments enable teachers, students and parents to know whether the attainment targets specified for the subjects of the National Curriculum have now been met.

12373 Course assessment and its role in the learning process.
GBR 1993
Research Date(s): 1988-1991
Cotton, R.; McDowell, L.
Inst: University of Central Lancashire, Corporation Street, Preston PR1 2TQ, United Kingdom; University of Northumbria at Newcastle, The Educational Development Service, Ellison Building, Ellison Place, Newcastle upon Tyne NE1 8ST, United Kingdom.
Fin: Council for National Academic Awards.
continuous assessment; assessment; learning process; learning strategy; higher education
contrôle continu; appréciation; apprentissage; stratégie d'apprentissage; enseignement supérieur
PROJECT DESCRIPTION
Learning styles and perceptions of the learning environment were investigated for the Higher National Diploma in Science (Applied Biology) students at Lancashire Polytechnic using a previously published questionnaire. The questionnaire was further developed to assess the relative merit of a variety of course work assessments in promoting learning. This was supported by student interviews. It was concluded that a diversity of assessment types is required to maximise learning from continual assessment.

Publ: Cotton, R. & McDowell, L. Student experiences of course assessment. In: Farmer, B.; Eastcott, D. & Lantz, B. *Making learning systems work - aspects of educational and training technology*, Vol 23, London: Kogan-Page, 1990.
McDowell, L. Course assessment and its role in the learning process. In: McDowell, L. (ed.). *Course evaluation: using students' experiences of learning and teaching.* Newcastle Polytechnic: The Educational Development Service, 1991.

12374 De invloed van effectief basisonderwijs op schoolloopbanen in het voortgezet onderwijs - fase II. (The influence of effective primary education on school careers in secondary education - phase II.)
NLD 1994
Research Date(s): 1992-1993
Hoeven-van Doornum, A.A. van der.
Sup: Jungbluth, P.
Inst: Instituut voor Toegepaste Sociale wetenschappen (ITS) (Institute for Applied Social Sciences), P.O. Box 9048, 6500 KJ Nijmegen, Netherlands. Katholieke Universiteit Nijmegen (Catholic University of Nijmegen), P.O. Box 9102, 6500 HC Nijmegen, Netherlands
Fin: SVO het Instituut voor Onderzoek van het Onderwijs.
school career; pupil; primary school; secondary school; performance; teacher role; expectancy
cursus scolaire; élève; école primaire; école secondaire; performance; rôle de l'enseignant; attente
PROJECT DESCRIPTION
Background: Depending on their personal judgment of pupils' abilities, teachers set higher-level or lower-level goals for their pupils. Pupils have a better chance of a successful school career if teacher expectations and target levels are high. Systematic differences in primary heads' recommendations regarding the most suitable type of secondary school lead to differential careers at different levels of secondary education. Earlier research has found differences in effectiveness between primary schools. This follow-up study examines the durability of school effectiveness.

Aim: To examine the relevance of measurable differences in effectiveness between primary schools for pupils' educational opportunities at the secondary level.

Design: The study used the same pupils who participated in the previous study on primary education and who have now moved on to secondary school. These pupils (n = 500 or over) will be asked about their careers in secondary school. Information on school characteristics will be obtained from maximally 200 schools. These data will be added to the existing data set resulting from the primary school study.

12375 Developing a portfolio of personal development.
GBR 1993
Research Date(s): 1990-1993
Saunders, D.
Inst: Glamorgan University, Enterprise Unit, Pontypridd, Mid Glamorgan CF37 1DL, United Kingdom.
Fin: Department of Employment.
student record; self-evaluation; achievement
dossier académique; auto-évaluation; rendement
PROJECT DESCRIPTION

A cross-section of students is engaged in a longitudinal study involving self-assessment of study and transferable skills. Academic and personal achievement are also recorded, and the final stage of the project involves the preparation of one-page profile sheets for use with curriculum vitae.

Publ: Saunders, D. The assessment of prior experiential learning. In: *Simulation Games for Learning*, Vol 20, No 1/1990, pp. 76-85.
Saunders, D. Profiling in higher education. In: *Journal of the National Association for Staff Development*, No 26/1992, pp. 51-57.

12376   Developing formative teacher assessment - as an example of the management of educational innovations.
GBR   1993
Research Date(s): 1984-1991
Harrison, I.
Sup: Christie, T.
Inst: Manchester University, School of Education, Centre for Formative Assessment Studies, Oxford Road, Manchester M13 9PL, United Kingdom.
assessment; teacher; further education of teachers; formative evaluation
appréciation; enseignant; perfectionnement des enseignants; évaluation formative
PROJECT DESCRIPTION
The national assessment system has been designed to serve several functions. It will be formative, summative, evaluative, informative, and helpful in promoting teachers' professional development. The basic proposition of this thesis, (and the major forms of the research) is that strategies to manage the required changes in teachers' assessment practices need to be developed. The 'change' literature, especially that relating to school effectiveness, identifies monitoring pupil progress as one characteristic of effective primary school organisation. However, further analysis of this body of literature reveals the apparent dichotomy between school effectiveness and improvement movements - the critical issue being the focus upon schools as organisations, or upon individuals. The empirical studies address this issue in order to provide evidence to support the development of strategies to promote teachers' formative assessment practice.

12377   The development of a computer-based system for records of achievement in science.
GBR   1993
Research Date(s): 1990-1991
McGarvey, B.; McMahon, H.; Creighton, N.
Inst: Ulster University, Department of Inservice Education, Cromore Road, Coleraine, County Londonderry BT52 1SA, United Kingdom.
assessment; computer; science education; student record
appréciation; ordinateur; éducation scientifique; dossier académique
PROJECT DESCRIPTION
A computer-based records of achievement system for the Northern Ireland Curriculum Key Stage 3 in Science has been developed, using the Hypercard software of the Apple Macintosh microcomputer. Records are held in the language of the classroom materials and are updated as and when necessary. The system includes the facility to translate records into AT statements of attainment and to display the summary record as a grid or histogram-type display. Trials of the system took place in schools, and an in-house operator manual has been produced.

12378   Development of Key Stage 1 Geography Standard Assessment Tasks.
GBR   1993
Research Date(s): 1991-1992
Boyle, W.; Davies, P.
Sup: Christie, T.
Inst: Manchester University, School of Education, Centre for Formative Assessment Studies, Oxford Road, Manchester M13 9PL, United Kingdom.
Fin: School Examinations and Assessment Council.
achievement test; assessment; geography; common core curriculum
test de rendement; appréciation; géographie; tronc commun
PROJECT DESCRIPTION
The Standard Assessment Tasks are to be developed as manageable for use by teachers and pupils, using resources normally available in primary schools. They are not extended curricular activities but used to provide valid and reliable assessments of pupils against the first four levels of attainment in each of the attainment targets for National Curriculum Geography. They will also enable teachers to identify pupils at the end of Key Stage 1 who are working towards level 1. Trialling of developmental Geography Task material will utilise Postgraduate Certificate of Education/B.Ed. students at three centres - Manchester University, Crewe and Alsager, Bangor Normal College - with more formalised Standard Assessment Tasks trialling in English and Welsh local education authorities during January, May and September 1992.

12379   Development of performance indicators for client satisfaction.
GBR   1993
Research Date(s): 1990-1992
Tymms, P.
Inst: Heriot-Watt University, Moray House Institute of Education, Holyrood Road, Edinburgh EH8 8AQ, United Kingdom.
performance; evaluation; satisfaction
performance; évaluation; satisfaction
PROJECT DESCRIPTION
The aims of the research are: (1) to develop instrument(s) for the regular monitoring of client satisfaction; and (2) consider the evaluation of teaching and learning.

12380   Development of Standard Assessment Tasks at the end of Key Stage 3 in the National Curriculum for English.
GBR   1993
Research Date(s): 1989-1992
Furlong, J.; Stubbs, M.
Inst: London University, Institute of Education, Department of English and Media Studies, 20 Bedford Way, London WC1H 0AL, United Kingdom.
Fin: School Examinations and Assessment Council.
assessment; achievement test; English language; test construction
appréciation; test de rendement; langue anglaise; construction de tests
PROJECT DESCRIPTION
The work requires the development of Standard Assessment Tasks for English. Standard Assessment Tasks will be constructed to include written and oral work, so that a pupil's performance can be set against any of the 10 levels associated with the National Curriculum attainment targets. Trialling in selected local education authorities will be carried out in 1989-1990, a pilot exercise on a broader sample in 1991, and a full scale unreported assessment in Summer 1992.

12381   Development of standard assessment tasks for pupils at the end of the first key stage of the National Curriculum.
GBR   1993
Research Date(s): 1989-1992
Sainsbury, M.; Christophers, U.; Ashby, J.; Clarke, J.
Sup: Whetton, C.
Inst: National Foundation for Educational Research, The Mere, Upton Park, Slough SL1 2DQ, United Kingdom.
Fin: School Examinations and Assessment Council.
assessment; primary education; achievement test; common core curriculum; further education of teachers
appréciation; enseignement primaire; test de rendement; tronc commun; perfectionnement des enseignants
PROJECT DESCRIPTION
A consortium consisting of NFER, Bishop Grosseteste College, NFER-Nelson and two local education authorities developed standard assessment tasks and associated INSET (Inservice Education and Training of Teachers) material. The standard assessment tasks provided valid, reliable assessments of attainment targets in mathematics, English (or Welsh) language and science, appropriate to seven year-olds. Issues such as the production of evidence for moderation, bias, special educational needs and the assessment of low and high achieving children were all addressed. INSET material was developed in order to ensure that national assessment and standard assessment tasks were fully understood. The project was extended to cover the production of standard assessment tasks for the first two years of full national assessment, 1991, 1992 and evaluations of its use in both these years.

12382   Development of standard assessment tasks in mathematics and science for pupils at the end of the first key stage of the National Curriculum for 1994-1996.
GBR   1993
Research Date(s): 1992-1995
Sainsbury, M.; Ashby, J.; Sizmur, S.; Hargreaves, E.; Evans, M.
Sup: Whetton, C.
Inst: National Foundation for Educational Research, The Mere, Upton Park, Slough SL1 2DQ, United Kingdom.
Fin: School Examinations and Assessment Council.
assessment; achievement test; common core curriculum; mathematics; science education
appréciation; test de rendement; tronc commun; mathématiques; éducation scientifique
PROJECT DESCRIPTION
A research team at the National Foundation for Educational Research (NFER) is developing standard assessment tasks in mathematics and science for pupils at the end of the first key stage of the National Curriculum. The tasks will provide valid, reliable assessments of attainment targets and be appropriate to seven-year-old children. Issues such as classroom manageability, comparability of judgements, bias and special educational needs will all be addressed. The tasks for each year will be monitored in operation and a commentary produced. The project will lead to the production of assessment materials to be used nationally in 1994, 1995 and 1996.

12383 Development of Standard Assessment Tasks in the core subjects for pupils at the end of the first Key Stage of the National Curriculum for 1993.
GBR 1993
Research Date(s): 1992
Sainsbury, M.; Ashby, J.; Sizmur, S.; Christophers, U.; Clarke, J.
Sup: Whetton, C.
Inst: National Foundation for Educational Research, The Mere, Upton Park, Slough SL1 2DQ, United Kingdom.
Fin: School Examinations and Assessment Council.
assessment; achievement test; test construction; common core curriculum
appréciation; test de rendement; construction de tests; tronc commun
PROJECT DESCRIPTION
A consortium led by the National Foundation for Educational Research (NFER) developed Standard Assessment Tasks to provide valid, reliable assessments of attainment targets in English (or Welsh), mathematics and science, appropriate to seven-year-olds. Issues such as classroom manage-ability, comparability of judgements, bias, special educational needs and low and high achieving children were all addressed. The project led to the production of Standard Assessment Tasks for use at Key Stage 1 in 1993, the third year of operation of National Curriculum assessment.

12384 Development of standard assessment tasks in Welsh for key stage 3 of the National Curriculum.
GBR 1993
Research Date(s): 1991-1993
Powell, R.; Lewis, G.; Jones, Ll.; Lewis, T.
Inst: National Foundation for Educational Research, Welsh Office, 39 St James Crescent, Abertawe, Swansea SA1 6DR, United Kingdom.
Fin: School Examinations and Assessment Council.
achievement test; assessment; common core curriculum; Welsh language
test de rendement; appréciation; tronc commun; langue galloise
PROJECT DESCRIPTION
This is an extension of the original contract for Welsh key stage 3 standard assessment tasks which ran from July 1989 to August 1991. The requirement is for the creation of standard assessment tasks to assess the range of attainment from Level 1 to Level 10 on both the Welsh and Welsh Second Language programmes contained in the Statutory Orders. Follow-ing pilots in 1991 and 1992 the first statutory assessment will be held in 1993. The standard assessment tasks comprise a long task for assess-ment of oracy and reading through oral response to be administrated in the classroom over three months, and written tests for assessment of writing and reading through written response.

12385 A diagnostic resource for technology.
GBR 1993
Research Date(s): 1989-1991
Black, H.; Turner, E.; Devine, M.; Schlapp, U.
Inst: Scottish Council for Research in Education, 15 St John Street, Edin-burgh EH8 8JR, United Kingdom.
Fin: Training, Enterprise and Education Directorate.
assessment; diagnostic test; technology
appréciation; test de diagnostic; technologie
PROJECT DESCRIPTION
The outcome of the project was a diagnostic resource which can be used in classroom assessment by teachers of technology within a range of subject areas across the curriculum. The assessment instruments result from collaborative work with practising teachers and relate to central and fundamental aspects of technology learning. They are appropriate for use in standard grade courses, short courses, National Certificate modules and General Certificate of Secondary Education.
Publ: Turner, E.; Black, H. & Devine, M. *Technology in home economics.* Edinburgh: SCRE/SARSU, 1989.
Turner, E.; Black, H. & Devine, M. *Technology: an annotated bibliography.* Edinburgh: SCRE/SARSU, 1990.

12386 Effectief onderwijs voor allochtone leerlingen. (Effective instruction for ethnic minority pupils.)
NLD 1994
Research Date(s): 1992-1994
Werf, M.P.C. van der; Reezigt, G.J.
Inst: RION Instituut voor Onderwijsonderzoek (RION Institute for Educa-tional Research), P.O. Box 1286, 9701 BG Groningen, Netherlands.
Rijksuniversiteit Groningen (State University of Groningen), P.O. Box 72, 9700 AB Groningen, Netherlands
Fin: SVO het Instituut voor Onderzoek van het Onderwijs.
achievement; primary school; ethnic minority; immigrant; teaching quality; compensatory education
rendement; école primaire; minorité ethnique; immigrant; qualité de l'en-seignement; éducation compensatoire
PROJECT DESCRIPTION
Background: The achievement levels of immigrant pupils are remaining far behind those of Dutch pupils. This can in part be explained by unfavourable background characteristics, but the school also makes a difference. At some schools, the instruction provided to immigrant pupils is

more effective than at others. The concept of "effectiveness" includes "quality" and "compensatory capacity". Analyses performed on data col-lected from 700 primary schools as part of the evaluation of the Educa-tional Priority (OVB) show that qualitative differences between schools are related to the proportion of immigrant pupils in these schools. The propor-tion of immigrant pupils does not explain differences in compensatory capacity between schools. In order to establish whether "black" schools are "bad" schools, secondary analyses have been performed. It appears that some black schools are more effective than others.
Aim: To determine how effective and less effective black primary schools differ in terms of educational characteristics.
Design: A number of schools that have participated in the first two phases of the OVB evaluation will be selected on the basis of the language test scores of their eighth-year pupils (12-year-olds). Schools with extremely high or extremely low scores on quality and compensatory capacity will be selected. Only those schools from the first and second phase that fall in the same catagory (n=25) will be studied in depth. At these schools observations will be carried out in the sixth, seventh and eighth forms. Each teacher will be observed three times with regard to: classroom climate, class work, emphasis on cognitive objectives, subject matter orientation and reaction to incorrect language usage by immigrant pupils. School work plans will be analysed for minimum objectives and their evaluation, relations with immigrant parents and regulations concern-ing Dutch language instruction for immigrant pupils. Head teachers will be asked to what extent the school work plans are being executed in practice. Teachers will be interviewed about the textbooks they use, the subject matter they select from these books and the way they test pupils' mastery of the material dealt with in class.

12387 The effects of the introduction of the GCSE on the work of a group of mathematics teachers: an ethnographic study.
GBR 1993
Research Date(s): 1986-1991
Weller, B.
Sup: Brown, M.; Davies, B.
Inst: London University, King's College, Centre for Education Studies, Cornwall House Annexe, Waterloo Road, London SE1 3TY, United Kingdom.
examination system; mathematics
régime des examens; mathématiques
PROJECT DESCRIPTION
The thesis forms a study of the effect of public examinations on the teaching of mathematics, with a particular focus on the way developments in mathematics education have been advanced or hindered by the presence of the public examination system.
The research took the form of an ethnographic study of a mathematics department in a comprehensive upper school (13-18 year old pupils) over a period of four years. The department was observed closely during this period as the General Certificate of Secondary Education (GCSE) examina-tion in mathematics was introduced.
The thesis makes a contribution to knowledge on the way departments function in secondary schools, the effect of external constraints on the work of teachers in classrooms, and on the whole process of teacher development in general.

12388 Erfolg des Studiums - Universitaet-Gesamthochschule Siegen. (Success at university: Siegen comprehensive university.)
DEU 1993
Research Date(s): 1991-1992
Menck, P.
Inst: Universitaet-Gesamthochschule Siegen, FB 02 Erziehungswissen-schaft, Psychologie, Sportwissenschaft, Fach Erziehungswissenschaft, LS Erziehungswissenschaft, Adolf-Reichwein-Strasse 2, D-5900 Siegen 21.
university studies; statistics; input-output analysis; success; university
études universitaires; statistique; analyse input-output; réussite; université
PROJECT DESCRIPTION
Inhalt: Nach einem einfachen Input-Output-Modell wird der Ausbildung-serfolg der Universitaet-Gesamthochschule Siegen fuer eine Stichprobe von Faellen und Jahrgaengen anhand der Daten der Hochschulstatistik ueber-prueft. Die Ausbildung gilt als erfolgreich, wenn innerhalb eines bestimmten Zeitrahmens ein bestimmter Prozentsatz einer Kohorte ein Examen abgelegt bzw. die Universitaet mit einem Examen verlassen hat.
Untersuchter Zeitraum: 1980-1991.
Vorgehensweise: Input (Studienanfaenger) - Output (Examinierte) - Modell der Ausbildungsleistung der Universitaet. Untersuchungsdesign: Panel.
Datengewinnung: Hochschulstatistik (Stichprobe: ca. 1500; Studienanfaenger in ausgewaehlten Studiengaengen einer Stichprobe von Semestern zwischen WS 80/81 und WS 80/85; Auswahlverfahren: Quota). Sekundaeranalyse bereits vorhandener maschinenlesbarer Datensaetze.
Auswertung: Deskription; Kontingenzstatistik. Datenaufbereitung: Verlaufsdaten (event history data).

12389 Evaluare formativă si sumativă: teste de cunostinte; bancă de teste. (Formative and summative evaluation: class tests; database of tests.)
ROM 1994
Research Date(s): 1992-1995
Novak, Cornelia; Toroiman, Emil; Mihail, Roxana; Bortă, Elena; Lisievici, Petru; Jigău, Mihaela; Popescu, Leonica.
Sup: Stoica, Adrian.
Inst: Institutul de Stiinte ale Educatiei (Institute for Educational Sciences), str. Stirbei Vodă 37, 70732 Bucharest, Romania.
Ministerul Învătământului (Ministry of Education), str. General Berthelot 28-30, Bucharest, Romania
continuous assessment; formative evaluation; summative evaluation; test; secondary education; test construction
contrôle continu; évaluation formative; évaluation sommative; test; enseignement secondaire; construction de tests
PROJECT DESCRIPTION
Background: The development of new curricula and, implicitly, of new assessment strategies are two of the major objectives of the educational reforms taking place in Romania. Assessment, regarded as part of the teaching-learning process, should give teachers, pupils and parents information that enables them to make a sound judgement of the pupil's achievement. National tests fulfill a complementary role in the assessment strategy in that they supply additional information on the results attained by pupils in different subjects.
Aims: To establish coherence, both in concept and in practice, in the way in which pupils' progress is assessed nationwide.
Design: The project has three stages that are closely interconnected. The first stage will define the methodology for formative and summative evaluation and will result in teacher guidelines for assessment in school. The second stage will be concerned with the elaboration of evaluation instruments, i.e. class tests for the fifth and ninth years for the following subjects: mathematics, physics, Romanian language and literature and English as a foreign language. The third stage will be concerned with storing these tests in a database.

12390 Evaluarea sistemului educational: indicatori si instrumente pentru evaluarea scolară. (Evaluation of the educational system: indicators and instruments for school evaluation.)
ROM 1994
Research Date(s): 1992-1995
Novak, Cornelia; Gheorghe, Adriana; Sandor, Maria.
Sup: Jigău, Mihaela.
Inst: Institutul de Stiinte ale Educatiei (Institute for Educational Sciences), str. Stirbei Vodă 37, 70732 Bucharest, Romania.
Ministerul Învătământului (Ministry of Education), str. General Berthelot 28-30, Bucharest, Romania
evaluation; teacher appraisal; education system; parent-school relation; school-community relation; school; family environment
évaluation; évaluation sur l'enseignant; système d'enseignement; relation parents-école; relation école-collectivité; école; milieu familial
PROJECT DESCRIPTION
Background: The project is based on the view that pupil achievement is not only influenced by curricula, textbooks, teaching methods, etc., but also by other factors, such as their intellectual level, health, family environment, school equipment and facilities, etc. Information on these factors is necessary for assessing pupils' progress. Within the framework of educational reforms that are now taking place in Romania, a national system of indicators will be developed which will include these factors. One of the main tasks in this context is the design and validation of appropriate instruments to evaluate these factors.
Aims: To elaborate an evaluation method for schools and the education system on the basis of a coherent system of indicators; to elaborate instruments that will assist decision-makers in taking decisions concerning educational policy.
Design: The first stage consists of the elaboration of a coherent and reliable system of indicators that represents, both in quantitative and in qualitative terms, the school and the education system in relation to pupils' socio-cultural, economic and family environments. The second stage concerns the elaboration of methods to (1) expand and maintain this system of educational indicators and to (2) evaluate schools and the education system on the basis of this information. The last stage will be concerned with the development of some instruments which, taking into account the results of the evaluations, will help decision-makers to devise or adjust educational policies.

12391 L'évaluation des connaissances par expert.
FRA 1993
Research Date(s): 1991-
Caverni, Jean-Paul; Péris, Jean-Luc.
Inst: Université d'Aix-Marseille I, UFR Psychologie Sciences de l'éducation, CNRS URA/182, Centre de recherche en psychologie cognitive, 29 av. Robert Schuman, 13621 Aix-en-Provence, France.

marking; docimology; examiner; skill; level of qualification; knowledge; evaluation
notation; docimologie; examinateur; compétence; niveau de qualification; connaissance; évaluation
PROJECT DESCRIPTION
Objectifs: Toute tâche d'évaluation de connaissances se résoud par la formulation d'un énoncé à propos d'un objet. La fonction de l'énoncé est de qualifier l'objet par rapport à un corps de connaissances à maîtriser. On s'intéresse ici au cas où la formulation de l'énoncé résulte de l'activité d'un opérateur humain expert dans l'enseignement d'un corps de connaissances reconnu comme tel par un diplôme et une pratique. L'objectif des recherches est de rendre compte des opérations mentales par lesquelles un expert humain élabore l'évaluation explicitée au terme de la tâche. La tâche particulière support aux travaux actuellement conduits est la notation (évaluation numérique) de productions scolaires (en l'occurence rédactions en langue maternelle). Un modèle de l'évaluation des connaissances est élaboré et les travaux expérimentaux mis en oeuvre sont destinés à sa validation.
Publ: Caverni, Jean-Paul & Péris, Jean Luc. Cognitive reality of multidimensional information processing in knowledge assessment by experts. In: *European Journal of Psychology of Education*, Juin 1992, Vol. 7, 2, pp. 109-122.

12392 Evaluation et pilotage de formations.
FRA 1993
Research Date(s): 1990-
Lecointe, Michel; Rebinguet, Michel.
Inst: Université de Pau, Centre universitaire de recherche, Laboratoire de didactique et communication pédagogique, SUFFO, Rue Jules Ferry, 64000 Pau, France.
Fin: Fonds interministériel pour la modernisation.
inspection; teacher appraisal; training of trainers
inspection; évaluation sur l'enseignant; formation des formateurs
PROJECT DESCRIPTION
Objectifs: (1) Analyse critique d'opérations d'évaluation (inspections, audit, effets de terrain); (2) mise au point de méthodologie d'action et d'analyse.
Méthodologie: (1) Typologie et effets des évaluations de formation; (2) l'évaluation dans le processus de construction des formations; (3) contribution à une théorie générale de l'évaluation comme production de sens et attribution de valeur.
Publ: Lecointe, Michel & Rebinguet, Michel. *L'audit de l'établissement scolaire.* Ed. des Organisations, 1990, 200p.

12393 The evaluation of school-initiated INSET in selected junior schools: teacher and headteacher perspectives.
GBR 1993
Research Date(s): 1989-1992
Hilliam, S.
Sup: Sutton, J.
Inst: Leicester University, School of Education, University Road, Leicester LE1 7RH, United Kingdom.
Fin: Leeds City Council.
evaluation; further education of teachers; in-service training; primary education; teacher; head teacher
évaluation; perfectionnement des enseignants; formation en cours d'emploi; enseignement primaire; enseignant; chef d'établissement
PROJECT DESCRIPTION
Although much has been written in general terms about evaluation, very little is known about teachers' concepts of inservice teacher education (INSET) evaluation. Particularly in view of the increasing and direct involvement of headteachers and teachers in the management and delivery of INSET, research into this area is of considerable significance.
This research will examine the concepts of evaluation of junior school headteachers and teachers and relate these findings to school-initiated INSET and teacher development. Two groups of fifteen schools will be randomly selected in two local education authorities (North Yorkshire and Leeds). The design of the research involves questionnaires to the headteacher and two colleagues plus interviews with the headteacher and a member of staff. Observations and documentation will be incorporated in the triangulation of the findings.

12394 Evaluation of teacher appraisal in Havering.
GBR 1993
Research Date(s): 1992-1993
McLaughlin, C.
Inst: Cambridge University, Institute of Education, Shaftesbury Road, Cambridge CB2 2BX, United Kingdom.
Fin: Havering Borough Council.
teacher appraisal; teacher; head teacher
évaluation sur l'enseignant; enseignant; chef d'établissement
PROJECT DESCRIPTION
The project aims to evaluate the training and implementation of teacher appraisal in a London Borough. The schools in the Borough were divided into two cohorts and the evaluation covers both cohorts. Headteacher

appraisal is also being evaluated. The methods used were as follows: questionnaires to all participants and then interviews in the sample schools. In Cohort 2 volunteers also kept diaries of the process. In Cohort 1 the interviewed sample was four out of a total of 20 primary schools, one special school and two out of a total of four secondary schools. The same sample was in Cohort 2.

12395 Evaluation of the programme of appraisal of teaching in the veterinary faculty at Liverpool University.
GBR   1993
Research Date(s): 1988-1991
Taylor, I.
Sup: Harlen, W.; Derricott, R.
Inst: Liverpool University, Department of Education, PO Box 147, Liverpool L69 3BX, United Kingdom.
Fin: Liverpool University; Universities Funding Council.
evaluation; university faculty; teaching
évaluation; faculté universitaire; enseignement
PROJECT DESCRIPTION
    A programme for evaluating teaching in the Faculty of Veterinary Science at Liverpool University was introduced in 1988. Two members of the Department of Education submitted a proposal to evaluate this innovation. The evaluation of the appraisal of teaching focuses on both the processes and the products of appraisal. Data are collected about the operation of teaching appraisal from students, academic staff and from 'official peers' who observe teaching.

12396 Evaluation of the Southampton University Pilot Appraisal Scheme.
GBR   1993
Research Date(s): 1991
Clift, P.; Turner, G.
Inst: Southampton University, Faculty of Educational Studies, Assessment and Evaluation Unit, Highfield, Southampton SO9 5NH, United Kingdom.
teacher appraisal; university
évaluation sur l'enseignant; université
PROJECT DESCRIPTION
    The aim of the project was to provide information to Southampton University Administration about the working of the pilot scheme for staff appraisal. The methods used were: (i) participant observation of training days; (ii) semi-structured interviews with a random sample drawn from departments involved; and (iii) questionnaires to all staff in the departments involved.
    The conclusions drawn were: (i) staff perceptions of appraisal and of the University's scheme were uncritical, but half-hearted; (ii) that the professional proximity of the appraisers to the appraisees resulted in little that was new being revealed; (iii) that there had been a lack of tangible and valued outcome; (iv) that the relationship between appraisal and pay and promotion needed urgently to be addressed; (v) that a 'University ethos' of collegial casualness had pervaded the whole exercise; (vi) that the objectives of appraisal were diverse and unclear. A list of ten recommendations for the future was put forward.
Publ: Clift, P. & Turner, G. *University of Southampton Pilot Appraisal Scheme: an evalution.* Assessment & Evaluation Unit, School of Education, University of Southampton, 1991 (mimeo).

12397 Examinations research programme.
GBR   1993
Research Date(s): 1983-
Delap, M.; Eason, S.; Macdonald, H.; Taylor, M.
Sup: Cresswell, M.
Inst: Associated Examining Board, Stag Hill House, Guildford, Surrey GU2 5XJ, United Kingdom.
examination; evaluation; common core curriculum; marking; standard
examen; évaluation; tronc commun; notation; norme
PROJECT DESCRIPTION
    The research and statistics group carries out a continuing programme of research into fundamental problems associated with educational measurement together with work on specific examinations. Particular areas of study pursued in 1992 and 1993 are: grading processes; reliability of moderation; gender differences; differentiated assessment; aggregation. The research group is also involved in development work associated with the assessment of the National Curriculum. A further aspect of the work involves collaborative studies with the other United Kingdom Examining Boards and Groups to ensure that all the General Certificate of Secondary Education (GCSE) and General Certificate of Education (GCE) examinations are set, marked and graded to comparable standards.
Publ: Good, F.J. & Cresswell, M.J. Can teachers enter candidates appropriately for examinations involving differentiated papers? In: *Educational Studies*, Vol 14, No 3/1988, pp. 289-297.
Good, F.J. & Cresswell, M.J. *Differentiated assessment: grading and related issues.* London: Secondary Examinations Council, 1988.
Good, F.J. & Cresswell, M.J. *Grading the GCSE.* London: Secondary Examinations Council, 1988.

Good, F.J. & Cresswell, M.J. Placing candidates who take differentiated papers on a common grade scale. In: *Educational Research*, Vol 30, No 3/1988, pp. 177-189.
Good, F.J. Setting common examination papers that differentiate. In: *Educational Studies*, Vol 15, No 1/1989, pp. 67-82.

12398 Factors relating to achievement of high school students in Kuching City, Malaysia.
GBR   1993
Research Date(s): 1988-1991
Ridzuan, A.
Sup: Wilkinson, J.
Inst: Hull University, School of Education, Cottingham Road, Hull HU6 7RX, United Kingdom.
Fin: Government of Malaysia.
achievement; learning conditions; learning strategy; secondary education; Malaysia
rendement; conditions d'apprentissage; stratégie d'apprentissage; enseignement secondaire; Malaisie
PROJECT DESCRIPTION
    This study aims to contribute towards a greater understanding of high school students' learning, with a view to determining remedial action to be taken to upgrade academic achievement, improving learning and teaching strategies and environment, and assisting in national curriculum development. The research used survey and demographic questionnaire techniques, looking at a sample study of 925 seventeen-year old lower sixth formers in the eight high schools of Kuching City, Sarawak, Malaysia. The data were analysed using t-tests, stepwise regression and correlation-statistical techniques to establish what correlation could be found between the educational achievements (SPM results) of the pupils in those groupings and the learning approaches, learning styles, school motivation and psychological attitudes (e.g. optimism, locus of control).
    It was found that there were considerable correlations between predictors and the overall achievement in each of the classification groups. However, the best predictors of achievement varied significantly from group to group. Achievement in individual subjects of the curriculum was also studied in relation to aspects of the teaching-learning environment, students' attitudes and demographic factors. This too provided evidence of significant correlations between achievement and certain factors for each discipline, but a wide range of variation between the predictors for achievement in different disciplines.
    On the basis of conclusions drawn from the analysis of the data, recommendations are made for remedial actions and strategic planning to be undertaken to improve students' achievement and enhance the institutional teaching-learning environment. Scope for further research comprising longitudinal studies, wider samples, and different methodologies is indicated, which could lead to a better understanding of high school students' learning in this developing Third World country.

12399 Formative assessments of reading.
GBR   1993
Research Date(s): 1990-1992
Owen, P.
Sup: Christie, T.
Inst: Manchester University, School of Education, Centre for Formative Assessment Studies, Oxford Road, Manchester M13 9PL, United Kingdom.
Fin: Leeds Local Education Authority.
formative evaluation; reading; further education of teachers; assessment
évaluation formative; lecture; perfectionnement des enseignants; appréciation
PROJECT DESCRIPTION
    The aim of this research is to develop procedures for the implementation of formative assessments of reading in the classroom and to design and evaluate the effectiveness of Inservice Education and Training (INSET) provision for monitoring reading standards. A literacy audit is made to: (i) describe the print environment to which children in Years 1-6 are exposed; and (ii) establish the degree of teachers' awareness of text types and 'readability' levels. This is followed by a survey of the range and type of reading purposes provided for children to inform current practice in relation to task setting.
    The results of the first phase are: (1) the beginnings of an acquisitions policy for schools; (2) an experimental set of guidelines for text selection; (3) an outline INSET programme for local education authority (LEA) intervention.
    The second phase of the research involves the development of internal (school) and external (LEA) procedures for monitoring reading performance. This involves the moderation of text selection and task definition within and across schools and the standardisation of teachers' judgements of levels of achievement. The sample is 30 schools (infant, junior and middle) with 15 operating as a lead group and 15 as a follow-up group. Experience with the lead group is encapsulated in trial INSET materials/activities for the follow-up group. The outcome is a long-term rolling programme for LEA-based INSET on the teaching and assessment of reading.

12400 Hodnocení žáka a efektivity školní výuky. (Evaluation of pupils and the effectiveness of teaching.)
CSK 1994
Research Date(s): 1993-1995
Půlpán, Zdeněk; Tachovský, Jaroslav; Trojovský, Pavel; Kebza, Vladimír.
Sup: Bartošek, M.
Inst: Vysoká škola pedagogická (Teacher Training College), Nám. Svobody 301, 501 91 Hradec Králové, Czech Republic.
Ministerstvo školství, mládeže a tělovýchovy ČR (Ministry of Education, Youth and Physical Education), Karmelitská 7, 118 13 Praha 1, Czech Republic
evaluation; didactics; mathematics; achievement measurement; test; test construction; achievement test; primary education; lower secondary; teaching quality
évaluation; didactique; mathématiques; mesure du rendement; test; construction de tests; test de rendement; enseignement primaire; secondaire premier cycle; qualité de l'enseignement
PROJECT DESCRIPTION
The aim is to prepare the evaluation of the primary and lower secondary school project. The project is designed by the Department of Education of the Czech Republic. Computer software is being prepared and tested and a questionnaire is being drawn up.

Publ: Půlpán, Z. & Langer, S. Vícenásobná souvislost nominálních znaků odhadovaná pomocí Shannovy míry informace. In: *Sborník Pedagogické fakulty Masarykovy univerzity v Brně*, 122/1993, pp. 83-98.
Půlpán, Z. Testový výkon a úspěšnost. In: *Pedagogika*, 4/1992.
Půlpán, Z.; Kuřina, F. & Kebza, Vl. *O představivosti*. Praha: Academia, 1992.

12401 I apopsis ton ekpedeftikon protovathmias ekpedefsis gia tis epidrasis ke ta apotelesmata tis aksiologisis tous apo ton epitheoriti - diefthindi. (Teachers' opinions about the effects and the results of their assessment by the school inspector and the headmaster.)
CYP 1993
Research Date(s): 1991
Gleka, Demetra; Florou, Roula.
Inst: Pedagogiko Instituto (Pedagogical Institute), P.O. Box 512, Nicosia, Cyprus.
assessment; teacher appraisal; teacher; evaluation
appréciation; évaluation sur l'enseignant; enseignant; évaluation
PROJECT DESCRIPTION
Background and aims: The assessment of primary school teachers in Cyprus is carried out by the school head and the school inspector. This research study examined the teachers' opinions about the effects and results of this assessment.
Methods: The research population consisted of all the teachers at primary and government nursery schools in Nicosia during the school year 1990-1991. A sample of 374 teachers was randomly selected. From the 374 questionnaires that were distributed, 240 were returned and analysed on the SPSS system (response rate: 64.17%).
Results: The subjects were given the four assessment criteria as used by the headmasters and inspectors: professional setting, adequacy at work, organization - administration - relations and general attitude. It was found that for all four criteria the teachers are not sure whether the assessment influences them positively or negatively. No statistically significant difference was found (1) between the opinions of male and female teachers about their assessment on the four criteria; (2) between the views of teachers with little experience and the views of teachers with more experience. For 76.7% of respondents, the current practice of assessment is a cause of stress and anxiety. For 66.7% it causes insincere relations with the headmaster. Moreover, the assessment leads to antagonism among the teachers. It is worth noting that three out of five teachers stated that the current practice of assessment does not promote teachers' professionalism. One out of two teachers believes that the assessment helps teachers to try harder and to use new methods and procedures.
One out of two teachers believes that the assessment is not helpful for the improvement of teaching and eight out of ten believe that the teachers' assessment is not valid and does not take account of the teachers' real ability. 75% of respondents believe that the assessment is not fair, that it is not based on facts (61.7%) and that it is predetermined (44.2%). One out of two teachers believes that self-assessment is possible. Three out of five teachers (60.8%) are in favour of abolishing current teacher assessment procedures.

12402 The IEA international reading literacy study in Ireland.
IRL 1994
Research Date(s): 1988-1994
Martin, Michael O.; Morgan, M.
Inst: Educational Research Centre, St Patrick's College, Dublin 9, Ireland.
achievement; cross-national research; literacy; reading
rendement; recherche transnationale; alphabétisation; lecture
PROJECT DESCRIPTION
The IEA Reading Literacy study is a large international comparative study being carried out in 32 countries under the auspices of the International Association for the Evaluation of Educational Achievement (IEA). The study involves an international comparison of reading literacy among 9-year-olds and 14-year-olds, and an analysis of the school, classroom and teacher factors related to literacy performance.
The study made use of large nationally-representative samples of students at each of the two age levels. Students were asked to respond to literacy tests and questionnaires, and information was also obtained in questionnaires from school principals and teachers. In Ireland, approximately 6,000 students in 270 schools took part in the study.
Analyses are examining such issues as levels of reading literacy in participating countries, gender differences in achievement, factors associated with the effective teaching of reading, and methods of teaching reading and their efforts on student achievement. A national report for Ireland is in preparation and will be completed in 1994.

12403 The IEA Third International Mathematics and Science Study in Ireland.
IRL 1994
Research Date(s): 1992-1996
Martin, Michael O.
Inst: Educational Research Centre, St Patrick's College, Dublin 9, Ireland.
achievement; cross-national research; mathematics; science education
rendement; recherche transnationale; mathématiques; éducation scientifique
PROJECT DESCRIPTION
The Third International Mathematics and Science Study (TIMSS) is a comparative study of student achievements in mathematics and science which is being conducted under the auspices of the International Association for the Evaluation of Educational Achievement (IEA).
The study consists of three major components: comparative analyses of national curricula in mathematics and science, comparisons of instructional approaches in these subjects, and a cross-national survey of student achievements. Curricula are being compared using a form of content analysis. Instructional approaches will be studied using questionnaires to principals, teachers and students. Student achievement will be studied using sample survey methods. There are three target populations in the study: 9-year-olds, 13-year-olds, and 17-year-olds. Intact adjacent grade-levels will be sampled to ensure both age and grade-level comparisons.
To date, content analysis of mathematics and science textbooks and curriculum guidelines has been completed. The results will be published early in 1994. Pilot-testing of questionnaires and tests is currently underway. In 1994 there will be a full-scale field trial of all procedures, tests and questionnaires. The main survey of student achievement will take place for northern hemisphere countries in the Spring of 1995.

12404 Ilkokullarda temel öğrenme ihtiyaçlarının karşılanması. (Meeting basic learning needs in primary schools.)
TUR 1994
Research Date(s): 1990-1991
Fidan, Nurettin; Baykul, Yaşar.
Inst: Hacettepe Üniversitesi (Hacettepe University), Beytepe, Ankara, Turkey; Milli Eğitim Bakanlığı (Ministry of Education), Kızılay, Ankara, Turkey. UNICEF Representative Office, Ankara, Turkey
achievement; primary education; educational need; aims of education; curriculum; knowledge level; comprehension
rendement; enseignement primaire; besoin d'éducation; finalité de l'éducation; programme d'études; niveau de connaissances; compréhension
PROJECT DESCRIPTION
The aims of the present study were: to specify basic learning needs in terms of knowledge, skills, values and attitudes; to evaluate to what extent primary schools are able to meet the basic learning needs of children; and to establish a basis for the improvement of primary school curricula and teaching practice.
The specification of learning needs was mainly based on a selection of objectives of Turkish National Education and the primary school curriculum. The selection of objectives focused on their importance in daily life and their relevance for further learning. The objectives were converted into pupil behaviours and test situations. Five achievement tests - Turkish language, mathematics, social studies, science, health and nutrition - and an attitude scale were constructed by a team of curriculum experts, educational measurement experts and primary school teachers. The tests were administered to 1,523 pupils.
About two thirds of pupils were unable to answer more than fifty percent of the questions correctly. Over two thirds of pupils gave incorrect answers to questions concerning comprehension and application. The scores on achievement tests and the attitude scale correlated strongly with Turkish language test scores. The lowest scores were found in reading comprehension, mathematics problem solving skills, economic activities in society, preventive health activities, first aid, and the application of scientific principles and rules to everyday problems.
The results of the study suggest that primary schools teach basic knowledge and skills, but not necessarily an understanding of the concepts required for their successful application. Schools should develop cognitive strategies, for instance through formal instruction. Teaching which aims at

the memorization of information for examinations does not benefit pupils' intellectual functioning. Primary schools should give attention to the quality of educational experiences and classroom interaction. Achievement tests give an indication of pupils' knowledge measured by an 'outside' criterion, but they reveal nothing about the strategies children use, the quality of instruction or the application of knowledge and skills to practical tasks in daily life. In the evaluation of the effectiveness of primary education the content and the quality of school experiences should be taken into consideration. Moreover, it can be concluded from the study that more emphasis should be given to mother tongue instruction, comprehension of knowledge and the application of generalized knowledge to everyday problems.

The main aim of this pilot study was to develop instruments for a nationwide survey. Emphasis was given to the development of the achievement tests and an attitude scale. The findings reported here are the by-products of the test construction process and should be interpreted as tentative conclusions or hypotheses for further research.

12405 The impact of the introduction of staff appraisal on women academics' career opportunities in higher education.
GBR 1993
Research Date(s): 1990-1995
Thomas, R.
Inst: Glamorgan University, Business School, Pontypridd, Mid Glamorgan CF37 1DL, United Kingdom.
teacher appraisal; teaching profession; women's profession; career development
évaluation sur l'enseignant; profession d'enseignant; profession féminine; déroulement de carrière
PROJECT DESCRIPTION

Staff appraisal is new to higher education and its introduction can be seen to reflect wider changes in public sector industrial relations. Stemming from the 23rd Report from Committee A (Committee of Vice-Chancellors and Principals (CVCP) (1987)), appraisal is being presented to staff as a formal procedure for staff development, "...directed towards developing staff potential, assisting in the improvement of performance and enhancing career and promotion opportunities..." (para 43). The assumption arising from this is that the introduction of staff appraisal will serve to improve women's opportunities of gaining senior positions due to the bureaucratisation of the promotion process and the provision of career planning. However, to some, its introduction is being heralded as an extension of managerial control which at best will have little impact on women's career opportunities and at worse will be detrimental to them, merely formalising and legitimising existing discriminatory practices.

Longitudinal research of in-depth case studies in higher education institutions, accompanied by wider questionnaire analysis, aims to establish women academics' experience of appraisal and its impact on their careers.

12406 The influence of teacher appraisal on secondary school management.
GBR 1993
Research Date(s): 1989-1993
Hazlewood, P.
Sup: Wragg, E.
Inst: Exeter University, School of Education, St Luke's, Heavitree Road, Exeter EX1 2LU, United Kingdom.
Fin: Wiltshire Local Education Authority; Pool School.
teacher appraisal; secondary school; educational administration
évaluation sur l'enseignant; école secondaire; administration de l'enseignement
PROJECT DESCRIPTION

The imminent introduction of formal teacher appraisal into schools, based on the premises that appraisal would monitor teacher performance, improve practice and enhance the overall management of schools, provides a platform for considerable debate. The principal aim of this investigation is to consider the influence that teacher appraisal has on the management of secondary schools. A range of hypotheses relating to management of schools are being tested. Based on case studies of four similar sized secondary schools (for 11-16 age group) in similar localities, the research used unstructured interview as the primary methodology. Validity is currently being established through group discussion and other methods. A detailed questionnaire is being utilized to test hypotheses arising from the interviews. Approximately 45 teachers in various management positions were interviewed and questionnaires were sent to a range of 198 teachers in six schools. The results are currently being analysed.

12407 The initial assessment of youth trainees with special needs: improving access to National Vocational Qualifications (NVQs) at level 1.
GBR 1993
Research Date(s): 1991
Smith, P.; Drysdale, D.; Lindley, P.
Inst: National Foundation for Educational Research, The Mere, Upton Park, Slough SL1 2DQ, United Kingdom.
Fin: Surrey Training and Enterprise Council.
initial assessment; trainee; unqualified young people; special education; learning difficulty
évaluation initiale; stagiaire; jeune sans qualification; enseignement spécial; difficulté de l'apprentissage
PROJECT DESCRIPTION

The project provided a 'module' or source document to assist Surrey Managing Agents in conducting the initial assessment of youth trainees with special needs (particularly Special Needs B, i.e. these with moderate learning difficulties). The module covered the range of assessments which might be needed and how to use the results of these in selecting appropriate NVQ Level 1 training opportunities in Surrey for such trainees. A survey of NVQ Level 1 provision in the Surrey area (including the nature of courses, entry requirements, etc.) was carried out. Potential assessment devices were reviewed for their suitability with this trainee group. The information drawn from these sources was then documented in a form which is practical for use by Managing Agents.

12408 An investigation into the calibration of GCSE grades and National Curriculum levels of attainment at Key Stage 3/4.
GBR 1993
Research Date(s): 1992
Owen, P.
Sup: Christie, T.
Inst: Manchester University, School of Education, Centre for Formative Assessment Studies, Oxford Road, Manchester M13 9PL, United Kingdom.
Fin: Northern Examinations Association.
achievement test; assessment; examination; marking
test de rendement; appréciation; examen; notation
PROJECT DESCRIPTION

The study was commissioned by the Northern Examinations Association (NEA) as a response to published guidance by the Schools Examinations and Assessment Council (SEAC) on the assessment of Key Stage 4 attainment through GCSE, and the pronouncement by the Secretary of State for Education and Science that examining bodies assessing performance of students at age 16 should be responsible for auditing the standards of pupils at age 14.

The development and trial of the assessment material led to the conclusion that: (1) external examination papers can be designed around statements of attainment (SoA) while retaining the integrity of the subject as a whole; (2) overlapping differentiated papers covering three National Curriculum profile components levels within bands as a viable structure; (3) assessment material suitable for students of the same chronological age but at widely differing levels of attainment can be devised following a set structure and relating to a single theme; (4) mark schemes can be constructed around SoA according to formula and recontextualised for different examining occasions; and (5) there is need for further investigation into calibration focusing on steps from strand to attainment target (AT) and AT to subject score. Data from all levels of specifity are currently being analysed to inform calibration rules.

12409 Item bank testing.
GBR 1993
Research Date(s): 1983-
Hagues, N.; Courtenay, D.
Inst: National Foundation for Educational Research, The Mere, Upton Park, Slough SL1 2DQ, United Kingdom.
achievement test; assessment
test de rendement; appréciation
PROJECT DESCRIPTION

An item bank is a large collection of pre-trialled questions, a small proportion of which can be selected to construct a test to the user's specification and to a pre-determined level of difficulty. Because these tests are custom-made, the test is unique and hence a very high level of security can be guaranteed. The National Foundation for Educational Research maintains item banks in verbal reasoning, non-verbal reasoning, mathematics and English, and these have been used in recent years with pupils aged 8 to 14 for attaimnent testing, monitoring, screening and selection.

12410 Key stage 1 non-mandatory standard assessment tasks.
GBR 1993
Research Date(s): 1991-1992
Jones, G.; Richardson, J.
Sup: Whetton, C.
Inst: National Foundation for Educational Research, The Mere, Upton Park, Slough SL1 2DQ, United Kingdom.
Fin: School Examinations and Assessment Council.
assessment; common core curriculum; achievement test; history
appréciation; tronc commun; test de rendement; histoire
PROJECT DESCRIPTION

Standard assessment tasks have been developed to assess pupils' attainment in National Curriculum history at key stage 1. Collectively, they will help teachers to make their end-of-key-stage assessments of pupils in the three attainment targets for history. There will be no statutory requirement for schools to use the standard assessment tasks. Separate standard assessment tasks have been developed for England and Wales, and Welsh standard assessment tasks are both English and Welsh medium. The standard assessment tasks are simple, straightforward and manageable for use by teachers and pupils, using resources normally available in primary schools. They provide valid and reliable assessment of pupils against levels 1-3 of each attainment target, and are appropriate for use with the widest possible ability range of pupils, including those with special educational needs.

The duration of the contract was from 1st October 1991 until 31st December 1992. In the first phase of development, informal trials took place in 20 schools in England and Wales and standard assessment task materials were produced cooperatively with teachers. In the second phase from January to March 1992 materials were formally trialled in a further 60 schools in England and Wales. Standard assessment task materials will be available for use in schools from early 1993.

12411 Leerlingbesprekingen in het basisonderwijs. (Evaluation of special needs pupils in ordinary primary schools.)
NLD 1994
Research Date(s): 1993-1994
Pijl, S.J.
Inst: RION Instituut voor Onderwijsonderzoek (RION Institute for Educational Research), P.O. Box 1286, 9701 BG Groningen, Netherlands.
Rijksuniversiteit Groningen (State University of Groningen), P.O. Box 72, 9700 AB Groningen, Netherlands
Fin: SVO het Instituut voor Onderzoek van het Onderwijs.
evaluation; pupil; special education; pupil integration; further education of teachers
évaluation; élève; enseignement spécial; intégration scolaire; perfectionnement des enseignants
PROJECT DESCRIPTION
Background: Current government policies, outlined in the policy paper "Together to school again", are aimed at keeping special needs pupils in ordinary schools. This requires teachers to develop their professional expertise, especially as regards the careful selection of subject matter contents and the regular evaluation of the outcomes of teaching. This can be done with the help of "pupil reviews", i.e. discussions of individual cases by the teaching team during regular staff meetings.

Aims: (1) To ascertain the extent to which and the way in which "pupil reviews" are taking place in primary schools; (2) to examine the feasibility of introducing pupil reviews in the entire primary sector; (3) to examine the effect of pupil reviews on teacher behaviour.

Methods: Case study; telephone survey.

Design: All school advisory services (OBDs) and 500 primary schools will be questioned by telephone to explore current practice in respect of pupil reviews and related activities or policies. The heads of 100 schools where pupil reviews take place will be asked to complete a questionnaire. Case studies will be made of year three and year six teachers at 30 schools. From this group 10 "trendsetting" schools will be selected of which the headteachers will be interviewed. Case studies will be conducted of five OBDs.

12412 Lehrplanbezogene Leistungsfeststellung im 3. Schuljahr. (Syllabus-based monitoring of achievement in the third year of school.)
DEU 1993
Research Date(s): 1991-1993
Schorch, G.; Treinies, G.
Sup: Rabenstein, R.
Inst: Universitaet Erlangen-Nuernberg, Erziehungswissenschaftliche Fakultaet, Lehrstuhl fuer Grundschuldidaktik 01, Regensburger Strasse 160, D-8500 Nuernberg.
assessment; primary education; achievement test; reading; mathematics; spelling; differentiation; achievement
appréciation; enseignement primaire; test de rendement; lecture; mathématiques; orthographe; différenciation; rendement
PROJECT DESCRIPTION
Inhalt: Feststellung des Leistungsstandes am Ende des 3. Schuljahres in den Lernbereichen Lesen, Rechtschreiben und Mathematik. Analyse und Auswahl der Testaufgaben im Hinblick auf jahrgangsuebergreifende Leistungserfassung als Basis fuer Beurteilung und ggf. Ausbau von Differenzierungsmassnahmen in der Grundschule.

Geographischer Raum: Nuernberg.

Vorgehensweise: Quantitative Erhebung mit kriterienbezogener Auswertung; Konsequenzen fuer die Unterrichtspraxis. Untersuchungsdesign: Querschnittserhebung; qualitative Forschung.

Datengewinnung: Schulleistungstest (Stichprobe: 152; Schueler der 3. Jahrgangsstufe; Auswahlverfahren: Zufall).

Auswertung: Itemanalyse; Varianzanalyse; Konfigurations-Frequenz-Analyse. Datenaufbereitung: Datenedition (z.B. Aufbau von Datenbanken); Verknuepfung verschiedener Datensaetze (record linkage).

12413 Leistungsprognosen bei Schihandelsschuelern. (Performance forecasts for pupils in upper secondary commercial schools with a focus on skiing instruction.)
AUT 1993
Research Date(s): 1988-1992
Rothschedl, Erich; Horn, Gerald.
Inst: Abteilung fuer Schulpsychologie und Bildungsberatung, Stifterstrasse 29, A-4020 Linz; Abteilung fuer Schulpsychologie Liezen, Koerblergasse 23, A-8010 Graz.
Landesschulrat fuer Oberoesterreich, Stifterstrasse 29, A-4020 Linz; Landesschulrat fuer Steiermark, Koerblergasse 23, A-8010 Graz
predictive evaluation; sport; individual characteristics; achievement; achievement motivation; success
évaluation prédictive; sport; caractéristique individuelle; rendement; motivation d'accomplissement; réussite
PROJECT DESCRIPTION
Bei diesem Projekt handelt es sich um eine Laengsschnittanalyse von 1988 bis 1992. Es wurden saemtliche AufnahmsbewerberInnen fuer das Schuljahr 1988/1989 mit psychologischen Tests ueberprueft. Im Anschluss wurden saemtliche aufgenommene SchuelerInnen ueber ihre gesamte Schulzeit hindurch bis zum Schuljahr 1991/1992 beobachtet. Als Kontrollgruppe diente dabei die angeschlossene regulaere Handelsschule. Bei den SportschuelerInnen wurden waehrend dieser vier Jahre folgende Daten erfasst: Persoenlichkeitsmerkmale, Veraenderung der Persoenlichkeitsmerkmale, Begabung, Konzentrationsleistungen, Motivation u.v.a. Es wurde weiters ein Vergleich angestellt zwischen den erfolgreichen AbsolventInnen und den sogenannten 'Dropouts', SchuelerInnen, die im Laufe der Schulzeit ausgeschieden sind. Ziel der Untersuchung war es, festzustellen, welche psychischen Voraussetzungen neben der sportlichen Eignung notwendig sind, um einen guenstigen Schulverlauf prognostizieren zu koennen.

Es erfolgte eine Laengsschnittanalyse 1988 bis 1991 an der Schihandelsschule Schladming. Als empirische Erhebungstechniken wurden Motivationstests, Persoenlichkeitstests, Begabungstests, Bales-Skalen, schriftliche Befragungen, Konzentrationsbestimmungstests und Soziogrammanalysen herangezogen.

Die Daten wurden mittels Prozentwertberechnung, Chi-Quadrat und Mittelwertanalysen ausgewertet.

Der Projektbericht liegt vor und ist bei den Autoren anzufordern.

12414 Lise III. sınıf öğrencilerinin ÖSYM I. Basamak sınavı öncesi ve sonrası kaygı düzeylerinin bazı faktörler yönünden karşılaştırılması. (A comparison of the anxiety levels of final-year secondary school pupils before and after university entrance examinations.)
TUR 1994
Research Date(s): 1988
Cengiz, Hanife Ferda.
Sup: Voltan-Acar, Nilüfer.
Inst: Hacettepe Üniversitesi, Eğitim Fakültesi, Psikolojik Hizmetler Bölümü (Hacettepe University, Faculty of Education, Department of Psychological Services), 06532 Beytepe, Ankara, Turkey.
competitive examination; anxiety; upper secondary; entrance examination; university
concours; angoisse; secondaire deuxième cycle; examen d'entrée; université
PROJECT DESCRIPTION
The research examined the effect of University Entrance Exams (UEE) on the levels of state and trait anxiety in male and female final-year secondary school pupils with varying levels of achievement.

The study used a 'single group pre-test post-test design'. The sample consisted of 49 girls and 64 boys who were in the final year of Sanakaya Secondary School of Ankara in the 1986-1987 school year. Pupils' anxiety levels were measured before and after the UEE with the help of the A-State A-Trait Anxiety Inventory. T-tests were performed and comparisons were made by gender and achievement level.

Before the UEE exam, pupils' trait and state anxiety levels are nearly identical. After the exam a decrease was observed in trait anxiety levels, but not in state anxiety levels.

The UEE had an effect on the anxiety levels of boys and girls, but the effect on girls was much stronger. After the examination the state anxiety level of both groups decreased. Furthermore, there was a strong decrease in level of trait anxiety among the boys, but not among the girls.

An important decrease was observed in the state anxiety levels of both successful and unsuccessful pupils, before and after UEE; trait anxiety levels decreased in unsuccessful pupils, but not significantly in successful pupils. Overall, the trait and state anxiety levels of unsuccessful pupils are higher than those of successful pupils.

The results show that the UEE leads to increased anxiety in all pupils. On the basis of the findings, several suggestions are offered relating to school guidance services and psychological counselling.

12415 The long-term influence of effective and ineffective A-level departments.
GBR 1993
Research Date(s): 1992-1994
Tymms, P.
Inst: Heriot-Watt University, Moray House Institute of Education, Holyrood Road, Edinburgh EH8 8AQ, United Kingdom.
Fin: Economic and Social Research Council.
examination programme; performance; school; quality of education; teaching quality
programme d'examen; performance; école; qualité de l'éducation; qualité de l'enseignement
PROJECT DESCRIPTION
The short-term effectiveness of schools can be measured by immediate outputs such as examination results, attitudes and aspirations. But what about the long-term effects of schools? The project will extend an existing database to answer that question.

12416 Measurement and accreditation of broad skills.
GBR 1993
Research Date(s): 1990-1993
Wolf, A.
Inst: London University, Institute of Education, Department of Mathematics, Statistics and Computing, 20 Bedford Way, London WC1H 0AL, United Kingdom.
Fin: Training, Enterprise and Education Directorate.
assessment; vocational education; skill
appréciation; enseignement professionnel; compétence
PROJECT DESCRIPTION
Over a three-year period the project will examine the types of assessment - both written and practical - which are most effective in predicting retention of skills, and ability to generalise to other more or less closely related areas. The work will be carried out with students (aged 16-20, and adult) who are nearing completion of vocational training courses. It will build upon previous research including a large study completed for the Training Agency (now Training, Enterprise and Education Directorate - TEED) by the Institute of Education. TEED has a strong interest in the current project, because of its implications for the development of assessment procedures for National Vocational Qualifications (NVQs), and for the design and regulation of training schemes receiving government funding. The policy implications of the research will therefore be of major concern to the team throughout the project.
The study will be longitudinal and will relate to: current mastery; success, at time of mastery, in generalising to related tasks; measured retention of skills at a later date; and success in generalising to related tasks at a later date. The use of definitions and measures of 'mastery' is central to the project, reflecting the criterion-referenced nature of current reforms in vocational standards and testing.

12417 Modelling school effectiveness.
NLD 1994
Research Date(s): 1993-1996
Bosker, R.J.; Werf, M.P.C.; Amelsvoort, H.W.C.H. van; Reezigt, G.J.
Sup: Scheerens, J.; Creemers, B.P.M.
Inst: Onderzoek Centrum Toegepaste Onderwijskunde (OCTO) (Research Centre of the Department of Educational Technology), P.O. Box 217, 7500 AE Enschede, Netherlands; RION Instituut voor Onderwijsonderzoek (RION Institute for Educational Research), P.O. Box 1286, 9701 BG Groningen, Netherlands.
Universiteit Twente (Twente University), P.O. Box 217, 7500 AE Enschede, Netherlands; Rijksuniversiteit Groningen (State University of Groningen), P.O. Box 72, 9700 AB Groningen, Netherlands
Fin: SVO het Instituut voor Onderzoek van het Onderwijs.
performance; secondary education; model; educational research
performance; enseignement secondaire; modèle; recherche en éducation
PROJECT DESCRIPTION
Background: The basis for this project is constituted by J. Scheerens' study entitled "Foundational and fundamental studies in school effectiveness: a research agenda". This study outlines three scenarios for the way in which knowledge about school effectiveness could develop. For several reasons, including pragmatic ones, the researchers have opted for the scenario of a quantitative synthesis of school effectiveness studies.
Aims: To examine the effect of actions aimed at improving school effectiveness, in terms of differences between schools and predictive factors; to establish the tenability of different models of school effectiveness and to explore alternative models.
Design: Four studies will be conducted. For the synthesis, international school effectiveness studies of the last five years will be studied in an international context. Supplementary data sets or research findings will be collected. The resulting information will be subjected to a meta-analysis. Literature on school effectiveness will be analysed. Secondary analyses will be performed on various models of school effectiveness that have emerged from the "VOCL" cohort study, which uses information on pupils, teachers and school characteristics of 320 secondary schools. In-depth studies will

be made of 24 schools, with a view to comparing different levels of effectiveness.

12418 Models and theories of self-regulation in higher education: a multi-national study.
GBR 1993
Research Date(s): 1990-1992
Kells, H.
Sup: Davies, J.
Inst: Anglia Polytechnic University, Anglia Business School, Centre for Higher Education Management, Danbury Park Conference Centre, Danbury Park, Chelmsford CM3 4AT, United Kingdom; Anglia Business School, Victoria Road South, Chelmsford CM1 1LR, United Kingdom.
self-evaluation; educational institution; higher education; cross-national research
auto-évaluation; établissement d'enseignement; enseignement supérieur; recherche transnationale
PROJECT DESCRIPTION
This is a multi-stage, fifteen year project to describe, understand and improve higher education self-regulation processes. Earlier stages were empirical; later stages qualitative and theory building. Focus was on North America and Western Europe. In the early stages, retrospective descriptive and correlational studies of self-evaluation processes were employed in North America. In the middle stages, qualitative case analyses, propositional in nature, were conducted in the Netherlands and North America.
Publ: Kells, H.R. The inadequacy of performance indicators. In: *Higher Education Management*, November 1990.
Kells, H.R. The use of incentives in programme review and planned change. Paper given at European Association for Institutional Research, Lyon, September. In: *Higher Education Management*, Vol 3, No 2, 1991.

12419 Moderation at National Curriculum Key Stage 1 across four local education authorities in 1992.
GBR 1993
Research Date(s): 1991-1992
James, M.; Conner, C.
Inst: Cambridge University, Institute of Education, Shaftesbury Road, Cambridge CB2 2BX, United Kingdom.
Fin: Four local education authorities.
assessment; marking; common core curriculum
appréciation; notation; tronc commun
PROJECT DESCRIPTION
The study was intended to focus upon the moderation of National Curriculum assessment at Key Stage One in four local education authorities (LEAs) in the Eastern Region, particularly addressing the issues of consistency and standards. Two moderators in each of the four LEAs were observed being trained, whilst training in their 'moderation schools' and during school visits. Interviews were undertaken with moderators, teachers and headteachers in the schools visited.
The evidence suggests that one of the major difficulties moderators faced was how to interpret and balance the various expectations placed upon them. Particular concern emerged regarding reliability and validity. Unless National Curriculum assessment is demonstrably reliable and valid it will have very little credibility and value. Current governmental concern stresses consistency (reliability) yet gives insufficient attention to the arguably more important question of validity.
Publ: James, M. & Conner, C. Are reliability and validity achievable in National Curriculum assessment? Some observations on moderation at Key Stage One in 1992. In: *The Curriculum Journal*, Vol 4, No 1/1993, Spring.

12420 Monitoring and evaluation in workplace nurseries.
GBR 1993
Research Date(s): 1990-1993
Hurst, V.; Blenkin, G.
Inst: London University, Goldsmiths' College, Faculty of Education, Lewisham Way, New Cross, London SE14 6NW, United Kingdom.
evaluation; day care; day nursery; child care
évaluation; mode de garde; crèche; aide à l'enfance
PROJECT DESCRIPTION
The project aims to gain an insight into the evaluation procedures used by workplace nurseries, in particular the role of the 'outsider'. Ethnographic action research, based on two nursery centres, will investigate how staff may be supported in the monitoring and evaluation of their practice.

12421 National standards for training and development within Master's programmes.
GBR 1993
Research Date(s): 1991-
Wolf, A.; Drake, P.; Eraut, M.; Holroyd, C.; Dunn, W.
Inst: London University, Institute of Education, 20 Bedford Way, London WC1H 0AL, United Kingdom; Sussex University, Institute of Continuing Education, Sussex House, Falmer, Brighton BN1 9RH, United Kingdom; Glasgow University, Department of Education, 8 University Gardens, Glasgow G12 8QQ, United Kingdom.
Fin: Department for Education.

masters degree; assessment; qualification; vocational training
diplôme universitaire (2e cycle); appréciation; qualification; formation professionnelle
PROJECT DESCRIPTION

A new structure of qualifications is being put in place to encourage employers and employees to raise standards of performance in the workplace. The qualifications are called National and Scottish Vocational Qualifications (NVQs and SVQs). The qualifications are based on standards of competence which are being set by Lead Bodies. National Standards for Training and Development were published by the Training and Development Lead Body, first in January 1991, then in revised form in March 1992. These National Standards are intended to cover all work roles that have a training and development content. The whole shift towards competence-based qualifications means there is a need for standards to which the assessors of competence must work; these are included. The National Standards have a number of uses: as a basis for job descriptions; to identify training needs; to develop training programmes; as a basis for assessment; as benchmarks for development; and to form vocational qualifications. The Lead Body has defined the key purpose of training as "to develop human potential to assist organisations and individuals to achieve their objectives". Given this broad definition, it is clear that National Standards can be applied to the work of teachers in schools and to the work of lecturers in colleges and universities. The extent to which they will be applied, and the rate of the application, is currently unpredictable.

A research study has been funded by the Department of Employment to explore the delivery of the National Standards for Training and Development within Master's Degree programmes. The project involves the Universities of London, Sussex and Glasgow. The three institutions involved have had distinct plans and priorities; however, the project was conceived as a consortium activity and each site has learned from the others. The first stage of the project has these aims: (1) To examine the feasibility of incorporating the National Standards for Training and Development within Masters Degrees; (2) To determine appropriate methods for achieving such incorporation; (3) To secure approval for, and then to prepare for the implementation of, pilot programmes; and (4) To integrate the parallel work of the three participating institutions, both internally and with other relevant developments.

Publ: *Recognition of TDLB key roles by M.Ed. students* (November 1991).
Staff views on basic issues (November 1991).*Recognition of TDLB units and elements by M.Ed. students* (September 1992).

12422 National standards for training and development within masters programmes in education: Glasgow University.
GBR 1993
Research Date(s): 1991-
Dunn, W.; Holroyd, C.
Inst: Glasgow University, Department of Education, Glasgow G12 8QQ, United Kingdom.
Fin: Department of Employment.
masters degree; assessment; qualification; standard; university studies
diplôme universitaire (2e cycle); appréciation; qualification; norme; études universitaires
PROJECT DESCRIPTION

The project aims to assess the appropriateness of incorporating the national standards for training and development with Master's Degrees in Education. Work at the feasibility stage has shown that students on M.Ed. courses recognise the Training and Development Lead Body (TDLB) key roles, units and elements of competence as applicable within their work as education professionals. In 1992-1993 two courses within the Glasgow M.Ed. programme will be developed in ways which allow students to demonstrate which of the TDLB standards they meet; it is intended that it will be clarified which parts of M.Ed. provision can NOT be described in terms of the TDLB competences/standards.

12423 A national survey of reading achievement in Irish primary schools.
IRL 1994
Research Date(s): 1993-1994
Martin, Michael O.; Forde, Patrick D.; Morgan, M.; Hickey, B.L.
Inst: Educational Research Centre, St Patrick's College, Dublin 9, Ireland.
achievement; evaluation; reading
rendement; évaluation; lecture
PROJECT DESCRIPTION

In May 1993, the Educational Research Centre conducted a national survey of reading achievement in primary schools in co-operation with the Department of Education. Earlier surveys were conducted in 1980 and 1988. The purpose of the series of studies is to monitor levels of student performance in reading in senior classes in primary school, and to study home, school, teacher, classroom and attitudinal factors related to reading achievement. Particular emphasis is being placed on the study of characteristics of students with low levels of achievement in reading.

The study consists of a national sample survey of students in fifth grade or who were born in the period September 1, 1981 to August 31, 1982.

Specially-developed tests of reading comprehension and general ability were administered to each student. The NS6 reading test, which was used in earlier surveys was also administered to permit comparison with the earlier surveys. Questionnaire information was collected from parents, school principals, teachers and pupils. Results of the survey will be available in early 1994. Initial reports will focus on the description of student reading levels and the social and educational contexts in which these are achieved. Later reports will investigate the factors which are related to reading achievement and, in particular, those which relate to low achievement levels.

12424 Ontwikkeling van een toetsservice systeem. (Development of an item banking system.)
NLD 1994
Research Date(s): 1985-1992
Werkhoven, R.F. van; Thio, K.D.; Linden, W.J. van der.
Sup: Klauw, C.F. van der; Scheerens, J.
Inst: Cito Instituut voor Toetsontwikkeling (National Institute for Educational Measurement), P.O. Box 1034, 6801 MG Arnhem, Netherlands.
Fin: SVO het Instituut voor Onderzoek van het Onderwijs.
test construction; data base; information system
construction de tests; banque de données; système d'information
PROJECT DESCRIPTION

Background: Evaluation in and of education are two fields where information technology can play a supportive role and open up new roads. Computers can provide support to teachers in the construction of learning tasks and test papers and the processing of test scores. At the national level it is possible to store large numbers of tasks and other relevant information in computers and to use this material for the construction of national tests. New roads that are being opened up by the computer are the individual testing of pupils and the integration of evaluation in computer-controlled or computer-assisted instruction. The computer also enables evaluations to be conducted within curricula. The National Institute for Educational Measurement (Cito) has undertaken two projects that were concerned with these new applications of information technology; one concerned with the development of an item banking system (TSS), the other the development of a school item banking system (STSS).

Methods: Structured interviews; content analysis; questionnaire survey; simulation; tests.

Results: Cito needs to abandon its original, somewhat "centralistic" development concept for item banking systems and replace it by a more flexible view. In the development of item banking systems account should be taken of internal and external needs. The development of an item banking system for schools will be the subject of a separate project which will partly build on the findings of the school item bank project. The project has resulted in a large number of products that can be seen as building blocks that can be used in the construction of item banking systems according to the needs of users.

Publ: Werkhoven, R.F. van; et al. *Eindverslag Project Toetsservicesystemen.* Arnhem: Cito, 1992, 68p.

12425 Opzet van de tweede fase van het school- en klaskenmerkenonderzoek in het voortgezet onderwijs ten behoeve van de evaluatie OVB/basisvorming. (A study of school and classroom characteristics in secondary schools in the context of the evaluation of the Educational Priority Policy programme and the introduction of a national curriculum in lower secondary education: phase two.)
NLD 1994
Research Date(s): 1991-1992
Driessen, G.W.J.M.; Werf, M.P.C. van der.
Inst: RION Instituut voor Onderwijsonderzoek (RION Institute for Educational Research), P.O. Box 1286, 9701 BG Groningen, Netherlands.
Rijksuniversiteit Groningen (State University of Groningen), P.O. Box 72, 9700 AB Groningen, Netherlands
Fin: SVO het Instituut voor Onderzoek van het Onderwijs.
evaluation; educational policy; equal opportunity
évaluation; politique de l'éducation; égalité de chances
PROJECT DESCRIPTION

Background: In the school year 1989-1990 the longitudinal study of the school careers of secondary school pupils entitled was launched under the name of "VOCL'89". The data gathered in this study will be used for the evaluation of the Educational Priority Policy programme (OVB) and the national core curriculum which will be introduced in August 1993 in the lower secondary sector. The measurements are repeated every other year. The data are collected by the Central Bureau of Statistics (CBS), the RION Institute for Educational Research at the University of Groningen and the ITS Institute for Applied Social Sciences at the University of Nijmegen. The second phase of the evaluation was concerned with pupils' achievement levels in Dutch language and mathematics in the third year at secondary school. As the data need to be analysed at various levels (pupil, teacher and school level), a specific approach is required.

Aim: To collect school and classroom data related to achievement levels in Dutch and mathematics in the third year of secondary school; to transform these data into variables that can be used in the planned analyses.

Design: Information was collected from three groups of respondents: teachers, management staff and the OVB "school contact person" (an intermediary between the school and ethnic minority pupils/parents). Teachers completed a questionnaire (response: 63%); the other respondents were interviewed.

Results: The collection of data went well. The response levels of management staff and school contact persons were particularly encouraging: 100%. The response of teachers was clearly lower, but this had nothing to do with teachers' willingness to cooperate. It proved to be a tall order to find out by whom the pupils in the study were being taught. This was probably the result of the many mutations that take place among teaching staff in the second half of the school year. As regards the operationalisation of school and classroom characteristics, the analyses generally show satisfactory results.

Publ: Driessen, G. et al. *Het functioneren van het voortgezet onderwijs: dataverzameling en operationalisatie van de school- en klaskenmerken in leerjaar 3*. Nijmegen/Groningen: ITS/RION, 1992, 84p.

12426   Oral assessment in modern languages.
GBR   1993
Research Date(s): 1990-1992
Richards, B.; Chambers, F.
Inst: University of Reading, Department of Arts and Humanities in Education, Bulmershe Court, Woodlands Avenue, Earley, Reading RG6 1HY, United Kingdom.
oral examination; assessment; foreign languages; French language
examen oral; appréciation; langues étrangères; langue française
PROJECT DESCRIPTION
The project is a study of oral testing in French. The aim is to compare the reliability and validity of different assessment criteria currently used by GCSE examining groups and to investigate whether characteristics of teacher-examiners influence their ratings of candidates' performance. The main focus is on the assessment of 'free conversation'. The project involves: (1) a literature review; (2) a review of the syllabuses, administrative practices and marking schemes of the GCSE examining groups; (3) a survey of current practices in selected schools; (4) development of three sets of criteria for assessing free conversation which reflect different approaches used by examining groups; (5) obtaining tape recordings of 75 children who were examined in the 1990 GCSE examination. This sample represents the full range of oral marks awarded at GCSE; (6) selection of a sub-sample of 30 children from the above to represent the middle ability range; (7) preparation of two versions (two different random orders) of a set of pre-recorded tapes of the 30 children completing a free conversation task; (8) piloting the three sets of assessment criteria and accompanying instructions and mark sheets; (9) assessment by four groups of six teachers representing native and non-native speakers in comprehensive and selective schools, of the 30 conversations on two separate occasions, one month apart; (10) assessment by 22 PGCE Modern Languages students of the 30 conversations; and (11) validation of the GCSE speaking task by using 15-year old children attending two schools in France. Statistical analysis will also be undertaken.

Publ: Chambers, F. & Richards, B. Criteria for oral assessment. In: *Language Learning Journal*, No 5/1992, pp. 5-9, September.

12427   Orientation des diplômé-e-s de l'Ecole de culture générale de Genève.
CHE   1994
Research Date(s): 1989-1991
Decarro, N. Marina.
Inst: Service de la recherche sociologique du Département de l'instruction publique, 8 rue du 31-Décembre, 1207 Genève, Suisse.
school career; post-compulsory education; vocational preparation
cursus scolaire; enseignement postobligatoire; initiation à la profession
PROJECT DESCRIPTION
L'Ecole de culture générale (ECG) de Genève existe depuis 1972. Elle a pour but de "dispenser un enseignement de culture générale et de préparer ses élèves à entreprendre des études ou un apprentissage dans diverses professions". Par son recrutement, ses objectifs et son mode de fonctionnement, elle fait partie des écoles de degré diplôme, qui occupent une place intermédiaire entre les écoles professionnelles et les gymnases. L'ECG genevoise s'adresse notamment aux jeunes filles et jeunes gens qui souhaitent entreprendre, une fois le diplôme obtenu, une formation professionnelle dans le domaine paramédical, le travail socio-éducatif, le commerce, etc. Actuellement, quelque 200 élèves obtiennent chaque année un diplôme de culture générale: que deviennent ces jeunes adultes par la suite? Entreprennent-ils des études et lesquelles? Jusqu'à quel point l'orientation effective correspond-elle à celle envisagée à l'école?

La recherche, entreprise pour répondre à une demande émanant de l'école, avait pour but de recenser et analyser les formations entreprises et terminées par les diplômé-é-s d'une volée pendant les quatre années qui ont suivi l'obtention du diplôme de culture générale.

La population étudiée était celle de 203 diplômé-e-s de juin 1985. La base de données de l'administration scolaire a permis de connaître les études suivies à Genève jusqu'en 1989. Un questionnaire a en outre été adressé aux diplômé-e-s pour compléter les informations manquantes. Les résultats montrent entre autres que, sur les 203 personnes considérées, 80% (162) ont suivi, à un moment ou un autre, un nouveau cursus public ou privé de formation. 66% (135) ont obtenu un nouveau diplôme et 10% étaient en cours de formation au moment de l'enquête. 6% (13 personnes) ont entamé une activité professionnelle sans formation supplémentaire, et 14% (28) n'ont pas pu être atteints ou n'ont pas retourné le questionnaire.

Publ: Decarro, N. Marina. *Après le diplôme de culture générale, quelles formations?* Genève: Service de la recherche sociologique, 1991, 81 pages (Cahier SRS; 33).

12428   Orientation des titulaires de maturité, à Genève, cinq ans après l'obtention du certificat.
CHE   1994
Research Date(s): 1991-1992
Decarro, N. Marina.
Inst: Service de la recherche sociologique du Département de l'instruction publique, 8 rue du 31-Décembre, 1207 Genève, Suisse.
school career; post-compulsory education; branch of study; school leaver
cursus scolaire; enseignement postobligatoire; filière d'études; élève sortant
PROJECT DESCRIPTION
Les écoles de maturité préparent en principe aux études supérieures universitaires et polytechniques. L'enquête annuelle qui est menée à Genève depuis 1968 montre que la proportion de jeunes s'engageant immédiatement dans les études supérieures est très différente selon le type de certificat obtenu. Une partie des nouveaux titulaires s'orientent vers des études non universitaires ou vers une activité professionnelle. Certains jeunes quittent les études supérieures après une ou plusieurs années. D'autres s'accordent une pause avant d'entrer dans une voie "définitive"; pendant cette période intermédiaire (qualifiée souvent d'année sabbatique), ils ou elles travaillent quelques mois et/ou effectuent des voyages (d'études ou d'agrément). Mais on ne sait que peu de choses sur le parcours à moyen terme après la maturité. C'est cette lacune que la présente étude tente de combler.

La recherche a pour but de recenser et d'analyser les parcours des titulaires de maturité de juin 1987 (études, activités professionnelles ou autres activités). L'observation portera sur cinq années. La population concernée est formée des 1100 titulaires de certificat de maturité de l'année 1987 issus des trois établissements d'enseignement public genevois qui préparent à la maturité: Collège de Genève, Ecole supérieure de commerce et Collège pour adultes (l'ancien Collège du soir).

12429   ÖSS ile yoklanan bilgi ve beceriler, farklı okul tür ve sınıflarında ne ölçüde kazanılmaktadır? (The acquisition of knowledge and skills (in years five to eleven) which are relevant in the Student Selection Examination.)
TUR   1994
Research Date(s): 1986-1989
Baykul, Yaşar.
Inst: Milli Eğitim Bakanlığı (Ministry of Education), Kızılay, Ankara, Turkey; Öğrenci Seçme ve Yerleştirme Merkezi (Student Selection and Placement Centre), Bilkent, Ankara, Turkey.
achievement; average achievement; primary education; secondary education; Turkish language; social sciences; mathematics; natural sciences
rendement; rendement moyen; enseignement primaire; enseignement secondaire; langue turque; sciences sociales; mathématiques; sciences naturelles
PROJECT DESCRIPTION
Aim: The aim of the study was to find out to what extent the achievement levels measured in the Student Selection Examination (ÖSS) - the first stage of the university entrance examination in Turkey - are the result of learning in years five to eleven, including various vocational schools at the last three year levels. Factors which might affect performance in this examination were also considered.

Design: The study was carried out in three typical provincial cities. A random sample of classes was used for each year level in each city. Data were collected using the tests administered in the 1986 examination selection. The entire examination was administered to the sample groups representing years nine to eleven. Pupils in years six to eight were randomly divided into two groups which were given either the verbal or the quantitative section of the examination. Pupils in year five were randomly divided into four groups of equal size, each of which was given one of the four following tests: Turkish language, social sciences (both subsections of the verbal section), mathematics, natural sciences (both subsections of the quantitative section). Each subsection of the Student Selection Examination was treated as a separate test in the study. The scores of the sample groups on each subsection were used to determine the extent to which the knowledge levels measured in this examination are acquired in years five to eleven.

Results: (1) The reliability of the tests is satisfactory. (2) Group mean scores on the Turkish subsection improve gradually, as expected, from year five to eleven. (3) Mean scores on the social sciences subsection, too, improve gradually, as expected, from year five to eleven. Some deviations from the expectations seem to occur, however, especially at the higher levels. (4) In the mathematics subsection, the group mean scores improve gradually among lycee students specializing in science and vocational school students specializing in industrial arts or religion. However, among students of literature in lycees and students in other disciplines in vocational schools the mean scores remain at the primary or middle school level. This unexpected finding may be due to deficiencies in mathematics instruction or to a negative selection occurring for these schools. (5) The mean scores on the natural sciences subsection rise with the years among lycee students specializing in science subjects. However, a steady decline occurs among a subgroup of literature students in lycees and among all vocational school students. This unexpected finding may be due to the poor quality of science education or to the positive selection for the science programs in lycees. (6) In the last years of lycees and vocational schools, the mean scores on all subsections are significantly higher than those obtained in the previous year. This may be the effect of college preparatory courses, among other factors.

12430 Parents and assessment at National Curriculum Key Stage 1.
GBR 1993
Research Date(s): 1991-1993
Desforges, C.; Hughes, M.
Inst: Exeter University, School of Education, St Luke's, Heavitree Road, Exeter EX1 2LU, United Kingdom.
Fin: Economic and Social Research Council.
assessment; student record; parent-school relation; parent-teacher relation
appréciation; dossier académique; relation parents-école; relation parents-enseignants
PROJECT DESCRIPTION
The aim of the proposed research is to study the effect that parents' conceptions of teaching, learning and assessment may have on the assessment and reporting procedures currently being introduced into schools, and to study the effect that these procedures may in turn have on parents. It is hypothesised that two important mediating factors could be the accuracy of teachers' perceptions of parents' views, and the extent to which parents are directly involved in the assessment process.

The specific research questions to be addressed are: (1) What are parents' conceptions of teaching, learning and assessment? (2) How accurately are these conceptions perceived by teachers? (3) How far do teachers' perceptions of parents influence their actual assessment behaviour? (4) How far do teachers actually involve parents in the assessment process, and to what effect? (5) What do teachers select to report to parents at the end of the assessment process? (6) What do parents make of these reports, and what effects do they have on their conceptions of teaching, learning and assessment, and on their relationship to the school? (7) What effects do the assessment and reporting processes have on teachers' perceptions of parents' conceptions, and on teachers' classroom practice?.

12431 Performance indicators project.
GBR 1993
Research Date(s): 1989-1992
Gray, J.; Jesson, D.; Booker, J.
Inst: Sheffield University, Division of Education, 388 Glossop Road, Sheffield S10 2TN, United Kingdom.
Fin: Local Education Authorities.
performance; quality of education; school
performance; qualité de l'éducation; école
PROJECT DESCRIPTION
More than one in ten of the country's local education authorities (LEAs) have requested specific help in the areas of shaping and implementing policy initiatives, particularly in the area of the evaluation of pupil and school performance. In one LEA a thorough review of secondary school examination performance has been undertaken, whilst elsewhere advisers and inspectors have sought assistance in developing comprehensive indicators of institutional performance. An increasing number of professional bodies (such as the the National Association of Inspectors and Advisers and the Association of Metropolitan Authorities) have turned to the group for advice and assistance.

Publ: Gray, J. & Jesson, D. The negotiation and construction of performance indicators, some principles, proposals and problems. In: *Evaluation and Research in Education*, Vol 4, No 2/1990, pp. 93-108.
Gray, J.; Jesson, D. & Sims, N. Estimating differences in the examination performances of secondary schools in six LEAs: a multilevel approach to school effectiveness. In: *Oxford Review of Education*, Vol 16, No 2/1990, pp. 137-158.
Gray, J. Performance indicators and the social organisation of evaluation: some proposals for change. In: Fitz-Gibbon, C.T. (ed.). *Performance indicators*. Clevedon: Multilingual Matters for British Educational Research Association, 1990.

12432 Performance measurement in higher education.
GBR 1993
Research Date(s): 1986-1991
Cave, M.; Hanney, S.; Kogan, M.
Inst: Brunel University, Faculty of Social Sciences, Uxbridge UB8 3PH, United Kingdom.
performance; achievement measurement; higher education
performance; mesure du rendement; enseignement supérieur
PROJECT DESCRIPTION
Against a background of growing interest in output and performance measurement in higher education (and the public sector in general) a need emerged for a critical analysis of the developing policy and practice being encouraged by the Government. The aims included: (i) to make a systematic and critical survey of the existing literature of performance indicators for higher education, within the context of more general literature of performance indicators; (ii) to analyse the range of models of performance indicators that might be applied. The literature review covered official reports and considerable material on subjects (including first destinations, bibliometrics and student evaluations of teaching) not specifically developed within the context of performance indicators (PIs). Some came from North America. The analysis therefore focused on how far it was appropriate to adopt this material to produce PIs which met the various criteria identified as being important in any successful model of PIs.

The research revealed weaknesses in the set of PIs that the Committee of Vice Chancellors and Principals and University Grants Committee had been persuaded to propose. However, provided PIs were developed for both the major functions of higher education - teaching and research - the analysis concluded they had a potential role within models of evaluation at several levels, including: (i) the funding body which makes inter-institutional comparisons; (ii) the institutions, where detailed and planning budgeting occurs.

The research has continued to monitor and analyse the rapid expansion of policy and practice in performance measurement in the United Kingdom and other western countries.

Publ: Cave, M.; Hanney, S.; Kogan, M. & Trevett, G. *The use of performance indicators in higher education: a critical analysis of developing practice*. London: Jessica Kingsley, 1988.
Cave, M.; Kogan, M. & Hanney, S. Performance measurement in higher education. In: *Public Money and Management*, Vol 9, No 1/1989, pp. 11-16, Spring.
Cave, M.; Kogan, M. & Hanney, S. The scope and effects of performance measurement in British higher education. In: Dochy, F. et al (eds.). *Management information and performance indicators in higher education: an international issue*. Van Gorcum, 1990.
Cave, M. & Hanney, S. Performance indicators for higher education and research. In: Cave, M.; Kogan, M. & Smith, R. *Output and performance measurement in government: the state of the art*. London: Jessica Kingsley, 1990.

12433 Les performances de l'enseignement primaire en Afrique sub-saharienne: comparaison des acquisitions en mathématiques dans quatre pays.
FRA 1993
Research Date(s): 1987-1989
Orivel, François; Perrot, Jean; Bakiyé, J.
Inst: Université de Dijon, UER Faculté des sciences économiques et de gestion, CNRS UPR/29 et GDR/996, Institut de recherche sur l'économie de l'éducation, BP 138, 21004 Dijon Cedex, France.
comparative achievement; Africa; Congo PR; Rwanda; France; teaching quality; mathematics; primary education; Central African Republic
rendement comparé; Afrique; Congo RP; Rwanda; France; qualité de l'enseignement; mathématiques; enseignement primaire; République Centrafricaine
PROJECT DESCRIPTION
Objectifs: Selon de nombreux observateurs, les taux de scolarisation dans l'enseignement primaire se sont généralement accrus dans les pays africains mais cette démocratisation s'est accompagnée d'une dégradation de la qualité de l'enseignement avec pour conséquence une baisse du niveau des élèves.

Méthodologie: Pour appréhender cette baisse de niveau on compare les résultats obtenus à un test standardisé en mathématiques dans 4 pays: Congo, République centrafricaine, Rwanda et France où ce test a été élaboré et étalonné. Dans chacun des trois pays africains, le test a été administré à un échantillon représentatif d'environ 1000 élèves appartenant à la 6e année du cycle primaire et inscrit dans des écoles de réputation différenciée.

Résultats: Les élèves rwandais obtiennent des résultats moyens à peu près identiques à ceux des élèves français alors que les élèves des deux autres pays africains obtiennent des résultats significativement inférieurs. D'une manière générale, les élèves africains réussissent relativement mieux dans les questions faisant appel à la mémoire mais plus mal dans les questions faisant appel au raisonnement. Le cas du Congo est plus grave dans la mesure où les élèves ne réussissent bien nulle part.

Publ: Orivel, François & Perrot, Jean. *Les performances de l'enseignement primaire en Afrique francophone: deux études de cas, le Congo et la République centrafricaine*. IREDU: document interne, 1989, 17p. et annexes.

12434 Pomiar sprawdzajacy wielostopniowy - ocenianie osiagnieć uczniów wedŁug wymagań programowych. (Graded criterion-referenced measurement: using curricular standards for grading achievement.)
POL 1994
Research Date(s): 1990-1995
Niemierko, BolesŁaw.
Inst: Instytut Pedagogiki Uniwersytetu Gdańskiego (Institute for Education, University of Gdansk), 80-952 Gdańsk-Oliwa, PO Box 628, Poland.
Komitet Nauk Pedagogicznych Polskiej Akademii Nauk (Education Committee, Polish Academy of Sciences), 60-568 Poznań, Szamarzewskiego 89, Poland
criterion-referenced test; achievement test; criterion-referenced evaluation; achievement measurement; test construction
test critériel; test de rendement; évaluation par objectifs; mesure du rendement; construction de tests
PROJECT DESCRIPTION
Aim: To identify theories and procedures that are useful in content-valid letter-grading of student achievement.
Hypotheses: (1) Reproducible subtest score patterns are obtained when a sequence of specified analytical and constructional steps of graded criterion-referenced measurement is followed. (2) Grade definitions across subject-matters and instructional systems are idiosyncratic with regard to the thinking level and content mastery required.
Sample: Incidental student and teacher samples are used.
Design: A series of curricular analyses and test specifications are performed. Multilevel criterion-referenced tests are constructed, applied and examined for gradability. Some highly gradable (gradability exceeding 90-95 percent) criterion-referenced tests in sciences are being constructed. Preconditions and procedures for graded measurement in humanities are still under consideration.
Publ: Niemierko, BolesŁaw. *Pomiar sprawdzajacy w dydaktyce.* Warszawa: PWN, 1991.
Niemierko, BolesŁaw. Using Criterion-Referenced Tests for Grading Achievement. In: Krope, Peter; Niemierko, BolesŁaw (eds.). *Proceedings of the 1992 Workshop on School Examinations.* Monographien zur Prüfungsforschung 15/1993. (Padagogische Hochschule Kiel).

12435 Primary science assessments.
GBR 1993
Research Date(s): 1989-1992
Sizmur, S.; Harris, S.
Sup: Ruddock, G.
Inst: National Foundation for Educational Research, The Mere, Upton Park, Slough SL1 2DQ, United Kingdom.
Fin: NFER/Nelson; Thomas Nelson U.K. Ltd.
assessment; science education; primary education
appréciation; éducation scientifique; enseignement primaire
PROJECT DESCRIPTION
Assessment materials for 'Science Assessment Modules' were developed to assist teachers to make teacher assessments of science for pupils' work at key stages 1 and 2 of the National Curriculum. They include worksheets and practical tasks, and cover all of the new statements of attainment in science at levels 1 to 5. They were published in December 1992 by NFER/Nelson.

12436 Profiling in the primary school: extension of self-assessment in primary schools 1989-1991 - collaborative approach to assessment.
GBR 1993
Research Date(s): 1993-
Towler, L.
Sup: Broadfoot, P.
Inst: Bath College of Higher Education, Newton Park, Newton St Loe, Bath BA2 9BN, United Kingdom.
student record; assessment; achievement
dossier académique; appréciation; rendement
PROJECT DESCRIPTION
This project investigates the background and issues surrounding the introduction of Records of Achievement, or profiles, to the primary school and, in particular, the principle of involving children and parents as partners, with teachers, in the assessment process. It explores the contribution made by the literature and research into Records of Achievement in the secondary context, in order to develop both a rationale for, and a critique of, self-assessment and examines ways in which these may prove applicable to primary children.
The issues examined inlcude the development of skills necessary for effective review and analysis of achievement and the extent to which young children may be empowered through ownership of their profile. The effect of individual differences in respect of age, gender, attainment and culture are also explored, and the implications for school policy on assessment considered. A qualitative case study of the introduction of profiling in one primary school was carried out in order to determine the extent to which children of ten and eleven years may be capable of taking responsibility for their own learning and benefit from involvement in their own self-assessment. The research also included using questionnaires and interviews, to gain the reaction and response of parents to the introduction of profiles as a method of reporting on achievement and to the request for their involvement in the process.
The conclusions drawn indicate that a coherent school policy for assessment, which is supported by the commitment of teachers and parents, can ensure that the principle of assessment as first and foremost the responsibility of the learner is both valid and can be realistically applied in education from the early years.

12437 Pupils as evaluators of textbooks.
GBR 1993
Research Date(s): 1987-1994
Wright, D.
Inst: University of East Anglia, School of Education, Norwich NR4 7TJ, United Kingdom.
evaluation; textbook; pupil; opinion
évaluation; manuel d'enseignement; élève; opinion
PROJECT DESCRIPTION
Textbooks for pupils are reviewed by teachers, not by pupils. Pupils are encouraged nowadays in school to express opinions and to evaluate evidence. The research seeks to experiment with pupils as reviewers of textbooks and other school books. Pupils in the United Kingdom and Australia are invited to review textbooks and information books. Their written observations are incorporated into articles discussing this new approach. Teachers are involved in evaluating pupils' observations. Results and conclusions will be illuminative, not definitive. The findings have implications for teachers and for educational publishers.
Publ: Wright, D.R. A pupil's perspective on textbooks: issues of motivation and racism. In: *Internationale Schulbuchforschung,* Vol 9, No 2/1987, pp. 137-142.
Wright, D.R. Applied textbook research in geography. In: Gerber, R. & Lidstone, J. (eds.). *Skills in geographical education.* International Geographical Union, 1988.
Wright, D.R. The role of pupils in textbook evaluation. In: *Internationale Schulbuchforschung,* Vol 12, No 4/1990.

12438 Quality of daycare provision in the United Kingdom.
GBR 1993
Research Date(s): 1992-1995
Caplan, M.; McGurk, H.
Inst: London University, Institute of Education, Thomas Coram Research Unit, 41 Brunswick Square, London WC1N 1AZ, United Kingdom.
Fin: Department of Health.
evaluation; day care; child care; day nursery
évaluation; mode de garde; aide à l'enfance; crèche
PROJECT DESCRIPTION
The goal of this project is to develop instruments and procedures that can contribute to the monitoring, evaluation, and enhancement of the quality of centre and family-based (childminding) childcare settings.

12439 Quantitative analysis for self-evaluation by schools.
GBR 1993
Research Date(s): 1993
Stradling, R.; Schagen, I.; Saunders, L.
Inst: National Foundation for Educational Research, The Mere, Upton Park, Slough SL1 2DQ, United Kingdom.
evaluation; school; measurement technique; model
évaluation; école; technique de mesure; modèle
PROJECT DESCRIPTION
This project will pilot test a self-evaluation package for schools which will help them to make use of the data they have to collect for the Department for Education for school management and evaluation purposes. The package will include access to a multilevel model which will be more sensitive than league tables of results. It will have a value-added element using tests and teacher assessments of student intake, and guidance to school managers on how to interpret the information.

12440 La reconnaissance des acquis.
FRA 1993
Research Date(s): 1988-1990
Liétard, Bernard; Chaput, Monique.
Sup: Pineau, Gaston.
Inst: Université de Tours, UFR Arts et sciences humaines, Laboratoire des sciences de l'éducation et de la formation, 3 rue des Tanneurs, bureau 405, 37041 Tours Cedex, France.
Fin: Délégation à la formation professionnelle.
recognition of qualifications; learning; research result
reconnaissance des qualifications; acquisition de connaissances; résultat de recherche
PROJECT DESCRIPTION
Objectifs: Il s'agit (1) d'opérer un bilan de la coopération franco-québe(coise dans le domaine de la reconnaissance des acquis; (2) d'iden-

tifier les principaux courants utilisant les approches personnalisées en reconnaissance des acquis.

Méthodologie: Un séminaire d'études avec appel à communications et travaux préparatoires.

Résultats: La reconnaissance des acquis est un réaménagement fondamental de la circulation des ressources humaines entre les organisations et leur environnement.

Publ: Pineau, Gaston; Liétard, Bernard & Chaput, Monique (coord.). *Reconnaître les acquis*. Paris: Editions universitaires, 1991, 227p.

12441 The role of informal assessment in teachers' practical action.
GBR 1993
Research Date(s): 1989-1994
Savage, J.
Sup: Desforges, C.
Inst: Exeter University, School of Education, St Luke's, Heavitree Road, Exeter EX1 2LU, United Kingdom.
assessment; teacher behaviour
appréciation; comportement de l'enseignant
PROJECT DESCRIPTION

The main aims of the research are to: (1) understand more about the way in which informal assessment is generated from teachers' intuitive theories; and (2) understand more about the way that this influences teaching acts. An opportunity sample of nine or ten teachers, who are working with 5-7 year olds, is being used. There will be several parts to the research. Firstly, the teachers will record some classroom action on videotape. Nine pieces of action of not more than 20 minutes in length will be recorded by each teacher. Secondly, each teacher will reflect upon this action, through the method of stimulated recall, in order to gain their informal assessments. Unstructured interviews will be used. Thirdly, these informal assessments will be organised and related to each teacher's views of teaching and learning. A more structured interview will then take place. Fourthly, the data will be analysed in terms of whether or not any action is taken as a result of the informal assessments. This data will include both the classroom action on videotape and teachers' reflections of that action on audiotape. The research is examining and analysing two types of process - teachers' thinking (the processes in their heads) and the processes that occur over a period of time in terms of action.

12442 School self-evaluation.
GBR 1993
Research Date(s): 1990-1992
MacBeath, J.; Thompson, W.; Arrowsmith, J.; Forbes, D.
Inst: Jordanhill College of Education, Division of Education and Psychology, Southbrae Drive, Glasgow G13 1PP, United Kingdom; Heriot-Watt University, Moray House Institute of Education, Holyrood Road, Edinburgh EH8 8AQ, United Kingdom; Craigie College of Education, Beech Grove, Ayr KA8 0SR, United Kingdom.
Fin: Scottish Office Education Department.
evaluation; school; performance
évaluation; école; performance
PROJECT DESCRIPTION

The aim of this project is to develop materials which can be used to gather parent, pupil and teacher perspectives on their own school.

12443 School self-evaluation: personnel training.
GBR 1993
Research Date(s): 1991-1992
Weir, A.
Inst: Jordanhill College of Education, Division of Secondary and Curricular Studies, Southbrae Drive, Glasgow G13 1PP, United Kingdom.
Fin: Grampian, Highland, Tayside Regions.
evaluation; in-service training; school; performance
évaluation; formation en cours d'emploi; école; performance
PROJECT DESCRIPTION

The aim of this project is to train and evaluate the senior personnel of schools in undertaking school self-evaluations.

12444 Schoolkwaliteit meten in het basisonderwijs; haalbaarheidsstudie. (Measuring the quality of primary schools.)
NLD 1994
Research Date(s): 1992-1994
Jungbluth, P.; Langen, A. van; Vierke, H.
Inst: Instituut voor Toegepaste Sociale wetenschappen (ITS) (Institute for Applied Social Sciences), P.O. Box 9048, 6500 KJ Nijmegen, Netherlands. Katholieke Universiteit Nijmegen (Catholic University of Nijmegen), P.O. Box 9102, 6500 HC Nijmegen, Netherlands
Fin: SVO het Instituut voor Onderzoek van het Onderwijs.
quality of education; primary school; achievement; achievement control; measuring instrument; data collection
qualité de l'éducation; école primaire; rendement; contrôle du rendement; instrument de mesure; rassemblement des données
PROJECT DESCRIPTION

Background: In educational policy there is a change taking place from government interference with the content of teaching to a "hard" type of quality control. Pupil achievement levels, controlled for factors on which the school has no influence, are regarded as indicators of school quality. In a recently published report the Advisory Council on Government Policy states that a model for testing, correction, aggregation and feedback is still lacking. This feasibility study is looking for the most practical solution to the problem of quality indicators.

Aim: To explore (a) the type of practical complications that occur in the operationalization of school quality and (b) practical solutions to the problem of quality indicators whereby the complications found under (a) can be avoided as much as possible.

Design: (I) Study of literature on experiences in other countries with the technical aspects of existing systems. (II) Simulation and secondary analysis of existing sets of data on: (1) longitudinal research on the influence of teacher expectations, (2) determinants of secondary school choice among pupils from "black" primary schools, and (3) achievement levels of three cohorts of pupils repeatedly tested as part of the evaluation of the Educational Priority Policy. (III) Study of 40 primary schools, some "white", some "black": in two successive years, tests will be administered five days a year to three year groups; once a year, parents will be interviewed. (IV) Experimental feedback study.

12445 Schools Assessment Research and Support Unit (SARSU).
GBR 1993
Research Date(s): 1983-
Black, H.; Devine, M.; Fenwick, N.; Gray, D.; Mingard, S.
Inst: Scottish Council for Research in Education, 15 St John Street, Edinburgh EH8 8JR, United Kingdom.
Fin: Local authorities; Scottish Council for Research in Education; Scottish Office Education Department.
assessment; action research; educational research
appréciation; recherche-action; recherche en éducation
PROJECT DESCRIPTION

The Schools Assessment Research and Support Unit (SARSU) carries out a rolling programme of action research and exploratory studies in assessment. It also encourages the dissemination of research findings and provides a support service for local authorities' inservice staff development programmes in assessment.

Publ: Black, H.D.; Devine, M.; Turner, E. & Harrison, C. *Standard Grade Assessment: a support package for schools*. Edinburgh: SCRE/SARSU, 1988; in collaboration with the Scottish Education Department.
Black, H.D. & Devine, M. *Mathematics checkpoint 7: assessment materials for primary 7 pupils*. Edinburgh: SCRE/SARSU, 1988.
Turner, E.; Black, H.D.; Hall, J. & Devine, M. *Technology in Home Economics*. Edinburgh: SCRE/SARSU, 1989.
Black, H.D.; Devine, M. & Turner, E. *Aspects of assessment: a primary perspective*. Edinburgh SCRE/SARSU, 1989.
Turner, E.; Black, H.D. & Devine, M. *Technology: an annotated bibliography*. Edinburgh: SCRE/SARSU, 1990.
A full list of publications is available from the researchers.

12446 Second International Assessment of Educational Progress (IAEP2).
GBR 1993
Research Date(s): 1989-1992
Foxman, D.
Sup: Burstall, C.
Inst: National Foundation for Educational Research, The Mere, Upton Park, Slough SL1 2DQ, United Kingdom.
Fin: Department of Education and Science.
assessment; cross-national research; test; achievement measurement
appréciation; recherche transnationale; test; mesure du rendement
PROJECT DESCRIPTION

In this research the National Foundation for Educational Research (NFER) acted as the agency for the participation of England and Wales in a second International Assessment of Educational Progress (IAEP) coordinated by the Centre for the Assessment of Educational Progress in the United States. The first IAEP, of 13 year-olds in mathematics and science in six countries (12 educational systems), was carried out in February 1988. The aim of reporting within a year was successfully achieved at both international and national levels early in 1989. The reports aroused a good deal of interest.

About 20 countries participated in the second assessment. In IAEP2 a second age group, 9 year-olds, was involved. There were also some questions on geography and an exploratory administration of practical items in mathematics and science for 13 year-olds. (England did not take part in the geography test.) Three international reports were published: one on the written tests of mathematics, a second on the written tests of science and the third on the results of the practical assessment. A national report on the findings in England was produced by the NFER.

12447 Secundaire analyses over de schoolloopbanen in het voortgezet onderwijs met het VOCL '89 cohort. (Secondary analyses on the school careers of secondary school pupils on the basis of data on the "VOCL '89" cohort.)

NLD 1994

Research Date(s): 1992-1993

Dronkers, J.; Jong, U. de; Roeleveld, J.

Sup: Meijnen, G.W.

Inst: Stichting Centrum voor Onderwijsonderzoek (SCO) (Centre for Educational Research), Grote Bickersstraat 72, 1013 KS Amsterdam, Netherlands.

Universiteit van Amsterdam (University of Amsterdam), P.O. Box 19268, 1000 GG Amsterdam, Netherlands

Fin: SVO het Instituut voor Onderzoek van het Onderwijs.

school career; lower secondary; denominational school; ethnic minority; achievement

cursus scolaire; secondaire premier cycle; école confessionnelle; minorité ethnique; rendement

PROJECT DESCRIPTION

Background: The study is part of a framework plan for a long-term analysis programme aimed at the first year of secondary education. This plan aims to establish the quality and the outcomes of education viewed from the perspective of "basic education" (the national core curriculum for lower secondary schools) and the aim of the Educational Priority Policy (i.e. to improve the school careers of disadvantaged pupils). The theoretical basis for the study is formed by theories on instructional and school effectiveness and selection and allocation mechanisms. The analyses of the first year of secondary education will be followed by investigations of the - potentially divergent - school careers of special categories of pupils.

Aim: To examine the relative significance of explanations for the educational disadvantages of immigrant pupils; to establish the relationship between, on the one hand, the regional dominance of a particular denomination, and, on the other, the effectiveness of schools of this denomination in terms of success rates per type of education. More particularly, the study examines: (a) the school careers of immigrant secondary school pupils as compared to those of native Dutch pupils; (b) the different effects of public-authority and denominational schools on individual pupils' school careers as a result of these schools' dominant or inferior position in their region; (c) the effectiveness of private non-denominational secondary schools.

Design: The VOCL '89 cohort comprises 19,000 pupils. Data are available on these pupils' school careers from the final year of primary education to the third year of secondary school. Secondary analyses will be performed to establish how far immigrant pupils are lagging behind and to determine the effectiveness of public-authority, denominational, and private non-denominational secondary schools. The analyses will be performed at pupil, parent, school and regional level.

12448 Special educational needs and the GCSE.

GBR 1993

Research Date(s): 1991-1993

Grant, M.; Came, F.; Bowker, P.; Noble, J.

Inst: Bristol University, School of Education, Centre for Assessment Studies, 22 Berkeley Square, Bristol BS8 1JA, United Kingdom.

Fin: School Examinations and Assessment Council.

examination; assessment; achievement; special education; learning difficulty

examen; appréciation; rendement; enseignement spécial; difficulté de l'apprentissage

PROJECT DESCRIPTION

A programme of research and development work will review the efficacy of existing General Certificate of Secondary Education (GCSE) provision for pupils with special educational needs and low-attaining pupils, and show how better access to assessment and certification can be achieved. In September 1991, the project was expanded to include approaches adopted by a sample of examining bodies, other than GCSE examining groups, to provision made for pupils with special educational needs.

Methods to be used include a questionnaire survey of 55 mainstream schools in England and Wales; interviews in 30 special schools; interviews with a range of representatives of examining groups, examining bodies, special educational needs (SEN) interest groups/interested parties and in-depth research and development work in two case study local education authorities (LEAs). The research report will identify developments in practice which have improved opportunities for pupils with special educational needs to gain accreditation at 16+. The report will be accompanied by support materials designed to provide techniques and procedures through which teachers and examiners can monitor and improve aspects of their assessment strategies. The project centres upon five National Curriculum subjects: English, mathematics, science, technology, and geography.

12449 Standard assessment tasks in design and technology and information technology at key stage 3 of the National Curriculum.

GBR 1993

Research Date(s): 1989-1992

Patterson, J.; Kimbell, R.; Baird, T.; Compton, J.; Farrell, A.; O'Hagan, P.

Inst: London University, Goldsmiths' College, Faculty of Education, Lewisham Way, New Cross, London SE14 6NW, United Kingdom.

Fin: School Examinations and Assessment Council.

assessment; test construction; art education; information technology; technology; lower secondary

appréciation; construction de tests; éducation artistique; technologie de l'information; technologie; secondaire premier cycle

PROJECT DESCRIPTION

The aim of the research is twofold. Firstly, to generate, test and evaluate teaching and learning materials that are a valid and reliable means of assessing the capability of 14 year olds in design and technology (D&T). Secondly, to generate, test and evaluate models of inservice teacher education (INSET) required to achieve suitably reliable assessment.

The design and technology schedule will involve a trial in 1990 of 3,000 pupils; a first pilot in 1991 of 15,000 pupils and a principal pilot in 1992 of 15,000 pupils. The Information Technology Schedule will involve a trial in 1990 of 500 pupils, and informal pilot in 1991 of 2,500 pupils and a pilot in 1992 of 15,000 pupils. The INSET schedule will involve approximately 175 teachers in 1990, approximately 500 teachers in 1991 and approximately 500 teachers in 1992. After each trial and pilot, a full report is to be written for the School Examinations and Assessment Council. This covers the appropriateness of the assessment materials and INSET and includes statistical data support for any recommendations that are made.

12450 Standard tests in English for pupils at the end of the second Key Stage of the National Curriculum in 1994, 1995, 1996.

GBR 1993

Research Date(s): 1992-1996

Whetton, C.; White, J.

Inst: National Foundation for Educational Research, The Mere, Upton Park, Slough SL1 2DQ, United Kingdom.

Fin: School Examinations and Assessment Council.

assessment; achievement test; common core curriculum; English language; reading; writing; test construction

appréciation; test de rendement; tronc commun; langue anglaise; lecture; écriture; construction de tests

PROJECT DESCRIPTION

The purpose of this work is to provide assessments of individual pupils' attainments in National Currciulum English at the end of Key Stage 2 (Year 6, typical age of pupils, 11 years). The assessments will be made in relation to the attainment targets English 2 (reading), English 3, 4 and 5 (writing, spelling and handwriting) in the statutory curriculum order for English. It is envisaged that the tests will be predominantly written and timed.

Developmental work leading up to the first full test of year 6 pupils in England and Wales in 1994 includes a pre-test carried out in December 1992 in about 70 schools. A range of materials and approaches were tried in the pre-test, from which a selection will be made for use in a national 2% pilot to be undertaken in May 1993. In advance of the pilot, the sponsoring agency, the School Examinations and Assessment Council, will be hosting several regional conferences to familiarise participating schools and teachers with the procedures to be adopted in the pilot test.

During the initial developmental stage of the work, the research team at the National Foundation for Educational Research worked intensively with teacher consultants, acting as material writers. Members of this panel will reconvene in successive stages of the project to revise and adapt material. Draft materials are scrutinised by an internally appointed vetting panel, while the work as a whole is under regular supervision by the committees of the School Examinations and Assessment Council.

12451 Standardization of a screening test of Greek-Cypriot speech and language.

CYP 1993

Research Date(s): 1991

Wilson, Margo.

Inst: Pedagogiko Instituto (Pedagogical Institute), P.O. Box 512, Nicosia, Cyprus.

test construction; speech; vocabulary; diction; expressivity; mother tongue; entry to school; diagnostic test

construction de tests; parole; vocabulaire; diction; expressivité; langue maternelle; entrée à l'école; test de diagnostic

PROJECT DESCRIPTION

Background and aims: Before children with communication disorders (disorders of articulation, language, fluency, voice) can be adequately served by the school system, there must be a means of reliably and validly identifying them upon entry into the school system. An initial step in such a process of evaluation is a standardized screening test which will identify children who need further testing and who may need treatment. Currently, no such test is available in the Greek language.

the purpose of this research was to develop the initial version of a Greek language speech and language screening test to be used with first-year Greek-speaking school children attending regular schools in Cyprus, to administer the test to a normative sample of children, to recommend modifications as needed, and to report tentative norms and numbers of children not passing the screening.

Methodology: The screening test was designed to provide a quickly administered, reliable and valid method of observing articulation in 35 selected samples and in sentences, as well as expressive vocabulary, expressive morphology and syntax, and comprehension of a variety of spatial and temporal terms, adjectives and clausal constructions. Informal evaluation of fluency and voice is done during the expressive language subtests.

Two hundred and thirty-six (236) subjects, 51% male, 49% female, were tested at three schools representing the range of socio-economic status backgrounds. Test administrators were native Greek-speaking trained speech-language pathologists. Retest data were obtained for 30 subjects. Subjects ranged in age from 67 to 88 months, with the mean and median age being 76.8 months.

Results: No significant differences were found for variables of gender, school or examiner. Therefore, data were pooled for normative scores. Test-retest correlations varied over subtests, but were acceptable for artic- ulation and language and total scores. Inter-examiner reliability was also acceptable. Cut-off scores were established at two standard deviations below the mean. Sounds misarticulated by more than 10% of the popula- tion were /s/, /z/, and blends containing these sounds. Sentences and commands containing question forms were most frequently missed by the subjects.

Thirty-one per cent (31%) of the children tested were referred for further testing based upon the information obtained during the administration of the screening test. Several recommendations were made for test revision and for further research to establish validity and check the norms against a more rural population.

Publ: Wilson, Margo. *Standardization of a Screening Test of Greek-Cypriot Speech and Language*, Nicosia: Research Report, Fulbright Commis- sion/Pedagogical Institute, 1991, 8p.

12452 Studeren in het hoger onderwijs: het eerstejaarsgebeuren modelmatig getoetst. (First-year students in higher education.)
BEL 1994
Research Date(s): 1990-1991
Bringmans, M.; Minnaert, A.; De Neve, H.
Sup: Janssen, P.
Inst: Centrum voor Schoolpsychologie (Centre for School Psychology), Tiensestraat 102, 3000 Leuven, Belgium.
Katholieke Universiteit Leuven (Catholic University of Leuven), Naamses- traat 22, 3000 Leuven, Belgium
Fin: Departement Onderwijs, Fonds voor Kollektief en Fundamenteel Onderzoek op Ministerieel Initiatief.
achievement control; achievement gain; achievement; dropout; student; motivation for studies; model construction
contrôle du rendement; progrès scolaire; rendement; abandon d'études; étudiant; motivation pour les études; construction de modèle
PROJECT DESCRIPTION
Background and aim: The high rate of failure in the first year of higher education in Belgium leads to the question: why and how do certain students achieve better than others? The aim of the project was therefore to explain differences in achievement in first-year students.

Methods: A general model has been constructed showing interrelation- ships between a number of relevant variables and between these variables and student performance. The underlying idea is that achievement at the end of the year is the result of a number of personal characteristics (i.e. capacity, motivation and self-confidence). These variables affect perform- ance directly or indirectly. In the latter case, students' study approach is very important: is it "meaning-oriented", "non-reproductive" or "achieve- ment-oriented"? (cf. Entwistle et al., 1979).

This model has been tested with the help of a LISREL programme, using data on 1,600 students gathered in an earlier project. These data include personal characteristics (social background, cognitive capacities, interest, secondary school career, choice of studies) and test results (motivation, intelligence, achievement). Only data on the following disciplines have been used (in each case a discipline at university level and one at non-university higher education level): psychology and pedagogy versus psychology and remedial education; applied sciences versus industrial engineering; German philology versus translating/interpreting and teacher training for modern languages.

Results: The model explained 22.3% of the achievement of the total research group. Subsequently, the model was tested separately for each discipline. There were some problems in three out of the eight disciplines. In the other disciplines 32.5%-62.6% of variation in achievement could be explained.

Publ: Bringsmans, M. et al. *Studeren in het hoger onderwijs: het eerstejaar- sgebeuren modelmatig getoetst op basis van in het OPFA-project verzamelde gegevens: rapport.* Leuven: KUL, Afdeling Psychodiagnostiek en psychologische Begeleiding, Centrum voor Schoolpsychologie, 1991, 150p.

12453 Studienverlauf und Uebergang ins Beschaeftigungssystem von Hochschulabsolventen 1988/1989. (Educational careers and occupational integration of university graduates from 1988/1989.)
DEU 1993
Research Date(s): 1989-1992
Nigmann, R.
Sup: Minks, K.
Inst: HIS Hochschul-Informations-System GmbH, Goseriede 9, D-3000 Hannover.
Fin: Bundesministerium fuer Bildung und Wissenschaft.
occupational integration; university studies; transition from school to work; graduate; school career
intégration professionnelle; études universitaires; passage à la vie active; étudiant diplômé; cursus scolaire
PROJECT DESCRIPTION
Inhalt: Analyse der Uebergangsverlaeufe in das Beschaeftigungssystem vor dem Hintergrund von Studienverlaufs- und -erfolgsmerkmalen bei Absolventen mit einem ersten Hochschulabschluss.
Geographischer Raum: Bundesrepublik Deutschland (alte Laender).
Vorgehensweise: Laengsschnittanalyse. Untersuchungsdesign: Panel.
Datengewinnung: Postalische Befragung (Stichprobe: 12000; Absolventen des Pruefungsjahres 1988/1989; Auswahlverfahren: Zufall). Primaererhebung: Feldarbeit von Mitarbeitern des Projektes durchgefuehrt.
Auswertung: Verschiedene bi- und multivariate Verfahren. Datenaufber- eitung: Datenedition (z.B. Aufbau von Datenbanken); Verlaufsdaten (event history data).

12454 Successful schooling.
GBR 1993
Research Date(s): 1990-1994
Brighouse, T.; Gough, G.; Johnson, M.; Glover, D.; Walton, W.
Inst: Keele University, Department of Education, Keele, Staffordshire ST5 5BG, United Kingdom.
Fin: Local Education Authorities.
achievement; performance; school; success
rendement; performance; école; réussite
PROJECT DESCRIPTION
The project aims to establish further information and knowledge about 'successful schooling', by means of questionnaires and in-depth interviews in 15-18 core study schools.

12455 Teacher appraisal in Malaysia: towards a strategy.
GBR 1993
Research Date(s): 1989-1993
Ahmed, S. ·
Sup: Reid, D.
Inst: Manchester University, School of Education, Oxford Road, Manchester M13 9PL, United Kingdom; Universiti Sains Malaysia, Pusat Pongajian, Ilmu Pendidikan, 11800 Nimden, Penang, Malaysia.
teacher appraisal; Malaysia; United Kingdom
évaluation sur l'enseignant; Malaisie; Royaume-Uni
PROJECT DESCRIPTION
Current trends in Malaysian secondary education are towards a national system of teacher appraisal. What has Malaysia to learn from the British model, and what features of the Malaysian teacher population demand special attention? A survey of 1,200 teachers in Malaysia is being used to determine the attitudes and opinions of secondary school teachers to appraisal. A strategy for appraisal will be developed on the basis of the survey.

12456 Teacher assessment in the National Curriculum core sub- jects: mathematics, science and English.
GBR 1993
Research Date(s): 1992-1993
Foxman, D.; Mason, K.
Inst: National Foundation for Educational Research, The Mere, Upton Park, Slough SL1 2DQ, United Kingdom.
assessment; common core curriculum; mathematics; science education; English language
appréciation; tronc commun; mathématiques; éducation scientifique; langue anglaise
PROJECT DESCRIPTION
In September 1989, following the Education Reform Act 1988, The National Curriculum was introduced in the core subjects of mathematics, science and English in all schools in England and Wales for the cohort of pupils in year 1. A year later saw the implementation of the National Curriculum in the core subjects in year 3; the first year of Key Stage 2. National Curriculum assessment arrangements include teacher assessment (TA) based on pupils' classroom work over the course of each key stage,

as well as statutory national assessments. Over the next two or three years, teachers of pupils at Key Stage 2 will be required to address a number of issues in their assessment practices, and to form and implement appropriate school policy.

The broad aims of this project are to study the various facets of teacher assessment in the three National Curriculum core subjects, as carried out by teachers in Key Stage 1 and 2 classrooms, and to identify good practice. The particular aims are to: (1) investigate if and how teachers use cross-curricular or topic work to make assessments in more than one subject; (2) determine the purposes to which teachers put the results of their assessments; (3) examine the range of procedures for recording pupil attainment; and (4) make recommendations on the professional development of teachers in teacher assessment practices, and the role of the local education authority (LEA) in this regard.

After an initial phase spent reviewing LEA and national documents on assessment, and contacting LEAs and primary schools, the project is to be carried out through a number of case studies of teachers. The case studies, which will take place during the school year 1992/1993, will involve the observation of the classroom work of teachers of years 1, 2, 3, and 4. A final report, to be written toward the end of the project, will point up good practice in teacher assessment, and make recommendations on the professional development of teachers in this area. A programme of dissemination will take place toward the end of the project within the LEAs participating in the research.

12457   Teacher assessment of the National Curriculum.
GBR   1993
Research Date(s): 1989-
Tanner, H.
Inst: University College of Swansea, Department of Education, Hendrefoilan, Swansea SA2 7NB, United Kingdom.
Fin: University of Wales; Association of Teachers of Mathematics.
assessment; common core curriculum
appréciation; tronc commun
PROJECT DESCRIPTION
A network of schools was established to conduct action research into the development of teacher assessment of the National Curriculum in key stage 3. Local education authority advisers were surveyed to establish the extent of guidance offered to teachers. Groups of teachers, trainers and advisers have been meeting to develop guidance materials.

12458   University examinations in science 1870-1900.
GBR   1993
Research Date(s): 1990-1993
Birley, G.
Inst: Wolverhampton University, Walsall Campus, Gorway Road, Walsall WS1 3BD, United Kingdom.
Fin: Royal Society; Wolverhampton University.
examination; science education; university; history of education
examen; éducation scientifique; université; histoire de l'éducation
PROJECT DESCRIPTION
This research will look at the content of science syllabuses and examination papers set by universities during the period 1870-1900, and relate this to examiners' interests and current scientific developments. The aim is to establish the role of the examinations and the extent to which the examination movement helped to codify scientific disciplines.

12459   Value-added measures.
GBR   1993
Research Date(s): 1991-1992
Quickfall, M.
Sup: Tymms, P.
Inst: Heriot-Watt University, Moray House Institute of Education, Holyrood Road, Edinburgh EH8 8AQ, United Kingdom.
performance; achievement; higher education; achievement measurement
performance; rendement; enseignement supérieur; mesure du rendement
PROJECT DESCRIPTION
Input and output measures are available for all students who have completed degrees in all colleges of education in Scotland. These data are being examined with a view to establishing value-added measures for courses in these colleges.

12460   Verbleibsanalyse Passauer Absolventen des Studiengangs Wirtschaftswissenschaften (BWL oder VWL). (Analysis of the destinies of graduates in economic sciences in Passau (business economics or economic science).)
DEU   1993
Research Date(s): 1988-1999
Luedeke, R.; Kleinhenz, G.
Inst: Universitaet Passau, Wirtschaftswissenschaftliche Fakultaet, Lehrstuhl fuer VWL, insb. Finanzwissenschaft, Innstr. 27, D-8390 Passau.
career; economics; branch of study; apprenticeship; school career; graduate
carrière; science économique; filière d'études; apprentissage professionnel; cursus scolaire; étudiant diplômé

PROJECT DESCRIPTION
Inhalt: Determinanten des Berufsverlaufs; Rueckschluesse auf die Lehre.
Vorgehensweise: Erhebung von Datenmaterial zur induktiven Verarbeitung bei der Theoriebildung. Untersuchungsdesign: Trend; Panel; retrospektive Daten.
Datengewinnung: Postalische Befragung (Stichprobe: 80; Absolventen Pruefungstermin November 1988; Auswahlverfahren: total. Stichprobe: 80; Absolventen Pruefungstermin Juni 1989; Auswahlverfahren: total). Primaererhebung: Feldarbeit von Mitarbeitern des Projektes durchgefuehrt.
Auswertung: Multiple Regression. Datenaufbereitung: Zeitreihe(n); Verlaufsdaten (event history data).

12461   Vergleich der Resultate von Lehrabschlussprüfungen nach Kantonen und nach Berufsgruppen.   (Comparaison des résultats obtenus aux examens de fin d'apprentissage selon les cantons et les métiers.)
CHE   1994
Research Date(s): 1990-1992
Martin, Margret; Klaghofer, Richard; Schläfli, André.
Inst: Schweizerische Gesellschaft für angewandte Berufsbildungsforschung (SGAB), Geschäftsstelle: R. Jörg, Ausstellungsstrasse 80, 8005 Zürich, Schweiz.
Bundesamt für Industrie, Gewerbe und Arbeit (BIGA), Abteilung Berufsbildung, Bundesgasse 8, 3003 Bern, Schweiz
final examination; apprenticeship; vocational education; vocational training; success
examen de sortie; apprentissage professionnel; enseignement professionnel; formation professionnelle; réussite
PROJECT DESCRIPTION
Das Bundesamt für Industrie, Gewerbe und Arbeit (BIGA) hat bei der Schweizerischen Gesellschaft für angewandte Berufsbildungsforschung (SGAB) eine Studie in Auftrag gegeben, mit welcher die Streuung von Noten und Ergebnissen in den Lehrabschlussprüfungen zwischen den Kantonen wie auch zwischen den Berufen untersucht werden soll. Die Untersuchung wird auf zwei Ebenen durchgeführt. In der Studie A werden die vom Bundesamt für Statistik seit 1984 jährlich zusammengetragenen Erfolgsquoten der Lehrvertragsstatistik ausgewertet. Die Studie B wird mehr im Detail Notenlisten der lokalen Prüfungsbehörden und somit Einzelresultate der Kandidatinnen und Kandidaten auswerten. Diese Forschungsphase wird sich auf fünf Kantone und drei ausgewählte Metiers beschränken.
Die Studie A beschlägt die sieben Jahre von 1984 bis 1990. Die globale Erfolgsquote weist über alle diese Jahre eine erstaunliche Stabilität auf. Bei einem Mittelwert aller Jahre von 93,39 Prozent betrug der Tiefstwert 93,00 Prozent (im Jahr 1988) und der Höchstwert 93,69 Prozent (1987). Grösser sind die Abweichungen zwischen den Kantonen. Was hier vorerst ins Auge springt, sind die Unterschiede zwischen der deutschsprachigen Schweiz und der französisch- oder italienischsprachigen Landesteilen. In der Deutschschweiz ist die Erfolgsquote generell höher; hier liegt einzig der Kanton Zürich unter dem gesamtschweizerischen Mittel (wobei er aufgrund seiner Bevölkerungsstärke natürlich mehr Kandidaten stellt als eine ganze Reihe kleiner deutschsprachiger Kantone zusammen). Die teifste Erfolgsquote (Mittelwert für die sieben Jahre) findet sich für den Kanton Genf (81,30 Prozent), die höchste für den Kanton Glarus (97,31 Prozent). Drückt im Falle Genfs z. B. der relativ hohe Anteil an Jugendlichen, die sich ein Maturitätszeugnis erwerben auf die durchschnittlichen, Leistungen der Lehrlinge? Oder ist die Latte für das Bestehen der Prüfung höher angesetzt? Auf Fragen dieser Art soll im Teil B der Untersuchung nach einer Antwort gesucht werden. Zuvor sollen allerdings die Ergebnisse der Phase A mit Expertinnen und Experten diskutiert werden; es wird gehofft, dass aus diesen Gesprächen noch Gesichtspunkte auftauchen werden, die für die Planung der zweiten Phase von Nutzen sein können.
Publ: Klaghofer, Richard; Martin, Margret & Schläfli, André. *Vergleich der Resultate von Lehrabschlussprüfungen: Studie A.* Zürich: Schweizerische Gesellschaft für angewandte Berufsbildungsforschung (SGAB), 1992, 65 Seiten (Berichte/Rapports; 6).

12462   Verifica della scheda sperimentale 1989-1990. (Evaluation of the new report card during the trial period 1989-1990.)
ITA   1993
Research Date(s): 1991
Coggi, C.; Del Gobbo, G.; Rastello, E.; Castro, W.; Belisario, C.; Bertola, A.
Sup: Calonghi, L.
Inst: Pontificio Ateneo Salesiano - PAS (Pontificial Salesian Atheneum), Piazza dell'Ateneo Salesiano 1, 00139 Roma, Italy.
Fin: Ministero della Pubblica Istruzione, Ufficio Studi e Programmazione.
student record; experimentation; assessment; evaluation criterion; criterion-referenced evaluation; achievement measurement
dossier académique; expérimentation; appréciation; critère d'évaluation; évaluation par objectifs; mesure du rendement
PROJECT DESCRIPTION
Aims: A number of lower secondary schools in Italy have experimented with a new kind of report card in the school year 1989-1990. The study

analysed the questionnaires administered to these schools in order to obtain feedback, to see what practical solutions have been devised, and to review the observations and proposals that have been put forward. It also aimed to probe the opinion of teachers and to stimulate reflection on problems of evaluation connected to the compilation of the new report card.

Methods: The responses were systematically examined and computerized according to uniform criteria.

Results: From the analysis of the first part of the questionnaire it appears that teachers face significant difficulties in the choice of information to include in Section 1 of the new report card. They are hesitant to label students and they meet obstacles in the collection of data. Schools are willing to gauge and adapt to individual characteristics of pupils. With regard to overall assessment, unresolved doubts and questions emerged, the main difficulties having to do with the problem of guidance. Parents seem to hold positive attitudes towards the new report card. Schools seem to be oriented toward developing individualized remedial teaching, but too often resort to stereotyped and standardized forms of evaluation. The Class Council, as a collegial body, is rarely in a position to face the problem of evaluation in a critical and constructive way and lacks the courage to start a debate on criteria that are already used in practice.

12463 Vooropleiding en schoolvorderingen in het MBO. (The relationship between previous education and school careers in senior secondary vocational education.)
NLD 1994
Research Date(s): 1990-1991
Batenburg, Th.A. van; Lokman, A.H.
Inst: RION Instituut voor Onderwijsonderzoek (RION Institute for Educational Research), P.O. Box 1286, 9701 BG Groningen, Netherlands.
Rijksuniversiteit Groningen (State University of Groningen), P.O. Box 72, 9700 AB Groningen, Netherlands
Fin: SVO het Instituut voor Onderzoek van het Onderwijs.
school career; achievement; dropout; vocational education
cursus scolaire; rendement; abandon d'études; enseignement professionnel
PROJECT DESCRIPTION

Background: A longitudinal study of the school careers and occupational careers of students on senior secondary education (MBO) courses has revealed that the success rates of these courses leave something to be desired. An explanation for this could be problems in the transfer from the previous school to the MBO institute. Most students entering MBO hold a junior vocational education (LBO) or junior general secondary education (MAVO) certificate. This study has examined the consequences of differences in the type of previous education for the school career in MBO.

The aim is to examine the influence of previous type of school (LBO or MAVO) on students' school careers in MBO. The project is part of a wider study of the school and occupational careers of the MBO students.

Results: The findings differ according to type of MBO course. In technical courses few differences exist between the success rates of former LBO and former MAVO pupils. In commercial courses former LBO pupils perform significantly lower than their colleagues from MAVO schools. The same holds for courses in personal social services and health care, but only in the first year. Differences in success rates in the first year are caused particularly by high dropout rates among former LBO pupils. A relatively high number of former LBO pupils find the courses too difficult or have chosen the wrong type of course. The relationship between level of previous school-leaving examination and degree of success in MBO is unclear. The hypothesis that a higher level of examination would be linked to a higher degree of success in MBO seems to hold only for personal social services and health care courses. After three years in MBO the number of former MAVO pupils with an MBO certificate is twice as high as the corresponding number of former LBO pupils.
(This is an updating of EUDISED no. 43/10261).

Publ: Batenburg, Th.A. van et al. *Vooropleiding en rendement in het MBO.* Groningen: RION, 1991, 49p.

12464 Was bleibt vom Schulbuchwissen bzw. vom Unterricht? Eine Untersuchung zu den 'Lerngegenstaenden' Geographie, Biologie und Geschichte anhand von Begriffs- und Fragetests. (What do pupils retain from textbooks and instruction? A study of the curriculum subjects geography, biology and history on the basis of tests and questionnaires.)
AUT 1993
Research Date(s): 1991-1993
Bamberger, Richard; Dillinger, Ernst; Gintenstorfer, Andrea; Jost, Joerg; Laske, Michael; Sirch, Christine.
Inst: Institut fuer Schulbuchforschung, Strozzigasse 2, A-1080 Wien.
Fin: Bundesministerium fuer Unterricht und Kunst.
knowledge level; concept formation; textbook; learning; achievement
niveau de connaissances; formation de concept; manuel d'enseignement; acquisition de connaissances; rendement
PROJECT DESCRIPTION

Forschungsansatz: Einblick in das Begriffsverstaendnis und das Merken von Lernfakten in den Gegenstaenden Geographie, Biologie und Geschichte anhand von einfachen Testverfahren (Erarbeitung, Einsatz, Auswertung): 650 SchuelerInnen der Hauptschulen/allgemeinbildenden hoeheren Schulen (30 Klassen, in Gruppen geteilt) wurden je 20 Begriffe bzw. Fragen vorgelegt, die von Paedagogen so ausgewaehlt worden waren, dass der betreffende Stoff mit Sicherheit vorher auch im Unterricht geboten wurde (Schulbuecher sind Grundlage fuer die Stoffauswahl im Unterricht).

Rund ein Viertel der gestellten Fragen/Begriffe wurde positiv beantwortet, 20% der Antworten waren teilweise richtig und 55% der Fragen/Begriffe konnten nicht oder nur falsch beantwortet werden. Als weiteres bestuerzendes Ergebnis (neben den vielen Rechtschreibfehlern) konnte die haeufig primitive Ausdrucksform bzw. die stilistische Unbeholfenheit (im Gegensatz zu den hochgestochenen Formulierungen des Lehrplans) festgestellt werden. Diese ersten Ergebnisse sollen durch die Einbeziehung der soziobiographischen Voraussetzungen sowie durch die Anwendung verschiedenster Untersuchungsmethoden ergaenzt werden.

In die Tests werden 650 SchuelerInnen von Hauptschulen/allgemeinbildenden hoeheren Schulen einbezogen. Es kommen zwei verschiedene Tests fuer je drei Gegenstaende zur Anwendung.

Die Daten werden mit statistischen Verfahren ausgewertet.

12465 Zittenblijven in het voortgezet onderwijs. (Repeating in secondary schools.)
NLD 1994
Research Date(s): 1993
Reezigt, G.J.
Inst: RION Instituut voor Onderwijsonderzoek (RION Institute for Educational Research), P.O. Box 1286, 9701 BG Groningen, Netherlands.
Rijksuniversiteit Groningen (State University of Groningen), P.O. Box 72, 9700 AB Groningen, Netherlands.
Fin: SVO het Instituut voor Onderzoek van het Onderwijs.
repeating; lower secondary; educational policy; pupil attitude; parental attitude
redoublement; secondaire premier cycle; politique de l'éducation; attitude de l'élève; attitude des parents
PROJECT DESCRIPTION

Background: Repeating is generally seen as an undesirable phenomenon, at least in as far as it can be avoided. In Dutch secondary schools it is a widespread phenomenon. In view of the principles of the pending national core curriculum for lower secondary schools, which aim at an uninterrupted learning route for all pupils, the Dutch Association of School Teachers (NGL) and a number of educational umbrella organizations have asked for a study of current practice regarding repeating years in secondary schools.

Aim: To examine the role of the school in the phenomenon of repeating as well as the way parents and pupils react to school policies regarding repeating.

Design: Secondary analyses will be performed on existing pupil, classroom and school data on 400 schools and over 20,000 pupils in the first three years of secondary school (the "VOCL" cohort). A survey will be conducted of 3,000 pupils who have been held back in the first three years and of staff at the schools they attend. In-depth studies will be conducted of schools that differ in respect of policies and repeater rates, involving interviews with parents, administrators, and pupils.

12466 Zweite Leistungsbeurteilung: Auswirkung von Leistungserwartung auf die Leistungsbeurteilung. (Performance evaluation: the impact of performance expectations on performance evaluation.)
AUT 1993
Research Date(s): 1992-1993
Rothschedl, Erich; Krenn, Boris.
Inst: Abteilung fuer Schulpsychologie und Bildungsberatung, Stifterstrasse 29, A-4020 Linz.
Landesschulrat fuer Oberoesterreich, Stifterstrasse 29, A-4020 Linz
achievement; achievement measurement; achievement motivation; performance
rendement; mesure du rendement; motivation d'accomplissement; performance
PROJECT DESCRIPTION

Anhand von Lehrer- und Schuelererwartungen bezueglich Schularbeitsnoten soll herausgefunden werden, inwieweit die Erwartungen an das Leistungsvermoegen Auswirkungen auf die tatsaechliche Leistung haben. Zudem soll mittels Motivationstest erhoben werden, welche Bedeutung Motivation fuer die Leistung hat und ob unterschiedliche Motivationstypen unterschiedliche Erwartungen an ihre Leistungen bei Schularbeiten haben. Ein weiteres Ziel dieser Arbeit ist es auch, herauszufinden, welche Bedeutung die Beziehung SchuelerInnen - LehrerInnen auf die Leistung bei Schularbeiten hat.

Es wird eine Befragung und eine Notenerhebung durchgefuehrt; einbezogen sind die vierten Klassen der Hauptschulen und die vierten Klassen der allgemeinbildenden hoeheren Schulen, insgesamt etwa 500 SchuelerInnen und 80 LehrerInnen.

07 BUILDING – BATIMENT – GEBAEUDE

12467 Aménagement de l'espace scolaire et projet d'établissement.
FRA 1993
Research Date(s): 1987-1990
Nouvelot-Gueroult, Marie-Odile; Pinot, Gérard.
Sup: Isambert-Jamati, Viviane; Conan, Michel.
Inst: Institut national de recherches et d'applications pédagogiques, 2 rue des Champs Prévois, 21100 Dijon, France.
Fin: Ministère de l'agriculture, Direction générale de l'enseignement et de la recherche; Ministère de l'équipement, Direction de l'architecture et de l'urbanisme.
space arrangement; agricultural training; educational institution; educational innovation
aménagement de l'espace; formation agricole; établissement d'enseignement; innovation pédagogique
PROJECT DESCRIPTION
   Objectifs: (1) Elaborer un projet global d'aménagement des espaces d'un établissement; (2) utiliser cette réflexion sur l'espace pour élaborer ou mettre à jour le projet d'établissement dans toutes ses composantes pédagogiques, éducatives et organisationnelles. Hypothèse principale: L'espace permet d'aborder un problème en partant de son inscription dans l'environnement et de le poser ensuite en terme d'organisation.
   Méthodologie: Démarche de recherche participante avec cinq établissements d'enseignement, quatre établissements d'enseignement agricole public et une école privée réunissant un collège d'enseignement général et un lycée agricole.
   Résultats: L'espace est une entrée tout à fait performante pour élaborer ou mettre à jour le projet d'établissement.
   Résultats très concrets: Réorganisation de l'espace et du travail, chantiers de construction... Nouveaux modèles de conduite suite à la formation méthodologique dispensée pendant tout le processus en particu-

lier pour ce qui concerne les méthodes d'analyse de la situation et de résolution de problèmes.

Publ: Nouvelot-Gueroult, Marie-Odile & Pinot, Gérard. *L'espace scolaire, support de recherche et de formation à l'évaluation du fonctionnement des établissements d'enseignement.* Colloque Culture technique et formation, Paris, déc. 1987, 14p.

Nouvelot-Gueroult, Marie-Odile. La programmation architecturale, une entrée en matière pour le projet d'établissement. In: *L'établissement, politique nationale ou stratégie locale?.* Actes du colloque de l'AECSE, 1989, pp. 136-143.

Nouvelot-Gueroult, Marie-Odile. *Les nouveaux enjeux de la décentralisation en matière de constructions et d'équipements scolaires.* Journées scientifiques: Penser le changement en éducation, organisées par le comité de recherche Modes et procès de socialisation de l'AISLF. Paris, janv. 1990, 11p.

Nouvelot-Gueroult, Marie-Odile & Pinot, Gérard. *Aménager, rénover, transformer des locaux: la programmation architecturale participative au service des établissements scolaires.* Document INRAP, mars 1990, 89p.

12468 Curriculum and staff development in small rural schools.
GBR 1993
Research Date(s): 1985-1991
Thorp, J.
Sup: Nisbet, J.
Inst: Aberdeen University, Department of Education, Taylor Building, King's College, Aberdeen AB9 2UB, United Kingdom.
small school; rural school; cooperation; further education of teachers; curriculum development
école de taille réduite; école rurale; coopération; perfectionnement des enseignants; élaboration de programmes d'études
PROJECT DESCRIPTION

In many areas of Britain the distribution of schools is at, or close to, the irreducible minimum. Small schools find themselves once again under threat resulting from both the requirement of the Education Reform Act 1988 to deliver the National Curriculum with the limited expertise of two or three teachers and from formula funding, which emphasises their high staffing costs. To meet their legal obligations it is widely thought that small schools need 'support'. Ten detailed case studies of support in action are presented, including Education Support Grant funded support projects, non-funded teacher self-help groups and individual school solutions. The case studies report the fieldwork undertaken in each of the ten areas and have been completed from interviews, observations and documentary analysis.

Analyses of individual cases reveal first a series of tensions among approaches to support, while further analysis indicates the substantive themes of the research, teacher empowerment, autonomy and control.

12469 Educational differentiation and social space.
GBR 1993
Research Date(s): 1990-
Shilling, C.
Inst: Southampton University, Department of Sociology and Social Policy, Highfield, Southampton SO9 5NH, United Kingdom.
space arrangement; differentiation; space perception
aménagement de l'espace; différenciation; perception de l'espace
PROJECT DESCRIPTION

The research consists, firstly, of a review of the literature on the role of social space in educational differentiation with particular reference to the place of space in structuration theory. Secondly, an ethnographic study has been conducted into the use of space in two school libraries. Particular attention is given to teacher and pupil attempts to colonise and regulate this educational space.

Publ: Shilling, C. & Cousins, F. Social use of the school library: the colonisation and regulation of educational space. In: *British Journal of Sociology of Education,* Vol 11, No 4/1990, pp. 411-430.

Shilling, C. Social space, educational differentiation and gender inequalities. In: *British Journal of Sociology of Education,* Vol 12, No 1/1991, pp. 23-45.

12470 The impact of pupil participation in playground design on pupil satisfaction with playtime and the incidence of bullying in school playgrounds.
GBR 1993
Research Date(s): 1991-1992
Beer, A.; Smith, P.; Higgins, C.; Sheat, L.
Inst: Sheffield University, Department of Psychology, Sheffield S10 2TN, United Kingdom.
Fin: Gulbenkian Foundation.
playground; recreational activities; bullying; antisocial behaviour; supervision
espace de jeu; activités récréatives; brimades; comportement antisocial; surveillance
PROJECT DESCRIPTION

Bullying has been found to be a pervasive as well as distressing phenomenon in many schools. Some 20% of pupils report some degree of involve-

ment in bullying over the previous term (Smith, 1991). Much of this bullying takes place in the playground, during lunch hour or mid-morning break.

A team of researchers at Sheffield University are currently examining both the incidence of bullying in a sample of some 24 junior/middle and secondary schools, and ways of intervening to reduce the extent of the problem. Various kinds of intervention will be negotiated with the schools, and to some extent resourced for them. These interventions will either be based on existing expertise, or in some cases developed by the research team. Work in playgrounds is one important intervention in this package, and one which is proving a popular option amongst the schools involved.

The main research project (funded by the DES) is planning to concentrate on producing a useful training course/materials for lunchtime supervisory assistants, who are often inadequately prepared or trained for the task of supervising large numbers of children, distinguishing bullying from more playful activities, and knowing how to respond appropriately.

The other main aspect of playground intervention is the design of the playground, facilities, and pupil involvement in these aspects of the playground environment. An attractive playground which allows a variety of activities of interest to children - when combined with informed supervision - is less likely to be a breeding ground for bullying. The Department of Psychology at Sheffield University is collaborating with the Department of Landscape Architecture to work on playground design and pupil participation. In the latter department, students usually carry out a small project in playgrounds, and a variety of methods and game formats have been devised to involve pupils in this activity.

The projects themselves are small-scale (lasting about a week) but the methods will be used on a larger scale, over a six-month period, to assist four schools which are seriously interested in involving their pupils in designing/changing/improving playground facilities. The design process will proceed in stages, culminating in a joint presentation of short-listed designs in February 1992.

The second phase of the project will be involved in assisting the implementation of these designs, and monitoring their impact, on behaviour in the playground generally and bully/victim problems in particular.

12471 The impact of pupil participation on playground design and school bullying.
GBR 1993
Research Date(s): 1991-1992
Higgins, C.; Sheat, L.
Sup: Smith, P.; Beer, A.
Inst: Sheffield University, Department of Psychology, Sheffield S10 2TN, United Kingdom.
Fin: Caloustie Gulbenkian Foundation (UK).
playground; recreational activities; bullying; antisocial behaviour; pupil attitude
espace de jeu; activités récréatives; brimades; comportement antisocial; attitude de l'élève
PROJECT DESCRIPTION

Four junior schools took part in this project. Initially students and staff from the Department of Landscape at Sheffield University worked with the pupils and staff of the schools, finding out which activities were done to which areas of the existing playgrounds, good and bad features, and then, with a series of games and exercises, what kind of playground they would like to have. Following this, a design brief was prepared for each school playground, together with applications for funding and implementation. These design briefs aimed towards a more diversified and challenging playground environment, which might reduce opportunities and incentives for bullying (a problem all these schools were working on).

During the second part of the project the school commenced implementing aspects of the design briefs. Feedback was obtained from both pupils and staff concerning (a) satisfaction about changes in the playground, and (b) levels of bullying.

12472 ISDN2 and computer networks to enhance initial teacher training.
GBR 1993
Research Date(s): 1991-1992
Davis, N.; Wright, B.; Tearle, P.
Inst: Exeter University, School of Education, St Luke's, Heavitree Road, Exeter EX1 2LU, United Kingdom.
Fin: Employment Department - Learning Technology Unit.
resource centre; didactic use of computer; teacher education; media technology; information technology
centre de matériel didactique; usage didactique de l'ordinateur; formation des enseignants; médiologie; technologie de l'information
PROJECT DESCRIPTION

Exeter University School of Education has recently built a Media and Resources Centre which contains a TV studio and three information technology (IT) rooms (two on 24 hour access), with extensive ethernet network and many of the PCs are on this network. The University of Virginia will provide computer conferencing and mail software (TIM) plus consultancy on its installation. Exeter will become the first international node in the emerging K12 network for the USA (Bull and Harris, 1990). British Telecom will install several ISDN2 nodes in this building and one in a local school's resource centre/library. Other nodes are in Martlesham and Anglia College of Higher Education's Xploratorium.

The second phase of the project during Lent and Trinity terms 1992 will trial these links with student teachers. These trials would be an assessed part of an IT course. At the same time the ISDN2 link will be in use with one or two students placed in the secondary school for teaching practice. Again this is an assessed part of their course. The project officers, who are experienced IT tutors with expertise in multimedia and communications including databases on CD, will assist permanent tutors implement this.

The third phase of the project will document these case studies in the form of published papers, video and student work. The database of IT applications discussed by large groups of students could provide stimulating reflections on future use of IT in education. At this stage the data gathered on costs and learning issues (using action research methods) will be carefully analysed.

12473 Small schools and pupil attitudes.
GBR   1993
Research Date(s): 1989-1992
Francis, L.
Inst: Trinity College, Carmarthen, Dyfed SA31 3EP, United Kingdom.
school size; small school; pupil attitude; attitude towards school; primary school
dimension de l'école; école de taille réduite; attitude de l'élève; attitude envers l'école; école primaire
PROJECT DESCRIPTION
The project is re-analysing data collected from 82% of the state maintained primary schools in a shire county in order to explore the relationship between school size and pupil attitude towards school. Attitudes are measured by means of semantic differential grids.

The data demonstrate that pupils attending schools of sixty or fewer children report a significantly more positive attitude towards school than pupils attending larger schools.
Publ: Francis, L.J. Primary school size and pupil attitudes: small is happy? *Educational Management and Administration*, Vol 20, No 2/1992, pp. 100-104.

08   EQUIPMENT – EQUIPEMENT – AUSSTATTUNG

12474 Design guidelines for electronic books.
GBR   1993
Research Date(s): 1990-1992
Barker, P.
Inst: Teesside University, School of Computing and Mathematics, Interactive Systems Research Group, Borough Road, Middlesbrough, Cleveland TS1 3BA, United Kingdom.
Fin: Training, Enterprise and Education Directorate.
optical storage; CD rom; compact disc; interactive video; educational technology; authoring system; didactic use of computer
mémoire optique; CD-ROM; disque compact; vidéo interactive; technologie de l'éducation; système-auteur; usage didactique de l'ordinateur
PROJECT DESCRIPTION
Electronic books based upon the use of digital optical storage (CD ROM) technology are capable of providing many new and novel approaches to the problems of disseminating knowledge and information. They are particularly useful for implementing a wide variety of different types of learning and training activities. Unfortunately, few guidelines currently exist to enable authors of such books to create effective page and book structures. This work is therefore intended to investigate this problem with a view to formulating a set of design guidelines and a collection of fabrication procedures.

Three basic optical storage technologies are being studied: basic CD ROM (compact disc read only memory); CD-I (compact disc interactive); and DVI (digital video interactive). Six different categories of electronic book are currently being studied: text books; static picture books; moving picture books; multi-media books; intelligent electronic books; and teleconferencing books. Authoring tools to enable authors to produce these different types of electronic book are also being investigated. To date a number

of books have been designed and fabricated. The group's most recent book template is called SPBAN (static picture books with audio narrations). The potential of this category of electronic book as a tool for promoting foreign language learning is currently being investigated.
Publ: Barker, P.G. Designing, authoring and fabricating electronic books. In: *Proceedings of the Seventh International Conference on Technology and Education*, Brussels, Belgium, 20-22 March 1990, pp. 291-293.
Barker, P.G. & Manji, K.A. Designing electronic books. In: *Educational and Training Technology International*, Vol 28, No 4/1991, pp. 273-280.

12475 Effects of introducing small equipment into primary schools for use at playtimes.
GBR   1993
Research Date(s): 1991-1992
Sleap, M.
Inst: Hull University, School of Education, Cottingham Road, Hull HU6 7RX, United Kingdom.
Fin: Learning Through Landscapes.
equipment; playground; recreational facilities; school environment
équipement; espace de jeu; installations récréatives; milieu scolaire
PROJECT DESCRIPTION
The physical environment of primary schools can provide an immense resource for the all-round development of children. At present only a fraction of the full potential is utilised. The aim of the project is to evaluate the effects of introducing a range of inexpensive, readily available items of small equipment into primary schools for use at playtimes. The sample consists of six different types of primary school. The project will last for 12 weeks during Autumn term 1991, with written evaluations and follow-up interviews conducted with children, teachers, and dinner supervisors.

12476 End-user interfaces to electronic books.
GBR   1993
Research Date(s): 1990-1993
Richards, S.
Sup: Barker, P.; Manji, K.
Inst: Teesside University, School of Computing and Mathematics, Interactive Systems Research Group, Borough Road, Middlesbrough, Cleveland TS1 3BA, United Kingdom.
Fin: Science and Engineering Research Council; Dean Associates.
optical storage; CD rom; compact disc; didactic use of computer; multimedia system; man-machine interface
mémoire optique; CD-ROM; disque compact; usage didactique de l'ordinateur; système multimédia; interface homme-machine
PROJECT DESCRIPTION
The term 'electronic book' is a metaphor which is used to describe an application which aims to deliver information in an electronic form. The rapid advances in storage technologies, for example Compact Disc Read Only Memory (CD ROM) and Magneto Optical Rewritable Optical Disk (MOROD), have allowed such books to deliver huge quantities of information in a wide variety of presentation media forms. Such developments, along with the advances in digital information presentation; video and audio compression and decompression in real-time; high resolution colour display devices; and hypermedia information networks, can facilitate the creation of extremely rich and stimulating information delivery environments. The very newness of these technologies has meant that the full capabilities and potentials as applied to electronic books, has as yet not been fully investigated.

The current research aims to develop extremely rich electronic book environments which are capable of tailoring the information which they deliver to individual user requirements. Information will be presented in the form of digital video, sound, animation, hypertext and hyperimages in order to assess the pedagogic impact of such information delivery strategies. This is to be effected by investigating the effectiveness of different page structures based upon the following models: simple page model; composite page model; overlay page model; and the viewport page model. Through the adoption of such a strategy it will then be possible to assess the efficacy of various page structures, presentation media and access techniques within learning and training environments.
Publ: Richards, S.M. & Barker, P.G. Page structures for electronic books. In: *Educational and Training Technology International*, Vol 28, No 4/1991, pp. 291-301.

12477 Evaluation of multisensory rooms in the education of children with profound and multiple learning difficulties.
GBR   1993
Research Date(s): 1980-1992
Gerard, M.
Sup: Fogelman, K.; Merry, R.
Inst: Leicester University, School of Education, University Road, Leicester LE1 7RH, United Kingdom.
Fin: Leicestershire County Council.
equipment; special education; multiple disability; handicapped
équipement; enseignement spécial; multihandicap; handicapé
PROJECT DESCRIPTION

Many schools for children with severe learning difficulties (SLD) have invested time, floor space, staffing and money for the purchase of equipment in constructing 'multisensory rooms'. The intention of the project is to find out the size of the investment made, the nature of the rooms, the equipment installed, the level of use, the client population and the teachers' evaluations of their installations in a number of areas such as development of visual skills, development of fine and gross motor skills, and general multisensory stimulation.

Analysis of the 75 responses (out of 100 sent to SLD schools in the English Midlands) to the questionnaire, alongside interviews with teachers and manufacturers of the specialist equipment and analysis of questionnaires submitted to peripatetic teachers for the visually impaired should help to answer some of the issues outlined above. At the same time some consideration is given to the theoretical justifications that are advanced for undertaking multisensory room work.

12478   I epidrasi tis didaskalias stin epidosi ton mathiton tou demotikou scholiou sti lisi tou mathimatikou provlimatos me ti chrisi ypologistikis michanis.   (The effect of calculators on pupils' problem solving abilities.)
CYP   1993
Research Date(s): 1992
Konstantinides, A.
Inst: Pedagogiko Instituto (Pedagogical Institute), P.O. Box 512, Nicosia, Cyprus.
calculator; mathematics; problem solving; achievement; sex difference
machine à calculer; mathématiques; résolution de problème; rendement; différence de sexe
PROJECT DESCRIPTION

Background and aims: The National Council of Teachers of Mathematics in the USA and the developers of the National Curriculum in the UK encourage and recommend the use of calculators in the teaching of mathematics. In Cyprus, the education system does not officially permit the use of calculators, but unofficially their use is encouraged in certain mathematics activities. These recommendations provided the framework for this study, which investigated the effectiveness of the use of calculators in the problem solving abilities of male and female pupils in the sixth year. It was moreover intended that the research findings would be useful for further research on the topic.

Methods: The study involved two sixth-year classes, one being the experimental group, the other the control group. Both groups had been taught the same concepts, skills and problems for months. The dependent variable was the performance of pupils in problem solving as measured by the posttest which was constructed by the researcher and which consisted of 57 items. The independent variables were the method used (use vs. non-use of calculators) and sex and socio-economic status of the pupils. A pretest was administered to all pupils at the beginning of the study, to determine whether the experimental and control groups differed significantly on the test.

Results: Pupils who used a calculator in solving problems attained higher scores than pupils who did not use a calculator. Pupils in the experimental group solved problems using a wide range of techniques and, most importantly, they used calculators to check their answers and to decide about the reasonableness of their answers. The experimental group performed better in solving geometry problems and in interpreting problems involving mathematical equations. The results also showed a significant correlation between sex and problem solving performance: boys scored higher than girls. No correlation was found between socio-economic status and performance in mathematics.

12479   Measurement in science in the primary classroom.
GBR   1993
Research Date(s): 1990-1992
Gott, R.; Phipps, R.; Feasey, R.
Inst: Durham University, School of Education, Leazes Road, Durham DH1 1TA, United Kingdom.
measuring instrument; science education; measurement
instrument de mesure; éducation scientifique; mesure
PROJECT DESCRIPTION

As part of work for the National Curriculum Council (NCC) on the implementation of the investigative work of Attainment Target 1 in Science, the issue of the availability of measuring equipment came to be seen as a matter of some concern to those interviewed as part of the research, and to the research team. As a consequence, the science team in Durham undertook a survey independently of the NCC, of the availability of such equipment in a sample of primary schools drawn from a nationwide random sample.

12480   Pre-School Activities Inventory.
GBR   1993
Research Date(s): 1988-1992
Golombok, S.; Rust, J.
Inst: City University, Northampton Square, London EC1V OBH, United Kingdom.

measuring instrument; role perception; pre-school child; sex role; child development
instrument de mesure; perception de rôle; enfant d'âge préscolaire; rôle sexuel; développement de l'enfant
PROJECT DESCRIPTION

The Pre-School Activities Inventory is a psychometrically constructed questionnaire for the measurement of sex-role behaviour in children. It is completed by the child's parents, teacher or nursery staff. The questionnaire contains 28 items, and is divided into three areas: toys and games, activities and characteristics. It has been validated by comparing parents' responses on the questionnaire with teachers' ratings of masculinity and femininity.

12481   A 'virtual' microscope.
GBR   1993
Research Date(s): 1993-1995
Whalley, P.; Williams, D.
Inst: Open University, Institute of Educational Technology, Walton Hall, Milton Keynes MK7 6AA, United Kingdom.
microscope; earth sciences; didactic use of computer
microscope; sciences de la terre; usage didactique de l'ordinateur
PROJECT DESCRIPTION

This project is concerned with developing a 'virtual' microscope which allows the student to choose, manipulate and examine rock samples on the computer screen. Embedding the 'virtual' microscope within a general multi-media database will provide the student with a powerful tool for enquiry and learning. The primary problems that the researchers intend to tackle are pedagogic, not technical: What does or does not aid student learning in the summer school environment, and how may computer-based materials be integrated with the other media being used? An important part of the project will be the developmental testing of the materials at Open University summer schools with the general aim of finding the right balance between questioning and support for the student. An immediate use of the materials will be to enrich the experience of the less mobile students attending these summer schools. Whilst other students go out collecting samples 'in the field', these students will be able to make detailed analyses of equivalent rock samples and consequently be able to make greater contributions to group discussions. A simple extension of the project on the lines of the well-known 'Eco-Disc' project would allow the student to 'move' around computer-based images and video clips of the hill or quarry and choose from where they would like a 'sample' to be taken. This would obviously empower disabled students to undertake courses and projects from which they would otherwise be blocked.

12482   WORM (Write-Once-Read-Many) and CD ROM (Compact Disc Read Only Memory) utility within a CAL (Computer-Asssisted Learning) workstation environment.
GBR   1993
Research Date(s): 1986-1992
Barker, P.
Inst: Teesside University, School of Computing and Mathematics, Interactive Systems Research Group, Borough Road, Middlesbrough, Cleveland TS1 3BA, United Kingdom.
optical storage; CD rom; compact disc; distance study; didactic use of computer
mémoire optique; CD-ROM; disque compact; enseignement à distance; usage didactique de l'ordinateur
PROJECT DESCRIPTION

Distance learning is concerned with the provision of learning facilities and resources at centres or sites that are remote from those at which these resources are produced. Distributed computer networks provide one mechanism by which distance learning may be realised. However, there are currently many severe limitations associated with the presently available telecommunications facilities with respect to the services available for high speed transmission of large volumes of text, sound and picture material. In due course (with the advent of ISDN (Integrated Service Digital Network)), these limitations are likely to be overcome. However, common access to ISDN over geographically large areas is likely to be some decades away.

This feasibility study is concerned with how Write-Once-Read-Many (WORM) and Compact Disc Read Only Memory (CD ROM) discs might be used to help realise some of the goals of distance learning. In particular, it is intended to study how such discs might be used within a CAL workstation learning environment to facilitate the storage of large volumes of textual information and digitised sound and pictorial material. Some of the aspects of optical disc technology (1,2,3) that would be considered in this feasibility study would therefore be the use of: (1) pre-mastered discs (such as conventional dictionaries, reference works, encyclopaedias, picture libraries, etc.) within CAL courseware; and (2) the use of discs created locally (containing image data, sound resources and so on). The first of these studies would involve the fabrication of a multi-media workstation to which is connected one or more CD ROM units. The second study would require the workstation to be enhanced through the addition of appropriate image/sound input peripherals, suitable digitisation equipment and, of course, a WORM unit. To support this work an investigation into interfaces and standards would also be necessary.

Publ: Barker, P.G. Video discs in libraries. In: *The Electronic Library*, Vol 4, No 3/1986, pp. 166-176.

09 CURRICULUM – PROGRAMME D'ETUDES – CURRICULUM

12483 5-14 Development Programme: coordination of the evaluation of its implementation.
GBR 1993
Research Date(s): 1991-1995
Harlen, W.
Inst: Scottish Council for Research in Education, 15 St John Street, Edinburgh EH8 8JR, United Kingdom.
Fin: Scottish Office Education Department.
curriculum development; quality of education; evaluation; primary education; secondary education
élaboration de programmes d'études; qualité de l'éducation; évaluation; enseignement primaire; enseignement secondaire
PROJECT DESCRIPTION
The work of coordinating the planning of the 5-14 education projects began in February 1991. The coordinated programme will cover all aspects of the new developments in the curriculum, assessment, use of test materials and reporting to parents as these are implemented during the next few years.

12484 Arbeitszeitverkuerzung fuer Schueler. (Reduction of pupils' working hours.)
AUT 1993
Research Date(s): 1992-1993
Mayr, Johannes.
Inst: Paedagogische Akademie der Dioezese Linz, Salesianumweg 3, A-4020 Linz.

Fin: Bundesministerium fuer Unterricht und Kunst.
leisure; behaviour; pupil; school day; recreational activities; learning time
loisir; comportement; élève; journée scolaire; activités récréatives; temps d'acquisition
PROJECT DESCRIPTION
Es wurde von den folgenden Fragestellungen ausgegangen: Wofuer verwenden Hauptschueler ihre Freizeit? Wie aendert sich das Freizeitverhalten im Zuge von Schulversuchen? Veraenderung des Ausmasses des haeuslichen Lernens durch den Schulversuch? Unterschiede zwischen Stadt- und Landhauptschule?
Es werden Schueler- und Elternfragebogen zum Freizeitverhalten ausgegeben. In die Erhebung werden alle Hauptschueler der Uebungshauptschule der Paedagogischen Akademie und der Hauptschule Andorf einbezogen.

12485 Charging for out of classroom activities in schools.
GBR 1993
Research Date(s): 1989-1991
Hale, M.; Hindon, J.
Inst: Council for Environmental Education, Reading University, Faculty of Education and Community Studies, National Environmental Resource Base, London Road, Reading RG1 5AQ, United Kingdom; Field Studies Council, Central Services, Preston Montford, Montford Bridge, Shrewsbury SY4 1HW, United Kingdom.
Fin: Field Studies Council; Council for Environmental Education; Department of Education and Science.
extra-curricular activities; out-of-school education; fees
activités hors programme; éducation extra-scolaire; droits de scolarité
PROJECT DESCRIPTION
The aim of the research is to discover the impact of the charging aspects of the Education Reform Act - 1988 on out of school activities, in particular, fieldwork related to geography and science. The investigation had three stages: (1) 1989/1990 - a questionnaire sent to approximately 400 Field Study Centres to assess the impact of charging; (2) 1990/1991 - a repeat of the 1989/1990 survey and (3) questionnaire sent to all schools in eight selected local education authorities.

12486 Classificatie van schoolvarianten. (Classification of school variants.)
NLD 1994
Research Date(s): 1988-1992
Bosker, R.J.
Inst: RION Instituut voor Onderwijsonderzoek (RION Institute for Educational Research), P.O. Box 1286, 9701 BG Groningen, Netherlands.
Rijksuniversiteit Groningen (State University of Groningen), P.O. Box 72, 9700 AB Groningen, Netherlands.
Fin: SVO het Instituut voor Onderzoek van het Onderwijs.
common core curriculum; secondary education; evaluation; research technique
tronc commun; enseignement secondaire; évaluation; technique de recherche
PROJECT DESCRIPTION
Background: One of the recommendations made by the Coordinating Committee for the Secondary Education Evaluation Plan (CCE) in its fourth advisory paper was to commission a research study that would examine the relationships between, on the one hand, the organizational, pedagogical and structural characteristics of schools, and, on the other, the schools' success in implementing the lower secondary core curriculum. Since a large number of school variables interact with the effect of the core curriculum (in terms of improved achievement levels and school careers), the CCE recommended a classification of schools into "variants" (based on a range of school characteristics), which would make it possible to determine the effect of the core curriculum per "school variant".
Aim: This preliminary study sought to answer the following questions: (1) Is it possible to classify secondary schools into a limited number of variants on the basis of a range of school characteristics, in such a manner that the differences within a variant are considerably smaller than those between variants? (2) What differences, if any, exist between these variants in terms of pupils' achievement levels and school careers?
Methods: Analysis of existing research data.
Results: It is not very well possible to classify schools on the basis of school type and combinations of school types within combined schools, due to the weak predictive validity of such a classification in terms of differences between schools as regards the achievement levels of their pupils. Neither is it possible to classify schools satisfactorily by looking at the presence or absence of inequality related to pupil background. A classification into variants on the basis of school development characteristics (pupil guidance, school work plan development, extended range of course offering, differentiation) enables a distinction to be made into four groups of schools, two of which lend themselves well to a workable interpretation: schools that are well ahead and schools that are remaining behind. A classification on the basis of "effectiveness" shows that the variant with the most favourable effect on pupils' affective functioning (well-being and motivation) does not have the most favourable effect on

achievement. In general it would seem that integrated variants are to be preferred. However, such integrated variants can give no guarantee as regards the reduction of inequality related to pupil background. Given the aims of the core curriculum, it would be wiser to develop a new typology; to relate this to both the cognitive and the affective functioning of pupils; and to include the necessary controlling for differences in the initial situation of pupils. It is advisable to develop and test this typology for use with combined schools.

Publ: Bosker, R.J. *Schoolvarianten: een empirisch onderzoek naar con-figuraties van schoolkenmerken ten behoeve van de evaluatie van de basis-vorming.* Groningen: RION, 1992, 62p.

12487 A comparative study of secondary school curricula in England and Wales and the Republic of Cameroon: issues of breadth, balance and relevance.
GBR   1993
Research Date(s): 1989-1991
Abangma, P.
Sup: Brock, C.
Inst: Hull University, School of Education, Cottingham Road, Hull HU6 7RX, United Kingdom.
curriculum development; comparative education; common core curriculum; aims of education; Cameroon; England; Wales
élaboration de programmes d'études; éducation comparée; tronc commun; finalité de l'éducation; Cameroun; Angleterre; Pays de Galles
PROJECT DESCRIPTION
Issues of breadth, balance and relevance seem to dominate educational debate in the twentieth century. These concepts are considered as curriculum planning principles which will lead to the development of every pupil (intrinsic values) and equip him/her with skills and knowledge of working life (extrinsic values), which will boost the economy of any nation. The problem is the controversy that surrounds the usage and application of these concepts. While it is very important to mention such issues, it is worth noting that no curriculum has ever existed without these concepts even if they are not mentioned; and also, their usage will differ within nations. An analysis of the existing literature and empirical data will reveal the relativity and limits within which they could be applied.

The following are to be considered: (1) the possibility of a country discovering the appropriate curriculum for future employment; (2) the stage/level at which one realises breadth, balance and relevance within the school curriculum; (3) areas of similarities or overlap and differences within the curricula of the countries in question.

The research centres on the secondary school curriculum in England/Wales and the Republic of Cameroon. This comparison is necessary especially as both countries operate a national curriculum.

12488 'Curriculum and Assessment in Scotland: A Policy for the 90s', impact of this initiative in a rural secondary and primary school.
GBR   1993
Research Date(s): 1990-1994
Percy, S.
Sup: Donn, G.; King, K.
Inst: Edinburgh University, Department of Education, 10-12 Buccleuch Place, Edinburgh EH8 9JT, United Kingdom.
curriculum; assessment; English language; language teaching; Scotland
programme d'études; appréciation; langue anglaise; enseignement des langues; Ecosse
PROJECT DESCRIPTION
This research aims to trace the process of change and the impact on assessment and teaching of English language in Scottish schools following the publication of Scottish Office Education Department (1987) Curriculum and Assessment in Scotland: A Policy for the 90s. Using a rural secondary school (510 pupils and 44 staff) and its feeder primary school (220 pupils and 11.8 staff) as a sample, the study involves oral history, ethnographic interviews, documentation and participant observation.

12489 Curriculum innovation, professional development and special educational needs.
GBR   1993
Research Date(s): 1988-1992
Hart, S.
Sup: Oliver, M.; Dalton, T.
Inst: Cambridge University, Institute of Education, Shaftesbury Road, Cambridge CB2 2BX, United Kingdom; Greenwich University, Avery Hill Campus, Bexley Road, Eltham, London SE9 2PQ, United Kingdom.
curriculum development; special education; integration; teaching method
élaboration de programmes d'études; enseignement spécial; intégration; méthode pédagogique
PROJECT DESCRIPTION
The research takes the form of a case study investigation of an instance of curriculum innovation which in principle presents the opportunity to combine the process of meeting 'special educational needs' with the process of improving curriculum provision on behalf of all pupils. The question which the research seeks to address is as follows: if general curriculum improvement is a means of meeting 'special educational needs', is there a

meaningful distinction to be maintained between 'ordinary' and 'special' education and, if so, on what basis is that distinction now to be made?

The area of new approaches to the teaching of writing has been selected as a focus for the investigation. Intensive fieldwork has been carried out in a 3rd-4th year junior class over a period of a year in order to monitor the writing development of six pupils representing a wide range of 'needs' and attainments. The material collected through participant observation together with samples of children's writing is being analysed in order to explore how individual needs are accommodated on a week by week basis and the significant features of individual development over time.

It is intended that the research should yield insights relating to children's learning in the substantive field of enquiry and also provide the basis for a rearticulation of the relationship between 'ordinary' and 'special' education grounded in sociological and curriculum theory, knowledge and research.

12490 Curriculumentwicklung eines Bildungsurlaubs zur Thematik "Leben lernen ohne Arbeit" fuer unterschiedliche Zielgruppen. (Development of a curriculum for educational leave devoted to "Learning to live without work" for various target groups.)
DEU   1993
Research Date(s): 1991-1992
Becker, S.; Hoffmann, E.; Theis, C.
Inst: Universitaet Saarbruecken, FB 06 Sozial- und Umweltwissen-schaften, Fachrichtung Erziehungswissenschaft, Stadtwald Bau 8, D-6600 Saarbruecken.
Fin: Arbeitskammer des Saarlandes.
curriculum development; educational leave; target groups of education; further training; unemployment
élaboration de programmes d'études; congé éducatif; destinataires de l'éducation; formation complémentaire; chômage
PROJECT DESCRIPTION
Inhalt: Curriculumentwicklung zum o.g. Thema; Teilnehmerorientierung (unterschiedliche Zielgruppen: Experten, psychosoziale Helfer, Erwerbslose und ihre Familien); Curriculum soll als Rahmen verschiedenen Traegern (Gewerkschaften, Bildungseinrichtungen, freie Traeger der Wohlfahrtspflege) die Moeglichkeit eroeffnen, nach dieser Konzeption zu arbeiten.

Vorgehensweise: Handlungsforschung. Untersuchungsdesign: qualitative Forschung.

Datengewinnung: Datenerstellung auf der Basis von bereits vorliegenden Materialien wie Texten, Akten, Statistiken.

12491 The demands for a teaching qualification in Outdoor Education.
GBR   1993
Research Date(s): 1991-1992
McWilliam, A.
Inst: Jordanhill College of Education, Division of PE, Sport and Outdoor Education, Southbrae Drive, Glasgow G13 1PP, United Kingdom.
open-air activities; qualification; teacher education
activités de plein air; qualification; formation des enseignants
PROJECT DESCRIPTION
A survey of headteachers of Scottish schools will be carried out to determine their attitudes towards the demands for a teaching qualification in Outdoor Education.

12492 Developing navigational skills in young children.
GBR   1993
Research Date(s): 1989-1993
Martland, J.; Stewart, R.; Walsh, S.
Inst: Liverpool University, Department of Education, PO Box 147, Liverpool L69 3BX, United Kingdom.
Fin: Sports Council/National Coaching Foundation.
navigation; open-air activities; skill
navigation; activités de plein air; compétence
PROJECT DESCRIPTION
Many geographical skills are taught to primary children but the learning fails when children use large-scale maps to plot route and to travel to a location. The research studied the natural behaviours of 300 children, aged 7-11 years, as they followed two routes across a uniform square grid of lines. The routes were of increasing complexity and involved turns of 180 degrees. The ability to keep the map orientated to the terrain, and to update one's position on the map, were major problems for the young. An analysis of the errors showed that children attempted to locate their route by using finger pointing to retrace their journey. Children below the age of 8 tended to locate their current position on the map, equivalent to saying 'I am here', but then moved randomly.

Following the initial research, 30 children aged 7+ years were introduced to the concept of orientation via landmarks and features and by using a compass. Two new routes were planned acrosss the grid layout. The results showed that children who used the compass maintained orientation and completed the task whereas children who became disorientated using the landmark strategy resorted to trial and error route finding. The landmark and compass strategies were also applied to a sample of 120 children and the results reinforced the finding that they use the compass to maintain orientation with greater facility than using landmarks.

The research has examined how the concepts and skill related to direction, for example, bearings can be taught. A sample of 148 children, aged 11, were taught to use a compass to take bearings from a map and apply them to the terrain. Fifty per cent received a skill-based, rote learning approach and fifty per cent received additional input highlighting the concept of a bearing. This approach was termed relational. In individual tests, in unfamiliar terrain, the relational group performed significantly better than the rote group in practical and applied situations.

Publ: Walsh, S.E.; Martland, J.R. & Stewart, R.R. The map orientation skills of young children - a preliminary investigation. In: *Scientific Journal of Orienteering*, Vol 7, No 1/2, 1991, pp. 90-103.
Martland, J.R.; Stewart, R.R. & Walsh, S.E. How do we teach our young orienteers to use the compass more effectively? In: *Scientific Journal of Orienteering*, Vol 7, No 1/2, 1991, pp. 104-114.
Stewart, R.R.; Martland, J.R. & Walsh, S.E. Personal and social dimensions of developing orienteering and self-navigation in primary schools: a turn for the better? In: *Social Science Teacher*, Vol 20, No 3/1991, pp. 95-96.
Martland, J.R.; Stewart, R.R. & Walsh, S.E. *Second Annual Report, 1990/91, 'Developing navigational skills with young children'*, Sport Science Education Programme, National Coaching Foundation.
A full list of publications is available from the researcher.

12493 The development, monitoring and evaluation of an advanced training course for part-time community education workers.
GBR 1993
Research Date(s): 1989-1993
Edwards, M.
Sup: Donald, A.
Inst: University of Wales College of Cardiff, School of Education, 42 Park Place, Cardiff CF1 3BB, United Kingdom.
training programme; community education
programme de formation; éducation sociale
PROJECT DESCRIPTION
This action research/case study concerns the development, monitoring and evaluation of an advanced training course for part-time youth and community workers in South East Wales. The study is designed to reflect on the participants' individual experiences in terms of personal and professional development in the circumstance of a Stage II training course. It attempts to place this innovative and unique course within the context of past and current local education authority training policy and practice. Qualitative data were gathered through participant observation; an analysis of student course journals; evaluation sheets; questionnaires; and tutor/participant meetings.

The thesis concludes that there is a need for Welsh statutory youth services to consider the development of progressive training models based on consultation, negotiation and an acceptance of part-time youth worker training needs.

Publ: Loudon, M. & Edwards, M. The identification of inservice needs of part-time community education workers - a case study. In: *Researching INSET*, pp. 104-109, September 1989.

12494 Economic and industrial awareness in the primary school.
GBR 1993
Research Date(s): 1987-1992
Roberts, R.; Dolan, J.
Inst: Derbyshire College of Higher Education, Western Road, Mickleover, Derby DE3 5GX, United Kingdom.
curriculum subject; economic studies; primary education; pupil attitude; student teacher
matière d'enseignement; études économiques; enseignement primaire; attitude de l'élève; élève-maître
PROJECT DESCRIPTION
Research is continuing into both the perceptions primary school children have of 'work' and the ways in which teachers can make use of these perceptions to design curricular responses. However, the publication of the National Curriculum Council's 'Education for economic and industrial understanding: curriculum guidance 3 and 4' has given an additional dimension to the research concerning the effective management of EIU (Economic and Industrial Understanding) as a cross curricular theme within the National Curriculum.

Over the past year a research base has been established in about 30 local primary schools whose headteachers have an interest in cross curricular themes in general and EIU in particular. It is proposed to investigate childrens' perceptions, school curricular responses and the management issues that these generate in the coming year. Additionally a group of 15 students completing initial teacher training will be undertaking exploratory research-based topics with the network. A comparison group and network is being established with Dr J. Ahier at Homerton College, Cambridge. Alongside this work with primary children, a parallel investigation is beginning into perception and awareness of EIU held by students training to be primary teachers with a view to establishing data which can then be reflected in the design of more effective EIU modules, and the further

development of cross curricularity within BEd (Bachelor of Education) and PGCE (Post Graduate Certificate of Education) courses.

Publ: Roberts, R.J. & Dolan, J. Childrens' perception of work. In: *Educational Review*, Vol 41, No 1/1989, pp. 19-28.
Dolan, J. & Roberts, R.J. Unpacking the knapsack. In: *Primary Teaching Studies*, Vol 4, No 3/1989, pp. 259-267, Summer.
Dolan, J. & Roberts, R.J. Consultancy led INSET: the case of economic awareness education. In: *British Journal of In-Service Education*, Vol 16, No 2/1990, pp. 91-96.

12495 Eesti üldkooli ôppekava. (A curriculum for general education in Estonia.)
EST 1994
Research Date(s): 1991-1992
Ruus, V.; Isok, H.; et al.
Inst: Tallinna Pedagoogikaülikool (Tallinn Pedagogical University), 0100 Tallinn, Narva mnt.25, Estonia.
Fin: EV Haridusministeerium.
common core curriculum; curriculum development; general education; primary education; secondary education; aims of education
tronc commun; élaboration de programmes d'études; enseignement général; enseignement primaire; enseignement secondaire; finalité de l'éducation
PROJECT DESCRIPTION
The aim of the research was to develop curriculum guidelines for compulsory and general secondary education in Estonia. More specifically, the aims were: (1) to work out an ideology of general education in terms of goals, aims and objectives as well as principles of curriculum policy; (2) to find a balance between key content areas of education and to establish links between these areas wherever appropriate; (3) to develop concepts for different subjects. The study was based on the view that the Estonian education system needs a new curriculum, based on the principle of permanent, long-term development.

The study is to result in a document in which the basic features of the curriculum are outlined. The development of curriculum guidelines takes place in cooperation with all interest groups in society and in schools. In 1993 the core curriculum will be presented to the Estonian Ministry of Culture and Education. At the same time, a start will be made with the development of curricula at the school level in consultation with teachers.

12496 Entwicklung medienpaedagogischer Curricula. (Development of media-pedagogic curricula.)
DEU 1993
Research Date(s): 1991-1996
Kohn, W.
Inst: Paedagogische Hochschule Leipzig, Institut fuer Kommunikations- und Medienpaedagogik, Karl-Heine-Strasse 22b, O-7031 Leipzig.
curriculum development; media education; German DR
élaboration de programmes d'études; éducation aux médias; Allemagne RDA
PROJECT DESCRIPTION
Geographischer Raum: Leipzig.
Untersuchter Zeitraum: 1990-1994.
Vorgehensweise: Untersuchungsdesign: Fallstudie.
Datengewinnung: Standardisiertes Interview (Stichprobe: 200; Grundschueler 1.-4. Klasse; Auswahlverfahren: Zufall). Gruppenbefragung (dito). Psychologischer Test (dito). Primaererhebung: Feldarbeit von Mitarbeitern des Projektes durchgefuehrt.

12497 Evaluation of National Curriculum Assessment at Key Stage Three in mathematics, science, English and technology.
GBR 1993
Research Date(s): 1991-1993
Ruddock, G.; Harris, D.; Tomlins, B.; Brooks, G.; Putman, K.
Sup: Whetton, C.; Foxman, D.
Inst: National Foundation for Educational Research, The Mere, Upton Park, Slough SL1 2DQ, United Kingdom; Brunel University, Department of Education and Design, Runnymede Campus, Cooper's Hill Lane, Egham TW20 0JZ, United Kingdom.
Fin: School Examinations and Assessment Council.
common core curriculum; assessment; evaluation; compulsory subject
tronc commun; appréciation; évaluation; matière obligatoire
PROJECT DESCRIPTION
The project will evaluate the first nationwide National Curriculum assessment of fourteen year olds in science and mathematics in 1992, and in English and technology in 1993. The results of these will be surveyed and the procedures used will be evaluated. The focus of evaluation is the validity and reliability of the results. Three elements make up the study: a statistical survey of results; case studies of schools' management of the assessment process and review of the assessment materials used.

Publ: Ruddock, G.; Tomlins, B.; et al. *Teacher assessment in mathematics and science at key stage 3*. London: SEAC.

12498 Freizeitpädagogik als Problem: eine theoretische und empirische Untersuchung. (Le problème de la pédagogie des loisirs: une étude théorique et empirique.)
CHE 1994
Research Date(s): 1989-1991
Herzog-Raschle, Yvonne.
Sup: Tuggener, Heinrich.
Inst: Universität Zürich, Pädagogisches Institut, Rämistrasse 74, 8001 Zürich, Schweiz.
leisure; leisure education; educational planning
loisir; éducation des loisirs; planification de l'éducation
PROJECT DESCRIPTION

Empirisches Kernstück dieser Dissertation war eine Untersuchung in der Stadt Zürich, in welcher eine Stichprobe von 805 Personen im Alter zwischen 15 und 74 Jahren mündlich zu ihrem faktischen Freizeitverhalten wie auch zu den ungestillten Bedürfnissen in diesem Bereich befragt wurden. Die Untersuchung wurde aufgrund einer Interpellation im städtischen Parlament vom Sozialamt der Stadt Zürich durchgeführt; die Autorin war im Rahmen ihrer beruflichen Tätigkeit im Sozialamt - die schwerpunktmässig in der Mitarbeit an einem Freizeitkonzept für Zürich bestand - für die Untersuchung verantwortlich. Wichtigstes Ziel war die Verbesserung der Informationslage im Hinblick auf planerische und politische Entscheidungen. Die Interviews wurden von der Firma Demoscope geführt, welche der Auftraggeberin die Ergebnisse in Form von Rohdaten auf einem Magnetband ablieferte. Die Auswertung wurde teils am Rechenzentrum der Universität Zürich vorgenommen, teils wertete die Projektverantwortliche die Daten am eigenen PC hinsichtlich sie speziell interessierender Fragestellungen aus.

Die Dissertation stellt die empirische Untersuchung in den weiteren Rahmen der Freizeitpädagogik. Das erste Kapitel gibt eine Einführung und diskutiert in Kürze Begriffe wie Erziehung und Bildung, mit einem speziellen Blick auf die Allgemeinbildung. Das zweite Kapitel geht in extenso auf die Freizeitpädagogik und ihren heutigen wissenschaftlichen Stand ein. Das dritte Kapitel fasst die Zürcher Untersuchung und ihre Ergebnisse zusammen. Im abschliessenden vierten Kapitel werden die theoretischen Ergebnisse der ersten beiden Kapitel mit den empirischen Daten des dritten verknüpft; das Ziel besteht darin, zu skizzieren, was eine bildungstheoretisch fundierte und den empirischen Daten Rechnung tragende Freizeitpädagogik zu erbringen hätte. Insbesondere wird von der Freizeitpädagogik verlangt, sie müsste mehr Realismus bezüglich der Lebenssituation und somit auch der Wünsche und Bedürfnisse ihres Zielpublikums aufbringen.

Publ: Herzog-Raschle, Yvonne. *Freizeitpädagogik als Problem: eine theoretische und empirische Untersuchung.* Zürich: ADAG, 1991, 336 + 28 Seiten (Dissertation zuhanden der Philosophischen Fakultät I der Universität Zürich).
Sozialamt der Stadt Zürich. *Freizeit und Lebensqualität in Zürich.* Zürich, Sozialamt, 1991, 104 + 28 Seiten.
Sozialamt der Stadt Zürich. *Strategien für die Freizeitgestaltung der Zürcher Bevölkerung.* Zürich, Sozialamt, 1991, 62 Seiten.

12499 An investigation of an interactive process model for implementing an English Language Teaching (ELT) syllabus in secondary schools in French-speaking Africa.
GBR 1993
Research Date(s): 1991-1994
Drame, M.
Sup: Dickinson, L.; McMichael, P.
Inst: Heriot-Watt University, Moray House Institute of Education, Holyrood Road, Edinburgh EH8 8AQ, United Kingdom.
Fin: The British Council.
curriculum development; language teaching; foreign languages; English language; teaching aid; Senegal; French-speaking Africa
élaboration de programmes d'études; enseignement des langues; langues étrangères; langue anglaise; moyen d'enseignement; Sénégal; Afrique francophone
PROJECT DESCRIPTION

In post-independence Africa there is concern about the mismatch between educational curricula and the teaching materials used to implement them. For example, in Senegal a national syllabus has been designed and yet the incongruity between this syllabus which teaches English as communication and the inappropriate audiolingual textbook used for its implementation remains an urgent issue to be addressed.

The project aims to address this issue and proposes to investigate an interactive process model for syllabus implementation. A draft set of materials appropriate to the Senegalese threshold level communicative syllabus will be designed. This package of materials will be trialled, revised and retrialled in Senegal with a view to investigating a proposed model for teacher development on syllabus implementation.

The project will include three stages: (1) a planning phase (1991-1992) in which a draft set of materials suitable to the Senegalese syllabus will be developed in addition to the data collection instruments (observation schedules, questionnaires, interviews) to be used during the implementation phase to take place in Senegal during the second year; (2) an imple-

mentation phase (1992-1993) in which the draft set of materials will be trialled, revised and retrialled in Senegal with a view to investigating the effectiveness of the proposed interactive process model for syllabus implementation; and (3) an evaluation and reporting phase (1993-1994) in which all data including questionnaires, interviews, observation schedules, teachers' diaries and samples of pupils' test scores will be collected and analysed qualitatively and quantitatively with the objective of assessing the empirical validity of the proposed procedure.

The research findings will be assessed and the possible applications considered with regard to the educational context in Senegal in particular and in French-speaking Africa in general.

12500 Konzeption und Entwicklung von Studienmaterialien zur Zusatzqualifikation fuer die Frauengleichstellungsarbeit. (Concept and development of study materials for a supplementary course on equal opportunities for women.)
DEU 1993
Research Date(s): 1991-1992
Schwertberger, S.
Sup: Begander, E.; Bruch, R.
Inst: Deutsches Institut fuer Fernstudien -DIFF- an der Universitaet, Konrad-Adenauer-Str. 40-44, D-7400 Tuebingen.
curriculum development; didactics; women's work; occupational qualification; self-instruction; woman; equal opportunity
élaboration de programmes d'études; didactique; travail des femmes; qualification professionnelle; auto-enseignement; femme; égalité de chances
PROJECT DESCRIPTION

Inhalt: Inhaltliches Ziel des Vorhabens ist die Entwicklung eines Curriculums fuer die Zusatzqualifizierung von kuenftigen Frauenbeauftragten im Selbststudium. Untersucht wird insbesondere, ob und in welcher Weise Frauen bestimmte didaktische Vermittlungsformen bevorzugen und nutzen, wenn sie sich in fachfremde, aber berufsrelevante Wissensgebiete einarbeiten muessen.

Geographischer Raum: Bundesrepublik Deutschland.

Vorgehensweise: Kompetenzerweiterung erwachsener Lernender. Untersuchungsdesign: Methodenforschung; Evaluationsstudie.

Datengewinnung: Gruppendiskussion (Stichprobe: 20; Studierende der Sozialwissenschaften; Auswahlverfahren: bewusst. Stichprobe: 10; Frauenbeauftragte; Auswahlverfahren: bewusst). Befragung (dito). Teilnehmende Beobachtung (dito). Nicht-standardisiertes Interview (Stichprobe: 10; Frauenbeauftragte; Auswahlverfahren: bewusst). Primaererhebung: Feldarbeit von Mitarbeitern des Projektes durchgefuehrt. Auswertung: Inhaltsanalyse. Datenaufbereitung: Evaluationsbericht.

12501 The Learn to Travel School's Project.
GBR 1993
Research Date(s): 1990-1994
Mason, P.
Sup: Hannan, A.; Essex, S.
Inst: Plymouth University, Rolle Faculty of Education, Douglas Avenue, Exmouth EX8 2AT, United Kingdom.
tourism; travel; curriculum development; primary education
tourisme; voyage; élaboration de programmes d'études; enseignement primaire
PROJECT DESCRIPTION

This research has three aims: (1) To examine the claims made for introducing travel and tourism into the primary school curriculum. The research explores arguments about the importance of knowledge of travel and tourism in primary schools; and the use of travel and tourism as a vehicle for developing values and attitudes and acquiring skills. (2) To undertake action research in curriculum development in these areas by the design and implementation of a 'Learn to Travel School's Project'. This is an attempt to test, in practice, the ideas of the first aim. The researcher, with a group of teachers in Devon, will design, produce, implement and evaluate curriculum resources for the 'Learn to Travel School's Project'. (3) To evaluate the impact of this contribution to primary school children's education, in relation to the first aim. This will involve the use of questionnaire surveys with children; and interviews with children and teachers.

Publ: Mason, P. *Learn to travel: activities in travel and tourism for primary schools.* Godalming: Worldwide Fund for Nature UK, 1992.

12502 The management of cross-curricular themes within the National Curriculum.
GBR 1993
Research Date(s): 1991-1994
Salkeld, T.
Sup: Sutton, R.
Inst: University of Wales College of Cardiff, School of Education, 42 Park Place, Cardiff CF1 3BB, United Kingdom.
integrated curriculum; common core curriculum; curriculum development; teaching method
programme d'études intégré; tronc commun; élaboration de programmes d'études; méthode pédagogique
PROJECT DESCRIPTION

Currently there are five cross-curricular themes which have been identified as being the most pre-eminent and it is the management of these which is being researched. Curriculum Guidance No. 3 - 'The Whole Curriculum' (National Curriculum Council 1990) points to the importance of the themes being planned and coherent to ensure 'continuity and progression'. The aim of this research is to investigate how schools in Wales are managing staff, structures, teaching and learning to ensure cohesion.

Questionnaires will be used to look at staffing structures and the methods used to manage the coordination of the themes. This in itself only indicates the presence of a framework and it will therefore also be necessary to research how learning is being managed. 'What takes place in the classroom?' will form an essential part of the research and will be investigated by a variety of methods. Interviews and questionnaires to both teachers and pupils will be used and examples of pupils' work will be sought.

It is recognised from the outset that in the current climate both schools and teachers may still be coming to grips with the necessary re-organisation to keep pace with the changes and therefore the findings of this research will not be finite, but will only reflect 'the current state of play'.

Publ: Salkeld, T. & Sutton, R.A. Introducing economic awareness. In: *Economic Awareness*, Vol 3, No 2/1991, pp. 22-25.

12503   Monitoring the implementation of the National Curriculum in primary schools.
GBR   1993
Research Date(s): 1990-
Silcock, P.
Inst: Nene College, Faculty of Education, Health and Science, Moulton Park, Northampton NN2 7AL, United Kingdom.
common core curriculum; primary education; educational reform
tronc commun; enseignement primaire; réforme de l'enseignement
PROJECT DESCRIPTION
The research aims to evaluate changes brought about in schools by the National Curriculum from the point of view of practitioners. The method of investigation used so far comprises an in-depth open-ended interview of a headteacher and at least one classteacher, in each school visited, involved with implementing and assessing pupils within the English National Curriculum. The only constraint set is that both positive and negative evaluates have to be elicited: i.e. practitioners are required, in so far as they are able, to describe the positive benefits accruing to the school through the introduction of the National Curriculum and any drawbacks they have discovered. This approach allows an interviewer to focus on changes occurring at the time of interview, since an important feature of the National Curriculum is its ongoing revision and development.

A small number of schools are sampled, representing a cross-section of primary schools within a single county. The outcome of the research is the publication of related articles. This is ongoing research. The project for 1991-1992 includes a case study of a school implementing change. The researcher will work with the staff of the school and investigate through observation, informal discussion, and interview.

Publ: Silcock, P.J. Implementing the National Curriculum: some teachers' dilemmas. In: *Education 3-13*, Vol 18, No 3/1990, pp. 3-10.
Silcock, P.J. The reflective practitioner in the year of the SAT. In: *Education 3-13*, Vol 20, No 1/1992, pp. 3-9.
Silcock, P.J. Primary school teacher-time and the National Curriculum: managing the impossible? In: *British Journal of Education Studies*, Vol XXXX, No 2/1992, pp. 163-173.

12504   National Coaching Centre.
GBR   1993
Research Date(s): 1987-1991
Lyle, J.; Lynn, A.; Messenger, G.; McLeod, C.
Inst: Heriot-Watt University, Moray House Institute of Education, Holyrood Road, Edinburgh EH8 8AQ, United Kingdom.
Fin: Scottish Sports Council; National Coaching Foundation; Reebok UK.
sport
sport
PROJECT DESCRIPTION
This is a consultancy service offered to coaches and coach educators. The services are grant-aided by the Scottish Sports Council and the National Coaching Foundation. Services include performance monitoring, courses, conferences and hire of facilities. A report is published annually.

12505   Návrh koncepce a osnov prvouky, vlastivědy a přírodovědy pro 1.stupen základních škol. (Conception and design of a course programme for national history, geography and natural sciences for use in primary schools.)
CSK   1994
Research Date(s): 1991
Pitha, P.; Hořejšová, D.; Hlaváčková, M.; Krákorová, M.; Pečinková, M.; Komanová, E.
Inst: Pedagogická fakulta Univerzity Karlovy (Charles University, Faculty of Education), M.D. Rettigové 4, 116 39 Praha 1, Czech Republic.
Ministerstvo školství, mládeže a tělovýchovy (Ministry of Education, Youth and Physical Education), Karmelitská 7, 118 00 Praha 1, Czech Republic

integrated curriculum; interdisciplinary approach; primary education; history; geography; natural sciences
programme d'études intégré; interdisciplinarité; enseignement primaire; histoire; géographie; sciences naturelles
PROJECT DESCRIPTION
Aims: The research examined how best to make the changes that are needed in the primary school curricula for national history and geography and how to link these curricula to the natural science curriculum.

Design: (1) Problem analysis, comparative study of foreign experiences, methodological preparation of cooperation between primary school teachers and specialists in the disciplines mentioned above; (2) choice of topics for the synthesis of the disciplines mentioned, from the angle of the individual disciplines (involving consultation with educationalists and practitioners); (3) allocation of the selected topics to individual subjects and grade levels, adjustment of teaching programmes, consultation; (4) processing of comments (including methodological comments), completion of the editorial work and preparation of examiners' reports.

Publ: *Návrh koncepce a osnov prvouky, vlastivědy a přírodovědy pro 1.stupen základní školy*. Praha, 1991, 119p.

12506   Onderzoek effectieve basisvorming innovatie voortgezet onderwijs. (A common core curriculum for lower secondary education.)
NLD   1994
Research Date(s): 1990-1993
Vilsteren, C.A. van; Kuiper, W.J.A.M.
Inst: Onderzoek Centrum Toegepaste Onderwijskunde (OCTO) (Research Centre of the Department of Educational Technology), P.O. Box 217, 7500 AE Enschede, Netherlands.
Universiteit Twente (Twente University), P.O. Box 217, 7500 AE Enschede, Netherlands
Fin: SVO het Instituut voor Onderzoek van het Onderwijs.
common core curriculum; educational innovation; educational administration; lower secondary
tronc commun; innovation pédagogique; administration de l'enseignement; secondaire premier cycle
PROJECT DESCRIPTION
Background: This study builds on an exploratory study of the implementation of a common core curriculum for 12-15 year-olds at 12 experimental schools. That study sought to identify the organizational and managerial conditions under which the core curriculum can be successfully implemented.

Aim: To elaborate the findings of the exploratory study; to collect additional data; to develop valid and reliable descriptive instruments.

Design: A thorough study was made of existing research instruments, which was followed by the construction of instruments that were needed for the study. Semi-structured interviews were conducted with senior management staff and the project leaders of the 12 schools. In addition, the heads of four subject departments were interviewed to gain an insight into the changing role of the subject departments. A pre-coded questionnaire was administered to all teachers in the departments concerned, to elicit information about classroom practice and changes that have taken place since the experiment was started. Case-studies were made of 12 teachers, divided between the four departments, involving classroom observation, interviews and analysis of instructional materials.

Results: The part of the study concerned with the school organization has revealed that schools have been successful in applying the main advisory guidelines. Differences between schools occur in between-class differentiation and in the way in which exemptions are granted. The findings of the part of the study concerned with the development of curricula for four subjects give rise to the assumption that the innovation of subject matter contents and teaching methods is still in an early stage. The description of the school organization and the curriculum shows that in the core curriculum the emphasis will be on pupil performance.

(This is an updating of EUDISED no. 41/9802).

Publ: Wal, G. van der. *De basisvorming in de praktijk: een tweede verkenning van de basisvorming in het dubbelproject basisvorming/primair beroepsonderwijs*. Enschede: OCTO, 1992, 292p.
Wal, G. van der. Een voorproefje op de basisvorming: vijf jaar experimenteren op het lbo. In: *Didaktief*, 2/1993, pp. 19-20.

12507   Out-of-school services survey and evaluation.
GBR   1993
Research Date(s): 1990-1993
Petrie, P.
Inst: London University, Institute of Education, Thomas Coram Research Unit, 41 Brunswick Square, London WC1N 1AZ, United Kingdom.
Fin: Department of Health.
recreational activities; play centre
activités récréatives; centre de jeu
PROJECT DESCRIPTION
The project consists of twelve case studies of playschemes, using a consultative approach with providers and staff, followed by a survey of

100 schemes looking at objectives and their realisation; organisation and resources.

12508 Personal, social, moral and religious education in primary schools: the impact and implications of the Education Reform Act 1988 and the National Curriculum.
GBR 1993
Research Date(s): 1989-1993
Bennett, J.
Sup: Webster, D.
Inst: Hull University, School of Education, Cottingham Road, Hull HU6 7RX, United Kingdom.
common core curriculum; religious education; moral education; primary education
tronc commun; éducation religieuse; éducation morale; enseignement primaire
PROJECT DESCRIPTION
The introduction of the National Curriculum and the implications of the Education Reform Act 1988 have serious consequences for the formal subject curriculum in primary schools, and for the informal curriculum defined to some degree as moral, personal and social education. This status of religious education in the basic currciulum, but not the National Curriculum, and the legal standing of the subject in the light of the Education Reform Act pose problems and possibilities for the subject within the curriculum as a whole. An analysis of these four interconnected areas of the curriculum will provide insights into their place and purpose in the primary school curriculum and a backdrop for an explanation of the impact of recent changes in education.

The following will be considered: (a) the natures of the four subject areas, aims, objectives and philosophical implications in primary schools; (b) the implications and effects of the Education Reform Act 1988; (c) the implications and effects of the National Curriculum; and (d) the interconnective nature of the four subject areas.

12509 Play provision for children and young people in Scotland aged 5-15: what is happening.
GBR 1993
Research Date(s): 1991-1992
Ovens, N.
Inst: Heriot-Watt University, Moray House Institute of Education, The National Centre for PLAY, Cramond Campus, Cramond Road North, Edinburgh EH4 6JD, United Kingdom.
play; recreational facilities; local government; social service
jeu; installations récréatives; administration locale; service social
PROJECT DESCRIPTION
Following the investigative study 'Working for PLAY' in 1988 in Scotland, and the research undertaken by the School for Advanced Studies at Bristol University and the production of the Action Plan 1991/1992 of Play Wales, there would appear to be a need to analyse the lack of comparable developments in Scotland. In Scotland, play is provided through both region and district local authority functions but in the local government restructuring, certain functions were not clearly allocated leading to some areas of confusion. Some authorities are single-purpose authorities. Voluntary agencies' local units therefore may lack clearly identified communication links with the local authorities. Interviews with key bodies such as the Scottish Office Education Department and Social Work Services Group, the Convention of Scottish Local Authorities, the Scottish Play Council and others, will be conducted. A report will be prepared on the findings.

12510 Primary assessment, curriculum and experience.
GBR 1993
Research Date(s): 1989-1993
Osborn, M.; Abbott, D.
Sup: Broadfoot, P.; Pollard, A.
Inst: Bristol University, School of Education, Centre for Assessment Studies, 22 Berkeley Square, Bristol BS8 1JA, United Kingdom; Bristol Polytechnic, Department of Education, Redland Primary Centre, Redland Hill, Bristol BS6 6UZ, United Kingdom.
Fin: Economic and Social Research Council.
common core curriculum; primary education; pre-school education; assessment; curriculum; pupil attitude; teacher behaviour; achievement test; educational reform
tronc commun; enseignement primaire; éducation préscolaire; appréciation; programme d'études; attitude de l'élève; comportement de l'enseignant; test de rendement; réforme de l'enseignement
PROJECT DESCRIPTION
The project aims to describe and analyse the responses of pupils and teachers in infant schools and infant departments to the National Curriculum and related innovations. This includes a consideration of the views of headteachers and teachers of the new reforms and their impact on the school and, in particular, an analysis and evaluation of the development of strategies for change. The study aims to contribute to theoretical perspectives on teacher professionalism and on the control and impact of educational change. It is also designed to consider the impact of the National Curriculum on the curriculum and pedagogy of the infant school. Issues of teacher aims and expectations, curriculum content and time allocation, teaching methods and pupil classroom experience, are being addressed. As well as considering the impact of the National Curriculum on teachers and pupils, the study will provide baseline data on contemporary infant practice. The project will also evaluate materials in action and their impact on pupils. The operation of the assessments in classrooms will be studied and pupil responses to the assessment tasks considered. Conflicting claims about pupil perceptions of and reactions to being tested are being considered.

The research involves interviews with 150 teachers drawn from 48 schools in 8 local education authorities plus four rounds of detailed classroom studies in a sub-sample of nine classrooms to study curriculum change and pupil experience in more depth. Classroom studies are also being conducted during the implementation of the first unreported and reported Standard Assessment Tasks in these nine schools.

Publ: Broadfoot, P.; Abbott, D.; Croll, P.; Osborn, M. & Pollard, A. *The conduct and effectiveness of primary school assessment*. (PACE Working Paper 6), AERA Conference, Chicago, 1991.
Broadfoot, P.; Abbott, D.; Croll, P.; Osborn, M.; Pollard, A. & Towler, L. Implementing national assessment: issues for primary teachers. In: *Cambridge Journal of Education*, Vol 21, No 2/1991.
Broadfoot, P.; Abbott, D.; Croll, P.; Osborn, M. & Pollard, A. *Look back in anger? Primary teachers' experience of SATs*. (PACE Working Paper 8), 1991.
Pollard, A. Balancing priorities: children and curriculum in the 90's. In: Campbell, R.J. (ed.). *Breadth and balance in the primary curriculum*. London: Falmer Press.

12511 Psychologicko pedagogický výzkum učiva a učení žáků základní školy. (Psychological and educational research on curriculum contents and the learning of primary school pupils.)
CSK 1994
Research Date(s): 1992-1994
Vyskočilová, Eva; Holubář, Zdeněk; Pech, Jiří; Matušková, Alena; Hájková, Eva; Sládečková, Zdena; Kotásková, Jarmila; et al.
Sup: Šourek, Vladimír; Zdeněk, Karel.
Inst: Pedagogická fakulta Univerzity Karlovy (Faculty of Education, Charles University), Rettigové 4, 116 39 Praha 1, Czech Republic.
Ministerstvo školství, mládeže a tělovýchovy (Ministry of Education, Youth and Physical Education), Karmelitská 7, 118 13 Praha 1, Czech Republic
curriculum; cognitive development; intellectual development; formal operational thinking; primary education
programme d'études; développement cognitif; développement intellectuel; pensée opératoire formelle; enseignement primaire
PROJECT DESCRIPTION
Aim: The aim is to study psychological conditions related to curriculum design for primary schools. The study of primary school pupils' abilities for learning in a later stage of education is to result in a definition of the criteria for curriculum evaluation in examined projects and the standards for the transition from primary to secondary school. The research will focus on history, economics, ecology, state legislation and geography.

Methods: Teaching experiments in schools that have voluntarily joined in the research; examination of the content of textbooks.

12512 Pupil attitudes to English, mathematics, science, technology and Welsh under the National Curriculum.
GBR 1993
Research Date(s): 1991-
Hendley, D.; Parkinson, J.; Stables, A.; Tanner, H.; Thomas, B.
Inst: University College of Swansea, Department of Education, Hendrefoilan, Swansea SA2 7NB, United Kingdom.
common core curriculum; secondary school; pupil attitude
tronc commun; école secondaire; attitude de l'élève
PROJECT DESCRIPTION
A questionnaire has been developed, using a Likert-type scale, to measure the attitudes of pupils in years 2 and 3 of secondary schools (years 8 and 9 of the National Curriculum) over a period of two years. The degree to which the implementation of the National Curriculum has affected attitudes will be ascertained.

12513 School, sport and society in Kenya.
GBR 1993
Research Date(s): 1990-1993
Sang, J.
Sup: Bale, J.
Inst: Keele University, Department of Education, Keele, Staffordshire ST5 5BG, United Kingdom.
sport; athletics; Kenya
sport; athlétisme; Kenya
PROJECT DESCRIPTION
This project seeks to explore the development of athletics in Kenya by adopting a world systems approach. The role of educational organisations both inside Kenya and abroad will be fully evaluated but it is recognised

168

that other agencies in a very wide range of cultures and nations cannot be ignored in explaining the emergence of sport in a 'developing' nation.

12514 Sport for all? An investigation into the factors that motivate a child not to participate in sport.
GBR 1993
Research Date(s): 1991-1994
Davis, J.
Sup: Donn, G.
Inst: Edinburgh University, Department of Education, 10-12 Buccleuch Place, Edinburgh EH8 9JT, United Kingdom.
Fin: Carnegie Trust.
sport; participation; physical education; motivation
sport; participation; éducation physique; motivation
PROJECT DESCRIPTION
At present there has been great concern by such organisations as the Sports Council that the number of school children taking up sport is falling. This study will attempt to discover how culture is involved when a child makes the everyday choice not to participate in sport at school and if the new educational policies that are being implemented by the Scottish Office are in any way reversing this process. By looking at what results in non-participation, this study will differ from previous ones in this field which have mostly been concerned with describing the process through which participation comes about (i.e. socialisation). That is, rather than recognising that children take everyday decisions concerning sports participation, previous works tend to view children's sports participation as being determined by external factors. Moreover, the research will investigate in what way, if any, educational policy changes affect the everyday choices of children in terms of sports participation.

12515 Sport und Bewegung als Foerderungshilfen zur schulischen und beruflichen Integration sozial benachteiligter Jugendlicher: Moeglichkeiten und Grenzen der Uebertragung in die Heimpaedagogik und Jugendberufshilfe. (Sport and movement as a means to promote the integration of socially deprived young people in education and work: opportunities and limitations in youth homes and in vocational guidance for young people.)
DEU 1993
Research Date(s): 1990-1994
Koch, J.
Inst: Universitaet Marburg, FB 21 Erziehungswissenschaften, Institut fuer Sportwissenschaft und Motologie, Barfuesserstr. 1, D-3550 Marburg.
Fin: Landeswohlfahrtsverband Hessen, Zweigverwaltung Darmstadt; Bundesministerium fuer Jugend, Familie, Frauen und Gesundheit.
sport; motion; adolescent; deprived; youth welfare; model
sport; mouvement; adolescent; défavorisé; aide à la jeunesse; modèle
PROJECT DESCRIPTION
Inhalt: Erprobung und Auswertung von neuen Modellen in der berufsbezogenen und schulbezogenen Jugendsozialarbeit (Heime); Erprobung und Auswertung von koerperbezogenen Angeboten fuer benachteiligte Jugendliche zur Foerderung der Schul- und Berufsreife; Erprobung und Auswertung von Modellen zur Verzahnung von Arbeit und Freizeitmassnahmen bei der Bildung benachteiligter Jugendlicher; Praxisbezug: Begleitforschung zu einem Modellprojekt in vier hessischen Kinder- und Jugendheimen.
Geographischer Raum: Nord- und Mittelhessen.
Untersuchter Zeitraum: 1.9.1990-31.12.1993.
Vorgehensweise: Untersuchung von koerperbezogenen Alltagsstrategien von Jugendlichen und Nutzbarmachung der strukturellen Beobachtungskriterien fuer paedagogische Angebote; lebensweltbezogener Ansatz, der Versuch die Rolle von koerperbezogenen Strategien bei der Selbstkriminalisierung zu reflektieren; "Weiche" Methoden der Forschung: Interviews, Sozialreportage, fotografische Dokumentationen etc.
Publ: Reihe Marburger Beitraege zur Sozialarbeit mit Sport und Bewegung, Nr. 1-5. Frankfurt, 1988-1991.
Koch, Josef. Gehalte einer Erlebnispaedagogik im Rahmen einer koerperbezogenen Jugendsozialarbeit. In: *AFET-Mitteilungen*, 1, 1991.
Koch, Josef. Koerperraeume - Bewegungsraeume - Erlebnisraeume. In: *Dokumentation der Kath. LAG der offenen Tuer "Maedchen koennen mehr"*. Koeln, 1991.

12516 Subject specialisation and the primary school curriculum.
GBR 1993
Research Date(s): 1986-1992
Thornton, M.
Sup: Young, M.
Inst: Hertfordshire University, School of Humanities and Education, Wall Hall Campus, Aldenham, Watford WD2 8AT, United Kingdom.
curriculum subject; specialization; teaching; curriculum research; primary education
matière d'enseignement; spécialisation; enseignement; recherche sur les programmes d'études; enseignement primaire
PROJECT DESCRIPTION
This is a critical examination of the effects of an increasing centralist emphasis upon subject specialism in the primary school and the implica-

tions this might have: (a) for the tradition of generalist class teaching in the primary school sector; (b) for the curriculum as experienced by primary aged pupils, and (c) the teaching methods and organisational features through which it is transmitted. School-based investigations took place in the autumn of 1988. The sample included 22 infant, junior and JMI (junior mixed infants) schools in one division of a local education authority. In each school curriculum guidelines were examined, the head teacher and a selection of teaching staff interviewed (determined by age of pupils taught) and classroom observations made on the basis of teaching staff interviewed.
Publ: Thornton, M. Primary specialism. In: *Early Years*, Vol 11, No 1/1990, pp. 34-38, Autumn.
Thornton, M. Why a full explanation is needed. In: *Times Educational Supplement*, 13 December 1991.

12517 Urban civic culture and the school curriculum.
GBR 1993
Research Date(s): 1991-
Coulby, D.; Jones, C.
Inst: Bath College of Higher Education, Newton Park, Newton St Loe, Bath BA2 9BN, United Kingdom; London University, Institute of Education, Department of International and Comparative Education, 20 Bedford Way, London WC1H OAL, United Kingdom.
curriculum; Europe; culture
programme d'études; Europe; culture
PROJECT DESCRIPTION
The research identifies two possible directions for curricular systems in the EC (European Community) in the light of developing European Civic Culture. The first of these - the traditional - seeks to identify European achievement in the arts and science and conflate these with human achievement per se. The second - the international - looks to the way in which European achievement in science and the arts has been influenced by forces beyond Europe. It further identifies scientific and artistic achievement entirely beyond Europe. The research seeks to investigate this polarity in curricular in EC countries. It seeks to establish ways in which international views of European civic culture may be encouraged.
Publ: Coulby, D. European civic culture and education. In: Coulby, D. & Jones, C. (eds.). *The world yearbook of education in 1992: urban education*. London: Kogan Page, 1992.

12518 The use of outdoor pursuits in schools in England and France.
GBR 1993
Research Date(s): 1991-1996
Dobson, N.
Sup: Aplin, R.; Wortley, A.
Inst: Leicester University, School of Education, University Road, Leicester LE1 7RH, United Kingdom.
open-air activities; recreational activities; physical education; cross-national research
activités de plein air; activités récréatives; éducation physique; recherche transnationale
PROJECT DESCRIPTION
Outdoor pursuits have grown greatly in importance in the educational programme of school children in England and France since World War Two. In 1951 the first local authority residential outdoor pursuits centre in England and Wales was opened, and the first class of elementary school children was taken to the Alps for a month of half-time skiing and half-time normal lessons. After a slow start the number of children being taken, through the education authorities of both countries, to experience outdoor pursuits, has expanded enormously. This study will attempt to describe this movement and to discover what value the authorities, parents, teachers and children ascribe to outdoor pursuit activities.

12519 Young women and leisure, 1920-1950.
GBR 1993
Research Date(s): 1990-1993
Tinkler, P.
Inst: Lancaster University, Department of Educational Research, Centre for Women's Studies, Cartmel College, Bailrigg, Lancaster LA1 4YW, United Kingdom.
Fin: British Academy.
leisure; girl; recreational activities; historical research
loisir; jeune fille; activités récréatives; recherche historique
PROJECT DESCRIPTION
This research has two aims. Firstly it explores the structural and ideological context within which young women's leisure was situated in terms of the social and economic conditions in which girls grew up and the influences which young women were exposed to through the family, schooling, paid work, formal leisure provision, media and popular culture. Secondly, it aims to uncover the actual leisure practices of young women during the period 1920-1950.
The research is structured in two parts reflecting the dual aims. The first part addresses the social, economic and ideological context of young women's leisure activity. It draws upon a range of sources including official documentation, academic and popular literature; census material and

Board/Ministry of Education statistics; a range of data relating to the conditions of life of young women including that pertaining to schooling, paid work, housing and home conditions, health, courtship and sexuality. Three main themes structure this part of the research: access to leisure, the temporal dimensions of leisure, and the question of suitable leisure activity. The second part of the research explores young women's experience and understanding of leisure using oral history sources as well as autobiographies, diaries, contemporary studies and material from the Mass Observation Archive (Sussex University).

12520 Zájmy dětí středního školního věku a možnosti jejich uplatnění. (The interests of lower secondary school pupils.)
CSK 1994
Research Date(s): 1992-1993
Steiniger, Bohumil (Svojšovická 2871/22, 140 00 Praha 4, Czech Republic); Jíra, Otakar.
Sup: Tomolya, Š.
Fin: Ministerstvo školství, mládeže a tělovýchovy České republiky.
leisure; interest; extra-curricular activities; parent role
loisir; intérêt; activités hors programme; rôle des parents
PROJECT DESCRIPTION
Aims: (1) To examine the structure of lower secondary school children's interests, the realization of these interests (including place and frequency) and children's satisfaction with the leisure activities offered by institutions; (2) to examine parents' perceptions of their children's leisure activities, parental influence on these activities, and parents' perceptions of the prices charged.
Methods: Questionnaire survey of 5th-7th year pupils in lower secondary schools and their parents.
Results: The subjects in the study displayed a wide variety of interests. A preference was found for sport activities, cultural and artistic activities and going out with friends. Interests realized in small groups are most frequent. Some of the children's interests are not realized. Most parents are interested in their children's leisure activities, but they do not have a decisive influence on the nature or the extent of their children's interests.
Publ: Steiniger, Bohumil. *Zájmy dětí středního školního věku a možnosti jejich uplatnění.* Praha: 1992, (mimeo) 56p.

10 CONTENT OF EDUCATION – CONTENU DE L'EDUCATION – BILDUNGSINHALT

12521 Achieving National Curriculum attainment targets in the primary school.
GBR 1993
Research Date(s): 1989-1992
Timmons, G.
Inst: Warwick University, Faculty of Educational Studies, Coventry CV4 7AL, United Kingdom.
science education; achievement; local studies; geography; history; teaching objective
éducation scientifique; rendement; études locales; géographie; histoire; objectif pédagogique
PROJECT DESCRIPTION

The aim of the research was to discover whether science attainment targets at key stage 2 of the National Curriculum can be achieved using a study of local history and geography, over a two-year period. The research began with 2 classes (9-10 years, 10-11 years), but only the younger class of 30 pupils experienced the full programme. The methods of teaching were those to be found in any good primary school: they were varied, but did involve a good deal of work outside at farms, factories, museums and other enterprises (e.g. a quarry and a brick factory). The children were tested five times in all.

About one third of the pupils could be said to have achieved all the targets up to the highest level for key stage 2. About one third achieved a satisfactory level. History and geography targets have also been aimed at, as have some in mathematics and technology.

Publ: Timmons, G.; Devine, J. & Murphy, A. Science attainment targets without tears. In: *Education 3-13*, Vol 19, No 3/1991, pp. 30-36.

12522 The aims of the Education Reform Act of 1988 for acts of worship in secondary schools.
GBR 1993
Research Date(s): 1991-1995
Watson-Broughton, A.
Sup: Copley, T.; John, M.
Inst: Exeter University, School of Education, St Luke's, Heavitree Road, Exeter EX1 2LU, United Kingdom.
Fin: College of St Hild and St Bede Durham Bursary.
religious education; educational legislation
éducation religieuse; législation scolaire
PROJECT DESCRIPTION

The aim of this research is to discover the most practical, sensitive, interesting, dynamic, relevant way to deliver the aims of the 1988 Education Reform Act with reference to daily acts of worship. To promote the spiritual aspects of a balanced curriculum in the secondary school, a working definition of 'spiritual' needs to be drawn. This needs to address the current secular nature of society. Since symbols have always played an important role in religion, it was thought useful to pursue research in the area of aesthetics. A study of National Curriculum art documents was made, which was very beneficial. Particular artists from history were highlighted and their ideas, aims and aspirations related to recent legislation on acts of worship in schools. A distinction was drawn at all times between ecclesiastical worship and educational worship.

12523 Art education in Japanese high schools: a case study.
GBR 1993
Research Date(s): 1990-1992
Mason, R.
Sup: Nakase, N.
Inst: De Montford University, Department of Education, Centre for Postgraduate Teacher Education, Scraptoft Campus, Scraptoft, Leicester LE7 9SU, United Kingdom; Joetsu University of Education, Joetsu-Shi, Niigata-Ken 943, Japan.
Fin: Ministry of Education, Japan.
art education; Japan; common core curriculum; secondary education
éducation artistique; Japon; tronc commun; enseignement secondaire
PROJECT DESCRIPTION

This project was carried out in a junior high school in Joetsu City over a three-month period in Autumn 1990. The aim was to describe and explain meanings and systems of organised behaviour making up a specifically Japanese culture of teaching and learning in art through ethnography. Fieldwork data are currently being analysed.

An ethnographic account of art teaching in a Japanese high school is thought to be of practical relevance for British art teachers for the following reasons: (1) Japan has a highly centralized education system with a National Curriculum which includes art. The high level of general education achievement is currently the envy of the developed world. Information derived from systematic observation of Japanese schooling is understood as having potential to generate useful comparative data about core curriculum content and standards of achievement in art. (2) Modern Japan provides a unique example of a culture which has adopted western ideals but to a remarkable degree has retained its unique artistic identity. An ethnog-raphy of Japanese art education is likely to be of practical assistance in contemporary debates about multicultural curriculum in art in the British educational context.

12524 Aspects of educational practice in the physical sciences and information technology.
GBR 1993
Research Date(s): 1970-1999
Jotham, R.; Ellis, M.
Inst: Nottingham University, Department of Adult Education, 14-22 Shakespeare Street, Nottingham NG1 4FJ, United Kingdom.
science education; physical sciences; information technology; teaching method
éducation scientifique; sciences physiques; technologie de l'information; méthode pédagogique
PROJECT DESCRIPTION

The aim of this project is to evaluate, comment upon and improve educational practice in science and information technology. The methodology involves direct experimentation work with student groups, followed by discussion with students and tutors. The research also includes extensive studies of statistical information on the extent, diversity and logistics of provision of adult education in this general area.

Publ: A list of publications is available from the researchers.

12525 Assessing achievement in the arts.
GBR 1993
Research Date(s): 1990-1991
Ross, M.
Sup: Radnor, H.
Inst: Exeter University, School of Education, St Lukes, Heavitree Road, Exeter EX1 2LU, United Kingdom.
Fin: Leverhulme Trust.
art education; assessment; teacher; pupil; interaction
éducation artistique; appréciation; enseignant; élève; interaction
PROJECT DESCRIPTION

This research report addresses the role of subjectivity in assessment in the arts. Perhaps it would be more accurate to speak of two, interacting, subjectivities: that of the pupil and that of the teacher. Subjectivity has traditionally been regarded as invalidating the legitimacy of aesthetic appraisal: on the one hand, the pupil's subjective experience has been seen both as inaccessible to the teacher and as private to the pupil. On the other hand, the subjective judgements of teachers have often been thought to be irrelevant and alien to their pupils' artistic purposes. Claims for validity and reliability in arts assessment are most often made to rest upon the twin notions of connoisseurship and consensus: teachers, by virtue of their experience and expertise, coming together to provide an agreed yardstick of aesthetic value, applied more or less exclusively to the impact of the pupil's artwork or product.

The researchers have sought to offer a contrary view: to focus upon process rather than product, upon pupil understanding rather than product impact, to promote the pupil as the principal assessor, and talk as a medium not only of aesthetic communication but of artistic insight and judgement. Above all the researchers argue the case for the recognition of the proper and indispensible function of subjectivity in artistic appraisal and have attempted to demonstrate, through the case studies, how the interplay of subjective responses, expressed in dynamic conversation, can yield substantial qualitative evidence for both formative and summative assessments in arts education.

The whole study rests upon a process model of aesthetic understanding that identifies a sequence of four transitional operations characterising each aesthetic encounter in terms of the two complementary dimensions of 'realization' and 'display'. This model (adapted from the work of Rom Harre) also serves as the instrument of data analysis and to articulate an argument in favour of qualitative assessment in the arts. Arts teachers are urged to make greater use of conversational talk in teaching and assessment and to allow greater emphasis upon contemplation and reflection in promoting aesthetic understanding in their classes. Incidentally, the study reveals the disturbing extent to which arts teachers currently may be neglecting children's aesthetic, creative and expressive development - those very elements they often claim to be their principal concerns. The arts encourage individual creative responses, whether in the course of art production or appreciation. These forms of response lend themselves to the assessment of individual achievement against personal past performance and within the context of an unfolding personal biography - rather than in more traditional normative and comparative terms. Much current practice is reductionist and fails to take account of the personal, expressive - as distinct from the collective, instructional - objectives of arts curricula.

The present project focuses upon National Curriculum Key Stage 3 and attempts: (i) to formulate an approach to assessment suitable for expressive and creative work in the arts at Key Stage 3 as a collective domain within the curriculum; (ii) to develop a framework for mapping the expressive and creative across the full range of the arts in education; (iii) to facilitate pupil self-assessment as a significant element in the formal assessment process. Work began in the schools in January 1990 and was concluded in June 1991. Field work was carried out in a number of secondary schools in Cornwall, Devon and Dorset.

12526 Assessment and examinations in physical education.
GBR 1993
Research Date(s): 1986-
Carroll, R.
Inst: Manchester University, School of Education, Centre for Physical Education, Oxford Road, Manchester M13 9PL, United Kingdom.
physical education; examination; assessment
éducation physique; examen; appréciation
PROJECT DESCRIPTION

Since the 1970s there has been a movement in schools into physical education examinations, first with Certificate of Secondary Education (CSE), later General Certificate of Secondary Education (GCSE) and A-levels. There has also been a similar movement by the further education sector into vocational qualifications such as City and Guilds and BTEC, and physical education has widened into the leisure industries. In addition there have been developments such as Records of Achievement (ROA) and the National Curriculum. The aim of the research has been to monitor such developments. The research has taken the form of a number of small projects and has been accumulative rather than one major project. Information has been collected from all the examination boards on statistics and structure, and from teachers and pupils on the functioning of examinations and assessment methods. Examples of Records of Achievement have also been collected, and questionnaires and interviews carried out.

The findings show the dramatic take-up of examinations in physical education. These statistics are continually updated and published. Analysis of GCSE and National Curriculum has been made to show the changes which will have to be undertaken in these examinations.

Publ: Carroll, R. Examinations and assessment in physical education. In: Armstrong, N. (ed.). *New Directions in Physical Education*. Human Kinetics, 1990, pp. 137-160.
Carroll, R. The twain shall meet: GCSE and the National Curriculum. In: *British Journal of Physical Education*, Vol 21, No 3/1990, pp. 29-32.
Carroll, R. & Jepson, J. ROA versus reports: what the pupils say. In: *British Journal of Physical Education*, Vol 22, No 2/1991, pp. 19-22.

12527 Assessment of work experience in relation to management learning.
GBR 1993
Research Date(s): 1991-1995
Lloyd, P.
Sup: Davies, J.
Inst: North Cheshire College, Padgate Campus, Fearnhead Lane, Warrington WA2 0DB, United Kingdom; Lancaster University, Department of Management Learning, Cartmel College, Bailrigg LA1 4YW, United Kingdom.
management education; university industry relationship; in-plant training; work experience
formation à la gestion; relation université-entreprise; stage en entreprise; expérience du travail
PROJECT DESCRIPTION

The aim of this research is to investigate and evaluate the validity of supervised work experience as a degree course component that: (1) enables students to acquire knowledge and skills; (2) enables students to complement the college based learning prior to the placement period; (3) enables students to develop appropriate and meaningful learning strategies following work experience periods; (4) facilitates course development through 'wash back' on existing learning programmes; (5) promotes staff development in terms of updating current practices within the industrial/commercial environment; (6) enhances host awareness and sympathy towards participation in supervised work experience programmes; (7) accurately assesses student development and performance in terms of: (a) personal/social skills; and (b) academic/cognitive skills.

A further aim is to test the above through a process of primary and secondary research into short- and long-term supervised work experience programmes in several institutions offering a range of vocational-related courses. It also aims to establish the theoretical concepts via primary and secondary sources of the notions underpinning: (1) experiential learning; (2) education and training; (3) teaching and learning methods; (4) assessment and profiling; and (5) competence and competition.

12528 Attitudes to and perceptions of Scottish primary school children to physical activities.
GBR 1993
Research Date(s): 1989-
Dick, A.
Inst: Heriot-Watt University, Moray House Institute of Education, Cramond Campus, Cramond Road North, Edinburgh EH4 6JD, United Kingdom.
physical education; pupil attitude
éducation physique; attitude de l'élève
PROJECT DESCRIPTION

The aims of this research are to: (i) set up an exploratory pilot study to clarify appropriate methodology for the collection of data; (ii) explore the data with reference to gender, multi-cultural issues, social class, environ-

ment and preferred physical activities amongst Scottish school children; and (iii) reflect on the implications of the above with regard to content of expressive arts, physical education (PE).

12529 Betriebliche Bildungsarbeit in der kaufmaennischen Ausbildung. (In-house training as part of commercial training courses.)
DEU 1993
Research Date(s): 1991-1992
Benteler, P.
Inst: Friedrich-Ebert-Stiftung Forschungsinstitut, Godesberger Allee 149, D-5300 Bonn 2.
Fin: Kloeckner Stahl; Bundesministerium fuer Bildung und Wissenschaft.
commercial training; enterprise; educational provision; vocational education; pilot project; trainer; work experience
formation commerciale; entreprise; scolarisation; enseignement professionnel; projet-pilote; formateur; expérience du travail
PROJECT DESCRIPTION

Inhalt: Bei der Uebertragung von Modellversuchsergebnissen auf der Basis eines Modellversuchs in der kaufmaennischen Berufsbildung werden wesentliche Ergebnisse aufbereitet und in Form eines Films, von Unterlagen fuer den Stand kaufmaennischer Ausbilder und durch Seminare uebertragen. Die realisierten Uebertragungsmedien werden evaluiert und revidiert.

Vorgehensweise: Curriculumentwicklung und Evaluation.

Datengewinnung: Standardisiertes Interview (Stichprobe: ca. 20; kaufmaennische Ausbilder). Gruppendiskussion (Stichprobe: ca. 20; Ausbilder). Expertengespraech.

12530 Building support for environmental education (Phase I).
GBR 1993
Research Date(s): 1991-1992
Midgley, C.
Inst: Council for Environmental Education, Reading University, Faculty of Education and Community Studies, National Environmental Resource Base, London Road, Reading RG1 5AQ, United Kingdom; Loughborough University of Technology, Department of Information and Library Studies, Loughborough LE11 3TU, United Kingdom.
Fin: Department of the Environment: Environmental Grant Fund; Esso UK plc.
environmental study; educational information; teaching aid; teacher; information need
étude du milieu; information pédagogique; moyen d'enseignement; enseignant; besoin d'information
PROJECT DESCRIPTION

The overall aim is to improve the provision and use of support for environmental education. The main objectives of the project are to: (1) increase awareness amongst practitioners of the sources of support; (2) encourage discerning use and evaluation of information by users; (3) improve and extend the means of dissemination of/access to information; (4) improve the applicability of the support provided; (5) establish mechanisms for maintaining the currency of information disseminated; and (6) recommend further initiatives, depending on the results of the research.

Phase I will focus on a survey of the information needs of environmental education practitioners which will be carried out by questionnaire and semi-structured interviews. The results of this survey will dictate the format of a subsequent survey of current provision, the findings of which will be used to compile a directory of information sources.

12531 Cambridge Business Studies Project.
GBR 1993
Research Date(s): 1967-
Dyer, D.; Lines, D.
Inst: London University, Institute of Education, 20 Bedford Way, London WC1H 0AL, United Kingdom.
Fin: Cambridge Business Studies Trust.
commercial training; curriculum development; teaching aid; post-compulsory education
formation commerciale; élaboration de programmes d'études; moyen d'enseignement; enseignement postobligatoire
PROJECT DESCRIPTION

This project has six objectives: (1) to foster the development of business education courses at 16+ and 18+ level, giving advice and support to teachers; (2) to develop and disseminate teaching aids and materials primarily of value for 16+ and 18+ courses; (3) to develop inservice training courses for intending teachers and others wishing to extend their expertise; (4) to liaise with examining bodies and others for appropriate curriculum development, to foster dialogue between teachers and others interested in business education; (5) to liaise with business and industry; and (6) to monitor work and interpret and report as required.

Publ: Dyer, D.M. & Chambers, I. *Business Studies: an introduction.* Harlow: Longman, 1987.
Whitehead, D. & Dyer, D.H. *New developments in economics and business education: handbook for teachers.* London: Kogan Page, 1991.
A list of teaching materials and syllabuses is available from the researchers.

12532 Children's perception of pitch relationships.
GBR 1993
Research Date(s): 1986-1992
Hodges, R.
Sup: Swanwick, K.
Inst: London University, Institute of Education, Department of Music Education, 20 Bedford Way, London WC1H OAL, United Kingdom; Derbyshire College of Higher Education, Kedleston Road, Derby DE3 1GB, United Kingdom.
music education; learning; cognitive development; music; perception; child
éducation musicale; acquisition de connaissances; développement cognitif; musique; perception; enfant
PROJECT DESCRIPTION

This study examines the perceptual and cognitive structures that children employ when listening to music. A number of chronometric studies use reaction time to attempt to identify developmental aspects of a schema theory of hierarchical music processing. A chronometrically measured forced-choice paired-comparisons experimental paradigm was used to test children's discrimination of same and different semitones presented dichotically by a computer-driven closed environment in context-free and various contextual presentations.

The results suggest that the maturation of children between the ages of six to twelve finds increasing ease in both context-free and contextual presentation in exhibiting fewer errors and decreasing reaction times with increasing age. No significant difference in mean reaction time for correct responses between the conditions of same and different suggest that the processing required for the mental translation of auditory stimuli into a verbal response is the same for both conditions. It is proposed that the observed differences in reaction time responses serve as a measure of the internalisation of cognitive structures such as tonality and responses may therefore be classified according to a perceptual hierarchy.

12533 Citizenship project.
GBR 1993
Research Date(s): 1991-1994
Fogelman, K.; Edwards, J.
Inst: Leicester University, School of Education, University Centre, Barrack Road, Northampton NN2 6AF, United Kingdom.
Fin: Barclaycard; ESSO.
content of education; citizen participation; common core curriculum
contenu de l'éducation; participation du citoyen; tronc commun
PROJECT DESCRIPTION

A centre has been established to investigate the teaching of citizenship, particularly in the National Curriculum. An annotated bibliography, inservice teacher education (INSET) work, teacher training and case studies are all in hand. A book is planned and market research will be undertaken.

12534 Communication and professional competencies in a modular humanities programme.
GBR 1993
Research Date(s): 1991-1993
Rice, J.; O'Sullivan, T.; Saunders, C.
Inst: De Montford University, School of Arts, PO Box 143, Leicester LE1 9BH, United Kingdom.
humanities; minimum competencies; open education; communication; university studies
études littéraires; fundamentum; éducation ouverte; communication; études universitaires
PROJECT DESCRIPTION

The Communication and Professional Studies (CPS) programme plays a key role in the degree scheme in arts and humanities (DSAH) at De Montford University. In brief, its function is two-fold: (1) it is designed to equip students with the core skills necessary to participate effectively within a flexible, modular arts degree; and (2) it begins to develop in students some of the key vocational and future career skills relevant to their undergraduate studies.

The aims of this project are to: (1) research, design and produce open learning packages for key elements of the CPS programme in the school of arts; (2) research and develop the necessary tutoring and student-centred delivery skills for staff teaching on the DSAH; (3) provide research evidence of the teaching and learning requirements generated by the DSAH; (4) provide staff development to support the teaching and learning requirements generated by the DSAH; (5) provide an opportunity to address broader issues of coherence and progression by developing CPS skills in the subject modules; and (6) provide a model for development for open learning packages on the Level 1 DSAH programme.

Project development will take two forms: (1) Curriculum audit and research - this will include research to identify the teaching and learning experiences of staff and students on the DSAH with reference to the CPS Level 1 module; and staff development workshops to address the issues identified in audit. (2) Open learning packs - this will include development of supported self-study packs for selected elements of the CPS course; and staff development workshops to disseminate the process of their genera-

tion (i.e. information technology skills) and the teaching skills necessary for their implementation.

12535 Comparative issues in science curriculum: USA & UK.
GBR 1993
Research Date(s): 1990-1992
Reid, D.
Inst: Manchester University, School of Education, Oxford Road, Manchester M13 9PL, United Kingdom.
science education; curriculum development; educational innovation; comparative education
éducation scientifique; élaboration de programmes d'études; innovation pédagogique; éducation comparée
PROJECT DESCRIPTION

Large amounts of currency have been spent on developing the science curriculum in both the USA & UK. In the USA the science curriculum has remained intransigent whilst in the UK a number of successful innovations have taken place since the late 1980s. Why, when the social and economic pressures for change have been the same in both countries, has one country been relatively successful and the other not? It is argued that the structure of the American High School is not conducive to collegiality and teacher empowerment. It is the highly developed department structure, with the head of department as mentorial, which has facilitated science curriculum innovation in the UK.

12536 Conceptual development in primary school science: the design of group tasks.
GBR 1993
Research Date(s): 1990-1992
Howe, C.; Tolmie, A.
Inst: Strathclyde University, Department of Psychology, Turnbull Building, 155 George Street, Glasgow G1 1RD, United Kingdom.
Fin: Leverhulme Trust.
sciences; group work; concept formation; primary education
sciences; travail par équipe; formation de concept; enseignement primaire
PROJECT DESCRIPTION

The National Curriculum for Science requires primary school teaching to both incorporate group work and focus on conceptual development. Previous studies with primary age groups have shown tasks which expose conceptual conflicts between participants to effectively promote conceptual advance, but there remains scope for additional task constraints which optimise conflict resolution.

Three task elements compatible with the prediction-test explanation format used previously, specifically address central aspects of the development of science concepts: (1) the provision of items which constitute critical tests for exclusion of irrelevant factors and isolation of relevant; (2) formulation of law-like statements through rule generation exercises; and (3) identification of law-like statements through rule selection. The two studies planned, in the areas of flotation and cooling, will assess the contribution of these task features to conceptual gain.

In each study 120 children between 8 and 12 will be pre-tested using clinical interview techniques to establish initial conceptions. They will then be randomly assigned to groups of four to work on prediction-test explanation problems under one of four conditions. A control condition will present groups with randomly ordered items and no additional constraints. A second condition will provide opportunities for critical tests, and the third and fourth conditions will combine critical tests with either rule generation or rule selection. Participants will subsequently be post-tested to obtain measures of conceptual change, in terms of broad level of understanding and movement towards classical conceptions of physical factors. In addition, group sessions will be videotaped to allow identification of on-task behaviours that mark successful learners.
Publ: Howe, C.J.; Rodgers, C. & Tolmie, A. Physics in the primary school: peer interaction and the understanding of floating and sinking. In: *European Journal of Psychology of Education*, Vol 5, No 4/1990, pp. 459-475.
Howe, C.J.; Tolmie, A. & Rodgers C. The acquisition of conceptual knowledge by primary school children: group interaction and the understanding of motion down an incline. In: *British Journal of Developmental Psychology*, Vol 10, Part 2, 1992, pp. 113-130.
Howe, C.J.; Tolmie, A. & Anderson, A. Information technology and group work in physics. In: *Journal of Computer Assisted Learning*, Vol 13, No 3/1991, pp. 133-143.

12537 Critical activity and its effect on the art and design curriculum.
GBR 1993
Research Date(s): 1990-1992
Grassie, M.
Inst: Heriot-Watt University, Moray House Institute of Education, Holyrood Road, Edinburgh EH8 8AQ, United Kingdom.
art education; critical sense; art activity; curriculum development
éducation artistique; sens critique; activité artistique; élaboration de programmes d'études
PROJECT DESCRIPTION

The aims of the research are to: (1) study the effect of the Scottish Certificate of Education new Standard Grade Critical Activity Units on the Art and Design Curriculum especially in S1 and S2; (2) prepare slide packs, display boards and appropriate visual material as backup for Critical Activity Units in Expressive and Design Areas and to see if these can be adapted for use in the common course; and (3) consider the new Higher Art and Design and the Critical Activity element proposed, in relationship to present Standard Grade development.

12538 Critical responses to recent developments in advertising and marketing.
GBR 1993
Research Date(s): 1989-1992
Masterman, L.
Inst: Nottingham University, School of Education, University Park, Nottingham NG7 2RD, United Kingdom.
media education; mass media; marketing; advertising
éducation aux médias; médias; mercatique; publicité
PROJECT DESCRIPTION
This research will attempt to: (1) describe the most up-to-date techniques used in marketing, especially via the mass media, e.g. product placement, industrial political marketing, public relations, manufacture and privatisation of information, (2) explore the central issues and questions raised by these developments, especially in relation to work in schools (traditionally, teachers of English and media studies have taught about advertising as it is more narrowly defined); (3) provide materials for use in schools - especially at General Certificate of Education (GCSE) level and A-level in media studies.

12539 Das Europabild im Schulbuch: zum Europabegriff in den oesterreichischen Geschichts- und Geographiebuechern der 8. Schulstufe. (Europe in school textbooks: the concept of Europe in Austria's history and geography textbooks for the 8th form.)
AUT 1993
Research Date(s): 1990-1991
Bamberger, Richard; Gattermann, Brigitte; Gintenstorfer, Andrea.
Inst: Institut fuer Schulbuchforschung, Strozzigasse 2, A-1080 Wien.
European dimension; textbook; history; geography
dimension européenne; manuel d'enseignement; histoire; géographie
PROJECT DESCRIPTION
Durch die politischen Umwaelzungen in Osteuropa und die Neuordnung Europas stellen sich neue Aufgaben hinsichtlich der Gestaltung der Schulbuecher. Ein Einblick in den Iststand soll die Herausforderungen fuer die Zukunft erschliessen. Gesichtspunkte der Untersuchung (begleitend zur Ausarbeitung von Analyserastern): Leitvorstellungen der gegenwaertigen Europadiskussion; Lehrplaninhalte der 8. Schulstufe; altersgemaesse Darstellung.
Auf eine quantitative Untersuchung (Datenerhebung, Raumanalyse) folgen verbale Erlaeuterungen und vergleichende Aussageanalysen. Sowohl in Geschichte als auch in Geographie gibt es nur wenige ueberzeugende und ausfuehrliche Darstellungen, eher nur Hinweise, eine Konfrontation mit Begriffen und Fachausdruecken ohne viele Erlaeuterungen (Erkennen von Zusammenhaengen). Man kann auch kaum von verschiedenen Zugaengen und Ansaetzen sprechen, besonders in Geschichte stellt sich (West-)Europa als lexikalisches Institutionsverzeichnis dar. Die begriffliche Ueberforderung der SchuelerInnen ist wenig geeignet, Verstaendnis fuer die Europaproblematik zu entwickeln bzw. Interesse fuer eine weitere Beschaeftigung mit diesem Gegenstand zu foerdern.
Es wurden Raumanalysen und Inhaltsanalysen durchgefuehrt.

12540 Developing European awareness: the role of local education authorities and schools in the 1990s.
GBR 1993
Research Date(s): 1993
Jamison, J.
Sup: Stradling, R.
Inst: National Foundation for Educational Research, The Mere, Upton Park, Slough SL1 2DQ, United Kingdom.
European dimension; curriculum development; educational policy; local government
dimension européenne; élaboration de programmes d'études; politique de l'éducation; administration locale
PROJECT DESCRIPTION
As part of the preparation for the creation of a single European Market by the end of 1992, the Council of the European Community passed a resolution in May 1988 aimed at promoting and strengthening the European dimension at all levels of education. Although a growing number of local education authorities (LEAs) and schools are now taking steps to incorporate the European dimension, research evidence on established practice and new developments is still limited.
The purpose of this evaluation is to update and extend the database on LEA-based and school-based initiatives on European awareness, and to evaluate the impact of established LEA programmes on school practice. In addition, the project will determine how LEAs are supporting these activities. Finally, the project will identify successful practices and establish which initiatives are appropriate to different educational phases, ability ranges and school contexts.
Methods employed will include a survey of all LEAs in England and Wales by questionnaire, concerning their policy documents and initiatives on European awareness, and a national survey of primary and secondary schools regarding the incorporation of European awareness into the curriculum. These will be accompanied by case study research in schools in selected LEAs. The research team plans to produce a written report on activities at LEA level and a handbook for schools and advisory staff with supporting materials which could be used for staff development.

12541 Devon Music Technology Project.
GBR 1993
Research Date(s): 1991-1992
Naughton, C.
Inst: Exeter University, School of Education, St Luke's, Heavitree Road, Exeter EX1 2LU, United Kingdom.
music education; didactic use of computer; educational technology; primary education
éducation musicale; usage didactique de l'ordinateur; technologie de l'éducation; enseignement primaire
PROJECT DESCRIPTION
The Devon Music Technology Project (DMTP) is a county-wide investigation based initially on a survey of what provision there is in the county. The use of 'Sampler' packages in primary schools in a cross-curricular manner is the basis of this project.

12542 Differentiated learning in science project.
GBR 1993
Research Date(s): 1992-1993
McGarvey, B.; Harper, D.; Day, J.
Inst: Ulster University, Department of Inservice Education, Cromore Road, Coleraine, County Londonderry BT52 1SA, United Kingdom.
Fin: Northern Ireland Curriculum Council.
science education; differentiated teaching; curriculum development
éducation scientifique; pédagogie differenciée; élaboration de programmes d'études
PROJECT DESCRIPTION
The aim of this project is to address the challenges of providing differentiated learning in science by developing and trialling suitable approaches to curriculum planning, teaching and assessing science at Northern Ireland Curriculum Key Stages 1, 2 and 3. Continuity and progression across the primary/secondary school interface will be a particularly important aspect. Two full-time project officers have been appointed and the work is proceeding through four phases: exploration of existing good practice; development work; trials and evaluation; production of guidelines, illustrative materials and INSET (Inservice Education of Teachers) materials.

12543 Drop out and progression in adult basic skills provision.
GBR 1993
Research Date(s): 1992-1993
Kambouri, M.
Sup: Francis, H.; Brain, S.
Inst: London University, Institute of Education, Department of Educational Psychology and Special Educational Needs, 20 Bedford Way, London WC1H 0AL, United Kingdom; Adult Literacy and Basic Skills Unit, 229/231 High Holborn, London WC1V 7DA, United Kingdom.
Fin: Department for Education; Adult Literacy and Basic Skills Unit.
basic education; adult education; dropout
éducation de base; éducation des adultes; abandon d'études
PROJECT DESCRIPTION
The main thrust of this report is a postal questionnaire sent to a sample of 1,500 former students plus limited interviews, together with a questionnaire to organising tutors, in a minimum of six local education authorities (LEA) areas. The data will be analysed using SSPX.

12544 Economic awareness as a curriculum entitlement for Welsh pupils.
GBR 1993
Research Date(s): 1990-1993
Jephcote, M.
Sup: Williams, M.
Inst: University College of Swansea, Department of Education, Hendrefoilan, Swansea SA2 7NB, United Kingdom.
Fin: Welsh Office; Esme Fairbairn Trust.
economic studies; curriculum development; curriculum research
études économiques; élaboration de programmes d'études; recherche sur les programmes d'études
PROJECT DESCRIPTION
The study is to facilitate the development of economic awareness in primary and secondary schools in Wales. The project has curriculum development and curriculum research aspects. On the research side the focus is on the preparation of case studies of individual schools and upon pupils' cognitive growth.

12545 The Economic Awareness Teacher Training Programme (EcATT).
GBR 1993
Research Date(s): 1986-
Hodkinson, S.; Thomas, L.
Inst: Manchester University, School of Education, Oxford Road, Manchester M13 9PL, United Kingdom; London University, Institute of Education, 20 Bedford Way, London WC1H OAL, United Kingdom.
Fin: BP; Banking Info Serv; DTI; Unilever; Esmee Fairbairn Charit Trust; Univ Grants Comm.
economic studies; curriculum research; teacher education
études économiques; recherche sur les programmes d'études; formation des enseignants
PROJECT DESCRIPTION
   The Economic Awareness Teacher Training Programme (EcATT) aims to promote and monitor the development and implementation of economic awareness programmes in schools, colleges and local education authorities (LEAs).
Publ: Hodkinson, S.R. & Thomas, L.M. (eds.). What is economic awareness? In: *Economic Awareness Journal*, Vol 1, No 1/1988, pp. 5-11, September.

12546 Economics and business studies education.
GBR 1993
Research Date(s): 1991-1994
Lines, D.
Inst: London University, Institute of Education, Department of Economics, Geography and Business Education, 20 Bedford Way, London WC1H OAL, United Kingdom.
Fin: Nuffield Foundation.
economic studies; curriculum development; post-compulsory education; teaching aid
études économiques; élaboration de programmes d'études; enseignement postobligatoire; moyen d'enseignement
PROJECT DESCRIPTION
   The aim of this project is to provide a comprehensive 16-19 curriculum package in economics and business studies, including teaching and learning aids and a post-16 assessment vehicle.

12547 Economics education 16-19 project.
GBR 1993
Research Date(s): 1991-1994
Thomas, L.
Inst: London University, Institute of Education, Department of Economics, Geography and Business Education, 20 Bedford Way, London WC1H OAL, United Kingdom.
Fin: Economics Association.
economic studies; post-secondary education; curriculum development
études économiques; enseignement postsecondaire; élaboration de programmes d'études
PROJECT DESCRIPTION
   This Economics Association project aims to stimulate and co-ordinate a fundamental review of the nature of economics thinking in response to the last decade's shift in the basic concerns of the discipline; by focusing on the full range of classroom contexts at 16-19, to help teachers to investigate the implications of this review for teaching, learning and assessment strategies; to develop and publish reports, materials and resources to provide access for other teachers to the expertise which will eventually be required by all.
Publ: Thomas, L. Project Briefing No 1 June 1991. In: *Economics*, Vol XXVII, Part 2, No 114/1991, Summer.
Thomas, L. Project Briefing No 2 November 1991. In: *Economics*, Vol XXVII, Part 4, No 116/1991, Winter.
Thomas, L. The Economics Education 16-19 Project: setting the scene. In: *Economics*, Vol XXVIII, Part 2, No 118/1992, Summer.
Thomas, L. *Working Paper No 1*. Economics Association, 1992.
Thomas, L. *Economics Education 16-19 Project, Newsletter No 1*, Oxford: Heinemann, 1992.

12548 Education management training and development in Europe.
GBR 1993
Research Date(s): 1990-1992
Braund, C.
Inst: Crewe & Alsager College of Higher Education, Department of Education Management, Hassall Road, Alsager, Stoke on Trent ST7 2HL, United Kingdom.
management education; educational administration; Europe
formation à la gestion; administration de l'enseignement; Europe
PROJECT DESCRIPTION
   The aim of this project is to chart education management training in Europe and to analyse different models in use. Research methodology will involve a literature survey, general survey and various visits.

12549 The education of the church and the pleasures of capitalism.
GBR 1993
Research Date(s): 1985-1993
Hull, J.
Inst: Birmingham University, School of Education, Centre for Religious Education Development and Research, Edgbaston, Birmingham B15 2TT, United Kingdom.
religious education; adult education; capitalism
éducation religieuse; éducation des adultes; capitalisme
PROJECT DESCRIPTION
   The project has to do with the education of the religious consciousness of adults under the conditions of industrial modernity and late capitalism. The approach is multi-disciplinary, drawing particularly upon sociology, social psychology and theology to create an understanding of the barriers to religious maturity for modern adults. Special emphasis is placed upon ideology and false consciousness, and resources are being drawn from Marxist and Freudian theory (critical theory).

12550 The effect of varied practice in instrumental teaching.
GBR 1993
Research Date(s): 1988-1992
Pacey, F.
Sup: Swanwick, K.
Inst: London University, Institute of Education, Department of Music Education, 20 Bedford Way, London WC1H OAL, United Kingdom.
Fin: Leeds City Council.
music education; musical instrument; psychomotor activity; learning strategy; teaching method
éducation musicale; instrument de musique; psychomotricité; stratégie d'apprentissage; méthode pédagogique
PROJECT DESCRIPTION
   The main research question is the applicability of Schmidt's focusing on the variable practice hypothesis which is that in learning a motor skill, many different ways of practising that skill are more efficient than repeating one way many times. Work has included background reading on the psychology of learning, on what the literature has to offer on musical ability in the aural sense as well as the expressive sense, on what constitutes a good learner, and the learning theories that preceded Schmidt's (1975) theory. The Leeds String Teaching Department has carried out field studies to discover whether variable practice is indeed useful in the real world. The first study, which aimed to help pupils learn to vary volume by using quicker and slower strokes of the bow, seemed to show positive results. The second study was concerned with achieving the asked for-tempo and a third small study was carried out by one teacher in the area of intonation.

12551 Emotivism, prescriptivism and moral education.
GBR 1993
Research Date(s): 1991-1994
Lee, F-J.
Sup: Straughan, R.
Inst: Reading University, Department of Arts and Humanities in Education, Bulmershe Court, Woodlands Avenue, Earley, Reading RG6 1HY, United Kingdom.
moral education; philosophy of education; China
éducation morale; philosophie de l'éducation; Chine
PROJECT DESCRIPTION
   The traditional Chinese moral education model places emphasis on authoritarian discipline dealing with heteronomy in behaviour training and doctrines of specific items, therefore less concern is placed on the education of moral autonomy and the capacities of making moral judgements. However, in view of the rapid changes in social structure and diversified value-judgement concepts of today, moral rules based solely on heteronomy are insufficient. On the other hand, the meta-ethics developed by the western world aim to clarify and justify the supporting claims beneath the traditional ethical theories, emphasising the analysis of moral languages and concepts, and investigating the logical frameworks of moral reasoning and decisions. This would contribute to the establishment of a rational and feasible theory in moral education. Since prescriptivism advocated by R.M. Hare and emotivism proposed by C.L. Stevenson play leading roles, this study attempts to investigate and compare them and to interpret their implications on moral education, such as decision of educational aims, selection of teaching contents, planning of curriculum organisation, methodology of moral education, and so on.
   The objectives to be achieved in this research are as follows: (1) to deal with the philosophical background of meta-ethics; (2) to investigate the theory of emotivism and elaborate its implications on moral education; (3) to investigate the theory of prescriptivism and elaborate its implications on moral education; (4) to compare and criticise the two theories, their limits and applicabilities; (5) to discuss Confucianism and its implication on moral education in Taiwan and (6) to propose recommendable ways to improve the theory and practice of moral education according to the research results. This study will deal with the philosophical background of emotiv-

ism and prescriptivism through a historical approach, and will apply theoretical analysis to elucidate them.

12552   Environmental Development Unit and Resources for Environmental and Social Studies Teaching (RESST).
GBR   1993
Research Date(s): 1983-
Masterton, T.; Simpson, A.
Inst: Heriot-Watt University, Moray House Institute of Education, Holyrood Road, Edinburgh EH8 8AQ, United Kingdom.
environmental study; social sciences; teaching aid
étude du milieu; sciences sociales; moyen d'enseignement
PROJECT DESCRIPTION
   The aims of the Environmental Development Unit are to: (1) act as a non-course related focus for environmental developments with the Institute; (2) create and manage an Institute environmental and social studies publications system; (3) assist with help - products specific to particular courses.
Publ: A full list of RESST publications and videos can be obtained from the researchers on request.

12553   Environmental education in primary teacher education.
GBR   1993
Research Date(s): 1991-1992
Bigger, S.
Inst: Westminster College, North Hinksey, Oxford OX2 9AT, United Kingdom.
Fin: Worldwide Fund for Nature UK.
environmental study; teaching aid; teacher education; further education of teachers
étude du milieu; moyen d'enseignement; formation des enseignants; perfectionnement des enseignants
PROJECT DESCRIPTION
   The aims of this research are to: (1) examine issues relating to environmental education as relevant to teacher education for the primary school; (2) design materials, in the form of a handbook, to disseminate to teacher education establishments; and (3) make these materials available to schools for inservice training. The focus of these materials is to combine local with global concerns and include economic and industrial understanding as a sub-theme.

12554   Ethical absolutism and education.
GBR   1993
Research Date(s): 1992-
Gardner, P.
Inst: Warwick University, Faculty of Educational Studies, Coventry CV4 7AL, United Kingdom.
moral education; ethics
éducation morale; éthique
PROJECT DESCRIPTION
   A consideration of the implications of ethical absolutism for moral education, especially in a multicultural society.
Publ: Gardner, P. Proportional attitudes and multicultural education, or believing others are mistaken. In: Horton, J. & Nicholson, P. (eds.). *Tolerance: philosophy and practice*. Aldershot: Avebury Press, 1992.

12555   Europe at school - European Schools Day Competition: an instrument to enhance the European dimension in education.
XCE   1993
Research Date(s): 1992
Bell, Gordon H.
Inst: Faculty of Education, Nottingham Polytechnic, Nottingham NG11 8NJ, United Kingdom.
European dimension; Europe; Council of Europe; European community; seminar
dimension européenne; Europe; Conseil de l'Europe; Communauté européenne; séminaire
COLLECTED WORKS - Conference proceedings
   Teacher Bursaries Scheme: European Teachers' Seminar on Europe at School - European Schools Day Competition: an instrument to enhance the European dimension in education, Portimão/Praia de Rocha (Portugal), 23-27 November 1991. This report begins by giving the background to the European Schools Day Competition (ESD-C), lists the problems, issues and opportunities discussed by the participants at the seminar and ends with the suggestions for further reading.
   The competition was created under the patronage of the Council of Europe, the Commission of the European Communities and the European Cultural Foundation in order to promote European awareness among pupils, students and teachers. The aim is not to identify a young European elite, but rather to incite as many Europeans as possible to explore and work on European themes. Themes adopted for the competition include subjects such as "The third election of the European Parliament" (1989) or the "Europe of tomorrow" (1991), "Environment and the quality of life - a challenge for Europe" (1992) and culminate in prize-giving ceremonies and a European prizewinners' gathering. All forms of written, manual and art

work including poems and radio plays are admitted. Activities and communication between the National Committees of Europe at School have intensified, especially in the field of individual, group and class work, team teaching and learning and projects. The greater part of these activities is run at local, regional and national levels with support from the Ministries of Education.
   The participants at this seminar, organized by the Centre for European Education and the Ministry of Education in Portugal, explored the experience of the ESD-C in the light of recent developments in European educational affairs.
   The report includes suggestions of how to promote and explore the European Dimension in Education through the ESD-C but notes that, in practice, introducing the idea of a "unifying Europe" implies that teachers must be trained and activities to promote co-operation between pupils, parents and teachers must be created. Problems concerning the structure and organization of the curriculum were identified throughout the seminar and are also presented in this paper, for example the anti-educational character of prejudices and bias, overloaded school curricula.
   The participants, mainly teachers from primary and secondary schools, concluded that the ESD-C is an activity of solidarity which expresses the reality of a unification process. It serves as an instrument of European awareness that needs to be linked more coherently to other activities with similar objectives. An inter-cultural pedagogy has to be formulated and re-examined in the light of school experience.

12556   Evaluating the effectiveness of a practitioner's use of a constructivist approach for developing scientific knowledge and understanding in primary students during their initial training and primary teachers on inservice courses.
GBR   1993
Research Date(s): 1989-1993
Ritchie, R.
Sup: Denley, P.
Inst: Bath University, School of Education, Claverton Down, Bath BA2 7AY, United Kingdom.
science education; student teacher; further education of teachers; teacher education; teaching method; primary education
éducation scientifique; élève-maître; perfectionnement des enseignants; formation des enseignants; méthode pédagogique; enseignement primaire
PROJECT DESCRIPTION
   Implementing the National Curriculum for Science requires primary teachers to develop pupils' knowledge and understanding in science, particularly through exploration and investigation, and assess their progress. For many teachers this is proving difficult because they lack appropriate background knowledge and understanding in science themselves. Recent research (Kruger & Summers, 1989) has confirmed that many primary teachers have no formal qualifications in science. Present recruits to teacher training are not required to have a qualification in science and existing cohorts in institutions include many students with limited scientific backgrounds. Consequently, the training of teachers and successful inservice education of teachers (INSET) requires trainers to adopt approaches that will develop scientific knowledge and understanding in teachers. Considerable research in the secondary sector, and limited research in the primary sector have shown the importance of adopting a constructivist approach to science education. The purpose of the research is to examine the effectiveness with adult learners of the use of such an approach. Focused observation and analysis of personal practice results in modifications to teaching and evaluation of changes. Effectiveness is assessed in terms of improved knowledge and understanding of scientific ideas. The project will look for evidence of improved understanding and the impact of this on the learning opportunities provided for children in the classroom. Formal and informal methods have been used to validate the research.

12557   Evaluation of implementation of science key stages 1-3.
GBR   1993
Research Date(s): 1991-1993
McGuigan, L.; Ewart, M.; Boyes, E.; Johnston, K.; Petrie, I.
Sup: Russell, T.; Qualter, A.
Inst: Liverpool University, Department of Education, Centre for Research in Primary Science & Technology, PO Box 147, Liverpool L69 3BX, United Kingdom.
Fin: National Curriculum Council.
science education; common core curriculum; evaluation
éducation scientifique; tronc commun; évaluation
PROJECT DESCRIPTION
   The project is evaluating the implementation of science in the National Curriculum at key stages 1, 2 and 3. In particular missing, deferred or overlooked areas of the curriculum - issues relating to conceptual progression and issues relating to meeting the needs of children of all abilities and achievements including those with special educational needs. The programme will collect information on a national basis in England. More intensive and qualitative work will be conducted in collaborative work with schools in a core sample having more restricted distribution.

12558   Evaluation of the Economic Awareness in Teacher Training project (EcATT).
GBR   1993
Research Date(s): 1990-1991
Jamieson, I.; Harris, A.
Inst: Bath University, School of Education, Claverton Down, Bath BA2 7AY, United Kingdom.
Fin: Department of Education and Science; Banking Information Service; Unilever.
economic studies; curriculum research; teacher education; evaluation
études économiques; recherche sur les programmes d'études; formation des enseignants; évaluation
PROJECT DESCRIPTION
   The evaluation uses a progressive focusing model to analyse the project's initial design, the local education authorities, with which it is involved, the schools with which it is working and finally the classrooms in which it operates. The evaluation should throw light on the concept of economic awareness, universities as centres for curriculum change and the operation of cross curriculum themes in the National Curriculum.

12559   Evaluation of the Health Education Authority's 'My Body' Integration Project.
GBR   1993
Research Date(s): 1992
Jamison, J.   Froud, K.
Sup: Stoney, S.
Inst: National Foundation for Educational Research, The Mere, Upton Park, Slough SL1 2DQ, United Kingdom.
Fin: Health Education Authority.
health education; human body
éducation sanitaire; corps humain
PROJECT DESCRIPTION
   The My Body Project is a Health Education Authority project designed for use in primary schools, and aims to teach pupils about the workings of the human body and to enable them to explore issues related to health education and to develop decision-making skills. The aim of the evaluation is to assess the impact of the My Body Project and identify a range of good practice at each level of delivery of the project material.
   A range of qualitative research methods will be employed within a broad case-study structure. Data will be collected from six local authorities and 24 schools (four within each). Within each of the case-study authorities, one school will be selected as a key school in which more detailed work will be undertaken. The My Body Project Team will be observed as they provide training and support. A final report will be submitted to the Health Education Authority which documents the main evaluation findings and identifies models and instances of good practice.

12560   Evaluation of the implementation of science in the National Curriculum.
GBR   1993
Research Date(s): 1991-1993
Russell, T.; Qualter, A.
Inst: Liverpool University, Department of Education, Centre for Research in Primary Science & Technology, PO Box 147, Liverpool L69 3BX, United Kingdom.
Fin: National Curriculum Council.
science education; common core curriculum; curriculum development; differentiated teaching
éducation scientifique; tronc commun; élaboration de programmes d'études; pédagogie differenciée
PROJECT DESCRIPTION
   The evaluation rests on a number of issues which have been raised by Her Majesty's Inspectorate, the National Curriculum Council, and by others. There are three main ones: (1) coverage; (2) progression; and (3) differentiation. In relation to coverage, it has been observed that teachers are to some extent failing to cover certain aspects of the National Curriculum in science; they may be overlooking them; or they may be deferring them. The reasons why this is the case are being explored with a focus on planning for teaching science. The second study, on progression, involves a consideration of the match between the levels in the National Curriculum intended to represent progression in learning, and the order in which pupils develop their understanding in science. The third issue involves the study of the appropriateness of the order for less able and more able and talented pupils.
   A mixture of individual interviews of teachers and pupils, national questionnaire, group interviews and classroom observation is used in meeting the challenges of this project.

12561   Evaluation of the Promoting Health in Primary Schools (PHIPS) project.
GBR   1993
Research Date(s): 1991-1992
Morris, B.; Turner, G.
Inst: Southampton University, Faculty of Educational Studies, Assessment and Evaluation Unit, Highfield, Southampton SO9 5NH, United Kingdom.

Fin: Health Education Authority.
health education; primary education
éducation sanitaire; enseignement primaire
PROJECT DESCRIPTION
   Promoting Health in Primary Schools (PHIPS) will plan and undertake a series of ten regional dissemination events focused on Curriculum Guidance 5 (CG5), Health Education Act 1990, which sets out the need for a coherent whole-school policy and programme for health education, supported by detailed curriculum guidelines. The aims of these events are to: (1) demonstrate how coherent health education programmes can be managed as an essential aspect of the whole school curriculum; (2) offer a unified response to CG5 through the integration of three major Health Education Authority (HEA) projects: Health for Life; My Body; Happy Heart; and (3) build on, and strengthen the existing dissemination network for health education in England.
   The evaluation will: (1) provide project teams, regional coordinators and the HEA with information about the effectiveness of each event; (2) provide project teams, regional coordinators and the HEA with information about the outcomes of each event; and (3) provide the HEA with an evaluation of the appropriateness of this model of dissemination for future activities. The regional events will be evaluated using a pre-coded questionnaire. Issues in planning, coordination and impact will be investigated through case studies of three of the regional events which represent the range of approaches chosen throughout the project. The case studies will involve interviews with project managers, team personnel and regional coordinators and the distribution of a more detailed questionnaire to a sample of participants.

12562   Evolution institutionnelle de l'enseignement agricole français.
FRA   1993
Research Date(s): 1988-1993
Boulet, Michel; Nouvelot-Gueroult, Marie-Odile.
Sup: Plaisance, Eric.
Inst: Institut national de recherches et d'applications pédagogiques, 2 rue des Champs Prévois, 21100 Dijon, France.
agricultural training; historical research; power; state; educational institution
formation agricole; recherche historique; pouvoir; Etat; établissement d'enseignement
PROJECT DESCRIPTION
   Objectifs: A travers l'étude de la mise en place du service public d'éducation et de formation agricoles (lois de juillet et décembre 1984) il s'agit d'analyser le partage du pouvoir entre l'Etat et les institutions éducatives.
   Méthodologie: Dans un premier temps, analyse d'ensemble du système de formation agricole par une approche socio-historique et analyse des interactions des instances sociales présentes au niveau local, l'établissement dans son milieu, par une approche s'appuyant sur la sociologie des organisations et l'anthropologie de l'éducation. Puis, travaux sur le processus d'élaboration du schéma prévisionnel national des formations et sur son articulation avec des schémas prévisionnels régionaux (comprenant trois sous-ensembles: enseignement public, enseignement privé à temps plein et par alternance). Enfin, comparaison internationale afin d'étudier le rôle de l'Etat et de l'initiative privée en matière d'enseignement agricole dans deux pays: l'Italie et la Pologne.

Publ: Boulet, Michel. *Le fonctionnaire et le paysan.* Dijon: INRAP, Coll. Recherches, 1991.
Boulet, Michel. Auguste Petit-Lafitte, premier professeur départemental d'agriculture. In: *Annales d'histoire des enseignements agricoles,* 1989, n° 3, pp. 7-21.
Boulet, Michel & Mabit, René. *De l'enseignement agricole au savoir vert.* Chapitre 1 et 2. Paris: L'Harmattan, 1991.

12563   Exeter Music Technology Project.
GBR   1993
Research Date(s): 1991-1992
Naughton, C.
Inst: Exeter University, School of Education, St Luke's, Heavitree Road, Exeter EX1 2LU, United Kingdom.
music education; didactic use of computer; educational technology
éducation musicale; usage didactique de l'ordinateur; technologie de l'éducation
PROJECT DESCRIPTION
   The Exeter Music Technology Project (EMTP) is an investigation into the use of a Roland 'Sampler' with a group of students from the School of Education and Exeter College of Further Education. The project is therefore concerned with students knowing how to use 'computer equipment'.

12564   Exploration of science.
GBR   1993
Research Date(s): 1990-1991
Gott, R.; Feasey, R.
Inst: Durham University, School of Education, Leazes Road, Durham DH1 1TA, United Kingdom.
Fin: National Curriculum Council.

science education; teacher behaviour; practical work; common core curriculum; curriculum development

éducation scientifique; comportement de l'enseignant; travaux pratiques; tronc commun; élaboration de programmes d'études

PROJECT DESCRIPTION

The research project has three aims. Firstly, a questionnaire survey to ascertain teachers' (in primary and secondary schools) perceptions of the nature and purpose of practical work in science. Secondly, a series of practical investigations which lead to information on progression in this key area of the National Curriculum. Finally, a series of case studies of curriculum elements in schools.

The work will result in a series of reports to the National Curriculum Council, INSET (Inservice Teacher Education) materials for schools and research publications.

12565 Forms of assessment in religious education (FARE).
GBR 1993
Research Date(s): 1989-1991
Copley, T.
Inst: Exeter University, School of Education, St Luke's, Heavitree Road, Exeter EX1 2LU, United Kingdom.
Fin: St Matthias Trust; Sarum St Michael Educ'n Charity; St Luke's Coll Found'n Trust; Jerusalem Trust; SW LEA's.
religious education; common core curriculum; assessment
éducation religieuse; tronc commun; appréciation
PROJECT DESCRIPTION

This is an action research topic carried out for South Western local education authorities, which uses teachers in the contributing authorities to investigate and trial appropriate ways of assessing religious education at each Key Stage compatible with current practice in National Curriculum subjects and current thinking in religious education.

Publ: Coddington, V.; Copley, T.; Priestley, J. & Wadman, D. A fare deal for RE. Exeter: School of Education, Exeter University, 1991.

12566 The functions, purposes and contributions of national education management centres.
GBR 1993
Research Date(s): 1993-
Gray, L.
Inst: Staff College, Coombe Lodge, Blagdon, Bristol BS18 6RG, United Kingdom.
educational administration; management education
administration de l'enseignement; formation à la gestion
PROJECT DESCRIPTION

The project will examine the work of national education management centres, in part through visits to a sample of such centres. It will compare their purposes, and relationships to national and local government systems, and funding sources. It will also examine their functions, with relation to training, consultancy, research, curriculum and management development; their client groups; and their links with other management capabilities across the education sectors. The project will examine the feasibility of building an international network of such centres; explore the likely costs and benefits; and seek possible sources of funding for such a network.

12567 Guidelines for political education.
GBR 1993
Research Date(s): 1987-1992
Davies, I.
Sup: Lister, I.
Inst: York University, Department of Educational Studies, Heslington, York YO1 5DD, United Kingdom.
political education; curriculum development; political science
éducation politique; élaboration de programmes d'études; science politique
PROJECT DESCRIPTION

There will be three main sections to this research. Firstly, a combination of narrative and analysis which shows the early call for guidelines for political education, the West German example, Department of Education and Science (DES) and Local Education Authority (LEA) guidelines. The researcher will be seeking to illuminate the nature of different guidelines, considering to what extent they address aims, content, methods, evaluation and to suggest how they relate to the recommendations made by key political educators. Secondly, the research will examine the perceptions of guidelines by the producers, by the political educators, by teachers and by gatekeepers who may include heads, governors, LEA officers and a sample of politicians. Finally, the research seeks to enquire how the guidelines help practice and focus on the relation between reality and theory in a number of Local Education Authorities.

Publ: Davies, I. Guidelines for political education. In: Social Science Teacher, Vol 18, No 2/1988, pp. 37-39, Spring.

12568 HIV/AIDS education within further education and tertiary colleges.
GBR 1993
Research Date(s): 1991
Hill, F.; Turner, G.
Inst: London University, King's College, Centre for Educational Studies, Cornwall House Annexe, Waterloo Road, London SE1 3TY, United Kingdom; Southampton University, Faculty of Educational Studies, Highfield, Southampton SO9 5NH, United Kingdom.
Fin: Health Education Authority.
health education; post-secondary education; sexually transmitted disease
éducation sanitaire; enseignement postsecondaire; maladie sexuellement transmissible
PROJECT DESCRIPTION

This is a case-study extension of a survey of Human-Immuno Virus/Acquired Immune Deficiency Syndrome (HIV/AIDS) Education in further education colleges and tertiary colleges catering for the 16-19 age range. The case studies have been selected to highlight good practice. Six colleges have been selected in order to describe and evaluate a range of different approaches to HIV/AIDS education. The case studies focus on: (a) the nature of college policies on HIV/AIDS, staff workshops, training and links with outside agencies; and (b) the effectiveness of a range of educational strategies, from lectures and tutorials to drama and student union activities. The latter is explored principally through group interviews with students in each college. Methods also include interviews with relevant staff, observation of appropriate activities and collection of materials. A report will be produced to highlight effective approaches to HIV/AIDS education which can be disseminated nationally.

12569 The impact of curriculum innovation in science in some small rural secondary schools.
GBR 1993
Research Date(s): 1988-1994
Mallon, P.
Sup: McGarvey, B.
Inst: Ulster University, Department of Inservice Education, Cromore Road, Coleraine, County Londonderry BT52 1SA, United Kingdom.
science education; curriculum development; rural school; secondary education
éducation scientifique; élaboration de programmes d'études; école rurale; enseignement secondaire
PROJECT DESCRIPTION

The aim is to identify the range of issues which science teachers in small rural schools were facing in implementing the new Northern Ireland science curriculum at Key Stage 3. Open-ended case studies were conducted initially and then more focused case studies of four schools were carried out over a two-year period. The final report will describe the challenges which the new Science Curriculum is posing to small science departments and the responses being made.

12570 The impact of the National Curriculum and Local Management of Schools (LMS) on the provision of sport and physical education in schools.
GBR 1993
Research Date(s): 1990-1994
Evans, J.; Penney, D.; Bryant, A.
Inst: Southampton University, Faculty of Educational Studies, Department of Physical Education, Highfield, Southampton SO9 5NH, United Kingdom.
Fin: Sports Council; Southampton University; Economic and Social Research Council.
physical education; sport; common core curriculum; educational reform
éducation physique; sport; tronc commun; réforme de l'enseignement
PROJECT DESCRIPTION

The research will be conducted over a three-year period to monitor the impact of the National Curriculum and Local Management of Schools (LMS) on the provision of sport and physical education (PE) in schools in England and Wales.

The research will be conducted in two phases. The first will employ a qualitative methodology to survey the impact of LMS on the levels and nature of physical education and sport provision for schools. The second will use a qualitative methodology to monitor the effects of LMS and a National Curriculum for PE on processes of teaching and learning in PE and sport in schools.

12571 Individualism and curriculum development in physical education.
GBR 1993
Research Date(s): 1986-1993
Laws, C.
Sup: Evans, J.
Inst: West Sussex Institute of Higher Education, Bishop Otter College, College Lane, Chichester PO19 4PE, United Kingdom; Southampton University, Faculty of Educational Studies, Highfield, Southampton SO9 5NH, United Kingdom.

physical education; individualism; teaching method; teaching style; individualized teaching
éducation physique; individualisme; méthode pédagogique; style pédagogique; enseignement individualisé
PROJECT DESCRIPTION

The word individualism is often used by educational writers and teachers without conscious precision as to its meaning. The research project attempts to discover whether teachers' commitment to individualism is expressed in their practice of teaching. Data have been utilized from a four year case study at one secondary school. The emphasis of the research focuses on the interpretative paradigm adopting the qualitative principles associated with ethnography.

Initial analysis of data indicates that while individualistic approaches are expressed in the formal intended curriculum, they are not always evident in the practice of teaching. Issues of equality of opportunity, equal worth, and value were recognised by teachers, but their practice did not express their commitment to these issues. The capacity of teachers to achieve an individualistic approach in their practice was also related to the distribution of power in schools and the limits inherent in the philosophy of individualism.

Publ: Laws, C.J. Individualism and teaching games: a contradiction of terms? In: *British Journal of Physical Education*, Vol 21, No 4/1990, Winter. Research supplement, No 8, pp. 2-6.

12572 Inovace didaktické činnosti ve školní tělesné výchově: odraz akcentovaných nároků na rozvoj koordinačních schopností v efektivitě plavecké výuky. (Innovation of physical education teaching methods: fostering the development of swimming skills through efficient teaching methods.)
CSK 1994
Research Date(s): 1991-1993
Bělková, Tatána.
Sup: Svaton, Vratislav.
Inst: Fakulta tělesné výchovy a sportu Univerzity Karlovy (Charles University, Faculty of Physical Education and Sport), Martího 31, 162 52 Praha 6, Czech Republic.
Ministerstvo školství, mládeže a tělovýchovy (Ministry of Education, Youth and Physical Education), Karmelitská 8, 118 00 Praha 1, Czech Republic
physical education; teaching method; swimming
éducation physique; méthode pédagogique; natation
PROJECT DESCRIPTION

Aim: To contribute to the development of didactic theory in the field of swimming instruction; to explore the possibilities of various methods of teaching swimming and their practical application.

Design: Methods used will include observation, experiment, and factual and statistical evaluation of results. The sample will consist of pre-school children and young school-age children.

Expected outcomes include a video programme (to be used as a teaching aid in the Faculty of Physical Education and Sport). The findings will also be disseminated through articles in journals, teacher guidelines and a seminar.

12573 Inservice Education of Teachers programmes in environmental education.
GBR 1993
Research Date(s): 1988-1992
Gayford, C.
Inst: Council for Environmental Education, Reading University, Faculty of Education and Community Studies, National Environmental Resource Base, London Road, Reading RG1 5AQ, United Kingdom.
Fin: Central Electricity Generating Board.
environmental study; further education of teachers; teaching aid; teaching method
étude du milieu; perfectionnement des enseignants; moyen d'enseignement; méthode pédagogique
PROJECT DESCRIPTION

This project involves the production of inservice teaching approaches suitable for use by local authorities, schools or colleges. The emphasis is on interactive methods both for educating teachers and giving suggestions for ways in which environmental education can be integrated into the curriculum. Extensive trialling will occur in several invited local authorities on a partnership basis. The following modules for inservice use will be available from 1992: (1) Introducing Environmental Education; (2) Science; (3) English.

12574 Interactive science in the primary school.
GBR 1993
Research Date(s): 1988-1991
Skelding, A.
Sup: Smith, L.
Inst: Lancaster University, Department of Educational Research, Cartmel College, Bailrigg, Lancaster LA1 4YW, United Kingdom.
science education; teaching method; technology; activity method; primary education
éducation scientifique; méthode pédagogique; technologie; méthode active; enseignement primaire

PROJECT DESCRIPTION

The project aims to evaluate an interactive, 'hands-on' approach to teaching science and technology in a primary school. Systematic classroom observation and interviews are being used to examine teachers' roles in this teaching approach, and to assess children's acquisition of scientific concepts and skills, and to consider the role of language and mathematics in their learning.

12575 Internationaler AGMOe (Arbeitsgemeinschaft der Musikerzieher Oesterreichs)-Kongress "Musik und Erziehung". (International symposium of the Working Group of Austrian Music Teachers on "Music and education".)
AUT 1993
Research Date(s): 1991-1992
Peschl, Wolf; Knaus, Herwig; Sulz, Josef; Gruebl, Reingard; Guertelschmied, Christine.
Inst: Arbeitsgemeinschaft der Musikerzieher Oesterreichs, Kundmanngasse 22, A-1030 Wien.
Fin: Stadt Wien; Bundesministerium fuer Unterricht und Kunst.
music education; cultural policy; congress
éducation musicale; politique culturelle; congrès
PROJECT DESCRIPTION

Musikpaedagoglnnen saemtlicher Schultypen aus dem In- und Ausland liefern eine umfassende Leistungsschau derzeitiger Lehr- und Unterrichtsmethoden. Um den Rueckgang des Musikunterrichtes, besonders auf elementarer Ebene, zu verhindern wird die Erstellung neuer Resolutionen angestrebt. Ziel des Kongresses ist es, eine Basis fuer die Positionierung jeglicher Musikerziehung fuer die Zukunft zu schaffen.

12576 Interreligieus onderwijs. (Interreligious education.)
NLD 1994
Research Date(s): 1993-1994
Ven, J.A. van der; Ziebertz, H.-G.; Biemans, B.
Inst: Instituut voor Toegepaste Sociale wetenschappen (ITS) (Institute for Applied Sciences), P.O. Box 9048, 6500 KJ Nijmegen, Netherlands.
Katholieke Universiteit Nijmegen (Catholic University of Nijmegen), P.O. Box 9102, 6500 HC Nijmegen, Netherlands
Fin: SVO het Instituut voor Onderzoek van het Onderwijs.
religious education; denominational school; primary education; teaching method
éducation religieuse; école confessionnelle; enseignement primaire; méthode pédagogique
PROJECT DESCRIPTION

Background: The increasing multi-ethnicity of Dutch society has prompted a reconsideration of the principles and the identity of denominational primary schools. The teaching method "Meetings in primary school" focuses on the relationship between Christian, Islamic and Hindu relgion, using the model of the interreligious dialogue.

Aim: (1) To explore the possibilities for using the dialogue model for interreligious learning in denominational schools; (2) to measure the effect of the dialogue model on pupils' knowledge, attitudes and communicative skills.

Design: The study will use a sample consisting of (1) the teachers and 300 pupils in year seven (10-year-olds) of ten primary schools with a high or low level of multi-ethnicity which use the method "Meetings in primary school" and (2) the teachers and 120 pupils of four primary schools with a high or low level of multi-ethnicity which do not provide religious education. Three themes will be selected from the method for the research. Data will be collected through teacher questionnaires, interviews and classroom observation. Pretests and posttests will be administered to pupils in order to determine learning effects. A non-equivalent control group design will be used.

12577 The introduction of 'Management' to the secondary curriculum.
GBR 1993
Research Date(s): 1990-1992
Wait, A.
Inst: Heriot-Watt University, Moray House Institute of Education, Holyrood Road, Edinburgh EH8 8AQ, United Kingdom.
management education; curriculum development; secondary education; curriculum subject
formation à la gestion; élaboration de programmes d'études; enseignement secondaire; matière d'enseignement
PROJECT DESCRIPTION

This two-year project seeks to examine the problems associated with the introduction of the new Scottish Certificate of Education higher grade course in 'Management and Information Studies', which commenced in 1991. This is a brand new subject area in secondary education and a stand-alone higher with no equivalent standard grade.

The aim is to research the preparedness and ability of Business Studies teachers to deliver the course, and to examine the problems associated with learning and teaching approaches and assessment structure. The research will establish: (a) the current level of preservice training; (b) the requirements for inservice training, and (c) the problems associated with the introduction of the course.

12578   Issues in science and decision making.
GBR   1993
Research Date(s): 1992-1993
Ratcliffe, M.; Fullick, P.
Sup: Kelly, P.
Inst: Southampton University, Faculty of Educational Studies, Highfield, Southampton SO9 5NH, United Kingdom.
science education; sciences; comprehension; reasoning
éducation scientifique; sciences; compréhension; raisonnement
PROJECT DESCRIPTION

With the implementation of the National Curriculum all pupils up to the age of 16 will be expected 'to study scientific controversies' and 'begin to understand the power and limitations of science in solving problems'. There is also a growing need to address the public understanding of science.

The objectives of this research are: (1) To identify some of the features of the role of the individual in collective decision making, and to identify the particular thinking skills and capacities which individuals need in order to take decisions about science-based issues. This objective to be met through (a) literature search from the fields of education, sociology, psychology and management; and (b) examination of case studies relating to decision making about science-based issues in the public domain. (2) To examine, through action research in classrooms, (a) the ways in which pupils make decisions about aspects of science which affect them personally, and scientific issues which, at the time, may have only a marginal impact on their daily lives; and (b) the ways in which teachers manage this decision making process.

Methodology will be observation in classes in the age range 14-18 in order to achieve objective 2. Techniques will include: observation schedules, video analysis, interviews and questionnaires involving both pupils and teachers. It is hoped to develop curriculum materials from this research.

12579   Kindlich-jugendliches Geschichtsbewusstsein in Ost- und Westdeutschland. (Awareness of history among children and young people in West and East Germany.)
DEU   1993
Research Date(s): 1991-1994
Grzeskowiak, S.; Schulz, S.
Sup: Borries, B.
Inst: Universitaet Hamburg, FB 06 Erziehungswissenschaft, Institut fuer Didaktik der Geographie, Geschichte, Politik und des Sachunterrichts, Von-Melle-Park 8, D-2000 Hamburg 13.
Fin: Bundesministerium fuer Bildung und Wissenschaft.
German DR; German DR; child; adolescent; political education; history; political socialization
Allemagne RDA; Allemagne RDA; enfant; adolescent; éducation politique; histoire; socialisation politique
PROJECT DESCRIPTION

Inhalt: Hauptgegenstand der Untersuchung sind Geschichtssozialisation und Geschichtsbewusstsein von Schuelern und Schuelerinnen im ost- und westdeutschem Vergleich. Dazu wird eine repraesentative Zufallsauswahl von Schuelern und Schuelerinnen der 6., 9. und 12. Klassen getroffen. Diese Auswahl soll dem Vergleich von mehreren Altersgruppen hinsichtlich der Entwicklungsstufen des Geschichtsbewusstseins dienen. Darueberhinaus soll ein Dreiecksvergleich zwischen dem Osten (der fuenf neuen Bundeslaendern), dem Norden (Nordrhein-Westfalen) und dem Sueden (Bayern/Baden-Wuerttemberg) durchgefuehrt werden. Durch die zusaetzliche Befragung der Lehrer, die eine Kombination mit der Schuelerbefragung ermoeglicht, werden auch Unterrichtsvariablen miteinbezogen (wie beispielsweise Methodenkonzepte und Zielvorstellungen der Lehrenden). Neben der Beruecksichtigung von Einflussvariablen auf die ausserschulischen Geschichtssozialisation der Schueler und Schuelerinnen sollen auch die Beziehungen zwischen dem Geschichtsbewusstsein und politischem Bewusstsein untersucht werden.

Geographischer Raum: Sachsen-Anhalt, Sachsen, Thueringen, Brandenburg, Mecklenburg-Vorpommern, Bayern, Baden-Wuerttemberg, Nordrhein-Westfalen.

Untersuchter Zeitraum: 1000 bis 1991.

Vorgehensweise: Repraesentative Umfrageforschung. Untersuchungsdesign: Querschnittserhebung.

Datengewinnung: Befragung (Stichprobe: 6300; Schueler und Schuelerinnen der 6., 9. und 12. Klasse; Auswahlverfahren: Zufall). Primaererhebung: Feldarbeit von Mitarbeitern des Projektes durchgefuehrt.

Auswertung: Haeufigkeitsverteilungen; Korrelationen; Varianzanalysen; Faktorenanalysen; Pfadanalysen; Cluster-Analysen.

12580   Konzeptentwicklung in der Sexualpaedagogik.   (Development of a concept for sex education.)
DEU   1993
Research Date(s): 1988-1992
Ziebertz, H.
Sup: Glueck, G.
Inst: Universitaet Koeln, Erziehungswissenschaftliche Fakultaet, Seminar fuer Paedagogik, Abt. Allg. Didaktik und Schulpaedagogik, Gronewaldstrasse 2, D-5000 Koeln 41.
sex education; curriculum; value system; autonomy
éducation sexuelle; programme d'études; système de valeurs; autonomie
PROJECT DESCRIPTION

Inhalt: In der Geschichte zeigt sich bis in die Nachkriegszeit (50er Jahre) eine Dominanz der Werteinbindung der Sexualpaedagogik in Ehe und Familie. Zugleich werden kognitiv-rezeptive bis heteronome Zielvorstellungen entwickelt. Seit den 60er Jahren gewinnt die multidimensionale Werteinbindung der Sexualpaedagogik an Bedeutung, zugleich wird verstaerkt Autonomie eingefordert. Die Untersuchung bildet eine Typologie, auf deren Basis die Einstellung der Befragten analysiert wird.

Geographischer Raum: BRD.

Untersuchter Zeitraum: empirischer Teil 1989.

Vorgehensweise: Survey N = 585. Untersuchungsdesign: Querschnittserhebung.

Datengewinnung: Postalische Befragung (Stichprobe: 585; 285 Religionslehre, 300 Jugendarbeiter; Auswahlverfahren: Zufall). Primaererhebung: Feldarbeit von Mitarbeitern des Projektes durchgefuehrt.

Auswertung: Frequenz; Korrelationen; Faktorenanalyse; Regression; Signifikanztests. Datenaufbereitung: Datenedition (z.B. Aufbau von Datenbanken).

12581   Learning resource centres for executive development.
GBR   1993
Research Date(s): 1991-1993
Holmes, G.
Sup: Gilding, D.; Peacock, A.
Inst: Bradford University, Management Centre, Emm Lane, Bradford BD9 4JL, United Kingdom.
management education; self-instruction; resource centre
formation à la gestion; auto-enseignement; centre de matériel didactique
PROJECT DESCRIPTION

This project will develop and evaluate different forms of flexible delivery of management education, that allow structured self-learning. A pilot 'Learning Resource Centre' will be established with an industrial partner. The project will study: (1) the place of student-centred learning in the management development process; (2) the design and production of suitable modules of learning material; (3) the 'learning and technology' required; (4) the physical facilities needed; (5) the management of learning resource centres.

12582   A local authority-based demonstration trial of 'good practice' in road safety education.
GBR   1993
Research Date(s): 1988-1993
Singh, A.; Spear, M.
Inst: Reading University, Faculty of Education and Community Studies, Bulmershe Court, Woodlands Avenue, Earley, Reading RG6 1HY, United Kingdom.
Fin: Department of Transport: Transport and Road Research Laboratory.
road safety education; primary education; secondary education
éducation à la sécurité routière; enseignement primaire; enseignement secondaire
PROJECT DESCRIPTION

The primary aim of the project is to develop, implement and evaluate policies of 'good practice' in road safety education for children aged 5-16. The initial phase of the project is being spent developing guidelines for the management and co-ordination of road safety education both at local authority and at school level in collaboration with educational advisers, teachers, road safety officers, health education officers and the police; and in conducting a pilot trial in one local authority.

During the second phase of the research, the revised policy document will be implemented through inservice training in all the primary and secondary schools (about 130 schools) within the selected areas of the two trial authorities.

The third phase of the research will be concerned with monitoring the implemented programmes closely in 20 primary and 10 secondary schools in order to assess the impact on educational outcomes over a given period of time, for example in pupils' knowledge, skills, attitudes, behaviour and future intentions regarding road safety. The research design will be quasi-experimental. The input, process and evaluation data will be obtained through visits, interviews, questionnaires, telephone calls, observation of lessons and unobtrusive observation of actual behaviour on the roads. The cost effectiveness of programmes including measures of changes in casualty rate will also be assessed.

The final phase of the research will comprise feedback to the participants, dissemination of the findings and the production of a report designed to assist local authorities and schools in implementing such policy(ies) effectively and economically.

12583   Look after yourself tutor training.
GBR   1993
Research Date(s): 1982-1992
Daines, J.; Graham, B.
Inst: Nottingham University, Department of Adult Education, 14-22 Shakespeare Street, Nottingham NG1 4FJ, United Kingdom.
Fin: Health Education Authority.
health education; training of trainers; teacher education; tutor
éducation sanitaire; formation des formateurs; formation des enseignants; tuteur de formation
PROJECT DESCRIPTION
The aim is to: (a) evaluate tutor training; (b) advise and consult on subsequent training and allied activities; and (c) develop a training strategy.

Publ: Daines, J. & Graham, B. *LAY report: innovations and outcomes 1978-1986*. Nottingham: University of Nottingham, Department of Adult Education, 1989.
Daines, J. & Graham, B. *Adult learning; adult teaching: a manual*. Nottingham: University of Nottingham, Department of Adult Education, 1989.

12584   Management and organisation of teaching 'The European Dimension' in schools (International network with representatives from The Netherlands, Belgium, Germany, Greece and Denmark).
GBR   1993
Research Date(s): 1990-1992
Peck, B.
Inst: Jordanhill College of Education, Division of Education and Psychology, Southbrae Drive, Jordanhill, Glasgow G13 1PP, United Kingdom.
Fin: European Community; Jordanhill College.
European dimension; comparative research; cross-national research
dimension européenne; recherche comparative; recherche transnationale
PROJECT DESCRIPTION
This is a comparative study of the introduction and teaching of 'The European Dimension' in schools, with particular focus upon management issues and organisation. The outcome will be the publication of a book on the experiences of the six participating countries.

12585   Management development centre: follow-up study.
GBR   1993
Research Date(s): 1992
Ouston, J.
Inst: London University, Institute of Education, Department of Policy Studies, 20 Bedford Way, London WC1N ONU, United Kingdom.
Fin: Baring Foundation.
management education; educational administration; in-service training; managerial staff
formation à la gestion; administration de l'enseignement; formation en cours d'emploi; personnel d'encadrement
PROJECT DESCRIPTION
A follow-up interview-based study of 22 participants in management development centre programmes, which explores the knowledge, skills and qualities needed by education managers and how these are acquired.

12586   Metodika výuky dopravní výchovy na vysokých školách. (Road safety teacher education.)
CSK   1994
Research Date(s): 1993
Fiala, Miloš; Papežová, Eliška; Václavík, Vladimír; Stojan, Mojmír; Bouřa, Václav.
Sup: Spička, Václav; Pospíšil, Karel.
Inst: Fakulta tělesné výchovy a sportu Univerzity Karlovy (Charles University, Faculty of Physical Education and Sport), Martího 31, 162 52 Praha 6, Czech Republic.
Ministerstvo školství, mládeže a tělovýchovy (Ministry of Education, Youth and Physical Education), Karmelitská 7, 118 00 Praha 1, Czech Republic
Fin: Ministry of the Interior.
road safety education; teacher education; further education of teachers
éducation à la sécurité routière; formation des enseignants; perfectionnement des enseignants
PROJECT DESCRIPTION
Aim: (1) To define a comprehensive goal for road safety teacher education for the nursery, primary, lower secondary and upper secondary levels and for traffic playgrounds; (2) to design a graduate-level road safety teacher education programme; (3) to design further education courses for road safety teachers and traffic playground teachers; (4) to design undergraduate-level driver education teacher training programmes.

Methods: A detailed analysis will be made of the roal safety teacher education system in the Czech Republic from different points of view. Analyses will also be made of training courses for driver education teachers.

12587   Monitoring of achievement in science.
GBR   1993
Research Date(s): 1991-1992
Stark, R.
Inst: Jordanhill College of Education, Division of Science, Southbrae Drive, Glasgow G13 1PP, United Kingdom.
Fin: Scottish Office Education Department.
science education; assessment; achievement
éducation scientifique; appréciation; rendement
PROJECT DESCRIPTION
This is a review of the Assessment of Achievement Programme (AAP) science survey linking it with the 5-14 Development Programme.

12588   Monitoring of achievement in science: second round.
GBR   1993
Research Date(s): 1989-1991
Bryce, T.; Stark, R.; Walker, A.; Dalziel, H.
Inst: Jordanhill College of Education, Division of Education and Psychology, Southbrae Drive, Glasgow G13 1PP, United Kingdom.
Fin: Scottish Office Education Department.
science education; achievement test; assessment
éducation scientifique; test de rendement; appréciation
PROJECT DESCRIPTION
The aim of this project was to assess the achievement of Scottish pupils at the P4, P7 and S2 stages in certain aspects of science. The approach and methodology was based on that of the monitoring exercises undertaken at Jordanhill College between 1985 and 1988. The exercise involved minor revision of the assessment framework; design and pilot testing of new and amended assessment materials; a testing programme carried out in summer 1990, marking and analysis of completed tests; writing a project report for the Scottish Office Education Department and draft dissemination materials for teachers. Advice and assistance on aspects of test design and data analysis was provided by the Assessment of Achievement Programme Central Support Unit. Account was taken of the 5-14 curriculum and assessment development programme.
Publ: *AAP Science* (based on the findings of the 1987 survey). Edinburgh: HMSO, 1990.
AAP Feedback. Science P4 and P7. SED/AAP, 1990.
AAP Feedback. Science P7 and S2. SED/AAP, 1990.
Stark, R.; Bryce, T.G.K.; Dalziel, H. & Walker, A. *Monitoring of Achievement in Science. Report of AAP Science (Second Round, 1990)* submitted to SOED, September 1991.

12589   Moral knowledge, moral principles and moral education.
GBR   1993
Research Date(s): 1987-1993
Phillips, G.
Sup: Gardner, P.
Inst: Warwick University, Faculty of Educational Studies, Coventry CV4 7AL, United Kingdom.
moral education; moral value; ethics; philosophy of education
éducation morale; valeur morale; éthique; philosophie de l'éducation
PROJECT DESCRIPTION
The research is philosophical. It is an inquiry into the possibility of objectivity in moral judgement, with particular reference to theories in moral realism; the nature of reasoning in morality; and the role of knowledge and reason in moral education.
Publ: Phillips, G. Personal, social and moral education. In: Entwhistle, N. (ed.). *A Handbook of Educational Ideas*. London: Croom Helm, 1990.

12590   Možnosti ďalšieho rozvoja výchovno-vzdelávacej sústavy so zameraním na stredné poľnohospodárske, lesnícke a potravinárske školy. (Possibilities for the further development of the education system, with particular reference to secondary schools of agriculture, forestry and food technology.)
CSK   1993
Research Date(s): 1991-1995
Kolenčík, Ladislav; Bakša, Ján; Pašková, Viera; Lörinčík, Jaroslav; Ivánek, Miroslav; Ondruška, František; Antošová, Margita.
Sup: Bátorová, Zdeňka.
Inst: Fakulta prevádzkovej ekonomiky-Katedra pedagogiky a sociológie (Operational-Economic Faculty, Department of Pedagogy and Sociology), Štefánikova tr. 13, 949 01 Nitra, Czech and Slovak Federal Republic.
Vysoká škola poľnohospodárska (University of Agriculture), Tr. A. Hlinku 1, 949 01 Nitra, Czech and Slovak Federal Republic
agricultural training; secondary education; curriculum; content of education
formation agricole; enseignement secondaire; programme d'études; contenu de l'éducation
PROJECT DESCRIPTION
The aim of the research was to determine the state and function of education, in particular of agricultural education. A theoretical-historical approach was used. Through interviews and questionnaires, the following results were obtained.

The present education system does not meet the needs of private enterprises. Agricultural education institutes need to set up interdisciplinary training courses and gear educational contents more strongly to the needs of those intending to set up a private enterprise. This would include retraining of graduates. Theory and practice should be linked more closely.

Methods used included: interviews, visits, statistical methods, questionnaires, discussions.

The outcomes of the questionnaire survey and the experts' statements can be summarized as follows. A majority of teachers point to the need to limit the content of subject matter in agricultural secondary schools to up to 55%. Also, the applicability of theory to practice is underlined. Critical comments were made on the overloading of curricula by general subjects. Specific attention should be given to subjects dealing with general production, vegetable and animal products and economics. Farmers should also have knowledge of veterinary problems. Teachers consider mathematics as it is currently taught to be of no practical use. Major shortcomings are observed in the gap between theory and practice and in the poor conditions of practical training (72% of respondents). The respondents attach great value to the motivation of the students.

The knowledge acquired through the research can serve as a basis for forecasting and for the development of agricultural education and training.

Publ: *Proceeding of the annual seminar on research projects*, University of Agriculture, Nitra, 1991, pp. 5-12.

12591 Možnosti tělovýchovy (s důrazem na školní TV) v rozvoji zájmu o cvičení i u sportovně nenadané a handicapované populace. (Physical training facilities in schools and the development of interest in physical exercise among less able or physically handicapped pupils.)
CSK 1994
Research Date(s): 1992-1993
Havlíčková, Ladislava; Bartůněk, Staša; Heller, Jan; Melichna, Jan; Jansa, Petr; Vránová, Jana; Vodička, Pavel.
Sup: Chválová, Olga.
Inst: Fakulta tělesné výchovy a sportu Karlovy Univerzity (Faculty of physical education, Charles University), José Martího 31, 162 52 Praha 6, Czech Republic.
Ministerstvo školství, mládeže a tělovýchovy (Ministry of Education, Youth and Physical Education), Karmelitská 7, 118 12 Praha 1, Czech Republic
physical education; physically handicapped; physical development; pupil attitude; health; motor development; pre-adolescence
éducation physique; handicapé physique; développement physique; attitude de l'élève; santé; développement moteur; préadolescence
PROJECT DESCRIPTION
Aims: (1) To investigate pupils' attitudes towards physical education in school and to examine the relationship between pupils' attitudes and physical constitution, motor activities, diet, physical efficiency and health (pre-adolescent subjects will be divided into three groups: hyperactive, normoactive, hypoactive); (2) to gather data on which to base a new conception of physical education which motivates pupils of lesser physical ability; (3) to evaluate the influence of physical education in school on the physical development of pre-adolescent children.
Design: Anthropometric, spiro-ergometric, biochemical and sensorimotor tests will be administered. Subjects' nervous system and health will be examined as well as the state of health of subjects' families.

12592 Music for the generalist primary teacher, with reference to the National Curriculum.
GBR 1993
Research Date(s): 1990-1995
Alston, P.; Ellis, V.; McQueen, A.; Derby, J.; Boxall, V.
Inst: Chester College of Higher Education, Cheyney Road, Chester CH1 4BJ, United Kingdom.
Fin: University of Liverpool Board of College Studies; Chester College.
music education; primary education; further education of teachers
éducation musicale; enseignement primaire; perfectionnement des enseignants
PROJECT DESCRIPTION
The aim of the project is to develop a model for combined skill, concept and affective learning in listening, performing and composing. This theoretical model will then be translated into classroom practice by the devising of materials to assist the generalist primary teacher to cope with the demands of the National Curriculum in Music at key stage 1 and key stage 2. All materials will be on trial in classrooms before being published. This work will then feed back into the theoretical model which will need to be revised and refined. A final report will comment on the practicability of teaching the National Curriculum in Music at key stage 1 and key stage 2 through a model of skill, concept and affective learning.

Publ: A list of publications is available from the researchers.

12593 National programme of training for primary school music consultants.
GBR 1993
Research Date(s): 1988-1993
Pegg, L.
Sup: Kemp, A.

Inst: Reading University, Department of Arts and Humanities in Education, Bulmershe Court, Woodlands Avenue, Earley, Reading RG6 1HY, United Kingdom.
Fin: Music Industries Association; Caloustie Gulbenkian Foundation.
music education; further education of teachers; in-service training
éducation musicale; perfectionnement des enseignants; formation en cours d'emploi
PROJECT DESCRIPTION
The purpose of the project is to provide a programme of inservice training for primary school music teachers who wish to develop consultancy skills. This training is offered on a national basis, organised in various locations throughout the country, and consists of four-week phased courses of the kind held at the University of Reading Music Education Centre since 1982. These courses offer teachers an updated view of recent developments in the primary music curriculum and training in the processes of consultancy work amongst colleagues. They also offer conferences for primary headteachers within their structure. A second important facet of the project will be the development of regional groups of music consultants to encourage on-going professional interchange and aftercare.

Publ: Kemp, A.E. Towards national adoption of music consultancy in primary schools. In: Barton, M. & Stewart, A. (eds.). *British Music Education Year Book 1988/89*. London: Rhinehold.
Kemp, A.E. & Wootton-Freeman, S. New tasks for music in primary schools and teacher training. In: *International Journal of Music Education*, No 11/1988, pp. 21-24.
Pegg, L.J. If music is for all pupils then it must be for all teachers. In: *Early Education*, No 7/1992, pp. 8.
Kemp, A.E. School within communities; are music opportunities being missed? In: Kemp, A.E. & Pegg, L.J. *Consultancy Matters*. Reading: Reading University, 1993.

12594 Ověřování dvouhodinové dotace pro výuku občanské výchovy na 2.stupni základních škol. (Verification of the need for two hours of civics teaching in lower secondary schools.)
CSK 1994
Research Date(s): 1990-1992
Pitha, P.; Hořejšová, D.; Peřich, V.; Peclinovská, M.; Heroutová, V.; Popélyová, A.; Hruška, A.
Inst: Pedagogická fakulta Univerzity Karlovy (Charles University, Faculty of Education), M.D. Rettigové 4, 116 39 Praha 1, Czech Republic.
Ministerstvo školství, mládeže a tělovýchovy (Ministry of Education, Youth and Physical Education), Karmelitská 7, 118 00 Praha 1, Czech Republic
civics; time-table; lesson; teaching time; lower secondary
instruction civique; emploi du temps; leçon; temps d'enseignement; secondaire premier cycle
PROJECT DESCRIPTION
Aim: To verfify whether there is a need for two hours of civics teaching a week in lower secondary schools.
Design: A one-year study was conducted of a sample of selected schools.
Results: The findings confirmed the need for two hours of civics teaching in every grade of lower secondary school.

Publ: Pitha, P.; et al. *Výchova k občanství*. AVED, 1992.

12595 Parents' understanding of science in the National Curriculum.
GBR 1993
Research Date(s): 1990-1993
Peacock, A.
Inst: Exeter University, School of Education, St Luke's, Heavitree Road, Exeter EX1 2LU, United Kingdom.
science education; common core curriculum; parent-school relation; primary education
éducation scientifique; tronc commun; relation parents-école; enseignement primaire
PROJECT DESCRIPTION
The research is a longitudinal study of parents of children entering school in Autumn 1989 in 11 representative primary schools in one local authority. The sample is identical to that being used for a larger study (Parents and the National Curriculum, sponsored by Leverhulme Trust, director Dr M. Hughes) and the current study works closely with Dr Hughes' team. The study uses semi-structured interviews on a serial basis with parents, teachers and head teachers, to ascertain the flow of information to parents about their children's science work at National Curriculum Key Stage 1, and to evaluate parents' understanding of the information received. The study has so far highlighted clear differences of perception between parents and teachers about what parents know and need to know; and is currently investigating parents' interpretations of the reports received after the 1991 Standard Assessment Tasks.

Publ: Peacock, A. & Boulton, A. Parents' understanding of science at Key Stage 1. In: *Education 3-13*, Vol 19, No 3/1991, pp. 26-29, October.

12596 Planning review and profiling in environmental education in the school curriculum.
GBR 1993
Research Date(s): 1991-1992
Dorian, C.
Sup: Gayford, C.
Inst: Reading University, Faculty of Education and Community Studies, Bulmershe Court, Woodlands Avenue, Earley, Reading RG6 1HY, United Kingdom; Council for Environmental Education, Reading University, Faculty of Education and Community Studies, National Environmental Resource Base, London Road, Reading RG1 5AQ, United Kingdom.
Fin: World Wide Fund for Nature; National Westminster Bank.
environmental study; curriculum development; common core curriculum
étude du milieu; élaboration de programmes d'études; tronc commun
PROJECT DESCRIPTION
    This project involves monitoring the ways in which schools are delivering environmental education in the National Curriculum. Models for achieving integration of cross-curricular elements in the whole curriculum will be investigated and approaches to profiling pupils' performance developed. Training materials suitable for providing appropriate Inservice Education and Training (INSET) will be produced.

12597 Political education, voluntary associations and civil society in state socialist countries.
GBR 1993
Research Date(s): 1989-
Morgan, W.
Inst: Nottingham University, Department of Adult Education, Centre for Research into the Education of Adults, 14-22 Shakespeare Street, Nottingham NG1 4FJ, United Kingdom.
Fin: British Council; Beatrice Webb Trust.
political education; socialism; Eastern Europe; voluntary organization; social change
éducation politique; socialisme; Europe orientale; organisation volontaire; changement social
PROJECT DESCRIPTION
    The research seeks to identify and analyse the relationship of adult political education and voluntary associations to the emergence of civil society in state socialist countries. The key concepts will be defined theoretically and examined empirically through a series of related historical and sociological studies.
Publ: Morgan, W.R. Homo-Sovieticus - political education and civil society in the Soviet Union. In: morgan, W.P. (ed) *Proceedings of the Standing Conference of University Teaching and Research into the Education of Adults.* Nottingham, 1989.
Morgan, W.P. Workers adult education in the Soviet Union. In: *Bulletin of the International Congress of University Adult Education,* Vol 2, No 1, Spring 1989.

12598 Politische Bildung fuer aeltere Menschen in den neuen Bundeslaendern. (Political education for senior citizens in the new German states.)
DEU 1993
Research Date(s): 1991-1992
Real, S.; Foerster, U.
Sup: Geissler, E.
Inst: Universitaet Bonn, Philosophische Fakultaet, Institut fuer Erziehungswissenschaft, Am Hof 3-5, D-5300 Bonn 1.
Fin: Bundeszentrale fuer politische Bildung (Berliner Freiheit 7, D-5300 Bonn 1).
political education; German DR; elderly person; didactics; further training; adult education; target groups of education
éducation politique; Allemagne RDA; personne âgée; didactique; formation complémentaire; éducation des adultes; destinataires de l'éducation
PROJECT DESCRIPTION
    Inhalt: In Zusammenarbeit mit der Bundeszentrale fuer politische Bildung werden Lehr-und Lernmaterialien zum Bereich "Politische Bildung fuer aeltere Menschen in den neuen Bundeslaendern" zusammengestellt. Die Situation der politischen Bildung in den neuen Bundeslaendern stellt sich zur Zeit aus mehreren Gruenden als sehr kompliziert dar. Fuer die Gruppe der juengeren Menschen (Schueler, Studenten) und die Gruppe der Berufstaetigen bestehen durchaus unterschiedliche Moeglichkeiten der politischen Weiterbildung im Gegensatz zur Gruppe der aelteren Menschen, die nicht mehr im Erwerbsprozess stehen. Sie naehern sich zwar quantitativ betrachtet der politischen Majoritaet, haben aber bisher kaum Moeglichkeiten gehabt, sich ueber politische Bedingungen eines freiheitlichen Rechtsstaates und seiner demokratischen Rahmenordnung zu informieren. Ziel ist daher die Entwicklung von entsprechend didaktisch aufbereiteten Materialien fuer Volkshochschulen, kommunale und kirchliche Traeger, die Weiterbildungsmassnahmen organisieren, auf der einen Seite, auf der anderen Seite fuer Aeltere als Moeglichkeit zur Selbstbildung.
    Geographischer Raum: neue Bundeslaender.
    Vorgehensweise: Untersuchungsdesign: Evaluationsstudie; Literaturanalyse.

12599 Primary school children's understanding of heat and temperature.
GBR 1993
Research Date(s): 1987-
Cowan, R.
Inst: London University, Institute of Education, Department of Educational Psychology and Special Educational Needs, 20 Bedford Way, London WC1H OAL, United Kingdom.
science education; comprehension; primary education
éducation scientifique; compréhension; enseignement primaire
PROJECT DESCRIPTION
    Assessment of Performance Unit surveys suggest that few 11-year-olds understand much about heat and temperature and how to measure them. Studies have been conducted to assess children's knowledge of temperature phenomena in connection with daily life; i.e. body temperature, ice cream and swimming pools. In addition, 9-11-year olds have been interviewed to assess their understanding of the two common temperature scales. Children between 7 and 12 have been tested on verbal and numerical versions of temperature prediction tasks. Confusion over temperature was found to be common even when no reference to numerical temperatures was made.
Publ: Cowan, R. & Sutcliffe, N. What children's temperature predictions reveal of their understanding of temperature. In: *British Journal of Educational Psychology,* Vol 61, Part 3/1991, pp. 300-309.

12600 Primary school teachers and science.
GBR 1993
Research Date(s): 1989-
Palacio, D.; Lenton, G.; Summers, M.; Kruger, C.
Inst: Westminster College, North Hinksey, Oxford OX2 9AT, United Kingdom; Oxford University, Department of Educational Studies, 15 Norham Gardens, Oxford OX2 6PY, United Kingdom.
Fin: Leverhulme Trust; University of Oxford; Westminster College.
science education; further education of teachers; teaching aid
éducation scientifique; perfectionnement des enseignants; moyen d'enseignement
PROJECT DESCRIPTION
    The aim of the project is to produce inservice materials for primary school teachers which will further develop their own understanding of those key conceptual areas of science which are known to be difficult, e.g. force, energy. A constructivist approach to the development of these materials has been adopted by the project team.
    Initially teachers' understanding in a particular conceptual area was elicited through one-to-one interviews (about 20 interviews per conceptual area) using a technique known as 'interview about instances'. The results of this phase of the project were then used to construct a questionnaire which was given to a larger sample of teachers (about 180 teachers per conceptual area). The results of this, the prevalence phase of the project, were used as a basis for the development of the inservice materials. These materials are designed for use by teachers, preferably in groups of four or five, without recourse to an 'expert' group leader or specialised science equipment.
Publ: A full list of working papers and publications is available from the researchers.

12601 Primary science: children planning investigations.
GBR 1993
Research Date(s): 1990-1991
Ellis, S.
Inst: Jordanhill College of Education, Division of Primary Education, Southbrae Drive, Glasgow G13 1PP, United Kingdom.
science education; discovery learning; teaching method; comprehension
éducation scientifique; apprentissage par la découverte; méthode pédagogique; compréhension
PROJECT DESCRIPTION
    The aims of this project are to look at teaching strategies which help children plan scientific investigations and how these relate to their scientific knowledge and understanding.

12602 Primary science processes and concept exploration project (Primary SPACE Project).
GBR 1993
Research Date(s): 1987-1991
Russell, T.; Osborne, J.; Longden, K.; McGuire, L.; Bell, D.; Wadsworth, P.
Sup: Harlen, W.; Black, P.
Inst: Liverpool University, Department of Education, Centre for Research in Primary Science & Technology, PO Box 147, Liverpool L69 3BX, United Kingdom; London University, King's College, Centre for Educational Studies, Cornwall House Annexe, Waterloo Road, London SE1 3TY, United Kingdom.
Fin: Nuffield Foundation 1987-1989; Nuffield-Chelsea Curriculum Trust 1989-1991.
science education; primary education; concept formation
éducation scientifique; enseignement primaire; formation de concept

PROJECT DESCRIPTION

The Primary SPACE (Science Processes and Concept Exploration) project is an action research project which aims to explore the ideas primary school children hold in the science concept areas of: changes in materials; evaporation/condensation; electricity; growth; forces and their effect on movement; light; living things and their adaptation to their environment; and sound.

Information is being collected by teachers and researchers through interview, discussion and analysis of children's written work and drawings. This information is then being used as a starting point for trying to influence the formation and development of children's ideas through application of process skills during classroom work.

The study involves forty-two classes in schools within London, Knowsley and Lancashire local education authorities, and covers the entire primary age range. The research is being continued into all areas of the National curriculum in Science and used as a basis for curriculum material development.

Publ: Harlen, W. *What is going on in SPACE.* University of Liverpool: Centre for Research in Primary Science and Technology, 1987.
Watt, D. Primary SPACE project phase one: an exploration of children's specific ideas. In: *Primary Science Review*, No 4/1987, pp. 27-28, Summer.
Research reports entitled 'Growth', 'Light', 'Evaporation and Condensation', 'Sound' and 'Materials' are available from Liverpool University Press.

12603 Primary teachers' perception of science concepts.
GBR   1993
Research Date(s): 1990-1992
Dockerty, A.
Inst: Sunderland University, School of Education, Hammerton Hall, Gray Road, Sunderland SR2 7EE, United Kingdom.
science education; primary education; further education of teachers; teacher; knowledge level
éducation scientifique; enseignement primaire; perfectionnement des enseignants; enseignant; niveau de connaissances
PROJECT DESCRIPTION

The work has evolved from an interest in children's perceptions of science concepts. It aims to discover the perceptions of primary school teachers of a range of concepts within the National Curriculum - Science.

The investigation uses questionnaires, designed with unambiguous questions, to discover any trends in misconception of important concepts. A pilot study has been completed and new questionnaires are under construction. It is hoped to sample 200-300 individual teachers within three local authorities.

Preliminary results have shown that most of the participants have serious misconceptions of particle theory and this is being extended to other areas of the National Curriculum. The result of the research will be used to design appropriate inservice packages for primary teachers.

12604 Psychological aspects of children and physical activity.
GBR   1993
Research Date(s): 1990-
Biddle, S.; Fox, K.; Armstrong, N.
Inst: Exeter University, School of Education, Physical Education Association Research Centre, St Luke's, Heavitree Road, Exeter EX1 2LU, United Kingdom.
Fin: Exeter University; Northcott Medical Foundation.
physical education; health; child psychology; sex difference
éducation physique; santé; psychologie de l'enfant; différence de sexe
PROJECT DESCRIPTION

11-12 year old children (N=250) have been tested on physical activity and psychological constructs to see if activity levels and choices can be related to the psychology of the child. Preliminary evidence indicated that more active boys were intrinsically motivated towards physical education and sport, whereas girls required more extrinsic motivation. Active and less active children could also be discriminated on the basis of motivational orientations and physical self-perceptions. Ongoing research is following up these findings and is investigating achievement cognitions and self-perceptions.

12605 Psychologie de l'éducation musicale.
FRA   1994
Research Date(s): 1985-
Mialaret, Jean-Pierre.
Inst: Université de Caen, UFR Sciences de l'homme, Centre d'études et de recherches en sciences de l'éducation, 14032 Caen Cedex, France.
child development; perceptual development; play; music education; pre-school education
développement de l'enfant; développement perceptif; jeu; éducation musicale; éducation préscolaire
PROJECT DESCRIPTION

Objectifs: Un travail d'articulation entre les caractéristiques des improvisations musicales et l'oeuvre d'Henri Wallon relative au développement psychologique a contribué à souligner le rôle de la fonction posturale dans l'élaboration de la productivité musicale chez l'enfant. Cette notion permet en effet d'éclairer les liens entre l'activité motrice et sensorielle en musique. Elle conduit à mieux comprendre comment s'ébauchent, par le jeu des attitudes, les différentes caractéristiques de l'activité musicale de chaque enfant. La nécessité d'intégrer les composantes émotives et l'appréhension cognitive de sons produits/perçus, au cours de l'acte musical, oblige à chercher des critères d'observation capables d'appréhender cette complexité et des indices capables d'élaborer les significations de ces phénomènes. Cette première approche précise également plusieurs orientations spécifiques d'investigation. L'accès à l'activité représentative en musique, comporte des modalités originales et influe sur les modes d'appropriation des langages musicaux. L'enfant au cours de son activité d'improvisation, exprime, semble-t-il dans la forme et l'organisation de ses gestes instrumentaux, la manière dont il éprouve le déroulement de la durée. Il est donc indispensable d'approfondir l'analyse et le sens de cette composante essentielle du développement et de la situer par rapport à d'autres modèles théoriques.

Méthodologie: Plusieurs études de cas d'improvisations musicales ont été entreprises afin de développer le travail d'articulation ébauché précédemment entre les problèmes soulevés par la description des improvisations et l'interprétation des événements musicaux en référence aux conduites psychologiques qui permettent de leur donner signification. La poursuite de ces études de cas doit permettre de repérer et préciser un itinéraire développemental au cours duquel chaque enfant élabore une productivité musicale instrumentale. Les caractéristiques de cette chronologie devront être ensuite validées sur un corpus plus important d'improvisations musicales. Ces études de cas permettront également de construire des hypothèses relatives à la production de nouveauté en musique chez l'enfant.

Publ: Mialaret, Jean-Pierre. Recherches sur l'improvisation musicale chez l'enfant. In: *Vibrations*, n° 6, Privat, 1988, pp. 108-123.
Mialaret, Jean-Pierre. *Composantes sensori-motrice et représentative de l'improvisation musicale enfantine. Essai de mise en perspective Wallonienne.* Documents du CERSE, n° 34, 1988, 53p.
Mialaret, Jean-Pierre. *Improvisation musicale de Florence. Etude de cas n° 1.* Documents du CERSE, 1989, n° 42, 33p.
Mialaret, Jean-Pierre. *Education musicale et psychologie de la musique.* In: *Les sciences de l'éducation -Pour l'ère nouvelle*, 1990, n°3-4.
(Une liste complète est disponible auprès du chercheur.).

12606 Relationships between works of literature and works of art with reference to interpretation theory and implications for school curricula.
GBR   1993
Research Date(s): 1985-
Rawding, M.
Sup: Mason, R.; Allison, B.
Inst: De Montford University, Department of Education, Centre for Postgraduate Teacher Education, Scraptoft Campus, Scraptoft, Leicester LE7 9SU, United Kingdom.
art education; curriculum development; literature
éducation artistique; élaboration de programmes d'études; littérature
PROJECT DESCRIPTION

The investigation seeks answers to three related questions. Firstly, what is available in art educational literature that relates both to the particular concept of artistic intention and the broader area of controversy which has arisen in connection with the theoretical relationship of art and criticism? Secondly, what insights can the study of the concept of artistic intention provide regarding conceptual issues associated with the theoretical relationship of art and criticism? Thirdly, what steps are required to 'bridge the gap' between philosophy of art (ref. critical theory) and the philosophy of education (ref. curriculum theory) in order to translate theoretical materials arising from the study of the concept of artistic intention into a coherent pedagogy of art criticism? It is anticipated that the study will render the nature of controversy in philosophical aesthetics more readily available to the field of education by providing a framework for a theoretically coherent and consistent pedagogy of criticism. Hence the study will conclude with recommendations for curriculum development that includes reference to the synthesis of subject content, methods of teaching and learning, and curricular aims and objectives.

12607 Religion in the Service of the Child (RiSC) project.
GBR   1993
Research Date(s): 1989-1992
Grove, J.; Spencer, L.
Sup: Hull, J.; Grimmitt, M.
Inst: Birmingham University, School of Education, Edgbaston, Birmingham B15 2TT, United Kingdom.
Fin: Church-related charitable trusts and industry.
religious education; teaching aid; teaching method; primary education
éducation religieuse; moyen d'enseignement; méthode pédagogique; enseignement primaire
PROJECT DESCRIPTION

Drawing upon phenomenological and hermeneutical theory, the Religion in the Service of the Child (RiSC) project has developed a strategy for teaching explicit religious material to primary pupils. The strategy has been developed through action research in classrooms. Many specific religious items, called numena, have been presented to pupils in National Curriculum Key Stages 1 and 2 in 39 schools in the West Midlands in a variety of situations. These trials have been closely observed, many through video recordings. Pupil reaction has been monitored and used to inform pedagogical development and to identify criteria for choice of content.

The strategy is designed to foster a deep approach to learning and encourages pupils to be their own meaning makers. Pupils are facilitated to make use of the religious material, presented to them in all its power and holiness, to illuminate their understanding of their own lives and experiences. Numena are chosen particularly for their potential to raise and address issues of concern to children. In the interaction between pupil and content facilitated by the strategy, those concerns, often unconscious, can be allowed to surface and be addressed with security. Such an encounter with the religious world can promote deep reflection on the child's part into his or her own life world.

The research has shown that, contrary to accumulated professional wisdom of the past 20 years, young pupils are able to respond imaginatively and holistically to the beauty and mystery of religious material in modes which are natural to them and in ways which benefit their development.

Publ: Grimmitt, M.H.; Grove, J.; Hull, J.M. & Spencer, L. *A gift to the child: Religious education in the primary school.* Hemel Hempstead: Simon & Schuster, 1991.
Grimmitt, M.H. *Religion in the Service of the Child: Interim Report.* CREDAR Lecture Series. University of Birmingham, 1991.
Hull, J.M. *God-talk with young children: notes for parents and teachers.* CEM, 1991.
Grimmitt, M.H. The use of religious phenomena in schools: some theoretical and practical considerations. In: *British Journal of Religious Education,* Vol 13, No 2/1991, pp. 77-88.
Grove, J.E. Religion in the Service of the Child: a new strategy for primary religious education. In: *Planning RE in Schools,* 1991.

12608 Religious education and primary school children.
GBR 1993
Research Date(s): 1991-1996
Ashton, E.
Sup: Minney, R.; Day, D.
Inst: Durham University, School of Education, Leazes Road, Durham DH1 1TA, United Kingdom.
religious education; primary education; concept formation; teaching aid
éducation religieuse; enseignement primaire; formation de concept; moyen d'enseignement
PROJECT DESCRIPTION

The research project arose out of observations of primary school children's modes of thinking and ways in which they conceptualize. Wide reading, at the moment, is being carried out in the fields of educational psychology, philosophy and theology. Practical teaching projects and schemes of work are to be planned and executed in the classroom, which will be assessed according to certain evaluation criteria. It is anticipated that the research will lead to the publication of educational material for both teachers and children.

12609 Renewal in music and education.
GBR 1993
Research Date(s): 1986-1993
Paton, R.
Sup: Cooper, B.
Inst: West Sussex Institute of Higher Education, Bishop Otter College, College Lane, Chichester PO19 4PE, United Kingdom; Sussex University, Institute of Continuing and Professional Education, Sussex House, Falmer, Brighton BN1 9RH, United Kingdom.
music education; music; learning
éducation musicale; musique; acquisition de connaissances
PROJECT DESCRIPTION

This is a theoretical and empirical study of musical learning and its role in the changing nature of musical functions and forms. It includes: epistemology of music, psychological aspects of musical learning, improvisation and "holding forms" (containment structures for improvised musical acts). There will be empirical back-up from workshops with students, children and people with learning disabilities, also study of new-style methods and courses elsewhere.

12610 The right place of music in education: a history of music education in England 1870-1927 with particular reference to the role of Her Majesty's Inspectorate (HMI).
GBR 1993
Research Date(s): 1988-1992
Cox, G.
Sup: Kemp, A.; Straughan, R.
Inst: Reading University, Department of Arts and Humanities in Education, Bulmershe Court, Woodlands Avenue, Earley, Reading RG6 1HY, United Kingdom.
music education; history of education; inspection
éducation musicale; histoire de l'éducation; inspection
PROJECT DESCRIPTION

The study focuses on the music curriculum during a period in which there was a steady advance away from the often irksome and uncongenial traditions associated with the revised code towards the cultivation of taste rather than the acquirement of technical proficiency. This broadening of scope was symbolized in the change of nomenclature in 1927 - from 'singing' to 'music'. The central concerns of the study include: the significance of Her Majesty's Inspectorate as agents of curriculum change; the original contributions to the development of music and education; notions of intrinsic and extrinsic values in music education.

The study is organised in three parts: (1) John Hullah and the decline of music in schools 1872-1883; (2) the utilitarian era of Stainer 1883-1901; (3) the liberalisation of the music curriculum and the contribution of Arthur Somervell 1901-1927. The research draws upon a considerable amount of unpublished materials, oral evidence, and texts of the period. It provides a detailed study of curriculum change and conflict which should lead to a greater knowledge of the process involved in 'becoming a subject'.

12611 The role of adult basic education in the re-education of brain injured adults: an investigation into student-specific re-learning programmes.
GBR 1993
Research Date(s): 1991-1996
Curtis, K.
Sup: Donald, A.
Inst: University of Wales College of Cardiff, School of Education, Senghennydd Road, Cardiff CF2 4AG, United Kingdom.
basic education; adult education; special education; brain injury; speech handicapped; learning difficulty; medical rehabilitation
éducation de base; éducation des adultes; enseignement spécial; lésion cérébrale; handicapé de la parole; difficulté de l'apprentissage; rééducation fonctionnelle
PROJECT DESCRIPTION

Although brain injuries are generally perceived to be the prerogative of the medical professions, this thesis presents a role for the adult basic education service in the re-education of dysphasic adults. The role model is the dysphasia project based in the Rhymney Valley district of Mid Glamorgan's community education service. Emphasis will be placed on the positive assessment of literacy and numeracy skills following brain injury and on student-specific re-learning programmes devised for each client. Research methods adopted are: literature surveys, interviews and study visits.

The thesis includes: (1) an outline of the history of the adult basic education service in England and Wales; (2) an explanation of the causes of the condition known as dysphasia and its effects on language skills; (3) an explanation of the efficacy of dysphasia therapy: the vital role of volunteers, their induction and training for this specialised tuition; (4) an examination of the range of assessment procedures used by medical practitioners and their applicability to adult literacy and numeracy; (5) the assessments devised by the author for use with dysphasics; (6) an explanation of the need for student-specific re-learning programmes and work materials, with particular reference to five case studies; and (7) an attempt to evaluate the success of dysphasia therapy and the ethical dilemma experienced by cross-professional approaches to re-education.

The various chapters of the thesis combine to guide the educational practitioners along an avenue of rehabilitation not previously explored for sufferers of stroke or head injury.

12612 The role of the college farm in the delivery of the curriculum in non-advanced further education.
GBR 1993
Research Date(s): 1990-1992
Harrison, R.
Sup: Kowalski, R.; Crocker, A.
Inst: Wolverhampton University, Walsall Campus, Gorway Road, Walsall WS1 3BD, United Kingdom.
agricultural training; vocational education
formation agricole; enseignement professionnel
PROJECT DESCRIPTION

A survey is being made of college farms. The intention of the survey is to establish the role of the farm in facilitating the teaching of practical skills and other aspects of curriculum development in the associated agricultural college.

12613 Science and religion project.
GBR 1993
Research Date(s): 1990-1992
Greer, J.
Inst: Ulster University, Department of Inservice Education, Cromore Road, Coleraine, County Londonderry BT52 1SA, United Kingdom.
sciences; religion; pupil attitude
sciences; religion; attitude de l'élève
PROJECT DESCRIPTION

The aim is to study the relationship between science and religion, with special reference to the problems faced by pupils at school. The sample was composed of 100 pupils from each of 24 grammar schools who completed original questionnaires, which were then revised. Preliminary analysis of data has been carried out and a first draft of a report has been written.

12614 Science teaching: supporting effective teacher change.
GBR 1993
Research Date(s): 1987-1991
Doubler, S.
Sup: Harlen, W.
Inst: Liverpool University, Department of Education, PO Box 147, Liverpool L69 3BX, United Kingdom.
science education; teacher; teacher behaviour; primary education; USA
éducation scientifique; enseignant; comportement de l'enseignant; enseignement primaire; Etats-Unis
PROJECT DESCRIPTION

This research is linked with the Science Teaching Action Research (STAR) Project which focuses on promoting effective learning and teaching of science in the primary school. This work is concerned more specifically with teachers and their experiences during the STAR Project. The main questions addressed by the study are: (1) Does thinking and practice change as a result of project efforts? (2) What are the significant factors in producing or inhibiting change?

The study is being conducted in the Boston, Massachusetts area, and involves 10 teachers from six school districts. The key factors in identifying members of the study group were: interest; involvement in process-based science; and three years participation in the STAR Project. The impact of intervention with teachers is determined by taking into consideration teachers' work situations, education, experience, thinking and current practice. As well as identifying changes within the entire study group, a case study of each teacher identifies individual change and its related causes.

Information has been collected through the use of two STAR Project research instruments, as well as other instruments designed specifically for this study. A questionnaire was used to collect baseline data about each teacher's work situation and background. Information about practice and the teacher's perception of change was gathered through interviews, surveys, formal student observations and documentation of teacher comments and writing over three consecutive years.

12615 Specific aspects of curriculum or Values Education and the understanding of Science.
GBR 1993
Research Date(s): 1991-1992
Crawford, E.
Inst: Heriot-Watt University, Moray House Institute of Education, Holyrood Road, Edinburgh EH8 8AQ, United Kingdom.
science education; value; teacher behaviour
éducation scientifique; valeur; comportement de l'enseignant
PROJECT DESCRIPTION

The project aims to explore the attitudes of science teachers which affect practice regarding teaching of science and understanding of the nature of science.

12616 Sport for all in education: an inquiry into PE and sport in schools, what constitutes good practice and its relation to the role of culture and cultures within schools.
GBR 1993
Research Date(s): 1991-1994
Davis, J.
Sup: Donn, G.; Thomson, G.
Inst: Edinburgh University, Department of Education, 10-12 Buccleuch Place, Edinburgh EH8 9JT, United Kingdom.
Fin: Carnegie Trust for Universities of Scotland; Scottish Office Education Department.
physical education; sport; culture
éducation physique; sport; culture
PROJECT DESCRIPTION

The project can be separated into two sections. The first is policy-based and aims to outline teaching methods, lesson structure, share of the curriculum, methods of evaluation and other areas that relate to physical education (PE) in schools. It will describe how these affect and are perceived by children of different age, sex and ethnic background. In doing so it will illustrate the present aim of PE policy, how this relates to children at different stages of development and how this is affected by issues such as time and resources. In short, the present practice existing in schools with regard to PE, will be brought forth with the aim of defining good practice in PE as viewed by parents, teachers and pupils. The second part of the proposal will use the first section as a practical core around which to develop the theoretical nature of the project. By viewing the school as a social microcosm the project will illustrate PE as it relates to other areas of the school and is affected by the structure of the school. Central to this will be the examination of the role of culture and cultures within the school.

12617 Student teachers' conceptions of the nature of science and learning.
GBR 1993
Research Date(s): 1992-1997
Rowlands, M.
Sup: Sutton, R.
Inst: Cardiff Institute of Higher Education, Faculty of Education, Cyncoed Centre, Cardiff CF2 6XD, United Kingdom; University of Wales College of Cardiff, School of Education, 42 Park Place, Cardiff CF1 3BB, United Kingdom.
science education; teacher education; student teacher
éducation scientifique; formation des enseignants; élève-maître
PROJECT DESCRIPTION

The aim of this research is to investigate any interrelationship between the construction of primary school student teachers' conceptions of the nature of science and the construction of their conceptions of teaching and learning.

Case studies will be carried out of a small number of primary school student teachers during the period of their four-year teacher training course. Triangulation will be achieved by employing several techniques, including: observation of classroom interactions; interviews; and analysis of journals and teaching materials. Results will generate theories grounded in the data and illuminated by developments in the history, philosophy and sociology of science and science education.

12618 Students' motivation in physical education classes perceived to have different goal perspectives.
GBR 1993
Research Date(s): 1990-1992
Papaioannou, A.
Sup: MacDonald, A.
Inst: Manchester University, School of Education, Centre for Physical Education, Oxford Road, Manchester M13 9PL, United Kingdom.
physical education; motivation; achievement motivation
éducation physique; motivation; motivation d'accomplissement
PROJECT DESCRIPTION

Based on recent theories of achievement motivation (Nicholls, 1989; Dweck, 1988) a questionnaire was developed in order to reveal physical education (PE) classes with different achievement orientations. Both exploratory and confirmatory factor analytic results deriving from three studies (in which were involved more than 2,000 students in 80 PE classes) revealed a solution of two learning-oriented and three performance-oriented factors with good internal consistency. The hypothesized relationships among these five factors and several self-related constructs as well as perceptions of classes' environments were established, suggesting validity for each scale of the questionnaire. Further, only the learning-oriented factors were positive predictors of intrinsic motivation, interest in the lesson, perceived usefulness of the lesson, attitudes towards exercise and intentions for involvement and effort expenditure in the class. Moreover, teachers' differential behaviour towards high and low achievers was negatively related with learning orientation but positively related with performance orientation. In addition, when learning orientation was salient in the class, both high and low perceived competence students were more willing to cooperate with either high or low athletic ability peers and low perceived competence students were less anxious to play with high achievers.

In the first two studies both between and within classes, differences were observed regarding perceptions of classes' goals. Results from the third study (394 students in 16 PE classes) revealed that the teacher, the particular class, students' personal orientations in sport, attitudes towards the specific teacher, and attitudes towards PE teachers in general, were significant predictors of perceptions of classes' goals. In a fourth study, eight PE classes were observed revealing that high learning-oriented classes were characterized by an emphasis on teaching issues of technique and students' skill practice, students' cognitive involvement, less game and less students' off-task behaviour. More teachers' orders/directions and students' unpredictable behaviours were recorded in high than in low performance-oriented classes.

All the results suggest that in order to increase motivation and achievement and to maintain equality in the PE classes, a learning orientation should be adopted. Suggestions for the creation of a learning-oriented climate in the class are offered.

12619 A study of the health education initiatives in physical education.
GBR 1993
Research Date(s): 1989-1991
Evans, J.
Inst: Southampton University, Faculty of Educational Studies, Department of Physical Education, Highfield, Southampton SO9 5NH, United Kingdom.
health education; physical education; secondary education
éducation sanitaire; éducation physique; enseignement secondaire
PROJECT DESCRIPTION

The aim of this research is to study the impact of health education initiatives in physical education (PE) on the curriculum and teaching of PE in secondary schools. The study focuses on the curriculum and teaching of PE in one large co-educational comprehensive school. The study is adopting a qualitative methodology (largely employing interview and observation techniques) and is sociological in theoretical orientation.

12620   A study of the rhetoric used in the public debates about religious education in England and Wales 1987-1990.
GBR   1993
Research Date(s): 1990-1991
Hull, J.
Inst: Birmingham University, School of Education, Edgbaston, Birminghm B15 2TT, United Kingdom.
religious education; intercultural education; food; conceptual imagery; symbol
éducation religieuse; éducation interculturelle; aliment; représentation mentale; symbole
PROJECT DESCRIPTION
   This research looked at the rhetoric used in debates about religious education in Britain. Examples of the imagery of mixed, inappropriate or disgusting food (mish-mash, hotch-potch) when describing the use of world religions in education were gathered from debates in the Houses of Parliament 1988 and from newspapers. The imagery of food disgust was traced back into childhood and through Western culture and the background of food distaste in biblical thought was studied. It is concluded that the use of these expressions indicates tribalistic and racist prejudice.

Publ: Hull, J.M. Mish-mash: religious education in multi-cultural Britain: a study in imagery. Derby: CEM, 1991.

12621   A survey of computer literacy in initial teacher education.
GBR   1993
Research Date(s): 1989-
Gilliland, J.; Steele, J.
Inst: Durham University, School of Education, Leazes Road, Durham DH1 1TA, United Kingdom.
computer literacy; teacher education; information technology; student teacher; training programme
initiation à l'informatique; formation des enseignants; technologie de l'information; élève-maître; programme de formation
PROJECT DESCRIPTION
   Nationally, information technology (IT) has been given an increasingly high profile in schools, from the early Department of Education and Science/Department of Trade and Industry initiatives and the Microelectronics in Education Project (MEP) to its inclusion now as a cross-curricular issue in the National Curriculum. Schools of Education are required therefore to offer computer literacy courses which meet professional school orientated needs and also enhance personal skills through IT in response to computer literacy programmes in higher education.
   This research is gathering survey data from students following courses of initial teacher education and students following some higher degree courses. Access, confidence and competence are assessed on entry to the course and the project seeks to monitor changes in these three aspects during and on exit from the course.
   First results from pre- and post-course surveys show differences between groups and positive effects of introductory courses and the IT environment made available to students in the School of Education of Durham University. The range of competence, confidence and experience on entry is extremely wide and creates educational and logistic problems for the delivery and management of courses in IT and the IT environment. Activities, responses and results to date suggest the need for an application of more sophisticated models of teaching and instruction.

Publ: Gilliland, J. & Steele, J. Computer literacy in an initial teacher training student population. In: McCartan, A. (ed.). *Computer literacy for every graduate - strategies and challenges for the early 1990s*, pp. 30-33. Oxford: CTISS Publications, 1990.

12622   Survey of health education policies in schools for the Health Education Authority.
GBR   1993
Research Date(s): 1992
Jamison, J.
Sup: Stradling, R.
Inst: National Foundation for Educational Research, The Mere, Upton Park, Slough SL1 2DQ, United Kingdom.
Fin: Health Education Authority.
health education; sex education; educational policy
éducation sanitaire; éducation sexuelle; politique de l'éducation
PROJECT DESCRIPTION
   Over the last decade there has been a growing recognition of the strategic and influential role which schools can play in the health education of the population and, as a result, a wide range of centrally funded initiatives has been implemented. A growing number of schools now have health education coordinators and written health education policies.

The research aims to evaluate the range, form and quality of written health education policies in schools, investigate the impact of policy on the organisation of the curriculum and classroom practice in schools, review the processes of policy implementation, and identify examples of good practice.
   A questionnaire will be sent to a sample of 900 schools in England, stratified to ensure adequate representation of different types of school and different regions and education authorities. From the responses, a selection will be made of 100 schools for more intensive qualitative research.
   A final report will be submitted to the Health Education Authority documenting the main findings and identifying examples of good practice suitable for adoption by other schools.

12623   Survey of HIV/AIDS education in secondary schools in the East Midlands to discover its curriculum organization, incidence and teaching strategies, the problems and INSET needs of teachers and the impact of the National Curriculum.
GBR   1993
Research Date(s): 1989-1993
Shepherd, D.; Ayres, D.
Inst: Loughborough University of Technology, Department of Education, Loughborough LE11 3TU, United Kingdom.
sex education; health education; sexually transmitted disease; prevention
éducation sexuelle; éducation sanitaire; maladie sexuellement transmissible; prévention
PROJECT DESCRIPTION
   This research will involve a survey of 150 headteachers and health education co-ordinators to discover their teaching and curriculum problems, needs and organization in HIV/AIDS (Human Immunodeficiency Virus/Acquired Immune Deficiency Syndrome), particularly in the context of DES Circular 11/87, 'Sex Education and National Curriculum Health Education' Cross-Curricular Theme. Methodology will be structured questionnaires with respondents providing basic data for subsequent analysis and report.

12624   Teacher Training for Economic Awareness.
GBR   1993
Research Date(s): 1986-1993
Thomas, L.; Hodkinson, S.
Inst: London University, Institute of Education, Department of Economics, Geography and Business Education, 20 Bedford Way, London WC1H OAL, United Kingdom; Manchester University, School of Education, Oxford Road, Manchester M13 9PL, United Kingdom.
Fin: Department of Trade & Industry; Banking Information Service; British Petroleum; Unilever.
economic studies; economics; further education of teachers; curriculum research
études économiques; science économique; perfectionnement des enseignants; recherche sur les programmes d'études
PROJECT DESCRIPTION
   The Economic Awareness Teacher Training Programme which began in 1986 is a response to calls for the introduction of economic awareness programmes into schools and colleges. The initiative is based upon a partnership between the Department of Education and Science, the Department of Trade & Industry, teacher training institutions, local education authorities and industrial and commercial organisations. British Petroleum, Banking Information Service, the Department of Trade & Industry, Unilever and the Esmee Fairbairn Trust Fund have provided funds to allow the appointment of academic and administrative staff.
   Initially, the Institute of Education and the University of Manchester will take responsibility for coordinating the programme, which will include: the development, piloting and evaluation of training programmes, schemes of work and training materials; the establishment of a forum to help local education authorities to identify their training needs and to devise strategies to meet these needs; promoting and supporting the development of teacher groups of advisers, coordinators and advisory teachers across local education authority boundaries as well as the development of links between training institutions, local education authorities and industry and commerce; the extension of the initiative to institutions in other areas of the country.

Publ: Dunhill, R. Three of a kind? A review of three LEA publications on Economic Awareness. In: *Economic Awareness*, Vol 2, No 2/1990.
Johnson, C. & Clarke, P. Coal: an economic awareness lesson in humanities. In: *Economic Awareness*, Vol 2, No 3/1990, pp. 15-19.
Davies, P. Industrial change - a lower school geography lesson. In: *Economic Awareness*, Vol 2, No 3/1990, pp. 20-22.
Thomas, L. & Wood, K. et al. What is slavery anyway? - the economic awareness implications of work on a theme in history. In: *Economic Awareness*, Vol 3, No 2/1991.
Hodkinson, S. Modern foreign languages and economic awareness: a comment. In: *Economic Awareness*, Vol 4, No 1/1991, pp. 7-9.
(A full list of publications is available from the researchers).

12625 Teacher Training for Economic Awareness: Welsh extension.
GBR 1993
Research Date(s): 1990-1992
Thomas, L.; Williams, M.
Inst: London University, Institute of Education, Department of Economics, Geography and Business Education, 20 Bedford Way, London WC1H OAL, United Kingdom; University College of Swansea, Singleton Park, Swansea SA2 8PP, United Kingdom.
Fin: Esmee Fairbairn Charitable Trust.
economic studies; economics; further education of teachers; curriculum research
études économiques; science économique; perfectionnement des enseignants; recherche sur les programmes d'études
PROJECT DESCRIPTION
   The Economic Awareness Teacher Training Programme (EcATT) aims to promote and monitor the development and implementation of economic awareness programmes in schools, colleges and LEAs (local education authorities). This project aims to extend the EcATT network to University College, Swansea.

Publ: Jephcote, M. Understanding economics or economics understanding? A case study for developing economics understanding as a pupil curriculum entitlement. In: Bloomer, G.; Brookes, K. & Jephcote, M. Putting the economics in EIU. EATE Research Report No 4, October 1992.
Jephcote, M. & Hendley, D. Design and technology and economic awareness. A guide to economic awareness in the National Curriculum 1992.

12626 Teaching and learning about food and nutrition in school: the nation's diet initiative.
GBR 1993
Research Date(s): 1993-1994
Burgess, R.; Morrison, M.
Inst: Warwick University, Faculty of Educational Studies, Centre for Educational Development, Appraisal and Research, Coventry CV4 7AL, United Kingdom.
Fin: Economic and Social Research Council.
nutrition education; health education; food; eating habit
éducation nutritionnelle; éducation sanitaire; aliment; habitude alimentaire
PROJECT DESCRIPTION
   The research is an exploratory case study on teaching and learning about food and nutrition in two primary and two secondary schools. The aim is to examine age, gender, ethnicity and social class in relation to food consumption. It will also contribute more broadly to studies on socialisation and attitude formation, and the use of case study methodology in the sociology of education. Included in the study will be an exploration of the implications of the research evidence for policy and practice on teaching and learning about food and nutrition in schools.

12627 Teaching art appreciation in the nursery school.
GBR 1993
Research Date(s): 1989-
Payne, M.
Inst: Roehampton Institute, Digby Stuart College, Roehampton Lane, London SW15 5PU, United Kingdom.
art education; aesthetic education; art activity; nursery school; child development
éducation artistique; éducation esthétique; activité artistique; école maternelle; développement de l'enfant
PROJECT DESCRIPTION
   The research considered the response of nursery school children to art appreciation when it was introduced into their curriculum. It explains how art appreciation was integrated into an intercurriculum approach and 'taught' through activities that are a 'normal' part of a nursery school day such as mime, movement, telling stories, expressing feelings, games and puzzles. This work stemmed from a question as to whether appreciation is a means to learning and whether young children develop in confidence and visual understanding as their awareness grows about the world of art 'outside the classroom'.
   The research aimed to discover how nursery school 3 and 4 year olds could be engaged in the activity; whether their involvement could be sustained; which works of art attracted their interest; and whether the activity could be a vehicle for building positive attitudes with regard to multicultural issues. With such questions in mind a programme of activities in the sample school (Eastwood Nursery School, Aubyn Square, London SW15) and at the Tate Gallery was planned. The research has included two exhibitions: (1) Eastwood Nursery School at the Tate Gallery, an educational display of text and visual material detailing the educational value of the visit. Exhibited at the Tate Gallery from September to December 1989. (2) Art Appreciation in a Multicultural Nursery School, an educational display - text and visuals. Exhibited at Spencer Park Teachers' Centre (ILEA), Summer 1989.
   Although the research is ongoing the findings suggest that critical appreciation of paintings and sculptures allows for reflective and physical partici-

pation, cognitive growth, observation, the development of vocabulary and can lead to children responding sensitively to stylistic similarities and being able to make cross-references between paintings.
Publ: Payne, M. Under fives at the Tate Gallery. In: Nursery World, Vol 89, No 3178/1989.
Payne, M. Teaching art appreciation in the nursery school: its relevance for 3 and 4 year olds. In: Early Child Development and Care, Vol 61/1990, pp. 93-106.

12628 Tělovýchova dětí, mládeže a dospělých z hlediska znečištění ovzduší. (Physical education and air pollution.)
CSK 1994
Research Date(s): 1992-1993
Doležal, Tomáš; Heller, Jan; Raifová, Ludmila; Havel, Zdeněk.
Sup: Přerovský, Jan.
Inst: Fakulta tělesné výchovy a sportu Univerzity Karlovy (Charles University, Faculty of Physical Education and Sport), Martího 31, 160 00 Praha 6, Czech Republic.
Ministerstvo školství, mládeže a tělovýchovy (Ministry of Education, Youth and Physical Education), Karmelitská 7, 118 00 Praha 1, Czech Republic
physical education; environment; pollution
éducation physique; environnement; pollution
PROJECT DESCRIPTION
   Aim: (1) To examine the effectiveness, in physiological and sociological terms, of the 1991 recommendation of the Czech Ministry of Education, Youth and Physical Education regarding the regulation of movement activities in physical education in case of high levels of air pollution; (2) to compare levels of air pollution of open-air playing fields and closed physical educational buildings (i.e. gymnasiums); (3) to conduct an experimental study of physical aspects of movement activities under conditions of air pollution.
Publ: Doležal, T. & Heller, J. Movement regime in relation to the environment. Konference IPCHER. Praha: 1992.

12629 A theological critique of Christian education, with special reference to developments in Northern Ireland since 1944.
GBR 1993
Research Date(s): 1988-1992
McCann, J.
Sup: Hulmes, E.
Inst: Durham University, Department of Theology, Abbey House, Palace Green, Durham DH1 3RS, United Kingdom.
Christian education; Northern Ireland; history of education
éducation chrétienne; Irlande du Nord; histoire de l'éducation
PROJECT DESCRIPTION
   The thesis has three principal aims: (1) to provide justification for a confident Christian education in an increasingly secular and agnostic world; (2) to evaluate the development and present status of Christian education in Northern Ireland in the light of its sectarian history and current situation of community conflict; (3) to consider the remit of Christian education and its role in promoting societal harmony.
   The thesis consists of seven chapters and includes: the issue of Christian education in the Northern Ireland context; a validation of Christian education; and a criticism of analytical philosophy and positivist influences in contemporary liberal education, especially where these have affected conceptions of religious education. In addition, it promotes Christian apologetics as both a viable and needed response to relativistic agnosticism. The scope of the thesis embraces considerations of Northern Ireland confessionalism; the influence of ideologies; the separate schools system; the question of integrated education; the historical background to the divided communities; the challenge of the great Christian imperatives of love and forgiveness in respect of community reconciliation and of implementing a Christian education fully alive to its responsibilities; the assumptions and values of Christian education; the nature of religious education; theistic belief and the Christian tradition. The concluding chapter confronts practical issues and suggest models and approaches in Christian education with outreach towards reconciliation.

12630 Undergraduate physicists' and post-graduate scientists' (undergoing teacher training) understanding of the nature of science.
GBR 1993
Research Date(s): 1991-
Parkhouse, P.
Inst: Keele University, Department of Education, Keele, Staffordshire ST5 5BG, United Kingdom.
science education; comprehension; student; student teacher; university studies
éducation scientifique; compréhension; étudiant; élève-maître; études universitaires
PROJECT DESCRIPTION
   The current research is concerned with students' understanding of the nature of science. It is in two principle parts: one concerned with undergraduate physicists and the other with post-graduate science students undergoing a course of training for teaching at Keele University. Some of the post-graduate science students will be followed during their teaching

practice to see if their teaching exemplifies their beliefs and whether the researcher is able to influence this by heightening their awareness through prolonged contact with them. The approach is ethnographic and the stimulus of a free-response questionnaire followed by recorded interviews elucidating their responses has been adopted. In addition, both samples have to interact with specially prepared practical materials designed to reveal further their philosophical standpoints.

12631   Use of official European Community information sources in schools and colleges.
GBR   1993
Research Date(s): 1991-
Chandler, H.
Sup: Bakewell, K.; McGarry, K.
Inst: Liverpool John Moores University, School of Information Science and Technology, Tithebarn Street, Liverpool L2 2ER, United Kingdom.
European dimension; curriculum; teaching aid; curriculum development
dimension européenne; programme d'études; moyen d'enseignement; élaboration de programmes d'études
PROJECT DESCRIPTION

At a time of increasing emphasis by the Department of Education and Science on the importance of the development of curricula and syllabuses for post-16 age groups to reflect the requirements of business and industry with the advent of the single European market, educational establishments are experiencing financial constraints imposed by Local Management of Schools and the implementation of the Community Charge, and the attendant difficulties in provision of additional resource materials to meet the demands of new courses. Merseyside is particularly affected by such problems. It is, however, an area which has a unique advantage in hosting the one regional European Depository Library in the United Kingdom which is accessible to the general public.

This research proposes to: (1) investigate both the extent to which national syllabuses reflect the European dimension and the extent to which support resources have already been developed; (2) evaluate these resources for identified post-16 student groups; and (3) concurrently, investigate the use, means and problems of access to official European Community information in various educational establishments on Merseyside.

The hypothesis is that problems of access obtain. If this is proven, the research would proceed to investigate types of learning programmes/packages which could meet local requirements, and, based primarily on the European Depository Library collection, develop and test such programmes using both quantitative and qualitative methodologies on student groups from collaborating establishments. Consequent on this would be the assessment, modifications and re-evaluation of processes and products. Potential outcomes of the research would be an educational product or products supporting post-16 courses in Merseyside, but with the potential for development on a broader scale; and the furtherance of the commitment of Liverpool John Moores University (previously Liverpool Polytechnic) to Service to the Community in contributing to the regional good through direct partnership of its staff with the public sector.

12632   Using management development packages in schools: an action research programme aimed at encouraging the wider use of school-managed training materials for professional development.
GBR   1993
Research Date(s): 1991-1992
Thomas, H.
Inst: Birmingham University, School of Education, Edgbaston, Birmingham B15 2TT, United Kingdom.
Fin: Department of Education and Science - School Management Task Force.
management education; educational administration; teaching aid; teaching method
formation à la gestion; administration de l'enseignement; moyen d'enseignement; méthode pédagogique
PROJECT DESCRIPTION

The aims of the project are to: (1) evaluate different training modes when using a package of materials for management development; (2) assess these training modes using two packages from a set identified by Task Force; (3) draw lessons from the use of these materials which would contribute to the development of nationally prepared guidelines, for dissemination to schools, on the use of management development packages; (4) use the project as a means for developing a regional support network of information and methodology on the use of packages of materials on the development of school management; (5) encourage local education authorities to support the maintenance of these networks beyond the lifetime of the project and the Task Force. The materials will be used in 10 schools, and data will be collected using an interview schedule.

Publ: Thomas, H. Using management development packages in schools: a report on the training materials project for the West Midlands consortium of the School Management Task Force. Birmingham: Birmingham University, 1992.

12633   Vooronderzoek naar het effect van kunstzinnige vorming in het voortgezet onderwijs op latere culturele participatie. (The effect of art education in secondary school on cultural participation later in life: a preliminary study.)
NLD   1994
Research Date(s): 1992
Haanstra, F.H.; Oud, W.C.M.; Ganzeboom, H.B.G.; Dronkers, J.
Sup: Meijnen, G.W.
Inst: Stichting Centrum voor Onderwijsonderzoek (SCO) (Centre for Educational Research), Grote Bickersstraat 72, 1013 KS Amsterdam, Netherlands.
Universiteit van Amsterdam (University of Amsterdam), P.O. Box 19268, 1000 GG Amsterdam, Netherlands
Fin: SVO het Instituut voor Onderzoek van het Onderwijs.
art education; culture; socialization; participation
éducation artistique; culture; socialisation; participation
PROJECT DESCRIPTION

Background: The Dutch government's cultural policies have since long aimed at promoting cultural participation. Insight is needed into the factors that determine cultural participation. There is research evidence that interest in participation in cultural activities develops at an early age. This interest can be enhanced through art education at school or cultural experiences at home or a combination of both. Information on these factors can be collected in a "retrospective" fashion by questioning a sample of the population about their current participation in culture and relating this to their past experiences. Alternatively, a "prospective" approach would involve the collection of data on art education programmes in school and an investigation of their effect on cultural participation after completion of the school career.

Aim: A research design will be outlined for both types of research. Following this, it will be attempted to determine which design and what instruments are the most appropriate to ascertain the effect of art education programmes in secondary schools on cultural participation later in life.

Methods: Analysis of existing research data; document analysis; structured interview.

Design and results: The feasibility study was in two stages: one explored whether the number of schools that offer art education at the upper secondary level would be sufficient for the main study; the other consisted of an analysis of existing research evidence concerning the effect of art education on cultural participation. On the basis of the findings, it is concluded that the main study is unconditionally feasible, including the various research phases.

Publ: Oud, W. et al. *Effecten van kunstzinnige vorming in het voortgezet onderwijs: verslag van een vooronderzoek.* SCO-Kohnstamm Instituut, 1992, 139p.

12634   Výchova k občanství na 2.stupni základních škol. (Citizenship education in lower secondary schools.)
CSK   1994
Research Date(s): 1990-1992
Pitha, P.; Blažková, M.; Hořejšová, D.; Cákiová, E.; Hlaváčková, M.; Kolář, Z.; Pečinková, P.; Peřich, V.
Sup: Helus, Z.
Inst: Pedagogická fakulta Univerzity Karlovy (Charles University, Faculty of Education), M.D. Rettigové 4, 116 39 Praha 1, Czech Republic.
Ministerstvo školství, mládeže a tělovýchovy (Ministry of Education, Youth and Physical Education), Karmelitská 7, 118 00 Praha 1, Czech Republic
civics; curriculum development; teaching method; lower secondary; curriculum research
instruction civique; élaboration de programmes d'études; méthode pédagogique; secondaire premier cycle; recherche sur les programmes d'études
PROJECT DESCRIPTION

Aim: To design a citizenship education curriculum for use in lower secondary schools.

Results: (1) Survey of current practice in civics teaching; (2) development of a new basic concept of civics teaching in a changing society; (3) construction of a civics curriculum for lower secondary schools (second-level primary schools); (4) development of teacher handbooks.

The curriculum includes: an introductory study, an outline of teaching methods for each year level under the headings of "Family", "Fatherland", "Man and Society", and a systematic survey of such disciplines as national history and geography, law, economy, anthropology, ecology and politics. It is intended to trial the curriculum in one four-year teaching cycle.

Publ: *Učební osnovy občanské výchovy pro 6.-9.ročník základní školy.* Schváleny MSMT v červnu 1991 s platností od 1.9.1991. Praha: Ministerstvo školství, mládeže a tělovýchovy, 1991.

12635   Wirtschaftskenntnisse von Maturanten. (Economic knowledge of secondary school leavers.)
AUT   1993
Research Date(s): 1991-1992
Freundlinger, Alfred.

Inst: Institut fuer Bildungsforschung der Wirtschaft, Rainergasse 38, A-1050 Wien.
Fin: Vereinigung Oesterreichischer Industrieller; Bundeswirtschaftskammer.
economic studies; knowledge level; comprehension; school leaver; secondary education; economics
études économiques; niveau de connaissances; compréhension; élève sortant; enseignement secondaire; science économique
PROJECT DESCRIPTION
Es wurde eine Befragung von rund 750 Studienanfaengern durchgefuehrt. Die acht Fragen zielen auf eine grundlegende Handlungs- und Orientierungsfaehigkeit in wirtschaftlichen Zusammenhaengen. Fuer die Auswertung wird nach Wirtschaftswissensgebieten (Weltwirtschaft, Volkswirtschaft, Geldwirtschaft und Betriebswirtschaft) und nach Fragetypen (Wissens- und Verstaendnisfragen) differenziert. Zusaetzlich erhoben wurden Berufsziele und das Interesse fuer wirtschaftliche Fragen.
Es wurde eine standardisierte Befragung mit multiple-choice Vorgaben durchgefuehrt.
Publ: Freundlinger, Alfred. *Wirtschaftskenntnisse von Maturanten.* Ibw-Schriftenreihe Nr. 88, Wien, 1992.

12636   Women and scientific literacy.
GBR   1993
Research Date(s): 1990–
Birke, L.; Barr, J.
Inst: Warwick University, Faculty of Educational Studies, Coventry CV4 7AL, United Kingdom.
Fin: Universities Funding Council.
science education; women's education; sciences; knowledge level; woman
éducation scientifique; éducation des femmes; sciences; niveau de connaissances; femme
PROJECT DESCRIPTION
The project is mapping the extent of understanding in science and science policy among women (with particular attention to ways in which women may have some scientific knowledge but do not identify it as such) and is identifying those issues within science which are of particular interest - actual and potential - to women who have no previous experience of higher education. Outcomes are oriented towards the development of policy and practice, and will be tested through a number of pilot courses.

11 SCIENCES AND TECHNOLOGY – SCIENCES ET TECHNOLOGIE – WISSENSCHAFTEN UND TECHNOLOGIE

12637 Les activités de résolution de problèmes renouvelées en physique.
FRA 1993
Research Date(s): 1989-
Dumas-Carré, Andrée; Goffard, Monique; Gomatos, L.; Gil Perez, Daniel.
Inst: Université de Paris VII et Université de Paris XI, UFR Physique, CNRS SDI/6207, Laboratoire interuniversitaire de recherche sur l'éducation scientifique et technologique, 2 Place Jussieu, Tour 23, 75251 Paris Cedex 05, France.
Fin: Ministère de l'éducation nationale, Action intégrée avec l'Espagne.
physics; upper secondary; problem solving; learning strategy
physique; secondaire deuxième cycle; résolution de problème; stratégie d'apprentissage
PROJECT DESCRIPTION
Objectifs: Il s'agit d'analyser les stratégies de résolution de problèmes et les arguments utilisés par les élèves lors de séquences de travail autonome en petits groupes. Après un apprentissage d'aides cognitives à la résolution de problème et pour des problèmes ouverts, sans données permettant des activités semblables à des activités de recherche.
Méthodologie: Enregistrement vidéo de séances en classe de 1ère S; analyse des transcripts de séances (enchaînement, et articulation des questions traitées par les élèves; type et finalité des arguments utilisés; relation entre les arguments et l'évolution des questions traitées). Un travail de confrontation des problématiques et d'évaluation des modèles de résolution de problème est mené en Espagne (Université de Valence).
Publ: Goffard, Monique. Modes de travail pédagogique et résolution de problèmes de physique. Université de Paris VII, Thèse, 1990.

Dumas Carré, Andrée; Gil Perez, Daniel & Goffard, Monique. Les élèves peuvent-ils résoudre des problèmes. In: *Bulletin de l'union des physiciens*, 1990, 728, pp. 1289-1299.

Dumas Carré, Andrée; Caillot, Michel; Martinez Torregrosa, J. & Gil, Daniel. Deux approches pour modifier les activités de résolution de problèmes dans l'enseignement secondaire. In: *Aster*, 1989, 8, pp. 135-160.

Gil Perez, Daniel; Dumas Carré, Andrée; Caillot, Michel & Martinez Torregrosa, J. Paper and pencil problem solving in the physical sciences as a research activity. In: *Studies in science education*, 1990, 18, pp. 137-151.

12638 Algebraic processes and the role of symbolism.

GBR 1993

Research Date(s): 1992-1993

Sutherland, R.

Inst: London University, Institute of Education, Department of Mathematics, Statistics and Computing, 20 Bedford Way, London WC1H OAL, United Kingdom.

Fin: Economic and Social Research Council.

mathematics; algebra; symbol; cognitive process

mathématiques; algèbre; symbole; processus cognitif

PROJECT DESCRIPTION

A seminar group is aiming to coordinate and synthesise the United Kingdom work on algebraic thinking in school mathematics. By working together the group aims to produce a set of clear questions and working hypotheses for future research collaboration with European colleagues.

12639 An alternative metaphor for teaching control technology.

GBR 1993

Research Date(s): 1990-

Whalley, P.

Inst: Open University, Institute of Educational Technology, Walton Hall, Milton Keynes MK7 6AA, United Kingdom.

control technology; computer science; logo; model; simulation; didactic use of computer

technologie de contrôle; informatique; logo; modèle; simulation; usage didactique de l'ordinateur

PROJECT DESCRIPTION

Control technology is viewed as a good way to provide practical experience of programmable systems that are familiar to children such as sliding doors, level crossings etc. Teachers using this technology usually also have the higher-level goals of encouraging 'systems thinking' and general problem-solving skills. Using a computer in this way to control physical micro-worlds can be an interesting and powerful educational experience. Unfortunately there is often a gulf between these aims and what happens in the classroom. The higher-order goals are frequently lost in the struggle to cope with the presently available control technology environments.

The project represents an attempt to create a graphic object-oriented control language for children. The underlying nature of environments like HyperTechnic is quite different from their procedural equivalents, and is in several ways intuitively more comprehensible. For example conditionals and loop-control are implicit in the way that the objects operate and do not have to be explicitly taught. The micro-worlds that the children are to explore and control are made up of plastic and cardboard models, rather than the purely screen-based, and hence necessarily more abstract, micro-worlds that are often provided for children.

The immediate practical goal of this research is to evaluate to what extent the level of description and explanatory metaphors used to describe control technology problems affects children's understanding of them. A longer-term aim is to foster understanding of how children comprehend the deeper conceptual problems underlying this form of task.

Publ: Whalley, P. HyperTechnic - a graphic object-oriented control language. Paper presented at the Seventh International Conference on Technology and Education, Brussels, March 1990.

Whalley, P. Level of description as a factor in children's interactions with computers. Paper presented at the Fourth European Conference for Research on Learning and Instruction (EARLI), Turku, Finland, August 1991.

Whalley, P. An alternative metaphor for teaching control technology. In: *Proceedings of the 'East-West Conference on Emerging Computer Technologies in Education*, Moscow, April 1992.

12640 Ambienti per la risoluzione interattiva di problemi. (Interactive problem-solving environments.)

ITA 1994

Research Date(s): 1992-

Culotta, Nadia; Oreste, Chiara.

Sup: Chioccariello, Augusto.

Inst: Istituto per le Tecnologie Didattiche - ITD (Institute for Educational Technology), Via dell'Opera Pia 11, 16145 Genova, Italy.

Consiglio Nazionale delle Ricerche - CNR (National Research Council), Piazzale Aldo Moro 7, 00185 Roma, Italy

information technology; programming language; logo; educational software; educational technology; mathematics; teaching method; didactic use of computer; problem solving; teacher education

technologie de l'information; langage de programmation; logo; didacticiel; technologie de l'éducation; mathématiques; méthode pédagogique; usage didactique de l'ordinateur; résolution de problème; formation des enseignants

PROJECT DESCRIPTION

Logo is the name of a philosophy of education in a family of programming languages still in evolution. The didactic innovation proposed by Logo and exemplified by the metaphor of "Mathland" - a learning environment in which students develop mathematical knowledge with the same ease with which they learn to speak - has evoked mixed reactions among educators. This may be explained by the different levels of support for the training of teachers and the variation in number of hours. The hypothesis of this research is that the cultural environment, in terms of the capacity and the support available to pupils, is essential to the success of Logo.

The aims of the study are: (1) to develop a model of teacher training that offers the cultural tools that are needed for the integration of Logo into the curriculum, with special attention to the use of Logo as an instrument for the development of problem solving skills; (2) to develop appropriate situations for the teaching of Italian and mathematics in the compulsory school.

The study will be conducted in collaboration with teachers in compulsory schools; the hypothesis will be tested in the classroom.

12641 Analyse des difficultés conceptuelles dans l'enseignement de la chimie-physique dans les premiers cycles universitaires.

FRA 1993

Research Date(s): 1989-

Dumon, Alain.

Inst: Université de Pau, Centre universitaire de recherche, Laboratoire de didactique et communication pédagogique, SUFFO, Rue Jules Ferry, 64000 Pau, France.

chemistry; physics; learning difficulty; undergraduate study; concept formation; cognitive process; abstraction

chimie; physique; difficulté de l'apprentissage; supérieur premier cycle; formation de concept; processus cognitif; abstraction

PROJECT DESCRIPTION

Objectifs: Pour identifier l'origine des difficultés de compréhension de ces concepts et analyser les structures cognitives et leur évolution deux techniques complémentaires sont utilisées: (1) "l'association de mots" qui conduit à la construction de diagrammes de proximité et de liaison entre mots et expression, (2) des questionnaires à choix de réponses permettant de préciser les observations issues des diagrammes et d'identifier les savoirs réellement assimilés.

Méthodologie: Echantillon: Etudiants des diplômes d'études universitaires générales (DEUG) et étudiants de maîtrise de chimie. Les concepts enseignés en première année de DEUG (modèle quantique, thermodynamique chimique) sont difficiles et abstraits. Comme il est impossible de développer dans le détail l'ensemble des concepts, les étudiants sont conduits à les accepter sans discussion et sans véritable compréhension. Les "bons" étudiants sont ceux qui sont capables de mémoriser des explications théoriques auxquelles ils n'ont rien compris. L'hypothèse est que ces notions, bien que difficilement perçues à leur niveau d'abstraction mathématique, doivent être introduites, même sous forme simplifiée, pour une bonne compréhension des notions introduites ultérieurement.

12642 Analyse et développement des apprentissages à réaliser au collège dans les travaux numériques, dans les travaux géométriques.

FRA 1993

Research Date(s): 1987-1992

Pluvinage, François; Rauscher, J.C.; Mathern, Claude; Maurette, Danielle; Ortheb, Monique; Roesch, Gabrielle; Keyling, Marie-Anne.

Inst: Université de Strasbourg I, Institut de recherche sur l'enseignement des mathématiques (Strasbourg), 10 rue du Général Zimmer, 67084 Strasbourg Cedex, France.

geometry; algebra; lower secondary; learning; logical thinking; mathematics

géométrie; algèbre; secondaire premier cycle; acquisition de connaissances; pensée logique; mathématiques

PROJECT DESCRIPTION

Objectifs: Les travaux ont deux objectifs complémentaires: (1) élaborer des instruments d'évaluation qui permettent de baliser des parcours d'apprentissage en collège (dans les domaines de la géométrie et de l'algèbre); (2) parallèlement élaborer et mettre en oeuvre des activités qui développent les compétences repérées comme nécessaires. L'hypothèse est que ces compétences ne réfèrent pas seulement à des contenus mathématiques mais aussi aux tâches à effectuer.

Méthodologie: Passations, observations, mises à l'épreuve des évaluations et des activités dans quatre collèges représentatifs de situations sociologiques de recrutements variées.

Résultats: (1) Travaux géométriques: distinction des difficultés liées à l'accès au raisonnement hypothético-déductif et détermination d'un parcours d'apprentissage de la sixième à la troisième pour surmonter ces difficultés; (2) travaux numériques: distinction des difficultés liées à l'accès au monde de la formalisation et du calcul littéral.

Publ: Articles dans les *Bulletins Inter-Irem* (Lyon).
En 5ème: Le développement des compétences pour la géométrie, 1987.
En 4ème: Vers l'apprentissage du raisonnement en géométrie, 1988.
En 3ème: La géométrie de la sixième à la troisième, 1989.
Calcul numérique et calcul algébrique au collège: quelles difficultés, 1992.

12643 Assessment of Achievement Programme (AAP) Mathematics: third round Monitoring Project.
GBR 1993
Research Date(s): 1990-1992
Meechan, R.; Robertson, I.; Clarke, D.
Inst: Jordanhill College of Education, Division of Mathematics, Southbrae Drive, Glasgow G13 1PP, United Kingdom.
Fin: Scottish Office Education Department.
mathematics; achievement test; assessment
mathématiques; test de rendement; appréciation
PROJECT DESCRIPTION
   The aim of this project is to assess achievement in various aspects of mathematics at the P4, P7 and S2 stages of Scottish schools, providing a description of what pupils know and can do at each stage and allowing valid comparisons to be made between stages and with results of the Scottish Office Education Department (SOED) Mathematics survey (1988). The exercise involves: a reappraisal of the assessment framework to take account of the 5-14 Development Programme and current curriculum; the development of new test items, both written and practical; a main programme of assessment in May/June 1991; marking completed tests; defining analyses to be undertaken; a project report for SOED with a summary for use in disseminating the results. Advice and assistance has been provided by the Assessment of Achievement Programme (AAP) Central Support Unit of the Scottish Council for Research in Education (SCRE) on aspects of test design, carrying out of data preparation and analysis, liaison with schools and distribution and collection of written tests.

12644 The attitudes and confidence of primary school teachers regarding mathematics education.
GBR 1993
Research Date(s): 1991-
Harries, D.
Inst: Reading University, Department of Science and Technology Education, Bulmershe Court, Woodlands Avenue, Earley, Reading RG6 1HY, United Kingdom.
Fin: Universities Funding Council.
mathematics; teacher behaviour; teaching style
mathématiques; comportement de l'enseignant; style pédagogique
PROJECT DESCRIPTION
   Many people have a suspicious and wary attitude to mathematics, viewing it as a highly abstract and difficult subject to master, even though they make effective use of 'everyday' mathematics. Some primary teachers who are not mathematics specialists exhibit these attitudes, and appear to have high anxiety levels regarding their own mathematical abilities. This can lead to a sterile teaching approach, whereas the National Curriculum requires a variety of approaches in the teaching of mathematics, including practical and investigative work.
   This study is intended to provide more precise information about attitudes to mathematics amongst primary school teachers, and the nature of any problems that may arise. Such information can be used to inform Inservice Education and Training (INSET) planning and development. Initially a questionnaire survey of a local sample of teachers will be carried out. Further in-depth work will be undertaken through selected individual interviews.

12645 Cabri geometry.
GBR 1993
Research Date(s): 1991
Rogers, L.
Inst: Roehampton Institute, Digby Stuart College, Mathematics Division, Roehampton Lane, London SW15 5PU, United Kingdom; Laboratoire LSDZ-IMAG, BP53X 38041 Grenoble Cedex, France; Institut für Didaktik der Mathematik, Universität Bielefeld, Postfach 8640, 4800 Bielefeld 1, Germany.
educational software; geometry; mathematics; didactic use of computer
didacticiel; géométrie; mathématiques; usage didactique de l'ordinateur
PROJECT DESCRIPTION
   Cabri geometry is a software package created by French mathematics educators at Grenoble, France. The package provides the student with a set of tools for the dynamic investigation of plane geometry. Research to date in France and Germany has considered the didactic applications of the material. The aim of the pilot project is to assess the suitability and potential for its use in England.

Publ: Mason, J. Pythagores in Cabri Geometre. In: *Micromath*, Vol 7, No 2/1991, pp. 15-17.

12646 Children's alternative ideas about earth science concepts, e.g. continental drift and plate tectonics.
GBR 1993
Research Date(s): 1989-1994
Marques, L.
Sup: Thompson, D.
Inst: Keele University, Department of Education, Keele, Staffordshire ST5 5BG, United Kingdom.
earth sciences; oceanography; physical sciences; comprehension
sciences de la terre; océanographie; sciences physiques; compréhension
PROJECT DESCRIPTION
   Children's alternative ideas relating to earth science concepts have been only modestly researched. Following work on children's ideas of the origin of the earth, the origin of life and the nature and origin of volcanoes, the research has now turned to children's views of the origin of continents, oceans and the possible wandering of the former. Following a pilot study with pupils and teachers and in-depth interviews with pupils, a questionnaire survey of the views of 300 Portuguese children has been administered. It is conjectured that the many garbled ideas of students accrue from watching television, reading newspapers and attempting to use ideas drawn from science and geography lessons at school. So far 30 or so alternative ideas have been noted and curriculum strategies which challenge many of them been developed and trialled.

12647 Children's 'application readiness with basic mathematics'.
GBR 1993
Research Date(s): 1981-
Ormell, C.; Abdel-Ghany, I.
Inst: University of East Anglia, School of Education, Norwich NR4 7TJ, United Kingdom; University of Minia, Department of Education, El Minia, Egypt.
Fin: Egyptian Bureau, London.
mathematics; test construction; comprehension
mathématiques; construction de tests; compréhension
PROJECT DESCRIPTION
   'Application Readiness' is a new idea in mathematics education. It signifies the condition in which a child has assimilated the applicative potency of a new mathematical concept so well that he/she is able spontaneously (without prompting or cueing) and unselfconsciously to recall and apply that concept to a practical situation needing that concept for its solution. The aims of the research are to clarify the idea of application readiness, to produce tests for it, to improve earlier tests, to trial such tests in schools and evaluate the results.
   Topics covered so far include basic (natural number) arithmetic up to 99, simple decimals and simple fractions. Recent research has centred on producing large numbers of 'rich, realistic contexts' of the kind needed to test for application readiness, including contexts where there is a mixed teaching/assessment use for the material.

Publ: Abdel-Ghany, I. & Ormell, C.P. *Problem solving with basic mathematics: ten lessons*. University of East Anglia: Mathematics Applicable Group, 1985.
Ormell, C.P. Application readiness in mathematics at 10/11. In: Blum, W. et al. *Applications and modelling in learning and teaching mathematics*. Maths and its Applications Series. Chichester: Ellis Horwood, 1989.
Ormell, C.P. Application readiness with fractions. In: Blum, W. et al. *Modelling applications, and applied problem solving*. Maths and its Applications Series. Chichester: Ellis Horwood, 1989.
Ormell, C.P. Why story maths? In: *I.M.A. Bulletin*, 1991.
Ormell, C.P. *Story maths*. Adelaide, Australia: AAMT, 1992.

12648 Chimie et enseignement médical.
FRA 1994
Research Date(s): 1979-1988
Davous, Dominique; Thibault, Janine; Vasseur, Alexis.
Sup: Gomel, Maurice.
Inst: Université de Paris VI, UFR Chimie-physique, Groupe de recherche en didactique de la chimie, 4 Place Jussieu, Bât. 72-73, 2ème étage, porte 228, 75252 Paris Cedex 05, France.
chemistry; content of education; medicine; course programme; undergraduate study
chimie; contenu de l'éducation; médecine; programme de cours; supérieur premier cycle
PROJECT DESCRIPTION
   Objectifs: Analyse du système d'enseignement de la première année du premier cycle médical (sélection-formation) (PCMEM-1); enquête visant à cerner la place et le rôle de la chimie (plus largement des disciplines fondamentales) souhaités par les médecins et les étudiants en médecine; expérimentation et évaluation d'un enseignement d'un type nouveau dont l'objectif est de mettre en évidence et d'expliquer le contenu chimique des examens de laboratoire les plus courants.
   Méthodologie: Entretiens non directifs (médecins hospitaliers, privés, des laboratoires pharmaceutiques, etc.); enquête (échantillonnage: 600 médecins, 450 étudiants en médecine, l'ensemble des chimistes et biochimistes médecin enseignant en PCEM-1); traitements des données et

mise au point d'outils pédagogiques pour les étudiants du PCEM-1; collaboration avec spécialistes en statistiques, en informatique, en sociologie, psychologie, sciences de l'éducation.

Résultats: La situation des 44 Centres hospitaliers universitaires de France est observée et analysée en termes de sélection et de formation. Une procédure de création d'outils d'enseignement fondant un enseignement de chimie en PCEM-1 sur des finalités médicales bien définies (les analyses médicales) est proposée puis concrétisée en totalité. On établit le fait qu'aucune matière n'est plus sélective qu'une autre: il n'est donc pas exact d'affirmer que la sélection des médecins est effectuée principalement sur leurs résultats (au concours) en sciences fondamentales. Le taux de réussite diffère selon les Centres Hospitaliers Universitaires (de 13 à 30%). L'ensemble de ces résultats est discuté. L'étude fait ressortir deux grandes tendances de formation caractérisant d'une part Paris et la région parisienne et d'autre part, le reste de la France. Ces deux tendances dégagées sont décrites. Comparé avec d'autres premiers cycles scientifiques, le PCEM-1 apparaît comme un hybride présentant l'organisation générale et l'horaire d'un enseignement universitaire de premier cycle classique, mais la finalité d'une classe préparatoire.

Publ: Davous, Dominique; Thibault, Janine; Gomel, Maurice & Vasseur, Alexis. Etude chimie-médecine, les modifications possibles d'un cursus universitaire. In: Revue française de pédagogie, 1988, 84, pp. 21-28.

Davous, Dominique & Thibault, Janine. Recherche et expérimentation sur l'enseignement de la chimie à finalité biomédicale. In: L'actualité chimique, 1989, 3, pp. 87-91.

Davous, Dominique. Analyse d'un système d'enseignement: le premier cycle des études médicales en France. Recherche et expérimentation sur l'enseignement de la chimie à finalité biomédicale. Université de Poitiers, Thèse de doctorat d'Etat, 1987.

(Une liste complète est disponible auprès du chercheur.).

12649 Chimie expérimentale en premier cycle universitaire.
FRA 1993
Research Date(s): 1987-1990
Pernot, Christiane; Larcher, Claudine; Frémont, Rolande; Viovy, Roger; Roletto, Ezio.
Sup: Caretto, Josette.
Inst: Université de Paris VII et Université de Paris XI, UFR Physique, CNRS SDI/6207, Laboratoire interuniversitaire de recherche sur l'éducation scientifique et technologique, 2 Place Jussieu, Tour 23, 75251 Paris Cedex 05, France.
chemistry; learning module; experimental education; upper secondary; undergraduate study
chimie; module d'enseignement; pédagogie expérimentale; secondaire deuxième cycle; supérieur premier cycle
PROJECT DESCRIPTION
Objectifs: Ce travail a consisté à mettre au point et effectuer des modules d'enseignement expérimental de chimie, mettant en oeuvre un apprentissage technique et méthodologique et prenant en compte les problèmes de communication et d'évaluation du travail des étudiants. L'expérimentation en lycée s'est faite par l'intégration complète des modules dans l'ensemble de l'enseignement du thème, celle du premier cycle universitaire a organisé ces modules comme enseignement indépendant. Cette réflexion tient compte des travaux de recherche concernant les théories de l'apprentissage, le rôle et le statut de l'expérimental, l'organisation en cycle d'apprentissage et cycle d'application.
Méthodologie: (1) Pour le lycée, expérimentation dans quatre classes de terminale à Rouen sur le thème "Acides-bases" après la réalisation d'une enquête sur les buts des travaux pratiques dans l'enseignement secondaire français; (2) Pour le premier cycle universitaire, ont été effectuées: une analyse de la situation existante, une analyse didactique du rôle de l'enseignement expérimental de chimie en premier cycle, une comparaison avec d'autres pays européens (programme ERASMUS), puis la mise en place de séquences d'enseignement pendant plusieurs années, dans trois modules de première année universitaire comprenant environ 500 étudiants de l'Université Paris XI.

Publ: Rapport au Ministère de l'éducation nationale, 1990.
Pernot, Christiane & Caretto, Josette. Travail expérimental en chimie. Université de Paris VII: LIREST, 1990 (document ronéoté).

12650 Cognitive model for the design of sketching systems.
GBR 1993
Research Date(s): 1983-1993
Fish, J.
Sup: Scrivener, S.
Inst: Loughborough University of Technology, Department of Computer Studies, Loughborough LE11 3TU, United Kingdom.
computer-assisted design; drawing
conception assistée par ordinateur; dessin
PROJECT DESCRIPTION
A model is proposed for the mental representation of artists' sketches. Evidence is presented to support the theory that artists' sketches are hybrid images consisting of visible precept and a cognitive component of a superimposed mental image. It is further argued that sketches amplify the mind's ability to generate imagery from long term memory by facilitating translation between descriptive and depictive modes of representation. The model is used to suggest new improved computer software packages, parts of which it is hoped to implement. The implication of the model for the way in which drawing is taught and the future use of sketching systems in education is analysed.

Publ: Fish, J.C.H. & Scrivener, S. Amplifying the mind's eye: sketching and visual cognition. In: Leonardo, Vol 23, No 1/1990.

12651 Comparative study of information technology training for disabled people in Britain and Portugal.
GBR 1993
Research Date(s): 1991-1993
Jotham, R.; Da Cunha, A.
Inst: Nottingham University, Department of Adult Education, 14-22 Shakespeare Street, Nottingham NG1 4FJ, United Kingdom; Associacao Portuguesa de Paralisia Cerebral, Rua Delfim Maia, 4300 Porto, Portugal.
Fin: Gulbenkian Foundation.
information technology; comparative education; handicapped; vocational training; Portugal; United Kingdom
technologie de l'information; éducation comparée; handicapé; formation professionnelle; Portugal; Royaume-Uni
PROJECT DESCRIPTION
A Portugese researcher will spend two months in the United Kingdom gathering information on the training of disabled people in information technology. This will be followed by gathering comparative data in Portugal and the results will be collated to generate a report which will be published in both English and Portugese.

12652 A competence framework in chemistry.
GBR 1993
Research Date(s): 1992
Dodd, J.
Sup: Goulding, K.
Inst: University of Central Lancashire, Corporation Street, Preston PR1 2TQ, United Kingdom.
chemistry; minimum competencies; curriculum development
chimie; fundamentum; élaboration de programmes d'études
PROJECT DESCRIPTION
Recent changes in Business and Technician Education Council (BTEC) policy towards 'competences and transferable skills' call for an urgent response from course teams. The Faculty has granted the researcher a six-month secondment (February-August 1992) to make progress in this area. The aim of the project is to develop a competence framework, primarily (but not exclusively) for HND/HNC courses in chemistry - along with supporting materials and delivery systems. The proposed activities are: liaison with other course teams in Faculty/University, and with the Faculty Support Group; visits to other institutions (to discover examples of good practice); consultations in industry to provide resource material, and to discuss joint assessment procedures in student placements and work-based projects; and the development of related student-centred learning materials.
The proposed outcomes of the research will be: a coherent strategy for a competence framework in BTEC chemistry/science courses; the development of quality materials for use in teaching/learning situations; and the facilitating (and assessment) of transferable skills within the curriculum. Evaluation will take the form of a written report, possibly an educational methods workshop, and some testing on student groups.

12653 Computer applications to special education.
GBR 1993
Research Date(s): 1985-
Seale, J.; Newberry-Tarrier, S.; Topping, M.
Sup: Hegarty, J.
Inst: Keele University, Department of Psychology, Keele, Staffordshire ST5 5BG, United Kingdom.
Fin: Various public and charitable sources.
computer application; special education; didactic use of computer; mentally handicapped; adult
application informatique; enseignement spécial; usage didactique de l'ordinateur; handicapé mental; adulte
PROJECT DESCRIPTION
The aim of the research is to support users of microcomputers in special education, particularly those who work with adults who have severe learning difficulties. The work combines research, development of software and hardware devices, consultancy and staff training. There are three major research projects: (1) Staff development - a detailed study of 11 centres using micros has revealed the dimensions of effective management of the computer as an educational resource. The research has produced a management profile (AMMASE) which can be used to identify weaknesses and strengths in management and create goals. (2) Expert Systems Project - detailed observational research of adults with a mental handicap whilst shopping for groceries has produced a specification for a computer aid which will help them produce their own shopping lists based on the grocery stocks normally required for their weekly needs. The software is

now written for a hand-held microcomputer with integral touch screen and printer which allows clients who cannot read or write to input the current grocery stocks and thus create a shopping list (which is graphical). Evaluation of the system is in progress. (3) A robotic device to allow people to eat unassisted has been developed. This low cost device is now in use and is being evaluated.

Publ: Collins, R. Computers and special education for adults. In: Hartley, J. & Branthwaite, J.A. (eds.). *The Applied Psychologist*. Buckingham: Open University Press, 1989.

Hegarty, J.R. *Into the 1990s: the Present and Future of Microcomputers for People with Learning Difficulties*. Market Drayton: Change Publications, 1991.

12654 La construction des savoirs en biologie par les élèves, les adultes, les maîtres de stage de l'enseignement agricole.
FRA 1993
Research Date(s): 1989-
Millot, Jacques; Caens, Sylvie; Rumelhard, Guy; Astolfi, Jean-Pierre; Jacobi, Daniel.
Inst: Institut national de recherches et d'applications pédagogiques, 2 rue des Champs Prévois, 21100 Dijon, France.
Fin: Ministère de l'agriculture, Direction générale de l'enseignement et de la recherche, Sous-direction de la recherche de l'animation et de la coopération internationale.
biology; agricultural training; concept formation
biologie; formation agricole; formation de concept
PROJECT DESCRIPTION

Objectifs: Etude des représentations des élèves et adultes de lycées agricoles sur le concept d'hormone animale. Le cadre de cette étude est celui des travaux, dans le domaine des représentations en biologie, menés à l'Institut national de recherche pédagogique, à l'Université de Paris VII et de Lyon I et à Genève.

Méthodologie: Construction d'un questionnaire d'enquête, passation, dépouillement et analyse des réponses à la lumière de l'histoire du concept d'hormone dans l'histoire et l'épistémologie de la biologie.

12655 The contribution of geography to environmental education.
GBR 1993
Research Date(s): 1991-1993
Fitzgerald, M.
Inst: Anglia Polytechnic University, Department of Geography, East Road, Cambridge CB1 1PT, United Kingdom.
geography; environmental study; rural development
géographie; étude du milieu; développement rural
PROJECT DESCRIPTION

The aim is to evaluate geography's contribution to education for sustainable development. The proposed method is an analysis of school syllabuses and assessment procedures in the United Kingdom and California. Initial research suggests that geography's separation of the 'human' and the 'physical' undermines its potential to synthesise ecology and environment in the ways needed to bring about new environmental ethics.

12656 Curriculum development in mathematics: using and applying mathematics.
GBR 1993
Research Date(s): 1989-1994
Miller, D.
Inst: Keele University, Department of Education, Keele, Staffordshire ST5 5BG, United Kingdom.
mathematics; curriculum development; teaching method; teaching aid
mathématiques; élaboration de programmes d'études; méthode pédagogique; moyen d'enseignement
PROJECT DESCRIPTION

The aims of this research are to extend the breadth of the secondary school mathematics curriculum, within the context of the National Curriculum, with particular reference to the use and application of mathematics, and to influence and enrich mathematics teachers' current methodologies. The nature of the research is to provide teachers of mathematics with new, or unfamiliar, activities and contexts for using and applying mathematics. These activities and contexts include mathematics as it is used by different cultures, topics from the history of mathematics, cross-curricular material and micro-computer and calculator applications. The results will be detailed in appropriate journals, the materials wil be published in a suitable format.

Publ: Miller, D.J. *Activity Maths, Level 5*. Ormskirk: Causeway Press Ltd, 1990.
Miller, D.J. *Activity Maths, Level 5, Teachers' Book*. Ormskirk: Causeway Press Ltd, 1990.
Miller, D.J. *Micromathematics, Levels 5 and 6*. Ormskirk: Causeway Press Ltd, 1990.
Miller, D.J. *Micromathematics, Levels 5 and 6, Teachers' Book*. Ormskirk: Causeway Press Ltd, 1990.
A full list of publications is available from the researcher.

12657 Curriculum materials for earth science teaching in the National Curriculum.
GBR 1993
Research Date(s): 1988-
Thompson, D.
Inst: Keele University, Department of Education, Keele, Staffordshire ST5 5BG, United Kingdom.
earth sciences; science education; teaching aid; physical sciences; common core curriculum; curriculum development
sciences de la terre; éducation scientifique; moyen d'enseignement; sciences physiques; tronc commun; élaboration de programmes d'études
PROJECT DESCRIPTION

Earth science is new to the science curriculum in the United Kingdom. Curriculum materials need to be written, trialled and published quickly. Trials are to be carried out on whole classes of 20-30 pupils. Materials are designed for variety and balance of approach and a concentration on pupil activity including practical experimental work. Publication is via the Earth Science Teachers' Association 'Science of the Earth' and 'Project Earth'.

12658 Data base di materiale didattico multimediale a supporto della riusabilità dei prodotti del processo di sviluppo di courseware. (Databases of multimedia learning materials to support the use of courseware development products.)
ITA 1994
Research Date(s): 1992-1994
Sarti, Luigi; Chioccariello, Augusto; Ulloa, Antonio; Lampignano, Sebastiano; Rada, Roy.
Sup: Persico, Donatella.
Inst: Istituto per le Tecnologie Didattiche - ITD (Institute for Educational Technology), Via all'Opera Pia 11, 16145 Genova, Italy.
Consiglio Nazionale delle Ricerche - CNR (National Research Council), Piazzale Aldo Moro 7, 00185 Roma, Italy
Fin: Comunit Economica Europea.
educational technology; information technology; educational software; software library; data base; teaching aid
technologie de l'éducation; technologie de l'information; didacticiel; logithèque; banque de données; moyen d'enseignement
PROJECT DESCRIPTION

This project represents the contribution of ITD/CNR (the Institute for Educational Technology/National Research Council) to the "D2006 - Open System for Collaborative Authoring and Reuse" project of the European DELTA programme. In the project, the Institute takes on the role of associate partner and will contribute to the implementation of a Database of Learning Material (DBLM), produced by the Institute itself under the auspices of the DISCOURSE project. The Institute will also contribute to the study of the skills needed by the author of learning material to put together a course, making use of existing material.

The DBLM is at the centre of the courseware development process and is a fundamental resource in this process, as it enables reusable material to be tracked down on the basis of precise specifications supplied by the author. Tracing, however, is a necessary but not a sufficient condition in the reusability of courseware development products. For example, the author will still need to have the appropriate tools to connect the various materials available and to adapt them to the new context.

The project is scheduled to span three years. In the first year, the Institute will define the specifications of the DBLM that satisfy the needs of both the DISCOURSE and the OSCAR projects. It will also initiate support for the implementation of a prototype of DBLM from its partner SYNTEX Spa. The implementation will continue into the second year. Research into the functionality of "reuse" is scheduled to be carried out in 1994.

12659 Database support for multi-media computer-assisted learning.
GBR 1993
Research Date(s): 1986-1992
Barker, P.
Inst: Teesside University, School of Computing and Mathematics, Interactive Systems Research Group, Borough Road, Middlesbrough, Cleveland TS1 3BA, United Kingdom.
data base management system; educational technology; multimedia system; didactic use of computer; distance study
système de gestion de bases de données; technologie de l'éducation; système multimédia; usage didactique de l'ordinateur; enseignement à distance
PROJECT DESCRIPTION

The multi-media approach to computer-assisted learning (CAL) necessitates the use of human-computer interaction environments which are capable of supporting highly parallel, mixed-mode dialogue. An environment that is able to meet these requirements is often referred to as multi-media workstation. Multi-media CAL workstations provide sophisticated interaction environments for a learner or trainee. These environments usually contain a wide range of interaction peripherals, including a light pen, a keyboard, a barcode reader, one or more concept keyboards, a digitiser, a touch screen, an image scanner, and so on. In addition to these interaction devices, the workstation might also contain a cluster of local storage peripherals.

This study investigates the potential utility of database technology as a support aid within a multi-media workstation environment. Both conventional and intelligent database software resources would be examined. A major objective of the study is to find appropriate means of simplifying both the use and control of a sophisticated workstation that is attached (as an active device) to a distributed wide-area computer network system. Such a workstation would be able to act both as a means of facilitating distributed courseware authoring and as a method for the effective realisation of distributed distance learning. In the latter context, it is important to realise that many of the resources used for instruction might either reside at remote host installations or be available locally. The database support facilities embedded within the workstation will therefore need to keep track of those resources which are held locally and those which must be accessed through remote sites. Obviously intelligence in the database will enable the workstation to be connected to the most appropriate host - where a selection exists.

Publ: Barker, P.G. *Author languages for CAL.* Basingstoke: Macmillan Press, 1986.
Barker, P.G. A practical introduction to authoring for computer assisted instruction. Part 8: multi-media CAL. In: *British Journal of Educational Technology*, Vol 18, No 1/1987, pp. 25-40.

12660 Daten- und Modellanalysen zum oesterreichischen Bildungssystem: Schulabbruch, Schulwechsel und Moeglichkeiten der Verbesserung im Informationssystem. (Data and model analyses of the Austrian educational system: dropout and transfer rates and ways to improve the information system.)
AUT 1993
Research Date(s): 1992-1993
Lassnig, Lorenz; Fraiji, Adelheid; Mueller, Karl H.; Haag, Guenther.
Inst: Institut fuer Hoehere Studien, Stumpergasse 56, A-1060 Wien.
Fin: Bundesministerium fuer Unterricht und Kunst, Abteilung fuer Bildungsoekonomie und Statistik.
statistical data; number of pupils; statistical model; dropout
données statistiques; effectifs scolaires; modèle statistique; abandon d'études
PROJECT DESCRIPTION
Auf der Basis eines Datensatzes zu den Schuelerbestandszahlen wird ein detaillierter Versuch unternommen, die jaehrlichen Veraenderungen im Schulwesen empirisch zu erfassen. Diese Analyse konzentriert sich auf das Problem der Schulabbrecher und bezieht die verschiedenen Formen 'nicht-regulaeren' Wechsels ein. Eine zureichende Erfassung und Analyse der Schulabbrecher impliziert, dass die 'nicht vorgesehenen Abgaenge' mit Zugaengen in andere Bereiche saldiert werden. Daher ist es erforderlich, auch die Schnittstellen zwischen den verschiedenen Bereichen des Schul- und Bildungswesens und die an diesen Stellen vorhandenen 'Wechsel-Stroeme' eingehend zu analysieren. In jenen Bereichen, fuer welche keine hinreichende Datenbasis zur Verfuegung steht, sollen analytische Schaetzverfahren Verwendung finden, welche im wesentlichen einen Rueckschluss auf die entsprechenden Stromdaten erlauben. Die vorhandenen Instrumente und Methoden der Datenerhebung im Rahmen der Schulstatistik sollen einer Evaluation unterzogen werden, um auf dieser Basis Vorschlaege fuer eine Weiterentwicklung erarbeiten zu koennen. Dieser Untersuchungsteil zielt darauf hin, wichtige Informationsluecken im System der statistischen Berichterstattung zu erfassen und Moeglichkeiten fuer ihre Schliessung zu explorieren.

Es werden die verfuegbaren Datenbestaende der Schulstatistik der Oesterreichischen Statistik (jaehrliche Schuelerbestaende, Vorbildung, Schulerfolge, 9. Pflichtschuljahr, Geburtenjahrgaenge) verwendet.

Die Auswertung erfolgt mittels explorativer Datenanalyse, konzeptionell-vergleichender Untersuchung, Modellschaetzung und Evaluation.

12661 Derde Internationale Wiskunde- en Science studie (TIMSS). (Third International Mathematics and Science Study (TIMSS).)
NLD 1994
Research Date(s): 1992-1993
Kuiper, W.A.J.M.
Sup: Plomp, Tj.
Inst: Onderzoek Centrum Toegepaste Onderwijskunde (OCTO) (Research Centre of the Department of Educational Technology), P.O. Box 217, 7500 AE Enschede, Netherlands.
Universiteit Twente (Twente University), P.O. Box 217, 7500 AE Enschede, Netherlands
Fin: SVO het Instituut voor Onderzoek van het Onderwijs.
mathematics; physical sciences; achievement; comparative research; cross-national research; secondary education
mathématiques; sciences physiques; rendement; recherche comparative; recherche transnationale; enseignement secondaire
PROJECT DESCRIPTION
Background: The Third International Mathematics and Science Study (TIMSS) is conducted under the auspices of the International Association for the Evaluation of Educational Achievement (IEA). Fifty countries are

participating in the study, including the USA, Japan, Russia, and various Western European countries. This project is concerned with the Dutch contribution to the first phase of the study (1991-1995). The TIMSS will produce baseline-data that are also important for the introduction of the national lower secondary basic education curriculum in the Netherlands and for the OECD educational indicators project.

Aim: To describe and analyse, for the purposes of the international comparative study, the context, contents, instructional practices and outcomes of education in science subjects (mathematics, physics, chemistry, biology, geography) at the primary and secondary level in the Netherlands.

Research questions: (1) What are the intended learning goals for mathematics and science (intended curriculum)? (2) How are mathematics and science taught in the classroom (implemented curriculum)? (3) What mathematics and science concepts, processes and attitudes do pupils learn (attained curriculum)? (4) How are the intended, the implemented and the attained curriculum related with respect to the context of education, the arrangements for teaching and learning and the outcomes of the educational process? (5) What similarities and differences occur between countries in respect of the questions above?

Design: In the international design of the TIMSS four populations are distinguished: 9-year-olds (pop1), 13-year-olds (pop2), pupils in the final year of secondary school (pop3a), and pupils in the final year of secondary school who take examinations in maths, physics, chemistry, biology and/or geography (pop3b). The Dutch contribution deals with populations 2 and 3a. The sample for each population consists of about 200 schools totalling 8,000 (pop2) and 4,000 (pop3a) pupils. It will be possible to establish links between data sets by making use of a sample that was used in earlier studies. Data will be collected with the help of participation questionnaires, curriculum analysis, cognitive tests, practical skills tests, attitude questionnaires (to pupils and teachers), opportunities for learning questionnaires (to teachers), classroom practice questionnaires (to teachers), and school organization questionnaires (school management staff).

12662 Development of microcomputer software for educational and vocational applications (for blind and partially sighted persons).
GBR 1993
Research Date(s): 1983-
Bozic, N.; Campbell, S.; Vallender, M.
Sup: Tobin, M.
Inst: Birmingham University, School of Education, Research Centre for the Education of the Visually Handicapped, Edgbaston, Birmingham B15 2TT, United Kingdom.
Fin: Royal National Institute for the Blind.
software; equipment; reading machine; blind; computer; teaching aid; visually handicapped
logiciel; équipement; appareil de lecture; aveugle; ordinateur; moyen d'enseignement; handicapé visuel
PROJECT DESCRIPTION
The Research Centre has a programme of individual research and development projects concerned with using and adapting microcomputer technology to allow visually handicapped children and adults to have access to databases, educational materials, and word processing systems. Software has been developed so that output can be produced in Braille, large print, computer graphics and synthetic speech. Details of software are provided by means of regular newsletters, information sheets, and software documentation, all of which is available on request from the Research Centre.

Publ: Spencer, S. & Ross, M. Visual stimulation using microcomputers. In: *European Journal of Special Needs Education*, Vol 3, No 3/1988, pp. 173-176.
Spencer, S. & Ross, M. Closing the gap, facilitating integration: microcomputer technology and the handicapped learner. In: *Special Children*, Vol 28/1989, pp. 20-21.
Spencer, S. & Ross, M. Assessing functional vision using microcomputers. In: *British Journal of Special Education*, Vol 16, No 2/1989, Research Supplement, pp. 68-70.
Spencer, S. & Ross, M. Software packages for the young visually handicapped. In: *Special Children*, No 31/1989, pp. 20-21.
Bozic, N.; Tobin, M.J. & Vallender, M. New developments in visual stimulation. In: *Visability*, Vol 3/1991, pp. 18-19, Autumn.

12663 Didactique de l'informatique.
FRA 1993
Research Date(s): 1986-1989
Rogalski, Janine; Rouchier, André; Balacheff, Nicolas; Capponi, Bernard; Dupuis, Claire; Guin, Dominique; Hoc, Jean-Michel; et al.
Inst: Ministère de la recherche, Centre national de la recherche scientifique, CNRS GDR/71, Didactique et acquisition des connaissances scientifiques, Laboratoire PSYDEE, Université de Paris V, 46 rue Saint-Jacques, 75005 Paris, France.
computer science; logical thinking; learning; cognitive development; programming
informatique; pensée logique; acquisition de connaissances; développement cognitif; programmation
PROJECT DESCRIPTION

Objectifs: Ce thème, selon le principe des groupements de recherche du CNRS est supporté par les travaux de plusieurs équipes. La didactique de l'informatique est abordée à partir de deux problématiques différentes: problématique de l'informatique comme "outil et aide à la pensée" et comme moyen de traitement d'objets mathématiques et problématique de l'enseignement de l'informatique comme discipline et domaine autonome.

Méthodologie: Les travaux entrepris sur la récursivité, sur les interactions entre concepts précurseurs et représentations du dispositif informatique, et sur le statut des méthodes de programmation reflètent l'existence de ces deux perspectives.

Résultats: Les analyses montrent deux phénomènes majeurs. (1) L'importance des prérequis liés à la notion même de variable et les relations étroites entre le codage des variables dans les procédures et la représentation du fonctionnement du dispositif informatique (distinction codage descriptif et codage analytique); (2) la lente évolution des modèles cognitifs engagés par les élèves (14-15 ans) dans l'écriture de programmes récursifs, depuis un modèle procédural, d'exécution simulée jusqu'à un modèle relationnel où les élèves établissent une relation entre la forme de l'appel récursif et les caractéristiques du résultat à obtenir. L'obstacle général est la coordination opératoire entre une représentation de type fonctionnel (ou relationnel) d'un programme comme relation statique "logique" entre données et résultats et une représentation de type procédural d'un programme comme succession de "calculs" faisant passer des données aux résultats, représentation dynamique "temporelle".

Publ: Dupuis, Claire; Egret, M.A. & Guin, Dominique. Présentation et analyse d'activités de programmation en LOGO. In: *Petit x*, 1988, n° 18, pp. 47-69.
Dupuis, Claire & Guin, Dominique. Gestion des relations entre variables dans un environnement de programmation LOGO. In: *Educational studies in mathematics*, 1989, vol. 20, n° 3.
Rouchier, André & Samurçay, Renan. Didactique de l'informatique. In: Vergnaud, Gérard et al. (Eds). *Didactique et acquisition des connaissances scientifiques*. Grenoble: La Pensée sauvage, 1988, pp. 339-360.
Rogalski, Janine & Samurçay, Renan. Acquisition of programming knowledge and skills. In: Hoc, Jean-Michel; Green, T.R.G.; Samurçay, Renan.; Gilmore, D. (Eds.). *Psychology of programming*. Londres: Academic Press Ltd, 1990.

12664 The differences in teaching and learning styles employed in primary and secondary schools with reference to developing information technology capability.
GBR 1993
Research Date(s): 1992
Kennewell, S.
Inst: University College of Swansea, Department of Education, Hendrefoilan, Swansea SA2 7NB, United Kingdom.
Fin: University of Wales.
information technology; didactic continuity; teaching method; primary education; secondary education
technologie de l'information; continuité didactique; méthode pédagogique; enseignement primaire; enseignement secondaire
PROJECT DESCRIPTION
This pilot project aims to: (1) identify current approaches to the teaching and learning of information technology (IT) in years 6 and 7 and establish an appropriate observation schedule; (2) examine the nature of changes in approach to learning IT for pupils transferring from primary to secondary school; (3) explore methods of evaluating teaching and learning where IT is involved; and (4) identify teaching approaches and learning materials which will help schools support continuity of learning and enhance progression.

The work will specifically consider the development of pupils' mental models for IT systems and processes through practical problem solving. The methods used will include: (1) a questionnaire to year 6 teachers in a sample of primary schools, and year 7 teachers whose pupils learn IT in their lessons in a sample of secondary schools; (2) an ethnographic study of a number of lessons in two secondary and two feeder primary schools; (3) interviews with pupils; and (4) analysis of learning resources.

12665 Earth science and physical geography in the secondary school curriculum: a study of current practice in one English local education authority.
GBR 1993
Research Date(s): 1985-1991
Trend, R.
Sup: Stephenson, J.; Chamberlain, P.
Inst: Exeter University, School of Education, St Luke's, Heavitree Road, Exeter EX1 2LU, United Kingdom.
earth sciences; curriculum research; physical geography; sciences
sciences de la terre; recherche sur les programmes d'études; géographie physique; sciences
PROJECT DESCRIPTION
This is a study of the geography/science interface, focusing on curriculum content, teacher co-operation, disciplines, school subjects and the relationships between the emerging National Curriculum and current practice in the schools of one English local education authority. The thesis is developed around the earth science and physical geography content of science and geography curricula at 11 to 14 years. Philosophical and historical elements are strongly represented. The empirical research initially involved a questionnaire survey of 270 geography and science teachers in the 67 schools of one English local education authority in order to examine content selection. Earth science was found to be closely associated with integrated science schemes, and physical geography with separate subject courses (as opposed to combined humanities). Fifteen "key schools" were identified from the questionnaire data, and 43 teachers were interviewed to identify critical factors in content selection. Various "models of" earth science content selection are proposed: one based on science, one on geography and one comprising a combined science/geography course, labelled "Earth Studies". National Curriculum content is used to develop a fourth "model for" earth studies at 11 to 14 years: it incorporates all relevant content from the geography and science curriculars. The conclusions address geography/science links in terms of both current practice and the opportunities provided by the National Curriculum. Earth science content selection is portrayed as essentially problematic because it straddles the geography/science interface.

12666 The effects of maturation on pupils' participation and achievement in mathematics.
GBR 1993
Research Date(s): 1992-1996
May, W.
Sup: Berry, J.; Mosley, P.
Inst: Plymouth University, Department of Mathematics and Statistics, Centre for Teaching Mathematics, Drake Circus, Plymouth PL4 8AA, United Kingdom.
mathematics; sex difference; maturity; achievement
mathématiques; différence de sexe; maturité; rendement
PROJECT DESCRIPTION
The purpose of this research is to investigate whether there are gender differences related to maturation and the particiation and achievement of pupils in mathematics, particularly of associated absences and any related psychological or physical factors.

12667 Entwicklung eines Beratungs- und Foerderangebots fuer technisch besonders kreative Jugendliche. (Development of a counselling and support programme for technically highly creative young people.)
DEU 1993
Research Date(s): 1988-1992
Geisler, H.; Facaoaru, C.
Sup: Heller, K.
Inst: Universitaet Muenchen, Fak. fuer Psychologie und Paedagogik, Institut fuer Empirische Paedagogik und Paedagogische Psychologie - Paedagogische Psychologie und Psychologische Diagnostik-, Leopoldstrasse 13, D-8000 Muenchen 40; DABEI-Institut fuer technische Kreativitaet e.V., Psychologische Beratungsstelle fuer Hochbegabtenfragen, Hansastrasse 39, D-8000 Muenchen 70.
Fin: Institution; Bundesministerium fuer Bildung und Wissenschaft.
technical education; adolescent; talent; highly gifted; creativity; remedial teaching; educational guidance
enseignement technique; adolescent; talent; surdoué; créativité; soutien pédagogique; orientation pédagogique
PROJECT DESCRIPTION
Inhalt: Themenbereich A: Einzelfallarbeit, Entwicklung und Einrichtung von Foerderangeboten. Allgemeine Zielsetzungen: Einzelfalldiagnose und Beratung zu Hochbegabungsfragen fuer Kinder und Jugendliche bzw. deren Bezugspersonen: Erprobung und Verbesserung von Diagnose- und Beratungsstrategien bzgl. Hochbegabungsdiagnose, Foerdermoeglichkeiten, Langeweile in der Schule, Leistungsstoerungen, Ueberspringen einer Jahrgangsstufe, soziale Entwicklung, Therapiebeduerftigkeit. Entwicklung und Organisation eines Kursprogrammes zur Foerderung des Lern- und Arbeitsverhaltens intellektuell besonders begabter Underachiever. Entwicklung und Organisation des Kursangebotes fuer besonders begabte Kinder und Jugendliche zur Foerderung der technischen Kreativitaet. Planung und Organisation eines Sommercamps fuer technisch besonders kreative Jugendliche. Planung und Durchfuehrung von Weiterbildungsveranstaltungen fuer Lehrer; Eltern- und Oeffentlichkeitsarbeit: Innere Differenzierung und Kreativitaetsfoerderung im Unterricht, Hinweise zum Ueberspringen, Anleitung von Elterngruppen usw. Themenbereich B: Evaluation der Foerderkurse zur technischen Kreativitaet in den Bereichen PC-Steuerung und -Regelung, Informatik und Elektronik sowie der Kurse zur Foerderung des Lern- und Arbeitsverhaltens besonders begabter Schueler/innen. Allgemeine Zielsetzungen: Evaluation der Lernvoraussetzungen: Identifikation der Begabungs-, Motivations- und Leistungsvoraussetzungen der Kursteilnehmer sowie deren Kenntnisstandes bezueglich der kursspezifischen Inhalte; Entwicklung bereichspezifischer Kenntnis-Checklisten und Kreativitaetstests mit standardisierten Auswertungskategorien; Evaluation der Lernergebnisse: Ermittlung von Veraenderungen im Bereich der kursspezifischen Fachkenntnisse, der Tiefe und Breite des technischen funktionsgebundenen Denkens, der kreativen Problemloesefaehigkeiten

und -strategien im Umgang mit fachspezifischen Inhalten; Ermittlung von Veraenderungen in der Leistungsmotivation, der Erfolgsorientiertheit, in der Breite und Tiefe der technisch-wissenschaftlichen Interessen und in den Einstellungen gegenueber Technik sowie von Veraenderungen des allgemeinen Lern- und Arbeitsverhaltens; Evaluation der Lernorganisation, der Arbeitsmethoden, der Lehrmaterialien, der Formen der Wissensvermittlung, der Kurseffektivitaet und -attraktivitaet.

Geographischer Raum: Sueddeutschland (Bayern)

Untersuchter Zeitraum: 1988 bis 1992.

Vorgehensweise: Beratungskonzepte, foerderliche und hemmende Entwicklungsbedingungen von Hochbegabung; Voraussetzungen der praktisch handwerklichen Kreativitaet und des theoretisch konstruktiven Denkens; Entwicklungsstufen technischen Denkens. Untersuchungsdesign: Evaluationsstudie; Querschnittserhebung.

Datengewinnung: Nicht-standardisiertes Interview, teilnehmende Beobachtung, Aktenanalyse (Stichprobe: 164; Kinder und Jugendliche im Alter von 2-20 Jahren bzw. deren Bezugspersonen). Befragung, postalische Befragung, psychologischer Test (Stichprobe: 164; Kinder und Jugendliche im Alter von 2-20 Jahren bzw. deren Bezugspersonen. Stichprobe: 70; Schueler/innen der 5. bis 13. Klasse. Stichprobe: 30; Schueler/innen der 9. und 10. Klasse). Beobachtung (Stichprobe: 92; Kinder und Jugendliche im Alter von 2-20 Jahren bzw. deren Bezugspersonen. Stichprobe: 70; Schueler/innen der 5. bis 13. Klasse. Stichprobe: 30; Schueler/innen der 9. und 10. Klasse). Inhaltsanalyse (Stichprobe: 70; Schueler/innen der 5. bis 13. Klasse; Stichprobe: 30; Schueler/innen der 9. und 10. Klasse). Primaererhebung: Feldarbeit von Mitarbeitern des Projektes durchgefuehrt; Datenerstellung auf der Basis von bereits vorliegenden Materialien wie Texten, Akten, Statistiken.

Auswertung: Korrelations-, Faktoren- und Varianzanalyse; F-Tests (fuer Paare); nichtparametrische Verfahren und Mittelwertsvergleiche. Datenaufbereitung: Datenedition (z.B. Aufbau von Datenbanken); Aggregierung oder Disaggregierung; Verknuepfung verschiedener Datensaetze (record linkage).

Publ: Facaoaru, C. Entwicklung und Erprobung veraenderungssensitiver Kenntnis- und Kreativitaetstests zur Erfassung des technischen Wissens und der technischen Kreativitaet. Beiheft Zeitschrift fuer Bildung und Erziehung. Koeln: Boehlau Verlag 1991.

Geisler, H.-J. Teil I: Einzelfallarbeit. Dritter Zwischenbericht zum Forschungsprojekt "Entwicklung eines Beratungs- und Foerderangebots fuer technisch besonders kreative Jugendliche". Muenchen: LMU 1990, 6-38.

Geisler, H.-J. Zusammenarbeit der Schulen mit der Psychologischen Beratungsstelle fuer Hochbegabtenfragen. Bericht an das Bayerische Staatsministerium fuer Unterricht und Kultus ueber den Einsatz staatlicher Lehrkraefte im Schuljahr 1989/90. 1990.

Geisler, H.-J. Zusammenarbeit der Schulen mit der psychologischen Beratungsstelle fuer Hochbegabtenfragen. Bericht ueber den Einsatz staatlicher Lehrkraefte im Schuljahr 1990/91 an das Bayerische Staatsministerium fuer Unterricht, Kultus, Wissenschaft und Kunst. Muenchen 1991. (Ein vollständiges Verzeichnis steht zur Verfügung.).

12668 Entwicklung eines didaktischen Konzeptes zur Vermittlung neuer Technologien in gewerblich-technischen Berufen, dargestellt am Beispiel der informationstechnischen Bildung im grafischen Gewerbe. (Development of a didactic concept for teaching new technologies in technical manufacturing occupations, with particular reference to information technology training in the graphic trade.)

DEU 1993

Research Date(s): 1990-1992

Loeffler, J.

Sup: Michelsen, U.

Inst: Technische Hochschule Aachen, Philosophische Fakultaet, Institut fuer Erziehungswissenschaft, LS Erziehungswissenschaft, Eilfschornsteinstrasse 7, D-5100 Aachen.

new technologies; didactics; technical education; vocational education; information technology; industrial training

nouvelles technologies; didactique; enseignement technique; enseignement professionnel; technologie de l'information; formation industrielle

PROJECT DESCRIPTION

Inhalt: Entwicklung eines Vorschlages zur inhaltlichen und methodischen Gestaltung einer informationstechnischen Bildung fuer die zur Zeit im Neuordnungsprozess befindlichen Berufe der Druckvorstufe des grafischen Gewerbes.

Publ: Michelsen, Uwe A. & Loeffler, Juergen. Ueberlegungen zur didaktischen Gestaltung einer informationstechnischen Grundbildung in der Bundesrepublik Deutschland. In: Szkola Zawodowa (Polen), 1990, Nr. 9.

Bindstadt, Peter; Henhagel, Wolfgang; Loeffler, Juergen & Michelsen, Uwe A. Konzeption einer informationstechnischen Grundbildung. Darmstadt: ZiT-Publik 1991.

Binstadt, Peter; Henhagel, Wolfgang; Loeffler, Juergen & Michelsen, Uwe A. Informationstechnische Grundbildung. Konzeptionen - Konkretionen - Gestaltungsvorschlaege. Alsbach: Leuchtturm-Verl. 1992.

12669 The Esprit project.

GBR 1993

Research Date(s): 1989-1992

Bliss, J.; Ogborn, J.; Martinand, J-L.; Jensen, J.

Inst: London University, King's College, 552 King's Road, London SW10 0UA, United Kingdom.

Fin: European Community.

expert system; information technology; didactic use of computer

système-expert; technologie de l'information; usage didactique de l'ordinateur

PROJECT DESCRIPTION

The aim of the research programme is to provide the specifications for explanation facilities intelligible to children within intelligent learning environments. The project was conceived in order to explore ways of closing the gap between recent research in cognitive science and education which construes explanation as a constructive act, and explanation as currently implemented in expert and knowledge-based systems.

The design of the study is fourfold: (1) to focus on children's and teachers' explanations for a given domain; (2) to examine the issues involved in implementing such explanations within an information technology learning environment; (3) to evaluate the acceptability of prototype explanation systems to children using microworld and simulation software; and (4) to specify the final prototype explanation systems.

The working group will fund individual research proposals submitted within these relevant areas. The outcomes will have both theoretical and practical significance. It will be possible to describe the explanations that satisfy children within a given domain and to compare these to those of the expert/teacher. Simultaneously, it will be possible to provide an analysis of the formal and practical problems of implementing explanation systems where explanations match both need and understanding.

12670 An evaluation of information technology development strategies in South Glamorgan schools.

GBR 1993

Research Date(s): 1991-1994

Bird, J.

Sup: Moss, G.

Inst: University of Wales College of Cardiff, School of Education, 42 Park Place, Cardiff CF1 3BB, United Kingdom.

information technology; common core curriculum; integrated curriculum; curriculum development

technologie de l'information; tronc commun; programme d'études intégré; élaboration de programmes d'études

PROJECT DESCRIPTION

The introduction of the National Curriculum has meant a change of course for information technology (IT) education. Information Technology is now statutory and designed to be taught on a cross-curricular basis.

The study will follow stages of implementation of IT into the curriculum. The research will be carried out at both primary and secondary levels and issues to be developed will be: local education authority (LEA) advisory roles; policy of school management; actual use; and attitudes of teachers. The research will need to be self-evolving in that the area is constantly undergoing change, and because of pressures of time, resources and attitudinal difficulties.

12671 Evaluation of National Curriculum Assessment at Key Stage 1 Technology.

GBR 1993

Research Date(s): 1991-1992

Harrison, I.; Dean, D.

Sup: Christie, T.

Inst: Manchester University, School of Education, Centre for Formative Assessment Studies, Oxford Road, Manchester M13 9PL, United Kingdom.

Fin: School Examinations and Assessment Council.

technology; achievement test; common core curriculum; assessment

technologie; test de rendement; tronc commun; appréciation

PROJECT DESCRIPTION

The major aim of the evaluation is to provide evidence to form the basis of an examination of National Curriculum Assessment (NCA) in Technology and to provide formative feedback to the Schools Examination and Assessment Council, the Standard Assessment Tasks development agency, local education authority trainers and moderators on the interpretation of NCA results.

12672 Evaluation von Systemdynamiksoftware. (Evaluation of systems dynamics software.)

AUT 1993

Research Date(s): 1991-1992

Ossimitz, Guenther; Schloeglhofer, Franz.

Inst: Institut fuer Mathematik, Universitaetsstrasse 65-67, A-9020 Klagenfurt.

Universitaet fuer Bildungswissenschaften, Universitaetsstrasse 65-67, A-9020 Klagenfurt

Fin: Bundesministerium fuer Unterricht und Kunst.

software; simulation; evaluation

logiciel; simulation; évaluation
PROJECT DESCRIPTION

Ziel der Untersuchung war es, fuenf fuer den schulischen Einsatz geeignete Softwareprogramme zur Systemdynamik auf ihre Eignung zur Modellierung und Simulation dynamischer Modelle zu ueberpruefen. Ausgewaehlt wurden fuenf relativ leistungsfaehige Produkte mit einem recht weit streuenden Spektrum an Leistungsmerkmalen, die unter dem Betriebssystem MS-DOS oder auf Apple-MacIntosh Computern laufen, und zwar konkret: Models (Lascaux Graphics, DOS und Apple); Vudynamo (Piet van Blokland, DOS); Modus (Comet Verlag, DOS); Stella II (High Performance Systems Inc., Apple); Supercalc 5 (Computer Associates, DOS). Um einen einheitlichen Untersuchungsraster zu erhalten, wurde zunaechst ein Kriterienkatalog entwickelt, der einerseits einen technischen Fragebogen und andererseits einen Satz von fuenf standardisierten praktischen Aufgaben umfasste, die mit den einzelnen Produkten moeglichst vollstaendig geloest werden sollten. Alle Produkte wurden anhand des Kriterienkatalogs ueberprueft und die Ergebnisse zusammengefasst. Es liegt ein Projektbericht im Umfang von 80 Seiten vor.

12673 An exploration into the notion of levels of attainment in mathematics.
GBR   1993
Research Date(s): 1989-1993
Melrose, J.
Sup: Schwarzenberger, R.
Inst: Loughborough University of Technology, Department of Education, Loughborough LE11 3TU, United Kingdom; Warwick University, Department of Science Education, Coventry CV4 7AL, United Kingdom.
mathematics; achievement; underachievement
mathématiques; rendement; rendement déficient
PROJECT DESCRIPTION

This research is a comparison of young children and older low-attainers in their thinking about mathematics topics including subtraction and three dimensional visualisation. The methods employed are principally individual interviews with the children together with reflections from their teachers.

12674 Exploratory Data Analysis (extension).
GBR   1993
Research Date(s): 1990-1991
Ogborn, J.; Hawkins, A.
Inst: London University, Institute of Education, Department of Science Education, 20 Bedford Way, London WC1H 0AL, United Kingdom.
Fin: Nuffield Foundation.
statistical data; statistical analysis; teaching method
données statistiques; analyse statistique; méthode pédagogique
PROJECT DESCRIPTION

In many areas of the school curriculum students come across quantitative data - in the form of tables, graphs, charts and so on. They are also confronted by data in newspapers and on television, and by arguments based on such data. This project is a small-scale experiment aimed at teaching ways of understanding and looking critically at such data. The material produced will be aimed primarily at the 16-18 age range, but much of it will also be appropriate at GCSE level.

Exploratory Data Analysis (EDA) may be used in a wide range of curriculum areas, and the materials will cover not only the concepts and techniques of EDA but also its applications in different subjects. It is hoped that students will gain greater confidence in the handling of quantitative data, and will be able to formulate and criticize arguments based on such data. They should develop skills of analysing and presenting data to the best effect.
Publ: Boohan, R. & Ogborn, J. *Making Sense of Data*. Harlow: Longman, 1991.
Ogborn, J. Making sense of data: Ein Projekt zur Entwicklung von Materialien zur Explorative Datenanalyse im Schulunterricht. In: *Der Mathematikunterricht*, Special issue, Explorative Datenanalyse im Mathematikunterricht, Journal 37, Heft 6/1991, pp. 54-63, November.

12675 Flexible learning approaches in sixth-form mathematics.
GBR   1993
Research Date(s): 1989-1991
Ahmed, A.; Oldknow, A.; Williams, H.
Inst: West Sussex Institute of Higher Education, The Dome, Upper Bognor Road, Bognor Regis PO21 1HR, United Kingdom.
Fin: Training, Enterprise and Education Directorate.
mathematics; teaching method; post-compulsory education
mathématiques; méthode pédagogique; enseignement postobligatoire
PROJECT DESCRIPTION

This project has identified an urgent need to seek ways of establishing long-term productive links with industry and commerce that are self-sustaining, and focus on what education and industry have to offer each other in the context of mathematics. In order that the efforts and resources committed by industry, commerce and education accrue maximum benefit, industry must become an integral resource for schools and vice-versa.

The central aim is to broaden teachers', students' and society's perception of what constitutes the effective learning of a crucial subject such as mathematics and to enable young people, particularly in the 16-19 age range, to gain maximum benefit from their education and training. In particular the strategies and publications developed are designed to: (1) motivate students by offering them access to mathematics being used in both abstract and real contexts; (2) encapsulate 'real-world' situations to encourage the natural interest of students; (3) encourage teachers and students to use resources more effectively, including a wide range of technological devices, databases etc.; (4) act as a catalyst for changing classroom approaches to using and applying mathematics; (5) offer students opportunities to encounter mathematics; (6) through challenging tasks, support teachers and students in diagnosis, self-evaluation and record keeping; (7) encourage teachers to become discerning users of support materials; (8) provide opportunities for exploiting the connections that already exist between mathematics and other subject areas; and (9) provide a basis and resource for staff development in order to involve a wider group of teachers in sustained professional development programmes.
Publ: Ahmed, A.; Oldknow, A.F. & Williams, H. *Sixth-form mathematics*. Bognor: West Sussex Institute of Higher Education, Mathematics Centre, 1990.
Ahmed, A.; Oldknow, A.F. & Williams, H. *Mathematics in context*. Bognor: West Sussex Institute of Higher Education, Mathematics Centre, 1990.
Ahmed, A.; Oldknow, A.F. & Williams, H. *Using resources*. Bognor: West Sussex Institute of Higher Education, Mathematics Centre, 1990.
Ahmed, A.; Oldknow, A.F. & Williams, H. *Using a microcomputer in sixth form mathematics classrooms*. Bognor: West Sussex Institute of Higher Education, Mathematics Centre, 1990.

12676 Fonctionnement et dysfonctionnements du système didactique en mathématique: échecs, thérapeutique et remédiations.
FRA   1993
Research Date(s): 1987-
Blanchard-Laville, Claudine; Chevallard, Yvon; Berdot, Pierre; Amigues, René; Mercier, Alain.
Inst: Ministère de la recherche, Centre national de la recherche scientifique, CNRS GDR/71, Didactique et acquisition des connaissances scientifiques, Laboratoire PSYDEE, Université de Paris V, 46 rue Saint-Jacques, 75005 Paris, France.
mathematics; learning difficulty; therapy; didactics; comparative analysis; compensatory education
mathématiques; difficulté de l'apprentissage; thérapie; didactique; analyse comparative; éducation compensatoire
PROJECT DESCRIPTION

Objectifs: Ce thème selon le principe des groupes de recherche du Centre national de la recherche scientifique est supporté par les travaux de plusieurs équipes. (1) De précédentes recherches ont mis en perspective les interactions auprès d'élèves en difficulté en mathématiques guidés par des approches à orientation psychanalytique ou didactique. Cette comparaison-confrontation a montré la nécessité pour chacune des approches d'expliciter le cadre conceptuel, les hypothèses de travail et les choix méthodologiques, et de rechercher leur compatibilité. (2) Un autre cycle d'échanges a pris appui sur l'analyse croisée d'un même corpus: une séquence d'un cours de mathématiques enregistrée en classe de première B. On a pu explorer par le biais de différentes théories de la communication, la dynamique des interactions de ce professeur avec ses élèves en lien avec sa fantasmatique personnelle et en fonction de son propre rapport au savoir mathématique; on a également examiné la discussion des erreurs mathématiques relevées dans les énoncés du discours de ce professeur.
Publ: Berdot, Pierre; Blanchard-Laville, Claudine & Mercier, Alain. Quelques éléments méthodologiques et théoriques issus de l'analyse de suivis individuels d'élèves en échec en mathématiques. In: Vergnaud, Gérard et al. (eds.). *Didactique et acquisition des connaissances scientifiques*. Grenoble: La Pensée sauvage, 1988.
Blanchard-Laville, Claudine & Obertelli, P. Rappport au savoir mathématique et médiation didactique. Etude clinique d'une situation didactique. In: Beillerot, Jacky; Bouillet, A.; Blanchard-Laville, Claudine; Mosconi, Nicole. *Savoir et rapport au savoir. Elaborations théoriques et cliniques*. Bégédis, Editions universitaires, 1989.
Blanchard-Laville, Claudine. Questions à la didactique des mathématiques. In: *Revue française de pédagogie*, 1989, n° 89, pp. 63-70.

12677 Formation et écologie.
FRA   1993
Research Date(s): 1983-1990
Pineau, Gaston.
Inst: Université de Tours, UFR Arts et sciences humaines, Laboratoire des sciences de l'éducation et de la formation, 3 rue des Tanneurs, bureau 405, 37041 Tours Cedex, France.
Fin: Université de Montréal (Québec), Centre de coopération interuniversitaire franco-québécoise.
ecology; training programme; environmental study
écologie; programme de formation; étude du milieu
PROJECT DESCRIPTION

Objectifs: Il s'agit de poser les bases pratiques et théoriques d'une auto-écoformation et de développer ce que Bachelard appelait une initiation aux éléments. Hypothèse: (1) La formation humaine passe par l'établissement d'un rapport personnel aux éléments matériels; (2) une société écologique ne se construira que par la prise de conscience des rapports vitaux, personnels et collectifs, aux éléments matériels. Cadre théorique: La théorie tripolaire de la formation et l'écosystémisme.

Méthodologie: (1) Groupe de travail interdisciplinaire et interprofessionnel combinant production personnelle et confrontation collective; (2) travail sur un premier élément: l'air.

Résultats: Respirer, aérer, s'aérer, habiter ciel et terre et s'aérodynamiser sont cinq apprentissages de base de l'auto-écoformation aérienne.

Publ: Pineau, Gaston (coord.). De l'air. Essai d'écoformation. Paris: Païdéia, Montréal: Sciences et culture, 1992, 269p.

12678 Formation par la recherche.
FRA 1993
Research Date(s): 1987-1989
Shinn, Terry.
Inst: Université de Paris IV, CNRS URA/886, Groupe d'études des méthodes de l'analyse sociologique, 54 bd Raspail, 75006 Paris, France.
engineering; electronics; electrical engineering; research project; in-plant training; graduate study; post-graduate study
ingénierie; électronique; électrotechnique; projet de recherche; stage en entreprise; supérieur deuxième cycle; supérieur troisième cycle
PROJECT DESCRIPTION
Objectifs: Dans le cadre d'une étude des innovations dans l'enseignement de l'ingénierie dans la France d'aujourd'hui, cette recherche s'est centrée dans le domaine de l'électronique et de l'électrotechnique sur deux établissements: l'Ecole supérieure d'ingénieurs en électrotechnique et électronique et l'Ecole supérieure d'électricité. La France possède deux systèmes de formation par la recherche depuis 1981: d'un côté un programme officiel, centralisé et co-dirigé par des professeurs et des bureaux d'études et de recherche des entreprises qui finance 600 jeunes ingénieurs pour suivre leurs études jusqu'au niveau du doctorat, de l'autre la formation par la recherche définie et organisée au sein de chaque école donc décentralisée et variable dans son fonctionnement, ne dépassant pas le niveau maîtrise.

Résultats: Les deux programmes se distinguent des enseignements traditionnels: (1) les ingénieurs-élèves se penchent sur de véritables problèmes de recherche; (2) les élèves sont autonomes, ils reçoivent un minimum de direction de leurs enseignants; (3) ils sont à mi-chemin entre les entreprises et les universités. L'évaluation des nouveaux programmes par les industriels se révèle assez contradictoire. La direction des grandes entreprises est très favorable à la formation par la recherche. Les cadres supérieurs des entreprises donnent des notes élevées aux travaux des diplômés des programmes de formation, néanmoins ils pensent que la formation par la recherche ne fait que désigner des personnes déjà motivées par la technologie et aptes à fournir un travail très supérieur.

Publ: Shinn, Terry. Ingénieurs et industriels face à la formation par la recherche. Paris: CNRS, rapport de recherche, avril 1989, 52p.

12679 The history of geological and earth science education in the United Kingdom.
GBR 1993
Research Date(s): 1970-
Thompson, D.
Inst: Keele University, Department of Education, Keele, Staffordshire ST5 5BG, United Kingdom.
physical sciences; history of education; earth sciences; geology; science education
sciences physiques; histoire de l'éducation; sciences de la terre; géologie; éducation scientifique
PROJECT DESCRIPTION
The history of geological and earth science education in the United Kingdom reveals the important part that geology, geologists and the geological profession played in the early days of the growth of science education from 1830 to 1900 in both schools and vocational courses, e.g. of the Department of Science and Arts. The wives of geologists were in the van of women's education and extra-mural education. A decline to a nadir in the 1930s has been followed by a steady rise in the growth of interest, culminating in the formation of the Association of Teachers of Geology (1967) (now the Earth Science Teachers' Association (1988)) and the acceptance of earth science in the National Science Curriculum (1989).

Publ: Thompson, D.B. MIMCU, Geoff Cox and the future of the Ecton Hill Education Centre. In: Geoscientist, Vol 1, No 5/1991, pp. 12-17.

12680 Humanities and information technology (Extension).
GBR 1993
Research Date(s): 1990-1992
Dickinson, A.; Kent, A.

Inst: London University, Institute of Education, Department of History, Humanities and Philosophy, 20 Bedford Way, London WC1H OAL, United Kingdom.
Fin: National Council for Educational Technology.
information technology; didactic use of computer; humanities
technologie de l'information; usage didactique de l'ordinateur; études littéraires
PROJECT DESCRIPTION
The project aims to support teachers' groups in history, humanities and geography who wish to explore ways in which information technology can be effectively used. It also aims to encourage collaboration between local education authorities and initial teacher training institutions and dissemination of good practice at local, regional and national levels.

Publ: NCET. Interpretations of women 1890-1914 - The Suffragettes. NCET/Longman, 1992.
NCET. Trading people. NCET/Longman, 1992.
NCET. A day in the life of a National Park. NCET/Longman, 1990.
NCET. Weather and people. NCET/Longman, 1990.

12681 I fabbisogni formativi nel settore della telematica nella prospettiva dell'istituzione di un indirizzo per le scienze informatiche e telematiche. (Educational needs in the telematic sector and prospects for creating a course in computer science.)
ITA 1993
Research Date(s): 1988-1989
Vitale, I.; Chinenti, R.; De Salvia, M.R.; Bianchini, V.
Sup: Scaglione, M.
Inst: Istituto di Ricerche Economiche e Sociali sul Mezzogiorno Europeo - IRESME (Institute of Economic and Social Research in Southern Europe), Via Molveno 87, 00135 Roma, Italy.
Fin: Ministero della Pubblica Istruzione, Ufficio Studi e Programmazione.
computer science; computer literacy; educational need; manpower need; upper secondary; curriculum development; training need
informatica; initiation à l'informatique; besoin d'éducation; besoin de main-d'oeuvre; secondaire deuxième cycle; élaboration de programmes d'études; besoin de formation
PROJECT DESCRIPTION
Aim: To determine, with the help of suitable instruments and methods: the interest of employers in computer science training; the kind of training that is needed; the skills acquired in this sector by those who have already taken courses; the practicability of a computer science course that is integrated with a course of general studies.

Methods: The six principal phases of the research were: bibliographic research; analysis of a number of teaching programmes identified in the literature; examination of relevant experiences abroad; surveys of the main Italian employers and workers trained in computer science; formulation of a hypothesis on an appropriate curriculum for upper secondary schools.

Results: Analysis of the questionnaire responses shows that a high percentage (around 87%) of companies organize computer science courses for their personnel. 94% of companies consider that secondary schools should provide basic training in this area. These skills should be accessible to all pupils in state schools, so that no one leaving school is functionally illiterate in the domain of computer science. It is moreover proposed that a minimum level of basic knowledge of the working environment be imparted to pupils through the use of a multidisciplinary approach. Given the prospect that compulsory education will be extended to 16 years, a proposal is made for a two-year curriculum for basic computer literacy and a three-year curriculum for further computer studies. The value of this type of instruction for the "recycling" of personnel is also emphasized. Teachers should be the first to be updated in this field.

12682 Iconic model maker.
GBR 1993
Research Date(s): 1990-1992
Ogborn, J.
Inst: London University, Institute of Education, Department of Science Education, 20 Bedford Way, London WC1H OAL, United Kingdom.
Fin: National Council for Educational Technology.
software; didactic use of computer; science education
logiciel; usage didactique de l'ordinateur; éducation scientifique
PROJECT DESCRIPTION
The aim was to develop a novel object-oriented computer modelling facility for early secondary and late primary use. The program is an extension of the concept of a cell automaton. Pupils and teachers can specify rules for how objects and backgrounds behave: movement, interaction, appearance, disappearance and change. These facilities make it possible to generate models from very simple games up to diffusion, crystal growth and ecological interactions.

Publ: Ogborn, J. A future for modelling in science education. In: Journal of Computer Assisted Learning, Vol 6, No 2/1990, pp. 103-112.
Ogborn, J. Modellizzazione con l'elaboratore: possibilita e prospettive. In: La Fisica nella Scuola, Anno XXIII, No 2/1990, pp. 32-43.

Ogborn, J. Modelacao com o computador: possibilidades e perspectivas. In: Teodoro V.D. & Freitas, J.C. (eds.). *Educacao e computadores*, Lisbon, Portugal: Ministerio da Educacao, 1991.

12683   Il concetto di data base per un sistema autore. (Database concept for the authoring workbench.)
ITA   1994
Research Date(s): 1992-1994
Persico, Donatella; Chioccariello, Augusto; Viarengo, Vittorio; Olimpo, Giorgio; Van Marke, Kris; Lousteau, Benoit.
Sup: Sarti, Luigi.
Inst: Istituto per le Tecnologie Didattiche - ITD (Institute for Educational Technology), Via all'Opera Pia 11, 16145 Genova, Italy.
Consiglio Nazionale delle Ricerche - CNR (National Research Council), Piazzale Aldo Moro 7, 00185 Roma, Italy
Fin: Comunit Economica Europea.
educational technology; information technology; educational software; authoring system; software library; multimedia system
technologie de l'éducation; technologie de l'information; didacticiel; système-auteur; logithèque; système multimédia
PROJECT DESCRIPTION
This project is workpackage 8 of the "D2008-DISCOURSE" project (Design and Interactive Specification of COURSEware) in which the Institute for Educational Technology participates as a partner under the auspices of the European DELTA programme.

The main objective of DISCOURSE is the development and testing of a multimedia authoring environment that includes support instruments for the author in the various phases of a project or the production of software.

The DBLM (Database of Learning Materials) is a data base which aims at the realization of the concept of "reusability", not only of completed multimedia materials but also of information related to the various phases of the cycle of courseware production (representation of the knowledge domain, teaching strategies, student models, etc.). Within the consortium, the Institute for Educational Technology will define the structure of DBLM that will constitute the common storehouse of a set of applied tools, each dedicated to the support of a specific activity pertaining to courseware development. The DBLM will assume, therefore, a central role in the architecture of the system, and will allow the various applications to communicate among themselves and to be integrated, guaranteeing a common base for the integration of the hardware-software platform.

12684   The implementation of the National Curriculum in mathematics: the effects of Key Stage 2 in primary schools.
GBR   1993
Research Date(s): 1990-1994
Koshy, V.
Sup: Ernest, P.
Inst: West London Institute of Higher Education, Gordon House, 300 St Margaret's Road, Twickenham TW1 1PT, United Kingdom; Exeter University, Northcote House, The Queen's Drive, Exeter EX4 4QJ, United Kingdom.
mathematics; primary education; common core curriculum; curriculum development
mathématiques; enseignement primaire; tronc commun; élaboration de programmes d'études
PROJECT DESCRIPTION
The aims of the study are to: (1) find out to what extent changes have been made to the teaching and learning of mathematics in schools as a result of the implementation of the National Curriculum; (2) monitor classroom practice in schools at present, in the National Curriculum context and compare it with what used to be the case, referring to curriculum development documents and surveys. The methodology employed includes questionnaires, interviews and case studies.

From the data so far collected the following are noted: (1) there is a marked difference between the responses to questions supplied by teachers on in-service courses in mathematics, and teachers who are not; (2) there is increased awareness of investigative work; (3) group work is being attempted by teachers who use a variety of styles of groups; (4) assessment and record keeping seem to be an area of concern; (5) there is an increased dependence on schemes.

12685   An individualised patient education programme for community pharmacy practice.
GBR   1993
Research Date(s): 1990-1994
Lindsay, G.; Hesketh, A.
Sup: Harden, R.
Inst: Dundee University, Centre for Medical Education, Ninewells Hospital and Medical School, Dundee DD1 9SY, United Kingdom.
Fin: Scottish Office, Home and Health Department.
medicine; pharmaceutics; patient; medical service
médecine; pharmacie; malade; service médical
PROJECT DESCRIPTION
This project aims to develop and study a practical system to provide patient education via the community pharmacy. This will involve the use of new technology to provide user-friendly interactive patient education materials. An important aspect of the project will look at ways of developing and studying a liaison between pharmacists, general practitioners, and patients.

12686   Informační systémy pro podporu a řízení výuky. (Information systems to support teaching and classroom management.)
CSK   1994
Research Date(s): 1992-1993
Cernochová, M.; Sinor, S.; Novák, J.; Slavík, J.; Fulková, M.; Kubínová, M.; Pastorová, D.; Solcová, A.
Sup: Helus, Z.
Inst: Pedagogická fakulta Univerzity Karlovy (Charles University, Faculty of Education), M.D. Rettigové 4, 116 39 Praha 1, Czech Republic.
Ministerstvo školství, mládeže a tělovýchovy (Ministry of Education, Youth and Physical Education), Karmelitská 7, 118 00 Praha 1, Czech Republic
information technology; class management; lesson preparation; further education of teachers
technologie de l'information; conduite de la classe; préparation des cours; perfectionnement des enseignants
PROJECT DESCRIPTION
Aim: (1) To develop an information system to support teaching and classroom management in primary and secondary schools; (2) to improve, with the help of this system, the quality of lesson preparation and evaluation.

The project incorporates elements from educational management theory, educational information theory and theories of teaching practice.

Results: So far, computer programs have been developed for art education and mathematics.
Publ: Cernochová, M. & Slavík, J. *Zpráva o řešení a výsledcích projektu: Informační systémy pro podporu a řízení výuky.* Praha: Pedagogická fakulta UK, 1993.
Slavík, J. *Informační systém jako podpora psychodidaktického rozhodování.* Praha: Pedagogická fakulta UK, 1993.
Cernochová, M.; Novák, J. & Sinor, S. *Technické a programové řešení informačního systému.* Praha: Pedagogická fakulta UK, 1993.
Cernochová, M.; Novák, J. & Sinor, S. *Příručka k obsluze informačního systému.* Praha: Pedagogická fakulta UK, 1993.
Novák, J. & Sinor, S. *Ukázka informačního systému pro podporu a řízení výuky matematiky a výtvarné výchovy. Programové řešení.*

12687   Information technology development programme for teachers.
GBR   1993
Research Date(s): 1989-1992
Winch, J.
Inst: Jordanhill College of Education, Division of Business & Computer Education, Southbrae Drive, Glasgow G13 1PP, United Kingdom.
Fin: Training, Enterprise and Education Directorate.
information technology; further education of teachers; teaching aid; didactic use of computer
technologie de l'information; perfectionnement des enseignants; moyen d'enseignement; usage didactique de l'ordinateur
PROJECT DESCRIPTION
This is a programme for staff development in schools dealing with awareness and perspectives on applying information technology (IT) in classrooms; managerial skills and classroom strategies in IT; and professional skills in the methodology of IT. Various booklets and education materials will be produced.

12688   Information technology in education and employment.
GBR   1993
Research Date(s): 1986-1992
Wellington, J.
Inst: Sheffield University, Division of Education, 388 Glossop Road, Sheffield S10 2TN, United Kingdom.
Fin: Training Agency; Universities Funding Council.
information technology; computer; training-employment relationship; occupational qualification; training need; industry
technologie de l'information; ordinateur; relation formation-emploi; qualification professionnelle; besoin de formation; industrie
PROJECT DESCRIPTION
This research carries on from the previous research project 'Skills for the Future'. The research has arisen from the increase in the use of microcomputers in both education and industry. In consequence, greater attention has been paid to the need for specific 'information technology skills' - skills which need to be taught in schools, colleges and training schemes to meet the needs of industry. This project draws on interviews with a sample of employers, questionnaire responses, in-depth interviews and case studies. By also considering previous research in the area, the project gives a detailed investigation into present provision, aims, and policy in training related to 'IT' (Information Technology) and discusses how this provision relates to employers' needs and requirements. The final publication gives a clear and accessible overview of the connection between IT and industry's needs.

Publ: Wellington, J.J. *Education for employment: the place of information technology*. Windsor: NFER-Nelson, 1989.

12689 Information technology in initial teacher training.
GBR 1993
Research Date(s): 1990-1991
Munro, R.; Ramsay, A.
Inst: Jordanhill College of Education, Division of Business & Computer Education, Southbrae Drive, Jordanhill, Glasgow G13 1PP, United Kingdom.
information technology; didactic use of computer; teacher education
technologie de l'information; usage didactique de l'ordinateur; formation des enseignants
PROJECT DESCRIPTION
This is an assessment of the impact on and influence of information technology in the delivery and methodology of Jordanhill College courses in initial teacher training and the formulation and refinement of strategies to exploit the education potential and enhance the educational effectiveness of this resource.

12690 The information technology in mathematics project.
GBR 1993
Research Date(s): 1989-
Tanner, H.
Inst: University College of Swansea, Department of Education, Hendrefoilan, Swansea SA2 7NB, United Kingdom.
Fin: University of Wales.
information technology; mathematics; didactic use of computer
technologie de l'information; mathématiques; usage didactique de l'ordinateur
PROJECT DESCRIPTION
This is a survey of the use of information technology for teaching mathematics in England and Wales. A network of schools has been set up to develop and trial materials and techniques for teaching elements from both the Mathematics and Information Technology (IT) National Curricula. It includes work on spreadsheets, logo and databases.

12691 Information technology: software in primary schools.
GBR 1993
Research Date(s): 1991-1992
Harris, S.
Sup: Whetton, C.
Inst: National Foundation for Educational Research, The Mere, Upton Park, Slough SL1 2DQ, United Kingdom.
Fin: National Foundation for Educational Research.
information technology; common core curriculum; technology; primary education; software; hardware
technologie de l'information; tronc commun; technologie; enseignement primaire; logiciel; matériel informatique
PROJECT DESCRIPTION
Information technology (IT) capability is one of the attainment targets of Technology in the National Curriculum. Within the non-statutory guidance provided by the National Curriculum Council, five strands of information technology capability are identified: communicating information; handling information; modelling; measurement and control; and applications and effects. The first four strands are related to types of software, the fifth is not.
The research aims to investigate the range of software in use in primary schools to support the first four strands of IT capability. In addition, the following areas will be investigated: the provision of hardware within schools; sources used by schools to obtain software; and the range of support services offered by local education authorities (LEAs).
Data will be collected from the following sources: (a) interviews with a small number of LEA IT advisers; (b) a questionnaire survey of all LEA IT advisers in England and Wales; (c) a questionnaire survey of a sample of 400 schools within the primary sector in England and Wales.
Publ: A report is available from the NFER.

12692 Initial teacher education and the new technology.
GBR 1993
Research Date(s): 1990-1992
Blackmore, M.; Clemson, D.
Inst: Liverpool John Moores University, School of Education and Community Studies, I.M. Marsh Campus, Barkhill Road, Liverpool L17 6BD, United Kingdom.
Fin: National Council for Educational Technology.
information technology; teacher education
technologie de l'information; formation des enseignants
PROJECT DESCRIPTION
This project has four main elements: (1) an evaluation of the explicit information technology inputs on all initial teacher training (ITT) courses in this institution; (2) an audit of current implicit use of information technology across all routes and areas of the ITT courses; (3) assessment of the status quo in schools in the region; and (4) suggestions for an institutional staff development programme.

12693 Integracja komputera z video w procesie kształcenia. (Integration of computer and video in the teaching process.)
POL 1993
Research Date(s): 1989-
Brelińska, Krystyna; Buda, Michał; Dylak, Stanisław; Kakolewicz, Mariusz; Kurkowski, Zdzisław; Michałowski, Marian; Łukaszewicz, Albert; et al.
Sup: Strykowski, Wacław.
Inst: Zakład Technologii Kształcenia Instytutu Pedagogiki Uniwersytetu im. Adama Mickiewicza (Adam Mickiewicz University, Institute of Pedagogy, Department of Educational Technology), Słowackiego 20, 60-823 Poznań, Poland.
Instytut Badań Edukacyjnych (Institute for Educational Research), Górczewska 8, 01-180 Warszawa, Poland
Fin: Ministry of National Education; Committee for Scientific Research.
educational technology; interactive video; computer; didactic use of computer
technologie de l'éducation; vidéo interactive; ordinateur; usage didactique de l'ordinateur
PROJECT DESCRIPTION
Aims: (1) To develop theoretical and methodological foundations for the integration of computer and video as a new interactive teaching aid; (2) to design a unified operational system integrating computer and video under the conditions of the Polish education system; (3) to design and test exemplary interactive programs.
Design: (1) Examination of relevant literature and technical equipment; (2) design of a unified operational system integrating computer and video; (3) design of interactive programs; implementation of programs on different types of computer; testing of programs in the educational process; (4) presentation of the results in the form of theoretical and methodological publications and interactive programs.
Hypothesis: The integration of computer and video will result in the development of a new interactive multimedia teaching aid of high quality.
Methods: (1) Pedagogical and technical analysis; (2) model construction and design; (3) pilot research; (4) pedagogical experiment.
Publ: Strykowski, Wacław (ed.). *Wideo interaktywne w kształceniu multimedialnym*. Poznań: Wyd. Zakład Technologii Kształcenia UAM, 1991.

12694 INTENT (Initial Teacher Education and New Technology).
GBR 1993
Research Date(s): 1990-1992
Somekh, B.
Inst: University of East Anglia, School of Education, Norwich NR4 7TJ, United Kingdom.
Fin: National Council for Educational Technology.
information technology; teacher education; training of trainers
technologie de l'information; formation des enseignants; formation des formateurs
PROJECT DESCRIPTION
Project INTENT has been set up as a response to the report 'Information Technology in Initial Teacher Training' (DES, HMSO 1989) and the revised criteria of the Council for Accreditation of Teacher Education (1989). It is concerned with supporting development work with information technology (IT) in Initial Teacher Training. It has four main foci: (1) developing the quality of teaching and learning with IT; (2) providing support for lecturers integrating IT across the curriculum for initial teacher training; (3) developing management strategies to enable (1) and (2) above; (4) monitoring the processes of institutional change.
In five initial teacher training establishments (two university departments, two colleges and a polytechnic department) a staff development tutor (with no teaching responsibility for the first year) and a senior manager are leading the development process and monitoring its impact. INTENT has an educational rather than a technological focus, and is adopting a research approach to development, believing research and formative evaluation to be essential components of successful development work. In addition to the action-focused research activities at the core of its work, INTENT is supporting individual tutors and lecturers engaging in IT-related research, using a range of methodologies.
Outcomes will include case studies and associated research reports. There will be an emphasis on sharing the practical and theoretical findings of the project with colleagues in other initial teacher training establishments.

12695 Internationale Vergleichbarkeit von Bildungsstatistiken: eine Untersuchung moeglicher Verzerrungen beim internationalen Vergleich von Hochschulstatistiken. (International comparability of education statistics: a study of possible distortions in international comparisons of university statistics.)
DEU 1993
Research Date(s): 1992
Schacher, M.
Sup: Kazemzadeh, F.
Inst: HIS Hochschul-Informations-System GmbH, Goseriede 9, D-3000 Hannover.

statistical data; university; Germany; USA; education system

données statistiques; université; Allemagne; Etats-Unis; système d'enseignement

PROJECT DESCRIPTION

Inhalt: Daten zur Darstellung von nationalen Bildungsleistungen und zu deren internationalem Vergleich werden mit Hilfe des UNESCO-Schluessels "International Standard Classification of Education" (ISCED) hierarchisch klassifiziert, d.h. u.a. dem primaeren, sekundaeren bzw. tertiaeren Sektor zugeordnet. Es wird angenommen, dass durch die besonderen Zuordnungskriterien des ISCED Verzerrungen in der Weise zustandekommen, dass vergleichbare Ausbildungsgaenge z.B. in den USA zum tertiaeren Sektor, in Deutschland aber zum sekundaeren gezaehlt werden.

Geographischer Raum: Deutschland, USA, UK.

Untersuchter Zeitraum: Ende der 1980er Jahre.

Vorgehensweise: Vergleichende Untersuchung. Untersuchungsdesign: Grundlage internationaler Datenvergleiche.

Datengewinnung: Datenerstellung auf der Basis von bereits vorliegenden Materialien wie Texten, Akten, Statistiken.

12696   An investigation into errors made in attempts to solve mathematical problems.

GBR   1993

Research Date(s): 1988-1992

De Medeiros, C.

Sup: Orton, A.

Inst: Leeds University, School of Education, Leeds LS2 9JT, United Kingdom.

Fin: Brazilian Government.

mathematics; arithmetic; error; teaching method; problem solving; primary education

mathématiques; arithmétique; erreur; méthode pédagogique; résolution de problème; enseignement primaire

PROJECT DESCRIPTION

The study aims to investigate teacher perceptions of pupils' errors in elementary arithmetic with a view to developing teacher training techniques which will enable teachers to improve their teaching methods. Selected groups of young pupils have been tested using simple problems and their errors have been classified by teachers in training, in a preparatory study aimed at clarifying the issues and problems. A further study of pupils' problem solving has yielded data which is currently being analysed.

12697   An investigation into the feasibility of presenting mathematics in the same form to pupils within National Curriculum key stages 2, 3 and 4.

GBR   1993

Research Date(s): 1993-1995

Graham, J.

Inst: Plymouth University, Rolle Faculty of Education, Douglas Avenue, Exmouth EX8 2AT, United Kingdom.

mathematics; assessment; teaching objective; achievement

mathématiques; appréciation; objectif pédagogique; rendement

PROJECT DESCRIPTION

Circular No. 17/91 (Department of Education and Science, 1991) states that "teachers are required to teach with a view to pupils achieving levels of attainment within the ranges specified for that key stage." The aim of the research is to ascertain how realistic it is to present pupils in different key stages with common 'teaching materials' aimed at giving them opportunities to achieve common levels of attainment.

It is envisaged that four different teaching 'units' will be employed and four different 'clusters' of schools will be sought comprising the following types: (a) primary - pupils aged 10/11, and middle - pupils aged 11 (key stage 2); (b) lower secondary - pupils aged 14 (key stage 3); (c) upper secondary - pupils aged 16 (key stage 4). In total, 16 groups/classes will be approached. The research will include a quantitative analysis of the effectiveness of the teaching materials used, using a two-way analysis of variance linked to a Latin square design.

12698   An investigation of teachers' mathematical subject knowledge and the processes of instruction in reception classes.

GBR   1993

Research Date(s): 1989-1992

Aubrey, C.

Sup: McNamara, D.

Inst: Durham University, School of Education, Leazes Road, Durham DH1 1TA, United Kingdom; Hull University, School of Education, Cottingham Road, Hull HU6 7RX, United Kingdom.

mathematics; early childhood education; teaching method; learning strategy; knowledge; primary education

mathématiques; éducation de la prime enfance; méthode pédagogique; stratégie d'apprentissage; connaissance; enseignement primaire

PROJECT DESCRIPTION

This research looks at the teaching of mathematics in infant classes. The main phase of the project (1991-1992) will be a direct follow-on to existing research which has been established for three years. The aims are to: (1) investigate teachers' pedagogical subject knowledge, in particular in terms

of its influence on beliefs and the content and processes of mathematical instruction in reception classes (this is an area with a small, but mainly US research interest, which has concentrated on addition and subtraction word problems); (2) take existing data on children's informal knowledge in key areas of mathematics at school entry, as a starting point for accessing teachers' understanding of how children think about mathematics, and knowledge about their own pupils' thinking (these data are available already from work carried out by the researchers with previous grants); (3) consider the co-ordination and utilisation of teacher and pupil knowledge within the complex world of classrooms (only limited research attention has been paid to this area); (4) consider the implications of the study for the mathematics curriculum for children's first year at school.

The early part of the project involved devising, piloting and revising complex mathematical assessment interviews for young children entering school. Data have been collected for around 90 children. The main phase of the project will entail observing some of the previously assessed children through their first year in school, using field notes, tape-recorded interactions, interviews with class teachers, and re-assessment of the children at the end of May, 1992. Observational data will allow generation of suitable categories, validation and interpretation. Audio recording will allow checking and validation of observer records and more detailed analysis of selected extracts of transcriptions of pupil and teacher discourse. All data collected from mathematics sessions will be transcribed and written up as a case record of the event. These will provide detailed descriptions of the content and processes of mathematics instruction in infant classrooms. The case records may form the basis for further analysis. The teacher interviews will document teachers' own descriptions of subject matter knowledge, their planning, their strategies and their means of instruction.

Data so far analysed suggest children bring into school a range of flexible, informal strategies and an overlapping, less stable conventional knowledge where a concern for accuracy is not always strong. Children's strategies suggest that, as in language acquisition, a rule-governed approach is operating from the start. Teachers' aims for early instruction seem, however, to be derived from a pre-school ideology which emphasises play, choice and practical activity rather than reflecting the way children think about mathematics.

Publ: A full list of publications is available from the researcher.

12699   Key Stage 1 of the National Curriculum in Mathematics as it relates to infant schools in Huddersfield.

GBR   1993

Research Date(s): 1989-1993

Bassett, J.

Sup: Wain, G.

Inst: Leeds University, Centre for Studies in Science and Mathematics Education, Leeds LS2 9JT, United Kingdom.

mathematics; assessment; achievement test; common core curriculum

mathématiques; appréciation; test de rendement; tronc commun

PROJECT DESCRIPTION

This research study will investigate the mathematics curriculum of 70 schools engaged in Key Stage 1 of the National Curriculum in Huddersfield. It will cover the background to the setting up of the National Curriculum and the philosophy which underpins it. It will involve looking at infant/first school models of the curriculum and, in particular, the mathematics curriculum and relating these to the National Curriculum. The content of Key Stage 1 of the National Curriculum will be analysed and compared with the pre-National Curriculum mathematics curriculum. Similarly the assessment component will be analysed in terms of assessment theory and pre-National Curriculum assessment procedures in school. The influence of the Standard Assessment Tasks of school internal curriculum assessments and approaches to teaching methods will be ascertained. The results of the first unreported Standard Assessment Tasks and the first reported Standard Assessment Tasks will be analysed in terms of what they mean in themselves and the effect on schools. The effects of the National Curriculum on the content of the mathematics curriculum in schools, internal assessment, and approaches to mathematics teaching will be assessed by means of a teacher questionnaire. This will be sent to all teachers involved in Key Stage 1 in 70 Huddersfield schools. A separate questionnaire will be sent to mathematics co-ordinators in the same schools. Selective interviews in a sample of the schools will be used to support the questionnaires. The questionnaires cover teacher opinions on effectiveness of National Curriculum INSET (Inservice Education of Teachers), areas where further training is needed, areas in which teachers feel confident/lacking confidence and resource needs to implement National Curriculum Mathematics.

12700   Key technologies - potential developments and their implications for vocational education and training.

GBR   1993

Research Date(s): 1990-1991

Clyde, A.

Inst: Further Education Unit, Citadel Place, Pinworth Street, London SE11 5EH, United Kingdom.

technology; vocational education; industry; curriculum development

technologie; enseignement professionnel; industrie; élaboration de programmes d'études

PROJECT DESCRIPTION

The aims of this project are to: (1) identify trends in the development of key technologies that might be incorporated into education and training curricula to prepare trainees for future developments; (2) identify methods whereby such trends can be reviewed regularly so that curricula can be updated by appropriate bodies (e.g. in the United Kingdom, by the examining and validating bodies, industrial lead bodies and education and training institutions); (3) support proposed research into key technologies at the Technical and Further Education (TAFE) National Centre for Research and Development in Australia.

The term 'key technologies' was used by the Engineering Council (EC) in 'A Call to Action' (EC, 1986), to describe those technologies which had a significant potential to increase 'added value' in industry. This document listed examples of key technologies under the general headings of materials, components and processes. These ideas and their curriculum implications were developed further in 'The Key Technologies - some implications for education and training' (FEU/EC, 1988). This report also indicated that potential key technologies varied with company circumstances, and could not always be easily recognised, although they were likely to have interdisciplinary implications. Subsequent FEU work, published as 'The Concept of Key Technologies' (FEU, 1989), suggested that an understanding of the 'added-value' and interdisciplinary aspects could best be fostered through student assignments. 'Training for the Future' (FEU, 1990) provides guidelines and model assignments.

Current work under the title 'Training in Context' aims to prepare and disseminate materials to assist in the delivery of the concept in industry, colleges and training centres. The FEU has also supported curriculum development in several potential key technology areas, e.g. transputers and quality assurance, but such work has not concentrated on this aspect of the technology. TAFE (in Australia) has also undertaken work in this area.

12701   Knowledge-based computer-assisted learning.

GBR   1993
Research Date(s): 1986-1992
Barker, P.
Inst: Teesside University, School of Computing and Mathematics, Interactive Systems Research Group, Borough Road, Middlesbrough, Cleveland TS1 3BA, United Kingdom.
expert system; authoring system; educational software; didactic use of computer
système-expert; système-auteur; didacticiel; usage didactique de l'ordinateur

PROJECT DESCRIPTION

In the past, most of the conventional approaches to the creation of software for computer-assisted learning (CAL) have suffered from a number of significant limitations. One of the most serious of these has been the need to embed the knowledge and skills (that are to be transferred to the student) within particular and discrete items of software. Embedding instructional material within courseware itself can be a source of many difficulties. For example, it leads to a very inflexible approach to the effective utilisation of instructional resources particularly with respect to the creation of software that is adaptable to the particular learning and training needs of individual students. In view of this, the research advocates that a better design principle would involve the creation of a computer resident, shared knowledge base that acts as a central repository for all the instructional material within a given teaching domain. The knowledge base is then used to service different types of 'presentation software' that does not embed any specific domain knowledge. Such an approach to the design of courseware could cater for multiple views of knowledge, and hence, the production of effective and adaptable courseware. This research is primarily concerned with an investigation into the potential utility of knowledge-based CAL and the development of appropriate knowledge engineering techniques to support this approach to the development of courseware for use in sophisticated interactive learning systems.

Publ: Barker, P.G. Knowledge-based CAL. In: *Proceedings of the Fifth Canadian Symposium on Instructional Technology*. Ottawa, Canada, 5-7 May 1986, pp. 137-143.
Barker, P.G. & Proud, A. A practical introduction to authoring for computer-assisted instruction. Part 10: knowledge-based CAL. In: *British Journal of Educational Technology*, Vol 18, No 2/1987, pp. 140-160.
Barker, P.G. Knowledge engineering for CAL. In: Louis, F.B. & Tagg, E.D. (eds.). *Computers in education: European Conference Proceedings*. North-Holland Publishing Company, 1988, pp. 529-535.

12702   Language and primary maths.

GBR   1993
Research Date(s): 1988-1991
Weeden, E.
Sup: Drever, E.
Inst: Stirling University, Department of Education, Stirling FK9 4LA, United Kingdom.

mathematics; textbook; language; verbal interaction; teacher; pupil; primary education
mathématiques; manuel d'enseignement; langage; interaction verbale; enseignant; élève; enseignement primaire

PROJECT DESCRIPTION

This is an investigation into the language used in primary mathematics texts and the interaction between teachers and pupils, with the emphasis on the pupils' perspective. An initial focus will be on the materials from the Scottish Primary Mathematics Group, and possibly from the School Mathematics Project.

12703   Logiciel d'aide à la résolution de problèmes arithmétiques par les élèves de cours élémentaire, première et deuxième années.

FRA   1993
Research Date(s): 1987-1988
Escarabajal, Marie-Claude; Kastenbaum, Michèle.
Sup: Richard, Jean-François.
Inst: Université de Paris VIII, CNRS URA/1297, Psychologie cognitive du traitement de l'information symbolique, 2 rue de la Liberté, 93526 Saint Denis Cedex 02, France.
arithmetic; primary education; problem solving; didactic use of computer; mathematics; educational software
arithmétique; enseignement primaire; résolution de problème; usage didactique de l'ordinateur; mathématiques; didacticiel

PROJECT DESCRIPTION

Objectifs: Il s'agit d'entraîner l'enfant à identifier la relation additive sous-jacente à l'énoncé linguistique d'un problème, puis à écrire l'équation numérique qui traduit cette relation.

Méthodologie: Construction d'un logiciel d'aide à la résolution de problèmes arithmétiques (SIPOS) et test de la validité du logiciel auprès de deux classes de cours élémentaire deuxième année (39 élèves).

Résultats: La comparaison classique pré-test/post-test des deux groupes "expérimental" et "contrôlé", effectuée en condition de classe, n'est pas probante, néanmoins une épreuve à long terme formulée dans les termes contextuels du logiciel montre une acquisition incontestable des notions visées par l'apprentissage; l'expérimentation de validation traduit la difficulté de transfert des acquisitions extra-scolaires à un contexte d'application scolaire.

Publ: Escarabajal, Marie-Claude. *SIPOS: Didacticiel d'aide à la résolution de problèmes arithmétiques au cours élémentaire*. Rapport de fin de contrat au Ministère de l'éducation nationale, 1988, 57p.

12704   Logo and the development of algebraic skills.

GBR   1993
Research Date(s): 1992-1995
Harries, T.
Sup: Sutherland, R.
Inst: Bath College of Higher Education, Newton Park, Newton St Loe, Bath BA2 9BN, United Kingdom; London University, Institute of Education, Department of Mathematics, Statistics and Computing, 20 Bedford Way, London WC1H OAL, United Kingdom.
logo; mathematics; algebra
logo; mathématiques; algèbre

PROJECT DESCRIPTION

The main aim of the research is to develop an understanding of the algebraic perceptions of pupils who are perceived to be 'low attainers' in mathematics. This involves investigating not only their algebraic perceptions but also their understanding of number and how this understanding can be used to articulate numerical algorithms.

Some of the specific questions being investigated are: (1) Is algebraic thinking closed to some pupils in school or is their lack of understanding more a reflection of the environment in which they are introduced to it? (2) Is the apparent lack of understanding of algebraic symbols due in part of a lack of facility with number? (3) Is it possible to create an environment within logo which will enable pupils to explore number, and naturally build up a facility to generalise and use variables?

The research is being carried out over a period of four terms, with year 8 pupils in two different schools. The progress of the pupils as they work through a series of activities will be monitored through observation and the use of 'dribble' files. Also there will be regular individual structured interviews.

12705   Mathematics 16-20.

GBR   1993
Research Date(s): 1991-1994
Searl, J.
Inst: Edinburgh University, Department of Mathematics and Statistics, James Clerk Maxwell Building, King's Buildings, Mayfield Road, Edinburgh EH9 3JZ, United Kingdom.
mathematics; post-secondary education; learning process; motivation for studies
mathématiques; enseignement postsecondaire; apprentissage; motivation pour les études

PROJECT DESCRIPTION

This project will analyse the different patterns of learning and teaching adopted in school and university (and polytechnics) for mathematics. The reasons for undergraduates abandoning their mathematical studies will be examined by means of personal interview and questionnaire. Students will be matched by sex, age and qualification in an attempt to elucidate the factors which contribute to success in mathematics in tertiary education.

12706 Mathematik in der Weiterbildung. (Mathematics in further education.)
AUT   1993
Research Date(s): 1992-1994
Schloeglmann, Wolfgang; Jungwirth, Helga; Maass, Juergen.
Inst: Institut fuer Mathematik, Altenbergerstrasse 69, A-4040 Linz.
Universitaet Linz, Altenbergerstrasse 69, A-4040 Linz
Fin: Fonds zur Foerderung der wissenschaftlichen Forschung.
mathematics; further training; post-compulsory education; educational provision; cultural change
mathématiques; formation complémentaire; enseignement postobligatoire; scolarisation; changement culturel
PROJECT DESCRIPTION
   Das vorliegende Forschungsprojekt zielt darauf, durch eine Analyse des Iststandes Perspektiven fuer eine Verbesserung der mathematischen Weiterbildung und damit zur Hebung der mathematischen Bildung insgesamt zu entwickeln. Dies soll durch empirische Erhebungen und durch theoretische Arbeiten geleistet werden. Die Theoriebasis des Forschungsvorhabens bilden gesellschaftstheoretische.
   Die empirischen Untersuchungen beziehen sich auf den Stand der mathematischen Bildung sowie auf die derzeitigen Weiterbildungsangebote auf verschiedenen Niveaus und mit verschiedenen Zielsetzungen. Zum ersten Aspekt, der mathematischen Bildung, werden bei TeilnehmerInnen an Weiterbildungskursen per Test Mathematikkenntnisse, bei TeilnehmerInnen an Weiterbildungskursen, KursleiterInnen und mit Kurskonzeption und -einrichtung befassten Personen per Fragebogen und Interview Sichtweisen von Mathematik und Haltungen gegenueber der Mathematik erhoben. Die Analyse des zweiten Aspekts betreffend die derzeitigen Weiterbildungsangebote bezieht sich auf die die Konzeption betreffenden Voraussetzungen, organisatorische Bedingungen, Erwartungen und Perspektiven von TeilnehmerInnen und KursleiterInnen sowie Probleme bei der Durchfuehrung der Kurse; eingesetzt wird wiederum die Methode der Befragung (schriftlich und muendlich). Darueber hinaus werden die Lehr-Lern-Prozesse innerhalb der Kurse untersucht. Diese Untersuchung, durchgefuehrt mittels teilnehmender Beobachtung mit gleichzeitiger Video- und Audiodokumentation der unterrichtlichen Prozesse, zielt auf die verstehende Rekonstruktion (im Sinne der Ethnomethodologie) der Deutung der Unterrichtssituationen durch die Lehrkraefte und KursteilnehmerInnen, auf ihre Handlungsweisen und entstehende Muster in ihrer Interaktion.
   Die theoretische Arbeit besteht in der Erstellung einer systemtheoretischen Analyse des Weiterbildungsbereichs in der Technologischen Formation auf der Basis von Literaturstudien und von erhobenen Daten. In diesem Rahmen soll der Frage nachgegangen werden, inwieweit sich der Weiterbildungsbereich als ein eigenes soziales Subsystem der Gesellschaft fassen bzw. wie er sich als solches charakterisieren laesst. Im Verlauf von zwei Workshops wollen wir unsere Forschungsergebnisse und -methoden (etwa Frageboegen und Interviewleitfaeden) mit einer internationalen Gruppe von WissenschaftlerInnen aus der Bundesrepublik Deutschland und aus Oesterreich diskutieren, mit denen wir kooperieren.
   Zur Sekundaeranalyse von Kenntnistests (Mathematik - Erwachsenenbildung) werden insgesamt 2000 bis 2500 Tests herangezogen; weiters werden zehn Tiefeninterviews zum Verstaendnis von Mathematik, 15 leitfadenorientierte Interviews mit KursplanerInnen, qualitative Erhebungen zur Struktur der mathematischen Erwachsenenbildung sowie eine exemplarische Analyse einzelner Kurse (Curriculum, Ziele, etc.) mit Interaktionsanalyse aufgrund von Video- Aufzeichnungen durchgefuehrt. Es kommen Frageboegen (20 Kurse) zu Motivation, Erwartungen, Erfolgen etc. zum Einsatz.
   Die Daten werden mittels Frageboegen, Interviews, qualitativer Analyse, Quellenstudium und Video- Aufzeichnungen gewonnen. Zugleich wird an der Theoriebildung gearbeitet.

12707 Mathimatikos alphavitismos sto dimotiko scholio. (Mathematical literacy in primary school.)
CYP   1993
Research Date(s): 1990
Constandinides, Aristides; Ioannides, Nakis.
Inst: Pedagogiko Instituto (Pedagogical Institute), P.O. Box 512, Nicosia, Cyprus.
mathematics; illiteracy; primary school
mathématiques; analphabétisme; école primaire
PROJECT DESCRIPTION
   Background and aims: The Cypriot Ministry of Education has stated as its main priority to reduce illiteracy rates among pupils at all levels of education. Mathematical illiteracy is a major problem facing schoolchildren. The purpose of this study was: to identify mathematically illiterate pupils in the Cornesios primary school and to find out which components of the

skills and knowledge prescribed in the curriculum mathematically illiterate pupils are unable to acquire.
   Methods: The sample was selected from a list of low achievers in mathematics which was constructed by the researchers on the basis of teachers' instructions and information. The study involved 25 pupils in years 2-6 of the Cornesios primary school. The researchers constructed three different tests, one for pupils in year 2, one for pupils in year 3 and one for the pupils in years 4, 5 and 6. The construction of tests was based on Cockcroft's recommendations. Descriptive statistics were used for the analysis of data (means and standard deviations).
   Results: Mathematically illiterate or partially illiterate pupils were found at each year level. However, the percentage of mathematically illiterate pupils was higher in year 2 than in years 3, 4, 5 and 6. No relationship was found between the pupils' gender and the degree of illiteracy. There were no mathematically illiterate pupils in years 3 and 6. It was also found that the subjects in the sample had difficulties in specific areas, such as recognizing geometrical figures and counting distance by non-compatible units. They were also unable to construct a graph or explain the data in a graph.

12708 Le nuove tecnologie nei processi formativi. (New technologies in educational processes.)
ITA   1993
Research Date(s): 1990-1991
Fierli, M.
Sup: Caputo, A.M.
Inst: Centro Europeo dell'Educazione - CEDE (European Centre for Education), Villa Falconieri, 00044 Frascati (Roma), Italy.
Fin: Ministero della Pubblica Istruzione, Ufficio Studi e Programmazione.
information technology; information science; didactic use of computer; primary education; secondary education
technologie de l'information; science de l'information; usage didactique de l'ordinateur; enseignement primaire; enseignement secondaire
PROJECT DESCRIPTION
   Aims: This study reports on the state of the art regarding the use of new technologies in Italian schools. The report is based on the analysis of documents produced in the context of the National Project for the Introduction of Computer Science in Schools, the results of the experimental project of IRIS and on the IEA study on computers in education.
   Methods: Collection, elaboration and analysis of data collected through questionnaires; construction of explanatory tables; definition of objectives of computer education, instructional procedures, and computer programs.
   Results: The conclusions are presented in the report under the following headings: the general situation of computer science in Italian schools with reference to the National Project of Introduction of Computer Science in Schools; the computer as a teaching tool and as a teacher; the evolution of teaching trends and of technical solutions; problems connected to the introduction of computer science in the educational process, such as the role of computers in the teaching of basic computer science, the choice of languages: BASIC (which experts consider to be too easy), LOGO (adapted for children), and PASCAL (for older students), the most appropriate school level at which to introduce computer science; analysis of the IEA Computers in Education study (1985) as a comparative study at the international level on the introduction of computers into schools (this takes place in two phases: 1987-1990 - observation of the state of computer science in schools and prospects for development; 1990-1993 - measurement of the educational results with the help of objective instruments).

12709 Optellen en aftrekken tot 100 in LOM en MLK: een hoofdrekenonderzoek. (Addition and subtraction in special education: a study of mental arithmetic.)
NLD   1994
Research Date(s): 1992-1993
Harskamp, E.G.; IJzendoorn, W.J.E.; Willemsen, T.F.W.P.
Inst: RION Instituut voor Onderwijsonderzoek (RION Institute for Educational Research), P.O. Box 1286, 9701 BG Groningen, Netherlands.
Rijksuniversiteit Groningen (State University of Groningen), P.O. Box 72, 9700 AB Groningen, Netherlands
Fin: SVO het Instituut voor Onderzoek van het Onderwijs.
arithmetic; special education; calculation; learning difficulty; remedial teaching; teaching method
arithmétique; enseignement spécial; calcul; difficulté de l'apprentissage; soutien pédagogique; méthode pédagogique
PROJECT DESCRIPTION
   Background: Special school pupils' numeracy skills are much poorer than those of pupils in ordinary schools. As regards mental arithmetic, about 60% of special school pupils can do addition and subtraction sums up to 20, but only 30% can do addition and subtraction sums up to 100. Proponents of constructivist teaching methods claim that these children can learn more with the help of constructivist methods; structuralist methods, they say, are too much focused on the solution of problems and too little on the pupils' problem solving processes. They recommend specific remedial instructional methods that take account of the most common errors in pupils' problem solving. At present, no remedial teaching materi-

als exist that are based on pupils' incorrect and partly correct problem solving procedures.

Aim: To examine whether a constructivist approach benefits special needs pupils who are having difficulties in mental arithmetic, especially in doing addition and subtraction sums up to 100.

Design: At 2 LOM schools (for pupils with learning and behavioural difficulties) and 2 MLK schools (for pupils with learning difficulties) addition and subtraction sums up to 100 will be given to pupils who have mastered the first principles of arithmetic. Interviews will be conducted with those pupils who have solved at least 80% of the sums up to 20 correctly, who have solved correctly nearly all sums whose solution does not pass the next ten, and who have completed at least 80% of the sums up to 100 incorrectly. Per school, the problem solving strategies of at least 10 pupils will be examined. Constructivist materials will be selected and presented for approval to a group of experts. The selected materials will be adjusted to the problem solving procedures of the pupils. The result will serve as a basis for experimental materials that will be tried out with 6 LOM pupils and 6 MLK pupils. The pupils' progress will be determined with the help of measurements carried out immediately after instruction and four weeks after instruction. For purposes of comparison, measurements will be made of the progress of pupils with the same initial level, but without remedial instruction.

12710   Permeating the learning of information technology across the secondary school curriculum.
GBR   1993
Research Date(s): 1991-1992
Kennewell, S.
Inst: University College of Swansea, Department of Education, Hendrefoilan, Swansea SA2 7NB, United Kingdom.
information technology; common core curriculum; integrated curriculum; didactic use of computer
technologie de l'information; tronc commun; programme d'études intégré; usage didactique de l'ordinateur
PROJECT DESCRIPTION
Attainment target 5 of the National Curriculum Technology requirement specifies that pupils should develop information technology (IT) capability. The non-statutory guidance suggests strongly that this should be achieved through subjects other than specialist IT/computing lessons.

This project aims to identify the extent to which IT had permeated the curriculum of all secondary schools in one Welsh county by mid-1990, and what short-term plans schools had for developing this aspect of the curriculum. Data on individual curriculum activities involving IT in all subjects were collected within the county and this is being analysed to compare the amount of IT use according to: (a) existing and planned provision; (b) ages of pupils; (c) subjects; (d) course units within each subject; (e) types of IT activity; (f) types of school; and (g) advisory support received.

12711   Place des humanités dans la formation médicale en Europe.
FRA   1993
Research Date(s): 1992-1993
Déchamp-Le Roux, Catherine.
Inst: Université de Paris XIII, UFR de médecine Bobigny, Département de pédagogie des sciences de la santé, 74 rue Marcel Cachin, 93012 Bobigny Cedex, France.
medicine; vocational training; social sciences; course programme; Europe; health service personnel; humanities
médecine; formation professionnelle; sciences sociales; programme de cours; Europe; personnel médical; études littéraires
PROJECT DESCRIPTION
Objectifs: La formation des soignants à la prise en compte de la dimension sociale de la maladie passe par l'initiation à des disciplines susceptibles de proposer les concepts et les outils adaptés. La place réservée à ces disciplines (sociologie, psychologie, éthique et philosophie) est variable selon les traditions médicales qui sont diverses en Europe. Le contenu de ces formations est un indicateur du statut de ces disciplines (marginal ou légitime).

Méthodologie: Inventaire de la littérature sociologique, pédagogique et éthique; enquête auprès des facultés de médecine en Europe; enquête auprès d'associations telles que "Association for Medical Education in Europe" et "European Society of Medical Sociology".

12712   Postavení a nezastupitelná úloha patofyziologie v systému výuky medicínských oborů. (The place and role of pathophysiology in medical education.)
CSK   1994
Research Date(s): 1993-1995
Vožeh, František; Mysliveček, Jaromír; Sobotka, P.; Záhlava, Jan; Barcal, Jan; Zalud, Václav; Safanda, Jiří.
Sup: Janoušek, Václav.
Inst: Lékařská fakulta Univerzity Karlovy Plzeň (Charles University, Faculty of Medicine, Institute of Pathophysiology), Lidická 1, 301 66 Plzeň, Czech Republic.
Ministerstvo školství, mládeže a tělovýchovy (Ministry of Education, Youth and Physical Education), Karmelitská 7, 118 00 Praha 1, Czech Republic

pathology; physiology; medicine; undergraduate study; post-graduate study
pathologie; physiologie; médecine; supérieur premier cycle; supérieur troisième cycle
PROJECT DESCRIPTION
Aim: (1) To foster awareness of the importance of pathophysiology as a "preclinical" discipline in medical education; (2) to design methods for teaching general pathophysiology as a necessary basis for medical professionals' thinking; (3) to apply the results in undergraduate and, possibly, postgraduate pathophysiology courses; (4) to define models of different pathophysiological states for use in practical teaching and demonstrations.

Method: The study will focus on the acquisition and use of special medical knowledge from the angle of pathophysiological mechanisms and their generalization to teaching.

12713   Practical work in the mathematics classroom.
GBR   1993
Research Date(s): 1990-1993
Triadafillidis, T.
Sup: Searl, J.; Entwistle, N.
Inst: Edinburgh University, Department of Mathematics and Statistics, James Clerk Maxwell Building, King's Buildings, Mayfield Road, Edinburgh EH9 3JZ, United Kingdom.
mathematics; practical work; lower secondary; teaching method
mathématiques; travaux pratiques; secondaire premier cycle; méthode pédagogique
PROJECT DESCRIPTION
This research arises from the oft-asserted claim that practical activities are an essential element in creating a learning environment in the mathematical classroom. A number of practical activities have been developed for pupils aged 12-14 and these, together with activities developed elsewhere, are being evaluated in a number of schools. The illuminative evaluation approach will be used.

12714   Problem solving in geometry in Greek schools.
GBR   1993
Research Date(s): 1990-1994
Zachos, I.
Sup: Orton, A.
Inst: Leeds University, School of Education, Leeds LS2 9JT, United Kingdom.
geometry; mathematics; problem solving; Greece
géométrie; mathématiques; résolution de problème; Grèce
PROJECT DESCRIPTION
The solution of Euclidean geometry problems is difficult for pupils in Greek schools, as it has always been for all pupils where Euclidean geometry has been taught. The aim is to produce a new scheme for teaching the subject, based on worked examples but theoretically underpinned by recent research on the writing of geometry proofs. Matched control and experimental groups will be used, the matching being carried out by using van Hiele levels and a specially constructed test. Pupils in Greek schools will be taught and tested in groups, with a large sample also having individual interviews.

12715   Procédures de validation et de vérification en mathématiques, physique et informatique et leur rôle dans l'apprentissage.
FRA   1993
Research Date(s): 1989-
Balacheff, Nicolas; Arsac, Gilbert; Coquin, Danièle; Dagdilelis, Vassilios; Margolinas, Claire; Tiberghien, Andrée; Grea, Jean.
Inst: Ministère de la recherche, Centre national de la recherche scientifique, CNRS GDR/71, Didactique et acquisition des connaissances scientifiques, Laboratoire PSYDEE, Université de Paris V, 46 rue Saint-Jacques, 75005 Paris, France; Ministère de la recherche, CNRS UPR/5411 et GDR/28, Institut de recherche en pédagogie de l'économie et en audiovisuel pour la communication dans les sciences sociales, 93 Chemin des Mouilles, BP 167, 69130 Ecully Cedex, France.
mathematics; physics; computer science; learning; demonstration; problem solving
mathématiques; physique; informatique; acquisition de connaissances; démonstration; résolution de problème
PROJECT DESCRIPTION
Objectifs: Ce thème, selon le principe des groupes de recherche du Centre national de la recherche scientifique est supporté par les travaux de plusieurs équipes. On pose le problème du statut et des modes de validation dans le cours de l'activité des étudiants ou des élèves, et leur rôle dans l'apprentissage. On réalise une synthèse des travaux pour en clarifier les problématiques et dégager les résultats marquants, la confrontation des différentes disciplines (mathématiques, physique et informatique) permettant de dégager des thèmes prioritaires, notamment: (1) le vocabulaire développé (vrai, conjecture, hypothèse, prémisse, justification, preuve, vérification, validation, spéculation...); (2) les types de validation acceptés (démonstration, méthode expérimentale, certification - validation de programme); (3) les rôles joués par les contenus sur lesquels portent les processus de validation dans le cadre de la résolution de problèmes; (4) les

conditions didactiques de l'apprentissage de la validation dans chacune des disciplines et leurs limites.

Publ: Balacheff, Nicolas. Treatment of refutations: aspects of the complexity of a constructivist approach of mathematics learning. In: Von Glaserfield, E. (ed.). *Radical constructivism in mathematics education.* Kleuwer press Publisher, 1991.

12716 Programming in Scottish Standard Grade Computing Studies.
GBR 1993
Research Date(s): 1990-1993
Kirkwood, M.
Inst: Jordanhill College of Education, Division of Business & Computer Education, Southbrae Drive, Jordanhill, Glasgow G13 1PP, United Kingdom.
computer science; teaching aid; programming
informatique; moyen d'enseignement; programmation
PROJECT DESCRIPTION
   The aim of this project is to develop and trial individualised learning materials on programming in Scottish Standard Grade Computing Studies within the framework of a staff development project.

12717 The role and value of A-level geography fieldwork: a case study.
GBR 1993
Research Date(s): 1984-1991
Harvey, P.
Sup: McPartland, M.; Saunders, A.
Inst: Durham University, School of Education, Leazes Road, Durham DH1 1TA, United Kingdom.
Fin: Economic and Social Research Council.
geography; field research; learning process; teaching method
géographie; recherche sur le terrain; apprentissage; méthode pédagogique
PROJECT DESCRIPTION
   The study aims to analyse the role and value of a residential fieldwork experience in geographical learning for advanced level geography students (i.e. students aged 16-19); to compare and contrast the respective assessments of the student and teacher of fieldwork's purpose; and to explore frameworks and methods for evaluating the effectiveness of field instruction as a learning process. The research uses qualitative research strategies in a case-study to describe and analyse the holistic process of learning in action from the perspectives of its participants. Four themes are explored in depth: skills-based learning; affective learning; learning transfer; and geography fieldwork as environmental education.
   Results show that learning is affected by a tension of purpose between teaching for theoretical exemplification, technical competency and investigative skills, and environmental awareness. Stage-management in hypothesis-testing aimed at developing students' conceptual understanding is the predominant teaching method but despite this emphasis successful transfer of learning is low. The technical competency emphasis is propositioned as moving fieldwork towards utilisation of a technocentric ideology in addressing environmental issues in geography. This is regarded as devaluing an individual's environmental experience, personal commitment, and political obligation which are seen as important aspects of an environmental education. Fieldwork is seen to be most valuable in the affective domain: producing self- and subject-motivation through inter alia novelty of milieu, self-concept enhancement, productive role-modelling, and changing students' 'scripts' for learning. The links between these affective dimensions and fieldwork's role in students' cognitive development offer profitable avenues for further research.

Publ: McPartland, M.F. & Harvey, P.K. A question of fieldwork? In: *Teaching Geography*, Vol 12, No 4/1987, pp. 162-164.

12718 Rôle de la formulation dans ce qu'on appelle une "bonne démonstration mathématique".
FRA 1993
Research Date(s): 1984-1989
Coquin-Viennot, Danièle.
Inst: Université de Poitiers, UER Sciences humaines, CNRS URA/666, Laboratoire de psychologie du langage, 95 av. du Recteur Pineau, 86022 Poitiers Cedex, France.
mathematics; demonstration; teacher behaviour; conceptual imagery; logical thinking; pupil attitude
mathématiques; démonstration; comportement de l'enseignant; représentation mentale; pensée logique; attitude de l'élève
PROJECT DESCRIPTION
   Objectifs: A travers une épreuve de jugement, on cherche à atteindre l'image qu'élèves et enseignants se donnent d'une "bonne démonstration".
   Méthodologie: On construit des démonstrations, solutions d'un même problème à partir de productions réelles d'élèves et selon quatre dimensions: deux dimensions atteignent la structure logique du système de déduction (ordre et présence de tous les maillons nécessaires), deux autres sont liées à la formulation (le type de codage des figures et l'utilisation ou non d'écriture symbolique). Une douzaine de démonstrations sont ainsi

ordonnées de la meilleure à la moins bonne par des enseignants (6e et 4e) et six sont ordonnées par des élèves de 4e.
   Résultats: Les enseignants privilégient les critères de structure logique dans leur classification; en ce qui concerne la forme, les démonstrations avec écriture symbolique sont mieux classées, le codage des figures par les lettres a leur préférence. L'aspect structure logique joue moins chez les élèves, ils classent mieux les démonstrations sans écriture symbolique et plébiscitent le codage des figures par des couleurs. On procède à l'analyse des démonstrations-type demandées par ailleurs à chaque enseignant. Afin de contrevalider le rôle de certaines marques dans la distinction "discours formels-discours naturels", on reprend le principe de l'expérience de jugement de démonstrations par des élèves et par des enseignants, mais les formulations des démonstrations à juger se distinguent par l'implication du locuteur, le type de connecteurs utilisés et les marques d'organisation textuelle.

Publ: Coquin-Viennot, Danièle. La notion de représentation-conception au service de l'enseignement d'un concept mathématique. In: Monteil, Jean-Marc & Fayol, Michel (éds.). *La psychologie scientifique et ses applications.* Grenoble: Presses universitaires, 1989.
Coquin-Viennot, Danièle. Le disours justificatif en mathématiques: l'implication du locuteur selon la représentation du référent. In: Verganud, G.; Rogalski, J. & Artigue, M. (éds.). *Psychology of mathematics education.* Paris: CNRS, 1989, pp. 188-195.

12719 The role of information technology in business, finance and management.
GBR 1993
Research Date(s): 1990-1991
Hall, J.
Sup: Williams, C.
Inst: Cheltenham & Gloucester College of Higher Education, Faculty of Business and Finance Management, Oxstalls Campus, Oxstalls Lane, Gloucester GL2 9HW, United Kingdom.
information technology; industry; commerce; hardware; software; skill; job requirements; commercial training
technologie de l'information; industrie; commerce; matériel informatique; logiciel; compétence; qualification requise pour l'emploi; formation commerciale
PROJECT DESCRIPTION
   The aims of this project are to: (1) ascertain the information technology skills and knowledge required by business and industry of a Business Studies graduate; (2) identify the types of hardware and software and the applications for which they are used in industry today, with particular reference to the micro-computer. The research will be carried out by semi-structured interviews with a selection of local organisations.

12720 Schulleistungen und Schulstrukturen: Separatauswertung des schweizerischen Beitrags zu IAEP II. (Structures et rendement scolaires: dépouillement séparé de la contribution suisse au projet international IAEP II.)
CHE 1994
Research Date(s): 1990-1992
Moser, Urs; von Waldkirch Scherer, Christina.
Inst: Amt für Bildungsforschung (ABF) der Erziehungsdirektion des Kantons Bern, Sulgeneckstrasse 70, 3005 Bern, Schweiz.
mathematics; natural sciences; knowledge level; public education; evaluation; achievement
mathématiques; sciences naturelles; niveau de connaissances; enseignement public; évaluation; rendement
PROJECT DESCRIPTION
   Im Jahr 1991 hat sich die Schweiz (bzw. fünfzehn ihrer Kantone) zusammen mit 19 anderen Ländern an einer internationalen Studie beteiligt, die sich zum Ziel setzte, die Leistungen von 13jährigen in den Bereichen Mathematik und Naturwissenschaften weltweit zu vergleichen und allfällige Unterschiede in Beziehung zu setzen mit Variablen wie Unterrichtsorganisation, Lehrmittel, Unterrichtsmethoden usw. Die Daten wurden vorerst auf internationaler Ebene ausgewertet, und die - für die Schweiz schmeichelhaften - Ergebnisse sind im ersten Halbjahr 1992 veröffentlicht worden.
   In einem zweiten Schritt sind nun die schweizerischen Daten separat ausgewertet worden. In dieser Auswertung wurden die Leistungen in Mathematik und Naturwissenschaften von fünf Schülerpopulationen verglichen: Schüler des Kantons Zürich, des Kantons Bern und des Tessins, dann eine gemischte Gruppe Deutschschweiz sowie eine gemischte Gruppe Welschschweiz. Insgesamt sind die Testergebnisse von 3600 Schülern aus rund 400 Klassen ausgewertet worden. Was die Ergebnisse im Bereich Naturwissenschaften betrifft, so ergaben sich kaum signifikante Unterschiede; die folgenden Aussagen beziehen sich deshalb auf die Mathematik.
   Hier ist festzustellen, dass sie Schüler aus der französisch- und der italienischsprachigen Schweiz allgemein bessere Ergebnisse erzielten. Dazu muss angemerkt werden, dass in diesen beiden Sprachregionen die Einschulung auch ein Jahr früher stattfindet und die geprüften Tessiner und Westschweizer Kinder deshalb in der Regel eine höhere Klasse

besuchten (7. oder 8.) als die Deutschschweizer Kinder (6. oder 7. Klasse). Innerhalb der deutschschweizerischen Gruppe erreichten die Zürcher Schülerinnen und Schüler klar die besseren Ergebnisse; im Vergleich zum Kanton Bern unterscheiden sich ihre um 8 Prozent besseren Resultate signifikant. Wie zu erwarten war, sind in anspruchsvolleren Schultypen auch die Leistungen besser. In den Grenzbereichen überlappen sich die Leistungen; gute Schüler des niedriger eingestuften Oberstufenzuges arbeiten somit ebenso gut oder besser als die Schwächsten des anspruchsvolleren Zuges. Dies darf sicher als Argument für die Durchlässigkeit zwischen Oberstufenzügen betrachtet werden. Interessant ist vor allem die Erkenntnis, dass integrierte Schulmodelle (Gesamtschulen) nicht zu einer Nivellierung der Leistungen nach unten führen. Die Zuweisung der Tessiner Schülerinnen und Schüler zu einem Niveaukurs in Mathematik innerhalb ihres Gesamtschulmodells führt zu denselben Ergebnissen wie die Zuteilung von Berner oder Zürcher Kindern zu separaten Oberstufentypen. Und im Kanton Zürich haben die Schülerinnen und Schüler der AVO-Schulen gar besser gearbeitet als ihre Kameradinnen und Kameraden aus den hierarchisch dreigegliederten Oberstufen.

Publ: Moser, Urs. *Was wissen 13jährige? Schulleistungen und Schulstrukturen: ein Vergleich in Mathematik und Naturwissenschaften bei 13jährigen Schülerinnen und Schülern verschiedener Schulstrukturen.* Bern: Amt für Bildungsforschung der Erziehungsdirektion des Kantons Bern, 1992, 29 Seiten.

12721   A social constructivist theory of mathematics.
GBR   1993
Research Date(s): 1991-1993
Ernest, P.
Inst: Exeter University, School of Education, St Luke's, Heavitree Road, Exeter EX1 2LU, United Kingdom.
Fin: Leverhulme Research Fellowship.
mathematics; philosophy of education
mathématiques; philosophie de l'éducation
PROJECT DESCRIPTION
This is a basic, theoretical research project extending a previous project which concerned the philosophical foundations of the mathematics curriculum and mathematical pedagogy (see Ernest, P. (1991). 'The philosophy of mathematics education'). The current project is intended to extend the theoretical foundations. The contributions of Imre Lakatos and Ludwig Wittgenstein form a basis, but parallels in educational, psychological, sociological theory (e.g. constructivism) are drawn upon and utilised. The central thesis is that mathematics is a human construction, which is fallible, corrigible and ever changing. The project concerns working out this theory rigorously.
Publ: Ernest, P. *The philosophy of mathematics education.* London: Falmer Press, 1991.

12722   Software reviews: what do teachers need to know?
GBR   1993
Research Date(s): 1989-1991
Drever, E.
Inst: Stirling University, Department of Education, Stirling FK9 4LA, United Kingdom; Scottish Council for Educational Technology, Downhill, 74 Victoria Crescent Road, Glasgow G12 9JN, United Kingdom.
educational software; didactic use of computer; teacher; teacher behaviour
didacticiel; usage didactique de l'ordinateur; enseignant; comportement de l'enseignant
PROJECT DESCRIPTION
The ways in which teachers gain information and form expectations about 12 to 15 widely used software packages will be studied. The research covers packages used in primary and secondary schools and assesses the extent to which expectations are borne out. Postal questionnaires, interviews and informal classroom observation will be used. Special attention will be given to teachers' views and practices in integrating the packages into the curriculum at classroom level.

12723   Sperimentazione di unità didattiche nella scuola. (Courseware experiments in school.)
ITA   1994
Research Date(s): 1991-1992
Ferraris, Maria; Innocenti, Carlo; Pieri, Federica.
Sup: Persico, Donatella.
Inst: Istituto per le Tecnologie Didattiche - ITD (Institute for Educational Technology), Via all'Opera Pia 11, 16145 Genova, Italy.
Consiglio Nazionale delle Ricerche - CNR (National Research Council), Piazzale Aldo Moro 7, 00185 Roma, Italy
information technology; educational software; evaluation; research method; experimentation
technologie de l'information; didacticiel; évaluation; méthode de recherche; expérimentation
PROJECT DESCRIPTION
The project, begun in 1991, has involved the study and analysis of methods for the formative evaluation of educational systems in general and methods for the experimentation of educational software material in particular. The methods examined can be divided roughly into quantitative and qualitative. The former are based on the collection of objective data about the experimental use of material and involve analysis of these data mostly through numerical methods. The qualitative methods, on the other hand, are fundamentally based on direct observation and on the indirect survey of non-quantifiable information.
The project is concerned with experiments to which both types of method apply. In particular, it uses the techniques and methods studied for the evaluation of two courseware packages developed by ITD: WordProf and Logiclandia. On account of the different characteristics of these packages, a purely qualitative approach was adopted for WordProf and a mixed approach, with a solid quantitative base, for Logiclandia.
The development and testing of assessment tools and an examination of the effectiveness of the educational material were planned in 1991. Toward the end of that year, the experimentation phase was initiated in a number of Italian schools. The experiments continued in 1992 and will be concluded with an analysis of the results and, consequently, a revision of the educational material.

12724   SPRITE (Supporting and Promoting Information Technology in Education).
GBR   1993
Research Date(s): 1991-1993
Munro, R.; Lamont, M.
Inst: Jordanhill College of Education, Division of Business & Computer Education, Southbrae Drive, Jordanhill, Glasgow G13 1PP, United Kingdom; Northern College of Education, Computer Education Department, Dundee Campus, Gardyne Road, Dundee DD5 1NY, United Kingdom.
Fin: Jordanhill College of Education; Northern College; Scottish Office Education Department.
information technology; didactic use of computer; higher education
technologie de l'information; usage didactique de l'ordinateur; enseignement supérieur
PROJECT DESCRIPTION
The aim of this project is to improve, enhance and encourage the use of information technology (IT) by college staff (throughout Scotland) and assist the permeation of IT use in college courses.

12725   Students' understanding of acceleration as a vector in the context of mechanics.
GBR   1993
Research Date(s): 1985-1992
Jagger, J.
Sup: Orton, A.
Inst: Leeds University, Centre for Studies in Science & Mathematics in Education, Leeds LS2 9JT, United Kingdom.
physics; mathematics; comprehension
physique; mathématiques; compréhension
PROJECT DESCRIPTION
This research aims to investigate the growth in students' understanding of acceleration as rate of change in velocity (as distinct from rate of change of speed) in the context of mechanics. Pupils' understanding was investigated by means of questionnaires administered to them three times during their A-level mathematics course. A questionnaire was also given to first year Honours mathematics undergraduates. The sample included: 120 lower sixth formers who had elected to study mathematics at A-level; 120 upper sixth formers who were studying mathematics at A-level; 60 first year Honours mathematics undergraduates. The school pupils were taken from three comprehensive schools in the north of England. About 40 of them have been followed through from lower sixth to upper sixth including an extra questionnaire.

Publ: Jagger, J.M. Introducing mechanics - a response. In: *Mathematics in School*, Vol 14, No 1/1985, pp. 24-26.
Jagger, J.M. A review of the research into the learning of mathematics. In: Orton, A. (ed.). *Studies in mechanics learning.* Leeds University, 1985.
Jagger, J.M. Students' understanding of acceleration. In: *Mathematics in School*, Vol 16, No 4/1987, pp. 24-25.

12726   Students' understanding of literal algebraic equations and formulae.
GBR   1993
Research Date(s): 1987-1993
Moncur, D.
Sup: Orton, A.
Inst: Leeds University, School of Education, Leeds LS2 9JT, United Kingdom.
algebra; mathematics; cognitive process; comprehension
algèbre; mathématiques; processus cognitif; compréhension
PROJECT DESCRIPTION
This research has been devised to compare the ability of pupils and students to solve numerical and literal equations in order to analyse why many learners find the step from numerical to literal so difficult. A preliminary study based on group testing was carried out using pupils from four schools in different parts of Britain. In some schools the literal equations

were placed before the numerical. The main part of the research is based on individual interviews with a large sample of pupils.

12727 A study of the information technology skills used by teachers in the first two years in the profession: comparison of these skills with the information technology content of Post-Graduate Certificate of Education courses.
GBR 1993
Research Date(s): 1990-1992
Wild, P.; Simmons, C.
Inst: Loughborough University of Technology, Department of Education, Loughborough LE11 3TU, United Kingdom.
information technology; computer science; teacher education; probationary teacher
technologie de l'information; informatique; formation des enseignants; enseignant stagiaire
PROJECT DESCRIPTION

During 1989-1990 a questionnaire survey was used to evaluate the effects of the Post-Graduate Certificate of Education courses on students' development of the use of information technology skills in teaching. The questionnaires were used at the start and end of their courses.

It will now be very useful to follow a sample of the students through their first two years of teaching to assess the impact of the teacher training course on the use of information technology (IT) within schools. The results of this survey will provide a useful contribution to the present debate on the models of IT coverage within teacher education and their relevance to the first years of teaching. It will also provide some preliminary evidence concerning the extent of IT use within the developing National Curriculum which could form the basis for further research in this area.

The research will be carried out by questionnaire and follow up visits to a sample of schools in the United Kingdom. Results will be disseminated through the Information Technology in Teacher Education Group, which is an active 'grass roots' body supporting IT developments in teacher education, as well as the relevant journals.
Publ: Wild, P. & Hodgkinson, K. Providing information technology competency in primary and secondary initial teacher training. In: *Proceedings of the Third National Conference in Design and Technology Education and Research.* Loughborough University, 1990.
Simmons, C. & Wild, P. Student teachers learning to learn through IT. In: *Educational Research*, Vol 33, No 3/1991, pp. 163-173.
Simmons, C. & Wild, P. New forms of student teacher learning. In: *Educational Review*, Vol 44, No 2/1991, pp. 31-40.
Wild, P. Information technology in teacher training and early years of teaching. 9th International Conference on Technology and Education, March 1992.

12728 Teachers' planning and evaluation of mathematics in Greek high schools.
GBR 1993
Research Date(s): 1988-1991
Serafingos, J.
Sup: Rogers, C.
Inst: Lancaster University, Department of Educational Research, Cartmel College, Bailrigg, Lancaster LA1 4YW, United Kingdom.
Fin: Greek Ministry of Education.
mathematics; Greece; lesson preparation; evaluation; teaching
mathématiques; Grèce; préparation des cours; évaluation; enseignement
PROJECT DESCRIPTION

This project is an examination of the ways in which a sample of Greek mathematics teachers think about their subject and their teaching, and how these understandings influence the kinds of experiences that are selected and presented to children in the mathematics curriculum. This is of particular interest in Greek education because of the high emphasis that is placed upon high school teachers' subject degree studies and the lack of any significant professional training for high school teaching.

12729 The teaching and learning of geography in schools in Gibraltar.
GBR 1993
Research Date(s): 1989-1992
Gonzalez, B.
Sup: Brock, C.
Inst: Hull University, School of Education, Cottingham Road, Hull HU6 7RX, United Kingdom.
geography; Gibraltar; curriculum subject; achievement
géographie; Gibraltar; matière d'enseignement; rendement
PROJECT DESCRIPTION

Examination results over the last 10 years have given much concern in Gibraltar with regard to geography. There have been several visible trends which suggest a decrease in importance and status of the subject in the school curriculum. The research aims to identify the factors which have been responsible for this downward trend. In British schools geography is one of the more popular subjects and the results obtained compare quite favourably with the results obtained in other diciplines. Why is there such a marked contrast with the results obtained in Gibraltar? The research will

concentrate on the learning of the subject and the importance of environmental stimulus or lack of it, and an in-depth analysis of the existing geographical curriculum taught in schools at all levels.

12730 Teaching and learning undergraduate mathematics.
GBR 1993
Research Date(s): 1990-1991
Burn, R.
Sup: Vamos, P.; Burghes, D.
Inst: Exeter University, School of Education, St Luke's, Heavitree Road, Exeter EX1 2LU, United Kingdom.
mathematics; higher education; teaching method; learning pace
mathématiques; enseignement supérieur; méthode pédagogique; rythme d'apprentissage
PROJECT DESCRIPTION

Although there is much current innovation in relation to other aspects of mathematics teaching in higher education, there is virtually none relating to the basic 'bread and butter' courses in the first and second year of an honours degree in mathematics. The research compared teaching and learning in the first and second year courses at an English university and an English polytechnic. The method was to conduct half-hour interviews, using one set of questions for staff and one for students. Sixty-eight students were interviewed and thirty-two staff, slightly more than half of each being from the university.

The results showed (in the students' opinion) significant advantages in two aspects of polytechnic practice (i.e. not making a sharp distinction between the use of class time for lectures or problems, and the prescription of a set book or lecture notes for the course). There were widespread complaints that lecturers went too fast and none that lecturers went too slowly. It also became clear that students following up recommendations for further reading in the library are frustrated and not helped by the recommendation. Finally there was a lack of awareness on the part of lecturers of the length of a student's working week; overestimated by university lecturers and underestimated by polytechnic lecturers.

12731 Techniek in het voortgezet onderwijs. (Technology in secondary schools.)
NLD 1994
Research Date(s): 1992-1993
Doornekamp, B.G.
Sup: Streumer, J.N.
Inst: Onderzoek Centrum Toegepaste Onderwijskunde (OCTO) (Research Centre of the Department of Educational Technology), P.O. Box 217, 7500 AE Enschede, Netherlands.
Universiteit Twente (Twente University), P.O. Box 217, 7500 AE Enschede, Netherlands
Fin: SVO het Instituut voor Onderzoek van het Onderwijs.
technology; curriculum subject; lower secondary; teaching method; problem solving
technologie; matière d'enseignement; secondaire premier cycle; méthode pédagogique; résolution de problème
PROJECT DESCRIPTION

Background: In 1982 the SLO National Institute for Curriculum Development developed a technology curriculum which has since been evaluated on a number of aspects related to its practical implementation. After revision of the proposed curriculum, the SLO developed a number of model teaching packages with a strong focus on problem solving skills. A theme that has been given little attention in the development of the teaching packages is the design of instructional trajectories for groups of pupils of different ability.

Aim: To evaluate the problem-solving components of the technology teaching packages; to establish how variants of the teaching packages for groups of different ability levels need to be designed so that pupils can use them without difficulty.

Design: Experimental schools that were involved in the development of the teaching packages and schools that have purchased the packages will be given a questionnaire asking whether they would be prepared to participate in the study. They will also be asked for information about the necessary equipment. Two instructional variants will be developed - one detailed, one less detailed - for each of the two different types of problem pupils will be asked to solve. At each school four groups of four pupils will participate. Per problem this involves 160 pupils on vocational/junior general secondary courses and 160 pupils on senior general secondary/pre-university courses. Technology teachers (N=20 per problem) will be interviewed.

12732 Technological aspects of interaction and effectiveness in the use of information networks and databases on higher education.
RUS 1994
Research Date(s): 1991-1992
Satunina, A.Y.
Inst: Research Institute for Higher Education, 103062, Moscow, K-62, Podsosensky per. 20, Russia.
State Committee for Higher Education Institutions, 113833, Moscow, M-230, Lysinovskja str. 51, Russia

information network; information system; information technology; higher education; data base
réseau d'information; système d'information; technologie de l'information; enseignement supérieur; banque de données
PROJECT DESCRIPTION

The study concerned the use of modern information technologies, especially the technical aspects of the interaction between Russian documentary databases on higher education and the TRACE information network.

Publ: Satunina, A.Y.; Kohanovich, Y.A. & Isayeva, N.Z. *Foreign data bases of higher education.* Information review. M., NIIVO, 1992.

12733 Technology for all: educational models for effective implementation.
GBR   1993
Research Date(s): 1990-1995
Goody, J.
Sup: Shipstone, D.; Selkirk, K.
Inst: Nottingham University, School of Education, University Park, Nottingham NG7 2RD, United Kingdom.
technology; technical education; curriculum development
technologie; enseignement technique; élaboration de programmes d'études
PROJECT DESCRIPTION

Design and technology activity is cross-curricular. This, and its relatively recent appearance in school curricula, has made consensus and clarity concerning its nature difficult to achieve and the introduction of the National Curriculum has led to new interpretations.

The study aims to establish a coherent theoretical framework to support the development of technology within the curriculum and to clarify the nature of technology and its role in education past, present and future.

The problems to be addressed are: (1) defining technology; (2) describing the nature of technology; (3) investigation of the role of human values in technology education; (4) identifying fundamental aims and objectives; (5) developing a descriptive model to demonstrate the central ideas of technological activity; (6) determining current organisational structures; (7) identifying the principles of learning and teaching technology; (8) developing models for implementing 1-7 above; (9) critique of the National Curriculum Orders in relation to 1-8 above; (10) issues relating to assessment and evaluation.

The methodology will include: literature surveys; structured interviews, e.g. with practitioners working with students in the 5-18 age range; classroom observation and case studies.

12734 Tecnologie informatiche nell'educazione linguistica. (Information technology in language teaching.)
ITA   1994
Research Date(s): 1992-
Caviglia, Francesco; Degl'Innocenti, Riccardo.
Sup: Ferraris, Maria.
Inst: Istituto per le Tecnologie Didattiche - ITD (Institute for Educational Technology), Via all'Opera Pia 11, 16145 Genova, Italy.
Consiglio Nazionale delle Ricerche - CNR (National Research Council), Piazzale Aldo Moro 7, 00185 Roma, Italy
information technology; computer science; language teaching; educational software; teaching method; didactic use of computer; composition; writing
technologie de l'information; informatique; enseignement des langues; didacticiel; méthode pédagogique; usage didactique de l'ordinateur; composition littéraire; écriture
PROJECT DESCRIPTION

For some years, the Institute for Educational Technology has been working on computer applications in the field of language teaching, especially composition writing. The Institute has developed an original courseware called WordProf, which aims at assisting beginners in the acquisition of communicative skills in writing. This courseware is presently in an experimental phase.

The knowledge that has been gained so far in this sector will be applied in 1992 in the anticipated extension of the Piano Nazionale Informatica (National Project for the Introduction of Computer Science in Curricula) in the discipline of linguistic science.

The activities planned for 1992 are directed towards a systematization of the materials and experiences and towards promoting their dissemination and their use as tools in teacher training. More specifically, the activities will include: revision of the WordProf software on the basis of the results of the experimental phase, and its successive marketing; development of a teaching package, including software and written material; offering support to teachers and pupils regarding the various uses of the computer in the teaching and learning of writing.

12735 TOSKA: Tools and Methods for a Sophisticated Knowledge Based Authoring Facility.
GBR   1993
Research Date(s): 1989-1991
Goodyear, P.
Inst: Lancaster University, Department of Educational Research, Cartmel College, Bailrigg, Lancaster LA1 4YW, United Kingdom.

Fin: European Community DELTA Programme.
authoring system; software; artificial intelligence
système-auteur; logiciel; intelligence artificielle
PROJECT DESCRIPTION

The main objectives of the TOSKA project are: (1) to define a generic framework for knowledge-based support of authoring interactive learning environments; and (2) to contribute to the standardization of an authoring methodology. The authoring framework must be able to support authors in building a wide variety of interactive learning systems (ranging from simple simulation systems to individualized tutorial instruction) in different domains. In its first phase the project has been searching for the generic components of instructional systems, domain representations, instructional methods and learner characteristics. Further, based on these generic components, it has developed some initial prototypes and methods to control the knowledge-based authoring process. In its second phase, the project is evaluating the applicability of the generic components and applying them in two selected test domains. The first concerns teaching the maintenance of aeroplane components; the second is training users in the use of a software package.

Publ: Goodyear, P. (ed.). Research on teaching and the design of intelligent tutoring systems, Chapter 1. In: *Teaching Knowledge and Intelligent Tutoring.* New Jersey: Ablex, Norwood, 1991.
Johnson, R. & Goodyear, P. Knowledge-based authoring of adaptive courseware. Paper for the 2nd European Congress on Artificial Intelligence and Training, Lille, France, September 1990.
Goodyear, P. & Johnson, R. Knowledge-based authoring of knowledge-based courseware. In: *Proceedings of the 7th International Conference on Technology and Education,* Vol 1/1990, pp. 379-381, Brussels, March.
Goodyear, P. Development of learning technology at the European level. In: *Educational and Training Technology International,* Vol 26, No 4/1989, pp. 335-341.

12736 La transmission et l'appropriation des connaissances dans les domaines de l'économie, de la physique et des mathématiques: le fonctionnement des connaissances chez l'apprenant.
FRA   1993
Research Date(s): 1987-
Balacheff, Nicolas; Belisle, Claire; Cicille, Patricia; Carluer, Claudine.
Sup: Albertini, Jean-Marie; Tiberghien, Andrée.
Inst: Ministère de la recherche, CNRS UPR/5411 et GDR/28, Institut de recherche en pédagogie de l'économie et en audio-visuel pour la communication dans les sciences sociales, 93 Chemin des Mouilles, BP 167, 69130 Ecully Cedex, France.
physical sciences; economics; mathematics; didactics; learning; secondary education
sciences physiques; science économique; mathématiques; didactique; acquisition de connaissances; enseignement secondaire
PROJECT DESCRIPTION

Objectifs: Dans le cadre des travaux de didactique trois thèmes sont développés: (1) étude des représentations économiques chez des élèves de classes de troisièmes et de terminales; (2) modélisation qualitative du fonctionnement des connaissances en physique d'élèves de 12 à 14 ans; (3) étude des problèmes de l'enseignement et de l'apprentissage des processus de validation en mathématiques et physique.

Méthodologie: (1) Une première enquête par questionnaire vidéotex accessible par minitel a été soumis à un échantillon représentatif des élèves de troisième, les résultats montrent que les représentations économiques se forgent dans la pratique extra-scolaire, leurs connaissances sont cohérentes mais peu complexe. Une enquête similaire porte sur un échantillon de 3000 élèves de terminales afin de déterminer s'il existe des différences sensibles entre les différentes filières (enseignement général littéraire et scientifique, baccalauréat technologique et professionnel). (2) Une modélisation permet d'élaborer des structures de connaissances en physique dans le champ d'application est constitué par l'ensemble des situations donnant lieu au même type d'interprétations, ces structures permettent d'interpréter les acquisitions des élèves au cours de l'enseignement et l'importance de la modification de l'organisation des connaissances (niveau explicatif, niveau théorique). (3) La confrontation entre deux disciplines amène à une analyse épistémologique à trois niveaux: discipline de référence, contenu de l'enseignement et élève. En mathématique la validation privilégiée est la démonstration, en physique la validation par la situation expérimentale est peu ou pas du tout pris en charge.

Publ: Albertini, Jean-Marie; Carluer, Claudine & Cicille, Patricia.
L'économie vue par les élèves de 3ème: des représentations justes mais parcellaires. In: *Education et formation,* 1989, n° 18, pp. 38-49.
Enquête sur les représentations économiques des élèves de 3ème. In: Coll. *Les dossiers éducation et formation,* Ministère de l'Education nationale, 1989, 140p.
Balacheff, Nicolas. Towards a problématique for research on mathematics teaching. In: *Journal for Research on mathematics Education,* 1990, 21, n° 4, pp. 258-272.

Balacheff, Nicolas. Beyond a psychological approach of the psychology of mathematics education. In: *For the learning of mathematics*, 1990, 10, n° 3, pp. 2-8.
(Une liste complète est disponible.).

12737 Tvorba a využití materiálních didaktických prostředků pro skoly základní a střední v rámci informační a komunikační technologie. (Construction and use of communication and information technology teaching aids in primary and secondary schools.)
CSK 1994
Research Date(s): 1991-1992
Kouba, L.; Rambousek, V.; Cernochová, M.; Fialová, I.; Jироušková, I.; Mlčková, M.; Novák, J.; Ohlídková, B.
Sup: Helus, Z.
Inst: Pedagogická fakulta Univerzity Karlovy (Charles University, Faculty of Education), M.D. Rettigové 4, 116 39 Praha 1, Czech Republic.
Ministerstvo školství, mládeže a tělovýchovy (Ministry of Education, Youth and Physical Education), Karmelitská 7, 118 00 Praha 1, Czech Republic
educational technology; information technology; development of education; teacher education
technologie de l'éducation; technologie de l'information; développement de l'éducation; formation des enseignants
PROJECT DESCRIPTION
Aim: The study is concerned with the potential contribution of information and educational technology to education in the Czech Republic. It seeks to develop a concept for educational technology from an interdisciplinary point of view and to define appropriate contents. The theoretical part of the study is concerned with the rational organization and management of education; the practical part addresses the effective use of information and educational technology to support teaching.
The study also addresses the optimal use of existing technological aids in teacher education for demonstration, training and diagnostic purposes. Teacher training courses in the field of information and educational technology will be developed and trialled.

12738 The use and practical application of mathematics in a cross-curricular context in National Curriculum key stage 4.
GBR 1993
Research Date(s): 1991-1992
Tanner, H.; Jones, S.
Inst: University College of Swansea, Department of Education, Hendrefoilan, Swansea SA2 7NB, United Kingdom.
Fin: Welsh Office.
mathematics; assessment; achievement test; common core curriculum; integrated curriculum
mathématiques; appréciation; test de rendement; tronc commun; programme d'études intégré
PROJECT DESCRIPTION
The research examines and develops approaches for teaching and assessing attainment target one of National Curriculum mathematics in Wales. The research is based initially on the techniques of mathematical modelling and subsequently on applications of mathematics in a cross-curricular context. A network of schools in South Wales is conducting action research into the teaching of mathematics through its practical applications.
The project aims to: (1) identify relevant approaches to teaching mathematics in a practical context; (2) establish the extent to which the techniques of modelling can be taught in key stage 4; (3) develop materials for use in schools to teach mathematics in a practical context; (4) develop assessment techniques and materials; and (5) consider ways of integrating practical approaches into programmes of study.

12739 The value of field residential courses in the teaching of earth sciences.
GBR 1993
Research Date(s): 1986-
Sutton, I.
Inst: Nottingham University, Department of Adult Education, 14-22 Shakespeare Street, Nottingham NG1 4FJ, United Kingdom.
earth sciences; study tour; open-air activities; study abroad; adult education
sciences de la terre; voyage d'étude; activités de plein air; études à l'étranger; éducation des adultes
PROJECT DESCRIPTION
The research is intended to investigate the value of field studies in the teaching of adults in the area of earth sciences. The study involves the investigation of the way field activities can be integrated into the teaching of earth sciences to adults with special reference to teaching methods, and day, weekend, longer residential and foreign study tours. The value of pre-course preparation for the field study is an important aspect of the research.

12740 The Wound Programme.
GBR 1993
Research Date(s): 1990-1994
Davis, M.
Sup: Harden, M.
Inst: Dundee University, Centre for Medical Education, Ninewells Hospital and Medical School, Dundee DD1 9SY, United Kingdom.
Fin: ConvaTec.
medicine; teaching aid; vocational education; undergraduate study
médecine; moyen d'enseignement; enseignement professionnel; supérieur premier cycle
PROJECT DESCRIPTION
The Wound Programme is a learning resource for medical undergraduates in the UK, Europe and North America. It comprises a resource book, a student study guide and a teachers' guide. It is designed to inform undergraduates about recent advances in the field of skin wound healing and can be employed by medical schools wishing to implement one or more of the following curriculum strategies: student-centred learning, problem-based learning and integration of the curriculum, both horizontal and vertical. The resource book employs a new format, based on a hypertext layout, and a new approach to the assessment of patients with wounds - the wound healing matrix.

Gap between arithmetical and algebraic thinking .... see no. 13130

Représentations dans l'apprentissage des sciences physiques .... see no. 13153

Affect and learning mathematics .... see no. 13206

Motivation von LehramtskandidatInnen in Mathematik (The motivation of mathematics student teachers)........................ see no. 13228

Alternatives to print for visually impaired students .... see no. 13295

Information technology and the learning needs of emotionally and behaviourally disturbed children.................................. see no. 13326

The logistics of provision of courses in information technology for adult students with physical and sensory disabilities .... see no. 13342

The logistics of provision of vocational training in information technology for adult students with physical and sensory disabilities .... see no. 13343

The use of information technology in adult basic education of students with physical and sensory handicaps .... see no. 13374

Spotkania a środowisko: rola teorii spotkania w nauczaniu przedmiotu środowisko społeczno-przyrodnicze (Encounters and the environment: the role of encounter theory in the teaching of the subject "Social and Natural Environment") .... see no. 13463

Evolution du système productif et appropriation des nouvelles technologies de formation .... see no. 13498

Technologie-indicatoren (Technology indicators) .... see no. 13514

Graduate numeracy.. see no. 13584

Problemi di formazione di operatori nel campo dello sviluppo delle infrastrutture di assistenza all'innovazione ed al trasferimento di tecnologie: problemi professionali, economici e legislativi (Professional, economic and legislative problems related to the training of officers working in the field of infrastructural development in support of educational innovation and the transfer of technology) .... see no. 13616

Qualifizierungsziel Ganzheitliche Arbeitsgestaltungskompetenz - Sozialvertraegliche Gestaltung von IuK-Systemen als Gegenstand der Aus- und Weiterbildung von DV-Fachkraeften (Holistic job engineering competence as a goal for qualifications: socially acceptable engineering of information and communications systems as a subject for basic and further training for computer specialists) .... see no. 13621

Technologie-indicatoren 1991 (Technology Indicators 1991).............. .... see no. 13743

12 SOCIAL SCIENCES – SCIENCES SOCIALE – SOCIALWISSENSCHAFTEN

12741 Alternatives in education: an investigation of past, present and future policies in education.
GBR 1993
Research Date(s): 1990-1992
Tomlinson, S.
Inst: University College of Swansea, Department of Education, Hendrefoilan, Swansea SA2 7NB, United Kingdom.
Fin: Leverhulme Trust.
history of education; educational policy; educational reform
histoire de l'éducation; politique de l'éducation; réforme de l'enseignement
PROJECT DESCRIPTION
The aim of this research is to lay the basis for suggesting alternatives to current educational policies by a critical analysis of historical and ideological developments in education from 1944 to 1992. It will include an examination of the nature of and purposes behind the Education Reform Act 1988; an analysis of how the Act and subsequent reforms are working out; and whose interests are being served.
The methodology is a library study and 'action research' with the researcher participating in various national political committees and associations concerned with changing educational policies.
Publ: Tomlinson, S. Yet another repeat. In: *Times Educational Supplement*, 1.11.91.
Tomlinson, S. & Ross, A.M. *Teachers and parents*. Education and Training Paper No 7. London: Institute for Public Policy Research, 1991.

12742 Analysis of reports on curriculum.
GBR 1993
Research Date(s): 1988-1992
Bain, W.
Inst: Heriot-Watt University, Moray House Institute of Education, Holyrood Road, Edinburgh EH8 8AQ, United Kingdom.
history of education; curriculum; educational reform; decision making
histoire de l'éducation; programme d'études; réforme de l'enseignement; prise de décision
PROJECT DESCRIPTION

The years between 1945-1990 have been a period of major change in school curriculum, assessment, and certificates as well as in advisory groups such as Her Majesty's Inspectorate (HMI) and the Scottish Examination Board (SEB), Scottish Vocational Education Council (SCOTVEC), Scottish Consultative Council on the Curriculum (SCCC) and the General Teaching Council (GTC). The researcher is analysing the processes of decision making which led to specific reports and their implementation or shelving, in both primary and secondary education. In addition, the analysis considers teachers' and others' involvement in working parties and bodies such as the GTC and SCCC, and the expanding of certification in secondary schools. A range of reports and primary sources are being studied for this work.
Publ: Bain, W.H. 29 steps to standard grade. In: *Times Educational Supplement Scotland*, No 1113, 4 March 1988, p. 12.
Bain, W.H. The Sera conference reports. In: *Times Educational Supplement Scotland*, 6 October 1989, p. 5.

12743 The Army Schoolmaster and the development of elementary education in the Army 1812-1920.
GBR 1993
Research Date(s): 1986-1992
Smith, E.
Sup: Gordon, P.
Inst: London University, Institute of Education, Department of History, Humanities and Philosophy, 20 Bedford Way, London WC1H OAL, United Kingdom; Ministry of Defence, Directorate of Army Education, Court Road, Eltham, London SE9 5NR, United Kingdom.
history of education; military school; teacher
histoire de l'éducation; école militaire; enseignant
PROJECT DESCRIPTION
This dissertation deals with a number of aspects of the Army Schoolmaster from the origins of Army education in 1812 until the establishment of the Royal Army Education Corps in 1920. It is concerned with the Army Schoolmasters training in the early times; the impact of educational reforms of the Gleig era, i.e. post 1846 and the service; the curriculum and examination for adult and children's schools; informal education; inspection of Army schools; the Army Schoolmaster's status and conditions of service; and the First World War and its impact on the nature of Army education.

12744 Assessment of National Curriculum History Key Stages 1-3.
GBR 1993
Research Date(s): 1990-1995
Knight, P.
Inst: Lancaster University, Department of Educational Research, Cartmel College, Bailrigg, Lancaster LA1 4YW, United Kingdom.
history; assessment; common core curriculum
histoire; appréciation; tronc commun
PROJECT DESCRIPTION
The English National Curriculum makes history a mandatory part of the curriculum for children in Key Stages 1-4 (ages 6-16). However, earlier research shows that this alone is an innovation in primary schooling. Moreover, the curriculum is to be assessment-led. Yet, not only is there little tradition of this sort of assessment in Key Stages 1 and 2 (ages 6-11) but it is not endemic in Key Stage 3 (ages 12-14). Lastly, there are doubts about the validity of the domain-specific developmental sequence underpinning both assessment and the curriculum.
This study builds on earlier, funded work. Two inter-related approaches will be taken: (1) with the aid of advisers, teachers and children, methods of teacher assessment which match National Curriculum requirements for history and which are compatible with the exigencies of classroom life will be devised, tested, refined and propagated; (2) using the data gained from the above and from clinical interviewing, a developmental account of children's historical reasoning will be offered.
Results from the research will be presented in two forms: (1) detailed "rich" guidelines for teachers; (2) a model of development.
Publ: Knight, P.T. Teaching as exposure: the case of good practice in junior school history. In: *British Educational Research Journal*, Vol 17, No 2/1991, pp. 129-140.

12745 Betriebswirtschaftslehre und Wirtschaftsdidaktik. (The science and didactics of business management.)
AUT 1993
Research Date(s): 1989-1992
Neuweg, Georg Hans.
Inst: Abteilung fuer Berufs- und Wirtschaftspaedagogik, Altenbergerstrasse 69, A-4040 Linz.
Universitaet Linz, Altenbergerstrasse 69, A-4040 Linz
economics; didactics; curriculum research; commercial training; business management
science économique; didactique; recherche sur les programmes d'études; formation commerciale; gestion des entreprises
PROJECT DESCRIPTION
Beitrag zur Klaerung des Problems der Auswahl und Begruendung von Lehrzielen und -inhalten in Betriebswirtschaftslehre-Curricula. Diskussion

des Verhaeltnisses von Fachwissenschaft und Fachdidaktik, Aufweisen von Bruchstellen in diesem Verhaeltnis und von Ansatzpunkten zu deren Ueberwindung. Evaluation der Betriebswirtschaftslehre im Hinblick auf die funktionale und emanzipatorische Qualifizierung auf dem Feld der kaufmaennisch-verwaltenden Berufe und auf dem Feld des Handelns in privaten Haushalten sowie im Hinblick auf die Bildung des muendigen Wirtschaftsbuergers. Aufriss von Bedingungen und Strategien zur Erweiterung des Qualifizierungs- und Bildungspotentials der Betriebswirtschaftslehre.

Die Theorien zur Auswahl und Begruendung von Lehrinhalten wurden evaluiert und weiterentwickelt, die ausgewaehlten metatheoretischen Konzeptionen der Betriebswirtschaftslehre analysiert und evaluiert.

Plaedoyer fuer wissenschaftsorierentierten Unterricht bei gleichzeitig kritischer Distanz zur Fachwissenschaft. Betriebswirtschaftliche Didaktik sollte sich auch auf ausserberufliche Lebenssituationen konzentrieren; insbesondere ist zielmonistischen und teilsystembezogenen Denkmustern entgegenzuwirken.

Publ: Neuweg, Georg Hans. *Betriebswirtschaftslehre und Wirtschaftsdidaktik. Fuer ein umfassendes Verstaendnis von oekonomischer Bildung im Betriebswirtschaftslehre- Unterricht.* Bergisch Gladbach: Th. Hobein 1992.
Neuweg, Georg Hans. Das Problemprinzip als wirtschaftsdidaktisches Innovationsparadigma. In: *Zeitschrift fuer Berufs- und Wirtschaftspaedagogik*, 1992, Heft 1, S. 3 ff.

12746 Binet's work and achievement: the first intelligence scales of 1905.
GBR 1993
Research Date(s): 1988-1993
Faber, D.
Sup: Lovie, A.
Inst: Liverpool University, Department of Psychology, PO Box 147, Liverpool L69 3BX, United Kingdom.
psychology; intelligence measurement; intelligence test; history of education
psychologie; mesure de l'intelligence; test d'intelligence; histoire de l'éducation
PROJECT DESCRIPTION

The area of this research is the history of psychology. Although Binet is recognised as the pioneer of intelligence testing and his influence has been very great, the genesis of his scales is often misrepresented. The researcher's aim is to explain the achievement of Alfred Binet (1857-1911) with reference to his Intelligence Scales of 1905, the first 'true' tests of intelligence.

The research involves identifying Binet's changing conceptions of intelligence and its developmental aspects, and tracing the origins of the test items in his experimental work in the 20 years preceding 1905. This also necessitates an examination of Binet's view of psychology as a science, his conception of a psychological experiment and the nature and role of introspections. The social and cultural contexts are important contributing factors to Binet's achievement, and are explained with reference to testing in other countries. In France, political forces and an immediate educational problem led to the Minister of Education's decision to have Paris school children tested or screened for ineducability. Binet's work, particularly that in association with the 'Société Libre pour L'Etude Psychologique de l'Enfant', was known by the authorities in 1904. The commission was entrusted to Binet; his earlier work and later collaboration with Simon resulted in the finally produced Scales of 1905, amply justifying their trust in the psychological work of Binet.

12747 Cambridge history project.
GBR 1993
Research Date(s): 1991-1992
Lee, P.
Inst: London University, Institute of Education, Department of History, Humanities and Psychology, 20 Bedford Way, London WC1H 0AL, United Kingdom.
Fin: Essex Local Education Authority; University of Cambridge Local Examinations Syndicate.
history; curriculum development; examination
histoire; élaboration de programmes d'études; examen
PROJECT DESCRIPTION

The research consists of two A and AS level projects, developing a new history course for the 16-19 age range. The projects include a radical assessment package. The courses are designed to follow GCSE in terms of progression, clear objectives, encouragement of active learning, and to overcome problems of content-coherence in concept/ability-led courses. Option 1 (People, Power and Politics) has been approved by the School Examinations and Assessment Council (SEAC), Option 2 (Technology and Society) has restricted approval from SEAC. This stage of the project follows an earlier one which ran from September 1988 to September 1991.

12748 Children's thinking and understanding in history, with special reference to the role of computer-assisted learning (CAL).
GBR 1993
Research Date(s): 1967-1995
Dickinson, A.
Sup: Gordon, P.
Inst: London University, Institute of Education, Department of History, Humanities and Philosophy, 20 Bedford Way, London WC1H 0AL, United Kingdom.
history; didactic use of computer; comprehension; thinking; pupil
histoire; usage didactique de l'ordinateur; compréhension; pensée; élève
PROJECT DESCRIPTION

The main aims of the research are to investigate further, children's conceptions of evidence and enquiry and to explore aspects of the contribution that computers can make to pupils' thinking and understanding in history (in particular their reflexive thinking, substantive understanding and notions of historical evidence and enquiry). A key principle underlying the work is that research into the learning and teaching of history requires analysis of the conceptual base of the discipline and empirical investigation of children's thinking and ideas (both explicit and tacit understandings). The work involves the use of video-recording techniques pioneered by the History Department at the Institute of Education with the aim of revealing the processes of children's thinking in history, pupils' strategies for making sense of the past and their understandings (explicit and tacit) of specific historical concepts (second order and substantive).

12749 Church, State and education: a study of the educational philosophy of Henry Edward Manning, 1865-1992.
GBR 1993
Research Date(s): 1990-1993
Pereiro, J.
Sup: McClelland, V.
Inst: Hull University, School of Education, Cottingham Road, Hull HU6 7RX, United Kingdom.
history of education; philosophy of education; Christian education
histoire de l'éducation; philosophie de l'éducation; éducation chrétienne
PROJECT DESCRIPTION

H.E. Manning's years as Archbishop of Westminster coincided with a renewed interest in the 'Education Question'. The civilizing value of education, the social and economic benefits which would follow from its wider extension, were themes dear to Victorian England. The interest in education and the rapid nationwide development of the educational structures soon led to an all important debate about the respective roles of the individual, the Church and the State in this area. H.E. Manning played a prominent part in the 'Education Question'. On the one hand, he made a considerable contribution to the setting up of the Catholic educational system. He also intervened quite decisively in the above-mentioned debate through his connections with men in power and his involvement in the official commissions set up to examine present policy and to offer solutions to the educational problems of the times. The research concentrates on the philosophical principles from which he draws his suggestions to solve the problems and tensions of the age, as well as for the setting up of the educational system on a proper basis to assure its greater effectiveness.

12750 A comparative study of student youth social and political lifestyles in Hungary and England.
GBR 1993
Research Date(s): 1991-1992
Cowen, H.; Rosie, A.; Gabor, K.
Inst: Cheltenham & Gloucester College of Higher Education, Faculty of Education and Health, The Park, Cheltenham GL50 2QF, United Kingdom; Attilar Joszef University, Department of Sociology, Saeged 6722, Petofi Sandor Str. 30/34, Hungary.
Fin: Hungarian Academy of Social Science.
student sociology; student life; cross-national research; student; Hungary; England
sociologie de l'étudiant; vie étudiante; recherche transnationale; étudiant; Hongrie; Angleterre
PROJECT DESCRIPTION

The research project builds upon an international youth study already carried out in Hungary, Germany and the Netherlands. Its focus is on the social profiles, social and political orientation and lifestyles of student youth in localities in Hungary and England, comparing how student youth are living through Europe's economic and political changes. Student bodies in Sopron and Kosseg, Hungary, and Cheltenham and Gloucester, England will be the subject of interviews by questionnaire. Students will be selected under three basic categories: older, secondary school students; further education and technical college students; students in higher education. They will be questioned on a series of central issues relating to: patterns of social orientation; most important life events; perspectives and attitudes towards personal and societal futures; political interest and participation; group activities. Findings will be compared and then considered in the light of current youth and educational policies in each country.

12751 Concepts of history and teaching approaches at National Curriculum Key Stages 2 & 3.
GBR 1993
Research Date(s): 1991-1995
Dickinson, A.; Lee, P.
Inst: London University, Institute of Education, Department of History, Humanities and Philosophy, 20 Bedford Way, London WC1H OAL, United Kingdom.
Fin: Economic and Social Research Council.
history; common core curriculum; teaching method; concept formation; primary education; lower secondary
histoire; tronc commun; méthode pédagogique; formation de concept; enseignement primaire; secondaire premier cycle
PROJECT DESCRIPTION
The project is concerned with the teaching and learning of history in National Curriculum Key Stages 2 and 3, and falls into three phases. In phase 1 the development of children's understandings of the concepts of evidence and explanation in history will be investigated. Phase 2 will seek to categorise teaching approaches according to their attention to progression in children's ideas. Phase 3 will explore relationships between teaching approaches and learning outcomes.

12752 De evaluatie van het SLO-onderwijsleerpakket "WO II, toen en nu". (Evaluation of the SLO teaching package "WO II, toen en nu" (World War II, Then and Now).)
NLD 1994
Research Date(s): 1992-1993
Vermeulen, A.C.A.M.; Gijtenbeek, J.; Eck, E. van.
Sup: Abram, I.B.H.
Inst: Stichting Centrum voor Onderwijsonderzoek (SCO) (Centre for Educational Research), Grote Bickersstraat 72, 1013 KS Amsterdam, Netherlands.
Universiteit van Amsterdam (University of Amsterdam), P.O. Box 19268, 1000 GG Amsterdam, Netherlands
Fin: SVO het Instituut voor Onderzoek van het Onderwijs.
history; social studies; curriculum development; learning kit; secondary education
histoire; études sociales; élaboration de programmes d'études; valise pédagogique; enseignement secondaire
PROJECT DESCRIPTION
Background: In the period 1988-1989 the National Institute for Curriculum Development (SLO) developed a teaching package entitled "World War II, Then and Now". A special feature of this package is that it focuses on the experiences of human beings rather than on military or political events. Moreover, links are made with the present wherever this is possible. To aid decision making with regard to the further development of teaching material in this field, this study examines how far the SLO package and the material developed by the Anne Frank Foundation (AFS) meet a need in the secondary schools.
Aim: The study seeks to identify any significant differences in teaching about World War II between teachers who use the SLO package and teachers who use other material. It will examine educational contents, objectives, teaching methods, the amount of instruction time devoted to the subject, teaching aids used, and the place of the subject in the history and civics curricula.
Design: Questionnaires will be presented to department heads of all types of secondary school to gather data on the distribution and the use of the SLO package. Information will also be collected on relevant school characteristics, (denomination, separate schools vs. combined schools, proportion of immigrant pupils) and teacher characteristics (subject, age/level of pupils, participation in conferences). This information will be linked to the distribution and usage of the SLO package. Questionnaires will be given to 147 teachers who participated in one of the four regional conferences at which the material was presented in order to elicit information on the distribution of the package and the considerations that played a role in the decision whether or not to start using it. Information on how the package is used and on teachers' perceptions of the package will be gained through two questionnaires to history teachers (two categories of school) and one to civics teachers. All questionnaires will first be judged by experts and be piloted. In each school two teachers will be interviewed about classroom practice and one about the context in which teaching takes place. Teachers will be asked to keep detailed diaries during teaching.

12753 Die Entkonfessionalisierung des Lehrerstandes im Reichsgau Salzburg. (The laicization of the teaching profession in the Reichsgau of Salzburg.)
AUT 1993
Research Date(s): 1989-1992
Rinnerthaler, Alfred.
Inst: Institut fuer kirchliche Zeitgeschichte, Moenchsberg 2a, A-5020 Salzburg; Institut fuer Kirchenrecht, Churfuerststrasse 1, A-5020 Salzburg.
Internationales Forschungszentrum fuer Grundfragen der Wissenschaften, Moenchsberg 2, A-5020 Salzburg; Universitaet Salzburg, Residenzplatz 1, A-5020 Salzburg

history of education; denominational school; Fascism; educational policy
histoire de l'éducation; école confessionnelle; fascisme; politique de l'éducation
PROJECT DESCRIPTION
Dargestellt wurde - an Hand einer Vielzahl von Quellenbelegen - die generelle Umgestaltung der LehrerInnenbildung in der Zeit von 1938 bis 1945 sowie die Errichtung einer staatlichen LehrerInnenbildungsanstalt in Salzburg. Der zweite Teil behandelte die Entfernung geistlicher Lehrer aus dem Unterricht in weltlichen Faechern. Der dritte Teil setzte sich mit sonstigen Entkonfessionalisierungsmassnahmen im Schulbereich auseinander. Dazu gehoerten das Verbot jeglicher Nebentaetigkeit im kirchlichen Bereich sowie eine intensive politische Schulung der Lehrerschaft. Zentrum der Schulungstaetigkeit war in Salzburg die 'Gauschulungsburg Hohenwerfen'. Wo die politischen Umschulungen keinen Erfolg erwarten liessen oder tatsaechlich erbrachten, griffen Amtsenthebungen und sonstige Disziplinierungen.
Ergebnis dieser regionalen Studie war, dass mindestens ein Drittel aller Erzieher in der nationalsozialistischen Zeit von dienstrechtlichen Massnahmen betroffen wurde, wobei in rund der Haelfte der Faelle die religioese Betaetigung der Betroffenen hiefuer ausschlaggebend war.
Es wurde eine historisch-kritische Quellenanalyse durchgefuehrt.
Publ: Rinnerthaler, Alfred. Die Entkonfessionalisierung des Lehrerstandes im Reichsgau Salzburg. In: *Oesterreich in Geschichte und Literatur mit Geographie*. 36. Jahrgang 1992, S. 277-311.

12754 Education and the working class: history, theory, policy and practice.
GBR 1993
Research Date(s): 1992-1996
McCulloch, G.
Inst: Lancaster University, Department of Educational Research, Cartmel Colleege, Bailrigg, Lancaster LA1 4YW, United Kingdom.
Fin: Leverhulme Trust.
history of education; educational policy; secondary education; working class
histoire de l'éducation; politique de l'éducation; enseignement secondaire; classe ouvrière
PROJECT DESCRIPTION
The project seeks to identify and explore a tradition of working class secondary education in modern Britain. It will assess its origins, its character, its wider influence, and its longer-term significance.
The working hypothesis is that this tradition has been related to different forms of educational provision that have been developed over the past century, especially in the higher grade schools, the central schools, and the secondary modern schools.
The aim is to study the curriculum, pedagogy, pupils, examinations and class relationships that developed in each of these types of schools, as well as changing policies and attitudes towards them. The underlying continuities are related to policy and provision especially in secondary education but also at other levels of educational provision in the 1990s, to examine how far the forms, assumptions and relationships that underlay these earlier types of provision have survived to play a part in our current outlooks and methods.

12755 Edukacja polityczna w państwach jednoczacej sie Europy. (Political education in the states of a uniting Europe (a glance from Poland).)
POL 1994
Research Date(s): 1992-1994
Mojsiewicz, Czesław; Robakowski, Kazimierz; Gill, Władysław; Borowczyk, Krzysztof.
Inst: Uniwersytet im. Adama Mickiewicza, Instytut Nauk Politycznych i Dziennikarstwa (Adam Mickiewicz University, Institute of Political Science and Journalism), Szamarzewskiego 89 A, Poznań, Poland.
political education; comparative education; Europe
éducation politique; éducation comparée; Europe
PROJECT DESCRIPTION
Aims: (1) Comparative analysis of political education theory and practice in Poland and Western Countries (USA, Germany); (2) definition of political education goals for the states of a uniting Europe; (3) formulation of principal values constituting a basis for political education objectives; (4) formulation of political education objectives in Poland in the period of transition to parliamentary democracy.
The research project consists of the following parts: (1) systemization of the categories of knowledge related to political education (model solutions); (2) analysis of the forms and content of political education from 1945; (3) comparative analysis of curricular contents and teaching methods; (4) verification of the model solutions on the basis of the views and attitudes of those traditionally receiving political training (youth circles, lecturers, political elites).
Methods: (1) Analysis of source materials and documents dealing with political education; (2) comparative analysis of political education goals, objectives and ways of implementation; (3) comparative research based on

behavioural methods of testing opinions, views and attitudes (model research).

The study is to result in a draft political education project for European countries - a perspective model - and a global political education project - including all stages from values to implementation - for the Polish education system.

12756   The elementary education of females in England 1800-1870, with particular reference to the lives and work of girls and women in industrial Lancashire and rural Norfolk and Suffolk.
GBR   1993
Research Date(s): 1983-1991
Gomersall, M.
Sup: Aldrich, R.
Inst: London University, Institute of Education, Department of History, Humanities and Philosophy, 20 Bedford Way, London WC1H OAL, United Kingdom.
history of education; social history; women's education; basic education
histoire de l'éducation; histoire sociale; éducation des femmes; éducation de base
PROJECT DESCRIPTION

The study explores the education and schooling of girls from the lower socio-economic ranks in the period between 1800 and 1870, with particular attention to the experiences of girls in the industrial regions of Lancashire and the agricultural districts of Norfolk and Suffolk. It aims both to reconstruct an area of the past hitherto 'hidden from history', and also to investigate critically the causes and consequences of girls' schooling and broader educational experiences through exploration of the wider socio-economic and cultural contexts in which that education was located. The study thus includes areas and issues beyond those conventionally explored in histories of education. It examines changes and continuities in the lives and work of women, and links these to the purposes and practices of female elementary schooling and the informal educational experiences of girls in the industrial and rural communities of the two regions.

The study is organised in two main sections, focusing firstly on responses to changing economic and social conditions before the 1830s, then moving to an examination of the contributory influences which led to the 'reformism and respectability' of the post-1850 period. Tensions and ambiguities are noted throughout; in relation to shifts and variations in the concept of the 'good' working-class wife and mother, and between the expressed ideals of elementary schooling and the realities of schooling provision and practices. Similarities and differences in the nature and quality of educational experiences across and within the selected regions are also noted, and it is through these dimensions that the key determinants of girls' educational experiences are clarified. The study then concludes with an assessment of the relative importance of schooling in the lives and work of women in the two regions, in an evaluation of the many educative influences which shaped their lives.

Publ: Gomersall, M. Ideals and realities: The education of working-class girls 1800-1870. In: *History of Education*, Vol 17, No 1/1988.
Gomersall, M. Women's work and education in Lancashire 1800-1870: a response to Keith Flett. In: *History of Education*, Vol 18, No 2/1989.

12757   Elementary education, society and politics in Hertfordshire 1918-1939.
GBR   1993
Research Date(s): 1988-1992
Parker, D.
Sup: Bell, R.; Sutherland, G.
Inst: Plymouth University, Rolle Faculty of Education, Douglas Avenue, Exmouth EX8 2AT, United Kingdom; Open University, School of Education, Walton Hall, Milton Keynes MK7 6AA, United Kingdom; Cambridge University, Newnham College, Cambridge CB3 9DF, United Kingdom.
Fin: Hertfordshire County Council.
history of education; educational policy; educational legislation
histoire de l'éducation; politique de l'éducation; législation scolaire
PROJECT DESCRIPTION

This research follows a Master of Philosophy thesis entitled 'The impact of the First World War upon elementary education in Hertfordshire'. Both studies examine the provision of elementary education locally in the light of national thought and trends. The primary research mainly involved source material in the Hertfordshire Record Office (County Council papers, parish files and school files), the Public Record Office (Board of Education files), the British Library, Colindale (county newspapers and national journals), the Census Office, private collections and local museums. Oral evidence was taken from local residents.

The PhD thesis will analyse the impact of new rapid residential and industrial development upon local society and public affairs, and the effect of national economic and political thought and trends upon education. The factors influencing curriculum change will be highlighted, in particular to shed light upon the growing vocational aspect of education for older elementary children (not least the attention given to technical and rural education in the county), the equivocal attitude towards the role of the central schools and the concern to determine an 'appropriate' expansion of secondary education. The impact of the three Hadow reports, especially that of 1926, will be examined, with its major implication for local reorganisation, parental attitudes, school meals, transport, the future of Dual Control and the role of the denominational schools. Research has been undertaken into the county's attempts to identify and provide for children suspected of mental deficiency and backwardness, and into the ambivalent attitudes towards the education of elementary schoolchildren after the age of eleven.

12758   Enquiry into teaching history to over sixteens (ETHOS).
GBR   1993
Research Date(s): 1987-1992
Fines, J.; Nichol, J.
Inst: Exeter University, School of Education, St Luke's, Heavitree Road, Exeter EX1 2LU, United Kingdom.
Fin: Nuffield Foundation.
history; curriculum development; examination; teacher role
histoire; élaboration de programmes d'études; examen; rôle de l'enseignant
PROJECT DESCRIPTION

Enquiry into teaching history to over sixteens (ETHOS) has developed an A and AS level syllabus consisting of 60% coursework. The syllabus gives control of the curriculum back to history teachers, and they mediate their courses from their perspective as trained academic historians. A new approach to resourcing which sees the student carrying on a dialogue with an academic has been produced. This is linked to initiatives in pedagogy.

12759   The European Studies project.
GBR   1993
Research Date(s): 1986-1992
Austin, R.
Inst: Ulster University, Faculty of Education, Cromore Road, Coleraine, County Londonderry BT52 1SA, United Kingdom.
Fin: Departments of Education: Northern Ireland and Eire; Departments for Education: England, France, Belgium and Germany.
international studies; European dimension; curriculum development; secondary education
études internationales; dimension européenne; élaboration de programmes d'études; enseignement secondaire
PROJECT DESCRIPTION

The European Studies project was set up as a six year curriculum development programme for schools in England, Northern Ireland and the Republic of Ireland. It has been developing programmes of joint work in the curriculum for pupils aged 11-18. Those involved in the 14-16 and 16-18 schemes are also linked to schools in France, Belgium, Denmark, Germany and Scotland. Schools have been using common resources and computer and satellite television links to work together across Europe. From the 93 schools involved in 1991 it is intended that a wider programme of dissemination will be undertaken in 1992.

Publ: A full list of project reports is available from the researcher.

12760   Global futures project.
GBR   1993
Research Date(s): 1989-1992
Hicks, D.
Sup: Gundara, J.
Inst: London University, Institute of Education, Centre for Multicultural Education, 20 Bedford Way, London WC1H OAL; United Kingdom.
Fin: Worldwide Fund for Nature.
international studies; environmental study; futurology; citizen participation; civics; primary education; secondary education; further education of teachers
études internationales; étude du milieu; futurologie; participation du citoyen; instruction civique; enseignement primaire; enseignement secondaire; perfectionnement des enseignants
PROJECT DESCRIPTION

If we are concerned about fully educating young people for the 21st century, what sort of preparation do they need and how will the National Curriculum provide it? To make sense of life in the 1990s contemporary trends and events need to be set in a context which is both globally and future orientated. This project focuses on the entitlement of pupils to preparation for responsible and active citizenship as future adult members of a global community. It arises out of, and builds on, much of the innovative work carried out in world studies during the last decade.

In particular, the project will help both teachers and pupils to (a) explore current concerns about the state of the planet; (b) clarify their choice of preferred futures at scales from the personal to the global; (c) envision alternative futures which are both just and ecologically sustainable; (d) develop their own personal and political skills; (e) exercise their rights responsibly as active citizens in the local and global community.

The project will be of interest to primary and secondary teachers concerned, for example, with English, science, design and technology, geography or religious education, and cross-curricular issues such as personal and social education, environmental education and citizenship. It will provide both appropriate in-service training programmes and also work with schools to produce relevant resource materials for teachers and pupils.

Publ: Hicks, D. *Exploring alternative futures: a teacher's interim guide.* Global Futures Project, University of London, Institute of Education, 1991.

Hicks, D. Preparing for the millennium: reflections on the need for futures education. In: *Futures,* Vol 23, No 6/1991.

12761 A headteacher dynasty: illuminating the history of education in England and Wales from the 1840s to the 1930s through the biographies of three generations of one teaching family.
GBR 1993
Research Date(s): 1990-1994
Marsden, W.
Inst: Liverpool University, Department of Education, PO Box 147, Liverpool L69 3BX, United Kingdom.
history of education; head teacher; England; Wales
histoire de l'éducation; chef d'établissement; Angleterre; Pays de Galles
PROJECT DESCRIPTION
In the course of previous educational history research, it became apparent that a large amount of, albeit widely scattered, archive material is available on a notable headteacher dynasty, the Adams family. The intention is to undertake a longitudinal study of this family, following through three generations of educational experience from the 1840s to the 1930s, a critical hundred years in the history of education in England and Wales. The range of institutions with which the family, at least six members of which were headteachers, was involved cover training, a National Society School; several British and Foreign Schools and training colleges; a works school; London Board schools; two universities; army education; 20th century 'Central' secondary schools; and a private school, in a wide range of geographical settings. The study will explore continuity and change in education in England and Wales; a range of educational trends and theories as applied in particular cases; and shifting social contexts and values as they interacted in various rural but mostly urban settings within the period under review.

Publ: Marsden, W.E. *Educating the respectable; a study of Fleet Road Board School, Hampstead, 1879-1903.* London: The Woburn Press, 1990.

12762 Historical analysis of the development of higher education in Russia.
RUS 1994
Research Date(s): 1991-1992
Hoteyenkov, V.F.
Sup: Momot, A.I.
Inst: Research Institute for Higher Education, 103062, Moscow, K-62, Podsosensky per. 20, Russia.
State Committee for Higher Education Institutions, 113833, Moscow, M-230, Lysinovskja str. 51, Russia
history of education; higher education; development of education
histoire de l'éducation; enseignement supérieur; développement de l'éducation
PROJECT DESCRIPTION
A systematic historical study was made of the origin and the development of the higher education system in Russia up to 1917. The study examined a range of aspects related to the development of higher education, such as teaching programmes and processes, the organization of education, financial aspects and scientific activity. Special attention was given to the characteristics of the university "codes" of 1804, 1863 and 1905, and to governmental policies in the field of higher education on the eve of the revolution of 1917.

Publ: Savelyev, A.Y.; Momot, A.I.; Hoteyenkov, V.F.; et al. *An outline of the history of Russian higher education.* Vol. 1. M., Vysshaya schoola, 1993.
Savelyev, A.Y.; Momot, A.I.; Hoteyenkov, V.F.; et al. *The history of university education in prerevolutionary Russia.* Information review. M., NIIVO, 1993.
Hoteyenkov, V.F. & Gospodarik, Y.P. Theory and practice of higher education management during the first 5-year plans. In: *Conceptual aspects of higher education development.* M., 1991.

12763 Historie ve škole: její možnosti při rozvíjení poznání, občanského vědomí, morálky a tvořivosti žáků a studentů a její potřeby. (History in school: possibilities for the development of knowledge, civic consciousness, morality and creativity in pupils and students.)
CSK 1994
Research Date(s): 1992-
Mandelová, Helena; Gladkovová, Eva; Kunstová, Eliška; Hrachovcová, Marie; Ulvr, Václav; Bezchlebová, Marie; Sedlmayerová, Milena; et al.
Sup: Fučíková, Jarmila.
Inst: Historický klub (Historical Club), Archiv UK, Ovocný trh, 110 00 Praha 1, Czech Republic.
Ministerstvo školství, mládeže a tělovýchovy České republiky (Ministry of Education, Youth and Physical Education of the Czech Republic), Karmelitská ul. 5, 110 00 Praha 1, Czech Republic
history; civics; democracy; moral education; curriculum research; cross-national research

histoire; instruction civique; démocratie; éducation morale; recherche sur les programmes d'études; recherche transnationale
PROJECT DESCRIPTION
Aims: (1) To describe the role of history teaching in the creation of a democratic society and to define its place in the modern school curriculum; (2) to examine literature on history teaching and relevant foreign experience; (3) to investigate current practice in schools and to further teaching, administration and curriculum development.
Design: A working group of teachers will evaluate experiences of Czech and foreign schools and will consider potential solutions (theoretical and practical) on the basis of theoretical literature, textbook analysis and team members' experiences.
Hypothesis: History teaching can enhance the development of knowledge, civic consciousness, morality and creativity in pupils and students.

12764 History of Cheltenham Training College 1847-1947.
GBR 1993
Research Date(s): 1990-1991
More, C.
Inst: Cheltenham & Gloucester College of Higher Education, Faculty of Education and Health, The Park, Cheltenham GL50 2AF, United Kingdom.
history of education; college of education; teacher education
histoire de l'éducation; centre de formation des enseignants; formation des enseignants
PROJECT DESCRIPTION
This research will trace the history of Cheltenham Training College (later the separate colleges of St Paul and St Mary), which was the largest Evangelical training college and at times the largest college in the country. The history will focus on eight areas: the foundation of the College; its management over the succeeding century in the light of national changes in the educational and religious framework; the qualifications, pay and conditions of staff; the origins and destinations of students; the syllabus; the expectations of students while training, and the formation and characteristics of the student ethos; sport and physical exercise; and the relationship between old students and the College. The study will use a full range of sources, e.g. annual reports, governors' minute books, inspectors' reports, staff and student registers, student magazines, reminiscences and photographs.

12765 History of educational psychology in Britain with special reference to university departments of education.
GBR 1993
Research Date(s): 1982-
Thomas, J.
Inst: Loughborough University of Technology, Department of Education, Loughborough LE11 3TU, United Kingdom.
educational psychology; history of education; teacher education
psychologie de l'éducation; histoire de l'éducation; formation des enseignants
PROJECT DESCRIPTION
This project includes the development of bibliographies on individual psychologists of education and case studies of individual university departments of education. It involves the use of primary and secondary historical services. The long term aim is a monograph on the history of educational psychology in Britain, including its clinical practice.

Publ: Thomas, J.B. J.A. Green, educational psychology and the Journal of Experimental Pedagogy. In: *History of Education Society Bulletin,* No 29/1982, pp. 41-45.

12766 History of the University of Liverpool 1981-1991.
GBR 1993
Research Date(s): 1989-1991
Harrop, S.
Inst: Liverpool University, Department of Education, PO Box 147, Liverpool L69 3BX, United Kingdom.
history of education; university
histoire de l'éducation; université
PROJECT DESCRIPTION
This project is to update and extend Thomas Kelly's History of Liverpool University 1981 to 1991, (Kelly, T. *For advancement of learning.* Liverpool: Liverpool University Press, 1981). The research will be based on documentary sources and oral evidence from past and present staff and students.

12767 Intercultural influence in adult/popular education: England and Germany 1890-1955.
GBR 1993
Research Date(s): 1988-1991
Marriott, J.; Coles, J.; Fretloh-Thomas, S.
Inst: Leeds University, School of Education, Leeds LS2 9JT, United Kingdom; Universität Tübingen, Institut für Erziehungswissenschaft II, FRG-7400 Tübingen, Germany.
Fin: Leverhulme Trust.
history of education; comparative education; adult education; workers' education; international education; intercultural education

histoire de l'éducation; éducation comparée; éducation des adultes; éducation ouvrière; éducation internationale; éducation interculturelle

PROJECT DESCRIPTION

The overall project involves a historical investigation of the intercultural 'reception' of ideas and institutional forms in the field of adult education. The present phase deals with reciprocal Anglo-German contacts at the periods: (1) 1890-1914 - emphasis on German interest in the university extension and settlement movements; (2) 1918-1933 - structure and effects of international contact with special reference to pacifism, women's and workers' education; (3) 1945-1955 - 'German educational reconstruction' and the contribution of English adult education and adult educators.

12768   Junior Certificate history in the Republic of Ireland: purpose, problems and potential.

GBR   1993

Research Date(s): 1991-1995

Austin, R.

Inst: Ulster University, Department of Inservice Education, Cromore Road, Coleraine, County Londonderry BT52 1SA, United Kingdom.

history; Ireland; curriculum development

histoire; Irlande; élaboration de programmes d'études

PROJECT DESCRIPTION

The aim of this study is to explore the ways in which a national curriculum change in the teaching of history in the Republic of Ireland is being implemented in the classroom. A sample of teachers are completing questionnaires, and resource materials are being designed, used and evaluated to measure student reaction to the proposed changes. The research is set in the wider context of the history of curriculum change in the Republic of Ireland and the perceived value and interest of history to young people.

12769   Ksiega Pamiatkowa Gimnazjum i Liceum Ziemi Kujawskiej we Włocławku wydana z okazji Jubileuszu 90-lecia. (Memory Book of Ziemia Kujawska Secondary School in Włocławek published on the occasion of the 90th anniversary.)

POL   1994

Research Date(s): 1989-1992

Gniazdowski, Marek; Gniazdowski, Włodzimierz; Gruszczyńska, Marianna; Kieloch, Tadeusz; Lenkiewicz, Teodor; Łecki, Wojciech; Nikonowiczowa, Olga; et al.

Sup: Pawlak, Marian.

Inst: Instytut Historii Wyższej Szkoły Pedagogicznej w Bydgoszczy (History Department, Higher School of Education, Bydgoszcz), 85 064 Bydgoszcz, Chodkiewicza 30, Poland.

Fin: Society of Ziemia Kujawska Secondary School Graduates.

history of education; publication; secondary school

histoire de l'éducation; publication; école secondaire

PROJECT DESCRIPTION

The aim of the project was to compile a Memory Book that would: (1) present the role of Ziemia Kujawska Secondary School in the education of children and youth; (2) present the role of former pupils in the life of the town, the district and the country.

The book contains articles on these subjects and includes 45 biographies of outstanding headmasters, teachers and former pupils, as well as lists of teachers and pupils in the periods 1900-1939 and 1945-1991.

Publ: Pawlak, Marian; et al. (eds.). Ksiega pamiatkowa Gimnazjum i Liceum Ziemi Kujawskiej we Włocławku. Włocławek: 1992, 276p.

12770   Locus of control beliefs in children with emotional and behavioural difficulties: an exploratory study.

GBR   1993

Research Date(s): 1988-1993

Elliott, J.

Sup: Coffield, F.

Inst: Sunderland University, School of Education, Hammerton Hill, Gray Road, Sunderland SR2 7EE, United Kingdom; Durham University, School of Education, Leazes Road, Durham DH1 1TA, United Kingdom.

child psychiatry; behavioural sciences; behaviour disorder; emotional disorder

psychiatrie infantile; sciences du comportement; trouble du comportement; trouble affectif

PROJECT DESCRIPTION

The study examines control-related beliefs of 240 children aged between nine and sixteen, and considers the implications of these beliefs for therapeutic intervention. All subjects have been referred to the educational psychology service because of perceived behavioural difficulties, and each child's behaviour is scored on nine behavioural dimensions. The data used for analysis are drawn from self-report scales, semi-structured interviews and case files. Both quantitative (using multivariate techniques) and qualitative modes of data analysis are employed and the stengths and weaknesses of each approach are noted.

The research challenges many assumptions contained within the locus of control literature and highlights the difficulty of adopting findings from nomothetic research for the purpose of clinical intervention.

12771   Marketing service industries: a comparative study of education and banking.

GBR   1993

Research Date(s): 1991-1992

Gray, L.

Inst: Staff College, Coombe Lodge, Blagdon, Bristol BS18 6RG, United Kingdom.

marketing; services; comparative analysis; school

mercatique; services; analyse comparative; école

PROJECT DESCRIPTION

This research will involve a comparative study of the education service and banking with reference to the organization of the marketing function, the preparation and use of marketing plans and the relevance of marketing to the development of intangible services.

Publ: Gray, L.S. Marketing Education. Buckingham: Open University Press, 1991.

12772   The Mechanics Institution movement in the North East of England.

GBR   1993

Research Date(s): 1990-1993

Stockdale, C.

Sup: French, M.

Inst: Durham University, School of Education, Leazes Road, Durham DH1 1TA, United Kingdom.

history of education; workers' education; England

histoire de l'éducation; éducation ouvrière; Angleterre

PROJECT DESCRIPTION

This research looks at the history of the development of the Mechanics Institutions in the North East of England between 1820 and 1902. It includes comparisons of contemporary and recent literature about the Movement. The Movement's activities will be evaluated within the context of the social and economic climate of the period, together with the legacy of educational, literary and social development in terms of failure and success.

The research includes consultation of contemporary records existing within the region and also those of institutions in other parts of the country. Standard texts have been used to support the political, social, economic and cultural background against which the Movement evolved.

12773   The order of knowledge.

GBR   1993

Research Date(s): 1988-1993

Powell, G.

Inst: Keele University, Department of Education, Keele, Staffordshire ST5 5BG, United Kingdom.

history of education; educational theory; philosophy

histoire de l'éducation; théorie de l'éducation; philosophie

PROJECT DESCRIPTION

The study will offer a radical re-assessment of the development of education, especially since the Renaissance. It will involve a new interpretation of the significance of Plato's analysis of the classical conceptual system which has dominated our education.

12774   The origins and destinations of Oxford University students and teachers 1900-1979.

GBR   1993

Research Date(s): 1988-1991

Harrison, B.; Howarth, J.; Greenstein, D.; Curthoys, M.; Pottle, M.

Inst: Oxford University, University Offices, Wellington Square, Oxford OX1 2JD, United Kingdom.

Fin: Leverhulme Trust; Economic and Social Research Council; Oxford University.

history of education; university; student; graduate; teaching personnel; social origin; school career; career; career development

histoire de l'éducation; université; étudiant; étudiant diplômé; corps enseignant; origine sociale; cursus scolaire; carrière; déroulement de carrière

PROJECT DESCRIPTION

The project has aimed at systematically recording and analysing data relating to the origins and destinations of students and dons at the university of Oxford in the twentieth century. The work on students has focused on a 10% sample of those who matriculated between 1900 and 1979. It has involved the collection and computerisation of data relating to pre-Oxford schooling and origins (father's occupation and address, place and date of birth, etc.); to university career - date and college of matriculation, performance in finals, scholarships won, degrees attained; and to post-Oxford career - location and nature of job, and career progression. The work on dons has focused on specific years - 1912, 1937, 1957 and 1976 and has recorded though not computerised data on undergraduate career, college membership and, where possible, career progression. The sample involved in the work on students, defined as junior members, has been randomly selected from the 133,000 who matriculated in between 1900-1979; it represents approximately 10% of the junior membership in the years in question. Data has been collected by two methods - traditional 'record search' involving scrutiny of published sources such as *Who's Who*, college and school registers, etc. and a postal survey questionnaire to those who matriculated after 1929. The research into the careers of Oxford dons has relied on the use of published sources, including those issued by the university. The sample has been comprehensive within the years specified, and an attempt has been made to include all teachers at the university, and not just those whose college membership and teaching commitment justified the description of 'don'.

12775   The origins, development and failure of the Day Continuation School Movement in England and Wales.
GBR   1993
Research Date(s): 1990-1995
Silto, W.
Sup: Gordon, P.
Inst: London University, Institute of Education, Department of History, Humanities and Philosophy, 20 Bedford Way, London WC1H OAL, United Kingdom.
history of education; adult education; continuing education; philosophy of education
histoire de l'éducation; éducation des adultes; éducation permanente; philosophie de l'éducation
PROJECT DESCRIPTION
   This research deals with the background behind the rise of Continuation Schools following the First World War. The importance of the 1918 Education Act and the Oxford school of idealist philosophers are described. The development and failure of the movement are traced in examination of local records of the seven local education authorities which implemented Day Continuation Schools: this will also involve a study of Public Record Office files in order to ascertain the views of the Board of Education as well as the political papers of the main supporters of the movement and other interest groups.

12776   Polska oświata pozaszkolna w rejencji opolskiej w latach 1922-1939. (Polish out-of-school education in the Opole regency in the years 1922-1939.)
POL   1994
Research Date(s): 1985-1989
Sapia-Drewniak, Eleonora.
Inst: Wyższa Szkoła Pedagogiczna (Pedagogical University), Oleska 48, Opole, Poland.
history of education; out-of-school education; continuing education
histoire de l'éducation; éducation extra-scolaire; éducation permanente
PROJECT DESCRIPTION
   Background: From the second half of the nineteenth century there were numerous cultural and educational institutions in Silesia. After the partitioning of Silesia in 1922 these forms of education, with a rich tradition, gained strong support from the Polish population in the Opole regency (i.e. the part incorporated by Germany). In this region, "germanization" affected all spheres of life, especially schools. Dissatisfaction with the quality of education increased the demand for the establishment of other institutions. Interesting extra-curricular forms of education, recreation and entertainment were the subject of this study.
   Aim: The purpose of this study was to provide a monographical presentation of the diversity of educational and cultural activities in the changing socio-political reality of the inter-war period in Opole, Silesia.
   Methods: The study was based on the analysis of archival documents.

Publ: Sapia-Drewniak, Eleonora. *Aktywność oświatowa i kulturalna kobiet* na Ślasku Opolskim w latach 1922-1939. Opole: 1991, 112p.
Sapia-Drewniak, Eleonora. *Polska oświata pozaszkolna w rejencji opolskiej w latach 1922-1939.* Opole: 1991, 142p.
Sapia-Drewniak, Eleonora. *Polski Uniwersytet Ludowy na Opolszczyźnie w latach 1932-1939.* In: *Dramat oświaty i szkolnictwa w latach faszyzmu hitlerowskiego.* Opole: 1988, pp. 127-135.
Sapia-Drewniak, Eleonora. *Zum wirken polnischer Vereine in Oberschlesien in den Jahren 1918-1932.* In: *Wissenschaftliche Zeitschrift Potsdam,* 4/1986, pp. 661-665.

12777   The Preparatory School experience 1918-1940.
GBR   1993
Research Date(s): 1991-1994
Austin, J.
Sup: Bell, R.; Low-Beer, A.
Inst: Open University, School of Education, Walton Hall, Milton Keynes MK7 6AA, United Kingdom; Bristol University, Senate House, Bristol BS8 1TH, United Kingdom.
history of education; private school; boys' school
histoire de l'éducation; école privée; école de garçons
PROJECT DESCRIPTION
   This is a historical study of the nature of preparatory school experience for boys and staff in the period between the wars. It will involve oral history methods as well as analysis of school magazines, autobiographies and other literary sources.

12778   Primary history project.
GBR   1993
Research Date(s): 1991-1994
Fines, J.; Nichol, J.
Inst: Exeter University, School of Education, St Luke's, Heavitree Road, Exeter EX1 2LU, United Kingdom.
Fin: Nuffield Foundation.
history; primary education; common core curriculum
histoire; enseignement primaire; tronc commun
PROJECT DESCRIPTION
   The primary history project is enquiring into possible approaches to implementing the national history curriculum in 25,000 primary schools where there is little expertise.

12779   Problèmes de sociologie de l'éducation.
CHE   1994
Research Date(s): 1986-1989
Girod, Roger (5 Chemin de la Boule, 1232 Confignon, Suisse).
educational sociology; knowledge level; teaching practice; teaching objective; equal opportunity
sociologie de l'éducation; niveau de connaissances; pratique pédagogique; objectif pédagogique; égalité de chances
PROJECT DESCRIPTION
   Cet ouvrage, rédigé pour la collection "Sciences de l'éducation" du Bureau international d'éducation (une institution dépendant de l'UNESCO), examine quelques-uns des principaux problèmes de la sociologie de l'éducation. Elle a aussi pour but d'expliquer quelques méthodes fréquemment utilisées dans cette discipline.
   Un premier problème concerne la différenciation entre les deux aspects du niveau d'instruction de la population auquel amènent l'enseignement et les autres instances impliquées. Le premier de ces aspects - souvent le seul pris en compte dans les statistiques et même dans beaucoup d'ouvrages de sciences de l'éducation - est le niveau formel d'instruction. Ce niveau renseigne, avec plus ou moins de précision, sur la durée et la nature des études et sur le genre de titre obtenu. L'autre aspect est le niveau réel d'instruction, qui porte sur ce que les individus savent effectivement. Niveau formel et niveau réel d'instruction sont loin d'aller de pair. Comme cette étude le relève, le premier ne peut servir d'indicateur satisfaisant du second, et leurs évolutions respectives ne concordent pas nécessairement.
   Les indications sur le niveau réel d'instruction sont très rares. Elles devraient donner une image d'ensemble du résultat du travail éducatif d'une société. Il faudrait donc, idéalement, qu'elles s'étendent à toute la population. Pour l'étude présentée ici, l'auteur a dû se limiter à un certain groupe d'âge. Il s'agit tout de même d'observations valables à l'échelle d'une génération entière, l'enquête ayant porté sur la totalité des recrues de l'armée suisse en 1984 (34'907 jeunes gens).
   Un autre aspect important abordé dans cette publication est l'inégalité des chances face aux études. Une liste des titres des chapitres illustre l'étendue de l'objet traité: Modernisation de la société et évolution du niveau réel d'instruction générale de la population - Origine social, études et degré réel d'instruction générale - Facteurs de l'inégalité des connaissances: sens de l'idée de dissociation de leurs influences et d'impact explicatif - L'analyse des impacts explicatifs - Inégalité des chances et impacts explicatifs - Sélection par les études et mobilité sociale.

Publ: Girod, Roger. *Problèmes de sociologie de l'éducation.* Neuchâtel: Delachaux & Niestlé, 1989, 139p. (série "Sciences de l'éducation" due BIE/UNESCO).

12780   Programmata tis UNESCO gia ti Diethni Ekpaidefsi (Ekpaidefsi gia ta Dikaiomata tou Anthropou kai tin Eirini) kai Scholika Vivlia Protovathmias kai Defterovathmias Ekpaidefsis stin Ellada. (UNESCO Projects on International Education (Education for Human Rights and Peace) and Greek primary and secondary school textbooks.)
GRC   1994
Research Date(s): 1989-
Papadopoulou, Dimitra.
Inst: Tmima Psychologias, Aristoteleio Panepistimio Thessalonikis (Department of Psychology, Aristotelian University of Thessaloniki), 54006 Thessaloniki, Greece.
peace studies; human rights; textbook; international education; UNESCO; primary education; secondary education
éducation à la paix; droits de l'homme; manuel d'enseignement; éducation internationale; UNESCO; enseignement primaire; enseignement secondaire
PROJECT DESCRIPTION
   This is an investigation of Greek primary and secondary school textbooks in relation to international education criteria set by UNESCO ("Recommendations concerning education for international understanding, co-operation and peace and for human rights and fundamental freedoms", UNESCO 1974). The research programme follows the research model initiated long ago by UNESCO in an effort to improve knowledge of other peoples and thereby to eliminate prejudice concerning differences among peoples and to promote mutual understanding and rapprochement.

The aim of the research is to show how school textbooks can be used to promote the principles of Human Rights and Peace Education. It has an interdisciplinary orientation, looking at textbooks for various curriculum subjects, such as history, modern Greek literature, Greek language, religion, foreign languages.

The part of the research concerning the history textbooks used in the three years of Gymnasium (lower secondary education) and the Greek language textbooks used in primary education has been completed. Another part, concerning the modern Greek literature textbooks and books on "Work Relations" used in Technological Education Institutions is at an advanced stage. The method used is content analysis.

The research programme is expected to show to what extent existing school textbooks can be used for teaching in the spirit of Peace and Human Rights Education. The findings will serve as a basis for proposals concerning the creation of textbooks in which the principles of the UNESCO and UNO recommendations for mutual understanding and rapprochement among peoples are implemented.

12781 Radical heroes: Gramsci, Freire and the Liberal Tradition in adult education.

GBR 1993

Research Date(s): 1985-1992

Coben, D.

Sup: McLellan, D.

Inst: London University, Goldsmiths' College, Department of Continuing and Community Education, Lewisham Way, New Cross, London SE14 6NW, United Kingdom; Kent University, Canterbury CT2 7NZ, United Kingdom.

history of education; adult education; ideology; philosophy of education
histoire de l'éducation; éducation des adultes; idéologie; philosophie de l'éducation

PROJECT DESCRIPTION

In the 1970s and 1980s many radical adult educators in Britain turned to the work of Antonio Gramsci and Paulo Freire for theoretical insights to support new initiatives in the education of adults in the wake of the Russell Report. The thesis considers the significance of the work of Gramsci and Freire on the development of theories of adult education in Britain in the period following the publication of the Russell Report. The thesis begins by charting the origins of the dominant tradition in British adult education, the Liberal Tradition, in the nineteenth century, starting with an analysis of the struggle for education and for emancipation by working class groupings. This is contrasted with the development of liberal adult education in the twentieth century with its emphasis on education for leisure as opposed to vocational education and an analysis of the origins and development of radical critiques of adult education in the period 1973-1990. Gramsci's writing on hegemony and the nature of education in a revolutionary process is considered, as is the development of Freire's analysis of the transformative role of adult education in liberating the oppressed. The relationship between Gramsci, Freire and the Liberal Tradition is explored, and the thesis looks at ways in which Gramsci and Freire have been used as 'Radical Heroes' in radical critiques and developments of the Liberal Tradition.

12782 Review of UK Social Science Research (Extension).

GBR 1993

Research Date(s): 1991-1992

Williams, G.; Loder, C.

Inst: London University, Institute of Education, Department of Policy Studies, Centre for Higher Education Studies, 20 Bedford Way, London WC1H OAL, United Kingdom.

Fin: Economic and Social Research Council.

social sciences; research; financial resources; financing; United Kingdom
sciences sociales; recherche; ressources financières; financement; Royaume-Uni

PROJECT DESCRIPTION

The study provides the first detailed analysis of the financial backers of the United Kingdom's social science research base. The Centre for Higher Education Studies surveyed research institutions throughout the UK to identify which organisations are supporting what kinds of research.

Publ: Loder, C. *Support for Social Science research: setting the scene.* CHES Policy series in association wtih ESRC, 1992.

Loder, C. *Support for Social Science research: examining the eighties.* CHES Policy series, 1992.

Loder, C. *Support for Social Science research: focus on funders.* CHES Policy series, 1992.

Loder, C. & Fry, H. Who supports Social Science research? In: Vincent, J. (ed.). *Critics and customers: the control of social policy research.* Aldershot: Gower Publishing, 1992.

12783 The role of the Church of England in the provision of education at Worfield Endowed Church of England (Aided) Primary School from 1546 to 1991 in the light of the 1988 Education Reform Act with particular reference to the governors' responsibility for curriculum, funding and building.

GBR 1993

Research Date(s): 1991-1993

Turnock, J.

Sup: Tolly, B.

Inst: Crewe and Alsager College of Higher Education, Hassall Road, Alsager, Stoke on Trent ST7 2HL, United Kingdom.

Fin: Shropshire Local Education Authority.

history of education; church; educational legislation; financing; reform
histoire de l'éducation; église; législation scolaire; financement; réforme

PROJECT DESCRIPTION

The aim of this research is to clarify the purpose and application of educational endowments from the Brierley Charity of 1609, Lloyd and Parker Charity of 1613 and other trust deeds which were later amalgamated into the Worfield United Charities. It will also try to establish the changing role of the Church of England and the provision of free education. The project will look at the changes which took place in local thinking and examine the influences of the major educational reform acts of the last 150 years. The researchers will establish whether the Foundation Governors' income from endowment is still regulated by the 1909 scheme, or whether subsequent variations have been legitimised by the Charity Commissioners. Links will be established between the elected Church Foundation Governors and their associated endowments with other members of the Governing Body in order to clarify responsibility for the curriculum and the ownership of the land and buildings of Worfield Primary School. It is also hoped to clarify the powers of the whole Governing Body in the light of new legislation under the 1988 Education Reform Act.

12784 Le savoir réel de l'homme moderne.

CHE 1994

Research Date(s): 1989-1991

Girod, Roger (5 Chemin de la Boule, 1232 Confignon, Suisse).

educational sociology; knowledge level; knowledge; adult; social change
sociologie de l'éducation; niveau de connaissances; connaissance; adulte; changement social

PROJECT DESCRIPTION

N'étant pas soumis aux contraintes de la rareté - quand quelqu'un acquiert une connaissance, il n'en prive personne d'autre -, le savoir devrait être parmi les choses les mieux partagées, du moins dans les sociétés développées, où les possibilités d'apprendre abondent. Là, chacun devrait avoir une bonne culture générale et de bonnes qualifications professionnelles. Longtemps la doctrine officielle a d'ailleurs donné à croire qu'il en était ainsi ou qu'il s'en fallait de peu. Récemment, diverses constatations, en particulier celles qui concernent l'"illettrisme" d'une fraction appréciable de la population, ont ébranlé ces convictions.

Le problème traité dans l'ouvrage présenté ici est celui du niveau réel des connaissances de la population adulte de pays industrialisés: situation actuelle, tendances futures. Les domaines retenus sont les suivants: raisonnement logique, instruction générale de base (lire, écrire, calculer), connaissances relatives à la politique, notions scientifiques élémentaires, niveau général des qualifications professionnelles, connaissance de l'informatique et des langues.

Une comparaison des indications - plutôt rares - dont on dispose sur le savoir réel d'adultes dans le monde moderne semble indiquer que les capacités de lecture, calcul et rédaction sont faibles et qu'elles ont baissé qu cours du 20e siècle, fait d'autant plus paradoxal que le "quotient d'intelligence" moyen est en hausse. La connaissance des langues étrangères s'améliore, et le niveau des connaissances mises en œuvre dans le travail paraît s'élever dans son ensemble. Les effets de l'informatique sont ambivalents. Quant aux connaissances politiques et scientifiques, elles stagnent au plus bas.

D'un point de vue d'une sociologie des connaissances (qui n'est pas à confondre avec la sociologie de la connaissance, mais est à voir plutôt comme une branche de l'étude de la communication), on peut postuler le caractère fonctionnel de toute acquisition de connaissances. L'idée consiste à reconnaître qu'à tout âge, l'individu n'apprend vraiment que ce qui répond à une motivation ressentie avec assez de force. Le désir est le ressort de l'apprentissage; la fréquence de l'utilisation des connaissances et la répétition des motifs de s'en servir contribuent à leur conservation et à leur approfondissement. Dans cette optique, les variations du niveau des connaissances de la population s'expliqueraient plus par les variations de la demande et par le changement des fonctions remplies par les différents types de connaissances que par des variables relatives à l'enseignement.

Publ: Girod, Roger. *Le savoir réel de l'homme moderne.* Paris: PUF, 1991, 235p. (série "Sociologies").

12785   Some aspects of historical understanding.
GBR   1993
Research Date(s): 1977-1995
Lee, P.
Sup: Gordon, P.
Inst: London University, Institute of Education, Department of History, Humanities and Philosophy, 20 Bedford Way, London WC1H OAL, United Kingdom.

history; comprehension; thinking; pupil
histoire; compréhension; pensée; élève
PROJECT DESCRIPTION

The research undertakes an analysis of concepts involved in the idea of historical understanding (rationality, intentionality, practical inference) and of related ideas (imagination, empathy, sympathy, identification, intuition, fellow-feelings, tolerance). An attempt is made to show that imagination (as supposal) is criterial to understanding in history. There is a discussion of major accounts of historical explanation (covering-law, explanation by rationale, narrativist and Marxist accounts). The relation between explanation, understanding and interpretation in history is examined, with particular attention to notions of meaning and significance.

The second part of the research is concerned to argue some implications of the earlier analysis for children's thinking and, in particular, the development of their ideas (explicit and tacit) about the nature and status of history (i.e. the ideas in question are second-order as opposed to substantive). Possible consequences for teaching will also be discussed. Previous work is examined, both from wider psychological research and from the more specific research undertaken within education, bearing directly upon children's abilities and thinking in history. The argument will draw upon empirical investigations performed by the author and by research projects in which he has been involved. It is anticipated that these will provide evidence bearing on children's ideas at all ages between 7 years and 19 years.

12786   Soviet/British curriculum development project.
GBR   1993
Research Date(s): 1989-1991
Simons, H.; Maw, J.
Inst: London University, Institute of Education, Department of Curriculum Studies, 20 Bedford Way, London WC1H OAL, United Kingdom.
Fin: Joseph Rowntree Charitable Foundation; Joseph Rowntree Social Service Trust; Elizabeth & Barrows Cadbury Foundation; Westcroft Trust.

history; international studies; USSR; international understanding; curriculum development; teaching
histoire; études internationales; URSS; compréhension internationale; élaboration de programmes d'études; enseignement
PROJECT DESCRIPTION

The purpose of this action research project is to examine ways in which teachers handle ethnocentrism in their teaching, focusing initially on the teaching of history. Working with a small group of schools, the research will document the strategies teachers employ in the teaching of history, encouraging teachers to conduct self-monitoring of their teaching strategies and jointly analyse the results. Classroom observation will be the major approach, supplemented by interviews with teachers and pupils and analysis of tapes, transcripts and observations of classroom practice. The project is part of a broader Soviet/British Curriculum Development Project sponsored collaboratively with colleagues from the Academy of Pedagogical Science in the USSR. The early part of the project involved an analysis of the image of each other's society in history textbooks at GCSE level. This current project takes up the crucial issue of how texts and teaching materials are mediated in the classroom.

12787   The State and women's schooling in France, 1815-1914.
GBR   1993
Research Date(s): 1988-1992
Gemie, S.
Inst: Cheltenham & Gloucester College of Higher Education, Faculty of Education and Health, The Park, Cheltenham GL50 2QF, United Kingdom.
history of education; France; government policy; state; women's education
histoire de l'éducation; France; politique gouvernementale; Etat; éducation des femmes
PROJECT DESCRIPTION

This research will test recent theoretical models of the State and women's relationships to public power structures by reference to the experience of schoolmistresses and schoolgirls in nineteenth century France. More specifically, the aims are: to assess the effects of the presentation of official role models of ideal feminine types on female students at teacher training colleges; to further understanding of the effects of limited entry into public positions on women's mentalities; and to analyse women's ability to re-formulate official ideas in the light of their experience - in particular, their relationship to feminist, anarchist and socialist subcultures following their entries into the teaching profession.

The research sample is based on archive research in Lyon, Caen, Bordeaux, Lille and Paris, and may involve reference to a database of the careers of some 200 schoolmistresses. Methods involve social and cultural

historical investigation, with some guidance from recent works by feminist and critical theorists.

Publ: Gemie, S. The schoolmistress's revenge: secular schoolmistresses, academic authority and village conflicts in France, 1815 to 1948. In: *History of Education*, No 20/1991, pp. 203-17.

12788   Studies of teacher education in the Victorian day training college.
GBR   1993
Research Date(s): 1978-
Thomas, J.
Inst: Loughborough University of Technology, Department of Education, Loughborough LE11 3TU, United Kingdom.
history of education; teacher education
histoire de l'éducation; formation des enseignants
PROJECT DESCRIPTION

The project aims to describe and analyse the work of education departments in universities from 1890 to 1918. It consists of case studies of individual institutions, biographical studies and investigations of related areas, for example, the development of the academic study of education and the greater opportunities for the professional education of women.

Publ: Thomas, J.B. Amos Henderson and the Nottingham Day Training College. In: *Journal of Educational Administration and History*, Vol 18, No 2/1986, pp. 24-33.
Thomas, J.B. University College, London, and the training of teachers. In: *History of Education Society Bulletin*, Vol 37/1986, pp. 44-49.
Thomas, J.B. Students, staff and curriculum in a day training college (Cardiff). In: *Collected Original Resources in Education*, Vol 10, No 3/1986, Fiche 1 A04.
Thomas, J.B. University College, Bristol: pioneering teacher training for women. In: *History of Education*, Vol. 17, No 1/1988, pp. 55-70.
Thomas, J.B. (ed.). *British universities and teacher education: a century of change*. London: Falmer Press, 1990.

12789   Teachers and the politics of gender 1800-1914: a comparative study of England and Scotland.
GBR   1993
Research Date(s): 1986-
Corr, H.
Inst: Durham University, Department of Sociology and Social Policy, Elvet Riverside II, New Elvet, Durham DH1 3JT, United Kingdom.
history of education; sex difference; teaching profession; sex role; educational policy
histoire de l'éducation; différence de sexe; profession d'enseignant; rôle sexuel; politique de l'éducation
PROJECT DESCRIPTION

The research is primarily designed to document historically the social construction of gender roles and inequalities in the teaching profession and within wider educational structures. It aims to show how successive state educational policies sought to promote gender differences in the curriculum and in the teacher training system as the nineteenth century progressed. The study compares and contrasts the position of the sexes under English and Scottish educational, religious, and political systems. Particular themes focus on the following: the feminisation of teaching 1800-1914; occupational and sex segregation in the teaching labour force; liberal upper and middle class feminism and the campaign to introduce the teaching of housework in state schools; sexual politics in teachers' unions - the National Union of Teachers (NUT) and the Educational Institute of Scotland (EIS). The research is based on archive sources, official parliamentary papers, school board records and church records.

12790   Teaching about European history and society in the 1990s.
XCE   1993
Research Date(s): 1991
Lang, Seán.
Inst: School of Education, University of Exeter, United Kingdom.
history; Europe; teaching method; curriculum; European dimension; seminar; Council of Europe
histoire; Europe; méthode pédagogique; programme d'études; dimension européenne; séminaire; Conseil de l'Europe
COLLECTED WORKS - Conference proceedings

Teacher Bursaries Scheme: European Seminar on teaching about European history and society in the 1990s, Tuusula (Finland), 4-9 August 1991. This conference dealt with the development of Europe, concentrating on the period since the changes in Eastern Europe in 1989-1990, and the development of new teaching and learning patterns to allow students more autonomy in their work.

There was a broad consensus that it is impossible to compile an exhaustive list of desirable human qualities which we would like to nurture in the young. However, there are some general points such as the development of individual initiative and enterprise, of a sense of independence and an appreciation of interdependence, which can be seen as major educational goals for students. Underlying all of these, is the idea of developing the attributes of an active citizen in a democracy.

Importance has been placed on employing a variety of teaching methods, above all the method of "Co-operative learning". This depends on altering the normal relationship of pupil and teacher, from one of master and disciple to one of partners in learning. The teacher's role is therefore no longer that of a fount of all knowledge, but that of a facilitator, whose responsibility includes designing and setting up the groups' tasks.

A wide-ranging discussion about Europe and the way in which it is developing has resulted in the definition of different "Europes". European unity is not the natural state of the continent. Any programme which aims to unite Europe must not ignore local identities, whether national or regional. Topics such as "Europeanness" and the national identity of European citizens formed the subject matter of individual national lectures.

The meeting in Finland concluded that it would be an over-simplification to pretend that designing education for the Europe of the 1990s would be easy. European countries feel the controversy that inevitably follows from changes in the national curriculum in history. Changes in society produce a need to revise national history, even to the point of calling in history books and writing new ones. The report ends with recommendations for action at both national and European level.

12791 The training and education of Froebelian teachers in England and Wales, 1889-1926.
GBR 1993
Research Date(s): 1984-1992
Smart, G.
Sup: Aldrich, R.
Inst: London University, Institute of Education, Department of History, Humanities and Philosophy, 20 Bedford Way, London WC1H 0AL, United Kingdom; Bedford College of Higher Education, Polhill Avenue, Bedford MK41 9AE, United Kingdom.
history of education; nursery school; curriculum research; teacher education; educational theory
histoire de l'éducation; école maternelle; recherche sur les programmes d'études; formation des enseignants; théorie de l'éducation
PROJECT DESCRIPTION
The research is concerned with the dissemination of child-centred theories and methods of education of young children in England and Wales between 1889 and 1926. The work is an investigation of the contribution of the Froebel movement to this process through the training and education of kindergarten teachers under the auspices of the National Froebel Union, whose previously unpublished archives form the basis of the source material. It considers the nature of the institutions concerned, the curricula followed by the students and the relationship between the Froebel movement and the maintained system.
Publ: Smart, R. The diffusion of Froebelian ideas and methods in England, 1882-1914. In: *Historia Infantiae* (Budapest), Vol 2/1985, pp. 29-48.

12792 The Tudors & Stuarts through information technology (IT): history & information technology in the primary school.
GBR 1993
Research Date(s): 1991-1992
Gomersall, M.
Inst: Bath College of Higher Education, Newton Park, Newton St Loe, Bath BA2 9BN, United Kingdom.
Fin: National Council for Educational Technology; Bath College of Higher Education.
history; curriculum; didactic use of computer; primary education
histoire; programme d'études; usage didactique de l'ordinateur; enseignement primaire
PROJECT DESCRIPTION
The project is concerned with the development of curriculum materials for primary school history, using information technology. Subject content is focused on the Tudors and Stuarts, a National Curriculum Core Study Unit for primary school history at key stage 2, and also recognises cross-curricular learning opportunities. The research is school-based, with materials being developed by curriculum tutors within the Faculty of Education at Bath College of Higher Education in association with local teachers and their pupils.

12793 'Vor und hinter dem Katheder: Lehrerinnen- und Maedchenerziehung in Oesterreich von Maria-Theresianischer Zeit bis zum Ende des Ersten Weltkriegs.' Ein Beitrag zur oesterreichischen Frauengeschichte. (The instruction of girls and the training of female teachers in Austria from Maria Theresa to the end of World War I: a contribution to the history of women in Austria.)
AUT 1993
Research Date(s): 1993-1995
Mazohl-Wallnig, Brigitte; Barth-Scalmani, Gunda; Friedrich, Margret.
Inst: Institut fuer Geschichte, Rudolfskai 42, A-5020 Salzburg.
Fonds zur Foerderung der wissenschaftlichen Forschung, Weyringergasse 35, A-1040 Wien; Universitaet Salzburg, Rudolfskai 42, A-5020 Salzburg
history of education; sex discrimination; women's education; teacher education
histoire de l'éducation; discrimination sexuelle; éducation des femmes; formation des enseignants

PROJECT DESCRIPTION
Ziel dieses Projekts ist eine Sozialgeschichte der Maedchenerziehung und der Berufsgruppe der Lehrerin, wobei die Situation der Maedchenerziehung und die Ausbildungs- und Berufssituation der Lehrerin analog zum Bild vor und hinter dem Katheder als zwei Teile des weiblichen Lebenszusammenhanges begriffen werden. Im Untersuchungsfeld der Maedchenerziehung werden die in der Habsburgermonarchie formulierten Erziehungsleitbilder eruiert und analysiert; die Massnahmen zur Maedchenbildung von staatlicher Seite (Studienhofkommission, Minister fuer Cultus und Unterricht, Behoerden der Laender und Kommunen) mit ihrem zugrundeliegenden Frauenbild, den ihnen vorausgehenden Diskussionen und Beeinflussungen durch verschiedene gesellschaftliche Gruppen und ihren schliesslichen Realisationen werden dargestellt; die Initiativen privater SchulgruenderInnen (fast alle Schulen und Kurse fuer Maedchen ausserhalb der Pflichtschulen wurden von Frauen als Privatpersonen, von Frauenvereinen oder Frauenorden eingerichtet) werden aufgezeigt, nach deren sozialem Hintergrund, ihren Gruendungsmotiven, Problemen bei der Schulerhaltung, Bildungszielen, Qualitaet des Lehrpersonals, nach ihrer Haeufigkeit und der jeweiligen Zahl und sozialen Herkunft der Schuelerinnen wird gefragt. Es wird die Schulwirklichkeit der Maedchen bezueglich verwendeter Lehrplaene, Stundenverteilung, Lerninhalten, der Moeglichkeit einer Abschlusspruefung und beruflicher Qualifikationen, der Bedeutung und Wertigkeit der Erziehungsleitbilder im Schulalltag, des Einflusses der subjektiven Schulerfahrung auf die Weckung des Selbstbewusstseins und der Reflexion der eigenen Situation dargestellt.

Die Sozialgeschichte der Lehrerin gliedert sich in drei Abschnitte, die durch die staatliche Rahmengesetzgebung bezueglich des weiblichen Lehrpersonals unterteilt sind (1. weibliche Lehrtaetigkeit vor 1804, 2. Zeit der geistlichen Schulaufsicht zwischen 1804 und 1869, 3. Institutionalisierung der LehrerInnenausbildung und der staatlichen Schulaufsicht nach der Einfuehrung des Reichsvolksschulgesetzes). Untersucht werden fuer 1. und 2. das Verhaeltnis zwischen den geistlichen und den in Frauenkloestern ausgebildeten weltlichen Lehrerinnen, ihre soziale Herkunft, die Methoden ihrer Ausbildung im Vergleich zu den staatlichen Praeparandenkursen, die allmaehliche Uebernahme dieser Methoden durch die Frauenkloester, ihre wichtiger werdende Funktion als Ausbildungsstaette weltlicher Lehrerinnen; fuer 3. werden untersucht das ungleiche Angebot von staatlichen und geistlichen Lehrerbildungsanstalten fuer Frauen und Maenner, die soziale Herkunft des Lehrpersonals, ihre Veraenderung im Rahmen der inneren sozialen Differenzierung des Buergertums, das Wechselspiel von Anwerbung und Verdraengung der Lehrerin je nach Anzahl der maennlichen Kollegen, der Einsatz buerokratischer Instrumente zur Verhinderung eines als uebermaessig stark empfundenen Eindringens der Frauen in den Lehrberuf (gleiche Startchancen - jedoch ungleiche Karriereverlaufsmuster, Zoelibatshandhabung der einzelnen Kronlaender), Erfassung der beruflichen Subkultur durch eine Darstellung des Vereinswesens und der damit verbundenen Publizistik.

Es handelt sich um eine historisch-kritische Untersuchung; es wurden Primaerquellen und Zeitungen ausgewertet.

12794 Vývoj pedagogického myšlení a vzdělání. (Development of educational philosophies and teacher education.)
CSK 1994
Research Date(s): 1991-1993
Stverák, V.; Vánová, R.; Vorlíček, Ch.; Palouš, R.
Sup: Helus, Z.
Inst: Pedagogická fakulta Univerzity Karlovy (Charles University, Faculty of Education), M.D. Rettigové 4, 116 39 Praha 1, Czech Republic.
Ministerstvo školství, mládeže a tělovýchovy (Ministry of Education, Youth and Physical Education), Karmelitská 7, 118 00 Praha 1, Czech Republic
history of education; teacher education; Czechoslovakia; philosophy of education; educational theory
histoire de l'éducation; formation des enseignants; Tchécoslovaquie; philosophie de l'éducation; théorie de l'éducation
PROJECT DESCRIPTION
The research consists of four subprojects. (1) The philosophical and theological basis of Jan Amos Komenský's thinking. This study is concerned with religiousness in Comenius' work - an aspect of Komenský's ideas that has been neglected both in Czech research and in research abroad. Methods include a through study of Comenius' work and its philosophical interpretations. (2) Karel Zitný and his attempts at educational innovation. This study will evaluate the importance of Karel Zitný's personality for the development of school practice, and his practical contribution in comparison with the work of other teacher personalities at that time. (3) The development of teacher education in Czechoslovakia and its impact on the Faculty of Education at Charles University. This study seeks to describe the most important experimental attempts at improving teacher education in Czechoslovakia before 1945. It also attempts to establish the impact of reforms in teacher education on the Faculty of Education at Charles University and to design criteria for the evaluation of the development of teacher education. (4) Pařízek and Wifling: the school and the teacher. This study is concerned with an investigation of the education system in the time of A.V. Pařízek and I.R. Wifling.

Publ: Vorlíček, Ch. K vývoji vysokoškolského vzdělání učitelů v Ceskoslovensku. In: *Pedagogika*, 42, 1992/3, pp. 345-352.

Palouš, R. Comenius the Chiliast. In: *Czechoslovak and Central European Journal*, 1991/1, pp. 1-13.

Palouš, R. Komenského harmonie a synkrize. In: *Filozofický časopis*, 39, 1991/5, pp. 723-736.

Palouš, R. Comenius redivivus. In: *Studia paedagogica*, 6/1991. Praha: Pedagogická fakulta UK, 1991, pp. 5-15.

Palouš, R. *The World of Comenius. Comenius in world science and culture*. Prague: Historical Institute of Academy, 1991.

Palouš, R. Comenius in Our Age. In: *Intecom-University of California*, vol. 14. Los Angeles, pp. 1-3.

Palouš, R. *Komenského Boží svět*. Praha: SPN, 1992, 142p.

13 LANGUAGE SCIENCES – SCIENCES DU LANGAGE – SPRACHWISSENSCHAFTEN

12795 "A toi de parler": méthode pour l'enseignement primaire du français à Madagascar.
FRA 1992
Research Date(s): 1985-1990
Garabédian, Michèle; Poulhès, Jean-Marie.
Inst: Ministère de l'éducation nationale, Ecole normale supérieure de Fontenay-St Cloud, Centre de recherche et d'étude pour la diffusion du français, Grille d'Honneur, 92211 Saint-Cloud, France.
Fin: Délégation générale de la langue française.
French language; language teaching; course programme; foreign languages; Madagascar; textbook; primary education
langue française; enseignement des langues; programme de cours; langues étrangères; Madagascar; manuel d'enseignement; enseignement primaire
PROJECT DESCRIPTION
Il s'agit de réaliser un cours de français, langue étrangère, pour les cycles dits "de base" de l'enseignement à Madagascar.

Méthodologie: Les options méthodologiques présidant à l'élaboration de ce cours tiennent compte de tous les aspects de la situation d'enseignement-apprentissage du français dans le contexte malgache: textes des instructions officielles, programmes pédagogiques, organisation de l'institution scolaire, statut et situation d'emploi du français à Madagascar (tout particulièrement du fait de l'Histoire), niveau de formation des enseignants, importance des effectifs scolaires. Ce matériel pédagogique s'adresse aux enfants de 7 à 11 ans et doit couvrir le cursus de cinq années de la scolarisation "de base". Sa réalisation est le fruit d'une collaboration entre les chercheurs du CREDIF et leurs collègues à Madagascar (six enseignants malgaches et deux attachés linguistiques en poste à Madagascar).

Résultats: L'ensemble est à ce jour réalisé et en cours d'édition par EDICEF. Le matériel est utilisé dans la majorité des écoles malgaches. Une évaluation critique au bout de quatre années se met en place afin de décrire les compétences langagières acquises par les apprenants, ainsi que le niveau de maîtrise au plan méthodologique et pédagogique, de ce matériel par les enseignants.

Publ: Poulhès, Jean-Marie & Garabédian, Michèle. *A toi de parler, T4, livre de l'élève.* Ouvrage collectif réalisé avec une équipe malgache. Paris: Hatier-Edicef, 1989.

Poulhès, Jean-Marie. *A toi de parler, T4, guide pédagogique.* Ouvrage collectif réalisé avec une équipe malgache. Paris: Hatier-Edicef/CNAPMAD, 1989.

Poulhès, Jean-Marie & Garabédian, Michèle. *A toi de parler, T5, livre de l'élève.* Ouvrage collectif réalisé avec une équipe malgache. Paris: Hatier-Edicef, 1990.

Poulhès, Jean-Marie. *A toi de parler, T5, guide pédagogique.* Ouvrage collectif réalisé avec une équipe malgache. Paris: Hatier-Edicef/CNAPMAD, 1990.

(Une liste complète est disponible auprès du chercheur.).

12796 "Les petits lascars": méthode pour l'enseignement précoce du français langue étrangère.
FRA 1992
Research Date(s): 1985-1990
Garabédian, Michèle; Lerasle, Magdeleine; Petreault-Vailleau, Françoise.
Inst: Ministère de l'éducation nationale, Ecole normale supérieure de Fontenay-St Cloud, Centre de recherche et d'étude pour la diffusion du français, Grille d'Honneur, 92211 Saint-Cloud, France.
foreign languages; early learning; French language; teaching method; pre-school education; textbook; audiovisual method
langues étrangères; apprentissage précoce; langue française; méthode pédagogique; éducation préscolaire; manuel d'enseignement; méthode audiovisuelle
PROJECT DESCRIPTION
Il s'agit d'élaborer du matériel pédagogique pour l'enseignement précoce du français, langue étrangère, à de jeunes enfants. On entend y prendre en considération les processus généraux du développement de l'enfant et de ses modes propres d'acquisition, tout en tenant compte des pratiques pédagogiques ayant cours à l'école maternelle.
Méthodologie: Le public visé est celui des enfants de l'école pré-élémentaire, d'origine non francophone et âgés de 3 à 6 ans. La mise à l'essai du matériel a été faite en classe au fur et à mesure de son élaboration. Des enregistrements vidéo des classes ont permis une analyse en continu des effets produits par l'utilisation du matériel en classe et facilité les réajustements nécessaires.
Résultats: Le matériel d'enseignement pour les deux premiers niveaux est publié. Le troisième niveau (élargissement aux 5-6 ans) est en cours d'édition.
Publ: Garabédian, Michèle; Lerasle, Magdeleine & Petrault-Vailleau, Françoise. *Les petits lascars niveau 1, les comptines, les histoires.* Paris: Didier, novembre 1988.
Garabédian, Michèle; Lerasle, Magdeleine & Petreault-Vailleau, Françoise. *Les petits lascars, le grand livre des comptines niveau 2.* Paris: Didier, déc. 1988.
Garabédian, Michèle; Lerasle, Magdeleine & Petrault-Vailleau, Françoise. Les petits lascars, un ensemble pédagogique pour l'enseignement/apprentissage du français langue étrangère. In: *Ici et là,* n°10, 1989, Madrid.
(Une liste complète est disponible auprès chercheur.).

12797 Adaptation in lecturing styles to audiences with English as a second language.
GBR 1993
Research Date(s): 1989-1994
Bilton, L.
Sup: Mitchell, R.
Inst: Southampton University, Faculty of Educational Studies, Centre for Language in Education, Highfield, Southampton SO9 5NH, United Kingdom.
English language; teaching style; lecture; foreign student; abroad; teaching language
langue anglaise; style pédagogique; exposé; étudiant étranger; à l'étranger; langue d'enseignement
PROJECT DESCRIPTION
Lecturing to audiences in an overseas context where English is a foreign language is expanding, as new universities adopt English as the medium of instruction for science and technology. Expatriate lecturers are on the whole unprepared for their undergraduates' low level of English and consequently much of their effort in planning and delivering lectures is wasted.
The aim of this research is to find out what goes on during lectures and where foreign students have particular difficulties in order to make recommendations about the adaptation of lecturing for audience needs.

12798 ALPS (Automated Language Processing Systems) computer-assisted translation system as a language learning tool.
GBR 1993
Research Date(s): 1985-1992
Corness, P.
Inst: Coventry University, School of International Studies and Law, Priory Street, Coventry CV1 5FB, United Kingdom.
language teaching; foreign languages; translation; computer; machine translation; higher education
enseignement des langues; langues étrangères; traduction; ordinateur; traduction automatique; enseignement supérieur
PROJECT DESCRIPTION
Computer-assisted translation (CAT) systems are being increasingly used in translation departments in business and industry. It is felt that it is vitally important to incorporate such advances in information technology into degree courses at this institution. In the BA Modern Languages Degree scheme, work with ALPS now features in the first year Approaches to Language Studies, in the Information Technology Option in the second and final year, in translation work at all levels, and the Translation Option includes a more advanced practical application of ALPS. Work with ALPS

is also incorporated into the language modules in European Engineering Studies and other degree courses. This is seen as a natural development of the successful Computer Assisted Language Learning programme. ALPS was selected from among a number of different systems because of its interactive approach, which makes possible new types of computer-assisted language learning activities and text analysis facilities, in addition to familiarising students with up to date tools of the modern practising translator.
Publ: Corness, P. The ALPS computer assisted translation system in an academic environment. In: Picken, C. (ed.). *Translating and the computer,* 7. London: ASLIB, 1986.

12799 An analysis of the sociolinguistics of the Creole-standard continuum and its relationship to education in a selected sample of secondary schools in Jamaica.
GBR 1993
Research Date(s): 1983-1991
Wright, L.
Sup: McLeod, A.
Inst: London University, Institute of Education, Department of English and Media Studies, 20 Bedford Way, London WC1H 0AL, United Kingdom; College of the Bahamas, PO Box No 8843, Nassau, Bahamas.
sociolinguistics; creole; dialect; Jamaica; official language; secondary education; pupil attitude; teacher education
sociolinguistique; langues créoles; dialecte; Jamaïque; langue officielle; enseignement secondaire; attitude de l'élève; formation des enseignants
PROJECT DESCRIPTION
This research involves 530 Grade 9 pupils aged 15+ and 54 Grade 9 teachers and the purpose is to: (1) determine and describe the nature of the sociolinguistic situation in a selected sample of Jamaican secondary schools by focusing on (a) the attitudes of pupils and their teachers to Jamaican Creole and Standard English, (b) pupils' perceptions of the role and status of both languages, (c) pupils' experience of, and their reactions to, criticism of Creole use at home and in school, (d) linguistic focusing and patterns of language use, (e) language variabiity evidenced by specimens of pupils' writing; (2) explore in some depth critical issues arising out of (1) above, e.g. the mesolect, or interlanguage; (3) assess the training levels and linguistic expertise of teachers in relation to national language goals set for this secondary sector; (4) criticize the gap between the rhetoric of avowed national goals and the realities of Grade 9 classrooms; and (5) make recommendations for language and linguistic training for teacher education, and in so doing, challenge traditionally held assumptions about language teaching and teacher education.

12800 An analysis of the structural relationships of narrative and argument in the writing of Year 8 schoolchildren.
GBR 1993
Research Date(s): 1987-1991
Andrews, R.
Sup: Protherough, R.
Inst: Hull University, School of Education, Cottingham Road, Hull HU6 7RX, United Kingdom.
written expression; writing; composition; argumentation
expression écrite; écriture; composition littéraire; argumentation
PROJECT DESCRIPTION
Research has shown that children in secondary school write argument less well than narrative, and that teachers concentrate on narrative forms in their teaching at the expense of argumentative forms. This study attempts to answer the question: Is there a path from narrative to argument via the structure of the two modes, so that children in schools might be helped to write argument? Traditionally, the two modes are seen as being at opposite poles of a rhetorical model. This study questions that model, and instead offers a model in which the two modes have much more in common than has been assumed.

12801 Ansätze zur wissenschaftlichen Begründung eines Kriterienrasters zur Beurteilung von Schülertexten. (Réflexions concernant un fondement scientifique d'une grille de critères pour évaluer des textes d'élèves.)
CHE 1994
Research Date(s): 1988-1990
Nussbaumer, Markus.
Sup: Sitta, Horst.
Inst: Universität Zürich, Deutsches Seminar, Rämistrasse 74, 8001 Zürich, Schweiz.
writing; written work; evaluation; linguistics
écriture; exercice écrit; évaluation; linguistique
PROJECT DESCRIPTION
Die vorliegende Dissertation enstand aus der Mitarbeit ihres Autors im vom Schweizerischen Nationalfonds finanzierten Projekt "Sprachfähigkeiten von Maturanden und Stuienanfängern in der deutschsprachigen Schweiz". Dieses Projekt war als empirische Arbeit im Bereich der angewandten Linguistik angelegt. Da die Bewertung von Fähigkeiten nun aber Werturteile impliziert, geht die Feststellung von Sprachfähigkeiten aber über reine Empirie hinaus. Für das Projekt "Sprachfähigkeiten" wurde

ein Analyseraster entwickelt: ein Set von Fragen, die an einen beliebigen Text gestellt werden können. Eine Anwendung dieses Rasters erlaubt es also, gewisse Merkmale des Textes zu erfassen; die Frage der Bedeutung aber, die diesen Merkmalen zuzuordnen ist, oder jene nach den Normen, welche den angewendeten Kriterien zugrunde liegen, lässt sich im Rahmen empirischer Forschung nicht beantworten. Diese Lücke zu füllen ist das Ziel der vorgestellten Dissertation: der Autor versucht, in acht Kapiteln etwas Gültiges darüber auszusagen, "was Texte sind", und Normen zu konstituieren, "wie sie sein sollen".

Nachdem im ersten Kapitel in die Arbeit eingeleitet worden ist, befasst sich das zweite mit dem Thema "Grammatik" und nennt notwendige Bestandteile von Texten, die jedoch noch nicht hinreichen, um Textualität zu konstituieren; Grammatik ist nichts Text-Spezifisches. Gleiches gilt vom Kapitel 3, zum Thema Schrift, das vor allem aufgenommen wurde, weil die Arbeit nur von schriftlichen Texten handelt. Im Kapitel 4, "Kohäsion", wird eine veraltete Position der Textlinguistik diskutiert; auch wenn mit der Kohäsionslinguistik Textualität nicht zu fassen ist, bringt sie doch wichtige Erkenntnisse zum Thema. Den Kern der Arbeit bilden die Kapitel 5 und 6 unter der Überschrift "Kohärenz", da die Kohärenz nach Ansicht der neueren Linguistik das grundlegende Merkmal von Texten ist. Die abschliessenden drei Kapitel (7-9) handeln von weiteren Textaspekten, nämlich von Metakommunikation, von Textsorten und von der (formellen und thematischen) Attraktivität von Texten.

Publ: Nussbaumer, Markus. *Was Texte sind und wie sie sein sollen: Ansätze zu einer sprachwissenschaftlichen Begründung eines Kriterienrasters zur Beurteilung von schriftlichen Schülertexten.* Tübingen: Niemeyer, 1991, 329 Seiten (Reihe Germanistische Linguistik; 119).

12802 Asessment of handwriting and its relationship to spelling and reading in six-and-a-half to seven-and-a-half year old children.
GBR 1993
Research Date(s): 1991-1993
Litt, L.; Pain, J.·
Inst: Open University, Chorlton House, 70 Manchester Road, Chorlton-cum-Hardy, Manchester M21 1PQ, United Kingdom; Underley Hall School, Kirkby Lonsdale, Carnforth LA6 2HE, United Kingdom.
writing; reading; spelling
écriture; lecture; orthographe
PROJECT DESCRIPTION
The research arises from the development of a dictation test for use with top infant (six-and-a-half to seven-and-a-half year old) children. Data (total scores) is available for several thousand children. From these, a sub-sample of some 500 scripts is being analysed in detail so that comparisons may be made between handwriting characteristics and attainments in spelling and reading. Anomalies identified in these comparisons will be investigated on an individual basis to identify causal factors.

12803 An assessment of teaching methodology in bilingual subject area situations in the secondary sector.
GBR 1993
Research Date(s): 1991-1994
Williams, C.
Sup: Baker, C.; Jones, G.
Inst: Y Coleg Normal Ffordd Caergybi, Bangor, Gwynedd LL57 2PX, United Kingdom; University College of North Wales, School of Education, Deiniol Road, Bangor, Gwynedd LL57 2UW, United Kingdom.
Fin: Awdurdod Addysg Gwynedd.
bilingualism; Welsh language; English language; bilingual education; teaching method
bilinguisme; langue galloise; langue anglaise; enseignement bilingue; méthode pédagogique
PROJECT DESCRIPTION
This is a study of successful teaching methods used in subject areas and within the bilingual (Welsh /English) context in the county of Gwynedd. The aim is to produce school-based inservice training material based on good practice observed in the classroom, combined with recent research findings in the fields of: (1) language across the curriculum in the bilingual setting; and (2) bilingual teaching.
The research will involve observation across a sample of 120 lessons in years 7-9 and in 15-18 secondary schools within the authority, with videotaped evidence of approximately one-third of the lessons. These have been chosen on the basis of: (1) following a Welsh-medium class for the whole day (in a variety of language medium settings); (2) following a group of Welsh learners for the whole day (either a whole teaching group or a smaller group within a bilingual class); and (3) observing a specifically stated policy for bilingual development, e.g. both languages within the same lesson, or bilingual development through modular monolingual teaching. Assessment of this variety of teaching methods in a range of bilingual situations will be included in the results and conclusions.

12804 Attitudes to the Welsh language and bilingualism.
GBR 1993
Research Date(s): 1988-1992
Baker, C.

Inst: University College of North Wales, School of Education, Deiniol Road, Bangor, Gwynedd LL57 2UW, United Kingdom.
Fin: Economic and Social Research Council.
Welsh language; bilingualism; language skill; attitude change; youth attitude
langue galloise; bilinguisme; aptitude linguistique; changement d'attitude; attitude de la jeunesse
PROJECT DESCRIPTION
The Welsh language has rapidly declined this century. At the turn of the century, some half of the population in Wales spoke Welsh. The Census of 1981 revealed that this figure had dropped to one in five residents in Wales. Attitude to the Welsh language is an important barometer of likely future language trends in Wales. In particular, previous research had indicated that attitudes to Welsh tend to decline during the early and middle teens.
The research aims to investigate the reasons for change in attitude to the Welsh language amongst 13 to 16 year olds. An attitude survey of first, second and third year secondary pupils in 1988 will be repeated with the same pupils in 1990. Change in the attitude to Welsh of some 800 pupils will be examined in terms of youth culture, use of mass media, identification models, language and background of the home as well as the school and neighbourhood, type of school attended, self-concept, achievement level, gender and age. In addition, the research will examine attitude to bilingualism as a concept importantly different from attitude to Welsh.

12805 Bakalářské studium komerční a průvodcovské ruštiny. (A Bachelor degree course in Russian for commerce and tourism.)
CSK 1994
Research Date(s): 1992-
Skácel, Josef; Lepilová, Květuše; Vavrečka, Mojmír; Rudincová, Blažena; Nováček, Pavel; Zidaro, Kounová.
Inst: Filosofická fakulta Ostravské univerzity (Ostrava University, Faculty of Arts), Reální 5, 701 00 Ostrava 1, Czech Republic.
Ministerstvo školství, mládeže a tělovýchovy České republiky (Ministry of Education, Youth and Physical Education of the Czech Republic), Karmelitská 8, 110 00 Praha 1, Czech Republic
language teaching; foreign languages; Russian language; commerce; tourism; curriculum development
enseignement des langues; langues étrangères; langue russe; commerce; tourisme; élaboration de programmes d'études
PROJECT DESCRIPTION
This research was set up in response to the need in the Ostrava region for translators, interpreters and suitably trained clerical staff (especially in the field of business correspondence) in the context of economic cooperation with Russia and other states of the Commonwealth of Independent States (CIS). In economic contacts with these states, Russian has the important role of intermediary language in business conversations, contracts, information exchange, etc.
The research is in two parts: (1) conceptualization of a Russian language course at Bachelor's degree level, specifically aimed at commerce and tourism; (2) preparation of teaching and learning materials for such a course.

12806 Bakalářské studium komerční průvodcovské němčiny (moderní profilace absolventa germanistiky na FF OU se zaměřením na potřeby regionu). (A Bachelor degree course in German for commerce and tourism: a modern profile of the German Studies graduate from Ostrava University Faculty of Arts.)
CSK 1994
Research Date(s): 1992-1995
Kyselá, M.; Jurajdová, P.; Sladovníková, Š.; Stupek, I.; Zajícová, P.; Sladovník, Z.
Sup: Schwarz, F.; Ehrhardt, H.
Inst: Katedra germanistiky, Filosofická fakulta Ostravské univerzity (Ostrava University, Faculty of Arts, Department of German Studies), Dvořákova 7, 701 03 Ostrava, Czech Republic.
language teaching; foreign languages; German language; commerce; tourism; curriculum development
enseignement des langues; langues étrangères; langue allemande; commerce; tourisme; élaboration de programmes d'études
PROJECT DESCRIPTION
This research is conducted in response to regional needs in the entrepreneurial sphere and the increasing pressure to make use of regional possibilities in the field of tourism.
The research is in two parts: (1) the conceptualization of a three-year German language course at Bachelor's degree level, specifically aimed at the fields of commerce and tourism; (2) the development of teaching and learning materials for such a course.

12807 Betrieblicher Fremdsprachenbedarf in Oberoesterreich. (Foreign language needs in companies in Upper Austria.)
AUT 1993
Research Date(s): 1991-1993
Stockinger, Josef; Wenidoppler, Heinrich; Zaller, Pia; Zinnagl, Robert.

Inst: Berufsfoerderungsinstitut Oberoesterreich, Raimundstrasse 3, A-4020 Linz.

Fin: Bundesministerium fuer Arbeit und Soziales.

foreign languages; job requirements; foreign relations; industry; commerce; manpower need; level of qualification

langues étrangères; qualification requise pour l'emploi; relations extérieures; industrie; commerce; besoin de main-d'oeuvre; niveau de qualification

PROJECT DESCRIPTION

Die zentralen Aufgabenstellungen des Projekts liegen im Erkennen wirtschaftlicher Trends oberoesterreichischer Betriebe, insbesondere im Bereich Export und internationale Wirtschaftsverflechtung, sowie in Grundlagenarbeiten zur Entwicklung betrieblicher Ausbildungskonzepte und von Loesungsansaetzen fuer eine verbesserte Bedarfsabdeckung. Die inhaltlichen Projektziele koennen in folgende Bereiche zusammengefasst werden: Grundlagenarbeiten in den Bereichen Fremdsprachendidaktik und -methodik, Psycho- und Soziolinguistik sowie Erstellung von Fallstudien; Analyse der Import-/Exportverflechtungen oberoesterreichischer Betriebe; Informationsbeschaffung auf nationaler und internationaler Ebene zu aehnlich gelagerten Forschungs- und Entwicklungsansaetzen; Durchfuehrung von Stellenanalysen im Hinblick auf die Relevanz von Fremdsprachenqualifikationen; Erkennen von Widerspruechen zwischen festgestelltem Bedarf und Bildungsangeboten durch eine Fremdsprachenerhebung auf Branchen- und Betriebsebene.

Es werden schriftliche Befragungen von rund .000 - nach Quoten ausgewaehlten - Unternehmen in Oberoesterreich durchgefuehrt, qualitative Interviews in etwa 50 Unternehmen und Arbeitsplatzbeobachtungen in sieben Unternehmen.

Das Untersuchungszenario baut auf einem dreistufigen, in sich geschlossenen deduktiven Modell auf, welches die Forschungsmethoden Fragebogenerhebung, qualitative Interviews sowie Arbeitsplatzbeobachtung zusammenfuehrt.

12808 Bildungspolitische Bedingungen des Unterrichts von Migrantenkindern in der Herkunftssprache. (Policy conditions for teaching immigrant children in their native language.)

DEU 1993

Research Date(s): 1991-1992

Poernbacher, U.

Sup: Reich, H.

Inst: Universitaet Koblenz-Landau, Abt. Landau, FB 06 Philologie, Studienbereich Lehrer fuer Kinder mit fremder Muttersprache, Auslaenderpaedagogik, Marktstr. 46, D-6740 Landau.

Fin: Deutsche Forschungsgemeinschaft.

mother tongue; teaching language; Sweden; France; educational policy; immigrant; United Kingdom; child of foreign national

langue maternelle; langue d'enseignement; Suède; France; politique de l'éducation; immigrant; Royaume-Uni; enfant d'étranger

PROJECT DESCRIPTION

Inhalt: Vergleich des "Muttersprachlichen Unterrichts" fuer Migrantenkinder in drei europaeischen Einwanderungslaendern, die sich aufgrund ihrer bildungspolitischen Positionen unterscheiden: Grossbritannien, Schweden und Frankreich. Zweck des Vergleichs ist es zu ermitteln, wieweit und in welcher Weise diese Positionen die konkrete Entwicklung dieses Unterrichtstyps bestimmen, und daraus bildungspolitische Kriterien oder Postulate abzuleiten.

Geographischer Raum: Frankreich, Grossbritannien, Schweden.

Vorgehensweise: Expertengespraeche; Unterrichtshospitationen (protokollierte Unterrichtsbeobachtungen); Analyse von Dokumenten.

12809 Bilingual learners and language provision in the National Curriculum.

GBR 1993

Research Date(s): 1991-1992

Mason, K.

Sup: Brumfit, C.

Inst: Southampton University, Faculty of Educational Studies, Centre for Language in Education, Highfield, Southampton SO9 5NH, United Kingdom.

multilingualism; bilingualism; sociolinguistics; minority language; ethnic minority

multilinguisme; bilinguisme; sociolinguistique; langue de minorité; minorité ethnique

PROJECT DESCRIPTION

The project surveys existing documentation on multilingual learners in Southampton, attemtping to build as complete as possible a picture of the distribution of multilingual learners and the range of languages represented. Following this survey, one school was chosen for detailed work. This project partly replicates the Linguistic Minorities Project studies on language use, and partly develops further studies on language patterns in the families of respondents. Some effort is made to explore possible future patterns of language distribution in relation to dispersal of speakers of minority languages. The research methodology of the project is carefully

described in a booklet (later to be accompanied by seminars and workshops) to enable teachers in other schools to develop similar projects.

12810 Bilinguale Kinder in monolingualen Schulen. (Bilingual children in monolingual schools.)

DEU 1993

Research Date(s): 1990-1992

Gogolin, I.; Neumann, U.

Inst: Universitaet Hamburg, FB 06 Erziehungswissenschaft, Institut fuer Didaktik der Geographie, Geschichte, Politik und des Sachunterrichts, Von-Melle-Park 8, D-2000 Hamburg 13.

Fin: Deutsche Forschungsgemeinschaft.

bilingualism; primary school; parental attitude; language development; child of foreign national

bilinguisme; école primaire; attitude des parents; développement du langage; enfant d'étranger

PROJECT DESCRIPTION

Inhalt: Das Projekt verfolgt das Ziel, die Institutionen sprachlicher Erziehung in der Einwanderungsgesellschaft in ihrer Verflechtung zu beschreiben: elterliche Anschauungen, Meinungen und Werthaltungen zur Spracherziehung, schulisches Spracherziehungshandeln von Lehrerinnen und Lehrern und das ausserunterrichtliche Sprachverhalten bilingualer Schueler und Schuelerinnen. Dies soll durch die Erarbeitung einer Schulfallstudie in Kooperation mit einer Hamburger Primarschule mit einem fuer den Stadtteil durchschnittlichen Anteil lebensweltlich zweisprachiger Schueler erreicht werden. Die Fallstudie ist im Hinblick auf moegliche Veraenderungen der Praxis der Beteiligten in der Schwellensituation des Uebergangs auf weiterfuehrende Schulen vergleichend angelegt. In die Untersuchung des unterrichtlichen Spracherziehungshandelns von Lehrkraeften wird ergaenzend eine international vergleichende Dimension einbezogen.

Geographischer Raum: Hamburg.

Vorgehensweise: Interkulturelle Bildung. Untersuchungsdesign: Fallstudie; Querschnittserhebung; Trend; qualitative Forschung.

Datengewinnung: Standardisiertes Interview, nicht-standardisiertes interview, teilnehmende Beobachtung, Beobachtung, Aktenanalyse (Stichprobe: ca. 150; Schueler und deren Eltern; Auswahlverfahren: total. Stichprobe: ca. 30; Lehrer einer Hamburger Schule; Auswahlverfahren: total).

12811 Bilinguisme, immigration et scolarisation.

FRA 1993

Research Date(s): 1986-

Pallaud, Berthille.

Inst: Université de Strasbourg I, UFR des Sciences du comportement, CNRS URA/668, Laboratoire de recherche Production et effets de la parole et du langage, Laboratoire de psycholinguistique, 12 rue Goethe, 67000 Strasbourg, France.

bilingualism; immigrant; school failure; compensatory education; language skill; primary education; official language; cultural identity

bilinguisme; immigrant; échec scolaire; éducation compensatoire; aptitude linguistique; enseignement primaire; langue officielle; identité culturelle

PROJECT DESCRIPTION

Objectifs: Le problème linguistique semble être au coeur de l'intrication des relations entre échec scolaire, milieu socio-professionnel et paramètres culturels. Ce qui n'est pas connu c'est le statut ou la nature de ce problème linguistique: simple difficulté de maîtrise d'une capacité à communiquer ou problèmes d'identité individuelle et socio-culturelle. Trois opérations de recherche correspondent à cette problématique: (1) le bilinguisme des enfants acquérant la langue française dans le cadre des classes d'initiation (CLIN), cours de rattrapage intégrés (CRI), classes ordinaires; (2) les conditions dans lesquelles l'acquisition de la langue nationale se fait par des enfants primo-arrivants non francophones.

Méthodologie: Enquête portant sur le niveau de compréhension des élèves en langues française et arabe et en calcul dans une école de Marseille (330 élèves environ).

Publ: Varro, Gabrielle & Pallaud, Berthille. Langues, langages et identités dans des contextes interculturels. In: *Langage et société, Saisons d'Alsace*, n° 106 (hiver), Le CNRS Alsace, des laboratoires tout terrain, 1989, pp. 196-198.

12812 Children's reading comprehension: self-image, attainments and attitudes. A cross-cultural study.

GBR 1993

Research Date(s): 1990-1992

Lewis, J.

Sup: Pumfrey, P.

Inst: Manchester University, School of Education, Centre for Educational Guidance and Special Needs, Oxford Road, Manchester M13 9PL, United Kingdom.

Fin: World Council of Churches; University of Manchester Bursory ORS Award Scheme.

reading; achievement; pupil attitude; cross-cultural research

lecture; rendement; attitude de l'élève; recherche transculturelle

PROJECT DESCRIPTION

This cross-cultural study is designed to identify changes in pupils' reading comprehension attainments and to consider these in relation to pupils' self-concepts as learners and their attitudes to reading. Samples of about 1,200 pupils will be tested in both Kingston/St Andrews in Jamaica and in an urban local education authority in the north-west of England. Each sample will comprise three year groups with average ages of 9, 11 and 13 years.

12813 Cognitive analysis of fluent reading and learning to read.
GBR 1993
Research Date(s): 1989-1992
Mitchell, D.
Inst: Exeter University, Department of Psychology, Washington Singer Laboratories, Exeter EX4 4OG, United Kingdom.
Fin: Economic and Social Research Council; Nuffield Foundation; British Council.
reading; cognitive process; comprehension; reading speed
lecture; processus cognitif; compréhension; vitesse de lecture
PROJECT DESCRIPTION

The aim of the research is to determine the cognitive processes underlying fluent reading and learning to read. The methods are experimental and often involve speeded responses and groups of words or sentences presented on a screen under the control of a microcomputer. Specific tasks that have been used include lexical decision tasks, subject placed reading tasks, tachistoscopic recognition tasks and mind-recall tasks. To date the researchers have carried out work on word recognition, sentence parsing and text integration with particular reference to the influence of context or prior knowledge at all levels. Some of the most recent work concerns the role of lexical and pragmatic effects of parsing. Contributions from PhD students include work on automatic processing of word meaning, the use of script knowledge in comprehension, the use of plans goals in comprehension, and individual differences in reading skills.

12814 Cognitive processes in reading and spelling.
GBR 1993
Research Date(s): 1979-
Underwood, G.
Inst: Nottingham University, Department of Psychology, University Park, Nottingham NG7 2RD, United Kingdom.
Fin: Medical Research Council; Science and Engineering Research Council.
reading; spelling; cognitive process; word recognition; comprehension
lecture; orthographe; processus cognitif; reconnaissance des mots; compréhension
PROJECT DESCRIPTION

The aim of the project is to identify the cognitive processes which enable us to read and spell - those processes through which written information must be transformed by the competent reader to reach understanding. Dependent measures of reading speed and accuracy are observed as a function of controlled variables. Measures are also used to observe eye movements. Experiments have been performed on skilled adult readers, young readers and latter with reading difficulties. Recognition of isolated words and the comprehension of coherent text have been investigated. The role of attention in recognition concerning isolated words has been studied and also the role of alternative processing routes (graphemic/phonological) by manipulating the orthographic regularity of the words presented. The role of regularity in spelling has also been investigated.

Findings suggest that for children of 10+ and adults, attention is not essential for isolated word recognition but is for measuring of sentences. Good and poor readers do not differ in their ability to recognise the meanings of isolated words so much as in their ability to use the meanings after recognition. Individual differences in reading ability are more associated with post-recognition processes such as those involved in the use of working memory than with initial encoding. One of the researcher's interests is in the patterns of eye movements (saccades, regressive saccades and fixation durations) made by skilled readers who are comprehending sentences, with specific interest in the cognitive mechanisms of eye guidance.

Computer-based learning support with classroom computers is currently being investigated. The questions being asked here are: How can computers be used to enhance the cognitive processes involved in reading and spelling, and what uses can teachers make of classroom computers with children of different ability background?.
Publ: A list of publications is available from the researcher on request.

12815 Cohesive ties in children's use of language in relation to the teaching of mathematics.
GBR 1993
Research Date(s): 1985-1992
Hargreaves, S.
Sup: Wain, G.; Beard, R.
Inst: Leeds University, Centre for Studies in Science and Mathematics Education, Leeds LS2 9JT, United Kingdom.
language; mathematics; language development; verbal interaction
langage; mathématiques; développement du langage; interaction verbale
PROJECT DESCRIPTION

A cohesive tie is defined as a semantic relation between items of a text, or between an item of a text and some feature of a broader context to which the textual item is perceived to be related. Cohesive ties may be recognised in all forms of text, including mathematics text and spoken or written discourse. Natural language communication is 'fuzzy', that is, characterised by probablistic structures and operations which are not fully delimited. Computer operations are taken to be logical, even when inputs and outputs are in the form of natural language signs or symbols, and therefore 'unfuzzy'.

Observations and video-recordings were made of children in pairs discussing with a view to problem solving an interactive mathematical computer-based game. The main purpose of the empirical work was to seek evidence to support a view that children's use of language is characteristic of particular stages or states of learning; and that their use of language, as learning progresses, becomes increasingly characteristic of a competent or expert user. As natural language is fuzzy there are problems in attempting any analysis of its manifestations if this is not to rely on purely formal definitions such as those of a dictionary. Therefore it was necessary to develop a systematic model which was somewhat removed from natural language description. Recorded discussions were analysed into categories of cohesive ties and this data subjected to cluster analysis and represented as hierarchical trees. An independent narrow measure of children's competence and efficiency in achieving the object of play was also used.

The recordings contained material which suggested, possibly, that children were responding differently to their task by reasons of variations in their past experience, their knowledge, mood and intention. Something of the influence of such matters was revealed more clearly by the clustering technique adopted suggesting that it may be an effective means of representing effects of non-observable entities. The method of analysis and modelling would seem to have useful application as a bridging technique between views held on the basis of general psychological or epistemological theory and records of performance based upon individual observation. The empirical study was seen upon analysis to reveal patterns of association in meaning which have implications for producers and users of educational software. Perhaps the form of modelling adopted and developed would be useful, with appropriate modifications, in exploring children's responses to methods and materials adopted by schools in their efforts to implement the National Curriculum.

12816 Communication between non-handicapped children and pupils with severe learning difficulties.
GBR 1993
Research Date(s): 1990-
Lewis, A.
Inst: Warwick University, Faculty of Educational Studies, Coventry CV4 7AL, United Kingdom.
communication; integration; mentally handicapped; interaction; learning difficulty
communication; intégration; handicapé mental; interaction; difficulté de l'apprentissage
PROJECT DESCRIPTION

This research is investigating the nature of communication between non-handicapped (NH) children and pupils with severe learning difficulties (SLD). The children interact in dyads or triads and each group comprises at least one NH and one SLD child. NH-SLD interaction has been video-recorded for approximately 60 minutes each week throughout a year of weekly integration sessions. Thirty-six NH children (ages ten years, one month to eleven years, one month at the start of the year) and nine pupils with SLD (ages twelve years, four months to fifteen years, eight months at the start of the year) have been involved. Analyses of data is being carried out utilising frameworks developed in an earlier study (Lewis and Carpenter, 1990; Lewis, 1990) involving younger children in NH-SLD dyads.

Publ: Lewis, A. Six and seven year old 'normal' children's talk to peers with severe learning difficulties. In: *European Journal of Special Needs Education*, Vol 5, No 1/1990, pp. 13-23.
Lewis, A. & Carpenter, B. Discourse, in an integrated school setting, between six and seven year old non-handicapped children and peers with severe learning difficulties. In: Fraser, W.I. (ed.). *Key issues in mental retardation*. London: Routledge, 1990.
Lewis, A. Entitled to learn together?. In: Ashdown, R.; Carpenter, B. & Bovair, K. (eds.). *Meeting the curriculum challenge*. Lewes: Falmer Press, 1991.

12817 Communication training via manual signing for non-speaking mentally handicapped children.
GBR 1993
Research Date(s): 1978-
Hewitt, J.
Sup: Remington, B.
Inst: Southampton University, Department of Psychology, Highfield, Southampton SO9 5NH, United Kingdom.
Fin: Economic and Social Research Council.
non-verbal communication; semiology; sign; mentally handicapped; speech handicapped

communication non-verbale; sémiologie; signe; handicapé mental; handi-capé de la parole
PROJECT DESCRIPTION

This is an ongoing research programme which aims to investigate the factors responsible for the development of effective communication in non-speaking children. Initially, the work focused both on children with a mental handicap and autistic children, but is now concerned primarily with mental handicap. Methods usually involve single-subject experimental designs. The role of receptive speech on expressive signing and the developments of novel sign combinations through specialised training methods have been investigated. The current interests of the research staff are in the communicative function of signing and symbol use and the investigation of transfer between requesting and naming functions.

Publ: Clarke, S.; Remington, B. & Light, P. The role of referential speech in sign learning by mentally retarded children: A comparison of total communication and sign-alone training. In: *Journal of Applied Behaviour Analysis*, No 21/1988, pp. 419-426.
Remington, B.; Watson, J. & Light, P. Beyond the single sign: A matrix-based approach to teaching productive sign combinations. In: *Mental Handicap Research*, No 3/1990, pp. 33-50.
Light, P.; Watson, J. & Remington, B. Beyond the single sign II: The significance of sign order in a matrix-based approach to teaching productive sign combinations. In: *Mental Handicap Research*, No 3/1990, pp. 161-178.
Remington, B. Why use single subject methods in AAC?. In: Brodin, J. & Bjorck-Akesson, E. (eds.). *Methodological issues in research in augmentative and alternative communication: Proceedings of the First International ISAAC Research Symposium in augmentative and alternative communication*. Stockholm: Swedish Handicap Institute, 1991.
Goodman, J. & Remington, B. Teaching communicative signing: Labelling, requesting and transfer of function. In: Remington, B. (ed.). *The challenge of severe mental handicap: A behaviour analytic approach*. Chichester: J. Wiley and Sons, 1991.

12818 Comparative study of writing development in French and English primary schools.
GBR 1993
Research Date(s): 1990-1996
Cotton, P.
Sup: McGuiness, J.; Gilliland, J.
Inst: Durham University, School of Education, Leazes Road, Durham DH1 1TA, United Kingdom.
Fin: Kingston University.
writing; comparative research; France; primary education
écriture; recherche comparative; France; enseignement primaire
PROJECT DESCRIPTION

This research will be looking at the effect of early visual exposure to cursive script on children's writing, and is a comparative study of writing development in England and France. From this it is hoped to add theoretical substance to the rapidly increasing desire for schools to change from print to joined writing when children begin school. Initially, theoretical aspects of the differences between print and cursive script will be investigated, looking at the theoretical rationale of French researchers such as Lilian Lurcat and her influence on children's writing in France. These will be compared with research that has influenced British children's writing, beginning with Edward Johnson in 1913, who wanted all children to print because he thought it would help with their reading. Practical aspects will be observed from school entry until the later primary years. Children will be carefully monitored in terms of their attitudes to writing and their self-image as writers. Specific areas to be targeted will be legibility, speed, accuracy, spelling, flow of ideas, creativity, and handwriting as part of the whole writing process. A small sample of about six schools will be monitored in detail over a period of about three years. This will necessitate involvement with all classes in all schools. Alongside this, a nationwide developmental survey will be conducted, and a National Register set up of all schools who are introducing or have already introduced joined writing on school entry. This development has been prompted by the numerous responses from an article written in *Child Education*.

Publ: Cotton, P. *Handwriting Review*, p. 57, 1990.
Cotton, P. *United Kingdom Reading Association Journal*, Vol 24, No 1, p. 2, April 1990.
Cotton, P. *United Kingdom Reading Association Journal*, Vol 25, No 1, p. 27, April 1991.
Cotton, P. *Child Education*, p. 53, April 1992.

12819 A comparison of linguistic performance in continuous assessment and unseen examination writing at undergraduate level.
GBR 1993
Research Date(s): 1982-1992
O'Brien, T.
Sup: Jordan, R.
Inst: Manchester University, School of Education, English Language Teaching Unit, Oxford Road, Manchester M13 9PL, United Kingdom.

linguistics; written expression; examination; undergraduate; student; performance
linguistique; expression écrite; examen; étudiant non-diplômé; étudiant; performance
PROJECT DESCRIPTION

The research aims to discover whether there is any basis to students' intuitive feeling that their linguistic performance deteriorates in examination conditions. Continuous assessment essays and examination questions written on the same areas and within a very short space of time of each other are being analysed in ignorance of the grades already awarded. Scope is limited to undergraduates in the Department of Psychology, writing in four special subject areas. The results of the analysis of linguistic performance up to and including discourse level, will eventually be compared with the grades that have been awarded.

Publ: O'Brien, T. Writing for continuous assessment or examinations: a comparison of style. In: *Proceedings of the Selmous Conference, 1985*. ELT Docs. Oxford: Pergamon Press, 1987.
O'Brien, T. Predictive items in student writing. In: *Written language* (published papers of the Annual Conference of the British Association of Applied Linguistics, Reading University, 1986). London: CILT/BAAL, 1987.

12820 A comparison of the internal organisation of proportions within English and French discourse and its bearings on the teaching of English to native speakers of French.
GBR 1993
Research Date(s): 1989-1992
Thornton, R.
Inst: Heriot-Watt University, Moray House Institute of Education, Holyrood Road, Edinburgh EH8 8AQ, United Kingdom.
language teaching; English language; foreign languages
enseignement des langues; langue anglaise; langues étrangères
PROJECT DESCRIPTION

This research aims to provide a basis for the production of learning activities and materials for native speakers of French learning English as a second language.

12821 Comprehension problems in children: the nature of the deficit.
GBR 1993
Research Date(s): 1989-1992
Stothard, S.
Sup: Hulme, C.
Inst: York University, Department of Psychology, Heslington, York YO1 5DD, United Kingdom.
Fin: Science and Engineering Research Council.
reading; comprehension; assessment; learning difficulty
lecture; compréhension; appréciation; difficulté de l'apprentissage
PROJECT DESCRIPTION

The aim of this study is to investigate the nature of the deficit underlying comprehension problems in children. Children aged 7-8 years were given a battery of tests designed to measure comprehension/semantic skills and decoding/phonological skills in an attempt to identify the underlying processes in these two components of reading. Different teaching methods aimed at remediating comprehension deficits will also be evaluated.

Publ: Stothard, S. & Hulme, C. A note of caution concerning the Neale Analysis of Reading Ability (Revised). In: *British Journal of Educational Psychology*, Vol 61, No 2/1991, pp. 226-229.

12822 A connectionist model of the development of visual word recognition.
GBR 1993
Research Date(s): 1990-1994
Hulme, C.; Rack, J.; Allinson, N.; Cohen, A.; Snowling, M.
Inst: York University, Department of Psychology, Heslington, York YO1 5DD, United Kingdom.
Fin: Economic and Social Research Council; Medical Research Council; SERC - Cognitive Science/Human Computer Interaction Initiative.
reading; dyslexia; word recognition; beginning learning
lecture; dyslexie; reconnaissance des mots; enseignement initial
PROJECT DESCRIPTION

The project will develop and evaluate a model of the processes involved in learning a sight vocabulary in the early stages of learning to read. The model will be evaluated and refined on the basis of data from studies of children's reading errors and will provide an explicit theoretical account of why good phonological skills aid the rapid learning of a sight vocabulary and how such learning may be impeded in dyslexic children. The research, which depends crucially on collaboration between different disciplines, will also contribute to the development of connectionist modelling techniques by advancing understanding of how to build a prior knowledge into such models, and in applying ideas taken from the study of self-organising neural maps to the modelling of higher level cognitive processes.

12823 La conoscenza delle lingue tra gli insegnanti della scuola elementare italiana. (Knowledge of languages among Italian primary school teachers.)
ITA 1993
Research Date(s): 1991
Sorcioni, M.; Donati, A.; Cataldi, G.F.
Sup: Cruciani, S.
Inst: Centro Studi Investimenti Sociali - CENSIS (Centre for Social Studies and Investments), Piazza di Novella 2, 00199 Roma, Italy.
Fin: Ministero della Pubblica Istruzione, Ufficio Studi e Programmazione.
language teaching; foreign languages; primary education; teacher; language skill
enseignement des langues; langues étrangères; enseignement primaire; enseignant; aptitude linguistique
PROJECT DESCRIPTION
Aims: Based on the results of the first large-scale survey of teachers' language competence, the study aimed to assess teachers' levels of competence for teaching foreign languages in primary school. It also sought to establish: teachers' levels of participation in the survey by geographical area; the geographical distribution of qualified language teachers; subcategories of participants in the survey according to average number of years of teaching experience.
Methods: The data were divided into four categories, corresponding to the four foreign languages which were the subject of the survey (English, French, Spanish and German).
Results: Analysis of the results shows a high level of participation: more than 14,000 tenured primary school teachers, without a college degree in a foreign language, participated in the test. Participation by geographical area was more or less homogeneous, with slightly higher levels in the North. English is most widely taught, especially in the North, followed by French, which enjoys a relatively strong popularity in the South. Levels of demand for German and Spanish are 3.6% and 1.2% respectively. The average number of years of teaching experience is higher in the South (14.5 years) than in the North (11.5). Aspiring English teachers have on average 11.5 years of teaching experience, while those aspiring to teach French have 14.3 years. Teachers seem to be better prepared overall in the North, with the exception of German teachers, who are qualitatively better in the South.
The percentages of teachers who passed the test administered in the survey are: English: 54% in the North, 50% in the Centre, 37% in the South; French: 59% in the North, 42% in the Centre, 31% in the South; Spanish: 89% in the North, 85% in the Centre, 79% in the South; German: 59% in the North, 52% in the Centre, 61% in the South.

12824 Constructing culture: a study of teacher-pupil talk in French language lessons.
GBR 1993
Research Date(s): 1986-1992
Taylor, S.
Sup: Byram, M.
Inst: Durham University, School of Education, Leazes Road, Durham DH1 1TA, United Kingdom.
foreign languages; language teaching; culture; verbal communication; French language; youth attitude
langues étrangères; enseignement des langues; culture; communication verbale; langue française; attitude de la jeunesse
PROJECT DESCRIPTION
This research was started as a result of work undertaken on an ESRC (Economic and Social Research Council) funded project to determine the effects of foreign language teaching on young people's perceptions of other cultures. The aims of this research are to: (1) apply the conversation analysis approach to the study of foreign language lessons; (2) explore and describe ways in which foreign culture is constructed through talk in foreign language lessons; (3) consider the implications of this process for children's perceptions of other cultures. The work is based upon detailed analysis of taped lessons using conversation analysis. The tapes were made over two terms and include lessons of first, second and third year pupils in a comprehensive school. This work is supported by observations and interviews with teachers in two schools.

12825 The cultural dimension of English as a foreign language in the Arabian Gulf States.
GBR 1993
Research Date(s): 1989-1993
Abu-Jalala, F.
Sup: Byram, M.
Inst: Durham University, School of Education, Leazes Road, Durham DH1 1TA, United Kingdom.
Fin: British Council in Doha.
language teaching; foreign languages; English language; Arab countries; secondary education
enseignement des langues; langues étrangères; langue anglaise; pays arabes; enseignement secondaire
PROJECT DESCRIPTION

The research aims to examine the possibility of introducing English as a foreign language (EFL) together with its western culture in an Arabic/Islamic culture, and to what extent. The study falls into two branches. Firstly, a study is made of the experts' (university staff, English language Inspectors, the curriculum planning department and teachers) opinion using the 'Delphi Technique' and questionnaires. Secondly, pupils at the secondary stage are involved in interviews and questionnaires asking their opinions about the same issue. The size of the sample is governed by the size of the population of teachers and pupils - this will include English language staff in secondary schools and the University of Qatar, and secondary school pupils.

12826 Culture and civilisation studies for advanced language learners - an experiment in French and English schools.
GBR 1993
Research Date(s): 1990-1993
Byram, M.
Inst: Durham University, School of Education, Leazes Road, Durham DH1 1TA, United Kingdom.
Fin: Leverhulme Trust.
language teaching; foreign languages; culture; civilization; French language; English language; curriculum development; international cooperation; cross-national research
enseignement des langues; langues étrangères; culture; civilisation; langue française; langue anglaise; élaboration de programmes d'études; coopération internationale; recherche transnationale
PROJECT DESCRIPTION
The purpose of the research is to develop curricula, teaching and assessment methods for advanced language learning with reference to cultural studies, i.e. acquiring knowledge and understanding of the way of life and thinking of a foreign people and country. The research takes place in England and France and is based on existing approaches to teaching culture at GCE 'A' level and Baccalaureat.
The design involves, in both countries, a team of teachers and researchers who develop, operate and evaluate an experimental curriculum and assessment. The curriculum has two main emphases: that learners should acquire knowledge and understanding of selected dimension of French/English culture (defined as above); and that learners should acquire the research tools - largely those of ethnography - to carry out their own investigations of a foreign culture.
The cooperation of teams working in parallels in France (at the Institut National de Recherche Pédagogique) and in England provides for mutual information on research and development methods, on teaching techniques and on evaluation. The report will include, as well as a description of the research process, a specimen curriculum and materials to illustrate the principles underpinning the experiment.

12827 Curriculum development and evaluation of Teaching English as a Second Language (TESOL) courses at foundation level in the United Arab Emirates.
GBR 1993
Research Date(s): 1991-
El-Laithy, S.
Sup: Smedley, D.
Inst: Loughborough University of Technology, Department of Education, Loughborough LE11 3TU, United Kingdom.
language teaching; foreign languages; English language; United Arab Emirates
enseignement des langues; langues étrangères; langue anglaise; Emirats arabes unis
PROJECT DESCRIPTION
The research will evaluate the effectiveness of the present curriculum for teaching English as a second language at foundation level in the six colleges of higher education in the the United Arab Emirates, and indicate what further developments might be appropriate. The methods used include questionnaires to students, staff and administrators, follow-up interviews of a selected sample, and documentary analysis.

12828 Das Spannungsfeld zwischen Mundart und Standardsprache in der Deutschschweiz: Einstellungen junger Deutsch- und Westschweizer. (La Suisse alémanique entre le dialecte et la langue standard: attitudes linguistiques de jeunes Suisses alémaniques et Romands.)
CHE 1994
Research Date(s): 1985-1991
Schläpfer, Robert; Gutzwiller, Jürg; Schmid, Beat.
Inst: Universität Basel, Deutsches Seminar, Nadelberg 4, 4051 Basel, Schweiz.
dialect; opinion; youth attitude; German-speaking Switzerland
dialecte; opinion; attitude de la jeunesse; Suisse alémanique
PROJECT DESCRIPTION
Die Pädagogischen Rekrutenprüfungen haben den Zweck, Aufschluss zu geben über den Stand der Information und der Ausbildung der dienstpflichtigen männlichen Jugend, insbesondere im staatsbürgerlichen Bereich; die Ergebnisse sollen der Grundlagenforschung für das schweizerische

Erziehungs- und Unterrichtswesen dienen und zur Schulplanung und Koordination beitragen. Die Teilnahme an den Prüfungen ist für die Rekruten obligatorisch; es gibt einen schriftlichen Teil (anonyme Fragebogen) und einen mündlichen mit Gruppengesprächen. Für die Rekrutenprüfungen ist die Schweiz in verschiedene Kreise aufgeteilt, und die Themen können von Kreis zu Kreis variieren.

Die Pädagogischen Rekrutenprüfungen 1985 hingegen befassten sich im ganzen Land mit demselben Thema: "Sprachen in der Schweiz". Die Wahl dieses Themas war keineswegs ein Zufall; vielmehr ist die Rekrutenbefragung zur Sprachenproblematik im Zusammenhang einer grösseren wissenschaftliche Untersuchung zu sehen, die im Rahmen des Nationalen Forschungsprogramms 21 ("Kulturelle Vielfalt und nationale Identität") durchgeführt wurde. Der Bericht über diese Rekrutenprüfungen besteht aus zwei Teilen.

Der erste Teil, eine von der Universität Basel unterdessen angenommene Dissertation, enthält die Resultate der Auswertung der Fragebogen, die den deutschschweizerischen Rekruten vorgelegt worden waren. Bei der Auswertung interessierten bloss die Verhaltensweisen der Jugendlichen im Spannungsfeld zwischen Dialekt und Hochsprache sowie die diesem Verhalten zugrunde liegenden Einstellungen. In diesem Teil zeigt sich, dass die Quasi-Gesamtheit der Deutschschweizer den Dialekt als Muttersprache betrachtet und wie sehr dieser Dialekt identitätsstiftende Funktion hat.

Der Autor des zweiten Teils hat sich nur mit den Antworten französischsprachiger Rekruten beschäftigt und versucht, eine "welsche Perspektive" zu synthetisieren. Die Rekruten aus der Romandie scheinen für die Sprachenproblematik in der Schweiz sensibilisiert zu sein, und nur ein Viertel von ihnen betrachten die Probleme als befriedigend gelöst (bei 35% Enthaltungen). Dagegen sieht es so aus, als hätte das in der Westschweiz verbreitete Malaise gegenüber den Deutschschweizern und ihrer Sprache nicht in erster Linie mit der Verwendung des Dialekts zu tun.

Publ: Schläpfer, Robert; Gutzwiller, Jürg & Schmid, Beat. *Das Spannungsfeld zwischen Mundart und Standardsprache in der deutschen Schweiz: Spracheinstellungen junger Deutsch- und Westschweizer.* Aarau: Sauerländer, 1991 (Pädagogische Rekrutenprüfungen; Bd. 12).

Schmid, Beat. Mundart und Standardsprache in der deutschen Schweiz. In: *Aktuelle pädagogische Probleme: Bericht über die Pädagogischen Rekrutenprüfungen 1991.* Bern: EDMZ, 1992, S. 135-142.

Gutzwiller, Jürg. Dialecte et langue officielle des Suisses alémaniques: le point de vue des romands. In: *Problèmes pédagogiques actuels: rapport sur les examens pédagogiques des recrues 1991.* Bern: EDMZ, 1992, S. 143-145.

12829   De la construction du sens à partir d'un support iconique.
FRA   1993
Research Date(s): 1987-
Kugler, Marie; Préneron, Christiane.
Inst: Université de Paris V, UFR Linguistique générale et appliquée, CNRS URA/1031, Laboratoire de recherches sur l'acquisition et la pathologie du langage chez l'enfant, 12 rue Cujas, 75230 Paris Cedex 05, France.
oral expression; written expression; behaviour disorder; meaning; language development; story telling
expression orale; expression écrite; trouble du comportement; signification; développement du langage; narration d'histoires
PROJECT DESCRIPTION
   Objectifs: La recherche porte sur l'élaboration et la restructuration langagière d'une référence chez des enfants présentant des troubles comportementaux, scolarisés dans un hôpital de jour (Hôpital de Montesson). En effet, de même "qu'on ne peut pas ne pas communiquer", "on ne peut pas ne pas référer", c'est à dire ne pas renvoyer à un monde au delà du discours. Et les différentes façons de référer, plus ou moins transparentes plus ou moins interprétables, peuvent être considérées comme différentes façons (non explicites) de montrer, de signifier une relation au monde et à autrui. Sachant qu'il n'y a pas une théorie préalable des modes de référence à appliquer telle quelle à la pathologie et que par ailleurs, le quid et le cur du langage du psychotique ne sont reliés ni simplement ni directement à la pathologie sous-jacente, on s'attache ici à préciser comment se construit ou ne se construit pas une référence dans différentes conditions d'élaboration.
   Méthodologie: Les enregistrements portent sur 35 enfants. Dans un premier temps on propose aux enfants de construire une histoire avec le support d'une bande dessinée. L'analyse des productions obtenues souligne que les enfants se distinguent dans leurs possibilités d'élaborer un enchaînement narratif prenant appui sur une succession d'images ordonnée. Parallèlement, on propose aux mêmes enfants une paraphrase de récits oraux ou, au delà de l'organisation narrative, on s'efforce de caractériser la relation à la référence initiale au travers des mécanismes de déplacement et d'accentuation des éléments constitutifs de l'histoire. Enfin, à partir du même texte, certains enfants ont élaboré une paraphrase écrite qui fait l'objet d'une comparaison avec la paraphrase orale à au moins deux niveaux de la structuration textuelle. Cette étude est approfondie en comparant les productions des enfants psychotiques ou état-limite à celles de deux autres populations répondant à la même tâche: enfants tout-venant de même âge et enfants présentant un retard de même âge également.

12830   Defining the role of metaphor in adult learning and development.
GBR   1993
Research Date(s): 1986-1992
Shorthouse, R.
Sup: Lawson, K.; Allman, P.
Inst: Nottingham University, Department of Adult Education, 14-22 Shakespeare Street, Nottingham NG1 4FJ, United Kingdom.
linguistics; adult education
linguistique; éducation des adultes
PROJECT DESCRIPTION
   The purpose of this research is to demonstrate, by means of a linguistic philosophical analysis, the central role of metaphor in adult learning, within the context of the diverse contemporary phenomena of post-modernism with particular regard to the epistemological issue in education.

12831   The demotivated pupil in the modern language classroom - a comparative study.
GBR   1993
Research Date(s): 1991-1995
Chambers, G.
Sup: Sugden, D.; Tomlinson, P.
Inst: Leeds University, School of Education, Leeds LS2 9JT, United Kingdom.
language teaching; foreign languages; motivation for studies; pupil attitude; cross-national research
enseignement des langues; langues étrangères; motivation pour les études; attitude de l'élève; recherche transnationale
PROJECT DESCRIPTION
   The National Curriculum heralds the implementation of the 'Language for All' policy, introduced in some schools in the course of the 1980s. Of great concern to teachers is how to cater for the disaffected or demotivated pupil. It is generally felt that German pupils are more motivated to learn English than British pupils are to learn German. Popular reasons for this include English as the language of the business world and pop-culture. How much of this is fact and how much is myth?
   The purpose of the study is to investigate the problem of demotivation in foreign language learners in Leeds and Kiel. The study will look at similar groups of 13-14 year olds in terms of ability and background in similar schools in Leeds and Kiel. This age range has been chosen as it is at this stage that demotivation commonly and significantly manifests itself. Surveys and subsequent interviews with pupils and teachers will try to identify the causes of demotivation and the strategies used to counter it.
   The study will examine several questions: (1) the effect on motivation of the attitude to language learning brought from home and friends; the influence of the media; the influence of the teacher and teaching methods; the influence of pupil perception of need; the influence of the language learning environment; (2) how teachers identify demotivated pupils; (3) how teachers deal with demotivated pupils.

12832   Deutsch kontrastiv: Probleme von Lernern mit verschiedenem muttersprachlichen Hintergrund beim Erlernen des Deutschen als Fremdsprache.   (Contrasting German: problems experienced by people with different native languages when learning German as a foreign language.)
DEU   1993
Research Date(s): 1992-1993
Grossner, R.; Schmidt, S.
Sup: Erdmenger, M.
Inst: Technische Universitaet Braunschweig, FB 09 Erziehungswissenschaften, Seminar fuer Englische und Franzoesische Sprache und deren Didaktik, Konstantin-Uhde-Strasse 16, D-3300 Braunschweig; Paedagogische Hochschule Magdeburg, Institut fuer Germanistik, Lehrbereich Deutsch als Fremdsprache, Postfach, O-3040 Magdeburg.
German language; mother tongue; foreign languages; learning; grammar; Europe; speech
langue allemande; langue maternelle; langues étrangères; acquisition de connaissances; grammaire; Europe; parole
PROJECT DESCRIPTION
   Inhalt: Ueberblickartige Zusammenstellung der Schwierigkeiten beim Erlernen der deutschen Sprache, die Sprecher verschiedener Muttersprachen haben, auf den Gebieten Aussprache und Intonation, Morphologie, Syntax, insbesondere auch Nominalflexion und Verblehre, kontrastiv jeweils: Deutsch-Englisch, Deutsch-Franzoesisch, Deutsch-Spanisch, Deutsch-Polnisch, Deutsch-Russisch, Deutsch-Tschechisch, Deutsch-Griechisch, Deutsch-Rumaenisch, eventuell weitere.
   Geographischer Raum: Europa.
   Vorgehensweise: Scanning kontrastiver Untersuchungen Deutsch-Ausgangssprache, hinsichtlich neuralgischer Punkte beim Lernprozess; Entwicklung einer Nachschlagesystematik; empirische Ergaenzungsuntersuchung. Untersuchungsdesign: Evaluationsstudie; qualitative Forschung; Erfassung von (egozentrierten) Netzwerken.
   Datengewinnung: Nicht-standardisiertes Interview (Primarschulen in Niedersachsen; Auswahlverfahren: Zufall). Expertengespraech (Sekundar-

schulen in Niedersachsen; Auswahlverfahren: bewusst). Gruppendiskussion (Sekundarschulen in Niedersachsen; Auswahlverfahren: bewusst. Institut der Erwachsenenbildung Niedersachsen; Auswahlverfahren: bewusst). Teilnehmende Beobachtung (Kindergaerten in Niedersachsen; Auswahlverfahren: total. Primarschulen in Niedersachsen; Auswahlverfahren: Zufall. Sekundarschulen in Niedersachsen; Auswahlverfahren: bewusst. Institut fuer Erwachsenenbildung Niedersachsen; Auswahlverfahren: bewusst). Datenerstellung auf der Basis von bereits vorliegenden Materialien wie Texten, Akten, Statistiken.

12833 The development and evaluation of online computer-assisted language learning materials for English for academic purposes.
GBR 1993
Research Date(s): 1992-1993
Nesi, H.; Tsai, C.
Inst: Warwick University, Faculty of Educational Studies, Centre for English Language Teaching, Coventry CV4 7AL, United Kingdom.
language teaching; foreign languages; language for special purposes; English language; didactic use of computer; foreign student
enseignement des langues; langues étrangères; langage de spécialité; langue anglaise; usage didactique de l'ordinateur; étudiant étranger
PROJECT DESCRIPTION
   The proposed project is to build up a coherent package of English language learning materials which can be accessed by non-native speaker students via the Warwick University network. The programs intended for use are commercially produced, but will be 'authored' by the Centre for English Language Teaching (CELT) staff, with due regard for the students' subject specialisms and levels of expertise. It is anticipated that students will be introduced to the first phase of materials at the beginning of the 1992-1993 academic session, and the use made of the materials will then be monitored by means of Warwick University's Novell 1.12 Netware package, supplemented by questionnaires and interviews with selected subjects.
   The aim is to discover which types of Computer-Assisted Language Learning (CALL) activity are (a) used most frequently; and (b) judged to be most effective by university-level learners of English for academic purposes. In further phases of the project the intention is to expand and modify the materials in accordance with these findings.

12834 Dialogisme et déplacement.
FRA 1993
Research Date(s): 1987-
Salazar-Orvig, Anne; Hudelot, Christian.
Inst: Université de Paris V, UFR Linguistique générale et appliquée, CNRS URA/1031, Laboratoire de recherches sur l'acquisition et la pathologie du langage chez l'enfant, 12 rue Cujas, 75230 Paris Cedex 05, France.
verbal communication; verbal interaction; dialogue; pre-school child; content analysis; verbal behaviour; language development; adult-child relation
communication verbale; interaction verbale; dialogue; enfant d'âge préscolaire; analyse de contenu; comportement verbal; développement du langage; relation adulte-enfant
PROJECT DESCRIPTION
   Objectifs: Il s'agit d'abord de préciser l'analyse des relations qu'entretiennent entre eux les discours des interlocuteurs et l'ensemble des facteurs qui font qu'un dialogue n'est pas toujours prévisible, ni homogène. Le déplacement, compris comme l'enchaînement qui comporte un certain degré de discontinuité avec ce qui précède permet d'aborder des problèmatiques relatives non seulement à l'interlocution stricto sensu mais également à la mise en mots et donc à l'élaboration du sens dans le discours. Cette étude est abordée par des biais méthodologiques complémentaires. Une étude longitudinale de jeunes enfants, (a) un enfant enregistré en milieu familial dans des situations de jeux et de conversations libres entre 18 et 36 mois, (b) une étude clinique de corpus d'enfants âgés de 2 à 4 ans en milieu familial dans des situations de jeu. Cette étude s'organise autour de l'établissement d'une double typologie conçue dans une perspective développementale: celle des enchaînements dans leurs modalités de réalisation et la diversité de leurs significations et celle des déplacements en mettant l'accent sur le jeu entre les diverses relations de continuité et de discontinuité.
   Résultats: Une première approche du corpus permet d'ores et déjà d'associer au premier objectif de typologie des enchaînements et des déplacements une réflexion sur l'acquisition de l'outil langue dans une perspective dialogique. Il s'agit moins de repérer la première apparition de tel ou tel élément linguistique que d'étudier les modalités de leur ancrage textuel et des valeurs qui leur sont peu à peu associées dans le discours de l'enfant.

Publ: Hudelot, Christian & Salazar-Orvig, Anne. Qu'est-ce que tu en penses toi de cette classe? Cinq dialogues parascolaires entre parents et enfants du milieu familial. In: *Cahiers d'acquisition et de pathologie du langage*, 1988, n° 3, pp. 137-180.
Salazar-Orvig, Anne & Hudelot, Christian. Enchaînements, continuités et déplacements dialogiques chez le jeune enfant. In: *Verbum*, 1989, tome XII, fasc.1, pp. 99-115.

12835 Dialogue corporel et verbal.
FRA 1993
Research Date(s): 1986-
Van der Sraten, Astrid.
Inst: Université de Paris V, UFR Linguistique générale et appliquée, CNRS URA/1031, Laboratoire de recherches sur l'acquisition et la pathologie du langage chez l'enfant, 12 rue Cujas, 75230 Paris Cedex 05, France.
language development; dialogue; verbal behaviour; physical expression; pre-school child; non-verbal communication
développement du langage; dialogue; comportement verbal; expression corporelle; enfant d'âge préscolaire; communication non-verbale
PROJECT DESCRIPTION
   Objectifs: Partant de l'hypothèse que le langage articulé s'acquiert sur les bases de la communication mise en place entre 0 et 2 ans, on montre comment le dialogue verbal se construit sur les fondements du dialogue corporel. Les hypothèses qui orientent la recherche sont les suivantes: l'enfant entre progressivement dans des genres discursifs différents, en acquérant des moyens de communiquer différents. Il y a un ordre d'acquisition des différentes composantes du langage articulé. Il y a un sens du développement qui va du corps au code. Il y a des modes préférentiels de communication apparaissant selon un ordre d'émergence donné.
   Méthodologie: On décrit les différentes conduites de communication d'un petit nombre d'enfants âgés de 0 à 2 ans avec leurs parents, dans un certain nombre de situations typiques. On recherche et on caractérise les significations portées: (a) par les comportements gestuel, postural, mimique, proxémique; (b) par le comportement verbal; (c) par les éléments motivés, fortement codés ou précodés (des moyens verbaux ou non verbaux); (d) par les enchaînements des conduites verbales et non verbales. On essaye alors de cerner l'ordre d'émergence des différents moyens utilisés par l'enfant pour communiquer.
   Résultats: A travers l'analyse de dialogues entre de jeunes enfants (de la naissance à l'âge des premiers mots) et leurs parents, l'étude met en évidence les facteurs entrant en jeu dans les relations interlocutives ainsi que leur ordre d'émergence; le développement des aspects mimo-posturo-gestuels y a une place de choix. Au delà de cette analyse, on s'interroge sur la question de l'élaboration de la signification.

Publ: Van der Straten, Astrid. A l'aube de la parole, ou le développement de la communication chez le petit enfant. In: *Bulletin de liaison de l'association des praticiens de la méthode verbo-tonale*, 1986, n° 2-3.
Van der Straten, Astrid. Communication non-verbale et développement du langage: évolution de la demande de la naissance à deux ans. In: Pierault-Le Bonniec (Ed.). *Connaître et le dire*. Bruxelles: Mardaga, 1987.
Van der Straten, Astrid. Heurs et malheurs de la communication précoce. In: François, Frédéric (Ed.). *La communication idéale*. Neuchâtel: Delachaux et Niestlé, 1990, pp. 13-31.
Van der Straten, Astrid. Parents-bébés. In: *Cahiers d'acquistion et de pathologie du langage*, 1990, n° 6, pp. 7-24.
Van der Straten, Astrid. *Premiers gestes, premiers mots. Les formes précoces de la communication*. Paris: Le Centurion, 1991, 315p.

12836 Education for international understanding through foreign language teaching: a German - British collaborative project.
GBR 1993
Research Date(s): 1990-1993
Byram, M.
Inst: Durham University, School of Education, Leazes Road, Durham DH1 1TA, United Kingdom.
Fin: Durham University; British Council.
language teaching; culture; German language; English language; international understanding; cross-national research; foreign languages
enseignement des langues; culture; langue allemande; langue anglaise; compréhension internationale; recherche transnationale; langues étrangères
PROJECT DESCRIPTION
   The purpose of the project is to investigate the contribution of foreign language teaching to international understanding through the images of a country purveyed in language teaching. The focus is on the images purveyed by textbooks for teaching English in Germany and German in England.
   The design involves a team of teachers and researchers at the Universities of Durham and Braunschweig (Germany). Working in German-English pairs, the teams analyse the images of German-English life portrayed in textbooks for secondary schools according to criteria including representativity, accuracy, realism and appropriateness to learners. Each textbook analysis includes a detailed account of the content of the book as well as an evaluation. The project also involves theoretical development of criteria for evaluation and discussion of the relationship between language teaching and teaching for international understanding or 'politische Erziehung'.

Publ: Doye, P. (ed.). *Grossbritannien: seine Darstellung in duetschen Schulbuchern fur den Englischunterricht*. Frankfurt: Deisterweg, 1990.

12837 Eesti ôpilaste emakeeletaseme diagnoosimisest. (Diagnosing the level of native language ability in Estonian pupils.)
EST 1994
Research Date(s): 1993-1995
Maanso, V.
Inst: Tallinna Pedagoogikaülikool (Tallinn Pedagogical University), Tallinn, Narva mnt.29, Estonia.
mother tongue; Baltic languages; language skill; measurement technique; test construction
langue maternelle; langues baltes; aptitude linguistique; technique de mesure; construction de tests
PROJECT DESCRIPTION
Aims: (1) To carry out a survey of the methods and means of assessing levels of native language ability in Estonian pupils; (2) to identify relevant subskills in the light of modern educational objectives; (3) to devise methods and tests to be used in the final year of different types of school for assessing pupils' levels of native language ability.

12838 Eesti pedagoogika ja psühholoogia terminoloogia koostamine ning terminite vôrdlev analüüs inglise-, saksa-, vene-, ja soomekeelsete vastetega. (Composition of Estonian educational and psychological terminology and a comparative analysis with English, German, Russian and Finnish terminology.)
EST 1994
Research Date(s): 1990-1994
Unt, I.; Maanso, V.; Erelt, T.; Rikberg, H.; Söerd, J.; Nilson, O.; Ollisaar, M.
Inst: Tallinna Pedagoogikaülikool (Tallinn Pedagogical University), 0102 Tallinn, Narva mnt. 25, Estonia.
Fin: EV Haridusministeerium.
terminology; lexicology; sciences of education; dictionary; English language; German language; Baltic languages; Finnish language
terminologie; lexicologie; sciences de l'éducation; dictionnaire; langue anglaise; langue allemande; langues baltes; langue finnoise
PROJECT DESCRIPTION
The aims of the project are: to collect existing Estonian educational and psychological terms; to form a system of educational and psychological terms; to conduct comparative analyses of Estonian, English, German, Russian and Finnish terminology; to create new terms in Estonian and to organize existing ones. The project is to result in a dictionary in five languages.

12839 Effective teaching in English as Foreign Language (EFL): a Greek case study.
GBR 1993
Research Date(s): 1988-1991
Zotou, V,.
Sup: Mitchell, R.
Inst: Southampton University, Faculty of Educational Studies, Centre for Language in Education, Highfield, Southampton SO9 5NH, United Kingdom.
Fin: Greek Ministry of Education.
language teaching; English language; foreign languages; Greece; teaching method
enseignement des langues; langue anglaise; langues étrangères; Grèce; méthode pédagogique
PROJECT DESCRIPTION
Given the dearth of descriptive studies of English as a Foreign Language (EFL) teaching in Greece, the aim of the researcher is to discover the extent to which classroom practice of teachers, judged 'effective' by their fellow professionals and superiors, conforms to a 'normative' model of effective teaching (conceptualised as 'communicative' language teaching), and what are the factors which have shaped their classroom behaviour.

Eight main case studies will be conducted in different parts of Greece. Classroom observation will be the main element of each case study. A systematic observation instrument, developed for the study of communicative language teaching, will be employed as the main classroom data gathering procedure.

The observations will be supplemented with teacher interviews seeking: (a) their views on the nature of effective teaching and the contextual factors promoting/inhibiting it; (b) accounts of practice; and (c) accounts of major influences on their own professional development. In addition, contextual data will be collected from pupils and institutions (including student achievement data).

It can be expected that a group of teachers selected in this way will vary considerably in degree of conformity to a normative model of communicative EFL teaching. If so, within-group comparisons will be necessary to establish: (a) what are the typical classroom practices of the most 'effective' sub-group; and (b) what professional influences and contextual factors have contributed substantially to greater and lesser degrees of 'effectiveness'. Finally, it is hoped to draw conclusions relevant to teacher training and the upgrading of more teachers to 'effective' levels of practice.

12840 Effizienz des Unterrichts in 'Lebende Fremdsprache' in der Grundschule. (Effectiveness of foreign language teaching in primary school.)
AUT 1993
Research Date(s): 1992-1994
Rohrauer, Christine; Rohrauer, Josef; Puehrer, Gerda Hermine.
Inst: Paedagogische Akademie des Bundes in Oberoesterreich, Kaplanhofstrasse 40, A-4020 Linz; Landesschulrat fuer Oberoesterreich, Steingasse 14, A-4020 Linz.
Fin: Bundesministerium fuer Unterricht und Kunst.
foreign languages; primary education; language teaching
langues étrangères; enseignement primaire; enseignement des langues
PROJECT DESCRIPTION
1. Inwieweit ist der Unterricht in 'Lebende Fremdsprache in der Grundschule' effizient? Werden die vom Lehrplan gesteckten Ziele mit den vom Lehrplan vorgegebenen Methoden auch tatsaechlich erreicht? 2. Welche Auswirkungen ergeben sich aus einem Unterricht mit verstaerktem Schriftbildeinsatz? Wird dadurch die kommunikative Kompetenz der Kinder im muendlichen Bereich wirkungsvoll gefoerdert, ohne dass eine Beeintraechtigung auf dem Gebiet der Aussprache gegeben ist? 3. Kann ein vermehrter Einsatz des Schriftbildes den Erwerb der graphischen Fertigkeiten (Leseverstaendnis, Schreiben) auf der Sekundarstufe wirkungsvoll vorbereiten?

Der Fremdsprachenunterricht an der Grundschule vollzieht sich hauptsaechlich in spielerischer Form; dabei werden aber vielfach die kognitiven Faehigkeiten des Kindes dieser Altersstufe vernachlaessigt. Aufgrund der Ueberbetonung des spielerischen, imitativ-reaktiven Sprachenlernens werden die vom Lehrplan sehr konkret formulierten Ziele zuwenig realisiert. Es wird davon ausgegangen, dass eine Einbindung des Schriftbildes das Behalten von Wortschatz und Redemitteln foerdert, wobei die Einfuehrung des Schriftbildes keinen negativen Einfluss auf das Einpraegen bzw. Behalten des Klangbildes hat.

Das Projekt zielt darauf ab, zu beweisen, dass zwar der spielerische Ansatz beim Fremdsprachenlernen in der Grundschule der Altersstufe der Kinder entgegenkommt, dass aber andererseits mehr als bisher kognitive Elemente in den Unterricht Eingang finden muessen.

Zweihundert VolksschuelerInnen werden Tests unterzogen.

12841 Emakeelse ôppekirjanduse jôukohasuse automaatanalüüs. (Assessing the appropriateness of textbooks with the help of the computer.)
EST 1994
Research Date(s): 1990-1992
Mikk, J.; Elts, J.; Orav, H.
Inst: Tartu Ülikool (Tartu University), 2400 Tartu, Ülikooli 18, Estonia.
Fin: EV Haridusministeerium.
mother tongue; readability; textbook; assessment; morphology; Baltic languages; software
langue maternelle; lisibilité; manuel d'enseignement; appréciation; morphologie; langues baltes; logiciel
PROJECT DESCRIPTION
The aim of the investigation is to develop computer programs for the assessment of text readability. An experiment is being carried out to elaborate readability formulae. Computer programs for morphological analyses of Estonian-language texts are being created.
Publ: Mikk, J. Tekstiredaktorid arvutis. In: *Keel ja Kirjandus,* 12/1991, pp. 727-731.
Elts, J. Bioloogiatekstide loetavusvalem. In: *Haridus,* 12/1992, pp. 23-26.

12842 Englisch als Arbeitssprache. (English as a working language.)
AUT 1993
Research Date(s): 1991-1995
Heindler, Dagmar; Abuja, Gunther; Kuchl, Irmtraud; Moran, Wolfgang; Pojer, Wolfgang; Weinhofer, Brigitte; Weiss, Martin.
Inst: Zentrum fuer Schulversuche und Schulentwicklung, Abt. I, Universitaetsstrasse 70, A-9020 Klagenfurt; Zentrum fuer Schulversuche und Schulentwicklung, Abt. III, Hans-Sachs-Gasse 14, A-8010 Graz.
Fin: Bundesministerium fuer Unterricht und Kunst.
English language; bilingual education; language skill; language teaching; teaching language
langue anglaise; enseignement bilingue; aptitude linguistique; enseignement des langues; langue d'enseignement
PROJECT DESCRIPTION
"Englisch als Arbeitssprache" soll grundsaetzlich der Intensivierung des Fremdsprachenunterrichts im Rahmen des oesterreichischen Schulwesens (mit Schwerpunkt auf der Sekundarstufe I, 10-14jaehrige) dienen. "Arbeitssprache" bedeutet, dass die Fremdsprache als ein "Werkzeug" zur Bewaeltigung vielfaeltiger sprachlicher und aussersprachlicher Lebenssituationen angesehen wird. Im Rahmen dieses Projektes werden unterschiedliche Formen des Einsatzes einer Fremdsprache (Englisch) im Fachunterricht theoretisch untersucht, methodisch-didaktisch entwickelt und in mehreren Phasen erprobt. In einem weitgespannten Bogen von Vorhaben sollen geeignete (Unterrichts-)Materialien erfasst werden, Lehrplaene analysiert

und die schulischen Anwendungsbedingungen entwickelt werden. Als Produkt dieser Bemuehungen sollen anwendungsfreundliche Arbeitsmaterialien mit modulaerem Charakter sowie Hilfen und Anleitungen fuer interessierte Lehrkraefte entstehen.

Es werden im Verlauf des Projekts schriftliche Befragungen, Unterrichtsbeobachtungen und Tests verwendet werden.

12843   English in the State of Qatar: an analysis of perceptions and attitudes.
GBR   1993
Research Date(s): 1987-1992
Galalah, A.
Sup: Byram, M.
Inst: Durham University, School of Education, Leazes Road, Durham DH1 1TA, United Kingdom; Ministry of Education, PO Box 80, Doha, Qatar, Arabian Gulf.
Fin: British Council.
English language; language teaching; Qatar; foreign languages; attitude; school age population; adult
langue anglaise; enseignement des langues; Qatar; langues étrangères; attitude; population d'âge scolaire; adulte
PROJECT DESCRIPTION

The research was conducted to verify the actual position of English in the Qatari society, among the student population in the Qatari school system, and among the adults who represent the Qatari workforce. The research addressed the fact-finding stage of syllabus design, which was considered the base for the other stages of specifying the objectives, tailoring the materials and then the evaluation of the final course material.

The study aimed at assessing the facts regarding the perception of the target language status in the society through the study of the attitudes of the respondents. The study sample consisted of three cross-sections, namely: 659 students from both the preparatory and secondary levels, 460 adults representing most professions and nationalities in the country. In addition, 10 interviews with prominent decision makers were undertaken. Two main areas were subject to assessment; facts and perceptions of respondents regarding the status of English and the attitudes regarding the target language and the peoples who speak it as a mother language.

Findings revealed that English is the language of wider communication in Qatar in addition to extremely positive attitudes. Non-parametric statistics were employed in data analysis. Nationality among other variables showed significant differences.

12844   English language curriculum development in Niger: Niger educational development 1960-1992 with particular reference to English language teaching.
GBR   1993
Research Date(s): 1990-1992
Goumandakoye, A.
Sup: Byram, M.; McPartland, M.
Inst: Durham University, School of Education, Leazes Road, Durham DH1 1TA, United Kingdom.
Fin: British Council.
language teaching; English language; curriculum development; French language; mathematics; comparative analysis; Niger
enseignement des langues; langue anglaise; élaboration de programmes d'études; langue française; mathématiques; analyse comparative; Niger
PROJECT DESCRIPTION

The present study concerns itself with a critical analysis of formal education in the Niger Republic from independence to the present, and the extent to which the experience gained in English language teaching could be beneficial for the rest of the curriculum, to the enhancement of the whole system. Hence, this piece of work should not only reveal achievements but also pinpoint the major setbacks of the educational system; more importantly, it should suggest ways and means which could lead to an improvement of the current system through a contrastive analysis of the major components, i.e. French, mathematics, and English, which is felt to be a dynamic and successful subject. The present study offers a comprehensive description of the evolution of Nigerian formal education, thus contributing to the enhancement of education awareness in Niger; it is hoped that the findings will not only give insight and provide skills useful to the Ministry, but also bring about positive change in one of the main components of any educational system, i.e. the curriculum.

12845   English language monitoring.
GBR   1993
Research Date(s): 1991-1993
Entwistle, N.; Napuk, A.; Dickie, S.; Normand, B.
Inst: Edinburgh University, Department of Education, Centre for Research on Learning and Instruction, 10-12 Buccleuch Place, Edinburgh EH8 9JT, United Kingdom.
Fin: Scottish Education Department.
mother tongue; English language; achievement test; assessment
langue maternelle; langue anglaise; test de rendement; appréciation
PROJECT DESCRIPTION

The main aim is to assess national standards of attainment across the language modes of reading, writing, listening, talking and interaction. A representative national sample will be drawn from P(primary)4, P7 and S(secondary)2 and assessed using appropriate test materials. Some tests used in the 1989 survey will be repeated to provide a basis of comparison.

12846   English language teaching - an evaluation of an industrial training programme.
GBR   1993
Research Date(s): 1988-1993
Qattous, K.
Sup: Byram, M.
Inst: Durham University, School of Education, Leazes Road, Durham DH1 1TA, United Kingdom.
language teaching; foreign languages; English language; language for special purposes; in-service training; industry; Saudi Arabia
enseignement des langues; langues étrangères; langue anglaise; langage de spécialité; formation en cours d'emploi; industrie; Arabie Saoudite
PROJECT DESCRIPTION

The English for Specific Purposes (ESP) course for workers in the Aramco petroleum company will be analysed and evaluated as an example of programme development and ESP in industrial settings.

12847   English language teaching in higher education in Jordan: syllabus design for English for Specific Purposes (ESP) courses.
GBR   1993
Research Date(s): 1990-1992
Khuwaileh, A.
Sup: Byram, M.
Inst: Durham University, School of Education, Leazes Road, Durham DH1 1TA, United Kingdom.
Fin: Jordanian Government.
language teaching; curriculum development; English language; language for special purposes; science education; technology; higher education; Jordan
enseignement des langues; élaboration de programmes d'études; langue anglaise; langage de spécialité; éducation scientifique; technologie; enseignement supérieur; Jordanie
PROJECT DESCRIPTION

A needs analysis in the use of English for learning science and technology in higher education in Jordan will be carried out, using questionnaires and interviews. This will lead to development of a syllabus and recommendations for curriculum change.

12848   Eskişehir Sağırlar Okulu ve Anadolu Üniversitesi IÇEM'de ortaokul sınıflarına devam eden 13-14 yaş işitme engelli öğrencilerin yazılı anlatım becerilerinin betimlenmesi. (A descriptive study of the writing skills of hearing-impaired children in two schools in Eskişehir.)
TUR   1994
Research Date(s): 1987-1989
Erdiken, Behram.
Sup: Konrot, Ahmet.
Inst: Anadolu Üniversitesi, IÇEM (University of Anatolia, Centre for Hearing-Impaired Children), Yunusemre Kampusu, Eskişehir, Turkey.
written expression; language skill; aurally handicapped; special school
expression écrite; aptitude linguistique; handicapé auditif; centre d'éducation spéciale
PROJECT DESCRIPTION

Hearing-impaired individuals are expected to make use of written forms of communication if they want to gain access to written media in order to improve their kowledge and to participate in the culture of the society of which they are a member.

The aim of the study was to describe the writing skills of hearing-impaired pupils aged 13-14 years, attending the Eskişehir School for the Deaf and the Centre for Hearing-Impaired Children (IÇEM) at Anadolu University. Considering the differences in approach to language and communication between these two educational environments, the study addressed the following question: What differences exist in pupils' writing skills (a) following an oral discussion with the teacher on a given topic for written work and (b) without an oral discussion preceding the written task?

Subjects in the study were eight pupils from the IÇEM and ten pupils from the Eskişehir School for the Deaf. The English as a Second Language (ESL) Composition Profile was used to analyse the written work produced by the pupils on a topic suggested by the teacher.

Results: Significant differences were found between the writing skills of the pupils who had been instructed through conventional oral communication and the skills of the pupils who had been instructed by a structured approach with an emphasis on written language in combination with spoken language. Another interesting finding was that the conversation with the teacher preceding the written work had a positive effect on the work produced by the pupils from the IÇEM, but not on that of the pupils from the Eskişehir School for the Deaf. The reason for this may be that the poor level of spoken language ability of these pupils limits the potential benefit they may derive from such oral instruction.

12849   Etude différentielle des performances communicatives et de leur stabilité chez le jeune enfant.
FRA   1993
Research Date(s): 1987-1989
Florin, Agnès; Testu, François.
Inst: Université de Poitiers, UER Sciences humaines, CNRS URA/666, Laboratoire de psychologie du langage, 95 av. du Recteur Pineau, 86022 Poitiers Cedex, France.
verbal communication; conversation; pre-school child; performance; verbal interaction
communication verbale; conversation; enfant d'âge préscolaire; performance; interaction verbale
PROJECT DESCRIPTION
   Objectifs: On se propose d'étudier les différences de performances communicatives des jeunes enfants dans leurs composantes "grammaticales" et "sociolinguistiques". A un premier niveau, il s'agit de préciser les liens entre ces deux composantes et les processus d'acquisition correspondants; à un deuxième niveau, la question est de savoir si les différences de participation à la conversation scolaire sont dépendantes des composantes grammaticales, des composantes sociolinguistiques ou de leur interaction; à un troisième niveau on s'intéresse aux variations journalières des performances communicatives et de leurs différentes composantes.
   Méthodologie: Ces problèmes sont étudiés dans des activités de compréhension et de production à partir d'enregistrements de conversations soumis à des enfants d'école maternelle.

Publ: Florin, Agnès. Développement du langage et de la participation à l'école maternelle et à l'école primaire: étude longitudinale. In: *Journal européen de psychologie de l'éducation*, 1988, n° spécial *Le fonctionnement de l'enfant à l'école*, pp. 205-207.
Florin, Agnès. *Pratiques du langage à l'école maternelle: Les conversations maîtresse-élève*. Université de Poitiers, thèse pour le Doctorat d'Etat (sous la direction de Stéphane Ehrlich) février 1989.

12850   Evaluatie project leesbevordering. (Evaluation of the reading promotion project.)
NLD   1994
Research Date(s): 1993-1994
Kok, W.A.M.; Veen, A.M.; Otter, M.E.; Erp, M. van; Poorthuis, G.M.T.
Sup: Glopper, K. de; Meijnen, G.W.
Inst: Interdisciplinair Sociaal-wetenschappelijk Onderzoeksinstituut, Afdeling Onderwijs (ISOR) (Interdisciplinary Research Institute for the Social Sciences, Department of Educational Research), P.O. Box 80140, 3508 TC Utrecht, Netherlands; Stichting Centrum voor Onderwijsonderzoek (SCO) (Centre for Educational Research), Grote Bickersstraat 72, 1013 KS Amsterdam, Netherlands.
Rijksuniversiteit Utrecht (State University of Utrecht), P.O. Box 80125, 3508 TC Utrecht, Netherlands; Universiteit van Amsterdam (University of Amsterdam), P.O. Box 19268, 1000 GG Amsterdam, Netherlands
Fin: SVO het Instituut voor Onderzoek van het Onderwijs.
reading; reading taste; reading aloud; parent role; pre-school child
lecture; intérêt de lecture; lecture à haute voix; rôle des parents; enfant d'âge préscolaire
PROJECT DESCRIPTION
   Background: In 1991, at the request of the Ministry of Welfare, Health and Cultural Affairs, a framework plan was established for the promotion of reading among children up to 6 years of age. The plan was accompanied by an evaluation plan for the evaluation of materials and instructional methods, the overall process and the outcomes of the project. In 1992 a start was made with the execution of a reading promotion project based on the framework plan. The present project is concerned with the evaluation of the implementation and the outcomes of the reading promotion project in the cities of Amsterdam, Tilburg and Emmen.
   Aims: (1) To examine the functioning of the project organization team, the project centres and the neighbourhood assistants; (2) to ascertain how far parents take heed of the suggestions of the project teams regarding their children's reading; (3) to establish how much time is devoted to silent reading or reading to children; (4) to determine the quality of parent-child interactions when parents read to their children.
   Design: The project plans will be analysed. On the basis of the analysis, every six months interviews will be conducted with the project coordinators. From the second interview onwards, the interviews will focus on the activities that are undertaken, the forms of cooperation that emerge and the problems that are encountered. Every six months, the institutions involved will be given a questionnaire asking for information about factors that promote or hinder the realization of the objectives of the project. Parental participation in activities will be registered and parents will be given questionnaires. Records will be kept of parents', project assistants' and professionals' involvement in reading aloud to children. Parents and teachers who do not participate in the project will be asked to form a control group.

12851   Evaluatie "Zorgverbreding/begrijpend lezen". (Evaluation of remedial reading programmes in the city of Utrecht.)
NLD   1994
Research Date(s): 1992-1995
Jacobs, E.
Inst: Interdisciplinair Sociaal-wetenschappelijk Onderzoeksinstituut, Afdeling Onderwijs (ISOR) (Interdisciplinary Research Institute for the Social Sciences, Department of Educational Research), P.O. Box 80140, 3508 TC Utrecht, Netherlands.
Rijksuniversiteit Utrecht (State University of Utrecht), P.O. Box 80125, 3508 TC Utrecht, Netherlands
Fin: SVO het Instituut voor Onderzoek van het Onderwijs.
reading; educational policy; primary education; remedial teaching; educational need
lecture; politique de l'éducation; enseignement primaire; soutien pédagogique; besoin d'éducation
PROJECT DESCRIPTION
   Background: The School Advisory Centre (SAC) in Utrecht has established close links between the Educational Priority Policy (OVB) and policies regarding special needs provision in ordinary schools: it has implemented innovatory special needs measures in the first instance in schools participating in the OVB. As a result, pupils in OVB target groups - i.e. pupils from disadvantaged backgrounds - can benefit from these measures to reduce their backwardness in reading. The SAC developed its guidance policies and the content of the innovatory programme "special needs provision in primary schools/reading for comprehension" (ZVB/BL) in the 1990-1991 school year. The programme has a scheduled duration of three years. The present study is concerned with its evaluation.
   Aim: To examine the effect of the ZVB/BL programme on teachers' actions concerning the identification and remediation of reading difficulties in pupils; to examine the effect of the programme on the number of pupils that are referred to special education.
   Design: Two quasi-experiments will be set up. In the first experiment one group will start with the ZVB/BL programme in September 1992 and the second in September 1993. Both groups will consist of six schools, with six teachers per school. The control group will consist of about 100 teachers. The teachers will be asked to complete questionnaires on the activities they have undertaken in the area of special needs provision. Information will be collected on guidance policies aimed at teachers and school heads. For the second experiment, use will be made of the first experimental group and the control group from the first experiment. Teachers will be asked to complete a checklist on the execution of planned remedial reading instruction in class. Pupils' levels of reading performance will be measured.

12852   Evaluating a programme for the teaching and learning of Welsh as a second language in year one and two infants.
GBR   1993
Research Date(s): 1991-1992
Bowen-Surtees, M.; Robertson, C.; Thomas, G.
Inst: North East Wales Institute of Higher Education, Clwyd Centre for Educational Development and Research, Cartrefle, Cefn Road, Wrexham, Clwyd LL13 9NE, United Kingdom.
Welsh language; language teaching; television programme
langue galloise; enseignement des langues; programme de télévision
PROJECT DESCRIPTION
   As today's children are growing up in a multicultural society and as Britain is increasingly recognising its place within Europe, there is a developing awareness of second language teaching. This research has been carried out in Wales as, for many years, learning a second language has been a feature of Welsh education even in the infant sector. As a result, many approaches and materials have been produced. The television programme 'Parablu' is one such approach, developed by Harlech Television and introduced into the primary schools of Clwyd with local education authority support in 1990. This project has been undertaken to evaluate the effectiveness of this programme and to extract from observations and research findings, principles of good practice in second language learning.

Publ: A detailed report is available from Clwyd Centre for Educational Development and Research.

12853   Evaluation of foreign language teaching objectives (with particular reference to the teaching of French).
GBR   1993
Research Date(s): 1986-1993
Tolley, J.
Sup: Wringe, C.
Inst: Keele University, Department of Education, Keele, Staffordshire ST5 5BG, United Kingdom.
foreign languages; French language; language teaching; teaching objective
langues étrangères; langue française; enseignement des langues; objectif pédagogique
PROJECT DESCRIPTION
   An empirical investigation of factors determining the choice of objectives for the teaching of French at school level. These include pupil motivation

and communication needs for the individual and for industry and commerce.

12854 Evaluation of national pilot projects: foreign languages in primary schools (Scotland).
GBR 1993
Research Date(s): 1991-1994
Low, L.; Duffield, J.; Bankowska, A.
Sup: Brown, S.; Johnstone, R.
Inst: Stirling University, Department of Education, Stirling FK9 4LA, United Kingdom.
Fin: Scottish Office Education Department.
modern languages; foreign languages; language teaching; primary education; pilot project; achievement
langues vivantes; langues étrangères; enseignement des langues; enseignement primaire; projet-pilote; rendement
PROJECT DESCRIPTION

As part of a major government initiative, pilot projects have been set up to test the feasibility of introducing foreign language teaching into the primary schools associated with twelve secondary schools. The commonest model involves collaboration between class teachers from P4 to P7 and visiting language teachers from the secondary school. The main aims of the evaluation are: (1) assessment of the linguistic attainments of children involved in the pilot projects, including comparisons with those children not involved; (2) evaluation of the project courses, including commentary on factors such as the nature of the course and pedagogical methods which influence the linguistic performance of the children involved.

The first aim has involved speaking and listening assessments carried out with pairs of pupils in the foreign language. In 1991 these compared 'project' and 'non-project' pupils in S1 and S2. In 1992 attention was on progression from Primary 7 onwards with 'project' pupils only. Within-class assessments carried out by teachers have also been analysed. The second aim has been addressed through an interview study with class teachers and others involved at every level in the management of the projects, and a lesson observation study of primary and secondary classes.

An extension of the evaluation will investigate the gains in linguistic attainments of pupils commencing their foreign language at different stages in the primary school, effective teaching approaches and various wider implications for the organisation of primary and secondary schools.

Publ: Interim report to Scottish Office Education Department, December 1991.

12855 Evaluation of the Basingstoke Language Awareness Project.
GBR 1993
Research Date(s): 1990-1991
Mitchell, R.; Grenfell, M.
Inst: Southampton University, Faculty of Educational Studies, Centre for Language in Education, Highfield, Southampton SO9 5NH, United Kingdom.
Fin: KPMG-Peat Marwick McLintock.
language teaching; foreign languages; foreign language assistant
enseignement des langues; langues étrangères; assistant en langues étrangères
PROJECT DESCRIPTION

The Basingstoke Language Awareness Project is a three-year project running from 1989 to 1992, which is providing 'taster' experience of modern language learning for primary school pupils in the six main feeder schools of a Basingstoke secondary school. The project is staffed with four foreign language assistants (FLAs), native speakers of French, German and Spanish. It is funded by local business sponsorship, from accountants KPMG-Peat Marwick McLintock.

In 1990-1991 KPMG also sponsored a small-scale interim evaluation of the project, by the University of Southampton. The evaluation assessed the aims, structure and methods of the project, and gathered qualitative data on attitudinal outcomes. The evaluation methodology mainly involved interviews with teachers, FLAs and pupils, plus observation of the FLAs at work in the classroom.

The evaluation concluded the project was operating successfully overall, thanks to good cross-pyramid cooperation, and documented favourable initial pupil reactions. The final report highlights the special needs of FLAs for systems of support and liaison, especially with class teachers; it also highlights needs for continuity and progression in the transition to secondary school.

Publ: Mitchell, R.; Martin, C. & Grenfell, M. *University of Southampton Evaluation of the Basingstoke Language Awareness Project: Final Report.* Centre for Language in Education Working Paper, University of Southampton, 1992.

12856 The evaluation of the management of English Language Teaching (ELT) overseas aid projects.
GBR 1993
Research Date(s): 1989-1992
Chambers, F.
Sup: Lewis, P.

Inst: West Sussex Institute of Higher Education, The Dome, Upper Bognor Road, Bognor Regis PO21 1HR, United Kingdom; Lancaster University, Department of Systems and Information Management, Cartmel College, Bailrigg, Lancaster LA1 4YW, United Kingdom.
language teaching; English language; foreign languages; development aid
enseignement des langues; langue anglaise; langues étrangères; aide au développement
PROJECT DESCRIPTION

Using Soft Systems methodology, the investigation develops a consensus model of the purpose of English Language Teaching (ELT) overseas aid which is then used to provide a source for a bank of evaluation questions.

12857 Evaluation of the National Curriculum assessment of Welsh (GWASG).
GBR 1993
Research Date(s): 1992-1994
Williams, I.; Baker, C.
Inst: University College of North Wales, School of Education, Deiniol Road, Bangor, Gwynedd LL57 2UW, United Kingdom.
Fin: The Welsh Office.
Welsh language; language teaching; assessment; achievement test
langue galloise; enseignement des langues; appréciation; test de rendement
PROJECT DESCRIPTION

The aim of this research is to carry out a comprehensive and detailed evaluation of National Curriculum assessment in first language (L1) and second language (L2) Welsh. The research issues can be summarised as: (1) The validity and reliability of teacher assessments (TAs). (2) Comparability, determining influences and patterning in TAs. (3) Variability in teacher interpretations of TAs. (4) Effects of aggregation on standard assessment task scores (SAs). (5) The validity of SAs. (6) Effects of sampling of SAs on assessment outcomes. (7) Comparability, determining influences and patterning in SAs across time. (8) Relationships between assessments and special educational needs pupils. (9) Relationships of assessments across key stages. (10) Quality of formative and summative information provided by the assessments. The process and effectiveness of teachers recording assessments and reporting to parents. (11) Effects of assessments on teaching and assessing L1 and L2 Welsh. (12) Comparability of TAs and SAs. Stability in patterns of difference. Commonality bases. (13) Comparability of assessments from two programmes at National Curriculum Key Stage 3. (14) The manageability of assessments for teachers. (15) Patterns in the take-up of non-statutory National Curriculum Key Stage 1 L2 Welsh materials. (16) Relationship between standardisation of assessment and School Examinations and Assessment Council (SEAC) (and preferably local education authority) training and guidance.

Three approaches are being employed. These approaches may be termed the statistical, the representative survey and the expert. First, the assessment data require considerable statistical analysis to investigate issues of validity, reliability, comparability across context and time, patterns and relationships in the data. Second, there are issues requiring a wide-scale survey of teacher, classroom and school practices. By stratified random sampling across Wales, a thoroughly representative elicitation of local procedures and individual viewpoints is necessary. This is achieved by interviewing and questionnaires. Third, the special insights of expert educationists provides a deep and perceptive sensitivity to complement wide consensus viewpoints. A careful and judicious 'purposeful sample' of experts will provide detailed qualitative information to complement the quantitative statistical analysis and the part-qualitative/part-quantitative approach of representative surveys. GWASG reports are available from SEAC.

Publ: *KS3 Welsh First Language Assessment (Cy): Analysis of Assessment Record Booklet Data.* Report for School Examinations and Assessment Council/Welsh Office. GWASG report, October 1992.
KS3 Welsh Second Language Assessment (Ca): Analysis of Assessment Record Booklet Data. Report for School Examinations and Assessment Council/Welsh Office. GWASG report, October 1992.
Evaluation of the Bridges Assessment Pack for KS1 Second Language Welsh. Report for School Examinations and Assessment Council/Welsh Office. GWASG report, October 1992.
KS1: An Analysis of Data from Assessment Record Booklets. Report for School Examinations and Assessment Council/Welsh Office. GWASG report, October 1992.
National Curriculum Assessment and Welsh Medium Education: Trends in Recent Results. Report for School Examinations and Assessment Council/Welsh Office. GWASG report October 1992.

12858 Evaluation of the National Curriculum core subjects (English) at key stages 1, 2 and 3.
GBR 1993
Research Date(s): 1991-1993
Raban, B.
Inst: Warwick University, Faculty of Educational Studies, Coventry CV4 7AL, United Kingdom.

Fin: National Curriculum Council.
English language; common core curriculum; evaluation; main subject
langue anglaise; tronc commun; évaluation; matière principale
PROJECT DESCRIPTION
The aim of this National Curriculum Council (NCC) monitoring programme is to ensure that problems which teachers are facing in implementing National Curriculum English are fully understood to discover: whether the difficulty lies in the Order; whether it is a question of teacher knowledge and understanding; or whether statement(s) of attainment are pitched inappropriately for pupils within a particular key stage.

An analysis of the English Orders will provide a conceptual and practical framework for fieldwork in schools. Between 70 and 80 schools will be visited in 10 local education authorities (LEAs) throughout England. Teachers, parents and governors will be interviewed. Classrooms will be observed and school documents inspected. Access to key stage 1 standard assessment task data, examples of pupils' work and interviews with LEA personnel will form the body of evidence required to address the issues specified by the NCC.

12859   Extent and correlates of variability among different groups of readers.
GBR   1993
Research Date(s): 1990-1993
McDougall, S.
Sup: Ellis, A.; Hulme, C.
Inst: York University, Department of Psychology, Heslington, York YO1 5DD, United Kingdom.
Fin: Economic and Social Research Council.
reading; reading difficulty; cognitive ability; performance
lecture; difficulté de lecture; aptitude cognitive; performance
PROJECT DESCRIPTION
The study has two principal aims. The first aim is to investigate whether different groups of readers matched on reading age show the same or different patterns of reading performance when latency as well as accuracy, and variability, as well as central tendency are taken into consideration. This should resolve current controversy over the extent to which dyslexic reading performance follows simply from reading age or includes a differential deficit in, for example, phonological processing. The groups concerned will be: (1) dyslexic children (high IQ) with specific and unexpected reading retardation; (2) poor readers (low IQ) with nonspecific learning difficulties; (3) precocious readers (high IQ) whose reading age is ahead of their chronological age; and (4) normal readers. If reading age is the sole determinant of group reading patterns, then these four groups should not differ from one another.

The second aim is to discover whether different reading patterns related to different patterns of strength and weakness in performance on tasks which do not involve reading per se, but tap aspects of cognition which may be relevant to the acquisition of reading. Different patterns of strength and weakness in reading skill will be related to different patterns of strength and weakness in basic visual and phonological processes. A broader subsidiary aim of this project is to evaluate the extent to which information-processing accounts of a skill such as reading can also provide the dimensions for characterising individual differences in cognitive ability.

12860   La faute de langue.
FRA   1993
Research Date(s): 1988-
Prieur, Jean-Marie.
Inst: Université de Strasbourg I, UFR des Sciences du comportement, CNRS URA/668, Laboratoire de recherche Production et effets de la parole et du langage, Laboratoire de psycholinguistique, 12 rue Goethe, 67000 Strasbourg, France.
language teaching; learning difficulty; learning
enseignement des langues; difficulté de l'apprentissage; acquisition de connaissances
PROJECT DESCRIPTION
Objectifs: La "faute de langue" est définie comme l'indice d'une précarité linguistique, d'une langue incertaine, provisoire toujours en constitution, dans des situations d'apprentissage ou de contact de langues.

Méthodologie: Une enquête auprès d'étudiants étrangers, français et d'enseignants de langue permet: (1) une description structurale des productions fautives, conçues comme moments intermédiaires dans l'apprentissage du français; (2) l'élucidation des fondements du sentiment de la faute en langue en tant qu'il est souvent indissociable d'un discours scolaire sur la faute; (3) une approche historique des figures de la faute (faute comme trouble du langage, invention poétique, péché de langue, interdit linguistique, bavure d'apprentissage et indice d'acquisition).

12861   Le fonctionnement des sujets comme récepteurs actifs de messages médiatisés: approche cognitive et psycho-sociale.
FRA   1993
Research Date(s): 1987-
Kouloumdjian, Marie-France; Belisle, Claire; Balacheff, Nicolas; Butheau, Robert; Jourdan, Robert; Rosado, Eliana; Chartier, Michèle.
Sup: Tiberghien, Andrée.

Inst: Ministère de la recherche, CNRS UPR/5411 et GDR/28, Institut de recherche en pédagogie de l'économie et en audio-visuel pour la communication dans les sciences sociales, 93 Chemin des Mouilles, BP 167, 69130 Ecully Cedex, France.
message reception; learning; televised teaching; technological change; vocational training; new technologies; cognitive psychology; didactic use of computer
réception de message; acquisition de connaissances; enseignement télévisé; changement technologique; formation professionnelle; nouvelles technologies; psychologie cognitive; usage didactique de l'ordinateur
PROJECT DESCRIPTION
Objectifs: Il s'agit d'étudier le fonctionnement des sujets comme récepteurs actifs de messages médiatisés en liaison avec les contextes de réception, les caractéristiques de la construction des messages et les conditions de leur production. Ces messages sont médiatisés en particulier par les nouvelles technologies. Le fonctionnement des sujets est abordé selon ses dimensions affective, sociale et cognitive.

Méthodologie: (1) Afin d'étudier les transferts de connaissances et de procédures en provenance de systèmes experts vers leurs utilisateurs respectifs, on observe professionnels et étudiants dans le secteur du bâtiment, dans leur traitement des connaissances à l'occasion de la résolution de problèmes professionnels puis en interaction avec lui. (2) Pour dégager les spécificités de la modélisation des connaissances de l'apprenant on explore les outils ou modèles disponibles en informatique et un projet est lancé pour réaliser un "environnement d'apprentissage" informatique pour la formation des techniciens de physique nucléaire au traitement du signal. (3) Pour l'étude de la pratique télévisuelle domestique on a créé un outil d'investigation: grille-liste de thèmes pertinents et discriminants pour un questionnement sur les activités des téléspectateurs, puis dans un deuxième temps conversion de cette grille en un questionnaire à réponses fermées en vue d'une enquête en vraie grandeur sur un échantillon représentatif. (4) Une étude d'impact des formations bureautiques met en évidence l'articulation de plusieurs champs représentationnels associés au départ à des contextes différents: les champs représentationnels du savoir, du travail et milieu professionnel et des nouvelles technologies plus particulièrement de la bureautique.
Publ: Belisle, Claire; Butheau, Robert; Jourdan, Robert & Rosado, Eliana. *Communication médiatisée: Etude de la pratique télévisuelle.* Rapport de recherche. IRPEACS-CNRS, 1988, 167p.
Belisle, Claire & Jourdan, Robert. L'expérience télévisuelle. In: *Hermès*, 1991.
Belisle, Claire & Rosado, Eliana. Bureautique et formation. In: *Informatique et différences individuelles.* Presses universitaires de Lyon, 1990, pp. 69-90.
Gréa, Jean; Sabatier, P. & Tiberghien, Andrée. Le rôle des utilisateurs dans l'élaboration d'environnements intelligents. Domaine de l'agriculture et de la physique appliquée. Ecully: IRPEACS, Rapport au programme régional *Systèmes experts et intelligence atificielle*, 1990, 48p.

12862   Forebygging av lese- og skrivevansker: pedagogiske utfordringer i arbeidet med 6-åringene.   (Preventing reading and spelling failure: the effects of various metalinguistic training programmes in nursery school on reading and spelling development.)
NOR   1994
Research Date(s): 1992-1994
Lyster, Solveig-Alma Halaas.
Inst: Universitetet i Oslo, Institutt for Spesialpedagogikk (University of Oslo, Institute for Special Education), PB 55, 1347 Hosle, Norway.
Fin: NAVF/RSF.
reading; spelling; linguistics; training programme; pre-school education; language development
lecture; orthographe; linguistique; programme de formation; éducation préscolaire; développement du langage
PROJECT DESCRIPTION
This study aims at exploring the effects of various metalinguistic training programmes in nursery school on reading and spelling development. It also aims at studying the predictive validity of linguistic and metalinguistic training on reading and spelling development.

A total of 273 monolingual Norwegian children were divided into two experimental groups and one control group and followed through their final pre-school year to the end of the first year in primary school. Experimental group 1 received a training programme that focused on the internal sound structure of words. Experimental group 2 received a training programme that focused on morphological parts of words (e.g. prefixes, suffixes). The control group received no training, but was regularly visited by the researcher. The children's abilities in various linguistic and metalinguistic areas were tested before and after the intervention. The children received weekly training periods of 25 minutes for 17 weeks. Mean age at the time of pretesting was 75.6 months. Reading and spelling levels were measured at the time of the pretest, at school entry and at the end of the first primary year.

The results of the intervention will be analysed using covariate designs with the mother's education and group as independent variables and Raven's Progressive Matrices and/or Vocabulary, Similarities and Digit

Span from Wechsler's Intelligence Scale for Children-Revised as covariates. The predictive validity of the training programmes will be analysed through multiple regression analyses.

Publ: Lyster, S.A.H. Forutsetninger for utvikling av gode lese- og skriveferdigheter. In: *Jotidligere, jo bedre. Tidlig forebygging av lese- og skrivevansker i forskole og tidlige skoleår.* Kompendium fra Norsk dysleksiforbunds faglige seminar, Sandvika, 2-3 April 1992.

Lyster, S.A.H. Prevention of reading and spelling failure. Is it possible? In: *Euro News Dyslexia*, the official journal of the European Dyslexia Association. 5th year (annual publication).

A full list of publications can be obtained on request from the research institute.

12863 Foreign language training for initial teacher training (ITT) students.

GBR 1993

Research Date(s): 1992-1993

Neather, E.

Inst: Exeter University, School of Education, St Luke's, Heavitree Road, Exeter EX1 2LU, United Kingdom.

Fin: Department for Education.

language teaching; foreign languages; teacher education; student teacher

enseignement des langues; langues étrangères; formation des enseignants; élève-maître

PROJECT DESCRIPTION

The aim of this project is to: (1) establish a detailed register of current language experience and competence amongst all undergraduate and Post-Graduate Certificate of Education (PGCE) students at the School of Education; (2) enquire into the aspirations and wishes of students in terms of foreign language learning, and their perception of the place of foreign languages in their careers, and in the future lives of the children they teach; (3) relate the pattern of such wishes and aspirations to the pattern of main subject courses followed by students, with a view to establishing what language courses could best be offered to which groups of students; (4) investigate the resources and timetabling of access courses for students wishing to pursue individual programmes of less common languages, such as Greek and Portuguese, for which class tuition might not be available; (5) discuss with course tutors the role and function of foreign languages in the course profile of students, with a view to integrating foreign language modules into the overall course structure on a rational and planned basis; (6) investigate the practice followed by other institutions of teacher training, and to make comparisons with foreign languages in teacher training establishments in other countries of the European Community; and (7) explore the needs and aims of foreign languages teaching in primary and middle schools in Devon.

It is proposed that the project should last three terms from October 1992. This would give time to carry out surveys and put in place a carefully considered pilot scheme at the start of the new academic year in October 1993. Proposals and recommendations would then be made in December 1993 for possible implementation of a full programme in October 1994. The research will involve questionnaire surveys and interviews with students (sample=420 post-graduate students and 917 undergraduate students) and staff colleagues; visits to other institutions and attendance at European conferences.

12864 Formative assessment of reading in the primary classroom: the Leeds Reading Project.

GBR 1993

Research Date(s): 1990-1992

Owen, P.

Sup: Christie, T.

Inst: Manchester University, School of Education, Centre for Formative Assessment Studies, Oxford Road, Manchester M13 9PL, United Kingdom.

Fin: Leeds Local Education Authority.

reading; assessment; achievement

lecture; appréciation; rendement

PROJECT DESCRIPTION

The aim of the Leeds Reading Project is to assist schools to develop procedures for the implementation of formative assessments of reading in the classroom and to design a framework for the development by schools of a guidance manual for monitoring reading standards. The sample comprised 30 schools (infant, junior and middle) with 15 operating as a lead group and 15 as a follow-up group. Experience with the lead group is encapsulated in trial Inservice Education and Training of Teachers (INSET) materials/activities for the follow-up group. The outcome is a long-term rolling programme for local education authority based INSET on the teaching and assessment of reading.

A literacy audit was conducted to: (1) describe the print environment to which children in Years 1-6 are exposed; and (2) establish the degree of teachers' awareness of text types and 'readability' levels. This was followed by a classification of the range and type of reading purposes provided for children and an analysis of reading difficulties to inform current practice in relation to task setting and instructional method.

Case studies tracking the progress of individual children in relation to types of texts, reading purposes and intervention strategies are currently being undertaken.

12865 Functionele geletterdheid van Turkse en Marokkaanse kinderen in Nederland en in de landen van herkomst. (Levels of functional literacy among Turkish and Moroccan children in the Netherlands and in the country of origin.)

NLD 1994

Research Date(s): 1992

Aarts, R.; Ruiter, J.J. de.

Sup: Extra, G.; Verhoeven, L.

Inst: Katholieke Universiteit Brabant, Faculteit der Letteren (Catholic University of Brabant, Arts Faculty), P.O. Box 90153, 5000 LE Tilburg, Netherlands.

Fin: SVO het Instituut voor Onderzoek van het Onderwijs.

bilingualism; functional literacy; immigrant; pupil; Turkish language; Arabic; Dutch language; mother tongue; first foreign language

bilinguisme; alphabétisation fonctionnelle; immigrant; élève; langue turque; langue arabe; langue néerlandaise; langue maternelle; première langue étrangère

PROJECT DESCRIPTION

Background: Research evidence shows that immigrant pupils are at risk of failing to reach the level of functional literacy in Dutch. Little is known about their levels of functional literacy in their own language. The present study is intended as a further elaboration of an earlier project entitled "Turkish and Arabic language tests at the end of primary school". That study was concerned with the development of test instruments for measuring Turkish and Moroccan pupils' mastery of their native language at the end of primary school. These children grow up in a bilingual environment. The two languages can each fulfill a specific communicative function. The present study examines the ability of Turkish and Moroccan pupils at the end of primary school to perform the reading and writing tasks they meet in everyday life in both languages.

Aim: To examine levels of functional literacy among Turkish and Moroccan pupils in their first and second language; to identify the relationships, if any, between literacy levels in the first and the second language; to investigate the connection between functional literacy and school literacy; to determine what factors have an influence on Turkish and Moroccan pupils' levels of literacy in both languages.

Design: The study uses a sample of 264 Turkish and 226 Moroccan children. The children are followed through secondary school. Levels of school literacy in Dutch will be measured with the help of relevant parts of the primary school-leaving test. Levels of school literacy in the mother tongue will be measured with the help of test instruments constructed in the earlier study. The functional literacy test will be administered in written form in Turkey (276 children), Morocco (242 children) and the Netherlands. For the operationalization of background characteristics use will be made of existing instruments. Questionnaires will be presented to pupils and teachers.

12866 The Gaelic Language Development Project.

GBR 1993

Research Date(s): 1992

Macneil, M.

Sup: Stoney, S.

Inst: National Foundation for Educational Research, The Mere, Upton Park, Slough SL1 2DQ, United Kingdom.

Fin: Gaelic Medium College of Further Education; Scottish Inter-Authority Standing Group for Gaelic.

Celtic languages; Scots Gaelic language; language teaching; mother tongue; bilingualism

langues celtiques; langue écossaise; enseignement des langues; langue maternelle; bilinguisme

PROJECT DESCRIPTION

As part of an expanding research programme, the Gaelic College (SMO) commissioned an investigation into the methods and effectiveness of school-based Gaelic language development, with the aims of identifying good practice and strategies for enhancing the current level of effectiveness. The scope of the research covers the development of Gaelic within both first and second language frameworks, and as a medium for the delivery of the curriculum in the primary and secondary sectors.

Three surveys are planned to cover: (1) all Scottish secondary schools which teach Gaelic as first and/or second language; (2) all Scottish primary schools which teach Gaelic as first and/or second language; and (3) all Gaelic medium and bilingual medium units. Additional information will be obtained from case-study work, currently underway in a sample of the kinds of schools described above. This element of the research will focus on teaching methods, resources, and the needs of children in the Gaelic and bilingual units, and be undertaken primarily through classroom observation and detailed interviews with key personnel.

12867   Genre theory and writing functions.
GBR   1993
Research Date(s): 1991-1995
Berry, J.
Sup: Evans, W.
Inst: Birmingham University, School of Education, Edgbaston, Birmingham B15 2TT, United Kingdom.
composition; writing; primary education
composition littéraire; écriture; enseignement primaire
PROJECT DESCRIPTION
   The research arises out of current debates about genre theory and its appropriateness to English education. The aim is to examine the theory and its applicability to English classroom situations. Examination of samples of writing done in classrooms in four or five contrasting schools will attempt to establish the number of functions of writing commonly covered by children at National Curriculum Key Stages 1 and 2 in those schools, and whether they can be related to any identifiable genres. Depending on these results, specific teaching ploys might be invented to test genre ideas and apply them to the teaching of writing. The usefulness of the ideas, the need for action (or otherwise) and the nature and outcome of the experiments will be discussed with statements of the National Curriculum (Writing) in mind. Australian genre teaching materials and the experience of Australian self-help groups will enter into the study for consideration and to provide a framework for experiment.

12868   Gestion et dynamique de la communication familiale en milieu bilingue ou multilingue.
FRA   1993
Research Date(s): 1986-
Hérédia (de)-Deprez, Christine.
Inst: Université de Paris V, UFR Linguistique générale et appliquée, CNRS URA/1031, Laboratoire de recherches sur l'acquisition et la pathologie du langage chez l'enfant, 12 rue Cujas, 75230 Paris Cedex 05, France.
bilingualism; multilingualism; family environment; language development
bilinguisme; multilinguisme; milieu familial; développement du langage
PROJECT DESCRIPTION
   Objectifs: La famille est vue comme lieu de genèse du bilinguisme précoce et comme lieu d'élaboration des conduites langagières permettant la gestion de l'asymétrie des compétences entre les différents membres et avec l'extérieur. La recherche s'est centrée sur, la transmission familiale des langues, les configurations dialogales et leur évolution.
   Méthodologie: Une enquête sur 300 questionnaires a permis de montrer que les langues d'origine étudiées sont largement transmises aux enfants dans les familles de la région parisienne, et que les couples "mixtes" ont un comportement fortement différencié des couples linguistiquement homogènes. Dans plus de 60 % des cas, les deux langues participent de la communication familiale et sont le plus souvent mélangées dans la conversation et chez le même individu, voire dans une même phrase. Il est alors apparu nécessaire d'approfondir ces questions avec des entretiens. Ces derniers font l'objet d'une analyse de contenu sur "attitudes et pratiques langagières" ainsi que d'une analyse de discours centrée sur les hésitations et les modalisations. Ces entretiens individuels permettent de dégager des profils de bilingues assez nuancés et de travailler à partir des ambivalences souvent manifestées chez les sujets. A travers eux on voit aussi comment se dégage et évolue une politique linguistique familiale qui se modifie au fil des ans et se (re)négocie en fonction d'événements clés (naissance, scolarisation, voyage(s) au pays, etc.). L'accent est mis sur la notion de répertoire linguistique individuel et familial. Les entretiens les moins sélectifs, proches des récits de vie, permettent de saisir le caractère évolutif des situations, et, mettant en évidence les différences de comportements entre différents enfants soumis globalement au même environnement, permettent de réaborder, sous un jour nouveau la dialectique des déterminismes linguistiques et de la liberté langagière.

Publ: Hérédia (de)-Deprez, Christine. Des enfants et des langues dans les villes. In: *Réalités africaines et langue française*, 1988, n° 22, pp. 41-59.
Hérédia (de)-Deprez, Christine. Le plurilinguisme urbain vu par les enfants: Paris. In: *Revue internationale des migrations européennes*, 1989. Hérédia (de)-Deprez, Christine. Le bilinguisme enfantin. Paris: PUF (Coll. L'éducateur), 1991.
Hérédia (de)-Deprez, Christine. Comment est-on bilingue en famille? Eléments de méthodologie. In: *La linguistique*, 1990, vol.26, 2, pp.95-105.
Hérédia (de)-Deprez, Christine. Le parler mélangé des familles bilingues. In: *Education et pédagogies*, 1990, n° 8, pp. 76-81.
Hérédia (de)-Deprez, Christine. Les représentations du plurilinguisme urbain contemporain: le cas parisien. In: *Le français dans le monde*, n° spécial *Vers le plurilinguisme? L'école et les politiques linguistiques*, 1991, pp. 131-142.

12869   Hearing children read.
GBR   1993
Research Date(s): 1980-
Campbell, R.
Inst: Hertfordshire University, School of Humanities and Education, Wall Hall Campus, Aldenham, Watford WD2 8AT, United Kingdom.

reading; beginning learning; reading aloud; teacher-pupil relation
lecture; enseignement initial; lecture à haute voix; relation maître-élève
PROJECT DESCRIPTION
   Now in its second phase, this study aims to explore the effectiveness of various teacher responses to the mistakes of early beginning readers. An in-depth case study of two children reading to their teacher throughout a school year has been conducted. Interactions were audio-recorded and subsequently transcribed. Results have suggested that a word cueing strategy was particularly helpful to the reader. However, effectiveness needs to be explored at various levels and recent articles have debated this topic.
Publ: Campbell, R. Social relationships in hearing children read. In: *Reading*, Vol 20, No 3, pp. 157-167, December 1986.
Campbell, R. Oral reading errors of two beginning readers. In: *Journal of Research in Reading*, Vol 10, No 2, pp. 144-155, September 1987.
Campbell, R. Is it time for USSR, SSR, SQUIRE, DEAR or ERIC? In: *Education*, Vol 16, No 2, pp. 3-13, June 1988.
Campbell, R. *Hearing children read.* London: Routledge, 1988.
Campbell, R. *Reading real books.* Buckingham: Open University Press, 1992.

12870   I didaskalia ton Aglikon sto Kipriako demotiko scholio: pragmatikotites - dinatotides - prooptikes. (The teaching of English in Cyprus primary schools: realities - potentialities - perspectives.)
CYP   1993
Research Date(s): 1991
Konstantinides, A.; Hatzitheodoulou, P.
Inst: Pedagogiko Instituto (Pedagogical Institute), P.O. Box 512, Nicosia, Cyprus.
English language; language teaching; foreign languages; self-confidence; teacher education; teacher
langue anglaise; enseignement des langues; langues étrangères; confiance en soi; formation des enseignants; enseignant
PROJECT DESCRIPTION
   Background and aims: The purpose of the study was twofold. First, to investigate whether teachers in primary schools feel confident in teaching English as a foreign language. Second, to investigate the effectiveness of the Pedagogical Academy's programme whereby teachers are prepared for teaching English.
   Methods: The study involved 80 teachers teaching English in primary schools in Cyprus, with up to five years of teaching experience. The teachers were asked to complete a questionnaire which was constructed by the investigators. Descriptive statistics were used for the analysis of data (means, standard deviations and frequencies).
   Results: The majority of teachers feel confident in their ability to teach English as a foreign language in primary schools. The teachers who had had English as their specialization during their training seemed to be more confident than the others. Most teachers believe that the Pedagogical Academy's programme is effective in providing teachers with an adequate number of teaching techniques appropriate for the teaching of English. On the other hand, most teachers believe that the Pedagogical Academy does not contribute effectively to the preparation of teachers in applying techniques for their daily lessons. In addition, a large number of teachers reported that they were not able to integrate songs in their lessons. Male teachers also reported that they did not consider games to be an important technique for teaching or practising language structures. Finally, some teachers reported that they had difficulties in pronouncing some English words because they had not had the opportunity to develop their ability to communicate in English during their studies at the Pedagogical Academy.

12871   Individual differences among poor readers and their implications for remediation.
GBR   1993
Research Date(s): 1988-1992
Hatcher, P.
Sup: Ellis, A.; Hulme, C.
Inst: York University, Department of Psychology, Heslington, York YO1 5DD, United Kingdom.
reading; remedial teaching; teaching method
lecture; soutien pédagogique; méthode pédagogique
PROJECT DESCRIPTION
   A battery of cognitive tests will be administered in order to discover the strengths and weaknesses of each of a sample of seven year old poor readers. Different remedial approaches will then be tried with different subgroups to discover whether the approaches differ in their overall effectiveness, and whether particular types of poor readers respond differently to different remediation procedures.

12872   Individuelles Lesen- und Schreibenlernen. (Individual learning: reading and writing.)
AUT   1993
Research Date(s): 1987-1992
Juna, Johanna.
Inst: Paedagogisches Institut der Stadt Wien, Burggasse 14-16, A-1070 Wien.

reading; writing; spelling; learning strategy; primary education

lecture; écriture; orthographe; stratégie d'apprentissage; enseignement primaire

PROJECT DESCRIPTION

Im Laufe der letzten Jahre wurde das 'Individuelle Lesen- und Schreiben-lernen' in Wien erprobt. Diese analytisch- synthetische Methode ist eine Weiterentwicklung der von Bergk propagierten Methode des 'Recht-schreibens von Anfang an'. Sieht man Zeichnen als eine Vorform des Schreibens an, dann koennen Kinder vom ersten Schultag an ihre Erlebnisse verschriften: sie zeichnen eben, was sie noch nicht schreiben koennen. Allmaehlich vereinfachen sie oft verwendete Zeichnungen, bis diese an logographische Schriftzeichen erinnern. Daneben erlernen die Kinder schrittweise das Schreiben und Lesen von Woertern, die an die Stelle der Zeichnungen treten. Anhand der Verschriftungen der Kinder wurde das Wiener Modell der Verschriftungsstufen erstellt, das eine Ein-schaetzung des Lernstandes eines Kindes erlaubt.

In fuenf Jahren wurden 13 Klassen einbezogen, in denen die Unterricht-sbeobachtungen stattfanden.

Die Evaluation erfolgt durch die Methode der Aktionsforschung (action research).

Genaue Analysen haben gezeigt, dass die Lernprozesse der Kinder so verschieden sind wie die Kinder selbst. Besonders das Hinterfragen von Fehlschreibungen ist aufschlussreich. Viele Fehler der Kinder lassen sich mit ihren Denkstrategien erklaeren, zum Beispiel mit dem Generalisieren. Dieses Forschungsprojekt findet seine Fortsetzung im 'Rechtschreiben in der Grundschule'.

Publ: Juna, Johanna. Die jungen Wiener schreiben wie die alten Griechen. In: Balhorn/Bruegelmann: *Jeder spricht anders.* Faude 1989.

Juna, Johanna. *Das Konzept der Betreuung schreib-leseschwacher Kinder im Bereich des Stadtschulrats fuer Wien.*

Juna, Johanna. Legasthenie, gibt's die? In: *Erziehung und Unterricht*, 5/92, Oesterreichischer Bundesverlag.

12873 Interdisziplinaeres Forschungsprojekt "Deutsch als Fremd-sprache: Ingenieurwissenschaftliche Fachsprachen". (Interdiscipli-nary research project: "German as a foreign language: technical engineering languages".)

DEU 1993

Research Date(s): 1991-1993

Goerts, W.; Monteiro, M.

Sup: Steinmueller, U.

Inst: Technische Universitaet Berlin, FB 22 Erziehungs- und Unterrichtswis-senschaften, Institut fuer Fachdidaktik Deutsch und Fremdsprachen, Franklinstr. 28-29, D-1000 Berlin 10.

German language; foreign languages; language teaching; engineer; interdis-ciplinary approach; university studies; language for special purposes; for-eign student

langue allemande; langues étrangères; enseignement des langues; ingénieur; interdisciplinarité; études universitaires; langage de spécialité; étudiant étranger

PROJECT DESCRIPTION

Inhalt: Auslaendische Studierende scheitern ueberproportional in ver-schiedenen ingenieurwissenschaftlichen Studiengaengen. Ursaechlich sind hierfuer u.a. fachsprachliche Anforderungen dieser Studiengaenge. Ziel des Projektes ist es, diese sprachlichen Anforderungen zu eruieren, darauf aufbauend sowohl spezifische Vorschlaege fuer die Veraenderung/Adap-tion einschlaegiger ingenieurwissenschaftlicher Lehrveranstaltungen zu erarbeiten wie auch Vorschlaege fuer Hochschuldidaktische Weiterbildung der Dozenten. Ausserdem sollen studiengangspezifische Sprachkurse und dafuer erforderliche Materialien erarbeitet werden. Diese Fragestellung und Ziele erscheinen dann besonders sinnvoll, wenn man die besondere Situa-tion der Technischen Universitaet Berlin beruecksichtigt - 17 Prozent aus-laendische Studierende (der Bundesdurchschnitt liegt bei 5,9 Prozent). Die grosse Mehrzahl von ihnen kommt aus Laendern der Dritten Welt. Etwa 70 Prozent der auslaendischen Studenten sind in den ingenieurwissenschaf-tlichen Studiengaengen eingeschrieben, in denen der Auslaenderanteil teilweise bis zu 38 Prozent betraegt. Die Ergebnisse, die an der TU-Berlin erzielt werden, koennen dazu beitragen, dass aehnliche Probleme an anderen Universitaeten durch Vorschlaege und besondere Massnahmen in Angriff genommen werden koennen.

Geographischer Raum: Berlin.

Untersuchter Zeitraum: 1.4.1991-31.3.1993.

Vorgehensweise: Ingenieurwissenschaftliche, sprachdidaktische und sprachwissenschaftliche Forschungsansaetze. Untersuchungsdesign: retrospektive Daten; qualitative Forschung; (Quasi-)Experiment.

Datengewinnung: Befragung (an der TU-Berlin immatrikulierte aus-laendische Studierende, WS 91/92; Auswahlverfahren: total). Teilnehmende Beobachtung (ausgewaehlte Vorlesungen an der TU-Berlin; Auswahlverfahren: bewusst). Experiment (an der TU-Berlin immatrikulierte auslaendische Studierende, WS 91/92; Auswahlverfahren: total). Primaer-erhebung: Feldarbeit von Mitarbeitern des Projektes durchgefuehrt.

12874 Internationale Projektierung: fachfranzoesische Aufbaugrammatik. ("International project work": advanced technical French grammar.)

DEU 1993

Research Date(s): 1990-1993

Forner, W.

Inst: Universitaet-Gesamthochschule, Siegen FB 03 Sprach- und Liter-aturwissenschaften, Fach Romanistik, Adolf-Reichwein-Strasse, D-5900 Siegen 21.

Fin: Bund; Land; Zukunftsinitiative Montanregion.

foreign languages; French language; grammar; language teaching; lan-guage for special purposes

langues étrangères; langue française; grammaire; enseignement des langues; langage de spécialité

PROJECT DESCRIPTION

Inhalt: "Fachsprache" wird verstanden als ein Funktionalstil, der sich von anderen Sprachvarianten durch die Anwendung spezifischer Elaboration-stechniken unterscheidet. Diese koennen systematisch (als Transforma-tionen) analysiert, gelehrt und geuebt werden.

Vorgehensweise: Observationeller Ausgangspunkt ist die -diaphasische-Sprachvariation einerseits, andererseits das geordnete Fachwissen. Die Bruecke zwischen beiden schlaegt eine "Grammatik", die auf Erhebung-swissen der Verb-, Kasus- und Tranformationsgrammatik aufbaut.

Publ: Fohrer, Werner. Vom Sinn zum Text. Vermittlung fachsprachlicher Vertextungsstrategien. In: *Fremdsprachen Lehren und Lernen*, 19, 1990, 82-96.

Fohrer, Werner. Ellipse und Adjunktion in franzoesischen fachsprachlichen Texten. In: Metzeltin, M.; Schmitt, Chr. (Hrsg.). *Grammatikographie der romanischen Sprachen.* 1992.

12875 Inventarizacija in analiza slovenske pedagoške terminologije. (Inventory and analysis of Slovenian terminology of education.)

SVN 1994

Research Date(s): 1980-1993

Pediček, Franc.

Inst: Pedagoški inštitut pri Univerzi v Ljubljani (Educational Research Insti-tute at the University of Ljubljana), Gerbičeva 62, 61111 Ljubljana, Slovenia.

Univerza v Ljubljani (University of Ljubljana), Kongresni trg 15, 61000 Ljubljana, Slovenia

Fin: Ministrstvo za znanost in tehnologijo.

terminology; sciences of education; information science

terminologie; sciences de l'éducation; science de l'information

PROJECT DESCRIPTION

Background: In Slovenia, as in most European countries, an inadequacy can be noted in the field of scientific educational terminology. That is why in 1980 the Development and System of Slovenian Educational Terminol-ogy project was started at the Educational Research Institute of the Univer-sity of Ljubljana. The research work continued with the Inventory and Analysis of Slovenian Terminological Signs in Education project and termi-nated in 1993 with a project entitled The Abridged Slovenian Version of European Education Thesaurus, which was part of the wider Language and Communication project.

Research questions: (1) What are the theoretical foundations of educa-tional terminology? (2) How can educational terminology be operational-ized? (3) How to participate in educational theory and research at the European level?

Hypothesis: (1) Research on scientific educational terminology is not only a matter of linguistics: it is part of a complex interdisciplinary and transdisciplinary field of research. (2) Educational terminology does not have a linear structure. An analysis of thematic concepts can show rele-vant aspects of structure. (3) Educational terminology is a component of educational information, which means that the languages of science and information are interconnected.

Methods: The study consisted of an examination of technical expres-sions from a sample of 25 educational texts written by 16 Slovenian educationalists and a theoretical synthesis of empirical material.

Results: (1) Like the study of scientific terminology, the study of educa-tional terminology requires an interdisciplinary science of terminology (Con-tributions to Theory of Terminology in Science, Ljubljana: Pedagoški Inštitut, 1990). (2) Educational terminology is closely related to educational information (Glossary of Educational terms for Slovenian Encyclopedia, Ljubljana: Pedagoški Inštitut, 1985; Slovenian Version of the Multilingual EUDISED Thesaurus, Ljubljana: Pedagoški Inštitut, 1986; Abridged Slove-nian Version of the European Education Thesaurus, Ljubljana: Pedagoški Inštitut, 1993). (3) The sign structure of educational terminology is triple: (a) the field of the word; (b) technical terms; (c) scientific terms (Develop-ment of Slovenian Terminology in View of Qualitative Analysis, Ljubljana: Pedagoški Inštitut, 1985).

Publ: Pediček, F. *Prispevki za teorijo terminologije v znanosti - tudi pedagoške.* Radovljica: Pedagoški inštitut; Didakta, 1990, 250p.

12876 Investigating teachers' assessment of children's writing at National Curriculum Key Stage 2.
GBR 1993
Research Date(s): 1991-1992
Fox, R.
Inst: Exeter University, School of Education, St Luke's, Heavitree Road, Exeter EX1 2LU, United Kingdom.
writing; assessment; primary education; software
écriture; appréciation; enseignement primaire; logiciel
PROJECT DESCRIPTION
The main aim of the project is to investigate primary teachers' methods of assessing the writing of children for National Curriculum Key Stage 2. A second aim is the production of computer software to enable teachers and students to practise such assessment within a framework provided. The investigation involves observation and interviews with local teachers in up to six primary schools in Devon. An important contextual feature is the need for teachers to develop their practice in this area in order to assess children in the National Curriculum for English at Key Stage 2.

12877 An investigation into the difficulties of introducing innovation in English language teaching in developing countries.
GBR 1993
Research Date(s): 1992-1993
Ahrens, P.
Inst: Heriot-Watt University, Moray House Institute of Education, Scottish Centre for Education Overseas, Holyrood Road, Edinburgh EH8 8AQ, United Kingdom.
language teaching; foreign languages; English language; developing country
enseignement des langues; langues étrangères; langue anglaise; pays en développement
PROJECT DESCRIPTION
This research grew out of work for a presentation at the British Council Dunford House Conference in 1990 on the topic of sustainability in the design of English language teaching projects. A database of difficulties was compiled in consultation with overseas Master of Arts (MA) students and used at the conference. This will be expanded and put into a hierarchy, in consultation with current overseas students, to form a questionnaire which will be sent to previous students, now seeking to introduce various innovative practices in their home systems. The results will be an ordered list of difficulties actually encountered by practitioners in the field. Later research might seek to identify ways of coping with these difficulties.

12878 An investigation into the present situation and problems of English language learning of adult Chinese immigrants in Nottingham and London.
GBR 1993
Research Date(s): 1992
Ling, J.; Jiangling, J.
Sup: Morgan, W.
Inst: Nottingham University, Department of Adult Education, Centre for Research into the Education of Adults, 14-22 Shakespeare Street, Nottingham NG1 4FJ, United Kingdom.
Fin: Nuffield Foundation.
language teaching; first foreign language; English language; immigrant; ethnic minority; adult
enseignement des langues; première langue étrangère; langue anglaise; immigrant; minorité ethnique; adulte
PROJECT DESCRIPTION
The proposed study will concentrate on the adult Chinese immigrants in London and Nottingham. Professionals and students will be excluded. The study aims at a thorough assessment of the actual level of English proficiency, the social, cultural or linguistic constraints that inhibit their English learning, the effects of their language disadvantage and the English second language (ESL) provisions that are available to them, with their effectiveness.

12879 An investigation of sustained silent reading in the primary school.
GBR 1993
Research Date(s): 1988-1992
Campbell, R.; Scrivens, G.; Mangan, M.
Inst: Hertfordshire University, School of Humanities and Education, Wall Hall Campus, Aldenham, Watford WD2 8AT, United Kingdom.
silent reading; reading; teaching method; primary education
lecture en silence; lecture; méthode pédagogique; enseignement primaire
PROJECT DESCRIPTION
Following the strong recommendations that there should be more emphasis on silent independent reading in primary schools there is limited evidence that the procedure defined as SSR (sustained silent reading) can have a beneficial effect on children's attitudes to reading and reading achievement when used with a course of reading instruction.
The aims of the study are: (i) to identify schools using SSR within the local division and/or county by means of a questionnaire; (ii) to explore and analyse how SSR is organised within some of these schools; (iii) to investi-

gate how the activity is perceived by teachers, children and parents by means of triangulation methods and interviews; (iv) to ascertain any possible gains in reading performance or attitudes to reading assessed within the schools; (v) to discover any particular problems these schools might experience in the use of SSR.
If this project is extended it will follow the form of an investigation of an adaption of SSR named 'Book-Time' which would be set up in one or more nursery schools or playgroups. There is very little evidence to date of the organisational difficulties which might occur or of the benefits to 3-5 year old children. This study would, therefore, be providing a contribution to knowledge about pedagogical practices.
Publ: Campbell, R. Is it time for USSR, SSR, SQUIRT, DEAR or ERIC? In: Education 3-13, Vol 16, No 2, pp. 22-25, June 1988.
Campbell, R. The teachers as a role model during sustained silent reading. In: Reading, Vol 23, No 3, pp. 179-183, November 1989.
Campbell, R. Reading together. Buckingham: Open University Press, 1990.
Campbell, R. Reading real books. Buckingham: Open University Press, 1992.

12880 'Knowledge about language', language learning and the National Curriculum.
GBR 1993
Research Date(s): 1991-1993
Brumfit, C.; Mitchell, R.
Inst: Southampton University, Faculty of Educational Studies, Centre for Language in Education, Highfield, Southampton SO9 5NH, United Kingdom.
Fin: Economic and Social Research Council.
language teaching; foreign languages; English language; language skill; knowledge
enseignement des langues; langues étrangères; langue anglaise; aptitude linguistique; connaissance
PROJECT DESCRIPTION
This project aims to investigate the nature of children's understanding of the nature of language and how it works, and how this is developed through experience of English/Modern Languages work in school. Teachers of English and Modern Languages have been encouraged by the Kingman Report, (Department of Education and Science Committee of Inquiry into the Teaching of English Language (1988). Report of the Committee of Inquiry into the Teaching of English Language. London HMSO), the Language in the National Curriculum (LINC) programme, and National Curriculum programmes for their subjects, to pay more attention to developing children's knowledge about language. Traditionally however, teachers in the different language subjects have dealt with 'Knowledge about Language' (KAL) in rather different ways. Moreover, in spite of much debate, little is known about school age children's resulting knowledge and beliefs about the nature of language, and the relationship between such knowledge and the development of children's practical language skills.
Fieldwork consists of case studies carried out during the school year 1991-1992 in the English and Modern Languages departments of three Hampshire schools. A period of approximately eight weeks is being spent in each school, spread over three terms. The focus is on pupils in Year 9; teachers of both subjects are being interviewed, and English/Modern Language classes are being observed and recorded, to learn how and when language matters are discussed, and in what terms. Children will also be interviewed, to explore their developing knowledge about language, and its relationship with classroom discussions and activities. The development of their language skills will also be monitored, through analysis of their day to day work, and possible links with their developing knowledge about language will be explored.

12881 The language learning experiences of Somalis and Eritreans in Britain and Italy.
GBR 1993
Research Date(s): 1991-1994
Loban, S.
Sup: Edwards, V.
Inst: Reading University, Faculty of Education and Community Studies, Bulmershe Court, Woodlands Avenue, Earley, Reading RG6 1HY, United Kingdom.
first foreign language; bilingualism; refugee; cross-national research
première langue étrangère; bilinguisme; réfugié; recherche transnationale
PROJECT DESCRIPTION
This is an investigation into the language learning of refugees in Europe. Somalis and Eritreans were chosen for this project as both Somalia and Eritrea were colonised by both Britain and Italy. The research will focus on the language learning needs of Somalis and Eritreans in Europe, and will address the following issues: (1) does language education meet needs; (2) attitudes towards bilingual education; (3) curriculum development and delivery; and (4) teaching methods.
The research will include participant observation; open-ended semi-structured interviews; and study of policy documents. Fieldwork will take

place in a college of further education in London and comparable institutions in Rome and Perugia, Italy.

12882   Language learning in large classes research project.
GBR   1993
Research Date(s): 1986-
Coleman, H.
Inst: Leeds University, School of Education, Overseas Education Unit, Leeds LS2 9JT, United Kingdom.
Fin: British Council; Bell Educational Trust; Centre for British Teachers.
language teaching; foreign languages; English language; class size
enseignement des langues; langues étrangères; langue anglaise; dimension de la classe
PROJECT DESCRIPTION

The project is primarily concerned with the learning and teaching of English as a second language or foreign language in the context of large classes. It has four aims: to develop links with individuals and institutions concerned with large classes, to organize meetings and other events for the purpose of discussing current research, undertake and promote research into specific aspects of language learning and teaching in large classes, and to develop and maintain a bibliography.

A series of project reports is now being published, and more reports will appear in the future. Colloquia have been organized in Chicago (1988), Warwick (1989), San Antonio (1989), Dublin (1990), San Francisco (1990), New York (1991) and Exeter (1991). A Specialist Conference was organised in Karachi, Pakistan, in 1991.

The specific issues being investigated include the following: (1) the aetiology of large classes, the definition of a 'large class', patterns of teacher and learner behaviour in large classes, teachers' perceptions of large classes, learners' perceptions of large classes, and approaches to the management of large classes; (2) relationship between class size and language acquisition, and teachers' and learners' strategies in large classes.

Publ: A complete list of publications is available from the researchers.

12883   Language medium teaching.
GBR   1993
Research Date(s): 1990-1993
Hamilton, J.
Inst: Heriot-Watt University, Moray House Institute of Education, Holyrood Road, Edinburgh EH8 8AQ, United Kingdom.
language teaching; foreign languages; teaching language
enseignement des langues; langues étrangères; langue d'enseignement
PROJECT DESCRIPTION

The aim of the research is to examine the effects of language medium teaching on learner motivation and foreign language proficiency within the Scottish context.

12884   Learners' language.
GBR   1993
Research Date(s): 1980-
Green, S.; Hecht, K.
Inst: York University, Language Teaching Centre, Heslington, York YO1 5DD, United Kingdom; Universität München, Lehrstuhl für die Didaktik der Englischen Sprache und Literatur, Schellingstrasse 3, D-8000 München 40, Germany.
Fin: British Council Academic Linking Scheme; European Community; EC Erasmus; York University.
language teaching; first foreign language; mother tongue; English language; comparative analysis; comparative achievement; cross-national research
enseignement des langues; première langue étrangère; langue maternelle; langue anglaise; analyse comparative; rendement comparé; recherche transnationale
PROJECT DESCRIPTION

This is an on-going project to investigate learners' language and compare it at all stages with the language of native peers. The project involves German school learners of English and English school pupils in performing three communicative tasks in English, and assessment by native and non-native teachers: (1) a letter writing task; (2) an oral narrative and (3) oral transaction.

To date there are 2,490 pupil productions from Germany and England. The productions are analysed from the following standpoints: (1) linguistic form; (2) content; (3) communicative effectiveness; (4) strategies; (5) self-correction/monitoring; (6) grammatical and lexical competence and performance; (7) the development of communicative competence; (8) assessment/reactions by natives and non-natives.

Publ: Green, P.S. & Hecht, Kh. The influence of accuracy on communicative effectiveness. In: *British Journal of Language Teaching*, Vol 25, No 2/1987, pp. 79-84, Autumn.
Green, P.S. & Hecht, Kh. The sympathetic native speaker - a GCSE role-play for the teacher. In: *Modern Languages*, Vol 69, No 1/1988, pp. 3-10. March.

12885   Learning outcomes and competences in English/Communication Studies.
GBR   1993
Research Date(s): 1989-1991
Beynon, W.; Middlehurst, R.
Inst: Glamorgan University, Department of Behavioural and Communication Studies, Pontypridd, Mid Glamorgan CF37 1DL, United Kingdom.
Fin: Department of Education and Science; Training Agency.
communication; learning; minimum competencies; job requirements
communication; acquisition de connaissances; fundamentum; qualification requise pour l'emploi
PROJECT DESCRIPTION

Since November 1989 there has been participation in a Department of Education and Science/Training Agency-funded research project organised by the Unit for the Development of Adult and Continuing Education (UDACE) and sited in Communication Studies, Polytechnic of Wales (now Glamorgan University); the English Department, Lancaster University; and the School of Humanities, Newcastle Polytechnic (now University of Northumbria at Newcastle). The research identified competences and learning outcomes associated with Communication/Cultural Studies (thus contextualised as 'English'). The research was of great significance both to students (who were fully involved in the research and were extensively interviewed, etc.) and staff teaching and planning courses in the area of Communication/Cultural Studies. The competences were arrived at after full liaison with prospective employers.

Publ: A list of working papers and reports is available from the researchers.

12886   Lesen von Sachtexten und kommunikatives Nutzen der Rezeptionsergebnisse.   (Reading factual texts and communicative use of the result.)
DEU   1993
Research Date(s): 1991-1994
Herrmann, H.
Inst: Paedagogische Hochschule Magdeburg, Institut fuer Germanistik, LS Fachdidaktik Deutsche Sprache und Literatur, Virchowstr. 24, O-3010 Magdeburg.
reading; pupil; cognitive ability; performance; comprehension
lecture; élève; aptitude cognitive; performance; compréhension
PROJECT DESCRIPTION

Inhalt: Erhellung schuelerbezogener Erschliessungs- und Verarbeitungsstrategien und Feststellung des erreichten Niveaus im Erschliessen und Verarbeiten; Gewinnung von Daten ueber die Art und Weise der Ueberfuehrung der Rezeptionsergebnisse in einen Zieltext, der gegenueber dem Ausgangstext eine andere Intention hat; Ermittlung des Niveaus im Schreiben von Texten auf der Grundlage von Texten durch Analyse von Schuelerarbeiten.

Geographischer Raum: Sachsen-Anhalt/Magdeburg.

Untersuchter Zeitraum: 1992-1994.

Vorgehensweise: Theoretisch-empirische Untersuchung. Untersuchungsdesign: Querschnittserhebung; Trend; qualitative Forschung; (Quasi-)Experiment.

Datengewinnung: Standardisiertes Interview (Stichprobe: 50; Schueler der 4. bis 9. Klasse; Auswahlverfahren: Zufall. Stichprobe: 100; Schueler der 4. bis 9. Klasse). Nicht-standardisiertes Interview (dito). Gruppenbefragung (dito). Experiment (dito). Primaererhebung: Feldarbeit von Mitarbeitern des Projektes durchgefuehrt.

Auswertung: Faktorenanalyse; Varianzanalyse.

12887   Lexical behaviour in a second language.
GBR   1993
Research Date(s): 1981-
Meara, P.
Inst: University College of Swansea, Centre for Applied Language Studies, Singleton Park, Swansea SA2 8PP, United Kingdom.
Fin: Eurocentres; Longmans; TVEI; University of Oxford Local Examinations Delegacy; BBC English.
foreign languages; language teaching; vocabulary
langues étrangères; enseignement des langues; vocabulaire
PROJECT DESCRIPTION

This project comprises a group of linked studies aimed at improving our understanding of vocabulary acquisition in foreign languages. The project includes: (1) a large-scale bibliographical survey; (2) development of lexical tests; and (3) a set of linked Ph.D. projects on lexical difficulties of second language speakers.

Publ: A list of publications is available from the researcher.

12888   The linguistic and discourse features of academic writing in English.
GBR   1993
Research Date(s): 1987-1992
Bloor, A.
Inst: Warwick University, Faculty of Educational Studies, Centre for English Language Teaching, Coventry CV4 7AL, United Kingdom.
writing; language for special purposes; author; research of academic literature

écriture; langage de spécialité; auteur; recherche sur documents
PROJECT DESCRIPTION

There is a need for objective studies into the nature of academic writing since existing handbooks, based largely on authors' intuitions, often fail to meet learners' needs. The main aims of the present research are to: (1) improve our descriptions of the genres of academic writing in English (for example, research or project reports, journal articles, dissertations); (2) investigate the writing processes employed by successful writers; and (3) (by application) analyse some of the writing problems encountered by inexperienced writers and assist teachers in the task of developing the writing skills of students in further and higher education.

The work is of particular relevance to speakers of other languages who are not used to writing in English. The methods employed involve the linguistic and discourse analysis of texts, the evaluation of support materials such as thesauri, and the collation and analysis of the results of previous research projects from around the world, many of which are not available to teachers in Britain.

Publ: Bloor, M. & St John, M.J. Project writing: the marriage of process and product. In: Robinson, P. (ed.). *Academic Writing: the Marriage of Process and Product.* ELT Documents 129. London: Modern English Publications and The British Council, 1988.
Bloor, M. & Bloor, T. Cultural expectations and sociopragmatic failure in academic writing. In: Heaton, B. (ed.). *Socio-cultural Issues in EAP.* ELT Documents. London: Modern English Publications and The British Council, 1991.
Nesi, H. Do dictionaries help students write? In: Bloor, T. & Norrish, J. (eds.). *Written Language.* British Studies for Applied Linguistics. London: Centre for Information on Language Teaching and Research, 1987.
Nesi, H. How many words is a picture worth? In: Tickoo, M. (ed.). *Learners' Dictionaries: State of the Art.* Singapore RELC Anthology Series 23, 1989.

12889 Metaphor as discourse strategy in teacher education.
GBR 1993
Research Date(s): 1990-1994
Packwood, A.
Sup: Raban, B.
Inst: Warwick University, Faculty of Educational Studies, Coventry CV4 7AL, United Kingdom.
verbal communication; teaching; verbal interaction; teacher education
communication verbale; enseignement; interaction verbale; formation des enseignants
PROJECT DESCRIPTION

A constructivist approach to metaphor has been used to develop an analytic framework. This is then being tested within the context of the discourse analysis of teachers in a classroom situation. The framework of metaphoric analysis will then be evaluated and refined.

12890 My Turn to Speak.
GBR 1993
Research Date(s): 1991-1992
Pennington, L.
Sup: McConachie, H.; Jolleff, N.
Inst: Institute of Child Health, The Wolfson Centre, Mecklenburgh Square, London WC1N 2AP, United Kingdom.
Fin: The Nuffield Foundation; The Baring Foundation.
communication; speech training; speech defect; physically handicapped; training workshop; special education; teaching aid
communication; éducation de la parole; trouble de la parole; handicapé physique; atelier de formation; enseignement spécial; moyen d'enseignement
PROJECT DESCRIPTION

My Turn to Speak is a workshop training package designed for use in schools for children with severe physical disabilities. The package is being developed in response to concern about the fragmented approach to communication development often observed in following up children assessed at The Communication Aids Centre, The Wolfson Centre, London. The workshop aims to facilitate the development of functional communication of users of communication aids in schools by creating a collaborative approach between teachers and therapists. The workshop is being trialled in four schools. Two children in each school are targeted for observation and intervention. The children use a variety of communication aids. Evaluation of their communication development is undertaken using objective techniques. Workshops are being undertaken and results will be given on their completion.

12891 Native and non-native use of English.
GBR 1993
Research Date(s): 1989-1992
Chappell, D.
Sup: Mitchell, R.
Inst: Southampton University, Faculty of Educational Studies, Centre for Language in Education, Highfield, Southampton SO9 5NH, United Kingdom.
Fin: Economic and Social Research Council.
verbal communication; English language; foreign languages; mother tongue

communication verbale; langue anglaise; langues étrangères; langue maternelle
PROJECT DESCRIPTION

This is an empirically based study focusing on the structure, nature and use of English by native and non-native speakers in the specific discourse type of information exchange. Data will be gathered from public arenas where transactions between: (i) native/native; (ii) native/non-native; (iii) non-native/non-native speakers take place and, in addition, from within the language learning classroom where activities of a like nature have been set up. The naturally occurring events and classroom tasks will then be analysed at an interactional level and characteristic features of each identified. The use of a psycholinguistic analysis endeavours not only to identify the reasons for participants' interpretive choice during interaction, but also to uncover any underlying relationships between use of these choices and their effect on the language learning process. In this way it is hoped that such descriptions may inform the understanding of: (1) particular points through and by which language learning takes place; (2) the elements that facilitate such learning; and (3) the conditions under which those elements are best served. The pedagogical implications related to any of the aforementioned aspects include a re-examination of teachers' own choices concerning aims, methodology and materials which may ultimately lead to a re-assessment of the evaluation process at all subsequent levels.

12892 Nederlands in de niet-taalvakken. (Dutch language in non-language subjects.)
BEL 1994
Research Date(s): 1990-1992
Geudens, V.
Sup: Daems, F.
Inst: Interfacultair Centrum voor Toegepaste Linguïstiek (Interfaculty Centre for Applied Linguistics), Rodestraat 14, 2000 Antwerpen, Belgium. Universitaire Faculteiten Sint-Ignatius Antwerpen, UFSIA (University Faculties St Ignatius Antwerp, UFSIA), Prinsstraat 13, 2000 Antwerpen, Belgium
Fin: Departement Onderwijs, Fonds voor Kollektief en Fundamenteel Onderzoek op Ministerieel Initiatief.
Dutch language; teaching language; language for special purposes
langue néerlandaise; langue d'enseignement; langage de spécialité
PROJECT DESCRIPTION

Aim: To gain insight into the use of Dutch in subject-specific conversations during lessons in non-language subjects in secondary education, concentrating on Dutch as a medium of instruction and as an instructional goal.

Method: The theoretical premises of the study have been described: (1) the different functions of language; (2) language acquisition; (3) the role of languages in school and in learning; (4) the phenomenon of subject-specific language. On basis of these premises an analysis scheme has been developed that will be of use for observations of lessons.

Publ: Daems, F. & Geudens, V. *Nederlands in de niet-taalvakken: wetenschappelijk verslag van het werkingsjaar 1990.* Antwerpen: UFSIA, Interfacultair Centrum voor Toegepaste Linguïstiek, 1991, 107p.

12893 A new dialect in a new city: children's and adults' speech in Milton Keynes.
GBR 1993
Research Date(s): 1990-1993
Kerswill, P.; Williams, A.
Inst: Reading University, Department of Linguistic Science, Whiteknights, Reading RG6 2AH, United Kingdom.
Fin: Economic and Social Research Council.
sociolinguistics; dialect; spoken language
sociolinguistique; dialecte; langage parlé
PROJECT DESCRIPTION

The research aims to examine the processes behind the formation of a new dialect in a city where the majority of the population originates from different parts of the country and to enquire how children develop 'sociolinguistic competence' - awareness of different accents and dialects in their community, and of their use. A range of sociolinguistic methods are used in the study of 48 children aged 4, 8 and 12.

Publ: Kerswill, P. & Williams, A. Some principles of dialect contact: evidence from the New Town of Milton Keynes. In: Warburton, I. & Ingham, R. (eds.). *Working Papers 1992.* Reading University, Department of Linguistic Science, 1992.

12894 The non-teacher directed peer-group classroom talk of nine-year olds.
GBR 1993
Research Date(s): 1984-1992
Brider, J.
Sup: Spencer, M.
Inst: London University, Institute of Education, Department of English and Media Studies, 20 Bedford Way, London WC1H 0AL, United Kingdom; West Sussex Institute of Higher Education, Bishop Otter College, College Lane, Chichester PO19 4PE, United Kingdom.

verbal communication; peer group; group learning; ex-cathedra teaching; primary education

communication verbale; groupe d'égaux; pédagogie de groupe; enseignement magistral; enseignement primaire

PROJECT DESCRIPTION

Observations and tape-recordings will be made of peer group non-teacher directed talk in an opportunity sample of classrooms of nine-year olds in the context of whole class and group teaching strategies. Analysis will be carried out using various historical methodologies of analysis of transcripts to isolate talk which others have ignored.

12895 Onderwijsaanbod, buitenschools lezen en leesvaardigheids-ontwikkeling van begin groep 5 naar eind groep 8. (Instruction, leisure time reading and development of reading skills from the beginning of primary year 5 (8-year-olds) to the end of year 8 (12-year-olds).)

NLD 1994

Research Date(s): 1993-1994

Otter, M.E.

Sup: Glopper, K. de.

Inst: Stichting Centrum voor Onderwijsonderzoek (SCO) (Centre for Educational Research), Grote Bickersstraat 72, 1013 KS Amsterdam, Netherlands.

Universiteit van Amsterdam (University of Amsterdam), P.O. Box 19268, 1000 GG Amsterdam, Netherlands

Fin: SVO het Instituut voor Onderzoek van het Onderwijs.

reading; skill; content of education; leisure; primary education

lecture; compétence; contenu de l'éducation; loisir; enseignement primaire

PROJECT DESCRIPTION

Background: Within the wider framework of the IEA Reading Literacy Study a national option is being conducted: a large-scale longitudinal study of the effects of reading instruction and leisure time reading on the development of reading skills. So far, two-yearly measurements have been conducted with pupils aged 8 to 10 years, focusing on the relationships between instruction, leisure time activities and achievement. This study proposes to prolong the duration of the survey by two years with a view to examining the development of reading skills up to the end of primary school (year 8).

Aim: To investigate the development of reading skills in primary school pupils from year 5 (8-9-year-olds) to year 8 (11-12-year-olds), focusing in particular on the instrumentation of instruction and leisure time activities.

Methods: Logs, tests.

Design: So far, the survey has covered pupils up to year 6 (9-10-year-olds). In the selection of schools for the extended survey, the original number of 40 schools will be reduced by half. Existing instruments (logs) will be used to collect data on the content of instruction and leisure time reading. At the end of year 7 and 8 reading proficiency will be measured with the help of the national Cito test of reading comprehension for end year 6 and 7, supplemented by the Cito reading comprehension test for end year 7 and 8. Thus it will be possible to compare the scores of different year groups on a measurement scale.

12896 Parental involvement in reading programmes.

GBR 1993

Research Date(s): 1985-1992

Macleod, F.

Sup: Hughes, D.; Bennett, S.

Inst: Exeter University, School of Education, St Luke's, Heavitree Road, Exeter EX1 2LU, United Kingdom.

reading; parent participation; parent role; achievement

lecture; participation des parents; rôle des parents; rendement

PROJECT DESCRIPTION

The study is investigating whether there are potentially important differences in parental involvement in reading programmes and that parental involvement in reading is causally related to increments in reading development as measured by reading tests and that this in turn is causally related to later scholastic achievement.

12897 Patterns of bilingualism in some families of Pakistani origin: implications for policy on language education.

GBR 1993

Research Date(s): 1989-1992

Khan, J.

Sup: Henderson, T.; Burgess, R.

Inst: Warwick University, Centre for English Language Teaching, Coventry CV4 7AL, United Kingdom.

bilingualism; minority language; mother tongue; ethnic minority; bilingual education; second generation migrant

bilinguisme; langue de minorité; langue maternelle; minorité ethnique; enseignement bilingue; deuxième génération

PROJECT DESCRIPTION

Despite much discussion at policy and institutional levels about the place of community languages in the curriculum, there are very few in-depth studies of the realities of bilingual language use outside the school in minority family or community settings in Britain. Most information available has been gathered by survey methods (e.g. Stubbs, M. (ed.). The Linguistic Minorities Project - the other languages of England. London: Routledge and Kegan Paul, 1985) and does not seek therefore to consider detailed individual profiles or language data. Furthermore, attention is rarely focused on second-generation minority group members who have no language problems, who are educationally successful and who do have a bilingual repertoire.

This study, is an ethnographic investigation of intergenerational developments in patterns of bilingualism within a number of families of Pakistani origin. Data are being gathered by extensive interviews, participant observation and recording of a language corpus. Analysis is focusing on patterns of language shift and maintenance, on the wide differences in the range of bilingual skills that exist between young people in different families and on the relationship between use of Punjabi and Urdu, cultural patternings and identity-related issues. Results are contributing to the development of a fine-grained analysis of individual bilingual repertoires. They are potentially very relevant to discussion of language policy in the school curriculum in Britain.

12898 Pencils with triangular barrels.

GBR 1993

Research Date(s): 1990-1991

Henderson, S.

Inst: London University, Institute of Education, Department of Educational Psychology and Special Educational Needs, 20 Bedford Way, London WC1H 0AL, United Kingdom.

Fin: Berol Ltd.

writing; teaching aid

écriture; moyen d'enseignement

PROJECT DESCRIPTION

The objective of this project was to evaluate the effectiveness of a triangular shaped pencil as a beginner's writing implement. Both the writing and pencil grip were examined in 100 5-6 year olds. A technical report has been produced for Berol.

12899 Perspektiven einer Deutschdidaktik für die Deutschschweiz. (Perspectives d'une didactique de l'allemand pour la Suisse alémanique.)

CHE 1994

Research Date(s): 1985-1989

Sieber, Peter.

Sup: Sitta, Horst.

Inst: Universität Zürich, Deutsches Seminar, Rämistrasse 74, 8001 Zürich, Schweiz.

mother tongue; language teaching; didactics; teaching method; dialect; German language

langue maternelle; enseignement des langues; didactique; méthode pédagogique; dialecte; langue allemande

PROJECT DESCRIPTION

Die vorliegende Dissertation beschäfigt sich mit der besonderen Situation des Muttersprachlernens und -lehrens in der Deutschschweiz, einer Situation also, die durch die Diglossie Mundart-Hochsprache gekennzeichnet ist. Der Autor hat längere Zeit in einem Forschungsprojekt mitgearbeitet, das sich mit dem Sprnnungsverhältnis zwischen Dialekt und Standardsprache im Unterricht beschäftigte; nach seinem Dafürhalten lassen die im Projekt gewonnenen Erkenntnisse eine detaillierte Auseinandersetzung mit Fragen der Muttersprachdidaktik für die besondere deutschschweizerische Situation als lohnend erscheinen.

Die Dissertation ist in sechs Teile gegliedert. Das erste Kapitel handelt von den neuen Vorstellungen über menschliches Lernen (kognitive Wende) und skizziert auf deren Basis ein Menschenbild, das nicht nur dem Sprachunterricht zugrunde gelegt werden kann. Kapitel 2 bietet einen Ausblick in die Spracherwerbsforschung und macht die Relevanz spracherwerbsorientierter Überlegungen für jegliche Sprachdidaktik deutlich. Insbesondere wird auch die Nützlichkeit des Konzepts der "Lernersprachen" (Zwischenstufen auf dem Weg der Aneignung voller sprachlicher Kompetenz) fúr die Analyse, die Bewertung und die Unterstützung von Spracherwerbsprozessen geschildert. Den veränderten Einschätzungen von Schriftlichkeit und Mündlichkeit geht das 3. Kapitel nach. Die Konsequenzen dieser Überlegungen machen die Forderung nach einer eigenständigen Entwicklung von Didaktiken der Mündlichkeit und der Schriftlichkeit plausibel. Eine Darstellung von einzelnen Aspekten der sprachlichen Situation will im 4. Kapitel die Chancen deutlich machen, die sich unter den besonderen sprachlichen Bedingungen in der Deutschschweiz für eine lernerorientierte Sprachdidaktik ergeben. Die Frage, wie weit eine solche Orientierung Anknüpfungspunkte in traditionellen Konzepten des Sprachunterrichts in der Deutschschweiz finden kann, ist Gegenstand des 5. Kapitels. Abschließend werden im Schlusskapitel aus den vorangehenden Überlegungen Perspektiven für zwei unterschiedliche Bereiche entworfen: für die wissenschaftliche Erforschung und Klärung von Fragen zum Sprachunterricht in der deutschsprachigen Schweiz sowie für die Weiterentwicklung sprachdidaktischer Konzept, welche die Besonderheiten, Schwierigkeiten und Chancen produktiv zu verwenden wissen.

Publ: Sieber, Peter. *Perspektiven einer Deutschdidaktik für die deutsche Schweiz.* Aarau: Sauerländer, 1990, 152 Seiten (Sprachlandschaften; 8).

12900   Phonological awareness of nursery-school children.
GBR   1993
Research Date(s): 1991-1993
Layton, L.
Sup: Upton, G.
Inst: Birmingham University, School of Education, Edgbaston, Birmingham B15 2TT, United Kingdom.
Fin: Department of Education and Science; Oak Foundation; Via Hereford and Worcester Dyslexia Association.
phonology; speech; sound; recognition; pre-school child; child development; training programme; pre-school education
phonologie; parole; son; reconnaissance; enfant d'âge préscolaire; développement de l'enfant; programme de formation; éducation préscolaire
PROJECT DESCRIPTION
   The project aims at the development and evaluation of a structured programme of phonological training materials designed to enhance phonological awareness in pre-school aged children in general and in particular those children whose phonological skills are under-developed.
   The first phase of the project involved assessing the phonological skills of a group of 50 pre-school aged children and a detailed examination of phonological training in a sample of 10 nursery schools.
   The second phase involves the development of the training pack and the evaluation of its effectiveness. The pack is being designed for use with all children but a particular focus of the study will be on its use with children whose phonological skills are under-developed and who are considered to be at risk of developing a specific learning difficulty. A follow-up of these children is planned two years after the completion of the present study.
Publ: Layton, L. & Upton, G. Phonological training and the pre-school child. In: *Links*, Spring 1991.
Layton, L. & Upton, G. In my view. In: *Child Education*, Vol 68, No 9/1991.

12901   A pilot study on the phonological acquisition of Turkish and its implications for phonological disorders.
TUR   1994
Research Date(s): 1990
Topbaş, S. Seyhun.
Inst: Anadolu Üniversitesi, Eğitim Fakültesi, Özel Eğitim Bölümü (Anadolu University, Faculty of Education, Department of Special Education), Yunusemre Kampusu, 26470 Eskişehir, Turkey.
phonology; infancy; speech handicapped; language development
phonologie; prime enfance; handicapé de la parole; développement du langage
PROJECT DESCRIPTION
   The purpose of this study was to investigate phonological processes in a case study of a phonologically disordered (PD) Turkish child in comparison with phonological processes in normal Turkish children. It is hoped that the study will contribute to our knowledge of speech and language pathology in Turkey and to the discussion on universal and language-specific factors in child phonology.
   The contrastive sample of Turkish children with normal phonological development consisted of 22 subjects. Two of these children were observed in a longitudinal design: one was observed from 1;0 to 3;0 years of age at 15-30 day intervals and in addition a diary was kept; the other child was observed at 1;3, 1;8, 2;0 and 2;5 years of age. The remaining speech samples were taken cross-sectionally from children between 1;3 and 3;0 years of age. The data from both the normal children and the PD child were obtained through picture-naming and spontaneous speech productions in dialogues. All the data were tape-recorded. A live phonetic transcription was made simultaneously and a complete transcription was made after each session.
   Three analytical procedures (Grunwell, 1985, 1987, 1992) were explored: phonetic inventory; contrastive system and phonotactic inventory; phonological process analysis and developmental status. The data were analysed by using a phonological framework of analysis based on selected procedures from the Phonological Assessment of Child Speech (Grunwell, 1985) with minor modifications necessitated by the characteristics of the Turkish language. The transcriptions were made with the help of the International Phonetic Alphabet (1989 revision) and the guidelines of the Working Party for the Phonetic Representation of Disordered Speech (1983).
   It was found that although the process patterns of the PD subject could also be found in normal development, the characteristics of the errors showed an idiosyncratic, variable and persistent process. Secondly, although there are individual differences, the phonetic tendencies and process patterns of normal children and the PD child coincide broadly with the universals of language. However, the data also enable us to agree on specificities of the language. It seems that certain aspects of Turkish phonology provide a challenge for children acquiring Turkish. Further longitudinal and cross-sectional research is needed to collect a wider range of data.

12902   A pilot study to test a programme for training nursery school children to attend to the sounds in words.
GBR   1993
Research Date(s): 1990-1991
Layton, L.
Sup: Upton, G.
Inst: Birmingham University, School of Education, Edgbaston, Birmingham B15 2TT, United Kingdom.
Fin: Children's Research Charity via Hereford & Worcester Dyslexia Association.
phonology; sound; recognition; diagnostic test; pre-school child
phonologie; son; reconnaissance; test de diagnostic; enfant d'âge préscolaire
PROJECT DESCRIPTION
   The objectives of this pilot study are: (1) to select, from existing techniques, a battery of tests which will assess certain phonological awareness skills in pre-school children who are currently attending nursery school classes or playgroups; (2) using these tests to identify about six children aged between three and a half to four years old with deficiencies in phonological awareness; (3) to design a set of graded procedures which can then be applied using the targeted group; and (4) to assess the suitability of the tests and procedures with a view to including them in a major training study. The object of this would be the improvement of phonological awareness skills in targeted children and an assessment of the effect of such improvement on the children's later written language skills. However it is hoped that the pilot study will also yield a set of games and activities which would have wider application within the typical nursery school routine.

12903   Putting training into practice: evaluating 'My Turn to Speak'.
GBR   1993
Research Date(s): 1993
Pennington, L.
Sup: McConachie, H.; Jolleff, N.
Inst: Institute of Child Health, The Wolfson Centre, Mecklenburgh Square, London WC1N 2AP, United Kingdom.
Fin: The Viscount Nuffield Auxiliary Fund.
communication; speech training; speech defect; physically handicapped; training workshop; special education; teaching aid
communication; éducation de la parole; trouble de la parole; handicapé physique; atelier de formation; enseignement spécial; moyen d'enseignement
PROJECT DESCRIPTION
   The current project has two parts to it. Firstly, the development team for 'My Turn to Speak' will run study days to familiarise speech therapists, teachers and others who might wish to use the published training package. The study days will include some of the activities of the workshop, and discussion on how best to implement the approach in various schools and with children who have various levels of severity of physical disorder.
   The second part of the current project involves evaluating the workshops that have been run by the development team, and comparing their process and outcome with workshops run by new tutors, often past participants. One aim of the package is to facilitate the setting up of a rolling programme of training throughout a school. In addition a multiple baseline, single case study is being undertaken to look at the implementation of the team approach to communication with one child.
Publ: Pennington, L.; Jolleff, N.; McConachie, H.; Wisbeach, A. & Price, K. *My Turn to Speak: A Team Approach to Augmentative Communication.* London: Institute of Child Health, 1993, distributed by Winslow Press.

12904   Reading and schema theory.
GBR   1993
Research Date(s): 1989-1991
Yazigy, A.
Sup: Cortazzi, M.
Inst: Leicester University, School of Education, University Road, Leicester LE1 7RH, United Kingdom.
Fin: Christian Aid.
language teaching; English language; reading; teaching method; first foreign language
enseignement des langues; langue anglaise; lecture; méthode pédagogique; première langue étrangère
PROJECT DESCRIPTION
   The aim of the research is to help students at primary levels, learning English as a second language, to be good readers (i.e. with a high level of comprehension) using the schema theory.

12905   Reading and writing in student learning.
GBR   1993
Research Date(s): 1989-1995
Rimmershaw, R.
Inst: Lancaster University, Department of Educational Research, Cartmel College, Bailrigg, Lancaster LA1 4YW, United Kingdom.
reading; student; study method; writing; higher education
lecture; étudiant; méthode de travail; écriture; enseignement supérieur

PROJECT DESCRIPTION

This research into students' reading and writing development is in two phases. In the first phase undergraduate students worked with the researcher to reflect on and analyse their own reading and writing development before and during their courses at Lancaster University. In the second phase a cohort of 16 non-traditional students were followed through the three years of their degree programme. The methods used include individual interviews, group discussions and deconstruction of particular reading and writing tasks as the students perform them.

12906   Reading standards in a local education authority: 1976-1991.
GBR   1993
Research Date(s): 1991-1992
Elliott, C.; Pumfrey, P.
Sup: Tyler, S.
Inst: Manchester University, School of Education, Centre for Educational Guidance and Special Needs, Oxford Road, Manchester M13 9PL, United Kingdom; Stockport Metropolitan Borough Council, Education Division, Schools' Psychological Service, Stopford House, Stockport, Cheshire SK1 3XE, United Kingdom.
reading; achievement test; cross-national research
lecture; test de rendement; recherche transnationale
PROJECT DESCRIPTION

The aim of the research was to identify a representative sample of pupils in National Curriculum Year 3 in a local education authority and to see whether reading standards had changed over a 15 year period. A comparison with American pupils was also undertaken. The relationship between objective test scores and AT2 Reading, as measured by Standard Assessment Tasks at Key Stage 1 was also examined. The pupils were tested on the British Ability Scales Word Reading Test and the Differential Ability Scales; the former was standardised in the United Kingdom in 1976 and the latter in the United States of America in 1989. In addition, information on the pupils' scores on National Curriculum (NC) English Attainment Target (AT) 2 Reading obtained in the Summer term, 1991, was collected. The sample was selected from all the primary schools in a local education authority. Twelve schools and 209 pupils were involved. The sample of schools selected was based on the proportion of pupils in receipt of free school meals. The tests (BAS & DAS) were administered individually with order of administration and pupil sex counterbalanced. The results include the means and ranges on both BAS and DAS word reading tests and on the Standard Assessment Test AT2 Reading for the total sample, and for children at each of the four levels of reading attainment recorded on the basis of the NC English Standard Assessment Task. The relationship between the three sets of reading tests scores are considered.

The results suggest that, in this particular LEA, standards of word reading have not changed significantly since 1976. The sample of pupils did not score as highly as American pupils on the DAS word reading test. An important finding was the high range of both BAS and DAS word reading scores associated with each of the four levels of reading attainment represented by Key Stage 1 Standard Assessment Tasks reading assessments.

12907   Rechtschreiben in der Grundschule. (Spelling in primary schools.)
AUT   1993
Research Date(s): 1992-
Juna, Johanna; Jung, Ingrid; Boran, Lieselotte; Teufel, Ingrid; Andlinger, Ulrike; Luebcke, Ursula; Mader, Eva.
Inst: Paedagogisches Institut der Stadt Wien, Burggasse 14-16, A-1070 Wien.
spelling; individualized teaching; primary education; learning strategy
orthographe; enseignement individualisé; enseignement primaire; stratégie d'apprentissage
PROJECT DESCRIPTION

Dieses Projekt hat sich aus der Analyse der Methode des 'Individuellen Lesen- und Schreibenlernens' ergeben. Die im Rahmen der Erprobung dieser Methode gemachten Beobachtungen zeigen nicht nur, dass die Lernwege der Kinder so verschieden sind wie die Kinder selbst, sondern auch, dass ein Teil ihrer Fehler sich mit den kindlichen Denkstrategien, wie z.B. dem Generalisieren, erklaeren lassen. Die Kinder entwickeln auf dem Weg zur richtigen Orthographie eine Fertigkeit, die als 'Hypothesentestendes Rechtschreiben' bezeichnet werden kann. Ziel des Forschungssprojekts ist die Beobachtung und Dokumentation des 'Hypothesentestenden Rechtschreibens' und dessen Verbindung zu Rechtschreibhilfen, die im Unterricht von LehrerInnen angeboten werden.

Es werden Unterrichtsbeobachtungen in zehn Klassen aus dem Grundschulbereich durchgefuehrt.

Die Evaluation erfolgt durch die Methode der Aktionsforschung (Action Research).

12908   The reform of English spelling by omission of redundant letters.
GBR   1993
Research Date(s): 1982-1992
Upward, C.

Inst: Aston University, Department of Modern Languages, Aston Triangle, Birmingham B4 7ET, United Kingdom.
Fin: Aston University; The Simplified Spelling Society.
English language; spelling; reform; literacy
langue anglaise; orthographe; réforme; alphabétisation
PROJECT DESCRIPTION

Proposals for rationalising English orthography date back to the sixteenth century. Modern proposals have assumed that reform merely required consistent representation of Received Pronunciation, but they took little account of the psychological and administrative practicalities of introducing a visually revolutionary system. One such proposal, the Simplified Spelling Society's 'New Spelling' (1948), formed the basis for Sir James Pitman's 'Initial Teaching Alphabet', which proved the educational benefits of regularised spelling, but was unsuited for a general reform of written English. In 1982, Valerie Yule published on the concept of 'Cut Spelling', which meant reform by omitting redundant letters rather than introducing new letters to words.

The aim of the project is to systematise the concept of Cut Spelling, explore its linguistic implications, and develop a coherent reform proposal based on it. The concept of Cut Spelling has been reduced to three main rules: (1) omission of letters irrelevant to pronunciation; (2) extended use of syllabographic l, m, n, r in post-accentual syllables, with morphophonemic regularisation of inflections; (3) simplification of doubled consonants. The implications of such a system have been explored under a number of headings: (i) degree of visual disruption resulting from different kinds of spelling change; (ii) reduction of grapheme-variety; (iii) avoidance of spelling error; (iv) economy of representation; (v) homophones and homographs; (vi) phonographic and graphotactic innovation; (vii) diachronic tendencies towards Cut Spelling in English and other European languages.

In conclusion, Cut Spelling offers a practicable new approach to the modernisation of English spelling, combining compatibility with traditional orthography, enhanced regularity, and significant economy in use.
Publ: Upward, C. Conflicting eficiency criteria in Cut Speling-2. In: *Journal of the Simplified Spelling Society*, Vol 3, No 1/1989, pp. 21-29.
Upward, C. The initial teaching alphabet and spelling reform. In: *UK i.t.a. Federation Newsletter*, pp. 13-18, Spring 1989.
Upward, C. Recent developments in 're-regulating' written German. In: *Journal of the Simplified Spelling Society*, Vol 3, No 1/1989, pp. 15-17.
Upward, C. & Gregersen, E. Morfemes and cut spelling. In: *Journal of the Simplified Spelling Society*, Vol 3, No 1/1989, pp. 25-29.
A full list of publications is available from the researcher.

12909   Relatieve moeilijkheid moderne vreemde talen. (The relative difficulty of foreign languages.)
NLD   1994
Research Date(s): 1992-1993
Schooten, E. van; Eiting, M.
Sup: Glopper, K. de.
Inst: Stichting Centrum voor Onderwijsonderzoek (SCO) (Centre for Educational Research), Grote Bickersstraat 72, 1013 KS Amsterdam, Netherlands.
Universiteit van Amsterdam (University of Amsterdam), P.O. Box 19268, 1000 GG Amsterdam, Netherlands
Fin: SVO het Instituut voor Onderzoek van het Onderwijs.
Spanish language; secondary education; foreign languages; language teaching
langue espagnole; enseignement secondaire; langues étrangères; enseignement des langues
PROJECT DESCRIPTION

Background: Since the effectuation of the School-Leaving Examinations Decree of 1990, secondary school pupils can take a final examination in the subject Spanish. In some types of secondary school pupils are obliged to take at least one other foreign language (English, French or German). According to the "Spanish in School" Association, the position of the subject Spanish in the curricula of Dutch general secondary schools is too marginal. This contrasts sharply with the situation in secondary and higher vocational education and non-formal education courses, where Spanish is an important and popular subject.

Aim: To test the hypothesis that Spanish is harder to learn than other foreign languages and thereby to inform the debate on the content of the pending national curriculum for lower secondary education and the content of teaching in upper secondary schools.

Design: A group of 1,000 pupils will be asked to compare the difficulty of the grammar, vocabulary, pronunciation, spelling, etc. of Spanish and other foreign languages. Two hundred teachers will be asked how much learning time (instruction time plus homework) is needed to attain previously specified levels of competence in the languages concerned. For Spanish, all Spanish language teachers will be questioned. Schools' arguments for and against offering Spanish language courses will be listed on the basis of a telephone survey of 300 management staff of schools that do not offer Spanish and the 20 management staff of the 18 schools that do offer Spanish. The findings will serve as a basis for the construction of a questionnaire that will be administered to school heads. Pupils' motivations for taking or not taking Spanish will be elicited through a questionnaire to two groups of 100 pupils who (a) are taking Spanish or (b) are not taking Spanish or who have dropped it.

12910 The relationship between the phonological strategies employed in the early stages of reading and spelling.
GBR 1993
Research Date(s): 1987-1992
Huxford, L.
Sup: Terrell, C.; Bradley, L.
Inst: Cheltenham & Gloucester College of Higher Education, Faculty of Education and Health, The Park, Cheltenham GL50 2QF, United Kingdom; Oxford University, Department of Experimental Psychology, Wellington Square, Oxford OX1 2JD, United Kingdom.
phonology; child development; reading; spelling; learning strategy
phonologie; développement de l'enfant; lecture; orthographe; stratégie d'apprentissage
PROJECT DESCRIPTION

This research comprises longitudinal and intervention studies aimed at examining young children's developing phonological strategies in reading and spelling. It contributes to the growing body of data on the connections between reading and spelling. Fifty-six children between three and a half and five and a half years, who had satisfied a minimum requirement of phonological ability were included in the sample for the longitudinal study. A combination of standardised tests and tasks specifically devised and refined for the study have been used. A battery of eight tests were constructed to compare reading and spelling, controlling for alphabet and use of visual and contextual strategies. In order to assess children's phonological development against other factors of experience and ability, measures of age, reading spelling, alphabetical knowledge, intelligence, memory and hearing were taken.

The pattern of results from forty-three of the children supports the claim that children appear to acquire a phonological strategy in spelling before an equivalent strategy.

Forty-two children in two experimental groups and a control group are taking part in the intervention study. The effects on reading acquisition of two different approaches to writing are being measured.

Publ: Huxford, L.; Terrell, C. & Bradley, L. The relationship between the phonological strategies in reading and spelling. In: *Journal of Research in Reading*, Vol 14, No 2/1991, pp. 99-105.

12911 The relationship between the use and understanding of narrative structures and general language development.
GBR 1993
Research Date(s): 1989-1992
Goodwyn, A.
Inst: Reading University, Faculty of Education & Community Studies, Bulmershe Court, Woodlands Avenue, Earley, Reading RG6 1HY, United Kingdom.
language sciences; narration; reading; writing; language development; language teaching
sciences du langage; narration; lecture; écriture; développement du langage; enseignement des langues
PROJECT DESCRIPTION

The project will investigate the links between children's general language competence and their ability to comprehend and use narrative structures. This will involve the study of children's reading and writing habits and the pedagogical implications for the way narratives are used in schools. The project will be chiefly of interest to teachers of language in primary schools and to teachers of English in secondary schools. In the early stages research will involve small scale studies of narrative work with children at primary and secondary level. These early studies will be used as the basis for more detailed work with a small number of children, mainly at secondary level.

It is hoped that the study will produce results that can help teachers and children to improve both their work with language and on narrative. Particular areas would include: the suitability of stories for specific age groups or development groups; the appropriateness of certain forms of narrative structure for particular age groups; the identification of staging points in pupils' development; the development of pedagogical strategies for improving children's engagement with narratives; identifying relationships between children's reading level and writing level; children's comprehension of visual narratives and their relationships to other forms.

12912 Schulversuch 'Englisch ab der Grundstufe 1'. (School experiment: English from primary level I.)
AUT 1993
Research Date(s): 1992-1994
Huber, Maria; Schmarl, Christoph; Katzlinger, Bernadette.
Inst: Uebungsvolksschule der Paedagogischen Akademie des Bundes, Pastorstrasse 5-7, A-6010 Innsbruck.
Paedagogische Akademie des Bundes in Tirol, Pastorstrasse 5-7, A-6010 Innsbruck; Paedagogisches Institut des Landes Tirol, Haymongasse, A-6020 Innsbruck

Fin: Bundesministerium fuer Unterricht und Kunst; Paedagogisches Institut des Landes Tirol.
first foreign language; experimentation; primary education; English language; foreign languages; language teaching
première langue étrangère; expérimentation; enseignement primaire; langue anglaise; langues étrangères; enseignement des langues
PROJECT DESCRIPTION

Die Projektziele sind Fragestellungen, zugrundeliegende Hypothesen, Folgerungen und Massnahmen. Wie kann 'Teaching English Across the Curriculum' als integrativer Bestandteil des Gesamtunterrichts auf der Grundstufe 1 eingebaut werden? Es soll keine zusaetzliche Unterrichtsstunde, sondern eine Integration in den Gesamtunterricht im Ausmass von einer Wochenstunde vorgesehen werden. Wie koennen die Lehrplaninhalte unter Beruecksichtigung der entwicklungspsychologischen und psycholinguistischen Gegebenheiten auf der Grundstufe 1 in fremdsprachliche Kurzsequenzen umgesetzt werden, sodass sie zu einer sprachlichen Vertiefung fuehren? Moeglichkeiten und Grenzen eines integrativen Englischunterrichts auf der Grundstufe 1 (und folglich auch auf der Grundstufe 2). Es wird von der Hypothese, basierend auf neuester Spracherwerbstheorie, ausgegangen (Beruecksichtigung der Forschungsergebnisse u.a. von Bruner und Vygotsky), dass der Spracherwerb ein komplexer Prozess ist, der im fruehen Grundschulalter begonnen werden soll (z.B. auch Betonung der Wichtigkeit des imitativen Lernens).

Erst im laufenden Schuljahr werden Untersuchungen durchgefuehrt, da der Schulversuch erst ab diesem Schuljahr angelaufen ist. Die Erhebungstechniken sind Befragungen, Frageboegen und Tests. Es werden insgesamt 90 VolksschuelerInnen der Grundstufe 1 einbezogen, und zwar aus vollgegliederten Volksschulen und aus weniggegliederten Volksschulen mit Abteilungsunterricht. Drei Schulen sind vollgegliedert: Uebungsvolksschule der Paedagogischen Akademie Innsbruck: 22 SchuelerInnen - 1. Klasse; Volksschule Reichenau/Innsbruck I: 23 SchuelerInnen - 1. Klasse; Volksschule St. Margarethen/Buch: 15 SchuelerInnen - 1. Klasse. Weniggegliederte Volksschulen mit Abteilungsunterricht sind: Volksschule Pertisau am Achensee: 21 SchuelerInnen, davon acht SchuelerInnen in der ersten Schulstufe und 13 SchuelerInnen in der zweiten Schulstufe, Volksschule Gattererberg/Gemeinde Kaltenbach (Zillertal): neun SchuelerInnen, davon drei in der ersten Schulstufe und sechs in der zweiten Schulstufe.

Es werden Befragungen, Beobachtungen und Tests zum Spracherwerb durchgefuehrt. Das Projekt wird einer handlungsorientierten Evaluation unterzogen.

12913 Scottish Standard Grade Beginners Latin Course: design of a course book.
GBR 1993
Research Date(s): 1988-1993
Williams, W.
Inst: Jordanhill College of Education, Division of Language and Literature, Southbrae Drive, Glasgow G13 1PP, United Kingdom.
Latin; teaching aid; textbook
latin; moyen d'enseignement; manuel d'enseignement
PROJECT DESCRIPTION

The aim of this project is to design a beginners Latin course book based on the elements of the Scottish Standard Grade.

12914 Second Language Acquisition (SLA): avoidance behaviour in Norwegian learners of English.
NOR 1994
Research Date(s): 1992-1994
Hasselgreen, Angela Maria.
Inst: Universitetet i Bergen, Engelsk Institutt (University of Bergen, Department of English), Sydnesplass 9, 5007 Bergen, Norway.
Fin: NAVF/RSF.
language teaching; first foreign language; English language; linguistics
enseignement des langues; première langue étrangère; langue anglaise; linguistique
PROJECT DESCRIPTION

Avoidance is linguistic behaviour involving the use of strategies which enable the second language learner to avoid certain words and structures, replacing them by less problematic or more familiar ones while the communicative goal is preserved.

The project has three main aims: (1) to establish areas of underproduction and overproduction in the interlanguage of adolescent Norwegian learners of English, which indicate the occurrence of avoidance behaviour; (2) to analyse this avoidance in terms of (a) strategies used, e.g. overgeneralisation, paraphrase, transfer, (b) influences, e.g. interlingual, intralingual, developmental, and (c) motivation for avoidance; (3) to demonstrate the effect of avoidance on the interlanguage and to relate this to current practice in English language teaching in schools in Norway.

The theoretical background to the project is based on recent SLA theory in the fields of communication strategies, lexical simplifications, developmental sequences, and cross-lingual influence.

12915 The significance of boundary negotiation between teachers and children from 'non-school-oriented backgrounds' in early school reading lessons.
GBR 1993
Research Date(s): 1985-1992
Gregory, E.
Sup: Spencer, M.
Inst: London University, Goldsmiths' College, Faculty of Education, Lewisham Way, New Cross, London SE14 6NW, United Kingdom; London University, Institute of Education, Department of English and Media Studies, 20 Bedford Way, London W21H OAL, United Kingdom.
reading; beginning learning; teacher-pupil relation; parent-school relation; social environment; attitude towards school; parental attitude; achievement
lecture; enseignement initial; relation maître-élève; relation parents-école; milieu social; attitude envers l'école; attitude des parents; rendement
PROJECT DESCRIPTION

The study originates in in-service work with teachers aiming to foster links with the families of children experiencing difficulty in learning to read in school. It aims to investigate the reasons behind the very different early reading progress of children from 'non-school-oriented backgrounds'. The sample studied are a group of reception-aged children of mixed social, cultural and linguistic background, their parents or caregivers and their teachers during the children's first eighteen months in school. Ethnographic and ethnomethodological approaches are being used.

Analyses so far point to a differential tuition which is taking place during individual 'shared reading' lessons and examine the form this takes.

Publ: Gregory, E. Do English eat octopus?: teacher and child negotiate reading in the multilingual classroom. In: *English in Education*, Vol 23, No 3, pp. 13-20, Autumn 1989.

12916 Social networks and ethnic identity in an urban nursery: a sociolinguistic analysis of preferred language use.
GBR 1993
Research Date(s): 1987-1992
Thompson, L.
Sup: Byram, M.
Inst: Durham University, School of Education, Leazes Road, Durham DH1 1TA, United Kingdom.
bilingualism; ethnic group; linguistics; nursery school
bilinguisme; groupe ethnique; linguistique; école maternelle
PROJECT DESCRIPTION

The aim of the research is to describe the preferred language use of a group of 12 Panjabi-English speaking children during their first term in nursery education where they constitute a linguistic minority. Data were gathered using audio-tape recorders. Three hours of naturally occurring discourse data were collected from each informant. These were complemented by observations of "thick" (Geertz, 1975) contextual data. The analysis describes the linguistic behaviour of these bilingual children in terms of Hymes' (1974) taxonomy of communicative competence: when they chose to speak; with whom; the preferred language (Panjabi or English) of each interaction; the contribution to the discourse as initiator, sustainer or terminator of the interaction.

Initial insights and observations from the analyses suggest that preferred language use functions as an act of ethnolinguistic identity (Le Page and Tabouret-Keller, 1985) that consolidates in-group membership of social networks. Social networks (Milroy, 1980) analysis offers a non-ethnocentric research method for observing language use.

12917 Sociocultural aspects of teaching English to Arabic speaking students.
GBR 1993
Research Date(s): 1989-1993
Hassan, F.
Sup: Byram, M.
Inst: Durham University, School of Education, Leazes Road, Durham DT1 1TA, United Kingdom; University of Qatar, Doha, PO Box 2713, Qatar.
language teaching; English language; foreign languages; international understanding; Arab countries; Qatar; student; university; attitude
enseignement des langues; langue anglaise; langues étrangères; compréhension internationale; pays arabes; Qatar; étudiant; université; attitude
PROJECT DESCRIPTION

In foreign language learning the learner's affective variables seem to be playing a crucial role. For example, the learner's own attitude towards learning the target language can be influenced by his/her attitudes towards the native speakers of this language and their culture. There is accumulating evidence that prejudice or active dislike diminishes motivation and interferes with learning.

The attitudes of the Arab students in the Gulf towards the English language people and culture have never been investigated before. In doing so, the present research aims to find out: (a) if these students come into the English language class with already acquired perceptions of the target language, people and culture and what these perceptions are; (b) what the students' attitudes towards the English people and culture are and whether these tend to be stereotypical; (c) if there is an association between these perceptions and attitudes and if the association is significant; and (d) investigate the relationship between the students' attitudes and perceptions on the one hand, and the learners' achievement in the target language on the other.

The study sample consists of 60 male and 120 female students starting their first year in Qatar University. The research tools are: self-report writing, questionnaires, interviews, semantic differential tests and results of final achievement examinations kept in the university records.

12918 The special oral language needs of low attaining pupils in mathematics.
GBR 1993
Research Date(s): 1985-1991
Jones, K.
Sup: Haylock, D.
Inst: University of East Anglia, School of Education, Norwich NR4 7TJ, United Kingdom; Cheltenham and Gloucester College of Higher Education, Faculty of Education and Health, The Park, Cheltenham GL50 2QF, United Kingdom.
verbal communication; underachievement; verbal learning; language; learning difficulty; mathematics; oral expression
communication verbale; rendement déficient; apprentissage verbal; langage; difficulté de l'apprentissage; mathématiques; expression orale
PROJECT DESCRIPTION

The research sets out to develop a theoretical framework to help teachers to understand the relationship between various kinds of verbal activity and learning in mathematics, thereby allowing them to determine, more accurately, the special oral language needs of pupils who experience learning difficulties in this area of the curriculum. This is achieved by examining ways in which researchers have analysed and described models of talk which predominate in mathematics classrooms; critically analysing research which claims that other models of talk facilitate learning in mathematics; enquiring, via a generative analysis of pupils' (N=40) natural language strategies, into the range of verbal activity which appears to promote the breadth of learning intended within recently stated aims of mathematics education. The study also evaluates (via technical action research) the effectiveness of such a framework in allowing teachers, on a principled basis, to plan activities specifically designed to develop children's oral language capabilities in mathematics and, subsequently, to assess the relative effectiveness of those activities from the point of view of their contribution to the growth of competence in mathematical language performance.

The particular focus of the research is the oral language needs of 8- to 10-year old low attaining pupils in numerical problem solving. Whilst supporting the notion that certain forms of discussion might facilitate learning in mathematics, the researcher argues that this is frequently tied to just one aspect of that process, notably the clarification of concepts. Recently stated aims of mathematics education (e.g. National Curriculum Council, 1989) demand a much greater range of learning, each facet of which might, arguably, have its own specialised language requirements. The research enquires into the kinds of verbal activity which appear to promote the full range of learning intended throughout the breadth of the mathematics curriculum.

Publ: Jones, K. & Charlton, T. The special oral language needs of low attaining children in mathematics. In: *Links*, Vol 12, No 2/1988, pp. 22-28.

12919 Spelling: teachers' perceptions, attitudes and expectations.
GBR 1993
Research Date(s): 1989-1992
Greig, S.
Sup: Brumfit, C.
Inst: Southampton University, Faculty of Educational Studies, Highfield, Southampton SO9 5NH, United Kingdom.
spelling; teacher behaviour; learning difficulty; teaching method
orthographe; comportement de l'enseignant; difficulté de l'apprentissage; méthode pédagogique
PROJECT DESCRIPTION

This research investigates persistent difficulty with spelling and teachers' perceptions of this. The researcher's hypothesis is that teachers misunderstand the spelling system and how it is learned and used by pupils, and that if the important features of the system could be explained to teachers with clear and easily followed advice on teaching, spelling, the correction of poor spelling and the marking of written work, their practice would improve and, with it their attitudes to their pupils and to the spelling skill. Higher expectations would follow and would spread to pupils with benefits all round.

The method will be to investigate these questions by interview and/or questionnaire with teachers in schools, student teachers and teacher trainers and perhaps try to introduce them to the practices mentioned above and observe the outcome of that.

12920 Sperimentazione di seconda lingua straniera nelle scuole medie di I grado. (An experiment with teaching a second foreign language in lower secondary schools.)
ITA 1994
Research Date(s): 1990
Verini, Antonio; et al.
Inst: Istituto Regionale Ricerca Sperimentazione Aggiornamento Educativi d'Abruzzo - IRRSAE (Regional Institute for Educational Research, Innovation, and Teacher Training - Abruzzo), Via Aldo Moro 30, 67100 L'Aquila, Italy.
Ministero della Pubblica Istruzione (Ministry of Education), Viale Trastevere 76, 00100 Roma, Italy
language teaching; foreign languages; second foreign language; lower secondary; further education of teachers
enseignement des langues; langues étrangères; deuxième langue étrangère; secondaire premier cycle; perfectionnement des enseignants
PROJECT DESCRIPTION
Background: The project was prompted by increasing demands to introduce a second foreign language in lower secondary schools and the need for information and training in this area.
Aims: To demonstrate how to carry out experimental projects, with particular reference to innovation in the areas of information, training and teaching methods; to raise awareness of the scientific and experimental logic of transferability, testing, publication and generalizability of the experiment; to make IRRSAE a point of reference, comparison and consultation for schools interested in teaching a second foreign language.
Methods: A survey was conducted with the help of a questionnaire developed in collaboration with the six schools in Abruzzo that experimented with the introduction of a second foreign language in the school year 1989/1990. The following IRRSAE divisions collaborated in the research: Research and Experimentation, Progetto Speciale Lingua Straniera (Special Foreign Languages Project), and Documentation. The project fell into four phases: (1) questionnaire survey; (2) data processing; (3) meetings for exchanges among schools; (4) publication of results.
Sample: All schools in the Abruzzo region that experimented with the introduction of a second foreign language in the 1989/1990 school year.
Results: The final results were used to inform schools in the region and to assist in the planning of an updating course for the teachers participating in the experiment.

12921 Sperimentazione di seconda lingua straniera nelle scuole medie di I grado. (An experiment with teaching a second foreign language in lower secondary schools.)
ITA 1994
Research Date(s): 1990
Verini, Antonio; et al.
Inst: Istituto Regionale Ricerca Sperimentazione Aggiornamento Educativi d'Abruzzo - IRRSAE (Regional Institute for Educational Research, Innovation, and Teacher Training - Abruzzo), Via Aldo Moro 30, 67100 L'Aquila, Italy.
Ministero della Pubblica Istruzione (Ministry of Education), Viale Trastevere 76, 00100 Roma, Italy
language teaching; foreign languages; second foreign language; lower secondary; further education of teachers
enseignement des langues; langues étrangères; deuxième langue étrangère; secondaire premier cycle; perfectionnement des enseignants
PROJECT DESCRIPTION
Background: The project was prompted by increasing demands to introduce a second foreign language in lower secondary schools and by the need for information and training in this area.
Aims: To demonstrate how to carry out experimental projects, with particular reference to innovation in the areas of information, training and teaching methods; to raise awareness of the transferability and generalizability of the experiment; to make IRRSAE a point of reference, comparison and consultation for schools interested in teaching a second foreign language.
Methods: A survey was conducted with the help of a questionnaire developed in collaboration with the six schools in Abruzzo that experimented with the introduction of a second foreign language in the school year 1989/1990. The following IRRSAE divisions collaborated in the research: Research and Experimentation, Progetto Speciale Lingua Straniera (Special Foreign Languages Project), and Documentation. The project fell into four phases: (1) questionnaire survey; (2) data processing; (3) meetings for exchanges among schools; (4) publication of results.
Sample: All schools in the Abruzzo region that experimented with the introduction of a second foreign language in the 1989/1990 school year.
Results: The final results were used to inform schools in the region and to assist in the planning of an updating course for the teachers participating in the experiment.

12922 Spoken English (Scottish Standard Grade) for pupils with language difficulties.
GBR 1993
Research Date(s): 1991
McGonigal, J.; Lawson, J.; Lovett, R.
Inst: Jordanhill College of Education, Division of Language and Literature, Southbrae Drive, Glasgow G13 1PP, United Kingdom.
Fin: Scottish Office Education Department.
language; speech defect; learning difficulty; teaching aid
langage; trouble de la parole; difficulté de l'apprentissage; moyen d'enseignement
PROJECT DESCRIPTION
This project will develop and test in field trials teaching and assessment materials for pupils with specific language difficulties who are to follow a proposed Scottish Standard Grade Course in Spoken English.

12923 Spoken language and new technology (SLANT).
GBR 1993
Research Date(s): 1990-1992
Fisher, E.; Elliott, J.; Mercer, N.
Inst: University of East Anglia, School of Education, Norwich NR4 7TJ, United Kingdom; Open University, Walton Hall, Milton Keynes MK7 6AA, United Kingdom.
Fin: Economic and Social Research Council.
verbal communication; didactic use of computer; information technology; language development; spoken language; new technologies
communication verbale; usage didactique de l'ordinateur; technologie de l'information; développement du langage; langage parlé; nouvelles technologies
PROJECT DESCRIPTION
This research aims to contribute to knowledge about the development of children's exploratory and argumentative talk through computer-based classroom activities. It is also intended to describe activities which serve this function and the range and quality of exploratory and argumentative talk and to provide information about the role of the teacher in mediating and supporting such activities. It is hoped that this work will make a contribution to educational policy and practice by generating practical suggestions for how computers may be used effectively to stimulate exploratory talk and reasoned arguments in the classroom, with particular reference to the curriculum goals of English and spoken language development across a range of curriculum areas. This research will adopt a social interactionist approach and will draw on Vygotskian perspectives.

12924 Sprachliche und kommunikative Bedingungen bilingualer Sozialisation russischer Kinder in Berlin. (Linguistic and communicative aspects of the bilingual socialization of Russian children in Berlin.)
DEU 1993
Research Date(s): 1991-1993
Leschber, C.; Dittmar, J.
Sup: Dittmar, V.; Reiter, N.
Inst: Freie Universitaet Berlin, Zentrale Universitaetsverwaltung Berlin-Forschung, Altensteinstrasse 48, D-1000 Berlin 33.
Russian language; German language; bilingualism; socialization; Berlin; child
langue russe; langue allemande; bilinguisme; socialisation; Berlin; enfant
PROJECT DESCRIPTION
Inhalt: In Auswertung der empirischen Daten sollen Aspekte des Spracherwerbs, der funktionalen Verwendung der Sprache und des Erzaehlerwerbs in der Zweitsprache beschrieben werden. Es sollen praxisrelevante Materialien fuer einen "Ratgeber zweisprachige Erziehung" erstellt werden.
Geographischer Raum: Berlin.
Untersuchter Zeitraum: 1991-1992.
Vorgehensweise: Untersuchungsdesign: Evaluationsstudie.
Datengewinnung: Standardisiertes Interview (Stichprobe: 2; Kinder - Alter 5-7 Jahre- sowjetischer Juden in Berlin). Teilnehmende Beobachtung (Stichprobe: 10X2; Kinder -Alter 5-7 Jahre- sowjetischer Juden in Berlin). Beobachtung (Stichprobe: 4X2; Kinder -Alter 5-7 Jahre- sowjetischer Juden in Berlin. Stichprobe: 3X3; Kinder -Alter 5-7 Jahre- sowjetischer Juden in Berlin). Primaererhebung: Feldarbeit von Mitarbeitern des Projektes durchgefuehrt.

12925 Standardisation of the LARR short-form test.
GBR 1993
Research Date(s): 1992-1993
Smith, P.
Sup: Whetton, C.
Inst: National Foundation for Educational Research, The Mere, Upton Park, Slough SL1 2DQ, United Kingdom.
Fin: NFER-Nelson; Wandsworth Local Education Authority.
reading; test; maturity; school entry age; test construction
lecture; test; maturité; âge d'entrée à l'école; construction de tests
PROJECT DESCRIPTION

The project has standardised a new version of the Canadian 'Linguistic Awareness in Reading Readiness (LARR) test' for use with British children at the start of formal schooling. The new version, 'The LARR short-form', will be published by NFER-Nelson.

The standardisation involved administering the test to nearly 500 nursery children and over 2,300 children in reception classes in schools throughout England and Wales during October 1992. The test was found to be too demanding for the nursery children but appropriate for the reception sample. Norms were created for the age range from 4 years 0 months to 5 years 3 months. The results, together with administration instructions and guidance on interpreting the test scores, were written for the test manual.

In parallel with the national standardisation, the test was also given to all reception age pupils in Wandsworth schools as part of the Local Education Authorities baseline assessment. The National Foundation for Educational Research (NFER) then carried out a local standardisation for Wandsworth.

12926 Les stéréotypes culturels dans l'apprentissage des langues. (Cultural stereotypes in language learning.)
BUL   1994
Research Date(s): 1990-1993
Simeonova, J.; Tzaneva, R.
Sup: Stefanova, P.
Inst: National Centre for Educational and Science Studies, Tzarigradsko Chossé 125, 1113 Sofia, Bulgaria; Commission de la République Française pour l'éducation, la science et la culture (UNESCO).
Fin: UNESCO; Ministry of Education and Science (Bulgaria).
language teaching; stereotype; culture; cross-national research
enseignement des langues; stéréotype; culture; recherche transnationale
PROJECT DESCRIPTION

Pupils in the 5th, 8th and 10th year studying German and English are investigated. The experiment compares cultural stereotypes among pupils in France, Bulgaria and Switzerland. Coordinated by France, the study is carried out in four stages, between September 1990 and February 1993.

Samples: Nine hundred pupils have been tested (300 pupils per year group).

Methods: The methods used for the experiment have been worked out by prior agreement between the three countries; they include association tests and essay writing.

The results are analysed qualitatively with the help of an accepted matrix. Comparisons will be drawn between the three countries that participate in the study. As a result of the study, it will be possible to establish differences and similarities in cultural stereotyping among Bulgarian, French and Swiss pupils, differentiated by level.

12927 Strategien, die zur Verwendung von Nonstandardmustern fuehren. (Strategies leading to the use of non-standard language patterns.)
DEU   1993
Research Date(s): 1991-1993
Will, A.; Lautenbach, A.; Koett, A.; Welz, C.; Mayer, M.
Sup: Henn-Memmesheimer, B.
Inst: Universitaet Mannheim, Fak. fuer Sprach- und Literaturwissenschaft, Seminar fuer Deutsche Philologie -Germanistische Linguistik-, Schloss Ehrenhof West, D-6800 Mannheim.
German language; dialect; spoken language; didactics; model
langue allemande; dialecte; langage parlé; didactique; modèle
PROJECT DESCRIPTION

Inhalt: Ziele: Beschreibung der Entwicklung der deutschen Dialekte: (Eliminierung bestimmter lautlicher und syntaktischer Merkmale, Verwendung anderer Merkmale als gruppensprachliche Identifikationssymbole); Bewertung nichtstandardsprachlicher Sprechweisen in einem kulturell polyzentrischen Land; Entwicklung von Modellen zur Beschreibung des Einflusses vom Nonstandard auf den Standard. Praxisbezug: Neuer Zugang zur Sprachkritik, zu Sprachnormierungsversuchen; Deutschdidaktik fuer Muttersprachler und Nichtmuttersprachler.

Geographischer Raum: Bundesrepublik Deutschland.

Vorgehensweise: Praxeologischer Ansatz (Pierre Bourdieu), der sich grundlegend von normtheoretischen Ansaetzen unterscheidet, Strategien und objektive Strukturen analysiert. Untersuchungsdesign: Methodenforschung; Fallstudie; qualitative Forschung.

Datengewinnung: Teilnehmende Beobachtung (Telefongespraeche; Auswahlverfahren: Zufall. Sprache in Institutionen; Auswahlverfahren: bewusst. Schueler; Auswahlverfahren: bewusst). Beobachtung (Sprache in Institutionen; Auswahlverfahren: bewusst. Schueler; Auswahlverfahren: bewusst). Sekundaeranalyse bereits vorhandener maschinenlesbarer Datensaetze; Datenerstellung auf der Basis von bereits vorliegenden Materialien wie Texten, Akten, Statistiken.

Auswertung: Interpretierende Fallanalysen.

Publ: Henn-Memmesheimer, B. Syntax auf der Basis von Standard und Nonstandard: Das Beispiel deiktischer Adverbsphrasen und die pragmatische Begruendung. In: Holtus, G.; Radtke, E. (Hrsg.). *Sprach-*

licher Substandard. Bd. II. Tuebingen 1989 (Konzepte der Sprach- und Literaturwissenschaft), S. 169-228.
Henn-Memmesheimer, B. Alltaegliche Dialektverwendung und das Spiel mit dialektalen Formen. In: *Jahrbuch fuer Internationale Germanistik XXI*, 1989, S. 38-58.
Henn-Memmesheimer, B. Nonstandard in "optimalen" Texten? In: Antos, G.; Augst, G. (Hrsg.). *Ausdrucksfaehigkeit und Textoptimierung.* Frankfurt/Bern/Las Vegas 1989, S. 38-51.
Henn-Memmesheimer, B. Normtheorie oder Praxeologie zur Erklaerung sprachlicher Varianz. In: Settekorn, W. (Hrsg.). *Sprachnorm und Sprachnormierung. Deskription, Praxis, Theorie.* Frankfurt 1990 (Pro lingua, Bd. 8), S. 153-164.

12928 Student supply and the expansion of Arabic studies in higher education.
GBR   1993
Research Date(s): 1989-1991
Guernina, Z.
Sup: Byram, M.; Lawless, R.
Inst: Durham University, School of Education, Leazes Road, Durham DH1 1TA, United Kingdom.
Fin: Economic and Social Research Council.
Arabic; higher education; choice of studies; motivation for studies; attitude
langue arabe; enseignement supérieur; choix des études; motivation pour les études; attitude
PROJECT DESCRIPTION

In 1986 the Parker Report ('Speaking for the future': a review of the requirements of diplomacy and commerce for Asian and African languages and area studies) University Grants Committee) drew attention to the need to increase available expertise in Oriental and African languages and associated area studies in order to meet the growing demands of industry, commerce and diplomacy. Yet the university system which has been the traditional source of this expertise has experienced difficulties and a gradual reduction of resources, especially in Arabic. Furthermore the Parker Report did not examine the implications of its recommendations with respect to the school system. Where are the increased numbers of students to come from? How are school pupils to be encouraged to take up Arabic Studies? How is the decline in applications for Arabic Studies over the last decade to be reversed?

The purpose of this project is therefore to examine the factors which influence school pupils' perceptions of Arabic Studies and their potential interest and to gather the information required to initiate change in Arabic Studies in higher education. The project includes a nation-wide survey of sixth formers, of undergraduates currently studying Arabic and of admissions tutors in Arabic departments. It also includes an analysis of sixth form curricula (Religious Education, Geography, History) which might have an influence on perceptions and attitudes towards the Arabic-speaking world. The project will thus provide data on the relationship between sixth form and university studies with respect to recruitment for Arabic Studies. It will also make recommendations as to possible changes which might promote an expansion of Arabic Studies in the future.

12929 A study of narrative and argument writing in three Beverley comprehensive schools.
GBR   1993
Research Date(s): 1987-1991
Andrews, R.
Sup: Protherough, R.
Inst: Hull University, School of Education, Cottingham Road, Hull HU6 7RX, United Kingdom.
written expression; writing; argumentation; composition
expression écrite; écriture; argumentation; composition littéraire
PROJECT DESCRIPTION

The aim of the study is to explore the connection between narrative and argument, with particular reference to the teaching of the 'essay' form. The hypothesis is that narrative structures underpin those of the argument and that a clarification of this relationship might well provide a basis for helping students of all ages to write essays more readily. The study will limit itself to writing in all the primary and secondary schools in one town: Beverley in East Yorkshire, where there are three large comprehensives. Methods used will include interviews, questionnaires and most importantly, analysis of scripts, as well as observation of teaching methods. The study will draw on the various disciplines of literature, psychology of child development, linguistics and education.

Publ: Andrews, R. *Narrative and argument.* Buckingham: Open University Press, 1989.

12930 A study of narrative and argument writing in three Beverley comprehensive schools.
GBR   1993
Research Date(s): 1987-1991
Andrews, R.
Sup: Protherough, R.
Inst: Hull University, School of Education, Cottingham Road, Hull HU5 2RX, United Kingdom.

written expression; argumentation; composition; writing
expression écrite; argumentation; composition littéraire; écriture
PROJECT DESCRIPTION

The aim of the study is to explore the connection between narrative and argument, with particular reference to the teaching of the 'essay' form. The hypothesis is that narrative structures underpin those of the argument and that a clarification of this relationship might well provide a basis for helping students of all ages to write essays more readily. The study will limit itself to writing in all the primary and secondary schools in one town: Beverley in East Yorkshire, where there are three large comprehensives. Methods used will include interviews, questionnaires and, most importantly, analysis of scripts, as well as observation of teaching methods. The study will draw on the various disciplines of literature, psychology of child development, linguistics and education.

Publ: Andrews, R. Narrative and argument. Buckingham: Open University Press, 1989.

12931 A study of the role and practice of the teacher of reading at National Curriculum key stage 1.
GBR 1993
Research Date(s): 1991-1994
Fisher, R.
Sup: Taylor, G.; Clibbens, J.
Inst: Plymouth University, Rolle Faculty of Education, Douglas Avenue, Exmouth EX8 2AT, United Kingdom.
reading; teaching method; primary education; teacher behaviour
lecture; méthode pédagogique; enseignement primaire; comportement de l'enseignant
PROJECT DESCRIPTION

The study aims to examine the decisions made by teachers of early reading as demonstrated by their responses to children. A pilot study examined the role of the teacher in four Reception/Year One classes and considered the relationship between what the teacher did to teach reading and what the children learned. This has led to a further study using video of infant teachers in the classroom. Teachers will be videoed in their interactions with children in relation to literacy. They will then be interviewed about their thinking at the time of interaction. This aims to develop an understanding of the cognitive processes involved in the spontaneous decisions related to the teaching of reading made by teachers in the classroom.

Publ: Fisher, R. Early Literacy and the Teacher. London: Hodder and Stoughton, 1992.

12932 Taalonderwijs Nederlands in meertalige onderwijssituaties. (Dutch language education in multilingual classrooms.)
NLD 1994
Research Date(s): 1992-1993
Gelderen, A. van.
Inst: Stichting Centrum voor Onderwijsonderzoek (SCO) (Centre for Educational Research), Grote Bickersstraat 72, 1013 KS Amsterdam, Netherlands.
Universiteit van Amsterdam (University of Amsterdam), P.O. Box 19268, 1000 GG Amsterdam, Netherlands
Fin: SVO het Instituut voor Onderzoek van het Onderwijs.
language teaching; Dutch language; primary education; immigrant; language skill; teaching language; textbook
enseignement des langues; langue néerlandaise; enseignement primaire; immigrant; aptitude linguistique; langue d'enseignement; manuel d'enseignement
PROJECT DESCRIPTION

Background: Increasing numbers of primary school pupils come from non-Dutch language backgrounds. This leads to problems in Dutch language instruction as well as instruction in factual subjects. For its project on multilingualism the SLO National Institute for Curriculum Development has asked for a study of the relationships between features of the language of instruction and the subject matter which is taught through that language. Such information would enable more informed choices to be made in the development of curriculum products.

Aim: To explore and define the gap between, on the one hand, the required receptive and productive language skills of pupils in instruction in factual subjects and, on the other, the objectives of language instruction.

Design: Data on the curricula used by primary schools will be obtained from the National Assessment of Educational Achievement study, which is conducted by the Cito National Institute for Educational Measurement. The seven most frequently used methods for history, geography and science in primary years 5 to 8 (ages 8-12) will be analysed regarding the vocabulary, grammatical structures and language functions they use. The two most commonly used Dutch language methods, two complementary reading comprehension methods and four popular methods for teaching Dutch as a second language used with ages 7-12 will be examined as to the relevant skills they teach. Data on the features of oral instruction will be gathered through tape-recordings of teachers in 60 primary schools: 20 with a low proportion of non-Dutch pupils, 20 with a moderate proportion of non-Dutch pupils and 20 with a high proportion of non-Dutch pupils.

12933 Teachers' perceptions of oracy and information technology project.
GBR 1993
Research Date(s): 1990-
Beverton, S.
Inst: New College Durham, Department of Education and Administration, Neville's Cross Centre, Darlington Road, Nevilles's Cross, Durham DH1 4SY, United Kingdom.
oral expression; information technology; common core curriculum; teacher behaviour
expression orale; technologie de l'information; tronc commun; comportement de l'enseignant
PROJECT DESCRIPTION

The aim of the research is to investigate teachers' perceptions of oracy and information technology (IT) in a number of local authorities. These two subject areas, although separate in themselves, were chosen because of two common factors: (1) both are 'new' in the sense of having acquired new status in the National Curriculum with little historical background as subjects per se; (2) the National Curriculum demands that all teachers address these themes.

The research aims to survey a wide range of perceptions to reflect the current position of oracy and IT in the curriculum in primary and secondary schools. A questionnaire has been designed and developed to be used in a pilot survey. Appropriate modifications will then be made before the questionnaire is distributed to schools in a number of local authorities. It is envisaged that a variety of perceptions in both areas will be revealed and that these might have implications for classroom practice. After analysis, the questionnaires will be followed up by more in-depth studies of particular teachers and schools, with the intention of revealing the nature of the relationship between perceptions and practice. The results will determine the current status of oracy and IT in terms of perceptions and practice. The dissemination of these results will inform and assist teachers' practice and also enable authorities to plan Inservice Education and Training of Teachers (INSET) courses appropriately.

12934 Teaching and testing Japanese and similar languages in schools.
GBR 1993
Research Date(s): 1991-1994
Neary, I.
Sup: Okazaki, T.
Inst: Essex University, Contemporary Japan Centre, Wivenhoe Park, Colchester CO4 3SQ, United Kingdom.
Fin: Department of Education and Science.
language teaching; Arabic; Chinese language; Japanese language; foreign languages; Oriental languages; teaching aid; teaching method
enseignement des langues; langue arabe; langue chinoise; langue japonaise; langues étrangères; langues orientales; moyen d'enseignement; méthode pédagogique
PROJECT DESCRIPTION

The aim of this research project is to undertake an investigation into methodologies appropriate for the teaching of 'hard languages', such as Japanese, Chinese and Arabic in schools in the UK. In the course of the research the Research Fellow will develop teaching materials, schemes of work and assessment techniques which will be used initially in the teaching of Japanese to groups of children from three schools in Colchester, namely the Sixth Form College, the Royal Grammar School and the County High School for Girls. The first stage of the research will consist of a survey of the courses already being used to teach Japanese, Chinese and Arabic in this country. New teaching materials for experimental Japanese classes will be devised according to the results of the preliminary survey, then they will be modified in response to the experiences within the classroom throughout the three year project.

12935 Teaching English in a multilingual classroom.
GBR 1993
Research Date(s): 1990-1993
Drever, M.
Sup: Richards, B.
Inst: Reading University, Department of Arts and Humanities in Education, Bulmershe Court, Woodlands Avenue, Earley, Reading RG6 1HY, United Kingdom.
multilingualism; English language; language teaching; teaching method; ethnic minority
multilinguisme; langue anglaise; enseignement des langues; méthode pédagogique; minorité ethnique
PROJECT DESCRIPTION

The research has two aims: (1) to carry out a survey of strategies used by class teachers in the teaching of the English language in a multilingual context, i.e. in a class composed of pupils from more than one linguistic home background, including English mother tongue, and (2) to suggest strategies which might benefit all pupils in attaining a competent level of English performance in order to cope with more sophisticated and subject specific language, semantically and structurally, as they move up the curriculum. The research will use classroom observation, interviews and questionnaires.

12936   Teaching foreign languages at primary level.
GBR   1993
Research Date(s): 1991-1993
Ahrens, P.; Dickinson, N.
Inst: Heriot-Watt University, Moray House Institute of Education, Scottish Centre for Education Overseas, Holyrood Road, Edinburgh EH8 8AQ, United Kingdom.
language teaching; foreign languages; teaching method; primary education; cross-national research
enseignement des langues; langues étrangères; méthode pédagogique; enseignement primaire; recherche transnationale
PROJECT DESCRIPTION
   This piece of research looks at English language teaching in Europe and at the teaching of foreign languages in Scotland at the primary level. It relates to the increased interest in and demand for foreign language learning at primary level. Data has been collected and is still in the process of being collected on the problems teachers of a foreign language at primary level face. From existing data a checklist of common difficulties has been designed. This has been trialled and refined. Copies of this checklist have been sent to contacts in various countries. The data from the checklists will be analysed. Visits have been made within Edinburgh to selected primary schools where a foreign language is being taught. A report will be written on the different models of teaching a foreign language at primary level in use and teachers will be asked to fill in a checklist about their specific problems. The analysis of the data should show the main areas that cause problems to teachers at this level. Further research will set out to identify and collect teachers' coping strategies.

12937   Teaching non-fiction in the secondary school.
GBR   1993
Research Date(s): 1990-1995
Middleton, R.
Sup: Richards, B.; Lockwood, M.
Inst: Reading University, Department of Arts and Humanities in Education, Bulmershe Court, Woodlands Avenue, Earley, Reading RG6 1HY, United Kingdom.
reading; secondary education; aims of education
lecture; enseignement secondaire; finalité de l'éducation
PROJECT DESCRIPTION
   This research will examine the question of why teachers use non-fiction. Is it for language development, reading and writing cross-fertilisation, or for helping pupils refine their knowledge of the world and themselves? What kinds of linguistic, intellectual and cultural demands do non-fiction texts make on pupils? Is non-fiction literature taught in the same way as fiction literature or does the case for using non-fiction rest partly on its difference from fiction? What kinds of teaching strategies are appropriate and is a specialist critical vocabulary necessary?
   Research methodology will include case studies/surveys of practice, lesson observation and interviewing of teachers and pupils and a survey of pupils' voluntary non-fiction reading. This will involve the co-operation of Berkshire's education library service and possible contributions of linguistic and literary theory.

12938   The teaching of English in Scottish secondary schools 1940-1990: a study of change and development.
GBR   1993
Research Date(s): 1986-1991
Northcroft, D.
Sup: Lloyd, J.; Peacock, C.
Inst: Northern College of Education, Aberdeen Campus, Hilton Place, Aberdeen AB9 1FA, United Kingdom.
English language; history of education; Scotland; curriculum research; language teaching
langue anglaise; histoire de l'éducation; Ecosse; recherche sur les programmes d'études; enseignement des langues
PROJECT DESCRIPTION
   This study follows the progress of a key school subject towards its slow, partial fulfilment of the 1940s aspiration for equality of educational opportunity within the post-war reconstruction of Scottish society. Its focus is on 'English' at both the level of public pronouncement and of day-to-day classroom experience - and on the intricate interactions between these two worlds. Therefore, in addition to analysis of official documentation and school materials, the personal testimony of twenty long-serving participants, practitioners as well as policy makers, is woven into the account. Two factors have helped to elucidate this history: (1) the centralised, uniform nature of the Scottish system; (2) the post-war inheritance of two articulated but competing models of English - (a) the initially dominant Scottish Education Department supported academic syllabus built on knowledge inculcation, national examination and institutional division into 'junior' and 'senior' secondary curricula as against (b) the progressivist alternative of the 'the full and harmonious development of the individual' to be sought in 'omnibus' schools.

Superficially, 1940-1990 may be viewed as the gradual, orderly movement towards Standard Grade English as a consensual acceptance of the progressivist version, a process facilitated by an opening up of decision making into a partnership between SOED (Scottish Office Education Department) and the profession through such bodies as the Consultative Council and a devolved examination board. A detailed investigation of actual practice shows a more ambiguous curricular reality in which pragmatic management and deeply embedded assumptions sustain a contradictory adherence to didactic methodology and rigid assessment procedure. The Scottish experience suggests that curricular change is a necessarily problematic process whose promotion depends upon a sensitive appreciation of its complex rhythms. In Scotland this means using the traditional authority of the centre to establish clear frameworks and appropriate assessment targets within and against which the individual teacher is freed to work out a matching pedagogy and to take control of in-course evaluations. Above all, the educational innovator must be alert to the power of historical inheritance in the construction of classroom practice.

12939   Teaching of reading in primary schools.
GBR   1993
Research Date(s): 1991-1992
Blatchford, P.; Ireson, J.; Francis, H.
Inst: London University, Institute of Education, Department of Educational Psychology and Special Educational Needs, 20 Bedford Way, London WC1H OAL, United Kingdom.
Fin: Esmee Fairbairn Charitable Trust.
reading; primary education; teaching method
lecture; enseignement primaire; méthode pédagogique
PROJECT DESCRIPTION
   Much of the present debate on the teaching of reading is based on false information about what is happening in schools and what approaches are effective. The basic aim of this project, therefore, is to describe current practice in a sample of schools in three local education authorities. There will be 60 schools in all, 20 in each authority, and they will be chosen to include children from a range of backgrounds, and schools with a range of approaches to reading. A range of research techniques will be used, including interviews with teachers and heads and classroom observations. One main aim is to develop a methodology capable of providing a reliable and comprehensive account of different components involved in the teaching of reading. This will provide the basis for a follow-up study which would seek to evaluate different approaches.

12940   TIGER project (Translating Industrial German) - Computer-based training in German technical translation.
GBR   1993
Research Date(s): 1990-1992
Corness, P.; Deepwell, F.
Inst: Coventry University, Priory Street, Coventry CV1 5FB, United Kingdom.
Fin: Training, Enterprise and Education Directorate.
machine translation; didactic use of computer; language teaching; German language; language for special purposes
traduction automatique; usage didactique de l'ordinateur; enseignement des langues; langue allemande; langage de spécialité
PROJECT DESCRIPTION
   Computer-assisted training packages in German-English translation are being developed for application in industry. The packages are at beginner's, intermediate and advanced (degree) levels. Design is based on contrastive analysis of German and English, and the learning materials focus on problems of translation from German to English caused by interference from native-language structures. At the advanced level, there is an additional module for training in the use of a computer-assisted translation system ('Alpnet TSS').
   The translation training, which will make use of an appropriate combination of computer-based and printed course materials, will be applied on courses in technical translation at Coventry University and will be supplied to similar institutions and to industry. On-line German-English technical glossaries, which are being developed in cooperation with industrial firms, and which are to form a component of the training course, will also be available as self-standing products.

12941   Training en transfer van leesstrategieën: moedertaalonderwijs en vreemde-talenonderwijs. (Training and transfer of reading strategies: mother tongue instruction and foreign language instruction.)
NLD   1994
Research Date(s): 1993-1995
Oostdam, R.J.; Bimmel, P.
Sup: Glopper, K. de; Westhoff, G.J.
Inst: Stichting Centrum voor Onderwijsonderzoek (SCO) (Centre for Educational Research), Grote Bickersstraat 72, 1013 KS Amsterdam, Netherlands.
Universiteit van Amsterdam (University of Amsterdam), P.O. Box 19268, 1000 GG Amsterdam, Netherlands
Fin: SVO het Instituut voor Onderzoek van het Onderwijs.

reading; learning strategy; transfer of learning; mother tongue; foreign languages
lecture; stratégie d'apprentissage; transfert pédagogique; langue maternelle; langues étrangères
PROJECT DESCRIPTION

Background: Research evidence shows that children from all age groups have difficulty in recognizing and understanding the structure of texts. On the other hand, reading strategies in the mother tongue or in a foreign language can be taught and learned. Little is known about the transfer of acquired mother tongue reading strategies to foreign languages.

Aim: To determine how and how far mother tongue reading strategies can be transferred to other languages.

Design: The experiment comprises ten 90 minutes' training sessions. Subjects are four groups of eight pupils in the second or third year of secondary school. Training will take place outside school hours. Pretests and posttests of pupils' skills in reading texts at paragraph and whole text level in Dutch and English and of pupils' use of reading strategies and metacognition will also be conducted outside school hours. The experimental group will receive training; the control group will only participate in the testing.

12942 Training en transfer van woordstrategieën: moedertaalonderwijs en vreemde-talenonderwijs. (Training and transfer of vocabulary acquisition strategies: mother tongue instruction and foreign language instruction.)
NLD 1994
Research Date(s): 1993-1995
Daalen-Kapteijns, M. van.
Inst: Stichting Centrum voor Onderwijsonderzoek (SCO) (Centre for Educational Research), Grote Bickersstraat 72, 1013 KS Amsterdam, Netherlands.
Universiteit van Amsterdam (University of Amsterdam), P.O. Box 19268, 1000 GG Amsterdam, Netherlands
Fin: SVO het Instituut voor Onderzoek van het Onderwijs.
vocabulary; transfer of learning; mother tongue; foreign languages
vocabulaire; transfert pédagogique; langue maternelle; langues étrangères
PROJECT DESCRIPTION

Background: Vocabulary acquisition is an essential aspect of learning a language. Pupils may benefit from a range of strategies and metacognitive skills when learning new words. The ability to deduce word meanings from context and to analyse word forms is related to the size of a pupil's vocabulary in Dutch and other languages. Research evidence suggests that vocabulary acquisition strategies and metacognitive skills can be improved through training. Little is known about the transfer of vocabulary acquisition in the mother tongue to other languages.

Aim: To determine how and how far vocabulary acquisition in the mother tongue can be transferred to other languages.

Design: The experiment involves ten training sessions of one and a half hours each. Subjects are 32 pupils in the final year of primary school or the first or second year of secondary school. The primary school pupils will receive training during school hours; the secondary school pupils will be trained outside school hours. The training programme comprises: clarifying, questioning, summarizing and predicting. In the primary school group, the pretests and posttests of pupils' mastery and application of strategies and metacognitive skills will be administered in class. In the other group testing will take place outside the classroom.

12943 Traitements de bas niveau et de haut niveau dans l'utilisation d'une langue étrangère.
FRA 1993
Research Date(s): 1987-
Gaonac'h, Daniel.
Inst: Université de Poitiers, UER Sciences humaines, CNRS URA/666, Laboratoire de psychologie du langage, 95 av. du Recteur Pineau, 86022 Poitiers Cedex, France.
foreign languages; learning; reading; cognitive process
langues étrangères; acquisition de connaissances; lecture; processus cognitif
PROJECT DESCRIPTION

Objectifs: De nombreux travaux ont montré que les facteurs textuels et contextuels qui facilitent normalement la lecture d'un texte (structure familière, énoncés thématiques, illustrations...) ont des effets beaucoup moins marqués en cas d'utilisation d'une langue étrangère, y compris pour des sujets de niveau avancé dans cette langue. On s'intéresse plus particulièrement au traitement de marques organisatrices de haut niveau (articulateurs textuels). L'efficacité de telles marques requiert en effet d'assurer de manière simultanée des traitements lexicaux (reconnaissance de ces marques) et des traitements d'ordre textuel (activation de représentations portant sur l'organisation du texte). L'accroissement de la charge cognitive liée à l'utilisation d'une langue étrangère conduit de manière générale à accorder une priorité aux traitements de bas niveaux (micro structuraux). (1) On cherche à montrer les conséquences de cette situation sur l'activation des représentations de haut niveau; (2) on recherche des techniques de

présentation de textes qui favorisent et exercent l'activation de telles représentations.

Publ: Gaonac'h, Daniel. Psychologie du langage et didactique des langues. In: Etudes de linguistique appliquée, 1988, 72, pp. 83-93.
Gaonac'h, Daniel. Apport de concepts vygotskyens à l'analyse de productions en langue étrangère. In: Enfance, 1989, 1-2, pp. 91-100.
Gaonac'h, Daniel. Psychologie cognitive et éducation: implications dans l'enseignement des langues étrangères. Université de Dijon, thèse d'Etat (sous la dir. de Michel Fayol), janv. 1987.
Gaonac'h, Daniel. Lire dans une langue étrangère: approche cognitive. In: Revue française de pédagogie, 1990, n° 93, pp. 75-100.

12944 Verbal discourse events and teaching styles of English language teachers in Kenyan secondary schools.
GBR 1993
Research Date(s): 1991-1994
Gathumbi, A.
Sup: Richards, B.; Goodwyn, A.
Inst: Reading University, Faculty of Education and Community Studies, Department of Arts and Humanities, Bulmershe Court, Woodlands Avenue, Earley, Reading RG6 1HY, United Kingdom.
Fin: International Development Research Centre.
language teaching; English language; teaching style; Kenya
enseignement des langues; langue anglaise; style pédagogique; Kenya
PROJECT DESCRIPTION

Kenyan English language teachers undergo pre-service and in-service training in the country's teacher training institutions, but there has not been any follow-up to find out what exactly goes on in the classrooms and the methods teachers use; therefore the effectiveness of the teacher training programmes is not known. Important as it is, classroom interaction research has been overlooked in Kenya. This is ironical bearing in mind that in recent years, claims have been made that standards of English are falling. It is important therefore that much more should be known about English language teaching in Kenya since it is the official language and the medium of instruction.

The aims of this research are to: (1) reveal the practised teaching styles and the cognitive level of questions used by a sample of English language teachers in Kenya through the study of teacher-pupil interaction; (2) compare the teaching styles of in-service and non in-service English language teachers; and (3) make recommendations for teacher training programmes, curriculum development, inspectorate and educational planning sectors. The target population for this study will comprise 12 English language teachers from public and private schools and also Form 3 students. The sample will be selected from a rural and an urban district. There will be a pilot study before the main study. This will enable the researcher to become familiar with data collection procedures and to make adjustments where necessary. The methods to be used are: unstructured observation notes, video and audio recording of teacher-pupil discourse, and a teachers' questionnaire.

12945 Verbal interaction in mathematics lessons in four secondary schools in Anglophone Cameroon.
GBR 1993
Research Date(s): 1990-1993
Breet, F.
Sup: Byram, M.; Thompson, L.
Inst: Durham University, School of Education, Leazes Road, Durham DH1 1TA, United Kingdom.
Fin: Overseas Development Administration.
English language; mathematics; teaching language; verbal interaction; Cameroon
langue anglaise; mathématiques; langue d'enseignement; interaction verbale; Cameroun
PROJECT DESCRIPTION

The study examines the role of classroom language in the learning of mathematics through English as a second language. Teachers of English and mathematics will be trained to work together and change classroom practices. Consequences for children's learning will be monitored.

12946 Vers une pédagogie du langage figuré: compréhension des métaphores et production d'images chez l'adolescent.
CHE 1994
Research Date(s): 1988-1991
Bonnet, Clairelise; Gardes-Tamine, Joëlle.
Inst: Centre vaudois de recherches pédagogiques (CVRP), rue Marterey 56, 1005 Lausanne, Suisse.
mother tongue; poetry; comprehension; image
langue maternelle; poésie; compréhension; image
PROJECT DESCRIPTION

Le sens figuré est un fait de langue propre à tous les registres, poétique ou scientifique, et à tous les niveaux, du plus populaire au plus élaboré. Il est pourtant rarement l'objet d'un enseignement spécifique. En psycholinguistique, il n'a jamais été reconnu comme une dimension de l'acquisition du langage.

Comment les enfants accèdent-ils au sens figuré? En ont-ils, quand ils abordent à l'adolescence biologie ou physique, textes littéraires ou textes journalistiques, une maîtrise suffisante?

Le présent rapport, issu d'une collaboration entre le Centre vaudois de recherches pédagogiques et l'Université de Provence, tente d'apprécier la capacité des adolescents à comprendre les métaphores de la poésie et à créer des images. Il devrait apporter aux enseignants quelques éléments susceptibles de nourrir leur pratique pédagogique.

Publ: Bonnet, Clairelise & Gardes-Tamine, Joëlle. *Vers une pédagogie du langage figuré: compréhension des métaphores et production d'images chez l'adolescent"*. Lausanne: CVRP, 1992, 24 pages (CVRP 92.6).

12947 Vocabulary rate in course materials for English as a second or foreign language.
GBR 1993
Research Date(s): 1989-
Scholfield, P.
Inst: University College of North Wales, School of English and Linguistics, College Road, Bangor, Gwynedd LL57 2DG, United Kingdom.
language teaching; vocabulary; English language; foreign languages; textbook
enseignement des langues; vocabulaire; langue anglaise; langues étrangères; manuel d'enseignement
PROJECT DESCRIPTION
The research consists of analysing the rate of introduction of new vocabulary items, lesson by lesson, in a sample of well-known course books for English as a second/foreign language. Using concepts of time series analysis, light is thrown on the patterns of rises and falls to be found. The results are interpreted in the light of learner needs and what the teacher can do when the rate in course materials is inappropriate.

Publ: Scholfield, P.J. Vocabulary rate in course books: living with an unstable lexical economy. In: *Proceedings of 5th International Linguistics Symposium*, Aristotle University, Thessaloniki, 1991.

12948 Vowel sounds in reading.
GBR 1993
Research Date(s): 1990-1992
Goswami, U.
Inst: Cambridge University, Department of Experimental Psychology, Downing Site, Downing Street, Cambridge CB2 3EB, United Kingdom.
Fin: Spencer Foundation.
phonetics; reading; word recognition
phonétique; lecture; reconnaissance des mots
PROJECT DESCRIPTION
The aim of this research is to discover whether a child's awareness of the linguistic units of the onset (initial consonants) and the rime (vowel and final consonants) affects learning about vowels in reading. The first phase of the project involved recognition of common vowels in spoken words when the vowel was either part of the rime (tap, LEG, pack), or constituted the entire rime (tree, flee, CLUE). Five and 6-year old children found it more difficult to recognise shared vowels within rimes, suggesting that it is hard to distinguish the vowel sound independently of the context provided by the final consonant/s. The second phase tested whether this recognition problem is reflected in learning to recognise vowel sounds in reading. The prediction was that shared vowels would be learned where rimes were common between words (e.g. beak-peak), but not where the vowel was shared but the rime differs (e.g. beak-heap). This prediction was found to hold true at all ages (5, 6 and 7-year-olds).

12949 Word recognition problems among Arabic-speaking learners of English.
GBR 1993
Research Date(s): 1987-1993
Meara, P.
Inst: University College of Swansea, Centre for Applied Language Studies, Singleton Park, Swansea SA2 8PP, United Kingdom.
English language; foreign languages; language teaching; Arabic; word recognition
langue anglaise; langues étrangères; enseignement des langues; langue arabe; reconnaissance des mots
PROJECT DESCRIPTION
The background of the research lies in the problems Arabic learners of English seem to have in distinguishing English words with similar consonant structure, e.g. broad/bread; curl/cereal. After several initial attempts to design test procedures which would replicate this type of error, a computer-based word-recognition test was developed in which firstly vowels and then secondly consonants were systematically deleted from word stimuli presented to the subjects. The test records response times and error rates for each subject.

Two initial experiments of this type indicated that there was a significant difference between the responses of, on the one hand, Arabic-speaking subjects and on the other, native speakers and speakers of European languages written in Roman script. This difference was maintained in the final experiment where Arabic-speaking subjects were compared with Jap-anese, Thai and European language speakers as well as native speakers of English, a total of 131 subjects.

In spite of the overall significance of the results of the Arabic-speaking group, there were considerable individual differences between subjects; this has prompted the final phase of the study in which it is hoped to design a simple diagnostic test to predict those subjects who are most likely to have word-handling difficulties of the type analysed here. Such a test would have considerable classroom value.

Publ: Ryan, A. & Meara, P. The case of the invisible vowels: Arabic speakers reading English words. In: *Reading in a Foreign Language*, Vol 7, No 2/1991, pp. 531-540.

12950 Writers' workshop leaders project.
GBR 1993
Research Date(s): 1992
Anderson, L.
Sup: Preston, P.; Hicks, D.
Inst: Nottingham University, Department of Adult Education, 14-22 Shakespeare Street, Nottingham NG1 4FJ, United Kingdom; East Midlands Arts, Mountfields House, Forest Road, Loughborough LE11 3HU, United Kingdom.
Fin: Arts Council of Great Britain; Gulbenkian Foundation; East Midlands Arts; Nottinghamshire County Council.
writing; composition; adult education; community education; trainer; training of trainers
écriture; composition littéraire; éducation des adultes; éducation sociale; formateur; formation des formateurs
PROJECT DESCRIPTION
The aim of the project is to investigate the training needs of leaders of writers' workshops in a variety of adult education and community contexts. In the first phase the project worker will visit groups and interview both leaders and group members, (this phase will be carried out in those geographical areas common to East Midlands Arts and the Extra-Mural Region of the University of Nottingham). Out of this investigation will arise an interim report and the preparation of a training programme. The second phase will involve the coordination, monitoring and evaluation of a training programme. The final phase will comprise the compilation of a training resource pack and the preparation of a final report.

12951 Writing exchange across the Atlantic: a study of secondary school students' writing, exchanged with peers in London and the Bay Area, California.
GBR 1993
Research Date(s): 1986-1992
McLeod, A.; Freedman, S.
Inst: London University, Institute of Education, Department of English and Media Studies, 20 Bedford Way, London WC1H 0AL, United Kingdom; University of California, School of Education, Centre for the Study of Writing, Berkeley, CA 94720, USA.
Fin: US National Writing Project.
writing; school correspondence; composition; cross-national research; USA; secondary education
écriture; correspondance scolaire; composition littéraire; recherche transnationale; Etats-Unis; enseignement secondaire
PROJECT DESCRIPTION
Following a survey of the teaching of writing in the USA and the UK, an exchange of secondary school student writing (age 12-15) was arranged between five classes in California and five classes in the London area in 1986/1987, the hypothesis being that an actual peer audience for student writing over a period of a whole school year would reveal changes in the quality, interest and commitment of the student writers. The 10 classroom teachers evaluated the outcome in the first instance. The principal researchers collaborated on a report 'Comparing the teaching and learning of writing in the United States and the United Kingdom: audience exchange', which has now been presented to the Office for Educational Research and Instruction, Washington DC.

12952 The York-Sheffield Russian Project.
GBR 1993
Research Date(s): 1988-1992
Pullin, R.; Rix, D.
Inst: Sheffield University, Division of Education, 388 Glossop Road, Sheffield S10 2TN, United Kingdom; York University, Language Teaching Centre, Heslington, York YO1 5DD, United Kingdom.
Fin: Nuffield Foundation.
Russian language; in-service training; language teaching; teaching aid; further education of teachers
langue russe; formation en cours d'emploi; enseignement des langues; moyen d'enseignement; perfectionnement des enseignants
PROJECT DESCRIPTION
The project aims to: (1) support a network of teacher-based teaching materials groups which will produce new materials to meet the changing needs of Russian at GCSE level and for 11+ beginners' courses; (2) to promote models of teacher development through exchange of ideas and experience, participation in the production of collaborative materials and a

series of national and regional inservice courses and (3) to monitor, evaluate and publicise new developments and initiatives for the consolidation and extension of Russian teaching in British secondary schools.

Publ: *Times Educational Supplement*, Modern Languages Extra, November 25th 1988.

12953 Zur bedingungsabhaengigen Akzentuierung spracherwerblicher Determinanten bei der Entwicklung der Schreibfaehigkeit im Fremdsprachenunterricht (bei Erwachsenen). (Aspects of foreign language instruction for adults.)
DEU 1993
Research Date(s): 1990-1994
Gebauer, C.
Sup: Lieber, G.
Inst: Universitaet Leipzig, Fachsprachenzentrum, LS Sprachdidaktik, Augustusplatz 9, O-7010 Leipzig.
foreign languages; language teaching; adult education; spelling; learning strategy; didactics; writing
langues étrangères; enseignement des langues; éducation des adultes; orthographe; stratégie d'apprentissage; didactique; écriture
PROJECT DESCRIPTION
Inhalt: Zur Domaenenspezifik fremdsprachlicher Schreibfaehigkeit; linguistische, didaktische, psycholingiustische Determinanten von Lernstrategien im Vergleich; Vorschlaege zur Praesentation von Sprachmaterial unter dem Aspekt der Erstellung lernbezogener Datenbanken.
Vorgehensweise: Hermeneutischer Zugang zu Theoremen und Phaenomenen; polymethodologische Ansaetze einschliesslich der Triangolierung.

12954 Zur Wirkung der Handlungsorientierung bei der zielgerichteten Informationsentnahme in fremdsprachigen Texten. (On the effect of action orientation in extracting specific information from foreign language texts.)
DEU 1993
Research Date(s): 1988-1992
Kallenbach, K.
Sup: Lieber, G.
Inst: Universitaet Leipzig, Fachsprachenzentrum, LS Sprachdidaktik, Augustusplatz 9, O-7010 Leipzig.
reading; adult education; foreign languages; language teaching; learning; comprehension
lecture; éducation des adultes; langues étrangères; enseignement des langues; acquisition de connaissances; compréhension
PROJECT DESCRIPTION
Inhalt: Ueber die Domaenenspezifik des fremdsprachigen Lesens; zum Einfluss uebergeordneter Taetigkeiten auf den Prozess der Informationsentnahme; Vorschlaege fuer Handlungsorientierungen im gesteuerten Fremdsprachenerwerb erwachsener Lerner.
Vorgehensweise: Analyse entsprechender theoretischer Erkenntnisse; empirische Forschung beruht auf polymethodologischem Ansatz (Hermeneutik, Triangolierung).

Publ: Das Lesen als Prozess des Problemloesens. In: *Theorie und Praxis des Fremdsprachenerwerbs*, 4, 1989.

12955 Zweisprachige Familien. (Bilingual families.)
AUT 1993
Research Date(s): 1993-1995
Larcher, Dietmar; Gubert, Renzo; Berghold, Joe; Modena, Emilio; Ottomeyer, Klaus.
Inst: Institut fuer Weiterbildung, Sterneckstrasse 15, A-9010 Klagenfurt. Alpha & Beta, Talfergasse 1A, I-39100 Bozen; Universitaet fuer Bildungswissenschaften, Universitaetsstrasse 65-67, A-9020 Klagenfurt
Fin: Assessorate fuer Unterricht und Kultur in deutscher und italienischer Sprache in Bozen.
bilingualism; intercultural education; family; family environment
bilinguisme; éducation interculturelle; famille; milieu familial
PROJECT DESCRIPTION
Erforschung der Familiendynamik und der Sprachkultur zweisprachiger Familien in Suedtirol; Untersuchung der Erziehungsstrategien, die sich zur Entwicklung zweisprachiger und bikultureller Persoenlichkeiten erfolgreich erwiesen haben.
Durch Beobachtung und Analyse von Gruppengespraechen werden Ergebnisse gewonnen.
Die Methode besteht in gleichschwebender Aufmerksamkeit und Tiefenhermeneutik.

14 PHILOSOPHY AND RELIGION – PHILOSOPHIE ET RELIGION – PHILOSOPHIE UND RELIGION

12956 A comparison of the main concepts in the philosophy of education used in Britain and China.
GBR 1993
Research Date(s): 1989-1992
Bin, L.
Sup: Morgan, W.; Lawson, K.

Inst: Nottingham University, Department of Adult Education, Centre for Research into the Education of Adults, 14-22 Shakespeare Street, Nottingham NG1 4FJ, United Kingdom.
philosophy of education; comparative education; China; United Kingdom
philosophie de l'éducation; éducation comparée; Chine; Royaume-Uni
PROJECT DESCRIPTION

The main concepts used in the philosophy of education in Britain and China will be defined, analysed and compared, with a view to establishing both universals and those that are bound within a cultural context.

12957 The curriculum as culture and ideology.
GBR 1993
Research Date(s): 1988-
Burt, G.
Inst: Open University, Institute of Educational Technology, Walton Hall, Milton Keynes MK7 6AA, United Kingdom.
philosophy of education; ideology; culture; curriculum
philosophie de l'éducation; idéologie; culture; programme d'études
PROJECT DESCRIPTION

According to the common-sense view, education is about indiviudal people 'learning' ideas and skills. It is an apolitical activity, which meets the needs of individuals and of society as a whole. The aim of the Curriculum as Culture and Ideology project is to challenge this view. Education is not about people learning ideas and skills; it is about cultural ideas and practices taking possession of people. Education then is simply one of a number of arenas in which different cultures and ideologies with differential powers seek to promote themselves, and hence come into conflict. Cultures seek to promote themselves in every sphere of society. Hence cultures demand education about every social sphere. The aim of the research project is to study educationale provision with a view to identifying the cultural and ideological promotions involved.

Currently under study are the areas of educational technology, educational computing, mathematics and technology education, management education and community education. Teaching materials in these areas involve cultural and ideological promotion relating to issues of gender, class, ethnicity, individualism, technicism and militarism. Proposals for how education might be redesigned to take account of this critique are also being developed.

Publ: Burt, G.J. Social forces and school computing. In: *British Journal of Educational Technology*, Vol 20, No 2/1989, pp. 140-141.
Burt, G.J. Computers in schools as culture and ideology. In: *International Council for Distance Education Bulletin*, Vol 20, 1989, pp. 19-24.
Burt, G.J. Beyond educational technology: the new discipline of cultural and ideological technology. In: *Research in Distance Education*, Vol 1, No 3/1989, pp. 9-11.
Burt, G.J. The message behind the medium. In: *Information Technology and Learning*, December 1989, pp. 55-56.
Burt, G.J. Culture and ideology in the training literature. In: *Educational Technology and Training International*, Vol 28, No 3/1991, pp. 229-237.
A full list of publications is available from the researcher.

12958 The educational influence of the Methodist church in the second half of the 19th century (1850-1902).
GBR 1993
Research Date(s): 1991-1995
Smith, J.
Sup: McClelland, V.
Inst: Hull University, School of Education, Cottingham Road, Hull HU6 7RX, United Kingdom.
religion; history of education; denominational school; state school; non-state school; educational legislation; church
religion; histoire de l'éducation; école confessionnelle; école de l'Etat; école non-étatique; législation scolaire; église
PROJECT DESCRIPTION

This is a survey of the influence of the Methodist church on education in the second half of the 19th century, with particular reference to the work of Dr J.H. Rigg. The influence of Methodist thought and pressure groups on the framing of legislation relating to education between 1870 and 1902 will be examined.

12959 Le forme dell'utopia - una ricerca comparata sulle filosofie di vita giovanile. (Forms of Utopia: a comparative investigation on the philosophies of life held by youth.)
ITA 1993
Research Date(s): 1990-1991
Fabretti, P.
Sup: Battisti, F.M.
Inst: Associazione Internazionale per gli Studi sulle Utopie (International Association for Studies on Utopia), Viale dei Quattro Venti 166, 00152 Roma, Italy.
Fin: Ministero della Pubblica Istruzione, Ufficio Studi e Programmazione.
philosophy; idealism; youth attitude; narcissism
philosophie; idéalisme; attitude de la jeunesse; narcissisme
PROJECT DESCRIPTION

Aims: To clarify the usage and the meanings of the term "Utopia" as they have developed historically; to clarify the social function and the concept of Utopia in the sociological and philosophical reflections of the 1990s; to analyse the forms of Utopia in the youth culture of the 1980s and early 1990s, with particular reference to: youth identity, the relationship between time and life, place of Utopia, future, Utopia and hope.

Methods: A research assistant was employed who took part in daily school life and who gave about 700 upper secondary school students a choice of five composition assignments in class. More than 1000 pages containing opinions and personal reflections were transcribed on computer. The present research is based on these compositions.

Results: The research shows the emergence of a narcissistic youth identity which gives more importance to the repressive aspects of narcissism than those of self-esteem, that is: to isolate oneself physically and psychologically and to look for exclusive relationships. The compositions reflect an anxiety related to the passing of time and the close relationship between time and life. For youth, daily life appears to constitute a moral oppression and a tangible limit to the realization of goals. The location of pupils' Utopia ranges from such classic examples as an "imaginary island" to a place outside the city, in contact with nature. Only a minority chose the city with certain characteristics. The concept of youth without a future is generally associated with drugs. As far as the relationship with Utopia is concerned, there appears to be a strong wish to realize the choices in life. However, the communal perspective is missing among youth, who argue that they do not have a major role to play in today's society. This notwithstanding, all recognize themselves to be unique and to have a future ahead of them.

12960   Freedom and indoctrination in education.
GBR   1993
Research Date(s): 1988-1992
Straughan, R.; Spiecker, B.
Inst: Reading University, Faculty of Education and Community Studies, Department of Arts and Humanities in Education, Bulmershe Court, Woodlands Avenue, Earley, Reading RG1 1HY, United Kingdom; Free University, Van der Boechorststraat 1, 1081 BT Amsterdam, Netherlands.
freedom; academic freedom; indoctrination; educational policy
liberté; franchises universitaires; endoctrinement; politique de l'éducation
PROJECT DESCRIPTION

Freedom and indoctrination are topics that have long dominated pedagogical and educational discourse in Europe and North America. On the national level, there have always been considerable differences in the way these topics are discussed. Now that the inner borders of the European countries are disappearing, supra-national structures will gradually change pedagogical ideologies and the demands on national, educational systems and institutions. As a result, freedom and indoctrination will become even more topical subjects for debate. The book, published as a result of the research, contains contributions from European and North American educationists.
Publ: Straughan, R.R. & Spiecker, B. (eds.). *Freedom and indoctrination in education: international perspectives.* London: Cassell, 1991.

12961   History of the Roman Catholic involvement in education in England and Wales since 1935.
GBR   1993
Research Date(s): 1989-1992
McClelland, V.
Inst: Hull University, School of Education, Cottingham Road, Hull HU6 7RX, United Kingdom.
Fin: The National Catholic Fund.
Catholicism; educational policy; history of education
catholicisme; politique de l'éducation; histoire de l'éducation
PROJECT DESCRIPTION

The project re-evaluates the origins of the dual system in education since 1944 and locates educational policy in the Roman Catholic church in England and Wales within the general ecclesiastical development of the period since 1935. The work will estimate the effect of the Second Vatican Council upon educational development and will examine the social upheaval within the Catholic community since 1965. It will also provide indications of the future of the current partnership between church and state in educational provision.
Publ: McClelland, V. Gravissimum Educationis. In: Hastings, A. (ed.). *Modern catholicism: Vatican II and after*, pp. 172-174. London: S.P.C.K., 1991.
McClelland, V. The effect of the Council on catholicism: Great Britain and Ireland. In: Hastings, A. (ed.). *Modern Catholicism: Vatican II and after*, pp. 365-376. London: S.P.C.K., 1991.

12962   Investigation of the relationship between education, politics, language and religion in Wales.
GBR   1993
Research Date(s): 1990-1992
Thomas, J.
Inst: Nottingham University, Department of Adult Education, 14-22 Shakespeare Street, Nottingham NG1 4FJ, United Kingdom.
nationalism; Wales; Welsh language; religion; politics
nationalisme; Pays de Galles; langue galloise; religion; politique
PROJECT DESCRIPTION

This is an intellectual analysis of the relationships between language, religion, politics and nationalism in Wales. It seeks to show that that the alleged aims of nationalism are counterproductive to the best aims and interests of Wales. It shows the tension between nationalism and internationalism which characterises Welsh history.

12963   Islamic education in the understanding of present day Muslim educationists.
GBR   1993
Research Date(s): 1988-1992
Ramzi, A.
Sup: Minney, R.; Day, D.
Inst: Durham University, School of Education, Leazes Road, Durham DH1 1TA, United Kingdom.
Islam; educational theory; religious education
islamisme; théorie de l'éducation; éducation religieuse
PROJECT DESCRIPTION

This study is an attempt to introduce a whole view of the understanding of present day Muslim educationists in respect of Islamic education within its Islamic context and Muslim conceptions. The problem the study explores and tries to underline is the kind of crisis that is hypothesized to exist in the understanding of Muslim educationists. The crisis is supposed to take the form of uncertainty and/or obscurity in the experience of Muslim educationists and thinkers that affects their understanding. The definition of this gap in conception, its existence, the factors that affect it and its exploration are present in the study. A historical background is given of both Islamic and non-Islamic education in the experience of Muslim educationists. The investigation has been conducted to answer one of the six questions raised in exploring the areas of thought in which the crisis appears more acute. The sample of respondents includes 100 Muslim educationists who were sent a questionnaire on four categories of concepts. Owing to its nature, the study suggests a certain set of strategies or broad lines of practicalities to help Muslim present day educationists bridge this gap in the light of what is changeable and unchangeable in Islamic thought.

12964   Manifeste Funktionen der von Max Weber analysierten "protestantischen Ethik" fuer die gegenwaertige Erziehung und Sozialisation. (Manifest functions of the "Protestant ethics" analysed by Max Weber for present-day education and socialization.)
DEU   1993
Research Date(s): 1990-1992
Looft, H.
Sup: Dieckmann, J.
Inst: Paedagogische Hochschule Kiel, Seminar fuer Soziologie, Olshausenstrasse 75, D-2300 Kiel.
ethics; capitalism; socialization; sciences of education
éthique; capitalisme; socialisation; sciences de l'éducation
PROJECT DESCRIPTION

Inhalt: Max Weber hat in seiner sehr verbreiteten Studie die Wechselwirkungen zwischen den Impulsen der puritanisch bestimmten Religion mit der von ihr geforderten reglementierten rational-asketischen Lebensfuehrung und dem modernen "Kapitalismus" untersucht. Ausgewaehlte Schulbuchliteratur wird mit den Mitteln der Dokumentenanalyse daraufhin untersucht, ob diese Ethik heute Spuren hinterlaesst.

Geographischer Raum: Schleswig-Holstein.

Untersuchter Zeitraum: Nachkriegszeit bis Gegenwart.

Vorgehensweise: Dokumentenanalyse, systemtheoretisch orientierte Interpretation. Untersuchungsdesign: qualitative Forschung.

Datengewinnung: Aktenanalyse (ausgewaehlte Schulbuchinhalte; Auswahlverfahren: bewusst). Inhaltsanalyse (ausgewaehlte Schulbuchinhalte; Auswahlverfahren: bewusst). Datenerstellung auf der Basis von bereits vorliegenden Materialien wie Texten, Akten, Statistiken.

12965   Mentale Modelle aus konstruktivistischer Perspektive. (Mental models from a constructive perspective.)
DEU   1993
Research Date(s): 1991-1992
Dinter, F.
Sup: Strittmatter, P.
Inst: Universitaet Saarbruecken, FB 06 Sozial- und Umweltwissenschaften, Fachrichtung Erziehungswissenschaft, Stadtwald Bau 8, D-6600 Saarbruecken.
epistemology; theory of science; sciences of education; model
épistémologie; théorie des sciences; sciences de l'éducation; modèle
PROJECT DESCRIPTION

Inhalt: Fortentwicklung eines theoretischen Ansatzes zur mentalen Modellbildung im Sinne einer konstruktivistischen Epistemologie; Erweiterung empirisch-analytischer Wissenschaftstheorie um eine erkenntnistheoretische Perspektive.

Vorgehensweise: empirisch-analytische Wissenschaftstheorie (speziell der Erziehungswissenschaft); Diskurs des (radikalen) Konstruktivismus.

12966 Parents' views on values in education.
GBR 1993
Research Date(s): 1992
Munn, P.; Allan, J.
Inst: Scottish Council for Research in Education, 15 St John Street, Edinburgh EH8 8JR, United Kingdom.
Fin: Gordon Cook Foundation.
value; parental attitude; parent-school relation
valeur; attitude des parents; relation parents-école
PROJECT DESCRIPTION
This project aims to: explore methods of eliciting parents' views about values; investigate how parents perceive values in education; and investigate parents' views on whether values should be explicitly transmitted by teachers and if so what these values should be.

12967 Philosophical inquiry in values education.
GBR 1993
Research Date(s): 1991-1993
McCall, C.; Ellis, S.; Grant, M.; Hughes, A.
Inst: Jordanhill College of Education, Division of Inservice Training, Southbrae Drive, Glasgow G13 1PP, United Kingdom.
Fin: Gordon Cook Foundation.
value; philosophy; moral education
valeur; philosophie; éducation morale
PROJECT DESCRIPTION
This project aims to disseminate the method of philosophical inquiry in values education and to use this in staff development in values education.

12968 Philosophie und Pädagogik bei Wilhelm Dilthey und Herman Nohl. (Les rapports entre philosophie et pédagogie chez Wilhelm Dilthey et Herman Nohl.)
CHE 1994
Research Date(s): 1988-1991
Thöny, Giosua.
Sup: Hager, Fritz-Peter.
Inst: Universität Zürich, Pädagogisches Institut, Rämistrasse 74, 8001 Zürich, Schweiz.
philosophy of education; history of philosophy; sciences of education
philosophie de l'éducation; histoire de la philosophie; sciences de l'éducation
PROJECT DESCRIPTION
Diese Dissertation versteht sich in forschungsmethodologischer Hinsicht als eine explizite Aufnahme der geisteswissenschaftlichen Forschungstradition, aber auch als eine aus der Auseinandersetzung mit ihr hervorgehende forschungskonzeptionelle Weiterentwicklung und methodologische Integration von Hermeneutik, Phänomenologie und Dialektik. Thematisch konzentriert sich dabei die Arbeit auf die Grundfragestellungen nach der Philosophie und Pädagogik sowie nach ihrem Begründungszusammenhang, die systematisch erforscht und mit jeweils spezifischen Fragestellungen herausgearbeitet werden; mit dem geisteswissenschaftlichen Forschungskonzept und den genannten Grundfragestellungen untersucht sie systematisch das historische Werk von Wilhelm Dilthey und Herman Nohl und stellt sich als eine historisch-systematische, komparative Problem-, Wirkungs- und Entwicklungsgeschichte dar.
Die Studie verfolgt hierbei folgende Ziele: Sie weist in ihrer historischen Ausrichtung die systematischen Zusammenhänge innerhalb der behandelten Werke zu den Autoren nach und zeigt deren je besondere Typik auf; sie untersucht weiter in begründungstheoretischer Hinsicht systematisch die Bedeutung der Philosophie für die Pädagogik im jeweiligen Werk, überprüft sodann komparativ mit spezifischen Fragestellungen sowie wirkungsgeschichtlich das Verhältnis von Dilthey zu Nohl und bestimmt sachlogisch die Entwicklung der beiden Autoren zueinander.
Das Hauptanliegen dieser Abhandlung besteht darin, in einer wissenschaftstheoretisch-forschungsmethodologisch reflektierten Weise eine historisch-systematisch orientierte Untersuchung zur Geistesgeschichte, insbesondere zur Geschichte der Pädagogik, vorzulegen, dann aber auch die Möglichkeit einer systematischen Philosophie der Erziehung aufzuzeigen, also insgesamt eine Philosophie der Pädagogik zu unternehmen; für dieses Wissenschaftsvorhaben will die vorliegende Studie eine paradigmatische Bedeutung einnehmen.
Die Studie ist - will man ihr eine real- oder sozial- und kulturgeschichtliche Forschungsrichtung gegenüberstellen - wesentlich durch eine geistes- oder ideengeschichtliche Orientierung gekennzeichnet, wobei sie sich in forschungsmethodologisch bestimmter Weise auf die ausgewählten Beispiele bezieht.
Publ: Thöny, Giosua. Der Erzieher oder die führende und bildende Kraft: Die Bedeutung des Erziehers in der Pädagogik von Nohl. In: *Pädagogische Rundschau*, 44. Jg., 2/1990, S. 181-192.
Thöny, Giosua. *Philosophie und Pädagogik bei Wilhelm Dilthey und Herman Nohl: eine geisteswissenschaftliche Studie als historisch-systematische, komparative Problem-, Wirkungs- und Entwicklungsgeschichte*. Bern; Stuttgart: Haupt, 1992, 613 S. (Studien zur Geschichte der Pädagogik und Philosophie der Erziehung, Band 14).

12969 Philosophy of the curriculum with particular reference to moral, religious, physical education and personal and social education.
GBR 1993
Research Date(s): 1973-
Meakin, D.
Inst: Liverpool University, Department of Education, PO Box 147, Liverpool L69 3BX, United Kingdom.
philosophy of education; moral education; religious education; physical education; curriculum
philosophie de l'éducation; éducation morale; éducation religieuse; éducation physique; programme d'études
PROJECT DESCRIPTION
This research has been within the area of the philosophy of the curriculum with particular reference to moral, religious, aesthetic and physical education. It has mainly been concerned with three questions: (i) how these kinds of education are to be characterised; (ii) how, if at all, they might be justified; (iii) whether any general criteria can be established for including subjects and activities in the school curriculum.
Publ: Meakin, D.C. On the justification of physical education. In: *Momentum*, Vol 8, No 3/1983, pp. 10-17.
Meakin, D.C. The moral status of competition: an issue of concern to physical educators. In: *Journal of Philosophy of Education*, Vol 20, No 1/1986, pp. 59-67.
Meakin, D.C. The justification of religious education reconsidered. In: *British Journal of Religious Education*, Vol 10, No 2/1988, pp. 92-96.
Meakin, D.C. Personal, social and moral education and religious education: the need for conceptual clarity. In: *British Journal of Religious Education*, Vol 11, No 1/1989, pp. 15-21.
Meakin, D.C. How physical education can contribute to personal and social education. In: *Physical Education Review*, Vol 13, No 2/1990, pp. 108-119.
A full list of publications is available from the researcher.

12970 Research on values education (ROVE).
GBR 1993
Research Date(s): 1991-1993
Francis, E.
Sup: Perfect, H.
Inst: Heriot-Watt University, Moray House Institute of Education, Holyrood Road, Edinburgh EH8 8AQ, United Kingdom.
Fin: Gordon Cook Foundation.
value; moral education
valeur; éducation morale
PROJECT DESCRIPTION
The project is concerned with the identification of approaches to teaching and learning which are beneficial to the development of values education for students over the age of 16 years. The aim of the project is to highlight the philosophical and methodological issues which should be addressed whenever the development of a values curriculum is contemplated. The focus will be the language currently used by educationalists in curriculum guidelines and educational settings which conveys a sense of values and approaches to teaching and learning which enable values education. The enquiry is being conducted with: teachers; lecturers in teacher education and other academic disciplines; curriculum developers; and educational adminstrators in central and local government. A network committed to the study of values in education will be created to enhance discussion of values education in Scotland for the 16+ age group. A number of unpublished working papers are available on request from the project team.

12971 Values education in Europe.
GBR 1993
Research Date(s): 1992-1993
Taylor, M.
Sup: Stoney, S.
Inst: National Foundation for Educational Research, The Mere, Upton Park, Slough SL1 2DQ, United Kingdom.
Fin: UNESCO; CIDREE; National Foundation for Educational Research.
value; moral education; international exchange; cross-national research
valeur; éducation morale; échange international; recherche transnationale
PROJECT DESCRIPTION
This project, the first collaborative exercise of the Consortium of Institutes of Development and Research in Education in Europe/Values Education in Europe Programme (CIDREE/VEEP), has been commissioned by United Nations Educational Scientific and Cultural Organisation (UNESCO). It has three parts: (1) to provide guidelines for Values Education in Europe (this work is being undertaken by Ian Barr, Chair of CIDREE/VEEP at the Scottish Consultative Council on the Curriculum, Dundee, Scotland); (2) to provide an annotated bibliography on Values Education in Europe from 1985 to 1992; (3) to provide an overview of the state of the art in Values Education in Europe. Parts (2) and (3) are being coordinated and undertaken by National Foundation for Educational Research (NFER).
The objectives of the project are to coordinate and facilitate the exchange of information and to build a foundation for undertaking further

collaborative projects on a European scale. Almost 30 countries are participating in the bibliography (up to 20 entries per country) and survey. Values Education has different emphases and scope in the education systems of Europe and the overview will seek to establish common ground, and review historical and ideological backgrounds, aims and objectives, aspects of provision, theoretical influences, current concerns, teacher training, teaching methods, curriculum development research and evaluation and aspects of informal education relating to Values Education.

There are likely to be three publications, corresponding to the three aspects of the project: guidelines, annotated bibliography and overview of state of the art. These will be launched by UNESCO at an international conference in Norway in September 1993.

15 ART – ART – KUNST

12972 Anglia Polytechnic University critical studies project.
GBR 1993
Research Date(s): 1990-1995
Tallack, M.
Sup: Baxter, D.
Inst: Anglia Polytechnic University, Department of Arts and Letters, East Road, Cambridge CB1 1PT, United Kingdom.
Fin: Caloustie Gulbenkian Foundation; Eastern Arts Association.
art; art education; art activity; critical sense; pupil
art; éducation artistique; activité artistique; sens critique; élève
PROJECT DESCRIPTION

Anglia Polytechnic University Art History Division staff at Cambridge are working with two hundred year 5 and year 6 pupils and their teachers, following these pupils through their school career until 1995. The staff provide: (1) expertise in and outside the classroom in critical studies work, working alongside the primary and secondary teachers in schools, galleries, museums and other locations; (2) in-service classes for primary and secondary teachers; (3) visual and other resources for cross-curricular critical studies work drawn from Anglia Polytechnic University's own due resources, galleries, museums and the community.

The aims of this critical studies research project are: (1) to introduce pupils to as wide a variety of art objects as possible in order to: (i) generate understanding of the cultural, historical, formal and other ways of engaging with art objects; (ii) improve their art work; (iii) extend their critical vocabulary to enable them to evaluate their own art work critically; (2) to familiarise teachers with the innumerable ways in which critical studies work can enrich many areas of the school curriculum; (3) to develop and extend teachers' confidence and abilities in relation to critical studies work; (4) to test, and refine, cross-curricular strategies, teaching methods and assessment procedures in relation to critical studies work in primary and secondary schools in the context of the National Curriculum.

12973 Anti-racism and children's literature.
GBR 1993
Research Date(s): 1989-
Pinsent, P.
Inst: Roehampton Institute, Digby Stuart College, Roehampton Lane, London SW15 5PU, United Kingdom.
children's literature; racism; race relations
littérature pour la jeunesse; racisme; relations raciales
PROJECT DESCRIPTION

This investigation into racism/anti-racism in children's literature is based on a belief in the influence of literature in the formation of attitudes, and a conviction that children should not be provided with sub-standard writing simply because the attitudes displayed in it are acceptable. Those writers who incorporate positive attitudes towards equality within quality children's books need discovering and supporting. The research includes personal reading and the evaluation of fiction.

Publ: Pinsent, P. Anti-racism and children's literature. In: *The School Librarian*, Vol 38, No 2/1990, pp. 45-50, May.

12974 Cathedrals through touch and hearing.
GBR 1993
Research Date(s): 1986-1993
Hull, J.; Reeve, J.
Inst: Birmingham University, School of Education, Centre for Religious Education Development and Research, Edgbaston, Birmingham B15 2TT, United Kingdom.
Fin: Industrial and charitable sources.
architecture; blind; equipment; teaching aid; visually handicapped
architecture; aveugle; équipement; moyen d'enseignement; handicapé visuel
PROJECT DESCRIPTION

The aim of the project is to explore the problems of presenting architecture to visually handicapped people. Cathedrals in England are being equipped with special facilites including wooden models, ground plans, tactile illustrations, cassette recordings and braille guides. The project was mainly confined to West Midlands cathedrals during 1988/1989 but will work in more than 20 cathedrals nationwide during the following years. The work is sponsored by the Archbishop of York.

Publ: Hull, J.M. *Touching the rock: an experience of blindness.* London SPCK (Society for the Promotion of Christian Knowledge), 1990.

Hull, J.M. On being a whole body seer: an epistemic condition for the education of the blind. In: *British Journal of Visual Impairment,* pp. 62-63, Summer 1990.

Hull, J.M. The God of the blind. In: *The New Beacon,* Vol 74, No 877/1990, pp. 200-204, June.

Reeve, J. Keeping in touch with cathedrals. In: *British Journal of Visual Impairment,* Autumn 1991.

12975   The Centre for the Study of the Arts in Primary Education (CENSAPE): development of resource collections of examples of good practice in primary arts education.
GBR   1993
Research Date(s): 1990-1992
Holt, D.
Inst: Plymouth University, Rolle Faculty of Education, Douglas Avenue, Exmouth EX8 2AT, United Kingdom.
Fin: Caloustie Gulbenkian Foundation.
art; art activity; primary education; art education
art; activité artistique; enseignement primaire; éducation artistique
PROJECT DESCRIPTION
The centre is an initiative of the expressive arts section of the Rolle Faculty of Education at Polytechnic South West (now Plymouth University). As well as drawing on the resources of this institution, The Centre for the Study of the Arts in Primary Education (CENSAPE) also works closely with schools and local education authorities (LEAs) in the South West of England. The principal concerns of the centre are to collect and disseminate examples of good practice in primary arts education and to undertake associated programmes of research and publication.

The current phase of the project is directed towards the establishment of a series of resource collections containing annotated examples of good primary practice in the areas of visual art, drama, dance and music, and with the development of a loan system to make such material available to schools, teachers and others with an interest in primary arts education. When this work is complete, CENSAPE will continue to pursue a variety of projects concerned with research and publication in this area of the curriculum.

Publ: Holt, D.A. CENSAPE: Centre for the Study of the Arts in Primary Education. In: *NFAE Journal,* No 6/1990, pp. 18-19.

12976   Činnosti hudebně pohybové v 1.-4.ročníku základní školy. (Music and movement education from the first to the fourth year in primary school.)
CSK   1994
Research Date(s): 1986-1990
Knopová, Blanka.
Sup: Čapek, Vratislav.
Inst: Ústřední ústav pro vzdělávání pedagogických pracovníků (Central Institute for Teacher Education), Myslíkova 7, 110 00 Praha 1, Czechoslovakia.
music and movement; physical expression; primary education; further education of teachers
rythmique; expression corporelle; enseignement primaire; perfectionnement des enseignants
PROJECT DESCRIPTION
Aims: To explore various components of music and movement expression as well as the conditions under which children develop and make use of active and creative movement skills in the classroom.

Hypothesis: The professional preparation of teachers, their instrumental and singing skills, their knowledge and understanding of the subject are the prerequisites for effective teaching.

Methods: Interviews and questionnaires with three types of questions: closed, open-ended and questions aimed at working out practical exercises.

Publ: Knopová, Blanka. *Hudebně pohybové činnosti a jejich realizace ve vyučovacím procesu u dětí mladšího školního věku.* Brno: 1989, 233p.
Knopová, Blanka. *Hudební slabikář.* Žďár nad Sázavou: 1992, 25p.
Knopová, Blanka. *Pohybová kretivita jako zdroj aktivního vnímání hudby.* Praha: Pedagogická fakulta Univerzity Karlovy, 1992, 5p.
Knopová, Blanka. *Funkce učebnice ve vyučovacím procesu.* Brno: Musica viva, 1992, 6p.

12977   Didaktika hudební výchovy jako studijní disciplína v učitelském vzdělání: hudební aktivizace učňovské mládeže. (Teaching methods in music education as a subject in teacher education: musical activities for apprentices in vocational training centres.)
CSK   1994
Research Date(s): 1986-1990
Polák, Jan.
Sup: Čapek, Vratislav.
Inst: Katedra hudební výchovy PDF MU (Institute of music education, Teacher Training Faculty, Masaryk University), Poříčí 31, 603 00 Brno, Czechoslovakia.

Ústřední ústav pro vzdělávání pedagogických pracovníků (Central Institute for Teacher Education), Myslíkova 7, 110 00 Praha 1, Czechoslovakia
music education; art activity; leisure; training centre; apprentice
éducation musicale; activité artistique; loisir; centre de formation; apprenti
PROJECT DESCRIPTION
Aim: To examine how the musical education of youth in vocational training centres may be improved (conditions, possibilities, teaching methods).

Hypotheses: The majority of tutors are not able to provide good musical activities for apprentices in their leisure time. Vocational training centres are lacking facilities for musical activities (educational techniques, electronic equipment). Apprentices hold no positive attitudes towards serious music and often have an uncritical admiration for one style of pop music.

Design: Questionnaires will be administered to tutors and apprentices. Questions will relate to their music education and interests and their opinion on the technical conditions for musical activities in leisure time.

Publ: Polák, Jan. *Hudební aktivizace učňovské mládeže.* Brno: 1989, 170p.

12978   Didaskalia tou paramythiou stin Kypro. (Teaching of fairy tales in Cyprus.)
CYP   1993
Research Date(s): 1992
Kyrou, Styliani.
Inst: Pedagogiko Instituto (Pedagogical Institute), P.O. Box 512, Nicosia, Cyprus.
fairy tale; narration; story telling; nursery school
conte de fées; narration; narration d'histoires; école maternelle
PROJECT DESCRIPTION
Background and aims: Fairy tales are part of the teaching programme in nursery schools in Cyprus. The aim of this research was to examine the frequency with which fairy tales are taught at nursery schools of all types, as well as the way they are selected and used in teaching. It was hypothesized that government nursery schools would display better practice in the teaching of fairy tales than communal and private nursery schools.

Methods: A questionnaire was distributed among the teachers of the sample of nursery schools. Using random sampling, 60 questionnaires were distributed, 28 of which were returned and analysed (response rate: 46.66%). The independent variable in the study was the type of the nursery school; the dependent variables were the criteria for the selection of fairy tales, the topics of the stories, the teaching aids used to present the story and the teaching method followed.

Results: All teachers, regardless of the type of the nursery school, use similar criteria when selecting fairy tales. Teachers at private schools place more emphasis on the childrens' interests and take them into account when choosing a fairy tale. Teachers at private schools are also more imaginative in choosing a story and they use the children's imagination to create their own stories as well. Teachers teach fairy tales with every-day topics and do not use their imagination the way they seem to believe. Respondents stated that at government nursery schools the topics are taken from Cypriot writers; at private schools the choice of topics depends on the circumstances; and at communal nursery schools the topics are derived from religious life or from aspects of the children's lives.

Teachers do not use teaching aids extensively to help children to concentrate on the story. Government teachers use plain narration as a technique for teaching fairy tales; the other teachers use more artificial teaching aids. Fairy tale teaching is generally not followed by creative activities.

12979   Drama in the English National Curriculum.
GBR   1993
Research Date(s): 1988-1993
Kempe, A.; Holroyd, R.
Inst: Reading University, Department of Arts and Humanities in Education, Bulmershe Court, Woodlands Avenue, Earley, Reading RG6 1HY, United Kingdom; Theale Green School, Bath Road, Reading RG7 5DA, United Kingdom.
drama; teaching aid; common core curriculum; curriculum development
art dramatique; moyen d'enseignement; tronc commun; élaboration de programmes d'études
PROJECT DESCRIPTION
The end product of the research will be two books for use in top primary/lower secondary classrooms. A pupil book will contain a range of resources on three separate topics. Literature, visual material, realia and research or creative tasks will be bound together by a linking narrative for each of the three topics. An accompanying teacher's book will outline how each individual resource may be used as part of an enactive learning programme and suggest various strategies by which the resources may be combined into dramatic structures.

Within the whole project, there will be opportunities to meet the stated attainment targets of English in the National Curriculum document and some reference will also be made to the history, science, and craft, design and technology (CDT) documents. Most of the material is being trialled at a comprehensive school in Reading. Other elements are being used on Inservice Education and Training (INSET) courses and a programme of primary school sessions.

The final publications will hopefully provide the basis for a more extensive and refined publishing programme aimed at meeting the needs of the National Curriculum without destroying current good practice.

Publ: Kempe, A. Enthusiastic beginners. In: *Drama*, Vol 1, No 1/1992, pp. 13-16.

12980 Group textual study of fiction in primary school.
GBR   1993
Research Date(s): 1983-1992
Hill, A.
Inst: Heriot-Watt University, Moray House Institute of Education, Holyrood Road, Edinburgh EH8 8AQ, United Kingdom.
children's literature; fiction; reading; primary education; group work
littérature pour la jeunesse; fiction; lecture; enseignement primaire; travail par équipe
PROJECT DESCRIPTION
   The aims of the project are: (1) to explore the potential for educational development in the group discussion of children's fiction texts; and (2) to make the resulting insights and developed expertise available to teachers. The project originated in a perceived need, in an area of Scotland, for the encouragement of oral work and the use of fiction as more than a Friday afternoon relaxation. It rests upon the following beliefs: (1) that imagination (defined as mental operation upon the possible, as distinct from the actual) is an important aspect of intelligence; (2) that good children's fiction, as a product of imagination, might have an important role in fostering imagination, and responses to imaginative stimuli, in children; (3) that structured discussion might: (a) expand children's understanding and appreciation of what is being read by enabling them to share insights and responses, developing their ability to take literal and inferred meaning from text; (b) enhance children's enjoyment of a text through sharing insights and responses; (c) actively motivate less committed readers by demonstrating the wider varieties of enjoyment and response contained within a text; and (d) promote children's language development, firstly by giving them an experience which is both common (the novel) and individually differentiated (subjective reading and responses), and secondly by presenting occasions when they need to express and articulate their own understandings and perceptions, and listen to and consider the responses and opinions of others in the group. To various extents, according to circumstances, observations by the researcher and by teachers suggest that these beliefs are valid. The resulting materials work well.

Publ: Hill, A.G. *Group textual study of fiction in the primary school.* Edinburgh: Moray House, 1985.
Hill, A.G. *Exemplar on, 'The battle of bubble and squeak'.* Edinburgh: Moray House, 1988.
Hill, A.G. Exemplar on, 'I am David'. Edinburgh: Moray House, 1989.
Hill, A.G. *Recommended titles for the group textual study of fiction in primary schools.* Edinburgh: Moray House, 1990.
Hill A.G. *Exemplar on Two Banana Books: 'Scaredy Cat' and 'Conker'.* Edinburgh: Moray House, 1991.
A full list of publications is available from the author.

12981 The hermeneutics of assessment: text interpretation and the assessment of writing.
GBR   1993
Research Date(s): 1987-1991
Owen, P.
Sup: Christie, T.
Inst: Manchester University, School of Education, Centre for Formative Assessment Studies, Oxford Road, Manchester M13 9PL, United Kingdom.
literary criticism; written expression; assessment
critique littéraire; expression écrite; appréciation
PROJECT DESCRIPTION
   The proposition is that the legitimacy of assessment practices can be established only by redefining validity in terms of the methods used to systematise formal procedures of interpretation. The focus of the research is the assessment of writing, with particular reference to the examining procedures pertaining to formative, progressive and criterion-referenced assessments such as those used in the Joint Matriculation Board's scheme of Staged Assessments In Literacy (SAIL). The assessment of writing is taken to be part of a more general process of criticism. Consideration is given to the methodology of criticism from the perspective of different schools of thought in literary theory. Hermeneutics, the study of the effects of signification, is taken to be of central importance in seeking to verify criterion-referenced assessments of writing. Taking the perspective that threats to validity derive from a lack of clarity in interpretative procedures and a failure to establish the legitimacy of readings of texts, it is argued that the quality of writing assessment schemes should be judged on the basis of the appropriacy of the inferential strategies and attributional reasoning used by the reader in relation to the structure of the text. Parallels are thereby drawn between the examining process and the reading process; both being represented as acts of interpretation governed by expectations about genre.

12982 Il cinema ed il teatro - quali fattori di integrazione di una armonica formazione culturale scolastica. (The use of film and drama in schools as a way to promote cultural awareness.)
ITA   1993
Research Date(s): 1991
Manna, E.; Maruffi, F.
Sup: Roma, G.
Inst: Centro Studi Investimenti Sociali - CENSIS (Centre for Social Studies and Investments), Piazza di Novella 2, 00199 Roma, Italy.
Fin: Ministero della Pubblica Istruzione, Ufficio Studi e Programmazione.
drama; film; educational film; visual learning; art education
art dramatique; film; film éducatif; apprentissage visuel; éducation artistique
PROJECT DESCRIPTION
   Aims: To identify and explore various schools of thought with regard to the use of film and drama as educational tools in school; to study interesting regional experiences in respect of the introduction of film and drama in school.
   Methods: Document analysis, interviews (with a selected panel of experts), and case-studies of some relevant experiences.
   Results: The study is a "pilot project". For this reason, its outcomes are not regarded as "results", but as "initial considerations". It is recognized that film and drama in school can complement school education and can make pupils familiar with these forms of cultural activity at an early age. It is felt that, notwithstanding the dominant position of television, film and drama can play an important role in the education of pupils.
   In schools, film and drama are not presented as regular subjects, but as innovative educational activities, especially at the experimental level. The updating of teachers focuses only on the theoretical level of visual education. Youth seem to appreciate viewing films greatly, but they complain about the lack of opportunity they are given to produce and stage theatrical works themselves. No less revealing is the finding that films are often played on video and not on a big screen, which strips films of the expressive characteristics of the cinematographic method.

12983 An investigation into techniques for the teaching of non-fiction in schools.
GBR   1993
Research Date(s): 1990-1992
Frame, B.
Inst: Heriot-Watt University, Moray House Institute of Education, Holyrood Road, Edinburgh EH8 8AQ, United Kingdom.
reading; document; primary education; teaching method
lecture; document; enseignement primaire; méthode pédagogique
PROJECT DESCRIPTION
   The first aim of this research is to describe the present use of non-fiction; to find out what non-fiction is used by teachers of pupils aged 9-12 years of age in two primary schools; to find out how the non-fiction is used by describing teaching methods and pupil tasks. The second aim is to compare this with the suggested programmes of study for reading as set out in Scottish Office Education Department (SOED) English language 5-14, comparing the findings of the first aim with what has been recommended in the SOED document under Reading: Strand 3 - Reading for Information; Strand 5 - Finding and handling information; and Strand 6 - Awareness of Genre - all under (1) programmes of study and (2) attainment targets. The comparison will draw out differences relating to teaching methods and pupil tasks.

Publ: *Non-fiction in Primaries 6-7 English Language 5-14: Report.* Edinburgh: Moray House.

12984 The nature of learning in educational drama.
GBR   1993
Research Date(s): 1989-1993
Somers, J.
Inst: Exeter University, School of Education, St Luke's, Heavitree Road, Exeter EX1 2LU, United Kingdom.
drama; learning; learning kit
art dramatique; acquisition de connaissances; valise pédagogique
PROJECT DESCRIPTION
   There is very little evidence of the nature of learning which takes place in the arts. At a time when the place of the arts in education is under scrutiny, it seems timely that we should attempt to discover what kind of learning takes place during and following specific drama experiences. Teachers have devised five lesson packages which they are reshaping as a result of using them within their own teaching. The next phase is for teacher-researchers to be brought out of their schools so that they can observe other teachers using the material. After final redrafting of the lesson packages, drama teachers across the country will be asked to use the material. Results will be collated in Exeter and published. The project uses attitude scales, observation schedules, interviews and analysis of written work to evaluate the nature of the pupils' experiences. Lessons are on (1) old age; (2) Downs Syndrome; (3) gender; (4) photograph as stimulus; (5) legend as stimulus.

12985 Optimising international links and exchange programmes between departments of photography.
GBR 1993
Research Date(s): 1988-1993
Smith, I.
Sup: Allen, W.
Inst: Southampton University, Department of Teaching Media, Highfield, Southampton SO9 5NH, United Kingdom.
Fin: Kodak Limited; ERASMUS.
photography; international exchange; post-secondary education
photographie; échange international; enseignement postsecondaire
PROJECT DESCRIPTION
   This project is concerned with the study of links and exchanges as mechanisms for promoting a greater mutual understanding of the nature and structure of college and university courses in photography in Europe. The investigation involves case studies of selected interchange programmes, the establishment of a data base of European courses in photography and an analysis of the characteristics of photographic courses with a view to identifying the potential for a European Scheme for credit accumulation and transfer. The project has reached the stage of having produced a published data base of European courses in photography through the 'Photolink International' scheme which is supported by Kodak Limited and ERASMUS.
   Publ: Smith, I.R. *Directory of photographic education: A European survey.* Photolink International, 1990.

12986 Perspective drawing in young children.
GBR 1993
Research Date(s): 1987-1991
Littleton, K.
Sup: Cox, M.
Inst: York University, Department of Psychology, Heslington, York YO1 5DD, United Kingdom.
drawing; art education; teaching aid
dessin; éducation artistique; moyen d'enseignement
PROJECT DESCRIPTION
   In order to draw an object in perspective, the artist must represent the projected shape of the object rather than its actual shape. Adults as well as children have difficulty in seeing the apparent shape, let alone drawing it. Even trained artists may need special aids such as the 'perspective frame', or 'Leonardo window' to enable them to draw what they see. This research project investigates the use of such aids with seven year old children.

12987 Shakespeare: from school to higher education.
GBR 1993
Research Date(s): 1992-1993
Gibson, R.
Inst: Cambridge University, Institute of Education, Shaftesbury Road, Cambridge CB2 2BX, United Kingdom.
literature; post-compulsory education; higher education
littérature; enseignement postobligatoire; enseignement supérieur
PROJECT DESCRIPTION
   A study of the continuity of the Shakespeare experience of students moving from school, sixth-form college or further education into higher education. The research arises out of the work of the Shakespeare and Schools project based at the University of Cambridge, Institute of Education. A considerable amount of data has been collected for the period 1986-1993. This will be analysed together with data on teaching methods and students' experience in the period April 1993-July 1994.
   Publ: Gibson, R. Teaching Shakespeare. In: Brindley, S. et al. *Teaching English.* Milton Keynes: Open University Press, 1993.

12988 The significance of dance in community-based projects.
GBR 1993
Research Date(s): 1987-
Bennett, R.
Sup: Allison, B.; Denscombe, M.
Inst: De Montford University, Department of Education, Scraptoft Campus, Scraptoft, Leicester LE7 9SU, United Kingdom.
dance; community
danse; collectivité
PROJECT DESCRIPTION
   Following a broad survey of the national, regional and local policies for the promotion of dance, the research follows a case study approach using a combination of observation, participant observation, and interview techniques to look at the effects of gender, race and class on the take-up of community-based dance initiatives.

12989 Towards a common form of assessment in drama as a methodology and as a performance art.
GBR 1993
Research Date(s): 1992-1995
Cabral, B.
Sup: Davis, D.; Cherrington, D.

Inst: University of Central England in Birmingham, Faculty of Education, Centre for Advanced Studies in Education, Westbourne Road, Edgbaston, Birmingham B15 3TN, United Kingdom.
Fin: Ministry of Education, Brazil.
drama; assessment
art dramatique; appréciation
PROJECT DESCRIPTION
   The aims of this research are to: (1) search for a model of assessment for drama in education, both as a methodology and as a performance mode, which represents achievement in drama, not excluding the possibility of achievement in other subject matters as well; (2) pinpoint the different ways in which both approaches deal with dramatic conventions and rules, and how these differences interfere in the assessment schemes; (3) analyse the performance of the reader (audience, self-spectator) as a main element in assessment schemes; (4) compare the assessment provided by the fellow student (audience) or by the student himself (self-spectator) with the one provided by the teacher; (5) analyse the links between the plurality of audience assessment and the possibility of open-ended productions, i.e. a non-closed conclusion to the art form.

12990 The use of resources in the development of learning through drama in education in primary schools.
GBR 1993
Research Date(s): 1990-1993
Abou El-Khir, M.
Sup: Perkin, R.; Long, J.
Inst: Leeds Metropolitan University, Department of Education, Faculty of Cultural and Education Studies, Beckett Park, Leeds LS6 3QS, United Kingdom.
Fin: Egyptian Education Bureau.
drama; learning; teaching aid; teaching method; primary education
art dramatique; acquisition de connaissances; moyen d'enseignement; méthode pédagogique; enseignement primaire
PROJECT DESCRIPTION
   The study seeks to examine the assertion that the use of theatre resources (such as lighting, costume, properties, sound effects etc.) enhances the symbolic fictitious world created in educational drama sessions, thereby influencing learning outcomes. A localised survey followed by selective interviews will provide data relating to the attitudes of primary teachers to the assertion. The assertion itself will be tested through action research and participant observation, culminating in a case study of drama practice with a particular class of primary children.

12991 The uses of playscripts in the secondary school curriculum.
GBR 1993
Research Date(s): 1993-1994
Kempe, A.
Inst: Reading University, Faculty of Education and Community Studies, Bulmershe Court, Earley, Reading RG6 1HY, United Kingdom.
drama; English language; secondary education
art dramatique; langue anglaise; enseignement secondaire
PROJECT DESCRIPTION
   The research will involve collating the responses to a questionnaire sent to a sample of English and Drama departments in secondary schools around the country. The questionnaire will ascertain the range and type of playscripts held in stock and the appeal of newly advertised titles. Furthermore, the research will try to gauge recent shifts in trends regarding the use of playscripts as either a stimulus for creative drama work or as a means of delivering the National Curriculum Orders for English at key stage 3. It is envisaged that articles reporting the research will be submitted to national English and Drama publications.

12992 Young children as musicians: a study of musical processes in the invented songs of children aged 3-7.
GBR 1993
Research Date(s): 1988-1992
Davies, C.
Inst: Durham University, School of Education, Leazes Road, Durham DH1 1TA, United Kingdom.
music; learning process; early learning; child
musique; apprentissage; apprentissage précoce; enfant
PROJECT DESCRIPTION
   The young child using language uses infantile forms of sentences, yet as soon as language is used at all it shows that the child is aware of relationships between elements of language and of the meanings conveyed by these relationships. But the view often taken of learning music is that young children acquire the 'building blocks' of music; and only at a later stage do they synthesise these and that not until then can it be said that they are making music. The researcher believes that in like manner, children are absorbing music holistically from the beginning, developing an intuitive awareness of the relationships inherent in music's structure.
   The research involves collecting invented songs of 33 children aged 5-7 and analysing them to see what evidence there is that children have a sense of the wholeness of music (as derived from Langer's account of music as time).

The analysis so far shows that even while they are still acquiring the materials for music-making, children are using these as musicians do.

12993 Zum Singverhalten der Zehn- bis Vierzehnjaehrigen: eine empirische Untersuchung zum Einfluss der Musikhauptschulen auf Singmotivation und Singart. (The singing behaviour of children aged 10-14: an empirical investigation of the influence of 'Musikhauptschulen' on motivation and forms of singing.)
AUT 1993
Research Date(s): 1985-1992
Hofer, Anton.
Inst: Abteilung Allgemeinbildende Pflichtschulen, Muehlgasse 67, A-2500 Baden.
Paedagogisches Institut des Bundes fuer Niederoesterreich, Dechant Pfeifer-Strasse 3, A-2020 Hollabrunn; Paedagogisches Institut des Bundes fuer Niederoesterreich, Muehlgasse 67, A-2500 Baden
singing; music education; lower secondary; motivation
chant; éducation musicale; secondaire premier cycle; motivation
PROJECT DESCRIPTION
Die Arbeit untersucht: Moeglichkeiten einer realistischen Beurteilung der Effektivitaet der Hauptschulen mit musikalischem Schwerpunkt; Moeglichkeiten zum Vergleich von 'Musik- Hauptschulen' und Regelschulen; Auswirkungen auf Liedvermittlung, Singaktivitaet und Singbereitschaft, auf Hoer- und Freizeitverhalten, auf Liedvorlieben und Liedwahl.

Es wird je ein Fragebogen fuer SchuelerInnen (der Musikklassen und der Regelklassen) und fuer LehrerInnen an Hauptschulen mit musikalischem Schwerpunkt entwickelt und eingesetzt.

Publ: Hofer, Anton. *Zum Singverhalten der Zehn- bis Vierzehnjaehrigen. Eine empirische Untersuchung zum Einfluss der Musikhauptschulen in Niederoesterreich auf Singmotivation und Singart.* Paedagogisches Institut des Bundes fuer Niederoesterreich, Abteilung Allgemeinbildende Pflichtschulen. Informationen, Schriftenreihe Nr. 30.

16 RESEARCH – RECHERCHE – FORSCHUNG

12994 Aspects of new paradigm research and nontraditional learning: innovative approaches to performance excellence in sport.
GBR 1993
Research Date(s): 1988-1992
McDonald, F.
Sup: Carlisle, B.; Adams, F.
Inst: Heriot-Watt University, Moray House Institute of Education, Cramond Campus, Cramond Road North, Edinburgh EH4 6JD, United Kingdom.
research; sport; performance; experimental education; teaching model
recherche; sport; performance; pédagogie expérimentale; modèle didactique
PROJECT DESCRIPTION
This study seeks to establish new parameters for training and performance in sport and the terms and conditions of a new paradigm research and development method in action.

The project aims to: (1) offer a critique of training theory; (2) analyse performance in terms of key concepts, underlying values and performance goals; (3) develop a methodology for working within the parameters of what has come to be known as 'New Paradigm Research'; (4) establish what is nontraditional as opposed to traditional learning; (5) spot emergent training parameters and consider general applications; (6) establish the broad features of a new training system.

12995 Cost-benefit analysis in education.
GBR 1993
Research Date(s): 1991-1992
Hough, J.
Inst: Loughborough University of Technology, Department of Education, Loughborough LE11 3TU, United Kingdom.
Fin: Overseas Development Administration (British Government).
cost-benefit analysis; education budget; developing country; economics of education
analyse coût-bénéfice; budget de l'éducation; pays en développement; économie de l'éducation
PROJECT DESCRIPTION
The research surveys educational cost-benefit analysis with particlar reference to Third World countries. The project covers the definition and development of cost-benefit analysis (CBA), methodology of CBA alternative approaches, comparison with other techniques in educational planning and extensive surveys of CBA results both in developed and in Third World countries. The research focuses particularly on problems relating to concepts, data, assumptions, methodology and interpretation of CBA results. Finally, the project will suggest ways in which CBA studies can become more practical and implementable.

12996 Das Mind-Modell: ein umfassendes Rahmenkonzept fuer Forschung und Praxis im paedagogisch-psychologischen Bereich. (The mind model: a comprehensive framework for educational- psychological research and practice.)
AUT 1993
Research Date(s): 1990-1992
Sedlak, Franz.
Inst: Abteilung fuer Schulpsychologie und Bildungsberatung, Minoritenplatz 5, A-1014 Wien.
Bundesministerium fuer Unterricht und Kunst, Minoritenplatz 5, A-1014 Wien
model construction; information processing; social change
construction de modèle; traitement de l'information; changement social
PROJECT DESCRIPTION
Die revolutionaere Entwicklung der Nachrichtentechnik und Medienelektronik bewirkt eine nie zuvor geahnte Moeglichkeit der Kommunikationsdichte, Informationsvernetzung und eines weltweiten Wissens- und Erfahrungsaustausches. Durch die gegenwaertigen gesellschaftlichen Umwaelzungen kommt es auch zu einem interkulturellen Assimilations- und Akkommodationsprozess, zu verschiedenen Integrationsbemuehungen einerseits, aber auch zu einer Pluralitaet von Konzepten andererseits. Diese Vielfalt birgt allerdings auch die Gefahr von Unuebersichtlichkeit und von unkoordinierten Parallelentwicklungen in sich. Ein umfassendes Rahmenmodell kann Gemeinsamkeiten verschiedener Ansaetze demonstrieren, Akzentsetzungen einordnen helfen und so den Iststand veranschaulichen. Ein umfassendes Rahmenkonzept wird sich aber nicht in der demonstrativen, veranschaulichenden Wirkung erschoepfen, sondern kann darueber hinaus sichtbar machen, wo Divergenzen, Einseitigkeiten oder Defizite bestehen. Ein umfassendes Rahmenmodell kann daher auch einen konstruktiv-kritischen Beitrag leisten, indem es durch die Aufstellung bestimmter inhaltlicher Kriterien Vergleichsstandards erstellt bzw. auf Problemstellen aufmerksam machen kann. Beide vorgenannten Zielsetzungen sind deskriptiv-praeskriptiv (letzteres in Verfolgung der logischen Konsequenzen aus dem kritisch- konstruktiven Ansatz), sie sind aber unbedingt zu ergaenzen durch eine weitere Intention. Kulturelle Verschmelzungsprozesse, Assimilations- und Akkommodationsvorgaenge in kultureller, gesellschaftspolitischer bzw. bildungspolitischer Hinsicht koennen vor neue Aufgaben stellen, fuer die bisherige Erfahrungsdaten

nicht ausreichen. Daher ist das Augenmerk auf Faktoren und Ebenen bzw. auf Zusammenhaenge zu richten, die bisher zu wenig beruecksichtigt wurden oder in einer neuen Hinsicht von besonders aktuellem Interesse sind.

Publ: Sedlak, Franz. *Das Mind-Modell*. Paedagogischer Verlag Eugen Ketterl, Wien 1992.

12997 De bruikbaarheid van multiniveau-analyse van longitudinale onderwijskundige data. (The usefulness of multilevel models for the analysis of longitudinal research data.)
NLD 1994
Research Date(s): 1993-1994
Kamp, L.J.Th. van der; Vooys, M.W.; Leeden, M. van der.
Inst: Faculteit der Sociale Wetenschappen, Vakgroep Methoden en Technieken van Psychologisch Onderzoek (Faculty of Social Science, Department of Psychological Research Methods and Techniques), Postbus 9555, 2300 RB Leiden, Netherlands.
Rijksuniversiteit Leiden (State University of Leiden), P.O. Box 9555, 2300 RB Leiden, Netherlands
Fin: SVO het Instituut voor Onderzoek van het Onderwijs.
model; multidimensional analysis; research technique
modèle; analyse multidimensionnelle; technique de recherche
PROJECT DESCRIPTION
  Background: Multilevel models are increasingly used to analyse data in educational research and other social science research. A major generalization is generalization to models for the analysis of longitudinal data. This application of multilevel models has advantages, but is only of an exemplary nature.
  Aim: To examine the usefulness of multilevel models for longitudinal research, in comparison with the often used longitudinal variants of variance analyses (MANOVA).
  Design: Secondary analyses will be performed on three data sets concerning reading proficiency. The results of multilevel analyses will be compared with those of univariate and multivariate variance analysis models for repeated measurements using the same data. The comparison will focus on the criteria of costs, comparability and interpretability of data, possibilities for hypothesis testing and model evaluation, the influence of sample size and the influence of unreliable measurements.

12998 Economic and Social Research Council Survey link scheme (2).
GBR 1993
Research Date(s): 1991-1992
Cohen, G.
Sup: McPherson, A.; Raffe, D.
Inst: Edinburgh University, Centre for Educational Sociology, 7 Buccleuch Place, Edinburgh EH8 9JT, United Kingdom.
Fin: Economic and Social Research Council.
measurement; achievement; model; performance; survey; socio-economic status
mesure; rendement; modèle; performance; enquête; statut socio-économique
PROJECT DESCRIPTION
  The research examined the problems of the measurement of socio-economic status using hierarchical linear models; missing data and modelling educational attainment.
Publ: A bibliography of published work is available.

12999 Elaborazione di strumenti di rilevamento situazionale. (Elaboration of survey instruments for the evaluation of in-service training courses.)
ITA 1994
Research Date(s): 1990-1991
Verini, Antonio; et al.
Inst: Istituto Regionale di Ricerca Sperimentazione e Aggiornamento Educativi d'Abruzzo - IRRSAE (Regional Institute for Educational Research, Innovation and Teacher Training of Abruzzo), Via Aldo Moro 30, 67100 L'Aquila, Italy.
Ministero della Pubblica Istruzione (Ministry of Public Education), Viale Trastevere 76, 00100 Roma, Italy
survey; questionnaire; evaluation; in-service training; training course; further education of teachers
enquête; questionnaire; évaluation; formation en cours d'emploi; cours de formation; perfectionnement des enseignants
PROJECT DESCRIPTION
  Aims: To define research tools for monitoring and evaluating the in-service training courses for nursery and primary school teachers run by IRRSAE-Abruzzo.
  Design: (1) Collection of documents and study of the questionnaires; (2) comparative analysis of the material collected; (3) identification of appropriate material; (4) elaboration of research tools.
  Method: Document analysis.
  Preliminary results: The first three phases of the project have been concluded. Three model questionnaires have been developed regarding course evaluation.

13000 Extending multilevel models.
GBR 1993
Research Date(s): 1990-1994
Goldstein, H.
Inst: London University, Institute of Education, Department of Mathematics, Statistics and Computing, 20 Bedford Way, London WC1H OAL, United Kingdom.
Fin: Economic and Social Research Council.
model; statistical method; research technique
modèle; méthode statistique; technique de recherche
PROJECT DESCRIPTION
  This project extends the work of the earlier projects entitled 'Developing the use of multilevel models' and 'Developing and disseminating multilevel models'. The three aims of the current project are: (1) to disseminate knowledge of multilevel modelling to the social science research community through conferences, seminars and training sessions in the use of statistical software developed for this form of analysis; (2) to extend existing methodology, especially in the area of time series and linear structural relations models; and (3) to study the practical application of the models to real data sets, especially with a view to increasing robustness and developing data diagnostic procedures.
  Work is in progress in many domains, including improving the operational efficiency of the 'Iterative Generalised Least Squares' (IGLS) algorithm used in fitting multilevel models; developing the theory of multilevel analysis with latent variables; comparing various methods for treating missing data in multilevel analysis; developing loglinear, time series and survival multilevel models.

13001 Foerderliche und hemmende Bedingungen fuer Innovationen an Schulen. (Factors that help or hinder innovation efforts in school.)
AUT 1993
Research Date(s): 1991-1993
Posch, Peter; Altrichter, Herbert; Messner, Elgrid; Rauch, Franz.
Inst: Institut fuer Schul- und Sozialpaedagogik, Universitaetsstrasse 65-67, A-9020 Klagenfurt.
Universitaet fuer Bildungswissenschaften, Universitaetsstrasse 65-67, A-9020 Klagenfurt
Fin: Universitaet fuer Bildungswissenschaften; Fonds zur Foerderung der wissenschaftlichen Forschung; Bundesministerium fuer Unterricht und Kunst; Landesschulrat fuer Steiermark; Paedagogisches Institut des Bundes in der Steiermark.
educational innovation; social change; working conditions; teacher; teacher role; role perception
innovation pédagogique; changement social; conditions de travail; enseignant; rôle de l'enseignant; perception de rôle
PROJECT DESCRIPTION
  Die Forschungsarbeit verfolgt das Ziel, Aufschluesse darueber zu gewinnen, wie LehrerInnen die Veraenderung gesellschaftlicher Anforderungen an ihre berufliche Taetigkeit wahrnehmen, durch welche Innovationen sie darauf antworten, welche Bedingungen sie als foerderlich bzw. hemmend wahrnehmen und wie sie damit umgehen.
  Methodischer Hintergrund ist die Aktionsforschung; dabei untersuchen Praktiker eigene berufliche Situationen, indem sie Reflexion und Handeln aufeinander beziehen und ihre Erfahrungen veroeffentlichen (Fallstudie). Die Forschungsarbeit der LehrerInnen wird von wissenschaftlichen BetreuerInnen unterstuetzt.
  Es liegen Arbeitsberichte, Seminarkonzeptionen, Literaturstudien zu Hypothesen hinsichtlich foerderlicher und hemmender Bedingungen fuer Innovationen, Manuskripte zu den Rollen und Dilemmas von BetreuerInnen u.a.m. vor.
Publ: Rauch, Franz & Messner, Elgrid. Aktionsforschung im Tandem. In: *Unser Weg*, 5/1992, Graz, 1993.
Herausgabe einer Projektzeitung *Innonet*, bisher fuenf Ausgaben.

13002 Genç anababa çatışma envanteri (GAÇE): geliştirilmesi, güvenirliği ve geçerliği. (The conflicts between adolescents and parents: development of a valid and reliable measuring instrument.)
TUR 1994
Research Date(s): 1992
Özgen, Çiğdem.
Sup: Dökmen, Üstün.
Inst: Ankara Üniversitesi, Sosyal Bilimler Enstitüsü (University of Ankara, Institute of Social Sciences), 06590 Ankara, Turkey.
test construction; reliability; validity; parent-child relation; test
construction de tests; fidélité; validité; relation parents-enfant; test
PROJECT DESCRIPTION
  The study aimed to develop a test for measuring the conflicts between adolescents and their parents and to examine its reliability and validity by various methods.
  The sample consisted of 452 students who were mainly from Ankara University (the Faculties of Languages, History, Geography and Educational Sciences) and the medical school of Hacettepe University.
  As a first step in the development of the test - the "Adolescent Parent Conflict Inventory (APCI)" - an experimental form comprising 43 items was

constructed. Item analysis was conducted in order to make it unidimensional. Two approaches were used. One considered the correlation between each item and the total score; the other focused on the t value of each item. On the basis of the findings, it was decided to eliminate three items from the test, leaving it with 40 items.

The reliability of the test was determined by three methods: the "split half" method, the "test-retest" method and the Cronbach Alfa test of reliability.

The validity of the test was determined by using two other tests: the Conflict Tendency Inventory (CTI) and the Family Atmosphere Inventory (FAI).

The study showed that there are differences between the conflicts adolescents have with their fathers and their mothers. This means that the conflicts between adolescents and their parents should be differentiated in the application of the APCI. As a whole the findings show that the APCI test is a valid and reliable measuring instrument. The fact that one inventory gives separate information about the conflicts of adolescents with their fathers and mothers adds to its value and applicability.

13003 Interdisziplinaere sozialwissenschaftliche Lehre und Forschung ueber Europa. (Interdisciplinary social scientific theory and research in Europe.)
DEU 1993
Research Date(s): 1991-1992
Schwarz, A.; Heinrich, M.; Hamm, B.
Inst: Universitaet Trier, FB 04 Wirtschafts- und Sozialwissenschaften, Mathematik, Fach Soziologie, Tarforst, D-5500 Trier.
interdisciplinary approach; research; social sciences; Europe
interdisciplinarité; recherche; sciences sociales; Europe
PROJECT DESCRIPTION
Inhalt: Erarbeitung eines Verzeichnisses von Personen/Institutionen, die sich interdisziplinaer-sozialwissenschaftlich mit Europa befassen.

13004 Konstruktvalidierung des Lerntest-Konzepts durch Untersuchungen beim Bearbeiten komplexer dynamischer Problemstellungen (Akronym: KOVALT). (Construct validation of the learning test concept through studies of complex problem solving (acronym: KOVALT).)
DEU 1993
Research Date(s): 1991-1993
Funke, J.; Guthke, J.
Inst: Universitaet Bonn, Philosophische Fakultaet, Psychologisches Institut, LS Allg. Psychologie, Roemerstrasse 164, D-5300 Bonn 1.
Fin: Deutsche Forschungsgemeinschaft.
intelligence measurement; learning test; problem solving; cognitive ability; learning; validity
mesure de l'intelligence; test d'acquisition; résolution de problème; aptitude cognitive; acquisition de connaissances; validité
PROJECT DESCRIPTION
Inhalt: Bisher gibt es lediglich Untersuchungen ueber den Zusammenhang von konventionellen Intelligenzparametern und sogenannten transparenten (vgl. etwa "Turm von Hanoi") bzw. intransparenten Problemloeseanforderungen (siehe die Arbeiten von Doerner, Putz-Osterloh, Lueer, usw.). Die Befundlage ist durchaus noch widerspruechlich (siehe u.a. die Arbeiten von Hussy, Funke, Wittmann). Ueberhaupt noch nicht untersucht wurde die Beziehung von Lerntests zu solchen Problemloeseanforderungen. Hierbei ist es zunaechst notwendig, genauer jene Parameter zu identifizieren (z.B. Aneignung von Systemwissen sensu Sternbergs "acquisition of knowledge" als wichtiger bisher wenig beachteter Intelligenzfaktor), die moeglicherweise mit Lerntests hoeher als mit konventionellen Statusintelligenztests korrelieren. Die geplanten Untersuchungen sollen einen Beitrag zur Konstruktvalidierung von Lerntests liefern (auch zum Nachweis ihrer groesseren oekologischen Validitaet) und gleichzeitig die differentialpsychologische Relevanz des Paradigmas des komplexen Problemloesens bzw. einzelner seiner Parameter erkunden.

Vorgehensweise: Experimentelle Forschung; Umgang mit Simulationsszenarien; computergestuetzte Intelligenzdiagnostik. Untersuchungsdesign: Methodenforschung; Computersimulation; Querschnittserhebung; (Quasi-)Experiment.

Datengewinnung: Psychologischer Test (Stichprobe: 80; Schueler der 7. Klasse; Auswahlverfahren: Zufall). Primaererhebung: Feldarbeit von Mitarbeitern des Projektes durchgefuehrt.

Auswertung: Multiple Regression, Varianzanalyse, t-Test, Cluster-analyse. Datenaufbereitung: Datenedition (z.B. Aufbau v. Datenbanken).
Publ: Funke, J. Solving complex problems: Human identification and control of complex systems. In: Sternberg, R.J.; Frensch, P.A. (Eds.). *Complex problem solving: Principles and mechanisms.* Hillsdale, N.J. Lawrence Erlbaum, 1991.

13005 Matching: an exact test procedure.
GBR 1993
Research Date(s): 1983-
Gillett, R.
Inst: Leicester University, Department of Psychology, University Road, Leicester LE1 7RH, United Kingdom.
statistical method; statistical model; validity
méthode statistique; modèle statistique; validité
PROJECT DESCRIPTION
Studies using the matching paradigm aim to establish whether a one-to-one pairing of objects or people from two groups contains more pairing of a particular kind than expected under the null hypothesis. By applying the combinatorial technique of Rook methodology, a flexible and general framework for constructing exact tests in the matching paradigm is being developed. Among the practical benefits of the approach are: (a) a more sensitive test of individual matching performance, (b) the assessment of broad agreement when raters are uncertain, and (c) a solution to the problem of infeasible pairings.
Publ: Gillett, R. The matching paradigm: an exact test procedure. In: *Psychological Bulletin,* Vol 97, No 1/1985, pp. 106-118.
Gillett, R. Nominal scale response agreement and rater uncertainty. In: *British Journal of Mathematical and Statistical Psychology,* Vol 38, No 1/1985, pp. 58-66.
Gillett, R. Allowing for infeasible pairings in the matching paradigm. In: *Psychometrika,* Vol 50, No 3/1985, pp. 265-274.

13006 Measurement of attitudes towards Christianity.
GBR 1993
Research Date(s): 1991-1992
Francis, L.
Inst: Trinity College, Carmarthen, Dyfed SA31 3EP, United Kingdom.
attitude scale; pupil attitude; Christianity; religion
échelle d'attitude; attitude de l'élève; christianisme; religion
PROJECT DESCRIPTION
This project is re-analysing data collected among primary and secondary pupils in England, Scotland and Ireland in order to perfect a reliable and valid short measure of attitude towards Christianity, building on Francis' well established longer Likert scale.

13007 Multilevel modelling for New York Project.
GBR 1993
Research Date(s): 1990-1992
Goldstein, H.
Inst: London University, Institute of Education, Department of Mathematics, Statistics and Computing, 20 Bedford Way, London WC1H OAL, United Kingdom.
Fin: New York City Public Schools.
model; statistical method; research technique; achievement measurement
modèle; méthode statistique; technique de recherche; mesure du rendement
PROJECT DESCRIPTION
The purpose of this project is to provide software support and professional advice to the New York Central Board of Education in a multilevel longitudinal analysis of test scores.

13008 Multiniveau-analyse van verschillen in het basisonderwijs. (Multi-level analysis of differences in primary education.)
NLD 1994
Research Date(s): 1992
Stokking, K.M.
Inst: Interdisciplinair Sociaal-wetenschappelijk Onderzoeksinstituut, Afdeling Onderwijs (ISOR) (Interdisciplinary Research Institute for the Social Sciences, Department of Educational Research), P.O. Box 80140, 3508 TC Utrecht, Netherlands.
Rijksuniversiteit Utrecht (State University of Utrecht), P.O. Box 80125, 3508 TC Utrecht, Netherlands
Fin: SVO het Instituut voor Onderzoek van het Onderwijs.
research technique; achievement; teaching method; primary school
technique de recherche; rendement; méthode pédagogique; école primaire
PROJECT DESCRIPTION
Background: In the Netherlands differences have been found to occur among primary classrooms within one school, among primary schools, and among geographical regions. So far, studies on the nature, the extent and the determinants of these differences have failed to take systematically account of the multi-level structure of education. Multi-level research is not a routine affair, as the methods for this type of research are still being developed. The present study uses various models and techniques for multi-level analysis.
Aim: (1) To determine the explanatory value of variables from various theoretical fields (school effectiveness, school improvement, utilization of knowledge, information processing, diffusion) for the differences mentioned above; (2) to gain a deeper insight into the usefulness of models and techniques for multi-level analysis.
Design: The study will focus on the following aspects of education: individualization, differentiation, and special needs provision in reading and writing instruction in ordinary schools. Differences will be examined at classroom, school and regional level. The usefulness of the models and techniques used will be determined by their application to empirical data.
At the outset, the study used a sample of 1,000 primary schools, dispersed across 20 regions, with a minimum of 100 pupils each. Questionnaires were given to the headmasters asking whether they would be

prepared to participate in the study. This was followed by a questionnaire survey of headmasters and teachers in the participating schools.

The regions, schools and classrooms will be described on the basis of 40 selected variables. The data will be analysed by various methods and models, using systematic variation.

13009 Performance measurement indicators in research in continuing education.
GBR 1993
Research Date(s): 1990-1991
Lovell, T.; Weller, P.
Sup: Field, J.
Inst: Warwick University, Faculty of Educational Studies, Department of Continuing Education, Continuing Education Research Centre, Coventry CV4 7AL, United Kingdom.
educational research; continuing education; researcher; performance; measurement technique; periodical
recherche en éducation; éducation permanente; chercheur; performance; technique de mesure; périodique
PROJECT DESCRIPTION
The project will seek to test the hypothesis that quantitative analyses of citations can be used to judge quality of research output, with respect to the field of continuing education. It will involve a citations count for two leading British-based journals (*Studies in the Education of Adults*, and the *International Journal of Lifelong Learning*).

13010 Planning for change in multiracial primary schools.
GBR 1993
Research Date(s): 1990-1992
Wallace, M.
Sup: Bolam, R.
Inst: Bristol University, School of Education, National Development Centre for Education Management and Policy, 35 Berkeley Square, Bristol BS8 1JA, United Kingdom.
Fin: Leverhulme Trust.
educational innovation; educational administration; intercultural education; educational planning; educational reform; school-community relation; expectancy
innovation pédagogique; administration de l'enseignement; éducation interculturelle; planification de l'éducation; réforme de l'enseignement; relation école-collectivité; attente
PROJECT DESCRIPTION
The aim of this research is: (1) to explore how multiracial schools in the primary sector plan to implement multiple innovations in a context of cultural diversity; and (2) to identify the processes and procedures which appear to be effective. Planning for change is likely to be especially problematic in a situation where different groups in the local community have different expectations about the direction for school development. The research will be conducted in three local education authorities (LEAs). In each LEA headteachers of eight schools will be interviewed and case studies will be carried out in two of these schools.

13011 Prognóza vývoja školstva v Slovenskej republike do roku 2010. (Prognosis of the development of education in the Slovak Republic up to the year 2010.)
SVK 1994
Research Date(s): 1990-1993
Majtán, M.; Rais, I.; Henrich, J.; Csicsayová, M.; Šebíková, R.
Sup: Harach, Ľ.
Inst: Ústav informácií a prognóz školstva, mládeže a telovýchovy (Institute of Information and Prognoses of Education, Youth and Sport), Staré grunty 52, 842 44 Bratislava, Slovak Republic.
Ministerstvo školstva a vedy SR (Ministry of Education and Science of the Slovak Republic), Hlboká 2, 813 30 Bratislava, Slovak Republic
forecasting; model construction; data base; statistical analysis; educational information
prévision; construction de modèle; banque de données; analyse statistique; information pédagogique
PROJECT DESCRIPTION
Aim: To elaborate a model on which to base prognoses for the development of the Slovak education system.

Method: The method was based on a procedure of complex prognostic modelling which was elaborated in detail. This is a modified version of the dynamic model of so-called "soft-systems", which includes the education system. The work took place in several stages. After the identification of the aims of the education system and the formalization of specific elements and relations, a quantitative mathematical model was created to be entered onto computer for making prognoses up to the year 2010 on the basis of about 200 educational indicators. Following the evaluation of preliminary results, a number of variants of educational development were constructed.

Objectives for the next stage of the research include: further elaboration of the model on the basis of mathematical-statistical analysis of the results; updating the database; examining the possibility to include qualitative aspects of education in the model.

Publ: Majtán, M. et al. *Prognóza vývoja školstva SR do r.2010: Úvodná štúdia.* (Prognosis of the development of education in the SR up to the year 2010: an introductory study.) ÚIP ŠMT, 1990, 31p.
Majtán, M.; Ondrejkovič, P.; Rais, I. & Herich, J. Stimulačný model školstva SR pre účely prognózovania. (Forecasting model for education in the SR.) In: *Modelovaní a simulace systému.* Vsetín, 14-16 May 1991, pp. 142-147.
Rais, I. *Parciálny prognostický model vysokých škôl.* (Partial forecasting model for higher education institutions.) ÚIP ŠMT, 1991, 7p. Research report.
Majtán, M. et al. *Prognostický model školstva v SR. Údajová základňa.* (Forecasting model for the education system in the SR. Data base.) ÚIP ŠMT, Bratislava, 1991, 55p.

13012 Questionnaire design project.
GBR 1993
Research Date(s): 1986-1993
Low, G.
Sup: Kyriacou, C.
Inst: York University, English Language Teaching Centre, Heslington, York YO1 5DD, United Kingdom.
questionnaire; linguistics; semantics; attitude
questionnaire; linguistique; sémantique; attitude
PROJECT DESCRIPTION
The object of the study is to explore the reactions of university students to linguistic aspects of the wording of Likert-type questionnaire items. Items of particular interest are those with 'AGREE/DISAGREE' as rating verbs and 'STRONGLY' or 'COMPLETELY' as adverbs. Three acceptability tests are being designed, involving closer and closer approximations to the task of actually completing a questionnaire. In addition a test has been devised to establish empirically the levels of certain types of salience attached by subjects to sentences in a questionnaire-type environment.

Publ: Low, G.D. The semantics of questionnaire rating scales. In: *Evaluation and Research in Education*, Vol 2, No 2/1988, pp. 69-79.
Low, G.D. Talking to questionnaires: pragmatic models in questionnaire design. In: Adams, P.; Heaton, B. & Howarth, P. (eds). *Review of English Language Teaching 1(2): Socio-Cultural Issues in English for Academic Purposes*, pp. 118-143. Modern English Publications in association with the British Council 1991.
Low, G.D.; Tasker, I. & Lu, H. The wording of bipolar attitude scales in Chinese. In: *Educational Research*, Vol 33, No 2/1991, pp. 141-150, Summer.

13013 Review of United Kingdom social science resources.
GBR 1993
Research Date(s): 1990-1991
Williams, G.; Loder, C.
Inst: London University, Institute of Education, Department of Policy Studies, 20 Bedford Way, London WC1H 0AL, United Kingdom.
Fin: Economic and Social Research Council.
research; social sciences; financial resources
recherche; sciences sociales; ressources financières
PROJECT DESCRIPTION
This is an examination of the sources, and distribution by institution, subject of research, and type of research, of United Kingdom social science research expenditure during 1988/1989.

13014 Sample size determination in replication attempts.
GBR 1993
Research Date(s): 1983-
Gillett, R.
Inst: Leicester University, Department of Psychology, University Road, Leicester LE1 7RH, United Kingdom.
research technique; reliability; sample
technique de recherche; fidélité; échantillon
PROJECT DESCRIPTION
A replication attempt is a study undertaken to establish whether an earlier finding represents a genuine effect. Sample size determination can prove difficult if the theory motivating the original experiment is insufficiently precise to provide strong predictions about the expected magnitude of the experimental effect.

A method is being developed to determine sample size in a replication attempt when there is uncertainty about the magnitude of the experimental effect. The method uses information provided by the original study to construct a distribution of probable effect sizes.

The sample size to be employed in a replication attempt is that which supplies an expected power of the desired amount over the distribution of probable effect sizes.

Publ: Gillett, R. Sample size determination in replication attempts: the standard normal Z test. In: *British Journal of Mathematical and Statistical Psychology*, Vol 39, No 2/1986, pp. 190-207.

13015   Validity and award-bearing teacher action research.
GBR   1993
Research Date(s): 1986-1991
Dadds, M.
Sup: Elliott, J.
Inst: Cambridge University, Institute of Education, Shaftesbury Road, Cambridge CB2 2BX, United Kingdom; University of East Anglia, School of Education, Centre for Applied Research in Education, Norwich NR4 7TJ, United Kingdom.
action research; further education of teachers; teacher; individual characteristics
recherche-action; perfectionnement des enseignants; enseignant; caractéristique individuelle
PROJECT DESCRIPTION
At the heart of this research is a case study of one inservice teacher. (A middle school teacher attending the action research based two-year part-time Advanced Diploma course at the Cambridge Institute of Education). The teacher's three assessed action research studies are analysed to show how they relate to her professional work in school. The impact of the research on her colleagues and on their curriculum development is also explored.
The case study shows the importance of this teacher's professional commitment and deep-rooted personal experiences in formulating, developing and using her research. It also shows the powerful effect of her personal qualities on her effectiveness as a change agent. Her influence on the research and on school colleagues was equally well supported by conducive management strategies and processes and by collegial attitudes towards curriculum and professional development. The case study explores the importance of these features of the receiving inservice climate and culture in school. Successful implementation of inservice is thus seen to be related to the context in which the teacher is working.
The research also considers the role of the written assessed text in action research based inservice work. Alternative ways of presenting research findings may, it is suggested, be crucial for developing texts for school audiences and school purposes. Alternative texts are shown to help teachers to develop further action outcomes from their award-bearing action research work.

Publ: Dadds, M. Thinking and being in teacher action research. In: Elliott, J. (ed.). *Reconstructing teacher education.* Lewes: Falmer Press, 1992.
Dadds, M. Can INSET essays change the world for children? In: Constable, H. *Change in classroom practice.* Lewes: Falmer Press, 1992.

13016   Vernieuwingsprojecten in het beroepsonderwijs.   (Innovation projects in vocational education.)
BEL   1994
Research Date(s): 1989-1990
Michiels, K.
Sup: Cossey, H.
Inst: Hoger Instituut voor de Arbeid, HIVA (Higher Institute of Labour Studies, HIVA), Van Evenstraat 2E, 3000 Leuven, Belgium.
Katholieke Universiteit Leuven (Catholic University of Leuven), Naamsestraat 22, 3000 Leuven, Belgium
Fin: Departement Onderwijs, Fonds voor Kollektief en Fundamenteel Onderzoek op Ministerieel Initiatief.
educational innovation; pilot school; head teacher; social perception; self-concept; pupil; school environment; social development; affective development
innovation pédagogique; école-pilote; chef d'établissement; perception sociale; conception de soi; élève; milieu scolaire; développement social; développement affectif
PROJECT DESCRIPTION
Aim: To evaluate, after 10 years of experimentation, innovations in secondary vocational education and to investigate to what extent pilot schools succeed in creating closer links between school life and the lifestyles of their pupils.
Method: A large-scale survey was conducted of 1,600 fourth-year pupils in 70 vocational secondary schools (pilot schools as well as other schools).
Results: The evolution of school participation in innovation processes is described, focusing on the way school heads react to innovation policies. As regards the effects of innovation upon the social and emotional lives of pupils (family perception, school perception and self-image), few significant differences were found between pupils in pilot schools and other schools. The only significant differences found between schools concerned teaching methods, i.e. the use (vs. non-use) of an open curriculum and of differentiated teaching methods.

Publ: Michiels, K. *Scholen en leerlingen en de vernieuwing in het BSO: de vernieuwingsexperimenten in het BSO bekeken vanuit de deelname van de scholen in de jaren '80 en vanuit de effecten op het sociaal-emotioneel functioneren van de leerlingen.* Leuven: HIVA, 1990, XIII, 140p. + summary (20p.).

13017   The work of the Scottish Council for Research in Education 1928-1992.
GBR   1993
Research Date(s): 1991-1994
Morris, J.
Sup: Entwistle, N.; McPherson, A.
Inst: Edinburgh University, Department of Education, 10-12 Buccleuch Place, Edinburgh EH8 9JT, United Kingdom.
educational research; history of education; Scotland
recherche en éducation; histoire de l'éducation; Ecosse
PROJECT DESCRIPTION
This is a study of the Scottish Council for Research in Education which was one of the earliest research councils to be found in Europe. Its history is traced from total independence relying on voluntary but professional labour, to that of a group of professional researchers still having independence but within the bounds of a market economy. The main themes will be testing shading into assessment; outreach i.e. dissemination of findings to the teaching force and in international activity; policy where customer-contractor and even negotiated research works within a range of constraints. The methodology will be that of archive search with the Founder Institutions, the Education Institute of Scotland and the Association of Directors of Education, Scotland, and other appropriate bodies such as the Scottish Office Education Department, the Public Record Office, West Register House, Edinburgh and the archive of the Council itself. It will include taped interviews with leading Council Members and officials, past and present. Four of its five Directors and all its Chairmen for the past 40 years are still alive.

Computer-based modelling across the curriculum .... see no. 11702

Einsatz von Fallstudien und Unternehmensplanspielen an Fachhochschulen im Fachbereich Wirtschaft (Use of case studies and management games in the economic departments of technical colleges)...... .... see no. 11730

De kwaliteit van het kleuteronderwijs: een onderzoek naar de samenhang tussen de pedagogisch-didactische aanpak, de processen en de ontwikkelingseffecten (The quality of pre-school education: an exploration of the relationships between teaching methods, process variables and outcomes) .... see no. 11926

Developing models of educational accountability .... see no. 11929

Developing tools to measure the outcomes of guidance .... see no. 11930

Forecasting the demand for higher education specialists.................. .... see no. 11952

Good schools, effective schools: judgements and their history......... .... see no. 11954

Het gebruik van "performance indicatoren" in het onderzoek van de overgangsproblematiek S.O.-H.O. en bij de evaluatie van het zelfstudiecentrum als begeleidingsinitiatief (The use of performance indicators in the study of problems in the transition from secondary to higher education and in the evaluation of the Centre for Self-Instruction as a guidance service)................................ see no. 11956

Internationale vergelijking onderwijsemancipatiebeleid met bijzondere aandacht voor het beleid van scholen (International comparison of equal opportunities policies in education with particular reference to school policies) .... see no. 11967

OECD (Organisation for Economic Co-operation and Development) education indicators on attitudes and expectations .... see no. 11991

Schulkultur - ein Schulversuch (School culture - a pilot project)....... .... see no. 12007

Annual survey of new Open University courses.......... see no. 12046

Begleitforschung zum Modellversuch 'Studienzirkel in Oberoesterreich' (Research on the pilot project 'A study circle in Upper Austria') .... see no. 12051

Das berufliche Bildungswesen in der Republik Oesterreich (Vocational education in the Republic of Austria) .... see no. 12071

The idea of 'university extension' across the English-speaking world, 1867-1914 .... see no. 12126

Lehrerarbeit auf dem Weg zur paedagogischen Professionalitaet (The teacher's work on the road to pedagogic professionalism) .... see no. 12153

Przygotowanie studentów kierunków nauczycielskich do twórczej pracy zawodowejstan aktualny i próby innowacji (Preparation of students in pedagogical faculties for creative work and attempts at innovation)... see no. 12198

Students, supervisors and the social science research training process .... see no. 12225

Forecasting student enrolments for further education colleges......... .... see no. 12313

17 INFORMATION SYSTEMS – SYSTEMES D'INFORMATION – INFORMATIONSSYSTEME

13018 Analýza výskumu mládeže v Slovenskej republike. (Review of youth research in the Slovak Republic.)
SVK 1994
Research Date(s): 1990-1992
Rimóczyová, K.; Slovíková, M.
Sup: Zubalová, M.
Inst: Ústav informácií a prognóz školstva, mládeže a telovýchovy (Institute of Information and Prognoses of Education, Youth and Sport), Staré grunty 52, 842 44 Bratislava, Slovak Republic.
Ministerstvo školstva a vedy SR (Ministry of Education and Science of the Slovak Republic), Hlboká 2, 813 30 Bratislava, Slovak Republic
information policy; research; youth; data base; information system
politique de l'information; recherche; jeunesse; banque de données; système d'information

PROJECT DESCRIPTION

Background: The research sought to chart the state of the art in youth research in Slovakia. The final report "Analysis of Youth Research in the Slovak Republic" presents a draft survey of the results that have been achieved so far. It is proposed to include relevant information (e.g. problems encountered) in the Slovak Information System on Youth. The present draft of the content and structure of youth research in the Slovak Republic should serve as a basis for the elaboration on a database of youth research that will be continuously updated. The permanent processing of data should also enable international comparisons to be made of programmes in the field of youth policy.

Aims: To list the institutions that are involved in youth research; to conduct a survey of analyses of youth research projects in the period 1985-1990; to outline possible prospects.

Methods: Semi-structured dialogue/interview; document analyses (research projects).

Results: A content analysis was realized with the help of the proposed model; the draft model was verified; the structure and content of youth research for a database within the framework of the Slovak Information System on Youth were worked out.

Publ: Rimóczyová, K. & Slovíková, M. Informácie - mládež. (Information - Youth.) Bratislava, ÚIP SMT, 1991, 8p. (Slov., Engl.).
Rimóczyová, K. & Slovíková, M. Výskum mládeže v SR. (Youth research in the SR.) In: Mládež a spoločnosť. Bratislava, ÚIP SMT, 1992, No. 4, pp. 16-17.

13019 The application of computer-aided learning to the development of information skills in further education.
GBR 1993
Research Date(s): 1990-1993
Robertson, J.
Sup: Williams, D.
Inst: Robert Gordon University, School of Librarianship and Information Studies, Hilton Place, Aberdeen AB9 1FR, United Kingdom.
information retrieval; post-secondary education; information source; student
dépistage de l'information; enseignement postsecondaire; source d'information; étudiant
PROJECT DESCRIPTION

The project seeks to examine the way in which further education (FE) students explore and utilise sources of information. The intial test group are National Diploma in Business Studies students at Telford College, Edinburgh and subsequently the students of similar courses in other Scottish FE colleges. A Hypertext system has been developed to guide students through information searches, and to log individual students' use of the system. These logs will be analysed to evaluate learning patterns.

13020 Biblioteca del software didattico - BSD. (Educational Software Library - ESL.)
ITA 1994
Research Date(s): 1992-
Trentin, Guglielmo; Tavella, Mauro; Ferlino, Lucia.
Sup: Ott, Michela.
Inst: Istituto per le Tecnologie Didattiche - ITD (Institute for Educational Technology), Via all'Opera Pia 11, 16145 Genova, Italy.
Consiglio Nazionale delle Ricerche - CNR (National Research Council), Piazzale Aldo Moro 7, 00185 Roma, Italy
software library; educational software; data base; information network; cataloguing; documentation; medicine; handicap
logithèque; didacticiel; banque de données; réseau d'information; catalogage; documentation; médecine; handicap
PROJECT DESCRIPTION

The Educational Software Library (ESL) catalogues, files and evaluates software products. Also, seminar activities take place, in particular with regard to the principal sectors of interest, identified through research. In this way, it is intended to strengthen the "handicap" and "medicine" sectors and to open a new sector dealing with psychology that will contain both teaching instruments and more typically clinical instruments which will be introduced in curricula of university level psychology courses. A similar strategy will be adopted for the choice of medical products. As regards the handicap sector, international ties will be strengthened (in particular with the Handynet project, a European network for the disabled, for which the ESL is the Italian contact for educational software material). National ties, with all the relevant institutions in the sector, will also be attended to. A new database is in the process of being developed with more functional characteristics that should be compatible with European standards. As part of the study, educational software products will be produced to bridge specific gaps in learning.

13021 Computer conferencing in distance education.
GBR 1993
Research Date(s): 1990-
Mason, R.; Kaye, A.
Inst: Open University, Institute of Educational Technology, Walton Hall, Milton Keynes MK7 6AA, United Kingdom.

Fin: Training, Enterprise and Education Directorate; Economic and Social Research Council; European Community DELTA project.
telecommunication; distance study; didactic use of computer; university studies
télécommunication; enseignement à distance; usage didactique de l'ordinateur; études universitaires
PROJECT DESCRIPTION

The Open University pioneered the use of computer conferencing in mass distance education on its Information Technology course in 1988. The University is now looking to rewrite that course and to offer it to students throughout Europe. Computer conferencing will form a major component of the course, both as a medium for supporting students and as a means of presenting and maintaining the course. Through a series of pilot schemes and other small applications, the researchers are refining the use of this medium as a tool for distance education.

Some of the areas under investigation are: (1) its integration with other media; (2) its use over ISDN links; (3) its use as a tool for collaborative writing of course material with other institutions; and (4) its application to training and continuing education. The focus of research by Open University Ph.D. students include: discourse analysis of conferencing interactions; and critical mass for successful conference interactions.

The researchers are also investigating the design of conferencing systems and front ends to provide low cost, easy to use access for home-based students throughout Europe.

Publ: Kaye, A.R. (ed.). Collaborative learning through computer conferencing. Heidelberg: Springer-Verlag, 1992.

13022 Conceptualisation design and orientation in complex multimedia structures.
GBR 1993
Research Date(s): 1989-1992
Bevan, R.
Sup: Richards, C.
Inst: Coventry University, School of Art & Design, Priory Street, Coventry CV1 5FB, United Kingdom.
Fin: Apple Computer UK Ltd.
multimedia system; computer-assisted design; concept formation
système multimédia; conception assistée par ordinateur; formation de concept
PROJECT DESCRIPTION

The aim of this research is to develop more intuitive and creative methods of designing and representing interlinked information in interactive, non-linear multimedia structures, providing simple and effective means of orientation and navigation within such structures.

13023 Elaboration of the foundations of the modern concept of informatics teaching and computer maintenance.
RUS 1994
Research Date(s): 1991-1992
Sazonov, B.A.
Inst: Research Institute for Higher Education, 103062, Moscow, K-62, Podsosensky per. 20, Russia.
State Committee for Higher Education Institutions, 113833, Moscow, M-230, Lysinovskja str. 51, Russia
information technology; computer science; teaching method; teaching programme; higher education
technologie de l'information; informatique; méthode pédagogique; programme d'enseignement; enseignement supérieur
PROJECT DESCRIPTION

The study examined the basic principles underlying the modern concept of informatics teaching. A structural framework was designed for the contents of various disciplines related to informatics teaching. A review was made of existing computer maintenance methods and informatics teaching methods. Teaching programmes were designed.

Publ: Sazonov, B.A. Modern concepts of teaching and the use of new information techniques in teaching informatics. Information review. M., NIIVO, 1992.

13024 Interactive video project for the hearing impaired.
GBR 1993
Research Date(s): 1989-1991
Jones, C.; Van der Kuyl, T.; Johnston, M.
Inst: Heriot-Watt University, Moray House Institute of Education, Holyrood Road, Edinburgh EH8 8AQ, United Kingdom.
Fin: Scottish Office Education Department.
interactive video; didactic use of computer; aurally handicapped; deaf
vidéo interactive; usage didactique de l'ordinateur; handicapé auditif; sourd
PROJECT DESCRIPTION

The project aims to research and identify the priority areas for development of education for the deaf and to produce high quality interactive courseware to meet the variety of needs of hearing-impaired children and adults. Due to problems faced by deaf children on their transfer from primary to secondary schools, the first multi-media courseware will be focused on the upper primary children (ages 8 to 12).

A Shopping Microworld is being designed and developed to enable children to organise their own shopping lists, and browse round the food and children's clothing departments of a large high street store. Various pedagogical activities and cognitive strategies are being incorporated into this Microworld. These include LOGO activities, unit pricing, money handling and conservation of measure.

13025   IRLME: Interactive Resources for Small and Medium Sized Enterprises.
GBR   1993
Research Date(s): 1990-1992
Goodyear, P.
Inst: Lancaster University, Department of Educational Research, Cartmel College, Bailrigg, Lancaster LA1 4YW, United Kingdom.
Fin: European Community COMETT Programme.
interactive video; didactic use of computer; small and medium entreprise; Europe
vidéo interactive; usage didactique de l'ordinateur; petite ou moyenne entreprise; Europe
PROJECT DESCRIPTION
  The goal of this project is to produce an interactive video (IV) about the uses of interactive video for training in small and medium sized enterprises (SMEs). The project involves research into methods of designing IV materials for use in SMEs in several European countries.

13026   Pilotprojekt Netzwerkuniversitaet.   (A pilot project on a computer network for university distance education.)
AUT   1993
Research Date(s): 1992-1994
Muehlbacher, Joerg; Steinparz, Franz; Kreuzeder, Ulrich; Kaineder, Hermann; Berger, Markus.
Inst: Forschungsinstitut fuer Mikroprozessortechnik, Altenbergerstrasse 69, A-4040 Linz.
Universitaet Linz, Altenbergerstrasse 69, A-4040 Linz
Fin: Bundesministerium fuer Wissenschaft und Forschung.
computer network; open university; didactic use of computer; distance study
réseau informatique; télé-université; usage didactique de l'ordinateur; enseignement à distance
PROJECT DESCRIPTION
  Gegenstand des Projekts ist die Erarbeitung von Grundlagen fuer eine Umsetzung des Konzepts einer Verteilten Universitaet. Das Konzept einer Verteilten Universitaet geht davon aus, dass StudentInnen ueber Arbeitsplatzrechner verfuegen, welche neben der klassischen Funktion solcher Rechner auch via Rechnerkommunikation eine Benutzerschnittstelle fuer den Studenten/die Studentin zu verschiedenen Dienstleistungen der Universitaet bieten. Telekommunikationstechniken im Verbund mit neuer Unterrichtstechnologie soll eingesetzt werden, um Studierenden die Moeglichkeit zu bieten 'von zuhause aus' an verschiedenen Lehrveranstaltungen teilzunehmen. Das Pilotprojekt dient dazu, Grundlagen zu erarbeiten und das Konzept anhand der Realisierung und Evaluation einzelner Kurse im Rahmen des Curriculums der Informatik praktisch zu erproben.

13027   The potential of computer-mediated communication for developing social and educational opportunities for adults with physical and sensory difficulties.
GBR   1993
Research Date(s): 1989-1993
Sherman, I.; Barnes, K.
Sup: Jotham, R.
Inst: Nottingham University, Department of Adult Education, 14-22 Shakespeare Street, Nottingham NG1 4FJ, United Kingdom.
Fin: Leverhulme Trust; Universities Funding Council.
telecommunication; computer network; information network; handicapped
télécommunication; réseau informatique; réseau d'information; handicapé
PROJECT DESCRIPTION
  The aim is to establish a communication network for training and related activities between disabled centres and individual users in the East Midlands with links through the Joint Academic Network and the Packet Switch system to researchers, practitioners and other disabled people in the United Kingdom and worldwide. The efficient use of the network will be evaluated by monitoring traffic and by consultation with disabled users and professionals working with them.

Publ: A list of publications is available from the researchers.

13028   Recommendations for state policy in the field of informatization of higher education in Russia.
RUS   1994
Research Date(s): 1991-1992
Kogdov, N.M.
Inst: Research Institute for Higher Education, 103062, Moscow, K-62, Podsosensky per. 20, Russia.
State Committee for Higher Education Institutions, 113833, Moscow, M-230, Lysinovskja str. 51, Russia

information technology; new technologies; development of education; higher education
technologie de l'information; nouvelles technologies; développement de l'éducation; enseignement supérieur
PROJECT DESCRIPTION
  The main concern of the study was the informatization of education in Russia. An examination was made of approaches towards the formation of an infrastructure for the education system. A prognosis was made of the development of informatization programmes and relevant technologies. Methodological and psychological aspects of education were considered, as well as the issue of a rational combination of teaching programmes and information technologies.
  An analysis was made of existing relations within the Commonwealth of Independent States in the field of the informatization of education; recommendations were made as to their further development. A methodological basis was provided for the assessment of the quality of new information technologies.

Publ: Tsevenkov, Y.M. *The use of computers in primary and secondary education.* Information review. M., NIIVO, 1992.
Kogdov, N.M. & Lobanov, Y.I. *Encyclopaedic dictionary for Automatic Educational Systems (AOC).* Ukrainian encyclopaedia. Kiev, 1992.
Savelyev, A.Y. & Kogdov, N.M. Training specialists in the sphere of informations and computer technology for different spheres of national economics. In: *Problems of informatics,* N2, VIMI, 1992.
Savelyev, A.Y.; Kogdov, N.M.; Sazonov, V.D.; et al. Practical manual *Computers,* 8 volumes, 2nd ed., 1992. M., Vysshaya shkola, 1992.

13029   RIE: design and evaluation of an interactive videodisc for small and medium sized enterprises.
GBR   1993
Research Date(s): 1990-1992
Goodyear, P.
Inst: Lancaster University, Department of Educational Research, Cartmel College, Bailrigg, Lancaster LA1 4YW, United Kingdom.
Fin: European Community COMETT Programme.
interactive video; didactic use of computer; simulation; videodisc; small and medium entreprise
vidéo interactive; usage didactique de l'ordinateur; simulation; vidéodisque; petite ou moyenne entreprise
PROJECT DESCRIPTION
  The goal of this project is to create and evaluate an interactive videodisc (IV) whose subject matter is the application of IV for training and information services in small and medium sized enterprises (SMEs). The project is led by the University of Barcelona. The design of the disc entailed the development of new techniques for modelling decision-making situations. Production is expected to be complete by early 1992. Field trials will be conducted in Spain, United Kingdom and Portugal.

13030   Sistemi per la cooperazione a distanza in ambito didattico. (Systems for long distance cooperation in education.)
ITA   1994
Research Date(s): 1992-
Tavella, Mauro; Banaudi, Giorgio; Chioccariello, Augusto; Ferlino, Lucia; Gibelli, Camillo; Sarti, Luigi.
Sup: Trentin, Guglielmo.
Inst: Istituto per le Tecnologie Didattiche - ITD (Institute for Educational Technology), Via all'Opera Pia 11, 16145 Genova, Italy.
Consiglio Nazionale delle Ricerche - CNR (National Research Council), Piazzale Aldo Moro 7, 00185 Roma, Italy
telecommunication; computer science; computer network; educational information; information service; system design; systems analysis
télécommunication; informatique; réseau informatique; information pédagogique; service d'information; analyse informatique; analyse de systèmes
PROJECT DESCRIPTION
  The project has as its central theme the study of the application of telematics in support of teaching activities, with a view toward the meeting existing needs for computer applications and training.
  The study explores: the organizational criteria and the functionality of telematic teaching systems in the training sector, exploring in particular the use of Bulletin Board Systems (BBS); the methods of access and use of educational information sources; the use of telematics instruments to support the drawing up of timetables and experimental support activities; the integration of telematics tools in computer science laboratories and the criteria of their usage.
  The study involves the planning and realization of a prototype telematics system, based on the BBS technique, that will initially be tested with the help of a network among the computer science laboratories of several schools.

13031 Steirische Wirtschafts-, Wissenschafts- und Bildungsdatenbanken. (Industrial, scientific and educational databases in Styria.)
AUT 1993
Research Date(s): 1992
Holzer, Franz; Adametz, Christoph.
Inst: Ausseninstitut der Technischen Universitaet Graz, Lessingstrasse 27, A-8010 Graz.
Technische Universitaet Graz, Lessingstrasse 27, A-8010 Graz
data base; educational information; information service; reference material
banque de données; information pédagogique; service d'information; instrument de référence
PROJECT DESCRIPTION
Im Auftrag der Ausbildungspartnerschaft Hochschule- Wirtschaft Suedoesterreich (APS), einer Institution, die das Bildungsprogramm Comett der Europaeischen Gemeinschaften in diesem Raum betreut, wurde das Angebot an oeffentlich und, soweit erfahrbar, intern zugaenglichen Datenbanken erfasst, welche die Themenkreise 'Wissenschaft und Bildung' sowie 'Wirtschaftsinformationen' im engeren und weiteren Sinne betreffen. Ziel dieses Kompendiums ist es, die regionale und zum Teil ueberregionale Datenbanklandschaft transparenter zu machen, um eine Grundlage fuer eine 'database of databases' zu schaffen. Die APS als regionale Plattform fuer Aus- und Weiterbildung stellt dieses Kompendium allen Mitgliedern zur Verfuegung und will so dazu beitragen, Doppelentwicklungen zu vermeiden und die Effizienz von Datenbankprojekten durch die Moeglichkeit fruehzeitiger Koordination zu erhoehen. Ein Ergebnis der Recherchen ist, dass auf dem Sektor der Weiterbildung und Bildung keine Institution umfassende, institutionsuebergreifende Informationen liefern kann, es also noch keine oeffentlich zugaengliche Datenbank gibt, die detaillierte Recherchen ueber Aus- und Weiterbildungsmoeglichkeiten zulaesst.

Es wurden in erster Linie Telefoninterviews mit den zustaendigen Mitarbeitern aller regionalen Bildungsorganisationen als Quelle verwendet.

Als Ergebnis liegt ein Verzeichnis aller Datenbanken (als Text und als Datenbank) vor, in welchem diese nach den Kriterien Charakteristik, geographische Abdeckung, Anzahl und Struktur der Datensaetze, inhaltliche Schwerpunkte, Quellen, Updating, Benutzer-Zielgruppe und Zugangsbedingungen dargestellt sind. Daneben sind die Zugriffsmoeglichkeiten der regionalen Institutionen auf externe, nicht selbst erstellte Datenbanken angefuehrt.

13032 System for accessing modular information project.
GBR 1993
Research Date(s): 1990-1991
Robertson, I.; Gordon, A.; Blake, J.
Inst: Jordanhill College of Education, Scottish School for Further Education, Southbrae Drive, Glasgow G13 1PP, United Kingdom.
Fin: Training, Enterprise and Education Directorate; Scottish Office Education Department.
information system; vocational information
système d'information; information professionnelle
PROJECT DESCRIPTION
The aims of the project are to: (1) develop, maintain, and market a computerised information system for Scottish vocational qualifications; and (2) develop an enhanced system for Youth Training (YT) and Employment Training (ET) provision.

13033 Teaching and learning by video-conferencing.
GBR 1993
Research Date(s): 1990-1993
Robinson, A.; Dallat, J.; Livingston, R.
Inst: Ulster University, Faculty of Education, Department of Adult and Continuing Education, Cromore Road, Coleraine, County Londonderry BT52 1SA, United Kingdom.
interactive video; distance study; higher education
vidéo interactive; enseignement à distance; enseignement supérieur
PROJECT DESCRIPTION
The University of Ulster installed a three-campus video-conferencing facility in 1990. The system is designed to permit technician-free operation, once the studios and equipment have been arranged, the tutor controlling robotic cameras on all sites by means of a touch-tablet. The purpose of the study is to evaluate the use of video-conferencing in the teaching of modules of study taken by adult students enrolled in the Postgraduate Diploma in Education (Professional Development) course, on two campuses separated by some 50 miles. Its aims are to consider the effectiveness of the learning that takes place, and the quality of interaction between tutors and students and among students themselves. Data are gathered through questionnaires, interviews and observation of classes.

Results confirmed expectations that tutor input would be largely unaffected by the new medium and also confirmed tutor fears on the difficulties of participant interaction and discussion as compared with conventional teaching. Tutors quickly mastered the operation of the equipment, but the effects of technical shortcomings in the system proved more difficult to overcome.

Initial findings are that video-conferencing provides a valuable additional medium of distance education, that it is not directly comparable to face-to-face teaching, and that it requires its own rules of procedure and method of assessment.
Publ: Dallat, J.; Fraser, G.; Livingston, R. & Robinson, A. Teaching and learning by video-conferencing in the University of Ulster. In: *Open Learning*, Vol 7, No 2/1992, pp. 14-22.

13034 Tecnologie ipermediali per l'educazione ambientale. (Hypermedia technology for environmental education.)
ITA 1994
Research Date(s): 1992-
Trentin, Guglielmo; Besio, Serenella; Doretti, Lorenzo; Frau, Elena.
Sup: Midoro, Vittorio.
Inst: Istituto per le Tecnologie Didattiche - ITD (Institute for Educational Technology), Via all'Opera Pia 11, 16145 Genova, Italy.
Consiglio Nazionale delle Ricerche - CNR (National Research Council), Piazzale Aldo Moro 7, 00185 Roma, Italy
Fin: Ministero dell'Ambiente.
telecommunication; computer network; multimedia system; information system; data base; teaching aid; environmental study
télécommunication; réseau informatique; système multimédia; système d'information; banque de données; moyen d'enseignement; étude du milieu
PROJECT DESCRIPTION
This project takes place in the context of a series of studies aimed at the establishment of teaching technology laboratories dedicated to environmental education and connected to a telematic network. Among the functions of these laboratories is the establishment of databases containing teaching materials and the production of hypermedia systems. The project is concerned with the definition of authoring methods and tools that will constitute the common know-how of various laboratories and that will guarantee standard approaches for the material developed. The project provides for the production of a prototype and a document that describes the various phases of the development process.

13035 Telekommunikation in Oesterreich. (Telecommunication in Austria.)
AUT 1993
Research Date(s): 1991-1992
Guenther, Johann.
Inst: Institut fuer Publizistik, Schopenhauerstrasse 32, A-1180 Wien.
Universitaet Wien, Dr. Karl Lueger-Ring 1, A-1010 Wien
Fin: Privatwirtschaft; Bundesministerium fuer oeffentliche Wirtschaft und Verkehr.
telecommunication; technological change; new technologies; didactic use of computer
télécommunication; changement technologique; nouvelles technologies; usage didactique de l'ordinateur
PROJECT DESCRIPTION
Es wird keine detaillierte Darstellung der einzelnen Medien vorgenommen, sondern es wird ihre Wirkung im gesamten unterstuetzt. Ein spezieller Abschnitt ist den 'Kommunikationstechnologien im oesterreichischen Bildungswesen' in Schulen und Universitaeten gewidmet. Der Iststand der Ausstattung oesterreichischer Schulen mit Kommunikationstechnologie wird erhoben. Wissenschaftsdatenbanken, die in Oesterreich zugaenglich sind, und die Erfahrungen beim Recherchieren in diesen werden untersucht.

Es wurden die Hauptschulen Wiens im Hinblick auf die Anwendung von Kommunikationstechniken sowie die Datenbanken fuer wissenschaftliche Zwecke in Oesterreich (paralleles Recherchieren an drei verschiedenen Schulen zum selben Thema) in die Untersuchung einbezogen.

In den Schulen wurde auf die Moeglichkeit der Anwendung von Kommunikationstechniken in allen Unterrichtsfaechern hingewiesen (Recherchen in oesterreichischen Datenbanken).

Verwendung wissenschaftlicher Datenbanken: Paralleles Recherchieren ergab unterschiedlichste Ergebnisse, unterschiedlichste Literaturangaben. Die Recherche in einer Datenbank war nicht ausreichend. Kommunikationstechnik im Unterricht ist noch stark abhaengig vom unterrichtenden Lehrer und dessen persoenlichem Engagement.

Publ: Guenther, Johann. *Telekommunikation in Oesterreich*. Wien - Paris, Literas Verlag, 1992.

13036 Toky informací mezi ministerstvem školství, mládeže a tělovýchovy, školou, školskými institucemi, žáky a rodiči. (Provision and dissemination of information among the Ministry of Education, schools, other educational institutions, pupils and parents.)
CSK 1994
Research Date(s): 1992-1993
Strádal, Jiří; Berný, Libor; Houfek, Ivan.
Sup: Krejčí, Jaromír.
Inst: Výzkumný ústav odborného školství (Research Institute of Vocational Education), Karlovo nám. 17, 120 00 Praha 2, Czech Republic.
Ministerstvo školství, mládeže a tělovýchovy ČR (Ministry of Education, Youth and Physical Education), Karmelitská 7, 118 13 Praha 1, Czech Republic

information; educational opportunities; educational information; information dissemination; software

information; chances d'éducation; information pédagogique; diffusion de l'information; logiciel

PROJECT DESCRIPTION

Aims: (1) To design the optimum form, content and structure of informative publications and software products; (2) to design a mechanism whereby information sources can be updated and information be transferred from these sources to the users.

The underlying hypothesis is that a democratic education system can only work well if it is transparent to its users, i.e. pupils and parents.

Methods: Elaboration of informative products; evaluation of how these products are developed and applied and transferred to users.

Publ: Strádal, Jiří. *Informační toky mezi MŠMT, školou, školskými institucemi, žáky a rodiči.* Praha: Výzkumný ústav odborného školství, 1992, 21p.

13037 TRACE: Transregional Academic Mobility and Credential Evaluation: Information Network - eine Studie zum Verfahren der Projekt-Implementierung. (TRACE: Transregional Academic Mobility and Credential Evaluation: Information Network - a study on the process of project implementation.)
DEU   1993
Research Date(s): 1991-1992
Schacher, M.
Sup: Kazemzadeh, F.
Inst: HIS Hochschul-Informations-System GmbH, Goseriede 9, D-3000 Hannover.
Fin: Institution; Deutscher Akademischer Austauschdienst.
information system; education system; university; data base; educational information
système d'information; système d'enseignement; université; banque de données; information pédagogique
PROJECT DESCRIPTION

Inhalt: TRACE ist ein internationales Projekt mit Beteiligung von derzeit 19 Laendern (ueberwiegend Mitglieder der OECD) zum Aufbau einer Informations-Datenbank ueber nationale Bildungs- und Hochschulsysteme sowie ueber Studiengaenge, akademische Grade und einzelne Hochschulen. Zur Erfassung der erforderlichen Informationen liegen 3 verschiedene Fragebogen vor: "Profile I - Higher Education System", "Profile II - Higher Education Institution", "Profile III - Higher Education Credential". Waehrend die Daten fuer die Fragebogen I und III zentral zusammengetragen werden, muss Fragebogen II zum Teil von den einzelnen Hochschulen bearbeitet werden. Im Rahmen des Projektes soll getestet werden, auf welche Art und Weise vor allem die Daten zum Fragebogen II mit Hilfe der einzelnen Hochschulen erhoben werden koennen.

Geographischer Raum: Deutschland.

Untersuchter Zeitraum: 1991/1992.

Vorgehensweise: Untersuchungsdesign: Nachbarkeitsstudie.

13038 Tvorba seznamů a sítí předškolních zařízení, škol a školských zařízení orgány státní správy. (Creation of lists and information networks on pre-school establishments, schools and other educational institutions by State Administration Boards.)
CSK   1994
Research Date(s): 1992
Strádal, Jiří; Berný, Libor; Houfek, Ivan.
Sup: Bezchleba, Jiří.
Inst: Výzkumný ústav odborného školství (Research Institute of Vocational Education), Karlovo nám. 17, 120 00 Praha 2, Czech Republic.
Ministerstvo školství, mládeže a tělovýchovy ČR (Ministry of Education, Youth and Physical Education), Karmelitská 7, 118 13 Praha 1, Czech Republic
information; educational information; data base; information network; information dissemination
information; information pédagogique; banque de données; réseau d'information; diffusion de l'information
PROJECT DESCRIPTION

Aim: Central Administration Boards should focus on updating the information networks on schools with the basic data necessary for the construction of exhaustive lists of information about schools with a view to: (1) enabling selection according to different criteria; (2) connecting other information sources to this network.

Hypothesis: The central elaboration of educational information will become increasingly difficult, due to increasing decentralization and the growing numbers of resources, compilers and users of educational information.

Intended outcomes: Design of: (1) the structure and the content of the network; (2) mechanisms for its updating and its extension by additional collections of information; (3) the coordination of activities undertaken by individual compilers.

13039 What dimensions are used to describe special educational needs?
GBR   1993
Research Date(s): 1992
Abraham, C.; Cross, J.; Smith, E.; Kirkaldy, B.
Inst: Dundee University, Department of Epidemiology and Public Health, Ninewells Hospital and Medical School, Dundee DD1 9SY, United Kingdom; Tayside Educational Psychology Service, St Mary's Lane, Lochee, Dundee, United Kingdom.
Fin: Scottish Office Education Department.
classification; special education; handicap; need
classification; enseignement spécial; handicap; besoin
PROJECT DESCRIPTION

There is evidence that, despite the recommendations of the Warnock Report, professionals continue to rely heavily on the use of handicap categories when describing children's special educational needs (SENs). This project aims to investigate current definitions of special educational needs by psychologists and doctors in Records of Needs within Tayside Region, with a view to evaluating progress towards a needs model.

A content analysis will be carried out on the 100 most recently opened Records of Needs in Tayside Region. A content analysis coding frame will be designed on the basis of a detailed analysis of a sub-sample of 25-30 records. The coding categories and method of analysis will be tested by independent coders and by deriving inter-coder reliability scores. There will also be comparison with the findings of other researchers.

18 INFORMATION SOURCE – SOURCE D'INFORMATION – INFORMATIONSQUELLE

13040 Amtliche Bildungsstatistik und empirische Sozialforschung. (Official education statistics and empirical social research.)
DEU 1993
Research Date(s): 1990-1992
Luettinger, P.; Schimpl-Neimanns, B.
Inst: Zentrum fuer Umfragen, Methoden und Analysen -ZUMA- e.V., Abt. Mikrodaten, Postfach 122155, D-6800 Mannheim 1.
information source; education system; statistics; social research; statistical data; population
source d'information; système d'enseignement; statistique; recherche sociale; données statistiques; population
PROJECT DESCRIPTION
Inhalt: Informationen ueber Datenquellen und Nutzungsmoeglichkeiten mit dem Schwerpunkt Individualdaten ueber gesamte Bevoelkerung, Bundesebene.
Geographischer Raum: Bundesrepublik Deutschland.
Untersuchter Zeitraum: 1945ff.
Vorgehensweise: Literaturstudie. Untersuchungsdesign: Methodenforschung; Forschungsuebersicht.
Datengewinnung: Datenerstellung auf der Basis von bereits vorliegenden Materialien wie Texten, Akten, Statistiken.

13041 Arbeidsmarktontwikkeling en vaktijdschriften. (Labour market development and professional journals.)
NLD 1993
Research Date(s): 1990-1991
Dam, J.W. van; Grip, A. de; Willems, E.J.T.A.
Inst: ROA Researchcentrum voor Onderwijs en Arbeidsmarkt, Universiteit Limburg (Research Centre for Education and the Labour Market, University of Limburg), P.O. Box 616, 6200 MD Maastricht, Netherlands.
Fin: ADP Adres Plus B.V.
periodical; labour market; information system
périodique; marché du travail; système d'information
PROJECT DESCRIPTION
ROA has conducted preliminary research for "ADP Adres-Plus" into the possibilities of developing a labour market information system to be used in the marketing programmes of companies publishing professional journals. This would include current labour market information as well as the expected developments. The information system is meant as a tool in determining the current and future market position of 'horizontal' and 'vertical' journals and, in combination with labour market information on a journal's readers, it could give an understanding of the market penetration of a journal.
Publ: *Arbeidsmarktinformatiesysteem vakbladen: AMIS* (Labour market information system for professional journals: AMIS), ADP-Adres Plus/ROA, 1991.

13042 Bibliografia dydaktyki geografii. (Bibliography on the didactics of geography.)
POL 1994
Research Date(s): 1972-1994
Piskorz, Sławomir; Furgała, Maria; Nowakowska, Alina; Potepa, Teresa; Szymański, Zdzisław; Zajac, Stanisław.

Inst: Wyższa Szkoła Pedagogiczna, Instytut Geografii, Zakład Dydaktyki Geografii (Higher School of Education, Geography Department, Unit of Geography Didactics), 30 084 Kraków, Podchorążych 2, Poland.
bibliography; didactics; geography
bibliographie; didactique; géographie
PROJECT DESCRIPTION
Aim: To collect exhaustive documentation on literature dealing with the didactics of geography which appeared between 1918 and 1994.
The bibliography that is being constructed covers the following topics: history of school geography and didactics of geography, aims and curricula of geography teaching, geography teaching on Poland, regional geography teaching on Poland, regional geography teaching on the world, physical geography teaching, social geography teaching, teaching methods, forms and systems of geography teaching, school trips, textbooks, supplementary reading, pupil notebooks, globes and maps in geography teaching, geography laboratory, evaluation, achievement testing, didactic devices, geography teachers, handbooks for didactics of geography and supplementary materials for teachers, conferences, symposia, congresses, exhibitions, courses in didactics of geography, list of abbreviations, index of people and subjects.
Methods: Examination of library collections, registration on cards, verification by correspondence with authors and by checking catalogues, document analysis.
Results: Two volumes (1918-1984) have been published, the third is in preparation.
Publ: Piskorz, Sławomir & Zajac, Stanisław. *Bibliografia dydaktyki geografii 1918-1974*. Kraków: Wydawnictwo Naukowe WSP, 1976, 226p.
Piskorz, Sławomir & Zajac, Stanisław. *Bibliografia dydaktyki geografii. Vol. II 1974-1984*. Kraków: Wydawnictwo Naukowe WSP, 1985, 124p.

13043 Bibliography of Scottish education 1970-1990.
GBR 1993
Research Date(s): 1991-1992
McLelland, D.; Millar, K.; Harrison, M.
Inst: Jordanhill College of Education, The Library, Southbrae Drive, Glasgow G13 1PP, United Kingdom.
Fin: Leverhulme Trust.
bibliography; data base; publication; education system; Scotland; data collection
bibliographie; banque de données; publication; système d'enseignement; Ecosse; rassemblement des données
PROJECT DESCRIPTION
The aim of this project is to collect and list on a computer database all material on Scottish education published or issued between 1970 and 1990.

13044 Biography and education.
GBR 1993
Research Date(s): 1990-
Erben, M.
Inst: Southampton University, Faculty of Educational Studies, Highfield, Southampton SO9 5NH, United Kingdom.
biography
biographie
PROJECT DESCRIPTION
The aim of the research is to offer a disquisition on the meaning of biography. This will be realised by supporting a view that the study of biography can develop a hermeneutical conceptualisation of how best knowledge that can be regarded as educational, is to be obtained and produced. Given that biography is a hermeneutical exercise, the manner in which the objective slides into the subjective and vice versa will be developed as the protocol for a successful treatise upon biographical method. The work of Dilthey, Ricoeur, Sartre, Benjamin, Samuel Johnson, and Lacan will be examined to elaborate this exercise in cultural sociology.
Publ: Erben, M. Geneology and sociology. In: *Sociology*, Vol 25, No 2/1991, pp. 275-292.

13045 Children and television.
GBR 1993
Research Date(s): 1988-
Crouch, C.
Inst: Ulster University at Jordanstown, Shore Road, Newtownabbey, County Antrim BT37 OQB, United Kingdom.
television; childhood; adolescence; child development
télévision; enfance; adolescence; développement de l'enfant
PROJECT DESCRIPTION
The research aims to provide a broad picture of children's use and understanding of television. To date, preferences of children of primary school age (i.e. 7 to 12) have been explored (sample of 3,700+ from Northern Ireland, England, Australia) and results have indicated early gender differences; females tending to prefer soap opera programmes increasingly by age.
A second wave of research (sample of 1,000 Australian, circa 1,000 Northern Ireland 12 to 16 year olds) involves survey by questionnaire on a

wide range of issues but with special emphasis on television and learning. These data remain to be analysed.

Publ: Crouch, C. Television and primary schoolchildren in Northern Ireland: 1: television programme preferences. In: *Journal of Educational Television*, Vol 15, No 13/1989, pp. 163-170.

Crouch, C. Soap in the eyes: primary schoolgirl TV preferences. In: *Metro: Media and Education Magazine*, (Australia), No 81/1989, pp. 18-22, Summer.

Crouch, C. The emergence of soap: primary schoolchildren's TV preferences in Northern Ireland, England and Australia. In: *Research in Education*, No 46/1991, pp. 73-83, November.

13046 Development of television literacy.
GBR 1993
Research Date(s): 1989-1991
Buckingham, D.
Inst: London University, Institute of Education, Department of English and Media Studies, 20 Bedford Way, London WC1H OAL, United Kingdom.
Fin: Economic and Social Research Council.
television; visual learning; comprehension
télévision; apprentissage visuel; compréhension
PROJECT DESCRIPTION

This research will investigate the development of children's competencies as television viewers between the ages of seven and twelve. The research will be primarily qualitative, and will concentrate particularly on the ways in which interpretations of the medium are established and negotiated in small group talk. It will also focus on the role of social class, gender and ethnic background in determining children's understanding and use of the medium.

A core sample of ninety children will be interviewed both individually and in small groups on a total of eight occasions over an 18 month period. Additional interviews will be held with their teachers and parents; and control groups will be used at appropriate stages. Interviews will be transcribed and analysed using techniques derived from social semiotics and discourse analysis. Particular aspects of study will include: the development of children's conceptions of television genres and narrative forms; their judgements about its representations of the social world and its degrees of realism; and their understanding of the processes of television production.

The project aims to provide an analysis of children's understanding of television which will enable broadcasters and educationalists to respond constructively to public concern about the 'effects' of the medium. In particular, it is hoped that the research will inform the development of media education within the National Curriculum.

Publ: Buckingham, D. What are words worth? interpreting children's talk about television. In: *Cultural Studies*, Vol 5, No 2/1991.

Buckingham, D. Media education: the limits of a discourse. In: *Journal of Curriculum Studies*, Vol 24, No 4/1992, pp. 297-313.

Buckingham, D. *Children talking television: the making of television literacy.* London: Falmer Press, 1993.

Moss, G. Children and television: gendered readings. In: *Women: an international Cultural Review*, Vol 2, 1991.

13047 Die Schulbuchbegutachtung in verschiedenen Laendern. (Textbook evaluation in different countries.)
AUT 1993
Research Date(s): 1991
Bamberger, Richard; Gattermann, Brigitte; Gintenstorfer, Andrea.
Inst: Institut fuer Schulbuchforschung, Strozzigasse 2, A-1080 Wien.
Fin: Bundesministerium fuer Unterricht und Kunst.
textbook; evaluation; content analysis; cross-national research
manuel d'enseignement; évaluation; analyse de contenu; recherche transnationale
PROJECT DESCRIPTION

Anfrage in mehr als dreissig Laendern, Auskuenfte liegen aus 25 Laendern vor, davon zwoelf aus der Bundesrepublik Deutschland (Beantwortungen der offiziellen Anfrage an die jeweiligen Schulbehoerden, Kontakte zu internationalen Schulbuchforschern). Schulbuchbegutachtung gibt es in Deutschland, USA (22 'adoption states'), Finnland, Norwegen, Japan und Oesterreich. Noch unklar ist die Situation in den Oststaaten, wo es frueher kein Begutachtungsverfahren gab, aber Forschungs- und Arbeitsstellen, die bei der Schulbuchproduktion den Staat vertraten. In einer Reihe von Laendern wird die Begutachtung vehement als staatliche Zensur und Einschraenkung der persoenlichen Freiheit abgelehnt. Besonders heftig waren die Diskussionen in Schweden, wo die Begutachtung im Juli 1991 abgeschafft wurde (Norwegen wird wahrscheinlich bald diesem Beispiel folgen). Die fuer Oesterreich interessantesten Hinweise stammen aus Deutschland, wo in den einzelnen Bundeslaendern teilweise unterschiedliche Richtlinien vorhanden sind. (In der Regel werden hier nicht Manuskripte, sondern die fertigen Buecher eingereicht, die Genehmigung erfolgt meist befristet.) In Laendern ohne Zulassungsverfahren (Frankreich, England, Schweden, teilweise USA) gibt es Beratungsstellen zur Gestaltung und Auswahl der Schulbuecher. In paedagogischen Zeitschriften finden sich Abhandlungen sowie kritische Besprechungen von Schulbuechern.

Es wurde die vergleichende Inhaltsanalyse verwendet.

13048 Evaluation of the response of teacher, parents and pupils to new forms of reporting introduced in the 5-14 development programme.
GBR 1993
Research Date(s): 1991-1995
MacBeath, J.; McAndrew, L.
Inst: Jordanhill College of Education, Division of Education and Psychology, Southbrae Drive, Jordanhill, Glasgow G13 1PP, United Kingdom.
Fin: Scottish Office Education Department.
student record; progress report; assessment; parent-pupil relation
dossier académique; rapport d'activité; appréciation; relation parents-élève
PROJECT DESCRIPTION

This project will examine the usefulness of new styles of reporting to parents, their implication for teachers and the degree to which pupils find them helpful and formative.

13049 Expert Meeting LDC. (Expert Meeting of the National Career Guidance Information Centre (LDC).)
NLD 1994
Research Date(s): 1990-1991
Grip, A. de; Berendsen, H.
Inst: ROA Researchcentrum voor Onderwijs en Arbeidsmarkt, Universiteit Limburg (Research Centre for Education and the Labour Market, University of Limburg), P.O. Box 616, 6200 MD Maastricht, Netherlands.
Fin: National Career Guidance Information Centre (LDC).
information need; labour market; regional administration
besoin d'information; marché du travail; administration régionale
PROJECT DESCRIPTION

Under a contract from the National Career Guidance Information Centre (LDC), a report was prepared concerning the need for and availability of regional labour market information, and on some recent initiatives towards improvement of the available information, in preparation for an expert meeting.

Publ: Grip, A. de. *Meer licht op de regionale arbeidsmarkt* (More light on the regional labour market), ROA-R-1991/4 (ISBN 90-5321-66-0).

Verslag van de Expert Meeting Regionale Arbeidsmarktinformatie (Report of the Expert Meeting on Regional Labour Market Information), 10 April 1991, LDC, The Hague, 1991.

13050 Footnotes in academic written discourse: a formal and functional analysis.
GBR 1993
Research Date(s): 1987-1991
El Sakran, T.
Sup: James, C.
Inst: University College of North Wales, School of English and Linguistics, College Road, Bangor, Gwynedd LL57 2DG, United Kingdom.
Fin: Egyptian Government Scholarship.
official text; document; language; comprehension
texte officiel; document; langage; compréhension
PROJECT DESCRIPTION

The aim of the study is to investigate the structures of footnotes in academic texts, their different types, their utility to the reader in understanding the texts they accompany, and their disruptive effect on reading comprehension.

13051 An international information and resources collection in adult education and training.
GBR 1993
Research Date(s): 1990-
Thompson, E.
Sup: Morgan, W.; Stock, A.
Inst: Nottingham University, Department of Adult Education, Centre for Research into the Education of Adults, 14-22 Shakespeare Street, Nottingham NG1 4FJ, United Kingdom.
Fin: Universities Funding Council.
data base; bibliography; adult education; vocational education; continuing education
banque de données; bibliographie; éducation des adultes; enseignement professionnel; éducation permanente
PROJECT DESCRIPTION

The aim of the research project is to establish an international information and bibliographical resources collection on adult education and training which will be of value to researchers engaged in international and comparative studies. The project involves the establishment of a database and production of a bibliography on comparative adult education and training.

13052 Local management of schools: database of research.
GBR 1993
Research Date(s): 1990-
Wallace, G.
Inst: Derbyshire College of Higher Education, Western Road, Mickleover, Derby DE3 5GX, United Kingdom.

Fin: Derbyshire College of Higher Education; British Educational Research Association.

information source; research; information dissemination; data base; educational administration

source d'information; recherche; diffusion de l'information; banque de données; administration de l'enseignement

PROJECT DESCRIPTION

The aim of this research is to establish and maintain a database of Local Management of Schools (LMS) related research with the objective of: (a) ensuring ready access to an overview of LMS research and findings for British Educational Research Association (BERA) members and other researchers; (b) widening such access beyond what is normally published, e.g. dissertations, and theses at Master's level; (c) identifying and disseminating successful practice; (d) identifying and disseminating issues of interest or concern to policy makers and the media.

Publ: Wallace, G. (ed.). *Local management of schools*. London: Multilingual Matters, 1991. British Educational Research Association. (BERA Dialogues Series, No 6).

13053 Television viewing among secondary school pupils.
GBR 1993
Research Date(s): 1990-1992
Francis, L.
Inst: Trinity College, Carmarthen, Dyfed SA31 3EP, United Kingdom.
television; pupil attitude; behaviour
télévision; attitude de l'élève; comportement
PROJECT DESCRIPTION

The project re-analyses data collected among over 5,000 secondary school pupils regarding television viewing habits. A sequence of analyses has led to a series of focused studies.

13054 Typologie a hodnocení variant tvorby učebnic v tržních podmínkách. (Examination and evaluation of approaches to textbook production under free market conditions.)
CSK 1994
Research Date(s): 1992-1993
Sirovátka, Jindřich; Dvořák, Dominik; Stretti, Mario; Frei, Václav; Obruča, Jan.
Sup: Peřtová, L.; Langová, J.
Inst: Portál, Klapkova 2, 180 00 Praha 8, Czech Republic.
Fin: Ministry of Education, Youth and Physical Education of the Czech Republic.
textbook; curriculum development; cross-national research; marketing
manuel d'enseignement; élaboration de programmes d'études; recherche transnationale; mercatique
PROJECT DESCRIPTION

Aim: (1) To examine the main approaches to textbook production in economically developed countries and to evaluate these from the angle of current educational reform in the Czech Republic; (2) to define the roles of social partners in the creation, authorization, financing and selection of textbooks.

Method: The study is based on book market marketing concepts.

13055 Untersuchung der Anpassung der oesterreichischen Schulbuecher an die Aufnahmekapazitaet, die Interessen und Beduerfnisse der Jugend. (A study of the extent to which Austrian school textbooks take account of the capacities, interests and needs of pupils.)
AUT 1993
Research Date(s): 1988-1992
Bamberger, Richard; Bamberger, Johannes; Gattermann, Brigitte; Gintenstorfer, Andrea; Hadrbolec, Hannelore; Laske, Michael.
Inst: Institut fuer Schulbuchforschung, Strozzigasse 2, A-1080 Wien.
Fin: Fonds zur Foerderung der wissenschaftlichen Forschung.
textbook; mental development; pupil; ability; interest; educational need
manuel d'enseignement; développement mental; élève; capacité; intérêt; besoin d'éducation
PROJECT DESCRIPTION

In Fortsetzung frueherer Arbeiten 'Die Lesbarkeit oder die Schwierigkeitsstufen von Texten in deutscher Sprache' und 'Zur Lesbarkeit und Lernbarkeit von Schulbuechern' legt dieses Projekt den Akzent auf die Schueleradaequatheit (Jugendgemaessheit). Um Rueckschluesse auf das oesterreichische Schulbuchwesen als Ganzes ziehen bzw. Auskuenfte ueber bestimmte Schulbuchgruppen erhalten zu koennen, wurde eine grosse Anzahl von Schulbuechern (150) verschiedener Schulstufen aus folgenden Gegenstaenden analysiert: Geschichte und Sozialkunde, Geographie und Wirtschaftskunde, Biologie und Umweltkunde, Physik sowie Schulbuecher des Polytechnischen Lehrgangs und der Berufsschule, die diese Unterrichtsfaecher abdecken. Anhand von Computeranalysen (rechnerisch bestimmte Lesbarkeitswerte), Analyseblaettern (u.a. Faktendichte, Begriffszahl, Kohaesionsgrad, Bekanntheitsgrad des Wortschatzes) und Besprechungen (vgl. Charakteristiken) wurden folgende Punkte besonders beleuchtet: sprachliche Schwierigkeit, Steigerung der inhaltlichen Anforderungen, Zahl der Fakten und Begriffe, Interpretation der quantitativen Ergebnisse, Gesichtspunkte der Ansprechbarkeit bezueglich der Schulbuchgestaltung

(u.a. Vorwort, Register, Glossar, Aufgaben, Beruecksichtigung des Vorwissens).

Die meisten Schulbuecher liegen um ein bis vier Schulstufen hoeher: Wenn man die hohen Anforderungen des Lehrplans und die noch hoeheren des Schulbuchs mit den Ergebnissen der Untersuchung vergleicht, ergibt sich die Forderung nach einer starken Reduzierung der Stoffuelle in den Schulbuechern, was auch eine schueleradaequate Gestaltung ermoeglichen wuerde. Die Besprechungen der Schulbuecher sind Grundlage und Hilfe fuer die Auswahl der Schulbuecher (in Planung: Schulbuchratgeber).

Es wurden Computeranalysen, Raumanalysen, Rundfragen und Inhaltsanalysen durchgefuehrt.

13056 Voraussetzungen und Resultate der begrifflichen Verarbeitung mediatisierte Erfahrungen. (Prerequisites and results of the conceptual processing of media-based experiences.)
DEU 1993
Research Date(s): 1989-1993
Schwarz, B.
Sup: Heid, H.
Inst: Universitaet Regensburg, Philosophische Fakultaet 02, Psychologie und Paedagogik, Institut fuer Paedagogik, LS Paedagogik, Gebaeude Pt, D-8400 Regensburg.
mass media; learning; communication; information source
médias; acquisition de connaissances; communication; source d'information
PROJECT DESCRIPTION

Inhalt: Ziel der Arbeit ist es zu pruefen, wieweit Massenmedien die kommunikative Kompetenz ihrer Rezipienten beeinflussen. Ausgangspunkt ist die Unterscheidung zwischen mediatisierter und nicht-mediatisierter Erfahrungen und deren Auswirkungen auf Begriffsbildungsprozesse. Im Kontext der Fragestellung wird eroertert, ob, wieweit und auf welche Weise informationsvermittelnde Institutionen begriffliches Lernen foerdern.

Vorgehensweise: Ideologiekritik; Literaturarbeit.

13057 Zur Sprache der Fibel. (The language of primers.)
AUT 1993
Research Date(s): 1988-1991
Bamberger, Richard; Mayer, Werner; Kaida, Ulrike; Oskamp, Irmtraud M.
Inst: Institut fuer Schulbuchforschung, Strozzigasse 2, A-1080 Wien.
Fin: Bundesministerium fuer Unterricht und Kunst.
textbook; reading; language development; pre-reading
manuel d'enseignement; lecture; développement du langage; préparation à la lecture
PROJECT DESCRIPTION

Forschungsansatz: Untersuchung der Sprache der Fibeln. Bisherige Untersuchungen konzentrierten sich hauptsaechlich auf die Methoden des Erstleseunterrichts. Mit Hilfe von drei eigens entwickelten Computerprogrammen wurden 24 Fibeln aus Oesterreich, der Bundesrepublik Deutschland, der Deutschen Demokratischen Republik und der Schweiz analysiert: 1. auf der Wortebene, 2. auf der Satzebene, 3. nach der Textform. Der Gesamtwortschatz liegt zwischen 1.900 und 16.000 Woertern. Die Zahl der verschiedenen Woerter liegt zwischen 587 und 3.100. Speicherungseffekt: 55% der Woerter kommen nur einmal vor. Wortartenverteilung: Ueberhang von Hauptwoertern, wenig Struktur- und Eigenschaftswoerter. Untersucht wurde auch das Verhaeltnis der Fibelsprache zur Kindersprache. Die meisten Fibelautoren betonen in den Lehrerheften, dass sie auf der Kindersprache aufbauen. Wenn das so waere, gaebe es in unserem Fall 24 Kindersprachen. Der Wortschatz der Fibeln unterscheidet sich sehr stark, er ist vor allem bestimmt von der Entwicklung des Buchstabenkanons, der zur Einfuehrung vieler seltener und unkindlicher Woerter fuehrt.

Es erfolgte die Entwicklung von eigenen Computerprogrammen.

Ksiega Pamiatkowa Gimnazjum i Liceum Ziemi Kujawskiej we Włocławku wydana z okazji Jubileuszu 90-lecia (Memory Book of Ziemia Kujawska Secondary School in Włocławek published on the occasion of the 90th anniversary)................................ see no. 12769

Programmata tis UNESCO gia ti Diethni Ekpaidefsi (Ekpaidefsi gia ta Dikaiomata tou Anthropou kai tin Eirini) kai Scholika Vivlia Protovathmias kai Defterovathmias Ekpaidefsis stin Ellada (UNESCO Projects on International Education (Education for Human Rights and Peace) and Greek primary and secondary school textbooks)..............
.... see no. 12780

Eesti pedagoogika ja psühholoogia terminoloogia koostamine ning terminite vôrdlev analüüs inglise-, saksa-, vene-, ja soomekeelsete vastetega (Composition of Estonian educational and psychological terminology and a comparative analysis with English, German, Russian and Finnish terminology)............................ see no. 12838

Emakeelse ôppekirjanduse jôukohasuse automaatanalüüs (Assessing the appropriateness of textbooks with the help of the computer)....
.... see no. 12841

Inventarizacija in analiza slovenske pedagoške terminologije (Inventory and analysis of Slovenian terminology of education) ....
.... see no. 12875

Scottish Standard Grade Beginners Latin Course: design of a course book.. see no. 12913

Vocabulary rate in course materials for English as a second or foreign language .... see no. 12947

Values education in Europe.. see no. 12971

Analýza výskumu mládeže v Slovenskej republike (Review of youth research in the Slovak Republic)................................... see no. 13018

The application of computer-aided learning to the development of information skills in further education........................ see no. 13019

Steirische Wirtschafts-, Wissenschafts- und Bildungsdatenbanken (Industrial, scientific and educational databases in Styria) ....
.... see no. 13031

Toky informací mezi ministerstvem školství, mládeže a tělovýchovy, školou, školskými institucemi, žáky a rodiči (Provision and dissemination of information among the Ministry of Education, schools, other educational institutions, pupils and parents) .... see no. 13036

Tvorba seznamů a sítí předškolních zařízení, škol a školských zařízení orgány státní správy (Creation of lists and information networks on pre-school establishments, schools and other educational institutions by State Administration Boards) .... see no. 13038

The mass media and the social construction of memory ....
.... see no. 13139

Reading, listening and television viewing: a study in children's cognition.. see no. 13152

Paedagogisches Wissen im Alltag: eine Explorationsstudie zum elterlichen Umgang mit paedagogischem Wissen am Beispiel der Einschulung (Pedagogic knowledge in everyday life: an exploratory study on parents' use of pedagogic knowledge, with particular reference to school choice).. see no. 13193

An evaluation of educational materials on HIV and AIDS for nurses
.... see no. 13316

Činnost' mládežníckych organizácií v Slovenskej republike (Activities of youth associations in the Slovak Republic) .... see no. 13419

Environmental education: a directory and review of research ....
.... see no. 13444

Technologie-indicatoren (Technology indicators) .... see no. 13514

Arbeidsmarktinformatie en arbeidsmarktdynamiek (Labour market information and labour market dynamics) .... see no. 13524

Arbeidsmarktmonitor voor het hoger beroepsonderwijs (Labour market monitor for higher vocational education) .... see no. 13525

Arbeidsmarktscanner Universiteit Limburg (Labour market scanner for the University of Limburg)....................................... see no. 13527

Arbeidsmarktscanner voor het hoger sociaal-agogisch onderwijs (Labour market scanner for the social work sector) ... see no. 13529

Arbeidsmarktvoorlichting en dynamiek op de arbeidsmarkt (Labour market information and labour market dynamics) .... see no. 13530

De actuele en toekomstige arbeidsmarktsituatie voor musici: haalbaarheidsonderzoek (The current and future labour market situation for musicians: a feasibility study)................................ see no. 13553

De vervangingsvraag naar beroepsklasse (Replacement demand by occupation).. see no. 13558

I-See! 1991 .... see no. 13588

Informatiesysteem onderwijs-arbeidsmarkt (Information system on education and the labour market)............................... see no. 13591

Inventarisatie van arbeidsmarktonderzoeken met betrekking tot het agrarisch onderwijs (Inventory of labour market research on agricultural training) .... see no. 13596

Onderwijs en arbeidsmarkt voor civiel ingenieurs (Education and the labour market for civil engineers)................................ see no. 13610

Occupational profiles of vocational counsellors............ see no. 13685

Technologie-indicatoren 1991 (Technology Indicators 1991)..............
.... see no. 13743

19 PERSONALITY DEVELOPMENT – DEVELOPPEMENT DE LA PERSONALITE – PERSOENLICHKEITSENTWICKLUNG

13058 Acquisition et gestion de la conduite de dialogue: la construction des finalités à travers le dialogue.
FRA 1993
Research Date(s): 1987-1990
Joulain, Michèle.
Inst: Université de Poitiers, UER Sciences humaines, CNRS URA /666, Laboratoire de psychologie du langage, 95 av. du Recteur Pineau, 86022 Poitiers Cedex, France.
language development; dialogue; pre-school child; mother-child relation; verbal behaviour
développement du langage; dialogue; enfant d'âge préscolaire; relation mère-enfant; comportement verbal
PROJECT DESCRIPTION
Objectifs: Cette étude, à caractère exploratoire, concerne l'investigation des comportements dialogiques du jeune enfant (24-30 mois) en situation dyadique, avec sa mère. On se propose de dégager les différents niveaux de traitement du même espace discursif, à travers l'analyse des réponses de l'enfant aux questions de l'adulte: (a) traitement des aspects linguistiques des questions (syntaxique, sémantique, pragmatique, discursif); (b) traitement de l'espace référentiel; (c) traitement de l'espace d'interaction sociale. L'utilisation contrôlée des types de questions permet de mettre en avant des stratégies de construction des réponses dans des situations déterminées, ainsi que des processus de planification et de contrôle de l'ensemble des opérations engagées.
Publ: Joulain, Michèle. Les dialogues enfants-maîtresse à l'école maternelle: un aspect du développement de la compétence à communiquer verbalement chez des enfants d'âge préscolaire. In: *Enfance*, 1988, 3-4, pp. 149-158.
Joulain, Michèle. Conversations maîtresse-enfants en maternelle: la circulation de la parole. In: *Revue française de pédagogie*, 1990, n° 91, pp. 59-67.

13059 L'adaptation à l'école maternelle des enfants issus de l'immigration maghrébine.
FRA 1993
Research Date(s): 1986-
Le Camus, Jean; Macary, Pascale; Beaumatin, Ania.
Inst: Université de Toulouse II, UFR Education Formation Insertion, CNRS URA /259, Département de psychologie - Laboratoire, personnalisation et changements sociaux, 5 allées Antonio Machado, 31058 Toulouse Cedex, France.
personality development; individualization; mother-child relation; socialization; social inequality; social adjustment; migrant worker's child; pre-school education; infancy
développement de la personnalité; individualisation; relation mère-enfant; socialisation; inégalité sociale; adaptation sociale; enfant de migrant; éducation préscolaire; prime enfance
PROJECT DESCRIPTION
Objectifs: Il s'agit de voir s'il existe des caractéristiques spécifiques de l'adaptation des enfants d'origine maghrébine à l'école maternelle. Cette adaptation est postulée comme directement liée, au vu de l'âge des sujets, aux types d'éducation familiale.
Méthodologie: L'étude comparative concerne une population de 60 enfants de 2-3 ans répartis selon trois groupes en fonction de leur origine socio-économique et socio-culturelle (a. enfants d'origine française-catégories défavorisées; b. enfants d'origine française-catégories moyennes; c. enfants d'origine maghrébine-catégories défavorisées). Les enfants sont filmés en récréation pendant leur première année de maternelle à raison de trois fois par trimestre (items comportementaux). Les maîtres évaluent les performances aux activités langagières, scolaires et sociales à partir d'un questionnaire. Un questionnaire oral sur les pratiques éducatives et les représentations est soumis aux mères des enfants.
Résultats: En ce qui concerne les enfants d'origine maghrébine en récréation, ils sont les moins sociaux et les plus dépendants du maître ou de leur fratrie. Au niveau de la classe ils ont des performances langagières meilleures que les enfants français de même catégorie sociale, leurs performances scolaires ne présentent pas d'homogénéité permettant de les caractériser. Les questionnaires aux mères maghrébines révèlent une éducation de type fusionnel avec leur enfant.

Publ: Le Camus, Jean. Modalités et facteurs de la transformation des rôles parentaux. In: *Bulletin de psychologie*, 1986-1987, 379, XI, pp. 423-429.

Le Camus, Jean. Les pratiques de nursing chez des parents d'enfants de crèche. In: *Enfance*, 1987, n° 3, pp. 245-261.

Macary, Pascale; Beaumatin, Ania & Philip, Carole. L'intégration de l'enfant à l'école, systèmes éducatifs et comportements d'adaptation: le cas des enfants migrants maghrébins. In: *Actes du colloque La Recherche en psychologie en Europe. Demandes sociales et réseaux scientifiques*, 1991, pp. 155-158.

13060 Bepaling beginsituatiekenmerken basisschoolleerlingen. (Determining the entry-level characteristics of primary school pupils.)

NLD 1994

Research Date(s): 1993-1995

Mooij, A.J.

Inst: Instituut voor Toegepaste Sociale wetenschappen (ITS) (Institute for Applied Social Sciences), P.O. Box 9048, 6500 KJ Nijmegen, Netherlands. Katholieke Universiteit Nijmegen (Catholic University of Nijmegen), P.O. Box 9102, 6500 HC Nijmegen, Netherlands

Fin: SVO het Instituut voor Onderzoek van het Onderwijs.

cognitive development; social development; pre-school child; entry to school; measuring instrument

développement cognitif; développement social; enfant d'âge préscolaire; entrée à l'école; instrument de mesure

PROJECT DESCRIPTION

Background: Children who develop at a relatively slow or fast rate run a greater risk of malfunctioning in school than their "average" class mates. These children benefit from suitable didactic stimulation as early as possible in their primary school career. School advisory services in the cities of Zoetermeer and Nijmegen are developing and using instruments and procedures whereby pupils' entry-level characteristics may be measured. These instruments have not been tested for validity and reliability; they partly overlap with existing instruments that have been tested for validity and reliability.

Aim: (1) To determine the validity and reliability of a number of instruments for measuring primary school pupils' entry-level characteristics; (2) to make recommendations as to the development of an "optimum" instrument.

Design: 12 schools will be using the Zoetermeer variant of the instrument and 12 schools will be using the Nijmegen variant. Administration of the instruments will be followed by measurements of the criterion variables. The cognitive and socio-communicative variables of the instruments will be measured per pupil four to seven months after school entry (4-5 year-olds). These variables give an estimate of the child's level of cognitive and socio-communicative development. The criterion variables are assessments based on extensive experience and standardized tests.

13061 Bio-Psychologie und Schule. (Bio-psychology at school.)

AUT 1993

Research Date(s): 1992-1994

Schachl, Hans.

Inst: Paedagogische Akademie der Dioezese Linz, Salesianumweg 3, A-4020 Linz.

Fin: Bundesministerium fuer Unterricht und Kunst.

brain; learning psychology; neurophysiology; learning; thinking

cerveau; psychologie de l'apprentissage; neurophysiologie; acquisition de connaissances; pensée

PROJECT DESCRIPTION

Es sollen wichtige Zusammenhaenge zwischen Lernvorgaengen und den biologischen Vorgaengen im Gehirn untersucht werden. Die dabei verwendete Methode, das sogenannte 'Brain- Mapping', ist in der Lage, die elektrischen Vorgaenge im Gehirn waehrend des Lernens und Denkens festzustellen. Es soll untersucht werden, wie weit bestimmte Lehr- und Lernmethoden, Methoden der Entspannung, etc. hirnbiologisch effizient sind.

Es wird ein Experiment an 100 SchuelerInnen der Uebungsvolksschule und Uebungshauptschule durchgefuehrt.

Es handelt sich um ein Experiment mit anschliessender statistischer Auswertung.

13062 Communication familiale et scolaire, articulation verbal-non verbal.

FRA 1993

Research Date(s): 1986-

Hudelot, Christian.

Inst: Université de Paris V, UFR Linguistique générale et appliquée, CNRS URA/1031, Laboratoire de recherches sur l'acquisition et la pathologie du langage chez l'enfant, 12 rue Cujas, 75230 Paris Cedex 05, France.

pre-school child; verbal communication; non-verbal communication; family environment; school environment; language development; verbal interaction; adult-child relation

enfant d'âge préscolaire; communication verbale; communication non-verbale; milieu familial; milieu scolaire; développement du langage; interaction verbale; relation adulte-enfant

PROJECT DESCRIPTION

Objectifs: La recherche s'articule sur deux axes. (a) Les travaux consacrés aux dialogues adulte-enfant en milieu familial ont permis en particulier une meilleure prise en compte de la circulation et de la restructuration de la référence dans les échanges adulte-enfant, ainsi qu'aux rôles de l'adulte dans ce type d'échange. (b) L'accent est mis maintenant sur la diversité des conduites d'interaction à l'école maternelle.

Méthodologie: Des enregistrements vidéo effectués régulièrement dans deux écoles de la proche banlieue parisienne permettent de s'interroger sur l'interrelation des conduites verbales et non verbales dans la communication chez des enfants de deux à quatre ans. Sont alors pris en compte le type d'activité, le thème de l'échange et la dimension du groupe.

Résultats: Deux constatations servent de fil conducteur à la recherche. D'abord une différence à la fois quantitative et qualitative des conduites des enfants en présence directe (active ou non) de la maîtresse, qui contraste avec celles des enfants en situation d'autonomie relative (présence de l'enquêteur et scolarité des tâches). Ces différences sont bien évidemment liées également à la dimension du groupe et à la propension des enfants à parler plutôt préférentiellement à deux, plus rarement à trois. Ce clivage conduit alors à rendre compte séparément des rôles de l'adulte dans l'étayage des conduites verbales ou des activités pratiques des enfants et sur la communication entre enfants pendant la réalisation de tâches pratiques (essentiellement peinture, dessin, activités manuelles), sans négliger les modes de relations qui s'établissent entre les enfants pendant les moments de "flottement", de changement d'activité. Dans sa seconde phase, cette recherche se centre sur le suivi longitudinal de quatre à cinq enfants de la section des deux à quatre ans et un travail transversal sur la relation à l'image mené en relation à un projet d'école sur la prélecture.

Publ: Hudelot, Christian. Organisateurs discursifs du dialogue inégalitaire. A propos de quelques dialogues adulte-enfant. In: *Modèles linguistiques*, 1987, IX, 1 (17), pp. 35-51.

Hudelot, Christian. Gestion de la différence dans le dialogue adulte-enfant et entre enfants. In: *Cahiers d'acquisition et de pathologie du langage*, 1988, n° 3, pp. 1-29.

Hudelot, Christian. Familiarité des interlocuteurs dans les dialogues adulte-enfant. In: *Protée*, 1990, vol. 18, n° 2, pp. 113-123.

Hudelot, Christian; Préneron, Christiane & Salazar-Orvig, Anne. Explications, distance et interlocution chez l'enfant de deux à quatre ans. In: *Cahiers d'acquisition et de pathologie du langage*, 1991, n° 7-8, pp. 241-255.

13063 The concerns of young people.

GBR 1993

Research Date(s): 1990-

Pumfrey, P.

Inst: Manchester University, School of Education, Centre for Educational Guidance and Special Needs, Oxford Road, Manchester M13 9PL, United Kingdom.

personality development; youth attitude; social behaviour; adolescent

développement de la personnalité; attitude de la jeunesse; comportement social; adolescent

PROJECT DESCRIPTION

This research concerns the psycho-social development of young persons aged from 11 to 18 years. The aim is to plot the changing concerns of males and females in relation to personal, educational and vocational issues. This is seen as a first step whereby young people can be helped to address their concerns in a variety of educational settings. Data are being collected from a variety of educational establishments using a specially devised checklist covering 15 major aspects of psycho-social development. In the present phase of the study, the current version of the Concerns Checklist is deliberately lengthy. To date, checklists from 3,000 pupils have been obtained. This database is being further extended.

13064 La construction de l'identité dans les trois premières années: un processus interactif producteur de transformations cognitives.

FRA 1993

Research Date(s): 1984-

Pinol-Douriez, Monique; Hurtig, Marie-Claude; Colas, Annie.

Inst: Université d'Aix-Marseille I, UFR Psychologie Sciences de l'éducation, CNRS URA/182, Centre de recherche en psychologie cognitive, 29 av. Robert Schuman, 13621 Aix-en-Provence, France.

personality development; identity; pre-school child; social interaction

développement de la personnalité; identité; enfant d'âge préscolaire; interaction sociale

PROJECT DESCRIPTION

Objectifs: Cette recherche sur la construction de l'identité chez les très jeunes enfants procède de l'hypothèse wallonnienne selon laquelle l'identité, comme ensemble bio-psycho-social, se construit au travers d'un réseau de dynamiques interactives qui implique et soutient l'activité cognitive; cette recherche s'inscrit dans le courant actuel des travaux sur les interactions précoces et sur l'émergence du self.

Méthodologie: Les données ont été recueillies par observation en crèche. Les observations longitudinales de six enfants (trois garçons et trois filles) ont été menées à partir de leur entrée à la crèche jusqu'à leur sortie de crèche et complétées par quelques observations au cours de la première année d'école maternelle. On dispose pour chaque enfant de 30 à 40 protocoles écrits, d'une demi-heure chacun, doublés d'un enregistrement vidéo à intervalles réguliers. La méthode de traitement des données est à deux niveaux d'analyse: l'une, molaire, s'appuie sur l'organisation séquentielle des conduites, l'autre se situe au niveau des unités de comportement (durée moyenne d'environ 15 secondes). Aux deux niveaux d'analyse les indicateurs retenus pour analyser le comportement de l'enfant et tenter de dégager les processus d'étayage en oeuvre dans la construction identitaire sont: la qualité d'engagement, les caractéristiques des articulations entre différenciation et dédifférenciation, la construction et la gestion des frontières du moi, les modalités de prise de contact dans les manifestations de ses intérêts.

Résultats: (1) Certaines modalités des premières différenciations mettent en évidence la précocité de l'activité catégorisante. (2) Dans l'élaboration de ces différenciations, les aspects cognitifs, conatifs, affectifs et émotionnels sont étroitement intriqués. (3) C'est dans le jeu sans cesse remanié des différenciations et des dédifférenciations que se dessinent les frontières de soi comme construction singulière du corps propre, du temps individuel, de l'autre. (4) Certaines modalités de régulation des tensions participent de la sémiotisation progressive de l'expérience. (5) Très précocément chaque enfant semble mettre en oeuvre un style interactif propre. La notion de processus d'étayage (R. Kaës, 1984) est un outil pour interpréter l'ensemble de ces résultats.

Publ: Pinol-Douriez, Monique; Hurtig, Marie-Claude & Colas, Annie. Médiations et transformations affectivo-cognitives: la construction de l'identité dans les trois premières années de la vie. *Actes du colloque européen: Construction et fonctionnement de l'identité*. Université d'Aix en Provence: CREPCO, 1988, pp. 143-152.

Pinol-Douriez, Monique; Hurtig, Marie-Claude & Colas, Annie. Dynamiques interactives de la construction de l'identité dans les trois premières années de la vie. In: B. Cramer (Ed.). *Psychiatrie du bébé. Nouvelles frontières*. Paris: ESHEL, 1988, pp. 363-390.

Pinol-Douriez, Monique; Hurtig, Marie-Claude & Colas, Annie. Gestion des tensions et gestion des frontières du moi dans les trois premières années: des processus fondamentaux pour la construction de l'identité. In: *Psychologie française*, n° spécial: L'identité de la personne, 1990, tome 35-1, pp. 25-33.

Colas, Annie; Pinol-Douriez, Monique & Hurtig, Marie-Claude. Processus d'étayage et autonomisation. In: *Le journal des psychologues*, Juin 1992.

13065 Critical assessment: Jean Piaget.
GBR   1993
Research Date(s): 1988-1991
Smith, L.
Inst: Lancaster University, Department of Educational Research, Cartmel College, Bailrigg, Lancaster LA1 4YW, United Kingdom.
intellectual development; intelligence; developmental psychology; history of education
développement intellectuel; intelligence; psychologie du développement; histoire de l'éducation
PROJECT DESCRIPTION

The aim of this collection is to survey, over the period 1950-1990, Piagetian commentary and criticism. The collection is in four volumes, each of which deals with a series of case-studies relevant to central issues in this Piagetian critique. The four volumes are: (1) understanding and intelligence; (2) children's thinking; (3) education and society; (4) intellectual development. Each volume includes an integral guide to the selected papers. A general introduction (in Volume 1) and a concluding assessment (in Volume 4) are also provided.

The papers have been selected with two features in mind. First, the issues in each volume have included contributions dealing with replication, elaboration, application and evaluation of Piaget's work at both empirical and theoretical levels. Second, mindful of the competing appraisals of Piaget's work, contributions have been selected with due attention to the successive dialogues which have been characteristic of the Piagetian critique over this period.

Piaget's work continues to attract the attention of developmentalists. There is every expectation that this will continue in the 1990s. This is not merely because Piaget's questions are fundamentally interesting to those with a concern for developmental theory, it is also because his work is still a fertile intellectual resource. Piagetian research is a vast and expanding body of inter-disciplinary writings. Those who are daunted by the prospect of thinking about Piaget's problems often turn to this research in their search for clarification and enlightenment. In fact, Piagetian research makes more, not less, demands on developmentalists.

Publ: Smith, L. (ed.). *Critical Assessment: Jean Piaget*. London: Routledge, 1992.

13066 Data analysis of the longitudinal research project: changes in general ability, personality, attitudes, values etc. of normal children from infancy to adolescence.
GBR   1993
Research Date(s): 1949-
Moore, T.
Sup: Hindley, C.
Inst: London University, Institute of Education, Department of Child Development and Primary Education, 20 Bedford Way, London WC1H OAL, United Kingdom.
Fin: Leverhulme Trust.
child development; personality development; child; adolescent
développement de l'enfant; développement de la personnalité; enfant; adolescent
PROJECT DESCRIPTION

The research began in 1949 as a collaborative project between the Institute of Education and the Department of Child Health at London University. There is thus a parallel research under Professor J.M. Tanner on the physical development of the same subjects. As representative a sample as possible of the London West Central 1 area was recruited from 1949 to 1952. 223 subjects were recruited, and 186 were in the sample at 18 months. For many purposes the researchers have around 110 subjects with records complete enough for general use up to 14 years; and 84 plus, up to 17 years. Subjects were seen at 8 days, 6 weeks, 3, 6, 9, 12 and 18 months, and then annually from 2 to 18 years.

The aim was to obtain reasonably comprehensive information, which includes: (1) regular interviews with mothers about their child's behaviour and parental methods; (2) testing of abilities, personality, etc; (3) assessment of interests, attitudes, personal values; and (4) interviews with adolescent subjects. Data on social and family background have been obtained throughout.

The researchers' interests have been: (i) comparison of child-rearing methods and early locomotion across collaborating European samples; (ii) infant sleep and the effects of anoxia at birth; (iii) effects of daily substitute care; (iv) stability and change in IQs and personality using individual curve fitting in addition to correlations etc.; (v) factors influencing development - family, social, life events, school etc.; and (vi) children's views of themselves or school, of their future and their correspondence with outcome.

Publ: A full list of publications is available from the researchers.

13067 The development of causal reasoning.
GBR   1993
Research Date(s): 1988-1992
Das Gupta, P.
Inst: Medical Research Council, Cognitive Development Unit, 17 Gordon Street, London WC1H OAL, United Kingdom.
cognitive development; reasoning; pre-school child
développement cognitif; raisonnement; enfant d'âge préscolaire
PROJECT DESCRIPTION

The main focus of this research has been the development of causal understanding in the pre-school years. The relationship between intelligence and causal reasoning has been explored with particular attention to causal inferences made by children with learning difficulties and autism. Although children with learning difficulties solve causal reasoning tasks correctly, they show considerable delay. This is also true of the autistic sample. Normal 4-year-olds are significantly better at causal reasoning tasks than children with learning difficulties whose mental age is below 5 years.

An attempt has been made to distinguish knowledge from inference and one strand of the research explores how knowledge of familiar transformations may be accessed to make appropriate inferences. Variations of the task and how these improve inferences have also been explored.

Publ: Das Gupta, P. & Bryant, P. Young children's causal inferences. In: *Child Development*, Vol 60, 1989, pp. 1138-1146.

13068 Différenciation intra et interindividuelle à l'adolescence.
FRA   1993
Research Date(s): 1988-
Massonnat, Jean; Lecacheur, Mireille.
Inst: Université d'Aix-Marseille I, UER Psychologie, Centre de recherche en psychologie du développement et de l'éducation, 29 av. de l'Arc de Meyran, 13100 Aix-en-Provence, France.
adolescence; personality development; individual characteristics; individualization; interpersonal relations
adolescence; développement de la personnalité; caractéristique individuelle; individualisation; relations interpersonnelles
PROJECT DESCRIPTION

Objectifs: Partant du constat fait par Rosenberg et Rodriguez-Tomé des progrès de la différenciation individuelle entre 12 et 18 ans, on envisage deux questions complémentaires: vérifier si cette tendance est mise en oeuvre par l'adolescent dans l'analyse de cas concernant autrui ou des événements de vie qui lui sont personnels, étudier le lien qui s'établit entre l'évolution du sentiment de différenciation intra-individuelle et celle du sentiment de différenciation interindividuelle.

Méthodologie: Une pré-enquête permet de choisir les cas concernant autrui et les événements de vie personnels à faire analyser au sujet. La tâche pour l'adolescent consiste à analyser les événements de vie le concernant et d'autre part ceux concernant autrui; dans ce dernier cas, on lui demande d'anticiper une action impliquant des relations à d'autres (individus ou groupes). La confrontation des deux analyses permet d'appréhender la covariation évoquée entre ces deux aspects de la différenciation.

Publ: Lecacheur, Mireille & Massonnat, Jean. Mémoire autobiographique et analyse rétrospective des changements identitaires: impact des différentes séquences d'évènements. In: *Technologies, idéologies et pratiques*, 1989, 3-4, pp. 253-259.

Massonnat, Jean & Lecacheur, Mireille. L'identité, un champ d'étude en construction. In: *Psychologie française*, 1990, 35, 1, pp. 3-6.

Massonnat, Jean & Lecacheur, Mireille. Le schéma de personne dans l'analyse des changements identitaires: approche expérimentale et son opérativité. In: *Psychologie française*, 1990, 35, 1, pp. 67-76.

13069 Dynamiques identitaires à l'épreuve de situations de formation.
FRA 1993
Research Date(s): 1987-
Dupuy, Raymond; Martineau, J.P.; Bordes, O.
Inst: Université de Toulouse II, UFR Education Formation Insertion, CNRS URA/259, Département de psychologie - Laboratoire, personnalisation et changements sociaux, 5 allées Antonio Machado, 31058 Toulouse Cedex, France.
personality development; continuing education; identity; adult; social development; social role
développement de la personnalité; éducation permanente; identité; adulte; développement social; rôle social
PROJECT DESCRIPTION

Objectifs: Les transformations socio-techniques, innovations technologiques, nouveaux rôles professionnels, affectent les individus aux divers plans cognitifs, psycho-socio-affectifs et idéologiques qui sont autant de dimensions entrant en jeu dans le sentiment d'identité. Cette recherche étudie les processus sollicités par les individus pour réguler les transformations auxquelles ils sont confrontés et restaurer ou maintenir une estime d'eux-mêmes satisfaisante, indicateur du sentiment d'identité. Ces travaux s'inscrivent dans le courant interactionniste qui fait de l'identité la résultante dynamique de l'influence réciproque individu-environnement social.

Méthodologie: Les formations d'adultes sont choisies comme classe de situations des recherches car elles présentent des caractéristiques d'amplification de ces processus: (1) processus identitaires en situation de communication à distance: visioconférence et audioconférence; (2) transformation des représentations de soi et du monde du travail au cours d'une formation qualifiante de longue durée (36 stagiaires en qualification universitaire sur trois ans).

Publ: Martineau, J.P. & Dupuy, Raymond. L'option transitionnelle à propos des situations de formation. In: *Revue internationale de psychologie sociale*, 1990, 3, 1, pp. 67-87.

13070 Eesti algkooliôpilaseareng ja seda môjutavad faktorid. (Factors influencing the development of primary school pupils in Estonia.)
EST 1994
Research Date(s): 1989-1992
Talts, L.; Nilson, O.; Kiili, J.; et al.
Sup: Hiie, E.
Inst: Tallinna Pedagoogikaülikool (Tallinn Pedagogical University), 0102 Tallinn, Narva mnt.25, Estonia.
Fin: EV Haridusministeerium.
child development; pupil; primary education
développement de l'enfant; élève; enseignement primaire
PROJECT DESCRIPTION

The study examines: indications as to the actual development of primary school children; developmental regularities in current Estonian society; aspects of the education system that are relevant for a more effective determination of children's development.

Research methods: Observation, sociological questionnaire, analysis of pupils' school work and school documents, standardized tests.

A total of 1,500 school children have been tested. The results will be used to study the effectiveness of school reform and to make recommendations for the improvement of primary schools.

13071 Effect of perceptuo-motor difficulty on early handwriting, speech and reading.
GBR 1993
Research Date(s): 1992-1995
Haines, C.
Inst: London University, Institute of Education, Department of Educational Psychology and Special Educational Needs, 20 Bedford Way, London WC1H OAL, United Kingdom.
Fin: Nuffield Foundation.
graphomotor activity; motor development; perceptual development; writing; reading; speech
graphomotricité; développement moteur; développement perceptif; écriture; lecture; parole
PROJECT DESCRIPTION

In an earlier study, children entering school routinely completed neurodevelopmental tasks in the entrant school medical examination. To study the effect of difficulties with these on later school activities in and around the classroom, teachers completed a questionnaire in final year infant and first year junior classes, and children copied a sentence from the blackboard. Some four thousand children were involved. Now the geometric shapes copied at school entry, and the sentence copied from the blackboard are being assessed in greater detail to test the effect of perceptuo-motor difficulties on early handwriting skills.

Publ: Haines, C. Young children's difficulty with capital letters. In: *Handwriting Review*, 1992, pp. 44-54.

13072 Etude développementale des premières capacités narratives.
FRA 1993
Research Date(s): 1987-
Sabeau-Jouannet, Emilie.
Inst: Université de Paris V, UFR Linguistique générale et appliquée, CNRS URA/1031, Laboratoire de recherches sur l'acquisition et la pathologie du langage chez l'enfant, 12 rue Cujas, 75230 Paris Cedex 05, France.
pre-school child; language development; pupil; oral expression; verbal behaviour; language skill; story telling
enfant d'âge préscolaire; développement du langage; élève; expression orale; comportement verbal; aptitude linguistique; narration d'histoires
PROJECT DESCRIPTION

Objectifs: La recherche porte sur deux périodes du développement des capacités narratives du jeune enfant: les débuts du récit oral chez l'enfant de trois à cinq ans et des récits écrits scolaires. On a déjà souligné que les débuts du récit oral étaient dans la dépendance étroite de l'étayage de l'adulte. Pour le découpage des faits et de leur articulation associative ou logique, l'enfant est soumis à la double problématique de la prégnance de son rapport au référent et à l'intérêt de/pour son interlocuteur: (1) au niveau de la tendance à synthétiser ou à détailler les événements; (2) au niveau de l'organisation et de la centration de leur déroulement.

Méthodologie: Les corpus ont été recueillis dans des écoles maternelles des 13e, 18e et 20e arrondissements de Paris. (1) Des reproductions de récits de conte; (2) des récits d'expérience personnelle: une journée de vacances; une bagarre, une expérience de découverte; (3) des récits de fiction et de rêves où le temps de la circularité et de la répétition demeurent, à cet âge, les plus importants.

Résultats: L'analyse s'oriente sur le traitement de l'évènement, la dimension de l'évènement, le degré de généralité porté par les catégories lexicales et grammaticales, l'établissement de scripts ou de saynettes dans des micro-continuités, les rôles et les statuts des personnages. La gestion du temps du récit s'articule au point de vue et au pathos. La continuité des enchaînements s'élabore au niveau local et au niveau global des grandes articulations du récit. Les deux niveaux de la continuité reposent bien sur l'intelligibilité des petites scènes de la vie quotidienne de l'enfant (scripts) mais aussi de l'imaginaire de la littérature enfantine (particulièrement les contes) mais encore les figures du pathos ("figures" des peurs et des angoisses enfantines ou des ressorts de son humour et de sa gaîté).

Si le développement des compétences narratives de l'enfant de trois à six ans manisfeste une tendance générale à aller du rapprochement de faits sur des caractéristiques liées à la situation, au rapprochement des évènements de caractères semblables puis à la séquence d'évènements reliés en chaînes, puis dans une relation de causalité, on peut dire qu'une grammaire de texte échouera à rendre compte de l'hétérogénéité et de l'inattendu des créations de l'enfant.

13073 An exploratory study on school readiness, with special reference to the school-aged children in Taiwan.
GBR 1993
Research Date(s): 1986-1991
Wu, L.
Sup: Entwistle, N.
Inst: Edinburgh University, Department of Education, 10-12 Buccleuch Place, Edinburgh EH8 9JT, United Kingdom.
Fin: Republic of China, Ministry of Education.
maturity; entry to school; Taiwan
maturité; entrée à l'école; Taiwan
PROJECT DESCRIPTION

The aim of the present research is twofold. First, to explore the reality of school readiness in progress, and second to discover the causes for the difference in children's readiness. The sample comprises thirty-six school-age entrants and their parents and four primary 1 teachers in Taiwan. Open-ended interviewing and fieldnote observations are the major methods employed in fieldwork.

13074 Fen Lisesi ile Ömer Seyfettin Lisesi öğrencilerinin denetim odağına göre bazı değişkenler yönünden karşılaştırılması. (The comparison of locus of control of pupils in two secondary schools.)
TUR 1994
Research Date(s): 1990
Giderer, Hakkı Engin.
Sup: Voltan-Acar, Nilüfer.
Inst: Hacettepe Üniversitesi, Eğitim Fakültesi, Psikolojik Hizmetler Bölümü (Hacettepe University, Faculty of Education, Department of Psychological Services), 06532 Beytepe, Ankara, Turkey.
individual characteristics; psychological characteristics; admission requirements; secondary school
caractéristique individuelle; caractéristique psychologique; conditions d'admission; école secondaire
PROJECT DESCRIPTION

The study examined whether pupils at Fen Secondary School, who are admitted after a special test, would attain lower scores on the Nowicki-Strickland Locus of Control Scale than the pupils of the Ömer Seyfettin Secondary School, who are admitted without any test.

Independent variables were: gender, achievement perception of primary and middle school, educational level of parents, pupils' environment, status of the mother (employed or unemployed).

The Nowicki-Strickland Locus of Control Scale and a questionnaire prepared by the researcher were administered to 200 pupils from both schools. In the statistical analysis t-tests were used.

The findings revealed that the pupils of the Fen Secondary School had higher internal locus of control than the pupils of the Ömer Seyfettin Secondary School.

13075 La formation du sens critique chez l'enfant et la construction du lien politique.
FRA 1993
Research Date(s): 1990-
Derouet, Jean-Louis.
Sup: Boltanski, Luc.
Inst: Ministère de l'éducation, Ecole des hautes études en sciences sociales, CNRS URA/1124, Groupe de sociologie politique et morale, 105 Bd Raspail, 75006 Paris, France.
political socialization; political behaviour; critical sense; social development; group membership; child development
socialisation politique; comportement politique; sens critique; développement social; appartenance au groupe; développement de l'enfant
PROJECT DESCRIPTION

Objectifs: On procède à une réflexion théorique et à la mise en place de procédures empiriques visant à analyser la formation des capacités critiques chez les enfants et, par là, à apporter une contribution à la sociologie de l'enfance en rapprochant la question reprise par la psychologie moderne, de la formation du jugement moral, d'interrogations portant plutôt sur la constitution du sens politique.

Méthodologie: Les études mises en place, en combinant des techniques expérimentales relevant d'une approche cognitiviste et des méthodes d'observation s'inspirant des travaux, surtout anglo-saxons, portant sur l'ethnographie de la vie scolaire, vise à analyser l'évolution, chez l'enfant, de la capacité à mettre en oeuvre une activité critique pour construire un lien plus ou moins durable avec les autres: le lien politique. Un travail est entrepris auprès de lycéens quant à leur participation comme délégués-élèves aux conseils dans les établissements scolaires.

13076 Gender differences in motor performance from infancy to adolescence.
GBR 1993
Research Date(s): 1990-1995
Lancey, K.
Sup: Durojaiye, S.
Inst: Cardiff Institute of Higher Education, School of Physical Education, Sport and Leisure, Cyncoed Centre, Cardiff, United Kingdom; University of Wales College of Cardiff, School of Education, Senghenaydd Road, Cardiff CF2 4AG, United Kingdom.
motor development; sex difference
développement moteur; différence de sexe
PROJECT DESCRIPTION

The aim of the research is to identify gender differences in the motor performance of children of primary school age, and to account for those differences.

13077 Genèse des processus argumentatifs.
FRA 1993
Research Date(s): 1985-1988
Caron, Jean; Caron-Pargue, Josiane.
Inst: Université de Poitiers, UER Sciences humaines, CNRS URA/666, Laboratoire de psychologie du langage, 95 av. du Recteur Pineau, 86022 Poitiers Cedex, France.
language development; argumentation; oral expression; verbal interaction; conversation

développement du langage; argumentation; expression orale; interaction verbale; conversation
PROJECT DESCRIPTION

Objectifs: L'étude de l'acquisition des marqueurs argumentatifs et de leur mise en oeuvre dans des situations d'interlocution est menée grâce au recueil de productions et à l'analyse des verbalisations d'enfants de 3 à 8 ans dans des situations de conversation libre ou semi-contrôlée. Les analyses portent sur trois points: (1) les étapes de l'acquisition de marqueurs argumentatifs (notamment des connecteurs) et de leurs conditions d'emploi; (2) la genèse des procédés argumentatifs, et notamment des procédures de réfutation; (3) l'analyse des productions verbales dans une situation de conflit socio-cognitif (le type de conflit étudié oppose des enfants pré-opératoires et opératoires dans un problème de conservation des quantités, selon un paradigme utilisé par Doise et Mugny).

Publ: Caron, Jean. Pour une approche psycholinguistique de l'argumentation. In: Pieraut-Le Bonniec, G. (éd.). *Connaître et le dire.* Bruxelles: Mardaga, 1987.
Caron, Jean. Processing connectives and the pragmatics of discourse. In: Verschueren, J. & Bertucelli Papi, M. (éds.). *The pragmatic perspective.* Amsterdam: J. Benjamins, 1987, pp. 567-580.
Caron, Jean. Comment aborder l'interaction verbale dans un modèle psycholinguistique. In: Cosnier, J. & Kerbrat Orecchioni, C. (éds.). *Echanges sur la conversation.* Paris: CNRS, 1988, pp. 123-134.
Caron-Pargue, Josiane & Caron, Jean. Towards a psycholinguistic approach of argumentative operators: the *thinking aloud* procedure. In: Van Eemeren, F.H.; Grootendorst, R.; Blair, J.A. & Villard, C.A. (éds.). *Argumentation, perpectives and approaches.* Dordrecht: Foris Publications, 1987, pp. 170-178.

13078 Geschlechtsspezifische Unterschiede im verbosensomotorischen Niveau bei Kindern im Alter von 4-6 Jahren und ihre Veraenderungen in der Schule der DDR. (Sex-specific differences in the verbal-sensorimotor development of children aged 4-6 in schools in the GDR.)
DEU 1993
Research Date(s): 1991-1993
Amse, C.
Sup: Rueckriem, G.; Breuer, S.
Inst: Hochschule der Kuenste Berlin, FB 10 Erziehungs- und Gesellschaftswissenschaften, Institut fuer Allg. Paedagogik WE 01, Bundesallee 1-12, D-1000 Berlin 15.
sensorimotor activity; school; German DR; pre-school child; sex difference; child; motor development
sensorimotricité; école; Allemagne RDA; enfant d'âge préscolaire; différence de sexe; enfant; développement moteur
PROJECT DESCRIPTION

Inhalt: Ueberpruefung der Geschlechtsspezifitaet der kindlichen Entwicklung im Bereich der Verbosensomotorik. Ueberpruefung der Auswirkung der Koedukation darauf.

Geographischer Raum: Greifswald.

Untersuchter Zeitraum: 1976-1987.

Vorgehensweise: Konzept der verbosensomotorischen Entwicklung nach Breuer und Weuffen. Untersuchungsdesign: Panel.

Datengewinnung: Screening (Stichprobe: ca. 800; alle Kindergartenkinder der Stadt Greifswald; Auswahlverfahren: total). Sekundaeranalyse bereits vorhandener maschinenlesbarer Datensaetze.

13079 Image de soi et interactions sociales.
FRA 1993
Research Date(s): 1987-1989
Meyer, Roger.
Inst: Université d'Aix-Marseille I, UER Psychologie, Centre de recherche en psychologie du développement et de l'éducation, 29 av. de l'Arc de Meyran, 13100 Aix-en-Provence, France.
self-esteem; self-concept; social interaction; performance; skill; child
estime de soi; conception de soi; interaction sociale; performance; compétence; enfant
PROJECT DESCRIPTION

Objectifs: On fait l'hypothèse que la confrontation des points de vue entre partenaires dépend en partie des images préalables de soi et du partenaire, en particulier en ce qui concerne le sentiment de compétence. Complémentairement, en se plaçant dans le cadre des théories sociales du concept de soi, ces situations d'interactions sociales peuvent entraîner des modifications sur les images de soi et de l'autre.

Méthodologie: Une expérimentation a consisté à observer le fonctionnement et la performance d'une soixantaine d'enfants en situation dyadique d'interaction dans la tâche de pesées fictives. Au pré-test et au post-test les enfants avaient à répondre à un questionnaire de description de soi et à un questionnaire d'évaluation du sentiment de valeur de soi en se comparant à l'autre membre de la dyade.

Résultats: L'analyse des résultats montre que le sentiment initial global de valeur de soi est en liaison avec la qualité du travail (actif-passif) dans la dyade et la qualité des échanges au cours de la réalisation de la tâche, et que le sentirnent initial de compétence cognitive est en liaison avec la qualité de la performance. Enfin, les dyades les plus efficaces dans la tâche proposée et les plus dynamiques dans leur fonctionnement (quantité des échanges) sont surtout celles qui sont constituées par des sujets qui se jugent d'une manière identique sur leurs compétences cognitives. L'étude des évolutions individuelles des images de soi montre de son côté une tendance à la valorisation de soi au post-test chez les enfants qui ont été particulièrement actifs dans les dyades et ont réalisé de bonnes performances.

Publ: Meyer, Roger. Image de soi et statut scolaire en éducation physique et sportive. In: *Infancia y aprendizage*, 1987, 37, pp. 45-56.
Meyer, Roger. Image de soi et statut scolaire: influence de déterminants familiaux et scolaires chez des élèves du cours moyen. In: *Bulletin de psychologie*, 1987, 40, pp. 933-939.
Meyer, Roger. Une approche des valeurs personnelles des adolescents: données générales et différentielles d'une enquête faite dans quelques collèges. In: *Enfance*, 1988, 41, pp. 75-86.
Meyer, Roger. Expérience éducative et positionnement de soi chez des élèves de collège. In: *Revue internationale de psychologie sociale*, 1989, 2, pp. 442-446.

13080 Individuatieprocessen bij Turkse, Marokkaanse, Chinese en Nederlandse jongvolwassenen. (Individuation processes among Turkish, Moroccan, Chinese and Dutch young adults.)
NLD 1994
Research Date(s): 1992-1993
Ledoux, G.; Deckers, P.
Sup: Meijnen, G.W.
Inst: Stichting Centrum voor Onderwijsonderzoek (SCO) (Centre for Educational Research), Grote Bickersstraat 72, 1013 KS Amsterdam, Netherlands.
Universiteit van Amsterdam (University of Amsterdam), P.O. Box 19268, 1000 GG Amsterdam, Netherlands
Fin: SVO het Instituut voor Onderzoek van het Onderwijs.
social adjustment; socialization; value system; immigrant; target groups of education; ethnic group
adaptation sociale; socialisation; système de valeurs; immigrant; destinataires de l'éducation; groupe ethnique
PROJECT DESCRIPTION
Background: A major goal of education in the Netherlands is to enable pupils to form an independent, individual judgement. This appears to pose problems for certain groups of pupils, such as Turkish and Moroccan pupils from an Islamic background. This may be due to specific aspects of child-rearing and socialization processes in Turkish and Moroccan families.
Aim: To investigate what factors have caused changes in the value systems or adjustment strategies of a number of selected, socially successful, Turkish, Moroccan and Chinese immigrants who have been raised in the Netherlands.
Design: A study will be made of relevant national and international literature. This is to result in a classification that can serve as a basis for in-depth interviews with Turkish, Moroccan, Chinese and Dutch young adults who have developed a "socially accepted" life style. Two interviews will be conducted per ethnic group in order to gain some first impressions and to test the hypotheses that have emerged from the literature survey. Following that, six in-depth interviews will be conducted per ethnic group. The subjects have an educational qualification at the level of senior secondary vocational education or higher vocational education and hold corresponding posts. The sample will contain equal numbers of males and females.

13081 Individuazione del contributo della scuola soluzione dei fenomeni di disagio giovanile. (The contribution of schools to remedying maladjustment among young people.)
ITA 1994
Research Date(s): 1990-1991
Giambattista, Vincenzo; Palumbo, Roberto.
Sup: Verini, Antonio.
Inst: Istituto Ricerca Sperimentazione Aggiornamento Educativi d'Abruzzo - IRRSAE (Regional Institute for Educational Research, Innovation and Teacher Training of Abruzzo), Via Aldo Moro 30, 67100 L'Aquila, Italy.
Ministero della Pubblica Istruzione (Ministry of Public Education), Viale Trastevere 76, 00100 Roma, Italy
Fin: Regione Abruzzo.
maladjustment; attitude towards school; pupil attitude; wastage; dropout; upper secondary
inadaptation; attitude envers l'école; attitude de l'élève; déperdition d'effectifs; abandon d'études; secondaire deuxième cycle
PROJECT DESCRIPTION
The aims of the project are: to study the phenomenon of maladjustment among youth and the way it manifests itself; to provide schools with information about the conditions for interventions aimed at reducing dropout and wastage.
Design: (1) Investigation in an upper secondary school in Aquila, taking into account students' social background; (2) a broad investigation of other upper secondary schools in the province; (3) identification of effective schools policies to prevent maladjustment.

Methods: Questionnaire survey, document analysis.

13082 L'intégration sociale des enfants de 4 à 7 ans: étude longitudinale.
FRA 1993
Research Date(s): 1988-
Prêteur, Yves; Lescarret, Odette; Beaumatin, Ania; Sublet, Françoise; Tap, Pierre; Louvet Schmauss, E.
Inst: Université de Toulouse II, UFR Education Formation Insertion, CNRS URA/259, Département de psychologie - Laboratoire, personnalisation et changements sociaux, 5 allées Antonio Machado, 31058 Toulouse Cedex, France.
socialization; pre-school child; identification; family environment; school environment; social integration; follow-up study
socialisation; enfant d'âge préscolaire; identification; milieu familial; milieu scolaire; intégration sociale; étude longitudinale
PROJECT DESCRIPTION
Objectifs: Etude longitudinale qui a pour objectif d'observer et d'expliquer le processus d'intégration-exclusion sociale chez les jeunes enfants (4 à 7 ans) en prenant en compte les trois principaux contextes éducatifs dans lesquels évoluent les enfants: la famille, l'école, les structures d'accueil du quartier. L'hypothèse est que les conceptions et les pratiques éducatives dans les principaux milieux de vie de l'enfant sont en relation dialectique avec les différents aspects des conduites des enfants de 4 à 7 ans.
Méthodologie: La population de départ est constituée de 260 enfants tout venant inscrits en moyenne section maternelle. (1) Dans le contexte familial sont appliqués des questionnaires et des épreuves projectives. (2) Dans le contexte scolaire: mesure des compétences en langage oral et écrit, des indicateurs des relations enfant-enseignant, enfant et milieu socio-familial (représentations que les parents ont de l'école, accompagnement scolaire de l'enfant). (3) Structures d'accueil du quartier: entretiens semi-directifs auprès des travailleurs sociaux, échelles de compétences sociales appliquée aux enfants, interactions entre enfants enregistrées.
Résultats: Il ressort la possibilité de dégager très tôt (chez des enfants de 4 ans) la variété des modes d'acquisition, des compétences sociales et des capacités d'affronter des situations conflictuelles inter- et intrapsychiques en relation avec les conceptions éducatives parentales et la pédagogie scolaire.

Publ: Prêteur, Yves; Sublet, Françoise; Tap, Pierre; Beaumatin, Ania & Lescarret, Odette. *Intégration sociale des enfants de 4 à 7 ans. Etude longitudinale*. Rapport de recherche 1988-1989, 1989.

13083 An investigation into the physical activity levels of primary school children.
GBR 1993
Research Date(s): 1991-1993
Warburton, P.
Sup: Sleap, M.
Inst: Durham University, School of Education, Leazes Road, Durham DH1 1TA, United Kingdom; Hull University, School of Education, Cottingham Road, Hull HU6 7RX, United Kingdom.
Fin: Health Education Authority.
motor activity; teaching aid; primary education; health education
motricité; moyen d'enseignement; enseignement primaire; éducation sanitaire
PROJECT DESCRIPTION
The aim of the research is to evaluate a two year dissemination programme presently being undertaken by the Happy Heart Resource project team at Hull University. This dissemination programme is centred on the resource materials produced by the project. The evaluation aims to: (1) establish views of teachers regarding usage of resource packs; (2) assess the activity levels of a sample of children experiencing Happy Heart resources in comparison to a matched group of children not involved in the project.

13084 An investigation of the relationship between perinatal risk factors and contingency learning and attentive behaviour in later infancy.
GBR 1993
Research Date(s): 1985-
Millar, W.; Weir, C.
Inst: London University, University College London, Department of Psychology, Gower Street, London WC1E 6BT, United Kingdom; Watford General Hospital, Shrodells Wing, Vicarage Road, Watford WD1 8HB, United Kingdom.
cognitive development; birth; brain injury; infancy; behaviour disorder; child development
développement cognitif; naissance; lésion cérébrale; prime enfance; trouble du comportement; développement de l'enfant
PROJECT DESCRIPTION
The research examines the relationship between specific major categories of perinatal risk and cognitive functioning in later infancy. Attentional and contingency analysis behaviours are examined in relation to several medical risk factors because of their potential central nervous system

(CNS) involvement; prematurity; the effects of oxygenation/respiratory problems.

Three groups of infants are established on the basis of clinical data and objective brain imaging data: (i) infants who revealed a normal brain scan and who at term were neurologically normal, i.e. no discernable CNS involvement; (ii) infants whose scan analysis revealed discrete but non-threatening injury; and (iii) infants whose scan revealed more complex and extensive injury. Behavioural measures on two attention/learning tasks were obtained from 6-12 month old infants who previously experienced the categories of perinatal risk in order to examine the effects of early CNS related risk/damage to later cognitive functioning.

The findings are expected to be relevant to early educative interventive strategies for basic skills acquisition in early infancy and early childhood.

13085 Is the sex-type of an individual an influencing factor in teacher-pupil interaction and motivational style amongst school children?
GBR 1993
Research Date(s): 1991-1996
Jackson, C.
Sup: Rogers, C.
Inst: Lancaster University, Department of Educational Research, Cartmel College, Bailrigg, Lancaster LA1 4YW, United Kingdom.
sex difference; teacher-pupil relation; motivation; sex role; role perception
différence de sexe; relation maître-élève; motivation; rôle sexuel; perception de rôle
PROJECT DESCRIPTION
Evidence demonstrating sex differences in motivational style and teacher-pupil interaction is now well documented. The aim of this research is to consider the importance of sex-type (masculine, feminine, androgynous or undifferentiated, as defined by the BEM Sex Role Inventory, 1978), on these two areas. Is sex-type a more useful and predictive concept than biological sex? The tests developed by Craske (1988) are the intended tool to identify motivational style amongst secondary school children in the two key areas of mathematics and English. The BEM Sex-Role Inventory is selected to identify sex-type. Teacher perceptions of the sex-type of children may be identified using a short pupil rating scale completed by the teacher.

13086 Jakość życia dzieci w zróżnicowanych środowiskach wychowawczych. (IEA Preprimary Project: Quality of Life Study.)
POL 1994
Research Date(s): 1991-1995
Karwowska-Struczyk, Małgorzata; Bieleń, Barbara; Trzeciak, Grażyna; Małkowska-Zegadło, Hanna.
Inst: Instytut Badań Edukacyjnych (Institute for Educational Research), Górczewska 8, 01-180 Warszawa, Poland.
High/Scope Educational Research Foundation, Ypsilanti, Michigan, U.S.A., 600 North River Street, Ypsilanti, Michigan 48 198, U.S.A
Fin: University of Michigan; Polish Ministry of Education; Institute for Educational Research.
child development; socialization; family environment; social environment
développement de l'enfant; socialisation; milieu familial; milieu social
PROJECT DESCRIPTION
Aim: The final aim of the study is to assess the significance of preschool socialization experiences for general development as well as for the adjustment to the social and academic demands of schooling. The study is designed to extend our scientific knowledge about early socialization and to evaluate models of early childhood policy intended to promote the well-being of children (national and cross-national analysis).

Design: The IEA Preprimary Project is a three-phase study of early childhood care and education that seeks to: (1) identify and characterize the variety of care and education settings used by families with 4-year-old children (household survey); (2) examine the "quality of life" for 4-year-old children in the major settings: extra-familial and familial (observation study); (3) assess the contribution of the experiences in various preschool settings to the general development of children at the age of 7 (follow-up study).

The study is guided by an ecological approach (e.g. U. Bronfenbrenner) that views the development of young children as the product of interactions between the child and the socialization settings of the immediate environment. The young child participates in a variety of settings that are significant for his/her development, including such settings as preschools, child care centres, the child's own home. These settings are in turn influenced by certain aspects of the broader social and cultural environment. This study will evaluate the effects of different socialization settings on child development by exploring the relationships among: (a) the structural features of settings; (b) the socialization processes occurring in the settings; (c) various features of the social and cultural background; (d) child developmental status.

Major questions: (1) What is the "Quality of life" for 4-year-old children in different settings? (2) How do the educational values and expectations of adults (caregivers, teachers, parents) concerning 4-year-old children affect the environment organization and activities for these children as well as their interactions with these children? (3) What is the relationship between specific structural features and/or interactional processes of the settings and children's developmental status? (4) What is the relationship between 4-year-old children's experiences in settings and their developmental status at the age of 7?

Methods: (1) records; (2) family interview; (3) adult questionnaire; (4) provider interview; (5) observation systems; (6) child assessment.

13087 Kehaline areng kasvatusüsteemis. (Physical development of pupils in school.)
EST 1994
Research Date(s): 1989-1993
Arvisto, M.; Unger, J.; et al.
Inst: Tallinna Pedagoogikaülikool (Tallinn Pedagogical University), 0102 Tallinn, Narva mnt. 25, Estonia.
Fin: EV Haridusministeerium.
physical development; physical characteristics; physical education; health education
développement physique; caractéristique physique; éducation physique; éducation sanitaire
PROJECT DESCRIPTION
The study examined the physical abilities of Estonian schoolchildren aged 13 years (n=1,015) and 15 years (n=1,015). Measurements were taken from pupils in 27 schools by the teaching staff of the Pedagogical University. Tests included: 60 m. race, 4 x 10 m. potato race, Cooper test, standing broad jump, push-ups, sit-ups and a flexibility test. Furthermore, the questionnaire "School, Sport, Life and I" was administered to a sample of pupils aged 13 years (n=1,038), 15 years (n=1,251) and 17 years (n=1,014), to collect information about participation in sport activities, attitudes towards sport, and pupils' motor skills and life styles.

The study can be used as a starting point for further monitoring and analyses of subjective factors related to participation in sports activities. The investigation was partly coordinated with the WHO Cross-National Survey - Health Behaviour in School-Age Children.

Publ: Arvisto, M. & Kannas, L. Noorte sportimisest. In: *Spordi Ilm*, 2/1992.

13088 Kognitiivsuse roll psühhomotoorsete tegevuste õppeprotsessis. (The role of cognition in psychomotor activities.)
EST 1994
Research Date(s): 1989-1992
Gross, H.; Gross, K-A.; Ulp, K.; Tomusk, H.; Hendre, J.; Bachmann, T.
Inst: Tallinna Pedagoogikaülikool (Tallinn Pedagogical University), 0102 Tallinn, Narva mnt. 25, Estonia.
Fin: EV Haridusministeerium.
psychomotor activity; motion; motor activity; cognitive ability; didactics
psychomotricité; mouvement; motricité; aptitude cognitive; didactique
PROJECT DESCRIPTION
The aim of the research is to study physical techniques used in sports as psychomotor activities and to describe them for didactic purposes. It is attempted to devise a cognition-based methodology. The study proceeds from the hypothesis that motor activities can be taught more efficiently if they are adequately integrated into learners' cognitive structures.

Methods: Recording and computerization of motor activities, data processing, analysis.

The development and structure of motor activities have been examined and analysed. Regularities and relevant criteria have been established. A method for assessing a range of cognitive images has been developed. Directions for describing sports techniques have been elaborated which can be used as a basis for the creation of an adequate system of cognitive images.

13089 Motor and perceptual competence in prematurely born children.
GBR 1993
Research Date(s): 1989-1993
Henderson, S.; Dubowitz, L.
Inst: London University, Institute of Education, Department of Educational Psychology and Special Educational Needs, 20 Bedford Way, London WC1H OAL, United Kingdom.
Fin: Medical Research Council; Nuffield Foundation.
child development; premature baby; brain injury; perceptual handicap; motor disorder
développement de l'enfant; enfant prématuré; lésion cérébrale; handicap sensoriel; trouble moteur
PROJECT DESCRIPTION
The focus of this study, which is being carried out jointly with the Royal Postgraduate Medical School, is on children who were born prematurely, both with and without brain damage. The study has two distinct objectives; the first is to investigate the progress of these children in school. The second is to investigate the specific perceptual and motor difficulties which many of the children experience.

13090 Musik- und tanzpsychologische Untersuchungen fuer Paedagogik und Therapie. (Psychological study of music and dance for pedagogics and therapy.)
DEU 1993
Research Date(s): 1991-1994
Muessgens, B.; Martin, K.; Weber, C.; Schwabowski, R.; Brank, R.; Lehmann, D.; Schurian, W.; Adamek, K.
Sup: Hoermann, K.
Inst: Deutsche Sporthochschule Koeln, FB 03 Sportdidaktik und - Methodik, Institut fuer Musik- und Tanzpaedagogik, Carl-Diem-Weg, D-5000 Koeln 41.
psychomotor development; motion; music; dance; music and movement; psychotherapy; psychomotor activity
développement psychomoteur; mouvement; musique; danse; rythmique; psychothérapie; psychomotricité
PROJECT DESCRIPTION
Inhalt: Untersuchung zu Musik und Bewegung unter Beruecksichtigung von psychomotorischen, lernpsychologischen, kuenstlerischen und therapeutischen Einflussfaktoren. (a) Vergleichende Studie zur Wirkung nicht grundtonbezogener und grundtonbezogener Musik auf Bewegungs- und Atemrhythmus in der musikalisch-motorischen Ausbildung von Sportstudenten. (b) Untersuchung zur Nutzung der emotionalen Wirkung musikalischer Parameter fuer die Choreographie. (c) Musikbedingte Angstreduktion zur Erhoehung der psychophysischen Stabilitaet. (d) Vergleich von Befindlichkeit und Einstellung verschiedener Studentenpopulationen mit und ohne taenzerische oder musikalische Ausbildung. (e) Musikpsychologische Grundlagenforschung (Konzentration, Kreativitaet und Motivation). (f) Altersspezifische Bedingungsanalyse in Paedagogik und Therapie bei Kindern, Jugendlichen und Erwachsenen.
Geographischer Raum: USA, Deutschland.
Vorgehensweise: Empirisch statistische Erhebung. Untersuchungsdesign: Fallstudie; Evaluationsstudie.
Datengewinnung: Primaererhebung: Feldarbeit von Mitarbeitern des Projektes durchgefuehrt.
Auswertung: SPSS.
Publ: Hoermann, Karl. *Durch Tanzen zum eigenen Selbst.* Muenchen: Goldmann 1991.
Schurian, Walter. *Kunst im Alltag.* Goettingen, Toronto, Zuerich: Verl. fuer Angew. Psychologie 1991.

13091 Parts de l'enfant et de la mère dans la gestion d'un récit produit conjointement.
FRA 1993
Research Date(s): 1988-
Espéret,Eric; Rondal, Jean-Adolphe; Crété, Marie-Françoise.
Inst: Université de Poitiers, UER Sciences humaines, CNRS URA/666, Laboratoire de psychologie du langage, 95 av. du Recteur Pineau, 86022 Poitiers Cedex, France.
language development; mother-child relation; oral expression; story telling; cognitive style; infant; pre-school child
développement du langage; relation mère-enfant; expression orale; narration d'histoires; style cognitif; enfant du premier âge; enfant d'âge préscolaire
PROJECT DESCRIPTION
Objectifs: Le cadre général est la mise en évidence de la genèse des premières conduites langagières complexes ainsi que les modalités de leur acquisition. Une première recherche a permis de suivre 6 dyades mère-enfant pendant 5 séances lorsque la mère dialogue avec son enfant âgé de 21 à 28 mois. Trois dimensions d'adaptation du langage de la mère (adaptation formelle, dialogique et fonctionnelle) et leur combinaison ont permis de caractériser trois styles maternels.
Une seconde recherche portant sur 3 dyades mère-enfant, correspondant aux trois styles, suivies de façon intensive (tous les 10 jours pendant 5 mois) s'intéresse au guidage de l'enfant par la mère dans la production du récit. Deux styles d'intervention de la mère existent: l'adaptation et l'adéquation.
Une troisième recherche porte sur trois groupes d'enfants (36, 48 et 60 mois) enregistrés à domicile dans leurs interactions verbales avec leur mère. Les analyses portent sur les types de "monitoring" textuel que la mère effectue sur le récit de son enfant et sur les énoncés ayant la même fonction chez l'enfant (corrections, ajouts...). Les résultats doivent permettre de préciser quand et de quelle façon s'effectue un transfert, de la mère à l'enfant, dans les processus de planification et de contrôle mis en oeuvre pour produire un texte "récit".
Publ: Espéret, Eric. Adaptation du langage de l'entourage et développement linguistique de l'enfant: la recherche de styles maternels interactifs. In: *Bulletin de psychologie*, 1988-1989, 61, n° spécial, pp. 57-65.
Rondal, Jean-Adolphe. Indications positives et négatives dans l'acquisition des aspects grammaticaux de la langue maternelle. In: *Cahiers de psychologie cognitive*, 1988, 8, pp. 383-398.

13092 Peer group counselling in upper primary.
GBR 1993
Research Date(s): 1990-1991
Jarvie, M.
Inst: Heriot-Watt University, Moray House Institute of Education, Holyrood Road, Edinburgh EH8 8AQ, United Kingdom.
personality development; guidance; peer group teaching; primary education
développement de la personnalité; orientation; enseignement mutuel; enseignement primaire
PROJECT DESCRIPTION
One of the issues identified in the Committee on Primary Education (Scotland) (COPE) Position Paper 'Primary Education in the Eighties' as not having been adequately addressed is 'the conscious and coherent development of aspects of Personal and Social Education'. The research will address this issue. Its aim is to ascertain if training P7 pupils in group counselling skills increases their ability to (a) listen to and be empathic with peers; (b) be confident and assertive; (c) engage in value clarification and decision-making, and (d) cope with change.

13093 Phonological and visuospatial processing at the left and right of the laterality distribution.
GBR 1993
Research Date(s): 1991-1994
Annett, M.
Inst: Leicester University, Department of Psychology, University Road, Leicester LE1 7RH, United Kingdom.
Fin: Wellcome Trust.
laterality; reading difficulty; visual perception; dyslexia
latéralité; difficulté de lecture; perception visuelle; dyslexie
PROJECT DESCRIPTION
The right shift (RS) theory of handedness has led to the hypothesis that there are specific risks for cognitive processing, associated with the rs-- and rs++ genotypes. The genotypes cannot be identified directly, but are more frequent at the left and right of the continuum of right minus left (R-L) hand skill. Those at the left are at risk because they lack something which assists the growth of speech in the left hemisphere. Those at the right are at risk because they carry a double dose of a factor which appears to work by handicapping the right hemisphere. Annett and Manning (1990) have shown that reading ability varies with laterality in normal school children such that children at both extremes are likely to be poorer readers than those in the centre.
The purpose of the research is to show that a double dissociation between people specifically at risk for phonological and visuospatial processing is associated with the left and right of the R-L hand skill distribution; and that this dissociation is relevant to subtypes of dyslexia. Among poorer readers, error patterns associated with 'phonological' versus 'surface' or 'dyseidetic' dyslexias could be more prevalent at the left and the right of the laterality distribution respectively.
Publ: Annett, M. Phonological processing and right minus left hand skill. In: *Quarterly Journal of Experimental Psychology*, No 44/1992, pp. 33-46.
Annett, M. Reading upside down and mirror text in groups differing for right minus left hand skill. In: *European Journal of Cognitive Psychology*, No 3/1991, pp. 363-377.

13094 Physical activity patterns of primary school children.
GBR 1993
Research Date(s): 1990-1992
Warburton, P.; Sleap, M.; Cale, L.
Inst: Durham University, School of Education, Leazes Road, Durham DH1 1TA, United Kingdom; Hull University, School of Education, Cottingham Road, Hull HU6 7RX, United Kingdom.
Fin: Health Education Authority.
motor activity; teaching aid; primary education; health education
motricité; moyen d'enseignement; enseignement primaire; éducation sanitaire
PROJECT DESCRIPTION
There is now wide recognition of the positive effect regular exercise can have on our health. The main aim of this observation study is to monitor the exercise activity levels of children aged between 5 and 11 years. This observation study forms part of a wider evaluation of the Happy Heart Resource Materials which was undertaken between February 1991 and June 1992.
The method of observation to be used will be based on a paper presented by O'Hara and Colleagues (1988) which validated a minute by minute observation procedure against heart rate. Between 60 and 70 children were observed in the spring of 1991 and again during the same period in 1992. Half of the children will act as a control group whilst the other half will receive regular input from the Happy Heart Resource Materials. The children will be observed both in school and at home.
The results from the study will be used to assess the impact of the Happy Heart Resource Materials with regard to possible changes in children's activity patterns.

13095 Piloting the personal competence model in secondary schools.
GBR 1993
Research Date(s): 1991-1992
Squirrell, G.
Sup: Broadfoot, P.
Inst: Bristol University, School of Education, Centre for Assessment Studies, 22 Berkeley Square, Bristol BS8 1JA, United Kingdom.
Fin: Department of Employment.
personality development; content of education; minimum competencies
développement de la personnalité; contenu de l'éducation; fundamentum
PROJECT DESCRIPTION
The project is in two phases. The first is concerned with evaluating the method of implementation and accessibility of a Model of Personal Competence commissioned by the Employment Department. This phase lasts from July 1991 to May 1992. During the second phase from May 1992 to August 1992 training and guidance materials for school staff and pupils will be written. The guidance materials arise from the findings of the early pilot project. Nine schools in England and Scotland are piloting the Model with young people in years 10 -13. The Model is used within pupils pursuing a personal and social education programme, general studies pre-employment and Certificate of Pre-Vocational Education (CPVE).
The research process is that of formative evaluation. A case study of implementation is being compiled for each institution piloting the Model. The Model aims to encourage greater personal effectiveness in young people in a number of areas; for example, handling emotions and stress, making effective use of information and getting on well with others. Four parallel projects are also piloting the Model in other educational institutions in further and higher education and with a number of employers.

13096 Prise en compte du partenaire dans les interactions de co-résolution.
FRA 1993
Research Date(s): 1985-1988
Fraysse, Jean-Claude.
Inst: Université d'Aix-Marseille I, UER Psychologie, Centre de recherche en psychologie du développement et de l'éducation, 29 av. de l'Arc de Meyran, 13100 Aix-en-Provence, France.
problem solving; cooperation; cognitive development; social behaviour; social interaction; child; adult-child relation
résolution de problème; coopération; développement cognitif; comportement social; interaction sociale; enfant; relation adulte-enfant
PROJECT DESCRIPTION
Objectifs: Trois expérimentations ont été conduites centrées sur l'étude de la prise en compte du partenaire dans des dyades adulte-enfant. (1) Des situations de répartition d'objets en classe d'équivalence proposées à des enfants de 3 à 8 ans ont permis de dégager des étayages mutuels qui renvoient à trois types de dominances fonctionnelles successives: centration sur l'aspect procédural, sur les échanges avec le partenaire, sur la maîtrise de la tâche et son intégration généralisatrice. (2) Une expérimentation conduite avec des enfants de quatre à huit ans a permis de préciser l'évolution des mécanismes de prise en compte du partenaire en liaison avec le niveau cognitif des sujets. Quatre périodes ont été dégagées: (a) syntonisation caractérisée par l'absence totale de prise en compte d'autrui; (b) premières structures de relations: apparition des premières intentions de communication; (c) imitation mimétique puis analytique; (d) coopération. (3) L'importance des prérequis dans l'organisation des échanges interactifs a été confirmée au cours d'une troisième expérimentation avec des enfants de 5-6 ans: les résultats ont montré que la dynamique interactive de type "conflit socio-cognitif" ne peut apparaître qu'à certaines conditions précises de prérequis développementaux et être alors source de progrès.
Publ: Fraysse, Jean-Claude. Relation entre niveaux fonctionnels et prise en compte d'un partenaire dans une tâche de tris d'objets. In: *Archives de psychologie*, 1985, 53, pp. 447-452.
Fraysse, Jean-Claude. Etude génétique de la prise en compte du partenaire dans la construction des opérations. In: *Bulletin de psychologie*, 1987, 40, pp. 915-922.
Fraysse, Jean-Claude. Nature des pré-requis et type d'interactions sociales. In: *Archives de psychologie*, 1988, 56, pp. 5-21.

13097 Processus de planification et de contrôle dans la production d'un texte procédural: évolution entre cinq et neuf ans.
FRA 1993
Research Date(s): 1987-
Espéret, Eric.
Inst: Université de Poitiers, UER Sciences humaines, CNRS URA/666, Laboratoire de psychologie du langage, 95 av. du Recteur Pineau, 86022 Poitiers Cedex, France.
language development; verbal communication; verbal interaction; child; written expression
développement du langage; communication verbale; interaction verbale; enfant; expression écrite
PROJECT DESCRIPTION

Objectifs: Il s'agit d'analyser la gestion des textes produits et non la communication elle-même. En particulier, on étudie à quel niveau structural (production de l'énoncé, d'une partie textuelle ou de l'ensemble) se situent d'une part, les moyens linguistiques mis en oeuvre (anaphores, connecteurs, marquage de l'opposition donné-nouveau), d'autre part, les traces spontanément émises d'un contrôle (reprises, corrections, ajouts...).
Méthodologie: Trois groupes d'enfants (5, 7 et 9 ans) sont placés dans une situation de communication référentielle, restreinte à la seule modalité verbale, par couple en alternant les rôles (émetteur, récepteur), ils doivent décrire (message unique ininterrompu) ou comprendre le fonctionnement d'un mécanisme simple.
Publ: Espéret, Eric. Micro-and macro-structural planning and control in production: approaches in story-telling situations. In: Mandl, H.; Corte (de), E.; Bennett, N. & Friedrich, H.F. (éds.). *Learning and instruction in an international context*. Oxford: Pergamon Press, 1989, vol. II, pp. 357-366.
Espéret, Eric & Piolat, Annie. Production: planning and control. In: Denhière, Guy & Rossi, Jean-Pierre (éds.). *Text and text processing*. Amsterdam: North-Holland, 1991.

13098 Processus de socialisation cognitive chez les femmes de bas niveau de qualification en formation.
FRA 1993
Research Date(s): 1989-
Debaisieux, Patricia.
Inst: Université de Lille I, Centre lillois d'études et de recherches sociologiques et économiques, CNRS URA/345, Laboratoire de sociologie du travail, de l'éducation et de l'emploi, Institut de Sociologie, 59655 Villeneuve d'Ascq Cedex, France.
cognitive development; trainee; women's education; occupational qualification; level of qualification
développement cognitif; stagiaire; éducation des femmes; qualification professionnelle; niveau de qualification
PROJECT DESCRIPTION
Objectifs: Evaluation de la mise en oeuvre et de la transférabilité des contenus des formations de type "remédiation cognitive" dans la vie privée et professionnelle chez les femmes de bas niveau de qualification et selon leur appartenance et leur type de socialisation professionnelle.
Méthodologie: Suivi des stages par observation participante, suivi des stagiaires par entretiens semi-directifs (avant le début du stage, pendant le stage, à la fin du stage et deux à trois mois après la fin du stage). L'échantillon est composé de quatre groupes de femmes de bas niveau de qualification (deux groupes de salariées, deux de demandeurs d'emploi).

13099 A psycholinguistic investigation into the underlying cause of specific language impairment in children.
GBR 1993
Research Date(s): 1991-1994
Van der Lely, H.
Inst: London University, Birkbeck College, Department of Psychology, Malet Street, London WC1E 7HX, United Kingdom.
Fin: British Academy.
language development; learning difficulty; psycholinguistics
développement du langage; difficulté de l'apprentissage; psycholinguistique
PROJECT DESCRIPTION
Specific language impaired (SLI) children suffer from language disorder in the absence of any other impairments. The underlying nature and cause of this disorder, affecting an estimated 500,000 children, is still poorly understood. This research proposes a hypothesis about the underlying deficit in SLI children based on the findings from expression and comprehension. The extent of the hypothesised 'domain specific' language deficit will be tested by investigating grammatical, general linguistic and non-linguistic (domain neutral) representations. This will give a better understanding of SLI children and of the mechanisms of language acquisition in general.

13100 Rôle des représentations sociales intergroupes dans la construction de l'identité.
FRA 1993
Research Date(s): 1986-1989
Massonnat, Jean; Lecacheur, Mireille.
Inst: Université d'Aix-Marseille I, UER Psychologie, Centre de recherche en psychologie du développement et de l'éducation, 29 av. de l'Arc de Meyran, 13100 Aix-en-Provence, France.
adolescence; identity; personality development; vocational training; individual characteristics; group membership; self-concept; occupational integration
adolescence; identité; développement de la personnalité; formation professionnelle; caractéristique individuelle; appartenance au groupe; conception de soi; intégration professionnelle
PROJECT DESCRIPTION
Objectifs: Le rôle des représentations sociales intergroupes dans la construction de l'identité a été examiné sur des échantillons de 100 adolescents de 16 à 18 ans insérés dans des groupes de formation dont la valorisation sociale est inégale (Lycée d'enseignement professionnel-LEP,

Centre de formation d'apprentis et Stages courts d'insertion professionnelle).

Méthodologie: Les adolescents avaient à se décrire, décrire autrui (in group et out group), et les différents groupes, sur des caractéristiques jugées nécessaires par les formateurs pour s'insérer professionnellement. Les premiers traitements ont conduit à retenir deux blocs de caractéristiques, celles actuellement possédées (aspect "présent") et celles que le sujet pense avoir dans l'avenir (aspect "anticipé").

La comparaison des différentes images entre elles sur les deux blocs dégagés: (a) va dans le sens des résultats relevés dans la littérature, à savoir que l'image propre est plus fortement estimée que l'image du groupe d'appartenance et des autres groupes; (b) montre que le phénomène général décrit par H. Tajfel de survalorisation de son groupe par rapport aux autres n'est pas confirmé pour les groupes qui sont le moins valorisés socialement (LEP et stages).

Publ: Massonat, Jean & Lecacheur, Mireille. Le schéma de personne dans l'analyse des changements identitaires: approche expérimentale de son opérativité. In: Massonat, Jean; Hurtig, Marie-Claude. *L'identité de la personne*. Psychologie française, 1990, tome 35, n° 1, pp. 67-76.
Massonnat, Jean; Serino, C. & Mailloux, F. Comparaison intergroupe, appartenance catégorielle, statut des groupes et point de référence. Colloque en Hommage à Jean-Paul Codol, *Cognition, cognition sociale et la question du soi*, Université d'Aix en Provence: CREPCO, 10-12 mars 1991.

13101 Sex-related differences in children's technological achievements in the middle years with special reference to the use of construction materials.
GBR 1993
Research Date(s): 1991-1995
Brown, C.
Inst: University of East Anglia, School of Education, Norwich NR4 7TJ, United Kingdom.
sex difference; technology; primary education; pupil attitude
différence de sexe; technologie; enseignement primaire; attitude de l'élève
PROJECT DESCRIPTION
A study by the Assessment of Performance Unit (APU) showed that experience with construction materials was markedly different in boys and girls. The rise in scientific and technological work in the primary curriculum has made the study of its nature and extent essential. The current study follows on from an initial study in which the gender gap was documented over a period of four years. In this study the quantity and quality of models produced by pupils across the first school age range as a result of specific arrangements facilitating equal access to materials was monitored.

Criteria for models made by each year group were drawn up to indicate the range of achievement. The criteria were used to support the teachers, not only in ensuring equal access to materials, but also to structure the work to enable the children to try to meet as many of the criteria as possible. Such structured opportunities were found to narrow the gender gap further than simply ensuring equal access for girls to the construction materials. Consequently, a programme offering suggestions for learning opportunities with construction materials was devised for each class in the school. In 1990/1991 a class of children who have received such structured opportunities throughout their entire time in the school were again monitored in their final year. The results showed that the gender gap had narrowed further but had not closed. It was decided therefore that the study of this cohort of children, for whom data exists from entry to school at 4+ years, should continue into the middle years.

A second phase of data collection began in 1991/1992 and findings from that academic year indicate that during that year the performance gap had closed according to the criteria used to assess implementation of science concepts in the models made. It was evident that in the variety of models made and the modification or origination of models the girls still lagged behind the boys.

These aspects in addition to the implementation of science concepts will continue to be monitored as the cohort progresses through 1992/1993.

Publ: Brown, C.A. What are little girls made of? A study of technology in the early years. In: *Educational Studies*, Vol 17, No 1/1991, pp. 107-113.
Brown, C.A. Using construction sets in a primary curriculum. In: *Primary Science Review*, No 17/1991, pp. 22-24.

13102 Social interaction and cognitive development in school-aged children.
GBR 1993
Research Date(s): 1979-
Light, P.
Inst: Open University, School of Education, Walton Hall, Milton Keynes MK7 6AA, United Kingdom.
Fin: Economic and Social Research Council; Foundation Fyssen (Paris); Open University; Leverhulme Trust.
cognitive development; interaction; reasoning; group work; didactic use of computer
développement cognitif; interaction; raisonnement; travail par équipe; usage didactique de l'ordinateur

PROJECT DESCRIPTION
An extensive programme of research (mostly in the form of small experimental projects) has addressed social aspects of children's cognitive development. Topics have encompassed social perspective taking, spatial perspective taking and drawing, conservation and logical reasoning. Current work is focused on the role of pragmatic schemes in deductive reasoning and the role of peer interaction in problem-solving, using computers.
Publ: Light, P. & Perret-Clermong, A.N. Social context effects in reasoning and testing. In: Gellatly, A. et al. (eds.). *Cognition and social worlds*. Oxford: Clarendon Press, 1989.
Light, P. & Blaye, A. Computer-based learning: the social dimensions. In: Foot, H.C.; Morgan, M.J. & Shute, R.H. *Children helping children*. Chichester: John Wiley & Sons Ltd, 1990.
Light, P.; Girotto, V. & Legrenzi, P. Childrens' reasoning on conditional promises and permissions. In: *Cognitive Development*, No 5/1990, pp. 369-383.

13103 Syntactic input and the acquisition of the verb lexicon.
GBR 1993
Research Date(s): 1990-1992
Fletcher, P.; Ingham, R.
Inst: Reading University, Department of Linguistic Science, Whiteknights, Reading RG6 2AH, United Kingdom.
Fin: Economic and Social Research Council.
language development; vocabulary; syntax; mother tongue
développement du langage; vocabulaire; syntaxe; langue maternelle
PROJECT DESCRIPTION
This research examines the relation between syntax and the lexical properties of verbs in children's acquisition of English as a first language. It is a hypothesis-based experimental study whose variables are motivated by recently published work in linguistic theory and language acquisition. It is expected that the results of this project will offer imporoved understanding of the relations between children's syntax and their lexical representations for verbs, on the one hand, and between adult syntax and children's lexical acquisition on the other.

13104 Trends and issues in gender and education in Scotland.
GBR 1993
Research Date(s): 1991-1992
Gerver, E.
Inst: Dundee University, Centre for Continuing Education, Dundee DD1 4HN, United Kingdom.
sex difference; educational administration; Scotland; trend; continuing education
différence de sexe; administration de l'enseignement; Ecosse; tendance; éducation permanente
PROJECT DESCRIPTION
This study will analyse patterns and trends in gender differences in Scottish education and training, including continuing education. It will focus on gender as an issue in education management.

13105 Wer wird (noch) Lehrer? (Who (still) wants to be a teacher?)
AUT 1993
Research Date(s): 1992-1993
Mayr, Johannes.
Inst: Paedagogische Akademie der Dioezese Linz, Salesianumweg 3, A-4020 Linz.
Fin: Bundesministerium fuer Unterricht und Kunst.
individual characteristics; student teacher; personality
caractéristique individuelle; élève-maître; personnalité
PROJECT DESCRIPTION
Die Arbeit untersucht folgende Fragen: Ursachen fuer die Veraenderungen in den Persoenlichkeitsmerkmalen von Studienanfaengern; Konsequenzen aus diesen Veraenderungen fuer Schule und Lehrerbildung; Unterscheiden sich Studierende der Paedagogischen Akademie hinsichtlich ihrer Persoenlichkeitsmerkmale von der Normalpopulation; Stellenwert von Persoenlichkeitsfrageboegen im Rahmen der Studienberatung.

Es werden Schueler- und Elternfragebogen zum Freizeitverhalten ausgegeben. In die Erhebung sind alle Hauptschueler der Uebungshauptschule der Paedagogischen Akademie und der Hauptschule Andorf einbezogen.

20 COGNITIVE PROCESS – PROCESSUS COGNITIF – KOGNITIVER PROZESS

13106 Acquisition des connaissances à partir du texte.
FRA 1993
Research Date(s): 1986-
Denhière, Guy; Poitrenaud, Sébastien; Tapiéro, Isabelle.
Inst: Université de Paris VIII, CNRS URA/1297, Psychologie cognitive du traitement de l'information symbolique, 2 rue de la Liberté, 93526 Saint Denis Cedex 02, France.
learning; didactic use of computer; cognitive development; scientific studies; expert system; educational software
acquisition de connaissances; usage didactique de l'ordinateur; développement cognitif; études scientifiques; système-expert; didacticiel
PROJECT DESCRIPTION
Objectifs: Etude du rôle des connaissances et croyances initiales, l'analyse des "domaines" à apprendre en termes de systèmes relationnels, transformationnels et téléologiques (fonctionnels et intentionnels). Pour chaque type de système, un domaine représentatif a été sélectionné: les mammifères marins pour le système relationnel, le moteur à explosion (systèmes de démarrage et de combustion) pour le système fonctionnel, des dépêches de presse relatant des détournements d'avion et un éditeur de texte pour le système intentionnel, et diverses expériences, suivant les mêmes principes méthodologiques, ont été réalisées.

Méthodologie: Les résultats de ces expériences sont utilisés pour construire des logiciels d'aide à l'acquisition de connaissances et à la formation au diagnostic des dysfonctionnements des systèmes.

Résultats: Les recherches réalisées ont conduit à trois types d'application: un logiciel interactif permettant la description de procédures sous le contrôle du formalisme de description élaboré; une batterie de diagnostic du fonctionnement cognitif dans la compréhension de textes dont la validation se fait en collaboration avec deux équipes de rééducateurs, l'une en France l'autre en Belgique; des logiciels éducatifs de diagnostic des connaissances initiales des apprenants et d'aide à l'acquisition individualisée des connaissances.

Publ: Tapiéro, Isabelle; Denhière, Guy & Poitrenaud, Serge. Individualized acquisition of knowledge with the computer: interrogation and learning guided by the structure of knowledge. In: *European journal of psychology of education*, 1988, n° spécial, vol. 3, 2, pp. 235-257.

Tapiéro, Isabelle. Apprentissage et transfert de connaissances à partir de textes. In: Denhière, Guy (éd.). Le traitement cognitif du texte. In: *Psychologie française*, 1991, 36, 2, pp. 106-212.

13107 L'acquisition des labels spatiaux chez l'enfant.
FRA 1993
Research Date(s): 1989-
Verjat, Isabelle; Tourrette, Catherine; Barbe, Valérie.
Inst: Université de Poitiers, UER Sciences humaines, CNRS URA/666, Laboratoire de psychologie du langage, 95 av. du Recteur Pineau, 86022 Poitiers Cedex, France.
space perception; language development; infancy; cognitive process; cognitive style
perception de l'espace; développement du langage; prime enfance; processus cognitif; style cognitif
PROJECT DESCRIPTION

Objectifs: L'utilisation des labels spatiaux chez l'enfant est déterminée par la structuration de l'espace, elle-même déterminée par les capacités cognitives des enfants: on peut donc, à partir des théories du développement cognitif (notamment néo-piagétiennes) faire certaines hypothèses sur l'acquisition de ces labels. Inversement, l'étude de cette acquisition peut éclairer certains aspects du développement cognitif.

(1) Une étape préparatoire de la recherche porte sur un inventaire des labels spatiaux utilisés par l'adulte, et une classification selon plusieurs critères (référent, domaine d'application, nature dichotomique ou non). (2) On cherche ensuite à établir l'ordre d'acquisition de ces labels spatiaux chez l'enfant en caractérisant notamment le type d'espace auxquel ils renvoient (limité-illimité, proche-lointain, etc.) et en confrontant l'ordre d'acquisition observé avec les prédictions des théories néo-piagétiennes. (3) On fait l'hypothèse que les styles cognitifs interviennent dans cette acquisition, plus précisément qu'il existe des liaisons entre la dépendance-indépendance à l'égard du champ (DIC), l'orientation spatiale et l'acquisition des premiers labels spatiaux.

Méthodologie: (1) Suivi longitudinal d'enfants entre 8 mois et 4 ans, comportant plusieurs épreuves: réactions au flux optique et à la transparence (DIC), orientation dans l'espace et repères spatiaux (espace), schéma corporel et différenciation (DIC et espace), compréhension et production des labels spatiaux (langage). (2) Compréhension du couple, devant-derrière, chez les enfants âgés de 4 à 6 ans. (3) Connaissance des principaux labels spatiaux chez des enfants de 4, 5 et 6 ans.

Publ: Verjat, Isabelle. Le statut cognitif des marqueurs *devant, derrière* chez l'enfant français. In: *L'année psychologique*, 1989, 89, pp. 277-289.

13108 Acquisitions des connaissances scolaires: apprentissage de la déduction en géométrie.
FRA 1993
Research Date(s): 1986-1989
Nguyen-Xuan, Ahn.
Inst: Université de Paris VIII, CNRS URA/1297, Psychologie cognitive du traitement de l'information symbolique, 2 rue de la Liberté, 93526 Saint Denis Cedex 02, France.
problem solving; reasoning; deductive method; geometry; demonstration
résolution de problème; raisonnement; méthode déductive; géométrie; démonstration
PROJECT DESCRIPTION

Objectifs: La construction d'une démonstration est un processus de recherche d'une chaîne déductive menant d'un ensemble d'hypothèses à une conclusion, en se servant des axiomes et des théorèmes déjà démontrés. Dans la phase de recherche d'un cheminement dans l'espace problème défini par l'énoncé du problème, les axiomes et théorèmes dont dispose le sujet peuvent être utilisées : prospective et rétrospective, mais seule la première est explicitée ensuite dans la démonstration.

Méthodologie: Trois expériences ont été menées: (1) en quatrième pour définir les conditions qui incitent l'élève à utiliser la stratégie de recherche rétrospective dans la recherche d'une chaîne déductive; (2) pour définir les conditions de mémorisation et de reproduction d'une démonstration proposée par le professeur; (3) pour apprendre la déduction à l'élève en l'incitant à verbaliser son raisonnement.

Publ: Nguyen-Xuan, Ahn. Deductive reasoning in geometry: search strategies and surface features. In: Mandl, H.; Corte (de), E.; Bennet, S.N. & Friedrich, H.F. (éds.). *Learning and instruction: European research in an international context*. Oxford: Pergamon Press, 1989.

13109 The analysis and use of spatial ability in educational contexts.
GBR 1993
Research Date(s): 1989-1993
Smith, P.
Sup: Whetton, C.
Inst: National Foundation for Educational Research, The Mere, Upton Park, Slough SL1 2DQ, United Kingdom.
Fin: MacFarlane Smith Bequest.
space perception; memory; assessment; test construction
perception de l'espace; mémoire; appréciation; construction de tests
PROJECT DESCRIPTION

This project has developed two paper and pencil tests of spatial memory, suitable for use as educational and psychological research tools. One uses a drawing response and is scored for correctness of shapes and proportions. The other uses multiple choice then shape-arranging on a grid and is scored for correctness of shape, position and orientation. An experimental computerised test, which runs on IBM compatibles, has also been developed. Evidence has been gathered to support the U.S. research literature which suggests that spatial memory is the key component of spatial ability. Differential validity studies have been carried out with the paper and pencil tests by testing large samples of eight, 12 and 16 year olds, then comparing their scores with performance measures in various school subjects. The tests are being prepared for publication by the NFER as research tools.

Publ: Smith, P. *Spatial Ability*, Topic, 5, 1991.

13110 Analysis of understanding as an educational aim and ways to detect its achievement.
GBR 1993
Research Date(s): 1978-
Ormell, C.
Inst: University of East Anglia, School of Education, Norwich NR4 7TJ, United Kingdom.
comprehension; learning process; cognitive test; learning test; evaluation; achievement measurement
compréhension; apprentissage; test cognitif; test d'acquisition; évaluation; mesure du rendement
PROJECT DESCRIPTION

The research is aimed at answering the question: How can we detect whether a child understands something, using objective behavioural methods? In most cases, 'understanding x' means 'having a fully assimilated model of x'. The chief assessment method consists of seeing whether children can apply the model swiftly and confidently to new circumstances. The central issue reduces to how to generate suitable 'new circumstances' in the numbers and variety required. To achieve reliability a lot of testing is needed, but this is only acceptable if the child's assessment experiences are also prime learning experiences. This means that the 'circumstances' used need to meet high standards of relevance, interest and memorability from the child's point of view. A major parameter is the degree to which the curriculum is 'liberal'. The more 'liberal' the curriculum, the more distant its topics from the child's immediate experience. This makes it harder to devise appropriate 'new circumstances', but unless this problem can be solved, the production of behavioural tests for understanding will fail. The problem has been solved (see Ormell 1988, 1991) by the use of counter-factual and counter-fictional contexts. The project 'Children's application readiness with basic mathematics' applies the general methods devised in this project to the example of mathematics.

Publ: Ormell, C.P. Is there a future for liberal education? In: *Cambridge Journal of Education*, Vol 18, No 2/1988, pp. 167-177.

Ormell, C.P. *Behavioural objectives in education*. Geelong, Australia: Deakin University Press, 1991.

Ormell, C.P. Behavioural objectives revisited. In: *Educational Research*, Vol 34, No 1/1992, pp. 23-33.

Ormell, C.P. Is content good for your health? In: *Cambridge Journal of Education*, Vol 22, No 2/1992, pp. 227-242.

13111 Children's development of number competence.
GBR 1993
Research Date(s): 1974-
Cowan, R.
Inst: London University, Institute of Education, Department of Educational Psychology and Special Educational Needs, 20 Bedford Way, London WC1H OAL, United Kingdom.
number concept; cognitive development; arithmetic; child
concept de nombre; développement cognitif; arithmétique; enfant
PROJECT DESCRIPTION

The research aims to develop an accurate account of how children's understanding of number develop from 4 to 7 years. Studies have been conducted to refine tasks used to assess children's understandings of number and procedures such as counting and sharing, to determine the causes of children's nonconserving responses, to explore whether children with severe language disorders show a qualitatively different pattern of development, and to identify what experiences make children more likely to count.

Publ: Cowan, R. The same number. In: Durkin, K. & Shire, B. (eds.). *Language in mathematical education: research and practice*. Milton Keynes: Open University, 1991.
(A full list of publications is available from the researcher).

13112   Cognitive components of experience in professional diagnosis and decision making, with implications for professional education.
GBR   1993
Research Date(s): 1987-1997
Boreham, N.
Inst: Manchester University, School of Education, Centre for Adult and Higher Education, Oxford Road, Manchester M13 9PL, United Kingdom.
cognitive process; decision making; teaching profession; higher education
processus cognitif; prise de décision; profession d'enseignant; enseignement supérieur
PROJECT DESCRIPTION
   Task analyses are being carried out of diagnosis and decision making in selected professions. Using protocol analysis techniques, computable models of the cognitive processes involved are being constructed. Comparisons between experts and novices are being made, and the results are being used to suggest improvements in current professional education and training.

Publ: Boreham, N.C. Modelling medical decision making under uncertainty. In: *British Journal of Educational Psychology*, Vol 59, Part 2/1989, pp. 187-199.
Boreham, N.C. Causal attributions by sensing and intuitive types during diagnostic problem solving. In: *Instructional Science*, Vol 16, 1987, pp. 123-136.

13113   Cognitive components of expertise in professional judgement, with reference to factors influencing acquisition of the relevant cognitive skills.
GBR   1993
Research Date(s): 1980-
Boreham, N.
Inst: Manchester University, School of Education, Centre for Adult and Higher Education, Oxford Road, Manchester M13 9PL, United Kingdom.
cognitive process; decision making; higher education
processus cognitif; prise de décision; enseignement supérieur
PROJECT DESCRIPTION
   The aim of this research is to analyse the knowledge and cognitive skills underpinning professional judgement, and to derive implications for higher education and continuing professional education. The fields encompassed include medical decision making, personnel management, fault finding and educational psychology. The methodology includes task analysis, skills analysis, cognitive simulation, expert-novice comparisons and learning experiments.
   The results point to the cognitive processes and structures crucial to cognitive skill acquisition, and lead to recommendations about teaching and learning.

Publ: Boreham, N.C.; Foster, R.W. & Mawer, G.E. The phenytoin game: its effect on decision skills. In: *Simulation and Games*, Vol 20, 1989, pp. 292-299.
Boreham, N.C. Modelling medical decision making under uncertainty. In: *British Journal of Educational Psychology*, Vol 59, Part 2, 1989, pp. 187-199.
Boreham, N.C. Models of diagnosis and their implications for adult professional education. In: *Studies in the Education of Adults*, Vol 20, 1988, pp. 95-108.
Boreham, N.C. Causal attribution by sensing and intuitive types during diagnostic problem solving. In: *Instructional Science*, Vol 16, 1987, pp. 123-136.

13114   Cognitive processes in student learning.
GBR   1993
Research Date(s): 1983-
Richardson, J.
Inst: Brunel University, Department of Human Sciences, Uxbridge UB8 3PH, United Kingdom.
cognitive process; learning psychology; memory; higher education; cognitive psychology; learning theory; learning process
processus cognitif; psychologie de l'apprentissage; mémoire; enseignement supérieur; psychologie cognitive; théorie de l'apprentissage; apprentissage
PROJECT DESCRIPTION
   Over the last 20 years, cognitive psychologists have made considerable advances in the development of theories of human learning and memory. Nevertheless, it is commonplace that such models cannot easily encompass the sort of learning that occurs in real life situations. During the same period, researchers into higher education have carefully investigated the knowledge and skills relevant to a variety of academic disciplines. Their findings have major implications for policy and practice in higher education, but they need to be interpreted within clearly articulated models of the cognitive processes underlying student learning. This research attempts to integrate these two areas of investigation. It will provide cognitive psychologists with a rich and qualitatively different body of evidence against which to evaluate the validity and generality of their theories of human learning and development; it will provide researchers into higher education with sophisticated theoretical descriptions of the strategies and processes employed in academic contexts; and it will provide teachers in higher education with statements of the practical applications of this research.

Publ: Richardson, J.T.E. Student learning in higher education. In: *Educational Psychology*, Vol 3, Nos 3 & 4/1983, pp. 305-311.
Richardson, J.T.E., Eysenck, M.W. & Piper, W.D. (eds.). *Student learning: research in education and cognitive psychology*. Guildford: SRHE & Open University Press, 1987.

13115   Cognitive skills in formal reasoning about programs.
GBR   1993
Research Date(s): 1991-1994
Bornat, R.; Reeves, S.; O'Shea, T.
Inst: Open University, Institute of Educational Technology, Walton Hall, Milton Keynes MK7 6AA, United Kingdom; Queen Mary and Westfield College, Mile End Road, London E1 4NS, United Kingdom.
Fin: Economic and Social Research Council; Science and Engineering Research Council; Medical Research Council.
cognitive process; reasoning; computer science; programming; teaching aid
processus cognitif; raisonnement; informatique; programmation; moyen d'enseignement
PROJECT DESCRIPTION
   The aim of the research is to test the hypothesis that with appropriate support, in particular with mechanical aids for symbolic calculation, a very much larger proportion of students can be made competent in formal techniques of reasoning about programs.
   In the Spring of 1991 and during the course of the academic year 1991 to 1992 a number of empirical studies were undertaken to assess the difficulties which students encounter in learning formal methods of reasoning. Information was obtained from 'diary' records kept by a selection of students. Exchanges on those electronic bulletin boards related to the programming course were noted and an informal electronic link was established between first-year computer science students at Queen Mary & Westfield College (QMW) and investigators at the Open University (OU). Sets of data based on answers, given by students, to questions on their backgrounds, their motivations for studying computer science and their expectations of the course were combined with video and audio interviews of them discussing their work.
   The results of these empirical studies have been used as feedback to researchers at QMW. During this period, the project members at QMW have investigated what graphical tools are currently available to help students learn formal reasoning methods and have designed and developed their own computer-based tools.
   A series of empirical studies are being undertaken from 1992 to 1993, during which students will be observed using the graphical tools developed in the first phase of the project. These studies will serve as the basis of an evaluation of the help such tools afford to students and will contribute to the further refinement of the tools themselves.

Publ: Fung, P. & O'Shea, T. Formal reasoning as a culture shock for computer science students. In: *Developments in the Teaching of Computer Science*. Proceedings of Conference at University of Kent, Canterbury, April 1992, pp. 26-34.
Fung, P. & O'Shea, T. Fear of formal reasoning. In: *Proceedings of the Fifth Psychology of Programming Workshop*, Paris, 1992, December, pp. 207-236.

13116   Cognitive style and learning mathematics.
GBR   1993
Research Date(s): 1989-1994
McAuley, J.
Sup: Orton, A.
Inst: Leeds University, School of Education, Leeds LS2 9JT, United Kingdom.
cognitive style; cognitive process; learning; mathematics; teaching style
style cognitif; processus cognitif; acquisition de connaissances; mathématiques; style pédagogique
PROJECT DESCRIPTION
   The implications of cognitive styles such as field dependence and field independence in learning mathematics have not been widely investigated. This study aims to focus on such styles and the implications in learning matrices. It is expected that pupils will be assessed and classified on a field dependence/field independence spectrum and the effects of different teaching styles will be measured.

13117 Computer-aided recognition of misconceptions about simple electrical circuits.
GBR 1993
Research Date(s): 1989-1992
Howe, J.; Brna, P.
Inst: Edinburgh University, Department of Artificial Intelligence, 80 South Bridge, Edinburgh EH8 9YL, United Kingdom.
Fin: Science and Engineering Research Council; Economic and Social Research Council; Medical Research Council.
comprehension; cognitive process; didactic use of computer; learning; science education; concept formation
compréhension; processus cognitif; usage didactique de l'ordinateur; acquisition de connaissances; éducation scientifique; formation de concept
PROJECT DESCRIPTION
It is desirable to have a more detailed understanding of how faulty beliefs (misconceptions) arise, how they are maintained, and how new beliefs effectively replace old ones. The long term goal is to use this understanding to guide the researchers in the development of exploratory regimes which can assist students to improve their grasp of some domain. Consequently, the ability is needed to recognize that one or more misconceptions are held by a given student and to characterize this set of beliefs.
This project is concerned with the problem of recognizing misconceptions as students are in the process of constructing simple electrical circuits. The method of investigation entails the construction of a number of student models. These are computational representations of the beliefs associated with simple electrical circuits. Various interpreters of these computational models are being constructed. The information obtained from the student's behaviour in constructing a circuit, the circuit's actual behaviour, and the student's exploratory activity will be the basis for exploring the diagnostic issues.

13118 Conceptual progression in science.
GBR 1993
Research Date(s): 1990-1991
Leach, J.
Sup: Driver, R.; Scott, P.
Inst: Leeds University, Centre for Studies in Science and Mathematics Education, Leeds LS2 9JT, United Kingdom.
Fin: National Curriculum Council.
concept formation; science education; common core curriculum; primary education; secondary education; teaching objective
formation de concept; éducation scientifique; tronc commun; enseignement primaire; enseignement secondaire; objectif pédagogique
PROJECT DESCRIPTION
This research project has been commissioned by the National Curriculum Council to undertake research into the progression of children's conceptual understanding in attainment target 2 (AT2) of the National Curriculum, The Variety of Life. This attainment target focuses upon classification of living things, the cycling of matter, flows of energy and interdependency in ecosystems.
Data will be collected, across the 5-16 age range at eight different sampling ages, using interview, paper and pencil and direct classroom techniques. These various approaches are designed to ascertain children's understanding of key ideas such as photosynthesis, respiration and decay at the different ages. The final report of the project will contain information about the progression in children's understandings relating to key ideas in this area. A review of existing research literature will be included and information about current approaches to teaching in this area will also be provided. A booklet for the use of teachers will be prepared and a package of in-service training material will also be produced.
Publ: Leach, J. *Progression in children's understanding from age 5-16 around AT2 in the Science National Curriculum: The Variety of Life.* Paper presented to the British Educational Research Association, Roehampton Institute, September 1990. Derby: British Educational Research Association.

13119 Development of a spatial ability handbook.
GBR 1993
Research Date(s): 1991-1993
Smith, P.
Sup: Whetton, C.
Inst: National Foundation for Educational Research, The Mere, Upton Park, Slough SL1 2DQ, United Kingdom.
Fin: Macfarlane Smith Bequest.
space perception; teaching aid; book
perception de l'espace; moyen d'enseignement; livre
PROJECT DESCRIPTION
This project was developed as a response to the belief that the education process does not currently attract sufficient attention to the development and use of spatial skills. It aims to produce a handbook for those educators who want to develop the spatial thinking and capitalise on the spatial strengths of their pupils, but who are not sure how best to do so.
The handbook will be in two parts. The first will describe the necessary background ideas in a non-technical way and will also include guidance on self-assessment and the role of parents and the home environment in developing spatial skills. The second part will include a wide range of teaching ideas and resource information, divided into four sections dealing with spatial memory, spatial thinking skills, spatial skills within specific subject areas and spatial presentation/study techniques. Some of the sub-sections within Part II will be written by external consultants.
Publ: Smith, P. & Traynelis, J.F. Keeping memory in shape. In: *Physics Education*, Vol 26, No 5/1991, pp. 262.

13120 The development of spatial awareness in children with physical handicaps, particularly those integrated in mainstream schools.
GBR 1993
Research Date(s): 1983-
Foreman, N.
Inst: Leicester University, Department of Psychology, University Road, Leicester LE1 7RH, United Kingdom.
space perception; cognition; physically handicapped; integration
perception de l'espace; cognition; handicapé physique; intégration
PROJECT DESCRIPTION
Children's spatial awareness has been tested using a variety of paradigms, and the development of cognitive mapping skills charted across the preschool and primary school age range. Using search tasks with groups of 10-20 infants, it has been shown that spatial awareness develops especially rapidly between 2 and 5 years (Foreman et al, 1984), and that reference memory develops in advance of working memory for visited places (Foreman, Warry & Murray, 1990). The research has also found, in groups of 30-40 able-bodied children, that independent spatial choice is necessary for the development of spatial awareness (Foreman, Foreman et al, 1990). In disabled children integrated in mainstream schools (N = 10) it was found that mobility status determined accuracy in using cognitive spatial representations of the classroom and school campus compared with a matched control group (Foreman et al, 1989; Foreman & Gell, 1990). This work was carried out collaboratively between the Psychology Department of Leicester University and the Advisory Service for Physically Impaired Pupils in Mainstream Schools, based at Westbrook Special School, Long Eaton, Derbyshire.
Current research is extending the earlier work, investigating whether locomotion in space and/or spatial choice in able-bodied pupils specifically affects working or reference components of spatial memory, and whether spatial skill relates to other areas of intellectual development such as reading, mathematical or technical ability. The research attempts to develop desk-top procedures and computerised tasks which measure spatial development. This will enable schools to identify spatial disabilities and offer appropriate remedial help. Within special education, the researchers are currently exploring the use of 'virtual reality' computerised environments as a possible means of remediating spatial difficulties in more severely disabled pupils, and in relating spatial difficulties to particular forms of cerebral dysfunction.
Publ: Foreman, N.; Arber, M. & Savage, J. Spatial memory in preschool infants. In: *Developmental Psychobiology*, Vol 17, 1984, pp. 129-137.
Foreman, N.; Foreman, D.; Cummings, A. & Ownes, S. Locomotion, active choice, and spatial memory in children. In: *Journal of General Psychology*, Vol. 117, 1990, pp. 215-232.
Foreman, N. & Berryman, M. Kids in space (Access, Mobility and Motability Section). In: *Special Children*, No 35/1990, pp. 20-21.
Foreman, N.; Orencas, C.; Nicholas, E.; Morton, P. & Gell, M. Spatial awareness in seven to 11-year-old physically handicapped children in mainstream schools. In: *European Journal of Special Needs Education*, Vol 4, No 3/1989, pp. 171-180.

13121 The development of visual memory strategies in children.
GBR 1993
Research Date(s): 1990-
Henry, L.; Norman, T.
Inst: Reading University, Department of Psychology, Whiteknights, Reading RG6 2AH, United Kingdom.
visual perception; memory; phonology; visual learning; verbal learning
perception visuelle; mémoire; phonologie; apprentissage visuel; apprentissage verbal
PROJECT DESCRIPTION
The aim of this research was to chart the development of verbal memory strategies in children. Previous research suggested that children progress from visual to verbal strategies of memory coding with age. However, this claim has not been adequately tested.
The first stage of the present research has been to test this claim with a wide age range (5, 7, 9, and 11 year olds). Children recalled sequences of pictures which were either visually similar (they looked the same) or phonemically similar (they sounded the same). Recall for these types of pictures was contrasted with recall for control pictures which were neither visually nor phonemically similar. The results showed that all age groups were poorer at remembering phonemically similar pictures, suggesting that they all used verbal memory strategies. There was very little evidence for the use of visual memory strategies in any group.

Further work with 4 year olds found that they did not appear to use any distinct strategy for remembering pictures. These findings conflicted with previous research which showed that 5-year olds used visual coding, and ongoing research is testing the competing claim of various hypotheses concerning the development of picture memory in children.

13122 Developmental concepts of Christianity in a person with a mental handicap.
GBR 1993
Research Date(s): 1991-1995
Warner, M.
Sup: Webster, D.
Inst: Hull University, School of Education, Cottingham Road, Hull HU6 7RX, United Kingdom.
belief; concept formation; religious education; Christian education; mentally handicapped
croyance; formation de concept; éducation religieuse; éducation chrétienne; handicapé mental
PROJECT DESCRIPTION

The majority of the research in this particular field, and to a large extent in the field of Christianity and education, has been done from a western, secular, academic approach. It is the intention of the study to 'plug this gap' by having the emphasis on Christianity and the development of thinking in terms of Faith, Jesus, God, Heaven, Hell, Holy Spirit, Salvation, death, angels, demons etc., in a person with a mental handicap. Gilliford, an authoritative work in this field, highlights the concern. He quotes in this work a study by D. Answorth (1961): 'it is likely that until 9 or 10 years of age, any story (biblical and in particular parables) will probably be interpreted literally, and that the details of the text and incidents of the story will be of paramount importance to the child'. The research hypothesises that this highlights a child's Faith; Matthew's Gospel chapter 18, v. 3 states: 'Assuredly, I say to you, unless you are converted and become as little children, you will by no means enter the Kingdom of Heaven' NKJ. This implies a simplicity of Faith uncomplicated by adult intellect and doubt.

The research starts from the premise that if a child can accept love, then they can accept the love of God. No child/adult, irrespective of the degree of intellectual handicap, is unable to receive love. Secondly, if we accept that we are body, soul and spirit in 'design', then a person with a mental handicap is injured in body and soul. However, God communicates through the spirit, hence the experience they have of God is as real as anyone else's. The problem is that they may be unable to express this experience. The intention of this research is to establish what is understood by such a person, to identify the development of thinking in this area, and propose ways in which we might teach and encourage their Beliefs and Faith.

13123 Développement de la mémoire opérationnelle chez l'enfant.
FRA 1993
Research Date(s): 1989-
Mendelsohn, Patrick; Roulin, Jean-Luc.
Inst: Université de Grenoble II, UFR Sciences de l'homme et de la société, CNRS URA/665, Laboratoire de psychologie expérimentale, psychologie cognitive et sciences de la cognition, BP 47 X, 38040 Grenoble Cedex, France.
memorizing; cognitive process; child
mémorisation; processus cognitif; enfant
PROJECT DESCRIPTION

Objectifs: On admet que l'empan (mesure classique de la capa cité de stockage de la mémoire à court terme) augmente avec l'âge. Deux courants de recherche rendent compte de cette constatation: (1) le courant développementaliste qui conçoit la mémoire de travail comme une entité unitaire où se déroule le traitement mais aussi le stockage de l'information et dont la capacité est déterminante dans les tâches de résolution de problème (Cf. Case); (2) la psychologie générale qui montre que la taille de l'empan verbal s'explique par la capacité à autorépéter le matériel (Cf. Baddeley). Le dispositif expérimental doit permettre de tester de telles hypothèses.

Méthodologie: Des enfants de 7, 9 et 11 ans sont soumis à deux types de tâches mnésiques, l'épreuve standard (consiste à mémoriser les noms des cases d'un tableau à double entrée -lettre, chiffre) et l'épreuve phonologique (consiste à mémoriser des couples lettre-chiffre présentés au centre de l'écran. Entre les deux épreuves varie le coût du traitement à effectuer avant la mise en mémoire de l'information (lecture dans le tableau à double entrée ou lecture simple de couples).

Résultats: (1) Ni l'efficacité du schème sollicité à l'encodage de l'information, ni l'efficacité du processus d'autorépétition ne sont de bons prédicteurs de l'empan en standard. (2) L'empan en standard est plus faible à tous les âges que l'empan en phonologie; or seul le traitement effectué lors de l'encodage diffère entre ces deux épreuves, le premier étant plus coûteux que le second. Ce résultat confirmerait les hypothèses développementalistes de type centrales comme celles de Case. (3) En ce qui concerne l'épreuve phonologique, l'efficacité du processus d'autorépétition parait un bon prédicteur de l'empan, ce qui irait dans le sens de

l'hypothèse de Baddeley. D'autres recherches en cours s'attachent à explorer la dynamique des sous-systèmes de la mémoire de travail.

13124 Diapistosi tou vathmou katanoisis vasikon ennion tou graptou logou ton mathiton tis A' taksis demotikou. (First-year primary school pupils' understanding of basic concepts of writing.)
CYP 1993
Research Date(s): 1991
Sotiriou, Elisavet.
Inst: Pedagogiko Instituto (Pedagogical Institute), P.O. Box 512, Nicosia, Cyprus.
comprehension; writing; written expression; spelling; concept; number concept; school entry age; pupil
compréhension; écriture; expression écrite; orthographe; concept; concept de nombre; âge d'entrée à l'école; élève
PROJECT DESCRIPTION

Aims: The aim of this study was to investigate first-year primary school children's understanding of basic concepts of writing, such as number, letter, capital letter, sentence. More specifically, it attempted to investigate any association between the children's gender/age and their understanding of these concepts. It also investigated how children discover the mechanism of writing.

Three hypotheses were stated: (1) children find it difficult to adopt the techniques of writing and reading, as well as to understand basic concepts of writing, (2) a child's age can be unsuitable for it to enter primary school; intellectual age and maturity are basic factors influencing understanding of writing, (3) gender influences the degree of understanding of basic concepts of writing.

Methods: The sample was randomly selected from all primary schools in Nicosia. The respondents were 97 children (53 boys and 44 girls) in the first primary school year. Several tests were used which were originally constructed by a research team at Toulouse University in France. Thirteen tests were used, one for each concept of writing. Each child was given the chance to give an answer by putting a circle on each test after having received verbal instructions from the researcher. The independent variables of the research were the children's gender, age and school; the dependent variables were their responses to the tests. The statistical analysis on the SPSS system used descriptive and inferential statistics.

Results: Girls proved to have a better grasp of the basic concepts of writing than did boys. The children's age was found to be unrelated to the understanding of the concepts of writing. The children found it more difficult to understand the concept of "sentence" (72.3%) than the concept of "first letter of a word" (56.4%). Generally, the children had more difficulty in manipulating letters than numbers. Each child appeared to have its own individual way of understanding reading and writing procedures.

13125 Education in active imagination: design and piloting of an open learning course for adult study.
GBR 1993
Research Date(s): 1984-1991
Angelo, M.
Sup: Abbs, P.
Inst: Sussex University, Institute of Continuing and Professional Education, Sussex House, Falmer, Brighton BN1 9RH, United Kingdom; Northbrook College of Design & Technology, Department of General and Community Education, Broadwater Road, Worthing BN14 8HJ, United Kingdom.
imagination; open education; curriculum development; aesthetic education; adult education
imagination; éducation ouverte; élaboration de programmes d'études; éducation esthétique; éducation des adultes
PROJECT DESCRIPTION

In the context of an educational system which emphasises the cognitive domain and skills training for business and technical applications, it has become the norm to be imaginally illiterate. Image intelligence is neither recognised nor educated: imagination is culturally stereotyped 'for children, artists or crazies', the expressive disciplines play a marginal role; self-expression, lacking the objective referencing of the traditional 'learning of the imagination', reduces to uncritical self-indulgence. Psychologies of image - Jungian, archetypal and transpersonal - characteristically place a therapeutic framework around their work with imagination. This includes both imagination as process and as place (the 'as if' location of autonomous content names the unconscious or the imaginal). Depth therapies of image are critical of a systematic educative approach, interpreting it as egotistical, manipulative and restrictive. The image of depth education is missing.

The research argues for a positive re-valuing of the educational mode, enabling the imaginal discipline of active imagination and guided fantasy to become valid aesthetic studies. It is suggested that a non-egoic directing pattern can be found in the traditional tree of life symbol system of the Renaissance polymath. Understood as the archetype of inter-relationships and drawing on the classical art of memory, intrinsic image connections open out for individual exploration.

A one-year open learning course has been designed on this basis to provide an imaginal apprenticeship. 24 practical sessions are on tape, guiding an imaginal journey. An accompanying 'traveller's diary' is written/drawn weekly. Regular personal tutorials discourage the over-familiar cognitive reductions of image into symptom and explore the cultural amplifications of 'depth-aesthetics'. There have been three piloting years involving small groups meeting on a monthly basis, together with qualitative, individual case studies.

13126 Espace, géométrie, graphismes scientifiques et techniques: étude didactique et psychologique.
FRA 1993
Research Date(s): 1989-
Maury, Sylvette; Rabardel, Pierre; Weil-Fassina, Annie.
Inst: Ministère de la recherche, Centre national de la recherche scientifique, CNRS GDR/71, Didactique et acquisition des connaissances scientifiques, Laboratoire PSYDEE, Université de Paris V, 46 rue Saint-Jacques, 75005 Paris, France.
space perception; graph; geometry; technical education; scientific studies; comprehension
perception de l'espace; graphique; géométrie; enseignement technique; études scientifiques; compréhension
PROJECT DESCRIPTION
Objectifs: Ce thème, selon le principe des groupements de recherche du Centre national de la recherche scientifique, est supporté par les travaux de plusieurs équipes. Il s'agit de l'étude didactique et psychologique des problèmes posés par la compréhension de l'espace concret (objet, environnement) et des formes symboliques de l'espace, exprimées et utilisées dans les graphismes scientifiques et techniques.
Méthodologie: Les travaux concernent plusieurs types de supports graphiques (perspectives, dessins en vues orthogonales, diagrammes, schémas, images de synthèse...) et des publics diversifiés: scolaires (enseignements généraux et techniques) et adultes (bas niveaux de qualification).
Publ: Rabardel, Pierre. Recherches en psychologie et didactique: un exemple d'interactions dans l'enseignement du dessin technique. In: *Revue française de pédagogie*, 1989, n° 89, pp. 55-62.

13127 Etude des verbalisations en situation de problème.
FRA 1993
Research Date(s): 1989-
Caron-Pargue, Josiane; Guillabert, Fabrice; Massé, Françoise.
Inst: Université de Poitiers, UER Sciences humaines, CNRS URA/666, Laboratoire de psychologie du langage, 95 av. du Recteur Pineau, 86022 Poitiers Cedex, France.
problem solving; cognitive process; oral expression
résolution de problème; processus cognitif; expression orale
PROJECT DESCRIPTION
Objectifs: L'étude des verbalisations simultanées à une résolution de problème constitue une situation méthodologiquement contrôlée, qui permet de dégager le fonctionnement cognitif des marqueurs linguistiques. Dans une première étape, ce fonctionnement peut s'exprimer en termes d'opérateurs relatifs à l'espace de problème (appréhendé du point de vue du sujet). Dans une deuxième étape, le rôle des marqueurs linguistiques peut être rapporté à l'environnement syntaxique et discursif.
Méthodologie: Les travaux portent sur les verbes et les termes fonctionnels (prépositions, connecteurs, modaux) et permettent de définir les représentations fonctionnelles du problème, leurs articulations et réorganisations progressives. Ces représentations commandent la planification du problème ainsi que la construction progressive des règles d'automatisations.
Publ: Caron-Pargue, Josiane & Caron, Jean. Processus psycholinguistique et analyse des verbalisations dans une tâche cognitive. In: *Archives de psychologie*, 1989, n° 57, pp. 3-32.

13128 Exploring the concept of 'formation' in adult learning.
GBR 1993
Research Date(s): 1985-1991
Fletcher, C.; Ruddock, R.
Inst: Manchester University, School of Education, Oxford Road, Manchester M13 9PL, United Kingdom; Cranfield Institute of Technology, School of Management, Cranfield, Bedfordshire MK45 4DT, United Kingdom.
concept; learning; terminology; adult education
concept; acquisition de connaissances; terminologie; éducation des adultes
PROJECT DESCRIPTION
The aim of the research is to establish the use of the term 'formation' in Anglophone educational discourse. The sense proposed is an extension of its general usage in European languages towards recognition of self-formation and learning in social systems, drawing upon the understandings of inter-actionism and critical sociology, with illustrations from life histories and observations in schools, adult and health education. A four-process model with a working diagram has been evolved, i.e. formation -- deformation -- reformation -- transformation.
Publ: Fletcher, C. & Ruddock, R. Key concepts for an alternative approach to adult education. In: *Convergence*, Vol XIX, No 2/1986.

13129 Frostig görsel algılama eğitim programının anaokulu çocuklarının görsel algılama ve zihinsel gelişmelerine etkisi. (The effect of the Frostig Visual Perceptual Training Programme on visual perception and the development of intelligence in a group of children in nursery school.)
TUR 1994
Research Date(s): 1989
Kaya, Özcan.
Sup: Baş, Mesut.
Inst: Hacettepe Üniversitesi, Eğitim Fakültesi, Psikolojik Hizmetler Bölümü (Hacettepe University, Faculty of Education, Department of Psychological Services), 06532 Beytepe, Ankara, Turkey.
visual perception; visual learning; intelligence level; pre-school child; training programme
perception visuelle; apprentissage visuel; niveau intellectuel; enfant d'âge préscolaire; programme de formation
PROJECT DESCRIPTION
The study examined the effect of the Frostig Visual Perceptual Training Programme on the development of visual perception and intelligence in nursery school children aged 4-5 years.
Mental maturity was tested by the Columbia Mental Maturity Scale. Visual perception was tested by the Frostig Visual Perception Scale. Development of visual perception was tested by the Frostig Visual Perception Training Programme.
The sample of the research consisted of 40 children aged 4-5 from the nursery of Ankara Numune Hospital. They were divided into experimental and control groups of ten children each.
For a period of two months the experimental groups were given the Frsotig Visual Perception Training Programme. The control group received no training. At the end of the training period the groups were tested for: eye-motor coordination; discernment of figures in a ground pattern, form constancy, position in space and spatial relations; and intelligence development. The differences between the experimental and control groups were evaluated by means of t-tests.
There was a considerable difference between pre-test and post-test scores of the experimental groups in respect of eye-motor coordination, discernment of figures in a ground pattern and form constancy elements of the Frostig Visual Perception Test. No significant difference was found between pre-test and post-test scores of the control groups.
In respect of perception of position in space and spatial relations, no important difference was found between pre-test and post-test scores of the control groups and the 4-year-olds in the experimental groups. A considerable difference did occur among the 5-year-olds in the experimental groups. The effect of the training programme on the development of intelligence was found not to be significant.
According to the findings of the research, the effectiveness of the Frostig Visual Perceptual Training Programme depends to an important extent on the age of the subject.

13130 Gap between arithmetical and algebraic thinking.
GBR 1993
Research Date(s): 1990-1992
Sutherland, R.
Inst: London University, Institute of Education, Department of Mathematics, Statistics and Computing, 20 Bedford Way, London WC1H OAL, United Kingdom.
Fin: Economic and Social Research Council.
thinking; problem solving; mathematics; arithmetic; algebra; didactic use of computer
pensée; résolution de problème; mathématiques; arithmétique; algèbre; usage didactique de l'ordinateur
PROJECT DESCRIPTION
The aim of this research project is to develop understanding of what is meant by arithmetical and algebraic approaches to problem solving. The underlying assumption being investigated is that certain computer-based experiences can help pupils bridge the gap between arithmetical and algebraic thinking. Longitudinal studies of pupils (ranging in age from 10 to 16) will be carried out in the classroom with some pupils being studied across the primary/secondary school divide.
Publ: Sutherland, R. Some unanswered research questions on the teaching and learning of algebra. In: *For the Learning of Mathematics*, Vol 11, No 3/1991.

13131 Güzel Sanatlar Fakültesi öğrencilerinin uzay ilişkileri yetenek testinden aldıkları puanla desen dersleri başarıları arasındaki ilişki. (The relationship between scores on the space relations aptitude test and scores in the subject "design" at the end of the first semester at the Faculty of Fine Arts.)
TUR 1994
Research Date(s): 1990
Çelik, Şule.
Sup: Kızıltan, Gonca.

Inst: Hacettepe Üniversitesi, Eğitim Fakültesi, Psikolojik Hizmetler Bölümü (Hacettepe University, Faculty of Education, Department of Psychological Services), 06532 Beytepe, Ankara, Turkey.
space perception; fine arts; aptitude test; comparative achievement
perception de l'espace; Beaux-Arts; test d'aptitude; rendement comparé
PROJECT DESCRIPTION

This study examined the relationship between the scores attained on the space relations aptitude test and those attained at the end of the first semester in the subject "design" by first-year students at the Faculty of Fine Arts at Hacettepe University. The study also examined the effect of branch of study and gender on space relations aptitude test scores. The primary objective was to determine the predictive validity of the space relations aptitude test scores for the scores obtained in "design" at the end of the first semester.

The sample of the study consisted of 64 students (30 males; 34 females) from the Departments of Painting and Sculpture of the Faculty of Fine Arts, the sections of graphical arts, interior architecture, landscaping, ceramics and glass of the Department of Applied Arts in the 1988-1989 academic year.

The data consisted of the scores students attained on the space relations aptitude test and the scores they attained at the end of the first semester in the subject "design". Data analysis techniques included the Pearson product-moment correlation coefficient technique, variance analysis and t-test.

Comparison of the space relations aptitude test scores and the scores in "design" at the end of the first semester for each department and branch showed no significant relationship between the two types of scores. Neither did analysis of the space relations aptitude test scores by department and branch of the Faculty of Fine Arts reveal significant differences. Analysis by gender showed that male students were more successful in the space relations aptitude test than females.

13132　Improving the quality of argument: schools.
GBR　1993
Research Date(s): 1991-1992
Costello, P.; Andrews, R.; Mitchell, S.
Inst: Hull University, School of Education, Cottingham Road, Hull HU6 7RX, United Kingdom.
Fin: Esmee Fairbairn Charitable Trust.
argumentation; critical sense; writing; primary education; secondary education
argumentation; sens critique; écriture; enseignement primaire; enseignement secondaire
PROJECT DESCRIPTION

This project is inter-related with 'Improving the quality of argument: sixth forms and higher education'. The project explores the learning and teaching of argument at key stages 2, 3 and 4 in the National Curriculum. Operating in ten primary and ten secondary schools in Humberside and Lincolnshire, its aim is to improve the quality of argument and to record evidence of this improvement. The approach is one of action research.
Publ: Andrews, R. Argument in the primary school. In: *Language Matters*, No 1, pp. 34-35, Autumn 1991.

13133　Improving the quality of argument: sixth forms and higher education.
GBR　1993
Research Date(s): 1991-1994
Costello, P.; Andrews, R.; Mitchell, S.
Inst: Hull University, School of Education, Cottingham Road, Hull HU6 7RX, United Kingdom.
Fin: Leverhulme Trust.
argumentation; writing; critical sense
argumentation; écriture; sens critique
PROJECT DESCRIPTION

This project is inter-related with 'Improving the quality of argument: schools'. The project is cross-curricular and runs for three years. In year one, the focus is on sixth forms; this shifts in years two and three to higher education (Humberside University and Hull University). The aim of this project is to explore argument action in various subjects and to devise materials to improve the qualtiy of arguing. The research is grounded to begin with and then is more focused and applied.

13134　Investigating effective reasoning models for students: what courses provide and what students concoct.
GBR　1993
Research Date(s): 1992-
Jones, A.; Petre, M.
Inst: Open University, Institute of Educational Technology, Walton Hall, Milton Keynes MK7 6AA, United Kingdom.
reasoning; computer application; information technology; teaching aid
raisonnement; application informatique; technologie de l'information; moyen d'enseignement
PROJECT DESCRIPTION

This research has two main aims: to investigate elements that contribute to the formation of mental models by novice users and to evaluate meta-phors by which models are suggested. A further aim is to consider practical issues for designing instructional material for independent study. A pilot project will investigate instructional elements that contribute to the formation of mental models by novice users.

Particular questions include: (1) Is there a generaliseable set of initial information that obstructs learning if it is absent or encourages learning if it is offered at the outset? (2) Do the principle metaphors work; where do they break down, when and in what circumstances do users reject them?

Practical issues for designing instructional material for independent study include the question of how people actually use the resources provided and when does the time it takes to become minimally competent with a system become prohibitive? The pilot study takes the form of a case study of a practical element of an Open University course. The domain is learning a computer application.

13135　Investigation of the development of social cognition and the subsequent effectiveness of cognitive curricular approaches to meeting individual needs.
GBR　1993
Research Date(s): 1987-
Powell, S.; Jordan, R.
Inst: Hertfordshire University, School of Humanities and Education, Wall Hall Campus, Aldenham, Watford WD2 8AT, United Kingdom.
Fin: Inge Wakehurst Trust.
social development; cognitive development; autism; curriculum research
développement social; développement cognitif; autisme; recherche sur les programmes d'études
PROJECT DESCRIPTION

This research investigates the development of social cognition with special regard to individuals who fall within the autistic continuum. The researchers have conducted experimental studies with individuals with autism on the development of a 'theory of mind'. Action research is being conducted into ways in which individual learning can be facilitated within the curriculum by means of cognitive approaches. Computer programs were used to derive principles that underpin the pedagogy of a 'cognitive curriculum', that encompasses the needs of all children. The programs were evaluated in an experimental study with autistic individuals and the principles are being evaluated through classroom-based action research in a variety of educational settings.

Publ: Powell, S.D. & Jordan, R.R. Thinking about autistic children thinking. In: *Collected Papers - International Conference on Experimental Psychology and the Autistic Syndromes*. (Durham) Sunderland: Sunderland Polytechnic, 1990.
Jordan, R.R. & Powell, S.D. Autism and the National Curriculum. In: *British Journal of Special Education*, Vol 17, No 4/1990, pp. 140-142.
Jordan, R.R. & Powell, S.D. Teaching thinking - the case for principles. In: *European Journal of Special Needs Education*, Vol 6, No 2/1991, pp. 112-124.
Riding, R.J. & Powell, S.D. *Learn to think - Stage two (Special Education Version)*, Birmingham, Learning and Training Technology, 1991.
Powell, S.D. & Jordan, R.R. A psychological perspective on identifying and meeting the needs of exceptional pupils. In: *School Pyschology International*, Vol 12, 1991, pp. 315-327.
A full list of publications is available from the researchers.

13136　Işitme engelli öğrencilerin benlik kavramlarının incelenmesi. (The self-concepts of hearing-impaired pupils.)
TUR　1994
Research Date(s): 1992
Ersek, Irfan.
Sup: Akçamete, Gönül.
Inst: Ankara Üniversitesi, Sosyal Bilimler Enstitüsü (University of Ankara, Institute for Social Sciences), 06590 Ankara, Turkey.
personality; self-concept; aurally handicapped
personnalité; conception de soi; handicapé auditif
PROJECT DESCRIPTION

The research examined the differences between the self-concepts of normal pupils and hearing-impaired pupils and studied these self-concepts in relation to such variables as: educational environment, sex, severity of hearing impairment, age of onset of the hearing impairment, level of communication, and academic success.

The sample consisted of 77 hearing-impaired pupils in year five of primary schools in the City of Ankara and the Ankara School for the Deaf in the school year 1990-1991 and 77 normal pupils. The Piers-Harris Self-Concept Inventory was used to collect data. Percentages, variance analysis and t-tests were employed in the statistical analysis of the data.

Results: The hearing-impaired pupils had more negative self-concepts with regard to: behaviour, intellectual and school performance, worries, popularity and feelings of happiness. No differences were observed in respect of body images. More positive self-concepts were found among: hearing-impaired pupils in ordinary classrooms (as opposed to pupils in more specialized educational facilities); pupils who were hard of hearing (as opposed to deaf pupils); pupils who were aged 5 or over at onset of the impairment (as opposed to pupils who were younger at onset of the impairment); and pupils with relatively good communication skills or relatively high academic achievement levels. No relationships seemed to exist between differences in self-concept and differences in gender, mathematics achievement or the educational environments provided by specialized educational institutions.

13137 Knowledge representation and information exchange in instruction.
GBR 1993
Research Date(s): 1986-1992
Hannabuss, C.
Sup: McAleese, R.
Inst: Robert Gordon University, School of Librarianship and Information Studies, Hilton Place, Aberdeen AB9 1FR, United Kingdom; Heriot-Watt University, Institute of Computer-Based Learning, Riccarton Campus, Currie, Edinburgh EH14 4AS, United Kingdom.
knowledge; management education; comprehension; epistemology; concept formation
connaissance; formation à la gestion; compréhension; épistémologie; formation de concept
PROJECT DESCRIPTION
This research aims to investigate knowledge representation in the context of knowledge paradigms and conceptual frameworks. It examines ways in which experts and novices know and come to know management concepts, and induce and undergo meta-positional change through the representation of canonical knowledge in idio-syncratic ways, epistemic and axiological, explicit and assumptive.

Publ: Hannabuss, C.S. Negotiating meaning. In: *Education Today*, Vol 37, No 1/1987, pp. 13-22.
Hannabuss, C.S. *Knowledge management*. Bradford: MCB University Press, 1987.
Hannabuss, C.S. Collaborating over meanings in management. In: *Personnel Review*, Vol 16, No 5/1987, pp. 34-39.
Hannabuss, C.S. Knowledge paradigms and change. In: *International Journal of Sociology and Social Change*, Vol 8, No 1/1988, pp. 23-31.

13138 Leerstijlen en sturen van leerprocessen in het hoger onderwijs. (Learning styles and regulation of learning in higher education.)
NLD 1993
Research Date(s): 1986-1992
Vermunt, J.D.H.M.
Inst: Faculteit Sociale Wetenschappen, Vakgroep Psychologie (Faculty of Social Sciences, Department of Psychology), P.O. Box 90153, 5000 LE Tilburg, Netherlands.
Katholieke Universiteit Brabant (Catholic University of Brabant), P.O. Box 90153, 5000 LE Tilburg, Netherlands
cognitive process; cognitive style; learning strategy; learning process; student
processus cognitif; style cognitif; stratégie d'apprentissage; apprentissage; étudiant
PROJECT DESCRIPTION
This doctoral dissertation deals with the quality of learning processes in higher education. The first part of the book outlines a theory on the regulation of learning processes and the design of instruction from a cognitive-psychological angle. It presents a new approach to learning and teaching, based on recent insights into the process of learning. This new educational concept, named "process-oriented instruction", refers to an instructional strategy in which the teaching of independent thinking strategies and domain-specific knowledge are combined.

The second part deals with eight empirical studies which investigated how students in the early stage of higher education learn. Over 1,600 regular education and distance education students participated in these studies. Four learning styles were identified: undirected, reproduction-directed, meaning-directed and application-directed. Learning processes appeared to be regulated above all by the students themselves. No connection was found between the external regulation of learning processes and students' use of deep and concrete cognitive strategies. These strategies were found to be related above all to students' mental models of learning and their usage of self-regulatory strategies. It was found that students' learning styles are of considerable stability, but not to the point of being unchangeable. The dominance of a particular learning style appeared to be linked to factors such as subject matter domain, previous education, learning experience, type of higher education, age and gender. Learning styles were found to explain a major proportion of the variance in examination results. It should be noted, however, that the examinations demanded little of students in terms of critical, analytical or concrete processing strategies. It was also found that process-oriented instruction can help students develop a more independent and constructive style of learning.

The third part discusses the relevance of the findings for theory and practice. One of the conclusions is that higher education curricula should pay more attention to the teaching of independent thinking strategies that may help students to construct, adapt and utilize knowledge. Examinations should be aimed more strongly at measuring to what extent students have acquired these strategies. Concrete suggestions are made as to how such an improvement of the quality of learning processes in higher education may be achieved.

Publ: Vermunt, J. *Leerstijlen en sturen van leerprocessen in het hoger onderwijs - naar procesgerichte instructie in zelfstandig denken.* Amsterdam/Lisse: Swets & Zeitlinger BV, 1992, 273p. (English summary) ISBN 90-265-1311-9.

13139 The mass media and the social construction of memory.
GBR 1993
Research Date(s): 1988-
Cox, D.
Inst: Nottingham University, Department of Adult Education, 14-22 Shakespeare Street, Nottingham NG1 4FJ, United Kingdom.
memory; mass media
mémoire; médias
PROJECT DESCRIPTION
The research will explore the ways in which many parts of people's memories are socially derived and will especially focus on those parts that are dependent on vicarious experience, learned about via the mass media (although the research will not ignore the importance of inter-personal vicarious experience).

Using a case study approach, the research will attempt to locate mass media influence in an historicised context. This is necessary because of: (a) the way we interpret present events will be affected by what we remember from the past; and (b) how we remember events from the past will be qualified by how new events are reported. As what we remember will also be filtered through the ideological positions of different people, then socially constructed memory has also to be seen in terms of ideological memory.

The case studies chosen for the research will examine the reporting of various types of industrial relations issues in national daily newspapers, but will not use conventional content analysis techniques alone. There will be an attempt to refine other qualitative measures. The research will also consider issues in the education of adults, especially how students' memory resources can be channelled, and how they have to be critically questioned and interpreted, rather than being simply accepted as evidence.

13140 Mathematics - shape & space: mathematics & art.
GBR 1993
Research Date(s): 1991-
Light, R.
Inst: Charlotte Mason College, Ambleside, Cumbria LA22 9BB, United Kingdom.
space perception; art; cognitive development; drawing; mathematics
perception de l'espace; art; développement cognitif; dessin; mathématiques
PROJECT DESCRIPTION
The project looks at cross-curricular links for mathematics and art, studying childrens' spatial development in the context of both their mathematics and drawing abilities, the development of spatial representation within art history and their relationship with cognitive development.

13141 Mentale activering door middel van vragen stellen. (Questioning and mental activity.)
NLD 1994
Research Date(s): 1992-1996
Meij, H. van der.
Sup: Pieters, J.M.
Inst: Onderzoek Centrum Toegepaste Onderwijskunde (OCTO) (Research Centre of the Department of Educational Technology), P.O. Box 217, 7500 AE Enschede, Netherlands.
Universiteit Twente (Twente University), P.O. Box 217, 7500 AE Enschede, Netherlands
Fin: SVO het Instituut voor Onderzoek van het Onderwijs.
thinking; learning; teaching method; cognitive process
pensée; acquisition de connaissances; méthode pédagogique; processus cognitif
PROJECT DESCRIPTION
Background: There is increasing research evidence showing the positive effects of teaching methods that capitalize on the active role of the learner in the learning process. Good learning results can be expected if learners themselves actively develop good learning activities. Few research projects have been concerned with the relationship between the questions learners pose and the outcomes of learning or with the direct ways in which learners can be encouraged to pose questions.
Aim: (1) To examine the relationships between learners' questioning behaviour, learning and thinking activities learning outcomes; (2) to determine what modes of stimulating learners' questioning behaviour mentally activate learners and thus lead to improved learning outcomes.
Design: Three experiments will be conducted with secondary vocational school pupils on mechanical engineering courses. A comparison will be made of the effects of studying an excerpt followed by questioning (with the pupils posing questions to the teacher) and studying an excerpt fol-

lowed by studying a longer text. Special attention will be paid to the effect of stimulating questioning behaviour on the achievement of pupils of lesser ability. The effects of compensatory stimulation and stimulation to reinforce questioning behaviour will be studied separately.

13142 Modellierung analysebasierten Wissenserwerbs und Entwicklung generativer Diagnosemodelle. (Model of analysis-based knowledge acquisition and development of generative diagnostic models.)
DEU 1993
Research Date(s): 1990-1993
Opwis, K.; Ploetzner, R.
Sup: Spada, H.
Inst: Universitaet Freiburg, Philosophische Fakultaet 01, Psychologisches Institut, Abt. Allg. Psychologie, Niemensstrasse 10, D-7800 Freiburg im Breisgau.
Fin: Deutsche Forschungsgemeinschaft.
knowledge; learning; learning theory; comprehension; model; cognitive process
connaissance; acquisition de connaissances; théorie de l'apprentissage; compréhension; modèle; processus cognitif
PROJECT DESCRIPTION
Inhalt: Die Genese individuellen Wissens wird verstanden als Zusammenspiel horizontaler und vertikaler Wissenserwerbungsprozesse im Sinne der Aneignung neuen bzw. der Modifikation vorhandenen Wissens und des Aufbaus adaequater Formen der mentalen Repraesentation eines Gegenstandsbereichs. Im Rahmen dieser Vorstellungen einer multiplen mentalen Repraesentation und bezogen auf den Gegenstandsbereich der Untersuchung, das qualitative und quantitative Verstaendnis funktionaler Beziehungen, werden analyse-basierte Wissenserwerbsmodelle entwickelt. Ein wichtiges Ziel ist die Rekonstruktion von Lernmechanismen, die nicht nur eine Vermehrung, sondern auch eine Umstrukturierung von Wissen ermoeglichen. Auch entwicklungspsychologische Gesichtspunkte werden bei der Theoriebildung beruecksichtigt. Weitere Ziele betreffen die Realisierung von Systemen zur automatisierten Diagnose von Wissensbestaenden auf verschiedenen Ebenen mentaler Repraesentation. Durch Einbeziehung der erarbeiteten Wissenserwerbsmodelle werden nicht nur die Voraussetzungen fuer eine theoretisch ueberzeugende Erfassung von Kenntnissen geschaffen, sondern auch fuer die Diagnose von Wissen im Verlauf seines Erwerbs (Prozessdiagnostik). Eine derartige on-line Diagnose mit automatisierter Generierung von Aufgaben ist eine Zielsetzung, der fuer die Gestaltung adaptiver tutorieller Systeme besondere Bedeutung zukommt.
Vorgehensweise: Entwicklung kognitiver Modelle / Computersimulation. Untersuchungsdesign: Computersimulation.
Datengewinnung: Psychologischer Test (Stichprobe: 30; Schueler der 5. Klasse. Stichprobe: 30; Schueler der 7. Klasse. Stichprobe: 30; Schueler der 9. Klasse. Stichprobe: 30; Schueler der 11. Klasse). Primaererhebung: Feldarbeit von Mitarbeitern des Projektes durchgefuehrt.
Auswertung: Varianzanalyse, Haeufigkeitsbestimmungen, testtheoretische Analysen.
Publ: Ploetzner, Rolf & Spada, Hans. *Analysis-based Learning on Multiple Levels of Mental Domain Representation*. Freiburg, 25 S.

13143 Öğretmen olarak yetişen öğrencilerin benlik kavramı ve işbaşında benlik kavramı arasındaki ilişkiyi etkileyen bazı faktörler. (Some factors affecting the agreement level between student teachers' self-concepts and vocational self-concepts.)
TUR 1994
Research Date(s): 1989
Altıntaş, Ersin.
Sup: Ersever, Oya.
Inst: Hacettepe Üniversitesi, Sosyal Bilimler Enstitüsü (Hacettepe University, Institute of Social Sciences), Beytepe Kampüsü, 06532 Ankara, Turkey.
self-concept; teacher education; teaching profession; student teacher
conception de soi; formation des enseignants; profession d'enseignant; élève-maître
PROJECT DESCRIPTION
The study examined the factors determining the agreement level between the self-concepts and vocational self-concepts of student teachers. Two checklists were used: "Identifying Oneself with Adjectives" and "Identifying Vocation with Adjectives".
It was hypothesized that the level of agreement between self-concept and vocational self-concept would be determined by personal characteristics, educational experience, perception of the teaching profession, and socio-economic and cultural characteristics.
The sample consisted of 400 senior students in the Faculties of Education, Science and Literature at Uludağ University in the academic year 1986-1987.
The findings show that the level of agreement between self-concept and vocational self-concept is more strongly determined by students' personal characteristics, educational experience and perception of the teaching profession than by socio-economic and cultural characteristics.

13144 Öğretmen yetiştiren fakülte öğrencilerinin benlik ve mesleki benlik kavramları arasındaki bağdaşım düzeylerini etkileyen bazı faktörler. (The effect of some factors on the agreement between self-concept and vocational self-concept of teacher training students.)
TUR 1994
Research Date(s): 1989
Altıntaş, Ersin.
Sup: Ersever, Oya G.
Inst: Hacettepe Üniversitesi, Eğitim Fakültesi, Psikolojik Hizmetler Bölümü (Hacettepe University, Faculty of Education, Department of Psychological Services), 06532 Beytepe, Ankara, Turkey.
self-concept; student teacher; teacher education; teaching profession
conception de soi; élève-maître; formation des enseignants; profession d'enseignant
PROJECT DESCRIPTION
Aim: The study investigated some factors affecting levels of agreement between the self-concepts and vocational self-concepts of teacher training students.
Design: In order to measure the dependent variable - agreement between self-concept and vocational self-concept - two specially developed tests were used: the "Identifying Oneself with Adjectives Checklist" and the "Identifying Vocation with Adjectives" test. Nineteen independent variables were included in the study which related to personal characteristics, educational and family background, and students' socio-economic and cultural characteristics. Data on these variables were collected with a questionnaire. The sample consisted of 400 fourth-year students in the faculties of Education, Science and Arts at Uldağ University in the academic year 1986-1987. The level of agreement between self-concept and vocational self-concept was calculated using the Kappa coefficient formula. Differences between Kappa coefficients were tested at a .05 level of significance.
Results: As regards students' personal characteristics, levels of agreement between self-concept and vocational self-concept were found to be significantly in favour of male students. A significant difference was found between those who scored above and those who scored below the median in the university entrance examination.
As regards the relationship between, on the one hand, agreement between students' self-concept and vocational self-concept and, on the other, students' educational experiences and their perception of the teaching profession, significant differences were found in favour of: students who had chosen their specialization by themselves (as opposed to those who had not); students whose interests and abilities were suitable for the teaching profession; students who perceived relations with their teachers as positive; students who identified themselves with their training institutions; students who were optimistic about the teaching profession; students who assigned high status to the teaching profession.
As regards socio-economic and cultural characteristics, a significant difference was found between self-concept and vocational self-concept in cases where the branch of education chosen by the student was in accordance with the expectations or hopes of one or both of the parents.
In the light of the findings, it is concluded that the agreement between self-concept and vocational self-concept is more strongly related to students' personal and educational characteristics and their perception of the teaching profession than to socio-economic or cultural characteristics. Recommendations are made on the basis of this conclusion.

13145 Personal competences in higher education.
GBR 1993
Research Date(s): 1991-1992
Prosser, J.
Inst: Westminster College, North Hinksey, Oxford OX2 9AT, United Kingdom.
Fin: Nottingham Polytechnic.
self-evaluation; skill; higher education; student
auto-évaluation; compétence; enseignement supérieur; étudiant
PROJECT DESCRIPTION
Westminster is one of five colleges / universities trialling a personal competences model for Nottingham Polytechnic (now The Nottingham Trent University). Twenty-five students are using the model, designed originally by the Department of Employment. Both students and supervisors will reflect on the qualities of the model.
Data are being collected via document analysis (students keep log books, supervisors keep diaries); semi-structured interviews; and questionnaires. The study has an external evaluator based at Nottingham Polytechnic.

13146 Processus d'acquisition étudié sous l'angle de la structuration de l'espace-problème.
FRA 1993
Research Date(s): 1986-1988
Poitrenaud, Sébastien; Richard, Jean-François.

Inst: Université de Paris VIII, CNRS URA / 1297, Psychologie cognitive du traitement de l'information symbolique, 2 rue de la Liberté, 93526 Saint Denis Cedex 02, France.

problem solving; learning; reasoning; logical thinking; cognitive development

résolution de problème; acquisition de connaissances; raisonnement; pensée logique; développement cognitif

PROJECT DESCRIPTION

Objectifs: L'acquisition des connaissances par la résolution de problèmes est examinée en termes de modifications de l'espace problème, défini par un ensemble d'états, des opérateurs (actions permises) et des contraintes d'application des opérateurs. (1) La modification des contraintes d'application des opérateurs a été étudiée en utilisant les différentes versions du problème de la Tour de Hanoï; (2) la modification de la structuration des états de l'espace-problème est étudiée en utilisant différentes versions du jeu de Nim.

Méthodologie: (1) On étudie les séquences d'erreurs dans la résolution du problème par des enfants de 7 à 10 ans, une étude du même type est menée également auprès d'adultes. (2) Une version simple du jeu de Nim est donnée à des enfants de 7 à 10 ans et des versions plus difficiles aux adultes. C'est un jeu à deux adversaires; résoudre un problème dans ce cas est jouer une partie avec un adversaire.

Résultats: (1) On a pu simuler la suite des actions de sujets résolvant une suite de trois problèmes; ceci a permis de conclure qu'il y a beaucoup d'incompréhensions concernant les actions permises et que les enfants transfèrent des procédures qui sont valables dans d'autres contextes mais sont inadaptées dans celui du problème; la planification ne devient possible qu'après élimination des contraintes inadéquates, c'est à dire à partir du moment où le sujet a une représentation correcte du problème. (2) Les mécanismes les plus fondamentaux, observés chez les enfants comme chez les adultes sont des mécanismes de génération, de test et de validation d'hypothèses. Des différences existent entre adultes et enfants au niveau de la structuration de l'espace-problème et au niveau du raisonnement mis en oeuvre. Les deux types de processus d'apprentissage chez l'enfant et chez l'adulte ont été modélisés.

Publ: Richard, Jean-François & Poitrenaud, Sébastien. Problématique de l'analyse de protocoles individuels d'observations comportementales. In: Caverni, Jean-Paul; Bastien, Claude; Mendelsohn, Patrick; Tiberghien, Geneviève (éds.). *Psychologie cognitive: méthodes et modèles.* Presses Universitaires de Grenoble, 1988.
Richard, Jean-François. Analyse des protocoles individuels et microgénèse de la représentation d'un problème. In: *Psychologie française*, 1989, 34, 2-3, pp. 207-211.

13147 Processus d'acquisition par transfert analogique.
FRA 1993
Research Date(s): 1986-
Nguyen-Xuan, Ahn; Richard, Jean-François; Escarabajal, Marie-Claude; Friemel, Edouard; Hoc, Jean-Michel.
Inst: Université de Paris VIII, CNRS URA / 1297, Psychologie cognitive du traitement de l'information symbolique, 2 rue de la Liberté, 93526 Saint Denis Cedex 02, France.
learning; reasoning; conceptual imagery; problem solving
acquisition de connaissances; raisonnement; représentation mentale; résolution de problème
PROJECT DESCRIPTION

Objectifs: Depuis une dizaine d'années le raisonnement et l'apprentissage par analogie sont considérés comme constituant un mécanisme adaptatif important. En effet, le transfert des connaissances d'une situation connue dans une situation nouvelle a l'avantage de réduire le coût mental nécessaire à la construction de la représentation de la situation de problème et de la procédure de solution. On s'intéresse dans cette étude aux mécanismes qui président à la modification d'une connaissance empruntée utile mais non totalement pertinente.

Méthodologie: Une première étude porte sur la modification des connaissances empruntées par auto-observation et contrôle métacognitif chez l'enfant (10-11 ans) et chez l'adulte (problèmes d'inclusion numérique); une seconde étude porte sur la modification des connaissances empruntées dans l'apprentissage des dispositifs de commande intéractifs par des étudiants (calculette, logiciel de traitement de données); un autre projet de recherche introduit le thème de la compréhension des phénomènes complexes par analogie multiple chez des adultes de niveau d'études secondaires (phénomènes électriques).

Publ: Escarabajal, Marie-Claude & Richard, Jean-François. Le transfert analogique de procédures dans l'interprétation et la résolution d'un problème d'inclusion chez des adultes. In: *Archives de psychologie*, 1986, 54, pp. 36-64.
Friemel, Edouard & Richard, Jean-François. Apprentissages de l'utilisation d'une calculette. In: *Hoc, Jean-Michel; Mendelsohn, Patrick (éds.).* Les langages informatiques dans l'enseignement, Psychologie française, *1987, n° 32-4, pp. 227-236.*

Nguyen-Xuan, Ahn. Le raisonnement par analogie. In: *Richard, Jean-François; Bonnet, Claude; Ghiglione, Rodolphe (éds.).* Traité de psychologie cognitive. 2. Traitement de l'information symbolique. *Paris: Dunod, 1990.*

13148 Production écrite de textes.
FRA 1993
Research Date(s): 1986-
Piolat, Annie.
Inst: Université d'Aix-Marseille I, UFR Psychologie Sciences de l'éducation, CNRS URA / 182, Centre de recherche en psychologie cognitive, 29 av. Robert Schuman, 13621 Aix-en-Provence, France.
written expression; information processing; composition; teaching method; word processing
expression écrite; traitement de l'information; composition littéraire; méthode pédagogique; traitement de texte
PROJECT DESCRIPTION

Objectifs: Produire un texte c'est planifier, contrôler et réviser afin de linéariser à l'aide des moyens disponibles dans la langue des suites d'informations sémantiques hiérarchisées et structurées en fonction de l'audience et du but que s'assigne le parleur ou le scripteur. Les contraintes auxquelles doit se plier le producteur sont diversifiées : procédurales, linguistiques, mnémoniques, pragmatiques. Trois questions retiennent l'attention: (1) Quels sont les types de connaissances déclaratives et procédurales qu'un scripteur utilise pour produire un texte? (2) Selon quels processus parvient-il, d'une part à séquentialiser les informations récupérées afin de les mettre en texte, et d'autre part à contrôler cette linéarisation? (3) Selon quels cheminements les jeunes scripteurs mettent-ils en place leurs compétences textuelles en production écrite?

Méthodologie: Deux aspects méthodologiques ont du être particulièrement approfondis: le mode de recueil des productions écrites et l'analyse des séquences d'activités qui concourent à la réalisation de ces tâches complexes que sont la production ou l'amélioration de texte écrit. Afin d'étudier la production écrite de texte en temps réel, des procédures de recherches "assistées" par ordinateur sont mises sur pied. Des recherches portent sur l'étude de la révision de textes qui implique aussi une importante activité de compréhension et qui suppose des retombées ergonomiques et pédagogiques (aide à l'amélioration de la rédaction de textes avec ou sans traitement de texte).

Résultats: Mise au point d'architectures rédactionnelles intégrant les aspects métacognitifs du contôle de la rédaction de texte. Mise en place de dispositifs favorisant l'enregistrement pas à pas de procédures rédactionnelles. Création d'un système informatique d'aide à la conception d'idées. Mise au point de tutoriel d'enseignement de l'écriture.

Publ: Piolat, Annie. Le retour sur le texte dans l'activité rédactionnelle précoce. In: *European journal of psychology of education,* n°spécial *Early literacy* 1988, 3(6), pp. 449-459.
Piolat, Annie; Farioli, Fernand & Roussey, Jean-Yves. La production de texte assistée par ordinateur. In: Monteil, Gérard; Fayol Michel (Eds.). *La psychologie scientifique et ses applications.* Grenoble: PUG, 1989.
Espéret, Eric & Piolat, Annie. Text production: planning and control. In: Denhière, Guy; Rossi, Jean-Pierre (Eds.). *Text and processing.* Amsterdam: North Holland, 1989.
Piolat, Annie & Roussey, Jean-Yves. Narrative and descriptive text revising strategies and procedures. In: Boscolo, Pietro; Espéret, Eric; Fayol, Michel. *Writing* N°spécial, *European Journal of Psychology of Education,* Juin 1991, vol. 6, 2, pp. 155-163.
(Une liste complète est disponible.).

13149 Psychische Befindlichkeit und Selbstbild bei Studierenden in den neuen und alten Bundeslaendern am Beispiel der Universitaeten Halle und Goettingen. (Mental condition and self-image of students in the old and new German states with particular reference to the universities of Halle and Goettingen.)
DEU 1993
Research Date(s): 1991-1992
Kuda, M.; Rueggeberg, J.
Sup: Schauenburg, H.
Inst: Universitaet Goettingen, FB Medizin, Zentrum Psychologische Medizin, Aerztlich-Psychologische Beratungsstelle fuer Studierende, Nikolausberger Weg 17, D-3400 Goettingen.
self-concept; Germany - Federal Republic; German DR; student; woman; psychological characteristics; university
conception de soi; Allemagne RFA; Allemagne RDA; étudiant; femme; caractéristique psychologique; université
PROJECT DESCRIPTION

Inhalt: Auswirkungen aktueller sozialer Verunsicherungen auf Studierende in den neuen Bundeslaendern in ausgewaehlten Fachbereichen. Hierbei wird eine Abhaengigkeit vom gewaehlten Fach und den damit verbundenen Zukunftsperspektiven postuliert. Untersucht werden psychovegetative Befindlichkeit, Selbstbild (Giessen-Text), Zukunftsperspektiven (eigener Fragebogen), Kontrollueberzeugungen (IPC-Fragebogen). Teilergebnisse: Eine deutliche Beeintraechtigung der Befindlichkeit findet sich nur unter den weiblichen Studenten der Universitaet Halle, hier insbesondere in den geisteswissenschaftlichen Faechern. Im Selbstbild gibt es Hinweise auf passive Orientierungen bei gleichzeitiger Hoeherbewertung sozialer Eigenschaften in Ostdeutschland.

Untersuchter Zeitraum: Fruehjahr 1991.

Vorgehensweise: Vergleichende gruppenstatistische Verfahren; Faktorenanalyse; Diskriminanzanalyse; Mittelwertvergleiche. Untersuchungsdesign: Querschnitterhebung.

Datengewinnung: Gruppenbefragung (Stichprobe: 440; Studenten von 5 Fachbereichen; Auswahlverfahren: Zufall) . Primaererhebung: Feldarbeit von Mitarbeitern des Projektes durchgefuehrt.

Auswertung: Dreifaktorielle Varianzanalyse (Land, Geschlecht, Studienfach); t-Tests; Faktorenanalyse. Datenaufbereitung: Datenedition (z.B. Aufbau von Datenbanken).

13150 Raisonnement temporel et raisonnement spatial.
FRA   1993
Research Date(s): 1983-
Crépault, Jacques.
Inst: Université de Paris VIII, CNRS URA/1297, Psychologie cognitive du traitement de l'information symbolique, 2 rue de la Liberté, 93526 Saint Denis Cedex 02, France.
time perception; space perception; reasoning; logical thinking; cognitive development
perception du temps; perception de l'espace; raisonnement; pensée logique; développement cognitif
PROJECT DESCRIPTION

Objectifs: Les recherches effectuées visent à étudier les modes d'organisation des inférences temporelles en dehors du contexte cinématique. Une première série de travaux concerne le domaine des relations durée-succession (raisonnements qualitatifs-quantitatifs); une deuxième série porte sur la représentation spatiale des relations temporelles, une dernière recherche concerne les relations spatiales (relations longueur, position initiale, position finale). L'ensemble de ces travaux s'insère dans la classe de problèmes à trois dimensions et le modèle des systèmes cognitifs stables-instables. Les informations sont présentées sous la forme d'énoncés hypothétiques (inférence sur la troisième dimension).

Méthodologie: Expériences auprès de sujets de 9 ans à l'âge adulte.

Publ: Crépault, Jacques & Warnaffe (de), A. Mémoire et raisonnement dans les problèmes de type durée-succession. In: *Canadian psychology*, 1987, n° 27.
Crepault, Jacques. *Temps et raisonnement. Développement cognitif de l'enfant à l'adulte*. Lille: Presses universitaires de Lille, 1989, 537p.
Crépault, Jacques & Nguyen, Ahn. Cognitive development: object, space, time, logico-mathematical concepts. In: *Hauert, C.-A. (ed.). Advances in Developmental Psychology: cognitive, perceptivo-motor and neuro-psychological perspectives. Amsterdam: North-Holland, 1990, pp. 231-272.*

13151 Rationalitaet als paedagogische Aufgabe: Moeglichkeiten und Gefahren. (Rationality as a pedagogic task: opportunities and risks.)
DEU   1993
Research Date(s): 1989-1993
Eckerle, G.
Sup: Kraak, B.
Inst: Deutsches Institut fuer Internationale Paedagogische Forschung, Abt. Paedagogische Psychologie, Schloss-Strasse, D-6000 Frankfurt am Main 90.
thinking; cognitive development; pupil; aims of education
pensée; développement cognitif; élève; finalité de l'éducation
PROJECT DESCRIPTION

Inhalt: Die Forderung nach Denkerziehung wird von Lehrern selten aufgegriffen. Viele fuerchten eine "Verkopfung" der Schueler. Dabei spielen Vorurteile ueber Rationalitaet eine Rolle. Untersucht werden soll, welche Auffassungen ueber Rationalitaet ihre Gegner und ihre Befuerworter haben und welche Auswirkungen von Rationalitaet erwartet werden. Untersucht werden soll auch die Geschichte dieser Kontroverse.

Vorgehensweise: Kritische Literaturauswertung. Untersuchungsdesign: Retrospektive Daten.

13152 Reading, listening and television viewing: a study in children's cognition.
GBR   1993
Research Date(s): 1988-1993
Afzalnia, M.
Sup: Hartley, J.
Inst: Keele University, Department of Psychology, Keele, Staffordshire ST5 5BG, United Kingdom.
Fin: Government of Iran.
cognition; television; reading; achievement
cognition; télévision; lecture; rendement
PROJECT DESCRIPTION

This research is concerned with the relationships between children's television viewing and their school performance with an emphasis on their reading, listening and viewing comprehension skills. Seventy-eight 9-10 year olds were selected from a local school to take part. Tests of reading, intelligence and listening skills, together with questionnaires, were used to collect information about the children's abilities and their parents' and teachers' attitudes towards their reading and listening habits.

While the results of the test studies supported the assumption that predicted that children's general reading and listening skills would relate to their viewing comprehension, the obtained data did not produce much support for the hypothesis that assumed a positive relationship between children's sensitivity to the audio channel of television and their verbal receptive achievements. The assumption that there would be a positive relationship between children's background variables and their reading, listening and viewing skills was mostly supported. However, the data indicated that some variables (such as library membership) were more important than the others. It was found that children with low achievements in reading and listening also had some difficulty with their overall cognition which was shown in their difficulty in general learning.

Publ: Afzalnia, M.R. Television literacy and young children's promotion of mental health. In: Trent, D. (ed.). *Promotion of mental health*, Aldershot: Avebury, 1993.

13153 Représentations dans l'apprentissage des sciences physiques.
FRA   1993
Research Date(s): 1986-1990
Amigues, René.
Inst: Université d'Aix-Marseille I, UFR Psychologie Sciences de l'éducation, CNRS URA/182, Centre de recherche en psychologie cognitive, 29 av. Robert Schuman, 13621 Aix-en-Provence, France.
problem solving; physics; cognitive process; learning; conceptual imagery; upper secondary
résolution de problème; physique; processus cognitif; acquisition de connaissances; représentation mentale; secondaire deuxième cycle
PROJECT DESCRIPTION

Objectifs: L'hypothèse de ce travail pose que le traitement des situations problèmes en physique est affecté simultanément par les "conceptions phénoménologiques" des élèves et par les données et la structure des situations présentées. Les recherches réalisées permettent d'avancer deux séries d'hypothèses: (a) différentes représentations d'un phénomène physique, des "unités phénoménologiques" sont regroupées de façon indifférenciée dans une conception unique (le "courant électrique"), elles constituent un ensemble de "premisses inférentielles" qui assurent l'interaction sujet-tâche mais qui s'avèrent être insuffisantes pour résoudre le problème posé; (b) ce système de représentations est associée une procédure familière qui se traduit par un traitement séquentiel des informations fondé sur l'organisation spatiale des données.

Méthodologie: Une première recherche réalisée auprès de lycéens de classe de seconde en sciences physiques montre que la déstabilisation de la procédure familière, observée dans des conditions bien particulières de dialogue entre élèves, entraîne une différenciation conceptuelle et l'élaboration d'une représentation plus fonctionnelle des phénomènes considérés. Une seconde expérimentation menée dans une situation de recherche de pannes dans un circuit électrique montre que l'organisation des informations fondée sur l'ordre de traitement généré par les conceptions phénoménologiques, favorise la structuration de la situation problème.

Résultats: Il a été mis en évidence que: (1) le contrôle est distribué sur les "espaces de problèmes" constitutifs de la situation et que la correction des erreurs par les élèves dépend des possibilités de réorganiser leur cadre interprétatif; (2) les modifications dans le contrôle exécutif dépendent de la stratégie en cours; à cet égard, les représentations graphiques semblent jouer un rôle prépondérant dans cette dynamique cognitive.

Publ: Amigues, René & Johsua, Samuel (Eds.). L'enseignement des circuits électriques: conceptions des élèves et aides didactiques. In: *Technologies, idéologies, pratiques*, 1988, n° 7, 2.
Amigues, René. Peer interaction in solving problems: sociocognitive confrontation and metacognitive aspects. In: *Journal of experimental child psychology*, 1988, n° 45, pp. 141-158.
Amigues, René & Caillot, Michel. Les représentations graphiques dans l'enseignement et l'apprentissage en électricité. In: *European journal of psychology of education*, N° spécial: Psychology of learning physics, 1990, vol. 5, 4, pp. 477-488.

13154 Samostatná činnost' detí pri poznávaní v základnej škole. (Independent work of children and cognitive processes in primary school.)
CSK   1993
Research Date(s): 1991-1993
Šimončičová, Marta; Dančová, Dagmar.
Sup: Holčík, Milan.
Inst: Ústav experimentálnej pedagogiky Slovenskej akadémie vied (Institute of Experimental pedagogy, Slovak Academy of Sciences), Mánesovo nám. 1, 851 01 Bratislava, Czech and Slovak Federal Republic.
Slovenská akadémia vied (Slovak Academy of Sciences), Štefánikova ul. 49, 811 04 Bratislava, Czech and Slovak Federal Republic
cognitive process; independent work; primary education; knowledge level; cognition; cognitive development; learning strategy

processus cognitif; travail indépendant; enseignement primaire; niveau de connaissances; cognition; développement cognitif; stratégie d'apprentissage

PROJECT DESCRIPTION

The project is based on theories aimed at improving the conditions for the development of pupils' independent cognitive abilities. The starting point for the research is the inability of the present education system to develop independent cognitive skills in primary school pupils, as a result of which many pupils have serious difficulties in adapting to the requirements of secondary school. Also important is the fact that in most cases the development of pupils' knowledge depends on empirical cognition rather than effective teaching techniques.

An educational experiment will be carried out in an attempt to stimulate pupils' cognitive independence. The experiment will be integrated with instruction in a regular curriculum subject under title of "Learning Strategy". The focus will be on changing the relation between the teacher and the pupils (humanization, freedom) and changing pupils' attitudes towards learning and cognition (creativity). In view of the importance of written media in modern society, the experiment will be mainly concerned with pupils' processing and understanding of written text. The experiment will be carried out in the second stage of primary school.

Hypotheses: (1) A direct relationship exists between the amount of training in different methods for studying texts and pupils' levels of cognitive independence; (2) pupils' ability to study a text independently enhances their overall school performance; (3) pupils' cognitive independence has a positive effect on the quality of their knowledge.

13155   Spatial cognition: children's pictorial representations.

GBR   1993

Research Date(s): 1990-1993

Tyler, S.

Sup: Light, P.

Inst: Open University, Walton Hall, Milton Keynes MK7 6AA, United Kingdom.

Fin: Economic and Social Research Council.

space perception; cognitive process; drawing; child

perception de l'espace; processus cognitif; dessin; enfant

PROJECT DESCRIPTION

Modern accounts of children's drawings still take intellectual/visual realism (or elaborations) as their focal point. The current research treats drawing as problem-solving, with solutions determined/constrained by factors such as lack of particular spatial concepts. However, Piaget's accounts of the child's construction of representational space, and his premise of perception in 2D are not accepted. Thus in the first experiments, which focused on inconsistencies in response when children are requested to draw an array in which one object is partly hidden by another, the dimensions of the objects were systematically varied (2D/3D).

Results showed that children aged 4-7 years are sensitive to object dimensions. When 2D equivalents of 3D objects are used children are less likely to segregate either outlines or 2D cutouts when drawing or arranging materials on paper, than when the objects are 3D. They are able to arrange 2D materials so that one is partially hidden, provided the arrangement is made 'in space' so that many gaps can be left to represent object depth. They can also match arrays, using identical materials. The findings show that children's difficulties are confined to the 2D drawing surface, and that they have no problems with understanding simple spatial relationships, with allowing objects to be partially hidden, or with viewpoint. Other findings showed that children will treat 3D objects as 2D provided object depth is not an essential feature (as it is in spheres, cones etc.).

A current experiment is investigating whether partial occlusion can be facilitated by triggering what may be schemas for drawing familiar objects - schemas that may be 2D in concept.

13156   The speed of tactile information processing for blind pupils.

GBR   1993

Research Date(s): 1990-1992

Mason, H.; Hull, T.

Inst: Birmingham University, School of Education, Edgbaston, Birmingham B15 2TT, United Kingdom.

Fin: Leverhulme Trust.

tactual perception; visually handicapped; blind; test construction; information processing

perception tactile; handicapé visuel; aveugle; construction de tests; traitement de l'information

PROJECT DESCRIPTION

The major aim of this research is to develop and field trial a tactile speed of information processing test based on a sighted version of the existing print version of the British Ability Scales. This is to be standardised on the blind population, aged 5-17, of England, Wales and Northern Ireland, Scotland and Eire.

13157   Studies of Attention Disordered - Hyperactive (ADHD) children.

GBR   1993

Research Date(s): 1989-

Brown, G.; Shaw, G.

Inst: University of East Anglia, School of Education, Norwich NR4 7TJ, United Kingdom; Georgetown College, Kentucky, KY 40324, USA.

cognition; cognitive ability; memory; attention; creativity; learning difficulty

cognition; aptitude cognitive; mémoire; attention; créativité; difficulté de l'apprentissage

PROJECT DESCRIPTION

A series of experiments is in progress to explore the cognitive skills of children with attention disorders and hyperactivity. In particular the research is investigating unusual facets of memory and high levels of non-verbal creativity in ADHD (Attention Disordered Hyperactive Children) children. There is also strong evidence of high levels of mixed laterality, left handedness and allergic conditions. Further work is aimed at improving selection procedures of subjects and refining the specially designed measures.

Publ: Shaw, G.A. & Brown, G. Laterality and creativity concomitants of attentional problems. In: Developmental Neuropsychology, Vol 6, No 1/1990, pp. 39-59.

Shaw, G.A. & Brown, G. Laterality, implicit memory and attention disorders. In: Educational Studies, Vol 17, No 1/1991, pp. 15-23.

Brown, G. Some more equal than others. The Vernon-Wall Lecture to the Education Section of the British Psychological Society, Blackpool, England, 1991.

13158   Teachers' strategies of self-evaluation.

GBR   1993

Research Date(s): 1986-1992

Hurst, V.

Sup: Kelly, A.

Inst: London University, Goldsmiths' College, Faculty of Education, Lewisham Way, New Cross, London SE14 6NW, United Kingdom.

self-evaluation; teacher; student teacher; curriculum development

auto-évaluation; enseignant; élève-maître; élaboration de programmes d'études

PROJECT DESCRIPTION

The project aims to gain an insight into classroom processes of evaluation and curriculum development. It is an ethnographic investigation through case studies of two infant classrooms, a group of initial teacher education (ITE) students on teaching practice, ITE students on college-based courses, collaborative work with a museum education department plus two nursery centres for the purpose of comparison.

13159   Teaching competence - a personal construct investigation.

GBR   1993

Research Date(s): 1990-1993

Johnson, G.

Sup: Harri-Augstein, S.; Thomas, L.

Inst: Brunel University, Centre for the Study of Human Learning, Uxbridge UB8 3PH, United Kingdom; Kingston University, Faculty of Education, Kingston Hill Centre, Kingston Hill, Kingston upon Thames KT2 7LB, United Kingdom.

self-evaluation; personality; teaching aptitude; minimum competencies; teacher education

auto-évaluation; personnalité; aptitude à l'enseignement; fundamentum; formation des enseignants

PROJECT DESCRIPTION

The research involves the elicitation of personal constructs of teaching competencies from teacher training staff and students with a view to re-designing teaching/school experience criteria for assessment. The major research tool is repertory grids and feedback for learning programmes linked to learning conversations between staff (ca 12) and students (ca 50).

13160   Temporal inference research project.

GBR   1993

Research Date(s): 1987-

Bancroft, D.

Inst: Open University, School of Education, Walton Hall, Milton Keynes MK7 6AA, United Kingdom.

time perception; cognitive development; reasoning; child

perception du temps; développement cognitif; raisonnement; enfant

PROJECT DESCRIPTION

It is arguably the case that much human reasoning and problem solving rests on an understanding of the temporal inter-relations between events. Early and effective development of temporal understanding may then make a considerable contribution to wider cognitive skills. There has been a considerable amount of European laboratory-based research investigation of the development of children's understanding of time. One outcome is the suggestion that the co-ordination of temporal concepts is problematic for children until late in childhood since it depends on considerable cognitive sophistication. Another possibility is that young children are capable of dealing with temporal concepts when not obstructed by 'interfering' factors. There is also evidence from the psycholinguistic tradition which suggests that children use the language of 'time' effectively from a very early age.

The aim of the project is to investigate children's ability to reason about, and manipulate the concepts of Order and Duration in order to resolve some of the theoretical issues and to identify means of encouraging the development of temporal reasoning. Children aged between 4 and 7 years are presented with temporal problems on a microcomputer. Children have either mouse or concept keyboard control of the computer, thus allowing a behavioural indication of comprehension.

Results to date indicate that, although not all temporal problems are of equal complexity, children of this age are capable of producing sophisticated solutions and that this ability can be developed and promoted.

13161 Theories and conceptions of change: a study in science education.
GBR 1993
Research Date(s): 1988-1992
Colinvaux, D.
Sup: Gilbert, J.; Pope, M.
Inst: Reading University, Faculty of Education and Community Studies, Bulmershe Court, Woodlands Avenue, Earley, Reading RG6 1HY, United Kingdom.
Fin: CPNQ - Brazil.
concept formation; science education
formation de concept; éducation scientifique
PROJECT DESCRIPTION

The thesis investigates people's understanding of change. Change is seen to be important within the context of science education. It is recognised that individuals have conceptions of change in relation to everyday theorising as well as in the public domain. Research studies in science education that investigate the learner's perspective are discussed and the implications of theories and conceptions of change for science education are addressed. The two dimensions, social/personal and formal/everyday life provide a framework for the study. The theoretical perspective underpinning the thesis is that of constructivism, and the methodological framework devised is consistent with this philosophical base. The fieldwork involved the use of questionnaires and interviews. An innovative instrument allowing participants to make comments about photographs in terms of the presence or absence of change was devised. The sample was drawn from 7 year olds, secondary school children, university students, and adults in Brazil.

The results provide information regarding participants' views of change, non-change, and their judgements regarding the nature of change. Several dimensions are identified. There is particular emphasis on the time dimension and how the various participants conceive the process of change on the basis of their understanding of the time dimension. Both qualitative and quantitative data will be presented and case studies drawing together several aspects of an individual's conceptions of change.

13162 Traitement cognitif des textes incluant la lecture, la compréhension, la mémorisation et la production de textes: la construction des représentations occurrentes.
FRA 1993
Research Date(s): 1987-
Denhière, Guy; Baudet, Serge; François, Jacques; Legros, Denis; Jhean-Larose, S.
Inst: Université de Paris VIII, CNRS URA/1297, Psychologie cognitive du traitement de l'information symbolique, 2 rue de la Liberté, 93526 Saint Denis Cedex 02, France.
Fin: Centre national de la recherche scientifique "Programme de recherche sur les sciences de la communication" et Ministères de la recherche et de l'éducation "Programme sciences de la cognition".
cognitive process; reading; memorizing; conceptual imagery
processus cognitif; lecture; mémorisation; représentation mentale
PROJECT DESCRIPTION

Objectif: Ces recherches sont menées dans le cadre du projet "Communication multimédias Intéractions texte et image" du Centre national de la recherche scientifique et du projet "Représentation: expression linguistique et réalisation de l'action" des Ministères de la recherche et de l'éducation. La construction des représentations occurrentes est analysée en fonction des types de textes (narratif, descriptif, énigme policière, explicatif), de leur cohérence locale (macrostructures et modèles de situations organisés en symboles).

Méthodologie: La méthode consiste (1) à administrer à des sujets de différents niveaux de connaissances initiales des épreuves différant par leurs exigences en activités de recouvrement de l'information en mémoire; (2) à construire des textes verbaux et figuratifs différant par la nature des relations établissant leur cohérence locale et globale et à évaluer leurs effets sur l'apprentissage.

Publ: Baudet, Serge & Denhière, Guy. Mental models and acquisition of knowledge from text: representation and acquisition of functional sys-

tems. In: Denhière, Guy & Rossi, Jean-Pierre (Eds.). *Text and text processing*. Amsterdam: North-Holland, 1991, vol. 79, pp. 155-188.
Denhière, Guy (Ed.). Le traitement cognitif du texte. In: *Psychologie française*, 1991, n° 36-2, pp. 106-212.
Baudet, Serge & Denhière, Guy. *Lecture, compréhension de texte et science cognitive*. Paris: PUF, 1992, 320p.

13163 Understanding in educational contexts.
GBR 1993
Research Date(s): 1991-1994
Smith, C.
Sup: Entwistle, N.
Inst: Edinburgh University, Department of Education, 10-12 Buccleuch Place, Edinburgh EH8 9JT, United Kingdom.
comprehension; learning
compréhension; acquisition de connaissances
PROJECT DESCRIPTION

Understanding is a much used term in education but what it is to understand in an educational context has received surprisingly little attention to date. If an aim of education is that students should achieve understanding, it seems that this deficit should be remedied. In fact, a growing interest in the nature of understanding is beginning to emerge. A difference in conceptualisation between authors can be detected in which understanding is described either as a phenomenon of personal experience or as a target set in some way by the contextual conditions around the individual. A more appropriate description for education seems to require some sort of combination of these two views in which the relationships between the targets for understanding set by the curriculum and the experiences of the students can be examined. Accordingly, an attempt has been made to develop a conceptualisation of understanding which enables this type of issue to be examined and attention is now being turned to examining the relationship between the target for understanding set by the curriculum (in terms of course outlines and aims, assessment materials and course delivery) and the understanding experiences of the students (probably by surveying responses to assessments and interviews).

13164 Understanding understanding.
GBR 1993
Research Date(s): 1990-1991
Entwistle, N.
Inst: Edinburgh University, Department of Education, Centre for Research on Learning and Instruction, 10-12 Buccleuch Place, Edinburgh EH8 9JT, United Kingdom.
Fin: Godfrey Thomson Trust Fund.
comprehension; learning; examination
compréhension; acquisition de connaissances; examen
PROJECT DESCRIPTION

This is an exploratory interview study in which the revision strategies of students who have recently finished their final examinations were discussed. In the context of revision, students explained how they had sought understanding, and how they used their understanding to answer examination questions. Qualitative analysis of the transcripts produced categories of description which elucidated the nature of understanding, the development of understanding, and the differing forms of understanding reached. These forms of understanding affected the ability of students to answer different kinds of question. Narrow, specific questions could be answered by reproducing the structure of the topic provided by the lecturer, while broader questions required a broader and more flexible, personal understanding. Complications for teaching and assessment in higher education are considered.

Publ: Entwistle, N.J. & Entwistle, A.C. Contrasting forms of understanding for degree examinations: the student experience and its implications. In: *Higher Education*, Vol 22/1991, pp. 205-227.

13165 Zur Repraesentation metakognitiver Wissensbereiche im Langzeitgedaechtnis am Beispiel der Semantik von Verben geistiger Taetigkeiten. (On the representation of metacognitive areas of knowledge in long-term memory with particular reference to the semantics of verbs concerning mental activities.)
DEU 1993
Research Date(s): 1990-1992
Hoffmann, B.
Sup: Esser, U.
Inst: Technische Universitaet Dresden, Fak. Geistes- und Sozialwissenschaften, Institut fuer Psychologie, Mommsenstr. 13, O-8027 Dresden.
knowledge; learning; cognitive ability; semantics; memory
connaissance; acquisition de connaissances; aptitude cognitive; sémantique; mémoire
PROJECT DESCRIPTION

Inhalt: Untersuchungen zum Verhaeltnis von Metakognition und Lernen.
Vorgehensweise: Untersuchungsdesign: Querschnittserhebung.
Datengewinnung: Primaererhebung: Feldarbeit von Mitarbeitern des Projektes durchgefuehrt.
Auswertung: Faktorenanalyse; Clusteranalyse.

Okres dorastania w Europie: życiowe perspektywy i akceptowane wartości młodzieży polskiej (Adolescence in Europe: accepted values and life perspectives of Polish adolescents) .... see no. 13458

The use of concepts as a planning framework for environmental studies .... see no. 13470

21 PERSONALITY – PERSONALITE – PERSOENLICHKEIT

13166 Animals and science education: pupils' knowledge, attitudes and behaviour with respect to animals and the uses which are made of them.
GBR 1993
Research Date(s): 1990-1991
Lock, R.; Millett, K.
Inst: Birmingham University, School of Education, Edgbaston, Birmingham B15 2TT, United Kingdom.
Fin: Research Defence Society Charitable Trust.
pupil attitude; animal; science education; knowledge level
attitude de l'élève; animal; éducation scientifique; niveau de connaissances
PROJECT DESCRIPTION
The aim of the research is to investigate the knowledge, attitudes and behaviour of 14-16 year old students towards the uses of animals. The findings of the research will inform the development of curriculum materials relevant to the use of animals as described by the National Curriculum (Science) with particular reference to Key Stage 4. Data will be gathered by means of a self-completion questionnaire to be completed by a sample of 14 year old students across the country. The questionnaire will survey student knowledge, attitudes and behaviour with respect to animals and their use both in the classroom and in the wider context of the students' everyday lives.

13167 Attitudes towards computers.
GBR 1993
Research Date(s): 1985-
Trueman, M.
Inst: Keele University, Department of Psychology, Keele, Staffordshire ST5 5BG, United Kingdom.
attitude; computer literacy; sex difference; computer
attitude; initiation à l'informatique; différence de sexe; ordinateur
PROJECT DESCRIPTION
A series of four studies has been carried out using the Lloyd and Gressard (1984) Computer Attitude Scale to measure computer anxiety, computer liking and computer confidence. A study of undergraduate students showed that males had more experience in using computers and liked computers more than females did. However, there were no sex differences in computer anxiety or computer confidence.
A second study of undergraduates found that males had more experience of using computers, liked computers more and were more confident with computers than females in the study. This study also showed a correlation between higher neuroticism scores and found that males were more likely to have access to a computer than females were.
The final study looked at the relationship between androgeny (as assessed by the Personal Attributes Questionnaire, Spence & Helmreich, 1978) and the Computer Attitude Scale in a sample of fourth form school children. There were no sex differences in computer anxiety, computer liking or computer confidence. However, androgynous individuals had higher computer liking scores than masculine, feminine or undifferentiated individuals. Also, there were a series of significant sex and androgeny interactions in which androgenous males and masculine females were less anxious, liked computers more and were more confident about computers than the other groups.
Publ: Trueman, M. Attitudes towards computers. Paper presented to the 5th Annual Wolverhampton Polytechnic Educational Research Conference. Ibiza: San Antonio, 1989.
Trueman, M. The effects of gender and computer experience on attitudes towards computers. In: *CORE* (Collected Original Resources in Education), Vol 14, No 3/1990. (Fr. B01 on No 1 of 9 microfiches).

13168 Badania nad postawami tolerancyjnymi młodzieży. (Attitudes of tolerance among adolescents.)
POL 1994
Research Date(s): 1991-1993
Karolczak-Biernacka, Barbara.
Inst: Instytut Badań Edukacyjnych (Institute for Educational Research), 01 180 Warszawa, Górczewska 8, Poland.
Ministerstwo Edukacji Narodowej (Ministry of National Education), 00 918 Warszawa, Aleja Szucha 25, Poland
tolerance; intolerance; youth attitude; ethics; value system
tolérance; intolérance; attitude de la jeunesse; éthique; système de valeurs
PROJECT DESCRIPTION
Background: The study takes place against the background of recent changes in the political system, which have led to increased intolerance, prejudice, hatred, xenophobia and chauvinism.

Aims: The study focuses on: (1) the meaning of the concept of "tolerance"; (2) the motivation for tolerant behaviour; (3) the motivation for intolerant behaviour; (4) typical reactions in Polish society towards differences as perceived by young people; (5) the intensity of tolerant and intolerant attitudes; (6) the motivation underlying pupils' own limited tolerance of differences among other people.
Design: Empirical data have been gathered and subjected to computer analyses.
Method: Questionnaire designed by the researcher.
Sample: 1,885 secondary school pupils.

13169 Choice of further studies at the end of compulsory education.
GBR 1993
Research Date(s): 1992-1993
Davies, P.
Inst: Staff College, Coombe Lodge, Blagdon, Bristol BS18 6RG, United Kingdom.
Fin: Commercial contract.
pupil attitude; post-compulsory education; choice of studies
attitude de l'élève; enseignement postobligatoire; choix des études
PROJECT DESCRIPTION
The research was based around focus groups and telephone interviews with 396 young people who took GCSEs (General Certificate of Secondary Education) during 1992, concerning the significant demographic and attitudinal factors which influenced their choice of further studies.

13170 Cinsiyet ve bazı sosyo-ekonomik değişkenlerin lise öğrencilerinin mesleki ilgilerine etkisi. (The effect of individual and socio-economic situational variables of secondary school pupils upon their vocational interests.)
TUR 1994
Research Date(s): 1988
Çimen, Mehmet.
Sup: Kızıltan, Gonca.
Inst: Hacettepe Üniversitesi, Eğitim Fakültesi, Psikolojik Hizmetler Bölümü (Hacettepe University, Faculty of Education, Department of Psychological Services), 06532 Beytepe, Ankara, Turkey.
interest; occupational aspiration; adolescent; sex difference; socio-economic status; level of education; parents; income; place of residence
intérêt; aspirations professionnelles; adolescent; différence de sexe; statut socio-économique; niveau d'enseignement; parents; revenu; lieu de résidence
PROJECT DESCRIPTION
Aim: This study explored the effect of individual and socio-economic characteristics of secondary school pupils on their vocational interests. Independent variables were: sex, family income, educational level of parents and the place where pupils had lived most of their lives. The dependent variable was pupils' vocational interests.
Sample: The subjects of the study were 445 eleventh-year Baskent High School pupils in the school year 1986-1987.
Methods: Data on pupils' vocational interests were gathered with the help of the Kuder Interest Inventory Form C. Data on the independent variables were obtained through a specially developed questionnaire. Variance analysis, the Tukey test and t-test analysis were used to analyse the data.
Results: The sex variable was found to have a significant effect on subjects' vocational interests. Levels of outdoor, mechanical, computational and scientific interest were higher among male pupils. Levels of artistic and social services interests were higher among female pupils. Family income appeared to have no significant effect on pupils' vocational interests. Pupils whose father or mother held a university degree displayed a higher level of interest in science than pupils whose parents were illiterate. The place where pupils had lived most of their lives has no significant effect on their vocational interests.
Conclusions: Studies exploring the effect of different factors on pupils' vocational interests should take place in different places and should use different sample groups. It is proposed that, taking current findings into consideration, normative studies be done on pupils' vocational interests. The effect of mass media could be included as an additional variable. The effect of the presence of a careers counsellor in school and the relationship between pupils' perceptions of societal values and their vocational interests would constitute interesting subjects for further research.

13171 Çocuk yuvasında ve ailesi yanında kalan 9, 10, 11 yaş çocuklarının özsaygı gelişimini etkileyen bazı faktörler. (The effects of adults' attitudes on the development of self-esteem in children aged 9-11 living with their parents or in institutions.)
TUR 1994
Research Date(s): 1989
Güçray, S. Sonay.
Sup: Ersever, Oya G.
Inst: Hacettepe Üniversitesi, Eğitim Fakültesi, Psikolojik Hizmetler Bölümü (Hacettepe University, Faculty of Education, Department of Psychological Services), 06532 Beytepe, Ankara, Turkey.

self-esteem; child development; parental attitude; home; adult-child relation

estime de soi; développement de l'enfant; attitude des parents; foyer; relation adulte-enfant

PROJECT DESCRIPTION

Aim: The study examined the effect of personal characteristics, institutional variables and children's perceptions of parental and carers' attitudes on the development of self-esteem in children aged 9-11 staying with their parents or living in institutions.

Sample: The population of the study consisted of children living with their parents and children living in Social Affairs and Child Protection institutions in Ankara, Adana and neighbouring areas. The children were randomly sampled from the primary schools they attended. The sample, which included able-bodied as well as handicapped children, consisted of 242 children living in an institution and 341 children living with both their parents.

Methods: The dependent variable was measured by the Coopersmith Self-Esteem Inventory. Children's perceptions of parental or carers' attitudes were measured with the help of an attitude scale on which adults' attitudes could be classified as "democratic", "authoritarian" or "indifferent". Data on the independent variables were collected with the help of two questionnaires. Multiple analysis of variance, one-way analysis of variance and t-test analysis were used to analyse the data.

Results: The findings showed that living in an institution has a negative effect on children's self-esteem. The variables of sex, age, number of siblings and birth order were found to have no significant impact on self-esteem. Neither did some of the factors related to living in an institution - duration of stay, visitors, reason for staying in an institution, number of siblings in the institution - affect levels of self-esteem significantly.

Democratic adult attitudes were found to have a positive effect on children's self-esteem, whereas authoritarian and indifferent attitudes had a negative effect. Children in institutions were more likely to perceive adults' attitudes as authoritarian or indifferent.

On the basis of the findings it is concluded that children in need of protection should only be committed to institutional care if no alternative is available. Institutional care needs to be reconsidered if it is to provide a sound basis for the protection and rearing of children.

13172 Dépréciation de soi et niveaux d'aspirations chez les jeunes toxicomanes.
FRA 1993
Research Date(s): 1988-
Tap, Pierre; Philip, Carole; Pern, F.; Ponce, N.
Inst: Université de Toulouse II, UFR Education Formation Insertion, CNRS URA/259, Département de psychologie - Laboratoire, personnalisation et changements sociaux, 5 allées Antonio Machado, 31058 Toulouse Cedex, France.
identity; self-concept; drug addiction; youth attitude; time perception; adolescence
identité; conception de soi; toxicomanie; attitude de la jeunesse; perception du temps; adolescence
PROJECT DESCRIPTION

Objectifs: La crise d'identité de l'adolescence perturbe les identifications antérieures et réactive chez les sujets angoisse et dépressivité, les poussant à rechercher de nouveaux modèles. La stratégie de relance la plus adaptée pour dépasser la crise est la projection de soi vers le futur et la mise en place de moyens pour atteindre les buts. Certains jeunes confrontés à la logique aliénante de la "perte et de l'abandon" répondent par une stratégie de "substitution et de remplissage". Une recherche préliminaire s'est centrée sur l'estime de soi et l'organisation temporelle.

Méthodologie: Cette étude compare un groupe de 19 toxicomanes rencontrés en centres de post-cure, en milieu hospitalier ou à l'association du Patriarche à un groupe témoin de 20 jeunes. Les sujets sont soumis à un test de phrases à compléter dont les items permettent d'exprimer les projets de vie. Sont utilisés également les tests de Coopersmith mesurant l'estime de soi et le test d'aspiration de Robaye permettant d'analyser les stratégies de dépassement et d'affirmation, le retrait temporel ou le projet utopique.

Résultats: Les résultats montrent que les jeunes toxicomanes ont dans l'ensemble un faible niveau d'estime de soi. L'hypothèse selon laquelle les toxicomanes vivent une crise d'identité plus forte que les jeunes du groupe témoin n'est vérifiée que pour les toxicomanes qui ne sont pas chez "Le Patriarche". Ces derniers semblent investir massivement l'institution qui les accueille et qui semble jouer le rôle de substitut parental.

Publ: Tap, Pierre & Malewska-Peyre, Hanna. Crise d'identité, dépression et toxicomanie à l'adolescence. In: Tap, Pierre & Malewska-Peyre, Hanna. (éds.). La socialisation de l'enfance à l'adolescence. Paris: PUF, Collection Psychologie d'aujourd'hui, 1991, 360p.

13173 Een landelijk onderzoek naar concentratieproblemen onder leerlingen van de basisschool: een herhaalde meting. (A nation-wide survey of attention problems among primary school pupils: a repeated measurment.)
NLD 1994
Research Date(s): 1993
Jong, P.F. de.
Inst: Faculteit der Psychologie en Pedagogische Wetenschappen (Faculty of Psychology and Educational Science), Van der Boechorststraat 1, 1081 BT Amsterdam, Netherlands.
Vrije Universiteit Amsterdam (Free University of Amsterdam), De Boelelaan 1105, 1081 HV Amsterdam, Netherlands
Fin: SVO het Instituut voor Onderzoek van het Onderwijs.
attention; pupil; primary education
attention; élève; enseignement primaire
PROJECT DESCRIPTION

Background: A nation-wide study conducted in 1988 revealed that, according to teachers, a fifth of 9-year-old primary school pupils have attention problems. The number of pupils with such problems is said to increase. In order to gain an understanding of the development of attention problems in primary school pupils over several years, the present project is concerned with a follow-up study of a sample comparable to that of the earlier study.

Aim: To collect data on the incidence of attention problems in primary school pupils and on developments in the incidence of such problems during the last five years.

Method: Tests.

Design: The same schools that participated in the 1988 study will be approached. Per school, one year six classroom (9-year-olds) will be selected (preferably the largest one) as well as five children from the remaining group of 9-year-olds. The Reading Comprehension Test and the Counting Test will be administered to the year six class. The behaviour of the pupils in this class will be assessed by their teacher with the help of the Amsterdam Child Behaviour Checklist (AKGL). No tests will be administered to the five selected 9-year-olds; data on their behaviour will be collected by the teacher with the help of the AKGL and a Dutch version of the Child Behaviour Checklist.

13174 Einstellungen von Oberschuelern zur geistigen Behinderung in Irland, Australien, Finnland und Deutschland. (Secondary school pupils' attitudes towards mental disability in Ireland, Australia, Finland and Germany.)
DEU 1993
Research Date(s): 1990-1992
Eggert, D.
Inst: Universitaet Hannover, FB Erziehungswissenschaften 01, Lehrgebiet Psychologie der Behinderten, Bismarckstrasse 2, D-3000 Hannover.
Fin: Alexander von Humboldt-Stiftung.
youth attitude; mentally handicapped; upper secondary; cross-national research
attitude de la jeunesse; handicapé mental; secondaire deuxième cycle; recherche transnationale
PROJECT DESCRIPTION

Inhalt: Australische Sekundarschulkinder wurden ueberprueft in bezug auf die Art ihrer Wahrnehmung von Personen mit geistiger Behinderung. Die erhobenen Daten bezogen sich auf: Reaktionen auf das Zusammentreffen mit einer Person mit Behinderung, das Helfen einer behinderten Person, die Reaktion auf spezifische Aussagen ueber behindernde Bedingungen, die Ursachen von Behinderung und das Beduerfnis nach weiterer Information ueber Behinderungen. Die Ergebnisse weisen auf einige Parallelen zwischen australischen und irischen Schulkindern hin, wobei beide Gruppen eine positive Wirkung widerspiegeln.

Geographischer Raum: Irland, Australien, Finnland, Bundesrepublik Deutschland.

Untersuchter Zeitraum: 1990-1992.

Vorgehensweise: Untersuchungsdesign: Fragebogen.

Datengewinnung: Standardisiertes Interview (Stichprobe: 955; Kinder).

Primaererhebung: Feldarbeit von Mitarbeitern des Projektes durchgefuehrt.

Publ: Berry, Paul & Eggert, Dietrich. Perceptions of mental handicap: a comparison of Australian and Irish school children. In: International Journal of Rehabilitation Research, 14, 1991, S. 187-194.

13175 Estime de soi et stratégies positionnelles à l'adolescence.
FRA 1993
Research Date(s): 1988-
Safont, Claire; Tap, Pierre; Leonardis, Myriam (de); Oubrayrie, Nathalie; Guitard, Lisiane.
Inst: Université de Toulouse II, UFR Education Formation Insertion, CNRS URA/259, Département de psychologie - Laboratoire, personnalisation et changements sociaux, 5 allées Antonio Machado, 31058 Toulouse Cedex, France.
self-esteem; self-concept; interpersonal relations; adolescence
estime de soi; conception de soi; relations interpersonnelles; adolescence
PROJECT DESCRIPTION

Objectifs: Après les travaux de Festinger et Ziller, on suppose que l'estime de soi se développe dans un contexte social, en interaction avec des personnes privilégiées et significatives pour le sujet. Le sujet adopterait des "stratégies de positionnement" associées à la mise en oeuvre de processus d'affirmation et de reconnaissance sociales.

Méthodologie: Cette problématique est traitée auprès de 640 adolescents de 13 à 20 ans dans le but d'analyser les effets d'âge et de sexe. Une échelle de 60 affirmations sur soi réparties en cinq dimensions (soi émotionnel, soi scolaire, soi social, soi physique, soi futur) permet au sujet de s'auto-évaluer (échelle ETES), des techniques proposées par Ziller sont transformées pour évaluer l'estime de soi sociale (épreuve ISIS).

Résultats: Dans le sens de l'hypothèse, il existe une corrélation positive quoique faible entre les scores bruts d'estime de soi et d'estime de soi sociale. Les deux dimensions font l'objet d'importantes variations en fonction du sexe et de l'âge. Sur l'ensemble de l'échantillon, la stratégie de conformité est plus fréquente que la stratégie d'affirmation. Dans le jeu des comparaisons sociales une auto-évaluation positive n'implique pas nécessairement l'affirmation positionnelle. En d'autres termes l'indépendance à l'égard du parent (surtout du même sexe) semble favoriser le rapprochement avec celui-ci.

Publ: Tap, Pierre; Oubrayrie, Nathalie & Guitard, Lisiane. Estime de soi et positions sociales à l'adolescence. Problèmes et techniques d'évaluation. In: *Actes du Congrès de la Société française de psychologie: L'évaluation: processus méthodes et pratiques, Bordeaux 10-12 mai 1990.*

Tap, Pierre. Estime de soi, stratégies positionnelles et valeurs à l'adolescence. In: *Actes du Colloque international Identités et Valeurs.* Centre de recherche interdisciplinaire de Vaucresson, octobre 1990.

13176 Estime de soi, stratégies de projet et compétences cognitives et sociales à l'adolescence.
FRA 1993
Research Date(s): 1991-
Leonardis, Myriam (de); Lescarret, Odette; Oubrayrie, N.; Tap, Pierre; Safont, Claire.
Inst: Université de Toulouse II, UFR Education Formation Insertion, CNRS URA /259, Département de psychologie - Laboratoire, personnalisation et changements sociaux, 5 allées Antonio Machado, 31058 Toulouse Cedex, France.
identity; adolescence; personality development; self-concept
identité; adolescence; développement de la personnalité; conception de soi
PROJECT DESCRIPTION

Objectifs: Il s'agit, dans une perspective dynamique et interactionniste, d'étudier les liens et les modalités d'articulation entre les processus de personnalisation par lesquels tout sujet peut actualiser ses potentialités et développer des conduites autonomes au cours de l'adolescence: on considère que le sujet construit son système de compétences autour: (1) du style de contrôle des informations, (2) de la croyance qu'il a en son pouvoir de contrôle (interne) des situations vécues ou au contraire du sentiment que rien ne dépend de lui (externalité), (3) de compétences sociales liées à la capacité de percevoir les stratégies d'autrui, à le comprendre et à communiquer plus facilement avec lui. Ce système de compétences est à l'oeuvre dans l'organisation des pratiques et dans l'investissement des activités, il influence le contrôle affectif, c'est à dire la gestion des émotions et le niveau d'estime de soi. L'estime de soi oriente les aspirations du sujet et influence l'élaboration des stratégies de projet par la médiation des réussites et des échecs antérieurs. Trois recherches sont successivement engagées à partir de ce modèle: (1) estime de soi et stratégies de projet étudiées chez 120 lycéens après la décision d'orientation en fin de seconde; (2) styles cognitifs et estime de soi; les styles cognitifs (dépendance du champ-indépendance du champ d'une part et contrôle interne-contrôle externe d'autre part) qui détermineraient l'estime de soi des sujets sont étudiés comme variable expérimentale auprès d'un échantillon de 240 enfants et adolescents; (3) compétences sociales, estime de soi et stratégies de projet sont étudiées chez 140 adolescents de 12-16 ans.

13177 Expectations of school health services: part 4 'What teenage students expect from the school health service'.
GBR 1993
Research Date(s): 1990-1991
Cutting, E.; Fahey, W.
Inst: Cheltenham & Gloucester College of Higher Education, Faculty of Education and Health, The Park, Cheltenham GL50 2QF, United Kingdom.
pupil attitude; school health services
attitude de l'élève; médecine scolaire
PROJECT DESCRIPTION

Given the current emphasis on making services 'more responsible to the consumer' (HMSO, 'Primary health care - an agenda for discussion'), and the client-centred approach of the Cumberlege report and other recent reports, the authors are examining a series of samples of parents, teachers and pupils as to their expectations of school health services. With the assistance of students on school nurse courses, the two authors are investigating the expectations of various groups of randomly chosen

respondents (up to 200). A two-part quantative and qualitative questionnaire is prepared each session.

13178 Factors influencing attitudes of secondary school pupils to aesthetic aspects of sport and dance.
GBR 1993
Research Date(s): 1984-1991
Sanderson, P.
Sup: Murray, C.
Inst: Manchester University, School of Education, Centre for Physical Education, Oxford Road, Manchester M13 9PL, United Kingdom.
pupil attitude; dance; sport; aesthetics; physical education
attitude de l'élève; danse; sport; esthétique; éducation physique
PROJECT DESCRIPTION

The development of aesthetic awareness is stated regularly in the physical education (PE) literature as a major objective, yet little research is available concerning its achievement. Attitude research could provide relevant information. This study investigates the relative influence of age, sex, social class, school type, pupils' and their families' interests in arts and sports. Attitude scales were developed in a pilot study, incorporated into a questionnaire along with measures of the independent variables, and administered to 1,668 pupils, aged between 11 and 16 supplied by 19 schools throughout England. Analyses of variance were employed to ascertain the effect of age, sex, social class and school type, and multiple regression analyses for the influences of pupils' and their families' interests in arts and sports.

Results show no effect of age on attitude; the impact of the sex factor is complex; generally more favourable attitudes are displayed by those from higher social classes, but for ballet, only for girls; family and pupil interests promote positive attitudes but on all scales but two, the influence is small; specialist arts education promotes positive attitudes only for girls towards ballet; extensive sports experience does not apparently promote positive attitudes.

Publ: Sanderson, P. Factors influencing attitudes of secondary school pupils towards aesthetic aspects of sport and dance. Dance: the study of dance and the place of dance in society. In: *Proceedings of the VIIIth Commonwealth and International Conference on Sport, Physical Education, Dance, Recreation and Health.* Glasgow. London: E. & F.N. Spon., 1986, pp. 137-143.
Sanderson, P. A methodology for measuring attitudes to dance. In: *Proceedings of the CORD Conference*, Canada, Toronto, 1988, pp. 161-167.
Sanderson, P. Secondary school pupils' attitudes to dance. In: *Proceedings of the DACI Conference*, London, Roehampton Institute, 1989, pp. 244-251.

13179 Indagine conoscitiva sulle opinioni degli studenti medi circa l'organizzazione scolastica. (Survey of secondary school pupils' perceptions of school organization.)
ITA 1993
Research Date(s): 1989
Brutti, M.
Sup: Di Giovan Paolo, R.
Inst: Ce.S.P. - Centro Studi e Programmazione Soc. Coop. a.r.l. (Centre for Studies and Planning), Via Pompeo Magno 27, 00192 Roma, Italy.
youth attitude; attitude towards school; upper secondary; work attitude; guidance
attitude de la jeunesse; attitude envers l'école; secondaire deuxième cycle; attitude envers le travail; orientation
PROJECT DESCRIPTION

Aims: The study analysed and evaluated the attitudes of students in Roman upper secondary schools with respect to fundamental themes and experiences, such as: school participation; the connection between school and work; the relation of youth to society; participation in associations and voluntary activities.

Methods: The sample was made up of 946 students aged 17-19 from schools in the city and the province of Rome. Data were collected through questionnaires. The data were analysed with the help of statistical analysis software. Cross-tabulation techniques were used for further elaboration, filtering the diverse responses and correlating them with the results of an earlier, similar investigation.

Results: The cultural profile of the Roman upper school student has changed: relations with the school are accepted and felt with intensity. However, there is also a great deal of criticism directed towards the system, the contents of education, and the teaching personnel. Students' expectations regarding study are highly personal and, in comparison with the 1980s, are characterized by more freedom of choice. Less space is given to undifferentiated criticisms. A strong need is expressed for an effective policy of guidance and information which would help students to find work that not only provides sufficient income but also an opportunity for self-realization.

The study confirms the decline in the desire of students to organize themselves as well as their detachment from strong social and political commitments. Attention to personal relationships not tied to organized groups prevails.

Conclusion: The way opens for intervention in three fields: (1) education: content of education, organization and methodology; (2) work: information, guidance, and the links between school and work; (3) culture and leisure: reference points responding to the demand for social participation.

13180 Indywidualne uwarunkowania postaw wobec pracy. (Individual determinants of the attitudes toward work.)
POL 1994
Research Date(s): 1989-1992
Oszustowicz, Barbara.
Sup: Maurer, Alicja.
Inst: Wyższa Szkoła Pedagogiczna (Pedagogical University), Podchorażych 2, 30-084 Kraków, Poland.
Ulsterski Uniwersytet w Coleraine (Ulster University at Coleraine), Coleraine, Co. Londonderry BT 52 ISA, Northern Ireland; Ministerstwo Edukacji Narodowej (Ministry of National Education), Al. I Armii Wojska Polskiego 25, 00-198 Warszawa, Poland
Fin: Government grant.
work attitude; industrial psychology; aspiration; university; student
attitude envers le travail; psychologie industrielle; aspiration; université; étudiant
PROJECT DESCRIPTION
Aim: The aim of the research carried out in 48 countries, and coordinated by Professor Richard Lynn from the Ulster University at Coleraine, was to define national determinants of work attitudes. In addition, the aim of the Polish research was to define individual determinants of these attitudes, i.e. determinants related to sex, temperament and intelligence.
Sample: The sample consisted of 300 students of the Cracow Pedagogical University (150 female students and 150 male students). 50% of each group were made up of younger students (of the 1st and the 2nd year) and 50% of undergraduate students (the 4th and the 5th year). 50% in each group were students of humanities and 50% were science students.
Methods: Use was made of the work attitudes questionnaire developed by Prof. Lynn on the basis of questionnaires measuring those psychological variables which, according to recognized theories, refer to economic progress: professional ethics, achievement motivation, aspiration for competitiveness, aspiration for mastery, aspiration for achievement through conformity, confidence in money, saving money, occupational preferences (physician, teacher, social worker, director, freeholder, entrepreneur). Additional methods applied were: Strelau's questionnaire of temperament, Raven's scale and Choynowski's vocabulary test.
Results: The subjects were similar as regards intellectual and temperamental traits. Sex appeared to be a factor strongly differentiating work attitudes; intellectual variables, however, did not exert a direct influence upon those attitudes. Interactions were found to occur between excitability and intelligence with regard to achievement motivation, as well as between sex, intelligence and excitability with regard to the confidence in money.
Publ: Lynn, Richard et al. *The secret of the miracle economy: Different national attitudes toward competitiveness and money.* London: Crowley Esmond, 1991.

13181 An inquiry into the role of skills in education.
GBR 1993
Research Date(s): 1990-1994
Johnson, S.
Sup: Gardner, P.
Inst: Warwick University, Faculty of Educational Studies, Coventry CV4 7AL, United Kingdom.
skill; basic education; problem solving; critical sense; philosophy of education
compétence; éducation de base; résolution de problème; sens critique; philosophie de l'éducation
PROJECT DESCRIPTION
This piece of research is a philosophical inquiry into the nature of skills and their prominent position in education with particular reference to general and transferable skills, e.g. problem solving and critical thinking skills, and into the extent to which personal qualities, disposition and virtues can be reduced to and taught as skills. The thesis will also include an inquiry into the role of skills in the teachings of the sophists and the emergence and dominance of skills in contemporary eductional recommendations.

13182 Insertion sociale et citoyenneté: une étude longitudinale auprès des 18-25 ans.
FRA 1993
Research Date(s): 1986-1995
Muxel-Douaire, Anne.
Inst: Fondation nationale des sciences politiques, CNRS URA/120, Centre d'étude de la vie politique française, 10 rue de la Chaise, 75007 Paris, France.
Fin: Mission Recherche Expérimentation; PIRTTEM-CNRS.
youth attitude; political behaviour; maturity; political socialization; citizen participation

attitude de la jeunesse; comportement politique; maturité; socialisation politique; participation du citoyen
PROJECT DESCRIPTION
Objectifs: Il s'agit de suivre une même classe d'âge ayant 18 ans lors de la première enquête jusqu'à ce qu'elle atteigne l'âge de 25 ans. Sept années qui définissent une période d'acquisition des attributs de la maturité; une période actuellement marquée par un certain report des calendriers scolaires, professionnels, résidentiels et matrimoniaux. Cette enquête veut atteindre un double objectif: (1) suivre les cheminements et les formes de la participation politique en fonction des itinéraires biographiques; (2) réaliser une observation des comportements politiques rythmée par la vie politique elle-même, c'est à dire par la succession des scrutins électoraux au cours d'une période donnée. L'hypothèse première s'appuie sur les nombreux travaux qui ont montré l'étroite corrélation qui existe entre les conditions de la participation politique et les conditions de l'insertion de l'individu dans la société.
Méthodologie: Enquête longitudinale; constitution d'un panel de jeunes interrogés à intervalles réguliers pendant 7 ans entre 18 et 25 ans.
Publ: Rapport de recherche remis à la MIRE et au PIRTTEM en décembre 1990.
Muxel, Anne. Les attitudes socio-politiques des jeunes issus de l'immigration maghrébine en région parisienne. In: *Revue française de science politique,* vol. 38, 6, décembre 1988.
Muxel, Anne. Le moratoire politique des années de jeunesse. In: Rémond, René; Percheron, Annick (Eds.). *Age et politique.* Paris: Ed. Economica, 1991.

13183 Jeugd en technologie. (Youth and Technology.)
NLD 1993
Research Date(s): 1992-1993
Grip, A. de; Willems, E.J.T.A.; Berendsen, H.
Inst: ROA Researchcentrum voor Onderwijs en Arbeidsmarkt, Universiteit Limburg (Research Centre for Education and the Labour Market, University of Limburg), P.O. Box 616, 6200 MD Maastricht, Netherlands.
Fin: Ministry of Economic Affairs.
youth attitude; opinion; technology; choice of studies; technical education
attitude de la jeunesse; opinion; technologie; choix des études; enseignement technique
PROJECT DESCRIPTION
In the context of the research programme "Technology and Society" of the Ministry of Economic Affairs, ROA examines young people's views regarding technological advancement. Three dimensions will be distinguished: (1) value judgements on technological developments (2) the image of technical occupations and (3) intentions for educational and vocational choices with respect to technology. A questionnaire survey was conducted of about 3,000 secondary school pupils in the autumn of 1992.
Apart from the separate analysis of the three elements mentioned above, the relationships between these elements will also be examined. Moreover, the image of technical education and work will be compared with the real situation. This will make it possible to identify problems that may be addressed by policies aimed at encouraging pupils to enrol in technical education courses.

13184 Jugend und Europa. (Young people and Europe.)
DEU 1993
Research Date(s): 1991-1994
Henschel, T.; Thimmel, A.; Tham, B.
Sup: Weidenfeld, W.
Inst: Universitaet Mainz, FB 12 Sozialwissenschaften, Institut fuer Politikwissenschaft, Colonel-Kleinmann-Weg 2, D-6500 Mainz.
Fin: Bundesministerium fuer Frauen und Jugend.
youth attitude; youth; Europe; educational policy; youth policy; Germany; political education
attitude de la jeunesse; jeunesse; Europe; politique de l'éducation; politique de la jeunesse; Allemagne; éducation politique
PROJECT DESCRIPTION
Inhalt: Wissenschaftliche Analyse der europaeischen Jugend- und Bildungspolitik; Untersuchung europapolitischer Entwicklungen in ihren Auswirkungen auf die Jugendlichen in der Bundesrepublik Deutschland. Konsequenzen hieraus fuer die Lebenswelt der Jugendlichen und ihrer Einstellungen zu Europa. Bestimmung des politischen Handlungsbedarfs auf kommunaler, Laender-, Bundes-und europaeischer Ebene. Inhaltliche und konzeptionelle Beratung zu europaeischen Themen in der politischen Bildung. Entwicklung und Durchfuehrung von Modellseminaren zu aktuellen Fragestellungen der europaeischen Integration. Organisatorische Hilfestellung fuer Bildungsmassnahmen.
Geographischer Raum: Europa.
Vorgehensweise: Untersuchungsdesign: Evaluationsstudie; Trend; Beratung; politische Bildung.
Datengewinnung: Standardisiertes Interview (Stichprobe: 1536; Jugendliche, 15-24 Jahre; Auswahlverfahren: Quota. Stichprobe: 288; Jugendliche, 14-26 Jahre; Auswahlverfahren: Quota). Nicht-standardisiertes Interview (Stichprobe: 180; Jugendliche, 8-28 Jahre; Auswahlverfahren: Quota. Stichprobe: 1000; Jugendliche, 14-26 Jahre; Auswahlverfahren:

Quota). Postalische Befragung (Stichprobe: 1000; Jugendliche, 14-26 Jahre; Auswahlverfahren: Quota). Befragung (dito).

Auswertung: Aufbau von Datenbanken.

Publ: Weidenfeld, Werner & Piepenschneider, Melanie. *Junge Generation und Europaeische Einigung. Einstellungen, Wuensche, Perspektiven.* Bonn: Europa Union Verl. 1990.

Piepenschneider, Melanie & Glaab, Manuela. Jugend und Europa. Zukunftsgut wird zum Pfeiler der Identitaet. In: *DUZ*, 24, 1991, S. 18-19.

Jugend in Europa. Hrsg. von der Landeszentrale fuer politische Bildung Rheinland-Pfalz unter Mitarb. der Forschungsgruppe Jugend und Europa der Universitaet Mainz. Reihe Europa, H. 2, 1991.

13185 Learned helplessness and self-worth motivation in children with special educational needs.
GBR 1993
Research Date(s): 1991-1993
Rogers, C.
Sup: Galloway, D.
Inst: Lancaster University, Department of Educational Research, Cartmel College, Bailrigg, Lancaster LA1 4YW, United Kingdom.
Fin: Economic and Social Research Council.
self-esteem; special education; motivation; achievement
estime de soi; enseignement spécial; motivation; rendement
PROJECT DESCRIPTION

The project aims to identify: (1) the prevalence of the motivational styles of mastery orientation, self-worth motive and learned helplessness in pupils in two secondary schools and their feeder primary schools; (2) the degree to which the distribution of stlyes varies in children with special needs contrasted to whole populations; (3) changes in prevalence of style over time in a longitudinal sample; (4) changes in prevalence across year groups with cross-sectional samples; (5) differences between curriculum areas with regard to the prevalence of motivational styles; and (6) the degree to which factors associated with school (e.g. school attended, teacher) influence the prevalence of each style. Theoretical developments by Weiner, Nicholls and Covington provide a general background to the research.

The sample consists of all children in the final year of 12 primary schools who are followed into years seven and eight in two secondary schools. Further cross-sectional samples are obtained with pupils in years nine and eleven in the secondary schools. Information about motivational style is obtained from analysis of children's performance on curriculum-related tasks in mathematics and English. Additional information is obtained from questionnaires completed by pupils and teachers. Pupil attainment data is used to identify children with special needs and also to allow comparisons between motivational style and achievement levels. A sub-sample of children have been interviewed.

Initial results suggest increases in maladaptive motivational styles consequent upon transfer to secondary schools, and differences in proportion of pupils showing maladaptive styles as a function of the curriculum subject.

13186 Lise öğrencilerinin özsaygı düzeyini etkileyen etmenler. (The effects of social and personal factors on levels of self-esteem in secondary school pupils.)
TUR 1994
Research Date(s): 1989
Güngör, Abide.
Sup: Kılıççı, Yadigar.
Inst: Hacettepe Üniversitesi, Eğitim Fakültesi, Psikolojik Hizmetler Bölümü (Hacettepe University, Faculty of Education, Department of Psychological Services), 06532 Beytepe, Ankara, Turkey.
self-esteem; family environment; socio-economic status; adolescent
estime de soi; milieu familial; statut socio-économique; adolescent
PROJECT DESCRIPTION

The aim of this study was to explore to what extent certain social and personal factors related to pupils and their families influence pupils' levels of self-esteem positively or negatively.

The sample included 1,000 secondary school pupils and was representative of the population in Ankara in the 1987-1988 school year. A special self-esteem scale was developed for the research and tested for validity and reliability. Data on the independent variables - pupils' personal characteristics and family characteristics - were gathered with the help of a questionnaire. Data analysis techniques included one-way analysis of variance and t-tests.

The main findings of the research can be summarized as follows. (1) No significant differences were found between boys and girls or between ninth and eleventh formers. (2) Levels of self-esteem in the first and last born children of families are higher than those of other children. (3) Levels of self-esteem of pupils who perceive themselves as successful are higher than those of pupils who perceive themselves as unsuccessful. (4) Levels of self-esteem rise with the level of family income. (5) Levels of self-esteem among children of parents with a medium to high level of education are higher than those of children of poorly educated parents. (6) Parental

occupation has an influence on pupils' self-esteem: the lowest levels of self-esteem were found among children of unemployed parents. (7) Levels of self-esteem in pupils from high socio-economic backgrounds are higher than those of pupils from low socio-economic backgrounds. (8) Levels of self-esteem among pupils from urban backgrounds are higher than those of pupils from rural backgrounds. (9) Levels of self-esteem among pupils who have good relations with their families and who perceive their parents as democratic are higher than those of pupils who have poor relations with their families and who perceive their parents as authoritarian.

In the light of the findings, it was concluded that socio-economic and cultural family characteristics as well as parental attitude have an important effect on secondary pupils' levels of self-esteem. Recommendations are made relating to healthy relations between parents and children and supportive educational settings.

13187 Memory, intelligence and talent.
GBR 1993
Research Date(s): 1987-1991
O'Connor, N.; Hermelin, B.
Inst: London University, Institute of Education, Department of Educational Psychology and Special Educational Needs, 20 Bedford Way, London WC1H 0AL, United Kingdom.
Fin: Medical Research Council.
cognitive ability; exceptional; gifted; cognitive development; mental retardation; memory; intelligence; developmental psychology
aptitude cognitive; atypique; doué; développement cognitif; retard intellectuel; mémoire; intelligence; psychologie du développement
PROJECT DESCRIPTION

This is a Medical Research Council developmental psychology project. The proposed experiments address questions concerning the nature of the specific talents found among idiots-savants and gifted normal children. One question is the degree to which the cognitive strategies used by such talented people are intelligence independent. A second is the nature of the impressive memory which seems to underlie their frequently surprising performance. Experiments will test whether this memory is predominantly rote or organized and, if the latter, whether organized 'semantically' or according to some 'syntactic' system as for logic or mathematics. In addition, the possible relevance of non-cognitive variables such as obsessive preoccupations will be assessed.

13188 Młodzież wobec wartości i zasad demokratycznych. (Youth attitudes towards values and democratic principles.)
POL 1994
Research Date(s): 1991-1993
Karolczak-Biernacka, Barbara.
Inst: Instytut Badań Edukacyjnych (Institute for Educational Research), 01 180 Warszawa, Górczewska 8, Poland.
Ministerstwo Edukacji narodowej (Ministry of National Education), 00 918 Warszawa, Aleja Szucha 25, Poland
youth attitude; value; value system; democracy; democratization
attitude de la jeunesse; valeur; système de valeurs; démocratie; démocratisation
PROJECT DESCRIPTION

Against the background of the political changes that have taken place in Poland, the project aims to examine: (1) present-day preferences regarding democratic values and their significance in modern Polish society; (2) preferences with regard to democratic and non-democratic principles in relation to 15 issues concerning the functioning of the State; (3) the extent to which democratic principles are currently being limited; (4) the effectiveness of democratic versus non-democratic principles; perceptions of the situation in Poland; (5) the development of democracy in Poland; (6) material changes in people's lives as a result of political change; (7) the influence of the government, the church and the mentality of Polish citizens on democratization processes; (8) the role of the school in the development of democratic attitudes.

Design: Empirical data have been gathered and subjected to computer analysis.

Methods: Questionnaire partly designed by the researcher and partly based on the H. McClosky and A. Brill's Worksheet of Attitudes towards Political System Rules.

Sample: 1,916 secondary school pupils.

13189 Modelli di socializzazione e variabili della dispersione scolastica nel Mezzogiorno. (Models of socialization and determinants of school failure in southern Italy.)
ITA 1993
Research Date(s): 1988-1989
Mattioli, F.; Bentivegna, S.
Sup: Lombardo, A.
Inst: Centro Studi Politico Economico Sociale - CESPES (Centre of Political, Economic and Social Studies), Via Aureliana 2, 00187 Roma, Italy.
Fin: Ministero della Pubblica Istruzione, Ufficio Studi e Programmazione.
youth attitude; attitude towards school; pupil attitude; dropout; wastage; teacher behaviour; interest profile; socialization

attitude de la jeunesse; attitude envers l'école; attitude de l'élève; abandon d'études; déperdition d'effectifs; comportement de l'enseignant; profil d'intérêt; socialisation

PROJECT DESCRIPTION

Aims: The study aimed to analyse and evaluate the problem of school failure in southern Italy. It examined the principal variables that come into play: family, school, mass media. The first part of the research also examined the aspirations, tendencies, and desires of youth and some models of socialization. In the second part, the roles of the school and the teacher were examined with respect to the problem of dissatisfaction and school dropout.

Methods: Questionnaires were administered and tables were elaborated with clarifications and comments. The investigation focused on compulsory and upper secondary schools in southern Italy.

Results: Three types of socialization emerged which correspond to three pupil profiles. The first, or "mixed" type, is generally shared by pupils in lower secondary schools and is a combination of two different conceptions of school: idealistic and instrumental. The second type is characteristic of students in technical, commercial, and teaching schools and is related to a strongly instrumental conception of school. The third type is characteristic of students in classical and scientific upper secondary schools and is related to an idealistic conception of school. A major finding of the research is that many youths find themselves in a position of uncertainty due to opposing forces: their own will to stay on in education and outside incentives luring them prematurely into the working world. The number of students who combine school with work exceeds the number of dropouts.

Regarding schools and teachers, the researchers add the following conclusions. Teachers appear not to have a definite role. Wide differences occur among teachers and many teachers are unmotivated. Teachers tend to be strictly tied to disciplinary teaching strategies and seem disillusioned in respect of the social recognition of their role; this attitude plays a relevant part in student alienation and dropout rates. Teachers are rarely disposed to self-criticism. Teachers' professionalism needs to be improved in order for them to be able to fulfil their social role more adequately.

13190   Monitoring attitudes towards Christianity among secondary school pupils in England.
GBR   1993
Research Date(s): 1974-1992
Francis, L.
Inst: Trinity College, Carmarthen, Dyfed SA31 3EP, United Kingdom.
pupil attitude; religion; Christianity; religious behaviour
attitude de l'élève; religion; christianisme; comportement religieux
PROJECT DESCRIPTION

A survey of secondary school pupils' attitudes towards Christianity, conducted originally in 1974 has been regularly replicated at four-yearly intervals. The data demonstrate the continued drift away from the Christian churches.

Publ: Francis, L.J. Monitoring changing attitudes towards Christianity among secondary school pupils between 1974 and 1986. In: *British Journal of Educational Psychology*, Vol 59, No 1/1989, pp. 86-91, February.
Francis, L.J. Monitoring attitudes towards Christianity: the 1990 study. In: *British Journal of Religious Education*.

13191   Noorukite hoiakud nende puuetega eakaaslaste suhtes. (The attitude of normal adolescents towards their handicapped peers.)
EST   1994
Research Date(s): 1988-1993
Veisson, M.
Sup: Tulviste, P.
Inst: Tallinna Pedagoogikaülikool (Tallinn Pedagogical University), 0102 Tallinn, Narva mnt. 25, Estonia.
attitude; empathy; physically handicapped; mentally handicapped; adolescent
attitude; empathie; handicapé physique; handicapé mental; adolescent
PROJECT DESCRIPTION

The aim of the present research was to investigate the attitude of normal upper secondary school pupils (aged 16-18 years) towards handicapped pupils of the same age. Until today, handicapped and nonhandicapped pupils in Estonia have always been taught in separate schools.

The method of K. Gillen and H. Gräser was adapted for use in Estonian schools. Pupils were given a questionnaire comprising 21 multiple-choice questions and were asked to write a short composition on handicapped people. A total of 923 pupils from 7 schools participated in the study.

Empathy with handicapped people was found to be an essential quality of many Estonian adolescents. Pupils showed an understanding of handicapped persons' problems and difficulties which Estonian society is unable to solve at once. Most pupils thought (485) that handicapped pupils are not ready for integration. It was concluded that the change of social attitudes towards the disabled will take a long time.

Publ: Veisson, M. Üldhariduskooli ôpilaste hoiakud puuetega laste suhtes. In: *Laps ja lasteaed*. Tallinn, 1992.

Veisson, M. Noorukite hoiakud puuetega eakaaslaste suhtes. In: *Haridus*, 6/1992.
The attitude of normal adolescents toward handicapped adolescents. Abstracts XIth Biennial Meetings of ISSBD, July 3-7, 1991, Minneapolis, U.S.A.

13192   Öğretim elemanı, öğrenci arası iletişimde istenilen öğretim elemanı davranışlarının gösterilmesini engelleyen faktörler. (Factors causing inadequate teacher behaviour in teacher-pupil communication.)
TUR   1994
Research Date(s): 1992
Deryakulu, Deniz.
Sup: Ergin, Akif.
Inst: Ankara Üniversitesi, Sosyal Bilimler Enstitüsü (University of Ankara, Institute of Social Sciences), 06590 Ankara, Turkey.
personality; teacher behaviour; teacher-pupil relation; communication
personnalité; comportement de l'enseignant; relation maître-élève; communication
PROJECT DESCRIPTION

Aim: This study examined, from the view point of participants in teacher certificate programmes, the factors causing inadequate teacher behaviour in the communication between teachers and pupils.

Design: A questionnaire survey was conducted among teachers taking part in teacher certificate programmes at Ankara University, Gazi University, Hacettepe University and Middle East Technical University.

Results: The two main causes of inadequate teacher behaviour in classroom communication were found to be the crowdedness of classes and undemocratic teacher behaviour. Other, less important, factors that were found included: lack of self-assurance in teachers, the composition of pupil groups, and teacher personality.

13193   Paedagogisches Wissen im Alltag: eine Explorationsstudie zum elterlichen Umgang mit paedagogischem Wissen am Beispiel der Einschulung. (Pedagogic knowledge in everyday life: an exploratory study on parents' use of pedagogic knowledge, with particular reference to school choice.)
DEU   1993
Research Date(s): 1991-1992
Fuechsle, U.
Sup: Lueders, C.
Inst: Universitaet der Bundeswehr Muenchen, Fak. fuer Paedagogik, Institut fuer Paedagogische Praxis und Erziehungswissenschaftliche Forschung, Werner-Heisenberg-Weg 39, D-8014 Neubiberg.
Fin: Deutsche Forschungsgemeinschaft.
parental attitude; parent-child relation; sciences of education; knowledge; knowledge level; entry to school; parents; choice of school
attitude des parents; relation parents-enfant; sciences de l'éducation; connaissance; niveau de connaissances; entrée à l'école; parents; choix d'une école
PROJECT DESCRIPTION

Inhalt: Welches Wissen verwenden Eltern, um in der Situation "Einschulung ihres Kindes" sich zu orientieren, zu handeln und Entscheidungen zu treffen, und welche Rolle spielt dabei paedagogisches Wissen? Wie gehen Eltern mit dem verfuegbaren Wissen um? Aus welchen Quellen speist sich das Wissen der Eltern?

Geographischer Raum: Muenchen, Oberbayern.

Vorgehensweise: Analyse von Wissensformen und Verwendungsprozessen von Wissen im Alltag; Qualitative Laengsschnittstudie, Mehrfachinterviews mit Eltern. Untersuchungsdesign: Fallstudie; qualitative Forschung; qualitativer Laengsschnitt.

Datengewinnung: Nicht-standardisiertes Interview (Stichprobe: 15; Eltern, deren Kinder im Herbst 1991 eingeschult wurden; Auswahlverfahren: bewusst. Dito; Auswahlverfahren: Zufall). Primaererhebung: Feldarbeit von Mitarbeitern des Projektes durchgefuehrt.

Publ: Lueders, Christian. Spurensuche. Ein Literaturbericht zur Verwendungsforschung. In: Oelkers, J.; Tenorth, H. E. (Hrsg.). *Paedagogisches Wissen; Beiheft der Zeitschrift fuer Paedagogik*. 1991, H. 27, S. 415-437.

13194   The personality and other attributes, qualities, abilities and opinions of A-level design students.
GBR   1993
Research Date(s): 1987-
Tyers, J.
Sup: Allison, B.
Inst: De Montford University, Department of Education, Centre for Postgraduate Teacher Education, Scraptoft Campus, Scraptoft, Leicester LE7 9SU, United Kingdom.
personality; art education; character; student; pupil attitude; ability
personnalité; éducation artistique; caractère; étudiant; attitude de l'élève; capacité
PROJECT DESCRIPTION

The project is designed to ascertain the personality characteristics of General Certificate of Education (GCE) students and to compare them with other A-level students. It is anticipated that the research will show the extent to which, if any, the design course affects attitudes and working processes.

13195 Psychologia zdrowia: modele teoretyczne normalności i zdrowia, mechanizmy zdrowia i zachowania zdrowotne. (Health psychology: theoretical models of normalcy and health, mechanisms of health and health behaviour.)

POL 1993

Research Date(s): 1990-1994

Sek, Helena; Ścigała, Ireneusz; Beisert, Maria; Stasiakiewicz, Michał; Pasikowski, Tomasz.

Inst: Instytut Psychologii, Uniwersytet im. A. Mickiewicza (Institute of Psychology, Adam Mickiewicz University), Szamarzewskiego 89, 60-568 Poznań, Poland.

Komitet Badań Naukowych (Committee for Scientific Research), Wspólna 1/3, 00-529 Warszawa, Poland

mental health; psychopathology; creativity

santé mentale; psychopathologie; créativité

PROJECT DESCRIPTION

Aims: The aim of the research is to develop, through approximations, theoretical foundations for health psychology. The main categories are: normalcy, mental health and health in the holistic and processual approach, individual subjective conceptions of health and health behaviour. As regards mechanisms of health, it is necessary to describe the role of creativity and processes of control (primary and secondary) in the management of mental stress. One of the questions addressed by the research is: To what extent do feelings of self-efficiency in the management of mental stress in social occupations prevent burnout? The approach applied is that of social cognitive psychology.

Design: Successive development of the elements of a theoretical model: health - subjective conceptions of health - mechanisms of health - health behaviour. Empirical research on subjective health conceptions and on the determinants of resistance to mental stress and other factors causing psychopathology, somatic pathology, psycho-somatic pathology and burnout.

Hypothesis: Health behaviour is determined by individual value systems and the subjective perception of health vs. ill-health. Among the mechanisms of health an important role is played by individual competences: control processes (primary and secondary), creativity in problem solving, creativity in everyday life, assertiveness.

Methods: Health Behaviour Questionnaire, Health Conviction Scale, measurement of perceptions of self-efficiency, Bryant's Control Questionnaire (S-R type), observation of aspects of creativity, experimental measurement of creativity in everyday life.

Publ: Sek, Helena. Psychologiczna prewencja jako obszar badań i zastosowań. In: Sek, Helena et al. *Zagadnienia psychologii prewencyjnej.* Poznań: UAM, 1991, pp. 1-34.

Ścigała, Ireneusz. Are people programmed to be normal? Psychological determinants of human normality. In: Ellis, E. & Maruszewski, T. (eds.). *Poznań Studies in the Philosophy of Sciences and Humanities.* Amsterdam: Rodopi, 1991.

Sek, Helena et al. *Twórczość i kompetencje życiowe a zdrowie psychiczne.* Poznań: UAM, 1991.

13196 Schueler-Media-Analyse. (Pupils-media analysis.)

DEU 1993

Research Date(s): 1991-1992

Bauer, J.; Gottschaller, E.

Inst: IJF Institut fuer Jugendforschung Markt- und Meinungsforschung GmbH, Arabellastr. 33, D-8000 Muenchen 81.

pupil; consumption; reading taste; youth attitude; literature

élève; consommation; intérêt de lecture; attitude de la jeunesse; littérature

PROJECT DESCRIPTION

Inhalt: Leserschaftsdaten und Konsumbewusstsein (Food u. Non-Food) bei 7-15 jaehrigen; Untersuchung wird seit 1984 jaehrlich durchgefuehrt; fuer 1992 werden erstmalig auch Jugendliche in der ehemaligen DDR befragt (hier nur Leserschaftsdaten, nicht Food bzw. Non-Food).

Geographischer Raum: Deutschland.

Untersuchter Zeitraum: 1991-1992.

Vorgehensweise: Repraesentativ CF-Random; face-to-face; geschlossene Fragen.

Datengewinnung: Standardisiertes Interview (Stichprobe: 2x1000; 7-15jaehrige BRD; Auswahlverfahren: Zufall. Stichprobe: 500; 7-15jaehrige ehemalige DDR; Auswahlverfahren: Zufall). Primaererhebung: Feldarbeit von Mitarbeitern des Projektes durchgefuehrt.

Auswertung: Datenaufbereitung: Verknuepfung verschiedener Datensaetze (record linkage).

13197 Secondary education during the transition towards a market economy: readiness for change (evaluation, adjustments and expectations of pupils, teachers and parents).

BUL 1994

Research Date(s): 1991-1994

Milovanova, V.; Ivanova, A.; Naidenov, G.

Sup: Kukusheva, V.

Inst: National Centre for Educational and Science Studies, Tzarigradsko Chossé 125, 1113 Sofia, Bulgaria.

Fin: Ministry of Education and Science.

pupil attitude; parental attitude; teacher behaviour; educational reform; education system

attitude de l'élève; attitude des parents; comportement de l'enseignant; réforme de l'enseignement; système d'enseignement

PROJECT DESCRIPTION

Background: The success of educational change depends on a certain knowledge of the degree of readiness for change in the people working within the education system and the groups concerned in society at large. That is why there is a need for research into the behaviour of the main groups that are involved in the educational change: pupils, teachers, parents.

Aims: (1) To establish the degree of readiness in different social groups involved in education for the realization of educational change; (2) to outline people's expectations of educational change during the transition towards a market economy.

Research questions: (1) What are the dynamics of assessment, adjustment and expectations in the groups under study? (2) Is the degree of readiness for educational change determined by the social group to which one belongs? (3) To what extent do the groups in the study support the various trends of change?

Design: The study focuses on the following groups: pupils in years 7 and 8; pupils in years 9 to 12; teachers in years 9 to 12. The inquiry uses four types of questionnaire: (1) for pupils in comprehensive schools and vocational schools; (2) for pupils in the years 7 and 8; (3) for teachers in comprehensive and vocational schools; (4) for parents.

Samples: The sample consists of 9,500 persons, including 1,500 teachers and about 2,000 parents.

13198 Secondary school pupils' attitudes towards science and religion (Northern Ireland).

GBR 1993

Research Date(s): 1992-1993

Francis, L.

Sup: Greer, J.

Inst: Trinity College, Carmarthen, Dyfed SA31 3EP, United Kingdom.

pupil attitude; sciences; religion

attitude de l'élève; sciences; religion

PROJECT DESCRIPTION

This project is re-analysing data collected from 2,000 secondary school pupils attending Catholic and Protestant schools in Northern Ireland in order to explore the relationship between attitudes to science, religion, creationism and scientism. Attitudes are measured by Likert-type scales.

13199 Secondary school pupils' attitudes towards science and religion.

GBR 1993

Research Date(s): 1989-1992

Francis, L.

Inst: Trinity College, Carmarthen, Dyfed SA31 3EP, United Kingdom.

pupil attitude; sciences; religion

attitude de l'élève; sciences; religion

PROJECT DESCRIPTION

This project is analysing data collected from 5,000 secondary school pupils in England to explore the relationships between attitudes to science, religion, creationism and scientism. Attitudes are measured by Likert scales. The findings are discussed against the background of Helmut Reich's theory of the development of complementarity, which enables people to coordinate apparently conflicting statements and to arrive at synoptic points of view.

Publ: Francis, L.J.; Gibson, H.M. & Fulljames, P. Attitudes towards Christianity, creationism, scientism and interest in science among 11-15 year olds. In: *British Journal of Religious Education*, Vol 13, No 1/1990, pp. 4-17, Autumn.

13200 Self-esteem and educational practice.

GBR 1993

Research Date(s): 1990-1991

Griffiths, M.

Inst: Nottingham University, School of Education, University Park, Nottingham NG7 2RD, United Kingdom.

self-esteem; personality; equal opportunity; achievement; philosophy

estime de soi; personnalité; égalité de chances; rendement; philosophie

PROJECT DESCRIPTION

This is a philosophical examination, which draws on psychological and feminist sources. The research considers the central concepts of achievement and belonging and their role in fostering self-esteem. Current influential theories emphasise the dependence of self-esteem on personal achievement, though others focus on belonging. The internal and mutual coherence of the two are being investigated. The theories are being considered in the light of philosophical theories of personal identity, and of feminist theories of identity politics. The implications for educational practice will be drawn out, with special reference to equal opportunities.

13201 Sociolinguistic factors affecting attitudes and motivation in foreign language learning at school: an Anglo-French comparative study.
GBR 1993
Research Date(s): 1991-1994
Young, A.
Sup: Ager, D.
Inst: Aston University, Department of Modern Languages, Aston Triangle, Birmingham B4 7ET, United Kingdom.
pupil attitude; foreign languages; comparative research; cross-national research; sociolinguistics; social environment
attitude de l'élève; langues étrangères; recherche comparative; recherche transnationale; sociolinguistique; milieu social
PROJECT DESCRIPTION
This study will attempt to identify the differing attitudes held by English and French school children towards foreign language learning, with particular reference to their sociolinguistic environment. The issue will be considered from a sociolinguistic, rather than from a psycholinguistic perspective, giving primary importance to environmental, as opposed to individual factors. In particular, emphasis will be placed upon the differing sociolinguistic environments of the two areas concerned (Mulhouse, France and Walsall, England), in an attempt to shed light upon the linguistic attitudes, orientations and motivation of the children living within these communities and to identify the underlying factors which may consequently affect motivation. Three aspects of the pupils' sociolinguistic environment - parental opinion; peer pressure and the learning environment - are believed to exert significant influence and will be given special attention, as it is believed that they play an important role in the formation of attitudes.

A structured sample drawn from pupils attending schools in Mulhouse and Walsall will supply the data base for this research. The main thrust of the study will be quantitative in approach, involving the distribution of about 500 questionnaires to pupils in both towns. This will be followed up by the use of qualitative methods, in the form of indepth interviews with an individually matched sample of 50 French/English pupils, whose purpose will be to modify and check the quantitative data.

13202 Students' environmental knowledge and attitude.
GBR 1993
Research Date(s): 1991
Walden, N.
Inst: Jordanhill College of Education, Division of PE, Sport and Outdoor Education, Southbrae Drive, Glasgow G13 1PP, United Kingdom.
attitude; environment; student teacher
attitude; environnement; élève-maître
PROJECT DESCRIPTION
The aim of this project is to examine the relationships between environmental knowledge and environmental attitude among student teachers in Jordanhill College.

13203 Symvola exousias: symperifores ton paidion apenanti sta symvola exousias. (Symbols of authority: children's attitudes towards the symbols of authority.)
GRC 1994
Research Date(s): 1992-
Terlexis, P.; Tanagia, Theano; Diomitsa, Lia; Gouga, Georgia; Kamarianos, John.
Inst: Panepistimio Thessalias, Sholi Anthropistikon Spoudon, Geniko Tmima (University of Thessaly, School of Humanities, Department of General Studies), Argonafton and Filellinon, 38221 Volos, Greece.
youth attitude; authority; family environment; school environment; political behaviour
attitude de la jeunesse; autorité; milieu familial; milieu scolaire; comportement politique
PROJECT DESCRIPTION
The basic question addressed by the research was: What are children's attitudes towards political symbols and existing structures of authority? A questionnaire was distributed to children aged 8, 12 and 16 years. The research took place in selected schools in the town of Volos, the seat of the University of Thessaly, and selected schools in Leucosia, Cyprus. For comparative reasons, 738 pupils (400 boys, 338 girls) participated in the research. The questionnaires were distributed in the period between September 1992 and February 1993.

Preliminary results: At home both girls and boys, despite trends of so-called "democratization", which some see as threatening the closeness of family relationships, are still expected to obey the commands of their parents without objection. At school the situation is totally different. In class a spirit of participation and mutual cooperation seems to be

encouraged. About eight out of ten pupils state that phrases they frequently hear from their teachers are: "Let's talk about it", "Express your opinion" or "Try again". Only two out of ten state that whenever they participate in classroom discussions, phrases such as "Don't talk nonsense" or "I'll throw you out" prevail. At the level of the political institutions and authority symbols, the findings are again different. The pupils' responses should be considered seriously by all those interested in democracy and the orderly political development of Greece. Pupils' responses to questions related to the concepts of "State", "government", "justice" and "law" were positive. However, their responses to questions concerning the political parties which are supposed to be agents of social development and free political expression give rise to questions about the future of the parliamentary system and of social and political democracy. These brief evaluations of children's political conceptions about specific political institutions seem to tell us that in the galaxy of the present Greek political system the stars of the parties no longer shine brightly enough. This comes from the most reliable source: the future clients of the old party system.

13204 Tolerance and education.
GBR 1993
Research Date(s): 1992-
Gardner, P.
Inst: Warwick University, Faculty of Educational Studies, Coventry CV4 7AL, United Kingdom.
tolerance; attitude
tolérance; attitude
PROJECT DESCRIPTION
An inquiry into the nature, value and relevance of tolerance in education today.
Publ: Gardner, P. Proportional attitudes and multicultural education, or believing others are mistaken. In: Horton, J. & Nicholson, P. (eds.). *Tolerance: philosophy and practice.* Aldershot: Avebury Press, 1992.

13205 Üniversite öğrencilerinin yalnızlık düzeyleri ve bazı değişkenlerin uyum düzeylerine etkisi. (The effects of university students' loneliness and some related variables on their adjustment.)
TUR 1994
Research Date(s): 1989
Bilgen, Suzan.
Sup: Kızıltan, Gonca.
Inst: Hacettepe Üniversitesi, Eğitim Fakültesi, Psikolojik Hizmetler Bölümü (Hacettepe University, Faculty of Education, Department of Psychological Services), 06532 Beytepe, Ankara, Turkey.
personality; adjustment; student; university
personnalité; adaptation; étudiant; université
PROJECT DESCRIPTION
Aim: This study examined the effect of university students' levels of loneliness on their levels of personal, social and general adjustment. In addition, the effects of class, specialization and sex on adjustment were investigated.

Sample: 90 female and 106 male students in the first and fourth years at the departments of Psychological Counselling and Guidance, Curriculum Development in Education and Measurement and Evaluation in Education at Hacettepe University.

Design: Data were gathered using the UCLA Loneliness Scale and the Hacettepe Personality Inventory. Means and standard deviations were calculated and t-test analyses performed.

Results: Increasing levels of loneliness are connected with decreasing levels of adjustment. No significant differences were found: among first-year students' personal adjustment levels; between social and general adjustment levels of fourth-year students; between the personal, social and general adjustment levels and loneliness levels of first-year and fourth-year students; between the personal, social and general adjustment levels and loneliness levels of male and female students.

Differences did occur in first-year students' levels of social and general adjustment and loneliness; these differences were in favour of the Department of Curriculum Development in Education. Differences were also found in fourth-year students' levels of personal adjustment (in favour of the Department of Psychological Counselling and Guidance) and loneliness (in favour of the Department of Curriculum Development in Education). Comparison of students' adjustment levels and loneliness (without considering class levels) by university department, shows that the findings are in favour of the Department of Curriculum Development in Education.

Proposals are made, emphasizing the importance of family education and of psychological counselling and guidance services in schools.

22 AFFECTIVITY AND FEELING – AFFECTIVITE ET SENTIMENT – AFFEKTIVITAET UND GEFUEHL

13206 Affect and learning mathematics.
GBR 1993
Research Date(s): 1986-
Zand, H.; Burt, G.
Inst: Open University, Institute of Educational Technology, Walton Hall, Milton Keynes MK7 6AA, United Kingdom.
affectivity; emotion; mathematics; student behaviour
affectivité; émotion; mathématiques; comportement de l'étudiant
PROJECT DESCRIPTION

Learners of mathematics experience a variety of emotions such as anxiety, raised/lowered self-image, depression, elation, etc. In this project, the researchers have been studying the emotional experiences of mathematics learners and their influence on the ability to learn. The researchers are also interested in questions such as how affects exert their influence and the implications for teaching mathematics; how affects influence memory and mathematical insight.

Publ: Zand, H. & Burt, G.J. Social and emotional aspects learning mathematics. In: Educational and Training Technology International, Vol 26, No 1/1989.

13207 Angst und Angstbewaeltigung. (Fear and coping.)
AUT 1993
Research Date(s): 1985-1992
Guttmann, Giselher; Beer, Franz; Huber, Gertrud; Kutalek, I.; Neumann, Ingrid.
Inst: Abteilung fuer Schulpsychologie und Bildungsberatung, Minoritenplatz 5, A-1014 Wien.
Bundesministerium fuer Unterricht und Kunst, Minoritenplatz 5, A-1014 Wien
anxiety; mental health; relaxation; therapy
angoisse; santé mentale; relaxation; thérapie
PROJECT DESCRIPTION

Es handelt sich um eine umfassende empirische Untersuchung zur Umsetzung eines neuen Zugangs zum Phaenomen der Angst im Schulalltag. Ziele sind die Erarbeitung unproblematischer, kindgerechter Entspannungstechniken sowie die spielerische Einuebung in Kooperation und Kommunikation. Tiefenpsychologische und existentialphilosophische Ueberlegungen zur Angst sind dafuer die Ausgangslage.

Publ: Sedlak, Franz (Hrsg.). Angst und Angstbewaeltigung. Paedagogischer Verlag Eugen Ketterl, Wien 1992.

13208 Job satisfaction in teaching.
GBR 1993
Research Date(s): 1990-1994
Mercer, D.
Sup: Constable, H.
Inst: Sunderland University, School of Education, Hammerton Hall, Gray Road, Sunderland SR2 7EE, United Kingdom.
occupational satisfaction; teaching profession; head teacher; theory
satisfaction professionnelle; profession d'enseignant; chef d'établissement; théorie
PROJECT DESCRIPTION

The research undertaken has involved the development of a methodology suitable for the study, the carrying out of fieldwork based on this methodology and the development of the data obtained into the beginnings of a grounded theory of job satisfaftion. In terms of the methodology, three approaches have been developed and made use of as a means of obtaining the data necessary to develop a grounded theory of job satisfaction, a methodological approach first fomulated by Glaser & Strauss. These three methods are Life History, Nominal Group Technique and Critical Incident Technique. Of these three, the Critical Incident Technique has proved to be the most productive in that after interviews with 23 secondary headteachers, important categories with regard to job satisfaction have begun to emerge, a crucial first step in the development of substantive and formal grounded theory. Examples of such categories are, for job satisfaction, a sense of personal achievement, the views of significant others, a sense of efficacy, and relations with governors. For job dissatisfaction, work pressure, role conflict, interpersonal relations and self-esteem have been identified as being of importance. In total, twenty-three and twenty-nine respectively of such categories have appeared so far and the next process has begun of condensing these into 'themes'.

The emergence of these themes is the second stage in the creation of a theoretical position which explains job satisfaction on the part of secondary headteachers. While data collection is well advanced, it is nevertheless anticipated that perhaps double this number of headteachers will be interviewed to allow for what Glaser & Strauss refer to as 'theoretical saturation'. The research programme has been planned on the assumption that saturation will be achieved by Easter 1993 with fieldwork due to be completed by July 1993. The future progress of the research is indicated by the degree to which the development of substantive theory has already begun. This process will continue as data collection and is guided by what Glaser & Strauss refer to as 'theoretical sampling', i.e. the process of data collection being determined by an analysis of the data already collected. Allied to this, use will be made of the related process of constant comparative analysis in which theoretical notions will be coded, analysed, and redesigned and re-integrated, with such re-design being constantly undertaken as the flow of data emerges from the fieldwork.

In this way it is anticipated that a formal theory of job satisfaction will emerge which will identify the key affective features of the job of headteacher. In view of the notable lack of research in this field, this will be a significant development which will increase understanding of a group which has a key part to play in our society.

Publ: Mercer, D. Professional myopia: job satisfaction and the management of teachers. In: School Organisation, Vol 11, No 3/1991.

13209 Üniversite öğrencilerinin kişisel bazı nitelikleri ile çeşitli problemlerinin kaygı düzeylerine etkisi. (The effects of personal traits and different problems of university students on their anxiety levels.)
TUR 1994
Research Date(s): 1989
Özyürek, Ragıp.
Sup: Kızıltan, Gonca.
Inst: Hacettepe Üniversitesi, Eğitim Fakültesi, Psikolojik Hizmetler Bölümü (Hacettepe University, Faculty of Education, Department of Psychological Services), 06532 Beytepe, Ankara, Turkey.
anxiety; undergraduate; mental stress; university studies; student
angoisse; étudiant non-diplômé; tension mentale; études universitaires; étudiant
PROJECT DESCRIPTION

The study investigated the effect of different problems of university students on their state and trait anxiety levels. The Problem Inventory was used to establish students' problem levels; and the State and Trait Anxiety Inventory was used to determine students' anxiety levels.

A total of 705 students from randomly selected departments of five faculties of Çukurova University participated in the study.

The independent variables in the study were: gender, class, socio-economic status and problem areas. The dependent variable was: level of anxiety.

In the statistical analysis of the data, students' scores were divided into two groups, corresponding to high and low Problem Inventory scores. The t-test was applied in order to examine the difference between problems levels and state/trait anxiety levels. Anxiety scores and Problem Inventory scores were also grouped according to gender, class, and socio-economic status; the t-test was applied to establish differences between groups.

The results show that students with high scores on problems related to studies, future, home, friendship, mental well-being, and health also have high levels of state/trait anxiety. Also, higher class levels corresponded with higher levels of trait anxiety. Moreover, students from lower socio-economic backgrounds were more likely to display a high level of trait anxiety.

The results indicated that students have an urgent need for an extensive psychological counselling and guidance service. These services should be put in place without delay in order to provide effective solutions to the problems of university students.

13210 Üniversite öğrencilerinin yalnızlık düzeylerini etkileyen bazı etmenler. (The effects of some variables on the loneliness levels of higher education students.)
TUR 1994
Research Date(s): 1990
Demir, Ayhan.
Sup: Özgüven, I. Ethem.
Inst: Hacettepe Üniversitesi, Eğitim Fakültesi, Psikolojik Hizmetler Bölümü (Hacettepe University, Faculty of Education, Department of Psychological Services), 06532 Beytepe, Ankara, Turkey.

dissatisfaction; student; interpersonal relations; personality; attitude
insatisfaction; étudiant; relations interpersonnelles; personnalité; attitude
PROJECT DESCRIPTION

The purpose of the study was to investigate the effect of various personal, social and familial variables on the loneliness levels of higher education students.

A total of 709 (280 females, 429 males) students from each of the four year levels participated in the study. Data on the subjects' personal, social and familial characteristics were collected through a questionnaire prepared for this purpose. The loneliness levels of the subjects were assessed by the UCLA Loneliness Scale. Subjects were grouped according to each independent variable. The mean loneliness scores were obtained for each group and were compared by using several one-way analyses of variance and Tukey's tests of significance.

Analysis of the data related to personal features indicated that: the relationships between loneliness levels and sex, academic achievement, the person with whom leisure time was spent and satisfaction with monthly income for social activities were significant, whereas the relationships between loneliness levels and age, department, year level, place where most of the life-time was spent, frequency of geographic mobility, type of residence, frequency of watching television were not significant. Analysis of the data related to social variables revealed that: the relationships between loneliness levels and the number of close friends, receipt of social support, desire for new social contacts, satisfaction with social skills, openness to others, satisfaction with the relation with the mother, father, siblings, opposite-sex and same-sex friends, were significant. The relationship between loneliness levels and romantic relations with the opposite sex was not significant.

Analysis of the data related to familial features revealed that the relationship between loneliness levels and satisfaction with the mother-father relationship was significant. The relationships between loneliness levels and the number of siblings, birth order and family structure were not significant.

The results were discussed in terms of the relationships between levels of loneliness and the groups of independent variables. Some important implications for the guidance and counselling area were discussed and recommendations were made for future research.

23 BEHAVIOUR INCENTIVE – MOTIVATION DU COMPORTEMENT – VERHALTENSAUSLOESENDER REIZ

13211 Aspects of academic underachievement in the gifted child.
GBR 1993
Research Date(s): 1990-1993
Jeavons, M.
Sup: Crocker, A.; Birley, G.
Inst: Wolverhampton University, Walsall Campus, Gorway Road, Walsall WS1 3BD, United Kingdom.

gifted; ability; underachievement
doué; capacité; rendement déficient
PROJECT DESCRIPTION

Five schools catering for a range of children of varying ability and varying socio-economic background have been selected from one local education authority and children in year three of these primary schools have been given a range of psychometric tests. Those identified as 'gifted' are being observed to measure their interaction with (a) the teacher and (b) their peers.

13212 Aufstiegserwartung als Motivation zur Weiterbildung bei berufstaetigen Erwachsenen. (Occupational advancement as motivation for further education in employed adults.)
DEU 1993
Research Date(s): 1989-
Lee, S.
Sup: Endruweit, G.
Inst: Universitaet Kiel, Wirtschafts- und Sozialwissenschaftliche Fakultaet, Institut fuer Soziologie, Wilhelm-Seelig-Platz 1, D-2300 Kiel 1.
motivation; vocational education; further training; employment opportunities; social success; occupational qualification
motivation; enseignement professionnel; formation complémentaire; chances d'obtenir un emploi; réussite sociale; qualification professionnelle
PROJECT DESCRIPTION

Inhalt: Hypothese: Je groesser die erwartete positive Sanktion, desto hoeher ist die Motivation zur Teilnahme an berufsqualifizierenden Weiterbildungsmassnahmen.

Geographischer Raum: Wuerttemberg.

Vorgehensweise: Verhaltenstheorie; Lerntheorie. Untersuchungsdesign: Querschnittserhebung.

Datengewinnung: Standardisiertes Interview (Gesamterhebung bei allen Absolventen einer Institution; Auswahlverfahren: total). Primaererhebung: Feldarbeit von Mitarbeitern des Projektes durchgefuehrt.

13213 Barrierer mot fullföring av voksenopplæring på videregående skoles nivå. (Deterrents to completing adult education at the upper secondary level: a theoretical and empirical analysis of factors determining adult student dropout in upper secondary level education.)
NOR 1994
Research Date(s): 1992-1996
Madsen, Björn-Emil.
Inst: Norsk Voksenpedagogisk Forskningsinstitutt (Norwegian Institute of Adult Education), Jonsvannsveien 82, 7035 Trondheim, Norway.
motivation; adult education; dropout; upper secondary
motivation; éducation des adultes; abandon d'études; secondaire deuxième cycle
PROJECT DESCRIPTION

Psycho-social traits (motivation, self-efficacy), pedagogical factors (in-school experiences, e.g. the degree of integration in class) and social factors (out-of-school experiences, e.g. conflict in use of time between studying and work or leisure activities) have all been identified as major factors affecting adult student dropout. Some research studies have pointed to the interaction between psycho-social traits and in-school experiences as a major factor. Using a survival analysis design, it will be possible to observe changes in psycho-social traits as students accumulate experiences both in and out of school throughout the school year. Testing will take place in four sessions, one just before the start of the school year, and three during the school year. Following each test, dropouts will be interviewed about their decision and the underlying motivation. Thus, it will be possible to compare their arguments for quitting with their profiles from previous tests. The project will also provide further insight into characteristics of persisters.

The sample will be drawn from participants in adult education at three major regional adult education institutes in southern Norway. By including psycho-social traits, in-school and out-of-school experiences in the analysis, it will be possible to determine whether dropout is determined by an interaction between these three factors and to identify which factor is the most important.

It is hoped that the knowledge gained can be used in adult education to prevent and reduce dropout in the future.

13214 Cultural bases of educational forms: an inquiry into the learning patterns of the 40 primary school children in an Indian village.
GBR 1993
Research Date(s): 1989-1992
Singh, A.
Sup: Little, A.
Inst: London University, Institute of Education, Department of International & Comparative Education, 20 Bedford Way, London WC1H OAL, United Kingdom.
motivation for studies; India; social environment; teaching method
motivation pour les études; Inde; milieu social; méthode pédagogique
PROJECT DESCRIPTION

The research examines a case of a very high incidence of absenteeism, stagnation and wastage in primary education among the tribal people in India (the Dhebar Commission, *All India Educational Survey 1986*). The study explores a case of contradiction prevailing between primary schooling and domestic routines especially in rural areas. For example, tribal children from the very beginning assume economic roles under parental guidance in the domestic settings. But the process of transmission of knowledge and skills in primary schools to the children is not effective as shown in their apathetic attitudes towards their school work.

The case in question is the domestic learning of raising silkworms and the classroom learning about them in a peasant village of Singhbhum, India. These issues need to be examined in the light of larger theoretical questions such as: Why are some educational forms more effective than others? What is the connection between children's learning and their current and emergent occupational roles? How do cultural discontinuities between two educational experiences affect the educational performance of a child and a community at large?

To analyse the case, the researcher uses the Theory of Activity based on the socio-cultural approach as developed by Vygotsky and his disciples. This approach has a large following in current educational research, especially in examining the role of cultural mediation in the current and emergent educational practices. The research is a case study of the Ho tribe in the peasant village of Singhbhum, where silk farming is the main subsidiary occupation. Intensive fieldwork includes: making full length direct observation of learning activities of raising silkworms; taking in-depth interviews of parents, teachers and children in the village and making a scientific content analysis of the textbooks taught in primary schools.

The research aims to make a critical analysis of the discontinuity between primary schooling and domestic routines (especially silk making) in the light of theoretical premises and the empirical evidence gathered which together will provide a meaningful insight into the problem of a very high incidence of absenteeism, stagnation and wastage among the Ho tribe in India.

13215 De ontwikkeling van motivatie en zelfregulatie bij leerlingen in de onderbouw. (The development of motivation and self-regulation in lower secondary school pupils.)
NLD 1994
Research Date(s): 1992-1994
Bergen, Th.C.M.; Lamberigts, R.J.A.G.; Amelsvoort, J.P.J. van; Setz, W.Ch.A.R.
Inst: Vakgroep Onderwijskunde (Department of Education), P.O. Box 9103, 6500 HD Nijmegen, Netherlands.
Katholieke Universiteit Nijmegen (Catholic University of Nijmegen), P.O. Box 9102, 6500 HC Nijmegen, Netherlands
Fin: SVO het Instituut voor Onderzoek van het Onderwijs.
motivation for studies; independent work; teaching quality; school career; teacher behaviour
motivation pour les études; travail indépendant; qualité de l'enseignement; cursus scolaire; comportement de l'enseignant
PROJECT DESCRIPTION
Background: In the first phase of the overall project "Motivation and Self-Regulation as Determinants of Educational Effects" several instruments have been adjusted or developed to measure the central concepts. The present longitudinal project has integrative function within the overall project. It aims to bring these instruments together and to examine: how the school careers, motivational orientations and self-regulation skills of pupils develop through time; how these developments are interrelated; and how these developments may be influenced by teachers' instructional behaviours. Seven non-task-specific measurement instruments will be included in the study.
Aim: To examine the development of lower secondary school pupils' motivational orientations and self-regulation skills as well as the influence of these variables of the pupils' school careers; to determine the effect, through the years, of instruction on pupils' motivational orientation and self-regulation skills in the subjects Dutch, French, mathematics, and history.
Design: For a period of four years, one cohort of pupils will be followed from the moment they entered secondary school in 1991-1992 up to the point where they have to choose their examination subjects. Measurements will be carried out in November and in May. Six schools with in all 45 first-year classes (1,300 pupils of all ability ranges) will participate in the study. Twice a year they will make three lesson periods available to enable measurements to be carried out of the quality of instruction as well as of pupils' perceptions of the subjects Dutch, French, mathematics and history. Pupils' subject preferences will be measured at the "even" measurement points. In the first year, an intelligence test will be administered instead of measuring pupils' subject preferences.

13216 Determinanter for individuelle forskjeller i valg og gjennomföring av utdanning. (Determinants of individual differences in educational choice and success.)
NOR 1994
Research Date(s): 1992-1995
Wichström, Lars.
Inst: Program for Ungdomsforskning (Norwegian Youth Research Centre), Gaustadalléen 21, 0371 Oslo, Norway.
Fin: NAVF/RSF.
aspiration; choice of studies; occupational choice; youth attitude
aspiration; choix des études; choix d'une profession; attitude de la jeunesse
PROJECT DESCRIPTION
This project is part of a larger project entitled "Young in Norway". Two main questions are asked: (1) What factors determine young people's educational and occupational aspirations? (2) What factors determine the course of education?
In 1992 some 5,000 pupils from all over Norway from year 7 (aged 13 years) to upper secondary year 3 (aged 18 years) responded to a questionnaire. The same subjects will be studied two years later. The research questions will be considered from a pedagogical, psychological and sociological angle.

13217 Le développement de la motivation à la réussite scolaire: premières approches.
FRA 1993
Research Date(s): 1989-1991
Forner, Yann.
Inst: Ministère de l'éducation, Conservatoire national des arts et métiers, Ecole pratique des Hautes Etudes et Université de Paris V, Institut national d'études du travail et d'orientation professionnelle - Service de recherche, 41 rue Gay-Lussac, 75005 Paris, France.
achievement motivation; success; lower secondary; course programme; evaluation
motivation d'accomplissement; réussite; secondaire premier cycle; programme de cours; évaluation
PROJECT DESCRIPTION
Objectifs: La motivation à la réussite est une combinaison de Besoin de réussite, de Locus de contrôle interne et de Perspective temporelle. Ses effets sur les conduites scolaires et pré-professionnelles sont souhaitables et il paraît intéressant de chercher à la développer selon des techniques relevant de divers cadres théoriques: l'impuissance acquise, l'efficacité personnelle, la modification des attributions. Cette recherche explore les possibilités de développement de cette motivation dans le premier cycle de l'enseignement secondaire.
Méthodologie: Une intervention expérimentale est réalisée dans un collège auprès d'un groupe de douze élèves de classe de troisième, dans une double intention afin: (1) d'évaluer les effets d'un court programme de développement de la motivation à la réussite chez des collégiens et l'on s'intéresse à leurs déclarations, à des évaluations réalisées par questionnaires et à des indices objectifs comme les résultats scolaires; (2) d'évaluer les conditions pratiques de la mise en place d'un tel programme par des conseillers dans un collège.
Résultats: (1) Le programme est bien accueilli et les élèves volontaires se caractérisent plus par une forte anxiété que par leur manque de motivation; (2) les participants sont plutôt satisfaits des activités et les évaluations par questionnaire de leur motivation à la réussite ne montrent qu'un développement non significatif, les effets à plus long terme sont évalués.
Publ: Forner, Yann. La motivation à la réussite à l'adolescence: l'influence parentale. In: *Nouvelles études psychologiques*, 1990, n° 2, pp. 151-156.
Forner, Yann. La motivation à la réussite et les examens: l'exemple du Brevet des collèges. In: *Enfance*, 1991, n° 45, pp. 191-204.
Forner, Yann. Validation d'un questionnaire de motivation à la réussite: premiers résultats. In: *Bulletin de l'Association des conseillers d'orientation de France*.

13218 Dierevnisi ton staseon ton sinithion ke ton tropon meletis ton mathiton ke tis schesis tous pros ti scholiki epidosi. (Investigation of study habits, learning strategies and students' attitudes toward study, and their relationship to student achievement.)
CYP 1993
Research Date(s): 1988-1992
Persianis, Panayiotis; Koutselini, Mary.
Inst: Pedagogiko Instituto (Pedagogical Institute), P.O. Box 512, Nicosia, Cyprus.
learning habit; learning strategy; study method; youth attitude; work attitude; achievement
habitude d'apprentissage; stratégie d'apprentissage; méthode de travail; attitude de la jeunesse; attitude envers le travail; rendement
PROJECT DESCRIPTION
This is an updating of EUDISED entry 36/8583.
Results: (1) Descriptive statistical analysis showed that pupils use a great number of self-control strategies - reviewing, organizing and transforming - as well as external assistance to overcome study difficulties and

to facilitate learning. (2) Pupils' attitudes towards studying are generally positive. A minority (37.3%) hold negative attitudes towards studying. (3) There is a positive, statistically significant correlation between study behaviour and academic performance as measured by the average final mark attained at the end of the third year at the Lyceum. There is also a significant correlation between the results of university entrance examinations and study behaviour, self-control strategies and valuation of study. There is a positive correlation between average school marks and the results obtained in university entrance examinations.

Regression analysis showed that study behaviour accounts for the results of university entrance examinations as follows: 55.8% for the Polytechnic Cycle, 26.43% for the Economic Cycle, and 88.08% for the Higher Technical Institute. Correlation between academic performance and each variable revealed a significant negative correlation between academic performance and study habits, learning strategies and attitudes. Comparisons between study behaviour and the results obtained per subject of the university entrance examinations showed significant positive correlations between: (a) self-control strategies and modern Greek, mathematics, chemistry, (b) organizing-transforming and mathematics, (c) reviewing and mathematics, (d) use of other books and modern Greek, (e) memorizing and chemistry, (f) use of external assistance and economics, (g) valuing study and modern Greek, mathematics, physics and biology.

Comparison of the study behaviours of high and low achievers showed a significant correlation between high achievers and specific study habits, learning strategies as well as attitudes towards study.

Of the demographic factors, gender has the strongest effect on pupils' study behaviours. Boys differ considerably from girls in study habits and learning strategies. In almost all cases, a statistically significant difference was found in favour of girls.

13219   L'échec à l'école: échec de l'école?

CHE   1994

Research Date(s): 1990-1992

Pierrehumbert, Blaise (Route de St-Cergue 96, 1260 Nyon, Suisse).

school failure; selection; achievement

échec scolaire; sélection; rendement

PROJECT DESCRIPTION

La collection des "Textes de base en pédagogie" s'adresse aux étudiants et à d'autres personnes intéressées en matière de pédagogie; elle a pour but de dresser l'état de questions spécifiques. Le livre "L'échec à l'école: échec de l'école?" traite d'un phénomène traité par de nombreux spécialistes. Si nous l'incluons dans les "Informations sur la recherche éducationnelle", c'est qu'il rassemble différents points de vue scientifiques sur le phénomène - sans forcément chercher à les concilier ni à en faire une synthèse. Des synthèses de recherche se trouvent plutôt à l'intérieur des différentes contributions, celle par exemple qui traite de l'attribution de l'échec scolaire. Les contributants sont dans leur majorité des chercheurs actifs en Suisse romande (ou au Tessin, mais formés en Suisse romande), auxquels viennent s'ajouter quelques chercheurs français.

Viviane Isambert-Jamati explique comment, au cours du 20e siècle, l'échec scolaire est devenu un problème social. Jean-Claude Deschamps s'intéresse aux attributions faites par l'élève de ses propres échecs ou réussites, illustrant le rôle de l'école dans la reproduction sociale, par une action qui passe au travers de l'individu. Philippe Perrenoud montre comment l'école fabrique l'échec, en privilégiant des domaines où les disparités entre élèves sont particulièrement fortes à un moment donné. André Inizan s'intéresse à la didactique et son rôle dans l'échec, insistant sur la nécessité de différencier les rythmes d'apprentissage. Blaise Pierrehumber montre la complexité psychologique de la norme et de la différence. Il explore son sujet à l'exemple de l'image de soi d'élèves vaudois en situation d'échec scolaire, fréquentant des classes spécialisées, tandis que Kathya Tamagni relate une étude tessinoise comparable, mais concernant des élèves qui suivent la classe normale, bénéficiant d'un appui pédagogique intégré. Bernard Gibello introduite une approche médico-psycho-pathologique. Walter Bettschart, avec le point de vue du psychiatre d'enfants, souligne la nécessité de l'investigation pluri-disciplinaire et montre l'importance, pour l'enfant, de pouvoir investir de façon autonome les moyens de la connaissance. Cet investissement passe par la fonction de plaisir, qui devrait s'exprimer à la fois dans l'exercice des instruments cognitifs pour eux-mêmes, et dans leur mise au service du désir de réussite.

Toutes les contributions sont accompagnées d'une brève note de lecture rédigée par un pair, qui a pour but de recentrer ou d'expliciter l'apport du texte dans le chanp global de l'échec scolaire. S'il y a un dénominateur commun à l'ensemble des contributions, c'est la certitude que les déterminants individuels et sociaux ne peuvent, isolément, expliquer l'échec.

Publ: Pierrehumbert, Blaise (éd.). *L'échec à l'école: échec de l'école?* Neuchâtel: Delachaux & Niestlé, 1992, 318p. (Collection "Textes de base en pédagogie").

13220   Een verrijkingsprogramma voor begaafde allochtone en begaafde kansarme basisschoolleerlingen.   (An enrichment programme for gifted immigrant and deprived primary school pupils.)

NLD   1994

Research Date(s): 1993

Mönks, F.J.; Ben-Michael, M.

Inst: Centrum voor begaafdheidsonderzoek (CBO) (Centre for Giftedness Research), P.O. Box 9104, 6500 HE Nijmegen, Netherlands.
Katholieke Universiteit Nijmegen (Catholic University of Nijmegen), P.O. Box 9104, 6500 HE Nijmegen, Netherlands

Fin: SVO het Instituut voor Onderzoek van het Onderwijs.

gifted; immigrant; deprived; compensatory education; primary education; pupil

doué; immigrant; défavorisé; éducation compensatoire; enseignement primaire; élève

PROJECT DESCRIPTION

Background: Teachers at primary schools with a high proportion of immigrant pupils spend a large part of their time trying to reduce the disadvantages of their pupils. Due to lack of time, they have to adjust their teaching constantly to the level of the average pupil. As a result, gifted immigrant and deprived pupils do not have the opportunity to realize their potential. That is why these underachieving pupils are said to constitute a double risk group.

Aim: To examine the effect of an Intervention Programme which aims at promoting the learning strategies and the cognitive and linguistic skills of gifted deprived pupils.

Design: The intervention programme will last the full length of the school year. It will be carried out in three schools in lower-class neighbourhoods in the city of Nijmegen for four hours a week. A "quasi experiment - nonequivalent control group" design will be adopted. The experimental group will consist of 50 gifted (underachieving) deprived pupils (aged 8 to 10 years) who will follow the Intervention Programme. Control group 1 (N=30) will not follow the programme; neither will the pupils in control group 2 (N=50), who have not been identified as being gifted.

13221   Embedded teacher development.

GBR   1993

Research Date(s): 1987-1994

Pinel, A.

Sup: Briggs, B.

Inst: West Sussex Institute of Higher Education, The Dome, Upper Bognor Road, Bognor Regis PO21 1HR, United Kingdom; Southampton University, Faculty of Educational Studies, Highfield, Southampton SO9 5NH, United Kingdom.

teacher role; teacher behaviour; role perception

rôle de l'enseignant; comportement de l'enseignant; perception de rôle

PROJECT DESCRIPTION

The central interest 'embedded teacher development' refers to processes through which teachers develop perceptions of their task, while continuing as classroom practitioners. The major concerns are how they learn more about the capabilities and powers of their pupils and how they attempt to provide more opportunities for the release of these powers through reflecting on and re-structuring their approaches to them and to their teaching material. The medium is (mainly) mathematics. The teachers are primary teachers.

13222   How do primary school teachers teach? An investigation into what the use of language by primary school teachers can tell us about their teaching strategies.

GBR   1993

Research Date(s): 1990-1992

Warham, S.

Inst: Plymouth University, Rolle Faculty of Education, Douglas Avenue, Exmouth EX8 2AT, United Kingdom.

teacher role; teacher-pupil relation; teaching method; communication; teaching style

rôle de l'enseignant; relation maître-élève; méthode pédagogique; communication; style pédagogique

PROJECT DESCRIPTION

This research for publication is based on 40 case studies of teachers working in their classrooms. Based on the assumption that communication is crucial to the process of teaching, it examines the communication strategies of different teachers working in their classrooms, and attempts to discover what the communication skills of teachers can tell us about how primary school teachers teach. An attempt is made to reconstruct the ways in which different teachers control and create learning experiences for their pupils.

The research finds that teachers set up different identities and power relationships with their pupils, and perform acts of hegemony. The differences in acts of hegemony are examined, and exploration of other aspects of teachers' work attempts to expose something of the complex power context in which teachers perform their professional activities, and how this affects their teaching. The research finally concludes that in order to carry out their professional activities teachers need to be professionally literate.

13223 Individual motivation and take-up of National Vocational Qualifications in the South West.
GBR 1993
Research Date(s): 1992
McHugh, G.; Fuller, A.
Sup: Saunders, M.
Inst: Lancaster University, Department of Educational Research, Centre for the Study of Education and Training, Cartmel College, Bailrigg, Lancaster LA1 4YW, United Kingdom.
Fin: Training, Enterprise and Education Directorate.
motivation; vocational education; occupational qualification; training-employment relationship
motivation; enseignement professionnel; qualification professionnelle; relation formation-emploi
PROJECT DESCRIPTION
This project aims to: (i) identify key factors which influence and motivate individuals to pursue and obtain National Vocational Qualifications (NVQs); (ii) to help Training and Enterprise Councils (TECs) identify ways of increasing take-up of NVQs.

13224 Intérêts et choix de filière post baccalauréat.
FRA 1993
Research Date(s): 1991-1993
Vrignaud, Pierre; Bernaud, Jean-Luc.
Inst: Ministère de l'éducation, Conservatoire national des arts et métiers, Ecole pratique des Hautes Etudes et Université de Paris V, Institut national d'études du travail et d'orientation professionnelle - Service de recherche, 41 rue Gay-Lussac, 75005 Paris, France.
motivation for studies; interest; undergraduate study; choice of studies; self-concept
motivation pour les études; intérêt; supérieur premier cycle; choix des études; conception de soi
PROJECT DESCRIPTION
Objectifs: L'objet de cette étude est d'établir des typologies d'intérêts pertinentes pour une approche différentielle de la motivation dans l'enseignement supérieur. Cette étude s'incrit dans le cadre des théories de l'appariement entre image de soi et prototype pour rendre compte des comportements motivés (Huteau et Vouillot, 1989). On se propose de mettre à l'épreuve les deux hypothèses suivantes: (1) Les réponses à des questionnaires d'intérêts permettent-elles d'établir des profils différenciés des étudiants de filières contrastées? Ces profils peuvent-ils servir à la construction de prototypes représentatifs de ces filières? (2) Dans quelle mesure la congruence entre l'image de soi de l'élève établie à partir de ces mêmes questionnaires et les prototypes peuvent-ils rendre compte du choix post-baccalauréat?
Méthodologie: Plusieurs questionnaires d'intérêts seront utilisés, en particulier le SVIB: "Strong Vocational Interest Blank". L'échantillon comprendra deux types de publics: lycéens de terminales toutes sections qui seront suivis au moins jusqu'à leur entrée dans l'enseignement supérieur; étudiants en seconde année de premier cycle (Diplôme d'études unversitaires générales, Diplôme universitaire de technologie, Brevet de technicien supérieur, Classes préparatoires aux grandes écoles).

13225 Kratos kai koinonia: morfes koinonikou eleghou sto sholiko perivallon. (State and society: modes of social control in the school environment.)
GRC 1994
Research Date(s): 1993-
Terlexis, P.; Tanagia, Theano; Diomitsa, Lia; Siamouris, Dimitris; Tzanetopoulou, Areti; Diamanti, Fotini.
Inst: Panepistimio Thessalias, Sholi Anthropistikon Spoudon, Geniko Tmima (University of Thessaly, School of Humanities, Department of General Studies), Argonafton and Filellinon, 38221 Volos, Greece.
teacher role; self-perception; social control; school environment
rôle de l'enseignant; perception de soi; régulation sociale; milieu scolaire
PROJECT DESCRIPTION
The research examines to what extent primary and secondary school teachers internalize their role. In an effort to complete the project on "Symbols of authority: children's attitudes towards the symbols of authority", the basic questions addressed in this project are related to: (a) the extent to which teachers identify with their teacher role and their perceptions of this role; (b) factors determining teachers' attitudes towards the class; (c) teachers' views of the "ideal" educational model. The theoretical framework of the research has been elaborated with these considerations in mind. Data will be collected with the help of questionnaires to teachers in all primary and secondary schools in the city of Volos.

13226 Leistungsmotivation unter besonderer Beruecksichtigung der kognitiven Komponente. (A study of achievement motivation, with particular reference to cognitive components.)
DEU 1993
Research Date(s): 1988-1992
Wulsch, I.
Inst: Universitaet Potsdam, FB Psychologie, Am Neuen Palais, O-1571 Potsdam.
achievement motivation; cognitive ability; history; secondary education; upper secondary
motivation d'accomplissement; aptitude cognitive; histoire; enseignement secondaire; secondaire deuxième cycle
PROJECT DESCRIPTION
Inhalt: (1) Lassen sich Zusammenhaenge nachweisen zwischen Qualitaetsparametern der kognitiven Struktur fuer Geschichte und der Motivationstendenz (He/Fm) fuer dieses Fach (in der Abiturstufe)? (2) Lassen sich Zusammenhaenge abbilden zwischen der Qualitaet des kognitiven Konzeptes und der entstehenden Motivationstendenz in der aktuellen Anforderungssituation? (3) Wie stark beeinflussen die verfestigten psychischen Komponenten der Leistungsmotivation wie Einstellungen, Wertorientierungen, Interessen, Beduerfnisse, Koennenskomponenten die Genese der Motivation in der aktuellen Anforderungssituation?
Geographischer Raum: Deutschland (ehem. DDR).
Untersuchter Zeitraum: 1989/1990.
Vorgehensweise: Im Theorieteil wird der Einfluss der kognitiven Komponente auf die Leistungsmotivation erlaeutert; die Konsistenzproblematik motivativer und kognitiver Komponenten wird methodisch mit Hilfe von Frageboegen, Leistungserhebungen sowie einem halbstandardisierten Interview erhellt. Untersuchungsdesign: Fallstudie; (Quasi-)Experiment; Erfassung von (egozentrierten) Netzwerken.
Datengewinnung: Gruppenbefragung (Stichprobe: 77; Schueler der Abiturstufe. Stichprobe: 23; Schueler der Abiturstufe; Auswahlverfahren: bewusst). Postalische Befragung (Stichprobe: 23; Schueler der Abiturstufe; Auswahlverfahren: bewusst). Nicht-standardisiertes Interview (dito). Experiment (dito). Leistungserhebungen (Stichprobe: 77; Schueler der Abiturstufe). Primaererhebung: Feldarbeit von Mitarbeitern des Projektes durchgefuehrt.
Auswertung: Faktorenanalyse; Korrelationen.

13227 Microscopisch schoolloopbaanonderzoek fase 2. (Microscopic school career research phase 2.)
NLD 1994
Research Date(s): 1993-1995
Kuyper, H.; Ferwerda, R.
Sup: Creemers, B.P.M.
Inst: RION Instituut voor Onderwijsonderzoek (RION Institute for Educational Research), P.O. Box 1286, 9701 BG Groningen, Netherlands.
Rijksuniversiteit Groningen (State University of Groningen), P.O. Box 72, 9700 AB Groningen, Netherlands
Fin: SVO het Instituut voor Onderzoek van het Onderwijs.
motivation; interest profile; school career; choice of studies; lower secondary
motivation; profil d'intérêt; cursus scolaire; choix des études; secondaire premier cycle
PROJECT DESCRIPTION
Background: In developmental psychology the age period 11-17 is seen as the period in which a person builds his/her identity. In this period major decisions are taken and plans for the future devised. With regard to the school career, too, almost daily major decisions are taken and choices made whose consequences influence motivational processes.
Aim: To examine (1) the interactions between motivational processes, tactic and strategic decisions and school achievement, (2) pupils' mental processing of these interactions and (3) the way other people influence these interactions.
Design: This phase concerns the collection of data on the remainder of the second secondary school year and the whole of the third school year of 900 pupils attending four combined schools which offer junior and senior general secondary education and pre-university education. Pupils have been given questionnaires asking about their expectations regarding new curriculum subjects (for all pupils: German and physics; for some: economics/commercial science, classical languages). Questionnaires on achievement motivation, stress, perceptions of curriculum subjects, perceptions of teachers, homework habits, important life events will be administered five times (instead of seven, as in the first phase). For the rest, the study is a replication of the first phase.
(This is an updating of EUDISED no. 43/10373).

13228 Motivation von LehramtskandidatInnen in Mathematik. (The motivation of mathematics student teachers.)
AUT 1993
Research Date(s): 1992-1994
Hanisch, Guenter; Ambros, Andra; Kmetc, Silva; Kokol-Volic, Vlasta.
Inst: Institut fuer Mathematik, Strudlhofgasse 4, A-1090 Wien.

Ludwig Boltzmann-Institut fuer Schulentwicklung und international vergleichende Schulforschung, Garnisongasse 3, A-1090 Wien; Universitaet Wien, Dr. Karl Lueger-Ring 1, A-1090 Wien

motivation; mathematics; teaching profession; student teacher; cross-national research

motivation; mathématiques; profession d'enseignant; élève-maître; recherche transnationale

PROJECT DESCRIPTION

Um die Motivationen von StudienanfaengerInnen fuer das Lehramt in Mathematik zu erforschen, werden StudentInnen in Wien (Universitaet und Technische Universitaet), in Salzburg, in Innsbruck, in Budapest, in Maribor und weiteren Orten mittels eines Fragebogens befragt. Insbesondere sollen Unterschiede in der Studienmotivation zwischen oesterreichischen, ungarischen und slowenischen StudentInnen entdeckt werden. Es ist geplant, die Studie auf eine Laengsschnittstudie auszuweiten.

Es werden ca. 1.000 LehramtskandidatInnen aus Oesterreich, Ungarn und Slowenien der Befragung unterzogen.

13229 Motivationele oriëntatie en metamotivatie als determinanten van leerintentie en inzet voor huiswerktaken. (Motivational orientation and meta-motivation as determinants of learning intention and effort in respect of homework tasks.)
NLD 1994
Research Date(s): 1992-1994
Boekaerts, M.; Otten, R.
Inst: Vakgroep Onderwijsstudies (Department of Educational Studies), P.O. Box 955, 2300 RB Leiden, Netherlands.
Rijksuniversiteit Leiden (State University of Leiden), P.O. Box 955, 2300 RB Leiden, Netherlands
Fin: SVO het Instituut voor Onderzoek van het Onderwijs.
motivation; homework; learning
motivation; devoirs; acquisition de connaissances
PROJECT DESCRIPTION

Background: The project builds on the findings of the project "Meta-Motivation and Effort". The first phase of that project focused on the development and testing of instruments for measuring meta-motivation. Preliminary findings showed that action control, as measured by Kuhl's action control scale, has an effect on pupils' learning intentions in respect of concrete tasks. More specifically, pupils who score low on the decision-oriented and the performance-oriented "daily routines" items of the action control scale appear to have difficulties in executing their learning intentions. The ability to deal with failure in a constructive fashion was not found to have any effect. A possible explanation for this could be that the tasks that were given had no consequences in school. Moreover, the teacher kept an eye on what the pupils were doing, which may have been perceived by the pupils as a sort of pressure. It seems important, therefore, to conduct further research using tasks that do have consequences for the pupils and to offer these tasks in a situation in which the pupils feel free to perform them with as much effort as they choose. It has been decided to use homework tasks, because these require both metacognitive and metamotivational skills. The study seeks to discover why pupils take or drop particular subjects during the second and third years of secondary schooling and to examine the influence of motivational orientation and meta-motivational skills on pupils' option choices.

Aim: To examine the effect of various aspects of motivational orientation, self-regulation and action control on pupils' homework efforts; to contribute to theory development in the field of motivational research.

Design: The model of the main variables and their interrelationships will be tested in a two-year longitudinal design. Pupils' subject perceptions will be measured by means of subject perception scales. Perceptions of the situation will be measured with the help of the "OMQ" list. Action control will be measured with the help of Kuhl's action control scale. Measurements will be carried out at the start of the second school year, after Christmas and at the start of the next school year. The study will examine effects per curriculum subject (French, history, Dutch, mathematics). Homework assignments will be given for each of these four subjects. At every measurement point the pupils will be asked to report - on the OMQ - their cognitions, emotions, and learning intentions in respect of the homework assignments for a period of two to three weeks. They will also be asked whether and why they would take the subject concerned as a final examination subject if they had to make their choice at that moment. The classes will be divided into four subgroups (n=200). Each subgroup will be asked to fill in the OMQ for two subjects before and after the homework assignments. Linear structural models will be formulated, which will first be tested per subject at one measurement moment. The subjects will be compared and changes through time will be identified.

13230 Odkrivanje nadarjenih učencev. (Identifying gifted pupils.)
SVN 1994
Research Date(s): 1986-
Jurman, Benjamin.
Inst: Pedagoški inštitut pri Univerzi v Ljubljani (Educational Research Institute at the University of Ljubljana), Gerbičeva 62, 61111 Ljubljana, Slovenia.

Univerza v Ljubljani (University of Ljubljana), Kongresni trg 15, 61000 Ljubljana, Slovenia
Fin: Ministrstvo za znanost in tehnologijo; Ministrstvo za šolstvo in šport.
gifted; creativity; measuring instrument; test construction; evaluation; intelligence
doué; créativité; instrument de mesure; construction de tests; évaluation; intelligence
PROJECT DESCRIPTION

Background: The Employment Service of the Republic of Slovenia has been awarding scholarships to gifted primary school pupils since 1987. The scholarships are awarded upon the recommendation of the primary schools. In 1993 more than 5,300 pupils were scholarship holders. Since the average population of primary school pupils is about 27,000 children, it is obvious that the number of scholarship holders exceeds the theoretically determined percentage of gifted pupils. This means that besides gifted pupils, average - but diligent - pupils are also taken into consideration. In previous psychological research on creativity the cognitive functions of personality were stressed. The present study is based on the view that the origin of creativity lies in the human energy potential which is determined by glands.

Aim: Analysis of literature on the concepts of intelligence, creativity, talent, giftedness, and academic giftedness; establishment of a new theory of giftedness; construction of an instrument to measure giftedness.

Research questions: (1) What is the basic difference between creativity, intelligence and giftedness? (2) Is it possible to construct a creativity test?

Design: The hypothesis is that it is possible to identify gifted pupils with the help of an appropriate measurement instrument. First of all, the basic concepts (intelligence, creativity, giftedness) were explored in the theoretical part of the research. As giftedness is considered from the angle of gestalt psychology, the research method was derived from the cognitive theory of the German philosopher Husserl and from some other perception laws of gestalt psychology. A new conception of giftedness was developed which formed the basis for test construction. The test has already been piloted with samples of seventh-year and eighth-year primary school pupils and first-year and second-year secondary school pupils in the Republic of Slovenia; 880 seventh-year primary school pupils are included in the research in order to test the basic hypothesis.

Publ: Jurman, Benjamin. Struktura bistrih ljudi. In: Zalaznik, Janez (ed.). *Stipendiranje in nadarjenost*. Ljubljana: Zveza skupnosti za zaposlovanje SR Slovenije, 1989, pp. 19-24.
Jurman, Benjamin. Problemi vrednotenja pri testih kreativnosti. In: *XVII. in XVIII. posvetovanje psihologov Slovenije*. Ljubljana: Društvo psihologov Slovenije, 1990, pp. 314-319.
Jurman, Benjamin. *Analiza inteligentnosti, ustvarjalnosti in nadarjenosti*. Ljubljana: Pedagoški inštitut pri Univerzi v Ljubljani, 1990, 298p.
Jurman, Benjamin. *Novo pojmovanje in merjenje nadarjenosti*. Ljubljana: Pedagoški inštitut pri Univerzi v Ljubljani, 1992, 297p.

13231 On-line Motivation: eine Laengsschnittstudie zur state-motivationalen Orientierung in schulischen Leistungssituationen. (On-line motivation: a cross-sectional analysis of emotional orientation in competitive situations in school.)
DEU 1993
Research Date(s): 1990-1993
Roell, A.
Sup: Schwarzer, C.
Inst: Universitaet Duesseldorf, Philosophische Fakultaet, Erziehungswissenschaftliches Institut, Abt. Bildungsforschung und Paedagogische Beratung, Universitaetsstrasse 1, D-4000 Duesseldorf 1.
motivation; pupil; performance; school; achievement motivation
motivation; élève; performance; école; motivation d'accomplissement
PROJECT DESCRIPTION

Inhalt: Vor dem Hintergrund eines State-Traitkonzeptes in der Motivationstheorie soll ueber ein gesamtes Schuljahr hinweg die Entwicklung leistungsmotivationaler Komponenten (Selbstkonzept der eigenen Faehigkeit, Wichtigkeit der Aufgabe, situative Handlungstendenz, emotionale Befindlichkeit, Aufgabenschwierigkeit etc.) in Abhaengigkeit vom Schultyp, Alter, Geschlecht, Lehrerpersoenlichkeit, Fach erfasst werden.

Geographischer Raum: Duesseldorf, Wuppertal.

Untersuchter Zeitraum: 1990-1994.

Vorgehensweise: Untersuchungsdesign: Querschnittserhebung; Trend; Laengsschnittstudie.

Datengewinnung: Befragung (Stichprobe: 325; Schueler der Klassen 5-10; Auswahlverfahren: willkuerlich. Stichprobe: 200; Schueler verschiedener Schultypen; Auswahlverfahren: willkuerlich). Primaererhebung: Feldarbeit von Mitarbeitern des Projektes durchgefuehrt.

Auswertung: Multiple Regression; Faktorenanalyse; Varianzanalyse; Pfadanalyse. Datenaufbereitung: Verknuepfung verschiedener Datensaetze (record linkage).

13232 Paedagogische und klinische Implikationen erlernter Hilflosigkeit. (Pedagogic and clinical implications of acquired helplessness.)
DEU 1993
Research Date(s): 1991-1993
Stiensmeier-Pelster, J.
Inst: Universitaet Bielefeld, Fak. fuer Psychologie und Sportwissenschaft, Abt. Psychologie, Postfach 100131, D-4800 Bielefeld.
Fin: Deutsche Forschungsgemeinschaft.
failure; underachievement; child; school failure; cognitive process; depression
échec; rendement déficient; enfant; échec scolaire; processus cognitif; dépression
PROJECT DESCRIPTION
Inhalt: Die Arbeiten stehen in der Tradition der Theorie der erlernten Hilflosigkeit. In einem ersten Teilprojekt werden unter einer eher paedagogisch-psychologischen Perspektive die psychologischen Prozesse, die zwischen wiederholtem Misserfolg bei einer Aufgabe und Leistungsdefiziten bei nachfolgenden Aufgaben vermitteln, untersucht. Insbesondere soll ein vom Autor entwickeltes Prozessmodell ueberprueft werden, welches die motivationalen und funktionalen (Aufmerksamkeits- bzw. Konzentrationsstoerungen) Folgen von Misserfolg sowie deren Auswirkungen auf die Leistung vorhersagt. In einem zweiten Teilprojekt werden unter einer eher klinisch-psychologischen Perspektive - ausgehend vom attributionstheoretischen Depressionsmodell der Theorie der erlernten Hilflosigkeit - Annahmen bezueglich der Entstehung und Aufrechterhaltung bestimmter Formen depressiver Stoerungen, sogenannter Hilflosigkeitsdepressionen, ueberprueft. Im Mittelpunkt des Untersuchungsinteresses stehen dabei die Auswirkungen schulischen Misserfolgs auf die Entstehung und Aufrechterhaltung depressiver Stoerungen bei Kindern.
Vorgehensweise: Laborexperimentelle Forschung; quasiexperimentelle Forschung im Feld. Untersuchungsdesign: Querschnittserhebung; Panel; (Quasi-)Experiment.
Datengewinnung: Gruppenbefragung (Stichprobe: ca. 300; GymnasiastInnen der 5. Klasse; Auswahlverfahren: Zufall. Stichprobe: ca. 800; SchuelerInnen 4.-8. Klasse alle Schulformen; Auswahlverfahren: Zufall). Experiment (Stichprobe: ca. 60; StudentInnen; Auswahlverfahren: Zufall. Stichprobe: ca. 300; Jugendliche; Auswahlverfahren: Zufall). Primaererhebung: Feldarbeit von Mitarbeitern des Projektes durchgefuehrt; Sekundaeranalyse bereits vorhandener maschinenlesbarer Datensaetze.
Auswertung: Varianzanalyse; multiple Regression; Faktorenanalysen; Itemanalysen.

13233 The place of reflection in teachers' processes of change.
GBR 1993
Research Date(s): 1986-1993
Cousins, J.
Sup: Desforges, C.; Hughes, M.
Inst: Exeter University, School of Education, St Luke's, Heavitree Road, Exeter EX1 2LU, United Kingdom.
teacher role; verbal communication; class management; teaching style; child development
rôle de l'enseignant; communication verbale; conduite de la classe; style pédagogique; développement de l'enfant
PROJECT DESCRIPTION
This is an ethnographic study of teachers' theories about the language of young children when they start school and how these influence their classroom practice. It is based on a piece of action research carried out with 10 reception teachers for a year and examines the development of their own theories and the courses of change.

13234 La première année de psychologie-sociologie à l'Université de Bourgogne.
FRA 1993
Research Date(s): 1987-1990
Duru-Bellat, Marie; Guégnard, Christine.
Inst: Université de Dijon, UER Faculté des sciences économiques et de gestion, CNRS UPR/29 et GDR/996, Institut de recherche sur l'économie de l'éducation, BP 138, 21004 Dijon Cedex, France.
failure; success; student sociology; choice of studies; undergraduate study; dropout
échec; réussite; sociologie de l'étudiant; choix des études; supérieur premier cycle; abandon d'études
PROJECT DESCRIPTION
Objectifs: Cette recherche prend sa place dans le débat plus général autour des déterminants de la réussite et de l'abandon dans les premiers cycles universitaires (redoublements, changements de filière, réorientations). Il a semblé utile de connaître les caractéristiques des étudiants quittant l'université dès la première année d'enseignement supérieur (1 sur 3 en première année de psychologie-sociologie) et surtout de recueillir de la part des anciens étudiants des informations sur les raisons de leur abandon.
Méthodologie: Les anciens étudiants ont été interrogés neuf mois après la fin de leur scolarité universitaire et l'année suivante, 135 questionnaires ont été recueillis représentant 70% de la population initiale interrogée et une trentaine d'entretiens a été effectuée.
Résultats: On ne peut assimiler systématiquement l'abandon des études à un échec, l'abandon ne sanctionne pas toujours un échec aux examens, il correspond fréquemment à l'accomplissement du projet de l'étudiant (réussite à un concours ou à une école spécialisée). La première année d'Université est alors une année d'orientation permettant aux étudiants de s'informer, de réfléchir, d'effectuer des choix professionnels.
Publ: Duru-Bellat, Marie & Guégnard, Christine. A l'Université de Bourgogne, 1 étudiant sur 3 en première année de DEUG de psychologie-sociologie ne renouvelle pas son inscription. Pourquoi? IREDU-CIA-CEREQ, Document de travail, octobre 1990, 25p.

13235 Propuneri de orientare si instruire a copiilor supradotati. (Proposals for the guidance and education of gifted children.)
ROM 1994
Research Date(s): 1990-1993
Stănescu, M.L.
Sup: Jigău, Mihai.
Inst: Institutul de Stiinte ale Educatiei (Institute for Educational Sciences), str. Stirbei Vodă 37, 70732 Bucharest, Romania.
Ministerul Învătământului (Ministry of Education), str. General Berthelot 28-30, Bucharest, Romania
gifted; high achievement; assessment; special education; grouping
doué; haut rendement; appréciation; enseignement spécial; groupement
PROJECT DESCRIPTION
Background: Giftedness is considered to show itself in two principal features: high intellectual ability and exceptional performance. The definition of giftedness focuses on the educational and psychological framework in the sense that it relates to the development of a high intellectual capacity. No matter what definition we accept, we have to acknowledge the existence of children who perform significantly better than others of their age level, an acknowledgement which will benefit both these children and society. This project is concerned with special forms of education for gifted children.
Aims: (1) To evaluate teachers' attitudes towards the special educational needs of gifted children in primary and secondary schools; (2) to elaborate psychological and educational tests for assessing the cognitive capacities of these children; (3) to develop appropriate guidance and special forms of education for gifted children in Romania.
Research questions: (1) Does a special type of education for gifted children increase these children's intellectual ability or does it only support it? (2) How can Romanian children with special educational needs, such as gifted children, be helped when there are still shortcomings in meeting even basic educational needs?
Design: The study focuses on two types of setting for gifted children: ability grouping (streaming) and mixed-ability classes (non-streaming). The children in the study are in the fourth year of primary school (10-11 years old) and in the third year of secondary school. In 1991 and 1992, 300 children were assessed through psychological (Raven and Mill Hill Vocabulary Scale) and educational tests; 19 were identified as being gifted. It is intended to extend the evaluation by selecting one school from each "judet". The survey will be enriched by evaluating teachers' attitudes towards this kind of education across the country.

13236 Sozial- und Motivationsstruktur von Kursleitern an Berliner Volkshochschulen: ein Vergleich der Jahre 1979 und 1990. (The social and motivational structure of course teachers at adult education institutes in Berlin: a comparison of the years 1979 and 1990.)
DEU 1993
Research Date(s): 1987-1992
Dieckmann, B.; et al.
Inst: Technische Universitaet Berlin, FB 22 Erziehungs- und Unterrichtswissenschaften, Institut fuer berufliche Bildung und Weiterbildungsforschung, Franklinstrasse 28-29, D-1000 Berlin 10.
motivation; training course; adult education; adult education institute; employment opportunities; working conditions
motivation; cours de formation; éducation des adultes; université populaire; chances d'obtenir un emploi; conditions de travail
PROJECT DESCRIPTION
Inhalt: Feststellung der Aenderung von Motiven und Strukturen in der Gruppe der Kursleiter, insbesondere in bezug auf Arbeitssituation als Inhaber ungesicherter Beschaeftigungsverhaeltnisse.
Geographischer Raum: Berlin - Bezirke des ehemaligen West-Berlin.
Untersuchter Zeitraum: 1979-1990.
Vorgehensweise: Das Erhebungsinstrument wurde sowohl 1979 als auch 1990 in engem Kontakt mit Praktikern entwickelt, fuer die die Mitarbeit am Forschungsprojekt forschendes Lernen war. Untersuchungdesign: Trend.
Datengewinnung: Postalische Befragung (Stichprobe: 577; Volkshochschuldozenten aller Bezirke Berlins; Auswahlverfahren: total. Stichprobe: 587; Volkshochschuldozenten aller Bezirke Berlins; Auswahlverfahren: total). Gruppendiskussion (dito). Aktenanalyse (dito). Primaererhebung: Feldarbeit von Mitarbeitern des Projektes durchgefuehrt.

Auswertung: Datenaufbereitung: Verknuepfung verschiedener Datensaetze (record linkage).

13237 Study of teacher effectiveness in the Malaysian secondary school.

GBR 1993

Research Date(s): 1991-1994

Konting, M.

Sup: Knight, P.

Inst: Lancaster University, Department of Educational Research, Cartmel College, Bailrigg, Lancaster LA1 4YW, United Kingdom.

Fin: Universiti Pertanian, Malaysia.

teacher role; teacher behaviour; teacher; teaching profession; teaching style; Malaysia

rôle de l'enseignant; comportement de l'enseignant; enseignant; profession d'enseignant; style pédagogique; Malaisie

PROJECT DESCRIPTION

Despite voluminous research findings in the literature on teacher effectiveness, its contribution, particularly from the theoretical and practical aspects is still being debated. This research is undertaken with the assumptions that teachers make a difference and that true knowledge of teaching is achieved by practice and experience in the classroom.

The objectives of the study are to: (a) identify and determine the constructs of teacher effectiveness; (b) examine and describe the effective teachers' teaching, and (c) study the planning and implementation of the teacher training programme, particularly on how the programme takes into account the construct of teacher effectiveness.

A total of 41 effective lower secondary school teachers, nominated by educational authorities, who teach national language (12 teachers), English (13 teachers), and mathematics (16 teachers) are asked, through open-ended questionnaire and interview, to identify and to list the characteristics of an effective teacher, and to explain why such a characteristic is important for the teacher to be an effective teacher. They are also asked about what they do and do not do in teaching, and why. Classroom teaching of the subjects is also observed using a systematic classroom observation schedule.

So far, the results of the study indicate that there exist peculiar characteristics of effective teachers and specific effective teachers' teaching styles.

13238 A survey of student expectations and perceptions of higher education.

GBR 1993

Research Date(s): 1990-1992

Noyes, P.

Inst: Cheltenham & Gloucester College of Higher Education, Faculty of Education and Health, The Park, Cheltenham GL50 2QF, United Kingdom.

expectancy; higher education; attitude; student

attente; enseignement supérieur; attitude; étudiant

PROJECT DESCRIPTION

This research was carried out to identify the nature of student expectations of the college. The major source of these expectations were discovered, and an investigation into how they had changed was conducted, especially at the time of most impact, i.e. the first two weeks at college, and after one year at college. Areas where the college fell short of student expectation were identified. Issues for further research and areas of college practice which needed to be adapted were recommended. Links were established with the quality assurance study of the induction process. The link between expectations, academic performance and satisfaction were investigated. There was also a contribution to the debate on the efficacy of expectation theory in explaining human behaviour.

All students who entered the college in September 1990 were surveyed by questionnaire. Firstly, before they arrived at college to monitor initial expectations, secondly, immediately after the induction process to ascertain immediate changes in perceptions after the initial impact of coming to college had been experienced and thirdly, after a year at college, to measure perceptions of that time. Expectation theory was used as a means of examining the process of attitude change that occurred during the year, and outcome measures were collected by means of satisfaction indices calculated from questionnaire responses and academic performance indicated by college grades.

13239 Transformation der Lehrerrolle in den neuen Bundeslaendern. (Transformation of the teacher's role in the new German states.)

DEU 1993

Research Date(s): 1991-1994

Lenhardt, G.; Stock, M.; Tiedtke, M.; Huebner, P.

Inst: Max-Planck-Institut fuer Bildungsforschung, Lentzeallee 94, D-1000 Berlin 33; Freie Universitaet Berlin, FB Philosophie und Sozialwissenschaften 01, Institut fuer Soziologie WE 02, Babelsbergerstrasse 14-16, D-1000 Berlin 31.

teacher role; teacher; teaching profession; German DR; Germany - Federal Republic; adaptability; social adjustment; social change

rôle de l'enseignant; enseignant; profession d'enseignant; Allemagne RDA; Allemagne RFA; adaptabilité; adaptation sociale; changement social

PROJECT DESCRIPTION

Inhalt: An den Anpassungsproblemen und politischen Implementierungsanstrengungen laesst sich in ungewoehnlicher Klarheit erkennen, welche sozialen Kraefte und normativen Ordnungen die westdeutsche Gesellschaft konstituieren. Das wird untersucht am Gegenstand der Lehrerrolle, die derzeit in Ostdeutschland reorganisiert wird. Schluesselbegriffe sind instrumentelle Rationalisierung und Professionalisierung der Lehrer. Sie bezeichnen Trends, die in unterschiedlicher Gewichtung beide deutsche Staaten kennzeichneten, mit groesserem Gewicht auf der Professionalisierung in Westdeutschland. Der Prozess wird konstituiert durch eine Vielfalt sozialer Kraefte, die jetzt auch in Ostdeutschland virulent werden.

Geographischer Raum: Ostdeutschland.

Vorgehensweise: Untersuchungsdesign: qualitative Forschung.

Datengewinnung: Nicht-standardisiertes Interview (Auswahlverfahren: bewusst). Expertengespraech (dito). Teilnehmende Beobachtung (dito). Aktenanalyse (dito). Primaererhebung: Feldarbeit von Mitarbeitern des Projektes durchgefuehrt; Datenerstellung auf der Basis von bereits vorliegenden Materialien wie Texten, Akten, Statistiken.

Auswertung: interpretative Bearbeitung.

13240 Üniversite öğrencilerinin cinsiyet rolleri ile ilgili kalıp yargılarının bazı değişkenler açısından incelenmesi. (University students' sex role stereotypes.)

TUR 1994

Research Date(s): 1988

Baykal, Sergin.

Sup: Kılıçcı, Yadigar.

Inst: Hacettepe Üniversitesi, Eğitim Fakültesi, Psikolojik Hizmetler Bölümü (Hacettepe University, Faculty of Education, Department of Psychological Services), 06532 Beytepe, Ankara, Turkey.

sex role; stereotype; university; student; self-concept; sex difference

rôle sexuel; stéréotype; université; étudiant; conception de soi; différence de sexe

PROJECT DESCRIPTION

The purpose of the present study was to determine university students' sex-role stereotypes and to examine these stereotypes in relation to such variables as sex, education, self-acceptance, parental level of education and maternal employment.

A total of 615 university students (349 female and 266 male) were given the Sex Role Stereotype Scale, the Self-Acceptance Inventory and a brief general questionnaire. The subjects were drawn from first-year and fourth-year students. The statistical data were processed by t-test techniques and analysis of variance.

Female students had higher sex-stereotyping scores than male students. Comparison of the self-acceptance levels of the traditional and non-traditional groups revealed that the self-acceptance level of the traditional group was higher. Further analysis showed that the observed significant difference between the groups was due to the mean self-acceptance of the males in the traditional and non-traditional groups. The effects of university education, parental level of education and maternal employment on students' sex-role stereotypes are far from being significant.

Recommendations were made in terms of counselling, social work, family counselling services.

13241 Wahl einer mathematisch-naturwissenschaftlich-technischen Studienrichtung und schulische Herkunft bei Frauen. (Women opting for a mathematically, scientifically or technically oriented course of studies and their educational background.)

AUT 1993

Research Date(s): 1991-1992

Jungwirth, Helga.

Inst: Bundesministerium fuer Unterricht und Kunst, Minoritenplatz 5, A-1014 Wien; Bundesministerium fuer Wissenschaft und Forschung, Bankgasse 1, A-1014 Wien.

motivation for studies; coeducational school; mathematics; girls' school; choice of studies; sciences

motivation pour les études; école mixte; mathématiques; école de filles; choix des études; sciences

PROJECT DESCRIPTION

Die vorliegende Studie ist ein Beitrag zur Koedukationsdebatte. Ihr Ziel war der Gewinn einer empirischen Basis zur Beantwortung der Frage, ob Maedchenschulen einen positiven Effekt auf die Zuwendung von Frauen zu Mathematik, Naturwissenschaften und Technik haben. Erhoben wurde erstens, zu welchen Anteilen Studienanfaengerinnen in den mathematisch-naturwissenschaftlich-technischen Richtungen aus koedukativen Schulen und aus Maedchenschulen kommen. Zweitens wurden die Schulerfahrungen in beiden Settings - koedukativ und nicht-koedukativ - erfasst und miteinander verglichen.

In die schriftliche Befragung wurden alle Studienanfaengerinnen des Wintersemesters 1991/1992 der ausgewaehlten (d.h. ohne Biologie und Bodenkultur) mathematisch-naturwissenschaftlich-technischen Studienrichtungen an den Universitaeten und Technischen Universitaeten Oesterreichs einbezogen.

Beschreibende und beurteilende Statistik wurden herangezogen.

Der Anteil der Absolventinnen von Maedchenschulen ist ueberproportional hoch. An den Maedchenschulen herrscht ein spezifisches, offenbar foerderndes Klima: der fachbezogene Kontakt zwischen Lehrkraeften und Schuelerinnen ist intensiver, die generelle Schul- und Leistungsorientierung ist hoeher, und es zeigt sich eine positive Hervorhebung mathematisch-naturwissenschaftlich-technisch interessierter und erfolgreicher Maedchen. In der sozialen Herkunft unterscheiden sich Absolventinnen von Maedchenschulen von denen aus koedukativen Schulen nicht signifikant.

24 BEHAVIOUR – COMPORTEMENT – VERHALTEN

13242 Academic dishonesty in students.
GBR 1993
Research Date(s): 1992-
Newstead, S.; Franklyn-Stokes, A.
Inst: Plymouth University, Department of Psychology, Drake Circus, Plymouth PL4 8AA, United Kingdom.
cheating; dishonesty; student behaviour
tricherie; malhonnêteté; comportement de l'étudiant
PROJECT DESCRIPTION

The purpose of the present project is to investigate the nature, frequency and causes of various forms of cheating behaviour. A general purpose questionnaire has been developed which has so far been given to staff and students at one 'new' and one 'old' university.

The results indicate that staff underestimate the frequency of cheating compared to students, and this is especially marked with coursework. Staff also rated most types of cheating behaviour as more serious than did students, but there were exceptions to this, notably cheating in group projects. Among the students, there were also interesting differences between mature students and others, with mature students responding more like staff.

Follow-up research will investigate self-reported frequency of cheating, the motives and causes of cheating, and cheating in other educational contexts.

13243 Active citizenship and adult learning.
GBR 1993
Research Date(s): 1990-1993
Field, J.
Sup: Duke, C.
Inst: Bradford University, Centre for Continuing Education, 12 Claremont, Bradford BD7 1DP, United Kingdom; Warwick University, Faculty of Educational Studies, Department of Continuing Education, Continuing Education Research Centre, Coventry CV4 7AL, United Kingdom; University of Wroclaw, Instytut Pedagogiki, 50 527 Wroclaw, Poland.
Fin: Universities Funding Council; Tempus, European Community.
citizen participation; adult education; community education; cross-national research
participation du citoyen; éducation des adultes; éducation sociale; recherche transnationale
PROJECT DESCRIPTION

Questions of citizenship are high on the political agenda, and are controversial conceptually. In Britain, initiatives such as the Speakers' Commission report 'Encouraging Citizenship', and the Guidance Note on 'Education for Citizenship' issued by the National Curriculum Council have sought to promote active citizenship through the formal schooling system. At the same time, developments within the framework of the European Community, and changes in the systems of government in Eastern and Central Europe, have highlighted the cognitive, behavioural and attitudinal prerequisites of active participation in public debate and decision-making among the adult population.

This project is concerned to examine citizenship within the adult education curriculum; learning within citizen movements; and the changing relation between civil society and state as manifested through the governance of the education system. Within the British context, this involves a series of case studies of citizen organisations (Womens' Institute, Credit Union Movement, Amnesty International, Greenpeace support groups,

Neighbourhood Watch, Football Supporters' Association) and of measures designed to delegate powers over the educational system (community education). Interviews with those involved are being supplemented by observation, literature review and small-scale surveys.

Comparative studies are being conducted in Poland, through the University of Wroclaw; negotiations are under way for a further comparative study in Sweden, conducted through the University of Linkoping as part of its inquiry into 'The Swedish Study Circle in the Year 2002'.

Publ: Field, J. (ed.). *Active Citizens as adult learners*. University of Warwick, 1991.

Payne, J. *Adult learning and active citizenship in Inner London*. University of Warwick, 1991.

Field, J. Questions about research that makes a difference. In: *Convergence*, Vol XXIV, No 3/1991, pp. 71-78.

13244 Alternativy adaptační výchovy a vzdělávání 14(15)-16(17) leté mládeže. (Alternative forms of education aiming at the social adjustment of youth in the 14-17 age range.)
CSK 1994
Research Date(s): 1992-
Fibichová, Naďa; Kašparová, Jana; Říhová, Marie; Hořejšová, Danuše.
Sup: Petrů, Eva.
Inst: Pedagogický výzkum (Educational Research), Na Pankráci 101, 140 00 Praha 4, Czech Republic.
Ministerstvo školství, mládeže a tělovýchovy ČR (Ministry of Education, Youth and Physical Education), Karmelitská 7, 118 13 Praha 1, Czech Republic
deviant behaviour; problem child; adolescent; social adjustment; teaching programme
comportement déviant; enfant perturbé; adolescent; adaptation sociale; programme d'enseignement
PROJECT DESCRIPTION
Aims: (1) To develop a framework for a flexible system of educational alternatives for underage youth who are experiencing social and personal difficulties in regular education and who run the risk of social marginalization after leaving compulsory education; (2) to elaborate one of the possible alternative education models, including a teaching programme.

The project is prompted by the need for a flexible non-traditional educational provision, specifically aimed at the social adaptation of specific groups of young people as well as the need for links between ninth form classes and alternative forms of education for unemployed youth.

Provisional results: A flexible system has been conceived, including the design of a teaching programme and a project for testing the programme in selected secondary schools.

13245 Analyse der Kompatibilitaet von Ausbilder- und Fuehrungsverhalten und aktuellen Situationskomponenten. (Analysis of the compatibility of training and management behaviours and of current situation components.)
DEU 1993
Research Date(s): 1990-1992
Schweer, M.
Sup: Rosemann, B.
Inst: Universitaet Bochum, Fak. fuer Philosophie, Paedagogik und Publizistik, Institut fuer Paedagogik, Universitaetsstrasse 150, D-4630 Bochum 1.
behaviour; managerial staff; trainer; enterprise
comportement; personnel d'encadrement; formateur; entreprise
PROJECT DESCRIPTION
Inhalt: Fragestellung: Erfassung der Bedingungen effektiven Ausbilder- und Fuehrungsverhaltens unter Beruecksichtigung der aktuellen Situationserfordernisse und individueller Verhaltensbereitschaften. Ziel: Entwicklung eines mehrdimensionalen Instruments zur Beschreibung von Ausbilder- und Fuehrungsverhalten.

Vorgehensweise: Untersuchungsdesign: Methodenforschung.

Datengewinnung: Standardisiertes Interview (Vorgesetzte und Mitarbeiter eines Wirtschaftsunternehmens; Auswahlverfahren: Zufall). Gruppenbefragung (Stichprobe: 150; Studenten der Paedagogik; Auswahlverfahren: Zufall. Stichprobe: 180; Auszubildende gewerblicher Berufe; Auswahlverfahren: Zufall. Vorgesetzte und Mitarbeiter eines Wirtschaftsunternehmens; Auswahlverfahren: Zufall). Primaererhebung: Feldarbeit von Mitarbeitern des Projektes durchgefuehrt.

Auswertung: Clusteranalyse, Faktorenanalyse, Varianzanalyse.

13246 Anti-bullying strategies.
GBR 1993
Research Date(s): 1991
Munn, P.; Johnstone, M.; Edwards, L.; Wake, R.
Inst: Scottish Council for Research in Education, 15 St John Street, Edinburgh EH8 8JR, United Kingdom.
Fin: Scottish Office Education Department.
bullying; discipline; antisocial behaviour; teaching aid; cross-national research
brimades; discipline; comportement antisocial; moyen d'enseignement; recherche transnationale

PROJECT DESCRIPTION
The aim of this research is to develop a package of ideas and information based on current research in Britain and in Scandinavia on the good practice of experienced teachers. The finished package will contain: a booklet outlining points to consider and steps to take; case-studies for teacher discussion; action plans for management/staff consideration and lists of information on resource and curricular materials.

Publ: Munn, P.; Johnstone, M. & Edwards, L. *Action against bullying: a support pack for schools*. Edinburgh: Scottish Council for Research in Education, 1992.

13247 Assessing and interviewing in problems of bullying with pupils with special needs.
GBR 1993
Research Date(s): 1991-1992
Smith, P.; Thompson, D.; Whitney, I.
Inst: Sheffield University, Department of Psychology, Sheffield S10 2TN, United Kingdom.
Fin: Economic and Social Research Council.
bullying; discipline; handicapped; pupil integration
brimades; discipline; handicapé; intégration scolaire
PROJECT DESCRIPTION
This project examined whether certain categories of statemented children with special educational needs (SENs) were more, or less likely to be involved in bully/victim problems at school. At total of 186 children from eight schools were interviewed. The three junior/middle schools had integrated resource units for children with moderate learning difficulties, mild learning difficulties and hearing impairments and for the five secondary schools the units were for children with hearing impairments, moderate learning difficulties, SENs physical handicaps and visual impairments. Ninety-three children with SENs and 93 mainstream (MS) children matched for age, ethnicity and gender were interviewed. A member of staff was also interviewed about the children with SENs. The interviews were semi-structured, designed to explore both the child's and the teacher's perception of their relationships with peers, their feelings about the school, and whether or not they were involved in bullying or being bullied. These interviews took place in between October and December 1991, and were repeated between May and July 1992. During this year, planned interventions designed to reduce bullying problems had taken place within these schools (via a DFE-funded project), so these second interviews focused on how these interventions affected the child, as well as whether any involvement in bully/victim problems had been reduced.

The main findings were that children with SENs were bullied more than MS children and had fewer friends in school. Teachers tended to underestimate how often children with SENs were being bullied. The number of children with SENs being bullied and bullying others had decreased over time and most children perceived that bullying had got better in their schools; these changes seemed attributable to effects of intervention rather than age per se.

Publ: Whitney, I.; Nabuzoka, D. & Smith, P.K. Bullying in schools: mainstream and special needs. In: *Support for Learning*, No 7/1992, pp. 3-7.

13248 Behavioural approach to teaching project.
GBR 1993
Research Date(s): 1980-
Merrett, F.
Inst: Birmingham University, School of Education, Edgbaston, Birmingham B15 2TT, United Kingdom.
behaviour; discipline; misconduct; teacher behaviour; class management
comportement; discipline; déviance scolaire; comportement de l'enseignant; conduite de la classe
PROJECT DESCRIPTION
Empirical research has been employed to investigate the kinds of behaviours that teachers find most troublesome and the sort of responses they make to these behaviours. This has been extended to include samples from Hong Kong and Singapore. Packages used to teach teachers' methods of classroom behaviour management based on surveys and on experimental work in primary and secondary classrooms have recently been revised and upgraded. Observational research is now being focused upon the differential response rates of male and female teachers to boys and girls and the effects brought about on pupil on-task behaviour by manipulation of teachers' response ratios (i.e. the ratio between their positive and negative response rates). Another new move is the application of correspondence training to the improvement of pupils' social behaviour at the secondary level.

Publ: Merrett, F. & Wheldall, K. *Positive teaching in the primary school*. (Research Paper). London: Paul Chapman, 1990.

Wheldall, K. & Merrett, F. *General manual for the positive teaching packages*. Cheltenham: Positive Products, 1991.

Wheldall, K. & Merrett, F. *Teaching manual for the positive teaching package (primary version)*. Cheltenham: Positive Products, 1991.

Merrett, F. & Wheldall, K. *Teaching manual for the positive teaching package (secondary version)*. Cheltenham: Positive Products, 1991.

13249 Citizenship and education.
GBR 1993
Research Date(s): 1991-1993
Demaine, J.
Inst: Loughborough University of Technology, Department of Education, Loughborough LE11 3TU, United Kingdom.
citizen participation; common core curriculum
participation du citoyen; tronc commun
PROJECT DESCRIPTION
A study of the concept of citizenship in the context of the National Curriculum requirement for teaching in schools.

13250 Comparative study of disruptive behaviour and discipline in schools in the United Kingdom and Kenya.
GBR 1993
Research Date(s): 1991-1994
Awiria, O.
Sup: Gilliland, J.; McGuiness, J.
Inst: Durham University, School of Education, Leazes Road, Durham DH1 1TA, United Kingdom.
Fin: St Christopher's Trust; British Foreign Schools Society; The Leather-sellers' Company.
behaviour; misconduct; discipline; comparative research; cross-national research
comportement; déviance scolaire; discipline; recherche comparative; recherche transnationale
PROJECT DESCRIPTION
This study, in its early stages, seeks to examine aspects of disruptive behaviour and discipline in selected secondary schools in the United Kingdom and Kenya. In both countries, disruption in schools is currently an issue of considerable concern to teachers, parents and government (e.g. *Discipline in schools*: report to the Committee of Enquiry chaired by Lord Elton, HMSO, 1989). The present study will examine aspects of definition, theory and explanation as they apply to different levels of organisation in the two countries. Data collection will be by means of sample surveys of attitudes among administrators, teachers, student teachers and pupils. It is hoped to include qualitative data obtained through individual and group interviews. Other research techniques are likely to be used as the project develops.

13251 A continued evaluation of 'Catch 'em Young'.
GBR 1993
Research Date(s): 1990-1995
Cleaver, H.
Sup: Millham, S.
Inst: Dartington Social Research Unit, Foxhole, Dartington Hall, Totnes, Devon TQ9 6EB, United Kingdom; Bristol University, Department of Social Policy and Planning, 8 Woodlands Road, Bristol BS8 1TN, United Kingdom.
Fin: Department of Education and Science.
behaviour; antisocial behaviour; delinquency
comportement; comportement antisocial; délinquance
PROJECT DESCRIPTION
The study will explore the possible long-term benefits for children who were involved in 'Catch 'em Young', a 3 year scheme established to prevent delinquency and behaviour problems in secondary school children. The report submitted to the Department of Education and Science in 1989 scrutinised children's behaviour as they transferred from primary to secondary school. The long term follow-up study allows us to focus on the study group of 495 children as they pass through school, make important career decisions and enter the adult world. The previously applied methodology, which used both extensive and intensive dimensions, will be utilised. Thus, the research will continue to combine an overview resulting from a survey of the experiences of the study children with insights and perceptions of a small group of children, their teachers and parents. When linked with the earlier research findings, it will provide an opportunity to explore how family, school and peer group influences interact in the transitions of adolescents.

Publ: Cleaver, H. *Vulnerable children in schools: a study of 'Catch 'em Young' - a project helping 10 year olds transfer school.* Aldershot: Dartmouth Publishing Company, 1991.

13252 Des arcanes du placement institutionnel à l'avènement de la juridiction des mineurs.
CHE 1994
Research Date(s): 1991-1994
Avvanzino, Pierre.
Inst: Ecole d'études sociales et pédagogiques (EESP), Isabelle-de-Montolieu 19, Case postale 70, 1000 Lausanne 24, Suisse.
Association vaudoise des œuvres privées (AVOP), 6 ch. Pré-Fleuri, 1000 Lausanne 13, Suisse
Fin: AVOP et EESP.
deviant behaviour; adolescence; history of education; social change; remedial instruction sciences
comportement déviant; adolescence; histoire de l'éducation; changement social; pédagogie spéciale
PROJECT DESCRIPTION
Cette recherche en histoire de l'éducation procède selon trois axes: le développement du contexte social et historique (suisse et particulièrement vaudois), l'émergence d'une pédagogie spéciale institutionnelle, l'avènement de la juridiction des mineurs.

Au cours du 19e siècle, à l'époque de l'industrialisation, la bourgeoisie prend conscience de la nécessité de mesures visant à former l'homme à la machine et au travail. Cette prise de conscience est activée par le développement de la mécanisation. Ce sont les cris d'alarme lancés par des médecins progressistes qui par humanisme ou par réalisme tentent de convaincre patrons et pouvoirs publics de prendre en considération la santé des travailleurs. Des moyens sont mis en place pour préserver cette santé qui devient un élément de calcul dans l'investissement.

C'est sur cet arrière-fond que se développent les pratiques de placement en institution d'enfants et adolescents définis comme déviants par rapport à certaines normes. On peut distinguer trois catégories d'enfants qui ont été soumis à un tel traitement: les enfants en état de pauvreté; les enfants à conduite répréhensible; les enfants appartenant à une catégorie sociale réprouvée. La mise en institution remplit une double fonction, l'une d'ordre répressif, visant à protéger la société de délinquants réels ou potentiels, l'autre d'un ordre plus utopique, cherchant à protéger ces jeunes des mauvaises influences de la société, mais aussi à les protéger d'eux-mêmes.

Il faudra attendre les deux dernières décennies du 19e siècle pour qu'un projet d'acculturation prenne de l'ampleur sous l'impulsion des républicains. Ils se méfient de la prison et lui préfèrent l'école obligatoire. Celle-ci, avec ses tris, sa sélection, ses classements occupera - et occupe toujours - une position centrale dans le système général de dépistage et de contrôle de la déviance.

Après la deuxième guerre mondiale, une nouvelle législation - comprenant pratiquement tous les aspects de la déviance juvénile, de la délinquance à la notion élastique d'enfant en danger moral - inaugure une collaboration prospère entre la justice des enfants et la psychiatrie infantile. Cette justice des enfants devient autonome. Le président de la Chambre pénale des mineurs fonctionne comme juge instructeur. Il doit connaître avant tout "la personnalité" du mineur. La psychiatrie infantile vient en aide dans le processus décisionnel, fournissant des "diagnostics exacts". En nommant l'ensemble des manifestations anormales chez l'enfant, elle se propose d'unifier ce qui est encore relativement composite. Elle rompt avec des appellations essentiellement répressives (enfant coupable) ou péjoratives (enfant anormal); elle préconise une approche psycho-pédagogique et médico-sociale comme fondement de l'hygiène mentale et définit un art moyen, syncrétique, simple, pratique et éclairé auquel sont conviés justice, éducateurs, parents et autres acteurs sociaux.

13253 The DFE Sheffield Bullying Project: a follow-up survey on bully/victim problems in one local education authority with monitoring and evaluation of the actions and interventions taken as a result of the survey.
GBR 1993
Research Date(s): 1991-1993
Smith, P.; Sharp, S.; Ahmad, Y.; Boulton, M.; Cowie, H.; Thomson, D.
Inst: Sheffield University, Department of Psychology, Sheffield S10 2TN, United Kingdom.
Fin: Department for Education.
bullying; antisocial behaviour; discipline
brimades; comportement antisocial; discipline
PROJECT DESCRIPTION
The Department for Education (DFE) Sheffield Bullying Project aims to identify through evaluation, ways in which schools can effectively tackle the problem of bullying. The project follows on from a survey conducted in November 1990 which monitored the nature and extent of bullying in 24 Sheffield schools (number of pupils = 6,758). Twenty-three of these schools, (16 primary, 7 secondary) wished to continue with the intervention project. All of the schools have at a minimum developed a whole-school anti-bullying policy which clarifies for staff, pupils and parents what bullying is and what can be done about it. Other interventions have also been explored. These include: strategies for tackling bullying through the curriculum; strategies for working directly with bullies and victims; and strategies for enhancing the playground environment. Data gathered through regular monitoring, pupil and staff interviews and observation will be combined with information gathered from a follow-up survey in November 1992 to indicate how successful schools have been in reducing levels of bullying, and which interventions work best.

Publ: Sharp, S. & Smith, P.K. Bullying in UK schools: the DES Sheffield Bullying Project. In: *Early Child Development Care*, No 77/1991, pp. 47-55.
Cowie, H. & Sharp, S. Students themselves tackle the problem of bullying. In: *Pastoral Care*, December 1992.
Cowie, H.; Sharp, S. & Smith, P.K. Tackling bullying in schools: the method of common concern. In: *BPS Education Section Review*, No 16/1992, pp. 55-57.

13254   Discipline in Scottish schools.
GBR   1993
Research Date(s): 1987-1991
Munn, P.; Johnstone, M.; Chalmers, V.
Inst: Scottish Council for Research in Education, 15 St John Street, Edinburgh EH8 8JR, United Kingdom.
Fin: Scottish Office Education Department.
discipline; behaviour; class management
discipline; comportement; conduite de la classe
PROJECT DESCRIPTION
   The main focus of this research into classroom and whole-school discipline was on 'effective discipline' in a range of different contexts. Case studies of primary and secondary schools were supplemented by surveys on secondary teachers' and headteachers' views on discipline.
Publ: Munn, P.; Johnstone, M. & Holligan, C. Pupils' perceptions of 'effective disciplinarians'. In: *British Educational Research Journal*, Vol 16, No 2/1990, pp. 191-198.
Johnstone, M. & Munn, P. *Discipline in Scottish secondary schools: a survey.* SCRE Research Report Series No 35, Edinburgh: Scottish Council for Research in Education.

13255   Disruptive behaviour in schools: post Elton Project Sandwell Initiative.
GBR   1993
Research Date(s): 1991-1993
Bovair, K.; Smith, C.; Watts, P.
Sup: Upton, G.
Inst: Birmingham University, School of Education, Edgbaston, Birmingham B15 2TT, United Kingdom; Sandwell Metropolitan Borough Council, Child Guidance Centre, 12 Grange Road, West Bromwich, West Midlands B70 8PD, United Kingdom.
misconduct; antisocial behaviour; discipline
déviance scolaire; comportement antisocial; discipline
PROJECT DESCRIPTION
   The aim of this project is to collect quantitative and qualitative data, in order to illuminate further the nature, causes and consequences of disruptive behaviour in schools. An assessment will be made of the impact of the Elton Report (*Discipline in schools*: the report of the Committee of Enquiry chaired by Lord Elton. Department of Education and Science, 1989) on responses to disruptive behaviour in schools.
   A detailed examination of developments in one local education authority (LEA) over a period of one school year will be carried out. The study will combine survey and case study analyses. The consequences of disruption will be examined in terms of school/LEA responses and subsequent pupil placements.

13256   Emotional and behavioural problems in reception class children.
GBR   1993
Research Date(s): 1989-1992
St James-Roberts, I.; Sing, G.; Papakyriakopoulos, C.
Inst: London University, Institute of Education, Department of Child Development and Primary Education, 20 Bedford Way, London WC1H OAL, United Kingdom.
Fin: Association of Commonwealth Universities; London University Central Research Fund.
behaviour disorder; emotional disorder; problem child; infant
trouble du comportement; trouble affectif; enfant perturbé; enfant du premier âge
PROJECT DESCRIPTION
   The first aim has been to develop instruments which enable reception class teachers to assess emotional and behavioural problems in their pupils. Contextually appropriate, reliable and valid procedures have been developed. The researchers are now studying factors in children, families and classroom contexts which lead to such problems.

13257   Etude longitudinale de l'intervention judiciaire éducative.
FRA   1993
Research Date(s): 1987-
Gazeau, Jean-François.
Inst: Ministère de la Justice, CNRS URA/412, Centre de recherche interdisciplinaire de Vaucresson, 54 rue de Garches, 92420 Vaucresson, France.
juvenile court; juvenile delinquency; decision making; social work; population trends
tribunal pour enfants; délinquance juvénile; prise de décision; travail social; tendances démographiques
PROJECT DESCRIPTION
   Objectifs: Recherche longitudinale suivie sur les décisions éducatives, pénales et civiles, provisoires et définitives, rendues à l'égard des mineurs, portant sur un échantillon exhaustif de mineurs relevant d'une même cohorte de naissance et connus pour décision éducative (c'est à dire qui mandate un travail social) au tribunal pour enfants de Nanterre (les décisions les concernant sont rendues à Nanterre ou ailleurs pendant toute leur minorité).

Méthodologie: Rapport entre nombre de décisions et nombre de mineurs concernés, étude des "doubles dossiers" et de l'interférence entre pénal et civil, analyse des cursus judiciaires, et analyse affinée des statistiques transversales officielles.

13258   Evaluatie van beloftevolle opvangprojecten voor voortijdig schoolverlaten.   (Evaluation of promising projects for early school leavers.)
NLD   1994
Research Date(s): 1992-1993
Eimers, A.
Sup: Hövels, B.
Inst: Instituut voor Toegepaste Sociale wetenschappen (ITS) (Institute for Applied Social Sciences), P.O. Box 9048, 6500 KJ Nijmegen, Netherlands. Katholieke Universiteit Nijmegen (Catholic University of Nijmegen), P.O. Box 9102, 6500 HC Nijmegen, Netherlands
Fin: SVO het Instituut voor Onderzoek van het Onderwijs.
truancy; dropout; guidance; care
école buissonnière; abandon d'études; orientation; soin
PROJECT DESCRIPTION
   Background: One of the results of the review study which the Institute of Applied Social Sciences (ITS) has conducted of the phenomenon of "early school leaving" is a description of promising local projects dealing with dropouts and early school leavers in both a preventive and curative manner. The description does not include information on the effectiveness of the projects.
   Aim: To make a comparison of the effectiveness of the individual projects, viewed in their local context, against the background of the new policy framework for tackling early school leaving described in the White Paper entitled "Profile of the second stage of secondary education".
   Design: An in-depth study will be made of each project as well as an overall comparative analysis. The quantitative part of the case studies will consist of standardized impact measurements among former participants in the projects with the help of questionnaires. Evaluative aspects will be included and the data collected from the former participants will be used to supplement the projects' own archives. The qualitative part of the case studies will focus primarily on the content, organization and structure of each project, the type of participants, and the way each project is embedded in its local environmental context. This involves per project document analyses as well as in-depth interviews with key persons within the project and with relevant people from the local environment.

13259   Family background factors characteristic of victims and bullies in middle childhood.
GBR   1993
Research Date(s): 1990-1991
Smith, P.; Binney, V.; Bowers, L.
Inst: Sheffield University, Department of Psychology, Sheffield S10 2TN, United Kingdom.
Fin: Medical Research Council.
bullying; antisocial behaviour; family environment
brimades; comportement antisocial; milieu familial
PROJECT DESCRIPTION
   Prevalence studies on bullying have emphasised the extent and severity of bully/victim problems in schools, with about 1 in 6 children in South Yorkshire secondary and middle schools reporting being bullied, and 1 in 12 pupils admitting to taking part in such bullying. The immediate and long-term consequences for both bullies and victims is of great concern. At extremes a victim may take his or her life to escape torment, and bullying has been associated with later violent crime and alcohol abuse. The role of family factors is thought to be crucial to the full understanding of the origins and maintenance of bully/victim relations in childhood and adolescence although little evidence exists to implicate a causal relationship between the two.
   The proposed investigation will aim to locate the structural and psychodynamic family factors thought to be characteristic of bullies and victims, as perceived by the children themselves. A sample pool of 170, 9-10 year old children will be used, from which after peer and teacher nominations, 20 children often proposed as bullies, 20 children often nominated as victims, and 20 controls will be selected for further data collection. This will measure the childrens' perceptions of family relations. This procedure will make use of the Family Relations Test, a modified version of the Parental Bonding Instrument, a modified version of the Separation Anxiety Test, and the FAST family sculpt test. Differences between the subject groups will be analysed and the data will be examined for possible subgroups of bullies and victims.

13260   Freedom of choice.
DEU   1993
Research Date(s): 1990-1993
Klemisch-Ahlert, M.
Inst: Universitaet Osnabrueck, FB Wirtschaftswissenschaften, Fachgebiet VWL, insb. Mikrooekonomische Theorie, Rolandstr. 8, D-4500 Osnabrueck.
decision making; freedom; concept; philosophy

prise de décision; liberté; concept; philosophie
PROJECT DESCRIPTION

Inhalt: In dieser Arbeit werden verschiedene bestehende und neu entwickelte Ansaetze zu "Freedom of Choice" verglichen, die den Begriff definieren. Mengen sozialer Alternativen oder Mengen von Entscheidungsmoeglichkeiten sollen im Hinblick auf die Freiheit der Auswahl miteinander verglichen werden.

Vorgehensweise: Axiomatische Charakterisierung des Vergleichs von Mengen sozialer Alternativen; Definition von Axiomensystemen, Existenz- und Eindeutigkeitsbeweise fuer Ordnungen und Mengen; oekonomische undphilosophische Diskussion der Axiome.

13261 The identification of the needs of lesbian and gay students in higher education.
GBR 1993
Research Date(s): 1991-1992
Fahey, W.
Inst: Cheltenham & Gloucester College of Higher Education, Faculty of Education and Health, The Park, Cheltenham GL50 2QF, United Kingdom.
homosexuality; higher education; need; student life
homosexualité; enseignement supérieur; besoin; vie étudiante
PROJECT DESCRIPTION

From a self-selected sample of at least 50 lesbians and gay students currently taking courses in 10 separate institutions of higher education, the authors in this study aim to: examine students' perceptions of their needs, explore the extent to which these needs are currently being met within educational institutions, and develop a strategy to reduce or eliminate inequalities in higher education related to student sexuality. Methodology will include a postal questionnaire followed by a selection of semi-structured interviews with quantitative and qualitative aspects.

13262 The influence of Church of England secondary schools on adolescents' attitudes towards the Church.
GBR 1993
Research Date(s): 1991-1992
Francis, L.
Inst: Trinity College, Carmarthen, Dyfed SA31 3EP, United Kingdom.
religious behaviour; church; pupil attitude; religion
comportement religieux; église; attitude de l'élève; religion
PROJECT DESCRIPTION

Five hundred and forty-six fourth-year pupils attending the four county and one Church of England voluntary schools within the same town completed a detailed questionnaire concerning their religious beliefs, practices and attitudes, together with some information regarding parental religiosity.

After taking into account the influence of sex, social class and parental religiosity, path analysis indicates that the Church of England school exerts neither a positive nor negative influence on the pupils' religious practice, belief or attitudes.

13263 The inter-relationship of cognitive abilities, attitudes, social interaction and performance in early logo learning.
GBR 1993
Research Date(s): 1990-1993
Greenhough, P.
Sup: Hughes, M.; Preece, P.
Inst: Exeter University, School of Education, St Luke's, Heavitree Road, Exeter EX1 2LU, United Kingdom.
Fin: Nuffield Foundation.
social behaviour; didactic use of computer; logo; interaction; cognitive ability; attitude; achievement
comportement social; usage didactique de l'ordinateur; logo; interaction; aptitude cognitive; attitude; rendement
PROJECT DESCRIPTION

This research investigates the inter-relationship of cognitive abilities, attitudinal factors, social interaction and performance in young children. The context of the research is paired learning with a computer and in the first instance focuses on early Logo activities. Seventy-two, Year 3 children worked either in same-sex or mixed pairs for five sessions with the floor Turtle on drawing or driving activities. They also worked for two sessions individually. Prior to the work with the Turtle, the children were assessed on five British Abilities Scales. Prior, during and after the sessions their attitudes to the task, their partner, and gender stereotypes were assessed. All sessions were videotaped and the social interaction transcribed.

13264 Knelpunten en psycho-sociale problematiek bij homo/lesbische adolescenten in onderwijssituaties: voorkomen en preventie. (Incidence and prevention of psycho-social problems among homosexual adolescents in schools.)
NLD 1994
Research Date(s): 1992-1993
Sandfort, Th.G.M.; Kersten, A.
Sup: Kok, W.A.M.
Inst: Interdisciplinair Sociaal-wetenschappelijk Onderzoeksinstituut, Afdeling Onderwijs (ISOR) (Interdisciplinary Research Institute for the Social Sciences, Department of Educational Research), P.O. Box 80140, 3508 TC Utrecht, Netherlands.
Rijksuniversiteit Utrecht (State University of Utrecht), P.O. Box 80125, 3508 TC Utrecht, Netherlands
Fin: SVO het Instituut voor Onderzoek van het Onderwijs.
homosexuality; adolescent; state school
homosexualité; adolescent; école de l'Etat
PROJECT DESCRIPTION

Background: One of the conclusions of a recently completed study on homosexuality in education is that a majority of school heads consider openness about homosexual life styles important. More openness is accompanied by an increased risk of problems for homosexual teachers and especially for gay and lesbian pupils, who find themselves still in the middle of development and identification processes. According to over three quarters of school heads, homosexual pupils are more vulnerable than heterosexual pupils. Research has shown that, in spite of the increasing tolerance of Dutch society, strong feelings of isolation exist among gay and lesbian adolescents. In schools, information about homosexuality and persons with whom homosexual pupils might identify are lacking. As a result, homosexual pupils are prone to feelings of uncertainty and they often feel unable to express their homosexuality. Research is needed to examine the experiences of these pupils.

Aim: To examine the nature, origin, and frequency of problems experienced by gay and lesbian pupils in public-authority schools and to investigate how these problems may lead to problems of a psycho-social nature; to determine to what extent the problems identified are incidental or structural and to what extent they are tied to a specific situation; to describe actions and methods that have been used to prevent or alleviate problems related to homosexuality in schools.

Design: Information will be obtained from 25 counsellors in public-authority secondary schools through questionnaires and interviews. They will be questioned about the incidence of psycho-social problems reported by homosexual pupils and about how the school deals with these problems. They will also be asked to help find pupils who would be prepared to participate in the investigation. Pupils aged 16-18 in vocational schools and academically-oriented schools will be given an anonymous questionnaire about the interaction between homosexual and heterosexual pupils. To gain insight into reactions to violations of group norms concerning sex role behaviour and sexuality, a number of school-context-related situations will be presented to pupils and the responses, in terms of behavioural intentions, will be registered. Thirty homosexual young people - up to 25 years of age - who have left education will be interviewed about the problems they experienced at school. Through self-selection of pupils who have completed the anonymous questionnaire and, if necessary, through advertisements in popular magazines and gay/lesbian magazines or personal appeals through contact persons, it will be attempted to recruit 30 gay/lesbian pupils for an interview.

13265 Lise öğrencilerinin alkol kullanımını etkileyen bazı değişkenler. (The effects of some variables on alcohol abuse among secondary school pupils.)
TUR 1994
Research Date(s): 1990
Tol, Canan.
Sup: Kılıççı, Yadigar.
Inst: Hacettepe Üniversitesi, Eğitim Fakültesi, Psikolojik Hizmetler Bölümü (Hacettepe University, Faculty of Education, Department of Psychological Services), 06532 Beytepe, Ankara, Turkey.
alcoholism; alcohol; family environment; school environment; behaviour
alcoolisme; alcool; milieu familial; milieu scolaire; comportement
PROJECT DESCRIPTION

This research investigated some important variables affecting alcohol abuse among secondary school pupils. The aim was to identify those social and individual characteristics of secondary school pupils and their families that affect the frequency of drinking by pupils.

The sample comprised 747 pupils, randomly chosen from two public secondary schools and one school teaching in a foreign language in Ankara. Data were collected by means of the 20-item questionnaire "The Consumption of Alcohol by High School Students" and a 22-item "Personal Data Sheet" developed by the researcher. Data analysis techniques included the Chi-square technique.

The results of the statistical analysis showed that secondary school boys drink more frequently than girls. Factors that did not affect the frequency of drinking or drinking behaviour were: age, having siblings, incompatibility between parents, peer group, being alone during the first experience with alcohol, feelings of regret after drinking. Factors that did affect drinking frequency or behaviour were: amount of pocket money, parental attitude (children of indifferent or authoritarian parents were more likely to drink alcohol than children of democratic parents), drinking alone (increases the frequency of drinking), the quantity of alcohol consumed each time, drinking to reduce anxiety and boredom (leads to more frequent drinking).

On the basis of the findings, a number of suggestions were made concerning the relations in the family and the school environment.

13266 The nature of relationships between teachers' attitudes and beliefs about educational change in Bermuda and other personal, psychological and educational variables.
GBR 1993
Research Date(s): 1989-1992
Hocking, C.
Sup: Burghes, D.; Harvard, G.
Inst: Exeter University, School of Education, St Luke's, Heavitree Road, Exeter EX1 2LU, United Kingdom; Bermuda Ministry of Education, Department of Education, PO Box HM 1185, Hamilton HM EX, Bermuda.
teacher behaviour; educational reform; Bermuda
comportement de l'enseignant; réforme de l'enseignement; Bermudes
PROJECT DESCRIPTION
The aim of this study is to determine whether there exists a relationship, and the nature of any possible relationship, between teachers' attitudes to educational changes taking place in Bermuda and other personal, psychological or educational variables. The research uses questionnaire investigation to gather data on teachers' age, experience, sex, training, etc., their current feelings about teaching as a job, their preferred psychological functioning and their attitudes to change. The background of educational change against which teachers' attitudes are assessed includes abolition of selection at 11+, introduction of middle level education, non-selective secondary education, and mainstreaming of special needs children.

13267 Negativní vlivy na osobnost učitele a možnosti jejich omezování. (Negative influences on teacher personality and how they may be reduced.)
CSK 1994
Research Date(s): 1992-1994
Paulík, Karel; Fialová, Ivana; Mlčák, Zdeněk; Pavlas, Ivan; Nevřala, Jan; Vašina, Bohumil; Záškodná, Helena.
Sup: Schneiderová, Anna.
Inst: Katedra psychologie Filosofické fakulty Ostravské Univerzity (Ostrava University, Faculty of Arts, Department of Psychology), Reální ul. 5, 701 03 Ostrava, Czech Republic.
Ministerstvo školství, mládeže a tělovýchovy České republiky (Ministry of Education, Youth and Physical Education of the Czech Republic), Karmelitská 8, 110 00 Praha 1, Czech Republic
teacher behaviour; adaptability; adjustment; mental stress
comportement de l'enseignant; adaptabilité; adaptation; tension mentale
PROJECT DESCRIPTION
Aim: This is a study of subjective perceptions of teachers' workloads as a negative factor influencing the professional and social functioning of teachers. Relationships between perceptions of workloads and other internal and external variables will also be examined.
Methods: Questionnaires, inventories, evaluation scales.

13268 Nieuwsgierigheid en exploratief gedrag. (Curiosity and exploratory behaviour.)
NLD 1994
Research Date(s): 1991-1992
Mellink, E.; Lokman, A.H.
Sup: Roede, E. de.
Inst: Stichting Centrum voor Onderwijsonderzoek (SCO) (Centre for Educational Research), Grote Bickersstraat 72, 1013 KS Amsterdam, Netherlands.
Universiteit van Amsterdam (University of Amsterdam), P.O. Box 19268, 1000 GG Amsterdam, Netherlands
Fin: SVO het Instituut voor Onderzoek van het Onderwijs.
behaviour; discovery learning; interest; learning process
comportement; apprentissage par la découverte; intérêt; apprentissage
PROJECT DESCRIPTION
Background: Curiosity and exploratory behaviour are needed to acquire information about the world. They initiate a learning process that is necessary to develop skills and competencies. Research findings suggest that teaching in schools does not stimulate curiosity and exploratory behaviour. Notwithstanding the importance of the concepts of curiosity and exploratory behaviour, they have been relatively neglected in educational research.
Aim: This exploratory study was concerned with a review of the literature on current definitions of the concepts of curiosity and exploratory behaviour. The results will be used for future research and instrument development.
Results: Children are by nature curious and interested in their environment. Teaching in school discourages the development of curiosity and exploratory behaviour. Curiosity is stimulated if there is an emphasis on the learning process itself, in which the pupils themselves can discover the answer to a problem and in which allowance is made for mistakes. Three questionnaires for pupils aged 10 to 12 years have been tested as to their validity and reliability. These questionnaires were found to be unsuitable for use in schools. In the construction of questionnaires measuring curiosity greater account should be taken of level of cognitive development of target group.
(This is an updating of EUDISED no. 43/10378).

Publ: Mellink, E. *Nieuwsgierigheid en exploratief gedrag: een oriënterend literatuuronderzoek naar definities en operationalisaties van de constructen nieuwsgierigheid en exploratief gedrag.* Amsterdam, SCO, 1992, 112p.
Mellink, E. *Nieuwsgierigheid als drijfveer voor leren op school: wat leerkrachten kunnen doen om hun leerlingen te motiveren.* In: *Didaktief,* 6/1992, pp. 29-30.

13269 Přínos tělesné výchovy pro reedukaci mravně narušené mládeže. (The contribution of physical education to the re-education of disruptive youth.)
CSK 1994
Research Date(s): 1992-1993
Vocilka, Miroslav; Švarcová, Iva; Kábrle, Josef.
Sup: Přerovský, Jan.
Inst: Výzkumný ústav pedagogický (Research Institute of Education), Strojírenská 386, 155 21 Praha 5 - Zličín, Czech Republic.
Ministerstvo školství, mládeže a tělovýchovy ČR (Ministry of Education, Youth and Physical Education), Karmelitská 7, 118 13 Praha 1, Czech Republic
juvenile delinquency; deviant behaviour; special education; sport; physical education
délinquance juvénile; comportement déviant; enseignement spécial; sport; éducation physique
PROJECT DESCRIPTION
Aims: (1) To contribute to the understanding of the role of physical education (PE) and sport in the re-education of disruptive youth; (2) to examine the present state of PE and sport in special education institutions; (3) to analyse the level of staff and facilities for PE and sport in these institutions; (4) to examine pupils' interest in PE and sport.
Hypotheses: (1) Levels of staff and facilities for PE in special education institutions are inadequate; (2) disruptive young people prefer team games; (3) disruptive youth have unrealistic aspirations.
Methods: (1) Questionnaire to PE teachers; (2) questionnaire concerning choices and priorities in sports and PE activities; (3) test of pupils' aspiration levels.

Publ: Vocilka, Miroslav. *Přínos tělesné výchovy pro reedukaci mravně narušení mládeže.* Etapová zpráva grantového úkolu MŠMT ČR č. 2 - II - 5 - 92. Listopad 1992. Praha: Výzkumný ústav pedagogický v Praze, 1992.

13270 Problem girls.
GBR 1993
Research Date(s): 1990-1992
Lloyd, G.
Inst: Heriot-Watt University, Moray House Institute of Education, Holyrood Road, Edinburgh EH8 8AQ, United Kingdom.
deviant behaviour; antisocial behaviour; discipline; adolescent; girl
comportement déviant; comportement antisocial; discipline; adolescent; jeune fille
PROJECT DESCRIPTION
The aim of the research is to explore the nature of school-based deviance in adolescent girls and the responses of schools to such deviant behaviour.
Publ: Lloyd, G. (ed.). Chosen with care? - Responses to disturbing and disruptive behaviour. Edinburgh: Moray House, 1992.

13271 Religion and attitude towards drug use among 13-15 year olds.
GBR 1993
Research Date(s): 1990-1992
Francis, L.
Inst: Trinity College, Carmarthen, Dyfed SA31 3EP, United Kingdom.
drug addiction; alcoholism; smoking; youth attitude; religion
toxicomanie; alcoolisme; tabagisme; attitude de la jeunesse; religion
PROJECT DESCRIPTION
A sample of 4,753 thirteen to fifteen year olds attending the third and fourth year classes of twenty-nine secondary schools completed a questionnaire concerned with attitude towards the use of alcohol, butane gas, glue, heroin, marijuana and tobacco, together with indices of religious affiliation, belief and practice.
The data demonstrate that young adolescents' attitudes towards drug use varies considerably from one substance to another and that religiosity is a significant predictor of attitude towards the use of each of the substances included in the survey.

13272 The role of education for citizenship with reference to Zambia.
GBR 1993
Research Date(s): 1985-1994
Small, N.
Sup: Bell, R.; Bown, L.
Inst: Open University, School of Education, Walton Hall, Milton Keynes MK7 6AA, United Kingdom; Glasgow University, Department of Adult and Continuing Education, 8 University Gardens, Glasgow G12 8QQ, United Kingdom.

citizen participation; educational policy; nationality; Zambia
participation du citoyen; politique de l'éducation; nationalité; Zambie
PROJECT DESCRIPTION

The research explores the informal area of education from which, and by which, adults develop a sense of identity at a national level. More positive is the idea and work of 'nation building' which can also arise from educational provision. The context is: What counts as citizenship in states formed in the last century in former British colonial territories in east and central Africa? This offers a comparative background to the main focus on Zambia. Zambia was administered by a chartered company for about a quarter of a century; was the responsibility of the British Colonial Office for forty years as Northern Rhodesia; and has been an independent state in the Commonwealth for a quarter of a century. In that last period, it has faced particular external difficulties, reflecting circumstances in Southern Rhodesia (now Zimbabwe); and from its position economically with regard to South Africa. Internally, copper mining has been the major supplier of exports and of foreign exchange; but a decline in demand and a fall in price have seriously affected the robustness of the economy to finance the expansion of desired infrastructure, and social, health and educational development. The researcher hopes to review the role of education among adults, and indicate if and how it contributes to a commitment of a sense of identity with the state; and whether the adult as citizen is a concept that is consciously pursued by formal and informal agencies.

13273 Schoolgrootte en probleemgedrag van VO-leerlingen. (The relationship between school size and problem behaviour among secondary school pupils.)
NLD 1994
Research Date(s): 1992-1993
Vries, A.M. de.
Inst: RION Instituut voor Onderwijsonderzoek (RION Institute for Educational Research), P.O. Box 1286, 9701 BG Groningen, Netherlands.
Rijksuniversiteit Groningen (State University of Groningen), P.O. Box 72, 9700 AB Groningen, Netherlands
Fin: SVO het Instituut voor Onderzoek van het Onderwijs.
deviant behaviour; pupil; school size; mental health
comportement déviant; élève; dimension de l'école; santé mentale
PROJECT DESCRIPTION

Background: The incidence of dropping out, demotivation, aggression, addiction to stimulants, decaying moral standards, and suicide attempts among secondary school pupils is taking on worrying proportions. The problems are said to occur more frequently in large schools and among immigrant pupils. Research results concerning the relationship between school size and pupil well-being are contradictory. Neither is there clear research evidence linking mental well-being and problem behaviour. This study attempts to cast a clearer light on these issues.

Aim: To examine the relationship between mental well-being and problem behaviour among secondary school pupils on the basis of an analysis of relevant literature; to determine what conditions in the school environment help to improve pupils' well-being.

Design: Relevant literature from various disciplines will be studied. If the findings do not offer a sufficiently sound basis for a clear conclusion, a research question will be formulated for further research.

13274 Schule (k)ein Ort der Gewalt? (Is the school a place of violence?)
AUT 1993
Research Date(s): 1992-1993
Niel, Gerhard.
Inst: Paedagogische Akademie der Dioezese Linz, Salesianumweg 3, A-4020 Linz.
Fin: Bundesministerium fuer Unterricht und Kunst.
violence; frustration; aggressiveness
violence; frustration; agressivité
PROJECT DESCRIPTION

Es werden die folgenden Themen problematisiert: Schulischer Leistungsdruck als Gewalterfahrung; Unterschiedlicher Umgang mit Gewalt in Stadt und Land; Formen der Gewalt in der Schule; Modelle zum Verstaendnis von Gewalt in der Schule.

Es werden Schueler- und Elternfragebogen zum Freizeitverhalten ausgegeben. In die Erhebung werden alle Hauptschueler der Uebungshauptschule der Paedagogischen Akademie und der Hauptschule Andorf einbezogen.

13275 The social context of prayer among 16 year olds.
GBR 1993
Research Date(s): 1990-1992
Francis, L.
Inst: Trinity College, Carmarthen, Dyfed SA31 3EP, United Kingdom.
religious behaviour; religion; family environment; pupil attitude; social environment
comportement religieux; religion; milieu familial; attitude de l'élève; milieu social
PROJECT DESCRIPTION

This study examined the influence of home, church and school on an attitudinal predisposition to pray among 711 sixteen year old adolescents attending Roman Catholic, Church of England and county state maintained schools in England. The results were compared with earlier findings among eleven year olds.

Among sixteen year olds the influence of church is stronger and the influence of parents is weaker.

Publ: Francis, L.J. & Brown, L.B. The predisposition to pray: a study of the social influence on the predisposition to pray among eleven year old children in England. In: Journal of Empirical Theology, Vol 3, No 2/1990, pp. 22-34.

13276 Soziale Kompetenz und Berufserfolg - Qualitaet und Quantitaet sozialer Kontakte und Beziehungen als Voraussetzung fuer beruflichen Erfolg unter den Bedingungen der technischen Entwicklung. (Social competence and occupational success: quality and quantity of social contacts and relations as a prerequisite for occupational success under conditions of technological progress.)
DEU 1993
Research Date(s): 1991-1993
Edinsel, K.; Feldhorst, A.; Koese, B.
Sup: Mackensen, R.
Inst: Technische Universitaet Berlin, FB 02 Gesellschafts- und Planungswissenschaften, Institut fuer Soziologie, Dovestr. 1, D-1000 Berlin 10.
Fin: Deutsche Forschungsgemeinschaft.
social behaviour; social integration; occupational success; occupational choice; career
comportement social; intégration sociale; réussite professionnelle; choix d'une profession; carrière
PROJECT DESCRIPTION

Inhalt: Gegenstand der vorgesehenen Untersuchung ist der Einfluss der sozialen Kompetenz "Kontaktsicherheit" sowie sozialer Kontakte und Beziehungen auf Berufswahl, Ausbildungs- und Arbeitsplatzsuche und auf den beruflichen/ betrieblichen Aufstieg. Die intervenierenden Variablen "Schulausbildung", "Herkunftsbedingungen", "Familientyp" und "Betriebszugehoerigkeit" moderieren die Fragestellung und sind ebenfalls Gegenstand der Untersuchung. Die Untersuchung ist subjektbezogen, handlungstheoretisch orientiert und berufsbiographisch angelegt. Zielgruppen der Untersuchung sind deutsche und tuerkische Arbeiter und Facharbeiter der Berliner Elektroindustrie im Alter von 18 bis 26 Jahren. Die Untersuchung soll methodische und theoretische Luecken der Qualifikations-, Arbeitsmarkt- und Berufsbildungsforschung sowie der Migrationssoziologie ausfuellen. Sie soll zeigen, wie formale, ethnische oder spezifische Barrieren im Berufsverlauf durch soziale Kompetenzen bzw. soziale Kontakte und Beziehungen ueberwunden und schulische und fachliche Defizite ausgeglichen werden (koennen). Es ist beabsichtigt, die Ergebnisse der Studie so zu formulieren, dass sie auch fuer Arbeitsmarkt- und Sozialplanung sowie fuer die Gestaltung von Aus-und Weiterbildungsmassnahmen verwendbar sind. Sie sollen ebenfalls verwendbar sein fuer die Optimierung der Massnahmen zur Kompetenzerhoehung sowie fuer Planung und Foerderung des qualifizierten jungen Nachwuchses der Industrie.

Geographischer Raum: Berlin.

Vorgehensweise: Subjektbezogen; handlungstheoretisch; qualitative Befragung, Typenbildung, quantitative Leitfadengespraeche. Untersuchungsdesign: retrospektive Daten; qualitative Forschung; Erfassung von (egozentrierten) Netzwerken; quantitative Befragung; Akten- und Dokumentenanalyse.

Datengewinnung: Standardisiertes Interview (Stichprobe: 300; deutsche und tuerkische Arbeiter und Facharbeiter; Auswahlverfahren: Zufall). Nichtstandardisiertes Interview (Stichprobe: 80; Typen der ersten Stichprobe; Auswahlverfahren: bewusst). Primaererhebung: Feldarbeit von Mitarbeitern des Projektes durchgefuehrt.

Auswertung: Das SPSS-Paket (SPSS PCplus).

13277 Student attitudes regarding effective teaching behaviours - a teaching practice study.
GBR 1993
Research Date(s): 1991-1993
Preece, P.
Inst: Exeter University, School of Education, St Luke's, Heavitree Road, Exeter EX1 2LU, United Kingdom.
teacher behaviour; teacher education; student teacher; attitude
comportement de l'enseignant; formation des enseignants; élève-maître; attitude
PROJECT DESCRIPTION

An anglicized version of the Teaching Behaviours Questionnaire is to be given to 200+ Post Graduate Certificate in Education (PGCE) secondary students before teaching practice (TP). After TP, quantitative ratings on each student for each category on the standard assessment schedule will be obtained. This should permit the investigation of the factorial structure of the instrument and provide TP performance scores for correlating with scores on the attitude inventory. In a related intervention exercise, half of the science student group will receive feedback on the research evidence concerning teaching behaviour covered in the inventory. By using the other half of the group as a control, the effect of the intervention on TP performance will be investigated.

13278 Teachers' attitudes towards children's behaviour problems in nursery classes in Greece and management strategies used.
GBR 1993
Research Date(s): 1991-
Papatheodorou, T.
Sup: Ramasut, A.
Inst: University of Wales College of Cardiff, School of Education, 42 Park Place, Cardiff CF1 3BB, United Kingdom.
Fin: Greek Government.
behaviour; misconduct; teacher behaviour; discipline; behaviour disorder; nursery school; Greece
comportement; déviance scolaire; comportement de l'enseignant; discipline; trouble du comportement; école maternelle; Grèce
PROJECT DESCRIPTION
This study investigates teachers' attitudes towards children's behaviour problems in nursery classes in Greece and the management strategies used by them. The research arose out of personal experiences as a nursery school teacher in Greece, together with data collected on behaviour problems in preschool children, which has now prompted this further investigation of teachers' attitudes and coping strategies.

From a review of the relevant literature it was found that the age at which children begin to present behavioural problems in schools is getting lower, and that a significant proportion of children who have difficulties on entering school are still having difficulties later in their school life. Furthermore, it is believed that the way teachers view and treat children is of crucial significance in the matter of disruptive behaviour. Additionally, the notion for early intervention which currently dominates education programmes - especially those of nursery education - makes the study of behaviour difficulties in early childhood an urgent and dominant issue in the field.

The aims of the study are to examine: (1) the types and prevalence of children's behaviour problems, according to the degree of seriousness; (2) the factors associated with teachers' attitudes towards children's behaviour problems; (3) how teachers manage children's behaviour problems; (4) what kind of help is available to nursery teachers, when children display serious and persistent behaviour problems; (5) how nursery teachers would like/wish to see their nursery school operating in order to prevent or to manage pupils' behaviour problems, more effectively; and (6) some of the theoretical and practical implications of the present study.

For the purpose of the study, a questionnaire was constructed, with items elicited from nursery teachers in Greece. The sample of teachers (N=225) was selected from nursery schools located in large urban, small urban and rural areas. Factors such as the type of school and the socioeconomic status of the location were also taken into consideration. Each nursery teacher will complete the questionnaire for the two pupils whom they perceived to exhibit the most serious behaviour problems in their classroom (pupil sample N=450).

13279 Teachers' morale and teachers' conditions of service.
GBR 1993
Research Date(s): 1988-1992
Saran, R.; Busher, H.
Inst: London University, Institute of Education, Department of Policy Studies, 20 Bedford Way, London WC1H 0AL, United Kingdom; Loughborough University of Technology, Department of Education, Loughborough LE11 3TU, United Kingdom.
Fin: Leverhulme Trust.
teacher behaviour; educational legislation; teaching profession; working conditions
comportement de l'enseignant; législation scolaire; profession d'enseignant; conditions de travail
PROJECT DESCRIPTION
The purpose of this research is to explore the impact of recent legislation on teachers. Methods used include interviews in different local education authorities (LEAs) at primary and secondary school level, and at LEA level, through the periods 1987/1988 and 1990/1991.

Conclusions reached are that: teachers are demoralised; the management style of headteachers makes a difference; the paradoxes of power, not least that of trade union power, has been strengthened at institutional level whilst being weakened at national level.

Publ: Busher, H. & Saran, R. Teachers' conditions of employment: a study in the politics of school management. London: Kogan Page, 1992.

13280 Verhaltensauffaellig. Was nun? (Abnormal behaviour. What to do?)
AUT 1993
Research Date(s): 1991-1992
Sedlak, Franz; Eder, Anselm; Fuerst, Jutta; Gruber, Gisela; Gold-Krautgartner, Claudia; Reinelt, Toni.
Inst: Abteilung fuer Schulpsychologie und Bildungsberatung, Minoritenplatz 5, A-1014 Wien.
Bundesministerium fuer Unterricht und Kunst, Minoritenplatz 5, A-1014 Wien

deviant behaviour; maladjusted; social behaviour
comportement déviant; inadapté; comportement social
PROJECT DESCRIPTION
Es wird geklaert, was unter Verhaltensstoerungen bzw. - auffaelligkeiten zu verstehen ist. Die Meinungen darueber sind naemlich aeusserst vielfaeltig und zum Teil auch oberflaechlich kontrovers. Insgesamt werden 16 verschiedene Beispiele dafuer angefuehrt, wie unterschiedlich das Verstaendnis von Verhaltensauffaelligkeiten und -stoerungen sein kann. Anschliessend wird dafuer plaediert, zunaechst nur von Verhaltensauffaelligkeiten und nicht gleich von Verhaltensstoerungen zu sprechen. Verhaltensauffaelligkeiten werden dabei als Beziehungspathologien angesehen. Es wird ein Ueberblick ueber die anthropologische, semantische, aetiologische und praktische Dimension von Verhaltensauffaelligkeiten gebracht.

Publ: Sedlak, Franz (Hrsg.). *Verhaltensauffaellig. Was nun?* Paedagogischer Verlag Eugen Ketterl, Wien 1992.

13281 Young people and illicit drugs.
GBR 1993
Research Date(s): 1991-1992
Ridley, L.
Sup: Coffield, F.
Inst: Durham University, School of Education, Leazes Road, Durham DH1 1TA, United Kingdom.
Fin: Department of Health; Northern Regional Health Authority.
narcotic; adolescence; drug addiction; health education; youth attitude; behaviour
drogue; adolescence; toxicomanie; éducation sanitaire; attitude de la jeunesse; comportement
PROJECT DESCRIPTION
The aims of the research are: (1) to produce a clear picture of young people's knowledge and attitudes towards illicit drug taking; (2) to identify the main sources of their information; (3) to assess the major influences in determining whether they accept offers of drugs and become engaged in experimental use. As a result of the information gained, a health promotion publicity campaign will be devised, aimed at the primary prevention of illicit drug use among young people. The method is ethnographic in principle and uses the research technique of single sex discussion groups. The participants are young people at three age levels of 12/13, 14/15 and 16/18. The discussion groups are taped and held in contrasting areas within Tyneside, Durham, Cumbria and Cleveland.

25 HEALTH – SANTE – GESUNDHEIT

13282 The assessment and statementing of children with emotional and behavioural difficulties: child and parent perspectives.
GBR 1993
Research Date(s): 1989-1993
Armstrong, D.
Sup: Galloway, D.
Inst: Lancaster University, Department of Educational Research, Cartmel College, Bailrigg, Lancaster LA1 4YW, United Kingdom.
personality assessment; behaviour disorder; emotional disorder
diagnostic de personnalité; trouble du comportement; trouble affectif
PROJECT DESCRIPTION
A sample of 29 children, who were being assessed under the Education Act 1981 because of emotional and behavioural difficulties, was identified for an in-depth case study of the assessment procedures. The research focused in particular on the perspectives of the children and their parents. The research had three aims: (1) to examine the perspectives of children and their parents on the procedures for assessing special educational needs; (2) to describe and provide a theoretical account of the concept of emotional and behavioural difficulties informed by the perspectives of children and their parents; (3) to describe and provide a theoretical analysis of sources of conflict and agreement between clients and professionals and to consider the implications of these for conceptualisations of the client-professional relationship.

Publ: Armstrong, D.; Galloway, D. & Tomlinson, S. Decision-making in psychologists' professional interviews. In: *Educational Psychology in Practice*, Vol 7, No 2/1991, pp. 82-87.
Armstrong, D. & Galloway, D. On being a client: conflicting persectives on assessment. In: Booth, T.; Swann, W.; Masterson, M. & Potts, P. (eds). *Policies for diversity in education*. London: Routledge/Open University, 1992.

13283 Les Centres médico-psycho-pédagogiques (CMPP), 1945-1975.
FRA 1993
Research Date(s): 1990-
Peyre, Vincent; Tétard, Françoise; Barral, Catherine; Mandelbaum, Françoise.
Inst: Ministère de la Justice, CNRS URA/412, Centre de recherche interdisciplinaire de Vaucresson, 54 rue de Garches, 92420 Vaucresson, France.
prevention; deviant behaviour; historical method; youth policy; psycho-educational method
prévention; comportement déviant; méthode historique; politique de la jeunesse; rééducation psychologique
PROJECT DESCRIPTION
Objectifs: Le centre psycho-pédagogique (qui deviendra centre médico-psycho-pédagogique) est une "création" institutionnelle de l'après-seconde guerre. Le premier, qui servira de modèle et de référence, est le CPP Claude Bernard, créé par André Berge et Georges Mauco en 1945. Dès le départ, le CMPP se place à l'interface entre Ministère de l'éducation nationale et Ministère de la santé. Il sera le creuset où collaboreront psychiatres, psychanalystes, puis psychologues, rééducateurs, orthophonistes, etc. Dès 1948 est créée l'Association française des CPP, elle sera reconnue d'utilité publique en 1963. A partir de 1971 démarre un organisme fédérateur concurrent du précédent: l'Association nationale des CMPP. A partir de 1964, le mode de financement est redéfini, et c'est le Vème Plan qui orchestrera le développement de cette structure. En 1972, les effets de la sectorisation se font sentir.

Méthodologie: Analyse historique et sociologique de la création des CMPP et de leur développement, à partir des archives des Associations des CMPP.

13284 Erevna anamesa stous Ellines Foitites stin opoia erevnate to epipedo ton gnoseon tous stis aities kai tin prolipsi tou karkinou. (A study of students' knowledge of cancer etiology and prevention.)
GRC 1994
Research Date(s): 1992-1993
Athanasiou, K.; Makris, G.; Charalampopoulos, K.A.
Inst: Paidagogiko Tmima Dimotikis Ekpaidefsis, Aristoteleio Panepistimio Thessalonikis (School of Education, Department of Elementary Studies, Aristotelian University of Thessaloniki), 54006 Thessaloniki, Greece.
Fin: EEC, Program "Europe against Cancer".
health; knowledge level; student; university; preventive medicine; disease
santé; niveau de connaissances; étudiant; université; médecine préventive; maladie
PROJECT DESCRIPTION
A 70-item questionnaire was distributed among 1,230 students of the Aristotelian University of Thessaloniki, Greece, to examine students' levels of knowledge of cancer etiology (which factors are considered as carcinogenic, how much do they contribute to cancer, etc.), and possibilities of prevention. The research also examined aspects of student behaviour that may be considered to reduce or increase the risk of cancer.

Analysis of the responses shows that 79.5% of students believe that cancer could be prevented. 7.8% believe nutrition to be one of the major factors related to cancer. 30.7% believe the major external factor related to carcinogenesis is radiation; 35.5% believe it is smoking; 5.9% believe it is the work environment. 5.2% believe cancer is usually inherited, while 3.1% relate cancer to viruses. 82.8% of students believe that air pollution is the most important factor contributing to lung cancer (compared to the actual figure of 1-2%), while 82.8% have never heard about radon risks. Nevertheless, 99.4% know about the depletion of the ozone layer and the implications it has for health, especially skin cancer. More than 96% know that sunbathing is dangerous, but 38.1% said to lie in the sun for up to one hour at a time, 16.55% for up to two hours and 8% for more than two hours. Nearly 100% of students correctly assumed that cancer is not contagious. Nearly 80% assumed correctly that the main cause of cancer is not genetic. Only 1% knew that drinking alcohol combined with smoking may cause cancer of the oesophagus and/or the pharynx. Other questions concerned eating, drinking and smoking habits.

The general conclusion of the research is that Greek students have a general and superficial knowledge of these matters, which they mostly get from newspapers and television. They lack the systematic information that could be provided through a health education course at school.

13285 Health care of primary school children.
GBR 1993
Research Date(s): 1991
Mayall, B.
Inst: London University, Institute of Education, Department of Policy Studies, Social Science Research Unit, 20 Bedford Way, London WC1H OAL, United Kingdom.
Fin: Nuffield Foundation.
health; primary school; parent role; teacher role
santé; école primaire; rôle des parents; rôle de l'enseignant
PROJECT DESCRIPTION
The project will study the perspectives of parents, teachers and children themselves on the division of labour and responsibility between children and adults for child health care.
Publ: Mayall, B. The health care of primary school children. Report to the Nuffield Foundation, 1991.

13286 I epidrasi tis didaskalias tou mathimatos tis Ikiakis Ikonomias sti diatrofi ton mathiton kata ta dialimata. (The impact of home economics on pupil nutrition during school breaks.)
CYP 1993
Research Date(s): 1991-1992
Choratta, Eleni.
Sup: Papanastasiou, Constantinos.
Inst: Pedagogiko Instituto (Pedagogical Institute), P.O. Box 512, Nicosia, Cyprus.
nutrition; food; girl; eating habit; home economics
nutrition; aliment; jeune fille; habitude alimentaire; économie domestique
PROJECT DESCRIPTION
This is an updating of the corresponding entry reported in issue 45 of the EUDISED R & D Bulletin.

The results of the research study on girl pupils' nutrition during school breaks are as follows. (1) During breaks at school, girls consume different kinds of food that contain colouring agents, for instance juice drinks, sweets, chewing gum. They eat many kinds of food that are basically made of minced meat. Over one third of the sample consumes food that contains a lot of sugar: sweets, ice-creams etc. (2) There is no difference between pupils in private schools and pupils in government schools as far as their food preferences are concerned. (3) The kind of food preferred by the pupils in the sample contains the necessary proteins for their development as well as the necessary carbohydrates for their energy and the protection of their organism. However, pupils take more of these compo-

nents than they need. They also take in more fat and sugar than they need and this may have a detrimental effect on their health. As pupils grow older, they spend more money on their nutrition.

13287 An investigation into the therapeutic relationship and implications for speech-language therapy training.
GBR 1993
Research Date(s): 1990-1995
Eastwood, J.
Sup: Mason, R.; Denscombe, M.
Inst: De Montford University, PO Box 143, Leicester LE1 9BH, United Kingdom; University of Central England in Birmingham, Perry Barr, Birmingham B42 2SU, United Kingdom.
speech therapy; speech training
orthophonie; éducation de la parole
PROJECT DESCRIPTION
Student training in speech-language therapy comprises theoretical and practical components. Theories are largely borrowed from other disciplines such as psychology, linguistics and medicine, but practical work with communicatively impaired individuals is an important part of training. The theory of therapy is, however, poorly understood.

This research will examine the theory or philososphy and practice of therapy in the literature and in a variety of in situ settings where communicatively impaired individuals receive treatment from speech-language therapists. The aim of the research is to analyse and clarify existing theories of therapy and to develop new systems and methods or models for training speech-language therapy students.
Publ: C.N.A.A. Briefing Paper No. 23. A survey of supervised work experience in speech therapy, 1990.

13288 Irrationalité des comportements: obstacle ou moteur d'une prévention efficace; l'approche des professionnels de la prévention du SIDA.
FRA 1993
Research Date(s): 1992-1993
Parisot, Denis.
Inst: Sciences de l'homme et de la société appliquées - Concept, Villa les Violettes, 66 Bd Edouard Herriot, 06200 Nice, France.
Fin: Agence nationale de recherche sur le SIDA.
prevention; sexually transmitted disease; sexual behaviour; health service personnel; high risk group
prévention; maladie sexuellement transmissible; comportement sexuel; personnel médical; groupe à risque
PROJECT DESCRIPTION
Objectifs: Il s'agit de connaître les conduites irrationnelles en matière de prise de risque pour intégrer les dimensions de la quête de sens dans les modèles d'action préventive et de communication.

Méthodologie: Enquête ethnographique par entretiens approfondis et analyse de documents écrits, supports de communication auprès des professionnels de la santé. Terrain: une vingtaine d'équipes de recherche-action en Europe du sud, au contact de publics à haut risque de contamination, une cinquantaine de médecins et infirmiers libéraux des Alpes Maritimes.

13289 Pratiques professionnelles des infirmières en milieu scolaire.
CHE 1994
Research Date(s): 1992-1993
Osiek-Parisod, Françoise; Pasche, Geneviève.
Inst: Service de la recherche sociologique du Département de l'instruction publique, 8 rue du 31-Décembre, 1207 Genève, Suisse.
school doctor; health service personnel; public education
médecin scolaire; personnel médical; enseignement public
PROJECT DESCRIPTION
Cette recherche vise à décrire et à comprendre certains aspects de l'expérience professionnelle des infirmières en milieu scolaire. Leur activité se situe en effet dans un champ relativement complexe, au carrefour de trois univers et donc de trois logiques qui peuvent être contradictoires, voire conflictuelles: l'univers de la profession (ensemble de savoirs, de valeurs et de pratiques spécifiques), l'univers de l'école (vue à la fois comme organisation et comme système éducatif), l'univers des usagers (de milieux et de cultures différents) auprès desquels elles interviennent. Pour s'orienter dans ces systèmes de contraintes, les infirmières mobilisent des représentations (notamment professionnelles), élaborent des stratégies de positionnement à l'intérieur du système scolaire, s'impliquent dans des interactions avec des enfants et des familles, où la dimension psychosociale est au premier plan.

La recherche s'inscrit dans le cadre théorique de la sociologie de l'action qui implique une méthode active (sociologie d'intervention) élaborée par Alain Touraine et ses collaborateurs, notamment François Dubet. Cette méthode pose pour principe que les acteurs doivent être partie prenante de la démarche d'analyse (passage d'un statut d'objet de recherche à celui de sujet), ce qui les amène à faire, avec les sociologues, l'auto-analyse de leurs pratiques.

Partir de l'expérience professionnelle des infirmières scolaires (personnes peu "étudiées" mais qui ont leur importance dans le système scolaire) pour "regarder" l'école, c'est aussi adopter un point de vue différent de celui des écoliers ou des enseignants. C'est une manière de nous renseigner sur l'organisation scolaire, dans son fonctionnement interne et dans ses rapports avec d'autres organisations, relevant - dans le cas présent - du système de santé.

13290 The psychological treatment of emotionally and behaviourally disordered children within a special school setting: a conceptual, experimental and survey analysis.
GBR 1993
Research Date(s): 1987-1991
Smith, A.
Sup: Thomas, J.
Inst: Loughborough University of Technology, Department of Education, Loughborough LE11 3TU, United Kingdom.
therapy; special education; special school; emotional disorder; behaviour disorder
thérapie; enseignement spécial; centre d'éducation spéciale; trouble affectif; trouble du comportement
PROJECT DESCRIPTION
After reviewing the residential treatment of emotionally and behaviourally disturbed children, the author surveys present provision and therapy in a national sample of schools and homes, and concludes with an analysis and evaluation of family therapy in a case study of one such school.

13291 Reading by the blind: Braille and Moon.
GBR 1993
Research Date(s): 1985-
Tobin, M.
Inst: Birmingham University, School of Education, Research Centre for the Education of the Visually Handicapped, Edgbaston, Birmingham B15 2TT, United Kingdom.
Fin: Birmingham University; Royal National Institute for the Blind.
finger reading; blind; braille
lecture tactile; aveugle; braille
PROJECT DESCRIPTION
A series of experiments are being undertaken on various aspects of tactile reading by blind children and adults. Experimental comparisons are being made among alternative letter shapes with the aim of producing a more legible tactile code for older adults and for those with poor tactual ability. For Braille, measurements are being made of Braille reading speed, accuracy, and comprehension among blind school children; experimental comparisons are also being made to evaluate alternative 'papers' on to which Braille can be embossed. Trials are also being conducted on methods to enable sighted adult volunteers to teach reading and writing of Moon-type to newly-blinded adults.
Publ: Cooper, A.; Davies, B.T.; Lawson-Williams, N. & Tobin, M.J. An examination of natural and synthetic papers for embossing Braille. In: *The New Beacon*, Vol LXIX, No 823/1985, pp. 325-328, November.
Tobin, M.J.; Burton, P.; Davies, B.T. & Guggenheim, J. An experimental investigation of the effects of cell size and spacing in Braille - with some possible implications for the newly-blind adult learner. In: *The New Beacon*, Vol LXX, No 829/1989, pp. 133-135, May.
Tobin, M.J. & Hill, E.W. Harnessing the community: Moonscript, the Moonwriter and sighted volunteers. In: *British Journal of Visual Impairment*, Vol VII, No 1/1989, pp. 3-5.

13292 Studio statistico sulla prevenzione carie dentale e menomazioni visive in Abruzzo. (Statistical study of compulsory school children in Abruzzo concerning the prevention of tooth decay and eye disorders.)
ITA 1994
Research Date(s): 1988-1992
Iorio, Paola; Marinucci, M.C.; Azzarita, F.; Ghirlanda, C.
Sup: Di Orio, Ferdinando.
Inst: Cattedra di Statistica Sanitaria, Dipartimento di Scienze, Tecnologie Biomediche e di Biometria (Health Statistics Institute, Department of Science, Biomedical Technology and Biometry), Collemaggio, 67100 L'Aquila, Italy.
Università degli Studi dell'Aquila (University of Aquila), Piazza Rivera 1, 67100 L'Aquila, Italy
Fin: Istituto Regionale di Ricerca Sperimentazione Aggiornamento Educativi d'Abruzzo - IRRSAE.
preventive medicine; prevention; health education; dental inspection; school health services; vision defect
médecine préventive; prévention; éducation sanitaire; contrôle dentaire; médecine scolaire; trouble de la vue
PROJECT DESCRIPTION
Aim: The project is aimed at early prevention and health education.
Hypothesis: Problems in dental and visual health can lead to poor school performance and social difficulties.
Design: (1) Epidemiological statistical research; (2) diagnosis; (3) planning of a rehabilitation programme; (4) checking of the results of rehabilitation after a period of time.

Sample: 1,500 children in compulsory schools in the provinces of Aquila, Chieti, Pescara, and Teramo in the region of Abruzzo.

26 HANDICAP – HANDICAP – BEHINDERUNG

13293 The aetiology and treatment of selective mutism (children who do not talk in school).
GBR 1993
Research Date(s): 1975-
Sluckin, A.; Foreman, N.; Herbert, M.
Inst: Leicester University, Department of Psychology, University Road, Leicester LE1 7RH, United Kingdom.
dumbness; speech handicapped; behaviour disorder
mutité; handicapé de la parole; trouble du comportement
PROJECT DESCRIPTION
This research analyses the phenomenon of the child who does not talk in school despite having age-appropriate speech at home. Data on 25 such cases, including details of home background, exposure to more than one language, age at referral and number of school terms spent mute, has been accumulated. The research also involves scrutinisation of the treatment programmes to which children were exposed, in particular the extent to which behavioural treatment methods were incorporated.
Statistical analysis revealed that those children having made little progress at follow-up were those having a clinical psychopathology in the immediate family (often maternal depression), and those having been given standard remedial programmes in school without a behavioural component. The results suggest that a subgroup of selective mute children can be identified that is likely to persist in selectivity of speaking, and that would benefit from the early application of treatment methods having a behavioural content.
Current research is aimed at extending the data to a larger sample, analysing more closely the quality of speech shown by selective mute children in the home environment, and assessing quality of speech in the school environment on recovery. It is hoped to develop procedures for assessing the possible role of behavioural inhibition in the aetiology of the condition. The work may have import for the testing of children who are reluctant to speak under National Curriculum arrangements.

13294 AIDS Education and Research Trust (AVERT) HIV/AIDS and Nursing project.
GBR 1993
Research Date(s): 1992-1994
Whitty, G.

Inst: London University, Institute of Education, Department of Policy Studies, Health and Education Research Unit, 20 Bedford Way, London WC1H OAL, United Kingdom.
Fin: AIDS Education and Research Trust (AVERT).
sexually transmitted disease; health service personnel; guidance; information
maladie sexuellement transmissible; personnel médical; orientation; information
PROJECT DESCRIPTION

Following Phase I of this project (a qualitative study of student nurses' lay beliefs of Human Immunodeficiency and Acquired Immune Deficiency Syndrome (HIV and AIDS) conducted between September 1991 and September 1992) Phase II will: (1) produce and disseminate policy recommendations detailing how HIV/AIDS might best be addressed on Project 2000 courses; (2) provide curriculum guidance for lecturers, nurse tutors and clinical teachers on how HIV/AIDS might best be addressed on Project 2000 courses and in allied clinical practice; (3) produce a booklet of information and guidance for student nurses.

13295 Alternatives to print for visually impaired students.
GBR 1993
Research Date(s): 1989-1991
Vincent, T.; Child, D.
Inst: Open University, Institute of Educational Technology, Walton Hall, Milton Keynes MK7 6AA, United Kingdom.
Fin: The Mercers' Company; Clothworkers' Foundation.
blind; visually handicapped; information technology; braille; teaching aid
aveugle; handicapé visuel; technologie de l'information; braille; moyen d'enseignement
PROJECT DESCRIPTION

This research will examine whether improved access to textual material could be provided to visually disabled students through use of new information technology. This project concerns investigation of three formats for material which could be produced easily with the aid of new technology. They are: enlarged print, braille and synthetic speech. The final result will be sets of guidelines relating to each of these possibilities indicating how best they can be exploited. This research has included an investigation into the use of compact disc technology (CD ROM) together with hypertext retrieval systems and synthetic speech environments to give interactive access to text in an electronic form.

13296 Ankara Eğitilebilir Çocuklar Mesleki Eğitim Okulu'ndaki çocukların mesleki eğitime yönelik tutumları. (The attitudes of pupils in the Ankara Vocational School for Educable Mentally Retarded Children towards vocational education.)
TUR 1994
Research Date(s): 1988-1990
Cavkaytar, Atilla.
Sup: Özsoy, Yahya.
Inst: Anadolu Üniversitesi, Sosyal Bilimler Enstitüsü (University of Anatolia, Institute of Social Sciences), Eğitim Fakültesi, Yunusemre Kampusu, Eskişehir, Turkey.
mental retardation; vocational education; educability; pupil attitude; special school
retard intellectuel; enseignement professionnel; éducabilité; attitude de l'élève; centre d'éducation spéciale
PROJECT DESCRIPTION

Mentally retarded children cannot benefit from normal educational provisions due to their impaired mental functions. In Turkey educational provision for such children is limited to pre-school, primary and post-primary levels. Post-primary education takes place at so-called "vocational schools for educable mentally retarded children". These schools offer vocational training programmes for mentally retarded children only.

This study aimed to investigate the attitudes of children attending these schools towards vocational training and to establish whether these attitudes are influenced by certain variables. The study was limited to the attitudes measured by an inventory developed for this purpose and to children attending the Ankara Eğitilebilir Çocuklar İş Okulu (Ankara Vocational School for Educable Mentally Retarded Children).

Results: (1) The pupils have a positive attitude towards their school, the staff, and the teaching methods used. Attitudes are less clear during workshop and school hours. (2) Pupils' attitudes towards vocational training are not influenced by age, sex or intelligence quotient. (3) Pupils perform better in home economics than in woodworking. (4) A relationship appears to exist between pupils' attitudes towards vocational training and achievement in home economics. No relationship was found between attitudes towards vocational training and performance in woodworking.

13297 Approche socio-linguistique et historique des emplois de la notion d'intégration dans le secteur professionnel de l'éducation spéciale.
FRA 1993
Research Date(s): 1986-1990
Rossignol, Christian.

Inst: Université de Strasbourg I, UFR des Sciences du comportement, CNRS URA/668, Laboratoire de recherche Production et effets de la parole et du langage, Laboratoire de psycholinguistique, 12 rue Goethe, 67000 Strasbourg, France.
handicapped; special education; social integration; concept analysis
handicapé; enseignement spécial; intégration sociale; analyse conceptuelle
PROJECT DESCRIPTION

Objectifs: Le maintien ou le retour des personnes qualifiées de "handicapés", "inadaptés" ou "marginaux" dans les institutions ordinaires de travail et de vie est devenu une nécessité pour la cohérence du corps social et un impératif économique. Cet objectif a été élevé au rang d'obligation nationale par la loi du 30 juin 1975. Une analyse des discours médico-sociaux construits autour de la notion d'intégration amène à faire l'hypothèse que ce discours intégratif, tant par les effets subjectifs qu'il produit chez ceux à qui il est proposé comme modèle et qui y adhèrent, que par les pratiques, les procédures administratives et les dispositifs institutionnels qu'il contribue à pérenniser, constitue l'un des obstacles majeurs à la réalisation de cet objectif.

Résultats: On observe que par glissement de sens et confusion des termes, l'objectif pratique qui était de permettre aux personnes en difficulté d'accéder à une maîtrise, relative mais réelle, de leur devenir, a été annexé sous forme de valeur et ennobli en forme de finalité en soi par une morale sociale. Il en est résulté un discours intégratif qui semble bien se situer en continuité et non en rupture par rapport aux discours antérieurs sur l'"assistance". Il tient lieu de théorie explicative et occupe la place d'une élaboration conceptuelle à laquelle il fait obstacle.

Publ: Rossignol, Christian. Recherche scientifique et travail social: Histoire d'une malédiction ou malédiction de l'histoire. In: *Les cahiers du CTNERHI*, 1988, 36, pp. 49-63.
Rossignol, Christian. Intégration de la dimension sociale du problème aux incidences subjectives du langage. In: *Media social*, 1988, n° 1, Hors série, pp. 18-34.
Rossignol, Christian. Quelques repères pour une approche sociolinguistique et historique des emplois de la notion d'intégration dans le secteur professionnel du travail social. In: *Avis de recherche*, 1990.

13298 The assessment of children with emotional and behavioural difficulties (EBD).
GBR 1993
Research Date(s): 1991-1992
Farrell, P.
Inst: Manchester University, School of Education, Centre for Educational Guidance and Special Needs, Oxford Road, Manchester M13 9PL, United Kingdom.
emotional disorder; behaviour disorder; diagnostic test; psychodiagnostics; assessment
trouble affectif; trouble du comportement; test de diagnostic; psychodiagnostic; appréciation
PROJECT DESCRIPTION

This is a case study using qualitative research methods, 16 cases in all. Professionals, parents and children were interviewed from receipt of referral until the conclusion. The main areas of the research are to look at the decision-making processes which affect the assessment and intervention of children's referral as having emotional and behavioural difficulties.

13299 Assessment of students with disabilities or learning difficulties.
GBR 1993
Research Date(s): 1992-1993
Dee, L.
Inst: London University, Institute of Education, 20 Bedford Way, London WC1H OAL, United Kingdom.
Fin: Further Education Unit.
handicapped; learning difficulty; special education; post-compulsory education; assessment
handicapé; difficulté de l'apprentissage; enseignement spécial; enseignement postobligatoire; appréciation
PROJECT DESCRIPTION

An investigation into current assessment procedures used by colleges of further education (FE) to identify the learning support needs of young people and adults with disabilities or learning difficulties, with a view to producing guidelines for good practice.

13300 AVERT AIDS: working with young people project.
GBR 1993
Research Date(s): 1992-1993
Whitty, G.; Aggleton, P.
Inst: London University, Institute of Education, Department of Policy Studies, Health and Education Research Unit, 20 Bedford Way, London WC1H OAL, United Kingdom.
Fin: AIDS Education and Research Trust (AVERT).
sexually transmitted disease; health education; teacher; training need
maladie sexuellement transmissible; éducation sanitaire; enseignant; besoin de formation
PROJECT DESCRIPTION

This project extends earlier work which researched the Human Immunodeficiency Virus/Acquired Immune Deficiency Syndrome (HIV/AIDS) training needs of adults who work with young people in youth service settings. A number of needs were identified. These ranged from information on social and medical issues to ways in which young people may be helped to learn about HIV infection and AIDS. The findings were disseminated via a resource for youth workers.

The current project aims to develop the work to include the needs of teachers in secondary schools. It will : (1) research the needs of teachers in relation to classroom-based activity on HIV and AIDS; (2) compare these needs with those of workers in youth service settings; (3) identify ways in which teachers might best support and enable pupils in learning about the medical and social issues associated with HIV and AIDS. The projects findings will be disseminated via an updated resource package which emphasises participatory training within a clearly defined equal opportunities framework.

13301 CD ROM as a curriculum delivery medium for blind and partially sighted learners.
GBR 1993
Research Date(s): 1991-1993
Vincent, T.
Inst: Open University, Institute of Educational Technology, Walton Hall, Milton Keynes MK7 6AA, United Kingdom.
Fin: Department for Education; Open University; Fund for Blind and Partially Sighted.
visually handicapped; blind; CD rom; didactic use of computer
handicapé visuel; aveugle; CD-ROM; usage didactique de l'ordinateur
PROJECT DESCRIPTION

The potential for using CD ROM has been explored within the Open University to provide blind students with access to course material and related books. A project funded by the Department for Education takes access to curriculum materials a step further and, by providing speech output and large character interfaces to existing CD ROM applications, enables learners to control the search for information as well as to read it. The process of identifying and using relevant material is required by most areas of the National Curriculum. Providing access to CD ROM publications offers a chance for this to be carried out independently.

Four schools and one college are involved in the project, covering a wide range of age and ability. Similar workstations are used in each location which are based on an IBM compatible PC with CD ROM drive, and enabling devices and software to produce large screen print and/or speech output. Each location has chosen a number of CD ROMs (such as *Times/Sunday Times* and *Grolier Encyclopaedia*) that are relevant to the curriculum. Enabling software has been prepared for each CD ROM, and training has been provided for teachers both in terms of the functionality of the hardware and software, as well as the most important aspect of how this technology can give new or enhanced access to the curriculum.

Publ: Hawkridge, D. & Vincent, T. *Learning difficulties and computers: access to the curriculum.* London: Jessica Kingsley Publishers, 1992.

13302 Communication problems of blind students in higher education.
GBR 1993
Research Date(s): 1990-1991
Hinton, R.; Wild, G.
Inst: Loughborough University of Technology, Department of Education, Loughborough LE11 3TU, United Kingdom.
Fin: Leverhulme Trust.
blind; visually handicapped; teaching aid; access to education
aveugle; handicapé visuel; moyen d'enseignement; accès à l'éducation
PROJECT DESCRIPTION

As a result of its experience in producing tactile diagrams, the department has in recent years been asked to help several blind students in higher education who are pursuing courses with a high content of visually orientated material. It has become apparent that not only are more blind students seeking to study courses which have an inherent visual content but also that courses which have in the past had a predominantly verbal structure are now making increasing use of visual resources. Resources which make it possible for a blind student to access visually orientated course work may exist but they are not always easily available or may require further development. Many existing students still struggle to obtain good quality resources and some students are refused entry to the courses of their choice partly because suitable resources are not available.

The present study is making detailed case studies of ten individual students pursuing a wide variety of courses with a significant visual content. Through maintaining contact with the students and their teaching and support staff over at least one complete academic year it sets out to: (1) identify academic subjects where such problems occur; (2) locate the causes of the problems; (3) develop more effective teaching resources where necessary and (4) provide for any necessary staff advice.

13303 A comparative, evaluative study of residential special schools for children with emotional and behavioural difficulties.
GBR 1993
Research Date(s): 1991-1992
Grimshaw, R.
Sup: Berridge, D.
Inst: National Children's Bureau, 8 Wakley Street, London EC1V 7QE, United Kingdom.
Fin: The Nuffield Foundation; The Healey Group and the National Children's Home.
behaviour disorder; emotional disorder; boarding school; special education; special school
trouble du comportement; trouble affectif; internat; enseignement spécial; centre d'éducation spéciale
PROJECT DESCRIPTION

This is an 18 month research study to investigate the processes by which children are defined as having emotional and behavioural difficulties (EBD) and being in need of residential experience. This will be approached with particular regard to the overlap between education and social service responsibilities. The work will analyse the treatment methods, social and educational functioning and impact on children of a sample of EBD residential schools. This will be located within the context of what is known to be good practice in residential child care. The researcher will be observing the schools for significant periods, noting daily activities and interviewing adults and pupils.

13304 Comparative study of children with a hearing impairment.
GBR 1993
Research Date(s): 1990-1992
Hosie, D.; Turner, M.
Inst: Heriot-Watt University, Moray House Institute of Education, Cramond Campus, Cramond Road North, Edinburgh EH4 6JD, United Kingdom.
aurally handicapped; deaf; teaching method
handicapé auditif; sourd; méthode pédagogique
PROJECT DESCRIPTION

This is a preliminary study to assess the merits of three distinct models of teaching children with a hearing impairment.

13305 Comparative study of the language development of children with Down's Syndrome placed in mainstream and special schools.
GBR 1993
Research Date(s): 1990-1994
Philps, C.
Sup: Crocker, A.; Thomas, N.
Inst: Wolverhampton University, Walsall Campus, Gorway Road, Walsall WS1 3BD, United Kingdom.
Fin: Down's Syndrome Association; Wolverhampton Polytechnic.
Down's syndrome; language development; special education; special school; pupil integration
mongolisme; développement du langage; enseignement spécial; centre d'éducation spéciale; intégration scolaire
PROJECT DESCRIPTION

This is a two-year longitudinal study of a sample of Down's Syndrome children, half of whom are in mainstream schools and half of whom are in Moderate Learning Difficulty (MLD) schools. The baseline measurements are IQ, language development, social skills and family details. An analysis is to be made of expressive language heard in the context of classroom interaction, playground interaction and, possibly, family interaction, with a view to testing the proposition that children placed in mainstream schools initiate more language than those in MLD schools.

Publ: Philps, C. & Alexander, P. *Mummy, why have I got Down's Syndrome?* Oxford: Lion, 1991.

13306 Constitution et analyse d'un ensemble documentaire sur l'intégration sociale et scolaire d'enfants et d'adolescents en difficulté dans les quartiers sud de Marseille.
FRA 1993
Research Date(s): 1986-1994
Rossignol, Christian; Loubié, Annie.
Inst: Université de Strasbourg I, UFR des Sciences du comportement, CNRS URA/668, Laboratoire de recherche Production et effets de la parole et du langage, Laboratoire de psycholinguistique, 12 rue Goethe, 67000 Strasbourg, France.
Fin: Association régionale pour l'intégration des personnes handicapées et en difficulté (ARI).
socially handicapped; social integration; pupil integration
handicapé social; intégration sociale; intégration scolaire
PROJECT DESCRIPTION

Objectifs: L'analyse d'un corpus, constitué à partir d'une enquête par entretiens et sur dossiers auprès de jeunes en difficulté, de leurs familles et de ceux qui s'occupent d'eux, vise à reconstruire les processus sociaux et langagiers qui ont contribué à écarter l'enfant ou l'adolescent des lieux ordinaires de travail et de vie. L'hypothèse principale est que les notions même de handicap et d'intégration ont des incidences telles sur ceux qu'elles concernent et sur leur entourage que le maintien ou le retour de ces personnes dans les conditions ordinaires de travail et de vie en est affecté.

Méthodologie: Etablissement du texte des entretiens et saisie sur ordinateur de cet ensemble. Analyse des éléments de l'histoire personnelle et des conditions actuelles de travail et de vie.

Publ: Rossignol, Christian. *Recherche sur l'intégration sociale et scolaire des enfants et adolescents en difficulté dans les quartiers sud de Marseille*. Rapport de recherche à l'ARI, Provence Côte d'Azur, 1988, 202p.
Rossignol, Christian. Mémoire familiale. In: *Enfance*, 1987, 40, 1-2, pp. 69-78.

13307 Contingency and breakdown: interactions with language-disordered children.
GBR 1993
Research Date(s): 1990-1992
Conti-Ramsden, G.
Inst: Manchester University, School of Education, Centre for Educational Guidance and Special Needs, Oxford Road, Manchester M13 9PL, United Kingdom.
Fin: March of Dimes Birth Defect Foundation, USA.
speech handicapped; verbal interaction; parent-child relation; verbal communication; sibling
handicapé de la parole; interaction verbale; relation parents-enfant; communication verbale; frères et soeurs
PROJECT DESCRIPTION

In this research the linguistic environment of severely language-disordered children will be studied. Mother and child; father and child; and sibling interactions will be video-recorded at home, transcribed and analysed. The study aims to identify conversational breakdown in dyadic interaction. The study will ask if fathers experience more conversational breakdown than mothers do with their language-disordered child; and what is the possible effect of language impairment on sibling interaction.

13308 Deprivation research - Phase 2.
GBR 1993
Research Date(s): 1991-1992
McPherson, A.; Raffe, D.; Bagnall, G.
Inst: Edinburgh University, Centre for Educational Sociology, 7 Buccleuch Place, Edinburgh EH8 9JT, United Kingdom.
Fin: John Watson's Trust.
deprived; socially handicapped; social status; social inequality
défavorisé; handicapé social; statut social; inégalité sociale
PROJECT DESCRIPTION

This project uses data from the Scottish Young People's Survey to investigate the effect of social disadvantages on education.

Publ: A full list of publications is available.

13309 Development of revised training materials for teaching people with severe learning difficulties - Education of the Developmentally Young (EDY).
GBR 1993
Research Date(s): 1990-1992
Farrell, P.
Inst: Manchester University, School of Education, Centre for Educational Guidance and Special Needs, Oxford Road, Manchester M13 9PL, United Kingdom.
Fin: Manchester University Press.
backwardness; slow learning; special education; teaching aid
retard; apprentissage lent; enseignement spécial; moyen d'enseignement
PROJECT DESCRIPTION

Evaluative research projects will assess the effectiveness of the revised training course in improving trainees' skills and knowledge and to see whether these techniques can be successfully applied in the classroom.

Publ: *Teaching people with severe learning difficulties, EDY Trainee's Workbook*. Manchester University Press, 1992.
Teaching people with severe learning difficulties, EDY Instructor's Handbook. Manchester University Press, 1992.

13310 The educational management of children with Usher Syndrome.
GBR 1993
Research Date(s): 1989-
Lynas, W.
Inst: Manchester University, School of Education, Centre for Audiology, Education of the Deaf and Speech Pathology, Oxford Road, Manchester M13 9PL, United Kingdom.
Fin: National Deaf-Blind and Rubella Association (SENSE).
multiple disability; visually handicapped; special education; deaf
multihandicap; handicapé visuel; enseignement spécial; sourd
PROJECT DESCRIPTION

The aim of the research is to develop sound principles for the educational management of children with Usher Syndrome. Diagnosed children and young people are observed in a variety of educational settings - special school for the deaf, unit, mainstream class, further education college and special provisions for deaf pupils/students with deteriorating vision are noted. The data collected include material from informal interviews with teaching staff and from the Usher pupils themselves. So far, 15 Usher children/young people have been observed.

Publ: Lynas, W. Deaf children with Usher Syndrome. In: *Journal of British Association of Teachers of the Deaf*, Vol 15, No 2/1991, pp. 33-39.
Lynas, W. *The educational management of children with Usher Syndrome*. London: SENSE, 1991.

13311 The effect of a thinking skills programme on the development of selected performance measures in prelingual deaf students.
GBR 1993
Research Date(s): 1989-1993
Finer, A.
Sup: Child, D.
Inst: Leeds University, School of Education, Leeds LS2 9JT, United Kingdom.
deafness; special education; curriculum development; teaching programme; thinking
surdité; enseignement spécial; élaboration de programmes d'études; programme d'enseignement; pensée
PROJECT DESCRIPTION

The aim of the present investigation is to utilize a course for deaf students that provides a conceptual framework which underpins the many curricula changes taking place in schools. The course consists of a series of visually based discussion tasks which highlight and develop many essential cross-curricular pupil resources. The course addresses a range of overlapping cognitive, linguistic, personal and social issues, all of which are relevant to the specific needs of deaf students. Samples of prelingual deaf students attending resourced mainstream schools will be used at primary and secondary levels. Assessment will be made of intellectual abilities, reading comprehension, social functioning, problem solving ability and educational measures similar to proposed standard attainment tasks in the context of the National Curriculum.

Subjects will follow a programme over the period of an academic year and rate and amount of improvement will be measured and comparisons made with control groups. Four schools will be used with experimental and control groups totalling 60 in each at both primary and secondary level. Stepwise regression analysis will be used to identify predictor variables for a number of criterion measures, prior to the use of multiple analysis of covariance. Teacher and educational interpreter effects will be examined on the development of the criterion measures.

Publ: Finer, A.R. The effectiveness of a thinking skills programme on the educational attainment of secondary age deaf students. In: *Proceedings of the 17th International Congress on Education of the Deaf, Rochester, New York*. National Technical Institute for the Deaf, 1990.

13312 Les enfants non-lecteurs; étude des impossibilités persistantes de l'activité de lecture chez des enfants âgés de neuf ans et plus.
FRA 1993
Research Date(s): 1985-
Netchine, Serge; Préneron, Christiane; Salazar-Orvig, Anne; Kugler, Marie; David, Jacques; Sprenger-Charolles, Liliane.
Inst: Université de Paris V, UFR Linguistique générale et appliquée, CNRS URA/1031, Laboratoire de recherches sur l'acquisition et la pathologie du langage chez l'enfant, 12 rue Cujas, 75230 Paris Cedex 05, France.
Fin: Institut national de la santé et de la recherche médicale (INSERM).
learning difficulty; reading; inaptitude; language skill; primary education; reading difficulty
difficulté de l'apprentissage; lecture; inaptitude; aptitude linguistique; enseignement primaire; difficulté de lecture
PROJECT DESCRIPTION

Objectifs: Cette recherche porte sur des enfants âgés de neuf ans ou plus, manifestant une impossibilité de lecture, qui ne présentent pas de pathologie neurologique ou psychiatrique et ont un niveau d'intelligence normale (avec un QI supérieur à 85 à au moins une des deux échelles du WISC-R). On examine une quarantaine d'enfants non-lecteurs ainsi qu'une trentaine d'enfants "mauvais lecteurs" qui constituent un des groupes de contrôle. Les enfants non-lecteurs sont revus après un intervalle de trois ans afin d'évaluer les modifications survenues à la fois dans leurs conduites langagières et dans leur capacité de lecture.

Ce travail s'est développé autour de deux axes: (1) les conduites de récit (récit paraphrasé, récit d'après bandes dessinées, récit spontané dicté à l'adulte et récit dicté d'après une série d'images séquentielles); (2) les conduites métalangagières (conscience phonique, définitions de mots).

Publ: David, Jacques & Sprenger-Charolles, Liliane. Phénomènes de distanciation dans les narrations écrites produites par des enfants en difficulté d'apprentissage de la lecture. In: *Langue française*, 1988, n° 80.
Salazar-Orvig, Anne; Preneron, Christiane & Kugler, Marie. Conduites de définition chez des enfants non lecteurs. In: *Langue française*, 1988, n° 80, pp. 83-97.
Netchine, Serge (dir.). *Etude des impossibilités persistantes de l'activité de lecture chez des enfants âgés de 9 ans et plus*. Rapport de fin de contrat, INSERM, 1988.

Salazar-Orvig, Anne. Coordination d'un n° spécial de *Perspectives psychiatriques*, 1990, n° 24/4.
(Une liste complète est disponible.).

13313 Entwicklung und Erprobung eines hochschuldidaktischen Konzeptes fuer die Vermittlung eines Handlungswissens zur Lehrerunterrichtssprache an der Schule fuer geistig Behinderte. (Development and testing of a didactic concept for transferring action knowledge relating to the teaching language of teachers at schools for the mentally disabled.)
DEU 1993
Research Date(s): 1991-1993
Meyer, H.
Inst: Universitaet Dortmund, FB Sondererziehung und Rehabilitation, Sonderpaedagogische Beratungsstelle, Emil-Figge-Strasse 50, D-4600 Dortmund 50.
mental handicap; university studies; didactics; teacher education; special school teacher; conversation
handicap mental; études universitaires; didactique; formation des enseignants; éducateur spécialisé; conversation
PROJECT DESCRIPTION
Inhalt: Auf der Grundlage von Untersuchungsergebnissen zur (verbalen) Kommunikation im Unterricht an der Schule fuer Geistigbehinderte wird ein hochschuldidaktisches Konzept entwickelt, das (zukuenftigen) LehrerInnen ein grundlegendes kommunikationsbezogenes Handlungswissen vermitteln soll. Im Mittelpunkt steht dabei die Lehrerunterrichtssprache, die in ihrer Bedeutung fuer das (schulische) Unterrichtsziel "Aufbau/Foerderung der Gespraechsfaehigkeit bei Geistigbehinderten" diskutiert wird. Dabei kann aufgrund der Heterogenitaet der geistigbehinderten SchuelerInnen im sprachlichen und kognitiven Bereich Lehrersprachverhalten nur situations- und individuumorientiert bewertet werden, so dass bei evaluativen Intentionen qualitative Verfahren (z.B. kommunikative Validierung) verwendet werden muessen.
Vorgehensweise: Untersuchungsdesign: Fallstudie; Evaluationsstudie; qualitative Forschung.
Datengewinnung: Teilnehmende Beobachtung, Inhaltsanalyse (Studierende - Lehramt Sonderpaedagogik -Schule- fuer Geistigbehinderte, Lerngruppen an Schulen fuer Geistigbehinderte).

13314 Erwachsenenbildung fuer Menschen mit geistiger Behinderung: Begleitforschungsprojekt zu einem Seminarprojekt der Bundesvereinigung Lebenshilfe. (Adult education for the mentally disabled: evaluation research for a seminar project run by the federal association "Lebenshilfe".)
DEU 1993
Research Date(s): 1992
Kane, J.; Rotter, B.
Inst: Bundesvereinigung Lebenshilfe fuer geistig Behinderte e.V., Raiffeisenstr. 18, D-3550 Marburg 7.
Fin: Bundesministerium fuer Bildung und Wissenschaft.
mentally handicapped; adult education; curriculum; self-esteem; conflict; social interaction
handicapé mental; éducation des adultes; programme d'études; estime de soi; conflit; interaction sociale
PROJECT DESCRIPTION
Inhalt: Das Projekt soll helfen, vorhandene Ansaetze zur Erwachsenenbildung geistig Behinderter zu objektivieren und weiter zu entwickeln. Hierzu dient die experimentelle Erprobung spezieller Curricula in Verbindung mit dem wissenschaftlichen Begleitprojekt, das die Auswirkungen von Erwachsenenbildungsseminaren zur Foerderung der Selbstsicherheit, Integrations- und Konfliktfaehigkeit im Arbeits- und Wohnbereich bei geistig behinderten Menschen in der Bundesrepublik Deutschland dokumentieren soll. Ueber die in den Seminaren vermittelten Bildungsinhalte bzw. die Erweiterung von allgemeinen Handlungskompetenzen hinaus sollen auch Veraenderungen der Persoenlichkeit im Sinne eines Zuwachses an Eigenstaendigkeit erfasst werden.
Vorgehensweise: Vergleichende einzelfallanalytische Forschung; Dokumentation. Untersuchungsdesign: Fallstudie; Trend; qualitative Forschung.
Datengewinnung: Standardisiertes Interview (Stichprobe: 20; Seminarteilnehmer; Auswahlverfahren: total). Nicht-standardisiertes Interview (Stichprobe: 20; Seminarteilnehmer; Auswahlverfahren: total). Teilnehmende Beobachtung (dito). Beobachtung (dito). Inhaltsanalyse (dito). Primaererhebung: Feldarbeit von Mitarbeitern des Projektes durchgefuehrt.
Auswertung: Datenaufbereitung: Verlaufsdaten (event history data); Verknuepfung verschiedener Datensaetze (record linkage).

13315 An evaluation of conductive education.
GBR 1993
Research Date(s): 1987-1992
Cochrane, R.
Sup: Bairstow, P.
Inst: Birmingham University, School of Psychology, Edgbaston, Birmingham B15 2TT, United Kingdom.
Fin: Department of Education and Science.
handicapped; special education; therapy; psychomotor development; cerebral palsy; motor disorder
handicapé; enseignement spécial; thérapie; développement psychomoteur; infirmité motrice cérébrale; trouble moteur
PROJECT DESCRIPTION
The Foundation for Conductive Education in conjunction with the Peto Institute in Budapest has set up a pilot project to bring the Hungarian system for treating children with cerebral palsy to Britain. An Institute has been set up in Birmingham which has admitted a number of children and trainee Conductors and exposed them to Conductive Education from 1 January 1988. A research evaluation of the effectiveness of Conductive Education in improving motor abilities, intellectual functioning and social functioning is being undertaken at the same time.
Three main questions are being addressed: (1) What are the key principles underlying Conductive Education? (2) Does the Birmingham Project faithfully replicate the original Hungarian scheme of Conductive Education? (3) Does Conductive Education produce more benefits for the disabled than traditional therapies?.

13316 An evaluation of educational materials on HIV and AIDS for nurses.
GBR 1993
Research Date(s): 1992
Sharp, C.; Baginsky, M.; Maychell, K.; Walton, I.
Sup: Bradley, J.
Inst: National Foundation for Educational Research, The Mere, Upton Park, Slough SL1 2DQ, United Kingdom.
Fin: Department of Health.
sexually transmitted disease; nurse; information need; information source
maladie sexuellement transmissible; infirmier; besoin d'information; source d'information
PROJECT DESCRIPTION
Human Immuno Virus/Acquired Immune Deficiency Syndrome (HIV/AIDS) presents major challenges to nurses and nurse educators. This reserch is aiming to evaluate the educational materials currently available and to discover the needs for new information presented in different formats. Methods include a mapping exercise (carried out by Anglia Polytechnic University (formerly Anglia Polytechnic)), a literature review, and interviews with nursing staff, students, nurse teachers and representatives from regional health authorities in six English regions.

13317 Evaluation of mobility education for young blind children.
GBR 1993
Research Date(s): 1990-1993
Spencer, C.; Blades, M.; Ungar, S.
Inst: Sheffield University, Department of Psychology, Sheffield S10 2TN, United Kingdom; Tapton Mount School for the Blind, 20 Manchester Road, Sheffield S10 5DG, United Kingdom.
Fin: Economic and Social Research Council.
visually handicapped; blind
handicapé visuel; aveugle
PROJECT DESCRIPTION
The researchers' previous work on the education for mobility of the visually handicapped has included: (1) development of spatial concepts; (2) the hierarchy of skills underlying successful mobility; (3) the evaluation of experimental programmes to improve aspects of training; and (4) the evaluation of tactile maps in learning a novel area. One such project - on the parental approach to independence and mobility skills for children prior to school - has led the researchers to embark upon the present project, which will study children through the years prior to entry to blind school, and their first few years of formal mobility training within the school. Research will be conducted in conjunction with Tapton Mount, the special school for the visually handicapped in Yorkshire and surrounding counties. The aim is to plan and test mobility training programmes designed to develop the child's techniques for (1) acquiring and storing knowledge of spatial layout; (2) updating one's position within a locale; and (3) applying systems of spatial concepts to plan routes.

Publ: Blades, M. & Spencer, C. The development of 3-6 year olds' map using ability: the relative importance of landmarks and map alignment. In: *Journal of Genetic Psychology*, No 151/1990, pp. 181-194.
Morsley, K., Spencer, C. & Baybutt, K. Is there any relationship between a child's body image and spatial skills? In: *British Journal of Visual Impairment*, No 9/1991, pp. 41-43.
Morsley, K.; Spencer, C. & Baybutt, K. Two techniques for encouraging movement and exploration in the visually impaired child. In: *British Journal of Visual Impairment*, No 9/1991, pp. 75-78.
Pike, E. Children's reactions to Nomad, an audio-tactile graphic processor. In: *British Journal of Visual Impairment*, No 9/1991, pp. 105-107.
Spencer, C.; Morsley, K.; Ungar, S.; Pike, E. & Blades, M. Developing the blind child's cognition of the environment: the role of direct experience and map-given experience. In: *Geoforum*, No 23/1992, pp. 191-197.

13318 Evaluation of quality and costs of services to people with multiple sensory impairments and severe learning difficulties provided by SENSE in the Midlands.

GBR 1993

Research Date(s): 1990-1992

Emerson, E.; Cooper, J.

Inst: Manchester University, Hester Adrian Research Centre, Oxford Road, Manchester M13 9PL, United Kingdom.

Fin: Department of Health.

multiple disability; blind; deaf; special education

multihandicap; aveugle; sourd; enseignement spécial

PROJECT DESCRIPTION

The project will examine the quality and costs of services provided by the residential further education facility operated by SENSE (The National Deaf-Blind and Rubella Association) in the Midlands. Comparisons will be made between a group of 18 current students and a matched waiting list control group with regard to: the range and costs of services received; nature of teacher-student interaction; nature of student activity; student participation in community activities.

13319 An evaluation study of the efficacy of 'Social Problem Solving Training', with people who have learning difficulties, living in residential and community settings.

GBR 1993

Research Date(s): 1990-1993

Loumidis, K.

Sup: Hill, A.

Inst: Keele University, Department of Psychology, Keele, Staffordshire ST5 5BG, United Kingdom.

mentally handicapped; special education; problem solving; training programme; adult

handicapé mental; enseignement spécial; résolution de problème; programme de formation; adulte

PROJECT DESCRIPTION

'Social Problem Solving Training' has been used with a variety of clinical and non-clinical populations. With learning difficulties, research has mainly focused on the mildly handicapped group living in the community, or in residential settings. Much of the work has had rather narrow objectives, e.g. to enhance the decision making of mothers with learning difficulties, to enhance dating skills and public transportation skills. The present study attempts to extend previous research by adapting 'Social Problem Solving Training' to give a more generic training, relevant to the needs of moderately handicapped people.

In Part 1 of the study, adults with learning difficulties living in the community as well as in a residential hospital, will be assessed to establish baseline measures of intellectual functioning, degree of psychological distress and ability to solve hypothetical but personally relevant problems. The second part of the research will consist of a period of six months training in social problem solving with one 75-90 minutes session each week. In the third part, the effects of training will be assessed by comparing performance on the problem solving test, used to establish baseline performance. Generalisation of training will also be evaluated on two parallel sets of new problems. Pre-post measures of dependent variables will be compared using 2 x 2 ANOVA (community/residential x time of assessment). Qualitative analyses of individual cases will also be carried out.

Publ: Loumidis, K.S. Can "Social Problem Solving Training" help people with a learning difficulty? In: *Proceedings of the First Annual Conference on the Promotion of Mental Health.* Avebury: Gower Publications, 1991.

13320 An examination of teaching and learning strategies for children with movement learning difficulties.

GBR 1993

Research Date(s): 1984-1991

Brown, B.

Sup: Sugden, D.

Inst: Cheltenham & Gloucester College of Higher Education, Faculty of Education and Health, The Park, Cheltenham GU50 2QF, United Kingdom; Leeds University, School of Education, Leeds LS2 9JT, United Kingdom.

motor disorder; learning difficulty; learning strategy; teaching method; motor development

trouble moteur; difficulté de l'apprentissage; stratégie d'apprentissage; méthode pédagogique; développement moteur

PROJECT DESCRIPTION

In this research, fifty children aged 2 to 11 years with movement learning difficulties have been examined for six years in a movement learning context whilst they have been engaged in developing rudimentary and fundamental movement abilities. The children's movement development has been examined in the context of their total development. The teaching considerations surrounding the teacher's role, curriculum content, teaching strategy and learning environment have been critically analysed in the context of the movement learning experience of the children. The children were taught in segregated and integrated settings.

13321 Factors influencing the successful integration of children with Down's Syndrome in mainstream education.

GBR 1993

Research Date(s): 1991-1996

Rovira-Garza, N.

Sup: Hinton, R.

Inst: Loughborough University of Technology, Department of Education, Loughborough LE11 3TU, United Kingdom.

Fin: National Mental Health Foundation.

Down's syndrome; pupil integration; special education

mongolisme; intégration scolaire; enseignement spécial

PROJECT DESCRIPTION

A study of the factors influencing successful integration of children with Down's Syndrome into mainstream classes, and in particular the influence of the teacher's attitude to the child and the quality and appropriateness of the pedagogic strategies.

13322 Fiziksel özürlü gençlerde benlik kavramı (aile kabul düzeyi açısından). (Self-concepts of physically handicapped adolescents (and family acceptance levels).)

TUR 1994

Research Date(s): 1991

Bıyıklı, Latife.

Inst: Ankara Üniversitesi, Eğitim Bilimleri Fakültesi (Ankara University, Faculty of Educational Sciences), Cebeci, Ankara, Turkey.

physically handicapped; self-concept; adolescent; family life; parent-child relation

handicapé physique; conception de soi; adolescent; vie familiale; relation parents-enfant

PROJECT DESCRIPTION

The purpose of this study was to determine the self-concepts of physically handicapped adolescents on a range of variables.

The study used a group of 16-year-olds, consisting of hearing-impaired, visually handicapped, and orthopaedically impaired adolescents from various boarding schools for handicapped children in Ankara. The "control group" consisted of able-bodied adolescents of the same age and socio-economic level.

Data were collected with the Piers-Harris Children's Self-Concept Scale (to measure subjects' self-concepts) and the Parents Acceptance-Rejection Questionnaire (to measure subjects' acceptance by their family). Variance analysis, t-test and correlation coefficients were used in the statistical analysis.

The results showed no significant differences between the self-concepts of orthopaedically impaired and normal adolescents. However, a significant difference was found between hearing-impaired and orthopaedically impaired children: the self-concepts of the latter group were higher.

As regards family acceptance level, no significant differences were found between physically handicapped and normal groups. However, among the impaired groups there were significant differences between the hearing-impaired group and the orthopaedically impaired group: the level of family acceptance was higher in the latter group. There was also a significant correlation between the family acceptance level and subjects' self-concepts. All correlation coefficients of physically handicapped groups were found to be statistically significant, except among hearing-impaired children. It can be concluded that self-concept levels increase with the family acceptance level.

13323 Graphic and perceptual development in autistic children and autistic savants.

GBR 1993

Research Date(s): 1989-1992

Eames, C.

Sup: Cox, M.

Inst: York University, Department of Psychology, Heslington, York YO1 5DD, United Kingdom.

Fin: Medical Research Council.

autism; Down's syndrome; exceptional; gifted; drawing

autisme; mongolisme; atypique; doué; dessin

PROJECT DESCRIPTION

The devlopment of depth representation in the drawings of normal children is now beginning to be understood. This research project was carried out to see whether the development of depth portrayal in the drawings of autistic children follows a 'normal' path.

Comparing autistic children with Down's Syndrome children and normal children, matched on non-verbal mental age, it was found that autistic children are developmentally delayed in their depth representation rather than showing anomalous strategies of depth portrayal. The work in progress is focusing upon the strategies of depth representation by autistic children who are gifted in the visual arts.

13324 Health Education Authority HIV/AIDS and homeless young people project.
GBR 1993
Research Date(s): 1990-
Warwick, I.
Sup: Aggleton, P.; Whitty, G.
Inst: London University, Institute of Education, Department of Policy Studies, Health and Education Research Unit, 20 Bedford Way, London WC1H OAL, United Kingdom.
Fin: Health Education Authority.
sexually transmitted disease; health education; vagrancy; deprived
maladie sexuellement transmissible; éducation sanitaire; vagabondage; défavorisé
PROJECT DESCRIPTION
This is a project to identify the Human Immunodeficiency Virus/Acquired Immune Deficiency Syndrome (HIV/AIDS) health education needs of young homeless people. Via a programme of national consultations involving workers from the statutory and non-statutory sectors, it will seek to access perspectives on the HIV/AIDS health education needs of young people who are homeless and rootless.

13325 The Health Education Authority HIV/AIDS local evaluation initiative.
GBR 1993
Research Date(s): 1990-
Aggleton, P.; Whittaker, M.
Inst: London University, Institute of Education, Department of Policy Studies, Health and Education Research Unit, 20 Bedford Way, London WC1H OAL, United Kingdom.
Fin: Health Education Authority.
sexually transmitted disease; health service personnel; evaluation; teaching aid; health education
maladie sexuellement transmissible; personnel médical; évaluation; moyen d'enseignement; éducation sanitaire
PROJECT DESCRIPTION
The Health Education Authority HIV/AIDS (Human Immunodeficiency Virus/Acquired Immune Deficiency Syndrome) Local Evaluation Support Initiative is a project to support and guide local HIV/AIDS workers in the monitoring and evaluation of HIV/AIDS health promotion activities. The project has developed a range of resources including a training manual for local HIV/AIDS workers, an edited collection of papers offering case studies in local monitoring and evaluation, and an HIV/AIDS and Sexual Health Programme Paper reporting on findings from a survey of HIV/AIDS monitoring and evaluation in practice. A national dissemination programme across England to alert local HIV/AIDS workers to the existence of the training resource will shortly commence, organised on a regional basis. The programme will offer workers the opportunity to examine comparative, survey and ethnographic styles of evaluation, and to consider the appropriateness of each of these techniques for work with which they are involved.

Publ: Moody, D.; Aggleton, P.J.; Kapila, M.; Pye, M. & Young, A. *Monitoring and evaluating local HIV/AIDS health promotion: a review of theory and practice, HIV/AIDS and Sexual Health Programme Paper 11.* London: Health Education Authority, 1991.
Aggleton, P.J.; Young, A.; Moody, D.; Kapila, M. & Pye, M. *HIV/AIDS health promotion - does it work?* London: Health Education Authority, 1991.
Aggleton, P.J.; Moody, D. & Young, A. *Evaluating local HIV/AIDS health promotion.* London: Health Education Authority, 1992.

13326 Information technology and the learning needs of emotionally and behaviourally disturbed children.
GBR 1993
Research Date(s): 1988-1992
Wood, G.
Sup: Jotham, R.; Dolan, T.
Inst: Nottingham University, Department of Adult Education, 14-22 Shakespeare Street, Nottingham NG1 4FJ, United Kingdom.
behaviour disorder; emotional disorder; didactic use of computer; information technology; special education; learning difficulty
trouble du comportement; trouble affectif; usage didactique de l'ordinateur; technologie de l'information; enseignement spécial; difficulté de l'apprentissage
PROJECT DESCRIPTION
The research will test the hypothesis that the learning inhibiting behaviours (classroom conformity, task orientation, acceptance of authority, peer relationships, emotional control, self-worth, self-responsibility and problem solving) emitted by the emotionally disturbed child can be significantly reduced by the use of computer-assisted learning/information technology (CAL/IT), providing the opportunity for a significant improvement in learning.
It will be necessary to: (1) measure and record the child's learning inhibiting behaviours in the presence and absence of CAL/IT; (2) measure and record the child's attainments and progress in the presence and absence of CAL/IT; and (3) ascertain reasons for this progress/lack of

progress in terms of (a) the child's academic abilities; (b) personality and attitude to CAL/IT; (c) the presentation model of the learning task; and (d) the learning environment of the hardware.

13327 Integracja społeczna dzieci niepełnosprawnych. (The social integration of handicapped children.)
POL 1994
Research Date(s): 1986-1993
Maciarz, Aleksandra.
Inst: Zakład Pedagogiki Opiekuńczej i Specjalnej, Wyższa Szkoła Pedagogiczna (Special Education Department, Higher School of Education), 65 625 Zielona Góra, Al. Wojska Polskiego 69, Poland.
handicapped; mentally handicapped; physically handicapped; pupil integration; social integration
handicapé; handicapé mental; handicapé physique; intégration scolaire; intégration sociale
PROJECT DESCRIPTION
Aims: (1) To define conditions for the social integration of handicapped children in ordinary schools; (2) to determine the effects of integration (degree of social adjustment in school, achievement levels of handicapped pupils, participation in extra-curricular activities, relations with other pupils); (3) to design a programme of activities aimed at promoting the social integration of handicapped children in ordinary schools.
Sample: 206 handicapped children in years 1-5 of ordinary primary schools in the Zielona Góra and Gorzów voivodships. The group was made up of 66 mildly mentally retarded children, 50 motor handicapped children, 50 children with vascular disease, and 40 children with epilepsy.
Methods: Case study, observation of children's behaviour with the help of a standardized list, sociometric test, psychological interview, teacher questionnaire, interview in the home and at school.
Results: Examination of the achievements of the handicapped children, the special help they are given in school, their school behaviour, their social adjustment and their relations with other children shows that there are many obstacles hindering the social integration of handicapped children in ordinary schools.

Publ: Maciarz, Aleksandra. *Integracja społeczna uczniów niepełnosprawnych.* Warszawa: WSiP, 1987.
Maciarz, Aleksandra. *Uczniowie niepełnosprawni w szkole powszechnej. Poradnik dla nauczycieli.* Warszawa: WSiP, 1992.

13328 Integrated education for children with special educational needs in physical education programmes in Nigerian primary schools.
GBR 1993
Research Date(s): 1990-1993
Okpanachi, J.
Sup: Mawer, M.; Hornby, G.
Inst: Hull University, School of Education, Cottingham Road, Hull HU6 7RX, United Kingdom.
handicapped; Nigeria; physical education; integration; primary education
handicapé; Nigeria; éducation physique; intégration; enseignement primaire
PROJECT DESCRIPTION
The 20th century has witnessed many educational innovations aimed at improving the quality of life for all children. A significant improvement among these is the education of handicapped children who for so long have been neglected and even forgotten. With several legislative acts and through the support of various philanthropic organisations, handicapped children are moving towards taking their proper place in society. To begin with, special schools were built to cater for the welfare of these children but with time it has been realised that special schools can only serve those with severe difficulties while others could be integrated into ordinary schools.
Children with special educational needs have greater problems in physical education than other school subjects because of difficulties in movement. The main concern of the research is to find out how best these children can be helped to overcome their movement difficulties and how others with different problems can also be helped. Participation and enjoyment are not the only goals for these children; their acceptance by others is another. Through integrated programmes all children should be able to work, play and learn together successfully.

13329 The integration experiences of hearing impaired children: the transition from primary to secondary schooling.
GBR 1993
Research Date(s): 1990-1992
Connors, M.
Sup: Fraser, B.
Inst: Birmingham University, School of Education, Edgbaston, Birmingham B15 2TT, United Kingdom.
Fin: National Deaf Children's Society.
aurally handicapped; integration; transitional class; special education
handicapé auditif; intégration; classe de transition; enseignement spécial
PROJECT DESCRIPTION
The project aims to describe the educational and social experiences of hearing-impaired pupils in mainstream settings as they transfer from pri-

mary to secondary schools and to identify those practices which facilitate transition.

Sample size will be not more than 12. These pupils will come from a variety of integrated settings, will be using a range of communication methods, will be from different ethnic backgrounds and will be situated in both rural and urban areas. An ethnographic approach will be used to study the following: pupils' own experiences and needs; access to the curriculum; social aspects of transfer; parental issues; implications for specialist and mainstream staff.

13330 The integration of visually impaired students in further education.

GBR 1993
Research Date(s): 1988-1993
Todd, N.
Sup: Hinton, R.
Inst: Loughborough University of Technology, Department of Education, Loughborough LE11 3TU, United Kingdom.
visually handicapped; post-compulsory education; vocational education; integration; guidance
handicapé visuel; enseignement postobligatoire; enseignement profession-nel; intégration; orientation
PROJECT DESCRIPTION

This research includes a survey by questionnaire of a large number of mainstream further education colleges in the Midlands to ascertain the numbers of visually impaired students studying in them. Further question-naires to individual students seek to examine the reasons for the students' choice of course and college and the quality of support they receive to allow comparison with the quality of support which college staff 'believe' they are providing. Recommendations will be made for improving the provision for visually impaired students in the future.

13331 Integration Schwerhoeriger an Regelschulen. (Integration of hearing-impaired pupils into mainstream education.)

DEU 1993
Research Date(s): 1993
Krepper, H.
Inst: Universitaet Muenchen, Fak. fuer Psychologie und Paedagogik, Institut fuer Sonderpaedagogik -Gehoerlosen- und Schwerhoer-igenpaedagogik-, Leopoldstrasse 13, D-8000 Muenchen 40.
hearing defect; handicapped; pupil integration
trouble de l'ouïe; handicapé; intégration scolaire
PROJECT DESCRIPTION

Inhalt: Moeglichkeiten und Grenzen der Integration Schwerhoeriger in der Praxis.

Geographischer Raum: Bayern.

Vorgehensweise: Am Kind mit seinen individuellen Faehigkeiten orientiert sowie an dessen Umfeld. Untersuchungsdesign: Fallstudie.

Datengewinnung: Primaererhebung: Feldarbeit von Mitarbeitern des Projektes durchgefuehrt; Datenerstellung auf der Basis von bereits vor-liegenden Materialien wie Texten, Akten, Statistiken.

13332 Integration und Muendigkeit: konzeptionelle Arbeit zur Gehoerlosenpaedagogik. (Integration and maturity: pedagogic con-cepts for the deaf.)

DEU 1993
Research Date(s): 1991-1994
Voit, H.
Inst: Universitaet Muenchen, Fak. fuer Psychologie und Paedagogik, Institut fuer Sonderpaedagogik -Gehoerlosen- und Schwerhoer-igenpaedagogik-, Leopoldstrasse 13, D-8000 Muenchen 40.
deafness; remedial instruction sciences; social integration; aims of educa-tion; language skill
surdité; pédagogie spéciale; intégration sociale; finalité de l'éducation; apti-tude linguistique
PROJECT DESCRIPTION

Inhalt: Reflexion vom Menschenbild und Erziehungszielen (Schlues-selbegriffe: Sprachfaehigkeit ist gleich Muendigkeit und Integration). Fall-studien zur Lebenswirklichkeit Gehoerloser (unterschiedliche Zuordnung zu Lebens-und Sprachwelten). Leitlinien einer Paedagogik, die auf selbstver-antwortete, grundsaetzliche und situativ bedingte Zuordnungsent-scheidungen zielt.

Vorgehensweise: Untersuchungsdesign: Fallstudie; qualitative Forschung.

Datengewinnung: Nicht-standardisiertes Interview (gehoerlose Erwach-sene; Auswahlverfahren: bewusst). Gruppendiskussion (dito). Teilnehmende Beobachtung (dito). Primaererhebung: Feldarbeit von Mitarbeitern des Projektes durchgefuehrt.

13333 Interdisziplinaere Betrachtungen zum Lernen und Lehren mit Schwerstbehinderten. (Interdisciplinary considerations on the learn-ing and teaching of severely disabled people.)

DEU 1993
Research Date(s): 1990-1992
Fornefeld, B.

Inst: Paedagogische Hochschule Ludwigsburg, FB 06 Sonderpaedagogik, Abt. 03 Koerperbehindertenpaedagogik, Postfach 2344, D-7410 Reutlingen.
handicap; multiple disability; didactics; learning; physical handicap; inter-disciplinary approach
handicap; multihandicap; didactique; acquisition de connaissances; handi-cap physique; interdisciplinarité
PROJECT DESCRIPTION

Inhalt: Unterricht als Prozess des Lehrens und Lernens mit Schwerstbehinderten bedarf sowohl einer vertieften anthropologisch-paedagogischen als auch didaktisch-methodischen Reflexion; einer Reflex-ion, die im interdisziplinaeren Austausch zwischen Geistig- und Koerperbehindertenpaedagogik, unter dem Einfluss aktueller systemthe-oretischer und phaenomenologisch-paedagogischer Erkenntnisse, schliesslich ueber den Bereich der Erziehung Schwerstbehinderter hinaus in die allgemeine Paedagogik reicht.

Geographischer Raum: Bundesrepublik Deutschland.

Untersuchter Zeitraum: von 1900 bis heute.

Vorgehensweise: Grundlage: phaenomenologische Paedagogik; hermeneutisch-phaenomenologische Vorgehensweise.

13334 An investigation into how pupils perceive and react to stressful situations in school.

GBR 1993
Research Date(s): 1987-1991
Macrae, S.
Inst: Heriot-Watt University, Moray House Institute of Education, Holyrood Road, Edinburgh EH8 8AQ, United Kingdom.
Fin: Health Promotion Trust; Economic and Social Research Council.
mental stress; pupil attitude; attitude towards school; behaviour
tension mentale; attitude de l'élève; attitude envers l'école; comportement
PROJECT DESCRIPTION

The study aims to find out how young people in school identify and respond to situations which they perceive as stressful. A longitudinal study was carried out with children from junior classes, from the transition from primary to secondary and from SIV. The researcher was involved with these pupils in discussions and in observing their behaviour to discover individual stressors. In the first year, the researcher concentrated on this identification process in a small number of schools. Thereafter, the task was to design appropriate measures so that stress might be alleviated. The research focused on children and their perceptions of stressful situations. The researcher was required to interact with children from different age groups and having identified stressors, conceptualise and implement mea-sures which would allow them to be reduced. The pupils themselves were encouraged to evaluate the new procedures.

13335 An investigation into the schedule control of stereotyped and self-injurious behaviours in young people with severe learning difficulties.

GBR 1993
Research Date(s): 1990-1991
Emerson, E.; Howard, D.
Inst: Manchester University, Hester Adrian Research Centre, Oxford Road, Manchester M13 9PL, United Kingdom.
Fin: Medical Research Council.
behaviour disorder; mentally handicapped; teaching method
trouble du comportement; handicapé mental; méthode pédagogique
PROJECT DESCRIPTION

The project is examining whether stereotyped behaviours shown by children and young people with severe learning difficulties may occur as 'side-effects' of teaching procedures based upon the systematic use of positive reinforcers. The project involves the observation of rates of stereo-typed and self-injurious behaviours shown by six young people in class-room settings and a number of experimental settings in which the schedul-ing of reinforcers is manipulated.

13336 Kinderen met het Down syndroom in het basisonderwijs. (Down's Syndrome children in primary schools.)

NLD 1994
Research Date(s): 1993-1994
Pijl, S.J.; Scheepstra, A.
Inst: RION Instituut voor Onderwijsonderzoek (RION Institute for Educa-tional Research), P.O. Box 1286, 9701 BG Groningen, Netherlands.
Rijksuniversiteit Groningen (State University of Groningen), P.O. Box 72, 9700 AB Groningen, Netherlands
Fin: SVO het Instituut voor Onderzoek van het Onderwijs.
Down's syndrome; pupil integration; primary education; admission
mongolisme; intégration scolaire; enseignement primaire; admission
PROJECT DESCRIPTION

Background: Policy makers, teachers and parents increasingly question the wisdom of referring handicapped children to special education. That is one of the reasons why Down Syndrome (DS) children are more and more integrated in ordinary schools. This places considerable demands on the schools. Little is known about schools' experiences with the registration and placement of DS children. School Counselling Services (SBDs) and

National Educational Advisory Centres (LPCs) can offer little guidance in setting suitable learning routes for DS children.

Aims: (1) To provide a picture of the possibilities and limitations of primary schools regarding the integration of DS children; (2) to identify the nature of the support desired by teachers and schools.

Design: A literature survey will be conducted on experiences in other countries with the integration of DS children in ordinary schools. In a field study interviews will be conducted with: parents, teachers, counsellors and headteachers of five schools with DS children; parents of five DS children who failed to obtain a place in an ordinary school and parents of five DS children whose placement was for some reason broken off; institutions and organizations that are active in this field. Questionnaires will be administered to the parents, teachers, counsellors and headteachers of all 220 DS pupils in primary schools. Observations will be conducted in 12 schools to find out how schools deal with DS children in the classroom.

13337 Lærestrategier i matematikk hos hörselshemmete grunn-skoleelever. (A study of arithmetic learning strategies in hearing-impaired children.)
NOR 1994
Research Date(s): 1992-1994
Frostad, Per.
Inst: Universitetet i Trondheim, Pedagogisk Institutt (University of Trondheim, Department of Education), 7055 Dragvoll, Norway.
Fin: NAVF/RSF.
aurally handicapped; learning strategy; arithmetic; achievement; sign; verbal communication; cognitive development; thinking
handicapé auditif; stratégie d'apprentissage; arithmétique; rendement; signe; communication verbale; développement cognitif; pensée
PROJECT DESCRIPTION
The development of arithmetic achievement of hearing-impaired children seems to follow a different pattern than that of their hearing peers. The rate of development seems to be slower and it seems to level out at a certain age.

This project will address the arithmetic achievement patterns among hearing-impaired Norwegian children aged 7-16 years. These children will be compared to hearing children of the same age. Differences in achievement level due to sex, type of school placement, and grade of hearing loss are also of interest. Another aim of the project is to describe the strategies used by hearing-impaired children when trying to solve arithmetic problems. The study will examine whether the use of sign language leads to different thinking strategies than the use of oral language. If this is the case, the study will go on to examine whether the thinking strategies developed by hearing-impaired children are less effective than those developed by hearing children. The metacognitive skills of hearing-impaired children and their use of control mechanisms will also be considered.

An experiment focused on training the process of choosing a particular strategy will be conducted as part of the project. The children will be trained to reflect on their choice of strategy with a view to enhancing their ability to choose an effective strategy for a particular problem.

13338 Laesst sich das Burnout-Syndrom bei kuenftigen LehrerInnen prognostizieren? (Can the burn-out syndrome be predicted with student teachers?)
AUT 1993
Research Date(s): 1992-1993
Urban, Wilhelm.
Inst: Paedagogische Akademie der Erzdioezese Wien, Mayerweckstrasse 1, A-1215 Wien.
overtaxing; student teacher; personality; individual characteristics
surmenage; élève-maître; personnalité; caractéristique individuelle
PROJECT DESCRIPTION
Mit Hilfe verschiedener Testmethoden und multivariater Analysetechniken werden Persoenlichkeitskonfigurationen herauszufiltern versucht, die durch hohe Stressbelastungen und nicht Erfolg versprechende Copingstrategien charakterisiert werden koennen, und bei denen gleichzeitig - auf Grund von Persoenlichkeitsuntersuchungen - vermittelt werden kann, dass Gegenmassnahmen seitens der Probanden (ohne fremde Hilfe) misslingen. Untersuchungen in dieser Richtung (Urban, 1992) stuetzen die Hypothese, dass erlebte Belastungen ihre Basis in einer 'unguenstigen' Persoenlichkeitskonstellation haben koennten: Die Praxis hat gezeigt, dass solche Probanden mit dem anstrengenden Beruf des Lehrers nicht zurechtkommen, was unter Umstaenden zum Burnout-Syndrom fuehren koennte. Das Ziel dieser Untersuchung liegt im Nachweis einer Verflochtenheit von grundlegenden Persoenlichkeitseigenschaften und Attribuierungsvariablen (Reagieren auf Erfolg und Misserfolg) einerseits und der subjektiven Verarbeitung von stressenden Situationen und der damit verbundenen Copingstrategien andererseits. In die Untersuchung wurden 250 Studierende der Paedagogischen Akademie einbezogen.

Es kommen diverse neuentwickelte Testverfahren zur Erfassung der Stressbelastung und der Copingstrategien fuer Studierende an Paedagogischen Akademien und Persoenlichkeitsverfahren nach W. Stangl von der Universitaet Linz, Stichprobengroesse: N = 250 (Studierende aus hoeheren Semestern, nach Quoten ausgewaehlt) zur Anwendung.

Die Auswertung erfolgt nach komplexen statistischen Analysemethoden.Erste Resultate bestaetigen die oben formulierte Hypothese.
Publ: Urban, Wilhelm. Untersuchungen zur Prognostizierbarkeit der Berufszufriedenheit und Berufsbelastung bei oesterreichischen Hauptschullehrern. In: *Zeitschrift fuer empirische Paedagogik*, Nr. 6, 1992, S. 131-148.

13339 Learning about AIDS project.
GBR 1993
Research Date(s): 1986-1991
Aggleton, P.
Inst: London University, Institute of Education, Department of Policy Studies, Health and Education Research Unit, 20 Bedford Way, London WC1H OAL, United Kingdom.
Fin: Health Education Authority.
sexually transmitted disease; health education; teaching aid
maladie sexuellement transmissible; éducation sanitaire; moyen d'enseignement
PROJECT DESCRIPTION
The Learning about AIDS (Acquired Immune Deficiency Syndrome) is an initiative to develop, produce and disseminate participatory training resources for use in local authorities, health authorities and voluntary organisations. Two training packages have already been produced and disseminated widely across England. In excess of 2,000 Human Immunodeficiency Virus/Acquired Immune Deficiency Syndrome (HIV/AIDS) workers have participated in one to two day training workshops using Learning about AIDS materials. These workshops have been externally evaluated by a consultant attached to the project. A third phase of development activity will result in the publication of a second edition of the existing Learning about AIDS training resource.
Publ: Homans, H.; Aggleton, P.J. & Warwick, I. *Learning about AIDS - Interim Materials.* Horsham: AVERT, 1987.
Aggleton, P.J.; Homans, H.; Mojsa, J.; Watson, S. & Watney, S. *AIDS: Scientific and Social Issues.* Edinburgh: Churchill Livingstone, 1989.
Aggleton, P.J.; Homans, H.; Mojsa, J.; Watson, S. & Watney, S. *Learning about AIDS.* Edinburgh: Churchill Livingstone, 1989.

13340 Learning about AIDS Project (continuation).
GBR 1993
Research Date(s): 1992-1994
Whitty, G.; Aggleton, P.
Inst: London University, Institute of Education, Department of Policy Studies, Health and Education Research Unit, 20 Bedford Way, London WC1H OAL, United Kingdom.
Fin: Health Education Authority.
sexually transmitted disease; health education; teaching aid; adult
maladie sexuellement transmissible; éducation sanitaire; moyen d'enseignement; adulte
PROJECT DESCRIPTION
This project aims to update earlier research on the training needs of adults who educate other adults about Human Immunodeficiency Virus (HIV) infection and Acquired Immune Deficiency Syndrome (AIDS). A series of national consultative meetings identified that adult HIV/AIDS trainers have had the following concerns: (1) relevant scientific and medical issues on HIV and AIDS should continue to be clarified; (2) psychological dimensions of HIV/AIDS should be explored; (3) there should be a greater attention to 'newer issues' in HIV/AIDS works (such as children and HIV); and (4) monitoring and evaluation, pre-course planning and post-course action should be further examined.

A series of interactive focus groups will be held across the country so that the above issues might be explored in greater detail. Attention will be focused on the need to develop accessible and relevant information as well as on the ways trainers might be supported in their work. Resource materials will be produced which will help trainers conduct effective HIV/AIDS education.

13341 Leer- en gedragsmoeilijkheden van leerlingen bij de overgang naar het secundair onderwijs: inventarisatie; kenschetsing, aanpak, consequenties voor de leerkractenopleiding. (Learning and behavioural difficulties in pupils transferring to secondary education: identification, definition, approach, consequences for teacher training.)
BEL 1994
Research Date(s): 1989-1990
Beine, A.; et al.
Sup: De Fever, F.
Inst: Eenheid Orthopedagogiek en Ortho-agogiek volwassensen (Unit for Remedial Education and Remedial Social Science), Pleinlaan 2, 1050 Brussel, Belgium.
Vrije Universiteit Brussel (Free University of Brussels), Pleinlaan 2, 1050 Brussel, Belgium
Fin: Departement Onderwijs, Fonds voor Kollektief en Fundamenteel Onderzoek op Ministeriel Initiatief.
behaviour disorder; learning difficulty; pupil; remedial teaching; guidance; lower secondary

trouble du comportement; difficulté de l'apprentissage; élève; soutien pédagogique; orientation; secondaire premier cycle

PROJECT DESCRIPTION

Aims: (1) To determine the nature and the extent of learning and behavioural difficulties observed by teachers in the first year of secondary education; (2) to catalogue initiatives in primary education to deal with these difficulties effectively; (3) to identify gaps, if any, in the field of remedial help and skills.

Methods: (1) Data were collected on 336 pupils from 20 public-authority schools by means of two questionnaires to secondary school teachers: one to identify learning difficulties and one to assess pupil behaviour. Besides this subjective information, an objective test was used measuring pupils' educational progress. (2) A questionnaire was given to guidance centres (PMS centres) to obtain information on how they deal with the difficulties of pupils. Another questionnaire was distributed to primary schools asking how they assist in remedying these difficulties.

Results: (1) The study revealed learning difficulties in arithmetics (problem solving, geometry and fractions) and in language (oral language proficiency and reading comprehension). A considerable percentage of pupils are classified by teachers as having behavioural difficulties. The most important difficulties are: lack of attention, (about 60%), poor work attitude (about 50%), and aggressive behaviour (about 15%). (2) The PMS centres prove to lack sufficient background information to deal with problem pupils. In primary schools there is some individual remediation, but the knowledge of remedial methods and techniques is very poor.

Publ: Beine, A. et al. *Leer- en gedragsmoeilijkheden van leerlingen bij de overgang naar het secundair onderwijs: inventarisatie, kenschetsing, aanpak, consequenties voor de lerarenopleiding: eindrapport.* Brussel: VUB, Eenheid Orthopedagogiek en Ortho-agogiek volwassenen, 1991, 165p. + summary (10p.).

13342 The logistics of provision of courses in information technology for adult students with physical and sensory disabilities.
GBR 1993
Research Date(s): 1985-
Green, P.; Naylor, M.; Lamerton, P.; Quinton, E.
Sup: Jotham, R.
Inst: Nottingham University, Department of Adult Education, 14-22 Shakespeare Street, Nottingham NG1 4FJ, United Kingdom.
Fin: Leverhulme Trust; Nottinghamshire County Council; Lincolnshire County Council; Derbyshire County Council.
handicapped; information technology; computer literacy; adult education handicapé; technologie de l'information; initiation à l'informatique; éducation des adultes
PROJECT DESCRIPTION

Centres with good disabled access have been equipped with computers and software for the provision of computer courses for disabled students and mixed groups of disabled and able-bodied students. As well as continually reviewing the logistics of such provision, including the need for special hardware aids, student progress is monitored and compared with progress of able-bodied adults attending similar computer courses at other centres. The number of disabled students involved in this educational programme is approximately 300.

Publ: A list of publications is available from the researchers.

13343 The logistics of provision of vocational training in information technology for adult students with physical and sensory disabilities.
GBR 1993
Research Date(s): 1988-
Sherman, I.; Naylor, M.; Green, P.; Vanaman, J.
Sup: Jotham, R.
Inst: Nottingham University, Department of Adult Education, 14-22 Shakespeare Street, Nottingham NG1 4FJ, United Kingdom.
Fin: Nottingham Task Force; European Social Fund; Nottinghamshire County Council.
handicapped; information technology; vocational training; computer literacy; adult education
handicapé; technologie de l'information; formation professionnelle; initiation à l'informatique; éducation des adultes
PROJECT DESCRIPTION

The aim is to establish and evaluate a model for the delivery of information technology (IT) training to disabled adults by direct experimentation. A key feature of the arrangement is that training operates in parallel with a workshop managed by disabled people with IT skills. The methodology involves regular consultation between staff, trainers and associated practitioners. The group of disabled people involved numbers approximately 70.

Publ: A list of publications is available from the researchers.

13344 Longitudinal investigation of cognitive development and educational achievement in blind and partially sighted children.
GBR 1993
Research Date(s): 1973-
Tobin, M.

Inst: Birmingham University, School of Education, Research Centre for the Education of the Visually Handicapped, Edgbaston, Birmingham B15 2TT, United Kingdom.
Fin: Birmingham University; Royal National Institute for the Blind.
blind; achievement; cognitive development; visually handicapped aveugle; rendement; développement cognitif; handicapé visuel
PROJECT DESCRIPTION

This investigation, begun in 1973, aims to monitor aspects of the psychological and educational development of blind and partially sighted children attending special schools for the visually handicapped in England and Wales. The sample of 120 is estimated as constituting some 47% of the age group, the visual activities of the children ranging upwards from nil to 4/36 plus (as measured on the Snellen chart). The subjects are tested at least once every year by the researcher and a team of assistants. Among the major variables being measured are: (1) print and Braille reading; (2) mathematics attainment; (3) short-term memory; (4) verbal and non-verbal reasoning; (5) speed of information processing; (6) various 'Piagetian' constructs; (7) personality and self-concept. Degree of residual vision, cause of visual defect, age of onset and social class constitute some of the major independent variables.

Publ: Tobin, M.J. A longitudinal study of blind and partially sighted children in special schools in England and Wales. In: *Insight*, Vol 1, No 1, Summer 1979.
Tobin, M.J. Visually handicapped teenagers' opinions about special and mainstream schooling. In: *The New Beacon*, January 1987.

13345 The measure of neuroticism among 15 and 16 year olds.
GBR 1993
Research Date(s): 1990-1992
Francis, L.
Inst: Trinity College, Carmarthen, Dyfed SA31 3EP, United Kingdom.
neurosis; personality test; sex difference névrose; test de personnalité; différence de sexe
PROJECT DESCRIPTION

Nearly two hundred 15-16 year old pupils completed four different editions of the Eysenck measures of personality. The data were analysed to examine for sex differences in neuroticism. The findings indicate that Eysenck's neuroticism scales clearly contain two sub-scales, one of which is sex-related and the other of which is not sex-related. This clarification of the construct of neuroticism enables clearer specification of the empirical correlates of scores recorded on the sub-scales.

Publ: Francis, L.J. & Pearson, P.R. Religiosity, gender and the two faces of neuroticism. In: *Irish Journal of Psychology*, No 12/1991, pp. 60-67.

13346 Meeting the needs of children with emotional and behavioural disorders.
GBR 1993
Research Date(s): 1991
Mittler, P.
Sup: Farrell, P.; Boreham, N.
Inst: Manchester University, School of Education, Centre for Educational Guidance and Special Needs, Oxford Road, Manchester M13 9PL, United Kingdom.
emotional disorder; behaviour disorder; diagnostic test; assessment trouble affectif; trouble du comportement; test de diagnostic; appréciation
PROJECT DESCRIPTION

This project aims to investigate decision-making processes in the assessment of children referred as having emotional and behavioural difficulties. Structured interviews are conducted with referring teachers, educational psychologists, parents and the pupils themselves. The aim is to match decisions made against a hypothetical decision-making model. Additional questionnaire research on larger samples will be conducted on: (1) assessment techniques used by particular groups, e.g. educational psychologists; (2) the perceptions of children who are placed in schools and units for children who have emotional and behavioural problems; (3) the range of provision which is currently offered in local authorities in England and Wales.

13347 The mobility of blind and visually impaired persons.
GBR 1993
Research Date(s): 1960-
Dodds, A.; Doyle, A.; Beggs, W.; Flannigan, H.; Ng, B.
Sup: Howarth, C.
Inst: Nottingham University, Department of Psychology, Blind Mobility Research Unit, University Park, Nottingham NG7 2RD, United Kingdom.
Fin: Department of Health.
visually handicapped; blind; medical rehabilitation; special education handicapé visuel; aveugle; rééducation fonctionnelle; enseignement spécial
PROJECT DESCRIPTION

The unit publishes its work in the national and international journals. Principal interests are investigation of the assessment of visual handicap and how trainers are taught to teach mobility of visually impaired people. A scale of adjustment is being developed.

Publ: Beggs, W.D.A. The psychological correlates of walking speed in the visually impaired. In: *Ergonomics*, Vol 34, No 1/1991, pp. 91-102.

Beggs, W.D.A. Goal setting in sport. In: Graham-Jones, J. & Hardy. L. (eds.). *Stress and performance in sport*. Chichester: John Wiley & Sons, 1990.

Dodds, A.G. Psychological assessment and the rehabilitation process. In: *New Beacon*, LXXV (885), 1991, pp. 101-106.

Dodds, A.G. The psychology of rehabilitation. In: *British Journal of Visual Impairment*, Vol 9, No 2/1991, pp. 38-40.

Dodds, A.G.; Bailey, P.; Pearson, A. & Yates, L. Psychological factors in acquired visual impairment: the development of a scale of adjustment. In: *Journal of Visual Impairment and Blindness*, Vol 85, No 7/1991, pp. 306-310.

A full list of publications is available.

13348 Model výchovné, vzdělávací a poradenské péče pro mládež a dospělé s tělesným a dalším postižením. (A model of educational guidance and care for handicapped youth and adults.)

CSK 1994

Research Date(s): 1992-1993

Svobodová, Jaroslava; Hon, Josef; Kubíčová, Zdena; Hadraba, Vojtěch; Doupovcová, Hana; Pahorecká, Blanka.

Sup: Teplá, Marta.

Inst: Arkadie regionální pedagogicko zdravotnické centrum (Arkadie Regional Educational and Medical Centre), Purkyňova 10, 415 00 Teplice, Czech Republic.

Ministerstvo školství, mládeže a tělovýchovy ČR (Ministry of Education, Youth and Physical Education), Karmelitská 7, 118 13 Praha 1, Czech Republic

handicapped; special education; educational provision; integration; information dissemination; guidance

handicapé; enseignement spécial; scolarisation; intégration; diffusion de l'information; orientation

PROJECT DESCRIPTION

Aim: To create regional centres based on cooperation between different disciplines, as a starting point for a new approach to the care of handicapped people; to provide information to handicapped people and their families with the help of databases located at the regional centres.

Adequate provisions for young handicapped children are particularly important because the first seven years are a crucial period in a child's development. The assistance of the parents of handicapped youth is needed to provide protected workshops, protected work environments and protected housing. Also, changes will be necessary in special and primary education.

The work is based on the view that integration is the only appropriate and natural way to educate physically handicapped people.

13349 Moon as a route to literacy for blind children with learning difficulties.

GBR 1993

Research Date(s): 1992-1994

McCall, S.; Stone, J.

Inst: Birmingham University, School of Education, Edgbaston, Birmingham B15 2TT, United Kingdom.

Fin: Leverhulme Trust.

blind; special education; teaching aid; finger reading; learning difficulty; literacy

aveugle; enseignement spécial; moyen d'enseignement; lecture tactile; difficulté de l'apprentissage; alphabétisation

PROJECT DESCRIPTION

The project is concerned with investigating the teaching of literacy to blind children with additional learning difficulties. Moon is an alternative to Braille, a tactile code based on a simplified raised line version of the Roman print alphabet rather tan on dots. The characters are large and bold and Moon has traditionally found a valuable role amongst elderly blind people, many of whom cannot cope with the demands of learning braille but go on to read fluently through Moon. There has been very little research done into the question of whether Moon presents access to literacy for blind children with learning difficulties who are unable to manage braille. Although a few teachers have attempted to experiment with Moon, their efforts have inevitably been hampered by the lack of appropriate material and information and the results of their efforts have not been evaluated.

The general aim of the project is to investigate whether Moon offers a viable alternative to braille in the teaching of literacy to educationally blind children and young people who have additional learning difficultes. Specifically, the project will address the following objectives: (1) to investigate current practices in the teaching of reading and writing to blind children with additional learning difficulties; (2) to develop packages of materials for the teaching and learning of Moon; (3) to trial and refine these materials with the assistance of teachers and children from a variety of educational settings; and (4) to evaluate the effectiveness of Moon in developing the literacy of blind children and young people with learning difficulties.

13350 Nachschulische Integration Schwerstbehinderter (NIS). (Out-of-school integration of the severely disabled (NIS).)

DEU 1993

Research Date(s): 1991-1993

Stadler, H.

Inst: Universitaet Dortmund, FB Sondererziehung und Rehabilitation, Fach Koerperbehindertenpaedagogik, Emil-Figge-Strasse 50, D-4600 Dortmund 50.

handicapped; occupational integration; physically handicapped; vocational training; commercial training

handicapé; intégration professionnelle; handicapé physique; formation professionnelle; formation commerciale

PROJECT DESCRIPTION

Inhalt: Untersucht wird die Situation einer Gruppe von 8 Schwerstkoerperbehinderten am Berufsbildungswerk Neuwied, die dort eine Ausbildung zum Buerokaufmann absolvieren. Zielsetzungen: Entwicklung von Konzepten und Materialien zur Verbesserung der sozialen Kompetenz und zur Sicherung des Ausbildungserfolges.

Vorgehensweise: Befragungen; Langzeitbeobachtungen; Selbst- und Fremdeinschaetzungen. Untersuchungsdesign: qualitative Forschung.

Datengewinnung: Nicht-standardisiertes Interview (Stichprobe: 8; Berufsausbildung; Auswahlverfahren: bewusst). Primaererhebung: Feldarbeit von Mitarbeitern des Projektes durchgefuehrt.

Auswertung: qualitative Analyse.

13351 The National Curriculum and language disorders.

GBR 1993

Research Date(s): 1990-1991

Conti-Ramsden, G.; Donlan, C.

Inst: Manchester University, School of Education, Centre for Educational Guidance and Special Needs, Oxford Road, Manchester M13 9PL, United Kingdom.

Fin: Education and Science Research Council.

speech handicapped; special education

handicapé de la parole; enseignement spécial

PROJECT DESCRIPTION

The project intends to study Year 2 language-disordered children who receive educational provision in the Greater Manchester area. The project aims to observe current practice and study the relationship between children's profiles and curricular opportunities.

13352 A new look at perceptuo-motor disorders in cerebral palsied children.

GBR 1993

Research Date(s): 1991-1993

Henderson, S.

Inst: London University, Institute of Education, Department of Educational Psychology and Special Educational Needs, 20 Bedford Way, London WC1H OAL, United Kingdom.

Fin: Spastics Society.

motor disorder; motor handicapped; perceptually handicapped; cerebral palsy

trouble moteur; handicapé moteur; handicapé sensoriel; infirmité motrice cérébrale

PROJECT DESCRIPTION

The focus of the project is on children who find it difficult to negotiate their way around in the environment i.e. children who cannot judge the size of doorways, who cannot perceive distances accurately etc. Such children are handicapped in a school setting because they need so much help from others with their wheelchairs, in physical education lessons, on the way to school etc. The aim of the study will be to try to establish what causes these problems - lack of motor experience, visual disorders such as squints which lead to absence of stereopsis and types of brain disorder will be investigated.

13353 Perceptions of children with special educational needs.

GBR 1993

Research Date(s): 1989-1991

Wade, C.

Inst: Birmingham University, School of Education, Edgbaston, Birmingham B15 2TT, United Kingdom.

Fin: Leverhulme Foundation Fellowship.

handicapped; special education; pupil attitude; educational need; cross-national research

handicapé; enseignement spécial; attitude de l'élève; besoin d'éducation; recherche transnationale

PROJECT DESCRIPTION

The clients in education are infrequently consulted; where the clients are designated as having special educational needs consultation is rare. The investigation presumes that what such pupils can tell us about their feelings and attitudes to their educational experiences will be of valid use in determining educational provision.

Approximately 135 children have answered (written, verbal, scribed) questionnaires and a similar number have answered a sentence completion instrument. This sample is a mix of hearing impaired, visually impaired, physically handicapped, mentally handicapped and learning difficulties pupils aged 7-16. In depth interviews complement the surveys and these are drawn from Australia and New Zealand as well as the United Kingdom.

13354   Post-school learning opportunities for people with profound intellectual and multiple impairments.
GBR   1993
Research Date(s): 1991-1993
Griffiths, M.
Sup: Hood, P.
Inst: MENCAP National Centre, 123 Golden Lane, London EC1Y ORT, United Kingdom; Further Education Unit, Spring Gardens, Citadel Place, Tinworth Street, London SE11 5EH, United Kingdom.
Fin: Department of Health; Further Education Unit.
mentally handicapped; adult education; educational opportunities; multiple disability; curriculum development
handicapé mental; éducation des adultes; chances d'éducation; multihandicap; élaboration de programmes d'études
PROJECT DESCRIPTION
The aim of the project is to identify existing practice and the current perceptions of learning opportunities for adults with profound intellectual impairment who are likely to have multiple disabilities and to produce a curriculum framework for these learners. The project will use the following methods: (a) a nationwide survey by questionnaire; (b) selection from the above and otherwise by a multi-disciplinary working group who will: (1) identify core learning experiences; (2) generate a curriculum framework; (3) produce and test learning material.

13355   Primary school children's understanding of severe learning difficulties.
GBR   1993
Research Date(s): 1990-
Lewis, A.
Inst: Warwick University, Faculty of Educational Studies, Coventry CV4 7AL, United Kingdom.
mentally handicapped; integration; comprehension; learning difficulty; age difference
handicapé mental; intégration; compréhension; difficulté de l'apprentissage; différence d'âge
PROJECT DESCRIPTION
This research investigated non-handicapped (NH) children's understanding of the nature of severe learning difficulties (SLD). The literature on social cognition was reviewed in order to identify developmental changes during middle childhood in understanding about others. As a result of this review two questions about children's understanding of SLD were identified. These two questions were: which cues of SLD are salient for NH children, and do NH children recognise the irrevocability of SLD?
Two age groups, 7 and 11 year olds, were selected for interview because research on social cognition (Aboud, 1988; Schneider, 1991) suggests that there will be marked differences between these two age groups in terms of their understanding of SLD. Nineteen 7 year olds (mean age seven years, two months) were interviewed individually. Thirty-two 11 year olds (mean age eleven years, one month) were interviewed in small friendship groups of four children. All children interviewed had participated in integration projects involving children with SLD.
Findings indicated that the 7 year olds were confused about the nature of SLD and tended to believe that children with SLD had transitory sensory, but not cognitive, impairments. The 11 year olds also misunderstood the nature of SLD although they were clearer than the younger children about the irrevocability of SLD. For the 11 year olds, intra-SLD group, as well as inter group (SLD-NH), differences were recognised.
These findings are consistent with research into the development of other aspects of social cognition, for example, children's understanding of gender and race.
Publ: Lewis, A. Group child interviews as a research tool. In: *British Educational Research Journal*, Vol 18, No 4/1992, pp. 413-421.
Lewis, A. Primary school children's understanding of severe learning difficulties. In: *Educational Psychology*, Vol 13, No 1/1993.

13356   Probleemgedrag bij intrede in het Basisonderwijs. (Problem behaviour in pupils entering primary school.)
NLD   1994
Research Date(s): 1992
Vergeer, M.M.; Roede, E.
Inst: Stichting Centrum voor Onderwijsonderzoek (SCO) (Centre for Educational Research), Grote Bickersstraat 72, 1013 KS Amsterdam, Netherlands.
Universiteit van Amsterdam (University of Amsterdam), P.O. Box 19268, 1000 GG Amsterdam, Netherlands
Fin: SVO het Instituut voor Onderzoek van het Onderwijs.
behaviour disorder; child development; entry to school; measuring instrument; validity; forecasting
trouble du comportement; développement de l'enfant; entrée à l'école; instrument de mesure; validité; prévision
PROJECT DESCRIPTION

Background: In 1991 researchers Koot and Verhulst published a study on the incidence of problem behaviour in 2-3-year-olds in a representative sample of the population of the province of South Holland. One of the conclusions of the study was that the Child Behaviour Checklist for 2-3-year-olds (CBCL/2-3) is a reliable and valid instrument. It is important to identify children with a potentially pathological development at the earliest possible stage, with a view to prevention of behaviour disorders. Little is known about the predictive value of such data for behavioural problems at a later age. The present study has been initiated to examine the feasibility of a study on this subject.
Aim: To collect research evidence on the continuity or discontinuity of problem behaviour in children and relevant factors in this context; to formulate a proposal for the design of a main study on the predictive validity of the CBCL/2-3.
Design: A bibliography will be compiled comprising publications from various disciplines, such as developmental psychology, educational theory, psychiatry, and developmental pathology. The publications will be analysed for: (1) information on the measurement of problem behaviour in children aged 4-7 and (2) information on the continuity and discontinuity of problem behaviour and on the effect of characteristics of the child, parents, family, school and health services on children's problem behaviour. On the basis of the two analyses a proposal will be made for the main study. External experts will be asked to judge the proposal.

13357   Psychological assessment of cochlear implantees.
GBR   1993
Research Date(s): 1989-1994
Aplin, D.
Inst: Manchester University, School of Education, Centre for Audiology, Education of the Deaf and Speech Pathology, Oxford Road, Manchester M13 9PL, United Kingdom.
aurally handicapped; deaf; psychological examination; medical rehabilitation
handicapé auditif; sourd; examen psychologique; rééducation fonctionnelle
PROJECT DESCRIPTION
A cochlear implant has important psychological implications for recipients and usually has a major impact on the lives of implantees and their families. There have been relatively few reports of psychological assessment of patients from cochlear implant projects world-wide. Psychological assessment has formed an integral part of the Manchester multi-channel cochlear implant programme. Subjects are seen in order to assess their psychological suitability pre-implant and the progress of implantees is reviewed at regular intervals post-implant. Cognitive, educational, personality, anxiety and depression assessments are carried out. The aim of the research is to assess and monitor intellectual and personality profiles of implantees and to evaluate the psychosocial benefits of implantation. Investigation of the possible psychological predictors of audiological outcome for implantees will also be carried out. The subjects will be all cochlear implantees in the Manchester programme. Up to December 1991 29 adults (of whom three are deaf and blind) and two children (aged nine years) have been implanted with multi-channel devices. As the project is on-going, the numbers in the research will continue to increase (with 12 adults per year and a smaller number of children receiving implants). In the adult programme subjects have ranged in age from 14 to 80.

13358   Reading with young deaf children in the home.
GBR   1993
Research Date(s): 1988-1992
Watson, J.; McAree, R.
Inst: Heriot-Watt University, Moray House Institute of Education, Holyrood Road, Edinburgh EH8 8AQ, United Kingdom.
deaf; aurally handicapped; reading; parent-pupil relation; early childhood education; family environment
sourd; handicapé auditif; lecture; relation parents-élève; éducation de la prime enfance; milieu familial
PROJECT DESCRIPTION
This research will examine the reading habits of young deaf children at home at the pre-school stage, with special attention given to what happens when parents and children read together. The transition from home to school will be monitored, reading at school will be observed if possible and an attempt will be made to determine difficulties and their causes - whether a deafness or teaching and learning issue.

13359   School stress.
GBR   1993
Research Date(s): 1987-1992
May, D.
Sup: Worrall, N.
Inst: London University, Institute of Education, Department of Educational Psychology and Special Educational Needs, 20 Bedford Way, London WC1H 0AL, United Kingdom.
Fin: Nuffield Foundation.
mental stress; teacher; secondary school
tension mentale; enseignant; école secondaire
PROJECT DESCRIPTION

The research uses focused interviews of some 100 secondary school teachers. Teachers are taken through a systematic hierarchical analysis of their 'life space' with a view to identifying major and minor stress episodes. These episodes are analysed for the effective, cognitive and bodily manifestations, before, during and after the episode. In addition, teachers' offered constructs and comparisons are incorporated into the analysis. Rather than aggregate across teachers, autoregressive response modelling is used to build a model of stress and coping patterns for each teacher. As a second stage, communality across teacher models can thus be examined, with a view to developing a more general picture of teacher stress-coping patterns in secondary schools.

Publ: Worrall, N. & May, D. Towards a person-in-situation model of teacher stress. In: *British Journal of Educational Psychology*, Vol 59/1988, Part 2; pp. 174-186.

13360 Scottish Centre for Children With Motor Impairment.
GBR 1993
Research Date(s): 1991-1994
MacKay, G.; McCartney, E.; Cheseldine, S.; McCool, S.
Inst: Jordanhill College of Education, Scottish Centre for Children with Motor Impairment, Southbrae Drive, Jordanhill, Glasgow G13 1PP, United Kingdom.
Fin: Scottish Office Education Department.
motor handicapped; special education; special school
handicapé moteur; enseignement spécial; centre d'éducation spéciale
PROJECT DESCRIPTION
  This project will undertake evaluation of children's progress, development of curriculum, implementation of policy, and costs/benefits of the Scottish Centre for Children with Motor Impairment.

13361 South East Thames regional HIV education and training evaluation project.
GBR 1993
Research Date(s): 1991-1993
Aggleton, P.; Whitty, G.
Inst: London University, Institute of Education, Department of Policy Studies, Health and Education Research Unit, 20 Bedford Way, London WC1H OAL, United Kingdom.
Fin: South East Thames Regional Health Authority.
sexually transmitted disease; health education; health service personnel; training programme; training need
maladie sexuellement transmissible; éducation sanitaire; personnel médical; programme de formation; besoin de formation
PROJECT DESCRIPTION
  This is a project to evaluate the implementation of the South East Thames Regional Human Immunodeficiency Virus (HIV) Education and Training Strategy at district level. It will seek to identify via interviews with Human Immunodeficiency Virus/Acquired Immune Deficiency Syndrome (HIV/AIDS) prevention coordinators, trainers, training providers, workers in relevant non-statutory agencies and other key informants.
  The aims of the project are to discover: (1) awareness of South East Thames Regional HIV Education and Training Strategy; (2) perceptions of its appropriateness and inclusiveness in meeting the HIV/AIDS training needs of relevant health authority personnel; (3) perceptions of the effectiveness and inclusiveness of this strategy in meeting the needs of clients and carers, for appropriate priorities for future HIV education and training; (4) appropriate ways in which the South East Thames Regional Health Authority might promote and support such work; and (5) appropriate strategies by which such education and training might be monitored and evaluated on an ongoing basis.

13362 The space within an interdisciplinary study of voluntary groups engaging with AIDS and HIV.
GBR 1993
Research Date(s): 1989-1993
Henson, C.
Sup: Mackie, K.; Parsons, W.
Inst: Nottingham University, Department of Adult Education, 14-22 Shakespeare Street, Nottingham NG1 4FJ, United Kingdom.
sexually transmitted disease; adult education; voluntary organization
maladie sexuellement transmissible; éducation des adultes; organisation volontaire
PROJECT DESCRIPTION
  The aim of the research is to discover a model for adult education based on voluntary groups engaging with Acquired Immune Deficiency Syndrome (AIDS) and Human-Immunodeficiency Syndrome (HIV); and to understand the ethical and theological implications of this model. The research will include interviews with selected voluntary groups and a comparative study of educational philosophies.

13363 Speed of visual information processing.
GBR 1993
Research Date(s): 1985-
Tobin, M.; Mason, H.

Inst: Birmingham University, School of Education, Research Centre for the Education of the Visually Handicapped, Edgbaston, Birmingham B15 2TT, United Kingdom.
Fin: Birmingham University; Royal National Institute for the Blind.
visually handicapped; cognitive process; visual perception; visual learning; information processing
handicapé visuel; processus cognitif; perception visuelle; apprentissage visuel; traitement de l'information
PROJECT DESCRIPTION
  The aim of this research is to measure the speed of visual information processing of partially sighted pupils on tasks similar to those used with their fully sighted peers. Preliminary findings have indicated a large discrepancy between the average performances of the partially sighted and the published norms for the fully sighted. Further work is now being undertaken with a larger sample of partially sighted children with a view to reducing normative data for the population of partially sighted pupils. Trials are also being conducted on a test to measure speed of tactile information processing.

Publ: Tobin, M.J. & Mason, H. Speed of information processing and the visually handicapped child. In: *British Journal of Special Education*, Vol 13, No 2/1986, pp. 69-70, June (Research Supplement).

13364 Spracherwerb bei blinden und gehoerlosen Kindern. (Language acquisition of blind and deaf children.)
AUT 1993
Research Date(s): 1992-1993
Peltzer-Karpf, Annemarie; Sireteanu, Ruxandra; Jantscher, Elisabeth; Kroissenbrunner, Anita; Posch, Hermine; Rauch, Astrid; Zangl, Renate; Rettenbach, Regina.
Inst: Institut fuer Anglistik, Heinrichstrasse 36, A-8010 Graz; Abteilung fuer Neurophysiologie, Deutschordenstrasse 46, D-6000 Frankfurt/Main. Universitaet Graz, Heinrichstrasse 36, A-8010 Graz; Max-Planck-Institut fuer Hirnforschung, Deutschordenstrasse 46, D-6000 Frankfurt/Main
Fin: Oesterreichische Nationalbank; Deutsche Forschungsgemeinschaft.
perceptual handicap; language development; perceptual training; aurally handicapped; visually handicapped
handicap sensoriel; développement du langage; éducation de la perception; handicapé auditif; handicapé visuel
PROJECT DESCRIPTION
  Das zentrale Thema des projekts ist die Anpassung des kindlichen Zentralnervensystems an eine unvollkommene Ausgangssituation. An Vorschulkindern soll untersucht werden, wie die Entwicklung von Funktionssystemen (und damit verbunden der Erwerb von Sprache) bei einem partiellen oder totalen Ausfall der visuellen oder auditiven Wahrnehmung verlaeuft. Erfasst werden sollen die Auswirkungen eines sensorischen Defekts auf andere Systeme mit dem Ziel, Unterschiede zu identifizieren, intersensorielle Kompensationsmechanismen zu foerdern und Teilleistungsstoerungen zu beheben. Ausgegangen wird vom Prinzip der Selbstorganisation, das die Entwicklung als einen Dialog der angeborenen Faehigkeiten mit der Umwelt sieht (der in speziellen Bereichen auch intensiviert werden kann). Die in Koordination mit psychophysischen Messungen durchgefuehrte sprachliche Untersuchung konzentriert sich auf die Entwicklung hoeher geordneter kognitiver Systeme und die aus den Defekten resultierende Beeintraechtigung der Kommunikationsfaehigtkeit. Die Daten werden mit den Erwerbsmustern nicht behinderter Kinder verglichen. Besonderes Augenmerk wird auf die Muster- und Kategorienbildung gelegt, die je nach Defekt auf der Basis visuell bzw. akustisch/taktil erfassbarer Merkmale erfolgen muss. Die Praezision und Latenz der Informationsverarbeitung wird durch Sehschaerfetests und akustische Perimetrie festgestellt.
  Es erfolgt eine Untersuchung der Spontansprache und des Kommunikationsverhaltens, gezielte linguistische Tests zu den sprachlichen Systemen (inklusive Textebene) kommen zur Anwendung. Beobachtungen, Audio- und Videoaufzeichnungen werden unter dem linguistischen Aspekt durchgefuehrt. Mit der Einzeluntersuchung von insgesamt ca. 100 Vorschulkindern (Kontrolluntersuchungen mit 8- bis 10jaehrigen Kindern) - in den Gruppen der Blinden, Gehoerlosen, Sehenden und Hoerenden - werden die Daten gewonnen. Benton-Test bei gehoerlosen Kindern, Reaktionszeitexperiment, Sehschaerfepruefung durch Landolt Ringe und Pruefung der Kontrastsensitivitaet und des Stereo- und Farbensehens zur Textursegmentierung dienen dem biophysikalischen Aspekt.
  Es werden sowohl linguistische Tests - Chi-Quadrat, Pearson-Analyse, t-Test, Computeranalyse der Spontansprache, Reynell-Skalen - als auch biophysikalische Untersuchungen - Auswertung des Benton-Tests und der visuellen Basisfunktionen nach Manualen, RT und hoehere visuelle Funktionen nach Computerprogramm und mit inferenzstatistischen Methoden - durchgefuehrt.

13365 Stress, coping en leren: een longitudinaal onderzoek. (Stress, coping and learning: a longitudinal study.)
NLD 1994
Research Date(s): 1992
Boekaerts, M.; Goor, J. van den.
Sup: Seegers, G.

Inst: Vakgroep Onderwijsstudies (Department of Studies of Education), P.O. Box 9555, 2300 RB Leiden, Netherlands.

Rijksuniversiteit Leiden (State University of Leiden), P.O. Box 9555, 2300 RB Leiden, Netherlands

Fin: SVO het Instituut voor Onderzoek van het Onderwijs.

mental stress; adjustment; behaviour; achievement; pupil; perception; absenteeism

tension mentale; adaptation; comportement; rendement; élève; perception; absentéisme

PROJECT DESCRIPTION

Background: Many pupils experience the transition from primary to secondary school as a stressful event which requires considerable adaptation. Data from an earlier project which examined the transition from primary to secondary school show that the relationships between perceived stress, pupils' coping behaviour, perceptions of social support, motivation and achievement are complex. One way to cast more light on these relationships is to examine their development through time. This is especially important for the timely identification of pupils who are at risk of getting into a problem situation.

Aim: To examine how the nature of stressors, the intensity of the levels of stress pupils experience and pupils' coping behaviours develop in time; to provide a basis, with the help of these longitudinal data, for the development of a preventive approach toward stress among pupils.

Design: The sample of the earlier study will be used: 861 pupils from 34 classes in 10 combined schools in the Doetinchem-Grave-Venlo region. The same four questionnaires will be administered: the Stress and Coping Questionnaire for First-Year Secondary School Pupils (SCVL-B), the Questionnaire on Stressful Life Events (VSL), the Social Support Questionnaire and the Motivation Questionnaire. Report card marks obtained in the first year will be used as a measure of pupils' ability. On the basis of repeated measurements a model will be constructed which will specify how the relationships between the variables determine the development of pupils' perceptions of stress and social support. Comparative analysis will be made of high-attaining vs. low-attaining pupils, pupils at academically-oriented schools vs. pupils at vocational schools, and pupils who are often absent vs. pupils who are seldom absent.

13366   Stress in children.

GBR   1993

Research Date(s): 1990-1995

Robson, M.

Sup: Cook, P.; Gilliland, J.

Inst: Durham University, School of Education, Leazes Road, Durham DH1 1TA, United Kingdom.

mental stress; adolescent; attitude; unconscious

tension mentale; adolescent; attitude; inconscient

PROJECT DESCRIPTION

The aim of this research is to investigate stress as it is perceived by adolescents in secondary schools and to build a paradigm of this perception. It is also proposed to design an intervention system that could be used in schools to teach adolescents to cope more successfully with stress. The cognitive paradigm that is useful in understanding the stress process seems incomplete without an acknowledgement of the role of unconscious learning and perception and this research aims to extend the model to include this. It is hoped that the role played by our unconscious in the perception of, and reaction to, stress may be incorporated in the model of the stress process as well as in the intervention system.

The size and composition of the sample has not yet been established although exploratory pilot studies suggest that stress is a meaningful concept in the adolescents' world. From these exploratory studies, stressors seem many and various and the individual's perception of the stress appears to rest upon factors which include learned responses, social support and personality. Coping strategies are also many and various and likewise appear to rest upon the same mediating factors, as well as the individuals' perceived control over the stressors.

13367   Stress on college lecturers working in the North East of England and its possible effects on student learning.

GBR   1993

Research Date(s): 1986-1991

Snape, J.

Sup: Child, D.

Inst: Leeds University, School of Education, Leeds LS2 9JT, United Kingdom.

mental stress; teaching personnel; teacher-pupil relation; post-compulsory education

tension mentale; corps enseignant; relation maître-élève; enseignement postobligatoire

PROJECT DESCRIPTION

This study presents the findings of research into aspects of stress among lecturers working in colleges of further education in the North East of England. The empirical work was carried out over one academic year with 130 lecturers and 213 of their students, all chosen at random, participating in the study. Seven instruments were used, namely: a 'stress' questionnaire; two types of logs, and a personality questionnaire for lecturers; and one 'annoyance' questionnaire and two types of logs for students. The study set out to address the broad question of whether stress among college lecturers affected the teaching process and, in turn, the students' learning.

The data highlighted that there were three broad problem areas or sources of stress for the lecturers: the teaching process; relationships; and other factors. These were further divided into the categories: resources; teaching; environment; students; staff; management; aspects external to the college; and administration. The effects of these stressors on the lecturers were demonstrated in feelings and actions which affected the role as a teacher, both inside and outside the classroom. Statistical analysis of all the responses revealed that similar stressors, and sources of annoyance, occurred throughout the academic year in all the colleges sampled. The lecturers with the most class-contact were found to have lower levels of self-esteem and higher levels of anxiety. This aspect was demonstrated particularly by female respondents, and those new to teaching. There were indications that the teaching process and students' learning were negatively affected by lecturers' stress, as perceived either directly or indirectly, by both students and lecturers. It was the potential learning experience that was seen to be most at risk.

13368   Study of the IBM Screen Reader for blind students in distance education.

GBR   1993

Research Date(s): 1989-1991

Vincent, T.

Inst: Open University, Institute of Educational Technology, Walton Hall, Milton Keynes MK7 6AA, United Kingdom.

Fin: IBM; Open University Development Fund.

blind; visually handicapped; distance study; computer; writing

aveugle; handicapé visuel; enseignement à distance; ordinateur; écriture

PROJECT DESCRIPTION

The study seeks to establish how the IBM PS/2 computer and Screen Reader can be used to meet the needs of blind Open University students studying from home for those activities where writing is an essential component of the course-related activities, such as assignment and essay writing. Three students are involved: two who are following Arts or Social Studies courses and have little or no computer literacy; one who will be following a computing, mathematics, science or technology course where a degree of computer literacy might be expected.

In each case, the students will have their individual needs assessed; and a programme of induction training arranged (using or supplementing training material provided with the Screen Reader) to provide the necessary skills in using the Screen Reader. Further advice and training will be provided to meet specific needs and applications.

The evaluation will focus on how quickly and easily a student can progress to independence in the various writing activities associated with distance education. Progress towards independence in using the Screen Reader and application software will be closely monitored. In particular, the relationship to the level of support (advice and training) provided will be examined.

13369   A study of the long-term foster care of children and young people with severe learning difficulties.

GBR   1993

Research Date(s): 1990-1992

Ames, J.

Sup: Berridge, D.

Inst: National Children's Bureau, 8 Wakley Street, London EC1V 7QE, United Kingdom.

Fin: Barnardo's.

adopted child; adoption; family life; learning difficulty; handicapped

enfant adopté; adoption; vie familiale; difficulté de l'apprentissage; handicapé

PROJECT DESCRIPTION

Barnardo's has been closely involved in establishing schemes to enable young people with a range of problems to live with families. This research programme focuses on the work of one such scheme, the Professional Fostering Project, based in Barnardo's northwest division in Liverpool. This project establishes and supports foster placements for around 70 young people with severe learning disabilities. Given the complex dynamics of foster-care placements, the general question addressed in the research is: how can Barnardo's fostering project staff secure and sustain successful foster placements for children and young people with severe learning disabilities? In addition to a broad evaluation of the current work of the fostering project, two aspects of the work are being examined in detail: (1) the experiences and feelings of the natural children of foster carers about sharing their homes with young people fostered through the project; (2) the impact of placing a second child from the project upon the life of a household.

13370 Survey of aphasia service provision.
GBR 1993
Research Date(s): 1990-1991
MacKenzie, C.
Inst: Jordanhill College of Education, Division of Speech Therapy, Southbrae Drive, Glasgow G13 1PP, United Kingdom.
aphasia; speech defect; special education; educational provision
aphasie; trouble de la parole; enseignement spécial; scolarisation
PROJECT DESCRIPTION
   This project aims to establish the nature and variation of aphasia service provision in the United Kingdom.
Publ: MacKenzie, C. Speech therapy services to aphasic adults in the United Kingdom. Paper presented at British Aphasiology Society Conference, September 1991, Sheffield.
MacKenzie, C. Pattern of aphasia services in the United Kingdom, with special reference to Scotland. Paper presented to joint study day of Care of the Elderly Special Interest Group/British Aphasiology Society, December 1991, Glasgow.

13371 Survey of communication practices in schools for the hearing impaired in the United Kingdom.
GBR 1993
Research Date(s): 1990-1992
Child, D.; Baker, R.
Inst: Leeds University, School of Education, Leeds LS2 9JT, United Kingdom.
Fin: Northern Counties School for the Deaf.
deaf; communication; aurally handicapped; special school; special education
sourd; communication; handicapé auditif; centre d'éducation spéciale; enseignement spécial
PROJECT DESCRIPTION
   In 1987 a survey was carried out with a number of schools for the hearing impaired in England and Scotland using a total communication approach. When the findings were circulated, suggestions were made by several headteachers for a further study to explore in more detail the ways in which different modes of communication are used, demand for resource materials, training of staff and parents in communication skills and the roles of deaf people in the schools. It has subsequently been suggested that a new survey be carried out to establish exactly what range of approaches are used throughout all the schools at the present time.
   A questionnaire was designed which asks for communication approaches in use, in order to provide a base of information for planning for future needs. At the same time, it goes more deeply into aspects of practices in schools using a total communication approach, in response to the requests already made by headteachers. The questionnaire has now been circulated and a 100% return obtained.

13372 Teacher stress and organisational climate.
GBR 1993
Research Date(s): 1989-1993
Reid, G.
Sup: Hinton, J.
Inst: Heriot-Watt University, Moray House Institute of Education, Holyrood Road, Edinburgh EH8 8AQ, United Kingdom; Glasgow University, Department of Psychology, Glasgow G12 8QQ, United Kingdom.
mental stress; teacher behaviour; school environment
tension mentale; comportement de l'enseignant; milieu scolaire
PROJECT DESCRIPTION
   The results from four pilot studies already undertaken show a need for examination of teacher stress from the perspectives of personal organisation, school organisation and organisational climate. The study will, therefore, develop some strands identified in the pilot studies including the following: (1) the implications of personal organisation for inservice programmes including aspects such as time management, staff support and staff training; (2) the effect of school organisation on communications, staff support, interpersonal links, role factors, curriculum development and curriculum and organisational changes; (3) the nature of the school organisational climate and its importance in relation to school management - staff morale, motivation, sociability and efficiency.
   Reading has revealed stress factors such as role overload; time management; administration; fragmentation; interpersonal relations; interpersonal support; openness of staff discussions; leadership skills; school communications network; role conflict and locus of control. The problem it appears with identifying stress contributory factors such as the list above, is that it is acknowledged that teacher stress is a multi-faceted phenomenon and the identification of isolated factors can be misleading and unhelpful for the development and delivery of a school inservice stress management programme.
   The study examines the theme of organisation, aiming to support the following hypotheses: (a) personal organisation, school organisation and organisational climate are influential factors in stress generation among teachers in schools; (b) stress management inservice programmes need to address these issues for enhanced effectiveness; and (c) the theoretical

model of psychological stress (Hinton 1991) is a valid model of examining perceived stress among teachers.
Publ: Reid, G. Supporting the support teacher: stress factors in teaching children with specific learning difficulties. In: *Links*, Vol 16, No 3/1991, pp. 18-20.

13373 Teaching under pressure.
GBR 1993
Research Date(s): 1993
Cockburn, A.
Inst: University of East Anglia, School of Education, Norwich NR4 7TJ, United Kingdom.
Fin: Nuffield Foundation.
mental stress; teacher behaviour; teaching profession
tension mentale; comportement de l'enseignant; profession d'enseignant
PROJECT DESCRIPTION
   Stress in the teaching profession is reaching critical proportions, yet there is very little comprehensible and comprehensive help and advice for teachers. The aim of this study is to produce a practical and insightful guide for trainee, beginning and experienced teachers, on the sources, responses and possible solutions to the negative aspects of stress in their lives. Using a sample of local primary teachers and structured and clinical interview techniques, this investigation will examine teachers' experiences of stress, their awareness of its effects and how, if at all, they manage it.

13374 The use of information technology in adult basic education of students with physical and sensory handicaps.
GBR 1993
Research Date(s): 1987-
Leicester, D.; Busby, M.; Green, P.
Sup: Jotham, R.
Inst: Nottingham University, Department of Adult Education, 14-22 Shakespeare Street, Nottingham NG1 4FJ, United Kingdom.
Fin: Leverhulme Trust; Nottinghamshire County Council; Lincolnshire County Council; Derbyshire County Council.
handicapped; computer literacy; basic education; information technology; adult education
handicapé; initiation à l'informatique; éducation de base; technologie de l'information; éducation des adultes
PROJECT DESCRIPTION
   Against a backcloth of computer courses for disabled adults in the University Adult Centre at Nottingham University, students whose educational needs lie primarily in the area of adult basic education, are working individually and/or in very small groups. Various teaching methods and materials are compared and contrasted, but the principle methodology is regular review of students' progress with tutors and Centre staff. The group of students under study numbers approximately 50.
Publ: A complete list of publications is available from the researchers.

13375 Visually impaired people in their mid-twenties: educational, vocational, and personal ambitions and needs.
GBR 1993
Research Date(s): 1990-
Tobin, M.; Hill, E.
Inst: Birmingham University, School of Education, Research Centre for the Education of the Visually Handicapped, Edgbaston, Birmingham B15 2TT, United Kingdom.
Fin: Guide Dogs for the Blind Association; Royal National Institute for the Blind; Birmingham University.
visually handicapped; educational need; ability; aspiration; adult
handicapé visuel; besoin d'éducation; capacité; aspiration; adulte
PROJECT DESCRIPTION
   This research forms part of a project concerning young visually handicapped people and those over the age of 60. It is a five year investigation into the changing skills, abilities, ambitions, life styles, and needs of such people with a visual handicap.
   The methodology consists of postal questionnaires, telephone and face-to-face interviews. Initially a core group of some 50 to 100 subjects will be assembled. The sample will be increased from time to time to deal with specific, ad hoc topics of concern to the population of visually impaired people.

13376 Visuelle Wahrnehmung bei Dyslexie: auf der Suche nach physischen Ursachen. (Perception visuelle des personnes dyslexiques: à la recherche de causes physiologiques.)
CHE 1994
Research Date(s): 1991-
Müller, Peter.
Sup: Groner, Rudolf.
Inst: Universität Bern, Psychologisches Institut, Laupenstrasse 4, 3008 Bern, Schweiz.
perceptual handicap; dyslexia; perception test
handicap sensoriel; dyslexie; test perceptif
PROJECT DESCRIPTION

Aufgrund von in Australien, Kanada und den USA gemachten Befunden ergibt sich die Vermutung, dass die Dyslexie (Lese-Rechschreib-Schwäche) in Verbindung stehen könnte mit gewissen Anomalien der visuellen Wahrnehmung. Im Rahmen seiner Dissertation will der Autor dieser Arbeit einerseits wissen, ob sich diese Befunde aus der angelsächsischen Welt anhand einer schweizerischen Stichprobe replizieren lassen; zum anderen will er zwei neue psychophysische Testverfahren einführen und überprüfen.

In einem zweiten Schritt wird es darum gehen, die Implikationen näher zu untersuchen, welche die diagnostizierte Schwäche auf den Lesevorgang hat. Beim Lesen bewegt sich das Auge in ruckartigen Bewegungen über den Text und bleibt zwischen diesen - Sakkaden genannten - schnellen Bewegungen jeweils für eine Dauer von 200 bis 300 Tausendstelsekunden stehen. Es wäre nun möglich, dass das Auge des dyslexischen Kindes nicht in der Lage ist, während dieser kurzen Ruhezeiten ein klares Informationspaket an das übergeordnete Verarbeitungssytem zu übermitteln. Eine andere Erklärungsmöglichkeit wäre die, dass das dyslexische Kind Mühe hat, sich im Text zu orientieren. Während der erwähnten Ruhephase ist das Auge nämlich funktional blind; nach jeder Phase muss es sich deshalb erneut im Text zurechtfinden.

Fragen der Behandlung stehen in diesem Projekt im Hintergrund. Die Forschungsresultate könnten jedoch klare Hinweise darauf erlauben, in welche Richtung eine Behandlung zu gehen hätte, wobei es Sache eines Folgeprojekts wäre, entsprechende Therapien zu entwickeln.

13377 Wissenschaftliche Begleitung des Foerderlehrganges fuer psychisch Behinderte als berufsvorbereitende Bildungsmassnahme nach Paragraph 40 AFG im Jugenddorf Blaesiberg. (Evaluation research on remedial teaching for the mentally disabled in Blaesiberg as a prevocational training programme in accordance with Section 40 of the Employment Promotion Act (AFG).)
DEU 1993
Research Date(s): 1991-1994
Schreifeldt, K.
Sup: Schaeuble, I.
Inst: Schaeuble Institut fuer Sozialforschung, Ickstattstr. 5, D-8000 Muenchen 5.
Fin: Bundesministerium fuer Arbeit und Sozialordnung.
handicapped; behaviour disorder; vocational preparation; adolescent; remedial teaching; occupational integration
handicapé; trouble du comportement; initiation à la profession; adolescent; soutien pédagogique; intégration professionnelle
PROJECT DESCRIPTION
Inhalt: Zur beruflichen Eingliederung von Rehabilitanden mit psychischen Stoerungen und anderen Verhaltensauffaelligkeiten muss das Instrumentarium noch ausgeweitet werden, um dem sozialrechtlichen Anspruch auf berufliche Rehabilitation gerecht zu werden. Im Jugenddorf Blaesiberg wird eine spezifische Vorbereitungsmassnahme durchgefuehrt, die die jungen Menschen auf die Anforderungen einer 3-jaehrigen Berufsausbildung oder die Einmuendung in ein Arbeitsverhaeltnis vorbereitet. Dabei wird den spezifischen Beduerfnissen dieser Zielgruppe Rechnung getragen und neuen Stigmatisierungsprozessen entgegengewirkt. Die wissenschaftliche Begleitung ist auf berufspaedagogische Kriterien ausgerichtet.
Geographischer Raum: Bundesrepublik Deutschland.
Untersuchter Zeitraum: 1991-1994.
Vorgehensweise: Untersuchungsdesign: Evaluationsstudie.
Datengewinnung: Expertengespraech (Gespraeche mit Betreuungspersonal, Leitung und ExpertInnen; Auswahlverfahren: total). Gruppendiskussion (mit Betreuungspersonal, Leitung und ExpertInnen; Auswahlverfahren: total). Personenzentrierte Gespraeche (Stichprobe: 40; Einzelfallstudien mit TeilnehmerInnen; Auswahlverfahren: total). Primaererhebung: Feldarbeit von Mitarbeitern des Projektes durchgefuehrt.

13378 Wissenschaftliche Begleitung des Modellversuchs "Gemeinsamer Unterricht mit unterschiedlicher Zielvorgabe fuer nichtbehinderte und behinderte SchuelerInnen im Bereich der Sekundarstufe I". (Evaluation research for the pilot project "Mixed classes with differential objectives for disabled and non-disabled pupils in lower-level secondary schools".)
DEU 1993
Research Date(s): 1990-1993
Schmidt, H.; Schnitzler, P.
Sup: Sander, A.
Inst: Universitaet Saarbruecken, FB 06 Sozial- und Umweltwissenschaften, Fachrichtung Erziehungswissenschaft, Stadtwald Bau 8, D-6600 Saarbruecken.
Fin: Bundesministerium fuer Bildung und Wissenschaft; Land Saarland Ministerium fuer Bildung und Sport.
handicapped; secondary education; primary education; teaching method; pupil integration; pupil
handicapé; enseignement secondaire; enseignement primaire; méthode pédagogique; intégration scolaire; élève
PROJECT DESCRIPTION
Inhalt: Uebergeordnete Fragestellungen: (1) Wie kann der Uebergang aus integrativen Klassen der Primarstufe in die Sekundarstufe paedagogisch

besser gestaltet werden? (2) Welche Spezifika der Sekundarstufe sind bei der zieldifferenten Integration behinderter Schueler/innen zu beruecksichtigen? (3) Welche Auswirkungen hat zieldifferente Integration in der Sekundarstufe I auf die Entwicklung der Schueler/innen?
Hypothesen: (1) Der Uebergang aus integrativen Klassen der Primarstufe in die Sekundarstufe I kann durch am Einzelfall orientierte paedagogische Unterstuetzung optimiert werden. (2) Das Team-Kleingruppen-Modell ist fuer zieldifferente Integration Behinderter in die Sekundarstufe I besser geeignet als traditionelle Formen der Unterrichtsorganisation. (3) Wenn zieldifferente Integration in der Sekundarstufe I einzelfallorientiert paedagogisch unterstuetzt wird, foerdert sie sowohl die Schulleistungsentwicklung als auch die soziale Entwicklung der betroffenen Schueler.
Geographischer Raum: Saarland.
Vorgehensweise: Oekosystemisch/entwicklungstheoretischer Ansatz; Elemente von Handlungsforschung; formative und summative Evaluation. Untersuchungsdesign: Evaluationsstudie; Trend; qualitative Forschung.
Datengewinnung: Befragung (Stichprobe: 38; Klassen der Sekundarstufe I; Auswahlverfahren: total. Stichprobe: 24; Kinder der Klassenstufe 5, die integrativ unterrichtet werden -"behinderte"-; Auswahlverfahren: total. Stichprobe: 18; Klassen der Klassenstufe 5; Auswahlverfahren: total. Weitere Bezugspersonen der beh. Kinder, insbesondere Eltern, ggf. Fachlehrer, Schulrat u.a.). Nicht-standardisiertes Interview (Stichprobe 18 KL, 18 SoL; die integrativ unterrichten in der Kl.-Stufe 5; Auswahlverfahren: total. Stichprobe: 24; Kinder der Klassenstufe 5, die integrativ unterrichtet werden -"behinderte"-; Auswahlverfahren: total. Weitere Bezugspersonen der beh. Kinder, insbesondere Eltern, ggf. Fachlehrer, Schulrat u.a.). Telefoninterview (Stichprobe: 18 KL, 18 SoL; die integrativ unterrichten in der Kl.-Stufe 5; Auswahlverfahren: total. Stichprobe: 24; Kinder der Klassenstufe 5, die integrativ unterrichtet werden - "behinderte"-; Auswahlverfahren: total). Teilnehmende Beobachtung, Beobachtung (Stichprobe: 18 KL, 18 SoL; die integrativ unterrichten in der Kl.-Stufe 5; Auswahlverfahren; total. Stichprobe: 24; Kinder der Klassenstufe 5, die integrativ unterrichtet werden -"behinderte"-; Auswahlverfahren: total. Stichprobe: 18; Klassen der Klassenstufe 5; Auswahlverfahren: total). Primaererhebung: Feldarbeit von Mitarbeitern des Projektes durchgefuehrt; Datenerstellung auf der Basis von bereits vorliegenden Materialien wie Texten, Akten, Statistiken.
Auswertung: Clusteranalyse bzw. Faktorenanalyse (geplant); multiple Chi-Quadrat-Analyse; spezielle Verfahren zur Soziogramm-Analyse. Datenaufbereitung: Verlaufsdaten (event history data); Verknuepfung verschiedener Datensaetze (record linkage).

13379 Wissenschaftliche Begleitung des Modellversuchs "Sonderpaedagogische Foerderzentren als Weiterentwicklung der Organisation Sonderpaedagogischer Arbeit fuer behinderte Schueler und Schuelerinnen. (Evaluation research for the pilot project "Special education promotion centres as a further development of the organization of special pedagogic work for disabled pupils".)
DEU 1993
Research Date(s): 1991-1994
Hoffmann, E.; Jung, J.; Raidt-Petrick, M.
Sup: Sander, A.
Inst: Universitaet Saarbruecken, FB 06 Sozial- und Umweltwissenschaften, Fachrichtung Erziehungswissenschaft, Stadtwald Bau 8, D-6600 Saarbruecken.
Fin: Bundesministerium fuer Bildung und Wissenschaft; Land Saarland Ministerium fuer Bildung und Sport.
handicap; pupil; remedial instruction sciences; pilot project; remedial teaching; social integration; general education
handicap; élève; pédagogie spéciale; projet-pilote; soutien pédagogique; intégration sociale; enseignement général
PROJECT DESCRIPTION
Inhalt: Uebergeordnete Fragestellungen: (1) Wie koennen Sonderschulen (Schulen fuer Behinderte) zu Sonderpaedagogischen Foerderzentren so weiterentwickelt werden, dass Uebergangsschwierigkeiten minimiert werden und. die Effektivitaet gesteigert wird? (2) Wie kann das Sonderpaedagogische Foerderzentrum (SFZ) die sonderpaedagogische Versorgung des bisherigen Sonderschul-Einzugsbereiches sicherstellen? (3) Welchen besonderen Beitrag kann das SFZ leisten zur Verbesserung der Integration von Kindern und Jugendlichen mit Behinderungen?
Hypothesen: (1) Schulen fuer Behinderte koennen durch gezielte und systematische Vorbereitungsmassnahmen, in denen eine intensive Kooperation mit den beteiligten Lehrpersonen erfolgt, zu effektiv arbeitenden Sonderpaedagogischen Foerderzentren weiterentwickelt werden. (2) Das Sonderpaedagogische Foerderzentrum kann die sonderpaedagogische Betreuung behinderter Schueler /innen in laendlichen Regionen zufriedenstellend gewaehrleisten. (3) Das Sonderpaedagogische Foerderzentrum ist geeignet, die schulische Integration behinderter Schueler/innen in den Regelschulen zu optimieren.
Geographischer Raum: Saarland.
Vorgehensweise: Elemente von Handlungsforschung, subjektorientierter Sozialforschung, Organisationsentwicklung/Prozessevaluation; qualitative, quantitative Methoden. Untersuchungsdesign: Evaluationsstudie; qualitative Forschung.

Datengewinnung: Standardisiertes Interview, Gruppendiskussion (Stichprobe: 5; LehrerInnen einer laendl. SS fuer Lernbehinderte; Auswahlverfahren: total. Stichprobe: 13; LehrerInnen der Schule fuer Sprachbehinderte des Saarl.; Auswahlverfahren: total). Expertengespraech (Stichprobe: 5; LehrerInnen einer laendl. SS fuer Lernbehinderte; Auswahlverfahren: total. Stichprobe: 13; LehrerInnen der Schule fuer Sprachbehinderte des Saarl.; Auswahlverfahren: total. LehrerInnen von Regelschulen, ggf. weitere Bezugspersonen der beh. Kinder - Eltern, ExpertInnen von Gesundheits-/Sozialeinrichtungen...). Primaererhebung: Feldarbeit von Mitarbeitern des Projektes durchgefuehrt; Datenerstellung auf der Basis von bereits vorliegenden Materialien wie Texten, Akten, Statistiken geplant.

Il ruolo delle condizioni ambientali nello stress lavorativo e nel burnout in professioni di aiuto (The role of environmental conditions in occupational stress and burnout in the helping professions) ....
.... see no. 13589
Integration von sehgeschaedigten Studierenden und Hochschulabsolventen in die Arbeitswelt (Integration of visually handicapped students and university graduates in working life) .... see no. 13594
AIDS Education and Research Trust (AVERT) HIV/AIDS and nursing project .... see no. 13648
The employment of disabled teaching staff .... see no. 13730
Législation de la jeunesse et institutions aujourd'hui: recherche comparative internationale.. see no. 13737

27 INTERRELATIONS – INTERRELATIONS – WECHSELBEZIEHUNGEN

13380 Bestandsaufnahme der Kooperation zwischen Betrieben und Einrichtungen der Erwachsenenbildung im Bereich Senioren-Weiterbildung. (Current state of cooperation between companies and adult education institutions in the field of further education for senior citizens.)
DEU 1993
Research Date(s): 1991-1993
Sutter, H.
Inst: Arbeitsgruppe fuer empirische Bildungsforschung e.V. -AFEB-, Werderstrasse 38, D-6900 Heidelberg.
Fin: Bundesministerium fuer Bildung und Wissenschaft.
cooperation; adult education; enterprise; educational institution; elderly person; employee; further training
coopération; éducation des adultes; entreprise; établissement d'enseignement; personne âgée; salarié; formation complémentaire
PROJECT DESCRIPTION
Inhalt: Moeglichkeiten der Kooperation zwischen Betrieben mittlerer Groessenordnung und Weiterbildungseinrichtungen bei der Erstellung von Weiterbildungsangeboten fuer aeltere Arbeitnehmer; Interessen, Bereitschaft, Probleme der Betriebe bei Fragen der Organisation, Finanzierung, Freistellung, Personalplanung u.a.
Geographischer Raum: Bundesrepublik Deutschland.
Vorgehensweise: Expertengespraeche; Fragebogenerhebung.

13381 Central Regional Council (Scotland) Youth Strategy - an evaluative study of school liaison groups.
GBR 1993
Research Date(s): 1990-1991
McCullough, D.
Inst: Jordanhill College of Education, Division of Social Work, Southbrae Drive, Glasgow G13 1PP, United Kingdom.
Fin: Central Regional Council; Jordanhill College.
school-community relation; group; cooperation
relation école-collectivité; groupe; coopération
PROJECT DESCRIPTION
The study aims to establish the extent to which school liaison groups are effective in helping to maintain children in their own communities, and in encouraging inter-agency co-operation for the assessment of children's needs and the provision of appropriate resources.
Publ: McCullough, D.R. *Developing a Strategy - a review of school liaison groups in Central Region.* Central Regional Council, December 1991.

13382 Clusters project.
GBR 1993
Research Date(s): 1991-1993
Wedell, K.; Norwich, B.; Lunt, I.; Evans, J.
Inst: London University, Institute of Education, Department of Educational Psychology and Special Educational Needs, 20 Bedford Way, London WC1H OAL, United Kingdom.
Fin: Economic and Social Research Council.
regional cooperation; special education; special school
coopération régionale; enseignement spécial; centre d'éducation spéciale
PROJECT DESCRIPTION
The project will describe the functioning of the cluster from an organisational point of view and look at the impact of the cluster organisation on special educational needs provision. Clusters of schools will be visited in four local education authorities (LEAs) and interviews of headteachers, teachers, educational psychologists and other LEA personnel will be carried out.

13383 Clusters Project (Extension).
GBR 1993
Research Date(s): 1993-1994
Wedell, K.; Lunt, I.; Norwich, B.; Evans, J.
Inst: London University, Institute of Education, Department of Educational Psychology and Special Educational Needs, 20 Bedford Way, London WC1H OAL, United Kingdom.
Fin: Waldburg Foundation.
regional cooperation; special education; special school
coopération régionale; enseignement spécial; centre d'éducation spéciale
PROJECT DESCRIPTION
This is an extension of the Clusters Project funded by the Economic and Social Research Council.

13384 Collaborative writing.
GBR 1993
Research Date(s): 1990-1993
Rimmershaw, R.
Inst: Lancaster University, Department of Educational Research, Cartmel College, Bailrigg, Lancaster LA1 4YW, United Kingdom.
cooperation; writing; author
coopération; écriture; auteur
PROJECT DESCRIPTION
This is a study of the collaborative writing practices of writers in the academic community. The main focus is on why they are involved, how they manage the collaboration, and how they deal with issues of identity and power in collaborating. The sample comprises 20 academic writers from eight disciplines, and from undergraduate to professional status. The main source of data is in-depth interviews. Additional sources used are observation and tape-recordings of collaborations in progress, and written reports by collaborators on the production of specific pieces of writing.
Publ: Rimmershaw, R.E. Collaborative writing practices and writing support technologies. In: Sharples, M. (ed.). *Computers and Writing: Issues and Implementations.* Dordrecht: Kluwer.

13385 Consumerist perspectives on education.
GBR 1993
Research Date(s): 1985-
Woods, P.
Sup: Mackay, H.; Cosin, B.
Inst: Open University, Walton Hall, Milton Keynes MK7 6AA, United Kingdom.
parent-school relation; parent-teacher relation; parent participation; governing body
relation parents-école; relation parents-enseignants; participation des parents; direction administrative
PROJECT DESCRIPTION
A study of the development of institutionalised forms of home-school links with particular reference to parent governors. These links are contextualised in notions of consumerism, which is considered in terms of its displacing the hitherto dominant approaches to the area of labourism and socialism.

13386 Der Beitrag der Kirche zum Zusammenleben der slowenischen und deutschen Volksgruppe in Kaernten: zur interkulturellen Verstaendigung im christlichen Kontext. (The contribution of the church to the coexistence of Slovenian and German ethnic groups in Carinthia: intercultural communication in a Christian context.)
AUT 1993
Research Date(s): 1989-1992
Marketz, Josef; Zulehner, Paul Michael; Virt, Guenter; Marketz, Friederike; Merkac, Janko; Oslak, Vinko; Perne, Maria; et al.
Inst: Institut fuer Pastoraltheologie, Schottenring 21, A-1010 Wien; Katoliska prosveta /Katholisches Bildungswerk, Viktringer Ring 26, A-9020 Klagenfurt.
Universitaet Wien, Schottenring 21, A-1010 Wien; Slowenischer Arbeitsausschuss der Katholischen Aktion, Viktringer Ring 26, A-9020 Klagenfurt
ethnic relations; intercultural education; church; bilingualism; religion
relations ethniques; éducation interculturelle; église; bilinguisme; religion
PROJECT DESCRIPTION
Nationale Spannungen zwischen der slowenischen und deutschen Volksgruppe in Kaernten werden vor allem auch auf kirchlicher Ebene abgehandelt und praegen weithin den pastoralen Alltag. Die Auseinandersetzungen werden allerdings meist mit pragmatischen oder disziplinaeren Argumenten gefuehrt; es scheint eine eigene, theologisch begruendete Position zu fehlen, die als Voraussetzung fuer einen gerechten Frieden immer wieder ins Spiel gebracht werden koennte. Die Arbeit ist vom Bestreben geleitet, in einer Art wissenschaftlichem Kommentar zur Vorlage ueber das Zusammenleben der Deutschen und Slowenen in der katholischen Kirche Kaerntens, die auf der Dioezesansynode der Dioezese Gurk-Klagenfurt von 1971 bis 1972 verabschiedet wurde, theologische Kriterien fuer kirchenamtliche Entscheidungen und die pastorale Alltagspraxis zu erarbeiten, die aber darueber hinaus von allgemeiner theologisch-ethischer Bedeutung sind. Ebenso wichtig wie ein handlungsleitender theologischer Hintergrund aber ist eine differenzierte Kenntnis der besonderen geschichtlich gewordenen, gesellschaftlichen und psychosozialen Situation, in die der einzelne Mensch gestellt ist und die seine Entscheidungs- und Handlungsfreiheit oft betraechtlich einengt. Die Arbeit traegt der Komplexitaet der Situation Rechnung, indem sie mittels einer umfassenden Situationsanalyse das Umfeld beschreibt, in dem pastorale Praxis in Suedkaernten stattfindet. Besonderes Augenmerk wird dabei der meist vernachlaessigten

Gruppe der zwischen den Volksgruppen stehenden 'Zwischenpositionellen' geschenkt.

Es wurde erstens eine persoenliche Befragung der Pfarrer aller 93 zweisprachigen Pfarrgemeinden der Dioezese Gurk- Klagenfurt ueber die pastorale Situation der Pfarren unter besonderer Beruecksichtigung des Gebrauchs der slowenischen Sprache in der Pastorale durchgefuehrt. Zweitens erfolgte eine qualitative Untersuchung mittels 19 Interviews und zehn schriftlichen Befragungen zum Glauben und zur Kirchenbeziehung bei den Menschen in Suedkaernten.

Es wurde eine Situationsanalyse erstellt. Die (Kirchen-) Geschichte des zweisprachigen Kaernten wurde dargestellt, eine Reflexion der kulturellen und politischen Beziehungen von Menschen und Voelkern sowie des Verhaeltnisses von Person und Volksgemeinschaft im Licht der Bibel und des kirchlichen Lehramtes wurde vollzogen; eine Handlungsvision fuer eine interkulturelle Verstaendigung in der Praxis der Kirche Kaerntens wurde entworfen.

Eine Kaerntner Kirchenvision: Aus einer Mystik schoepfend, die als Gottsuche gerade auch in der je eigenen Kultur die religioese Dimension erkennen laesst und sie einbringt in eine lebendige Kommunikation mit anderen, die in der Feier der Eucharistie als der gemeinsamen Versammlung der beiden Volksgruppen auf 'anschauliche' Weise die biblische Endzeitvision einer multikulturellen Gesellschaft vorwegnimmt, erwaechst der Kirche als erste Frucht die taegliche Zusammenleben praegende Geschwisterlichkeit. Diese orientiert sich am Modell der 'gegenseitigen Integration', das zwei Beduerfnissen gerecht zu werden versucht: der existentiellen und kulturellen Gemeinschaft der Minderheit mit der Mehrheit und zugleich der Bewahrung der eigenen ethnisch-kulturellen Identitaet. Als zweite Frucht der Mystik erwaechst der Kirche die als Diakonie verstandene Politik, die in Kaernten ein eindeutiges, aus der Kraft der Gewaltfreiheit schoepfendes oeffentliches Eintreten gegen die gesellschaftlichen Assimilationstendenzen zum Inhalt hat, um ueber eine Chancengleichheit an kulturellen Entfaltungsmoeglichkeiten ein friedliches Miteinander der Volksgruppen zu erreichen.

13387 Developing deep-processing strategies in academic interaction.
GBR 1993
Research Date(s): 1989-1991
Carver, D.; Dickinson, L.
Inst: Heriot-Watt University, Moray House Institute of Education, Holyrood Road, Edinburgh EH8 8AQ, United Kingdom.
verbal interaction; student behaviour; student participation; higher education
interaction verbale; comportement de l'étudiant; participation de l'étudiant; enseignement supérieur
PROJECT DESCRIPTION
This research at Moray House Institute of Education is in three phases and involved in 1988-1989 creating and trialling a set of materials designed to enable academic counselling to proceed on a structured basis; and in 1989-1990 analysing transcripts of academic oral interaction in order to classify strategies and sources of breakdown. The aim of this research is to create and test a teaching module designed to develop students' ability to interact in the academic setting.

13388 Developing successful learning.
GBR 1993
Research Date(s): 1990-
Ainscow, M.; Hart, S.
Inst: Cambridge University, Institute of Education, Shaftesbury Road, Cambridge CB2 2BX, United Kingdom.
Fin: Bedfordshire Local Education Authority; Sharnbrook School; Samuel Whitbread School; Cambridge University.
cooperation; teaching personnel; further education of teachers
coopération; corps enseignant; perfectionnement des enseignants
PROJECT DESCRIPTION
This is an action research project which is seeking to develop effective approaches to school-based staff development. The work was prompted by concerns about how to support teachers in meeting the needs of all pupils within the National Curriculum. Specifically, the research is exploring the use of partnerships within which teachers support one another in reflecting upon and developing their professional practice.

The findings of the research are currently being introduced into a further group of schools using materials that have been developed. Experience so far suggests that adopting a partnership approach to professional development helps to create a collaborative culture in schools.
Publ: Ainscow, M. & Hart, S. Moving practice forward. In: Support for Learning, Vol 7, No 3/1992, pp. 115-120.

13389 Education for sustainable development in the Third World.
GBR 1993
Research Date(s): 1987-
Fitzgerald, M.
Inst: Anglia Polytechnic University, Department of Geography, East Road, Cambridge CB1 1PT, United Kingdom.
development aid; developing country; environmental study; Ethiopia
aide au développement; pays en développement; étude du milieu; Ethiopie

PROJECT DESCRIPTION
The aims are to determine the origin of and reasons for environmental education programmes (EEPs) and to assess their contribution to sustainable development and disaster mitigation. A pilot EEP in Ethiopia has been evaluated. A 45% sample of participating centres has been visited and interviews conducted with students, farmers, teachers and education officers at district, regional and ministerial level.

It is concluded that there are contradictions between the centralisation of programme planning and the need for environmental education to be location-specific and between the goals of providing relevant education and meeting the demand for qualifications. These arise from northern-inspired interpretations of sustainable development. They limit the potential of environmental education to produce the values and behaviour required for sustainable development.
Publ: Fitzgerald, M. Education for sustainable development: decision-making for environmental education in Ethiopia. In: The International Journal of Educational Development, Vol 10, No 4/1990, pp. 289-302.
Fitzgerald, M. Environmental education in Ethiopia: the sources of decision-making. In: Bandhu, D.; Singh, H. & Maitra, A.K. Environmental education and sustainable development. New Delhi: Indian Environmental Society, 1990.
Fitzgerald, M. Education for sustainable development: a long-term strategy for famine prevention in Ethiopia. In: Occasional Paper in Rural Studies, No 9, Anglia Polytechnic, Division of Geography, 1991.

13390 Edukační prostředí české základní školy: pedagogicko-psychologické a sociální determinanty. Život ve škole: analýza metodami pedagogické etnografie. (Life in school: an analysis using methods of educational ethnography.)
CSK 1994
Research Date(s): 1991-1992
Bittnerová, Dana; Kasíková, Hana; Klusák, Miroslav; Pavlica, Karel; Rendl, Miroslav; Štech, Stanislav; Viktorová, Ida; Škaloudová, Alena.
Sup: Kučera, Miloš.
Inst: Ústav pedagogických a psychologických výzkumů, Pedagogická fakulta Univerzity Karlovy (Institute of Educational and Psychological Research, Charles University), M.D. Rettigové 4, 116 39 Praha 1, Czech Republic.
Ministerstvo školství, mládeže a tělovýchovy ČR (Ministry of Education, Youth and Physical Education), Karmelitská 7, 118 13 Praha 1, Czech Republic
ethnic relations; school environment; primary school; teacher-pupil relation; parent-pupil relation; parent-school relation; interaction; identity; comparative research
relations ethniques; milieu scolaire; école primaire; relation maître-élève; relation parents-élève; relation parents-école; interaction; identité; recherche comparative
PROJECT DESCRIPTION
Aims: (1) To conduct a holistic study of cultural, social and anthropological aspects of life in primary school; (2) to make intercultural comparisons.

Methods: Educational research workers, psychologists from different fields and ethnographers-folklorists used a combination of quantitative and qualitative methods to make a holistic description of the cultural and socio-anthropological aspects of primary school life. The research was of a longitudinal nature and was carried out in several schools in one part of Prague. Intercultural comparisons were included in the study.
Publ: "Co se v mládí naučíš...". Zpráva z terénního výzkumu. Praha: Ústav pedagogických a psychologických výzkumů, Pedagogická fakulta University Karlovy, 1992, 456p.

13391 The effectiveness of implementing a multicultural and antiracist education.
GBR 1993
Research Date(s): 1988-1992
Reid, J.
Sup: Thomas, J.; Down, B.
Inst: Brunel University, Department of Education and Design, Runnymede Campus, Englefield Green, Egham TW20 0JZ, United Kingdom.
racial integration; intercultural education; educational policy
intégration raciale; éducation interculturelle; politique de l'éducation
PROJECT DESCRIPTION
The research reviews the effective changes in school practices of the LEAs' (local education authorities) policies. It traces the changing trends and concerns regarding the amount of take-up, the process and impact of which are qualitatively and quantitatively assessed. The research objectives are threefold: to establish what is recognized as multicultural and antiracist education in local education authorities and schools; to establish whether there are differences in provisions between the LEAs and schools; and to establish whether multicultural and antiracist education practices at the primary level help the performances/achievements at secondary level.

The introductory section, a historical perspective, discusses the rise of multicultural and antiracist education awareness. Issues on prejudices and institutional racism are included. A survey of the literature and a review of other researches are undertaken in order to base the similarities and differences of this research. The investigation is three-dimensional, analyzing the LEAs' policies, the primary and secondary schools' policies and comparing/contrasting the schools objectives according to needs.

The methodologies are ethnographic - the 'involved' observer, questionnaires and interviews. The implications of the Education Reform Act 1988 are also discussed, particularly equal opportunity and education for all in relation to cross-curricular dimensions - is it a policy which will permeate an education for a multicultural society? The results are assessed, the outcomes discussed and summarized according to the underlying hypothesis - have LEAs' and schools' policies affected positive changes?.

13392 Enterprising higher education: links between higher education institutions and industrial, commercial sectors.
GBR   1993
Research Date(s): 1989-1993
Ding, D.
Sup: Fulton, O.
Inst: Lancaster University, Department of Educational Research, Cartmel College, Bailrigg, Lancaster LA1 4YW, United Kingdom.
Fin: Overseas research studentship; Lancaster University studentship.
cooperation; educational institution; higher education; enterprise; industry; China
coopération; établissement d'enseignement; enseignement supérieur; entreprise; industrie; Chine
PROJECT DESCRIPTION
As a comparative study, this research focuses on mapping out the main trends over the past decade of higher education institutionsl (HEIs) links with industrial and commercial sectors in Britain and China, examining the rationales and attempting to find appropriate models for each.

Through interviews with a selective sample of personnel numbering nearly 60 in HEIs in both countries; together with documentation review, this qualitative study illustrates a diversified picture of the present links respectively, where some interesting similarities are found. Meanwhile, differences of the links are also paid attention and probed, as obvious gaps remain between the two nations' fundamental social structures as well as educational systems.

In sum, the current linkage at all levels would, against resistance, continue to exist since there is a growing recognition that this link is not only a channel eventually generating funds for the much needed HEI pool, particularly in a time when its main, central funding sources are dwindling in real terms, but also a vitality which animates higher education progress. However, at present the links have formulated a challenge in both HE frameworks, since its behaviours are generally alien, unfamiliar to many, and still on a trial base. This controversy has inevitably confronted traditional ethos long established in higher education. Currently found issues show that unless some all-round strategies and policies are available and in effect, the links for some HEIs would cause quality problems and put the health of those linking institutions in jeopardy.

13393   An evaluation of a home-school-community liaison project.
IRL   1994
Research Date(s): 1990-
Ryan, Sandra.
Inst: Educational Research Centre, St Patrick's College, Dublin 9, Ireland.
Fin: Department of Education.
school-community relation; parent-school relation; deprived
relation école-collectivité; relation parents-école; défavorisé
PROJECT DESCRIPTION
In 1990, the Department of Education initiated a programme of home-school-community liaison in 56 primary schools in designated areas of socio-economic disadvantage. In 1991, the programme was extended to an additional 24 primary schools and to 13 second-level schools. A key feature of the project was the provision of the services of a teacher to participating schools who had as a major responsibility the co-ordination of activities between schools, homes, and communities. The purposes of the evaluation are to examine how the project is constructed and implemented in schools; to monitor specified outcomes of project activity; and to identify models of good practice.

A good deal of variation was found between schools in the range and number of activities which were initiated. Schools became more open to parents, many of whom become more involved in educational activities, both at home and in school. The community dimension of the project proved difficult to develop.

13394   Facteurs psychologiques de l'insertion professionnelle des jeunes de niveau V et l'emploi.
FRA   1993
Research Date(s): 1990-
Wach, Monique.
Sup: Huteau, Michel.
Inst: Ministère de l'éducation, Conservatoire national des arts et métiers, Ecole pratique des Hautes Etudes et Université de Paris V, Institut national d'études du travail et d'orientation professionnelle - Service de recherche, 41 rue Gay-Lussac, 75005 Paris, France.

occupational integration; maturity; personality development; social adjustment; occupational environment; predictive evaluation
intégration professionnelle; maturité; développement de la personnalité; adaptation sociale; milieu professionnel; évaluation prédictive
PROJECT DESCRIPTION
Objectifs: Cette recherche veut tenter d'éclairer les mécanismes psychologiques et psychosociologiques qui facilitent l'insertion des jeunes de niveau V. L'employabilité ferait appel à une compétence sociale, c'est à dire à une capacité de l'individu à s'adapter à un certain nombre de normes sociales dominantes dans son environnement. Des styles de conduite mobilisés, des aspirations à la consommation, le maintien des réseaux familiaux et sociaux, une certaine centralité du travail, tout comme une dissonnance, pas trop importante, entre sa personnalité, son système de valeurs et les caractéristiques de l'environnement constitueraient, mis ensemble, cette "qualification sociale" permettant l'accès à l'emploi. C'est ce faisceau d'hypothèses concernant l'insertion professionnelle des jeunes que nous proposons de vérifier dans cette enquête. On prend en compte non seulement le fait d'avoir ou non un emploi, mais aussi les stratégies de recherche d'emploi et les changements intervenus dans les modes de vie. Pour ceux ayant un emploi, on s'attache à décrire qualitativement le type d'emploi ainsi que les autres formes de socialisation des jeunes (famille, loisirs). Si les résultats de l'enquête le permettent, on propose des actions éducatives destinées à améliorer la capacité des jeunes à trouver un emploi.

Méthodologie: L'ensemble des indicateurs sont rassemblés en fin de Brevet d'enseignement professionnel dans huit lycées professionnels à Paris, en banlieue et en province. On interroge des sections industrielles (électrotechnique et de mécanique de maintenance) et tertiaires. La méthode utilisée est un questionnaire proposé à une population d'environ 600 élèves. Pour ceux qui cherchent à s'insérer, les données sont complétées par des informations sur les comportements en cours d'insertion.

13395   Gemeinsam geht alles besser.   (Together, all things are easier.)
AUT   1993
Research Date(s): 1980-1990
Sedlak, Franz; Gruber, Heinz; Chiba, Renate; Kozdera, Eva; Stari, Margarete.
Inst: Abteilung fuer Schulpsychologie und Bildungsberatung, Minoritenplatz 5, A-1014 Wien.
Bundesministerium fuer Unterricht und Kunst, Minoritenplatz 5, A-1014 Wien
pupil integration; handicapped; individualized teaching; aims of education; personality development; equal opportunity
intégration scolaire; handicapé; enseignement individualisé; finalité de l'éducation; développement de la personnalité; égalité de chances
PROJECT DESCRIPTION
Verfolgt man die Diskussion um die schulische Integration Behinderter und Nichtbehinderter, dann kann man sehr leicht feststellen, dass zwei Werte miteinander in Streit geraten: die Entfaltung von Faehigkeiten und des vorhandenen Begabungspotentials, die Ausnutzung von latenten Ressourcen usw., kurzum die optimale Individualfoerderung einerseits, die berechtigte Sorge um die Chancengleichheit fuer alle, die Verbundenheit mit den Benachteiligten, der engagierte Einsatz fuer die Schwaecheren und ihre Lebensqualitaet in einer vorurteilsbefreiten Gesellschaft, kurz die praktizierte Solidaritaet andererseits. Es wird die aktuelle Situation der integrativen Schulversuche beschrieben und ein umfassender Ueberblick ueber Ansaetze, Chancen, Probleme und Weiterentwicklungen der integrativen Bemuehungen geboten. Soll wirkliche Integration und nicht bloss oberflaechliche Scheinanpassung erreicht werden, muss mit masshaltenden Schritten und mit einem die Grenzen respektierenden Tempo gegen die Abwertung einer Personengruppe vorgegangen werden.

Publ: Sedlak, Franz (Hrsg.). *Gemeinsam geht alles besser. Praktizierte Solidaritaet und optimale Individualfoerderung als Brennpunkte der schulischen Integrationsdiskussion.* Oesterreichischer Bundesverlag, Wien 1990.

13396   Gendered expectations and the primary school curriculum.
GBR   1993
Research Date(s): 1987-1991
King, J.
Sup: Wallace, G.; Weiner, G.
Inst: Derbyshire College of Higher Education, Western Road, Mickleover, Derby DE3 5GX, United Kingdom; South Bank University, Department of Education, Diary House, 77-79 Borough Road, London SE1 OAA, United Kingdom; Liverpool University, Department of Education, PO Box 147, Liverpool L69 3BX, United Kingdom.
sex discrimination; primary education; sex difference; teacher behaviour; pupil attitude
discrimination sexuelle; enseignement primaire; différence de sexe; comportement de l'enseignant; attitude de l'élève
PROJECT DESCRIPTION
The central question of this project was whether gender discrimination continues to operate in primary schools in the planning and delivery of topic work. The research examined whether there was: gender bias in the

topic choices of teachers and pupils; gender bias in the reasons teachers give about their topic choices; gender bias in the organisation and delivery of topic lessons; and gender bias in the value given to achievements by pupils. Gender bias is defined as any consistent pattern of differentiated behaviour in the way pupils are treated.

The research was conducted in two parallel junior school classes in a rural and suburban primary school. The methods used included participant observation, interviews, questionnaires, and records, children's work and documents.

The evidence shows that in spite of equal opportunities rhetoric, differential gender expectations condition teachers' reactions to pupils' work. Teachers have the power to convert these expectations into graded hierarchies of ability that continue to affect pupils' life chances.

Publ: *Gendered expectations and the primary school curriculum.* Paper presented at British Educational Research Association (BERA) Conference, August 1990.

13397   Genèse des relations affinitaires chez des jeunes enfants de moins de trois ans.
FRA   1993
Research Date(s): 1988-1991
Le Camus, Jean; Espinoza, Odile.
Inst: Université de Toulouse II, UFR Education Formation Insertion, CNRS URA/259, Département de psychologie - Laboratoire, personnalisation et changements sociaux, 5 allées Antonio Machado, 31058 Toulouse Cedex, France.
social interaction; pre-school child; interpersonal relations; social development; friendship
interaction sociale; enfant d'âge préscolaire; relations interpersonnelles; développement social; amitié
PROJECT DESCRIPTION

Objectifs: Il s'agit d'étudier les premières relations affinitaires s'établissant entre jeunes fréquentant régulièrement une collectivité afin d'éclairer certains aspects de la fonction des relations affinitaires dans le développement social du jeune enfant.

Méthodologie: Le recueil des données (enregistrement en continu des activités sociales et non sociales de chaque enfant, descriptions des conduites et interactions sociales intervenant au sein du groupe, enregistrement vidéo de l'ensemble du groupe) s'effectue sur trois périodes successives d'un mois et demi chez 38 dyades de moyenne section et 26 dyades de grande section.

Résultats: L'hypothèse de l'existence des relations affinitaires et préférentielles au sein de groupes de très jeunes enfants est donc étayée par ce travail. La comparaison entre enfants de 1-2 ans et enfants de 3-4 ans montre l'intensification des échanges sociaux, l'attention plus grande portée aux partenaires. L'étude des épisodes conflictuels suggère une diminution, chez les grands, des conduites franchement agressives au profit de stratégies plus subtiles.

Publ: Le Camus, Jean. Ethopsychologie de l'enfant et pédagogie coopérative à l'école maternelle. In: *Animation et éducation*, n° 71, pp. 11-16.
Espinoza, Odile. Genèse et formes de l'amitié chez les jeunes enfants. In: *Dossiers de l'éducation*, 1988, 4, 13, pp. 7-9.
Le Camus, Jean & Espinoza, Odile. Les relations interpersonnelles précoces. In: Malewska-Peyre, Hanna & Tap, Pierre (éds.). *La socialisation de l'enfance à l'adolescence.* Paris: PUF, 1991.

13398   The identification of prerequisites for effective teacher mobility between Germany and the United Kingdom.
GBR   1993
Research Date(s): 1989-1993
Alker, D.
Sup: Postle, M.
Inst: Charlotte Mason College, Development Unit, Ambleside, Cumbria LA22 9BB, United Kingdom.
Fin: Department of Education and Science.
teacher exchange; teacher abroad; free movement; training programme; Germany; United Kingdom
échange d'enseignants; enseignant à l'étranger; libre circulation; programme de formation; Allemagne; Royaume-Uni
PROJECT DESCRIPTION

The project will develop, implement, monitor and evaluate a training programme in consultation with local education authorities (LEAs) for the induction and transfer training of European Community (EC) trained teachers. The aims of the training programme are: (1) to introduce an appropriate range of teaching methods and styles to obtain a better match in teaching approaches; (2) to familiarise EC teachers with the National Curriculum; (3) provide support in meeting the language demands in both general communication skills and the language of the classroom; (4) develop confidence in coping with the demands of cultural and social difference. A major focus of the training programme will be school-based training in association with participating schools and LEAs.

13399   Integration and responsibility for learning in mainstream primary schools.
GBR   1993
Research Date(s): 1991-1993
Piotrowski, J.
Sup: Pumfrey, P.
Inst: Manchester University, School of Education, Centre for Educational Guidance and Special Needs, Oxford Road, Manchester M13 9PL, United Kingdom.
integration; special education; social learning
intégration; enseignement spécial; apprentissage social
PROJECT DESCRIPTION

This study is set within the theoretical framework of social learning theory. It comprises a cross-sectional study of about four hundred 6-11 year old boys and girls. Hypotheses concerning the relationships between the independent variables (year group, sex and special educational needs) and the dependent variables (locus of control, belief, self-concept and attendance) will be tested. The study will examine the implications of the results for integration policies and practices in mainstream primary schools.

13400   The integration of deaf and partially hearing children in Berkshire schools.
GBR   1993
Research Date(s): 1991-1992
Sellers, M.; Palmer, B.
Inst: Reading University, Faculty of Education and Community Studies, Bulmershe Court, Woodlands Avenue, Earley, Reading RG6 1HY, United Kingdom.
integration; special education; deaf; aurally handicapped
intégration; enseignement spécial; sourd; handicapé auditif
PROJECT DESCRIPTION

Largely as a result of legislation such as the 1976 and 1981 Education Acts, 'special needs' children, including 90% of those with a hearing disability, are now taught 'wherever possible' in ordinary schools. What is uncertain is how well hearing-impaired children are faring, especially since the 1988 Education Reform Act with its introduction of the National Curriculum and Local Management of Schools, and with possible changes in local education authority (LEA) 'statementing' practices.

This project is designed as a pilot for a larger multinational study. Its aims are to: (a) establish a database which will list all children with a hearing disability in Berkshire schools and partially hearing units, together with relevant details such as their audiometric profile; the communication support and resources available to each individual child; and the children of Berkshire residents at schools for the deaf outside the county; (b) review 'statements' and the 'statementing' process in principle and in practice; (c) conduct case studies in which the progress of a sample number children will be explored in depth; (d) identify specific research questions and strategies for the major study.

The survey will be carried out by reference to published data and Berkshire LEA documentation; interviews with children, parents and teachers in relation to the case studies; and interviews with LEA staff involved in 'statementing' and with a sample of professional staff submitting advice.

It is intended that the results of this intitial survey will be publised in different forms in educational journals and in more popular specialist publications for deaf people. The survey will act as the basis for an application for European funding for the major project.

13401   Inter-ethnic relationships in secondary schools.
GBR   1993
Research Date(s): 1990-1992
Verma, G.; Zec, P.
Inst: Manchester University, School of Education, Centre for Ethnic Studies, Oxford Road, Manchester M13 9PL, United Kingdom; Canterbury Christchurch College of Higher Education, North Holmes Road, Canterbury CT1 1QU, United Kingdom.
Fin: Leverhulme Trust.
ethnic relations; intergroup relations; secondary school
relations ethniques; relations intergroupes; école secondaire
PROJECT DESCRIPTION

Among issues highlighted by the Swann Report (Education for All, HMSO, 1985) was the state of inter-ethnic relationships in schools and the potential impact of school policy and practice on such relationships. The project is investigating the nature of pupil relationships in nine multiethnic schools through the use of surveys, observation and interviews with pupils and staff. The factors influencing these relationships (including school policy and practices) will be assessed and compared.

13402   An investigation of the collaborative interaction and talk of children in relation to their perception of teacher audience, task purpose and learning context.
GBR   1993
Research Date(s): 1987-1991
Corden, R.
Sup: Evans, T.

Inst: Keele University, Department of Education, Keele, Staffordshire ST5 5BG, United Kingdom.

interaction; verbal communication; teacher-pupil relation; group work; learning process; verbal interaction

interaction; communication verbale; relation maître-élève; travail par équipe; apprentissage; interaction verbale

PROJECT DESCRIPTION

The study is of task-related, or work-focused discourse of small groups of 12 to 13 year old pupils working within the naturalistic settings of the classroom. The research is concerned with the way in which children engage in a variety of tasks using spoken language to interact and collaborate in the learning process when the teacher is not in a central, authoritative position (physically), and when the discussion has the 'potential' to be negotiable and not dominated by one omnipotent figure. The study will attempt to identify the way in which pupils engage in discussion in relation to their perception of teacher audience and the subsequent perceptions of contextual learning conditions and task purpose.

The study adopts an ethnographic, or ethnomethodological approach and makes extensive use of audio and video recordings. The use of retrospective analysis and triangulation will be adopted in order to try and encompass the 'whole' group interaction and to be sensitively aware of contextual factors and particularly, the way in which the pupils' perceptions of 'audience' (as projected by the teacher) affects the interactional process and use of language in the learning process.

13403 The management and development of mechanisms of university/industry collaboration in European and Latin American universities.

GBR 1993

Research Date(s): 1989-1991

Davies, J.; Kells, H.

Inst: Anglia Polytechnic University, Anglia Business School, Centre for Higher Education Management, Danbury Park Conference Centre, Danbury Park, Chelmsford CM3 4AT, United Kingdom.

Fin: EC; UNESCO; European Rectors' Conference, Geneva (CRE); Participating universities.

university industry relationship; comparative research; Europe; Latin America

relation université-entreprise; recherche comparative; Europe; Amérique latine

PROJECT DESCRIPTION

The research aims to: (1) assess the state of the art university/industry relations in terms of technology transfer and continuing education in 14 European universities; (2) identify and evaluate the significance of factors facilitating and inhibiting these developments; (3) develop perspectives on the strategics and processes needed to improve universities' adaptability and responsiveness to industry and the internal mechanisms of managing and sustaining such change; and (4) assess the relevance of these findings to developments in this field in Latin America.

The research is based on 14 European universities in Spain, Portugal, Italy, France, Switzerland, Netherlands, Belgium and the United Kingdom. The analysis is carried out by teams of visiting Latin American rectors and academics using a tightly structured framework based on prior research by the principal researcher carried out for the Organisation for Economic Cooperation and Development (OECD). This case study method draws on institutions of different sizes, traditions, disciplinary configurations, and environmental stimuli.

Publ: Managing quality and the links with the productive sector. In: *In the Wake of Columbus*. European Rectors' Conference, Geneva, 1990.

13404 Medarbeidersamtaler som veiledningsstrategi (modell LIS). ("Clarification" as a strategy for guidance in teacher training.)

NOR 1994

Research Date(s): 1992-1993

Statle, Sturla Ravn.

Inst: Alta Lærerhögskole (Alta College of Education), Postboks 1200, 9501 Alta, Norway.

teacher-pupil relation; guidance; teacher education; personality development

relation maître-élève; orientation; formation des enseignants; développement de la personnalité

PROJECT DESCRIPTION

The aim is to foster communication and cooperation between teachers of pedagogy and students at the start of their teaching training by developing receptivity and self-confidence. The paramount target will be students' professional and personal development. It will be attempted to establish whether guidance in the form of "clarification" can contribute to achieving these aims.

The following questions will be addressed: (1) Does this type of guidance further communication and cooperation between students and teachers? (2) Does it further professional understanding and does it produce results, e.g. pertaining to pedagogy as an element of teacher training? (3) Does it develop students' insight into themselves and develop their integrity?

The study may involve a division of the class in two, to enable one half of the class to function as a governing body. Evaluation data will derive from personal talks, questionnaires and individualized tests.

Publ: A full list of publications can be obtained on request from the research institute.

13405 Organising academic-industry liaison: theory and evidence.

GBR 1993

Research Date(s): 1985-1991

Connor, S.

Sup: Young, A.; Wylie, J.

Inst: Paisley College, High Street, Paisley PA1 2BE, United Kingdom.

university industry relationship; higher education; cooperation

relation université-entreprise; enseignement supérieur; coopération

PROJECT DESCRIPTION

The main aim of this research is an attempt to determine the most effective strategies and forms of organisation which academic institutions should adopt to facilitate and encourage liaison with industry, commerce and the public sector. Empirical work relating to the organisation forms and strategies operating in higher education institutions has been completed. This involved surveys (by personal interview) of the perceptions of over 400 academics and members of senior management groups in 11 Central Institutions throughout Scotland. These interviews were conducted by a team led by the researcher who was also responsible for the survey design.

Preliminary results of the research suggest that a system of delegated control, together with guidelines for liaison activities, contribute towards the instigation, maintenance and extension of liaison activities in Scottish Central Institutions. At this stage an analysis of the empirical study data and at the theoretical level will be carried out and an attempt will be made to construct and test models of 'best practice' of college-industry liaison.

Publ: Connor, S.; Wylie, J. & Young, A. Academic-industry liaison in the United Kingdom: economic perspectives. In: *Higher Education*, Vol 5, No 5/1986, pp. 407-420.

Connor, S. & Wylie, J. Post-experience vocational education: an investigation of its role in linking colleges, universities and business. In: *Scottish Journal of Adult Education*, Vol 7, No 2/1985.

Connor, S. & Wylie, J. Driving a hard bargain. In: *Times Higher Education Supplement*, 4.7.86.

13406 Paedagogisches Handeln in der beruflichen Bildung - zum Zusammenhang von Koordination, Kooperation und Integration. (Pedagogic action in vocational training: on the relationship between coordination, cooperation and integration.)

DEU 1993

Research Date(s): 1991-1994

Thiele, H.

Sup: Paetzold, G.

Inst: Universitaet Dortmund, FB Erziehungswissenschaften und Biologie, Institut fuer Allg., Vgl. und Berufspaedagogik, Emil-Figge-Str. 50, D-4600 Dortmund 50.

cooperation; vocational education; integration; sciences of education

coopération; enseignement professionnel; intégration; sciences de l'éducation

PROJECT DESCRIPTION

Geographischer Raum: Bundesrepublik Deutschland.

Vorgehensweise: Qualitativ-hermeneutisch. Untersuchungsdesign: Qualitative Forschung.

13407 Parents and the National Curriculum.

GBR 1993

Research Date(s): 1989-1992

Hughes, M.

Inst: Exeter University, School of Education, St Luke's, Heavitree Road, Exeter EX1 2LU, United Kingdom.

Fin: Leverhulme Trust.

parent-school relation; common core curriculum; parental attitude

relation parents-école; tronc commun; attitude des parents

PROJECT DESCRIPTION

The focus of the research is on the relationship between parents and schools as the National Curriculum is implemented in the early years of school. The research has two main objectives: (1) to obtain baseline data on the perceptions of parents and teachers as the first children entered Key Stage 1; (2) to monitor the changing perceptions of parents and teachers as these children progress through Key Stage 1, culminating in the first national standardised assessments of 7-year-olds in 1991. In order to achieve these objectives a cohort of 150 children in 11 schools has been followed through Years 1 and 2 of the National Curriculum. Annual interviews have been carried out with their parents and teachers. Further information has been obtained from a wider sample of 80 headteachers who have also been interviewed annually.

Publ: Hughes, M.; Wikely, F. & Nash, T. Business partners. In: *Times Educational Supplement*, pp. 20-21, 5 January 1990.

Hughes, M. Parents and the National Curriculum. In: *Early Education*, No 3/1991, pp. 8-9.

Hughes, M. Parents and the National Curriculum. In: *Proceedings of the Conference, 'Young Children Learning'*, Thames Polytechnic, 1991.

13408   Prejudice, isolation and bullying: intervention in ethnically mixed classes.
GBR   1993
Research Date(s): 1990-1993
Smith, P.; Laver, R.; Cowie, H.
Inst: Sheffield University, Department of Psychology, Sheffield S10 2TN, United Kingdom.
Fin: Economic and Social Research Council.
intergroup relations; ethnic relations; cooperation; group behaviour; antisocial behaviour; bullying; intervention
relations intergroupes; relations ethniques; coopération; comportement de groupe; comportement antisocial; brimades; intervention
PROJECT DESCRIPTION
   Research has shown that racial prejudice, social isolation and bullying are far from uncommon during the middle school period. The first aim of the project is to document the extent and inter-relationship of these problems on a large sample of classes. At present, for example, it is not known whether racial prejudice and bullying are related, and if so, whether in some cases the former may be a cause of the latter.
   In a previous one-year Economic and Social Research Council (ESRC) funded project, the research team found that prejudice could be ameliorated to some extent, and liking of peers increased, in classes where teachers were trained in and used cooperative group work (CGW). The central feature of this approach is the opportunity to learn through the expression and exploration of diverse ideas and the cooperative solution of problems, in groups formed across ethnic and gender barriers.
   In the present project, the CGW curriculum will be refined and more focused in some respects, based on previous experience. The second aim of the project is that it should provide a more definitive test of the efficacy of this form of school-based intervention programme. The extent to which the preliminary results from the one-year project can be replicated will be assessed on a larger sample and over a longer time period. Periodic assessments, both quantitative and qualitative, will be made of the nature of social relationships in the participating classes.
Publ: Boulton, M.J. & Smith, P.K. Bullying and withdrawn children. In: Varma, V.P. (ed.). *Truants from life: theory and therapy*. London: David Fulton, 1991.
Cowie, H.; Boulton, M.J. & Smith, P.K. Bullying: pupil relationships. In: Jones, N. & Jones, E.B. (eds.). *Learning to behave: curriculum and whole school management approaches to discipline*. London: Kogan Page, 1992.

13409   Race and education: perspectives of primary B.Ed. students.
GBR   1993
Research Date(s): 1980-1994
Gaine, C.
Sup: Ball, S.
Inst: West Sussex Institute of Higher Education, The Dome, Upper Bognor Road, Bognor Regis PO21 1HR, United Kingdom; London University, King's College, Centre for Educational Studies, Cornwall House Annexe, Waterloo Road, London SE1 3TY, United Kingdom.
race relations; racism; student teacher; teacher behaviour
relations raciales; racisme; élève-maître; comportement de l'enseignant
PROJECT DESCRIPTION
   This is a study of the perspectives about race and education held by primary Bachelor of Education (B.Ed.) students, and whether these change in any way during their course, and whether critical or anti-racist perspectives persist after two years of working as teachers.
Publ: Gaine, C. *No problem here*. London: Hutchinson Publishing Co., 1987.
Gaine, C. On getting equal opportunities policies. In: Cole, M. (ed.). *Education for equality*. Basingstoke: Falmer Press, 1989.
Gaine, C. The effect of LMS on black children. In: *Multicultural Teaching*, Vol 9, No 2/1991, pp. 21-22, Spring.

13410   Régulations socio-cognitives des interactions paritaires à la crèche.
FRA   1993
Research Date(s): 1987-
Flament, Fanny.
Inst: Université d'Aix-Marseille I, UFR Psychologie Sciences de l'éducation, CNRS URA/182, Centre de recherche en psychologie cognitive, 29 av. Robert Schuman, 13621 Aix-en-Provence, France.
pre-school child; social interaction; cognitive development
enfant d'âge préscolaire; interaction sociale; développement cognitif
PROJECT DESCRIPTION
   Objectifs: Un ensemble d'une vingtaine de recherches s'applique à l'étude des interactions entre enfants de première, deuxième et troisième années. Les situations sont construites pour décrire les réorganisations successives d'interactions, le fonctionnement paritaire dyadique y a statut de révélateur de compétence cognitivo-motrice. Les recherches s'articulent autour d'une hypothèse cognitiviste: les transformations d'interactions paritaires observables s'articulent avec les réorganisations développe-mentales et sont donc tributaires des capacités manipulatoires, locomotrices, affectives et communicationnelles en cours d'acquisition. La présence du pair signale en retour les limites des ressources d'attention des sujets dans une situation donnée.
   Méthodologie: On met en place une tâche cognitive complexe combinée à divers aspects de sa présentation perceptivo-motrice afin d'observer l'émergence et les transformations des interactions paritaires précoces. Les observations standardisées et vidéo-filmées en crèche font l'objet d'un double codage à deux niveaux de segmentation: (1) évaluation de "l'état d'attention sociale" de l'enfant et de ses communications vocales ou verbales; (2) description de la dépendance signifiante des émissions des partenaires.
   Résultats: A la fin de la première année l'attention du bébé est orientée vers l'action de l'autre; à 18 mois le compagnon-objet est devenu compagnon-partenaire; entre 30 et 36 mois émergence de la coopération.
Publ: Flament, Fanny. D'où procèdent les imitations perceptivo-motrices du bébé? In: *Psychologie française*, 1988, 33, pp. 19-28.

13411   La sfida multiculturale e il sistema formativo. (The multicultural challenge and the educational system.)
ITA   1993
Research Date(s): 1990-1991
Mazza, A.
Sup: Magni, V.
Inst: Cooperativa Insegnanti di Iniziativa Democratica - CIID (Teacher Cooperative for Democratic Initiatives), Piazza Sonnino 13, 00153 Roma, Italy.
Fin: Ministero della Pubblica Istruzione, Ufficio Studi e Programmazione.
integration; cultural integration; social integration; immigrant; educational need; educational provision; intercultural education
intégration; intégration culturelle; intégration sociale; immigrant; besoin d'éducation; scolarisation; éducation interculturelle
PROJECT DESCRIPTION
   Aims: The study aimed to analyse and evaluate national and international experiences during the past five years in respect of the education of immigrants from outside the EC and the intercultural education of Italian pupils. It also aimed to establish the needs of adult immigrants for permanent education and vocational training. Finally, it examined the educational needs of immigrant pupils and the contents of activities directed at immigrant pupils and activities directed at Italian pupils.
   Methods: Identification of objectives; elaboration of a framework for the classification and evaluation of innovative experiences; specification of essential terminology; study of relevant literature; questionnaire survey (seven questionnaires sent to public and private bodies, associations, teachers and workers in the sector).
   Results: The educational needs of those concerned are still to a large extent unexpressed or disregarded. On the other hand, there is a growing commitment on the part of interested public and private agencies. These new educational responsibilities are largely placed in the hands of the schools. The reality of current practice presents a mixed picture, with limited interventions and resources. Immigrant children are having difficulties due to the use of two languages: their mother tongue and the language of the host country. In-service training courses for teachers are scarce, but are also hard to provide, given the diversity of demands. Moreover, there are juridical difficulties in the recruitment of qualified foreign personnel. Little weight has been given to the diffusion of the culture of origin of immigrants.
   The research concludes with proposals for urgent interventions, ranging from the introduction of a general law to the revision of curricula from an intercultural perspective.

13412   Social identity in adolescence.
GBR   1993
Research Date(s): 1988-1992
Back, L.
Sup: Tizard, B.; Phoenix, A.
Inst: London University, Institute of Education, Thomas Coram Research Unit, 41 Brunswick Square, London WC1N 1AZ, United Kingdom.
Fin: Department of Health.
group membership; identity; ethnic group; social environment; social class; cultural identity; urban environment
appartenance au groupe; identité; groupe ethnique; milieu social; classe sociale; identité culturelle; milieu urbain
PROJECT DESCRIPTION
   This project is concerned with the social identities of young Londoners. The researchers aim to describe the range of social groups they feel they belong to, the strength of the affiliation they feel towards each group, and what they see as the important characteristics of each group. It is also intended to describe which of these identities are most central in their lives. The social identities in which the researchers are particulary interested are the neighbourhood, church, gender, social class, ethnic group and nationality. Interest is also being shown in the extent to which young people in schools of different ethnic composition have developed multiracial friendships, and the extent to which their skin colour is an important

organising identity in their lives. In relation to this, the researchers aim to explore their attitude to, and experience of, racial discrimination, and the extent to which their attitudes and coping strategies have been influenced by families and friends.

Publ: Tizard, B. & Phoenix, A. Black identity and transracial adoption. In: *New Community*, Vol 15, No 3/1989, pp. 427-437.

13413   Social interactions around microcomputers between children with severe learning difficulties.
GBR   1993
Research Date(s): 1987-1992
Earp, P.
Sup: Ware, J.; Norwich, B.
Inst: London University, Institute of Education, Department of Educational Psychology and Special Educational Needs, 20 Bedford Way, London WC1H OAL, United Kingdom.
interaction; learning difficulty; special education; didactic use of computer interaction; difficulté de l'apprentissage; enseignement spécial; usage didactique de l'ordinateur
PROJECT DESCRIPTION
It is known that pupils working with a microcomputer not only interact with the micro but also with each other. Pupils with severe learning difficulties are also known to interact more with each other when adults take a less dominant role. The study has already investigated the extent to which children with severe learning difficulties spontaneously interact when using a micro without the presence of an adult.

An alternating treatments design was used to compare the effectiveness of the two conditions: computer and non-computer activities for improving the social interaction of two children with severe learning difficulties. The computer condition reliably increased the task-relevant social responses of both children, whereas the non-computer condition increased responses although many of these were non-task relevant. Subsequent experiments have developed ideas based on the original studies, these have continued to use quasi-experimental designs.

13414   Social skills training in the classroom: effects on sociometric status.
GBR   1993
Research Date(s): 1992-1997
Brooks, R.
Sup: Cherrington, D.; Rowley, K.
Inst: University of Central England in Birmingham, Faculty of Education, Centre for Advanced Studies in Education, Westbourne Road, Edgbaston, Birmingham B15 3TN, United Kingdom.
social interaction; social behaviour; child; interpersonal relations; friendship; social adjustment
interaction sociale; comportement social; enfant; relations interpersonnelles; amitié; adaptation sociale
PROJECT DESCRIPTION
The aims of this research are: (1) to present a review of current sociometric research and materials in the area of children's friendship choices and social adjustment in the classroom; (2) use sociographic techniques to assess the patterns of specific friendship choices which exist in classes (e.g. popular children, reciprocated pairs, isolates, etc.); (3) assess the personality and behavioural characteristics of specific 'types' of children (as identified in (2)) using the Junior Eysenck Personality Inventory and behavioural observations; (4) intervene to coach the identified 'isolated' children in specific social skills, e.g. asking questions, offering directions to peers; (5) ascertain what effect/s the social skill training (as in (4)) has on overall peer acceptance and popularity within the class; (6) provide an in-depth examination of individual isolates, including the perceptions of friendship, and reasons for sociometric choices made; (7) for individual isolates (as in (6)) examine the family structure, number of siblings, contact with other social networks (e.g. clubs, church) which affect their social experience and competence.

13415   Student experience of European exchange.
GBR   1993
Research Date(s): 1991-1992
French, D.; Richards, M.
Inst: Coventry University, Centre for Communication Studies, Gosford Street, Coventry CV1 5RZ, United Kingdom; Worcester College of Higher Education, Henwick Grove, Worcester WR2 6AJ, United Kingdom.
student exchange; study abroad; international exchange; attitude change échange d'étudiants; études à l'étranger; échange international; changement d'attitude
PROJECT DESCRIPTION
The project examines, using individual and group interviews, students' perceptions of the changes in their attitude and competences consequent upon the experience of study abroad. Results, even provisional, are not yet available but should be of importance in formulating future policies on student mobility. Initial interviews are with students from Britain and Belgium and the initial sample is small.

13416   Teacher-pupil relationships in the primary classroom.
GBR   1993
Research Date(s): 1987-
Worrall, N.
Inst: London University, Institute of Education, Department of Educational Psychology and Special Educational Needs, 20 Bedford Way, London WC1H OAL, United Kingdom.
teacher-pupil relation; primary school; follow-up study
relation maître-élève; école primaire; étude longitudinale
PROJECT DESCRIPTION
This is continuing research being carried out with colleagues and research students. The sample size of a given study varies from 30 to 100. Methods have been mainly questionnaires/rating scales, increasingly supplemented by interviews. Topics explored range from child autonomy through differential curricular experiences and the development of mutual regard between children and teachers.

Publ: Ingram, J. & Worrall, N. The negotiating classroom. In: *Early Child Development and Care*, Vol 28/1987, pp. 401-415.
Worrall, N. & Tsarna, H. Teachers' reported practices towards boys and girls in science and languages. In: *British Journal of Educational Psychology*, Vol 57/1987, pp. 300-312.
Worrall, N.; Worrall, C. & Meldrum, C. Children's reciprocations of teacher evaluations. In: *British Journal of Educational Psychology*, Vol 58/1988, pp. 78-88.
Thirkell, B. & Worrall, N. Differential ethnic bias in Asian and white children. In: *Educational Research*, Vol 31/1989, pp. 181-188.
Ingram, J. & Worrall, N. Children's self-allocation and use of classroom curricular time. In: *British Journal of Educational Psychology*, Vol 62, No 1/1992, pp. 45-55.

13417   Towards a reconceptualisation of support teaching.
GBR   1993
Research Date(s): 1990-1993
Sweetingham, P.
Sup: Rouse, M.; Ainscow, M.
Inst: Cambridge University, Institute of Education, Shaftesbury Road, Cambridge CB2 2BX, United Kingdom.
integration; special education; special school teacher; teaching personnel; cooperation
intégration; enseignement spécial; éducateur spécialisé; corps enseignant; coopération
PROJECT DESCRIPTION
This thesis covers the ways in which special needs and subject specialist teachers work together in secondary schools. It explores through a series of case studies the developmental process through which relationships grow or are inhibited from growing. The study has implications for special needs provision in all ordinary schools and will suggest ways in which there needs to be a reconceptualisation of roles and responsibilities in mainstream education.

cational training programme in accordance with Section 40 of the Employment Promotion Act (AFG)) .... see no. 13377

Wissenschaftliche Begleitung des Modellversuchs "Gemeinsamer Unterricht mit unterschiedlicher Zielvorgabe fuer nichtbehinderte und behinderte SchuelerInnen im Bereich der Sekundarstufe I" (Evaluation research for the pilot project "Mixed classes with differential objectives for disabled and non-disabled pupils in lower-level secondary schools") .... see no. 13378

Church schools in an urban environment .... see no. 13418

An investigation into parent-teacher association activities and their effectiveness in secondary schools in Kwara State, Nigeria .... see no. 13422

Les relations entre la famille et l'école: le point de vue des parents d'élèves; les fédérations de parents d'élèves dans la société et la vie politique françaises .... see no. 13424

Družbene spremembe in izobraževanje (Social changes and education).. see no. 13440

Interaction between the school and the cultural environment for the education of the pupils .... see no. 13450

Lebenslaeufe im Wandel (Changing life careers) .... see no. 13452

Mature students and higher education .... see no. 13454

Parents and teenagers: understanding and improving communication about Human Immunodeficiency Virus/Acquired Immune Deficiency Syndrome (HIV/AIDS).. see no. 13486

Berufliche Lebensplaene sozial deprivierter Jugendlicher (im Vergleich alte - neue Bundeslaender) (Occupational plans of socially deprived young people (comparison of old and new German states)) .... see no. 13538

Education-Business Partnerships (EBPs): targets and stocktake........ .... see no. 13565

Etude de la relation maître d'apprentissage-apprenti: quelles difficultés de communication? .... see no. 13575

Integration von sehgeschaedigten Studierenden und Hochschulabsolventen in die Arbeitswelt (Integration of visually handicapped students and university graduates in working life) .... see no. 13594

Orientamento scolastico e professionale nella scuola dell'obbligo: verifica di una esperienza (Evaluation of an educational and vocational guidance initiative in compulsory school) .... see no. 13612

The role of the female deputy headteachers: an investigation into the role and profiles of female deputy headteachers in co-educational comprehensive schools in one local education authority .... see no. 13697

Reforming school governing bodies: a sociological investigation .... see no. 13717

A sociological evaluation of the relationship between expectations and outcomes concerning parental inclusion on School Boards......... .... see no. 13722

Three primary school boards: the first years.............. see no. 13725

Berufsschule als Feld von Jugendarbeit (The part-time vocational school as a field for youth work) .... see no. 13728

28 GROUPS AND ORGANIZATIONS – GROUPES ET ORGANISATIONS – GRUPPEN UND ORGANISATIONEN

13418 Church schools in an urban environment.
GBR 1993
Research Date(s): 1989-1992
Francis, L.
Inst: Trinity College, Carmarthen, Dyfed SA31 3EP, United Kingdom.
church; urban school; Christian education
église; école urbaine; éducation chrétienne
PROJECT DESCRIPTION
This project is re-analysing data collected from over 7,150 Anglican churches to explore the impact of urban church schools on a range of features of urban church life. The presence of a church school is shown to augment slightly the urban church's contact with under 14 year olds through membership of the choir and team of servers. The presence of a church school also increases slightly the number of young confirmands under the age of 14 and the number of 14-17 year olds contacted through church youth groups. There is also a higher number of infant baptisms in parishes which contain a church school.

13419 Činnost' mládežníckych organizácií v Slovenskej republike.
(Activities of youth associations in the Slovak Republic.)
SVK 1994
Research Date(s): 1991-1993
Rohál'-Il'kiv, I.; Slovíková, M.
Sup: Schmit, M.

Inst: Ústav informácií a prognóz školstva, mládeže a telovýchovy (Institute of Information and Prognoses of Education, Youth and Sport), Staré grunty 52, 842 44 Bratislava, Slovak Republic.
Ministerstvo školstva a vedy SR (Ministry of Education and Science of the Slovak Republic), Hlboká 2, 813 30 Bratislava, Slovak Republic
youth organization; youth attitude; socio-cultural activities; youth group; youth club; data base
organisation de jeunesse; attitude de la jeunesse; activités socioculturelles; groupe de jeunes; club de jeunes; banque de données
PROJECT DESCRIPTION
Aim: The research project aims to chart the activities of Slovak youth associations and other national institutions catering for children and young people. At the present stage, about 80 associations (member organizations of the Council of Youth of Slovakia as well as others) have been examined. The information about individual associations has been elaborated in such a way that it can be used for the database on children's organizations and youth organizations in the Slovak Republic.
Design: Documents of individual organizations (statutes, programmes, materials concerning the internal organization, guidelines, evaluations, etc.) have been collected and analysed. Information was gathered on: the seat of the organization; address; name of a representative; characteristics and objectives of the organization's activities; size of the organization; membership; admission criteria; organizational structure; competence of the association. In addition, basic information was collected on material and financial aspects of each association's activities (from journals, bulletins, brochures, etc.) and about the nature of the association's foreign contacts. The data served as a basis for the construction of typologies of the associations from various perspectives (objectives, orientation, target groups, territorial competence, membership, etc.). Furthermore, a description was made of the administrative and organizational structures of the associations and the legal conditions for their establishment.
Methods: Semi-structured interviews with representatives of associations; document analysis (statutes and other documents pertaining to the organizations as well as relevant laws and legal regulations); literature survey.
Publ: Macháček, L. & Rohál'-Il'kiv, I. *Youth Work in the Slovak Republic.* Information on Youth in Slovak Republic. Bratislava, Ministry of Education, Department of Youth, 1992, 54p.
Rohál'-Il'kiv, I. Mládežnícke organizácie na Slovensku a náčrtok typológie. (Youth Organizations in Slovakia.) In: *Mládež a spoločnost'*, Bratislava, UIP ŠMT, 1992, No. 4, 14p.

13420 Educational impact of voluntary organisations.
GBR 1993
Research Date(s): 1990-1995
Elsdon, K.; Stewart, S.; Reynolds, J.
Inst: Nottingham University, Department of Adult Education, 14-22 Shakespeare Street, Nottingham NG1 4FJ, United Kingdom.
Fin: Universities Funding Council.
voluntary organization; adult education; community education; social development
organisation volontaire; éducation des adultes; éducation sociale; développement social
PROJECT DESCRIPTION
The project aims to investigate the learning effects of local voluntary organisations on their members as individuals, and through them on their catchment population. An intensive study is planned of a representative sample of about 25 organisations chosen to take account of factors such as purpose, activities, size, ethnicity, geographical area, sex and age range of members. Each study will rest on the organisation's records and structured interviews and questionnaires administered individually or in groups as appropriate. Independent sources of evidence in the community will also be tapped.
The individual case studies will be published on completion and will form the basis of evidence on which the final report will rest; together they will also form a thesaurus of good practice. The analysis and interpretation of the case studies will be used to arrive at any general principles and practical applications.
Publ: Elsdon, K.T. *Adult learning in voluntary organisations: Vol 1: case studies 1 and 2.* Nottingham: University of Nottingham, Department of Adult Education, 1991.
Elsdon, K.T. Voluntary organisations and the White Paper. In: *Educational Centres Association Annual Report 1991.*
Elsdon, K.T. Voluntary organisations, learning and democracy. In: *Adult Education and Development.* February 1992.

13421 The interface of feminism, education and the Church: a study of power.
GBR 1993
Research Date(s): 1990-1994
Harrison, B.
Sup: Parsons, W.; Hay, J.
Inst: Nottingham University, School of Education, University Park, Nottingham NG7 2RD, United Kingdom.

religious organization; church; power; sexism
organisation religieuse; église; pouvoir; sexisme
PROJECT DESCRIPTION

This research looks at definitions of power and at what are regarded as the structures of authority in the Church of England. A case has been made for the existence of patriarchy but little can be found on the mechanisms by which it works. This research proposes to look further into the theory of the management of complex organisations, and will involve working with a group from a church congregation on the language used for the experience of God. The management language used by church bureaucrats will also be studied. The researcher also may work with a group from another parish. Study sessions for clergy on inclusive language and the liturgy, have been conducted, and the aim is to provide material for a deanery synod to work with.

13422 An investigation into parent-teacher association activities and their effectiveness in secondary schools in Kwara State, Nigeria.
GBR   1993
Research Date(s): 1989-1992
Lanade, J.
Sup: Spence, B.
Inst: Hull University, School of Education, Cottingham Road, Hull HU6 7RX, United Kingdom.
parents' association; parent-school relation; teachers' organization; development of education; Nigeria
association de parents; relation parents-école; organisation d'enseignants; développement de l'éducation; Nigeria
PROJECT DESCRIPTION

The concept of parents and teachers working together for the mutual benefit of the schools and the pupils has only recently been applied formally to the administration of secondary schools in Nigeria. This study of a sample of secondary schools in Kwara State, Nigeria, by means of a battery of questionnaires for school principals, teachers, parents and pupils, aims to develop criteria for the more effective development of the associations, and to determine the relationship, if any, between currently active parent-teacher associations and the general educational welfare and development of the pupils and the schools' academic success and reputation in the community.

13423 Pédagogie du militantisme dans les mouvements de jeunesse.
FRA   1993
Research Date(s): 1990-1991
Poujol, Geneviève; Romer, Madeleine.
Inst: Ministère de la recherche, CNRS UPR/31, Laboratoire de sociologie du changement des institutions, Institut de recherche sur les sociétés contemporaines, 59-61 rue Pouchet, 75849 Paris Cedex 17, France.
Fin: Fonds national de développement de la vie associative.
youth movement; citizen participation; social learning; social behaviour
mouvement de jeunesse; participation du citoyen; apprentissage social; comportement social
PROJECT DESCRIPTION

Objectifs: Approche historique et sociologique destinée à cerner la participation des mouvements de jeunesse actuels dans l'apprentissage à l'engagement social des jeunes. L'hypothèse est qu'il n'y a pas transmission d'un modèle et que les approches de cet apprentissage sont différentes selon les mouvements laïques et les mouvements confessionnels.

Méthodologie: Enquête auprès des responsables actuels des mouvements de jeunesse et des anciens militants issus des mouvements de jeunesse.

Publ: Poujol, Geneviève. Le journal d'une bénévole. In: *Vie sociale*, 1990.
Poujol, Geneviève. Demain les militants? In: Levasseur, Roger (ed.). *De la sociabilité*. Québec: Editions Boréal, 1991.
Poujol, Geneviève. *Rôle des mouvements de jeunesse dans l'apprentissage du militantisme*. Rapport au Fonds national de la vie associative, 1991.

13424 Les relations entre la famille et l'école: le point de vue des parents d'élèves; les fédérations de parents d'élèves dans la société et la vie politique françaises.
FRA   1993
Research Date(s): 1988-1993
Barthélémy, Martine.
Inst: Fondation nationale des sciences politiques, CNRS URA/120, Centre d'étude de la vie politique française, 10 rue de la Chaise, 75007 Paris, France.
Fin: Mission Recherche Expérimentation.
parents' association; parent-school relation; parent participation; political affiliation; value system
association de parents; relation parents-école; participation des parents; affiliation politique; système de valeurs
PROJECT DESCRIPTION

Objectifs: (1) Etude des relations entre les parents et l'école, compte tenu de leur institutionnalisation progressive depuis 20 ans, et du discours produit sur le système éducatif par les parents d'élèves; (2) Etude de trois grandes associations de parents d'élèves: identité, action et fonction de représentation, et interrogation sur la notion de militantisme associatif.

On considère (1) que les associations de parents d'élèves sont un lieu stratégique de rencontre entre famille et école, où s'expriment de manière privilégiée attentes et représentations, (2) que les projets d'école et images de son fonctionnement se développent à partir de conceptions divergentes du rôle de la famille (droits du père, droits de l'enfant), il faut donc prendre la mesure à la fois des filiations idéologiques et des évolutions. Enfin on fait l'hypothèse d'une multiplicité de critères de mobilisation dans le mouvement parents d'élèves et de formes d'action collective.

Méthodologie: Entretiens non directifs; enquête postale par questionnaire auprès d'un échantillon national de 2720 parents d'élèves membres de la PEEP, de la FCPE et de l'UNAPEL dans dix académies réparties géographiquement; étude des publications des trois organisations sur la période 1958 à nos jours ; analyse des élections aux conseils d'établissement (lycées et collèges) depuis 1968-1969 et aux conseils d'école (écoles maternelles et élémentaires) depuis 1977-1978.

Résultats: Elaboration de différents "modèles" de parents d'élèves à partir de l'exploitation des entretiens non directifs: les militants politiques, les "utopistes", les "parents militants", les "représentants", les "cogestionnaires", les "militants catholiques", les "participationnistes", les "militants associatifs".

13425 Training for the part-time youth service.
GBR   1993
Research Date(s): 1990-1993
Howells, M.
Sup: Donald, A.
Inst: University of Wales College of Cardiff, School of Education, Senghennydd Road, Cardiff CF2 4AG, United Kingdom.
youth organization; training programme; part-time work
organisation de jeunesse; programme de formation; travail à temps partiel
PROJECT DESCRIPTION

Most of the face-to-face work in the youth service is carried out by part-time workers. Therefore one way of ensuring good youth work is through the training of the part-time work force. This study describes the development of training for part-time youth work from the Albemarle report to the present, and sets it in the context of the aims of the youth service. Common elements in training are analysed. The social, economic and geographic background of Mid Glamorgan as an example, and the relationship of this with youth service provision are outlined. An investigation, based on a questionnaire and follow-up interview, of the perceptions of their training of 101 participants in the initial training course provided by the county over a period of four years is described. Issues such as the relationship between training and policies and practices; equal opportunities; and communications are discussed.

Main findings were that for many of the respondents, the training increased self-confidence and paved the way to new opportunities in employment or in personal life; that the part-time workers concerned brought into the youth service a wide variety of skills which were not always used as fully as they might have been; and that, although there are interesting developments in new forms of training, course-based provision still has a valuable place.

Publ: Howells, M.J. & Donald, A. *The contribution made to the youth service by the interests and activities of part-time youth workers*. Wales Youth Agency, Occasional Paper, March 1992.

13426 Youth work curriculum in Wales.
GBR   1993
Research Date(s): 1992-1993
Loudon, M.; Williamson, H.
Sup: Davies, B.
Inst: University of Wales College of Cardiff, School of Education, Senghennydd Road, Cardiff CF2 4YG, United Kingdom.
Fin: Welsh Office.
youth organization; youth attitude
organisation de jeunesse; attitude de la jeunesse
PROJECT DESCRIPTION

The aim of this project is to inform the debate on the youth work curriculum in Wales. Twenty-five youth work settings were visited to elicit the views of youth workers and young people on current and future provision.

13427 Youth work management policy to practice.
GBR   1993
Research Date(s): 1991-1993
Rose, J.
Sup: Donald, A.
Inst: University of Wales College of Cardiff, School of Education, 42 Park Place, Cardiff CF1 3BB, United Kingdom.
youth organization; youth policy
organisation de jeunesse; politique de la jeunesse
PROJECT DESCRIPTION

This study is an investigation into how youth work managers and full-time and part-time youth workers within an identified local education authority translate their organisation's youth work policy into practice. It will be concerned with examining the consistency of practice throughout the organisation by trying to determine how quality standards are established and maintained for core elements of the youth work curriculum. It attempts to do this by identifying the political process by which policy is developed and then follows the interpretation of that policy through to the point of delivery with young people.

Data are being collected from historical documents relating to policy discussion by the education sub-committee responsible for youth work; and through interviews with the chair of the relevant education sub-committee, assistant director of youth work, county adviser, part-time youth worker and young people. Questionnaires will also be used to obtain data from area youth workers, full-time youth workers, part-time youth workers and young people.

The supplementary school and its role in inner-city London..............
.... see no. 12229

The role of the Church of England in the provision of education at Worfield Endowed Church of England (Aided) Primary School from 1546 to 1991 in the light of the 1988 Education Reform Act with particular reference to the governors' responsibility for curriculum, funding and building.. see no. 12783

Social networks and ethnic identity in an urban nursery: a sociolinguistic analysis of preferred language use .... see no. 12916

Central Regional Council (Scotland) Youth Strategy - an evaluative study of school liaison groups.. see no. 13381

Policy and practice in community education: a study of the youth service and ethnic minority girls and young women in Peterborough .... see no. 13740

29 SOCIO-CULTURAL ENVIRONMENT – ENVIRONNEMENT SOCIO-CULTUREL – SOZIO-KULTURELLE UMWELT

13428 Adolescents' responses to short stories as representations of other cultures.
GBR 1993
Research Date(s): 1990-1992
Hayhoe, M.
Inst: University of East Anglia, School of Education, Norwich NR4 7TJ, United Kingdom.
cultural pluralism; youth attitude; fiction
pluralisme culturel; attitude de la jeunesse; fiction
PROJECT DESCRIPTION
The International Poetry Response Project undertook as one of its themes the investigation of adolescents' means of coping with poems from other cultures which also used English as the main language. The Short Story Response Project will investigate adolescents' understanding of and response to stories from Canada and India which were written in English. Comparison will be made between the views of United Kingdom students and students from the countries from which the stories originate. It is hoped that this pilot study will lead to a major one in two years time.

13429 Arbeitertoechter und ihr sozialer Aufstieg: zum Verhaeltnis von Klasse, Geschlecht und Technikkompetenz. (Working-class daughters and their social uprise: on the relationship between class, sex and technical competence.)
DEU 1993
Research Date(s): 1990-1994
Schlueter, A.; Metz-Goeckel, S.
Inst: Universitaet Dortmund, Hochschuldidaktisches Zentrum, Rheinlanddamm 199, D-4600 Dortmund 1.
woman; working class; natural sciences; social success; occupational status; student; social mobility; social origin
femme; classe ouvrière; sciences naturelles; réussite sociale; statut professionnel; étudiant; mobilité sociale; origine sociale
PROJECT DESCRIPTION
Inhalt: Es werden Studentinnen aus Arbeiterfamilien befragt, die sich fuer ein Naturwissenschafts- und Technikstudium entschieden haben. Zentral ist die Fragestellung nach den Integrations- und Differenzierungsleistungen, die Arbeitertoechter fuer einen sozialen Aufstieg ueber ein Studium erbringen muessen. Die Kontrollgruppe sind Paedagogikstudentinnen.
Geographischer Raum: Ruhrgebiet.
Untersuchter Zeitraum: 1960 und spaeter.
Vorgehensweise: Es wird mit dem Ansatz von P. Bourdieu gearbeitet.
Untersuchungsdesign: Fallstudie; Querschnittserhebung; qualitative Forschung.
Publ: Schlueter, A. Ueber den Zusammenhang von sozialer Herkunft - Technikstudium und Geschlechtszugehoerigkeit. In: Wetterer, A. (Hrsg.). *Profession und Geschlecht.* Frankfurt: Campus 1992.
Schlueter, A. (Hrsg.). *Arbeitertoechter und ihr sozialer Aufstieg.* Weinheim: Deutscher Studien Verl. 1992.

Metz-Goeckel, S. Bildung; Lebensverlauf und Selbstkonzepte von Arbeitertoechtern. In: Schlueter, A. (Hrsg.). *Arbeitertoechter und ihr sozialer Aufstieg.* Weinheim: Deutscher Studien Verl. 1992.

13430 Le attese informative e formative dei giovani nei confronti della scuola e delle altre agenzie formative. (The educational and informative expectations of youth with regard to school and other educational institutions.)
ITA 1994
Research Date(s): 1991-1992
De Angelis, Tiziana.
Sup: Del Corn, Lucio.
Inst: Arciragazzi Nazionale - Associazione Ricreativa Culturale Italiana (Italian Recreational and Cultural Association, Youth Department), Via G. Battista Vico, 22, 00196 Roma, Italy.
Fin: Ministero della Pubblica Istruzione, Ufficio Studi e Programmazione.
pre-adolescence; value; value system; youth attitude; information need
préadolescence; valeur; système de valeurs; attitude de la jeunesse; besoin d'information
PROJECT DESCRIPTION
A study of what is known about children and youth in Italy was conducted on the basis of investigations and interviews with pre-adolescents and adolescents aged 11-17 (both individually and in groups - organized by Arciragazzi, one of the most important youth organizations in Italy). These interviews and investigations allowed for a broad overview of the expectations of pre-adolescents with respect to information and training. This was followed by a study of pre-adolescents' needs for information about the real world.

Pre-adolescents express a need for guidance and information, either from peers or from adults (parents, teachers, social service workers, or adults they meet in associations). They have a need for practical non-ideological values, related to tolerance, a peaceful and cooperative disposition (for example, regarding relations between different countries, ethnic groups, and races), non-violence, understanding of others and of other points of view (from other cultures as well), civil rights, conscientious objection, solidarity, respect for and safeguarding of the quality of life, sexuality, physical expression and the physical health, attitudes towards science and technology in modern society, and attitudes towards new knowledge and foreign languages.

Publ: Del Corn, L.; Parrello, S. & De Angelis, T. Dossier: Adolescenza. In: *Nuovo Albero ad Elica,* no. 4a. VII, luglio-agosto 1991, pp. 35-56.

13431 Časový režim a využívanie vol'ného času jednotlivých vekových a sociálnych skupín nezamestnanej mládeže. (Time regime and use of leisure time by unemployed youth of different ages and from different social backgrounds.)
SVK 1994
Research Date(s): 1991-1992
Bieliková, M.; Kadlecová, B.
Sup: Zubalová, M.
Inst: Ústav informácií a prognóz školstva, mládeže a telovýchovy (Institute of Information and Prognoses of Education, Youth and Sport), Staré grunty 52, 842 44 Bratislava, Slovak Republic.
Ministerstvo školstva a vedy SR (Ministry of Education and Science of the Slovak Republic), Hlboká 2, 813 30 Bratislava, Slovak Republic
youth; youth unemployment; employment opportunities; graduate unemployment; job search; leisure
jeunesse; chômage des jeunes; chances d'obtenir un emploi; chômage des diplômés; recherche d'emploi; loisir
PROJECT DESCRIPTION
Aims: (1) To obtain a picture of trends in the development of leisure activities of unemployed youth, especially unemployed university graduates; (2) to analyse on the basis of empirical research the structure and scope of the activities of unemployed youth and university graduates; (3) to make recommendations for the management of youth organizations in the Slovak Republic regarding the efficient use of time by unemployed graduates from the perspective of self-realization and self-assertion.

Research question: What are the key problems in the use of time by unemployed youth in comparison with the use of time by economically active youth?

Design: Data were collected with the help of diaries kept by employed and unemployed young people and university graduates in the Slovak Republic in the academic year 1990/1991. Activities were divided into four basic categories: satisfying biological-physiological needs; job searching (by unemployed graduates) or work activities (by employed graduates); leisure activities; idle time. The data were supplemented by information collected by questionnaire and supplementary questions.

The information thus collected will provide an insight into the activities of young people, the quality of their free time and any tendencies in the development and orientation of their free-time activities.

Publ: Bieliková, M. Mládež a jej vol'ný čas. (Youth and Leisure.) In: *Informačný bulletin.* ÚIP ŠMT, 1993, No. 1, pp. 10-14.

13432   Chancen, Risiken und Konflikte von Jugendlichen beim Berufseinstieg: Lebensperspektiven und Wertorientierungen von Jugendlichen in den neuen Bundeslaendern.   (Opportunities, risks and conflicts faced by young people entering employment: perspectives and value orientations of young people in the new German states.)
DEU   1993
Research Date(s): 1991-1993
Preuss, H.
Inst: Projektgruppe Chancen, Konflikte, Potentiale in den ostdeutschen Bundeslaendern, Jaegerstr. 10-11, O-1086 Berlin.
youth; transition from school to work; German DR; youth attitude; value system; self-concept
jeunesse; passage à la vie active; Allemagne RDA; attitude de la jeunesse; système de valeurs; conception de soi
PROJECT DESCRIPTION
Inhalt: Die vorgesehene soziologische Laengsschnitt-Untersuchung hat das Ziel, den Zusammenhang von Ausbildungsprozessen und der weiteren Lebens- und Berufsentwicklung bei Jugendlichen im Land Brandenburg zu erfassen, zu beschreiben und zu erklaeren. Fuer die Realisierung des Projektes ist einerseits die Darstellung der objektiven Situation der Jugendlichen in der differenzierten Berufsausbildungsstruktur im Land Brandenburg erforderlich. Andererseits sollen Wertorientierungen, Zukunftserwartungen und bildungspolitische Vorstellungen der Jugendlichen untersucht werden. Schwerpunkte der empirischen Untersuchung sollen sein: allgemeine Einstellungen; generelle Lebenswerte; Arbeits- und Leistungsmotivation; Selbstkonzept/ Zukunftserwartungen; Einstellungen zur Gesellschaft; bildungspolitische Auffassungen; Geschlechtsrollenorientierungen.
Geographischer Raum: neue Bundeslaender.
Vorgehensweise: Laengsschnittanalyse: Dokumentenanalyse, standardisierte schriftliche Befragung, Gruppendiskussion, Expertengespraeche, Tiefeninterviews.
Datengewinnung: Gruppendiskussion. Expertengespraech.

13433   Communities in crisis: an adult education and resource programme for local groups and community leaders.
GBR   1993
Research Date(s): 1983-
Bryant, R.; Addy, T.
Inst: Ruskin College, Ruskin Hall, Old Headington, Oxford OX3 9BZ, United Kingdom; William Temple Foundation, Manchester, United Kingdom.
local community; adult education; community education; voluntary organization
collectivité locale; éducation des adultes; éducation sociale; organisation volontaire
PROJECT DESCRIPTION
The project has two aims: (1) to provide local activists/volunteers with the opportunity to reflect on their experiences and share ideas across different localities, towns and regions by linking groups in the north-west with groups in the southern regions; (2) to undertake project-based learning which, (a) will be of value to the participants, (e.g. confidence, writing skills etc.), and (b) will yield socially useful knowledge for local groups, e.g. data for jobs and applications.
Research and evaluation are concerned with: (a) recording the organisation of the programme, (b) monitoring the experiences of the participants, (c) evaluating the use of the project material by local groups.
Publ: Addy, T. & Bryant, R. et al. *Communities in crisis.* Ruskin College/William Temple Foundation, 1985.
Bryant, R. *Learning from experience: project work with community groups.* Ruskin College/William Temple Foundation. 1989.

13434   Componenten van sociaal milieu.   (Components of the social environment.)
NLD   1994
Research Date(s): 1993
Diederen, J.
Inst: Instituut voor Toegepaste Sociale wetenschappen (ITS) (Institute for Applied Social Sciences), P.O. Box 9048, 6500 KJ Nijmegen, Netherlands. Katholieke Universiteit Nijmegen (Catholic University of Nijmegen), P.O. Box 9102, 6500 HC Nijmegen, Netherlands
Fin: SVO het Instituut voor Onderzoek van het Onderwijs.
social environment; career; school career; family environment
milieu social; carrière; cursus scolaire; milieu familial
PROJECT DESCRIPTION
Background: The longitudinal survey "From Year to Year" monitors the educational and occupational careers of men and women who completed primary school in 1965. The present project is concerned with a secondary analysis of the data collected in this survey. The project examines the influence of social background on people's school, work and life careers. It is a sequel to the "Social environment and Careers" project, which also involved a secondary analysis of the data collected in the "From Year to Year" survey.

Aims: (1) To chart the interrelationships between a range of environmental indicators and, if possible, to reduce these to a limited number of components; (2) to determine whether and, if so, to what extent the relationships between social environment variables change in the course of time.
Design: The study starts from the view that the respondents themselves now represent a social environment. Social environment variables will be measured on five occasions that together encompass a period of three generations. The following variables will be measured: grandparents' variables; parents' variables at the start of their occupational career; parents' variables in 1970, when one of their children (the respondent in the study) reached the age of 17; respondents' variables in 1978 and 1987, at the respective ages of 25 and 35 years. The interrelationships between a maximum number of core variables will be looked at and subsequently be extended by variables that further concretize the family situation and family climate. This will result in a model with a maximum number of variables at each measurement point.

13435   Cultural studies in advanced language learning: the year abroad in under-graduate courses.
GBR   1993
Research Date(s): 1990-1993
Roberts, C.; Byram, M.
Inst: Thames Valley University, Faculty of Humanities and Languages, 1 The Grove, London W5 5DX, United Kingdom; Durham University, School of Education, Leazes Road, Durham DH1 1TA, United Kingdom.
Fin: Economic and Social Research Council.
study abroad; foreign languages; culture; language teaching; undergraduate study
études à l'étranger; langues étrangères; culture; enseignement des langues; supérieur premier cycle
PROJECT DESCRIPTION
The aim of this research is to develop a more integrated approach to language and culture on four year language degree courses. At the Thames Valley University this will be done by introducing principles of ethnography in the second year of the degree course. Students will write ethnographies of the target culture while abroad, which will then be evaluated. Two language staff will learn ethnographic approaches and their learning will be documented. They will then develop a new course for the language students.

13436   The development and application of socio-spatial indices.
GBR   1993
Research Date(s): 1990-1993
Reid, I.
Inst: Loughborough University of Technology, Department of Education, Loughborough LE11 3TU, United Kingdom.
Fin: Bradford Metropolitan Council, Directorate of Education.
social environment; social inequality; performance; school; pupil
milieu social; inégalité sociale; performance; école; élève
PROJECT DESCRIPTION
This project looks at the use of commercially-based post code applications to school populations to allow for comparisons, and the construction and application of the derived scale of social advantage/social deprivation to school and pupil performance.

13437   Didaktische Wege zur Motivation und Qualifizierung lernungewohnter Erwachsener.   (Didactic methods for the motivation and qualification of adults who are not accustomed to learning.)
DEU   1993
Research Date(s): 1991-1994
Belgrad, J.
Inst: Paedagogische Hochschule Ludwigsburg, Diplomaufbaustudiengang Erziehungswissenschaft, Forschungsgruppe Spiel- und Theaterpaedagogik, Reuteallee 46, D-7140 Ludwigsburg.
Fin: Land Baden-Wuerttemberg Ministerium fuer Wissenschaft und Kunst.
adult; learning difficulty; didactics; qualification; motivation for studies; place of work; teaching method
adulte; difficulté de l'apprentissage; didactique; qualification; motivation pour les études; lieu de travail; méthode pédagogique
PROJECT DESCRIPTION
Inhalt: Ermittlung und Vermittlung notwendiger Qualifikationen fuer neue, geaenderte Arbeitsplaetze z.B. (a) Abbau von Einzelarbeitsplaetzen zugunsten von Gruppenarbeitsplaetzen (Teamarbeit statt Einzelarbeit); (b) keine festen Arbeitsinhalte, sondern verschiedene Arbeiten (manuell) incl. selbstaendiger Qualitaetskontrolle; (c) kleine Stueckproduktionen (10-15 Stueck) statt grosser Serien.
Geographischer Raum: Baden-Wuerttemberg.
Vorgehensweise: Experten- und Anwenderbefragung, um danach didaktisches Material erstellen zu koennen. Untersuchungsdesign: qualitative Forschung.
Datengewinnung: Nicht-standardisiertes Interview (Stichprobe: 40; Arbeiter; Auswahlverfahren: Quota). Expertengespraech (Stichprobe: 10; Ausbildungsleiter grosser Betriebe -MB, ABB, SEL-; Auswahlverfahren: bewusst). Primaererhebung: Feldarbeit von Mitarbeitern des Projektes

durchgefuehrt; Datenerstellung auf der Basis von bereits vorliegenden Materialien wie Texten, Akten, Statistiken.

Auswertung: Faktorenanalyse.

13438 Die politische Verarbeitung sozialstrukturell-lebensweltlichen Wandels und ethno-kulturelle Pluralisierung in Nordamerika insbesondere am Beispiel der Bildungspolitik. (Political management of sociostructural change and ethno-cultural pluralization in North America, with particular reference to education policy.)
DEU 1993
Research Date(s): 1991-1993
Thunert, M.
Sup: Joas, H.
Inst: Freie Universitaet Berlin, ZI John-F.-Kennedy-Institut fuer Nordamerikastudien, Abt. Soziologie Nordamerikas, Lansstrasse 5-9, D-1000 Berlin 33.
Fin: Deutsche Forschungsgemeinschaft; Land Berlin.
social change; USA; Canada; educational policy; social structure; cultural pluralism; cultural change
changement social; Etats-Unis; Canada; politique de l'éducation; structure sociale; pluralisme culturel; changement culturel
PROJECT DESCRIPTION
Inhalt: Seit nunmehr zwei Jahrzehnten konstatiert die nordamerikanische Sozialwissenschaft einen fundamentalen sozialstrukturellen Wandel in den USA und Kanada. Charakteristisch fuer die heraufziehende postindustrielle Gesellschaft ist nach D. Bell der Bedeutungsanstieg des Dienstleistungssektors und des wissenschaftlich-technologischen Wissens. Gleichzeitig vollzieht sich die Aufloesung lebensweltlicher Realitaeten und Sicherheiten, die einem diffusen Pluralismus von Lebenschancen und Klassenlagen weichen. Begleitet wird dieser Wandlungsprozess von einer zunehmenden ethnischen Heterogenisierung und der Ausdifferenzierung kultureller Sinnstiftungsangebote. Wie verarbeiten die demokratischen Institutionen der USA (und Kanadas), denen ein normatives Demokratiemodell basierend auf individuellem Gleichheitsrecht und individueller Leistung zugrunde liegt, diese Erosion der tradierten sozialen Gussformen der Industriegesellschaft? Diese "grosse" Frage soll am Beispiel des (1) sozialphilosophischen Diskurses zwischen "Kommunitaristen" und "Liberalen" sowie neuen Ansaetzen der politischen Theorie und (2) neueren Entwicklungen und aktuellen Streitfragen in der Bildungspolitik einer Antwort naeher bringen.

Geographischer Raum: Nordamerika.

Untersuchter Zeitraum: seit 1970.

Vorgehensweise: Eklektisch; (1) interpretativ - deutende Rezeption der amerikanischen/nordamerikanischen Debatte; (2) Fallstudien, sekundaere Auswertung von US-Forschern erhobenen Daten, Texten; Policy-Analyse; teilnehmende Beobachtung am kongressionalen Gesetzgebungprozess. Untersuchungsdesign: Fallstudie; Evaluationsstudie; qualitative Forschung.

Datengewinnung: Beobachtung (Stichprobe: ca. 10; innovative Bildungssprojekte auf lokaler, regionaler und Bundesebene; Auswahlverfahren: bewusst). Expertengespraech (Stichprobe: ca. 25; bildungsrelevante Bundes- und Einzelstaatsgesetze zwischen 1989 und 1992; Auswahlverfahren: total. Stichprobe: ca. 10; innovative Bildungsprojekte auf lokaler, regionaler und Bundesebene; Auswahlverfahren: bewusst). Teilnehmende Beobachtung (dito). Inhaltsanalyse (dito). Primaererhebung: Feldarbeit von Mitarbeitern des Projektes durchgefuehrt; Datenerstellung auf der Basis von bereits vorliegenden Materialien wie Texten, Akten, Statistiken.

13439 Die Rolle der Grosstaedte im neuentstehenden Mitteleuropa. (The role of metropolitan areas in newly emerging central Europe.)
AUT 1993
Research Date(s): 1991-1992
Pohoryles, Ronald; Galehr, Claudia; Betz, Fritz.
Inst: Interdisziplinaeres Forschungszentrum Sozialwissenschaften, Hamburgerstrasse 14/20, A-1050 Wien.
Fin: Bundesministerium fuer Wissenschaft und Forschung.
town; modernization; urban area; economic development
ville; modernisation; zone urbaine; développement économique
PROJECT DESCRIPTION
Da der Modernisierungsprozess in den ostmitteleuropaeischen Wirtschaften von den Zentralraeumen ausgeht, werden diese anhand von vier ausgewaehlten Staedten (Wien, Budapest, Prag, Krakau) untersucht. Von speziellem Interesse ist hiebei die Kooperation sowie Konkurrenz zwischen diesen Staedten unter Beachtung historischer bzw. aktuell vorhandener Netzwerke.

Es werden Literaturanalysen, Akten- und Dokumentenanalysen, Expertengespraeche und eine Sekundaerdatenanalyse durchgefuehrt.

13440 Družbene spremembe in izobraževanje. (Social changes and education.)
SVN 1994
Research Date(s): 1993-1995
Štrajn, Darko; Kolenc, Janez; Bahovec, Eva; Kodelja, Zdenko; Milharčič-Hladnik, Mirjam; Šimenc, Marjan.

Inst: Pedagoški inštitut pri Univerzi v Ljubljani (Educational Research Institute at the University of Ljubljana), Gerbičeva 62, 61111 Ljubljana, Slovenia.
Univerza v Ljubljani (University of Ljubljana), Kongresni trg 15, 61000 Ljubljana, Slovenia
Fin: Ministrstvo za znanost in tehnologijo.
social change; educational reform; social interaction
changement social; réforme de l'enseignement; interaction sociale
PROJECT DESCRIPTION
Background: Although the problem of the relationship between social change and education is not new, especially when viewed from the angle of educational science, it is obvious that it has recently become more urgent. Indeed, it is becoming one of the central questions related to social reproduction. The difficulty in coping with social changes is that, even though everyone is aware of them, it is hard to grasp their "rationality", to sense their direction or to gain control over them through the mechanisms we install in society to avoid chaos.

Aim: The aim is to construct a theory which would make it possible to distinguish more relevant social changes from more ephemeral ones and to explain the reactions of the education system to changes in society. This theory would take account of the accomplishments of social philosophy, sociology (and a range of subdisciplines), psychoanalytical theory and educational science.

Research questions: (1) What does the transition from an industrial to a post-industrial society mean for the education system? (2) How can political changes be understood and what is their influence on school reform? (3) To what extent does cultural development (a transformation of values, mentalities and life styles, and a changing role of culture in the narrow sense of the term) affect changes in the education system?

Design: Special attention will be given to the role of the national Slovenian tradition in the development of education as a key "aggregate" of economic, social and cultural development. The study will make use of: (1) a comparative approach (at several levels); (2) a critical analysis of discourses; (3) a "typology" of phenomena, which will be useful to explore the sociological dimension of the problem.

13441 The effects of the Education Reform Act 1988 on black communities.
GBR 1993
Research Date(s): 1992-1993
Hyder, K.
Inst: Warwick University, Centre for Research in Ethnic Relations, Coventry CV4 7AL, United Kingdom.
Fin: Economic and Social Research Council.
ethnic minority; equal opportunity; educational reform; assessment; achievement; underachievement
minorité ethnique; égalité de chances; réforme de l'enseignement; appréciation; rendement; rendement déficient
PROJECT DESCRIPTION
Pupils of Caribbean background have a long history of educational disadvantage in Britain. The main aim of the study is to examine developments in local authorities and their schools which arise from the Education Reform Act 1988 and which may further disadvantage black pupils. Advantages, disadvantages and the overall effect of the Act will be investigated using a questionnaire to be circulated to all local education authorities in 1993.

A second aim of the study is to look in detail at the process of assessment. This is one of the few aspects of the Act with potential benefits for black pupils. The project will examine the hypothesis that the structures and networks developed for assessment will be used by authorities and schools to monitor and respond to inequalities.

The third aim is to observe classroom teaching and assessment in order to clarify the more controversial causes of 'underachivement/achievement'. Particular attention will be paid to the role of teacher knowledge and awareness of black children's backgrounds and the mechanisms through which these inform teaching processes and influence academic success.

For the second and third aims, the research will focus on a sample of Year 2 learners in schools in two authorities. Research methods will include classroom observations and interviews of teachers, pupils and parents.

13442 Einstellungen zu aktuellen Problemen der Innenpolitik 1991. (Attitudes towards current problems of domestic policy in 1991.)
DEU 1993
Research Date(s): 1991-
Berger, M.; Jung, M.; Roth, D.; Schulte, W.
Inst: Institut fuer praxisorientierte Sozialforschung -ipos-, N7, 13-15, D-6800 Mannheim 1.
foreigner; politics; nationalism; German DR; Germany - Federal Republic; attitude; racial discrimination; delinquency
étranger; politique; nationalisme; Allemagne RDA; Allemagne RFA; attitude; discrimination raciale; délinquance
PROJECT DESCRIPTION

Inhalt: politische und gesellschaftliche Grundeinstellungen; Links- und Rechtsextremismus; Kriminalitaet; Nationalstolz; Probleme in Ostdeutschland; auslaendische Mitbuerger; Asylrecht; EG; NATO; UNO.

Geographischer Raum: neue und alte Bundeslaender.

Untersuchter Zeitraum: 1991.

Vorgehensweise: Untersuchungsdesign: Querschnittserhebung.

Datengewinnung: Standardisiertes Interview (Stichprobe: 1500; Wahlberechtigte Westdeutschland; Auswahlverfahren: Zufall. Stichprobe: 1000; Wahlberechtigte Ostdeutschland; Auswahlverfahren: Zufall). Primaererhebung: Feldarbeit als Auftrag an kommerzielle Umfrageinstitute vergeben.

Auswertung: Tabellenauswertung; Korrelationsverfahren; Varianzanalyse.

13443 Emergent environmentalism: subject knowledge and concern for the environment.
GBR 1993
Research Date(s): 1991-1994
Palmer, J.
Inst: Durham University, School of Education, Leazes Road, Durham DH1 1TA, United Kingdom.
environment; natural resources; environmental study; citizen participation; curriculum development
environnement; ressources naturelles; étude du milieu; participation du citoyen; élaboration de programmes d'études
PROJECT DESCRIPTION

Phase One of this project has led to the accumulation of a substantial amount of data. Questionnaires have been circulated to environmental educators throughout the UK asking for information and supporting autobiographical statements explaining key factors influencing the development of personal concern for the environment. The aim is to identify significant life events/life experiences which have contributed towards people's concern for and interest in environmental matters. If a major goal of environmental education is to produce informed and environmentally active citizens, then presumably environmental educators should know the kinds of learning experiences which help to influence the development of environmental care and concern. Statements have been collected from a sample of over 200 educators. They will be used to make recommendations on the implications of significant learning experiences for the designing of educational programmes and approaches to the inclusion of environmental education in the formal curriculum.

The pilot study for Phase Two of the project will involve the collection of autobiographical (audio-taped) statements/discussion from nursery children in the USA on their understanding of common environmental issues (ranging from the immediate environment to global concerns). Analysis of this should reveal issues for further investigation, suggest preliminary categories of response and allow for subsequent comparison with nursery age children in the UK.

13444 Environmental education: a directory and review of research.
GBR 1993
Research Date(s): 1993
Tomlins, B.
Sup: Stoney, S.
Inst: National Foundation for Educational Research, The Mere, Upton Park, Slough SL1 2DQ, United Kingdom.
environmental study; educational research; directory
étude du milieu; recherche en éducation; répertoire
PROJECT DESCRIPTION

There is currently a widespread and diverse research community in the field of environmental education research but little in the way of formal networking to aid communication between groups. This project aims to collate a directory of members of the research community, listing basic information such as name, address and area of interest/activity. This would facilitate communication and a more coordinated approach to the development of research in environmental education.

A form will be devised to collect this information and will be circulated to all relevant institutions. A review of existing and, as far as possible, ongoing environmental education research will be conducted in order to identify the main themes and findings. Gaps in the research would also be highlighted.

The directory and review will initially cover the United Kingdom but could be expanded to include a representative range of European institutions. It will focus on research involving the teaching of 5-18 year-olds and will be produced in a format which facilitates updating. A directory and review of environmental education research in the United Kingdom will be produced.

13445 Environmental training policy.
CHE 1993
Research Date(s): 1991-
Alfthan, T.; Gagliardi, R.
Sup: Lee, E.

Inst: Training Policy and Programme Development Branch, Training Department, International Labour Office, 1211 Geneva, Switzerland.
Fin: Ministry of Education and Science, Federal Republic of Germany; ILO.
environmental study; environment; ecology; educational need; curriculum development; training programme; cross-national research
étude du milieu; environnement; écologie; besoin d'éducation; élaboration de programmes d'études; programme de formation; recherche transnationale
PROJECT DESCRIPTION

Background: The Training Policy and Training Programmes Branch of the ILO prepared the background paper for an ILO Tripartite Meeting on Employment and Training Implications of Environmental Policies in Europe, held in Geneva in 1989. As a result of the meeting, it was considered opportune to gather more information in the environmental training area and, since the Government of the Federal Republic of Germany was also interested in the subject, they expressed willingness to finance a study. It seemed apparent from desk studies of literature on environmental subjects that there was little mention of the need for training.

Aims: To assist policy makers and planners to identify priorities in environmental protection so as to design relevant training programmes. Further, to contribute to the integration of training into mainstream occupational training and also to discuss environmental education with a view to creating responsible environmental attitudes and behaviour as well as a new environmental ethic.

Design: In addition to a literature survey, case studies of training for environmental protection in a number of European countries have been undertaken as an initial step in data collection. These data will be used as background information for a book covering: (1) The meaning of a desirable environment; (2) The environmental impacts of human activities: the implications for training; (3) Corrective vs. preventive environmental policies: training needs differ; (4) Environmental literacy training for everybody; (5) Job-related environmental literacy training; (6) Environmental training for people engaged in environmental protection jobs; (7) The labour market: matching the supply and demand for environmental skills; (8) The cultural context of environmental training; (9) The multi-disciplinary nature of environmental training; (10) The complexity of interactions between environmental phenomena and human activities; (11) Environmental protection: managing situations of conflict; (12) Skill and knowledge background of students entering environmental training programmes; (13) Developing an environmental ethic; (14) Training modes and methods; Matching training to learners' conceptions; (15) Training for major actors in the environmental area: enterprises; environmental administration and management; training farmers for sustainable agriculture; trade unions; training environmental trainers; environmental organisations; (16) The role of international organisations; Conclusions and recommendations.

Publ: Gagliardi, R. Training for environmental protection in the Lombardy and Umbria regions. ILO, Geneva, 1991 (Training Policies Branch Discussion Paper No. 74).

13446 Ethnic minorities in higher education.
GBR 1993
Research Date(s): 1991-1993
Taylor, P.
Inst: Warwick University, Centre for Research in Ethnic Relations, Coventry CV4 7AL, United Kingdom.
Fin: Economic and Social Research Council.
ethnic minority; higher education; access to education
minorité ethnique; enseignement supérieur; accès à l'éducation
PROJECT DESCRIPTION

The main aims of the project are to: (1) obtain greater knowledge of ethnic minority participation in higher education; (2) study the perceptions formed by these students and (3) consider the role of higher education institutions in the continuation of discrimination.

In order to pursue these aims several different institutions are being studied. Data obtained from various sources (including the Universities Central Council for Admissions (UCCA)) were used to study participation. Consideration of students' experiences and perceptions of higher education will be facilitated by interview and survey material.

These studies are to be placed in the context of the institutional policies and practices which affect students, in particular ethnic minorities.

Publ: Taylor, P. Ethnic group data and application to higher education. In: Higher Education Quarterly, Autumn 1992.
Taylor, P. Ethnic group data for university entry. Project report for the Committee of Vice-Chancellors and Principals, Coventry: Centre for Research in Ethnic Relations, 1992.

13447 Evaluation of English Nature's School Grants Scheme.
GBR 1993
Research Date(s): 1991-1992
Tomlins, B.; Harris, S.
Sup: Stoney, S.
Inst: National Foundation for Educational Research, The Mere, Upton Park, Slough SL1 2DQ, United Kingdom.
Fin: English Nature.

nature conservation; garden; environment; natural resources; environmental study
conservation de la nature; jardin; environnement; ressources naturelles; étude du milieu
PROJECT DESCRIPTION

Nature areas in the school grounds can assist in the teaching of required knowledge, skills and understanding and cultivate desirable attitudes towards the natural environment and living things. They can be used as a resource for aspects of science and geography in the National Curriculum. The Nature Conservancy Council (NCC) now English Nature (EN) has, since 1985, awarded grants to assist schools in the setting up of nature areas.

The aims of the research project are to: (1) assess the extent to which grant-aided nature areas have raised both the quality of environmental education and children's levels of awareness of conservation issues; (2) investigate how far the School Grants Scheme has stimulated interest in the creation of nature areas; (3) examine the range of strategies employed by schools for the management of nature areas; (4) investigate the range and extent of support provided to schools for nature areas by local education authorities (LEAs); (5) assess the extent to which educational institutions are aware of the School Grants Scheme and whether the activities of other organisations are seen to be in competition; and (6) investigate cost/benefit relationships in schools where grants have been awarded.

Questionnaires have been circulated to 750 schools which have applied to English Nature for a grant and 400 schools which have not, both samples including primary and secondary schools. A separate questionnaire has been sent to all LEA Advisers with responsibility for environmental education. The research also includes 40 school visits, 20 of these constituting case-studies.

13448   How does bereavement affect spiritual and moral thinking in children?
GBR   1993
Research Date(s): 1993-1995
Clark, V.
Sup: Halstead, M.; Hannan, A.
Inst: Plymouth University, Rolle Faculty of Education, Douglas Avenue, Exmouth EX8 2AT, United Kingdom.
death; moral development; child development; religious behaviour
mort; développement moral; développement de l'enfant; comportement religieux
PROJECT DESCRIPTION

The general principles established in the first section of the Education Reform Act 1988 (ERA) ensure that the education received "promotes the spiritual, moral (and) cultural...development of pupils at school and of society". Such principles, however, may be affected by personal rather than educational circumstances - such as the loss by death of a significant person in the child's life. Despite steady increase in research into the effects of bereavement in the adult population, less has been written about bereaved children's reactions and, in particular, of the links that may exist with spiritual and/or moral development.

The aim of this research is: (a) to review the literature concerning spiritual, moral (and religious) development and bereavement reactions and to identify common themes, particularly regarding children; (b) to analyse the responses obtained through interviews and questionnaires from children, adolescents and adults concerning their thinking and behaviour following childhood/adolescent bereavement; and (c) to indicate what the implications of these findings are for the implementation of ERA.

Respondents, who will be contacted through schools, colleges, bereavement counselling groups and national networks, will provide information through taped interviews and questionnaires, thus providing both breadth and depth of response. It is anticipated that some correlation between childhood bereavement and spiritual and/or moral thinking/development will appear, despite variations in its frequency and intensity and in individual awareness of it. Adults are likely to provide a longer-term perspective of their development in this respect; children and adolescents will be asked for information as to how their educational life is/was affected by bereavement.

13449   IEA Prosholiki erevna, Fasi 2, Poiotita Zois. (IEA Preprimary Study, Phase 2, Quality of Life.)
GRC   1994
Research Date(s): 1992-
Frangos, Christos; Smaragda-Tsiantzi, Marika; Evangelou, Demetra; Tsitouridou, Melpomeni.
Inst: Paidagogiko Kentro Erevnon kai Epimorfosis (Educational Research and In-Service Training Centre - EDURIT), PO Box 1664, 540 06 Thessaloniki, Greece; Paidagogiko Tmima Nipiagogon, Aristoteleio Panep. Thessalonikis (Department of Early Childhood Education, Aristotelian University of Thessaloniki), PO Box 1664, 540 06 Thessaloniki, Greece.
pre-school age; target groups of education; expectancy; teacher behaviour; family environment; socialization; child development
âge préscolaire; destinataires de l'éducation; attente; comportement de l'enseignant; milieu familial; socialisation; développement de l'enfant
PROJECT DESCRIPTION

This study is part of the IEA Preprimary Project, which consists of a large-scale longitudinal study of early childhood education settings and children in 14 countries. 240 4-year-old children in 58 early childhood settings from Athens and Thessaloniki are participating in the study. The research is concerned with the quality of life of preschool children in Greece. Quality of life is assessed through a range of research methods investigating the role of different socialization agents in the development of preschool children. Detailed parent questionnaires investigate the family background, living conditions and caretaking arrangements for children. Extensive interviews with directors of day care centres and nursery schools are part of the research as well. In addition, parents' and teachers' expectations regarding child development are explored. Child development is assessed through a battery of developmental tests in different areas. Direct classroom observation of child activities, teacher behaviour and management of time are also part of the research. The research aims at the development of a model of child development through careful description of the position, strength and interrelation of different socialization agents in the life of preschool children.

13450   Interaction between the school and the cultural environment for the education of the pupils.
BGR   1994
Research Date(s): 1991-1993
Ivanova, A.; Lazarov, P.; Mircheva, V.
Inst: National Centre for Education and Science Studies, Tzarigradsko Chossé 125, 1113 Sofia, Bulgaria.
Fin: Ministry of Education and Science.
culture; cultural environment; cultural exchange; philosophy of education; humanism
culture; milieu culturel; échange culturel; philosophie de l'éducation; humanisme
PROJECT DESCRIPTION

Background: The period 1988-1997 has been proclaimed a world decade for the development of culture. The research conforms to the main tasks outlined in the UNESCO's plan of activities. Participants from the following countries have taken part in the research during the various phases: Belgium, Finland, Germany, Netherlands, Norway, Poland, Romania and Russia.

Aims: The overall concern of the project is the education of free human beings with wide cultural interests and human interrelations in society and with nature, on the basis of interaction between the school and the cultural environment, with the help of national and worldwide accomplishments. More specifically, the project aims at: (1) discovering the possibilities of schools and the opportunities for the harmonious development of pupils on the basis of humanistic values, rights and freedom of the individual; (2) determining the main areas of culture which offer possibilities for interaction with the schools; (3) the application of effective pedagogical approaches and methods fostering interaction between the school and the cultural environment in accordance with the peculiarities and the individual interests of pupils of different ages; (4) directing the school work towards the formation of an interest and a necessity in pupils to communicate with the cultural environment and to participate in the activities of cultural institutions; (5) promoting teacher training programmes fostering active, creative and effective work for the realization of interaction between schools and their cultural environment and of an education for pupils in the spirit of humanism and universal virtue.

Hypothesis: When there is interaction between the school and the cultural environment and when pupils have an active personal attitude towards this interaction, pupils will adopt certain national and international values; under these circumstances it will be possible for them to be educated in humanistic values and universal virtue, to have a harmonic relation with nature and to get to know the cultures of different countries.

Methods: Analyses, empirical research, pedagogical experiments, sociological research, etc. The concrete approaches and methods are determined according to the peculiarities of the education systems of the countries participating in the study and of the working conditions in each school and its cultural environment.

Population: The research deals with primary and secondary school pupils.

13451   Internationales Oeffentliches Umweltschutzrecht. (International legislation on environmental protection.)
AUT   1993
Research Date(s): 1992-1994
Bodo, Bernhardt.
Inst: Institut fuer Voelkerrecht und Internationale Beziehungen, Innrain 52, A-6020 Innsbruck.
Universitaet Innsbruck, Innrain 52, A-6020 Innsbruck
environment; community law; legislation
environnement; droit communautaire; législation
PROJECT DESCRIPTION

Problembezogene Darstellung voelkerrechtlicher Vertraege zum Umweltschutz mit Beteiligung Oesterreichs sowie der bestehenden Kompetenzen der Europaeischen Gemeinschaft in sektoriellen Bereichen des Umweltschutzes in Ausrichtung auf einen kuenftigen EG-Beitritt Oesterreichs unter dem Aspekt der Gefahr eines kuenftigen Abbaues inlaendischer Schutz- und Qualitaetsstandards. Zunaechst sollen die einzelnen primaerrechtlichen Grundlagen und sekundaerrechtlichen sektoriellen Ausfuehrungsbestim- mungen des EG-Rechts im Bereich des Umweltschutzes dargestellt wer- den. Dem schliesst sich die Analyse der derzeit geltenden Abkommen im Umweltschutzbereich an, denen die EG als Internationale Organisation als Vertragspartner beigetreten sind. Im dritten Hauptteil soll - auf der Grun- dlage der oesterreichischen Verfassungs- und Binnenkompetenzstruktur - ein nach geschuetzten Medien und erfassten Regelungsgegenstaenden gegliederter systematischer Ueberblick ueber die gegenwaertigen Oester- reichischen Umweltschutzstandards gegeben werden - und zwar in qualita- tiver und quantitativer Dimension. In einem vierten Hauptteil sollen auf der Grundlage einer synoptischen qualitativen normativen Auswertung die einzelnen Schutzstandards des EG-Rechts mit den - soweit wech- selbezueglich existierenden und kompatiblen - einschlaegigen oesterreichis- chen Standards verglichen werden. Aus diesem Vergleich sollen sich unmittelbare Rueckschluesse ueber den Anpassungsbedarf der oester- reichischen Standards fuer den Fall eines EG- Beitritts, insbesondere in den Bereichen Gewaesserschutz, Luftreinhaltung, Laermbekaempfung, Abfallbehandlung und saubere Technologien, nukleare Sicherheit und radioaktive Abfaelle, chemische und gefaehrliche Stoffe, Schutz von Fauna und Flora sowie im Hinblick auf Umweltvertraeglichkeitspruefungen ergeben. Daneben soll geklaert werden, in welchen Sektoren Oesterreich durch Beibehaltung hoeherer als der insoweit verbindlich zu stellenden EG- Standards Wettbewerbsverzerrungen zu den internationalen, insbesondere europaeischen Maerkten, vor allem in Ausrichtung auf den EG-Bin- nenmarkt, zu gewaertigen haette.

13452   Lebenslaeufe im Wandel. (Changing life careers.)
DEU   1993
Research Date(s): 1991-1992
Watzinger, D.; et al.
Sup: Schulze, G.
Inst: Universitaet Bamberg, Fak. Sozial- und Wirtschaftswissenschaften, Soziologisches Forschungspraktikum, Feldkirchenstrasse 21, D-8600 Bamberg.
social change; school; occupation; leisure; family; social interaction; life cycle
changement social; école; profession; loisir; famille; interaction sociale; cycle de vie
PROJECT DESCRIPTION
   Inhalt: Aufzeigen von sozialem Wandel, der sich in Lebenslaeufen, und zwar in den Bereichen Schule/Beruf; Familie: Partnerschaft - Ehe -Kinder; soziale Kontakte; Freizeit, manifestiert. (Individualisierungstendenzen; Insti- tutionalisierung/Alters-, Kohorten-, Periodeneffekte).
   Geographischer Raum: Bamberg.
   Vorgehensweise: Individualisierung - Institutionalisierung; quantitative und qualitative Lebenslaufforschung; Kohortenanalyse. Untersuchung- sdesign: retrospektive Daten; qualitative Forschung.
   Datengewinnung: Standardisiertes Interview (Stichprobe: 300; 60- 65jaehrige, Bamberg, deutsch; Auswahlverfahren: Zufall. Stichprobe: 300; 40-45jaehrige, Bamberg, deutsch; Auswahlverfahren: Zufall. Stichprobe: 300; 20-25jaehrige, Bamberg, deutsch; Auswahlverfahren: Zufall). Nicht- standardisiertes Interview (Stichprobe: ca. 50; Auswahlverfahren: Quota). Primaererhebung: Feldarbeit von Mitarbeitern des Projektes durchgefuehrt.
   Auswertung: Deskription; 2-dimensionale Auswertung (Tab., Korrela- tionen); multivariate Verfahren (klassische Testtheorie; Faktorenanalyse; multiple Regression). Datenaufbereitung: Verlaufsdaten (event history data).

13453   Lifestyle, values and educational participation among adults.
GBR   1993
Research Date(s): 1992-1993
Field, J.
Inst: Bradford University, Centre for Continuing Education, 12 Claremont, Bradford BD7 1DP, United Kingdom.
adult; life cycle; participation; adult education; value
adulte; cycle de vie; participation; éducation des adultes; valeur
PROJECT DESCRIPTION
   Most studies of participation in adult education focus upon socio-eco- nomic and demographic factors, such as social class, age or gender. However, participation rates also vary widely within categories, and this study is concerned to discover whether lifestyle patterns can be related to educational participation among the adult population.
   Two major methods will be used to explore the extent to which educa- tional participation can be explained with reference to life cycle patterns. They are: (a) surveys of adult learners in personal development courses and in craft-based courses, using an established lifestyle analysis; and (b) semi- structured interviews to explore the degree of inner-directedness within adult learners' value systems, and to investigate the role of material factors in influencing decisions to participate.

Outcomes will be analysed using a conceptual framework that will draw upon the work of Pierre Bourdieu as well as of market research theorists and critics of post-modernist sociology.

13454   Mature students and higher education.
GBR   1993
Research Date(s): 1992-
Gardner, P.; Pickering, J.
Inst: Warwick University, Faculty of Educational Studies, Coventry CV4 7AL, United Kingdom.
adult; university; interpersonal relations
adulte; université; relations interpersonnelles
PROJECT DESCRIPTION
   The research examines how mature students at university perceive younger undergraduates; how they get on in halls of residence; and how course selectors view mature students.

Publ: Gardner, P. & Pickering, J. Learning to live with Madonna: or mature students on campus. In: *Pastoral Care in Education*, Vol 10, No 4/1992, pp. 3-8.
Pickering, J. & Gardner, P. Access: a selector's perspective. In: *Journal of Access Studies*, Vol 7, No 2/1992, pp. 220-233.

13455   Mobiliteit van leraren in primair en voortgezet onderwijs. (Teacher mobility in primary and secondary education.)
NLD   1994
Research Date(s): 1992
Gennip, J. van; Spruit, L.; Helderman, J.
Sup: Pouwels, J.
Inst: Instituut voor Toegepaste Sociale wetenschappen (ITS) (Institute for Applied Social Sciences), P.O. Box 9048, 6500 KJ Nijmegen, Netherlands. Katholieke Universiteit Nijmegen (Catholic University of Nijmegen), P.O. Box 9102, 6500 HC Nijmegen, Netherlands
Fin: SVO het Instituut voor Onderzoek van het Onderwijs.
occupational mobility; teacher; career change; motivation
mobilité professionnelle; enseignant; changement de carrière; motivation
PROJECT DESCRIPTION
   Background: The Minister of Education and Science has commissioned the Future of the Teaching Profession Committee to prepare an advisory report on the future of teachers in the Netherlands. The Committee intends to make use of the outcomes of research of the mobility of teachers in primary and secondary education. Two main types of mobility are distin- guished: external mobility (into and out of education) and internal mobility (change of school, employer, post, geographical region).
   Aim: To examine the attitudes and motivations underlying internal and external teacher mobility.
   Design: The sample will consist of 1,050 primary school teachers (500 schools) and 1,400 secondary school teachers (500 schools) who were employed by a school in May 1992. Schools will be asked for the teachers' addresses and some additional information. Data on mobility will be col- lected through a telephone survey of the teachers. Pre-structured question- naires will be used. Qualitative data will be collected through 10 in-depth interviews.

13456   Musikalische Verhaltensweisen von 'Gastarbeiter'-Kindern in Wien. (Children of migrant workers and their musical behaviour.)
AUT   1993
Research Date(s): 1991-1992
Smudits, Alfred; Bailer, Noraldine; Emir, Mehmet; Horak, Roman; Huber, Harald; Ratkovic, Vlasta.
Inst: Institut fuer Musiksoziologie, Schubertring 14, A-1010 Wien.
Hochschule fuer Musik und darstellende Kunst, Lothringerstrasse 18, A-1030 Wien
Fin: Bundesministerium fuer Unterricht und Kunst.
cultural environment; host country; ethnic origin; immigrant; music; child of foreign national; music education; intercultural education
milieu culturel; pays d'accueil; origine ethnique; immigrant; musique; enfant d'étranger; éducation musicale; éducation interculturelle
PROJECT DESCRIPTION
   Ausgangsthese ist, dass die musikalischen Verhaltensweisen von 'Gas- tarbeiter'-Kindern im Spannungsfeld der Stammkultur, der musikalischen Kultur des Gastlandes und der anglo- amerikanischen Pop- und Rock- Musikkultur stehen. Ziel der Untersuchung war es, einen ersten Einblick zur Klaerung dieser spezifischen Akkulturationsproblematik zu liefern, u.a. auch um Grundlagen fuer musikpaedagogische Initiativen im schulischen und ausserschulischen Bereich zu erstellen. Speziell wurde der Frage nachge- gangen, welche Arten von Musik welche Bedeutungszuschreibungen von seiten der Jugendlichen erhalten.
   Es wurden Gruppendiskussionen (fuenf Gruppen mit jeweils zehn Jugen- dlichen) und Expertengespraeche (vier Lehrerinnen, vier Jugendbetreuer) durchgefuehrt. Die Schulstatistik wurde einer Sekundaeranalyse unterzogen.
   Es handelt sich um eine explorative Untersuchung.
   Jugendliche Migranten bewegen sich (vordergruendig gar nicht so problematisch) zwischen zwei kulturellen Welten: der Kultur des Herkunft-

slandes (Heimat, Volksmusik, zu Hause) und der Kultur des Gastlandes Oesterreich (anglo- amerikanisch gefaerbte Jugendkultur).

Publ: Bailer, Noraldine; Horak, Roman & Smudits, Alfred. *Musikalische Verhaltensweisen von 'Gastarbeiter'-Kindern in Wien. Bericht ueber eine Untersuchung* (Manuskript), Wien, August 1992.

Bailer, Noraldine; Horak, Roman & Smudits, Alfred. 'Gastarbeiter'-Kinder zwischen Volksmusik und Popmusik. In: *SWS-Rundschau*, 32. Jahrgang, Heft 3/1992, S. 375-384.

13457   The needs and individual coping responses of adolescents in the United Arab Emirates.
GBR   1993
Research Date(s): 1986-1991
Alnajjar, A.
Sup: Gilliland, J.; McGuiness, J.
Inst: Durham University, School of Education, Leazes Road, Durham DH1 1TA, United Kingdom.
Fin: United Arab Emirates Embassy.
adolescent; need; Arab countries
adolescent; besoin; pays arabes
PROJECT DESCRIPTION
   This research consists of a survey of models of adjustment and coping relevant to the investigation of adolescents' perceived needs and coping responses. The research includes a pilot study and the main study of adolescents in the United Arab Emirates (UAE).
   The pilot study involving approximately 60 students elicited a range of perceived needs and responses by means of written replies to open-ended statements. A questionnaire based on the results of the pilot study has been administered to approximately 700 students throughout all of the States of the UAE.

13458   Okres dorastania w Europie: życiowe perspektywy i akceptowane wartości młodzieży polskiej. (Adolescence in Europe: accepted values and life perspectives of Polish adolescents.)
POL   1994
Research Date(s): 1991-1992
Liberska, H.; Botcheva, L.; Csapo, B.; Flanagan, C.; Gootkina, N.; Macek, P.; Noack, P.; et al.
Sup: Flammer, August; Grob, Alexander.
Inst: Instytut Psychologii, Uniwersytet Adama Mickiewicza (Psychological Institute, Adam Mickiewicz University), 60 568 Poznań, Szamarzewskiego 89, Poland.
Universität Bern, Psychologisches Institut (University of Bern, Psychological Institute), Gerbaunde 2, Laupenstrasse 4, 3008 Bern, Switzerland
adolescent; self-perception; social change; Europe; cross-national research; youth attitude
adolescent; perception de soi; changement social; Europe; recherche transnationale; attitude de la jeunesse
PROJECT DESCRIPTION
   The research is carried out in co-operation with universities in: Bern, Brno, Bologna, Helsinki, Michigan, Manheim, Moscow, Rennes, Sofia, Szeged.
   Aims: To identify specific features of adolescence in the period of radical socio-economic change in Europe; to establish the relationships between social conditions and the mental development of young people; to determine the psychological consequences of the "social revolution" for the young generation; to collect data on which to base predictions regarding entry into adulthood by adolescents in Europe today; to examine the mental development of youth in different cultures.
   Hypotheses: (1) The values accepted by Polish youth are of a universal nature. (2) Young people's perceptions of their life prospects depend on social changes. Radical and rapid changes hinder young people's mental adjustment to the new conditions, which manifests itself for example in a different view of one's life prospects for the near future. Differences are expected in the perceptions of adolescents growing up under different conditions in Eastern, Western, Northern, Southern and Central Europe.
   Methods: Interviews, questionnaires and assessment scales are used to collect information on everyday activities, future expectations, coping strategies, subjects' well-being, background variables, intercultural attitudes, personal control.
   The findings of the project will be presented at the European ISSBD Conference in Seville, Spain.

13459   Ontwikkelingen in theoretische inzichten en empirische bvindingen omtrent de schoolcarrières van kinderen uit diverse sociaal-economische en etnisch-culturele groepen. (Unequal opportunities: a review.)
NLD   1994
Research Date(s): 1990-1992
Meijnen, G.W.; Riemersma, F.S.J.
Inst: Stichting Centrum voor Onderwijsonderzoek (SCO) (Centre for Educational Research), Grote Bickersstraat 72, 1013 KS Amsterdam, Netherlands.
Universiteit van Amsterdam (University of Amsterdam), P.O. Box 19268, 1000 GG Amsterdam, Netherlands

Fin: SVO het Instituut voor Onderzoek van het Onderwijs.
social origin; social inequality; deprived; achievement; school career
origine sociale; inégalité sociale; défavorisé; rendement; cursus scolaire
PROJECT DESCRIPTION
   Background: Research on in-school and out-of-school determinants of school careers is traditionally closely linked to research on unequal educational opportunities. To date, no empirically grounded theory exists of the causes of unequal opportunities. However, connections have been found to exist between the ethnic and socio-economic background of pupils and their success at school. The view that pupils who begin to lag behind will have increasing difficulty to catch up has steadily been gaining ground. This has led to a growing interest in research and policy circles for the pre-school period and the early years of primary education (4-7 year-olds). The research programme "School careers from 4 to 7 years" is concerned with empirical research on the family situation of school pupils, instructional characteristics during the first three years in school and context characteristics of effective instruction.
   Aim: To provide an interpretative framework for the study of the school careers of children aged 4-7, on the basis of a literature survey on school careers in the period up to 18 years.
   Results: The longer a child has lived in the Netherlands, the less the influence of the ethnic factor on school achievement. The relatively poor achievement levels of ethnic minority pupils should be atttibuted above all to the socio-economic status of the family, which has an influence on the school career throughout the school years. Differences between children are caused by differences in knowledge, intelligence, learning style, social intelligence, motor skills, health, behaviour and motivation. The development of these qualities takes place to a large extent during the early years. An important factor in this context is the social interaction in the family, especially the relation between mother and child. Also, the first years at school may have a crucial influence on a child's future school career. In order for children to attain a steady, high level of academic performance, they need to experience "success in learning" as early in their school career as possible. Intervention programmes for disadvantaged children are mainly effective in the long term.
   (This is an updating of EUDISED no. 43/10400).

Publ: Meijnen, G.W. et al. *Schoolcarrières: een klassenkwestie?* Amsterdam/Lisse: Swets & Zeitlinger, 1992, 140p. (FORUM 21).

13460   Re-storying the landscape.
GBR   1993
Research Date(s): 1990-1992
Dyer, A.
Inst: Plymouth University, Rolle Faculty of Education, Douglas Avenue, Exmouth EX8 2AT, United Kingdom.
Fin: National Trust; Plymouth University.
environmental study; open-air activities; story telling
étude du milieu; activités de plein air; narration d'histoires
PROJECT DESCRIPTION
   This is an environmental education project aimed at using all of the arts in the interpretation and discovery of the natural world. Children are encouraged to rediscover some of the stories about particular or nearby landscapes, or invent new ones. The experimental phase of the project took place at Killerton Park near Exeter in Devon, with a group of children taking part in a 'Dragon Quest'. Twenty-eight children met with the organisers every other Saturday and came together for regular weekend camps. The results are being written up and will be published in a handbook for teachers, leaders and parents.

13461   Returning to learning: mature students in higher education.
GBR   1993
Research Date(s): 1990-1993
Betts, S.; Garland, P.
Inst: University College of North Wales, School of Sociology and Social Policy, College Road, Bangor, Gwynedd LL57 2DG, United Kingdom.
adult; higher education; sex difference; school career
adulte; enseignement supérieur; différence de sexe; cursus scolaire
PROJECT DESCRIPTION
   This research investigates the transitions of students returning to higher education. It considers the pathways and turning points as well as the experiences of mature students in higher education. Most importantly the research highlights gender differences in the pathways and experiences of mature students and seeks to explain these in the wider context of gender divisions in society.

13462   Sociaal milieu en loopbanen: de effecten van gezinsachtergrond op school-, beroeps- en levensloopbaan. (Social environment and career: the effect of family background on careers through school, work and life.)
NLD   1994
Research Date(s): 1992
Diederen, J.
Inst: Instituut voor Toegepaste Sociale wetenschappen (ITS) (Institute for Applied Social Sciences), P.O. Box 9048, 6500 KJ Nijmegen, Netherlands.

Katholieke Universiteit Nijmegen (Catholic University of Nijmegen), P.O. Box 9102, 6500 HC Nijmegen, Netherlands

Fin: SVO het Instituut voor Onderzoek van het Onderwijs.

social environment; family environment; parents; career; school career

milieu social; milieu familial; parents; carrière; cursus scolaire

PROJECT DESCRIPTION

Background: This study is a continuation of the analysis of the effects of social background on careers in school, work and life which was conducted as part of the fourth phase of the "From Year to Year" project. Additional work is required, because the analysis was not complete. The "From Year to Year" project follows the careers of men and women who left primary school in 1965.

Aim: A more complete analysis will be made of the effects of social background on the course of the subjects' careers in education, work and life.

Design: Besides direct effects, this study will also consider indirect effects of social background that are reflected in performance at primary school. The study will also consider, besides the effect of the father's occupational level in 1970: the effect of the father's type of occupation (employment sector), the mother's occupation, the grandparents' occupations, the educational level of the other family members and the parents' perceptions and attitudes.

13463 Spotkania a środowisko: rola teorii spotkania w nauczaniu przedmiotu środowisko społeczno-przyrodnicze. (Encounters and the environment: the role of encounter theory in the teaching of the subject "Social and Natural Environment".)

POL 1994

Research Date(s): 1985-1992

Chymuk, Maria.

Inst: Wyższa Szkoła Pedagogiczna w Krakowie (Higher School of Education, Cracow), 30 084 Kraków, Podchorażych 2, Poland.

environment; natural sciences; primary education; philosophy

environnement; sciences naturelles; enseignement primaire; philosophie

PROJECT DESCRIPTION

Pupils have a range of possibilities to have meaningful encounters (in philosophical terms), such as: man with man, man with other man's work (art, music, literature, tradition, etc.), man with nature. This study examined how pupils can be prepared for an encounter with nature through the primary school subject "Social and Natural Environment".

Methods: Participant observation, interview, survey, pupil questionnaire (for pupils in years 1, 2 and 3), teacher questionnaires (to teachers of the subject "Social and Natural Environment"), questionnaires to fourth-year students of Initial Education at the Pedagogical University.

Sample: 330 teachers, 370 university students, 2,542 primary school pupils.

Results: The research shows that although "encounter philosophy" is known only to a limited group of specialists in Poland, a good, devoted teacher can often, even unconsciously, lead his or her pupils to encounters with the highest values. Conditions which would allow teachers to perform this task were explored.

Publ: Chymuk, Maria. Przygotowanie nauczycieli do nauczania przedmiotu: "Srodowisko społeczno przyrodnicze" i jego realizacja. In: *Ruch Pedagogiczny*, 5/1987.

Chymuk, Maria. Przygotowanie studentów do nauczania przedmiotu środowisko społeczno-przyrodnicze. In: *Rocznik Nauk Ped*, T.XL Kraków: PAN, 1985.

Chymuk, Maria. Zeszyt do przedmiotu środowisko społeczno-przyrodnicze jako forma pracy z uczniem. In: *Życie Szkoły*, 11/1988.

Chymuk, Maria. Rola wycieczek w nauczaniu przedmiotu środowisko społeczno-przyrodnicze. In: *Życie Szkoły*, 9/1989.

Chymuk, Maria. *Srodowisko społeczno-przyrodnicze w kl.III. Przewodnik metodyczny.* Warszawa: WSiP, 1992.

13464 Strukturmerkmale von Jugendlichen und jungen Erwachsenen ohne Berufsausbildung - Bildungsverhalten, berufliche Erfahrungen und Orientierungen. (Structural characteristics of young people and adults without a vocational qualification: educational motivation, job experience and orientation.)

DEU 1993

Research Date(s): 1991-1994

Davids, S.; Jurisch, M.; Kloas, P.; Puhlmann, A.; Selle, B.; Spree, B.

Inst: Bundesinstitut fuer Berufsbildung, Fehrbelliner Platz 3, D-1000 Berlin 31.

youth; German DR; unemployment; unqualified young people

jeunesse; Allemagne RDA; chômage; jeune sans qualification

PROJECT DESCRIPTION

Inhalt: Die berufliche und soziale Situation von Jugendlichen und jungen Erwachsenen in den alten Bundeslaendern, die ohne Berufsausbildung geblieben sind, ist relativ gut bekannt. Dagegen weiss man sehr wenig ueber die Lage der "Unqualifizierten" aus den neuen Bundeslaendern. Unklar ist, wieviele Jugendliche in der ehemaligen DDR keine Berufsausbildung aufnehmen bzw. abschliessen konnten, welche Qualifikationen in den "Teilausbildungen" vermittelt wurden, worin sich vor allem Niedrigklassen- und Sonderschulabgaenger/ innen befanden. Fraglich ist, ob und wie diese jungen Erwachsenen unter gegenwaertigen Bedingungen (Uebernahme des Berufsbildungsgesetzes, Anerkennung der Bildungsabschluesse aus der DDR, steigende Zahl von Betriebsstillegungen und der Arbeitslosen) ihre beruflichen Qualifikationen verwerten koennen.

Ziel der Auftragsforschung ist deshalb, auf repraesentativer Basis in den neuen Bundeslaendern unter der Altersgruppe der 20- bis 24jaehrigen eine Erhebung durchzufuehren.

Es sollen muendliche Interviews gefuehrt werden. Es soll ein zweistufiges Verfahren angewandt werden. Als Vorerhebung sollen als repraesentativer Bevoelkerungsquerschnitt ca. 4000 Personen zu wenigen soziodemographischen Merkmalen (Schulabschluss, Ausbildung, gegenwaertige Situationen etc.) befragt werden. Daran schliesst sich die Haupterhebung bei folgenden Gruppen an: Untersuchungsgruppe sind 1600 Personen, die keine Berufsausbildung (der Anteil wird auf ca. 5 Prozent geschaetzt) oder eine Teilausbildung (ca. 7 Prozent eines Altersjahrganges) abgeschlossen haben. Kontrollgruppe sind 1600 Personen, die ueber eine abgeschlossene Berufsausbildung verfuegen oder sich derzeit in Ausbildung befinden.

13465 A study of the perceptions and responses of young women of South Asian origin to a single-sex access Youth Training Scheme.

GBR 1993

Research Date(s): 1989-1991

Robinson, J.

Sup: Skeggs, B.

Inst: York University, Department of Educational Studies, Heslington, York YO1 5DD, United Kingdom.

cultural environment; target groups of education; women's education; access to education; ethnic minority; training programme; vocational training

milieu culturel; destinataires de l'éducation; éducation des femmes; accès à l'éducation; minorité ethnique; programme de formation; formation professionnelle

PROJECT DESCRIPTION

This study is based on a college-based Youth Training Scheme set up in 1987 which was aimed specifically at bilingual young women who were seriously under-represented on existing language-supported courses within a college, situated in a large city of the North of England. The scheme included in the initial stages a number of special provisions to enable the trainees to participate, and has normally involved a gradual transition to 'mainstream' courses during the two-year scheme. The aim of the study is to investigate and analyse the trainees' perceptions of and responses to this kind of provision.

The data is being collected by observation of the present trainees and semi-structured interviews with both past (where possible) and present trainees.

The findings will be related to the published literature concerning race, gender, education and training. The results and conclusions are expected to relate to the issues surrounding the achievement of equality of opportunity in education and training for young women of South Asian origin.

13466 Subjektívne prežívanie života mládeže. (Young people's subjective perceptions of life.)

SVK 1994

Research Date(s): 1991-1992

Zubalová, M.; Bieliková, M.; Zvalová, M.

Sup: Dvorský, J.

Inst: Ústav informácií a prognóz školstva, mládeže a telovýchovy (Institute of Information and Prognoses of Education, Youth and Sport), Staré grunty 52, 842 44 Bratislava, Slovak Republic.

Ministerstvo školstva a vedy SR (Ministry of Education and Science of the Slovak Republic), Hlboká 2, 813 30 Bratislava, Slovak Republic

youth; aspiration; occupational satisfaction; social status; graduate; dissatisfaction

jeunesse; aspiration; satisfaction professionnelle; statut social; étudiant diplômé; insatisfaction

PROJECT DESCRIPTION

Aim: To investigate Slovak university graduates' perceptions of specific aspects of their personal and social lives; to examine graduates' ideas of "quality of life" and, on the basis of comparisons, to identify those spheres of life where quality is lacking and in where dissatisfaction and critical attitudes may manifest themselves; to make recommendations to decision-makers regarding youth policy.

Research questions: What is the level of satisfaction with life among employed and unemployed graduates? What factors influence young people's perceptions of life?

Methods: A questionnaire was used which elicited information on demographic characteristics, satisfaction with life and happiness in respect of specific aspects of life in the past, present and future. Data were analysed using differential and statistical techniques.

Publ: Zubalová, M. et al. *Subjektívne prežívanie kvality života mládeže.* (Subjective perceptions of the quality of youth's life.) Bratislava, ÚIP ŠMT, 1992, 109p.

Zubalová, M. & Bieliková, M. *Mládež - Informácia, listovka.* (Youth - Information, records/card catalogue.) UIP ŠMT, 1993, 6p.

Zubalová, M. Absolventi vysokých škôl v SR a ich subjektívna reflexia kvality života. (University graduates in the SR and their perceptions of the quality of life.) In: *Proceedings of the International Conference of the 30th anniversary of KIP MTF STU,* 1993, 6p.

13467   To noima tou graptou kodika stin proscholiki ilikia: simasio-logia i fonitiki.   (Making sense of writing at pre-school age: semantics or phonetics.)
GRC   1994
Research Date(s): 1992-
Papoulia-Tzelepi, P.
Inst: Panepistimio Patron, Tmima Dimotikis Ekpaidefsis (Patras University, Department of Education), 261 10 Patra, Greece.
pre-school age; literacy; reading; writing
âge préscolaire; alphabétisation; lecture; écriture
PROJECT DESCRIPTION
This research is conducted from the perspective of writing acquisition as a "psychogenesis" (Ferreiro, Tolskinsky, Pontecorvo, etc.) in the context of Greek orthography and Greek society. It attempts to reveal how Greek pre-school age children conceptualize the conventionality of written text: (a) as related to the semantics of the language; or (b) as related to the phonetics of the language. It is attempted to answer the following questions: Is there a sequential developmental pattern for (a) and (b)? Is (b) a regres-sion/deviation (Pontecorvo) or are (a) and (b) alternatives? Is (a) necessary but not sufficient for the (b) condition to emerge?

Subjects are 100 pre-schoolers who are tested individually before the formal teaching of reading and writing. Test materials are figurative, i.e. images of objects varying in size, number, gender and linguistic features. Children's responses are recorded in written form and analysed by a team consisting of the researcher and teachers.

13468   La trasversalità dell'educazione ambientale nei curricoli della scuola secondaria di primo grado: obiettivi, contenuti (conoscenze e valori), metodi.   (The transversality of environmental education in lower secondary school curricula: objectives, contents (knowledge and values), and methods.)
ITA   1994
Research Date(s): 1992-
Bonelli, Alba; Bachiorri, Antonella; Giubellini, Marino; Ferrari, Ireneo; Soliani, Lamberto; et al.
Sup: Moroni, Antonio.
Inst: Centro Italiano di Ricerca ed Educazione Ambientale - CIREA (Italian Centre for Research and Environmental Education), Via Cavestro 14/A, 43100 Parma, Italy.
Università degli Studi di Parma (University of Parma), Via Università 12, 43100 Parma, Italy
Fin: Ministero dell'Ambiente, Enti Pubblici e Privati.
environment; environmental study; lower secondary; educational innova-tion; curriculum research
environnement; étude du milieu; secondaire premier cycle; innovation pédagogique; recherche sur les programmes d'études
PROJECT DESCRIPTION
A recent study promoted by the Centre for Studies and Planning of the Ministry of Public Education and carried out under the auspices of the CIREA has shown that there is a great deal of activity in the area of environmental education in schools at all levels. Although these activities are generally referred to as "environmental education", most of them are really to do with nature observation or, at most, ecological education; only in some cases do they assume the characteristics of a more broadly interpreted environmental education.

The present project aims to develop an innovative environmental educa-tional model. In this regard, the objective of "transversality in environmen-tal education" calls for the realization of three significant aspects: the meaning of environmental education, transversality, and interdisciplinarity.

The research project will be limited to the three-year period of lower secondary school, as this period occupies a pivotal position between basic education and the two-year period in upper secondary school. The investi-gation may be extended to other school levels at a later date. The study focuses on schools in five areas of the city and Province of Parma: a town in the mountains, a town in the hills, a town in the countryside, a neighbourhood on the periphery of the city, and one in the city centre. For each area, an experimental class and a control class will be selected, coordinated by a designated teacher.

The study will last four years: three for the research and one for the compilation of a theoretical manual and an exercise workbook.

13469   Umweltschutz im Ruhrgebiet: Materialien zur Umwelterziehung in der Schule und an ausserschulischen Lernorten. (Environmental protection in the Ruhr area: materials for environ-mental education in schools and out-of-school educational settings.)
DEU   1993
Research Date(s): 1990-1993
Stichmann, W.; Kersberg, H.

Inst: Universitaet Dortmund, FB Erziehungswissenschaften und Biologie, Fach Biologie, Emil-Figge-Strasse 50, D-4600 Dortmund 50.
Fin: Kommunalverband Ruhrgebiet.
environment; teaching objective; teaching programme; nature conserva-tion; out-of-school education
environnement; objectif pédagogique; programme d'enseignement; conser-vation de la nature; éducation extra-scolaire
PROJECT DESCRIPTION
Inhalt: Inhaltliche Ziele/Praxisbezug: Darstellung oekologischer Frages-tellungen der Region und deren Behandlung im Unterricht. Materialien zu den Themen: Naturschutzgebiete brauchen Pflege; mit Baeumen leben; Gewaesser in Bergsenkungsgebieten.

Geographischer Raum: Ruhrgebiet, NRW.

Vorgehensweise: Entwicklung von Unterrichtsmaterialien fuer einen Unterricht "vor Ort": grundlegende allgemeine Sachverhalte an konkreten Einzelbeispielen vermittelt.
Publ: Wildkraeuter. Hrsg. von Wilfried Stichmann. In: *Unterricht Biologie,* Jg. 15, H. 165, 1991.
Kersberg, Herbert & Stichmann, Wilfried. *Umweltschutz im Ruhrgebiet. Materialien zur Umwelterziehung in der Schule und an ausserschulischen Lernorten.* Essen 1991. Standort: UuStB Koeln (38)-920109134.

13470   The use of concepts as a planning framework for environ-mental studies.
GBR   1993
Research Date(s): 1991
Graham, I.
Inst: Jordanhill College of Education, Division of Primary Education, South-brae Drive, Glasgow G13 1PP, United Kingdom.
environmental study; concept; primary education
étude du milieu; concept; enseignement primaire
PROJECT DESCRIPTION
This project will show how a concept framework can be used in the selection of knowledge, skills and attitudes to be developed in an environ-mental study in the primary classroom.

13471   Young families now: a focus for learning in the community.
GBR   1993
Research Date(s): 1986-1991
Flett, M.; Watt, J.; Nisbet, J.
Inst: Aberdeen University, Department of Education, Taylor Building, King's College, Aberdeen AB9 2UB, United Kingdom.
Fin: Bernard Van Leer Foundation.
local community; community education; family education; mother; women's education; early childhood education; child care; educational provision
collectivité locale; éducation sociale; éducation par la famille; mère; éduca-tion des femmes; éducation de la prime enfance; aide à l'enfance; scolarisation
PROJECT DESCRIPTION
'Young Families Now' is an action research project based in an area of rapid social change within the city of Aberdeen. The focus of the work is the development of educational opportunities for young children and their parents, particularly their mothers. The project aims to respond to educa-tional needs as these are defined by the community. It supports existing groups in the field of early childhood care and education and helps local people identify new needs and establish new forms of provision for children and their mothers. The project also aims to bring together parents and professionals to look at new ways of working and to open up discussion on how local childcare services in health, social work and education can better meet the needs of young families. As an action research project it also tries to bring together the community's expertise in developing an action pro-gramme with the University's expertise in research.

13472   Zwischen zwei Welten: kulturelle Verhaltensweisen jugend-licher Migranten in Wien unter besonderer Beruecksichtigung der Musik.   (Between two worlds: the cultural behaviour of young migrants in Vienna with particular reference to music.)
AUT   1993
Research Date(s): 1992-1993
Smudits, Alfred; Bailer, Noraldine; Emir, Mehmet; Horak, Roman; Huber, Harald; Ratkovic, Vlasta.
Inst: Institut fuer Musiksoziologie, Schubertring 14, A-1010 Wien.
Hochschule fuer Musik und darstellende Kunst, Lothringerstrasse 18, A-1030 Wien
Fin: Bundesministerium fuer Unterricht und Kunst.
adolescent; music education; intercultural education; immigrant; child of foreign national; cultural environment; host country; ethnic origin
adolescent; éducation musicale; éducation interculturelle; immigrant; enfant d'étranger; milieu culturel; pays d'accueil; origine ethnique
PROJECT DESCRIPTION
Jugendliche Migranten stehen im Spannungsfeld von zwei Welten: der Welt der 'Stammkultur', die 'Heimat' bedeutet, und der Welt der anglo-amerikanisch gepraegten Kultur des Gastlandes. Am Beispiel der Musik soll die Akkulturationsproblematik jugendlicher Migranten untersucht werden,

wobei allerdings auch einige andere - religioese, familiaere, erziehungsbezogene, geschlechtsspezifische - Faktoren mitzuberuecksichtigen sind. Ziel ist es u.a., Anregungen fuer schulische und ausserschulische musikpaedagogische Initiativen zu erarbeiten.

Es werden standardisierte Interviews mit ca. 100 Jugendzentrums-BesucherInnen, Gruppendiskussionen, Einzelinterviews (Tiefeninterviews) und eine Musikanalyse von ca. fuenf Pop-Hits und fuenf Volksliedern durchgefuehrt.

Es handelt sich um eine explorative Untersuchung.

Urspruengliche Absicht war es, einen intensiven Kontakt mit einer Gruppe von fuenf bis zehn Jugendlichen herzustellen. Dies erschien in der kurzen Zeit als wenig zielfuehrend. Daher schien eine Orientierung auf eine Fragebogenaktion sinnvoll.

Publ: Bailer, Noraldine; Horak, Roman & Smudits, Alfred. 'Gastarbeiter'-Kinder zwischen Volksmusik und Popmusik. In: *SWS-Rundschau*, 32. Jahrgang, Heft 3/1992, S. 375-384.

13473 Zwischenmenschliches Verhalten im TV-Kinderprogramm: ein interkultureller Vergleich Wien - Beograd. (Interpersonal behaviour on children's TV programmes: an intercultural comparison Vienna - Belgrade.)
AUT 1993
Research Date(s): 1987-1990
Otalora, Zora (Am Heumarkt 9/16, 1030 Wien, Österreich); Plavsic, Prvoslav; Mijatovic, Branislav.
Inst: Centar za istrazivanje programa i auditorijuma TV Beograd, Kneza Milosa 7, 11000 Beograd, Jugoslawien.
Fin: Institut fuer Publikumsforschung der Oesterreichischen Akademie der Wissenschaften; Zentrum zur Erforschung des Programms und Auditoriums von Radio-Television Beograd; Zora Otalora.
cultural pattern; cross-cultural research; television programme; cross-national research
modèle culturel; recherche transculturelle; programme de télévision; recherche transnationale
PROJECT DESCRIPTION
Ausgehend von einer Kritik der bisherigen Erforschung des kindlichen Fernsehverhaltens und der Inhaltsanalyse von Kinder- und Jugendprogrammen, welche eine Vergleichsmoeglichkeit unterschiedlich strukturierter Programme auf universaler Grundlage ausschliesst, orientierten sich die Verfasser bei der Erarbeitung eines neuen Forschungsmodells an den Ergebnissen der Entwicklungspsychologie und der Ethnopsychoanalyse. Eine wichtige Stuetze in diesem Projekt eines interkulturellen Vergleichs wurde in morphologischen Studien ueber Mythen und Maerchen gefunden und dabei besondere Aufmerksamkeit Interaktionen gewidmet, in welche bestimmte Akteure beim Vollzug bestimmter Aktivitaeten eintreten. So wurde mit Hilfe einer qualitativen Methode und mittels eines entsprechenden mathematischen Apparats ein Modell der Signierung 'kulturimmanenter' TV-Sendungen sowie des Vergleichs relativ stabiler 'Verhaltensmodelle' entwickelt, hinter denen definierte psychische, das heisst kognitive und emotionale Konstituenten einer Kultur stehen (in diesem Fall in Wien und Beograd). Bereits die Resultate der ersten Realisationsphase des Projekts bestaetigen die Relevanz einer solchen Vorgangsweise und gleichzeitig auch die Moeglichkeit einer breiten Anwendung dieses Interaktionsmodells sowohl bei der Analyse anderer TV- Sendungen als auch von Handlungen in Film und Theater.

Es wurde eine Interaktionsanalyse der Aktivitaeten von Akteuren in Filmen des Kinder- und Jugendprogramms des Oesterreichischen Rundfunks und des RTV Beograd und die Signierung dieser Interaktionen mittels eines nach entwicklungspsychologischen und ethnopsychoanalytischen Parametern eigens entwickelten Rasters durchgefuehrt. Daraus resultierend wurde sowohl eine qualitative Evaluierung als auch eine mathematisch-statistische Auswertung und Verifizierung des Materials und der Ergebnisse erstellt.

Es wurden deutliche nationale Unterschiede in der Verteilung der Interaktionen im jeweiligen TV-Kinder- und Jugendprogramm festgestellt. Das Modell beruecksichtigt insofern die Kulturimmanenz national ausgestrahlter Programme auch internationaler Provenienz, da die TV-interne Programmauswahl jeweils nach kulturspezifischen Kriterien erfolgt. Das neuentwickelte Modell, das sowohl zur Feststellung der Altersadaequatheit von Programmen als auch fuer Kulturvergleiche anwendbar ist, kann ausserdem auch fuer die altersadaequate Programmgestaltung im Fernsehen operationalisiert werden. Damit ist eine universale Anwendungsmoeglichkeit der Methode gegeben.

Publ: Otalora, Zora; Plavsic, Prvoslav & Mijatovic, Branislav. *Zwischenmenschliches Verhalten im TV-Kinderprogramm. Ein interkultureller Vergleich Wien - Beograd (in serbokroatischer Sprache)*. Berichte und Studien, Zentrum zur Erforschung des Programms und Auditoriums, Radio-Television Beograd. Beograd 1990. 185 Seiten. Mejduljudsko ponasanje u tv-programu za decu. Interkultralno poredjanje Bec-Beograd.

30 DEMOGRAPHIC ENVIRONMENT – ENVIRONNEMENT DEMOGRAPHIQUE – DEMOGRAPHISCHE UMWELT

13474 The experience of working class men in further and higher education.
GBR 1993
Research Date(s): 1991-1996
Neville, C.
Sup: Glandon, N.
Inst: Bradford University, Department of Social & Economic Studies, Richmond Road, Bradford BD7 1DP, United Kingdom.

man; working class; recurrent education; adult education; attitude change; self-concept

homme; classe ouvrière; éducation récurrente; éducation des adultes; changement d'attitude; conception de soi

PROJECT DESCRIPTION

The research aims to explore the backgrounds and motivations of working-class men who choose to return to non-vocational education via Access Courses. It will explore their experiences on the Access Courses, particularly how they deal with topics that may challenge or threaten their self-images, e.g. gender/race. It will chart their progress from Access Course into higher education and explore changes in values/attitudes that may result. The research will attempt to summarise the range of traits and motivations for study displayed by the same group.

The methods include a survey of all Access students in West Yorkshire via questionnaires to highlight gender differences; discussion with Access Course tutors; and individual/group discussion with male Access students. The results may have implications for (a) marketing Access Courses and (b) teaching mixed groups of adults.

13475 Feminisation of teaching: a comparative study of Israel and Chile.

GBR 1993

Research Date(s): 1991-

Lapidot, R.

Sup: Loudon, M.

Inst: University of Wales College of Cardiff, School of Education, Senghennydd Road, Cardiff CF2 4AG, United Kingdom.

woman; teaching profession; comparative education; Israel; Chile

femme; profession d'enseignant; éducation comparée; Israël; Chili

PROJECT DESCRIPTION

The mechanisms of feminisation will be examined and the effects on schools' socialising systems will be explored.

13476 Gender roles in adolescent girls.

GBR 1993

Research Date(s): 1984-1993

McDonald, M.

Inst: University of Central Lancashire, Department of Psychology, Preston PR1 2TQ, United Kingdom; Wolverhampton Polytechnic, Department of Psychology, Molineux Street, Wolverhampton WV1 1SB, United Kingdom.

Fin: Lancashire Polytechnic.

sex; sex role; sex difference; girl; adolescent; stereotype

sexe; rôle sexuel; différence de sexe; jeune fille; adolescent; stéréotype

PROJECT DESCRIPTION

A sample of 43 girls aged 10-15 years from the northwest of the United Kingdom were interviewed about their own, and other girls' preferences and choices regarding sports, school subjects, occupations and leisure interests. Their gender-role attitudes were also examined by means of two other methods: (1) responses to vignettes involving gender-role dilemmas; (2) repertory grids involving supplied and elicited elements. Grids were represented a year later to provide a limited longitudinal design. The interview data has been analysed separately in relation to the four topics.

Quantitative analysis showed that the answers for both sports and school subjects departed from established stereotypes. There was little support for the hypothesis that gender-role activities become accentuated at adolescence. Qualitative analysis revealed a number of gender-related themes in these answers.

The remaining data from the project is being analysed. Supplementary studies have been provided by rating-scale investigations of the gender-stereotyping of school subjects (Archer & Freedman, 1989; Archer & Macrae, 1991), and the research has been integrated into more general theoretical work on gender-role development (Archer, 1984, 1989).

Publ: Archer, J. & Freedman, S. Gender-stereotypic perceptions of academic disciplines. In: British Journal of Educational Psychology, No 59/1989, pp. 306-313.

Archer, J. & Macdonald, M. Gender roles and school subjects in adolescent girls. In: Educational Research, Vol 33, No 1/1991.

Archer, J. Childhood gender roles: structure and development. In: The Psychologist, No 9/1989, pp. 367-370.

Archer, J. & Macdonald, M. Gender roles and sports in adolescent girls. In: Leisure Studies, No 9/1990, pp. 225-240.

13477 Mature students in higher education.

GBR 1993

Research Date(s): 1989-1992

Adams, S.

Sup: Harris, C.

Inst: University College of Swansea, Department of Sociology and Anthropology, Singleton Park, Swansea SA2 8PP, United Kingdom.

woman; adult education; higher education; women's education; sex difference; sex role

femme; éducation des adultes; enseignement supérieur; éducation des femmes; différence de sexe; rôle sexuel

PROJECT DESCRIPTION

The research aims to look into the possible source of insight mature students (especially women) may offer into changing gender relations in the family and in society. There is also the question of why the number of mature women students is rising. This can be partly explained by the fact that, due to demographic changes, more mature women are needed in the labour market and access to university is now being made easier for them. It can also be partly explained by women now having more control over their fertility and by changes in women's employment patterns and economic participation rates. The rising numbers may also be partly explained by a change in women's self-perceptions due partially to two decades of activity by the Women's Movement.

The researcher is interested in how mature women, particularly those who have experienced a change in self-perception, get on in university. Does higher education deal equitably with the needs of mature male and female students? The research will look at changes in life courses and whether men's life courses affect women's to a far greater extent than vice-versa. It will also investigate how women experience directly the pressures imposed on them to be good wives, mothers, daughters, etc.; how they negotiate their own social and sociological reality in this situation; how they negotiate this reality as mature students; and what changes and of what type may occur. Related to this is an analysis of the way in which women are inscribed in unequal, passive and subordinate relations by the State, the law and all the other spheres which have the ability to shape their lives.

13478 Soziale Entwicklung und Lebenssituation der Muenchner Buerger. (Social development and life situation of Munich citizens.)

DEU 1993

Research Date(s): 1991-1992

Bremer, H.

Sup: Romaus, R.

Inst: Gruppe fuer sozialwissenschaftliche Forschung, Oberanger 34, D-8000 Muenchen 2.

Fin: Stadt Muenchen, Referat fuer Stadtplanung und Bauordnung.

urban population; Bavaria; Germany - Federal Republic; population; population trends; housing; unemployment; poverty

population urbaine; Bavière; Allemagne RFA; population; tendances démographiques; logement; chômage; pauvreté

PROJECT DESCRIPTION

Inhalt: Sekundaerstatistische Analyse: Entwicklung in den '80er Jahren: Bevoelkerung, insbesondere Haushalte; Wohnverhaeltnisse, Wohnversorgung; soziale Probleme: Armut, Obdachlosigkeit, Arbeitslosigkeit. Primaererhebung: Haushaltsbefragung im Hinblick auf soziodemografische Struktur, soziooekonomische Lage, Bildungsniveau und Bildungsbeteiligung, berufliche Situation, Wohnen, Morbiditaet, Pflegebeduerftigkeit, Kommunikation, soziale Netze, Lebensorientierung, Lebensstile.

Geographischer Raum: Stadt Muenchen.

Untersuchter Zeitraum: 1980-1990 (Querschnitt 1991).

Vorgehensweise: Untersuchungsdesign: Fallstudie; Trend.

Datengewinnung: Standardisiertes Interview (Stichprobe: 2000; Huashalte in Muenchen; Auswahlverfahren: Zufall). Primaererhebung: Feldarbeit als Auftrag an kommerzielle Umfrageinstitute vergeben; Sekundaeranalyse bereits vorhandener maschinenlesbarer Datensaetze; Datenerstellung auf der Basis von bereits vorliegenden Materialien wie Texten, Akten, Statistiken.

Auswertung: Faktorenanalyse; Diskriminanz-; Varianzanalysen; MDS. Datenaufbereitung: Datenedition (z.B. Aufbau von Datenbanken); Zeitreihe(n).

**Migration und Erziehung in multikulturellen Gesellschaften: europäische Modelle im Wandel (Migration et éducation dans les sociétés multiculturelles: les modèles européens en changement) ....
.... see no. 11981**

**A study of the relationship between intentions and outcomes of policy initiatives related to women's education and training ....
.... see no. 12016**

Exploring the gender gap in primary schools .... see no. 12112

Secundaire analyses over de schoolloopbanen in het voortgezet onderwijs met het VOCL '89 cohort (Secondary analyses on the school careers of secondary school pupils on the basis of data on the "VOCL '89" cohort) .... see no. 12447

Politische Bildung fuer aeltere Menschen in den neuen Bundeslaendern (Political education for senior citizens in the new German states) .... see no. 12598

Women and scientific literacy .... see no. 12636

The elementary education of females in England 1800-1870, with particular reference to the lives and work of girls and women in industrial Lancashire and rural Norfolk and Suffolk ..... see no. 12756

**The State and women's schooling in France, 1815-1914 ....
.... see no. 12787**

An investigation into the present situation and problems of English language learning of adult Chinese immigrants in Nottingham and London .... see no. 12878

The language learning experiences of Somalis and Eritreans in Britain and Italy .... see no. 12881

Amtliche Bildungsstatistik und empirische Sozialforschung (Official education statistics and empirical social research) ...... see no. 13040

Een verrijkingsprogramma voor begaafde allochtone en begaafde kansarme basisschoolleerlingen (An enrichment programme for gifted immigrant and deprived primary school pupils) ....
.... see no. 13220

Üniversite öğrencilerinin cinsiyet rolleri ile ilgili kalıp yargılarının bazı değişkenler açısından incelenmesi (University students' sex role stereotypes) .... see no. 13240

Arbeitertoechter und ihr sozialer Aufstieg: zum Verhaeltnis von Klasse, Geschlecht und Technikkompetenz (Working-class daughters and their social uprise: on the relationship between class, sex and technical competence) .... see no. 13429

Emploi et modes de vie: passages à la vie professionnelle, passage à la vie adulte en Région Provence-Alpes-Côte d'Azur ... see no. 13569

Formation et mobilité: la gestion de la main-d'oeuvre féminine ....
.... see no. 13580

The higher education route to the labour market for women returners .... see no. 13586

Lehrlinge und Facharbeiter am Arbeitsmarkt: Prognose bis zum Jahr 2005/2007 (Apprentices and skilled workers on the labour market: a forecast up to the years 2005/2007) .... see no. 13600

Motherhood and teaching: a life history investigation ....
.... see no. 13680

Kinder- und Familienforschung im Rahmen kommunaler Jugendhilfeplanung fuer die Stadt Osnabrueck (Youth and family research within the framework of municipal youth welfare planning in Osnabrueck) .... see no. 13736

Social and psychological adjustment of educated married women in Mauritius .... see no. 13766

31 FAMILY ENVIRONMENT – MILIEU FAMILIAL – FAMILIENMILIEU

13479 L'adolescence en crise à travers quelques auto-portraits de jeunes romanciers.
FRA 1993
Research Date(s): 1987-1989
Grimanelli, Anne; Fize, Michel.
Inst: Ministère de la Justice, CNRS URA/412, Centre de recherche interdisciplinaire de Vaucresson, 54 rue de Garches, 92420 Vaucresson, France.
novel; family environment; parent-child relation; adolescence; written expression; youth attitude
roman; milieu familial; relation parents-enfant; adolescence; expression écrite; attitude de la jeunesse
PROJECT DESCRIPTION
Objectifs: Dans le cadre plus général d'une recherche sur les représentations romanesques des relations intra-familiales entre parents et adolescents, l'étude, privilégiant le point de vue des jeunes, porte sur des journaux intimes publiés. La problématique centrale était: l'adolescence est-elle nécessairement une période de crise, avec des conflits intrapsychiques et interrelationnels importants, ou bien au contraire cette période de croissance peut-elle être harmonieuse?
Méthodologie: Recherche et analyse des documents pertinents, par dépouillement systématique du "Livre-Hebdo" de 1980 à 1986. Analyse thématique de contenu de romans autobiographiques, de journaux intimes publiés.
Résultats: Le matériel utilisé n'a pas permis de répondre à la question posée au départ: il s'est avéré, en effet, que les familles décrites dans les romans représentaient presque toujours des familles parisiennes, à hauts revenus. L'analyse était donc limitée à une population particulière. De plus, les autobiographies décrivaient toujours des situations de malaise, de tension extrême, ce qui tendait à confirmer l'hypothèse de l'existence d'une crise d'adolescence. Mais il est impossible de savoir si ce n'est pas parce que ces représentations confortent un stéréotype très bien établi socialement qu'elles ont été retenues par les éditeurs: en effet, les résultats obtenus par questionnaire sont différents.
Publ: Grimanelli, Anne. L'adolescence en crise à travers quelques auto-portraits de jeunes romanciers. In: Annales de Vaucresson, 1988, n° 28, pp. 89-108.
Grimanelli, Anne. Adolescence et conformisme: la fugue à travers un auto-portrait d'adolescente. In: Droit de l'enfance et de la famille, 1989, n° 27, pp. 126-138.

Grimanelli, Anne. L'adolescent écrivain. In: Bulletin du CIEP, 1989, n° 3, pp. 41-47.

13480 De invloed van sociale hulpbronnen op schoolprestaties. (The influence of social resources on achievement.)
NLD 1994
Research Date(s): 1993
Dijkstra, A.B.
Inst: Vakgroep Sociologie (Department of Sociology), Grote Rozenstraat 31, 9712 TG Groningen, Netherlands.
Rijksuniversiteit Groningen (State University of Groningen), P.O. Box 72, 9700 AB Groningen, Netherlands
Fin: SVO het Instituut voor Onderzoek van het Onderwijs.
family environment; socio-economic status; social environment; achievement; school career
milieu familial; statut socio-économique; milieu social; rendement; cursus scolaire
PROJECT DESCRIPTION
Background: This project fits in with the Dutch tradition of longitudinal school careers research which is concerned with finding specifications for the influence of social background on school careers. Although the status position of the family appears to be a strong indicator of school success, status as such offers no insight into the factors that are responsible for the ways in which school career and family characteristics are interconnected.
Aims: (1) To examine: (a) to what extent Coleman's assumptions concerning mechanisms related to social resources can be operationalized; and (b) to what extent Coleman's proposed explanation is empirically tenable; (2) to assess the contribution that can be attributed to these mechanisms in Dutch school careers research.
Methods: Secondary analysis.
Design: The research population consists of a cohort of 4,000 primary school pupils (aged 10 to 12 years) whose skills in language and mathematics were tested in an earlier study. In 1990 a questionnaire survey was conducted among the parents of these pupils, asking for information about the family and about the child's school career in the first years at secondary school. The data thus collected between 1987 and 1991 constitute a sizeable longitudinal data set which contains information about pupils' school careers in the final years of primary school and the first years of secondary school. The design of the study enables analyses to be made of the effects of social capital (in the first instance operationalized at the family level), measured by the level of achievement attained later in the school career.

13481 Education and the family in Taiwan and China.
GBR 1993
Research Date(s): 1991-
Stafford, C.
Inst: Brunel University, Department of Human Sciences, Uxbridge UB8 3PH, United Kingdom.
Fin: Wenner-gren Foundation; Taiwan History Field Research Project; University of London Central Research Fund.
family life; religious behaviour; value system; ideology; China; Taiwan
vie familiale; comportement religieux; système de valeurs; idéologie; Chine; Taiwan
PROJECT DESCRIPTION
Anthropological fieldwork was carried out in Taiwan to investigate the relationship between families and the state. Particular attention was paid to education and to family religion as competing discourses within a small fishing village.
The schools promote identification with the nation, and encourage sacrifice to the point of martyrdom for national goals. Families, through religious practices involving spirit mediums, seek to protect children from all harm for the sake of the family goals.
The researcher is in the process of writing articles based on this fieldwork, and in the next year will expand the project to include material from mainland China.

13482 The educational progress of children in care.
GBR 1993
Research Date(s): 1987-1991
Aldgate, P.; Heath, A.
Inst: Oxford University, Department of Applied Social Studies and Social Research, Barnett House, Wellington Square, Oxford OX1 2ER, United Kingdom.
Fin: Economic and Social Research Council.
child placement; adopted child; achievement; underachievement
placement d'enfant; enfant adopté; rendement; rendement déficient
PROJECT DESCRIPTION
This research has identified factors contributing to the educational success or difficulties of middle school-aged children in long-term foster care. To this end the researchers studied the school-aged children in foster care in one local authority, together with their parents and carers over a period of three years. The educational attainment of these children in reading ability, mathematics and vocabulary was compared with a contrast group of children of the same age and from similar backgrounds who were living

with their own families, known to Social Services Departments, and who were receiving social work help (usually under Section 1 of the 1980 Child Care Act). A combination of longitudinal and cross-sectional research design was used. Children's educational progress was charted over three years.

Both groups of children were low achievers by national standards. Factors influencing the foster children's attainment included their early histories, and the stability of the current foster home. Contact with families of origin had no effect on children's achievement or behaviour. There was an interaction between children's behaviour and their educational attainment. Social workers place educational attainment low on their agenda of activities in relation to children in foster care.

Publ: Heath, A.F.; Colton, M. & Aldgate, J. The education of children in and out of care. In: *British Journal of Social Work*, No 19/1989, pp. 447-460.

Aldgate, J. Foster children at school: success or failure? In: *Adoption and Fostering*, Vol 14, No 4/1990, pp. 38-49.

Colton, M.; Aldgate, J. & Heath, A.F. Behavioural problems among children in and out of care. In: *Social Sciences Review*, Vol 2, No 3/1991, pp. 177-191.

13483 Een permanent systeem inzake registratie van migrantenkinderen in het Nederlandstalig onderwijs. (A permanent system for the registration of immigrant pupils in the Dutch-speaking part of Belgium.)
BEL 1994
Research Date(s): 1989
Van Meensel, R.; Dumon, W.
Inst: Departement Sociologie (Department of Sociology), Van Evenstraat 2B, 3000 Leuven, Belgium.
Katholieke Universiteit Leuven (Catholic University of Leuven), Naamsestraat 22, 3000 Leuven, Belgium
Fin: Departement Onderwijs, Fonds voor Kollektief en Fundamenteel Onderzoek op Ministerieel Initiatief.
migrant worker's child; data collection; statistical data; registration
enfant de migrant; rassemblement des données; données statistiques; inscription
PROJECT DESCRIPTION
Aim: The study was conducted in response to a request from the government for an elaborate statistical method to map the situation of immigrant children in the Flemish education system. A registration instrument, it was felt, could serve as an evaluation instrument for educational policy. The aim of this project was therefore to develop such a registration instrument.

Method: Existing sources of data were listed. These sources were evaluated in terms of accuracy, usefulness, accessibility and periodicity. Existing data bases were described. On the basis of official registration methods used in the French-speaking part of Belgium (Wallonia) and in the neighbouring countries, registration forms were elaborated and their possibilities explored.

Results: The registration instrument has been evaluated in primary schools and during the "social priority area" project in the region of Mechelen.

Publ: Van Meensel, R. & Dumon, W. *Een permanent systeem inzake registratie van migranten-kinderen in het Nederlandstalig onderwijs.* Leuven: KUL, Departement Sociologie, 1991, 146p. + appendix.

13484 Familiäre Erziehung, Fremdbetreuung und generatives Verhalten. (Education familiale, prise en charge extra-familiale et comportements procréatifs.)
CHE 1994
Research Date(s): 1991-1993
Herzog, Walter; Schröder, Inge; Guldimann, Joana; Böni, Edi.
Inst: Universität Bern, Pädagogisches Seminar, Abteilung Pädagogische Psychologie, Muesmattstrasse 27, 3012 Bern, Schweiz; Universität Zürich, Pädagogisches Institut, Aussenstation Kronenstrasse 48, 8006 Zürich, Schweiz.
Fin: Schweizerischer Nationalfonds zur Förderung der wissenschaftlichen Forschung.
family planning; day care; social change; working mother
planification de la famille; mode de garde; changement social; mère exerçant un emploi
PROJECT DESCRIPTION
Die gesellschaftlichen Veränderungen der letzten Jahre haben bedeutende Auswirkungen auf die Familien und die familiäre Erziehung. Im Vordergrund steht eine zunehmende Beteiligung der Frauen an Bildung und Erwerbstätigkeit. Dem damit einhergehenden Abbau geschlechtsspezifischer Rollenzuteilung steht eine auf traditionelle geschlechtliche Arbeitsteilung ausgerichtete Schule gegenüber. Erschwerend kommt hinzu, dass sich der Lebensraum für Kinder zusehends verengt. Vier Kinder von fünf wachsen in der Schweiz heute allein oder mit höchstens einem Geschwister auf. Alle diese Dinge erschweren die familiäre Erziehungsarbeit.

Dei geringe Dichte an Institutionen, welche die Eltern in der familiären Erziehung unterstützen, bewirkt zusätzlichen Druck auf Eltern, die sich nicht an herkömmliche Formen der Geschlechtsrollenzuweisung halten wollen. Es sieht so aus, als wäre vor allem die Geburt eines zweiten Kindes dazu angetan, die Familie auf alte Rolle zurückgreifen zu lassen. Umgekehrt kann man sich denken, dass auf ein zweites Kind verzichtet wird, weil man sich vorstellen kann, dass ein solches Ereignis um den Preis etwa einer Erwerbsaufgabe der Mutter erkauft werden müsste. Eine Bestätigung dieser Hypothese wäre auch geeignet, die Diskrepanz zwischen der hohen Zahl an Einkindfamilien und der weiten Verbreitung des Ideals der Familie mit zwei Kindern zu erklären.

Das hier vorgestellte Projekt wird der Frage nachgehen, wie weit der soziale Wandel in Familie und Gesellschaft mit vermehrten Ansprüchen an Institutionen der Fremdbetreuung verbunden ist und ob das Vorhandensein bzw. die tatsächliche Nutzung von Fremdbetreuung sich auf die Familien (etwa auf die Entscheidung, ein weiteres Kind zu haben) auswirkt. In der ersten Projektphase werden die Eltern interviewt, die 1990 in der Stadt Zürich für ihr Kind einen Tagesschulplatz beantragten, wobei insbesondere die Eltern, deren Kind einen Platz bekam, verglichen werden mit jenen, deren Kind abgewiesen wurde. Die Ergebnisse der ersten Phase werden helfen, den Fragebogen für die zweite Phase zu gestalten. Dieser wird sich an eine repräsentative Stichprobe von Stadtzürcher Eltern richten, deren ältestes Kind seit einem Jahr eingeschult ist; die Fragen werden sich um die familiäre und erzieherische Situation, den Bedarf an Fremdbetreuung und das generative Verhalten drehen.

13485 Paragontes pou epireazoun tin epidosi ton mathiton. (Factors influencing pupils' performance at school.)
CYP 1993
Research Date(s): 1992
Hatgigeorgiou, Androula.
Sup: Papanastasiou, Constantinos.
Inst: Pedagogiko Instituto (Pedagogical Institute), P.O. Box 512, Nicosia, Cyprus.
family environment; parent role; pupil; performance
milieu familial; rôle des parents; élève; performance
PROJECT DESCRIPTION
Background and aims: Educators and parents often claim that a relationship exists between pupils' performance at school on the one hand and their family situation and individual characteristics on the other. The aim of this study was to investigate whether the factors "family" and "pupil" have any influence on pupils' performance at school. More specifically, it examined whether the parents' financial and educational situation and their expectations of their children affect pupils' performance at school. It also examined pupils' achievement levels in modern Greek and mathematics as well as the influence of gender, maturity and study time on performance in these two subjects.

Methods: A questionnaire was distributed to the pupils in the sample. Specific tests were constructed to establish pupils' competence in modern Greek and mathematics, taking the syllabus of the fifth and sixth class of primary school as a basis. The sample comprised 140 pupils in the sixth and fifth years of a primary school in Nicosia.

Results: Parental occupation and the parents' interest for their children are the most important factors influencing pupils' performance in both modern Greek and mathematics: 42.50% of the pupils' performance is influenced by the parents' occupation and interest. As regards the parents' financial situation, it was found that 66.4% of the parents are in a "good" financial situation; 11.4% are "rich". However, the parents' financial situation was not found to be an important factor influencing performance. It was also found that the pupils' maturity, gender and study time are not related to their performance levels. In both mathematics and modern Greek, boys and girls showed similar capacities and their performance was found to be satisfactory. It is worth mentioning that a combination of several other factors influence 57.0% of pupils' school performance.

13486 Parents and teenagers: understanding and improving communication about Human Immunodeficiency Virus/Acquired Immune Deficiency Syndrome (HIV/AIDS).
GBR 1993
Research Date(s): 1991-1992
Stronach, I.; Frankham, J.
Inst: University of East Anglia, School of Education, Norwich NR4 7TJ, United Kingdom.
Fin: AIDS Education and Research Trust (AVERT).
parents; parent-child relation; sexually transmitted disease; interpersonal relations; communication; sexual behaviour
parents; relation parents-enfant; maladie sexuellement transmissible; relations interpersonnelles; communication; comportement sexuel
PROJECT DESCRIPTION
The project will investigate whether and how parents and teenagers discuss matters relating to Human Immunodeficiency Virus/Acquired Immune Deficiency Syndrome (HIV/AIDS) and sexual behaviour. It aims to improve communication within families through the generation of research-based educational materials and advice. The study will involve an initial

survey of parental attitudes (sample size = 50) and reported behaviour, followed by detailed and voluntary case studies (sample size = 10) of parent/teenager relations in the area. These data will form the basis for the development of educational materials.

32 ECONOMIC ENVIRONMENT – ENVIRONNEMENT ECONOMIQUE – WIRTSCHAFTSMILIEU

13487 The curricular impact of the Teachers into Industry Project.
GBR 1993
Research Date(s): 1991-1992
Wallis, J.
Inst: Nottingham University, Department of Adult Education, 14-22 Shakespeare Street, Nottingham NG1 4FJ, United Kingdom.
industry; economic factor; educational policy; teacher
industrie; facteur économique; politique de l'éducation; enseignant
PROJECT DESCRIPTION
The research addresses the recent initiative in the social policy directed at creating closer links between education and the economy. The research is based upon interviews with teachers in one county. The sample will be drawn from all teachers who have taken part in the scheme. The sample size is approximately 50. The findings should reveal examples of 'good' practice for dissemination in the field and that the degree to which components of a 'hidden' curriculum are being constructed.

13488 De begeleiding van de introductie van Fries in het primair en voortgezet onderwijs. (Support of the introduction of Frisian language in primary and secondary education.)
NLD 1994
Research Date(s): 1992-1993
Brandsma, H.P.
Sup: Scheerens, J.
Inst: Onderzoek Centrum Toegepaste Onderwijskunde (OCTO) (Research Centre of the Department of Educational Technology), P.O. Box 217, 7500 AE Enschede, Netherlands.
Universiteit Twente (Twente University), P.O. Box 217, 7500 AE Enschede, Netherlands
Fin: SVO het Instituut voor Onderzoek van het Onderwijs.
financing; subsidy; minority language; educational policy
financement; subvention; langue de minorité; politique de l'éducation
PROJECT DESCRIPTION
Background: For ten years, the government has financially supported the introduction of Frisian language in Frisian schools. As part of wider government plans for cutting public spending, these funds are going to be reduced. This is to take place in such a way that the total of support provision remains equal. To realize this, the State Secretary for Education has asked for a study of the effects of the additional resources, which would facilitate future policy making in this area.
Aim: (1) To examine how additional state subsidies for the introduction of Frisian language in schools have been used by the Corporate Centre for School Counselling (GCO) since 1982; (2) to describe the results of the support provided as well as the need for support expressed by schools.
Design: Analyses will be made of the contracts between the Minsitry of Education and the Corporate Centre for School Counselling (GCO) and of relevant policy documents. Two representatives from the Ministry and two from the GCO will be interviewed. Annual reports and project plans of the GCO will be analysed and talks will be had with key staff at the GCO. A questionnaire survey will be conducted in order to determine what use is being made of the support that is offered and to identify users' needs for support. Interventions that have been carried out in schools will be described; activities that are currently being developed by the GCO will be charted. A sample of 572 primary schools, 101 secondary schools and 41 special schools will be asked what concrete services and/or products they need.

13489 Design of a job evaluation system for use in further education corporations.
GBR 1993
Research Date(s): 1992-1994
Saunders, R.
Sup: Gray, L.
Inst: Staff College, Coombe Lodge, Blagdon, Bristol BS18 6RG, United Kingdom.
job description; job requirements; salary; post-compulsory education
description d'emploi; qualification requise pour l'emploi; traitement; enseignement postobligatoire
PROJECT DESCRIPTION
Incorporation of further education (FE) colleges will deprive them of the services of local authority job evaluation units. Equal Pay claims where support staff cite academic staff comparators become increasingly likely. This research aims to design and test a job evaluation system capable of measuring the comparative value of all the jobs in a further education corporation to produce an integrated salary structure. Relevant factors have been selected, defined and provisionally weighted by analysis of benchmark job descriptions obtained from four colleges. The resulting job evaluation manual now needs to be tested in practice by applying it to a range of jobs in one or more colleges. Outcomes will be described by papers in The Staff College Mendip Paper series.

Publ: Saunders, R.C. *Job analysis and the preparation of job descriptions.* Mendip Paper No 37. Bristol: The Staff College, 1992.

13490 Education and training of property valuers in China.
GBR 1993
Research Date(s): 1991-1993
Plimmer, F.; Jiang, L.
Sup: Hibberd, P.; Gronow, S.
Inst: Glamorgan University, Department of Property and Development Studies, Pontypridd, Mid Glamorgan CF37 1DL, United Kingdom.
Fin: Royal Institution of Chartered Surveyors.
property; vocational education; China; didactic use of computer
propriété; enseignement professionnel; Chine; usage didactique de l'ordinateur
PROJECT DESCRIPTION
In the light of China's economic reform and the development of an 'open policy', the emergence of a property market has produced the need for property valuation skills in China. The research has investigated the needs of China for property valuation skills and, based on United Kingdom experience, is investigating ways in which computer-aided teaching can be used

to provide appropriate professional education and training for valuers in China.

13491 The education policies of large companies.
GBR 1993
Research Date(s): 1989-
Richardson, W.; Finegold, D.
Inst: Warwick University, Faculty of Educational Studies, Centre for Education and Industry, Coventry CV4 7AL, United Kingdom.
Fin: British Petroleum; Department for Education; Department of Employment.
industry; training-employment relationship; workers' education; educational policy
industrie; relation formation-emploi; éducation ouvrière; politique de l'éducation
PROJECT DESCRIPTION
The project is an analysis of the education policies of large companies in the United Kingdom. Research methods include literature reviews (general and that of specific companies) and interviews with companies' managers. The research characterises the development of companies' education policies, how they are formulated and who is responsible for their operation.

Analyses of results is presented in two ways: (a) stages of evolution in a company's relationship with education; (b) variables which shape company behaviour.

Publ: Richardson, W. & Finegold, D. *Making education our business.* (Interim report). Warwick: Warwick University, 1991.

13492 English local education authorities' schemes of local financial management.
GBR 1993
Research Date(s): 1990-1991
Atkinson, D.
Inst: Staff College, Coombe Lodge, Blagdon, Bristol BS18 6RG, United Kingdom.
education budget; financial resources; educational planning; local government; post-compulsory education
budget de l'éducation; ressources financières; planification de l'éducation; administration locale; enseignement postobligatoire
PROJECT DESCRIPTION
This research is a comparative analysis of English local education authority funding schemes (schemes of local financial management) for maintained further education colleges which have been prepared in accordance with the Education Reform Act 1988 and the Department of Education and Science Circular 9/88.

13493 Enterprise in higher education: evaluation.
GBR 1993
Research Date(s): 1988-1993
Fulton, O.
Inst: Lancaster University, Department of Educational Research, Cartmel College, Bailrigg, Lancaster LA1 4YW, United Kingdom.
Fin: Training, Enterprise and Education Directorate.
enterprise; higher education
entreprise; enseignement supérieur
PROJECT DESCRIPTION
This is a rolling evaluation of enterprise in higher education at Lancaster University. The first year investigated organisational and implementation issues, using interviews with staff. The second year focused on student experiences, using interviews with students. The third year looked at institutional diffusion and impact using staff and student interviews and student questionnaires.

13494 The enterprising college.
GBR 1993
Research Date(s): 1991-
Whyte, G.
Sup: Bennett, S.; Shipstone, D.
Inst: Nottingham University, School of Education, University Park, Nottingham NG7 2RD, United Kingdom.
enterprise; training-employment relationship; post-secondary education
entreprise; relation formation-emploi; enseignement postsecondaire
PROJECT DESCRIPTION
The aims of this research project are to: (1) propose an overall definition of the terms 'enterprise' and 'enterprising' and to identify the characteristics associated with enterprising people; (2) identify good practice in the techniques used by employers to develop an enterprising work force; (3) evolve a series of training events to enable managers to apply these techniques within further education and evaluate both the effectiveness of these techniques and the methods of importing them; (4) develop a mechanism for introducing enteprise approaches into the work of students and evaluate the effectiveness of these approaches; and (5) make recommendations for further applications of enterprise approaches within further education.

This research requires the integration of academic disciplines in that it combines approaches to both educational research and to management

development in the field of enterprise. The methodology falls into three distinct phases: (1) review of the literature; (2) project activity; and (3) evaluation.

13495 Entwicklung, Durchfuehrung und Auswertung eines bundesweiten Leistungswettbewerbs fuer hauswirtschaftliche Berufe zur Schaffung einer Basis fuer neue Inhalte und Strukturen in der hauswirtschaftlichen Berufsausbildung. (Development, implementation and assessment of a nation-wide performance competition for home economics occupations with the aim of creating a basis for new contents and structures in home economics education.)
DEU 1993
Research Date(s): 1991-1993
Biermann.
Sup: Bober, S.; Arens-Azevedo, U.
Inst: Fachhochschule Hamburg, FB Ernaehrung und Hauswirtschaft, Lohbruegger Kirchstrasse 65, D-2000 Hamburg 80.
home economics; occupation; vocational training; comparative achievement; competition; curriculum
économie domestique; profession; formation professionnelle; rendement comparé; concurrence; programme d'études
PROJECT DESCRIPTION
Inhalt: Entwicklung eines bundesweiten Leistungswettbewerbs fuer hauswirtschaftliche Berufe unter Beruecksichtigung oekologischer und gesellschaftlicher Bedingungen. Anregung der TeilnehmerInnen zur Entwicklung von zukunftsweisenden Loesungsvorschlaegen. Foerderung der Kreativitaet und Selbstaendigkeit der TeilnehmerInnen. Evaluierung der Konzeptionen und Durchfuehrung im Hinblick auf eine regelmaessige Wiederholung. Evaluierung der Ergebnisse als Grundlage fuer Ueberlegungen zur strukturellen Veraenderung hauswirtschaftlicher Berufsausbildung.

Vorgehensweise: Workshop; Wettbewerb; Evaluierung des Wettbewerbs; Vergleich zu Ausbildungsgaengen und -strukturen hauswirtschaftlicher Berufe.

13496 Evaluatie invoering nieuwe bekostigingssystematiek nascholing. (Evaluation of a new funding system for in-service training.)
NLD 1994
Research Date(s): 1993-1994
Karstanje, P.N.
Inst: Stichting Centrum voor Onderwijsonderzoek (SCO) (Centre for Educational Research), Grote Bickersstraat 72, 1013 KS Amsterdam, Netherlands.
Universiteit van Amsterdam (University of Amsterdam), P.O. Box 19268, 1000 GG Amsterdam, Netherlands
Fin: SVO het Instituut voor Onderzoek van het Onderwijs.
financing; reform; further education of teachers; in-service training; evaluation
financement; réforme; perfectionnement des enseignants; formation en cours d'emploi; évaluation
PROJECT DESCRIPTION
Background: From August 1993, the in-service training of primary and secondary school teachers will no longer be financed from the supply side (training providers, i.e. teacher training institutes), but from the demand side (school governing bodies). After a short transition period, schools will be free in their choice of training providers. The new funding system will be introduced over a period of four years. The present study concerns the evaluation of the first year.

Aim: (1) To examine the consequences of transferring the in-service training budget to school governing bodies; (2) to gain insight into successful and less successful school policies and into the conditions under which policies may be successfully realized.

Design: An analysis will be made of policy documents dealing with the new in-service training policies. Reactions to these new policies will be examined. A questionnaire survey will be made of the coordinators in 18-23 in-service training institutions and representatives from a total of 685 primary and secondary schools (including special and agricultural schools) and 15 junior vocational schools (MBO). In-service training courses on offer will be listed. Depending on when exactly the new funding system will be introduced, either new investigations will be conducted to enable comparisons to be made with the situation in 1991-1992, or in-depth studies will be made of 10 primary and 10 secondary schools. Five case-studies will be made of successful schools. Methodology includes two panel studies.

13497 Evaluation of the Construction Industry Training Board's curriculum centre initiative.
GBR 1993
Research Date(s): 1991-1993
Sims, D.
Sup: Stoney, S.
Inst: National Foundation for Educational Research, The Mere, Upton Park, Slough SL1 2DQ, United Kingdom.
Fin: Construction Industry Training Board.
construction industry; vocational education
industrie de la construction; enseignement professionnel

PROJECT DESCRIPTION

The Construction Industry Training Board (CITB) is establishing up to 50 Curriculum Centres around the country with the aim of: (1) establishing 'construction' as a genuine context for cross-curricular learning; (2) providing practical facilities which will simulate real-work situations; and (3) providing a platform for a continuing dialogue between education and industry.

The National Foundation for Educational Research is providing advice and devising materials for the self-evaluation of the initiative by the CITB and the Centres themselves. It will also conduct periodic evaluative reviews of the self-evaluation outputs and of data collected independently by the Foundation. The evaluation is proceeding in a series of phases. A preliminary phase (when a self-evaluation strategy and materials were devised) was completed in August 1991. The first phase of the main evaluation was completed in February 1992 and resulted in a report, published by the CITB, on the progress and outcomes of the initiative to date. During the remainder of 1992 further work (Phase 2) was conducted and resulted in an evaluation up-date report, a report on the employers' contribution to the initiative and an evaluation handbook. During Phase 3, in 1993, a series of evaluation workshops are being organised in order to disseminate the evaluation findings and to promote local self-evaluation.

13498   Evolution du système productif et appropriation des nouvelles technologies de formation.
FRA   1993
Research Date(s): 1987-
Silem, Ahmed; Auvolat, Michel; Barcet, André; Mayère, Anne; Bonamy, Joël; Cicille, Patricia.
Sup: Albertini, Jean-Marie.
Inst: Ministère de la recherche, CNRS UPR/5411 et GDR/28, Institut de recherche en pédagogie de l'économie et en audio-visuel pour la communication dans les sciences sociales, 93 Chemin des Mouilles, BP 167, 69130 Ecully Cedex, France.
services; technological change; vocational training; economics of education; qualitative analysis; new technologies
services; changement technologique; formation professionnelle; économie de l'éducation; analyse qualitative; nouvelles technologies
PROJECT DESCRIPTION

Objectifs: Le développement des nouvelles technologies pour la formation fait partie du développement plus général des nouvelles technologies de l'information dans le système productif, les recherches socio-économiques permettent de mieux comprendre les conditions du développement des nouvelles technologies de la formation.

Méthodologie: (1) On analyse comment et pourquoi les nouvelles technologies de la formation entraînent une modification de la structure de formation: deux séries de travaux, l'une sur la définition du concept et la création des outils d'un centre de ressources informatiques, l'autre sur la mise au point d'un outil d'évaluation de didacticiels dans le cadre du réseau européen "Fondation des régions européennes pour la recherche en éducation et formation (FREFEF)". (2) On analyse l'éducation non comme une institution mais comme un service, cette approche amène à appliquer dans le domaine de l'économie de la formation les concepts et démarches de l'économie des services. Une recherche présentée à l'appel d'offre de la Délégation à la formation professionnelle étudie les rapports entre la démarche qualité dans la formation et l'économie des services. Elle permet grâce à l'analyse de cas d'accroître les connaissances permettant: (1) à partir des démarches analysées à la lumière de l'économie des services d'aboutir ultérieurement à une démarche prescription, (2) dans le cadre des recherches sur l'économie des services d'analyser la valeur d'usage, l'efficacité et l'évolution de la structure de la formation.

Publ: Barcet, André & Bonamy, Joël. *Services et transformation des modes de production.* In: *Revue d'économie industrielle,* 1988, n° 43, pp. 206-217.
Barcet, André. *La montée des services: vers une économie de la servuction.* Université de Lyon II: CEDES, thèse d'Etat, 333p.
Barcet, André et al. *La qualité des services: de l'analyse économique aux processus de qualification des services intellectuels.* Ecully: CEDES, 89p.
Albertini, Jean-Marie; Bonamy, Joël; Cicille, Patricia & Mayère, Anne. *Les producteurs de nouvelles technologies de formation.* Ecully: IRPEACS, 2 tomes, 1991.
(Une liste complète est disponible.).

13499   Financial circumstances of adult/mature students.
GBR   1993
Research Date(s): 1986-
Bryant, R.; Noble, M.
Inst: Ruskin College, Ruskin Hall, Old Headington, Oxford OX3 9BZ, United Kingdom.
financial resources; student loan; adult education; student
ressources financières; prêt d'études; éducation des adultes; étudiant
PROJECT DESCRIPTION

This is a long-term evaluation of the financial circumstances of adult students at Ruskin College, with particular reference to students on the CQSW/Social Work course. The research aims to: (1) monitor the financial

difficulties experienced by mature/adult students; (2) compile data on how financial problems impact upon recruitment and the course work of students; and (3) evaluate the impact of the student loans scheme on students at Ruskin.
Publ: Bryant, R. & Noble, M. *Reflections on Social Work Education.* Oxford: Ruskin College, 1988.
Bryant, R. & Noble, M. *Education on a Shoestring.* Oxford: Ruskin College, 1989.

13500   La formation comme variable d'efficience économique.
FRA   1993
Research Date(s): 1988-
Bourdon, Jean.
Inst: Université de Dijon, UER Faculté des sciences économiques et de gestion, CNRS UPR/29 et GDR/996, Institut de recherche sur l'économie de l'éducation, BP 138, 21004 Dijon Cedex, France.
Fin: Communauté économique européenne.
economic factor; vocational training; manpower; regional development; international exchange; competition; France; achievement measurement
facteur économique; formation professionnelle; main-d'oeuvre; développement régional; échange international; concurrence; France; mesure du rendement
PROJECT DESCRIPTION

Objectifs: Des travaux récents tendent à remettre en cause l'efficacité d'une analyse fonctionnelle des diverses mains d'oeuvre et réactivent la mesure de l'efficience du facteur éducatif en utilisant des indicateurs de nombres moyens d'années de scolarité de la main d'oeuvre. Deux tentatives de vérification sont entreprises.

Méthodologie: (1) On reprend l'analyse selon laquelle le niveau de formation générale de la population active d'une zone géographique donne un avantage absolu au commerce international pour cette région (Bela Balassa). L'analyse est réalisée sur les régions françaises pour la période 1970-1984 et valide l'hypothèse que les régions où le capital-formation s'est accru le plus rapidement sont celles qui connaissent les plus fortes percées sur les marchés extérieurs. (2) On recherche l'impact de la formation scolaire sur l'évolution des grands équilibres régionaux. Partant d'une formalisation prenant en compte une relation d'offre de travail, de demande de travail et de mobilité géographique de la main d'oeuvre, on réalise des tests en coupe croisée (22 régions X date de recensements: 1968, 1975, 1982).

Résultats: Les tests montrent un gain explicatif de ces trois relations si les variables de population active et de main d'oeuvre prennent en compte cet effet de formation régionale. Ce type d'analyse nécessite une généralisation, certains résultats pouvant être contestés en fonction des bases statistiques utilisées au niveau régional. Est entreprise également une analyse de l'avantage absolu à l'exportation dû à la formation des mains d'oeuvre sur l'espace européen.

13501   Funding for special educational needs - post-school provision.
GBR   1993
Research Date(s): 1992
Dee, L.
Inst: London University, Institute of Education, 20 Bedford Way, London WC1H OAL, United Kingdom.
Fin: Further Education Unit.
financing; cost of education; special education; post-compulsory education; adult education; economics of education; education budget; access to education; handicapped
financement; coût de l'éducation; enseignement spécial; enseignement postobligatoire; éducation des adultes; économie de l'éducation; budget de l'éducation; accès à l'éducation; handicapé
PROJECT DESCRIPTION

This is a survey of funding arrangements and unit costs in three local authorities in order to establish costs for students with disabilities and learning difficulties in colleges of further education (FE) and adult education. Recommendations on interim and long-term funding arrangements will be made.
Publ: Dee, L. *The funding and costing of provision for learners with learning difficulties or disabilities in colleges and adult education institutes.* FEU Report 725, 1992.

13502   "Human capital" en exportconcurrentie. (Human capital and export competitiveness.)
NLD   1993
Research Date(s): 1992-1996
Cörvers, F.
Sup: Grip, A. de; Heijke, J.A.M.
Inst: ROA Researchcentrum voor Onderwijs en Arbeidsmarkt, Universiteit Limburg (Research Centre for Education and the Labour Market, University of Limburg), P.O. Box 616, 6200 MD Maastricht, Netherlands.
competition; industry; level of education; worker; training supply; know-how
concurrence; industrie; niveau d'enseignement; travailleur; offre de formation; savoir-faire

PROJECT DESCRIPTION

This Ph.D. research project focuses on the relationship between the export competitiveness of a sector of industry and the human capital of that sector. The purpose of the research project is to explain the international competitiveness of sectors of industry in a Heckscher-Ohlin setting by differentiating between four kinds of human capital: the educational level of workers in a sector; the firm-specific or general training efforts per sector; the experience level or specific knowledge per sector; the technological knowledge per sector.

An important part of the study deals with empirical research on the relationship between the international competitiveness of sectors of industry and the various kinds of human capital in the Netherlands, Great Britain and Germany.

13503 Impact macroéconomique de la formation professionnelle.
FRA 1993
Research Date(s): 1988-
Bourdon, Jean.
Inst: Université de Dijon, UER Faculté des sciences économiques et de gestion, CNRS UPR/29 et GDR/996, Institut de recherche sur l'économie de l'éducation, BP 138, 21004 Dijon Cedex, France.
vocational training; continuing education; state; enterprise; regional planning; training supply; in-plant training; economic factor
formation professionnelle; éducation permanente; Etat; entreprise; planification régionale; offre de formation; stage en entreprise; facteur économique
PROJECT DESCRIPTION

Objectifs: Cet axe de travail entend mesurer les liens de la formation professionnelle continue avec la dynamique économique. Trois sous thèmes sont élaborés: (1) modélisation de l'effort de formation professionnelle dispensée tant par l'Etat, les régions que par les entreprises; (2) analyse de la dotation des entreprises à la formation professionnelle; (3) analyse des offres de stage comme facteur explicatif des entrées-sorties de chômage.

Méthodologie: (1) L'effort de formation professionnelle est modélisé à partir de données rétrospectives 1972-1987 pour la France; (2) la participation des entreprises à la formation professionnelle continue (FPC) est étudiée à partir de la nomenclature T40; (3) on introduit l'offre de stage dans la modélisation des entrées-sorties du chômage.

Résultats: (1) Au niveau de l'Etat, les indicateurs qualitatifs montrent que devant le flux de la demande on a sacrifié aux objectifs quantitatifs du traitement social du chômage; (2) la participation à la FPC est fortement différenciée selon les secteurs soit comportement passif (suivre les obligations légales), soit remise en cause de la FPC, à des fins de rentabilité, soit progression forte de la FPC; (3) l'offre de stage n'est pas neutre sur le niveau d'offre de travail et ceci peut en partie restreindre l'effet attendu des politiques de traitement social basé sur l'offre de formation.

13504 International group for the study of language standardisation and the vernacularisation of literacy.
GBR 1993
Research Date(s): 1986-
Warner, A.; Russell, J.; Verma, M.; Christie, P.; Devonish, D.
Sup: Le Page, R.; Tabouret-Keller, A.
Inst: York University, Department of Language and Linguistic Science, Heslington, York YO1 5DD, United Kingdom; University of the West Indies, Mona Campus, Mona, Kingston 7, Jamaica; Université Louis Pasteur, Institute Le Bel, 4 rue Blaise Pascal, 67007 Strasbourg, France.
Fin: ESRC; Nuffield Foundation; York University; CNRS - Paris; British Academy; British Council.
developing country; literacy; mother tongue; linguistics; cross-national research
pays en développement; alphabétisation; langue maternelle; linguistique; recherche transnationale
PROJECT DESCRIPTION

Biennial workshops bring together research workers concerned with the language-related educational problems of developing countries, particularly with former colonies of France and Britain, in order to monitor progress with these problems while at the same time using them to refine linguistic, sociolinguistic and psycholinguistic insights, theory and stereotypes generally. At each workshop short presentations are made on the application of points in a position paper, and circulated beforehand, to the particular area of each participant. Most of the participants are concerned in some way with teacher training, the formulation of policy and the preparation of descriptions of vernaculars and of teaching materials in the vernaculars.

The 1986 York workshop was concerned with the stereotypes concerning 'standardisation', and the volume of abstracts and transcription of discussions was concerned with English, French, German, Italian, Greek, Hindi, Punjabi, Chinese, Swahili, Malay, Bislama, Creole English, Creole French and Sango. The 1988 workshop was concerned with literacy and orthographies for these same language communities with the exception of Italian. The 1990 workshop was concerned with evaluations of historical progress in literacy. In each case the history of the older 'standard lan-

guages' will be compared with linguistic evolution in the developing countries in order to illuminate stereotypes about both.

The 1992 workshop to be held at Sevres will be concerned with the preparation of chapters for a book seeking to find possible ways forward from the various disasters which have overtaken many of the UNESCO initiatives since publication in 1953 of Monograph VIII 'The use of vernacular languages in education'.

Publ: Le Page, R.B. (ed.). *Abstract of the proceedings of the April 1986 Workshop of the International group for the study of Language Standardisation and the Vernacularisation of Literacy.* York: University of York, Department of Language and Linguistic Science, Mimeo, 1986, 139p. Idem (1988), 154p. Idem (1990) 136p.

13505 Investment appraisal of Education Support Grant XXX for the training of youth leaders in the inner cities in England and in the valleys in Wales.
GBR 1993
Research Date(s): 1991-1993
Thompson, Q.
Sup: D'Armenia, M.
Inst: Coopers & Lybrand Deloitte, Plumtree Court, London EC4A 4HT, United Kingdom.
Fin: Department of Education and Science.
economics of education; training cost; youth policy
économie de l'éducation; coût de la formation; politique de la jeunesse
PROJECT DESCRIPTION

The Department of Education and Science has commissioned Coopers and Lybrand Deloitte to carry out an investment appraisal of Education Support Grant (ESG) XXX for the training of youth leaders in the inner cities in England and in the valleys in Wales. The appraisal will: estimate the total investment in the local scheme; assess the extent of support from other sources; compare costs with those of other forms of youth worker training; assess the costs and benefits of the schemes; and evaluate the efficiency of the ESG mechanism.

This is one of a number of evaluation exercises of the ESG, the combined results of which will allow the Department to assess the overall value of the programme and its viability as a model for future youth training.

13506 Návrh metodiky rozpisu investičných a neinvestičných prostriedkov na vysoké školy v SR na rok 1993. (Proposal for the allocation of resources to higher education institutes in the Slovak Republic for 1993.)
SVK 1994
Research Date(s): 1991-1993
Bláhová, E.; Dzurko, J.
Sup: Majtán, M.
Inst: Ústav informácií a prognóz školstva, mládeže a telovýchovy (Institute of Information and Prognoses of Education, Youth and Sport), Staré grunty 52, 842 44 Bratislava, Slovak Republic.
Ministerstvo školstva a vedy SR (Ministry of Education and Science of the Slovak Republic), Hlboká 2, 813 30 Bratislava, Slovak Republic
financial resources; education budget; resource allocation; wage
ressources financières; budget de l'éducation; affectation des ressources; salaire
PROJECT DESCRIPTION

Aim: The aim of the research was to elaborate a methodology and criteria for the "objective" allocation of the state budget for higher education institutions. The definition of objective criteria focused on investment and non-investment funds, salaries and institutional funds for science and technology. Two associated aims were: to determine the objective performance of individual higher education institutions as well as the objective expenditures related to unit performance.

Results: Two alternative methods were proposed for the allocation of the salary budget: (1) a relatively global method for which it is recommended to relate the average wage development to the qualification level of staff (this method was elaborated in two variants); (2) an individualized method which requires a complete stock-taking of basic staff salaries, extra allowances and bonuses for management.

As regards the institutions' budgets for science and technology, two criteria were formulated: the planned capacity and demands for scientific research and the consequent demands of individual scientific branches for financial resources.

Publ: Majtán, M. & Cabajová, M. Možnosti zobjektívnenia riadenia vývoja miezd a mzdových prostriedkov na vysokých školách SR. In: *Problémy a perspektívy VŠ a vedy*, 1991, No. 1.
Majtán, M.; et al. *Návrhy objektivizácie rozpisu rozpočtových prostriedkov na vysoké školy v SR na rok 1993 - tézy.* Bratislava, ÚIP ŠMT, May 1992.
Dzurko, J. & Hajtš, V. *Návrh postupu prác na tvorbe kritérií pre rozpis rozpočtu ma vysoké školy. Pracovný materiál.* Bratislava, ÚIP ŠMT, September 1991.

13507 Onderwijs en ondernemerschap: analytisch onderzoek van de aandacht voor ondernemerschap in het Nederlandstalig onderwijs. (Education and entrepreneurship: an analytical study of the attention given to entrepreneurship in education (in Dutch-speaking Belgium).)
BEL 1994
Research Date(s): 1988-1991
Segers, J.-P.; Courtmans, A.; Lambrecht, J.
Sup: Donckels, R.
Inst: KMO-studiecentrum (Study centre of small and medium enterprises), Vrijheidslaan 17, 1080 Brussel, Belgium.
Universitaire Faculteiten Sint-Aloysius, UFSAL (University Faculties St Aloysius, UFSAL), Vrijheidslaan 17, 1080 Brussel, Belgium
Fin: Departement Onderwijs, Fonds voor Kollektief en Fundamenteel Onderzoek op Ministerieel Initiatief.
university industry relationship; training-employment relationship; enterprise; small and medium entreprise; commercial training; economic studies
relation université-entreprise; relation formation-emploi; entreprise; petite ou moyenne entreprise; formation commerciale; études économiques
PROJECT DESCRIPTION
Background: The study is conducted in answer to requests from policy makers for practical suggestions aimed at fostering a spirit of entrepreneurship in pupils and students.
Research questions: (1) What attention do schools give to self-employment? (2) What is the attitude of economy and trade teachers towards entrepreneurship? (3) What initiatives can be taken to stimulate a spirit of entrepreneurship in secondary and higher education?
Methods and results: A literature survey was conducted of such terms as "entrepreneurship", "entrepreneur", "self-employer" and of the relationship between education and entrepreneurship. A survey was conducted of economy, trade and business administration teachers in secondary and higher vocational education schools. Information was collected on: (1) teachers' attitudes towards enterprises and entrepreneurship, (2) their views of the characteristics and skills of a good entrepreneur, (3) their perceptions regarding links between schools and enterprises. A second survey was conducted of 176 higher education students and graduates in applied economics. This survey revealed students' perceptions of self-employment and showed what proportion of graduates become entrepreneurs themselves. The final report proposes the organization of a course in "self-employment" in secondary and higher vocational schools. At the university level, a "multidisciplinary university entrepreneurship school" is needed.
Publ: Donckels, R. et al. *Onderwijs en ondernemerschap: eindverslag.* Brussel: UFSAL, KMO-studiecentrum, 1991, 207p.

13508 Prévision des dépenses d'éducation primaire à l'horizon 2000 dans les pays en développement.
FRA 1993
Research Date(s): 1987-1989
Lassibille, Gérard.
Inst: Université de Dijon, UER Faculté des sciences économiques et de gestion, CNRS UPR/29 et GDR/996, Institut de recherche sur l'économie de l'éducation, BP 138, 21004 Dijon Cedex, France.
developing country; cost of education; forecasting; primary education; Africa; Latin America; Caribbean; Asia; Oceania
pays en développement; coût de l'éducation; prévision; enseignement primaire; Afrique; Amérique latine; Caraibes; Asie; Océanie
PROJECT DESCRIPTION
Objectifs: Il s'agit de fournir une évaluation chiffrée de la dépense que devraient supporter les pays en développement pour satisfaire la demande d'éducation primaire qui est prévue en l'an 2000 et d'estimer également le coût qu'entraînerait pour eux la généralisation de l'enseignement primaire à cette même époque.
Méthodologie: Les données proviennent des informations recueillies annuellement par l'UNESCO qui permettent de déterminer les composantes de la dépense pour un échantillon de 111 pays en développement observés au cours de l'année 1985.
Résultats: (1) Description de l'évolution anticipée des effectifs d'élèves dans le premier degré et des implications de l'objectif d'éducation primaire universelle en l'an 2000; ces charges financières liées à la réalisation de cette scolarisation future sont évaluées sur la base d'un modèle de simulation des dépenses par pays. (2) Les dépenses d'enseignement primaire à l'horizon 2000 sont simulées au niveau des grandes régions géographiques (Afrique, Amérique latine et Caraïbes, Asie et Océanie), selon trois scénarios: maintien de la structure actuelle, amélioration de la qualité de l'enseignement, couverture des besoins d'éducation par des personnels moins qualifiés.
Publ: Lassibille, Gérard & Navarro-Gomez, Lucia. *Prévisions des dépenses d'éducation primaire à l'horizon 2000 dans les pays en développement.* Rapport à l'Office des statistiques de l'UNESCO, sept. 1989, 27p.

13509 Rural social development: education, literacy and organisation in the Third World.
GBR 1993
Research Date(s): 1989-1992
Turner, J.
Sup: Carmen, R.
Inst: Manchester University, School of Education, Centre for Adult and Higher Education, Oxford Road, Manchester M13 9PL, United Kingdom.
developing country; economic development; rural development; social development
pays en développement; développement économique; développement rural; développement social
PROJECT DESCRIPTION
After the previous four decades (since World War II) of economic development with directive, top-down strategies and non-directive efforts known under 'community development' and 'integrated rural development', we are now in the 1980s and 1990s, entering the era of self-directed, autonomous development. The very term 'autonomy' does not figure on current development and education library indexes, therefore there is an urgent need for compilation and research.

13510 Scottish Enterprise Consortium: Moray House Institute of Education.
GBR 1993
Research Date(s): 1989-1991
Francis, E.; Jackson, S.; Morrison, A.
Inst: Heriot-Watt University, Moray House Institute of Education, Holyrood Road, Edinburgh EH8 8AQ, United Kingdom.
Fin: Training, Enterprise and Education Directorate.
enterprise; higher education
entreprise; enseignement supérieur
PROJECT DESCRIPTION
The aim of the research is to develop a range of enterprise projects within a centrally funded college and across a consortium of higher education institutions. These will include: (i) a process innovative network; (ii) an enterprise model for the Postgraduate Certificate of Education (PGCE); (iii) a video project on enterprise awareness; and (iv) consultancy for an evaluation project.

13511 Sponsorship in Scottish colleges of further and higher education.
GBR 1993
Research Date(s): 1990-1991
Weir, A.; Mair, J.
Inst: Jordanhill College of Education, Division of Secondary and Curricular Studies, Southbrae Drive, Glasgow G13 1PP, United Kingdom.
Fin: Scottish Office Education Department.
financial resources; industry; higher education
ressources financières; industrie; enseignement supérieur
PROJECT DESCRIPTION
The aim of this project is to investigate the entrepreneurial activities of colleges with particular reference to their success in attracting commercial sponsorship. In particular it will examine: (1) how funding is attracted; (2) what are the objectives of customers and contractors and what benefits they perceive; (3) what particular or distinctive activities result and what are the consequences of these for the contractor's institutional profile; and (4) what internal structures characterise contractors who are successful in attracting sponsorship.
Publ: Mair, J.D. *Colleges and sponsorship.* Glasgow: Jordanhill College, 1991.

13512 Studentenjobs - eine repräsentative Untersuchung bei Studierenden an der Universität Bern. (Enquête représentative sur les activités rémunérées des étudiants à l'Université de Berne.)
CHE 1994
Research Date(s): 1991-1992
Arber, Daniel; Pasquier, Martial.
Inst: Universität Bern, Institut für Marketing und Unternehmensführung, Sennweg 2, 3012 Bern, Schweiz.
income; student life; university; money; part-time work
revenu; vie étudiante; université; argent; travail à temps partiel
PROJECT DESCRIPTION
Der vorliegende Bericht stellt in verdichteter Form die Daten zusammen, die im Rahmen einer Lizentiatsarbeit an der Universität Bern erhoben worden sind. Die (schriftliche) Befragung lieferte Antworten von 636 Personen (davon 255 weiblichen Geschlechts). 50 dieser Personen arbeiteten bereits an ihrer Dissertation; sie wurden für die meisten der folgenden Aussagen ausgeklammert. Durchschnittsalter war 25, wobei 63,5 Prozent der Befragten jünger als 25 waren. 52 Antwortende hatten eines oder mehrere Kinder. 95 Prozent waren schweizerischer Nationalität; von den 31 Ausländern hatten 18 eine Arbeitsbewilligung. Nachfolgend einige Ergebnisse.
Die meisten Antwortenden waren im Lauf ihrer bisherigen Studienzeit mindestens einmal erwerbstätig. Von den 74 anderen sind mehr als die Hälfte im ersten Semester, wo weniger Zeit zur Verfügung zu stehen

scheint. Während der Semesterferien arbeiten nahezu alle; 85 Prozent gehen aber auch während des Semesters einem Erwerb nach - im Mittel etwa während 16 Stunden pro Woche. Bei diesen Studenten liegt der gesamte zeitliche Aufwand für Studium und Erwerbsarbeit bei 44,7 Stunden die Woche, wovon rund 19 für das Studium. Studierende ohne Erwerbsarbeit dagegen widmen ihrem Studium gegen 38 Stunden pro Woche.

Der mittlere Stundenlohn beträgt sFr. 25.70; vernachlässigt man die Lehrtätigkeiten, so sinkt der Betrag auf sFr. 21.90. Im Mittel steht den Antwortenden monatlich eine Summe von 1414 Franken zur Verfügung. 37,6 Prozent dieses Geldes stammt aus regelmässiger eigener Arbeit, weitere 10,8% werden in Ferienjobs verdient. Die eigene Erwerbsarbeit ist somit die wichtigste Quelle und deckt nahezu die Hälfte der finanziellen Mittel. (Im zweiten Rang folgen die Eltern mit 36,1%; quantitativ weniger bedeutend sind die Stipendien mit 6,2% die Beiträge von Partnerin/Partner mit 4,6% und die Darlehen mit 1,6%.) Eine Analyse nach der besuchten Fakultät fördert recht grosse Unterschiede zutage: so verfügen etwa die Studenten der Philosophisch-Historischen Fakultät mit 1794 Franken im Monat über deutlich mehr Mittel als die Medizinstudenten mit ihren monatlich 1033 Franken. Dies hat einerseits damit zu tun, dass viele Phil.-hist.-Studenten unterrichten, was eine lukrative Beschäftigung ist; andererseits gehören die Mediziner zu jener Kategorie, die es von Stundenplan und Stoffmenge her am schwersten haben, neben dem Studium noch einer bezahlten Arbeit nachzugehen.

Publ: Arber, Daniel. *Studentenjobs: Eine repräsentative Untersuchung über die Erwerbstätigkeit von Studierenden an der Universität Bern.* Bern: Universität Bern, Institut für Marketing und Unternehmensführung, Dez. 1991, 47 Seiten (Arbeitsbericht des Instituts für Marketing und Unternehmensführung; Nr. 13).

13513 Teachers' pay and bargaining machinery in four European countries.
GBR 1993
Research Date(s): 1991-1992
Scribbins, K.
Inst: Staff College, Coombe Lodge, Blagdon, Bristol BS18 6RG, United Kingdom.
Fin: Central Bodies Advisory Group/The Staff College.
salary; comparative research; teacher; Europe; cross-national research
traitement; recherche comparative; enseignant; Europe; recherche transnationale
PROJECT DESCRIPTION
   This is a study of the effects of educational reform on pay bargaining machinery and the output of negotiations. Pay scales and approaches as well as relativities with other professions will be studied on a comparative basis.

13514 Technologie-indicatoren. (Technology indicators.)
NLD 1993
Research Date(s): 1989
Dam, J.W. van; Ramaekers, G.W.M.
Inst: ROA Researchcentrum voor Onderwijs en Arbeidsmarkt, Universiteit Limburg (Research Centre for Education and the Labour Market, University of Limburg), P.O. Box 616, 6200 MD Maastricht, Netherlands.
Fin: Maastricht Economic Research Institute on Innovation and Technology (MERIT); Ministry of Economic Affairs, Directorate for General Technology Policy.
economic development; technology; technological change; manpower; statistical data
développement économique; technologie; changement technologique; main-d'oeuvre; données statistiques
PROJECT DESCRIPTION
   The Dutch Ministry of Economic Affairs has developed a data bank of indicators on the international economic position of the Netherlands with regard to the implementation of technology. One category of indicators in this data bank refers to the technological potential of the labour force as an indication of the societal breeding ground for technological development.
   In this context, ROA annually carries out research to update a number of internationally comparable "key indicators" regarding population, labour and schooling, mostly on the basis of the international statistical data sources of the ILO, UNESCO, Eurostat, and the OECD. In addition, ROA asks some 60 statistical offices, research institutes and/or researchers every year for new figures to extend the existing key indicators and to explore the possibility of developing new indicators. The research project also includes an annual search for relevant incidental surveys by other agencies.

Publ: Dam, J.W. van & Ramaekers, G.W.M. *Technology Indicators: Population, Labour and Schooling, 1992 report,* ROA-R-1992/5E (ISBN 90-05321-091-1).

13515 Towards the integration of education, science and industrial production under the conditions of a decentralized market economy.
RUS 1994
Research Date(s): 1991-1992
Ashkerov, Y.V.
Sup: Tsesnek, L.S.
Inst: Research Institute for Higher Education, 103062, Moscow, K-62, Podsosensky per. 20, Russia.
State Committee for Higher Education Institutions, 113833, Moscow, M-230, Lysinovskja str. 51, Russia
economic development; higher education; sciences; industry; integration
développement économique; enseignement supérieur; sciences; industrie; intégration
PROJECT DESCRIPTION
   The overall aim of the study was to contribute to the integration of education, science and industrial production. More specifically, the study developed a systematic approach to regional aspects of managing the development and use of higher education know-how as part of a national economic complex, which involved the integration of national statistical data. Forecasts were made on the basis of calculations using an economic model for the development of productive activity.
Publ: Savelyev, A.Y.; Zuyev, V.M. & Tsesnek, L.S. *The conversion of military production and higher education.* M., NIIVO, 1992.
Savelyev, A.Y.; Zuyev, V.M.; Tsesnek, L.S.; et al. *Regional problems of higher education development.* M., NIIVO, 1992.
Gorelik, B.Y.; Rusakovskaya, M.; Mamonova, Y.I.; et al. *Prognosis of the development of scientific disciplines in higher education.* M., NIIVO, 1992.

13516 The transferability of current insurance qualifications within the European Community.
GBR 1993
Research Date(s): 1990-1992
Bray, S.
Inst: Cheltenham & Gloucester College of Higher Education, Oxstalls Campus, Oxstalls Lane, Gloucester GL2 9HW, United Kingdom.
insurance; occupational qualification; recognition of qualifications; European community
assurances; qualification professionnelle; reconnaissance des qualifications; Communauté européenne
PROJECT DESCRIPTION
   The aim of this research is to investigate: the various insurance qualifications within the European Community; their level; the recognition they receive within individual member states; and how they compare with the insurance qualifications elsewhere in the European Community. It is also intended to enquire: how transferable these qualifications are in the light of 1993; how qualifications which have been gained in the United Kingdom can be applied to jobs in the European Community and the implications for business studies/language courses; and how qualifications which have been gained in other European countries apply to work in the United Kingdom insurance industry.
   The investigation will be carried out in European countries where insurance features most prominently. Methodology will include desk research, data collection, contacting professional bodies from each country, insurance companies, Chamber of Commerce and The National Council for Vocational Qualifications (NCVQ).

33 LABOUR ENVIRONMENT – ENVIRONNEMENT DU TRAVAIL – ARBEITSUMWELT

13517   16-19 Initiative: Liverpool.
GBR   1993
Research Date(s): 1986-1991
Roberts, K.; Strivens, J.; Derricott, R.
Inst: Liverpool University, Department of Sociology, PO Box 147, Liverpool L69 3BX, United Kingdom.
Fin: Economic and Social Research Council.
transition from school to work; occupational choice; youth employment; school leaver
passage à la vie active; choix d'une profession; emploi des jeunes; élève sortant
PROJECT DESCRIPTION
Random samples, totalling 1,600, of 15 and 17 year old cohorts from Liverpool schools were surveyed by questionnaire in 3 successive sweeps. Interview surveys with sub-samples were also conducted.
The aim was to identify different career trajectories from education into the labour market, and to relate career paths to economic and political socialisation, the development of social representation, social attributions, self-concepts and efficacy.

13518   Adult employment training in Nottinghamshire: case studies.
GBR   1993
Research Date(s): 1990-1993
McCarthy, J.
Sup: Morgan, W.; Bayliss, F.
Inst: Nottingham University, Department of Adult Education, Centre for Research into the Education of Adults, 14-22 Shakespeare Street, Nottingham NG1 4FJ, United Kingdom.
Fin: National Westminster Bank Research Fund; Department of Employment.
training-employment relationship; employment; training supply; vocational training; adult education
relation formation-emploi; emploi; offre de formation; formation professionnelle; éducation des adultes
PROJECT DESCRIPTION
Shortcomings in training are at the core of the National Skills and Training debate. What are the causes of these shortcomings? This enquiry attempts to answer this question and to indicate how firms local to the Nottinghamshire area seek to overcome them. Semi-structured interviews are undertaken with key providers and consumers of training. These are accompanied by a series of case studies, both of major employers and of small to medium sized industries.
Publ: McCarthy, J.; Morgan, W.J. & Bayliss, F.J. *Adult employment training in Nottinghamshire*. Nottingham: University of Nottingham, Department of Adult Education, 1992.

13519   Allochtonen in het BBO zonder leerovereenkomst (LOK). (Immigrant apprentices without an apprenticeship contract.)
NLD   1994
Research Date(s): 1992-1993
Brandsma, T.F.; Velden, L.F.J. van der.
Sup: Scheerens, J.
Inst: Onderzoek Centrum Toegepaste Onderwijskunde (OCTO) (Research Centre of the Department of Educational Technology), P.O. Box 217, 7500 AE Enschede, Netherlands.
Universiteit Twente (Twente University), P.O. Box 217, 7500 AE Enschede, Netherlands
Fin: SVO het Instituut voor Onderzoek van het Onderwijs.

training-employment contract; apprenticeship; apprentice; immigrant; equal opportunity

contrat emploi-formation; apprentissage professionnel; apprenti; immigrant; égalité de chances

PROJECT DESCRIPTION

Background: Immigrants are in a weak position on the Dutch labour market. Many immigrants enter the labour market without a basic vocational qualification. To improve this situation, it is being attempted to stimulate participation in apprenticeship training. Statistical figures show not only that participation in apprenticeship training is poor, but also that many immigrant pupils on theoretical apprenticeship training courses do not have an apprenticeship contract for practical training.

Aim: To examine the causes of the relatively high number of immigrant pupils on apprenticeship training courses without an apprenticeship contract; to propose measures for a better balance between the number of apprenticeship contracts and the number of immigrant pupils attending theoretical apprenticeship training.

Design: To ascertain the proportion of immigrant apprentices without an apprenticeship contract, use will be made of data available from the Ministry of Education and Science. A survey will be made of consultants from national organizations in the field of apprenticeship training (n = ca. 100), focusing on (a) policies regarding the recruitment of immigrant apprentices and (b) measures that may help raise the number of immigrants with an apprenticeship contract. Questionnaires will be presented to officials who are responsible for the supply of apprenticeship training places and the selection of apprentices in about 100 companies that take apprentices. The regional consultants (n = ca. 30) will be asked about their tasks regarding the guidance of apprentices and the contacts between the theoretical training institutes and the companies providing practical training.

13520 Analyse de la relation formation-emploi, applications aux jeunes sortant des formations initiales.

FRA   1993

Research Date(s): 1984-1988

Houzel, Yvette; Vernières, Michel; Pasqualini, Esther; Levaillant, Marc.

Inst: Université de Paris I, UFR Analyse et politique économiques, CNRS URA/941 et GDR/996, Laboratoire d'économie sociale-Equipe Emploi, Formation, Développement, 90 rue de Tolbiac, 75634 Paris Cedex 13, France.

Fin: Centre d'études et de recherches sur les qualifications.

youth employment; labour market; vocational education; secondary education; higher education; occupational integration; training-employment relationship; transition from school to work; urban environment; rural area

emploi des jeunes; marché du travail; enseignement professionnel; enseignement secondaire; enseignement supérieur; intégration professionnelle; relation formation-emploi; passage à la vie active; milieu urbain; zone rurale

PROJECT DESCRIPTION

Objectifs: Dans le cadre des enquêtes de l'Observatoire national des entrées dans la vie active (ONEVA) réalisées par le CEREQ, deux volets d'études sont mis en oeuvre au niveau de l'Ile de France: (1) le premier porte sur le recueil d'information statistique concernant les formations technologiques de niveau V, IV, III et l'apprentissage grâce à la mise en perspective des enquêtes rétrospectives décrivant le fonctionnement du marché du travail des débutants et des enquêtes de cheminement interrogeant périodiquement des cohortes d'anciens élèves; (2) le deuxième porte sur l'analyse de l'insertion des étudiants en droit et sciences économiques grâce à deux enquêtes. Une comparaison systématique des situations Paris-Province est menée.

Résultats: Il existe des différences significatives et favorables aux parisiens quant à la nature de l'insertion, cette différenciation apparaissant aussi bien à l'examen des taux de chômage qu'à celle de la nature des emplois occupés.

Publ: Kerleau, M. & Pasqualini, Esther. Données régionales relatives à l'entrée dans la vie active des jeunes issus de l'enseignement technique. Mai 1984, document établi pour le recteur de l'académie de Paris (Groupe de travail pour l'évolution des enseignements technologiques).

Corbet, G. & Randon de Grollier, O. Analyse de la relation formation-emploi. Enquête d'insertion professionnelle des diplômés de maîtrise de sciences économiques de l'Université de Paris I. Université de Paris I: Mémoire pour le DEA d'économie du travail et de ressources humaines, novembre 1988.

13521 Analyse des effets induits par un dispositif de réapprentissage destiné aux salariés peu qualifiés.

FRA   1993

Research Date(s): 1990-1992

Silvestre, Jean-Jacques; Brochier, Damien; Froment, Jean-Pierre; Coppi, Marylène.

Sup: Arliaud, Michel.

Inst: Ministère de la recherche, CNRS UPR/7511, Laboratoire d'économie et de sociologie du travail, 35 av. Jules Ferry, 13626 Aix-en-Provence Cedex, France.

occupational qualification; training centre; social integration; occupational integration; retraining; career change

qualification professionnelle; centre de formation; intégration sociale; intégration professionnelle; recyclage; changement de carrière

PROJECT DESCRIPTION

Objectifs: Il s'agit d'analyser en quoi le dispositif requalification est porteur d'une réduction du risque d'exclusion professionnelle et sociale, à partir de deux éléments importants: (1) le dispositif intervient dans une organisation structurée; (2) le dispositif prend en compte la socialisation, la trajectoire individuelle, la position dans l'organisation, les représentations qu'en ont les employeurs. On analyse également l'incidence de ces facteurs sur les rapports des personnes concernées à la compétence, à l'apprentissage, à l'organisation. On prend en compte le fait que le dispositif requalification est une relation.

Méthodologie: Observations sur le terrain des entreprises du secteur industriel qui ont mis en place le dispositif requalification; entretiens.

13522 Analyse des formations en alternance: apprentissage et contrats de qualification.

FRA   1993

Research Date(s): 1984-

Pasqualini, Esther; Vernières, Michel.

Inst: Université de Paris I, UFR Analyse et politique économiques, CNRS URA/941 et GDR/996, Laboratoire d'économie sociale-Equipe Emploi, Formation, Développement, 90 rue de Tolbiac, 75634 Paris Cedex 13, France.

Fin: Région Ile de France.

youth employment; alternating training; occupational integration; vocational training

emploi des jeunes; formation alternée; intégration professionnelle; formation professionnelle

PROJECT DESCRIPTION

Objectifs: Les contrats de qualifications créés en 1982 par le dispositif de la formation en alternance destiné aux 16-18 ans occupent une part croissante dans le dispositif d'insertion professionnelle des jeunes comme l'avaient mis en évidence les enquêtes menées en mars 1983 et mars 1988 auprès d'anciens apprentis ayant quitté leur Centre de formation d'apprentis. L'étude menée actuellement conjointement par le CEREQ, le LES, l'IRED (Rouen), le LEST (Aix en Provence) et le GREE (Nancy) sur les contrats de qualification a pour principaux objectifs: l'analyse quantitative et qualitative des contenus, des durées, des niveaux, des modalités d'organisation (tuteurs) et de reconnaissance (diplôme, homologation ...) des formations incluses dans les contrats de qualification; l'étude s'attache également à révéler les phénomènes de complémentarité et de substitution avec les autres types de formation en alternance, l'apprentissage en particulier.

Publ: Kerleau, Monique & Pasqualini, Esther. Aspects de l'insertion professionnelle des anciens apprentis en région Ile de France. Etude réalisée à la demande de la Région Ile de France, 1984.

Coutinet, N. & Pasqualini, Esther. Aspects de l'insertion professionnelle des anciens apprentis en région Ile de France. Etude réalisée à la demande de la Région Ile de France, 1989.

Vernières, Michel. L'apprentissage: forme du passé ou de l'avenir. In: L'évolution des formes d'emploi. Paris: La Documentation française, 1989, pp. 342-350.

13523 Analyse qualitative des procédures de mise en oeuvre des contrats de qualification au niveau local.

FRA   1993

Research Date(s): 1989-1990

Brochier, Damien; Lamanthe, Annie.

Inst: Ministère de la recherche, CNRS UPR/7511, Laboratoire d'économie et de sociologie du travail, 35 av. Jules Ferry, 13626 Aix-en-Provence Cedex, France.

Fin: Centre d'études et de recherches sur les qualifications.

occupational qualification; training-employment contract; youth employment; local community; occupational integration

qualification professionnelle; contrat emploi-formation; emploi des jeunes; collectivité locale; intégration professionnelle

PROJECT DESCRIPTION

Objectifs: Le développement quantitatif du contrat de qualification, comme mesure d'insertion professionnelle des jeunes (plus de 125000 jeunes sous contrat début 1990) conduit à constater que cette mesure est de plus en plus utilisée par les entreprises. En s'appuyant sur les recherches menées autour du concept de transition professionnelle, la recherche se donne pour objectif de s'interroger sur les effets de cette mesure sur l'évolution de la relation formation-emploi au niveau local.

Méthodologie: L'étude est issue d'une collaboration d'un an et demi avec le réseau des missions locales pour l'insertion professionnelle sociale des jeunes des régions Provence Alpes Côte d'Azur. Une série de rencontres et d'échanges avec des partenaires publics et privés (organismes agréés, directions du travail, formateurs...) sur deux zones précises (Avignon et La Seyne sur mer) a permis de cerner les pratiques et les stratégies des acteurs locaux dans la perspective de mise en oeuvre de cette mesure.

Résultats: Le développement du contrat de qualification se situe aujourd'hui au coeur de l'enjeu d'un repositionnement de la relation formation-emploi sur des bases décentralisées et partenariales. L'analyse de ses principales caractéristiques permet en particulier de faire émerger le rôle-clé joué au niveau local par les acteurs institutionnels intermédiaires agissant à l'interaction des jeunes et des entreprises. Grâce à la régulation conjointe de ces acteurs, le dispositif semble évoluer progressivement d'une stricte préoccupation pour l'emploi vers des logiques d'offre de travail incluant une dimension de formation qualifiante.

Publ: Brochier, Damien & Lamanthe, Annie. *La mise en oeuvre des formations en alternance des jeunes au niveau local: le cas du contrat de qualification dans la région Provence Alpes Côte d'Azur.* Aix en Provence: LEST, 1990, 49p.

Lamanthe, Annie. *Les contrats de qualification sur les zones d'intervention des missions locales d'Avignon (Vaucluse) et de La Seyne sur Mer (Var).* Aix en Provence: LEST (Rapport d'étude pour les missions locales), 1990, 74p.

13524 Arbeidsmarktinformatie en arbeidsmarktdynamiek. (Labour market information and labour market dynamics.)
NLD 1993
Research Date(s): 1992-1996
Borghans, L.
Sup: Heijke, J.A.M.
Inst: ROA Researchcentrum voor Onderwijs en Arbeidsmarkt, Universiteit Limburg (Research Centre for Education and the Labour Market, University of Limburg), P.O. Box 616, 6200 MD Maastricht, Netherlands.
labour market; choice of studies; expectancy; employment opportunities; vocational information; information dissemination; university studies
marché du travail; choix des études; attente; chances d'obtenir un emploi; information professionnelle; diffusion de l'information; études universitaires
PROJECT DESCRIPTION
This Ph.D. research project adopts a theoretical economic perspective in investigating the extent to which the labour market will change as a result of publicizing labour market forecasts. One of the aims of the research is to offer a new understanding of the manner in which the information system can function well. The research comprises theoretical as well as empirical analyses.

In order to examine the extent to which the educational choices of students change as a result of labour market forecasts, a model has been constructed in which choice behaviour is dependent on the quality of the available forecasts. A "welfare economics" analysis of the effects of such a change has also been carried out. Beginning with a base model, the project has examined the results of students with diverse labour market expectations, the relationship between specialized and more general training types, and other topics.

Publ: Borghans, L. *Errors in Rational Expectations Matter*, ROA-RM-1992/4E (ISBN 90-5321-089-X).
Borghans, L. *Histo-topographic Map of Dutch University Studies*, ROA-W-1992/5E (ISBN 90-5321-086-5).

13525 Arbeidsmarktmonitor voor het hoger beroepsonderwijs. (Labour market monitor for higher vocational education.)
NLD 1993
Research Date(s): 1991-
Velden, R.K.W. van de; Lodder, B.J.H.; Loo, P.J.E. van de; Ramaekers, G.W.M.
Inst: ROA Researchcentrum voor Onderwijs en Arbeidsmarkt, Universiteit Limburg (Research Centre for Education and the Labour Market, University of Limburg), P.O. Box 616, 6200 MD Maastricht, Netherlands.
Fin: Higher Vocational Education Council.
employment opportunities; graduate; labour market; career
chances d'obtenir un emploi; étudiant diplômé; marché du travail; carrière
PROJECT DESCRIPTION
A labour market monitor was developed for all sectors of Higher Vocational Education (except Higher Agricultural Education), under a contract from the Higher Vocational Education Council. The object of this monitor is to generate every year reliable, national data on the market position of graduates from Higher Vocational Education and its fit with professional practice, by means of a partly sector-specific basic questionnaire.

In the autumn of 1991 16,000 graduates of the 1989/1990 academic year were surveyed. In the last months of 1992 the basic questionnaire was sent to more than 20,000 graduates of the 1990/1991 academic year.

The Service Bureau for School-leavers' Information takes care of the data processing and the drafting of separate reports for each participating school. ROA is charged with the analyses and reports on the national level and the coordination and evaluation of the project.

Publ: Loo, P.J.E. van de; et al. *De arbeidsmarktpositie van afgestudeerden van het hoger beroepsonderwijs, 1991* (The labour market position of graduates of Higher Vocational Education, 1991), Higher Vocational Education Council (HBO-Raad), The Hague, 1992.

13526 Arbeidsmarktscanner Universiteit Limburg. (Labour market scanner for the University of Limburg.)
NLD 1993
Research Date(s): 1989-1991
Heijke, J.A.M.; Ramaekers, G.W.M.
Inst: ROA Researchcentrum voor Onderwijs en Arbeidsmarkt, Universiteit Limburg (Research Centre for Education and the Labour Market, University of Limburg), P.O. Box 616, 6200 MD Maastricht, Netherlands.
employment opportunities; graduate; career; labour market; survey
chances d'obtenir un emploi; étudiant diplômé; carrière; marché du travail; enquête
PROJECT DESCRIPTION
ROA has set up a system for periodic labour market research among graduates of the University of Limburg. The object of the monitoring system is to obtain information on the labour market position and careers of graduates available at regular intervals.

The core of the project is an annual standard questionnaire through which a file of basic data on graduates and their position on the labour market is produced and up-dated. Less frequently, more specific additional questions investigate the correspondence of education with the demands which graduates encounter in professional practice.

In 1990 graduates from four previous years, 1986 up to 1989, were questioned for the first time in a mail survey. In 1991 it was decided to continue the project for at least three more years.

Publ: *Arbeidsmarktscanner Rijksuniversiteit Limburg; afgestudeerden 1986-1989* (Labour market scanner of graduates of the University of Limburg 1986-1989), ROA-R-1991/6.

13527 Arbeidsmarktscanner Universiteit Limburg. (Labour market scanner for the University of Limburg.)
NLD 1993
Research Date(s): 1989-
Ramaekers, G.W.M.; Heijke, J.A.M.; Velden, R.K.W. van .der.
Inst: ROA Researchcentrum voor Onderwijs en Arbeidsmarkt, Universiteit Limburg (Research Centre for Education and the Labour Market, University of Limburg), P.O. Box 616, 6200 MD Maastricht, Netherlands.
employment opportunities; graduate; career; labour market; survey
chances d'obtenir un emploi; étudiant diplômé; carrière; marché du travail; enquête
PROJECT DESCRIPTION
ROA has set up a system for monitoring the labour market position and careers of graduates of the University of Limburg. The information is obtained annually through two postal questionnaires. The first is the basic questionnaire, used to survey all of the previous year's students approximately one year after their graduation. The second is the annual questionnaire, which is sent each year as a follow-up to the basic questionnaire. With this form respondents can report changes in their labour market position over the past year, for instance a change of jobs.

The first application of the labour market scanner related to students who graduated in the years 1986 to 1989. As of 1992, the previous year's graduates are surveyed each year for the first time about one year after graduation, and information on earlier students is updated from year to year. The Office of Student Affairs of the University handles the administrative aspects of the data collection, while ROA is responsible for the research methodology and contents of the project.

Publ: Heijke, J.A.M. & Ramaekers, G.W.M. *Labour Market Position of University of Limburg Graduates*, ROA-RM-1992/2E (Paper for the European Symposium on Labour Market Developments, held 21st-22nd May 1992 at the University of Warwick) (ISBN 90-5321-082-2).
Heijke, J.A.M.; et al. De arbeidsmarktpositie van afgestudeerden van de Rijksuniversiteit Limburg 1986-1989, op basis van de arbeidsmarktscanner (The labour market position of graduates of the University of Limburg 1986-1989, on the basis of the labour market scanner). In: *Tijdschrift voor Hoger Onderwijs*, Vol. 10, no. 3, 1992, pp. 168-188.

13528 Arbeidsmarktscanner voor de sector sociaal werk. (Labour market scanner for the social work sector.)
NLD 1993
Research Date(s): 1991-1992
Loo, P.J.E. van de; Velden, R.K.W. van der.
Inst: ROA Researchcentrum voor Onderwijs en Arbeidsmarkt, Universiteit Limburg (Research Centre for Education and the Labour Market, University of Limburg), P.O. Box 616, 6200 MD Maastricht, Netherlands.
Fin: Groningen Education-Employment Liaison Centre.
employment opportunities; graduate; social work; labour market
chances d'obtenir un emploi; étudiant diplômé; travail social; marché du travail
PROJECT DESCRIPTION
As part of the monitoring system for Higher Social Work Education, ROA is in charge of a labour market scanner for the welfare sector. By means of this scanner those working in practical and educational fields can be kept up to date with relevant labour market developments. The labour market scanner fits in with the Higher Vocational Education monitor developed for the Higher Vocational Education Council, as well as with the labour market

scanner used at the University of Limburg under a contract from the University's Board of Governors.

The Higher Social Work Scanner contains a number of elements. In monitoring the supply side, ROA has developed a nationally applicable basic questionnaire and an annual follow-up card. These enable the labour market position and professional careers of graduates of Higher Social Work Education to be mapped. The graduates will be questioned around one year after their graduation by means of the basic questionnaire and after that every year, by means of the annual card with which they can report any changes. To measure the demand side, ROA is compiling a questionnaire for employers in the field. Apart from a number of items of quantitative data on the staff structure of the organization, this questionnaire will have questions on the expected changes in staff structure.

13529 Arbeidsmarktscanner voor het hoger sociaal-agogisch onderwijs. (Labour market scanner for the social work sector.)
NLD   1993
Research Date(s): 1991-1993
Velden, R.K.W. van der; Dekker, R.J.P.; Loo, P.J.E. van de.
Inst: ROA Researchcentrum voor Onderwijs en Arbeidsmarkt, Universiteit Limburg (Research Centre for Education and the Labour Market, University of Limburg), P.O. Box 616, 6200 MD Maastricht, Netherlands.
Fin: Groningen Education-Employment Liaison Centre.
employment opportunities; graduate; career; labour market; survey; social work
chances d'obtenir un emploi; étudiant diplômé; carrière; marché du travail; enquête; travail social
PROJECT DESCRIPTION

As part of the monitoring system for the social-work sector, ROA is in charge of developing a labour market scanner. With the help of this scanner, practitioners and educators can be kept up-to-date on relevant labour market developments.

The labour market scanner contains a number of elements. To monitor the supply side, ROA has developed a nationally applicable basic questionnaire to map the labour market position of graduates of Higher Socio-cultural Education one year after graduation and an annual follow-up card to report any changes in their professional careers.

To measure the demand side, ROA has conducted a panel survey among employers in the public health and welfare sector in the North of the Netherlands. Apart from a number of items on developments in the staff structure of the organization, the employers were questioned on the changes expected in the staffing structure and the training facilities within and outside the organization.

The project will be rounded off with the publication of a report on the survey among the graduates of Higher Socio-cultural Education, a report on the results of the panel survey, an explanation of the instruments of this labour market scanner in a handbook, and a conference.

Publ: Loo, P.J.E. van de; et al. *De arbeidsmarktpositie van afgestudeerden van het hoger sociaal-agogisch onderwijs, 1991* (The labour market position of graduates of Higher Socio-Cultural Education, 1991), Higher Vocational Education Council (HBO-Raad), The Hague, 1992 (ISBN 90-6390-157-7).

13530 Arbeidsmarktvoorlichting en dynamiek op de arbeidsmarkt. (Labour market information and labour market dynamics.)
NLD   1993
Research Date(s): 1991-
Borghans, L.
Sup: Heijke, J.A.M.
Inst: ROA Researchcentrum voor Onderwijs en Arbeidsmarkt, Universiteit Limburg (Research Centre for Education and the Labour Market, University of Limburg), P.O. Box 616, 6200 Maastricht, Netherlands.
labour market; forecasting; choice of studies; information system
marché du travail; prévision; choix des études; système d'information
PROJECT DESCRIPTION

This doctoral research project adopts a theoretical economic perspective in investigating the extent to which the labour market will change as a result of making labour market forecasts public. One of the objects of this research is to offer a new understanding of the manner in which the information system can function well. The research comprises theoretical as well as empirical analyses.

In order to examine the extent to which the choices of students change as a result of labour market forecasts, a model has been constructed in which students' "choice behaviour" is dependent on the quality of the available forecasts. A "welfare economics" analysis of the effects of such a change has been carried out. Beginning with a base model, the project has examined the results of students with diverse labour market expectations, the relationship between specialized and more general training varieties, and other topics.

Publ: *The value of Public Labour market Information: The Case of Dispersed Predictions*, ROA-RM-1991/2E.
Occupational Choice: The Market of Primary School Teachers, ROA-RM-1991/3E.
The Cobweb Theorem: A Rational Interpretation, ROA-RM-1991/7E.

(A full list can be obtained from the research institute).

13531 Arbeidsmarktvooruitzichten en opleidingsaanbod in de provincie Limburg. (Labour market prospects and training possibilities in the province of Limburg.)
NLD   1994
Research Date(s): 1991
Berendsen, H.; Velden, R.K.W. van der.
Fin: National Civil Pension Fund (ABP).
labour market; forecasting; employment opportunities; training supply
marché du travail; prévision; chances d'obtenir un emploi; offre de formation
PROJECT DESCRIPTION

The study was conducted in response to a request by the National Civil Pension Fund (ABP) for information on expected changes in the labour market for categories of occupations and occupational positions at MBO (senior secondary vocational education) and HBO (higher vocational education) levels in the province of Limburg. Apart from that, the ABP asked for a survey of the training opportunities available for those categories with favourable labour market prospects.

ROA conducted the two-phase study. In the first phase, the expected labour market situation in the province of Limburg was outlined on the basis of a literature survey and interviews with regional labour market experts. In the second phase a selection was made from the occupational and job categories with good prospects, for which an overview of the training opportunities was then drawn up, focusing especially on part-time training.

13532 Arbeitsmarktentwicklung und Hauptschulabschluss. (Development in the labour market and in the qualifications of general secondary school-leavers.)
DEU   1993
Research Date(s): 1991-1993
Sandner, S.; Conrad, M.
Sup: Sandner, H.
Inst: Institut fuer angewandte paedagogische Forschung e.V., Heinrich-Besenstr. 8, D-3016 Seelze 6.
school leaving; labour market; job requirements; level of qualification; secondary education
fin de scolarité; marché du travail; qualification requise pour l'emploi; niveau de qualification; enseignement secondaire
PROJECT DESCRIPTION

Inhalt: Es soll ermittelt werden, ob die vorhandenen Qualifikationsstrukturen in der Hauptschule ausreichen, um der Arbeitsmarktentwicklung und dem Qualifikationsbedarf in den traditionellen beruflichen Aufnahmefeldern von Hauptschuelern gerecht zu werden. Dazu soll mit Hilfe von Vergleichsstudien untersucht werden, ob die Qualifikationsstruktur und die Anforderungsstruktur kompatibel sind oder ob notwendige Umstrukturierungen stattfinden muessen. Ferner werden die Auswirkungen politischer Schul- und Abschlussvorstellungen auf die Entwicklung der Schuelerzahlen in der Hauptschule untersucht.

Vorgehensweise: Sekundaeranalysen; Expertengespraeche; Auswertung von Bildungs- und Ausbildungsstatistik; systematischer Vergleich von Richtlinien einzelner Faecher und Qualifikationsanforderungen in der Wirtschaft und im Handwerk.

13533 Arbeitsmarktperspektiven fuer Absolventinnnen des Lehramtes der beruflichen Fachrichtung Sozialpaedagogik, Sekundarstufe II, in NRW und BRD. (Job prospects of female graduates from teacher education courses in social pedagogics, upper-level secondary education, in North Rhine-Westphalia and the Federal Republic of Germany.)
DEU   1993
Research Date(s): 1990-1992
Beher, K.; Knauer, D.
Sup: Rauschenbach, T.
Inst: Universitaet Dortmund, FB Erziehungswissenschaften und Biologie, Institut fuer Sozialpaedagogik, Erwachsenenbildung und Paedagogik der fruehen Kindheit, Rheinlanddamm 199, D-4600 Dortmund 1.
Fin: Bundesanstalt fuer Arbeit.
labour market; teacher; employment opportunities; sciences of education; secondary education
marché du travail; enseignant; chances d'obtenir un emploi; sciences de l'éducation; enseignement secondaire
PROJECT DESCRIPTION

Inhalt: Nach wie vor unbefriedigend und ungeklaert ist die Situation des hauptamtlich beschaeftigten Lehrpersonals an den sozialpaedagogischen Fach- und Berufsfachschulen zur Ausbildung von Kinderpflegerinnen und Erzieherinnen. Das Projekt erarbeitet - vor dem Hintergrund, dass die Universitaet Dortmund als einzige Hochschule des Landes Nordrhein-Westfalen einen eigenen Lehramtsstudiengang "Berufliche Fachrichtung Sozialpaedagogik" anbietet -anhand eigener empirischer Studien und Sekundaeranalysen Datenmaterial und verschiedene Aspekte dieses Themas: durch eine Absolventinnenbefragung zum beruflichen Verbleib, durch eine Schulleiterinnenbefragung der sozialpaedagogischen Fach- und

Berufsfachschulen sowie durch eine Befragung zum Fachpersonal in Kindertageseinrichtungen in den 20 groessten Staedten der Bundesrepublik Deutschland.

Geographischer Raum: Dortmund, Nordrhein-Westfalen.

13534 Arbeitsplatznahe Qualifizierung von un- und angelernten Arbeitskraeften in kleinen und mittleren Betrieben unter Einbezug computergestuetzter Lernmedien. (Job-based training for unskilled and semi-skilled workers in small and medium-sized companies using computer-aided resources.)
DEU 1993
Research Date(s): 1991-1995
Schmidt, H.
Sup: Severing, E.
Inst: Berufliche Fortbildungszentren der Bayerischen Arbeitgeberverbaende e.V., Zentralabt. Forschung und Entwicklung, Moltkestr. 7, D-8500 Nuernberg 80.
Fin: Bundesinstitut fuer Berufsbildung.
qualification; didactic use of computer; enterprise; unqualified young people; model construction; learning; unskilled worker; small and medium entreprise
qualification; usage didactique de l'ordinateur; entreprise; jeune sans qualification; construction de modèle; acquisition de connaissances; travailleur non-qualifié; petite ou moyenne entreprise
PROJECT DESCRIPTION
Inhalt: Das Modellvorhaben entwickelt und erprobt neue organisatorische, methodische und inhaltliche Weiterbildungsformen von An- und Ungelernten zu kompetenten Fachkraeften. Um den besonderen Bedingungen in kleinen und mittleren Betrieben gerecht zu werden, strebt das Projekt die Realisierung von Konzepten des arbeitsplatznahen Lernens, eine Verschraenkung von Arbeiten und Lernen und die Gestaltung einer aktiven Lernumwelt an. Insbesondere sollen neue Erkenntnisse zum Einsatz von computeruntersteutzten Lernmodellen in der An- und Ungelerntenqualifikation gewonnen werden.
Vorgehensweise: Modellvorhaben in 3-5 KMU in Bayern; Aktionsforschung; qualitative und quantitative Untersuchungen zum Bereich "Weiterbildung von Un- und Angelernten".
Datengewinnung: Nicht-standardisiertes Interview (Stichprobe: ca. 70; An- und Ungelernte in kleinen und mittleren Betrieben). Gruppendiskussion (dito). Befragung (Stichprobe: 70; An- und Ungelernte in kleinen und mittleren Betrieben. Fragebogen zur Leistungsmotivation).

13535 Ausbildung, berufliche Integration und Weiterqualifizierung von Berufsanfaengern. (Training, occupational integration and further qualification of entry workers.)
DEU 1993
Research Date(s): 1991-1996
Boenisch, I.; Feher, K.; Feller, G.; Hoecke, G.; Schoengen, K.; Schulte, B.
Sup: Herget, H.
Inst: Bundesinstitut fuer Berufsbildung, Fehrbelliner Platz 3, D-1000 Berlin 31.
occupational integration; vocational training; further training; initial employment
intégration professionnelle; formation professionnelle; formation complémentaire; premier emploi
PROJECT DESCRIPTION
Inhalt: Ziele des Projekts sind: (1) Eine empirische Basis zu schaffen, die einen Zusammenhang von der ersten ueber die zweite Schwelle bis zu den ersten fuenf Berufsjahren herstellt. Erreicht wird dies ueber eine Panelstudie, die aktuelle und repraesentative Daten ueber die Absolventen 1990 - 1992 bereitstellt und zwar zum Prozess des Uebergangs an der zweiten Schwelle; zum gesamten beruflichen Verlauf und der weiteren Qualifizierung bis zu fuenf Jahre nach der Lehre (sowie einer Vergleichsgruppe von Ausbildungsabbrechern); zu Faktoren, die Verlauf und Erfolg ihres Berufsweges und ihr Weiterbildungsverhalten erklaeren. (2) Eine umfassende Darstellung von Ausbildung und beruflicher Integration aus der Sicht der Absolventen fuer die neugeordneten industriellen Metall- und Elektroberufe und (3) strukturelle Veraenderungen im Uebergang und im Berufsverlauf ermitteln (Zeitvergleich mit frueherem BIBB-Absolventenpanel). Forschungshypothese ist, dass wirtschaftliche und gesellschaftliche Rahmenbedingungen und der technisch-arbeitsorganisatorische Wandel die Verwertbarkeit beruflicher Erstqualifikation und die berufliche Integration der Berufsanfaenger bestimmen. Wie erfolgreich der einzelne dabei ist, haengt zunehmend von den Bedingungen beim Berufsstart ab, wie er sich beruflich bewaehrt und ob er sich durch Weiterbildung auf neue Qualifikationserfordernisse einstellen kann. Ueberpruefen lassen sich die qualifikatorischen Auswirkungen des Wandels und die Prozesse der Eingliederung sowie die Verwertung und Erweiterung der Qualifikation, indem man ihre Folgen kontinuierlich in den Berufsverlaeufen von Absolventen erfasst und untersucht. Die Kenntnis der Veraenderungen und das darauf bezogene Verhalten der Absolventen ist Grundlage fuer eine gezielte Berufsbildungspolitik.
Vorgehensweise: Laengsschnittuntersuchung als Panelstudie mit fuenf Befragungsrunden, ueberwiegend als schriftlich-postalische Befragung;

Termine: 1988/1989-1989/1990-1991-1993-1995; zwei Stichproben: (1) Repraesentativ - S. fuer Ausbildungsbeginner der Jahre 1987 bis 1989; (2) disproportionale S. von Ausbildungsbeginnern 1987-1989 industrielle Metall- und Elektroberufe.
Datengewinnung: Gruppendiskussion (Teilnehmerkreise; Auswahlverfahren: Quota). Expertengespraech (Befragungsteilnehmer, Lehrer, Ausbilder, Ausbildungsleiter, Verbaende). Befragung (Lehrerbeginner der Jahre 1987-1989, neu geordneter industrieller Metall- und Elektroberufe). Sekundaeranalyse (amtliche Statistik).

Publ: Herget, Hermann. Beitraege zu den: *Berufsbildungsberichten*, 1990, S. 46 ff; 1991, S. 46-49; 1992, Kapitel 3.3 und 4.3.1.
Feller, Gisela & Herget, Hermann. *Ausbildung - Abbrecher - Absichten nach der Lehre: Das BIBB-Lehrlingspanel 1987-1989.* (Berichte zur beruflichen Bildung) Berlin u. Bonn: BIBB.

13536 Baccalauréats professionnels (Bac-Pro): description d'une première promotion.
FRA 1993
Research Date(s): 1987-
Dauty, Françoise; Fourcade, Bernard.
Inst: Université de Toulouse I, UFR Sciences économiques, CNRS URA/921 et GDR/996, Centre d'études juridiques et économiques de l'emploi, Place Anatole France, 31042 Toulouse Cedex, France.
employment opportunities; training-employment relationship; upper secondary; vocational education; final examination; branch of study; occupational integration; certificate
chances d'obtenir un emploi; relation formation-emploi; secondaire deuxième cycle; enseignement professionnel; examen de sortie; filière d'études; intégration professionnelle; diplôme
PROJECT DESCRIPTION
Objectifs: Le système éducatif a un rôle de formation et de différenciation des jeunes, son évolution est liée à celle des emplois et des qualifications. Dans cette double optique, on étudie les conséquences des transformations récentes de l'enseignement technique et professionnel notamment l'arrivée de nouveaux diplômés sur le marché du travail et la place d'une nouvelle filière de formation dans le système éducatif. Cette recherche s'appuie sur une étude relative aux baccalauréats professionnels.
Méthodologie: Lancement d'une enquête auprès de la première cohorte d'élèves terminant leur cycle de formation dans trois régions (Midi-Pyrénées, Aquitaine, Rhône-Alpes). Une réinterrogation des mêmes individus est effectuée 18 mois plus tard.
Résultats: La première interrogation auprès de 100 personnes fait ressortir que la majorité des jeunes est convaincue, aux termes de ces études, que les chances de trouver un emploi et de réussir dans la vie professionnelle sont très dépendantes du niveau de diplôme obtenu, d'où le désir de poursuivre jusqu'au Brevet de technicien supérieur. Modalités de recherche d'emploi et aspirations professionnelles sont également étudiées. Il apparaît que (1) le Bac-Pro est au coeur d'un processus de transformation de l'enseignement technique et professionnel car il implique à terme la disparition des anciennes filières courtes, (2) avec le Bac-Pro on assiste à une nouvelle façon de gérer les relations formation-emploi dans la mesure où désormais les emplois visés sont des cibles mouvantes et où les instances de concertation entre acteurs jouent un rôle accru d'ajustement entre formations et emplois.

Publ: Dauty, Françoise & Fourcade, Bernard. Le baccalauréat professionnel: une nouvelle étape de l'évolution du système éducatif. Université de Toulouse II: CEJEE, 1989, note n° 87.

13537 Bedarf an Technikern und Naturwissenschaftern in Westoesterreich. (The demand for engineers and scientists in Western Austria.)
AUT 1993
Research Date(s): 1992
Schedler, Klaus; Loibl, Elisabeth.
Inst: Institut fuer Bildungsforschung der Wirtschaft, Rainergasse 38, A-1050 Wien.
Fin: Bundesministerium fuer Wissenschaft und Forschung.
manpower need; scientific personnel; engineer; regional development
besoin de main-d'oeuvre; personnel scientifique; ingénieur; développement régional
PROJECT DESCRIPTION
Untersucht wird in diesem Bericht das regionale Absolventenangebot (in Tirol, Vorarlberg und Salzburg) mit technisch-naturwissenschaftlicher Berufsvorbildung der letzten zehn Jahre sowie die Struktur der Beschaeftigungslage von Technikern und Naturwissenschaftern. Auf diesen Analysen beruht eine Prognose ueber den kuenftigen Bedarf der Wirtschaft an Absolventen der betreffenden - ausgewaehlten - Studienrichtungen unter besonderer Beruecksichtigung der regionalen Besonderheiten des Arbeitsmarktes in Westoesterreich.

Es werden Experteninterviews, Fragebogenerhebungen und sekundaerstatistische Analysen durchgefuehrt.

13538 Berufliche Lebensplaene sozial deprivierter Jugendlicher (im Vergleich alte - neue Bundeslaender). (Occupational plans of socially deprived young people (comparison of old and new German states).)
DEU 1993
Research Date(s): 1991-1992
Woelfel, I.
Inst: Universitaet Greifswald, Abt. Neubrandenburg, Institut fuer Erziehungswissenschaften, Brodaer Str. 2, O-2000 Neubrandenburg.
Fin: Alexander von Humboldt-Stiftung.
occupational integration; Germany - Federal Republic; German DR; adolescent; vocational preparation; occupational aspiration; socially handicapped
intégration professionnelle; Allemagne RFA; Allemagne RDA; adolescent; initiation à la profession; aspirations professionnelles; handicapé social
PROJECT DESCRIPTION
Inhalt: In der ehemaligen DDR bestanden fuer sozial deprivierte Jugendliche relativ guenstige Bedingungen bei der Integration in den Arbeitsprozess, da aufgrund der spezifischen Produktionsformen und Versorgungssituation eine grosse Nachfrage nach niedrig qualifizierten Arbeitskraeften bestand. Fuer die gesellschaftlichen Veraenderungen im Prozess der deutschen Einheit sind diese Sozialisationserfahrungen in der sozialen Arbeit unbedingt zu beruecksichtigen, um Konfliktlagen adressatengerecht begegnen zu koennen. Eine empirische Vergleichsstudie bei randomisierten Stichproben (Jugendliche in berufsvorbereitenden Massnahmen/ in ausbildungsbegleitenden Hilfen/in Heimen) soll die Gemeinsamkeiten und Unterschiede bei Jugendlichen mit aehnlicher Lebenslage aber sehr unterschiedlicher Sozialisation (Alt-BRD - DDR) abbilden. Besondere Beruecksichtigung finden geschlechtsspezifische Besonderheiten.
Geographischer Raum: Niedersachsen - Mecklenburg/Vorpommern.
Vorgehensweise: Erhebung der Daten ueber strukturierte Interviews und drei standardisierte Verfahren (Berufsinteressentest, Problemfragebogen, Motivtest nach Mullet). Untersuchungsdesign: Querschnittserhebung; retrospektive Daten; qualitative Forschung.
Datengewinnung: Nicht-standardisiertes Interview (Stichprobe: 2x100; Jugendliche in abH; Auswahlverfahren: Quota. Stichprobe: 2x30; Jugendliche in berufsvorbereitenden Massnahmen; Auswahlverfahren: Quota. Stichprobe: 2x20; Jugendliche in Heimen -elternlos bzw. familiengeloest-; Auswahlverfahren: Quota). Psychologischer Test (dito). Primaererhebung: Feldarbeit von Mitarbeitern des Projektes durchgefuehrt.
Auswertung: Clusteranalyse; Diskriminanzanalyse; in erster Linie qualitative Auswertung. Datenaufbereitung: Datenedition (z.B. Aufbau von Datenbanken).

13539 Beruflicher Werdegang von DiplomsportlehrerInnen. (Professional development of graduate sports teachers.)
DEU 1993
Research Date(s): 1991-1993
Hartmann-Tews, I.; Mrazek, J.
Inst: Deutsche Sporthochschule Koeln, FB 01 Erziehungs-, Geistes- und Sozialwissenschaften, Institut fuer Sportsoziologie, FG Freizeitpaedagogik, Carl-Diem-Weg 6, D-5000 Koeln 41.
career; teacher; sport; job requirements; occupational qualification; unemployment; sex difference
carrière; enseignant; sport; qualification requise pour l'emploi; qualification professionnelle; chômage; différence de sexe
PROJECT DESCRIPTION
Inhalt: Ausgangspunkt der Studie sind die veraenderten Angebots- und Nachfragestrukturen im Sport (Stichwort Dienstleistungsmarkt) und damit verbundene Qualifikationsforderungen der Absolventen von Sportstudiengaengen. Zentrale Aspekte der Untersuchung sind: Struktur und Anforderung von Berufsfeldern, Relevanz der Studieninhalte fuer den Beruf, Stellenwert von Arbeitsbeschaffungsmassnahmen, Gruende fuer und Strategien gegen Arbeitslosigkeit. Aus analytischer Perspektive sind vor allem Merkmale geschlechtsspezifischer Differenzierung interessant.
Vorgehensweise: Untersuchungsdesign: Querschnittserhebung.
Datengewinnung: Postalische Befragung (Vollerhebung aller AbsolventInnen der DSHS der Abschlussjahrgaenge 1986-1990; Auswahlverfahren: total). Primaererhebung: Feldarbeit von Mitarbeitern des Projektes durchgefuehrt.
Auswertung: Faktorenanalyse; Varianzanalyse.

13540 Berufs- und Arbeitssituation von Frauen in der ehemaligen DDR (Berufliche Weiterbildung fuer Frauen in den neuen Bundeslaendern). (The employment situation of women in the former GDR (further vocational training for women in the new German states).)
DEU 1993
Research Date(s): 1990-1992
Deutschmann-Temel, D.; Herget, C.; Puhlmann, A.; Panzig, C.; Engel, H.; Voth, H.
Sup: Gensior, S.
Inst: Berliner Institut fuer Sozialforschung und sozialwissenschaftliche Praxis e.V., Pfalzburger Strasse 72, D-1000 Berlin 15.
Fin: Institution; Bundesinstitut fuer Berufsbildung; Bundesministerium fuer Bildung und Wissenschaft.

women's work; German DR; level of qualification; employment opportunities; women's employment; occupational qualification; further training; training-employment relationship
travail des femmes; Allemagne RDA; niveau de qualification; chances d'obtenir un emploi; emploi des femmes; qualification professionnelle; formation complémentaire; relation formation-emploi
PROJECT DESCRIPTION
Inhalt: Um die Berufs-, Arbeits- und Beschaeftigungssituation von Frauen in Berufen unterhalb akademischer Abschluesse in den neuen Bundeslaendern und Ost-Berlin zu erfassen, wurde eine Repraesentativbefragung in Betrieben und bei dort Beschaeftigten vorgenommen. Vertiefend wurden zusaetzlich 40 Interviews gefuehrt. Die Untersuchung fand im Zeitraum von Oktober-Dezember 1990 statt. Auf Basis einer geschichteten Stichprobe wurden an 115 Betriebe in 16 Branchen Betriebs- und Personenfragebogen (1500) versandt. 86 Betriebe (rund 75 Prozent) beteiligten sich an der Erhebung und 675 Frauen (45 Prozent) sandten den an sie verteilten Fragebogen zurueck.
Ergebnisse: Zusammengefasst nach Bereichen verteilen sich die Frauen wie folgt ueber die Berufe: Handelsberufe (33,9 Prozent), gewerblichtechnische Berufe (31,7 Prozent), kaufmaennisch-verwaltende Berufe (29,5 Prozent), sozialpflegerische Berufe (11,1 Prozent), technische Berufe (11,1 Prozent) und landwirtschaftliche Berufe (10,3 Prozent). Die Analyse der Taetigkeitsmerkmale, Arbeitsmittel und der erstellten Produkte bzw. erbrachten Leistungen ergab, dass der ueberwiegende Teil der Frauen mit Berufsabschluss auch qualifikationsadaequate oder sogar hoeherwertige Taetigkeiten ausuebte. Letzteres insbesondere dann, wenn noch eine zusaetzliche Qualifikation, z.B. durch Weiterbildung oder einen Fachschulabschluss, erworben wurde. Die guenstige Situation der Uebereinstimmung zwischen den formalen Qualifikationen eines vorhandenen Berufsabschlusses und den tatsaechlich im Arbeitsprozess geforderten und erbrachten Leistungen betrifft rund drei Viertel der befragten Frauen. Wir haben unsere Zielgruppe mit Hilfe einer repraesentativen, geschichteten Stichprobe erreicht; es handelt sich bei den Befragten also nicht um eine bevorzugte Gruppe von Frauen. Die Ausgangsbedingungen sind strukturelle stark unterschiedlich, verglichen mit denen in den alten Bundeslaendern. Dies wurde bei der Formulierung unserer Empfehlungen beruecksichtigt: Kuenftige Weiterbildungspolitik sollte das Hauptgewicht auf den Erwerb von "Zusatzqualifikationen" legen und diese als Fortbildung anbieten. Umschulung im Sinne von "Nachqualifizierung", zum Erwerb eines Berufsabschlusses, sollte hierbei keinen programmatischen bildungspolitischen Schwerpunkt bilden. Die Entscheidung fuer eine eventuelle Umschulung sollte der individuellen Entscheidung der Frauen ueberlassen bleiben und/oder den Betrieben, die dies fuer notwendig erachten.
Geographischer Raum: ehem. DDR (neue Bundeslaender).
Untersuchter Zeitraum: 70er Jahre bis einschliesslich 08/1992.
Vorgehensweise: Auf Basis einer geschichteten Stichprobe wurden in der Ex-DDR branchenweit 115 Betriebe und 1500 Personen (Frauen mittlerer Alterjahrgaenge) befragt (quantitative Erhebung) sowie aufbauend darauf 40 Interviews mit Frauen an ihren Arbeitsplaetzen untersucht (qualitative Untersuchung). Untersuchungsdesign: Methodenforschung; Fallstudie; Trend; retrospektive Daten; qualitative Forschung.
Datengewinnung: Postalische Befragung, Befragung (Stichprobe: 115; Betriebe -ehem. DDR - branchenweit-). Aktenanalyse (Stichprobe: 115; Betriebe -ehem. DDR - branchenweit-. Stichprobe: 1500; Personen in Betrieben -branchenweit- der ehem. DDR - erwerbstaetige Frauen mittlerer Alterjahrgaenge-). Standardisiertes Interview, nicht-standardisiertes interview (Stichprobe: 1500; Personen in Betrieben -branchenweit- der ehem. DDR - erwerbstaetige Frauen mittlerer Altersjahrgaenge-). Primaererhebung: Feldarbeit von Mitarbeitern des Projektes durchgefuehrt; Datenerstellung auf der Basis von bereits vorliegenden Materialien wie Texten, Akten, Statistiken.
Auswertung: Datenaufbereitung: Verlaufsdaten (event history data).
Publ: Gensior, Sabine; u.a. *Berufliche Weiterbildung fuer Frauen in den neuen Laendern. Ergebnisse eines Forschungsprojektes zur Arbeitssituation und zum beruflichen Weiterbildungsverhalten.* In: Reihe Bildung - Wissenschaft - Aktuell 11/91, hrsg. v. Bundesminister fuer Bildung und Wissenschaft. Bonn 1991.

13541 Berufsorientierungsseminare fuer Jugendliche und Erwachsene. (Career guidance seminars for adolescents and adults.)
AUT 1993
Research Date(s): 1992-1993
Salzgeber, Gabriele; Pranger, Veronika.
Inst: Berufsorientierungszentrum, Leipziger Platz 1, A-6020 Innsbruck. Berufsfoerderungsinstitut Tirol, Salurnerstrasse 1, A-6020 Innsbruck
vocational guidance; unemployed; vocational information
orientation professionnelle; chômeur; information professionnelle
PROJECT DESCRIPTION
Untersuchung und Evaluation eines Konzeptes zur Durchfuehrung von Berufsorientierungsseminaren fuer jugendliche und erwachsene Arbeitslose. Dabei soll die Legitimation von betriebswirtschaftlichen, wirtschaftspaedagogischen und psychologischen Aspekten in der Arbeit mit den betreffenden Klientengruppen erarbeitet werden. Ausserdem wird eine Erhebung der bisherigen Verlaeufe von Berufsorientierungskursen stich-

probenartig bei ehemaligen TeilnehmerInnen, Trainern und Bediensteten des Berufsfoerderungsinstituts durchgefuehrt. Ergebnis der Diplomarbeit sind konkrete, wissenschaftlich untersuchte Massnahmen zur Verbesserung der Berufsorientierung mit Praxisschwerpunkt.

Es handelt sich um eine kritische Untersuchung auf der Basis von empirischen Erhebungen, dokumentiertem Material und den Ergebnissen von Primaerevaluationen. Es soll die wirtschaftspaedagogisch-didaktische Entwicklung eines Modulsystems fuer Berufsorientierung geleistet werden.

13542 Berufswuensche und Arbeitsmarktrealitaet bei Abgaengern allgemeinbildender hoeherer Schulen. (Career aspirations and employment opportunities of general secondary school leavers.)
AUT 1993
Research Date(s): 1991-1994
Amann, Anton; Hohenbalken, Walther; Papouschek, Ulrike; Nowak, Guenter; Nemeth, Guenther; Koeltringer, Richard; Leitgeb, Egon.
Inst: Wiener Institut fuer Sozialwissenschaftliche Dokumentation, Schelleingasse 12/10, A-1040 Wien.
Fin: Bundesministerium fuer Arbeit und Soziales.
training-employment relationship; vocational information; occupational aspiration
relation formation-emploi; information professionnelle; aspirations professionnelles
PROJECT DESCRIPTION

Dieses Projekt dient einer Analyse der Berufswuensche und der Arbeitsmarktrealitaet von MaturantInnen (Allgemeinbildende hoehere Schule, Handelsakademie, Hoehere Lehranstalt fuer wirtschaftliche Berufe) in Oesterreich. Das Endprodukt dieses Projekts werden - neben dem Bericht ueber die Forschungsergebnisse - speziell aufbereitete Informationsmaterialien sein: in Broschuerenform fuer mehr als 15000 AbsolventInnen; ein computerunterstuetztes Such- und Lernspiel fuer die AbsolventInnen und SchuelerInnen der 6. bis 8. (3. bis 5.) Klassen; und die schematische Darstellung des im Laufe des Projekts zu entwickelnden "Informationskonzepts".

Es wird eine schriftliche Befragung von Abschlussklassen allgemeinbildender hoeherer Schulen, Hauptschulen und Kollegs sowie von berufstaetigen MaturantInnen durchgefuehrt. Mit Personalchefs, BildungsberatungslehrerInnen und AMV-MitarbeiterInnen werden Interviews durchgefuehrt.

13543 Beschäftigungssituation der Neuabsolventen der schweizerischen Hochschulen 1991. (La situation de l'emploi des jeunes universitaires suisses en 1991.)
CHE 1994
Research Date(s): 1991-1992
Diem, Markus (Jungstrasse 14, 4056 Basel, Schweiz).
Schweizerische Arbeitsgemeinschaft für akademische Berufs- und Studienberatung (AGAB), Hirschgraben 28, 8001 Zürich, Schweiz
Fin: Schweizerische Hochschulkonferenz; Bundesamt für Bildung und Wissenschaft (BBW).
employment; transition from school to work; openings; graduate; graduate unemployment; employment opportunities
emploi; passage à la vie active; débouchés; étudiant diplômé; chômage des diplômés; chances d'obtenir un emploi
PROJECT DESCRIPTION

Im Auftrag der Schweizerischen Hochschulkonferenz und des Bundesamts für Industrie, Gewerbe und Arbeit führt die Schweizerische Arbeitsgemeinschaft für akademische Berufs- und Studienberatung (AGAB) alle zwei Jahre (seit 1977) eine Untersuchung zur Frage durch, wie den jungen Akademikern der Einstieg in die Berufswelt gelingt. Es handelt sich diesmal um die achte Auflage dieser schriftlichen Befragung; sie betraf wiederum alle Hochschulabsolventen, die im Kalenderjahr vor der Befragung ihr Studium abgeschlossen hatten (Abschlussjahrgang 1990).

Der Begriff der Arbeitslosigkeit wird in den AGAB-Studien weiter gefasst als in den offiziellen Statistiken: während letztere nur die als arbeitslos registrierten Personen betreffen, werden hier alle einbezogen, die angeben, auf der Suche nach einer Erwerbstätigkeit zu sein.

Während sich die letzten Umfragen vor dem Hintergrund eines anhaltenden wirtschaftlichen Wachstums abspielten, war das Jahr 1991 durch eine Abschwächung der wirtschaftlichen Konjunktur gekennzeichnet. Dies hat sich auch prompt in den Ergebnissen der Untersuchung niedergeschlagen: lag der Prozentsatz der arbeitslosen Neuabsolventen nach AGAB-Definition 1989 noch bei 3,0 Prozent, so ist er innert zweier Jahre um gleich 60 Prozent gestiegen und lag 1991 bei 4,8 Prozent. Von der Verschlechterung der Arbeitsmarktlage war vor allem die französischsprachige Schweiz betroffen, wo sich die Quote der arbeitsuchenden Jungakademiker von 4,2 auf 8,8 Prozent mehr als verdoppelt hat, während die Deutschschweiz mit einer Steigerung von 2,3 auf 3,1 Prozent vergleichsweise glimpflich davonkam.

Wie schon in den früheren Untersuchungen wurden beträchtliche Unterschiede je nach Studienbereich festgestellt. Während sich die Situation für Theologen und Mediziner nicht verändert oder gar leicht verbessert hat, ist die Situation für alle anderen Bereiche ungünstiger als zwei Jahre zuvor. Die höchsten Beschäftigungslosenquoten findet man für Sozial- (9%), Wirt-

schafts- (7,2%) und Geisteswissenschafter (6,2%). Die Schwierigkeiten für Ökonomen auf dem Weg in den Arbeitsmarkt sind ein neues Phänomen. Durchschnittliche Arbeitslosenquoten weisen Naturwissenschafter (4,2%) und Ingenieure (4,1%) auf. Unter dem Durchschnitt liegen die Werte für Juristen sowie für die bereits erwähnten Theologen (2,7%) und Mediziner (1,8%).

Ein überraschendes Ergebnis der Studie ist zum Schluss zu vermelden. Man hatte sich einigermassen an das Phänomen gewöhnt, dass sich bei rezessiven wirtschaftlichen Tendenzen die Schwierigkeiten für Frauen auf dem Arbeitsmarkt überproportional vergrössern. Dies ist 1991 nicht eingetroffen: trotz ungünstigeren wirtschaftlichen Rahmenbedingungen haben sich die beiden Kurven, welche die jeweiligen Arbeitslosenquoten beschreiben, im Jahr 1991 getroffen und waren somit nicht mehr Neuabsolventinnen beschäftigungslos als Neuabsolventen.

Publ: Diem, Markus. *Die Beschäftigungssituation der Neuabsolventen der Schweizer Hochschulen 1991.* Bern: (BBW), 1992, 156 Seiten (Reihe Beihefte zu "Wissenschaftspolitik"; 56).
Diem, Markus. *La situation de l'emploi des jeunes universitaires en 1991.* Berne: (OFES), 1992, 160p. (série "Politique de la science", suppléments; 56).

13544 BP Exploration Fellowship in vocational education and guidance.
GBR 1993
Research Date(s): 1990-1992
Semple, S.
Inst: Jordanhill College of Education, Division of Inservice Training, Southbrae Drive, Glasgow G13 1PP, United Kingdom.
Fin: BP Exploration plc.
vocational guidance; transition from school to work; occupational choice; educational guidance; school leaver; teaching aid
orientation professionnelle; passage à la vie active; choix d'une profession; orientation pédagogique; élève sortant; moyen d'enseignement
PROJECT DESCRIPTION

The overall aim of this project is to improve the preparation young people receive for their transition from school to employment and further and higher education. Specifically, it aims to: devise and pilot careers education materials for pupils and their parents; develop careers education and information videos where needed; provide inservice support to teachers using careers education and involved in vocational guidance and education/industry links; provide inservice support to careers service staff and others working in the field; influence the content of initial teacher training to ensure student teachers are briefed on vocational education and guidance; and contribute to staff development in the college on vocational education and guidance.

The outcome of the project will be the production of six briefing papers on young people's views of transition issues; a video and teaching pack 'Going to College' on non-advanced further education; a careers education resource base; materials for inservice courses in: (a) careers education; (b) evaluating careers interviews; (c) work related curriculum; (d) influencing the curriculum; and materials for preservice courses in careers and the work-related curriculum.

13545 Career guidance in Avon: encouraging collaboration.
GBR 1993
Research Date(s): 1991
Davies, P.; McHugh, G.
Inst: Lancaster University, Department of Educational Research, Centre for the Study of Education and Training, Cartmel College, Bailrigg, Lancaster LA1 4YW, United Kingdom.
Fin: Avon Training and Enterprise Council.
vocational guidance; occupational choice; cooperation
orientation professionnelle; choix d'une profession; coopération
PROJECT DESCRIPTION

The aim of the study was to obtain a clear understanding of the expectations and needs of guidance users so that careers guidance provision in Avon is made more appropriate and effective. The research was undertaken on the basis of 300 questionnaires completed by students, 100 individual interviews and eight group interviews. The report for Avon Training and Enterprise Council concluded that although guidance users were satisfied with the guidance provision, greater collaboration and networking by guidance providers would enhance the overall provision of careers guidance.

13546 Career guidance in Birmingham: a preliminary study.
GBR 1993
Research Date(s): 1991-1992
Davies, P.
Inst: Lancaster University, Department of Educational Research, Centre for the Study of Education and Training, Cartmel College, Bailrigg, Lancaster LA1 4YW, United Kingdom.
Fin: Birmingham Training and Enterprise Council.
vocational guidance; occupational choice; cooperation
orientation professionnelle; choix d'une profession; coopération
PROJECT DESCRIPTION

The aim of the study was to map the career guidance provision for young people in schools and colleges in Birmingham and to identify the principal providers. Of particular importance was the investigation of the potential for partnership agreements to be drawn up between the main guidance providers. The research was based on a study of documentary evidence and interviews with key personnel. It was concluded that the partnership approach offered considerable scope for the improvement of careers guidance in schools and colleges. A report was produced for Birmingham Training and Education Council.

13547 Career outcomes of engineers and their relationships to education, training and early work experiences.

GBR 1993

Research Date(s): 1992-1994

Keenan, A.

Inst: Herriot-Watt University, Department of Business Organisation, Riccarton Campus, Currie, Edinburgh EH14 4AS, United Kingdom.

Fin: Science and Engineering Research Council.

career; engineer; career development; training-employment relationship

carrière; ingénieur; déroulement de carrière; relation formation-emploi

PROJECT DESCRIPTION

The research follows up a sample of several hundred professional engineers into mid career. Extensive data are already held on them from a previous study covering the first five years at work. The investigation will look at the predictive power of the earlier data in terms of a variety of career outcomes.

13548 Careers service analyses.

GBR 1993

Research Date(s): 1984-

Reece, D.

Inst: Berkshire County Council, Education Department, Information Technology Management, Shire Hall, Shinfield Park, Reading RG2 9XD, United Kingdom.

youth employment; employment opportunities; occupational choice; vocational guidance; career

emploi des jeunes; chances d'obtenir un emploi; choix d'une profession; orientation professionnelle; carrière

PROJECT DESCRIPTION

A cohort study is made annually to study the experiences of young people in finding employment and to provide information about their career preferences and outcomes.

13549 Community education graduates at Jordanhill - survey of appointments.

GBR 1993

Research Date(s): 1991-1992

Rowlands, C.

Inst: Jordanhill College of Education, Division of Community Education, Southbrae Drive, Glasgow G13 1PP, United Kingdom.

initial employment; graduate; community education; employment opportunities

premier emploi; étudiant diplômé; éducation sociale; chances d'obtenir un emploi

PROJECT DESCRIPTION

This study began out of an interest to acquire an accurate picture of the employment of past students especially when related to the present national employment figures. Similar research has been completed each year since 1981. Within Scotland as a whole and especially within the colleges of education, much concern has been expressed at the numbers of newly qualified teachers who have been unable to obtain employment in their chosen profession. Within the Jordanhill Division of Community Education it has always been assumed that ex-students have been more fortunate in this respect. In an effort to gain a realistic assessment of the situation, this research was undertaken.

The purpose of the research was: (1) to investigate the employment situation of youth and community work students who qualified from June 1981 onwards from Jordanhill; (2) to investigate the jobs obtained by students according to certain criteria, i.e. sex, length of course followed; (3) to investigate the degree of difficulty experienced by students in gaining employment; and (4) to investigate the types of employment accepted.

13550 Comparative research on career guidance between Britain and China.

GBR 1993

Research Date(s): 1991-1994

Weiyuan, Z.

Sup: King, K.; Thomson, G.

Inst: Edinburgh University, Department of Education, 10-12 Buccleuch Place, Edinburgh EH8 9JT, United Kingdom.

vocational guidance; occupational choice; comparative research; Scotland; China

orientation professionnelle; choix d'une profession; recherche comparative; Ecosse; Chine

PROJECT DESCRIPTION

Career guidance is increasingly becoming an important task in a changing world. The aim of this research is to compare students' career needs, including students' value criteria and choices of various occupations; the relationship between their career goals and school activities; and their needs with regard to career choice.

In China, the researcher has selected and surveyed four junior-senior secondary schools (grades 7-12) and two junior secondary schools (grades 7-9). In each of these schools, classes were randomly chosen from each grade level. The total participants in the study were 674 students, 722 parents, and 127 teachers. A further study will select and survey using the same questionnaire, similar schools and students, parents and teachers, in Scotland.

Through comparative research on need assessment between British students and Chinese students, the study will discuss problems and give recommendations on how career guidance can be best implemented.

Publ: A full list of publications is available from the researcher.

13551 Competency-based vocational qualifications in the labour market.

GBR 1993

Research Date(s): 1990-1991

Weller, P.

Sup: Field, J.

Inst: Warwick University, Faculty of Educational Studies, Department of Continuing Education, Continuing Education Research Centre, Coventry CV4 7AL, United Kingdom.

Fin: Universities Funding Council.

occupational qualification; training-employment relationship; labour market; vocational education; skill

qualification professionnelle; relation formation-emploi; marché du travail; enseignement professionnel; compétence

PROJECT DESCRIPTION

This project investigates the responses of labour market organisations to the introduction of competency-based vocational qualifications in the United Kingdom. Its chief concerns are with trade unions, lobbying bodies and advisory organisations, all of whom play a role as partners in the labour market, and are reacting to a standards-based qualifications system which is intended to be employer-led.

Publ: Field, J. Competency and the pedagogy of labour. In: Studies in the Education of Adults, Vol 23, No 1/1991, pp. 41-52.

13552 Das Verhalten von Interessenten fuer eine Zweitausbildung aus der Landwirtschaft. (Conflict of interests among farmers seeking a second occupation.)

DEU 1993

Research Date(s): 1991-1992

Geiger, I.; Moritz, R.

Sup: Haris, J.; Kromka, F.

Inst: Universitaet Hohenheim, Fak. 04 Agrarwissenschaften, 02 Institut fuer Agrarsoziologie, Landwirtschaftliche Beratung und Angewandte Psychologie, FG Agrar- und Landsoziologie, Postfach 700562, D-7000 Stuttgart 70.

Fin: Institution; Verein zu Foerderung von Zweiteinkommen in der Landwirtschaft der Region Bodensee-Oberschwaben e.V.

retraining; agriculture; pilot project; Baden-wurtemberg; vocational education; social change; employment opportunities

recyclage; agriculture; projet-pilote; Bade-Wurtemberg; enseignement professionnel; changement social; chances d'obtenir un emploi

PROJECT DESCRIPTION

Inhalt: Der permanente Strukturwandel in der Landwirtschaft fuehrt dazu, dass ein grosser Anteil der Landwirte in ihren Betrieben keine volle Existenz mehr finden wird. In vielen Faellen wird jedoch die berufliche Umorientierung von starken, psychisch bedingten Hemmfaktoren (Einstellungen, Vorurteilen, Motiven) blockiert. Ohne die Kenntnis der Art, der Staerke und der Verbreitung der Hemmfaktoren ist aber eine fruchtbare Hilfe (sei es durch Information, Beratung, Alternativangebote, finanzielle Hilfeleistungen usw.) kaum moeglich. In der vorliegenden Untersuchung soll der Versuch unternommen werden, detaillierte Kenntnisse ueber die hemmenden und treibenden Kraefte landwirtschaftlicher Betriebsleiter bei der beruflichen Zweitausbildung im Rahmen des Ravensburger-Modellprojektes (das 1988 gestartet wurde) zu erarbeiten.

Geographischer Raum: Regionen Ravensburg, Sigmaringen und Biberach.

Untersuchter Zeitraum: 1988 bis 1991.

Vorgehensweise: Untersuchungsdesign: Evaluationsstudie.

Datengewinnung: Standardisiertes Interview (Stichprobe: 140; Interessenten fuer eine Zweitausbildung; Auswahlverfahren: bewusst). Primaererhebung: Feldarbeit von Mitarbeitern des Projektes durchgefuehrt.

Auswertung: uni- und bivariate Analysen.

13553   De actuele en toekomstige arbeidsmarktsituatie voor musici: haalbaarheidsonderzoek. (The current and future labour market situation for musicians: a feasibility study.)
NLD   1993
Research Date(s): 1992
Grip, A. de; Berendsen, H.
Inst: ROA Researchcentrum voor Onderwijs en Arbeidsmarkt, Universiteit Limburg (Research Centre for Education and the Labour Market, University of Limburg), P.O. Box 616, 6200 MD Maastricht, Netherlands.
Fin: Ministry of Welfare, Health and Cultural Affairs.
employment opportunities; graduate; music school; labour market; forecasting
chances d'obtenir un emploi; étudiant diplômé; école de musique; marché du travail; prévision
PROJECT DESCRIPTION
   This feasibility study examined how an analysis of the current and future situation in the labour market for graduates from schools of music could be prepared. The focus was on whether any future oversupply or shortage of graduates from such courses could be quantified.
   It was proposed that a medium-term forecast should be made for the total labour market for graduates from schools of music. This would be supplemented by an indication of the market segments in which shortages or absorption problems might arise in the near future. The forecast for the total market can be constructed on the basis of the expected numbers of graduate music students entering the labour market and the supply of unemployed qualified musicians. Every element of the forecast has been related to the availability and the usefulness of the relevant data.
Publ: Berendsen, H. & Grip, A. de *De actuele en toekomstige arbeidsmarktsituatie voor musici: haalbaarheidsonderzoek* (The current and future labour market situation for musicians: a feasibility study), ROA-R-1992/6 (ISBN 90-5321-091-1).

13554   De arbeidsmarkt in de Euro-regio Maas-Rijn. (Labour market of the Euro-region Maas-Rhine.)
NLD   1994
Research Date(s): 1991
Dam, J.W. van; Heijke, J.A.M.; Grip, A. de.
Inst: ROA Researchcentrum voor Onderwijs en Arbeidsmarkt, Universiteit Limburg (Research Centre for Education and the Labour Market, University of Limburg), P.O. Box 616, 6200 MD Maastricht, Netherlands.
Fin: Province of Dutch Limburg.
labour market; occupational mobility
marché du travail; mobilité professionnelle
PROJECT DESCRIPTION
   In preparation for a Euro-regional Congress on labour mobility in the Maas-Rhine Euro-region on 28 November 1991, a study was carried out into impediments to international labour mobility within the Euro-region. Furthermore, current initiatives which aim to correct or reduce the problems observed were listed. An indication was given of necessary and promising policy initiatives which could be further developed. The research results were presented at the Euro-regional Congress.
Publ: Dam, J.W. van & Grip, A. de. *De Euregionale arbeidsmarkt: Van fictie naar werkelijkheid* (The euro-regional labour market: from fiction to reality), ROA-R-1991/10 (ISBN 90-5321-068-7).

13555   De kosten van het niet opleiden. (The costs of not training.)
NLD   1993
Research Date(s): 1992
Grip, A. de; Heijke, J.A.M.; Willems, E.J.T.A.
Inst: ROA Researchcentrum voor Onderwijs en Arbeidsmarkt, Universiteit Limburg (Research Centre for Education and the Labour Market, University of Limburg), P.O. Box 616, 6200 MD Maastricht, Netherlands.
Fin: Institute of Employment Research, University of Warwick (UK).
labour market; vocational training; skill
marché du travail; formation professionnelle; compétence
PROJECT DESCRIPTION
   As part of the research project "The costs of not training", carried out on behalf of the EC Task Force on Human Resources, Education, Training and Youth, ROA catalogued the most relevant Dutch studies with regard to (1) skill structures and training levels, (2) forecasts of the future labour market and the use of labour market models and (3) training activities.

13556   De positie van vrouwen op de Limburgse arbeidsmarkt: het ATHENA project. (The position of women on the Limburg labour market: the ATHENA project.)
NLD   1993
Research Date(s): 1992-1993
Velden, R.K.W. van der; Dam, J.W. van.
Inst: ROA Researchcentrum voor Onderwijs en Arbeidsmarkt, Universiteit Limburg (Research Centre for Education and the Labour Market, University of Limburg), P.O. Box 616, 6200 MD Maastricht, Netherlands.
Fin: EC Task Force on Human Resources, Education, Training and Youth.
labour market; government policy; women's employment; regional development

marché du travail; politique gouvernementale; emploi des femmes; développement régional
PROJECT DESCRIPTION
   As part of the ATHENA project, ROA has conducted research into the position of women on the Limbourg labour market. The study was funded by the EC Task Force on Human Resources, Education, Training and Youth. The same project is being carried out in five other EC countries.
   The goals of the project are to provide information on factors that influence the success or failure of policy measures, to describe examples of good practice which could be copied in one of the other regions, and to formulate concrete recommendations for the most relevant actors in the region of Limburg, in the five other regions involved and for the European Commission. The project should stimulate the regional network of relevant actors and initiate new projects and measures by taking over interesting ideas from other regions.
Publ: Dam, J.W. van. *The position of women on the Limburg labour market*, ROA-R-1992/7E.

13557   De toekomstige arbeidsmarkt voor de sector gezondheidszorg. (The future labour market for the health care sector.)
NLD   1993
Research Date(s): 1992-1994
Grip, A. de; Willems, E.J.T.A.; Loo, P.J.E. van de.
Inst: ROA Researchcentrum voor Onderwijs en Arbeidsmarkt, Universiteit Limburg (Research Centre for Education and the Labour Market, University of Limburg), P.O. Box 616, 6200 MD Maastricht, Netherlands.
Fin: Ministry of Welfare, Health, and Cultural Affairs.
labour market; health service personnel; employment opportunities; manpower need
marché du travail; personnel médical; chances d'obtenir un emploi; besoin de main-d'oeuvre
PROJECT DESCRIPTION
   Under a contract from the Ministry of Welfare, Health and Cultural Affairs, ROA prepares estimates of the future employment levels, the replacement demand, and the number of labour market entrants in the health care sector. These estimates, differentiated by specific sectors and occupational groups, will be based on the three long-term scenarios drawn up by the Central Planning Bureau: "Global shift", "European Renaissance" and "Balanced Growth". The scenarios will be elaborated for the period 1993-2005, giving both a medium-term and a long-term forecast.

13558   De vervangingsvraag naar beroepsklasse. (Replacement demand by occupation.)
NLD   1993
Research Date(s): 1990-1991
Grip, A. de; Willems, E.J.T.A.
Inst: ROA Researchcentrum voor Onderwijs en Arbeidsmarkt, Universiteit Limburg (Research Centre for Education and the Labour Market, University of Limburg), P.O. Box 616, 6200 MD Maastricht, Netherlands.
Fin: Organization for Strategic Labour Market Research.
manpower need; forecasting; labour market
besoin de main-d'oeuvre; prévision; marché du travail
PROJECT DESCRIPTION
   Replacement demand is an important component of the future demand for labour. In this inquiry a forecasting methodology was developed to determine the future replacement demand for each occupational class. The replacement demand for each occupational class indicates the numbers of workers withdrawing from a given occupational class. A distinction can be made between permanent withdrawals, such as retirements, and withdrawals due to mobility to other occupational classes. As part of this research, forecasts were drawn up of the expected replacement demand in the period 1990-2000 for 93 occupational classes defined in ROA's 1990 occupational classification. A separate analysis was made of the replacement demand for nurses.

13559   Dealing with knowledge in the Museums Sector Standards: an evaluation of an approach using carefully chosen examples.
GBR   1993
Research Date(s): 1991-1992
Black, H.; Hall, J.; Martin, S.
Inst: Scottish Council for Research in Education, 15 St John Street, Edinburgh EH8 8JR, United Kingdom.
Fin: Department of Employment.
job requirements; knowledge level; standard; museum
qualification requise pour l'emploi; niveau de connaissances; norme; musée
PROJECT DESCRIPTION
   This research is an investigation of the best ways in which to describe the knowledge base which underpins standards within the Department of Employment's Standards Programme. Using 'examples' of typically competent performance within the Museums Sector, the project will seek to: (1) explore the potential of an 'examples' approach to knowledge clarification; (2) describe and evaluate the process by which standards developers might use such an approach; and (3) investigate the extent to which industry experts feel it is likely that sound assessments would result if the

existing draft standards statements, supported by examples of knowledge, were all that were available to them.

13560 Determinanten der beruflichen Orientierung und Entwicklung: Untersuchung im Rahmen einer Laengsschnittstudie. (Determinants of occupational orientation and development: study within the framework of a cross-sectional investigation.)
DEU 1993
Research Date(s): 1991-1993
Haase, K.
Sup: Fisseni, H.; Trost, G.
Inst: Universitaet Bonn, Philosophische Fakultaet, Psychologisches Institut, Roemerstrasse 164, D-5300 Bonn 1.
Fin: Institution; Studienstiftung des deutschen Volkes e.V.
career; occupational aspiration; occupational satisfaction; secondary school; upper secondary; occupational choice; occupational success; transition from school to work
carrière; aspirations professionnelles; satisfaction professionnelle; école secondaire; secondaire deuxième cycle; choix d'une profession; réussite professionnelle; passage à la vie active
PROJECT DESCRIPTION
Inhalt: Zusammenhang von Berufswuenschen, konkreten Berufsabsichten, sowie dem tatsaechlich ausgeuebten Beruf. Welche Variablen beeinflussen die Konsistenz der beruflichen Entwicklung? Beeinflusst eine konsistente berufliche Entwicklung ihrerseits den spaeteren Berufserfolg bzw. die Berufszufriedenheit? In welchem Masse lassen sich Berufserfolg und berufliche Zufriedenheit aus kognitiven, motivationalen, sozio-oekonomischen und weiteren Variablen, die mit Ende der Sekundarstufe II erhoben wurden, vorhersagen? Analyse der Karrieremobilitaet dieser Kohorte von Berufsanfaengern.
Geographischer Raum: alte Bundeslaender.
Vorgehensweise: Bildungs- und Berufswegforschung als ein Beitrag zur laengsschnittlichen Beschreibung und Analyse der beruflichen Entwicklung anhand einer repraesentativen Stichprobe; Identifizierung von Determinanten, die den Erfolg bzw. die Zufriedenheit im Ausbildungs- bzw. Berufsweg beeinflussen. Untersuchungsdesign: Panel; retrospektive Daten.
Datengewinnung: Postalische Befragung (Stichprobe: 9.029; Abiturjahrgang 1974; Auswahlverfahren: Quota). Sekundaeranalyse bereits vorhandener maschinenlesbarer Datensaetze; Datenerstellung auf der Basis von bereits vorliegenden Materialien wie Texten, Akten, Statistiken.
Auswertung: Deskriptive Statistiken; parametrische und non-parametrische Gruppenvergleiche; Clusteranalyse; Diskriminanzanalyse; DEL-Analyse. Datenaufbereitung: Aggregierung oder Disaggregierung; Verlaufsdaten (event history data).

13561 Developing an industrial relations training programme for Greek supervisors and trade union representatives in simultaneous process research into training needs.
GBR 1993
Research Date(s): 1988-1992
Chadwick, A.; Fisher, J.; Protopapas, G.
Inst: Surrey University, Department of Educational Studies, Guildford GU2 5XH, United Kingdom.
Fin: European Community COMETT Programme.
labour relations; trade unionism; Greece; training programme; managerial staff
relations industrielles; syndicalisme; Grèce; programme de formation; personnel d'encadrement
PROJECT DESCRIPTION
This project is intended to help to develop an industrial relations training system in Greece for trade union representatives and managers. It involves: (1) identifying training needs; (2) developing the framework for a training programme; and (3) the implementation of that programme in Greece 'in simultaneous process'.
Needs identification is mainly through consultation with all interested parties and organisations. Programme design and development is ongoing, and evaluation will be by participation and observation, as well as by response of involved parties. The project is supported by the Greek government, companies' unions and training organisations.

13562 Didaktische Konzeption fuer ein Qualifizierungsprogramm im AuT-Projekt, CAD- und EDV-gestuetzte Informationssysteme in einer Konstruktionsabteilung im Anlagen- und Spezialmaschinenbau. (Didactic concept for a training programme in an "AuT" project, CAD-based and computer-aided information systems in a design department for plant construction and special purpose machines.)
DEU 1993
Research Date(s): 1989-1992
Tilch, H.
Sup: Rauner, F.
Inst: Universitaet Bremen, FB 11 Arbeits- und Bildungswissenschaften, Institut Technik und Bildung, Grazer Str. 2, D-2800 Bremen 33.
Fin: Deutsche Forschungsanstalt fuer Luft- und Raumfahrt -DLR- Projekttraeger des Programms "Arbeit und Technik".

qualification; information system; electronic data processing; in-service training; didactics; mechanical engineering
qualification; système d'information; traitement électronique des données; formation en cours d'emploi; didactique; construction mécanique
PROJECT DESCRIPTION
Inhalt: Mit den Qualifizierungsmassnahmen sollen alle Mitarbeiter der Konstruktionsabteilung eines Mittelbetriebes im Anlagen- und Spezialmaschinenbau in die Organisationsentwicklung und EDV-Qualifizierung einbezogen werden. Die zentrale Aufgabe fuer die Entwicklung der Qualifizierungskonzeption besteht in der didaktischen Analyse des Arbeitsfeldes unter den Gesichtspunkten der Organisationsentwicklung und EDV-Unterstuetzung (CAD/CAM).
Vorgehensweise: Empirische Erforschung der Lernvoraussetzungen und Anforderungen im Bereich Konstruktion und Entwicklung des Projektfeldes; Didaktische Analyse.
Datengewinnung: Gruppendiskussion (Stichprobe: 70; Mitarbeiter im konstruktiven Bereich im Maschinenbau-Mittelbetrieb). Befragung (Stichprobe: 70; Mitarbeiter im konstruktiven Bereich im Maschinenbau-Mittelbetrieb).
Publ: Klingenberg, H. & Tilch, H. Arbeitsorganisation, Qualifizierung und EDV in einem Technischen Buero. Modell fuer veraenderte Maerkte. In: Frese, M.; et al (Hg.). *Software fuer die Arbeit von morgen* (Ergaenzung zum Tagungsband). Bonn: Projekttraeger "Arbeit und Technik" 1991, S. 75-89.

13563 Diplom-Paedagogen im Beruf: Berufstaetigkeit, Berufseinmuendung, Bildungsbiographie und retrospektive Beurteilung des Studiums. (Education graduates at work: occupation, career start, educational biography and retrospective assessment of the university course.)
DEU 1993
Research Date(s): 1991-1992
Kuckartz, U.; Lukas, H.
Sup: Skiba, E.
Inst: Freie Universitaet Berlin, FB Erziehungs- und Unterrichtswissenschaften, Institut fuer Sozialpaedagogik und Erwachsenenbildung WE 05, Arnimallee 12, D-1000 Berlin 33.
transition from school to work; sciences of education; career; university studies; occupational choice; branch of study; graduate
passage à la vie active; sciences de l'éducation; carrière; études universitaires; choix d'une profession; filière d'études; étudiant diplômé
PROJECT DESCRIPTION
Inhalt: Die empirische Studie ist als Totalerhebung aller Absolventen des Studienganges Diplom-Paedagogik (Studienrichtung Sozialpaedagogik) an der FU Berlin seit der Einrichtung des Studienganges zu Beginn der 70er Jahre konzipiert. Zweck der Befragung ist es, einen moeglichst praezisen Ueberblick ueber den Verbleib der ca. 400 Absolventen zu erhalten. Der Prozess der Berufseinmuendung wird erfasst, die Zusammenhaenge zwischen der Bildungsbiographie, dem Studierverhalten und der Berufskarriere sind Gegenstand detaillierter Analysen.
Geographischer Raum: Berlin (West).
Untersuchter Zeitraum: 1973-1991.
Vorgehensweise: Explorative Studie; gezielter Einsatz von offenen Fragen; verstehende Soziologie. Untersuchungsdesign: Querschnittserhebung; Trend.
Datengewinnung: Postalische Befragung (Stichprobe: 400; Dipl.-Paed. Absolventen der FU Berlin; Auswahlverfahren: total). Primaererhebung: Feldarbeit von Mitarbeitern des Projektes durchgefuehrt.
Auswertung: Faktorenanalyse; Clusteranalyse; computergestuetzte Auswertung von offenen Fragen. Datenaufbereitung: Datenedition (z.B. Aufbau von Datenbanken); Verknuepfung verschiedener Datensaetze (record linkage).

13564 Dritte Gemeinsame BIBB/IAB-Repraesentativ-Befragung zu Qualifikationserwerb, -verwertung und Arbeitsmitteleinsatz in Ost- und Westdeutschland. (Third representative BIBB/IAB survey on attainment and utilization of qualifications, as well as the use of working materials in East and West Germany.)
DEU 1993
Research Date(s): 1991-1994
Stooss, F.; Parmentier, K.; Plicht, H.; Troll, L.
Inst: Institut fuer Arbeitsmarkt- und Berufsforschung der Bundesanstalt fuer Arbeit -IAB-, Regensburgerstrasse 104, D-8500 Nuernberg; Bundesinstitut fuer Berufsbildung, Fehrbelliner Platz 3, D-1000 Berlin 31.
occupational qualification; further training; unemployment; retraining; Germany - Federal Republic; German DR
qualification professionnelle; formation complémentaire; chômage; recyclage; Allemagne RFA; Allemagne RDA
PROJECT DESCRIPTION
Inhalt: Erhebung von grund- und Strukturdaten zum Erwerb und zur Nutzung von Qualifikationen sowie zum Arbeitsmitteleinsatz in einer mit den bisherigen BIBB/IAB-Erhebungen voll kompatiblen Form in den alten Bundeslaendern. Ziel ist es, zu gesamtdeutschen Strukturen zu kommen und zentrale Variablen zwischen West- und Ostdeutschland vergleichen zu

koennen. Im Zentrum stehen die Beziehungen zwischen Ausbildung, Weiterbildung und Berufstaetigkeit bzw. beruflicher Stellung sowie im Kontext damit der Arbeitsmitteleinsatz einschliesslich der Durchsetzung neuer Techniken. Aufgrund der besonderen Situation in Ostdeutschland wurden dort auch Arbeitslose und Personen in Fortbildungs- und Umschulungsmassnahmen in die Erhebung mit einbezogen.

Geographischer Raum: Ostdeutschland, Westdeutschland.

Datengewinnung: Standardisiertes Interview (Stichprobe: 12.000; Erwerbstaetige durch Infratest Sozialforschung und Marplan in Westdeutschland. Stichprobe: 5.000; Erwerbspersonen durch Infratest und das Ostberliner Institut EMMAG/ISS in Ostdeutschland).

13565 Education-Business Partnerships (EBPs): targets and stocktake.
GBR 1993
Research Date(s): 1988-1993
Bennett, R.; Wicks, P.
Inst: London University, London School of Economics and Political Science, Department of Geography, Houghton Street, London WC2A 2AE, United Kingdom.
Fin: Shell UK; Confederation of British Industry.
training-employment relationship; transition from school to work; school; industry; cooperation
relation formation-emploi; passage à la vie active; école; industrie; coopération
PROJECT DESCRIPTION

The objective of the report is to provide a stocktake of the current development of Education-Business Partnerships (EBPs). This has the purpose of acting like a 'church tower appeal' in that a visual impression is to be given of the current level of development in EBPs in different local education authorities (LEAs). The purpose of the stocktake is to provide a measure of the current development of EBPs against which future evolution and progress can be judged. It is intended that this will encourage existing effective EBPs whilst setting clear targets for the LEAs which have not yet developed full EBPs, and that further assessments will be made annually to stimulate the development of EBPs. The analysis assesses the progress in development of EBPs against a five level classification.

Publ: Bennett, R.J. *Education-Business Partnerships*. London: Confederation of British Industry, 1991.
Bennett, R.J.; McCoshan, A. & Sellgren, J. *The organisation of Business/Education links: further findings from the CBI Schools Questionnaire*. (Department of Geography Research Papers). London: London University, 1989.

13566 Educational responses to adult unemployment.
GBR 1993
Research Date(s): 1990-1993
Edwards, R.
Inst: Open University, School of Education, Walton Hall, Milton Keynes MK7 6AA, United Kingdom.
Fin: Canadian High Commission.
unemployment; adult education; vocational training; educational policy
chômage; éducation des adultes; formation professionnelle; politique de l'éducation
PROJECT DESCRIPTION

The aim of this research is to examine critically the policies and practices which produce and respond to adult unemployment in contemporary society and the role of education and training discourse and programmes in overcoming and/or reproducing adult unemployment. This is pursued through desk research and interviews with policy makers, practitioners and participants in the field. Conclusions are always provisional, dependent on the changing constellation of policy and practice.

Publ: Edwards, R. The Canadian jobs strategy. In: *Unemployment Bulletin*, Autumn 1991, pp. 8-13.
Edwards, R. The inevitable future? post-Fordism and open learning. In: *Open Learning*, Vol 6, No 2/1991, pp. 36-43.
Edwards, R. Guidance and unemployment in Canada. In: *Adults Learning*, Vol 2, No 10/1991, pp. 279-282.
Edwards, R. Winners and losers: the education and training of adults. In: Raggatt, P. & Unwin, L. (eds.). *Change and intervention: vocational education and training*. London: Falmer Press.

13567 Einstellungen/Haltungen sozialer Fachkraefte in den neuen Bundeslaendern. (Attitudes/approaches of female social workers in the new German states.)
DEU 1993
Research Date(s): 1991-1992
Koch, U.
Inst: Fachhochschule Ostfriesland Emden, FB Sozialwesen, Constantiaplatz 4, D-2970 Emden.
social worker; woman; unemployment; German DR; further training
travailleur social; femme; chômage; Allemagne RDA; formation complémentaire
PROJECT DESCRIPTION

Inhalt: Darstellung der Situation der Sozialarbeiterinnen unter den neuen Bedingungen: (a) soziale Lage, (b) Einstellungen bezueglich Arbeitslosigkeit, Zukunft, staatlichen Fuersorgeleistungen, (c) Einschaetzung eines Weiterbildungskurses und dessen Nuetzlichkeit (Kurs Winter/ Fruehjahr 1990/91 und 1991).

Geographischer Raum: Sachsen/ Region Mittweida.

Vorgehensweise: Untersuchungsdesign: Trend; Panel; 2 Querschnitte selbe Gruppe.

Datengewinnung: Postalische Befragung (Stichprobe: 66; Teilnehmerinnen Weiterbildungskurs fuer soziale Fachkraefte Mittweida/ Sachsen; Auswahlverfahren: total). Befragung (dito). Primaererhebung: Feldarbeit von Mitarbeitern des Projektes durchgefuehrt.

Auswertung: Signifikanzen.

Publ: Koch, Ursula. Weiterbildung fuer soziale Fachkraefte in den neuen Bundeslaendern. In: *Blaetter der Wohlfahrtspflege - Deutsche Zeitschrift fuer Sozialarbeit*, 10 u. 11, 1991, S. 244-247.

13568 Emploi et formation dans les processus de développement économique.
FRA 1993
Research Date(s): 1986-
Vernières, Michel.
Inst: Université de Paris I, UFR Analyse et politique économiques, CNRS URA/941 et GDR/996, Laboratoire d'économie sociale-Equipe Emploi, Formation, Développement, 90 rue de Tolbiac, 75634 Paris Cedex 13, France.
labour market; economic development; developed country; developing country; cross-national research; training supply
marché du travail; développement économique; pays développé; pays en développement; recherche transnationale; offre de formation
PROJECT DESCRIPTION

Objectifs: Il s'agit d'une recherche synthétique visant à analyser, dans les pays de structures économiques et de traditions culturelles différentes, la dynamique de l'évolution de l'emploi dans les processus de développement de ces sociétés, ce qui exige une analyse simultanée des systèmes de formation. Le travail s'organise autour de deux axes: (1) une réflexion sur l'apport des théories du développement et des travaux actuels d'économie du développement; (2) une étude de l'évolution des structures d'emploi et de l'appareil de formation dans la France contemporaine et comparaisons internationales.

Publ: Vernières, Michel. Notes sur la formation des ressources humaines en Asie. In: *Asies Recherches*, n° 6, 1989.
Vernières, Michel. Les ressources humaines dans le devenir des Tiers-Mondes. In: *Cahier GEM DEV*, n° 9, 1988, pp. 9-19.
Vernières, Michel & Gambier, Dominique. Participation aux ouvrages collectifs: *Economie des Tiers-Mondes*, PUF, 1991.
Collectif GEM DEV. *L'avenir des Tiers-Mondes*, PUF, 1991.

13569 Emploi et modes de vie: passages à la vie professionnelle, passage à la vie adulte en Région Provence-Alpes-Côte d'Azur.
FRA 1993
Research Date(s): 1986-1989
Godard, Francis.
Inst: Ministère de l'éducation, Ecole des hautes études en sciences sociales, CNRS URA/377, Centre d'enquête et de recherche sur la culture, la communication, les modes de vie et la socialisation, Centre pluridisciplinaire de la Vieille Charité, 2 rue de la Charité, 13002 Marseille, France.
Fin: Programme interdisciplinaire de recherche sur la technologie, le travail, l'emploi et les modes de vie (PIRTTEM).
women's employment; transition from school to work; vocational training; family life; social change
emploi des femmes; passage à la vie active; formation professionnelle; vie familiale; changement social
PROJECT DESCRIPTION

Objectifs: L'hypothèse de base de cette recherche est que les années 1972-1975 constituent une rupture du point de vue des modes de passage à l'état adulte. Cette rupture s'opère sur le plan économique avec le développement du chômage et l'instauration progressive d'un type de rapport salarial; elle s'opère sur le plan démographique et familial avec notamment les transformations des calendriers de nuptialité et de fécondité; elle s'opère sur le plan idéologique et le plan culturel avec ce que l'on pourrait appeler la "période 68". Si cette hypothèse est exacte on peut supposer que les calendriers et les diverses modalités de passage à l'état adulte vont se modifier entre les cohortes qui ont connu leurs passages au cours des années 1960 et celles qui les ont connu au cours des années 1970.

Méthodologie: On choisit deux cohortes de femmes. La première est constituée des femmes nées en 1947, la seconde des femmes nées en 1959. Ces deux cohortes sont considérées comme représentatives de deux générations. L'enquête a été conçue suivant trois grandes dimensions: (1) on analyse les divers cheminements de ces femmes à partir des calendriers résidentiels, familiaux, professionnels et de formation, (2) on situe ces cheminements sur l'histoire de la parentèle, (3) on analyse les cheminements de ces cohortes en relation avec les évolutions du marché de l'emploi, de l'urbanisation, de l'appareil de formation d'une zone déterminée (la zone Cannes-Grasse, Antibes). Cette enquête porte sur un échantillon de 1500 femmes. Le recensement de 1982 constitue la base de sondage.

Publ: Coninck (de), Frédéric & Godard, Francis. *Itinéraires féminins. Les calendriers familiaux, professionnels et résidentiels de deux générations de jeunes femmes dans les Alpes maritîmes.* Rapport remis au PIRTTEM, 1989.

Coninck (de), Frédéric & Godard, Francis. Les stratégies temporelles des jeunes adultes. In: *Enquête, Cahiers du CERCOM,* n° 6, *La socialisation de la jeunesse,* juin 1991.

13570 Employees' attitudes to learning at work.
GBR 1993
Research Date(s): 1990-1992
Saunders, M.; Fuller, A.; Lobley, D.
Inst: Lancaster University, Department of Educational Research, Centre for the Study of Education and Training, Cartmel College, Bailrigg, Lancaster LA1 4YW, United Kingdom.
Fin: United Distillers.
employee; vocational training; in-service training; attitude
salarié; formation professionnelle; formation en cours d'emploi; attitude
PROJECT DESCRIPTION
This research has been commissioned by an international drinks company. The company is going through a period of rapid change following a take-over in the late eighties. Senior managers are reviewing all aspects of the business including human resource development. As a consequence, the Centre for the Study of Education and Training was asked to provide independent research on employees' attitudes to training and learning and work as well as to qualifications. Surveys and case studies have been conducted.

13571 Entrée des jeunes dans la vie active (enquêtes EVA).
FRA 1993
Research Date(s): 1984-
Guégnard, Christine; Chenin, J.F.; Labopin, M.A.
Inst: Université de Dijon, UER Faculté des sciences économiques et de gestion, CNRS UPR/29 et GDR/996, Institut de recherche sur l'économie de l'éducation, BP 138, 21004 Dijon Cedex, France.
youth employment; occupational integration; follow-up study; regional development; transition from school to work
emploi des jeunes; intégration professionnelle; étude longitudinale; développement régional; passage à la vie active
PROJECT DESCRIPTION
Objectifs: Depuis 1984, le centre assure un suivi permanent des enquêtes décentralisées dans l'Académie de Dijon. Ces enquêtes décentralisées donnent une image de la situation des sortants du système éducatif d'une région, permettent de connaître l'évolution des conditions d'entrée des jeunes dans la vie active, par niveaux de formation, par spécialités.
Méthodologie: 10 000 jeunes, diplômés ou non, quittent chaque année l'enseignement secondaire, un sur trois intègre directement un emploi. Sept ans d'enquêtes permettent de caractériser l'évolution de l'insertion.
Résultats: Trois dates-repères caractérisent l'évolution de l'insertion, suivant d'ailleurs assez bien les évolutions économiques régionales. La Bourgogne a connu de 1984 à 1990 une période d'évolution rapide des conditions d'insertion des jeunes, caractérisée par une hausse du niveau de formation des jeunes sortants, une baisse du chômage grâce aux mesures jeunes et une progression des emplois.

Publ: Guégnard, Christine. *L'entrée des jeunes dans la vie active, des disparités.* Dijon: Publication SAIO/CIA-CEREQ, mars 1989, 4p.
Guégnard, Christine; Chenin, J.F. & Dumontet, O. *L'insertion professionnelle des jeunes après une formation technologique en Bourgogne.* Dijon: Document SAIO-SSR-CEREQ-ONISEP, mars 1989, 4p.
Guégnard, Christine & Chenin, J.F. *Les inégalités d'insertion en Bourgogne après une formation technologique.* Dijon: Document SAIO-SSR-CEREQ-ONISEP, février 1990, 8p.
Guégnard, Christine. *L'entrée des jeunes dans la vie active en février 1990.* Dijon: Document SAIO-SSR-CEREQ-ONISEP, octobre 1990, 4p.
Guégnard, Christine. *Après une formation complémentaire d'initiative locale.* Dijon: IREDU, janvier 1991, 4p.
Labopin, M.A. *L'insertion professionnelle des jeunes après un BTS en Bourgogne.* Dijon: IREDU, juin 1991.

13572 Entwicklung und Erprobung eines Modells fuer die betriebliche Weiterbildung des Lager- und Umschlagspersonals in der Spedition. (Development and testing of a model for in-company further training for warehouse and handling personnel in forwarding agencies.)
DEU 1993
Research Date(s): 1991-1994
Alleweldt, K.; Hilbers, J.
Sup: Char, H.
Inst: Rhein-Ruhr-Institut fuer Sozialforschung und Politikberatung e.V. - RISP- an der Uni, Heinrich-Lersch-Str. 15, D-4100 Duisburg 1.

Fin: Thyssen-Haniel-Logistic GmbH Magdeburg; Deutsche Forschungsanstalt fuer Luft- und Raumfahrt -DLR- Projekttraeger des Programms "Arbeit und Technik".
vocational training; further training; enterprise; in-service training; transport; qualification; curriculum development
formation professionnelle; formation complémentaire; entreprise; formation en cours d'emploi; transport; qualification; élaboration de programmes d'études
PROJECT DESCRIPTION
Inhalt: Im Zentrum stehen Beschaeftigte in den derzeit neu entstehenden Transport-, Lagerei- und Umschlagsunternehmen auf dem Gebiet der neuen Bundeslaender. Insbesondere geht es um die Qualifizierung des Lager- und Umschlagspersonals. Die Qualifikation richtet sich zum einen auf die Vermittlung von Kenntnissen und Faehigkeiten fuer ein Arbeiten unter marktwirtschaftlichen Rahmenbedingungen. Zum anderen geht es um die Herausbildung fachspezifischer Grundqualifikationen. Soweit es die fachlichen Inhalte betrifft, soll ein uebertragbares Konzept entwickelt werden, d.h. ein Modell, das ggf. in Form betriebsuebergreifender Angebote auch in Klein- und Mittelbetrieben Anwendung finden kann. Es soll darueber hinaus als Kernmodul konzipiert werden. Das bedeutet, es geht um die Entwicklung eines Basismoduls, mit dem anderen Qualifikationsmassnahmen, z.B. auf dem Gebiet der EDV oder zum Erwerb spezieller Zertifikate (Fuehrerscheine, Gefahrgutscheine) inhaltlich miteinander verknuepft und fundiert werden. Es sind folgende Arbeiten vorgesehen: Projektkoordination und Ermittlung des Bedarfs im Unternehmen; Ermittlung der besonderen mitgebrachten Leistungsvoraussetzungen bei Arbeitnehmern in den neuen Bundeslaendern; Entwicklung eines provisorischen Rahmenplans fuer explorative Schulungen; Durchfuehrung explorativer Schulungen; Erstellung eines Rahmencurriculums und einzelner Schulungseinheiten.
Geographischer Raum: Vorrangig neue Bundeslaender.
Vorgehensweise: Untersuchungsdesign: qualitative Forschung.
Datengewinnung: Gruppendiskussion (Stichprobe: 100; gewerbl. Arbeitnehmer; Auswahlverfahren: bewusst). Datenerstellung auf der Basis von bereits vorliegenden Materialien wie Texten, Akten, Statistiken.

13573 Equitable staffing policies in further and higher education.
GBR 1993
Research Date(s): 1991-1994
Powney, J.; Weiner, G.; McPake, J.
Inst: Scottish Council for Research in Education, 15 St John Street, Edinburgh EH8 8JR, United Kingdom; South Bank University, 103 Borough Road, London SE1 OAA, United Kingdom.
Fin: Economic and Social Research Council.
equal opportunity; employment opportunities; higher education; teaching post; teaching profession
égalité de chances; chances d'obtenir un emploi; enseignement supérieur; poste d'enseignement; profession d'enseignant
PROJECT DESCRIPTION
This project will explore the strategies deployed by further and higher educational institutions committed to developing and implementing equitable staff policies and practices. Further it will disseminate examples of good practice for information to other institutions.
The specific aims of the project are to: (1) develop understanding of the policies and practices which enhance the promotion of under-represented groups, e.g. female and black and ethnic minority staff in educational institutions; (2) encourage wider implementation and evaluation of such policies and practices; (3) develop understanding of processes of change by drawing together theoretical and empirical work in the fields of equal opportunities and the study of organisations; and (4) contribute to understanding and utilisation of evaluative case-study methodologies.

13574 Ergebnisse aus dem Modellversuch "Berufliche Qualifizierung von Frauen" als Teil der Modellversuchsreihe "zur beruflichen Qualifizierung von Erwachsenen, die keine abgeschlossene Berufsausbildung haben und ein besonderes Arbeitsmarktrisiko tragen". (Results of the pilot project "Vocational qualification of women" as part of the series of projects "On vocational qualifications for adults who have not completed their vocational training and who are particularly at risk on the labour market".)
DEU 1993
Research Date(s): 1986-1992
Horstmann, M.
Sup: Weindel, K.
Inst: Neue Arbeit Saar gGmbH, Berta-Von-Suttner-Str. 1, D-6600 Saarbruecken 3.
Fin: Bundesinstitut fuer Berufsbildung; Land Saarland Ministerium fuer Wirtschaft.
women's education; occupational qualification; vocational education; retraining; vocational preparation; occupational integration
éducation des femmes; qualification professionnelle; enseignement professionnel; recyclage; initiation à la profession; intégration professionnelle
PROJECT DESCRIPTION

Inhalt: Erprobung unterstuetzender Massnahmen, die Frauen ohne oder ohne verwertbare Berufsausbildung dazu befaehigen sollen, einen qualifizierten Abschluss (Umschulung) zu erlangen, um ihre (Wieder-)Eingliederung in das Erwerbsleben zu ermoeglichen. Aus regionalen arbeitsmarktpolitischen Gruenden finden die Umschulungen in Betrieben unterschiedlicher Groesse in unterschiedlichen Branchen statt. Favorisiert werden zukunftstraechtige Berufe, insbesondere im gewerblich-technischen Bereich. Der Modellversuchstraeger stellt die flankierenden Massnahmen und fungiert als Koordinator zwischen Teilnehmerinnen und Betrieben. Flankierende Massnahmen: berufliche Orientierungs- und Vorbereitungskurse; sozialpaedagogische Betreuung, insbesondere Organisation der Kinderbetreuung; Stuetz- und Foerderunterricht; finanzielle Hilfen: Aufstockung des Unterhaltsgeldes; Zuschuss bei Kinderbetreuungskosten; Nachbetreuung; Schwerpunkt des 1. Durchgangs: Lebenssituation und Lernumfeld der Teilnehmerinnen (Wissenschaftliche Begleitung: Karin Weindel, Dipl. Soz.); Schwerpunkt des 2. Durchgangs: Qualifizierung der Ausbilder im Hinblick auf eine zielgruppenspezifische Didaktik (Wissenschaftliche Begleitung: Marina Horstmann, Erziehungsw. M.A.).

Geographischer Raum: Saarbruecken und Umgebung.

Untersuchter Zeitraum: Der Modellversuch erstreckt sich auf 6 Jahre: 1. Durchgang 1986-1989, 2. Durchgang 1989-1992.

Vorgehensweise: Ergebnisse: Die flankierenden Massnahmen haben sich als unverzichtbare Voraussetzung zum erfolgreichen Bestehen der Kammerpruefungen erwiesen. Die Abbruchquoten liegen unter denen ueblicher FuU-Massnahmen. 75 Prozent der Teilnehmerinnen konnten in Arbeit vermittelt werden. Untersuchungsdesign: Evaluationsstudie; retrospektive Daten; qualitative Forschung.

Datengewinnung: Standardisiertes Interview, nicht-standardisiertes Interview, Gruppendiskussion (Stichprobe: 90; Teilnehmerinnen der versch. Jahrgaenge; Auswahlverfahren: total, Zufall). Expertengespraech (Stichprobe: 20; Ausbilder der Umschulungsbetriebe; Auswahlverfahren: bewusst). Primaererhebung: Feldarbeit von Mitarbeitern des Projektes durchgefuehrt, von der wiss. Begleitung durchgefuehrt; Datenerstellung auf der Basis von bereits vorliegenden Materialien wie Texten, Akten, Statistiken.

13575 Etude de la relation maître d'apprentissage-apprenti: quelles difficultés de communication?
FRA 1993
Research Date(s): 1990-
Savy, Françoise; Maubant, Philippe.
Sup: Chaix, Marie-Laure.
Inst: Ministère de l'Agriculture, Institut national de recherches et d'applications pédagogiques, 2 rue des Champs Prévois, 21100 Dijon, France.
Fin: Délégation à la formation professionnelle.
apprentice; apprenticeship; teacher-pupil relation; agricultural training; learning process
apprenti; apprentissage professionnel; relation maître-élève; formation agricole; apprentissage
PROJECT DESCRIPTION
Objectifs: Le développement de l'apprentissage à tous les niveaux de formation fait apparaître aujourd'hui le rôle crucial du maître d'apprentissage dans la formation des jeunes. La relation pédagogique qui va s'installer entre les deux partenaires dépend d'un certain nombre de facteurs psycho-affectifs. Si l'on veut agir sur la relation pédagogique afin de l'améliorer, il convient de bien appréhender l'ensemble de ces facteurs. Le premier volet de l'étude a permis cette approche globale. Le deuxième volet a pour objectif de voir quelles sont les difficultés particulières de communication qui se posent. L'analyse transactionnelle est utilisée comme cadre thématique.

Méthodologie: Entretiens semi-directifs auprès de maîtres d'apprentissage et d'apprentis de niveaux différents: apprentis en Certificat d'aptitude professionnelle agricole, Brevet d'enseignement professionnel agricole et Brevet de technicien agricole. Tous sont dans des entreprises horticoles: productions florales, pépinières ou maraîchères.

Résultats: Le premier volet de l'étude a montré la quantité des facteurs qui interviennent dans la relation maître d'apprentissage-apprenti et la complexité de leurs rapports. Notamment on a mis en évidence l'importance des représentations des acteurs: sur le métier, l'avenir professionnel, la formation. On a pu également constater la rupture culturelle qu'introduisent les apprentis de niveau IV auprès de leur maître d'apprentissage lorsque celui-ci a un niveau de formation inférieur, ce qui peut provoquer des difficultés relationnelles importantes.

Publ: Savy, Françoise. *Un dispositif de formation à la communication pour les maîtres d'apprentissage.* Dijon: INRAP, décembre 1990.

13576 An evaluation of career development courses in higher education.
GBR 1993
Research Date(s): 1991-1995
Bray, R.
Sup: Fulton, O.
Inst: Lancaster University, Department of Educational Research, Cartmel College, Bailrigg, Lancaster LA1 4YW, United Kingdom.

vocational guidance; occupational choice; higher education
orientation professionnelle; choix d'une profession; enseignement supérieur
PROJECT DESCRIPTION
There is evidence of a significant growth in careers education provision in higher education in recent years. Contributory causes may include: transfer from the experiences of secondary and further education (e.g. Technical and Vocational Education Initiative); influence of the Enterprise in Higher Education project with its focus on transferable personal skills; and policy responses to graduate unemployment.

This research aims to identify the reasons for such growth, the nature of the provision and likely future trends. The research will involve two stages. Stage 1 involves a questionnaire to all United Kingdom institutions of higher education investigating extent of careers education content and aims. Stage 2 uses Stage 1 results to select a sample (6-10) of institutions for in-depth follow-up: interviews with management, teaching staff and students concerning course aims, content and outcomes.

13577 Evaluation verschiedener Ansaetze zur Teilnehmergewinnung fuer Qualifizierungs- und Beschaeftigungsangebote, die durch den Europaeischen Sozialfonds (ESF) gefoerdert werden. (Evaluation of various approaches in attracting participants to the training and employment programmes promoted by the European Social Fund (ESF).)
DEU 1993
Research Date(s): 1991-1993
Hagemann, O.
Inst: Stiftung Berufliche Bildung Arbeitslosenbildungswerk, Abt. Forschung, Statistik, Wendenstrasse 493, D-2000 Hamburg 26.
Fin: Europaeische Gemeinschaft Sozialfonds.
access to employment; employment policy; job creation; unemployment; employment opportunities; Europe; evaluation
accès á l'emploi; politique de l'emploi; création d'emploi; chômage; chances d'obtenir un emploi; Europe; évaluation
PROJECT DESCRIPTION
Inhalt: vor dem Hintergrund einer positiven Arbeitsmarktentwicklung wurde beobachtet, dass sich die Arbeitsmarktchancen von Angehoerigen sogenannter Problemgruppen kaum verbessern. Sie sind von Langzeit- und Dauerarbeitslosigkeit sowie von haeufiger Arbeitslosigkeit, die nur von instabilen Beschaeftigungen unterbrochen wird, betroffen. Herkoemmliche arbeitsmarktpolitische Reintegrationsprogramme erreichen diese Gruppen kaum. Eine Vielzahl sozialer und persoenlicher Probleme, Qualifizierungsverluste und weiteres schaffen Barrieren und Schwellen vor der Teilnahme an "normalen" Reintegrationsangeboten. Durch den ESF werden deshalb neue Angebote der Qualifizierung bzw. der Beschaeftigung und Qualifizierung gefoerdert, fuer die eine eigene Teilnehmergewinnung, die von vier Teams mit unterschiedlichen Ansaetzen betrieben wird, eingerichtet wurde. Der Effekt dieser Teilnehmergewinnung soll evaluiert werden.

Vorgehensweise: Die Evaluation erfasst sowohl den Input der Teilnehmergewinnungsaktivitaeten in einem Berichtssystem Teilnehmergewinnung als auch den Output mittels Befragungen von Teilnehmern und Teilnehmerinnen, Multiplikatoren sowie der Massnahmentraeger. Durch einen Vorher-Nachher-Vergleich sozialstatistischer Daten wird die strukturelle Zusammensetzung der Teilnehmer/innen in den gefoerderten Massnahmen analysiert, um die Auswirkungen der Teilnehmergewinnung zu ueberpruefen. Zusaetzlich sollen Experteninterviews Aufschluss ueber eher qualitative Aspekte ergeben. Die Auswertung umfasst eine quanitative und qualitative Analyse der verschiedenen Aktivitaeten, die Bewertung derselben durch die Multiplikatoren sowie eine Trendanalyse der Teilnehmerdaten von entsprechend ESF-gefoerderten Qualifizierungs- und Arbeitsmassnahmen

Datengewinnung: Expertengespraech; Befragung; Sekundaeranalyse.

13578 FHW-Studierende zwei Jahre danach: empirische Analyse des AbsolventInnenverbleibs und des Berufsstarts. (Polytechnic students two years after graduation: empirical analysis of their destination and career start.)
DEU 1993
Research Date(s): 1991-1992
Bischoff, G.; Huss, J.; Penrose, V.
Sup: Kadritzke, U.
Inst: Fachhochschule fuer Wirtschaft Berlin, Facheinheit 06, Unternehmensfuehrung und Personalwesen, Badensche Strasse 50-51, D-1000 Berlin 62.
Fin: Land Berlin Senatsverwaltung fuer Wissenschaft und Forschung.
economics; transition from school to work; career; initial employment; occupational integration; graduate
science économique; passage à la vie active; carrière; premier emploi; intégration professionnelle; étudiant diplômé
PROJECT DESCRIPTION
Inhalt: (1) Gewinn empirischer Befunde ueber den sozialen und beruflichen Status von FHW-AbsolventInnen nach dem Studium, vor allem bezueglich des sektoralen, taetigkeitsfeldspezifischen und fachlichen Zuschnitts der beruflichen Qualifikationsanforderungen. (2) Gewinn empirischer Befunde zur Einschaetzung der FHW-Ausbildung durch die

AbsolventInnen im Lichte der ersten Berufserfahrungen. (3) Rueckschluesse aus der empirischen Untersuchung auf die Struktur und das inhaltliche Profil der FHW-Ausbildung (Grundwissen, Vermittlung wesentlicher Faehigkeiten funktionaler und extrafunktionaler Art, Praxisbezug, Taetigkeitsfelder).

Geographischer Raum: Berlin (West).

Vorgehensweise: Die Forschung versteht sich unter anderem als Beitrag zur bildungssoziologischen Debatte zum Verhaeltnis von Theorie- und Praxisbezuegen, von fachlich-spezialisierten zu ueberfachlich-extrafunktionalen Studieninhalten. Untersuchungsdesign: Querschnittserhebung; retrospektive Daten.

Datengewinnung: Postalische Befragung (Stichprobe: 590; FHW-AbsolventInnen ueber 5 Semester; Auswahlverfahren: total). Primaererhebung: Feldarbeit von Mitarbeitern des Projektes durchgefuehrt.

Auswertung: Multiple Regression; Varianzanalyse. Datenaufbereitung: punktueller Vergleich mit Ergebnissen vergleichbarer Studien.

13579 Final analysis of the data collected on the work experience of graduate engineers.

GBR 1993
Research Date(s): 1979-1991
Newton, T.
Sup: Keenan, A.
Inst: Heriot-Watt University, Department of Business Organisation, Riccarton Campus, Currie, Edinburgh EH14 4AS, United Kingdom; Edinburgh University, Department of Business Studies, William Robertson Building, 50 George Square, Edinburgh EH8 9JY, United Kingdom.
Fin: Economic and Social Research Council.
training-employment relationship; engineer; graduate; employment
relation formation-emploi; ingénieur; étudiant diplômé; emploi
PROJECT DESCRIPTION

The project analysed the engineering education, business training of engineers, work difficulties and work experience of young graduate engineers. The study was based on a longitudinal analysis of the work of 798 engineers, who were followed up from their penultimate term at university until four years into employment. Data collection was through questionnaire and semi-structural interview. Good response rates were obtained throughout the study.

The findings suggest: (1) notable mis-matches between the career expectations of engineering students and their subsequent work experience; (2) deficiencies in the higher education of engineers, particularly in relation to management studies; (3) a dissatisfaction with the business training of graduate engineers, again particularly in relation to managerial skills; (4) that work difficulties in relation to report writing, information handling and dealing with people were more common than those relating to lack of technical expertise.

Publ: A full list of publications is available from the researcher.

13580 Formation et mobilité: la gestion de la main-d'oeuvre féminine.

FRA 1993
Research Date(s): 1988-1990
Engrand, Sylvie; Gadrey, Nicole; Charlon, Elisabeth; Feutrié, Michel.
Inst: Université de Lille I, Centre lillois d'études et de recherches sociologiques et économiques, CNRS URA/345, Laboratoire de sociologie du travail, de l'éducation et de l'emploi, Institut de Sociologie, 59655 Villeneuve d'Ascq Cedex, France.
Fin: Ministère des affaires sociales, Mission Recherche et expérimentation.
women's employment; vocational training; business management; personnel management; sex discrimination; level of qualification
emploi des femmes; formation professionnelle; gestion des entreprises; gestion du personnel; discrimination sexuelle; niveau de qualification
PROJECT DESCRIPTION

Objectifs: Cette recherche s'intéresse au type de relations existant entre le mode de construction sociale de la flexibilité en entreprise et la composition sexuelle de la main d'oeuvre.

Méthodologie: Exploitation de données statistiques et enquêtes en entreprises.

Résultats: Les données statistiques confirment l'existence d'inégalités entre les secteurs masculins et féminins aussi bien au niveau de la précarité de l'emploi qu'à celui des salaires ou des possibilités de promotion; les enquêtes en entreprises montrent comment les directions tiennent compte de la composition de leur main d'oeuvre quand elles élaborent des politiques de formation et de flexibilité; elles mettent en évidence des tendances contradictoires: développement de la précarité et sous-qualification, mais aussi création de nouveaux types d'emplois et de nouvelles trajectoires professionnelles.

Publ: Engrand, Sylvie & Gadrey, Nicole. Mobilité et formation: la gestion de la main d'oeuvre féminine. Rapport de recherche MIRE, Université de Lille, CLERSE, 1990.

13581 Frauen mit Hoch- bzw. Fachschulabschluessen der ehemaligen DDR und ihre spezifischen Probleme auf dem Arbeitsmarkt. (Female graduates of universities and polytechnics in the former GDR and their specific problems on the labour market.)

DEU 1993
Research Date(s): 1992-1993
Waehlisch, B.
Inst: KOBRA Koordinierungs- und Beratungszentrum fuer die Weiterbildung von Frauen, Knesebeckstr. 33-34, D-1000 Berlin 12.
labour market; woman; German DR; employment opportunities; occupational status; graduate
marché du travail; femme; Allemagne RDA; chances d'obtenir un emploi; statut professionnel; étudiant diplômé
PROJECT DESCRIPTION

Inhalt: Wie wirkt sich die Anerkennungsproblematik von Bildungsabschluessen der ehemaligen DDR auf die realen Arbeitsmarktchancen der Frauen aus? Wie greifen Anpassungsqualifizierungen und wo fehlen geeignete Massnahmen? Fuer welche Frauen spielt Aufstieg/ Karriere/Fuehrungsposition eine Rolle? Welche Frauen sind bereit einen Abstieg in beruflicher Hinsicht zu akzeptieren? Welche Veraenderungen der Lebenssituation wirken sich hemmend bzw. foerdernd auf die Berufstaetigkeit aus? Spielt die Vereinbarkeit von Familie und Beruf eine andere Rolle als zu DDR-Zeiten?

Geographischer Raum: Berlin.

Vorgehensweise: Problemstudie aufgrund der Auswertung von Beratungen.

13582 Gender, training and employment: an historical analysis 1939-1950.

GBR 1993
Research Date(s): 1990-1992
Summerfield, P.
Inst: Lancaster University, Department of Educational Research, Cartmel College, Bailrigg, Lancaster LA1 4YW, United Kingdom.
Fin: Economic and Social Research Council.
women's employment; history of education; training-employment relationship; women's education
emploi des femmes; histoire de l'éducation; relation formation-emploi; éducation des femmes
PROJECT DESCRIPTION

This is a study of the relationships between the training and employment of women during the Second World War and the immediate post-war period. The central research question is whether wartime training altered the position of women in the labour market on either a temporary or a permanent basis. In pursuit of answers the research scrutinizes the formulation and outcomes of training and employment policy in the period 1939-1950.

13583 La gestion de la reconversion des salariés: une forme de transition professionnelle.

FRA 1993
Research Date(s): 1986-
Villeval, Marie-Claude; Chaskiel, P.; Méhaut, Philippe.
Inst: Université de Nancy II, CNRS URA/1167 et GDR/996, Emploi et politiques sociales - Groupe de recherche sur l'éducation et l'emploi, 23 bd Albert 1er, BP 3397, 54015 Nancy Cedex, France.
career change; occupational mobility; personnel management; industry; employment policy
changement de carrière; mobilité professionnelle; gestion du personnel; industrie; politique de l'emploi
PROJECT DESCRIPTION

Objectifs: Le cadre des recherches sur ce thème est celui des processus de mobilité au sein des fractions de main d'oeuvre insérées de longue date dans le salariat, qui produisent de nouveaux dispositifs institutionnels de mobilité, notamment par le recours à la formation: (1) un groupe de travail pluridisciplinaire a effectué un bilan des connaissances sur l'évolution des politiques de reconversion de la main d'oeuvre depuis les années cinquante en France et sur la transformation des problématiques des économistes, sociologues, juristes et spécialistes des sciences de l'éducation en ce domaine; (2) une évaluation du fonctionnement interne et des effets externes du dispositif conventionnel de la sidérurgie sur les trajectoires de reconversion de l'ensemble des salariés d'un site sidérurgique (enquête auprès de 1300 salariés). Ces travaux ont fait l'objet de plusieurs confrontations avec des chercheurs européens notamment sur les spécificités nationales des politiques; les perspectives s'orientent dans trois directions: une confrontation France-RFA sur les politiques de reconversion et leurs effets en termes de transformation des rapports à l'emploi avec un éclairage sur les politiques européennes de formation de reconversion, une réflexion sur l'imbrication des stratégies de reconversion interne selon les fractions du système productif, dans la dynamique de transformation du rapport salarial.

Publ: Villeval, Marie-Claude; Enclos, P.; Marraud, C.; Chassey (de), Francis; Dupuis, P.A.; Fath, Gérard & Higelé, Pierre. La reconversion de la main d'oeuvre. Bibliographie sélective (1950-1988). In: *Formation-emploi*, 1990, n° 29, pp. 82-92.

Villeval, Marie-Claude. Reconversions et mobilités. In: *Bref-CEREQ*, juin 1990, n° 55, pp. 1-4.

Villeval, Marie-Claude. *Se former ou capitaliser? Dynamique conventionnelle et trajectoire de reconversion dans une entreprise sidérurgique.* GREE-UNIMETAL-MRT-Préfecture de Lorraine, 1990, 130p.

Villeval, Marie-Claude; Chassey (de), Francis & Receveur, D.*Contribution à l'évaluation du dispositif de reconversion dans la sidérurgie lorraine.* GREE-Laboratoire de sociologie du travail-UNIMETAL-MRT-Préfecture de Lorraine, 1990, 30p.

(Une liste complète est disponible.).

13584 Graduate numeracy.

GBR 1993

Research Date(s): 1990-

Cornelius, M.

Inst: Durham University, School of Education, Leazes Road, Durham DH1 1TA, United Kingdom.

Fin: Enterprise in Higher Education.

employment; graduate; arithmetic; job requirements

emploi; étudiant diplômé; arithmétique; qualification requise pour l'emploi

PROJECT DESCRIPTION

This is an investigation into the mathematical needs of new graduates in employment. The methods used include a sample of new graduates being investigated through employers via questionnaires and interviews to ascertain what mathematical skills are needed in employment and what deficiencies exist. The conclusions are likely to be of interest to both institutions of higher education and employers.

Publ: Cornelius, M.L. Numeracy in a university and beyond. In: *Education and Training*, Vol 33, No 3/1991, pp. 28-31.

Cornelius, M.L. Just a few questions. In: *Times Higher Education Supplement*, April 1991.

Cornelius, M.L. Degree of panic. In: *Times Educational Supplement*, May 1991.

Cornelius, M.L. Graduate numeracy. In: *Teaching Mathematics and its Applications*, Vol 10, No 4/1991, pp. 151-153.

13585 Guidance aspects of the Enterprise in Higher Education programme.

GBR 1993

Research Date(s): 1990-1992

Watts, A.; Hawthorn, R.

Inst: National Institute for Careers Education and Counselling, Sheraton House, Castle Park, Cambridge CB3 0AX, United Kingdom.

occupational choice; higher education; vocational guidance; training-employment relationship

choix d'une profession; enseignement supérieur; orientation professionnelle; relation formation-emploi

PROJECT DESCRIPTION

The aim of the project is to examine ways in which institutions involved in the Training, Enterprise and Education Division's EHE (Enterprise in Higher Education) programme can help students to establish linkages between the competencies and skills they are developing and their possible futures. The project is preparing case studies of examples of existing practice in five institutions, feeding back the case studies to the institutions concerned in ways which will be likely to foster further development work, and disseminating examples of good or interesting practice to other institutions involved in the EHE initiative. The case studies will be made available in published form as part of a document including recommendations for policy and guidelines for practice.

Publ: Watts, A.G. & Hawthorn, R. *Careers educationa and the curriculum in higher education*, Cambridge: CRAC/Hobsons, 1992.

13586 The higher education route to the labour market for women returners.

GBR 1993

Research Date(s): 1990-1991

Macauley, C.

Sup: Brown, A.; Webb, J.

Inst: Edinburgh University, Department of Business Studies, William Robertson Building, 50 George Square, Edinburgh EH8 9JY, United Kingdom.

Fin: Universities Funding Council.

labour market; adult education; women's education; higher education; employment opportunities; sex; age

marché du travail; éducation des adultes; éducation des femmes; enseignement supérieur; chances d'obtenir un emploi; sexe; âge

PROJECT DESCRIPTION

The project explored the aspirations and achievements of those women returners who re-enter the labour market via the higher education route; and compared the labour market experience of mature women graduates from Scottish universities with men who also gain a university degree for the first time at the same age. Preliminary research using data from the Universities Statistical Records Office had already been conducted before the project began. This was supplemented by a postal questionnaire for all contactable Scottish university graduates who entered university at the age of 25 or over and graduated in the period 1985-1990. The response rate was 51.2%. 541 usable responses were received.

The majority (90%) of respondents were satisfied with their university course. A relatively high proportion (one third) however graduated with ordinary degrees. Significantly more women than men had other domestic commitments while at university. Older graduates were successful in attaining occupational mobility, although more men than women obtained the highest status jobs (11.4% women; 27.7% men). Mature graduates were more likely than young graduates to work in the public sector. The private sector was more likely to recruit younger graduates and mature male graduates than mature female graduates. One third of respondents felt that they had been discriminated against on grounds of age.

Publ: Brown, A. & Webb, J. The higher education route to the labour market for mature students. In: *British Journal of Education and Work*, Vol 4, No 1/1990, pp. 5-21.

13587 Hilfen zum Uebergang Schule - Beruf im regionalen Kontext (Koordination und wissenschaftliche Begleitung). (Facilitating the transition from school to employment in a regional context (coordination and evaluation research).)

DEU 1993

Research Date(s): 1991-1995

Preiss, C.; Raab, E.; Meier, U.; Schmid, B.

Sup: Rademacker, H.

Inst: Deutsches Jugendinstitut e.V., Freibadstrasse 30, D-8000 Muenchen 90.

Fin: Institution; Bundesministerium fuer Bildung und Wissenschaft.

transition from school to work; German DR; Germany - Federal Republic; priority area; vocational guidance

passage à la vie active; Allemagne RDA; Allemagne RFA; zone prioritaire; orientation professionnelle

PROJECT DESCRIPTION

Inhalt: Auswertung vorliegender Laengsschnittdaten aus Muenchen und Duisburg fuer die Umsetzung in regionalen Kontexten unter Einbeziehung von Standorten der neuen Bundeslaender. Organisation und Entwicklung von Erfahrungsaustausch. Durchfuehrung eigener Erhebungen.

Geographischer Raum: Muenchen, Duisburg, Brandenburg (Stadt), Berlin, Jena.

Untersuchter Zeitraum: 1993-1995.

Vorgehensweise: Evaluation von Unterstuetzungsleistungen im Uebergang Schule - Beruf im regionalen Kontext; Begleitforschung. Untersuchungsdesign: Evaluationsstudie.

Auswertung: Datenaufbereitung: Datenedition (z.B. Aufbau von Datenbanken); Verlaufsdaten (event history data); Verknuepfung verschiedener Datensaetze (record linkage).

13588 I-See! 1991.

NLD 1993

Research Date(s): 1990-1991

Dekker, R.J.P.; Grip, A. de; Beekman, T.B.J.; Loo, P.J.E. van de; Wieling, M.H.; Willems, E.J.T.A.; et al.

Inst: ROA Researchcentrum voor Onderwijs en Arbeidsmarkt, Universiteit Limburg (Research Centre for Education and the Labour Market, University of Limburg), P.O. Box 616, 6200 MD Maastricht, Netherlands.

Fin: National Career Guidance Information Centre (LDC).

labour market; trend; forecasting; employment; employment opportunities

marché du travail; tendance; prévision; emploi; chances d'obtenir un emploi

PROJECT DESCRIPTION

As in previous years, ROA has been responsible for providing the labour market module of "I-See!" This covers current data, development trends, risk indicators and labour market forecasts by economic sectors, occupational classes and types of education. On behalf of the third I-See! product, a new occupational classification developed by ROA was used, which offers a better match than the current CBS (Central Bureau of Statistics) classification with the occupational classification used in educational and vocational guidance fields. Furthermore, a first move has been made towards the extension of the system with regional labour market information with an analysis of unemployment among school leavers, divided by types of education, at regional level. Other adjustments concern the employment of data from the Labour Force Survey for the calculation of risk indicators and for the determination of the replacement demand, the further improvement of the forecasting models for expansion demand and continuing refinement of the supply forecast methodology.

From 1992 the research project I-See! will be integrated with another information system, and the two will become one project charged with maintaining and further developing the information system on education and the labour market.

I-See! has appeared on CD rom.

13589 Il ruolo delle condizioni ambientali nello stress lavorativo e nel burnout in professioni di aiuto. (The role of environmental conditions in occupational stress and burnout in the helping professions.)
ITA 1994
Research Date(s): 1990-
Sirigatti, Saulo; Stefanile, Cristina; Menoni, Ezio.
Inst: Istituto di Psicologia Generale e Clinica (Institute of General and Clinical Psychology), Pian dei Mantellini 35, 53100 Siena, Italy.
Università degli Studi di Siena (University of Siena), Pian dei Mantellini 35, 53100 Siena, Italy
Fin: Consiglio Nazionale della Ricerche.
occupational environment; working conditions; social worker; teaching personnel; health service personnel; occupational disease; mental stress; fatigue; overtaxing
milieu professionnel; conditions de travail; travailleur social; corps enseignant; personnel médical; maladie professionnelle; tension mentale; fatigue; surmenage
PROJECT DESCRIPTION
Findings of research on burnout in the helping professions show the importance of a systematic study of the role of personal characteristics and environmental conditions in burnout in the helping professions and in the coping styles adopted. Initially, qualitative information on the incidence of burnout among public health workers and educators was collected through thematic interviews. On the basis of the information collected, a preliminary questionnaire was prepared which dealt with various areas of burnout (role conflict and ambiguity; work motivation; anxiety; hostility; etc.). The questionnaire was administered to 300 public health workers (doctors, psychologists, head nurses, professional nurses, professional educators, and volunteers) in various hospital divisions, outpatient clinics, and therapy communities, to 200 professional nursing students, and to 270 public health workers representing various helping professions. The data collected underwent qualitative and quantitative analysis to test the congruity of the information and the characteristics of the measurement scales.
Early indications suggest connections between levels of burnout and certain aspects of the organizational climate (role conflict and ambiguity). A plan of action was prepared to identify, through univariate and multivariate techniques, the possible connections between burnout and personality traits and socio-environmental conditions in the workplace.
Further research on the most effective coping styles and the most useful interventions for the prevention and control of burnout is envisaged.
Publ: Sirigatti, Saulo; Stefanile, C. & Menoni, E. Maslach Burnout Inventory in Italy. XIII Congresso Nazionale della Società Italiana di Medicina Psicosomatica, Bologna, 2-4 maggio 1991.
Sirigatti, Saulo; Stefanile, C. & Menoni, E. The Maslach Burnout Inventory in Italy: uncertainties about its factor structures. 5th Permanent Conference of Italian-Polish Psychology. Amalfi, 1991.
Sirigatti, Saulo & Stefanile, C. Maslach Burnout Inventory (MBI Alla luce dell'analisi fattoriale confirmatoria). In: *Bollettino di Psicologia Applicata*, 200, pp. 39-45.

13590 Impact de la mesure "Travaux d'utilité collective" (TUC) en région Lorraine.
FRA 1993
Research Date(s): 1991-
Rose, José; Poret, Bernard; Gérardin, Frédéric; Meyer, J.L.
Inst: Université de Nancy II, CNRS URA/1167 et GDR/996, Emploi et politiques sociales - Groupe de recherche sur l'éducation et l'emploi, 23 bd Albert 1er, BP 3397, 54015 Nancy Cedex, France.
Fin: Direction régionale à la formation professionnelle.
occupational integration; youth employment; in-plant training; socialization; vocational training; work experience
intégration professionnelle; emploi des jeunes; stage en entreprise; socialisation; formation professionnelle; expérience du travail
PROJECT DESCRIPTION
Objectifs: Il s'agit de mettre à jour les diverses formes de travaux d'utilité collective comme situations constitutives de modes de transition professionnelle et de repérer le jeu des variables différenciant les pratiques de formation, de mise au travail et de socialisation des jeunes et de les analyser au regard des trajectoires des jeunes et des "stratégies" des structures d'accueil.
Méthodologie: Deux axes méthodologiques sont retenus: (1) une enquête postale auprès d'environ 500 organismes pour repérer les conditions de mobilisation et d'usage de cette "fraction particulière de main d'oeuvre"; (2) un questionnaire passé auprès de 160 jeunes pour cerner les conditions et modalités d'accès aux travaux d'utilité collective, la place et le rôle tenus par les jeunes au sein des organismes et la contribution de ce passage à leur professionnalisation.

13591 Informatiesysteem onderwijs-arbeidsmarkt. (Information system on education and the labour market.)
NLD 1993
Research Date(s): 1986-
Grip, A. de.

Inst: ROA Researchcentrum voor Onderwijs en Arbeidsmarkt, Universiteit Limburg (Research Centre for Education and the Labour Market, University of Limburg), P.O. Box 616, 6200 MD Maastricht, Netherlands.
Fin: National Career Guidance Information Centre (LDC); Ministry of Education and Science; Central Employment Board.
labour market; information system; educational guidance; vocational guidance
marché du travail; système d'information; orientation pédagogique; orientation professionnelle
PROJECT DESCRIPTION
1992 was the first year of the second phase of a long-term project on education and the labour market. The aim of the project is to create an information system to be used in vocational guidance for pupils and students in secondary and higher education. In this second phase the project is commissioned by the National Career Guidance Information Centre, the Ministry of Education and Science and the Central Employment Board.
In the beginning of 1992 the third complete version of the information system was published in the first bi-annual report *The Labour Market by Education and Occupation to 1994*. At the end of the year a first update of the statistical appendix to the report was made. In addition work continued on a programme aimed at the gradual expansion and improvement of the information system. Among other things, regional labour market information has for the first time been published in addition to the national data.
Publ: ROA, *De arbeidsmarkt naar opleiding en beroep tot 1994* (The labour market by education and occupation to 1994), ROA-R-1992/1 (ISBN 90-5321-077-6).
ROA, *De arbeidsmarkt naar opleiding en beroep tot 1994, Statistische bijlage* (The labour market by education and occupation to 1994, statistical appendix), ROA-R-1992/1B (ISBN 90-5321-078-4).
Berendsen, H. et al. *Regionale arbeidsmarktinformatie naar opleiding en beroep. Een verkenning vanuit het ROA-informatiesysteem onderwijs-arbeidsmarkt* (Regional labour market information by education and occupation. An investigation using the ROA Information System on Education and the Labour Market), ROA-R-1992/2 (ISBN 90-5321-071-7).

13592 Informatiesysteem voor onderwijs en arbeidsmarkt. (Information system for education and the labour market.)
NLD 1993
Research Date(s): 1986-1991
Grip, A. de; Heijke, J.A.M.
Inst: ROA Researchcentrum voor Onderwijs en Arbeidsmarkt, Universiteit Limburg (Research Centre for Education and the Labour Market, University of Limburg), P.O. Box 616, 6200 MD Maastricht, Netherlands.
Fin: Ministry of Education and Science.
labour market; transition from school to work; educational guidance; vocational guidance; information system
marché du travail; passage à la vie active; orientation pédagogique; orientation professionnelle; système d'information
PROJECT DESCRIPTION
The year 1991 was the last year of the first phase of the long-term project on education and the labour market. The project was aimed at the development of an information system on education and the labour market suitable to be used in giving educational and vocational guidance to pupils and students in secondary and higher education.
In 1991 the third complete version of the information system was ready. This is reported in "The labour market by education and occupation to 1994" and the corresponding statistical appendix. In addition work continued on a programme aimed at the gradual expansion and improvement of the information system.
Publ: *Werkloosheidsindicatoren voor schoolverlaters* (Unemployment indicators for school leavers), ROA-RM01991/1.
The information system on education and the labour market developed by ROA, ROA-W-1991/2E.
De arbeidsmarkt naar opleiding en beroep tot 1994 (The labour market by education and occupation to 1994), ROA-R-1992/1.
In- en uitstroom op de markt voor leerovereenkomsten (Inflows and outflows in the market for apprenticeships), ROA-RM-1992/1.

13593 L'insertion professionnelle des élèves issus des écoles d'arts plastiques.
FRA 1993
Research Date(s): 1985-1989
Archambault, Edith; Barthe, Marie-Annick; Lallement, Jérôme; Le Vaillant, Marc; Houzel, Yvette.
Inst: Université de Paris I, UFR Analyse et politique économiques, CNRS URA/941 et GDR/996, Laboratoire d'économie sociale-Equipe Emploi, Formation, Développement, 90 rue de Tolbiac, 75634 Paris Cedex 13, France.
Fin: Ministère de la culture et de la communication, Direction des arts plastiques et Délégation aux enseignements.
training-employment relationship; occupational integration; graduate; fine arts
relation formation-emploi; intégration professionnelle; étudiant diplômé; Beaux-Arts

PROJECT DESCRIPTION

Objectifs: Il s'agit d'étudier le cheminement et l'insertion des élèves sortis des écoles d'arts plastiques relevant du Ministère de la culture.

Méthodologie: Enquête par questionnaire en fonction de variables spécifiques liées à la formation reçue (école, filière, année d'étude, diplôme) auprès de 2000 étudiants sortis diplômés ou non, en 1984. L'enquête porte sur les conditions d'insertion professionnelle et les modalités de déroulement de leur vie professionnelle sur quatre ans.

Résultats: 928 questionnaires ont été exploités. Les modalités d'insertion, les cheminements professionnels et les situations d'emploi ont été décrits en fonction des variables socio-démographiques et des variables de formation. Les élèves issus des écoles d'arts plastiques connaissent un processus d'insertion peu différent de celui des autres étudiants et comme eux, ils se déplacent vers des emplois stables. Les emplois occupés correspondent dans la grande majorité à la formation et même à la spécialisation reçues. Le taux de chômage est du même ordre que celui des étudiants littéraires. Les deux principales spécificités semblent être le maintien prolongé de certains dans des emplois précaires et l'absence d'influence du diplôme sur la situation d'emploi.

Publ: Archambault, Edith; Barthe, Marie-Annick; Houzel, Yvette; Lallement, Jérôme; Pasqualini, Esther & Sagot-Duvauroux, Dominique. Etude préalable à l'enquête d'insertion professionnelle des élèves issus des écoles d'arts plastiques. Rapport remis au Ministère de la culture, 1988, 65p. et annexes.

Archambault, Edith; Barthe, Marie-Annick; Houzel, Yvette; Lallement, Jérôme & Le Vaillant, Marc. L'insertion professionnelle des élèves issus des écoles d'arts plastiques. Rapport au Ministère de la culture, 1990.

13594 Integration von sehgeschaedigten Studierenden und Hochschulabsolventen in die Arbeitswelt. (Integration of visually handicapped students and university graduates in working life.)
DEU 1993
Research Date(s): 1991-1993
Lehnerer, U.
Sup: Klaus, J.
Inst: Universitaet Karlsruhe, Fak. fuer Informatik, Modellversuch Informatik fuer Blinde, Engesserstr. 4, D-7500 Karlsruhe 1.
Fin: Kommission der Europaeischen Gemeinschaften.
occupational integration; job creation; practical work; stay abroad; visually handicapped
intégration professionnelle; création d'emploi; travaux pratiques; séjour à l'étranger; handicapé visuel
PROJECT DESCRIPTION

Inhalt: Im 1. Jahr werden konkrete Formen der Zusammenarbeit zwischen Partnerhochschulen und Partnerfirmen entwickelt, die auf einer Tagung im Maerz diskutiert werden; werden schwerpunktmaessig Praktika im jeweiligen Heimatland vorbereitet und durchgefuehrt (Mitarbeiterschulung, Bewerbertraining fuer Praktikanten etc.). Im 2. Jahr erfolgt eine Auswertung der Praktika des 1. Jahres; werden Vorbereitungen fuer Auslandspraktika getroffen (Sprachkurse, Beruecksichtigung von landesspezifischen Besonderheiten etc.), die in die Durchfuehrung von Praktika im europaeischen Ausland muenden. Im 3. Jahr werden auf der Grundlage der Auswertung der Auslandspraktika die Auswirkungen auf Studium/Studienplaene, arbeitsspezifische Bedingungen, landesspezifische Bedingungen deutlich gemacht; wird ein Konzept fuer eine Umwandlung des Praktikantenplatzes in einen moeglichen Dauerarbeitsplatz erstellt; werden Ueberlegungen zur Uebertragbarkeit auf andere Studiengaenge und entsprechende Arbeitsplatzgestaltung vorgenommen; wird die Moeglichkeit einer Einbindung in ein Weiterbildungskonzept ueberprueft.

13595 Interact/Job hop: Pilotstudie zu einer medienunterstuetzten, aktivierenden Berufsberatung. (Interact/job hop: a pilot study on a media-supported career counselling scheme.)
AUT 1993
Research Date(s): 1992-1994
Steinhardt, Gerald; Wagner, Ina; Birbaumer, Andrea; Purgathofer, Peter.
Inst: Abteilung fuer gesellschaftswissenschaftliche Grundlagen, Argentinierstrasse 8/187, A-1040 Wien.
Institut fuer Gestaltungs- und Wirkungsforschung, Argentinierstrasse 8/187, A-1040 Wien
Fin: Bundesministerium fuer Arbeit und Soziales.
occupational choice; youth attitude; interactive video; vocational guidance; computer game
choix d'une profession; attitude de la jeunesse; vidéo interactive; orientation professionnelle; jeu informatique
PROJECT DESCRIPTION

Ausgehend von den Schwierigkeiten, mit denen sich herkoemmliche Formen der Jugendlichen motivierenden Berufsberatung konfrontiert sehen, wird il diesem Projekt ein Modell entwickelt, das die Moeglichkeiten der neuen Technologien nutzbar macht, um bei den Jugendlichen im Vorfeld konkreter Berufsentscheidung Reflexionen ueber den Berufswahlprozess anzustossen, sich in realistischer Weise mit Varianten beruflicher Alltagswirklichkeit auseinanderzusetzen, ueber eigene Wuensche und Vorstellungen zum kuenftigen Beruf nachzudenken und angemessene Kriterien

fuer die eigene Berufswahl zu entwickeln. Diese Beratungsanliegen wurden auf der Grundlage paedagogisch- psychologischer Ueberlegungen in ein Computerspiel umgesetzt, das an der gegenwaertigen Medienrealitaet Jugendlicher und deren attraktiven Momenten ansetzt und sich an einer jugendkulturellen Erfahrungswelt orientiert.

Als Erhebungstechniken werden halbstrukturierte Interviews, teilnehmende Beobachtung und Expertengespraeche herangezogen.

Die Daten werden mit qualitativen Verfahren, hermeneutischen Techniken und Inhaltsanalyse ausgewertet.

13596 Inventarisatie van arbeidsmarktonderzoeken met betrekking tot het agrarisch onderwijs. (Inventory of labour market research on agricultural training.)
NLD 1993
Research Date(s): 1991
Dam, J.W. van; Heijke, J.A.M.
Inst: ROA Researchcentrum voor Onderwijs en Arbeidsmarkt, Universiteit Limburg (Research Centre for Education and the Labour Market, University of Limburg), P.O. Box 616, 6200 MD Maastricht, Netherlands.
Fin: Ministry of Agriculture and Fisheries.
labour market; research; agricultural training; information source
marché du travail; recherche; formation agricole; source d'information
PROJECT DESCRIPTION

In preparation for a study day organized by the Agricultural Education Department of the Ministry of Agriculture, Nature Management and Fisheries, a list was made of labour market research which has been carried out in the agricultural sector. In addition to this catalogue, some recommendations were made for increasing the comparability of the data collected.

Publ: *Inventarisatie van arbeidsmarktonderzoeken onder afgestudeerden van het agrarisch onderwijs* (Inventory of labour market research among graduates from agricultural education), ROA-W-1991/1.

13597 Kansen voor herintreedsters met een opleiding aan de Universiteit van Limburg. (Re-entry opportunities for women with higher education at the University of Limburg.)
NLD 1993
Research Date(s): 1992-1993
Velden, R.K.W. van der; Loo, P.J.E. van de.
Inst: ROA Researchcentrum voor Onderwijs en Arbeidsmarkt, Universiteit Limburg (Research Centre for Education and the Labour Market, University of Limburg), P.O. Box 616, 6200 MD Maastricht, Netherlands.
employment opportunities; women's employment; graduate; woman; university
chances d'obtenir un emploi; emploi des femmes; étudiant diplômé; femme; université
PROJECT DESCRIPTION

Under a contract from the Board of Governors of the University of Limburg, ROA investigates the conditions facing women (or men) with higher education wishing to work as a staff member or researcher at the University of Limburg after having left the labour market for several years.

For this investigation the directors and some professors of the faculties are being interviewed to collect information about their opinion of researchers and staff members re-entering the labour market and about their ideas regarding solutions to problems which may occur.

13598 Konzeptentwicklung fuer den Qualifizierungsbedarf geringer qualifizierter Arbeitnehmer in ausgewaehlten Regionen. (Development of a concept concerning the need for qualifications among workers with low qualifications in selected regions.)
DEU 1993
Research Date(s): 1992-1993
Hoefkes, U.
Inst: Berufsbildungsstaette Westmuensterland, GmbH Planung und Entwicklung, Weidenstr. 2, D-4422 Ahaus.
Fin: Land Nordrhein-Westfalen, Ministerium fuer Arbeit, Gesundheit und Soziales.
qualification; demand for education; employment opportunities; job requirements; unqualified young people; regional development; manpower need; small and medium entreprise
qualification; demande d'éducation; chances d'obtenir un emploi; qualification requise pour l'emploi; jeune sans qualification; développement régional; besoin de main-d'oeuvre; petite ou moyenne entreprise
PROJECT DESCRIPTION

Inhalt: Foerderung des regionalen Strukturwandels bei KMU; Schliessen der Qualifikationsluecke (Fachkraefte-/Lehrlingsmangel); Verbesserung der Chancen fuer Un-/Angelernte.

Geographischer Raum: Westmuensterland und angrenzende niederlaendische Region.

Vorgehensweise: Basisqualifikationen muessen auf einer zeitlichen Laengsschnittachse angesiedelt werden statt auf einer Querachse; von Angelernten werden vielfach qualifizierte Taetigkeiten wahrgenommen, die sonst von Fachkraeften durchgefuehrt werden. Untersuchungsdesign: Fallstudie; Evaluationsstudie; qualitative Forschung.

Datengewinnung: Postalische Befragung (Stichprobe: 1.000; Unternehmen -KMU-; Auswahlverfahren: bewusst. Stichprobe: 1.000;

Unternehmen; Auswahlverfahren: bewusst). Standardisiertes Interview (Stichprobe: 80; Unternehmen -KMU-; Auswahlverfahren: bewusst). Expertengespraech (Stichprobe: 20; Ausbilder etc.; Auswahlverfahren: bewusst). Primaererhebung: Feldarbeit von Mitarbeitern des Projektes durchgefuehrt.

Auswertung: Faktorenanalyse; Varianzanalyse. Datenaufbereitung: Datenedition (z.B. Aufbau von Datenbanken); Aggregierung oder Disaggregierung.

13599 Kool ja elukeskkond. (School and environment.)
EST 1994
Research Date(s): 1993-1994
Hanschmidt, S.; Pavelson, M.; Lehtlaan, H.; Roots, M.; Pärnapuu, E.
Inst: Tallinna Pedagoogikaülikool (Tallinn Pedagogical University), 0102 Tallinn, Narva mnt.25, Estonia.
labour market; social integration; occupational integration; vocational education; motivation for studies; training-employment relationship; parent role
marché du travail; intégration sociale; intégration professionnelle; enseignement professionnel; motivation pour les études; relation formation-emploi; rôle des parents
PROJECT DESCRIPTION
The aim of the research is to study the mismatch between the education system and the needs of the labour market. The study consists of the following parts: (1) interviews with school heads and teachers as experts concerning the role of the school as an institution fostering social integration (1993); (2) analysis of vocational education programmes carried out in urban comprehensive schools; (3) research of (a) the connections between motivation and work habits of vocational school pupils; (b) the careers of former vocational school pupils on the labour market and their participation in retraining programmes (analysis of clients of job centres; interviews with former pupils); (4) a study of the connections between work and achievement motivation in vocational and comprehensive school pupils (analysis of pupils' choices); (5) interviews with parents about parental expectations and cooperation with schools as factors determining pupils' motivation and attitudes towards work.

13600 Lehrlinge und Facharbeiter am Arbeitsmarkt: Prognose bis zum Jahr 2005/2007. (Apprentices and skilled workers on the labour market: a forecast up to the years 2005/2007.)
AUT 1993
Research Date(s): 1992
Hofstaetter, Maria; Hruda, Hans.
Inst: Oesterreichisches Institut fuer Berufsbildungsforschung, Kolingasse 15, A-1090 Wien.
apprentice; economic development; population trends; manpower need; forecasting; labour market
apprenti; développement économique; tendances démographiques; besoin de main-d'oeuvre; prévision; marché du travail
PROJECT DESCRIPTION
Es soll die zukuenftige Entwicklung der Zahl der Lehrlinge in Oesterreich beleuchtet werden. In einem kurzfristigen Ansatz wird die Nachfrage nach Lehrlingen sowie das Angebot an Lehrlingen unter Einbeziehung der wirtschaftlichen Gesamtsituation fuer die Jahre 1992 und 1993 prognostiziert, waehrend in einem langfristigen Ansatz die moegliche Entwicklung der Zahl der Lehrstelleneintritte aufgrund der demographischen Entwicklung einerseits und der Veraenderungen des Bildungswahlverhaltens der Pflichtschulabgaenger andererseits bis zum Jahr 2005 dargestellt wird. Diese Ergebnisse der Lehrlingsprognose sind die Basis fuer eine Abschaetzung der voraussichtlichen Entwicklung des jaehrlichen Facharbeiterneuzugangs bis zum Jahr 2007.
Die Daten wurden mittels Datenbankenabfragen (ISIS, SAMIS etc.) gewonnen.
Es wurden sekundaerstatistische Analysen des Arbeitsmarktes fuer Jugendliche, sekundaerstatistische Analysen des Lehrstellenmarktes, des Bildungsverhaltens und der Bildungsabbrecher sowie eine Prognose der Lehrstelleneintritte bzw. des Lehrstellenangebotes erstellt.
Publ: Oesterreichisches Institut fuer Berufsbildungsforschung. *Lehrlinge und Facharbeiter am Arbeitsmarkt - Prognose bis zum Jahr 2005/2007.* Wien 1992.

13601 Maedchenarbeit im Verbund: Bestandsaufnahme und Entwicklung von Foerdermoeglichkeiten fuer Maedchen und junge Frauen in Freiburg. (Girls working in teams: state of the art and development of support for girls and young women in Freiburg.)
DEU 1993
Research Date(s): 1991-1993
Mayer, B.
Inst: Universitaet Freiburg, Rechtswissenschaftliche Fakultaet, Wissenschaftliches Institut des Freiburger Jugendhilfswerk, Erwinstrasse 10, D-7800 Freiburg im Breisgau.
Fin: Stiftung Deutsche Jugendmarke e.V., Deutsche Bank Stiftung Alfred Herhausen "Hilfe zur Selbsthilfe".
social work; girl; woman; vocational preparation; deprived

travail social; jeune fille; femme; initiation à la profession; défavorisé
PROJECT DESCRIPTION
Inhalt: Ziel der Arbeit ist, das bestehende Angebot im berufsvorbereitenden und Ausbildungsbereich, im beraterischen/ therapeutischen Bereich und im Freizeit- und Wohnbereich in Freiburg zu erheben und zu dokumentieren, auf seine Nutzbarkeit und Entwicklungsmoeglichkeit fuer Maedchen und junge Frauen zu untersuchen und strukturelle Benachteiligung aufzudecken. Auf der Grundlage von Expertinnen- und Betroffeneninterviews und Gruppengespraechen sollen Angebotsluecken aufgedeckt und Foerdermoeglichkeiten entwickelt werden, wobei der Schwerpunkt auf der Vernetzung bereits vorhandener und der Entwicklung neuer, niedrigschwelliger Angebote liegen soll.
Geographischer Raum: Freiburg im Breisgau.
Untersuchter Zeitraum: 1991-1993.
Vorgehensweise: Handlungsorientierter Forschungsansatz im Rahmen der Prinzipien der Frauenforschung; d.h. aktive Mitwirkung an der konzeptionellen Planung, Beteiligung an der sozialen und politischen Praxis, Parteilichkeit und Orientierung an Alltag und Lebenslage von Maedchen und Frauen. Untersuchungsdesign: qualitative Forschung.
Datengewinnung: Nicht-standardisiertes Interview (Stichprobe: 17; Massnahmetraeger im beruflichen Bereich; Auswahlverfahren: total. Stichprobe: 17; Massnahmetraeger im beruflichen Bereich; Auswahlverfahren: Quota). Gruppendiskussion (dito). Befragung (Stichprobe: 17; Massnahmetraeger im beruflichen Bereich; Auswahlverfahren: total. Stichprobe: 17; Massnahmetraeger im beruflichen Bereich; Auswahlverfahren: Quota. Stichprobe: 68; Beratungsstellen, Freizeiteinrichtungen, Heime; Auswahlverfahren: total). Primaererhebung: Feldarbeit von Mitarbeitern des Projektes durchgefuehrt.
Auswertung: Deskriptive Verfahren (Haeufigkeiten etc.); Inhaltsanalyse (qualitativ).

13602 La métis professionnelle: savoirs et savoir-faire.
FRA 1993
Research Date(s): 1985-
Cornu, Roger; Bonnault (de)-Cornu, Phanette.
Inst: Université de Nantes, UFR Institut d'histoire et de sociologie, CNRS URA/889 et GDR/55, Laboratoire d'études et de recherches sociologiques sur la classe ouvrière, Chemin de la Sensive-du-Tertre, BP 1025, 44036 Nantes Cedex, France.
know-how; learning; trainer; enterprise; worker; vocational training; training-employment relationship
savoir-faire; acquisition de connaissances; formateur; entreprise; travailleur; formation professionnelle; relation formation-emploi
PROJECT DESCRIPTION
Objectifs: Cette étude vise à cerner un ensemble de qualités (intelligence des situations, capacités, aptitude à s'adapter, modes de pensée, formes de mentalités) qui sont à la base de l'acquisition et de la mise en oeuvre des savoirs et savoir-faire. Elle consiste à étudier les différentes formes professionnelles et historiques, à décrire les lieux, les modes de développement et les moments privilégiés de la mise en oeuvre de cette métis.
Méthodologie: La recherche s'est déroulée en privilégiant trois groupes: les formateurs, les entreprises et les ouvriers; quatre corpus ont été constitués: (1) données sur les entreprises à partir de documents d'archives, d'entretiens biographiques ou non, de dépouillement d'un journal d'entreprise, de séquences filmées tournées dans trois entreprises; (2)entretiens avec des jeunes ouvriers (entre 22 et 28 ans) et biographies collectées par d'autres chercheurs ou autobiographies publiées; ce corpus couvre une période historique d'une centaine d'années; (3) archives sur la formation professionnelle, livres publiés par des formateurs et enquêtes sur la formation professionnelle; (4) études sur les savoirs et savoir-faire réalisées par des sociologues, anthropologues, ou psychologues, et articles de revues et de presse sur les savoir-faire et la culture technique.
Résultats: La métis professionnelle ne s'enseigne pas mais s'acquiert, apparaît donc une interrogation sur les voies d'accès à la connaissance et sur le passage école-travail.

Publ: Cornu, Roger. Le savoir-y-faire. In: *Bulletin du CILAC*, 1985, n° 5.
Cornu, Roger. La noblesse ouvrière et la maîtrise de l'ouvrage. In: *Le travail: marché, règles, conventions.* Paris: Ed. Economica-INSEE, 1986.
Cornu, Roger. La métis professionnelle. In: *Formes de socialisation de la jeunesse populaire et métis professionnelle.* Rapport intermédiaire au PIRTTEM, janv. 1988, 211p.
Cornu, Roger. Changements techniques, changement des mentalités: une enquête à Nantes en 1938. In: *Formation et emploi*, Juillet-Septembre 1989, n° 27-28, pp. 101-114.
Cornu, Roger. Voir et savoir. In: *Savoir-faire et pouvoir transmettre.* Paris: Maison des sciences de l'homme, 1991.
Bonnault-Cornu, Phanette (de) & Cornu, Roger. Savoir-faire, savoir mesurer. In: *Terrain*mars 1991, pp. 51-61.

13603 Modèles et problématiques de la reconversion.
FRA 1993
Research Date(s): 1988-1990
Villeval, Marie-Claude.

Inst: Université de Nancy II, CNRS URA/1167 et GDR/996, Emploi et politiques sociales - Groupe de recherche sur l'éducation et l'emploi, 23 bd Albert 1er, BP 3397, 54015 Nancy Cedex, France.

Fin: Ministère de la recherche, Programme "Homme, travail, technologies".

career change; personnel management; manpower; model construction; educational theory; economics of education

changement de carrière; gestion du personnel; main-d'oeuvre; construction de modèle; théorie de l'éducation; économie de l'éducation

PROJECT DESCRIPTION

Objectifs: Il s'agit de produire un bilan de connaissances sur l'évolution des politiques de reconversion de la main d'oeuvre depuis les années cinquante en France et sur la transformation des problématiues des économistes, sociologues, juristes et spécialistes des sciences de l'éducation en ce domaine.

Résultats: (1) Jusqu'à la fin des années soixante la reconversion est un simple problème d'ajustement sur le marché et ne constitue pas en soi un objet d'analyse, les difficultés constatées sont expliquées par le comportement irrationnel des salariés et l'analyse est renvoyée aux psycho-sociologues pour analyser les problèmes psychologiques; (2) Dans les années soixante-dix la politique de reconversion est analysée dans le cadre des stratégies sociales et économiques des groupes industriels, introduisant des redivisions au sein du segment primaire du marché du travail; (3) Aujourd'hui trois types d'approche économique de la reconversion coexistent: approche par la différenciation de la gestion des flux de main d'oeuvre, approche par la gestion de la qualification mettant en évidence la nécessaire production de nouveaux instruments institutionnels pour activer la mobilité; et enfin approche par la transformation des modes de régulation et des rapports salariés à l'emploi.

Publ: Villeval, Marie-Claude. Restructuring of an industry and local changes in the wage earning relationship. In: *Labour and society*, 1988, vol. 13, n° 4, pp. 359-374.
Villeval, Marie-Claude. La reconversion de la main d'oeuvre, réflexions autour d'un analyseur des recompositions du travail et de l'emploi. Synthèse du rapport *La reconversion de la main d'oeuvre. Bilan des problématiques (1950-1988)*. Nancy: GREE, 1989, 52p.
Villeval, Marie-Claude; Enclos, P.; Marraud, C.; Chassey (de), F.; Dupuis, P.A.; Fath, G. & Higelé, P. La reconversion de la main d'oeuvre, bibliographie sélective (1950-1988). In: *Formation-Emploi*, 1990, n° 29, pp. 82-92.

13604   Modellversuch 'LehrerInnen in die Wirtschaft'. (Pilot project 'Making the transition from teaching to business'.)
AUT   1993
Research Date(s): 1992-1993
Reiter, Walter; Hausegger, Trude; Lechner, Ferdinand.
Inst: L&R Sozialforschung, Proschkogasse 1/12, A-1060 Wien.
Fin: Bundesministerium fuer Unterricht und Kunst.
career change; in-plant training; teacher; industry; occupational mobility
changement de carrière; stage en entreprise; enseignant; industrie; mobilité professionnelle
PROJECT DESCRIPTION

Der Modellversuch 'LehrerInnen in die Wirtschaft' hat das Ziel, den befristeten oder dauerhaften Umstieg von LehrerInnen in die Wirtschaft zu foerdern und zu einer besseren Beziehung zwischen Schule und Wirtschaft beizutragen. In der Vorbereitungsphase entwickeln die am Modellversuch teilnehmenden Unternehmen ein Anforderungsprofil fuer einen oder mehrere Praktikumsplaetze (bis Mitte Dezember 1992). Die Adressaten des Modellversuches sind Volksschul-, Hauptschul- und AHS- LehrerInnen. Aus den berufsbildenden Schulen zaehlen nur LehrerInnen der allgemeinbildenden Faecher zur Zielgruppe.

Es werden Interviews mit PersonalchefInnen aus groesseren Unternehmen durchgefuehrt.

Publ: *Option Wirtschaft? Alternativen zum Schuldienst aus der Sicht von LehrerInnen und Unternehmen.* Reihe Bildungsforschung, Band 2.

13605   Monitor voor het hoger beroepsonderwijs. (Higher Vocational Education monitor.)
NLD   1993
Research Date(s): 1991-1993
Lodder, B.J.H.; Loo, P.J.E. van de; Ramaekers, G.W.M.; Velden, R.K.W. van der.
Inst: ROA Researchcentrum voor Onderwijs en Arbeidsmarkt, Universiteit Limburg (Research Centre for Education and the Labour Market, University of Limburg), P.O. Box 616, 6200 MD Maastricht, Netherlands.
Fin: Higher Vocational Education Council.
employment opportunities; graduate; labour market; career
chances d'obtenir un emploi; étudiant diplômé; marché du travail; carrière
PROJECT DESCRIPTION

A labour market monitor was developed for all sectors of Higher Vocational Education (excluding Higher Agricultural Education), under a contract from the Higher Vocational Education Council. The object of the monitor is to generate reliable, national data on the labour market position of gradu-

ates from Higher Vocational Education and its fit with professional practice, by means of a partly sector-specific basic questionnaire.

In the autumn of 1991 the graduates of the 1989/1990 academic year were surveyed. To increase the response, these graduates were approached through their "own" school. The National Information Service Bureau for School Leavers takes care of the data processing. ROA is charged with the analyses and the drafting of separate reports for each participating school - reports which can be compared to national sector data.

After an interim evaluation, the graduates of 1990/1991 will be approached, which will result in new reports. This will be followed by an evaluation of the entire project.

13606   Multimediale Lernsysteme in der fertigungs- und verfahrenstechnischen Planung und Produktion. (Multimedia learning systems in production and process engineering and planning.)
DEU   1993
Research Date(s): 1991-1992
Burgwald, M.; Schmidt, E.
Sup: Behrendt, E.; Kromrey, H.
Inst: Institut fuer Medien und Kommunikation, Friederikastrasse 111, D-4630 Bochum.
Fin: Bundesinstitut fuer Berufsbildung.
enterprise; further training; place of work; learning; in-service training
entreprise; formation complémentaire; lieu de travail; acquisition de connaissances; formation en cours d'emploi
PROJECT DESCRIPTION

Inhalt: Darstellung und Analyse erfolgreicher Modelle fuer die Integration von multimedialen Lernsystemen und Bedienhilfen in die arbeitsplatznahe Weiterbildung.

Geographischer Raum: Deutschland.

Untersuchter Zeitraum: 1991.

Vorgehensweise: Untersuchungsdesign: Fallstudie.

Datengewinnung: Expertengespraech (Stichprobe: 45; Anwendungsfaelle; Auswahlverfahren: Quota). Aktenanalyse (dito). Standardisiertes Interview (Stichprobe: 6; Fallstudien; Auswahlverfahren: Quota). Teilnehmende Beobachtung (dito). Primaererhebung: Feldarbeit von Mitarbeitern des Projektes durchgefuehrt; Datenerstellung auf der Basis von bereits vorliegenden Materialien wie Texten, Akten, Statistiken.

13607   National evaluation of Compacts.
GBR   1993
Research Date(s): 1990-1994
Stoney, S.; Saunders, L.; Morris, M.
Inst: National Foundation for Educational Research, The Mere, Upton Park, Slough SL1 2DQ, United Kingdom.
Fin: Department of Employment.
training-employment relationship; vocational education; transition from school to work
relation formation-emploi; enseignement professionnel; passage à la vie active
PROJECT DESCRIPTION

The Compacts initiative, funded by the Department of Employment from 1988, has the main aim of raising the attainment of young people in education, training and work by guaranteeing a job with training for all young people aged 14 and over who meet their personal goals. Each Compact is a contract between employers, schools, colleges, training providers and young people, where each party makes a commitment to achieve agreed goals such as: (a) schools, colleges and training providers work with young people to improve levels of achievement; (b) young people make a commitment to attend school regularly and to complete their course work on time and to the best of their ability; (c) employers agree to provide jobs with training, or training leading to a job, for young people who achieve their goals. There are currently over 50 Compacts in existence based in Urban Programme Authority areas in England and priority areas in Scotland and Wales.

The National Foundation for Educational Research (NFER) has been commissioned by the Department of Employment to carry out a national evaluation in England and Wales, the overall aim of which is to establish whether the Compacts initiative is being effective in meeting its stated objectives with respect to students, schools and employers. The evaluation will take place over the period 1990-1994 and has a nation-wide focus.

Although individual schemes are not being evaluated, most Compacts are being asked to provide information for the study in some way by assisting with one or more of the following: (a) an annual questionnaire to key decision-makers (Compact directors and Compact school staff), to collect factual information on the management and performance of Compacts; (b) a series of questionnaires to key participants (Compact students, parents, employers and training providers) to gather a range of viewpoints of the programme's impact; (c) questionnaires to students participating in Compacts during the four years to look at the longer-term outcomes of the programme for young people's decisions, qualifications and destinations; (d) questionnaires to non-Compact students and schools to provide comparisons. Additionally, 'case studies' in four contrasting travel to work areas are under way which will identify key issues and collect in-depth data concerning the operational effectiveness of Compacts in different kinds of labour markets.

Annual reports will be produced with an overview report in 1994.

Publ: Morris, M.; Saunders, L. & Schagen, I. *The impact of Compact 1991* (together with a summary). Sheffield: Department of Employment, 1992.

Saunders, L.; Morris, M. & Froud, K. *Compact: the contributions and views of employers*. Sheffield: Department of Employment, 1992.

Morris, M.; Schagen, I. & Stradling, B. *Compact Technical Report 1991*. Sheffield: Department of Employment, 1992.

Saunders, L. & Morris, M. et al. *Motivating young people for success in the inner cities*. Sheffield: Department of Employment, 1992.

13608   Neue Anforderungen an die Berufsbildung: die Aufgaben der Ausbildner. (New requirements in vocational education: the tasks of trainers.)
AUT   1993
Research Date(s): 1991-1992
Hofstaetter, Maria; Moshammer, Friedrich; Denk, Guenther; Hruda, Hans; Rosenthal, Ewald.
Inst: Oesterreichisches Institut fuer Berufsbildungsforschung, Kolingasse 15, A-1090 Wien.
Fin: Anton Benya Stiftungsfonds.
level of qualification; social change; technological change; vocational training; training of trainers; apprenticeship; training-employment relationship
niveau de qualification; changement social; changement technologique; formation professionnelle; formation des formateurs; apprentissage professionnel; relation formation-emploi
PROJECT DESCRIPTION

Rasche Veraenderungen der betrieblichen Ausbildungserfordernisse und -bedingungen infolge der technischen und wirtschaftlichen Entwicklung stellen heute immer hoehere Anforderungen an die Arbeitnehmer. Um die Qualitaet der Ausbildung zu heben und dadurch auch den Mangel an Facharbeitern zu lindern, ist eine Verbesserung der dualen Ausbildung notwendig. Ziel des Forschungsprojekts war es, auf Grund einer Bestandsaufnahme der aktuellen Entwicklung der Berufs- und Betriebspaedagogik, wie sie vergleichbar in Deutschland zu verfolgen ist, die Situation in Oesterreich zu durchleuchten. Dazu diente sowohl eine Untersuchung von Ausbildungsmaterialien fuer AusbildnerInnen und entsprechender Kursangebote als auch eine Befragung von AusbildnerInnen in ganz Oesterreich.

Nach dem Quotenverfahren wurden 200 AusbildnerInnen, drei Bildungsexperten des Oesterreichischen Gewerkschaftsbundes und 15 Ausbildungsleiter von Grossbetrieben ausgewaehlt und in die Untersuchung einbezogen.

Nach der Analyse relevanter Literatur wurde eine statistische Analyse und ein Vergleich der rechtlichen Grundlagen durchgefuehrt. Dann erfolgte die Erstellung des Befragungsinstrumentariums, die Auswahl der Stichprobe und die Durchfuehrung der Befragung.

Im Alltag werden Lehrlinge nicht allein von qualifiziertem Ausbildungspersonal betreut. In 62,9% der Betriebe wirken andere Fachkraefte an der Ausbildung mit. In rund zwei Drittel der befragten Betriebe werden die Lehrlinge dort eingesetzt, wo gerade Arbeit anfaellt. Nur rund 40% der befragten Betriebe haben einen eigenen Ausbildungsplan fuer Lehrlinge.

Publ: Oesterreichisches Institut fuer Berufsbildungsforschung. *Neue Anforderungen an die Berufsbildung - Die Aufgabe der Ausbildner*. Wien, 1993.

13609   La notion de qualification.
FRA   1993
Research Date(s): 1987-
Dadoy, Mireille.
Inst: Université de Paris VII, UFR Sciences sociales, CNRS UPR/16, Groupe de sociologie du travail, 2 Place Jussieu, Tour centrale, 75251 Paris Cedex 05, France.
occupational qualification; manpower; personnel management; labour market; training-employment relationship
qualification professionnelle; main-d'oeuvre; gestion du personnel; marché du travail; relation formation-emploi
PROJECT DESCRIPTION

Objectifs: La problématique est centrée sur l'analyse des politiques de gestion de main d'oeuvre, plus largement sur l'analyse des modes de gestion de la force de travail et organisée dans le concept de "système social du travail": notions de qualification, professionnalité, métier, système de travail, polyvalence. La notion de qualification a donné lieu à trois axes de recherche: la notion de qualification dans la sociologie du travail française depuis 1936, un modèle d'analyse de la qualification au centre des modes de production et des rapports sociaux du travail, une bibliographie thématique sur la qualification.

Publ: Dadoy, Mireille. La notion de qualification chez Georges Friedmann. In: *Sociologie du travail*, 1987, vol. 29, n° 1, pp. 15-34.

Dadoy, Mireille. Rôle et place de l'analyse du travail dans les systèmes d'évaluation de la qualification du travail. In: *Le travail humain*, 1991, n° 2, pp. 97-112.

Dadoy, Mireille. Bibliographie thématique de la sociologie du travail française. Université de Paris VII: Groupe de sociologie du travail, 1987, 500p.

13610   Onderwijs en arbeidsmarkt voor civiel ingenieurs. (Education and the labour market for civil engineers.)
NLD   1993
Research Date(s): 1992-1993
Ramaekers, G.W.M.; Dekker, R.J.P.; Velden, R.K.W. van der.
Inst: ROA Researchcentrum voor Onderwijs en Arbeidsmarkt, Universiteit Limburg (Research Centre for Education and the Labour Market, University of Limburg), P.O. Box 616, 6200 MD Maastricht, Netherlands.
Fin: Faculty of Civil Engineering, Delft University of Technology.
employment opportunities; training-employment relationship; graduate; career; civil engineering
chances d'obtenir un emploi; relation formation-emploi; étudiant diplômé; carrière; génie civil
PROJECT DESCRIPTION

In the quality control system for university education, set up by the Association of Universities in the Netherlands (VSNU), increasing emphasis is placed on labour market issues. This research project is carried out in this framework. The aim is to generate information on the labour market position of Civil Engineers and the match between their education and the labour market. The necessary information is obtained through a postal survey among those who graduated in Civil Engineering since 1986.

13611   L'organisation de la transition professionnelle des jeunes en voie d'intégration dans le salariat.
FRA   1993
Research Date(s): 1984-
Rose, José; Méhaut, Philippe; Monaco, Antonio; Chassey (de), Francis; Lhotel, Hervé; Poret, Bernard.
Inst: Université de Nancy II, CNRS URA/1167 et GDR/996, Emploi et politiques sociales - Groupe de recherche sur l'éducation et l'emploi, 23 bd Albert 1er, BP 3397, 54015 Nancy Cedex, France.
Fin: Délégation régionale à la formation professionnelle; Délégation régionale de l'emploi; Communauté européenne; CEDEFOP.
occupational integration; youth employment; vocational training; labour market; initial employment; access to employment
intégration professionnelle; emploi des jeunes; formation professionnelle; marché du travail; premier emploi; accès á l'emploi
PROJECT DESCRIPTION

Objectifs: L'analyse de l'organisation sociale de l'accès à l'emploi des jeunes a été approfondie sous trois angles: (1) analyse de l'usage par le système productif de dispositifs d'insertion des jeunes: (a) pratiques de formation des jeunes de niveau VI, Vbis et V mises en oeuvre par les entreprises dans le cadre des dispositifs de formation en alternance; (b) analyse des formes, conditions et effets de l'usage des contrats de qualification du point de vue tant des modalités d'insertion et de qualification d'une fraction de la main d'oeuvre "jeune" que des modalités de gestion de l'emploi et de la qualification dans les entreprises (enquêtes auprès d'organismes mutualisateurs agréés professionnels et interprofessionnels, d'organismes de formation et d'un échantillon de 300 entreprises); (2) etude des trajectoires de transition et leur structuration par les dispositifs: (a) étude sur les bénéficiaires de Congés individuels de formation (CIF): formes nouvelles de prolongation de la scolarité au delà de 16 ans pour les publics dits de bas niveau, (b) étude des travaux d'utilité collective (TUC) comme situations constitutives de modes de transition professionnelle (enquête postale auprès de 500 organismes et questionnaire passé auprès de 160 jeunes); (3) analyse internationale de l'insertion des jeunes grâce à une confrontation des dispositifs statistiques concernant le lien entre formation initiale et marché du travail et un bilan critique des données et enquêtes disponibles dans les divers pays européens.

Publ: Rose, José. L'évaluation de la politique de transition professionnelle en France: jugement de valeur ou mise en valeur. In: *Revue de l'Institut de sociologie*, Bruxelles, 1988, n° 1-2.

Gérard, D.; Lhotel, Hervé & Monaco, Antonio. Alternance et formation des jeunes en entreprise en France. In: *Les dossiers de l'Institut des sciences du travail*, 1988, 3ème trimestre, pp. 161-175.

Monaco, Antonio. Formation alternée des 16-18 ans et système productif: enjeux et contradictions. In: *Travaux et mémoires - Théories et pratiques sociales*, t.3, Nancy: PUN, 1986, pp. 167-177.

Poret, Bernard; Bestion, Francis; Collet, F.; Faria de Oliveira, F.; Fourcade, Bernard; Galode, G. & Paul, Jean-Jacques. *Le congé individuel de formation: quel impact sur la trajectoire professionnelle du salarié*. Rapport d'étude COPACIF-CEREQ-DFP, 1988, 353p. + ann. 265p.

(Une liste complète est disponible.).

13612 Orientamento scolastico e professionale nella scuola dell'obbligo: verifica di una esperienza. (Evaluation of an educational and vocational guidance initiative in compulsory school.)
ITA 1993
Research Date(s): 1988-1989
Attanasio, A.M.; Falciatore, M.G.; Filigheddu, G.; Barattolo Ferrone, E.
Sup: Sgobino, L.
Inst: Istituto di Recerche e Studi sull'Educazione e la Famiglia - IRSEF (Institute for Research and Study on Education and the Family), Via Soana 22, 00183 Roma, Italy.
Fin: Ministero della Pubblica Istruzione, Ufficio Studi e Programmazione.
guidance service; vocational guidance; educational guidance; training-employment relationship; occupational choice; choice of studies; cooperation; school; industry
service d'orientation; orientation professionnelle; orientation pédagogique; relation formation-emploi; choix d'une profession; choix des études; coopération; école; industrie
PROJECT DESCRIPTION
Aims: To evaluate at least two guidance initiatives conducted by schools and by the Provincial Employment Office; to create a guidance model which can serve as a model of cooperation between the two administrations; to assess, through a brief investigation, the level of satisfaction of users (youth and their parents). The research examined the educational reality in the city and province of Nuoro and in two schools in Naples in the period November-June, 1988-1989.
Methods: Examination of the situation in the areas under study, questionnaire survey, evaluation of experiences, assessment of responses, conclusions.
Results: The problem of academic guidance is strongly felt by parents, pupils, and teachers. Apart from a few experimental initiatives on the part of public and private bodies, Italy lacks a public guidance service like the services that have existed for over a decade in other EC countries. Insufficient and inadequate information leads to erroneous choices, as is demonstrated by the large number of university students that change faculties after the first year, that abandon their studies, or that do not complete their studies within the normal time schedule.
Dramatic changes can be seen in occupational structures and in the characteristics of individual professions: the fixed, secure and stable workplace is giving way to more flexible and independent work environments. The collaboration that take place between schools and business is noticed and appreciated by families, students, and teachers. They hope that information on the workplace and the labour market will come to be furnished by appointed, competent public institutions that operate at the national level.
A strong need was expressed for more personal contacts between youth, educators, and experts. Youth do not disdain computers or mass media, but when it comes to their future they need a direct human relationship in which they are given security and trust. It is hoped that the Ministries involved will strengthen their guidance activities. Cooperation between the two administrations may improve the efficiency of the services of the various institutions - local, regional, and national.

13613 Ostdeutsche Jungakademiker im Beschaeftigungssystem der Bundesrepublik Deutschland 1991/1992. (Young East German academics in the employment system of the Federal Republic of Germany in 1991/1992.)
DEU 1993
Research Date(s): 1991-1992
Bathke, G.
Sup: Minks, K.
Inst: HIS Hochschul-Informations-System GmbH, Goseriede 9, D-3000 Hannover.
Fin: Bundesministerium fuer Bildung und Wissenschaft.
German DR; occupational integration; employment opportunities; economic conditions; university studies; graduate
Allemagne RDA; intégration professionnelle; chances d'obtenir un emploi; conditions économiques; études universitaires; étudiant diplômé
PROJECT DESCRIPTION
Inhalt: Ermittlung von Angebot, Nutzung und Bedarf von Weiterbildung fuer Hochschulabsolventen der ehemaligen DDR (Absolventenjahrgang '87) vor dem Hintergrund fach- und geschlechtsspezifischer Probleme bei der Integration in das Beschaeftigungssystem unter marktwirtschaftlichen Bedingungen.
Geographischer Raum: Bundesrepublik Deutschland.
Vorgehensweise: Quer- und Laengsschnittanalyse. Untersuchungsdesign: Querschnitterhebung; Panel.
Datengewinnung: Postalische Befragung (Stichprobe: 3500; Hochschulabsolventen der ehemaligen DDR; Auswahlverfahren: Quota). Primaererhebung: Feldarbeit von Mitarbeitern des Projektes durchgefuehrt.
Auswertung: Verschiedene bi- und multivariate Verfahren. Datenaufbereitung: Datenedition (z.B. Aufbau von Datenbanken); Verlaufsdaten (event history data).

13614 Pathways 16-19: the youth cohort study of England and Wales.
GBR 1993
Research Date(s): 1985-1992
Gray, J.; Jesson, D.; Courtenay, G.; Hedges, B.
Inst: Sheffield University, Division of Education, 388 Glossop Road, Sheffield S10 2TN, United Kingdom; Social and Community Planning Research, 35 Northampton Square, London EC1V OAX, United Kingdom.
Fin: Training Agency; Department of Education and Science; Department of Employment.
transition from school to work; post-compulsory education; vocational education; school leaver; youth; youth employment; school career
passage à la vie active; enseignement postobligatoire; enseignement professionnel; élève sortant; jeunesse; emploi des jeunes; cursus scolaire
PROJECT DESCRIPTION
The Youth Cohort Study is a collaborative project researched by Sheffield University, Division of Education and Social and Community Planning Research. The project is surveying nationally representative samples from five cohorts of young people in England and Wales. Each respondent is contacted on three occasions, at ages 16+ and 18+ years, by means of a postal questionnaire. Data from the surveys will provide a comprehensive framework of information to illuminate the processes of transition from school to work. The intention is that those responsible for policy on education, training and employment provision for young people over 16 years of age will have, for the first time, a common database to inform aspects of their decision-making and planning.
A basic concern of the study is to learn more about the 'routes' young people take through the framework of 16-19 provision. At the same time, another major aim of the monitoring exercise is to produce detailed data which are sufficiently flexible, not merely to test hypotheses formulated at the outset of the project, but to address a range of issues and questions which may occur as the project proceeds. The study will, for example, enable the evaluation of: (1) the various routes for transition from school to further education, training and employment; (2) the relevance of education and qualifications to subsequent training and occupations (and progress within these occupations); and (3) the extent and nature of training and its usefulness across a variety of job types.
Publ: A full list of publications is available from the researchers.

13615 Potentieel aanbod van onderzoekers. (The potential supply of researchers.)
NLD 1993
Research Date(s): 1990-1991
Berendsen, H.; Grip, A. de; Willems, E.J.T.A.
Inst: ROA Researchcentrum voor Onderwijs en Arbeidsmarkt, Universiteit Limburg (Research Centre for Education and the Labour Market, University of Limburg), P.O. Box 616, 6200 MD Maastricht, Netherlands.
Fin: Ministry of Economic Affairs.
labour market; researcher; employment opportunities; manpower need; forecasting
marché du travail; chercheur; chances d'obtenir un emploi; besoin de main-d'oeuvre; prévision
PROJECT DESCRIPTION
This study was carried out as part of the Ministry of Economic Affairs' research programme entitled "Technology-Economy Policies Studies" (BTE). It examined to what extent the future supply of "hard-science" researchers (R & D personnel) in the Netherlands could constitute a bottle neck for overall economic growth, which is expected to become ever more dependent on knowledge, and, in particular, for the accelerating process of putting new technologies into practice.
Changes in the employment levels for researchers were forecast for three sectors: universities, research institutes and enterprises. When combined with the expected replacement demand, this gives the total demand for newcomers. Comparison of total demand with the total supply of existing and new researchers gives a forecast of the future labour market situation for researchers. A long forecasting period was chosen: 1990-2010. A sensitivity analysis was made of the results, on the basis of alternative figures for expected economic growth, investments in R & D activities, replacement demand and changes in the labour supply.
The policy implications of the research results were examined.
Publ: *De arbeidsmarkt voor onderzoekers 1990-2000* (The labour market for researchers 1990-2000), Beleidsstudies Technologie Economie nr. 13, The Hague: Ministry of Economic Affairs, 1991.

13616 Problemi di formazione di operatori nel campo dello sviluppo delle infrastrutture di assistenza all'innovazione ed al trasferimento di tecnologie: problemi professionali, economici e legislativi. (Professional, economic and legislative problems related to the training of officers working in the field of infrastructural development in support of educational innovation and the transfer of technology.)
ITA 1993
Research Date(s): 1989
Remotti, L.; Luzzi, L.
Sup: Facci, R.

Inst: Fondazione per la Ricerca sulla Migrazione e sulla Integrazione delle Tecnologie - FORMIT (Foundation for Research on Migration and Integration of Technology), Via G. Gemelli Careri 11, 00147 Roma, Italy.

Fin: Ministero della Pubblica Istruzione, Ufficio Studi e Programmazione.

occupational qualification; innovation; technology transfer; career profile; manpower need; training type

qualification professionnelle; innovation; transfert de technologie; monographie de carrière; besoin de main-d'oeuvre; type de formation

PROJECT DESCRIPTION

Aims: The study examined problems related to technological transfer in Italy. More specifically, it identified and defined the skills that are needed for the creation of new professional profiles which fall under the heading of "officers for infrastructural development in support of innovation in education". In addition, the study examined what educational, economic, and legislative instruments are conducive to the attainment of the levels of professionalism that are required in the field of support of educational innovation and transfer of technology in Italy.

Methods: Analysis of the existing situation and definition of the problem; investigation of Italian workers; cataloguing of legislative measures and interventions in Italy and in the European Community; preparation of explanatory tables and graphs.

Results: Due to the lack of appropriate skills and the meagreness of economic resources, Italy is lagging behind its European partners in the field of infrastructural development in support of innovation in education and in the transfer of technology. Small and medium-sized enterprises, which represent 97.83% of industry in Italy, are more receptive to innovation. They make use of their adaptability and flexibility to implement innovation in production more rapidly. Formal education must adapt itself and make available specialized teaching and multidisciplinary support. This points to the primary role of post-graduate business-oriented courses.

A project for the training of experts in the transfer of technologies is being planned. The principal phases, objectives, and procedures for its execution are being determined. Two major professional profiles are outlined: technical-scientific and technical-economic consultants. The training method (which alternates between full-time study and work experience) and organizational structures are indicated. The criteria of selection and the prerequisites are outlined. The creation of specific National Training Projects is recommended in order to promote the growth of small and medium-sized enterprises. They would be dynamic and up-to-date in their use of modern technologies. They would be able to serve as models in the national economic and scientific context.

13617 Problemy i potrzeby w zakresie kadr wykwalifikowanych dla życia muzycznego w Polsce. (Professionals in music institutions in Poland: problems and issues in professional training and careers.)

POL 1994

Research Date(s): 1988-1990

Jankowska, Mirosława; Ludkiewicz, Zofia; Hnidec, Ligia; Misiak, Tomasz.

Inst: Instytut Pedagogiki Muzycznej, Akademia Muzyczna im. F. Chopina (Institute for Research in Music Education, Frederic Chopin Academy of Music), Okólnik 2, 00-368 Warszawa, Poland.

Ministerstwo Edukacji Narodowej (Ministry of National Education), Al. I Armii Wojska Polskiego 25, 00-582 Warszawa, Poland

Fin: Ministry of National Education; Ministry of Culture and Art.

career; music school; music; educational sociology; occupation

carrière; école de musique; musique; sociologie de l'éducation; profession

PROJECT DESCRIPTION

Background: Polish publications lack general information about the situation of musicians, music institutions and music education in Poland. Neither do they mention changes that occur in this field. This type of information, however, could be a good point of departure for research and a frame of reference for decision makers and managers in this field.

Aims: (1) To gather information about professional musicians in Poland (classified by: sex, age, education, post), employed in different institutions (symphony orchestras, philharmonics, opera houses, schools of music); (2) to analyse changes in the situation of the staff of music institutions - a comparison of the late 1970s to the 1980s; (3) to collect statistical data concerning music education in Poland after the Second World War; (4) to make an attempt at the creation of a system of information about musicians, music institutions and music education in Poland; (5) to lay the foundations for a sociological analysis of the perception of music; a survey of different typologies (psychological, sociological and aesthetic) of the perception of music; (6) to compare, considering different aspects, the situation of musicians and music institutions in Poland with the situation in other European and non-European countries.

Results: (1) A set of statistical data related to professional musicians, music education and music institutions in Poland; (2) a list of deficiencies and information needs in this field; (3) an analysis of selected topics; (4) a bibliography of musical culture in Poland; (5) a bibliography of the social status of professional musicians in selected countries.

Publ: Jankowska, Mirosława (ed.). *Szkolnictwo muzyczne w Polsce. Zebrane materiały statystyczne.* Warszawa: AMFC, 1990, 170p.

Misiak, Tomasz. *Muzyka jako wspólnota. Kulturowe wzory odbioru muzyki w europejskiej kulturze muzycznej XX w.* Warszawa: AMFC, 1990, 165p.

13618 Psychologiczne i organizacyjne determinanty osiagnieć zawodowych u osób z wyższym wykształceniem technicznym zatrudnionych w zespołach badawczorozwojowych firm elektronicznych i chemicznych. (Psychological and organizational determinants of R and D professionals' performance.)

POL 1994

Research Date(s): 1991-1993

Henzel-Korzeniowska, Alina.

Inst: Katedra Psychologii Wyższej Szkoły Pedagogicznej (Department of Psychology, Pedagogical University), Podchorażych 2, 30-084 Kraków, Poland.

Centrum Innowacji i Personelu Badawczego (CIPRES) (Centre for Innovation and Personnel Research), Catholic University of Nijmegen, Department of Psychology, Section of Work and Organizational Psychology, Montessorilaan 3, Nijmegen, Netherlands; Zakład Psychologii Pracy, Uniwersytet Jagielloński (Department of Psychology of Work, Jagiellonian University), Gołebia 13, 31-007 Kraków, Poland

Fin: Pedagogical University; Committee for Scientific Research; Tempus project.

career development; job description; career profile; industrial psychology; personality

déroulement de carrière; description d'emploi; monographie de carrière; psychologie industrielle; personnalité

PROJECT DESCRIPTION

Background and aims: R and D personnel (scientists and engineers in Research and Development departments of Polish companies) constitute an economic group where traditional management tools are sometimes inadequate and often not sufficient. Creative production cannot be forced to occur, only facilitating conditions can be improved. In this way, advanced knowledge of personnel management could develop productivity in R and D. Unfortunately, knowledge of modern human resources management is insufficient in Polish firms. The present study fills this gap by offering new knowledge for a more fact-based career management. Furthermore, the study has relevance to stress prevention, as it addresses a crucial source of stress in the creative professions: obsolescence, the lack of ideas at a certain stage in one's career (the "plateau"). With adequate career management, productivity can be improved, and stress can be prevented.

Design: Data have been collected from 250 R and D employees of 30 firms. The data are currently being analysed; they will be published in four articles, written in English. A two-day workshop with company directors will be planned where the results of the study will be presented. On the Dutch side, CIPRES members will participate as supervisors of the study and as West-European experts.

Hypothesis: There is a relationship between several dimensions of individual performance and personality (cognitive style, career orientation), job (diversity, challenge) and career characteristics (career pattern), among scientists and engineers in R and D departments of the Polish companies.

Sample: 250 persons with tertiary education have been examined in R and D groups of electronic (25) and chemical (5) firms. The majority were men (66%). The average age of the sample was 38 years. The majority of subjects (73.9%) were employed in government firms; 22% were employed by Limited Liability Companies; only 1.6% were employed by private businesses. 153 persons (61%) worked for electronic firms; 38% worked for chemical firms. The most common type of tertiary education was training at an Institute of Technology (70% of the persons examined).

Methods: The questionnaire included several scales (e.g. Hall and Lawler's job challenge instrument; the CIPRES instrument on building knowledge, etc.) which have been validated in other studies. Methods also included the assessment of perceived career steps, as developed by Prof. van Assen at Philips, Lighting Division, in the Netherlands. Moreover, performance was measured by self-assessment and management ratings.

Publ: Aryee, S. & Leong, C.C. Career Orientations and Work Outcomes among Industrial R and D Professionals. In: *Group and Organization Studies*, 2/1991, pp. 193-205.

13619 Qualifikationsfragen im ostdeutschen Braunkohlenbergbau im Vergleich. (Comparison of qualification structures in lignite mining in East Germany.)

DEU 1993

Research Date(s): 1991-1992

Vollmer, H.

Inst: Landesinstitut Sozialforschungsstelle Dortmund, Rheinlanddamm 199, D-4600 Dortmund 1.

Fin: Kommission der Europaeischen Gemeinschaften.

occupational qualification; German DR; further training; training need; industry

qualification professionnelle; Allemagne RDA; formation complémentaire; besoin de formation; industrie

PROJECT DESCRIPTION

Inhalt: Vergleich der Qualifikationsstrukturen des ost- und westdeutschen Braunkohlenbergbaus; Abschaetzung der Entwicklung des ostdeutschen Braunkohlenbergbaus; Formulierung des Weiterbildungsbedarfs.

Geographischer Raum: Bundesrepublik Deutschland.

Vorgehensweise: Untersuchungsdesign: Fallstudie; qualitative Forschung.

Datengewinnung: Expertengespraech (Experten des Braunkohlenbergbaus; Auswahlverfahren: bewusst). Primaererhebung: Feldarbeit von Mitarbeitern des Projektes durchgefuehrt.

13620 Qualifizierungsverbund mit Qualifikationsplanung und - durchfuehrung sowie Qualifikationsberatung im Rahmen eines umzustrukturierenden Qualifizierungszentrums zur Begleitung des Strukturwandels in der Region (Rheinhausen). (Planning, implementation and consultation on qualifications in the context of the reorganization of a training centre prompted by structural changes in the region (Rheinhausen).)
DEU 1993
Research Date(s): 1989-1992
Koch, J.
Inst: Friedrichsdorfer Buero fuer Bildungsplanung, An der Schoelke 5, D-3320 Salzgitter 1.
Fin: Bundesministerium fuer Bildung und Wissenschaft.
in-service training; North Rhine-Westphalia; employment opportunities; further training; industry; training centre; regional planning
formation en cours d'emploi; Rhénanie du Nord-Westphalie; chances d'obtenir un emploi; formation complémentaire; industrie; centre de formation; planification régionale
PROJECT DESCRIPTION
Inhalt: In der Region Duisburg soll ein betriebliches Ausbildungszentrum, das angelegt war auf die Beduerfnisse der Stahlindustrie und bereits die neuen industriellen Metall- und Elektroberufe sowie buerowirtschaftliche Berufe ausbildet, so umstrukturiert werden, dass eine bildungspolitische Potentialstrategie in der Erst- und Weiterbildung fuer Jugendliche und Erwachsene entwickelt und dadurch ein kreativer Impuls fuer Qualifizierung und Beschaeftigung gegeben wird. Mit Betrieb und Bildungstraegern in der Region soll eine Abstimmung ueber Qualifizierungsziele und Qualifizierungsmassnahmen getroffen werden. Fuer das Qualifizierungszentrum kommt es darauf an, fuer die regionale Wirtschaftsstruktur bedeutsame Nischen zu besetzen, die von anderen Einrichtungen nicht abgedeckt werden. Ein solcher zusaetzlicher Bedarf wird vor allem in der Qualifizierung fuer kleine und mittlere Unternehmen in der Region erwartet, die aufgrund der strukturellen Veraenderungen teilweise gezwungen sind, sich neue Maerkte zu erschliessen und dazu neue Qualifikationen benoetigen. In dem Verbund soll das Qualifizierungszentrum sowohl Aus- und Weiterbildung fuer die Betriebe als auch mit ihnen durchfuehren.

13621 Qualifizierungsziel Ganzheitliche Arbeitsgestaltungskompetenz - Sozialvertraegliche Gestaltung von IuK-Systemen als Gegenstand der Aus- und Weiterbildung von DV-Fachkraeften. (Holistic job engineering competence as a goal for qualifications: socially acceptable engineering of information and communications systems as a subject for basic and further training for computer specialists.)
DEU 1993
Research Date(s): 1991-1993
Baukrowitz, A.
Sup: Boes, A.; Boss, C.
Inst: Institut fuer Sozialwissenschaftliche Forschung, Uferstrasse 11, D-3550 Marburg.
Fin: Land Nordrhein-Westfalen Ministerium fuer Arbeit, Gesundheit und Soziales.
working conditions; new technologies; computer application; qualification; social development; information technology
conditions de travail; nouvelles technologies; application informatique; qualification; développement social; technologie de l'information
PROJECT DESCRIPTION
Inhalt: Die Mikroelektronik ist die Schluesseltechnologie der aktuellen und sozialen Entwicklung. Die Einsatzdichte der darauf basierenden Computertechnologie hat sich im Laufe des zurueckliegenden Jahrzehnts rapide erhoeht. Mit dieser quantitativen Veraenderung ging ein qualitativer Umbruch der Rationalisierungsentwicklung einher. Diese Entwicklung beruehrt in neuer Qualitaet das Arbeitshandeln und die Arbeitsbedingungen der Beschaeftigten. Die wirtschaftliche Potenz moderner Industriegesellschaften hat in der qualifizierten Anwendung dieser Technologie eine ihrer wichtigsten Grundlagen. Die Datenverarbeitungs-(DV-)Fachkraefte sind aufgrund ihrer Gestaltungsfunktion fuer computergestuetzte Arbeitssysteme eine "Schluesselgruppe" fuer die wirtschaftliche und soziale Entwicklung. Ihre Qualifikationen sind gefragt: bei der Festlegung der DV-technischen Hardware- und Softwarekonzeption, die nachhaltig auf die konkrete Arbeitsorganisation und die Arbeitseinsatzkonzepte wirkt; bei der fruehzeitigen Beteiligung von (spaeteren) Benutzern, um deren Erfahrungswissen und ihre Gestaltungsinteressen in qualifizierter Formzum Gegenstand der Systementwicklungsprozesse zu machen; bei der humanen Gestaltung von DV-Benutzeroberflaechen; bei der Festlegung von Weiterbildungsmassnahmen fuer die Benutzer und nicht zuletzt bei der humanen Gestaltung ihrer eigenen Arbeitsbedingungen. Ueber das Qualifizierungsziel "Ganzheitliche Arbeitsgestaltungskompetenz" werden die relevanten Qualifikation-sbestandteile von DV-Fachkraeften (soziale Qualifikationen, DV-fachliche Qualifikationen und fachuebergreifende Qualifikationen) fuer ein ganzheitliches Qualifizierungskonzept operationalisiert. Diese Operationalisierung erfolgt gemeinsam mit vier Kooperationspartnern aus den Bereichen DV-Hersteller, DV-Anwender, DV-Ausbildung und DV-Forschung. Gemeinsam mit diesen Partnern werden modellhaft konkrete Vorhaben in einem uebergreifenden Kooperationsprozess in die Aus- und Weiterbildungsmassnahmen umgesetzt und adaequate Prozesse der Organisations- und Personalentwicklung initiiert. Ziel des Projekts ist die modellhafte Entwicklung und Erprobung eines Qualifizierungskonzepts fuer die "Schluesselgruppe" der DV-Fachkraefte. Durch den kontinuierlichen zielgruppengerechten Transfer der verallgemeinerbaren Ergebnisse in die (Fach-)Oeffentlichkeit wird der Anstoss zu entsprechenden gesellschaftlichen Initiativen gegeben.

13622 The relationship of curriculum and workplace change.
GBR 1993
Research Date(s): 1990-
Richardson, W.; Finegold, D.
Inst: Warwick University, Faculty of Educational Studies, Centre for Education and Industry, Coventry CV4 7AL, United Kingdom.
Fin: British Telecom; Department for Education; Department of Employment.
training-employment relationship; transition from school to work; employment; curriculum; skill; job requirements
relation formation-emploi; passage à la vie active; emploi; programme d'études; compétence; qualification requise pour l'emploi
PROJECT DESCRIPTION
The research poses broad questions about the relationship between curriculum change and changes in skill deployment in the workplace. Specific stress is laid upon the need to incorporate research literature from a number of disciplines (political science, management studies, labour market studies, educational studies); and the main concern is closer analysis of the supply of skilled labour from education and the employers' demand for skilled labour.

Publ: Richardson, W. The changing nature of work: responses from education. In: Wellington, J. (ed.). *The education-work relationship for the future.* London: Kogan Page, 1993.

13623 Research and development in National Vocational Qualifications (NVQs) and the identification of various competencies in teaching and management.
GBR 1993
Research Date(s): 1989-1991
Burke, J.
Inst: Sussex University, Institute of Continuing and Professional Education, Sussex House, Falmer, Brighton BN1 9RH, United Kingdom.
Fin: National Council for Vocational Qualifications.
qualification; vocational training; skill; minimum competencies
qualification; formation professionnelle; compétence; fundamentum
PROJECT DESCRIPTION
The National Council for Vocational Qualifications (NCVQ) set up a two-year research fellowship in April 1989; its three objectives are to: (1) pursue research and development in competency-based learning in support of the emerging model of National Vocational Qualifications (NVQs); (2) publish, disseminate and generally promote research and developments in respect of the above area; and (3) provide consultancy to NCVQ on research and development on specific projects.

The major focus of the work in the first year has been on generic competences or core skills. Three papers, dealing with the reconceptualisation of generic competence and aspects of problem solving, were published by the NCVQ in Jessup, G. (1990); several other publications have been produced.

The focus of the research in the second year continues on generic competences and involves: (a) supporting the work of the NCVQ in collaboration with the National Curriculum Council (NCC) and School Examinations and Assessment Council (SEAC) and others; (b) working with the Open University Enterprise in Higher Education Project; and (c) providing consultancy for Education Management South East's project on competency in educational management. A fourth area of interest is National Vocational Qualifications and special needs.

Publ: Burke, J. Research in competency-based education and training. In: *Competency and Assessment*, No 8/1989, pp. 12-13.
Burke, J. *Competency-based education and training.* London: Falmer Press, 1989.
Burke, J. Problem solving. In: Jessup, G. *Common learning outcomes: core skills in A/AS levels and NVQs.* London: National Council for Vocational Qualifications, (NCVQ R & D Report No 6), 1990.
Burke, J. Generic units. In: Jessup, G. *Common learning outcomes: core skills in A/AS levels and NVQs.* London: National Council for Vocational Qualifications, (NCVQ R & D Report No 6), 1990.
Burke, J. Towards a framework for problem solving as a common learning outcome. In: Jessup, G. *Common learning outcomes: core skills in A/AS levels and NVQs.* London: National Council for Vocational Qualifications, (NCVQ R & D Report No 6), 1990.

13624   Reviewing the economic benefits of careers guidance.
GBR   1993
Research Date(s):   1991
Killeen, J.; White, M.
Sup: Watts, A.
Inst: National Institute for Careers Education and Counselling, Sheraton House, Castle Park, Cambridge CB3 OAX, United Kingdom; Policy Studies Institute, 100 Park Village Street, London NW1 3SR, United Kingdom.
Fin: Department of Employment.
career; vocational guidance; economics of education; evaluation
carrière; orientation professionnelle; économie de l'éducation; évaluation
PROJECT DESCRIPTION
   The project aims to develop conceptual models for evaluating the economic benefits of careers guidance, and to review the existing research literature on the effects of careers guidance in the light of these models.

Publ: Killeen, J.; White, M. & Watts, G. *The economic value of careers guidance.* London: Policy Studies Institute, 1992.
Economic benefits of careers guidance. NICEC Briefing. Cambridge: NICEC, 1992.

13625   RUBS (Registratie Uitstroom en Bestemming van School-verlaters).   (RUBS '92 (registration of the further careers of school leavers).)
NLD   1993
Research Date(s):   1991-
Velden, R.K.W. van der; Dekker, R.J.P.; Loo, P.J.E. van de; Ramaekers, G.W.M.; Wieling, M.H.
Inst: ROA Researchcentrum voor Onderwijs en Arbeidsmarkt, Universiteit Limburg (Research Centre for Education and the Labour Market, University of Limburg), P.O. Box 616, 6200 MD Maastricht, Netherlands.
Fin: National Career Guidance Information Centre (LDC); National Consultative Body on Education-Employment Liaison Centres (LCB).
labour market; transition from school to work; school leaver; career; employment opportunities
marché du travail; passage à la vie active; élève sortant; carrière; chances d'obtenir un emploi
PROJECT DESCRIPTION
   The RUBS project (registration of the outflow and destination of school-leavers), carried out annually, is a national postal survey among school-leavers (whether as drop-outs or with qualifications) from general secondary education and junior and senior vocational education). RUBS generates an up-to-date picture of the destination of school-leavers, their labour market position and the match between education and the labour market, differentiated by type of education and vocational specialization.
   The schools participating in the sample are charged with distributing the questionnaires and the Service Bureau for School-leavers' Information takes care of the processing of the survey data. The project management lies in the hands of ROA, which is also charged with the analysis and the writing of the national reports. As part of the fourth RUBS survey (RUBS '92) a general national report and a national report on school-leavers from Senior Secondary Technical Schools (MTO) have been written.

Publ: ROA, *De uitstroom en bestemming van schoolverlaters, RUBS '92* (The outflow and destination of school-leavers, RUBS '92).
ROA, *De uitstroom en bestemming van schoolverlaters van het Middelbaar Technisch Onderwijs, RUBS '92* (The outflow and destination of school-leavers from Intermediate Technical Education, RUBS '92).

13626   RUBS '91.   (RUBS '91 (registration of the further careers of school leavers).)
NLD   1993
Research Date(s):   1991
Lodder, B.J.H.; Ramaekers, G.W.M.; Velden, R.K.W. van der.
Inst: ROA Researchcentrum voor Onderwijs en Arbeidsmarkt, Universiteit Limburg (Research Centre for Education and the Labour Market, University of Limburg), P.O. Box 616, 6200 MD Maastricht, Netherlands.
Fin: National Service Bureau for School Leavers' Information.
labour market; transition from school to work; school leaver; employment opportunities
marché du travail; passage à la vie active; élève sortant; chances d'obtenir un emploi
PROJECT DESCRIPTION
   The RUBS project (Registration of the further careers and destinations of school leavers) concerns a large-scale survey of skilled and unskilled school leavers from general secondary education and senior secondary vocational education. The participating schools are charged with distributing the questionnaires and the National Service Bureau for School Leavers' Information takes care of the processing of the survey data.
   With the aid of RUBS, an up-to-date picture is obtained of the position of school leavers on the labour market and the match between education and the labour market, differentiated by type of education and vocational specialization. As part of the third RUBS survey (RUBS '91), ROA is charged with the analysis and the national report regarding school leavers from senior secondary commercial education courses.

Publ: Lodder, B.J.H.; Ramaekers, G.W.M. & Velden, R.K.W. van der. *De Arbeidsmarktpositie van schoolverlaters van het Economisch en Administratief (K)MBO: RUBS'91* (The labour market position of school leavers from senior secondary commercial education, RUBS'91), ROA-R-1991/11 (ISBN 90-5321-072-5).

13627   Schluesselqualifikationen.   (Key qualifications.)
AUT   1993
Research Date(s):   1991-1992
Freundlinger, Alfred.
Inst: Institut fuer Bildungsforschung der Wirtschaft, Rainergasse 38, A-1050 Wien.
Fin: Wirtschaftsfoerderungsinstitut der Bundeswirtschaftskammer.
qualification; personality development; learning aptitude
qualification; développement de la personnalité; aptitude aux études
PROJECT DESCRIPTION
   Durcharbeitung von verfuegbarer Literatur zum Thema Schluesselqualifikationen und Vertiefung in ausgewaehlte Ansaetze zur Persoenlichkeitstheorie (Mead, Piaget, Aebli) mit dem Ziel einer begrifflichen Klaerung, einer Dokumentation der aktuellen Diskussion und bestehender Ansaetze zur Foerderung und Entwicklung von Schluesselqualifikationen und der Entwicklung einer eigenstaendigen Didaktik der Schluesselqualifikationen.

Publ: Freundlinger, Alfred. *Schluesselqualifikationen - Der interaktionsorientierte Ansatz.* Ibw-Schriftenreihe Nr. 90, Wien, 1992.

13628   Schreibkraefte und elektronische Textverarbeitung.   (Typists and electronic word processing.)
DEU   1993
Research Date(s):   1991-1992
Odebrett, E.
Sup: Dippelhofer-Stiem, B.
Inst: Institut Frau und Gesellschaft, Walter-Gieseking-Str. 14, D-3000 Hannover 1.
Fin: Arbeitsamt Hannover.
clerical worker; electronic data processing; word processing; enterprise; women's work; further training
employé de bureau; traitement électronique des données; traitement de texte; entreprise; travail des femmes; formation complémentaire
PROJECT DESCRIPTION
   Inhalt: In dem Projekt sollen anhand einer Befragung von betroffenen Schreibkraeften unterschiedlichen Alters aus unterschiedlichen Betrieben die Probleme und Schwierigkeiten der Arbeit mit elektronischen Textverarbeitungsprogrammen, aber auch die Vorteile und Arbeitserleichterungen erfragt werden. Ferner werden die Art, Dauer und Qualitaet der betrieblichen bzw. privaten Einarbeitungen in die EDV-Systeme thematisiert, sowie die kognitiven effektiven und sozialen Anforderungen und Kompetenzen analysiert. Ziel der Untersuchung ist eine Problemanalyse aus der Sicht der Betroffenen und die Formulierung von praktischen Folgerungen fuer die betriebliche und ausserbetriebliche Aus- und Weiterbildung dieser Frauen.
   Datengewinnung: Standardisiertes Interview (Stichprobe: ca. 30; Schreibkraefte, differenziert nach Alter und Ausbildungsplatztyp; Auswahlverfahren: Quota).

13629   Schulische Berufsorientierung: Jugendliche vor der Berufswahl.   (Vocational orientation at school: adolescents facing the choice of a career.)
AUT   1993
Research Date(s):   1990-1992
Dichatschek, Guenther.
Inst: Institut fuer Erziehungswissenschaften, Garnisongasse 3, A-1096 Wien.
Universitaet Wien, Garnisongasse 3, A-1096 Wien
occupational choice; vocational information; educational guidance; vocational guidance
choix d'une profession; information professionnelle; orientation pédagogique; orientation professionnelle
PROJECT DESCRIPTION
   Vordringliche Aufgabe ist es, von verschiedenen vorhandenen Berufswahltheorien als Grundlage fuer die Entwicklung eines Modells eines Berufswahlunterrichts in der allgemeinbildenden Pflichtschule ausgehend gezielte Vorschlaege zu einer inhaltlichen Gestaltung eines effizienten Berufswahlunterrichts zu entwerfen. Dabei sollen die bereits vorliegenden Ergebnisse in der Berufspaedagogik (Vorberufliche Bildung) mit den vorhandenen Lehrplaenen in 'Berufsorientierung und Bildungsinformation' (Berufsorientierung und Bildungsinformation/Hauptschule und allgemeinbildende hoehere Schule-Unterstufe) sowie 'Berufskunde und praktische Berufsorientierung' (Berufskunde/Polytechnischer Lehrgang) Beachtung finden.
   Mit Hilfe von Inhaltsanalyse, Unterrichtserprobung und Realbegegnungen wurden die Daten gewonnen.
   Schulische Berufsorientierung ist ein aktuelles und dringendes Problem geworden. Die Gruende liegen in der Situation und den verschaerften Orientierungsproblemen Jugendlicher beim Uebergang in die Arbeits- und

Berufswelt sowie in der Einseitigkeit und damit mangelhaften Objektivitaet von Theorie und Praxis in der schulischen Berufsorientierung. Ansatzpunkte einer solchen Berufsorientierung (auch fuer Maedchen mit ihren speziellen Problemen) sollen deutlich machen, dass dieser Bereich auf objektive Grundlagen gestellt werden kann. Bildungspolitische Forderungen zeigen die Relevanz fuer die paedagogische Praxis auf.

Publ: Dichatschek, Guenther. Schulische Berufsorientierung von Maedchen - Probleme, didaktische Ansaetze und bildungspolitische Forderungen. In: *Erziehung und Unterricht*, 7-8/1991, S. 631-637.
Dichatschek, Guenther. Vorberufliche Bildung im Schulversuch Landhauptschule - Berufsorientierung und Bildungsinformation. In: *Schule und Leben*, 2/1992, S. 20-26.
Dichatschek, Guenther. Vorberufliche Bildung unter dem Aspekt von Geographie/Wirtschaftskunde in der allgemeinbildenden Pflichtschule. In: *Unterricht*, 40/1990, S. 10-16.
Dichatschek, Guenther. Aspekte und Probleme der Berufsfindung in der allgemeinbildenden Pflichtschule. In: *Arbeitsmarkt*, 4/1990, S. 18-23.
Dichatschek, Guenther. Berufswahlunterricht in der allgemeinbildenden Pflichtschule. In: *Arbeitsmarkt*, 5/1992, S. 8-13.
Dichatschek, Guenther. Das Berufsinformationszentrum - ein Lernort in der vorberuflichen Bildung. In: *Arbeitsmarkt*, 5/1992, S. 17-18.

13630 Scottish Young People's Survey.
GBR   1993
Research Date(s): 1971-
Paterson, L.; Lamb, J.; Howieson, C.; Croxford, L.; Middleton, L.; Raffe, D.
Sup: McPherson, A.
Inst: Edinburgh University, Centre for Educational Sociology, 7 Buccleuch Place, Edinburgh EH8 9JT, United Kingdom.
Fin: Scottish Office, Education Department; Industry Department for Scotland; Department of Employment; Economic and Social Research Council.
transition from school to work; youth employment; vocational training; higher education; post-secondary education; career; school career; survey; Scotland
passage à la vie active; emploi des jeunes; formation professionnelle; enseignement supérieur; enseignement postsecondaire; carrière; cursus scolaire; enquête; Ecosse
PROJECT DESCRIPTION
    Regular multi-purpose surveys of school leavers and young people in Scotland, which collect data on their secondary, further and higher education, training, employment and unemployment, and on the various transitions among them. The surveys also cover the family backgrounds of young people, their household formation and other aspects of the transition to adulthood, and various attitudes. A postal survey, the Scottish Young People's Survey (SYPS) currently comprises two arms: a biennial survey, conducted in the spring of each odd-numbered year, of school leavers from the previous session; and a biennial series of longitudinal surveys of school year groups, each of which is first contacted in the spring after fourth year and followed up after about 30 months at age 19-plus. Samples for the leavers' survey and the (first-sweep) year-group survey overlap. Sample fractions are usually 10% giving target samples of about 7,000 for each survey arm, and achieved samples of about 5,500. The basic survey design is periodically enhanced to boost coverage in particular regions or for groups of interest.

13631 Scottish Young People's Survey - transition issues.
GBR   1993
Research Date(s): 1990-1991
Semple, S.
Inst: Jordanhill College of Education, Division of Inservice Training, Southbrae Drive, Glasgow G13 1PP, United Kingdom.
Fin: BP Exploration plc.
transition from school to work; school leaver; higher education; youth attitude
passage à la vie active; élève sortant; enseignement supérieur; attitude de la jeunesse
PROJECT DESCRIPTION
    The purpose of this project was to create briefing papers on young people's views on further and higher education, manufacturing industry and reasons for leaving school. The study used data already existing in the Scottish Young People's Survey that had not been previously assessed. The six briefing papers on transition issues created are: (1) Further Education: Scottish School Leavers' Views; (2) Higher Education: Scottish School Leavers' Views; (3) Returning to School: Scottish School Leavers' Views; (4) Making Decisions: Scottish School Leavers' Views; (5) Parents and Young People: Some Perceptions of Parental Influence; and (6) Manufacturing Industry: Scottish School Leavers' Views.

13632 Skill shortages in Limburg.
NLD   1994
Research Date(s): 1990-1991
Dam, J.W. van; Ramaekers, G.W.M.; Velden, R.K.W. van der.

Inst: ROA Researchcentrum voor Onderwijs en Arbeidsmarkt, Universiteit Limburg (Research Centre for Education and the Labour Market, University of Limburg), P.O. Box 616, 6200 MD Maastricht, Netherlands.
Fin: EC Task Force on Human Resources, Education, Training and Youth.
manpower need; skill; labour shortage
besoin de main-d'oeuvre; compétence; pénurie de main-d'oeuvre
PROJECT DESCRIPTION
    As part of an EC study on skill shortages, ROA has conducted research into the part education and training can play in reducing discrepancies on the Limburg labour market. The study was funded by the EC Task Force on Human Resources, Education, Training and Youth.
    Five case-studies were carried out in different fields: customs clearance, office automation, printing, metallurgic industry and health care. The research project was brought to a conclusion with a seminar entitled "Technology, Qualifications, and Education". This was organised by ROA for interested parties from the policy-making and research fields, and from private enterprise.
    On the basis of this research and similar studies carried out in other EC countries, the Task Force organised an international conference on the theme of "Skill Needs in Europe - 1992 and Beyond".

Publ: Dam, J.W. van; Ramaekers, G.W.M. & Velden, R.K.W. van der. *Skill shortages in Limburg*, ROA-R-1991/3E (ISBN 90-5321-052-0).
Dam, J.W. van & Velden, R.K.W. van der. *New Technologies, Skill Shortages and Training Policy: a Comparative Approach Between Branches of Industry*, ROA-W-1991/3E (ISBN 90-5321-079-9).

13633 Study of factors affecting students' success and drop-out rates in hotel management courses.
GBR   1993
Research Date(s): 1986-1993
Ineson, E.
Sup: Kempa, R.
Inst: Manchester Metropolitan University, Department of Hotel, Catering and Tourism Management, Hollings Faculty, Old Hall Lane, Manchester M14 6HR, United Kingdom; Keele University, Department of Education, Keele, Staffordshire ST5 5BG, United Kingdom.
job requirements; qualification; skill; tourism; management education
qualification requise pour l'emploi; qualification; compétence; tourisme; formation à la gestion
PROJECT DESCRIPTION
    Students' success in hotel management courses is frequently judged by employers in terms of a range of qualities other than academic ones. The research aims at identifying these non-academic qualities and, thereafter, will focus on the extent to which their development can be predicted before or at the commencement of students' courses. Central to the study is the administration of personality and related inventories to students on hotel management training courses. Data obtained in this way will be supplemented by information from interviews.

13634 A study of probationers.
GBR   1993
Research Date(s): 1988-1991
Draper, J.; Fraser, H.; Taylor, W.; Smith, D.
Inst: Heriot-Watt University, Moray House Institute of Education, Holyrood Road, Edinburgh EH8 8AQ, United Kingdom.
Fin: Scottish Office Education Department.
initial employment; teacher education; student teacher; probationary teacher
premier emploi; formation des enseignants; élève-maître; enseignant stagiaire
PROJECT DESCRIPTION
    The project was designed to collect data on views of training held by beginning teachers, and on the experience of those teachers of their induction, support and assessment. Data was also collected on their recruitment experiences. The data was collected over a two-year period from a national sample of over 300 probationer teachers employed across Scotland, and from their headteachers. A longitudinal database on the experiences of probationer teachers was constructed. This was analysed in conjunction with data from an end-of-training profile, and reports compiled by headteachers after one year and after two years of probationary teaching.
    The results suggest that there is a broad range of views of training, and varied experiences of recruitment, induction support and assessment. The project report highlights experiences found by probationers to support their professional development and identifies issues requiring debate and resolution. Implications of the findings for appraisal and the evaluation of probation 'as an experience' fostering development are key concerns in the project.

Publ: Draper, J.; Fraser, H.; Smith, D.J. & Taylor, W. Shaping the new teacher in school: the insider's view. In: *Report of 5th meeting of the Forum of Educational Research in Scotland*. Scottish Council for Research in Education, 1989.
Draper, J.; Fraser, H.; Smith, D. & Taylor, W. The induction of probationer teachers: implications of an industrial model. In: *Scottish Educational Review*, Vol 23, No 1/1991, pp. 23-31.

Draper, J. & Smith, D. Primary probationers and discipline. In: *Summary reports from Control and Discipline Seminar*, Craigie College, Ayr, June 1991, pp. 7-8.

13635 Survey of older graduates.
GBR 1993
Research Date(s): 1990-1991
Graham, B.
Inst: Strathclyde University, Careers Advisory Service, 16 Richmond Street, Glasgow G1 1XQ, United Kingdom.
choice of studies; job search; career; employment opportunities; graduate; student; adult; occupational choice
choix des études; recherche d'emploi; carrière; chances d'obtenir un emploi; étudiant diplômé; étudiant; adulte; choix d'une profession
PROJECT DESCRIPTION
This is a national survey, by questionnaire, of mature graduates' (25+ on graduation) previous experience and qualifications. This includes their reasons for choice of course and career, experience of job seeking; destinations after employment, opinions of careers services and of employers' attitudes to older graduates.

13636 Le système de formation dans la dynamique locale de l'emploi.
FRA 1993
Research Date(s): 1990-
Vernières, Michel; Beaumert, François.
Inst: Université de Paris I, UFR Analyse et politique économiques, CNRS URA/941 et GDR/996, Laboratoire d'économie sociale-Equipe Emploi, Formation, Développement, 90 rue de Tolbiac, 75634 Paris Cedex 13, France.
Fin: Centre d'études et de recherches sur les emplois et les qualifications.
training-employment relationship; regional development; vocational training
relation formation-emploi; développement régional; formation professionnelle
PROJECT DESCRIPTION
Objectifs: Dans le cadre des Observatoires régionaux emploi-formation le CEREQ a souhaité élaborer une grille de lecture des dispositifs existants. En premier lieu, on précise le questionnement méthodologique sur le rôle de la formation dans la dynamique locale de l'emploi, ensuite la recherche s'articule autour de deux axes: (1) Comment appréhender la liaison emploi-formation dans les régions polarisées par une grande métropole? (2) Comment les stratégies de localisation des entreprises intègrent-elles la variable "formation de la main d'oeuvre locale"?.

13637 Teacher training and teacher recruitment in the inner city.
GBR 1993
Research Date(s): 1991
Varlaam, A.; Walker, A.
Sup: Nuttall, D.
Inst: London University, London School of Economics and Political Science, Centre for Educational Research, Houghton Street, London WC2A 2AE, United Kingdom.
Fin: Department of Education and Science.
teaching post; initial employment; appointment; probationary teacher; urban school
poste d'enseignement; premier emploi; nomination; enseignant stagiaire; école urbaine
PROJECT DESCRIPTION
The research consists of four parts: (1) a questionnaire survey of a sample of about 600 final-year Bachelor of Education (B.Ed.) and Postgraduate Certificate in Education (PGCE) students selected from a cross-section of training institutions, supplemented by group interviews in four institutions; (2) group discussions at six training institutions with first-year B.Ed. students and PGCE students early in their year of study, to investigate whether their views are more malleable; (3) an identification of the local education authorities that were the first destination of students acquiring Qualified Teacher Status (QTS) in 1988 and 1989, possibly supplemented by an analysis of the home addresses, by institution and of applicants successfully entering a B.Ed. or a PGCE course in 1991; and (4) a questionnaire survey of a sample of about 300 teachers in their first three years of service, supplemented by group interviews.

13638 Theoretische en empirische aspecten van arbeidskrachtanalyse. (Theoretical and empirical aspects of manpower analysis.)
NLD 1993
Research Date(s): 1992-1996
Eijs, P.W.L.J. van.
Sup: Heijke, J.A.M.; Grip, A. de.
Inst: ROA Researchcentrum voor Onderwijs en Arbeidsmarkt, Universiteit Limburg (Research Centre for Education and the Labour Market, University of Limburg), P.O. Box 616, 6200 MD Maastricht, Netherlands.
labour market; manpower need; forecasting
marché du travail; besoin de main-d'oeuvre; prévision

PROJECT DESCRIPTION
Manpower analysis deals with the prediction of occupational and skill structures. In the past this analysis has been used mainly as an aid in educational planning. Today it is seen in the first place as a source of information for the participants on the labour market. The most widely used method in manpower analysis is the "manpower requirements approach". One disadvantage of this simple approach is that no allowance is made for adaptive mechanisms within the labour market as the result of factors such as technological progress, educational discrepanices, immobility, etc. If the process of adaption were taken into account, the informational value of the analysis would be increased.
This Ph.D research project examines whether and how far it is possible to increase the informational value of manpower analysis in general and the "manpower requirements approach" in particular. Three questions are addressed: (1) How can the traditional manpower requirements approach be related to equilibrium or disequilibrium theory and so be given a better theoretical foundation? (2) How can developments in occupational and skill structures be related to economic theory? (3) Are predictions made with theoretically based models better than those using traditional models?.

13639 Typologie des relations formation-emploi: effets sur la stabilité des emplois des jeunes ouvriers et employés.
FRA 1993
Research Date(s): 1988-
Affichard, Joëlle; Combes, Marie-Christine; Grelet, Yvette.
Inst: Centre d'études et de recherches sur les qualifications, 9 rue Sextius Michel, 75732 Paris Cedex 15, France; Commissariat général au Plan, Service des études et de la recherche, 18 rue de Martignac, 75007 Paris, France.
training-employment relationship; occupational integration; apprenticeship; technical education
relation formation-emploi; intégration professionnelle; apprentissage professionnel; enseignement technique
PROJECT DESCRIPTION
Objectifs: Confrontation des conditions d'entrée dans la vie professionnelle de jeunes formés dans l'enseignement technique scolaire et par l'apprentissage. Mise en évidence de différents modèles d'insertion professionnelle, mettant en cause le schéma dualiste. Réinterprétation, dans le cadre théorique d'une pluralité de modes de coordination, des phénomènes de stabilité des emplois.
Méthodologie: Analyses statistiques sur un échantillon de 9300 anciens élèves de lycées professionnels et de 4250 anciens apprentis, interrogés dans le cadre de l'Observatoire des entrées dans la vie active du Centre d'études et de recherches sur les qualifications.
Résultats: Quatre types d'insertion professionnelle ont pu être dégagés pour les jeunes ouvriers et employés, combinant selon des modalités diverses les liens de nature domestique, industrielle et marchande.

13640 Unge gutters vandring i arbeid og utdanning fra 1985 til 1990. (The careers of boys in work and education from 1985 to 1990.)
NOR 1994
Research Date(s): 1992
Grögaard, Jens B.
Inst: Fagbevegelsens Senter for Forskning, Utredning og Dokumentasjon (Norwegian Trade Union Centre for Social Science and Research), Fossveien 9, 0551 Oslo, Norway.
Fin: NAVF/RSF.
career; school career; transition from school to work; success; school failure; boy; unemployment
carrière; cursus scolaire; passage à la vie active; réussite; échec scolaire; garçon; chômage
PROJECT DESCRIPTION
The project seeks to describe the careers of boys in school and work from the end of primary school to the age of 20-22 during the last half of the 1980s. It is attempted to construct a flow chart outlining as precisely as possible pupils' subject choices in upper secondary school, school careers in upper secondary school, "gap" years and periods of waiting, work experience and unemployment. Thus, it is intended to establish who are the winners and the losers in the competition for education and work, in a social, cognitive, ideological and socio-medical sense. The main questions addressed are: Who are the "regulars" in upper secondary school? Who are the unemployed? To what extent do practical subjects in upper secondary education lead to an apprenticeship contract?.

Publ: A full list of publications can be obtained on request from the research institute.

13641 Verbesserung des Innovationsmanagements in kleinen und mittleren Unternehmungen. (Improving innovation management in small and medium-sized companies.)
DEU 1993
Research Date(s): 1990-1993
Schaeper, C.
Sup: Boehler, H.; Wossidlo, P.

Inst: Betriebswirtschaftliches Forschungszentrum fuer Fragen der Mittelstaendischen Wirtschaft e.V. an der Uni, Friedrichstrasse 19a, D-8580 Bayreuth.

Fin: Freistaat Bayern, Bayerisches Staatsministerium fuer Wirtschaft und Verkehr.

managerial staff; business management; interplant training; innovation; small and medium entreprise

personnel d'encadrement; gestion des entreprises; formation interfirmes; innovation; petite ou moyenne entreprise

PROJECT DESCRIPTION

Inhalt: Modellvorhaben zur Zusammenarbeit mehrerer bayerischer, mittelstaendischer Unternehmen und Technologie-Transfer-(TT)-Stellen bei der betriebsuebergreifenden Ausbildung von Fuehrungskraeften im Innovationsmanagement; Dokumentation und Erfolgsmessung; Entwicklung und wissenschaftliche Begleitung neuartiger Massnahmen von TT-Stellen zur Foerderung von Innovationen in kleinen Unternehmen.

Geographischer Raum: Bayern.

Vorgehensweise: Aktionsforschung; explorative Einzelfallstudien. Untersuchungsdesign: Fallstudie; Trend; qualitative Forschung.

Datengewinnung: Telefoninterview, teilnehmende Beobachtung (Stichprobe: ca. 9; Geschaeftsleitungen von Unternehmen; Auswahlverfahren: total. Stichprobe: ca. 15; Nachwuchs-Fuehrungskraefte; Auswahlverfahren: total). Primaererhebung: Feldarbeit von Mitarbeitern des Projektes durchgefuehrt.

Auswertung: Datenaufbereitung: Zeitreihe(n).

13642 Weiterbildung und Beschaeftigung von Hochschulabsolventen in informationsverarbeitenden Berufen. (Further training and employment of university graduates in information-processing occupations.)

DEU 1993

Research Date(s): 1990-1993

Rolf, W.

Sup: Timmermann, D.; Sommer, M.

Inst: Universitaet Bielefeld, Fak. fuer Paedagogik, Fach Bildungsplanung und Bildungsoekonomie, Postfach 100131, D-4800 Bielefeld 1.

employment opportunities; graduate; further training; higher education; qualification; information processing

chances d'obtenir un emploi; étudiant diplômé; formation complémentaire; enseignement supérieur; qualification; traitement de l'information

PROJECT DESCRIPTION

Inhalt: Entwicklung und Eroerterung von Qualitaetskriterien der DV-Weiterbildung; Analyse von Zusammenhaengen zwischen der Qualitaet der DV-Weiterbildung und den Beschaeftigungschancen der Absolventen.

Vorgehensweise: Expertengespraeche (DV-Schulungsleiter, DV-Personalverantwortliche, Berater der Arbeitsverwaltung); schriftliche Befragung von Lehrgangsteilnehmern an DV Schulen; exemplarisch.

13643 Werkgelegenheid en voortijdig (ongediplomeerd) schoolverlaten. (Employment and early school leaving.)

NLD 1994

Research Date(s): 1993

Batenburg, Th.A. van.

Sup: Hoeben, W.Th.J.G.

Inst: RION Instituut voor Onderwijsonderzoek (RION Institute for Educational Research), P.O. Box 1286, 9701 BG Groningen, Netherlands.

Rijksuniversiteit Groningen (State University of Groningen), P.O. Box 72, 9700 AB Groningen, Netherlands

Fin: SVO het Instituut voor Onderzoek van het Onderwijs.

employment; dropout; vocational training; recruitment; work experience

emploi; abandon d'études; formation professionnelle; recrutement; expérience du travail

PROJECT DESCRIPTION

Background: It is suspected that a considerable number of young people leave training because employers offer them a job during their work experience period. In the long term, this "skimming phenomenon" has a detrimental effect on the labour market position and mobility of these early school leavers. Current policies are aimed at further developing the "dual" training system, with alternating periods of theoretical and practical training, as a result of which the incidence of skimming may increase. The present project is a preliminary study seeking empirical evidence of the incidence of skimming. If such evidence is found, the project will be followed by a major study of skimming practices.

Aim: To investigate whether the skimming phenomenon described above exists.

Design: The study will use a sample of early school leavers from a wide range of training courses: mechanical engineering, construction engineering, electrotechnology, commercial training, secretarial training, accountancy, and social work. A distinction will be made between the Randstad (the urban agglomeration of Western Holland) and the remainder of the Netherlands. Use will be made of the information in two data banks and a telephone survey to trace 102 early school leavers that have been "skimmed off" and their employers. In-depth interviews will be conducted with both parties.

13644 Work socialisation of youth (WOSY): a cross-national study.

GBR 1993

Research Date(s): 1988-1992

Banks, H.; Parkinson, B.

Inst: Sheffield University, Department of Psychology, Medical Research Council, Sheffield S10 2TN, United Kingdom.

transition from school to work; cross-national research; work attitude; occupational integration; youth employment

passage à la vie active; recherche transnationale; attitude envers le travail; intégration professionnelle; emploi des jeunes

PROJECT DESCRIPTION

This is a collaborative cross-national research approach that seeks to describe and explain work role development of youth in ten countries, through a common theoretical and methodological framework. A minimum of two samples are drawn in each country, representing jobs selected to emphasise work with either 'data' or 'things'. The samples will comprise 200 young people beginning jobs with information systems such as word processors, and 200 machine operators in manufacturing companies. Interviews will be carried out on three occasions: within six months of starting the job or training scheme, nine to twelve months later, and two years after the first interview. Interviews will gather information about education, early career, and job characteristics. Motivational variables include employment commitment, job attitudes, and information about the personal meanings of work. Young people's perceptions of the personal impact on their job and their colleagues and the match between prior expectations and later circumstances, will also be assessed. In addition, several indices of career advancement and satisfaction will be obtained.

The aim is to determine individual, organisational and societal factors which underlie successful entry into the labour market. Changes across time will be identified, and these will be examined in relation to previously gathered data. Cross-national comparisons will permit evaluation of characteristic educational and training arrangements within each country.

13645 Youth Development Projects.

GBR 1993

Research Date(s): 1989-1992

Squirrell, G.

Sup: Broadfoot, P.

Inst: Bristol University, School of Education, Centre for Assessment Studies, 22 Berkeley Square, Bristol BS8 1JA, United Kingdom.

Fin: Department of Employment.

transition from school to work; occupational choice; youth employment; vocational preparation; vocational guidance; vocational information

passage à la vie active; choix d'une profession; emploi des jeunes; initiation à la profession; orientation professionnelle; information professionnelle

PROJECT DESCRIPTION

Forty-seven Youth Development Projects (YDPs) have been funded by the Employment Department for a three year period 1989-1992. These YDPs were funded to develop increased awareness of working life, enhanced careers guidance and higher level skills. The overall aim for all YDPs was to consider mechanisms for, and the barriers to, increasing the coherence of young people's experiences of the various sectors of education, training and employment. The YDPs are run and delivered by Careers Service staff, school and college teachers, training providers and employers. The young people involved are aged 14-19 taking mainstream school, college and training courses and those receiving special education and training needs provision.

Publ: Squirrell, G. *Individual action planning: development work with 14-19 year olds.* CAS/TEED, 1991.

Squirrell, G. *Youth Development Project Directory.* TEED, 1991.

Squirrell, G. *Report on the Youth Development Project Initiative,* TEED, 1992.

13646 Zur Evaluation betrieblicher Weiterbildung: Bewertungsrelevanz der Auspraegungen und Zusammenhaenge erfragter bzw. eingeschaetzter Merkmale. (On the evaluation of in-service training in industry: relevance of the features and relationships between surveyed and estimated characteristics.)

DEU 1993

Research Date(s): 1989-1992

Haeusle, K.

Inst: Universitaet Saarbruecken, FB 06 Sozial- und Umweltwissenschaften, Fachrichtung Erziehungswissenschaft, Stadtwald Bau 15, D-6600 Saarbruecken.

further training; enterprise; in-service training; evaluation

formation complémentaire; entreprise; formation en cours d'emploi; évaluation

PROJECT DESCRIPTION

Inhalt: (1) Traegt betriebliche Weiterbildung zum Erfolg des Betriebes bei und wie muss sie bzgl. Planung, Durchfuehrung und Kontrolle gestaltet sein? (2) Welche betrieblichen Bedingungen erleichtern den Transfer? (3) Wie ist der Zusammenhang zwischen Weiterbildung, Personalentwicklung und Organisationsentwicklung in Betrieben?

Vorgehensweise: Eine prozessorientierte Auffassung der Weiterbildung erfordert eine Erfolgskontrolle von der Planung bis zur Durchfuehrung und die Eingebundenheit in ein strategisches Gesamtkonzept der Personalentwicklung. Untersuchungsdesign: Evaluationsstudie; Querschnittserhebung; (Quasi-)Experiment.

Datengewinnung: Standardisiertes Interview (Stichprobe: 20-30; mittelstaendische und grosse Betriebe; Auswahlverfahren: bewusst). Expertengespraech (dito). Befragung (dito). Aktenanalyse (dito). Primaererhebung: Feldarbeit von Mitarbeitern des Projektes durchgefuehrt.

13647 Zweite Befragung von Hochschulabsolventen westdeutscher Hochschulen des Jahrganges 1988/1989. (Second survey of West German university graduates from 1988/1989.)
DEU 1993
Research Date(s): 1991-1992
Minks, K.
Inst: HIS Hochschul-Informations-System GmbH, Goseriede 9, D-3000 Hannover.
Fin: Bundesministerium fuer Bildung und Wissenschaft.
occupational integration; university studies; transition from school to work; graduate; school career
intégration professionnelle; études universitaires; passage à la vie active; étudiant diplômé; cursus scolaire
PROJECT DESCRIPTION
Inhalt: Analyse der Uebergangsverlaeufe und der beruflichen Integration vor dem Hintergrund von Studienverlaufs- und Studienerfolgsmerkmalen bei Absolventen mit einem ersten Hochschulabschluss.
Geographischer Raum: Bundesrepublik Deutschland (alte Laender).
Vorgehensweise: Laengsschnittanalyse. Untersuchungsdesign: Panel.
Datengewinnung: Postalische Befragung (Stichprobe: 7000; Hochschulabsolventen ausgewaehlter Studiengaenge; Auswahlverfahren: total). Primaererhebung: Feldarbeit von Mitarbeitern des Projektes durchgefuehrt.
Auswertung: Verschiedene bi- und multivariate Verfahren. Datenaufbereitung: Datenedition (z.B. Aufbau von Datenbanken); Verlaufsdaten (event history data).

34 PROFESSION AND PERSONNEL – PROFESSION ET PERSONNEL – BERUF UND PERSONAL

13648 AIDS Education and Research Trust (AVERT) HIV/AIDS and nursing project.
GBR 1993
Research Date(s): 1991-1992
Walker, R.
Sup: Aggleton, P.
Inst: London University, Institute of Education, Department of Policy Studies, Health and Education Research Unit, 20 Bedford Way, London WC1H 0AL, United Kingdom.
Fin: AVERT (AIDS Education and Research Trust).
nurse; attitude; anxiety; sexually transmitted disease; vocational education
infirmier; attitude; angoisse; maladie sexuellement transmissible; enseignement professionnel
PROJECT DESCRIPTION
This is a project to examine the interface between professional, scientific and biomedical understandings of Human Immunodeficiency Virus/Acquired Immune Deficiency Syndrome (HIV/AIDS) and nurses' awareness, attitudes, beliefs and anxieties about HIV disease. It is broadly exploratory in nature. Data will be collected by means of semi-structured small group interviews so as to identify respondents' recurrent concerns, beliefs and anxieties. Fieldwork will be carried out in six colleges of nursing involving student nurses in their first and final year of training. Two of these colleges will be linked to hospitals and/or community settings in which there is considerable experience of care for people with HIV/AIDS. Two will be

institutions without such links, and two will be colleges with intermediate levels of experience.

13649 Akademische Laufbahn und Geschlecht. (Carrière universitaire et sexe.)
CHE 1994
Research Date(s): 1989-1992
Nadai, Eva (Heidwiesen 25, 8051 Zürich, Schweiz).
Bundesamt für Statistik, Sektion Hochschule und Wissenschaft, Hallwylstrasse 15, 3003 Bern, Schweiz
teacher; university; sexism; recruitment; woman; discrimination
enseignant; université; sexisme; recrutement; femme; discrimination
PROJECT DESCRIPTION
Bis zum Jahr 2005 werden an den schweizerischen Hochschulen über die Hälfte der gegenwärtigen Professoren in den Ruhestand treten und zu ersetzen sein. Die Besetzung dieser freiwerdenden Lehrstühle wird sich stark darauf auswirken, wie die universitäre Forschung und Lehre im ersten Viertel des nächsten Jahrhunderts aussehen wird. Der entsprechende Nachwuchs darf nicht automatisch als gesichert gelten; Nachwuchsförderungsmassnahmen könnten sich als wünschbar oder notwendig erweisen. Die Tatsache, dass sich unter den Studierenden der Frauenanteil auf etwa 40 Prozent beläuft, aber nur etwa auf 4 Prozent bei den Professoren, verdient in diesem Zusammenhang Beachtung; sie lässt etwa vermuten, dass der Selektionsmechanismus Elemente aufweist, die gezielt auf die Erhaltung des Status quo und auf den Ausschluss von Gruppen von "Neuankömmlingen" ausgerichtet sind. Welches sind die Initiationsriten, die den Weg zu einem Lehrstuhl öffnen? Nach welchen Mechanismen geschieht die Selektion für einen Lehrstuhl? Welche (unter anderem geschlechtsspezifischen) Faktoren bestimmen überhaupt die akademische Karriere?
Diese Analyse von Forschungsliteratur zum Thematik der Situation und Förderung von wissenschaftlichen Nachwuchskräften an Schweizer Hochschulen wurde vom Bundesamt für Statistik in Auftrag gegeben. Die Autorin präsentiert zu Beginn Befunde und Überlegungen zu den bedingenden Faktoren für eine akademische Laufbahn und verweilt dann insbesondere bei den spezifischen Problemen der Akademikerinnen und ihrer Untervertretung in den hierarchisch höheren Bereichen des Hochschulwesens. Sie äussert die Vermutung, dass Professoren (aber auch Professorinnen) bei der Förderung ihrer latenten Nachfolger (und Nachfolgerinnen) via intuitive Wiedererkennungsprozesse eine Auswahl treffen. Der dritte Teil ist den in der Schweiz angewandten Massnahmen zur Nachwuchsförderung gewidmet. Zum Schluss wird auf Forschungslücken hingewiesen; in diesem Zusammenhang unterstreicht die Autorin die Notwendigkeit, empirische Studien zur Nachwuchsproblematik auf allen Stufen der Laufbahn zu unternehmen, insbesondere qualitative empirische Untersuchungen, die sich mit individualbiographischen Prozessen beschäftigen und die in einer umfassenden Perspektive nach den Bedingungen von Scheitern oder Erfolg von Wissenschafterinnen und Wissenschaftern fragen, ohne dabei den Faktor Geschlecht als Strukturierendes Merkmal aus den Augen zu verlieren.

Publ: Nadai, Eva. *Akademische Laufbahn und Geschlecht: Situation und Förderung von wissenschaftlichen Nachwuchskräften an Schweizer Hochschulen: eine Analyse der Forschungsliteratur.* Bern: Bundesamt für Statistik, 1992, 44 Seiten.

13650 Arbeitssituation, berufliches Selbstverstaendnis und Qualifikation ausbildender Fachkraefte. (Work situation, occupational self-image and qualification of specialist instructors.)
DEU 1993
Research Date(s): 1992-1995
Hoge, E.; Neubert, R.; Selka, R.; Steinborn, H.
Sup: Schmidt-Hackenberg, B.
Inst: Bundesinstitut fuer Berufsbildung, Fehrbelliner Platz 3, D-1000 Berlin 31.
trainer; apprentice; in-service training; role perception; qualification
formateur; apprenti; formation en cours d'emploi; perception de rôle; qualification
PROJECT DESCRIPTION
Inhalt: Jeder sechste Erwerbstaetige ist an der Qualifizierung des betrieblichen Facharbeiter-und Sachbearbeiternachwuchses beteiligt (repraesentative IAB/BIBB-Befragung 1985/1986). Einen Auszubildenden anzuleiten ist Teil ihrer Arbeitsaufgabe; ein selbstverstaendlicher Teil oder ein konfliktreicher? In welcher Rolle sehen sich Fachkraefte, die ausbilden? Welche Bedingungen bestimmen das Lernpotential von Arbeitsplaetzen? Welche Hilfen koennten ausbildenden Fachkraeften die Aufgabe erleichtern?
Geographischer Raum: Deutschland (Ost und West).
Vorgehensweise: Die betriebliche Ausbildung am Arbeitsplatz ist Bildung in einer bildungsfernen Institution. Untersuchungsdesign: Fallstudie; Evaluationsstudie; Querschnittserhebung; qualitative Forschung.
Datengewinnung: Primaererhebung: Feldarbeit von Mitarbeitern des Projektes durchgefuehrt; Primaererhebung: Feldarbeit als Auftrag an kommerzielle Umfrageinstitute vergeben; Datenerstellung auf der Basis von bereits vorliegenden Materialien wie Texten, Akten, Statistiken.

13651 Art therapists and their art.
GBR 1993
Research Date(s): 1983-1991
Gilroy, A.
Sup: Smith, P.
Inst: London University, Goldsmith's College, Art Psychotherapy Unit, Lewisham Way, New Cross, London SE14 6NW, United Kingdom; Sussex University, Faculty of Social Sciences, Sussex House, Falmer, Brighton BN1 9RH, United Kingdom.
therapist; art; student; teacher; occupational choice
thérapeute; art; étudiant; enseignant; choix d'une profession
PROJECT DESCRIPTION
This research outlines the processes of career choice and occupational development of art therapists, focusing on their own art practice and the varying influences upon it, from early childhood through to the present. The study is survey based, using questionnaires and supplemented by interviews. Two consecutive academic years of postgraduate art therapy students (44) and art teacher students (38), and 217 practising art therapists were the respondents.

A route is traced from art therapy and art teacher students' interest in art, through to entry into postgraduate education. Although the two groups were found to have much in common with each other, the art therapy students were distinguished by stressful experiences during their childhoods and early adult lives. Art therapy students' learning in experiential groups was seen to promote increases in self-awareness and spontaneity in art, as well as a more honest engagement with personal imagery. It is demonstrated that most art therapists continue with some form of art, although its frequency diminishes upon entry into the profession. The nature of art therapists' art is seen to vary and the influence of clinical practice may be positive or negative, but the activity itself remains of critical importance in their lives. That their own art enables art therapists to sustain a sense of personal and professional well being implies that art therapists should not neglect their art practice, and that art therapy educators should pay attention to students' art practice during their professional education.
Publ: Gilroy, A.J. On occasionally being able to paint. In: *Inscape*, pp. 2-9, Spring 1989.

13652 Artists-in-education training project.
GBR 1993
Research Date(s): 1990-1991
Mason, R.; Maughan, C.; Bruntlett, S.
Inst: De Montford University, PO Box 143, Leicester LE1 9BH, United Kingdom.
Fin: Arts Council of Great Britain.
artist; art; art education; teaching
artiste; art; éducation artistique; enseignement
PROJECT DESCRIPTION
This pilot project was set up in 1990 by the Arts Council working with three regional arts associations and Leicester Polytechnic (now De Montford University). The aims were "to provide performing artists, visual artists, craftspeople, writers and composers with the skills and knowledge they need to work with confidence in education today". The programme developed and implemented early in 1991 covered a ten day period and included residential training weekends staffed by a combination of artists, teachers and educators, and six day placements in primary or secondary schools. The progress of the project was systematically documented and evaluated by a project officer specifically appointed for this purpose. His evaluation report identified strengths and weaknesses of the training programme and of the residencies in terms of their contribution to teachers' and pupils' learning in the arts and the impact of artists on school arts programmes.
Publ: Illsley, R. *The Artists-in-Education Training Project: an evaluative report*, Leicester Polytechnic, 1991.

13653 Aspetti e problemi inerenti all'applicazione della normativa sul fondo di incentivazione e sulle nuove figure professionali. (Aspects and problems inherent to the application of legislation on monetary incentives for teachers and on new professional profiles.)
ITA 1993
Research Date(s): 1990-1991
De Bella, A.; Magni, V.
Sup: Chiaramonte Fo, B.
Inst: Cooperativa Insegnanti di Iniziativa Democratica - CIID (Teacher Cooperative for Democratic Initiatives), Piazza Sonnino 13, 00153 Roma, Italy.
Fin: Ministero della Pubblica Istruzione, Ufficio Studi e Programmazione.
teaching profession; teaching personnel; educational legislation; career; reward; career profile
profession d'enseignant; corps enseignant; législation scolaire; carrière; récompense; monographie de carrière
PROJECT DESCRIPTION
Aims: The research had three main objectives: (1) assessment of the levels of information and knowledge with regard to legislation on monetary incentives for teachers and new professional profiles; (2) evaluation of the application of this legislation and the results; (3) the collection of proposals for the modification and/or integration of existing legislation.

Methods: Identification of objectives, questionnaire survey (first of a limited sample, subsequently to 167 schools); cross-analysis.

Results: School staff were found to react in two different ways to these two innovations - monetary incentives for teachers and new professional profiles: on the one hand, they were suprised, on the other, they recognized the need for them. These two reactions can be explained by the difficulties that exist in applying this legislation, by inexperience and by the uncertain work prospects of teachers. The changes introduced are too rigid and do not take account of particular needs or available competencies. The legislation appears to be confusing and rigid at the same time. Examination of the data reveals the necessity to change decision-making procedures at the centre without first passing through an experimental phase. Schools appear to be quite heterogeneous, but not completely closed to innovation. They hover between centralism and autonomy, and are therefore incapable of managing innovative processes.

13654 Assessment of the educational needs of health professionals in palliative care of patients with advanced cancer, and their families.
GBR 1993
Research Date(s): 1986-1992
Abdel-Fattah, A.; Thomas, M.
Sup: Harden, R.
Inst: Dundee University, Centre for Medical Education, Ninewells Hospital and Medical School, Dundee DD1 9SY, United Kingdom.
Fin: Cancer Relief Macmillan Fund.
health service personnel; continuing education; vocational education; educational need
personnel médical; éducation permanente; enseignement professionnel; besoin d'éducation
PROJECT DESCRIPTION
The aim of this project is to assess the learning needs of the health care professionals in palliative care of patients with advanced cancer, and their families. The first phase, concluded in 1990, has targeted general practitioners and included a print programme, patient management challenges and a computer program. The current phase is targeting junior hospital doctors in a hospital ward environment. Different educational strategies are being used to facilitate the learning needs in this area.

13655 Berufsverbleib von Ingenieurinnen aus den ostdeutschen Laendern unter den Bedingungen des Uebergangs zu einem marktwirtschaftlichen Beschaeftigungssystem. (The employment situation of female engineers from the new German states during the transition to a market economy.)
DEU 1993
Research Date(s): 1991-1992
Bathke, G.
Sup: Minks, K.
Inst: HIS Hochschul-Informations-System GmbH, Goseriede 9, D-3000 Hannover.
Fin: Institution; Bundesministerium fuer Bildung und Wissenschaft.
German DR; engineer; further training; retraining; employment opportunities; woman; economic conditions
Allemagne RDA; ingénieur; formation complémentaire; recyclage; chances d'obtenir un emploi; femme; conditions économiques
PROJECT DESCRIPTION
Inhalt: Analyse des Verbleibs von in der ehemaligen DDR ausgebildeten Ingenieurinnen; Angebot, Bedarf und Nutzung von Weiterbildungs- und Umschulungsmassnahmen. Befindlichkeit. Ueberpruefung der Hypothese von Tendenzen zur Annahme nicht ausbildungsadaequater Beschaeftigungen und Umschulungen sowie der Vermutung des verstaerkten drop out aus dem Beschaeftigungssystem im Zuge der Umstellung der Wirtschaft.

Geographischer Raum: Bundesrepublik Deutschland (neue Laender).

Vorgehensweise: Untersuchungsdesign: Querschnittserhebung.

Datengewinnung: Postalische Befragung (Stichprobe: 2500; Ingenieurinnen aus ostdeutschen Laendern; Auswahlverfahren: Quota. Stichprobe: 1000; Ingenieure -Kontrollgruppe- aus ostdeutschen Laendern; Auswahlverfahren: Quota) .Primaererhebung: Feldarbeit von Mitarbeitern des Projektes durchgefuehrt.

Auswertung: Verschiedene bi- und multivariate Verfahren. Datenaufbereitung: Datenedition (z.B. Aufbau von Datenbanken).

13656 Brede inzetbaarheid van onderwijsgevenden. (Broad deployability of teachers.)
NLD 1994
Research Date(s): 1993-1994
Amelsvoort, H.W.C.H. van.
Inst: Onderzoek Centrum Toegepaste Onderwijskunde (OCTO) (Research Centre of the Department of Educational Technology), P.O. Box 217, 7500 AE Enschede, Netherlands.
Universiteit Twente (Twente University), P.O. Box 217, 7500 AE Enschede, Netherlands

Fin: SVO het Instituut voor Onderzoek van het Onderwijs.

teacher; primary education; qualification; teaching; teacher role
enseignant; enseignement primaire; qualification; enseignement; rôle de
l'enseignant

PROJECT DESCRIPTION

Background: After all the debates that have been conducted, also in policy circles, a well-founded answer is needed to the question of whether and to what extent primary school teachers may be expected to be "broadly deployable", i.e. capable of performing a wide variety of tasks in relation to: the classes they teach (the entire 4-12 age range); the subjects they teach (the national core curriculum); the teaching strategies they use in various roles (stimulating cognitive processes in pupils, improving pupils' self-regulation, developing the "zone of proximal development", designing powerful learning environments); and management tasks (managerial work, administrative tasks, organizing instruction in mixed-age classes).

Aim: To investigate the tension that exists between, on the one hand, the desired "broad deployability" of teachers and, on the other, the need for specialization (given statutory professional requirements), the educational needs of pupils and the needs and possibilities of the teacher as an employee.

Design: On the basis of a survey of relevant literature, the concepts of "broad deployability" and "specialization" will be defined. In phase one of the research, a questionnaire survey will be conducted among teachers to determine how far they consider themselves capable of performing a variety of tasks. A second survey, of 2,000 primary schools, will aim to establish to what extent teachers are deployed for a wide variety of tasks. Phase two will consist of case studies. First, a valid and reliable instrument will be constructed with which it will be possible to measure the quality of teachers. Subsequently, 16 teachers from the survey will be asked to participate in a study of instructional effectiveness. These teachers will be observed in the classroom while giving instruction in language, arithmetic and factual subjects.

13657 The changing role of secondary headteachers.

GBR 1993
Research Date(s): 1990-1995
Drane, J.
Sup: Lofthouse, M.
Inst: Leicester University, School of Education, University Centre, Barrack Road, Northampton NN2 6AF, United Kingdom.

head teacher; educational administration; role conflict; educational legislation
chef d'établissement; administration de l'enseignement; conflit de rôles; législation scolaire

PROJECT DESCRIPTION

This research focuses upon the changing role of secondary headteachers following the Education Reform Act (1988). The main area of interest is the centralisation versus decentralisation conflict within recent legislation and the effect this has had on the role of the headteacher. Questions of interest are: (1) headteachers and governors - their working relationship; (2) headteachers or chief executives; (3) headteachers and power/authority - enhanced or diminished; and (4) headteachers and their senior management teams - real or imagined team work.

13658 Committee of Vice-Chancellors and Principals of the UK: a study of its development and role.

GBR 1993
Research Date(s): 1991-1993
Howell, D.
Inst: London University, Institute of Education, Department of Policy Studies, 20 Bedford Way, London WC1H 0AL, United Kingdom.
Fin: Nuffield Foundation.

managerial staff; higher education; university; committee; educational policy
personnel d'encadrement; enseignement supérieur; université; comité; politique de l'éducation

PROJECT DESCRIPTION

A study of the Committee of Vice-Chancellors and Principals of the UK (CVCP) from a political science perspective, concentrating on its current role in the higher education policy making process and its relationship with other organisations involved therein.

13659 The constructs teachers use to evaluate their own classroom practice.

GBR 1993
Research Date(s): 1986-1991
Hopkins, S.
Sup: Thomas, D.
Inst: Bishop Grosseteste College, Newport, Lincoln LN1 3DY, United Kingdom; Liverpool University, Department of Education, PO Box 147, Liverpool L69 3BX, United Kingdom.

teacher; student teacher; self-evaluation; performance; teaching
enseignant; élève-maître; auto-évaluation; performance; enseignement

PROJECT DESCRIPTION

The research is aimed at eliciting the constructs used by primary teachers when they evaluate a teaching/learning episode as successful and/or unsuccessful. 120 teachers and 120 student teachers completed an open-ended questionnaire which was used to elicit, from a content analysis, indicators which teachers or student teachers use to categorise teaching/learning as successful and/or unsuccessful, and the influences which determine, in their view, the presence or absence of these indicators. A comparison of teachers and student teachers is related to the expert-novice literature. A model to support reflective-pedagogy, generated from the empirical findings of the study, is suggested.

13660 Current developments in the preparation and support of principals in the United States.

GBR 1993
Research Date(s): 1991
Weindling, R.
Inst: Create Consultants, 109 West End Lane, London NW6 4SY, United Kingdom.
Fin: Department of Education and Science.

head teacher; management education; USA
chef d'établissement; formation à la gestion; Etats-Unis

PROJECT DESCRIPTION

The study consisted of a review of the current literature concerning United States school principals' management roles, functions and competencies. The aim was to present a description of research and practice, together with critical comment and recommendations to assist the Department of Education and Science School Management Task Force. The first section of the study covered the phases of pre-service prior to being appointed as a principal including State certification; induction - the support given during the first years of the principalship; and in-service - the various types of management development for established principals. The second section examined various national initiatives such as the 'Lead' programme which established a leadership centre in each State. Two national research centres have also been established. Section three looked at competency-based approaches, particularly assessment centres. (The first UK one has been opened in Oxford). The elaborate and detailed system in Florida is described, as well as a summary of the research on which it is based. The fourth section provides details of six methods of supporting principals, including mentoring and shadowing. The study also offers recommendations about the applicability of the various systems to the UK.

13661 Der Alltag des Sonderschullehrers im Spannungsfeld gesellschaftlicher Akzeptanz und eigener Idealvorstellungen. Wirkt eine psychodramatische Begleitung stabilisierend? (Everyday life of special school teachers caught between social acceptance and personal ideals. Can psychodramatic support have a stabilizing effect?)

DEU 1993
Research Date(s): 1991-1995
Roeber, S.
Sup: Kriwet, I.
Inst: Universitaet Hannover, FB Erziehungswissenschaften, 01 Lehrgebiet Lernbehindertenpaedagogik, Bismarckstr 2, D-3000 Hannover.

teacher; special school; occupational status; occupational choice; disease; psychodrama; mental stress
enseignant; centre d'éducation spéciale; statut professionnel; choix d'une profession; maladie; psychodrame; tension mentale

PROJECT DESCRIPTION

Inhalt: Vorlaeufige Gliederung: (1) Gesellschaftliche Bedingungen des Lehrers; Soziologie des Berufsstandes; (2) Alltagssituation des Lehrers/ Realitaet im Unterricht und Kollegium; (3) Individuelle Bedingungen des Lehrers; Warum wird Mann/ Frau LehrerIn?; (4) Die Krise des Lehrers als Folge des Spannungsverhaeltnisses zwischen den oben genannten Faktoren: Krankheitsstand, Therapiebeduerfnis, Fruehpensionierung. Kann die Begleitung des Lehrers durch eine selbsterfahrungsorientierte Gruppe dieses Spannungsverhaeltnis loesen, damit sein individuelles Wohlbefinden verbessern und folglich der Dequalifizierung des Lehrers entgegenwirken? (1) Moeglichkeiten der supervisorischen Begleitung von Lehrern; (2) Psychodrama als Technik in der Supervision; (3) Beobachtung von zwei Psychodrama-Gruppen mit Sonderschullehrern.

Geographischer Raum: Bundesrepublik Deutschland.

Vorgehensweise: Langzeitbeobachtung; Gruppenbeobachtung; Interviews; Frageboegen; Falldarstellung. Untersuchungsdesign: Fallstudie; Evaluationsstudie; qualitative Forschung.

Datengewinnung: Nicht-standardisiertes Interview (Stichprobe: 15; Studenten der Sonderpaedagogik der Uni Hannover; Auswahlverfahren: Zufall. Stichprobe: 15; Sonderschullehrerinnen aus Hannover und Umgebung; Auswahlverfahren: Zufall. Stichprobe: 8; Supervisionsgruppe ohne besonderes Konzept mit Sonderschullehrerinnen eines Schulkollegiums; Auswahlverfahren: Quota). Teilnehmende Beobachtung (dito). Primaererhebung: Feldarbeit von Mitarbeitern des Projektes durchgefuehrt.

13662 Determinanten van de professionaliteit van leraren voortgezet onderwijs. (Determinants of secondary school teachers' professionalism.)
NLD 1994
Research Date(s): 1993
Sleegers, P.; Gennip, J.W.M.G. van.
Sup: Pouwels, J.; Giesbers, J.
Inst: Vakgroep Onderwijskunde (Department of Education), P.O. Box 9103, 6500 HD Nijmegen, Netherlands.
Katholieke Universiteit Nijmegen (Catholic University of Nijmegen), P.O. Box 9102, 6500 HC Nijmegen, Netherlands
Fin: SVO het Instituut voor Onderzoek van het Onderwijs.
teacher; teaching profession; work environment; skill
enseignant; profession d'enseignant; milieu de travail; compétence
PROJECT DESCRIPTION
Background: Changes in society and in education place increasing demands on teachers. More and more teachers are expected to function in an organization with bureaucratic traits. In the debate on the nature of teacher professionalism the personal characteristics of the teacher and the teacher's working conditions are a central issue. There is a lack of research evidence on the influence of both these factors on teacher professionalism.
Aim: To examine the influence of personal characteristics and employment conditions on the level of professionalism of secondary school teachers.
Method: Secondary analysis.
Design: Secondary analyses will be performed on data that have been collected in a study on teacher mobility, which involved 334 schools and 1,400 teachers. Levels of professionalism will be measured on the basis of teachers' perceptions of the main tasks of the teaching profession, the variety of duties teachers perform, and the duties teachers say they would like to perform. Consistency of professionalism can be measured at the level of the actual duties performed by teachers. General occupational satisfaction will be used as a criterion variable in order to validate the concept of "professionalism" with the help of another criterion than those mentioned above.

13663 Diploma in advanced nursing studies.
GBR 1993
Research Date(s): 1990-
Thomson, L.
Sup: Harden, R.
Inst: Dundee University, Centre for Medical Education, Ninewells Hospital and Medical School, Dundee DD1 9SY, United Kingdom.
Fin: University of Dundee; Tayside Health Board.
nurse; vocational education
infirmier; enseignement professionnel
PROJECT DESCRIPTION
The Diploma Course aims to equip the individual with the knowledge and ability necessary to provide a high standard of individualised nursing care which is research based and reinforces individual accountability of the practitioner. Furthermore, the course aims to embrace the dynamics of change and emphasise the necessity for continuing professional updating and educational development.

13664 Educating 'desirable attitudes' in nurses.
GBR 1993
Research Date(s): 1989-1992
Rolfe, G.
Sup: Weare, K.
Inst: Southampton University, Faculty of Educational Studies, Highfield, Southampton SO9 5NH, United Kingdom.
nurse; health service personnel; attitude
infirmier; personnel médical; attitude
PROJECT DESCRIPTION
This research attempts to discover what attitudes are thought to be 'desirable' in nurses and ways in which desirable attitudes in nurses can be taught and assessed.

13665 Les enseignants des lycées professionnels (LEP).
FRA 1993
Research Date(s): 1986-1988
Tanguy, Lucie; Agulhon, Catherine; Poloni, Arlette.
Inst: Université de Paris VII, UFR Sciences sociales, CNRS UPR/16, Groupe de sociologie du travail, 2 Place Jussieu, Tour centrale, 75251 Paris Cedex 05, France.
teaching profession; occupational research; vocational education; level of qualification; level of qualification; recruitment
profession d'enseignant; recherche relative aux professions; enseignement professionnel; niveau de qualification; niveau de qualification; recrutement
PROJECT DESCRIPTION
Objectifs: Cette recherche procède à l'étude de la morphologie sociale des enseignants de lycées professionnels, de leurs cursus scolaires, de leurs itinéraires professionnels antérieurs, des modes d'accès à la profession enseignante et des pratiques de conversion à cette profession.

Méthodologie: La démarche de recherche combine certaines méthodes et instruments d'une sociologie des professions avec celles d'une sociologie de curricula.
Résultats: L'analyse de l'identité des enseignants montre les effets du renouvellement des modes de recrutement sur l'intégration de ce corps. La notion de générations se trouve ainsi placée au coeur de cette analyse; on s'attache à saisir les changements produits par le renouvellement de génération en matière de formation de compétences et de modes de socialisation accomplis dans les lycées professionnels et à les mettre en rapport avec les politiques de redéfinition des modes de formation professionnelle.
Publ: Tanguy, Lucie; Agulhon, Catherine & Poloni, Arlette. *Des ouvriers de métiers aux diplômés du technique supérieur: le renouvellement d'une catégorie d'enseignants en lycées professionnels.* Université de Paris 7: Groupe de sociologie du travail, janv. 1988, 468p. (Rapport remis au Ministère de l'éducation nationale).
Tanguy, Lucie; Agulhon, Catherine & Poloni, Arlette. Les institutions d'enseignement technique court en France: genèse et évolution. In: *Revue française de pédagogie*, 1987, 78, pp. 43-64.

13666 Evaluation of a mentor scheme for headteachers.
GBR 1993
Research Date(s): 1992-1994
Bradley, H.
Inst: Cambridge University, Institute of Education, Shaftesbury Road, Cambridge CB2 2BX, United Kingdom.
Fin: School Management Task Force; Department for Education; Local Education Authorities.
head teacher
chef d'établissement
PROJECT DESCRIPTION
There are three phases, containing 16, 32 and 96 mentor/mentee pairs respectively. By questionnaire and interview, the mentors are followed through their training. Then by interview of a sample of both mentors and mentees, the implementation of the mentor programme will be monitored. In Phase 1 about a 50% sample is being followed for evaluation purposes, reducing to about 25% in Phase 2 and 10% in Phase 3.

13667 Gender and headship: career contexts and strategies.
GBR 1993
Research Date(s): 1990-1992
Evetts, J.
Inst: Nottingham University, School of Social Studies, University Park, Nottingham NG7 2RD, United Kingdom.
head teacher; teaching profession; career development; career profile; sex difference
chef d'établissement; profession d'enseignant; déroulement de carrière; monographie de carrière; différence de sexe
PROJECT DESCRIPTION
This is a study of how details of individuals' life histories and career biographies can contribute to educational and sociological understanding about teachers' careers and about gender differences in career building. Using career history interviews from a sample of twenty headteachers, ten men and ten women, from two Midlands educational authorities, the research has considered what were the external structural conditions and the characteristics of the labour market for constructing careers in teaching. The research has also considered what strategies men and women have devised to manage and negotiate such contexts.
The researcher has argued that one can demonstrate that career histories illustrate both structural conditions, in particular labour markets and the strategies of individuals' developing careers.
Publ: Evetts, J. The experience of secondary headship selection: continuity and change. In: *Educational Studies*, Vol 17, No 3/1991, pp. 285-294.
Evetts, J. When promotion ladders seem to end: the career concerns of secondary headteachers. In: *British Journal of Sociology of Education*, Vol 13, No 1/1992, pp. 37-49.
A complete list of publications is available from the researcher.

13668 The headteacher's role in the implementation of National Curriculum.
GBR 1993
Research Date(s): 1991-1992
Peers, I.
Sup: Ray, R.
Inst: Manchester University, School of Education, Centre for Formative Assessment Studies, Oxford Road, Manchester M13 9PL, United Kingdom.
Fin: Council for Educational Technology.
head teacher; common core curriculum; educational administration; curriculum development
chef d'établissement; tronc commun; administration de l'enseignement; élaboration de programmes d'études
PROJECT DESCRIPTION
Beginning with a pilot group of three headteachers, a log was kept to establish how a headteacher's time is spent. The activities were coded and time spent on National Curriculum was established. Other headteachers are

now being recruited into the project. Fifteen headteachers took part in a structured interview as part of a needs analysis exercise. The role of the headteacher as facilitator of National Curriculum implementation will be defined with a view to producing a report and training materials.

13669   Headteachers: the impact of radical reform upon senior professionals.
GBR   1993
Research Date(s): 1990-1994
Grace, G.; McGuiness, J.
Inst: Durham University, School of Education, Leazes Road, Durham DH1 1TA, United Kingdom.
head teacher; leadership; educational administration
chef d'établissement; commandement; administration de l'enseignement
PROJECT DESCRIPTION
   An empirical and theoretical study of changing conceptions of leadership in English schooling with reference to transitions from the headteacher as moral leader, the headteacher as senior professional and the headteacher as chief executive. The study is based upon taped interviews with a sample of infant, junior and secondary headteachers in the north-east of England. A target sample of 100 is proposed. Accounts will be analysed in relation to LEA (local education authority) locations, level of school and possible gender differences in reaction to the development of managerialism in education.

13670   Il corpo insegnante della scuola italiana. (Teaching personnel in Italian schools.)
ITA   1993
Research Date(s): 1990-1991
De Lillo, A.; Gattullo, M.; Martinelli, A.; Moscati, R.; Trivellato, P.
Sup: Cavalli, A.
Inst: Associazione per la Ricerca Sperimentale sui Problemi dei Giovani - IARD (Association for Experimental Research and Problems of Youth), Via Soncino 1, 20123 Milano, Italy.
Fin: Ministero della Pubblica Istruzione, Ufficio Studi e Programmazione.
teaching profession; teaching personnel; teacher behaviour; role perception; teacher role; motivation; teacher status; self-perception; occupational satisfaction
profession d'enseignant; corps enseignant; comportement de l'enseignant; perception de rôle; rôle de l'enseignant; motivation; statut de l'enseignant; perception de soi; satisfaction professionnelle
PROJECT DESCRIPTION
   Aims: This extensive survey of Italian teaching personnel aimed to remedy the lack of information about teachers in Italy and to offer insight into the profound differences that exist within this professional category.
   Methods: With the help of a questionnaire, 90 interviewers conducted interviews with 5,000 teachers (1000 primary, 1,500 lower secondary and 2,500 upper secondary school teachers) in four areas: northwest, northeast, south-central, and islands. The interviews took place in the period November 1989 - February 1990.
   Results: The general characteristics of Italian teachers can be summarized as follows. Teachers have a strong feeling of belonging to the academic environment. They have long - but not always smooth - careers. They derive most satisfaction in their work from personal relationships with pupils, while dissatisfaction mainly comes from relationships with colleagues, head teachers, collegial bodies, and external support teams. There is a general lack of interest in computers and in specializing in computer science. Teachers display a critical judgement regarding pre-service training in educational theory and teaching methods. They would like to see changes in the initial training of teachers and they are open towards in-service training. Many see an erosion of the teacher's professional prestige and image. Teachers oppose criticisms that they lack social awareness, that they have a low level of cultural awareness, that they are conservative, that they have short work hours and excessively long holiday time, that they are authoritarian, etc. Regarding these criticisms, teachers tend to defend themselves as a group. Wide gaps exist between the desired teacher role, the actual role, and the role considered necessary. A contradiction is seen to exist between secretarial duties and the demand for professional capacities and autonomy.
   The role attribute about which the strongest consensus exists is the capacity to communicate with others. Expectations are related to a relevant social role on the basis of a specialized competence. Diverse opinions exist regarding the reform of upper secondary school. There is confusion and discomfort regarding educational and vocational guidance and a lack of trust in managerial staff. Approval of labour unions is declining. There is sympathy for grassroots movements and a preference for a unified labour union. Participation in group activites is low and there is a tendency not to use free time for cultural purposes. An "ethic of pessimism" exists among teachers, caused by an awareness of the decline in certain fundamental moral values, such as honesty, altruism, religiousness, family values, etc.

13671   Information needs and information seeking behaviour of nurses.
GBR   1993
Research Date(s): 1991
Wakeham, M.
Inst: Anglia Polytechnic University, Faculty of Health and Social Work, Victoria Road South, Chelmsford CM1 1LL, United Kingdom.
Fin: British Library.
nurse; student; information need; information
infirmier; étudiant; besoin d'information; information
PROJECT DESCRIPTION
   The objectives of the study are to identify the kinds of information sought by student nurses, trained staff and students on post-basic courses. The researchers have sought by means of a questionnaire, to investigate the ways in which information is sought, particularly in libraries. One thousand questionnaires were distributed within the four health districts with which Anglia Polytechnic University has links via its Departments of Nursing and Midwifery Education. A response rate of around 50% was obtained. The replies have been analysed through the SPSS PC program and the results are being collated.

13672   Innovative uses of non-teaching staff in primary and secondary schools.
GBR   1993
Research Date(s): 1991-1992
Mortimore, P.; Mortimore, J.
Inst: London University, Institute of Education, The Directorate, 20 Bedford Way, London WC1H 0AL, United Kingdom.
Fin: Department of Education and Science.
non-teaching staff; educational administration; personnel management
personnel non-enseignant; administration de l'enseignement; gestion du personnel
PROJECT DESCRIPTION
   The efficient and cost-effective use of trained staff is crucial to any enterprise. The implementation of the Education Reform Act (1988) is likely to have resulted in a re-examination of the traditional roles of both teaching and non-teaching staff. The research aims to identify examples of innovatory uses of non-teaching staff; to draw up a typology of staffing models and to estimate cost benefits (and disbenefits) of different models.
Publ: Mortimore, P. & Mortimore, J. et al. *The innovative uses of non-teaching staff in primary and secondary schools project*. London: DFE/Institute of Education, 1992.

13673   Les instituteurs: leurs formations, leurs trajectoires sociales et professionnelles, leurs pratiques professionnelles.
FRA   1992
Research Date(s): 1985-1989
Peyronie, Henri.
Sup: Marmoz, Louis.
Inst: Université de Caen, UFR Sciences de l'homme, Centre d'études et de recherches en sciences de l'éducation, 14032 Caen Cedex, France.
primary education; teacher education; teaching practice; pre-school education; regional development
enseignement primaire; formation des enseignants; pratique pédagogique; éducation préscolaire; développement régional
PROJECT DESCRIPTION
   Objectifs: Approche des effets de la formation des enseignants dans son articulation aux autres facteurs du devenir professionnel, par une étude pluri-référentielle des manières de faire professionnelles d'instituteurs rapportées à leurs trajectoires sociales, professionnelles et de formation.
   Méthodologie: Etude pluri-référentielle d'enseignants de l'école élémentaire du Calvados. Le travail de recherche se développe sur deux axes méthodologiques et épistémologiques: (1) Une étude principalement descriptive à partir du traitement quantitatif d'un certain nombre d'indicateurs concernant la population étudiée (trajet de formation initiale et continuée, demande de formation continuée, ancienneté dans les postes, proximité éventuelle entre les lieux de naissance et les lieux d'exercice professionnel, entre ceux-ci et les lieux d'habitation...). Cette étude a donné lieu à des représentations cartographiques favorisant une lecture sociologique en terme d'approche locale différentielle de ces données. (2) Une étude socio-anthropologique du corps des instituteurs du Calvados, de ses "manières de faire" professionnelles, et de ses représentations (étude des rôles des acteurs professionnels de l'enseignement vis-à-vis de la fonction démocratisante de l'institution scolaire).
Publ: Peyronie, Henri (en coll. M. Altet). *Une convergence possible? Styles d'enseignements - Typologie d'enseignants*. Documents du CERSE, n° 28, 1988, 64p.
Peyronie, Henri. Recherches scientifiques et formation des enseignants et des formateurs. In: *Actes du VIe Congrès international de l'AIPELF*. Université de Caen, 1989, pp. 107-132.
Peyronie, Henri. La pédagogie Freinet serait-elle devenue une pédagogie pour les enfants des nouvelles classes moyennes? In: *Actualité de la pédagogie Freinet*, sous la dir. de P. Clanche et J. Testanière. Presses Universitaires de Bordeaux, 1989, pp. 97-118.

Peyronie, Henri. Les stages en entreprise: passerelle vers la culture technique pour les enseignants de disciplines générales, ou objet mythique? In: *Culture technique et formations*. Presses Universitaires de Nancy, 1990.

(Une liste complète est disponible auprès du chercheur.).

13674   Integrated interdisciplinary learning of the behavioural sciences in the health and social care professions: a feasibility study.
GBR   1993
Research Date(s): 1991-1994
Tope, R.
Sup: Sutton, R.
Inst: University of Wales College of Medicine, Institute of Health Care Studies, Advanced Nursing Section, Heath Park, Cardiff CF4 4XW, United Kingdom; Cardiff Institute of Higher Education, Faculty of Health & Community Studies, Llandaff Centre, Western Avenue, Cardiff CF5 2SG, United Kingdom; University of Wales College of Cardiff, School of Education, Senghennydd Road, United Kingdom.
Fin: S.E. Wales Inst. of Nursing and Midwifery Education and Cardiff Inst. of Higher Education; Smith & Nephew Edcuation Scholarship; Welsh Office Grant.
health service personnel; behavioural sciences; interdisciplinary approach; vocational training
personnel médical; sciences du comportement; interdisciplinarité; formation professionnelle
PROJECT DESCRIPTION

Integrated interdisciplinary education in health care and social care is a global issue. Maintaining health, preventing disease and caring for the sick is now so complex a problem that it is impossible for any single health profession to deliver quality care in isolation.

In order to enhance an integrated interdisciplinary approach to health care a feasibility study has commenced which examines the behavioural sciences component within the curriculum of 14 health professions. Action research has been adopted as the appropriate methodology. To date a content analysis of the 14 curricula has been completed, which has revealed many potential areas for shared learning. A 'random' stratified sample of teaching staff (N=31) from each discipline, and a student from each year of each discipline (N=42) have been interviewed in order to ascertain their opinions of the potential for shared learning between all the professions.

The information obtained from the literature review, the content analysis and the data generated from the structured interviews with the teaching staff and students has formed the basis of a questionnaire which will be distributed to all teaching staff (400) and all students (1,600) in March 1993. It is anticipated that the study will be completed by January 1994.

13675   Investors in People in post-16 institutions.
GBR   1993
Research Date(s): 1992-1993
Havard, R.; Warrender, A.-M.
Inst: Staff College, Coombe Lodge, Blagdon, Bristol BS18 6RG, United Kingdom.
personnel; career development; post-compulsory education
personnel; déroulement de carrière; enseignement postobligatoire
PROJECT DESCRIPTION

The aim of this research is to identify: the extent to which post-16 institutions are committed to Investors in People; perceptions of connection with total quality management and British Standard 5750; and perceptions of support institutions have or are likely to receive from Training and Enterprise Councils.

13676   Learning psychiatric nursing skills: the contribution of the ward environment.
GBR   1993
Research Date(s): 1987-1994
Chambers, M.
Sup: McGarvey, B.
Inst: Ulster University, Department of Inservice Education, Cromore Road, Coleraine, County Londonderry BT52 1SA, United Kingdom.
nurse; learning conditions; psychiatric service
infirmier; conditions d'apprentissage; service psychiatrique
PROJECT DESCRIPTION

The aim of this study is to ascertain those factors which facilitate student psychiatric nurses in the learning of psychiatric nursing skills. A pilot study of an open-ended nature was conducted on wards, using the Delphi technique, interview and participant observation. The main study involved more closely focused case studies of the learning experiences of eight students. The final report will compare and contrast the aims of the ward experience and the actual learning opportunities, and will discuss the roles of nursing and nurse education staff in supporting student learning on the ward.

13677   Management issues in nursing/midwifery education.
GBR   1993
Research Date(s): 1991-1992
Niven, S.; McQueenie, E.; Finlay, I.
Inst: Jordanhill College of Education, Scottish School of Further Education, Southbrae Drive, Glasgow G13 1PP, United Kingdom.
Fin: Jordanhill College; Scottish Office Home and Health Department.
nurse; management education
infirmier; formation à la gestion
PROJECT DESCRIPTION

The aim of this project is to promote active research into management issues in nursing/midwifery education for the directors of nursing/midwifery education.

13678   The management of teacher probation and induction in primary schools.
GBR   1993
Research Date(s): 1987-1992
Turner, M.
Sup: Lacey, C.; Lewin, K.
Inst: Anglia Polytechnic University, Sawyers Hall Lane, Brentwood CM15 9BT, United Kingdom; Sussex University, Institute of Continuing and Professional Education, Sussex House, Falmer, Brighton BN1 9RH, United Kingdom.
probationary teacher; primary school; teacher education; probation period
enseignant stagiaire; école primaire; formation des enseignants; période d'essai
PROJECT DESCRIPTION

The pilot and main study investigated approaches to the management of teacher probation and induction in five local education authorities, chosen to represent rural, suburban and urban perspectives. Overall, 11 schools were used and interviews were conducted with all participants within them of the management of probation and induction on five occasions during a year (headteacher, deputy, designated support teachers, probationers). The methodology was of partially structured but open-ended interviews which were recorded by the interviewer, and transcribed and analysed for key factors. The research analysis aims to identify significant patterns and models in the management of probation and induction.

13679   Młode pokolenie nauczyciele w Polsce w okresie transformacji ustrojowej.   (The young generation of teachers in Poland under conditions of structural change.)
POL   1994
Research Date(s): 1992-1993
Dróżka, Wanda.
Inst: Instytut Pedagogiki, Wyższa Szkoła Pedagogiczna w Kielcach (Institute of Pedagogy, Higher School of Education in Kielce), 25-029 Kielce, Krakowska 11, Poland.
Fin: Wyższa Szkoła Pedagogiczna w Kielcach; Ministerstwo Edukacji Narodowej.
teacher; teacher status; social change; teacher role; occupational aspiration; life cycle; self-perception
enseignant; statut de l'enseignant; changement social; rôle de l'enseignant; aspirations professionnelles; cycle de vie; perception de soi
PROJECT DESCRIPTION

Aim: To conduct a survey of the young generation of teachers in Poland in the early 1990s. Aspects to be considered include: (a) the identity of young teachers and their perception of the values that make their lives and work worthwhile; (b) ambitions, aims, expectations and personal problems; (c) likes and dislikes; (d) experiences that have influenced their personalities; aspects they would like to change (how and why). The investigation should make it possible to define the social, moral and professional status of young teachers as well as their position and role in society under conditions of structural change.

Design: Investigations were started in November 1992 with a nationwide competition for diaries and reports by young teachers (aged under 35) from all types of school. In September-October 1993 a nation-wide survey will be made of this young generation of teachers.

The investigations will cover a wide range of personal and professional problems, starting from teachers' personalities and their individual, professional and social biographies. The development of their individual, professional and generation identity under different conditions will be considered as well. Two approaches will be applied in the analysis and interpretation of the data: one will focus on the concept of "generation" and will therefore include the theoretical and analytical category of "generation"; the other will focus on the concept of "developing together" and will include the category of "life cycle" and E.H. Erikson's concept of "phase-crisis identity development".

13680   Motherhood and teaching: a life history investigation.
GBR   1993
Research Date(s): 1991-1993
Sikes, P.
Inst: Warwick University, Faculty of Educational Studies, Coventry CV4 7AL, United Kingdom.

teaching profession; women's profession; teacher; teacher behaviour; mother; working mother; woman

profession d'enseignant; profession féminine; enseignant; comportement de l'enseignant; mère; mère exerçant un emploi; femme

PROJECT DESCRIPTION

Traditionally, it has been seen as 'natural' for women teachers to work with young chldren and to adopt a mother/teacher role. The research focuses on the perceptions and experiences of female primary school teachers and asks such questions as: how do mother teachers perceive their role; do they feel there are any links between being a mother and being a teacher; if so, what are these and do they affect the way they do their job?

The research uses life history method. The sample consists of approximately 15 women. Around one-third are mature students with children on a teacher training course. The reason for including them is to discover whether motherhood had, in any way, motivated them to become teachers. The rest of the sample are practising teachers who were childless when they started teaching.

13681 Motivatie en demotivatie van leerkrachten in het secundair onderwijs. (Motivation and demotivation among secondary school teachers.)
BEL 1994
Research Date(s): 1989-1991
Lens, W.; Schops, L.
Inst: Onderzoekscentrum voor motivatie en tijdsperspectief (Research Centre on Motivation and Time Perspective), Tiensestraat 102, 3000 Leuven, Belgium.
Katholieke Universiteit Leuven (Catholic University of Leuven), Naamsestraat 22, 3000 Leuven, Belgium
Fin: Departement Onderwijs, Fonds voor Kollektief en Fundamenteel Onderzoek op Ministerieel Initiatief.
teaching profession; occupational satisfaction; motivation; occupational choice
profession d'enseignant; satisfaction professionnelle; motivation; choix d'une profession
PROJECT DESCRIPTION

The aim is to investigate the problem of demotivation and dissatisfaction among secondary school teachers. The study seeks to answer two main questions: (1) To what degree are these teachers demotivated? (2) What is the cause of this demotivation?

Methods: An extensive questionnaire was sent to 2,038 secondary school teachers. 720 responses (53% from male and 47% from female teachers) were useful for analysis.

Results: The final report summarizes all relevant information under 18 headings, such as positive and negative aspects of the teaching profession, stress, effort, job satisfaction, causes of motivation and demotivation, career choice, etc. Some interrelationships between factors are analysed: job satisfaction and effort, age and sex and effort, education type and effort.

Motivation stimuli are mostly expected from the highest policy level (Ministry of Education or educational organizations): wage increase, greater job security, improved promotion prospects, good education inspectors, etc. Reforms are needed in the work situation: improved curricula and evaluation systems, better facilities, participation in school management. 50.7% of teachers would choose again for a teaching career. This number approximates the 53% of a similar study in the Netherlands (Van Ginkel, 1987).

Publ: Lens, W. & Schops, L. Motivatie en demotivatie van leerkrachten in het secundair onderwijs: een exploratief onderzoek. Leuven: KUL, Onderzoekscentrum voor Motivatie en Tijdsperspectief, 1991, 128p. + bijlage (58p.).

13682 Newly-qualified entrants to the speech therapy profession.
GBR 1993
Research Date(s): 1990-1991
McCartney, E.
Inst: Jordanhill College of Education, Division of Speech Therapy, Southbrae Drive, Glasgow G13 1PP, United Kingdom.
Fin: Scottish Office Home and Health Department; Jordanhill College.
speech therapist; initial employment
orthophoniste; premier emploi
PROJECT DESCRIPTION

The aims of this project are to: (1) investigate the experiences of newly-qualified graduates entering speech therapy services in Great Britain; (2) implement a package of supportive measures for Grade A therapists in conjunction with one Area Health Board (Ayrshire and Arran, the 'Good Practice' Area); and (3) relate the performance (management objectives) and morale (personal objectives) of Grade A therapists to their first post experiences.

13683 Nieuwe rollen en taken voor onderwijsgevenden. (New roles and tasks for teachers.)
NLD 1994
Research Date(s): 1993
Brandsma, T.F.
Inst: Onderzoek Centrum Toegepaste Onderwijskunde (OCTO) (Research Centre of the Department of Educational Technology), P.O. Box 217, 7500 AE Enschede, Netherlands.
Universiteit Twente (Twente University), P.O. Box 217, 7500 AE Enschede, Netherlands
Fin: SVO het Instituut voor Onderzoek van het Onderwijs.
teaching profession; teacher role; social change; technological change; occupational research
profession d'enseignant; rôle de l'enseignant; changement social; changement technologique; recherche relative aux professions
PROJECT DESCRIPTION

Background: Due to social developments (the need to prepare pupils for a role in society, the fading distinction between initial and post-initial education and between education and work), technological developments (the use of modern media) and scientific developments (changing insights into teaching/learning processes), there is a growing need for new occupational profiles for the teaching profession.

Aim: To develop a valid instrument whereby both the existing and the "desirable" occupational profiles of primary school teachers can be established and described.

Design: The project falls into the following parts: (a) analysis of relevant social, technological and scientific developments (literature survey and interviews with experts); (b) analysis of the current roles and tasks of teachers and of ways in which these can be established (literature survey, document analysis, observations and interviews with teachers); (c) development of instruments whereby current and desirable profiles can be determined; (d) establishment of current occupational profiles (survey); (e) establishment of desirable occupational profiles (Delphi procedure); (f) analysis and report.

13684 Nurse selection project - United Kingdom Central Council for Nursing, Midwifery and Health Visiting (UKCC).
GBR 1993
Research Date(s): 1987-1992
Child, D.; Borrill, C.; Ciechanowski, A.; Michaud, A.
Inst: Leeds University, School of Education, Nurse Selection Project, Leeds LS2 9JT, United Kingdom.
Fin: United Kingdom Central Council for Nursing, Midwifery and Health Visiting; Department of Health.
nurse; recruitment; occupational qualification; occupational choice; career
infirmier; recrutement; qualification professionnelle; choix d'une profession; carrière
PROJECT DESCRIPTION

The project is concentrating on two main research areas: monitoring the career choices of adolescents and a validation study of the DC test series, an alternative entry route into nurse training. The study of young people's career choices is cross-sectional and longitudinal and is exploring how and why they become interested in nursing as a career, and why it is they change their minds. The insights from this work will be used to make recommendations about how to encourage and keep young people interested in nursing.

A sample of 648 school pupils and college students in three regions of England are being followed over a period of four to five years using questionnaires and a subsample of 20% interviewed each year. The validation study of the DC test series is following the progress of 629 entrants to nurse training. The performance of 315 students who entered training with five O-levels or more is being compared with 314 who passed a DC test to enter. Further research has been carried out on the test, such as a study of the effect of age on performance and the effect of practice and coaching on performance. The project also carries out short term research at the request of the funding bodies.

Publ: Child, D. et al. Selection for nurse training; making decisions. Leeds: University of Leeds Press, 1988.
Borrill, C.S. Cultivating an interest in nursing. In: Nursing Times, pp. 44-45, December 14th, 1988.
Borrill, C.S. Nursing an ambition. In: Nursing Times, Vol 85, No 34/1989, pp. 30-32.
Child, D. et al. Taking the DC test - a guide for candidates. Leeds: University of Leeds Press, 1990.

13685 Occupational profiles of vocational counsellors.
GBR 1993
Research Date(s): 1991-1992
Watts, A.; Hawthorn, R.
Inst: National Institute for Careers Education and Counselling, Sheraton House, Castle Park, Cambridge CB3 OAX, United Kingdom.
Fin: European Centre for the Development of Vocational Training (CEDEFOP).

guidance officer; job description; vocational guidance; educational guidance; Europe; cross-national research; directory

orienteur; description d'emploi; orientation professionnelle; orientation pédagogique; Europe; recherche transnationale; répertoire

PROJECT DESCRIPTION

This is one of a series of studies of various occupations, designed to build into a European Directory of Occupational Profiles. Its objectives are to: (1) identify the main occupational groups involved in education and/or careers guidance work with young people and/or adults; (2) analyse the main tasks carried out by each of them; and (3) examine the training provided for them.

Publ: Watts, A.G. *Occupational profiles of vocational counsellors in the European Community: a synthesis report.* Berlin: CEDEFOP, 1992.

Hawthorn, R. & Butcher, V. *Guidance workers in the UK: their work and training.* Cambridge: CRAC/Hobsons, 1992.

13686 Personalentwicklung und aktueller Personalbestand der Sozialpaedagogik an den wissenschaftlichen Hochschulen der Bundesrepublik Deutschland. (Personnel development and current level of social pedagogic personnel in the scientific universities in the Federal Republic of Germany.)

DEU 1993

Research Date(s): 1990-1992

Knobel, R.; Wilschrei, S.

Sup: Rauschenbach, T.

Inst: Universitaet Dortmund, FB Erziehungswissenschaften und Biologie, Institut fuer Sozialpaedagogik, Erwachsenenbildung und Paedagogik der fruehen Kindheit, Rheinlanddamm 199, D-4600 Dortmund 1.

Fin: Deutsche Forschungsgemeinschaft.

personnel; teaching personnel; university; sciences of education; social work

personnel; corps enseignant; université; sciences de l'éducation; travail social

PROJECT DESCRIPTION

Inhalt: Als Teildisziplin der Erziehungswissenschaft kann fuer die universitaere Sozialpaedagogik bis heute keine differenzierte Angabe ueber Personalentwicklung und -bestand gemacht werden. Dies erschwert ihre Konturierung und ihre disziplinimmanente Gruppierungsplanung im Kontext anderer Teildisziplinen der Erziehungswissenschaft ebenso wie vor dem Hintergrund einer ausgebauten Sozialpaedagogik/Sozialarbeit an den bundesdeutschen Fachhochschulen. Das Projekt erarbeitet hierzu erste Analysen.

13687 Pressure on primary headteachers during and following the implementation of Local Management of Schools.

GBR 1993

Research Date(s): 1989-1992

Simpson, T.

Sup: Fidler, B.

Inst: Reading University, Faculty of Education and Community Studies, Centre for Education Management, Bulmershe Court, Woodlands Avenue, Earley, Reading RG6 1HY, United Kingdom.

Fin: Berkshire County Council.

head teacher; primary school; mental stress; educational administration; educational reform

chef d'établissement; école primaire; tension mentale; administration de l'enseignement; réforme de l'enseignement

PROJECT DESCRIPTION

The investigation focuses on pressures on primary headteachers in Berkshire during the historically significant early stages of the receipt of delegated budget management (Local Management of Schools) by their schools. Research is by questionnaire, interview and diary completion. Perceptives of (a) pressure, (b) role change, (c) Type 'A'/'B' behaviour characteristics, (d) psychoneurotic states (using the Middlesex Hospital questionnaire) and time management skills are being assessed while a small pilot group has carried out a heart rate monitoring exercise, the results of which have been measured against a diary of daily work based activity.

Results so far suggest that the major source of pressure on the respondents relates to a perception of lack of time to achieve their objectives and that their major predicted pressure (as forecast prior to the receipt of LMS) was the 'need to read and absorb an increasing flow of papers, documents etc.'. Over the first year of LMS, respondents (in 1989 and 1990) noted a modification of role toward that of 'Communicator and Budget Manager'. Psychoneurotic scores were compared with general population norms and the results of previous headteacher findings, with the largest representative group that was surveyed in April 1991, females scored similarly to the general population and males compared closely with previous primary headteacher scores. Continuing research is examining more closely the relationship between pressure and management of time.

13688 Prieskum názorov učiteľskej verejnosti na vybrané aktuálne problémy v školstve (sociálna analýza). (Survey of teachers' views of specific problems in education: a social analysis.)

SVK 1994

Research Date(s): 1992

Zvalová, M.; Zubalová, M.; Bieliková, M.; Kadlecová, B.; Roháľ, I.; Slovíková, M.; Rimóczyová, K.; Sehnal, P.

Sup: Dvorský, P.

Inst: Ústav informácií a prognóz školstva, mládeže a telovýchovy (Institute of Information and Prognoses of Education, Youth and Sport), Staré grunty 52, 842 44 Bratislava, Slovak Republic.

Ministerstvo školstva a vedy SR (Ministry of Education and Science of the Slovak Republic), Hlboká 2, 813 30 Bratislava, Slovak Republic

teacher; occupational status; educational administration; interpersonal relations; teacher-pupil relation; occupational satisfaction; teacher behaviour

enseignant; statut professionnel; administration de l'enseignement; relations interpersonnelles; relation maître-élève; satisfaction professionnelle; comportement de l'enseignant

PROJECT DESCRIPTION

Aims: The research aimed to describe the attitudes and opinions of primary and secondary school teachers in respect of school management, interpersonal relations, the social status of the teaching profession, teacher-pupil relations, etc. Three areas were distinguished: (1) opinions and attitudes regarding the present administrative structure of the education system (Ministry of Education, local authorities, school heads); (2) opinions and attitudes regarding occupational satisfaction (relations among teachers, teacher-pupil relations, social recognition, working conditions, etc.); (3) opinions on other aspects of education, for instance perceptions of school boards, "methodical centres", and the integration of handicapped children.

Methods: A questionnaire survey was made of a selected sample of primary and secondary school teachers (n = 1,220).

Results: Teachers display critical attitudes towards the present system of educational administration. Closer relations with the management lead to greater satisfaction on the part of the teacher. As regards working conditions, teachers are particularly critical of the low socio-economic status of their profession. Awareness of a low social status is a cause of mental stress for teachers. There is a permanent feeling of frustration which has a detrimental effect on teachers' views and their relations with their environment and their pupils.

Publ: Zvalová, M. et al. *Prieskum názorov učiteľskej verejnosti na vybrané aktuálne otázky v školstve.* (A survey of the opinions of teachers on questions in education.) Bratislava, ÚIP ŠMT, 1992, 53p.

Zvalová, M. *Výskum verejnej mienky v školstve - informácia Listovka.* (Gallup poll in education - information sheets.) Bratislava, ÚIP ŠMT, 1992, 8p.

13689 Primary school headship: an analysis derived from an ethnographic study of a single headteacher.

GBR 1993

Research Date(s): 1987-1993

Southworth, G.

Sup: Nias, J.; Macdonald, B.

Inst: Cambridge University, Institute of Education, Shaftesbury Road, Cambridge CB2 2BX, United Kingdom; University of East Anglia, School of Education, Centre for Applied Research in Education, Norwich NR4 7TJ, United Kingdom.

head teacher; teaching profession; power

chef d'établissement; profession d'enseignant; pouvoir

PROJECT DESCRIPTION

An ethnographic study was conducted into the work of a single, male headteacher. Using participant observation and interviews over the course of a school year (one day per week) data were collected and then analysed and written up as a case study.

The case study offers a portrait of the headteacher at work. Whilst a number of themes emerge from the study, the main issue centres upon the power of the headteacher. The researcher is critical of the headteacher's power in the school and analyses why the headteacher is powerful and how this might be altered and headship reconceptualised.

13690 The Principal's role in innovation in schools.

GBR 1993

Research Date(s): 1989-1992

Bakioglu, A.

Sup: Day, C.; Adey, K.

Inst: Nottingham University, School of Education, University Park, Nottingham NG7 2RD, United Kingdom.

Fin: Turkey.

head teacher; teaching profession; career development; career profile

chef d'établissement; profession d'enseignant; déroulement de carrière; monographie de carrière

PROJECT DESCRIPTION

This study attempts to answer the following questions: (1) Do headteachers experience some career stages during the time they are in post? (2) What difficulties does each stage have? (3) How do these stages influence the development of their professional life?

A questionnaire was developed to investigate three aspects of the headteacher's role, i.e. internal, external, staff and staffing issues. Each category was divided into two sections: (a) questions related to change and innovation and (b) questions related to administrative matters. A Likert Scale was used which contained five levels of difficulty ranging from 'very serious' to 'not a problem'. Of the 305 surveys sent to the secondary school headteachers in Nottinghamshire, Derbyshire, Lincolnshire and Leicestershire, 196 were returned (overall response rate of 64.2%).

The most significant items related to previous headteachers' actions, with less experienced headteachers having greater difficulty with this issue. Headteachers with 4-8 years of experience seem to be the most successful and feel least difficulty in internal issues, although headteachers with 1-3 years and over 8 years of experience have great problems. In order to investigate further, a semi-structured interview schedule was designed, and all data received illustrated on tables and charts.

13691 Processus d'émergence de professions nouvelles: les formateurs d'adultes.
FRA 1993
Research Date(s): 1984-1987
Jobert, Guy.
Inst: Ministère de la recherche, CNRS UPR/31, Laboratoire de sociologie du changement des institutions, Institut de recherche sur les sociétés contemporaines, 59-61 rue Pouchet, 75849 Paris Cedex 17, France.
trainer; occupational research; know-how; training of trainers
formateur; recherche relative aux professions; savoir-faire; formation des formateurs
PROJECT DESCRIPTION
Objectifs: La sociologie des professions est ici abordée sous l'angle des processus et non des caractéristiques structurelles des professions. A propos des formateurs d'adultes, on a isolé la question de la constitution d'un savoir propre. D'abord lié aux pratiques et à leurs développements, ce savoir est repérable grâce à une perspective diachronique: la recherche reconstitue sur les vingt-cinq dernières années l'évolution des pratiques et des lieux institutionnels de leur mise en oeuvre, les référentiels multiples qu'elles ont mobilisés et ceux qu'elles ont produits.

Méthodologie: Le choix s'est porté sur l'approche biographique, le récit de vie étant considéré comme récit de pratique. La contextualisation s'appuie sur la littérature propre au milieu professionnel étudié.

Résultats: Etayage du primat de la connaissance comme enjeu et moyen de lutte pour la professionnalisation, la recherche constitue une contribution à la constitution du savoir identitaire des formateurs.

Publ: Jobert, Guy. *Processus de professionnalisation des formateurs d'adultes.* Paris: LSCI-CNRS, 1986 (rapport intermédiaire).
Jobert, Guy. Une nouvelle professionnalité pour les formateurs d'adultes. In: *Education permanente,* Projet action-formation, 1987, n° 87, pp. 19-33.
Jobert, Guy (ed.). Identité professionnelle et formation continue des enseignants. In: La formation continue des enseignants, *Education permanente,* 1988, n° 91, pp. 39-52.

13692 Professional development of private music teachers.
GBR 1993
Research Date(s): 1991-1992
Gibbs, L.
Inst: London University, Goldsmiths' College, Department of Continuing and Community Education, Lewisham Way, New Cross, London SE14 6NW, United Kingdom.
Fin: Universities Funding Council.
teacher; music education; teacher education; private tutor; further education of teachers; certification
enseignant; éducation musicale; formation des enseignants; précepteur; perfectionnement des enseignants; certification
PROJECT DESCRIPTION
It is likely that private music teachers exert the most extensive influence upon musical life and development in this country and yet we know very little of their activities beyond casual anecdotal evidence. (A private music teacher is anyone teaching music on a self-employed basis, whether in a studio, at home, or under the aegis of an educational agency or institution). In the absence of any research in the area, the project has the general aim of gaining an impression of the scope and state of private music teaching, and a more specific aim of looking at the professional development of training, if any, of individual private music teachers.

A comprehensive questionnaire has been circulated nationally which addresses the issues of: teaching experience, preparation for teaching, musical training and education, current musical activities, perceived effectiveness of preparation for teaching, certification, and teacher training priorities. From the collected information, 50 questionnaire respondents are selected for interview so that a qualitative picture of the data can be drawn. One specific task of the data is to relate preparation/training for teaching or lack of it to perceived teaching effectiveness.

Publ: Gibbs, L. Research into the professional development and training of private music teachers. In: *Journal of the European Piano Teachers Association,* Vol 12, No 36/1991, p. 36.

13693 Professional development of teachers.
GBR 1993
Research Date(s): 1990-1994
Gates, J.
Sup: Smith, R.
Inst: Durham University, School of Education, Leazes Road, Durham DH1 1TA, United Kingdom.
teacher; teaching profession; attitude; personality development; career development
enseignant; profession d'enseignant; attitude; développement de la personnalité; déroulement de carrière
PROJECT DESCRIPTION
This is a qualitative research project using case study method. It focuses upon a small group of primary school teachers at varying career stages and in differing cultural settings. Using research strategies of action research, biographical and journal writing and career profiles, the growth of reflectivity is examined. The research aims to identify the explicit and implicit values, attitudes and assumptions that govern the rationale of teachers in both their 'talk about teaching' and their practice. From an analysis of these it is planned to move to a consideration of implications in terms of initial and inservice teacher training.

13694 A programme to encourage and facilitate doctors' participation in clinical audit.
GBR 1993
Research Date(s): 1991-1992
McAleer, S.
Sup: Harden, R.; Laidlaw, J.
Inst: Dundee University, Centre for Medical Education, Ninewells Hospital and Medical School, Dundee DD1 9SY, United Kingdom.
Fin: Scottish Office, Home and Health Department.
doctor; participation; distance study; bookkeeping; training programme
médecin; participation; enseignement à distance; comptabilité; programme de formation
PROJECT DESCRIPTION
The need for audit as one aspect of clinical practice is now generally accepted throughout the medical profession. Its adoption requires a change in behaviour of doctors - one which will be successful and long lasting. This distance learning programme intends to provide a more in-depth training about audit by using a five-stage approach - awareness, interest, appraisal, trial and adoption. The programme will be designed to relate audit to the doctor's (both hospital and community) day to day practice and encourage further learning about audit on-the-job. It comprises a resource book which contains key information about audit. In addition participants will receive a series of 'doctors' diaries' in which audit activities will be described in a problem-based format. Responses to these problems will be collected and feedback provided - using comparisons between decisions made and those of colleagues. There will also be a number of practical audit activities linked to the diaries. The programme will be offered on a national basis.

13695 Returners to teaching.
GBR 1993
Research Date(s): 1989-1991
Munn, P.
Inst: Scottish Council for Research in Education, 15 St John Street, Edinburgh EH8 8JR, United Kingdom.
Fin: Scottish Office Education Department.
teaching profession; teacher; recruitment; supply of teachers; demand for teachers; career change
profession d'enseignant; enseignant; recrutement; offre d'enseignants; besoin d'enseignants; changement de carrière
PROJECT DESCRIPTION
The research aims to explore the factors affecting the career choice of different groups of non-practising teachers and to assess whether there are practical measures to encourage these groups to return to teaching. Stage One of the research consisted of face-to-face interviews with over 40 teachers about the factors affecting their non-return. Stage Two involved telephone interviews with 500 non-practising teachers using the information from the first stage to construct a telephone interview schedule.

Publ: Robinson, R.; Munn, P. & MacDonald, C. *Once a teacher always a teacher? Encouraging return to teaching.* SCRE Research Report Series, No 36. Edinburgh: Scottish Council for Research in Education, 1992.

13696 A review of management education for librarians.
GBR 1993
Research Date(s): 1990-1991
Johnson, I.; Hannabuss, C.; Wildgoose, D.
Inst: Robert Gordon University, School of Librarianship and Information Studies, Hilton Place, Aberdeen AB9 1FR, United Kingdom.

Fin: Library and Information Services Committee (Scotland).
librarian; management education; in-service training; job requirements
bibliothécaire; formation à la gestion; formation en cours d'emploi; qualification requise pour l'emploi
PROJECT DESCRIPTION

The review arises out of recent general interest in the extent and quality of management education and training, and particular concern about the nature of management training for librarians. The aim of the study is to investigate the need for the provision of management education for mid-career professional librarians in all types of library and concentrates on middle and senior management levels.

The objectives are: (1) to identify management competencies and skills necessary at different career levels, relating these to exisiting and likely future job needs; (2) review existing provision - examining what is available and what can be provided by external agencies, e.g. NBA, DMS programmes, Local Government Unit, Industrial Society etc.; (3) study the profession's perceptions of provision, and the pattern of uptake; (4) identify gaps in existing provision; (5) make recommendations as to future provision, and propose a development plan.

A review of existing and planned courses in Scottish institutions leading to management qualifications, and short courses in Scotland in management topics was undertaken. In addition a survey of provision of short courses in management for librarians was undertaken. The enquiry also elicited the profession's perception of provision and the pattern of uptake, information on resources available for staff development, and the relative priorities attached to management development.

13697 The role of the female deputy headteachers: an investigation into the role and profiles of female deputy headteachers in co-educational comprehensive schools in one local education authority.
GBR 1993
Research Date(s): 1988-1992
Litawski, R.
Sup: Thomas, J.
Inst: Loughborough University of Technology, Department of Education, Loughborough LE11 3TU, United Kingdom.
head teacher; teaching profession; sex discrimination; equal opportunity; woman; sex role
chef d'établissement; profession d'enseignant; discrimination sexuelle; égalité de chances; femme; rôle sexuel
PROJECT DESCRIPTION

This research examines sexual discrimination and/or role differentiation in comprehensive schools using a theory of micropolitics of the school, use of survey, case studies, and structured interview methodology.

13698 Selbstverstaendnis und Funktion bayerischer Schulpsychologen. (Self-image and function of Bavarian school psychologists.)
DEU 1993
Research Date(s): 1990-1993
Lehmeier, H.
Sup: Hischer, E.
Inst: Katholische Universitaet Eichstaett, Philosophisch-Paedagogische Fakultaet, Fachgebiet Paedagogik, LS Sozialpaedagogik, Ostenstrasse 26-28, D-8078 Eichstaett.
school psychologist; Bavaria; self-concept; self-perception
psychologue scolaire; Bavière; conception de soi; perception de soi
PROJECT DESCRIPTION

Inhalt: Analyse des beruflichen Selbstverstaendnisses bayerischer Schulpsychologen (Schwerpunkte der Arbeit, Konzipierung der Arbeit, Zielperspektiven der Arbeit) im Rahmen einer Eroerterung des Funktionszusammenhangs von Schule und Psychologie.

Geographischer Raum: Bayern.

Untersuchter Zeitraum: 1989-1990.

Vorgehensweise: Problemzentriertes Leitfadeninterview. Untersuchungsdesign: Querschnittserhebung.

Datengewinnung: Nicht-standardisiertes Interview (Stichprobe: ca. 80 Prozent; bayerischer Schulpsychologen, Volksschule, Realschule-,Gymnasium; Auswahlverfahren: total). Primaererhebung: Feldarbeit von Mitarbeitern des Projektes durchgefuehrt.

Auswertung: qualitative Inhaltsanalyse; deskriptive Statistik. Datenedition (z.B. Aufbau von Datenbanken).

13699 Socio-political attitudes of teacher trainers in the United Kingdom.
GBR 1993
Research Date(s): 1991-1993
Demaine, J.
Inst: Loughborough University of Technology, Department of Education, Loughborough LE11 3TU, United Kingdom.
trainer; teacher education; teacher behaviour; political behaviour; social behaviour
formateur; formation des enseignants; comportement de l'enseignant; comportement politique; comportement social
PROJECT DESCRIPTION

This is an investigation into the socio-political attitudes of teacher trainers in the United Kingdom.

13700 A study of mature entrants to the teaching profession.
GBR 1993
Research Date(s): 1989-1991
Kennard, R.; Adamson, F.
Inst: Sunderland University, School of Education, Hammerton Hall, Gray Road, Sunderland SR2 7EE, United Kingdom.
Fin: Department of Education and Science.
teaching profession; student teacher; probationary teacher; teacher education; maturity
profession d'enseignant; élève-maître; enseignant stagiaire; formation des enseignants; maturité
PROJECT DESCRIPTION

Given their extensive experience of industry, commerce and life in general, it is popularly assumed that mature students have much to offer the teaching profession. To what extent is this belief rooted in reality? Using both qualitative and quantitative approaches for the collection of data from mature entrants, other school staff and LEA (local education authority) advisers, the research will attempt to identify and evaluate the problems they face in training and in school during the early years of their teaching career. The research team hope to provide recommendations for institutions with responsibility for the recruitment and training of mature students and for 'good practice' regarding the support of mature probationary teachers in school.

13701 Supply workers in state schools and the National Health Service.
GBR 1993
Research Date(s): 1988-1991
Shilling, C.
Inst: Southampton University, Department of Sociology and Social Policy, Highfield, Southampton SO9 5NH, United Kingdom.
teaching profession; visiting teacher; health service personnel; nurse; supply of teachers; employment
profession d'enseignant; enseignant associé; personnel médical; infirmier; offre d'enseignants; emploi
PROJECT DESCRIPTION

This project is concerned with the organisation and work of supply workers in state schools and the National Health Service, and is based on interviews with over 70 head/senior teachers, nurse managers, supply teachers and bank nurses. Research also includes a review of literature into supply teachers, which is being published by *Educational Research*.

Publ: Shilling, C. The organisation of supply workers in state schools and the National Health Service: a comparison. In: *Journal of Education Policy*, Vol 5, No 2/1991, p. 127-141.
Shilling, C. Permanent supports or temporary props? Supply workers in state schools and the National Health Service. In: *Gender and Education*, Vol 3, No 1/1991, pp. 61-80.
Shilling, C. Supply teachers: working on the margins. In: *Educational Research*, Vol 33, No 1/1991, pp. 3-12.

13702 Taakprofielen docenten secundair beroepsonderwijs. (Professional profiles of teachers in vocational secondary schools.)
NLD 1994
Research Date(s): 1993-1994
Streumer, J.N.; Stoel, W.G.R.
Sup: Nijhof, W.J.
Inst: Onderzoek Centrum Toegepaste Onderwijskunde (OCTO) (Research Centre of the Department of Educational Technology), P.O. Box 217, 7500 AE Enschede, Netherlands.
Universiteit Twente (Twente University), P.O. Box 217, 7500 AE Enschede, Netherlands
Fin: SVO het Instituut voor Onderzoek van het Onderwijs.
teacher; job description; job requirements
enseignant; description d'emploi; qualification requise pour l'emploi
PROJECT DESCRIPTION

Background: Drastic changes are taking place in the secondary education sector as a result of a number of new laws coming into effect. It is expected that the developments will have consequences for the teaching profession. No clear views exist regarding the professional requirements of "new style" teachers.

Aim: To examine current professional profiles of teachers in secondary education; to ascertain what developments are taking place and what developments are desirable.

Design: The formal and the actual professional profile of secondary school teachers will be investigated on the basis of document analysis, a study of relevant literature and a questionnaire survey among the head teachers and teachers of 196 schools. The questionnaire will ask specifically for the way in which teachers perceive various aspects of the profession. A Delphi procedure, involving the participation of 30-50 teachers and 30-50 experts, will be used to examine "new style" profiles and to identify gaps between the actual and the desirable situation. Twenty teachers and experts will participate in a conference to discuss aspects on which they hold diverging views.

13703 Training in communication skills and counselling techniques and its influence on participants' personal constructs.
GBR 1993
Research Date(s): 1989-1994
Dexter, G.
Sup: Gilliland, J.; McGuiness, J.
Inst: Durham University, School of Education, Leazes Road, Durham DH1 1TA, United Kingdom.
guidance officer; training course; evaluation
orienteur; cours de formation; évaluation
PROJECT DESCRIPTION
This is a study of the effectiveness of counsellor training, involving a review of intentions, content and processes involved in counsellor training courses. The research, in its early stages, will sample a range of short and long courses. The effects and effectiveness of courses will be evaluated by use of a range of qualitative measures including structured interviews, personal diaries, with some pre and post-structured assessment, possibly involving the use of repertory grid techniques and where appropriate, case studies.

13704 Tutorenausbildung an den bayerischen Fachhochschulen. (Training of instructors at 'Fachhochschulen' (colleges for higher professional training) in Bavaria.)
AUT 1993
Research Date(s): 1991-1993
Hoffmann, Manfred; Leitner, Erich; Webler, Wolf-Dietrich; Wagemann, Hellmuth.
Inst: Kontaktstelle Hochschuldidaktik, Weihenstephan, D-8825 Weidenbach; Abteilung fuer Hochschulpaedagogik, Universitaetsstrasse 65-67, A-9020 Klagenfurt.
Fachhochschule Weihenstephan, Weihenstephan, D-8825 Weidenbach; Universitaet fuer Bildungswissenschaften, Universitaetsstrasse 65-67, A-9020 Klagenfurt
tutor; post-secondary education; curriculum development; higher education; training of trainers; teacher education; vocational education
tuteur de formation; enseignement postsecondaire; élaboration de programmes d'études; enseignement supérieur; formation des formateurs; formation des enseignants; enseignement professionnel
PROJECT DESCRIPTION
Entwicklung von Zielen, Inhalten und Methoden eines Ausbildungsganges fuer Tutoren an den bayerischen Fachhochschulen. Arbeitsanleitung fuer die Tutorenausbilder, Arbeitsunterlagen fuer die Tutoren, Kursentwicklung fuer Ausbildungssequenz (eintaegig).
Auf der Basis der Auswertung einschlaegiger internationaler Erfahrungen auf dem Gebiet der Tutorenausbildung und unter Einschluss des Erkenntnisstandes zum Beziehungsverhaeltnis von Lehren und Lernen an der Hochschule erfolgt die Entwicklung eines Ausbildungspaketes.
Bereits vorliegende Ergebnisse sind in den Referaten zur Tutorenbetreuung und Tutorenausbildung zusammengefasst, die auf der Tagung der Didaktikbeauftragten der bayerischen Fachhochschulen im Bildungszentrum Kloster Banz, 1992, gehalten wurden.

13705 Une promotion d'éducateurs de l'Education surveillée.
FRA 1993
Research Date(s): 1988-1991
Peyre, Vincent.
Inst: Ministère de la Justice, CNRS URA/412, Centre de recherche interdisciplinaire de Vaucresson, 54 rue de Garches, 92420 Vaucresson, France.
special school teacher; correctional education; vocational training; career; identity
éducateur spécialisé; éducation surveillée; formation professionnelle; carrière; identité
PROJECT DESCRIPTION
Objectifs: Enquête par questionnaire auprès des anciens élèves de la promotion 1968-1970, portant sur leur formation, leur trajectoire professionnelle et leurs opinions et attitudes sur ces questions.
Méthodologie: Analyse en terme d'identité professionnelle générationnelle renvoyant à la sociologie des professions. Analyse statistique et analyse de contenu des réponses au questionnaire soumis à l'ensemble des élèves éducateurs d'une promotion nationale de l'Ecole nationale de formation des personnels de l'éducation surveillée.
Résultats: Cette contribution à une sociologie de l'identité professionnelle des éducateurs met en lumière certaines caractéristiques propres aux éducateurs de l'éducation surveillée ainsi que la forte dimension générationnelle.
Publ: Peyre, Vincent. *Promo 68. Eléments pour un auto-portrait.* Vaucresson: CRIV, Rapport de recherche, 1991.

13706 Verbesserung der Weiterbildung von Fach- und Fuehrungskraeften in den fuenf neuen Bundeslaendern. (Improving further training for specialists and executives in the five new German states.)
DEU 1993
Research Date(s): 1991-1994
Engelbracht, P.; Schepanski, N.; Viefhaus, T.; Moeller, R.
Sup: Staudt, E.
Inst: Universitaet Bochum, Institut fuer Arbeitswissenschaft, LS Arbeitsoekonomie, Postfach, D-4630 Bochum.
Fin: Bundesministerium fuer Bildung und Wissenschaft.
managerial staff; further training; educational provision; German DR; occupational qualification
personnel d'encadrement; formation complémentaire; scolarisation; Allemagne RDA; qualification professionnelle
PROJECT DESCRIPTION
Inhalt: Erarbeitung von Erkenntnissen ueber bestehende Defizite und Schwachstellen in der Weiterbildung von Fuehrungs- und Fachkraeften im Gebiet der ehemaligen DDR; Ansaetze bzw. Loesungsstrategien fuer die Durchfuehrung eines mittel- und langfristig tragfaehigen Weiterbildungsangebotes; Entwicklung von Kriterien und Ansaetzen zur Evaluation ausgewaehlter Weiterbildungsmassnahmen.
Geographischer Raum: 5 neue Bundeslaender.
Vorgehensweise: Vorbereitende Untersuchungen zur Erarbeitung eines Konzepts zur formativen Evaluation.

13707 Weiterbildungsbedarf bei technischen Fach- und Fuehrungskraeften. (Further training needs of technical specialists and executives.)
DEU 1993
Research Date(s): 1991-1992
Vogler-Ludwig, K.; Hofmann, H.·
Inst: Ifo-Institut fuer Wirtschaftsforschung e.V., Poschingerstrasse 5, D-8000 Muenchen 86.
Fin: Rationalisierungs-Kuratorium der Deutschen Wirtschaft e.V. -RKW-.
further training; managerial staff; demand for education; technical personnel; technical education; qualification
formation complémentaire; personnel d'encadrement; demande d'éducation; personnel technique; enseignement technique; qualification
PROJECT DESCRIPTION
Inhalt: Das Rationalisierungskuratorium der deutschen Wirtschaft (RKW) fuehrt traditionsgemaess Weiterbildungsmassnahmen fuer technische Fach- und Fuehrungskraefte durch. Um die zur Verfuegung stehenden Mittel bedarfsorientiert einzusetzen, ist eine systematische Bedarfsermittlung und Bedarfspriorisierung erforderlich. Es soll daher mit Methoden der Marktforschung der Weiterbildungsbedarf fuer technische Fach- und Fuehrungskraefte nach Inhalt, Vermittlungsformen und Bedeutung transparent gemacht werden, damit (a) die Mittel des RKW so nutzbringend wie moeglich eingesetzt werden koennen; (b) Empfehlungen an Foerderstellen und andere Weiterbildungstraeger gegeben werden koennen; (c) eine moeglichst grosse oeffentliche Beachtung erzielt werden kann. Die Bedarfsermittlung soll insbesondere auch unter Beruecksichtigung der Zukunftsorientierung und der Vorwegnahme technischer Trends erfolgen. Dabei ist die notwendige Abstimmung der Qualifizierungsmassnahmen mit der technologischen Entwicklung im Rahmen der Personalentwicklung zu beruecksichtigen. Die Untersuchung hat den Weiterbildungsbedarf im gesamten Bundesgebiet zu ermitteln. Dabei ist besonderes Augenmerk auf die neuen Bundeslaender zu legen.
Geographischer Raum: Ostdeutschland.
Datengewinnung: Muendliche Befragung (Stichprobe: 80-100; Industrieunternehmen bis 1000 Beschaeftigte). Befragung (Stichprobe: 1500; Industrieunternehmen bis 1000 Beschaeftigte. Stichprobe: 3000; technisch Fach- und Fuehrungskraefte).

13708 Zmiany miedzypokoleniowe w zawodzie nauczycielskim w latach 90tych w Polsce. (Intergenerational changes in the teaching profession in the 1990s in Poland.)
POL 1994
Research Date(s): 1989-1990
Dróżka, Wanda.
Inst: Instytut Pedagogiki, Wyższa szkoła Pedagogiczna w Kielcach (Institute of Pedagogy, Higher School of Education in Kielce), 25-020 Kielce, Krakowska 11, Poland.
teaching profession; life cycle; cultural environment; value system; teacher; self-perception
profession d'enseignant; cycle de vie; milieu culturel; système de valeurs; enseignant; perception de soi
PROJECT DESCRIPTION
Aim: The aim was to study the range and causes of intergenerational changes in the teaching profession in the 1990s. The investigations were based on an inventory and a comparative analysis of personal values and ambitions set against the biographies of three generations of teachers.
Design: The data were analysed and interpreted at two levels: the level of "history and generation", which included the category of "generation",

and the level of "developing together", which included the category of "life cycle" and E.H. Erikson's concept of "phase-crisis identity development" in a life cycle. The empirical inquiry focused on such aspects as: universal values and ambitions; values and ambitions in everyday life; values and ambitions regarding work. The autobiographical method used teachers' compositions entitled "The Meaning and Dignity of my Life and Career".

Results: The investigations show considerable differences and changes in personal values systems and ambitions within each generation of teachers, resulting from different cultural and historical conditions. Some of these changes are more clearly dependent than others upon development factors related to the age group and different qualities of individual phases in a life cycle. Considerable differences were found between the older generation and the younger generation, and partly in the intermediary one, with regard to professional values and ambitions, social activities, and material values and aspirations. Career perceptions of teachers in the cross-section of generations range from a predominant system of social and moral values, pro-social attitudes and a view of the teaching profession as a social service (typical of the older generation), to an inclination towards professional and individual values and towards the subjective fulfillment of professional duties (typical of the younger generation). Personal values and ambitions that dominated all three generations concerned private affairs, family life, stabilization, the meaning of work and its results, relations between people, and a feeling of usefulness, approval and satisfaction. A community spirit and a cross-generational continuity were observed in the area of universal values and ambitions.

Publ: Dróżka, Wanda. *Pokolenia nauczycieli*. Kielce: WSP, 1993, 348p.
Dróżka, Wanda. Wartości i cele życiowe nauczycieli. In: *Edukacja*, 1/1992, pp. 49-68.
Dróżka, Wanda. Pokolenia nauczycieli. In: *Edukacja*, 2/1993.

35 ADMINISTRATION – ADMINISTRATION – VERWALTUNG

13709 The devolved management of schools: a comparative study of the impact of parental participation and the local management of schools in Scotland and England.
GBR 1993
Research Date(s): 1992-1995
Arnott, M.
Sup: Adler, M.; Munn, P.
Inst: Edinburgh University, Edinburgh Centre for Social Welfare Research, 23 Buccleuch Place, Edinburgh EH8 9JT, United Kingdom; Scottish Council for Research in Education, 15 St John Street, Edinburgh EH8 8JR, United Kingdom.
Fin: Economic and Social Research Council.
governing body; board of Governors; educational administration; comparative education
direction administrative; conseil d'administration; administration de l'enseignement; éducation comparée
PROJECT DESCRIPTION
Separate legislation in Scotland and England provides a strategic opportunity for comparative research on parental participation and the local management of schools. In Scotland, every school is expected to establish its own School Board. Parents have a majority of places but the Board's 'baseline' powers are quite limited. This contrasts with the situation in England where parents have one-third of the places on governing bodies but these have more extensive powers. For example, they receive budgets from the local authority to cover most of their running costs which they are free to spend as they wish.

The research will attempt to examine and inform the arguments of supporters and critics of these developments by studying the management of four secondary schools in each of three education authorities. These authorities have contrasting policies towards devolved management: Authority 1 has sought to retain a dominant position in the management of its schools; Authority 2 is experimenting with a greater degree of delegated managment of resources; while Authority 3 is strongly committed to devolved school management.

The research will be based upon documentary analysis, observation of meetings, interviews with key actors in the policy process at national, local and school levels, and a parents survey.

13710 Effects of emotion and sexuality in the organizational processes of management.
GBR 1993
Research Date(s): 1990-1993
Civil, J.
Sup: Fineman, S.
Inst: Staff College, Coombe Lodge, Blagdon, Bristol BS18 6RG, United Kingdom.
management; sexuality; emotion
gestion; sexualité; émotion
PROJECT DESCRIPTION
  This research will look at the effect of emotions and sexuality in the organizational processes of management. Particular issues of interest are: appraisal, management, structures, interviews, promotions and divisions of labour.

13711 Europaeische Integration und Anerkennung von Hochschuldiplomen. (European integration and the recogniton of university diplomas.)
AUT 1993
Research Date(s): 1991-1992
Hoellinger, Herwig.
Inst: Institut fuer Bildungsforschung der Wirtschaft, Rainergasse 38, A-1050 Wien.
Fin: Bundesministerium fuer Wissenschaft und Forschung.
community law; recognition of qualifications; post-secondary education; European community
droit communautaire; reconnaissance des qualifications; enseignement postsecondaire; Communauté européenne
PROJECT DESCRIPTION
  In einem ersten Abschnitt werden Stellenwert, praktische Relevanz und Inhalt der Regeln zur Anerkennung beruflicher Befaehigungsnachweise im Gemeinschaftsrecht dargestellt. Hiezu werden die legislativen Aktivitaeten der Gemeinschaftsorgane, vor allem die beiden Richtlinien zur Anerkennung beruflicher Befaehigungsnachweise und die Jurisdiktion des Europaeischen Gerichtshofes eingehend analysiert.
  Im zweiten Abschnitt wird untersucht, ob und - bejahendenfalls - welche Anforderungen der acquis communautaire an Bildungseinrichtungen des Tertiaersektors stellt, deren Diplome zu beruflichen Zwecken anerkannt werden sollen. Hiezu werden die Zugangsbedingungen zu den Institutionen des nichtuniversitaeren Sektors in ausgewaehlten Mitgliedsstaaten dargestellt. Aufschlussreich ist in diesem Zusammenhang eine Bewertung der diesbezueglich in der Schweiz angestellten Ueberlegungen. Die Frage der notwendigen Mindeststudiendauer wird an Hand der juengsten Judikatur des Europaeischen Gerichtshofes eingehend eroertert. Breiter Raum wird der Frage der Moeglichkeit der Anerkennung facheinschlaegiger Kenntnisse in weiterfuehrenden Studiengaengen gewaehrt. In diesem Zusammenhang wird das an britischen Polytechnics gehandhabte System der Anerkennung von Kenntnissen dargestellt und analysiert.
  Die bei der praktischen Umsetzung der Diplomanerkennungsrichtlinien sich ergebenden Fragen und moeglichen Loesungsansaetze werden in einem dritten Abschnitt an Hand der Berufe des 'Rechtsanwaltes' und des 'Ziviltechnikers' untersucht.
  Es wurde eine Literaturrecherche durchgefuehrt.

13712 Evaluation of further education college governor training.
GBR 1993
Research Date(s): 1990-1992
Stoker, S.; Reece, I.
Inst: Durham University, School of Education, Leazes Road, Durham DH1 1TA, United Kingdom; Northern Council for Further Education, 5, Grosvenor Villa, Grosvenor Road, Newcastle upon Tyne NE2 2RU, United Kingdom.
board of Governors; training programme; evaluation
conseil d'administration; programme de formation; évaluation
PROJECT DESCRIPTION
  The aim of the project is to evaluate the Further Education Governor Training Programme run by the Northern Council for Further Education at Newcastle upon Tyne based on: observation of teaching sessions; assessment of materials used; and interviews with governors and tutors.

13713 Further education governing bodies and their contribution to a quality learning service.
GBR 1993
Research Date(s): 1992-1993
Graystone, J.; Reece, I.; Bayliss, J.; Evans, S.; Warrender, A.-M.
Sup: Coleman, J.
Inst: Staff College, Coombe Lodge, Blagdon, Bristol BS18 6RG, United Kingdom; Further Education Unit, Spring Gardens, Citadel Place, Tinworth Street, London SE11 5EH, United Kingdom.
governing body; post-compulsory education; educational administration; skill
direction administrative; enseignement postobligatoire; administration de l'enseignement; compétence
PROJECT DESCRIPTION

This project for the Further Education Unit: (1) maps the current composition and characteristics of governing bodies in further education, with particular interest in their potential for an impact on curriculum issues; (2) identifies governors' current (a) expertise and experience, relevant to further education governance; and (b) individual commitment to curriculum issues and ways of working which contribute to the effectiveness of the college as a learning service; and (3) makes recommendations to further education (FE) colleges for incorporation, having regard for the wider responsibilities of governing bodies in the future.
  A short literature search was carried out, followed by a questionnaire completed by 214 FE colleges in England and Wales. Interviews were then held with over 50 governors from selected colleges, and five governing body meetings were observed.

13714 The new governing bodies for further education colleges.
GBR 1993
Research Date(s): 1990-1991
Graystone, J.
Inst: Staff College, Coombe Lodge, Blagdon, Bristol BS18 6RG, United Kingdom.
governing body; post-compulsory education; board of Governors; training need
direction administrative; enseignement postobligatoire; conseil d'administration; besoin de formation
PROJECT DESCRIPTION
  This research will involve an investigation of instruments and articles of government of further education colleges in England and Wales, and an analysis of the development needs of the new governors.
Publ: Graystone, J.A. & Williams, D. *Development programmes for further education governors: a guide for providers.* London: Further Education Unit, 1990.

13715 Perspectives on the government of schools at local level.
GBR 1993
Research Date(s): 1986-
Golby, M.
Inst: Exeter University, School of Education, St Luke's, Heavitree Road, Exeter EX1 2LU, United Kingdom.
Fin: Leverhulme Trust; Universities Funding Council; Exeter University Research Fund; Exeter Society for Curriculum Studies.
governing body; board of Governors; educational administration; parent participation; local government
direction administrative; conseil d'administration; administration de l'enseignement; participation des parents; administration locale
PROJECT DESCRIPTION
  The School Governors Research Group and the Governors Support Centre mounts a range of research conducted both by individual members of the Group and as a collective. The research includes local studies, regional studies and international comparative studies. Central interests are in the extent of parental involvement, the internal processes of deliberation and judgement and the relation to local education authorities. Theoretical work on key constructs underpins the work.
Publ: Golby, M. *The new governors speak: Exeter papers in school governorship No 1.* Tiverton: Fairway Publications, 1990.
Golby, M. In their own words. In: *School Governors*, pp. 11-18, April 1990.
Golby, M. & Appleby, R. *School governors today: in good faith.* Tiverton: Fairway Publications, 1991.

13716 Provision and take-up of School Board training.
GBR 1993
Research Date(s): 1990-1991
Munn, P.; Arney, N.; Holroyd, C.
Inst: Scottish Council for Research in Education, 15 St John Street, Edinburgh EH8 8JR, United Kingdom.
Fin: Scottish Office Education Department.
board of Governors; governing body; educational administration; parent participation; training supply
conseil d'administration; direction administrative; administration de l'enseignement; participation des parents; offre de formation
PROJECT DESCRIPTION
  The research concentrates on four main areas: (1) Board members' views on the information and training available to them; (2) their preferences for particular forms of training; (3) the factors affecting the take-up and selection of forms of training provision; (4) gaps in available provision. The research design combines depth with breadth and is in three strands. Strand One consists of a telephone survey of 100 Boards. Strand Two involves case studies of 15 Boards. Strand Three involves a survey of 1,000 Board members.
Publ: Munn, P.; Arney, N. & Holroyd, C. *The provision and take-up of School Board Information and Training: a summary.* SCRE Spotlights Series, No 29, Edinburgh: Scottish Council for Research in Education, 1990.

13717 Reforming school governing bodies: a sociological investigation.

GBR 1993

Research Date(s): 1990-1993

Deem, R.; Brehony, K.

Inst: Lancaster University, Department of Educational Research, Cartmel College, Bailrigg, Lancaster LA1 4YW, United Kingdom; Reading University, Department of Education Studies and Management, Bulmershe Court, Woodlands Avenue, Earley, Reading RG6 1HY, United Kingdom.

Fin: Economic and Social Research Council.

governing body; educational administration; board of Governors; parent-school relation

direction administrative; administration de l'enseignement; conseil d'administration; relation parents-école

PROJECT DESCRIPTION

School governing bodies in England and Wales were reshaped in the autumn of 1988 as a result of the 1986 (No 2) Education Act, with greater parental representation and more co-opted governors (including those from the business community). The 1986 Act and the 1988 Education Act have also given governors more power over schools than previously.

The project is an in-depth study of ten school governing bodies (four primary and six secondary) in two local education authorities. A pilot study ran from October 1988 to July 1992. The research has monitored what coping strategies governing bodies are using to deal with the tasks and responsibilities given to them by the new educational legislation and has also focused on the identification of power relations (including gender and race/ethnicity), decision-making processes and networks of influence operating in the eight governing bodies. The project also, in addition, seeks to discover whether co-opted governors and parent governors (widely described as 'consumer') come to predominate over those sometimes termed 'producer' governors (teacher and local education authority representative) and headteachers. The work has been done through observation of formal, informal and sub-committee meetings, questionnaires and interviews.

Publ: Brehony, K.J.B. Neither rhyme nor reason - primary schooling and the National Curriculum. In: Flude, M. & Hammer, M. (eds.). *The 1988 Education Act.* London: Falmer Press, 1990.
Deem, R. The reform of school governing bodies - the power of the consumer over the producer? In: Flude, M. & Hammer, M. (eds.). *The 1988 Education Act.* London: Falmer Press, 1990.
Deem, R. & Brehony, K.J.B. The long and the short of it. In: *Times Educational Supplement,* 13 July 1990.
Hemmings, S. Determined to see it through. In: *Times Educational Supplement,* 21 July 1990.

13718 School governorship as democratic participation.

GBR 1993

Research Date(s): 1990-1992

Viant, R.

Sup: Golby, M.

Inst: Exeter University, School of Education, St Luke's, Heavitree Road, Exeter EX1 2LU, United Kingdom.

governing body; board of Governors; participation

direction administrative; conseil d'administration; participation

PROJECT DESCRIPTION

This work seeks to illuminate how far school governorship can be a democratic and participatory activity undertaken as a public service through 'active citizenship'. Recent legislation has opened up such possibilities even though it has not been unequivocally intended to do so. The introductory section places the work in context and attention is initally directed towards the historical origins of school governorship and shows how, through the post war period, it became a merely cermonial institution. The legal, educational and philosophical contexts are then explored. The empirical work forms a detailed case study of one governing body - 'The Everyday Story of Governorfolk'. The research programme which supports the case study is qualitative in style, and centres round non-participant observation of governors' meetings and in-depth interviews with four governors. As the research proceeds the focus is progressively refined to concentrate on emerging issues which relate to key democratic principles - participation, responsibility, representation, independence of mind and accountability. There emerges a picture of one example of governorship which is subsequently compared and contrasted with different governing bodies by means of a review of other research in this field. The findings from the case study reveal that in certain respects opportunities for democratic participation exist and are taken up. In many other respects this governing body is not found to be particularly democratic. The work concludes with recommendations for changes in governors' training and for amendments to the legislation.

Publ: Appleby, R. & Golby, M. *School governors: end of term report.* Tiverton: Fairway Publications, 1992.

13719 The secondment of professional staff between education and industry.

GBR 1993

Research Date(s): 1988-1993

Huddleston, P.

Sup: Woolhouse, J.; Tomlinson, J.

Inst: Warwick University, Faculty of Educational Studies, Centre for Education and Industry, Coventry CV4 7AL, United Kingdom.

Fin: Goldsmiths' Company of London.

secondment; teacher; industry

détachement; enseignant; industrie

PROJECT DESCRIPTION

The research is concerned with the professional development of outcomes of teacher secondments/placements into business and industry at both individual and institutional level. In particular, the impact of placement experiences on curriculum development is being investigated.

The methodology includes questionnaire and personal interviews of teachers who have undertaken placements; longitudinal studies; core studies; and evaluation of placement studies.

13720 Sekretariat der Zukunft: zukuenftige Qualifizierung und Entwicklung inhaltlicher und organisatorischer Gestaltungsempfehlungen fuer den Sekretariatsbereich. (Tomorrow's secretarial office: future qualifications and development of the factual and organizational recommendations for secretarial work.)

DEU 1993

Research Date(s): 1990-1992

Bonnet, P.; Scharer, H.; Schneider, U.; Hahn, H.

Sup: Klein, B.

Inst: Fraunhofer-Institut fuer Arbeitswirtschaft und Organisation -IAO-, Abt. Unternehmensfuehrung, Nobelstr. 12c, D-7000 Stuttgart 80.

Fin: Deutsche Forschungsanstalt fuer Luft- und Raumfahrt -DLR- Projekttraeger des Programms "Arbeit und Technik".

secretariat; further training; personnel; qualification; secretary

secrétariat; formation complémentaire; personnel; qualification; secrétaire

PROJECT DESCRIPTION

Inhalt: Entwicklung von Empfehlungen fuer die Ueberarbeitung der Rechtsverordnung "gepruefte Sekretaerin/gepruefter Sekretaer; Entwicklung von inner- und ueberbetrieblichen Weiterbildungskonzepten; Entwicklung inhaltlicher und organisatorischer Gestaltungsempfehlungen.

Geographischer Raum: Bundesrepublik Deutschland.

Vorgehensweise: Untersuchungsdesign: Fallstudie; qualitative Forschung; arbeitswissenschaftliche Analyse; computergestuetzte Befragung; Repraesentation; Befragung; Einsatz von Szenario-Technik.

Datengewinnung: Standardisiertes Interview (Stichprobe: 20; Sekretaerinnen; Auswahlverfahren: willkuerlich. Stichprobe: 20; Unternehmensfallstudien; Auswahlverfahren: willkuerlich. Stichprobe: 180; computerunterstuetzte Erhebung auf der Messe "Sekretaerin '91"; Auswahlverfahren: willkuerlich. Stichprobe: 33; LeiterInnen von Aus- und Weiterbildungsinstitutionen, Gewerkschafts- und VerbandsvertreterInnen, Personal- und ArbeitsvermittlerInnen; Auswahlverfahren: willkuerlich). Nicht-standardisiertes Interview (Stichprobe: 20; Sekretaerinnen; Auswahlverfahren: willkuerlich. Stichprobe: 20; Unternehmensfallstudien; Auswahlverfahren: willkuerlich. Stichprobe: 33; LeiterInnen von Aus- und Weiterbildungsinstitutionen, Gewerkschafts- und VerbandsvertreterInnen, Personal- und ArbeitsvermittlerInnen; Auswahlverfahren: willkuerlich). Expertengespraech (Stichprobe: 20; Sekretaerinnen; Auswahlverfahren: willkuerlich. Stichprobe: 20; Unternehmensfallstudien; Auswahlverfahren: willkuerlich. Stichprobe: 33; LeiterInnen von Aus- und Weiterbildungsinstitutionen, Gewertschafts- und VerbandsvertreterInnen, Personal- und ArbeitsvermittlerInnen; Auswahlverfahren: willkuerlich). Gruppendiskussion (Stichprobe: 20; Unternehmensfallstudien; Auswahlverfahren: willkuerlich). Postalische Befragung (Stichprobe: 3000; Sekretaerinnen, Auftraggeber; Auswahlverfahren: Zufall. Stichprobe: 78; IHKs; Auswahlverfahren: total. Stichprobe: 40-50; Aus- und Weiterbildungsinstitutionen im Sekretariatsbereich; Auswahlverfahren: willkuerlich. Stichprobe: 20-40; Aus- und Weiterbildungsabteilungen von Unternehmen; Auswahlverfahren: willkuerlich). Befragung (Stichprobe: 180; computerunterstuetzte Erhebung auf der Messe "Sekretaerin '91"; Auswahlverfahren: willkuerlich). Fragebogen (Stichprobe: 52; Arbeitswissenschaftliche Analyse eingesetzt bei Sekretaerinnen; Auswahlverfahren: willkuerlich). Primaererhebung: Feldarbeit von Mitarbeitern des Projektes durchgefuehrt.

Auswertung: qualitative Auswertung ueber ATLAS; Faktorenanalyse; Clusteranalyse; Varianzanalyse. Datenaufbereitung: Datenedition (z.B. Aufbau von Datenbanken); Verknuepfung verschiedener Datensaetze (record linkage).

Publ: *Sekretariat der Zukunft.* Projektnachrichten. 1. Ausg. 1991.
Sekretariat der Zukunft. Projektnachrichten. Messeausg. 2. Ausg. 1991.
Sekretariat der Zukunft. Projektnachrichten. 3. Ausg. 1991.
Bullinger, Hans-Joerg; Froeschle, Hans-Peter & Klein, Barbara. *Telearbeit: Schaffung dezentraler Arbeitsplaetze unter Einsatz von Teletex.* (AIT - Angewandte Informationstechnik, Bd. 2) Hallbergmoos, AIT-Verl. GmbH 1987, 182 S.

Human aspects in computing. Design and use of interactive systems and information management. Proceedings of the Fourth International Conference on Human-Computer Interaction, Stuttgart, 1-6.9.1991. Ed. by Hans-Joerg Bullinger. Amsterdam, London, New York, Tokyo: Elsevier, 1991.
(Ein vollständiges Verzeichnis steht zur Verfügung.).

13721 Short-term secondments.
GBR 1993
Research Date(s): 1991-1992
McMichael, P.; Draper, J.
Inst: Heriot-Watt University, Moray House Institute of Education, Holyrood Road, Edinburgh EH8 8AQ, United Kingdom.
Fin: Scottish Office Education Department.
secondment; teaching profession; career development
détachement; profession d'enseignant; déroulement de carrière
PROJECT DESCRIPTION
Stimulated by an increase in short-term (23 months) appointments to college lectureships together with a policy of secondments to posts at both regional and national level from within the teaching profession, this project aims to examine the experience of secondment and to discover ways in which transitions from job to job can be facilitated in order to maximise a sense of personal control as well as productivity. The project will attempt to discover: (1) why secondees apply for secondments and what their expectations about secondment might be; (2) what form of induction was provided; (3) how this was perceived; (4) how initial adjustments were made; (5) what balance was achieved between fitting the job and developing the job; (6) whether exiting from secondment was 'managed' and, if so, how; (7) what effects the secondment had on perceptions of self and on future employment.
Interviews will be conducted with 25 secondees completing full-time secondments during 1991 in colleges, the Scottish Office Education Department, the Scottish Consultative Council on the Curriculum, and regional authorities. Questionnaires based on analysis of the interviews will be circulated to a wider sample of secondees. Selected secondees are: teachers, headteachers, advisers and college lecturers.

13722 A sociological evaluation of the relationship between expectations and outcomes concerning parental inclusion on School Boards.
GBR 1993
Research Date(s): 1990-1993
Littlewood, P.
Inst: Glasgow University, Department of Sociology, Lilybank House, Glasgow G12 8RT, United Kingdom.
board of Governors; parents; parent-school relation; educational administration; reform; Scotland
conseil d'administration; parents; relation parents-école; administration de l'enseignement; réforme; Ecosse
PROJECT DESCRIPTION
The establishment of School Boards in Scotland under the Education Reform Act 1988 took place amid considerable controversy as to the possible consequences of so increasing the participative role of parents in decision-making and policy formulation of schools. The study seeks to assess the nature and extent of the impact of this increased participation, and how the perceptions of the principal actors have been affected by the first two years of School Board activity.
The study is based on a sample of 6 secondary schools in Glasgow, and involves: (a) sustained observation of their meetings; (b) interviews and questionnaires with all members and head teachers of the school in the sample; and (c) collection of data from the Regional and Scottish Education Departments regarding policies relating to School Boards.

Publ: Littlewood, P. The return of the board? 'Parent power' and participation in the Scottish school system. In: *Critical Social Policy*, No 27, pp. 96-109, Winter 1990.

13723 Study of School Boards in Scotland.
GBR 1993
Research Date(s): 1990-1992
MacBeath, J.; Thompson, W.
Inst: Jordanhill College of Education, Division of Education and Psychology, Southbrae Drive, Glasgow G13 1PP, United Kingdom.
Fin: Scottish Office Education Department.
governing body; educational administration; Scotland
direction administrative; administration de l'enseignement; Ecosse
PROJECT DESCRIPTION
The aim of this project is to evaluate the work of School Boards in Scotland.

13724 Survey of recruitment and staffing difficulties in secondary schools.
GBR 1993
Research Date(s): 1986-
Reece, D.

Inst: Berkshire County Council, Education Department, Information Technology Management, Shire Hall, Shinfield Park, Reading RG2 9XD, United Kingdom.
recruitment; secondary school; demand for teachers; supply of teachers; teaching personnel
recrutement; école secondaire; besoin d'enseignants; offre d'enseignants; corps enseignant
PROJECT DESCRIPTION
The need to form a full picture of the staffing problems in schools has prompted the development of a systematic monitoring of the recruitment process and the resulting teaching force. A system is in place for incorporating the collection of information on attempts to recruit into the routine of administration.

13725 Three primary school boards: the first years.
GBR 1993
Research Date(s): 1989-1991
Andrews, J.
Inst: Jordanhill College of Education, Division of Primary Education, Southbrae Drive, Jordanhill, Glasgow G13 1PP, United Kingdom.
governing body; Scotland; school-community relation
direction administrative; Ecosse; relation école-collectivité
PROJECT DESCRIPTION
This project will use three case studies to establish how a school and its community perceive: (a) their role in the new school board, and its functions; (b) their feelings of preparedness for participation in the boards; and (c) how these perceptions alter over the first year of school boards.

13726 Umsetzungsprobleme bei EG-Richtlinien im Falle eines oesterreichischen Beitritts. (Problems in the implementation of EC directives in the case of Austria's admission to the EC.)
AUT 1993
Research Date(s): 1992-1994
Bodo, Bernhardt.
Inst: Institut fuer Voelkerrecht und Internationale Beziehungen, Innrain 52, A-6020 Innsbruck.
Universitaet Innsbruck, Innrain 52, A-6020 Innsbruck
directive (European Communities); constitution; Austria
directive (Communauté européenne); constitution; Autriche
PROJECT DESCRIPTION
Analyse von Strukturdivergenzen zwischen Verordnung und Richtlinie als Rechtsaktsformen des ausfuehrenden, sekundaeren Rechts der Europaeischen Gemeinschaft; der Mitgliedsstaat als Normadressat der Richtlinie und Probleme aus dem Umsetzungsgebot aus der vertraglichen Verbindlichkeit des primaeren EG-Rechts; Rangfragen und Rechtsaktsformenprobleme in der Umsetzung von EG-Richtlinien im Rahmen des nationalen, innerstaatlichen Rechts der Mitgliedsstaaten; Masstaebe und Mechanismen der rechtlichen Kontrolle der Durchfuehrung von Richtlinien durch den Europaeischen Gerichtshof im Rahmen der Gruendungsvertraege der EG; Umsetzungsverweigerung als Akt der Vertragsverletzung in Ausrichtung auf die Gemeinschaftsvertraege; Substitution der innerstaatlichen Durchfuehrung von EG-Richtlinien durch Erkenntnisse des Europaeischen Gerichtshofes bis zum Erlass des nationalen, mitgliedsstaatlichen Rechts; Rang- und Geltungsprobleme zwischen Verordnungen und Richtlinien des EG-Rechts (Derogation nationaler Durchfuehrungsbestimmungen von EG-Richtlinien durch nachfolgende, unmittelbar durchgreifende EG-Rechtsverordnungen); horizontale Kompetenzprobleme im Rechtsgrundlagenbezug auf das Primaerrecht beim Erlassen diverser Rechtsaktssetzungsformen des sekundaeren Gemeinschaftsrechts.

Cognitive components of expertise in professional judgement, with reference to factors influencing acquisition of the relevant cognitive skills.. see no. 13113

Consumerist perspectives on education .... see no. 13385

Internationales Oeffentliches Umweltschutzrecht (International legislation on environmental protection)............................... see no. 13451

Dealing with knowledge in the Museums Sector Standards: an evaluation of an approach using carefully chosen examples ....
.... see no. 13559

Verbesserung des Innovationsmanagements in kleinen und mittleren Unternehmungen (Improving innovation management in small and medium-sized companies)............................... see no. 13641

Returners to teaching.. see no. 13695

Bedingungen und Blockierungen demokratischer Kultur, Politik, Wissenschaft und Bildung in der DDR (Conditions and obstacles in democratic culture, politics, science and education in the GDR) ....
.... see no. 13727

Optimálny model školskej správy (Optimum model of a local education authority) .... see no. 13739

Tower Hamlets project: communication between Tower Hamlets Local Education Authority and school governing bodies....................
.... see no. 13744

Utdanningspolitikken i forhandlingssamfunnet (Educational policy in the negotiating society).. see no. 13747

36 PUBLIC ADMINISTRATION – ADMINISTRATION PUBLIQUE – OEFFENTLICHE VERWALTUNG

13727 Bedingungen und Blockierungen demokratischer Kultur, Politik, Wissenschaft und Bildung in der DDR. (Conditions and obstacles in democratic culture, politics, science and education in the GDR.)
DEU 1993
Research Date(s): 1992
Gebhardt, B.; Grunwald, S.
Sup: Zak, C.
Inst: Kautsky-Bernstein Kreis e.V., Islaendische Str. 4, O-1071 Berlin.
Fin: Bundesanstalt fuer Arbeit.
politics; democracy; culture; sciences; democratization; historical research; German DR
politique; démocratie; culture; sciences; démocratisation; recherche historique; Allemagne RDA
PROJECT DESCRIPTION
Inhalt: Untersuchung von Ausgangspunkten fuer den Transformationsprozess politischer Kultur in den neuen Bundeslaendern und ihren Wurzeln in der Hinterlassenschaft der DDR. Zusammenhaenge von sozialer Differenzierung und politischer Kultur. Wissenschaft zwischen Freiraum und Vereinnahmung. DDR-Schule, Anliegen und Wirklichkeit.
Geographischer Raum: DDR.
Untersuchter Zeitraum: 1949-1989.
Vorgehensweise: Dokumentenanalyse; Archivstudien.
Datengewinnung: Einzelinterview. Aktenanalyse.

13728 Berufsschule als Feld von Jugendarbeit. (The part-time vocational school as a field for youth work.)
DEU 1993
Research Date(s): 1989-1992
Mueller, C.; Lindemann, H.
Inst: Technische Universitaet Berlin, FB 22 Erziehungs- und Unterrichtswissenschaften, Institut fuer Sozialpaedagogik, Fraenklinufer, D-1000 Berlin 10.
Fin: Deutscher Gewerkschaftsbund Bundesvorstand.
youth welfare; vocational school; adolescent; out-of-school education; apprentice; cooperation
aide à la jeunesse; école professionnelle; adolescent; éducation extrascolaire; apprenti; coopération
PROJECT DESCRIPTION
Inhalt: Es handelt sich um ein Projekt der experimentellen Jugendforschung. Berufsschule und verbandliche Jugendbildungsarbeit bzw. Jugendarbeit haben sich in den letzten Jahren gegenseitig nicht wahrgenommen. Beide haben sich mehr oder weniger weit von der Lebensmitte der Jugendlichen entfernt. Das Projekt als Zwischeninstanz entwickelt Kooperationsmoeglichkeiten fuer Jugendliche (Azubis) in der Berufsschule. Jugendliche sollen in ausserschulische Jugendarbeit einbezogen werden.
Geographischer Raum: Berlin/Herford, NRW.
Untersuchter Zeitraum: 1985 bis heute.
Vorgehensweise: Handlungsforschung in der Tradition Kurt Lewins. Untersuchungsdesign: Handlungsforschung.
Datengewinnung: Primaererhebung: Feldarbeit von Mitarbeitern des Projektes durchgefuehrt.
Auswertung: Datenaufbereitung: Verlaufsdaten (event history data).

13729 Der Fachhochschulstandort Spittal an der Drau. (Spittal an der Drau as a location for a 'Fachhochschule' (college of higher professional training).)
AUT 1993
Research Date(s): 1992
Leitner, Erich.
Inst: Abteilung fuer Hochschulpaedagogik, Universitaetsstrasse 65-67, A-9020 Klagenfurt.
Universitaet fuer Bildungswissenschaften, Universitaetsstrasse 65-67, A-9020 Klagenfurt
Fin: Stadt Spittal an der Drau.
educational planning; post-secondary education; regional development
planification de l'éducation; enseignement postsecondaire; développement régional
PROJECT DESCRIPTION
Untersuchung der Eignung der Stadt Spittal an der Drau als Fachhochschulstandort nach den Kriterien: Regionalisierung, Bildungsnachfrage, Qualifikationsbedarf, Standortqualitaeten.
Es handelt sich um ein Projekt aus dem Bereich Bildungsplanung; der empirische Teil wird unter Nutzung verfuegbarer Daten der oesterreichischen Raumplanung, der Hochschulstatistik und der Statistiken der Laender errechnet.
Es kommen empirische und analytische Methoden zur Anwendung.

13730 The employment of disabled teaching staff.
GBR 1993
Research Date(s): 1990-1992
Simpson, P.
Inst: Royal Association for Disability and Rehabilitation (RADAR), 25 Mortimer Street, London W1N 8AB, United Kingdom.
employment policy; access to employment; teaching post; physically handicapped; teacher
politique de l'emploi; accès á l'emploi; poste d'enseignement; handicapé physique; enseignant
PROJECT DESCRIPTION
This research aims to update a previous Royal Association for Disability and Rehabilitation (RADAR) survey which interviewed disabled members of the teaching profession. This national quantitative survey assesses data provided by 51 local education authorities in the United Kingdom on their recruitment; retention policies, and practices regarding disabled teachers. The postal questionnaire will provide information on the numbers of disabled teachers employed in the primary, secondary and tertiary sectors; support services for disabled staff (including newly disabled people); facilities provided and measures taken to recruit disabled staff.

13731 An examination of the factors that promote the development of an integrated child care strategy.
GBR 1993
Research Date(s): 1990-1993
Kendrick, A.; Fraser, A.
Inst: Dundee University, Department of Social Work, Dundee DD1 4HN, United Kingdom.
Fin: Social Work Services Group.
social service; child protection; child care
service social; protection de l'enfance; aide à l'enfance
PROJECT DESCRIPTION
This is an overview study of current policies and developments in Scottish Social Work Departments which relate to the integration of residential and community child care services between agencies (particularly Social Work and Education) and with Social Work Departments. The study will be carried out by content analysis of policy and planning documents and by interviews with key social work personnel. In three selected local authorities the nature of the integration of child care services will be studied in more detail over two years. A cohort study will look at career patterns of children in care and will focus on the outcomes of particular social work placements. Collection of data will be by questionnaire, analysis of case files and interviews with children and young people. Interviews will be carried out with personnel involved with the cohort of children to examine the relationship between organisational structures, policies and practice as perceived by social work staff, Children's Panel Members and Reporters to the Children's Panel. To provide information about the level of inter-agency integration, educational staff will be interviewed. A questionnaire survey of residential establishments used for children in the care of Social Work Departments will be carried out to establish the extent and range of residential services in Scotland and their links with complementary child care services.

13732 Fortbildung fuer Polizeidienststellen im Bereich Gewalt gegen Frauen. (Further education for police personnel on the subject of violence against women.)
DEU 1993
Research Date(s): 1990-1993
Marth, D.; Kochskaemper, B.
Sup: Frehsee, D.

Inst: Universitaet Bielefeld, Fak. fuer Rechtswissenschaft, Lehrstuhl fuer Strafrecht, Strafprozessrecht und Kriminologie, Universitaetsstrasse 25, D-4800 Bielefeld 1.

Fin: Bundesministerium fuer Frauen und Jugend.

further training; police; woman; violence; deviant behaviour; aggressiveness; training course

formation complémentaire; police; femme; violence; comportement déviant; agressivité; cours de formation

PROJECT DESCRIPTION

Inhalt: Bestandsaufnahme polizeilicher (Aus- und) Fortbildungen zum Thema Gewalt gegen Frauen; Entwicklung einer Lehrgangskonzeption fuer die Polizei zum Thema Gewalt gegen Frauen; konzeptionelle Ueberlegungen zur Supervision polizeilicher Arbeit im Bereich Gewalt gegen Frauen; Bestandsaufnahme der Zusammenarbeit zwischen Polizei und Hilfseinrichtungen und Sozialbehoerden.

Geographischer Raum: Bundesgebiet mit den Schwerpunkten Schleswig-Holstein, Mecklenburg-Vorpommern.

Vorgehensweise: Interpretatives Paradigma; Interviews und Befragungen bei Innenministerien, polizeilichen Aus- und Fortbildungsinstitutionen, PolizeilehrerInnen, polizeilichen Fortbildungen, Schutz- und KriminalpolizistInnen, ueber schutz- und kriminalpolizeiliche Arbeit, mit von Gewalt betroffenen Frauen, Hilfseinrichtungen, Gleichstellungsbeauftragten, Arbeitskreisen, Frauenministerien, General- und SonderstaatsanwaeltInnen. Untersuchungsdesign: qualitative Forschung.

Datengewinnung: Nicht-standardisiertes Interview. Telefoninterview. Befragung.

13733 Government intervention and policy change in higher education: a comparative study. Stage 1.

GBR 1993

Research Date(s): 1990-1991

Fulton, O.

Inst: Lancaster University, Department of Educational Research, Cartmel College, Bailrigg, Lancaster LA1 4YW, United Kingdom.

Fin: Ministry of Education, Finland.

government policy; higher education; comparative education; educational policy; cross-national research

politique gouvernementale; enseignement supérieur; éducation comparée; politique de l'éducation; recherche transnationale

PROJECT DESCRIPTION

This is a large scale comparative study (up to 11 'Organisation for Economic Co-operation and Development' countries) of the intended and unintended effects of government intervention in policy-making and implementation for higher education. It focuses particularly on issues such as diversification or integration of higher education in a context of expanding numbers and contracting resources during the 1980s. The first stage is a review of broad policy developments in each country, contributed by a local "expert". Further empirical investigations may follow.

Publ: Fulton, O. Slouching towards a mass system: society, government and institutions in the United Kingdom. In: *Higher Education*, Vol 21, No 4/1991, pp. 589-606.

13734 Impact of school development plans in primary schools.

GBR 1993

Research Date(s): 1991-1994

Mortimore, P.; MacGilchrist, B.; Savage, J.; Beresford, C.

Inst: London University, Institute of Education, The Directorate, 20 Bedford Way, London WC1H 0AL, United Kingdom.

Fin: Economic and Social Research Council.

educational planning; educational administration; development of education; primary school

planification de l'éducation; administration de l'enseignement; développement de l'éducation; école primaire

PROJECT DESCRIPTION

School development plans provide a mechanism to link the planning of improvements with the financial and staff development planning of the school as a whole. This project aims to investigate whether these plans - and the process of planning - are having positive impacts. Schools in contrasting areas make up the sample. A mixture of research methods has been chosen for this three year study.

Publ: Beresford, C.; Mortimore, P.; MacGilchirst, B. & Savage, J. School development planning in the U.K.. In: *Unicorn*, Vol 18, No 2/1992, pp. 12-16.

13735 The implementation of local education authority curriculum policies in two metropolitan authorities.

GBR 1993

Research Date(s): 1984-1991

Bennett, N.

Sup: Kogan, M.

Inst: Brunel University, Department of Government, Uxbridge UB8 3PH, United Kingdom.

educational planning; curriculum development; local government; teaching practice

planification de l'éducation; élaboration de programmes d'études; administration locale; pratique pédagogique

PROJECT DESCRIPTION

This study examines the impact of local education authority (LEA) curriculum policies on teachers' practice in two metropolitan LEAs, working from literature on policy-making and implementation, curriculum theory and school improvement. Sixty-six teachers in six schools, three from each LEA, discussed in extended semi-structured interviews the influences they took account of, or were aware of as an influence, when deciding on programmes of study, setting work or working in the classroom. The six headteachers and the two LEA Chief Inspectors were also interviewed. The sample of teachers was stratified by seniority and subject area, and balanced so far as possible for gender across seniority. The schools were selected as 'matched pairs' across the LEAs, which were themselves selected for their comparable size, location, and socio-political character.

LEA curriculum policies were found to have little impact, due to their general character but more importantly to the low professional status and lack of policing authority of their advisers/inspectors. Public examinations were more important, and had caused major reviews of departmental and individual practice. Parental interest in examination results was seen to have influenced this. Most significant were internal school factors. Departmental characteristics influenced its importance and impact as a basic unit of institutional allegiance. The degree of trust between senior and junior staff affected how far teachers would surrender their perceived classroom privacy, autonomy and discretion.

The study concludes that external requirements need strong policing or strong internal support if they are to have a significant impact on teacher practice.

13736 Kinder- und Familienforschung im Rahmen kommunaler Jugendhilfeplanung fuer die Stadt Osnabrueck. (Youth and family research within the framework of municipal youth welfare planning in Osnabrueck.)

DEU 1993

Research Date(s): 1991-1992

Wicher, M.; Schneider, D.; Knobel, M.; Holste, J.; Bensmann, E.

Sup: Gries, J.; Otten, D.

Inst: Deutsches Institut zur Erforschung der Informationsgesellschaft e.V., Kamp 10, D-4500 Osnabrueck.

Fin: Stadt Osnabrueck.

youth welfare; community development; family; child care; life cycle; value system

aide à la jeunesse; développement des collectivités; famille; aide à l'enfance; cycle de vie; système de valeurs

PROJECT DESCRIPTION

Inhalt: Ziel der Untersuchung ist es, die Lebensstile und Lebensperspektiven von jungen Familien, ihre Einstellungen zu Familie, Wohnumfeld, Schule, Beruf, Freizeit, Konsum, Umweltschutz, Politik/ politische Parteien etc. in Osnabrueck zu erfassen und fuer die Problemfrueherkennung fruchtbar zu machen. Dazu wird das vom DII entwickelte WAFFEL-Cluster-Verfahren eingesetzt, das von einem sechsdimensionalen Erklaerungsmodell des Alltagshandelns ausgeht. Die Dimensionen sind Wohnumfeld, Alltagskultur, Familiensituation, Freizeitverhalten, Einstellungsprofile (Werthaltungen, Normen, Ethiken etc.) und Lebenszyklus.

Geographischer Raum: Osnabrueck.

Untersuchter Zeitraum: 1991/1992.

Vorgehensweise: Untersuchungsdesign: Methodenforschung; Fallstudie; Querschnittserhebung.

Datengewinnung: Standardisiertes Interview (Stichprobe: ca. 1500; Familien mit Kindern im Alter bis 12 Jahren; Auswahlverfahren: Quota). Primaererhebung: Feldarbeit von Mitarbeitern des Projektes durchgefuehrt.

Auswertung: Cluster-Analyse.

13737 Législation de la jeunesse et institutions aujourd'hui: recherche comparative internationale.

FRA 1993

Research Date(s): 1990-1993

Charvin, Monique.

Inst: Ministère de la Justice, CNRS URA/412, Centre de recherche interdisciplinaire de Vaucresson, 54 rue de Garches, 92420 Vaucresson, France.

youth protection; prevention; official text; cross-national research; juvenile court; legislation; Europe

protection de la jeunesse; prévention; texte officiel; recherche transnationale; tribunal pour enfants; législation; Europe

PROJECT DESCRIPTION

Objectifs: Recherche comparative à partir de la notion de jeunesse, en prenant en compte les notions de protection (sociale et judiciaire), de prévention, de décentralisation, confrontation en Allemagne, France, Italie des textes et de la pratique articulée autour des tribunaux des trois capitales: Berlin, Paris, Rome.

Méthodologie: Comparaison internationale fondée sur l'analyse des textes législatifs et réglementaires et des pratiques judiciaires.

13738 London Plan (London Record of Achievement).
GBR 1993
Research Date(s): 1990-1992
Bradley, G.; Green, W.
Inst: London University, Institute of Education, Department of Curriculum Studies, 20 Bedford Way, London WC1H 0AL, United Kingdom.
Fin: Training, Enterprise and Education Directorate.
educational planning; post-compulsory education
planification de l'éducation; enseignement postobligatoire
PROJECT DESCRIPTION
The aim of the project is to develop the formative processes of individual action planning through case studies across a range of programmes in further education and with managing agents and employers, involving students of different ages and abilities.

13739 Optimálny model školskej správy. (Optimum model of a local education authority.)
SVK 1994
Research Date(s): 1991-1992
Malá, E.; Szabová, V.
Sup: Gabčo, P.
Inst: Ústav informácií a prognóz školstva, mládeže a telovýchovy (Institute of Information and Prognoses of Education, Youth and Sport), Staré grunty 52, 842 44 Bratislava, Slovak Republic.
Ministerstvo školstva a vedy SR (Ministry of Education and Science of the Slovak Republic), Hlboká 2, 813 30 Bratislava, Slovak Republic
regional administration; governing body; school district; school autonomy; decentralization; local government
administration régionale; direction administrative; district scolaire; autonomie scolaire; décentralisation; administration locale
PROJECT DESCRIPTION
Aim of research: To outline the optimum model of a local educational authority in the light of the various proposals that have been made for the territorial structure of the Slovak Republic. Starting points for the project were the fact that local educational authorities have become less functional since some of their powers were devolved to the community, local authorities and head teachers as well as the fact that some activities, particularly in the field of professional management, which are currently not performed by local education authorities, could be delegated to them under the new conditions.
Methodology: An analysis was made of existing problems in primary and secondary schools with the help of a questionnaire, structured interviews, document analysis, and model development and optimization. Proposals were made for changes in the powers of administrative bodies, changes in administrative mechanisms and changes in legislative and economic domains.
Results: Within the framework of the research project the following drafts were prepared: a draft of the major activities of the local education authority as a body at the second level of primary and secondary education management and criteria for positioning education authorities in a network within the territory of the Slovak Republic; a draft of alternative models for the management of primary and secondary schools linked to the various proposals for the territorial structure of the Slovak Republic.
The research project should be followed up by research work oriented towards concrete activities and the structure and position of second-level administrative bodies in the primary and secondary education sectors under the conditions of the new territorial structure of the Slovak Republic.
Publ: Malá, E. & Szabová, V. *Optimálny model školskej správy.* (The optimum model of a local educational authority.) Bratislava, ÚIP ŠMT, 1992, 40p.

13740 Policy and practice in community education: a study of the youth service and ethnic minority girls and young women in Peterborough.
GBR 1993
Research Date(s): 1988-1992
Ali, R.
Sup: Wallis, J.; Allman, P.
Inst: Nottingham University, Department of Adult Education, 14-22 Shakespeare Street, Nottingham NG1 4FJ, United Kingdom.
youth policy; youth organization; ethnic group; community education; women's education; value system
politique de la jeunesse; organisation de jeunesse; groupe ethnique; éducation sociale; éducation des femmes; système de valeurs
PROJECT DESCRIPTION
The research centres on studies of social and cultural issues among young Asians with a view to identifying patterns of conflict, continuity and change in their emerging value systems.
The information is being gathered via: a questionnaire completed by over 100 adolescents; in-depth interviews with over 50 of these respondents and their parents; group discussions with young people; informal discussions with Asian community leaders, youth workers, teachers etc.; and participant observation. The findings are aimed at eliciting the circumstances, experiences and views of young people of Asian ethnic origin in an inner-city area. Where necessary the questions are translated into Asian languages or dialects. A small number of representative case studies will be drawn up to illustrate the various forms of conflict revealed by the research. The use of a computerised database programme will be incorporated into the system for collecting and recording data.

13741 Politique de prévention et acteurs de la protection judiciaire de la jeunesse, 1983-1986.
FRA 1993
Research Date(s): 1985-1988
Chauvin, Monique; Pineau, Joseph; Tetard, Françoise; Kalunszinski, Martine.
Sup: Peyre, Vincent.
Inst: Ministère de la Justice, CNRS URA/412, Centre de recherche interdisciplinaire de Vaucresson, 54 rue de Garches, 92420 Vaucresson, France.
Fin: Ministère de la justice, Conseil de la recherche.
social policy; special school teacher; justice; correctional education
politique sociale; éducateur spécialisé; justice; éducation surveillée
PROJECT DESCRIPTION
Objectifs: Analyse empirique de la politique de prévention de la délinquance mise en oeuvre dans les années 1983-1986 et de ses effets: déplacements, recompositions des modes d'action et des rôles des différents partenaires, particulièrement dans le domaine de l'intervention auprès des jeunes relevant de la protection judiciaire, dans le contexte de la territorialisation de l'action sociale.
Méthodologie: Approche du déploiement actuel des dipositifs et de ses effets par référence aux modes antérieurs d'intervention préventive et à l'évolution des constructions et représentations grâce à une enquête dans quatre départements différenciés quant à leur population, les dispositifs présents et la place de la protection judiciaire de la jeunesse.
Résultats: Dans le double contexte de la mise en place d'une politique de prévention et d'une territorialisation de l'action sociale, deux types principaux d'effets sont à prendre en considération: (1) modification des relations entre partenaires institutionnels et redistribution partielle des rôles; (2) évolution des représentations de l'action et de ses perspectives, des rôles professionnels, des partages de territoires.
Publ: Peyre, Vincent et al. *Politique de prévention et acteurs de la protection judiciaire de la jeunesse, 1983-1986.* Vaucresson: CRIV, rapport de recherche, 1987, 183p.
Peyre, Vincent. Prévention, pouvoir local-pouvoir central, position des acteurs et des institutions. In: *Cahiers du CRIV*, 1988, n° 4, pp. 123-130.
Peyre, Vincent. La prévention de la délinquance: une nouvelle politique en France. In: *Le groupe familial*, juillet-septembre 1987, n° 116, pp. 87-91.
Peyre, Vincent. Prévention, pouvoir local-pouvoir central, position des acteurs et des institutions. In: *Cahiers du CRIV*, janvier 1988, n° 4, pp. 123-130.
Peyre, Vincent. La politique de prévention et les acteurs de la protection judiciaire de la jeunesse de 1983 à 1986. In: *Hommes et migrations*, janvier 1990, n° 1128, pp. 7-14.

13742 Schoolmaatschappelijk werk in het regulier voortgezet onderwijs. (School social work in secondary schools.)
NLD 1994
Research Date(s): 1992-1993
Peetsma, T.T.D.; Vermeulen, M.
Sup: Roede, E.; Karstanje, P.
Inst: Stichting Centrum voor Onderwijsonderzoek (SCO) (Centre for Educational Research), Grote Bickersstraat 72, 1013 KS Amsterdam, Netherlands.
Universiteit van Amsterdam (University of Amsterdam), P.O. Box 19268, 1000 GG Amsterdam, Netherlands
Fin: SVO het Instituut voor Onderzoek van het Onderwijs.
social work; social worker; school
travail social; travailleur social; école
PROJECT DESCRIPTION
Background: An increasing number of secondary school pupils have individual problems that affect their life at school. These problems may cause truancy, delinquency, addiction to stimulants or gambling, etc. Parents, welfare institutions, judicial authorities and policy-makers are asking schools to do something about these problems. However, the schools' possibilities are limited, in spite of the work of class mentors and pupil counsellors. That is why a number of secondary schools are now deploying school social workers. Various institutions are involved in the appointment and financing of school social workers. This is likely to have an effect on the degree to which school social work is integrated in the school organization as well as on its development, its continuity and its ultimate results. As there is a lack of information about school social work, the present study seeks to gather information on current practice in this field.
Aim: To explore current practice and results in the field of school social work; to pool information and expertise of individual school social workers

421

with a view to facilitating policy-making and informing school administrators, school governing bodies and government officials.

Design: The number of social workers working in secondary schools will be determined on the basis of information available from the National Association of Social Workers and an advertisement in relevant professional periodicals. Seventy schools with and 70 schools without a school social worker will be approached for comparative data on the way they perceive, practice and organize pastoral care. A questionnaire will be presented to senior management staff and school social workers. Schools with a social worker will be questioned about the results of social work and developments in the field. To supplement these quantitative data, case studies will be made of three schools where school social work is well integrated into the whole of school services and three schools where school social work occupies a "marginal" position. Interviews will be conducted with pupils, parents, management staff, teachers and social workers.

13743 Technologie-indicatoren 1991. (Technology Indicators 1991.)
NLD 1994
Research Date(s): 1991
Dam, J.W. van; Lodder, B.J.H.; Ramaekers, G.W.M.
Inst: ROA Researchcentrum voor Onderwijs en Arbeidsmarkt, Universiteit Limburg (Research Centre for Education and the Labour Market, University of Limburg), P.O. Box 616, 6200 MD Maastricht, Netherlands.
Fin: Ministry of Economic Affairs.
government policy; technology; data base
politique gouvernementale; technologie; banque de données
PROJECT DESCRIPTION
Every year ROA conducts research for the up-dating of a data bank that is used as a basis for the Ministry of Economic Affairs' policies regarding technology. In 1991 the research was split up into a fixed part carried out every year, in which a number of "basic indicators" regarding population, labour and schooling are up-dated, and a variable part. The variable part of the research covered two topics: the percentage of women among trainees in technical training courses and the coordination of education and the labour market in Sweden.
Publ: Dam, J.W. van; Lodder, B.J.H. & Ramaekers, G.W.M. Technology indicators: population, labour and schooling, 1991 Report, ROA-R-1991/9E (ISBN 90-5321-076-8).

13744 Tower Hamlets project: communication between Tower Hamlets Local Education Authority and school governing bodies.
GBR 1993
Research Date(s): 1991-1992
Treharne, D.
Inst: Exeter University, School of Education, St Luke's, Heavitree Road, Exeter EX1 2LU, United Kingdom.
Fin: London Borough of Tower Hamlets.
local government; educational planning; governing body
administration locale; planification de l'éducation; direction administrative
PROJECT DESCRIPTION
Now in the second year of research, this project is evaluating communication between the Tower Hamlets Education Aurthority, schools and governing bodies. The particular focus of this study has been a primary school and a secondary school, both in different neighbourhoods. The interim report dealt with the period of transition between Tower Hamlets as part of division five of the Inner London Education Authority, and Tower Hamlets Local Education Authority in its first year of operation. It outlined the problems encountered by the local authority establishing a working network for information, and the difficulties encountered by governing bodies in promoting this as practice. Phase two of the study will evaluate the change from the provision of centrally based services, to provision through neighbourhoods. It will also focus on the relationship between a new headteacher, the governing body, and the newly devolved neighbourhood services.

13745 Un objet: l'enfant en danger moral; une expérience: la société de patronage.
FRA 1993
Research Date(s): 1987-1991
Kaluszinski, Martine; Tétard, Françoise; Dupont-Bouchat, Sylvette.
Inst: Ministère de la Justice, CNRS URA/412, Centre de recherche interdisciplinaire de Vaucresson, 54 rue de Garches, 92420 Vaucresson, France.
Fin: Ministère des Affaires sociales et de l'Emploi, Mission Recherche et expérimentation.
youth policy; historical method; youth protection; social development; child at risk; social history
politique de la jeunesse; méthode historique; protection de la jeunesse; développement social; enfant à risque; histoire sociale
PROJECT DESCRIPTION
Objectifs: Nécessité de définir le champ d'intervention des sociétés de patronage. Celles qui ont été étudiées dans le rapport se réfèrent explicitement au pénal. Elles apparaissent au début du XIXème siècle et viseront à réinsérer les libérés sortant de prison. A la fin du XIXème siècle, ces sociétés se transforment, se développent et se diversifient. Beaucoup vont se spécialiser sur l'enfant et plus particulièrement sur l'enfant en danger moral, devenant solutions alternatives, en amont de la punition par enfermement. Trois parties chronologiques: la préhistoire du patronage (1819-1880), le temps de l'essor et de la maturité (1880-1914), le déclin d'un modèle dans une société en recomposition (l'entre-deux-guerres). La démarche suivie dans ce rapport a été double: saisir "l'institution en soi", l'archéologie de sa création, son processus de développement et d'extension; mesurer l'inscription politique et sociale de cette institution dans la société républicaine.
Méthodologie: Recherche d'archives (difficulté d'accès aux archives privées) et constitution d'un corpus à partir des documents disponibles sur les sociétés de patronage en France et en Belgique.
Résultats: C'est une recherche qui reste exploratoire. Le manque d'archives de première main a été un handicap. Les sociétés de patronage sont un terrain d'observation du milieu des notables de la fin XIXème siècle, un décrypteur du rapport public-privé dans le régime républicain (ici la IIIème République) et un indicateur du traitement de la question sociale, et plus particulièrement de la question de l'enfance. C'est une institution qui joue le rôle de médiation.
Publ: Kaluszinski, Martine; Tétard, Françoise; Dupont, Sylvie; Pierre, Eric & Strimelle, Véronique. Rapport remis à la Mission recherche et expérimentation du Ministère des affaires sociales et de l'emploi, CRIV, 1991.

13746 Untersuchung zur Situation der sozialwissenschaftlichen Forschung in der Schweiz (Projekt SOWI). (Enquête sur la situation de la recherche en sciences sociales en Suisse (Projet SOWI), projet partiel "Recherche en éducation".)
CHE 1994
Research Date(s): 1990-1993
Gretler, Armin; Grossenbacher, Silvia (Schweizerische Koordinationsstelle für Bildungsforschung, Entfelderstrasse 61, 5000 Aarau, Schweiz).
Inst: Schweizerischer Wissenschaftsrat (SWR), Wildhainweg 9, 3003 Bern, Schweiz.
science policy; social sciences; organization of research; research policy
politique scientifique; sciences sociales; organisation de la recherche; politique de recherche
PROJECT DESCRIPTION
Im März 1990 hat der Schweizerische Wissenschaftsrat (SWR) eine Gruppe von Vertretern verschiedener sozialwissenschaftlicher Fachgesellschaften eingeladen, ihn über Entwicklungstendenzen und Probleme in den Sozialwissenschaften im allgemeinen und speziell in den Bereichen Politologie, Psychologie, Bildungsforschung und Soziologie zu informieren. In der Folge beschloss der Wissenschaftsrat, den Stand und die Entwicklungsperspektiven in diesen Bereichen genauer abzuklären und unter Beteiligung ausländischer Experten evaluieren zu lassen. Zu diesem Zweck wurde eine Arbeitsgruppe Sozialwissenschaften (AG SOWI) gegründet, die das Projekt SOWI ausarbeitete. Ziele dieses Projekts sind folgende: Anregung der Diskussion zwischen den interessierten Kreisen; Bestandesaufnahme und Evaluation der Entwicklungstendenzen und Probleme der Sozialwissenschaften; Vorbereitung von Strategien und forschungspolitischen Massnahmen zur Weiterentwicklung der Sozialwissenschaften.
In der ersten, nun abgeschlossenen Projektphase wurde in den obenerwähnten vier Wissenschaftsbereichen eine Bestandesaufnahme der sozialwissenschaftlichen Forschungsstrukturen und -entwicklungen sowie der Rahmenbedingungen durchgeführt. Parallel dazu waren die Beteiligten aufgefordert, konkrete Massnahmen zur Weiterentwicklung der je eigen Disziplin zu formulieren. In der zweiten Phase wird eine Gruppe unabhängiger ausländischer Experten die Resultate der ersten Phase evaluieren. Die dritte Phase wird der Synthese der Ergebnisse aus den ersten beiden dienen, aber auch der Formulierung von Vorschlägen zuhanden des Bundesrates und der wissenschaftspolitischen Instanzen.
Der Bericht Bildungsforschung gliedert sich in zwei Teile; der eine davon beschreibt Geschichte, Stand und Perspektiven der schweizerischen Bildungsforschung, während der zweite Teil die Ergebnisse der Fragebogenuntersuchung wiedergibt. Letztere diente der Erfassung der personellen und finanziellen Ressourcen, der wissenschaftlichen Aktivitäten, der Projekte, der Kooperationszusammenhänge, der Forschungsschwerpunkte und -methoden sowie der Probleme des Forschungsalltags.
Publ: Grossenbacher, Silvia & Gretler, Armin. Untersuchung zur Situation der sozialwissenschaftlichen Forschung in der Schweiz: Bericht der Bildungsforschung. Bern: Schweizerischer Wissenschaftsrat, 1992, 87 Seiten (Forschungspolitik, FOP 1/1992).

13747 Utdanningspolitikken i forhandlingssamfunnet. (Educational policy in the negotiating society.)
NOR 1994
Research Date(s): 1992-1995
Rasch, Björn Erik.
Inst: Institutt for Samfunnsforskning (Institute for Social Research), Munthesgate 31, 0260 Oslo, Norway.
Fin: NORAS.
government policy; educational policy; decision making

politique gouvernementale; politique de l'éducation; prise de décision
PROJECT DESCRIPTION

The aim is to inform the debate on conditions for political decision-making in educational affairs. The project will analyse the decision-making process in educational policy at a national level. A major part of the work will be an empirical examination of the hypothesis of segmentation within the area of education and to reveal mechanisms that work in other directions than the dominating triangle.

Hypothesis: The idea of a triangle (the Standing Committee on Church and Education, the authorities and interest groups) forming educational policy after its own "inner logic" has taken root within social sciences and dominates the public debate about decision-making processes. This idea has been accepted too easily and has not been proved.

The results of the study would be relevant for decision-makers (politicians, administrators, professionals) as well as for the social debate in general.

13748   Výchova a práva diet'at'a. (Education and the rights of the child.)
CSK   1993
Research Date(s): 1990-1995
Holkovič, Ľubomír; Samuhelová, Magdaléna; Štepanovič, Rudolf; Kalnická, Ľubica; Obrcian, Daniel.
Sup: Hart, S.N.
Inst: Ústav experimentálnej pedagogiky SAV (Institute of Experimental pedagogy, Slovak Academy of Sciences), Mánesovo nám. 1, 851 01 Bratislava, Czech and Slovak Federal Republic.
Slovenská akadémia vied (Slovak Academy of Sciences), Štefánikova ul. 49, 811 04 Bratislava, Czech and Slovak Federal Republic
rights of the child; child protection; socialization; family environment; school environment
droits de l'enfant; protection de l'enfance; socialisation; milieu familial; milieu scolaire
PROJECT DESCRIPTION

The research is conducted as part of an international research project on child development and is coordinated by the ISPA board at Indiana University, USA.

The research studies the development of children, focusing in particular on comparative aspects of the rights of the child and observing socialization techniques used in school and in families. The research is carried out in three stages. The first stage consists of a survey of perceptions of the rights of the child as well as teachers' and children's views on the importance and the existence of individual rights for children. The second and third stages examine the observance of the rights of the child in, respectively, schools and families.

Early results suggest that there is a poor level of knowledge of the rights of the child in educational theory and practice, where these rights are mainly seen as a means to protect children. Children's rights to express their personality and to have access to all kinds of activities in life are insufficiently understood by teachers and children. Furthermore, in educational practice these aspects of children's rights are not sufficiently observed. This is confirmed by the fact that in the Czech and Slovak Federal Republic a child is viewed as an object that needs to be protected, which emphasizes the proprietary nature of the adult-child relation. The respondents in the research do not attach sufficient importance to the personality of the child.
Publ: *The child and its rights*, Institute of Experimental pedagogy, Slovak Academy of Sciences, 1991, 49p.
Education and the rights of the child, (initial review of the literature), Institute of Experimental pedagogy, Slovak Academy of Sciences, 1991, 103p.

37 INTERNATIONAL ORGANIZATIONS – ORGANISATIONS INTERNATIONALES – INTERNATIONALE ORGANISATIONEN

13749 Anwendung des humanitaeren Voelkerrechts auf peace-keeping operations. (The application of humanitarian international law to peace- keeping operations.)
AUT 1993
Research Date(s): 1992-1993
Bodo, Bernhardt.
Inst: Institut fuer Voelkerrecht und Internationale Beziehungen, Innrain 52, A-6020 Innsbruck.
Universitaet Innsbruck, Innrain 52, A-6020 Innsbruck
UN; international law; human rights
ONU; droit international; droits de l'homme
PROJECT DESCRIPTION
Darstellung von humanitaetsrechtlichen Problemen der Beteiligung oesterreichischer Truppenkontingente bei friedenserhaltenden Operationen der Vereinten Nationen; Analyse der Defizite im System des konventionalen Humanitaetsrechtsschutzes und besondere Beruecksichtigung der fehlenden vertragsfoermlichen Einbindung der Vereinten Nationen als internationale Organisation und ihre praktische Relevanz in der Durchfuehrung von peace-keeping operations; Frage nach der Bindungswirkung aufgrund bestehender nationaler Disziplinar- und Strafgewalt ueber die staatliche Einbindung in das System des konventionalen Humanitaetsrechts (vier Genfer Abkommen 1949 samt den beiden Zusatzprotokollen 1977); Abgrenzung zwischen friedensschaffenden Zwangsmassnahmen nach Kapitel VII SVN und freiwilligen Blauhelmeinsaetzen aus der Perspektive des humanitaeren Voelkerrechts; neue Sonderformen des 'humanitaeren Einsatzes' durch Mitgliedsstaaten der Vereinten Nationen mit weitgestellter Ermaechtigung des Sicherheitsrates gemaess Art. 39.42 SVN im Spannungsverhaeltnis zu 'humanitaetsrechtlicher' Bindung im Humanitaetseinsatz als bewaffnetem internationalem Konflikt; Hervorhebung besonderer Aspekte oesterreichischer Beteiligung an internationalen Kontingenten in der Grauzone zwischen peace-keeping und enforcement measures am Beispiel von UNIKEM unter dem Aspekt der doppelten Zurechnung von Massnahmen und Fragen der doppelten Verbindlichstellung humanitaetsrechtlicher Normen; Spannungsfaelle zwischen peace-keeping/Zwangsmassnahmen und humanitaerem Voelkerrecht.

Berufliche Weiterbildung und Europaeische Integration (Further vocational training and European integration) .... see no. 12054

38 AFRICA – AFRIQUE – AFRIKA

13750 The export of the British extramural model to Africa 1945-1960.
GBR 1993
Research Date(s): 1990-1992
Steele, G.
Sup: Titmus, C.
Inst: Leeds University, Department of Adult Continuing Education, Leeds LS2 9JT, United Kingdom.
Fin: Universities Funding Council.
Africa; continuing education; adult education; colonialism; history of education
Afrique; éducation permanente; éducation des adultes; colonialisme; histoire de l'éducation
PROJECT DESCRIPTION
The aim is to describe and analyse the development of British extramural education in Africa during the immediate pre-independence and post-independence period. The research examines the role of education within British colonial policy under the Labour government and especially the parts played by the Fabian Colonial Bureau and the Colonial Secretary Creech-Jones; the original initiative of the University of Oxford Delegacy and its secretary Thomas Hodgkin; the relationship of the initial courses to African nationalist movements; the establishment of African university adult education departments; the role of Sidney Raybould and other leading British adult educationists in Africa; the subsequent Africanisation of university extramural departments; the roles of American and European influences in countering the British model; the comparison with 'mass education' and the origins of 'community development'.
The intention is to conclude with some firm observations on the nature of cultural borrowing. Sources of material used are mostly archival including universities in Britain and Africa and the Public Records Office, but interviews and correspondence with exponents will add significant detail.

Publ: Steele, T. Metropolitan extensions: a comparison of two moments in the export of British University Adult Education, Europe 1890-1910 and Africa 1945-1955. In: Marriott, J.S.M. & Hake, B. (eds.). *Leeds Studies in the Education of Adults, Proceedings of the Leiden Conference of Intercultural Adult Education,* 1992.

13751 Public construction of the status of teachers and teaching in Nigeria with special interest in vocational teachers: a case study of the Delta and Edo States of Nigeria.
GBR 1993
Research Date(s): 1990-1993
Nwaokolo, P.
Sup: Saunders, M.
Inst: Lancaster University, Department of Educational Research, Cartmel College, Bailrigg, Lancaster LA1 4YW, United Kingdom.
Fin: European Community.
Nigeria; teaching profession; teacher; teacher behaviour; teacher status
Nigeria; profession d'enseignant; enseignant; comportement de l'enseignant; statut de l'enseignant
PROJECT DESCRIPTION
This study arose following complaints as evidenced in the literature about poor public image and poor status of teachers in Nigeria. Its aim is to ascertain the extent of the problem, explore its nature and why it exists, with a view to proffering suggestions for the solution of the problem.
The enquiry was carried out as a case study of the Edo and Delta States of Nigeria between January 1991 and September 1992. A total of 171 teachers, student teachers, educational administrators, business and public administrators, professionals, clerks/artisans and typical village peasant farmers were interviewed in nine major towns of Edo and Delta States. A questionnaire was also administered on 150 subjects, mainly to teachers and student teachers. Its principal aim was to locate the teacher and the teaching profession on an occupational prestige ladder. Secondly, it aimed at identifying the social standing of the vocational teacher among colleagues in the same secondary school system. Data on the subject matter was also generated through documents, and more unobtrusive means such as monitoring radio commentaries and casual discussion with members of the public. Provisional results show that the poor status of teachers in Nigeria is traceable to unattractive conditions of service such as poor pay; salary irregularity; the unhelpful attitude of civil servants implementing policies that favour teachers; poor working environment; presence of a large number of unqualified teachers in the system; poor promotion, denial and/or delayed fringe benefits; and non-professionalisation of teaching. Other factors which are a consequence of the earlier ones include poor teacher dedication to duty and unimpressive appearance and attitude that portray teaching as synonymous with poverty.

39 AMERICA – AMERIQUE – AMERIKA

Die Nachhaltigkeit von Vorhaben der beruflichen Bildung (The permanence of vocational training projects)...................... see no. 11720

Die Wettbewerbsfaehigkeit der amerikanischen Wirtschaft und das System der beruflichen Bildung in den USA (The competitive capacity of American industry and the vocational training system in the USA) .... see no. 11722

Continuing education practice in Canada and the United Kingdom: a case study of Calgary and Leeds Universities .... see no. 12070

Towards the effective inclusive school.......................... see no. 12250

International recruiting of student-athletes by American universities .... see no. 12323

Science teaching: supporting effective teacher change...................... .... see no. 12614

An analysis of the sociolinguistics of the Creole-standard continuum and its relationship to education in a selected sample of secondary schools in Jamaica .... see no. 12799

Writing exchange across the Atlantic: a study of secondary school students' writing, exchanged with peers in London and the Bay Area, California .... see no. 12951

The nature of relationships between teachers' attitudes and beliefs about educational change in Bermuda and other personal, psychological and educational variables....................................... see no. 13266

Die politische Verarbeitung sozialstrukturell-lebensweltlichen Wandels und ethno-kulturelle Pluralisierung in Nordamerika insbesondere am Beispiel der Bildungspolitik (Political management of sociostructural change and ethno-cultural pluralization in North America, with particular reference to education policy) .... see no. 13438

Feminisation of teaching: a comparative study of Israel and Chile .... see no. 13475

Current developments in the preparation and support of principals in the United States.. see no. 13660

40 ASIA/MIDDLE EAST/OCEANIA – ASIE/MOYEN-ORIENT/OCEANIE – ASIEN/MITTELOST/OZEANIEN

13752 The conceptual ecology of 'health' and its significance for the science education system in Pakistan.
GBR 1993
Research Date(s): 1985-1991
Zufar, K.
Sup: Pope, M.
Inst: Surrey University, Department of Educational Studies, Guildford GU2 5XH, United Kingdom; Reading University, Faculty of Education and Community Studies, Bulmershe Court, Woodlands Avenue, Earley, Reading RG6 1HY, United Kingdom.
Pakistan; health education; science education; health; concept
Pakistan; éducation sanitaire; éducation scientifique; santé; concept
PROJECT DESCRIPTION
   This study deals with the conceptual ecology of science students of Pakistan, aged 15-17 years, and their teachers and parents. The concept of health was elicited from the students, their parents and their science teachers by using a technique called 'Interview about pictures'. This involved discussion about the instances and non-instances of health as depicted in line drawings on cards. The repertory grid technique was used to elicit the teachers' concepts of good teaching and various science teaching methods. A series of semi-structured interviews was conducted with parents, teachers, health educators, health personnel, religious leaders and community elders. The questions asked were about science and science education, health and health education, religious influence upon education, expectations, problems and suggested solutions. The teachers were selected to represent the male and female population and rural and urban backgrounds. They were also asked to complete an open-ended questionnaire at the end of the field work to ascertain feedback on the effects of the research methods in which they participated.

13753 Curriculum reform in Japanese art education: the case of multiculturalism.
GBR 1993
Research Date(s): 1989-1992
Iwano, M.
Sup: Mason, R.; Denscombe, M.
Inst: De Montford University, Department of Education, Centre for Postgraduate Teacher Education, Scraptoft Campus, Scraptoft, Leicester LE7 9SU, United Kingdom.
Japan; art education; cultural pluralism; intercultural education
Japon; éducation artistique; pluralisme culturel; éducation interculturelle
PROJECT DESCRIPTION

   This research will investigate, analyse and evaluate Japanese art curriculum at primary, secondary and high school levels. It will explore the possibility of curriculum reform in Japanese art education with reference to theory and practice of multicultural education. Since multicultural education has been applied in non-western societies, the study will aim also to identify key principles which might be taken into account or underpin an international concept and application of multicultural education.

13754 Educational resources allocation to primary schools in Saudi Arabia.
GBR 1993
Research Date(s): 1991-1994
Al-Bassam, A.
Sup: Richards, J.
Inst: University of Wales College of Cardiff, School of Education, Senghennydd Road, Cardiff CF2 4AG, United Kingdom.
Fin: Saudi Arabian Government.
Saudi Arabia; quality of education; primary school; resource allocation
Arabie Saoudite; qualité de l'éducation; école primaire; affectation des ressources
PROJECT DESCRIPTION
   This is an investigation into the sources of education resources to state primary schools in Saudi Arabia, and the relationship with school quality.

13755 Evaluation of the process of curriculum design of technical and vocational education in Hong Kong.
GBR 1993
Research Date(s): 1989-1993
Wong, K.
Sup: Morgan, W.; Shipstone, D.
Inst: Nottingham University, Department of Adult Education, Centre for Research into the Education of Adults, 14-22 Shakespeare Street, Nottingham NG1 4FJ, United Kingdom.
Hong Kong; vocational education; technical education; training-employment relationship; curriculum research
Hong-Kong; enseignement professionnel; enseignement technique; relation formation-emploi; recherche sur les programmes d'études
PROJECT DESCRIPTION
   An evaluation of the process of curriculum design in technical and vocational education in Hong Kong will be undertaken. Special reference will be made to the interaction between education, training, employment and economic outcomes. It is also intended to identify present and likely difficulties, and to suggest ways of linking technical and vocational education with the general education system in order to ensure an adequate supply of competent technical personnel for the 1990s and beyond 1997.

13756 An examination of the inter-relationship between the development of adult education, Gandhian philosophy, the Congress Party, and the legacy of the British Raj, in India between 1935 and 1955, and an analysis of subsequent developments in adult education in the period up to the 1980s.
GBR 1993
Research Date(s): 1989-1992
Taylor, R.; Steele, G.
Inst: Leeds University, Department of Adult Continuing Education, Leeds LS2 9JT, United Kingdom.
Fin: Universities Funding Council.
India; adult education; history of education
Inde; éducation des adultes; histoire de l'éducation
PROJECT DESCRIPTION
   This project concerns the influence of British cultural values, practices and structures on the development of adult education in India from the 1930s to the 1980s. British cultural legacy was not homogeneous, as with the industrial British society from which it sprang, its imperial strands were diverse and often conflicting. A major theme of the study will be to disentangle these various elements and to match them up both to the empirical development of adult education structures in India, and to the political dimensions of British culture in the UK. An essential concern will be the relationship between Gandhian philosophy and adult education development. Linked to this will be a study of the educational dimension to the emerging Congress Party as the dominant political force in India before, during and after Indian independence.

13757 Leadership training in Chinese adult education.
GBR 1993
Research Date(s): 1988-1993
Stephens, M.
Sup: Daines, J.; Graham, B.
Inst: Nottingham University, Department of Adult Education, 14-22 Shakespeare Street, Nottingham NG1 4FJ, United Kingdom.
Fin: Leverhulme Trust.
managerial staff; leadership; China; adult education
personnel d'encadrement; commandement; Chine; éducation des adultes
PROJECT DESCRIPTION

The Department of Adult Education at Nottingham University is helping to establish China's first institute of research and training in adult education at Jinan. Three members of staff have been seconded to Nottingham from Jinan for three years to train for leadership roles in Chinese adult education. They will read for Ph.D. degrees in adult education, review policy and practice throughout the United Kingdom, and the programme will be assessed in the final year of the research funding. This project is part of an interconnecting programme of initiatives.

13758 The provision of education in the middle school years in Cyprus.
GBR   1993
Research Date(s): 1983-1992
Constantinides, A.
Sup: Booth, I.
Inst: Durham University, School of Education, Leazes Road, Durham DH1 1TA, United Kingdom.
Cyprus; lower secondary; education system; educational provision
Chypre; secondaire premier cycle; système d'enseignement; scolarisation
PROJECT DESCRIPTION

The aim of this study is to examine the type of education offered during the middle school years in Cyprus. At first an attempt is made to define middle school years and relate this concept to the educational system of Cyprus and other countries. The history of education in Cyprus is briefly surveyed to set the background against which the Gymnasium, a distinct educational unit catering for the middle school years, has evolved and reached its present form. The aims, objectives, structure and content of the Gymnasium are examined in detail. The role of the Gymnasium within the educational system and the degree to which this role is successfully accomplished are investigated in two studies conducted among students and teachers of the Gymnasium. The results reveal that on the whole the role, content and time span of the Gymnasium are satisfactory. There is, however, a strong feeling that there is scope for improvement in the content of the curriculum in order to make it more effective. Finally, certain recent developments in the educational system of Cyprus and their implications for the future of the Gymnasium are discussed.

13759 The role and development of technical and vocational education in Qatar.
GBR   1993
Research Date(s): 1989-1992
Al-Marzooki, A.
Sup: Stoker, S.; Lawless, R.
Inst: Durham University, School of Education, Leazes Road, Durham DH1 1TA, United Kingdom.
Qatar; vocational education; technical education
Qatar; enseignement professionnel; enseignement technique
PROJECT DESCRIPTION

This research is examining the social, political and religious environment of Qatar in the context of its changing economic situation. It will also look at past policies of vocational education and training in Qatar in an attempt to assess the compatibility of such schemes with the country's manpower requirements and will pay special attention to the pace of industrialisation in Qatar.

13760 The role of foreign experts in the development of Chinese universities.
GBR   1993
Research Date(s): 1988-1992
Kai, J.
Sup: Morgan, W.; Stephens, M.
Inst: Nottingham University, Department of Adult Education, Centre for Research into the Education of Adults, 14-22 Shakespeare Street, Nottingham NG1 4FJ, United Kingdom.
Fin: British Council; Nottingham University.
China; university; development of education; foreign relations
Chine; université; développement de l'éducation; relations extérieures
PROJECT DESCRIPTION

The aims of this project are to: (1) evaluate the work that foreign experts have done in Chinese universities since 1978 when China adopted the open door policy; (2) measure the benefits of these undertakings for China's educational reform; and (3) assess the effect of recent policital changes.

13761 School education and young people in Japan.
GBR   1993
Research Date(s): 1987-1991
Simmons, C.
Inst: Loughborough University of Technology, Department of Education, Loughborough LE11 3TU, United Kingdom.
Japan; comparative research; cross-cultural research; pupil attitude; value; attitude towards school
Japon; recherche comparative; recherche transculturelle; attitude de l'élève; valeur; attitude envers l'école
PROJECT DESCRIPTION

This project compares the results of two surveys, the main aim of which was to portray what young people think, feel and believe about important aspects of their lives, using as evidence their own written statements. The subjects comprised 820 fifteen-year-olds in six schools in England in 1981 and 283 fourteen-year-olds at two schools in Japan in 1986. The open-ended questionnaire comprised ten prompts designed to elicit responses concerning ideals and least ideals, most and least preferred companions, use of solitude, summum bonum, most and least desired outcomes to life and nascent philosophies. Two methods of analysis were used. First, references to dominant themes were totalled; second, responses were assigned to six categories according to the dominant values expressed from materialistic to altruistic.

Similarities but also significant differences were found in the dominant themes and significant differences were also apparent between the values expressed by the two samples. Most marked was the tendency for the Japanese sample to place a higher valuation on education than the English but to express less regard for their parents and family.
Publ: Simmons, C.V. *Some comparisons between English and Japanese young people: a report on two surveys.* Research Report 15. Tokyo: National Institute for Educational Research, 1987.
Simmons, C.V. & Wade, W. Contrasting attitudes to education in England and Japan. In: *Educational Research*, Vol 30, No 2/1988, pp. 146-152.

13762 School education and young people in Saudi Arabia.
GBR   1993
Research Date(s): 1991-1993
Simmons, C.
Inst: Loughborough University of Technology, Department of Education, Loughborough LE11 3TU, United Kingdom.
Saudi Arabia; comparative research; cross-cultural research; pupil attitude; value
Arabie Saoudite; recherche comparative; recherche transculturelle; attitude de l'élève; valeur
PROJECT DESCRIPTION

This project compares the results of two surveys, the main aim of which was to portray what young people think, feel and believe about important aspects of their lives, using as evidence own written statements. The subjects comprised 89 Saudi Arabian and 107 English adolescents aged between 13 and 15 years. The open-ended questionnaire comprised ten prompts designed to elicit responses concerning ideals and least ideals, most and least preferred companions, use of solitude, summun bonum, most and least desired outcomes to life and nascent philosophies. Two methods of analysis were used. First, references to dominant themes were totalled; second, responses were assigned to six categories according to the dominant values expressed from materialistic to altruistic.

Significant differences were found in the dominant themes and between the values expressed by the two samples. Most marked were the pervasive religious values in the Saudi Arabian sample and the absence of these in the English sample.

13763 Women and education in Nepal.
GBR   1993
Research Date(s): 1988-1993
Saunders, K.
Sup: Aspinall, M.
Inst: University of Wales College of Cardiff, School of Education, 42 Park Place, Cardiff CF1 3BB, United Kingdom.
Nepal; women's education; equal opportunity; educational policy
Népal; éducation des femmes; égalité de chances; politique de l'éducation
PROJECT DESCRIPTION

The study examines teacher education and the structure of education in Nepal and questions whether policies will lead to equality in education and employment opportunities for girls and women. The research, spanning the years 1988-1990, investigates the situation of female teachers living in Karnali Zone, a remote mountainous region of Mid-West Nepal. In addition, the lives of young girls from the Karnali area are highlighted. Restrictions in attendance at full-time formal school and the introduction of non-formal classes to meet the educational needs of 'out-of-school' girls are discussed.

The researcher argues that traditional structures can obstruct equality and suggests that development agencies and educational policy makers sometimes perpetuate the status quo of inequality.

Making efficient use of microcomputers in teaching mathematics to gifted children in the Jordanian primary schools .... see no. 11777

The use of microcomputers in Saudi secondary schools ....
.... **see no. 11830**

Access to higher education in Xinjiang Uyghur Autonomous Region, China, 1949-1987 .... **see no. 11904**

Abstimmung und Steuerung von Bildung und Beschaeftigung in Japan (im Rahmen des Projektverbundes: Wechselbeziehungen zwischen Bildungs- und Beschaeftigungssystem in Japan in vergleichender Perspektive) (Coordination and control of education and employment in Japan (as part of the series of projects: "Interrela-

41 EUROPE – EUROPE – EUROPA

13764 Musisch interkulturelle Erziehung in Europa. (Intercultural education in the fine arts in Europe.)
DEU 1993
Research Date(s): 1990-1996
Boehle, R.
Inst: Hochschule der Kuenste Berlin, FB 08 Musikerziehung und Musikwissenschaft, Fasanenstr. 1b, D-1000 Berlin 12.
intercultural education; music; Europe; general education; didactics; model
éducation interculturelle; musique; Europe; enseignement général; didactique; modèle
PROJECT DESCRIPTION
Inhalt: Erstellung eines didaktischen Modells zur Musikerziehung in allgemeinbildenden Schulen.
Geographischer Raum: Europa.

13765 United Kingdom professions and the European challenge.
GBR 1993
Research Date(s): 1990-1993
Todd, F.; Neale, P.
Inst: Leeds University, Department of Continuing Professional Education, Leeds LS2 9JT, United Kingdom.
Fin: Universities Funding Council.
European community; directive (European Communities); occupational qualification; professional association
Communauté européenne; directive (Communauté européenne); qualification professionnelle; association professionnelle
PROJECT DESCRIPTION
This research arises out of the European Community Directive on rights of establishment which was implemented from 1991, together with the various sectoral directives already in force. Professional groups in the United Kingdom are faced with the need to develop new policies, practices and requirements in regard to Europe. These formal and public moves are being made in the context of changing attitudes toward the Directive, and complex developments in cross-national working relations between partner professional institutions and their members.
This is a three year, real-time study of British professionals, their employers and their institutions in a period of change. It is examining the extent and nature of the links being established with other professional organisations within the European Community to analyse developing policies and practices towards Europe and how these might be affected by cross-national working relations. An assessment will be made of the implications for continuing professional education.
The first phase of this project has been a comprehensive study of the 77 professional institutions whose members are affected by the First General Directive on the Mutual Recognition of Qualifications. The response rate to this recently completed exercise has been 70%.
The second phase will involve a series of case studies of selected professional institutions and particular issues raised by the professions' response to Europe.
The preliminary computer data analysis suggests that the advent of the single European market is not as significant as one might have predicted for all the professions surveyed. Many have taken an international stand on their professional activities on behalf of their members for a substantial number of years. Nonetheless, professional institutions are aware of the opportunities and problems that may arise for their practitioners in the next few years and they are becoming increasingly active on behalf of their members, and of the publics they serve.

42   REGIONS – REGIONS – REGIONEN

13766   Social and psychological adjustment of educated married women in Mauritius.
GBR   1993
Research Date(s): 1987-1993
Gukhool, P.
Sup: Aspinall, M.
Inst: University of Wales College of Cardiff, School of Education, 42 Park Place, Cardiff CF1 3BB, United Kingdom.
Mauritius; attitude; women's employment; equal opportunity; women's education
Île Maurice; attitude; emploi des femmes; égalité de chances; éducation des femmes
PROJECT DESCRIPTION
The work concerns a study of the attitudes towards, and difficulties encountered by, educated working women in Mauritius. The investigation involved participatory observation, questionnaire and in-depth questioning of some of the 120 respondents. These were women representing the different racial groups in Mauritius with the emphasis being upon those whose ancestors came from the Indian Sub-Continent, as for historic reasons family attitudes towards their participation in professional work has been slowest to change.

Whilst it is being established that attitudes are changing, women are still meeting family and male hostility.

Index of names
Index des noms cités

Subject index

An examination of the factors that promote the development of an integrated child care strategy. EN 13731

child psychiatry
Locus of control beliefs in children with emotional and behavioural difficulties: an exploratory study. EN 12770

child psychology
Psychological aspects of children and physical activity. EN 12604

childhood
Children and television. EN 13045

children's literature
Anti-racism and children's literature. EN 12973
Group textual study of fiction in primary school. EN 12980

Chile
Feminisation of teaching: a comparative study of Israel and Chile. EN 13475
The transition to democracy and educational change in contemporary Chile and post-Franco Spain. EN 12018

China
Access to higher education in Xinjiang Uyghur Autonomous Region, China, 1949-1987. EN 11904
Adult education in the United Kingdom and China. EN 12035
Comparative research on career guidance between Britain and China. EN 13550
A comparison of the main concepts in the philosophy of education used in Britain and China. EN 12956
Education and the family in Taiwan and China. EN 13481
Education and training of property valuers in China. EN 13490
Emotivism, prescriptivism and moral education. EN 12551
Enterprising higher education: links between higher education institutions and industrial, commercial sectors. EN 13392
Leadership training in Chinese adult education. EN 13757
The role of foreign experts in the development of Chinese universities. EN 13760

Chinese language
Teaching and testing Japanese and similar languages in schools. EN 12934

choice of school
Motives determining choice of school in the transfer from primary to secondary education. EN 12347
Parental choice of school. EN 12339
Parents and National Curriculum: criteria of parental choice of primary school. EN 12340
Pedagogic knowledge in everyday life: an exploratory study on parents' use of pedagogic knowledge, with particular reference to school choice. DE 13193
School career decisions in the fourth year (a follow-up survey among parents in Graz). DE 12290
School-home collaboration in pupil guidance. EN 12274

choice of studies
Accès des bacheliers à l'enseignement supérieur. FR 11902
Choice of further studies at the end of compulsory education. EN 13169
Determinants of individual differences in educational choice and success. EN 13216
Evaluation of an educational and vocational guidance initiative in compulsory school. EN 13612
Intérêts et choix de filière post baccalauréat. FR 13224
Labour market information and labour market dynamics. EN 13524
Labour market information and labour market dynamics. EN 13530
Microscopic school career research phase 2. EN 13227
La première année de psychologie-sociologie à l'Université de Bourgogne. FR 13234
School-home collaboration in pupil guidance. EN 12274
Student supply and the expansion of Arabic studies in higher education. EN 12928
Survey of older graduates. EN 13635
Une approche multimédia pour l'orientation scolaire et professionnelle. FR 12020
Women opting for a mathematically, scientifically or technically oriented course of studies and their educational background. DE 13241
Youth and Technology. EN 13183

choice of training
Comparison of further vocational training courses to facilitate choice of training. DE 12301

Christian education
Church schools in an urban environment. EN 13418
Church, State and education: a study of the educational philosophy of Henry Edward Manning, 1865-1992. EN 12749
Developmental concepts of Christianity in a person with a mental handicap. EN 13122
Economy, education and ecumenism 1931-1984. EN 12292
A theological critique of Christian education, with special reference to developments in Northern Ireland since 1944. EN 12629

Christianity
Measurement of attitudes towards Christianity. EN 13006
Monitoring attitudes towards Christianity among secondary school pupils in England. EN 13190

church
Church schools in an urban environment. EN 13418
The contribution of the church to the coexistence of Slovenian and German ethnic groups in Carinthia: intercultural communication in a Christian context. DE 13386
Economy, education and ecumenism 1931-1984. EN 12292
Education for senior citizens in a church setting (Schleswig-Holstein). DE 11808
The educational influence of the Methodist church in the second half of the 19th century (1850-1902). EN 12958
The influence of Church of England secondary schools on adolescents' attitudes towards the Church. EN 13262
The interface of feminism, education and the Church: a study of power. EN 13421
Protestant adult education in urban and rural communities. DE 11750
The role of the Church of England in the provision of education at Worfield Endowed Church of England (Aided) Primary School from 1546 to 1991 in the light of the 1988 Education Reform Act with particular reference to the governors' responsibility for curriculum, funding and building. EN 12783

citizen participation
Active citizenship and adult learning. EN 13243
Citizenship and education. EN 13249
Citizenship project. EN 12533
Emergent environmentalism: subject knowledge and concern for the environment. EN 13443
Global futures project. EN 12760
Insertion sociale et citoyenneté: une étude longitudinale auprès des 18-25 ans. FR 13182
Pédagogie du militantisme dans les mouvements de jeunesse. FR 13423
The role of education for citizenship with reference to Zambia. EN 13272

civics
The beginnings of reorientation in political education in the GDR 1989/1990. DE 11719
Citizenship education in lower secondary schools. EN 12634
Global futures project. EN 12760
History in school: possibilities for the development of knowledge, civic consciousness, morality and creativity in pupils and students. EN 12763
Verification of the need for two hours of civics teaching in lower secondary schools. EN 12594

civil engineering
Education and the labour market for civil engineers. EN 13610

civilization
Culture and civilisation studies for advanced language learners - an experiment in French and English schools. EN 12826

class management
Behavioural approach to teaching project. EN 13248
Discipline in Scottish schools. EN 13254
Information systems to support teaching and classroom management. EN 12686
The Leverhulme Primary Project. EN 12157
Management in the primary school class. EN 11778
The place of reflection in teachers' processes of change. EN 13233

class size
Language learning in large classes research project. EN 12882
Teaching strategies in heterogeneous classes - ideals and realities. EN 11826

classification
What dimensions are used to describe special educational needs? EN 13039

classroom
Life in post-compulsory classrooms. EN 12159

classroom arrangement
Changes in the classroom experience of Inner London pupils. EN 11919

clerical worker
Typists and electronic word processing. DE 13628

coeducational school
Exploring the gender gap in primary schools. EN 12112
Women opting for a mathematically, scientifically or technically oriented course of studies and their educational background. DE 13241

cognition
Cognitive structures and language skills in vocational training. EN 11882
The development of spatial awareness in children with physical handicaps, particularly those integrated in mainstream schools. EN 13120
Independent work of children and cognitive processes in primary school. EN 13154
Reading, listening and television viewing: a study in children's cognition. EN 13152
Studies of Attention Disordered - Hyperactive (ADHD) children. EN 13157

cognitive ability
Confirmatory study and teaching experiment for overcoming difficulties in complex texts in primary years 3 and 5. DE 11773
Construct validation of the learning test concept through studies of complex problem solving (acronym: KOVALT). DE 13004
Extent and correlates of variability among different groups of readers. EN 12859
The inter-relationship of cognitive abilities, attitudes, social interaction and performance in early logo learning. EN 13263
Memory, intelligence and talent. EN 13187
On the representation of metacognitive areas of knowledge in long-term memory with particular reference to the semantics of verbs concerning mental activities. DE 13165
Primary school pupils' ability to understand tables and schematic drawings. DE 11690
Reading factual texts and communicative use of the result. DE 12886
The role of cognition in psychomotor activities. EN 13088
Stimulation and support of learning processes in illiterate adults working with computers. DE 11910
Studies of Attention Disordered - Hyperactive (ADHD) children. EN 13157
A study of achievement motivation, with particular reference to cognitive components. DE 13226
Suggestions for a CNC turning course as the outcome of a pilot project and CNC learning material for basic and further training. DE 11756
Training and promotion of technical creativity among gifted young people at the intermediate secondary school level. DE 11715

cognitive development
Acquisition des connaissances à partir du texte. FR 13106
Children's development of number competence. EN 13111
Children's perception of pitch relationships. EN 12532
Cognitive assessment of maladjusted children. EN 12371
Cognitive impairments in children with arithmetical learning disabilities. EN 11854
Cognitive structures and language skills in vocational training. EN 11882
Day care and later development. EN 12072
Determining the entry-level characteristics of primary school pupils. EN 13060
The development of causal reasoning. EN 13067
Didactique de l'informatique. FR 12663
Independent work of children and cognitive processes in primary school. EN 13154
Investigation of the development of social cognition and the subsequent effectiveness of cognitive curricular approaches to meeting individual needs. EN 13135
An investigation of the relationship between perinatal risk factors and contingency learning and attentive behaviour in later infancy. EN 13084
Longitudinal investigation of cognitive development and educational achievement in blind and partially sighted children. EN 13344
Mathematics - shape & space: mathematics & art. EN 13140
Memory, intelligence and talent. EN 13187
Prise en compte du partenaire dans les interactions de co-résolution. FR 13096
Processus d'acquisition étudié sous l'angle de la structuration de l'espace-problème. FR 13146

Le développement de la motivation à la réussite scolaire: premières approches. FR 13217

Models of the primary teacher in use in primary B.Ed. courses. EN 12170

Place des humanités dans la formation médicale en Europe. FR 12711

craft

Assessment of Performance Unit in design and technology: aimed at monitoring the performance of 15 year old pupils in design and technology. EN 12365

creative activities

The effects of information technology on the sequencing and development of concept acquisition, particularly in open-ended, creative situations. EN 11727

creativity

Development of a counselling and support programme for technically highly creative young people. DE 12667

Health psychology: theoretical models of normalcy and health, mechanisms of health and health behaviour. EN 13195

Identifying gifted pupils. EN 13230

Preparation of students in pedagogical faculties for creative work and attempts at innovation. EN 12198

Studies of Attention Disordered - Hyperactive (ADHD) children. EN 13157

Training and promotion of technical creativity among gifted young people at the intermediate secondary school level. DE 11715

credits

Evaluation of the second year of the Training Credits pilot: three case studies. EN 11748

La qualité du dispositif rénové de formation professionnelle continue en agriculture. FR 12002

Work-based learning for academic credit. EN 11841

creole

An analysis of the sociolinguistics of the Creole-standard continuum and its relationship to education in a selected sample of secondary schools in Jamaica. EN 12799

crisis of education

L'impact de la crise économique sur les systèmes éducatifs. FR 12320

criterion-referenced evaluation

Evaluation of the new report card during the trial period 1989-1990. EN 12462

Graded criterion-referenced measurement: using curricular standards for grading achievement. EN 12434

criterion-referenced test

Graded criterion-referenced measurement: using curricular standards for grading achievement. EN 12434

critical sense

Anglia Polytechnic University critical studies project. EN 12972

Critical activity and its effect on the art and design curriculum. EN 12537

La formation du sens critique chez l'enfant et la construction du lien politique. FR 13075

Improving the quality of argument: schools. EN 13132

Improving the quality of argument: sixth forms and higher education. EN 13133

An inquiry into the role of skills in education. EN 13181

cross-cultural research

Children's reading comprehension: self-image, attainments and attitudes. A cross-cultural study. EN 12812

Interpersonal behaviour on children's TV programmes: an intercultural comparison Vienna - Belgrade. DE 13473

School education and young people in Japan. EN 13761

School education and young people in Saudi Arabia. EN 13762

cross-national research

Active citizenship and adult learning. EN 13243

Adolescence in Europe: accepted values and life perspectives of Polish adolescents. EN 13458

Analysis of foreign experiences in dealing with problem situations in higher education. EN 12041

Anti-bullying strategies. EN 13246

Comparaisons des inégalités sociales de scolarisation dans quatre pays européens et en France au cours des trente dernières années. FR 11922

Comparative studies of educational management in Russia and the Baltic republics. EN 12324

Comparative study of disruptive behaviour and discipline in schools in the United Kingdom and Kenya. EN 13250

A comparative study of student youth social and political lifestyles in Hungary and England. EN 12750

Comparative study on the teaching of information technology in compulsory schools in Italy, France and England. EN 11804

Coût et financement de l'enseignement supérieur en France. FR 12276

Cultural stereotypes in language learning. EN 12926

Culture and civilisation studies for advanced language learners - an experiment in French and English schools. EN 12826

The demotivated pupil in the modern language classroom - a comparative study. EN 12831

Education for international understanding through foreign language teaching: a German - British collaborative project. EN 12836

The effectiveness of new curriculum models for initial vocational training. EN 11726

Emploi et formation dans les processus de développement économique. FR 13568

Environmental training policy. EN 13445

Equality versus quality: the dilemma of primary schools in today's Europe. EN 11975

Ethnicité et multilinguisme: recherche fondamentale dans le domaine de la pédagogie interculturelle. DE 11947

Examination and evaluation of approaches to textbook production under free market conditions. EN 13054

The Freinet Movement in its international context. EN 11953

Government intervention and policy change in higher education: a comparative study. Stage 1. EN 13733

History in school: possibilities for the development of knowledge, civic consciousness, morality and creativity in pupils and students. EN 12763

The IEA international reading literacy study in Ireland. EN 12402

The IEA Third International Mathematics and Science Study in Ireland. EN 12403

International comparison of equal opportunities policies in education with particular reference to school policies. EN 11967

International education in international schools: developing a consensus of opinion. EN 12139

International group for the study of language standardisation and the vernacularisation of literacy. EN 13504

Interpersonal behaviour on children's TV programmes: an intercultural comparison Vienna - Belgrade. DE 13473

The language learning experiences of Somalis and Eritreans in Britain and Italy. EN 12881

Learners' language. EN 12884

Législation de la jeunesse et institutions aujourd'hui: recherche comparative internationale. FR 13737

Management and organisation of teaching 'The European Dimension' in schools (International network with representatives from The Netherlands, Belgium, Germany, Greece and Denmark). EN 12584

Models and theories of self-regulation in higher education: a multi-national study. EN 12418

Models of effective management in schools. EN 12334

The motivation of mathematics student teachers. DE 13228

Occupational profiles of vocational counsellors. EN 13685

The pedagogical knowledge base in teacher education. EN 12183

Perceptions of children with special educational needs. EN 13353

PINGIST PINKI: normative orientations for teacher trainers and teachers. DE 11887

Policy and practice in multicultural education in Canada and Great Britain. EN 11994

Professional bodies: education and training and the labour market. EN 12196

Reading standards in a local education authority: 1976-1991. EN 12906

Reducing the cost of technical and vocational education. EN 12343

The role of the workplace in the work experience triangle with particular reference to transferable skills. EN 11806

Second International Assessment of Educational Progress (IAEP2). EN 12446

Secondary school pupils' attitudes towards mental disability in Ireland, Australia, Finland and Germany. DE 13174

Sociolinguistic factors affecting attitudes and motivation in foreign language learning at school: an Anglo-French comparative study. EN 13201

Special needs in the classroom. EN 12220

Teachers' pay and bargaining machinery in four European countries. EN 13513

Teaching foreign languages at primary level. EN 12936

Textbook evaluation in different countries. DE 13047

Third International Mathematics and Science Study (TIMSS). EN 12661

The use of microcomputers in British schools, the implications for their use in Turkish schools and the improvement of computer-assisted learning in Turkish schools. EN 11829

The use of outdoor pursuits in schools in England and France. EN 12518

Values education in Europe. EN 12971

Work socialisation of youth (WOSY): a cross-national study. EN 13644

Writing exchange across the Atlantic: a study of secondary school students' writing, exchanged with peers in London and the Bay Area, California. EN 12951

cultural change

Mathematics in further education. DE 12706

Political management of sociostructural change and ethno-cultural pluralization in North America, with particular reference to education policy. DE 13438

cultural environment

Between two worlds: the cultural behaviour of young migrants in Vienna with particular reference to music. DE 13472

Children of migrant workers and their musical behaviour. DE 13456

Interaction between the school and the cultural environment for the education of the pupils. EN 13450

Intergenerational changes in the teaching profession in the 1990s in Poland. EN 13708

A study of the perceptions and responses of young women of South Asian origin to a single-sex access Youth Training Scheme. EN 13465

cultural exchange

Inter-cultural meetings on language trips to England for young people. DE 11966

Interaction between the school and the cultural environment for the education of the pupils. EN 13450

cultural identity

Bilinguisme, immigration et scolarisation. FR 12811

Institutional ethos. EN 12138

Social identity in adolescence. EN 13412

cultural integration

The multicultural challenge and the educational system. EN 13411

Multicultural education: images at primary level. EN 11987

cultural pattern

Interpersonal behaviour on children's TV programmes: an intercultural comparison Vienna - Belgrade. DE 13473

cultural pluralism

Adolescents' responses to short stories as representations of other cultures. EN 13428

Curriculum reform in Japanese art education: the case of multiculturalism. EN 13753

Expanding horizons: multicultural and international education in the South West of England. EN 11950

Political management of sociostructural change and ethno-cultural pluralization in North America, with particular reference to education policy. DE 13438

cultural policy

International symposium of the Working Group of Austrian Music Teachers on "Music and education". DE 12575

culture

Conditions and obstacles in democratic culture, politics, science and education in the GDR. DE 13727

Constructing culture: a study of teacher-pupil talk in French language lessons. EN 12824

Cultural stereotypes in language learning. EN 12926

Cultural studies in advanced language learning: the year abroad in under-graduate courses. EN 13435

Culture and civilisation studies for advanced language learners - an experiment in French and English schools. EN 12826

The curriculum as culture and ideology. EN 12957

Education for international understanding through foreign language teaching: a German - British collaborative project. EN 12836

The effect of art education in secondary school on cultural participation later in life: a preliminary study. EN 12633

Interaction between the school and the cultural environment for the education of the pupils. EN 13450

Sport for all in education: an inquiry into PE and sport in schools, what constitutes good practice and its

youth homes and in vocational guidance for young people. DE 12515

Suggestions for a CNC turning course as the outcome of a pilot project and CNC learning material for basic and further training. DE 11756

Unequal opportunities: a review. EN 13459

developed country

Emploi et formation dans les processus de développement économique. FR 13568

School management in conditions of stringency. EN 12346

developing country

Apprenticeship training in Nigeria. DE 11774

Cost-benefit analysis in education. EN 12995

Education for sustainable development in the Third World. EN 13389

Educational management in developing countries. EN 12294

Emploi et formation dans les processus de développement économique. FR 13568

Equity aspects of training policy. EN 11945

Financial management in education. EN 12312

The identification of the feasibility of the preparation of Master of Arts (MA) Dissertations in distance mode in developing countries. EN 12127

International group for the study of language standardisation and the vernacularisation of literacy. EN 13504

An investigation into the difficulties of introducing innovation in English language teaching in developing countries. EN 12877

The permanence of vocational training projects. DE 11720

Prévision des dépenses d'éducation primaire à l'horizon 2000 dans les pays en développement. FR 13508

Reducing the cost of technical and vocational education. EN 12343

Rural social development: education, literacy and organisation in the Third World. EN 13509

School management in conditions of stringency. EN 12346

development aid

Education for sustainable development in the Third World. EN 13389

The evaluation of the management of English Language Teaching (ELT) overseas aid projects. EN 12856

The permanence of vocational training projects. DE 11720

development of education

Construction and use of communication and information technology teaching aids in primary and secondary schools. EN 12737

Demographic change and the loss of resources in the education system. EN 12309

Development of education in the Czech and Slovak Federal Republic in the period 1991-1992. EN 12006

The development of primary and secondary education: analysis and prognosis. EN 12045

Development of the educational level of the population in the Slovak Republic by the year 2000. EN 12021

Education in the United Arab Emirates: an examination of selected themes and issues with reference to the 'small country' context. EN 12293

The future of education in a renewed democratic society and a united Europe. EN 11917

Historical analysis of the development of higher education in Russia. EN 12762

Identification and evaluation of innovatory curriculum development approaches in higher education. EN 11959

Impact of school development plans in primary schools. EN 13734

Improving the quality of education for all. EN 11965

An investigation into parent-teacher association activities and their effectiveness in secondary schools in Kwara State, Nigeria. EN 13422

Managing the implementation of the National Curriculum. EN 12332

Organization and economic foundations for the development of scientific technical education. EN 12179

Recommendations for state policy in the field of informatization of higher education in Russia. EN 13028

Research on the pilot project 'A study circle in Upper Austria'. DE 12051

The role of foreign experts in the development of Chinese universities. EN 13760

School as an instrument in the education of the young generation. EN 12012

developmental psychology

Critical assessment: Jean Piaget. EN 13065

Memory, intelligence and talent. EN 13187

deviant behaviour

Abnormal behaviour. What to do? DE 13280

Alternative forms of education aiming at the social adjustment of youth in the 14-17 age range. EN 13244

Care for children with learning and behavioural difficulties. EN 11873

Les Centres médico-psycho-pédagogiques (CMPP), 1945-1975. FR 13283

The contribution of physical education to the re-education of disruptive youth. EN 13269

Des arcanes du placement institutionnel à l'avènement de la juridiction des mineurs. FR 13252

Further education for police personnel on the subject of violence against women. DE 13732

Problem girls. EN 13270

The relationship between school size and problem behaviour among secondary school pupils. EN 13273

diagnosis

Care for children with learning and behavioural difficulties. EN 11873

diagnostic test

The assessment of children with emotional and behavioural difficulties (EBD). EN 13298

A diagnostic resource for technology. EN 12385

Meeting the needs of children with emotional and behavioural disorders. EN 13346

A pilot study to test a programme for training nursery school children to attend to the sounds in words. EN 12902

Standardization of a screening test of Greek-Cypriot speech and language. EN 12451

diagram

Primary school pupils' ability to understand tables and schematic drawings. DE 11690

dialect

An analysis of the sociolinguistics of the Creole-standard continuum and its relationship to education in a selected sample of secondary schools in Jamaica. EN 12799

A new dialect in a new city: children's and adults' speech in Milton Keynes. EN 12893

Perspectives d'une didactique de l'allemand pour la Suisse alémanique. DE 12899

Strategies leading to the use of non-standard language patterns. DE 12927

La Suisse alémanique entre le dialecte et la langue standard: attitudes linguistiques de jeunnes Suisses alémaniques et Romands. DE 12828

dialogue

Acquisition et gestion de la conduite de dialogue: la construction des finalités à travers le dialogue. FR 13058

Dialogisme et déplacement. FR 12834

Dialogue corporel et verbal. FR 12835

diction

Standardization of a screening test of Greek-Cypriot speech and language. EN 12451

dictionary

Composition of Estonian educational and psychological terminology and a comparative analysis with English, German, Russian and Finnish terminology. EN 12838

didactic continuity

The differences in teaching and learning styles employed in primary and secondary schools with reference to developing information technology capability. EN 12664

Local education authority support for continuity and progression in the 5-16 curriculum. EN 11978

didactic use of computer

Acquisition des connaissances à partir du texte. FR 13106

Adapting tutoring systems to students' learning styles. EN 11684

An alternative metaphor for teaching control technology. EN 12639

Cabri geometry. EN 12645

CD ROM as a curriculum delivery medium for blind and partially sighted learners. EN 13301

Children's thinking and understanding in history, with special reference to the role of computer-assisted learning (CAL). EN 12748

Classroom-based multimedia authoring tools. EN 11696

Comparative study on the teaching of information technology in compulsory schools in Italy, France and England. EN 11804

"CompReha": computer-aided teaching for rehabilitation. DE 11700

Computer-aided recognition of misconceptions about simple electrical circuits. EN 13117

Computer applications to special education. EN 12653

Computer-assisted learning in the teaching of reading. EN 11701

Computer-based modelling across the curriculum. EN 11702

Computer conferencing in distance education. EN 13021

Computers in nursery schools. EN 11706

Computers in teaching history. EN 11707

Computing in physical education. EN 11708

The construction of dynamic documents by children. EN 11709

The creation of interactive instructional programs for multimedia systems. EN 11823

Database support for multi-media computer-assisted learning. EN 12659

Design guidelines for electronic books. EN 12474

Design of Electronic Performance Support Systems. EN 11711

The development and evaluation of online computer-assisted language learning materials for English for academic purposes. EN 12833

Development of an extended concept of learning tasks for experience-based activities in computer-aided work. DE 11733

Development of complex educational contents. DE 11862

Devon Music Technology Project. EN 12541

Didactique de l'informatique en pédagogie curative. DE 11704

DISCOURSE: Design & Interactive Specification of Courseware. EN 11723

Distributed knowledge-based CBT. DE 11834

Education and training of property valuers in China. EN 13490

The effects of information technology on the sequencing and development of concept acquisition, particularly in open-ended, creative situations. EN 11727

End-user interfaces to electronic books. EN 12476

The Esprit project. EN 12669

An evaluation of home computers in adult distance education. EN 11746

Exeter Music Technology Project. EN 12563

Features of powerful learning environments. EN 11772

Feedback: its effects on procedural and conceptual knowledge for problem solving strategies. EN 11752

Feedback, peer interaction and adult intervention in initial logo learning. EN 11863

Le fonctionnement des sujets comme récepteurs actifs de messages médiatisés: approche cognitive et psycho-sociale. FR 12861

Gap between arithmetical and algebraic thinking. EN 13130

Gender differences in educational computing in the humanities. EN 11755

Group work with computers. EN 11864

How do computers best help children and adults to overcome learning difficulties? EN 11867

Human-computer interfaces to reactive graphical images. EN 11759

Humanities and information technology (Extension). EN 12680

Iconic model maker. EN 12682

Improving methods of teaching and learning swimming. EN 11825

Information technology and the learning needs of emotionally and behaviourally disturbed children. EN 13326

Information technology development programme for teachers. EN 12687

Information technology in initial teacher training. EN 12689

Information technology in language teaching. EN 12734

The information technology in mathematics project. EN 12690

L'informatique au service des jeunes en formation professionnelle élémentaire. FR 12135

Informatique et formation: les nouvelles technologies de l'information (NTI). FR 11763

Intégration de l'outil informatique dans l'enseignement des disciplines. FR 11765

Integration of computer and video in the teaching process. EN 12693

The inter-relationship of cognitive abilities, attitudes, social interaction and performance in early logo learning. EN 13263

Interactive problem-solving environments. EN 12640

Interactive video project for the hearing impaired. EN 13024

Economic knowledge of secondary school leavers. DE 12635

Polytechnic students two years after graduation: empirical analysis of their destination and career start. DE 13578

The science and didactics of business management. DE 12745

Teacher Training for Economic Awareness. EN 12624

Teacher Training for Economic Awareness: Welsh extension. EN 12625

La transmission et l'appropriation des connaissances dans les domaines de l'économie, de la physique et des mathématiques: le fonctionnement des connaissances chez l'apprenant. FR 12736

University studies as a factor for success. DE 11740

Use of case studies and management games in the economic departments of technical colleges. DE 11730

economics of education

Attitudes towards 'economic course' provision in the public further education sector. EN 12271

A conceptual model for the functioning of higher education during the transition to a market economy. EN 12275

Cost-benefit analysis in education. EN 12995

Demographic change and the loss of resources in the education system. EN 12309

Economic decision-making models on non-advanced further education. EN 12291

Economy, education and ecumenism 1931-1984. EN 12292

The effects of the Education Reform Act 1988: formula funding of schools. EN 12298

Evolution du système productif et appropriation des nouvelles technologies de formation. FR 13498

Financial management in education. EN 12312

Funding for special educational needs - post-school provision. EN 13501

The funding of schools after the 1988 Education Reform Act. EN 12315

Investment appraisal of Education Support Grant XXX for the training of youth leaders in the inner cities in England and in the valleys in Wales. EN 13505

Local management in schools: the three year review. EN 12326

Modèles et problématiques de la reconversion. FR 13603

Monitoring and evaluation of new funding mechanisms in higher education. EN 12336

The new government and management of education. EN 11990

Organization and economic foundations for the development of scientific technical education. EN 12179

Resourcing Sheffield schools. EN 12344

Reviewing the economic benefits of careers guidance. EN 13624

educability

The attitudes of pupils in the Ankara Vocational School for Educable Mentally Retarded Children towards vocational education. EN 13296

education budget

Analyse comparative des systèmes scolaires des pays d'Asie. FR 12039

La comparaison des systèmes d'enseignement supérieur français et espagnol. FR 12062

Cost-benefit analysis in education. EN 12995

Coût et financement de l'enseignement supérieur en France. FR 12276

Les coûts de l'enseignement pré-scolaire au Brésil. FR 12277

Coûts et efficacité dans l'enseignement supérieur malien. FR 12278

Les dépenses publiques pour l'enseignement universitaire et le taux de rendement fiscal. FR 12285

English local education authorities' schemes of local financial management. EN 13492

Le financement de l'enseignement post-obligatoire. FR 12310

Le financement de l'enseignement supérieur espagnol. FR 12311

Financial management in education. EN 12312

Funding for special educational needs - post-school provision. EN 13501

The funding of schools after the 1988 Education Reform Act. EN 12315

L'impact de la crise économique sur les systèmes éducatifs. FR 12320

Proposal for the allocation of resources to higher education institutes in the Slovak Republic for 1993. EN 13506

Resourcing Sheffield schools. EN 12344

School management in conditions of stringency. EN 12346

education system

Analyse comparative des systèmes scolaires des pays d'Asie. FR 12039

Analysis of the demand for education and the functioning of the education system. EN 11909

Bibliography of Scottish education 1970-1990. EN 13043

La comparaison des systèmes d'enseignement supérieur français et espagnol. FR 12062

Comparaisons des inégalités sociales de scolarisation dans quatre pays européens et en France au cours des trente dernières années. FR 11922

Comparison of schools in the Federal Republic of Germany and the Soviet Union. DE 12217

The competitive capacity of American industry and the vocational training system in the USA. DE 11722

Coordination and control of education and employment in Japan (as part of the series of projects: "Interrelationships between education and employment systems in Japan, a comparative view"). DE 12029

Developing models of educational accountability. EN 11929

Development of education in the Czech and Slovak Federal Republic in the period 1991-1992. EN 12006

The development of primary and secondary education: analysis and prognosis. EN 12045

The education system in England and Wales. EN 11935

Elaboration of didactic aspects of the reform of higher education. EN 11941

Evaluation of the educational system: indicators and instruments for school evaluation. EN 12390

Fonctionnement des établissements scolaires et efficacité d'ensemble du système. FR 12117

Further vocational training and European integration. DE 12054

International comparability of education statistics: a study of possible distortions in international comparisons of university statistics. DE 12695

International education in international schools: developing a consensus of opinion. EN 12139

Knowledge of "education" and "pedagogics" in the pedagogic debate in Germany 1945-1989. DE 12025

New trends in educational administration and teacher training in a democratic society and their implications for the role of the teacher. EN 12337

Official education statistics and empirical social research. DE 13040

The problem of the efficiency/effectiveness of the education system: organizational solutions for upper secondary schools. EN 12128

The provision of education in the middle school years in Cyprus. EN 13758

Reorganization of the education system in the new German states. DE 12077

School as an instrument in the education of the young generation. EN 12012

Secondary education during the transition towards a market economy: readiness for change (evaluation, adjustments and expectations of pupils, teachers and parents). EN 13197

Structure and development of the supply of trainee places in selected regions in the new German states. DE 11814

Teachers' perceptions of computer education and computer-assisted instruction (CAI). EN 11694

TRACE: Transregional Academic Mobility and Credential Evaluation: Information Network - a study on the process of project implementation. DE 13037

Vocational education in the Republic of Austria. DE 12071

educational administration

The applicability of total quality management to the management of schools. EN 12270

Attitudes towards 'economic course' provision in the public further education sector. EN 12271

The changing role of secondary headteachers. EN 13657

A common core curriculum for lower secondary education. EN 12506

Comparative studies of educational management in Russia and the Baltic republics. EN 12324

Decision-making and school policy: a case study of a primary school at a time of rapid change. EN 12284

Demographic change and the loss of resources in the education system. EN 12309

Deregulation: needs and possibilities for school management. EN 12286

The development of managerialism in Scottish education since 1945. EN 12288

Devolved management of schools. EN 12289

The devolved management of schools: a comparative study of the impact of parental participation and the local management of schools in Scotland and England. EN 13709

Economy, education and ecumenism 1931-1984. EN 12292

Education management training and development in Europe. EN 12548

Educational management in developing countries. EN 12294

Educational management, teacher evaluation and teacher autonomy. EN 12295

The effects of the Education Reform Act 1988: formula funding of schools. EN 12298

Evaluation of information technology systems used to support administration in schools. EN 12306

Evolution of the role, structure and operations of senior management groups in universities. EN 12308

Financial management in education. EN 12312

The framework for Local Management of Schools: a study of local education authorities' approved Local Management of Schools schemes. EN 12314

The functions, purposes and contributions of national education management centres. EN 12566

The funding of schools after the 1988 Education Reform Act. EN 12315

Further education governing bodies and their contribution to a quality learning service. EN 13713

Going grant-maintained: a case study of change from a management perspective. EN 12317

Governance and corporatism in the Norwegian school system. EN 12318

The headteacher's role in the implementation of National Curriculum. EN 13668

Headteachers: the impact of radical reform upon senior professionals. EN 13669

Humboldt Universitaet - Freie Universitaet: a comparison of the development of the different functions and the restrictions of the autonomy and the shortcomings of the two Berlin universities. DE 12125

The impact of local management of schools. EN 11961

Impact of school development plans in primary schools. EN 13734

The influence of teacher appraisal on secondary school management. EN 12406

Innovative uses of non-teaching staff in primary and secondary schools. EN 13672

The introduction of central management teams in secondary schools. EN 12282

Learning styles and education management. EN 11878

Local management in schools: the three year review. EN 12326

Local Management of Schools. EN 12327

Local management of schools and racial equality. EN 11979

Local management of schools: database of research. EN 13052

Local management of secondary schools in Berkshire - an evaluation. EN 12328

Management cultures within primary schools. EN 12329

Management development centre: follow-up study. EN 12585

Management information services. EN 12330

The management of politically, or financially expedient change in a college of further education. EN 12162

The management of the Technical and Vocational Education Initiative within post-16 institutions in Hampshire. EN 12163

Managing the implementation of the National Curriculum. EN 12332

Models of effective management in schools. EN 12334

Models of organization and management of pre-school provision and their effects on the child's development in Great Britain, Sweden and the USA. EN 12169

The new government and management of education. EN 11990

New trends in educational administration and teacher training in a democratic society and their implications for the role of the teacher. EN 12337

Opting for grant-maintained status: a study of policy-making in education. EN 11993

L'ordinateur dans l'enseignement: la Suisse en comparaison avec 18 autres systèmes éducatifs. DE 11703

Perspectives on the government of schools at local level. EN 13715

educational reform

Alternatives in education: an investigation of past, present and future policies in education. EN 12741

Analysis of reports on curriculum. EN 12742

Assessment of the school inspectorate by teachers. DE 12299

The beginnings of reorientation in political education in the GDR 1989/1990. DE 11719

Bringing teachers to the centre of the stage: a study of secondary school teachers' responses to curriculum change in mathematics. EN 11916

Change in teacher education: an Anglo-Soviet study. EN 12059

Changes in the classroom experience of Inner London pupils. EN 11919

Changing modes of professionalism? A case study of teacher education in transition. EN 12060

Comparative studies of educational management in Russia and the Baltic republics. EN 12324

Competence-based teacher training for the primary years: a comparative approach. EN 12065

A conceptual model for the functioning of higher education during the transition to a market economy. EN 12275

Decision-making and school policy: a case study of a primary school at a time of rapid change. EN 12284

Development of an educational technology for the preparation of university students for the teaching profession. EN 12184

Development of education in the Czech and Slovak Federal Republic in the period 1991-1992. EN 12006

The education system in England and Wales. EN 11935

The effects of the Education Reform Act 1988 on black communities. EN 13441

Elaboration of didactic aspects of the reform of higher education. EN 11941

L'enseignement des branches de culture générale dans les écoles professionnelles des arts et métiers en Suisse. DE 12038

Equal opportunities policies in schools and colleges post local management developments from the 1988 Education Act. EN 11944

Evaluation of the three-year training course in primary teacher training colleges. EN 12099

Forecasting the demand for higher education specialists. EN 11952

The future of education in a renewed democratic society and a united Europe. EN 11917

The impact of local management of schools. EN 11961

The impact of the Education Reform Act - 1988 on the further education curriculum. EN 11962

The impact of the National Curriculum and Local Management of Schools (LMS) on the provision of sport and physical education in schools. EN 12570

Implementing educational changes in primary schools with particular reference to small schools. EN 11963

The in-service teacher education system and the regional service centres for teachers. EN 12233

Local Management of Schools. EN 12327

Local management of secondary schools in Berkshire - an evaluation. EN 12328

The management of politically, or financially expedient change in a college of further education. EN 12162

Monitoring the implementation of the National Curriculum in primary schools. EN 12503

The nature of relationships between teachers' attitudes and beliefs about educational change in Bermuda and other personal, psychological and educational variables. EN 13266

The new government and management of education. EN 11990

New trends in educational administration and teacher training in a democratic society and their implications for the role of the teacher. EN 12337

Non-university higher education in Slovakia: an international cooperative project. EN 12000

Opting for grant-maintained status: a study of policy-making in education. EN 11993

Planning for change in multiracial primary schools. EN 13010

Preparing teachers for organisational change: an evaluation of a programme of compulsory inservice training in readiness for the re-organisation of a school system. EN 12191

Pressure on primary headteachers during and following the implementation of Local Management of Schools. EN 13687

Primary assessment, curriculum and experience. EN 12510

Problems and possibilities of managing small secondary schools (circa 400) as a result of the Education Reform Act 1988. EN 11998

Problems with right wing education policy. EN 11999

Processes and outcomes of the introduction of comprehensive schools in England and Wales. EN 12195

La qualité du dispositif rénové de formation professionnelle continue en agriculture. FR 12002

Réforme de l'enseignement des branches de culture générale dans les écoles professionnelles. FR 12203

Reorganising further education: the tertiary option. EN 12204

Reorganization of the education system in the new German states. DE 12077

School as an instrument in the education of the young generation. EN 12012

The Scottish educational reforms and teachers' theories of teaching and learning. EN 12009

Secondary education during the transition towards a market economy: readiness for change (evaluation, adjustments and expectations of pupils, teachers and parents). EN 13197

Self-managing schools - a practical way forward for secondary schools. EN 12348

Social changes and education. EN 13440

A study of the management and implementation of educational change in primary schools. EN 12015

Theory and concept of primary education. EN 12246

The transition to democracy and educational change in contemporary Chile and post-Franco Spain. EN 12018

educational research

Central Support Unit: the Assessment of Achievement Programme. EN 12370

The continuing education market: patterns and functions. EN 12073

Environmental education: a directory and review of research. EN 13444

Good schools, effective schools: judgements and their history. EN 11954

Modelling school effectiveness. EN 12417

OECD (Organisation for Economic Co-operation and Development) education indicators on attitudes and expectations. EN 11991

Performance measurement indicators in research in continuing education. EN 13009

Schools Assessment Research and Support Unit (SARSU). EN 12445

The work of the Scottish Council for Research in Education 1928-1992. EN 13017

educational sociology

New Directions in Education Policy Sociology. EN 11989

Problèmes de sociologie de l'éducation. FR 12779

Professionals in music institutions in Poland: problems and issues in professional training and careers. EN 13617

Le savoir réel de l'homme moderne. FR 12784

educational software

Acquisition des connaissances à partir du texte. FR 13106

Adapting tutoring systems to students' learning styles. EN 11684

Cabri geometry. EN 12645

Courseware experiments in school. EN 12723

Database concept for the authoring workbench. EN 12683

Databases of multimedia learning materials to support the use of courseware development products. EN 12658

DISCOURSE: Design & Interactive Specification of Courseware. EN 11723

Distributed systems for telework and group work. DE 11833

Educational Software Library - ESL. EN 13020

Human-computer interfaces to reactive graphical images. EN 11759

Information technology in language teaching. EN 12734

Interactive problem-solving environments. EN 12640

Knowledge-based computer-assisted learning. EN 12701

Logiciel d'aide à la résolution de problèmes arithmétiques par les élèves de cours élémentaire, première et deuxième années. FR 12703

The MEDA project (Méthodologie d'Evaluation des Didacticiels pour les Adultes). EN 11781

Methods for the management and development of adaptive education systems. EN 11784

Open learning methods in chemistry. EN 11992

Software reviews: what do teachers need to know? EN 12722

Tools for exploratory learning programme. EN 11898

educational technology

Construction and use of communication and information technology teaching aids in primary and secondary schools. EN 12737

Database concept for the authoring workbench. EN 12683

Database support for multi-media computer-assisted learning. EN 12659

Databases of multimedia learning materials to support the use of courseware development products. EN 12658

Design guidelines for electronic books. EN 12474

Design of Electronic Performance Support Systems. EN 11711

Development of an educational technology for the preparation of university students for the teaching profession. EN 12184

Devon Music Technology Project. EN 12541

Exeter Music Technology Project. EN 12563

Features of powerful learning environments. EN 11772

Integration of computer and video in the teaching process. EN 12693

Interactive problem-solving environments. EN 12640

The trainer's workbench. EN 11821

educational theory

Developing emancipatory curricula in primary schools. EN 11928

Development of educational philosophies and teacher education. EN 12794

Education and humanities: teachers' and pupils' educational competence. EN 11936

The Freinet Movement in its international context. EN 11953

The Gramscian theory of education: a critical study of the development of educational theory. EN 11955

Islamic education in the understanding of present day Muslim educationists. EN 12963

Modèles et problématiques de la reconversion. FR 13603

The order of knowledge. EN 12773

The pedagogical knowledge base in teacher education. EN 12183

School as an instrument in the education of the young generation. EN 12012

Theory and concept of primary education. EN 12246

The training and education of Froebelian teachers in England and Wales, 1889-1926. EN 12791

educationalist

Hudson Shaw and the university extension movement. EN 12124

elderly person

Current state of cooperation between companies and adult education institutions in the field of further education for senior citizens. DE 13380

Development and testing of curricular elements for a model of further and advanced training for voluntary geriatric work. DE 11739

Education for senior citizens in a church setting (Schleswig-Holstein). DE 11808

On the situation of further and advanced training in geriatric care: current situation, evaluation and development of quality standards. DE 11849

Political education for senior citizens in the new German states. DE 12598

electrical engineering

Evaluation research for the pilot project "Cross-curricular teaching at vocational schools". DE 11838

Formation par la recherche. FR 12678

electronic data processing

Didactic concept for a training programme in an "AuT" project, CAD-based and computer-aided information systems in a design department for plant construction and special purpose machines. DE 13562

Distributed systems for telework and group work. DE 11833

The quality of further vocational training. DE 11798

Typists and electronic word processing. DE 13628

electronics

Formation par la recherche. FR 12678

elite

Socialisation of elites. EN 12013

emancipation

Developing emancipatory curricula in primary schools. EN 11928

emotion

Affect and learning mathematics. EN 13206

Effects of emotion and sexuality in the organizational processes of management. EN 13710

emotional disorder

The assessment and statementing of children with emotional and behavioural difficulties: child and parent perspectives. EN 13282

The reform of English spelling by omission of redundant letters. EN 12908

School experiment: English from primary level I. DE 12912

Second Language Acquisition (SLA): avoidance behaviour in Norwegian learners of English. EN 12914

Sociocultural aspects of teaching English to Arabic speaking students. EN 12917

Standard tests in English for pupils at the end of the second Key Stage of the National Curriculum in 1994, 1995, 1996. EN 12450

Teacher assessment in the National Curriculum core subjects: mathematics, science and English. EN 12456

Teaching English in a multilingual classroom. EN 12935

The teaching of English in Cyprus primary schools: realities - potentialities - perspectives. EN 12870

The teaching of English in Scottish secondary schools 1940-1990: a study of change and development. EN 12938

The uses of playscripts in the secondary school curriculum. EN 12991

Verbal discourse events and teaching styles of English language teachers in Kenyan secondary schools. EN 12944

Verbal interaction in mathematics lessons in four secondary schools in Anglophone Cameroon. EN 12945

Vocabulary rate in course materials for English as a second or foreign language. EN 12947

Word recognition problems among Arabic-speaking learners of English. EN 12949

enterprise

Analysis of the compatibility of training and management behaviours and of current situation components. DE 13245

Current state of cooperation between companies and adult education institutions in the field of further education for senior citizens. DE 13380

Development and testing of a model for in-company further training for warehouse and handling personnel in forwarding agencies. DE 13572

Development and testing of a seminar concept for on-the-job instructors. DE 11735

Development and testing of holistic learning concepts for environmental education programmes for vocational school-industry partnerships. DE 11738

Development of an extended concept of learning tasks for experience-based activities in computer-aided work. DE 11733

Education and entrepreneurship: an analytical study of the attention given to entrepreneurship in education (in Dutch-speaking Belgium). EN 13507

Enterprise Education: Scottish Enterprise funded package writing. EN 11731

Enterprise in higher education: evaluation. EN 13493

The enterprising college. EN 13494

Enterprising higher education: links between higher education institutions and industrial, commercial sectors. EN 13392

Further training for in-house instructors in companies in the new German states. DE 11835

Impact macroéconomique de la formation professionnelle. FR 13503

In-company further training for training personnel (BeWAP). DE 11693

In-house training as part of commercial training courses. DE 12529

In-house vocational training: learning and behavioural difficulties. DE 11692

Job-based training for unskilled and semi-skilled workers in small and medium-sized companies using computer-aided resources. DE 13534

Learning and manufacturing. DE 11880

La métis professionnelle: savoirs et savoir-faire. FR 13602

Multimedia learning systems in production and process engineering and planning. DE 13606

On the evaluation of in-service training in industry: relevance of the features and relationships between surveyed and estimated characteristics. DE 13646

Organization of further vocational training for CIM and flexible work systems. DE 11790

Problems in reorganizing further vocational/in-house training for people with lower and middle level qualifications in the five new German states. DE 12194

Scottish Enterprise Consortium: Moray House Institute of Education. EN 13510

Typists and electronic word processing. DE 13628

Visual and practical learning in the combined educational setting of museums - companies - schools. DE 11851

entrance examination

A comparison of the anxiety levels of final-year secondary school pupils before and after university entrance examinations. EN 12414

entry to school

Baseline assessment at age 4+. EN 12366

Determining the entry-level characteristics of primary school pupils. EN 13060

An exploratory study on school readiness, with special reference to the school-aged children in Taiwan. EN 13073

Pedagogic knowledge in everyday life: an exploratory study on parents' use of pedagogic knowledge, with particular reference to school choice. DE 13193

Problem behaviour in pupils entering primary school. EN 13356

Standardization of a screening test of Greek-Cypriot speech and language. EN 12451

Transition from pre-school to primary school. EN 12357

environment

Development and testing of a curriculum for the integration of ecology in economics training. DE 11736

Development and testing of holistic learning concepts for environmental education programmes for vocational school-industry partnerships. DE 11738

Ecological awareness and behaviour: on the social vacuum in environmental education and training. DE 12019

Emergent environmentalism: subject knowledge and concern for the environment. EN 13443

Encounters and the environment: the role of encounter theory in the teaching of the subject "Social and Natural Environment". EN 13463

Environmental protection in the Ruhr area: materials for environmental education in schools and out-of-school educational settings. DE 13469

Environmental training policy. EN 13445

Evaluation of English Nature's School Grants Scheme. EN 13447

International legislation on environmental protection. DE 13451

Learning programme for environmental education at commercial colleges (LUKAS). DE 11776

Physical education and air pollution. EN 12628

Students' environmental knowledge and attitude. EN 13202

The transversality of environmental education in lower secondary school curricula: objectives, contents (knowledge and values), and methods. EN 13468

environmental study

Building support for environmental education (Phase I). EN 12530

Continuous innovation of environmental education in chemistry teacher education. EN 12185

The contribution of geography to environmental education. EN 12655

Developing teaching materials on the international politics of the environment. EN 11713

Development of curriculum-based resources. EN 11714

Education for sustainable development in the Third World. EN 13389

Emergent environmentalism: subject knowledge and concern for the environment. EN 13443

Environmental Development Unit and Resources for Environmental and Social Studies Teaching (RESST). EN 12552

Environmental education: a directory and review of research. EN 13444

Environmental education in primary teacher education. EN 12553

Environmental training policy. EN 13445

Evaluation of English Nature's School Grants Scheme. EN 13447

Formation et écologie. FR 12677

Global futures project. EN 12760

Hypermedia technology for environmental education. EN 13034

Inservice Education of Teachers programmes in environmental education. EN 12573

Learning programme for environmental education at commercial colleges (LUKAS). DE 11776

Planning review and profiling in environmental education in the school curriculum. EN 12596

Re-storying the landscape. EN 13460

The transversality of environmental education in lower secondary school curricula: objectives, contents (knowledge and values), and methods. EN 13468

The use of concepts as a planning framework for environmental studies. EN 13470

epistemology

Knowledge representation and information exchange in instruction. EN 13137

Mental models from a constructive perspective. DE 12965

equal opportunity

Access to higher education in Xinjiang Uyghur Autonomous Region, China, 1949-1987. EN 11904

Collaborative learning and equal opportunities. EN 11855

Comparaisons des inégalités sociales de scolarisation dans quatre pays européens et en France au cours des trente dernières années. FR 11922

Concept and development of study materials for a supplementary course on equal opportunities for women. DE 12500

Les coûts de l'enseignement pré-scolaire au Brésil. FR 12277

Education and social change with special reference to Nigerian women (particularly the Igbo). EN 11934

The effects of the Education Reform Act 1988 on black communities. EN 13441

Equal opportunities and social justice. EN 11943

Equal opportunities policies in schools and colleges post local management developments from the 1988 Education Act. EN 11944

Equality versus quality: the dilemma of primary schools in today's Europe. EN 11975

Equitable staffing policies in further and higher education. EN 13573

Equity aspects of training policy. EN 11945

Immigrant apprentices without an apprenticeship contract. EN 13519

International comparison of equal opportunities policies in education with particular reference to school policies. EN 11967

Labour market indicators for equal opportunity policies. EN 11912

Local management of schools and racial equality. EN 11979

Moray House Institute of Education policy on equal opportunities (disability and race): curricular implementation. EN 11985

The position in education of the 88-8 Educational Priority Policy cohort in the third secondary school year. EN 11927

Preparation for life: TVEI and equal opportunities (gender). EN 11997

Problèmes de sociologie de l'éducation. FR 12779

Racial equality and initial teacher education. EN 12201

The role of the female deputy headteachers: an investigation into the role and profiles of female deputy headteachers in co-educational comprehensive schools in one local education authority. EN 13697

Self-esteem and educational practice. EN 13200

Social and psychological adjustment of educated married women in Mauritius. EN 13766

A study of school and classroom characteristics in secondary schools in the context of the evaluation of the Educational Priority Policy programme and the introduction of a national curriculum in lower secondary education: phase two. EN 12425

Together, all things are easier. EN 13395

Widening access to human resources disciplines: developing opportunities for ethnic minority students at the University of Leeds. EN 12024

Women and education in Nepal. EN 13763

equipment

Cathedrals through touch and hearing. EN 12974

Development of microcomputer software for educational and vocational applications (for blind and partially sighted persons). EN 12662

Effects of introducing small equipment into primary schools for use at playtimes. EN 12475

Evaluation of multisensory rooms in the education of children with profound and multiple learning difficulties. EN 12477

error

An investigation into errors made in attempts to solve mathematical problems. EN 12696

ethics

Attitudes of tolerance among adolescents. EN 13168

Ethical absolutism and education. EN 12554

Manifest functions of the "Protestant ethics" analysed by Max Weber for present-day education and socialization. DE 12964

Moral knowledge, moral principles and moral education. EN 12589

Ethiopia

Education for sustainable development in the Third World. EN 13389

ethnic group

Access to higher education in Xinjiang Uyghur Autonomous Region, China, 1949-1987. EN 11904

Improving access to education for young black adults. EN 11964

Individuation processes among Turkish, Moroccan, Chinese and Dutch young adults. EN 13080

Policy and practice in community education: a study of the youth service and ethnic minority girls and young women in Peterborough. EN 13740

Racism and multicultural education. EN 12003

Social identity in adolescence. EN 13412

Social networks and ethnic identity in an urban nursery: a sociolinguistic analysis of preferred language use. EN 12916

The supplementary school and its role in inner-city London. EN 12229

ethnic minority

Bilingual learners and language provision in the National Curriculum. EN 12809

Effective instruction for ethnic minority pupils. EN 12386

The effects of the Education Reform Act 1988 on black communities. EN 13441

Ethnic minorities in higher education. EN 13446

An investigation into the present situation and problems of English language learning of adult Chinese immigrants in Nottingham and London. EN 12878

Multicultural education: images at primary level. EN 11987

Patterns of bilingualism in some families of Pakistani origin: implications for policy on language education. EN 12897

Secondary analyses on the school careers of secondary school pupils on the basis of data on the "VOCL '89" cohort. EN 12447

A study of the perceptions and responses of young women of South Asian origin to a single-sex access Youth Training Scheme. EN 13465

Teaching and learning strategies in multi-ethnic further education classrooms. EN 11897

Teaching English in a multilingual classroom. EN 12935

Third phase of the primary education cohort studies conducted as part of the evaluation of the Educational Priority Policy (OVB). EN 11925

Widening access to human resources disciplines: developing opportunities for ethnic minority students at the University of Leeds. EN 12024

ethnic origin

Between two worlds: the cultural behaviour of young migrants in Vienna with particular reference to music. DE 13472

Children of migrant workers and their musical behaviour. DE 13456

ethnic relations

The contribution of the church to the coexistence of Slovenian and German ethnic groups in Carinthia: intercultural communication in a Christian context. DE 13386

Inter-ethnic relationships in secondary schools. EN 13401

Life in school: an analysis using methods of educational ethnography. EN 13390

Multicultural education after ERA: concerns and challenges for the 1990s. EN 11986

Prejudice, isolation and bullying: intervention in ethnically mixed classes. EN 13408

Europe

Adolescence in Europe: accepted values and life perspectives of Polish adolescents. EN 13458

Contrasting German: problems experienced by people with different native languages when learning German as a foreign language. DE 12832

Education management training and development in Europe. EN 12548

Europe at school - European Schools Day Competition: an instrument to enhance the European dimension in education. EN 12555

Evaluation of various approaches in attracting participants to the training and employment programmes promoted by the European Social Fund (ESF). DE 13577

The future of education in a renewed democratic society and a united Europe. EN 11917

Intercultural education in the fine arts in Europe. DE 13764

Interdisciplinary social scientific theory and research in Europe. DE 13003

"International learning" - Changes in the life situation and orientation of young people in the context of European development: youth research as a basis for improving educational work. DE 11767

IRLME: Interactive Resources for Small and Medium Sized Enterprises. EN 13025

JITOL: Just In Time Open Learning. EN 12145

Législation de la jeunesse et institutions aujourd'hui: recherche comparative internationale. FR 13737

The management and development of mechanisms of university/industry collaboration in European and Latin American universities. EN 13403

Occupational profiles of vocational counsellors. EN 13685

Place des humanités dans la formation médicale en Europe. FR 12711

Political education in the states of a uniting Europe (a glance from Poland). EN 12755

Professional bodies: education and training and the labour market. EN 12196

School links and exchanges in Europe. EN 11807

Teachers' pay and bargaining machinery in four European countries. EN 13513

Teaching about European history and society in the 1990s. EN 12790

Urban civic culture and the school curriculum. EN 12517

Young people and Europe. DE 13184

European community

Educators - training in Lower Saxony. DE 11741

Europe at school - European Schools Day Competition: an instrument to enhance the European dimension in education. EN 12555

European integration and the recogniton of university diplomas. DE 13711

The transferability of current insurance qualifications within the European Community. EN 13516

United Kingdom professions and the European challenge. EN 13765

European dimension

Developing European awareness: the role of local education authorities and schools in the 1990s. EN 12540

Europe at school - European Schools Day Competition: an instrument to enhance the European dimension in education. EN 12555

Europe in school textbooks: the concept of Europe in Austria's history and geography textbooks for the 8th form. DE 12539

The European Studies project. EN 12759

Management and organisation of teaching 'The European Dimension' in schools (International network with representatives from The Netherlands, Belgium, Germany, Greece and Denmark). EN 12584

School links and exchanges in Europe. EN 11807

Teaching about European history and society in the 1990s. EN 12790

Use of official European Community information sources in schools and colleges. EN 12631

evaluation

5-14 Development Programme: coordination of the evaluation of its implementation. EN 12483

Analysis of understanding as an educational aim and ways to detect its achievement. EN 13110

The changing impact of a policy initiative: a multilevel analysis of TVEI. EN 11920

Classification of school variants. EN 12486

Courseware experiments in school. EN 12723

Descriptive analyses of the "VOCL" cohort: year three. EN 12368

Development of performance indicators for client satisfaction. EN 12379

Le développement de la motivation à la réussite scolaire: premières approches. FR 13217

Education for senior citizens in a church setting (Schleswig-Holstein). DE 11808

Effectiveness of different kinds of literacy provision. EN 12297

Elaboration of survey instruments for the evaluation of in-service training courses. EN 12999

Evaluation and monitoring at local education authority level. EN 12303

L'évaluation des connaissances par expert. FR 12391

Evaluation of a new funding system for in-service training. EN 13496

Evaluation of Derbyshire College B.Ed (Hon) Initial Degree. EN 12103

Evaluation of further education college governor training. EN 13712

Evaluation of implementation of science key stages 1-3. EN 12557

Evaluation of National Curriculum Assessment at Key Stage Three in mathematics, science, English and technology. EN 12497

Evaluation of pupils and the effectiveness of teaching. EN 12400

The evaluation of school-initiated INSET in selected junior schools: teacher and headteacher perspectives. EN 12393

Evaluation of special needs pupils in ordinary primary schools. EN 12411

Evaluation of systems dynamics software. DE 12672

Evaluation of "tailored instruction" in primary schools. EN 11742

Evaluation of the Economic Awareness in Teacher Training project (EcATT). EN 12558

Evaluation of the educational system: indicators and instruments for school evaluation. EN 12390

Evaluation of the National Curriculum core subjects (English) at key stages 1, 2 and 3. EN 12858

Evaluation of the programme of appraisal of teaching in the veterinary faculty at Liverpool University. EN 12395

Evaluation of various approaches in attracting participants to the training and employment programmes promoted by the European Social Fund (ESF). DE 13577

Examinations research programme. EN 12397

The Health Education Authority HIV/AIDS local evaluation initiative. EN 13325

Identification and evaluation of innovatory curriculum development approaches in higher education. EN 11959

Identifying gifted pupils. EN 13230

The MEDA project (Methodologie d'Evaluation des Didacticiels pour les Adultes). EN 11781

Methods for the management and development of adaptive education systems. EN 11784

Monitoring and evaluation in workplace nurseries. EN 12420

A national survey of reading achievement in Irish primary schools. EN 12423

On the evaluation of in-service training in industry: relevance of the features and relationships between surveyed and estimated characteristics. DE 13646

Pupils as evaluators of textbooks. EN 12437

Quality assurance in continuing professional education. EN 12199

Quality in initial teacher training - an examination of course structure within selected institutions. EN 12200

Quality of daycare provision in the United Kingdom. EN 12438

The quality of teaching at Kaiserslautern university. DE 11799

Quantitative analysis for self-evaluation by schools. EN 12439

Réflexions concernant un fondement scientifique d'une grille de critères pour évaluer des textes d'élèves. DE 12801

Research Station - Primary Education Information Technology. EN 11795

Reviewing the economic benefits of careers guidance. EN 13624

School self-evaluation. EN 12442

School self-evaluation: personnel training. EN 12443

Structures et rendement scolaires: dépouillement séparé de la contribution suisse au projet international IAEP II. DE 12720

A study of school and classroom characteristics in secondary schools in the context of the evaluation of the Educational Priority Policy programme and the introduction of a national curriculum in lower secondary education: phase two. EN 12425

Teachers' opinions about the effects and the results of their assessment by the school inspector and the headmaster. EN 12401

Teachers' planning and evaluation of mathematics in Greek high schools. EN 12728

Textbook evaluation in different countries. DE 13047

Third phase of the primary education cohort studies conducted as part of the evaluation of the Educational Priority Policy (OVB). EN 11925

Training in communication skills and counselling techniques and its influence on participants' personal constructs. EN 13703

TVEI local evaluation. EN 12256

The use of performance indicators in the evaluation of educational institutions. EN 12261

The use of performance indicators in the study of problems in the transition from secondary to higher education and in the evaluation of the Centre for Self-Instruction as a guidance service. EN 11956

The use of special media in graduate correspondence courses: a comparative study. DE 11811

evaluation criterion

Evaluation of the new report card during the trial period 1989-1990. EN 12462

first foreign language
An investigation into the present situation and problems of English language learning of adult Chinese immigrants in Nottingham and London. EN 12878

The language learning experiences of Somalis and Eritreans in Britain and Italy. EN 12881

Learners' language. EN 12884

Levels of functional literacy among Turkish and Moroccan children in the Netherlands and in the country of origin. EN 12865

Reading and schema theory. EN 12904

School experiment: English from primary level I. DE 12912

Second Language Acquisition (SLA): avoidance behaviour in Norwegian learners of English. EN 12914

flexibility
Transfer ability and instruction. EN 11899

follow-up study
Entrée des jeunes dans la vie active (enquêtes EVA). FR 13571

L'intégration sociale des enfants de 4 à 7 ans: étude longitudinale. FR 13082

Teacher-pupil relationships in the primary classroom. EN 13416

food
The impact of home economics on pupil nutrition during school breaks. EN 13286

A study of the rhetoric used in the public debates about religious education in England and Wales 1987-1990. EN 12620

Teaching and learning about food and nutrition in school: the nation's diet initiative. EN 12626

forecasting
Apprentices and skilled workers on the labour market: a forecast up to the years 2005/2007. DE 13600

Berkshire school pupil forecasting system. EN 12273

Coût et financement de l'enseignement supérieur en France. FR 12276

The current and future labour market situation for musicians: a feasibility study. EN 13553

Development of the educational level of the population in the Slovak Republic by the year 2000. EN 12021

Forecasting student enrolments for further education colleges. EN 12313

Forecasting the demand for higher education specialists. EN 11952

I-See! 1991. EN 13588

L'impact de la crise économique sur les systèmes éducatifs. FR 12320

Labour market information and labour market dynamics. EN 13530

Labour market prospects and training possibilities in the province of Limburg. EN 13531

The potential supply of researchers. EN 13615

Prévision des dépenses d'éducation primaire à l'horizon 2000 dans les pays en développement. FR 13508

Problem behaviour in pupils entering primary school. EN 13356

Prognosis of the development of education in the Slovak Republic up to the year 2010. EN 13011

Replacement demand by occupation. EN 13558

Theoretical and empirical aspects of manpower analysis. EN 13638

foreign language assistant
Evaluation of the Basingstoke Language Awareness Project. EN 12855

foreign languages
"A toi de parler": méthode pour l'enseignement primaire du français à Madagascar. FR 12795

"Les petits lascars": méthode pour l'enseignement précoce du français langue étrangère. FR 12796

ALPS (Automated Language Processing Systems) computer-assisted translation system as a language learning tool. EN 12798

Aspects of foreign language instruction for adults. DE 12953

A Bachelor degree course in German for commerce and tourism: a modern profile of the German Studies graduate from Ostrava University Faculty of Arts. EN 12806

A Bachelor degree course in Russian for commerce and tourism. EN 12805

A comparison of the internal organisation of proportions within English and French discourse and its bearings on the teaching of English to native speakers of French. EN 12820

Constructing culture: a study of teacher-pupil talk in French language lessons. EN 12824

Contrasting German: problems experienced by people with different native languages when learning German as a foreign language. DE 12832

The cultural dimension of English as a foreign language in the Arabian Gulf States. EN 12825

Cultural studies in advanced language learning: the year abroad in under-graduate courses. EN 13435

Culture and civilisation studies for advanced language learners - an experiment in French and English schools. EN 12826

Curriculum development and evaluation of Teaching English as a Second Language (TESOL) courses at foundation level in the United Arab Emirates. EN 12827

The demotivated pupil in the modern language classroom - a comparative study. EN 12831

The development and evaluation of online computer-assisted language learning materials for English for academic purposes. EN 12833

Education for international understanding through foreign language teaching: a German - British collaborative project. EN 12836

Effective teaching in English as Foreign Language (EFL): a Greek case study. EN 12839

Effectiveness of foreign language teaching in primary school. DE 12840

English in the State of Qatar: an analysis of perceptions and attitudes. EN 12843

English language teaching - an evaluation of an industrial training programme. EN 12846

Evaluation of foreign language teaching objectives (with particular reference to the teaching of French). EN 12853

Evaluation of national pilot projects: foreign languages in primary schools (Scotland). EN 12854

Evaluation of the Basingstoke Language Awareness Project. EN 12855

The evaluation of the management of English Language Teaching (ELT) overseas aid projects. EN 12856

An examination of Language Experience Approach (LEA) to teaching reading development and its use in second language learning. EN 11751

An experiment with teaching a second foreign language in lower secondary schools. EN 12920

An experiment with teaching a second foreign language in lower secondary schools. EN 12921

Foreign language needs in companies in Upper Austria. DE 12807

Foreign language training for initial teacher training (ITT) students. EN 12863

Interdisciplinary research project: "German as a foreign language: technical engineering languages". DE 12873

"International project work": advanced technical French grammar. DE 12874

An investigation into the difficulties of introducing innovation in English language teaching in developing countries. EN 12877

An investigation of an interactive process model for implementing an English Language Teaching (ELT) syllabus in secondary schools in French-speaking Africa. EN 12499

'Knowledge about language', language learning and the National Curriculum. EN 12880

Knowledge of languages among Italian primary school teachers. EN 12823

Language learning in large classes research project. EN 12882

Language medium teaching. EN 12883

Lexical behaviour in a second language. EN 12887

Native and non-native use of English. EN 12891

New perspectives of English language teaching at the Tallinn Pedagogical University. EN 11832

On the effect of action orientation in extracting specific information from foreign language texts. DE 12954

Oral assessment in modern languages. EN 12426

The relative difficulty of foreign languages. EN 12909

School experiment: English from primary level I. DE 12912

Sociocultural aspects of teaching English to Arabic speaking students. EN 12917

Sociolinguistic factors affecting attitudes and motivation in foreign language learning at school: an Anglo-French comparative study. EN 13201

Teaching and testing Japanese and similar languages in schools. EN 12934

Teaching foreign languages at primary level. EN 12936

The teaching of English in Cyprus primary schools: realities - potentialities - perspectives. EN 12870

Training and transfer of reading strategies: mother tongue instruction and foreign language instruction. EN 12941

Training and transfer of vocabulary acquisition strategies: mother tongue instruction and foreign language instruction. EN 12942

Traitements de bas niveau et de haut niveau dans l'utilisation d'une langue étrangère. FR 12943

Vocabulary rate in course materials for English as a second or foreign language. EN 12947

Word recognition problems among Arabic-speaking learners of English. EN 12949

foreign relations
Foreign language needs in companies in Upper Austria. DE 12807

The role of foreign experts in the development of Chinese universities. EN 13760

foreign school
Investigation of Italian schools abroad. EN 12133

foreign student
Adaptation in lecturing styles to audiences with English as a second language. EN 12797

The development and evaluation of online computer-assisted language learning materials for English for academic purposes. EN 12833

An evaluation of current British policy concerning postgraduate overseas students. EN 12102

Evaluation of international occupational pedagogics courses, with particular reference to a group of stipendiaries from Yemen. DE 12110

Interdisciplinary research project: "German as a foreign language: technical engineering languages". DE 12873

foreign worker
Further education for immigrants, with particular reference to cross-disciplinary competencies. DE 11836

foreigner
Attitudes towards current problems of domestic policy in 1991. DE 13442

formal operational thinking
Psychological and educational research on curriculum contents and the learning of primary school pupils. EN 12511

formative evaluation
Developing formative teacher assessment - as an example of the management of educational innovations. EN 12376

Formative and summative evaluation: class tests; database of tests. EN 12389

Formative assessments of reading. EN 12399

France
Analyse des disparités géographiques de scolarisation en France. FR 12269

La comparaison des systèmes d'enseignement supérieur français et espagnol. FR 12062

Comparative study of writing development in French and English primary schools. EN 12818

Coût et financement de l'enseignement supérieur en France. FR 12276

La formation comme variable d'efficience économique. FR 13500

Les performances de l'enseignement primaire en Afrique sub-saharienne: comparaison des acquisitions en mathématiques dans quatre pays. FR 12433

Policy conditions for teaching immigrant children in their native language. DE 12808

The State and women's schooling in France, 1815-1914. EN 12787

free movement
The identification of prerequisites for effective teacher mobility between Germany and the United Kingdom. EN 13398

freedom
Freedom and indoctrination in education. EN 12960

Freedom of choice. DE 13260

French language
"A toi de parler": méthode pour l'enseignement primaire du français à Madagascar. FR 12795

"Les petits lascars": méthode pour l'enseignement précoce du français langue étrangère. FR 12796

Constructing culture: a study of teacher-pupil talk in French language lessons. EN 12824

Culture and civilisation studies for advanced language learners - an experiment in French and English schools. EN 12826

English language curriculum development in Niger: Niger educational development 1960-1992 with particular reference to English language teaching. EN 12844

Evaluation of foreign language teaching objectives (with particular reference to the teaching of French). EN 12853

"International project work": advanced technical French grammar. DE 12874

Oral assessment in modern languages. EN 12426

training in readiness for the re-organisation of a school system. EN 12191

Problems and development perspectives in the cooperation between vocational training institutions. DE 11794

Problems in reorganizing further vocational/in-house training for people with lower and middle level qualifications in the five new German states. DE 12194

The quality of further vocational training. DE 11798

A review of management education for librarians. EN 13696

The role of the workplace in the work experience triangle with particular reference to transferable skills. EN 11806

School self-evaluation: personnel training. EN 12443

Training female "multiplicators" in the new German states. DE 12216

Work situation, occupational self-image and qualification of specialist instructors. DE 13650

The York-Sheffield Russian Project. EN 12952

inaptitude

Les enfants non-lecteurs; étude des impossibilités persistantes de l'activité de lecture chez des enfants âgés de neuf ans et plus. FR 13312

income

The effect of individual and socio-economic situational variables of secondary school pupils upon their vocational interests. EN 13170

Enquête représentative sur les activités rémunérées des étudiants à l'Université de Berne. DE 13512

independent work

The development of motivation and self-regulation in lower secondary school pupils. EN 13215

Improving self-regulation skills through isolated and integrated training. EN 11865

Independent work of children and cognitive processes in primary school. EN 13154

India

Cultural bases of educational forms: an inquiry into the learning patterns of the 40 primary school children in an Indian village. EN 13214

An examination of the inter-relationship between the development of adult education, Gandhian philosophy, the Congress Party, and the legacy of the British Raj, in India between 1935 and 1955, and an analysis of subsequent developments in adult education in the period up to the 1980s. EN 13756

individual characteristics

Can the burn-out syndrome be predicted with student teachers? DE 13338

The comparison of locus of control of pupils in two secondary schools. EN 13074

Différenciation intra et interindividuelle à l'adolescence. FR 13068

Performance forecasts for pupils in upper secondary commercial schools with a focus on skiing instruction. DE 12413

Rôle des représentations sociales intergroupes dans la construction de l'identité. FR 13100

Validity and award-bearing teacher action research. EN 13015

Who (still) wants to be a teacher? DE 13105

individual work

An investigation into the social and educational impact of project work in GCSE. EN 11770

individualism

Individualism and curriculum development in physical education. EN 12571

individualization

L'adaptation à l'école maternelle des enfants issus de l'immigration maghrébine. FR 13059

La collaboration des enseignant-e-s dans les classes enfantines et primaires intégratives: chances et problèmes. DE 12058

Différenciation intra et interindividuelle à l'adolescence. FR 13068

individualized teaching

Individualism and curriculum development in physical education. EN 12571

Making efficient use of microcomputers in teaching mathematics to gifted children in the Jordanian primary schools. EN 11777

School-centred in-service training of teachers. DE 12218

Spelling in primary schools. DE 12907

Together, all things are easier. DE 13395

indoctrination

Freedom and indoctrination in education. EN 12960

industrial psychology

Individual determinants of the attitudes toward work. EN 13180

Psychological and organizational determinants of R and D professionals' performance. EN 13618

industrial training

Development of a didactic concept for teaching new technologies in technical manufacturing occupations, with particular reference to information technology training in the graphic trade. DE 12668

Internal differentiation into specialized classes in part-time vocational schools. DE 11764

Learning by workers (aged above 35) with a low level of education. EN 12156

Marketing PICKUP in Europe. EN 11779

industrialization

Retraining under conditions of industrial restructuring. EN 11803

industry

Comparison of qualification structures in lignite mining in East Germany. DE 13619

The curricular impact of the Teachers into Industry Project. EN 13487

Development of a course for users of integrated software for production planning and control. DE 11732

Education-Business Partnerships (EBPs): targets and stocktake. EN 13565

The education policies of large companies. EN 13491

English language teaching - an evaluation of an industrial training programme. EN 12846

Enterprising higher education: links between higher education institutions and industrial, commercial sectors. EN 13392

Evaluation of an educational and vocational guidance initiative in compulsory school. EN 13612

Evaluation research for the pilot project "Materials for the cross-disciplinary training of educators and learners in the chemical industry, with a special focus on ecology and social learning". DE 11839

Foreign language needs in companies in Upper Austria. DE 12807

La gestion de la reconversion des salariés: une forme de transition professionnelle. FR 13583

Human capital and export competitiveness. EN 13502

Information technology in education and employment. EN 12688

Key technologies - potential developments and their implications for vocational education and training. EN 12700

Pilot project 'Making the transition from teaching to business'. DE 13604

Planning, implementation and consultation on qualifications in the context of the reorganization of a training centre prompted by structural changes in the region (Rheinhausen). DE 13620

The role of information technology in business, finance and management. EN 12719

School/Industry Compacts: the translation of an American model to England. EN 12214

The secondment of professional staff between education and industry. EN 13719

Sponsorship in Scottish colleges of further and higher education. EN 13511

Towards the integration of education, science and industrial production under the conditions of a decentralized market economy. EN 13515

infancy

L'acquisition des labels spatiaux chez l'enfant. FR 13107

L'adaptation à l'école maternelle des enfants issus de l'immigration maghrébine. FR 13059

An investigation of the relationship between perinatal risk factors and contingency learning and attentive behaviour in later infancy. EN 13084

A pilot study on the phonological acquisition of Turkish and its implications for phonological disorders. EN 12901

infant

Emotional and behavioural problems in reception class children. EN 13256

Parts de l'enfant et de la mère dans la gestion d'un récit produit conjointement. FR 13091

information

AIDS Education and Research Trust (AVERT) HIV/AIDS and Nursing project. EN 13294

Comparison of further vocational training courses to facilitate choice of training. DE 12301

Creation of lists and information networks on pre-school establishments, schools and other educational institutions by State Administration Boards. EN 13038

Information needs and information seeking behaviour of nurses. EN 13671

Provision and dissemination of information among the Ministry of Education, schools, other educational institutions, pupils and parents. EN 13036

information dissemination

Creation of lists and information networks on pre-school establishments, schools and other educational institutions by State Administration Boards. EN 13038

Informatique et formation: les nouvelles technologies de l'information (NTI). FR 11763

Labour market information and labour market dynamics. EN 13524

Local management of schools: database of research. EN 13052

A model of educational guidance and care for handicapped youth and adults. EN 13348

Provision and dissemination of information among the Ministry of Education, schools, other educational institutions, pupils and parents. EN 13036

information need

Building support for environmental education (Phase I). EN 12530

The educational and informative expectations of youth with regard to school and other educational institutions. EN 13430

An evaluation of educational materials on HIV and AIDS for nurses. EN 13316

Expert Meeting of the National Career Guidance Information Centre (LDC). EN 13049

Information needs and information seeking behaviour of nurses. EN 13671

information network

Creation of lists and information networks on pre-school establishments, schools and other educational institutions by State Administration Boards. EN 13038

Educational Software Library - ESL. EN 13020

The potential of computer-mediated communication for developing social and educational opportunities for adults with physical and sensory difficulties. EN 13027

Technological aspects of interaction and effectiveness in the use of information networks and databases on higher education. EN 12732

information policy

Review of youth research in the Slovak Republic. EN 13018

information processing

Further training and employment of university graduates in information-processing occupations. DE 13642

The mind model: a comprehensive framework for educational- psychological research and practice. DE 12996

Production écrite de textes. FR 13148

The speed of tactile information processing for blind pupils. EN 13156

Speed of visual information processing. EN 13363

information retrieval

The application of computer-aided learning to the development of information skills in further education. EN 13019

information science

Inventory and analysis of Slovenian terminology of education. EN 12875

New technologies in educational processes. EN 12708

To initiate a distance learning undergraduate degree course in information and library studies. EN 12249

information service

Industrial, scientific and educational databases in Styria. DE 13031

Systems for long distance cooperation in education. EN 13030

information source

The application of computer-aided learning to the development of information skills in further education. EN 13019

An evaluation of educational materials on HIV and AIDS for nurses. EN 13316

Inventory of labour market research on agricultural training. EN 13596

Local management of schools: database of research. EN 13052

Official education statistics and empirical social research. DE 13040

Prerequisites and results of the conceptual processing of media-based experiences. DE 13056

information system

CHECK (Continuing Higher Education Consulting Kit). DE 11695

Development of an item banking system. EN 12424

Didactic concept for a training programme in an "AuT" project, CAD-based and computer-aided information systems in a design department for plant construction and special purpose machines. DE 13562

Hypermedia technology for environmental education. EN 13034

Information system for education and the labour market. EN 13592

Information system on education and the labour market. EN 13591

Labour market development and professional journals. EN 13041

Labour market information and labour market dynamics. EN 13530

Review of youth research in the Slovak Republic. EN 13018

System for accessing modular information project. EN 13032

Technological aspects of interaction and effectiveness in the use of information networks and databases on higher education. EN 12732

TRACE: Transregional Academic Mobility and Credential Evaluation: Information Network - a study on the process of project implementation. DE 13037

Une approche multimédia pour l'orientation scolaire et professionnelle. FR 12020

information technology

Alternatives to print for visually impaired students. EN 13295

Aspects of educational practice in the physical sciences and information technology. EN 12524

Comparative study of information technology training for disabled people in Britain and Portugal. EN 12651

Construction and use of communication and information technology teaching aids in primary and secondary schools. EN 12737

Courseware experiments in school. EN 12723

Database concept for the authoring workbench. EN 12683

Databases of multimedia learning materials to support the use of courseware development products. EN 12658

Developing information technology in a primary Post-Graduate Certificate of Education course. EN 12080

Development of a didactic concept for teaching new technologies in technical manufacturing occupations, with particular reference to information technology training in the graphic trade. DE 12668

The differences in teaching and learning styles employed in primary and secondary schools with reference to developing information technology capability. EN 12664

Elaboration of the foundations of the modern concept of informatics teaching and computer maintenance. EN 13023

The Esprit project. EN 12669

An evaluation of information technology development strategies in South Glamorgan schools. EN 12670

Evaluation of information technology systems used to support administration in schools. EN 12306

Evaluation of information technology teacher training development programme. EN 12105

Gender differences in educational computing in the humanities. EN 11755

Holistic job engineering competence as a goal for qualifications: socially acceptable engineering of information and communications systems as a subject for basic and further training for computer specialists. DE 13621

Humanities and information technology (Extension). EN 12680

Information systems to support teaching and classroom management. EN 12686

Information technology and the learning needs of emotionally and behaviourally disturbed children. EN 13326

Information technology development programme for teachers. EN 12687

Information technology in education and employment. EN 12688

Information technology in initial teacher training. EN 12689

Information technology in language teaching. EN 12734

The information technology in mathematics project. EN 12690

Information technology: software in primary schools. EN 12691

Informatique et formation: les nouvelles technologies de l'information (NTI). FR 11763

Initial teacher education and the new technology. EN 12692

INTENT (Initial Teacher Education and New Technology). EN 12694

Interactive problem-solving environments. EN 12640

Investigating effective reasoning models for students: what courses provide and what students concoct. EN 13134

ISDN2 and computer networks to enhance initial teacher training. EN 12472

The logistics of provision of courses in information technology for adult students with physical and sensory disabilities. EN 13342

The logistics of provision of vocational training in information technology for adult students with physical and sensory disabilities. EN 13343

Management information services. EN 12330

New technologies in educational processes. EN 12708

PALM (Pupil Autonomy in Learning with Micros) Extension. EN 11791

Permeating the learning of information technology across the secondary school curriculum. EN 12710

Recommendations for state policy in the field of informatization of higher education in Russia. EN 13028

The role of information technology in business, finance and management. EN 12719

The role of information technology in the education of socially handicapped children. EN 11805

Spoken language and new technology (SLANT). EN 12923

SPRITE (Supporting and Promoting Information Technology in Education). EN 12724

Standard assessment tasks in design and technology and information technology at key stage 3 of the National Curriculum. EN 12449

A study of the information technology skills used by teachers in the first two years in the profession: comparison of these skills with the information technology content of Post-Graduate Certificate of Education courses. EN 12727

A survey of computer literacy in initial teacher education. EN 12621

Teachers' perceptions of oracy and information technology project. EN 12933

Technological aspects of interaction and effectiveness in the use of information networks and databases on higher education. EN 12732

The use of computers to teach mathematics. EN 11827

The use of information technology in adult basic education of students with physical and sensory handicaps. EN 13374

initial assessment

Baseline assessment at age 4+. EN 12366

The initial assessment of youth trainees with special needs: improving access to National Vocational Qualifications (NVQs) at level 1. EN 12407

initial employment

Community education graduates at Jordanhill - survey of appointments. EN 13549

Follow-up study on the initial training of newly qualified teachers - a feasibility study. EN 12116

Newly-qualified entrants to the speech therapy profession. EN 13682

L'organisation de la transition professionnelle des jeunes en voie d'intégration dans le salariat. FR 13611

Polytechnic students two years after graduation: empirical analysis of their destination and career start. DE 13578

A study of probationers. EN 13634

Teacher training and teacher recruitment in the inner city. EN 13637

Training, occupational integration and further qualification of entry workers. DE 13535

innovation

Improving innovation management in small and medium-sized companies. DE 13641

Professional, economic and legislative problems related to the training of officers working in the field of infrastructural development in support of educational innovation and the transfer of technology. EN 13616

Referral of pupils to special education and returning of special education pupils to mainstream education in the city of Utrecht. EN 12355

The role of a change agent in the introduction of a new curriculum in technical teacher training. EN 12207

input-output analysis

Success at university: Siegen comprehensive university. DE 12388

inspection

Assessment of the school inspectorate by teachers. DE 12299

Evaluation and monitoring at local education authority level. EN 12303

Evaluation et pilotage de formations. FR 12392

Evaluation of a local education inspectorate. EN 12305

An evaluation of the Dorset Local Education Authority Inspectorate. EN 12307

The modern inspectorate: HM Inspectorate of schools 1944-91. EN 12335

The right place of music in education: a history of music education in England 1870-1927 with particular reference to the role of Her Majesty's Inspectorate (HMI). EN 12610

inspector

Assessment of the school inspectorate by teachers. DE 12299

insurance

Evaluation research for the pilot project "Development and testing of holistic learning concepts in further commercial training, with particular reference to the occupation of insurance clerk". DE 11840

The transferability of current insurance qualifications within the European Community. EN 13516

integrated curriculum

Conception and design of a course programme for national history, geography and natural sciences for use in primary schools. EN 12505

An evaluation of information technology development strategies in South Glamorgan schools. EN 12670

Evaluation research for the pilot project "Cross-curricular teaching at vocational schools". DE 11838

The management of cross-curricular themes within the National Curriculum. EN 12502

Managing the implementation of the National Curriculum. EN 12332

Permeating the learning of information technology across the secondary school curriculum. EN 12710

The use and practical application of mathematics in a cross-curricular context in National Curriculum key stage 4. EN 12738

The workings of multidisciplinary teams in special education. EN 11843

integration

L'appui pédagogique: résultats d'une enquête dans la partie alémanique du canton de Fribourg. DE 12121

La collaboration des enseignant-e-s dans les classes enfantines et primaires intégratives: chances et problèmes. DE 12058

Communication between non-handicapped children and pupils with severe learning difficulties. EN 12816

Curriculum innovation, professional development and special educational needs. EN 12489

The development of spatial awareness in children with physical handicaps, particularly those integrated in mainstream schools. EN 13120

Effets à long terme de la ségrégation scolaire. DE 12151

Integrated education for children with special educational needs in physical education programmes in Nigerian primary schools. EN 13328

Integration activities in learning. EN 11871

Integration and responsibility for learning in mainstream primary schools. EN 13399

The integration experiences of hearing impaired children: the transition from primary to secondary schooling. EN 13329

The integration of deaf and partially hearing children in Berkshire schools. EN 13400

The integration of visually impaired students in further education. EN 13330

A model of educational guidance and care for handicapped youth and adults. EN 13348

The multicultural challenge and the educational system. EN 13411

Pedagogic action in vocational training: on the relationship between coordination, cooperation and integration. DE 13406

Primary school children's understanding of severe learning difficulties. EN 13355

Special needs in primary schools. EN 12219

Special needs in the classroom. EN 12220

Towards a reconceptualisation of support teaching. EN 13417

Towards the effective inclusive school. EN 12250

Towards the integration of education, science and industrial production under the conditions of a decentralized market economy. EN 13515

intellectual

Educating teachers to be intellectuals: a study of an attempt to enable preservice primary teachers to develop as critically reflective practitioners. EN 12090

intellectual development

Critical assessment: Jean Piaget. EN 13065

Relationships between works of literature and works of art with reference to interpretation theory and implications for school curricula. EN 12606

Shakespeare: from school to higher education. EN 12987

local community

Analyse qualitative des procédures de mise en oeuvre des contrats de qualification au niveau local. FR 13523

Communities in crisis: an adult education and resource programme for local groups and community leaders. EN 13433

Young families now: a focus for learning in the community. EN 13471

local government

Les coûts de l'enseignement pré-scolaire au Brésil. FR 12277

Developing European awareness: the role of local education authorities and schools in the 1990s. EN 12540

English local education authorities' schemes of local financial management. EN 13492

Evaluation of a local education inspectorate. EN 12305

An evaluation of the Dorset Local Education Authority Inspectorate. EN 12307

The funding of schools after the 1988 Education Reform Act. EN 12315

Governance and corporatism in the Norwegian school system. EN 12318

The implementation of local education authority curriculum policies in two metropolitan authorities. EN 13735

Local education authority policy and practices in supporting special education provision in schools. EN 12160

Local management in schools: the three year review. EN 12326

The modern inspectorate: HM Inspectorate of schools 1944-91. EN 12335

Multi-professional support for young adults with special needs. EN 12172

Optimum model of a local education authority. EN 13739

Patterns of local education authority inservice education and training of teachers (INSET) organisation. EN 12182

Perspectives on the government of schools at local level. EN 13715

Play provision for children and young people in Scotland aged 5-15: what is happening. EN 12509

The role of the local education authority in the professional development of new teachers. EN 12208

Special needs in primary schools. EN 12219

Tertiary education in West Glamorgan Local Education Authority. EN 12248

Tower Hamlets project: communication between Tower Hamlets Local Education Authority and school governing bodies. EN 13744

local studies

Achieving National Curriculum attainment targets in the primary school. EN 12521

logical thinking

Analyse et développement des apprentissages à réaliser au collège dans les travaux numériques, dans les travaux géométriques. FR 12642

Didactique de l'informatique. FR 12663

Processus d'acquisition étudié sous l'angle de la structuration de l'espace-problème. FR 13146

Promotion of deductive and inductive judgment. DE 11753

Raisonnement temporel et raisonnement spatial. FR 13150

Rôle de la formulation dans ce qu'on appelle une "bonne démonstration mathématique". FR 12718

logo

An alternative metaphor for teaching control technology. EN 12639

Feedback: its effects on procedural and conceptual knowledge for problem solving strategies. EN 11752

Feedback, peer interaction and adult intervention in initial logo learning. EN 11863

The inter-relationship of cognitive abilities, attitudes, social interaction and performance in early logo learning. EN 13263

Interactive problem-solving environments. EN 12640

Logo and the development of algebraic skills. EN 12704

Lower Saxony

Educators - training in Lower Saxony. DE 11741

lower secondary

Analyse et développement des apprentissages à réaliser au collège dans les travaux numériques, dans les travaux géométriques. FR 12642

Citizenship education in lower secondary schools. EN 12634

A common core curriculum for lower secondary education. EN 12506

Concepts of history and teaching approaches at National Curriculum Key Stages 2 & 3. EN 12751

Consortium for assessment and testing in schools - English key stage 3. EN 12372

Curriculum development for secondary school teacher training. EN 12187

Descriptive analyses of the "VOCL" cohort: year three. EN 12368

The design of education in primary and lower secondary schools. EN 11988

Le développement de la motivation à la réussite scolaire: premières approches. FR 13217

Differentiation according to ability in seventh form mathematics classes. DE 11734

Elaboration of a simulation game for educational and vocational guidance in lower secondary schools. EN 11942

Evaluation of pupils and the effectiveness of teaching. EN 12400

An experiment with teaching a second foreign language in lower secondary schools. EN 12920

An experiment with teaching a second foreign language in lower secondary schools. EN 12921

Learning and behavioural difficulties in pupils transferring to secondary education: identification, definition, approach, consequences for teacher training. EN 13341

Microscopic school career research phase 2. EN 13227

Practical work in the mathematics classroom. EN 12713

Promotion of deductive and inductive judgment. DE 11753

The provision of education in the middle school years in Cyprus. EN 13758

Repeating in secondary schools. EN 12465

Secondary analyses on the school careers of secondary school pupils on the basis of data on the "VOCL '89" cohort. EN 12447

The singing behaviour of children aged 10-14: an empirical investigation of the influence of 'Musikhauptschulen' on motivation and forms of singing. DE 12993

Standard assessment tasks in design and technology and information technology at key stage 3 of the National Curriculum. EN 12449

Technology in secondary schools. EN 12731

The transversality of environmental education in lower secondary school curricula: objectives, contents (knowledge and values), and methods. EN 13468

L'utilisation des logiciels de traitement de texte pour le développement de la maîtrise de la production écrite. FR 11831

Verification of the need for two hours of civics teaching in lower secondary schools. EN 12594

machine translation

ALPS (Automated Language Processing Systems) computer-assisted translation system as a language learning tool. EN 12798

TIGER project (Translating Industrial German) - Computer-based training in German technical translation. EN 12940

Madagascar

"A toi de parler": méthode pour l'enseignement primaire du français à Madagascar. FR 12795

main subject

Degree specialism and pedagogic understanding in primary PGCE courses. EN 12075

Evaluation of the National Curriculum core subjects (English) at key stages 1, 2 and 3. EN 12858

The place and role of core cultural subjects in the secondary school curriculum. EN 12180

maladjusted

Abnormal behaviour. What to do? DE 13280

maladjustment

Cognitive assessment of maladjusted children. EN 12371

The contribution of schools to remedying maladjustment among young people. EN 13081

Malaysia

Factors relating to achievement of high school students in Kuching City, Malaysia. EN 12398

Study of teacher effectiveness in the Malaysian secondary school. EN 13237

Teacher appraisal in Malaysia: towards a strategy. EN 12455

Mali

Coûts et efficacité dans l'enseignement supérieur malien. FR 12278

man

The experience of working class men in further and higher education. EN 13474

man-machine interface

End-user interfaces to electronic books. EN 12476

Human-computer interfaces to reactive graphical images. EN 11759

management

The applicability of total quality management to the management of schools. EN 12270

Competence-based teacher training for the primary years: a comparative approach. EN 12065

Deregulation: needs and possibilities for school management. EN 12286

The development of managerialism in Scottish education since 1945. EN 12288

Effects of emotion and sexuality in the organizational processes of management. EN 13710

Evolution of the role, structure and operations of senior management groups in universities. EN 12308

Models of effective management in schools. EN 12334

Strategic management and development in educational organisation. EN 12349

management education

Assessment of work experience in relation to management learning. EN 12527

Current developments in the preparation and support of principals in the United States. EN 13660

Distance learning in Central Nervous Systems (CNS) psychiatry. EN 12087

Education management training and development in Europe. EN 12548

The functions, purposes and contributions of national education management centres. EN 12566

The introduction of 'Management' to the secondary curriculum. EN 12577

Knowledge representation and information exchange in instruction. EN 13137

Learning resource centres for executive development. EN 12581

Learning styles and education management. EN 11878

Management development centre: follow-up study. EN 12585

Management issues in nursing/midwifery education. EN 13677

Management training needs of technical institutions in Africa. EN 12331

A review of management education for librarians. EN 13696

Study of factors affecting students' success and drop-out rates in hotel management courses. EN 13633

Using management development packages in schools: an action research programme aimed at encouraging the wider use of school-managed training materials for professional development. EN 12632

managerial staff

Analysis of the compatibility of training and management behaviours and of current situation components. DE 13245

Committee of Vice-Chancellors and Principals of the UK: a study of its development and role. EN 13658

Developing an industrial relations training programme for Greek supervisors and trade union representatives in simultaneous process research into training needs. EN 13561

Evaluation of an in-service training programme "Management activities in day nurseries". DE 11744

Evolution of the role, structure and operations of senior management groups in universities. EN 12308

The expectations of pupils, teachers, counsellors and administrators of the service for psychological counselling and guidance. EN 11913

Further training needs of technical specialists and executives. DE 13707

Improving further training for specialists and executives in the five new German states. DE 13706

Improving innovation management in small and medium-sized companies. DE 13641

The introduction of central management teams in secondary schools. EN 12282

Leadership training in Chinese adult education. EN 13757

Learning styles and education management. EN 11878

Management development centre: follow-up study. EN 12585

The role of the senior management team in secondary schools. EN 12345

manpower

La formation comme variable d'efficience économique. FR 13500

Modèles et problématiques de la reconversion. FR 13603

La notion de qualification. FR 13609

Technology indicators. EN 13514

manpower need

Apprentices and skilled workers on the labour market: a forecast up to the years 2005/2007. DE 13600

The demand for engineers and scientists in Western Austria. DE 13537

Development of a concept concerning the need for qualifications among workers with low qualifications in selected regions. DE 13598

Educational needs in the telematic sector and prospects for creating a course in computer science. EN 12681

Forecasting the demand for higher education specialists. EN 11952

Foreign language needs in companies in Upper Austria. DE 12807

The future labour market for the health care sector. EN 13557

The potential supply of researchers. EN 13615

Professional, economic and legislative problems related to the training of officers working in the field of infrastructural development in support of educational innovation and the transfer of technology. EN 13616

Replacement demand by occupation. EN 13558

Retraining under conditions of industrial restructuring. EN 11803

Skill shortages in Limburg. EN 13632

Theoretical and empirical aspects of manpower analysis. EN 13638

marketing

Critical responses to recent developments in advertising and marketing. EN 12538

Examination and evaluation of approaches to textbook production under free market conditions. EN 13054

Marketing PICKUP in Europe. EN 11779

Marketing service industries: a comparative study of education and banking. EN 12771

Parental choice of school. EN 12339

marking

L'évaluation des connaissances par expert. FR 12391

Examinations research programme. EN 12397

An investigation into the calibration of GCSE grades and National Curriculum levels of attainment at Key Stage 3/4. EN 12408

Moderation at National Curriculum Key Stage 1 across four local education authorities in 1992. EN 12419

mass media

Critical responses to recent developments in advertising and marketing. EN 12538

Doing homework in front of the television or sound media: a descriptive preliminary study. EN 11758

The mass media and the social construction of memory. EN 13139

Prerequisites and results of the conceptual processing of media-based experiences. DE 13056

masters degree

National standards for training and development within Master's programmes. EN 12421

National standards for training and development within masters programmes in education: Glasgow University. EN 12422

mastery learning

Improving the quality of education through mastery learning. EN 11900

mathematics

16-19 mathematics support materials project. EN 11683

Achievements and competence of Standard Grades 3-6. EN 12358

The acquisition of knowledge and skills (in years five to eleven) which are relevant in the Student Selection Examination. EN 12429

An action research study into the role of a mathematics coordinator in a primary school. EN 12034

Affect and learning mathematics. EN 13206

Algebraic processes and the role of symbolism. EN 12638

Analyse et développement des apprentissages à réaliser au collège dans les travaux numériques, dans les travaux géométriques. FR 12642

Assessment of Achievement Programme (AAP) Mathematics: third round Monitoring Project. EN 12643

The attitudes and confidence of primary school teachers regarding mathematics education. EN 12644

Cabri geometry. EN 12645

Children's 'application readiness with basic mathematics'. EN 12647

Cognitive style and learning mathematics. EN 13116

Cohesive ties in children's use of language in relation to the teaching of mathematics. EN 12815

The creation of interactive instructional programs for multimedia systems. EN 11823

Curriculum development in mathematics: using and applying mathematics. EN 12656

Development of materials for basic directives for mathematics in the field of stochastic theory for teachers and pupils. DE 12302

Development of standard assessment tasks in mathematics and science for pupils at the end of the first key stage of the National Curriculum for 1994-1996. EN 12382

Differentiation according to ability in seventh form mathematics classes. DE 11734

Dyslexia and mathematics. EN 11859

The effect of calculators on pupils' problem solving abilities. EN 12478

The effects of maturation on pupils' participation and achievement in mathematics. EN 12666

The effects of the introduction of the GCSE on the work of a group of mathematics teachers: an ethnographic study. EN 12387

English language curriculum development in Niger: Niger educational development 1960-1992 with particular reference to English language teaching. EN 12844

Evaluation of basic instruction in reading and writing. EN 11749

Evaluation of pupils and the effectiveness of teaching. EN 12400

An exploration into the notion of levels of attainment in mathematics. EN 12673

Flexible learning approaches in sixth-form mathematics. EN 12675

Fonctionnement et dysfonctionnements du système didactique en mathématique: échecs, thérapeutique et remédiations. FR 12676

Further development on interactive video. EN 11754

Gap between arithmetical and algebraic thinking. EN 13130

The IEA Third International Mathematics and Science Study in Ireland. EN 12403

The implementation of the National Curriculum in mathematics: the effects of Key Stage 2 in primary schools. EN 12684

The information technology in mathematics project. EN 12690

Inquiry into key psychological concepts used to characterise features of learning and teaching, especially in mathematics. EN 11870

Interactive problem-solving environments. EN 12640

Investigating a framework for mathematics teacher education: an action research study. EN 12142

An investigation into errors made in attempts to solve mathematical problems. EN 12696

An investigation into the feasibility of presenting mathematics in the same form to pupils within National Curriculum key stages 2, 3 and 4. EN 12697

An investigation of teachers' mathematical subject knowledge and the processes of instruction in reception classes. EN 12698

Key Stage 1 of the National Curriculum in Mathematics as it relates to infant schools in Huddersfield. EN 12699

Language and primary maths. EN 12702

Logiciel d'aide à la résolution de problèmes arithmétiques par les élèves de cours élémentaire, première et deuxième années. FR 12703

Logo and the development of algebraic skills. EN 12704

Making efficient use of microcomputers in teaching mathematics to gifted children in the Jordanian primary schools. EN 11777

Mathematical literacy in primary school. EN 12707

Mathematics 16-20. EN 12705

Mathematics in further education. DE 12706

Mathematics - shape & space: mathematics & art. EN 13140

The motivation of mathematics student teachers. DE 13228

Les performances de l'enseignement primaire en Afrique sub-saharienne: comparaison des acquisitions en mathématiques dans quatre pays. FR 12433

Practical work in the mathematics classroom. EN 12713

The principle of economy in learning and teaching mathematics. EN 11889

Priorities of the new mathematics curriculum for problem solving in primary school. EN 11792

Problem solving in geometry in Greek schools. EN 12714

Procédures de validation et de vérification en mathématiques, physique et informatique et leur rôle dans l'apprentissage. FR 12715

Promotion of deductive and inductive judgment. DE 11753

Rôle de la formulation dans ce qu'on appelle une "bonne démonstration mathématique". FR 12718

A social constructivist theory of mathematics. EN 12721

The special oral language needs of low attaining pupils in mathematics. EN 12918

A stochastics teaching method for intermediate schools. DE 11716

Structures et rendement scolaires: dépouillement séparé de la contribution suisse au projet international IAEP II. DE 12720

Students' understanding of acceleration as a vector in the context of mechanics. EN 12725

Students' understanding of literal algebraic equations and formulae. EN 12726

A study of the experiment in Abruzzo with mathematics and physics programmes developed as part of the National Computer Science Project (PNI). EN 12132

Syllabus-based monitoring of achievement in the third year of school. DE 12412

Teacher assessment in the National Curriculum core subjects: mathematics, science and English. EN 12456

Teachers' planning and evaluation of mathematics in Greek high schools. EN 12728

Teaching and learning undergraduate mathematics. EN 12730

Third International Mathematics and Science Study (TIMSS). EN 12661

Transfer in mathematical problem solving. EN 11971

La transmission et l'appropriation des connaissances dans les domaines de l'économie, de la physique et des mathématiques: le fonctionnement des connaissances chez l'apprenant. FR 12736

Tutoring from colleges to schools. EN 11822

The use and practical application of mathematics in a cross-curricular context in National Curriculum key stage 4. EN 12738

The use of computers to teach mathematics. EN 11827

Use of games in the teaching of mathematics. EN 11828

Verbal interaction in mathematics lessons in four secondary schools in Anglophone Cameroon. EN 12945

Women opting for a mathematically, scientifically or technically oriented course of studies and their educational background. DE 13241

maturity

The effects of maturation on pupils' participation and achievement in mathematics. EN 12666

An exploratory study on school readiness, with special reference to the school-aged children in Taiwan. EN 13073

Facteurs psychologiques de l'insertion professionnelle des jeunes de niveau V et l'emploi. FR 13394

Insertion sociale et citoyenneté: une étude longitudinale auprès des 18-25 ans. FR 13182

Standardisation of the LARR short-form test. EN 12925

A study of mature entrants to the teaching profession. EN 13700

Une approche multimédia pour l'orientation scolaire et professionnelle. FR 12020

Mauritius

Social and psychological adjustment of educated married women in Mauritius. EN 13766

meaning

De la construction du sens à partir d'un support iconique. FR 12829

measurement

Economic and Social Research Council Survey link scheme (2). EN 12998

Measurement in science in the primary classroom. EN 12479

The use of performance indicators in the study of problems in the transition from secondary to higher education and in the evaluation of the Centre for Self-Instruction as a guidance service. EN 11956

measurement technique

Developing models of educational accountability. EN 11929

Developing tools to measure the outcomes of guidance. EN 11930

Diagnosing the level of native language ability in Estonian pupils. EN 12837

Performance measurement indicators in research in continuing education. EN 13009

Quantitative analysis for self-evaluation by schools. EN 12439

measuring instrument

Determining the entry-level characteristics of primary school pupils. EN 13060

Identifying gifted pupils. EN 13230

Measurement in science in the primary classroom. EN 12479

Measuring the quality of primary schools. EN 12444

Pre-School Activities Inventory. EN 12480

Problem behaviour in pupils entering primary school. EN 13356

mechanical engineering

Didactic concept for a training programme in an "AuT" project, CAD-based and computer-aided information systems in a design department for plant construction and special purpose machines. DE 13562

media education

Critical responses to recent developments in advertising and marketing. EN 12538

Development of media-pedagogic curricula. DE 12496

Media education in nurseries: pedagogic principles and practical activities. DE 11782

On the psychology of teaching literature (from the psychology of teaching literature to its dramaturgy). DE 11848

media technology

ISDN2 and computer networks to enhance initial teacher training. EN 12472

medical rehabilitation

The mobility of blind and visually impaired persons. EN 13347

Psychological assessment of cochlear implantees. EN 13357

The role of adult basic education in the re-education of brain injured adults: an investigation into student-specific re-learning programmes. EN 12611

medical service

An individualised patient education programme for community pharmacy practice. EN 12685

Possibilities and limitations of academicizing teacher training in the nursing sector in relation to the development of nursing as a science. DE 11787

medical treatment

Possibilities and limitations of academicizing teacher training in the nursing sector in relation to the development of nursing as a science. DE 11787

medicine

Assessment of competence in general practice. EN 12364

Chimie et enseignement médical. FR 12648

Educational Software Library - ESL. EN 13020

An individualised patient education programme for community pharmacy practice. EN 12685

The place and role of pathophysiology in medical education. EN 12712

Place des humanités dans la formation médicale en Europe. FR 12711

Three longitudinal studies of medical student selection. EN 12353

The Wound Programme. EN 12740

memorizing

Développement de la mémoire opérationnelle chez l'enfant. FR 13123

Traitement cognitif des textes incluant la lecture, la compréhension, la mémorisation et la production de textes: la construction des représentations occurrentes. FR 13162

memory

The analysis and use of spatial ability in educational contexts. EN 13109

Cognitive processes in student learning. EN 13114

The development of visual memory strategies in children. EN 13121

Integration activities in learning. EN 11871

The mass media and the social construction of memory. EN 13139

Memory, intelligence and talent. EN 13187

On the representation of metacognitive areas of knowledge in long-term memory with particular reference to the semantics of verbs concerning mental activities. DE 13165

Studies of Attention Disordered - Hyperactive (ADHD) children. EN 13157

mental development

A study of the extent to which Austrian school textbooks take account of the capacities, interests and needs of pupils. DE 13055

mental handicap

Development and testing of a didactic concept for transferring action knowledge relating to the teaching language of teachers at schools for the mentally disabled. DE 13313

mental health

Fear and coping. DE 13207

Health psychology: theoretical models of normalcy and health, mechanisms of health and health behaviour. EN 13195

The relationship between school size and problem behaviour among secondary school pupils. EN 13273

School psychology - educational counselling. DE 12008

Well-being and education. EN 12023

mental retardation

The attitudes of pupils in the Ankara Vocational School for Educable Mentally Retarded Children towards vocational education. EN 13296

Memory, intelligence and talent. EN 13187

mental stress

The effects of personal traits and different problems of university students on their anxiety levels. EN 13209

Everyday life of special school teachers caught between social acceptance and personal ideals. Can psychodramatic support have a stabilizing effect? DE 13661

An investigation into how pupils perceive and react to stressful situations in school. EN 13334

Negative influences on teacher personality and how they may be reduced. EN 13267

Pressure on primary headteachers during and following the implementation of Local Management of Schools. EN 13687

The role of environmental conditions in occupational stress and burnout in the helping professions. EN 13589

School stress. EN 13359

Stress, coping and learning: a longitudinal study. EN 13365

Stress in children. EN 13366

Stress on college lecturers working in the North East of England and its possible effects on student learning. EN 13367

Student teachers' perceptions of stressful situations in schools. EN 12224

Teacher stress and organisational climate. EN 13372

Teaching under pressure. EN 13373

mentally handicapped

Adult education for the mentally disabled: evaluation research for a seminar project run by the federal association "Lebenshilfe". DE 13314

The attitude of normal adolescents towards their handicapped peers. EN 13191

Care for children with learning and behavioural difficulties. EN 11873

Communication between non-handicapped children and pupils with severe learning difficulties. EN 12816

Communication training via manual signing for non-speaking mentally handicapped children. EN 12817

Computer applications to special education. EN 12653

Developmental concepts of Christianity in a person with a mental handicap. EN 13122

Establishing access to the tertiary curriculum for adults with special educational needs. EN 11946

An evaluation study of the efficacy of 'Social Problem Solving Training', with people who have learning difficulties, living in residential and community settings. EN 13319

An investigation into the schedule control of stereotyped and self-injurious behaviours in young people with severe learning difficulties. EN 13335

Post-school learning opportunities for people with profound intellectual and multiple impairments. EN 13354

Primary school children's understanding of severe learning difficulties. EN 13355

Secondary school pupils' attitudes towards mental disability in Ireland, Australia, Finland and Germany. DE 13174

The social integration of handicapped children. EN 13327

Special education: concepts and issues. EN 12147

message reception

Le fonctionnement des sujets comme récepteurs actifs de messages médiatisés: approche cognitive et psycho-sociale. FR 12861

methodology

Méthodologie des histoires de vie et formation de formateurs. FR 11783

Supervision as a pedagogic activity in in-service further training processes. DE 11818

microcomputer

An evaluation of home computers in adult distance education. EN 11746

Microcomputer use in the primary school. EN 11785

The use of microcomputers in Saudi secondary schools. EN 11830

L'utilisation des logiciels de traitement de texte pour le développement de la maîtrise de la production écrite. FR 11831

microscope

A 'virtual' microscope. EN 12481

migrant

Migration et éducation dans les sociétés multiculturelles: les modèles européens en changement. DE 11981

migrant worker's child

L'adaptation à l'école maternelle des enfants issus de l'immigration maghrébine. FR 13059

A permanent system for the registration of immigrant pupils in the Dutch-speaking part of Belgium. EN 13483

military school

The Army Schoolmaster and the development of elementary education in the Army 1812-1920. EN 12743

minimum competencies

Communication and professional competencies in a modular humanities programme. EN 12534

A competence framework in chemistry. EN 12652

Description and evaluation of an educational intervention to assist learning-disabled adults into employment and independent living. EN 12078

Learning outcomes and competences in English/Communication Studies. EN 12885

Piloting the personal competence model in secondary schools. EN 13095

Research and development in National Vocational Qualifications (NVQs) and the identification of various competencies in teaching and management. EN 13623

Teacher competencies and professional development. EN 12237

Teaching competence - a personal construct investigation. EN 13159

minority language

Bilingual learners and language provision in the National Curriculum. EN 12809

Patterns of bilingualism in some families of Pakistani origin: implications for policy on language education. EN 12897

Support of the introduction of Frisian language in primary and secondary education. EN 13488

misconduct

Behavioural approach to teaching project. EN 13248

Comparative study of disruptive behaviour and discipline in schools in the United Kingdom and Kenya. EN 13250

Disruptive behaviour in schools: post Elton Project Sandwell Initiative. EN 13255

Pupils' misbehaviour reported as discipline problems conceptually interpreted by headmasters, teachers and pupils in secondary schools. EN 11958

Teachers' attitudes towards children's behaviour problems in nursery classes in Greece and management strategies used. EN 13278

model

An alternative metaphor for teaching control technology. EN 12639

Computer-based modelling across the curriculum. EN 11702

Developing models of educational accountability. EN 11929

Development of complex educational contents. DE 11862

Distributed knowledge-based CBT. DE 11834

Economic and Social Research Council Survey link scheme (2). EN 12998

Extending multilevel models. EN 13000

Intercultural education in the fine arts in Europe. DE 13764

Internal differentiation into specialized classes in part-time vocational schools. DE 11764

Mental models from a constructive perspective. DE 12965

Model of analysis-based knowledge acquisition and development of generative diagnostic models. DE 13142

Modelling school effectiveness. EN 12417

Multilevel modelling for New York Project. EN 13007

Quantitative analysis for self-evaluation by schools. EN 12439

Sport and movement as a means to promote the integration of socially deprived young people in education and work: opportunities and limitations in youth homes and in vocational guidance for young people. DE 12515

Strategies leading to the use of non-standard language patterns. DE 12927

Supervision as a pedagogic activity in in-service further training processes. DE 11818

The usefulness of multilevel models for the analysis of longitudinal research data. EN 12997

Visual and practical learning in the combined educational setting of museums - companies - schools. DE 11851

model construction

First-year students in higher education. EN 12452

Job-based training for unskilled and semi-skilled workers in small and medium-sized companies using computer-aided resources. DE 13534

Learning and the pace of lessons. EN 11877

The mind model: a comprehensive framework for educational- psychological research and practice. DE 12996

Modèles et problématiques de la reconversion. FR 13603

Prognosis of the development of education in the Slovak Republic up to the year 2010. EN 13011

modern languages

Evaluation of national pilot projects: foreign languages in primary schools (Scotland). EN 12854

modernization

The role of metropolitan areas in newly emerging central Europe. DE 13439

modular training

The effectiveness of new curriculum models for initial vocational training. EN 11726

Modular vocational courses: types and effects. EN 11786

Young people's experience of National Certificate Modules. EN 11845

Young people's experience of National Certificate Modules. EN 12267

money

Enquête représentative sur les activités rémunérées des étudiants à l'Université de Berne. DE 13512

moral development

How does bereavement affect spiritual and moral thinking in children? EN 13448

moral education

Emotivism, prescriptivism and moral education. EN 12551

Ethical absolutism and education. EN 12554

History in school: possibilities for the development of knowledge, civic consciousness, morality and creativity in pupils and students. EN 12763

Moral knowledge, moral principles and moral education. EN 12589

Personal, social, moral and religious education in primary schools: the impact and implications of the Education Reform Act 1988 and the National Curriculum. EN 12508

Philosophical inquiry in values education. EN 12967

Philosophy of the curriculum with particular reference to moral, religious, physical education and personal and social education. EN 12969

Research on values education (ROVE). EN 12970

Values education in Europe. EN 12971

moral value

Moral knowledge, moral principles and moral education. EN 12589

morphology

Assessing the appropriateness of textbooks with the help of the computer. EN 12841

mother

Motherhood and teaching: a life history investigation. EN 13680

Young families now: a focus for learning in the community. EN 13471

mother-child relation

Acquisition et gestion de la conduite de dialogue: la construction des finalités à travers le dialogue. FR 13058

L'adaptation à l'école maternelle des enfants issus de l'immigration maghrébine. FR 13059

Parts de l'enfant et de la mère dans la gestion d'un récit produit conjointement. FR 13091

mother tongue

Assessing the appropriateness of textbooks with the help of the computer. EN 12841

Contrasting German: problems experienced by people with different native languages when learning German as a foreign language. DE 12832

Diagnosing the level of native language ability in Estonian pupils. EN 12837

English language monitoring. EN 12845

The Gaelic Language Development Project. EN 12866

International group for the study of language standardisation and the vernacularisation of literacy. EN 13504

Learners' language. EN 12884

Levels of functional literacy among Turkish and Moroccan children in the Netherlands and in the country of origin. EN 12865

Native and non-native use of English. EN 12891

Patterns of bilingualism in some families of Pakistani origin: implications for policy on language education. EN 12897

Perspectives d'une didactique de l'allemand pour la Suisse alémanique. FR 12899

Policy conditions for teaching immigrant children in their native language. DE 12808

Standardization of a screening test of Greek-Cypriot speech and language. EN 12451

Syntactic input and the acquisition of the verb lexicon. EN 13103

Training and transfer of reading strategies: mother tongue instruction and foreign language instruction. EN 12941

Training and transfer of vocabulary acquisition strategies: mother tongue instruction and foreign language instruction. EN 12942

Vers une pédagogie du langage figuré: compréhension des métaphores et production d'images chez l'adolescent. FR 12946

motion

Psychological study of music and dance for pedagogics and therapy. DE 13090

The role of cognition in psychomotor activities. EN 13088

Sport and movement as a means to promote the integration of socially deprived young people in education and work: opportunities and limitations in youth homes and in vocational guidance for young people. DE 12515

motivation

Deterrents to completing adult education at the upper secondary level: a theoretical and empirical analysis of factors determining adult student dropout in upper secondary level education. EN 13213

Further development on interactive video. EN 11754

Individual motivation and take-up of National Vocational Qualifications in the South West. EN 13223

Is the sex-type of an individual an influencing factor in teacher-pupil interaction and motivational style amongst school children? EN 13085

Learned helplessness and self-worth motivation in children with special educational needs. EN 13185

Microscopic school career research phase 2. EN 13227

Motivation and collaboration in computer-assisted learning of chemistry. EN 11788

Motivation and demotivation among secondary school teachers. EN 13681

The motivation of mathematics student teachers. DE 13228

Motivational orientation and meta-motivation as determinants of learning intention and effort in respect of homework tasks. EN 13229

Occupational advancement as motivation for further education in employed adults. DE 13212

On-line motivation: a cross-sectional analysis of emotional orientation in competitive situations in school. DE 13231

Protestant adult education in urban and rural communities. DE 11750

The singing behaviour of children aged 10-14: an empirical investigation of the influence of 'Musikhauptschulen' on motivation and forms of singing. DE 12993

The social and motivational structure of course teachers at adult education institutes in Berlin: a comparison of the years 1979 and 1990. DE 13236

Sport for all? An investigation into the factors that motivate a child not to participate in sport. EN 12514

Students' motivation in physical education classes perceived to have different goal perspectives. EN 12618

Supervision of science research students in Belgium and other European countries. EN 12367

Teacher mobility in primary and secondary education. EN 13455

Teaching personnel in Italian schools. EN 13670

motivation for studies

Cultural bases of educational forms: an inquiry into the learning patterns of the 40 primary school children in an Indian village. EN 13214

The demotivated pupil in the modern language classroom - a comparative study. EN 12831

The development of motivation and self-regulation in lower secondary school pupils. EN 13215

Didactic methods for the motivation and qualification of adults who are not accustomed to learning. DE 13437

First-year students in higher education. EN 12452

Intérêts et choix de filière post baccalauréat. FR 13224

Learning by workers (aged above 35) with a low level of education. EN 12156

Mathematics 16-20. EN 12705

Modular vocational courses: types and effects. EN 11786

Participation in education and training: age group 16-19. EN 12181

School and environment. EN 13599

Student supply and the expansion of Arabic studies in higher education. EN 12928

Women opting for a mathematically, scientifically or technically oriented course of studies and their educational background. DE 13241

motor activity

An investigation into the physical activity levels of primary school children. EN 13083

Physical activity patterns of primary school children. EN 13094

The role of cognition in psychomotor activities. EN 13088

motor development

Effect of perceptuo-motor difficulty on early handwriting, speech and reading. EN 13071

An examination of teaching and learning strategies for children with movement learning difficulties. EN 13320

Gender differences in motor performance from infancy to adolescence. EN 13076

Physical training facilities in schools and the development of interest in physical exercise among less able or physically handicapped pupils. EN 12591

Sex-specific differences in the verbal-sensorimotor development of children aged 4-6 in schools in the GDR. DE 13078

motor disorder

An evaluation of conductive education. EN 13315

An examination of teaching and learning strategies for children with movement learning difficulties. EN 13320

Motor and perceptual competence in prematurely born children. EN 13089

A new look at perceptuo-motor disorders in cerebral palsied children. EN 13352

motor handicapped

A new look at perceptuo-motor disorders in cerebral palsied children. EN 13352

Scottish Centre for Children With Motor Impairment. EN 13360

multidimensional analysis

The usefulness of multilevel models for the analysis of longitudinal research data. EN 12997

multilingualism

Bilingual learners and language provision in the National Curriculum. EN 12809

Gestion et dynamique de la communication familiale en milieu bilingue ou multilingue. FR 12868

Policy and practice in multicultural education in Canada and Great Britain. EN 11994

Teaching English in a multilingual classroom. EN 12935

multimedia method

Informatique et formation: les nouvelles technologies de l'information (NTI). FR 11763

Multi-media course in Italian language. EN 11789

Une approche multimédia pour l'orientation scolaire et professionnelle. FR 12020

multimedia system

Classroom-based multimedia authoring tools. EN 11696

Conceptualisation design and orientation in complex multimedia structures. EN 13022

The creation of interactive instructional programs for multimedia systems. EN 11823

Database concept for the authoring workbench. EN 12683

Database support for multi-media computer-assisted learning. EN 12659

nurse

AIDS Education and Research Trust (AVERT) HIV/AIDS and nursing project. EN 13648

Diploma in advanced nursing studies. EN 13663

Educating 'desirable attitudes' in nurses. EN 13664

Effectiveness of nurse teacher training related to experience since qualifying. EN 12093

An evaluation of educational materials on HIV and AIDS for nurses. EN 13316

The implications for nursing education in Cyprus commensurate with joining the European Community: a problem study. EN 12130

Information needs and information seeking behaviour of nurses. EN 13671

Learning psychiatric nursing skills: the contribution of the ward environment. EN 13676

Management issues in nursing/midwifery education. EN 13677

Nurse selection project - United Kingdom Central Council for Nursing, Midwifery and Health Visiting (UKCC). EN 13684

Supply workers in state schools and the National Health Service. EN 13701

nursery school

Changes in the classroom experience of Inner London pupils. EN 11919

Children in mixed-age groups (0 to 6 years) in the Sebastianstrasse day care centre in Ingolstadt. DE 12146

Computers in nursery schools. EN 11706

The effects of the National Curriculum on infant teachers and their practice. EN 11728

Evaluation of an in-service training programme "Management activities in day nurseries". DE 11744

Media education in nurseries: pedagogic principles and practical activities. DE 11782

Social networks and ethnic identity in an urban nursery: a sociolinguistic analysis of preferred language use. EN 12916

Structure d'accueil pour la petite enfance dans la région morgienne. FR 12350

Teachers' attitudes towards children's behaviour problems in nursery classes in Greece and management strategies used. EN 13278

Teaching art appreciation in the nursery school. EN 12627

Teaching of fairy tales in Cyprus. EN 12978

Territorial justice and nursery education provision in England and Wales. EN 12247

The training and education of Froebelian teachers in England and Wales, 1889-1926. EN 12791

nutrition

The impact of home economics on pupil nutrition during school breaks. EN 13286

nutrition education

Teaching and learning about food and nutrition in school: the nation's diet initiative. EN 12626

occupation

Changing life careers. DE 13452

Development, implementation and assessment of a nation-wide performance competition for home economics occupations with the aim of creating a basis for new contents and structures in home economics education. DE 13495

Professionals in music institutions in Poland: problems and issues in professional training and careers. EN 13617

occupational aspiration

Career aspirations and employment opportunities of general secondary school leavers. DE 13542

Determinants of occupational orientation and development: study within the framework of a cross-sectional investigation. DE 13560

The effect of individual and socio-economic situational variables of secondary school pupils upon their vocational interests. EN 13170

Occupational plans of socially deprived young people (comparison of old and new German states). DE 13538

Socialisation of elites. EN 12013

The young generation of teachers in Poland under conditions of structural change. EN 13679

occupational choice

16-19 Initiative: Liverpool. EN 13517

Art therapists and their art. EN 13651

BP Exploration Fellowship in vocational education and guidance. EN 13544

Career guidance in Avon: encouraging collaboration. EN 13545

Career guidance in Birmingham: a preliminary study. EN 13546

Careers service analyses. EN 13548

Comparative research on career guidance between Britain and China. EN 13550

Determinants of individual differences in educational choice and success. EN 13216

Determinants of occupational orientation and development: study within the framework of a cross-sectional investigation. DE 13560

Development of an interactive system for career guidance. EN 11940

Education graduates at work: occupation, career start, educational biography and retrospective assessment of the university course. DE 13563

Evaluation of an educational and vocational guidance initiative in compulsory school. EN 13612

An evaluation of career development courses in higher education. EN 13576

Everyday life of special school teachers caught between social acceptance and personal ideals. Can psychodramatic support have a stabilizing effect? DE 13661

Guidance aspects of the Enterprise in Higher Education programme. EN 13585

Interact/job hop: a pilot study on a media-supported career counselling scheme. DE 13595

Motivation and demotivation among secondary school teachers. EN 13681

Nurse selection project - United Kingdom Central Council for Nursing, Midwifery and Health Visiting (UKCC). EN 13684

Social competence and occupational success: quality and quantity of social contacts and relations as a prerequisite for occupational success under conditions of technological progress. DE 13276

Survey of older graduates. EN 13635

Une approche multimédia pour l'orientation scolaire et professionnelle. FR 12020

Vocational orientation at school: adolescents facing the choice of a career. DE 13629

Young people and vocational training in Germany. DE 11771

Youth Development Projects. EN 13645

occupational disease

The role of environmental conditions in occupational stress and burnout in the helping professions. EN 13589

occupational environment

Facteurs psychologiques de l'insertion professionnelle des jeunes de niveau V et l'emploi. FR 13394

The role of environmental conditions in occupational stress and burnout in the helping professions. EN 13589

occupational integration

Analyse de la relation formation-emploi, applications aux jeunes sortant des formations initiales. FR 13520

Analyse des effets induits par un dispositif de réapprentissage destiné aux salariés peu qualifiés. FR 13521

Analyse des formations en alternance: apprentissage et contrats de qualification. FR 13522

Analyse qualitative des procédures de mise en oeuvre des contrats de qualification au niveau local. FR 13523

Baccalauréats professionnels (Bac-Pro): description d'une première promotion. FR 13536

Educational careers and occupational integration of university graduates from 1988/1989. DE 12453

Les enseignements moyens général et technique au Bénin. FR 12300

Entrée des jeunes dans la vie active (enquêtes EVA). FR 13571

Evaluation research on remedial teaching for the mentally disabled in Blaesiberg as a prevocational training programme in accordance with Section 40 of the Employment Promotion Act (AFG). DE 13377

Facteurs psychologiques de l'insertion professionnelle des jeunes de niveau V et l'emploi. FR 13394

Further education for immigrants, with particular reference to cross-disciplinary competencies. DE 11836

Impact de la mesure "Travaux d'utilité collective" (TUC) en région Lorraine. FR 13590

L'insertion professionnelle des élèves issus des écoles d'arts plastiques. FR 13593

Integration of visually handicapped students and university graduates in working life. DE 13594

Learning to be a natural science teacher. EN 12149

Occupational plans of socially deprived young people (comparison of old and new German states). DE 13538

L'organisation de la transition professionnelle des jeunes en voie d'intégration dans le salariat. FR 13611

Out-of-school integration of the severely disabled (NIS). DE 13350

Polytechnic students two years after graduation: empirical analysis of their destination and career start. DE 13578

Results of the pilot project "Vocational qualification of women" as part of the series of projects "On vocational qualifications for adults who have not completed their vocational training and who are particularly at risk on the labour market". DE 13574

Rôle des représentations sociales intergroupes dans la construction de l'identité. FR 13100

School and environment. EN 13599

Second survey of West German university graduates from 1988/1989. DE 13647

Training, occupational integration and further qualification of entry workers. DE 13535

Typologie des relations formation-emploi: effets sur la stabilité des emplois des jeunes ouvriers et employés. FR 13639

Work socialisation of youth (WOSY): a cross-national study. EN 13644

Young East German academics in the employment system of the Federal Republic of Germany in 1991/1992. DE 13613

occupational mobility

La gestion de la reconversion des salariés: une forme de transition professionnelle. FR 13583

Labour market of the Euro-region Maas-Rhine. EN 13554

Pilot project 'Making the transition from teaching to business'. DE 13604

Teacher mobility in primary and secondary education. EN 13455

occupational qualification

Aide à domicile: emplois et formation en Bourgogne. FR 11686

Analyse des effets induits par un dispositif de réapprentissage destiné aux salariés peu qualifiés. FR 13521

Analyse qualitative des procédures de mise en oeuvre des contrats de qualification au niveau local. FR 13523

Apprenticeship training in Nigeria. DE 11774

Comparison of qualification structures in lignite mining in East Germany. DE 13619

Competency-based vocational qualifications in the labour market. EN 13551

Concept and development of study materials for a supplementary course on equal opportunities for women. DE 12500

Development and testing of a seminar concept for on-the-job instructors. DE 11735

Development of an interactive system for career guidance. EN 11940

The employment situation of women in the former GDR (further vocational training for women in the new German states). DE 13540

Improving further training for specialists and executives in the five new German states. DE 13706

Individual motivation and take-up of National Vocational Qualifications in the South West. EN 13223

Information technology in education and employment. EN 12688

Interplant training centre "Oberes Erzgebirge". DE 11824

La notion de qualification. FR 13609

Nurse selection project - United Kingdom Central Council for Nursing, Midwifery and Health Visiting (UKCC). EN 13684

Occupational advancement as motivation for further education in employed adults. DE 13212

Processus de socialisation cognitive chez les femmes de bas niveau de qualification en formation. FR 13098

Professional development of graduate sports teachers. DE 13539

Professional, economic and legislative problems related to the training of officers working in the field of infrastructural development in support of educational innovation and the transfer of technology. EN 13616

Results of the pilot project "Vocational qualification of women" as part of the series of projects "On vocational qualifications for adults who have not completed their vocational training and who are particularly at risk on the labour market". DE 13574

A study on 'Fachakademien' (vocational academies). DE 11691

Third representative BIBB/IAB survey on attainment and utilization of qualifications, as well as the use of working materials in East and West Germany. DE 13564

The transferability of current insurance qualifications within the European Community. EN 13516

L'adaptation à l'école maternelle des enfants issus de l'immigration maghrébine. FR 13059

Children in mixed-age groups (0 to 6 years) in the Sebastianstrasse day care centre in Ingolstadt. DE 12146

Les coûts de l'enseignement pré-scolaire au Brésil. FR 12277

Defining high-quality preschool provision in Belgium and Britain. EN 12074

Didactic materials for pre-school road safety education. DE 11717

Les instituteurs: leurs formations, leurs trajectoires sociales et professionnelles, leurs pratiques professionnelles. FR 13673

Jardins d'enfants bilingues-biculturels et multiculturels: accompagnement scientifique d'une expérience-pilote à Bâle. DE 11915

Models of organization and management of pre-school provision and their effects on the child's development in Great Britain, Sweden and the USA. EN 12169

Phonological awareness of nursery-school children. EN 12900

Playgroups' study. EN 12186

Preventing reading and spelling failure: the effects of various metalinguistic training programmes in nursery school on reading and spelling development. EN 12862

Prevention of learning problems in nursery school children. EN 12193

Primary assessment, curriculum and experience. EN 12510

Psychologie de l'éducation musicale. FR 12605

The quality of pre-school education: an exploration of the relationships between teaching methods, process variables and outcomes. EN 11926

The share-a-book project. EN 11809

A study of pre-school education in the Republic of Ireland with particular reference to those pre-schools which are listed by the Irish Pre-School Playgroups Association in Cork City and County. EN 12227

predictive evaluation

Facteurs psychologiques de l'insertion professionnelle des jeunes de niveau V et l'emploi. FR 13394

Improving student achievement through promoting effective learning. EN 11869

Performance forecasts for pupils in upper secondary commercial schools with a focus on skiing instruction. DE 12413

premature baby

Motor and perceptual competence in prematurely born children. EN 13089

prevention

Les Centres médico-psycho-pédagogiques (CMPP), 1945-1975. FR 13283

Irrationalité des comportements: obstacle ou moteur d'une prévention efficace; l'approche des professionnels de la prévention du SIDA. FR 13288

Législation de la jeunesse et institutions aujourd'hui: recherche comparative internationale. FR 13737

Statistical study of compulsory school children in Abruzzo concerning the prevention of tooth decay and eye disorders. EN 13292

Survey of HIV/AIDS education in secondary schools in the East Midlands to discover its curriculum organization, incidence and teaching strategies, the problems and INSET needs of teachers and the impact of the National Curriculum. EN 12623

preventive medicine

Statistical study of compulsory school children in Abruzzo concerning the prevention of tooth decay and eye disorders. EN 13292

A study of students' knowledge of cancer etiology and prevention. EN 13284

primary education

"A toi de parler": méthode pour l'enseignement primaire du français à Madagascar. FR 12795

5-14 Development Programme: coordination of the evaluation of its implementation. EN 12483

The acquisition of knowledge and skills (in years five to eleven) which are relevant in the Student Selection Examination. EN 12429

An action research study into the role of a mathematics coordinator in a primary school. EN 12034

Bilinguisme, immigration et scolarisation. FR 12811

Broad deployability of teachers. EN 13656

The Centre for the Study of the Arts in Primary Education (CENSAPE): development of resource collections of examples of good practice in primary arts education. EN 12975

Comparative study of writing development in French and English primary schools. EN 12818

Computer-assisted learning in the teaching of reading. EN 11701

Conception and design of a course programme for national history, geography and natural sciences for use in primary schools. EN 12505

Concepts of history and teaching approaches at National Curriculum Key Stages 2 & 3. EN 12751

Conceptual development in primary school science: the design of group tasks. EN 12536

Conceptual progression in science. EN 13118

Confirmatory study and teaching experiment for overcoming difficulties in complex texts in primary years 3 and 5. DE 11773

The contribution of social education to primary and secondary education. EN 11957

Cross phase continuity and progression project: transition from primary to secondary school. EN 12280

A curriculum for general education in Estonia. EN 12495

The design of education in primary and lower secondary schools. EN 11988

Developing emancipatory curricula in primary schools. EN 11928

The development of primary and secondary education: analysis and prognosis. EN 12045

Development of standard assessment tasks for pupils at the end of the first key stage of the National Curriculum. EN 12381

Development of the educational level of the population in the Slovak Republic by the year 2000. EN 12021

Devon Music Technology Project. EN 12541

The differences in teaching and learning styles employed in primary and secondary schools with reference to developing information technology capability. EN 12664

Down's Syndrome children in primary schools. EN 13336

Dutch language education in multilingual classrooms. EN 12932

Economic and industrial awareness in the primary school. EN 12494

Effectiveness of foreign language teaching in primary school. DE 12840

Encounters and the environment: the role of encounter theory in the teaching of the subject "Social and Natural Environment". EN 13463

Les enfants non-lecteurs; étude des impossibilités persistantes de l'activité de lecture chez des enfants âgés de neuf ans et plus. FR 13312

An enrichment programme for gifted immigrant and deprived primary school pupils. EN 13220

Enterprise Education: Scottish Enterprise funded package writing. EN 11731

Equality versus quality: the dilemma of primary schools in today's Europe. EN 11975

Evaluating the effectiveness of a practitioner's use of a constructivist approach for developing scientific knowledge and understanding in primary students during their initial training and primary teachers on inservice courses. EN 12556

Evaluation de la double vacation au primaire: l'exemple du Niger. FR 12304

Evaluation of a development project on primary teacher education. EN 12262

Evaluation of national pilot projects: foreign languages in primary schools (Scotland). EN 12854

Evaluation of pupils and the effectiveness of teaching. EN 12400

Evaluation of remedial reading programmes in the city of Utrecht. EN 12851

The evaluation of school-initiated INSET in selected junior schools: teacher and headteacher perspectives. EN 12393

Evaluation of "tailored instruction" in primary schools. EN 11742

Evaluation of the Promoting Health in Primary Schools (PHIPS) project. EN 12561

Evaluation of the three-year training course in primary teacher training colleges. EN 12099

Evaluation research for the pilot project "Mixed classes with differential objectives for disabled and non-disabled pupils in lower-level secondary schools". DE 13378

Factors influencing the development of primary school pupils in Estonia. EN 13070

Gendered expectations and the primary school curriculum. EN 13396

Genre theory and writing functions. EN 12867

Global futures project. EN 12760

Group textual study of fiction in primary school. EN 12980

The implementation of the National Curriculum in mathematics: the effects of Key Stage 2 in primary schools. EN 12684

Improving the quality of argument: schools. EN 13132

Independent work of children and cognitive processes in primary school. EN 13154

Individual learning: reading and writing. DE 12872

Information technology: software in primary schools. EN 12691

Les instituteurs: leurs formations, leurs trajectoires sociales et professionnelles, leurs pratiques professionnelles. FR 13673

Instruction, leisure time reading and development of reading skills from the beginning of primary year 5 (8-year-olds) to the end of year 8 (12-year-olds). EN 12895

Integrated education for children with special educational needs in physical education programmes in Nigerian primary schools. EN 13328

Interactive science in the primary school. EN 12574

Interreligious education. EN 12576

Investigating teachers' assessment of children's writing at National Curriculum Key Stage 2. EN 12876

An investigation into errors made in attempts to solve mathematical problems. EN 12696

An investigation into techniques for the teaching of non-fiction in schools. EN 12983

An investigation into the physical activity levels of primary school children. EN 13083

An investigation of sustained silent reading in the primary school. EN 12879

An investigation of teachers' mathematical subject knowledge and the processes of instruction in reception classes. EN 12698

Investigation of the effects of different Inservice Education and Training of Teachers (INSET) experiences on teachers' understanding and perception of their role in teaching science at the elementary level (in US schools). EN 12144

Knowledge of languages among Italian primary school teachers. EN 12823

Language and primary maths. EN 12702

The Learn to Travel School's Project. EN 12501

A local authority-based demonstration trial of 'good practice' in road safety education. EN 12582

Local education authority support for continuity and progression in the 5-16 curriculum. EN 11978

Logiciel d'aide à la résolution de problèmes arithmétiques par les élèves de cours élémentaire, première et deuxième années. FR 12703

Management in the primary school class. EN 11778

Meeting basic learning needs in primary schools. EN 12404

Monitoring the implementation of the National Curriculum in primary schools. EN 12503

Music and movement education from the first to the fourth year in primary school. EN 12976

Music for the generalist primary teacher, with reference to the National Curriculum. EN 12592

A nation-wide survey of attention problems among primary school pupils: a repeated measurment. EN 13173

New technologies in educational processes. EN 12708

The non-teacher directed peer-group classroom talk of nine-year olds. EN 12894

L'ordinateur dans l'enseignement: la Suisse en comparaison avec 18 autres systèmes éducatifs. DE 11703

Parents' understanding of science in the National Curriculum. EN 12595

Peer group counselling in upper primary. EN 13092

Les performances de l'enseignement primaire en Afrique sub-saharienne: comparaison des acquisitions en mathématiques dans quatre pays. FR 12433

Personal, social, moral and religious education in primary schools: the impact and implications of the Education Reform Act 1988 and the National Curriculum. EN 12508

Physical activity patterns of primary school children. EN 13094

Planning for differentiation in the primary classroom. EN 11793

Prévision des dépenses d'éducation primaire à l'horizon 2000 dans les pays en développement. FR 13508

Primary assessment, curriculum and experience. EN 12510

Primary history project. EN 12778

Primary school children's understanding of heat and temperature. EN 12599

Primary school pupils' ability to understand tables and schematic drawings. DE 11690

Primary science assessments. EN 12435

Sociocultural aspects of teaching English to Arabic speaking students. EN 12917

qualification

Broad deployability of teachers. EN 13656

The demands for a teaching qualification in Outdoor Education. EN 12491

Development and testing of a model for in-company further training for warehouse and handling personnel in forwarding agencies. DE 13572

Development of a concept concerning the need for qualifications among workers with low qualifications in selected regions. DE 13598

Didactic concept for a training programme in an "AuT" project, CAD-based and computer-aided information systems in a design department for plant construction and special purpose machines. DE 13562

Didactic methods for the motivation and qualification of adults who are not accustomed to learning. DE 13437

Evaluation of an in-service training programme "Management activities in day nurseries". DE 11744

Evaluation of the project "Students and the world of work". DE 11743

Evaluation research for the pilot project "Cross-curricular teaching at vocational schools". DE 11838

Further training and employment of university graduates in information-processing occupations. DE 13642

Further training needs of technical specialists and executives. DE 13707

Holistic job engineering competence as a goal for qualifications: socially acceptable engineering of information and communications systems as a subject for basic and further training for computer specialists. DE 13621

Job-based training for unskilled and semi-skilled workers in small and medium-sized companies using computer-aided resources. DE 13534

Key qualifications. DE 13627

National Council for Vocational Qualifications (NCVQ) Fellowship. EN 12173

National standards for training and development within Master's programmes. EN 12421

National standards for training and development within masters programmes in education: Glasgow University. EN 12422

Rationalization of the preparation of university graduates for the teaching profession. EN 12210

Research and development in National Vocational Qualifications (NVQs) and the identification of various competencies in teaching and management. EN 13623

Study of factors affecting students' success and drop-out rates in hotel management courses. EN 13633

Tomorrow's secretarial office: future qualifications and development of the factual and organizational recommendations for secretarial work. DE 13720

Work situation, occupational self-image and qualification of specialist instructors. DE 13650

qualitative analysis

Evolution du système productif et appropriation des nouvelles technologies de formation. FR 13498

quality of education

5-14 Development Programme: coordination of the evaluation of its implementation. EN 12483

Analysis of the demand for education and the functioning of the education system. EN 11909

An analysis of vocational schools. DE 12040

Annual survey of new Open University courses. EN 12046

The applicability of total quality management to the management of schools. EN 12270

The application of quality management principles to learning. EN 11911

A comparative study of outcomes and process in English higher education. EN 12063

Continuous innovation of environmental education in chemistry teacher education. EN 12185

Defining high-quality preschool provision in Belgium and Britain. EN 12074

Demographic change and the loss of resources in the education system. EN 12309

Descriptive analyses of the "VOCL" cohort: year three. EN 12368

Developing models of educational accountability. EN 11929

Educational resources allocation to primary schools in Saudi Arabia. EN 13754

The effectiveness of Access courses. EN 11937

Effectiveness of nurse teacher training related to experience since qualifying. EN 12093

Equality versus quality: the dilemma of primary schools in today's Europe. EN 11975

An evaluation of distance learning Inservice Education and Training of Teachers (INSET) in Wales. EN 12104

Good schools, effective schools: judgements and their history. EN 11954

Identification and evaluation of innovatory curriculum development approaches in higher education. EN 11959

Identifying and developing a quality ethos for teaching in higher education. EN 11960

Improving access to education for young black adults. EN 11964

Improving the quality of education for all. EN 11965

Improving the quality of education through mastery learning. EN 11900

Law improvement project. EN 11972

Leicestershire Technical and Vocational Education Initiative Extension evaluation consultancy. EN 12155

The long-term influence of effective and ineffective A-level departments. EN 12415

Making your way through secondary school: pupils' experiences of teaching and learning. EN 11980

Measuring the quality of primary schools. EN 12444

Performance indicators project. EN 12431

Positive approaches to discipline in inner-city schools. EN 12188

The problem of the efficiency/effectiveness of the education system: organizational solutions for upper secondary schools. EN 12128

Quality assurance in continuing professional education. EN 12199

Quality in initial teacher training - an examination of course structure within selected institutions. EN 12200

The quality of further vocational training. DE 11798

Research Station - Primary Education Information Technology. EN 11795

Socialization to learning: how students learn and learn to learn at the university. EN 11892

Tertiary education in West Glamorgan Local Education Authority. EN 12248

Transition from pre-school to primary school. EN 12357

The use of performance indicators in the evaluation of educational institutions. EN 12261

questionnaire

Elaboration of survey instruments for the evaluation of in-service training courses. EN 12999

Fonctionnement des établissements scolaires et efficacité d'ensemble du système. FR 12117

Questionnaire design project. EN 13012

race

Moray House Institute of Education policy on equal opportunities (disability and race): curricular implementation. EN 11985

race relations

Anti-racism and children's literature. EN 12973

Race and education: perspectives of primary B.Ed. students. EN 13409

racial discrimination

Attitudes towards current problems of domestic policy in 1991. DE 13442

Local management of schools and racial equality. EN 11979

Racial equality and initial teacher education. EN 12201

racial integration

The effectiveness of implementing a multicultural and antiracist education. EN 13391

Local management of schools and racial equality. EN 11979

Racial equality and initial teacher education. EN 12201

Racism and multicultural education. EN 12003

racism

Anti-racism and children's literature. EN 12973

Race and education: perspectives of primary B.Ed. students. EN 13409

Racism and multicultural education. EN 12003

readability

Assessing the appropriateness of textbooks with the help of the computer. EN 12841

reading

Asessment of handwriting and its relationship to spelling and reading in six-and-a-half to seven-and-a-half year old children. EN 12802

Children's reading comprehension: self-image, attainments and attitudes. A cross-cultural study. EN 12812

Cognitive analysis of fluent reading and learning to read. EN 12813

Cognitive processes in reading and spelling. EN 12814

Comprehension problems in children: the nature of the deficit. EN 12821

Computer-assisted learning in the teaching of reading. EN 11701

Confirmatory study and teaching experiment for overcoming difficulties in complex texts in primary years 3 and 5. DE 11773

A connectionist model of the development of visual word recognition. EN 12822

Effect of perceptuo-motor difficulty on early handwriting, speech and reading. EN 13071

Effective instructional methods for reading and writing in secondary schools. EN 11725

Les enfants non-lecteurs; étude des impossibilités persistantes de l'activité de lecture chez des enfants âgés de neuf ans et plus. FR 13312

Evaluation of basic instruction in reading and writing. EN 11749

Evaluation of remedial reading programmes in the city of Utrecht. EN 12851

Evaluation of the reading promotion project. EN 12850

An examination of Language Experience Approach (LEA) to teaching reading development and its use in second language learning. EN 11751

Extent and correlates of variability among different groups of readers. EN 12859

Formative assessment of reading in the primary classroom: the Leeds Reading Project. EN 12864

Formative assessments of reading. EN 12399

Functional illiteracy and adult basic education in Romania. EN 11908

Group textual study of fiction in primary school. EN 12980

Hearing children read. EN 12869

The IEA international reading literacy study in Ireland. EN 12402

Individual differences among poor readers and their implications for remediation. EN 12871

Individual learning: reading and writing. DE 12872

Instruction, leisure time reading and development of reading skills from the beginning of primary year 5 (8-year-olds) to the end of year 8 (12-year-olds). EN 12895

An investigation into techniques for the teaching of non-fiction in schools. EN 12983

An investigation of sustained silent reading in the primary school. EN 12879

The language of primers. DE 13057

Making sense of writing at pre-school age: semantics or phonetics. EN 13467

A national survey of reading achievement in Irish primary schools. EN 12423

On the effect of action orientation in extracting specific information from foreign language texts. DE 12954

Parental involvement in reading programmes. EN 12896

Preventing reading and spelling failure: the effects of various metalinguistic training programmes in nursery school on reading and spelling development. EN 12862

Reading and schema theory. EN 12904

Reading and writing in student learning. EN 12905

Reading factual texts and communicative use of the result. DE 12886

Reading, listening and television viewing: a study in children's cognition. EN 13152

Reading standards in a local education authority: 1976-1991. EN 12906

Reading with young deaf children in the home. EN 13358

The relationship between the phonological strategies employed in the early stages of reading and spelling. EN 12910

The relationship between the use and understanding of narrative structures and general language development. EN 12911

Segmentation ability and patterns of reading failure: the nature of the relationship. EN 11890

The share-a-book project. EN 11809

The significance of boundary negotiation between teachers and children from 'non-school-oriented backgrounds' in early school reading lessons. EN 12915

Standard tests in English for pupils at the end of the second Key Stage of the National Curriculum in 1994, 1995, 1996. EN 12450

Standardisation of the LARR short-form test. EN 12925

Stimulation and support of learning processes in illiterate adults working with computers. DE 11910

The effects of the Education Reform Act 1988: formula funding of schools. EN 12298

Evaluation and monitoring at local education authority level. EN 12303

Evaluation of an educational and vocational guidance initiative in compulsory school. EN 13612

Evaluation of the educational system: indicators and instruments for school evaluation. EN 12390

Fitting into institutions. EN 12113

The long-term influence of effective and ineffective A-level departments. EN 12415

Marketing service industries: a comparative study of education and banking. EN 12771

The modern inspectorate: HM Inspectorate of schools 1944-91. EN 12335

On-line motivation: a cross-sectional analysis of emotional orientation in competitive situations in school. DE 13231

Performance indicators project. EN 12431

Practical learning at school. DE 11888

The problem of the efficiency/effectiveness of the education system: organizational solutions for upper secondary schools. EN 12128

Quantitative analysis for self-evaluation by schools. EN 12439

School/Industry Compacts: the translation of an American model to England. EN 12214

School self-evaluation. EN 12442

School self-evaluation: personnel training. EN 12443

School social work in secondary schools. EN 13742

Sex-specific differences in the verbal-sensorimotor development of children aged 4-6 in schools in the GDR. DE 13078

Successful schooling. EN 12454

Visual and practical learning in the combined educational setting of museums - companies - schools. DE 11851

school activities

Pupils' workloads in years 1-12. EN 11797

school age population

English in the State of Qatar: an analysis of perceptions and attitudes. EN 12843

school autonomy

Civic schools as alternative educational institutions. EN 12236

Deregulation: needs and possibilities for school management. EN 12286

The framework for Local Management of Schools: a study of local education authorities' approved Local Management of Schools schemes. EN 12314

Going grant-maintained: a case study of change from a management perspective. EN 12317

Independence in further education. DE 12272

Optimum model of a local education authority. EN 13739

Opting for grant-maintained status: a study of policy-making in education. EN 11993

Self-governance, grant-maintained schools and educational identities. EN 12011

Self-managing schools - a practical way forward for secondary schools. EN 12348

school career

Analysis of the destinies of graduates in economic sciences in Passau (business economics or economic science). DE 12460

The careers of boys in work and education from 1985 to 1990. EN 13640

Components of the social environment. EN 13434

Descriptive analyses of the "VOCL" cohort: year three. EN 12368

The development of motivation and self-regulation in lower secondary school pupils. EN 13215

Educational careers and occupational integration of university graduates from 1988/1989. DE 12453

Educational careers in youth. DE 12369

Enquête sur les apprentis des cinq départements de la Région Pays de Loire. FR 11861

The influence of effective primary education on school careers in secondary education - phase II. EN 12374

The influence of social resources on achievement. EN 13480

Making your way through secondary school: pupils' experiences of teaching and learning. EN 11980

Microscopic school career research phase 2. EN 13227

Orientation des diplômé-e-s de l'Ecole de culture générale de Genève. FR 12427

Orientation des titulaires de maturité, à Genève, cinq ans après l'obtention du certificat. FR 12428

The origins and destinations of Oxford University students and teachers 1900-1979. EN 12774

Pathways 16-19: the youth cohort study of England and Wales. EN 13614

The position in education of the 88-8 Educational Priority Policy cohort in the third secondary school year. EN 11927

The relationship between previous education and school careers in senior secondary vocational education. EN 12463

Returning to learning: mature students in higher education. EN 13461

Scottish Young People's Survey. EN 13630

Second survey of West German university graduates from 1988/1989. DE 13647

Secondary analyses on the school careers of secondary school pupils on the basis of data on the "VOCL '89" cohort. EN 12447

Social environment and career: the effect of family background on careers through school, work and life. EN 13462

Spring 1991 and autumn 1991 Scottish Young People's Surveys. EN 12222

Unequal opportunities: a review. EN 13459

school-community relation

Central Regional Council (Scotland) Youth Strategy - an evaluative study of school liaison groups. EN 13381

The City Technology College initiative with particular reference to the establishment of a City Technology College on Teesside. EN 12061

Conditions for learning and Estonian educational reality: the social environment as the background to social education. EN 11884

An evaluation of a home-school-community liaison project. EN 13393

Evaluation of the educational system: indicators and instruments for school evaluation. EN 12390

Models of organization and management of pre-school provision and their effects on the child's development in Great Britain, Sweden and the USA. EN 12169

Planning for change in multiracial primary schools. EN 13010

Three primary school boards: the first years. EN 13725

school correspondence

Writing exchange across the Atlantic: a study of secondary school students' writing, exchanged with peers in London and the Bay Area, California. EN 12951

school day

Experiences with extended school time in the lower secondary schools in Campania. EN 12319

Reduction of pupils' working hours. DE 12484

school distribution

Effects of the discontinuation of the special education planning procedure. EN 12092

Effects of the discontinuation of the special education planning procedure. EN 12296

school district

Optimum model of a local education authority. EN 13739

school doctor

Pratiques professionnelles des infirmières en milieu scolaire. FR 13289

school entry age

Baseline assessment at age 4+. EN 12366

First-year primary school pupils' understanding of basic concepts of writing. EN 13124

Standardisation of the LARR short-form test. EN 12925

Term of birth and special educational placement: the impact of assessment procedures in a local education authority. EN 12352

school environment

Communication familiale et scolaire, articulation verbal-non verbal. FR 13062

Education and the rights of the child. EN 13748

Effects of introducing small equipment into primary schools for use at playtimes. EN 12475

The effects of some variables on alcohol abuse among secondary school pupils. EN 13265

Innovation projects in vocational education. EN 13016

L'intégration sociale des enfants de 4 à 7 ans: étude longitudinale. FR 13082

Life in school: an analysis using methods of educational ethnography. EN 13390

Management cultures within primary schools. EN 12329

State and society: modes of social control in the school environment. EN 13225

Symbols of authority: children's attitudes towards the symbols of authority. EN 13203

Teacher stress and organisational climate. EN 13372

Transition from pre-school to primary school. EN 12357

school exchange

School links and exchanges in Europe. EN 11807

school failure

Bilinguisme, immigration et scolarisation. FR 12811

The careers of boys in work and education from 1985 to 1990. EN 13640

L'échec à l'école: échec de l'école? FR 13219

Pedagogic and clinical implications of acquired helplessness. DE 13232

school health services

Expectations of school health services: part 4 'What teenage students expect from the school health service'. EN 13177

Statistical study of compulsory school children in Abruzzo concerning the prevention of tooth decay and eye disorders. EN 13292

school leaver

16-19 Initiative: Liverpool. EN 13517

Assessing the ability of school leavers in Swaziland to use process skills. EN 12047

BP Exploration Fellowship in vocational education and guidance. EN 13544

Continuation of Scottish Young People's Survey. EN 12067

Continuation of Scottish Young People's Survey. EN 12068

Economic knowledge of secondary school leavers. DE 12635

Orientation des titulaires de maturité, à Genève, cinq ans après l'obtention du certificat. FR 12428

Pathways 16-19: the youth cohort study of England and Wales. EN 13614

RUBS '91 (registration of the further careers of school leavers). EN 13626

RUBS '92 (registration of the further careers of school leavers). EN 13625

Sample enhancement for the 1991 Scottish Young People's Survey. EN 12212

Scottish Young People's Survey - transition issues. EN 13631

Spring 1991 and Autumn 1991 Scottish Young People's Surveys. EN 12221

Spring 1991 and autumn 1991 Scottish Young People's Surveys. EN 12222

Survey of 50% of Grampian Leavers. EN 12232

Unqualified school leaver. EN 12260

school leaving

Dealing with transitional situations in adolescence. DE 11914

Development in the labour market and in the qualifications of general secondary school-leavers. DE 13532

school psychologist

School psychology - educational counselling. DE 12008

Self-image and function of Bavarian school psychologists. DE 13698

school size

Implementing educational changes in primary schools with particular reference to small schools. EN 11963

Problems and possibilities of managing small secondary schools (circa 400) as a result of the Education Reform Act 1988. EN 11998

The relationship between school size and problem behaviour among secondary school pupils. EN 13273

Small schools and pupil attitudes. EN 12473

A study of the management and implementation of educational change in primary schools. EN 12015

school system

Tripartism and education in 20th century Britain. EN 12254

Uniformity and differentiation in the school system. DE 12095

school travel

School links and exchanges in Europe. EN 11807

school visit

School links and exchanges in Europe. EN 11807

schooling

Demographic change and the loss of resources in the education system. EN 12309

schooling rate

Analyse des disparités géographiques de scolarisation en France. FR 12269

Comparaisons des inégalités sociales de scolarisation dans quatre pays européens et en France au cours des trente dernières années. FR 11922

science education

Achieving National Curriculum attainment targets in the primary school. EN 12521

Animals and science education: pupils' knowledge, attitudes and behaviour with respect to animals and the uses which are made of them. EN 13166

Official education statistics and empirical social research. DE 13040

Success at university: Siegen comprehensive university. DE 12388

stay abroad

Integration of visually handicapped students and university graduates in working life. DE 13594

stereotype

Cultural stereotypes in language learning. EN 12926

Exploring the gender gap in primary schools. EN 12112

Gender roles in adolescent girls. EN 13476

University students' sex role stereotypes. EN 13240

story telling

De la construction du sens à partir d'un support iconique. FR 12829

Etude développementale des premières capacités narratives. FR 13072

Parts de l'enfant et de la mère dans la gestion d'un récit produit conjointement. FR 13091

Re-storying the landscape. EN 13460

Teaching of fairy tales in Cyprus. EN 12978

student

The application of computer-aided learning to the development of information skills in further education. EN 13019

Art therapists and their art. EN 13651

Becoming a postgraduate science student. EN 12050

A comparative study of student youth social and political lifestyles in Hungary and England. EN 12750

A comparison of linguistic performance in continuous assessment and unseen examination writing at undergraduate level. EN 12819

The effects of personal traits and different problems of university students on their anxiety levels. EN 13209

The effects of some variables on the loneliness levels of higher education students. EN 13210

The effects of university students' loneliness and some related variables on their adjustment. EN 13205

Evaluation of the project "Students and the world of work". DE 11743

Evaluation of the three-year training course in primary teacher training colleges. EN 12099

Financial circumstances of adult/mature students. EN 13499

First-year students in higher education. EN 12452

Identification and support of gifted engineering students. DE 11760

Individual determinants of the attitudes toward work. EN 13180

Information needs and information seeking behaviour of nurses. EN 13671

Learning styles and regulation of learning in higher education. EN 13138

Life in post-compulsory classrooms. EN 12159

Mature students' perceptions and performance of polytechnic degree courses. EN 12333

Mental condition and self-image of students in the old and new German states with particular reference to the universities of Halle and Goettingen. DE 13149

Methods for the acquisition, evaluation and optimization of learning and working techniques for first-year students at technical colleges. DE 11879

The needs of mature entrants in higher and further education. EN 12176

The origins and destinations of Oxford University students and teachers 1900-1979. EN 12774

Personal competences in higher education. EN 13145

The personality and other attributes, qualities, abilities and opinions of A-level design students. EN 13194

Reading and writing in student learning. EN 12905

Sociocultural aspects of teaching English to Arabic speaking students. EN 12917

Student and peer tutoring in Wales. EN 11815

Students, supervisors and the social science research training process. EN 12225

A study of students' knowledge of cancer etiology and prevention. EN 13284

Survey of older graduates. EN 13635

A survey of student expectations and perceptions of higher education. EN 13238

Three longitudinal studies of medical student selection. EN 12353

Transition to college. EN 12253

Undergraduate physicists' and post-graduate scientists' (undergoing teacher training) understanding of the nature of science. EN 12630

University students' sex role stereotypes. EN 13240

The use of performance indicators in the study of problems in the transition from secondary to higher education and in the evaluation of the Centre for Self-Instruction as a guidance service. EN 11956

A working arrangement: student work experience placements. EN 11842

Working-class daughters and their social uprise: on the relationship between class, sex and technical competence. DE 13429

student behaviour

Academic dishonesty in students. EN 13242

Affect and learning mathematics. EN 13206

B.Ed. Primary and Scottish Wider Access Programme - monitoring student progress. EN 12049

Developing deep-processing strategies in academic interaction. EN 13387

Development of students' situations and orientations. DE 12097

Investigation into what factors pre-dispose students to seek counselling with special reference to: subject bias, special categories of college entry and history of mental instability. EN 11968

Mature students' perceptions and performance of polytechnic degree courses. EN 12333

Mature women entrants to teaching: an analysis of the process of adjustment to the student role in the four-year B.Ed. course. EN 12167

Socialization to learning: how students learn and learn to learn at the university. EN 11892

Student teachers' perceptions of stressful situations in schools. EN 12224

Transition to college. EN 12253

student exchange

Student experience of European exchange. EN 13415

student life

A comparative study of student youth social and political lifestyles in Hungary and England. EN 12750

Development of students' situations and orientations. DE 12097

Enquête représentative sur les activités rémunérées des étudiants à l'Université de Berne. DE 13512

The identification of the needs of lesbian and gay students in higher education. EN 13261

Mature women entrants to teaching: an analysis of the process of adjustment to the student role in the four-year B.Ed. course. EN 12167

Observatoire de la vie étudiante. FR 12338

Transition to college. EN 12253

student loan

Financial circumstances of adult/mature students. EN 13499

student participation

Developing deep-processing strategies in academic interaction. EN 13387

student record

Developing a portfolio of personal development. EN 12375

The development of a computer-based system for records of achievement in science. EN 12377

Evaluation of the new report card during the trial period 1989-1990. EN 12462

Evaluation of the response of teacher, parents and pupils to new forms of reporting introduced in the 5-14 development programme. EN 13048

Parents and assessment at National Curriculum Key Stage 1. EN 12430

Profiling in the primary school: extension of self-assessment in primary schools 1989-1991 - collaborative approach to assessment. EN 12436

Teacher competencies and professional development. EN 12237

student sociology

Accès des bacheliers à l'enseignement supérieur. FR 11902

L'allocation du temps en cours d'études: le cas des étudiants espagnols. FR 12268

A comparative study of student youth social and political lifestyles in Hungary and England. EN 12750

Observatoire de la vie étudiante. FR 12338

La première année de psychologie-sociologie à l'Université de Bourgogne. FR 13234

student teacher

Action research in initial teacher training. EN 12033

B.Ed. Primary and Scottish Wider Access Programme - monitoring student progress. EN 12049

Can the burn-out syndrome be predicted with student teachers? DE 13338

Cardiff Collegiate Faculty of Education: provision of routes to graduate status for certificated teachers. EN 12056

The constructs teachers use to evaluate their own classroom practice. EN 13659

Developing information technology in a primary Post-Graduate Certificate of Education course. EN 12080

The development, implementation and evaluation of a model of practice in art and design teacher education. EN 12083

Economic and industrial awareness in the primary school. EN 12494

The effect of some factors on the agreement between self-concept and vocational self-concept of teacher training students. EN 13144

Evaluating the effectiveness of a practitioner's use of a constructivist approach for developing scientific knowledge and understanding in primary students during their initial training and primary teachers on inservice courses. EN 12556

Evaluation of the licensed teacher route to Qualified Teacher Status. EN 12108

Fitting into institutions. EN 12114

Focused mentoring for the National Curriculum. EN 12115

Follow-up study on the initial training of newly qualified teachers - a feasibility study. EN 12116

Foreign language training for initial teacher training (ITT) students. EN 12863

Graduates becoming primary teachers: a study of the development of reflective professionalism by graduates following a school-based one-year primary course in initial teacher education. EN 12120

Initial teacher training and professional development within dimensions of classroom activity ambiguity. EN 12136

Investigating a framework for mathematics teacher education: an action research study. EN 12142

Learning strategies in teacher education. EN 11876

Learning to be a natural science teacher. EN 12149

Life history and initial teacher education. EN 12158

Mature women entrants to teaching: an analysis of the process of adjustment to the student role in the four-year B.Ed. course. EN 12167

The motivation of mathematics student teachers. DE 13228

Preparation of students in pedagogical faculties for creative work and attempts at innovation. EN 12198

Preparing teachers for student placement. EN 12192

Race and education: perspectives of primary B.Ed. students. EN 13409

School-based teacher training: a comparative case study of an Articled Teacher course and a one-year Post-Graduate Certificate in Education (PGCE) course. EN 12213

Some factors affecting the agreement level between student teachers' self-concepts and vocational self-concepts. EN 13143

Student attitudes regarding effective teaching behaviours - a teaching practice study. EN 13277

Student teachers' conceptions of the nature of science and learning. EN 12617

Student teachers' perceptions of stressful situations in schools. EN 12224

Students' environmental knowledge and attitude. EN 13202

Study of mature entrants to teaching. EN 12226

A study of mature entrants to the teaching profession. EN 13700

A study of probationers. EN 13634

Support of mentors in the classroom. EN 12230

A survey of computer literacy in initial teacher education. EN 12621

Teacher competencies and professional development. EN 12237

Teacher preparation for compulsory schools in Linköping University. EN 12148

Teachers' strategies of self-evaluation. EN 13158

The Two Degrees - a comparative study of former students and first post headteacher satisfaction with initial teacher education at Charlotte Mason College. EN 12257

Undergraduate physicists' and post-graduate scientists' (undergoing teacher training) understanding of the nature of science. EN 12630

Who (still) wants to be a teacher? DE 13105

study abroad

Cultural studies in advanced language learning: the year abroad in under-graduate courses. EN 13435

Investigation of Italian schools abroad. EN 12133

Student experience of European exchange. EN 13415

The value of field residential courses in the teaching of earth sciences. EN 12739

study method

Improving self-regulation skills through isolated and integrated training. EN 11865

Investigation of study habits, learning strategies and students' attitudes toward study, and their relationship to student achievement. EN 13218

Methods for the acquisition, evaluation and optimization of learning and working techniques for first-year students at technical colleges. DE 11879

An analysis of vocational schools. DE 12040

The application of quality management principles to learning. EN 11911

Baccalauréats professionnels (Bac-Pro): description d'une première promotion. FR 13536

Career aspirations and employment opportunities of general secondary school leavers. DE 13542

Career outcomes of engineers and their relationships to education, training and early work experiences. EN 13547

Competency-based vocational qualifications in the labour market. EN 13551

Education and entrepreneurship: an analytical study of the attention given to entrepreneurship in education (in Dutch-speaking Belgium). EN 13507

Education and the labour market for civil engineers. EN 13610

Education-Business Partnerships (EBPs): targets and stocktake. EN 13565

The education policies of large companies. EN 13491

The employment situation of women in the former GDR (further vocational training for women in the new German states). DE 13540

The enterprising college. EN 13494

Evaluation of an educational and vocational guidance initiative in compulsory school. EN 13612

Evaluation of the process of curriculum design of technical and vocational education in Hong Kong. EN 13755

Final analysis of the data collected on the work experience of graduate engineers. EN 13579

Gender, training and employment: an historical analysis 1939-1985. EN 13582

Guidance aspects of the Enterprise in Higher Education programme. EN 13585

Individual motivation and take-up of National Vocational Qualifications in the South West. EN 13223

Information technology in education and employment. EN 12688

L'insertion professionnelle des élèves issus des écoles d'arts plastiques. FR 13593

Labour market relevance and output of adult education courses. EN 11689

La métis professionnelle: savoirs et savoir-faire. FR 13602

National evaluation of Compacts. EN 13607

New requirements in vocational education: the tasks of trainers. DE 13608

La notion de qualification. FR 13609

The relationship of curriculum and workplace change. EN 13622

Reviewing post-16 provision in four occupational sectors. EN 12206

School and environment. EN 13599

Le système de formation dans la dynamique locale de l'emploi. FR 13636

Technical and Vocational Education Initiative (TVEI) local evaluation. EN 12244

Typologie des relations formation-emploi: effets sur la stabilité des emplois des jeunes ouvriers et employés. FR 13639

training need

AVERT AIDS: working with young people project. EN 13300

Comparison of qualification structures in lignite mining in East Germany. DE 13619

Educational needs in the telematic sector and prospects for creating a course in computer science. EN 12681

The future of apprenticeship training. EN 12283

In-company further training for training personnel (BeWAP). DE 11693

Information technology in education and employment. EN 12688

Management training needs of technical institutions in Africa. EN 12331

Mentors in education and training. EN 12168

Multi-professional support for young adults with special needs. EN 12172

The new governing bodies for further education colleges. EN 13714

New perspectives of English language teaching at the Tallinn Pedagogical University. EN 11832

Retraining under conditions of industrial restructuring. EN 11803

South East Thames regional HIV education and training evaluation project. EN 13361

Training for special educational needs in Sandwell and Coventry. EN 12251

training of trainers

An action project designed to promote the development of mentors in the context of initial teacher training (ITT) teaching practice. EN 12032

Development and testing of a further training programme for vocational trainers in the new German states. DE 11737

Development and testing of a seminar concept for on-the-job instructors. DE 11735

Effectiveness of nurse teacher training related to experience since qualifying. EN 12093

Evaluation et pilotage de formations. FR 12392

Evaluation research for the pilot project "Materials for the cross-disciplinary training of educators and learners in the chemical industry, with a special focus on ecology and social learning". DE 11839

Further training for in-house instructors in companies in the new German states. DE 11835

In-company further training for training personnel (BeWAP). DE 11693

INTENT (Initial Teacher Education and New Technology). EN 12694

Look after yourself tutor training. EN 12583

Mentors in education and training. EN 12168

Méthodologie des histoires de vie et formation de formateurs. FR 11783

New requirements in vocational education: the tasks of trainers. DE 13608

Processus d'émergence de professions nouvelles: les formateurs d'adultes. FR 13691

Quel dispositif de formation pour les maîtres d'apprentissage. FR 11801

Training of instructors at 'Fachhochschulen' (colleges for higher professional training) in Bavaria. DE 13704

The training the trainers approach to staff development project. EN 12252

Writers' workshop leaders project. EN 12950

training personnel

Development and testing of a further training programme for vocational trainers in the new German states. DE 11737

Focused mentoring for the National Curriculum. EN 12115

training programme

Developing an industrial relations training programme for Greek supervisors and trade union representatives in simultaneous process research into training needs. EN 13561

The development, monitoring and evaluation of an advanced training course for part-time community education workers. EN 12493

The effect of the Frostig Visual Perceptual Training Programme on visual perception and the development of intelligence in a group of children in nursery school. EN 13129

Environmental training policy. EN 13445

Evaluation of a teacher training package designed to enhance pupils' self-image. EN 12101

Evaluation of further education college governor training. EN 13712

An evaluation study of the efficacy of 'Social Problem Solving Training', with people who have learning difficulties, living in residential and community settings. EN 13319

Formation et écologie. FR 12677

The identification of prerequisites for effective teacher mobility between Germany and the United Kingdom. EN 13398

INSET for school reorganisation in Hull: analysis and evaluation. EN 12137

Phonological awareness of nursery-school children. EN 12900

Preparing teachers for organisational change: an evaluation of a programme of compulsory inservice training in readiness for the re-organisation of a school system. EN 12191

Preventing reading and spelling failure: the effects of various metalinguistic training programmes in nursery school on reading and spelling development. EN 12862

A programme to encourage and facilitate doctors' participation in clinical audit. EN 13694

Retraining under conditions of industrial restructuring. EN 11803

South East Thames regional HIV education and training evaluation project. EN 13361

A study of the perceptions and responses of young women of South Asian origin to a single-sex access Youth Training Scheme. EN 13465

A survey of computer literacy in initial teacher education. EN 12621

Training for the part-time youth service. EN 13425

training supply

Adult employment training in Nottinghamshire: case studies. EN 13518

Analyse des disparités géographiques de scolarisation en France. FR 12269

Emploi et formation dans les processus de développement économique. FR 13568

The future of apprenticeship training. EN 12283

Human capital and export competitiveness. EN 13502

Impact macroéconomique de la formation professionnelle. FR 13503

Labour market prospects and training possibilities in the province of Limburg. EN 13531

Patterns of local education authority inservice education and training of teachers (INSET) organisation. EN 12182

Provision and take-up of School Board training. EN 13716

Structure and development of the supply of trainee places in selected regions in the new German states. DE 11814

Training for special educational needs in Sandwell and Coventry. EN 12251

training type

Design of Electronic Performance Support Systems. EN 11711

Informatique et formation: les nouvelles technologies de l'information (NTI). FR 11763

Professional, economic and legislative problems related to the training of officers working in the field of infrastructural development in support of educational innovation and the transfer of technology. EN 13616

The training the trainers approach to staff development project. EN 12252

training workshop

41st European Teachers' Seminar on education against violence: the potential of fair play in sport. EN 12028

My Turn to Speak. EN 12890

Putting training into practice: evaluating 'My Turn to Speak'. EN 12903

transfer of learning

Analysis and effects of fellow pupils' and teachers' explanations in the performance of complex tasks. EN 11688

Improving self-regulation skills through isolated and integrated training. EN 11865

The reconstruction and transfer of learning: teaching for effective learning in higher education. EN 12004

The role of the workplace in the work experience triangle with particular reference to transferable skills. EN 11806

Training and transfer of reading strategies: mother tongue instruction and foreign language instruction. EN 12941

Training and transfer of vocabulary acquisition strategies: mother tongue instruction and foreign language instruction. EN 12942

Transfer ability and instruction. EN 11899

Transfer in mathematical problem solving. EN 11971

transition from school to work

16-19 Initiative: Liverpool. EN 13517

Analyse de la relation formation-emploi, applications aux jeunes sortant des formations initiales. FR 13520

Assessing the ability of school leavers in Swaziland to use process skills. EN 12047

BP Exploration Fellowship in vocational education and guidance. EN 13544

The careers of boys in work and education from 1985 to 1990. EN 13640

The changing impact of a policy initiative: a multilevel analysis of TVEI. EN 11921

Continuation of Scottish Young People's Survey. EN 12067

Continuation of Scottish Young People's Survey. EN 12068

Determinants of occupational orientation and development: study within the framework of a cross-sectional investigation. DE 13560

Education-Business Partnerships (EBPs): targets and stocktake. EN 13565

Education graduates at work: occupation, career start, educational biography and retrospective assessment of the university course. DE 13563

Educational careers and occupational integration of university graduates from 1988/1989. DE 12453

Emploi et modes de vie: passages à la vie professionnelle, passage à la vie adulte en Région Provence-Alpes-Côte d'Azur. FR 13569

Entrée des jeunes dans la vie active (enquêtes EVA). FR 13571

Evaluation of the second year of the Training Credits pilot: three case studies. EN 11748

Facilitating the transition from school to employment in a regional context (coordination and evaluation research). DE 13587

Youth and family research within the framework of municipal youth welfare planning in Osnabrueck. DE 13736

Youth attitudes towards values and democratic principles. EN 13188

verbal behaviour

Acquisition et gestion de la conduite de dialogue: la construction des finalités à travers le dialogue. FR 13058

Dialogisme et déplacement. FR 12834

Dialogue corporel et verbal. FR 12835

Etude développementale des premières capacités narratives. FR 13072

verbal communication

Communication familiale et scolaire, articulation verbal-non verbal. FR 13062

Constructing culture: a study of teacher-pupil talk in French language lessons. EN 12824

Contingency and breakdown: interactions with language-disordered children. EN 13307

Dialogisme et déplacement. FR 12834

Etude différentielle des performances communicatives et de leur stabilité chez le jeune enfant. FR 12849

An investigation of the collaborative interaction and talk of children in relation to their perception of teacher audience, task purpose and learning context. EN 13402

Metaphor as discourse strategy in teacher education. EN 12889

Native and non-native use of English. EN 12891

The non-teacher directed peer-group classroom talk of nine-year olds. EN 12894

The place of reflection in teachers' processes of change. EN 13233

Processus de planification et de contrôle dans la production d'un texte procédural: évolution entre cinq et neuf ans. FR 13097

The special oral language needs of low attaining pupils in mathematics. EN 12918

Spoken language and new technology (SLANT). EN 12923

A study of arithmetic learning strategies in hearing-impaired children. EN 13337

verbal interaction

Cohesive ties in children's use of language in relation to the teaching of mathematics. EN 12815

Communication familiale et scolaire, articulation verbal-non verbal. FR 13062

Contingency and breakdown: interactions with language-disordered children. EN 13307

Developing deep-processing strategies in academic interaction. EN 13387

Dialogisme et déplacement. FR 12834

Etude différentielle des performances communicatives et de leur stabilité chez le jeune enfant. FR 12849

Genèse des processus argumentatifs. FR 13077

An investigation of the collaborative interaction and talk of children in relation to their perception of teacher audience, task purpose and learning context. EN 13402

Language and primary maths. EN 12702

Metaphor as discourse strategy in teacher education. EN 12889

Processus de planification et de contrôle dans la production d'un texte procédural: évolution entre cinq et neuf ans. FR 13097

Verbal interaction in mathematics lessons in four secondary schools in Anglophone Cameroon. EN 12945

verbal learning

The development of visual memory strategies in children. EN 13121

The interrelationship of verbal and visual narrative: its importance as a teaching tool. EN 11768

The special oral language needs of low attaining pupils in mathematics. EN 12918

videodisc

RIE: design and evaluation of an interactive videodisc for small and medium sized enterprises. EN 13029

videorecording

Improving methods of teaching and learning swimming. EN 11825

violence

Further education for police personnel on the subject of violence against women. DE 13732

Is the school a place of violence? DE 13274

vision defect

Statistical study of compulsory school children in Abruzzo concerning the prevention of tooth decay and eye disorders. EN 13292

visiting teacher

Supply workers in state schools and the National Health Service. EN 13701

visual learning

Development of television literacy. EN 13046

The development of visual memory strategies in children. EN 13121

The effect of the Frostig Visual Perceptual Training Programme on visual perception and the development of intelligence in a group of children in nursery school. EN 13129

The interrelationship of verbal and visual narrative: its importance as a teaching tool. EN 11768

Picture-text interaction in children's learning of science. EN 11886

Speed of visual information processing. EN 13363

The use of film and drama in schools as a way to promote cultural awareness. EN 12982

visual perception

The development of visual memory strategies in children. EN 13121

The effect of the Frostig Visual Perceptual Training Programme on visual perception and the development of intelligence in a group of children in nursery school. EN 13129

Phonological and visuospatial processing at the left and right of the laterality distribution. EN 13093

Speed of visual information processing. EN 13363

visually handicapped

Alternatives to print for visually impaired students. EN 13295

Cathedrals through touch and hearing. EN 12974

CD ROM as a curriculum delivery medium for blind and partially sighted learners. EN 13301

Communication problems of blind students in higher education. EN 13302

Development of microcomputer software for educational and vocational applications (for blind and partially sighted persons). EN 12662

The educational management of children with Usher Syndrome. EN 13310

Evaluation of mobility education for young blind children. EN 13317

Integration of visually handicapped students and university graduates in working life. DE 13594

The integration of visually impaired students in further education. EN 13330

Language acquisition of blind and deaf children. DE 13364

Longitudinal investigation of cognitive development and educational achievement in blind and partially sighted children. EN 13344

The mobility of blind and visually impaired persons. EN 13347

The speed of tactile information processing for blind pupils. EN 13156

Speed of visual information processing. EN 13363

Study of the IBM Screen Reader for blind students in distance education. EN 13368

Visually impaired people in their mid-twenties: educational, vocational, and personal ambitions and needs. EN 13375

vocabulary

Lexical behaviour in a second language. EN 12887

Standardization of a screening test of Greek-Cypriot speech and language. EN 12451

Syntactic input and the acquisition of the verb lexicon. EN 13103

Training and transfer of vocabulary acquisition strategies: mother tongue instruction and foreign language instruction. EN 12942

Vocabulary rate in course materials for English as a second or foreign language. EN 12947

vocational education

Access to learning and accreditation in Work-Related Further Education. EN 12031

Adult employment training in four regions (East Midlands, South Wales, Bremen, and Baden Wurttemberg). EN 12037

AIDS Education and Research Trust (AVERT) HIV/AIDS and nursing project. EN 13648

Analyse de la relation formation-emploi, applications aux jeunes sortant des formations initiales. FR 13520

Analysis of the Semi-Higher Education Colleges. EN 12044

An analysis of vocational schools. DE 12040

The application of quality management principles to learning. EN 11911

Assessment of the educational needs of health professionals in palliative care of patients with advanced cancer, and their families. EN 13654

The attitudes of pupils in the Ankara Vocational School for Educable Mentally Retarded Children towards vocational education. EN 13296

Baccalauréats professionnels (Bac-Pro): description d'une première promotion. FR 13536

The changing impact of a policy initiative: a multilevel analysis of TVEI. EN 11920

The changing impact of a policy initiative: a multilevel analysis of TVEI. EN 11921

Characteristics of leavers from Adult Elementary Vocational Education projects. EN 12253

Cognitive structures and language skills in vocational training. EN 11882

Comparaison des résultats obtenus aux examens de fin d'apprentissage selon les cantons et les métiers. DE 12461

Comparison of further vocational training courses to facilitate choice of training. DE 12301

Competency-based vocational qualifications in the labour market. EN 13551

The competitive capacity of American industry and the vocational training system in the USA. EN 11722

Conditions for vocational retraining. DE 11802

Conflict of interests among farmers seeking a second occupation. DE 13552

Curriculum development in technical and vocational education in Saudi Arabia related to students' needs, perceptions and expectations. EN 12281

Development of a didactic concept for teaching new technologies in technical manufacturing occupations, with particular reference to information technology training in the graphic trade. DE 12668

Diploma in advanced nursing studies. EN 13663

Education and training of property valuers in China. EN 13490

Educators - training in Lower Saxony. DE 11741

Les enseignants des lycées professionnels (LEP). FR 13665

L'enseignement des branches de culture générale dans les écoles professionnelles des arts et métiers en Suisse. DE 12038

Enterprise in vocational education and training. EN 12096

Evaluation of information technology teacher training development programme. EN 12105

Evaluation of international occupational pedagogics courses, with particular reference to a group of stipendiaries from Yemen. DE 12110

Evaluation of Technical & Vocational Education Initiative developments. EN 12106

Evaluation of the Construction Industry Training Board's curriculum centre initiative. EN 13497

Evaluation of the Lothian Region Technical and Vocational Education Initiative (TVEI) Extension. EN 12109

Evaluation of the process of curriculum design of technical and vocational education in Hong Kong. EN 13755

Evaluation research for the pilot project "Cross-curricular teaching at vocational schools". DE 11838

Further training for unskilled and semi-skilled workers in small and medium-sized companies in Wuppertal, Remscheid and Solingen. DE 11837

The impact of the Education Reform Act - 1988 on the further education curriculum. EN 11962

The implications for nursing education in Cyprus commensurate with joining the European Community: a problem study. EN 12130

Improving access to education for young black adults. EN 11964

Improving the problem solving skills of learners in vocational programmes. EN 12131

In-house training as part of commercial training courses. DE 12529

Individual costs and benefits of further vocational training. DE 12321

Individual motivation and take-up of National Vocational Qualifications in the South West. EN 13223

L'informatique au service des jeunes en formation professionnelle élémentaire. FR 12135

Innovation and mergers in senior secondary vocational education. EN 12316

The integration of visually impaired students in further education. EN 13330

Internal differentiation into specialized classes in part-time vocational schools. DE 11764

An international information and resources collection in adult education and training. EN 13051

Key technologies - potential developments and their implications for vocational education and training. EN 12700

Lancaster Technical and Vocational Education Initiative evaluation programme. EN 12150

Leicestershire Technical and Vocational Education Initiative Extension evaluation project. EN 12154

Leicestershire Technical and Vocational Education Initiative Extension evaluation consultancy. EN 12155

Local evaluation of Technical and Vocational Education Initiative (TVEI), TVEI-Related Inservice Training

Index des matières

Picture-text interaction in children's learning of science. EN 11886

The principle of economy in learning and teaching mathematics. EN 11889

Qualitative thinking in tertiary education. EN 11800

The quality of pre-school education: an exploration of the relationships between teaching methods, process variables and outcomes. EN 11926

The role and value of A-level geography fieldwork: a case study. EN 12717

School content knowledge and pupils' subjective learning processes. EN 11891

Stimulation and support of learning processes in illiterate adults working with computers. DE 11910

A survey of learner training for language learning. EN 11896

Technical training and ecological learning in youth. DE 11819

Use of CBT (Computer-Based Training) as a multimedia learning component in adult education. DE 11729

Young children as musicians: a study of musical processes in the invented songs of children aged 3-7. EN 12992

apprentissage fortuit

Youth - leisure - technology: acquisition of competence in everyday use of technology, with particular reference to leisure as an educational setting. DE 11872

apprentissage lent

Development of revised training materials for teaching people with severe learning difficulties - Education of the Developmentally Young (EDY). EN 13309

Differential provision for children with special educational needs in ordinary schools. EN 12085

apprentissage par la découverte

Curiosity and exploratory behaviour. EN 13268

The nature of teacher-student interaction in active and student-centred approaches: an inservice course in a college of further education. EN 11881

PALM (Pupil Autonomy in Learning with Micros) Extension. EN 11791

Practical learning at school. DE 11888

Primary science: children planning investigations. EN 12601

Tools for exploratory learning programme. EN 11898

Visual and practical learning in the combined educational setting of museums - companies - schools. DE 11851

apprentissage par la pratique

Enterprise in vocational education and training. EN 12096

Experiential learning in initial teacher education. EN 12111

Outcomes of experiential learning. EN 11885

Practical learning at school. DE 11888

Work-based learning for academic credit. EN 11841

apprentissage précoce

"Les petits lascars": méthode pour l'enseignement précoce du français langue étrangère. FR 12796

Young children as musicians: a study of musical processes in the invented songs of children aged 3-7. EN 12992

apprentissage professionnel

Analyse de l'apprentissage et évaluation des activités de remédiation. FR 11687

Analysis of the destinies of graduates in economic sciences in Passau (business economics or economic science). DE 12460

An analysis of vocational schools. DE 12040

Apprenticeship training in Nigeria. DE 11774

Comparaison des résultats obtenus aux examens de fin d'apprentissage selon les cantons et les métiers. DE 12461

Didactic development of training support resources; modification and updating of such resources. DE 11718

Enquête sur les apprentis des cinq départements de la Région Pays de Loire. FR 11861

Etude de la relation maître d'apprentissage-apprenti: quelles difficultés de communication? FR 13575

The future of apprenticeship training. EN 12283

Immigrant apprentices without an apprenticeship contract. EN 13519

Modular vocational courses: types and effects. EN 11786

New requirements in vocational education: the tasks of trainers. DE 13608

Quel dispositif de formation pour les maîtres d'apprentissage. FR 11801

Transfer from bridging courses to elementary apprenticeship training. EN 11724

Typologie des relations formation-emploi: effets sur la stabilité des emplois des jeunes ouvriers et employés. FR 13639

apprentissage social

Cognitive assessment of maladjusted children. EN 12371

Evaluation research for the pilot project "Materials for the cross-disciplinary training of educators and learners in the chemical industry, with a special focus on ecology and social learning". DE 11839

Integration and responsibility for learning in mainstream primary schools. EN 13399

Pédagogie du militantisme dans les mouvements de jeunesse. FR 13423

apprentissage verbal

The development of visual memory strategies in children. EN 13121

The interrelationship of verbal and visual narrative: its importance as a teaching tool. EN 11768

The special oral language needs of low attaining pupils in mathematics. EN 12918

apprentissage visuel

Development of television literacy. EN 13046

The development of visual memory strategies in children. EN 13121

The effect of the Frostig Visual Perceptual Training Programme on visual perception and the development of intelligence in a group of children in nursery school. EN 13129

The interrelationship of verbal and visual narrative: its importance as a teaching tool. EN 11768

Picture-text interaction in children's learning of science. EN 11886

Speed of visual information processing. EN 13363

The use of film and drama in schools as a way to promote cultural awareness. EN 12982

aptitude

Identification and support of gifted engineering students. DE 11760

aptitude à l'enseignement

Education and humanities: teachers' and pupils' educational competence. EN 11936

Teaching competence - a personal construct investigation. EN 13159

aptitude aux études

Education and humanities: teachers' and pupils' educational competence. EN 11936

Key qualifications. DE 13627

aptitude cognitive

Confirmatory study and teaching experiment for overcoming difficulties in complex texts in primary years 3 and 5. DE 11773

Construct validation of the learning test concept through studies of complex problem solving (acronym: KOVALT). DE 13004

Extent and correlates of variability among different groups of readers. EN 12859

The inter-relationship of cognitive abilities, attitudes, social interaction and performance in early logo learning. EN 13263

Memory, intelligence and talent. EN 13187

On the representation of metacognitive areas of knowledge in long-term memory with particular reference to the semantics of verbs concerning mental activities. DE 13165

Primary school pupils' ability to understand tables and schematic drawings. DE 11690

Reading factual texts and communicative use of the result. DE 12886

The role of cognition in psychomotor activities. EN 13088

Stimulation and support of learning processes in illiterate adults working with computers. DE 11910

Studies of Attention Disordered - Hyperactive (ADHD) children. EN 13157

A study of achievement motivation, with particular reference to cognitive components. DE 13226

Suggestions for a CNC turning course as the outcome of a pilot project and CNC learning material for basic and further training. DE 11756

Training and promotion of technical creativity among gifted young people at the intermediate secondary school level. DE 11715

aptitude linguistique

Attitudes to the Welsh language and bilingualism. EN 12804

Bilinguisme, immigration et scolarisation. FR 12811

A descriptive study of the writing skills of hearing-impaired children in two schools in Eskişehir. EN 12848

Diagnosing the level of native language ability in Estonian pupils. EN 12837

Dutch language education in multilingual classrooms. EN 12932

Les enfants non-lecteurs; étude des impossibilités persistantes de l'activité de lecture chez des enfants âgés de neuf ans et plus. FR 13312

English as a working language. DE 12842

Etude développementale des premières capacités narratives. FR 13072

Integration and maturity: pedagogic concepts for the deaf. DE 13332

'Knowledge about language', language learning and the National Curriculum. EN 12880

Knowledge of languages among Italian primary school teachers. EN 12823

Arabie Saoudite

Curriculum development in technical and vocational education in Saudi Arabia related to students' needs, perceptions and expectations. EN 12281

Educational resources allocation to primary schools in Saudi Arabia. EN 13754

English language teaching - an evaluation of an industrial training programme. EN 12846

An open university for women in Saudi Arabia: problems and prospects. EN 12178

School education and young people in Saudi Arabia. EN 13762

The use of microcomputers in Saudi secondary schools. EN 11830

architecture

Cathedrals through touch and hearing. EN 12974

argent

Enquête représentative sur les activités rémunérées des étudiants à l'Université de Berne. DE 13512

argumentation

An analysis of the structural relationships of narrative and argument in the writing of Year 8 schoolchildren. EN 12800

Genèse des processus argumentatifs. FR 13077

Improving the quality of argument: schools. EN 13132

Improving the quality of argument: sixth forms and higher education. EN 13133

A study of narrative and argument writing in three Beverley comprehensive schools. EN 12929

A study of narrative and argument writing in three Beverley comprehensive schools. EN 12930

arithmétique

Addition and subtraction in special education: a study of mental arithmetic. EN 12709

Children's development of number competence. EN 13111

Cognitive impairments in children with arithmetical learning disabilities. EN 11854

Gap between arithmetical and algebraic thinking. EN 13130

Graduate numeracy. EN 13584

An investigation into errors made in attempts to solve mathematical problems. EN 12696

Logiciel d'aide à la résolution de problèmes arithmétiques par les élèves de cours élémentaire, première et deuxième années. FR 12703

A study of arithmetic learning strategies in hearing-impaired children. EN 13337

arrangement de la salle de classe

Changes in the classroom experience of Inner London pupils. EN 11919

art

Anglia Polytechnic University critical studies project. EN 12972

Art therapists and their art. EN 13651

Artists-in-education training project. EN 13652

The Centre for the Study of the Arts in Primary Education (CENSAPE): development of resource collections of examples of good practice in primary arts education. EN 12975

The effects of information technology on the sequencing and development of concept acquisition, particularly in open-ended, creative situations. EN 11727

Mathematics - shape & space: mathematics & art. EN 13140

A socio-historical and psychoanalytical view of museums. DE 11924

art dramatique

Drama and special needs. EN 12088

Drama in the English National Curriculum. EN 12979

The nature of learning in educational drama. EN 12984

Towards a common form of assessment in drama as a methodology and as a performance art. EN 12989

The use of film and drama in schools as a way to promote cultural awareness. EN 12982

The use of resources in the development of learning through drama in education in primary schools. EN 12990

The uses of playscripts in the secondary school curriculum. EN 12991

Sachregister

Abordnung   EN 13719, EN 13721
Abschlußprüfung   DE 12461, FR 13536
Abschlußzeugnis   EN 13692
Abstraktion   FR 12641
Adoleszenz   EN 13045, FR 13068, FR 13100,
   FR 13172, FR 13175, FR 13176, FR 13252,
   EN 13281, FR 13479
Adoption   EN 13369
Adoptivkind   EN 13369, EN 13482
Adreßbuch   EN 12098, EN 13444, EN 13685
Affektive Entwicklung   EN 13016
Affektivität   EN 13206
Afrika   EN 12331, FR 12342, FR 12433, FR 13508,
   EN 13750
Aggressivität   DE 13274, DE 13732
Akademikerarbeitslosigkeit   EN 13431, DE 13543
Akademische Freiheit   EN 12960
Akademischer Grad   DE 11787, EN 12127,
   EN 12363
Aktivierende Methode   EN 11710, EN 11881,
   EN 12574
Algebra   EN 12638, FR 12642, EN 12704, EN 12726,
   EN 13130
Alkohol   EN 13265
Alkoholismus   EN 13265, EN 13271
Allgemeinbildendes Schulwesen   EN 11988,
   FR 12017, DE 12038, FR 12203, DE 12217,
   EN 12279, FR 12300, EN 12495, DE 13379,
   DE 13764
Allgemeinbildung   DE 12022
Alphabetisierung   EN 11685, EN 11976, EN 11977,
   EN 12014, EN 12026, EN 12297, EN 12402,
   EN 12908, EN 13349, EN 13467, EN 13504
Alter Mensch   EN 11739, DE 11808, DE 11849,
   DE 12598, DE 13380
Alternativschule   DE 12215, EN 12236
Alternierende Weiterbildung   EN 11949, EN 13474
Altersunterschied   EN 13355
Amtssprache   EN 12799, FR 12811
Analphabetismus   EN 11908, DE 11910, FR 11983,
   FR 11984, EN 12707
Anerkennung von Bildungsabschlüssen   EN 11949,
   FR 12440, EN 13516, DE 13711
Anfangsunterricht   EN 11749, EN 12822, EN 12869,
   EN 12915
Ängstlichkeit   EN 12414, DE 13207, EN 13209,
   EN 13648
Anmeldung   EN 12313, EN 13483
Anpassung   EN 13205, EN 13267, EN 13365
Anpassungsfähigkeit   DE 13239, EN 13267
Anpassungsschwierig   EN 13187, EN 13323
Anwerbung   EN 12226, EN 13643, DE 13649,
   FR 13665, EN 13684, EN 13695, EN 13724
Anwesenheit   EN 12309
Aphasie   EN 13370
Arabische Länder   EN 12825, EN 12917, EN 13457
Arabische Sprache   EN 12865, EN 12928,
   EN 12934, EN 12949
Arbeiter   EN 13502, FR 13602
Arbeiterbildung   EN 12055, EN 12124, EN 12152,
   EN 12259, EN 12767, EN 12772, EN 13491
Arbeiterklasse   FR 11932, EN 12754, DE 13429,
   EN 13474
Arbeitgeber   EN 11842
Arbeitnehmer   EN 11685, DE 11880, FR 12129,
   EN 12152, EN 12156, DE 13380, EN 13570
Arbeitsbedingungen   EN 12166, EN 12255,
   DE 13001, DE 13236, EN 13279, EN 13589,
   DE 13621
Arbeitsbeschreibung   EN 13489, EN 13618,
   EN 13685, EN 13702
Arbeitsbeziehungen   EN 13561
Arbeitserfahrung   EN 11762, EN 11806, EN 11841,
   EN 11842, DE 11880, EN 12263, EN 12527,
   DE 12529, FR 13590, EN 13643
Arbeitshaltung   EN 12013, EN 13179, EN 13180,
   EN 13218, EN 13644
Arbeitskräfte   FR 13500, EN 13514, FR 13603,
   FR 13609

Arbeitskräftebedarf   EN 11803, EN 11952,
   EN 12681, DE 12807, DE 13537, EN 13557,
   EN 13558, DE 13598, EN 13600, EN 13615,
   EN 13616, EN 13632, EN 13638
Arbeitskräftemangel   EN 13632
Arbeitsloser   EN 12091, FR 12129, DE 13541
Arbeitslosigkeit   DE 12490, DE 13464, DE 13478,
   DE 13539, DE 13564, EN 13566, DE 13567,
   DE 13577, EN 13640
Arbeitsmarkt   EN 11912, EN 11940, DE 12029,
   EN 12222, EN 12232, EN 12258, EN 13041,
   EN 13049, FR 13520, EN 13524, EN 13525,
   EN 13526, EN 13527, EN 13528, EN 13529,
   EN 13530, EN 13531, DE 13532, DE 13533,
   EN 13551, EN 13553, EN 13554, EN 13555,
   EN 13556, EN 13557, EN 13558, FR 13568,
   DE 13581, EN 13586, EN 13588, EN 13591,
   EN 13592, EN 13596, EN 13599, DE 13600,
   EN 13605, FR 13609, FR 13611, EN 13615,
   EN 13625, EN 13626, EN 13638
Arbeitsmarktpolitik   DE 12029, DE 13577,
   FR 13583, EN 13730
Arbeitsmilieu   EN 11711, EN 13662
Arbeitsplatz   EN 11814, DE 13437, DE 13606
Arbeitsplatzsuche   EN 13431, EN 13635
Arbeitstechnik   DE 11790, DE 11819, EN 11865,
   DE 11879, EN 11956, EN 12905, EN 13218
Arbeitszeit   EN 12354, EN 12356
Architektur   EN 12974
Arithmetik   EN 11854, EN 12696, FR 12703,
   EN 12709, EN 13111, EN 13130, EN 13337,
   EN 13584
Armut   DE 13478
Arzt   EN 12364, EN 13694
Asien   FR 12039, FR 13508
Asoziales Verhalten   EN 12470, EN 12471,
   EN 13246, EN 13251, EN 13253, EN 13255,
   EN 13259, EN 13270, EN 13408
Assistent   EN 12231
Ästhetik   EN 13178
Ästhetische Erziehung   DE 11924, EN 12627,
   EN 13125
Äthiopien   EN 13389
Audiovisuelle Methode   FR 12020, FR 12796
Aufbaustudium   EN 12050, EN 12075, EN 12134,
   FR 12678, EN 12712
Aufmerksamkeit   EN 13157, EN 13173
Aufnahme   EN 12323, EN 12352, EN 12355,
   EN 13336
Aufnahmeprüfung   EN 12414
Aufsatz   EN 12014, EN 12734, EN 12800, EN 12867,
   EN 12929, EN 12930, EN 12950, EN 12951,
   FR 13148
Aufsicht   DE 11818, EN 11907, EN 12001,
   EN 12032, EN 12115, EN 12142, EN 12168,
   EN 12192, EN 12209, EN 12225, EN 12230,
   EN 12470
Ausbilder   EN 12168, FR 12202, EN 12529,
   EN 12950, DE 13245, FR 13602, DE 13650,
   FR 13691, EN 13699
Ausbildung der Ausbilder   DE 11693, DE 11735,
   DE 11737, FR 11783, FR 11801, EN 11835,
   DE 11839, EN 12032, EN 12093, EN 12168,
   EN 12252, FR 12392, EN 12583, EN 12694,
   EN 12950, DE 13608, FR 13691, DE 13704
Ausbildungsangebot   DE 11814, EN 12182,
   EN 12251, FR 12269, EN 12283, EN 13502,
   FR 13503, EN 13518, EN 13531, FR 13568,
   EN 13716
Ausbildungsart   EN 11711, FR 11763, EN 12252,
   EN 13616
Ausbildungsbedarf   DE 11693, EN 11803,
   EN 11832, EN 12168, EN 12172, EN 12251,
   EN 12283, EN 12331, EN 12681, EN 12688,
   EN 13300, EN 13361, DE 13619, EN 13714
Ausbildungseinrichtung für Militärberufe
   EN 12743
Ausbildungseinrichtung für Musik   EN 13553,
   EN 13617
Ausbildungskosten   EN 12233, EN 13505

Ausbildungskurs   EN 11724, EN 11779, EN 11789,
   DE 11798, EN 12999, DE 13236, EN 13703,
   DE 13732
Ausbildungspersonal   DE 11737, EN 12115
Ausbildungsprogramm   EN 11803, EN 12101,
   EN 12137, EN 12191, EN 12493, EN 12621,
   FR 12677, EN 12862, EN 12900, EN 13129,
   EN 13319, EN 13361, EN 13398, EN 13425,
   EN 13445, EN 13465, EN 13561, EN 13694,
   EN 13712
Ausbildungsvertrag   EN 13519, FR 13523
Ausbildungswahl   DE 12301
Ausbildungszentrum   DE 11824, EN 12078,
   EN 12977, FR 13521, DE 13620
Ausländer   DE 13442
Ausländerkind   DE 11915, DE 11981, DE 12808,
   DE 12810, DE 13456, DE 13472
Ausländischer Arbeitnehmer   DE 11836
Ausländischer Student   EN 12102, DE 12110,
   EN 12797, EN 12833, DE 12873
Auslandsaufenthalt   DE 13594
Auslandsbeziehungen   DE 12807, EN 13760
Auslandslehrer   EN 13398
Auslandsschule   EN 12133
Auslandsstudium   EN 12133, EN 12739, EN 13415,
   EN 13435
Auslese   EN 12176, EN 12323, EN 12353, FR 13219
Ausleseprüfung   EN 12414
Ausschuß   EN 13658
Außerhäusliche Kinderbetreuung   DE 12048,
   EN 12072, EN 12420, EN 12438, DE 13484
Außerschulische Bildung   DE 12048, EN 12485,
   EN 12776, DE 13469, DE 13728
Ausstattung   EN 12475, EN 12477, EN 12662,
   EN 12974
Auswendiglernen   FR 13123, FR 13162
Autismus   EN 13135, EN 13323
Autonomie   DE 12125, DE 12580
Autor   EN 12014, EN 12888, EN 13384
Autorensystem   EN 11696, EN 11810, EN 12474,
   EN 12683, EN 12701, EN 12735
Autorität   EN 13203

Bachelor's Degree   EN 12103, EN 12257
Baden-Württemberg   DE 13552
Baltische Sprachen   EN 12837, EN 12838,
   EN 12841
Bauindustrie   EN 13497
Bauingenieurwesen   EN 13610
Bayern   DE 13478, DE 13698
Bedeutung   FR 12829
Bedürfnis   EN 13039, EN 13261, EN 13457
Befriedigung   EN 11909, EN 12257, EN 12379
Befriedigung im Beruf   EN 13208, EN 13466,
   DE 13560, EN 13670, EN 13681, EN 13688
Begabter   EN 11777, DE 12360, EN 13187,
   EN 13211, EN 13220, EN 13230, EN 13235,
   EN 13323
Begleitende Kontrolle   EN 12373, EN 12389
Begriff   EN 11870, EN 12066, EN 13124, EN 13128,
   DE 13260, EN 13470, EN 13752
Begriffsanalyse   FR 13297
Begriffsbildung   EN 11698, EN 11727, DE 12464,
   EN 12536, EN 12602, EN 12608, FR 12641,
   FR 12654, EN 12751, EN 13022, EN 13117,
   EN 13118, EN 13122, EN 13137, EN 13161
Behinderter   EN 11697, EN 11827, EN 11867,
   EN 11985, EN 12250, EN 12477, EN 12651,
   EN 13027, EN 13247, FR 13297, EN 13299,
   EN 13315, EN 13327, EN 13328, DE 13331,
   EN 13342, EN 13343, EN 13348, DE 13350,
   EN 13353, EN 13369, EN 13374, EN 13377,
   DE 13378, DE 13395, EN 13501
Behinderung   EN 13020, EN 13039, DE 13333,
   DE 13379
Beihilfe   EN 11993, EN 12005, EN 12011
Belgien   EN 11762, EN 12074
Belohnung   EN 13653

Indice de materias

Onderwerpsregister

Sagregister

åben pædagogik EN 11992, EN 12145, EN 12534, EN 13125
åbent universitet EN 11746, EN 12046, EN 12086, EN 12178, DE 13026
abstraktion FR 12641
adfærd DE 11692, EN 12188, DE 12484, EN 13053, DE 13245, EN 13248, EN 13250, EN 13251, EN 13254, EN 13265, EN 13268, EN 13278, EN 13281, EN 13334, EN 13365
adfærdsforstyrrelse EN 12082, EN 12770, FR 12829, EN 13084, EN 13256, EN 13278, EN 13282, EN 13290, EN 13293, EN 13298, EN 13303, EN 13326, EN 13335, EN 13341, EN 13346, EN 13356, DE 13377
adfærdsvidenskaber EN 12770, EN 13674
adgang EN 12323, EN 12352, EN 12355, EN 13336
adgang til beskæftigelse DE 13577, FR 13611, EN 13730
adgang til uddannelse DE 11816, EN 11901, FR 11902, EN 11903, EN 11937, EN 11946, EN 11949, EN 11964, EN 11985, EN 11995, EN 12010, EN 12016, EN 12024, EN 12030, EN 12031, EN 12036, EN 12049, EN 12078, EN 12181, FR 12277, EN 13302, EN 13446, EN 13465, EN 13501
adgangsbetingelser DE 11816, EN 11901, EN 12353, EN 13074
administrerende organ EN 12292, EN 13385, EN 13709, EN 13713, EN 13714, EN 13715, EN 13716, EN 13717, EN 13718, EN 13723, EN 13725, EN 13739, EN 13744
adoption EN 13369
adoptivbarn EN 13369, EN 13482
ældre menneske DE 11739, DE 11808, DE 11849, DE 12598, DE 13380
æstetik EN 13178
æstetisk opdragelse DE 11924, EN 12627, EN 13125
Ætiopien EN 13389
afasi EN 13370
affektivitet EN 13206
afgangselev EN 12047, EN 12067, EN 12068, EN 12212, EN 12221, EN 12222, EN 12232, EN 12260, FR 12428, DE 12635, EN 13517, EN 13544, EN 13614, EN 13625, EN 13626, EN 13631
afgangsprøve DE 12461, FR 13536
Afrika EN 12331, FR 12342, FR 12433, FR 13508, EN 13750
afspænding DE 13207
afvigende adfærd EN 11873, EN 13244, FR 13252, EN 13269, EN 13270, EN 13273, DE 13280, FR 13283, DE 13732
aggressivitet DE 13274, DE 13732
akademikerarbejdsløshed EN 13431, DE 13543
akademisk frihed EN 12960
akademisk grad DE 11787, EN 12127, EN 12363
aktionsforskning EN 12445, EN 13015
aktivitetsmetode EN 11710, EN 11881, EN 12574
alder EN 13586
aldersforskel EN 13355
algebra EN 12638, FR 12642, EN 12704, EN 12726, EN 13130
alkohol EN 13265
alkoholisme EN 13265, EN 13271
almen uddannelse EN 11988, FR 12017, DE 12038, FR 12203, DE 12217, EN 12279, FR 12300, EN 12495, DE 13379, DE 13764
almendannelse DE 12022
alternativ skole DE 12215, EN 12236
amtsstyre FR 12311, EN 13049, EN 13739
analfabetisme EN 11908, DE 11910, FR 11983, FR 11984, EN 12707
anden generation EN 12897
andet fremmedsprog EN 12920, EN 12921
åndssvaghed EN 13187, EN 13296
anerkendelse af eksamen EN 11949, FR 12440, EN 13516, DE 13711
angst EN 12414, DE 13207, EN 13209, EN 13648
anlægstest EN 13131

arabisk sprog EN 12865, EN 12928, EN 12934, EN 12949
arabiske lande EN 12825, EN 12917, EN 13457
arbejder EN 13502, FR 13602
arbejderbevægelse EN 13561
arbejderklasse FR 11932, EN 12754, DE 13429, EN 13474
arbejderuddannelse EN 12055, EN 12124, EN 12152, EN 12259, EN 12767, EN 12772, EN 13491
arbejdsbeskrivelse EN 13489, EN 13618, EN 13685, EN 13702
arbejdserfaring EN 11762, EN 11806, EN 11841, EN 11842, DE 11880, EN 12263, EN 12527, DE 12529, FR 13590, EN 13643
arbejdsforhold EN 12166, EN 12255, DE 13001, DE 13236, EN 13279, EN 13589, DE 13621
arbejdsgiver EN 11842
arbejdskraft FR 13500, EN 13514, FR 13603, FR 13609
arbejdskraftbehov EN 11803, EN 11952, EN 12681, DE 12807, DE 13537, EN 13557, EN 13558, DE 13598, DE 13600, EN 13615, EN 13616, EN 13632, EN 13638
arbejdskraftmangel EN 13632
arbejdsløs EN 12091, FR 12129, DE 13541
arbejdsløshed DE 12490, DE 13464, DE 13478, DE 13539, DE 13564, EN 13566, DE 13567, DE 13577, EN 13640
arbejdsmarked EN 11912, EN 11940, DE 12029, EN 12222, EN 12232, EN 12258, EN 13041, EN 13049, FR 13520, EN 13524, EN 13525, EN 13526, EN 13527, EN 13528, EN 13529, EN 13530, EN 13531, DE 13532, EN 13533, EN 13551, EN 13553, EN 13554, EN 13555, EN 13556, EN 13557, EN 13558, FR 13568, DE 13581, EN 13586, EN 13588, EN 13591, EN 13592, EN 13596, EN 13599, DE 13600, EN 13605, FR 13609, FR 13611, EN 13615, EN 13625, EN 13626, EN 13638
arbejdsmarkedets forhold EN 13561
arbejdsmiljø EN 11711, EN 13662
arbejdsplads DE 11814, DE 13437, DE 13606
arbejdspsykologi EN 13180, EN 13618
arbejdssøgning EN 13431, EN 13635
arbejdstager EN 11685, DE 11880, FR 12129, EN 12152, EN 12156, DE 13380, EN 13570
arbejdstid EN 12354, EN 12356
argumentation EN 12800, EN 12929, EN 12930, FR 13077, EN 13132, EN 13133
aritmetik EN 11854, EN 12696, FR 12703, EN 12709, EN 13111, EN 13130, FR 13337, EN 13584
arkitektur EN 12974
Asien FR 12039, FR 13508
asocial adfærd EN 12470, EN 12471, EN 13246, EN 13251, EN 13253, EN 13255, EN 13259, EN 13270, EN 13408
aspiration DE 11771, EN 13180, EN 13216, EN 13375, EN 13466
assistent EN 12231
at fortælle historie FR 12829, EN 12978, FR 13072, FR 13091, EN 13460
atypisk EN 13187, EN 13323
audiovisuel metode FR 12020, FR 12796
autisme EN 13135, EN 13323
automatiseret undervisning DE 11862
autonomi DE 12125, DE 12580
autonomi i skoleenhed EN 11993, EN 12011, EN 12236, DE 12272, EN 12286, EN 12314, EN 12317, EN 12348, EN 13739
autoritet EN 13203

bachelorgrad EN 12103, EN 12257
Baden-Württemberg DE 13552
baltiske sprog EN 12837, EN 12838, EN 12841
barn EN 11863, DE 11888, EN 11889, EN 12532, DE 12579, DE 12924, EN 12992, EN 13066, DE 13078, FR 13079, FR 13096, FR 13097,

EN 13111, FR 13123, EN 13155, EN 13160, DE 13232, EN 13414
barndom EN 13045
Bayern DE 13478, DE 13698
befolkning DE 13040, DE 13478
begavet EN 11777, DE 12360, EN 13187, EN 13211, EN 13220, EN 13230, EN 13235, EN 13323
begreb EN 11870, EN 12066, EN 13124, EN 13128, DE 13260, EN 13470, EN 13752
begrebsanalyse FR 13297
begrebsdannelse EN 11698, EN 11727, DE 12464, EN 12536, EN 12602, EN 12608, FR 12641, FR 12654, EN 12751, EN 13022, EN 13117, EN 13118, EN 13122, EN 13137, EN 13161
begynderundervisning EN 11749, EN 12822, EN 12869, EN 12915
behov EN 13039, EN 13261, EN 13457
Belgien EN 11762, EN 12074
belønning EN 13653
Benin FR 12300
Berlin DE 11816, DE 12125, DE 12924
Bermudaøerne EN 13266
beskæftigelse DE 12029, EN 12255, EN 12258, EN 13518, DE 13543, EN 13579, EN 13584, EN 13588, EN 13622, EN 13643, EN 13701
beskæftigelsepolitik DE 12029, DE 13577, FR 13583, EN 13730
beskatning FR 12285
beskyttelse af unge FR 13737, FR 13745
beslutningstagning EN 11939, EN 12169, EN 12284, EN 12291, EN 12318, EN 12742, EN 13112, EN 13113, FR 13257, DE 13260, EN 13747
bestyrelse EN 13709, EN 13712, EN 13714, EN 13715, EN 13716, EN 13717, EN 13718, EN 13722
betydning FR 12829
bevægelse DE 12515, EN 13088, DE 13090
bevis FR 12002, FR 12300, FR 13536
bibliografi EN 13042, EN 13043, EN 13051
bibliotekar EN 13696
biblioteksvidenskab EN 12249
billedbånd EN 11714
biografi FR 11783, EN 12124, EN 13044
biologi DE 11847, EN 12367, FR 12654
blind EN 12662, EN 12974, EN 13156, EN 13291, EN 13295, EN 13301, EN 13302, EN 13317, EN 13318, EN 13344, EN 13347, EN 13349, EN 13368
blindeskrift EN 13291, EN 13295
bog EN 13119
bogholderi EN 13694
bogtrykkerkunst EN 12245
bolig DE 13478
bopæl EN 13170
borgernes medbestemmelse EN 12533, EN 12760, FR 13182, EN 13243, EN 13249, EN 13272, FR 13423, EN 13443
børne- og ungdomslitteratur EN 12973, EN 12980
børneforsorg EN 12420, EN 12438, EN 13471, EN 13731, DE 13736
børnehave EN 11706, EN 11728, DE 11744, DE 11782, EN 11919, DE 12146, EN 12247, FR 12350, EN 12627, EN 12791, EN 12916, EN 12978, EN 13278
børnepsykiatri EN 12770
børnepsykologi EN 12604
børneværn EN 13731, EN 13748
børns pasning uden for hjemmet DE 12048, EN 12072, EN 12420, EN 12438, DE 13484
børns rettigheder EN 13748
børns udvikling EN 11873, EN 12072, EN 12366, EN 12480, FR 12605, EN 12627, EN 12900, EN 12910, EN 13045, EN 13066, EN 13070, FR 13075, EN 13084, EN 13086, EN 13089, EN 13171, EN 13233, EN 13356, EN 13448, EN 13449
Brasilien FR 12277
budget EN 12298

Indice analitico

Indice de matérias

Ευρετήριο θεμάτων

Country index
Index par pays

EN 12155, EN 12157, EN 12158, EN 12159,
EN 12160, EN 12161, EN 12162, EN 12163,
EN 12166, EN 12167, EN 12168, EN 12170,
EN 12171, EN 12172, EN 12173, EN 12174,
EN 12176, EN 12177, EN 12178, EN 12181,
EN 12182, EN 12186, EN 12188, EN 12190,
EN 12191, EN 12192, EN 12195, EN 12196,
EN 12197, EN 12199, EN 12200, EN 12201,
EN 12204, EN 12206, EN 12207, EN 12208,
EN 12209, EN 12211, EN 12212, EN 12213,
EN 12214, EN 12219, EN 12220, EN 12221,
EN 12222, EN 12223, EN 12224, EN 12225,
EN 12226, EN 12227, EN 12228, EN 12229,
EN 12230, EN 12231, EN 12232, EN 12237,
EN 12238, EN 12239, EN 12240, EN 12241,
EN 12242, EN 12243, EN 12244, EN 12245,
EN 12247, EN 12248, EN 12249, EN 12250,
EN 12251, EN 12252, EN 12253, EN 12254,
EN 12256, EN 12257, EN 12259, EN 12260,
EN 12261, EN 12263, EN 12265, EN 12266,
EN 12267, EN 12270, EN 12271, EN 12273,
EN 12279, EN 12280, EN 12281, EN 12284,
EN 12287, EN 12288, EN 12289, EN 12291,
EN 12292, EN 12293, EN 12294, EN 12295,
EN 12297, EN 12298, EN 12303, EN 12305,
EN 12306, EN 12307, EN 12308, EN 12312,
EN 12313, EN 12314, EN 12315, EN 12317,
EN 12323, EN 12325, EN 12326, EN 12327,
EN 12328, EN 12329, EN 12330, EN 12331,
EN 12332, EN 12333, EN 12334, EN 12335,
EN 12336, EN 12339, EN 12340, EN 12341,
EN 12343, EN 12344, EN 12345, EN 12346,
EN 12348, EN 12349, EN 12351, EN 12352,
EN 12353, EN 12354, EN 12356, EN 12358,
EN 12359, EN 12361, EN 12362, EN 12363,
EN 12364, EN 12365, EN 12366, EN 12370,
EN 12371, EN 12372, EN 12373, EN 12375,
EN 12376, EN 12377, EN 12378, EN 12379,
EN 12380, EN 12381, EN 12382, EN 12383,
EN 12384, EN 12385, EN 12387, EN 12393,
EN 12394, EN 12395, EN 12396, EN 12397,
EN 12398, EN 12399, EN 12405, EN 12406,
EN 12407, EN 12408, EN 12409, EN 12410,
EN 12415, EN 12416, EN 12418, EN 12419,
EN 12420, EN 12421, EN 12422, EN 12426,
EN 12430, EN 12431, EN 12432, EN 12435,
EN 12436, EN 12437, EN 12438, EN 12439,
EN 12441, EN 12442, EN 12443, EN 12445,
EN 12446, EN 12448, EN 12449, EN 12450,
EN 12454, EN 12455, EN 12456, EN 12457,
EN 12458, EN 12459, EN 12468, EN 12469,
EN 12470, EN 12471, EN 12472, EN 12473,
EN 12474, EN 12475, EN 12476, EN 12477,
EN 12479, EN 12480, EN 12481, EN 12482,
EN 12483, EN 12485, EN 12487, EN 12488,
EN 12489, EN 12491, EN 12492, EN 12493,
EN 12494, EN 12497, EN 12499, EN 12501,
EN 12502, EN 12503, EN 12504, EN 12507,
EN 12508, EN 12509, EN 12510, EN 12512,
EN 12513, EN 12514, EN 12516, EN 12517,
EN 12518, EN 12519, EN 12521, EN 12522,
EN 12523, EN 12524, EN 12525, EN 12526,
EN 12527, EN 12528, EN 12530, EN 12531,
EN 12532, EN 12533, EN 12534, EN 12535,
EN 12536, EN 12537, EN 12538, EN 12540,
EN 12541, EN 12542, EN 12543, EN 12544,
EN 12545, EN 12546, EN 12547, EN 12548,
EN 12549, EN 12550, EN 12551, EN 12552,
EN 12553, EN 12554, EN 12556, EN 12557,
EN 12558, EN 12559, EN 12560, EN 12561,
EN 12563, EN 12564, EN 12565, EN 12566,
EN 12567, EN 12568, EN 12569, EN 12570,
EN 12571, EN 12573, EN 12574, EN 12577,
EN 12578, EN 12581, EN 12582, EN 12583,
EN 12584, EN 12585, EN 12587, EN 12588,
EN 12589, EN 12592, EN 12593, EN 12595,
EN 12596, EN 12597, EN 12599, EN 12600,
EN 12601, EN 12602, EN 12603, EN 12604,
EN 12606, EN 12607, EN 12608, EN 12609,
EN 12610, EN 12611, EN 12612, EN 12613,
EN 12614, EN 12615, EN 12616, EN 12617,
EN 12618, EN 12619, EN 12620, EN 12621,
EN 12622, EN 12623, EN 12624, EN 12625,
EN 12626, EN 12627, EN 12629, EN 12630,
EN 12631, EN 12632, EN 12636, EN 12638,
EN 12639, EN 12643, EN 12644, EN 12645,
EN 12646, EN 12647, EN 12650, EN 12651,
EN 12652, EN 12653, EN 12655, EN 12656,
EN 12657, EN 12659, EN 12662, EN 12664,
EN 12665, EN 12666, EN 12669, EN 12670,
EN 12671, EN 12673, EN 12674, EN 12675,
EN 12679, EN 12680, EN 12682, EN 12684,
EN 12685, EN 12687, EN 12688, EN 12689,
EN 12690, EN 12691, EN 12692, EN 12694,

EN 12696, EN 12697, EN 12698, EN 12699,
EN 12700, EN 12701, EN 12702, EN 12704,
EN 12705, EN 12710, EN 12713, EN 12714,
EN 12716, EN 12717, EN 12719, EN 12721,
EN 12722, EN 12724, EN 12725, EN 12726,
EN 12727, EN 12728, EN 12729, EN 12730,
EN 12733, EN 12735, EN 12738, EN 12739,
EN 12740, EN 12741, EN 12742, EN 12743,
EN 12744, EN 12746, EN 12747, EN 12748,
EN 12749, EN 12750, EN 12751, EN 12754,
EN 12756, EN 12757, EN 12758, EN 12759,
EN 12760, EN 12761, EN 12764, EN 12765,
EN 12766, EN 12767, EN 12768, EN 12770,
EN 12771, EN 12772, EN 12773, EN 12774,
EN 12775, EN 12777, EN 12778, EN 12781,
EN 12782, EN 12783, EN 12785, EN 12786,
EN 12787, EN 12788, EN 12789, EN 12791,
EN 12792, EN 12797, EN 12798, EN 12799,
EN 12800, EN 12802, EN 12803, EN 12804,
EN 12809, EN 12812, EN 12813, EN 12814,
EN 12815, EN 12816, EN 12817, EN 12818,
EN 12819, EN 12820, EN 12821, EN 12822,
EN 12824, EN 12825, EN 12826, EN 12827,
EN 12830, EN 12831, EN 12833, EN 12836,
EN 12839, EN 12843, EN 12844, EN 12845,
EN 12846, EN 12847, EN 12852, EN 12853,
EN 12854, EN 12855, EN 12856, EN 12857,
EN 12858, EN 12859, EN 12863, EN 12864,
EN 12866, EN 12867, EN 12869, EN 12871,
EN 12876, EN 12877, EN 12878, EN 12879,
EN 12880, EN 12881, EN 12882, EN 12883,
EN 12884, EN 12885, EN 12887, EN 12888,
EN 12889, EN 12890, EN 12891, EN 12893,
EN 12894, EN 12896, EN 12897, EN 12898,
EN 12900, EN 12902, EN 12903, EN 12904,
EN 12905, EN 12906, EN 12908, EN 12910,
EN 12911, EN 12913, EN 12915, EN 12916,
EN 12917, EN 12918, EN 12919, EN 12922,
EN 12923, EN 12925, EN 12928, EN 12929,
EN 12930, EN 12931, EN 12933, EN 12934,
EN 12935, EN 12936, EN 12937, EN 12938,
EN 12939, EN 12940, EN 12944, EN 12945,
EN 12947, EN 12948, EN 12949, EN 12950,
EN 12951, EN 12952, EN 12956, EN 12957,
EN 12958, EN 12960, EN 12961, EN 12962,
EN 12963, EN 12966, EN 12967, EN 12969,
EN 12970, EN 12971, EN 12972, EN 12973,
EN 12974, EN 12975, EN 12979, EN 12980,
EN 12981, EN 12983, EN 12984, EN 12985,
EN 12986, EN 12987, EN 12988, EN 12989,
EN 12990, EN 12991, EN 12992, EN 12994,
EN 12995, EN 12998, EN 13000, EN 13005,
EN 13006, EN 13007, EN 13009, EN 13010,
EN 13012, EN 13013, EN 13014, EN 13015,
EN 13017, EN 13019, EN 13021, EN 13022,
EN 13024, EN 13025, EN 13027, EN 13029,
EN 13032, EN 13033, EN 13039, EN 13043,
EN 13044, EN 13045, EN 13046, EN 13048,
EN 13050, EN 13051, EN 13052, EN 13053,
EN 13063, EN 13065, EN 13066, EN 13067,
EN 13071, EN 13073, EN 13076, EN 13083,
EN 13084, EN 13085, EN 13089, EN 13092,
EN 13093, EN 13094, EN 13095, EN 13099,
EN 13101, EN 13102, EN 13103, EN 13104,
EN 13109, EN 13110, EN 13111, EN 13112,
EN 13113, EN 13114, EN 13115, EN 13116,
EN 13117, EN 13118, EN 13119, EN 13120,
EN 13121, EN 13122, EN 13125, EN 13128,
EN 13130, EN 13132, EN 13133, EN 13134,
EN 13135, EN 13137, EN 13139, EN 13140,
EN 13145, EN 13152, EN 13155, EN 13156,
EN 13157, EN 13158, EN 13159, EN 13160,
EN 13161, EN 13163, EN 13164, EN 13166,
EN 13167, EN 13169, EN 13177, EN 13178,
EN 13181, EN 13185, EN 13187, EN 13190,
EN 13194, EN 13198, EN 13199, EN 13200,
EN 13201, EN 13202, EN 13204, EN 13206,
EN 13208, EN 13211, EN 13214, EN 13221,
EN 13222, EN 13223, EN 13233, EN 13237,
EN 13238, EN 13242, EN 13243, EN 13246,
EN 13247, EN 13248, EN 13249, EN 13250,
EN 13251, EN 13253, EN 13254, EN 13255,
EN 13256, EN 13259, EN 13261, EN 13262,
EN 13263, EN 13266, EN 13270, EN 13271,
EN 13272, EN 13275, EN 13277, EN 13278,
EN 13279, EN 13281, EN 13282, EN 13285,
EN 13287, EN 13290, EN 13291, EN 13293,
EN 13294, EN 13295, EN 13298, EN 13299,
EN 13300, EN 13301, EN 13302, EN 13303,
EN 13304, EN 13305, EN 13307, EN 13308,
EN 13309, EN 13310, EN 13311, EN 13315,
EN 13316, EN 13317, EN 13318, EN 13319,
EN 13320, EN 13321, EN 13323, EN 13324,
EN 13325, EN 13326, EN 13328, EN 13329,

EN 13330, EN 13334, EN 13335, EN 13339,
EN 13340, EN 13342, EN 13343, EN 13344,
EN 13345, EN 13346, EN 13347, EN 13349,
EN 13351, EN 13352, EN 13353, EN 13354,
EN 13355, EN 13357, EN 13358, EN 13359,
EN 13360, EN 13361, EN 13362, EN 13363,
EN 13366, EN 13367, EN 13368, EN 13369,
EN 13370, EN 13371, EN 13372, EN 13373,
EN 13374, EN 13375, EN 13381, EN 13382,
EN 13383, EN 13384, EN 13385, EN 13387,
EN 13388, EN 13389, EN 13391, EN 13392,
EN 13396, EN 13398, EN 13399, EN 13400,
EN 13401, EN 13402, EN 13403, EN 13405,
EN 13407, EN 13408, EN 13409, EN 13412,
EN 13413, EN 13414, EN 13415, EN 13416,
EN 13417, EN 13418, EN 13420, EN 13421,
EN 13422, EN 13425, EN 13426, EN 13427,
EN 13428, EN 13433, EN 13435, EN 13436,
EN 13441, EN 13443, EN 13444, EN 13446,
EN 13447, EN 13448, EN 13453, EN 13454,
EN 13457, EN 13460, EN 13461, EN 13465,
EN 13470, EN 13471, EN 13474, EN 13475,
EN 13476, EN 13477, EN 13481, EN 13482,
EN 13486, EN 13487, EN 13489, EN 13490,
EN 13491, EN 13492, EN 13493, EN 13494,
EN 13497, EN 13499, EN 13501, EN 13504,
EN 13505, EN 13509, EN 13510, EN 13511,
EN 13513, EN 13516, EN 13517, EN 13518,
EN 13544, EN 13545, EN 13546, EN 13547,
EN 13548, EN 13549, EN 13550, EN 13551,
EN 13559, EN 13561, EN 13565, EN 13566,
EN 13570, EN 13573, EN 13576, EN 13579,
EN 13582, EN 13584, EN 13585, EN 13586,
EN 13607, EN 13614, EN 13622, EN 13623,
EN 13624, EN 13630, EN 13631, EN 13633,
EN 13634, EN 13635, EN 13637, EN 13644,
EN 13645, EN 13648, EN 13651, EN 13652,
EN 13654, EN 13657, EN 13658, EN 13659,
EN 13660, EN 13663, EN 13664, EN 13666,
EN 13667, EN 13668, EN 13669, EN 13671,
EN 13672, EN 13674, EN 13675, EN 13676,
EN 13677, EN 13678, EN 13680, EN 13682,
EN 13684, EN 13685, EN 13687, EN 13689,
EN 13690, EN 13692, EN 13693, EN 13694,
EN 13695, EN 13696, EN 13697, EN 13699,
EN 13700, EN 13701, EN 13703, EN 13709,
EN 13710, EN 13712, EN 13713, EN 13714,
EN 13715, EN 13716, EN 13717, EN 13718,
EN 13719, EN 13721, EN 13722, EN 13723,
EN 13724, EN 13725, EN 13730, EN 13731,
EN 13733, EN 13734, EN 13735, EN 13738,
EN 13740, EN 13744, EN 13750, EN 13751,
EN 13752, EN 13753, EN 13754, EN 13755,
EN 13756, EN 13757, EN 13758, EN 13759,
EN 13760, EN 13761, EN 13762, EN 13763,
EN 13765, EN 13766

GRC EN 12780, EN 13203, EN 13225, EN 13284,
EN 13449, EN 13467

IRL EN 12112, EN 12402, EN 12403, EN 12423,
EN 13393

ITA EN 11784, EN 11804, EN 11909, EN 11942,
EN 12128, EN 12132, EN 12133, EN 12193,
EN 12274, EN 12309, EN 12319, EN 12462,
EN 12640, EN 12658, EN 12681, EN 12683,
EN 12708, EN 12723, EN 12734, EN 12823,
EN 12920, EN 12921, EN 12959, EN 12982,
EN 12999, EN 13020, EN 13030, EN 13034,
EN 13081, EN 13179, EN 13189, EN 13292,
EN 13411, EN 13430, EN 13468, EN 13589,
EN 13612, EN 13616, EN 13653, EN 13670

LAT EN 12183, EN 12184

NLD EN 11688, EN 11689, EN 11724, EN 11725,
EN 11742, EN 11757, EN 11758, EN 11772,
EN 11786, EN 11795, EN 11856, EN 11865,
EN 11871, EN 11882, EN 11899, EN 11907,
EN 11912, EN 11925, EN 11927, EN 11967,
EN 11971, EN 11973, EN 12073, EN 12092,
EN 12141, EN 12156, EN 12164, EN 12165,
EN 12258, EN 12262, EN 12282, EN 12283,
EN 12296, EN 12316, EN 12347, EN 12355,
EN 12368, EN 12374, EN 12386, EN 12411,
EN 12417, EN 12424, EN 12425, EN 12444,
EN 12447, EN 12463, EN 12465, EN 12486,
EN 12506, EN 12576, EN 12633, EN 12661,
EN 12709, EN 12731, EN 12752, EN 12850,
EN 12851, EN 12865, EN 12895, EN 12909,

EN 12932, EN 12941, EN 12942, EN 12997,
EN 13008, EN 13041, EN 13049, EN 13060,
EN 13080, EN 13138, EN 13141, EN 13173,
EN 13183, EN 13215, EN 13220, EN 13227,
EN 13229, EN 13258, EN 13264, EN 13268,
EN 13273, EN 13336, EN 13356, EN 13365,
EN 13434, EN 13455, EN 13459, EN 13462,
EN 13480, EN 13488, EN 13496, EN 13502,
EN 13514, EN 13519, EN 13524, EN 13525,
EN 13526, EN 13527, EN 13528, EN 13529,
EN 13530, EN 13531, EN 13553, EN 13554,
EN 13555, EN 13556, EN 13557, EN 13558,
EN 13588, EN 13591, EN 13592, EN 13596,
EN 13597, EN 13605, EN 13610, EN 13615,
EN 13625, EN 13626, EN 13632, EN 13638,
EN 13643, EN 13656, EN 13662, EN 13683,
EN 13702, EN 13742, EN 13743

NOR   EN 11749, EN 11812, EN 11826, EN 11876,
EN 11891, EN 11892, EN 11939, EN 11975,

EN 12149, EN 12205, EN 12318, EN 12324,
EN 12862, EN 12914, EN 13213, EN 13216,
EN 13337, EN 13404, EN 13640, EN 13747

POL   EN 11936, EN 12027, EN 12148, EN 12169,
EN 12198, EN 12235, EN 12236, EN 12434,
EN 12693, EN 12755, EN 12769, EN 12776,
EN 13042, EN 13086, EN 13168, EN 13180,
EN 13188, EN 13195, EN 13327, EN 13458,
EN 13463, EN 13617, EN 13618, EN 13679,
EN 13708

ROM   EN 11908, EN 11940, EN 12389, EN 12390,
EN 13235

RUS   EN 11698, EN 11868, EN 11941, EN 11952,
EN 12041, EN 12179, EN 12275, EN 12732,
EN 12762, EN 13023, EN 13028, EN 13515

SVK   EN 12000, EN 12006, EN 12021, EN 13011,
EN 13018, EN 13419, EN 13431, EN 13466,
EN 13506, EN 13688, EN 13739

SVN   EN 12357, EN 12875, EN 13230, EN 13440

TUR   EN 11694, EN 11844, EN 11913, EN 12180,
EN 12255, EN 12404, EN 12414, EN 12429,
EN 12848, EN 12901, EN 13002, EN 13074,
EN 13129, EN 13131, EN 13136, EN 13143,
EN 13144, EN 13170, EN 13171, EN 13186,
EN 13192, EN 13205, EN 13209, EN 13210,
EN 13240, EN 13265, EN 13296, EN 13322

XCE   EN 11807, EN 12028, EN 12555, EN 12790